Plevnik

D1599368

MARK

A Commentary on His Apology for the Cross

MARK

A Commentary on His Apology for the Cross

Robert H. Gundry

WILLIAM B. EERDMANS PUBLISHING COMPANY
GRAND RAPIDS, MICHIGAN

Library of Congress Cataloging-in-Publication Data

Gundry, Robert Horton.
Mark: a commentary on his apology for the cross / Robert H. Gundry.
p.   cm.
Includes bibliographical references and indexes.
ISBN 0-8028-3698-4
1. Bible. N.T. Mark — Commentaries.   I. Title.
BS2585.3.G85   1992
226.3′07 — dc20   92-39055
CIP

Contents

Acknowledgments

My thanks go above all to my wife Lois, who not only entered almost all my original longhand and many revisions into a word-processor but also with her penetrating questions brought clarity to my thinking on a number of difficult questions. To her I affectionately dedicate this book.

Thanks also to my daughter Judith Gundry-Volf, who gave the manuscript a critical reading and offered many a helpful correction and suggestion,

To my son Mark, who advised me on some matters of style,

To my daughter Connie Gundry Tappy, who entered part of my original longhand into a word-processor and tracked down several obscure references,

To my son-in-law Ron Tappy, who also tracked down several obscure references and gained me access to the Widener Library at Harvard University,

To Cory Weiss, rabbinic student at the Hebrew Union College (Los Angeles), who helped me track down some passages in rabbinic literature,

To David Cole, professor of molecular cell biology at the University of California at Berkeley, who gained me access to the main research and legal libraries at his institution,

To Ned Divelbiss, who as a member of the library staff at Westmont College procured for me many books and articles on interlibrary loan,

To the librarians who opened their doors to me at the University of California at Santa Barbara, the University of California at Los Angeles, the University of California at Berkeley, Harvard University, Harvard Divinity School, Weston College, the Graduate Theological Union, the Hebrew Union College (Los Angeles), the Claremont Graduate School of Theology, and Fuller Theological Seminary,

To the administration, trustees, and alumni of Westmont College for grants, a half year's sabbatical, and a half year's leave of absence,

To Steffan Sherman, an alumnus of Westmont College and former student of mine, and to anonymous donors and El Montecito Presbyterian Church who joined him in providing financial support during my leave,

And to all those at Wm. B. Eerdmans Publishing Co. who helped turn a manuscript and computer disks into a book.

Robert H. Gundry

Abbreviations

AAR	American Academy of Religion
AB	Anchor Bible
'Abod. Zar.	*'Aboda Zara*
'Abot R. Nat.	*'Abot de Rabbi Nathan*
Ach. Tat.	Achilles Tatius
Acts Pet.	Acts of Peter
Acts Phil.	Acts of Philip
Acts Pil.	Acts of Pilate
Acts Thom.	Acts of Thomas

Adamantius
  Dial. contra
  Marcion
	Dialogue against Marcion

Ael.	Aelianus
VH	*Varia Historia*
Ael. Arist.	Aelius Aristides
Or.	*Orationes*
Aesch.	Aeschylus
PV	*Prometheus Vinctus*
AGJU	Arbeiten zur Geschichte des antiken Judentums und des Urchristentums
AJSL	*American Journal of Semitic Languages and Literatures*
AJT	*American Journal of Theology*
AnBib	Analecta Biblica
ANET	J. B. Pritchard (ed.), *Ancient Near Eastern Texts*
ANRW	*Aufstieg und Niedergang der Römischen Welt*
Ap. Jas.	Apocryphon of James
Apoc. Abr.	Apocalypse of Abraham
2-3 Apoc. Bar.	Syriac, Greek Apocalypse of Baruch

Apoc. Elijah	Apocalypse of Elijah
Apoc. Ezra	Apocalypse of Ezra
Apoc. Mos.	Apocalypse of Moses
Apoc. Zeph.	Apocalypse of Zephaniah
Apul.	Apuleius
Met.	*Metamorphoses*
Aq	Aquila
Ar.	Aristophanes
Ach.	*Acharnenses*
Plut.	*Plutus*
Ran.	*Ranae*
Vesp.	*Vespae*
ʿ*Arak.*	ʿ*Arakin*
Arist.	Aristoteles
Eth. Nic.	*Ethica Nicomachea*
Insomn.	*De Insomniis*
Ph.	*Physica*
Poet.	*Poetica*
Arr. *Epict. Diss.*	Arrianus *Epicteti Dissertationes*
Artem.	Artemidorus Daldianus
Oneir.	*Oneirokritika*
As. Mos.	Assumption of Moses
Asc. Isa.	Ascension of Isaiah
ASNU	Acta Seminarii Neotestamentici Upsaliensis
ASTI	*Annual of the Swedish Theological Institute*
ATANT	Abhandlungen zur Theologie des Alten und Neuen Testaments
Ath.	Athenaeus Grammaticus
Deipn.	*Deipnosophistai*
ATR	*Anglican Theological Review*
Augustine	
Ev. Joh.	*Exposition of the Gospel of John*
b.	Babylonian Talmud
B. Bat.	*Baba Batra*
B. Meṣ.	*Baba Meṣiʿa*
B. Qam.	*Baba Qamma*
BA	*Biblical Archaeologist*
BAGD	W. Bauer, W. F. Arndt, F. W. Gingrich, and F. W. Danker, *Greek-English Lexicon of the New Testament*
BAR	*Biblical Archaeologist Reader*
Barn.	Barnabas
BB	*Bible Bhashyam*
BBB	Bonner Biblische Beiträge
BBET	Beiträge zur biblischen Exegese und Theologie

B.C.E.	before the Common Era (traditionally designated B.C.)
BDB	F. Brown, S. R. Driver, and C. A. Briggs, *Hebrew and English Lexicon of the Old Testament*
BDF	F. Blass, A. Debrunner, and R. W. Funk, *A Greek Grammar of the New Testament*
Bek.	*Bekorot*
Ber.	*Berakot*
BETL	Bibliotheca Ephemeridum Theologicarum Lovaniensium
BEvT	Beiträge zur Evangelischen Theologie
BFCT	Beiträge zur Förderung Christlicher Theologie
BGBE	Beiträge zur Geschichte der Biblischen Exegese
BGU	*Berliner Griechische Urkunden (Ägyptische Urkunden aus den Königlichen Museen zu Berlin)*
Bib	*Biblica*
Bib. Ant.	Pseudo-Philo, Biblical Antiquities
BibLeb	*Bibel und Leben*
BJRL	*Bulletin of the John Rylands University Library of Manchester*
BJS	Brown Judaic Studies
BK	*Bibel und Kirche*
BKAT	Biblischer Kommentar: Altes Testament
BLit	*Bibel und Liturgie*
BN	*Biblische Notizen*
BR	*Biblical Research*
BSac	*Bibliotheca Sacra*
BT	*Bible Translator*
BTB	*Biblical Theology Bulletin*
BTS	*Bible et Terre Sainte*
BU	Biblische Untersuchungen
Bultmann, *HST*	R. Bultmann, *History of the Synoptic Tradition*
BWANT	Beiträge zur Wissenschaft vom Alten und Neuen Testament
BZ	*Biblische Zeitschrift*
BZNW	*Beihefte zur ZNW*
CAD	*Assyrian Dictionary of the Oriental Institute of the University of Chicago*
Cath	*Catholica*
CBQ	*Catholic Biblical Quarterly*
CBQMS	Catholic Biblical Quarterly — Monograph Series
CD	Cairo (Genizah text of the) Damascus (Document)
C.E.	the Common Era (traditionally designated A.D.)
CEP	Contemporary Evangelical Perspectives
chap(s).	chapter(s)
Chrys.	John Chrysostom
Hom. on Matt.	*Homilies on Matthew*

Cic.	Cicero
Att.	*Epistulae ad Atticum*
De Or.	*De Oratore*
Div.	*De Divinatione*
Lig.	*Pro Ligario*
Rab. Post.	*Pro Rabirio Postumo*
Rep.	*De Republica*
Top.	*Topica*
Tusc.	*Tusculanae Disputationes*
Verr.	*In Verrem*
1–2 Clem.	1–2 Clement
Clem.	Clemens Alexandrinus
Adumbr.	*Adumbrationes*
Paed.	*Paedagogus*
Q.d.s.	*Quis dives Salvetur*
Strom.	*Stromateis*
CNT	*Christian News From Israel*
Cod(d).	Codex(-ices)
col(s).	column(s)
ConBNT	Coniectanea Biblica, New Testament
Conc	*Concilium*
ConNT	*Coniectanea Neotestamentica*
Corp. Herm.	*Corpus Hermeticum*
CPR	*Corpus Papyrorum Raineri Archiducis Austriae,* vol. 1, *Griechische Texte*
CR	*Clergy Review*
CRBR	*Critical Review of Books in Religion*
CSR	*Christian Scholar's Review*
CTM	*Concordia Theological Monthly*
CTR	*Criswell Theological Review*
Cyr. H.	Cyril of Jerusalem
Catech.	*Catechetical Lectures*
Dalman, *SSW*	G. Dalman, *Sacred Sites and Ways*
Daube, *NTRJ*	D. Daube, *The New Testament and Rabbinic Judaism*
DCG	*Dictionary of Christ and the Gospels*
Deissmann, *LAE*	A. Deissmann, *Light from the Ancient East*
Dem.	Demosthenes
Did.	Didache
Dio Cass.	Dio Cassius
Dio Chrys.	Dio Chrysostomus
Orat.	*Orationes*
Diod. Sic.	Diodorus Siculus
Diog. Laert.	Diogenes Laertius
Dion. Com.	Dionysius Comicus
Dion. Hal.	Dionysius Halicarnassenis

Ant. Rom.	*Antiquitates Romanae*
Comp.	*De Compositione Verborum*
Dioscor. Ped.	Dioscorides Pedanius
De mater. med.	*De materia medica*
DJD	Discoveries in the Judean Desert
DownRev	*Downside Review*
EBC	Expositor's Bible Commentary
EBib	Études Bibliques
EcumRev	*Ecumenical Review*
ʿEd.	ʿEduyyot
EDNT	*Exegetical Dictionary of the New Testament*
EH	Europäische Hochschulschriften
EKKNT	Evangelisch-Katholischer Kommentar zum Neuen Testament
EncJud	*Encyclopaedia Judaica* (1971)
1–2–3 Enoch	Ethiopic, Slavonic, Hebrew Enoch
Ep. Arist.	Epistle of Aristeas
Epiph.	Epiphanius
De mens. et pond.	*De mensuris et ponderibus*
Haer.	*Adversus Haereses*
ErThSt	Erfurter Theologische Studien
ʿErub.	ʿErubin
EstBib	*Estudios Biblicos*
ETL	*Ephemerides Theologicae Lovanienses*
Eunap.	Eunapius
VS	*Vitae Sophistarum*
Eur.	Euripides
Alc.	*Alcestis*
El.	*Electra*
Hipp.	*Hippolytus*
IT	*Iphigenia Taurica*
Tro.	*Troades*
Eus.	Eusebius
Chron.	*Chronicon*
H.E.	*Historia Ecclesiastica*
EvE	*Evangelische Erzieher*
EvQ	*Evangelical Quarterly*
EvT	*Evangelische Theologie*
ExpTim	*Expository Times*
f(f).	following (page[s], verse[s], etc.)
FB	Forschung zur Bibel
FBBS	Facet Books, Biblical Series
FFLF	Foundations & Facets: Literary Facets
frg(s).	fragment(s)

Frg. Tg.	*Fragmentary Targum*
FRLANT	Forschungen zur Religion und Literatur des Alten und Neuen Testaments
FS	Festschrift
FTS	Frankfurter Theologische Studien
FV	*Foi et Vie*
GBS	Guides to Biblical Scholarship
GCS	Griechische Christliche Schriftsteller
Geopon.	*Geoponica*
Giṭ.	*Giṭṭin*
GKC	*Gesenius' Hebrew Grammar,* ed. E. Kautzsch, tr. A. E. Cowley
GNS	Good News Studies
Gos. Barth.	Gospel of Bartholomew
Gos. Naz.	Gospel of the Nazarenes
Gos. Nic.	Gospel of Nicodemus
Gos. Pet.	Gospel of Peter
Gos. Thom.	Gospel of Thomas
Greg	*Gregorianum*
GTJ	*Grace Theological Journal*
Ḥag.	*Ḥagiga*
Hatch and Redpath	E. Hatch and H. A. Redpath, *A Concordance to the Septuagint and the other Greek Versions of the Old Testament (including the Apocryphal Books)*
HDR	Harvard Dissertations in Religion
Hdt.	Herodotus Historicus
Herm. Man.	Hermas, Mandate
Herm. Vis.	Hermas, Vision
Hes.	Hesiodus
Th.	*Theogonia*
HeyJ	*Heythrop Journal*
HibJ	*Hibbert Journal*
Hippoc.	Hippocrates
Morb. Sacr.	περὶ ἱερῆς νούσου
Hippol.	Hippolytus
Trad. Ap.	*Apostolic Tradition*
HKNT	Handkommentar zum Neuen Testament
HNT	Handbuch zum Neuen Testament
Hom.	Homerus
Il.	*Ilias*
Od.	*Odyssea*
Hor.	Horace
Carm.	*Carmina* or *Odes*
Epist.	*Epistulae*
Epod.	*Epodi*

HTKNT	Herders Theologischer Kommentar zum Neuen Testament
HTR	*Harvard Theological Review*
HTS	Harvard Theological Studies
HUCA	*Hebrew Union College Annual*
Iambl.	Iamblichus
VP	*De Vita Pythagorica*
IBS	*Irish Biblical Studies*
ICC	International Critical Commentary
IDB	G. A. Buttrick (ed.), *Interpreter's Dictionary of the Bible*
IEJ	*Israel Exploration Journal*
Ign.	Ignatius
Eph.	*Letter to the Ephesians*
Magn.	*Letter to the Magnesians*
Rom.	*Letter to the Romans*
Smyrn.	*Letter to the Smyrnaeans*
Int	*Interpretation*
Iren.	Irenaeus
Haer.	*Adversus Haereses*
IRT	Issues in Religion and Theology
ISBE	*International Standard Bible Encyclopedia*
Isoc.	Isocrates
Ant.	*Antidosis*
Arch.	*Archidamus*
Phil.	*Address to Philip*
JAAR	*Journal of the American Academy of Religion*
JANESCU	*Journal of the Ancient Near Eastern Society of Columbia University*
JAOS	*Journal of the American Oriental Society*
JBL	*Journal of Biblical Literature*
JBLMS	Journal of Biblical Literature Monograph Series
Jerome	
Comm.	*Commentarius*
De Vir. Inl.	*De Viris Inlustribus*
JETS	*Journal of the Evangelical Theological Society*
JJS	*Journal of Jewish Studies*
Jos. Asen.	Joseph and Asenath
Josephus	
Ag.Ap.	*Against Apion*
Ant. (or *AJ*)	*Jewish Antiquities*
J.W. (or *BJ*)	*Jewish War*
JPOS	*Journal of the Palestine Oriental Society*
JQR	*Jewish Quarterly Review*
JR	*Journal of Religion*

JSJ	*Journal for the Study of Judaism in the Persian, Hellenistic and Roman Period*
JSNT	*Journal for the Study of the New Testament*
JSNTSup	Journal for the Study of the New Testament — Supplement Series
JSOT	*Journal for the Study of the Old Testament*
JSOTSup	Journal for the Study of the Old Testament — Supplement Series
JSS	*Journal of Semitic Studies*
JTS	*Journal of Theological Studies*
JTSA	*Journal of Theology for Southern Africa*
Jub.	Jubilees
Justin	Justin Martyr
1 Apol.	*First Apology*
Dial.	*Dialogue with Trypho*
Juv.	Juvenal
Sat.	*Satirae*
KBANT	Kommentare und Beiträge zum Alten und Neuen Testament
Ker.	*Keritot*
Ketub.	*Ketubot*
Kil.	*Kil'ayim*
l(l).	line(s)
LBS	Library of Biblical Studies
LCL	Loeb Classical Library
LD	Lectio Divina
LHD	Library of History and Doctrine
LingBib	*Linguistica Biblica*
Liv.	Livius
Ab urbe cond.	*Ab urbe condita*
LL	Lutterworth Library
LQHR	*London Quarterly and Holborn Review*
LSJ	Liddell-Scott-Jones, *Greek-English Lexicon*
LUÅ	Lunds Universitets Årsskrift
Luc.	Lucianus
Asin.	*Asinus*
Catapl.	*Cataplus*
Cont.	*Contemplantes*
Demon.	*Demonax*
Deor. Conc.	*Deorum Concilium*
Mer. Cond.	*De Mercede Conductis*
Nec.	*Necyomantia*
Peregr.	*De Morte Peregrini*
Philops.	*Philopseudes*

LXX	Septuagint
m.	Mishna
Macrob.	Macrobius
Sat.	*Saturnalia*
Mak.	*Makkot*
Marc. Ann. Luc.	Marcus Annaeus Lucanus
Marc. Aurel.	Marcus Aurelius
Mart. Con.	Martyrdom of Conon
Mart. Isa.	Martyrdom of Isaiah
Mart. Pol.	Martyrdom of Polycarp
Meg.	*Megilla*
Meʿil.	*Meʿila*
Mek.	*Mekilta*
Menaḥ.	*Menaḥot*
MeyerK	H. A. W. Meyer, Kritisch-Exegetischer Kommentar über das Neue Testament
Mid.	*Middot*
Midr.	*Midraš;* cited with a usual abbreviation for a biblical book; but *Midr. Qoh.* = *Midraš Qohelet*
Miqw.	*Miqwaʾot*
MM	J. H. Moulton and G. Milligan, *Vocabulary of the Greek Testament*
MNTC	Moffatt New Testament Commentary
Moʿed Qaṭ.	*Moʿed Qaṭan*
MS(S)	manuscript(s)
MT	Masoretic Text
MTZ	*Münchener Theologische Zeitschrift*
Mur	Wadi Murabbaʿat texts
MVAG	Mitteilungen der Vorderasiatisch-Ägyptischen Gesellschaft
n(n).	notes(s)
N-A	Nestle-Aland, *Novum Testamentum Graece*
N.B.	nota bene (note well)
NCB	New Century Bible
Ned.	*Nedarim*
NedTTs	*Nederlands Theologisch Tijdschrift*
Neg.	*Negaʿim*
Neot	*Neotestamentica*
nf	neue folge
NICNT	New International Commentary on the New Testament
Nid.	*Niddah*
NIGTC	New International Greek Testament Commentary
no(s).	number(s)
NovT	*Novum Testamentum*
NovTSup	Novum Testamentum, Supplements

ns	new series
NT	New Testament, Neue Testament
NTAbh	Neutestamentliche Abhandlungen
NTL	New Testament Library
NTS	*New Testament Studies*
NTT	*Nieuwe Theologisch Tijdschrift*
NTTS	New Testament Tools and Studies
NVBS	New Voices in Biblical Studies
O	Origen's recension of the Septuagint
OBO	Orbis Biblicus et Orientalis
ÖBS	*Österreichische Biblische Studien*
Odes Sol.	Odes of Solomon
Ohol.	*Oholot*
Or.	Origen
Cels.	*Against Celsus*
Joh.	*Commentary on the Gospel of John*
Matt.	*Commentary on the Gospel of Matthew*
os	old series
OT	Old Testament
ÖTKNT	Ökumenischer Taschenbuch-Kommentar zum Neuen Testament
OTL	Old Testament Library
OTM	Oxford Theological Monographs
Ov.	Ovid
Ars Am.	*Ars Amatoria*
Fast.	*Fasti*
Her.	*Heroides*
Met.	*Metamorphoses*
p(p).	page(s)
par(r).	parallel(s)
PEger.	Egerton Papyrus
PEGLBS	*Proceedings: Eastern Great Lakes Biblical Society*
PEQ	*Palestine Exploration Quarterly*
Pesaḥ.	*Pesaḥim*
Pesh	Peshitta
Pesiq. R.	*Pesiqta Rabbati*
Petr.	Petronius
Sat.	*Satura*
PFlor.	*Papiri Fiorentini*
PGM	K. Preisendanz (ed.), *Papyri Graecae Magicae*
Philo	
Abr.	*De Abrahamo*
All.	*Legum Allegoriarum*
Cher.	*De Cherubim*
Conf.	*De Confucione Linguarum*

De sacr. A. et C.	*De Sacrificiis Abelis et Caini*
Decal.	*De Decalogo*
Flac.	*In Flaccum*
Hypoth.	*Hypothetica*
Imm.	*Quod Deus sit Immutabilis*
Jos.	*De Josepho*
Legat.	*De Legatione ad Gaium*
Migr.	*De Migratione Abrahami*
Mos.	*De Vita Mosis*
Mut.	*De Mutatione Nominum*
Opif.	*De Opificio Mundi*
Praem.	*De Praemiis et Poenis*
Prov.	*De Providentia*
Sobr.	*De Sobrietate*
Som.	*De Somniis*
Spec.	*De Specialibus Legibus*
Virt.	*De Virtute*
Philostr.	Philostratus
Ep.	*Epistulae*
VA	*Vita Apollonii*
Phld.	Philodemus
Vol. Rhet.	*Volumina Rhetorica*
pl(s).	plate(s)
Pl.	Plato
Euthphr.	*Euthyphro*
Phd.	*Phaedo*
Phdr.	*Phaedrus*
Prt.	*Protagoras*
Resp.	*Respublica*
Symp.	*Symposium*
Tht.	*Theaetetus*
PL	J. Migne, Patrologia Latina
Plaut.	Plautus
Cas.	*Casina*
Mil. Glor.	*Miles Gloriosus*
Trucul.	*Truculentus*
PLille	Papyrus graecs de Lille
Plin.	Plinius (the Elder)
HN	*Naturalis Historia*
Plin.	Plinius (the Younger)
Ep.	*Epistulae*
PLond.	*Greek Papyri in the British Museum*
Plot.	Plotinus
Enn.	*Enneades*

Plut.	Plutarchus
Alex.	*Alexander*
Arat.	*Aratus*
Cat. Mai.	*Cato the Elder*
Cat. Min.	*Cato the Younger*
Cleom.	*Cleomenes*
Coriolan.	*Coriolanus*
Crass.	*Crassus*
De def. or.	*De defectu oraculorum*
De Pyth. or.	*De Pythiae oraculis*
Mor.	*Moralia*
Pel.	*Pelopidas*
Per.	*Pericles*
Pomp.	*Pompeius*
Sull.	*Sulla*
Pol. *Phil.*	Polycarp to the Philippians
Polyb.	Polybius
Porph.	Porphyrius Tyrius
VP	*Vita Pythagorae*
POxy.	*Oxyrhynchus Papyri*
Ps.-Callisth.	Pseudo-Callisthenes
Pss. Sol.	Psalms of Solomon
pt.	part
PTebt.	*Tebtunis Papyri*
Ptol.	Ptolemaeus Mathematicus
Geog.	*Geographia*
PW	Pauly-Wissowa, *Real-Encyclopädie der classischen Altertumswissenschaft*
PWSup	Supplement to PW
1QapGen, 4QFlor, etc.	*Genesis Apocryphon* from Qumran Cave 1, *Florilegium* from Qumran Cave 4, etc. (see J. A. Fitzmyer, *The Dead Sea Scrolls: Major Publications and Tools for Study* [2nd ed.] 3-93, for further standard abbreviations)
QD	Quaestiones Disputatae
QDAP	*Quarterly of the Department of Antiquities in Palestine*
Qidd.	*Qiddušin*
QL	Qumran Literature (also called the Dead Sea Scrolls)
Quint.	Quintillianus
Inst.	*Institutio Oratoria*
Rab.	*Rabbah* (following an abbreviation for a biblical book: *Gen. Rab.* = *Genesis Rabbah*)
RAC	*Reallexikon für Antike und Christentum*
RAT	*Revue Africaine de Théologie*

RB	*Revue Biblique*
RechBib	Recherches Bibliques
Reitzenstein, *Poim.*	R. Reitzenstein, *Poimandres*
REJ	*Revue des Études Juives*
RevExp	*Review and Expositor*
RevQ	*Revue de Qumran*
RHPR	*Revue d'Histoire et de Philosophie Religieuses*
RHR	*Revue de l'Histoire des Religions*
RIDA	*Revue Internationale des Droits de l'Antiquité*
RJ	*Reformed Journal*
RJV	*Rheinisches Jahrbuch für Volkskunde*
RNT	Regensburger Neues Testament
Roš Haš.	*Roš Haššana*
RSPT	*Revue des Sciences Philosophiques et Théologiques*
RSR	*Recherches de Science Religieuse*
RTL	*Revue Théologique de Louvain*
Sall.	Sallustius
Cat.	*Bellum Catilinae* or *De Catilinae coniuratione*
Šabb.	*Šabbat*
Sanh.	*Sanhedrin*
SANT	Studien zum Alten und Neuen Testament
SBB	Stuttgarter Biblische Beiträge
SBEC	Studies in the Bible and Early Christianity
SBFLA	*Studii Biblici Franciscani Liber Annuus*
SBL	Society of Biblical Literature
SBLDS	SBL Dissertation Series
SBLMS	SBL Monograph Series
SBLSBS	SBL Sources for Biblical Study
SBM	Stuttgarter Biblische Monographien
SBS	Stuttgarter Bibelstudien
SBT	Studies in Biblical Theology
ScEs	*Science et Esprit*
Scr	*Scripture*
SE	*Studia Evangelica I, II, III* (= TU 73 [1959], 87 [1964], 88 [1964], etc.)
SEÅ	*Svensk Exegetisk Årsbok*
Šeb.	*Šebiʿit*
Šebu.	*Šebuʿot*
SecCent	*Second Century*
Sem.	*Semaḥot*
Sen.	Seneca, L. Annaeus
De consol. ad	
Marc.	*De consolationes ad Marciam*
Ep.	*Epistulae*

QNat.	*Quaestiones Naturales*
Šeqal.	*Šeqalim*
SFEG	Schriften der Finnischen Exegetischen Gesellschaft
SGM	Secret Gospel of Mark
Sib. Or.	Sibylline Oracles
SIG	*Sylloge Inscriptionum Graecarum*
SJLA	Studies in Judaism in Late Antiquity
SJT	*Scottish Journal of Theology*
SNTSMS	Society for New Testament Studies Monograph Series
SNTU	Studien zum Neuen Testament und seiner Umwelt
SNTW	Studies of the New Testament and its World
SO	Symbolae Osloenses
Sop.	*Soperim*
Soph.	Sophocles
Aj.	*Ajax*
El.	*Electra*
OT	*Oedipus Tyrannus*
Phil.	*Philoctetes*
SPap	*Studia Papyrologica*
SPB	Studia Postbiblica
SPIB	Scripta Pontificii Instituti Biblici
ST	*Studia Theologica*
STDJ	Studies on the Texts of the Desert of Judah
Str-B	[H. Strack and] P. Billerbeck, *Kommentar zum Neuen Testament*
Suet.	Suetonius
Aug.	*Augustus*
Calig.	*Gaius Caligula*
Dom.	*Domitianus*
Vesp.	*Vespasianus*
Sukk.	*Sukka*
SUNT	Studien zur Umwelt des Neuen Testaments
s.v.	sub verbo
SVTP	Studia in Veteris Testamenti Pseudepigrapha
SWJT	*Southwestern Journal of Theology*
Sym	Symmachus
t.	Tosepta
T. Abr., T. Adam, T. Benj., etc.	Testament of Abraham, Testament of Adam, Testament of Benjamin, etc.
Taʿan.	*Taʿanit*
Tac.	Tacitus
Ann.	*Annales*
Hist.	*Historiae*

Tanḥ.	*Tanḥuma*
TDNT	G. Kittel and G. Friedrich (eds.), *Theological Dictionary of the New Testament*
TDOT	G. J. Botterweck and H. Ringgren (eds.), *Theological Dictionary of the Old Testament*
Ter.	*Terumot*
Tert.	Tertullian
Apol.	*Apology*
Pudic.	*On Modesty (De Pudicitia)*
Tg. Esth I, II	*First* or *Second Targum of Esther*
Tg. Ket.	*Targum of the Writings*
Tg. Neb.	*Targum of the Prophets*
Tg. Neof.	*Targum Neofiti 1*
Tg. Onq.	*Targum Onqelos*
Tg. Ps.-J.	*Targum Pseudo-Jonathan*
Tg. Yer. I	*Targum Yerušalmi I*
TGl	*Theologie und Glaube*
THAT	*Theologisches Handwörterbuch zum Alten Testament*
Theod	Theodotion
Theoph.	Theophilus of Antioch
Autol.	*To Autolycus (ad Autolycum)*
THKNT	Theologischer Handkommentar zum Neuen Testament
Thphr.	Theophrastus
HP	*Historia Plantarum*
Thuc.	Thucydides
Tib.	Tibullus
TLZ	*Theologische Literaturzeitung*
TrinJourn	*Trinity Journal*
TRu	*Theologische Rundschau*
TSFBul	Theological Students Fellowship Bulletin
TSK	*Theologische Studien und Kritiken*
TTZ	*Trierer Theologische Zeitschrift*
TU	Texte und Untersuchungen
TynBul	*Tyndale Bulletin*
TZ	*Theologische Zeitschrift*
UBSGNT	United Bible Societies *Greek New Testament*
UNT	Untersuchungen zum Neuen Testament
UP	University Press
v(v)	verse(s)
Val. Max.	Valerius Maximus
Varro	
Rust.	*Res Rusticae*
Verg.	Vergilius
Aen.	*Aeneid*
Geor.	*Georgics*

VF	*Verkündigung und Forschung*
Vit. Proph.	*Vitae Prophetarum* (Lives of the Prophets)
v.l., vv.ll.	varia(e) lectio(nes) (variant reading[s])
VS	Verbum Salutis
VT	*Vetus Testamentum*
WBC	Word Biblical Commentary
WD	*Wort und Dienst*
WMANT	Wissenschaftliche Monographien zum Alten und Neuen Testament
WTJ	*Westminster Theological Journal*
WUNT	Wissenschaftliche Untersuchungen zum Neuen Testament
Xen.	Xenophon
An.	*Anabasis*
Cyr.	*Cyropaedia*
Mem.	*Memorabilia*
Oec.	*Oeconomicus*
Xen. Eph.	Xenophon Ephesius
y.	Jerusalem Talmud
Yad.	*Yadayim*
Yal.	*Yalquṭ*
Yebam.	*Yebamot*
ZahnK	Kommentar zum Neuen Testament, ed. T. Zahn
ZAW	*Zeitschrift für die alttestamentliche Wissenschaft*
ZDPV	*Zeitschrift des deutschen Palästina-Vereins*
Zebaḥ.	*Zebaḥim*
ZKT	*Zeitschrift für katholische Theologie*
ZNW	*Zeitschrift für die neutestamentliche Wissenschaft*
Zonar.	Zonaras
ZTK	*Zeitschrift für Theologie und Kirche*

Bibliography of Books Referred To

*(Excluding most primary sources
and well known books of reference)*

À cause de l'Évangile. J. Dupont FS. LD 123. Paris: Cerf, 1985.
Abraham unser Vater. O. Michel FS. Ed. O. Betz et al. AGJU 5. Leiden: Brill, 1963.
Abrahams, I. *Studies in Pharisaism and the Gospels.* LBS. New York: Ktav, 1967.
Achtemeier, P. J. *Mark.* 2nd ed. Proclamation Commentaries. Philadelphia: Fortress, 1986.
Aland, K. *Did the Early Church Baptize Infants?* LHD. Philadelphia: Westminster, 1963.
Aland, K. *Synopsis Quattor Evangeliorum.* 2nd ed. Stuttgart: Württembergische Bibelanstalt, 1964.
Aland, K. *Vollständige Konkordanz zum griechischen Neuen Testament.* Arbeiten zur neutestamentlichen Textforschung 4. Berlin: Walter de Gruyter, 1983.
Albertz, M. *Die synoptische Streitgespräche.* Berlin: Trowitzsch, 1921.
Allison, D. C., Jr. *The End of the Ages Has Come.* Philadelphia: Fortress, 1985.
Almquist, H. *Plutarch und das Neue Testament.* ASNU 15. Uppsala: Appelberg, 1946.
Alsup, J. E. *The Post-Resurrection Appearance Stories of the Gospel Tradition.* Calwer theologische Monographien: Reihe A, Bibelwissenschaft 5. Stuttgart: Calwer, 1975.
Alt, A. *Where Jesus Worked.* London: Epworth, 1961.
Alternative Approaches to New Testament Study. Ed. A. E. Harvey. London: SPCK, 1985.
Ambrozic, A. M. *The Hidden Kingdom.* CBQMS 2. Washington: Catholic Biblical Association of America, 1972.
Anderson, H. *The Gospel of Mark.* NCB. London: Oliphants, 1976.
Anfänge der Theologie. J. Bauer FS. Ed. N. Brox et al. Graz: Styria, 1987.
Annen, F. *Heil für die Heiden.* FTS 20. Frankfurt: Knecht, 1976.
L'Apocalypse johannique et l'Apocalyptique dans le Nouveau Testament. Ed. J. Lambrecht. BETL 53. Leuven: Leuven UP, 1980.

Apocalyptic in the New Testament. J. L. Martyn FS. Ed. J. Marcus and M. L. Soards. JSNTSup 24. Sheffield: JSOT, 1989.

Archer, G. L., and G. C. Chirichigno. *Old Testament Quotations in the New Testament.* Chicago: Moody, 1983.

Arens, E. *The ΗΛΘΟΝ-Sayings in the Synoptic Tradition.* OBO 10. Göttingen: Vandenhoeck & Ruprecht, 1976.

Attridge, H. W. *The Epistle to the Hebrews.* Hermeneia. Philadelphia: Fortress, 1989.

Aune, D. E. *The New Testament in its Literary Environment.* Library of Early Christianity 8. Philadelphia: Westminster, 1987.

Aune, D. E. *Prophecy in Early Christianity and the Ancient Mediterranean World.* Grand Rapids: Eerdmans, 1983.

Aus, R. *Water into Wine and the Beheading of John the Baptist.* BJS 150. Atlanta: Scholars, 1988.

Avi-Yonah, M. *The Holy Land.* 2nd ed. Grand Rapids: Baker, 1977.

Avigad, N. *Discovering Jerusalem.* Nashville: Nelson, 1983.

Baarlink, H. *Anfängliches Evangelium.* Kampen: Kok, 1977.

The Background of the New Testament and Its Eschatology. C. H. Dodd FS. Ed. W. D. Davies and D. Daube. Cambridge: Cambridge UP, 1956.

Bacon, B. W. *The Beginnings of the Gospel Story.* New Haven: Yale, 1909.

Bacon, B. W. *The Gospel of Mark.* New Haven: Yale, 1925.

Bagatti, B., and J. T. Milik. *Gli scavi del "Dominus Flevit."* Gerusalemme: Tipigrafia dei PP. Francescani, 1958.

Bailey, K. E. *Through Peasant Eyes.* Grand Rapids: Eerdmans, 1980.

Baird, J. A. *The Justice of God in the Teaching of Jesus.* Philadelphia: Westminster, 1963.

Baltensweiler, H. *Die Verklärung Jesu.* ATANT 33. Zürich: Zwingli, 1959.

Baly, D. *Geographical Companion to the Bible.* New York: McGraw-Hill, 1963.

Barclay, W. *Introduction to John and the Acts of the Apostles.* Philadelphia: Westminster, 1975.

Barclay, W. *Introduction to the First Three Gospels.* 2nd ed. Philadelphia: Westminster, 1975.

Barrett, C. K. *The Holy Spirit and the Gospel Tradition.* London: SPCK, 1966.

Barrett, C. K. *Jesus and the Gospel Tradition.* Philadelphia: Fortress, 1968.

Barrett, C. K. *New Testament Essays.* London: SPCK, 1972.

Barrett, C. K. *The Signs of an Apostle.* Cato Lecture. Philadelphia: Fortress, 1972.

Batey, R. A. *Jesus & the Forgotten City.* Grand Rapids: Baker, 1991.

Bauckham, R. J. *Jude, 2 Peter.* WBC 50. Waco: Word, 1983.

Bauernfeind, O. *Die Worte der Dämonen im Markusevangelium.* BWANT 44. Stuttgart: Kohlhammer, 1927.

". . . Bäume braucht man doch!" Ed. H. Schweizer. Sigmaringen: Thorbecke, 1986.

Bayer, H. F. *Jesus' Predictions of Vindication and Resurrection.* WUNT 2/20. Tübingen: Mohr, 1986.

Beasley-Murray, G. R. *Baptism in the New Testament.* Grand Rapids: Eerdmans, 1988.

Beasley-Murray, G. R. *A Commentary on Mark Thirteen.* New York: Macmillan, 1957.

Beasley-Murray, G. R. *Jesus and the Future.* New York: St. Martin's, 1954.

Beasley-Murray, G. R. *Jesus and the Kingdom of God.* Grand Rapids: Eerdmans, 1986.

Beavis, M. A. *Mark's Audience.* JSNTSup 33. Sheffield: JSOT, 1989.

Begegnung mit dem Wort. H. Zimmermann FS. Ed. J. Zmijewski and E. Nellessen. BBB 53. Bonn: Hanstein, 1980.

Beginnings of Christianity. Ed. F. J. Foakes-Jackson and K. Lake. Grand Rapids: Baker, 1979.

Ben-David, A. *Talmudische Ökonomie.* Hildesheim: Olms, 1974.

Benoit, P. *Jesus and the Gospel.* New York: Herder, 1973-74.

Berg, W. *Die Rezeption alttestamentlicher Motive im Neuen Testament — dargestellt an den Seewandelerzählungen.* HochschulSammlung Theologie, Exegese 1. Freiburg: HochschulVerlag, 1979.

Berger, K. *Die Amen-Worte Jesu.* BZNW 39. Berlin: Walter de Gruyter, 1970.

Berger, K. *Die Gesetzesauslegung Jesu.* Teil I: *Markus und Parallelen.* WMANT 40. Neukirchen-Vluyn: Neukirchener Verlag, 1972.

Best, E. *Disciples and Discipleship.* Edinburgh: T. & T. Clark, 1986.

Best, E. *Following Jesus.* JSNTSup 4. Sheffield: JSOT, 1981.

Best, E. *Mark: The Gospel as Story.* SNTW. Edinburgh: T. & T. Clark, 1983.

Best, E. *The Temptation and the Passion.* 2nd ed. SNTSMS 2. Cambridge: Cambridge UP, 1990.

Betz, H. D. *Lukian von Samosata und das Neue Testament.* TU 76. Berlin: Akademie, 1961.

Betz, O. *Jesus. Der Messias Israels.* WUNT 42. Tübingen: Mohr, 1987.

Betz, O., and W. Grimm. *Wesen und Wirklichkeit der Wunder Jesu.* Arbeiten zum Neuen Testament und Judentum 2. Frankfurt: Lang, 1977.

Beyer, K. *Die aramäischen Texte vom Toten Meer.* Göttingen: Vandenhoeck & Ruprecht, 1984.

Beyer, K. *Semitische Syntax im Neuen Testament* 1/1. 2. Aufl. SUNT 1. Göttingen: Vandenhoeck & Ruprecht, 1968.

The Bible and the Narrative Tradition. Ed. F. McConnell. New York: Oxford, 1986.

Biblical Studies: Essays in Honor of W. Barclay. Philadelphia: Westminster, 1976.

Bieler, L. *ΘΕΙΟΣ ANHP.* Verzeichnis der Abkürzungen in den Literaturangagen 1. Darmstadt: Wissenschaftliche Buchgesellschaft, 1967.

Bilezikian, G. G. *The Liberated Gospel.* Baker Biblical Monograph. Grand Rapids: Baker, 1977.

Bishop, E. F. F. *Jesus of Palestine.* London: Lutterworth, 1955.

Black, C. C. *The Disciples according to Mark.* JSNTSup 27. Sheffield: JSOT, 1989.

Black, M. *An Aramaic Approach to the Gospels and Acts.* 3rd ed. Oxford: Clarendon, 1967.

Black, M. *The Book of Enoch* or *I Enoch.* SVTP 7. Leiden: Brill, 1985.

Blackburn, B. *Theios Anēr and the Markan Miracle Traditions.* WUNT 2/40. Tübingen: Mohr, 1991.

Blass, F., A. Debrunner, and F. Rehkopf. *Grammatik des neutestamentlichen Griechisch.* 14. Aufl. Göttingen: Vandenhoeck & Ruprecht, 1976.

Blau, L. *Das altjüdische Zauberwesen.* Westmead, Farnborough, Hants., England: Gregg International, 1970.

Blinzler, J. *Der Prozess Jesu.* 4. Aufl. Regensburg: Pustet, 1969.

Blomberg, C. L. *Interpreting the Parables.* Downers Grove: InterVarsity, 1990.

Böcher, O. *Christus Exorcista.* BWANT 96. Stuttgart: Kohlhammer, 1972.

Böcher, O. *Dämonenfurcht und Dämonenabwehr.* BWANT 90. Stuttgart: Kohlhammer, 1970.

Böcher, O. *Das Neue Testament und die dämonischen Mächte.* SBS 58. Stuttgart: KBW, 1972.

Bode, E. L. *The First Easter Morning.* AnBib 45. Rome: Pontifical Biblical Institute, 1970.

Boman, T. *Jesus-Überlieferung im Lichte der neueren Volkskunde.* Göttingen: Vandenhoeck & Ruprecht, 1967.

Booth, R. P. *Jesus and the Laws of Purity.* JSNTSup 13. Sheffield: JSOT, 1986.

Booth, W. C. *A Rhetoric of Irony.* Chicago: University of Chicago, 1974.

Borg, M. J. *Conflict, Holiness & Politics in the Teachings of Jesus.* SBEC 5. New York: Mellen, 1984.

Boring, M. E. *Sayings of the Risen Jesus.* SNTSMS 46. Cambridge: Cambridge UP, 1982.

Boring, M. E. *Truly Human/Truly Divine.* St. Louis: CBP, 1984.

Bornhäuser, K. B. *Die Gebeine der Töten.* BFCT 26/3. Gütersloh: Bertelsmann, 1921.

Bornkamm, G. *Geschichte und Glaube.* BEvT 48. München: Kaiser, 1968.

Bornkamm, G. *Jesus of Nazareth.* New York: Harper, 1960.

Boucher, M. *The Mysterious Parable.* CBQMS 6. Washington: Catholic Biblical Association of America, 1977.

Bousset, W. *Kyrios Christos.* Nashville: Abingdon, 1970.

Bousset, W. *Die Religion des Judentums im späthellenistischen Zeitalter.* HNT 21. Tübingen: Mohr, 1926.

Bowker, J. W. *Jesus and the Pharisees.* London: Cambridge UP, 1973.

Bowker, J. W. *Religious Imagination and the Sense of God.* Oxford: Clarendon, 1978.

Bowman, J. W. *The Gospel of Mark.* SPB 8. Leiden: Brill, 1965.

Brandenberger, E. *Markus 13 und die Apokalyptik.* FRLANT 134. Göttingen: Vandenhoeck & Ruprecht, 1984.

Brandon, S. G. F. *Jesus and the Zealots.* New York: Scribner, 1967.

Branscomb, B. H. *The Gospel of Mark.* MNTC. New York: Harper, n.d.

Braude, W. G. *The Midrash on Psalms.* Yale Judaica Series 13. New Haven: Yale, 1959.

Braun, F.-M. *Jean le Théologien.* EBib. Paris: Gabalda, 1959-72.

Braun, H. *Qumran und das Neue Testament.* Tübingen: Mohr, 1966.

Breytenbach, C. *Nachfolge und Zukunftserwartung nach Markus.* ATANT 71. Zürich: Theologischer Verlag, 1984.

Brown, C. *Miracles and the Critical Mind.* Grand Rapids: Eerdmans, 1984.

Brown, R. E., and J. P. Meier. *Antioch and Rome.* New York: Paulist, 1983.

Brown, R. E. *The Birth of the Messiah.* Garden City: Doubleday, 1977.

Brown, R. E. *New Testament Essays.* 3rd ed. New York: Paulist, 1982.

Brown, R. E. *The Semitic Background of the Term "Mystery" in the New Testament.* FBBS 21. Philadelphia: Fortress, 1968.

Brown, R. E. *The Virginal Conception and Bodily Resurrection of Jesus.* New York: Paulist, 1973.

Brown, W. N. *The Indian and Christian Miracles of Walking on the Water.* Chicago: Open Court, 1928.

Bruce, F. F. *New Testament Development of Old Testament Themes.* Grand Rapids: Eerdmans, 1968.

Bruce, F. F. *The "Secret" Gospel of Mark.* Ethel M. Wood Lecture. London: Athlone, 1974.

Buchanan, G. W. *Jesus, the King and His Kingdom.* Macon: Mercer, 1984.

Buck, C. D. *A Dictionary of Selected Synonyms in the Principal Indo-European Languages.* Chicago: University of Chicago, 1949.

Bultmann, R. *The History of the Synoptic Tradition.* 2nd ed. Oxford: Blackwell, 1968.

Bultmann, R. *Jesus and the Word.* New York: Scribner, 1962.

Bureth, P. *Les Titulatures impériales dans les papyrus, les ostraca et les inscriptions d'Égypte (39 a.C.–284 p.C.).* Brussels: Fondation Égyptologique Reine Élisabeth, 1964.

Burger, C. *Jesus als Davidssohn.* FRLANT 98. Göttingen: Vandenhoeck & Ruprecht, 1970.

Burkill, T. A. *Mysterious Revelation.* Ithaca: Cornell UP, 1963.

Burkill, T. A. *New Light on the Earliest Gospel.* Ithaca: Cornell UP, 1972.

Burney, C. F. *The Aramaic Origin of the Fourth Gospel.* Oxford: Clarendon, 1922.

Busemann, R. *Die Jüngergemeinde nach Markus 10.* BBB 57. Königstein/Ts.-Bonn: Hanstein, 1983.

Cadbury, H. J. *The Making of Luke-Acts.* 2nd ed. London: SPCK, 1958.

Caird, G. B. *The Language and Imagery of the Bible.* Philadelphia: Westminster, 1980.

Cameron, R. *Sayings Traditions in the Apocryphon of James.* HTS 34. Philadelphia: Fortress, 1984.

Campenhausen, H. F. von. *Tradition and Life in the Church.* Philadelphia: Fortress, 1968.

Cangh, J.-M. van. *La multiplication des pains et l'Eucharistie.* LD 86. Paris: Cerf, 1975.

Caragounis, C. C. *Peter and the Rock.* BZNW 58. Berlin: Walter de Gruyter, 1989.

Caragounis, C. C. *The Son of Man.* WUNT 38. Tübingen: Mohr, 1986.

Carlston, C. E. *The Parables of the Triple Tradition.* Philadelphia: Fortress, 1975.

Carrington, P. *According to Mark.* Cambridge: Cambridge UP, 1960.

Casey, M. *Son of Man.* London: SPCK, 1979.

Catchpole, D. R. *The Trial of Jesus.* SPB 18. Leiden: Brill, 1971.

Childs, B. S. *Exodus.* OTL. London: SCM, 1974.

Chilton, B. D. *A Galilean Rabbi and His Bible.* GNS 8. Wilmington: Glazier, 1984.

Chilton, B. D. *God in Strength.* SNTU B/1. Freistadt: Plöchl, 1979.

Chilton, B. D. *Profiles of a Rabbi.* BJS 177. Atlanta: Scholars Press, 1989.

Christ the Lord. D. Guthrie FS. Ed. H. H. Rowdon. Downers Grove: Inter-Varsity, 1982.

Christian History and Interpretation. J. Knox FS. Ed. W. R. Farmer et al. Cambridge: Cambridge UP, 1967.

Christianity, Judaism and Other Greco-Roman Cults. M. Smith FS. SJLA 12. Leiden: Brill, 1975.

Christie, W. M. *Palestine Calling.* London: Pickering & Inglis, n.d.

Christology and a Modern Pilgrimage. Ed. H. D. Betz. Missoula: Society of Biblical Literature, 1971.

Church, I. F. *A Study of the Marcan Gospel.* New York: Vantage, 1976.

Clark, K. W. *The Gentile Bias and Other Essays.* NovTSup 54. Leiden: Brill, 1980.

Clarke, W. K. L. *New Testament Problems.* New York: Macmillan, 1929.

Clévenot, M. *Materialist Approaches to the Bible.* Maryknoll: Orbis, 1985.

Cole, R. A. *The Gospel According to St. Mark.* Tyndale New Testament Commentaries. Grand Rapids: Eerdmans, 1961.

Colin, J. *Les villes libres de l'Orient gréco-romain et l'envoi au supplice par acclamations populaires.* Collection Latomus 82. Bruxelles-Berchem: Latomus, Revue d'Études Latines, 1965.

Colloquy on New Testament Studes. Ed. B. C. Corley. Macon: Mercer UP, 1983.

Cook, M. J. *Mark's Treatment of the Jewish Leaders.* NovTSup 51. Leiden: Brill, 1978.

Coulot, C. *Jésus et le disciple.* EBib ns 8. Paris: Gabalda, 1987.

Craig, W. L. *The Historical Argument for the Resurrection of Jesus during the Deist Controversy.* Texts and Studies in Religion 23. Lewiston: Mellen, 1985.

Cranfield, C. E. B. *The Gospel according to Saint Mark.* Cambridge Greek Testament Commentary. Cambridge: Cambridge UP, 1959 (1960).

Critical History and Biblical Faith: New Testament Perspectives. Ed. T. J. Ryan. Annual Publications of the College Theological Society. Villanova: College Theological Society, 1979.

Crossan, J. D. *Cliffs of Fall.* New York: Seabury, 1980.

Crossan, J. D. *The Cross That Spoke.* San Francisco: Harper & Row, 1988.

Crossan, J. D. *Four Other Gospels.* Minneapolis: Winston, 1985.

Crossan, J. D. *In Fragments.* San Francisco: Harper & Row, 1983.

Cullmann, O. *Baptism in the New Testament.* SBT 1/1. London: SCM, 1950.

Cullmann, O. *Vorträge und Aufsätze, 1925-1962.* Tübingen: Mohr/Zürich: Zwingli, 1966.

Dalman, G. H. *Grammatik des·jüdisch-palästinischen Aramäisch.* Darmstadt: Wissenschaftliche Buchgesellschaft, 1960.

Dalman, G. H. *Jesus-Jeshua.* New York: Ktav, 1971.

Dalman, G. H. *Sacred Sites and Ways.* New York: Macmillan, 1935.

Dalman, G. H. *The Words of Jesus.* Edinburgh: T. & T. Clark, 1902.

Dana, H. E., and J. R. Mantey. *A Manual Grammar of the Greek New Testament.* New York: Macmillan, 1927.

Danby, H. *The Mishnah.* Oxford: Oxford UP, 1933.

Danker, F. W. *Benefactor.* St. Louis: Clayton, 1982.

Daube, D. *Appeasement or Resistance.* Berkeley: University of California, 1987.

Daube, D. *The New Testament and Rabbinic Judaism.* Salem, NH: Ayer, 1984.

Dautzenberg, G. *Sein Leben bewahren.* SANT 14. München: Kösel, 1966.

Davies, W. D. *Christian Origins and Judaism.* Philadelphia: Westminster, 1962.

Davies, W. D. *The Gospel and the Land.* Berkeley: University of California, 1974.

De Jésus aux Évangiles. Ed. I. de la Potterie. BETL 25. Gembloux: Duculot, 1967.

De la Tôrah au Messie. H. Cazelles FS. Ed. M. Carrey et al. Paris: Desclée, 1981.

De Septuaginta. J. W. Wevers FS. Ed. A. Pietersma and C. Cox. Mississauga: Benben, 1984.

Deissmann, A. *Bible Studies.* 2nd ed. Edinburgh: T. & T. Clark, 1909.

Deissmann, A. *Light from the Ancient East.* 2nd English ed. New York: Doran, 1927.

Derrett, J. D. M. *Jesus's Audience.* New York: Seabury, 1973

Derrett, J. D. M. *Law in the New Testament.* London: Darton, Longman & Todd, 1970.

Derrett, J. D. M. *The Making of Mark.* Shipston-on-Stour: Drinkwater, 1984.

Derrett, J. D. M. *An Oriental Lawyer Looks at the Trial of Jesus and the Doctrine of Redemption.* London: School of Oriental and African Studies, 1966.

Derrett, J. D. M. *Studies in the New Testament.* Vols. 1, 4. Leiden: Brill, 1977, 1986.

Dewey, J. *Markan Public Debate.* SBLDS 48. Chico: Scholars, 1980.

Diakonia. B. Stogiannos Memorial Volume. Thessalonica: University of Thessalonica, 1988.

Dibelius, M. *Botschaft und Geschichte.* Vol. 1. Tübingen: Mohr, 1953.

Dibelius, M. *From Tradition to Gospel.* Library of Theological Translations. Cambridge: James Clarke, 1971.

Dieterich, A. *Abraxas.* H. Usener FS. Leipzig: Teubner, 1905.

Dieterich, A. *Eine Mithrasliturgie.* 3. Aufl. Leipzig: Teubner, 1966.

Discipleship in the New Testament. Ed. F. F. Segovia. Philadelphia: Fortress, 1985.

Dodd, C. H. *Historical Tradition in the Fourth Gospel.* London: Cambridge UP, 1963.

Dodd, C. H. *The Interpretation of the Fourth Gospel.* Cambridge: Cambridge UP, 1960.

Dodd, C. H. *The Parables of the Kingdom.* New York: Scribner, 1958.

Dodds, E. R. *The Greeks and the Irrational.* Sather Classical Lectures 25. Berkeley: University of California, 1951.

Donahue, J. R. *Are You the Christ?* SBLDS 10. Missoula: SBL, 1973.

Donahue, J. R. *The Gospel in Parable.* Philadelphia: Fortress, 1988.

Donahue, J. R. *The Theology and Setting of Discipleship in the Gospel of Mark.* The 1983 Père Marquette Theology Lecture. Milwaukee: Marquette, 1983.

Donaldson, T. L. *Jesus on the Mountain.* JSNTSup 8. Sheffield: JSOT, 1985.

Donum Gentilicium. D. Daube FS. Ed. E. Bammel et al. Oxford: Clarendon, 1978.

Dormeyer, D. *Evangelium als literarische und theologische Gattung.* Erträge der Forschung 263. Darmstadt: Wissenschaftliche Buchgesellschaft, 1989.

Dormeyer, D. *Die Passion Jesu als Verhaltensmodell.* NTAbh nf 11. Münster: Aschendorff, 1974.

Dormeyer, D. *Der Sinn des Leidens Jesu.* SBS 96. Stuttgart: KBW, 1979.

Doudna, J. C. *The Greek of the Gospel of Mark.* JBLMS 12. Philadelphia: Society of Biblical Literature, 1961.

Dowd, S. E. *Prayer, Power, and the Problem of Suffering.* SBLDS 105. Atlanta: Scholars, 1988.

Downing, F. G. *Christ and the Cynics.* JSOT Manuals 4. Sheffield: JSOT, 1988.

Dschulnigg, P. *Sprache, Redaktion und Intention des Markus-Evangeliums.* SBB 11. Stuttgart: KBW, 1984.

Dungan, D. L. *The Sayings of Jesus in the Churches of Paul.* Philadelphia: Fortress, 1971.

Dunn, J. D. G. *The Evidence for Jesus.* Philadelphia: Westminster, 1985.

Dunn, J. D. G. *Jesus and the Spirit.* NTL. London: SCM, 1975.

Dunn, J. D. G. *Romans 1–8, Romans 9–16.* WBC 38a, 38b. Dallas: Word, 1988.

Dunn, J. D. G. *Unity and Diversity in the New Testament.* 2nd ed. London: SCM/Philadelphia: Trinity, 1990.

Dupont, J. *Études sur les évangiles synoptiques.* BETL 70-A. Leuven: Leuven UP, 1985.

Dürr, L. *Die Wertung des göttlichen Wortes im Alten Testament und im antiken Orient.* MVAG (E.V.) 42/1. Leipzig: Hinrichs, 1938.

Dynamik im Wort. Stuttgart: KBW, 1983.

Early Jewish and Christian Exegesis. Studies in Memory of W. H. Brownlee. Ed. C. A. Evans and W. F. Stinespring. Homage Series 10. Atlanta: Scholars, 1987.

Ebeling, H. J. *Das Messiasgeheimnis und die Botschaft des Marcus-Evangelium.* BZNW 19. Berlin: Töpelmann, 1939.

Edwards, R. A. *The Sign of Jonah in the Theology of the Evangelists and Q.* SBT 2/18. London: SCM, 1971.

Egger, W. *Frohbotschaft und Lehre.* FTS 19. Frankfurt: Knecht, 1976.

Egger, W. *Nachfolge als Weg zum Leben.* ÖBS 1. Klosterneuberg: KBW, 1979.

Eissfeldt, O. *Kleine Schriften.* Vols. 2-3. Tübingen: Mohr, 1963-66.

Eitrem, S. *Some Notes on the Demonology in the New Testament.* 2nd ed. SO Fasc. Supplet. 20. Oslo: University Press, 1966.

Elliott, J. K. *Questioning Christian Origins.* London: SCM, 1982.

Ernst, J. *Das Evangelium nach Markus.* RNT. Regensburg: Pustet, 1981.

Ernst, J. *Johannes Taufer.* BZNW 53. Berlin: Walter de Gruyter, 1989.

Der Erzähler des Evangeliums. Ed. F. Hahn. SBS 118/119. Stuttgart: KBW, 1985.

Essays in Honour of Yigael Yadin. Ed. G. Vermes and J. Neusner. Totowa: Allan-held, Osmun, 1983. (= *JJS* 33 [1982])

Essays on the Love Commandment. Philadelphia: Fortress, 1978.

Essays presented to Chief Rabbi Israel Brodie on the occasion of his seventieth Birthday. Ed. H. J. Zimmels et al. Jew's College Publications ns 3. London: Soncino, 1967(1968).

L'Évangile selon Marc. Ed. M. Sabbe. BETL 34. Leuven: Leuven UP, 1974.

Evangelienforschung. Ed. J. B. Bauer. Graz: Styria, 1968.

Das Evangelium und die Evangelien. Ed. P. Stuhlmacher. WUNT 28. Tübingen: Mohr, 1983.

Evans, C. A. *To See and Not Perceive.* JSOTSup 64. Sheffield: JSOT, 1989.

Evans, C. F. *Resurrection and the New Testament.* London: SCM, 1970.

Evans-Pritchard, E. E. *Nuer Religion.* Oxford: Clarendon, 1956.

Fanning, B. M. *Verbal Aspect in New Testament Greek.* OTM. Oxford: Clarendon, 1990.

Farla, P. J. *Jezus' Oordeel over Israel.* Kampen: Kok, 1978.

Farmer, W. R. *The Last Twelve Verses of Mark.* SNTSMS 25. Cambridge: Cambridge UP, 1974.

Farmer, W. R. *The Synoptic Problem.* New York: Macmillan, 1964.

Farrer, A. M. *The Glass of Vision.* Bampton Lectures. Westminster: Dacre, 1948.

Fee, G. D. *The First Epistle to the Corinthians.* NICNT. Grand Rapids: Eerdmans, 1987.

Feldmeier, R. *Die Krisis des Gottessohnes.* WUNT 2/21. Tübingen: Mohr, 1987.

Festschrift für Ernst Fuchs. Ed. G. Ebeling et al. Tübingen: Mohr, 1973.

Feuillet, A. *L'agonie de Gethsémani.* Paris: Gabalda, 1977.

Fiebig, P. *Der Erzählungsstil der Evangelien.* UNT 11. Leipzig: Hinrichs, 1925.

Fiebig, P. *Jüdische Wundergeschichten des neutestamentlichen Zeitalters.* Tübingen: Mohr, 1911.

Fiedler, W. *Antiker Wetterzauber.* Würzburger Studien zur altertumswissenschaft . . . 1. Stuttgart: Kohlhammer, 1931.

Field, F. *Notes on the Translation of the New Testament.* Cambridge: Cambridge UP, 1899.

Finegan, J. *Hidden Records of the Life of Jesus.* Philadelphia: Pilgrim, 1969.

Finkel, A. *The Pharisees and the Teacher of Nazareth.* 2nd ed. AGJU 4. Leiden: Brill, 1974.

Finney, C. G. *Memoirs.* New York: Barnes, 1876.

Fiorenza, E. S. *In Memory of Her.* New York: Crossroad, 1984.

Fitzmyer, J. A. *The Dead Sea Scrolls: Major Publications and Tools for Study.* SBLSBS 20. Missoula: Scholars 1990.

Fitzmyer, J. A. *Essays on the Semitic Background of the New Testament.* SBLSBS 5. Missoula: Scholars, 1974.

Fitzmyer, J. A. *The Gospel According to Luke.* AB 28, 28A. Garden City: Doubleday, 1981-85.

Fitzmyer, J. A. *To Advance the Gospel.* New York: Crossroad, 1981.

Fitzmyer, J. A. *A Wandering Aramean.* SBLMS 25. Missoula: Scholars, 1981.

Flusser, D. *Jesus.* New York: Herder, 1969.

Flusser, D. *Jewish Sources in Early Christianity.* New York: Adama, 1987.

Ford, D. *The Abomination of Desolation in Biblical Eschatology.* Washington, D. C.: University Press of America, 1979.

The Four Gospels 1992. F. Neirynck FS. Leuven: Leuven UP, 1992.

Fowler, R. M. *Loaves and Fishes.* SBLDS 54. Chico: Scholars, 1981.

France, R. T. *Jesus and the Old Testament.* London: Tyndale, 1971.

Frankemölle, H. *Evangelium — Begriff und Gattung.* SBB 15. Stuttgart: KBW, 1988.

Freedman, H., and M. Simon. *Midrash Rabbah.* London: Soncino, 1961.

Frey, J.-B. *Corpus Inscriptionum Iudaicarum.* Vol. 1: *Europe.* Roma: Pontificio Istituto di Archeologia Cristiana, 1936.

Freyne, S. *Galilee from Alexander the Great to Hadrian 323 B.C.E. to 135 C.E.* Wilmington: Glazier/Notre Dame: Notre Dame UP, 1980.

Fridrichsen, A. J. *The Problem of Miracle in Primitive Christianity.* Minneapolis: Augsburg, 1972.

Fructus Centesimus. G. J. M. Bartelink FS. Ed. A. A. R. Bastiaensen et al. Instrumenta Patristica 19. Dordrecht: Kluwer, 1989.

Fuller, R. H. *The Formation of the Resurrection Narratives.* Philadelphia: Fortress, 1980.

Fuller, R. H. *Interpreting the Miracles.* Philadelphia: Westminster, 1963.

Fuller, R. H. *The Mission and Achievement of Jesus.* SBT 1/12. London: SCM, 1967.

Funk, R. W. *Jesus as Precursor.* Semeia Supplements 2. Philadelphia: Fortress, 1975.

Funk, R. W. *The Poetics of Biblical Narrative.* FFLF. Sonoma: Polebridge, 1988.

Furnish, V. P. *The Love Command in the New Testament.* Nashville: Abingdon, 1972.

The Future of Our Religious Past. R. Bultmann FS. New York: Harper & Row, 1971.

Garrucci, R. *Storia della Arte Cristiana.* Prato: Guesti, 1872-81.

Gaston, L. *No Stone on Another.* NovTSup 23. Leiden: Brill, 1970.

Geddert, T. J. *Watchwords: Mark 13 in Markan Eschatology.* JSNTSup 26. Sheffield: JSOT, 1989.

Georgi, D. *The Opponents of Paul in Second Corinthians.* Philadelphia: Fortress, 1986.

Gerhardsson, B. *The Ethos of the Bible.* Philadelphia: Fortress, 1981.

Gerhardsson, B. *The Gospel Tradition.* ConBNT 15. Malmö: Gleerup, 1986.

Gerhardsson, B. *Tradition and Transmission in Early Christianity.* ConNT 20. Lund: Gleerup, 1964.

Gerleman, G. *Esther.* 2. Aufl. BKAT 21. Neukirchen-Vluyn: Neukirchener Verlag, 1982.

Gese, H. *Essays on Biblical Theology.* Minneapolis: Augsburg, 1981.

Giesen, H. *Glaube und Handeln.* EH 23/205. Frankfurt: Lang, 1983.

Glaube im Neuen Testament. H. Binder FS. Ed. F. Hahn and H. Klein. Biblisch-theologische Studien 7. Neukirchen-Vluyn: Neukirchener Verlag, 1982.

Glaube und Eschatologie. W. G. Kümmel FS. Ed. E. Grässer and O. Merk. Tübingen: Mohr, 1985.

Glaube und Gerechtigkeit. In memoriam R. Gyllenberg. Ed. J. Kiilunen et al. SFEG 38. Helsinki: Vammalan Kirjapaino Oy, 1983.

Glöckner, R. *Neutestamentliche Wundergeschichten und das Lob der Wundertaten Gottes in den Psalmen.* Walberger Studien der Albertus-Magnus-Akademie, Theologische Reihe 13. Mainz: Grünewald, 1983.

The Glory of Christ in the New Testament. Studies in memory of G. B. Caird. Ed. L. D. Hurst and N. T. Wright. Oxford: Clarendon, 1987.

Gnilka, J. *Das Evangelium nach Markus.* EKKNT II/1, 2. Zürich: Benziger/Neukirchen-Vluyn: Neukirchener Verlag, 1978-79.

God's Christ and His People. N. A. Dahl FS. Ed. J. Jervell and W. A. Meeks. Oslo: Universitetsforl., 1977.

Goldin, J. *The Song at the Sea.* New Haven: Yale UP, 1971.

Goodspeed, E. J. *Problems of New Testament Translation.* Chicago: University of Chicago, 1945.

Goppelt, L. *Jesus, Paul, and Judaism.* London: T. Nelson, 1964.

Goppelt, L. *Theology of the New Testament.* Grand Rapids: Eerdmans, 1981-82.

Goppelt, L. *Typos.* Grand Rapids: Eerdmans, 1982.

Gospel Perspectives 1-2. Studies of History and Tradition in the Four Gospels. Ed. R. T. France and D. Wenham. Sheffield: JSOT, 1980-81.

Gospel Perspectives 5. The Jesus Tradition Outside the Gospels. Ed. D. Wenham. Sheffield: JSOT, 1985.

Gospel Perspectives 6. The Miracles of Jesus. Ed. D. Wenham and C. Blomberg. Sheffield: JSOT, 1986.

Gospel Traditions in the Second Century. Ed. W. L. Petersen. Christianity and Judaism in Antiquity 3. Notre Dame: University of Notre Dame, 1989.

Gould, E. P. *A Critical and Exegetical Commentary on the Gospel according to St. Mark.* ICC. Edinburgh: T. & T. Clark, 1912.

Gourges, M. *À la droite de Dieu.* EBib. Paris: Gabalda, 1978.

Grant, F. C. *The Earliest Gospel.* The Cole Lectures for 1943. Nashville: Abingdon, 1943.

Grant, R. M., and D. N. Freedman. *The Secret Sayings of Jesus.* Garden City: Doubleday, 1960.

Greco-Roman Literature and the New Testament. Ed. D. E. Aune. SBLSBS 21. Atlanta: Scholars, 1988.

Green, J. B. *The Death of Jesus.* WUNT 2/33. Tübingen: Mohr, 1988.

Gregg, D. W. A. *Anamnesis in the Eucharist.* Grove Liturgical Study 5. Bramcote: Grove, 1976.

Grelot, P. *Les Paroles de Jésus Christ.* Introduction critique au Nouveau Testament 7. Paris: Desclée, 1986.

Gressmann, H. *Altorientalische Texte zum alten Testament.* 2. Aufl. Berlin: Walter de Gruyter, 1926.

Grimm, W. *Die Verkündigung Jesu und Deuterojesaja.* 2. Aufl. Arbeiten zum Neuen Testament und Judentum 1. Frankfurt: Lang, 1983.

Grundmann, W. *Das Evangelium nach Markus.* 2. Aufl., 7. Aufl. THKNT 2. Berlin: Evangelische Verlaganstalt, 1959, 1977.

Guelich, R. A. *Mark.* WBC 34a. Dallas: Word, 1989.

Gundry, R. H. *Matthew.* Grand Rapids: Eerdmans, 1982.

Gundry, R. H. *Sōma in Biblical Theology.* SNTSMS 29. Cambridge: Cambridge UP, 1976.

Gundry, R. H. *The Use of the Old Testament in St. Matthew's Gospel.* NovTSup 18. Leiden: Brill, 1967.

H. L. Ginsberg Volume. Ed. M. Haran. Eretz-Israel 14. Jerusalem: Israel Exploration Society in cooperation with the Jewish Theological Seminary of America, 1978.

Haenchen, E. *Die Bibel und wir.* Tübingen: Mohr, 1968.

Haenchen, E. *Gott und Mensch.* Tübingen: Mohr, 1965.

Haenchen, E. *Der Weg Jesu* [= a commentary on Mark]. Sammlung Töpelmann 2/6. Berlin: Töpelmann, 1966.

Hahn, F. *Mission in the New Testament.* SBT 1/47. London: SCM, 1965.

Hahn, F. *The Titles of Jesus in Christology.* LL. New York: World, 1969.

Hammerton-Kelly, R. *God the Father.* Overtures to Biblical Theology. Philadelphia: Fortress, 1979.

Hare, D. R. A. *The Son of Man Tradition.* Minneapolis: Fortress, 1990.

Hare, D. R. A. *The Theme of Jewish Persecution of Christians in the Gospel according to St. Matthew.* SNTSMS 6. Cambridge: Cambridge UP, 1967.

Harner, P. B. *The "I Am" of the Fourth Gospel.* FBBS 26. Philadelphia: Fortress, 1970.

Harrington, W. *Mark.* New Testament Message 4. Wilmington: Glazier, 1979.

Harris, M. J. *Raised Immortal.* Grand Rapids: Eerdmans, 1983.

Harry M. Orlinsky Volume. Ed. B. A. Levine and A. Malamat. Eretz-Israel 16. Jerusalem: Israel Exploration Society, 1982.

Hartman, L. *Prophecy Interpreted.* ConBNT 1. Lund: Gleerup, 1966.

Harvey, A. E. *Jesus and the Constraints of History.* Philadelphia: Westminster, 1982.

Hatch, E. *Essays in Biblical Greek.* Amsterdam: Philo, 1970.

Hay, D. M. *Glory at the Right Hand.* SBLMS 18. Nashville: Abingdon, 1973.

Heil, J. P. *Jesus Walking on the Sea.* AnBib 87. Rome: Pontifical Biblical Institute, 1981.

Helm, R. *Die Chronik des Hieronymus.* 2. Aufl. GCS 7. Berlin: Akademie-Verlag, 1956.

Hemer, C. J. *The Book of Acts in the Setting of Hellenistic History.* WUNT 49. Tübingen: Mohr, 1989.

Hempel, J. *Heilung als Symbol und Wirklichkeit im biblischen Schriften.* 2. Aufl. Göttingen: Vandenhoeck & Ruprecht, 1965.

Hengel, M. *Acts and the History of Earliest Christianity.* Fortress: Philadelphia, 1980.

Hengel, M. *The Atonement.* Philadelphia: Fortress, 1981.

Hengel, M. *Between Jesus and Paul.* Philadelphia: Fortress, 1983.

Hengel, M. *The Charismatic Leader and His Followers.* New York: Crossroad, 1981.

Hengel, M. *Crucifixion in the Ancient World and the Folly of the Message of the Cross.* Philadelphia: Fortress, 1977.

Hengel, M. *Judaism and Hellenism.* Philadelphia: Fortress, 1974.

Hengel, M. *The Son of God.* Philadelphia: Fortress, 1976.

Hengel, M. *Studies in the Gospel of Mark.* Philadelphia: Fortress, 1985.

Hengel, M. *The Zealots.* Edinburgh: T. & T. Clark, 1989.

Herzog, R. *Die Wunderheilungen von Epidauros.* Philologus Supplement 22/3. Leipzig: Dieterich, 1931.

Higgins, A. J. B. *Jesus and the Son of Man.* Philadelphia: Fortress, 1964.

Higgins, A. J. B. *The Tradition About Jesus.* Scottish Journal of Theology Occasional Papers 15. Edinburgh: Oliver & Boyd, 1969.

Hill, D. *New Testament Prophecy.* New Foundations Theological Library. Atlanta: Knox, 1979.

Historicity and Chronology in the New Testament. Theological Collections 6. London: SPCK, 1965.

Der historische Jesus und der kerygmatische Christus. 3. Aufl. Ed. H. Ristow and K. Matthiae. Berlin: Evangelische Verlaganstalt, 1964.

Hock, R. F., and E. N. O'Neill. *The Chreia in Ancient Rhetoric.* Vol. I. *The Progymnasmata.* Texts and Translations 27; Graeco-Roman Series 9. Atlanta: Scholars, 1986.

Hoehner, H. W. *Chronological Aspects of the Life of Christ.* CEP. Grand Rapids: Zondervan, 1977.

Hoehner, H. W. *Herod Antipas.* SNTSMS 17. London: Cambridge UP, 1972.

Holleran, J. W. *The Synoptic Gethsemane.* Analecta Gregoriana 191. Rome: Gregorian University, 1973.

Holtzmann, H. J. *Die Synoptiker-Die Apostelgeschichte.* 2. Aufl. HKNT 1. Freiburg: Mohr, 1892.

Hooker, M. D. *Jesus and the Servant.* London: SPCK, 1959.

Hooker, M. D. *The Message of Mark.* London: Epworth, 1983.

Hooker, M. D. *The Son of Man in Mark.* London: SPCK, 1967.

Hopfner, T. *Griechisch-ägyptischer Offenbarungszauber.* Studien zur Palaeographie und Papyruskunde 21. Amsterdam: Hakkert, 1974.

Horsley, R. A., and J. S. Hanson. *Bandits, Prophets, and Messiahs.* NVBS. Minneapolis: Winston, 1985.

Horstmann, M. *Studien zur Markanischen Christologie.* 2. Aufl. NTAbh nf 6. Münster: Aschendorff, 1973.

Houlden, J. L. *Backward into Light.* London: SCM, 1987.

Hübner, H. *Das Gesetz in der synoptischen Tradition.* Witten: Luther, 1973.
Huck, A., and H. Greeven. *Synopsis of the First Three Gospels.* 13th ed. Tübingen: Mohr, 1981.
Hull, J. M. *Hellenistic Magic and the Synoptic Tradition.* SBT 2/28. London: SCM, 1974.
Hultgren, A. J. *Jesus and His Adversaries.* Minneapolis: Augsburg, 1979.
Iersel, B. M. F. van. *Reading Mark.* Collegeville: Liturgical Press, 1988.
The Interpretation of Mark. Ed. W. Telford. IRT 7. Philadelphia: Fortress/London: SPCK, 1985.
Intertextuality in Biblical Writings. B. M. F. van Iersel FS. Ed. S. Draisma. Kampen: Kok, 1989.
Jastrow, M. *A Dictionary of the Targumim, the Talmud Babli and Yerushalmi, and the Midrashic Literature.* Brooklyn: Shalom, 1967.
Jeremias, J. *Abba.* Göttingen: Vandenhoeck & Ruprecht, 1966.
Jeremias, J. *The Central Message of the New Testament.* New York: Scribner, 1965.
Jeremias, J. *The Eucharistic Words of Jesus.* London: SCM, 1990.
Jeremias, J. *Heiligengräber in Jesu Umwelt (Mt. 23, 29; Lk. 11, 47).* Göttingen: Vandenhoeck & Ruprecht, 1958.
Jeremias, J. *Infant Baptism in the First Four Centuries.* LHD. Philadelphia: Westminster, 1962.
Jeremias, J. *Jerusalem in the Time of Jesus.* 3rd ed. London: SCM, 1969.
Jeremias, J. *Jesus' Promise to the Nations.* 2nd ed. SBT 1/24. London: SCM, 1967.
Jeremias, J. *Jesus als Weltvollender.* BFCT 33/4. Gütersloh: "Der Rufer" Evangelischer Verlag, Herman Werner Nachf., 1929.
Jeremias, J. *New Testament Theology.* New York: Macmillan, 1971.
Jeremias, J. *The Parables of Jesus.* 2nd English ed. New York: Scribner, 1963.
Jeremias, J. *Unknown Sayings of Jesus.* New York: Macmillan, 1957.
Jerusalem Revealed. Ed. Y. Yadin. New Haven: Yale UP/London: Israel Exploration Society, 1976.
Jesu Rede von Gott und ihre Nachgeschichte im frühen Christentum. W. Marxsen FS. Ed. D.-A. Koch et al. Gütersloh: Mohn, 1989.
Jesus and the Politics of His Day. Ed. E. Bammel and C. F. D. Moule. Cambridge: Cambridge UP, 1984.
Jésus aux origenes de la christologie. 2nd ed. BETL 40. Leuven: Leuven UP, 1989.
Jesus Christus in Historie und Theologie. H. Conzelmann FS. Ed. G. Strecker. Tübingen: Mohr, 1975.
Jesus und der Menschensohn. A. Vögtle FS. Ed. R. Pesch and R. Schnackenburg. Freiburg: Herder, 1975.
Jesus und Paulus. W. G. Kümmel FS. 2. Aufl. Ed. E. E. Ellis and E. Grässer. Göttingen: Vandenhoeck & Ruprecht, 1978.
Jewett, P. K. *Infant Baptism and the Covenant of Grace.* Grand Rapids: Eerdmans, 1978.

The Jewish People in the First Century. Ed. S. Safrai and M. Stern in co-operation with D. Flusser and W. C. van Unnik. Philadelphia: Fortress, 1974.

Jirku, A. *Materialen zur Volksreligion Israels.* Leipzig: Deichert, 1914.

Jones, A. H. M. *The Cities of the Eastern Roman Provinces.* 2nd ed. Oxford: Clarendon, 1971.

Joüon, P. *L'Évangile de Notre-Seigneur Jésus-Christ.* VS 5. Paris: Beauchesne, 1930.

Joüon, P. *Grammaire de l'hébreu biblique.* Rome: Pontifical Biblical Institute, 1965.

The Joy of Study. F. C. Grant FS. Ed. S. E. Johnson. New York: Macmillan, 1951.

Judentum, Urchristentum, Kirche. J. Jeremias FS. Ed. W. Eltester. BZNW 26. Berlin: Töpelmann, 1964.

Juel, D. *Messiah and Temple.* SBLDS 31. Missoula: Scholars, 1977.

Juel, D. *Messianic Exegesis.* Philadelphia: Fortress, 1988.

Kahle, P. *The Cairo Geniza.* 2nd ed. Oxford: Blackwell, 1959.

Kahle, P. *Masoreten des Westens.* Stuttgart: Kohlhammer, 1927-33.

Kallas, J. *Jesus and the Power of Satan.* Philadelphia: Fortress, 1968.

Kato, Z. *Die Völkermission im Markusevangelium.* EH 23/252. Bern: Lang, 1986.

Kazmierski, C. R. *Jesus, the Son of God.* 2. Aufl. FB 33. Würzburg: Echter, 1982.

Kealy, S. P. *Mark's Gospel: A History of its Interpretation.* New York: Paulist, 1982.

Kearns, R. *Das Traditionsgefüge um den Menschensohn.* Tübingen: Mohr, 1986.

Kee, H. C. *Community of the New Age.* Philadelphia: Westminster, 1977.

Kee, H. C. *Medicine, Miracle, and Magic in the New Testament Times.* SNTSMS 55. Cambridge: Cambridge UP, 1988.

Kee, H. C. *Miracle in the Early Christian World.* New Haven: Yale UP, 1983.

Keil, C. F., and F. Delitzsch. *Biblical Commentary on the Books of Samuel.* Grand Rapids: Eerdmans, 1956.

Kelber, W. H. *The Kingdom in Mark.* Philadelphia: Fortress, 1974.

Kelber, W. H. *Mark's Story of Jesus.* Philadelphia: Fortress, 1979.

Kelber, W. H. *The Oral and Written Gospel.* Philadelphia: Fortress, 1983.

Kenyon, F. G., and H. I. Bell. *Greek Papyri in the British Museum.* London: British Museum, 1893-1917.

Kermode, F. *The Genesis of Secrecy.* The Charles Eliot Norton Lectures. Cambridge, MA: Harvard UP, 1979.

Kertelge, K. *Die Wunder Jesu im Markusevangelium.* SANT 23. München: Kösel, 1970.

Kiilunen, J. *Das Doppelgebot der Liebe in synoptischer Sicht.* Suomalaisen Tiedeakatemian Toimituksia Annales Academiae Scientiarum Fennicae Sarja-ser. B nide-tom. 250. Helsinki: Suomalainen Tiedeakatemia, 1989.

Kiilunen, J. *Die Vollmacht im Widerstreit.* Annales Academiae Scientiarum Fennicae Dissertationes Humanarum Litterarum 40. Helsinki: Suomalainen Tiedeakatemia, 1985.

Kim, S. *The "Son of Man" as the Son of God.* Grand Rapids: Eerdmans, 1985(1983).

The Kingdom of God in the Teaching of Jesus. Ed. B. Chilton. IRT 5. Philadelphia: Fortress, 1984.

Kingsbury, J. D. *The Christology of Mark's Gospel.* Philadelphia: Fortress, 1983.

Kingsbury, J. D. *Conflict in Mark.* Minneapolis: Fortress, 1989.

Kirche. G. Bornkamm FS. Ed. D. Lührmann and G. Strecker. Tübingen: Mohr, 1980.

Kirschenbaum, A. *Self Incrimination.* New York: Burning Bush, 1970.

Klauck, H.-J. *Allegorie und Allegorese in synoptischen Gleichnistexten.* NTAbh nf 13. Münster: Aschendorff, 1978.

Klauck, H.-J. *Gemeinde–Amt–Sakrament.* Würzburg: Echter, 1989.

Klauck, H.-J. *Judas, ein Jünger des Herrn.* QD 3. Freiburg: Herder, 1987.

Klausner, J. *Jesus of Nazareth.* New York: Macmillan, 1927.

Klein, G. *Ärgernisse.* München: Kaiser, 1970.

Klein, G. *Rekonstruktion und Interpretation.* BEvT 50. München: Kaiser, 1969.

Kleist, J. A. *The Gospel of Saint Mark.* Milwaukee: Bruce, 1936.

Kleist, J. A. *The Memoirs of St. Peter.* Science and Culture Series. Milwaukee: Bruce, 1932.

Kloppenborg, J. S. *The Formation of Q.* Studies in Antiquity and Christianity. Philadelphia: Fortress, 1987.

Klostermann, E. *Das Markusevangelium.* 4. Aufl. HNT 3. Tübingen: Mohr, 1971.

Knox, W. L. *The Sources of the Synoptic Gospels.* Vol. I. *St. Mark.* Cambridge: Cambridge UP, 1953.

Koch, D.-A. *Die Bedeutung der Wundererzählungen für die Christologie des Markusevangeliums.* BZNW 42. Berlin: Walter de Gruyter, 1975.

Köhler, L. *Kleine Lichter.* Zwingli-Bücherei 47. Zürich: Zwingli, 1945.

Kopp, C. *The Holy Places of the Gospels.* New York: Herder, 1963.

Körtner, U. H. J. *Papias von Hierapolis.* FRLANT 133. Göttingen: Vandenhoeck & Ruprecht, 1983.

Kratz, R. *Rettungswunder.* EH 23/123. Frankfurt: Lang, 1979.

Krauss, S. *Griechische und Lateinische Lehnwörter im Talmud, Midrasch und Targum.* Hildesheim: Olms, 1964.

Krauss, S. *Talmudische Archäologie.* Grundriss der Gesamtwissenschaft des Judentums. Hildesheim: Olms, 1966.

Kremer, J. *Die Osterevangelien — Geschichten um Geschichte.* 2. Aufl. Stuttgart: KBW, 1981.

Kuhn, H.-W. *Ältere Sammlungen im Markusevangelium.* SUNT 8. Göttingen: Vandenhoeck & Ruprecht, 1971.

Kühner, R., and B. Gerth. *Ausführliche Grammatik der griechischen Sprache.* 4. Aufl. Leverkusen: Gottschalk, 1955.

Kühschelm, R. *Jüngerverfolgung und Geschick Jesu.* ÖBS 5. Klosterneuberg: Österreichisches Katholisches Bibelwerk, 1983.

Kümmel, W. G. *Introduction to the New Testament.* 2nd English ed. Nashville: Abingdon, 1986.

Kümmel, W. G. *Promise and Fulfillment.* SBT 1/23. London: SCM, 1957.

Kümmel, W. G. *The Theology of the New Testament according to its Major Witnesses.* NTL. Nashville: Abingdon, 1973.

Kunzi, M. *Das Naherwartungslogion Markus 9,1 par.* BGBE 21. Tübingen: Mohr, 1977.

Kürzinger, J. *Papias von Hierapolis und die Evangelien des Neuen Testaments.* Eichstätter Materialien 4. Regensburg: Pustet, 1983.

Lachs, S. T. *A Rabbinic Commentary on the New Testament. The Gospels of Matthew, Mark, and Luke.* Hoboken: Ktav, 1987.

Ladd, G. E. *Presence of the Future.* Grand Rapids: Eerdmans, 1974.

Lagrange, M.-J. *Évangile selon Saint Marc.* EBib. Paris: Gabalda, 1966.

Lambrecht, J. *Die Redaktion der Markus-Apokalypse.* AnBib 28. Rome: Pontifical Biblical Institute, 1967.

Lane, W. L. *The Gospel according to Mark.* NICNT 2. Grand Rapids: Eerdmans, 1974.

Latourette, K. S. *History of the Expansion of Christianity.* New York: Harper, 1937-45.

Laufen, R. *Die Doppelüberlieferungen der Logienquelle und des Markusevangeliums.* BBB 54. Königstein/Ts.-Bonn: Hanstein, 1980.

Lauterbach, J. Z. *Mekilta de-Rabbi Ishmael.* JPS Library of Jewish Classics. Philadelphia: The Jewish Publication Society of America, 1976.

Le Bon, G. *The Crowd.* London: Unwin, 1914.

Leben und Taten Alexanders von Makedonien, Der griechische Alexanderroman nach der Handschrift L. Ed. H. van Thiel. 2. Aufl. Texte zur Forschung 13. Darmstadt: Wissenschaftliche Buchgesellschaft, 1983.

Lee, M. Y.-H. *Jesus und die jüdische Autorität.* FB 56. Würzburg: Echter, 1986.

Légasse, S. *L'appel du riche.* EBib. Paris: Beauchesne, 1966.

Leivestad, R. *Jesus in His Own Perspective.* Minneapolis: Augsburg, 1987.

Lémonon, J.-P. *Pilate et le gouvernement de la Judée.* EBib. Paris: Gabalda, 1981.

Lentzen-Deis, F. *Die Taufe Jesu nach den Synoptikern.* FTS 4. Frankfurt: Knecht, 1970.

Léon-Dufour, X. *Resurrection and the Message of Easter.* New York: Holt, Rinehart and Winston, 1974.

Lightfoot, J. B. *Saint Paul's Epistle to the Galatians.* New York: Macmillan, 1900.

Lightfoot, R. H. *The Gospel Message of St. Mark.* Oxford: Clarendon, 1950.

Lightfoot, R. H. *History and Interpretation in the Gospels.* The Bampton Lectures. London: Hodder and Stoughton, 1935.

Lightfoot, R. H. *Locality and Doctrine in the Gospels.* New York: Harper, n.d.

Lindars, B. *Jesus, Son of Man.* Grand Rapids: Eerdmans, 1984.

Lindars, B. *New Testament Apologetic.* Philadelphia: Westminster, 1961.

Lindsey, R. L. *A Hebrew Translation of the Gospel of Mark.* Jerusalem: Dugith, 1969.

Linnemann, E. *Studien zur Passionsgeschichte.* FRLANT 102. Göttingen: Vandenhoeck & Ruprecht, 1970.

Loewe, H. *"Render Unto Caesar."* Cambridge: Cambridge UP, 1940.

Logia. J. Coppens Mémorial. Ed. J. Delobel. BETL 59. Leuven: Leuven UP, 1982.

Lohfink, G. *Die Himmelfahrt Jesu.* SANT 26. München: Kösel, 1971.

Lohmeyer, E. *Das Evangelium des Markus.* MeyerK 1/2. *Ergänzungsheft,* 2. Aufl. Göttingen: Vandenhoeck & Ruprecht, 1963.

Lohmeyer, E. *Galiläa und Jerusalem.* FRLANT 52. Göttingen: Vandenhoeck & Ruprecht, 1936.

Lohmeyer, E. *Urchristliche Mystik.* 2. Aufl. Darmstadt: Genter, 1956.

Lohse, E. *History of the Suffering and Death of Jesus Christ.* Philadelphia: Fortress, 1967.

Lohse, E. *Märtyrer und Gottesknecht.* FRLANT 64. Göttingen: Vandenhoeck & Ruprecht, 1955.

Loisy, A. *L'évangile Marc.* Paris: Nourry, 1912.

Loos, H. van der. *The Miracles of Jesus.* NovTSup 9. Leiden: Brill, 1965.

Lövestam, E. *Spiritual Wakefulness in the New Testament.* LUÅ n.f. Avd. 1, Bd. 55, Nr. 3. Lund: Gleerup, 1963.

Lührmann, D. *Das Markusevangelium.* HNT 3. Tübingen: Mohr, 1987.

McCarter, P. K., Jr. *I Samuel.* AB 8. Garden City: Doubleday, 1979.

McConnell, R. S. *Law and Prophecy in Matthew's Gospel.* Theologische Dissertationen 2. Basel: Reinhardt, 1969.

Macdonald, J. *Theology of the Samaritans.* NTL. Philadelphia: Westminster, 1964.

McGinley, L. J. *Form-Criticism.* Woodstock: Woodstock College, 1944.

McGuckin, J. *The Transfiguration of Christ in Scripture and Tradition.* SBEC 9. Lewiston: Mellen, 1986.

Mack, B. L. *A Myth of Innocence.* Philadelphia: Fortress, 1988.

Mack, B. L., and V. K. Robbins. *Patterns of Persuasion in the Gospels.* FFLF. Sonoma: Polebridge, 1989.

McKelvey, R. J. *The New Temple.* OTM. London: Oxford, 1969.

Mackowski, R. M. *Jerusalem, City of Jesus.* Grand Rapids: Eerdmans, 1980.

McNamara, M. *Targum and Testament.* Grand Rapids: Eerdmans, 1972.

Madden, F. W. *History of Jewish Coinage and of Money in the Old and New Testaments.* Chicago: Argonaut, 1967.

Magness, J. L. *Sense and Absence.* Semeia Studies. Atlanta: Scholars, 1986.

Mahnke, H. *Die Versuchungsgeschichte im Rahmen der synoptischen Evangelien.* BBET 9. Frankfurt: Lang, 1978.

Mahoney, R. *Two Disciples at the Tomb.* Theologie und Wirklichkeit 6. Bern: H. Lang/Frankfurt: P. Lang, 1974.

Maisch, I. *Die Heilung des Gelähmten.* SBS 52. Stuttgart: KBW, 1971.

Malbon, E. S. *Narrative Space and Mythic Meaning in Mark.* NVBS. San Francisco: Harper & Row, 1986.

Maloney, E. C. *Semitic Interference in Marcan Syntax.* SBLDS 51. Chico: Scholars, 1981.

Manicardi, E. *Il cammino di Gesù nel Vangelo di Marco.* AnBib 96: Rome: Pontifical Biblical Institute, 1981.

Mann, C. S. *Mark.* AB 27. Garden City: Doubleday, 1986.

Manns, F. *Essais sur le Judéo-Christianisme.* Studium Biblicum Franciscanum Analecta 12. Jerusalem: Franciscan, 1977.

Mansfield, M. R. *"Spirit and Gospel" in Mark.* Peabody: Hendrickson, 1987.

Manson, T. W. *The Sayings of Jesus.* London: SCM, 1957.

Manson, T. W. *The Servant-Messiah.* Grand Rapids: Baker, 1977.

Manson, T. W. *Studies in the Gospels and Epistles.* Ed. M. Black. Manchester: Manchester UP, 1962.

Manson, T. W. *The Teaching of Jesus.* 2nd ed. Cambridge: Cambridge UP, 1935.

Marcel, L. *La sagesse africaine.* Paris-Fribourg: Editions Saint-Paul, 1983.

Marcus, J. *The Mystery of the Kingdom of God.* SBLDS 90. Atlanta: Scholars, 1986.

Mariadasan, V. *Le triomphe messianique de Jésus et son entrée à Jérusalem.* Tindivanam, India: Catechetical Centre, 1978.

Markus-Philologie. Ed. H. Cancik. WUNT 33. Tübingen: Mohr, 1984.

Marshall, C. D. *Faith as a Theme in Mark's Narrative.* SNTSMS 64. Cambridge: Cambridge UP, 1989.

Marshall, I. H. *The Gospel of Luke.* NIGTC. Grand Rapids: Eerdmans, 1978.

Marshall, I. H. *Last Supper and Lord's Supper.* Grand Rapids: Eerdmans, 1980.

Marshall, I. H. *The Origins of New Testament Christology.* Downers Grove: InterVarsity, 1990.

Martin, E. L. *Secrets of Golgotha.* Alhambra, CA: ASK, 1988.

Martin, R. A. *Syntax Criticism of the Synoptic Gospels.* SBEC 10. Lewiston/Queenston: Mellen, 1987.

Martin, R. P. *Mark: Evangelist and Theologian.* CEP. Grand Rapids: Zondervan, 1973.

Mary in the New Testament. Ed. R. E. Brown et al. Philadelphia: Fortress, 1978.

Marxsen, W. *Mark the Evangelist.* Nashville: Abingdon, 1969.

März, C.-P. *"Siehe, dein König kommt zu dir. . . ."* ErThSt 43. Leipzig: St. Benno, 1980.

Massaux, É. *Influence de l'évangile de saint Matthieu sur la littérature chrétienne avant saint Irenée.* BETL 75. Leuven: Leuven UP, 1986.

Masson, C. *Vers les sources d'eau vive.* Publications de la faculté de théologie Université de Lausanne 2. Lausanne: Librairie Payot, 1961.

Matera, F. J. *The Kingship of Jesus.* SBLDS 66. Chico: Scholars, 1982.

Matera, F. J. *What Are They Saying About Mark?* New York/Mahwah: Paulist, 1987.

Mauser, U. W. *Christ in the Wilderness.* SBT 1/39. London: SCM, 1963.

Meagher, J. C. *Clumsy Construction in Mark's Gospel.* Toronto Studies in Theology 3. New York: Mellen, 1979.

Meagher, J. C. *Five Gospels.* Minneapolis: Winston, 1983.

Medicine and the Bible. Ed. B. Palmer. Exeter: Paternoster, 1986.

Medicus Viator. R. Siebeck FS. Tübingen: Mohr/Stuttgart: Thieme, 1959.

Mélanges Bibliques. B. Rigaux FS. Gembloux: Duculot, 1970.

Mélanges Dominique Barthélemy. Ed. P. Casetti et al. OBO 38. Göttingen: Vandenhoeck & Ruprecht, 1981.

Mélanges Syriens offerts à Monsieur René Dussaud. Bibliothèque archéologique et historique 30. Paris: Geuthner, 1939.

The Messianic Secret. Ed. C. Tuckett. IRT 1. Philadelphia: Fortress/London: SPCK, 1983.

Metzger, B. M. *A Textual Commentary on the Greek New Testament.* New York: United Bible Societies, 1971.

Meye, R. P. *Jesus and the Twelve.* Grand Rapids: Eerdmans, 1968.

Meyer, B. F. *The Aims of Jesus.* London: SCM, 1979.

Meyer, H. A. W. *Critical and Exegetical Handbook to the Gospels of Mark and Luke.* New York: Funk & Wagnalls, 1884.

Mikra. Ed. M. J. Mulder. The Literature of the Jewish People in the Period of the Second Temple and the Talmud 1. Philadelphia: Fortress, 1988.

Minear, P. S. *Commands of Christ.* Nashville: Abingdon, 1972.

Minette de Tillesse, G. *Le secret messianique dans l'évangile de Marc.* LD 47. Paris: Cerf, 1968.

Miscellanea Neotestamentica. Ed. T. Baarda et al. NovTSup 47-48. Leiden: Brill, 1978.

Die Mitte des Neuen Testaments. E. Schweizer FS. Ed. U. Luz and H. Weder. Göttingen: Vandenhoeck & Ruprecht, 1983.

Mohr, T. A. *Markus- und Johannespassion.* ATANT 70. Zürich: Theologischer Verlag, 1982.

Montefiore, C. G. *The Synoptic Gospels.* LBS. New York: Ktav, 1968.

Montefiore, H. *Josephus and the New Testament.* Contemporary Studies in Theology 6. London: Mowbray, 1962.

Moo, D. J. *The Old Testament in the Gospel Passion Narratives.* Sheffield: Almond, 1983.

Moore, A. L. *The Parousia in the New Testament.* NovTSup 13. Leiden: Brill, 1966.

Moore, G. F. *Judaism in the First Centuries of the Christian Era.* Cambridge, MA: Harvard UP, 1955-58.

Morgenstern, J. *Some Significant Antecedents of Christianity.* SPB 10. Leiden: Brill, 1966.

Morris, L. *The Gospel According to John.* NICNT. Grand Rapids: Eerdmans, 1971.

Moule, C. F. D. *An Idiom-Book of New Testament Greek.* Cambridge: Cambridge UP, 1963.

Moulton, J. H. *A Grammar of New Testament Greek.* Vol. I: *Prolegomena.* 3rd ed. Edinburgh: T. & T. Clark, 1908.

Moulton, J. H., and W. F. Howard. *A Grammar of New Testament Greek.* Vol. II: *Accidence and Word-Formation.* Edinburgh: T. & T. Clark, 1919-29.

Mudiso Mbâ Mundla, J.-G. *Jesus und die Führer Israels.* NTAbh nf 17. Münster: Aschendorff, 1984.

Myers, C. *Binding the Strong Man.* Maryknoll: Orbis, 1988.

Neirynck, F. *Duality in Mark.* 2nd ed. BETL 31. Leuven: Leuven UP, 1988.

Neirynck, F. *Evangelica.* BETL 60. Leuven: Leuven UP, 1982.

Neotestamentica et Patristica. O. Cullmann FS. NovTSup 6. Leiden: Brill, 1962.

Neotestamentica et Semitica. M. Black FS. Ed. E. E. Ellis and M. Wilcox. Edinburgh: T. & T. Clark, 1969.

Neuenzeit, P. *Das Herrenmahl.* SANT 1. München: Kösel, 1960.

Neugebauer, F. *Jesu Versuchung.* Tübingen: Mohr, 1986.

Neusner, J. *From Politics to Piety.* 2nd ed. New York: Ktav, 1979.

Neusner, J. *The Idea of Purity in Ancient Judaism.* SJLA 1. Leiden: Brill, 1973.

Neusner, J. *Judaism, the Evidence of the Mishnah.* Chicago: University of Chicago, 1981.

Neusner, J. *The Rabbinic Traditions about the Pharisees before 70.* Part III: *Conclusions.* Leiden: Brill, 1971.

Neutestamentliche Aufsätze. J. Schmid FS. Ed. J. Blinzler et al. Regensburg: Pustet, 1963.

Neutestamentliche Studien für Rudolf Bultmann. 2. Aufl. Ed. W. Eltester. BZNW 21. Berlin: Töpelmann, 1957.

A New Commentary on Holy Scripture. Ed. C. Gore et al. New York: Macmillan, 1929.

New Dimensions in New Testament Study. Ed. R. M. Longenecker and M. C. Tenney. Grand Rapids: Zondervan, 1974.

New Documents Illustrating Early Christianity. North Ryde: The Ancient History Documentary Research Centre, Macquarie University, 1981-.

Neues Testament und Geschichte. O. Cullmann FS. Ed. H. Baltensweiler and B. Reicke. Zürich: Theologischer Verlag, 1972.

Neues Testament und Kirche. R. Schnackenburg FS. Ed. J. Gnilka. Freiburg: Herder, 1974.

New Synoptic Studies. Ed. W. R. Farmer. Macon: Mercer UP, 1983.

The New Testament Age. B. Reicke FS. Ed. W. C. Weinrich. Macon: Mercer UP, 1984.

The New Testament and Gnosis. R. M. Wilson FS. Ed. A. H. B. Logan and A. J. M. Wedderburn. Edinburgh: T. & T. Clark, 1983.

New Testament Essays. Studies in memory of T. W. Manson. Ed. A. J. B. Higgins. Manchester: Manchester UP, 1959.

The New Testament in Early Christianity. Ed. J.-M. Sevrin. BETL 86. Leuven: Leuven UP, 1989.

The New Testament in Historical and Contemporary Perspective. Essays in memory of G. H. C. Macgregor. Ed. H. Anderson and W. Barclay. Oxford: Blackwell, 1965.

New Testament Textual Criticism. B. M. Metzger FS. Ed. E. J. Epp and G. D. Fee. Oxford: Clarendon, 1981.

Nielsen, H. K. *Heilung und Verkündigung.* Acta Theologica Danica 22. Leiden: Brill, 1987.

Nineham, D. E. *Saint Mark.* Pelican Gospel Commentaries. Baltimore: Penguin, 1963.

Norden, E. *Agnostos Theos.* Stuttgart: Teubner, 1956.

Nützel, J. M. *Die Verklärungserzählung im Markusevangelium.* FB 6. Würzburg: Echter, 1973.

Oakman, D. E. *Jesus and the Economic Questions of His Day.* SBEC 8. Lewiston/Queenston: Mellen, 1986.

Oberlinner, L. *Historische Überlieferung und christologische Aussage.* FB 19. Stuttgart: KBW, 1975.

Oikonomia. O. Cullmann FS. Ed. F. Christ. Hamburg-Bergstedt: Reich, 1967.

The Old Testament Pseudepigrapha. Ed. J. H. Charlesworth. Garden City: Doubleday, 1983-85.

Orchard, B., and H. Riley. *The Order of the Synoptics.* Macon: Mercer UP, 1987.

Orientierung an Jesus. J. Schmid FS. Ed. P. Hoffmann et al. Freiburg: Herder, 1973.

Orr, W. F., and J. A. Walther. *I Corinthians.* AB 32. Garden City: Doubleday, 1976.

Osborne, G. R. *The Resurrection Narratives.* Grand Rapids: Baker, 1984.

Otto, R. *The Idea of the Holy.* 2nd ed. New York: Oxford, 1950.

Otto, R. *The Kingdom of God and the Son of Man.* 2nd ed. LL 9. London: Lutterworth, 1951.

Pannenberg, W. *Jesus — God and Man.* 2nd ed. Philadelphia: Westminster, 1987.

Pape, W., and G. E. Benseler. *Wörterbuch der griechischen Eigennamen.* 3. Aufl. Handwörterbuch der Griechische Sprache 3. Braunschweig: Friedr. Vieweg & Sohn, 1911.

La Pâque du Christ. F.-X. Durrwell FS. LD 112. Paris: Cerf, 1982.

Les Paraboles évangeliques. Ed. J. Delorme. LD 135. Paris: Cerf, 1989.

Paschen, W. *Rein und Unrein.* SANT 24. München: Kösel, 1970.

The Passion in Mark. Ed. W. H. Kelber. Philadelphia: Fortress, 1976.

Patsch, H. *Abendmahl und historischer Jesus.* Calwer Theol. Monographien A, 1. Stuttgart: Calwer, 1972.

Patte, D. *Structural Exegesis.* Philadelphia: Fortress, 1978.

Peabody, D. B. *Mark as Composer.* New Gospel Studies 1. Macon: Mercer UP, 1987.

Perkins, P. *Love Commands in the New Testament.* New York: Paulist, 1982.

Perrin, N. *The Kingdom of God in the Teaching of Jesus.* Philadelphia: Westminster, 1963.

Perrin, N., and D. C. Duling. *The New Testament, an Introduction.* 2nd ed. New York: Harcourt Brace Jovanovich, 1982.

Perrin, N. *Rediscovering the Teaching of Jesus.* New York: Harper & Row, 1976.

Perrin, N. *The Resurrection according to Matthew, Mark, and Luke.* Philadelphia: Fortress, 1977.

Perspectives on Language and Text. F. I. Andersen FS. Ed. E. W. Conrad and E. G. Newing. Winona Lake: Eisenbrauns, 1987.

Pesch, R. *Das Abendmahl und Jesu Todesverständnis.* QD 80. Freiburg: Herder, 1978.

Pesch, R. *Der Besessene von Gerasa.* SBS 56. Stuttgart: KBW, 1972.

Pesch, R. *Das Markusevangelium.* HTKNT II/1 (2. Aufl.)-2. Freiburg: Herder, 1977.

Pesch, R. *Naherwartungen: Tradition und Redaktion in Mk 13.* KBANT. Düsseldorf: Patmos, 1968.

Peter in the New Testament. Ed. R. E. Brown et al. Minneapolis: Augsburg/New York: Paulist, 1973.

Petersen, N. R. *Literary Criticism for New Testament Critics.* GBS: NT Series. Philadelphia: Fortress, 1978.

Piper, J. *"Love Your Enemies."* SNTSMS 38. Cambridge: Cambridge UP, 1979.

Piper, R. A. *Wisdom in the Q-Tradition.* SNTSMS 61. Cambridge: Cambridge UP, 1989.

Poland, L. M. *Literary Criticism and Biblical Hermeneutics.* AAR Academy Series 48. Chico: Scholars, 1985.

Porter, S. E. *Verbal Aspect in the Greek of the New Testament, with Reference to Tense and Mood.* Studies in Biblical Greek 1. New York: Lang, 1989.

Preuss, J. *Biblical and Talmudic Medicine.* New York: Sanhedrin, 1978.

Probleme der Forschung. Ed. A. Fuchs. SNTU A/3. Wien: Herold, 1978.

Promise and Fulfilment. S. H. Hooke FS. Ed. F. F. Bruce. Edinburgh: T. & T. Clark, 1963.

Protocol of the Center for Hermeneutical Studies in Hellenistic and Modern Culture. Colloquy 18 (1976). The Center for Hermeneutical Studies in Hellenistic and Modern Culture, 2465 Le Conte Ave., Berkeley, CA 94709.

Der Prozess gegen Jesus. 2. Aufl. Ed. K. Kertelge. QD 112. Freiburg: Herder, 1989.

Pryke, E. J. *Redactional Style in the Marcan Gospel.* SNTSMS 33. Cambridge: Cambridge UP, 1978.

Quesnell, Q. *The Mind of Mark.* AnBib 38. Rome: Pontifical Biblical Institute, 1969.

Qumrân. Sa piété, sa théologie et son milieu. BETL 46. Leuven: Leuven UP, 1978.

Rabin, C. *The Zadokite Documents.* 2nd ed. Oxford: Clarendon, 1958.

Rad, G. von. *Old Testament Theology.* London: SCM, 1975.

Räisänen, H. *Das "Messiasgeheimnis" im Markusevangelium.* SFEG 28. Helsinki, 1976.

Räisänen, H. *Die Parabeltheorie im Markusevangelium.* SFEG 26. Helsinki, 1973.

Räisänen, H. *The Torah and Christ.* Suomen Eksegeettisen Seuran julkaisuja 45. Helsinki: Finnish Exegetical Society, 1986.

Rawlinson, A. E. J. *St Mark.* Westminster Commentaries. London: Methuen, 1925.

Rechtfertigung. E. Käsemann FS. Ed. J. Friedrich. Tübingen: Mohr/Göttingen: Vandenhoeck & Ruprecht, 1976.

Redaktion und Theologie des Passionsberichtes nach den Synoptikern. Ed. M. Limbeck. Weg der Forschung 481. Darmstadt: Wissenschaftliche Buchgesellschaft, 1981.

Reiser, M. *Syntax und Stil des Markusevangeliums.* WUNT 2/11. Tübingen: Mohr, 1984.

Reitzenstein, R. *Hellenistiche Wundererzählungen.* Leipzig: Teubner, 1906.

Reitzenstein, R. *Poimandres.* Darmstadt: Wissenschaftliche Buchgesellschaft, 1966.

Religion, Science, and Magic. Ed. J. Neusner et al. New York: Oxford UP, 1989.

Renan, E. *The Life of Jesus.* New York: Carleton, 1880.

Reploh, K.-G. *Markus — Lehrer der Gemeinde.* SBM 9. Stuttgart: KBW, 1969.

Resurrexit. Citta del Vaticano: Libreria editrice vaticana, 1974.

Reumann, J. *The Supper of the Lord*. Philadelphia: Fortress, 1985.

Rhoads, D. M. *Israel in Revolution, 6-74 C.E.* Philadelphia: Fortress, 1976.

Richter, G. *Studien zum Johannesevangelium*. BU 13. Regensburg: Pustet, 1977.

Ridderbos, H. *The Coming of the Kingdom*. Philadelphia: Presbyterian and Reformed, 1975.

Riesenfeld, H. *The Gospel Tradition*. Philadelphia: Fortress, 1970.

Riesenfeld, H. *Jésus transfiguré*. ASNU 16. Copenhagen: Munksgaard, 1947.

Riesenfeld, H. *Zum Gebrauch von ΘΕΛΩ im Neuen Testament*. Arbeiten und Mitteilungen aus dem neutestamentlichen Seminar zu Uppsala 1. Uppsala: Akademisk Maskinskrift, 1936.

Riessler, P. *Altjüdisches Schrifttum ausserhalb der Bibel*. 6. Aufl. Freiburg: Kerle, 1928.

Robbins, V. K. *Jesus the Teacher*. Philadelphia: Fortress, 1984.

Robertson, A. T. *A Grammar of the Greek New Testament in the Light of Historical Research*. Nashville: Broadman, 1934.

Robinson, G. *New Testament Detection*. New York: Oxford, 1964.

Robinson, J. A. *St. Paul's Epistle to the Ephesians*. 2nd ed. London: James Clarke, 1904.

Robinson, J. A. T. *Jesus and His Coming*. London: SCM, 1957.

Robinson, J. A. T. *Twelve New Testament Studies*. London: SCM, 1962.

Robinson, J. M. *The Problem of History in Mark and Other Marcan Studies*. Philadelphia: Fortress, 1982.

Rochais, G. *Les récits de résurrection des morts dans le Nouveau Testament*. SNTSMS 40. Cambridge: Cambridge UP, 1981.

Rohde, E. *Psyche*. The Library of Religion and Culture. New York: Harper & Row, 1966.

Rohde, J. *Rediscovering the Teaching of the Evangelists*. NTL. Philadelphia: Westminster, 1968.

Roloff, J. *Das Kerygma und der irdische Jesus*. 2. Aufl. Göttingen: Vandenhoeck & Ruprecht, 1973.

Ropes, J. H. *The Synoptic Gospels*. Cambridge, MA: Harvard UP, 1934.

Rossé, G. *The Cry of Jesus on the Cross*. New York: Paulist, 1987.

Rowland, C. *The Open Heaven*. New York: Crossroad, 1982.

Rückfrage nach Jesu. 2. Aufl. Ed. K. Kertelge. QD 63. Freiburg: Herder, 1977.

Ruhland, M. *Die Markuspassion aus der Sicht der Verleugnung*. Eilsbrunn: Ko'amar, 1987.

Ruppert, L. *Jesus als der leidende Gerechte?* SBS 59. Stuttgart: KBW, 1972.

Ruppert, L. *Der leidende Gerechte und seine Feinde*. Würzburg: Echter, 1973.

Saldarini, A. J. *Pharisees, Scribes and Sadducees in Palestinian Society*. Wilmington: Glazier, 1988.

Salvación en la Palabra: Targum, Derash, Berith. In memory of A. D. Macho. Madrid: Ediciones Cristiandad, 1986.

Sanders, E. P. *Jesus and Judaism*. Philadelphia: Fortress, 1985.

Sanders, E. P. *Jewish Law from Jesus to the Mishnah*. London: SCM/Philadelphia: Trinity, 1990.

Sanders, E. P. *The Tendencies of the Synoptic Tradition.* SNTSMS 9. London: Cambridge UP, 1969.

Sanders, J. A. *Canon and Community.* GBS. Philadelphia: Fortress, 1984.

Schanz, P. *Commentar über das Evangelium des heiligen Marcus.* Freiburg: Herder, 1881.

Schenk, W. *Der Passionsbericht nach Markus.* Gütersloh: Mohn, 1974.

Schenke, L. *Auferstehungsverkündigung und leeres Grab.* 2. Aufl. SBS 33. Stuttgart: KBW, 1969.

Schenke, L. *Der gekreuzigte Christus.* SBS 69. Stuttgart: KBW, 1974.

Schenke, L. *Studien zur Passionsgeschichte des Markus.* FB 4. Würzburg: Echter, 1971.

Schenke, L. *Die Wundererzählungen des Markusevangeliums.* SBB. Stuttgart: KBW, 1974

Schillebeeckx, E. *Christ.* New York: Crossroad, 1981.

Schlatter, A. *Markus.* 2. Aufl. Stuttgart: Calwer, 1984.

Schlatter, A. *Der Evangelist Matthäus.* Stuttgart: Calwer, 1948.

Schlosser, J. *Le Dieu de Jésus.* LD 129. Paris: Cerf, 1987.

Schlosser, J. *Le règne de Dieu dans les dits de Jésus.* EBib. Paris: Gabalda, 1980.

Schmahl, G. *Die Zwölf im Markusevangelium.* Trier Theologische Studien 30. Trier: Paulinus, 1974.

Schmid, J. *The Gospel according to Mark.* RNT. Cork: Mercier, 1968.

Schmidt, K. L. *Der Rahmen der Geschichte Jesu.* Darmstadt: Wissenschaftliche Buchgesellschaft, 1964.

Schmidt, T. E. *Hostility to Wealth in the Synoptic Gospels.* JSNTSup 15. Sheffield: JSOT, 1987.

Schmithals, W. *Das Evangelium nach Markus.* ÖTKNT 2/1-2. Gütersloh: Mohn/Würzburg: Echter, 1979.

Schnackenburg, R. *The Gospel according to St. John.* Vol. 1. London: Burns & Oates/New York: Herder, 1968.

Schnackenburg, R. *Schriften zum Neuen Testament.* München: Kösel, 1971.

Schneider, G. *Das Evangelium nach Lukas.* ÖTKNT 3/2. Gütersloh: Mohn, 1984.

Scholem, G. *Jewish Gnosticism, Merkabah Mysticism, and Talmudic Tradition.* New York: Jewish Theological Seminary, 1960.

Schottroff, L., and W. Stegemann. *Jesus von Nazareth.* Urban-Taschenbücher 639. Stuttgart: Kohlhammer, 1978.

Schottroff, W. *"Gedenken" im Alten Orient und im Alten Testament.* WMANT 15. Neukirchen: Neukirchener Verlag, 1964.

Schrage, W. *Das Verhältnis des Thomas-Evangeliums zur synoptischen Tradition und zu den koptischen Evangelienübersetzungen.* BZNW 29. Berlin: Töpelmann, 1964.

Schreiber, J. *Der Kreuzigungsbericht des Markusevangeliums Mk 15,20b-41.* BZNW 48. Berlin: Walter de Gruyter, 1986.

Schreiber, J. *Theologie des Vertrauens.* Hamburg: Furche, 1967.

Schroeder, H.-H. *Eltern und Kinder in der Verkündigung Jesu.* Theologische Forschung 53. Hamburg-Bergstedt: Reich, 1972.

Schultze, V. *Altchristliche Städte und Landschaften. II. Kleinasien.* Gütersloh: Bertelsmann, 1926.

Schulz, S. *Q.* Zürich: Theologischer Verlag, 1972.

Schulz, S. *Die Stunde der Botschaft.* Hamburg: Furche, 1967.

Schürer, E. *The History of the Jewish People in the Age of Jesus Christ (175 B.C.-A.D. 135).* A new English version revised by G. Vermes et al. Vols. 1-3. Edinburgh: T. & T. Clark, 1973-87.

Schürmann, H. *Der Abendmahlsbericht Lucas 22,7-38 als Gottesdienstordnung-Gemeindeordnung-Lebensordnung.* Paderborn: Schoningh, 1963.

Schürmann, H. *Der Einsetzungsbericht Lk. 22,19-20.* 2. Aufl. NTAbh 20/4. Münster: Aschendorff, 1970.

Schürmann, H. *Jesu Abschiedsrede Lk. 22,21-38.* 2. Aufl. NTAbh 20/5. Münster: Aschendorff, 1977.

Schürmann, H. *Jesu ureigener Tod.* Freiburg: Herder, 1975.

Schürmann, H. *Der Paschamahlbericht Lk. 22,(7-14.)15-18.* 2. Aufl. NTAbh 19/5. Münster: Aschendorff, 1968.

Schürmann, H. *Traditionsgeschichtliche Untersuchungen zu den synoptischen Evangelien.* KBANT. Düsseldorf: Patmos, 1968.

Schwankl, O. *Die Sadduzäerfrage (Mk 12,18-27 parr).* BBB 66. Frankfurt: Athenäum, 1987.

Schwarz, G. *Jesus und Judas.* BWANT 123. Stuttgart: Kohlhammer, 1988.

Schweitzer, A. *The Quest of the Historical Jesus.* New York: Macmillan, 1968.

Schweizer, E. *The Good News according to Mark.* Richmond: Knox, 1970.

Schwyzer, E., and A. Debrunner. *Griechische Grammatik.* Handbuch der Altertumswissenschaft 2/1. München: Beck, 1934-71.

Scott, B. B. *Hear Then the Parable.* Minneapolis: Fortress, 1989.

Scott, B. B. *Jesus, Symbol-Maker for the Kingdom.* Philadelphia: Fortress, 1981.

Scott, W. *Hermetica.* Oxford: Clarendon, 1924-36.

The Scrolls and the New Testament. Ed. K. Stendahl. New York: Harper, 1957.

Segundo, J. L. *The Historical Jesus of the Synoptics.* Jesus of Nazareth, Yesterday and Today 2. Maryknoll: Orbis, 1985.

Selvidge, M. J. *Woman, Cult, and Miracle Recital.* Lewisburg: Bucknell UP, 1990.

Senior, D. *The Passion of Jesus in the Gospel of Mark.* Passion Series 2. Wilmington: Glazier, 1984.

Sherwin-White, A. N. *Roman Society and Roman Law in the New Testament.* Sarum Lectures 1960-61. Oxford: Clarendon, 1963.

The Significance of the Message of the Resurrection for Faith in Jesus Christ. Ed. C. F. D. Moule. SBT 2/8. Naperville: Allenson, 1968.

Simpson, E. K. *Words Worth Weighing in the Greek New Testament.* London: Tyndale, 1946.

Sloyan, G. S. *Jesus on Trial.* Philadelphia: Fortress, 1973.

Smith, M. *Clement of Alexandria and a Secret Gospel of Mark.* Cambridge, MA: Harvard UP, 1973.

Smith, M. *Jesus the Magician.* San Francisco: Harper & Row, 1978.

Smith, M. *Tannaitic Parallels to the Gospels.* JBLMS 6. Philadelphia: Society of
    Biblical Literature, 1968.
Snodgrass, K. *The Parable of the Wicked Tenants.* WUNT 27. Tübingen: Mohr,
    1983.
Söding, T. *Glaube bei Markus.* SBB 12. Stuttgart: KBW, 1985.
Sperber, D. *Nautica Talmudica.* Bar-Ilan Studies in Near Eastern Languages and
    Culture. Leiden: Brill, 1987.
Spicq, C. *Notes de Lexicographie néo-testamentaire.* Vol. 1. OBO 22. Göttingen:
    Vandenhoeck & Ruprecht, 1978.
Spirit Within Structure. G. Johnston FS. Ed. E. J. Furcha. PTMS 2/3. Allison Park:
    Pickwick, 1983.
Standaert, B. H. M. G. M. *L'évangile selon Marc.* Nijmegen: Stichting Studen-
    tenpers, 1978.
Stanton, G. H. *Jesus of Nazareth in New Testament Preaching.* SNTSMS 27.
    London: Cambridge UP, 1974.
Stauffer, E. *Christ and the Caesars.* London: SCM, 1955.
Stauffer, E. *Jerusalem und Rom im Zeitalter Jesu Christi.* Dalp-Taschenbücher
    331. Bern: Francke, 1957.
Stauffer, E. *Jesus and His Story.* New York: Knopf, 1959.
Steck, O. H. *Israel und das gewaltsame Geschick der Propheten.* WMANT 23.
    Neukirchen-Vluyn: Neukirchener Verlag, 1967.
Steichele, H.-J. *Der leidende Sohn Gottes.* BU 14. Regensburg: Pustet, 1980.
Stein, R. H. *An Introduction to the Parables of Jesus.* Philadelphia: Westminster,
    1981.
Stein, R. H. *The Proper Methodology for Ascertaining a Marcan Redaktions-
    geschichte.* Ann Arbor: University Microfilms, 1969.
Steinhauser, M. G. *Doppelbildworte in den synoptischen Evangelien.* FB 44.
    Würzburg: Echter, 1981.
Stock, A. *Call to Discipleship.* GNS 1. Wilmington: Glazier, 1982.
Stock, A. *The Method and Message of Mark.* Wilmington: Glazier, 1989.
Stock, K. *Boten aus dem Mit-Ihm-Sein.* AnBib 70. Rome: Pontifical Biblical
    Institute, 1975.
Stonehouse, N. B. *Witness of Matthew and Mark to Christ.* 2nd ed. Grand Rapids:
    Eerdmans, 1958.
Strobel, A. *Die Stunde der Wahrheit.* WUNT 21. Tübingen: Mohr, 1980.
Structural Analysis and Biblical Exegesis. PTMS 1/3. Pittsburgh: Pickwick, 1974.
Studia Biblica 1978 II. Ed. E. A. Livingstone. Sheffield: Dept. of Biblical Studies,
    University of Sheffield, 1979.
Studien zum Text und zur Ethik des Neuen Testaments. H. Greeven FS. Ed.
    W. Schrage. BZNW 47. Berlin: Walter de Gruyter, 1986.
Studies in Early Christianity. Ed. S. J. Case. New York: Century, 1928.
Studies in New Testament Language and Text. G. D. Kilpatrick FS. Ed. J. K.
    Elliott. NovTSup 44. Leiden: Brill, 1976.
Studies in the Gospels. Essays in memory of R. H. Lightfoot. Ed. D. E. Nineham.
    Oxford: Blackwell, 1955.

Studies in the New Testament and Early Christian Literature. A. P. Wikgren FS. Ed. D. E. Aune. NovTSup 33. Leiden: Brill, 1972.

Stuhlmacher, P. *Reconciliation, Law, and Righteousness.* Philadelphia: Fortress, 1986.

Stuhlmacher, P. *Schriftauslegung auf dem Wege zur biblischen Theologie.* Göttingen: Vandenhoeck & Ruprecht, 1975.

Stuhlmann, R. *Das eschatologische Mass im Neuen Testament.* FRLANT 132. Göttingen: Vandenhoeck & Ruprecht, 1983.

Suffering and Martyrdom in the New Testament. G. M. Styler FS. Cambridge: Cambridge UP, 1981.

Suhl, A. *Die Funktion der alttestamentlichen Zitate und Anspielungen im Markusevangelium.* Gütersloh: Mohn, 1965.

Sundwall, J. *Zusammensetzung des Markusevangeliums.* Acta Academiae Aboensis. Humaniora IX: 2. Åbo: Åbo Akademi, 1934.

Swete, H. B. *The Gospel according to St. Mark.* London: Macmillan, 1908.

The Synagogue in Late Antiquity. Ed. L. I. Levine. Philadelphia: ASOR, 1987.

Tagawa, K. *Miracles et Évangile.* Études d'histoire et de philosophie religieuses 62. Paris: Presses universitaires de France, 1966.

Talbert, C. H. *Reading Luke.* New York: Crossroad, 1982.

Tannehill, R. C. *The Sword of His Mouth.* Semeia Supplements 1. Philadelphia: Fortress, 1975.

Taylor, V. *The Gospel according to St. Mark.* 2nd ed. London: Macmillan/New York: St. Martin's, 1966.

Telford, W. R. *The Barren Temple and the Withered Tree.* JSNTSup 1. Sheffield: JSOT, 1980.

Text and Interpretation. M. Black FS. Ed. E. Best and R. McL. Wilson. Cambridge: Cambridge UP, 1979.

Text and Testimony. A. F. J. Klijn FS. Ed. T. Baarda et al. Kampen: Kok, 1988.

Text-Wort-Glaube. K. Aland FS. Ed. M. Brecht. Arbeiten zur Kirchengeschichte 50. New York: Walter de Gruyter, 1980.

Thayer, J. H. *A Greek-English Lexicon of the New Testament.* 4th ed. Edinburgh: T. & T. Clark, 1901.

Theissen, G. *The Miracle Stories of the Early Christian Tradition.* SNTW. Philadelphia: Fortress, 1983.

Theissen, G. *Sociology of Early Palestinian Christianity.* Philadelphia: Fortress, 1978.

Theologia Crucis — Signum Crucis. E. Dinkler FS. Ed. C. Andresen and G. Klein. Tübingen: Mohr, 1979.

Theologie und Leben. G. Söll FS. Ed. A. Boden and A. M. Kothgasser. Biblioteca di Scienze Religiose 58. Roma: Libreria Ateneo Salesiano, 1983.

Theologisches Handwörterbuch zum Alten Testament. Ed. E. Jenni and C. Westermann. München: Kaiser, 1971-76.

Thiede, C. P. *Die älteste Evangelien-Handschrift?* Wuppertal: Brockhaus, 1986.

Thissen, W. *Erzählung der Befreiung.* FB 21. Würzburg: Echter, 1976.

Thompson, M. R. *The Role of Disbelief in Mark.* New York: Paulist, 1989.

Thompson, R. C. *The Devils and Evil Spirits of Babylonia*. Luzac's Semitic Text and Translation Series 14-15. London: Luzac, 1903-4.

Thompson, R. C. *Semitic Magic*. Luzac's Oriental Religions Series 3. New York: AMS, 1976.

Thrall, M. E. *Greek Particles in the New Testament*. NTTS 3. Grand Rapids: Eerdmans, 1962.

Tilborg, S. van. *The Jewish Leaders in Matthew*. Leiden: Brill, 1972.

To Touch the Text. J. A. Fitzmyer FS. Ed. M. P. Horgan and P. J. Kobelski. New York: Crossroad, 1989.

Tödt, H. E. *The Son of Man in the Synoptic Tradition*. NTL. Philadelphia: Westminster, 1965.

Tolbert, M. A. *Sowing the Gospel*. Minneapolis: Fortress, 1989.

Torrey, C. C. *Our Translated Gospels*. New York: Harper, 1936.

Tradition and Interpretation in the New Testament. E. E. Ellis FS. Ed. G. F. Hawthorne and O. Betz. Grand Rapids: Eerdmans/Tübingen: Mohr, 1987.

Tradition und Glaube. K. G. Kuhn FS. Ed. G. Jeremias et al. Göttingen: Vandenhoeck & Ruprecht, 1971.

Traktellis, D. *Authority and Passion*. Brookline: Holy Cross Orthodox Press, 1987.

Trautmann, M. *Zeichenhafte Handlungen Jesu*. FB 37. Würzburg: Echter, 1980.

The Trial of Jesus. C. F. D. Moule FS. Ed. E. Bammel. SBT 2/13. London: SCM, 1970.

Trocmé, E. *The Formation of the Gospel according to Mark*. Philadelphia: Westminster, 1975.

Trocmé, E. *The Passion as Liturgy*. London: SCM, 1983.

Turner, N. *Christian Words*. Nashville: Nelson, 1982.

Turner, N. *Grammatical Insights into the New Testament*. Edinburgh: T. & T. Clark, 1966.

Turner, N. *Style*. Edinburgh: T. & T. Clark, 1976. (= Vol. IV of *A Grammar of New Testament Greek* by J. H. Moulton)

Turner, N. *Syntax*. Edinburgh: T. & T. Clark, 1963. (= Vol. III of *A Grammar of New Testament Greek* by J. H. Moulton)

Understanding the Sacred Text. M. S. Enslin FS. Ed. J. Reumann. Valley Forge: Judson, 1972.

Unnik, W. C. van. *Sparsa Collecta*. NovTSup 29-30. Leiden: Brill, 1973-80.

The Use of the Old Testament in the New and Other Essays. W. F. Stinespring FS. Ed. J. M. Efird. Durham: Duke UP, 1972.

Vansina, J. *Oral Tradition*. Chicago: Aldine, 1965.

La Venue du Messie. Ed. É. Massaux et al. RechBib 6. Bruges: Desclée de Brouwer, 1962.

Verborum Veritas. G. Stählin FS. Ed. O. Böcher and K. Haacker. Wuppertal: Brockhaus, 1970.

Vermes, G. *Jesus the Jew*. Philadelphia: Fortress, 1973.

Vermes, G. *Post-Biblical Jewish Studies*. SJLA 8. Leiden: Brill, 1975.

Vermes, G. *Scripture and Tradition in Judaism*. 2nd ed. SPB 4. Leiden: Brill, 1973.

Via, D. O. *The Ethics of Mark's Gospel — in the Middle of Time.* Philadelphia: Fortress, 1985.

La vie de la Parole. P. Grelot FS. Paris: Desclée, 1987.

Vielhauer, P. *Aufsätze zum Neuen Testament.* Theologische Bücherei 31, 65. München: Kaiser, 1965-79.

Views of the Biblical World. Ed. M. Avi-Yonah and A. Malamat. Chicago: Jordan, 1959-61.

Vogler, W. *Judas Iskarioth.* Theologische Arbeiten 42. Berlin: Evangelische Verlagsanstalt, 1983.

Vögtle, A. *Offenbarungsgeschehen und Wirkungsgeschichte.* Freiburg: Herder, 1985.

Vom Urchristentum zu Jesus. J. Gnilka FS. Ed. H. Frankemölle and K. Kertelge. Freiburg: Herder, 1989.

Vom Wort des Lebens. M. Meinertz FS. Ed. N. Adler. NTAbh 1. Münster: Aschendorff, 1951.

Vos, G. *The Self-Disclosure of Jesus.* Grand Rapids: Eerdmans, 1954.

Vouga, F. *Jésus et la loi selon la tradition synoptique.* Le Monde de la Bible. Genève: Labor et Fides, 1988.

Waard, J. de. *A Comparative Study of the Old Testament Text in the Dead Sea Scrolls and in the New Testament.* STDJ 4. Grand Rapids: Eerdmans, 1966.

Wachsmann, S. *The Excavations of an Ancient Boat in the Sea of Galilee (Lake Kinneret).* 'Atiqot, English Series 19. Jerusalem: Israel Antiquities Authority, 1990.

Waetjen, H. C. *Reordering of Power.* Minneapolis: Fortress, 1989.

Wanke, J. *Beobachtungen zum Eucharistieverständnis des Lukas auf Grund der lukanischen Mahlberichte.* ErThSt 8. Leipzig: St. Benno, 1973.

Wanke, J. *"Bezugs- und Kommentarworte" in den synoptischen Evangelien.* ErThSt 44. Leipzig: St. Benno, 1981.

Warfield, B. B. *Christology and Criticism.* Grand Rapids: Baker, 1981.

Weder, H. *Die Gleichnisse Jesu als Metaphern.* 2. Aufl. FRLANT 120. Göttingen: Vandenhoeck & Ruprecht, 1980.

Weeden, T. J. *Mark — Traditions in Conflict.* Philadelphia: Fortress, 1971.

Weinacht, H. *Die Menschenwerdung des Sohnes Gottes im Markusevangelium.* Hermeneutische Untersuchungen zur Theologie 13. Tübingen: Mohr, 1972.

Weinreich, O. *Antike Heilungswunder.* Religionsgeschichtliche Versuche und Vorarbeiten 8/1. Giessen: Töpelmann, 1909.

Weinreich, O. *Religionsgeschichtliche Studien.* Tübinger Beiträge zur Altertumswissenschaft 5, 18. Stuttgart: Kohlhammer, 1968.

Weiss, J. *Das älteste Evangelium.* Göttingen: Vandenhoeck & Ruprecht, 1903.

Weiss, J. *Die Schriften des Neuen Testaments.* Bd. 1: *Die drei älteren Evangelien.* 4. Aufl. Göttingen: Vandenhoeck & Ruprecht, 1929.

Weiss, W. *"Eine neue Lehre in Vollmacht."* BZNW 52. Berlin: Walter de Gruyter, 1989.

Wellhausen, J. *Einleitung in die drei ersten Evangelien.* 1. Aufl. Berlin: Reimer, 1905.

Wellhausen, J. *Das Evangelium Marci.* 1. Aufl., 2. Aufl. Berlin: Reimer, 1905, 1909.

Wendling, E. *Die Entstehung des Marcus-Evangeliums.* Tübingen: Mohr, 1908.

Wengst, K. *Pax Romana.* Philadelphia: Fortress, 1987.

Wenham, D. *The Rediscovery of Jesus' Eschatological Discourse.* Sheffield: JSOT, 1984. (= *Gospel Perspectives* 4)

Wenham, J. W. *Christ and the Bible.* Grand Rapids: Baker, 1984.

Wenham, J. W. *Easter Enigma.* 2nd ed. CEP. Grand Rapids: Zondervan, 1984.

"Wenn nicht jetzt, wann dann?" H.-J. Kraus FS. Ed. H.-G. Geyer et al. Neukirchen-Vluyn: Neukirchener Verlag, 1983.

Wer ist unser Gott? Ed. L. Schottroff and W. Schottroff. München: Kaiser, 1986.

Westerholm, S. *Jesus and Scribal Authority.* ConBNT 10. Lund: Gleerup, 1978.

Wettstein, J. *Novum Testamentum Graecum.* Graz: Akademische Druck- und Verlagsanstalt, 1962.

"Wie gut sind deine Zelte, Jaakow. . . ." R. Mayer FS. Ed. E. L. Ehrlich and B. Klappert with U. Ast. Gerlingen: Bleicher, 1986.

Wilcken, U. *Urkunden der Ptolemäerzeit.* Berlin: Walter de Gruyter, 1927.

Wilckens, U. *Resurrection.* Atlanta: Knox, 1977.

Williams, J. G. *Gospel Against Parable.* Bible and Literature Series 12. Decatur: Almond, 1985.

Williams, S. K. *Jesus' Death as Saving Event.* HDR 2. Missoula: Scholars, 1975.

Wilson, S. G. *The Gentiles and the Gentile Mission in Luke-Acts.* SNTSMS 23. Cambridge: Cambridge UP, 1973.

Wimmer, J. F. *Fasting in the New Testament.* Theological Inquiries. New York: Paulist, 1982.

Wink, W. *John the Baptist in the Gospel Tradition.* SNTSMS 7. London: Cambridge UP, 1968.

Winter, P. *On the Trial of Jesus.* 2nd ed. Studia Judaica 1. Berlin: Walter de Gruyter, 1974.

Witherington, B., III. *Women in the Ministry of Jesus.* SNTSMS 51. Cambridge: Cambridge UP, 1984.

Wohlenberg, G. *Das Evangelium des Markus.* 1.-2. Aufl. ZahnK 2. Leipzig: Deichert, 1910.

Wort in der Zeit. K. H. Rengstorf FS. Ed. W. Haubeck and M. Bachmann. Leiden: Brill, 1980.

Das Wort und die Wörter. G. Friedrich FS. Stuttgart: Kohlhammer, 1973.

Wrede, W. *The Messianic Secret.* Library of Theological Translations. Cambridge: Clarke, 1971.

Wrege, H.-T. *Die Gestalt des Evangeliums.* BBET 11. Frankfurt: Lang, 1978.

Wuellner, W. H. *The Meaning of "Fishers of Men."* NTL. Philadelphia: Westminster, 1967.

Wunsche, A. *Der Kuss in Bibel, Talmud und Midrasch.* Breslau: Marcus, 1911.

Yadin, Y. *The Temple Scroll.* Jerusalem: Israel Exploration Society, 1983.

Zahn, T. *Acta Joannis.* Erlangen: Deichert, 1880.

Zahn, T. *Das Evangelium des Matthäus.* 3. Aufl. ZahnK 1. Leipzig: Deichert, 1910.

Zahn, T. *Introduction to the New Testament.* Minneapolis: Klock, 1977.

Die Zeit Jesu. H. Schlier FS. Ed. G. Bornkamm and K. Rahner. Freiburg: Herder, 1970.

Zerwick, M. *Biblical Greek.* SPIB 114. Rome: Pontifical Biblical Institute, 1963.

Zerwick, M. *Untersuchungen zum Markus-Stil.* SPIB. Rome: Pontifical Biblical Institute, 1937.

Zimmermann, F. *The Aramaic Origin of the Four Gospels.* New York: Ktav, 1979.

Zur Geschichte des Urchristentums. R. Schnackenburg FS. Ed. G. Dautzenberg et al. QD 87. Freiburg: Herder, 1979.

Zwick, R. *Montage im Markusevangelium.* SBB 18. Stuttgart: KBW, 1989.

Introduction

The Gospel of Mark contains no ciphers, no hidden meanings, no sleight of hand:

No messianic secret designed to mask a theologically embarrassing absence of messianism from the ministry of the historical Jesus. No messianic secret designed to mask a politically dangerous presence of messianism in his ministry. No freezing of Jesuanic tradition in writing so as to halt oral pronouncements of prophets speaking in Jesus' name. No Christology of irony that means the reverse of what it says. No back-handed slap at Davidic messianism. No covert attack on divine man Christology. No pitting of the Son of man against the Christ, the Son of David, or the Son of God.

No ecclesiastical enemies lurking between the lines or behind the twelve apostles, the inner three, and Jesus' natural family. No mirror-images of theological disputes over the demands and rewards of Christian discipleship. No symbolism of discipular enlightenment in the miracles. No "way"-symbolism for cross-bearing. No bread-symbolism for the Eucharist. No boat-symbolism for the Church. No voyage-symbolism for Christian mission. No other-side-of-Galilee symbolism for a mission to the Gentiles. No Galilee-symbolism for salvation or for the Second Coming. No Jerusalem-symbolism for Judaism or Judaistic Christianity.

No apocalyptic code announcing the end. No de-apocalyptic code cooling down an expectation of the end. No open end celebrating faith over verifiability. No overarching concentric structure providing a key to meaning at midpoint. No riddle wrapped in a mystery inside an enigma.

None of those. Mark's meaning lies on the surface. He writes a straightforward apology for the Cross, for the shameful way in which the object of Christian faith and subject of Christian proclamation died, and hence for Jesus as the Crucified One.

Though spelled out much more fully in later comments and accompanying notes, the thesis formed by the foregoing denials and affirmation needs both partial substantiation and more positive statement in advance. These will provide a

1

roadmap for the long, labyrinthian journey to follow. Though they may also leave an impression that the thesis was imposed on Mark from the start, in fact the thesis evolved through multiple readings of Mark combined with the reading of other primary literature and of secondary literature. One may not lay claim to having begun with a blank mind. Otherwise no questions of interpretation could have risen. But despite the claims of some that all interpretation consists in no more than an effort at political domination (in which case this very interpretation of interpretation loses its credibility), we can make the effort to attune and retune our thoughts to external data. Scholarly enterprise demands such an effort. Readers will have to decide whether the present one has proved successful. The decision should grow out of their own efforts at tuning and retuning, however; for a writer does not bear this responsibility alone.

Here then is the thesis spelled out more positively and provided with partial substantiation. The Gospel of Mark poses a literary problem in that two disparate kinds of material make up its contents. The first kind describes the successes of Jesus which make him look like others admired in the Greco-Roman world for their divine powers of wisdom, clairvoyance, exorcism, thaumaturgy, and personal magnetism — men such as Pythagoras, Empedocles, Philo's Moses, Simon Magus, Apollonius of Tyana, and even Barnabas and Paul. Jesus attracts disciples, draws crowds, exorcises demons, works miracles, teaches with authority, bests his opponents in debate. We may say that this material teaches a theology of glory. The second kind of material portrays quite a different Jesus, a persecuted one. He predicts his passion. One of his closest disciples betrays him. The rest forsake him. The leading one of the rest denies him. The Jewish authorities condemn him. The crowd yell for his crucifixion. He undergoes that most shameful of executions. And so on till in closing, the women flee from the martyr's empty tomb too bewildered and afraid to say anything to anyone. We may say that this material teaches a theology of suffering. To many, the theology of glory seems to concentrate in the first part of the gospel, the theology of suffering in its last part — though the passion predictions start as early as chap. 8 and Jesus' forensic victories extend into chap. 12. The basic problem in Marcan studies is how to fit together these apparently contradictory kinds of material in a way that makes sense of the book as a literary whole.

The regnant view has it that Mark corrects the theology of glory with the theology of suffering. Does Mark castigate the theology of glory so as to deny it altogether, or does he only qualify it? Does he cast the Apostles in an antagonistic role of bearing the theology of glory, or does he take a kinder, developmental view of them? For now, these intramural differences need not occupy us. Enough to know that at its core this regnant view hypothesizes that Mark wrote for a Christian audience, that his audience held to a tradition which glorified Jesus as a thaumaturgist and teacher, that the audience expected to see in their own lives evidence of similar power and authority and saw weakness, failure, and persecution instead. Experience seemed to contradict the theology of glory in their cherished tradition about Jesus. To resolve this problem of cognitive dissonance, Mark incorporated the tradition containing the theology of glory, but corrected that theology by putting it in the framework of the theology of suffering, the theology of the Cross — the cross of Jesus and that of his disciples: following him requires self-denial and taking up one's own cross. Not only did Mark add the chapters on the Passion. He also intruded into earlier chapters, containing the theology of glory, several passion predictions — not to detail other redaction, all designed to prick the balloon of what would nowadays be called a health-and-wealth view of Christian discipleship.

One should not deny that this reconstruction contains theological truth such as appears elsewhere in the NT (2 Corinthians 10–13, for instance). But does it contain historico-literary truth so far as the writing of Mark is concerned? Troubling questions arise: If Mark wants to lower Christian expectations of glory, why do only two passages (in chaps. 8 and 10) relate the sufferings of Jesus to similar experience on the part of his disciples, and why does each of those passages end on the note of glory ("the glory of his Father with the holy angels. . . . some of the ones standing here will by no means taste death till they see the rule of God as having come with power" — 8:38–9:1; "but to sit on my right and left will be given to those for whom it has been prepared" — 10:40)? Why does the Marcan Jesus not carry his cross (15:21), as in the fourth gospel (John 19:17), to provide an example of cross-carrying for the disciples? More broadly, why does Mark retain *so much* material representing the theology of glory? In sheer bulk that material far exceeds its counterpart on the side of suffering. Why does Mark not curtail it? Why does he write half his gospel before bringing in the supposed correction? By that time has not the theology of glory become so firmly established that a program of correction can hardly be carried out with much success? And is it really true that he deflates glory in his presentation of the thaumaturgic-didactic tradition? For that matter, does he present suffering as a corrective to glory, or glory as a counterbalance to suffering?

This last question telegraphs the present thesis, which turns the regnant view on its head by saying that Mark does not pit the suffering and death of Jesus against his successes, but that Mark pits the successes against the suffering and death, and then uses the passion predictions, writes up the passion narrative, and caps his gospel with a discovery of the empty tomb in ways that cohere with the success-stories, in ways that make the passion itself a success-story. Thus all the materials in the gospel attain a unity of purpose. Competition ceases, and the point of the book turns Christological instead of parenetic, rather as in Peter's Pentecostal sermon (and we might remember the pre-Papian tradition that Mark wrote up Peter's reminiscences — see pp. 1026-45): "Jesus the Nazarene, a man attested to you by God with miracles and wonders and signs which God did through him . . . this man, delivered up by the predetermined plan and foreknowledge of God, you nailed to a cross by the hands of lawless men and put him to death, whom God raised by loosing the pangs of death, because it was impossible for him to be held by it. . . . God has made him both Lord and Christ — this Jesus whom you crucified" (Acts 2:22-24, 36; cf. 10:34-43, also attributed to Peter [though even apart from a Petrine origin these cross-references exhibit a Christian way of overcoming the scandal of the Cross];

John 20:30-31; 21:25; Rom 1:16; 15:18-19; 1 Cor 2:4-5 with 1:18, 23; Gal 3:1-5; 1 Thess 2:13; Justin *Dial.* 32-34).

The success of any interpretation depends on its explanatory power, on its ability to make more complete, coherent, and natural sense of textual data than other interpretations do (cf. M. A. Tolbert, *Sowing the Gospel* 10-13); so to the text of Mark we must go, paying attention to the selection and arrangement of material, recurring themes, word order, editorial comments, summaries, and such like. Mark starts with a superscription that identifies Jesus as Christ and Son of God (1:1). Immediately this identification transforms the coming crucifixion from the shameful death of a common criminal into the awe-inspiring death of a divine being who is God's appointed agent. The episode concerning the centurion at the foot of the Cross will confirm this transformation (15:39). Meanwhile, a prophetic quotation sets the career of Jesus in the framework of a divine plan (1:2-3): nothing is going to happen by accident, not even his death, as the passion predictions will further show. Mark stresses the divine plan by putting the quotation before the Baptist narrative to which it corresponds, and within the quotation by putting Exod 23:20 before Isa 40:3 to get a divine "I," which Isa 40:3 lacks — "behold, I am sending my messenger" — and this despite the mention of Isaiah in the introductory formula. The initial outworking of God's plan through John the Baptizer reaches a climax in John's description of his successor as the Stronger One who will baptize people in the superior element of Holy Spirit (1:7-8). Strength of divine magnitude — this will characterize Jesus, supercharged by the Holy Spirit in his dealings with others. Mark includes none of John's preaching of repentance (Matt 3:7-10; Luke 3:7-14), only what John has to say about Jesus that will forestall any impression of weakness when the Crucifixion takes place.

It makes sense, then, that in Jesus' first appearance Mark should show him receiving the Spirit, who descends into him (1:9-11). The comparison of the Spirit with a dove headlines the divinity of the Spirit, for the Hellenistic world regarded the dove as a divine bird. Since Spirit connotes power, Mark has prepared us doubly — by John's description of Jesus and by the Spirit's descent — to expect that Jesus will act with a power no less than divine. The heavenly voice, "You are my beloved Son; in you I am well pleased," confirms this significance in the Spirit's descent, confirms Mark's initial identification of Jesus as God's Son, and rules out ahead of time any misinterpretation of the Crucifixion as a sign of God's displeasure.

The temptation narrative brings the introduction of Jesus to a climax (1:12-13). But it is hardly a narrative of temptation. Mark does not detail so much as one temptation, let alone three (contrast Matt 4:1-11; Luke 4:1-13). He does not even tell whether Jesus overcame the temptation. He says only that the Spirit expelled Jesus into the wilderness, that Satan's temptation lasted forty days, that Jesus was with wild beasts, and that angels were waiting on him. The length of the temptation shows him to be Satan's archfoe (a point that defangs in advance the charge that he enjoys an alliance with Satan — 3:22-30). Jesus' ability to stay with the wild beasts for so long a time shows him to be the Stronger One — they cannot harm him. And the angels' waiting on him shows him to be God's beloved

Son, well pleasing to God. What we have, then, is not the story of a moral victory, but a series of narrative statements each pregnant with a Christology of power and divine sonship.

From here on, spatial limitations force us to proceed thematically rather than serially. Having introduced Jesus, Mark now portrays him as magnetic, authoritative, powerful, insightful, and dignified, just as one would expect of God's Son and appointed agent. Jesus starts preaching. His magnetism proves so attractive that some people follow him fulltime, and others repeatedly come to him in droves. At his command, Simon and Andrew leave their trade, right in the middle of practicing it. They do not even haul in their fishing nets. James and John leave their father as well, and do so despite the strength of patriarchalism in that society. Jesus' magnetism proves stronger, and will prove so to others, too — the twelve apostles (1:16-20; 3:13-19).

Crowds flock to Jesus at lakeshore in Galilee, in the city of Capernaum, from the whole of Galilee (1:33, 45; 2:1-2, 13; 5:21). His magnetism knows no bounds. He attracts crowds from as far away as Judea, Jerusalem, Idumea, Transjordan, and Tyrian and Sidonian territory (3:7-8). These crowds are large, sometimes superlatively large (πλεῖστος — 4:1). They make a multitude. In 3:7-8 the use of cognates in the phrase πολὺ πλῆθος, "a multitudinous multitude," the repetition of the phrase, and the chiastic reversal of word order in its second occurrence put all possible emphasis on Jesus' power of attraction. More than one crowd comes to him at the same time (10:1). They run to him (9:25). Once they run by foot so fast that they arrive at his landing site before he does (6:32-33). They acclaim him before the very gates of Jerusalem (11:1-10).

Jesus attracts all sorts of people in these crowds, even toll collectors and sinners, and *many* of them (2:15). Not only religious people, then, but irreligious people, too. One toll collector leaves his office to follow him (2:13-14). Jesus attracts whole populations: "*All* are seeking you," his disciples report (1:37). For privacy he has to get up very early and go to a deserted place (1:35). Even there the crowds pursue him (6:32-34). A crowd of four thousand are so enthralled that they stay with him three days in the wilderness (8:1-2, 9). He and his disciples have no leisure even to eat (3:20; 6:31). The crowds press in on him so eagerly that they threaten to crush him to death (3:9; 5:24). To keep that from happening, he tells the unclean spirits not to shout, "You are the Son of God" (3:11). By an apotropaic use of his divine title, they are trying to defend themselves from exorcism; but he is defending himself from being crushed to death by a crowd that will press in on him all the more eagerly if any more of them learn about his divine sonship. One crowd is so huge that he has to teach them from a boat offshore (4:1-2). People fill not only the house where he is staying, but also the street outside (2:1-2). They are packed so tightly that nobody can get through to him (2:3-4). Even though he enters incognito, he cannot stay hidden for long (2:1-2; 7:24).

The crowds hang on Jesus' words because he teaches them with authority. The teaching of Christ God's Son is bound to carry supreme authority, but Mark goes further by remarking the effect and recognition of that authority. "They were

knocked out at his teaching, for he was teaching them as one who had authority
and not as the scribes" (1:22). This is the effect, and for the moment it is all that
Mark is interested in. He does not tell what Jesus taught. The shadowboxing of
the scribes only highlights the impact of his teaching. When the audience came
to, they asked, "What is this?" and answered their own question, "A new teaching
with authority!" This answer spells a recognition of Jesus' authority. Nobody
missed it. All of them (ἅπαντες) were astonished (1:27).

Mark puts the authority of Jesus on display also in 2:1–3:6, a section made
up largely of so-called controversy stories. In fact, these stories deal not so much
in controversy as in Jesus' authority, his authority to forgive sins, to eat with toll
collectors and sinners, to let his disciples neglect fasting, to let them pluck grain
on the Sabbath, and himself to heal on the Sabbath. In 2:1-12 his enemies say
nothing aloud, not even to each other. In 2:13-17 they make no accusation, not
even silently and privately. They only ask "why?" and direct their question to the
disciples, not to Jesus himself. In 2:18-22 the questioners are not enemies at all;
so their question "why?" may carry not even an implied accusation, and it has to
do with the disciples' behavior, not with Jesus' behavior. In 2:23-28 an accusatory
"why?" — the first one spoken aloud — again has to do only with the disciples'
behavior. 3:1-6 starts with Jesus' enemies looking for an accusation and ends with
their murderous plot, but they ask no question and issue no challenge. What binds
these stories together, then, is the overwhelming effect of Jesus' sayings, whether
or not a controversy in the normal sense of the word evoked those sayings. This
effect illustrates the authority with which he speaks. In two of the stories his
authority forms the very nub of the argument by breaking down two pillars of
Jewish piety, fasting and Sabbath-keeping. His presence or removal determines
whether or not the disciples *can* fast, not merely the appropriateness or inappropriateness of their fasting; and as Lord of the Sabbath, he can and does let his
disciples violate the Sabbath law (2:19-20, 28).

The intensifying of opposition, seen especially in the murderous plot at 3:6,
does not merely anticipate the death of Jesus. It acts as a foil to the increasingly
mighty exercise of his authority. The greater the opposition, the greater his
mastery. First century Mediterranean society lay great store by honor and shame.
Mark has Jesus shame his opponents. Shaming them forestalls the shame that
would otherwise attach to his crucifixion. It also justifies the honor that Mark
pays to him in this gospel.

The didactic authority of Jesus also gives a favorable interpretation of his
death. He teaches in parables to desensitize outsiders — purposefully (telic ἵνα —
4:12) — lest they convert and be forgiven. So his death will stem, not from failure
to achieve a goal of universal discipleship, but from the successful achievement of
his goal to separate out his true family from outsiders. The whole section on parables
(4:1-34), coming on the heels of the section concerning Jesus' true family (3:31-35),
makes this apologetic point. The last verse in the parabolic section (4:34) sharpens
the point with κατ᾽ ἰδίαν, "privately," with the emphatic forward position of the
phrase, and with the attachment of ἰδίοις to μαθηταῖς to produce "his own disciples"
— "his *own*" as opposed to outsiders, by now successfully desensitized.

In 7:1-23 Jesus exhibits his authority over the elders of the Pharisees and over the OT law itself by pronouncing all foods clean. The intrusiveness and awkwardness of the editorial phrase, "cleansing all foods" (v 19) — it breaks into the middle of Jesus' words and modifies the "he" in "he says" five clauses back — shows to what lengths Mark goes to make his point, as already in the editorial hyperbole that made "*all* the Jews" join the Pharisees in supererogatory rites of purification (7:3-4).

In 8:10-12 Mark narrates the demand for a sign as a contest between the Pharisees and Jesus. "Groaning in his spirit" indicates that Jesus audibly gives force to his following refusal, the authority of which will shut down the Pharisees' attempt to embarrass him. The perfective ἀνα-, "deeply," intensifies the forcefulness of his groaning; and the archaicness of the Hebrew ἀμήν and of the Hebrew way of expressing solemn denial, "If this generation will be given a sign!" adds further strength.

It has become evident that just as Mark started by emphasizing the authority of Jesus' teaching without revealing its contents, where later he does reveal its contents he does so not for ecclesiastical application but for Christological enhancement. In fact, the initial emphasis on didactic authority apart from didactic content gives us the clue to Mark's principle of selection when he does come round to include content. He chooses only those teachings that exhibit the authority of Jesus to upset established norms and the establishment itself. In this light we should view 9:33–10:45, which many have taken in whole or in part as a handbook for life in the church. Running like a red thread throughout this section is the iconoclasm of Jesus' teachings. Mark punctuates this iconoclasm with periodic notations of the disciples' befuddledness and amazement. These notations show where Mark's interest lies, in an iconoclasm that demonstrates overawing authority. Startlingly, Jesus teaches that you must lose your life to save it, that Elijah has already come, that anybody who wants to be first has to be last, that a maimed body in God's kingdom is better than a whole body in hell, that divorce is wrong and remarriage adulterous, that God's kingdom belongs to children, that wealth is a disadvantage more than impossible for anyone but God to overcome, and that you should enter a life of voluntary servitude.

Barely have Mark's audience caught their breath in the healing of Bartimaeus and the Triumphal Procession — two more successes (10:46–11:10) — but Mark quotes some further strong words. Jesus curses a fig tree and despite its having leaves, it has withered before twenty-four hours have passed (11:11-14, 19-21). Meanwhile, he "teaches" in the temple that it shall be called a house of prayer for all the nations but that the authorities have made it a den of bandits (11:17). In response to this teaching, those authorities seek how to destroy him because they fear him, "for all the crowd were knocked out by his teaching" (11:18). The pericope ends there; so even the cleansing of the temple serves the point of Jesus' didactic power. On discovering that the fig tree has withered, he continues to make pronouncements uncomfortably startling: Faith without doubt can cause the Mount of Olives to be taken up and thrown into the Dead Sea. All that you ask for is yours if you pray with faith. Forgive instead of praying for vindication and retribution. God's forgiving you requires you to forgive others even though they are in the wrong (11:22-25).

The following confrontation with the Sanhedrin, who challenge Jesus' authority, starts a series of four verbal victories that he wins over his opponents, the last of whom turns into an admirer (11:27-33; 12:1-12, 13-17, 18-27, 28-34). Here are the real controversy stories in Mark. The Sanhedrin fail to embarrass Jesus with two questions (11:28). He embarrasses them with only one: "I will ask you *one* word" (11:29). They retire when he tells a parable against them (12:12). When next he escapes the horns of a dilemma on taxes, even the Pharisees and Herodians who came to trap him in his speech marvel at him (12:17). The Sadducees take their turn, but to no avail. Jesus closes by telling them, "You are much deceived" (12:27). Asyndeton gives such force to this putdown that in the textual tradition variant readings have developed to soften its impact. When even a scribe comes to recognize the truth of Jesus' teaching, no one dares to ask Jesus any more questions (12:34).

Having cleared the field of his opponents and won over one of them, Jesus exposes to a large crowd his opponents' ignorance with regard to "the Son of David" (12:35-37) and their dangerousness ("Beware!") and their doom ("These will receive very abundant judgment" — 12:38-40). Having earned the admiration of the crowd (they "heard him gladly" — 12:37), he displays to the disciples his insight, which upsets popular opinion on the size of gifts ("this poor widow has thrown [money] into the treasury to a greater extent than all those who have been throwing [money into the treasury]" — 12:41-44) and his foresight (the eschatological discourse of chap. 13). With this preparation, Mark's audience will understand the following passion of Jesus to be, not a penalty deserved by him for any danger that he posed to society, but the outcome of a backlash against his having defeated opponents who were dangerous to society as well as to him.

Closely interwoven with Jesus' authority and magnetism are his powerful deeds. They fall into two classes: exorcisms and miracles. The interweaving starts as early as the first episode in the long day at Capernaum: ". . . a new teaching with authority. He commands even the unclean spirits, and they obey him" (1:27); "and a multitudinous multitude followed . . . hearing how many things he was doing" (3:7-8). Though Jesus has just said only that he came forth to preach (1:38), Mark adds that Jesus cast out demons as well (1:39). He cast them out even though they knew his name and title and used their knowledge in a way that should have shielded them with magical protection: "Jesus of Nazareth. . . . I know you, who you are, the Holy One of God" (1:24). At this point a Hellenistic audience think the unclean spirit has gained an upper hand. But success in the exorcism will display the divine potency of Jesus. He does not have to counter with any names, appeals to deity, incantations, or potions. "Shut up" (1:25) does not impose a messianic secret; it starts the exorcism itself. Jesus penetrates the magical defense as though it were missing. The loudness of the spirit's last outcry demonstrates the success of the exorcism. The inarticulateness of the outcry proves the effectiveness of Jesus' command to stop the self-defensive use of his name and title. Mark's audience are to share in the amazement of all who saw and heard the exorcism (1:26-27).

Mark presents a particularly difficult case in the Gergasene demoniac (5:1-20). The detail with which he describes the demoniac's untameability makes the exorcism all the more remarkable once it occurs. Indirectly, so also does the failure of Jesus' first attempt: "for he had been saying to it [the spirit], 'Come out,'" but using "Jesus," "Son of God," and "God," it adjured Jesus not to torment it — and did not come out. When he forced it to reveal *its* name, "Legion," the reason for initial failure became apparent: he had been addressing the spirit as though it were one instead of many. So they seized a temporary advantage by using his name and title and adjuring him in the name of God. Forced to reveal their large number, however, and despite their large number, they are reduced to grovelling supplication. To exorcise them, Jesus does not even have to use their name. He only has to address them accurately in the plural. Add to the exorcism the drowning of the pigs and what started as a stubborn case turns into a humorously crushing defeat of the spirits. The imperfect tense of ἐπνίγοντο, "were drowning," dramatizes the defeat, as in slow motion playback: Mark's audience can visualize the pigs gradually going under (5:13). "And all [who came to see the ex-demoniac] marveled" (5:20).

In another difficult case, at which the disciples failed utterly, the question of Jesus' ability is raised; and he answers it decisively by exorcising without prayer a spirit that the disciples could have exorcised only with prayer (9:14-29). On another occasion, he exorcises a demon at a distance without so much as a command (7:24-30). The asyndeton in "go, the demon has gone out . . ." (we would have expected "go, *for* the demon has gone out . . .") underscores Jesus' ability to exorcise at a distance, and also his supernatural knowledge in announcing the distant exorcism (7:29).

A mere word of Jesus brings healing (2:11-12; 3:5; 10:52). His mere touch brings it (1:31, 41; 6:5). Even that little effort is unnecessary. Jesus is so charged with healing power that people have only to touch him (3:9-10; 5:27-34). Even the fringe of his garment will do, for his skin cannot contain the radiant energy (6:56). Power goes out from him (5:30). It is not just an attribute that enables him to work a miracle. The power (δύναμις) *is* the miracle (again δύναμις, by definition an act of power). Jesus is so charged with power that it goes out from him even apart from a particular act of his will (5:30 again) as well as by such an act (1:41 again). When he himself touches people to heal them, his hands become instruments through which acts of power take place (6:2).

The leper does not even have to ask for cleansing. He only affirms that Jesus has the abililty to cleanse him. Jesus proves him right (1:40-41). This ability inspires such vigorous faith that people dig through a roof (2:4-5) and run around cities, towns, and hamlets to bring their sick to Jesus (6:54-56). However many the kinds of diseases, he never fails at a healing (1:34); and Mark's summaries make the point that there were many more healings and exorcisms than he can recount in his gospel (1:32-34; 3:7-12; 6:53-56).

To explain these deeds Herod Antipas joins in the opinion of those who say that Jesus is John the Baptizer raised from the dead (6:14-16). The account of John's martyrdom does not merely fill a temporal gap between the commission of the Twelve and the completion of their mission. It makes the point that even a king who himself had ordered the beheading of John and with his own eyes had seen John's head delivered on a platter to his own dining room went so far as to infer a resurrection of John — so many and mighty were the miracles at work in Jesus (6:17-29).

He heals what physicians cannot heal (5:25-34). He even raises a dead person (5:35-43). So astonishing are his miracles that they invalidate unbelief even when they are few (6:1-6a). Mark turns their sparsity in Nazareth into a testimony to their numerousness elsewhere. "And he was wondering on account of their unbelief" rules out lack of power as the reason for Jesus' inability to perform very many miracles when visiting his hometown. He marvels that unbelief can coexist with the Nazarenes' astonishment at his wisdom and miracles, which make their unbelief a marvel of its own kind.

Specially difficult miracles call for the use of extraordinary means — extraordinary at least for Jesus: application of spittle, sticking of fingers into a patient's ears, looking up to heaven, groaning, a second laying on of hands (7:31-37; 8:22-26). The effects are stupendous: a deaf mute speaks plainly, a blind man sees all things distinctly even at a distance (τηλαυγῶς, "far-shiningly"). Likewise, Bartimaeus follows sightfully on the very road beside which he has blindly begged (10:46-52). Peter's mother-in-law serves as hostess in the house where she has just been bedridden with a fever (1:29-31). With everybody looking on, the paralytic gets up and carries out his pallet (2:1-12).

Not only does the power of Jesus show itself through his own activities. It also multiplies itself through those of his disciples. With it, they heal the sick and cast out demons just as he does (6:12-13). But he remains supreme: only he multiplies bread and fish (6:35-44; 8:1-9), stills a storm (4:35-41), and walks on water (6:45-52). In these episodes the disciples' ignorance and fear magnify his majesty. Only the dullest sensibilities, writes Mark, could have failed to detect the miraculous element in the feedings and consequently have failed to apply to present need the surfeit of Jesus' power (6:52; 8:13-21).

Lacing his power is compassion (1:41). He does not destroy life; he saves it (3:4). Even his anger, justified as it was, is tempered with sorrow (3:5). He shows mercy to Bartimaeus though the crowd try to shush the beggar (10:46-52). Mark makes his audience sympathetic toward Jesus. They should not take offense at the Crucifixion; for Jesus was no criminal deserving to be crucified, but a healer and savior worthy of honor.

Added to magnetism, authority, and power are clairvoyance, insight, and, above all, foresight. Jesus says that he will turn fishers of fish into fishers of human beings (1:16-21), and so it happens on their mission (6:6b-13, 30-31). He reads the thoughts of the scribes (2:8). He predicts his coming death and resurrection and the fate of his followers (8:27–9:1). He predicts that some standing in his audience will not die till they see God's rule as having come with power (9:1), and in the next episode (the Transfiguration) they do see it so (9:2-8). Jesus can accurately predict his resurrection even against the seemingly contradictory implications of the scribes' correctly biblical expectation concerning Elijah's coming first (9:12). The disciples' failure to understand yet another passion prediction makes Jesus' foresight stand out all the more, and their fear to ask him what he means implies the awesomeness of a divine being who knows his own fate (9:30-32). He says that the first will be last, the last first, the great person a servant, the person in first position a slave of all. He promises that the disciples will receive a hundredfold in this life, with persecutions, and eternal life hereafter (9:33-37; 10:17-31, 35-45). The predictions of his passion increase in detail (delivery to the Gentiles, mockery, spitting, whipping — 10:32-34) and interpret the passion as self-sacrificial: "to give his life as a ransom in place of many" (10:45). Here, the apologetic of predictive power metamorphoses into an apologetic of beneficial service. No felon this!

He predicts small events as well as large. The disciples will find a colt. They will find it as soon as they enter a village. It will be male, tied, previously unsat upon. Someone may ask why they are untying it (11:1-6). Delicious detail. Jesus predicts the fate of the temple, the fate of the world, the fate of the elect, the coming of the Son of man — again with details galore: not one stone on another, wars, persecution, abomination of desolation, unprecedented tribulation, false christs, false prophets, celestial disasters (chap. 13). Since a number of these predictions have yet to be fulfilled, the repeated command to watch stresses the already proved reliability of Jesus as a forecaster. Parenesis serves Christology. We make a mistake to isolate chap. 13 from the many other predictions that pepper the pages of Mark, and then to tease out of that chapter a historical setting. Put alongside the other predictions, those in chap. 13 tell us more about Jesus than about the setting of Mark's church. We should note in particular that persecution does not stand out, but only lines up in a row with other predicted events and conspicuously fails to appear on the schedule of the unprecedented tribulation; for that tribulation threatens "all flesh," not especially the elect.

The double reference in 14:1-2, 10-11 to the chief priests' plot to kill Jesus makes an inclusion highlighting that his passion predictions are beginning to take effect. The anointing of his body for burial, which intervenes, shows the same. In the story of the anointing occurs yet another passion prediction, plus a prediction that the deed of anointing will be published wherever the gospel is preached in the whole world (14:6-9). Mark's very writing examples the fulfilment of this prediction. The preparation of the Passover features a prediction by Jesus that two of his disciples will meet a man carrying a jar of water, and their being shown a room in which to make preparation (14:13-15). The prediction includes details describing the room: large, upstairs, furnished, ready for use. "And they found just as he had told them" (14:16). There is the point: Jesus' foresight.

At the Last Supper (14:17-25) he predicts that one of the Twelve will betray him and that his death will entail the outpouring of his blood from his body. The unlikelihood that one of the Twelve should betray Jesus contributes to the impressiveness of fulfilment. An appeal to the OT strengthens the reliability of his prediction. And a pronouncement of woe on the betrayer exposes him, not Jesus, as the true criminal. The passage closes with yet another prediction, that of Jesus' not drinking till kingdom come. This prediction continues to be fulfilled as Mark writes.

Jesus proceeds to predict all the disciples' deserting him. "All" increases the unlikelihood of fulfilment and therefore again the impressiveness of fulfilment. Once more the OT supports the prediction by fitting the event into God's plan. Mark's appetite for Jesus' predictions is insatiable. Jesus says that after his resurrection he will go ahead of the disciples to Galilee. In the meantime, the one most likely to falsify the prediction of desertion by all the disciples — viz., Peter, the first-listed apostle, the one whose added name means "stone," the leading confessor of Jesus' messiahship, the one who rebuked Jesus for predicting the Passion, the one who repeats his present protest and adds vehemence to it (ἐκπερισσῶς) — this one will not only desert Jesus. He will do worse. He will deny him. "Today," "this night," "before the cock crows twice," "three times" — bitter details, but no less astonishing. The quick fulfilment of the predictions that stuff the paragraph in 14:26-31 will fortify Mark's apology for the Cross (14:32-52). Fulfilment starts already in the garden of Gethsemane. Mark does not show much interest in Jesus' prayers. He quotes only the first one, barely refers to the second, and does not refer at all to the third. But he does take care to note that when Jesus was arrested "they left him and fled — all" (πάντες, in emphatic last position), just as Jesus had said they would (14:50).

By now we have moved well into the passion narrative, where the apologetic interpretation receives its acid test; and we are already seeing that here, too, Mark chooses and shapes his materials and comments on them in ways that glorify the Passion, not in ways that passionize the earlier glory. The meeting of "*all* the chief priests and elders and scribes" (14:53), of "the *whole* Sanhedrin" (14:55), stresses the completeness with which Jesus' prediction is being fulfilled (cf. 8:31; 10:33). Failure to find true testimony against him shows that he does not deserve crucifixion (14:55-59). That the false witnesses are "many" stresses this point. In line with Mark's superscription (1:1), "I am" affirms Jesus' christhood and divine sonship (14:62). There follow his predictions of session at the right hand of the Power and of his coming with the clouds of heaven. Jesus is giving further predictions right as his earlier predictions are coming to pass.

The fulfilment of Jesus' prediction that he would be rejected gains in impressiveness from the details of condemnation and mockery (14:64-65). A similiar gain accrues to the fulfilment of his prediction that Peter will deny him three times: it takes only a lowly maid to elicit the first and second denials. Not even an exit of Peter into the forecourt before the second denial has worked an escape from Jesus' prediction. After the third denial Peter's weeping dramatizes the fulfilment in its entirety (14:66-72). Then comes a fulfilment of Jesus' prediction that the chief priests and the scribes would give him over to the Gentiles (15:1-15; cf. 10:33). So also with the soldiers' mocking him and spitting on him (15:16-20a; cf. 10:33-34). "The *whole* cohort" makes the fulfillment large-scale. The Crucifixion and Resurrection bring the theme of fulfilment to a climax. "Just as he told you" are the last words spoken at the empty tomb (16:7).

But let us back up, for Mark has glorified the Passion also in other ways, which may be loosely described as the dignifying of Jesus. "The spirit is willing, but the flesh is weak" (14:38). Since Jesus stays awake in Gethsemane while his disciples fall asleep, his flesh is strong just as his voice will be strong at the very moment of his death. The swords and clubs carried by the gang who arrest him contrast his submission to the Father's will with the hellbent animosity of the Sanhedrin (14:36, 43). Jesus' accepting the title "King of the Jews" as a given designation but rejecting it as a self-designation ("*You* say [so]") avoids insurrectionism (15:2). Pilate marvels at Jesus' silence in the face of vigorous accusations (15:3-5). This silence makes Pilate's offer to release Jesus all the more remarkable (15:6-9). For if Pilate sees no crime in him despite his refusal to defend himself, how flimsy must be the case against him. Barabbas's association with murders committed during a rebellion makes a foil against which Jesus' innocence stands out. Even Pilate recognizes the envy which gives rise to animosity against Jesus (15:10), and he avers Jesus' innocence (15:14). "Wanting to satisfy the yelling crowd" attributes the Crucifixion to a miscarriage of justice (15:15).

Jesus is Christ, Son of God — a figure of great dignity; so someone else takes up his cross (15:21). The soldiers' attempt to give him wine mixed with myrrh increases his dignity, for such wine is a delicacy (15:23). His refusal exhibits fortitude (15:23). His innocence having been established, the crucifixion with him of two bandits throws that innocence into bold relief (15:27). Mark describes the vilification of Jesus as blasphemous, i.e. as slanderous — undeserved (15:29). The Sanhedrin even ridicule Jesus with the false charge which at his trial they themselves dismissed (the Temple-accusation [15:29-32]). In answer, a supernatural darkness hides him from their leering (15:33). Twice Mark notes the loudness of Jesus' last outcry: he dies in a burst of strength, not with a whimper. Nor does he lapse into the usual unconsciousness (15:34, 37). The rending of the veil from top to bottom adds to the awesomeness of the event (15:38). It is seeing that Jesus' died "in this way" (οὕτως, adverbial form of οὗτος) which causes the centurion to exclaim, "Truly this man was God's Son" (15:39). For emphasis, Mark puts "God's Son" ahead of the copula. Even in the Crucifixion Jesus' divine sonship is dramatically evident.

Quick burial by a distinguished councilor showers unexpected honor on Jesus' corpse (15:42-47). The councilor's piety ("waiting for God's kingdom") and courage ("taking a risk") enhance the honor, and Pilate's marveling that Jesus is already dead minimizes the shame of his crucifixion. Now we see why Mark carefully counted out the hours during which Jesus hung on the Cross, from the third hour to the sixth to the ninth: he hung there only a short time, an amazingly short time, not the usual two, three, or four days. The linen used to wrap Jesus' corpse adds decency to the burial. So also does the tomb used for his interment, especially in view of Roman regulations forbidding such interment to executed criminals, particularly those executed like Jesus for high treason. A description of the tomb as "hewn out of rock," i.e. as of high grade, further enhances the honor accorded to his corpse. Just as quick removal from the Cross exempted the corpse from a Roman custom of leaving victims on crosses while the corpses decomposed in plain view and predatory beasts and birds of prey savaged them, so the stone that blocks the tomb protects Jesus' corpse from such indignities.

Discovery that the stone has been rolled away telegraphs the marvel of his resurrection (16:1-4). Mark's omitting to tell who rolled it away shows that he is interested only in the marvel as such. "For it was exceedingly large" heightens the marvel. The presence of a young man, sitting on the right (the favorable side), his long white robe, and the women's extreme amazement play up the marvel (16:5-7). The young man's announcement says that resurrection has undone crucifixion. The further announcement that Jesus is going ahead into Galilee and that there the disciples will see him brings us back to his predictive power and to the fulfilment of his very most unlikely prediction, that of his resurrection after three days. No wonder the women flee away trembling, astonished, and awestruck beyond words.

We know the shamefulness of crucifixion in the Greco-Roman world. M. Hengel has detailed it in his book *Crucifixion*. We know the consequent folly and scandal of early Christian preaching of the Cross. "The word of the Cross is folly to those who are perishing . . . to the Jews a scandal and to Gentiles folly" according to Paul (1 Cor. 1:18, 23), "madness" according to Justin Martyr (*1 Apol.* 13.4). With crude mockery the graffito that portrays Jesus as having the head of an ass as he hangs on the Cross illustrates this folly, this scandal, this madness (R. Garrucci, *Storia della Arte Cristiana* 6, pl. 483). H.-W. Kuhn (in *ANRW* II 25/1. 648-793) argues that the scandal of preaching the Cross consisted not in crucifixion as such; rather, in preaching the Cross as God's way of salvation. A fine distinction, yet it is hard to shake off the impression that there was something about crucifixion itself, its shamefulness, that made the preaching of the Cross foolish, scandalous, and mad. For an honorable manner of death (take Socrates' drinking of hemlock, for example) would have evoked plaudits rather than slurs, and "even death on a cross" (Phil 2:8) makes no sense apart from the shamefulness of crucifixion (N.B. the replacement of an expected ascensive καί with the even stronger adversative δέ for "even," death on a cross being so humiliating that it contrasts with every other kind of death).

On the other side and as mentioned earlier, we know that the Greco-Roman world highly estimated the ability of great men to attract disciples, draw large crowds, work miracles, cast out demons, and forecast the future, especially the circumstances of their own death, all as evidence of their divinity. Right within the NT, and not many miles from where Jesus grew up, the Samaritans "from small to great" hailed Simon Magus as "the Power of God which is called Great" for Simon's extended and astonishing practice of the magical arts (Acts 8:9-11). When in Lystra Paul healed a lame man, the reaction of the city was to identify Barnabas and Paul with the gods (Acts 13:8-13). Empedocles said, "But I go about among you as an immortal god, no longer as a mortal, honored by all. . . . When I come . . . into the busy towns to men and women, I am honored by them; however, they follow after me in their thousands . . . some requiring sayings from the oracle, others seeking to experience a word that brings healing in their manifold sicknesses . . ." (*Purifications* 102[112]). Pythagoras is said to have so enthralled a crowd of over two thousand men with one of his lectures that along with their wives and children they stayed with him instead of returning home

(Iambl. *VP* 6; cf. ibid. 30; Porph. *VP* 19-20). When Apollonius of Tyana arrived in Ephesus, we are told, not even the artisans remained at their handicrafts, but followed him (Philostr. *VA* 4.1; cf. 4.24). A notably large and enthusiastic band of youths joined themselves to him (ibid. 8.21); and he performed miracles and exorcisms (passim). A miracle performed by the emperor Vespasian made up for his lack of other prestige that would have qualified him for emperorship (Suet. *Vesp.* 7.2-3), and the mighty deeds of Sarapis made up for his lacking a myth about himself (Ael. Arist. *Hymn to Sarapis;* cf. G. Petzke in *NTS* 22 [1975-76] 202-3). Philo describes the falling of the divine spirit on Moses so that Moses, while still alive, prophesied with discernment the story of his own death — and Philo revels in the detailedness of the prophecy (Philo *Mos.* 2.290-91; cf. Suet. *Dom.* 15.3; Artapanus according to Clem. *Strom.* 1.23). The prominence and mixture of such elements in the Gospel of Mark combine with his attention to Jesus' crucifixion to favor that Mark wrote his gospel as an apology for the Cross. For he appeals to exactly those elements in the career of Jesus which for Greco-Roman readers would most likely suffuse the shame of crucifixion in a nimbus of glory (see B. Blackburn, *Theios Anēr,* against assuming that the said elements had no basis in Jesus' career but made their way from Greco-Roman culture into the tradition about him.)

This thesis and its substantiation grow out of the following interests, listed in a descending order of importance: (1) the Gospel of Mark itself, what it says and how it speaks; (2) the external subject matter to which it refers, almost solely the ministry of Jesus; (3) the author of the gospel (whether John Mark or someone else); and (4) its audience, i.e. those whom the author wanted to hear it read (private reading being comparatively unusual prior to the invention and use of the printing press — cf. Rev 1:3). Primary attention will go to the Gospel of Mark itself, because the present work is a commentary on that gospel, not a life of Jesus (which would require that primary attention go to the external subject matter) or a biography of the author (which would require that primary attention go to what might be gleaned about him from his gospel) or a homily or a history of religion based on the gospel (either one of which would require primary attention to its audience or audiences).

The devotion of primary attention to the Gospel of Mark itself will entail a careful examination of its text vis-à-vis that of comparable literature. But texts are not autonomous. If they were, they would carry no meaning (cf. L. M. Poland, *Literary Criticism* 86). So secondary attention will go to the external subject matter of Jesus' ministry. Such attention will keep the Gospel of Mark from meaninglessness with regard to its contents. Tertiary attention to him as its author will keep it from meaninglessness with regard to the intention with which it was written. Quaternary attention to the audience will keep it from meaninglessness with regard to its relevance to and effect on them.

We will look for the meaning of Mark's gospel primarily in its text to avoid the referential fallacy of thinking that we can discern its meaning outside the text in the subject matter to which it refers. For the text itself is our main source of information concerning the external subject matter to which it refers. Yet an author hardly chooses to write about a subject matter that does not provide the raw materials for what the author wants to say; so we can be reasonably sure that by and large the subject matter, though external to the text, does contribute to its meaning. The author's ways of referring to this subject matter will tend to correct anything in it that the author deems inimical to the meaning desired for the text. The subject matter to which Mark refers, then — i.e. the ministry of Jesus as known through Mark's text and parallel sources of information — will be brought in view to the extent that this subject matter may contribute to an understanding of the text, but not to the extent of overpowering its most natural meaning when considered apart from the underlying ministry of Jesus.

We will look for the meaning of Mark's gospel primarily in its text also to avoid the intentional fallacy of thinking that we can discern its meaning in the author behind the text. For the text itself is our main source of information concerning the author's intention. Though an unskilfully written text may convey that intention inadequately (sometimes an author will miswrite or write less well than desired), a skilfully written text will convey it adequately — and to the extent that we lack other texts by the same author or reliable and sufficient third-party information about that author, it becomes hard to judge the adequacy or inadequacy with which the text conveys authorial intention. But presumption lies on the side of adequacy, because a person would ordinarily neither write nor publish unless reasonably well satisfied that the produced text conveys authorial intention adequately. Furthermore, the preponderant meaning of a text will serve to make up for inadequacies here and there. As author, then, Mark will be brought in view to the extent that data concerning his person, background, and situation as known outside the text of his gospel may contribute to an understanding of this text, but not to the extent of overpowering its most natural meaning when considered apart from those data.

We will look for the meaning of Mark's gospel primarily in its text also to avoid the affective fallacy of thinking that we can discern its meaning in the response that an audience gives it. For their response might be determined partly, largely, or in theory even wholly by factors outside the text. To some extent, on the other hand, we may presume that an audience listen to a text to learn what it has to say, not to make it say what they want. The counter tendency to make it say what they want admittedly makes audience-response the weakest kind of evidence for meaning inherent to a text. But this tendency produces interpretations so various that they tend to cancel out each other, except for dominant interpretations, which because of their very dominance deserve to be considered as possibly true to the text. We do not know the response of Mark's intended audience, however. Under the supposition of their having heard his gospel read, we may chalk up in favor of the gospel that at least they did not suppress or destroy it. But its survival and circulation offer virtually no interpretative help. At most we may assume that Mark knew his intended audience reasonably well, anticipated the ways they might respond to this or that sort of writing, and wrote so as to insure as best he could the response he wanted to elicit. The responses of audiences other than the one intended by Mark lie outside the purview of this commentary except as the commentary itself and other secondary literature with which it interacts may count as such responses. Audience-response will be brought in view, then, to the extent that we may infer it from Mark's manner of writing and thus use it as a contribution to an understanding of his text as he wanted it to be understood, but not to the extent of overpowering its natural meaning when considered apart from inferences concerning the response of his intended audience.

To speak of the natural meaning of the text is to put a wild card in the deck. For how do we go about determining that natural meaning if not by examining our own and others' responses to the text, asking questions about its author, and comparing parallels to it? The answer is: by examining the text itself, by asking questions about it, and by comparing its elements with one another. This method will prove superior to those other means of determining the natural meaning. To be sure, our own subjectivity affects the avenues we take for examination, the questions we ask, the comparisons we make. But unless our thoughts and deeds are wholly determined — in which case we should no longer think of dialogue as meaningful — both writer and reader can will to shift the magnetic pole of interpretation from their respective subjectivities to the text, and can do so with some success. In fact, the objectivities of the text may well mold the subjectivities of writer and reader as curiosity, interest, and engagement build up. There can be no clean separation between what a text meant at first and what it now means; for none of us, including the writer and the readers of a commentary like the present one, can jump out of our skin into that of the author whose work is being interpreted. But there can develop a conformity of what the text means to what it originally meant, for through interpretation all of us subject ourselves to influence from the text that we are interpreting.

To mount a philosophical argument for the possibility of meaningful dialogue and against the ineluctability of solipsism would burst the boundaries of a biblical commentary (though commentators on the Bible, like literary critics, do well to learn from their colleagues in philosophy). Therefore be it only noted that this commentary proceeds on a belief in the possibility of meaningful dialogue. Higher critically, it also proceeds on a belief in the priority of Mark so far as the synoptic problem is concerned. The case for Marcan priority and against other solutions has been made well enough elsewhere and so will not be repeated there. Though referenced for the convenience of readers, parallels to Marcan passages will accordingly go undiscussed except as they may help to illuminate the text of Mark. Where Mark and Q appear to overlap, the position will not be taken that Mark knew Q itself. Otherwise, his emphasis on Jesus as a teacher would likely have led to inclusion of much more didactic material such as Q contained (R. H. Stein, *Proper Methodology* 196-97). Rather, Mark must have known some traditions which made their way into Q — hence "pre-Q," though we might hypothesize that Q pre-dated Mark but that after the writing of Q these other traditions continued to circulate independently from Q and thus came one by one to Mark's attention. Apart from investigating the possibility of an earlier stage of tradition as reflected in or represented by Q, the present commentary will seldom engage in a quest for the history of pre-Marcan traditions. It will often engage in criticism of attempts to trace such a history, however. With notorious frequency those attempts have reached mutually contradictory conclusions (C. C. Black, *Disciples;* F. Neirynck, *Evangelica* 618-36), and the homogeneity of Mark's style as brought out in a number of recent studies (F. Neirynck, *Duality;* idem, *Evangelica* 83-142; M. Reiser, *Syntax und Stil;* idem in *BZ* nf 30 [1986] 132-34; P. Dschulnigg, *Sprache;* G. Lüderitz in *Markus-Philologie* 165-203; C. Breytenbach, *Nachfolge* 40-47, 68-74; C. C. Black in *JSNT* 33 [1988] 19-39 — take E. J. Pryke, *Redactional Style,* for a contrary example) combines with our lack of pre-Marcan sources to make a quest for the history of pre-Marcan traditions largely impracticable. Even if we could trace this history by way of diachronic analysis, it is appropriate that by way of synchronic analysis a commentary on Mark pay most attention to Mark's text as it stands.

We will discover that synchronic analysis leaves so few loose ends that the need for diachronic analysis nearly vanishes anyway. Moreover, pre-Papian tradition says that Mark wrote up Peter's reminiscences of Jesus' ministry. If this tradition seems trustworthy (see pp. 1026-45 that it does) and if an interpretation given from the standpoint of its trustworthiness displays a superiority of explanatory power, the need to posit multiple stages of traditioning between Jesus and Mark diminishes considerably. The very possibility of such stages diminishes considerably. For though Peter may have shaped what he had seen and heard of Jesus' ministry to suit both his own interests and the needs of those who were listening to his sermons and though Mark may have shaped that sermonic material to suit both *his* own interests and the needs of those who were to hear his gospel read, Peter's having eyewitnessed Jesus' ministry and Mark's having earwitnessed Peter's ministry make unlikely any further stages of traditioning-cum-shaping. And we will see in the comments and notes to follow that those elements of Mark's text which are often adduced to prove such stages fail to do so.

Under a reasonable assumption that the present text of Mark made sense to the evangelist who authored it, we will see more particularly that inconcinnities provide keys to understanding it and therefore need not derive from its prehistory, i.e. from disparities between various sources and successive shapings (cf. W. Egger, *Nachfolge* 184-86; D. Zeller in *TLZ* 110 [1985] 736). On the contrary, the successive shapings of Mark in Matthew and Luke and of all the gospels and the rest of the NT in the textual tradition tend to smooth out inconcinnities (hence the text critical rule, for example, that other things being equal we should prefer a more difficult reading), so that inconcinnities can equally well look early and original rather than late and derivative. Nor will we find it necessary to think that Mark assumed his audience's prior knowledge of Jesuanic tradition and their consequent ability to fill gaps in his presentation. Failing that assumption, he may have been writing for non-Christian ignoramuses rather than for Christian know-it-alls.

The form critical attempt to recapture the oral tradition prior to Mark and prior to whatever written sources he may have used, if any, is foredoomed. All we have is texts. Once the oral tradition faded away, so also did the opportunity to study it with a degree of precision that could pass for scientific method. For an evolution of the oral tradition would not necessarily have matched the evolution of a written tradition. Evolution within each kind of tradition may have taken any number of different turns. And Mark may have drawn on oral tradition so primitive (whether Petrine or not) that too little space is left between Jesus and Mark for the critical mass of oral traditioning necessary to the practice of form criticism.

Misleading is the form critical tendency to assume that stereotypicality signals earliness whereas non-stereotypicality signals lateness; for non-stereotypicality may equally well derive from the rawness of early data, and stereotypicality may equally well derive from a lengthy process of retelling and assimilation to like materials in the tradition.

Also misleading is the form critical tendency to assume that materials linked by catchwords but not by linear logic have been combined secondarily. Perhaps they have been, but it is equally possible that Jesus and his partners in dialogue did not always speak according to the standards of linear logic, that their speech sometimes proceeded according to association by catchwords. After all, if later traditioners and redactors could have used such association, so also could the original speakers. Nor do events always take place in lock step. Real life is characterized by disorder as well as order. And differences in the order and association of materials among the gospels may be due to non-Marcan as well as to Marcan editorial activity. Unknown traditioners, Q, the other evangelists, and the Gospel of Thomas may have divided a tradition that appears whole in Mark — and vice versa.

Yet again misleading is the form critical tendency to assume the secondariness of what can be detached from a pericope without leaving it nonsensical, most commonly an introductory setting of time and place. That many Jesuanic incidents, sayings, dialogues, and speeches could easily have been set at a large number of different times and places does not undermine the historicity of the times and places at which these incidents, sayings, dialogues, and speeches were in fact set. The detachability of such information does not imply its inauthenticity. It is just as probable that eyewitnesses related temporal and topographical details from the very start and that traditioning, especially local traditioning, preserved such details as that those details were immediately lost only to be later fabricated. Of course, synoptic studies and comparisons between the synoptics and John and non-canonical gospels prove that new settings came into existence in the writing of later gospels. But Marcan settings were often maintained, too; and pre-Papian tradition says that Mark recorded the teachings of Peter, an eyewitness. So we have good reason to leave open the possibility that original historical settings were maintained before and in the writing of Mark, our first written gospel. Even if later evangelists had always changed the Marcan settings, it would not follow that Mark anticipated the later evangelists by always fabricating the settings in his gospel. This line of reasoning applies also to other kinds of detachables.

Perhaps most misleading of all is the tendency in form criticism to judge historicity according to the criterion of dissimilarity, i.e. to call in question the historicity of any tradition that agrees with the Judaism of Jesus' time or with later Christian beliefs and practices. Users of this criterion acknowledge that he shared beliefs and practices with his fellow Jews and influenced the beliefs and practices of his followers. But disturbed by the possibility that Jewish and Christian beliefs and practices have been falsely attributed to him, users of the criterion seek to vault from probabilism to certitude in a charmed core of historical critical judgments. Unfortunately, the criterion proves faulty. It rests on the wrong presupposition that we know enough about first century Judaism and early Christianity to achieve certitude in saying that such-and-such a dominical tradition differs from first century Judaism and early Christianity, and on the doubtful presupposition that even if we were omniscient of first century Judaism and early Christianity we could say with certitude that Jesus was the only one in the world of the NT capable of something different, something new. The thought is preposterous. But if others were capable of difference, of novelty — and whatever of the Jesuanic tradition may be different and new requires *someone* to have exercised such a capability — then it is always possible that their differences and novelties were falsely attributed to Jesus; and historical critical certitude evaporates. Discoveries such as those of the QL, of an unexpectedly high degree of Hellenization in NT Palestine, and of the Nag Hammadi library keep reminding us that our knowledge of first century Judaism and early Christianity remains fragmentary. We ought to use the criterion of dissimilarity — yes. But it deserves no pride of place, brings no certitude, and has no value for a denial of historicity. A dominical tradition agreeing with first century Judaism or early Christianity is none the worse for that agreement, for Jesus is at least as likely to have drawn from first century Judaism and contributed to early Christianity as he is to have differed from them. The criterion of dissimilarity has value only as an argument *for* historicity, and then only to a degree of probability that rates evenly with other historical critical arguments.

Likewise relatively useless for an understanding of Mark is redaction criticism. As usually practiced on this gospel, it rests on false presuppositions and takes insufficient account of factors that hinder a convincing distinction between redaction and tradition. It is false not only to presuppose that inconcinnity signals redaction (see the foregoing). It is false also to presuppose that a tradition originally carried only one emphasis or point, so that more than one emphasis or point signals redaction. If a redactor can make more than one, so also can an original speaker. In fact, speakers and writers of all times and places regularly do so. Nor should we presuppose that interruption of a line of thought or narrative signals redaction. Who has not started down such a line, digressed, and then resumed the line? To deny the originality of intervening material as to its placement or content merely because a good connection can be gained by omitting that material does not pay due to the realities of normal speech. Indeed, the informality of speech lends itself to stops and starts, turns and twists. One might expect secondary writing to contain fewer of them in that a writer has greater leisure than a speaker has to iron them out. Their presence could therefore indicate faithfulness to a tradition of speech.

Acknowledgedly unredacted writing contains stops and starts, twists and turns. Take, for example, Gal 2:6, where Paul interrupts his own narrative with personal and theological statements, equally his own. This example also illustrates the error of presupposing that repetition signals redaction, as though Paul's repetition of "the ones seeming [to be something]" implies that a non-Pauline redactor added the intervening personal and theological statements. Nor does the kind of repetition in which an item occurs again and again necessarily indicate redaction. Mark's habitually writing that Jesus went to, taught alongside, and sailed across the Sea of Galilee, to take but one example, could just as easily be due to Jesus' actually having done so (or, more sceptically, to a traditioner's having made him do so) as to Mark's redaction. Repetition characterizes oral communication and, especially in a Semitically rooted culture, original writing as well. So whatever repetition we find in Mark — whether of words, phrases, or themes — may be due to Jesus' actions and way of speaking, to a traditioner's interests and way of speaking, to Mark's interests and way of writing, or to a combination of these factors. As such, repetition does not help us decide between these possibilities (cf. F. Neirynck, *Duality*). The reduction of repetition by later evangelists need not imply their knowledge of unrepetitive tradition more original than Mark. They may simply prefer the greater efficiency of non-repetition or shrink Marcan material to make room for non-Marcan material (mainly Q). Conversely, the multiplication of a locution or saying in later gospels does not imply fabrication by Mark or, for that matter, by a Christian before him. An authentically Jesuanic locution or saying may simply have attained increasing popularity in Christian circles. Yet neither does infrequency imply tradition. A hapax legomenon, for example, may have come equally well from Mark, a traditioner before him, or Jesus. From one side we might ask why Mark does not use a hapax more often if he likes it. From another side we might ask why it does not occur more often if traditioners or Jesus liked it (see M. Goulder in *Alternative Approaches to NT Study* 14-16 for a very good exposé of the fallacy of supposing that hapaxes necessarily signal tradition).

Parallelism is a kind of repetition, and redaction critics of Mark will often presuppose that looseness of parallelism signals redaction whereas closeness of parallelism signals originality. They will likewise presuppose that looseness of connection signals redaction whereas closeness of connection signals originality. Not necessarily; for events often take place haphazardly in real life, and informality characterizes extemporaneous speech. Though redaction may produce intrusions, then, it is equally possible that looseness may signal originality, or at least primitiveness, rather than redaction (cf. the text critical preference for awkward readings, Matthew's apparent habit of tightening the parallels and connections that he finds in Mark, and J. Vansina, *Oral Tradition* 57-65, esp. 64: "[Field research shows that] the more perfect the structure of a text, the more likely it is that it has been altered for artistic reasons"). It is even possible that Mark himself intruded material into a pre-published version of his text, for "it was customary for authors to give readings from their productions before invited audiences in order to gather useful criticisms and be able to insert corrections before the final version was issued" (F. G. Downing in *Alternative Approaches to NT Study* 98 with references to primary literature).

Quotation of and allusion to the OT would not signal redaction unless we could correctly presuppose that neither Jesus nor a pre-Marcan traditioner is likely to have quoted the OT or alluded to it. That presupposition does not deserve the time of day. A use of the LXX might seem to betray redaction, but even here we should exercise caution. The redaction may go no further than assimilation of a Jesuanic or traditional OT quotation to the LXX. Or the quotation may represent Jesuanic or pre-Marcan traditional use of a non-Massoretic text-type of the Hebrew OT. We might even think of Jesuanic or pre-Marcan traditional use of the LXX itself; for the Naḥal Ḥever Greek scroll and Greek fragments of the Minor Prophets show that the LXX was used in Palestine at the time of Jesus; and the Hellenization of Palestine by his time makes it probable that at least occasionally he used Greek, including the LXX (for recent summaries of the evidence, see J. M. Ross in *IBS* 12 [1990] 41-43; P. Grelot, *Paroles* 45-47; B. Schwank in *Anfänge der Theologie* 61-62; and an earlier treatment by R. H. Gundry in *JBL* 83 [1964] 404-8; cf. also the preponderance of Greek inscriptions in Jewish burial catacombs near Sepphoris, only four miles from Nazareth, where Jesus grew up). On the other hand, Semitisms do not prove authenticity; for a pre-Marcan traditioner or Mark would have been as capable of a Semitism as Jesus was. Because of increasingly thorough Hellenization of much Christianity, however, the presence of Semitisms in Jesuanic tradition tends toward authenticity by favoring an early date and thus lowering the likelihood of fabrication.

Nor should we presuppose that agreements of Matthew and Luke against Mark rest on non-Marcan tradition more original than Mark. For Matthew and Luke may have independently hit upon the same or similar redaction of Mark, and Luke may have been influenced by Matthew despite using Mark and Q as his main sources (see R. H. Gundry in *The Four Gospels 1992*). Even though we could successfully use this and other phenomena of the text to distinguish Marcan redaction from pre-Marcan tradition, our understanding of Mark should not alter appreciably; for textual meaning is not determined by redaction alone, but by the whole text, whatever the proportions and degrees of redaction within it. To know those proportions and degrees would sharpen our focus, as it does in the study of Matthew and Luke at the same time that it there poses the danger of undervaluing the adoption of tradition and of overvaluing the practice of redaction; but a holistic reading of Mark's text will have to suffice, and the closer this reading, the less our disadvantage in not knowing the proportions and degrees of redaction (cf. Q. Quesnell in *JBL* 105 [1986] 155-56).

Not only do false presuppositions invalidate redaction criticism of Mark. Certain factors would make it difficult to carry out even under the truest of presuppositions. We have already noted our lack of any sources that Mark might have used. Take Matthew by way of contrast. Through comparison with Mark you can determine specially Matthean diction, style, and theology with good accuracy, through comparison with Luke with fair accuracy (but only fair because of the necessity of reconstructing Q), and through analysis of peculiarly Matthew passages with considerably reduced accuracy. What accuracy does attach to analysis of peculiarly Matthean passages rests for the most part on agreement with the results reached through comparisons of the other passages with Mark and Luke. A few possible overlaps with Q excepted, however, Mark contains material comparable in its peculiarity only with peculiarly Matthean passages.

Another hindrance to redaction criticism of Mark is to be found in the possibility of Mark's writing up traditional material according to his own tastes. If we knew his sources, thereby discovered his special diction, style, and theology, and came across passages in his gospel where only that diction, style, and theology were represented, a strong argument for redaction, indeed for fabrication, would emerge (as in some peculiarly Matthean passages). As it is, however, the possibility of Mark's writing up traditional material according to his own tastes always remains open.

Conversely again, we have to consider the possibility that traditional diction, style, and theology influenced Mark even when he was not writing up tradition but was fabricating material, if ever he did so. Thus, fabricated material could look traditonal just as traditional material could look fabricated. These considerations apply to the so-called seams between pericopes as well as to the bodies of pericopes (cf. P. Dschulnigg, *Sprache* 264-65 with 241-57).

Posing another hindrance is the possibility that tradition and redaction shared diction, style, and theology, not because one had influenced the other or because they had influenced each other, but because the tradition offered what the redactor already liked. On the one hand, moreover, some things can hardly be said without using locutions foreign to one's favorite diction whether or not one is passing on tradition, redacting it, or fabricating new material. On the other hand, variations may be found in the diction, style, and theology both of a redactor and of tradition at the redactor's disposal. If we drew redactional conclusions from variations in Paul's epistles the way such conclusions are drawn from variations in Mark, the results would be laughed off the stage. Think, for example, what redactional hay would be made of Paul's switching in Gal 4:1-7 from the first person singular (v 1) to the first person plural (v 3), next to the third person plural (v 5a) and back to the first person plural (v 5b), then to the second person plural (v 6a), back again to the first person plural (v 6b), and finally to the second person singular (v 7). In Gal 4:10 the contrast between the pre-verbal position of ἡμέρας, "days," and the post-verbal position of the remaining direct objects would be taken as a sign that the remainder were added later. The shifts in 1 Corinthians 15 from "body" (vv 35-38) to "flesh" (v 39) to "bodies" (v 40) and from seeds (vv 36-38) to the animal kingdom (v 39) to heavenly luminaries (vv 40-41) would provide grist for the redactional mill. So also would the repetitiousness of "it is necessary to boast" (2 Cor 12:1) after "if it is necessary to boast" (2 Cor 11:30) and the intervention of boasting in visions and revelations (2 Cor 12:1-5a) between boastings in weakness (2 Cor 11:30-33; 12:5b-10). In the practice of redaction criticism on Mark, such phenomena would inspire theories of redactional insertions, redactional changes of traditional diction, etc. But we would do better to refrain from propounding such theories. In the comments and notes to follow, therefore, references to Mark's style and diction will have to do with the whole gospel rather than distinguishing supposedly redactional material from supposedly traditional material. Individual questions of redaction, tradition, and historicity will be discussed in the framework of these larger methodological considerations.

Structural criticism can hone one's ability to read a text closely, but abstractness keeps this kind of criticism from contributing very much to an exposition of Mark's originally intended meaning in its historical specificity. Because this commentary aims at such an exposition, then, structural criticism will suffer neglect. In a way, the interpretation of Mark as an apology for the Cross strikes a sociological note, but not an economic-political one — rather, a cultural-psychological note with respect to the scorn to which Christians were subject for preaching the Cross. We might draw parallels between Mark's response to such scorn and the response of modern Pentecostalists to the scorn of an establishment that considers them sectarian, unsophisticated, and insignificant. Their response consists in an emphasis on crowds, miracles, exorcisms, clairvoyance (commonly called "the gift of knowledge" by Pentecostalists after 1 Cor 12:8; 14:25), power over content in preaching, iconoclasm where content does become important (N.B. the applause drawn by Pentecostalist preachers when making iconoclastic points), and predictive prophecy. But again because this is a commentary on the text of Mark, neither the sociology of Mark's community nor that of Jesus and his band of followers will receive very much attention.

The commentary contains an attempt to make interpretative capital out of Mark's grammar and style. Thus, emphases will be drawn out of asyndeton (where used for rhetorical effect), word order (where differing from the usual — e.g., from the predominant Marcan [and Semitic] order of verb–subject), chiasm (but not on the grand scale, for such chiasm seems imposed on Mark's text rather than inherent in it), and tenses (with particular attention to the historical present). There is no implication that Mark always thought out these phenomena. At times he probably did so. At other times his desire to emphasize this or that probably led him to use appropriate patterns of speech with little or no deliberation. It is both impossible and unnecessary for us to decide between the deliberate and the spontaneous. The resultant emphases stay the same.

This commentary stresses neither philology (for that, see V. Taylor's commentary, *TDNT,* and *EDNT*) nor textual criticism (though some important text critical questions are discussed). Excurses on topics such as "gospel," "kingdom of God," "parables," "Pharisees," and "Son of man" (to list but a few that one regularly finds in commentaries on Mark) are notable by their absence here. Limitations of space prohibit dealing with these topics in the detail that they deserve. Readers need to examine full-length treatments of them in monographs, articles, and relevant sections of topical books. Context will dictate the switching back and forth between "kingdom of God" and "rule of God," between "gospel" and "good news." For the benefit of beginning students who may use this commentary and except for references to verbal forms that appear in primary texts, Greek verbs will be cited according to their first-listed forms in lexicons, not according to their present active or (in the case of deponents) middle-passive infinitive forms.

Cross-references to primary literature that appear in secondary literature, sometimes commonly, but that lack relevance, as they do surprisingly often, have here been weeded out. A good many truly relevant such cross-references remain, and some new additions have been made to their number. Most of these cross-references appear in the notes, where matters of lower and higher criticism and of competing interpretations tend to concentrate, as distinct from the comments, where exegesis holds sway. Though older secondary literature receives some consideration, the preponderance of interactive discussion deals with newer secondary literature. It is hoped that this preponderance will make the commentary up-to-date and at the same time provide readers with an avenue through which to pursue the older secondary literature, often listed in the newer. An attempt has been made to include both older and newer secondary literature that has suffered neglect though containing items worthy of consideration. The present author has surveyed far more secondary literature than he cares to remember and far more than he could have discussed within the limits of his commentary, but he does not claim to have surveyed all such literature. Readers will have to guess what he surveyed but chose not to include and what he did not survey at all. He has chosen not to include some secondary literature which he considers overrated by others. And he apologizes for fairly frequent citations of his own previously published works. These citations save space by avoiding repetition; and, in some instances, they offer self-corrections.

Other commentaries on Mark are cited simply by the names of their authors. Except when occurring in the same paragraph, authors' initials are usually repeated since readers may often dip into this commentary here and there rather than reading it in continuity. For books, abbreviated titles are often used. Even the abbreviations OT and NT are used in those titles. The titles of articles are omitted, only their locations given. At the beginning is included full bibliographical information for books, but not for articles. For the latter, the information given in the body of the commentary suffices. The University of Leuven Press is publishing a bibliography on Mark which will dominate the field.

Postscript: R. M. Fowler's *Let the Reader Understand* (Minneapolis: Fortress, 1991) appeared too late for detailed engagement on the following pages. The monograph, oriented as it is to reader-response criticism, pays special attention to Marcan gaps (what Mark did not write that raises questions about what he did write), treats the gaps as indicative of deliberate mystification on Mark's part, and concludes from this mystification that Mark wrote a figurative gospel much more or even rather than a realistically referential one. To the extent that Fowler is merely telling about his experience in the reading of Mark, one can counter only by telling about one's own different experience of finding that Mark left gaps, not because he had an interest in them, but because other interests occupied him. To the extent that Fowler shifts from reader-response criticism to philological-historical criticism by passing judgment on authorial intention (for example: "Mark's persistent and insistent turn to indirection, that is, to doubleness, incongruity, and uncertainty, *is calculated* to make a deep and lasting impression upon us" — p. 225, italics added; cf. the talk on p. 222 of Mark's design and "trying to do something to the audience"), one can counter that it is far more difficult to exegete the intentions of authors by what they did not write than by what they did write. From there on, the argument turns to interpretation of particular texts, except for saying that the pre-Papian tradition of Mark's writing down the reminiscences of Peter concerning Jesus' ministry adds historical difficulty to the exegetical one of believing that Mark did not write in realistic reference to that ministry.

MARK

THE GOOD NEWS ABOUT JESUS CHRIST: ITS START IN THE PROCLAMATION OF JOHN THE BAPTIZER

1:1-8 (Matt 1:1; 3:1-6, 11-12; 11:10; Luke 1:1-4; 3:1-6, 15-18; 7:27; John 1:1-28)

According to very early tradition, Mark depends on Peter's teachings (see Eus. *H.E.* 3.39.15 and pp. 1026-45 below on the reliability of that tradition). Peter's association with Jesus did not start till their adulthood; so Peter's preaching probably omitted Jesus' earlier life. Thus also Mark omits it. Besides, it is only certain activities of Jesus as an adult that will lead to his death by crucifixion, the scandal of which Mark writes his gospel to overcome. It is therefore those activities and the Crucifixion itself that Mark needs to interpret in a way that overcomes the scandal.

His starting with John the Baptizer ("the Baptizer" representing ὁ βαπτίζων, often considered redactional here and in 6:14, 24, as distinct from ὁ βαπτιστής, "the Baptist," often considered traditional in 6:25; 8:28) agrees with indications in John 1:35-51; Acts 1:21-22 that Peter followed Jesus from the time of John's ministry onward. It also agrees with indications that Jesus himself regarded John as a pivotal figure (Matt 11:11-15; Luke 7:24-35; 16:16; for further considerations, see J. Ernst in *Dynamik im Wort* 163-82 and J. Drury in *Alternative Approaches to NT Study* 34, the latter of whom questionably presupposes, however, that Mark writes for a Christian audience). The first pericope in Mark deals therefore with John and starts with a superscription that concludes with quotations of the OT (vv 1-3). Mark then notes the appearance and activities of John that correspond with those quotations (vv 4-8). This second subsection divides further into a description of John's baptizing ministry (vv 4-6) and his preaching about someone else who is coming (vv 7-8).

Though we have identified and subdivided the first eight verses of Mark as its first pericope, the first fifteen verses bristle with interpretative and textual questions, some of which affect the identification and subdivision of the first eight verses as Mark's first pericope. In v 1, for example, does ἀρχή mean "beginning" as to time, as to content, or as to both time and content? Does τοῦ εὐαγγελίου mean "the good news" as such, as preached, or as written up in Mark's gospel? Does Ἰησοῦ Χριστοῦ, "of Jesus Christ," mean that Jesus Christ preached the good news (subjective genitive) or that he was preached as good news (objective genitive)? Does υἱοῦ θεοῦ, "Son of God," belong in the original text? Does "beginning of the good news of Jesus Christ" refer to the subject matter of the whole gospel or to the subject matter only of the first verses? If to only that of the first verses, how many of them does it include? (The most usual answers to this last question take the "beginning" through v 8, v 11, v 13, or v 15.) In vv 2-3, do the καθώς-clause, "according as . . . ," and the OT quotations depending on it go with v 1 as part of the non-sentential superscription, or with v 4 as part of the first complete sentence in the gospel? To ask the same question in a different way, does ἐγένετο in v 4 continue a sentence begun in v 2 or start the first sentence in the gospel, the independent clauses quoted from the OT depending on the superscription and therefore not counting as sentences in Mark's grammatical structure? (For other, less likely possibilities, see P. Schanz 59-62; A. Wikgren in *JBL* 61 [1942] 11-20; C. E. B. Cranfield 34-35.) In vv 14-15, will "the good news of God" mean the same good news that Jesus preached according to the subjective genitival interpretation of v 1, or good news that differs in that vv 14-15 refer to good news preached *by* Jesus whereas v 1 refers to good news preached *about* him? Does the parallel between "the good news of Jesus Christ" in v 1 and "the good news of God" in vv 14-15 form an inclusion that binds together vv 1-15 into a single pericope, or do differences between "the good news of Jesus Christ" and "the good news of God" plus topographical movements in vv 9, 12, 14 and other considerations prohibit treating vv 1-15 as a unity?

1:1-3 *(Matt 1:1; 3:1-3; Luke 3:1-6; 7:27; John 1:1-23)* For a number of reasons we should take vv 2-3 with v 1 rather than with v 4: (1) Elsewhere in Mark, καθώς-clauses always depend on the preceding, as they usually do in other, associated literature, particularly when followed as here by γέγραπται, "it is written" (see 4:33; 9:13; 11:6; 14:16, 21; 15:8; 16:7; Matt 26:24; Luke 2:23; Acts 7:42; 15:15; Rom 1:17; 2:24; 3:4, 10; 4:17; 9:13, 33; 10:26; 11:8; 15:3, 9, 21; 2 Cor 8:15; 9:9; 4 Kgdms 14:6; 23:21 LXX; 2 Chr 23:18; 25:4 LXX; Tob 1:6; *T. Levi* 5:4; cf. Mark 7:6; John 6:31; 12:14; 1QS 5:17; 8:14; CD 7:19; 4QFlor 1:2, 12; on the other side, Dan 9:13 Theod). (2) A connection with v 1 provides an easier identification of "your" (singular, bis in v 2) with "Jesus Christ" (v 1), its being understood from the designation of Isaiah as "the prophet" that God is the "I" speaking through him. (3) Similarly, the substitution of "his" (v 3) for "of our God" (Isa 40:3 LXX; cf. "for our God" in the MT) seems to identify the "Lord" (κυρίου) of the preceding line with "Jesus Christ" in v 1. A grammatical link between vv 2-3 and v 1 makes this identification easier. (4) A link with v 4 instead of v 1 would seem to require οὕτως (or ὁμοίως) at the start of v 4 for the regular construction, "just as . . . , so [or 'likewise'] . . ." (see καθώς[d] in K. Aland, *Vollständige Konkordanz*). (5) The asyndeton at the start of v 4 (contrast the καί, "and," that usually precedes ἐγένετο, "appeared on the scene") would get a good explanation if vv 2-3 went with v 1; for then the non-sentential character of vv 1-3, consisting of a phrase from which dangle dependent OT quotations, makes v 4 the first sentence. A first sentence does not need an introductory conjunction, because there is no preceding sentence to which it can be connected. Especially in Semitic books, the first sentence often does start with a conjunction ("and") despite the lack of a preceding sentence and whether or not a superscription precedes; but even in Semitic books the first sentence starts with asyndeton about equally as often, again whether or not a superscription precedes (see the beginnings of the OT, apocryphal, and pseudepigraphal books for examples of all possible permutations, too numerous to list; for two examples of asyndeton with ἐγένετο, as in Mark 1:4, outside the biblical sphere, see Philostr. *VA* 1.3.1; Hdt. 1.96.1). (6) Superscriptions often consist of phrases on which hang danglers of various sorts, including clauses (see again the OT, apocryphal, and pseudepigraphal books; cf. the comment of J. A. Kleist [181] that ἀρχή and ἀρχήν often function as predicates, though unlike Mark 1:1 the passages that he quotes from Pl. *Phd.* 58C and Isoc. *Ant.* 117 have a verb).

Since καθώς in v 2a defines "beginning of the good news of Jesus Christ" as in accordance with the OT quotations in vv 2b-3, the phrase covers only those verses whose subject matter corresponds to the OT quotations, i.e. vv 4-8, which tell how John the Baptizer's activities correspond to the quoted passages (cf. Acts 1:21-22; 13:24-25 and the special attention paid to John at the start of Jesus' public ministry also in Matthew, Luke, and John; J. C. Meagher, *Five Gospels* 21-22). To extend the beginning by including further verses, and perhaps the whole of Mark, would violate the definition of the beginning by the καθώς-clause. This definition spoils the appeal to Acts 1:1-2; Heb 2:3-4 for interpreting the beginning more broadly as a reference to Jesus' whole ministry. An extension would also violate the use of ἀρχή, "beginning," and its cognate ἄρχομαι, "begin," in comparable literature for the first subject matter of a book, or of its main section as distinguished from preliminary comments, never for the whole subject matter (see Isoc. *Phil.* 1; Philo *Sobr.* 1 §1; idem *Spec.* 1 §1; Diod. Sic. 11.1.1; Tac. *Hist.* 1.1.1 [Latin]; Polyb. 1.5.1, 4-5; Dion. Hal. *Ant. Rom.* 1.8.1, 4; Josephus *J.W.* 1.12 §30 with 1.6 §18; *Leben und Taten Alexanders von Makedonien, Der griechische Alexanderroman nach der Handschrift L* [ed. H. van Thiel] p. 2 for 1.1.2 — canvassed by G. Arnold in *ZNW* 68 [1977] 123-27; cf. Aristotle's use of ἀρχή for the beginning of a dramatic plot [*Poet.* 7.1-7]). Since this use has to do with subject matter, not with form, the non-Marcan examples provide good parallels to Mark's use of ἀρχή in connection with the good news as preached, not with the gospel as a book (against T. Söding, *Glaube* 225, n. 77; cf. the following comments on εὐαγγέλιον, "good news"). That the non-Marcan examples of this use occur in complete sentences, whereas Mark's ἀρχή does not, makes no difference to the coverage of ἀρχή; and the verbal character of its meaning justifies the dependence on it of an adverbial clause such as καθώς γέγραπται κτλ. (against H. Baarlink, *Anfängliches Evangelium* 292, n. 32). Hos 1:2a LXX (ἀρχὴ λόγου κυρίου πρὸς Ὡσῆε, "[the] beginning of [the] word of [the] Lord to Hosea") provides another and very striking example in that it distinguishes itself as a superscription for the first subject matter of Hosea from the immediately preceding superscription (1:1) for all the subject matter of Hosea. Mark's ἀρχή matches the superscription for the first rather than that for all.

Yet again, an extension of the beginning beyond v 8 would violate indications in every phrase of v 9a that a new pericope begins there. After the pattern of ἐγένετο in v 4, καὶ ἐγένετο, "and it came to pass," makes a new start. "In those days" sets a temporal frame for it. "Jesus came" shifts attention from John to Jesus. The description of Jesus as "from Nazareth of Galilee" calls attention to this shift. We will see that Mark regularly starts new pericopes with topographical movement; hence, the verb "came" also indicates a break between vv 8 and 9 (as the verbs of motion in vv 12 and 14 will indicate further breaks).

Since the "beginning of the good news of Jesus Christ . . ." covers only vv 4-8, the genitive cannot be subjective; for Jesus does not preach good news in those verses. On the contrary, Mark will take care to note that Jesus did not start preaching good news till "after" (μετά) the end of John's ministry (see vv 14-15 with 6:17; cf. Acts 10:37, where similar care is taken to locate the beginning of Jesus' ministry after the baptism that John preached). John's preparing for and preaching about the coming "stronger one" who would baptize people "in Holy Spirit" then constitutes the "beginning of the good news of Jesus Christ," for Jesus quickly turns out to be the stronger one. Thus the genitive is objective. For the subjective genitive we would expect "the good news of God," because vv 2-3, which relate to v 1 by way of καθώς, go on to speak of what God said in the OT (cf. the similar comment, only in reverse, on v 14, where "the good news of God" does appear but by context with an objective, not subjective, genitive). The objective genitive, however, fits the fact that by the time Mark wrote "it had long been accepted that Jesus Christ was himself the central object of the gospel, of the apostolic preaching" (J. Schmid 17, with a cornucopia of NT references cited). Furthermore, the very close association of Jesus and the good news in Mark 8:35; 10:29 ("on account of me and the good news") coupled with the disciples' preaching the good news during the church age in Mark 13:10; 14:9 favors good news told about Jesus rather than good news told by him in those passages, and therefore an objective genitive here. The addition of "Son of God" to "Jesus Christ" also favors the Christological emphasis carried by an objective genitive. Even though we were to accept the v.l. that omits "Son of God" (but see the following discussion), Mark devotes the bulk of his book to Christology rather than to theology. From time to time Jesus will proclaim God's rule; but Mark himself will constantly write about Jesus — and 1:1 represents Mark himself. Though we must beware of limiting the meaning of a Greek genitive, then, there is no convincing reason in either the immediate or the larger context of Mark to see anything more than the objective meaning.

Since Jesus is the object of John's preparation and preaching in vv 4-8, "the good news of Jesus Christ" in v 1 differs from "the good news of God" in v 14. For Jesus will not proclaim himself; rather, as v 15 goes on to say, he will proclaim the nearness of *God's* rule. That nearness will constitute "the good news" in which he will call on people to believe. John's preaching, which constitutes the "beginning of the good news of Jesus Christ," carries no such content. No fundamental disagreement exists (for Jesus will turn out to be the agent for bringing God's rule), but the differences between "of Jesus Christ" and "of God" and between the Christological content of John's preaching and the theocratic content of Jesus' preaching rule out an inclusion that would clamp together vv 1-15 into a single pericope.

Since the "beginning of the good news of Jesus Christ" consists in John's preparing for and preaching about the stronger one before the stronger one begins his own preaching, we have no need to take ἀρχή as meaning "fundamental principle" (which it can mean in other contexts — see A. Feuillet in *NTS* 24 [1977-78] 167 for references) in addition to or instead of "temporal beginning." The purely temporal meanings of ἀρχή and ἄρχομαι at the beginning of books and sections thereof (see the literature cited above) and of the only other occurrences of ἀρχή in Mark (10:6; 13:8, 19) support this understanding. So also do the purely temporal meanings of ἀρχή in connection with gospel materials at Luke 1:2; 1 John 1:1 and the closest parallel to Mark 1:1, i.e. Phil 4:15, where ἐν ἀρχῇ τοῦ εὐαγγελίου, "in [the] beginning of the good news," refers to the start of preaching good news in a geographical region (see the context and cf. the geographical notations in Mark 1:1-8). As a result, τοῦ εὐαγγελίου carries the connotation of good news as preached, not just good news as such, much less good news as written in a book (cf. G. Minette de Tillesse, *Le secret messianique* 400-401, for the Isaianic as opposed to Greek background of the active connotation). The non-bookish meaning of εὐαγγέλιον elsewhere in Mark and the NT further rules out a bookish connotation here (again cf. Hos 1:2 LXX, where "[the] beginning of [the] word of [the] Lord to Hosea" consists in an oral word spoken long before the written report of it). The later bookish meaning (first in Marcion — see H. Koester in *NTS* 35 [1989] 361-81) will grow out of an association of the oral proclamation with the books where that proclamation was recorded.

"Son of God" is missing in ℵ* Θ 28ᶜ *al.* The external evidence favoring inclusion of the phrase looks much better, however: "the combination of B D W *al* in support of υἱοῦ θεοῦ is extremely strong" (B. M. Metzger, *Textual Commentary* ad loc.). Admittedly, the internal criterion of favoring a shorter reading speaks for omission. But the greater the number of possible explanations for secondary omission, the weaker the appeal to this criterion. In the present case, several possible explanations for secondary omission present themselves: (1) "Son of God" may have seemed otiose to some scribes since "the gospel of Christ" was becoming, or had become, a stereotyped phrase; and Mark's inclusion of "Jesus" before "Christ" had already loaded the phrase. Therefore, despite the tendency of scribes "to expand titles and quasi-titles of books" (ibid.), they had reason here to omit "Son of God." (2) Scribes may have omitted "Son of God" to avoid the linguistically ugly sight and sound of six successive words ending with -ου (cf. the omission of Ἰησοῦ Χριστοῦ by Epiphanius). (3) Scribes may have omitted "Son of God" by oversight because of six successive endings in -ου. (4) Scribes often abbreviated sacred names. Here, the abbreviated longer reading IY- XYYYΘY might easily have been shortened to IYXY by homoioteleuton.

The argument in favor of "Son of God" that the title reappears at important points in 3:11; 5:7; 15:39 (cf. 1:11; 9:7; 12:6; 13:32; 14:61) is only slightly weakened by the apparently traditional rather than redactional character of the title at those points. For it may appear redactionally in 1:1 because the tradition that Mark later incorporates suits his purpose in writing the book. Furthermore, if he redacts the body of his materials as well as supplies editorial appendages, later occurrences of the title may owe something to his Christological interest. If then "Son of God" belongs in 1:1, we have here the second part of Mark's first, double move toward overcoming the scandal of Jesus' crucifixion: the identification of Jesus (a) as Christ and (b) as Son of God changes his coming crucifixion from the shameful death of a common criminal into the awe-inspiring death of a divine being who is God's appointed agent. It remains for Mark to provide evidence that Jesus is Christ and Son of God.

"Christ" means "anointed" (in a literal sense) but has also developed the metaphorical sense "appointed" (so already in Isa 45:1 — see M. de Jonge in *TDNT* 9. 504; G. Vermes, *Jesus the Jew* 158-59). We may take "Christ" either as a personal name along with "Jesus" or as a title along with "Son of God." The anarthrousness of "Christ," which contrasts with the arthrousness of "the Christ" in 8:29; 14:61; 15:32, counts against the titular understanding no more than the anarthrousness of "Son of God" (so also 15:39), which contrasts with the arthrousness of "the Son of God" in 3:11; 5:7 (cf. 1:11; 9:7; 14:61), counts against its titular meaning. Rather, the absence of the definite article emphasizes the qualities of divine appointment and divine sonship. The editorial use of "Christ" in a superscription, the follow-up with an undeniably titular and similarly anarthrous "Son of God," Mark's habit of putting parallel expressions side by side without a connecting "and" (cf. 1:32, 35; 4:28; 10:14; 12:23; 13:33; 14:3; 16:2), and the pairing of "the Christ" and "the Son of the Blessed One" in obviously titular senses at 14:61 all favor a titular use of "Christ" here in 1:1.

"Son of God" does not necessarily imply divinity, much less preexistence in heaven; for the phrase can denote a purely human king and messiah (2 Sam 7:14; Ps 2:7; 4QFlor 1:10-12; and possibly 4QpsDan A^a = 4Q243) and therefore say little or nothing more than "Christ" (as perhaps in 14:61 according to a meaning that the high priest may have intended — though see the comments and notes ad loc.). But Mark's doublings regularly sharpen and heighten the meaning of what precedes (F. Neirynck, *Duality* 96-97, 107-8); and unclean spirits will call Jesus God's Son because they recognize his divine power, not merely because they recognize his messiahship (3:11; 5:7; cf. 1:24). Gentiles would certainly respond to "Son of God" with thoughts of divinity (contrast Jewish usage for a mere charismatic — G. Vermes, *Jesus the Jew* 206-10), and Mark writes for Gentiles (see esp. 7:2-4). It is hard not to think that he is aware of the way they would understand "Son of God" and that he therefore adds the phrase to prompt thoughts of divinity, especially since he will add masses of material dealing with Jesus' exorcisms, miraculous healings, nature miracles, magnetic attraction of crowds, predictive ability, overpowering authority in teaching, irresistible skill in debate, exercise of the divine prerogative of forgiving sins, dying to the accompaniment of supernatural events, and being raised from the dead — all of which will fortify such an understanding (cf. the high Christology of Paul, Mark's companionship with Paul, and the tradition that Mark wrote this book; also C. Breytenbach, *Nachfolge* 254-63; M. E. Boring in *Semeia* 30 [1984] 131-32 and in *JBL* 104 [1985] 734-35; H. Baarlink, *Anfängliches Evangelium* 203-24, 242-69; and see the notes on 14:61).

Quotations of the OT make the ministry of John the Baptizer, which introduces Jesus' ministry, correspond to God's plan from ages past. But Mark puts the quotations in the superscription that precedes the narrative rather than at the close of the narrative, where quotations indicating correspondence would naturally appear. As a result, the emphasis falls not so much on correspondence at the time of John as on God's planning things out long before the time of John (cf. A. Suhl, *Funktion* 133-37). This emphasis gains further strength from the fact that only here does Mark explicitly quote the OT in an openly editorial passage, and yet further strength from his putting first the OT quotation which has God's "I" and "my" — this despite Mark's deriving that passage, against his introductory reference to Isaiah, from outside Isaiah. Already he is starting to show that Jesus' crucifixion will happen "by the predetermined plan and foreknowledge of God" (a statement of Peter, according to Acts 2:23). There is no shame to be seen in it, then; rather, God's working out his plan so as to make the good news that Mark writes about.

The name of Isaiah the prophet stands in the introductory formula because the longest quotation comes from his book and perhaps because Isaiah, along with the Book of Psalms, attained the greatest popularity among OT books in the early church (and perhaps at Qumran, too, if we may judge by volume of manuscripts; see R. H. Gundry, *Use of the OT* 125, on the Jewish practice of naming only one author in a composite quotation). "Behold, I am sending my messenger before your face" comes, however, from Exod 23:20. There the pronoun "your" refers to the nation of Israel. Here it refers to Jesus. "Messenger" refers to John the Baptist, and "I" and "my" to God. The similarity of "behold, I am sending my messenger" to Mal 3:1, which in the MT and LXX differs only slightly from Exod 23:20, leads to the quotation of "who will prepare your way" from Mal 3:1. "Your" replaces "my," which appears there, and comes into the quotation from similar phraseology in Exod 23:20, an earlier part of which Mark has just quoted. "My" refers to the Lord in Mal 3:1; "your" refers to Jesus here. These combinations of first and second person singular pronouns prepare for God's addressing Jesus in v 11: "You are my beloved Son; in you I am well pleased."

The preparation of a way in Mal 3:1 now leads to a quotation of Isa 40:3, which also speaks of preparing a way: "Ready the way of [the] Lord; straight make his paths." An emphatic forward position puts emphasis on εὐθείας, "straight"; and the present tense of the imperative ποιεῖτε, "make," intensifies the emphasis (contrast the preceding unemphatic aorist imperative ἑτοιμάσατε, "ready"; also the aorist imperative ποιήσατε in Matt 3:8 par. Luke 3:8). The MT construes "in the wilderness" with "make ready" (so also 1QS 8:14; 9:19-20) whereas the evangelists, LXX, Targum, OT Peshitta, Vulgate, *Barn.* 9:3, and rabbinic expositors (Str-B 1. 96-97; 2. 154) construe it with "a voice of one crying." It is hard to know whether Mark writes that "John the Baptizer appeared in the wilderness" (v 4) to conform to a traditional understanding of the syntax in Isa 40:3, or whether Mark chooses the syntax in the LXX and its supporters to make the correspondence of John to Isa 40:3 more exact. Either way, the correspondence is exact at the level of Mark's text and apologetic in its implication that from the very start, what will lead up to Jesus' crucifixion happens according to the plan of God, who sends John to prepare for Jesus' coming just as he sends his messenger in the OT. The asyndeton caused at the start of v 3 by the jamming together of different OT passages highlights this exactness of correspondence and its apologetic implication. So also does the lack of a verb for which "a voice" could be the subject. The MT may be understood either as "the voice crying" or as "the voice of one crying." The latter understanding, adopted by Mark in agreement with the LXX, puts a bit more emphasis on the messenger, i.e. on John.

Mark's context requires that "Lord" refer to Jesus and thus identify him by means
of a divine title (see 12:35-37; cf. 2:28; 7:28; 11:3; 13:35 and the Christian use
of κύριος for Jesus, a use already common in Mark's time — see esp. Paul's
epistles). Hence again, the Crucifixion changes from the shameful death of a
common criminal into the awe-inspiring death of a divine being (cf. the comments
on v 1). Along with the use of "your" for Jesus where the OT used it for the Lord
(v 2), the identification of Jesus as "Lord" may lend some weight to the view that
the divine title "Son of God" belongs to the original text of 1:1. The putting of
"his" (v 3) in place of "for our God" (Isa 40:3) keeps the word "God" for later
use in reference to the Father of Jesus (cf. v 11 with vv 14-15) and keeps Mark's
audience from misunderstanding "the Lord" as God the Father rather than as
Jesus. Αὐτοῦ, "his," is the last of a long string of words (thirteen of them) ending
in -ου (cf. M. A. Tolbert, *Sowing the Gospel* 111). The concentration of these
words in only three verses produces a euphony which welds vv 1-3 together and
stresses the goodness of the news about Jesus.

   1:4-6 *(Matt 3:4-6)* Verses 4-5 start to narrate the outworking of God's plan
written in Isaiah the prophet. John's appearance on the scene (ἐγένετο) matches
the sending of God's messenger (v 2). John's activity of baptizing matches the
messenger's preparing the way of the Lord (i.e. of Jesus — v 2). The location "in
the wilderness" matches the location of "one crying in the wilderness" (v 3).
John's preaching matches the crying out of the voice (v 3). The "baptism of
repentance," which starts with confession of sins (cf. 1QS 1:21-25) and ends in
their forgiveness, matches the making ready of the Lord's way and the making
straight of his paths (v 3). (We should note the distinction between the preparatory
work of the messenger and that of his audience in response.) The detailedness of
these match-ups adds great weight to Mark's emphasis on God's working out his
plan. The double "all" that describes the Judean region and the Jerusalemites that
are making ready by baptism and confession shows abundance as well as detailedness of correspondence. "All the Judean region" comes before "all the Jerusalemites" to stress wide extent. "All the Jerusalemites" gets special mention to
stress large number, for Jerusalem was the capital city of heaviest population in
Judea (cf. the particularizations in 13:34; 16:7). The chiastic order in which "all"
is placed — "all the Judean region and the Jerusalemites all" according to the
word order of the Greek text — intensifies the emphasis on wide extent and large
number by putting "all" both first and last in the compound phrase. Comparison
with Luke 7:29-30 brings out Mark's hyperbole (and cf. with his personification
of the Judean region Gen 41:57 LXX; John 3:22). John's magnetism and the
mighty impact of his ministry anticipate the greater magnetism and mightier
impact of Jesus the coming stronger one (v 7) and of his ministry (a main emphasis
in Mark — cf. esp. 3:7-8), just as John's death will anticipate the death of Jesus
(see 1:14; 6:14-29; and esp. 9:9-13). "The forgiveness of sins" begins to show
why "the news of Jesus Christ" is "good" (1:1). The absence of John's ethical
and judgmental message (contrast Matt 3:7-10; Luke 3:7-14) keeps the focus on
the gospel of Jesus Christ, Son of God, as the coming stronger one.

   The description of John as wearing "a leather belt around his waist" comes from 4 Kgdms 1:8 LXX, which agrees with 2 Kgs 1:8 MT. The description of him as "clothed with camel's hair" comes from 2 Kgs 1:8, but with an understanding of the Hebrew (literally, "a man, an owner of hair") that disagrees with the translation in 4 Kgdms 1:8 LXX, which means "a hairy man." Apparently a tradition that John wore a leather belt led to this disagreement. The immediate mention of a belt in the OT passage as well as in Mark favors the Marcan understanding as the original meaning of the Hebrew (as does also the rather different description of Esau in Gen 27:11 as "a man of hair," i.e. a hairy man [cf. Gen 27:23] as distinct from a man who owns a hair-garment). A tradition probably contributes also to the description of John's diet as consisting of "locust and wild honey." For Mark, this piece of information harks back to John's being "in the wilderness" and thus reemphasizes correspondence to God's plan as written in Isaiah the prophet. Because Mark does not make explicit the allusion to 2 Kgs 1:8 and Elijah (contrast 9:13), the description of John's clothing likewise furthers the emphasis on wilderness and thus on correspondence to the OT (cf. the wilderness dress and diet of Bannus — and his ablutions, which are at least somewhat comparable to John's baptism [Josephus *Life* 2 §11; also 2 Macc 5:27; *Mart. Isa.* 2:8-12; J. J. Hess in *ZAW* 35 (1915) 131]).

1:7-8 *(Matt 3:11-12; Luke 3:15-18; John 1:24-28)* In contrast with Matt 3:7-10; Luke 3:7-14, which give extensive quotations of John's ethical and judgmental message, Mark quotes only that part of John's proclamation which focuses on the good news about Jesus. It describes him as the one stronger than John. In the context of Mark's gospel, the definite article identifies the stronger one anaphorically with "Jesus Christ, Son of God" (v 1) and "Lord" (v 3); and the description fits Mark's apology by counteracting in advance the apparent weakness of Jesus on the cross (cf. the element of power in portraits of the Messiah at Isa 9:5[6]; 11:2, 4b; *Pss. Sol.* 17:21–18:9; *1 Enoch* 45-46, 47-49 and Mark's coming emphasis on Jesus' display of strength in the Passion as well as of thaumaturgic power in the public ministry). Elsewhere in Mark ὀπίσω invariably carries the locative meaning, "behind" (1:17, 20; 8:33, 34; 13:16 — all passages which may easily be taken as traditional rather than Marcanly redactional). This is the usual though not unexceptionable meaning in other literature, too. Originally, then, John may have meant that the stronger one was a follower of his ("is coming behind me" as a progressive present tense). Jesus' submission to the baptism of John supports this view (cf. C. H. Dodd, *Historical Tradition* 272-75; J. Murphy-O'Conner in *NTS* 36 [1990] 337-58; but also J. Ernst in *Vom Urchristentum zu Jesus* 13-33 against discipleship in a technical sense). Yet the statement in v 9 that Jesus came will retrospectively change an erstwhile declaration by John concerning the present into a prediction concerning the future ("is coming after me" as a futuristic present tense, on the vividness of which usage see S. E. Porter, *Verbal Aspect* 230-32; cf. the LXX of 3 Kgdms 1:6, 24; Eccl 10:14 for ὀπίσω in a chronological sense). The motifs of a beginning and of preparation (vv 1-3) have laid the groundwork for this change (so J. M. Gundry-Volf in private communication). Also in respect of prediction, then, John anticipates Jesus; for Mark will later display with all possible prominence the predictive power of Jesus and will detail the fulfilments of his predictions (bearing in mind Mark's writing for Gentiles, cf. the references in M. Smith, *Clement* 225, to Hellenistic fascination with knowing the future, though some of those references are weakened by their having to do with a helping angel's granting of foreknowledge in consequence of magical rites, of which kind of angel and rites Mark writes nothing).

John says that he is not fit to do for the stronger one even the menial service of loosening the strap of his sandals. The statement contributes to Mark's program of dignifying Jesus, a program that will pervade even the account of Jesus' passion. So great is the dignity of the stronger one that John, despite his being God's messenger (v 2), is not fit to do for the stronger one what was so menial that Hebrew slaves were prohibited from doing for their masters, though a son or a pupil might do it (*Mek.* Exod 21:2 [J. Z. Lauterbach 3. 5-6]), and what at least one later rabbi (R. Joshua ben Levi, c. 250 C.E.) said even a pupil was exempt from doing despite the pupil's obligation to do all other kinds of slave-service for his master (*b. Ketub.* 96a; cf. D. Daube, *NTRJ* 266-67, 277).

The stronger one's future baptism of people "in Holy Spirit" will surpass John's past baptism of people "with water"; for "Spirit" connotes power (see Judg 14:6, 19; 15:14; 1 Sam 11:6; Isa 31:3; Mic 3:8; Zech 4:6; Luke 1:17; 4:14; Acts 1:8; 10:38; Rom 15:19; 1 Cor 2:4; 2 Tim 1:7; Josephus *Ant.* 8.15.4 §408), and "Holy" acts as a prophylactic against the scribes' error of thinking that an unclean spirit lies behind Jesus' power (3:22, 30; cf. J. H. Neyrey in *Semeia* 35 [1986] 106). Asyndeton at the start of v 8, an adversative δέ, "but," strongly contrastive pronouns in ἐγώ, "I," and αὐτός, "he," and the anarthrousness of "Holy Spirit" emphasize these points, which again counteract in advance the apparent weakness of Jesus on the cross.

What does baptism in Holy Spirit mean? Nowhere in Mark do we read about a promise by the risen Jesus that the disciples will receive the Holy Spirit shortly after his departure, as in Luke 24:49; Acts 1:4-5; 11:16 (cf. Luke 11:13) and as fulfilled on the Day of Pentecost (Acts 2:1-4), or about an Easter gift of the Holy Spirit, as in John 20:22. This omission is the more striking in view of the prediction in Mark 13:11 that after Jesus' death and resurrection the Holy Spirit will speak through the disciples. Already during Jesus' ministry their exorcisms and miraculous healings (6:13) match those that he performed after the Spirit descended into him (1:10), but Mark will make no mention of the disciples' having received the Spirit. It appears, then, that Mark is not interested in Jesus' giving the Holy Spirit to his disciples. For him, rather, Jesus' baptizing people in Holy Spirit represents the way Jesus will deal with the masses of repentant people whom John has baptized with water. Having himself received the Spirit, Jesus will teach them with authority, heal their sick, and, most pertinently to the present prediction, cast unclean spirits out of their demon-possessed (cf. Acts 10:38). The fact that Mark immediately follows up John's prediction with an account of Jesus' receiving the Spirit at his baptism (vv 9-11; contrast the intervening material in Matt 3:12; Luke 3:17-20) and then narrates the Spirit's acting on Jesus and Jesus' acting in the power of the Spirit (1:12 and esp. 3:22-30) supports this view. More particularly, so also does the emphasis in 3:28-29 on the unpardonableness of attributing the Spirit's power, which Jesus exercises, to an unclean spirit. John was not a water-giver but a water-user when he baptized people. By the same token, the stronger one will not be a Spirit-giver but a Spirit-user when he baptizes people (cf. the v.l. in v 8 that lacks ἐν, "in," before πνεύματι ἁγίῳ and thereby gives an instrumental rather than locative emphasis, "with Holy Spirit," though an instrumental ὕδατι, "with water," may add an instrumental sense even to the better attested ἐν πνεύματι ἁγίῳ). Thus, John's prediction of the stronger one's baptizing people in Holy Spirit will have its fulfilment recorded in this gospel. The absence of baptism in fire, which is connected with judgment in Matt 3:11-12; Luke 3:16-17, leaves the accent on the good news with which the pericope started.

NOTES

So far as our hard evidence goes, Mark is the first to have included in the Christian "good news" materials about Jesus that reach back earlier than his death and resurrection. We should not make too much of this supposed theological achievement, however; for Mark's dependence on oral traditions (Peter's teachings, according to Papias's elder in Eus. *H.E.* 3.39.15) holds out the possibility that "gospel" already included such materials. With the narrative connotation of εὐαγγέλιον in Mark, cf. the association of εὐαγγελίζομαι in Isa 52:7 LXX (bis) with ἀναγγέλλω, "report," in Isa 52:15 LXX and with διηγέομαι, "relate, recount," in Isa 53:8 LXX. For surveys of research on εὐαγγέλιον, see H. Frankemölle and D. Dormeyer in *ANRW* II 25/2. 1543-1704; H. Frankemölle, *Evangelium;* D. Dormeyer, *Evangelium.*

For the originality of "Son of God" in v 1, T. A. Burkill (*Mysterious Revelation* 9-10) argues that as "Christ" represents the Jewish confession of Peter (8:29), "Son of God" represents the Gentile confession of the centurion (15:39). This argument falters on the intervening uses of "Son of God" by others, including demons (3:11; 5:7). More convincingly, R. Schnackenburg (in *Orientierung an Jesus* 321-23) argues that the anarthrousness of both nouns in 15:39 (υἱὸς θεοῦ) combines with the text critical certainty of the phrase there to favor the originality of the same doubly anarthrous phrase here. The already listed other Marcan occurrences of the phrase offer various permutations of arthrousness and anarthrousness, and a later addition of "Son of God" in 1:1 would probably have conformed to the Attic grammatical standard of writing the definite article with both nouns or at least with one of them (A. Globe in *HTR* 75 [1982] 209-18). It is unlikely that an orthodox scribal addition of "Son of God," designed to scotch adoptionistic Christology, would have permeated the textual tradition widely and left an original shorter reading with relatively weak attestation; for not many scribes would have recognized the anti-adoptionistic point of the addition or have independently struck on so subtle a way of defending orthodox Christology. We may also suspect that an addition of "Son of God" would not have scotched adoptionistic Christology, anyway; for the title might be understood from a post-baptismal standpoint which anticipates adoption to divine sonship at baptism. The title does not necessarily imply preexistence. The lack of "Son of God" in the original text of 1:1 would leave "my beloved Son" in 1:11 for a much less closely matching inclusion with "Son of God" in 15:39.

We should carefully note that the beginning of the good news is not the word of God written in Isaiah the prophet; rather, it *accords* with that word. The anarthrousness of ἀρχή suits a superscript (see A. T. Robertson, *Grammar* 781, 793, and for other examples, Matt 1:1; Rev 1:1; and the LXX of Prov 1:1; Eccl 1:1; Cant 1:1; Hos 1:1, 2; Tob 1:1;

2 Esdr 11:1). It is weak to argue that inclusion of Mark's whole gospel would require "the good news of . . ." rather than "beginning of the good news of . . ."; for Mark could think that the good news got its start in the whole of Jesus' ministry, not just in John's ministry. On the other hand, the common use of ἀρχή for only the first subject matter in a book cancels out the argument that the superscript in 1:1 must cover the whole subject matter because no later section of Mark has a superscript. It also makes otiose the theological interpretation of ἀρχή as a new creation after the pattern of Gen 1:1, for which meaning we should expect Mark to write "in the beginning . . ." (cf. John 1:1). The "beginning of the good news" relates to "from [the] beginning of creation" in 10:6; 13:19 no more than it does to the "beginning of birth pangs" in 13:8. In 10:6; 13:19, "from" and "of creation" plus a following quotation in 10:6 from Gen 1:27; 2:24 make the allusion unmistakable. There are no such pointers in 1:1. P. Pokorný (in *NTS* 32 [1986] 395-96 and in *ANRW* II 25/3. 1986-88, 1994-96) argues that the beginning of the good news includes all the contents of Mark because Jesus Christ cannot be proclaimed without mention of his resurrection, which comes at the end. This argument pays insufficient attention to the limitation inherent in "beginning" and to the definition of "beginning" by the καθώς-clause plus OT quotations.

The attempt by J. Gnilka (1. 39) to make vv 9-11 (God's voice) correspond to vv 2-3 (God's speaking to Isaiah), vv 12-13 (Jesus' temptation by Satan) to vv 4-6 (John's work), and vv 14-15 (Jesus' preaching) to vv 7-8 (John's preaching) overlooks the important element in vv 9-11 of Jesus' enduement with the Spirit (which has no counterpart in vv 2-3) and the fundamental dissimilarity between Jesus' temptation by Satan and John's work of preaching and baptizing. So no valid argument follows for treating vv 1-15 as a carefully constructed pericope, and Gnilka's otherwise correct rejection of R. Pesch's view that vv 1-15 formed a pre-Marcan unit (What function could it have had apart from Mark's book?) falls to the ground as needless.

R. Pesch (in *Die Zeit Jesu* 108-44) mounted an earlier, similar attempt to weld together vv 1-15 into a carefully constructed pericope bound together by inclusion through occurrences of εὐαγγέλιον in vv 1 and 15 and consisting of two parts, vv 1-8 on John and vv 9-15 on Jesus, each part consisting of three subparts (vv 1-4, 5-6, 7-8 and 9-11, 12-13, 14-15, respectively), containing an attestation by God's word (vv 2-3 and 11), and reaching a climax in preaching (vv 7-8 and 14-15). But we have already noted reasons to deny an inclusive use of εὐαγγέλιον and to affirm major breaks, not minor subdivisions, between vv 8 and 9, 11 and 12, 13 and 14. As for subdivisions, a line should be drawn between vv 3 and 4, not between vv 4 and 5. The foregoing criticisms of Gnilka's view apply also to Pesch's view.

R. A. Guelich (in *BR* 27 [1982] 7-11) supports Pesch and Gnilka by arguing that a beginning which closes with v 8 puts too much emphasis on John the Baptizer and too little on Jesus (in disagreement with "the good news *of Jesus*" in 1:1), and that vv 9-15 as well as vv 4-8 carry forward the OT themes of vv 2-3. But Isaiah speaks only of preparing the way of the Lord ahead of him, not of the Lord's arrival. John does the former: he prepares the way of Jesus. And preparation suits "beginning" very well, particularly when the preparation includes the first preaching about Jesus. Mark's writing that Jesus was in the wilderness (vv 12-13) does indeed parallel John's appearance there (v 4), but not in the manner of the OT quotation. For being tested by Satan for forty days in the wilderness hardly represents a smooth, straight road; and passages from Isaiah that have nothing to do with the work of preparation and that may or may not be alluded to in vv 9-13 but are certainly neither quoted nor alluded to in vv 2-3 — viz., Isa 11:6-8; 42:1; 65:25 — hardly support an extension of the beginning of the good news to include vv 9-15. Rather, John's proclamation of the coming stronger one constitutes the beginning of the good news and thus brings the first pericope to a close with v 8.

That Paul can write "my [or 'our'] gospel" with reference to his preaching of it —
hence, a subjective genitive (Rom 2:16; 16:25; 2 Cor 4:3; 1 Thess 1:5; 2 Thess 2:14; 2 Tim
2:8) — does not argue strongly for the same kind of genitive here. The contexts differ.
Moreover, since the gospel that Paul preaches consists of good news about Jesus Christ,
one can reverse the argument to favor an objective genitive in Mark 1:1.

G. Dautzenberg (in *Kairos* 18 [1976] 290) argues to the contrary that if "of Jesus
Christ" represented an objective genitive, v 15 would report Jesus as calling on people to
believe in him. As it is, the call is to believe in the good news of God; so we must have
a subjective genitive in 1:1. But the call to believe in v 15 relates to the good news of God
in v 14, not to the good news of Jesus Christ in v 1. And despite the phrase "the good
news of God" in v 14, v 15 relates no call to believe in God; hence, nothing is to be made
out of the corresponding lack of a call to believe in Jesus Christ.

Since Mark's context has nothing of battle (the vocabularies of testing in vv 12-13
and of exorcism and debate throughout the rest of Mark do not equate with the vocabulary
of warfare), it may read too much into εὐαγγελίου to see the elsewhere frequent connotations
of victory and the peace it brings (cf. G. Friedrich in *TDNT* 2. 707-27). Yet the widespread
claim of Caesar to be a son of God (see P. Bureth, *Les Titulatures impériales* 23-25) links
with the use of εὐαγγέλιον for good news about Caesar to suggest a Christian counter claim
in 1:1 (P. H. Bligh in *ExpTim* 80 [1968-69] 51-53). Mark will not use the vocabulary of
anointing for Jesus' reception of the Spirit, nor will the baptismal voice use "Christ"
alongside "my beloved Son" (vv 9-11). So far as Mark is concerned, then, "Christ" may
have nothing to do with that reception. The doctrine of Jesus' heavenly preexistence appears
in earlier Christian literature (see esp. Gal 4:4; 2 Cor 8:9; Phil 2:6-7); so Mark may
presuppose the doctrine in calling Jesus God's Son. Or he may by-pass it to call speculative
Christology back to the historical Jesus. But since neither the sometimes bumbling disciples
nor any other negatively portrayed character in Mark represents a Christology of heavenly
preexistence, it seems better to say that the doctrine does not appear simply because Mark
writes to apologize for the Cross.

The distinctions made by J. A. Kleist (182) between a futuristic present and an
aoristic present for ἀποστέλλω, and between a simple future and a final (or volitive) future
for κατασκευάσει, may be too fine for Mark. Kleist's statement rings truer, however, that
the aorist ἑτοιμάσατε views the preparation "as a whole and finished product (τὴν ὁδόν;
sing.!); the pres. [ποιεῖτε] looks to the ever recurring details of repair . . . (τὰς τρίβους;
plur.!)" (183). On the other hand, see S. E. Porter, *Verbal Aspect* 326, 354-55 et passim,
that the present tense does not indicate linear action so much as it "presents" an action
more forcefully, more emphatically. Of course, linear action is one of the possible reasons
for putting a verb or verbal in this more forceful, emphatic form, as for example in the
command ὕπαγε/-ετε, "go" (1:44; 2:11; 5:19, 34; 6:38 et passim). Normally, the forcefulness
of the present tense will not be noted where the meaning in context makes it obvious (as
usually in ὕπαγε/-ετε, to take the foregoing example). The non-theological uses of ὁδός in
2:23; 4:4, 15; 6:8; 8:3 cast doubt on the interpretation of "your way . . . the way of the
Lord" in vv 2-3 as the ministry of Jesus, particularly his way to the Cross starting in 8:27
(cf. 9:33, 34; 10:17, 32, 46, 52; 11:8; 12:14; and E. Manicardi, *Il cammino* 148-70). The
baptism of repentance which John proclaims does not prepare for Jesus' going to Jerusalem
for Crucifixion. That journey will not start till after a considerable interval; and the
Crucifixion will take place because the Jewish leaders *fail* to prepare the way of the Lord.
We will discover further reasons not to theologize the occurrences of ὁδός.

M. A. Tolbert (*Sowing the Gospel* 239-48) identifies the messenger sent to prepare
the way of the Lord primarily as Jesus, only secondarily as John the Baptizer, and thus
"the way of the Lord" primarily as the way of God, only secondarily as the way of Jesus.
She reasons, for example, that if John were the messenger, then God would be addressing

Jesus in the OT quotation and that Jesus but not John has been introduced to Mark's audience. But this reasoning overlooks that God will address Jesus with OT phraseology in v 11. And it is unsurprising that someone in the OT quotation should not be identified till the narrative corresponding to it (here, till v 4, which immediately introduces John in phraseology parallel to the quotation). Even in Tolbert's view "your" (singular) remains unidentified till the following narrative if the pronoun refers to the nation of Israel in Mark as well as in the OT. A reference to Mark's audience, also considered by her, would cut vv 2-3 entirely off from their context; for neither Jesus nor John preached to Mark's audience. And to say that "your" refers to the nation of Israel or to Mark's audience destroys the parallel between "your way" and "the way of the Lord . . . his paths."

K. R. Snodgrass (in *JSNT* 8 [1980] 34) suggests that in v 3 the substitution of "his" for "of [or 'for'] our God" may merely represent an avoidance of the divine name, as in 1QS 8:13. But Mark and his traditions do not hesitate to use "God" elsewhere, even in other OT quotations (12:26, 29-30; 15:34); and in the quotation of Isa 40:3 at 1QS 8:14 (1QS 8:13 making only an allusion) we read "for our God." 1QS 8:13-14 avoids only the tetragrammaton (יהוה), for which Mark, without avoidance, writes χυρίου so far as we can tell (though G. Howard [in *JBL* 96 (1977) 63-83, esp. 78] uses the retention one way or another of יהוה [as opposed to a translation with χύριος] in pre-Christian manuscripts of the LXX to hypothesize that Mark 1:3 originally read יהוה instead of χυρίου — yet see N. A. Dahl and A. F. Segal in *JSJ* 9 [1978] 5-6 for Philo's reading Septuagintal manuscripts that translated יהוה with χύριος already in the first century; also H. Stegemann in *Qumrân* 195-217 and the notes on 12:36-37). The occurrences of "Jesus Christ," "God," and "Isaiah the prophet" in vv 1-2a undermine the statement that "the antecedent of the pronouns in vs. 2-3 is uncertain on any reading" (Snodgrass, loc. cit.). The immediate context in Mark, not distant contexts in the OT, determines the referents; for the evangelist is not giving a grammatical historical exegesis of the OT passages. The non-vocative χύριος will twice occur for the Christ in 12:36-37, and 8:29; 14:61-62; 15:32 as well as 1:1 will identify Jesus as the Christ. So the greater frequency of the vocative χύριε for Jesus does not rule out another non-vocative χύριος referring to Jesus Christ in 1:1-3 (against M. A. Tolbert, *Sowing the Gospel* 245).

The presence of v 2b in all our texts of Mark, the redactional reason for its coming ahead of v 3 (see the foregoing comments), and the Jewish practice of naming only one author in a composite quotation militate against the conjectures that v 2b is a later redactional or scribal gloss and that vv 2-3 come from a Testimony Book. Matt 3:3; Luke 3:4-6 may omit Mark 1:2b in anticipation of later inclusion of the same OT passage in Matt 11:10; Luke 7:27. W. Schenk (in *ZNW* 70 [1979] 158-59) argues for the influence of Q on Mark. See R. H. Gundry, *Use of the OT* 9-12, for further details on the text of the OT quotation.

The need to introduce John into the narrative at v 4 favors the translation "John . . . appeared preaching" over the translation "John . . . was preaching." Even in 9:3, 7 ἐγένετο should probably not be treated periphrastically: thus, "became shining" and "appeared overshadowing," respectively, rather than "were shining" and "was overshadowing" (again cf. Philostr. *VA* 1.3.1; Hdt. 1.96.1). The brevity of Mark's identification of John ("the Baptizer") does not necessarily imply that the intended audience already know about John. Mark might expect them to pick up information as the narrative proceeds. On first introduction of other characters, too, he gives only a brief identification and fails to give background information — even with regard to Jesus (v 1), but also with regard to Isaiah (v 2), Simon and Andrew (v 16), James and John (v 19), et al. We might suppose that an intended audience of Christians already know the backgrounds of these other characters as well as of John. But it is an open question whether Mark writes his book for Christians; and even if he does, it is hard to think that a Roman Christian audience consisting of

Gentiles (again see 7:2-4) would know background information about Herod Antipas, whom Mark will introduce with similar brevity (6:14). (Herod's contest with Archelaus took place in Rome many decades earlier [Josephus *Ant.* 17.9.4-17.11.4 §§224-320; idem *J.W.* 2.2.3-2.6.3 §§20-100].) The putting of τινα, "a certain," with Simon the Cyrenian, the father of Alexander and Rufus (15:21), favors that Mark does not care to clutter his story of Jesus with background information; for "a certain" will imply that the audience know no more about Simon than the little that Mark tells them in the text.

Toward the beginning of v 4 the most difficult v.l. is not that of Cod. א and its supporters, which yields a smooth statement: "John appeared, the one baptizing in the wilderness and preaching a baptism of repentance . . ." (against M. Reiser, *Syntax und Stil* 134-36). The most difficult v.l. is that of Cod. B and its supporters: "John appeared, the one baptizing, in the wilderness, preaching a baptism of repentance. . . ." For by itself this v.l. leaves unclear whether "in the wilderness" tells where John was baptizing people or where he made his appearance. We should therefore prefer this reading. The preceding reference to crying in the wilderness (v 3) and the following reference to baptism in the Jordan River favor that in v 4 the phrase "in the wilderness" tells where John appeared preaching. J. K. Elliott (in *TZ* 31 [1975] 14-15 and in *NT Textual Criticism* 49-50) argues that Mark uses ὁ βαπτίζων titularly and that the titular use favors the v.l. of Cod. B and its supporters (cf. G. D. Kilpatrick in *NovT* 27 [1985] 100).

It is doubtful that Mark meant or his first audience understood an allusion to the Exodus in the references to the wilderness. For despite such an allusion in Isaiah, neither preaching in the wilderness nor baptism nor repentance nor confession of sins corresponds to the Exodus (the passage through the Reed Sea having to do with deliverance, not with repentance and confession — similarly with regard to the Isaianic exodus from Babylonia). John may baptize and preach in the wilderness because he shares a Jewish belief that God's rule will be inaugurated there (cf. 1QS 8:13-14; Matt 24:26; Acts 21:38) or simply because he grew up in the wilderness (Luke 1:80). J. Wright (in *Perspectives on Language and Text* 269-89) draws a line from the association of the wilderness with wind to the Holy Spirit, represented by wind. But only baptism with water took place in the wilderness. Nothing indicates that baptism in Holy Spirit will take place there.

Though the lower Jordan flows through the wilderness, with the result that John's baptizing in the Jordan River need not imply a shift from the wilderness where he is preaching (see R. W. Funk in *JBL* 78 [1959] 209-10, 212; U. W. Mauser, *Christ in the Wilderness* 78; W. Wink, *John the Baptist* 4-5), Mark's later statement that the Spirit thrusts Jesus "into the wilderness" (v 12) is jarring. For at the Jordan, Jesus is already in the wilderness! Mark obviously means that the Spirit thrusts Jesus out into the wilderness surrounding the lower Jordan, but it looks as though he mentions the surrounding wilderness in v 4 to emphasize correspondence with Isa 40:3 in v 3 — and mentions it at the expense of narrative smoothness in v 12, so strong is his emphasis on the correspondence. This correspondence determines his use of ἐρημός as a feminine substantive in vv 3, 4, 12, 13. Elsewhere he uses it as a masculine adjective modifying τόπος for "a deserted place" (1:35, 45; 6:31, 32, 35). We do not need to posit two different traditions, one of John's preaching in the wilderness and another of his baptizing in the Jordan.

The baptism and confession of all those living in Judea and Jerusalem may set the stage for a tragic reversal in the passion narrative, but Mark's later stress on the Sanhedrin's responsibility for Jesus' passion weakens this possibility. "Confessing their sins" defines "baptism of repentance" as a baptism that arises out of repentance (a genitive of source or cause in μετανοίας) or as a baptism characterized by repentance (a genitive of description). Since confession of sins accompanies baptism, the forgiveness of sins may relate to repentance-cum-confession as effect to cause, and to baptism as symbol to reality. An alternative view would keep baptism and repentance-cum-confession indivisible and thus include baptism in cause as well as in symbol. 1QS 3:4-6, 9; 4:21; 5:13-14; Josephus *Ant.* 18.5.2 §§116-17 and OT prophetic passages excoriating ritual without repentance favor divisibility, but do not decide whether or not baptism contributed to forgiveness when repentance accompanied baptism. For the phrase "for the forgiveness of sins" may go with "baptism," with "repentance," or with the two of them taken together; and εἰς may indicate purpose, result, or both. Since Mark writes that John baptized people, we should reject the interpretation of E. Lohmeyer (12-13, n. 4) that John preached baptism instead of repentance because baptism is God's work and forgiveness his gift. Rather, John preached that people ought to get baptized by him in connection with their repentance and forgiveness. He was aiming for national restoration; so we must think of national repentance and forgiveness. But baptism with confession of sins implies individual repentance and forgiveness, too, as does John's distinction in Q between the wheat and the chaff (Matt 3:7-12; Luke 3:7-17). His warning in Q to flee from the coming wrath seems to imply present forgiveness as insulation against the last judgment rather than future forgiveness as acquittal at the last judgment. Being baptized by John (ὑπό plus the genitive, which makes ἐβαπτίζοντο passive rather than middle) also militates against self-baptism, in relation to which John would have only the function of a witness, as in proselyte baptism (so J. Jeremias, *NT Theology* 1. 51). The designation of John as the Baptizer further militates against self-baptism. The passive is permissive: "were letting themselves be baptized." See J. Gnilka 1. 40, 45-46 for a brief survey and bibliography concerning possible backgrounds of John's baptism: Essene ritual washings, proselyte baptism, and ritual washings in the temple. Among others, see also M. Smith, *Clement* 205-8.

Mark's concern to stress the wilderness for correspondence with Isa 40:3 supports the interpretation of John's dress and diet as normal for living in the wilderness. Connotations of poverty, asceticism, trust in divine provision, vegetarianism, ritual purity (cf. Lev 11:22; CD 12:13-14), and prophetic garb (cf. Zech 13:4) do not enter the picture at the level of Mark's text, and perhaps not at the earlier level of the historical John, either. Through application of internal criteria a fair argument can be made for reading δέρριν καμήλου, "camel's skin" (so D a), instead of τρίχας καμήλου, "camel's hair," and for omitting καὶ ζώνην δερματίνην περὶ τὴν ὀσφὺν αὐτοῦ, "and a leather belt around his waist" (with D it — see R. H. Gundry, *Use of the OT* 131-32). But the external evidence strongly favors the usual reading. It is better, then, to see the influence of Zech 13:4 LXX both in δέρριν and in the omission. And it is easier to see influence from Zech 13:4 LXX on a relatively careless scribe than it is to see such influence on Mark himself (as we should probably have to explain his text if the Western readings were original). For Mark wants to portray John as a true prophet (cf. 11:32); yet Zechariah is portraying false prophets.

For Elijah as a forerunner, see Str-B 4/2. 779-98. But in Jewish literature Elijah first appears as forerunner of God (Mal 3:1). So far as hard evidence is concerned, the NT is the first to portray Elijah as forerunner of the Messiah (see the notes on 9:4, 11-13). But in the second century Trypho states that Jews commonly believe in Elijah as forerunner of the Messiah (Justin *Dial.* 8:4; 49:1). We might infer that the belief antedated the NT period; for later, non-Christian Jews would hardly have accepted a belief like that of Christians, much less have borrowed a belief from them. Nevertheless, the argument remains speculative. The agreement of the LXX with the MT of 2 Kgs 1:8 where Mark agrees with the LXX in the matter of a belt and the disagreement of Mark with the LXX in the matter of a garment weaken the argument of P. Vielhauer (*Aufsätze* 47-54) that Mark's agreement with the LXX shows the historical John not to have been Elijah-like.

E. Klostermann (7) suggests that the definite article in "the stronger one" is a Semitism. If so, we should translate with an indefinite article: "a stronger one." On the possibilities that John had in mind God, the Messiah, the Son of man, an eschatological prophet, or an unknown eschatological figure, see R. A. Guelich 1. 22-24. In addition to the arguments that "the one stronger than I" favors a human referent and disfavors a divine one, for which we should expect a non-comparative "the strong one," and that John would hardly assign sandals to God, we should note that John's later question whether Jesus was the coming one (Matt 11:3 par. Luke 7:19) implies a human rather than divine referent. The authenticity of this question is supported by the unlikelihood that Christians would have made John doubt the identity of Jesus as the stronger one whom he expected to come. On the locative meaning of ὀπίσω, see K. Grobel (in *JBL* 60 [1941] 397-401), who errs, however, in thinking that John is referring only to a genius of a pupil. Cod. B omits μου after ὀπίσω probably because of the μου right before ὀπίσω. On Semitic interference in the redundant αὐτοῦ, see E. C. Maloney, *Semitic Interference* 116-18. The aorist ἐβάπτισα either stands for the Hebrew stative perfect, having a present meaning, or looks back on the baptisms which John has performed up to this point. It goes too far to think that the aorist implies the finish of his activity, however; for he has yet to baptize Jesus (vv 9-11) and the phrase "after John's being given over" (v 14) lacks Mark's favorite εὐθύς, which would have closed down John's activity "immediately" after the baptism and testing of Jesus. Nor does the aorist reflect the standpoint of Mark rather than that of John (so G. Lüderitz in *Markus-Philologie* 196-97), for then the following future tense would imply that baptism in Holy Spirit is yet future to Mark.

The foregoing interpretation of baptism in Holy Spirit in Mark (for which see also E. Manicardi, *Il cammino* 166-69; C. Brown, *Miracles* 300-310; B. L. Mack, *Myth* 234-35) invalidates the debate between N. R. Petersen, who thinks that this baptism looks beyond the life of Jesus to what 13:11 talks about (*Literary Criticism* 71), and E. Best, who thinks that Mark presupposes his audience's knowledge of what happened on the Day of Pentecost (*Gospel as Story* 120). The foregoing interpretation also has the advantages of not requiring a referent outside the life of Jesus or text of Mark and of not leaving the fulfilment of a prediction unnoted by Mark (cf. the comments on 16:8). If Jesus uses rather than gives the Holy Spirit in Mark, the commonly cited cross-references to the Holy Spirit as an eschatological gift do not apply (cf. Isa 32:15; 44:3; Ezek 11:19; 18:31; 36:25-27; 37:14; Joel 3:1-2 [2:28-29]; Zech 12:10; 1QS 4:21; *T. Levi* 18:11; *T. Judah* 24:2-3). The objection that John cannot have made the stronger one the giver of the Holy Spirit because the cross-references attribute this gift to God also falls away if John means that the stronger one will use rather than give the Holy Spirit (just as in Q he will use rather than give fire). Luke-Acts then represents an advance in making Jesus as well as God the giver (see esp. Acts 2:33). With the alternation between the simple dative ὕδατι and the dative preceded by ἐν in ἐν πνεύματι ἁγίῳ, cf. 2:8.

B. M. F. van Iersel (in *Text and Testimony* 132-41) identifies baptism in Holy Spirit as the exhalation of Jesus' last breath, identified with the Spirit that descended into him at his baptism, and therefore as a veil-rending judgment on the temple because of those who were baptized by John without repenting (15:37-39). To support this identification, van Iersel notes the cognateness of πνεῦμα, "Spirit," and -έπνευσεν, "breathed" (15:37, 39), the complementarity of εἰς, "into" (1:10), and ἐξ-, "out" (15:37, 39), the presence of φωνή, "voice," in both passages (1:3, 11; 15:34, 37; cf. φωνεῖ, "he is calling," in 15:35), and the rejection of Jesus by Judeans and Jerusalemites (3:22; 7:1-5; 10:33; 11:18, 27-12:34; 14:1-2, 10-11, 43-15:15, 29-32) despite John's having baptized "all the Judean region and all the Jerusalemites" (1:5). We will see, however, that the veil-rending does not signify judgment on the temple. In neither substance (the cry of dereliction) nor volume (loud) will Jesus' voice correspond to the voices of John and God the Father. No holiness will be attributed to Jesus' last breath, as though it were the Holy Spirit that descended into him at his baptism; and he had been breathing long before the Holy Spirit descended into him. According to 1:5 all the Judean region and all the Jerusalemites were confessing their sins as John was baptizing them. Surely this confession unites with the baptismal submission itself to indicate that the people, all of them, did repent. If he thought at all about the problem posed by the later rejection of Jesus, Mark may have wanted his audience to suppose that at least some of the Judeans and Jerusalemites backslid. Or perhaps he does not regard submission to John's baptism of repentance as having guaranteed belief in Jesus. Or the double "all" in 1:5 represents a hyperbole which leaves room for some who did not submit to that baptism and thus turned into Jesus' enemies. In any case, 3:20-30 links baptism by Jesus in Holy Spirit with his ministry of preaching, teaching, healing, and exorcism rather than with his last breath.

Drawing a parallel with the water-baptism of repentance for forgiveness of sins, some have interpreted baptism in Holy Spirit as cleansing by the Holy Spirit (so R. A. Guelich 1. 25-26 and others cited there). Thus the two baptisms become essentially synonymous. John draws a strong contrast between them, however. This contrast resists synonymity; and for baptism in Holy Spirit to represent an advance, the water-baptism of repentance could only promise forgiveness in the future — but not so far in the future as the last judgment unless baptism in Holy Spirit is likewise delayed till then. For otherwise the Holy Spirit would be cleansing people before their sins were forgiven. But forgiveness seems to have taken effect at the baptism of repentance, and baptism in Holy Spirit will apparently take place at the coming of the stronger one. To equate baptism in Holy Spirit with Q's baptism in fire and thus to interpret baptism in Holy Spirit in terms of the judgment that will burn up "the chaff," the unrepentant (cf. Matt 3:10, 12 par. Luke 3:9, 17), honors the strong contrast that John draws between water-baptism for the forgiveness of sins and baptism in Holy Spirit. But baptism in Holy Spirit seems rather to correlate with the gathering of "the wheat" into the granary, i.e. with the gathering of the repentant into the kingdom. Even the supposition of an original baptism "in wind and fire" does not provide such a correlation, for wind blows away the chaff for burning. It does not blow the wheat into the granary. Therefore we should think of a twofold baptism by the stronger one. In it he will use the Holy Spirit to deal salvifically with the repentant, and fire to deal judgmentally with the unrepentant. The "you" of John's audience according to Q included the unrepentant "offspring of vipers" needing to produce "fruits worthy of repentance" (Matt 3:7-8 par. Luke 3:7-8) as well as the repentant. Mark's lack of the phrase "and fire" and of sayings that speak about judgment limits "you" to the repentant, though in other respects the sayings that appear in vv 7-8 may show more originality than do their synoptic parallels. The attempt of H. Fleddermann (in *SBL 1984 Seminar Papers* 381-84) to demonstrate that in vv 7-8 Mark redacts a Q-saying more thoroughly than Matthew or Luke does (cf. also W. Schenk in *ZNW* 70 [1979] 160) suffers from underestimation of Matthew's redaction and from failure to consider the possibility of Luke's secondary use of Matthew (see R. H. Gundry, *Matthew* 47-49).

A DOUBLE ATTESTATION OF JESUS BY THE SPIRIT'S ENDUEMENT AND GOD'S ACKNOWLEDGMENT

1:9-11 (Matt 3:13-17; Luke 3:21-22; John 1:29-34

Jesus' coming opens this short pericope with a topographical movement characteristic of the way Mark makes a new start (v 9a). Next, Jesus is baptized (v 9b) and sees the Spirit descending into him (v 10). Finally, a heavenly voice acknowledges him (v 11). The double attestation by Spirit and heavenly voice does not interpret Jesus' baptism; it interprets Jesus himself. His baptism simply provides the occasion for the double attestation.

"And it came to pass" prepares for the bringing of Jesus on stage. "In those days" alludes to the beginning of the good news about him in John's prediction: "The one stronger than I is coming after me [and so forth]." "Jesus came" notes the quick fulfilment of that prediction and identifies the stronger one as Jesus. Mark does not explicitly state fulfilment. It is not his style to do so; rather, he narrates the fulfilment so as to let his audience discover it for themselves. Leaving no doubt about it are the textual juxtaposition of vv 9-11 with vv 1-8, the solemn Semitism "and it came to pass," the temporal clamping of vv 9-11 together with vv 1-8 by means of "in those days" (cf. 8:1), the repetition of the verb ἔρχομαι, "come," the naming of Jesus after John's prediction concerning the stronger one, the verbal interrelating of vv 9-11 with vv 1-8 through repetition of baptism "by John into the Jordan" (cf. the phraseology of vv 5b and 9b), the descent of the Spirit into Jesus after John's prediction concerning baptism in Holy Spirit, and the narrating of Jesus' Spirit-empowered exorcisms, miracles, and teaching throughout the rest of the book.

If "from Nazareth of Galilee" modified "Jesus," a definite article would precede the phrase, as in John 1:45; Acts 10:38; and similarly and above all in the better supported text of Mark 15:43 ("Joseph the one [ὁ] from Arimathea"). Therefore the phrase modifies "came" (against N. Turner, *Syntax* 166-67; idem, *Grammatical Insights* 28-29; G. D. Kilpatrick in *JSNT* 15 [1982] 4-5). The city-name "Nazareth" stands against "Jerusalemites" in v 5 and prepares for the later designations of Jesus as "the Nazarene" (1:24; 10:47; 14:67; 16:6). The regional name "Galilee" stands over against "the Judean region" in v 5 and prepares for Jesus' ministry in Galilee (1:14-15 and onward). As a whole, Jesus' coming from Nazareth of Galilee contrasts with the going out of all the Judean region and all the Jerusalemites. This contrast makes it appear that Jesus is the only Nazarene and Galilean to get baptized by John (contrast Luke 3:7, 10, 15, 18, and esp. 21; John 1:35-41). Thus attention concentrates on Jesus. The further contrast between his coming (ἦλθεν) and the Judeans' and Jerusalemites' going out (ἐξεπορεύετο) adds to the fulfilment of John's prediction that the stronger one was coming (ἔρχεται). Now that John no longer stands in the spotlight, "into the Jordan" moves ahead of "by John" in connection with Jesus' baptism (contrast v 5); and John's name loses the anaphoric definite article that gave it some prominence in v 6 and will yet give it some prominence on reintroduction in v 14 after a hiatus (vv 12-13). "River" (v 5) needs no remention; but ἐν, "in" (v 5), gives way to εἰς, "into," to prepare for Jesus' coming up "out of" (ἐκ) the water.

At the beginning of v 10, "immediately" emphasizes the following points of real interest, i.e. the Spirit's enduement and God's acknowledgment of Jesus, which strikingly replace what v 5 led us to expect, i.e. "confessing his sins." Since an immediate coming up out of the water is to be expected in baptism (which would otherwise be tantamount to drowning), "immediately" does not modify "coming up out of the water" so much as it modifies the whole of the following vision and audition. The present tense of the participle ἀναβαίνων indicates that the vision and audition happen as Jesus is coming up out of the water. Mark's taking care to mention this circumstance suggests that he does not want anyone to think of water-baptism by John as effecting the immediately subsequent enduement of Jesus with the Spirit. In agreement with the contrast between water-baptism and Spirit-baptism in v 8, the Spirit descends into Jesus only on emergence, not on immersion (a more contextual explanation than D. Daube's appeal to coming up as the decisive moment in proselyte baptism [b. Yebam. 47b] and his suggestion of a new coming up into the promised land [cf. Josh 4:15-24] — NTRJ 111-12, 243). Since "Holy Spirit" in v 8 has made it clear what spirit is in view, "Holy" now drops out to leave the stress exclusively on the connotation of power (see the comments on vv 7-8 and cf. Isa 9:5[6]; 11:2, 4b; Pss. Sol. 17:21–18:9; 1 Enoch 45-46, 47-49 on the power of the Messiah). The Spirit's enduement thus shows that Jesus truly is stronger than John, with the result that Jesus will baptize people in the Spirit that he himself has.

The splitting (σχιζομένους) of the heavens shows that the Spirit is no less than God's Spirit, whose power is awesome (cf. the awesome power of Yahweh who can split the heavens and come down in Isa 63:19[64:1]; see also Isa 63:14 LXX for the descent of the Spirit from the Lord; R. H. Gundry, Use of the OT 28-29). Mark means his audience to understand that Jesus has that very omnipotence (cf. Acts 10:38). The violence implied in splitting connotes an act of power such as only God can perform when it is the heavens that are split (cf. the rending of the veil of the temple from the top downward in the only other Marcan occurrence of σχίζομαι at 15:38-39, where again there is seeing and a declaration of Jesus as Son of God). The usual reference to the heavens' being "opened" (see Jos. Asen. 14:2-3 for the only other exception) is tame by comparison. The placement of σχιζομένους, "being split," before τοὺς οὐρανούς, "the heavens," contrasts chiastically with the normal placement of καταβαῖνον, "coming down," after τὸ πνεῦμα, "the Spirit," and thereby stresses the transmission of heavenly power to Jesus (against F. Lentzen-Deis [Die Taufe Jesus 48-49] and C. R. Kazmierski [Jesus, the Son of God 30-31], whose appeal to Mark's usual placement of finite verbs before their subjects neglects the participial character of σχιζομένους and the function of τοὺς οὐρανούς as a direct object). The contrast between the Spirit's coming down and Jesus' coming up likewise stresses this transmission of heavenly power.

Jesus' seeing the heavens being split and the Spirit descending into him makes him aware of receiving heavenly power. This awareness will lead him to use the power throughout the rest of Mark. Though Jesus is the only one who is said to see the Spirit descending into him (thus the visionary character of the seeing), Mark's letting his audience see the event through the narrative gives them in advance the correct interpretation of Jesus' future words and deeds, stupendously powerful as they will be, and of the Crucifixion and Resurrection. Since εἰς bears its proper sense "into" everywhere else in vv 1-13, even in v 5 (see the following notes), and since throughout Mark εἰς normally has this sense with verbs of motion, we should probably reject the possible alternative meanings "to" (= πρός) and "on" (= ἐπί). If so, Mark seems to mean that Jesus sees the Spirit descend and disappear into himself (i.e. into Jesus).

The seeing of the Spirit and the placement of ὡς περιστεράν after τὸ πνεῦμα rather than after καταβαῖνον favor that "like a dove" modifies "the Spirit" rather than "descending." Since οὐρανός means "sky" as well as "heaven," the splitting of the οὐρανούς and descent of the Spirit make appropriate the appearance of a bird that flutters down out of the sky. And what bird so appropriate as the dove, pure and innocent (Matt 10:16), the only bird fit for sacrifice (Lev 1:14)? More importantly for Mark and his Gentile audience, however, the dove is regarded in the Hellenistic world as a divine bird (see the abundant citations of primary and secondary literature by G. Sellin in *Kairos* 25 [1983] 243, 249-50, n. 25, though in suggesting that Mark has transformed into a secret epiphany an earlier account lacking the heavenly voice and having only the Spirit's visible descent, witnessed by John [as in John 1:29-34; cf. also G. Richter, *Studien* 326], Sellin underestimates the fourth evangelist's redactional activity — by way of heightening the role of John as a witness, for example).

The acknowledgment by God, "You are my beloved Son; in you I am well pleased," adds audition on top of vision to heighten Jesus' awareness and once again to inform Mark's audience for the correct interpretation of Jesus' future words, deeds, crucifixion, and resurrection. Not as usual, Mark puts the introductory subject φωνή, "a voice," before its verb to emphasize the acknowledgment conveyed by the voice (contrast esp. 9:7, which does not form the climax of its pericope as 1:11 does; cf. M. Zerwick, *Untersuchungen* 76-81). The absence of a transitional λέγουσα, "saying," adds further emphasis to the acknowledgment (cf. 9:7; Luke 3:22; John 12:28; 2 Pet 1:17, but contrast Matt 3:17; 17:5; 27:46; Luke 9:35; Acts 9:4; 11:7; 14:11; 16:28; 19:34; 22:7, 22; 26:14; Rev 1:10-11; 5:11-12; 6:6, 7; 10:4, 8; 11:12, 15; 12:10; 14:13; 16:1, 17; 18:4; 19:1, 5, 6; 21:3). The first half of the acknowledgment probably comes from Ps 2:7b. There, both the MT and the LXX put "my son" first and lack the definite article with "son" — thus: "A son of mine (are) you." Mark puts σύ, "you," in first position to accent the identification of Jesus as God's Son and thus avoid an ugly σύ, ἐν σοί, "you, in you." He also adds a definite article before "my Son" and another definite article plus the adjective "beloved" after "my Son" (ὁ υἱός μου ὁ ἀγαπητός) to accent the love that God has for Jesus. Though ἀγαπητός has come to mean "only" (יחיד in Hebrew) because an only son is naturally beloved (see esp. C. H. Turner in *JTS* os 27 [1926] 113-29; 28 [1927] 152; A. Souter in *JTS* os 28 [1927] 59-60; and J. Barr in *The Glory of Christ in the NT* 15-16), the primary meaning "beloved" has not disappeared, as the second half of the assurance makes clear: "in you I am well pleased" (see also the copious evidence cited by N. Turner, *Christian Words* 266-68, and Philo's addition of μόνος, "only," to ἀγαπητός, apparently because the latter retains its primary meaning [*Imm.* 1 §4; *Som.* 1.34 §§194-95; cf. *All.* 3.72 §203; 3.74 §209; *Migr.* 25 §140]).

The second half is illative: "You are my beloved son; *therefore* I am well pleased in you," just as 9:7 means, "This is my beloved son; *therefore* hear him" (T. A. Burkill, *Mysterious Revelation* 19-20). It probably comes from Isa 42:1b, since the aorist εὐδόκησεν corresponds to the stative perfect in Isa 42:1b, since the next clause in Isaiah ("I have put my Spirit on him") ties in with the descent of the Spirit into Jesus, and since Matt 12:18-21 quotes Isa 42:1-4 (cf. *Tg. Isa* 41:8-9; 43:4, 10, 20; 44:1-2). Other possible sources include 2 Kgdms 22:20 LXX; Isa 62:4 LXX v.l. "In you I am well pleased" informs Mark's audience as well as Jesus that God considers Jesus an obedient son, whatever impression to the contrary the coming crucifixion might give. Asyndeton, the forward position of "in you," and the parallel with the forward position of σύ, "you," in the preceding clause all highlight this piece of information. The question whether Jesus was God's Son before his baptism does not come into view. As an omniscient narrator Mark is simply telling his audience of Jesus' true identity, as already indicated by Mark in v 1 but now as acknowledged by none other than God, and is setting the stage for Jesus' exercise of divine power. The descent of the Spirit endues him with that power, but does not necessarily make him God's Son (whatever the original meaning of Ps 2:7).

NOTES

On καὶ ἐγένετο, see E. C. Maloney, *Semitic Interference* 81-85, and for the combination, "And it came to pass in those days," Exod 2:11 MT LXX. Context determines whether or not "in those days" is eschatological. Here it is not. Not even John's preaching sounded an eschatological note in Mark (cf. R. H. Gundry, *Matthew* 41). Since Mark does not quote the OT to theologize Galilee the way he quoted it in vv 2-3 to theologize the wilderness (contrast Matt 4:14-16), we should beware of loading Galilee with theological freight. Baptism will refer to death in 10:38 (cf. 14:23-24, 36), but it hardly does so here; for 10:38 is too far away for easy anticipation or reflection, and 10:38 will speak of a baptism even farther in the future. The redactional reasons noted above for Mark's repeating the names of John and the Jordan, for omitting the definite article with John's and Jesus' names, and for omitting "River" after "the Jordan" (cf. v 9 with vv 4-6) do away with the need to posit originally independent traditions.

Against C. H. Turner in *JTS* os 26 (1924-25) 14-20, see J. J. O'Rourke in *JBL* 85 (1966) 349-51 that in v 9 εἰς probably bears its proper meaning "into" rather than the meaning of ἐν, "in." O'Rourke notes that in vv 12-13 these prepositions contrast with each other and that the use of εἰς for ἐν in v 9 would be the only exception to the proper use of the prepositions in vv 1-13. According to H. C. Waetjen (*Reordering of Power* 67-69), the shift from ἐν (v 5) to εἰς (v 9) implies that only Jesus truly repented, the Judeans and Jerusalemites not having submitted themselves to the full depth of John's baptism. It is strange, then, that these are said to have been confessing their sins while undergoing baptism but that Jesus is not said to have been doing so.

Neither by content nor by context can we say that Jesus' vision is apocalyptic. For the opening (but not splitting) of the heavens, see Ezek 1:1; John 1:51; Acts 7:56; 10:11; Rev 4:1; 11:19; 19:11; *T. Levi* 2:6; 5:1; 18:6-7 (probably with a Christian interpolation); *T. Judah* 24:2; 2 *Apoc. Bar.* 22:1; 3 Macc 6:18. The truly apocalyptic visions represented in some of these passages either postdate Mark or have uncertain dates (so H.-J. Steichele, *Der leidende Sohn Gottes* 119, n. 36).

D. Ulansey (in an unpublished paper) argues that apart from the rending of the heavens, Isa 63:19 MT and Mark 1:10 do not correspond to each other. The OT passage contains a prayer that God might rend the heavens and come down in judgment on the enemies of God and of God's people, whereas in Mark the Spirit comes down while God stays in heaven and speaks from there. The frequent disregard of context in NT usage of the OT weakens Ulansey's argument, however; and the nearby reference in Isa 63:14 LXX to the descent of the Spirit from the Lord (κατέβη πνεῦμα παρὰ κυρίου — cf. Mark 1:10: τὸ πνεῦμα . . . καταβαῖνον) combines with the unusualness of rending the heavens to support the possibility of conscious borrowing from Isaiah 63. Ulansey's own suggestion that Mark combines the inaugural vision of Ezekiel with the portrayal in Isa 40:22 of the heavens as a curtain, which can be opened only by rending it, suffers from the lack of rending in either of those OT passages, from the Spirit's not descending in Ezekiel (on the contrary see 1:20-21; 3:12, 14, 24 for the Spirit's work of lifting and setting up), from the lack of both the Spirit and descent in Isa 40:22 and its immediate context (though v 13 refers to the Spirit of Yahweh, the verses right around v 22 portray God as sitting far above the earth), and from a bit of the same judgmental context that Ulansey finds problematic with regard to Isa 63:19 (God "blows" on the princes and judges of the earth, "they wither, and the whirlwind takes them away like stubble" — Isa 40:23-24).

Many times in the OT the Spirit of God came mightily on certain people (see Judg 3:10; 6:34; 11:29; 13:25; 1 Sam 10:6; 11:6; 19:20, 23; Isa 42:1; 61:1; cf. Luke 4:18). Here we have both vision ("he saw . . . the Spirit like a dove") and enduement ("descending into him"). V. Taylor (160) argues against enduement that the Spirit's immediate action of thrusting Jesus out (ἐκβάλλει — vv 12-13) shows Jesus to be constrained by an external force, not by an internal one. But the Spirit's descent looks much like his "coming on" or being "put on" certain people in the OT, where enduement is unquestionable. The probable meaning of εἰς as "into" may even intensify the thought of enduement in Jesus' case. And Mark 3:22-30 will brook no question about his enduement.

Interpretations of the dove-symbolism are manifold. Besides the already cited article by Sellin, see representative treatments by L. E. Keck in *NTS* 17 (1970-71) 41-67 and F. Lentzen-Deis, *Die Taufe Jesu* 170-83, 265-70 (with a criticism of Lentzen-Deis by G. Richter, *Studien* 317-18). It looks as though Palestinian Jewish Christian material regarding Jesus' baptism has taken on something of a Hellenistic cast in the comparison of the Spirit to a dove — but not necesarily in the use of "Spirit" without "Holy," as shown by the absolute use of "Spirit" in 1QS 4:6; 1QH 12:11 with 12; 13:18-19; 16:11 with 13; *1 Enoch* 91:1; *2 Apoc. Bar.* 21:4 and by a likely anaphoric use of τό, "the," in Mark 1:10 to refer back to "Holy Spirit" in v 8 (against G. Dalman, *Words* 202-3). Though accepting the apocalyptic evidence, E. Ruckstuhl (in *Die Mitte des NT* 198) discounts the evidence in QL because there the Spirit appears as God's gift. But so also does the Spirit appear as God's gift to Jesus here. H.-J. Steichele (*Der leidende Sohn Gottes* 110-12) argues against an absolute use of "Spirit" for God's Spirit outside Hellenistic circles that 1QS 4:6 represents an abbreviated form of "the Spirit of truth" earlier in its context. He admits that Mark 1:10 could represent a similar abbreviation of v 5, but argues that the passage in 1QS is unitary whereas a break occurs between Mark 1:5 and 10. But if Mark is writing up traditions partly in his own words, he may mean "the Spirit" in one pericope to refer back to "Holy Spirit" in the preceding pericope, just as definite articles with the names of John and Jesus in v 14 will refer back to John and Jesus as introduced anarthrously in vv 1, 4, 9, even though a new pericope will have started with v 14. And just as Mark has dropped the initial descriptions of Jesus as "Christ, Son of God" and of John as "the Baptizer," so he drops the initial description of "Spirit" as "Holy." Though the splitting of the heavens and the descent of the Spirit as Jesus is coming up out of the water speak favorably of Jesus, it does not follow that the absence of such special phenomena at the baptisms of Judeans and Jerusalemites invalidated their baptisms (so W. Harrington 5-6). The statement that those people were confessing their sins (v 5) provided validation enough, and the ordinariness of those people as contrasted with Jesus' divine sonship accounts for the absence of special phenomena from their baptisms.

Since Mark writes about a "voice," not about "a daughter of the voice" (*bath-qol,* i.e. an echo of God's voice), we should probably not interpret v 11 in the light of rabbinic parallels (against I. Abrahams, *Studies* 1. 47-50; cf. G. Vermes, *Jesus the Jew* 205-6, and see the collection of materials in Str-B 1. 125-35). Nor was "a daughter of the voice" accompanied by an epiphany as the voice in Mark is accompanied by one. The advantages of treating Ps 2:7 as the source of Mark 1:11b lie in the shared direct address to the son (as in *Tg. Isa* 41:8-9, which has "servant" instead of "son," however; contrast the third person in the other suggested sources Gen 22:2, 12, 16; Exod 4:22; 2 Sam 7:14; Isa 42:1a; Mark 12:6) and the explicit quotation of Ps 2:7 in other parts of the NT (Acts 13:33; Heb 1:5; 5:5). C. R. Kazmierski (*Jesus, the Son of God* 38) argues that since the explicit quotations keep the word order of the psalm, which stresses adoption and enthronement, Mark's divergence militates against an allusion. But we have seen Christological and stylistic purposes in the divergence. The stylistic purpose of avoiding an ugly σύ, ἐν σοι does not apply to the other NT passages, where a quotation of Isa 42:1b fails to follow. Besides, divergence is to be expected in allusive quotations. It is explicit quotations of the OT in the NT that are more notable for sticking close to the LXX.

The advantage of seeing an allusion to Genesis 22, especially in the LXX, lies in the occurrences there of ἀγαπητός, preceded by the definite article, the both of them following the arthrous υἱός as in Mark (on this word order, see E. C. Maloney, *Semitic Interference* 56-57). But not only is there no direct address to the beloved son; it is also doubtful whether the rest of the NT alludes to this passage (see, e.g., D. R. Schwartz in *JBL* 102 [1983] 264-65 and esp. P. R. Davies and B. D. Chilton in *CBQ* 40 [1978] 514-46, responding to R. J. Daly in *CBQ* 39 [1977] 45-75). Further appeals to the Targums of Genesis 22 (so A. R. C. Leaney in *Historicity and Chronology* 28-34 and W. R. Stegner in *BR* 1 [1985] 36-46, building on G. Vermes, *Scripture and Tradition* 222-23) — in particular, the appeals to Isaac's consenting to be sacrificed, his asking to be bound lest by struggling he make the sacrifice unfit and be cast into eternal punishment, his seeing "the angels of the height" and the glory of the "Lord's Shekinah" as he lies bound on the altar, and his hearing a voice that says, "Come, see the two elect individuals in the world" — overlook that Mark 1:9-11 says nothing about sacrifice, consent, binding, eternal punishment, angels, or Shekinah glory. In the Targums neither the angels nor the Shekinah descends, as the Spirit does in Mark. The voice speaks to Jesus in Mark, but not to Isaac in the Targums. And the voice in the Targums speaks about two elect ones, in Mark to a single son.

Seeing an allusion to Isa 42:1a enjoys the advantage of a possible allusion to Isa 42:1b immediately following. But again there is no direct address to the "servant" (as he is called); and we have to suppose that the ambiguous παῖς, "servant, child," of the LXX was changed to υἱός, "son," despite the retention of παῖς in Matt 12:18, where Isa 42:1a *is* quoted. Furthermore, the possibility of an allusion to Isa 42:1b is no stronger than the possibility of an allusion to Isa 42:1a (see H.-J. Steichele, *Der leidende Sohn Gottes* 131-33). The other suggested sources need no further comment (but see R. H. Gundry, *Use of the OT* 29-32; I. H. Marshall in *NTS* 15 [1968-69] 326-36; Steichele, op. cit. 135-48).

Tg. Ket. Ps 2:7 has "beloved," but only in an analogy: "Beloved as a son to his father are you to me." It is hard to tell whether Mark imports the term from an early targumic tradition while keeping the direct statement of sonship in the psalm itself, whether the targumic tradition postdates Mark and exhibits a reaction against Christian use of Ps 2:7 (a weakening of divine sonship to mere analogy could equally well have come about in reaction to paganism either before, during, or after the NT era), whether there is any relation at all between Mark 1:11 and *Tg. Ket.* Ps 2:7, or — looking away from the Targum — whether Mark may have overlaid his primary text Ps 2:7 with Genesis 22 (in respect of ὁ ἀγαπητός). The parallels in Genesis 22 make it doubtful that ὁ ἀγαπητός is a separate title, "the Beloved One" (cf. G. D. Kilpatrick in *NovT* 5 [1962] 111-14). The lack of ὁ υἱός in Matt 12:18 (cf. Eph 1:6) lessens the value of that passage as evidence for a titular meaning. The pathos of losing a son or daughter who is beloved because he or she is an only child permeates passages such as Genesis 22; Judg 11:34; Jer 6:26; Amos 8:10; Zech 12:10; Mark 12:6 (cf. J. Swetnam in *Bib* 65 [1984] 414); but pleasure, not pathos, permeates the present text. Ὁ ἀγαπητός μου in Matt 12:18 probably echoes the baptismal voice rather than vice versa.

The thoroughness with which OT phraseology permeates the statement of God to Jesus makes doubtful that Mark has substituted "my beloved Son" for an older title (as thought by J. Zmijewski in *SNTU* A/12. 5-34), but the fact that Mark quotes God as calling Jesus "my beloved Son" does at least show Mark's approval of Son-of-God Christology. The aorist of εὐδόκησα, "I am well pleased," expresses the pleasure that God took in Jesus' getting baptized or the pleasure that God constantly takes in him (see S. E. Porter, *Verbal Aspect* 126-29, that this aorist need not carry a temporal reference). The advancement of σύ, "you," to the front shifts the point from adoption and enthronement (so Ps 2:7) to identification and acknowledgment. So also does the omission of the clause, "Today have I begotten you." As 9:7 will not imply a second adoption, so 1:11 does not imply a first adoption. Nor is Jesus called and commissioned to his messianic task. He is endued and acknowledged.

See H.-J. Steichele, *Der leidende Sohn Gottes* 292-94, against the appeal to an Egyptian ceremony of enthronement. We should even beware of reading the ideologies of kingship and servanthood from Psalm 2 and Isaiah 42 into the heavenly voice; for Mark can hardly expect his Gentile audience to know those passages, and he himself does not introduce those ideologies into the pericope. Emphasis falls instead on belovedness and pleasingness. The appeal of F. Lentzen-Deis (*Die Taufe Jesu* 249ff.) to interpretative visions in the Targums suffers from the late date of the Targums, from the uncertain date of the traditions in them, and from the failure of the targumic visionaries to be addressed by God as Jesus is addressed by God. Lentzen-Deis thinks that the account of Jesus' vision is not meant to be taken as historical, but A. J. B. Higgins (*Tradition* 10) wonders why Jesus could not have related his visionary and auditory experiences to the disciples as Isaiah did to his disciples. But if so, asks A. Vögtle (*Offenbarungsgeschehen und Wirkungsgeschichte* 86-87), why is Jesus not quoted as speaking in the "I"-style (cf. Luke 10:18, 21-22 par.; 11:20 par.), and why does Mark say nothing of a discipular reaction to Jesus' report? An answer to these questions comes easily. Mark is narrating Jesus' baptism. Only if he were narrating a later report by Jesus to the disciples would the "I"-style become appropriate and a reaction by the disciples possible. At the time of baptism, Jesus had no disciples. The suggestion that Christians fabricated the Spirit's descent and God's voice to portray Jesus as superior to John even though baptized by him (ibid. 96-100) suffers from the lack of a comparison between Jesus and John (contrast vv 7-8), from the seeing of the Spirit's descent only by Jesus, and from the addressing of God's voice only to Jesus. A fabricator would likely have made the descent observed by others or another, as redactionally in John 1:32-34, and would likely have made God's voice speak to others or another about Jesus, as redactionally in Matt 3:17 and again John 1:32-34 (cf. Mark 9:2-8 parr.). Since Jesus receives no commission and offers no reaction, we cannot think of a call-story. And the lack of emphasis on his baptism as such, which provides only the hinge between his coming in fulfilment of John's prediction on the one hand and enduement by the Spirit and acknowledgment by God on the other hand, prohibits our treating the pericope as a paradigm of Christian baptism.

ACKNOWLEDGMENTS OF JESUS BY SATAN, WILD BEASTS, AND ANGELS

1:12-13 (Matt 4:1-11; Luke 4:1-13)

This short pericope begins characteristically with topographical movement: the Spirit thrusts Jesus out into the wilderness (v 12). Jesus is there forty days being tempted by Satan (v 13a), is with the wild beasts (v 13b), and the angels serve him (v 13c). Because the parallels in Matthew and Luke run much longer and differ in other respects as well, we will take up what Mark says, what he does not say that Matthew and Luke do say, the implications of what Mark does and does not say for the main interpretations of his text, and the interpretation favored by the comparative data.

As noted, what Mark says is contained in four clauses having to do with Jesus. In the first, "the Spirit thrusts him out into the wilderness," and does so "immediately" after coming into him at his baptism. The forward position of τὸ πνεῦμα stresses Jesus' having "the Spirit" to thrust him out into the wilderness, for the position of a subject before its verb is comparatively unusual in Mark. Normally it follows the verb (M. Zerwick, *Untersuchungen* 76-81). The placement of the direct object αὐτόν, "him," before its verb likewise gives prominence to Jesus. Moreover, the vivid historical present tense of ἐκβάλλει, "thrusts," and the forcefulness of this verb in its very meaning highlight the activity of the Spirit in Jesus (on the vividness of the historical present tense in Mark, see E. C. Maloney in *To Touch the Text* 67-78 and, more generally and sophisticatedly from the linguistic standpoint, S. E. Porter, *Verbal Aspect* 189-98, esp. 195-96, and B. M. Fanning, *Verbal Aspect* 226-39 [though on pp. 231-33 Fanning denies the vividness in Mark's verbs of speaking without seriously considering whether Mark is emphasizing the quotations following them]).

According to the second clause, Jesus "was in the wilderness forty days." "Being tempted by Satan" is only a participial phrase, not part of a periphrastic verbal construction. There are two reasons for saying so. One is that καὶ ἦν, "and he was," stands in parallel with the same phrase in the next clause, where we find no participle that could go with it to form a periphrastic verbal construction. Another reason is that "in the wilderness" and "forty days" separate "being tempted" from "was" too far for a periphrastic construction to be likely. But though the temptation merits only a participial phrase, it lasts the whole forty days that Jesus is in the wilderness, because the present tense of a participle such as "being tempted" indicates linear action concurrent with the action or state of being expressed by the indicative verb in its clause, here the durative imperfect ἦν. So the accent falls, not on the temptation as such, but on the length of time that Jesus was in the wilderness being tempted by Satan. The position of "forty days" before "being tempted" confirms and increases this accent on length of time.

Third, Jesus "was with the wild beasts." The parallelism with his being in the wilderness forty days (note again the repetition of καὶ ἦν) implies that he was with the wild beasts forty days. What is rarely if ever remarked is that Mark does not put the wild beasts with Jesus; rather, Jesus with them. Since τῶν θηρίων connotes wildness, his being with them without harm, or even attack, carries Mark's point (cf. the story of Daniel in the lion's den [Dan 6:1-28], the reputed divine power of Pythagoras to soothe wild beasts [Iambl. *VP* 60-62], and stories of wild beasts' not attacking Apollonius of Tyana [Philostr. *VA* 5.42; 6.43; 8.30] and, in early Christianity, of wild beasts' obeying exemplary monks [W. A. Schulze in *ZNW* 46 (1955) 280-83]; see also Philo *Praem.* 15 §§88-90; idem *Opif.* 28 §§83-86).

Fourth, "the angels were serving him." Since the setting is a wilderness and since no mention is made of Jesus' fasting, presumably the angels are serving him food. Serving food is the most common meaning of διηκόνουν, anyway (as probably also in 1:31; 15:41; and much other literature; see 6:35; 8:4 on the need for food in a deserted place and wilderness). Since διηκόνουν is in the imperfect tense, paralleling the imperfect tense of ἦν, this serving of food to Jesus takes place throughout the forty days that he is in the wilderness being tempted by Satan and being with the wild beasts. The position of the subject οἱ ἄγγελοι before its verb διηκόνουν emphasizes that they are no less than the angels who give Jesus food-service throughout this period.

What does Mark not say that Matthew and Luke do say? He does not say that Jesus was led around by the Spirit forty days, as in Luke. He does not say that Jesus fasted forty days or hungered after fasting, as in both Matthew and Luke. We learn nothing from Mark about the character of the temptation. Was it testing by ordeal? Was it enticement to sin? Was it a combination of both? In Mark, no dialogue takes place between Satan and Jesus. Satan does not challenge him to presume on his divine sonship — does not challenge him to make stones into bread, for example. Jesus has not been fasting. The angels have been spreading his table throughout; so he is not hungry. Furthermore, there is no topographical movement, as from the wilderness to Jerusalem and then to a mountain in Matthew and, with a different order, in Luke. There is no challenge that Jesus throw himself down from the pinnacle of the temple to let angels catch him in mid-air, for in Mark the angels are already on the scene and have been serving Jesus the whole while. There is no offer of the kingdoms and glory of the world if Jesus will worship Satan, because in a way Jesus is the object of homage: he is with the wild beasts yet they do him no harm. He does not overcome the temptation by using scripture, as in Matthew and Luke. Most strikingly, he is not said to overcome the temptation at all. Nor does Satan leave him, as in Matthew and Luke; for in Mark he has not approached Jesus. We are not told that Satan finishes each and every temptation, as Luke tells us; nor do the angels approach and serve Jesus after Satan leaves, as Matthew tells us. Again, the angels have been there serving him all along.

What are the implications of what Mark does and does not say for the main interpretations of his text? According to one such interpretation, he wrote his gospel in general for the hortatory purpose of teaching discipleship through following Jesus' example and therefore wrote 1:12-13 in particular to portray

Jesus as an example of overcoming temptation. Against this interpretation, we read of no moral, psychological, or physical struggle, much less of a corresponding victory on Jesus' part. He is entirely passive. He is just there. Not even 3:27 will supplement 1:12-13 by way of a delayed announcement that he overcomes temptation here (as thought by E. Best, *Temptation* 14-15). The whole passage 3:22-30 will offer, not an announcement of past victory over temptation, but an exercise in logic with regard to exorcism: How can Satan cast out Satan? If a kingdom or royal household is divided against itself, it cannot survive. Only by binding a strong man first can anyone seize the articles in the strong man's house. Jesus' exorcisms will not *follow* on the binding. They will *be* the binding, which will then enable Jesus to seize demoniacs from Satan's control (cf. the binding of Satan in Rev 20:2 and the use of δέω, "bind," in the magical papyri for exercising supernatural mastery over a variety of objects). So the binding of the strong man will not contain a backward allusion to the present temptation; rather, an allusion to exorcisms that Jesus is performing at the time.

A contrastive parallel with Israel's succumbing to temptation in the wilderness would support the interpretation that Mark presents Jesus as an example of overcoming temptation. But such a parallel does not exist in Mark. To be sure, the forty days as well as the wilderness match up. But again, and quite differently from Matthew and Luke, Mark's non-mention of Jesus' overcoming the temptation leaves a contrast with Israel's succumbing wholly unexpressed and therefore unlikely. Moreover, Jesus' presence with the wild beasts and the angels' serving him seem extraneous to the temptation and therefore point away from this interpretation. The wild beasts are sometimes said to be Satan's means of terrifying Jesus into succumbing. But the text does not relate the wild beasts to Satan or to the temptation in that way, and tempting and trying to frighten do not make a natural combination found elsewhere in the NT. Nor does Mark say that Jesus refuses to be frightened.

T. Naph. 8:4 combines Satan, wild beasts, and angels: "If you achieve the good, my children, humans and angels will bless you; and God will be glorified through you among the Gentiles. Satan will flee from you. Wild animals will flee from you, and the angels will stand by you." *T. Benj.* 5:2 is similar. But in those passages there is no temptation by Satan, no wilderness, no serving by the angels; whereas in Mark there is no achieving of the good, no fleeing of Satan, no fleeing of the wild beasts, and the angels do not stand by Jesus, but serve him. So the Testaments do not support a centrality of the temptation.

Other interpreters try to maintain its centrality by holding that the wild beasts are, so to speak, only the furniture of the wilderness and therefore have no importance in themselves. But the devotion of a whole clause, one quarter of the grammatical construction of the narrative, to Jesus' being with the wild beasts speaks against this interpretation. So also does the intervention of being tempted by Satan between being in the wilderness and being with the wild beasts. To subordinate being in the wilderness and being with the wild beasts to being tempted by Satan violates Mark's grammar, which does the reverse by subordinating the temptation.

Yet other interpreters say that Mark omits the character and details of the temptation and Jesus' overcoming it to indicate that it continues throughout Jesus' ministry. But he does not stay in the wilderness (see v 14) or go back into it to be tempted again. Nor does Satan tempt him again elsewhere. He does not even confront him again. (In 8:33 "Satan" will stand for Peter, but not to indicate that Satan has appeared in the person of Peter; for Peter will have been minding "the things of human beings," not "the things of Satan.") Nor do the wild beasts follow Jesus out of the wilderness to threaten him elsewhere; and after leaving the wilderness he no longer enjoys food-service from the angels (see 1:31; 2:15 et passim). So the view that Mark portrays Jesus as an example of overcoming temptation, an example to be imitated by those who take up their crosses and follow him, does not pass muster.

Another view is that Mark wrote his gospel for the proclamatory purpose of portraying Jesus as a cosmic warrior for God's kingdom; and here Jesus wins an initial, decisive victory in the eschatological war against the satanic forces that have thus far held sway. But not only does Satan fail to reappear later on in Mark for this war to continue (as J. M. Robinson [*Problem* 28-32] thinks it continues). Even here Jesus does not go on the attack against Satan; nor does he defend himself against the wild beasts, which under this view are sometimes supposed to represent demons in league with Satan. Jesus is acted on by the Spirit and then by Satan and by the angels. He is the subject only of the verb *to be,* which is not a verb of action. Mark does not portray demons as wild beasts (as in the copious but often doubtfully relevant materials cited by O. Böcher, *Christus Exorcista* 36-42; idem, *Dämonenfurcht* 81-98; idem, *Mächte* 26-28: e.g., in *T. Iss.* 7:7; *T. Naph.* 8:4, 6; *T. Benj.* 5:2 demons and beasts are paralleled but not equated, and in Luc. *Philops.* 31 an attacking spirit successively takes the shape of different beasts but apparently has its own proper appearance). For when Mark elsewhere refers to such beings, he uses the term "demons" or the term "unclean spirits." Nor does Mark portray the wilderness as a haunt of demons (as do Matt 12:43; Luke 8:29; 11:24; *b. Pesaḥ.* 112b; and perhaps Isa 13:21-22; 34:14; cf. Böcher, *Christus Exorcista* 28-30; Str-B 4/1. 515-16). For Mark, the wilderness is associated with John the Baptizer in accordance with scripture (vv 1-8). The parallel between Jesus' being in the wilderness and John's being there links Jesus with God's plan as stated by Isaiah the prophet and worked out through John. The wilderness has as little to do with an eschatological battle against satanic forces as it has to do with enticement to sin. Nor should we think that the angels were serving Jesus by protecting him from demons in the form of wild beasts (cf. Ps 91:11-13; Dan 10:10-13, 20-21; 12:1; Heb 1:14). Not only is the representation of demons by wild beasts to be questioned, but also we need evidence that διηκόνουν means protection. The doubling of "the wilderness" supports the most common meaning of this verb, i.e. serving food (cf. 6:35-44, esp. 35; 8:1-9, esp. 4). We should not think that Jesus fasted before the angels served him food and that his purpose in fasting was to protect himself from demonic wild beasts (as thought by Böcher, *Dämonenfurcht* 273-84; cf. Str-B 4/1. 82-83). Mark fails to mention any fasting; and mere mention of the wilderness does not imply fasting, for John lived there but ate food (v 6). An implication that the angels served Jesus food does not require preliminary fasting. The conjunction of "the wilderness" (bis) and διηκόνουν suffices for that implication.

Yet another view is that Mark writes his gospel for the promissory purpose of portraying Jesus as the apocalyptic restorer of human good, and that here he portrays Jesus as restoring paradise by overcoming temptation (cf. *Barn.* 6:13b: "Behold, I make the last things like the first things"; see, e.g., H. Mahnke, *Versuchungsgeschichte* 28-50; E. Grässer in *Studien zum Text und zur Ethik des NT* 144-57; H. Sahlin in *ST* 41 [1987] 12-13; E. Fascher in *TLZ* 90 [1965] 567-68; U. Holzmeister in *Vom Wort des Lebens* 87-88). An examination of the supposed parallels between the temptation of Jesus in Mark and the first temptation in Genesis 3 undermines this view, however (see also H.-G. Leder in *ZNW* 54 [1963] 188-216). The ἐκβάλλει of Mark 1:12 hardly draws on Gen 3:24 LXX; for there God thrust Adam and Eve out of Eden after the temptation, but here the Spirit thrusts Jesus out before the temptation. Furthermore, this is not a garden, but a wilderness; and Jesus does not transform it into a garden. Forty days has no association with the Garden of Eden. The reference to forty days in *Adam and Eve* 6:1, 3 comes after the expulsion of Adam and Eve and has to do with subsequent repentance from the original sin. The temptation would figure prominently, not subordinately, if an allusion to Genesis 3 were intended. The serpent, later associated with Satan, tempted Eve, not Adam (not only according to Gen 3:1-6 but also according to *Adam and Eve*, which is often mined for parallels to support the paradisic interpretation of the temptation in Mark). The absence of any statement to the effect that Jesus overcomes his temptation militates against the view that he wins back paradise by overcoming whereas Eve succumbed. Temptation would not enter the picture at all if the eternal state of perfection were in view. Nor is there anything of a victory over Satan that might issue in a new creation (as in Rom 16:20; 2 Thess 2:3-12; Rev 19:19-21; 20:1-3, 10). One could say that Mark assumes his audience's knowledge of Jesus' victory over Satan (cf. E. Lohmeyer 28; E. Best, *Gospel as Story* 48), but Mark does not neglect to spell out the other successes of Jesus. Why neglect this one? Besides, a mere assumption could not provide the point of a narrative. Verses 12-13 do not show that God was well pleased with Jesus at his baptism because Jesus now overcomes satanic temptation. God was well pleased with him before the temptation, and Jesus does nothing in Mark's version of the temptation to earn God's good pleasure.

In Eden the Lord God brought to Adam all the animals, domestic as well as wild, and the birds to boot; but Jesus is with only the wild beasts. For the friendly subjection of the wild beasts to Jesus in a restored paradise (cf. Gen 1:24-31; 2:19-20; 3:15; Job 5:22-23; Isa 11:6-9; 65:25; Hos 2:20[18]; Luke 10:19; Mark 16:18; *Sib. Or.* 3:787-95; *T. Naph.* 8:4; *T. Iss.* 7:7; *T. Benj.* 5:2; *2 Apoc. Bar.* 73:6; *'Abot R. Nat.* 1) we would expect Mark to write, "And the wild beasts were with him," as he will later write that the disciples were with Jesus in such a relation, not he with them (3:14; 14:67; cf. 5:18). The reverse order, "And he was with the wild beasts," suggests therefore that Jesus was an object of the wild beasts' unfriendly threat just as he was an object of Satan's unfriendly temptation (cf. 2:19, where the being of the bridegroom with the sons of the bridal chamber makes him the object of their behavior).

Rabbinic tradition speaks of God's telling angels to worship Adam and of Satan's leading the rebellion of refusing to worship him (*b. Sanh.* 59b). But Mark writes of angels' serving Jesus, not of their worshiping him. In the text of Genesis, Adam is to gather food for himself (1:29; 3:2). In *Adam and Eve* 4:1-2, on the other hand, Adam and Eve are said to have eaten angels' food in Paradise, whereas after the fall they had to eat animals' food. But that text says nothing about angels' having served their own kind of food to Adam and Eve in Paradise, and Mark's text says nothing about an angelic kind of food. It says nothing about any kind of food. Διηκόνουν only implies food. The emphasis falls on service as such, because that is what dignifies Jesus as God's Son. *B. Sanh.* 59b and *'Abot R. Nat.* 1 (Recension A), unlike *Adam and Eve*, do have angels serving Adam in the Garden of Eden. But the angels serve him flesh and wine, not an angelic kind of food. In fact, they not only have to roast the flesh; they even have to strain and cool the wine. And the contextual point of the talmudic passage has nothing to do with apocalyptic. It is to prove that Adam was permitted to eat flesh prior to the Noahic covenant. Apart from context, the point lies in the dignity accorded to Adam by the angels' food-service: "thereupon the serpent looked, saw his glory [i.e. Adam's glory], and became envious of him."

What we truly have in Mark 1:12-13, then, is not an apocalyptic restoration of Paradise or an eschatological or moral victory, but purely and simply a dignifying of Jesus as God's Son in accordance with Mark 1:1 and in a follow-up on what happened at Jesus' baptism, i.e. on the Spirit's coming into Jesus and on the pronouncement of Jesus as God's beloved Son in whom God is well pleased. Thus in Mark's version of the so-called temptation the Spirit's immediate thrusting of Jesus out into the wilderness gives instant evidence of Jesus' Spirit-endued divine sonship. His being tempted by none less than Satan, the archdemon, carries an acknowledgement of Jesus' stature as the very Son of God. The wildness of the beasts with which Jesus is present without harmful consequence bears witness to his being God's Son, the stronger one of whom John the Baptizer spoke. That even the angels serve Jesus adds a final touch to Mark's portrayal of him as no less a personage than the Spirit-endued Son of God. That he was in the wilderness being tempted by Satan, that he was with the wild beasts, that the angels were serving him — all for so long a time as forty days — enhances the portrayal as a whole.

The archdemon's spending no fewer than forty days tempting Jesus contrasts with the limitation of the temptation in Matthew to what happened after the forty days — likewise in Luke, except that Luke conflates the forty days of temptation in Mark with the temptation following the forty days in Matthew, or Q. The length of the temptation in Mark also contrasts with the small number of temptations in Matthew and Luke. Only three temptations would look ridiculous in a marathon of forty days. Jesus is with the wild beasts all that time — they must be salivating over him — and still no harm comes to him. Nor does God allow his beloved Son to go hungry in the wilderness. Unlike John the Baptizer, Jesus does not even

have to forage food (contrast v 6; also 2 Macc 5:27, which describes Judas
Maccabeus and his companions as foraging food in the wilderness as wild beasts
do). The word order makes these very same emphases: it is no less than the Spirit
who thrusts Jesus into the wilderness, Jesus is in the wilderness no fewer than
forty days being tempted by Satan, it is no less than the angels who are serving
him. Thus Mark 1:12-13 adds to the twin divine attestations of Jesus in vv 9-11
(the descent of the Spirit and the voice of God) a triple recognition from the
creaturely world, ranging from the demonic realm through the animal kingdom
to the angelic sphere (cf. D. Traktellis, *Authority and Passion* 9).

Does Mark redact a version of Jesus' temptations such as we have in
Matthew and Luke because he knows Q or a pre-Q tradition? If he does, his
redaction speaks loudly concerning what is and is not his purpose in writing both
this pericope and the gospel to which it belongs. We must be cautious, however.
Mark may have only a short tradition, Q a long one; or Matthew may expand
Mark, and Luke reflect both Mark and Matthew. Furthermore, vv 12-13 form
only a small part of Mark's gospel; so one should not generalize very confidently
from them. Nevertheless, they do come toward the beginning; and first impres-
sions are often lasting. For what they are worth, then, these two verses fail to
support an interpretation of Mark as a gospel that teaches Christian discipleship
after the moral pattern of Jesus, fail to support an interpretation of Mark as a
gospel that proclaims the victory of Jesus over Satan in an eschatological war,
and fail to support an apocalyptic interpretation of Mark as a gospel that promises
the restoration of Paradise through Jesus' making up for the failure of Adam and
Eve in the Garden of Eden. All that we have is a dignifying of Jesus, a series of
acknowledgments — a backhanded acknowledgment by Satan, a pacifistic acknowledgment by the wild beasts, and a ministerial acknowledgment by the angels
— in recognition of the status of Jesus as God's beloved Son. Mark 1:12-13 is
neither exemplary nor proclamatory nor promissory, but Christological. The high-
ness of its Christology suits an apology for the Cross.

NOTES

The reasons usually given for regarding this pericope as originally independent from the
story of Jesus' baptism lack cogency. The historical present tense in v 12 proves nothing;
for it characterizes Mark's writing style in general, not just seams between originally
independent traditions. The putting of subjects before their verbs in vv 12-13 may have a
redactional purpose and has occurred already in the preceding pericope (v 11); so independence cannot be deduced from this phenomenon. The wilderness is presented as Jesus'
destination even though he was already in the wilderness at his baptism. True, but the
baptismal story did not mention the wilderness; and we might infer a redactional intrusion
of the wilderness into vv 2-4 as readily as an original independence of vv 9-11, 12-13 from
vv 1-8. The natural progression from the Spirit's descent into Jesus to his thrusting Jesus
out, the geographical proximity of the wilderness to the Jordan River, and the falling of
the antecedent of αὐτόν, "him," into the baptismal story favor that that story and this one
belonged together from the start (and see F. Neirynck, *Duality* 94-96, on the redundancy
of "into the wilderness . . . in the wilderness" as characteristic of Mark).

If among other ways Mark redacts Q by radically shortening the temptation, he does not do so to reject divine man Christology (as thought by S. Schulz, *Q* 182); for a Jesus acknowledged by Satan, wild beasts, and angels fits a divine man Christology better than a merely moral hero does. For topographical movement under the power of the Spirit, see 1 Kgs 18:12; 2 Kgs 2:16; Ezek 3:12, 14-15; 8:3; 11:24; Acts 8:39-40 (cf. Philostr. *VA* 4.10; 8.10ff.). But such movement does not necessarily imply ecstasy, either here or in the cross-references, which therefore remain relevant (against C. E. B. Cranfield [56], whose suggestion of "moral compulsion" in the present passage fails to take account of Mark's disinterest in any moral side of the temptation).

C. R. Kazmierski (*Jesus, the Son of God* 65-66) correctly notes that Mark does not attribute to the Spirit a purpose of getting Jesus tempted. But he incorrectly reads into the text a purpose of meeting God in the wilderness. The cross-references fail: 1:35 speaks of "a deserted place," not of the wilderness; 6:31-32 does likewise and has to do with rest, not with meeting God; 1:2-3 portrays the wilderness as a place of proclamation, not as a place where one meets God; and right within our present pericope Jesus meets Satan, wild beasts, and angels — but not God. Equally, Mark does not portray the wilderness as a place of loneliness and remoteness. For that idea he writes ἔρημος τόπος, "a deserted place." Here, the wilderness seems well stocked with a population drawn from heaven, hell, and the zoo; and of that population, the angels provide Jesus with good company. From Mark's neglecting to say anything like Matt 4:11 ("then the Devil left him"; cf. Luke 4:13) we should not deduce that the temptation lasts throughout the whole book (so U. W. Mauser, *Christ in the Wilderness* 100). Mark is not interested enough in the temptation per se to bother with such a statement. "Forty days" suffices to imply a termination. This length of time appears often in the Bible and with a variety of associations (see, e.g., Gen 7:12; Exod 24:18; 34:28; Deut 9:9, 18; 1 Kgs 19:8; Jonah 3:4; Acts 1:3; cf. forty years in Deut 2:7; Judg 13:1; Ps 95:10; Acts 7:23, 30).

Since Mark does not quote Satan as enticing Jesus and since elsewhere in Mark πειράζω means "test" (8:11; 10:2; 12:15), one might argue for the latter meaning here and dispense with the traditional translation "tempt." On the other hand, any Satanic test has the purpose of inducing a lapse that is sinful in one way or another. At this point, then, the distinction in meaning becomes artificial and the traditional translation acceptable.

J. Carmignac (in *ASTI* 7 [1968-69] 70) detects a Hebrew wordplay in an underlying והיה עם החיה, "and he was with the wild beasts" (החיה being a collective singular). Aramaic would provide the same wordplay. The difference between the generality of wild beasts and the specificity of snakes spoils the parallel drawn by F. Neugebauer (*Versuchung* 32-33) with the snakes that destroyed Israelites in the wilderness (Num 21:6; 1 Cor 11:9); and that destruction was a single incident during forty years, whereas Jesus is with the wild beasts for the whole of forty days. The present setting of a wilderness determines that τῶν θηρίων does not include domesticated animals (against E. Fascher in *TLZ* 90 [1965] 567). The suggestion that v 13b draws on the friendliness of formerly wild beasts in Isa 11:6-9 struggles against a difference in locale. Mark speaks of the wilderness. Isa 11:9 speaks of Mount Zion: "they will not hurt or destroy in all my holy mountain." People are living on the mountain. Children are playing there. It is not a wilderness. The wilderness does appear in Isaiah 35; but in that passage the wild beasts are not friendly. They are absent: "No lion will be there, nor will any ravenous beast . . ." (v 9). With beasts' posing a threat, as implied by their wildness, cf. Deut 8:15-16; Isa 13:21-22; Job 5:22; Pss 22:12-22[11-21]; 91:13; Jer 15:3; Ezek 14:21; 33:27; 34:5, 8, 25; Dan 7:3-8; 2 Tim 4:17; 1 Pet 5:8; Rev 11:7; 13:1-18; *T. Naph.* 8:6; *Adam and Eve* 37:1–38:3; *Apoc. Mos.* 10:1–11:3; 24:4. With their remaining docile, as implied by the relaxed atmosphere of angelically served meals, cf. 1 Kgs 19:4-8; *T. Naph.* 8:4 (see also Deut 8:2-3; Ps 78:23-29). In Isa 13:21-22; 34:11, 13-15 wild beasts are a sign of desolation due to judgment, but judgment does not come into Mark 1:12-13. Jesus' suffering no harm undermines any allusion to Christians' being devoured by wild beasts in the arena during Roman persecution. Matthew's parallel does not enable us to understand the angels' service in Mark (against B. Reicke in *ANRW* II 25/2. 1781); for in Matthew the angels serve Jesus only after he has fasted forty days and forty nights and the devil has left, whereas in Mark they serve Jesus the whole while rather than by way of enabling him to break his fast.

It seems doubtful that vv 12-13 are the remnant of a larger myth reflected in the *Apocalypse of Adam* in the Nag Hammadi Codices V 77:21–82:28. The similarity of angelic nourishment in the wilderness offers only a slim base, for one might just as well think that the similar nourishment of Elijah in the wilderness lies at the base of vv 12-13 (but against Elijah-typology see H. Mahnke [*Versuchungsgeschichte* 25], who notes that in contrast with Jesus, Elijah is traveling, gets only one meal served by one angel, is not tempted, and is not with the wild beasts, and that Mark does not mention forty nights as 1 Kgs 19:8 does; see also J. Jeremias in *ZNW* 54 [1963] 278-79). The question of A. J. B. Higgins (*Tradition* 10) why Jesus could not tell his disciples about the visionary and auditory experience which he had at baptism if Isaiah could tell his visions and auditory experiences to his disciples applies to Jesus' temptation as well (cf. the autobiographical revelations of Jeremiah's private and inner life, apparently to Baruch).

JESUS' OVERPOWERING WORD OF COMMAND TO FOLLOW HIM

1:14-20 *(Matt 4:12-22; Luke 4:14-15; 5:1-11; John 4:1-3, 43-46a; 21:1-14)*

Now Jesus goes into Galilee and preaches (vv 14-15). There he makes Simon and Andrew into his disciples (vv 16-18) and then James and John, too (vv 19-20). We are not to imagine a sharp break between vv 15 and 16. Rather, the participial phrases "going along to the side of the Sea of Galilee" (v 16a) and "going on a little" (v 19) carry forward the topographical movement begun in v 14: "Jesus went into Galilee." Thus the stories in vv 16-20 tell in further detail how Jesus begins to take action in the power of the Spirit with whom he has been endued. He now appears as acting rather than as acted on. For him, the drawing near of God's rule makes it urgent to get helpers in order that as many people as possible may prepare themselves by repentance and faith (cf. v 15 with "fishers of human beings" in v 17). For Mark, however, the center of gravity does not lie in an eschatological crisis, but in the overpowering authority of Jesus' command, which compensates in advance for his seeming helplessness on the cross.

1:14-15 *(Matt 4:12-17; Luke 4:14-15; John 4:1-3, 43-46a)* Μετὰ δέ, "but after," signals a break. Ordinarily Mark makes connections with καί, "and." Comparatively seldom does he use δέ; so when he does we can see an adversative meaning that sets off the following material more radically than usual. Here, δέ marks a shift from the wilderness to Galilee. In v 44 it will mark a shift from synagogues (v 39) to deserted places, in 7:24 to the Gentile region of Tyre, in 10:32 to Jerusalem as a destination of travel, in 14:1 to the Passion, in 15:16 to the Crucifixion, and in 15:40 to the Resurrection (for which is needed an introduction of certain women and an account of Jesus' burial). We can see further justification, then, for our earlier decision not to regard vv 14-15 as the close of a pericope encompassing vv 1-15. The sharing of considerable vocabulary between vv 14-15 and vv 1-13 (Ἰωάννης, ἔρχομαι, Ἰησοῦς, Γαλιλαία, κηρύσσω, κηρύσσω + λέγω, εὐαγγέλιον + a genitive, θεός, μετανοέω/-νοία) may show a reflection of vv 1-13 in vv 14-15, but it need not show a unity between them. In fact, the repetitions may indicate a new start rather than inclusion.

Jesus' coming into Galilee after John was given over carries forward the fulfilment of John's prediction that a stronger one would come after him (v 7; cf. Acts 10:37). Mark's not telling how long after Jesus' temptation John was given over leaves room for concurrent ministries, as in John 3:22-24; 4:1-2. But the chronological placement of the call of the disciples remains a problem, since in the fourth gospel they begin to follow Jesus while John is still free and active (John 1:35–4:2). To say that Jesus starts his ministry before John's beheading requires Mark 1:14 to refer to John's imprisonment and makes sense of his asking Jesus about that ministry during the imprisonment (Matt 11:2-3; Luke 7:18-19); but it makes nonsense of people's thinking that Jesus is John risen from the dead (6:14; 8:28; Matt 14:1-2; 16:14; Luke 9:7-9, 19), for they should very well understand that two men whom they knew as contemporaries in public life must be distinct from each other. And to say that Jesus does not start his ministry till after John's beheading would contradict Jesus' engaging in the ministry that John asked him about before losing his head. It therefore seems that at the cost of historical chronology Mark's "after" (v 14) has the purpose of giving John's prediction, "The one stronger than I is coming after me," a chronological fulfilment as well as a locative one. The locative took place when Jesus came behind John for baptism "in those days" (v 9), i.e. during the period that John was still preaching and baptizing, not later. Now a chronological fulfilment takes place "after"-wards. Thus ὀπίσω (v 9) reaches fulfilment both in its usual locative sense, "after" as "behind," and in its rare chronological sense, "after" as "subsequent to" (μετά — v 14). In conjunction with this move and in contrast with Luke and the fourth evangelist, Mark seems also to delay the call of the first disciples. So in Mark Jesus comes to start his own ministry after the close of John's. Again Mark wants his audience to understand that everything is happening according to plan. The Cross will likewise come as no surprise and therefore as no scandal. Mark omits to indicate both the length of time, if any, between Jesus' temptation and John's being given over, the reason for John's being given over (contrast 6:14-29), the person or persons who gave him over, the person or persons to whom he was given over, and even the purpose for which he was given over (whether for imprisonment or beheading, etc.). These omissions keep interest focused on the point of Jesus' carrying out God's plan.

It is doubtful, however, that παραδοθῆναι, "was given over," represents a divine passive carrying the implication that God's plan lay behind John's death. K. Stock (*Boten* 157-58) argues to the contrary that this passive must be divine because no human being is identified as the one who gave John over. But the argument proves too much, for it leads to the absurdity that all passives lacking a human agent are divine. Did God clothe John in camel's hair, for example (v 6)? The passive of παραδίδωμι will occur four times in Mark with regard to Jesus, at

9:31; 10:33; 14:21, 41. But after the statement in 3:19 that Judas Iscariot was the one who gave Jesus over, Mark can hardly expect his audience to think of a divine passive in those passages. Furthermore, in 10:33 the giving over will be "to the chief priests and scribes," just as Judas Iscariot will give Jesus over to them (14:10-11, 41b-47; cf. "into the hands of men" in 9:31 for an emphasis on merciless violence, and "into the hands of sinners" in 14:41 for a condemnatory judgment on the chief priests and scribes). The passive in 14:21 will follow on the heels of Jesus' statement to the Twelve, "One of you will give me over" (14:18), and be modified by "that man [Judas] through whom" the Son of man is being given over. The passive in 14:41 will be immediately followed by a reference to Judas as "the one who is giving me over" (vv 42-44). Everywhere else in Mark the verb occurs in the active for a human giving over (3:19; 10:33c; 13:9, 11, 12; 14:10, 11, 18, 42, 44; 15:1, 10, 15; cf. 4:29; 7:13 and the notes on 9:31; contrast the theological developments in Rom 8:32, according to which God gave his Son over for us, and Gal 2:20; Eph 5:2, 25, according to which Christ gave himself over for us). Mark's using παραδοθῆναι for John's being given over even though the verb will not appear in the presumably traditional account of John's arrest, imprisonment, and beheading (6:14-29) suggests that Mark is starting to set up a parallel between the deaths of John and Jesus (see esp. 9:11-13), just as between their prior ministries. To mention that John was given over for imprisonment and beheading would spoil the parallel; for Jesus was tried, not imprisoned, and crucified, not beheaded (contrast the use of παραδίδωμι with εἰς φυλακήν, "into prison," in Acts 8:3; 22:4). The passive παραδοθῆναι in v 14 is designed not to allude to divine action, then, but to put off as long as possible those elements in John's story that mismatch the story of Jesus.

Jesus goes into Galilee simply because he came from Nazareth of Galilee (v 9). Mark has geography, not theology, in view (contrast Matt 4:14-16). He goes on to report the specific content of Jesus' preaching, but nothing about his exorcisms and miracles, which will play a very large role in the immediately following pericopes. Thus vv 14-15 form a hinge, not a generalizing summary of the following pericopes or a structural peg on which to hang a whole section of Mark's book (see J. Schlosser, Le règne de Dieu 96-97; C. W. Hedrick in NovT 26 [1984] 294-95). "Preaching the good news of God" means announcing that "the time is fulfilled and the rule of God has drawn near" (cf. the MT, LXX, and Targum of Isa 40:9-10; 52:7; 56:1; 61:6). But just what does this combination of fulfilment and nearness indicate, the nearness of imminent arrival or the nearness of an arrival that has taken place (cf. the linguistic arguments summarized by R. A. Guelich 1. 43-44 and further literature cited there plus N. Perrin, Kingdom 64-68; B. D. Chilton in The Kingdom of God in the Teaching of Jesus 14-15)? A number of considerations favor an arrival that has taken place: (1) the connotation of καιρός as an appropriate or fixed time and more especially its use in the singular to indicate the arrival of a point in time characterized by a certain event (as, for example, in 13:33; Luke 1:20 [N.B. the preceding singular of "day"]; John 7:6, 8 [cf. Jesus' "hour" in John 2:4; 7:30 et passim]; Rev 11:18; Lam 4:18 LXX [bis]; cf. Gal 4:4) rather than indicating imminence caused by the fulfilment of a preceding period of time (as in passages where the plural of καιρός and of other temporal nouns is used: Gen 25:24 LXX; 29:21 LXX; Esth 2:12 LXX [bis]; Lam 4:18 LXX [with respect to ἡμέραι, "days"]; Luke 21:24; Eph 1:10; Tob 14:5; 4 Ezra 4:36-37; 2 Apoc. Bar. 40:3). (2) Parallelism favors that if an appropriate or fixed time has been fulfilled, the drawing near of God's rule means a fulfilment of God's rule, not just its imminent arrival. (3) The precedence of fulfilment over nearness favors the stronger meaning of nearness in consequence of an arrival that has already taken place, for imminence that leads up to but stops short of fulfilment in arrival would seem to require the reverse order. (4) The sense of accomplishment conveyed by the perfect tense of πεπλήρωται, "is fulfilled," and of ἤγγικεν, "has drawn near," suits nearness in consequence of an arrival that has already taken place better than it would suit anticipation of an imminent arrival (contrast Rev 1:3, where mere imminence is noted with the simple adjective ἐγγύς, "near"). (5) The arrival (παραγίνεται) of Judas Iscariot while Jesus was still speaking the words, "Behold, the one who is giving me over has drawn near (ἤγγικεν)" (14:42-43), shows that having drawn near denotes arrival (C. D. Marshall, Faith 35). (6) The parallelism of John 7:6 (ὁ καιρὸς ὁ ἐμὸς οὔπω πάρεστιν, "my time is not yet present [i.e. 'has not yet arrived']") and John 7:8 (ὁ ἐμὸς καιρὸς οὔπω πεπλήρωται, "my time is not yet fulfilled") supports the meaning of fulfilment as arrival rather than as imminence, and therefore the same meaning for the Marcan parallel to fulfilment, i.e. nearness. (7) The parallelism in Lam 4:18 LXX (ἤγγικεν [N.B. the perfect tense, as in Mark 1:15] ὁ καιρὸς ἡμῶν, ἐπληρώθησαν αἱ ἡμέραι ἡμῶν, πάρεστιν ὁ καιρὸς ἡμῶν, "our time has drawn near, our days have been fulfilled, our time is present [i.e. 'has arrived']" — in the context of the already accomplished destruction of Jerusalem and captivity of Judah) likewise supports nearness as arrival rather than as imminence (and note that the arrival of a point in time is consequent on the fulfilment of a preceding period of time, "our days"). (8) To make Jesus prepare people for an imminent arrival would confuse his role with that of John the Baptizer (cf. vv 1-8).

Though the passive voice may elsewhere express temporal fulfilment without implying that God effects it (yet he may effect a concomitant event — see, e.g., Gen 25:24; 29:21; Esth 2:12 [bis in the LXX]), Jesus' reference to the rule of God favors a divine passive here: God has brought about the fulfilment of the time (cf. Luke 21:24; John 7:8; Gal 4:4; Eph 1:10; Tob 14:5; 4 Ezra 4:36-37; 2 Apoc. Bar. 40:3; and, more generally, Ezek 7:12; Dan 7:22; 12:4, 9; Mark 13:7-8, 13, 20, 33; Acts 1:7; 1 Pet 1:11; 1QpHab 7:12-14; T. Naph. 7:1; 4 Ezra 11:44). The connotation of καιρός as an appropriate or fixed time may allude to John's prediction in vv 7-8 (cf. E. Wendling, Entstehung 3), especially if Mark has given ὀπίσω the temporal meaning "after" in that prediction (see the comments on v 14). Mark is then implying that God's rule begins to show itself through Jesus' baptizing people in Holy Spirit (cf. the foregoing interpretation of v 8). The fulfilment of time insures a temporal meaning for the kingdom's drawing near (against C. E. B. Cranfield [67-68], who sees only spatial nearness in the person of Jesus — cf. 12:34). But the predominant use of ἐγγίζω for drawing near in space and Mark's using the verb in that sense twice elsewhere (11:1; 14:42) favor the spatial meaning as well. The two meanings complement each other. The betrayer's having drawn near to Gethsemane in 14:42 will be followed in 14:43 by his "immediate" (εὐθύς) appearance "while he [Jesus] is still speaking." Similarly, in 11:1 the drawing near to Jerusalem, to Bethphage and Bethany, will be followed by the immediate (εὐθύς) finding of a colt in the village and procession to the city. So also the kingdom's having drawn near means that God has drawn near (see J. Jeremias, *NT Theology* 1. 102, for evidence of "the rule of God" as a periphrasis for God) and that God's rule is going to take effect immediately (cf. Rom 13:12). The immediacy of its effect makes repentance and belief urgent (cf. Isa 56:1). The dynamic side of βασιλεία, "kingdom" — i.e. "rule" — highlights the outworking of God's plan and power as Mark exhibits it in Jesus' preaching, teaching, exorcisms, miracles, death, and resurrection (more broadly on the kingdom in Mark, including a remaining futuristic aspect, see T. Söding, *Glaube* 150-97, and for an up-to-date treatment not limited to Mark, G. R. Beasley-Murray, *Jesus and the Kingdom of God*).

In an a-b-a'-b' construction, Jesus' call to repent probably relates back to the fulfilled time, and the call to believe back to the neared kingdom: "Repent *because* the time is fulfilled; believe in the good news *because* God's rule has drawn near." The greater length of b and b' as compared with a and a' adds solemnity and explicitness: "The time is fulfilled *with the result that* the rule of God has drawn near; repent *with the result of* believing in the good news" (cf. T. Söding, *Glaube* 142-49). The absolute use of "the good news" is clear in its meaning because Jesus has just announced the nearness of God's rule. The call to repent links up with John's baptism of repentance (v 4) to provide continuity in the carrying out of God's plan. Asyndeton sharpens the command to repent. The new command to believe in the good news carries God's plan farther forward and in the larger scope of Mark's gospel means: do not disbelieve because of Jesus' crucifixion, but believe because of the fulfilled time and the nearness of God's rule (see C. D. Marshall, *Faith* 49-56, that belief includes trust and commitment as well as assent). The present tense of both imperatives does not demand a continuation of repentance and belief so much as it emphasizes their necessity (cf. the notes on v 3; contrast the unemphatic aorist and subjunctive forms of these verbs in Matt 24:23; Luke 8:50; Acts 2:38; 3:19; 8:22; 16:31; Rev 2:5, 16; 3:3, 19).

1:16-18 *(Matt 4:18-20; Luke 5:1-11; John 1:35-51)* Jesus' "going along to the side of the Sea of Galilee" carries forward the journey "into Galilee" (v 14). Mark might have used "the Sea of Chinnereth" (Num 34:11), "the Sea of Chinroth" (Josh 12:3), "the Lake of Gennesaret" (Luke 5:1), "the Sea of Tiberias" (John 21:1; cf. 6:1; *t. Sukk.* 3:9), or "the Lake of Gennesar" (Josephus *J.W.* 3.10.7 §506; Plin. *HN* 5.15.71 [". . . Genesarum"]), but none of those phrases would have linked up so well with the Galilean designation of the adjoining land mass. Jesus' seeing Simon and Andrew and telling them to follow him show him to be a man of initiative, rather like a "divine man" in the pagan sphere but unlike a Jewish rabbi, to whom disciples attach themselves at *their* initiative (cf. Matt 8:18-22 par. Luke 9:57-62). "Casting nets into the sea, for they were fishers" prepares for emphasis on the force of Jesus' command. Its force will prove so compelling that the brothers will forsake their occupation right in the midst of practicing it. "Hither! Behind me!" stresses Jesus' leadership (cf. 4 Kgdms 6:19 LXX in a different kind of setting, and see G. Kittel in *TDNT* 1. 212-13; M. Aberbach in *Essays presented to Chief Rabbi Israel Brodie on the occasion of his seventieth Birthday* 14 on the Jewish discipular practice of following behind a teacher — at a little distance, for closeness would indicate arrogance [*b. Yoma* 37a]). "And I will make you to become fishers of human beings" stresses Jesus' power to make the fishers capable of catching human beings, a far more difficult task than catching fish. The statement also contains a prediction, the first of a number of predictions that Mark will highlight to display Jesus' power of foretelling the future. Nor will Mark neglect to narrate fulfilments of those predictions. In the present pericope, the distinguishing of two pairs of brothers anticipates the fulfilment of this prediction in Jesus' sending them and the rest of the twelve disciples two by two for preaching, healing, and exorcism (3:13-19; 6:7-13, 30). Thus the fulfilment will define the figure of fishing for human beings as getting them to repent and saving them from sickness and demonic possession. "Immediately" stresses the impact of Jesus' words. The suddenness of their impact coupled with the lack of any preparation — Jesus is not portrayed as telling the brothers why they should follow him, nor did the repentance and faith that he preached to the general public prompt this kind of following — marks him out as superhuman (contrast Elisha's following Elijah only after going home to kiss his parents goodbye and after treating his fellow townspeople to dinner — 1 Kgs 19:19-21). "Leaving their nets" highlights the impact that Jesus' words have on the brothers (cf. 10:28-30). Jewish rabbis and their disciples keep up a trade, but at Jesus' word the brothers stop practicing their trade. They do not even bother to haul in their nets. Moreover, Jewish rabbis attract their disciples to a sedentary life of study, but Jesus' command carries so much force that the brothers follow him in an itinerant life of ministry.

1:19-20 *(Matt 4:21-22; Luke 5:1-11; John 1:35-51)* "And going on a little" — Jesus travels only a bit more and repeats the miracle of sudden persuasion. This time Mark mentions the name of the brothers' father to prepare for their leaving him. Likewise, Jesus' seeing them "in the boat" prepares for leaving their father "in the boat." Just as "casting nets into the sea" exhibited Jesus' power to tear the first pair of brothers from the practice of their trade, so also does "preparing [i.e. cleaning, mending, and folding] their nets." So forceful is this power that it brooks no delay: "and immediately he called them." "Called" (ἐκάλεσεν) adds a note of authority (cf. 2:17) and means more than "called to." As shown by Mark's omitting to quote what Jesus says in his call (contrast v 17, which does not use this verb) and by the effect that Jesus' call has (James' and John's leaving their father Zebedee), "called" means "summoned." It is one thing to leave an occupation, but to leave one's father, especially to do so despite the patriarchalism of ancient Jewish society — how great must be the power of Jesus to induce that kind of conduct! So "leaving their father Zebedee" intensifies the impact of Jesus' call. "In the boat" points up the immediacy of its impact. "With the hired men" makes a foil against which the brothers' leaving their father stands out. Not even the closest, most obligatory family tie can keep the brothers there, so powerful is Jesus' call. The prefix ἀπ-, "away," with -ῆλθον, "went," fits this emphasis. "After him" brings the thought back to Jesus' leadership (cf. v 17; 8:24).

NOTES

An acceptance of the v.l. καὶ μετά, "and after" (B D a ff² boᵖᵗ) would not rule out the start of a new pericope with v 14; for καί introduces new pericopes most commonly in Mark. Did δέ, "but," replace καί to distinguish Jesus more sharply from John the Baptizer? Or did the monotonous parataxis leading up to v 14 foster a scribal assimilation of δέ to preceding instances of καί?

Here in v 14 would be the place for a subjective genitive Ἰησοῦ after εὐαγγέλιον, for Jesus is preaching as he did not preach in the verses immediately following v 1. Indeed, the whole of v 1 might well have replaced v 14 if the genitive were subjective in v 1 (cf. the foregoing comments on v 1). Likewise, a genitive of author or source in τὸ εὐαγγέλιον τοῦ θεοῦ, "the good news from God," would have been more appropriate in place of v 1, which is immediately followed by God's speaking through Isaiah the prophet. The definition of the good news of God in v 15 as featuring the nearness of God's rule favors an objective genitive: "the good news about God." The qualification of Jesus' message in this way (καὶ λέγων being epexegetic) shows that Mark possesses enough historical sensitivity to distinguish between what John preached about Jesus (v 1) and what Jesus preached about God's rule (vv 14-15). As noted before, efforts to equate the occurrences of "the good news" in vv 1 and 14-15 labor unsuccessfully under the contrast in qualifying phrases. Even if Mark has taken up the term εὐαγγέλιον from earlier Christian or particularly Pauline usage, where it had to do with the message about Jesus, and applied it to the message preached by Jesus, synonymity does not follow — only Mark's desire to show how the present message about Jesus grows out of the past message proclaimed by him about someone else, viz., God. Later occurrences of εὐαγγέλιον will tend by association to bring Jesus into its content, as already in 1:1 (see 8:35; 10:29; 13:9-10; 14:9). It is another question whether Jesus brought himself into such association, or whether later Christian traditioners did so. His regarding himself as God's agent for bringing the kingdom does not justify our saying that when he preaches the good news of God he is preaching about himself. Self-proclamation is conspicuously missing throughout the ministry of Mark's Jesus (see H. Giesen, *Glaube und Handeln* 1. 116; also T. Söding [*Glaube* 198-251], whose discussion suffers somewhat from reading later Marcan connotations into earlier passages).

The connotation of victory that often characterizes εὐαγγέλιον elsewhere (see the notes on 1:1) may have a foothold here in the following reference to the nearness of God's rule, but not in the preceding accounts of Jesus' baptism and temptation. For in those accounts Jesus remained passive; and Mark revealed no outcome of the temptation, much less did he emphasize a victorious outcome. See O. Betz in *Das Evangelium und die Evangelien* 56-65, 69-75 on a connection between the good news and the kingdom; D. E. Aune in *NovT* 11(1969) 26 on a messianic implication (cf. *Pss. Sol.* 11:1-9; 1QH 18:14; 11QMelch 15); and E. Lemcio in *NTS* 32 (1986) 203, n. 20, against a parallel with Rom 1:1, where vv 3-4 define the good news of God Christologically in contrast with the theocratic definition in Mark 1:15. It is possible to take ὅτι in v 15 as causal, "*Because* the time is fulfilled and the rule of God has come near, repent and believe . . . ," and thus eliminate the superfluity of καὶ λέγων, "and saying," before a recitative ὅτι. But Mark likes to use double participles (here, "preaching . . . and saying"; F. Neirynck, *Duality* 82-84; contrast the omission of καὶ λέγων in א * c sy^s Or) and also the recitative ὅτι (G. Wohlenberg 51; cf. M. Reiser, *Syntax und Stil* 132-33).

"The good news of God" corresponds to pre-Marcan terminology in the Hellenistic Christian mission (Rom 1:1; 15:16; 2 Cor 11:7; 1 Thess 2:2, 8, 9; 1 Pet 4:17; but see G. Dautzenberg in *BZ* nf 22 [1978] 76 that "the gospel of God" does not come from a pre-Pauline preaching of monotheism). Yet we have just noted that there it was not associated with the message of God's kingdom (which meant less to Gentiles than to Jews — see 1 Thess 2:12, however), so that "of God" meant "from God," whereas here Mark defines "the good news of God" as the message of God's rule, so that "of God" means "about God." Mark prefers to use "the good news" absolutely, but the redactional non-absolute use in v 1 should keep us from surprise at his borrowing a non-absolute use in v 14 and filling it with content from the Jesuanic tradition. For Mark, "the good news" in v 15 is shorthand for "the good news of God" in v 14; but if v 15 reflects authentic tradition, the absolute phrase may go back to Jesus' own usage growing out of the cognate verb as used in the latter part of Isaiah (yet see H. Frankemölle, *Evangelium* 58-161; idem in *Vom Urchristentum zu Jesus* 34-67, on the many uncertainties attending the evolution of this term into Christian usage). Though what Jesus said in his time may translate into a message that Mark wants to convey to a later generation, we should not hastily interpret the perfect tense of πεπλήρωται and ἤγγικεν, "has been fulfilled" and "has drawn near," as indicating a present relevance for Mark's audience. The perfect tense may stress the completion of an action without implying present relevance; and since Jesus is speaking, a present relevance might be limited to the time of his speaking.

Against Mark's carving v 15 out of thin air, πληρόω, "fulfil," has a different, scriptural rather than temporal meaning in 14:49 (and 15:28 v.l.). The only other similar use of καιρός, "time," i.e. the one in 13:33, is likely traditional. It is also futuristic and therefore damaging to the interpretation of J. Marcus (in *Apocalyptic in the NT* 49-56) that here in 1:15 "the time" that is fulfilled refers to "the previous epoch [dominated by Satan] . . . pictured as a container that has been filling up and is now full, so that the eschaton is imminent." Ἐγγίζω, "draw near," occurs for God's rule also in Q (Matt 10:7; Luke 10:9, 11). God's rule is a characteristic theme in Jesus' message. Mark will use μετανοέω, "repent," in a narrative statement at 6:12, but probably as an echo of 1:15, which may therefore be traditional. Some have argued to the contrary that he inserts repentance into Jesus' preaching for a link with John's preaching a baptism of repentance (v 4), that the canonical gospels do not consistently represent Jesus as preaching or inducing repentance, and that despite much criticism he and his followers behave as celebrants, eating and drinking, rather than as penitents (M. Smith, *Clement* 211; W. Egger, *Frohbotschaft* 52; E. P. Sanders in *JSNT* 19 [1983] 5-36). But there are other references to Jesus' demanding and inducing repentance (Matt 11:21; 12:41; Luke 10:13; 11:32; 13:3, 5; 15:7, 10; 16:30; cf. Luke 15:17-19; 18:9-14; 19:1-10), and the ethical imperative runs too deeply throughout all strata of the NT to believe that Jesus did not demand repentance. Probably the Pharisees lodged criticism not because he failed to demand repentance but because he offered forgiveness, with joyful celebration following, on the basis of a repentance not entailing the usual ritual or restitution (N. H. Young in *JSNT* 24 [1985] 73-75). The very sparsity of references to repentance in Mark and other contemporary or earlier Christian literature speaks against redactional insertion of the theme into Jesus' preaching: the theme was not considered important enough to insert (S. McKnight in *TrinJourn* ns 6 [1985] 223-24). Matthew assimilates John's message to that of Jesus (cf. 3:2 with 4:17; also 10:7); so it does not seem likely that Mark would assimilate Jesus' message to that of John, especially since Mark reports John as preaching, not repentance itself, but a baptism of repentance. Jesus' submitting to John's baptism and thus showing his belief in John's message make it probable that in his own preaching the element of repentance would enter, especially at first. See also D. C. Allison, Jr., in *JSNT* 29 (1987) 68-74.

Further against Mark's carving v 15 out of thin air, πιστεύω ἐν, "believe in," is un-Marcan. In fact, though πιστεύω occurs ten more times in Mark, ἐν follows it nowhere else in Mark or the rest of the NT (except John 16:30) or classical Greek literature or the Greek papyri (J. C. Doudna, *Greek* 23, 79; contrast the occurrences of τὸ εὐαγγέλιον as an accusative of direct object after πιστεύω in Gal 2:7; 1 Thess 2:4). Both here and in John 16:30 the combination probably represents the Hebraism of belief as taking place in the sphere of that which is its object (cf. the MT and LXX of 1 Sam [1 Kgdms] 27:12; 2 Chr 20:20; Pss 78[77]:22, 32; 106[105]:12; Jer 12:6; Mic 7:5 plus Dan 6:24 Theod; Sir 32:21 LXX). This understanding seems more natural than taking ἐν in an instrumental or causal sense, which would yield believing by means of the good news or because of it. The fact that only here in the NT is the good news made the explicit object of belief (cf. implicit statements in Rom 1:16-17; Mark 16:15-16, however) works against the hypothesis that the expression came into the tradition after Easter (against L. Schenke, *Studien* 112-13).

On the other hand, the three dualities in the parallel participles "preaching . . . and saying," in the parallel declarative clauses concerning the time and the kingdom, and in the imperative clauses commanding repentance and belief betray a compositional technique. If it is Mark's, we might conclude that he writes up the tradition in his own style and that to universalize Jesus' message for an audience of Gentiles he omits the Palestinian element of preaching to the poor, which looms large in Q (G. Dautzenberg in *Kairos* 18 [1976] 286-87). J. Schlosser (*Le règne de Dieu* 96-97) calls attention to similarities with Rom 13:11-14 and suggests a common catechetical tradition; but if there is any relation at all, Rom 13:11-14 may simply reflect the same Jesuanic tradition that Mark uses.

Simon Peter, James, and John will form an inner circle among the twelve disciples; and Andrew will appear with the trio again at 13:3. Perhaps their importance is the reason for the preservation of this story in the tradition. Or is it that Mark heard the story from Simon Peter's own lips and put it at the head of the stories concerning Jesus' activities because his gospel depends on the taught reminiscences of Peter?

Not only does the command to follow differ from the rabbinic pattern. It also differs from the prophetic pattern; for a prophet did not call people to follow him, but called on them to follow God. So Jesus stands not merely in place of the Law (so W. Grundmann [7. Aufl.] 55-56), but in place of God. No wonder his disciples do not engage in theological disputations or aspire to succeed him, as rabbinic students do in relation to one another and to their masters. The often-cited parallel with Elijah's "call" of Elisha (1 Kgs 19:19-21) is more instructive by its differences than by its similarities. True, Elisha was engaged in daily work as are the two pairs of brothers in vv 16-20. But not only did Elisha request and get a delay, in contrast with our story. Elijah issued no command to follow. He only made the gesture of casting his mantle on Elisha, whereas Jesus issues a command without a gesture. Elijah did not even seem to intend that Elisha follow him, for he went on and Elisha had to run and catch up — only to hear Elijah say that he should go back again. Elijah's subsequent question, "For what have I done to you?" is enigmatic. It looks as though he intended that Elisha await the coming of God's Spirit on him when Elijah passed off the scene ("you shall anoint Elisha . . . as a prophet in your place" — 1 Kgs 19:16). In any event, Elisha finally went after Elijah, but as a servant ministering to his mundane needs, not as a disciple learning from his master and representing him as Jesus' disciples will do (see V. K. Robbins, *Jesus the Teacher* 98-101; idem in *NTS* 28 [1982] 228-29; A. J. Droge in *SBL 1983 Seminar Papers* 249-50). This model of a prophetic call does not work, then, for Jesus' calling his first disciples. We know too little about the disciples of Isaiah the prophet (Isa 8:16) to make them useful here. We do not even know that Isaiah *called* them to be his disciples.

It would be a mistake to homogenize Hellenistic divine men as to their activities and characteristics and the terms used to describe them, but perhaps the closest parallel to Jesus' calling his first disciples appears in Diog. Laert. 2.48, where Socrates is reported as having very forcefully said to Xenophon, "Then follow me and learn" (cf. ibid. 7.2-3). The parallels in Pl. *Prt.* 310D-319A, 328B-E; Xen. *Mem.* 1.2.2-3, 48-52; 4.1.5-4.2.40 lack an authoritative call, but they do show some initiative on Socrates' part and stress being with the master constantly (cf. V. K. Robbins [in *NTS* 28 (1982) 221, 226, 230], whose additional cross-reference Gen 12:1-4 LXX lacks the elements of following and constant companionship). Mark's emphasis on Jesus' predictive power also looks like an appeal to Hellenistic admiration of such ability on the part of divine men (cf. Philostr. *VA* 1.2-3; 4.24; 8.7.9; idem *Ep.* 68 *To the Milesians; Treatise of Eusebius . . . Against the Life of Apollonius* 23). Perhaps then there is some value in Droge's suggestion (loc. cit.) that Mark writes up this story in accordance with the Cynic ideal of discipleship (but see J. R. Butts in *Early Jewish and Christian Exegesis* 199-219 for important corrections of Droge's overall discussion). Pagan parallels to Jesus' initiative and to the disciples' adopting his self-denying life of itineration do not disprove historicity, however; for we have no reason to think that Jesus could not have gone beyond Jewish teachers. If he had not, the Christian religion would hardly have been born. Palestine had been Hellenized by the time of Jesus, anyway; so that from the standpoint of historical analogy his taking initiative and making the disciples itinerate with him should not seem incredible (cf. M. Hengel, *Charismatic Leader* 16-37, esp. 28-30, on Greek philosophical discipleship as entailing renunciation of property and breaking with one's own family, and on other possible backgrounds for following Jesus). At the same time, a similarity to the Cynic ideal of discipleship does not give adequate grounds for denying a Jewish eschatological proclamation by Jesus. We should respect the mix of cultures caused by the Hellenization of Palestine.

The double duality of two call-stories each featuring a pair of brothers recalls a double duality in vv 14-15, again betrays a compositional technique, and therefore opens the possibility that Mark is the first to unite the two call-stories, especially since fishing takes place at night and mending nets during the day (Luke 5:2-5; John 21:3). On the other hand, fishing takes place also during the day; the partnership of James and John with Simon (Luke 5:10) favors the original unity of vv 16-18 and 19-20; and the compositional rhythm and careful avoidance of repetitiousness may support an original unity (so J. Gnilka 1. 72). These very features may be due to a Marcan penchant for duality, however, regardless of original unity or disunity. Also betraying a compositional technique is the use of a compound verb plus the preposition of the compound in the phrase παράγων παρὰ τὴν θάλασσαν, which probably ought to be translated "going along to the seaside" (rather than "going along beside the sea") to carry Jesus' journey forward from entrance into Galilee (vv 14-15) to arrival at the Sea of Galilee. The accusative following παρά then retains its proper sense of motion toward an object (cf. 2:13, the only other passage where παρὰ τὴν θάλασσαν is construed with a verb of motion, in contrast with 4:1; 5:21; see similar compound constructions in 1:21, 26, 29, 42; 2:1, 26; 3:1, 34 et passim). This particular example is striking because παράγω should take a simple accusative, not a prepositional phrase (see LSJ s.v.), and because "the sea" at the beginning of v 16 anticipates "the sea" at its close. Mark often writes an explanatory γάρ-clause such as "for they were fishers"; and εὐθύς, "immediately" (vv 18, 20), and introductory circumstantial participles such as those in vv 16, 18, 19, 20b may characterize his style (though lacking his sources, we also lack certainty).

But the remainder gives little reason to be regarded as Marcan. "The Sea of Galilee" belongs to the actual geography of Jesus' main activity, its theological value for Mark being much overestimated in modern scholarship (cf. the comments on 14:28; 16:7 and J. Ernst 56-57, 60-61). Elsewhere he shows no special interest in Andrew. ᾿Αμφιβάλλοντας must come from tradition, for the ambiguity of its meaning leads to an explanatory γάǫ-clause even though an unambiguous ἁλιεύοντας, "fishing," might have substituted (see E. Best in *L'Évangile selon Marc* 25-26; idem, *Following Jesus* 166-74). The difference between preparing nets and fishing (contrast everybody's preparing nets followed by everybody's fishing in Luke 5:1-11, and everybody's fishing in John 21:1-14) and the circumstantial detail of the hired men in v 20 undermine the hypothesis that Mark formulated vv 19-20 after the pattern of vv 16-18 and after the analogy of 2:13-14 to give James and John the same outstanding call that Simon received and thus to substantiate their belonging with him in the innermost trio. See W. Schmithals 106 for a recent presentation of that hypothesis. Under it, we might also ask why Mark will not present an innermost quartet that includes Andrew instead of a trio that excludes him? Later mentions of Simon's house (1:29; cf. 2:1, 15; 9:33) and of the disciples' access to a boat or boats (3:9; 4:1, 36; 6:45-52) do not disprove the historicity of the disciples' leaving all to follow Jesus. For the owners of the boats will not be named; the present boat presumably belongs to Zebedee; sudden following leaves no time to dispose of possessions; boats, houses, and family can be left with family; and 10:29 will describe the actual leaving of family and possessions (T. E. Schmidt, *Hostility* 104-5). Mark is making Christological capital out of historical data.

In view of many other uses of εἶδον for simple seeing, we should not interpret Jesus' look as elective in vv 16, 19 and elsewhere (against E. Schweizer 48). The repetition of "Simon" in v 16, where we might expect "his," forestalls our thinking of Andrew as Jesus' brother. Now that Mark has established the pattern of a pair of fishers who are brothers to each other, he can write "his brother" rather than "the brother of James" in v 19. By itself, fishing for human beings is an ambiguous figure of speech. Though it often carries the connotation of judgment because of what happens to fish when they are caught (see, e.g., Jer 16:16; Ezek 38:4; Amos 4:2; Hab 1:14-15; 1QH 3:26; 5:7-8), it can also carry the connotation of salvation (see Matt 13:47-50, where the two connotations coexist) and persuasion (see W. H. Wuellner, *Meaning*, esp. 64-133, for a host of references containing these and a wide variety of other positive and negative connotations). It has been suggested that Jesus meant the figure judgmentally and that Mark or an earlier traditioner made it salvific in conformity to its Hellenistic use for the activities of philosophers, teachers, and wise men (E. Best, *Following Jesus* 170). But the Hellenization of Palestine and the use of the figure in a positive (as well as negative) but undidactic sense at Matt 13:47-50 make the suggestion unnecessary (see S. T. Lachs in *JQR* 74 [1983] 162-63; idem, *Rabbinic Commentary* 58-59, for a linguistic argument running along this line and based on the shift from the Hebrew דוג to the Hebrew צוד and the Aramaic צדי, which have wider connotations). And Jesus' overall purpose of restoring Israel makes the suggestion improbable. As noted above, 3:13-19 and 6:7-13, 30 will define the figure positively, salvifically. To the best of our knowledge, Jesus intended it to be taken that way, though J. Mánek (in *NovT* 2 [1958] 138-41) may go too far in making the waters from which human beings are rescued represent the underworld of sin and death. Nothing is said about the perishing of human beings in the waters. See M. Hengel, *Charismatic Leader* 76-78, against the hypothesis that the present narrative setting was spun out of the saying on fishing for human beings.

Καὶ αὐτούς might refer to the hired men: "and them" (cf. R. H. Gundry, *Matthew* 62). But such a reference is unlikely; for then αὐτούς would become awkwardly prospective, leaving the audience to discover the identity of "them" not till the end of the next verse. Furthermore, a reference to the hired men would spoil the parallel between preparing nets and casting them, and would ill fit Mark's emphasis on the power of Jesus' calling the two pairs of brothers to immediately leave what they are doing in order that they might come after him. Therefore we should understand an ellipsis after καί, fill it with εἶδεν, and translate, "And he saw them" (i.e. James and John, not others — cf. Luke 1:36; Acts 15:27,

32). Or we may dismiss an ellipsis and translate καί with "even" (cf. the epexegetic καί in 3 Kgdms 19:19 LXX). See D. E. Nineham 73 for interpretations of the hired men that do not link up very well with Mark's interests.

JESUS' OVERPOWERING WORD OF EXORCISM

1:21-28 (Luke 4:31-37)

Verses 16-20 have exhibited the authority of Jesus' word in calling disciples. Verses 21-28 now exhibit the authority of his word in teaching and exorcism. Jesus goes into Capernaum (v 21a) and teaches in the synagogue there (v 21b). Mark notes the awe-inspiring effect of the teaching on the audience (v 22). A demoniac then confronts Jesus in the synagogue (vv 23-24), and Jesus performs an exorcism (vv 25-26). Mark notes again the awe-inspiring effect of Jesus' teaching, adds the awe-inspiring effect of the exorcism, and closes with the publicity that comes to Jesus as a result (vv 27-28).

1:21-22 *(Luke 4:31-32)* "And they go into Capernaum" particularizes the going of Simon and Andrew, James and John after Jesus (v 20). An indefinite "they" would not make good sense either in the context of vv 16-20 or independently. Mark's sudden switch to the historical present tense, which he abandons immediately afterwards, may underline the effect of Jesus' call as well as highlight the start of a new pericope with topographical movement. The switch from "they" to "he" and the associated entry into the synagogue and teaching of the people there exhibit the initiative of Jesus. "Immediately" stresses the quickness with which he didactically takes charge. The authority (ἐξουσία) with which he teaches counteracts in advance his apparent helplessness on the cross (see also 1:27; 2:10; 3:15; 6:7; 11:28, 29; 13:34 for this important theme in Mark). The facts that Jesus' authority comes up first in an editorially explanatory γάρ-clause (contrast v 22b with v 27 in this respect) and precedes the participle of which it is the direct object (see the word order in the Greek text) show the narrative point of view to focus on that authority. And the fact that Mark does not tell what feature of Jesus' teaching displays authority shows that the point lies in authority as such. The strong verb ἐξεπλήσσοντο, "they were astounded" or, to preserve the metaphor, "they were being knocked out with astonishment," lays great emphasis on the overwhelming power of Jesus' authority (see also 6:2; 7:37; 10:26; 11:18). The imperfect tense of ἐδίδασκεν (usually taken as inceptive, "he began to teach") is due to the linear nature of teaching and is common in other verbs of speaking, too. The non-specification of content and the emphasis instead on authoritative manner favor a dynamic meaning for τῇ διδαχῇ αὐτοῦ, "his activity of teaching," over a static meaning, "what he taught" (cf. the comments on v 27). The imperfect tense of ἐξεπλήσσοντο makes the audience's astonishment match Jesus' activity of teaching: as long as he taught, astonishment overwhelmed them. It probably goes too far to see a connotation of fear and alarm in ἐξεπλήσσοντο, for neither the present context nor other Marcan contexts make detection of that connotation

very easy (but see G. Bertram in *TDNT* 3. 4-7). Mark likes to exalt Jesus' stature
by portraying him as a teacher (see also 1:27; 2:13; 4:1, 2; 6:2, 6, 34; 8:31; 9:31;
10:1; 11:17, 18; 12:14, 35, 38; 14:49), for teachers enjoy high respect in Mark's
environment. But with the phrase "not as the scribes" he has Jesus vault far higher
than other teachers. We might think that in their teaching they *appeal* to authority
whereas in his teaching he *assumes* authority. In fact, however, Mark tells what
feature of the scribes' teaching betrays a lack of authority no more than he tells
what feature of Jesus' teaching exhibits authority. Only the contrast as such
between authority and lack thereof interests him as a means of exalting the figure
of Jesus. We might also think that Jesus is teaching what he has been preaching,
i.e. the nearness of God's reign, repentance, and faith (v 15; cf. v 21 with v 39
and 6:12 with 6:30 for the closeness of διδάσκω and κηρύσσω in Mark, against
the strict distinction made by H. Riesenfeld, *Gospel Tradition* 59-64); but to think
so would only blunt Mark's point — the overpowering authority with which Jesus
teaches. Contributing even further to that point are the piling up of references to
that teaching (one in each of three successive clauses) and the escalation of the
last reference to an emphatic periphrastic construction.

1:23-24 *(Luke 4:33-34)* Mark includes in his book only half as many
complete stories of exorcisms as he does of miraculous healings (besides the
present passage, see 5:1-20; 7:24-30; 9:14-29 for exorcisms; 1:29-31, 40-45;
2:1-12; 3:1-6; 5:21-43 [two intertwined stories]; 7:31-37; 8:22-26; 10:46-52 for
miraculous healings, plus 4:35-41; 6:35-44, 47-52; 8:1-9; 11:12-14, 20-25 for
nature-miracles). Perhaps no more stories of exorcisms were available to him. In
any case, he includes four in full, multiplies them in summaries (1:34, 39; cf.
3:11-12, 15, 22-23; 6:13; 9:38), makes the present story of an exorcism the first
of Jesus' mighty acts, and combines with the exorcism the authoritative teaching
of Jesus. The result of this combination is not a subordination of exorcism to
teaching (much less a criticism of exorcism), but a coordination in which the two
support each other (cf. 2:10-11; 6:2; Acts 13:6-12; Gal 3:5; Heb 2:1-4 et passim).
For the last statements in the story proper — "even the unclean spirits he commands, and they obey him" — form an independent sentence, not a subordinate
clause introduced by a characteristically Marcan γάρ, "for" (as we would expect
for a subordination of exorcism to teaching). The final emphasis thus rests on
exorcism, and it is a double-barreled emphasis since the sentence is compound.
A diachronic analysis of the text that sees evidence of Mark's adding the element
of Jesus' teaching to an originally bare story of an exorcism is liable to mislead
us into thinking of a devaluation of exorcism as compared with teaching. We must
read the text as it stands. It goes too far to *equate* the exorcistic command with
the authoritative teaching, however; for Jesus teaches in vv 21-22 before he casts
out an unclean spirit in vv 23-26. Verse 27 simply coordinates the two, and follows
the order of vv 21-22 and 23-26 in doing so.

Another "immediately" shows Mark's eagerness to give proof of Jesus'
didactic authority. The adverb probably modifies the whole of the following story
rather than ἦν, in the improbable sense "came to be," or ἀνέκραξεν, "he shouted
out," which seems too far away. In view of Mark's attention to the Gentileness

of his audience (see esp. 7:2-4), the attachment of "their" to "synagogue" may set Jews apart from Gentiles as well as describe the synagogue as that of people living in Capernaum (contrast Matthew's multiplication of the phrase to distinguish church from synagogue because he is writing for Jewish Christians — see 9:35; 10:17; 12:9; 13:54; 23:34 in addition to 4:23). Primitive tradition is reflected in the characteristically Jewish expectation that the messianic age will bring destruction to the demonic world (see esp. *1 Enoch* 55:4; other references in Str-B 4/1. 527) and in Semitic textual features such as ἐν for בְּ in the sense "with" (v 23; cf. 5:2, 25) and the expressions "unclean spirit" (vv 23, 26, 27 — though the alternative "demon" would not necessarily indicate an un-Jewish origin of material, for Jews adopted the term from the Greeks), "shouting with a loud shout" rather than "shouting loudly," "the Holy One of God" (cf. 4 Kgdms 4:9 LXX; Ps 106[105]:16; Isa 40:25; 57:15), and probably τί ἡμῖν καὶ σοί . . . ; "Why are you interfering with us . . . ?" (cf. the LXX of Josh 22:24; Judg 11:12; 2 Kgdms 16:10; 19:23; 3 Kgdms 17:18; 4 Kgdms 3:13; 2 Chr 35:21; Jer 2:18; Hos 14:9 — though the expression occurs in purely Greek literature with the slightly milder meaning, "What do we and you have to do with each other?"; cf. M. Reiser, *Syntax und Stil* 20-21; E. C. Maloney, *Semitic Interference* 183-85; see also Mark 5:7; Matt 8:29; 27:19; Luke 4:34; 8:28; John 2:4). Likewise, ἄνθρωπος, "a man," may originally have represented Semitic usage for τις, "someone." But for Mark's Gentile audience such a usage would require an attributive participle or an adjective or a noun to which ἄνθρωπος could be appositive (ibid. 131-34). The Hellenistic context of Mark's audience and the terminological context of the immediately following story therefore combine to create the possibility (but only a possibility in view of Mark's other uses of ἄνθρωπος) that "a man" here provides a merely human foil for "the Holy One of God" (v 24), earlier identified as God's beloved Son (v 11).

The unclean spirit that possesses a man in the synagogue contrasts with the Holy Spirit, who took control of Jesus in vv 10, 12 and with whom he is baptizing people (v 8). Since "spirit" connotes power (see the comments on vv 7-8), the outcome of the present contest will show that by the Holy Spirit Jesus has greater power than that of the unclean spirit (cf. 3:22-30). The perfective preposition in ἀνέκραξεν, "shouted out," a compound verb that Mark uses elsewhere only at 6:49 whereas he usually contents himself with the unintensified κράζω (3:11; 5:5, 7; 9:24, 26; 10:47, 48; 11:9; 15:13, 14, 39 v.l.), emphasizes the force of the unclean spirit in the attempt of the man to defend himself against Jesus (cf. the magical effectiveness of shouting in *PGM* XII. 160-78). Thus Jesus' force will appear all the greater when he silences the spirit.

"Why are you interfering with us, Jesus of Nazareth?" puts Jesus on the opposite side from the unclean spirit. "Us" might include the man along with the spirit (especially in the oral stage of the story, but not according to the modern psychological sense of schizophrenia) or the people in the synagogue along with the spirit (a less likely possibility, since the spirit does not control them). In view of the plural "unclean spirits" in v 27, however, Mark probably means that this unclean spirit speaks on behalf of all unclean spirits, so that the present exorcism demonstrates Jesus' power over all of them. "Jesus of Nazareth" harks back to v 9 and marks the beginning of the spirit's attempt to defend himself against Jesus by showing how much he knows about him — here, his personal name and his hometown. Taken as a declaration, ἦλθες ἀπολέσαι ἡμᾶς, "You have come to destroy us," shows further knowledge on the part of the unclean spirit. Taken as a question, "Have you come to destroy us?" the words show fear as well as further knowledge. Either way, we catch a foregleam of the destruction about to take place. It will consist in being cast out of the possessed man. "Have you come . . . ?" does not refer merely to Jesus' entry into the synagogue, but to his coming on the scene in general, as made clear by the probable reference in "us" to all unclean spirits and the further uses of ἦλθον for Jesus' coming (e.g., in 1:39; 2:17; 10:45). Historically, since Jesus spoke and acted on behalf of God's rule (cf. vv 14-15), the verb carried a hint of divine commission. Literarily, since Mark has written of Jesus as God's Son, the verb carries a hint of divine origin (E. Arens, ΗΛΘΟΝ-Sayings 219-20). The unclean spirit's reference to destruction signals that the spirit does not make its following statement as an ingenuous acknowledgment of Jesus' superiority, much less as a backhanded confession; rather, as a defensive maneuver. Jesus' aggressive reaction will confirm this understanding.

It is appropriate that as an agent and teacher of magic the unclean spirit should try to use it on Jesus (O. Bauernfeind, Worte 12-13). The unclean spirit's knowledge of Jesus and attempt to use that knowledge in self-defense reach their peak in the statement, "I know you, who are you, the Holy One of God." At this point a Hellenistic audience think that the unclean spirit has gained the upper hand and is going to adjure Jesus not to torment it (as will actually happen in 5:7). But this same audience think in terms of the part of Mark's gospel that they have thus far heard as well as in terms of pagan magic associated with unclean spirits. In terms of Mark's gospel the designation "the Holy One of God" contrasts with the character of the spirit as unclean; it agrees with Jesus' being possessed by the Holy Spirit in that possession by such a spirit makes Jesus holy, too; and it refutes in advance the charge in 3:30 that Jesus has an unclean spirit rather than the Holy Spirit (cf. A. Fridrichsen, Problem 111-12, on the distinguishing of Jesus from magicians; also J. H. Neyrey in Semeia 35 [1986] 105-6). The antagonism of the source adds weight to the truth of the designation "the Holy One of God": what was for the unclean spirit an attempt to gain control over Jesus becomes for Mark and his intended audience an unintended admission by the spirit of Jesus' true identity. The spirit knew this identity, Mark is saying; so do not let the crucifixion of Jesus mislead you to a false identification. Bauernfeind's failure to recognize that Mark writes and his audience listen in two frames of reference at the same time — Hellenistic paganism and the Christian contents of Mark's gospel — leads him to argue unnecessarily that the reputed deceitfulness of unclean spirits would keep Mark from using their identification of Jesus positively (op. cit. 78-79). Mark's audience would recognize that this unclean spirit has everything to lose by a false identification, which would insure a failure of the defensive maneuver. The first identification, "Jesus the Nazarene," was true enough. So also is "the Holy One of God."

1:25-26 *(Luke 4:35)* Jesus breaks in before an adjuration can be spoken (cf. the demoniac's apparent interruption of Jesus' teaching), by-passes the man who shouted out, and rebukes the unclean spirit by telling it to "shut up" (φι-μώθητι). The rebuke does not have the purpose of dampening publicity (cf. Mark's only other use of φιμόω at 4:39, where there can be no question of publicity), but of stopping the spirit's attempt to reduce him to helplessness through uttering his knowledge of Jesus' name, hometown, intention, and title. Thus the silencing of the spirit starts the process of exorcism, shows the superiority of Jesus, and goes with the immediately following command to come out (see *PGM* IX. 4, 9; XXXVI. 164, and cf. E. Rohde, *Psyche* 2. 603-5 on the later, somewhat different use of φιμόω and its cognate φιμωτικόν in exorcisms of the dead). Together, the silencing and the command to come out (cf. 5:8; 9:25; *PGM* IV. 1243, 1245, 3013) make up the rebuke. The verb of rebuke, ἐπετίμησεν, corresponds to רעג in 1QM 14:10; 1QapGen 20:28-29, where the rebuke effects the departure of evil spirits (but with respect to a sickness of sexual disability and to wickedness in general, not to demonic possession in the strict sense; cf. the non-exorcistic but magical uses of ἐπιτιμάω in *PGM* I. 254; VII. 332; XII. 316). The lack of an adjuration, of an incantation, of an appeal to some deity or supernatural power, of a physical manipulation — all techniques normally used in exorcisms — lets all the emphasis fall on the authority of Jesus' own simple but effective command (cf. Eus. *H.E.* 1.13.1-20). By putting the convulsion and shout after that command, Mark makes the convulsion and shout a visible and audible demonstration that the command has indeed effected an exorcism (cf. the distinction in 9:20, 26 between convulsions and outcries prior to Jesus' command as proof of demonic possession, and after his command as proof of exorcism). The loudness of the shout leaves no doubt, and its inarticulateness shows the effectiveness of Jesus' command to stop using his name and title in self-defense. The cognate construction, "shouting with a loud shout," adds emphasis.

1:27-28 *(Luke 4:36-37)* Mark returns to the people's amazement with ἐθαμβήθησαν, a synonym of ἐξεπλήσσοντο (v 22). "All" emphasizes the universality of their amazement and thereby the impressiveness of the exorcism. The very fact that the amazement prompts discussion among the onlookers further emphasizes the impact of the exorcism on them. The interrogative form of "What is this?" demonstrates their amazement. A similar "Who is this?" will appear in 4:41. But there it will be a question of Jesus' identity; here it is a question of his teaching. The repetition of "teaching" and "authority" (cf. vv 21-22) completes the framing of the exorcism so as to make it support Jesus' authority as a teacher. Continued omission of the content of his teaching and modification of "teaching" by the phrase "with authority" (κατ᾽, "with," indicating the authoritative manner according to which Jesus taught) again tend to favor teaching as activity rather than as subject matter. We might attach "with authority" to "he commands even the unclean spirits," but that syntax would disagree with v 22 and produce a less natural rhythm. The newness of Jesus' teaching lies in the overwhelmingly authoritative manner with which he gives it. Thus καινή keeps its proper connotation of newness in kind, not just in time (νέα), and indicates that such authoritative

teaching surpasses anything the audience have heard or seen before. The ellipsis
of a verb to go with "a new teaching" and, in the two following clauses, the
ascensive καί, "even," the forward position of τοῖς πνεύμασι τοῖς ἀκαθάρτοις, "the
unclean spirits," and the pairing of "commands" (cf. 9:25 and the comments ad
loc.) and "obey" (cf. 4:41) all stress the personal authority of Jesus rather than
the marvel of his exorcisms as such. So also do the generalizing plural in the
reference to unclean spirits and the equally generalizing present tense of the verbs.
(In fact, Jesus has exorcised only one unclean spirit.) Mark's audience know from
1:1-11 how it is that Jesus can exercise authority over the unclean spirits despite
their attempt to overcome him — he is Christ, the one stronger than John, the
Spirit-endued Son of God — and they can only smile at the astonishment of the
congregation in the synagogue. Better yet, the hearing of this story replaces
ignorant astonishment with knowledgeable admiration.

The report about Jesus carries forward the emphasis on his authority. The
interruption of what would otherwise be a smooth transition from the astonishment
of the people in the synagogue (v 27) to Jesus' and the disciples' going out of the
synagogue (v 29) contributes to the emphasis. But so also does every detail
concerning the spread of the report: (1) the report's going out "immediately";
(2) its going into "the surrounding region of Galilee"; (3) its going into the
"whole" of that surrounding region; and (4) its going out "everywhere," with no
part missed, in the whole surrounding region. Thus far in Mark, then, Jesus' word
has proved so powerful that it has compelled people to leave their occupation and
their father to follow him; so powerful that it has transcended the teaching of the
scribes; so powerful that it has defeated a demonic force; and so powerful that
Jesus has become the talk of the whole territory. Next it will prove powerful over
illness and disease.

NOTES

It is often thought that vv 21-31 present a typical or ideal day in Jesus' ministry, "the day
in Capernaum," which was a Sabbath, and that Simon Peter is at least the ultimate source
of the information concerning it. We might extend the day through v 34 to include the last
part of a Roman legal day, i.e. evening; but Mark's mentioning the Sabbath, which ends
at sunset, disfavors such an accommodation. And extending the day through v 38 or v 39
to include the whole night disagrees with both the Jewish and the Roman legal methods
of reckoning a day of twenty-four hours (cf. L. Morris, *John* 158, n. 90). "Typical" or
"ideal" may read too much into the format, however; and we may even doubt that Mark
means the temporal progression to demarcate one day as a discrete unit centered in
Capernaum. The paratactic καί, "and," at the start of v 21 and another one at the start of
v 35 do not forestall demarcation, but neither do they favor it. And vv 21-22 and 33-34
hardly offer the kind of summarizing statements that would set off the whole passage (vv
21-34) from its surroundings; for vv 21-22 speak of a particular sermon, and vv 33-34
speak of healings and exorcisms on a particular occasion. Chronology and topography are
incidental to the power that Jesus displays in his activities. Mark's interest lies in the power.

Opinions differ widely on distinguishing between tradition and redaction in vv
21-28, and arguments often lack cogency. For example, the form critical canon that a story
like that of this exorcism originally circulated without indications of time and place suggests

that only the exorcism in vv 23-26 is traditional, Mark adding the rest because of his interest in Jesus' teaching. But canon is not proof. We should consider the possibility that stories *lost* original indications of time and place, as happens in the written gospels (cf. the loss of Capernaum and the change of the comparatively specific "after some days" to the quite general "on one of the days" in Luke 5:17 as compared with Mark 2:1, to take but one example). Perhaps some stories did circulate from the start without indications of time and place. But there is no sure way of knowing whether this story ever circulated in that way. Even if it did, we might suppose that Mark clamped two traditions together rather than adding fabricated material to traditional material. Or we might suppose in the opposite direction that even some of vv 23-26, too, comes from Marcan fabrication, not only his favorite εὐθύς (v 23), but also "in their synagogue" (v 23), because "their" lacks a referent apart from the characteristically Marcan indefinite third person plural "they" who were astounded in v 22. We might also reason that a demoniac's attendance at synagogue is historically unlikely but redactionally possible on account of Mark's desire to link Jesus' teaching with an exorcism, either for the purpose of letting the authority displayed in the exorcism rub off on the teaching or for the purpose of subordinating the exorcism to the teaching.

Perhaps Mark also fabricated v 24 ("Why are you interfering with us . . . ? Have you come to destroy us? . . . the Holy One of God") after the pattern of 3 Kgdms 17:18 LXX ("Why are you interfering with me, man of God? Have you come . . . to put my son to death?"; cf. the proof of Jesus' teaching in his miracle of exorcism and the proof of Elijah's speaking the word of the Lord in his miracle of raising the widow's son — see esp. 3 Kgdms 17:24 LXX), all to carry over an Elijah-typology from John the Baptist (Mark 1:6) to Jesus (cf. Mark 9:11-13; 15:35-36). Or, since Mark is writing for Gentiles whom he can hardly expect to recognize such allusions to the OT, was it an earlier traditioner who added these elements? Or, in favor of original tradition, are the allusions too subtle to be accepted as real allusions? Perhaps Jesus and his first disciples really did go into Capernaum, especially if Simon and Andrew had their home there and Jesus called them on the northwest shore of the Sea of Galilee where Capernaum stood, so that v 21a is traditional rather than redactional. But perhaps the entry into the synagogue in v 21b is redactional rather than traditional because of the shift from "they" to "he," the synagogue being suggested by the teaching which Mark intends to introduce.

Elsewhere, on the other hand, Mark almost always has Jesus teaching outside the synagogue (2:13; 4:1-2; 6:6, 34; 8:31; 9:31; 10:1; 11:17; 12:35; 14:49 — the sole exception: 6:2); so perhaps entry into the synagogue is traditional rather than redactional, especially since we might expect the awkwardness of a demoniac's attendance at synagogue to keep Mark from introducing his presence without traditional support. And perhaps v 21a is redactional, since the "they" who go into Capernaum refers back to Jesus and the four fishers, the story of whose call by him may have been first put with the present pericope by none other than Mark (contrast Matt 4:18-22; Luke 5:1-11; John 1:35-51; 21:1-23). But then why Capernaum, for Mark usually has Jesus teaching and performing exorcisms and other miracles in nameless places? Even the house of Simon and Andrew in the following pericope (vv 29-34) does not demand the name of a town or city which Mark may have transferred from that pericope to the present one, for the house of Jairus will lack any indication of the town or city where it is located (5:21-24a, 35-43). And if Jesus did enter the synagogue, is it so hard to accept as traditional that he taught there? But perhaps Mark borrows teaching in a synagogue from the tradition behind 6:2 (complete with the use of ἐξεπλήσσοντο). On the other hand again, who is to say that 6:2 does not reflect 1:21-22 rather than vice versa? And how do we know whether the Marcan style and diction seemingly apparent in the verses on Jesus' teaching represent the redaction of old tradition or the fabrication of new tradition? Our lack of Mark's sources and the consequent and increasingly recognized difficulty of distinguishing between tradition and redaction leave us in the lurch (see esp. F. Neirynck, *Duality;* M. Reiser, *Syntax und Stil;* P. Dschulnigg, *Sprache;* C. C. Black, *Disciples*).

So round and round we go with unanswerable questions and inconclusive arguments. Larger considerations having to do with the historicity of dominical traditions, with the roles of eyewitnesses and of other traditioners in the early church, with the dates and authorship of the gospels, with the reliability of Papias's elder, etc., determine our treatment of textual details more than exegetical discussions seem at first to reveal. To say so is not to make philosophical presuppositions swallow up exegesis. After all, the larger considerations have to do with historical questions whose answers are not wholly determined by philosophical presuppositions. Rather, it is to give these larger considerations their due so as to keep all sides open to mutual influence in a process of adduction.

The two pairs of brothers in vv 16-20 would not be working on the Sabbath. Yet they appear to go into Capernaum with Jesus immediately after he calls them. Mark does not write, "And it was the Sabbath," however; so "on the Sabbath" seems to introduce another day, either the next day or a later one (cf. 6:1-2). Otherwise "on the Sabbath" would be otiose; for teaching in the synagogue would suffice to imply the Sabbath, and its being the Sabbath plays no role in the story (cf. 1:39 and esp. 3:1; 6:2). Even when its being the Sabbath does play a role, mention of entry into a synagogue suffices to get things started (3:1-6). Since "on the Sabbath" seems to introduce the next day or a later one, then, there is no question of the first disciples' having been working on the Sabbath, and certainly no polemic against Sabbath-keeping (as thought by J. Schreiber, *Theologie des Vertrauens* 101-2). On the contrary, the implication of another day may have the purpose of ruling out any thought that the two pairs of brothers were working on the Sabbath during which Jesus taught in the synagogue. Mark's "immediately" tells how soon Jesus enters the synagogue on the Sabbath or, more likely since it suits Mark's emphasis on Jesus' teaching, how soon Jesus starts teaching once he enters the synagogue on the Sabbath. See H. P. Rüger in *Markus-Philologie* 80-82 on Καφαρναούμ and τὰ σάββατα.

It is no more superfluous to mention Capernaum as the city of the synagogue than it would be to mention it as the city of Simon's and Andrew's house in vv 29-34 (against the argument of L. Schenke [*Wundererzählungen* 109] for Mark's transferring Capernaum to v 21 from an original position in v 29). Since Mark regularly starts a pericope with topographical movement and since v 21a presents the main movement, v 21b only a minor one, we should not regard v 21a as a tailpiece of the preceding pericope. Likewise, v 22 does not close a short pericope consisting of vv 21-22 (so W. Grundmann [2. Aufl.] 41); for v 23 does not mention the topographical movement with which Mark regularly opens a new pericope. The omission of εἰσελθών, "having entered," and putting of ἐδίδασκεν, "he began to teach," before εἰς τὴν συναγωγήν, "into the synagogue," by א and some supporters give a smoother reading than the overloaded introduction that makes Mark's audience wait till the end of the clause for the main verb. He likes to use circumstantial participles like εἰσελθών; in fact, he likes this one in particular (see also 2:1; 3:27; 5:39; 6:25; 7:24, 25; 11:15; 15:43; 16:5; and for other considerations, B. M. Metzger, *Textual Commentary* ad loc.).

We should not think that "synagogue" means "gathering" without reference to a building specially used for worship and instruction (as thought by H. C. Kee in *NTS* 36 [1990] 1-24). Already by 66 C.E., according to Josephus *J.W.* 2.14.4-5 §§285, 289, "the Jews in Caesarea had a synagogue alongside a plot" whose owner left them only a narrow passage on their way to "assemble in the synagogue" (cf. the next-door relationship of a house and a synagogue in Acts 18:7). Even earlier, according to Josephus *Ant.* 19.6.3 §§300, 305, an image of Caesar was set up "in a synagogue" as opposed to "his own sanctuary." These statements can hardly be understood in a non-architectural sense. Their wording is not satisfied even by a private house used for gatherings. Luke 7:5 goes so far as to say that a Gentile centurion "had built" (ᾠκοδόμησεν) a synagogue for the Jews in Capernaum (cf. the Theodotus inscription, found near Jerusalem and referring to the building of a synagogue, though Kee questions the dating of this inscription to a period before 70 C.E. despite the arguments of A. Deissmann, *LAE* 439-41). And right here in Mark 1 the parallels between going into Capernaum, a city consisting in buildings, and entering into the synagogue there (v 21) and between going out of the synagogue and into the house of Simon and Andrew (v 29) favor an architectural understanding of "synagogue" (cf. similar parallels between synagogues and the temple, the city, streets, street-corners, marketplaces, and prisons in 12:38-39 parr.; Matt 6:2, 5; Luke 21:12; John 18:20; Acts 17:17; 24:12; and see E. P. Sanders, *Jewish Law* 341-43, nn. 28-29, for devastating criticisms of Kee's position; also 76-77, 340-41, n. 24; L. I. Levine in *The Synagogue in Late Antiquity* 7-31).

It misses the point to say that here and elsewhere in Mark the amazement of people does not carry an entirely positive connotation because of lack of commitment to Jesus himself, limitation to his wonder-working, ignorance of his true identity, and such like (so T. Söding, *Glaube* 398-400, citing 6:2, 51-52; 7:31-37; 10:24, 26, 32; 12:17; 15:5, 44; 16:8 as well as 1:22, 27). Notations of amazement are designed to build up its object, not to tear down those who are amazed. Furthermore, disciples are amazed, too (6:51; 10:24, 26; 16:8 with 15:40-41). Amazement extends to Jesus' authoritative, wise, and unconventional teaching (1:22, 27; 6:2; 10:24, 26; 12:17), his heading up to Jerusalem (10:32), his silence under interrogation (15:5), and the rapidity of his death (15:44) as well as to his wonder-working (1:27; 6:2, 51; 16:8). M. R. Thompson (*Role of Disbelief* 49) argues that the "admittedly strong" vocabulary of amazement is "made much weaker by consistent use." But if Mark had not used such vocabulary so often — eighteen times by Thompson's own count — she would doubtless have argued for "a practice of negating laudatory incidents" from infrequency (cf. her similarly weak attempts to denigrate the miraculous in Mark by noting that only "many" are healed in 1:34, that only three disciples and two parents saw the raising of Jairus's daughter in 5:40-43, that only three disciples saw the Transfiguration in 9:2-13, and so on).

P. J. Achtemeier (75-77) argues unconvincingly that it is awkward of Mark to let his emphasis on Jesus' didactic authority lead him to portray Jesus as a teacher in the context of miracles. On the contrary, it is only natural that Jesus should teach in the synagogue whether or not he performs an exorcism there. "Teacher" will seem natural at 4:38 because of his parabolic teaching during the preceding hours of daylight; and further references to him as a teacher will hardly seem awkward once he has established himself in the role, no matter what the immediate circumstances (5:35; 6:34; 9:5, 17, 38; 10:51; 11:21; 14:45; cf. the Twelve's teaching in 6:30 with their preaching and miracle-working in 6:7, 12-13). The generality of the present audience weakens the suggestion of R. A. Guelich (1. 60) that by following up the making of the first disciples (vv 16-20) with a portrayal of Jesus as teacher, Mark is setting the tone for Jesus' didactic ministry to the disciples. See J. D. Kingsbury in *NTS* 36 (1990) 42-65 on Mark's developing the theme of Jesus' authority over against the religious leaders of the Jews.

We should not distinguish sharply between ἐξουσία as inherent divine authority, like that of a Hellenistic divine man, and ἐξουσία as delegated divine authority, like that of a Hebrew prophet; for Jesus is not only God's agent, "Christ," but also God's Son, who does not need to say, "Thus saith the Lord," or to quote scripture to establish a point (though he does quote it in Mark to illustrate a point). A limitation to delegated authority would be lost on Mark's Gentile audience, and his portraying Jesus as divine forbids such a limitation. Jesus' audience do not say whether the scribes appeal to scripture or to tradition passed on from earlier scribes, but 7:1-13 suggests the latter. See A. W. Argyle in *ExpTim* 80 (1968-69) 343;

R. H. Stein, *Proper Methodology* 133-34, and W. L. Lane 72, n. 11, against the view of D. Daube (*NTRJ* 205-16 and in *JTS* os 39 [1938] 45-59) that Mark means to portray Jesus as an authoritative rabbi in contrast with a mere village teacher. The scribes in 3:22; 7:1, 5; 8:31; 10:33; and chaps. 11ff., where Jesus arrives in Jerusalem and encounters the scribes who belong to the Sanhedrin, can hardly have been village teachers.

In v 23 the omission of εὐθύς, "immediately," by A C D W Θ 0135 *f*¹³ Majority Text latt sy is due to parallel influence from Luke 4:33 or, as in Luke, to a desire to rid the text of the awkward combination of εὐθύς and ἦν, "he was." The adverb normally goes with a verb of action; elsewhere in Mark it always does. Surrounding Jewish features favor that the Hebrew בְּ in the sense "with" stands behind ἐν in relation to "unclean spirit." But for Mark's Hellenistic audience ἐν carries the merely Greek sense "under the special influence of" (BAGD s.v. I5d). "Unclean spirit" may mean that (1) the spirit itself is unclean; (2) the spirit makes its victim unclean; or (3) both. The masculine gender of λέγων, "saying," at the beginning of v 24 shows that it is the man (ἄνθρωπος — masculine) who shouts out, but he does so under the impulse of the unclean spirit (ἐν πνεύματι ἀκαθάρτῳ — neuter).

"The Holy One of God" (v 24) does not occur in ancient Jewish literature as a messianic title, and in the rest of the NT (outside the parallel Luke 4:34) it occurs only at John 6:69. But holiness is ascribed to Jesus also in John 10:36; Acts 3:14; 4:27, 30 (cf. a synonym in Acts 2:27; 13:35); 1 John 2:20; Rev 3:7; and in John 10:36 it is ascribed to Jesus as the Son of God (cf. the proximity of "the Holy One of God" in Mark 1:24 to "Son of God" and "my beloved Son" in Mark 1:1, 11; also to unclean spirits' shouting in 3:11; 5:17 that Jesus is the Son of God). Some have hypothesized that "the Holy One of God" comes in two steps by association of "Nazarene" (v 24) with "a Nazirite of God" in Judg 13:7; 16:17 MT LXX^A and then by association with "a holy one of God" in Judg 13:7; 16:17 LXX^B as an alternative translation of "a Nazirite of God" (see, e.g., E. Schweizer in *Judentum, Urchristentum, Kirche* 90-93). Against this hypothesis stand half a dozen considerations: (1) the subtlety of the allusion (which would be lost on Mark's Gentile audience); (2) the tortuousness of the trail from Jesus as a "Nazarene" to "Nazirite" and on through more than one textual tradition of the LXX to "the Holy One of God"; (3) our uncertainty about the Septuagintal textual tradition (or traditions) known to Mark and earlier traditioners; (4) the differences between ι and α and between -αιος and -ηνος in the Greek behind "Nazirite" and "Nazarene," respectively (Matt 2:23 proving that a NT writer can attach -αιος to a stem representing Nazareth, as Mark does *not* do); (5) the difference between the double definite article in Mark and the complete anarthrousness of the phrase in Judges; and (6) the likelihood that Jesus' reputation for living in no way as a Nazirite would keep his kind of holiness from being associated with "Nazirite" (see Matt 11:19; Luke 7:34; R. H. Gundry, *Use of the OT* 97-104).

According to E. S. Malbon (*Narrative Space* 25-26), Jesus is designated a Nazarene to reaffirm his humanity when his actions seem superhuman. Not so in 14:67, however; for there Jesus will be standing trial. And here in 1:24 he has not yet done anything superhuman, nor will he have yet done anything superhuman within the pericope at 10:47. The designation carries no Christological freight, but only identifies Jesus from the topographical standpoints of Capernaum (1:24) and Judea (10:47; 14:67; 16:6).

Because of the similarity between the widow's "Why are you interfering with me?" in 1 Kgs 17:18 (= 3 Kgdms 17:18 LXX) and the demoniac's "Why are you interfering with us?" it has also been suggested that her addressing Elijah as a "man of God" (i.e. a charismatic) led via Elisha's being called "a holy man of God" in 2 Kgs 4:9 (= 4 Kgdms 4:9 LXX) to the unclean spirit's addressing Jesus as "the Holy One of God." We might suppose that Mark or an earlier traditioner dropped "man" out of the OT expression because "man" has just occurred in v 23 for the demoniac. Nevertheless, we might also suppose that τις, "a certain one," should occur in v 23 so as to reserve "man" for an OT allusion in v 24. An allusion to 1 Kgs 17:18 is otherwise uncertain, too. The question, "Why are you interfering . . . ?" is common both inside and outside the Bible (besides the biblical references cited above, see also extrabiblical references cited in BAGD s.v. ἐγώ [toward the end]). Bringing the widow's sins to remembrance and slaying her son may or may not be analogous to the destruction of unclean spirits; but the pathos of her grief and Elijah's raising her son back to life stand miles apart from Jesus' exorcism, for Mark presents it as a mighty overcoming of the demoniac-cum-unclean spirit, not as a merciful deliverance of the demoniac from the unclean spirit. The generally acknowledged lack of high priestly messiahship in Mark and pre-Marcan tradition militates against derivation from the calling of Aaron "[the] holy one of [the] Lord" (Ps 106[105]:16 LXX; see further H. Braun, *Qumran* 1. 62; F. Hahn, *Titles* 231-35). Perhaps it is best simply to see the holiness of God associated through the Holy Spirit with Jesus God's Son for a contrast with the spirit's uncleanness.

J. D. Kingsbury (*Christology of Mark's Gospel* 86-87) detects a contrapuntal pattern of demoniacal cries regarding Jesus' true identity (1:24, 34; 3:11; 5:7) and human questions regarding it (1:27; 2:7; 4:41; 6:3). The pattern is not quite so neat as presented, however. 1:27 does not carry a question about Jesus' true identity, but about the kind of teaching he gives. 1:34 mentions no demoniacal cries, only Jesus' not allowing the demons to speak. Perhaps less damagingly, the question of his true identity in 2:7 arises in reaction to his forgiveness of sins, not to an exorcism or a healing; and considerable distance, occupied by whole pericopes, usually several of them, separates the cries and questions in 1:34 and 2:7, in 3:11 and 4:41, and in 5:7 and 6:3.

M. Reiser (*Syntax und Stil* 14-15) cites plenty of non-Jewish literature to show that the proleptic σε in the demoniac's and unclean spirit's outcry (v 24) is not necessarily Semitic. Cf. also the proleptic σε in the most often cited parallel: "I know you, Hermes, who you are and whence you are and what your city is, Hermopolis" (οἶδά σε, Ἑρμῆ, τίς εἶ κτλ. — *PGM* VIII. 13, in a love-spell; cf. "Jesus of Nazareth," too, in Mark 1:24). Since the use of divine names permeates the Greco-Roman world (for examples of the frequent formulas "I know it" and "you are . . ." in addressing a divine being, see *PGM* III. 449-500, 623-25; IV. 1500, 2251-52, 2287ff., 2343ff., 2984-88; V. 100-103; VIII. 6-7, 13, 20; XII. 60-66; and for "you have come . . ." IV. 2340), Hellenistic readers cannot help but understand vv 23-24 in terms of attempted self-defense on the part of the demoniac, inspired by the unclean spirit. True, the magical texts in *PGM* date from the third century onward, and we have no Hellenistic example of a demoniac or a demon trying to use a divine name in self-defense against an exorcist. But the NT itself tells us that the use of divine names in exorcism, prayer, etc., was already current (see, e.g., Mark 9:38; Acts 19:13, and note in the latter passage the demon's verbal as well physical resistance; cf. ancient Mesopotamian evidence cited by E. Yamauchi in *Gospel Perspectives* 6. 101; *ANET* 12-14; and the first century exorcistic use of Solomon's name according to Josephus, who divinizes him Hellenistically in *Ant.* 8.2.5 §§45-49); and the Hellenistic use of divine names is so varied — for adjuring, summoning, dismissing, expelling, invoking for good or ill with respect to others, with respect to oneself, and so on (see *PGM* passim) — that this lack of a perfectly parallel example poses no problem. Knowledge of divine names and titles is powerful for whatever purpose anyone has. Unlike Jesus' name, moreover, the names of ordinary Hellenistic people who try to exorcise demons are not divine; so naturally a demoniac or a demon does not try to use those names in self-defense. Most of all, the magical papyri are written for the self-serving purposes of human beings, not as manuals of self-defense for demons. Doubtless a Hellenistic *Screwtape Letters* would offer examples of demonic use of divine names for self-defense, and Mark 5:7 gives us an indubitable example of using a divine name in demoniacal self-defense.

On the other hand, τί ἡμῖν καὶ σοί . . . ; usually lacks a magical connotation and carries such a connotation here only by association with the following apotropaic use of a divine name (cf. P. Guillemette's refutation of O. Bauernfeind on 3 Kgdms 17:18 LXX in *ScEs* 30 [1978] 83-89). Similarly, ἐπετίμησεν carries an exorcistic connotation only by association with the following command to shut up and come out. By the same token this verb does not in and of itself connote divine reproof (see concordances and lexicons against the tendency of E. Stauffer in *TDNT* 2. 624-26 and of his followers). Modern linguistics has taught us to seek the meaning of a word primarily in its contextual associations. Here ἐπετίμησεν connotes divine reproof to the extent that Jesus the speaker is portrayed as divine. Neither originally nor in the context of Mark's gospel do the words of the demoniac-cum-unclean spirit express capitulation; for then Jesus' rebuke becomes unnecessary, indeed inappropriate. The demoniac's words set a resistant, not a capitulatory, tone (contrast the citation in H. Gressmann, *Altorientalische Texte* 78). The argument against self-defense that the demoniac knows the futility of resistance modernistically attributes too much rationality to an unclean spirit and mistakes the spirit's knowledge of Jesus' purpose for prescience of Jesus' success (against G. Minette de Tillesse, *Le secret messianique* 75-77, with reference to H. J. Ebeling and E. Percy, whose other arguments do not merit refutation; see further T. A. Burkill, *Mysterious Revelation* 72-76; J. Marcus in *JBL* 103 [1984] 558-59).

H. C. Kee (in *NTS* 14 [1967-68] 232-46) notes that ἐπετίμησεν never occurs in Hellenistic exorcistic literature, and interprets the word in terms of גער as an effective word of command that represents the exercise of God's sovereignty in bringing evil powers under control. But the OT and other passages that Kee surveys show that the word can also refer to reprimands without regard to effectiveness or the question of God's sovereignty; so it is the context, not the word itself, that determines whether the rebuking succeeds or has to do with the rule of God. In other words, we do not have a technical term that carries such connotations by itself (cf. D. E. Aune in *ANRW* II 23/2. 1530-31). From the modern standpoint it might seem ironic after the identifications of Jesus in 1:1, 11 as Christ and Son of God that he should hush up an unclean spirit that calls him "the Holy One of God." But Mark's audience — in particular his historically intended Gentile audience, well acquainted as they were with the magical use of divine names and titles for self-defensive and other self-serving purposes — would not initially think of Christological irony in the hushing up, but of Christological authority (against R. M. Fowler in *PEGLBS* 1 [1981] 26-36).

For the same reason we should not think that Mark makes Jesus try to keep his messiahship secret. Besides, Mark has not given his audience any reason to think that Jesus wants to dampen publicity for purposes of avoiding misunderstanding, criticism, attack, or anything else of that sort. Mark portrays him, rather, as stopping the apotropaic use of his name and titles (see also the comments on 1:34; 3:12; 8:30). Mark's audience have a long way to go before arriving at any of the passion predictions, which might make them think that he wants to qualify titles such as "Christ," "Son of God," and "Holy One of God" by the Cross. And on arrival at the passion narrative, the audience will discover that Mark qualifies the Cross with the miraculous rather than qualifying the miraculous with the Cross. His emphasis on the wide publication of Jesus' miracles and the comparative infrequency of commands to silence about miracles of healing weaken the argument that those commands will interpret the shutting up of unclean spirits in terms of a messianic secret rather than apotropaically, and they suggest that those commands themselves will need an explanation different from a messianic secret. It is hard to understand how J. D. Kingsbury (*Conflict in Mark* 38) can write that "Mark forbids the reader to imagine that these shouts [of unclean spirits] ever reach the ears of humans" but that "on the contrary, these shouts are either suppressed by Jesus or occur in a place where they cannot be heard."

Jesus suppresses the shout here, but the demoniac's presence in the synagogue and the audience's amazement at the exorcism make it impossible for the reader *not* to imagine that this shout reached the ears of human beings.

R. Pesch (1. 118, 124; in *BibLeb* 9 [1968] 118, 123-24; and in *Evangelienforschung* 254) thinks that Mark adds the item of authority in v 27 as he obviously did in v 22, with the result that he changes an original "Who is this?" (as in 4:41) to "What is this?" But other possibilities make the suggestion unsure: (1) in v 22 Mark may have editorially anticipated a traditional reference to authority in v 27; (2) the story may originally have ended with the exit of the unclean spirit in v 26 (cf. 7:30 and 8:26-27, where a crowd [8:15-17] that is already running together [8:25] might have expressed admiration), so that the entirety of v 27 comes from Mark, not from tradition; (3) a traditional expression of admiration may have included only astonishment at exorcism, so that the question "What is this?" as well as the reference to a new teaching with authority comes from Mark. More seriously, Mark's concern throughout with Jesus' identity (see esp. 1:1, 11; 3:11; 8:27-29; 14:61-62; 15:2, 39) and "I know you, who you are . . . ," which appeared recently in the present pericope, would lead us to expect just the opposite sort of change (from an original "What is this?" to "Who is this? He teaches with authority" — cf. v 22) or at least the retention of an original "Who is this?" The one other NT occurrence of "new teaching" in Acts 17:19 does not make a technical missionary term. We could even surmise that Luke uses the expression there to make up for his omitting it in his parallel to Mark 1:27, i.e. Luke 4:36.

At v 27 we should not follow J. K. Elliott (in *NT Textual Criticism* 50-52) in favoring the v.l. of (A) C (f¹³ 565^mg) Majority Text lat sy^p,h: "What [is] this new teaching?" It is easier and therefore unoriginal, not to mention the weightier external evidence of ℵ B L 33 (f¹ 28* 565*) on the side of "What is this? A new teaching . . ." (see B. M. Metzger, *Textual Commentary* ad loc.; also C. E. B. Cranfield [80-81] for construing authority with the new teaching, not with Jesus' commanding of unclean spirits). In the newness of Jesus' teaching R. H. Stein (*Proper Methodology* 137-38) sees reflected the Jewish belief that the messianic age will bring new teaching of the Law. Perhaps so originally, but Mark's accent rests solely on authority as such; and he can hardly expect his Gentile audience to fill in Jewish legal content. Similarly, the accent on authority means that at least on the plane of Mark's text we should not equate the newness of Jesus' teaching with the nearness of God's rule. In view is didactic style, not a temporal element of content.

At Matt 3:5 πᾶσα ἡ περίχωρος τοῦ Ἰορδάνου must mean "all the region *around* the Jordan," for "all the surrounding region *of* the Jordan" (genitive of apposition) would not make good sense (the Jordan does not surround any region). Hence, Mark's εἰς ὅλην τὴν περίχωρον τῆς Γαλιλαίας may mean "into the whole region *around* Galilee" (cf. Matt 4:24). But the oddity of leapfrogging the Galilean region around Capernaum (contrast 3:7-8) combines with Jesus' going soon into the whole of Galilee (v 39) to favor the genitive of apposition: "into the whole surrounding region *of* Galilee" (cf. Deut 3:13 LXX and Luke's omitting Galilee in his parallel 4:37: "into every spot of the surrounding region").

See R. Pesch 1. 119 for form criticism of vv 21-28. Whether the form of the pericope is due to earlier oral use in missionary work (as Pesch and others think) or to Mark's authorial concerns (as suggested by the suitability of the details to his overall emphases and purpose) is another question. On form critical and historical issues surrounding stories of miracles, including exorcisms, in general, see H. K. Nielsen in *Probleme der Forschung* 59-66; and on differences between NT descriptions of demonic possession and what modern psychiatrists diagnose as severe mental illness, see J. Schmid 47-48.

ONE HEALING, MANY HEALINGS, AND MANY EXORCISMS

1:29-34 (Matt 8:14-17; Luke 4:38-41)

Verses 29-31 and 32-34 go together to form a single pericope. The adversative δέ, "but," that introduces evening in v 32 marks a shift of time in one and the same locale: everything in vv 29-34 happens at the home of Simon and Andrew. The healing of Simon's mother-in-law leads up to and gives a particular instance of the many healings that Jesus performs on this occasion. Thus the pericope breaks down into entering the home of Simon and Andrew (v 29), the illness of Simon's mother-in-law (v 30a), the drawing of Jesus' attention to her illness (v 30b), his healing her (v 31), and further healings plus exorcisms (vv 32-34). The healing of Simon's mother-in-law also complements the exorcism in vv 21-28: the former had to do with a man, the latter has to do with a woman; the first occurred in public at synagogue, the second occurs in private at home.

1:29-31 *(Matt 8:14-15; Luke 4:38-39)* The immediacy of Jesus' going from the synagogue in Capernaum to the home of Simon and Andrew, where he will heal Simon's mother-in-law, hurries him to another display of his saving power. The frequency of Mark's use of εὐθύς, "immediately," does not mean that the adverb has lost its vitality for him; rather, he wants to portray a ministry full of powerful activity. The position of ἐκ τῆς συναγωγῆς, "from the synagogue," before ἐξελθόντες, "going out," strengthens the linkage of this pericope with the preceding one and helps create a chiasm with ἦλθον εἰς τὴν οἰκίαν Σίμωνος καὶ Ἀνδρέου, "into the house of Simon and Andrew." The addition of James and John as also going with Jesus implies the continued effectiveness of his calling all four to follow him (vv 16-20). An adversative δέ, "but," and the position of the subject "the mother-in-law of Simon" before its verb shift attention to the mother-in-law, because she is suffering from a fever. Her lying down instead of serving the men, especially the guests, shows how severe the fever is (cf. 2:4). We should not allow modern advances in medicine to lead us into underestimating the seriousness of fever in ancient times (see John 4:46-54). The immediacy of others' speaking to Jesus about the fever of Simon's mother-in-law and the historical present tense of λέγουσιν, "they speak," underline her plight. Jesus' approaching, grasping her hand, and raising her up show him exercising power over the fever. Elsewhere in Mark, grasping and otherwise touching are sometimes absent (2:10-12; 3:1-6; 10:46-52). But where present (cf. 6:5) they have a certain appropriateness: here Jesus grasps a woman's hand to raise her from a prone position; in 1:40-44 he will touch a leper to show that healing makes this untouchable touchable; in 5:39-42 he will grasp a girl's hand (contrast the laying on of hands requested in 5:23, when she was still alive) to get her up from "sleep"; in 7:33 he will put his fingers in a deaf mute's ears and touch his tongue with spittle to give him hearing and speech (cf. 7:32); in 8:22, 24 he will spit on a blind man's eyes and touch them to give him sight; in 9:26-27 he will grasp a boy's hand to raise him to a standing position from a paroxysm that has left him looking dead; in 3:10 people will touch Jesus for healing because they are too numerous for him to touch them;

in 5:25-34 a woman will touch Jesus' garment out of fear as well as faith; and in 6:56 people will touch the fringe of his garment because he is not bent on ministering in the region (cf. 6:45; 7:14). Though suitable to the transmission of healing power, then (cf. 2 Kgs 13:20-21; Acts of Paul; H. Wagenvoort in *RAC* 3. 404-21), touching is fundamentally incidental and therefore unnecessary. Here the fever leaves, and the mother-in-law's serving those present proves that Jesus' power has in fact made it leave. Since ancient people used many home remedies and magical means to get rid of fever (see the literature cited by Str-B 1. 479-80; K. Weiss in *TDNT* 6. 956-58; H.-J. Horn in *RAC* 7. 877-909, esp. 880-86), the simplicity of Jesus' gesture makes this healing very impressive (cf. H. K. Nielsen, *Heilung* 14-20, where the relative absence of magical manipulation is made an argument for historical memory of Jesus' healing ministry; also L. J. McGinley, *Form-Criticism* 48-154, on the differences that distance Jesus' healings from rabbinic and Hellenistic healings, and B. Blackburn, *Theios Anēr* 24-38, on miraculous healers in general).

1:32-34 *(Matt 8:16-17; Luke 4:40-41)* The purpose of the summary in these verses is to play up the healing and exorcistic power of Jesus. An adversative δέ, "but," sets off the evening from the preceding hours of daylight. The addition of "when the sun had set" to "when a late [hour] had come" specifies more clearly and exactly that the Sabbath has ended in accordance with a Jewish method of reckoning days from sunset to sunset. For both Mark and the pre-Marcan tradition, some think, this bit of information has the purpose of indicating that the people do not break the Sabbath by carrying and otherwise bringing their sick and demon-possessed to Jesus and that he does not break it by working cures and exorcisms. But observance of the Sabbath has not yet arisen as an issue; it does not arise as an issue in this pericope; it will not till 2:23–3:6; and when it does, Mark and his tradition will portray Jesus as lording it over the Sabbath, not try to protect him from the charge of breaking it. Therefore Mark and the traditioner before him are hardly concerned to exculpate the people and Jesus from breaking the Sabbath. Rather, they offer the Christ-glorifying point that the people bring their sick and demon-possessed as soon as possible after the Sabbath (cf. v 21) so great is his magnetic power (cf. 16:1-2). Whether both temporal expressions occurred in the tradition or Mark adds one or the other we can hardly tell. For how do we know whether the frequency in Mark of "when evening came" favors tradition or redaction? (The expression, which can refer to late afternoon or evening, will occur again in 4:35; 6:47; 14:17; 15:42 [cf. 11:11].) And how do we know whether the singularity of "when the sun had set" favors tradition or redaction? (Except for Luke's parallel to 1:32, the expression occurs nowhere else in Mark or in the entire NT.) We do not even know whether the frequency of dual expressions in Mark is due to tradition or redaction (for other dual temporal notes of time, see also 1:35; 14:12; 15:42; 16:1-2 and F. Neirynck, *Duality* 45-53, 94-96). Whether or not Mark created one or both sides of the present expression, its duality and introduction with an adversative δέ, "but," stress the alacrity with which the people bring their sick and demon-possessed once the Sabbath has ended (against the view of L. Schenke, *Wundererzählungen* 124-25, that Mark separates vv 32-34 sharply from vv 29-31). In view of an upcoming report about Jesus' healing on the Sabbath despite Pharisaic objections (3:1-6), we can hardly think that Mark is highlighting Jesus' observance of the Sabbath. Instead, "all" and "whole" highlight the magnitude that Jesus' reputation has already attained (v 28). "The city" refers back to Capernaum (v 21). Inclusion of both the sick and the demon-possessed points up the broad reach of Jesus' power. Additionally, the mention of demon-possessed people recalls the man with an unclean spirit (vv 21-28). His deliverance, perhaps also the healing of Peter's mother-in-law, has caused people to bring their sick and demon-possessed. The whole of the city (v 33) corresponds to the whole of the surrounding region of Galilee (v 28). That the whole city is gathered "at the door" not only provides a realistic detail relating to the house of Simon and Andrew (v 29); it joins the other features of the text that highlight Jesus' magnetism (cf. the flocking of young men around Pythagoras because of a miracle he was supposed to have performed [though it was not a healing or an exorcism] — Iambl. *VP* 37).

"Many" (bis) stresses how much power Jesus has to heal and to perform exorcisms. It does not weaken the "all" that describes those who are brought to Jesus, as though he succeeds on many but not all of them; rather, it points up that the all whom he delivers are numerous. In particular, the forward position of the direct object δαιμόνια πολλά, "many demons," in v 34b empha- sizes the large number of the "all" (cf. T. Snoy in *RTL* 3 [1972] 69 on the interchange of "all" and "many" in Mark and, more generally, J. Jeremias in *TDNT* 6. 540-42). "Various" (with "diseases") highlights the wide range of Jesus' ability to heal. He does not prohibit the healed people from speaking — only the demons. Why them? Because he does not want publicity from such a source? Or because Mark or an earlier traditioner wants to keep Jesus' messi- ahship secret — i.e. wants to produce a ministry of secret epiphanies — till the account of his passion and resurrection (and to do so for one of several possible and mutually exclusive reasons, such as covering up a theologically embar- rassing *absence* of messianism in his public ministry or a politically dangerous *presence* of messianism in it)? No, for Mark gives a different answer: "because they [the demons] knew him." In v 24 the unclean spirit said, "I know you, who you are," to gain control over Jesus (see the comments and notes ad loc.). His "shutting up" the unclean spirit showed his greater power. So also in v 34 Jesus' not allowing the demons to speak means his not allowing them to speak in self-defense. Again his power crushes the attempt to gain control over his actions by uttering knowledge of him. Since this purpose fits Mark's constant emphasis on Jesus' power, we have no need to introduce a messianic secret which, at the time of Mark's writing or earlier, reinterpreted the tradition (cf. 3:11-12; 5:7). The emphasis on Jesus' power comes out in repetition, allitera- tion, and assonance:

v 32: πάντας τοὺς κακῶς ἔχοντας καὶ τοὺς δαιμονιζομένους

v 33: πόλις . . . πρός . . .

v 34: πολλοὺς κακῶς ἔχοντας ποικίλαις . . . δαιμόνια πολλά.

Also adding to this emphasis is inclusion: (a) the bringing of the ill and demon-possessed; (b) the gatheredness of the whole city at the door; and (a') the healing of the ill and exorcism of demons.

NOTES

Because Jesus had just called the first disciples to follow him (vv 16-20), Mark used the plural for going into Capernaum (v 21a). But because only Jesus was going to teach in the synagogue there, Mark switched to the singular for entering it (v 21b). Now he switches back to the plural for leaving the synagogue, because the plural becomes appropriate to Jesus' entering Simon's and Andrew's house along with them, James, and John. The "they" who leave the synagogue and come into the house includes Jesus, but the "they" who speak to him about the mother-in-law naturally excludes him and refers only to the four disciples or, alternatively and indefinitely, to other people perhaps already in the house with her. The failure of Jesus' name to reappear between v 25 and 2:5 shows the extent to which Mark or someone before him has "composed" the materials in the etymological sense of the word. The resultant flow of narrative makes it easy to understand that the dominant "he" refers to Jesus. The singular of his entering the synagogue in v 21b seems to have led to the vv.ll. in v 29 that mention Jesus alone as leaving the synagogue and entering the house.

The house is Simon's and Andrew's (hence, the subordination of James and John in a "with"-phrase), but we do not know whether both or either of Simon's and Andrew's parents has ever lived there or still lives there or whether Andrew is married. That Simon's mother-in-law cooks and serves a meal there (the probable meaning of διηκόνει in v 31) favors but does not require that she lives in the house rather than that she is only being cared for there. It also favors that Simon is widowed (otherwise, why does Simon's wife not serve the men from the start?), though if so he will marry again (1 Cor 9:5). We do not know whether his mother-in-law is widowed or still married. The belonging of the house to Andrew as well as to Simon disfavors that it belongs or has ever belonged to her husband, and also disfavors that Simon moved into the house of his parents-in-law when he married. It has been argued that the improbability of several families' living in the same Palestinian house betrays some unhistorical redactional additions of names by Mark (for the purpose of emphasizing discipleship). The argument founders on the possibility that very few people live there (it is theoretically possible that only the mother-in-law lives there now that Simon and Andrew are following Jesus — if Simon is widowed, childless, and parentless and Andrew unwedded or widowed, childless, and parentless) and rests on overconfidence in our knowledge of first century Palestinian living conditions in general and of the size of Simon's and Andrew's house in particular. Excavations of what may have been their house in Capernaum show a size large enough to handle more than one family (J. F. Strange and H. Shanks in *BAR* 8 [1982] 26-37). Of course, the listing of the first disciples' names may simultaneously forge a literary link with vv 16-20, carry a theological point concerning discipleship, and reflect a historical datum. Whether an earlier version of the story had only Simon's name we cannot tell, though the view is often expressed with confidence.

The awkwardness of implying but not stating that the disciples enter the synagogue is no greater than would be the awkwardness (to say nothing about historical improbability) of leaving the impression that the first disciples, despite vv 16-20, do *not* follow Jesus in and out of the synagogue (so the singular vv.ll. in v 29). Similarly, the awkwardness of saying "with James and John" despite their already belonging to the "they" who come out of the synagogue and go to the home of Simon and Andrew is no greater than would be the awkwardness of leaving Simon and Andrew out of the journey by saying that "he" (Jesus) comes out and goes with James and John to the home of Simon and Andrew. Mark chooses the awkwardness that he does for the literary and theological reasons already indicated. Therefore nothing stands in the way of the suggestion that he originally heard Peter tell this story in the first person and then changed "we" to "they" and substituted "Simon's" for "my." Only the presupposition that the story in vv 29-34 was originally told without the background of the story in vv 16-20 would lead one to infer a secondary addition of Andrew, James, and John. The identification of Bethsaida rather than Capernaum as "the city of Andrew and Peter" in John 1:44 might support an original independence of the story in vv 29-34 from that in vv 21-28 (set in Capernaum), but not from that in vv 16-20 (set anywhere alongside the Sea of Galilee). On the other hand, see R. A. Guelich 1. 62 for the possibilities of a move from Bethsaida to Capernaum and, in connection with the fishing business, of dual residence.

The interpretation that in v 30 those who speak to Jesus about the mother-in-law's fever are apologizing for her absence and resultant failure to serve a meal would nicely make her serving a meal after her cure a matter of amends as well as of proof. The text suggests only an explanation of the reason why she is lying down, however, not of her absence from the room that Jesus and the disciples have entered. In fact, προσελθών, "approaching," implies her presence in the room (instead of Jesus' entering another room to heal her in accordance with the different wording of 5:38-40) more probably than speaking to Jesus about her is said to imply her lying in another room. Since she is bed-ridden and so close to Jesus that it would not make sense for anyone to carry her to him, he approaches her. Mark does not write that they ask Jesus to heal her. Why should they? Jesus has not yet performed a healing, only an exorcism; so a request for healing would look strange at this point in Mark's narrative. W. Grundmann (2. Aufl., 46) thinks that originally they expected Jesus to visit, perhaps to pray over, the mother-in-law (cf. Matt 25:36; Jas 5:14). Our inability to confirm or disconfirm such a suggestion or to answer questions of detail arising out of historical curiosity highlights the theological concerns of Mark that limit him by and large to more significant matters of salvation-history.

The paralleling of 1QapGen 20:28-29 suffers somewhat from several differences: (1) Jesus' grasping the hand of the mother-in-law does not equate with Abraham's laying his hands on Pharaoh; (2) Jesus does not pray for the mother-in-law as Abraham prays for Pharaoh; and (3) Jesus does not drive away a spirit by means of a rebuke as Abraham does in Pharaoh's case. See 4 Kgdms 5:11 LXX for an even earlier reference to healing with the laying on of hands; Acts 28:8 for a combination of prayer and laying on of hands (as in 1QapGen 20:28-29) for curing a fever (as in Mark 1:29-31) and dysentery; b. Ber. 4b for curing a fever by prayer; and B. Blackburn, Theios Anēr 188, for discussion of healings of fever. D. E. Aune (in ANRW II 23/2. 1553-54) describes touching by pagan healers as rare and late in date (from the third century onward; cf. E. R. Dodds, The Greeks and the Irrational 22, n. 52). So we may be dealing with an especially Semitic style of healing (see also b. Ber. 5b). On the other hand, see Suet. Vesp. 7; Tac. Hist. 4.81; Philostr. VA 3.39; 4.45; and, for further material, O. Weinreich, Antike Heilungswunder 1-37, 45-48; Blackburn, op. cit. 112-17. J. Kopas (in RR 44 [1985] 914-16) thinks it a risk for Jesus to have grasped a female here and in 5:41, but in each case the specification of her hand and the purpose of raising her up from a bed rather than luring or forcing her down on one make his gesture unobjectionable. The lack of any reference to a demon, the absence of a rebuke (contrast Luke 4:39), and the mere gesture of raising up Simon's mother-in-law disfavor any thought of a demonically induced fever (contrast Plin. HN 8.32.50; 22.14.16; R. Reitzenstein, Poim. 18.8; R. and M. Hengel in Medicus Viator 341; cf. the non-demonic aetiology of diseases as discussed by E. Yamauchi in Gospel Perspectives 6. 101-3 et passim).

Since the definition of discipleship as service lies a long way off in 9:35; 10:43-45, it seems unlikely that the mother-in-law's serving a meal means anything more than her proving the reality of her cure by doing the work expected of a woman. The coordination of healing and serving in v 31bc favors that Mark has his eye on proof of healing, not on the nature of discipleship. It is possible that in 15:41 the coordination of certain women's following Jesus with their serving him says something about discipleship. But there Jesus alone will be the object of following and serving. Here it is a group of people. And the story in Luke 10:38-42 should give pause to those who see discipleship entailed in women's serving food, for there Jesus demotes women's kitchen service and promotes their sitting at his feet to hear his word. Against J. Ernst (68-69), the very normality of a woman's serving food contributes to the proof of healing; otherwise the activity would not merit any mention. We must not let the opinion of a single rabbi in *b. Qidd.* 70a that a man should not use the services of a female, young or adult, deceive us into thinking that serving men was not normal woman's work. On the contrary, see Luke 8:3; 10:38-42; John 12:2, to take three outstanding examples. The rabbinic tradition dates from the third or fourth century and emanates from Babylonia. See the comments on 10:34 regarding suggested relationships between vv 29, 31 and the Secret Gospel of Mark, and R. Pesch 1. 129 for form critical comments. Perhaps the preservation and early narration of this story owes something to the patient's relationship to no less an ecclesiastical figure than Simon Peter.

The preceding stories (vv 21-28, 29-31) gave only two examples out of many that might have been cited. The chiastic order in vv 32-34 of healings and then exorcisms after the stories of an exorcism (vv 21-28) and then a healing (vv 29-31) may indicate that Mark is taking over earlier tradition and perhaps adding the reference to exorcisms in reflection of vv 21-28. But it is equally possible that the chiastic order represents a simple stylistic touch (hardly beyond the capability of even so rough a writer as Mark) or that in composing the summary Mark simply works backward through his text. It would be surprising if Jesus' activity did not include exorcisms as well as healings on an occasion when the general public bring him their oppressed loved ones and friends. Mark uses the noun "demon" with the verb "go out" three times (7:26, 29, 30), and the phrase "unclean spirit" with the same verb four times (1:26; 5:8, 13; 7:25). But he usually puts "demon" with or near "cast out" (1:34, 39; 3:15, 22; 6:13; 7:26; 9:38) and never puts "unclean spirit" with "cast out" (see 1:23, 27; 3:11, 30; 5:2; 7:25; and esp. 6:7, where we expect "authority to cast out unclean spirits" [cf. 3:15: "authority to cast out demons"] but actually read "authority *of* the unclean spirits" [an objective genitive meaning authority *over* them]). These combinations and non-combinations sometimes occur in the same pericope (3:22-30; 5:1-20; 7:24-30). "Demoniac" occurs as the short way to refer to "a man with an unclean spirit" (1:32; 5:15, 16, 18). It appears, then, that the choice between "demon" and "unclean spirit" depends on linguistic habits having to do with associated verbs and economy of expression rather than on a difference between Jewish Christian tradition (using "unclean spirits") and Hellenistic Christian redaction (using "demon" and "demoniac"). The phenomena thus blunt the argument that the use of "demoniacs" and "demons" indicates a late Hellenistic insertion by Mark of exorcisms which pre-Marcan Jewish Christian tradition lacked. In other words, we do not have convincing reasons to think that he fabricates exorcisms here to match the exorcism in vv 21-28. The absence of Jesus' teaching argues for Mark's taking over a pre-formed tradition, since he emphasized Jesus' teaching in vv 21-28. On the other hand, he may compose the summary and leave out Jesus' teaching because Jesus has just taught in the local synagogue, because it seems impossible for him to teach just outside the door with throngs of people bringing their sick and demon-possessed for deliverance (2:2 has him speaking the word to crowds at the door, but no large numbers of sick and demon-possessed are there — only a lone paralytic), or simply because the oral form of the tradition lacks a reference to teaching. On the whole, it seems best to think that Mark composes the summary but follows oral tradition (Peter's teachings according to Papias's elder — Eus. H.E. 3.39.15), with the result that the wording represents both the tradition and his interests and linguistic habits (see Matt 11:20-24; Luke 10:13-15 in favor of historicity; for attempts to decide between tradition and redaction with references to other secondary literature, J. Verheyden in *ETL* 64 [1988] 415-20; R. A. Guelich 1. 63-65).

It is sometimes urged that elsewhere Mark implies the non-Jewish methods of reckoning a day from midnight to midnight and from sunrise to sunrise (11:11-12; 14:12; 15:42) and that this implication rules out his own and his Gentile audience's knowing the Jewish method of reckoning a day from sunset to sunset. But see the notes on 14:12 that Jews reckon a day from sunrise to sunrise as well as from sunset to sunset (also the notes on 14:17), and Jewish practices in observing the Sabbath are so well known even among the Gentiles (see R. Goldenberg in *ANRW* II 19/1. 414-47; M. J. Borg, *Conflict* 334, n. 2; E. Lohse in *TDNT* 7. 17-18 and contrast the need in Mark 7:2-4 to explain less obvious Jewish practices) that Mark can presume Gentiles' appreciation of the point that the Jewish people brought their afflicted to Jesus as soon as possible. In Mark, φέρω refers to bringing by more means than carrying (see the concordance s.v. and C. H. Turner in *JTS* os 26 [1924-25] 12-14). The third person plural of ἔφερον is indefinite ("they" in the sense of people in general). The imperfect tense is used because of the linearity of bringing. Mark does not portray the bringing of the ill and demon-possessed to Jesus as bad. Seeking the salvation of such people is not to be equated with the sign-seeking that grows out of unbelief. In 3:22-30 Mark will quote Jesus as condemning only the misinterpretation of his miracles (in particular, his exorcisms). Misinterpretation of his miracles invalidates or devalues them no more than misunderstanding of his teaching (4:10-13) invalidates or devalues that.

W. Egger (*Frohbotschaft* 67) argues that in v 34b Mark's putting the command to silence after the exorcisms contrasts with v 25 and shows that here we have the messianic secret rather than part of the exorcisms. But ᾔδεισαν αὐτόν, "they knew him," has all the appearance of a deliberate allusion to οἶδα σε, "I know you," and therefore favors an understanding in terms of demonic self-defense, as earlier. The change in order may have a simple stylistic reason behind it, viz., avoidance of a ὅτι-clause between coordinate main clauses, as would result if Mark had put the command to silence, on which the ὅτι-clause depends, before the casting out of demons. But not only style is involved; so also is emphasis. Mark wants to highlight the large number of exorcisms. So he shoves forward not only the direct object δαιμόνια πολλά, "many demons," and thereby produces an emphatically chiastic order (cf. the order of verb and then direct object in the preceding clause); he also shoves forward the whole clause that features the large number of demons that Jesus casts out. The imperfect tense of ἤφιεν in the statement, "And he was not allowing the demons to speak," contrasts with the aorist of ἐξέβαλεν, "he cast out," and seems to indicate what Jesus was doing in the course of and therefore by way of casting out demons, not something that he did afterward by way of imposing a messianic secret (for which we would expect both verbs to be in the aorist).

JESUS' MAGNETISM AND ABILITY TO CLEANSE A LEPER

1:35-45 (Matt 4:23; 8:1-4; Luke 4:42-44; 5:12-16)

Mark has narrated Jesus' city-wide activity in Capernaum (vv 21-34). Now he narrates Jesus' region-wide activity throughout Galilee (vv 35-45). Thus the power of Jesus becomes evident not only in its effect but also in it compass. The pericope divides into a stage-setting for his wider activity (vv 35-38) and his preaching throughout Galilee and cleansing a leper in the course of that preaching (vv 39-45). The stage-setting subdivides into his departure (v 35), the disciples' finding him (vv 36-37), and the announcement of his intention to preach elsewhere (v 38). The wider activity subdivides into his carrying out that intention to the accompaniment of exorcisms (v 39), a leper's confronting him (v 40), his cleansing the leper (vv 41-42) and thrusting him out with certain instructions (v 43-44), and the leper's going out, preaching, and publishing the word with the result that people flock to Jesus even in otherwise deserted places (v 45). His cleansing the leper in the course of preaching and casting out demons is reminiscent of his casting out an unclean spirit in the course of teaching (vv 21-28). By recalling Jesus' going out to preach in vv 35-38, the ex-leper's going out to preach in v 45 completes a verbal inclusion which ties together the whole passage into a single pericope.

1:35 *(Luke 4:42a)* The reference to evening after sunset (v 32) has prepared for the present reference to morning before dawn. The doubling of temporal expressions in πρωὶ ἔννυχα, "[so] early [it was still] nighttime" (cf. the comments on v 32), and the adding of the intensifier λίαν, "exceedingly" (cf. 6:51; 9:3; 16:2), emphasize the attractive power of Jesus by indicating how early he must get up and leave to avoid the crowds (a better explanation than saying that Mark is trying to set the following material apart from a preceding "ideal day" in Capernaum, for then why the focus on earliness?). Ἐξῆλθεν, "he went out," refers to Jesus' exit from Capernaum and from the house of Simon and Andrew there (cf. vv 21, 29); for Mark uses this verb primarily and perhaps exclusively for exit from enclosed spaces, such as a house (1:35, 38; 2:12, 13; 6:1, 10; 9:30; cf. "getting up from there" [ἐκεῖθεν ἀναστάς] for exit from a house [7:24 with 7:17; 10:1 with 9:33]), a room (6:24; 14:26), a courtyard (14:68), a tomb (16:8), the temple (11:11), a synagogue (1:28, 29, 45 [cf. 39]; 3:6), a city (1:35, 38), a boat (5:2; 6:54), a human body (1:25, 26; 5:8, 13, 30; 7:29, 30; 9:25, 26, 29), and regional boundaries (7:31). It remains unclear whence some exits are made; but presumably Jesus' natural family go out from their house or town (3:21), the sower goes out from his house (4:3), the Twelve go out from a house into which Jesus summoned them (6:12 with 7), the Pharisees from their houses or towns (8:11), Jesus and his disciples from Bethsaida and Bethany or whatever house they may have been staying in there (8:27; 11:12; 14:16; cf. 14:3), and Jesus' arresters from the temple or the city of Jerusalem (14:48; cf. 14:10, 26, 49). Ἀπῆλθεν, "he went away," refers to Jesus' departure from the crowd (cf. vv 32-34), for Mark consistently uses this verb for going away from people (see the concordance s.v. ἀπέρχομαι). The doubling of verbs and the adding of the phrase, "to a deserted place," increase the emphasis on Jesus' magnetism by underscoring the distance he must put between himself and the crowds if he is to pray. Mark may mention Jesus' praying but omit its content to underline the closeness of Jesus as Son to God as Father. Or Mark may want his audience to see in Jesus' praying (cf. 6:46) some evidence of godliness, as opposed to dying a criminal's death by crucifixion; but that point is much more certain in Luke's parallel. Or

Mark may want this evidence of Jesus' piety to forestall suspicion that Jesus is a charlatanic magician (see the following notes).

1:36-37 *(Luke 4:42bcd)* "Simon and the ones with him" (apparently Andrew, James, and John — cf. vv 16-20, 29) do not speak on behalf of the crowd. They simply report, "All are seeking you." Jesus' saying to them, "Let us go elsewhere . . . ," presumes that they are already his disciples. Thus their hunting him down gives evidence of the continuing effect of his call to follow him (cf. vv 17, 21, 29 and extrabiblical materials cited by V. K. Robbins, *Jesus the Teacher* 106-7). It also prepares for the main point, viz., that the people's seeking Jesus demonstrates his magnetism, which is due to the authority of his teaching and the wonder of his healings and exorcisms, already described. That "all" are seeking him emphasizes the extent of his magnetism in Capernaum. The position of the subject πάντες, "all," before its verb intensifies this emphasis; and the historical present tense of λέγουσιν, "they say," dramatizes the statement concerning his magnetism by drawing readers into the event, by making it seem as though they were there at the time. The power to attract large crowds of people characterizes divine men (see Philostr. *VA* 4.1, 24; 8.21; Iambl. *VP* 6, 30; Porph. *VP* 19-20; Empedocles *Purifications* 102[112]; and other passages cited by L. Bieler, *ΘΕΙΟΣ ANHP* 1. 122-29, esp. 122-23; M. Hengel, *Charismatic Leader* 25-27; but avoid the passages in *PGM* cited in this connection by M. Smith, *Clement* 224, for all of them contain charms for attracting a lover and therefore do not match Jesus' attraction of large crowds).

1:38 *(Luke 4:43)* Jesus' statement, "Let us go elsewhere to the neighboring market towns in order that I may preach there, too; for to this purpose I came out," indicates again that he refuses to let his power lie dormant. But this time the accent stresses his widening the sphere of his powerful activity outside Capernaum rather than his concentrating that activity in Capernaum (cf. the comments on v 29). The historical present tense of λέγει, "he says," and the forward position of "to this purpose" strengthen this accent. As usual, the hortatory subjunctive of ἄγω takes the present tense (ἄγωμεν, "let us go"), strengthening the accent yet further (contrast the unemphatic aorist hortatory subjunctive διέλθωμεν, "let us go through," in 4:35; also 9:5, and cf. the notes on 1:3). After pericopes concerning the powerfulness of Jesus' call (vv 16-20), of his teaching and exorcism (vv 21-28), and of his healings and exorcisms (vv 29-34), Mark now comes back to Jesus' preaching (cf. v 14), but by-passes its subject matter to concentrate exclusively on its magnetic effect (contrast v 15).

1:39 *(Matt 4:23; Luke 4:44)* Now that Jesus has come out of Capernaum, Mark drops ἐξ-, "out of," from -ἦλθεν, "came" (cf. v 39 with vv 35, 38), to produce an echo of v 14 (cf. ἦλθεν κηρύσσων . . . εἰς ὅλην τὴν Γαλιλαίαν, "he came preaching . . . in the whole of Galilee" [v 39], with ἦλθεν . . . εἰς τὴν Γαλιλαίαν κηρύσσων, "he came . . . into Galilee preaching" [v 14]). Along with Jesus' preaching go exorcisms, just as an exorcism went along with his authoritative teaching in vv 21-28. Since Jesus did not mention exorcisms in his preceding statement of purpose (v 38), their addition here in a narrative statement shows that they constitute an editorially important demonstration of his power. The chiastically forward position of τὰ δαιμόνια, "the demons" (contrast the rearward position taken by the complements of "preaching"), highlights this demonstration. "In their synagogues in the whole of Galilee" provides a further link with vv 21-28 (see the comments on vv 23-24 for the meaning of "their" with "synagogues"). As in v 28, the addition of "whole" to "Galilee" underscores the breadth of Jesus' powerful activity. So also does the asyndetic pairing of "in the whole of Galilee" with "in their synagogues."

1:40 *(Matt 8:1-2; Luke 5:12; cf. Matt 10:8; 11:5; Luke 7:22; 17:12-21)* The remarkable cleansing of a leper now joins the just-mentioned preaching and exorcisms to demonstrate Jesus' authority and power. The omission of particulars concerning place and time focuses attention on the cleansing as such. The historical present tense of ἔρχεται, "comes," stresses the leper's desperate plight. "Beseeching him and falling on his knees" adds a double pathos that prepares for Jesus' compassion. Additionally, these participles imply the authority of Jesus as a figure to whom another makes supplication and shows reverence. "If you will" points to Jesus' authority, "you are able to cleanse me" to his ability (cf. Wis 12:18 with respect to God's ability to do what he wills; also Pss 115:3[113:11]; 135:6). The forward position of με, "me," increases the pathos yet again. "To cleanse" means "to *make* clean," as only Jesus can do, not "to *declare* clean," as only a priest can do (*m. Neg.* 3:1 — but without any exercise of miraculous power). We should note that the leper's words do not themselves make a request that Jesus cleanse him (the notion of request being only implied in παρακαλῶν, "beseeching"); rather, they make a statement that Jesus has the ability to cleanse him (contrast the element of doubt, which Jesus will have to overcome, in 9:22-23). Here lies Mark's interest — in Jesus' ability. The view that leprosy is like death and that cleansing a leper (Num 12:15 LXX; 4 Kgdms 5:14 LXX) is as marvelous as raising the dead, something that only God can do (Num 12:10-12; 2 Kgs 5:7; Josephus *Ant.* 3.11.3 §264; *b. Sanh.* 47a; Str-B 4. 750-51), shows how great this ability must be, and that to have it Jesus must be the Son of God.

1:41-42 *(Matt 8:3; Luke 5:13)* Mark now begins to show that the leper's confidence in Jesus' ability to cleanse him is well founded. The reference to Jesus' compassion portrays him in a light that will reveal his coming crucifixion to be undeserved. The narrator is using his omniscience of Jesus' inner feelings to put across a point of view sympathetic to Jesus, which is literarily more important than Jesus' compassion toward the leper. Jesus' stretching out his hand gestures his will to cleanse the leper (cf. numerous occurrences of this gesture in the story of the Exodus [Exodus 1–15]). Asyndeton in the coordination of compassion and stretching out the hand lends emphasis to both (M. Reiser, *Syntax und Stil* 158-60). Jesus' touching the leper exhibits his power to cleanse him (cf. the comments on v 31). Jesus has power so great that Mark does not even bother to note that contact with a leper ordinarily transfers uncleanness and is therefore prohibited (Lev 5:3; 13:1-46; Num 5:2; Josephus *Ag.Ap.* 1.31 §281). "I will" gives oral confirmation of Jesus' compassion. "Be cleansed" adds his powerful word to his powerful touch. The historical present tense of λέγει, "he says," emphasizes this powerful word. "Immediately" furthers the emphasis by describing the departure of the leprosy: it cannot stay even an instant more, the cleansing takes place quick as a flash (cf. O. Weinreich, *Antike Heilungswunder* 197-98; M. Wojciechowski in *BZ* nf 33 [1989] 118-19; B. Blackburn, *Theios Anēr* 221-22). After the leper's plea for cleansing and Jesus' command, "Be cleansed," the statement, "And he was cleansed," might seem to suffice. But the intervening statement, "And immediately the leprosy left him," certifies a physical miracle as distinct from a ritual purification. The duality of the statements concerning the leprosy's departure and the leper's cleansing underlines the miracle (for similar duality, see 3:5; 4:39; 5:29; 6:42; 7:35; 8:25; cf. 1:31; 2:12; 5:42; 10:52).

1:43-44 *(Matt 8:4; Luke 5:14)* Jesus' growling (ἐμβριμησάμενος) stresses the forcefulness with which he now instructs and sends the healed leper to the priest. The growling hardly represents Jesus' working himself up to perform a miracle (cf. the following note on the v.l. ὀργισθείς, "becoming angry," in v 41), for the miracle has already taken place (contrast John 11:33-38). To think that Jesus growls in anticipation of the ex-leper's disobeying the command not to tell anybody is to read foreknowledge into the text without other support. Besides, the command to silence appears to be consequent on Jesus' growling rather than his growling consequent on violation of the command. The suggestion that he growls because the leper breaks the Law by coming close to him founders on Jesus' willingness to heal the leper by touching him, as does also the suggestion that Jesus growls because contamination from the leper has made him unable to enter any city openly. Verse 45 will attribute this inability to fame, not to uncleanness; and it would be strange if people were to flock to a man so unclean that he cannot enter their cities. He hardly growls because the incident has put a stop to his ministry in the city of the leper, for it was Jesus' purpose to itinerate anyway. Growling at the results of sin as seen in leprosy resonates with nothing else in the passage; and such growling should have come before the healing, not afterward. Likewise, growling at miracle-mongering as opposed to cross-taking would have come at the time of the leper's plea. The granting of a miracle looks the opposite of such growling, anyway; and it is too early in Mark to introduce the theme of cross-taking as a backdrop (contrast 8:34 and onward). We do best, therefore, to say that just as Mark here uses ἐξέβαλεν not in the negative sense of expulsion (as in 1:34, 39; 3:15, 22, 23; 5:40; 6:13; 7:26; 9:18, 28, 38, 47; 11:15; cf. 12:8) but in the positive sense of thrusting out (as already in v 12), so also he uses ἐμβριμησάμενος, which goes with ἐξέβαλεν and λέγει, not to express displeasure but to emphasize the forcefulness of the thrusting out and of the instructions which accompany it (v 44). "Immediately" and the historical present tense of λέγει, "he says," increase this emphasis. So also do numerous features of the directly quoted words: (1) the unnecessary and therefore emphatic ὅρα, "see [that]," which goes with εἴπῃς, "you say"; (2) the present tense of the imperative in ὅρα; (3) the double negative μηδενὶ μηδέν, "nothing to no one" (or, in good English, "nothing to anyone"); (4) the putting of this double negative before its verb εἴπῃς; (5) the strong adversative ἀλλά, "rather"; (6) the present tense (as usual) of the imperative ὕπαγε, "go" (cf. the notes on 1:3); (7) the asyndetic combination of "go" and "show yourself to the priest" (see M. Reiser, *Syntax und*

Stil 152-54; cf. 6:38 ℵ B D L W *f*¹ 33 *pc* b c ff² sy^s,p; 10:21; 16:7; and contrast 5:19, 34; 6:38 A Θ *f*¹³ Majority Text lat sy^h); and (8) the position of σεαυτόν, "yourself," before δεῖξον, "show." Why does Mark lay so much emphasis on Jesus' forcefulness? The answer is that the greater the forcefulness, the more startling the ex-leper's doing better than Jesus instructed him to do — and therefore the greater the glory that accrues to Jesus.

Offering sacrifices would not constitute evidence to support the ex-leper's cleanness in the eyes of the priest. Rather, showing himself to the priest, who will inspect his body, would provide that evidence (for the phraseology cf. Lev 13:49 LXX, but with regard to showing a mark of leprosy to the priest). The offering of sacrifices is to come about because the priest would be convinced by the inspection. For others, who would not have inspected the ex-leper's body, the offering of sacrifices would constitute a testimony that the inspecting priest had pronounced him clean. Hence, we read of a testimony "to them" rather than "to him." The indefinite third person plural refers to people in general; for Jesus makes no reference to other priests, and at this point in a miracle story we expect a general audience of admirers to see an authentication of the miracle. Thus the testimony that people would receive in the form of Mosaically prescribed sacrifices offered by an ex-leper whom a priest will have declared clean — this testimony would authenticate to people the miracle of cleansing that Jesus has performed, just as the convulsing of the demoniac and the inarticulate loud cry of the unclean spirit authenticated to those in the synagogue the exorcism in vv 23-26 and just as the serving at table of Simon's mother-in-law authenticated to those in the house her miraculous healing in vv 29-31 (not to mention other examples from later in Mark and from the other gospels). The command to silence, then, has the purpose of hurrying up the testimony — i.e. of drawing an authentication of the miracle as close as possible to the miracle itself — for effect (cf. 2 Kgs 4:29; Luke 10:4b; and extra-biblical parallels cited by H. J. Ebeling, *Messiasgeheimnis* 136-39, but not for holy silence as thought by Ebeling). Ultimately, this purpose runs exactly counter to keeping the cleansing secret till the death and resurrection of Jesus. Mark does not write *"till* you go show yourself to the priest . . . ,"* not because he wants to make the command to silence last till Jesus' death and resurrection in accordance with a messianic secret, but because to write such a "till"-clause would put the accent on silence whereas Mark wants it to fall on testimony. The length of the journey from Galilee to the temple in Jerusalem gives point to the avoidance of delay by saying nothing to anyone. The quicker the authentication, the better.

1:45 *(Luke 5:15-16)* As everywhere else in Mark, the definite article (or a pronoun) plus δέ, "but," indicates a change in subject, here from Jesus as speaker (v 44) to the ex-leper as preacher and publisher (see K. Aland, *Vollständige Konkordanz* s.v. δέ c-f for Mark). Ἐξελθών, "going out," complements ἐξέβαλεν, "thrust out" (v 43). That the object of thrusting out is the subject of going out also in 7:26, 29-30; 9:18, 25-26, 28-29 confirms the identity of the one who goes out in v 45 as the ex-leper, whom Jesus thrust out in v 43, not as Jesus, whom some have taken as the one who goes out. Ἐξελθών also implies that the cleansing of the leper took place in a synagogue; for v 39 located Jesus' activities in synagogues, and Mark uses ἐξέρχομαι for exit from enclosed spaces (see the comments on v 35). Lev 13:46; Num 5:2 to the contrary notwithstanding, b. Neg. 13:12 shows the possibility of a leper's attendance at synagogue (cf. ἐξέβαλεν, "thrust out" [v 43], which fits a setting indoors though 1:12 shows that it does not require one). "Began to preach" recalls Jesus' going out to preach in v 38 (cf. vv 35, 39). But the ex-leper's preaching is strengthened by πολλά, "much," and by διαφημίζειν τὸν λόγον, "to publish the word." Formally, preaching and publishing represent disobedience to Jesus' preceding instruction; but materially they represent a spontaneous effect of his healing power, the cure being so happy a demonstration of it that the ex-leper cannot contain himself despite the forcefulness of Jesus' instructions (so also 5:20 and esp. 7:36, both using κηρύσσω, "preach," as here). Thus the offering of sacrifices for a testimony is replaced by a more glowing testimony. In 2:2; 4:14, 15 (bis), 16, 17, 18, 19, 20, 33, "the word" will occur as an alternative for "the good news" with verbs other than "preach." The good news is that God's rule has drawn near (1:14-15). But in 5:36; 8:32; 9:10; 10:22; 11:29; 14:39 "the word" will occur for various individual statements that do not proclaim this good news (cf. 12:13). The present text gives us no reason to think that the ex-leper preaches the good news about the nearness of God's rule. Hence, he must be publishing the powerful statement that Jesus spoke to him, "I will; be cleansed" (v 41). (Mark's usage does not favor "the matter" as the meaning of τὸν λόγον [see 9:10 for a possible but unlikely exception]; and it would not make good sense for the ex-leper to publish Jesus' instruction to him.)

"So that he was no longer able to go openly into a city, but was outside in deserted places; and people kept coming to him from everywhere" brings the pericope back to Jesus' magnetism. The introduction of αὐτόν, "he," as the subject of μηκέτι . . . δύνασθαι, "was no longer able," reconfirms that the ex-leper has been the preacher and publisher; for in accordance with Greek grammar, Mark elsewhere introduces an accusative subject into infinitival phrases beginning with ὥστε, "so that," only to indicate a different subject from that of the main verb (2:2 [if τά, "the things [area]," is a subjective accusative], 12; 3:20; 4:1, 32, 37; 9:26; 15:5; cf. 3:10) whereas he does not introduce an accusative subject of the infinitive when the subject of the main verb carries over, as it would do here if Jesus had been the preacher and publisher (1:27; 2:2 [if τά is an adverbial accusative]). The placement of αὐτόν before δύνασθαι emphasizes the change in subjects (cf. 4:1; 9:26, but contrast 2:2 [if τά is a subjective accusative], 12; 3:20; 4:32, 37; 15:5; cf. 3:10; and see J. Swetnam in Bib 68 [1987] 245-49 for literature supporting Jesus as the continuing subject and for refutation of the arguments in that literature). "Deserted places" recalls the "deserted place" where Jesus prayed in v 35, and people's coming to him from everywhere recalls Simon's statement in v 37 that all are seeking Jesus and the statement in v 40: "a leper comes to him." The imperfect tense of ἤρχοντο, "kept coming," heightens the effect of the statement that even though Jesus stays outside the cities, people are still coming to him (cf. 2:13). Mark delights in publicity, not in secrecy, for publicity magnifies the impact of Jesus' activities. At first, "no longer . . . openly" seems to imply that Jesus does enter cities incognito. But the strong adversative ἀλλ', "rather," indicates that he does not enter cities at all. Therefore "no longer . . . openly" does not apply to the period during which he was staying in deserted places. Instead, it anticipates the way in which he will enter Capernaum incognito at the end of that period. The emphatic forward position of the adverb in the Greek text stresses his magnetism, which will lead him not to enter the city openly lest he be mobbed. Meanwhile, the deserted places where he is staying turn into centers of population because of the throngs that stream to him (cf. 6:32-33; 7:24). (Whether the inconcinnity of "no longer . . . openly" in its own sentence arises out of late addition to that sentence, regarded as originally independent from 2:1, or belongs to the original version of the sentence in anticipation of 2:1, regarded as tied to 1:45 from the very start, we cannot tell. Taking 1:45 as purely redactional would allow the latter.) Staying in deserted places does not contradict going into synagogues to preach in 1:39; rather, it demonstrates the success of Jesus' preaching in synagogues. Mark wants his audience to think in terms of chronological succession: one thing leads to another.

NOTES

As teaching was followed by exorcism and then by healing (see vv 21-22, 23-28, 29-34), so now preaching is followed by exorcism and then by healing (vv 35-39a, 39b, and 40-45). For Romans, πρωΐ, "early [morning]" (v 35), could refer to the last of the four watches of the night and ὀψία, "evening" (mentioned in v 32), to the first of them (cf. 13:35). The disparity between "nighttime" in 1:35 and "when the sun had risen" in 16:2 blocks an association of the two passages because of their sharing πρωΐ and λίαν, "exceedingly." Also, "nighttime" (ἔννυχα) defines ἀναστάς here in v 35 as getting up from sleep. Therefore the present passage does not foreshadow the resurrection of Jesus (against W. Schmithals 133-34).

Against S. E. Dowd (*Prayer* 117-22), it is doubtful that Mark wants his audience to think of Jesus as praying for power to perform miracles and exorcisms. Jesus has already performed many of them, apparently without prayer (vv 23-34). The descent of the Spirit into him would seem to have already supplied him with the requisite power (v 11; cf. 3:22-30), and the only Jesuanic prayer whose content Mark records does not contain a request for power (14:32-42). Dowd (op. cit. 130-45) may stand on firmer ground to argue that Mark's portrayal of Jesus as a man of prayer implies that he is no magician trying to force God's hand to do a magician's will. It does not follow, however, that Jesus is portrayed as praying for God to will the performance of miracles and exorcisms through Jesus. In fact, when a leper appeals to Jesus' will, Jesus asserts it, not God's will (1:40-41).

The omission of Jesus' praying in the parallel Luke 4:42 does not provide enough support for the suggestion that this element is a late gloss in Mark, for Luke does not omit it so much as he delays it till 5:16, perhaps to rivet attention in 4:42 solely on extension of the good news, a very prominent theme in Luke-Acts. It is not Jewish custom to pray so early in the morning as Jesus does here; hence, the usual cross-references to Pss 5:4; 88:14, which speak of prayer in the morning but not so extremely early that it is still nighttime, are not entirely appropriate (cf. Gen 22:3, where prayer, too, is missing; but see Ps 119:147a for praying before dawn in an emergency). "There" links the clause, "and there he was praying," with the preceding one, "and he went away [ἀπ-] into a deserted place." Thus v 35 does not say or imply that Jesus "went out" (ἐξ-) for the purpose of praying, and there is not even the slightest contradiction with the statement in v 38 that he "went out" (ἐξ-) for the purpose of preaching. That he preaches throughout the whole of Galilee (v 39) makes it uncontradictory of his purpose to preach elsewhere that he should be back in Capernaum at 2:1. By then he *has* preached elsewhere, and extensively at that. From these standpoints, then, we need not see anything more than exit from Capernaum and a house there in "I have come out" (cf. the following notes).

If Jesus has come out to preach elsewhere, why has he not taken the two pairs of brothers with him, for he told them to follow him (vv 16-20)? They do follow him. They hunt him down. He sets the course and pace. They must catch up and keep up (cf. 10:32). Mark is uninterested in answering whether they know a deserted place where Jesus habitually prays, whether his praying aloud helps them find him, and like questions. Because the compound subject Σίμων καὶ οἱ μετ' αὐτοῦ, "Simon and the ones with him," follows its verb κατεδίωξεν, "hunted down," the verb is singular to agree with the first member of the compound (see the notes on 13:3 and L. Morris, *John* 592, n. 63). The two subsequent verbs, having the same compound subject, take the plural (εὗρον, "[they] found," and λέγουσιν, "[they] say"). In and of itself κατεδίωξεν does not carry a hostile or otherwise negative connotation (see, e.g., good connotations in the LXX of Pss 22:6; 37:21; cf. Polyb. 6.42.1 — against M. A. Tolbert, *Sowing the Gospel* 138, 196). The present context does not favor a hostile or otherwise negative connotation. Jesus does not react against being hunted down. In fact, we might even think that Mark uses the strong verb διώκω and prefixes a perfective κατά to emphasize that Jesus has such a hold on those whom he has told to follow him that when he slips away they go after him till they find him.

Because of other negative uses of ζητέω in Mark, a number of observers see a negative connotation in everybody's seeking Jesus (v 37) and tease a Marcan polemic against miracle-mongering out of that connotation (see, e.g., R. Schlarb in *ZNW* 81 [1990] 155-70, esp. 158-59). But in every other use except one, the negative connotation comes from associated expressions (seeking to test, seize, betray, destroy, kill — 3:32 with 21; 8:11-12; 11:18; 12:12; 14:1, 11, 55); and the remaining use is not negative, for the seeking is rewarded with the happy announcement of Jesus' resurrection and with a commission to go and tell (16:6). In support of a negative connotation here, D. E. Nineham (84-85) argues from Mark's "pointed" avoidance of the term "disciples." But Mark will not use that term till 2:15. Are we to imagine, then, that every preceding reference to Simon and Andrew, James and John is incriminating? And if Nineham's argument is correct, how is it that they will definitely come in for criticism after Mark has started using "disciples"? And if Mark means that Jesus' leaving to preach elsewhere implies his rejection of people's seeking him as a wonder-worker, or even implies a subordination of wonder-working to preaching, it is passing strange that Mark immediately associates Jesus' preaching with more exorcisms (v 39) and follows up with another miracle-story (vv 40-45). "Simon and the ones with him" simply avoids mentioning all the names a third time (cf. vv 16, 29), though it also agrees with the Papian tradition that Mark got his information from Simon Peter.

By echoing ἐξῆλθεν, "he went out," in v 35, ἐξῆλθον, "I have come out," in v 38 refers to Jesus' having come out from Capernaum and the house of Simon and Andrew there (though some interpreters read into the expression larger meanings, such as coming out of obscurity, coming forth as a prophet from God [cf. Luke 4:43], or even coming forth from a preincarnate being with God [cf. John 8:42; 13:3; 16:27-30; 17:8]). Moreover, since Jesus' having come out in v 38 refers to his coming out in v 35, no tension exists between two different exits, the first for prayer in a deserted place, the second for preaching in neighboring market towns. Praying in a deserted place is associated with Jesus' coming *away* (ἀπ-), not with his coming *out* (ἐκ-; see the foregoing notes), and thus leaves the latter to be associated with preaching. The purpose to preach elsewhere suffices to explain why Jesus left Capernaum; there is no need to cast any aspersion on the seeking of Jesus by all in Capernaum. The text does not.

Though topographical movement normally starts a new pericope in Mark, such movement in v 39 carries out the intention expressed in v 38 and carries on a movement already begun in v 35. Therefore we should probably not see a paragraph-break between vv 38 and 39. Ἐξῆλθον, "I have come out," in v 38 may favor the reading ἦλθεν, "he went," in v 39 to carry the thought forward. A scribe would probably have hesitated to replace an original ἦν, "was" (so the v.l.), with ἦλθεν very soon after ἐξῆλθον. The echo of v 14 in v 39 likewise favors ἐξῆλθον to the disadvantage of ἦν. Mark's liking the periphrastic verbal construction (ἦν plus κηρύσσων would produce "was preaching") provides scant support for the v.l., for that construction never appears in his eleven other uses of κηρύσσω. Hence, the v.l. looks like parallel influence from Luke 4:44, where ἦν leaves all the emphasis on preaching rather than dividing it with going.

The use of "there" with "preach" in v 38, the placement of the εἰς-phrases regarding synagogues and Galilee in v 39 (contrast the placement in 1:14), and the use of locative εἰς-phrases with "preach" also in 13:10; 14:9; Luke 4:44; 1 Thess 2:9 (see the notes on 13:10) favor a construal of the εἰς-phrases in v 39 with κηρύσσων ("and he came preaching in their synagogues in the whole of Galilee") rather than a construal with ἦλθεν ("and he came, preaching, into their synagogues into the whole of Galilee") or an assignment of the first phrase to the second verbal and the second phrase to the first verbal ("and he came, preaching in their synagogues, into the whole of Galilee"). Matt 4:23; 9:35; Luke 4:44 construe the synagogues with preaching (though Matthew substitutes teaching and delays preaching); but to construe Galilee with Jesus' travel, Matthew advances "in the whole of Galilee" to a position right after "he was going around" and ahead of "teaching." Luke sticks by Mark's association of Galilee with preaching, but substitutes Judea. The asyndetic pairing of εἰς-phrases typifies the penchant for duality evident throughout Mark, and this particular instance of duality favors an adverbial construal of "in the whole of Galilee" with "preaching" instead of an adjectival construal with "their synagogues." The notion that because preaching in synagogues characterized Christian preaching in the Diaspora, v 39 reflects this practice rather than what Jesus actually did runs into problems with his teaching in the synagogues at Capernaum (vv 21-28) and Nazareth (6:1-6a parr.; cf. also 3:1 parr.; Matt 9:35; Luke 13:10; John 18:20). If he taught in those synagogues — and it would take an excessively sceptical spirit to deny that he did — we have no reason to deny that he preached and taught in others. Of course, preaching and teaching in synagogues does not rule out preaching and teaching elsewhere, too (see 1:4; 2:13; 4:1; 6:34; 8:31; 9:31; 10:1; 11:17; 12:35; 14:49 for locales in the wilderness and deserted places, at the seaside, on the road, and in the temple). There is no rhythmic alternation of positive and negative in the stories of 1:21–2:12, for the first three feature the negative leaving of an unclean spirit, a fever, and leprosy, whereas the fourth story features the positive restoration of a hand but also the negative leaving of sins (ἀφίημι; cf. 1:31).

The distance of Galilee from the temple in Jerusalem need not imply an originally Judean setting for the story of the leper. To reenter society a healed leper has to do the necessaries at that temple wherever he lives, and this one does not go to the temple. Biblical leprosy includes skin diseases besides Hansen's disease (see references in R. H. Gundry, *Matthew* 139), but the desperation of the man in the present story favors that Hansen's disease is here in view (cf. the difference of opinion between D. A. Bennahum [in *Koroth* 9 (1985) 86-89], who doubts that biblical leprosy includes Hansen's disease, and J. Zias [ibid. 242-48], who takes the opposite view). See Leviticus 13–14 for the law of leprosy, in particular 13:45-46 for the requirement that lepers keep their distance from other people and yell, "Unclean! Unclean!" (see further W. L. Lane 84-86; J. Gnilka 1. 92). Mark pays no attention to this leper's breaking that requirement in approaching Jesus. That the only healing of a leper in the OT took place at the word of a prophet (Elisha — 2 Kgs 5:1-14; see B. Blackburn, *Theios Anēr* 188-89, on other healings of leprosy) need not imply that the present leper's healing portrays Jesus as a prophet. Though Mark does not make the cleansing of the leper an explicit symbol of cleansing from sin, the belief that leprosy is a punishment for sin (Num 12:9-12; 2 Kgs 5:27; 15:5; 2 Chr 26:19-23; Str-B 1. 228-29; 2. 136, 196-97; 3. 767, 794; 4. 747-50; G. F. Moore, *Judaism* 2. 149, 248), the requirement of a guilt offering and a sin offering in the rite of cleansing a leper (Lev 14:10-32), the use of "cleanse" for removal of sin (Ps 51[50]:4; Acts 15:9; 2 Cor 7:1; Eph 5:26; 1 John 1:7, 9 et passim), and Mark's repeating the matter of Jesus' ability with regard to cleansing and forgiveness (1:40; 2:7) may well have led to putting the present story where it is as an appropriate lead into the controversy over Jesus' forgiving the sins of a paralytic (2:1-12).

As in the case of fever, the going away of the leprosy does not imply that the disease has a demonic cause (contrast *b. Ketub.* 61b); for Mark mentions no demon or unclean spirit (contrast his practice elsewhere), and an exorcistic command is missing (cf. 1:42 with 1:31). The theory of E. Lohmeyer (44-46) that Mark has conflated two earlier versions, one featuring Jesus' angry expulsion of a leprous spirit plus sending the man to a priest, the other his compassionate healing by touch and word plus a command to secrecy, has suffered enough at the hands of other commentators. See E. Haenchen (94-95) against the hypothesis that in the original story the leper asked Jesus to *declare* him clean even though he was still suffering from leprosy. The evidence cited by C. H. Cave in *NTS* 25 (1978-79) 245-50 for a layman's declaring a leper clean requires a priest to announce the cleansing even though the layman is prompting him (CD 13:5-7; *m. Neg.* 3:1; *b. Neg.* 3:1). F. Neirynck (in *ETL* 61 [1985] 153-60) and D. F. Wright in *Gospel Perspectives* 5. 207-21, esp. 216-17) show that *PEger.* 2, frg. 1 recto (text in K. Aland, *Synopsis* 60; A. Huck and H. Greeven, *Synopsis* 44, n. 57), does not reflect pre-Marcan non-canonical tradition, but the synoptics.

In v 40 we may need to omit καὶ γονυπετῶν (καί), "and falling on his knees (and)," with B D W *al.* But 10:17 favors retention. Under the hypothesis of Marcan priority, Matt 8:2 and Luke 5:12 also favor retention; for the similar but different expressions there look like redactions of the phrase here. Scribes would likely have conformed to Matthew's or Luke's wording had they been inserting the phrase into Mark's text. The abundance of καί's and of parallel endings in -ων increases the possibility of homoioteleuton (see also M. Wojciechowski in *BZ* nf 33 [1989] 114).

In v 41 the reading ὀργισθείς, "becoming angry," in place of σπλαγχνισθείς, "feeling compassion," has the support of only D it[a,d,ff2,r1] Ephraem. B. M. Metzger (*Textual Commentary* ad loc.) also notes that although the ascription of anger to Jesus might have offended copyists and led them to change an original ὀργισθείς to σπλαγχνισθείς, they did not change Jesus' anger to compassion in 3:5; 10:14 (so that it is unlikely they did so here); and ἐμβριμησάμενος, taken in the sense of indignation (v 43), may have suggested anger as more compatible with indignation than compassion is (cf. 10:14). Metzger also notes the possibility that similar Aramaic words were confused (cf. G. Dalman, *Words* 65). The occurrence of σπλαγχνίζομαι in 6:34; 8:2; 9:22 may favor that word here, too, though it could be argued that copyists were influenced by those passages. Such influence would have to be prospective, however. The agreement of the parallels Matt 8:2-4; Luke 5:12-16 in omitting any sort of emotion does not imply their objection to an original ὀργισθείς, for this kind of agreement against Mark is common with regard to unobjectionable terminology. Right here, Matthew and Luke agree in omitting v 43, too (see R. H. Gundry, *Matthew* 139, for the possibility of Matthean influence on Luke and for a possible reason behind Matthew's omitting the compassion even though he usually keeps it).

The understanding of ὀργισθείς as Jesus' working himself up to perform a miracle does not favor this v.l., for the ascription of such behavior to Jesus might just as easily come from copyists who expect a miracle-worker to act that way as from Mark or the tradition behind him (against R. Pesch [1. 144], who refers to Mark 7:34; John 11:33, 38; *Acts Phil.* 84; Philostr. *VA* 4.20). In view of Jesus' own prayer to God, "Not what I will; rather, what you [will]" (14:36), anger at the leper's "if you will" seems unlikely. Nowhere else in Mark or the rest of the NT do we read of anger at disease as the result of sin, the verbs in 7:34 and John 11:33, 38 being different and subject to other interpretations. But if after all we should read ὀργισθείς, the word would add to Mark's emphasis on the authority of Jesus. Even so, it would overinterpret the passage to say that Mark presents the leprosy as a demonic scourge overcome by that authority. No demon is mentioned. No exorcistic command is quoted. And the leprosy goes "away" (ἀπῆλθεν; cf. the fever's leaving, ἀφῆκεν, in v 31); it does not come "out" (ἐξ-), as a demon does.

The leper's anonymity, like the anonymity of Peter's mother-in-law in vv 29-31, leaves the spotlight on Jesus. For the translation of ἐμβριμησάμενος by "growling," see H. C. Kee in *JBL* 92 (1973) 418, n. 123. E. F. F. Bishop (*Jesus of Palestine* 89-90) thinks somewhat similarly of an inarticulate "rapid breathing out between the teeth." Either way, a negative kind of body-language backs up the verbal negatives to follow. The association with Jesus' growling favors a connotation of forcefulness and eliminates any need to suppose that ἐμβριμησάμενος αὐτῷ inadequately translates an Aramaic substratum referring to Jesus' becoming angry within himself (cf. M. Jastrow, *Dictionary* s.v. זעף; John 11:33 and esp. 38; see M. Wojciechowski in *BZ* nf 33 [1989] 116; M. H. Marco in *EstBib* 31 [1972] 420-21). He thrusts out the healed leper (αὐτόν, "him" — cf. 1:12; 5:40; 11:15; 12:8); he does not cast out the leprosy (which would require αὐτήν, "it," to agree in gender with λέπρα, "leprosy") or a leprous demon (which would require αὐτό, "it," to agree in gender with δαιμόνιον, "demon"). Nowhere in Mark is growling associated with exorcism, and here growling comes after the departure of the leprosy. So once again we can hardly think of the emotionally charged exorcism of a leprous demon, unless for the sake of the demonic hypothesis an earlier version is imagined that lacked the departure of the leprosy (or noted the departure of a demon instead) and put the pronoun in a different gender (cf. S. Eitrem, *Some Notes* 51-53).

On the non-Semitic construction ὅρα . . . εἴπῃς in v 44, see E. C. Maloney, *Semitic Interference* 75. The commanded silence comes too soon to be interpreted as holy silence in the presence of the Lord. It is a matter of haste, not of holiness. D.-A. Koch (*Bedeutung* 73, n. 3) observes that since v 44 functions as a demonstration of the healing, Jesus' respect for the Law need not provide the point of the verse. We may add that though a portrayal of Jesus as respectful of the Law might shield him in advance from criticisms lodged by the scribes and Pharisees in 2:1–3:6, the emphasis in 2:23–3:6 on his lordship over the Law and in 7:19 (in an editorial phrase) on his reversing the Law does not sit easily on this interpretation of Mark's present point. Besides, we have to wait till 2:23–3:6 for the question of the Law to arise. J. Gnilka (1. 91) thinks that Mark adds v 45 to change an originally apothegmatic story about Law-keeping into a missionizing miracle story. But Jesus' using a legally prohibited touch to heal the leper does not fit the allegedly original purpose very well. The leper's pleading and Jesus' compassion (or anger) fit the norms of a miracle story much better.

Elsewhere in the gospels "for a testimony" does not refer to a written statute (contrast Ps 80:5-6 LXX); therefore we should not take the phrase closely with the preceding subordinate clause as follows: "which Moses commanded for a statute to them." It is hard to accept the interpretation that Moses prescribed offerings as a testimony to Jesus (cf. John 5:45-47); for Jesus' sacrificial death, his predictions of it, and the Words of Institution will come much later in Mark's book (and, so far as we can tell, in Jesus' life as well).

Therefore the ex-leper's action of offering what Moses commanded, not Moses' command itself, would constitute the testimony. Since the testimony would go to people in general, not to the priest or to the priesthood, and since the people have done nothing bad or good or indeed anything at all, we have no reason to take αὐτοῖς either in the negative sense, "against them," or in the positive sense, "in their favor." The present context requires only the neutral sense, "to them." Even the putting of εἰς μαρτύριον αὐτοῖς shortly before a batch of controversy stories (2:1–3:6) does not favor the negative sense; for in those stories it will be the scribes, Pharisees, and Herodians who will oppose Jesus and plot against his life. By contrast, it is people in general who are to receive the testimony. To say that the priesthood is to receive it would still not require the negative sense, "against them"; for thus far they have done nothing against Jesus, nor will they in the upcoming controversy stories. The context of 6:11 will require the negative sense (cf. Luke 9:5; Jas 5:3; but see Gen 21:30 LXX for the positive sense). The meaning at 13:9 is uncertain, though the reference in the next verse to preaching the good news among all the nations will tend toward the meaning "to them" rather than "against them." Furthermore, it is questionable that Jesus means his disciples to testify before governors and kings against those who give them over to those authorities rather than preaching the good news to those authorities, too. C. E. B. Cranfield (95) surveys other views.

Since the main controversy over the Mosaic Law in the early church has to do with whether *Gentiles* must keep it, we may doubt that Mark or an earlier traditioner puts forward the present story in favor of Law-keeping. Moreover, the context of the story is more Christological than ecclesiastical or soteriological. The purpose of avoiding delay in authentication renders irrelevant or wrong various other suggestions, too, such as that the healed leper is to keep it quiet how the healing took place (E. Haenchen 95), that the healed leper is to keep the identity of Jesus as the miracle-worker secret rather than the miracle itself secret (A. Pilgaard as reported in *TLZ* 110 [1985] 734), and that the healed leper is to keep it quiet that Jesus has pronounced him clean so as to be able to get such pronouncement from a priest (G. Theissen, *Miracle Stories* 146, overlooking that Jesus' word of command, "Be cleansed," does not equate with a pronouncement of cleanness, "You are clean"). The ritual cleansing naturally has to follow the physical one (cf. esp. Lev 14:1-32; *b. Neg.* 8:2; J. D. M. Derrett, *Studies* 4. 5-6; and, for moral cleansing through the offering of sacrifice, Job 1:15 LXX). Other commands to silence will appear in 3:12; 5:43; 7:36; 8:26, 30; 9:9-10, and another breaking of such a command in 7:36. See R. A. Guelich 1. 76 against the attempt of U. Luz in *ZNW* 56 (1965) 9-30 to distinguish between a broken secret of Jesus' miracles and a kept secret of his true identity.

In v 45 K. L. Schmidt (*Rahmen* 66-67) ascribes ὥστε through ἦν to redactional addition. Others see the whole verse as redactional. There are other opinions, too. Ἤρξατο plus an infinitive, "he began to . . . ," is an Aramaism or a feature of κοινή Greek (J. C. Doudna, *Greek* 111-17) which Mark likes to use and in which the notion of beginning has no independent significance but makes some ado about the new thought of the following infinitive (J. A. Kleist 154-61; idem, *Memoirs* 169; M. Y.-H. Lee, *Jesus und die jüdische Autorität* 160). Mark also likes to use πολλά as an adverbial accusative, usually with verbs of speaking (see also 3:12; 4:2; 5:10, 23, 38, 43; 6:20, 34; 8:31; 9:12, 26; 15:3). R. A. Guelich (1. 72, n. g) uses 4:2; 6:34 to argue for an accusative of direct object; but there, too, we should see an adverbial accusative (cf. the comments ad loc.). Guelich (1. 73, 78, 79, 96) also detects a "suggestion of conflict" in "the rather ominous comment about Jesus' inability to enter any city publicly," and thus a setting of the stage for the controversy stories to follow in 2:1–3:6. But there is no such suggestion and the comment is not ominous; for Jesus' inability to enter any city publicly is due to adulation, not opposition.

According to a reconstruction by C. Myers (*Binding the Strong Man* 152-54), the leper had already gone to the priests, "who for some reason had rejected his petition [to be declared clean]," so that Jesus' command is a command to go back as a witness against them inasmuch as they control the entire apparatus of purity — but the strategy backfires when publication of his having incurred uncleanness through contact with leprosy makes it impossible for him to enter any city. This reconstruction requires too much imagination, especially in the positing of an earlier visit by the leper to the priests. Moreover, it overlooks the distinction between the singular of "the priest" and the plural of "them," which therefore appears not to refer to priests in general (cf. the foregoing comments). And once again it would be strange if people were to flock to a Jesus so unclean that he cannot enter their cities.

EXCURSUS ON 2:1–3:6

The five stories that now follow are usually dubbed "controversy [or 'conflict'] stories" (2:1–3:6). They are sometimes compared to five later controversy stories set in Jerusalem (11:27–12:37); but the comparison suffers from the facts that 12:1-12 will look more parabolic than controversial, that 12:28-34 will turn into a very friendly conversation between Jesus and a scribe, and that 12:35-37 will contain only a soliloquy by Jesus. Many scholars have taken 2:1–3:6 as a pre-Marcan collection that Mark inserts here at the cost of interrupting his story line (and M. J. Cook [*Mark's Treatment* 46-47] includes 7:1-23 in the collection). Not only will 3:7 pick up where 1:45 left off, it is said; but also Jesus' entering Capernaum in 2:1 disagrees with his staying outside cities in 1:45. Against this argument, however, Jesus' withdrawal in 3:7 follows on the plot of the Pharisees and Herodians in 3:6 as easily as it does on people's coming to him in 1:45 — more easily, in fact, for (1) in 1:45 Jesus is already in deserted places; (2) the seaside in 3:7a is hardly a better place to escape the crowds (as 3:7b-8 shows); and (3) withdrawal from a synagogue in the city (3:1-6) to the sea (3:7a) makes perfectly natural sense. To be sure, 1:45 says that Jesus avoids cities. But the avoidance can scarcely last very long (see 6:1-2; 7:31; 8:22, 27; 9:33, to say nothing of homes and populated areas in general); and the statement in 2:1 that Jesus enters again into Capernaum δι' ἡμερῶν, "after [some] days," indicates that it does not.

But other arguments are adduced for a pre-Marcan collection behind 2:1–3:6. It is said that the hint of Jesus' death in 2:20 and the plot against his life in 3:6 arise too early in the overall plan of Mark's gospel and therefore derive from an earlier document; that "the Son of man" in 2:10, 28 likewise arises too early and, additionally, does not conform to its later use for a suffering and then exalted figure; and that the stories lack the characteristically Marcan temporal and topographical interconnections already found, for example, in 1:9, 12, 14, 16, 21, 29, 35, 39. But the allusiveness of the hints at Jesus' death saves them from prematurity. The very fact that nothing comes of the plot against his life makes it also only a hint, and would make a poor conclusion to a pre-Marcan collection. For what would be the purpose of a collection of stories that ends only in a plot? As it is, the hints and plot prepare Mark's audience for the coming passion predictions and the passion narrative (H.-W. Kuhn, *Ältere Sammlungen* 18-24; J. Dewey,

Markan Public Debate 46-47), just as the Sanhedrin's seeking to destroy Jesus (11:18) and trying to seize him by using the Pharisees and Herodians (see 12:12-13 with 11:27) will capitalize on the Pharisees' and Herodians' already having plotted in 3:6 and will set the stage for a final plot in 14:1-2 (against A. J. Hultgren [*Jesus and His Adversaries* 153], who thinks that 12:12-13 "neutralizes" 3:6 because in the end the Pharisees turn into tools of the Sanhedrin).

If Mark will later use "the Son of man" with two different associations, suffering and exaltation, what is to prevent him from using the phrase with another association now? Indeed, it would be to his advantage to establish that the Jesus who presently acts with authority is the Son of man who will undergo suffering and then enjoy exaltation (ibid. 123-25).

The stories in 2:1–3:6 are *not* devoid of temporal and topographical interconnections: "and having entered again into Capernaum" (2:1; cf. 1:21); "and he went out [cf. 1:29, 35, 38, 45] again to the seaside [cf. 1:16] . . . and going along [cf. 1:16] . . . and it came to pass [cf. 1:9] he was reclining at table in his house [cf. 1:29]" (2:13-15); ". . . and they come" (2:18; cf. 1:29, 39); "and it came to pass [cf. 1:9] he was traveling along [cf. another compound of πορεύομαι in 1:21] through the grainfields on the Sabbath [cf. 1:21]" (2:23); "and he entered again into the synagogue" (3:1; cf. 1:21). We seem to be reading the Mark who wrote chap. 1! Of course, one might hypothesize that these interconnections represent Mark's redaction of an earlier source. But to do so is to admit at this point the lack of an argument for such a source. Given the weakness of the other arguments adduced for it, the similarity of the interconnections in 2:1–3:6 to those in chap. 1 favor that Mark himself has collected these stories to further his emphasis on Jesus' authority and that in accordance with 1:21-28, 39 he has put stories with a miracle both first and last to support the authority of Jesus' teaching over against its rejection by Jewish authorities (cf. A. B. Kolenkow in *ANRW* II 23/2. 1493-94; D.-A. Koch, *Bedeutung* 30-39; M. D. Hooker, *Message* 22; Dewey, op. cit. 52-55, 181-97 [but see E. Best, *Gospel as Story* 104-6, for strictures on the ring composition that Dewey sees in 2:1–3:6; and the separating out of declarations on the Son of man [2:10-12, 27-28] to produce a more complicated ring composition [so W. Harrington 24-25] overlooks that the cure of the paralytic occurs in 2:12, not in 2:1-9). Notably, the miracles in these stories lack the element of touch or grasp (again cf. 1:21-28, 39), take place through Jesus' sheer speaking (cf. esp. 2:11: "I say to you"), and thus suit their purpose to support Jesus' teaching (2:13). The counter argument that a Hellenist like Mark would not put two stories about the Sabbath at the climax of the collection (J. Roloff, *Kerygma* 73) rests on neglect of widespread Gentile knowledge and mockery of the Jewish Sabbath (see the notes on 1:32).

The charge of blasphemy in the first story (2:7) and the plot against Jesus' life in the last story (3:6) lie too far apart to be regarded as a foreshadowing of the same combination in the passion narrative. For that, we would expect the plot to occur at the end of the story containing the charge of blasphemy, or at least the story with the charge to immediately precede the story with the plot. In the passion narrative a plot (14:1-2) will precede a charge of blasphemy (14:64), but Jesus will be executed under a completely different charge (15:26).

The growingly popular reduction of a pre-Marcan collection through lopping off 2:1-12 (and 2:13-14, which is widely regarded as a redactional intrusion also by believers in a full collection) or 3:1-6 or both or even more (see R. A. Guelich 1. 82-83 and D. Lührmann 56 with references) loses at least one of the primary arguments that first led to the hypothesis of a pre-Marcan source, i.e. the interruption of a supposedly original smooth connection between 1:45 and 3:7. And lopping off 3:6 loses the argument from the supposedly inappropriate earliness of the plot in 3:6 as well. More and more, proponents of a shorter collection appeal to the content of the stories as justification for a pre-Marcan date of collection. In particular, they appeal to the stories' dealing with ecclesiastical issues, such as table fellowship, fasting, and Sabbath observance, whose import has faded by the time and in the place that Mark writes for a Gentile audience.

Let us take R. Pesch's view as a representative example (1. 149-51). He excludes 2:1-12 from the pre-Marcan collection, which deals with the Christological question of Jesus' right to forgive sins, not with the church's right to declare sins forgiven (cf. J. Kiilunen, *Vollmacht* 112-13). According to Pesch, the story of Levi's call in 2:13-14 makes a redactional bridge from the originally isolated story in 2:1-12 to a pre-Marcan collection incorporated in 2:15–3:6. The prefixing of 2:1-12 to this collection is supposed to shift the point from ecclesiastical problems (so the pre-Marcan collection with regard to controversies between Jewish and Gentile Christians over table fellowship [2:15-17]; over the right day for fasting [2:18-22]; and over freedom from Sabbath restrictions [2:23–3:6]) to Jesus' authority (the leading motif in 2:1-12). Support for a shorter pre-Marcan collection comes from the absence of the Pharisees in 2:1-12 over against their presence in each story throughout 2:15–3:6, from the greater specificity of Pharisaical scribes in 2:16 as compared with the scribes in general in 2:1-12, from the failure of the disciples to play a role in 2:1-12 in contrast with their role in 2:15–3:6, and — when 2:1-12 and 2:13-14 are excluded — from the balance between feasting and fasting (2:15-17, 18-22), between plucking grain on the Sabbath and healing on the Sabbath (2:23-28; 3:1-6), and from the framing of two stories regarding the disciples' practice (2:18-22, 23-28) with two stories regarding Jesus' practice (2:15-17; 3:1-6).

But we need convincing evidence that Levi's call did not in fact issue in a meal at which Jesus ate with publicans and sinners; otherwise 2:13-14 need not be considered an addition to 2:15-17. The beginning of v 15 with καὶ γίνεται, "and it comes to pass," starts a new episode but does not necessarily imply that Mark prefixes vv 13-14 redactionally, especially since the antecedent or antecedents of "he" and "his" in v 15a are totally obscure without vv 13-14. In 4:4 the phrase, with the aorist, will continue something already begun. The present tense in 2:15 makes an even tighter connection with 2:13-14. It is doubtful that Jesus' eating with presumably circumcised toll collectors and sinners from among the Jewish people would ever have spoken to the later issue of table fellowship between Jewish Christians and uncircumcised Gentile Christians (and we have no evidence that Jewish Christians ever debated among themselves or with non-Christian Jews whether or not it is proper to eat with *Jewish* sinners — against

J. D. G. Dunn in *NTS* 30 [1984] 395-415). Besides, an eye to the later issue of table fellowship would probably have brought the disciples as well as Jesus into the observation and question of the Pharisaical scribes (2:16; J. Kiilunen, *Vollmacht* 150-51). Jesus' saying that the disciples will fast "when the bridegroom has been taken away from them" favors their fasting at least on one occasion in the church age, but where is the evidence that NT Christians, Gentile or Jewish, argued with one another or with non-Christian Jews over the question whether or when they should fast (cf. the absence of such evidence in Matt 6:16-18; Acts 10:30; 13:21; 14:23; 27:9; 1 Cor 7:5; 2 Cor 6:5; 11:27; contrast the disagreement over the days of weekly fasting in *Did.* 8:1)? Disputes did arise over the question whether they ought to keep the Sabbath, but the stories in 2:23–3:6 do not speak to the question of accepting the Sabbath so much as to the question of interpreting it: what to do in cases of hunger and illness (and once more against Dunn we do not have any evidence that even Jewish Christians ever debated among themselves or with non-Christian Jews over degrees of strictness in keeping the Sabbath). The nearly complete absence in the NT epistles — all of them, not just Paul's — of explicit appeals to Jesus' words and deeds casts serious doubt on the common notion that Mark 2:1 (or 15)-28 (or 3:6) and similar passages in the gospels are the result of preserving such stories and arranging them for ecclesiastical purposes before the gospels were written. Even though these stories did speak directly to ecclesiastical issues, their speaking thus would not need to imply a pre-Marcan collection — only their *individual* preservation for ecclesiastical purposes, Mark being the first to bring them together and his doing so for the Christological purpose of emphasizing Jesus' authority (W. Thissen, *Erzählung* 27-28, 105-8; Kiilunen, op. cit. 249; W. Weiss, *"Eine neue Lehre in Vollmacht"* 19-31).

Every one of the stories displays Jesus' authority: to forgive sins (2:1-12), to eat with toll collectors and sinners (2:13-17), to let his disciples dispense with fasting (2:18-22), to let them pluck grain the Sabbath (2:23-28), and to heal on the Sabbath (3:1-6). Controversy takes a back seat to this theme of authority and does not come in for so much prominence as is usually thought (but see R. H. Lightfoot, *Locality* 118). In 2:1-12 Jesus' enemies are present but do not say anything aloud, not even to one another. Rather, he reads their thoughts and goes on the attack. In 2:13-17 there is no accusation (as there was silently and privately in 2:1-12), but only a question "why?" — and it is directed to Jesus' disciples, not to him. 2:13-17 is stronger than 2:1-12 in that Jesus' enemies do speak out, but "why?" is weaker than the charge of blasphemy. 2:18-22 is weaker yet in that the questioners are not enemies at all. Their question "why?" may therefore carry not even an implied accusation; and it deals with the behavior of Jesus' disciples, not with his own behavior. The first accusatory "why?" appears in 2:23-28; but again it deals with the disciples' behavior, not with that of Jesus. 3:1-6 starts with his enemies looking for an accusation and ends with their plot, but they ask no question and issue no challenge. So we can speak of controversies only in a highly qualified sense. What binds the stories together is the overwhelming effect of Jesus' sayings (which Mark probably presents as part of Jesus' "new teaching with authority" [1:27] by inserting a reference to his teaching early in the collection [2:13]) whether or not a controversy in the normal sense of the term evokes those sayings (cf. W. Thissen, *Erzählung* 116-46, on the Christological argumentation in 2:1–3:6). We should reject the objection against this view that 3:1-6 is not overtly Christological, for Jesus' raising the issue of what is permissible (ἔξεστιν) to do on the Sabbath (3:4) interconnects with the Pharisees' raising the same issue in the preceding story (2:24: ἔξεστιν) and thereby makes the overtly Christological statement that the Son of man is Lord also of the Sabbath (2:28) apply to both stories. In fact, this statement applies better to 3:1-6 than to 2:23-27, for 3:1-6 has to do with Jesus' own behavior whereas 2:23-27 has to do only with the disciples' behavior.

If collecting the stories himself, Mark may gather together those stories concerning the Pharisees and move by stages from "the scribes" in general (2:1-12) to "the scribes of the Pharisees" (2:13-17) to "the Pharisees" (2:18–3:6). But we must not simplify the pattern in the interests of contrasting 2:1-12 with 2:15–3:6. Let it be noted that "the scribes of the Pharisees" in the first pericope of 2:15–3:6 contrast with "the Pharisees" in the remaining pericopes of that section as much as with "the scribes" in 2:1-12. Furthermore, "the Pharisees" in 2:18-22 appear alongside "the disciples of John," are differently referred to as "the disciples of the Pharisees" the second time around, and do not engage in a controversy with Jesus. They do not even seem to be present. It is others who ask Jesus a question about fasting. And in 3:1-6 the Pharisees team up with the Herodians. A very mixed picture indeed! The disciples play a role in 3:1-6 no more than they do in 2:1-12 (so that Pesch must take 3:1-6 with 2:23-28, which does mention the disciples, to keep alive the supposed contrast with 2:1-12). And surely Mark is capable of arranging stories so as to produce a balance between feasting and fasting, between plucking grain on the Sabbath and healing on the Sabbath, and capable of framing two stories regarding the disciples' practice with two stories regarding Jesus' practice (though we should note that Jesus' practice of eating with toll collectors and sinners is the practice of his disciples, too [see 2:15]).

Jesus' preaching, exorcisms, and healings came to something of a climax by the end of chap. 1. Mark is now in a position to start again. We can see a progression from silent accusation against Jesus (2:6-7) to a questioning of his disciples (2:16) to a questioning of Jesus himself by neutral people (2:18) to a questioning of him by his enemies (2:24) to a lying in wait for the purpose of accusing him (3:2) and finally to a plot to do away with him (3:6). Thus the present section will come to something of a climax, just as chap. 1 did. The intensifying opposition does not merely prepare for Jesus' coming crucifixion, however; it acts as a foil to the increasingly mighty exercise of his authority. The greater the opposition, the greater his mastery (cf. the comment of B. J. Malina [in *CBQ* 43 (1981) 132-33] that in terms true to first century Mediterranean society the stories deal with honor versus shame as Jesus puts to shame his hostile challengers and thereby justifies the grant of honor to him). To heighten the stakes, moreover, Mark puts first the only story in which Jesus is recognized to exercise a divine prerogative, that of forgiving sins (2:1-12, though see the comments on 2:27 for Jesus' assuming the role of Yahweh in lording it over the Sabbath). As in the last story (3:1-6), it is a miracle that puts down his enemies. In the intervening stories his words put them down (cf. the characteristic of Hellenistic divine men that they overcome their enemies in debate — H. D. Betz, *Lukian* 110-11).

JESUS' AUTHORITY AS THE SON OF MAN
TO FORGIVE SINS ON THE EARTH

2:1-12 (Matt 9:1-8; Luke 5:17-26; John 5:8-9a)

Jesus enters Capernaum, and the news circulates that he is at home (2:1). Many people gather (2:2a). Jesus speaks to them (2:2b). A paralytic is brought (2:3-4), and Jesus forgives his sins (2:5). Some scribes think that Jesus is blaspheming (2:6-7). His response is twofold: (1) he asks them a double question (2:8-9) and (2) commands the paralytic to get up and go (2:10-11). The obedience of the paralytic demonstrates his healing and thus his forgiveness (2:12a). The onlookers are amazed (2:12b).

2:1-2 *(Matt 9:1; Luke 5:17)* Jesus' entering Capernaum brings to an end his staying "outside in deserted places" (1:45). "Again" harks back to his going into Capernaum for the first time (1:21). The unmodified plural "days" need not be restricted to several (see, e.g., 2:20; Matt 2:1). If we do not so restrict it and if we attach δι' ἡμερῶν, "after [a number of] days," to "having entered," the span of days covers the period of time spent away from Capernaum (1:35-45). Taking "after [a number of] days" differently with "it was heard" might seem to disagree with Mark's emphasis on Jesus' magnetic power by allowing that Jesus can enter Capernaum and stay there for a while without immediately drawing a crowd (contrast 7:24-25; also 1:35-37; 3:20; 6:32-33, 54-55). On the other hand, the inconcinnity of "openly" in 1:45, where he stays in deserted places and therefore does not appear to enter cities at all, favors that "openly" interpreted 2:1 in advance: Jesus does succeed in staying hidden for some days in Capernaum because he does not enter it openly. Then δι' ἡμερῶν attaches to the following "it was heard" (just as in 14:58 διὰ τριῶν ἡμερῶν, "after three days," will attach to the following "I will build . . ." — cf. the notes ad loc.) and may bear a possibly more natural sense of several days rather than a prolonged period; and this sense will suit Mark's emphasis: even though entering Capernaum incognito, Jesus attracts people so magnetically that he cannot stay hidden very long (cf. 1:33; 2:13; 3:7-8; 4:1-2; 5:21; 6:34; 8:1; also 1:5). Ὅτι may introduce an indirect quotation ("it was heard that he was at home") or a direct one ("it was heard, 'He is at home' "). In view of 1:29, ἐν οἴκῳ, "at home," probably refers to the house of Simon and Andrew and reflects Simon's standpoint in the telling of the story, which Mark may have heard from him (see Eus. *H.E.* 3.39.15 and cf. 3:20; 7:17; 9:28; also 8:3, 26; BAGD s.v. οἶκος 1aα; G. Minette de Tillesse, *Le secret messianique* 243-46 for the anarthrous use in the sense of one's own home). The forward position of the phrase gives the news that Jesus is at home a note of excitement.

That "many gathered together" shows again his magnetic power. "At the door" harks back to 1:33, where "the whole city was gathered at the door" (cf. 3:9, 20; 4:1; 6:31). But here Jesus' magnetic power has increased the size of the crowd. Not as before, they fill the house or courtyard. They also fill the area outside the door, which by itself held the whole city on the previous occasion. (Does Mark want his audience to think that people are streaming in from outside the city, too?) But there is still not room enough. "Not even" stresses the over-crowding, and "no longer" indicates that the area outside the door used to be adequate (cf. the use of μηκέτι in 1:45, a similar statement concerning the effect of Jesus' words and deeds). This emphasis does not merely prepare for v 4, for the crowding of the space within the house or courtyard would alone be enough to prepare for the inability of the four to bring the paralytic to Jesus. Rather, we are supposed to see an intensification of Jesus' magnetism. This intensification gains from the chiasm of vv 1-2 as compared with 1:45: (1) the first-mentioned entry into Capernaum (v 1) corresponds to the last-mentioned non-entry into any city (1:45); (2) the construction ὥστε μηκέτι, "so that no longer," plus an infinitive takes a middle position in both passages; and (3) the last-mentioned speaking of the word (v 2) corresponds to the first-mentioned publishing of the word (1:45; cf. C. D. Marshall, *Faith* 83). Likewise, the phrase with εἰς, "into," follows the verbal of entry in v 1 but precedes it at 1:45; and in the present ὥστε μηκέτι-construction the subject of the infinitive follows the infinitive (if we are to take τά, "the things [= area]," as a subjective accusative — see the following notes) whereas the subject of the infinitive precedes the infinitive in the earlier instance of this construction. Jesus' "speaking the word" indicates that the following miracle will give evidence for the truth of the good news, which his word of forgiveness in the middle of the story will epitomize.

2:3-5 *(Matt 9:2; Luke 5:18-20)* The historical present tense of ἔρχονται, "they come," stresses the power of Jesus that attracts people to come bringing a paralytic. "Being carried by four" underlines the severity of this case. The phrase, "and not being able to bring [him] to him [v.l.: 'to come near to him'] on account of the crowd," not only sets the stage for further development of the story. Again it emphasizes Jesus' magnetic power, in particular, his speaking the word so powerfully as to cause overcrowding. The removal of part of the roof by digging out a hole in it dramatizes this emphasis. The cognateness of "unroofed the roof" and the duality of that expression plus "having dug out" heighten the dramatiza-tion. The historical present tense in the statement that the four "let down" the pallet, the parallel between "where he [Jesus] was" and "where the paralytic was lying," and the placement of ὁ παραλυτικός, "the paralytic," before its verb add further drama to the men's act of faith, which counts as a nonverbal request for healing. Mention of the pallet and of the paralytic's lying on it prepares for the contrastive demonstration of healing in v 12a. In accordance with the editorial comment that Jesus sees their faith, the action of the four in digging through the roof magnifies Jesus' power to heal by showing what vigorous faith it inspires (cf. the association of faith and impediments as noted by G. Theissen, *Miracle Stories* 52-53, 129-40). The editorial comment implies an "omniscient narrator" who knows the reason why Jesus says what he says (cf. Acts 14:9). Since Jesus sees the faith of the four on the roof but speaks only to the paralytic before him on the floor, "their faith" may refer to the faith of the four, not including faith on the part of the paralytic.

Τέκνον, "child," puts Jesus in a position of superiority over the paralytic. The historical present tense of λέγει, "he says," highlights Jesus' authority to say that the paralytic's sins are being forgiven. The passive voice of ἀφίενται, "are being forgiven," could imply God's forgiveness, which Jesus knows about and reports to the paralytic (cf. Isa 6:7). But the implication is unnecessary, and the scribes will understand Jesus himself to be the forgiver (v 7). (This statement holds true even though one regards vv 5b-10 or 6-10 as a later intrusion into the story; for under this view only the occasion, not the substance, of the scribes' understanding Jesus himself to be the forgiver would shift; and whoever made the insertion will have agreed with the scribes' understanding that Jesus is the forgiver.) Similarly, v 10 will portray Jesus as the Son of man forgiving sins on the earth (contrast 2 Sam 12:13, where Nathan explicitly identified the Lord as the forgiver). The present tense of ἀφίενται most naturally means that Jesus pronounces the forgiveness as taking place at this very moment and therefore as being effected by his pronouncement (cf. Acts 9:34). So we do not have a miracle — at least not yet — but a word, an authoritative word of sins being forgiven on the spot. This word anticipates vv 13-17, where Jesus comes forward as the friend of sinners. The emphatic position of σου, "your," marks off the paralytic's sins from those of the four who brought him or from those of everyone else present (cf. v 9).

2:6-7 *(Matt 9:3; Luke 5:21)* In 1:22, 27 Jesus' display of didactic authority contrasted with the scribes' lack of such authority. So now they make their appearance, but not merely as unauthoritative; worse yet, as antagonistic and wrong (N.B. the adversative δέ, "but"). Their sitting contrasts with the activity of the four men of faith: coming, bringing and carrying the paralytic, digging a hole in the roof, letting down the pallet. The scribes appear as sceptical observers rather than as active believers in Jesus' power. Mark's attributing sceptical reasoning to them and knowing exactly what they are thinking "in their hearts" show him to be writing yet again as an omniscient narrator who makes his point in an editorial aside (for reasoning in Mark that is *not* inward, see 8:16-17; 9:33-34; and probably [because of πρὸς ἑαυτοὺς λέγοντες, "saying to themselves (in the sense, 'to one another')," and a following "we"] 11:31). Οὗτος may be contemptuous: "this fellow" (cf. the references in BAGD s.v. 1aα), but only by context (for an admiring use, see 4:4). The assonance in οὗτος οὕτως, "this one thus," emphasizes the scribes' scepticism. The successive references to speaking thus, to blaspheming, and to God alone form a crescendo of increasing criticism. "He is blaspheming" specifies what the scribes mean by "speaking thus," and "Who is able to forgive sins except one, [viz.] God?" gives a basis for the charge of blasphemy. Together, the charge and its basis set the stage for an implied claim to deity on Jesus' part. Thus, it is no ordinary man, much less a criminal, who will die on the Cross. He is a divine figure unrecognized as such by those who will put him there (cf. Ov.

Met. 8.626-720). The scribes raise a question of ability. Jesus has already shown ability to cleanse a leper (1:40-45). Now he will show ability to forgive sins, which is a divine prerogative (Exod 34:6-7; 2 Sam 12:13; Pss 32:1-5; 51:3-4[1-2], 9-11[7-9]; 103:3; 130:4; Isa 43:25; 44:22; Dan 9:9; Zech 3:4; 1QS 2:9; CD 3:18; 20:34; cf. Str B 1. 495). According to Jewish belief, not even the Messiah is going to forgive sins (*Tg. Isa* 53:5b; K. Koch in *JSJ* 3 [1972] 117-48). Yet Jesus' ability to forgive sins will turn out to be authority, i.e. legitimately exercised ability. Here in v 7 and also in v 10 the absolute "sins," where we might have read "his sins" to correspond to "your sins" in vv 5 and 9, generalizes this authority of Jesus.

    2:8-9 *(Matt 9:4-5; Luke 5:22-23)* Again Mark writes as an omniscient narrator: he knows what Jesus knows without Jesus' having said what the scribes are thinking. In Jesus' question ταῦτα, "these things," has its antecedent only in an editorial comment, not in anything he has said about the scribes' inward thoughts. Hence, it is an important point to Mark that among Jesus' other powers is the power of clairvoyance which characterizes God himself (see 1 Sam 16:7; 1 Kgs 8:39; 1 Chr 28:9; Pss 7:10[9]; 139:1-2, 6, 23; Jer 11:20; 17:9-10; Sir 42:18, 20; *Pss. Sol.* 14:8; Luke 16:15; John 2:24-25 with 1:1; Acts 1:24; 15:8; Rom 8:27; 1 Thess 2:4; Rev 2:23; cf. 2 Kgs 5:25-26; 6:8-14; Mark 14:65 parr.; Luke 7:39; John 4:19 on the clairvoyance of God's prophets; and L. Bieler, ΘΕΙΟΣ ΑΝΗΡ 1. 87-94, on the clairvoyance of Hellenistic "divine men," though their clairvoyance tends toward knowledge of future events, the secrets of nature, and other things hidden from ordinary human beings rather than the antagonistic thoughts of enemies [W. Weiss, *"Eine neue Lehre in Vollmacht"* 138-39, n. 46]). Mark emphasizes this power with the adverb "immediately": Jesus' clairvoyance needs no time to figure things out. Further emphasis comes from the historical present tense λέγει, "he says," and just possibly from the perfective use of ἐπι- with γνούς. Though the compound form of the verb refers to simple recognition in 6:33 (where B* D *f*¹ have the simplex form, however), 54, Mark will use the simplex in 8:17 for Jesus' easily knowing the disciples' reasoning because they express it aloud in talking with one another, and in 15:10 for Pilate's unspectacular knowledge of the chief priests' envy. Yet Mark will use the compound form again in 5:30 for Jesus' supernatural knowledge that healing power has gone from him (on the other side, see MM s.v. ἐπιγινώσκω; J. A. Robinson, *Ephesians* 248-54). "His" with "spirit" rules out the Holy Spirit (cf. 8:12). "With his spirit" contrasts with "in their hearts" (v 6) and with "in themselves" and "in your hearts" (v 8; cf. the parallelistic alternation in the preferable vv.ll. at 1:8 between a simple dative, as here in τῷ πνεύματι αὐτοῦ, "with his spirit," and the dative preceded by ἐν, "in," as here [bis]). Perhaps Mark shifts from "heart" to "spirit" because "spirit" connotes power (see the comments on 1:7-8) and because he wants to emphasize Jesus' power of clairvoyance. The repeated use of "reason" and "in your [or 'their'] hearts" adds to the emphasis (cf. v 8 with v 6). It does not take much to "see" the obvious faith of the four (v 5). But to perceive the inward reasoning of the scribes requires divine power. Armed with such power, Jesus now takes the initiative by asking why the scribes are reasoning as they do. The οὕτως, "thus," in his reference to their reasoning echoes the οὕτως in their inward question (v 7) and will be topped by the οὕτως of their and everyone else's exclamation in v 12: "We have never seen thus!"

The easier thing is to say, "Your sins are being forgiven"; for no human being can falsify that statement. The position of σου ahead of αἱ ἁμαρτίαι, "your sins" (contrast the position of σου after τὸν κράββατον, "the pallet of yours"), echoes v 5 and highlights that it is the paralytic's sins which are being forgiven. To give verifiable evidence of the invisible effectiveness of the easier statement and thus to belittle his silent accusers, Jesus will proceed to say the less easy thing, "Rise and take up the pallet of yours and walk." "Rise" might have sufficed. The adding of "take up the pallet of yours and walk" amplifies the demonstration of Jesus' power. The use of αἴρω in the active voice, "take up," points out that the man *being* carried in v 3 (αἰρόμενον, passive voice) will turn into a man who, thanks to Jesus' act of power, *does* the carrying in vv 9-12. Now we see the reason for the addition of "being carried" to "bringing" in v 3.

2:10-11 *(Matt 9:6; Luke 5:24; John 5:8)* An adversative δέ, "but," contrasts the preceding abstract question with the following concrete demonstration. Knowing contrasts with the scribes' sceptical reasoning, and Mark wants his audience to know what Jesus wants the scribes to know. It is Jesus' authority to do what the scribes have said in their hearts that only God is able to do: forgive sins. The emphatic position of the ἵνα-clause — ordinarily it comes after the main clause, but here it comes first — underscores the need to recognize that authority. So also does the forward position of ἐξουσίαν, "authority," within the clause. The earlier question, "Who can forgive sins except one, [viz.] God?" carried the implied answer, "Nobody." Jesus now reverses that answer by saying that the Son of man, i.e. he himself as a human being, can. And he can do so on the earth, as opposed to heaven, the dwelling place of the only one who the scribes think can forgive sins. "But in order that you [plural] may know . . ." goes with "I say to you [singular]. . . ." "He says to the paralytic" intervenes for the sake of the shift from second person plural (in addressing the scribes) to the second person singular (in addressing the paralytic). This editorial interruption takes the place of Jesus' physically turning from the scribes to the paralytic in the actual event. Thus disappear the supposed awkwardness and the consequent need to take the ἵνα in an unusual imperatival sense, "But know that the Son of man has authority . . . ," which mistakes the emphatic first position of the ἵνα-clause for an indication of imperatival use, misses the indication of Jesus' purpose (telic ἵνα) in speaking words of healing, and makes Mark himself call Jesus "the Son of man" whereas neither Mark nor anyone else besides Jesus does so in the rest of the gospel (or, nearly, in the rest of the NT). The historical present tense of λέγει, "he says," stresses those powerful words. "I say to you" highlights the dominant social position of the speaker, Jesus (cf. 5:41 and see D. E. Aune, *Prophecy* 164-65). The emphatic forward position of σοι, "to you," contributes to a chiasm: (a) "He says"; (b) "to the paralytic"; (b′) "To you"; (a′) "I say." This chiasm at once underlines the change of address from the scribes to the paralytic and implies that even so desperate a case as the paralytic's does not lie beyond the range of Jesus' power to heal (cf. the placement of σου before αἱ ἁμαρτίαι in vv 5, 9). "Rise, take up your pallet" echoes v 9, except that Mark omits an intervening "and." The staccato-like effect of the resulting asyndeton sounds a note of authority that stresses the miracle-working power of the command. But to avoid undue awkwardness Mark keeps "and" before the last part of the command, which changes from "walk" (v 9) to "go to your home." This change creates a balance with the paralytic's having been brought (presumably from his home — v 3) and thus shows the completeness of his healing (cf. the healed leper's going to the priest in 1:44; also 5:19, 34; 7:29; 8:26; 10:52; John 5:8-9; Acts 3:8; 9:34; 14:10; Luc. *Philops.* 11; Cic. *Div.* 1.26.55; Liv. *Ab urbe cond.* 2.36.1-8; Plut. *Coriolan.* 24.1-3; R. Herzog, *Wunderheilungen* nos. 15, 37, 57, 70). The present tense of the imperative in ἔγειρε (vv 9, 11), περιπάτει (v 9), and ὕπαγε lends emphasis to the paralytic's rising, walking, and going home as a demonstration of Jesus' power (cf. the notes on 1:3).

2:12 *(Matt 9:7-8; Luke 5:25-26; John 5:9a)* Verse 12 exhibits the power of Jesus' less easy saying to accomplish itself and thus to give evidence for the effectiveness of his word of forgiveness. "He went out in front of them all" replaces an expected "he walked" (cf. v 9) or "he went home" (cf. v 11) to shift emphasis to observedness. "All" stresses undoubtedness — even the sceptical scribes see the evidence. To put all possible weight on this indubitable observedness, Mark repeats the vocabulary of getting up and taking up the pallet and attaches "immediately" to the paralytic's taking up his pallet and going out rather than to his getting up, and then repeats "all" in his statement concerning the crowd's amazement. Thus even the scribes are amazed (ἐξίστασθαι; cf. 5:42; 6:51; 16:8; also 1:22, 27). The good news of God is true (1:14). The rule of God has taken effect (1:15). The glorification of God because of Jesus' miraculous deed reverses the earlier accusation that he blasphemed God by his word of forgiveness. To argue that if the story originally included vv 5b-10 or 6-10 the people would glorify Jesus as the forgiver of sins rather than God as the enabler of this miracle is to miss the suitability of this reversal. It is also to forget that the miracle has verified the forgiveness. And it is only natural that the people concentrate on what they have seen instead of the invisible forgiveness verified by it. Were the forgiveness of their own sins in view and had they suffered a heavy conscience over them — now that would be another matter. "Thus have we never seen" indicates that Jesus' miracle exceeds anything the onlookers have observed before. The pericope ends, then, with a recognition of his power as God-given. Mark's audience are to infer that the Crucifixion will therefore be unjustified.

NOTES

T. Söding (*Glaube* 407-14) thinks that the larger context of Mark expands "their faith" (v 5) to include, not only faith for a miracle, but also faith in Jesus as the Son of God and bringer of God's rule. Except for the disciples, however, people misidentify Jesus (6:14-16; 8:29-30); so the faith of the four who brought the paralytic seems limited to faith for a miracle (though not criticized for that limitation). The reference to their faith hardly makes the healing portion of the pericope into an example story of faith that overcomes obstacles; for Jesus himself does not commend the faith, and the acclamation that brings the story to a climax centers on his deed, not on the men's faith (against I. Maisch, *Heilung* 74-75). By the same token, the motif of faith is hardly strong enough to validate the argument that it has ridden roughshod over the historical improbability of the owner's letting the four men dig a hole in his roof. If the four could not get through the crowd to Jesus, presumably the owner could not get through the crowd to stop the four. The text does not say that Jesus continued teaching calmly and that the crowd continued listening silently as the four dug the hole. In attacking historical probability E. Haenchen (100-101) reads into the text imaginative features worthy of rabid harmonizers (who exercise their imaginations with quite a different aim, of course). The fact is that often we do not know enough to adjudicate questions of historical detail. Apparently somebody acquainted with mud-roofs thought it possible to dig through them; otherwise we would not have the story in its present form (against D. Daube, *NTRJ* 383-86, and against the argument of J. Wellhausen [1. Aufl., 16] that since an opening can be made only in a tile-roof, digging through a mud-roof arises by mistranslation of underlying Aramaic; see also F. Schulthess in *ZNW* 20 [1921] 220 against Wellhausen, and H. van der Loos, *Miracles* 441-42, n. 3, for quotations from other ancient literature that make the action of the four look realistic). The present story has to do with the authority of Jesus himself to forgive sins, not with the authority of the church to declare sins forgiven by God, of which authority the pericope says absolutely nothing. O. Hofius (in *"Wenn nicht jetzt, wann dann?"* 115-27) has shown that the Jewish high priest could not perform an act of absolution, or even give a promise of forgiveness, either for individuals or for the people; hence, the pericope does not attack a claim by the priesthood in Jerusalem to have an exclusive authority to forgive sins over against an ecclesiastical counter claim. A Jewish diviner forgives the sins of Nabonidus in 4QprNab; but he forgives them for God (לה, "for him," not לי, "for me [Nabonidus]") and immediately tells Nabonidus to give glory to God, so that no question of blasphemy arises (cf. J. A. Fitzmyer in *JBL* 99 [1980] 15-16). Here, Jesus does not tell the paralytic to give God glory; rather, the people spontaneously glorify God instead of joining in the charge of blasphemy (see also H.-J. Klauck in *BZ* nf 25 [1981] 239-40; B. Blackburn, *Theios Anēr* 138-40).

Unless ἠκούσθη is taken personally in v 1 ("he was heard that he is at home," which seems intolerably awkward), εἰσελθών, "having entered," has nothing to modify. Thus we have anacoluthon. Capernaum is often considered unhistorically redactional because it relates to 1:21 but has no relevance to anything else in 2:1–3:6. But it *is* relevant to "at home," also in v 1 (cf. 1:29). At the same time, relevance is not a necessity; so we should grant at least the point that nothing in 2:1–3:6, not even a home, necessitates a location in Capernaum. This very lack of necessity argues for the traditional origin of the location, however; for it would have been much easier for Mark to avoid even the appearance of inconcinnity with 1:45 by not creating the entry into Capernaum than by inserting "openly" (1:45) and "after [some] days" (2:1) under the duress of his own fabrication.

On the v.l. εἰς οἶκον, see B. M. Metzger, *Textual Commentary* ad loc. For "the word," see the comments on 1:45; also BAGD s.v. λόγος 1bβ; G. Kittel in *TDNT* 4. 114-17; H.-W. Kuhn, *Ältere Sammlungen* 133-34. We may take τά as the subject of χωρεῖν ("so that not even the area at the door had room any more") or as an accusative of respect ("so that no longer did they [the many who had gathered] have room even with respect to the area at the door"). It would not be surprising if the area just inside the door of the courtyard were filled; therefore "not even" seems to imply that Mark is referring to the area just outside the door and facing it. Jesus' speaking the word to many does not imply that he has stepped outside; rather, "not even" implies that so many are trying to get in that the area outside the door is packed — with the result that the four cannot bring the paralytic inside and have to take him up an outside staircase to the rooftop. Jesus' speaking the word in a home may have appealed to first century Christians who normally met in homes for instruction and worship (E. Best, *Gospel as Story* 54, 63, 91).

In vv 3-4, the indefinite third person plural of "they come" is striking, because the "many" who have gathered and to whom Jesus has been speaking would seem to provide a definite antecedent yet the last phrase in the sentence, "by four," identifies "they" rather differently and proves "they come" to have been indefinite at first (see C. H. Turner in *JTS* os 25 [1923-24] 379). The addition of αἰρόμενον, "being carried," to φέροντες, "bringing," shows that by itself bringing would not need to imply carrying. The roof seems to be flat and constructed of rafters spaced far enough apart to allow passage of the paralytic once a hole has been dug through the mud-plastered branches that are spread over the rafters (cf. G. Dalman, *SSW* 69; F. W. Deichmann in *RAC* 3. 524-29). "They unroofed the roof" is ambiguous: it could equally well refer to taking away tiles (cf. Luke 5:19) or anything else of which the roof might be constructed. But "having dug out" defines the unroofing as digging a hole in a mud-roof (cf. Mark's love of dual expressions in which the second member is more specific). H. Jahnow (in *ZNW* 24 [1925] 155-58) thinks that originally a hole was dug in the roof to let a demon out by a way that would be closed up if and when it tried to return at a later date — and it would not know any other way in. This view labors against the absence of a demon in the story and overestimates the extent to which ancient people attributed illness to demons without mentioning them (against this overestimation, see E. Yamauchi in *Gospel Perspectives* 6. 89-183). The address, "Child," does not sound like the story of an exorcism (see the following discussion against subtracting this part of the story from its original form).

On κράβαττος, "pallet," a late loanword avoided in the parallels Matt 9:1-8; Luke 5:17-27, see BAGD s.v. Cf. Ps 103:3; 4QprNab; *b. Ned.* 41a for the connection between forgiveness and healing (also 2 Sam 12:13; 2 Chr 7:14; 30:13-20; Ps 41:5[4]; Isa 6:10; 19:22; 38:16-17; 57:18-19; Jer 3:22; Hos 14:5[4]; Mark 4:12; *b. Ned.* 41a). It goes too far, however, to say that forgiveness and healing are synonymous in vv 1-12 as they seem to be in 4QprNab (against G. Vermes, *Jesus the Jew* 68); for in vv 1-12 one provides evidence for the other. We have no explicit indication whether the present paralysis is considered a result of sin in general or a punishment for some particular sin committed by the paralytic (cf. Job 4:1-21 et passim; John 5:14; 9:2; Acts 28:3-4). We might think that the latter would entail immediate, automatic healing instead of a healing tacked on for its evidential value, i.e. tacked on only incidentally from the standpoint of the theological question concerning the interrelation of sin and sickness. A loose connection between the paralysis and sin in general gains some support from the Christological rather than soteriological emphasis in vv 5b-11: the healing proves that Jesus has authority to forgive more than that the man has received forgiveness. In any case, every argument presupposing some particular sin as the cause of paralysis — e.g., the argument against the integrity of vv 1-12 that Jesus nowhere else attributes sickness to a particular sin — perches on a pinhead (cf. H.-J. Klauck in *BZ* nf 25 [1981] 241-42). Apparently it is the faith of the four who brought the paralytic that prompts Jesus to forgive the paralytic's sins rather than proceeding directly to the healing.

J. Carmignac (in *ASTI* 7 [1968-69] 70) sees a Hebrew wordplay, יושבים וחושבים, underlying καθήμενοι καὶ διαλογιζόμενοι, "sitting and reasoning" (v 6). Aramaic would offer the same wordplay. M. Black (*Aramaic Approach* 65-66, 122) takes τί as rhetorical: "Why, . . . this fellow is blaspheming!" (v 7). But under this view, "is speaking thus," which is not at all awkward in the usual understanding, awkwardly intrudes before the reference to blasphemy. And against Black's view, "Who is able to forgive sins . . . ?", which gives the ground for the charge of blasphemy, is a question, not an exclamation. The question means that nobody except God is able to forgive sins. See also E. C. Maloney, *Semitic Interference* 142-44. Blasphemy is too strong a charge for Jesus' merely taking a prophetic prerogative of reporting God's forgiveness. God is the implied object of the blasphemy. For such blasphemy death is prescribed, but only if the blasphemy has included a pronunciation of "Yahweh" (see Lev 24:10-16; *m. Sanh.* 7:5; and the notes on 14:61b-64 with further literature cited there; cf. 1 Kgs 21:13). Εἰ μὴ εἷς ὁ θεός, "except one, [viz.] God," occurs also in 10:18 and may carry an overtone of monotheism as expressed in Deut 6:4. If so, the scribes see in Jesus' arrogating to himself the divine prerogative of forgiving sins an undermining of monotheism. But the anarthrousness of θεός in the clearly mono-theistic statements of 1 Cor 8:6; Eph 4:6; 1 Tim 2:5 and the possibility of a pleonastic use of εἷς (on which see K. Beyer, *Semitische Syntax* 1/1. 126-29) disfavor such an overtone.

Some commentators think that at a deeper level, and paradoxically, it is less easy to say, "Your sins are being forgiven," because a prophet might perform a healing but only God can forgive sins. Yet Jesus appears to be speaking simply on the level of observability versus unobservability (also against U. Luck [in *Vom Urchristentum zu Jesus* 107-8], who interprets "easier" to mean "less blasphemous"). Still others think that forgiveness and healing are equally hard, for it takes God to accomplish either one (Ps 103:3). But for this we would expect, "Isn't it as hard to say, 'Arise . . . ,' as to say, 'Your sins are forgiven'?" "What is easier?" more naturally implies that one of the two is easier (cf. 10:25: "it is easier . . . than . . ." — against J. Kiilunen [*Vollmacht* 120, n. 25], who strangely uses 10:25 to deny a question of relative ease). C. D. Marshall (*Faith* 186-87) accepts all three interpretative possibilities — speaking a word of forgiveness as less easy, a word of healing as less easy, and both as equally hard — and thereby treats the saying as a polemical riddle. But in proceeding to speak a word of healing, Jesus seems to take the challenge of doing the less easy thing (contrast his leaving polemical riddles unsolved in 11:29-33; 12:35-37). T. L. Budesheim (in *ZNW* 62 [1971] 191-92) thinks that the question is purely rhetorical: the issue is not one of ease, but one of Jesus' authority to make both statements. But the text says that he performed the miracle to demonstrate his authority to forgive sins, not to demonstrate his authority to speak a word of healing, which is an enabling command rather than an authoritative statement.

Whether we treat ἵνα as telic or as imperatival, it is possible to take v 10 as a parenthetical address to Mark's audience: "but in order that you [the audience of my book] may know . . . , he says to the paralytic" or "but know [as a command to the audience]. . . . he says to the paralytic." Since Jesus has just been addressing the scribes, however, the second person plural more naturally continues to refer to them (see further arguments by D. R. A. Hare, *Son of Man Tradition* 53). "The Son of man" occurs now for the first time in Mark's gospel, but he does not explain the phrase. Perhaps it comes to him through the tradition but he has no special interest in it. Here it can hardly mean human beings in general, for their authority to forgive sins would not fit the contextual issue of Jesus' individual authority. Nor would *his* miracle prove *their* authority to forgive sins. Elsewhere he does not teach a general human authority of this sort, nor do we find such a doctrine in Jewish literature or the rest of the NT (though John 20:23 does teach forgiveness by Jesus' disciples [cf. Matt 16:19; 18:18; R. H. Gundry, *Matthew* 165]). And since forgiving someone who has sinned against you is not in view, such a doctrine would seem pointless in the first place.

On the other hand, "the Son of man" does not seem to be a recognized title, for the phrase never evokes opposition, surprise, or even curiosity, as such a title would be expected to do (J. L. Segundo, *Historical Jesus* 52-53, quoting the *Nueva Biblia Española*). Jesus never says, "I am the Son of man," or "yes" to a question whether he is; nor does the phrase appear in direct addresses to him or in confessions of him or (as noted in the comments) on the lips of anyone besides him (the two or three apparent exceptions occurring outside Mark), as again such a title would be expected to do. Only Jesus uses the phrase, and he uses it in statements about what he does. In contrast with "the Son of

God," "the Christ," and "the Son of David," "the Son of man" does not occur in statements that tell who Jesus is (J. D. Kingsbury, *Conflict in Mark* 58-61; E. Lemcio in *NTS* 32 [1986] 194-95). Therefore his claim to authority does not insure a titular usage recognizable to his or Mark's audiences (cf. similar arguments by C. Tuckett in *JSNT* 14 [1982] 62-64). Therefore again, "the Son of man" is not a Christological title by which Mark's Jesus corrects "the Son of God," "the Christ," and "the Son of David." Rather, he uses "the Son of man" for himself as a human being who is also "the Son of God," "the Christ," and "the Son of David" whom some others recognize him to be, or simply for himself as a human being without regard to any further identity (against P. J. Achtemeier 59-60).

Some have treated the definite articles in ὁ υἱὸς τοῦ ἀνθρώπου, literally "the Son of the man," as reflecting the Aramaic emphatic state used indefinitely (P. M. Casey in *JSNT* 29 [1987] 27-36; B. Chilton, *Profiles* 91-92). But this treatment revives the aforementioned problems adhering to an interpretation in terms of human beings in general. We should rather recognize that the double arthrousness of Jesus' ὁ υἱὸς τοῦ ἀνθρώπου makes the phrase self-referentially definite — "I as a human being distinct from other human beings" — and rests on a self-referentially definite use of whatever Semitic phrase underlies the Greek one. But why should Jesus have used the phrase so often as he did here and elsewhere in exclusive references to himself? By context and outside the NT בר אנשא, "a son of man," might refer exclusively to the speaker of the phrase. But this usage stands in considerable doubt and comes forward seldom, if at all. Normally the phrase carries a generic meaning which may include but does not particularize the speaker (for discussion, see D. R. A. Hare, *Son of Man Tradition* 231-56, and further literature cited there). Hence, other usage explains neither the frequency with which Jesus uses his phrase for exclusive self-references nor the limitation of his use to exclusive self-references. The best explanation remains that he identified himself with the figure described in Dan 7:13-14 as "like a son of man" and that this self-identification led him to use בר אנשא or a similar phrase often and only in referring exclusively to himself. The borrowing of other phraseology from Dan 7:13-14 in Mark 8:38; 13:26; 14:62 and parr. supports this explanation (for the failure of early Christians to use "the Son of man" in their own statements about Jesus discourages the view that they put the phraseology of Dan 7:13-14 on his lips), and the authority of the Son of man to forgive sins in the place of God tallies with the Danielic figure's reception of sovereignty, glory, and a kingdom from the Ancient of Days (cf. also Jesus' taking a central role in the coming of God's kingdom). To be sure, the reception of these items does not correspond exactly to Jesus' authority to forgive sins. But this sort of difference characterizes other NT uses of the OT (cf. the use of a passage concerning Isaiah's preaching for Jesus' teaching in parables [4:12], the use of statements about creation and marriage to argue against divorce [10:6-8], the use of a statement about the God of Moses' ancestors to argue for a future resurrection [12:26], etc.). To say that Jesus drew on Dan 7:13-14 does not entail that others had already derived an apocalyptic Son of man from that OT passage — only that that passage inspired him to use "the Son of man" in exclusive self-references whether or not the surrounding subject matter reflected Dan 7:13-14 in other respects. The probability that "the Son of man" was not yet used as the title of an apocalyptic figure (Hare, op. cit.) and the obliqueness of the phrase when used in self-references save Jesus from a prematurely transparent revelation of his superhuman and messianic dignity, a revelation that would have conflicted with his reserve when it comes to "the Son of God," "the Christ," and "the Son of David." Besides the afore-cited book by Hare, the following might be fished from the ocean of literature on the topic — they are recent and helpful by way of survey and evaluation: R. J. Bauckham in *JSNT* 23 (1985) 23-33; J. R. Donahue in *CBQ* 48 (1986) 484-98; D. C. Allison, Jr., *End* 128-37; W. Horbury in *JTS* ns 36 (1985) 34-55; I. H. Marshall, *Origin* 63-82.

C. Tuckett (in *JSNT* 14 [1982] 64-65) associates the charge of blasphemy (v 6) with the same charge in the passion narrative (14:64) to get a Marcan connotation of suffering in v 10. But the present text mentions authority, not suffering, whereas 14:62, which will lead up to the later charge of blasphemy, will not mention authority (so also against the attempt of J. Kiilunen, *Vollmacht* 177, to draw a parallel between 2:10 and 14:62 and deduce a fabrication and interpolation of 2:10 by Mark). The present narrative provides as good a setting as any for a saying on authority to forgive sins, and such a saying needs a narrative setting. For occasionless, the saying and within it the phrase "on the earth" lack relevance. Since the rest of synoptic tradition does not portray Jesus as forgiving sins, an originally isolated saying on the Son of man's authority to forgive them could not have gotten its relevance from a generally known practice of Jesus to forgive sins. His eating with toll collectors and sinners does not entail his forgiving their sins (see Luke 7:36-50); so we should not suppose that the saying in v 10 derives from a more original setting of table fellowship. See T. L. Budesheim (in *ZNW* 62 [1971] 193) on the dynamic rather than static connotation of ἐξουσία, "authority," but also D. Daube, *NTRJ* 218, on the underlying connotation of legitimacy (though not in a rabbinically technical sense, as Daube thinks).

The textual tradition varies between placing "on the earth" after "to forgive sins," after "the Son of man," and between "to forgive" and "sins." The uncertainty of placement has apparently caused the most weakly attested tradition to omit "on the earth" (W *pc* b q). In any of its textually supported positions, this phrase looks too distant from "authority" to modify it, and the position right after "the Son of man" looks influenced by Matt 9:6. "On the earth" might modify "sins," but what would be the point of describing sins as located on the earth? In 9:3 "on the earth" will contrast with glory that originates in heaven, but nobody thinks that the paralytic has sinned in heaven (or in hell). We are left, then, with adverbial possibilities: (1) "have . . . on the earth" (so Luke 5:24); (2) "to forgive . . . on the earth"; and (3) "have . . . to forgive . . . on the earth" (i.e. a modification of the entire verbal structure). The third possibility seems most natural. The implied contrast is spatial (over against the exercise of authority in heaven), not temporal (over against the exercise of authority at the last judgment [so E. Best, *Temptation* 137-38], for which we would expect "now" rather than the locative phrase "on the earth"). In and of itself "on the earth" would not necessarily imply a contrast with heaven, but the scribes' conviction that only God can forgive sins implies such a contrast here. In a pre-Marcan stage and on the lips of Jesus an allusion to the man-like figure coming with the clouds of heaven in Dan 7:13 also implies such a contrast. Without the contrast, "on the earth" seems otiose. Even in Luke 18:8; John 17:4, heavenly origin hovers in the background to give point to "on the earth."

For ὥστε, "so that," as a Marcan introduction to the effect of Jesus' words and deeds, see 1:27, 45; 2:2, 12; 3:10, 20; 4:1; 15:5. The earlier antagonism of the scribes may exclude them from the "all" who are amazed and glorify God (so J. A. Kleist [146], who misinterprets Quint. 8.2.19 as writing that good speakers leave some things to the intelligence of their hearers; rather, Quintillian is attacking verbal obfuscation). For the same exclusion, J. Dewey (*Markan Public Debate* 74-75) argues that in the concentric structure of the pericope v 12 corresponds to the first part, where the scribes have not yet entered the picture; and C. D. Marshall (*Faith* 82) argues that in 1:27 "all" excluded the scribes. But in 1:21-28 the scribes were not said to have been present; and since Jesus has addressed his questions and his authenticating miracle to the scribes in the present passage (see vv 8a, 10a), the scribes should be the last ones excluded. The doubling of "all" in v 12 favors their inclusion with everybody else. Cf. Pss 86:8-10; 113:1, 4-5, 7; 145:5-6, 11-12, 14. Since the paralytic did not die and since Mark does not intend his book to be read backwards, the occurrence of ἠγέρθη, "he got up," also in 16:6 (cf. 5:41; 6:14, 16; 12:26; 14:28) does not make the present healing an anticipation of Jesus' resurrection. Elsewhere in Mark the verb occurs a number of times with no conceivable allusion to the Resurrection.

The same considerations apply to the occurrences of ἐξίστασθαι, "were amazed," in v 12 and its cognate ἔκστασις, "amazement," in 16:8. In favor of reading backwards, so to speak, M. A. Beavis (in *CBQ* 49 [1987] 592-96) supposes that in virtue of studying their texts ahead of time, public readers introduced later material by way of explanation and answers to questions during the course of reading. To capitalize on such a practice, however, authors would have had to know what explanations were going to be offered and what questions were going to be asked and answered. Their ignorance at these points would have kept them from capitalizing on the practice.

The hypothesis that the original story lacked vv 5b-10 or 6-10 deserves some consideration and criticism. It is argued that the repetition of "he says to the paralytic" (v 10; cf. v 5) is mechanical and therefore favors this hypothesis. But the repetition is necessary and natural, not mechanical, since between vv 5 and 10 Jesus has been speaking to the scribes ("he says to them," v 8) and now the address needs to return to the paralytic (cf. the observation of R. Tannehill [in *ANRW* II 25/2. 1810] that the unvoiced objection of the scribes, far from making an awkward intrusion, heightens tension in the story). The peculiar construction in v 10 is also supposed to favor the hypothesis. But taking vv 5b-10 or 6-10 as an insertion by Mark or someone prior to him does nothing to remove the peculiarity. Furthermore, the peculiarity vanishes if we take v 10 with v 11 — i.e. v 10 as expressing the purpose of Jesus' command in v 11 — and the editorial parenthesis, "he says to the paralytic," as the literary equivalent of Jesus' turning physically from the scribes to the paralytic. It is further argued for the hypothesis that the failure of v 11 to take from v 9 the reference to walking shows that vv 5b-10 or 6-10 come from an originally different source. But if v 11 *had* taken over that reference from v 9, advocates of the hypothesis would doubtless argue once again from mechanical repetition! As it is, v 12 speaks of going out in front of them all instead of taking the reference to home-going from v 11 even though the two verses come from the same source. So why should v 11 have to repeat v 9? We have already seen that the variations have a purpose. Taking vv 6-10 (instead of vv 5b-10) as an insertion relieves the problem of the shift from what looks at first like a divine passive in v 5 (God forgives the sins) to Jesus' forgiving the sins in vv 7, 10. But even apart from vv 6-10 the present tense in "your sins are being forgiven" indicates forgiveness effected by Jesus' pronouncement more naturally than forgiveness reported as a result of communication from God in heaven, for which we would expect the perfect tense, as in Luke 7:47-48; John 20:23 (cf. Matt 16:19).

It is hard to know what to make of other arguments for the hypothesis of insertion, such as the failure of the scribes to voice their objection in vv 6-8 (How does that argue for an insertion?), the failure of the acclamation in v 12 to refer to the supposed insertion (But what is there in it that should be referred to more specifically than by the summarizing "thus"?), and the lack of an adverse reaction by the scribes (cf. 3:1-6) coupled with their inclusion in the acclamation (But none of the other controversy stories before 3:1-6 closes with an adverse reaction). And how do we know that the scribes do react adversely on this occasion? Who is to say that they do not react in amazement with the rest of the crowd, or at least that Mark suppresses an adverse reaction on their part in favor of general amazement? In 12:28, 32 he will note that a scribe recognizes the beauty and truth of Jesus' answers. The argument that because Jesus nowhere else claims authority to forgive sins (with the dubious exception of Luke 7:47-48, which has the perfect rather than the present tense) vv 5b-10 must be an inauthentic insertion — this argument can cut the other way, too: in accordance with the criterion of dissimilarity, the uniqueness of the claim speaks in favor of its authenticity. The Jews do not expect the Messiah to forgive sins; and though other passages in the NT make Jesus the channel of God's forgiveness, only the present passage makes him the forgiver (see R. Bultmann in *TDNT* 1. 511-12; for other considerations, H.-J. Klauck in *BZ* nf 25 [1981] 242). The argument that nowhere else does Jesus claim to be the Son of man misreads the passage: Jesus does not say, "I am the Son of man." As elsewhere he leaves it to be inferred that he is referring to himself because the statement has relevance only with that understanding (see, e.g., 8:31; 9:9, 12, 31; 10:33, 45; 14:21, 41). The argument that a pre-Marcan traditioner made an insertion because Mark himself does not regard miracles as proof of Jesus' authority mistakes Mark's view of miracles as well as wrongly accepts the hypothesis of an insertion. In 8:11-12 Jesus will reprove the sign-seeking that springs from the Pharisees' unbelief; but it is a sign "from heaven," not a miracle or an exorcism, that they will seek, and in Matt 11:4-6, 20-24; 12:29; Luke 7:22-23; 10:13-15; 11:20 Jesus positively appeals to his miracles and exorcisms as evidence regarding his own person as well as God's rule (cf. John 3:2; Acts 2:22; 10:38). Since forgiveness of sins plays a major role in the coming of God's rule, the interrelating of miracles and forgiveness harmonizes with the interrelating of miracles and the coming of that rule.

The argument that the contrast between the abstract diction in vv 5b-10 or 6-10 and the concrete terms in the surrounding narrative favors a later insertion offers a non sequitur. Why should not an abstract discussion take place in concrete circumstances? It happens all the time. Where else *can* an abstract discussion take place? The argument that subtraction of vv 5b-10 (but not merely of vv 6-10) produces a form critically perfect healing story backfires: since traditioners tend to assimilate historical data to standard forms (see F. Hahn in *Rückfrage nach Jesu* 20-23), the atypicality of having vv 5b-10 in the story may just as easily derive from primitive brute facts as from later contrived insertion. Neither vv 5b-10 nor vv 6-10 could stand by themselves; so advocates of their insertion have to posit either an earlier framework, now lost, or a redactional fabrication of the present framework. The first position faces the unlikelihood of transfer from one story to another. The second position faces the unlikelihood that material so dissimilar from the rest of Mark and the NT in its interrelating of forgiveness and healing is the product of wholesale fabrication. The "if"-clause in Jas 5:15 makes that passage only a partial exception. Furthermore, it is strange that a creative redactor would like "the Son of man" well enough to put it on Jesus' lips but not on the lips of others or in his own frankly editorial passages.

In favor of literary unity W. L. Lane (97) traces "the homogeneous development" of the pericope from the announcement of pardon (v 5) through the question (vv 6-9) and the validation (v 11) to the recognition (v 12). As noted above, however, v 10 goes with v 11 as part of the validation rather than offering an editorial address to readers. Nowhere else in the NT or other Hellenistic materials does pronouncing the forgiveness of sins act as an encouragement to the seeking of help (J. Gnilka in *Jesus und der Menschensohn* 199-200). Therefore it seems unlikely that Jesus is here trying to encourage the paralytic with a merely prophetic assurance of God's forgiveness. O. Hofius (in *Diakonia* 131) goes on to argue that in other healing stories the word of Jesus accomplishes itself (see 5:41; Luke 7:14; 8:54; 13:12; John 11:43) and that subtracting vv 6-10 leaves "Child, your sins are forgiven" parallel with "Get up . . ." (the parenthetical "I say to you" being considered a redactional addition). Therefore, just as the word about getting up accomplishes a getting up, so also the word about forgiveness accomplishes a forgiveness, so that the passive is not divine: mere announcement of God's forgiveness is no more in view than is mere announcement of getting up. The difference between the indicative mood of the word about forgiveness and the imperative mood of the word about getting up weakens this argument. Nevertheless, the unlikelihood that the word about forgiveness acts as an encouragement leaves that word without purpose when vv 6-10 are subtracted. Those verses seem to go with v 5b, then. And Hofius (ibid. 129, n. 23) correctly notes a difficulty in the view that v 5b as well as vv 6-10 belongs to an insertion: this view leaves it unclear why material about forgiveness of sins is inserted into a pure healing story that originally did not even hint at the topic of forgiveness (see also J. Kiilunen, *Vollmacht* 94-99; C. D. Marshall,

Faith 78-86; and cf. 4:41; 7:37 with Gen 1:31; Ps 65:8[7]; 89:10[9]; 104:7; 107:23-32; Isa 35:4-6 for Jesus' doing other sorts of things that only God is supposed to do; plus B. Blackburn, *Theios Anēr* 1899, on healings of paralysis).

JESUS' POWER TO ATTRACT TOLL COLLECTORS AND SINNERS AND HIS AUTHORITY TO EAT WITH THEM

2:13-17 (Matt 9:9-13; Luke 5:27-32)

The story of Levi gets a general introduction in Jesus' departure to the seaside (v 13a), the crowd's coming (v 13b), and his teaching them (v 13c). The call of Levi occurs next (v 14) and issues in toll collectors' and sinners' eating with Jesus and his disciples (v 15), the scribes' raising a question about such table fellowship (v 16), and Jesus' reply (v 17).

2:13 *(Luke 5:27a)* Having shown Jesus' authority to forgive sins (vv 1-12), Mark can appropriately introduce a story about Jesus' calling sinners. Jesus' going "out" means out from Capernaum and a house there (v 1). "Again" attaches to his going out, harks back to his going out from Capernaum in 1:35, 38, and portrays him as continuing to fulfil the purpose of extending his powerful activity as expressed in 1:38 (cf. the use of "again" in 2:1). But "again" modifies the rest of the predicate, too, including "to the seaside," and thus recalls 1:16, which started the first story of a call to discipleship beside the Sea of Galilee (1:16-20). A number of other parallels with that story will also appear. "The crowd" may refer to the crowd mentioned in the preceding pericope (v 4; cf. 4:1; 9:15), especially since the adjective "all" that goes with it seems to carry forward the "all" who were twice mentioned at the very close of the preceding pericope (v 12). Their coming to Jesus — all of them — emphasizes his magnetic power. Wherever he goes, even to the seaside, the crowd is drawn. The forward position of πᾶς ὁ ὄχλος, "all the crowd," intensifies this emphasis. So also does the imperfect tense of ἤρχετο, "kept coming," by indicating that they came to him wave upon wave (cf. 1:45). Mark does not identify the subject matter of Jesus' teaching. As before, he is more interested in portraying him as an authoritative figure (cf. 1:21-22, 27).

2:14 *(Matt 9:9; Luke 5:27b-28)* "And going along he saw" again matches 1:16. "He saw Levi the [son] of Alphaeus" recalls "he saw James the [son] of Zebedee" in 1:19. "Sitting at the toll booth" recalls "casting nets into the sea" in 1:16 and "preparing their nets" in 1:19 and thereby reemphasizes the forcefulness of Jesus' command: the command will prove so forceful that Levi, like Simon and Andrew, James and John, will forsake his occupation right in the middle of pursuing it (see fuller comments on 1:16-20). The historical present tense of λέγει, "he says," highlights this forcefulness. Above and beyond the repetition of this earlier emphasis, "sitting at the toll booth" prepares for the effectiveness of Jesus' calling a whole crowd of toll collectors and other sinners in vv 15-17. "Follow me" (cf. John 1:43) echoes the statement in 1:18 that Simon and Andrew "followed him" and takes the present tense, emphatic in the imperative (ἀκολούθει; contrast the unemphatic aorist imperative of this verb in 14:13, where following somebody other than Jesus is in view, and cf. the notes on 1:3). Levi's "standing up" contrasts with his "sitting" earlier in the verse, corresponds to "leaving their nets" and "leaving their father Zebedee" in 1:18, 20, and again highlights Jesus' power to induce the giving up of an occupation. The match between ἠκολούθησεν αὐτῷ, "he followed him," and ἀκολούθει μοι, "Follow me" (which replaces the somewhat different δεῦτε ὀπίσω μου, "Hither! After me!" of 1:17), stresses the exact obedience that Jesus' command is able to effect even on a toll collector (again cf. 1:18). "He followed him" also prepares for the even more astounding report that "many" toll collectors and sinners were following Jesus (see v 15 with comments). Levi is the first of a large number of fellow sinners thus to give evidence of Jesus' magnetism.

2:15 *(Matt 9:10; Luke 5:29)* The historical present tense of "and it comes to pass" (contrast the past tense of this expression in 1:9; 2:23; 4:4) ties the following episode of a banquet to the preceding episode of Levi's call (cf. the excursus on 2:1–3:6). The "he" who "was sitting" might refer to Levi. But the second half of this verse makes "he" refer more naturally to Jesus, for otherwise there is no preparation for his even being in the house where toll collectors and sinners dine with him and his disciples. In either case, by saving Jesus' name for toll collectors' and sinners' dining with him, Mark emphasizes the magnetism of Jesus. "His house" probably means Levi's house (cf. 14:3; Luke 19:1-10), since Mark has not said that Jesus has a house in Capernaum but has portrayed him as a wandering preacher, and since "at home [Simon's and Andrew's — or Jesus', for that matter]" would most likely have been ἐν οἴκῳ, as in 2:1 (cf. 1:29; against M. Theobald in *BZ* nf 22 [1978] 175; E. S. Malbon in *NTS* 31 [1985] 282-92). For the first time in Mark the term "disciples" appears. The evangelist apparently refers to Simon and Andrew, James and John (1:16-20, 21, 29-31, 36-38), and now perhaps to Levi as well. The reference prepares for the question addressed to the disciples in v 16. As to those reclining at table with Jesus and his disciples, "toll collectors" links up with Levi's just-relinquished occupation; and "sinners" broadens Jesus' attractive power to include wicked people of other sorts, too. As often, "many" magnifies that power, as does also the position of the subject πολλοὶ τελῶναι καὶ ἁμαρτωλοί, "many toll collectors and sinners," before its verb συνανέκειντο, "were reclining with. . . ." "For they were many" may seem redundant. In fact, it is emphatic, as are "for"-clauses in 6:50 vis à vis 6:49; 7:21 vis à vis 7:20; 12:23 vis à vis 12:20-22; 16:8bd vis à vis 16:8ac (cf. 13:35 vis à vis 13:33). Such clauses regularly stress an authorial point of view. That toll collectors and sinners should follow Jesus as well as recline at table with him provides staggering evidence for the effectiveness of his word — his teaching and his call. That *many* of them follow him is more than staggering, and it counterbalances the growth of opposition to Jesus. Mark cannot stress too much that Jesus' power is so great that it draws not only religious people who attend synagogues (cf. 1:21-28, 39), but also irreligious, downright wicked people whom one might think to lie outside his magnetic field. "And they were following him" may refer to their reclining at meal with Jesus; for along with ἦσαν, "they were," the two verbs συνανέκειντο, "were reclining," and ἠκολούθουν, "were following," are imperfect and parallel. But since reclining does not equate with following, Mark may refer back to their having followed Jesus to the house. Then the conjunction γάρ, "for," governs their following Jesus as well as their being many. Mark is hardly referring forward to their following Jesus subsequently; for the imperfect indicative points to past time, and Mark makes no later reference to such following. Whether equivalent to reclining or retrospective of going to the house, the reference to following looks intrusive (cf. the omissions in Matt 9:10; Luke 5:29). This very intrusiveness — or the forced nature of the equation between following and reclining at table, if we accept such an equation — shows the strength of Mark's desire to stress that Jesus' magnetic power draws people who ordinarily would have little or nothing to do with religion.

Some think that the many who follow Jesus are his disciples as distinct from the toll collectors and sinners and that Mark describes them as many to indicate at his first use of "disciples" that the term includes a larger number than Simon, Andrew, James, John, and Levi. But other interpreters question whether "disciples" in Mark means more than the Twelve, and nowhere else does Mark emphasize a large number of disciples (see esp. R. P. Meye, *Jesus and the Twelve* 140-45). In the present context, since the conjunction "for" makes the clause give a reason for the dining of many toll collectors and sinners with Jesus and his disciples, the "they" who are "many" and "follow him" more easily points to the "many toll collectors and sinners," exclusive of the disciples, in the preceding clause. It would not make good sense for Mark to write that many toll collectors and sinners were eating with Jesus and his disciples because his *disciples* were many. The magnetism of Jesus, not the number of the disciples, is what attracts the toll collectors and sinners. But a reference to the toll collectors and sinners makes good sense of the "for"-clause: many of them eat with Jesus and the disciples because there *are* many toll collectors and sinners, and they cannot resist following him. Furthermore, since the representative toll collector and sinner Levi has followed Jesus in v 15, it is only natural that those who are many and follow him in v 15 are other toll collectors and sinners (see also F. Vouga in *Jesu Rede von Gott und ihre Nachgeschichte im frühen Christentum* 60-61). To take the "and" before "they were following him" as Semitic parataxis for "who" (producing "for there were many who were following him") tends to miss the distribution of emphasis between the large number and the following (and see M. Reiser, *Syntax und Stil* 128-30, against treating the construction necessarily as a Semitism).

2:16 *(Matt 9:11; Luke 5:30)* "The scribes" harks back to vv 6-7. "Of the Pharisees" is added because of the Pharisees' moral concern plus their ritual concern to extend the laws of purity, which Jesus is violating by eating with toll collectors and sinners (cf. Acts 23:9 for Pharisaical scribes). The repetitiveness of "sinners and toll collectors" where a simple "with them" would have sufficed in the editorial introduction (a reference to them has just preceded and another will immediately follow in direct quotations) makes for a striking contrast with "the scribes of the Pharisees" who ask a question. Though a v.l. has the usual order, the better reading puts "sinners" before "toll collectors" in the introduction to the scribes' question. This forward position prepares for v 17, where the scribes do not merely take second place but drop out altogether. Why do the scribes ask the disciples instead of Jesus? Perhaps because of the preceding demonstration of his power over against the scribes' criticism (vv 1-12). If so, their fear to ask Jesus directly makes another tribute to the awesomeness of his authority. Because of their special hatred of toll collectors they mention them first in the question. We might take the second ὅτι in v 16 as recitative and therefore their words as an accusatory statement: "He is eating with toll collectors and sinners" (cf. the charge of blasphemy in v 7; see, e.g., W. Thissen, *Erzählung* 63, n. 60). In view of 9:11, 28; Matt 9:11; Luke 5:30; and the vv.ll. here in Mark 2:16, however, the ὅτι may be interrogatory: "Why does he eat with toll collectors and sinners?" (but see BAGD s.v. ὅστις 4b). As a question the words are still accusatory. In the Greek text the emphatic position of the phrase "with toll collectors and sinners" (contrast the order of words in the introduction to the question) sharpens the accusatory tone.

2:17 *(Matt 9:12-13; Luke 5:31-32)* Jesus' "hearing" corresponds to the scribes' "seeing" (v 16). He takes the initiative. He does not wait for the disciples to relay the question. He directs his statement to the scribes, not to the crowd, and defends his action. The first part, "The strong have no need of a physician, but the sick [have need of a physician]," represents proverbial wisdom. The second half, "I did not come to call righteous people, but [I came to call] sinners," represents Jesus' application of that wisdom to answer the question brought against him. Toll collectors have dropped out to make a cleaner contrast with righteous people, i.e. to limit the contrast to one expression on each side. But Mark is not interested in the reason for Jesus' eating with sinners so much as in the way that Jesus' statement ends the argument almost before it begins. There is no see-sawing. With one verbal blow he knocks out his critics. His word is final, its truth self-evident. He can call sinners. He does call them. Nobody can stop him from doing so, or even make him look bad when he does, ritual laws notwithstanding. Underscoring this point are the historical present tense of λέγει, "he says," the asyndeton between the two parts of his statement, the parallelism of the construction οὐ . . . ἀλλά, "not . . . but," in each of them, the strength of the adversative ἀλλά (bis), and the ellipsis in each ἀλλά-clause.

NOTES

We should avoid overinterpreting the sea as here symbolizing the forces of evil and chaos, as though Jesus goes out to look his foe in the face. We should likewise avoid the conjecture that the call of Levi occurred at a time and place different from Mark's location of it. W. H. Wuellner (*Meaning* 43-44) thinks that as a toll collector Levi had fishers working for him. "Son of Alphaeus" leads to the presumption that Levi is a brother of James the son of Alphaeus (3:18 parr.; Acts 1:13b), unless against Matt 9:9 Levi is the same as that James (cf. Mark 2:14 D Θ *f*¹³ 565 *pc* it Tat). In view of Jesus' going out of the city to the seaside in v 13, the toll booth appears to be located on a commercial road along the sea for the purpose of taxing goods in transport. H. Simonsen (in *ST* 26 [1972] 7-9) thinks that "sitting at the toll booth" implies the unworthiness of Levi to be called. But vv 15-17 stress not so much the unworthiness of toll collectors and sinners as Jesus' power and authority to call them just as he tore the two pairs of brothers away from their occupations in 1:16-20.

The non-appearance of Levi the son of Alphaeus elsewhere in Mark favors that the name comes from tradition, for a fabricator would likely have picked the name of one of the Twelve as listed in 3:16-19. Jesus went to the house of Simon and Andrew and was served there even though Simon and Andrew were following him (1:16-18, 29-31); so Jesus' dining in Levi's house even though Levi is following him offers no handle for arguing that Mark fabricates vv 13-14 and overlooks a disagreement between Levi's following and Jesus' eating in Levi's house (so E. Best, *Following Jesus* 175). If Mark were fabricating 2:13-14 with the help of 1:16-20 and a traditional reference to Levi the son of Alphaeus in 2:15 (now replaced by αὐτοῦ, "his," because of Mark's transferring it to 2:14 — so R. Pesch in *ZNW* 59 [1968] 43-45), we would expect Mark to include a γάρ-clause, "for he [Levi] was a toll collector," to match "for they were fishers" in 1:16b; and we would expect him to write that Jesus said, "Hither! After me!" as in 1:17 or, especially if Mark were fabricating vv 13-14 to illustrate Jesus' "calling" sinners in 2:17c, to write "he called him," after the pattern of 1:19, instead of writing that Jesus said, "Follow me." Even the much later "Follow me" in 10:21 is preceded by "Hither!" Moreover, it seems unlikely that Mark would disrupt the series of controversy stories by fabricating and inserting a call-story in vv 13-14. Far simpler for him to pass directly from the controversy in vv 1-12 to the one in vv 15-17 just as he passes directly from one controversy to another at every other juncture in 2:1–3:6. The controversy in vv 15-17 already has an adequate setting in the meal. To affirm the original unity of vv 13-14 with vv 15-17 is not to deny a correspondence between vv 13-14 and 1:16-20. But the circumstances are much the same, and on similar occasions Jesus is likely to have called disciples in much the same way. A traditional connection of vv 13-14 with vv 15-17 damages the view that according to an earlier version which lacked vv 13-14 the meal took place in Jesus' house. Though "and it comes to pass" may start a new pericope and therefore favor that vv 15-17 did not originally carry on from vv 13-14 (see 1:9; 2:23), the expression does not have to start a new pericope (see 4:4). The historical present tense differs from 1:9; 2:23; 4:4 and, as noted in the foregoing comments, ties vv 15-17 closely to vv 13-14. One could attribute the historical present to redaction, but then an argument turns into a hypothesis. And even in 1:9, though "and it came to pass" started a new pericope, "in those days" linked the following baptism of Jesus to its probably historical setting in the ministry of John the Baptizer (1:1-8). M. Zerwick (*Untersuchungen* 65) argues against an emphatic historical present tense in λέγει, "he says," on the ground that the parallel in 1:17 has the aorist εἶπεν, "he said." But lack of emphasis in 1:17 forestalls emphasis in 2:14 no more than the comparatively mild "Follow me" in 2:14 retrospectively evacuates "Hither! After me!" of its vigor in 1:17.

The view that the ambiguity of the pronouns in v 15a is due to a transfer of Levi's name from the position of its substitute "his" (αὐτοῦ) in v 15a to the newly fabricated vv 13-14 not only runs into the aforementioned objections to Mark's fabricating vv 13-14, but also overlooks that for the sake of clarity he does not hesitate to repeat a name quickly (see 1:29-30). Perhaps Mark thinks that since Simon followed Jesus but Jesus entered Simon's house and ate there (1:29-31), it ought to be clear enough by precedent that Levi follows Jesus but Jesus goes to Levi's house for a meal. The varied associations of "house" that we have already met in Mark — with healing (1:29-34), with speaking the word and healing (2:1-12), and now with dining and controversy (2:15-17) — should warn us against reading too much theology into the term, in particular, against regarding "house" as a code-word for withdrawal-cum-messianic secret. On reclining at special meals and in the open, but not at ordinary meals, see J. Jeremias, *Eucharistic Words* 48-49. Eating in the house of a toll collector-sinner is liable to bring ritual defilement from contact with unclean dinnerware, furniture, and garments, less likely from food not butchered and prepared according to the Mosaic Law, for a Palestinian Jewish host would be unlikely to serve such food (R. P. Booth, *Jesus and the Laws of Purity* 80-81, 110-11). Then there is the danger of moral defilement. On the disciples and the crowd as well as on the later-mentioned twelve and others in relation to Jesus, see E. S. Malbon in *NovT* 28 (1986) 104-30 (though she does not recognize that Mark means his treatment of them to make Christological points rather than to teach lessons of discipleship). For toll collectors, see J. Jeremias, *Jerusalem* 303-12; H. W. Hoehner, *Herod Antipas* 77-79; J. R. Donahue in *CBQ* 33 (1971) 49-61; F. Herrenbrück in *ZNW* 72 (1981) 178-94, and on "sinners" as very wicked people, not just "the people of the land" who make up the more or less religious but by Pharisaic standards careless bulk of the population, E. P. Sanders, *Jesus and Judaism* 174-211, and earlier literature cited there.

It is often suggested that the use of "sinners" for Gentiles as well as for some Jews made this story seem applicable to the question of table fellowship between Jewish and Gentile Christians in the early church (Acts 11:3; Rom 14:1–15:13; Gal 2:11-14) and thus led to preservation of the story (cf. the association of "sinners" and "Gentiles" in Matt 5:46-47; 18:17; Luke 6:33-34; Gal 2:15). But in the present story the transfer from Jewish to Gentile sinners remains conjectural at best, and the association of "sinners" with Jewish toll collectors (like Levi, as Jewish a name as can be imagined — cf. M. Stern in *The Jewish People in the First Century* 2. 599) makes the transfer quite doubtful. It is even more conjectural and doubtful that "sinners" was not an original part of the tradition; for the compound phrase appears in different contexts (Matt 11:19 par. Luke 7:34; Luke 15:1), and the presence of "sinners" without "toll collectors" in 2:17c speaks for the origin of "sinners" in tradition.

To say that in v 15c Mark refers to disciples and expands their number to prepare for the selection of the Twelve in 3:13-19 stumbles over the failure of any of the diction in the present passage ("his disciples," "many," "were following him") to anticipate any of the diction in the later passage ("summons," "whom he himself willed," "went away to him," "apostles"). Conversely, the later passage will not reflect the present one. "Were following him" does not necessarily refer to discipleship (see 3:7; 5:24; 9:38 [N.B. the plural object "us"]; 11:9; 14:13). E. Arens (*ΗΛΘΟΝ-Sayings* 33) is wrong to argue against identifying the many who were following Jesus with the toll collectors and sinners by saying that another subject comes between them and ἦσαν, "they were." There is no intervening subject at all. In v 15b Jesus and his disciples are only the objects of συν-, "with." Taking v 15c as referring to the toll collectors and sinners avoids a shift in subjects.

After the καί which means "and" and introduces "were following" in v 15c, the καί in v 16a would mean "and" more naturally than "also," as it would have to mean under the v.l. supported by (P[88]) ℵ L Δ 33 *pc* b bo[mss] and producing "and also the scribes of the Pharisees were following him; and seeing . . . , they were saying" (vv 15-16). Moreover, toll collectors' and sinners' attraction to Jesus suits following him better than the Pharisaic scribes' opposition to Jesus would suit following him. C. M. Martini (in *Text–Wort–Glaube* 31-39) argues for omitting the definite article before "scribes" but keeping "of the Pharisees, seeing," though no textual tradition reads quite that way in v 16a. See B. M. Metzger, *Textual Commentary* ad loc., on text critical questions in vv 15-16. Since Mark does not mention the Pharisaic scribes among those who eat with Jesus and his disciples, one presumes that he portrays the Pharisaic scribes as onlookers. Hence, there is no conflict between eating with the toll collectors and sinners and Pharisaic scruples against doing so. Besides, the Pharasaic scribes are hardly doing what they criticize Jesus for doing. It is normal near eastern custom for people to stand around observing a banquet, as the scribes do here (Luke 7:37; *b. Ta'an.* 23ab; K. E. Bailey, *Through Peasant Eyes* 4-5). The Pharisees make their first appearance at this point in Mark. See D. R. Schwartz in *JSJ* 14 (1983) 157-71; A. J. Saldarini, *Pharisees* 128-32, on their strong influence even prior to 70 C.E. (against the view that the NT and Josephus [in the *Antiquities*] exaggerate it greatly). On the other hand, evidence of their activity in Galilee is sparse. Yet they are known to have been included in at least one delegation sent to Galilee (Josephus *Life* 38-39 §§189-98 et seqq.); so perhaps Pharisaic scribes come from Judea to Galilee to investigate Jesus' activities (cf. 3:22; for brief surveys of the evidence, see G. Vermes, *Jesus the Jew* 56-57; S. Freyne, *Galilee* 319-23; Saldarini, op. cit. 291-93 and, for Mark's tendency to use "Pharisees" in connection with Galilee and "scribes" in connection with Jerusalem, D. Lührmann in *ZNW* 80 [1989] 266-68). The modifying of both toll collectors and sinners by only one definite article (bis) reflects that toll collectors belong to the larger class of sinners. The imperfect tense of ἔλεγον, "were saying," and of other verbs of speaking reflects without emphasis the linear character of speech.

That Mark does not consistently use the historical present λέγει, "he says," to introduce Jesus' answers to antagonistic questions does not imply that it lacks emphasis (so M. Zerwick, *Untersuchungen* 65). One might argue to the contrary that it is consistency of use that would betray an authorial habit lacking emphasis. Those who argue that the saying about the strong and the sick (v 17b) has no bearing on the controversy over eating with toll collectors and sinners have suffered a lapse of the imagination it takes to appreciate metaphorical language. Even under their view, a redactor saw such a bearing. If a redactor, why not Jesus? Are we to suppose that originally the saying could have referred only prosaically to Jesus' healing ministry? Why would he have needed to defend such a ministry? Who would have criticized his healings as such? And what purpose besides defense might the saying have had? Such questions cause E. Arens (*ΗΛΘΟΝ-Sayings* 39-43) to think that this saying originally belonged to the story, but he denies that the saying about coming to call sinners did (cf. F. Vouga in *Jesu Rede von Gott und ihre Nachgeschichte im frühen Christentum* 68-69). His argument arbitrarily rules out the possibilities of original asynedeton, asyndetic redaction of originally syndetic sayings, and original mixture of metaphors. He also interprets "call" too passively. To say that because *POxy.* 1224 has been broken off before the canonical reference to not calling the righteous but sinners, that reference must have been added later as an aphoristic conclusion (so J. D. Crossan, *In Fragments* 215-16) is weaker than an argument from silence. Since we do not know what the missing portion of the papyrus said, it is an argument from only the *possibility* of silence. The additional argument that a pericope would not originally have ended with more than one saying (see also B. M. F. van Iersel in *De Jésus aux Évangiles* 217) depends on the circular reasoning of ruling out the originality of more than one saying at the ends of other pericopes, too (e.g., in the very next two controversy stories).

For the proverbial wisdom represented in v 17b, see Plut. *Mor.* 230F; Dio Chrys. *Orat.* 8.5; Diog. Laert. 2.70; 6.1.6; Luc. *Demon.* 7; and other literature cited by J. Wettstein 1. 358-59. But Hellenistic proverbial wisdom stresses the duty and habit of physicians to be with the diseased. Jesus' emphasis falls on the need of the sick to have a physician (see also H. Braun in *Festschrift für Ernst Fuchs* 100-101). It is hypercritical to think that the sick in the first part of the statement ill fit the toll collectors in the story. Surely the toll collectors' need of forgiveness (a kind of healing) is as great as that of the other sinners, whose misdeeds (a kind of sickness) seem not to exceed those of the toll collectors. Besides, the toll collectors do not even appear in the second part of the statement, yet that part belongs to the story as its climax. Does Jesus not call the righteous because they trust in their own righteousness, which is only apparent (cf. Luke 16:15), or because they do not need to be called since they are indeed righteous (cf. Luke 15:7, which may be taken as ironic, however)? The bad light in which Jesus elsewhere casts the scribes and Pharisees favors the former view, which does not make him ironically include them in his call. Rather, it makes him judgmentally exclude them. But the difficulty of interpreting the parallel phrase "the strong" to mean only those who think they are strong, but are not, stands against an interpretation in terms of self-righteousness. Perhaps "not righteous people but sinners" is meant comparatively rather than exclusively: "not righteous people so much as sinners" (see Hos 6:6 for the best known example of this sort of hyperbole; M. Zerwick, *Biblical Greek* §445; cf. the view of H. B. Swete [43] that with neither affirmation nor irony, "righteous" describes certain people as they profess to be; also the view of H. Ridderbos [*Coming* 219-22] that "righteous" and "sinful" mirror the relativity of human standards, though the righteous need to consider themselves sinners, as God does, for the purpose of hearing Jesus' call). W. Weiss (*"Eine neue Lehre in Vollmacht"* 93-94) uses Matt 5:19; 10:34-35; Mark 10:45 to argue that οὐκ . . . ἀλλά, "not . . . but," disallows the comparative meaning. But Matt 5:19 does not contain the construction. Matt 10:34-35 might be taken comparatively ("not peace so much as a sword") in view of Mark 5:34; Luke 2:14, 29; 7:50; 8:48; 19:42; 24:36; John 14:27; 16:33; 20:19, 21, 26. And thus also might Mark 10:45 be taken comparatively ("not to be served so much as to serve") in view of Mark 1:13 ("and the angels were serving him"), 31 ("and she [Simon's mother-in-law] was serving them [including Jesus]"). But since the Greek word order emphasizes "no need" and since in most double-edged sayings emphasis falls on the second member (here, on "sinners"; C. E. Carlston, *Parables* 113-14), identifying the exact nuance of "righteous" may be unnecessary and inappropriate in the first place. The righteous would be neither excluded nor required to repent of self-righteousness; they would simply provide a foil for Jesus' calling of sinners. The use of "sinners" for especially wicked people militates against saying that toll collectors drop out for the sake of a generalizing description of all human beings (or at least of all the Jews to whom Jesus is ministering — see M. Trautmann, *Zeichenhafte Handlungen* 162-64) and therefore also against the theory that early Christians fabricated the second half of the saying out of their being drawn almost entirely from the general population, hardly at all from the scribes and Pharisees (cf. Matt 11:19; 18:12-14; Luke 7:34, 36-50; 15:1-32; 19:1-10; and C. E. B. Cranfield 105-7 against the suggestion of D. E. Nineham 98).

Concerning "I have come," cf. the comments on 1:38; and BAGD s.v. 2 on καλέω. Jesus may mean his "call" to be an invitation to share in an anticipation of the messianic banquet (on which see the references listed by R. H. Gundry, *Matthew* 70), the present banquet being itself such an anticipation. In favor of this view, Jesus almost seems to be the host in v 15, since the toll collectors and sinners are dining with him. But they are also dining "with his disciples," and Levi is probably acting as the host. So the argument passes muster only if we suppose that Jesus is comparing his invitation to sinners with Levi's invitation to toll collectors and sinners. But that supposition seems far-fetched, because Jesus makes no mention of such an invitation by Levi, because Levi belongs to the class of toll collectors and sinners as Jesus does not, and because καλέω cannot mean "invite" but must mean "call" in 1:16-20, which provides numerous parallels to the present passage. Neither does Mark mention an invitation by Levi to his fellow toll collectors and sinners; so it seems doubtful that he is portraying Levi as a fisher of human beings. Omission of an invitation by Levi puts the emphasis instead on Jesus' magnetic call. Luke's οἱ ὑγιαίνοντες, "the healthy" (5:31), makes a better contrast in Greek with οἱ κακῶς ἔχοντες, "the sick" (both Mark and Luke); so Mark's οἱ ἰσχύοντες, "the strong," may rest on the Aramaic בְּרִיא, which carries both meanings. This possibility undermines the view that v 17b comes from Greek peripatetic philosophers rather than from Jesus. On the other hand, see the classical Greek references cited in LSJ s.v. ἰσχύω 1 for strength in the sense of health. The observation about physicians is common enough; and first century Palestine, especially

Galilee, where Jesus lived, is Hellenized anyway. So there is no need to deny the authenticity of v 17b. In favor of authenticity R. Pesch (in *Mélanges Bibliques* 81-82) also notes contrasts between the above-mentioned centrality of the physician in comparable Hellenistic sayings and that of the sick in v 17b and between the pairing of ὑγιαίνοντες and νοσοῦντες, "ailing," in those sayings and the pairing of ἰσχύοντες and κακῶς ἔχοντες here.

C. E. Carlston (*Parables* 114-15) argues against the authenticity of v 17 that had Peter heard Jesus use such a saying to defend eating with toll collectors and sinners, Peter would not have stopped eating with Gentile Christians in Antioch (see Gal 2:11-14 plus the reference to Gentiles as "sinners" in v 15). But Jesus' example should by itself have kept Peter from stopping his practice of eating with Gentile Christians. Yet Carlston does not dispute Jesus' eating with toll collectors and sinners; so there is no more reason to doubt the authenticity of Jesus' saying than to doubt the authenticity of his example. The reason for Peter's withdrawal from table-fellowship is to be found where Paul puts it, i.e. in the influence of "certain ones from James."

JESUS' AUTHORITY TO ALLOW NON-FASTING

2:18-22 *(Matt 9:14-17; Luke 5:33-39)*

Now Mark demonstrates Jesus' authority to overturn prevailing practices of piety, in particular, to turn the sorrow of fasting into the joy of feasting. Along with prayer and almsgiving, fasting forms one of the three main pillars of Jewish piety (see, e.g., Tob 12:8). The Mosaic Law requires fasting only once a year, on the Day of Atonement (Lev 16:1-34; 23:26-32; Num 29:7-11; cf. CD 6:19; 1QpHab 11:8); but the Pharisees fast weekly on Mondays and Thursdays as well (Luke 18:12; *Did.* 8:1; *m. Taʿan.* 1:4-6; 2:9; *b. Taʿan.* 10a; Str-B 2. 243; see ibid. 4. 77-114; J. Behm in *TDNT* 4. 927-31; W. L. Lane 108, n. 57, for other Jewish fasts). The presence of Jesus breaks down even this pillar of Jewish piety, however; and so great will be the loss when he is taken away that his disciples will fast once again. Mark lays the groundwork for this pericope by mentioning that John's disciples and the Pharisees were fasting (v 18a). Then comes the question why Jesus' disciples are not fasting (v 18b). His reply utilizes three analogies: (1) a wedding (vv 19-20); (2) a patch (v 21); and (3) new wine (v 22).

2:18 *(Matt 9:14; Luke 5:33)* Mention of John's disciples (see also 6:29) naturally follows the first mention of Jesus' disciples (v 15). Likewise, mention of the Pharisees naturally follows a reference to the scribes of the Pharisees (v 16). And a question about fasting naturally follows a story about eating (vv 13-17). The eating in vv 13-17 makes it unnecessary to indicate in v 18a that the disciples are eating in contrast with the fasting of John's disciples and the Pharisees.

The "they" who come and ask the question why John's disciples and the disciples of the Pharisees are fasting but Jesus' disciples are not hardly refers to John's disciples and the Pharisees unless they speak of themselves in the third person — an unlikely possibility (as shown in Matt 9:14 by the change to "we" for John's disciples and by the retention of the third person for the Pharisees). Of course, we might think that Mark or an earlier traditioner makes up the introduction to the question (v 18ab) with a view to equating the questioners with those who are fasting. But such an editor would probably put "the disciples of the Pharisees" in the introduction to the question to make an equation with "the disciples of the Pharisees" in the question itself. Instead, the introduction simply reads, "the Pharisees." If "they" meant "the scribes of the Pharisees" mentioned in v 16, the question would probably refer to "our disciples" rather than to "the disciples of the Pharisees" (see also the following notes). Therefore we should take "they" as indefinite, meaning "people" (so also Luke 5:33 and elsewhere in Mark; cf. C. H. Turner in *JTS* os 25 [1923-24] 379). "The *disciples* of the Pharisees" complements "the *scribes* of the Pharisees" in vv 16-17. In turn, "the disciples *of John* and the disciples *of the Pharisees*" stands over against "*your* disciples" (i.e. the disciples *of Jesus*) in the question. The use of the possessive dative σοι, "your" (instead of the expected genitive), and its position before μαθηταί, "disciples," stress the contrast. Because of earlier incarceration (1:14), John is not mentioned as fasting along with his disciples. But the Pharisees in general are fasting according to v 18a. In the following question, then, "the disciples of the Pharisees" does not refer to a group different from the Pharisees (as though the Pharisees as such have disciples — they do not), but distinguishes the Pharisees who are *not* scribes from those who *are* scribes and who as such teach the non-scribal ones to fast along with them. The distinction makes possible a parallel with John's disciples and a contrast with the disciples of Jesus (against a loose interpretation of the disciples of the Pharisees as people influenced by the Pharisees' ideals and practices even though they do not belong to the Pharisaic sect; cf. K. H. Rengstorf in *TDNT* 4. 443; W. L. Lane 108).

We may presume that in failing to fast the disciples of Jesus follow his example (cf. vv 15-16; Matt 11:19 par. Luke 7:34), just as the fasting of John's disciples may reflect a practice of his (cf. Matt 11:18 par. Luke 7:33). But neither John's nor Jesus' own practices come into view here. Thus, the question does not deal with fasting so much as with the relative authority of John, of the Pharisees, and of Jesus: Does Jesus have authority to suspend fasting for his disciples despite John's and the Pharisees' requiring that their disciples fast? The present historical tense of ἔρχονται, "they come," and of λέγουσιν, "they say," highlights this question of authority.

2:19-20 *(Matt 9:15; Luke 5:34-35)* In language that is at once figurative and cryptic, Jesus answers by pointing to himself as a kind of bridegroom whose presence makes fasting not just inappropriate but impossible, and whose coming removal will make his disciples fast. His authority transcends any comparison of his interpretative skill with that of John and the Pharisaic scribes. He is in a class by himself. His personal presence or removal determines whether his disciples can fast or not. The mention of inability at the beginning and at the end of Jesus' words in v 19 and the use of "day" at the beginning and at the end of his words in v 20 form inclusions. These inclusions stress the difference that his presence and absence make between the present time of non-fasting and the future day of fasting (cf. J. Dewey, *Markan Public Debate* 91). The delay of νηστεύειν, "to fast," in his counter question, "The sons of the wedding hall are not able . . . to fast, are they?" gives emphasis to "while the bridegroom is with them"; and within this clause the delay of ἐστιν, "is," allows the accent to fall on the bridegroom's presence. The following up of this counter question with a declaration that repeats the notes of presence and inability, "So long a time as they have the bridegroom with them they are not able to fast," doubles the emphasis on the overpowering effect of his presence. And the predictions of his removal and of his disciples' fasting on that day exhibit the power he has to foretell the future — a theme that will become increasingly prominent in Mark.

The striking redundancy of "on that day" after "then" and the equally striking shift from the plural "days" to the singular "on that day" demand explanation. The demonstrative "that" makes it difficult to think of a collective singular for the days of Jesus' absence as a time of fasting (cf. the contrast in Luke 17:22-24 between "days" and "one of the days," "in his day"). The contrast between the singular and the plural (unlike the singular alone of "day" for the church age in John 14:20; 16:23, 26) and the backward reference of the singular to the removal of the bridegroom make it difficult to think of repeated days of fasting during the church age (Wednesdays and Fridays according to *Did.* 8:1; see H.-W. Kuhn, *Ältere Sammlungen* 66-70, on the further possibilities of a reference to fasting every Friday, every Good Friday, every Saturday following Good Friday, and every Passover; and C. E. Carlston, *Parables* 120, n. 15, against the widely accepted reference to fasting every Friday). Besides, evidence for such regular fasting in the church postdates the NT. The presupposition that v 20b refers to an ongoing practice of fasting in the church hinders the most natural understanding of the text. It is that the disciples will fast on the day of the bridegroom's removal, after which will follow an indefinite number of days. In other words, "on that day" makes "then" refer to the time of the bridegroom's removal rather than to the days following (as "then" would do without "on that day"; cf. John 16:16-22, esp. 20; H. Simonsen in *ST* 26 [1972] 9-10). Thus the statement does not point to an ongoing practice of fasting in the church, but centers on the person of Jesus. One could say that originally v 20b lacked "on that day" and referred to fasting for a number of days and that Mark adds "on that day" to make a Christological point. If so, a prediction of fasting for a number of days turns out to be early (pre-Marcan) rather than late (cf. the view of E. Lohmeyer [60] that under the expectation of a soon coming kingdom, the days were few and all given over to fasting [*As. Mos.* 9:1-7], but that with the physical impossibility of fasting any longer and with the redactional addition of "on that day" the days of fasting became occasional; also the rather similar eschatological interpretation of G. Braumann in *NovT* 6 [1963] 264-67). See the LXX of 1 Kgdms 2:31; Jer 19:6; 28:52-58; Amos 4:2; and Luke 17:22; 19:43; 21:6; 23:29 for other examples of "days will come [or 'are coming']" used ominously, but Jer 16:14-15; 23:5-6; 38:27-30, 31-36 for contrastively hopeful uses. Non-fasting and fasting may express joy and sorrow, but there is no need to treat them as metaphorical of joy and sorrow.

2:21-22 *(Matt 9:16-17; Luke 5:36-39)* A wedding requires good clothes on the part of the guests (Matt 22:11-14) and an ample supply of wine on the part of the host (John 2:1-11). So it is natural that this pericope should close with two more figurative sayings, the first dealing with clothes, the second with wine (cf. the verbal echo of the bridegroom's being "taken away" [2:20] in the "taking away" from the old garment [2:21]). The two sayings deal with the contrastive phenomena of shrinkage and expansion. Just as the saying about a wedding stressed, not the incompatibility of fasting with the festivity of a wedding, but the inability of the guests to fast in the presence of the bridegroom, so the sayings on clothes and wine stress, not the incompatibility of a new patch and an old garment and of new wine and old wineskins, but the irresistible shrinkage of a new patch and the irresistible expansion of new wine. An old garment cannot help but rip when a patch of unshrunken cloth shrinks after the next washing of the garment. Old wineskins, already stretched to their limits, cannot help but burst when new wine swells in them. For Mark, these irresistible forces illustrate Jesus' "new teaching with authority," "not as the scribes" (1:22, 27).

The triple parallelism of the two illustrative sayings heaps enormous emphasis on the irresistibility of Jesus' new teaching: (1) "no one sews a patch of unshrunken cloth on an old garment" is paralleled by "no one puts new wine into old wineskins"; (2) "otherwise, the fulness takes away [something] from it, the new [takes away something] from the old" is paralleled by "otherwise, the wine bursts the wineskins"; (3) "and a worse rip comes about" is paralleled by "and the wine is lost, also the wineskins [are lost]." Further emphasis accrues to the irresistibility of Jesus' new teaching from the capping clause, "rather, [one puts] new wine into new wineskins," which at once pays respect to that irresistibility, antithetically parallels "no one puts new wine into old wineskins," and provides a contrastive counterpart to the development of a worse rip in the preceding saying. This capping clause does not spoil the parallelism; it adds to the parallelism and aided by the strength of the adversative ἀλλά brings it to a climax. (So the argument against originality from a falsely supposed spoilage falls to the ground.) Yet further emphasis accrues to the irresistibility of Jesus' new teaching from the repetitive explanation, "the new from the old," from the additional subject, "also the wineskins," from the multiple ellipses (which add vigor), and from the emphatic forward positions in the Greek text of "a patch of unshrunken cloth," "a worse rip," and "the wine" before "is lost" (against Mark's usual placement of a subject after its verb). The point does not consist in the destruction of the old. In fact, the new is subject to destruction, too: the destruction of the wine, which is new, is mentioned even before the destruction of the wineskins, which are old; and the worse ripped garment now includes the new patch. The point consists in the power of the new. And since the destruction of the old is mentioned alongside that of the new and nothing is said about preserving either one (contrast the synoptic parallels and *Gos. Thom.* 47), the point consists *solely* in the power of the new. Mark means the sayings to indicate again that Jesus' authoritative pronouncements end all discussion. They brook no contradiction. They slam the door against all doubt. The story ends without debate (cf. the comments on v 17).

NOTES

See R. H. Gundry, *Matthew* 169, on Matthew's and Luke's reasons for reshaping the introductions to this pericope. The redactional character of these reasons forestalls the argument that Matthew's and Luke's introductions rest on a shorter, pre-Marcan tradition. J. Kiilunen (*Vollmacht* 165-68) argues that the identification of Jesus' opponents in the surrounding pericopes favors a reference to "the scribes of the Pharisees" (v 16) in the "they" who come and speak to Jesus (v 18). But the surrounding pericopes all contain an identification within themselves (2:6, 16, 24; 3:6), and "they come" (v 18) would disagree with the presence already of the Pharisaic scribes (v 16) if "they" were to refer back to them. "The disciples of the Pharisees" (cf. Matt 12:27; Luke 11:19; and esp. Matt 22:15-16) is hardly a later intrusion for the purpose of tying the story to surrounding stories having to do with Pharisees; for then we would expect in the question a simple reference to "the Pharisees," as in the immediately preceding introduction (v 18a) and in v 24, or to "the scribes of the Pharisees," as in v 16, rather than a reference to "the disciples of the Pharisees." The fact that elsewhere the disciples of the Pharisees do not stand alongside the disciples of John makes no argument against the authenticity of the Pharisees' disciples here; for elsewhere we do not find the Pharisees' disciples standing by themselves, either. To say that in v 18a "the Pharisees" is a tertiary correction of a secondary "the disciples of the Pharisees" leaves unexplained why the same correction is not made later in the verse. Appeal to parallel influence from "the disciples of John" fails, because that influence should have forestalled a correction in the first part of the verse, too.

Some suggest that John's disciples are fasting to mourn his death (the account of it appearing out of chronological order in 6:17-29), in which case Jesus' disciples are not fasting because they are not John's disciples and because Jesus is still with them. But this view trivializes the question by making it deal with a passing occasion rather than with a regular practice; it makes Jesus' answer uncharacteristically callous toward the memory of John (contrast 9:11-13; Matt 11:7-15; 17:10-12; Luke 7:24-35; cf. A. Kee in *NovT* 11 [1969] 164); and it leaves the Pharisees' disciples out of account or forces itself to regard them as an inauthentic addition. So others suggest that John's disciples and the Pharisees have the same purpose in fasting, i.e. to hasten the arrival of the messianic kingdom. If so, Jesus' following allusion to a wedding feast may indicate that that kingdom has already arrived. Mark makes nothing of this possibility, however. Though the singling out of John's disciples and the Pharisees points away from a fast required of all good Jews and might therefore seem to allow that the disciples of Jesus did join in generally required fasts (so J. O'Hara in *Scr* 19 [1967] 85-86), Jesus' answer casts doubt on such an allowance. For he is as much with his disciples during times of generally required fasts as he is on the present occasion.

The question why Jesus' disciples are not fasting assumes that a teacher like him is responsible for the conduct of his disciples (see D. Daube in *NTS* 19 [1972-73] 1-16, esp. 4-8; cf. the fasting of John's disciples with his neither eating nor drinking — Matt 11:18; cf. Luke 7:33). That the question deals with failure to fast by Jesus' disciples rather than by Jesus himself does not imply that he fasts. To say that it does would be to argue from silence, to overlook the rule that disciples follow their master's example, and to neglect the seemingly contrary implication of Matt 11:18-19 par. Luke 7:33-34. That Jesus' practice does not appear in the question leaves him free to speak of his presence and removal as the reasons for non-fasting and fasting. The absence of his practice from the question does not imply an early Christian milieu rather than Jesus' lifetime; for the main point of the pericope is the reason why his disciples are not fasting — an irrelevant point after his lifetime, when they do fast and when nobody appears to question why they do even though they did not during his lifetime (Acts 13:2-3; 14:23; 1 Cor 7:52 ℵ² Majority Text sy; *Did.*

8:1). Verses 21-22 would not stand at the close of the pericope if in an early Christian milieu the reference in v 20 to later fasting were considered the main point (and see the foregoing comments on the exclusion from that reference of an ongoing practice of fasting).

Νυμφών means either "wedding hall" or "bridal chamber" (BAGD s.v.). "The sons of the bridal chamber" would mean the groomsmen and has in its favor the contextual reference to Jesus' disciples, those closest to him. "The sons of the wedding hall" would mean the wedding guests and has in its favor the custom of feasting instead of fasting on the part of all the wedding guests, not just on the part of the groomsmen. The expression would still distinguish the disciples as those who are Jesus' guests in contrast with non-disciples, who are not his guests (E. Lohmeyer 59-60, n. 4). J. Ernst (99) rightly rejects as unconvincing the attempt to differentiate v 19a as pictorial from v 19b as allegorical and assign them to successive stages of tradition (see, e.g., J. Gnilka 1. 114). Instead, he emphasizes the synonymous parallelism of v 19ab. C. E. B. Cranfield (109) notes some allegory already in v 19a, for "while the bridegroom is with them" anticipates the bride-groom's future departure whereas in real life it is the guests who will depart. By now we have learned not to let the presence of some allegory rule out authenticity (see the notes on 3:23). H. Anderson (106) suggests that the omission of v 19b in Matt 9:15; Luke 5:34 rests on pre-Marcan tradition which shows v 19b to be Mark's redactional addition, or rests on an original Marcan text that shows v 19b to be a post-Marcan gloss (cf. D W f^{13} 33 700 it vg^{mss} [sy^p]). But Matt 9:15 combines v 19b with v 19a rather than omitting v 19b (R. H. Gundry, *Matthew* 169-70); Luke drops v 19b because of his redactional shift from "they are not able to fast" to "you are not able to make them fast"; and the v.l. represents the parallel influence that is rife in D and its partners.

Too much attention goes to the bridegroom in vv 19-20 to make acceptable the interpretation that "while the bridegroom is with them" means no more than "at the wedding" (so J. Jeremias, *NT Theology* 1. 105; idem in *TDNT* 4. 1101-3). But the cryp-ticness of the messianic claim in vv 19-20 speaks in favor of authenticity. We would expect an outright claim to messiahship in a redactional fabrication. So much vagueness attaches to the figure of a bridegroom, in fact, that quotation marks belong around the word "messianic." Though W. H. Brownlee (in *NTS* 3 [1956-57] 205) has argued that 1QIsa^a of Isa 61:10 portrays the coming Aaronic Messiah as a bridegroom, it seems that up through the first century the Jewish people did not think of the coming Davidic Messiah as a bridegroom (cf. J. Gnilka in *TTZ* 69 [1960] 298-301). Hence, it looks unlikely that the comparison would have been made by a Christian traditioner trying to portray Jesus as the Davidic Messiah (cf. R. H. Gundry, *Matthew* 170; also Jeremias, loc. cit.; but see Str-B 1. 517-18 for rabbinic portrayals of the days of the Messiah as a wedding feast). H. Riesenfeld (*Gospel Tradition* 152-54) argues cogently that since Jesus ascribes to himself activities of Yahweh and since the OT portrays Yahweh as a bridegroom (Isa 61:10; 62:5; cf. Matt 22:1-14; OT passages listed by C. E. B. Cranfield [110] on Yahweh as Israel's husband; and Str-B loc. cit.), it would be natural for Jesus to portray himself as a bridegroom. On the other hand, though John 3:22-30 is usually thought to represent late redaction, we might consider the possibility that John the Baptist's explicit identification of Jesus as the Messiah and his comparison of him with a bridegroom in John 3:28-29 enshrine a historical tradition that gives the source of Jesus' cautious comparison. Nevertheless, in John 3:28-29; 2 Cor 11:2; Eph 5:22-33; Rev 19:7; 21:2, 9 weight falls, not on the bridegroom, but on the bride of the groom. She plays no role whatever here in Mark (so also in Matt 25:1-13, due to redaction by Matthew, who may draw partly on the present Marcan tradition — see Gundry, *Matthew* 497-502). Probably, then, those passages do not indicate the source of the present comparison. S. Schulz (in *SE II/1*. 152-53) asks why we should allow Paul or Mark or an unknown traditioner but not Jesus to hit on the metaphor of a bridegroom. The instructions on fasting in Matt 6:16-18 come from Matthew's redaction (see Gundry, op.

cit. 110-11) and therefore do not historically contradict Jesus' saying that his disciples cannot fast while he is with them. Besides, even in Matthew those instructions apply only to the time after Jesus' departure (cf. Matt 9:14-17). Hence, Matt 6:16-18 does not imply the inauthenticity of Mark 2:19-20. Removal of the bridegroom hardly points to the end, especially since an indefinite number of days will follow; therefore "in that day" does not carry an eschatological connotation.

The view of R. Pesch (1. 171-76) is fairly typical. He accepts the authenticity of v 19a, but rejects the authenticity of vv 19b-20. To him, "as long a time as" seems to reflect the ever increasing number of "days" in the church age rather than the eschatological crisis of Jesus' ministry. Similarly, a reference to his death ("when the bridegroom is taken away") would have puzzled his audience, but not later Christians (cf. 14:7). Against this view, ὅσον χρόνον need not imply a lengthy period. In fact, it certainly does not with respect to the time of not being able to fast (its direct and only reference). Neither the question in v 18 nor Jesus' answer in vv 19-22 deals with how to fast; rather, with whether to fast. Since then the practice of fasting was undisputed in the early church (see the excursus on 2:1–3:6), there was no reason to create vv 19b-20. Actually, if vv 19b-20 were a fabrication of the early church, we would expect a dispute to have arisen between Christians who opposed fasting on the ground that the risen Jesus was still present with his people through the Holy Spirit and Christians who practiced fasting because of his bodily absence.

But not only is a dispute missing and the length of time for fasting left completely undefined. So also is the reference to Jesus' death quite ambiguous. To be "taken away" (ἀπαρθῇ) does not necessarily mean to die, much less to be killed. It does mean to be killed in Isa 53:8 LXX, but there the wording very clearly states that "*his life* is being taken *from the earth.*" By way of contrast, παρρησίᾳ, "openly," in 8:32a may allude to crypticness in an earlier reference to Jesus' death here in 2:20. But the account of his death will not allude to the present passage or borrow from its phraseology, and opposition to him is already building up. Why should he not refer to a coming period of absence and leave the reason unstated? The question whether he already knows exactly what will happen to him, or whether such knowledge will come to him later, does not affect the authenticity of vv 19b-20. Only the unjustified assumption that Jesus has no premonition of removal from his disciples would rule out authenticity. C. E. B. Cranfield [111] entertains the possibility that this story appears earlier in Mark's gospel than it took place in Jesus' life. And we should not overlook the possibility that ἀπαρθῇ is deponent and therefore even more ambiguous than a true passive: "Pass. verbs often require an active rendering, as πορευ-θῆναι, to march, travel. Ar. *Vesp.* 51, ἀρθεὶς ἀφ' ἡμῶν, 'after leaving us.' So here: 'when he departs from them' " (J. A. Kleist 191; cf. *Gos. Thom.* 104; Venetian Diatessaron). To get an active meaning, therefore, it is unnecessary to posit with J. B. Muddimann (in *Jésus aux origines* 278-79) an original allusion to Joel 2:16 ("let the bridegroom go out of his chamber"), whose contextual call to repentance bears no resemblance to the present passage. An active meaning would hardly allow a reference to Jesus' departure from Galilee for Jerusalem, however, because the preceding references to the bridegroom's being with the wedding guests demands a departure from them — yet the disciples will accompany Jesus to Jerusalem (against Muddimann, loc. cit.). The double meaning of the Aramaic ענה עני in the *ithpᵉel*, "be sad" and "fast" (cf. *Tg. Neb.* 1 Kgs 2:26 and *Tg. Neb.* Zech 7:5), does not justify an elimination from the present passage of fasting in favor of the more general notion of sorrow. The context prohibits such an elimination (cf. J. F. Wimmer, *Fasting* 99; R. H. Gundry, *Matthew* 170; J. Jeremias in *TDNT* 4. 1103, n. 41); and Wimmer (loc. cit.) notes that the LXX never puts πενθέω, "be sad," for the Hebrew verb corresponding to the Aramaic one, viz., אנה "be sad."

According to J. Jeremias (*Parables* 117-18), the sayings on clothing and wine mean that the old age has run out and the new age has arrived. This temporal interpretation runs into the problem that the sayings do not stress replacement of the old with the new. New wineskins are not the center of attention in the second saying, and a new garment is not even mentioned in the first. Rather, the stress falls on the power of the new, a power that could lead to the destruction even of the new. V. Taylor (213) sees a distinction between καινόν for a new kind of cloth, i.e. unshrunken cloth, and νεόν for temporally new wine, i.e. recently made wine; but he admits that the distinction does not loom large in the papyri. That "also the wineskins" looks like an afterthought does not insure later redactional addition. Afterthoughts of this sort are part of original, everyday speech. So efforts to regain an original version by stripping away everything that looks like an afterthought or a redundancy or a slight shift in thought are misplaced. These phenomena are the bread and butter of oral discourse. J. Carmignac (in *ASTI* 7 [1968-1969] 70) suggests that a rip is described as "worse" rather than "bigger" to get a Hebrew wordplay on רַע, "worse," and קָרַע, "rip." Aramaic would provide the same wordplay. See R. H. Gundry, *Matthew* 170, on αἴρει τὸ πλήρωμα ἀπ᾽ αὐτοῦ as meaning that the shrinking patch of new cloth pulls the part of it that overlaps (τὸ πλήρωμα) onto the old garment away from the old garment; and E. C. Maloney, *Semitic Interference* 110-11, for the translation, "And a worse rip comes about," instead of the translation, "And the rip becomes worse" (so M. Black, *Aramaic Approach* 94-95).

P. Trudinger (in *BTB* 5 [1975] 311-15) argues that new wine was not always put into new wineskins, that old wineskins were reused after being moistened, so that the point of the analogy has to do with preparation of the old for reuse, not with discarding the old. True, the point does not have to do with discarding the old. But it has to do with the power of the new, not with preparation of the old for reuse; for neither the moistening of old wineskins nor the preshrinking of a new patch comes into the picture. And preshrinking would prepare the new for first use, not the old for reuse. In the opinion of G. Brooke (in *ExpTim* 95 [1984] 175-76), Jesus' answer implies that the celebration by the Essenes of their festival of the first fruits of new wine is taking place at the time and makes fasting inappropriate. But according to 11QTemple 19:11-21; 21:4-7, the new wine was offered to the Lord and drunk by the celebrants, whereas Jesus speaks about storing new wine, and does so in connection with a wedding feast involving himself, not a feast of first fruits involving a Jewish sect. The limitation of emphasis to the power of the new rules out interpreting the sayings as a warning against the eternal loss of one's salvation (cf. 8:35-38 parr. Matt 10:39; Luke 17:33), as a description of the before and after of conversion (Rom 7:6; Eph 4:22-24; Col 3:9-10), and as a replacement of the old covenant with the new (Heb 8:13). See M. G. Steinhauser, *Doppelbildworte* 42-53, 56-58, against seeing a reflection of Q in the synoptic parallels and against a reflection of pre-synoptic tradition in *Gos. Thom.* 47.

We might think that the sayings about clothing and wine originated on a different occasion. They appear in reverse order in *Gos. Thom.* 47 and at some distance from the wedding sayings (*Gos. Thom.* 104; cf. 75). But the Gospel of Thomas may have broken up an original unity to make a whole collection of impossibilities (mounting two horses at once, stretching two bows at once, serving two masters at once, liking new wine after drinking old wine, putting new wine in old wineskins without their bursting, putting old wine in a new wineskin without the wine's spoiling, putting an old patch on a new garment without the result of a rip when the garment is washed), and it is hard to identify a better setting for the sayings than the one in which they here appear. The suitability of sayings about clothing and wine to a wedding feast (see the comments on vv 21-22) favors an original unity. If the fasting in question is some voluntary fasting unprescribed by the OT, Jesus' conservatism with regard to the OT (see, e.g., 7:8-10; Luke 16:17) offers no ground to suppose that the sayings originally referred to another topic. Besides, that conservatism may have exceptions when it comes to ritual practices, the exceptions being only apparent in that Jesus does not reject them anti-ritualistically so much as he radicalizes them pro-morally. The lack of a characteristically Marcan καὶ ἔλεγεν αὐτοῖς, "and he was saying to them," at the head of vv 21-22 does not prove a pre-Marcan redactional attachment of these verses to the preceding unless it is first proved that these verses are a redactional attachment at all (and see the comments on 2:27 regarding that introductory clause). If according to the theory of original disunity Mark or an earlier traditioner was able to apply these sayings, which state a general principle, to the specific question of fasting, we can hardly deny the possibility that Jesus himself formulated the sayings as statements of general principle applicable to the specific question of fasting. After all, we have no pre-Marcan document in which the sayings appear separated from the question of fasting. Statements of general principle usually arise out of particular cases; in fact, at 12:18-27 Jesus goes on to make a general statement about resurrection after taking up the particular case of a woman who will have had seven husbands at the resurrection. So the question stays open. Confidence in our ability to trace tradition history is especially ill-advised when we try to peer behind the earliest extant documents. The omission of the last clause in v 22 by D it bo^ms may be accidental (e.g., by the skipping of a line) or due to scribal offense at the ellipsis of the verb (cf. the other vv.ll., which betray the same offense, and B. M. Metzger, *Textual Commentary* ad loc.).

JESUS' LORDING IT OVER THE SABBATH

2:23-28 (Matt 12:1-8; Luke 6:1-5)

Mark's mentioning that the disciples are plucking grain on a Sabbath as Jesus is going through some grainfields (v 23) lays the groundwork for this pericope. The Pharisees' accusatory question (v 24) leads to Jesus' reply (vv 25-28), which divides into two parts: (1) an appeal to David's actions with regard to the question of permissibility in general (vv 25-26); (2) a deduction from the humanitarian reason for the Sabbath to the Son of man's lordship over the Sabbath with regard to the question of the Sabbath in particular (vv 27 28).

   2:23 *(Matt 12:1; Luke 6:1)* The fasting discussed in vv 18-22 was a religious observance (cf. vv 18-22). Hence, it is natural that a question regarding another religious observance, i.e. Sabbath-keeping, should now arise, especially since Jesus' answer to the question refers to eating. Mark starts by noting Jesus individually in order that the disciples of Jesus may next enter the picture. The use of a pronoun instead of Jesus' name ties this story to the preceding one, where his name did appear (v 19). The fact that it is not his practice but the practice of his disciples that comes into question yet again makes the question not simply (and, so far as Mark is concerned, not mainly) one of the legitimacy of an action, but a question of Jesus' authority: Does he have authority to let them pluck ears of grain on the Sabbath (cf. the comments on v 18)? The forward position of ἐν τοῖς σάββασιν, "on the Sabbath," highlights this question.

   In the next clause the position of the subject before its verb switches attention to the disciples. Ὁδὸν ποιεῖν τίλλοντες τοὺς στάχυας means either "to make a path by plucking ears of grain" or "to make their way [i.e. to journey along a path] plucking ears of grain [as they go]." At first glance, the active voice of ποιεῖν appears to favor the first possibility. For normally the middle voice of ποιεῖν would be used with a direct object to put across the verbal meaning inherent in the direct object; i.e. the second possibility would seem to require ὁδὸν ποιεῖσθαι. But Jdg 17:8 LXX uses the active voice in the sense of the second possibility. "To make a path" would make no sense in that passage. Mark has a penchant for Latinisms (see pp. 1043-45), and the Latin phrase *iter facere* corresponds to the Greek phrase using the active voice in the sense of journeying. Add to these grammatical and stylistic considerations the practical consideration that a path is not made by plucking ears of grain — at the very least the stalks would have to be trodden or cut down, and perhaps removed as well, to say nothing about the incongruity of the disciples' making a path *behind* Jesus, whom presumably they are following as usual — and one has to favor the second possibility. Passages such as 1:45; 2:4, 21-22; 3:9, 20, 31-32, 34; 4:1, 34 (see the comments ad loc.), 37b-38, and others, but especially 7:2-4, show that Mark thinks pragmatically as well as theologically. But what is the purpose of using the fulsome expression, "began to make their way," instead of integrating the disciples alongside Jesus as the compound subject of παραπορεύεσθαι, "was going along"? It is to make a clean separation between Jesus' going along *without* plucking ears of grain and the disciples' making their way *while* plucking ears of grain; for the Pharisees will not raise a question about Jesus' conduct, but only about the conduct of his disciples, and he will defend their conduct, not his own. The putting of ὁδόν before ποιεῖν (contrast Jdg 17:8 LXX but cf. the Latin phrase) slightly separates the plucking of ears of grain from the notion of a way or path. This separation gives the plucking a somewhat independent conceptual status that tends to make up for its grammatical subordination (cf. M. Zerwick, *Biblical Greek* §§263, 376; J. A. Kleist 191, on the presence of the main thought in a participle rather than in a finite verbal expression). The Pharisees will object, then, to the plucking, not to the making of a path. Nor should we think that they accuse the disciples of violating the limitation of distance to be traveled on the Sabbath (one or two thousand cubits — see C. Rabin, *Zadokite Documents* 52-53, n. 5 on CD 10:20, for a brief discussion of the primary literature and archeological evidence), for then the Pharisees who happen to be along would be caught in the same violation.

2:24 *(Matt 12:2; Luke 6:2)* The position of the subject before its verb now switches attention to the Pharisees at the start of v 24. In v 16 the scribes of the Pharisees asked Jesus' disciples a question about his conduct. Here the Pharisees, who are keeping the Sabbath just as they were fasting in v 18, ask him a question about his disciples' conduct just as people in general were asking him about his disciples' conduct in v 18. For the Sabbath prohibition of harvesting (as the disciples are doing by plucking ears of grain), see Exod 34:21; *Jub.* 2:29-30; 50:6-13; CD 10:14–11:18; *m. Šabb.* 7:2 (and E. P. Sanders, *Jewish Law* 6-23, for a general survey of Sabbath-observance in the NT era).

2:25-26 *(Matt 12:3-7; Luke 6:3-4)* The historical present tense of λέγει, "he says," emphasizes the overpowering authority of Jesus' counter question (cf. the note on v 16). The construction οὐδέποτε plus the indicative verb ἀνέγνωτε,

"Have you never read . . . ?" implies that the Pharisees have indeed read the OT passage to which Jesus is going to refer (1 Sam 21:2-7[1-6]) and therefore should know better than to criticize the disciples' behavior (cf. 12:10, 26; D. Daube, *NTRJ* 432-36). In Jesus' question αὐτός, "he himself" (David), and the last καί, "also" (introducing "the ones who were with him"), do not imply that Jesus as well as his disciples is plucking ears of grain on the Sabbath, much less that he is giving grain to his disciples as David gave the loaves of the presentation to his companions. Neither in the editorial introduction nor in the question put to Jesus did his own conduct come under review any more than it had done in v 18. Therefore his argument does not depend on any typological correspondence between him and David. Rather, David as well as his companions represents only Jesus' disciples; and the need, hunger, and action of David and his companions correspond to the disciples' plucking ears of grain, not to any need, hunger, and action of Jesus. "Which it is not permitted to eat, with the exception of the priests" implies that Jesus' disciples are indeed breaking the Sabbath just as David and his companions broke the law concerning the loaves of the presentation.

To strengthen his argument, Jesus adds a number of features not found in the OT passage: (1) David's having companions with him (contrast 1 Sam 21:2-3[1-2]); (2) his having need; (3) his and his companions' being hungry; (4) the house of God and David's entering it rather than merely asking for bread; (5) Abiathar's being a "high priest," not just a "priest"; (6) David's eating the loaves of presentation, either while he is still inside the house of God or after he has come out; and (7) his giving some of the loaves to his companions. Moreover, the OT passage speaks of Ahimelech, not of Abiathar. Though elsewhere we have some reason to suspect a textual confusion of the two (see, e.g., P. K. McCarter, Jr., *II Samuel* 252-53; yet Keil and Delitzsch [*Samuel* 365-67] demur), no such confusion seems to characterize 1 Sam 21:2-7(1-6). Apparently, then, Jesus not only adds a number of features. He also replaces Ahimelech with Abiathar the son of Ahimelech for a link with the added house of God, which for Jesus and his audience stands in Jerusalem, where Abiathar officiated (2 Sam 15:24, 35; 17:15; 19:12[11]), not in Nob, where Ahimelech gave bread to David.

Since only David illegally enters the house of God, since he is the one who illegally gives some loaves to his companions, and since he is the only one whose illegal eating of the sacred loaves is actually mentioned, he parallels the disciples in law-breaking more than his companions do. The forward position of τοὺς ἄρτους τῆς προθέσεως, "the loaves of the presentation," emphasizes his breaking the Law just as the forward position of χρείαν, "need," emphasizes the reason for his breaking the Law. In contrast with the heavy role that Jesus makes David play, Ahimelech the priest not only changes to Abiathar the high priest but also becomes totally inactive, his name merely identifying the section of the OT where the story is found (see also 12:26 for ἐπί plus the genitive as indicative of an OT section). This locative interpretation of the reference to Abiathar contrasts with the temporal interpretation, "at the time of Abiathar." Mark uses ἐπί in a temporal sense nowhere else, no matter what case follows. A v.l. in 15:1 does use ἐπί temporally, but with a following accusative rather than a genitive, as here. Jesus delays his reference to Abiathar rather than putting it close to "Have you never read?" (so 12:26), because there it would compete for attention with David's name; and the writer of 1 Samuel does not introduce Abiathar till the close of the next chapter, and even then not as an important figure in the narrative (cf. W. L. Lane 115-16). But these facts do not undermine a locative interpretation so much as they show the extent to which David is pushed forward as a Law-breaker. The fact that when Abiathar does appear in 1 Sam 22:20-23 he does so in connection with the foregoing incident at the house of God makes it easy for Jesus to use his name in blotting out Ahimelech for the sake of a link with Jerusalem.

In 1:44 Jesus told an ex-leper to carry out a Mosaic commandment. But here Jesus goes on to explain that his disciples' action is not violating the humanitarian purpose of the Sabbath law even though it may be violating that law as such. Mark is satisfied with the explanation, for it suits his emphasis on Jesus' authority. Strikingly, Mark resists what must have been an almost overpowering urge to mention need, hunger, and eating on the part of the disciples to correspond with the mentioned need, hunger, and eating on the part of David and his companions (so Matthew and Luke). Mark never states that the disciples plucked ears of grain because they were hungry or that they ate what they plucked! Only their breaking the Sabbath by plucking ears of grain comes into the picture. Thus no emphasis falls on the humanitarian purpose of the Sabbath. Instead, the emphasis builds up Jesus' authority as Lord of the Sabbath to pronounce on its humanitarian purpose.

2:27 Jesus now states the humanitarian purpose of the Sabbath: "the Sabbath came into being for the sake of human beings [literally: 'on account of the man'] and not human beings for the sake of the Sabbath" (cf. a similar rabbinic statement cited in Str-B 2. 5 but applying only to life-threatening situations; also 1 Macc 2:39-41; 2 Macc 5:19). Chiastic form gives flair to Jesus' pronouncement, and ellipsis gives it vigor. (Filled out and translated literally the second clause would read, "and the man did not come into being on account of the Sabbath.") Ἐγένετο, "came into being," alludes to the creation (cf. John 1:3). Jesus seems to infer his dictum from the establishment of the Sabbath not till God had created Adam and Eve (Genesis 1–2; cf. *Jub.* 2:16-17 and Jesus' overriding the Mosaic law on divorce with an appeal to the creation story — Mark 10:1-12).

The introduction to the dictum, "And he was saying to them," is often taken as indicating that the sayings in vv 27-28 did not originally belong to this pericope. The same phrase does break into the middle of Jesus' words also in 4:13, 21, 24, 26, 30 (in the last two passages without "to them"; cf. the notes on 4:1-34). But in each of those passages it introduces a new parable instead of interrupting a series of sayings; and because of its length and unity a parable tends to need an editorial introduction to a degree an individual saying or two within a larger pericope do not. In 4:2, 11; 6:4; 7:14; 8:21; 9:31; 11:17 (cf. 3:23) the phrase comes at the start, not in the middle, of Jesus' speaking; at least something of another nature precedes and makes the introduction appropriate, sometimes necessary, so that it is gratuitous to infer an importation of material from elsewhere. Only 6:10; 7:9; 9:1 are truly comparable with 2:27 in that the phrase interrupts a series of sayings. But instructions for the disciples' Galilean mission surround the phrase in 6:10, so that it appears merely to introduce a new batch of instructions (concerning the acceptance of hospitality) after an earlier batch (concerning what to take and what not to take), both given on the same occasion. Similarly, references to "the tradition of men" come right before and right after the phrase in 7:9, so that it appears not to introduce material imported from elsewhere, but a new accusation based on Exod 20:12; 21:17; Deut 5:16 after an earlier accusation based on Isa 29:13. And in 9:1 the phrase seems to separate the next saying literarily (but not historically) from the preceding sayings to relate it to the Transfiguration (vv 2-8) as prediction to fulfilment. So we do not have convincing evidence to suppose that in 2:27 the phrase indicates the importation of sayings into a pericope that lacked them before (cf. a similarly interruptive phrase in Gen 15:2-3).

I. Maisch (*Heilung* 119) argues that the singular of σάββατον betrays that Mark has added vv 27-28 because it contrasts with the plural in 2:23-24; 3:2, 4. But the singular has a grammatical explanation that makes a tradition historical explanation superfluous. Σάββατον takes the plural wherever in Mark it is used as a temporal adverb or with the meaning "week" (1:21; 2:23, 24; 3:2, 4; 16:2). Elsewhere and otherwise it takes the singular, as here and in 6:2; 16:1. Here, a plural would have diverted attention from the Sabbath as such to individually successive Sabbaths. In 6:2; 16:1 a plural participle agreeing with a plural of σάββατον would have made Mark's audience think of more than one Sabbath, whereas the context points to a particular Sabbath.

It appears that Mark wants his audience to understand both of the following sayings as spoken by Jesus (for the reason why, see later comments). But the "so then" with which the saying in v 28 will begin could easily mislead readers into thinking of an editorial comment (as shown by some modern commentators' actually thinking so, believing v 28 to draw a deduction not from v 27 but from the whole story). To guard against this misunderstanding, Mark inserts a reference to Jesus' speaking, but he inserts it before both sayings because an editorial interruption between the two sayings would spoil the "so then" which makes the second saying grow out of the first (cf. the comment of P. J. Achtemeier [in *JBL* 109 (1990) 21] that when read aloud, "and he was saying [to them]" would help listeners understand a continuation of the scene in following material).

2:28 *(Matt 12:8; Luke 6:5)* Mark does not want the pericope to end on a humanitarian note, but with an emphasis on Jesus' authority. The saying in v 28 certainly provides such an emphasis. Reinforcing it are not only the meaning of κύριος, "Lord," but also its anarthrousness, which highlights the quality of lordship, its emphatic first position after the introductory conjunction (ὥστε, "so then"), the wordplay between "the Son of the man" (v 28) and "the man" (v 27 [bis], to adopt a literal translation of both expressions), and the καί, "also," before the reference to the Sabbath. We might take the καί ascensively ("*even* of the Sabbath"). If so, it implies that the Sabbath offers the supreme test of Jesus' lordship over religious practice — and he passes (see G. Vos, *Self-Disclosure* 53-54, against the minimizing statement of J. D. Crossan [*In Fragments* 80]: "the 'even' makes this power seem just barely achieved"). But there is a rhetorical parallel with v 10: κύριός ἐστιν, "is Lord," corresponds to ἐξουσίαν ἔχει, "has authority," in v 10; ὁ υἱὸς τοῦ ἀνθρώπου, "the Son of man," matches v 10 exactly; and καὶ τοῦ σαββάτου, "also of the Sabbath," corresponds to ἀφιέναι ἁμαρτίας ἐπὶ τῆς γῆς, "to forgive sins on the earth," in v 10. Thus it seems that Jesus' lordship over the Sabbath is something in addition to his authority to forgive sins (καί as "also"). Since v 10 has recently indicated that the Son of man has authority on the earth, the audience of v 28 will naturally understand that the Son of man exercises his lordship on the earth.

Mark wants this saying to be understood as spoken by Jesus. As in vv 17 and 19-22, Jesus' pronouncement ends debate before it can start. His opponents get only the chance to raise an initial question before his answers crush them. Whether modern scholars know enough to deny that Jesus speaks the words of v 28 is doubtful. For Mark it goes without saying that Jesus refers to himself when using the phrase "the Son of man" (here for the second time in Mark; cf. v 10). The obliqueness of the self-reference favors the authenticity of the saying. Reference to a third party — in particular, to an apocalyptic Son of man different from Jesus — would make the saying irrelevant to the question at hand (and probably irrelevant to the question of Sabbath-keeping in any other incident in Jesus' life, so that we do not need to think of this saying as transferred from another incident, known or unknown).

How then does the deduction that the Son of man is Lord also of the Sabbath stem from the Sabbath's coming into being for the sake of human beings rather than human beings for the sake of the Sabbath? Should we think that Jesus means "the Son of man" to be taken generically, so that "the man" in v 27 (bis) and "the son of the man" in v 28 synonymously refer to human beings (cf. Ps 80:17)? If so, Jesus is saying that any human being may violate the Sabbath to meet a legitimate need that keeping the Sabbath would leave unmet. Though the lordship of Jesus as the unique Son of man would fade out of the saying, such a meaning would leave intact Mark's main point, i.e. the authority with which Jesus' pronouncements end all discussion. Or Mark may understand Jesus as the Son of man and Lord of the Sabbath, whereas Jesus himself intends the generic meaning.

On the other hand, κύριος seems too strong for an ordinary human being in relation to the Sabbath. But it fits the exalted position of the unique Son of man who appears elsewhere in Jesus' sayings, e.g., in the only preceding saying in Mark that mentions him. There this Son of man, who can be none other than Jesus, had authority like that of God to forgive sins (v 10). An authority of Jesus to lord it over the Sabbath by letting his disciples pluck ears of grain, i.e. work, on the Sabbath looks very similar. In v 28, then, he goes beyond what he has said in v 27. He deduces ("so then") that if the Sabbath is subordinate to the needs of a human being, as "the Son of man" he is its Lord.

This deduction requires some unpacking. As seen in the note on v 10, "the Son of man" leads a simultaneously double life on Jesus' lips: (1) it refers self-referentially to Jesus as a human being; (2) it alludes to the human-like figure in Dan 7:13. Here, its self-referential use provides the link between a logical deduction from v 27 and an exegetical deduction from Dan 7:13. The logical deduction entails a wordplay on "man" as "human being" and on Jesus' use of "the Son of man" instead of "I." The exegetical deduction entails a reminiscence of the Son of man's authority in v 10 as well as an allusion to the authority given to the figure like a son of man in Dan 7:13. The logical deduction: if the Sabbath came into being on account of human beings, then it came into being on account of me. The exegetical deduction: but since I am no ordinary human being, but the figure like a son of man in Dan 7:13, I am more than a beneficiary of the Sabbath. I am also its Lord, who can let my disciples break the Sabbath (contrast J. D. Crossan [*In Fragments* 80], who can write that "the 'so' gives this [lordship] to Jesus almost as a subordinate consequence, as being simply one man among many" only by neglecting v 10 and the background of Dan 7:13). We should note well that v 28 is not simply a Christological narrowing of v 27. It is a Christo-logical advance on v 27, for lordship (v 28) goes far beyond benefit (v 27). A Christological point has grown out of an anthropological one, and outgrown it. The pericope ends, then, at some remove from the initial question concerning the disciples' conduct. It ends on the note of Jesus' authority.

NOTES

See J. Kiilunen, *Vollmacht* 75-77, for criticism of the attempt to draw close parallels between vv 23-28 and vv 13-17. On καὶ ἐγένετο, "and it came to pass," plus the infinitive (v 23), see E. C. Maloney, *Semitic Interference* 85-86. For παραπορεύομαι, "go along," plus διά with the genitive, "through," see also 9:30. Concerning the auxiliary use of ἤρξατο, see the notes on 1:45. The standing grain with ears of mature kernels implies the season around May or June. For the allowance of plucking grain on a journey through a field not one's own, see Deut 23:26(25), though *Tg. Neof.* Deut 23:26 and the discussion in *b. B. Meṣ.* 87b treat the allowance narrowly with regard to the privilege of laborers harvesting a crop. Since stealing breaks the law on any day of the week, the Sabbath would scarcely come into the picture were the charge that the disciples were stealing, not breaking the Sabbath. The Pharisees' question contains an ellipsis: "Why are they doing on the Sabbath what is not permissible [to do on the Sabbath]?" (against Kiilunen, op. cit. 209-10). D. Daube (in *NTS* 19 [1972-73] 1-15) discusses the responsibility of a master for the conduct of his disciples, a responsibility presupposed here. The argument in vv 25-26 that David and his companions acted illegally militates against the suggestion of A. Schlatter (74-75) that Mark wants to present the disciples as on the move, not illegally standing still while plucking ears of grain. It also militates against the minimizing interpretation of D. J. Moo (in *JSNT* 20 [1984] 7-9) that Jesus is only criticizing a non-humanitarian tendency in the *oral* law. S. Westerholm (*Jesus and Scribal Authority* 98-99) correctly discerns that according to Jesus the Scripture countenances David's breaking of the *written* law. Likewise, M. Gourges (in *La vie de la Parole* 200) correctly summarizes Jesus' argument: How can you excuse David's action despite Scripture but accuse my disciples on the ground of Scripture? The suggestion of D. Flusser (*Jesus* 46) and M. Lowe and Flusser (in *NTS* 29 [1983] 30-33) that Jesus follows a Galilean tradition which allows the rubbing of fallen (not plucked) ears of grain between the hands (not just between the fingers as in Judean halakah) does not suit Mark's mention of only the plucking; so Flusser posits a pre-Marcan version that lacked "plucking" (so also Tatian's Diatessaron and "a newly discovered Christian text"). Dependence on post-canonical texts weakens the hypothesis, as does also the limitation to spices of the distinction between hand-rubbing and fingertip-rubbing (*b. Šabb.* 128a), whereas the present question deals with grain. A churchly fabrication of the story to justify Christian disregard for the Sabbath would almost certainly have made Jesus himself, not just his disciples, an example of such disregard (see E. Haenchen 122-23; J. Roloff, *Kerygma* 55).

On the Sabbath, as noted in the foregoing comments, Pharisees allowed themselves to travel from town only one or two thousand cubits, about three-tenths or three-fifths of a mile. But we have no way of knowing that these Pharisees had overstepped that limitation. From this standpoint, then, no valid argument can be mounted against the historicity of their part in the story or of the story as a whole. The view of J. D. M. Derrett (*Studies* 1. 85-100) that Jesus was avoiding the quadrilateral Sabbath limit surrounding towns and cities has some merit in view of Mark's using παραπορεύομαι in the sense of going past when he uses it elsewhere (9:30; 11:20; 15:29). But it does not necessarily follow that the disciples were *making* a path to avoid the roads that would lead him into the limit.

M. Black (*Aramaic Approach* 122) takes the τί in v 24 as exclamatory ("why!") and regards the preceding ἴδε as strengthening it. One should think instead that the doubtlessly exclamatory force of ἴδε, "look!" favors the more usual interrogative τί ("why?"); for two successive exclamations would be quite unlikely. Since a teacher bears responsibility for the conduct of his disciples (see the note on v 18), the question, "Why are they doing on the Sabbath what is not permitted?" amounts to a warning the violation of which in 3:1-5 will constitute a capital crime leading the Pharisees to plot Jesus' death in 3:6. Their watching in 3:2 to see whether he will ignore the warning confirms this legal progression from warning to capital charge and plot (see Exod 31:14; *m. Šabb.* 7:2; *m. Sanh.* 5:1; 7:4, 8; *m. Mak.* 1:8-9; cf. H. Danby, *Mishnah* 562, n. 16; J. Jeremias, *NT Theology* 1. 278-79 with further references); and the progression favors a historical connection between the two incidents, for a Christian traditioner or writer would hardly want to fabricate a legally valid procedure on the Pharisees' part. L. Schenke (*Wundererzählungen* 161, n. 516) objects that independently from 2:23-28 the deliberateness of the violation in 3:1-5 would give ground for the plot in 3:6. But this objection neglects the Pharisees' watching for a violation of the Sabbath, which implies a preceding violation that excited their anticipation of another one. The objection also neglects the purpose of the legal procedure to make sure that a violation is deliberate.

To argue that because the scriptural argument in vv 25-26 is not Christological it comes from Jesus rather than from the church wrongly posits that only non-Christological statements are historically acceptable on his lips. To argue that because the scriptural argument is not eschatological it comes from the church rather than from Jesus wrongly posits that only eschatological statements are historically acceptable on his lips. Easy formulas do not decide historical questions. J. Bowker (*Jesus and the Pharisees* 40, n. 1) detects in the replacement of Ahimelech with Abiathar a pointed polemic aimed against the Sadducean-Zadokite claim to the priesthood. But why would Jesus attack the Sadducees when he is speaking to Pharisees? Is he trying to get on their good side? The reproachful tone of "Have you never read?" and the bold attack on the inviolability of the Sabbath dictate a negative answer. The view of J. D. M. Derrett (*Studies* 1. 91-92; cf. J. W. Wenham, *Christ and the Bible* 75-77) that ἐπὶ ᾿Αβιαθὰρ ἀρχιερέως means "in the presence of Abiathar [who later became the] high priest" has in its favor a similar use of ἐπί with the genitive at 13:9, but suffers from the lack of any indication in 1 Sam 21:2-7(1-6) that Abiathar was present and from the necessity of supposing that "high priest" is meant prospectively. Whether topographical or scriptural in its referent, the locative interpretation is usually taken to avoid a mistake on the part of Jesus, a pre-Marcan traditioner, or Mark; but it need not be taken with that purpose in mind (see the foregoing comments for a deliberate replacement of Ahimelech with Abiathar).

On the loaves of the presentation see Exod 25:30; Lev 24:5-9; Heb 9:2, and on Jesus' inferences from 1 Sam 21:2-7(1-6), see R. H. Gundry, *Matthew* 223. Judg 18:31 uses "the house of God" for the tabernacle. A formal rabbinic debate would have called for Jesus to make a halakic appeal to a definite command in the OT (see esp. D. M. Cohn-Sherbock in *JSNT* 2 [1979] 31-41). The informal setting of a journey through the countryside justifies his haggadic argument, which merely draws an inference from the OT. The argument shows no trace of a rabbinic notion that the incident in David's life, like the present one in Jesus' life, took place on a Sabbath (*b. Menaḥ.* 95b; *Yal. Šimʿon* 1 Sam 21:5 §130).

The characterization of David's companions as those who were "with him" (bis) does not portray him as a type of Christ, who also has companions with him. For in this passage Mark does not comparably describe Jesus' disciples as those who are with him, even though he will so describe them elsewhere (3:14; 5:40; 14:33, 67; cf. 5:18; 14:18, 20 and a number of passages where he describes Jesus as with his disciples). For the same reason it is improbable that Mark adds the references to those who were "with" David. In that case we would expect him to describe Jesus' disciples parallelistically in the same fashion, as the other passages show he is quite capable of doing. "With him" simply emphasizes that David was not alone, so that the plurality of him and his companions matches the plurality of the disciples, not including Jesus, who as we have seen is not said to be doing what his disciples are doing. It is untrue that for a parallel with his disciples Jesus makes David's companions more prominent than the writer of 1 Samuel does, for the question of the ritual cleanness of David's young men occupies a fair amount of space in 1 Sam 21:3b, 5b-6(2b, 4b-5) even though that passage makes them absent at the moment and even though David may be lying about them to get bread. Because of the common but mistaken appeal to David-Jesus typology, it bears repeating that only Jesus' disciples are said to break the Law in a way that corresponds especially to David's breaking of the Law. (Whether Davidic typology appears in the synoptic parallels is another question.) David's giving bread provides too thin a thread from which to hang a eucharistic interpretation pointing to Jesus' giving his disciples bread at the Last Supper. Ἄρτος, "bread," takes the plural here, the singular in Mark 14:22; and for a hint of the Eucharist we would expect Mark or an earlier traditioner to have included here at least a reference to breaking the bread before giving it, perhaps also to blessing it.

Since elsewhere in Mark ὥστε, "so then, so that," always introduces a consequence of one sort or another (1:27, 45; 2:2, 12; 3:10, 20; 4:1, 32, 37; 9:26; 10:8; 15:5), we should not treat it here in v 28 as loosely transitional rather than logically deductive. Nor should we think of v 28 as more radical than v 27, as though Christians fabricated v 28 to justify their non-observance of the Sabbath whereas v 27 merely slackens such observance (as thought by M. Gourges in *La vie de la Parole* 202-4). Apart from the present context, neither the Sabbath's coming into being for the sake of human beings rather than vice versa nor the Son of man's lordship also over the Sabbath would tell to what extent the Sabbath should or should not be observed; and in the present context each statement equally well justifies Sabbath-breaking on the present occasion. Only in another context could the Son of man's lordship over the Sabbath be used to justify regular non-observance.

For the view that v 28 is an editorial comment on the whole story, see among others W. L. Lane 119-20; E. Lohmeyer 66; E. Lohse in *TDNT* 7. 22; and on the omission of v 27 by Matthew, followed as often by Luke, to avoid siphoning attention from Jesus' lordship to the humanitarian purpose of the Sabbath, see R. H. Gundry, *Matthew* 224-25 and 650, s.v. "Luke's being influenced by Matthew" (also M. D. Hooker, *Son of Man* 98). This redactional reason for omission makes doubtful the inference (and deductions based on it) that Matthew and Luke found one saying but not the other in pre-Marcan tradition. A. J. Hultgren (in *JBL* 91 [1972] 42-43) also defends the originality of v 27 on the grounds that "and he was saying to them" in Luke 6:5a seems to reflect part of Mark 2:27 and that v 27 contains the only saying which speaks to the action of the disciples in breaking the Sabbath (for vv 25-26 do not deal with the Sabbath, and v 28 features the Son of man). According to Lev 23:3 the Sabbath is for Yahweh (τῷ κυρίῳ, "for the Lord," in the LXX). By making himself "Lord (κύριος) of the Sabbath," then, Jesus assumes Yahweh's role (but see the notes on v 10 concerning the obliqueness of self-reference in "the Son of man"). To treat τοῦ σαββάτου temporally ("on [i.e. during] the Sabbath"; so J. D. M. Derrett, *Studies* 1. 91-92) misses the point.

The evident allusion in v 27 to the story of creation makes attractive the suggestion that in v 28 "the man" (τοῦ ἀνθρώπου) refers to Adam, whose very name means "man, mankind, human race." But then "the son of" becomes problematic, for it incorporates Jesus into the first Adam rather than making him into another Adam — "the last Adam" or "the second man" of Paul — as those who take this view think (J. B. Cortés and F. M. Gatti in *Bib* 49 [1968] 494-95; cf. R. Leivestad in *NTS* 18 [1971-72] 258-59). Also, "the Son of Adam" would not provide the oblique self-reference that the present passage and other uses favor. On the other hand, the lordship of the original human beings Adam and Eve over the physical creation (Gen 1:26, 28; Ps 8:6-9[5-8]; 4 Ezra 6:54; *2 Apoc. Bar.* 14:18) supports "also" as the meaning of καί. The argument against authenticity that nowhere else does Jesus claim to abrogate the Law in virtue of his messianic status (so H. Anderson 106-7) mistakes "the Son of man" for a recognized messianic title. "The sons of men" will mean ordinary human beings in Mark 3:28, but there the expression is plural. Here we have the singular. In Matt 8:20; 11:19; Luke 7:34; 9:58 the singular refers more naturally to the Son of man than to an ordinary human being. For more detailed discussion, see the comments and notes on v 10; R. H. Gundry, *Matthew* 152-53, 213, and esp. 237-39; G. R. Beasley-Murray, *Jesus and the Kingdom of God* 230-34.

The woods are full of mutually destructive theories regarding stages of tradition-history leading up to the present pericope. Some examples: (1) vv 23-26 + vv 27-28; (2) vv 23-26 + v 27 + v 28; (3) vv 23-26 + v 28 + v 27; (4) vv 23-24, 27 + vv 25-26 + v 28; (5) vv 23-24 + v 27 + vv 25-26 + v 28; (6) vv 23-24, 27 + v 28 + vv 25-26; (7) vv 27-28 + vv 25-26 + vv 23-24; (8) v 27 + vv 23-24 + vv 25-26, 28. Sometimes parts of verses are late-dated, e.g., "and the ones with him" in v 25, "and he gave [the loaves] also to the ones who were with him" in v 26, etc. Perhaps the point most often agreed upon is the inappropriateness, inauthenticity, and therefore later addition of vv 25-26 because their appeal to the OT does not suit Jesus' way of arguing elsewhere in 2:1–3:6 and because the OT passage to which appeal is made does not even deal with the Sabbath.

But that reasoning is reversible. We would expect an adder-on to choose an OT passage which does deal with the Sabbath; and if contrariwise the adder-on did choose the present OT passage, we would expect that adder-on to make David and Jesus parallel with each other rather than making David match the disciples but not Jesus, who only defends his disciples whereas David is said to lead his companions in breaking the Law. The very lack of arguments from the OT in the other controversy stories of 2:1–3:6 might lead us to affirm the originality and authenticity of the present such argument. A traditioner or redactor would not have been conditioned by the other stories to think of adding an argument from the OT. It is just as likely that a question about the Sabbath law would prompt Jesus to think in terms of the OT as that it would prompt a later traditioner or redactor to do so. The sermonically free (i.e. haggadic) rather than legally technical (i.e. halakic) nature of the OT argument increases the chances of originality and authenticity. At the very start of the comments on this pericope we noted that vv 25-26 do not by-pass the question of the Sabbath so much as they prepare for Jesus' answer in vv 27-28 by taking up the general question of permissibility. If the point most often agreed upon by tracers of tradition-history lacks cogency, the points on which they disagree lack it all the more. The use of a typically rabbinic counter question appealing to the OT in 12:10, 26, too, further increases the chances of originality and authenticity (cf. P. Fiebig, *Erzählungs-stil* 109). Only by the circular reasoning of rejecting the historicity of those passages as well as this one because of their OT argumentation can the evidence be dismissed.

JESUS' AUTHORITY TO HEAL ON THE SABBATH

3:1-6 (Matt 12:9-14; Luke 6:6-11)

The story of Jesus' healing a withered hand on the Sabbath shows that he ignores the warning in the preceding story against violating the Sabbath (see the notes on 2:24). Thus the two stories belong together. As a result of his ignoring the warning, the present story issues in a conspiracy to do away with him. The stage-setting consists of his entering a synagogue (v 1a), the presence of a man with a withered hand (v 1b), and the scrutinizing of Jesus to catch him in an act of breaking the Sabbath (v 2). His remarks make up the central part of the story: telling the man to get up (v 3), asking the Pharisees whether it is permissible to perform a healing on the Sabbath (v 4), and telling the man to stretch out his hand (v 5). The second remark silences the Pharisees, the third one effects a healing. The story ends with a conspiracy to destroy Jesus (v 6).

3:1 *(Matt 12:9; Luke 6:6)* "And he entered again into the synagogue" recalls 1:21, "and . . . entering into the synagogue," and thus implies the synagogue in Capernaum, since 1:21 began with Jesus' and the disciples' going into Capernaum (contrast the lack of "enter" as well as the plural of "synagogues" and the addition of "their" in 1:39; cf. also Jesus' going to the sea, beside which Capernaum is located, in 3:7). The backward reference to 1:21 favors that at this point Mark is composing his text rather than following an earlier collection of controversy stories that he started to incorporate at 2:1 or 2:15 (cf. the excursus on 2:1–3:6). "And a man was there" echoes "a man was in the synagogue" at 1:23 ("there" replacing "in the synagogue" because in the present passage no interruption requires a repetition of the prepositional phrase, as in 1:23). This echo again favors that Mark is composing with reminiscence of 1:21-28 rather than following an earlier collection of controversy stories. Ἄνθρωπος, "a man," points to the sort of being for whose sake Jesus has just said the Sabbath came into existence (2:27) and hence for whose healing the Sabbath might well be violated. (Hence, ἄνθρωπος is not merely the Semitic equivalent of τις, "some-one"; see also M. Reiser, *Syntax und Stil* 20-21, against treating ἄνθρωπος as a Semitism.) Ἐξηραμμένην, "withered," advances away from its noun χεῖρα, "hand," to play up the power that Jesus will display in the following miracle (so also the position of τὴν ξηρὰν χεῖρα, "the withered hand," before the participle whose object it is in v 3).

3:2 *(Matt 12:10; Luke 6:7)* "And they were observing him carefully" means keeping a close eye on Jesus to see whether he will violate the warning that the Pharisees gave in 2:24 (cf. Luke 13:10-16). The disciples do not come

into view (as they did in 2:24), because only Jesus is the healer who may break
the Sabbath by healing the man's withered hand. In 2:23-28 Jesus bore the
responsibility for his disciples' conduct on the Sabbath. Here he bears the responsibility for his own conduct on the Sabbath. A violation of the earlier warning
will expose him to the possibility of capital punishment. In a foreshadowing of
chief priestly action in 15:3-4, "that they might lay charge against him" exposes
the Pharisees' purpose to take legal action which will lead to his judicial death.
Throughout v 2 "they" might refer to the general audience in the synagogue (cf.
the indefinite "they" thus far in 1:22-23, 30[?], 32, 44, 45; 2:3-5, 18). But the
Pharisees were Jesus' antagonists in 2:23-24. As the present pericope has to do
with the Sabbath question, so 2:23-28 had to do with the same question. There
the Pharisees issued a legal warning. Here they end up deliberating against him
for the purpose of destroying him (v 6). Hence, the "they" who observe Jesus
carefully with the purpose of accusing him refers more likely and particularly to
the Pharisees. Τοῖς σάββασιν, "on the Sabbath," not only relates to the same phrase
in 2:24 but also echoes 1:21 and again suggests that Mark is composing the present
pericope with some reminiscence of the only previous pericope set in a synagogue.
Both pericopes feature an example of Jesus' wonder-working power: an exorcism
there, a healing here.

   3:3-4 *(Matt 12:11-12; Luke 6:8-9)* In v 3 the present historical tense of
λέγει, "he says," stresses the authority of Jesus' command that the man with the
withered hand get up in the midst of the onlookers. Lending force to the command
itself is the present tense of the imperative ἔγειρε, "get up" (contrast the unemphatic aorist imperative of this verb in Matt 17:7; cf. the notes on 1:3). The
command prepares for a demonstration of Jesus' power to them, but at the moment
gives some hope to the man (cf. 10:49). Notably, Jesus starts things going despite
malevolent scrutiny. He risks himself to exercise his power for human benefit. In
v 4 the present historical tense of λέγει stresses the forcefulness of his following
question, which keeps his scrutinizers silent. Their silence itself testifies to the
forcefulness of his question: they intended to accuse him. Now they can only
keep their mouths shut and, at the end of the story, go out and conspire against
him (cf. 4:39; 9:34; 11:33; 12:17, 34). Meanwhile, he seizes the initiative from
them (cf. 12:35). *They* raised a question of permissibility in 2:24 (ἔξεστιν). Now
he does (ἔξεστιν again). As in v 2, the third plural pronoun probably refers to the
Pharisees, not to the audience in general. Τοῖς σάββασιν, "on the Sabbath," is to
be construed with ἀγαθὸν ποιῆσαι κτλ., "to do good [and so on]," not with ἔξεστιν
(see 2:24). Therefore the forward position of τοῖς σάββασιν stresses the point at
issue. Stressing the same point are the forward position of ἀγαθόν, "good," the
prefixing of κακο-, "evil," and the forward position of ψυχήν, "life."

   Saving life defines doing good in physical terms (but a moral connotation
does not evaporate as a result; see R. H. Fuller, *Interpreting the Miracles* 52-53,
on the salvific connotation of "doing good"). The Pharisees believe that saving
the life of a whole man on the Sabbath is not illegal (*m. Yoma* 8:6 and much other
literature cited in Str-B 1. 622-29). But in a withered hand they see no threat to
life; therefore the healing can wait for a day (cf. Luke 13:14; also CD 11:10; *m.*

Šabb. 14:3-4; *t. Šabb.* 12:8-14, cited by E. P. Sanders, *Jewish Law* 13). For Jesus, however, a medical estimate does not define the saving of life. Doing good defines that, and nobody denies the legality of doing good at any time (cf. Matt 19:16; Rom 13:3; and R. Pesch [1. 192], who rightly brings under consideration Jesus' emphasis on loving your neighbor as yourself). Since healing the withered hand of a man for whose sake the Sabbath came into being would surely count as doing good, then, let the Sabbath be violated for the healing. The moral robustness of Jesus' question reduces to absurdity the medically casuistic opinion of the Pharisees. His question calls for a halakic answer (one derived from a definite command in the OT), but he has outflanked the only consideration — viz., a differentiated medical diagnosis — to which a halakic argument could be applied. Jesus regards the withered hand as threatened by death, perhaps as already dead. Therefore restoring it to health counts as saving life and doing good, no matter what the threat to the life of the whole man.

On the negative side, killing defines doing evil in physical terms (though again a moral connotation does not evaporate as a result). But doing harm and killing represent destructive actions, not merely the neglect of someone in need of healing; and it is not permissible to do harm and kill on *any* day of the week. Furthermore, Jesus doubtless knows that a violation of the Pharisees' earlier warning is liable to prompt capital proceedings against him. Therefore, doing harm and killing do not refer to neglect of the man's need for healing, but set out the alternative of killing Jesus, if possible. The Pharisees will try to take this illegal alternative as a result of Jesus' taking the legal alternative of saving life. In an advance on 2:20 (see the notes ad loc.), he may now be thinking of the violent fate of the OT prophets as his own, too (cf. 12:1-12; Matt 23:29-39; Luke 11:47-51; 13:31-34; Acts 7:51-52; O. H. Steck, *Israel und das gewaltsame Geschick der Propheten;* L. Ruppert, *Der leidende Gerechte;* idem, *Jesus als der leidende Gerechte?*).

3:5 *(Matt 12:13; Luke 6:10)* Jesus' looking around with anger at the Pharisees comes in response to their failure to answer his question. He need not say anything more to them. They are beaten. The asyndeton between participial phrases emphasizes his angry look and sorrow-stricken emotion. As a narrator omniscient of both Jesus' emotions and the heart condition of his enemies, Mark displays Jesus' anger and deep sorrow in the light of his enemies' murderous design and callousness of heart to make readers sympathetic toward Jesus, so sympathetic that they will not take offense at his crucifixion. His anger grows out of his enemies' murderous design. His deep sorrow grows out of their callousness of heart, for that callousness will work to their own detriment. One expects the reverse, viz., that the sorrow would relate to the possibility of his death through their murderous design, now betrayed by silence, and the anger to their callousness of heart, richly deserving of judgment. But here is no sword-wielding rebel worthy of a Roman cross, but a man who grieves deeply over his enemies (συλ- is a perfective preposition prefixed to -λυπούμενος) and who gets angry to save life, not kill, to do good, not harm. By contrast, the Pharisees have hearts callous enough to harm, to kill, even on the Sabbath. Their callous hearts are worse than a withered hand. Not only would they fail to do the good of saving life on the Sabbath. They would actually use the Sabbath to kill Jesus (v 6).

The present historical tense of λέγει, "he says," stresses the powerful word of healing, "Stretch out the hand." Since in the healing of the paralytic Jesus told him to do what he could not do unless healed (2:10-11; see other healings, too, throughout the gospels and Acts) and since in 1 Kgs 13:4 a hand that suddenly withered in an extended position could not be drawn back, the statement, "And he stretched [it] out," is probably synonymous with the accompanying statement, "And his hand was restored." That is to say, the restoration occurs in the very act of stretching out the hand. Conversely, that very act demonstrates restoration. Before, the man could not stretch it out. It was stiff, immobile. But stretching it out exhibits the effectiveness of Jesus' word. By defining the healing as doing good and as saving life, he has already defended the breaking of the Sabbath to heal a withered hand. By performing the healing with a mere word, which does not count as work, he now trumps even those who would not accept his defense (cf. D. Flusser, *Jesus* 49-50; E. P. Sanders, *Jewish Law* 21).

3:6 *(Matt 12:14; Luke 6:11)* "Having gone out" balances the entrance with which the pericope began (v 1). "The Pharisees" confirms the natural identification of Jesus' would-be accusers as the same as those in 2:23-28. "Immediately," delayed till after the participle "having gone out" so as to modify the predicate "were giving consultation," indicates that the Pharisees use this very Sabbath, on which Jesus has done good by saving life, to plot the destruction of his life, which as Jesus has pointed out is unlawful. The Herodians are probably supporters of Herod Antipas, who under Roman aegis rules Galilee at this time. Therefore, "with the Herodians" highlights the Pharisees' failure to fabricate a theological accusation with respect to Sabbath-breaking. They must go to the Herodians for political help (cf. 8:15; 12:13-17). "Giving consultation against him" (v 2) fore-shadows the chief priestly action of "making consultation" so as to engineer the crucifixion of Jesus (15:1), but it does not fulfil the Pharisees' original purpose to "bring [legal] charge against him." The placement of μετὰ τῶν Ἡρῳδιανῶν συμβούλιον, "with the Herodians consultation," before ἐδίδουν, "were giving," underscores this shift. The revised purpose of the Pharisees to "destroy him," which foreshadows the plot of the chief priests and scribes in 11:18 (cf. 12:12; 14:1) and defines the Pharisees' "giving consultation against him," ironically casts them in the role of assassins who deserve the kind of death that Jesus will unjustly suffer because he saves life rather than killing people. Again ironically, the guardians of the Sabbath conspire to destroy the Lord of the Sabbath (cf. 2:20; 11:18; 12:12; 14:1). The forward position of αὐτόν, "him," heightens the irony. In summary, the conspiracy at once testifies to the miracle that Jesus has per-formed, provides a foil against which he stands out as a doer of good and savior of life, and displays his ability to frustrate the Pharisees' plan to accuse him of breaking the Sabbath.

NOTES

א B bo lack the definite article before συναγωγήν, "synagogue." We might think that the article comes into Mark by parallel influence from Matt 12:9; Luke 6:6. On the other hand, it is better to think that Matt 12:9; Luke 6:6 reflect Mark's original text and that the article drops out through scribal inattention to the back reference to 1:21, where the presence of the article favors its presence in 3:1, too. The Hellenistic practice of increasingly omitting the article in prepositional phrases (M. Zerwick, *Biblical Greek* §182) may have abetted this inattention. A withered hand may mean a paralyzed hand, but we have no way of choosing between different possibilities (H. van der Loos, *Miracles* 438-39). The perfect tense of ἐξηραμμένην, "withered," does not have to imply a congenital malady, and in view of ἀπεκατεστάθη, "was restored," probably does not carry that implication. *Gos. Naz.* 10 (according to Jerome, *Comm. Matt.* 2 [on Matt 12:13]) makes the man with a withered hand into a mason whose livelihood depends on its use (text in K. Aland, *Synopsis* 158; A. Huck and H. Greeven, *Synopsis* 66).

E. Schweizer (73-74) sceptically asks whether Pharisees would really think that Jesus can heal. But Jesus' reputation, the Pharisees' attributing his exorcisms to satanic power rather than denying them (vv 22, 30), and later rabbis' accepting the reality of Jesus' miracles dictate the answer "yes." See M. Reiser (*Syntax und Stil* 17) on ἔγειρε εἰς τὸ μέσον as good Greek. Εἰς may be pregnant with motion: "Get up [and come] into the midst" (cf. J. J. O'Rourke in *JBL* 85 [1966] 349; J. A. Kleist 192).

The contrasts in v 4 seem to come from Deut 30:15. But there, according to the MT, the synonymous pair "life and good" contrasts with the synonymous pair "death and evil." Since Deut 30:19 MT selects the first in each of these pairs to produce a new, antithetical pair "life and death," the LXX of v 15 anticipates v 19 by putting first the same antithetical pair and then following up with a second antithetical pair "good and evil." In agreement with Sir 33:14 except for the order of words within each pair, Jesus adopts the antithetical pairs but reverses their order to end on the climactic contrast between life and death. Furthermore, whereas the passage in Deuteronomy sets forth good and evil, life and death as blessings and judgments from the hand of God, Jesus' saying sets them forth as alternatives in human behavior. Thus we read of "*doing* good," "*doing* evil," "*saving* life," and "*killing*" (against the abstractness of the contrasts in Sir 33:14).

"To save life" does not come up to the level of raising the dead; so we should avoid overinterpreting the phrase as an allusion to the Resurrection. An ethical interpretation that exalts the doing of good merely at the expense of ritual observance does not satisfy the strong language in the contrast between saving life and killing. In Jesus' view, healing a withered hand counts as saving life; but neglecting to heal the hand would by no means count as killing it (for the hand is already dead or dying of its own accord), much less as killing the whole man. Hence, we should refuse the objections of D. E. Nineham (108-10) and H. Anderson (113-14) against an allusion to the Pharisees' murderous design, an allusion that does not diminish the theology of Jesus' argument by being ad hominem (see the foregoing comments on vv 3-4). M. J. Borg (*Conflict* 156-61) thinks that Jesus appeals to Jewish allowance of warfare on the Sabbath to preserve the life of God's people: if it is lawful to kill on the Sabbath, then how much more to heal. But Jesus' phrase "to kill" is stronger than the phrases "to fight" and "to resist" in the passages cited to support this view (1 Macc 2:29-41; Josephus *Ant.* 12.6.2 §§274-77; 14.4.2 §63); and he sets out alternatives with "or," not an argument with "if . . . , then. . . ."

R. Pesch (1. 193) suggests that Jesus argued from Gen 2:7: since God created Adam a living ψυχήν ("soul" — so the LXX), one ought to save a ψυχήν ("life" — so Mark 3:4), Sabbath day or not. To make Jesus' silencing of the storm in 4:39 an indication that the present silence of the Pharisees implies their representation of the powers of chaos is to forget that hearers of 2:4 do not yet have 4:39 in mind (cf. the notes on 2:12). Perhaps they will recall 2:4 when they hear 4:39 read to them. But will the silence of the disciples, embarrassed because Jesus asks them about their disputing who of them is the greatest, imply that *they* represent the powers of chaos (see 9:33-34)? Περιβλέπομαι, "look around," appears often in Mark (3:5, 34; 5:32; 9:8; 10:23; 11:11) but nowhere else in the NT except for the present Lucan parallel. The association of Jesus' anger with his looking around at the Pharisees militates against our seeing the anger as the excitement which enables a charismatic to work a miracle. So also does the contrastive sorrow of Jesus. Ordinarily, συλ- with -λυπέω changes grieving to grieving "with" someone else, i.e. sympathizing. M.-J. Lagrange (59) suggests that συλ- here refers to a mixture of grief "with" anger, and C. F. D. Moule (*Idiom-Book* 192) compares the Latin *contristari,* which means simply "to grieve." See BAGD s.v. συλλυπέω for the perfective meaning. In 10:5 Jesus will refer to the hardheartedness of the Pharisees with the word σκληροκαρδίαν. The phrase used here, ἐπὶ τῇ πωρώσει τῆς καρδίας αὐτῶν, will reappear in cognate form to describe the disciples' callous hearts at 6:52; 8:17, where lack of understanding defines it. Perhaps the callousness of the Pharisees' hearts in the present passage means their failure to understand Jesus' statements about the Sabbath. For healings similar to this one, see 1 Kgs 13:6; *T. Sim.* 2:12-13; Tac. *Hist.* 4.81; Suet. *Vesp.* 7; Dio Cass. 65.8.1; Philostr. *VA* 3.39; B. Blackburn, *Theios Anēr* 189-90. W. Weiss (*"Eine neue Lehre in Vollmacht"* 125) draws a parallel between 3:1-6 and 1:21-28 and argues that just as 1:21-28 presents Jesus not as an exorcist but as a teacher whose authority an exorcism confirms (sic — for teaching and exorcism enjoy equal billing), so also 3:1-6 presents him not as a miraculous healer but as a teacher whose authority a miraculous healing confirms. Unfortunately for this view, his teaching is not even mentioned in 3:1-6 as it was mentioned repeatedly and emphatically in 1:21-28; and the question in 3:4 can hardly be construed as teaching.

On the Herodians, see Josephus *J.W.* 1.16.6 §319 (Ἡρῴδειοι), set in Galilee as is Mark 3:6, and idem *Ant.* 14.15.10 §450 (τοὺς τὰ Ἡρῴδου φρονοῦντας), set in Judea as Mark 12:13 will be, and the secondary literature cited in BAGD s.v. Ἡρῳδιανοί plus C. Daniel in *RevQ* 6 (1967) 31-53; H. W. Hoehner, *Herod Antipas* 331-42; W. J. Bennett, Jr., in *NovT* 17 (1975) 9-14; K. Wengst, *Pax Romana* 195-96, n. 14. In the Josephan passages the Herodians appear as supporters of Herod the Great, father of Herod Antipas. The Pharisees could be playing on the later Herodians' fear that Jesus might lead a messianic revolt which would threaten their favored position. Given the public falling out between Herod Antipas and Herod Agrippa I and their struggle for power, in which Antipas lost his tetrarchy and property to Agrippa (Josephus *Ant.* 18.6.2 §§148-50; 18.6.10–18.7.2 §§237-54; idem *J.W.* 2.9.6 §§181-83), the popular view that the supporters of Agrippa (41-44 C.E.) anachronistically crept into the gospel tradition as supporters of Antipas in consequence of Agrippa's persecuting the Palestinian church (Acts 12:1-19) seems doubtful. Our sources do not put Agrippa in partnership with the Pharisees. Acts 12:1-19 says only that he persecuted Christians to please the Jews. The obscurity and figurativeness of "the leaven of Herod" in 8:16 and the appropriateness of the Herodians' presence in 12:13-17 to the pilgrimatic character of the Passover Festival and to one horn of the dilemma posed to Jesus, i.e. the horn of paying tax to Caesar, support the historicity of the Herodians' role in each passage where they appear in Mark. A common enemy makes strange bedfellows: this historical truism deprives of its cogency the argument that because the Pharisees and the Herodians disliked each other they would not have teamed up. One could argue that the general unpopularity of Antipas would make meaningful the use of his name to designate a party consisting of a minority who did favor him and thereby gained favor from him, as in the Josephan passages cited above. The frustration of the Pharisees' purpose to accuse Jesus, their being silenced by him and having to go instead to the Herodians and hatch a plot with them, undermines the view that v 6 portrays Jesus as a righteous sufferer (so L. Schenke, *Wundererzählungen* 171-72). He seems rather to be in control.

We have noted various features of the pericope that point to its compositional unity with preceding pericopes. By themselves, however, these features do not tell us whether Mark or an earlier traditioner imposed this unity or whether they reflect a historical connection of incidents, especially of 3:1-6 with 2:23-28. To some, 3:1-6 looks like a Marcan or pre-Marcan addition to illustrate the Son of man's lordship over the Sabbath (2:28). Thus, unless Mark has added "again" in 3:1 to allude to Jesus' entering the synagogue at Capernaum for the first time in 1:21, the adverb in the pre-Marcan version of the story alluded to Jesus' visiting a synagogue in an unknown earlier context, carried a transitional rather than temporal meaning, or referred to Jesus' habit of attending synagogue. But to note Jesus' habit, we would expect Mark to write ὡς εἰώθει, "as he was accustomed," as in 10:1, not πάλιν, "again," which refers to a single repetition but hardly to the number of repetitions required for a habit. A non-temporal transitional use would require an unknown earlier context just as a temporal use would. But what advantage does an unknown earlier context have over the known context of Mark? It seems better to treat "again" as a Marcan touch. More importantly, to regard 3:1-6 as a Marcan or pre-Marcan addition makes it easy to regard the plotting of the Pharisees in 3:6 as an addition to 3:1-5 to forge a link with the antagonistic Pharisees in 2:24, perhaps also to bring to a climactic conclusion all the preceding controversies (and also the material from 1:21 onward, which prepared for the controversies, according to D.-A. Koch, *Bedeutung* 51). Form critically, it is argued, a miracle-cum-controversy story should not end on the defeatist note of a plot against Jesus' life; 3:5 makes a good and sufficient conclusion by describing the healing that took place; and plotting against Jesus' life in 11:18; 12:12; 14:1 will combine with the plotting in 3:6 to form a theme that Mark or a prior traditioner has added to earlier materials. The non-mention of Pharisees in the body of the story (3:1-5) confirms the hypothesis that 3:6 is a later addition. If that verse falls away from the original version of the story, the purpose to accuse Jesus (v 2b) looks unoriginal, too; for without v 6 that purpose leads nowhere, not even to frustration. If the purpose falls away, the scrutinizing of Jesus to see whether he will heal on the Sabbath (v 2a) either becomes innocent rather than antagonistic or, if still antagonistic, unoriginal and therefore subject to falling away with the other antagonistic additions. With no antagonism left in the story, the question of permissibility, the strength of the language setting out the alternatives of doing good and bad, of saving life and killing, the silence of Jesus' addressees, and his angry and sorrowful reactions (vv 4-5a) look like Marcan or pre-Marcan additions growing out of the antagonism imposed on the story.

At this point doubts about the foregoing line of reasoning can no longer be held at bay. For we are left with an emaciated story of healing. The healing itself has nothing to prompt it either by way of a request, a presentation of the patient to Jesus, or a challenge of any kind. And the successful healing does not generate admiration such as we expect to be mentioned when an audience is present (as here and in the synagogue at 1:21-28, esp. 27-28). So perhaps we should reconsider earlier points along the line. The aggressiveness shown by Jesus in raising the question of permissibility and the strength of his language in setting out alternatives typify the charismatic figure portrayed in our most probably authentic traditions. But where better would the question and the language fit than in the present story of a healing on the Sabbath? But if they belong to the story, the aggressiveness of Jesus and the strength of his language favor a setting of antagonism over one of innocent curiosity. Besides, "watching to see whether he will heal on the Sabbath" implies antagonism more naturally than it implies innocent curiosity. A setting of antagonism leads us to rehabilitate the purpose to accuse Jesus, the silence of his addressees, and his reactions of anger and sorrow as original parts of the story. Verse 6 comes back, too, as an appropriate conclusion taking the place of the admiration that we expect on the part of a non-antagonistic audience (cf. F. W. Danker, *Benefactor* 405). Unless we are willing to pare down the story despite the foregoing considerations, v 6 is form critically incongruous no more than is the mixture of miracle and polemic in vv 1-5. Canons of form criticism may help us discern the stereotyped shape that a story tended to take when told over and over again, but they make poor instruments for discerning its earliest shape, determined more by historical data and less by the oral conventions of later storytellers and the needs of their audiences. Form critical incongruities may therefore point to the earliest historical shape as easily as to the latest literary tampering with oral conventions.

Adding to our confidence in the originality and authenticity of v 6 is the non-appearance of the Pharisees and Herodians in the passion narrative (chaps. 14–16). Why would anyone falsely implicate them in a plot against Jesus' life when they will play no role in the actual taking of it? Furthermore, v 6 lacks the key verb ζητέω, "seek," which will characterize the later description of plots against his life; it will be others who "accuse" Jesus during his trial (cf. v 2 with 15:3-4); and the Latinism συμβούλιον ἐδίδουν, "were giving consultation" (*consilium dederunt;* cf. a similar Latinism in 15:1), occurs only here (see V. Taylor 224; J. D. M. Derrett, *Studies* 4. 28-29, for different explanations). So it does not seem that anyone has added v 6 purely in anticipation of 11:18; 12:12; 14:1, or that Mark brings in the Herodians to set up a kind of parallel between Herod Antipas's execution of John the Baptist (6:21-29) and the Herodians' joining the Pharisees to plot Jesus' death (as thought by W. J. Bennett, Jr., in *NovT* 17 [1975] 9-14). The rehabilitation of v 6 carries with itself the original connection of the story with 2:23-28, which mentioned the Pharisees and quoted their warning question with the result that Mark does not need to mention them in 3:1-6 until they form an alliance with another group, the mention of whose name "the Herodians" makes desirable the recurrence of "the Pharisees." The scrutiny and the purpose to accuse Jesus of deliberate Sabbath-breaking presuppose 2:23-28. For this reason we should also reject the suggestion that Mark tore 3:1-6 away from an earlier connection with 12:13 (K. Kertelge, *Wunder* 83; E. A. Russell in *SE VI* 466-72). See W. Thissen, *Erzählung* 74-79, for a fullscale attack on the exclusion of 3:1-6 from a pre-Marcan collection of controversy stories (so H.-W. Kuhn, *Ältere Sammlungen* 88); J. Dewey, *Markan Public Debate* 100-101, on rhetorical parallels between 3:1-6 and 2:1-12; and J. Kiilunen, *Vollmacht* 73-75, against drawing such parallels. All in all, we do best to think of original Marcan composition based on traditional reports that already included a connection between 3:1-6 and 2:23-28.

JESUS' MAGNETISM

3:7-12 (Matt 4:24-25; 12:15-16; Luke 6:17-19)

In this pericope Jesus withdraws to the sea (v 7a), but a large multitude follows him and comes to him (vv 7b-8) with the result that he commands a boat to be readied (v 9). Mark then identifies two reasons why so large a multitude follows and comes that Jesus has to take this extraordinary precaution: (1) his having performed many healings (v 10); (2) repeated acknowledgments by unclean spirits of his divine sonship (v 11). Closing out the pericope is his having to shut up the spirits to avoid further publicity (v 12).

3:7-8 *(Matt 4:24-25; Luke 6:17-18a)* The mention of Jesus' name and its placement before the verb set him over against the Pharisees and Herodians who were conspiring against him (v 6). The conspiracy now leads to his withdrawal. "Flight" may be too strong a word, for he will come back. But at least he gets away from the immediate threat. "With his disciples" prepares for a request that he will make of them in v 9. There is no indication that he withdraws with them to get away from the multitude, as in 4:36; 6:32, 45; rather, the multitude follows him after he withdraws. "To the sea" tells how far he goes before pausing to minister to their needs. He will next go up into a mountain (v 13), whether via the lakeshore or because of a change in plan — or whether there is no continuity between his going to the sea and his going up into a mountain — we cannot tell. If there is no continuity, we are left wondering whether he intends to withdraw farther than the lakeshore and perhaps does so. Or is the point on the lakeshore where he heals many people already far enough away from the conspirators (who may or may not be consulting with one another in Capernaum)? The πρός, "to," before τὴν θάλασσαν, "the sea," may suggest the intention or actuality of a further withdrawal, since in 1:16; 2:13; 4:1; 5:21 παρά occurs for a simple journey to the sea or for a position alongside it.

The following of Jesus by a large multitude renews and heightens attention to his magnetism and gives a popular answer to the conspiracy of the Pharisees and Herodians (v 6). Usually Mark writes about a "crowd" (ὄχλος). "Multitude" (πλῆθος) puts even greater emphasis on numerousness, and this emphasis increases severalfold with placement before the verb and the prefixing, cognateness, and consequent assonance of πολύ, "multitudinous." The large number of the multitude prepares for selection of the Twelve to act as Jesus' apostles, helpers in an oversized ministry (vv 13-19). Not only did this multitude follow him "from Galilee," where he had been ministering. They also came to him "from Judea [the south] and from Jerusalem [the capital city there] and from Idumea [even farther to the south] and Transjordan [to the east] and around Tyre and Sidon [to the north — the west being omitted because the Mediterranean Sea is there]." Mark has mentioned no ministry in those places. It is "hearing *how many* things he was doing" that draws the more distant ones from the three possible points of the compass; and the present tense of ἀκούοντες, "hearing," makes their going to him contemporaneous with their hearing how many things he was doing. They no sooner hear than they go, so great is his attraction. Those from Galilee "followed" him to the sea because they were already with him in Galilee. Those from other regions had to "come." Mark repeats "a multitudinous multitude" for those from regions outside Galilee and by this means reinforces his main point, viz., Jesus' magnetism, which far exceeds that of John the Baptizer, who drew only from the Judean territory and Jerusalem within it (1:5). Emphasis on the large number of the multitude increases not only by means of the inclusion which the repetition effects but also by means of the chiastic placement of πολύ, "multitudinous," after πλῆθος, "multitude" (cf. the reverse order in v 7).

3:9-10 *(Matt 12:15; Luke 6:18b-19)* Jesus' request that a boat be readied for him underscores his attractive power by pointing to the severity of the danger that the crowd is so large they will crush him (cf. 2:4; 5:24, 31). The forward position of πλοιάριον, "boat," and the present tense of the subjunctive in προσκαρτερῇ, "be readied," and θλίβωσιν, "crush," accentuate the need for this pre-caution (cf. the notes on 1:3). Can such a man be dangerous, vile, the kind that usually hangs on a cross? Hardly, for the reason they nearly crush him to death before his enemies can crucify him is that "he had healed many" — so many, in fact, that now others "were falling on him in order that as many as had lashes might touch him." As a figure for suffering the torments of disease, εἶχον μάστιγας, "had lashes," intensifies κακῶς ἔχοντας ποικίλαις νόσοις, "were ill with various diseases" (1:34), to stress neediness. In 1:34 καὶ ἐθεράπευσεν πολλούς, "and he healed many," referred to Jesus' healing many *at the time.* Here, πολλοὺς γὰρ ἐθεράπευσεν refers back, as shown by the similarity of phraseology, to those many healings as the reason for the present onrush: "for he *had* healed many." Not as in 1:34, however, the object πολλούς, "many," advances ahead of its verb for special emphasis. The placement of αὐτοῦ, "him," before ἅψωνται, "might touch," combines with the preceding ἐπιπίπτειν αὐτῷ, "to fall on him," to produce a chiasm that highlights Jesus as the object of an onrush. "As many as [ὅσοι] had lashes" corresponds to "as many things as [ὅσα] he had been doing" and refers to victims of illness among the crowd. Merely touching Jesus brings healing, so great is his power (cf. 5:27-34; 6:56). It works for good, not for ill. He is a hero, not a villain. As usual, the γάρ-clause, "for . . . ," puts across Mark's point of view.

3:11-12 *(Matt 12:16)* The forward positions of τὰ πνεύματα τὰ ἀκάθαρτα and of αὐτόν emphasize the acknowledgement by "the unclean spirits" of "him" (Jesus) as God's Son. Mark also emphasizes the repetitiveness and consistency with which the unclean spirits fall prostrate toward Jesus and shout to him that he is God's Son: "whenever they saw him" (ὅταν plus the imperfect indicative). Without exception they find themselves irresistibly drawn to acknowledge by gesture and outcry his divine sonship. He has a magnetic hold on them just as he has on the large multitude. The wordplay of προσέπιπτον in v 11 with ἐπιπίπτειν in v 10 enhances the point: as the sick "were falling *on*" Jesus to touch him, so the unclean spirits "were falling *toward*" him to acknowledge his divine sonship. But Mark writes nothing about the unclean spirits' coming out of people, or even mentions the people afflicted by them. So exorcism is not his point. On the other hand, had he wanted to make the identity of Jesus as God's Son the point, he would probably not have allowed Jesus' rebuking the unclean spirits that they should not make him manifest to stand at the close of the pericope. The pericope reaches its climax in that very rebuking (ἐπετίμα).

In 1:25 the rebuking of an unclean spirit that was trying to ward off Jesus by shouting Jesus' divine title, "the Holy One of God," included not only a command to shut up but also a command to come out (cf. 4:39 and esp. 9:25, yet see the notes on 1:24-25 against an overly technical interpretation of ἐπιτιμάω). We may suspect that tradition behind 3:11 showed the same purpose of Jesus to overcome demonic self-defense by shutting up the unclean spirits. But Mark's stopping short of quoting an exorcistic command and of describing an expulsion relates the rebuke solely to Jesus' supersuccessful attraction of the large multitude, which threatens to crush him (a danger not present in the synagogue at Capernaum — 1:21-28; but cf. φανερόν, "manifest," with the use of φανερῶς, "openly," in

1:45, where supersuccessful attraction of people was already in view). The imperfect tense of ἐπετίμα (cf. 10:48) indicates that he has to issue his rebuke time after time so successful a crowd-drawer is he. The adverbial πολλά, "much" or "vigorously," which occurs often in Mark (see the note on 1:45), indicates the strength of the rebuke. The emphatic forward position of the adverb makes the rebuke even stronger. This emphasis on the strength of the rebuke reinforces the point of Jesus' magnetism. It is not keeping a messianic secret of his divine sonship for theological reasons which is in view any more than people's rebuking Bartimaeus to silence him will have a deeper theological purpose of keeping a messianic secret of his Davidic sonship (10:46-48). The preceding context dictates otherwise. It is that Jesus attracts so large a multitude that he must have a boat ready and insist that the unclean spirits not publicize him as God's Son lest the throngs crush him (the true parallels being 1:45; 9:30 rather than 8:30; 9:9). Consequently, the following ἵνα-clause may indicate not only the content of the rebuke (epexegetic ἵνα), but also its purpose (telic ἵνα; so also ἐπιτιμάω plus ἵνα in 8:30; 10:48; cf. 5:10, 18, 43; 6:8-9, 12, 56; 7:26, 32, 36; 8:22; 13:34; 15:11). In 1:25, λέγων, "saying," introduced the content of Jesus' rebuke. Therefore, the shift to ἵνα in the present passage again favors a statement of purpose as well as of content.

All in all, then, this pericope portrays a strong Jesus before whom unclean spirits fall every time they see him and whose true identity they shout out. Their testimony to Jesus is visible, audible, and invariable. But to keep the large multitude from crushing him, he repeatedly has to insist that they not publicize his divine sonship any further; and he has to tell his disciples to ready a boat because the press of the multitude has become so great as to threaten his life. His not having to use the boat as a way of escape shows that he succeeds in dampening the unwanted publicity.

NOTES

After an indication of topographical movement, this pericope offers a fairly general statement of Jesus' activity and its effect. The statement summarizes neither the preceding (since the element of controversy in most of 2:1–3:6 is missing) nor the following (since the immediately following pericopes will not speak of healings and confrontations with unclean spirits, as do vv 7-12, and since vv 7-12 do not speak of teaching, as the immediately following pericopes will do — an exorcism and healings not coming up till chap. 5, after the appointment of the Twelve, after the charges concerning Beelzebul, after the teaching of Jesus about his new family, after a number of didactic parables, and after the calming of a storm).

The evidence that Mark or an earlier traditioner writes vv 7-12 by pirating words and ideas from a pre-Marcan collection of miracle stories underlying 4:35–5:43; 6:32-52 (cf. R. Pesch 1. 198-202, 277-81) does not look impressive. The disciples' accompaniment of Jesus (3:7) need not have been drawn from 4:35-41; 5:21-43; 6:32-44, 45-52, for they have already accompanied Jesus in 1:20, 21, 29, 36-38; 2:15, 23 and will do so in later parts of Mark, too. The thronging of people to Jesus in 3:7 might just as well reflect 1:5, 32-34, 45; 2:2, 13 as come by anticipation from 5:14-15, 21; 6:32-33; and the same phenomenon will occur outside the supposed field of borrowing in 8:1; 9:25 (and in

6:53-56, too; but that is supposed to be a concluding summary of the pre-Marcan collection of miracle stories). The use of ἠκολούθησεν, "followed," in a non-discipular sense (3:7) need not have been drawn from 5:24; for it may well have occurred with that sense in 2:15, and it will do so certainly in 11:9 and perhaps also in 10:32. It is just as easy to think that ὅσα ἐποίει, "how many things he was doing" (3:8), affects later phraseology in 5:19, 20; 6:30 as to think that it comes from that phraseology by way of anticipation (cf. also 9:13, which stands outside the field of supposed borrowing).

The boat in 3:9 is said to have come from 4:1, 36, 37; 5:2, 18, 21; 6:32, 45, 47, 51. But again the boat will appear outside the field (see 8:10, 13, 14; also 6:54, in the supposed concluding summary). Jesus does not use the boat in 3:7-12; it only stands ready in case of need. He will not use a boat till 4:1, where he will "again" begin to teach alongside the sea. In the meantime we will find him on a mountain (3:13) and in a house (3:20). One might think that Mark disarranges material, i.e. that 4:1 originally followed 3:7-12. But since Jesus does not teach here in 3:7-12, the statement in 4:1 that "he again began to teach alongside the sea" harks back to 2:13, where he did the same. Therefore it does not look as though 3:7-12 and 4:1 are related by anticipation or in any other way. Furthermore, in 4:1 Mark will not mention the danger of Jesus' being crushed by the multitude, as he does in 3:9-10; and 3:9 has the diminutive πλοιάριον for "boat," whereas 4:1 has the non-diminutive πλοῖον. The difference between diminutive and non-diminutive forms does not have to be significant (C. H. Turner in *JTS* os 29 [1927-28] 349-52); but it is striking that despite the frequency of diminutives in Mark (see 5:23, 39, 41; 6:9; 7:25, 27, 28; 8:7; 14:47), this diminutive is hapax at 3:9 and the non-diminutive form of the word occurs everywhere else. Yet further, πλοῖον will have no anaphoric definite article in 4:1, as we would expect it to have if Mark or his source meant 3:9 to introduce the boat referred to in 4:1. All subsequent occurrences of πλοῖον do, in fact, have an anaphoric definite article.

The danger that Jesus *might* be crushed (θλίβωσιν) could anticipate 5:24, 31; but there the crowd will *actually* crush Jesus and the verb will be compound (forms of συνθλίβω). Here in 3:9, moreover, the phrase διὰ τὸν ὄχλον, "on account of the crowd," echoes 2:4 exactly and thus shows a backward reference in addition to the possible forward reference. Similarly, πολλούς . . . ἐθεράπευσεν, "he had healed many," makes a backward reference to 1:34, where the same statement occurred. People's touching Jesus to be healed (3:10) crops up in the supposed concluding summary (6:56) as well as in the supposed field of borrowing (5:27, 28, 30, 31; cf. Jesus' touching people in 1:41; 7:33; 8:22; 10:13), but the progression in the three passages from touching Jesus to touching his garment and finally to touching the hem of his garment leads us to suspect a backward-looking intensification in the second and third passages rather than an anticipative borrowing in the first passage. For this reason we can think that μάστιγας, "lashes" (3:10), represents an intensification of the similar statement in 1:34 rather than an anticipation of 5:29, 34 (see the foregoing comments). Such a use of μάστιγας in connection with ἅψωνται, "touch," may be helped along by a wordplay on the root נגע, for which the LXX uses both of these Greek words (cf. J. Carmignac in *ASTI* 7 [1968-69] 70). The wordplay need be no more than mental on the part of a Greek writer thinking Semitically, however. "Unclean spirits" have populated Mark's text already (1:23, 26, 27) and will yet populate it outside a supposed pre-Marcan collection of miracle stories (3:30; 6:7; 7:25; 9:25); hence, there is no need to think that in 3:10 they derive from 5:2, 8, 13. Forms of θεωρέω, "see" (cf. 3:11), will occur in 12:41; 15:40, 47; 16:4 as well as in 5:15, 38. Forms of προσπίπτω, "fall before" (cf. 3:11), will occur not only in 5:33 but also in 7:25. The shouting (ἔκραζον — 3:11) of unclean spirits is mentioned in 1:23; 9:26 as well as in 5:5, 7. Their knowledge of Jesus as God's Son could echo 1:1, 11, 24 as well as anticipate 5:7. His rebuking them (3:12) could echo 1:25 and anticipate 9:25 more easily than it could anticipate 4:39, where he will rebuke the wind, not an unclean spirit as in the other passages.

Since then the phraseology in 3:7-12 has appeared and will appear outside the boundaries of a supposed pre-Marcan collection of miracle stories incorporated into chaps. 4–6, and since the subject matter in 3:7-12 differs significantly from that in 3:13–4:34 (esp. with respect to performing healings and exorcisms versus teaching), we should doubt that 3:7-12 summarizes the following. If it were meant to summarize the miracle stories beginning later in 4:35, we would expect it to appear right before 4:35. And if the summary were pre-Marcan, we would again expect Mark to keep it right before the miracle stories; for a transition from synagogue (3:1-6) to mountain (3:13-19) would be as easy as the transition from synagogue to sea (3:7-12). Furthermore, the conjunction γάρ in v 10a helps give the aorist ἐθεράπευσεν the force of a pluperfect, "for he had healed," which explains why a dangerously large multitude has gathered; i.e. Mark refers to the many *prior* healings of 1:34 and stops short of saying that any healings or exorcisms take place here, so that attention concentrates solely on Jesus' magnetism. Verses 7-12 do not look like the introduction to a pre-Marcan collection of miracle stories, then. Better to think that from the start Jesus' withdrawal to the sea was related to the conspiracy against his life (3:6) and that the following statements summarize according to tradition what occurs at the present time and place on account of what he has been doing earlier and elsewhere (cf. the extensive criticisms by R. M. Fowler [*Loaves and Fishes* 5-37] not only of Pesch's hypothesis, which is here treated as representative, but also of similar hypotheses put forward by Jenkins, Taylor, Keck, Kuhn, and Achtemeier).

This pericope has its own discrete significance. Its link with the immediately foregoing conspiracy and the difference in subject matter from the immediately following pericopes militate against our seeing it as the start of a new main section of Mark. The subject matter of the summary in 1:14-15 (Jesus' preaching) did not match the subject matter of 3:7-12 (Jesus' deeds). As a result, the parallel between the subsequent call of the first four disciples in 1:16-20 and the subsequent appointment of the Twelve in 3:13-19 becomes less impressive. Similarly, the summaries in 1:32-34 and 1:39 bring single pericopes to a climax. In truth, the whole of 3:7-12 is not a summary. Only vv 10-12 are a summary. And after the earlier pattern, these verses simply bring to a climax a pericope that concerns Jesus' withdrawal with crowds following and coming.

Since Mark regularly uses topographical movement to open new pericopes rather than to close old ones, v 7a does not belong to vv 1-6. Furthermore, v 7a and v 7b belong together, because the multitude's following Jesus in v 7b is consequent on his withdrawal in v 7a. By arguing that ἀνεχώρησεν probably does not connote withdrawal from danger because Jesus' enemies reappear in v 22, J. Gnilka (1. 134) overlooks that the description of those enemies as "the scribes who had come down from Jerusalem" seems to distinguish them from the Pharisees and Herodians who conspired against Jesus in 3:6. To interpret his withdrawal in v 7 as an attempt to escape the crowds would require an original preceding context of crowds, which none of the three immediately preceding pericopes provide. Nor does the theory that 3:7-12 originally introduced a pre-Marcan collection of miracle stories allow for such a preceding context.

Cf. 2:13 for an earlier going to the sea after a healing and a silencing of opponents (though the silencing is only implied, not stated as in 3:4). There, however, Jesus "went out"; here Mark says that Jesus "withdrew." The sea does not represent antagonistic forces of chaos, then. On the contrary, it is a safe haven because of its distance from those who conspire to destroy Jesus. For Judea and Jerusalem, paired in that order, cf. 1:5 and see F. Neirynck, *Duality* 96-97. The prepositional construction περὶ Τύρον καὶ Σιδῶνα, "around Tyre and Sidon," seems to be patterned after the immediately preceding πέραν τοῦ Ἰορδάνου, "across the Jordan" (contrast 7:24, 31). The repetition of ἀπό, "from," typifies Semitic style (M. Black, *Aramaic Approach* 114-15). As yet, we have seen no reason to believe that Mark thinks of a vanguard of Gentile "Christians" from outside Galilee (as thought by Z. Kato, *Völkermission*

30-31, and others). Why would he add Judea and Jerusalem, which are even more Jewish than Galilee, as well as Idumea, Transjordan, and the territory around Tyre and Sidon? And why would he omit Samaria, the steppingstone to evangelism of Gentiles (Acts 1:8; 8:4-40) and the Decapolis, which he will mention later (5:20; 7:31)? Kato *(loc. cit.)* suggests that Mark did not know of Samaria or included it in Judea (cf. its omission in 10:1) and included the Decapolis in Transjordan. But the two later mentions of the Decapolis will disfavor its inclusion in Transjordan, and the mention of Transjordan alongside Judea in 10:1 will favor a route skirting Samaria rather than an inclusion of Samaria in Judea. We do better to say that Mark omits Samaria and the Decapolis because few if any Jews live there. The coming of Jews from farther regions stresses what by now we know to be a prominent theme in Mark, viz., Jesus' power of attraction. The sufficiency of this theme undercuts the theory that the place-list honors the claims of Christian churches existing in those places at the time of Mark or of an earlier traditioner.

The use of πλῆθος, "multitude," for the church in Acts 4:32; 6:2, 5; 4:1; 15:12, 30; 17:4; 21:22 v.l. does not recommend an allusion to the church in the present passage. For Mark's multitude does not consist of disciples; his usage (or that of an earlier traditioner) need not match Luke's; and immediate contextual references to Christian belief and the like always qualify the use of πλῆθος for the church in Acts, whereas the word occurs without a Christian connotation about an equal number of times in Acts (and in Luke as well). Whatever the make-up of the multitude, Luke wants to stress largeness of number by using πλῆθος. Though it may be historically true that the large multitude came "from an innate instinct for sensationalism and a desire to be freed from their bodily needs" (J. Schmid 77), this does not represent Mark's point, which is Christological.

See B. M. Metzger, *Textual Commentary* ad loc., on the "nest of variant readings" in vv 7-8. The greater smoothness to which C. E. B. Cranfield (124) appeals in favor of the vv.ll. is precisely what casts text critical doubt on them. The roughness of the preferable text makes punctuation difficult. Perhaps Mark starts with only Galilee in mind, then thinks to add the other place-names after "followed" (so that the καί after ἠκολούθησεν is best translated "also"), and finally decides that the list of place-names has grown so long that he had better repeat "multitudinous multitude" and provide it with the verb "came" to bring the thought to completion.

"Lest they crush him" is not redundant; it clarifies the meaning of "on account of the crowd." Since here Jesus and his disciples do not even get into the boat, much less set sail, it does not separate Jesus and his disciples from the multitude. Moreover, the present readying of the boat does not prepare for later use in 4:1ff., for Jesus will in the meantime have gone up a mountain (3:13) and into a house (3:20). Thus fails the symbolic interpretation of the boat as representing the church (against E. Best, *Following Jesus* 230-34). See the note on 2:12 concerning ὥστε, "so that," as a Marcan term introducing the effects of Jesus' ministry. It is a modern judgment to say that "the price Mark pays" for portraying Jesus as a Hellenistic divine man is that Jesus appears as a mana-bearer whose power works automatically, independently of his will, when sick people touch him (S. Schulz, *Stunde* 70-71). Of course, this phenomenon is found also outside the Hellenistic sphere (see, e.g., 2 Kgs 13:20-21). Original meanings of words do not determine current meanings; so even though we assume that μάστιξ, "lash," originally implied a demon's whipping its victim with disease (cf. *PGM* V. 170; XVIIa. 16, 24), it does not follow that the present text attributes diseases to demons. On the contrary, it distinguishes between the diseased and the possessed (cf. S. Eitrem, *Some Notes* 35-36). And though μάστιξ might imply that God inflicts disease by way of punishment (W. Grundmann [7. Aufl.] 100 with references to Homer; Aesch. *PV* 682; and the LXX of Ps 72:4-5; Jer 5:3 et passim), C. Schneider (in *TDNT* 4. 518-19) writes that "after Aesch. the term loses it religious significance and is used generally for 'suffering' or even 'want.'"

We should not take προσέπιπτον, "were falling toward," in v 11 as connoting an attack against which Jesus has to protect his ministry to the disciples (a suggestion by O. Bauernfeind, *Worte* 66). Private ministry to them has not yet started, and will not till some time after the choice of the Twelve. The drift of the whole pericope is toward Jesus' magnetism, which the aforementioned wordplay with ἐπιπίπτειν, "to fall upon," points up. Προσέπιπτον connotes neither attack nor worship, but servility, and so will be associated with fear, trembling, and supplication in 5:33; 7:25. To say that the demoniacs are "imprecisely identified with the unclean spirits themselves" (J. Schmid 78; cf. C. E. B. Cranfield 126) misses the point that here Mark omits to mention demoniacs because their deliverance lies off the track of his emphasis on Jesus' magnetism. The v.l. λέγοντα, "saying," looks like a scribal grammatical improvement that makes the participle agree in gender with the neuter πνεύματα, "spirits." The probably original λέγοντες, "saying," implies the personality of the unclean spirits. For Jesus as God's Son in Mark, see the comments and notes on 1:1. The suggestion of H. Boers (in *SBL 1987 Seminar Papers* 262) that Jesus did not want his divine sonship revealed lest the revelation keep him from crucifixion (cf. 1 Cor 2:7-8) stumbles over a later self-revelation of divine sonship to his very judges (Mark 14:61-62). Far from deterring them, the self-revelation will provoke their condemning him as deserving the death penalty (14:63-64). Likewise, the explanation that he did not want people to think of him as God's Son apart from the Crucifixion and the Resurrection, which had yet to take place (R. A. Guelich 1. 149 and others cited there), stumbles over God's own proclamation of Jesus' divine sonship to disciples who were still unaccepting of those events (cf. 9:7 with 8:31-33; 9:33-37; 10:35-40). The adverbial use of πολλά elsewhere in Mark favors intensity ("much"), not repetition ("many times"; see 1:45; 4:2; 5:10, 23, 26, 38, 43; 6:20, 23, 34; 8:31; 9:12, 26; 12:41[?]; 15:3).

THE APPOINTMENT OF TWELVE APOSTLES AS EVIDENCE OF JESUS' OVERWHELMING MAGNETISM

3:13-19 (Matt 10:1-4; Luke 6:12-16)

As usual, a noting of topographical movement signals the start of a new pericope. This pericope deals with the appointment of the Twelve. Jesus' going up a mountain and issuing a summons and the response of the summoned (v 13) prepare for the appointment. The appointment follows, first with reference to its purpose (vv 14-15) and then with reference to the names of the Twelve (vv 16-19). Since Mark will not mention the Twelve again till 4:10 (and then not very prominently) and after that not till 6:7 and then not till 9:35, the point lies in Jesus' attracting so many people to himself that he has to have helpers (cf. vv 7-12).

3:13 *(Matt 10:1a; Luke 6:12-13a)* Jesus' going up a mountain relates loosely to his withdrawal to the sea in the preceding pericope (v 7) and perhaps to his dampening of publicity in the very preceding verse (12). The mountain sets him in a position of sovereignty. The present historical tense of ἀναβαίνει, "goes up," and of προσκαλεῖται, "summons," emphasizes this position and his exercise of sovereignty (cf. God's summoning Moses up Mount Sinai). For Jesus' authoritative summons, see also 3:23; 6:7; 7:14; 8:1, 34; 10:42; 12:43. Only once does

Mark use the verb for someone else's summoning. At 15:44 it will occur for Pilate's summoning the centurion, but this too will exhibit an exercise of authority. "Whom he willed" reveals the selectivity of Jesus' summons and further emphasizes his sovereignty. The emphatic αὐτός, "he himself," intensifies this emphasis. "And they went away to him" points to the powerful effect of his summons. 'Απ-, "away," implies that those who are summoned leave the multitude (vv 7-12) to heed the summons (cf. 1:19-20 with comments). Since we might expect "after him" (as in 1:20) or "with him" (cf. 5:24), the phrase "to him" suggests that Jesus is already on the mountain. If so, the going away does not mean accompanying him up the mountain, but heeding his summons from a distance, going up to him after he has gone up, and thus testifying all the more to the authority of his summons. Similar phraseology in 14:10 will support this understanding, which implies that Jesus goes up the mountain, not to get away from the large multitude or to commune with God, but to survey the crowd in preparation for his summons. Mark's interest in the authority of Jesus' summons leaves him disinterested in practical questions concerning the timing and means of the summons vis-à-vis Jesus' going up the mountain ahead of the others.

3:14-15 *(Matt 10:1b; Luke 6:13b)* "And he appointed [literally, 'made,' ἐποίησεν] twelve" again calls attention to Jesus' exercising an elective prerogative. The lack of any rationale for the number twelve leaves attention focussed solely on that exercise. "Whom also he named 'apostles'" offers a further emphasis on Jesus' exercise of authority, since naming is a function of authority and shows superiority (cf. Adam's naming the animals in Gen 2:18-20, God's giving Jacob a new name in Gen 32:23-33[22-32], and so on). "Whom also he named 'apostles'" awkwardly intrudes between "and he appointed twelve" and "in order that they might be with him . . . ," which go together grammatically and conceptually. But the very awkwardness of the intrusion, which speaks against omission of the clause in a comparatively weak part of the textual tradition, demonstrates the strength of Mark's emphasis on the authority which Jesus exercises in the act of naming. "Apostles" implies that his authority will be multiplied in the activities of the Twelve, for the connotation of full representation attaches to the term. Καί, "also," and the forward position of ἀποστόλους, "apostles," underline this multiplication. The chiasm of "in order that *they* might be with *him* and in order the *he* might send *them*" highlights the purpose of Jesus to multiply his authority. Neither here nor in 6:7-13 does Mark mention where or to whom Jesus sends the apostles (contrast Matt 10:1-6; Luke 9:1-6; 10:1); so nothing diverts attention from the multiplication. "To preach" indicates that the authority of Jesus' preaching will be multiplied in the apostles' preaching (for his preaching, see 1:14, 38, 39, 45). "To have authority to cast out demons" indicates that his exorcistic authority will be multiplied in their casting out demons (cf. 1:21-28; 6:7 for the association of authority with exorcism). "Send . . . to preach" makes smooth sense. "Send . . . to cast out demons" would make smooth sense. But "send . . . *to have authority* to cast out demons" is appallingly awkward: "One is sent . . . to perform an action, not to have an ability (Matt 21:34; 22:3; Luke 1:19; 4:18; 9:2; 1 Cor 1:17 . . .)" (R. A. Guelich 1. 159, comma added). Again, however, the very awkwardness points up the strength of Mark's concentration on the multiplying of Jesus' authority. Being with Jesus will qualify the apostles educationally (cf. 5:18, 40; 14:33). His sending them will qualify them commissionally (cf. 9:37; John 17:18; 20:21). His power is so great that he can exercise it through those whom he chooses. See 6:7-13 for the fulfilment of his purposes, and contrast following him for the sake of one's own discipleship with being with him and sent by him for the sake of representing him to others. The present tense of the subjunctive and infinitival verbal forms throughout vv 14-15 lend a certain prominence to the companionship, sending, preaching, and exorcistic authority (cf. the notes on 1:3).

3:16-19 *(Matt 10:2-4; Luke 6:13c-16)* "And he appointed the Twelve" signals the second half of the pericope by restating Jesus' exercise of his elective prerogative. The restatement stands in an awkward position, not in relation to the preceding relative and telic clauses (for it picks up what they interrupted), but in relation to the following clause (where we expect the beginning of a list instead of the renaming of Simon). This awkwardness at once shows the strength of Mark's emphasis on Jesus' exercising an elective prerogative and teams up with the better quality of the textual tradition containing restatement to overturn the textual tradition omitting it. Mark is known for his repetitiveness (cf. the repetition of the renaming-clause in vv 16-17). Addition of "the" to "Twelve" points back to the anarthrous "twelve" in v 14 and forward to the following list of names (cf. the anaphoric use of the definite article also with the name of Simon because of his past mention and future prominence). But the list does not start before Mark breaks in with another emphasis on Jesus' exercise of authority, this time in pinning the new name "Peter" on Simon (with the resultant stylistic disasters that Σίμων, "Simon," does not go into the accusative case, as do the other names because of their appositive relation to the accusative τοὺς δώδεκα, "the Twelve," and that Πέτρον, "Peter," is in the accusative not as one of the appositives to τοὺς δώδεκα but as an appositive to ὄνομα, "name"). In fact, then, neither "Simon" nor "Peter" is part of the delayed list. We can tell from the word order of Mark's interruptive statement that emphasis falls, not on the meaning of the new name for its significance to Simon, but on the act of renaming for its signifying Jesus' authority: ὄνομα comes right after the verb and Πέτρον does not appear till after the following τῷ Σίμωνι. Thus: "and he put a name on the [aforementioned] Simon, [i.e.] Peter." The greater bestows a name on the lesser.

Though Andrew's name would naturally come next because he is Simon's brother and the one whom Jesus initially called with Simon before he called James and John (see 1:16-20, 29), Mark brings forward James and John to make another point of Jesus' showing his superiority through the exercise of authority to give new names. (We would make a mistake to let the order depend entirely on tradition.) Again the clauses about renaming wreak havoc with the list and thereby show the strength of Mark's emphasis. "James the [son] of Zebedee and John the brother of James" matches 1:19 exactly — except for the repetition of James's name in place of the earlier "his." This repetition has the purpose of putting "John" and "James" as close as possible to the clause about Jesus' renaming them, or has

the purpose of avoiding an ambiguity that would allow Mark's audience to think
mistakenly of Simon Peter rather than of James (cf. 5:37). Mark translates into
Greek the Aramaic new names "Boanerges." Because "Peter" is already Greek
and probably because Peter has become prominent among Greek-speaking Christians throughout the Roman Empire and in Rome itself, where Mark may be
writing, that new name needs no translation. (Originally, of course, this form of
it derived from the Aramaic "Cephas," which for the most part means "stone,"
not "rock" or "bedrock" — see C. C. Caragounis, *Peter and the Rock;* P. Lampe
in *NTS* 25 [1978-79] 227-45; also J. A. Fitzmyer, *To Advance the Gospel* 115-18,
on "Cephas" as a proper name already in use rather than as a newly minted
descriptive title). In comparison with the position of ὄνομα, "name," in v 16, Mark
delays ὀνόματα, "names," here in v 17 to highlight its plural number by putting
it alongside the further plural, "Boanerges, which means 'Sons of Thunder.'"
Mark's audacity in using the plural "names" for a single name whose plural form
merely enables it to cover both James and John (contrast the singularizing v.l. in
B D 28 *pc* bo^ms, which takes offense at this audacity) doubles the emphasis on
Jesus' authoritative act of renaming them.

Mark does not give a rationale for these new names, because his interest
lies in the act of renaming. This interest also keeps him from pairing up the
apostles' names in accordance with Jesus' sending them out "two by two" in 6:7
(contrast Matt 10:2-4). The rest of the list simply strings out the repetitions of
καί, "and," with three additions: (1) "the son of Alphaeus" to distinguish the two
Jameses; (2) "the Cananaean" to distinguish the two Simons (Mark is not interested in the meaning of this Aramaic designation, because it does not represent
an exercise of Jesus' authority in the giving of a new name); and (3) "who also
betrayed him" to hint that Jesus' will and choice (cf. vv 13-14) will contribute to
his betrayal. Thus the Crucifixion will take place not only according to God's
plan (cf. the comments on 1:2-3), but also by Jesus' own doing. There is no need
to be scandalized by it, then.

NOTES

Though singular in number, τὸ ὄρος may refer to mountainous terrain rather than to a
particular mountain (BAGD s.v.). Mark uses the plural for mountainous terrain in 5:5;
13:14, however; and in such terrain Jesus would of course be located on a particular
mountain at the time of the event described. At 9:2 Mark will introduce a particular
mountain without a definite article, which is present here; but addition of the adjective
"high" will make up for the lack. Naturally, "Mount of Olives" will take the definite article
(11:1; 13:3; 14:26; cf. 11:23). On the whole, then, it seems best to think that here Mark is
referring to a particular mountain (cf. T. L. Donaldson, *Jesus on the Mountain* 10-11).
Jesus' frequent shifts in location represent a narrative style and the presumably historical
actualities of an itinerant ministry, not theological symbolism (see R. A. Guelich 1. 156-57
against interpreting the mountain as a place of divine revelation [absent here] or of secrecy
[absent in 5:11]).

The prefix προσ- and the middle voice of προσκαλέομαι give it the meaning, "call
to oneself," whereas the active voice and simplex form of καλέω give it the unadorned

meaning, "call." The hypothesis that Mark composes v 13 according to the threefold scheme of a call-story — viz., setting, call, and response (cf. 1:16-20; 1 Kgs 19:19-21; so G. Schmahl in *TTZ* 81 [1972] 206-8) — comes to grief over the use of "summons" rather than "calls," over a second summons in 6:7 (whereas a call is once for all), and over the probable distinction between the summons and the appointment, including the preliminariness of the summons, and the occurrence of the appointment not till after the summoned ones have responded by coming away to Jesus. Nowhere else in Mark does προσκαλέομαι mean selection. If it did in 6:7, we would have two different selections of the Twelve. And if Jesus summons more people than he appoints to the band of twelve (Luke 6:13), these problems are exacerbated for the hypothesis.

The verb ἤθελεν can denote wishing, but here the stronger notion of willing suits the emphasis on Jesus' initiative and choice. The nominative form αὐτός regularly carries some weight throughout Mark (see the comments on 1:8; 2:25; 3:13; 4:27, 38; 5:40; 6:17, 45, 47; 8:29; 12:36, 37; 14:15, 44; 15:42; cf. the comment of C. H. Turner in *JTS* os 28 [1926-27] 356 that here αὐτός adds the element of personal choice to an otherwise colorless [sic] ἤθελεν). E. Best (*Following Jesus* 181-82) observes that normally and redactionally Mark uses εἰς, "into," after ἀπέρχομαι, "go away," whereas in v 13 we read πρός, "to"; but the observation overlooks that in every instance of the combination with εἰς a place follows whereas this combination never occurs when a person follows, as here and in 1:20; 5:24; 14:10.

In connection with the number twelve, ἐποίησεν refers to the formation of a group (cf. the LXX of Isa 43:1; 44:2), i.e. to appointment (cf. the LXX of Exod 18:25; 36:1; 1 Kgdms 12:6; 3 Kgdms 12:31; 13:33; 2 Chr 2:17 and 1 Macc 1:51; Acts 2:36; Heb 3:2; Rev 5:10; see E. Best, *Following Jesus* 186, n. 7, on the possibilities of an Aramaism, a Septuagintalism, and a Latinism). "Made" in the sense "created" and thus as an allusion to Gen 1:1 LXX goes too far, because that would probably have produced a "the" in front of "Twelve" (ibid. 187-88). Mark 1:17 had something of the same combination of summons and formation ("Hither! Behind me! And I will make you fishers of human beings"). But the connotation of appointment does not work backwards onto "summons," especially if Jesus appoints twelve out of a larger number. Even otherwise, summoning only sets the stage for appointment (against ibid. 180).

The Twelve whom Jesus appoints may be the same as those whom he summoned, not a selection out of a larger group whom he summoned (R. P. Meye, *Jesus and the Twelve* passim). If so, v 14a means that Jesus makes the Twelve whom he summoned into a band of apostles. On the other hand, the lack of a definite article with "twelve" makes it look as though Jesus chooses twelve out of a larger number to be his apostles; and in 4:10, where the Twelve will next appear, a larger number of insiders will be with them. Indeed, Mark will subordinate the Twelve to that larger number. See also 10:32; 15:40-41 (but not 2:15, which referred to many toll collectors and sinners, not to many disciples). From this point onward in Mark, "the Twelve" will usually distinguish the apostles from nearby larger circles of disciples: in 4:10 from "the ones around him [Jesus]"; in 6:7 from "his disciples" (6:1); in 9:35 from "his disciples" (9:31); in 10:32 from "the ones following"; in 11:11 from "his disciples . . . the ones going before and the ones following" (11:1, 9); and in 14:17 from "his disciples" (14:12; against E. Best [*Disciples and Discipleship* 131-61], who says that for Mark "the Twelve" and "the disciples" are often interchangeable). In 14:10, 20, 43 the Twelve are not a small group of apostles selected out of a larger group of disciples so much as they are a small group of apostles out of which a single selection is made, that of the betrayer. Historically, the number twelve follows the pattern of Jacob's twelve sons, the patriarchs of the twelve tribes of Israel, and represents either Jesus' establishing a new messianic community within Israel or his attempt to restore the whole of old Israel. The breadth of his own ministry and of the Twelve's mission in 6:7-13,

30-31 favors the latter (see K. Stock, *Boten* 35-41; J. Gnilka 1. 139). The mention of apostles in 6:30 favors the textual tradition that includes them here in v 14. Otherwise their mention in 6:30 will have had no preparation and will mystify readers. Mark's emphasis on Jesus' renaming Simon, James, and John favors the originality of a like emphasis on Jesus' giving the name "apostles" to the Twelve (and see M. Hengel, *Charismatic Leader* 82-83; F. H. Agnew in *JBL* 105 [1986] 75-96 for a background in God's sending the OT prophets, not in a later Jewish institution or in Gnosticism). Against the possibility of scribal interpolation from Luke 6:13 we may put the possibility of scribal omission to get rid of the interruption, and the likelihood of Luke's borrowing from Mark. The external evidence for inclusion outweighs that for omission.

It would make no sense to say that Jesus gives the name "apostles" to the Twelve in order that they might be with him. But we might consider the possibility of an a-b-a′-b′ pattern in vv 14-15: Jesus appoints twelve in order that they might be with him, and names them apostles (ἀποστόλους) in order that he might send them as such (ἀποστέλλῃ). This construal is probably oversubtle, however. It also neglects the subordinate role of the "whom"-clause, where the suggested pattern would probably have put a coordinate clause. Yet again, appointing twelve to send them makes better sense than naming them whom to send them. So both telic clauses depend on Jesus' appointing twelve, and the intrusiveness of "whom also he named 'apostles'" stands firm. See J. Carmignac in *ASTI* 7 (1968-69) 70 on the possibility of an underlying Hebrew (or Aramaic, we might add) wordplay between שׁלח, "send," שׁלט, "have power," and שׁלך, "cast (out)." An assignment of v 15 to Mark's redaction (R. A. Guelich 1. 159-60) tends away from such a wordplay, however, unless we suppose that Mark was thinking in Hebrew or Aramaic while dictating in Greek.

Jesus' sending the apostles will follow their being with him; so we have no reason to see a contradiction between their following and his sending and therefore an indication of different sources (cf. 1:17). Already in 1:16–3:12 disciples have been with Jesus as much as they will be with him in 3:20–6:6a. But not so the Twelve in particular and as a group; hence, we should not deny that being with Jesus from here on will specially prepare them for their mission in 6:7-13, 30-31 (against E. Best, *Following Jesus* 188-89, n. 32). Though outside the indicative mood ἀποστέλλω normally occurs in the aorist (5:10; 6:17, 27; 9:37), we should not stress the present tense of the subjunctive ἀποστέλλῃ too much, as though it looks forward to sendings on different occasions. Rather, it betrays influence from the present tense in the parallel subjunctive verb ὦσιν, which is strongly linear, and perhaps anticipates the iterative kind of linearity represented in 6:7 by the present infinitive ἀποστέλλειν for Jesus' sending the Twelve "two by two" on a single occasion. Initially, during his lifetime, the Twelve had a temporary mission to carry out. The outcome of his life led them to a permanent kind of apostleship in the life of the church. But Mark's stress on Jesus' authority makes it doubtful that the world-wide mission of the church motivates him to omit as too restrictive the places and people to whom Jesus will shortly send the Twelve (as thought by K. Stock, *Boten* 90).

Against the attempt of E. Best (*Temptation* 187-88) and R. H. Stein (*Proper Methodology* 101) to make Mark minimize the role of exorcism by having Jesus send the Twelve, not to cast out demons, but to have authority to cast them out, Mark's description of the fulfilment of Jesus' purpose will say that the Twelve did cast out demons — many of them (6:13). With "cast out" Mark likes to use "demon" rather than "unclean spirit" (cf. the notes on 1:34). See 9:14-27 for a difficult case of exorcism that will go beyond the apostles' ability (a factor that will favor the historicity of the story in that it will compete with Mark's desire to portray Jesus' power as multiplied in the ministry of the Twelve), and cf. Exod 18:13-27 for a somewhat distant parallel (Moses' choice of administrative helpers).

The clauses about renaming force Mark's audience to supply "he appointed" each time the list picks up again. The accusative case of the names on the list does not help the hypothesis that the list was originally an independent unit; but had Mark made up the list, most likely he would have included Levi (cf. 2:13-14). If he wants the Twelve to represent the church nuclearly, he may be apologizing for the Cross by implying that Jesus anticipates it and even plans for it in the appointment of twelve apostles to take his place. We might understand Mark to imply that Jesus renames Simon and the sons of Zebedee on this occasion (R. A. Guelich 1. 160), but the text does not demand this understanding (cf. Matt 10:2; 16:17-19; John 1:42). It is the authority exercised in renaming, not the time of renaming, which stands in the forefront. The renaming of these three appears to indicate Jesus' special liking of them. They make up an inner circle among the Twelve (cf. 5:37; 9:2; 14:33; also 13:3, where Andrew will come back into the picture, but in fourth place as here, not in second place as in 1:16-20). Cf. the LXX of 4 Kgdms 24:17; 2 Esdr 19:7; Dan 1:7 for ἐπέθηκεν ὄνομα as renaming; also the discussion in K. Stock, *Boten* 29-33.

"Sons of Thunder" may represent rashness of disposition (cf. 9:38; 10:35-40; Luke 9:51-56; O. Betz in *RevQ* 3 [1961-62] 41-52). The association of Nathaniel with Philip in John 1:45 has led to the equation of Nathaniel with Bartholomew, who comes right after Philip in Mark 3:18. James the son of Alphaeus may have been a brother of Levi the son of Alphaeus (cf. 2:14); but more than one man may have had the name Alphaeus, and in a sense the Western Text of 2:14 identifies James the son of Alphaeus with Levi by substituting James for Levi (cf. 15:40). In Matt 9:9 the substitution of Matthew for the Levi of Mark 2:14 has led to the equation of the Matthew of Mark 3:18 with the Levi of Mark 2:14 (R. H. Gundry, *Matthew* 166, 620-21). Some have thought that Mark does not translate the Aramaic "the Cananaean" because it means "the Zealot" and because, though referring originally to a religious zealot (Acts 22:3; 2 Macc 4:2; Josephus *Ant.* 12.6.2 §271), it has come to refer to an insurrectionist by the time Mark writes — and he does not want anyone to infer that Jesus tolerated, much less taught, insurrectionism. The explanation given in the foregoing comments makes this explanation unnecessary, however. Mark does not hesitate to give a translation of Boanerges that might arouse suspicions of insurrection-ism. If he writes before 66 C.E. (see pp. 1041-43), the term "Zealot" may not yet have acquired a political connotation (see R. A. Horsley in *NovT* 28 [1986] 159-92; M. Borg in *JTS* ns 22 [1971] 504-12; T. L. Donaldson in *JSJ* 21 [1990] 19-40); but M. Hengel (*Zealots* 62-66, 69-70, 388-404 et passim) argues strongly in favor of an earlier date for this connotation.

"Iscariot" may be attached to Judas's name to distinguish this Judas from Judas the son of James (Luke 6:16; Acts 1:13; cf. John 14:22), or from Judas the brother of James the brother of Jesus (Mark 6:3; Matt 13:55; Jude 1). In English we traditionally distinguish the betrayer and the brother of James the brother of Jesus by spelling the one's name "Judas" and the other's name "Jude" even though the names are identical in Greek (cf. 14:10-11, 43-45 and see R. H. Gundry, *Matthew* 183, on "the Cananaean" and "Iscariot"). "Who also betrayed him" adds betrayal of Jesus to appointment by him; it does not imply betrayal by others, too. Παρέδωκεν gets the connotation of betrayal only from its context, here the larger context of Judas Iscariot's giving Jesus over to the antagonistic Sanhedrin (cf. the consequent shift in Luke 6:16 to προδότης, which quite specifically denotes a betrayer). Elsewhere the verb can refer to a different kind of giving over. The aorist tense and description as a whole do not have to imply that Mark wrote for a Christian audience already knowledgeable of Jesus' betrayal by Judas (so D. Lührmann 72). Only Mark's knowledge is necessarily implied. He may be preparing an ignorant audience for what is yet to be narrated rather than presupposing a knowledgeable audience for whom the description would be needless. W. Vogler *(Judas Iskarioth)* thinks that Judas followed Jesus after Easter as well as before, but was the first to apostatize and so was blamed for Jesus' death.

See commentaries such as those by W. L. Lane, R. Pesch, and R. A. Guelich ad loc.

for further details and voluminous literature on the apostles; the literature cited in BAGD s.v. on the various names; plus H. P. Rüger in *Markus-Philologie* 74-80; D. R. G. Beattie in *IBS* 5 (1983) 11-13; G. Schwarz, *Jesus und Judas* 6-12. "Boanerges" presents special difficulties of derivation, transliteration, and usage. It will not replace "James" and "John" as "Peter" will replace "Simon" (except for 14:37), perhaps because its use for two apostles would have left them indistinguishable from each other (see esp. 9:38), perhaps because the Greekness of "Peter" would sit well with Mark's audience but the Semiticness of "Boanerges" would not. The unimportance of the Twelve as a body in the early church and the inclusion of so dastardly a character as Judas Iscariot among them make it unlikely that the early church fabricated this story of their appointment. See J. Gnilka 1. 141-43 for a convenient summary of arguments for and against historicity, and Guelich 1. 154-55 on questions of tradition and redaction.

THE HOLY SPIRIT AS THE TRUE SOURCE OF JESUS' POWER

3:20-35 (Matt 9:32-34; 12:22-32, 46-50; Luke 8:19-21; 11:14-15, 17-23; 12:10; John 15:14)

Again as usual, this pericope starts with a topographical shift; thus everything in the pericope will take place "at home" (v 20a). The charges that Jesus "has Beelzebul" and "casts out the demons by the ruler of the demons" (v 22) occupy center stage. Mark puts the pericope here, then, as a follow-up on Jesus' appointing the Twelve in order that he might send them not only "to preach" but also "to have authority to cast out the demons" (v 15). Where does this authority come from? That is the question now discussed. The charges against Jesus and his responses to them (vv 22-30) are sandwiched between the starting out of his family to seize him because they think he has gone berserk (vv 20b-21) and their arrival and his response (vv 31-35). The quotation at the close of this middle part, "He has an unclean spirit" (v 30), forms an inclusion with the quotation at the head of the middle part, "He has Beelzebul" (v 22). The intervening responses of Jesus consist of an argument (vv 23-27) and a warning (vv 28-29). In v 8 Mark did not insert anything to fill up the time between hearing and arrival from a distance (cf. also 2:1-2; 5:27; 6:29; 7:25); therefore a merely chronological interpretation of Mark's insertion of vv 22-30 looks inadequate. Rather, he sticks the scribes' charge in the middle of the pericope to give a theological interpretation of the story concerning the attempt of Jesus' mother and brothers to seize him. According to this interpretation Jesus has the Holy Spirit, not the unclean spirit Beelzebul, and therefore has the authority to form a supernatural family rather than having to submit to search and seizure by his natural family.

3:20-21 The historical present tense of ἔρχεται, "he comes [home]," and of συνέρχεται, "[the crowd] comes together," emphasizes the magnetism of Jesus. Wherever he comes, even though it is only to a private home, the crowd comes together. "Again" points back to the gathering together of "the whole city" at the door of Simon's and Andrew's home in 1:29-34 and to the gathering together of "many," also called "the crowd," apparently at the same home in 2:1-2, 4, where "again" has already appeared in the text (cf. 2:13; 3:7-9). Therefore εἰς οἶκον probably refers to the same home yet again and reflects Simon Peter's standpoint (under the view that Mark is writing up that apostle's sermonic reminiscences of Jesus' ministry — see pp. 1026-45). Therefore also, if we are to read the definite article before ὄχλος, "crowd," with א¹ A B D et al. instead of omitting it with א* C L* W et al., the article anaphorically recalls attention to the large number of people mentioned in 1:29-34; 2:1-2, 4, 13; 3:7-9. "So that they were not (μή) able even (μηδέ) to eat bread" puts all possible stress on Jesus' attractive power, especially with the forward position and double negativity of μηδὲ ἄρτον, "not even bread" (cf. esp. 6:31; also 1:45; 2:2, 4; 3:10; 4:1; 7:24). "They" brings the just-appointed apostles back into the picture and implies the carrying out of Jesus' purpose "that they might be with him" (v 14). Mark does not mention the reason why the crowd kept Jesus and the apostles from eating. Presumably it was his activites of healing the sick and exorcising demons, or perhaps just teaching (cf. the crowd's sitting around him in vv 32, 34). But omission of the reason centers attention on his magnetism alone.

The idiom οἱ παρ' αὐτοῦ, which has a wide range of possible meanings (one's immediate family, extended family, confederates, envoys — see 1 Macc 9:44 v.l. [cf. 9:32]; 13:52-53; Sus 33; Josephus *Ant.* 1.10.5 §193; BAGD s.v. παρά I4bβ), here refers to Jesus' immediate family, as will be indicated by "his mother and his brothers" in v 31 plus the commonness in Mark of dual expressions in which the second specifies the first (cf. F. Neirynck, *Duality* 96-97). This sort of duality eliminates any reason to infer from the difference in phraseology a difference in sources and therefore in occasions and meanings. Since Mark has written that Jesus hailed from Nazareth (1:9), his family's coming forth (ἐξῆλθον) means their coming from Nazareth to Capernaum, where the home of Simon Peter and Andrew is located. The underlying reason for their coming forth — viz., the belief that Jesus has gone berserk — implies that they have heard of his going into a private home and being cooped up by a crowd and that they plan on catching him there so as to bring him under control. "To seize him" sets up a contest of power, which will turn out in his favor and to their frustration (see the comments on vv 34-35 and 4:10; cf. 6:17; 11:18; 12:12; 14:1, 11, 44, 46, 49, 51, 55).

Who were saying, "He has gone berserk"? Not the crowd, for Jesus will pronounce them his true family (vv 31-35). Not the scribes from Jerusalem, either; for Mark will give them their own thing to say about Jesus and will parallelistically introduce it with ἔλεγον, "they were saying," as here (see v 22). Because of the crowd's and the scribes' proximity, "they" can hardly be indefinite even though Mark likes that usage. In the text, Jesus' family stand closest to "they"; so it is his family who were saying, "He has gone berserk." Thus Mark begins to set up a parallel between them and the scribes, both of whose statements about Jesus set them outside the circle of those who do God's will (vv 31-35). Jesus' responses to the statements make the parallel so important to Mark that he neglects to reveal the reason why Jesus' family were saying that he had gone berserk. (Going into a house and attracting an admiring crowd do not count as signs of berserkness.)

3:22 *(Matt 9:34; 12:24; Luke 11:15)* Literarily, the scribes' charge that Jesus has Beelzebul implies that Beelzebul fills the void left in Jesus according to his family by his "standing outside himself" (the literal meaning of ἐξέστη, "gone berserk" — cf. E. Rohde, *Psyche* 2. 259-60, 274-75). Thus Jesus is the biggest demoniac of all — but not as a victim; rather, as one who has a demon at his disposal (see P. Samain in *ETL* 15 [1938] 468-70). The charge that he has Beelzebul also explains how it comes about that he is able to cast out demons by their ruler. Thus, "Beelzebul" and "the ruler of the demons" (and in vv 23, 26 "Satan" as well) are the same (cf. *T. Sol.* 2:8–3:6; 6:1-11; J. A. Fitzmyer, *Luke* 920-21; H. Kruse in *Bib* 58 [1977] 39-41). The emphatic positions of Βεελζεβούλ, "Beelzebul," and of ἐν τῷ ἄρχοντι τῶν δαιμονίων, "by the ruler of the demons," stress the seriousness of the charges.

"From Jerusalem" distinguishes the scribes who lay these charges against Jesus from the scribes mentioned in 2:6, 16 (1:22 refers to scribes in general) and perhaps looks forward to the scribes in Jerusalem who will help engineer his crucifixion (8:31; 10:33; 11:18, 27-28; 14:1, 43, 53; 15:1, 31; cf. also 7:1). The present appearance of scribes from Jerusalem should not surprise us, for according to vv 7-8 part of the great multitude that flocked to Jesus came "from Jerusalem." That the scribes came "down" from Jerusalem reflects the topography of Palestine and may anticipate Jesus' going "up" to Jerusalem, where the scribes will help engineer his crucifixion (10:32-33; S. M. Smith in *NTS* 35 [1989] 170). Just as the purpose of Jesus' family to seize him sets up a contest of power, so also the charges that he has Beelzebul and casts out the demons by the ruler of the demons set up a contest of didactic authority (cf. 1:22, 27). Jesus will prove to be more than a match both for his family and for the scribes.

3:23-26 *(Matt 12:25-26; Luke 11:17-18)* Taking up the charges in chiastic order, Jesus now answers the second charge that he casts out the demons by their ruler. "And summoning them" recalls v 13, where he summoned those whom he willed, and again alludes to his authority (see the comments on 3:13-15). But there he exercised that authority over his followers. Here, apparently, he exercises it over the scribes from Jerusalem; for they have just been mentioned (v 22) and the crowd have already pressed around him so closely that he and his disciples cannot take a meal — i.e. the crowd are sitting around him in the house and do not need to be summoned (cf. vv 32-35). The vagueness of the scribes' whereabouts between arrival and summons leaves attention focussed solely on the Christological implication of the summons (cf. E. Wendling, *Entstehung* 22).

Having commandeered the scribes to be his audience, Jesus now forces them to listen to some parables that reduce their charge to absurdity. Hence, "he was speaking to them" means that he was speaking to the scribes. The forward position of "in parables" (see the Greek text; cf. 4:11, 13, 30, 33; 12:1, 12 and contrast 4:2; 13:28) highlights the parabolic form of speech. The parables start with a question: "How is Satan able to cast out Satan?" In its first occurrence "Satan" identifies "Beelzebul" and "the ruler of the demons" of v 22. In its second occurrence "Satan" incorporates the demons in their ruler and takes a position before the infinitive of which it is the direct object — and therefore right after the first "Satan," which is the subject of the main verb (see the Greek word order) — to highlight the point of absurdity. Satan as "ruler" points to the figure of a kingdom. Satan as "Beelzebul," which can be taken to mean "master of the house" (see W. Foerster in *TDNT* 1. 605-6; R. H. Gundry, *Matthew* 195; and, more complicatedly, L. Gaston in *TZ* 18 [1962] 247-55), points to the figure of a house. We might think that Satan's kingdom stands opposite God's kingdom. But we have here an axiom that applies to any kingdom; and Satan's house hardly provides a parallel contrast with God's house, for only one house will come into view in v 27, which will elaborate the figure of a house. The question in v 23b points up an interpersonal impossibility based on the unity of Satan and the demons whom he rules. Jesus is not arguing for the psychological impossibility of thinking that Satan would not use him to cast out the demons because they serve Satan and because Satan is too smart to work against his own cause. The impossibility has to do with Satan's action, not with our thinking. Satan is one with his demons, and he cannot cast himself out. By definition of casting out, somebody else would have to do that.

The interpersonal impossibility changes to a political one in the statement about a kingdom: "And if a kingdom should be divided against itself, that kingdom is not able to stand." Civil war makes a kingdom easy prey for invaders. In the same vein, "if a house should be divided against itself, that house will not be able to stand." The context of a kingdom defines the house as a royal family, not an ordinary household, much less a building. Strife within a royal family will open the door to usurpers. The placements in the underlying Greek text of "a kingdom against itself" and "a house against itself" before "should be divided" (bis) reemphasize the absurdity of thinking that Satan is casting out Satan. Though Jesus is arguing against Satan's doing so (therefore καί at the start of v 24 may · have a causal force — M. Reiser, *Syntax und Stil* 126-28; C. E. B. Cranfield 137; cf. BDB s.v. ו 1k), the suggestions of take-over from outside point in the direction of Jesus' success in exorcisms and thus anticipate the next parable (v 27). The following of the gnomic present tense, "is not able" (v 24), with the predictive future, "will not be able" (v 25), furthers this anticipation. The subjunctive mood of "should be divided" sets out a weak hypothesis. In v 26 Mark strengthens the hypothesis by switching to the indicative mood. We may paraphrase as follows: if, as you scribes say, Satan really has risen up in rebellion against himself and suffered a split, he cannot survive but is now coming to the end of his career. This time the present tense is not gnomic, but progressive; i.e. Satan is suffering disability and demise right now. The conclusion that he "is not able to stand but is having an end [in the sense 'is at his end']" is true even though the supposition in the preceding "if"-clause is absurd. Therefore v 27 will follow up with a parabolic indication of the real reason for Satan's downfall, i.e. Jesus' exorcistic invasion of Satan's domain. The repetition of "Satan" in v 26 makes an inclusion with "Satan" in v 23; and the strength of the adversative ἀλλά, "but," combines with the placement of the direct object τέλος, "end," before its verb ἔχει, "has," to stress Satan's downfall.

3:27 *(Matt 12:29; Luke 11:21-22)* The parable of a strong man's house

completes Jesus' answer to the charge that he casts out the demons by their ruler
(v 22b). It completes Jesus' answer, not by telling through whom else he casts
out demons, but by putting their ruler in the role of his antagonist as opposed to
the role of partner in the charge. Furthermore, the focus shifts from Satan as the
one who is absurdly thought to act against himself to Jesus as the one who really
does act against Satan. It is not a messianic secret (as thought by G. Minette de
Tillesse, *Le secret messianique* 102-3) but the figurativeness of parabolic speech
which leaves Jesus standing anonymously in the shadow of the binder who is
able to take spoils, for Satan's standing equally anonymously in the shadow of
the bound strong man leads no one to speak of a Satanic secret. 'Αλλ', "but,"
does not contradict Jesus' preceding statements (vv 23b-26), but aims at the charge
that he casts out demons by their ruler. The strength of this adversative and its
reuse after its use in the immediately preceding clause underline the following
denial. "No one is able . . . unless . . ." implies that Jesus *has* been able . . .
because. . . . This fifth occurrence of δύναμαι in vv 23-27 puts enormous weight
on his ability. In a wordplay, "the house" now means a building (contrast v 25).
"The strong man" who owns the house represents Satan, but the house does not
represent a demoniac; for the strong man is not thrown out of the house as Satan,
who is one with his demons, is cast out of demoniacs. Rather, the strong man is
bound. The placement of "into the house of the strong man" before "having
entered" (see the word order of the Greek text) highlights the strength of the
house-owner so as to play up the even greater strength of the robber who binds
him. The house represents Satan's domain, or kingdom, as a whole (cf. vv 24-25).
The robber represents Jesus. His binding the strong man stands for Jesus' exorcising demons (thus we need not look back to 1:12-13 for a binding of Satan at
the temptation — Mark wrote nothing about Jesus' resisting temptation or overcoming Satan, anyway), and the placement of the direct object "the strong man"
before its verb "bind" (so the Greek word order) again highlights the strength of
the house-owner Satan so as to play up the even greater strength of Jesus the
robber. This greater strength gains further emphasis from the forward position of
πρῶτον, "first," which describes the binding. Similarly, the placement of the direct
objects "his articles" and "his house" before "to plunder" and "will plunder,"
respectively (again see the Greek text), highlights Satan's ownership so as to play
up Jesus' success as a robber. The taking of articles from the house represents
Jesus' take-over of demoniacs once he has tied up Satan through exorcisms (cf.
the implied take-overs in vv 24-25). Now the articles belong to Jesus. Hence,
they rather than the house represent demoniacs. The plundering of the house is
defined by the plundering of the articles in it and therefore does not mean a taking
over of the whole house. We read "and then he will plunder his house" instead
of the expected "and then he will *be able* to plunder his house" (cf. the first part
of the verse). In other words, actuality takes the place of ability in order that the
emphasis may now shift to what is in fact happening through Jesus' ministry (a
point missed by J. A. Kleist [147-50] in his desire to see a modal use of the
indicative for ability). The implication that Jesus is stronger than the strong one,
stronger even than Satan, suits Mark's purpose of counteracting the notion that

Jesus was crucified as a weakling (cf. esp. Luke 11:22, but also Mark 1:7; Isa 49:24-25; 53:12 and the comments on Mark 14:38; 15:33-39).

3:28-30 (Matt 12:31-32; Luke 12:10) Jesus has shown the scribes the absurdity of their second charge that he casts out demons by the ruler of the demons (vv 23-27). Now he shows them the seriousness of their first charge that he has Beelzebul (see esp. J. D. G. Dunn, *Jesus and the Spirit* 53). The Q-form of the saying would not fit the editorial comment in v 30: the possibility of forgiveness for the person "who will speak a word against the Son of man" (Luke 12:10; cf. Matt 12:32) would contradict the equation of the unforgivable sin with the scribes' saying that Jesus "has an unclean spirit" (v 30). If *that* is not speaking against Jesus, what is? To suit the equation and avoid the contradiction, therefore, the possibility of forgiveness for the person who will speak a word against the Son of man is generalized into the possibility of forgiveness for human beings who speak all sorts of slanders. Thus "the Son of man" as an object of slander changes into "the sons of men" as speakers of slander. It may have oiled this change that Christian piety easily takes offense at the possibility of forgiveness for the person who will speak a word against the Son of man but not so easily for the one who does the same against the Holy Spirit (cf. D. Flusser in *"Wie gut sind deine Zelte, Jaakow . . ."* 140-41; H. E. Tödt, *Son of Man* 120; B. B. Warfield, *Christology and Criticism* 92-93). We are dealing, then, not with a Greek translation of an ambiguous Aramaic substratum, a Greek translation alternative to the one in Q (more or less like Luke 12:10), but with a redactional change due to an insertion into the context of the scribal charge that Jesus has Beelzebul, the unclean spirit who rules the demons, and due to an equation of that charge with the unforgivable sin (see R. H. Gundry, *Matthew* 238-39, against the painful attempts to extract Mark and Q from a common Aramaic substratum).

"Truly I say to you" may belong to the original version of the saying, Luke having omitted the clause (but see ibid. 79). The Semitic "everyone who" (πᾶς ὅς — so Luke) becomes "all" (πάντα) to go with the added "sins." Together, they generalize the original speaking against the Son of man; and the position of πάντα before ἀφεθήσεται, "will be forgiven," reinforces the generalization. The original speaking against the Son of man becomes in turn the plural "slanders" in a furtherance of the generalization. "However many [sins] they slander" completes the generalization with another addition. The clause does not mean that sins are the objects of slander. In view of the hendiadys "the sins and the slanders" for "the sinful slanders," it means "however many sins they commit by slandering" (see R. A. Guelich 1. 167, n. g, for other, less likely explanations of the neuter ὅσα, where we might have expected the feminine ὅσας, "however many [slanders]" [so the v.l.]). Because ὅσα ἐάν plus the subjunctive of βλασφημέω has just occurred, "but to the person who slanders [= 'blasphemes'] the Holy Spirit it will not be forgiven [that he has done so]" (Luke 12:10b) or "everyone who will speak a word against the Holy Spirit, it will not be forgiven him" (as it may have originally run in parallel with Luke 12:10a if in 12:10b Luke adopts Mark's verb "slanders" for stylistic variation) changes to ὅς δ' ἄν plus the subjunctive of βλασφημέω κτλ.: "but whoever slanders the Holy Spirit does not have forgiveness."

Three additions stress the seriousness of this slander: (1) "eternally" (cf. *y. B. Bat.* 6c); (2) "rather, he is guilty of eternal sin"; and (3) "because they were saying, 'He has an unclean spirit.'" The compositional style characteristic of Mark's gospel shines out in the dualities of "the sins" plus "the slanders," of "the sins and the slanders" plus "however many [sins] they slander," of "however many [sins] they slander" plus "whoever slanders the Holy Spirit," and of "does not have forgiveness eternally" plus "is guilty of eternal sin." The overall result is a largely chiastic structure:

    a) "Truly I say to you"
       b) "that all the sins and the slanders will be forgiven to the sons of men"
          c) "however many [sins] they slander"
          c') "but whoever slanders the Holy Spirit"
       b') "does not have forgiveness eternally"
    a') "rather, he is guilty of eternal sin."

Only the introductory a) and the concluding a') do not match.

To "speak a word against" (so Luke 12:10a; Matt 12:32a) is a Semitism that Mark's version, followed in part by Matthew and Luke, Graecizes with the verb βλασφημέω (M. Black, *Aramaic Approach* 194-95; H. E. Tödt, *Son of Man* 315-17). Mark's version also gets rid of the Semitic casus pendens, "everyone who," picked up by "to him" (Luke 12:10a; cf. Matt 12:32; E. C. Maloney, *Semitic Interference* 86-90). "To the sons of men" not only effaces "against the Son of man" but also replaces "to him." And an original, Semitic "it will not be forgiven to him" behind Luke 12:10b (= אֵין לוֹ מְחִילָה — G. Dalman, *Words* 147) has probably been Graecized with "does not have forgiveness," which J. A. Kleist (195) describes as "splendid Greek." The sayings in vv 28-29 rest on the obvious implication that Jesus does not have Beelzebul, as the scribes have said he does (v 22), but that he has the Holy Spirit (from the literary standpoint of Mark's book, cf. 1:8, 10, 12) and that therefore the attributing of Jesus' power of exorcism to the ruler of the demons constitutes a slander against the true source of Jesus' power, viz., the Holy Spirit (cf. Matt 12:28; Luke 11:20; *Did.* 11:7b; *Gos. Thom.* 44).

"Truly I say to you" stresses the seriousness of the charge that Jesus has Beelzebul. "You" continues to refer to the scribes (cf. v 23 with comments). "Will be forgiven" means "can be forgiven"; for Jesus is hardly predicting the forgiveness of all sins and blasphemies, and the future tense corresponds to the imperfect tense in Galilean Aramaic, where the imperfect usually has a virtual rather than a future meaning (see J. Jeremias, *NT Theology* 1. 150, n. 2; cf. J. A. Kleist 147-50). Given the subject matter, however, it is hard to lose all sight of a futuristic reference to the last judgment. The passive is divine, meaning "God will forgive." "The sons of men" means human beings. The repetitiousness of "all the sins and the slanders, however many [sins] they slander" and the emphatic "all" and "however many" intensify the seriousness of the one *other* slander that is unforgivable (cf. Exod 23:21). "Whoever" aims at the scribes to whom Jesus is speaking; for they have committed the unforgivable sin, which consists in "slandering the Holy Spirit." The false accusation of some earlier scribes that Jesus had blasphemed (2:6-7) has given way to his true accusation that the present scribes have committed blasphemy. So serious is this sin that the slanderer "will never have forgiveness [literally, 'does not have release eternally']; rather, he is guilty of eternal sin." The repetitiousness of these judgmental phrases carries great emphasis; and their parallelism defines "eternal sin" as the opposite of release of sin from the sinner, i.e. as the permanent sticking of sin to the sinner. The consequence goes without saying (except in the vv.ll.). The adversative δέ, "but," the more strongly adversative ἀλλά, "rather," and the forward position of ἔνοχος, "guilty," intensify yet further the judgmental tone.

"Because" signals Mark's editorial identification of the reason why Jesus speaks the statements in vv 28-29. That Mark closes this subdivision of the pericope by noting this reason — viz., the scribes' charge that Jesus has an unclean spirit — shows strength of concern not only that nobody fail to know the fact of Jesus' power, but also that nobody mistake its source. "An unclean spirit" replaces "Beelzebul" for contrast with the holiness of the just-mentioned Holy Spirit and takes an emphatic position for emphasis on the unforgivability of the sinful charge. Thus, "he has an unclean spirit" interprets "he has Beelzebul" (v 22). The scribes should have been saying, "He has the Holy Spirit" (M. D. Hooker, *Message* 37). But Jesus has reduced them to speechlessness. As always, he triumphs before a real debate can start (cf. esp. 2:1–3:6; 11:27–12:37).

3:31-32 *(Matt 12:46-47; Luke 8:19-20)* The parallel between what Jesus' natural family were saying about him in v 21 (ἔλεγον γὰρ κτλ.), "He has gone berserk," and what the scribes were saying about him in v 30 (ὅτι ἔλεγον κτλ.), "He has an unclean spirit," has set the stage for an identification of his new family. The historical present tense of ἔρχεται, "comes," makes the attempt of his mother and brothers to seize him more dramatic (cf. v 21). Now that they have arrived, the prefix ἐξ-, "out, forth," drops off the verb (contrast v 21). "Standing outside" literally means standing outside the house (cf. v 20) and theologically means that they do not belong to the circle of Jesus' followers (cf. 4:10-12). The forward position of ἔξω, "outside," stresses this lack of belonging. ᾿Απέστειλαν πρὸς αὐτὸν καλοῦντες αὐτόν, "they sent for him [or 'sent (word) to him'], calling him," again stresses their not belonging to the circle and, in something of a reversal of Jesus' summoning and appointing the Twelve "in order that he might send them" (ἵνα ἀποστέλλῃ αὐτούς — v 14), shows his mother and brothers trying to exercise authority over him. The crowd is the same one that came together in v 20. The lack of a definite article with ὄχλος does not point to a new crowd any more than it does in 5:24; 9:25 (cf. 5:21; 9:14-15, 17), but reflects a fresh start within the overall story. The crowd's sitting around Jesus marks them off from the scribes and the outsiders (the latter being his mother and brothers, who are only "from the side of him" [παρά plus the genitive — v 21]); or, to put the matter positively, it portrays the crowd as belonging to him (cf. 4:10-11). The placement of περὶ αὐτόν, "around him," before ὄχλος, "a crowd," underlines this significance of their position. The historical present tense of λέγουσιν, "they say," further dramatizes the attempt of Jesus' mother and brothers to seize him; and "outside" reemphasizes their not belonging to his circle. We might think that the "they" who speak to him are the just-mentioned crowd. But since Jesus has been addressing the scribes (see vv 22-23, 28 with 30) and since he will speak to them *about* the crowd (vv 33-35), it looks as though "they" and "them" are the scribes. Thus they and Jesus' natural family act in concert. Of course, the scribes do not tell him that his natural family have come to seize him, but only that they seek him. "Behold," the repetition of ἔξω even though "standing" is absent (contrast v 31), and the forward position of ἔξω stress once again the natural family's lack of belonging to him.

3:33-35 *(Matt 12:48-50; Luke 8:21; John 15:14)* The historical present tense of λέγει, "he says," stresses the rhetorical question that follows (v 33). The question itself, "Who is my mother and [who are] my brothers?" prepares not only for a surprising answer, but also for Jesus' "looking around at those sitting in a circle around him" (v 34a). "Sitting . . . around him" identifies these sitters with the crowd that was sitting around him in v 32 and again emphasizes the contrast between their closeness to Jesus and the standing outside on the part of his mother and brothers. "In a circle" implies a closed group, which his mother and brothers have failed to penetrate. That is to say, their attempt to seize Jesus has failed. Instead, the pericope ends with a pronouncement whose astoundingness is again emphasized with the historical present tense of λέγει, "he says," and also by the exclamatory character of "Look, my mother and my brothers!" (v 34b).

In the pronouncement Jesus identifies a new family for himself. Its astoundingness consists in his disregard (if not disowning) of natural family ties, which first century Palestinian Jews consider extremely important; and its astoundingness exhibits his authority to upset established mores (cf. esp. 10:1-31). The omission of the definite articles before "brother," "sister," and "mother" in the following explanation (v 35) adds emphasis to the new relationships by stressing their quality (P. B. Harner in *JBL* 92 [1973] 77-78). "For" (γάρ) identifies those who are sitting around Jesus with those who do God's will. Even if we omit "for" (only B [W] b e bo have it), the juxtaposition of those who are sitting around Jesus and those who do God's will identifies them with each other. But we read nothing that spells out what the will of God is that the surrounding crowd are doing (and cross-taking lies in the temporal future just as the call to cross-taking lies in the textual future [8:34], whereas Jesus identifies the surrounding crowd as already his true family — against J. R. Donahue, *Theology and Setting* 35-37). This omission concentrates attention on Jesus' astonishing identification as such (and prompts R. Bultmann, *HST* 29-30, to think that vv 31-34 portray "some imaginary situation" — which, of course, does not necessarily follow). Casus pendens plus an emphatic resumptive οὗτος, "this," underlines the identification. Unless we should read "and your sisters" in v 32 (but see the notes on vv 31-32), the adding of "sister" here in v 35 expands Jesus' true family to include younger women. Their non-mention in the exclamation of v 34 simply followed the pattern set by vv 31-33. The sisters, then, have not come with Jesus' mother and brothers to seize him. But while making his exclamation he noticed younger women in the crowd and therefore includes them in his present explanation. The sequence brother–(sister–)mother chiastically reverses the sequence mother–brothers in vv 33-34 (bis). This reversal emphasizes "mother" — even the closest of natural ties, that to your mother, is subject to Jesus' redefinition — and prepares for the sequence in 10:29-30. The placement of the predicate nominatives before ἐστιν, "is," and the omission of "my" once it has occurred with "brother" (contrast vv 31, 32, 33, 34) add further emphasis to the redefinition as such rather than to the belonging of this family to Jesus. Thus his authority to engage in this redefinition stands out.

NOTES

R. A. Guelich (1. 168-72) surveys source and redaction critical theories of vv 20-35 and offers his own judgments. Such theories often depend on questionable presuppositions, e.g., that differences in literary form imply differences of historical occasion, that the introduction of a new theme reflects a different historical occasion instead of a development on one and the same such occasion, that different contexts for an event or saying in Matthew, Luke, Q, Didache, Gospel of Thomas, or what-have-you favor Mark's or his source's amalgamation of originally separate materials rather than others' fracturing of originally unitary materials, that the sandwiching of one event between earlier and later segments of another event derives from literary manipulation rather than from the way things happened, that specially Marcan diction forecloses the possibility of underlying tradition, and that we can detect specially Marcan diction without knowing Mark's sources. The presence of a saying in both Mark and Q does provide a valid basis for source and redaction critical judgments, however. See L. Oberlinner, *Historische Überlieferung* 176-78, against Mark's depending on Q and using the tradition behind 6:1-6a for the construction of 3:20-21, 31-35.

J. D. Crossan (in *NovT* 15 [1973] 83) argues that v 20 belongs to the preceding pericope, because 1:16-20, 29-31; 2:13-16 have shown that Mark wants to conclude elections with a common meal. But considerable material came between the election in 1:16-20 and the meal in 1:31b, and 1:31b did not describe a common meal so much as it noted the serving of a meal as evidence of healing. Furthermore, 3:20 does not refer to any following of Jesus (contrast 1:20b; 2:14c); four of the Twelve have already been called and have eaten with him; 3:13-19 described, not a call for the purpose of discipleship, but a summoning and appointment for the purpose of service; and 3:20b stresses the magnetism of Jesus rather than an attempt to have a common meal. As usual, therefore, the topographical shift in 3:20a signals a new pericope.

Ἔρχονται, "they come" (v 20), is read by ℵ² A C D (with εἰσ- prefixed) L Θ 0133 0134 f[1,13] Majority Text lat sy[p,h]. Ἔρχεται, "he comes," is read by ℵ* B W Γ 1241 pc b sy[s] sa bo[pt]. Besides having somewhat better external testimony, the singular reading ties in with Mark's using the singular at 1:35, 39; 2:1, 13, 23; 3:1, 7, 13; 4:1, 10 even though the disciples are sometimes accompanying Jesus in these passages and even though in passages farther distant from 3:20 Mark uses the plural for the topographical movements of Jesus and his disciples (see, e.g., 1:21, 29; 4:35-36; 5:1). The singular also links up with Mark's emphasis in the next clause on Jesus' magnetism. The answer to the question whether Mark has redactionally added the house (so L. Oberlinner, *Historische Über-lieferung* 154-59) depends a great deal on whether one accepts the pre-Papian tradition that Mark is writing up Peter's reminiscences of Jesus' ministry (see pp. 1026-45).

"The Twelve" and the others who were "summoned" in vv 13-19 do not appear as such in vv 20-35. Rather, we read in v 32 about "a crowd" that "was sitting around him [Jesus]" and that he identifies as his new family because they do God's will. Therefore we might think that in v 20 those who cannot eat are Jesus and "the crowd" which has just been mentioned. If so, that such a large number of people could not eat because of the press of humanity contributes further to Mark's point concerning Jesus' magnetism. Nevertheless, the initial reference to entering a house and the preceding appointment of "the Twelve . . . in order that they might be with him" (vv 13-19, esp. v 14) favor that the gathering of the crowd makes it impossible for Jesus and the Twelve to eat in the house. Cf. the unbelief of Jesus' brothers in John 7:1-9 with their and their mother's saying that he has gone berserk; and with Jesus' leaving his family, cf. his demand that others do so (Matt 8:21-22; 10:34-37 par. Luke 9:59-62; 12:51-53; 14:25-26).

In v 21 ὅτι may be recitative ("He has gone berserk") or epexegetic ("that he had gone berserk"). The parallel with v 22, where the present tense of the quoted verbs almost demands a recitative ὅτι, favors the recitative in v 21, too. Does the adverbial πολλά, "much" or "vigorously," which describes Jesus' rebuking of unclean spirits in v 12 underlie the charge of ecstatic behavior? The suggestion that the natural family of Jesus want him to take up his family responsibilities because Joseph the father has died does not agree with their reason as stated in v 21, viz., their saying that Jesus has gone berserk. It seems likely that Christian piety would have kept Mark or an earlier traditioner from fabricating such a charge (cf. the softening in Matt 12:46-47 par. Luke 8:19-20 as compared with Mark 3:31-32, and the softening vv.ll. in v 21 for ἐξέστη, "he has gone berserk": ἐξέσταται αὐτούς, "he has escaped" [Θ 565 pc]; ἐξέσταται αὐτούς, "he has escaped them" [D it]; ἐξήρτηνται αὐτοῦ, "they were related to [or 'dependent on'] him" [W 28]). Even a hypothesized concern by the family for Jesus' well-being or for their own honor (see E. von Dobschütz in *ZNW* 27 [1928] 196 and esp. D. M. Hay in *BTB* 17 [1987] 83-87) would leave the contextual implication intact: they do not belong to the circle of those who do God's will. See J. Lambrecht in *NovT* 16 (1974) 244-45, n. 6; E. Best, *Disciples and Discipleship* 49-63; L. Oberlinner, *Historische Überlieferung* 165-67, against identifying οἱ παρ᾽ αὐτοῦ as Jesus' adherents and against saying that they went out from the house where he was to calm the crowd, who had become ecstatic (so H. Wansbrough in *NTS* 18 [1971-72] 233-35, supported in part by D. Wenham in *NTS* 21 [1974-75] 295-300; also H.-H. Schroeder, *Eltern und Kinder* 110-16). Apart from identifying the ecstatic αὐτόν with the crowd, the suggestion that οἱ παρ᾽ αὐτοῦ originally meant Jesus' adherents rather than his family suffers the problem of explaining how adherents could charge him with berserkness and remain his adherents. That οἱ παρ᾽ αὐτοῦ "hear" of the crowd's coming together again with the result of Jesus' and the disciples' inability to eat becomes very awkward if as adherents of Jesus οἱ παρ᾽ αὐτοῦ are none other than his disciples themselves. So also does a use of οἱ παρ᾽ αὐτοῦ for them right after a simple "they." And the preceding context narrates nothing that would favor an understanding of ἐξέστη as ecstasy in the sense of amazement on the crowd's part (contrast 2:12; 5:41-42; 6:51).

J. R. Edwards (in *NovT* 31 [1989] 209-10) suggests that Mark inserts vv 22-30 to imply that the attempt of Jesus' family to seize him was as bad as charging that "he has an unclean spirit" (cf. 8:33). But the statement that only that charge is unforgivable (vv 28-29) makes this point very doubtful. Comparison with Luke 11:14-15 (par. Matt 9:32-34; 12:22-24) suggests that Mark omits an introductory story about the exorcism of a dumb demon (as he can afford to do because of his earlier reporting of exorcisms [1:21-28, 34; cf. 3:11-12]) to attach the following charges to the foregoing charge that Jesus has gone berserk, and that Mark therefore constructs the next charge, "He has Beelzebul," out of the phrase "by Beelzebul" (Luke 14:15b) to link the charge of berserkness with the charge that Jesus casts out demons by their ruler. On the other hand, the plural of "demons," which all the synoptics share, suggests a general charge which in Matthew and Luke has attracted an exemplary story of exorcism; and the apposition of "(the) ruler of the demons" to "Beelzebul" in Matt 12:24b; Luke 11:15b makes the single charge there look like a conflation of the two charges here in Mark 3:22bc (cf. R. H. Gundry, *Matthew* 230-33).

To say that "the two charges of Mk. 3:22 are mutually exclusive: one who is possessed by a demon is the *object*, not the *subject*, of an exorcism" (C. E. Carlston, *Parables* 131) is to neglect the possibility of presupposing a hierarchy and conflict in the demonic world. In substituting a cohesive demonic world for a chaotic one, Jesus accepts the presupposition of a hierarchy but attacks the presupposition that Beelzebul wants some of his demons cast out (J. Kallas, *Jesus and the Power of Satan* 139-40). Though Beelzebul is not known as ruler of the demons in Jewish literature of the period, a hierarchy or organization of demons is well known.

One often reads that the charge, "He has Beelzebul," receives no answer and is therefore fabricated to anticipate the importation of vv 28-29, which will imply that Jesus has the Holy Spirit rather than the unclean spirit Beelzebul (see v 30). More likely, the charge that Jesus has Beelzebul attracts the saying in vv 28-29 and explains how it is that Jesus can cast out demons by their ruler: he *has* their ruler. If the first charge merely prepares for the second, an answer to the second (so vv 23-27) leaves the first without need of an answer. Verses 28-29 will imply that Jesus has the Holy Spirit, however — otherwise the sayings are irrelevant to their context — and v 30 will stress the implication. Whether Beelzebul's inhabiting Jesus entails Jesus' using Beelzebul's name for exorcisms (P. Samain in *ETL* 15 [1938] 464-72, followed by D. E. Aune in *ANRW* II 23/2. 1540-41) remains uncertain. "By Beelzebul" may be shorthand for "by the name of Beelzebul"; but neither the charge nor Jesus' answer to it makes explicit mention of a name, and the parallel expression in Jesus' answer, "by the finger (or 'Spirit') of God" (Luke 11:20 par. Matt 12:28), hardly means "by the *name* of the finger (or 'Spirit') of God." Furthermore, the stories of Jesus' exorcisms contain nothing which could be distorted into a charge that he used Beelzebul's name. On the contrary, those stories are notable for Jesus' nonuse of any divine name, though the magical papyri are full of divine names used for exorcism and other purposes. Cf. the charge in John 7:20; 8:48, 52; 10:20 that Jesus has a demon and is mad; the charge against a righteous man in Wis 5:1-5 that he is mad; and the possibility that the scribes come down from Jerusalem to determine for the Sanhedrin whether Jesus has "seduced" the city of Capernaum (W. L. Lane 141; E. Stauffer, *Jesus and His Story* 74; Acts 5:27-40; Deut 13:13-19[12-18]; *Bib. Ant.* 25:3-6, 8; *m. Sanh.* 10:4; Josephus *Life* 39 §§196-97; cf. Jer 11:21; 12:6; Zech 13:3; *b. Sanh.* 43a; *Midr. Qoh.* 1:1 [quoted in Str-B 1. 691]; Justin *Dial.* 69.6-7). See R. H. Gundry, *Matthew* 195, on Matthean redaction in Matt 10:25, redaction which undermines the view of M. Limbeck (in *Wort Gottes in der Zeit* 31-42) that Beelzebul was originally a Jewish name for Jesus which Jewish exorcists used in their trade.

In v 23 we are looking at Mark's first use of "parables." Its forward position carries emphasis. Here the word does not mean "illustrative stories," but "figurative sayings." In chap. 4 it will mean "enigmatic stories" and "enigmatic sayings," because the dullness of Jesus' audience will keep them from deciphering the figures (see R. H. Stein, *Introduction to the Parables of Jesus* 15-16, on the range of meanings). By contrast the present scribes are too keen not to decipher the figures (see also 12:1-12 with 11:27).

J. Lambrecht (in *NovT* 16 [1974] 247) sees an a-b-b'-a' pattern in vv 23b-26. But though a kingdom's and a house's division and inability to stand correspond to each other (b-b') and though Satan appears in both v 23b and v 26 (i.e. in a and a'), v 23b is a question about casting out whereas v 26 is a conditional sentence that comes much closer in structure and diction to the conditional sentences in vv 24-25.

It is often thought that Mark constructs the question, "How is Satan able to cast out Satan?" (v 23a), by taking "Satan" from v 26 (parr. Matt 12:26; Luke 11:18) and "cast out" from the sayings that he otherwise omits but which appear in Matt 12:27-28 par. Luke 11:19-20. But see R. H. Gundry, *Matthew* 230-35, esp. 233-34, for arguments favoring Matthean omission and secondary influence of Matthew on Luke. Among others, D.-A. Koch (*Bedeutung* 142) likewise suggests that the question, "How is Satan able to cast out Satan?" is secondary because it anticipates the application to Satan in v 26. One might just as well suggest that the application is secondary. But an inclusion does not necessarily imply the secondariness of either of its members; so the occurrence of "Satan" in both the question and the application makes no argument for any position. With the incorporation of demons in their ruler, cf. the incorporation of Peter in Satan at 8:33.

A kingdom's being divided against itself differs from a kingdom's being divided for distribution by an outside force, as in Dan 2:34-35, 41-45; 5:25-28; 11:4. Though Jesus may be speaking Aramaic rather than Greek (as the Aramaic term "Satan" suggests but does not demand, since the term occurs outside Jesus' sayings in 1:13, where it could represent Mark's own diction, and since Mark never uses the Greek equivalent διάβολος, "Devil"), the subtleties in change of mood and tense presumably derive from Mark or his source, not from Jesus. With τέλος ἔχει, "has an end," cf. Heb 7:3; *As. Mos.* 10:1. For the view that Satan's having an end in v 26 represents a Marcan redaction of his kingdom's not standing, see M. G. Steinhauser, *Doppelbildworte* 139-40); and for a contrary view, R. H. Gundry, *Matthew* 234. Apparently Mark does not know the sayings in Matt 12:27-28 par. Luke 11:19-20. They do not reveal a messianic secret; their emphasis on Jesus' authority would appeal to Mark; and their denying that Jesus casts out demons by Beelzebul would provide a direct refutation of the charges in Mark 3:22 that Jesus has Beelzebul and that he casts out demons by the ruler of the demons (J. Wanke, *"Bezugs- und Kommentarworte"* 89).

R. H. Gundry, *Matthew* 236 (fine print), gives background for the taking of spoils from a strong man. Matt 12:43-45 par. Luke 11:24-26 speaks of demons' inhabiting a human house. On binding in a figurative sense, sometimes with reference one way or another to Satan, see 7:35; Luke 13:16; Rev 20:1-3; *T. Levi* 18:12; *1 Enoch* 10:4-5, 11-12; 18:16; 21:3-4, 6; 54:4-5; *Jub.* 10:7; 48:15; cf. *T. Zeb.* 9:8; *T. Dan* 5:11; *Pesiq. R.* 36 (161a); Tob 8:3. It is wrong to say that Matt 12:28 par. Luke 11:20 favors God as the binder in the other synoptics; for even there Jesus is the actor, God's Spirit or finger only the means. M. A. Tolbert (*Sowing the Gospel* 100-101) interprets the binding of the strong man as the binding of Jesus (15:1) and the plundering of the strong man's household articles as the flight of Jesus' disciples (14:43-50) and as Peter's denials (14:66-72). But for this interpetation to stand, Jesus would need to be bound before that flight and before those denials, in accordance with the emphatically positioned "first" of the strong man's being bound.

The measure of allegorical interpretation adopted in the foregoing comments makes the present parable more relevant to the issue of Jesus' exorcisms, about which issue the parable speaks in all three synoptics. We should not resist allegory when the details of a parable combine with its occasion to support allegory (cf. J. Drury in *JTS* ns 24 [1973] 367-79; G. B. Caird, *Language* 160-67; H.-J. Klauck, *Allegorie* 1-147 et passim; K. Snodgrass, *Parable* 12-30; C. L. Blomberg, *Interpreting the Parables* 29-69). That this parable belonged from the start to the issue of Jesus' exorcisms is favored by the observation of J. Wanke (*"Bezugs- und Kommentarworte"* 92) that without v 27 the preceding sayings might only prove that Satan's kingdom has nothing to fear. R. Meynet (in *RB* 90 [1983] 334-37, 348-50) understands the stronger one as the Holy Spirit. Such a referent would prepare for vv 28-29; but in the charge that Jesus is answering, he is the actor. The Holy Spirit stands opposite the unclean spirit Beelzebul only as Jesus' enabling agent. Therefore the robber who is stronger than the strong house-owner is Jesus.

R. Laufen (*Doppelüberlieferungen* 133) argues that the present parable did not originally belong to this context (cf. Luke 11:21-22; *Gos. Thom.* 35), because the parable relates only indirectly to the charge that Jesus casts out demons by their ruler. But putting Satan in the role of antagonist rather than partner does not look so indirect; and we must allow for an argument to progress beyond what initially prompted it, especially since we are dealing with the free-wheeling thought of the ancient Near East, not with the carefully measured logic of the modern West. It is doubtful that we can find or even imagine a better context for the parable.

To interpret the blasphemy of the Holy Spirit as a sin committed in the church age after the coming of the Holy Spirit flies in the face of the context at hand, especially v 30. Eternal sin as sin that will never be released makes unnecessary the suggestions of E. P. Gould (66) that the unforgivable sin is eternal in its character as a fixed state of opposition to the Holy Spirit, and of M. Black (*Aramaic Approach* 140, n. 3) that "eternal sin" arises from understanding the Aramaic חִיּוּבָא as "sin" rather than as "condemnation." Moreover, the Aramaic word means "condemnation" as the passing of a negative verdict, not as the suffering of a punishment, which would be needed for the suggestion. On Jesus' use of ἀμήν, "truly," see the bibliography in BAGD s.v. Since Mark does not show rabbinic interests, his redactional responsibility for "all the sins and the slanders" would make it unlikely that the forgivability of all of them except one denies the rabbis' long lists of unforgivable sins (as thought by J. Jeremias, *NT Theology* 1. 149-50). Jeremias (op. cit. 261) interprets sins as against men and blasphemies as against God; but this interpretation requires an unlikely contrast between blaspheming God and blaspheming the Holy Spirit, nor does it sit easily with the concentration on blasphemy alone in the last clause of v 28. This concentration gives "sins" the force of an adjective — hence, hendiadys: "sinful slanders." The one unforgivable sin that Jesus recognizes appears to have arisen out of a hardened determination to interpret in the worst possible way the Holy Spirit's working through him, and this so as to avoid becoming his disciples. Therefore apostasy, which only professing disciples can commit, has nothing to do with the unforgivable sin; and desire to become a disciple stands at the opposite end of the spectrum. Lev 24:15-16 prescribes death by stoning for the one who slanders God and pronounces "Yahweh" in so doing (see the notes on 14:61b-62; contrast Matt 6:9 par. Luke 11:2), and D. Flusser (in *"Wie gut sind deine Zelte, Jaakow . . ."* 139-44) draws parallels between blaspheming the Holy Spirit and blaspheming God, and between one's relation to God and one's relation to fellow human beings. But Jesus stresses the difference between blaspheming the Holy Spirit and all other slanderous sins. There is no good reason to deny that he could have pronounced a "sentence of holy law" such as v 29 sets forth.

We might consider the possibility that Jesus himself adapted his saying in Matt 12:32 par. Luke 12:10 to the historical context surrounding Mark 3:28-29. But despite the likelihood that he occasionally used Greek, the Graecizing which accompanies the adaptation favors a later redactor. We might then consider the possibility of a pre-Marcan redactor. But the dualities in the adaptation typify the style of Mark's gospel throughout, and the editorial comment in v 30 favors his responsibility for the adaptation. That is to say, there is no reason to distinguish between him and an earlier redactor. The need to avoid an equation between the scribes' charge against Jesus and the forgivable sin of speaking a word against the Son of man neutralizes the argument that " 'the sons of men' . . . is unlikely to have been introduced once the more familiar phrase 'the son of man' had become established" (J. D. G. Dunn, *Jesus and the Spirit* 50). So far as this passage is concerned, nothing favors that Mark drew the saying from Q rather than that he knew the saying from another source. On the whole, though, it is likely that Mark knew sayings which Q incorporated, it is unlikely that he knew Q (W. G. Kümmel, *Introduction to the NT* 70).

See J. D. G. Dunn, *Jesus and the Spirit* 50-52; idem in *NTS* 24 (1977-78) 194-96; D. E. Aune, *Prophecy* 240-42, for refutation of the arguments put forward by M. E. Boring

(*Sayings* 159-64) and others in favor of Christian prophecy as the matrix for the saying on the unforgivable sin (cf. esp. R. Scroggs in *JBL* 84 [1965] 360-65). In addition, Boring's selection of forgiveness as the topic of vv 28-29 does not favor Christian prophetic origin, for Jesus spoke of forgiveness (see, e.g., 2:5, 9-10; 11:26; Matt 6:12 par. Luke 11:4). Besides, it would be more accurate to select blasphemy as the topic of vv 28-29. Nor does a change in tone from reasoning (vv 23a-27) to pronouncement (vv 28-29) favor Christian prophetic origin, for Jesus and other speakers may change their tone on one and the same occasion. Introduction of the Holy Spirit as a new element in vv 28-29 does not imply a non-dominical origin, for Jesus spoke of the Holy Spirit (see, e.g., 12:36; 13:11; Luke 11:13). "Truly I say to you" (v 28a) may favor rather than disfavor a dominical origin (see the summary by R. A. Guelich 1. 177-78 of the debate whether or not this locution distinguishes the authentic speech of Jesus). Boring neglects to deal with the offensiveness of vv 28-29, as shown by the vv.ll. which soften the sayings by subtracting "eternally" after "not have forgiveness," by changing present guilt or judgment into future guilt, and (as just implied) by changing eternal sin into the more traditional and manageable concept of eternal judgment. This offensiveness argues against later Christian origin, prophetic or other.

The argument that ὃς ἐάν, "whoever" (Matt 12:32), rather than πᾶς ὅς, "everyone who" (Luke 12:10), represents Q because Matthew tends to retain ὃς ἐάν and Luke to change it (so M. E. Boring in *NovT* 18 [1976] 265-66) fails to take account of Matthew's having the phrase eighteen times in parallel material, apparently by insertion or revision much of the time. Here, Mark's πάντα, "all [sins]," seems to reflect πᾶς ὅς. The argument of Boring (op. cit. 269-70) that Mark would not have revised the saying to include as forgivable the very sin that he wants to remain unforgivable (πάντα!) rests on a failure to read the first half of the saying (v 28) with the second half (v 29 and parr.), a failure that Boring later makes up without renouncing his argument (op. cit. 273). Even if someone before Mark were responsible for πάντα in v 28, the adversative δέ, "but," in v 29 (and parr.) would qualify it. Only by denying that v 28 was originally followed by v 29 can one maintain Boring's argument (cf. ibid. 277); but the theological harshness of v 29, demonstrated by the softening vv.ll., favors an original connection.

A. Stock (in *Emmanuel* 92 [1986] 18-19) treats vv 28-29 not as one harmonious statement but as contradictory and originally independent statements set side by side, as in the Mishnah and other early Jewish literature: (a) all sins are forgivable (v 28) versus (b) one sin is unforgivable (v 29). But the largely chiastic pattern of these verses (see the foregoing comments) militates against treating them as contradictory and originally independent, and even Stock has to admit that rabbinic literature indicates a difference in speakers when citing contradictory statements. B. M. F. van Iersel (in *NedTTs* 24 [1980] 27-28) thinks that v 29 should be translated, "But whoever blasphemes *Jesus* against the Holy Spirit [i.e. abjures Jesus in court against the voice of the Holy Spirit]" (cf. 13:11 and Stock, *op. cit.* 20-21). But speaking a word against the Son of man in Matt 12:32a par. Luke 12:10a and speaking against the Holy Spirit in Matt 12:32b do not tolerate the supplying of a personal direct object. Therefore we should probably not supply one in Mark, either. The difference between blaspheming the Holy Spirit and grieving the Holy Spirit militates against taking vv 28-29 as a pesher on Isa 63:3-11 (against C. K. Barrett, *Holy Spirit* 104-5).

J. Lambrecht (in *NovT* 16 [1974] 247-48) suggests that "an unclean spirit" in v 30 comes from the parable of the unclean spirit and its house in Q (Matt 12:43-45 par. Luke 11:24-26). But apart from the question whether Mark knows Q, for this suggestion to work we need to know why he omits the parable as a whole. It seems, rather, that had he known it he would have used it instead of importing the saying on the unforgivable sin; for the parable would have carried on the motif of a house and could easily have applied to the scribes in a condemnatory fashion. Since he identifies Beelzebul (v 22) as an unclean spirit (v 30) to contrast him with the Holy Spirit (v 29), there is no need to infer from "an unclean spirit" that Beelzebul differs from Satan. As one with his demons (v 23), Satan too is an unclean spirit. Having Beelzebul so as to use him in casting out his subjects (v 22) makes such an intimate connection between having him and using him that the supposed problem of the difference between the unforgivable sin as charging Jesus with having an unclean spirit (so Mark) and the unforgivable sin as charging Jesus with using Beelzebul for exorcisms (so Matthew and Luke) evaporates. See O. J. F. Seitz in *SE VII* 456 for the possibility that having an unclean spirit alludes to Zech 13:2 and therefore implies the charge of being a false prophet.

The suggestion that in pre-Marcan tradition divorced from vv 20-21 Jesus' mother and brothers seek him to see him, not to seize him (vv 31-32), makes it all the more difficult to explain why Christian piety did not keep the charge of berserkness in vv 20-21 from being fabricated or preserved. J. Gnilka (1. 147) mistakenly distinguishes between standing outside the house in pre-Marcan tradition and standing outside the circle of the people sitting around Jesus in Mark. To stand outside the house is to stand outside the circle. And since the circle does not come into view till v 32, standing outside in v 31 must refer even in Mark to standing outside the house mentioned in v 20. The contrast between distance and the closeness of sitting around Jesus inside the house (cf. v 20) seems to have determined Mark's use of the idiom οἱ παρ᾽ αὐτοῦ, "the ones from the side of him" (v 21). Does the v.l. that includes Jesus' sisters in v 32 represent influence from v 35 (cf. 6:3), or does the v.l. that omits them represent influence from v 31 and Matt 12:47 par. Luke 8:20? Verse 31 and Matt 12:47 par. Luke 8:20, none of whose textual traditions mention his sisters, probably reflect the original text of v 32. The external evidence also favors omission of the sisters in v 32 (see B. M. Metzger, *Textual Commentary* ad loc.; *Mary in the NT* 51-52, n. 90; contrast 10:29-30). Ἔξω, "outside," may go with Jesus' mother and brothers or with the verb "are seeking," probably the former since in v 31 they are standing outside.

The omission of "father" in vv 33-34 is due to the failure of Jesus' father to come with Jesus' mother and brothers. The practice of Jewish men's marrying girls younger than they makes it likely that Joseph has died by now (against L. Oberlinner, *Historische Überlieferung* 75-78). In addition, however, the fatherhood of God may rule out any mention of a father "who does God's will" (cf. 10:30, where the omission of "fathers," in contrast with the preceding verse, is probably due to the same theological reason — against E. S. Fiorenza, *In Memory of Her* 147). Since it is the crowd who are sitting around Jesus in v 32, we would make a mistake to limit to the Twelve his new family who are sitting in a circle around him in v 34. "Whoever" (v 35) also favors a wider reference than the Twelve. The generality of the apothegm in v 35 favors neither inauthenticity nor secondary application to a particular situation nor fabrication of an ideal scene to display the apothegm. A particular historical situation may prompt general as well as specific comments. Form critical canons that dictate otherwise are too hidebound. True, it is unclear how the crowd sitting around Jesus are doing God's will, and this unclarity has been used to argue for the original independence of the apothegm (cf. E. Best, *Disciples and Discipleship* 57-58). But the Marcan setting of the apothegm does not require that the crowd be doing God's will at the moment. Jesus may be implying that they would not be sitting around him except for their being the sort that do God's will. Nor does "the will of God" necessarily point to Mark's creativity under the influence of Paul, who often uses the phrase. Paul may have picked it up from this saying or from Christian diction influenced by it. Mark may have changed an original reference to the Father's will (so Matt 12:50). But Matthew often refers to the Father's will where the parallels lack it (6:10; 7:21; 18:14; 21:31; 26:42); so he looks like the redactor. J. Lambrecht (in *NovT* 16 [1974] 249-50) thinks that Mark constructs v 35 out of Q (Luke 11:28; cf. *Gos. Thom.* 99; *2 Clem.* 9:11).

But again we need to know why Mark omits the hearing of God's word in Q (cf. Mark 4:15, 16, 18, 20), the rest of the pericope (Luke 11:27), and intervening material, too (cf. Mark 3:23-30 with Luke 11:14-26). Far from redefining Jesus' new family according to a condition that might exclude some or all of the crowd sitting around him and that therefore implies an original independence or an originally different occasion, "whoever does the will of God" includes them by describing them as doers of God's will. If this clause did not originally describe them, the saying as a whole might have circulated independently or belonged to a different occasion without losing its meaning, but the redefinition of Jesus' new family would be scaled down to merely physical posture, configuration, and location: sitting in a circle around him. A good joke, perhaps; but dominical tradition seems to pass on theologically significant materials. Moreover, "whoever does the will of God" descriptively distinguishes the crowd sitting around Jesus from his natural family and therefore does not open the possibility that his natural family belong to his new family. Rather, his natural family's coming to seize him and standing outside contrast with the doing of God's will (cf. the parallel beween their saying that he has gone berserk [v 21] and the scribes' saying that he has Beelzebul [vv 22, 30]). "Whoever" plus the subjunctive has the purpose of roping in the present crowd, not of opening the possibility that Jesus' natural family might be converted (against the attempt of D. Dormeyer in *Vom Urchristentum zu Jesus* 122 to make vv 32-35 a metaphorical broadening of Jesus' family rather than a substitution for them).

JESUS' SPEAKING IN PARABLES TO ESTABLISH GOD'S RULE AMONG THE DISCIPLES AND TO SHUT OUT NON-DISCIPLES

4:1-34 (Matt 5:15; 7:2; 10:26; 13:1-23, 31-32, 34-35; Luke 8:4-18; 13:18-19)

Jesus' use of parables in the preceding pericope (particularly in 3:23-27) now leads Mark to bring in a larger batch of parables. The long pericope containing it subdivides into an editorial introduction (vv 1-2), the parable of the seeds (vv 3-9), the meaning and the purpose of the parables (vv 10-12), the explanation of the parable of the seeds (vv 13-20), the parable of the lamp (vv 21-23), the parable of the measure (vv 24-25), the parable of the growing seed (vv 26-29), the parable of the mustard seed (vv 30-32), and an editorial conclusion (vv 33-34). Practical considerations dictate the alternation of comments and notes subdivision by subdivision.

NOTES

It is commonly thought that much of the parabolic material in vv 1-34 existed in scattered places or as isolated units in the oral tradition and that Mark or someone or others before him collected the material (cf. the differing contexts of v 24b and Matt 7:2 par. Luke 6:38, for example, or those of v 25 and Matt 13:12 par. 25:29 par. Luke 19:26). Probably so, but sometimes it is hard to tell whether originally scattered or isolated units were collected, or whether units originally associated (because they go back to the same historical occasion) became scattered in Q because of its lack of narrative structure (cf. the Gospel of Thomas). It is likewise hard to tell whether linking words, such as "sow," "seed," "come up," "soil," "fruit," and "yield," attracted different parables to each other in the mind of a collector or whether they reflect the workings of Jesus' mind on a single occasion. We have already discovered that καὶ ἔλεγεν αὐτοῖς, "and he was saying to them," does not necessarily point to importation from another setting (see the comments on 2:27; also the notes below). In principle, then, some of the parabolic material may have cohered from the start.

J. Dupont (*Études* 264, n. 12) sets up a concentric outline for vv 1-34, but it requires the lumping together of the discretely separated parables in vv 21-23 and 24-25, and in vv 26-29 and 30-32. The similarly concentric outline of D. O. Via (*Ethics* 183) depends on failure to recognize vv 21-25 as parabolic (cf. V. Fusco in *Les Paraboles évangéliques* 225) as well as on lumping together vv 2b-9, 10-12, and 13-20, and vv 26-29 and 30-32. In another, similar attempt F. G. Lang (in *ZTK* 74 [1977] 8, n. 18) commits the same error with regard to vv 26-29 and 30-32 but also lumps together vv 10-12, 13-20, 21-23, and 24-25 on the ground that καὶ ἔλεγεν αὐτοῖς in vv 11, 13, 21, and 24 points to esoteric teaching of the disciples, whereas the dropping of αὐτοῖς in vv 26, 30 brings back Jesus' public teaching (cf. G. Lüderitz in *Markus-Philologie* 194-95). But the earlier dropping of αὐτοῖς in v 9 did not bring back the public teaching of Jesus, because still earlier in v 2 καὶ ἔλεγεν αὐτοῖς had already referred to it *with* αὐτοῖς. Moreover, αὐτοῖς (with ἐλάλει, "was speaking") will twice refer to non-disciples in vv 33-34; and v 13 reads the present instead of imperfect tense of λέγω. Yet again, 7:14-23 has a structure similar to that of the present passage. There, Jesus speaks a parable to a crowd, the disciples ask about it in private, and καὶ λέγει αὐτοῖς introduces his explanation (cf. 4:13; W. Marxsen in *ZTK* 52 [1955] 258-59, 262); yet additional explanation is introduced in 7:20 by ἔλεγεν without αὐτοῖς — not to indicate a return to the crowd, for Jesus is still explaining the parable, as he does only to his disciples. So καὶ ἔλεγεν αὐτοῖς is not a technical phrase for esoteric teaching. Jesus returns to teaching the huge crowd in 4:21; for according to vv 10-12, 33-34 he speaks in parables to the huge crowd but adds explanations for the disciples only in private, whereas he leaves explanations and returns to parables in v 21.

A survey of the occurrences of ἔλεγεν in Mark produces the following probable results: (1) καὶ ἔλεγεν derives from tradition concerning Jesus' words and compares to הוּא הָיָה אוֹמֵר, "he was saying," in *m. 'Abot* passim, but with a characteristically Semitic "and" prefixed (see 4:9, 26, 30; 14:36; cf. W. G. Essame in *ExpTim* 77 [1965-66] 121); (2) the addition of αὐτοῖς (for examples in vv 1-34, see vv 2, 11, 13, 21, 24; cf. vv 33, 34) and of other expressions (e.g., "in his teaching" at v 2; but see also 5:30; 8:24; 12:35, 38 for examples of additions without αὐτοῖς) represents Mark's tying of dominical words to their narrative contexts; (3) the present tense of λέγει (see v 13 for an example in the pericope at hand) represents Mark's changing the traditional imperfect tense for the sake of emphatic vividness (cf. his liking the historical present of other verbs, too); and (4) the presence of δέ instead of καί (7:20) represents a pre-Marcan or Marcan adversative interpretation, "but," of the original Semitic "and." Despite these probabilities, it is hard to be sure whether Mark is expanding or otherwise changing a traditional short introductory clause or composing the entirety of the introductory clause by imitation plus expansion and other changes when he writes more than or differently from καὶ ἔλεγεν.

To take one example of evidence for the traditionality of καὶ ἔλεγεν, Mark introduces the parable of the mustard seed with that clause (v 30a). Yet Q seems to have done so, too; for Luke 13:18a reads ἔλεγεν οὖν (see the comments and notes on Mark 4:30-32 for the derivation of Luke 13:18-19 from Q rather than from Mark and for Mark's using a pre-Q tradition). Apparently Luke changes "and" to "therefore," and Mark reflects the tradition also in v 26a: καὶ ἔλεγεν. Should we then think of a pre-Marcan collection of the three parables about seed and growth (vv 3-8, 26-29, 30-32; cf. R. Otto, *Kingdom* 113-14; D. W. Riddle in *JBL* 56 [1937] 77-83; J. Jeremias, *Parables* 14, n. 11; W. Marxsen in *ZTK* 52 [1955] 258-63; H.-W. Kuhn, *Ältere Sammlungen* 130-31)? Such an earlier grouping would explain why we read καὶ ἔλεγεν in vv 9, 26, 30 but the same phrase plus αὐτοῖς, "to them," or the same phrase except for a characteristically Marcan shift to the historical present plus αὐτοῖς or to ἐλάλει plus αὐτοῖς everywhere else in vv 1-34 (vv 2, 11, 13, 21, 24, 33, 34). Then we have to decide whether any or all of the intervening material (vv 10-25) was inserted prior to Mark or whether he is the first to insert it. (Whether the intervening material represents dominical tradition or churchly fabrication or both is another question not decided by answering questions concerning insertion.)

One wonders, however, whether Mark or an earlier traditioner would have broken up the unity of three parables that have in common the sowing and growth of seed. Perhaps so for the sake of explaining the parable of the seed, but far less likely so for the sake of introducing the quite different materials concerning the lamp and the measure. We would expect those materials, and perhaps also the private explanation of the seeds, to have been appended at the close of the earlier unit. Moreover, in surveying Marcan introductions to sayings of Jesus (and to statements of others), one is struck by variety of expression rather than by any phraseological fixity. Λέγω occurs not only in the imperfect, but also in the present and second aorist. Usually καί precedes, but not always. Sometimes other expressions will intervene. Elsewhere, too, αὐτοῖς is lacking, and ὅτι may follow — not to detail the use of other verbs of speaking. There is variety even in vv 1-2, 10-25, 33-34. One can, of course, attribute different phrases to different sources. But the greater the variety, the larger the number of sources; and the larger the number of sources, the less likely the hypothesis and the more likely we are dealing with authorial variation. Smallness of difference also argues for authorial variation. Καὶ ἔλεγεν may well come from tradition, but so also may other forms of the introduction, only with Marcan or pre-Marcan supplementation and revision. One cannot argue consistently from the lack of αὐτοῖς in vv 26a, 30a for a pre-Marcan collection of three parables concerning seed and growth when the introduction to the first of them does *not* lack αὐτοῖς (v 2b). That is to say, the argument leads us to expect καὶ ἔλεγεν in v 2b as well as in vv 26a, 30a. Instead, we find it in v 9a and read in v 2b καὶ ἔλεγεν αὐτοῖς ἐν τῇ διδαχῇ αὐτοῦ, "and he was saying to them in his teaching" (not to quote a preceding parallel clause). If Mark is expanding an original καὶ ἔλεγεν, we could rest comfortably on the hypothesis of an earlier collection of those three parables. But if he is composing v 2b on his own, the case for such a collection weakens, and perhaps reduces to the two later parables of the growing seed and of the mustard seed (cf. E. Lohmeyer 86). Since Q paired the parable of the mustard seed with that of the leaven, however (see Matt 13:31-33 par. Luke 13:18-21), even the hypothesis of a pre-Marcan pairing of the parables of the growing seed and of the mustard seed lacks certainty. For Mark may be the first to have paired them. The bareness of καὶ ἔλεγεν may favor an origin of the clause in tradition, but the clause does not indicate whether or not the materials so introduced were or were not interrelated prior to Mark's writing.

M. Zerwick (*Untersuchungen* 34-38) suggests that Mark omits αὐτοῖς when καὶ ἔλεγεν introduces a conclusion. But this suggestion improbably requires a double conclusion in 4:26, 30; 12:35, 38; and by limiting itself to these passages and 4:9, it overlooks several non-concluding passages where Mark omits αὐτοῖς after καὶ (. . .) ἔλεγεν (5:30; 8:24; 14:36). The closeness in wording of 4:2, which has αὐτοῖς, to 12:38, which does not, should warn us against drawing distinctions between tradition and redaction on the ground of αὐτοῖς alone (H. Räisänen, *Parabeltheorie* 89-113, esp. 108-9). At the same time, the unusualness of καὶ ἔλεγεν for introducing direct speech (with or without αὐτοῖς and other additions and changes) and the large number of possibilities for other introductions of direct speech point to a locution that Mark likes whether he finds it in the tradition or writes it on his own (P. Dschulnigg, *Sprache* 86-87, 103-4; see the comments on 2:27 concerning the question whether the formula of introduction necessarily indicates importation of material from another setting).

P. Sellew (in *NTS* 36 [1990] 254-55) adopts some further suggestions of Zerwick

— viz., that καὶ ἔλεγεν αὐτοῖς introduces a new saying within a discourse (i.e. without a change of speaker) and that καὶ λέγει αὐτοῖς introduces a saying in a dialogue (i.e. with a change of speaker). Then Sellew explains the anomaly in 4:13, where καὶ λέγει αὐτοῖς presently introduces a new saying within a discourse rather than a saying in a dialogue, by hypothesizing that in earlier tradition v 13 followed v 10 and thus introduced a saying in a dialogue. As admitted by Sellew, however, both v 11 (where καὶ ἔλεγεν αὐτοῖς intro- duces a saying in a dialogue) and v 35 (where καὶ λέγει αὐτοῖς introduces a continuation of Jesus' speaking) remain anomalous. In fact, the anomalies are so much more numerous that we should give up the whole enterprise of maintaining the suggested distinctions. Καὶ ἔλεγεν αὐτοῖς introduces the very start of Jesus' speaking or a response by him in 3:23 (with an inserted participial phrase); 4:2 (with an added prepositional phrase); 6:4 (with an addition of his name); 8:21; 9:31; 11:17. Καὶ λέγει αὐτοῖς introduces the very start of his speaking or a continuation of it in 3:4; 5:39 (with an inserted participle); 6:50; 9:35; 10:23 (with an inserted participle and the substitution of τοῖς μαθηταῖς αὐτοῦ, "to his disciples," for αὐτοῖς), 24 (with δέ, "but," instead of καί, and the insertions of Jesus' name, an adverb, and a participle), 42 (with the insertions of a participial phrase and Jesus' name); 11:2; 12:16; 14:27 (with an addition of Jesus' name), 32 (with the substitution of τοῖς μαθηταῖς αὐτοῦ for αὐτοῖς), 34, 41 (cf. 16:6). This list of anomalies would grow very much longer if we included further instances where δέ, ἀλλά, "but," or γάρ, "for," appears instead of καί, where no conjunction at all is used, where someone or ones different from Jesus do the speaking, where the speaking comes in response to something unuttered or spoken to others than the speaker, and where the dative disappears, occurs in the singular, or is replaced by a prepositional phrase. Again, we see variety of expression, not precision in the use of formulas, a mistaken supposition of which precision Sellew uses to argue for a pre-Marcan written rather than oral source.

B. H. M. G. M. Standaert (*L'évangile selon Marc* 202) adds that according to an- cient rhetoric καὶ ἔλεγεν αὐτοῖς carries more emphasis than καὶ λέγει αὐτοῖς or καὶ ἔλεγεν does, because καὶ ἔλεγεν αὐτοῖς contains more syllables than the shorter expressions do. But the passages to which Standaert appeals (Dion. Hal. *Comp.* passim; Cic. *De Or.* 3.174-321, esp. 199-201; Quint. *Inst.* 9.4) do not support this conclusion. Rather, they speak of long and short syllables, describe the long as beautiful and dignified, the short as vigorous, and recommend a mixture of long and short clauses. We may safely stay with the view that the present tense even of verbs of speaking carries more emphasis by virtue of vividness.

4:1-2 (Matt 13:1-3a; Luke 8:4) "And again he began to teach beside the sea" harks back to 2:13: "And he went out again to the seaside, and all the crowd was coming to him, and he was teaching them." But in 2:13 "again" referred to his going out to the seaside; here, "again" refers to his teaching. In 2:13 παρά plus the accusative indicated a shift to the seaside in association with a verb of motion. Here, lack of a verb of motion leaves the motion from house (3:20) to seaside to be inferred (cf. 5:21b with 5:21a) and puts the emphasis entirely on Jesus' teaching, which comes forward (in comparison with 2:13) and connotes his authority (cf. esp. 1:22, 27). Instead of the simple verb, "he was teaching" (so 2:13), Mark uses the compound expression, "he began to teach" (cf. the comments and notes on 1:45), to leave room for the simple verb in v 2 (cf. esp. 6:2, 34; 8:31). Instead of ἤρχετο, "was coming" (so 2:13), Mark writes συνάγεται, "gathers together." The prefix συν-, "together," may echo his recent statement at 3:20:

"And again the crowd comes together (συνέρχεται)." As there, the historical present tense emphasizes Jesus' magnetism. For the use of συνάγω in connection with a crowd, see also 2:2; 5:21. "All the crowd" (2:13) here becomes "a huge crowd." By preparing for the distinction between a smaller crowd, who with the Twelve constitute Jesus' new family (cf. 3:31-35), and a larger crowd including outsiders as well (cf. 4:10-12; P. Minear in *NT und Geschichte* 82-84), the elative superlative πλεῖστος, "huge," adds to the emphasis on Jesus' magnetism. Πρὸς αὐτόν, "to him," stays the same as it was in 2:13.

In 3:9-10, which dealt with another occasion, Jesus ordered that the disciples ready a small boat for him lest the crowd crush him. But that passage did not say he used it then (or, for that matter, whether the disciples carried out the order — see the comments on 3:7-12). Now he does get into a boat, and he sits "in the sea" to teach "all the crowd" (finally the latter phrase comes in from 2:13). They are "on the land [facing] toward the sea." "All" indicates that though the crowd is huge, Jesus captures the attention of everybody in it. Underlining this point is the placement of "all the crowd toward the sea on the land" before "were" (see the Greek text). The seated posture of Jesus befits his teaching the crowd. Here, then, he does not use the boat to avoid being crushed to death (so the motive behind the precaution in 3:9-10), but to wield his didactic authority (on sitting as the authoritative posture of a teacher, see the notes below). The oddity of saying that he sat in the sea instead of in the boat into which he had gotten provides a foil for the crowd's being "on the land." Mark is anticipating the parable of the seeds and its meaning: by his teaching, Jesus sows the seed of the word on the land (i.e. on the earth or soil — forms of γῆ in vv 1, 5 [bis], 8, 20), where all the crowd are located.

"And he was teaching them" echoes 2:13 again. The repetitiveness of the statement (cf. 4:1a) adds to the emphasis on Jesus' exercise of didactic authority. "In parables" echoes 3:23 and looks forward to the further contents of chap. 4. The adverbial πολλά, "much" in the sense of "extensively" (till evening, it will turn out according to v 35), fills this day with the exercise of didactic authority (cf. esp. 6:34-35). "And he was saying to them" echoes 3:23 again. But having already borrowed "in parables" from 3:23, Mark now writes "in his teaching" (cf. 1:22, 27; 11:18; and esp. 12:38) for yet another emphasis on Jesus' exercise of didactic authority. The command, "Hear" (v 3), will reverberate with that authority. In summary, Mark might simply have written at this point καὶ ἐν παραβολαῖς ἔλεγεν αὐτοῖς, "and in parables he was saying to them," just as in 3:23. Instead, he constructs two clauses, distributes ἐν παραβολαῖς and ἔλεγεν αὐτοῖς between them, adds a verbal reference to Jesus' teaching, strengthens it with an adverbial πολλά, and adds a nominal reference to Jesus' teaching — all to lay massive emphasis on didactic authority (cf. 9:31; 11:17; 12:35).

NOTES

The evident parallel between v 1 and 2:13 gives "again" its full temporal force, over against the view that Mark uses it as a mere link-word. S. T. Lachs (in *JQR* 69 [1978] 99-101 and

74 [1983] 171-72) argues that teachers of the Law did not adopt the sitting posture till after the mid-first century (*b. Meg.* 21a; cf. *b. Ber.* 27b). But M. Aberbach (in *JQR* 52 [1960] 168-74) allows for a more gradual change and notes that the talmudic texts are dealing with formal study on the part of rabbis and their students. It seems doubtful that we can attribute the sitting posture of teachers in all such texts as Matt 5:1-2; 13:1-2; 23:2; 24:3; 26:55; Luke 4:20-21; 5:3; Acts 22:3; *m. 'Abot* 1:4 (not to list many later passages) to a development that entirely postdates the lifetimes of Jesus and Mark. Does "sitting in the sea" imply his control over the powers of chaos (Ps 29:10)? Probably not (see the notes on 3:7-8).

Verse 35 and Mark's predilection for the adverbial use of πολλά (see the note on 1:45) combine to disfavor taking the word in v 1 as a direct object: "many things." "In his teaching" probably refers to the activity rather than to the content of teaching; for αὐτοῦ, "his," is most naturally taken as a subjective genitive. M.-J. Lagrange (94) disagrees on account of "un pléonasme intolérable" thus produced. But what for us is an intolerable pleonasm is for Mark a happily emphatic duality, and the lack of pleonasm in 12:38 will leave no excuse to take "in his teaching" unnaturally as a reference to content. "In parables" has the instrumental sense, "by means of parables." See J. W. Sider in *NTS* 31 (1985) 1-23 and further literature cited there for correction of some recent non-referential views concerning parables.

4:3-9 (Matt 13:3b-9; Luke 8:5-8) In view of his emphasis on Jesus' exercise of didactic authority, Mark's interest must lie mainly on the introductory command, "Hear" (v 3), and on the closing command, "Let the one who has ears to hear, hear" (v 9), which both use the emphatic present tense of the imperative (contrast the unemphatic aorist imperative of this verb in 7:14; Matt 13:18; 21:33; Rev 2:7, 11, 17, 29 et passim; cf. the notes on 1:3) and together form an inclusion. In fact, whether by retention of tradition or by his own composition, the setting off of this closing command with the intrusive introduction, "And he was saying" (cf. v 2b), carries forward the emphasis on Jesus' exercise of didactic authority (again see the comments on 2:27 and the introductory notes on 4:1-34 that this formula does not necessarily point to importation from an originally different setting). As vv 10-12 and 13-20 will show, Mark uses the parable of the seeds as a parable about parables to explain the rejection of Jesus by some people and the acceptance of him by others. Since the interpretation of the parable will highlight the theme of hearing (see vv 15, 16, 18, 20; also vv 12, 23, 24, 33), it is appropriate that the first word of the parable itself should be "hear" (cf. Judg 9:7; Isa 28:23; Ezek 20:47 for commands to hear right before figurative language).

"Behold!" grabs attention. "A sower went out to sow" sets the stage. In the first act, the coming of the birds and their devouring the seed on the edge of the path are presented straightforwardly. In the next act, "where"- and "when"-clauses balance each other, relate chiastically to their main clauses, and leave yet another, intervening clause to occupy center stage: "and immediately it rose up out of [the soil] on account of not having depth of soil." "Immediately" adds to the emphasis already apparent in the central position. Yet further emphasis accrues from the echo and extension of "on account of not having depth of soil" in the last clause of this act: "and on account of not having root, it withered." The phrases beginning "on account of" are chiastically related to their verbs; thus the second phrase comes before its verb to stress the reason for the withering (against the view of M. Wojciechowski [in *BN* 28 (1985) 38], which destroys the chiasm and creates an extremely harsh asyndeton by dividing the sentence after ἐξανέτειλεν instead of γῆς). The wordplay between ἐξανέτειλεν, "rose up out of [the soil]," and ἀνέτειλεν, "rose up," likewise stresses the immediate sprouting of the seed and the sun's rising to scorch it. The third act of the parable presents a dramatic reversal: the thorns come up rather than the seed and choke it so that it does not give fruit. The placement of καρπόν, "fruit," before οὐκ ἔδωκεν, "it did not give," underscores the failure to produce what was hoped for. Even more dramatically, in the last act the giving of fruit is mentioned before the coming up of the seed. Jesus cannot wait to reach the good part. Then he steps back to mention the coming up and to add the growing (cf. Col 1:6, 10; also Acts 6:7; 12:24; 19:20). Coming up means breaking through the soil; growing means developing into a mature plant. But those actions stay in the subordinate form of participles in order that the last accent in the story may fall on another reference to fruit-bearing, this time expanded into the increasingly productive "thirtyfold and sixtyfold and a hundredfold." No longer do we read simple aorist indicative verbs, as at the close of the other acts, but imperfect verbs, accompanied by present participles, all of which combine to form a moving picture of ongoing emergence, growth, and productivity. The amount of attention given to failures is surprising and therefore emphatic. So also is the progression in failure from no growth through little growth to much growth, but of the thorns rather than of the seed. Yet this progressive, threefold failure is overmatched by a threefold success. After "thirtyfold and sixtyfold" we expect "and ninetyfold." So the unexpectedly larger yield of "a hundredfold" stresses a productivity that more than compensates for the failures.

Interpreters continue to debate whether the parable is realistic or not, why the sower sowed on the edge of the path, on the rocky soil, and among the thorns, whether he had already plowed or was going to plow after sowing, and whether the yields of thirtyfold, sixtyfold, and a hundredfold were realistically good or eschatologically fantastic. The questions clear up when we pay attention to the contrast between the singular expressions ὃ μέν . . . ἄλλο . . . ἄλλο, "one [seed] . . . another [seed] . . . another [seed]," and the plural ἄλλα, "other [seeds]." The other seeds turn out to be three in number — (1) ἕν, "one" that was bearing thirtyfold; (2) ἕν, "one" that was bearing sixtyfold; and (3) ἕν, "one" that was bearing a hundredfold (so *1 Clem.* 24:5; Infancy Gospel of Thomas 12:1; cf. *Ap. Jas.* 8:10-27; 12:30-31) — three seeds that fell into good soil to match the three seeds that fell on poor soils. The singulars are not collective. When Mark later uses a collective singular for a batch of seed he writes the masculine noun σπόρος (vv 26-27) rather than the neuter noun σπέρμα, implied here by the neuter pronouns ὃ μέν . . . ἄλλο . . . ἄλλο . . . ἄλλα. The first one of the singular pronouns implies that the sower did not deliberately sow on the whole path and plan to plow it later. No, a single seed chanced to fall on its edge (παρά, not the ἐπί that we would expect for deliberate sowing "on" the path — see the more extensive discussion in R. H. Gundry, *Matthew* 253). Likewise, the sower did not deliberately sow on the rocky ground and among the thorns. No, another seed chanced to fall on the rocky ground and yet another among the thorns. The rocky ground means ground with rock just underneath the surface, not ground strewn with stones; so it had no visible edge, as the path did, and it is quite realistic that the sower did not know exactly where the underlying rock came close to the surface and therefore that a seed accidentally fell "on" it (ἐπί). The fact that the thorns "came up" (as the seeds in good soil "came up") after a seed fell among them shows that only the seeds of the thorns were in the ground at the time of sowing; the sower did not throw the seed of grain among already growing or grown thorns, or even among withered or cut-back thorns from the previous season.

Thus Jesus is speaking realistically not only about what happened when seeds fell from the hand of the sower, but also about the yields of individual seeds, thirty-, sixty-, and a hundredfold being good but not fantastic (cf. Gen 26:12), not exaggeratedly about the yields of the whole field, for which those yields *would* be fantastic (though not nearly so fantastic as those in Eus. *H.E.* 3.39.13). Anyhow, one cannot assess the yield of a field, or of parts thereof, in three different ways. We still have unrealism, but of a different sort: the unrealism of so small a number of seeds as six and of assessing the yields of the three that fell into the good soil. This unrealism highlights the yields in contrast with the failures. For discussions, see P. B. Payne in *Gospel Perspectives* 1. 181-86; idem in *NTS* 25 (1978-79) 123-29; F. Hahn in *Text and Interpretation* 135-36; J. D. Crossan, *Cliffs* 41-42; H.-J. Klauck, *Allegorie* 190-91; K. D. White in *JTS* ns 15 (1964) 300-307; J. Jeremias in *NTS* 13 (1966-1967) 48-53; J. Drury in *JTS* ns 24 (1973) 367-71; D. E. Oakman, *Economic Questions* 63; R. H. Gundry, *Matthew* 253-54.

NOTES

H. Baarlink (*Anfängliches Evangelium* 163) thinks that "and he was saying to them in his teaching" (v 2b) introduces the following command to hear (v 3a), but not the parable following that command (vv 3b-8); for that parable tells how to hear, not what to hear. Thus Jesus issues the command to hear during the course of his teaching (temporal ἐν) rather than as part of it (locative ἐν). But a command issued during the course of teaching may form part of that teaching, and telling how to hear does not rule out a command to hear a parable that tells how. Unless you hear the parable about hearing, the parable will do your hearing no good — hence, the repetition and expansion of the command to hear at the close of the parable (v 9). And v 33 will refer to the hearing of parables, not just to the hearing of the command to hear.

Cf. Justin *Dial.* 125.1-2. The definite article in ὁ σπείρων is usually taken as generic — hence, "a sower" — and thus as reflective of Aramaic influence. On the other hand, we may see an indirect though not exclusive reference to Jesus. Since according to 1:38 his very purpose was to go out (ἐξῆλθον) to preach (cf. 1:35, 39; 2:13, 17) and since this parable has to do with preaching the word (vv 14-20), as Jesus has done (2:2), the sower's going out (ἐξῆλθεν) may represent Jesus' going out to preach the word. But his disciples, too, will go out to preach (6:12); and the role of the sower remains minor both in the parable and later in the explanation. H.-J. Klauck (*Allegorie* 186-87) gives a conveniently up-to-date list of the many Semitisms that have been seen in the parable. E. C. Maloney (*Semitic Interference;* see the pages listed on p. 303 for 4:1ff.) notes that most of the

supposed Semitisms represent normal Greek. Their concentration favors a Semitic substratum, however. J. A. L. Lee (in *NovT* 27 [1985] 1-8) thinks that Mark or an earlier
traditioner dignified Jesus' speech with the stylish construction ὁ μέν . . . καὶ ἄλλο, which
occurs relatively seldom in Hellenistic Greek and only on Jesus' lips in Mark (see also
9:12; 12:5; 14:21, 38). This possibility fits a Marcan apologetic.

J. D. Crossan (*Cliffs* 31-34) sees a discrepancy between instant scorching because
of the sun and slow withering from lack of root, and infers that Mark inserts the scorching
to symbolize affliction and persecution (which he is thought to insert in v 17b) and then
repeats the construction διά plus an articular infinitive when he returns to the tradition (cf.
F. C. Synge in *ExpTim* 92 [1980-81] 329). But lack of a good root system follows naturally
from insufficient depth of soil. Scorching by the sun follows naturally from lack of a good
root system. (Otherwise, sunshine is likely to enhance growth.) And though withering can
occur apart from scorching, it follows scorching naturally and quickly. So it is hard to see
a discrepancy. Not having much soil and not having depth of soil already look like
characteristically Marcan duality in which the second member specifies more closely the
meaning of the first (cf. F. Neirynck, *Duality* 96-97). The twin occurrences of διὰ τὸ μὴ
ἔχειν, "on account of not having," plus a direct object also look like such duality in that
not having root is the effect of not having depth of soil. The dual statement concerning
scorching and withering parallels the dual statements concerning the other end-results, i.e.
concerning the birds' coming and devouring the seed, the choking and failure to give fruit,
and the fruit-giving and bearing of thirtyfold, sixtyfold, and a hundredfold. Mark's love
of duality suggests that throughout the parable he puts the tradition in dualistic form and
that we cannot tell where he adds to the tradition and where he simply divides it to achieve
duality of expression. The likelihood that sunshine will enhance the growth of a plant
having a good root system also militates against the argument of P. Sellew (in *NTS* 36
[1990] 244) that the present lack of a good root system stems from redaction because the
sun as an active opponent corresponds to the birds and to the thorns whereas the lack of
a good root system, being passive, does not.

Since the bad soils are hard, thin, and thorny, respectively, the good soil must be
constrastively soft, deep, and free of thorns (cf. Jer 4:3-4; 12:13; Isa 5:2-6; 7:23-25; 32:13).
The Aramaic use of חד as a sign of multiplication underlies ἕν (E. C. Maloney, *Semitic
Interference* 150-52). But that use is strange to the Greek language, and ἑκατονταπλασίονα,
"a hundredfold," in 10:30 shows that Mark knows the proper Greek way of expressing
multiplication. Therefore his over-literalistic ἕν highlights the oneness of each fruit-bearing
seed to make a contrast with each seed that did not bear fruit. J. G. Williams (*Gospel
Against Parable* 43) misses the limitation on the number of seeds when he paraphrases
the meaning of Jesus, "I could keep on enumerating if there were time." Except for the
division into three rates of fruit-bearing, the underlying Aramaic would have allowed more
than three fruit-bearing seeds. Naturally, the underlying Aramaic favors reading ἕν all the
way through rather than ἐν or the vv.ll. (B. M. Metzger, *Textual Commentary* ad loc.). The
commands to hear (vv 3, 9) may seem at first to call for understanding the deeper meaning
of the parable (J. M. Robinson in *The Future of Our Religious Past* 104-9). But it is difficult
to take the hearing at v 33 in the sense of understanding (see the comments ad loc.); and
the command to hear in the simple sense of listening appears often in non-parabolic
contexts, too (see Deut 6:4; 9:1; 20:3; Matt 11:15; Rev 2:7, 11, 17, 29; 3:6, 13, 22; 13:9;
and other passages cited by H. Räisänen [*Parabeltheorie* 84-86], who contrasts the differently stated command to deeper understanding in Rev 13:18; see also E. F. F. Bishop, *Jesus
of Palestine* 33, for an ordinary call to silence). The commonness of the command to hear
in different kinds of material also makes doubtful a special allusion to the Shema ("Hear,
O Israel, . . ." — Deut 6:4-5). Since the command in v 9 appears almost verbatim in other
gospel settings, too — in particular, at Luke 14:35 (for its occurrences in Matt 11:15; 13:43

are probably redactional) — Mark may be importing it here. But Jesus may well have spoken the command in connection with the parable and repeated it in other connections (cf. 7:14 and the frequency of commands to hear in Jewish teaching by means of מְשָׁלִים, παραβολαί or "parables," as noted by M.-J. Lagrange [95] with references to Prov 5:1; 22:17; Sir 3:1; 16:24 et passim). J. Gnilka (1. 156) rejects the originality of the command to hear in v 3 because that command supposedly clashes with the immediately following command to look; but he may underestimate the extent to which ἰδού has lost its imperative force to become an exclamatory particle ("behold!"), for "the sower" does not go into the accusative case as the direct object of a verbally understood ἰδού. Besides, any awkwardness in the juxtaposition of "hear" and "behold!" could represent original forcefulness instead of secondary clumsiness (cf. the command in v 24 to *"watch* out how you *hear"*). Unredacted speech is at least as full of clumsiness as is redacted speech, and one speaker's clumsiness is another's forcefulness. Having ears to hear is descriptive, not restrictive. One can hear and not understand and thus fail to be converted and forgiven (v 12; cf. Aesch. *PV* 447-48). One can hear the word in ways that frustrate it (vv 15, 16, 18). And non-disciples as well as disciples hear the word (vv 33-34). Therefore having ears to hear is not limited to the elect (see Jer 5:21, which Mark 4:9 appears to parody — against J. Starobinski in *Structural Analysis and Biblical Exegesis* 76; J. Marcus in *JBL* 103 [1984] 562; idem, *Mystery* 57-59). The call to hear needs following up, *is* followed up, with an indication of bad and good ways of hearing.

The suggestion of H. Koester (in *NT and Gnosis* 195-97) that "the soil" may be the subject of "was giving fruit . . . and bearing" (as possibly in *Gos. Thom.* 9) runs afoul of the neuter participles ἀναβαίνοντα and αὐξανόμενα, "coming up" and "growing," which show that the neuter ἄλλα, "other [seeds]," is still the subject. On *Gos. Thom.* 9, see A. Lindemann in *ZNW* 71 (1980) 214-43; P. B. Payne in *Gospel Perspectives* 1.187-93; C. L. Blomberg in *Gospel Perspectives* 5.184-86; J. Marcus, *Mystery* 33-34; J. Horman in *NovT* 21 (1979) 326-43. Horman argues that the omission of "to you has been given the mystery of God's kingdom" in *Gos. Thom.* 9 must go back to pre- or extra-canonical tradition because a Gnostic writer would not have omitted it from the tradition. But this argument fails to take account of the facts that *Gos. Thom.* 9 occurs in the middle of a string of parables and figurative sayings which are offered without indication of meaning and that motives for omitting canonical indications of meaning are to be found in the introduction of the kingdom as a matter of knowledge (more specifically, of self-knowledge) at *Gos. Thom.* 3, in the bewilderment and marveling caused by finding the explanation of Jesus' secret words at *Gos. Thom.* 1-2, and in the hiddenness of the light despite its manifestation at *Gos. Thom.* 83. Gnostics are to find the explanation by themselves, in themselves. Horman also argues that the shorter version in *Gos. Thom.* 9, "Others fell on the rock and did not send a root down into the earth and did not send an ear up to heaven," shows up an allegorical expansion in Mark 4:5-6. This argument neglects that sending an ear up to heaven represents Gnostic aspiration for immaterial heavenly existence (cf. the later phrase, "brought forth good fruit up to heaven") and therefore gives motive for replacing canonical material unuseful for representing that aspiration (cf. R. M. Grant and D. N. Freedman, *Secret Sayings* 127-28).

4:10-12 (Matt 13:10-17; Luke 8:9-10) At 9:28; 13:3 Mark will use κατ' ἰδίαν, "privately," with the imperfect of ἐπερωτάω, "inquire" (cf. 4:34). Here, he reserves κατ' ἰδίαν for the explaining of the parables in v 34, drops ἐπ- from the imperfect verb, and writes that Jesus ἐγένετο κατὰ μόνας, "came to be alone," to separate him from outsiders (cf. the combination κατ' ἰδίαν μόνους in 9:2; also

6:47; 9:8). Thus the presence of "the ones around him with the Twelve" (cf. 8:34) does not contradict his being alone (again cf. 9:2, 8) so much as it lays greater than usual emphasis on their distinctness from outsiders (and the locution is to be taken as due to Mark's concerns, not to a pre-Marcan source — cf. J. Lambrecht in *L'Évangile selon Marc* 277-82). Mark mentions "the Twelve" as well as "the ones around him" to make it clear that the Twelve, too, whom Jesus chose to be "with him" and to send out to preach (3:14), receive the following explanation. "The ones around him" means the crowd sitting around Jesus and declared by him to be his new family, those who do God's will (3:31-35). We see here why Mark described the intervening crowd in 4:1 as "huge" (πλεῖστος): it included many others, too, i.e. others who did not belong to Jesus' new family because they were not doing God's will. That the smaller crowd plus the Twelve are with him in his separation from outsiders is due to the membership of the smaller crowd plus the Twelve in his new family. So also is their inquiring about the parables (cf. 7:17; 9:28; 10:10); for doing God's will, which defines them as Jesus' new family, requires a knowledge of that will as hidden in the parables.

Though Jesus spoke in parables on an earlier occasion (3:23-27), he has spoken only one parable to the huge crowd on the present occasion (4:1-9); and his answer to an inquiry will feature the outsiders who help make up the huge crowd but who did not hear the earlier parables (v 11). So those earlier parables do not come in view (against G. H. Boobyer [in *NTS* 8 (1961-62) 59-70], who under a very wide definition of "parables" also includes Jesus' other sayings and deeds in chaps. 1–3 and the saying in 4:9 as distinct from the parable in 4:3-8). But more parables will follow (vv 21-32) and have already been referred to (v 2). The present plural reference to "the parables" implies, then, that in vv 10-20 Mark inserts tradition out of its original order. Four more factors strengthen this implication: (1) the perfect tense of δέδοται, "has been given," which points to action completed in the past (v 11); (2) the distinction between Jesus' explaining the parables privately to his disciples and his speaking many parables to the people in general (vv 33-34) and the consequent implication that he speaks the parables in vv 21-32 to a general audience and later explains them to his disciples in private; (3) his still being in the boat at v 36 (cf. v 1); and (4) the contrastive use of the singular "parable" in the very similarly phrased statement at 7:17.

But why does Mark disregard chronology by advancing Jesus' coming to be alone with his true family? He does so to emphasize Jesus' answer to their inquiry; for the answer shows that just as Jesus predetermines his own death partly by healing on the Sabbath despite the Pharisees' watching him with murderous intent (see 3:1-6 with comments) and partly by choosing the betrayer (see 3:16-19 with comments), so also he predetermines his own death partly by speaking in parables. His parabolic speaking desensitizes outsiders purposefully (telic ἵνα) "lest they should convert and it should be forgiven them" (cf. the yelling of "the crowd" to crucify Jesus [15:6-15]). *In part, then, his crucifixion will stem not from failure to achieve a goal of universal discipleship but from the successful achievement of a goal to keep outsiders from conversion and forgiveness.*

Jesus has just issued a command to hear (v 9). Because they have heard, his new family — "the ones around him with the Twelve" — ask him about the parables (v 10; see J. Marcus [*Mystery* 91], who cites 1QH 4:23-24; 1QS 5:11-12 to support the appropriateness of the disciples' inquiry). The generality of the inquiry leaves the way open for Jesus to answer in terms of the purpose behind the parables (cf. Matthew's interpreting the question as asking why Jesus speaks in parables [Matt 13:10] or in terms of their meaning (so Luke's interpretation of the question [Luke 8:9]). He will do both. Because of the figurativeness of parables, it is natural to think first of meaning (cf. 7:17). So Jesus answers first that in the parables the mystery of God's rule has been given to the disciples. If this were a statement of purpose, we would have to conclude that the disciples' failure to understand the parable of the seeds (v 13) frustrated the purpose. But "given," which carries a stronger meaning than "happen" in the next clause, implies that if they do not understand the parable, Jesus will make them understand by explaining it, as in fact he does (vv 14-20). It is unsurprising that they should need an explanation, since it is not God's rule itself, but "the mystery" of it, that has been given them in the parables — and because of human ignorance, including that of disciples, mysteries need explanations. The forward position of τὸ μυσ-τήριον, "the mystery" (Mark usually puts a subject after its verb), and its separation from the dependent phrase τῆς βασιλείας τοῦ θεοῦ, "of the rule of God," stress the element of mystery (cf. Josephus *J.W.* 1.24.1 §470 on the mysteriousness of a mystery).

"Has been given" instead of the expected "has been revealed" (cf. A. E. Harvey in *JTS* ns 31 [1980] 335-36) states privilege but stops short of implying that the disciples understand the mystery (cf. B. M. F. van Iersel, *Reading Mark* 79-80; idem in *Semeia* 48 [1989] 91-92) and thereby leaves the way open to their non-understanding and Jesus' explanation. Hence, there is no contradiction between vv 11-12 and 13-20 that would favor Mark's interposing vv 11-12 between an originally united vv 10, 13-20 (but Harvey [loc. cit.] may err in thinking that the combination of "has been given" with "mystery" is peculiarly Greek rather than Semitic; for his only Greek cross-reference, Arr. *Epict. Diss.* 3.21.17, combines "give" with the matter of becoming a philosophical lecturer, not with a mystery, the passive voice of "has been given" in Mark may represent a typically Semitic divine passive [cf. the following notes], and *1 Enoch* 51:3; 68:1 provide a similar un-Greek combination of "give" with "the mysteries of wisdom" and "the teaching of all the mysteries"). Nonetheless, the parables *contain* the mystery; they *mean* God's rule; and they have been given to the disciples *for* that meaning. After all, the disciples are those around Jesus who do God's will and thereby show themselves to be subjects of God's rule (cf. 3:34-35). The mystery's dealing with this rule (cf. 1:15) shows that the disciples are subjects in God's kingdom as well as family members in God's royal household (cf. 3:24-25 with comments).

The question of meaning in the disciples' inquiry is answered. Jesus proceeds to the question of purpose. As he limited his answer to the question of meaning to his disciples, so he limits his answer to the question of purpose to non-disciples, "the outsiders" as opposed to "the ones around him." The forward positions of ὑμῖν, "to you," and of ἐκείνοις . . . τοῖς ἔξω, "to those outside," and an adversative δέ, "but," emphasize the contrast between the two groups. "Those" is not a redundant addition to "the ones outside"; rather, "those" contrasts the distance from Jesus of "the ones outside" with the closeness of his true family "around him" (cf. 12:7; E. C. Maloney, *Semitic Interference* 124-26). Jesus will not explain the parables to the distant outsiders. So in the antithetically parallel v 11c (as against v 11b) no "mystery" is "given" in the parables; instead, "the all things" that are in them merely "happen" because they will remain enigmatic (cf. J. Jeremias, *Parables* 16, on parables as riddles in Semitic speech). Τὰ πάντα, "the all things," takes a prominent position before its verb to emphasize the completeness of Jesus' judgment on outsiders. Ἐν παραβολαῖς, "in parables," takes an even more prominent forward position to emphasize the means of judgment. These riddling parables are meaningless to the outsiders. To make up for this lack of meaning with a statement of purpose, there now comes a ἵνα-clause, which has nothing corresponding to it in Jesus' telling what the parables mean for insiders. The ἵνα-clause tells the purpose of the parables so far as outsiders are concerned. In this clause Jesus says that behind the telling of parables to outsiders lies the purpose of keeping the outsiders from insight, understanding, conversion, and forgiveness. Insight and understanding carry moral as well as intellectual connotations. The quotation of Isa 6:9-10 (besides the parallels in Matt 13:13; Luke 8:10, see also Mark 8:17-18 with comments; Matt 13:14-15; John 12:40; Acts 28:26-27) might seem to fit Jesus' purpose into God's purpose as expressed through an OT prophet (see also Deut 29:3[4]; Jer 5:21; Ezek 12:2; cf. Philo *All.* 2.17 §69; Aesch. *PV* 446; Dem. 25.89), with the result that the outcome of Jesus' life — viz., his death by crucifixion — need not cause any scandal: that death was God-willed as well as self-willed by Jesus. But Mark does not inform his audience that the OT language of God is being used (contrast 1:2-3; 7:6-7; 14:27); so the emphasis rests solely on obscurative purpose as such. "Lest . . . it should be forgiven them" agrees with the Targum and the OT Peshitta against the Hebrew of Isa 6:10 ("lest . . . one heals them"; similarly the LXX) so as to identify the outcome of judgment by parabolic speaking, i.e. the outcome of no forgiveness (cf. 3:28-30, and see C. A. Evans, *To See* 92, 105, for further deviations from the LXX and MT and for contacts with the Targum). "Lest . . . it should be forgiven them" also contains a divine passive, which means, "lest . . . God should forgive them."

NOTES

Because of the linear nature of speaking, verbs of speaking often take the imperfect tense; so we have no reason to think that the imperfect of ἐρωτάω, "ask," expresses typical action (cf. esp. 5:9; 7:17, 26; 8:5, 23, 27, 29; 9:11, 28, 33; 10:2, 10, 17; 12:14 [linear present], 18; 13:3; 14:61; 15:4; against C. F. D. Moule in *Neotestamentica et Semitica* 101-2). A. M. Ambrozic (in *CBQ* 29 [1967] 224-25) thinks that ἠρώτων plus a double accusative means that the disciples were asking for more parables, not for the meaning of the parables. But then the rest of vv 10-12 loses its relation to the question. Luke 14:32 and extra-NT passages cited in BAGD s.v. ἐρωτάω 1 show that the second accusative can mean "about" (cf. Mark 7:17). The infrequency in Mark of ἐρωτάω as compared with ἐπερωτάω is sometimes taken as evidence for the traditionality of v 10 or of vv 10-12. So also with regard to κατὰ μόνας, "alone," as compared with κατ' ἰδίαν, "privately." We need not quarrel with traditionality; but a redactor may use an expression as infrequently as a tradition does, and a tradition may use an expression just as often as a redactor does.

Nowhere else does Mark use "the ones around Jesus" for Peter, James, and John, or for them plus Andrew (against R. P. Meye in *SE II* 211-18 and in *Oikonomia* 62-65; idem, *Jesus and the Twelve* 152-56). Identifying the ones around Jesus as the Twelve or as a smaller number among them runs into the problem that 3:31-35 identified the ones around Jesus as a "crowd" of people consisting of "whoever does the will of God." And it is hard to escape the impression that Mark is responsible for the expression with περὶ αὐτόν, "around him," in 3:32, 34; 4:10 and that he uses it to interrelate the materials in which he puts it. If so, his addition of "with the Twelve" is not an appendage tacked onto a previously existing formulation, but part of his original composition (cf. E. Best, *Disciples and Discipleship* 137-40). "With the Twelve" does not mean "including the Twelve" (cf. the use of "with" [σύν] for accompaniment rather than inclusion in 2:26; 8:34; 9:4; 15:27, 32). See the notes on 3:14, 16 that throughout Mark "the Twelve" distinguishes the apostles from a large group of disciples and in 14:10, 20, 43 identifies the apostles as a small group out of which Jesus' betrayer is named. Since Mark writes several times of Jesus' going into a house with his disciples (1:29; 2:15-16; 7:17; 9:28, 33) and even puts a crowd in the house with Jesus (2:1-4, 15-16; 3:20-35), the absence of a house in v 10 favors that he is working on a tradition that did not include such a locale (cf. G. Wohlenberg 125).

According to B. M. F. van Iersel (in *Semeia* 48 [1989] 92-93), the disciples remain ignorant of the mystery even after Jesus explains the parable of the seeds (vv 13-20), because in line with the messianic secret his explanation will omit an identification of the sower with himself. But the mystery has to do with God's rule, the nature of which the following explanation will describe. So it is gratuitous to introduce a messianic secret. And because it introduces the explanation, the question, "If you don't understand this parable, then how will you understand the rest of the parables?" (v 13), seems to imply that the explanation will make the disciples understand.

C. M. Tuckett (in *Bib* 69 [1988] 15-16) argues that the mystery of God's rule cannot have been given to the disciples in parables, because Jesus spoke the parables to outsiders, too. (Tuckett also proceeds to give the mystery a Christological twist.) This argument overlooks the distinction between disciples' being given the mystery and the mere happening of all things to outsiders (see the foregoing comments).

The outsiders to whom all things happen in parables cannot be Jesus' mother and brothers, who stood outside a house in 3:31-35 (cf. 3:20). On the one hand, they did not arrive in time to hear the parables that he spoke in 3:23-27, so that those parables could not be in view at 4:11 even though his mother and brothers were the outsiders at 4:11 as well as in 3:31-35. On the other hand, the scene shifted in 4:1. As a result, his mother and brothers have disappeared and been replaced by the part of the huge crowd that is not around him. A parallel remains: both groups are outsiders (contrast J. Coutts in *SE II* 155-57).

The plural of "parables" at 12:1, where only a single parable will follow, might seem to favor a generalizing plural or plural of category in 4:2, 10-12 for the parable of the seeds alone (N. Turner, *Grammatical Insights* 47). But "began to speak" at 12:1 will suggest that Mark means his audience to understand the following parable as one chosen from among other, unreported parables; and the distinction in 4:13 between "this parable" and "all the parables" insures that the plural in 4:2, 10-11 refers to more parables than the one concerning seeds. We can hardly think that in either v 10 or v 11 Mark changes an original singular of "parable" into a plural (so, e.g., H. Räisänen, *Parabeltheorie* 68-69); for then he would be violating his own context, where the plural has only one parable as a referent. Therefore the plural favors again that he is working on a tradition. According to 1:14-15, Jesus publicly preached the nearness of God's rule; but the private mystery of God's rule will not turn out to deal with its nearness. So there is no contradiction from which to argue against the authenticity of 4:11-12 and for a reflection therein of the experience of early Christians in having their message rejected.

G. Minette de Tillesse (*Le secret messianique* 169) gives two reasons for thinking that Mark inserts vv 11-12 between a previously united vv 10, 13-20: (1) the implication in v 13 that the disciples should have understood the parable almost contradicts the statement in vv 11-12 that the mystery has been given to them; (2) vv 11-12 state the purpose of the parables, whereas v 10 asks for their meaning. Against this reasoning, we have seen in the comments that the wording of the disciples' inquiry is general enough to be taken both as a question concerning the purpose of the parables and as a question concerning their meaning (and even general enough to allow the interpretation that the disciples were asking for more parables — so A. M. Ambrozic in *CBQ* 29 [1967] 220-23; against whom, however, see H. Räisänen, *Parabeltheorie* 31-32, n. 12). Jesus' first statement does answer the question of meaning. The fact that in the parables it is a mystery which is given to the disciples makes their ignorance in v 13 unproblematic; for any mystery needs explaining, and giving a mystery is not equivalent to explaining it (again see the foregoing comments).

In favor of the intrusiveness of vv 11-12, D. Wenham (in *TynBul* 23 [1972] 19-20) adds that the imperfect ἔλεγεν, "he was saying," does not normally introduce a reply in Mark; but he has to admit exceptions at 7:27; 8:23 (cf. 9:33). His explaining these exceptions as cases where the reply will introduce what follows fits vv 11-12 perfectly (see vv 13-20), and his driving a wedge between vv 11-12 as didactic and 7:27; 8:23 as non-didactic misses a definitely didactic element in 7:27. In 7:20, moreover, ἔλεγεν will introduce the continuation of a didactic reply.

The further argument that vv 11-12 intrude because without them the structure of vv 1-20 would match that of 7:14-23 would be convincing only if it could be shown that both passages come from a pre-Marcan source. Otherwise, we can attribute the similarity quite simply to Mark's writing 7:14-23 in reminiscence of 4:1-20 yet not having in 7:14-23 any tradition that corresponds to 4:11-12. Notably, the structural argument for the intrusiveness of vv 11-12 also requires several assumptions: (1) that the tradition behind 4:10 had the singular "parable" so as to provide the same singular in 7:17; (2) that Mark changes the traditional singular to a plural disagreeing with Jesus' having thus far spoken only one parable on this occasion (an unlikely assumption); and probably (3) that because of its plural, "Then how will you understand any of the parables?" (v 13) did not stand in the tradition but that Mark fabricates it despite the disagreement of its plural with the context (again unlikely). So an appeal to 7:14-23 does not produce a perfectly straightforward case.

If the reasons for thinking that Mark imported vv 11-12 from elsewhere are not good, the attempt to make these verses refer originally to Jesus' whole ministry (as an aggregate of enigmas to outsiders) fails. Besides, that attempt suffers from a non-recognition that γίνεται, "happens," which can refer to the occurrence of nearly any kind of event, is here limited to verbal events by ἐν παραβολαῖς, "in parables," which refers consistently in the gospels to certain kinds of speech. We then have to take as enigmas the parables alone — but these parables in chap. 4 concerning the kingdom (cf. also 7:14-23; 13:28-29, 34-37, all of which have explanations), not others whose meaning is evident even to outsiders and the understanding of whose meaning does no good (3:23-27; 12:1-12); and τὰ πάντα, "the all things," will refer not to everything in Jesus' ministry, much less to everything in general, but to everything in the parables (cf. v 34), as favored by the anaphoric definite article (cf. B. Reicke in *TDNT* 5. 888; BAGD s.v. πᾶς 2bβ). The variant omission of the definite article is to be rejected as easier and less well supported than is its inclusion.

Verse 11b and c are antithetically parallel, but this fact does not require that "the all things" in 11c carries a wider reference than does "the mystery of God's rule" in 11b. The contrast lies between giving to insiders and happening in parables to outsiders, not between narrow and wide subjects of these actions. The following OT quotation refers to the entire activity of the prophet Isaiah. But this fact does not require that "the all things" refer widely to the entirety of Jesus' activity (which would still include speaking in parables and therefore not alleviate the problem of obscurative parables) rather than narrowly to his giving the mystery to insiders through parables plus explanations, for the meaning of an OT passage in its original context does not determine its meaning in the NT when quoted there. It overinterprets the perfect tense of δέδοται to say that the mystery was given as early as the call to discipleship in 1:16-20 (against A. Stock, *Call* 120). The ones around Jesus with the Twelve include many more than the four called in 1:16-20; and the alleged parallel with the binding of Satan as early as the Temptation rests on a misalignment of the Temptation and the binding of Satan (see the comments and notes on 1:12-13; 3:27).

In Isa 6:9, hearing comes before seeing. Why do we have the reverse order here? Because Jewish eschatological hope was primarily an object of seeing? Perhaps so, but it may be better to think that hearing is put second to stand closer to the emphasis on hearing in the immediately following explanation. Notably, in Isa 6:10 the order hearing–seeing is at first maintained in the order ears–eyes, but is then reversed in the order eyes–ears. In any case, the reversal in Mark does not imply that Mark has inserted vv 11-12 into a previously united vv 10, 13-20; for the reversal could have been made in an original continuity of vv 10, 11-12, 13-20. According to the text, the mystery has to do with God's rule, not with Jesus' messiahship, with the speaking of the word, not with the person of Jesus. Whether or not there is any chronological development in Mark, the disciples' manifestation in 8:29 of knowledge that Jesus is the Christ is textually far removed from the present reference to the mystery's having been given to them. It is not Jesus' keeping his messiahship hidden in a *mystery* but his speaking about God's rule in *parables* that prevents the conversion of outsiders. There is no equation between parables and mystery, for parables are a mode of speaking whereas a mystery is a form of doctrine. For all these reasons we should disregard vv 11-12 in discussions of Mark's so-called "messianic secret" (cf. S. Brown in *JBL* 92 [1973] 60-74).

The argument that Jesus' expecting the disciples to have understood the parable of the seeds shows that the parables cannot have been enigmatic underestimates the rhetorical purpose of the questions in v 13 to introduce the explanation in v 14. The condemnatory language in 8:17-18 is much stronger than are the questions in 4:13. The illustrative purpose of some parables located elsewhere does not forestall the obscurative purpose of the parables located here. Differences in subject matter and occasion may make some parables illustrative, others obscurative (cf. C. M. Tuckett in *Bib* 69 [1988] 13 on the difference between vv 11-12, where understanding would have led to conversion, and 12:12, where understanding will lead to a murderous plot).

Matt 11:25-27 par. Luke 10:21-22 blunts the argument that Jesus would not hide the truth from outsiders, for he would only be following the example of God his Father as he sees it. If it be asked why he speaks at all to outsiders, why he does not spare himself the trouble of having to obscure the truth in parables and then having to clarify it to his disciples in private, we may answer that he is only following the example of Isaiah, not in respect of obscuring the truth, but in respect of speaking to people who he knows ahead of time will be lost. Besides, telling parables to a general audience gives reason to explain them privately to disciples who have made up part of that audience.

The paralleling of a trajectory from the parables as Jesus' sermon illustrations to the parables as Mark's enigmas with a trajectory from Jewish "sayings of the sages" to Gnostic "secret sayings" (so J. M. Robinson, *Problem* 46-47) will stand only if each trajectory can be proved. We have seen no sufficient reason to accept the first one; and even acceptance of the second would not provide a valid argument favoring the first, for we cannot simply assume that what happened in the one case happened in the other as well.

The purposed judgment comes in response to failure to do God's will. But we should reject attempts to evade the telic ἵνα, "in order that"; for the combination with μήποτε, "lest," comes as close as possible to insuring the telic meaning. See C. A. Evans, *To See* 92-99; idem in *NovT* 24 (1982) 127-33 for a summary and criticism of those attempts (ἵνα as ecbatic, "with the result that"; as causal, "because"; as a mistranslation of the Aramaic ִּד, "who"; as imperative, "let [as a command, not as a permission] . . ."; as followed by an implied πληρωθῇ, "that it might be fulfilled" — to which suggestions we need to add ἵνα as epexegetic of τὰ πάντα, "the all things happen in parables in that seeing, they see . . ." [so P. Lampe in *ZNW* 65 (1974) 140-50] — and μήποτε as "unless" or "perhaps") and for arguments favoring the telic meaning. The changes made by Matthew and Luke make it apparent that they did not see a way of softening the telic meaning apart from dropping the μήποτε-clause as well as making earlier changes. (The μήποτε-clause in the unparallel Matt 13:14-15; Acts 28:26-27 tells the purpose of *non*-disciples, not of God or of Jesus.) Mark omits "make the heart of this people fat . . ." (Isa 6:10), not to avoid the telic meaning, but to bind the intermediate purpose of preventing discernment and understanding more closely to the ultimate purpose of preventing conversion and forgiveness. The argument that the targumic characteristics of the OT quotation combine with the non-telic meaning of *Tg. Isa* 6:9-10 to disprove a telic μήποτε in Mark (ibid. 146) fails to note Mark's using ἵνα instead of the Targum's ִּד, "who," his adopting Septuagintal verbs, and his reversing the order of clauses. That is to say, Mark does not limit himself to the Targum.

R. M. Fowler (in *Semeia* 48 [1989] 126-29) argues that Jesus' public preaching of God's rule (1:14-15; cf. 1:4) forces an ironic meaning on ἵνα . . . μήποτε. But his attempt to avoid a judgmental purpose fares no better than the other such attempts. For it trivializes the contrast between insiders and outsiders. It leaves unmotivated the refusal of Jesus to explain the parable of the seeds to outsiders as well as insiders. And it overlooks the failure of outsiders to have heeded his public preaching of God's rule. This failure makes appropriate a judgmental purpose behind obscurative parables.

It is likewise both illegitimate and unavailing to import the notion of scriptural fulfilment right after ἵνα to avoid a judgmental purpose ("in order that [what is written in Isaiah the prophet might be fulfilled]"). Such an importation leaves the following subjunctive verbs and the μήποτε-clause without a grammatical base. Moreover, A. Suhl *(Funktion)* has shown that Mark does not emphasize fulfilment of the OT. Even where it becomes plain that OT language is being used, Mark's audience hear of correspondence and causation, not of fulfilment (again see 1:2-3; 7:6-7; 14:27); and in the only Marcan passage that talks of OT fulfilment, the language of the OT is not even borrowed without acknowledgment, much less quoted explicitly (14:49; cf. 14:21a; against M. A. Beavis, *Mark's Audience* 140-51). Here, not only does Mark omit to inform his audience that OT language is being used (see the foregoing comments); but also a fulfilment of the OT would still look judgmental with respect to the parables vis-à-vis outsiders.

The argument that Jesus' application of Jer 5:21 ("You have eyes and do not see; you have ears and do not hear") to the disciples in Mark 8:18 requires the possibility of forgiveness and therefore the meaning "unless" or "perhaps" in 4:12 (so R. A. Guelich 1. 211-12) overlooks that the context of 8:18 will transform Jeremiah's declarations into questions implying affirmative answers ("Having eyes you see, don't you? [Yes] And having ears you hear, don't you? [Yes]" — οὐ plus the indicative in questions; cf. the question, "And you remember, don't you?" with the disciples' answering *correctly* how many baskets of leftovers they had picked up [8:18-19]). K. Romaniuk (in *NovT* 23 [1981] 196-99) suggests that we should read a question, "But do all things happen in parables to those outsiders in order that . . . ?" which retains the natural telic meaning but gets rid of the telic problem. The suggestion dies for want of a μή, which is needed with the indicative γίνεται for a negative answer. Moreover, OT citations are ordinarily used for affirmations, not for questions (a point made by M. Wojciechowski in *BN* 28 [1985] 36, n. 2).

Since Jesus does not tell the parables to divide between insiders and outsiders, but to give the mystery to those who are *already* inside and to hide everything from those who are *already* outside (cf. 3:20-35), vv 10-12 have little to say about predestination and human responsibility. The hiding for the purpose of preventing later conversion and forgiveness tends toward predestinarianism, but the definition of insiders as those who are already doing God's will (3:35) tends toward human responsibility (cf. the appeal of F. W. Danker [in *CTM* 44 (1973) 92-93] to the Pharisees' self-made hardness of heart in 3:5-6).

Though the Marcan Jesus predetermines his crucifixion in part by successfully achieving his aim to keep outsiders from conversion and forgiveness (see the foregoing comments), it might be asked whether the historical Jesus aimed to exclude outsiders. If we understand "outsiders" to mean those who did not believe his message and act on it (cf. 3:34-35), little reason exists to deny such an aim. The achievement of this aim then becomes a deliberately taken step toward what turned out to be crucifixion even though Jesus would doubtless have preferred that none remain outside to oppose and destroy him.

On the Twelve, see 4:10; on μυστήριον, R. E. Brown, *Semitic Background;* A. E. Harvey in *JTS* ns 31 (1980) 332-36. It is possible to take δέδοται, "has been given," as a divine passive, like ἀφεθῇ, "should be forgiven." But if giving the mystery consists in telling the parables, we must think either that Jesus' telling the parables rules out a divine passive or that God uses Jesus to give the mystery by means of Jesus' telling them. Several factors favor a genitive of reference in τῆς βασιλείας, the mystery *"concerning* the rule," over a genitive of apposition, the mystery "which *is* the rule": (1) "mystery" denotes a kind of truth, not a kind of action; (2) the context refers to explanations which set forth this kind of truth; (3) "has been given" suits a kind of truth better than it does the action of ruling; (4) the giving of a certain kind of truth makes a better contrast to the happening of all things in riddling parables than does the "giving" of the action of ruling (cf. G. Dautzenberg in *BZ* nf 34 [1990] 42).

Whether we translate ἐν παραβολαῖς "in parables" (local ἐν, telling where all things take place for outsiders) or "by means of parables" (instrumental ἐν, telling the means used by Jesus to make all things happen for outsiders) is unimportant. For outsiders as non-disciples, unbelievers, cf. 1 Cor 5:12-13; Col 4:5; 1 Thess 4:12; Rev 22:15. "In order that seeing they may see . . . and hearing they may hear" represents Semitic idiom meaning "in order that they may look and look . . . and hear and hear." In distinction from βλέπωσιν, "see" in the sense of "look," μὴ ἴδωσιν here means "not see" in the sense of "not perceive" (as confirmed by the progression from hearing to understanding in the next, parallel line). The third person of the plural verbs in the OT quotation agrees with Jesus' own words in v 11 and with *Tg. Isa* 6:9 against the MT and the LXX. The participles in the OT quotation also agree with the Targum. For more discussion of the OT quotation, see R. H. Gundry, *Use of the OT* 33-35, and especially C. A. Evans, *To See.* On hearing and understanding, see 7:14; also 6:52; 8:17, 21. As usual, Mark seems to be using tradition for his own purposes (e.g., by advancing the tradition behind vv 10-20 to its present location).

A. M. Ambrozic (*Hidden Kingdom* 86-88) argues for the greater originality of Matt 13:11; Luke 8:10 over Mark 4:11; but see R. H. Gundry, *Matthew* 255-57, for evidence of redaction in Matthew. Additionally, it is easier to think that the plural of "mysteries" in the QL and the connection of mysteries with knowledge in the QL reflect a common usage that has led Matthew to shift from an original singular than it is to think that an original common usage has been changed by Mark (under Paul's influence, according to L. Cerfaux in *NTS* 2 [1955-56] 240-41). The singular appears also in *SGM* 1; but if there is any relation at all, the singular there may reflect the present singular in canonical Mark as easily as vice versa. The occurrence of the singular for a particular mystery in Dan 2:18, 19, 27, 30, 47 LXX Theod; 4:9 Theod; Tob 12:7, 11; Jdt 2:2; Sir 22:22 proves that the use of the singular in Mark 4:11 for the particular mystery of God's rule is not at all odd, despite some scholarly statements to the contrary. The use in v 13 of the plural "parables" in opposition to the single "parable" of the seeds upsets the attempt by P. Lampe (in *ZNW* 65 [1974] 141) to refer vv 11b-12 as a whole to the parable of the seeds alone, and the plural "parables" within these verses to the individual points in that overall parable ("happen" = sowing; "see" = receiving the fallen seed; "not understand" = the unproductivity of the bad kinds of soil; "perhaps . . . convert and be forgiven" = fruit-bearing).

4:13-20 *(Matt 13:18-23; Luke 8:11-15)* Jesus continues to speak in private to his new family. But "and he says to them" marks a switch to the explanation of the parable concerning the seeds (cf. the foregoing comments on 2:27 and notes on 4:1-34). Since Jesus has already answered in vv 11-12 the disciples' question in v 10, we are not to think of this explanation as another or as the original answer to their question. They asked about parables in general and Jesus answered about parables in general. What follows here is an explanation of a particular parable. The historical present tense of λέγει, "he says," stresses Jesus' exercise of didactic authority in explaining the parable (cf. the comments on vv 1-2 and 3-10). If we were to take the following οὐκ οἴδατε τὴν παραβολὴν ταύτην as a question by itself, the construction οὐκ plus an indicative verb would imply an affirmative answer: "You understand this parable, don't you?" (cf. 7:18; 8:18-20 with comments). But an implied affirmative would contradict both the insiders' asking about the parables in v 10, the continuation in v 13 ("and how will you understand all the parables?"), and the offering of an explanation in vv 14-20. Therefore we should take the quoted words in v 13 as a single question characterized by a remarkable instance of parataxis and meaning, "If you don't understand this parable [as evidently you don't], then how will you understand the rest of the parables?" (alternatively: "You don't understand this parable! Then how will you understand any of the parables?" [M. Reiser, *Syntax und Stil* 112-13]). The question implies that the parable of the seeds is a parable about different ways of hearing other parables. The chiasm of putting "this parable" after "you don't understand" and "all the parables" ahead of "will you understand" (see the Greek text) and the further chiasm in τὴν παραβολὴν ταύτην . . . πάσας τὰς παραβολάς, literally "the parable this . . . all the parables," highlights this interrelation. The chronological displacement of vv 10-20 shows that Mark uses the interrelation to stress the necessity of Jesus' explanation, a necessity that supports one of Mark's explanations of Jesus' death, viz., that Jesus determined his own death partly by hiding the truth from outsiders (see the comments on vv 10-12). Therefore the rebuking tone of the question does not impugn the disciples so much as it provides a foil against which his explaining the mystery contained in the parable will stand out in bold relief (cf. 4:40; 6:52; 7:18; 8:32-33; 9:32 with comments; H. J. Ebeling, *Messiasgeheimnis* 156-65). "The word" is the good news concerning God's rule (cf. 1:14-15 and see the comments on 1:45). So if you do not understand the parable that tells you how to hear the word, how will you understand the parables which tell you what that word says? You have to know how to hear it before you can understand it.

Τὸν λόγον, "the word," gets emphasis by virtue of placement before σπείρει, "sows." Since the sower sows the word, the seed represents the word. But since the seed fell into the soil and became one with it, the seed-cum-soil also represents different kinds of hearers. Hence, the explanation quickly switches to the four kinds of soil which, with the seed, represent different kinds of hearers. Because they receive the word in different ways, the explanation identifies them with different kinds of soil. Thus the seed represents the word and melds figuratively with the people who receive it. The soils represent their hearing the word in different ways and melds figuratively with the people who hear thus. The hearers, then, are the middle term that makes sense out of what appears at first glance to be a confusion between the seed as the word ("the sower sows the word") and the seed as hearers ("these are the ones alongside the road . . . the ones sown on rocky places . . . the ones sown among the thorns . . . the ones sown on the good soil"; for similar combinations of symbolism, see Col 1:6, 10; 4 Ezra 8:41; 9:31). The masculine plural οὗτοι, "these," refers to people who are like the seed sown in different kinds of soil. To correspond with οὗτοι, the masculine plural οἱ, "the ones," personalizes and pluralizes the seed (contrast the neuter singulars ὃ μέν . . . ἄλλο . . . ἄλλο, "one [seed] . . . another [seed] . . . another [seed]," in vv 4, 5, 7). An adversative δέ, "but" (v 15a), signals this personalization and pluralization.

To stress the identification of the seed with the word (v 14), the further parts of the explanation mention "being sown" four times (vv 15, 16, 18, 20), each time in replacement of the verb "fell" in the parable (vv 4, 5, 7, 8). The four additions of "hearing the word" (vv 15, 16, 18, 20) indicate that seed-sowing means preaching a message that needs to be heard (cf. v 9). In v 15 the addition of "immediately," which is missing in the corresponding part of the parable (v 4), indicates that any delay in acting on the heard word gives Satan time to take it away. His taking it away interprets the devouring of the seed. Notably, Satan appears as the enemy in the first kind of soil (contrast the charge in 3:22-23 that Jesus is in league with him), and his coming and taking away the word may provide Mark with a further explanation for the end of Jesus' ministry in death by crucifixion: many people rejected Jesus because Satan snatched his message away from them before they acted on it. The implication in 3:23 that demons are so united with Satan as to form a corporate Satan favors a corporate reference here.

The plural of the rocky places (v 16) substitutes for the singular (v 5) to conform with the plural of "those who are sown." The explanation omits the parabolic references to not having much soil and to not having depth of soil, but retains the note of immediacy in those references (cf. v 16 with v 5). The lack of root, i.e. of a sufficient root system, comes over from the parable — but with the added phrase "in themselves" (v 17a). Some do not have root in themselves because they themselves are the soil in which the word ought to take root. "But they are temporary" (v 17a) gives a general interpretation of the effect of not having a sufficient root system, i.e. of the scorching and withering in the parable. Underlining this effect are the strength of the adversative ἀλλά, "but," and the placement of πρόσκαιροι, "temporary," ahead of εἰσιν, "they are." The scorching and the withering get a more detailed explanation in the following reference to "being tripped up" by "affliction or persecution because of the word" (v 17b). The initial acceptance of the word with joy, emphasized by "immediately" and by the placement of "with joy" before "receive," shows that apostasy under pressure (θλίψεως) of persecution (διωγμοῦ) is in view. Sadly, the immediacy of the apostasy matches and cancels the immediacy of the joyful reception of the word.

In v 18 ἄλλοι, "others," temporarily replaces οὗτοι, "these" (vv 15, 16), in reminiscence of the parable (v 7; cf. vv 5, 8). But the number has changed from singular to plural and the gender from neuter to masculine for a reference to people. Then Mark quickly switches back to οὗτοι. The entrance of "the cares of the world and the deceitfulness of wealth and the lusts for everything else" (v 19) interprets the coming up of the thorns. These items get emphasis from their placement before the verb "choke." Emphasis likewise accrues to ἄκαρπος, "un-fruitful," from its placement before γίνεται, "becomes."

To set the people represented by the good soil in a class by themselves, Mark shifts from οὗτοι, "these," to ἐκεῖνοι, "those," substitutes the aorist participle σπαρέντες, "having been sown," in place of the earlier present participle σπειρόμε-νοι, "being sown" (vv 16, 18), and uses οἵτινες, "who are such that," for emphasis on their character as good hearers (v 20). The insertion of καὶ παραδέχονται, "and they welcome [the word]," interprets "coming up and growing" (v 8) as opposite the fate of the seeds that fell on the first three kinds of soil. Welcoming is stronger, more favorable than mere receiving (λαμβάνουσιν — v 16). Καρποφοροῦσιν, "they bear fruit," combines ἐδίδου καρπόν, "it was giving fruit," and ἔφερεν, "it was bearing," in the parable (v 8) and contrasts with the statement about the third kind of soil, "and it became unfruitful (ἄκαρπος)" (v 19). By its abundance, the threefold success of thirtyfold, sixtyfold, and a hundredfold more than cancels out the threefold failure of the seeds that fell on bad soils.

In summary, the good hearers welcome the word immediately, so that Satan cannot snatch it away. They welcome it deeply, so that persecution because of it cannot induce them to apostatize. They welcome it exclusively, so that other concerns do not stifle it. The understanding that results from this kind of reception goes beyond the intellectual to touch conduct, commitment, and devotion. In this light, though the abundant fruit-bearing of the good soil is commonly interpreted as a reference to the eschatological harvest when God fully imposes his rule on earth, the vocabulary of harvesting is completely missing and the vocabulary of fruit-bearing seems rather to represent the life of discipleship (cf. Matt 3:8, 10; 7:16-20; 12:33; Luke 3:8-9; 6:43-44; John 15:1-17; Rom 6:22; 7:4-5; 15:28; Gal 5:22-23; Eph 5:9; Phil 1:11, 22; 4:17; Col 1:10; Heb 12:11; 13:15; Jas 3:17-18; Pol. *Phil.* 1:2; *Barn.* 11:11). The fruit consists in obedience to the word of the kingdom (see further R. H. Gundry, *Matthew* 261). Thus the mystery turns out to be that God's rule is established, not by conquest, but by speaking; and that a person participates in God's rule, not by joining an army, but by hearing the message in right ways (cf. H. Giesen in *La Pâque du Christ* 107-9; contrast 1QM).

NOTES

Mark includes the rebuking of the disciples' ignorance, not to show that they were saved by grace (so, e.g., M. Hengel, *Studies* 43-44), but to urge his audience to heed the following explanation. A number of commentators (e.g., H. B. Swete [77], E. Lohmeyer [84], and V. Taylor [258]) think that the proper distinction between οἴδατε as knowing by intuition or insight and γνώσεσθε as knowing through experience or being taught is here maintained. But why would inability to intuit the meaning of one parable imply inability to learn the meaning of other parables by being taught their meanings? We should not think of different means of understanding, but of different amounts: some understanding is necessary for more.

"This parable" (v 13) would not refer to the parable of the seeds if other parables originally intervened. Moreover, "all the parables" seems to look forward to future parables (in contrast with looking backward to past parables, as "the other parables" would have implied) and therefore ill fits the disciples' asking about more than one parable already spoken (as in v 10). Thus it seems that although Mark has kept the traditional plural of parables in vv 10, 13, he has suited the tradition to the forward position into which he has advanced it. He has done so by forging a particular reference to the parable of the seeds ("this parable"), which as a result of the advancement is now the only parable already told on this occasion, and by fostering an anticipation of more parables to come ("all the parables"). The progressive duality of v 13 characterizes his style (F. Neirynck, *Duality* 57-58), and the follow-up by an explanation of the parable of the seeds undercuts the identification of "this parable" with the saying in vv 11-12 (against G. H. Boobyer in *NTS* 8 [1961-62] 66-68). See also 9:12 for καὶ πῶς in the sense "then how?"; and 11:18; 12:41; 14:1, 11 for πῶς in editorial statements. In 2:2 Jesus was hardly telling the story of the healed leper as "the word"; so "the word" hardly refers to that story here, either (against M. Clévenot, *Materialist Approaches* 64).

It is difficult to imagine how the parable as explained would make sense unless the seed represents both the word and its hearers. For without the word, there can be no hearers; without the hearers, the word has no purpose; and the figure of sowing demands a union of seeds and soils. Therefore we should not assign the seed as hearers to OT tradition and the seed as word to Greek tradition (so H.-J. Klauck, *Allegorie* 202-3; cf. the criticism below of G. Lohfink). R. Pesch (1. 244-45) suggests that σπαρέντες, "having been sown," indicates a completed action having reached a satisfactory result; that its aorist tense contrasts with the present tense for incomplete action having failed to reach a satisfactory result (vv 15, 16, 18); that the present tense of ἀκούουσιν is iterative ("they keep on hearing [the word]"); and that this present tense contrasts with the aorist in earlier occurrences of the same verb for only one hearing (vv 15, 16, 18). But the present tense of σπείρω in v 14 (bis) covers successful as well as unsuccessful sowing; the perfect participle of σπείρω in v 15 more naturally indicates completed action than does the aorist; the completion of an action says nothing one way or the other about a successful result; the completed action of the perfect participle in v 15 leads to an unsuccessful result; the aorist tense of ἀκούω may be constative as easily as it may be iterative; and the present tense of ἀκούω, especially in the indicative, does not have to be iterative. Furthermore, why should the present tense of σπείρω be thought to imply an unsatisfactory result, but the present tense of ἀκούω a satisfactory one?

For the word as sown, cf. 4 Ezra 9:31. For teaching as sowing seed, cf. Philo *All.* 3.59 §170; Antiphon frg. 60 in Diels-Kranz; Hippoc. *Lex* 3; Pl. *Phdr.* 61 (276E-277A); Plut. *De Pyth. or.* 1 (394E); Quint. *Inst.* 5.11.24; Sen. *Ep.* 38.2; *Corp. Herm.* 1. 29). For people as sown, cf. Matt 13:24-30, 36-43; Isa 6:13; Jer 31:27-28; Hos 2:23; Zech 10:9; 4 Ezra 5:48; 8:41; *1 Enoch* 62:8; *2 Apoc. Bar.* 70:2; and other passages cited by G. Lohfink in *À cause de l'Évangile* 219-20 and J. Jeremias, *Parables* 79, n. 35. For Satan as a bird, cf. Rev 18:2; *Jub.* 11:11; *1 Enoch* 90:8-13; *Apoc. Abr.* 13:3-14; *T. Job* 27:1; *b. Sanh.* 107a; and as a hinderer of the gospel, 2 Cor 11:3; 1 Thess 2:18; 3:5. For the enthusiasm of first belief, cf. 1 Thess 1:6; for the figurative sense of "root," Eph 3:17; Col 2:7; for θλῖψις, "affliction," and διωγμός, "persecution," in combination, Rom 8:35; 2 Cor 4:8-9; 2 Thess 1:4; and for σκανδαλίζομαι as apostasy, G. Stählin in *TDNT* 7. 340-57 (though Mark 14:27-29; 16:7 show that σκανδαλίζομαι does not have to mean the kind of apostasy that results in eternal judgment). 'Απάτη may mean "delight." If so, τοῦ πλούτου expresses the object of delight, viz., "wealth." But in the preceding phrase, "of the age" identifies the sources of "the anxieties," not their object; and the following construction, "the lusts for (περί) everything else," differs. So we should take wealth as the source of ἀπάτη and use "deceitfulness" to translate the term, as it is most probably to be translated everywhere else in the NT (Matt 13:22; Eph 4:22; Col 2:8; 2 Thess 2:10; Heb 3:13; 2 Pet 2:13). In Hellenistic Greek οἵτινες may be the equivalent of the simple οἵ, "who." But Mark often uses the simple relative (eighty-six times), the compound form only seldom (five times). And where he does use the compound form, it easily has the emphatic force, "who are [or 'is'] such that" (see also 8:34 v.l.; 9:1; 12:18; 15:7; cf. 6:23).

In 14:66-72 Peter ("Stone") will exemplify the explanation of the rocky soil (though in 8:33, where Jesus will call him "Satan," Peter will not be acting as Satan acts in 4:15). On the other hand, it may go too far to adopt the suggestion of M. A. Tolbert (*Sowing the Gospel* 145-46, 154-56) that vv 16-17 give a religious explanation of the otherwise unexplained new name "Peter" (3:16). That the paired new name "Boanerges" (3:17) gets no such explanation makes this suggestion at least questionable. To be sure, Mark translated "Boanerges" with "Sons of Thunder," but only because "Boanerges" is Aramaic in contrast with "Peter," which he did not translate because its being Greek eliminated any need for translation; and the translation of "Boanerges" is not a religious explanation. The forbidding of the strange exorcist will not count as such an explanation, because John's "we" (9:38) will include the rest of the Twelve (9:35), not just James the other one of the "Sons of Thunder." Nor will James' and John's request for seats at the right and left of Jesus provide a religious explanation of "Boanerges"; for Mark will identify James and John as "the sons of Zebedee," not as "the Sons of Thunder," and the request will contain no obviously thunderous element (10:35; see the comments on 3:16-17 concerning Mark's sole interest in the authority that Jesus displayed in giving new names).

The suggestion of B. Gerhardsson (*Ethos* 38-39) that in accordance with Deut 6:4-5 thirtyfold means loving God with all your heart, sixtyfold with all your possessions, and a hundredfold with your very life (i.e. to the point of martyrdom) not only fails to have a solid basis in the text but also runs aground on the contrastive kinds of bad soil, where the thorny soil of worldly cares and wealth ought to come second as a contrast with the sixtyfold of loving God with all your possessions and where the rocky soil of affliction and persecution ought to come third as a contrast with the hundredfold of loving God to the point of sacrificing life itself. Similarly, the three nets of Belial in CD 4:15-18 (whoredom, wealth, and conveying uncleanness to the sanctuary) do not correspond very well to the three bad kinds of soil.

Usually, Mark's redaction of an already redacted pre-Marcan collection of parables (if not of their original dominical form) is seen in the addition of v 9 to the parable and therefore also in the introductory command to hear (v 3a); in the sower's "going out" to sow (v 3b; cf. 1:38); in the supposedly redundant "where it did not have much soil" (v 5), "and on account of not having root it withered" (v 6), and "was bearing" (v 9); in the Marcan favorite "immediately" (vv 5, 15, 16); in the dual phrase "coming up and growing" (v 8); in v 17ab, the omission of which would leave a good connection between vv 16 and 17c; in "on account of the word" (v 17c; cf. 8:35; 10:29); and in the generalizing "and the lusts for everything else" (v 19). Perhaps so, but we scarcely know enough to deny that Jesus told the parable to emphasize correct hearing, that he saw his own going out to preach in the sower's going out to sow, that he was capable of redundancy (which characterizes all oral speech), that the Christian technical use of "the word" derived from his own use of it, and that he generalized from particulars. The strongest case for Marcan or pre-Marcan redaction can be built in v 17, because disciples were not yet suffering "affliction and persecution on account of the word" at the time Jesus spoke the parable. But we need to bear in mind the possibilities that he foresaw such suffering for his disciples along with his own sufferings (H. Riesenfeld, *Gospel Tradition* 156-57) and that the present tense in the explanation of the parable is customary, representing what "may be reasonably expected to occur" (H. E. Dana and J. R. Mantey, *Manual Grammar* 183) rather than what is actually going on at the time Jesus speaks. If we were to regard rootlessness in the interpretation as inauthentic (v 17) and as fostering a Marcan or pre-Marcan redactional addition to vv 5-6 of immediate springing up for lack of deep soil and of withering for lack of root, the question would arise: What prompted the fabrication of rootlessness in the interpretation? If the answer is supplied by rockiness in the original version of the parable, then we need to ask why the teller of the parable may not have rootlessness in mind? The structural arguments of R. Cameron (*Sayings Traditions* 25-27) and others for redactional additions in the corresponding part of the parable (vv 5-6) rest on the presupposition that textual tidiness, balance, and smoothness (as, e.g., in a reconstructed triadism) imply originality, and the lack thereof, unoriginality. The opposite is at least as likely to be true (cf. the text critical principle that greater smoothness bespeaks unoriginality).

In contrast with the parable, the explanation displays much hypotaxis. Πρόσκαιροι, "temporary," is said to have no Aramaic equivalent; and the changes of tense in the explanation make sense only in Greek (see H.-J. Klauck, *Allegorie* 200-209; H.-W. Kuhn, *Ältere Sammlungen* 144; J. Dupont, *Études* 236-58, esp. 248-51; J. Jeremias, *Parables* 77-79). H. Räisänen (*Parabeltheorie* 72-73), P. B. Payne (in *Gospel Perspectives* 1. 177-81), and M. Krämer (in *Theologie und Leben* 41-43) correct the usual appeal to later Christian vocabulary in the explanation, however; and we may suspect the Graecizing of Semitic tradition as easily as wholesale invention of the explanation. Moreover, the absence of Semitisms may not be so complete as is usually thought. Πρόσκαιροι may go back to קצר (Aramaic) or זבנא (Syriac). The awkward juxtaposition of seed-as-word and seed-as-people possibly derives from an Aramaic substratum (Payne, op. cit. 172-77). The occurrence of two adversative καί's close to each other at the beginnings of vv 17a and 19, the frequency of redundant definite articles in vv 15-16, 18, 20, and the threefold ἔν in v 20 all favor an Aramaic substratum. The absolute use of τοῦ αἰῶνος, "of the age" (v 19), appears only here in the NT but recalls *2 Apoc. Bar.* 54:21; 69:4; 83:7. And τὰ λοιπά (v 19) looks like a literalistic translation of the Aramaic יתר, which has to do with "excess, superfluity" as well as with "leftovers" (F. Zimmermann, *Aramaic Origin* 87). A mistaking of שְׂאָר, flesh" (producing "lusts of the flesh"), for שְׁאָר, "remaining" (so H. Sahlin in *ST* 24 [1970] 104-6), seems less likely. Hortatory application of the explanation makes it only natural that the explanation should undergo heavier Graecizing than did the parable. R. W. Funk (in *God's Christ and His People* 43-50) holds that even the narrative *parables* were composed in Greek, not in Aramaic, and that Jesus himself may have spoken them in Greek.

R. A. Guelich (1. 218) finds most persuasive against authenticity the argument that the present interpretation changes the basic structure of the parable from a contrast between three unproductive seeds and three productive ones to a contrast between three groups of unproductive hearers and one group of productive ones. But "those" amalgamates the productive hearers no more than "others" amalgamated the three productive seeds, and "one . . . one . . . one" distinguishes the three productive hearers just as much as "one . . . one . . . one" distinguished the three productive seeds. The contrast remains as balanced in the interpretation as in the parable.

B. Gerhardsson (*Tradition and Transmission* 37) notes that ancient texts, oral as well as written and especially those of the type *mashal*, were often accompanied by an original commentary; and E. E. Lemcio (in *JTS* ns 29 [1978] 323-38) notes that most of vv 3-20 follows a long-established pattern of dialogue: (1) ambiguity (vv 3-8); (2) incomprehension (v 10); (3) surprised or critical rejoinder (v 13); and (4) explanation (vv 14-20). The strong emphasis on esoteric teaching among rabbis (J. Jeremias, *Jerusalem* 237-42) and in the QL (1QS 4:6; 8:11-12; 9:17, 21-22; 10:24-25; see also Josephus *J.W.* 2.8.7 §141; Pl. *Tht.* 152C) gives a historically credible framework for private explanation on Jesus' part. Christians' "going public" with the mysteries of the gospel (see esp. Paul and cf. the Prologue of Sirach) disfavors our finding the source of private explanations in the church rather than in Jesus' ministry. He wanted his disciples to avoid falling away through failure to take immediate action, through desire to avoid persecution, and through worldly concerns (cf. W. L. Lane 161-63; H. Riesenfeld, *Gospel Tradition* 156-57). J. W. Bowker (in *JTS* ns 25 [1974] 300-317) and C. A. Evans (in *RB* 88 [1981] 234-35 and in *CBQ* 47 [1985] 464-68) argue that the "holy seed" spared by God in Isa 6:13 links with the seed-like word of God in Isa 55:10-11 to provide both the basis of the parable and of its explanation and the hinge between them by way of Isa 6:9-10, quoted in Mark 4:12. But Isa 55:10-11 compares the word of God, not to seed, but to rain and snow that produce seed for the sower (see G. Lohfink in *À cause de l'Évangile* 216). As we have seen in the comments, vv 14-20 do not merely explain the parable point by point. They develop the parable by means of additions, subtractions, and the like as the explanation progresses, just as in the vision of Ezek 37:1-10 the dry bones lie strewn about a valley unburied but the explanation in Ezek 37:11-14 makes the people of Israel, whom the bones represent, come out of graves. It is natural for hearers to be identified with the seed that they take in and respond to (cf. W. Schmithals 232). Therefore the identification offers no support for regarding the explanation as secondary.

On the other hand, G. Lohfink (in *À cause de l'Évangile* 223-28) argues that the identification of the seed with the word stems from Greek rather than old Oriental thinking (cf. the non-Jewish references cited above) and that therefore the parable originally dealt with the restoration of Israel as God's planting. But 4 Ezra 9:31, a Jewish document of the NT era, compares the words of the Law to sown seed. There is nothing about the comparison that would make it distinctively Greek or unsuitable to old Oriental thinking. The comparison might arise easily and independently in any culture characterized by seed-sowing and teaching. Besides, Palestine was Hellenized by Jesus' time. The distinction in the parable between different kinds of soil does not sit well with the collectivity of Israel as God's planting in the OT. The first three kinds of soil do not present merely intermediate threats overcome by final success (so Lohfink). They present ultimate failures and therefore point to different individual responses to the word about the kingdom. The differentiating between thirtyfold, sixtyfold, and a hundredfold likewise points to individual differences of response.

See the notes on 3:27 against fear of allegory. The argument that an allegorical interpretation like the present one could have come into existence only after the parable of vv 3-9 had been reduced to writing so as to allow piecemeal scrutiny and parenetic application (so P. Sellew in *NTS* 36 [1990] 235 with dependence on A. N. Wilder) lacks conviction. For it seems doubtful that the allegorical interpretation in Judg 9:16-20 did not come into existence till after the parable in vv 7-15 had been reduced to writing, or that the allegorical interpretation in Isa 5:7ff. did not come into existence till after the parable in vv 1-6 had been reduced to writing (to take but two contrary examples). The present allegorical interpretation does not go so far as to identify the sower with Jesus, as might be expected in a later Christian fabrication.

It has often been said that the whole section vv 1-34 and especially the present parable aim to assure discouraged disciples of the final success of God's rule despite temporary hindrances (see J. H. Ropes, *Synoptic Gospels* 11-12, 18-19; R. H. Lightfoot, *Gospel Message* 40; H.-W. Kuhn, *Ältere Sammlungen* 122-27, and many others). But the fruit-bearing in the parable of the seeds represents the life of discipleship, not the harvest of the consummation. The hiddenness in the later parable of the lamp will not be the same as hindrance; and in fact the lamp will *not* be hidden, even at first. The parable of the measure will be more minatory than assuring. Neither the growing seed nor the mustard seed that becomes large will suffer any hindrance. Nor is there any sign of discouragement on the part of the present sower because three of his seeds do not produce, on the part of the later man because of the time it takes for his seed to turn into a crop, or on the part of the planter because of the smallness of his mustard seed — as we would expect if encouragement were the aim. Mystification will come into v 27, but discouragement will not. And the planter will not even appear in vv 30-32; so his psychological state will not come under treatment.

Though alone the explanation of the parable concerning the seeds "is more descriptive than prescriptive" (R. A. Guelich 1. 224), the commands to hear which framed this parable combine with the frequent references in its explanation to hearing the word, including hearing it in wrong ways, to make the parable hortatory; and we are in no position to dress the parable in an older suit of clothing (see H. Anderson 128-29 for a summary of different understandings of the original meaning, to which understandings add that of D. E. Oakman [*Economic Questions* 103-9], who, overlooking the absence of any reference to food or to the eating of it, says that the parable teaches eschatological divine providence in the giving of food despite difficulties). It is not a question of soil changing itself, but of human beings making sure by the way they hear that they are good soil rather than bad (cf. 1 Thess 3:5). H.-W. Kuhn (*Ältere Sammlungen* 117-19) identifies apocalyptic elements in "Satan" (v 15), "affliction" (v 17), "the age" (v 19), and the dualism of those who do not bear fruit (outsiders) versus those who do (insiders). Then he argues against a hortatory purpose by noting that apocalyptic literature does not contain exhortation to outsiders. But the explanation of the parable is addressed to insiders, so that it can carry a hortatory point without contradicting apocalyptic in the least. And are the elements which Kuhn identifies as apocalyptic necessarily so? If they are, consistency would demand that John 15:1-8 also count as apocalyptic because of its dualism with respect to those who bear fruit and those who do not! A concordance will turn up many equally unlikely examples.

4:21-23 *(Matt 5:15; 10:26; 11:15; 13:43; Luke 8:16-17; 11:33; 12:2)* Though the editorial introduction, "And he was saying to them," does not necessarily indicate the importation of material from another setting, it does call attention to the newness of the next item (see the notes on vv 1-34 and the comments on 2:27; 4:9). Since Mark advanced vv 10-20 chronologically (see the comments on vv 10-12) and now shifts from interpretation, given only to the disciples, back to parables, spoken to the huge crowd (vv 1-2, 10-12, 13ff., 33-34), Jesus is speaking again to the huge crowd. In the question, "The lamp doesn't come in order that it may be put under the peck-measure or under the couch, does it?" μήτι calls for the answer, "No." In the question, "[The lamp comes] in order that it may be put on the lampstand, doesn't it?" οὐχ calls for the answer, "Yes." The definite articles that accompany each of the nouns may reflect the emphatic state of nouns in underlying Aramaic (for an Aramaic noun may occur in the emphatic state even where the noun is indefinite in meaning) or may represent the deictic use of the definite article in Greek (E. C. Maloney, *Semitic Interference* 104-9). Therefore the definite article with "lamp" does not argue strongly for a portrayal of Jesus as "*the* lamp" (cf. Rev 21:23). Likewise, though we may think it odd that the lamp "comes," the Greek verb ἔρχεται may reflect the Aramaic verb אתא, "come," which in the ittaphal means to be caused to come, i.e. to be brought (cf. W. C. Allen in *ExpTim* 13 [1901-2] 30; J. Jeremias, *Abba* 100); and even in Greek uninfluenced by Aramaic, ἔρχομαι sometimes occurs in the sense "be brought" (BAGD s.v. I1cβ). Since light may symbolize teaching along with a teacher (cf. H. Conzelmann in *TDNT* 9. 344; J. Marcus, *Mystery* 141-42) and since the Marcan context has to do with Jesus and his teaching, the coming of the lamp likewise has to do with Jesus and his teaching (cf. Luke 11:33, where the context favors an application to "the person and preaching of Jesus as the light" [J. A. Fitzmyer, *Luke* 939], and Matt 5:15, where the application is transferred from Jesus to the doxological good works of his disciples). The parable of the lamp does not speak of Jesus' teaching the huge crowd in parables, however; for his purpose in that exercise was obscuration, to which the coming of a lamp to be put under a peck-measure or a couch *would* correspond, whereas the lamp comes to be put on a lampstand, i.e. on display. Hence, the parable of the lamp speaks of Jesus' explaining the parables to the disciples, as he has just done in vv 14-20.

Generally speaking, people do not hide things for the purpose of revealing them; they hide them to keep them from being revealed. Therefore, we might take ἵνα in v 22 (bis) as indicating result rather than purpose and as referring to the exposure of all hidden things at the last judgment, as in Luke 12:2-3. Correspondingly, we might take ἵνα in v 21 (bis) as indicating result rather than purpose and interpret the coming of the lamp and its being put on the lampstand as a figure for the exposure of hidden things at the last judgment. Then, however, vv 21-22 would not relate very well to the preceding context, which has to do with present responses to Jesus' teaching, not with future judgment. Apparently Mark has imported the sayings into a setting where the original judgmental meaning of at least the saying on hiddenness and manifestation is not at home (cf. a similar change in Matt 10:26-27 [R. H. Gundry, *Matthew* 196], whereas Luke 8:16-17 follows Mark). To accommodate the new setting of parables, whose explanation would not be well described by the apocalyptic language of revelation, Mark shifts from that language to the ordinary language of manifestation.

As the parable of the lamp naturally carried on the theme of Jesus' teaching, so in its Marcan setting the saying about hiddenness and manifestation naturally means that nothing is hidden in a parable spoken to the huge crowd that will not be made manifest to Jesus' disciples in a private explanation. This pattern reflects vv 10-20 and anticipates vv 33-34. Therefore we may keep the full purposive force of each ἵνα in vv 21-22: Jesus hides truth in parables from outsiders "in order that" he may reveal it to insiders. This purpose is the reason why he used figurative language not only in vv 3b-8 but also in v 21 (v 22 begins with γάρ, "for") and continues to use it through v 32. Numerous features of the text emphasize the triumph of manifestation over hiddenness, i.e. of private explanation over public obscuration: (1) the unrealism of a lamp's coming to be put under a peck-measure, which would extinguish the lamp, or under a bed, which the lamp would set on fire; (2) the rhetorical questioning; (3) the ellipsis of the lamp's coming in the first rhetorical question so as to focus attention on the purpose of putting the lamp on the lampstand; (4) the doubling of the rhetorical questioning; (5) the antithetic parallelism in the resultant rhetorical questions; (6) the synonymous parallelism in the following pair of declarations; (7) the embedding of a ἵνα-clause in each of the rhetorical questions and in each of the declarations; (8) the strength of the adversative ἀλλ', "but," introducing the last ἵνα-clause; (9) the inclusion formed by ἔρχεται and ἔλθη for "come"; (10) the repetition of τεθῇ, "it might be put"; (11) the placement of ὑπὸ τὸν μόδιον, "under the peck-measure," ahead of its τεθῇ; (12) the placement of ἐπὶ τὴν λυχνίαν, "on the lampstand," ahead of its τεθῇ; and (13) the cognateness of λύχνος and λυχνίαν, "lamp" and "lampstand." Despite saying that Jesus "was explaining all things to his disciples in private" (v 34), Mark feels no need to record a further explanation here, because the explanation of the parables in general (vv 11-12) and that of the parable of the seeds in particular (vv 13-20) have already explained it (cf. the suggestion in the question at v 13, "If you don't understand this parable, then how will you understand any of the parables?" that understanding the parable of the seeds also brings an understanding of the other parables collected here). Furthermore, vv 33-34 will editorially explain the present parable in the same way.

The command to hear in v 23 relates the parable of the lamp to the parable of the seeds and its explanation. The change from the relative construction, "he who has ears to hear" (v 9), to the conditional construction, "if anyone has ears to hear," differs from all other NT parallels (Matt 11:15; 13:43; Luke 14:35; Rev 2:7, 11, 17, 29; 3:6, 13, 22) and anticipates the limit on ability to hear that v 33 will express. This anticipation will lead to the warning in v 24b. But "if" does not distinguish people who have ears (insiders) from those who do not (outsiders). Even outsiders have ears; they just do not understand what they hear with them (vv 11-12, 13-19). Neither do the insiders (v 13). But since they hear in the right way by allowing the word to penetrate them immediately, by letting it go deep, and by keeping it free from worldly competition, Jesus will explain the word to them. As often, "if" means "since": since a person has ears for hearing, let that person use them for their intended purpose. But though hearing is necessary, it is not sufficient. So a warning to hear in the right way will follow the present exhortation simply to hear (see v 24ab). Yet even hearing in the right way is not equivalent to understanding the parables (again see v 13). *That* takes Jesus' private explanations. What right hearing does do, however, is to guarantee the granting of those explanations. See the comments on v 3 for the present tense of the imperative ἀκουέτω, "let him hear."

NOTES

J. Marcus (*Mystery* 130-36) summarizes the arguments for Mark's redaction of pre-Q tradition in vv 21-22. We might think that Mark or someone before him added "or under the couch," but not only does Luke 8:16 share it with Mark. The dual expression in a non-Marcan context at Luke 11:33, though not mentioning a couch, seems to reflect the duality of a peck-measure and a couch in Q as well as in Mark.

To extinguish a lamp, you put a peck-measure over it; you do not put it under a peck-measure (though doing so would extinguish it). Therefore, in accord with putting a lamp under a couch (which would not extinguish the lamp) and in accord with v 22, the point of putting the lamp under the peck-measure has to do with hiding the lamp, not with extinguishing it (for a summary of more extensive discussion on this matter, see R. A. Guelich 1. 229).

A. Dupont-Sommer (in *Mélanges Syriens offerts à Monsieur René Dussaud* 2. 789-92) thinks that ὑπὸ τὸν μόδιον does not mean "under the peck-measure," but "under the grain-container"; for a grain-container stands 3-4 feet tall whereas a peck-measure is too small to put a lamp under. But the height of the open space beneath a couch corresponds more closely to the height of a peck-measure than to the 3-4 feet of a grain-container; and μόδιος seems not to be used for a grain-container, but regularly to mean a peck-measure (cf. G. Schneider in *ZNW* 61 [1970] 189-90, n. 29). Besides, a lamp such as one sets on a lampstand does not take 3-4 feet of height (see K. Galling in *ZDPV* 46 [1923] 1-50 on lamps and lampstands). J. Carmignac (in *ASTI* 7 [1968-69] 70) suggests a wordplay between אֵיפָה, "ephah," and אֵיכָה, "is it?" But an ephah is about three times larger than a peck.

The suggestion that originally the lamp-saying meant that Jesus' mission prevented him from hiding to save himself (J. Jeremias, *Parables* 120-21; E. Schweizer 99) gets some weak support from the reference to Jonah's ministry, which parallels that of Jesus, just before Luke 11:33. But there, the connection with the following reference to the eye as "the lamp of the body" seems much closer. If Mark knew a form of the lamp-saying like the forms in Matthew and Luke, we might expect him to have kept the reference to the lamp's shining for the ones in the house (so Matthew) or for the ones entering it (so Luke). For that would harmonize with his emphasis on the privileged insiders, whom he sometimes portrays as inside a house with Jesus (see, e.g., 3:20-35). C. E. Carlston (*Parables* 151-53) surveys various interpretations of the parable concerning the lamp.

Verse 22 rests on a universal proverb that nothing can remain forever hidden: sooner or later, truth will out. The added τι, "anything," in the v.l. represented by ℵ A C L Δ 0133 33 892 1010 1241 *pm* lat sy gives back the general meaning that the proverb originally had (as in Matt 10:26 par. Luke 12:2). But we should prefer the omission of τι as more difficult, more liable to be changed, better attested by B D K W Θ *f*[1,13] 28 565 700 *pm* it co, and supported by the parallel Luke 8:17. The omission leaves "the lamp" of v 21 to be the contextual subject of the verbs in v 22: the lamp is not hidden except that it might be made manifest, and so on. In other words, the parables are not meant to remain obscure to the disciples, but are meant to be explained to them just as a lamp comes to be put on a lampstand.

Mark's importing the proverb behind v 22 into a setting of parables and revising the proverb accordingly does not make the resultant saying paradoxical so as to raise the question why you hide something if your purpose is to make it manifest. Rather, the importation and revision add significance to the hiddenness. In the original proverb, hiddenness was only the necessary backdrop for manifestation. Now it refers to the judgmental hiddenness of these parables (as to their meaning) from outsiders. But as we have already learned from vv 10-12, 13-20 and will learn again from vv 33-34, Jesus hides the mystery of God's rule in these parables only to bring it out into the open through his explanations to insiders, the disciples. The immediacy of those explanations rules out a salvation historical interpretation according to which his ministry was a riddle at the time and became manifest in its meaning only after his death and resurrection. Besides, the lamp that comes is not hidden even for a short while. Mark's stressing that Jesus limited his explanations to the disciples means that Mark does not want the manifestation of the hidden to be understood as the universal proclamation of the gospel. For that thought other passages are more appropriate. Whereas vv 10-12 emphasized the judgmental hiddenness of meaning from outsiders, v 22 unites with v 21 to emphasize the explanations of meaning with which Jesus privileges his disciples. The parallel with vv 10-12 remains, nonetheless; and just as those verses were followed by a section on how to hear (vv 13-20), so also vv 24-25 follow up vv 21-23 with a new section on how to hear. The undeniably hortatory cast of the new section makes this parallel support our having taken the explanation in vv 13-20 as hortatory (if such a confirmation be needed after the command to hear at the opening and closing of the parable of the seeds [vv 3, 9]).

The generality of the proverb underlying v 22 casts some doubt on the possibility of a divine passive in φανερωθῇ, "God will make [it] manifest," though in Matt 10:26 par. Luke 12:2 we may think of a divine passive in the application of the proverb to the last judgment. Here in Mark, it is Jesus rather than God who makes manifest the meaning of the parables through his explanations.

The view that vv 21-22 put a temporal limit on Jesus' obscuring the truth in parables pays insufficient attention to the context. There is nothing of a contrast between obscurative parables here and plain speech at some point in the future; rather, the contrast lies between obscurative parables and clarifying explanations, both of which Jesus speaks on the present occasion. See H. Räisänen, *Parabeltheorie* 79-80, against W. Wrede's generalization of 9:9, which properly refers only to the Transfiguration. Wrede tries to postpone till after Jesus' resurrection the revelation of a messianic secret that supposedly resides in the parables (contrast 14:62, where such a revelation takes place before the Resurrection).

A deliberate assimilation to the ἵνα in vv 11-12 would eliminate the need, though not the possibility, of seeing an accidentally mistranslated Aramaic relative pronoun ‏ד‎ behind the two ἵνα's of v 22 (against E. Lohmeyer 84, 86; C. F. Burney, *Aramaic Origin* 75-76; cf. M. Black, *Aramaic Approach* 76-77). According to the theory of mistranslation, the original meaning was "except that which will be revealed" (cf. the relative pronouns in Matt 10:26 par. Luke 8:17). Similarly, the reminiscence eliminates the need, though not the possibility, of seeing behind Mark's subjunctive of purpose and Luke's and Matthew's simple future tense an Aramaic imperfect (so M. Wilcox in *TLZ* 110 [1985] 101).

The synonymous parallelism in v 22 and the exceptive and adversative meanings of a possibly underlying אלא (Aramaic) make doubtful any significant distinction between ἐστιν, "is," and ἐγένετο, "became," and between ἐὰν μὴ ἵνα, "except that," and ἀλλ' ἵνα, "but that" (against H. B. Swete 82; see the discussion by V. Taylor 263 with references to earlier literature; also M. Black, *Aramaic Approach* 113-14; E. C. Maloney, *Semitic Interference* 93-99, esp. 98-99). Though ἐστιν is present tense and ἐγένετο aorist, what "has become" hidden "is" hidden. The interpretation of A. Stock (*Call* 100-101) that the parables paradoxically manifest the truth by hiding it overlooks the contrastive setting of the lamp on the lampstand — just the opposite of hiding — which is part of what v 22 is supposed to explain. T. A. Burkill (*Mysterious Revelation* 110-11) says that reading v 21 with v 22 leads to the implication that the lamp is hidden for a limited period of time. But the implied answers to the questions in v 21 forestall such an implication and demand that v 22 refer to immediate exposure (as indeed Jesus immediately explains his parables to the disciples).

Since in Mark the hiding describes putting a lamp under a peck-measure or under a couch, it hardly alludes to hiding seed in soil in order that the seed may come out into the open as a plant growing above ground (so R. Pesch 1. 250). Hence, the parable does not encourage evangelism by promising fruit. Nor did Jesus mean to discourage his followers from keeping his message secret among themselves. That meaning would require a reversal of the wording in v 22, as follows: "for nothing is made manifest in order that it may be hidden, nor does anything come out into the open in order that it may be secret." The command to hear in v 23 makes vv 21-22 a parable about people's hearing the word, not about disciples' proclaiming it.

The lack of a parallel to v 23 after Luke 8:17 may arise out of the added words peculiar to Luke 8:16: "in order that those who enter may see the light." That is to say, the added words stress seeing rather than hearing and therefore may lead Luke to omit as inappropriate the Marcan exhortation to hear. Or Luke may omit the exhortation as superfluous in view of the immediately following command to "watch out how you hear," perhaps also in view of an intention to use the exhortation to hear in 14:35 (see R. H. Gundry, *Matthew* 261, on Matthew's procedure). Otherwise, Luke knows and follows a non-Marcan tradition lacking the exhortation; and Mark or his source imports the exhortation from a different setting or fabricates it out of v 9 to link the parable of the lamp with the parable of the seeds, which has already talked about hearing, and perhaps also to link the parable of the lamp with the immediately following command to "watch out how you hear" (unless Mark will import that command, too, or fabricate it out of v 12ab [cf. J. Dupont, *Études* 429] — but Luke does have a parallel to the command). It is possible, then, either that Jesus spoke the exhortation to hear in v 23 at the time he spoke the sayings in vv 21-22 or that the exhortation first came together with those sayings in pre-Marcan tradition or in the composition of Mark itself. The exhortation has protean capabilities of application; therefore its use in other settings leaves open the possibilities of multiple use by Jesus and of single use by him followed by multiple use on the part of others. At least we can say with confidence that Mark uses the exhortation to hear for emphasis on Jesus' didactic authority. This emphasis contributes to Mark's omitting the individual explanations of each parable (after that of the sower) even though he refers to them (v 34): he is more interested in the authority of Jesus' teaching than in its content, except as that content highlights the authority.

Since hearing does not equate with understanding (see vv 12b, 15, 16, 18), the command to hear in v 23 does not imply that Jesus meant these parables to be understood by everybody. Understanding depends on his explanations of the parables, and he explains them only to those who hear well — hence, the following warning on *how* to hear (v 24ab). See J. M. Robinson, *Problem* 44, for a long list of references to passages where the command to hear appears. To say that hearing and seeing are Marcan themes is not to decide that he makes them up. Their prominence may be due to the traditions that Mark uses rather than to his creativity.

4:24-25 *(Matt 7:2; 13:12; 25:29; Luke 6:38; 8:18; 19:26)* Again Mark calls attention to the newness of the next item by using the introduction, "And he was saying to them" (see the comments on 2:27; 4:9, 21-23 and cf. the introductory notes on 4:1-34) and follows with a parable consisting of a figurative saying plus a supportive statement beginning with γάǫ, "for." This time, however, an imperative about hearing comes before the parable rather than afterwards. By standing back to back, the imperatives clamp the two parables together. Furthermore, τὸν μόδιον in the first parable (vv 21-23) meant a vessel containing a peck and therefore used to measure out that amount. This meaning probably led to the present parable about measuring, whether in Jesus' mind and message or in those of a later oral traditioner or scribal redactor is hard to say, since in principle Mark rather than Q (or Luke or Matthew) may preserve the original context. The combination of βλέπετε, an emphatic present imperative meaning "watch out" (cf. the notes on 1:3), and τί ἀκούετε, "how you hear," makes a wordplay. In it, Jesus commands people to use their sense of sight to help their sense of hearing (cf. v 3). Again his didactic authority receives emphasis. Thus "the measure with which you measure" refers to the ways in which people hear his parabolic word. "It will be measured to you" refers to the treatment of hearers according to their ways of hearing. Asyndeton at the start of the statement about measuring highlights the importance of the way people hear. "And it will be added to you" takes up first the good example of people who hear well and promises to such people the adding of an explanation to the parable. This clause is missing in the parallels Matt 7:2; Luke 6:38 and, by parallel influence or homoioteleuton, in a Marcan v.l. Mark's shifting the saying, which looks like another proverb, from a context of treating others generously (so Luke and Matthew) to one of hearing parables leads him to append the clause as an indication that things do not stop with a favorable measurement of the quality of hearing: that kind of measurement brings the addition of explanations. Thus the appended clause anticipatively reinterprets "it will be given to him" in v 25a, which originally had to do with reward at the last judgment. For the appended clause, did Mark draw on the tradition behind Matt 6:33 par. Luke 12:31, where the added things are food and clothing (cf. J. Lambrecht in *L'Évangile selon Marc* 290)?

Verse 25a supports the promise in v 24cd with what looks like an economic truism, yet again probably proverbial: "For the person who has — it will be given to him" (cf. v 11). The rich get richer. Just as it takes money to make money, it takes a good hearing of these parables to get an added explanation of them (cf. Prov 1:5; 9:9; Dan 2:20-22; 4 Ezra 7:25; Str-B 1. 660-62; G. Lindeskog in *ST* 4 (1950) 149; J. Marcus, *Mystery* 154-56). The continuation of the apparent truism brings in the person who hears poorly: "and the person who does not have — even what he has will be taken away from him" (v 25b). The poor get poorer. If you do not have money enough to invest, you will lose what little money you do have by spending it on necessities (cf. *Gos. Thom.* 41). Similarly, the person who does not hear parabolic speech in the right way will lose the parable in the sense of missing out on its explanation (cf. the use of αἴρω, "take away," both here and in v 15, where it referred to Satan's taking away the word). But to describe the saying as an economic truism probably foists on it a modern capitalistic interpretation full of challenge. We might better describe it as a sociological truism full of resignation, for in ancient oriental society (as in parts of modern oriental society) the already rich are plied with gifts while the last penny is extracted from the destitute (M.-J. Lagrange 114). Whether economic or sociological, the effect is the same; and Jesus' use of the truism is more challenging than resigned. At the beginning of each member of the truism, casus pendens plus an unemphatic resumptive pronoun probably displays Semitic interference (E. C. Maloney, *Semitic Interference* 88-90) and underlines the fatefulness of having and not having.

So the two parables in vv 21-25 have to do with hearing the parables of Jesus just as the parable of the seeds and its interpretation had to do with this same topic. As before, the necessity of good listening plays up the authority of the speaker, Jesus. And as before, the mystery turns out to be that God's rule is being established with persuasion, not force, with the word, not weaponry. The understanding of this mystery is what is taken away from outsiders but added to insiders. These points gain emphasis from the reciprocal parallelism in v 24c that features a tripling of the vocabulary of measurement in the clause ἐν ᾧ μέτρῳ μετρεῖτε μετρηθήσεται ὑμῖν, "with the measure with which you measure it will be measured to you," from the antithetic parallelism in v 25, from the tripling of ἔχει, "has," in v 25, from the ascensive καί, "even," before the last ἔχει in v 25b, and from the assonance of four verbs ending in -θήσεται throughout vv 24cd-25.

NOTES

Βλέπετε τί ἀκούετε hardly means, "Pay attention to what you hear" (cf. *Mek.* Exod 15:26), as though τί were an accusative of direct object (so J. Wellhausen [2. Aufl.] 33); for in commands βλέπετε usually has the warning connotation of "watch out, beware" (as, e.g., in 8:15; 12:38; 13:5, 9, 23, 33); and in the non-commanding statement of v 12 the verb occurred for poor seeing, not for the good seeing that would be commanded here if τί were an accusative of direct object. Instead, we should take τί as an adverbial accusative, "how" (cf. πῶς, "how," in Luke 8:18). See R. H. Gundry, *Matthew* 120-21, 254-58, on the meanings of not judging one another and of final judgment by God in Matthew and Luke, and on the addition of parables to reward true disciples as opposed to false ones with further knowledge because they already understand a little (so Matthew) rather than the addition of explanations to enable disciples as opposed to non-disciples to understand parables that they do not yet understand at all (so Mark).

The second person plural pronouns in v 24 rule out the thought of an eschatological measurement of time, which would promise the arrival of the end at a set time. As with the passive of φανερωθῇ, "be made manifest" (v 22), the passive of verbs in vv 24-25 shifts from a divine passive in the original context of the last judgment to a passive regarding the present actions of Jesus in deciding to whom he will and will not give explanations of his parables. In its literal sense, v 24c means that the very same measuring device that you use in selling your goods to others shall be used when they sell their goods to you (B. Couroyer in *RB* 77 [1970] 366-70). The text critical argument of J. B. Bauer (in *ZNW* 71 [1980] 248-51) for omitting the clause, "and it will be added to you," with D W 565 *pc* b e l sa^ms vg^mss suffers not only from weak external evidence and the strong possibilities of parallel influence and homoioteleuton, but also from Mark's love of duality and emphasis on Jesus' explaining the parables to disciples, both of which are well served by the clause.

The anaphoric αὐτῷ, "to him," in the conditional relative clause of v 25a (so also Matt 13:12; Luke 8:18) is Semitic and therefore more original than the Graecized form that we find in Matt 25:29; Luke 19:26 (K. Beyer, *Semitische Syntax* 1/1. 214). Apparently Mark knows the saying in a form that partly and perhaps fully antedates Q. Because taking away implies possession, the second half of the proverb underlying v 25 applies less naturally to the withholding of explanations from outsiders than the first half applies to the adding of explanations to insiders. But analogies usually break down at one point or another; rarely does a proverb apply fully to a situation. C. E. Carlston (*Parables* 156) sees a principial contradiction between vv 24 and 25: the one who does not have will be given according to what little he does have (v 24), but even this little will be taken away rather than used as a basis of recompense (v 25). The contradiction holds under rules of arithmetic; but real life bends such rules, and the proverbs underlying vv 24-25 reflect the contradictions of real life (see the foregoing comments).

In Matt 25:29; Luke 19:26, having and not having represent good works and the lack thereof. Mark's importation of the saying into its present setting shifts the representation to hearing well and hearing badly. Likewise, the future tense of verbs in both v 24 and v 25 originally pointed to the last judgment (see Matt 7:2; Luke 6:38 for the parallels to v 24), but now point to the explanations which follow parables in the experience of disciples and which do not follow parables in the experience of non-disciples. With the saying on measurement, cf. *Tg. Isa* 27:8 and other literature laid out and discussed by H. P. Rüger in *ZNW* 60 (1969) 174-82.

That the sayings in vv 21-25 can count as Marcan parables despite their lack of narrative is shown by 3:23-27. Therefore we should not regard vv 21-25 as mere comment. The question of V. Taylor (262), "Why should the sayings be grouped so artificially unless the Evangelist was hampered by an existing arrangement?" only pushes the problem one step back. Why should the author of a supposed pre-Marcan collection have grouped the sayings so artificially? Someone is responsible for grouping the sayings thus. Similarity of subject matter unites vv 21 and 22 just as the similarity between being added to and being given more unites vv 24cd and 25. But who is to say whether such unity finds its origin in the original speaker or in a later redactor?

4:26-29 On καὶ ἔλεγεν, "and he was saying," see the first comment on vv 21-23 with further cross-references. Like the parables in vv 21-25, the parable of the growing seed has no explanation, because the explanation of the parable concerning the seeds (vv 13-20) carries over well enough to eliminate the need for another explanation and because Mark has more interest in Jesus' didactic authority than in explanations as such (cf. v 13 and the comments on vv 21-23). Essentially, the present parable rehashes the parable of the seeds by taking over the sowing and fruit-bearing, omitting the bad soils, expanding the description of growth on the good soil, and adding some OT color at the close. "Thus is the rule of God" harks back to "the mystery of the rule of God" in v 11. "As if a man should throw the seed on the soil" points to preaching the word (cf. vv 3, 14). Since only good growth and fruitful harvest occur, there is no thought of contrasting the fates of individual seeds; so Mark switches from the neuter noun σπέρμα/-ατα, implied by ἄλλο (ter) and ἄλλα in vv 3-8, to the masculine noun σπόρος, "sowing" and thus "seed" in a collective sense. So also "the soil" matches the good soil in the parable of the seeds. "The seed" stands before its verb to shift attention from "a man" (see the Greek word order), and again it represents the word about the kingdom. But the man's later ignorance rules out his standing for Jesus the sower-teacher of the seed-word (as implicitly in vv 3-20; against P. Stuhlmacher [*Schriftauslegung* 156-57], who supposes that "a man" goes back to "the Son of man" as a self-designation of Jesus); and the point of the parable switches from the need to hear well to the incomprehensibility of marvelous growth, which is doubly detailed in progressive states, following the order of seed-soil in v 26: (1) "the seed sprouts and becomes long"; (2) "the soil bears fruit, first blade, then ear, then full grain in the ear. And whenever the fruit is ripe . . ." (contrast the single, general phrase, "coming up and growing," in v 8; cf. v 20). By matching the threeness of the man's throwing, sleeping, and rising the threeness of blade, ear, and full grain in the ear highlights the element of progression. The resultant emphasis on growth illustrates the power of the taught word.

The daily round of sleeping at night and rising at day not only provides the passage of time necessary to growth, but also distances the man from the growth; for no tilling or other farmwork comes in view, and "by itself" excludes such efforts. Adding to the sense of distance is the a-b-a'-b' arrangement of "sleeps and rises night and day" and the stair-step arrangement in which (if we bracket out the ὡς-clause, discussed below, as parenthetical) the subject shifts from the man who throws the seed on the soil to the seed which he throws on the soil and then to the soil on which he throws the seed. Similarly, the fruit borne by the soil becomes the subject of being ripe, which then leads to harvest (B. B. Scott, *Hear* 366). So far as we can tell from the parable, the man scarcely deserves to be called a sower or a farmer. He is called neither, in fact. He does not effect the growth. He does not even help it along. He is merely "a man" (ἄνθρωπος), a Semitism for the indefinite "someone" (τις — see E. C. Maloney, *Semitic Inter-ference* 134), who only "throws" seed on the soil (cf. the comments on v 30 with Luke 13:19). In contrast, it was "the sower" who, like Jesus, "went out" for the express purpose of "sowing" (see v 3 with comments). Moreover, the time of harvest is determined by the readiness of the fruit rather than attributed to the decision of the man (see esp. E. Lohmeyer 86-87). As much as possible, the diction deemphasizes the man's contribution. The accent falls rather on "by itself" (αὐτομάτη), which modifies "the soil," takes a first, predicate position in its clause, and elsewhere describes volunteer plants (i.e. those that are not sown — see BAGD s.v. for references). "By itself" goes beyond anything that we found in the parable of the seeds and its explanation, and it gives the reason for the man's ignorance. The ὡς underlying the first word in "how, he himself does not know" has become a point of discussion (see, e.g., A. M. Ambrozic, *Hidden Kingdom* 115-16; H.-J. Klauck, *Allegorie* 218-19; and, among older treatments, E. Loh-meyer 86-87; G. Wohlenberg 137). Most probably, we should think of the way ὡς is used in indirect questions (cf. BAGD s.v. I2d), where it blends together the element of fact and an adverbial element, as required here. In Luke 8:47, for example, ὡς blends together the fact and immediacy of healing; in Luke 23:55 the fact and fashion of the placement of Jesus' body in a tomb (cf. v 53); in Luke 24:35 the fact and occasion of the risen Jesus' manifestation "in the breaking of bread"; in Acts 10:38 the fact and means of his anointing "with Holy Spirit and power"; in 2 Cor 7:15 the fact and manner of Titus's coming "with fear and trembling"; and so on. But the ὡς in Mark 4:27 does not blend together the fact and manner of the man's not knowing; rather, it blends together the fact and manner of the seed's growth as the object of the man's not knowing, just as ὡς-clauses are the objects of stated verbs in the cross-references just cited. We need, then, to recognize an ellipsis after ὡς, but an ellipsis easily filled from the immediately preceding clause, the repetition of which would have been pedantic:

"How [the seed sprouts and becomes long] he himself does not know." Filling the ellipsis makes obvious that a new sentence begins with ὡς. The asyndeton with which it begins, the forward position of the ὡς-clause within it, the assonance and wordplay made by this ὡς in relation to οὕτως ("thus") . . . ὡς ("as if") in v 26, the further asyndeton at the start of the next sentence, which answers the indirect question with αὐτομάτη, "by itself," and the forward position of αὐτομάτη all stress the mystery that in those who hear well God's rule has taken hold through Jesus' teaching. Therefore the crucified Jesus is to be regarded, not as an executed revolutionary, but as a martyred teacher whose teaching proved so authoritative that it had an "automatic" effect (cf. the comments on vv 13-20). Αὐτός, "himself," and the wordplay that it makes with αὐτομάτη stress the man's ignorance. So also does the starting of that ignorance with the very first two evidences of growth (sprouting and becoming long). Similarly, what human being knows how Jesus' teaching effects the rule of God as seen in the fruit of discipleship that Mark has already detailed (1:16-20; 2:13-17; 3:13-19, 31-35; 4:10-12) and will return to right after the present parable (4:36)?

As in the parable of the seeds and its explanation, fruit-bearing stands for discipleship. Καρποφορέω harks back to the explanation in v 20, where it occurred in this sense, and needs no further explanation here (see the comments on v 20). The four stages of growth — blade, ear, full grain in the ear, and ripeness — replace the four kinds of soil in the parable of the seeds to underscore, not good hearing, but the unknown power by which the word of the kingdom achieves a happy result in people who hear well. This emphasis gains from the switch to the indicative mood, which is stronger than the subjunctive mood used five times in vv 26-27, and comes out with great clarity in the expansion of the fourth stage: "but whenever the fruit is ripe, immediately he sends the sickle, because the harvest has arrived" (v 29). The adversative δέ, "but," the "whenever" of the fruit's ripeness, the immediacy of the sickle's being thrust in, and the arrival of harvest highlight the shift from growth to fruit but do not look forward to the future consummation. Rather, they emphasize the actuality of present discipleship, which the fruit represents (cf. Isa 5:2, 4 with 7; contrast the failures of growth and maturation in Mark 4:4-7, 15-19). Ὅταν, "whenever," has already appeared in the explanation of the parable concerning the seeds (vv 15, 16; cf. also vv 31, 32). Καρπός, "fruit," has already appeared in that same parable (vv 7, 8). And εὐθύς, "immediately," has already appeared in vv 5, 15, 16, 17. These links show again that this parable needs no further explanation. Like all three earlier parables in chap. 4, then, the present one deals with the heard word. The parable of the seeds stressed different ways of hearing it. The parable of the lamp stressed the purpose of manifestation to those who hear well. The parable of the measure stressed the means of manifestation, i.e. the adding of explanations to parables for those who hear well. Now the parable of the growing seed stresses the marvelous process of fruition resulting from the well heard and consequently explained word. The incomprehensibility of this process forms the centerpiece in an alternating rhythm that starts with a man, leaves him, returns to him, leaves him again, and ends with him: (a) a man throws . . . sleeps . . . and rises . . . ;

(b) the seed sprouts and grows long; (c) the man does not know how; (b') the earth bears fruit by itself; (a') the man sends the sickle whenever the fruit is ripe, because the harvest has arrived.

Since the parable has to do with the heard and explained word, the odd use of ἀποστέλλει for "sending" the sickle — i.e. thrusting it in — may echo Jesus' purpose of "sending" (ἀποστέλλῃ) the apostles to multiply his ministry (3:14; cf. 6:7, 12). More probably, however, the odd use reflects the Hebrew phraseology of Joel 4(3):13: "send a sickle" (LXX: ἐξαποστείλατε δρέπανα, "send out sickles"; cf. Deut 16:9). Given the allusion, Jesus forsook the imperative in Joel to suit the parable and probably used the Aramaic emphatic state (so the Targum), which underlies the definite article with "sickle" but does not correspond to the MT or LXX. Mark or his source shows no influence from ἐξ- or the plural of δρέπανα in the LXX; but the following clause in the LXX, ὅτι παρέστηκεν ὁ τρυγητός, "because the vintage [or 'harvest'] has arrived," may well have influenced Mark or his source. For παρέστηκεν translates בָּשַׁל nowhere else in the LXX; and Mark's text corresponds verbatim, except for his using θερισμός (reading קָצִיר and clarifying the reference to a grain harvest) rather than τρυγητός (reading בָּצִיר and referring possibly to a grape vintage — see OT commentaries for different interpretations of the Hebrew). Such a clarification and the derivation of "the harvest" from the OT, whose meaning does not determine the NT meaning (see the following notes), would eliminate any need to see an eschatological harvest here. The emphasis falls on harvesting fruit, which stands for discipleship, not on the coming of the harvest as such, which stands only in a subordinate causal clause; and the immediate context of discipleship as evidence of God's present rule weighs heavier than distant references to his future cosmic triumph and bars the door against Joel's emphasis on judgment. The success of God's present rule in the disciples of Jesus helps neutralize the scandal of the Crucifixion (cf. J. H. Ropes, *Synoptic Gospels* 11-12, 18-19, though he thinks of neutralization through a future cosmic triumph).

NOTES

See J. Marcus, *Mystery* 165-70, on *1 Clem. 23:4; Ap. Jas.* 12:22-31; *Gos. Thom.* 21. The shoving of the man to the fringes of the parable and the putting of emphasis instead on αὐτομάτη ἡ γῆ, "the soil by itself," suggests that divine power is at work in the teaching of Jesus as in the process of fruition, usual though it is (cf. the use of αὐτόματος in Lev 25:5, 11 LXX for volunteer growth during sabbatical years, when human beings do not work the land but acknowledge Yahweh's lordship over it; in 4 Kgdms 19:29 LXX for a divinely given sign; in Acts 12:10 for a divine deliverance; and Philonic passages cited and discussed by R. Stuhlmann in *NTS* 19 [1972-73] 154-56). The point of the parable does not lie in a contrast between throwing seed on the ground and sending the sickle at harvest-time, for then the staging of the fruition would be superfluous.

God does not enter the picture as the sickle-sender, as we might expect in a parable of apocalyptic judgment. Much less does God enter the picture as the seed-thrower and ignoramus. Yet if God were the sickle-sender God would be the seed-thrower and ignoramus as well, for one and the same man is all three. No emphasis falls on the figure of the seed-thrower and sickle-sender. Hence, a contrast between the man's inactivity during the period of growth and his activity at seed-time and harvest-time does not form the heart of the parable. The seed and soil do the work. So also does the sickle. The man only sends it, and sending it at the end amounts to no more than throwing the seed at the beginning. The power of the seed-cum-soil all the way through successive stages of growth to ripeness captures the limelight. On display is the power of Jesus' word to produce the fruit of discipleship, not the power of God to bring about the final judgment; for then we would expect a reference to winnowing, burning the chaff, storing the grain, treading out the grapes, and the like. Therefore lessons of patience and confidence, calmness and composure, are not to be drawn from the parable in its present form and context. The parable portrays the man as ignorant, not as patient, confident, calm, or composed. And the parable is far from portraying him as a negative example of trying to hasten the harvest through hyper-activity such as would correspond to Zealotic rebellion, apocalyptic calculation and preparation, and Pharisaic keeping of the Law. We have no convincing reasons to hypothesize an earlier form and context that would substitute the virtue of patience and its sisters for the man's present ignorance. It is true that "by itself" describes the soil rather than the seed. But the soil is seeded, and it is the seed's sprouting and becoming long that the man does not understand and that the parable mentions ahead of the soil's bearing fruit by itself. The position of ὁ σπόρος, "the seed," before its verb goes against Mark's usual order of verb–subject and by so doing puts emphasis on the seed. Therefore it is wrong to pit the soil against the seed and decide in favor of the soil. We need to speak of seed-cum-soil and soil-cum-seed. Only when it is implanted in people does the word produce the fruit of discipleship, and only when people are seeded with the word do they produce the fruit of discipleship. The relationship between seed and soil, between word and disciple, is complementary. On the other side, it is the incomprehensibility of the power of the seed-cum-soil, of the implanted word, not slowness of growth, which the parable emphasizes. The stages of organic development do not point to the graduality of church growth during the Christian era, but to the irresistible growth of discipleship during Jesus' ministry — by virtue of his teaching (cf. Mark's apologetic use of Jesus' power of attraction, by word as well as by miracle and exorcism). The harvest is presented neither as slow in coming nor as impending. It is simply mentioned as the reason for sickling the ripe fruit. So it is wrong to distinguish between Jesus' meaning to teach passivity and patience to disciples endangered by Zealotic, apocalyptic, and Pharisaic influences and Mark's meaning to teach confidence to Christians discouraged by persecution and rejection of their witness.

J. Lambrecht (in *L'Évangile selon Marc* 293-94, esp. n. 111) suggests that "to them" is missing from v 30a, and therefore from v 26a and perhaps v 9a as well, because Q lacked it (cf. Luke 13:18, 20). His suggestion would rule out the hypothesis that Mark draws on an earlier collection of three parables concerning seed and growth, for Q neither included all three nor paired the two that it did include. We might salvage the hypothesis by supposing that Mark does not know Q (against Lambrecht's suggestion), but draws on a collection of the three parables earlier than Q and partly reflected in Q as well as in Mark (hence, the lack of "to them" in Luke 13:18, 20 as well as in Mark 4:26, 30). But then it becomes problematic why Q, as reflected especially in Luke, breaks up the unity of the earlier collection, i.e. fails to put the parables of the seeds and of the mustard seed in proximity to each other, tears the parable of the mustard seed away from the parable of the growing seed, and omits the latter parable. R. Otto (*Kingdom* 113-14) argues that οὕτως, "thus" (v 26), presupposes something preceding; that by virtue of content, this something must be the parable of the seeds; and that therefore the two parables used to stand side by side. The argument overlooks the prospective use of οὕτως.

It is commonly stated that ὡς plus the subjunctive mood without ἄν, ἐάν, or ὅταν is grammatically intolerable, as shown by the presence of those additional words in the vv.ll. (see, e.g., BAGD s.v. ὡς II4c; BDF §380[7]). Some commentators surmise an accidental loss of one of those additional words. But C. F. D. Moule (*Idiom-Book* 23) has pointed to the similarly used subjunctive verb εἴη (bis) in Luke 11:5, 7, where ἄν, ἐάν, and ὅταν are likewise missing. Of course, ὡς does not appear in that passage; and there the aorist subjunctive alternates with the future indicative in a fashion normal to Hellenistic Greek. But the passage in Luke lacks ὡς because the parable starts with a question rather than with a comparison; and it would be truer and more pertinent to say that because of the parabolic character of that passage the future indicative carries the hypothetical force of the aorist subjunctive, which therefore looks quite like the aorist subjunctive of βάλη in Mark 4:26. Here, other verbs follow in the present subjunctive to express linear actions; but the hypothetical force of the subjunctive, which suits the hypothetical character of the parable, remains the same. J. H. Moulton (*Prolegomena* 185-86) goes the other direction by positing a futuristic element in the subjunctive mood. Such an element would suit Mark's aorist subjunctive verb well enough, but hardly his present subjunctive verbs. Taking us too far into the realm of conjecture is the suggestion of H.-J. Klauck (*Allegorie* 218-27) that a dative originally stood after ὡς, that it was mistakenly changed to the present nominative, and that out of this change came a half-hearted realized conditional construction and the necessary addition of οὕτως at the very beginning of the parable. Actually, οὕτως . . . ὡς (plus yet another ὡς in v 27) makes a nice wordplay, the value of which may have struck Mark as greater than the price of an unusual grammatical construction. He could have tamely written, "The rule of God is like a man who. . . ." Cf. T. Muraoka in *NovT* 7 (1964) 55.

According to v 11, the mystery of God's rule is only for insiders; yet in speaking to outsiders (cf. vv 33-34) Jesus identifies God's rule as the referent of the parable. S. Brown (in *JBL* 92 [1973] 67-68) solves the problem by saying that Mark can assume his audience's inferring from v 11 a distinction between the mention of God's rule, a mention made only to insiders, and the telling of the parables proper to outsiders as well. But in each case, the ὡς-clause that starts the parable proper demands the earlier reference to God's rule. The solution lies, rather, in the outsiders' lack of understanding what each parable says about God's rule. Because Jesus will not explain the parables to them, the mystery has not been given to them even though it has been spoken to them (cf. the comments on vv 10-12).

The subjunctive after ὡς favors the translation "as if." God's rule is not like the man alone, but like the whole hypothesis that starts with the man: "as if a man should throw. . . ." The present subjunctive of καθεύδη and ἐγείρηται for repeated sleeping and getting up contrasts with the aorist subjunctive of βάλη for one-time sowing. The mention of night before day (so also 5:5; Luke 2:37) reflects a Jewish method of reckoning the twenty-four hour day from sunset to sunset. It may also reflect that the interim between sowing and harvest began with the man's sleeping the night after he sowed the seed. If the man's supposed patience originally stood for God's patience in not intervening to bring his rule (so J. Dupont, *Études* 310-11), what does the man's ignorance stand for?

On αὐτομάτη, "by itself," see C. Spicq, *Notes* 1. 162-65. B. B. Scott (*Symbol-Maker* 86; *Hear* 368-70) thinks that this term alludes to the sabbatical year, when only volunteer plants grow. But though it occurs in connection with the sabbatical year at Lev 25:5, 11 LXX, not even so much as a man's throwing seed on the soil should be mentioned if such an allusion were intended. The collective character of "the seed" intensifies the problem that Jesus does mention the seed-throwing. A. N. Wilder (in *JBL* 102 [1983] 499) objects that Scott goes "far afield outside the anecdote." D. O. Via (*Ethics* 185) interprets "by itself" as the preunderstanding of hearers which makes them hear in certain ways. But preunderstanding hardly causes the man in the parable not to know how the seed sprouts and lengthens. Because v 29 mentions the man's work of harvesting, R. Stuhlmann (in *NTS* 19 [1972-73] 153-62) interprets αὐτομάτη, not as meaning "without human assistance," but as meaning "without visible cause," i.e. "by God's wondrous work." But we have seen that even the phraseology of v 29 deemphasizes the man's work. The same deemphasis comes from "threw" (as opposed to a possible "sowed") and from "slept and rose night and day" (vv 26-27). Moreover, the mention of harvesting does not shift αὐτομάτη to a meaning compatible with human assistance; for αὐτομάτη describes the soil, not in relation to planting or harvesting, but in relation to the process of growth and maturation. In this process the man plays no role whatever.

According to H. Baltensweiler (in *Oikonomia* 69-75), Jesus portrays the man as not believing the seed would grow and as not knowing *that* (not *how*) it was growing, i.e. as a disciple who is falling away through disbelieving ignorance that God's rule has started in Jesus' ministry. Limited though it is, the man's participation through throwing the seed and sending the sickle does not fit this interpretation. Nor does the emphasis on the absence of his supportive activity during the process of growth. Of course he will not contribute to the process if he represents one who is falling away. All that needs emphasis is the growth despite his disbelieving ignorance. It is not as though he would be contributing to the process if he were not falling away.

Since χόρτος means "meadow-grass" but the Latin *herba* means both that and a blade, the present use of χόρτος for a blade seems to betray Latin influence (E. Lohmeyer 86, n. 2). See R. Le Déaut (in *Bib* 49 [1968] 393) for criticism of M. Black's choice of alliterative Aramaic words thought to underlie v 29a (cf. Black, *Aramaic Approach* 163-65; also T. W. Manson in *JTS* os 38 [1937] 399-400 for a different retroversion). Παραδοῖ literally means "gives over," then "permits, allows," in this context with regard to ripeness (see BAGD s.v. παραδίδωμι 4). H.-W. Kuhn (*Ältere Sammlungen* 104-12) sees redundancy between the full grain in the ear and the ripeness of the fruit. Getting rid of this redundancy leads him to denude the original form of the parable of other features, too — viz., the farmer's sleeping, rising, and not knowing, and the soil's bearing fruit through successive stages of growth. The remainder is supposed to teach the lesson of patience. But full grain in the ear still has to ripen; so there is no redundancy. And we again miss any hint of or reason for impatience on the part of the man. The center of gravity lies in the sending of the sickle, to which the ripening of fruit and the arrival of harvest are subordinate. Therefore the point of the parable does not consist in the certainty of a harvest or in its arrival at the right time (as though the text said that the harvest arrived when the fruit ripened), but in the sickling of the fruit, which represents Jesus' reaping in his disciples the results of his teaching and explaining the parables to them.

See J. Gnilka (1. 183) against the opposite tendency to jettison v 29 from the original form of the parable. Some would jettison it because of its probable allusion to the OT. Others would accept the originality of v 29 in an earlier form uninfluenced by OT phraseology. It is hard to understand, much more to share, the presupposition that Jesus did not allude to the OT. Even Septuagintal influence on an OT allusion may only say that a non-Septuagintal allusion by Jesus was conformed partly or wholly to the LXX by later Christians. In places where an allusion depends on the LXX as opposed to the MT, we must keep in mind the possibilities of a Hebrew text differing from the MT and giving rise to the LXX, of Semitic interpretative tradition distorting the MT and giving rise to the LXX, and of Jesuanic use of the LXX. According to Gnilka, v 29 shows its originality by carrying out the artistic alternation of subjects begun and developed earlier in the parable: man–seed–man–soil (vv 26-28)/fruit–man–harvest (v 29). A later addition would probably have discontinued the pattern. The pattern in v 29 lacks the elegance of the stair-step pattern in vv 26-28 (on which see the foregoing comments). Nevertheless, Gnilka's argument retains some force, and we might add that deemphasis on the man's work even in v 29 (again see the foregoing comments) is of one piece with the rest of the parable. The judgmental meaning in Joel 4(3):13 does not demand a judgmental meaning in the parable, for OT phraseology often occurs in the NT with meanings different from those in the OT — even in explicit quotations, all the more in allusive ones. The references in Jas 5:7 to patient waiting and to early and latter rains probably imply that that passage and the present parable have no relation to each other. Otherwise we would have to say quite gratuitously that a lean parable was fleshed out in extremely different ways.

Against the suggestion that v 29 borrows phraseology from the v.l. in Hab 3:17 LXX, ἡ συκῆ οὐ μὴ παραδῷ τὸν καρπὸν αὐτῆς, "the fig tree will by no means yield its fruit," H.-J. Klauck (*Allegorie* 219) notes that Mark has no direct object as the OT text has. Moreover, "the fig tree" ill suits Mark's sickled harvest of grain. Klauck also notes the necessity of the harvest as a conclusion to the parable and therefore rules out a later, allegorical addition of the harvest to the parable; but he allows the possibility of later assimilation to the language of Joel 4(3):13. See A. M. Ambrozic, *Hidden Kingdom* 108-14, for a convenient survey of various interpretations and of their strengths and weaknesses, plus references to the copious literature on the parable. J. Schmid (105) notes a number of detailed allegorizations that transgress the boundaries of contextual exegesis. P. Carrington (112-13) interprets the parable in terms of Jesus' death, resurrection, departure from the world, and return for the eschatological harvest (cf. 1 Cor 15:36; *1 Clem.* 24:1-5). But this interpretation turns Jesus into the man as well as the seed, finds it difficult to understand how the man's ignorance could apply to Jesus, makes Jesus the ripe fruit as well as the harvester, and wavers between regarding the harvest as Jesus' resurrection and regarding it as the last day and therefore also between regarding the interval between sowing and harvest as the interval between Jesus' death and resurrection and regarding it as the interval between his first and second comings. Though J. Marcus (*Mystery* 171-85) correctly rejects identifications of the man with God and with Christian disciples, he wrongly defends an identification with Jesus by appealing to 5:30, where Jesus does not know who touched him; to 6:6, where he is amazed at people's unbelief; to 14:35-36, where "he acknowledges that the cup/hour is in God's hands, not his" (p. 184); and to 15:34, where his cry implies that God's abandonment of him "is something that he has not expected" (ibid.). But none of these passages speak to the matter at hand in chap. 4, i.e. the power of Jesus' parables and explanations to effect the fruit of discipleship. The activity of the man is minimized so much that we should not even ask whom he represents. He does not represent anyone. Again D. E. Oakman (*Economic Questions* 109-14) interprets the parable of God's providing food at no cost of human labor in the kingdom, but again a reference to harvest stops short of any reference to food or eating (cf. the notes on vv 13-20). See J. O'Callaghan (in *Bib* 53 [1972] 97-99; idem in *Supplement to JBL* 91/2 [1972] 10-12) for the view that 7Q6, 1 represents Mark 4:28 (but see also the notes on 6:52-53).

4:30-32 *(Matt 13:31-32; Luke 13:18-19)* The occurrence of the parable concerning the mustard seed in a completely different context at Luke 13:18-19 favors that Q as well as Mark contained this parable. Matthew's agreements with Luke against Mark, which are more extensive than those which elsewhere can be explained by secondary influence of Matthew on Luke (cf. R. H. Gundry in *The Four Gospels 1992*), confirm Matthew's use of the Q-version. But since he uses Mark's version, too, and in a context parallel to Mark's, we need to make Luke, which seems not to reflect Mark, our basis of comparison with Q (cf. H. Fleddermann in *SBL 1989 Seminar Papers* 216-23).

The general improbability that Mark knows Q (W. G. Kümmel, *Introduction to the NT* 70) suggests that Mark uses a pre-Q version that Q incorporated. Furthermore, since he includes parables not having to do with seed and growth in vv 21-25, it would be hard to explain his omitting the parable of the leaven if he knew Q, which pairs the parables of the mustard seed and of the leaven. The emphasis on power in the parable of the leaven would have greatly appealed to Mark, and the parable of the growing seed hardly substitutes for the parable of the leaven.

Though not always, the differences between Mark and Luke often look due to Mark's redaction for reasons of new context and theological emphasis. Thus it appears that he imports the parable from another context. As with the parable of the growing seed, the parable of the mustard seed does not need interpretation, because the explanation of the parable of the seeds carries over well enough to eliminate the need for another interpretation (cf. the comments on vv 26-29). In particular, the themes of hearing the word and of large result from good hearing carry over from the parable of the seeds and its explanation (vv 1-20).

The parataxis of Mark's καί, "and," looks more original than Luke's οὖν, "therefore." The absence of αὐτοῖς, "to them," after ἔλεγεν, "he was saying," matches Luke (and Mark 4:26). Πῶς, "how?" echoes the question in v 13, which only Mark had. That πῶς does not properly go with ὁμοιώσωμεν, "should we liken," which requires a dative (here τίνι, "to what?" — see Luke and the concordance s.v. ὁμοιόω), shows the extreme to which Mark goes to assimilate the parable to its new context. Ὁμοιώσωμεν advances ὁμοιώσω, "shall I liken" (Luke), to make room for a reference to the particular speech-form "parable" in the next question. The "we" in ὁμοιώσωμεν also pluralizes ὁμοιώσω to tie in with the new context of Jesus' family, "the ones around him with the Twelve" (v 10; cf. 3:31-35). The outsiders are listening in, but his illuminative purpose aims at the insiders alone.

"The rule of God" comes from the tradition (so Luke), but also links with vv 11, 26. Thus all three parables concerning seed and growth are expressly tied to God's rule (contrast vv 21-23, 24-25). Mark changes καί, "and" (Luke), to ἤ, "or," to make his following reference to the particular speech-form "parable" an alternative to the more inclusive category of a comparison. Though the tradition has two questions (cf. Luke 13:18), Marcan duality sometimes makes the second member more specific, as here (cf. F. Neirynck, *Duality* 45-53, 96-97). The insertion of παραβολῇ, "parable" (not in Luke 13:18; *Gos. Thom.* 20), ties the comparison to the collection of parables into which Mark has imported the comparison. He portrays Jesus as teaching one parable after another (see vv 33-34; R. Laufen, *Doppelüberlieferungen* 177). The insertion of παραβολῇ necessitates the exchange of ὁμοιώσω, "shall I liken" (Luke), for θῶμεν, "should we put," which echoes the double use of τίθημι in v 21, and a consequent insertion of ἐν, "in," before τίνι, "what?" The questions display a parallelism of clauses and a chiastic order of verb–object–object–verb. The chiasm comes even at the expense of intruding the object αὐτήν, "it," between ἐν τίνι (which as an interrogative needs to come first) and παραβολῇ.

The ellipsis of ἐστίν, "is," which Luke has, may be traditional and is certainly vigorous. Ὡς, "like," replaces ὁμοία, also meaning "like," for a wordplay with πῶς. It also echoes two instances of ὡς in the preceding parable (vv 26, 27) and anticipates yet another parabolic ὡς in 13:34. But in those passages a nominative properly follows; here, improperly, a dative because of the traditional dative κόκκῳ, "a grain" (so Luke), which relates properly to ὁμοία (cf. T. Muraoka in *NovT* 7 [1964] 58). That Mark would write ὡς despite his keeping the traditional dative shows again the extreme to which he goes to assimilate the parable to its new setting. Κόκκῳ σινάπεως, "a grain of mustard," comes from the tradition, κόκκῳ referring to an individual grain (contrast the collective singular ὁ σπόρος, "the seed," in vv 26-27 [bis]).

Ὅταν, "whenever," plus the subjunctive links this parable to the preceding one (see v 29; cf. also vv 15, 16) and transforms a narrative of fact (so Luke and most of Jesus' narrative parables) into a hypothesis, just as the preceding parable was hypothetical ("as if a man should throw seed on the soil" [v 26]). Consequently, the throwing of a single seed into a garden, which looks unrealistic in a narrative such as Luke's version of the parable, turns into a comparison in which the seed might be realistically understood as one of many mustard seeds thrown on the soil. The greater ease of Mark's version speaks against, not for, its originality.

At first, Luke's ἔβαλεν εἰς κῆπον ἑαυτοῦ, "threw into his own garden," looks like adaptation to a non-Palestinian setting. True, *m. Kil.* 3:2; *b. Kil.* 2.8 disallow sowing mustard in a garden. But throwing seed may not be the same as sowing it. In fact, even though a crop came about in Mark 4:26-29, the overall inactivity of the man there suggested that "throw" unrealistically — and therefore emphatically — effaced a normal act of sowing. And in the traditional form of the present parable, a man's throwing a grain of mustard into his garden would contrast with sowing mustard seeds in his field and would highlight the surprising result all the more. If we may suppose so, Mark's differences look like redactional assimilations to the new context into which he has imported the parable and therefore favor the traditionality of Luke's throwing into a garden (cf. B. B. Scott, *Hear* 375-79).

In Mark, throwing changes to sowing to recollect in this last parable of the series the sowing in the first one (vv 3-9), i.e. to make an inclusion that stresses Jesus' teaching in parables the mystery of God's rule. "Sow" (σπείρω) also recalls the cognate noun "seed" (σπόρος) in vv 26-27. The verb changes from active to passive to put all emphasis on the grain of mustard, to whose smallness Mark will add a large amount of attention. This change effects the further change of ὅν to ὅς and the elimination of "a man." Though retention of "a man" and of "threw" would have tied this parable to the preceding one, the association of "a man" and of "threw" with ignorance in that parable is not an item which Mark could make good use of here. "A man" and "threw" thus disappear together. For another inclusion and emphasis on Jesus' teaching in parables the mystery of God's rule, "on the soil" replaces "into his own garden" (cf. vv 1, 20; also vv 8, 26 — all with vv 11, 14). The omission of "a man" makes it easy to replace the individualistic reference to his own garden (E. Wendling, *Entstehung* 36-37). We expect ἐπί, "on," to be followed by the accusative τὴν γῆν, "the soil," in accordance with the accusative objects of ἐπί in vv 5, 16, 20. But despite his present avoidance of the man's throwing that occurred in v 26, Mark echoes the genitival ἐπὶ τῆς γῆς which appeared there.

The smallness of the mustard grain was proverbial in Palestine (C.-H. Hunzinger in *TDNT* 7. 288). But Mark is probably writing for non-Palestinians. So to emphasize smallness as a foil to later bigness, he inserts a long participial phrase completely lacking in Luke (though Matthew, under Mark's influence, has it; so also *Gos. Thom.* 20). Luke might have made the same sort of insertion for the benefit of his non-Palestinian audience, but he sticks to Q. Mark's emphasis on smallness begins with a jarring switch of attention from the masculine κόκκῳ, "grain" (the antecedent of ὅς, "which"), whose meaning includes grains from which come small as well as large plants, to the neuter σινάπεως, "of mustard" (which the neuter participial phrase μικρότερον ὄν, "being smaller," and the neuter predicate adjective μεῖζον, "greater," modify), whose meaning is limited to a large plant that grows from a very small grain. The switch is all the more jarring in that the nominative case of the participial phrase makes it seem as though the phrase modifies the nominative ὅς, which refers to κόκκῳ, though the difference in genders prohibits such a modification. The switch requires a leap from ὅς to an unstated ὅ, also meaning "which" but referring to σινάπεως. The mental gymnastics required for this leap and for following the double switch in genders and antecedents dramatize the smallness to which Mark devotes his insertion. The difficulty of finding an antecedent for the closing participial phrase in 7:19, which almost certainly derives from Mark's redactional activity, supports our taking the present difficulty as due to his redactional activity. The forward position of μικρότερον, "smaller," adds further emphasis; and the use of the comparative "smaller" in a superlative sense, the modification of "the seeds" with "all," and the addition of ἐπὶ τῆς γῆς, which echoes the first part of the parable, absolutize the smallestness of the mustard seed. A shift in the meaning of ἐπὶ τῆς γῆς from "on the soil" to "on the earth" underscores this absolutization.

The insertion of the long participial phrase concerning smallestness has delayed the verb of ὅς so long that Mark makes a new start. The resultant anacoluthon and repetition of "whenever it is sown" reemphasize sowing, which represents Jesus' powerful teaching, as the means by which God's rule has been established. For "grew" (so Luke) Mark substitutes "comes up," which links this parable yet again with its new context, in particular, with the parable of the seeds (vv 7-8 [bis]). Of course, that parable used "grow" as well as "come up" (v 8). But the pairing of them there triggers the shift from one to the other here. Mark makes the shift because the first thing a sown seed does is to "come up" out of the soil and because that first coming up makes a sharper contrast with the largeness of the final product. Growing covers the whole intervening process, but Mark has paid enough attention to that in the preceding parable (vv 26-29). The tense of the verb changes from a narrative aorist (so Luke) to a present to agree with the hypothetical character of the parable in Mark. The aorist would not agree with it (cf. the present tense of the participle "coming up" in v 8). For the same reason the following verbs, "becomes" and "makes," take the present tense (contrast Luke's "became").

Mark changes becoming a tree to becoming "larger than all the vegetable plants" for an antithetic parallel with "smaller than all the seeds on the earth," which he inserted earlier. It would be glaringly untrue to say that the grown mustard is larger than all the trees (though see Thphr. *HP* 1.3.1-4 on the imprecision of the boundary between trees and shrubs). Again a use of the comparative for the superlative and an addition of "all" to the noun absolutize the thought. Since not all vegetable plants have branches, as trees do, Mark advances "branches" from its last position (cf. Luke) and adds a necessary verb, viz., "makes." The further addition of "large" (not in Luke) doubles the emphasis on largeness and helps make up for the reduction of "tree" to "vegetable plant." The "and" that introduces the birds (see Luke) changes to "so that" to point up the result of largeness. The addition of "are able" increases this emphasis with the implication that the birds of the sky would not be able to take their shelter here were it not for the largeness of the plant and of its branches. Naturally, the addition necessitates the changing of the following verb to an infinitive.

The traditional references to branches and birds remind Mark of Ezek 17:23; so he borrows "under its shade" from the LXX of that passage (contrast the MT: "in the shade of its branches") to substitute for "in its branches" (so Luke) now that he has just referred to branches in his preceding insertion. As a result of the substitution, the meaning of κατασκηνοῦν changes from nesting to taking shelter from the sun. The forward position of this new phrase contrasts with the last position of the original, corresponding phrase (see Luke) and thus puts another accent on largeness. The traditional phraseology concerning the settling of the birds of the sky comes from Dan 4:9(12), 18(21), to which Ezek 17:23 comes close except that Daniel associates shade with beasts and branches with birds (so Luke and Matthew for branches with birds; cf. Ezek 31:5-6), and Ezek 17:23 associates shade with birds (so Mark; for the various texts, see R. H. Gundry, *Use of the OT* 35; and G. R. Beasley-Murray, *Jesus and the Kingdom of God* 122-23, against an allusion to Ps 104:12). Thus Mark intensifies an already existing emphasis.

The large size of the grown mustard and its branches corresponds to and expands on the large yields of the good soil in the parable of the seeds. Because of the aforementioned links with that parable and its explanation, the large size, like the large yields, does not stand in Mark's text for the future magnitude of God's rule (including the Gentiles, perhaps represented by the birds as in Daniel and Ezekiel; cf. Zech 2:11 LXX; *1 Enoch* 90:30; *Jos. Asen.* 15:6 v.l.; *Midr. Ps.* 104:13); nor does it stand for the magnitude of the mixed church as the present locale of God's rule (as in Matt 13:31-32). Rather, it stands for the magnitude of God's rule in the disciples during the time of Jesus (see the comments on vv 13-20), a magnitude that derives from Jesus' powerful teaching and counteracts the scandal of his coming crucifixion (see the comments on vv 26-29).

NOTES

It might be argued against Mark's redacting a pre-Q version of the parable of the mustard seed that the version in *Gos. Thom.* 20 looks Marcan but does not derive from Mark (cf.

C.-H. Hunzinger in *TDNT* 7. 290, n. 35). But do we know that it does not derive from Mark? Most of it is easily derived therefrom, and the rest from Matthew, Luke, and Gnosticizing tendencies (W. Schrage, *Verhältnis* 61-66; C. L. Blomberg in *Gospel Perspectives* 5. 186-87; H. Fleddermann in *SBL 1989 Seminar Papers* 228-29, 235). As in Mark but not Luke or Matthew, it occurs beside the parable of the growing seed (*Gos. Thom.* 21). These data suggest that the five trees in Paradise (*Gos. Thom.* 19) led the author or compiler of the Gospel of Thomas to the parable of the mustard seed, that he took it primarily from Mark, that he brought along its mate, the parable of the growing seed, and that he reversed their Marcan order to bring the parable of the mustard seed that produced "a large branch" next to the five trees in Paradise.

The separation of the parables of the mustard seed and of the leaven in *Gos. Thom.* 20, 96 implies their original independence from each other no more than does the absence from Mark of the parable of the leaven, and no more than Matthew's frequent repositioning of Marcan materials negates their original connections in Mark (similarly with regard to Matthew's repositioning of Q-material so far as we can tell from comparison with Luke). The apparent haphazardness of the arrangement of materials in the Gospel of Thomas may be due to piecemeal selection from the tradition (be it canonical or extra-canonical) rather than to their order in extra-canonical tradition. We have seen, however, that the placement of the parable of the mustard seed is not haphazard.

G. D. Kilpatrick (in *Neotestamentica et Semitica* 201-2) favors the v.l. ἐν τίνι παραβολῇ παραβάλωμεν αὐτήν; "In what parable should we make it a parable?" because of the non-Semitic but emphatically Greek position of αὐτήν in the usually accepted reading — also because of the not-so-Greek cognate construction in the v.l. But the verb παραβάλωμεν strikes one as more Greek, not less Greek, than θῶμεν, "should we put," which looks like Marcan assimilation (see the foregoing comments). The cognate παραβολῇ simply carries over from the original text of Mark rather than combining with παραβάλωμεν to form any sort of Semitic idiom favoring the v.l. And from the standpoint of κοινή Greek the position of αὐτήν in the usually accepted reading cries out for scribal change. Kilpatrick's additional emending of τίνι, "what?" to ποίᾳ, "what sort of?" and then explaining τίνι as a v.l. resulting from assimilation to Isa 40:18 LXX (cf. H.-W. Bartsch in *TZ* 15 [1959] 126-28) pays too little heed to the stronger possibility that τίνι derives from dominical tradition (cf. Luke).

Comparison with rabbinic introductions to parables (see Str-B 2. 7-9; J. Jeremias, *Parables* 100) shows that Luke 13:18bc lies closer to the rabbinic introductions than does Mark 4:30bc, particularly in the singular of the first person rather than Mark's plural and in "be like" and "liken," both with the dative, rather than Mark's "how . . . liken" and "put . . . in a parable," both with the accusative. This fact supports our taking Luke's version as a more traditional standard of comparison and Mark's version as more heavily redacted to suit the new context into which the parable has been imported. Luke's second ὁμοία ἐστιν, "is like" (13:19a), is sometimes suspected of replacing an original bare dative or ὡς plus a nominative, and his ἑαυτοῦ, "his own," of replacing an original αὐτοῦ, "his" (see, e.g., R. Laufen in *Begegnung mit dem Wort* 107, 109). It is puzzling why Jeremias (op. cit. 101, n. 53) thinks ὁμοία ἐστιν, "is like," should easily give the erroneous impression of an identification, as opposed to referring to a subject about to be described. He makes this opinion a basis for describing ὁμοία ἐστιν as more Graecized than ὁμοιώσω αὐτήν, "shall [or 'should'] I liken it" (both in Luke).

Jesus would not have started with a mustard seed if he had wanted merely to create a parable culminating in a tree with branches for nesting (cf. H. K. McArthur in *CBQ* 33 [1971] 204); but he wanted also to set up a contrast between smallness and bigness, for which the mustard is very useful. R. Laufen (in *Begegnung mit dem Wort* 109-10) argues that because Luke's "man" plays no essential role and that because the parable has to do with God's rule, Mark's making the mustard seed the subject (ὅς) reflects the original and Luke's man reflects assimilation to the woman in the parable of the leaven, with which parable Laufen thinks Q secondarily paired the present one. But Mark's ὅς does not get a verb till "comes up," by which time the mustard seed is the subject in Luke's version, too; and we have seen reasons for Mark's replacing "a man" with the passive voice of a verb. It is another question whether Jesus used the word "man," whether he himself paired it with "woman" by speaking the parables of the mustard seed and of the leaven one after the other (so B. Witherington III, *Women* 40-41), whether an original "man" and an original "woman" helped attract separately spoken parables to each other, or whether "man" made its way into the parable of the mustard seed as the result of a later pairing of the parables. The suggestion that "garden" replaced "soil" at the time the two parables were paired and for the purpose of assimilating the parable of the mustard seed to the domesticity of the parable of the leaven overlooks the possibility that Jesus himself paired them — and the possibility that if he did not, an original domesticity in both of them helped draw them together. Moreover, a man hardly sows a single mustard seed in his field. His "taking" the seed suits its singleness; and his "throwing" it suits the garden, where sowing a mustard seed is prohibited so far as Palestine is concerned. Thus Luke's version is self-consistent. This self-consistency argues against explaining Luke's version as the result of later assimilation to the parable of the leaven.

According to B. B. Scott (*Hear* 380-87), Mark's motive in substituting soil for a garden is to keep Jesus from approving a possible transgression of the law requiring separation of plants (Lev 19:19; Deut 22:9-11). But for that motive we would expect an explanation of the law such as Mark writes in 7:2-4, 11b; for an audience that does not know about Jewish ceremonial washings and "Corban" will hardly know about the law of horticultural separation and therefore will not need Jesus to be protected from approving a possible transgression of it. Besides, Mark lets Jesus approve his disciples' transgression of the Sabbath law (2:23-28) and even calls attention to his abrogation of the dietary law (7:19).

D. Wenham (in *TynBul* 23 [1972] 21, n. 50) criticizes attempts to explain the redundant "whenever it is sown" (bis in Mark) by mistranslated Aramaic. H.-J. Klauck (*Allegorie* 210) argues that Mark would have kept the active voice of σπείρω, "sows," and would not have jettisoned ἄνθρωπος, "a man," if his tradition had contained those elements, and that Luke 13:19 betrays an assimilation to Luke 13:21 in the construction of a relative pronoun plus a participle plus a nominative noun plus a finite verb plus εἰς, "into." But we have noted redactional reasons for Mark's not keeping the active voice and for his jettisoning ἄνθρωπος; and the similarity between Luke 13:19 and 21 may as easily stem from Jesus' way of speaking (whether or not he spoke these two parables one after the other) as from later assimilation, while Mark 7:19 supports a Marcan origin for the grammatical difficulties in 4:31 (see the foregoing comments). M. Black (*Aramaic Approach* 189, n. 3) detects a wordplay between זרע and זער, which he thinks stand behind "sow" and "smaller." Since Mark's frequent translations of Aramaic exhibit a knowledge of that language, such a wordplay may have originated with him rather than with an earlier traditioner or Jesus (cf. the foregoing comments on the Marcan redactional origin of "being smaller . . ."). The plural of πάντων τῶν σπερμάτων, "than all the seeds," keeps its neuter gender from explaining the neuter of μικρότερον ὄν, which is singular. W. Schenk (in *ZNW* 70 [1979] 144-46) attributes Luke's lack of emphasis on the contrast between smallness and bigness to Q's assimilating this parable to that of the leaven and making the grown mustard plant into a tree. For the grown mustard plant is far from the largest of trees. But in the Palestinian setting represented by Q, people did not need to have the smallness of the mustard seed pointed out; and Mark's emphasis on the contrast more probably derives from his non-Palestinian setting and from his need to make up for correcting the classification "tree," a hyperbole more typical of Jesus than of Mark.

It is puzzling why R. Laufen (in *Begegnung mit dem Wort* 124) regards Luke's (Q's) ηὔξησεν, "grew," as abstract and therefore unoriginal. Growing is hardly less pictorial than coming up (ἀναβαίνει — so Mark). We might suspect that Luke substitutes "grew" for "comes up" to symbolize the growth of God's word in the growth of the church (Acts 6:7; 12:24; 19:20; cf. 7:17; Luke 1:80; 2:40). But Matthew's agreement with Luke favors that Luke depends on a tradition, for Matthew hardly borrows the verb from Luke. H.-W. Kuhn (*Ältere Sammlungen* 103) thinks that the present tense of Mark's indicative verbs points to what is happening in Mark's community. But the preceding subjunctive verbs have set a hypothetical tone that does not support an allusion to contemporary history. Laufen (in *Begegnung* 112) and G. Lohfink (in *". . . Bäume braucht man doch!"* 114-16) regard Mark's "vegetable plant" as original because it correctly describes the grown mustard and because Luke's (Q's) incorrect "tree" looks like an assimilation to "the branches" in the OT allusion with which the parable closes. But the correctness of "vegetable plant" might as easily be a pedestrian correction of "tree," and the originality of the OT allusion (supported by Mark as well as Luke!) would make "tree" more suitable than "vegetable plant" to the original version of the parable (cf. B. B. Scott, *Hear* 375-79). A possible underlying wordplay between הזרעים, "the seeds," and הזרעונים, "the vegetables" (so J. Carmignac in *ASTI* 7 [1968-69] 71), or their Aramaic equivalents might as easily come from Mark, thinking Semitically while dictating in Greek, as from Jesus, speaking in Semitic. In the LXX, moreover, λάχανον does not stand for זרעון.

The context in Luke gives no clue to the original meaning of the parable. The context in Matthew points to the magnitude of the mixed church (see R. H. Gundry, *Matthew* 265-69, where some of the comments need revision in view of Mark's redacting a Q-like version of the parable). The theme of God's rule, a theme that overarches the message of Jesus, suggests that the parable originally pointed from a small beginning in Jesus' ministry to a final triumph in the world at large rather than in the parabolically taught disciples (so Mark). If so, the seed would not have connoted the parabolic word, as it does in Mark's context.

But in Luke no emphasis falls on smallness. Only by inference from the typically dominical hyperbole of the grown mustard plant as "a tree" (a hyperbole not unknown elsewhere — see C.-H. Hunzinger in *TDNT* 7. 289) and from the proverbially recognized but unstated smallness of the mustard plant do we get a balanced contrast between smallness and largeness. Though the mustard seed was proverbial for its smallness, the large size of the grown mustard was not proverbially contrasted with that smallness (ibid. 288). Therefore, since Luke's version leads up to an emphasis on largeness without having emphasized smallness and since his version seems far less redacted than Mark's or Matthew's, it looks as though the parable started out with only an implication of smallness and that the original emphasis on largeness led Mark to make explicit the proverbial emphasis on smallness — this for the sake of heightened contrast. Jesus wanted mainly to emphasize the ultimate universality of God's rule. It then becomes easy to think not only that the birds' nesting in the branches of the tree belonged to the original form of the parable but also that their nesting captures the originally main point, i.e. inclusion of the nations of the world. For that is what their nesting refers to in the Danielic passage alluded to, and in this instance the meaning of the OT text suits the features of the NT text into which the OT text is fit. Then also, Jesus did not aim to convince doubters or encourage the discouraged so much as to teach people concerning the wide significance of what was happening in their midst. In any case, we must beware of overdrawing the psychological state of Jesus' and Mark's audiences, and of drawing it overconfidently. Jesus' and Mark's speaking and writing such a parable might as easily have been prophylactic of doubt and discouragement as indicative and corrective of already existing such states.

R. W. Funk (in *Int* 27 [1973] 3-9) thinks that the lowly mustard plant contrasts with the high and mighty cedar of Lebanon (Ezekiel 17) to portray God's kingdom as a refuge that is quite modest from a worldly standpoint. But the parable gives as the standard of comparison, not the high and mighty cedar of Lebanon, but the mustard's own seed. By this standard the size of the grown mustard plant is astonishingly large. That the parable of the growing seed likewise ended with phraseology drawn from the prophetic portion of the OT (v 29) helps further to clamp together these two parables about seed. Cf. the notes on vv 26-29 against automatically denying the authenticity of an OT allusion. Yet again D. E. Oakman [*Economic Questions* 123-27], overlooking the absence of any reference to food or to the eating of it, interprets the parable to teach God's eschatological providence in providing food at no cost of labor. But birds have never worked for their food (Matt 6:26 par.; cf. the notes on vv 13-20, 26-29).

4:33-34 *(Matt 13:34-35)* "And with many such parables he was speaking" implies the telling of more parables than Mark records here. The forward position of the phrase "with many such parables" emphasizes the abundance of Jesus' powerful teaching. So also does the word "many" within the phrase (cf. the adverbial πολλά, "much," with reference to parabolic teaching in v 2); and the forward position of τοιαύταις, "such," emphasizes that the unquoted parables carried a similar point, i.e. that they highlighted his authority by teaching the importance of hearing him well. "To them" points to the huge crowd, including non-disciples as well as disciples (see v 1 with comments). "The word" means the good news of God's rule, here only in its parabolic form (see the comments on 1:45 and 2:1-2, where the phraseology, "And he was speaking the word to them," exactly matches the present phraseology). A comparison with vv 14-20 shows that Jesus was sowing seed by speaking the word. "As they were able to hear" refers simply to their attention span or to the amount of time they could spend listening to Jesus. Since he is speaking to a mixed audience, the qualification does not distinguish good hearing from bad. Mark does not intend to say, "As they were able to understand"; for the very next sentence indicates that even for disciples it takes private explanations to bring understanding, and vv 12b, 15-18 have emphatically distinguished between hearing and understanding (cf. the notes on vv 3-9, particularly on v 9). That Jesus speaks in accordance with the huge crowd's ability to hear implies a superabundance of words full of life-force. He had more to say. Here lies Mark's point, which typifies his interest in the power of Jesus' teaching and therefore invalidates the assignment of v 33 to pre-Marcan composition and of v 34 to Mark, or vice versa, as though v 34 corrects a tradition of parables as inherently understandable by means of a notion of parables as inherently obscurative and therefore as requiring esoteric explanations, or as though v 33 corrects v 34 in the opposite direction. The intricacy of the interrelationships in vv 33-34 argues against separate origins for the two verses. The limit on ability to hear balances the speaking in many parables. Private explanations to the disciples balance the exclusivity of parabolic speech to the general audience. Not speaking apart from parables restates in a negative way the positive reference to speaking with many such parables. And Jesus' privately explaining "all things" to his disciples corresponds negatively to the limited ability of the general audience even to hear.

"But apart from a parable he was not speaking to them" revives the judgmental emphasis which Mark uses as an apology for the Cross (see vv 10-12 with comments). The adversative δέ, "but," contrasts Jesus' refusal to say anything at all in ordinary speech with the large number of his parables. The forward position of "apart from a parable" stresses the contrast. "But privately to his own disciples" shows that "speaking to them" means speaking to the huge, mixed crowd of v 1. The further adversative δέ contrasts Jesus' private speech with his public speech. Since vv 10-12 anticipated his private explanations (see the comments ad loc.), "the disciples" here seems to collapse into a single expression the twofold designation, "the ones around him with the Twelve" (v 10; cf. C. M. Tuckett in *Bib* 69 [1988] 14). In both passages the people referred to stand in contrast with outsiders, non-disciples, who receive no explanations. Mark switches from κατὰ μόνας, "alone" (v 10), to κατ' ἰδίαν, "privately," for a match with ἰδίοις, "his own." The emphatic first position of κατ' ἰδίαν stresses Jesus' success in forming a new family around himself (cf. 3:31-35; 4:10-12). So also does the strong ἰδίοις, where we might expect an ordinary αὐτοῦ, "his." In Hellenistic Greek the emphasis in ἰδίοις sometimes weakens, but here the contrast with the crowd as a whole and Mark's use everywhere else of an ordinary pronoun with μαθηταί, "disciples," favor the strong meaning. Thus, Jesus' success counteracts the scandal of his crucifixion by demonstrating the fruit-bearing power of the seed-like word which he sows in the soil of those who hear well. His explaining "all things" to them shows how abundantly the good soil bears, how brightly the light shines, how wealthy the rich grow, how forcefully the seed matures, how big the plant becomes (vv 1-20, 21-23, 24-25, 26-29, 30-32, respectively). The explaining of "all things" to the disciples contrasts with the obscuring of "all things" from outsiders in v 11 and thus makes an inclusion that brings the parabolic discourse to a close. By context both here and there, "all things" means all things taught in the parables (against Tuckett, op. cit. 18-19).

NOTES

The foregoing comments which speak for the unity of vv 33-34 militate against assigning these verses to different pre-Marcan traditions (so H. Räisänen, *Parabeltheorie* 56) as well as against assigning one verse to pre-Marcan tradition and the other to Mark (see C. M. Tuckett in *Bib* 69 [1988] 6-8 for a survey of six different apportionments of vv 33-34 to tradition and redaction). Besides, the contrast is not between public speaking with parables in v 33 and public speaking only with parables in v 34a. Those two statements complement each other. The contrast is between them taken together and private explanations in v 34b. We have seen good reasons to regard vv 33-34 as coming from the same hand, Mark's. But we can go further: neither does v 33 make sense when taken with the preceding context but apart from v 34, nor do vv 33-34 make sense when taken together if we violate the earlier distinction between hearing and understanding. According to the terms of v 33, if the huge crowd were not able to hear in the sense of understanding, Jesus would not have spoken to them with parables at all. For according vv 10-13 neither the huge crowd nor the disciples among them understood, yet the wording of v 33 has it that their ability to hear conditioned his speaking. Moreover, the wording of v 34a limits his speaking to the parables which according to v 33 he was not speaking except on condition that they could hear. Only hearing as listening stays within the limits of the text. Hearing as understanding makes nonsense of the text as well as violating the earlier distinction between hearing and understanding.

On the other hand, if to reconstruct a hypothetical earlier collection of seed-parables one strips away vv 9-25, 34, which contain the distinction between hearing and understanding, it would make sense to say that in v 33 hearing includes understanding (so, e.g., H.-W. Kuhn, *Ältere Sammlungen* 134). But we have seen the questionableness of this reconstruction. Moreover, "according as they were able to hear" sets a limit. In fact, "were able" highlights it; for "according as" (καθώς) would set a limit even if that verb were not part of the text, i.e. if the text were to say "according as they were hearing." Whatever the following verb, "according as" sets a limit (cf. the way "according as it is written" sets a scriptural limit). Here, the limit is presumably not due to the parables as such; for according to the interpretation we are discussing, they make understanding easier. Nor is the limit due to divine hardening; for according to the interpretation, vv 10-12 did not belong to the pre-Marcan collection and God's hardening of human hearts would contradict Jesus' telling parables to win people over. Nor is the limit self-imposed through people's hardening of their own hearts; for "were able" not only emphasizes the limit. It also removes the limit from the sphere of moral choice. At least there is no contextual indication of blameworthiness in the reconstructed pre-Marcan collection. The interpretation is left with the simple creaturely limit on understanding that all human beings have. But this does not differ very much from the simple creaturely limit on attention span and the like under the interpretation that hearing means listening, not understanding. At least there is nothing more theologically profound in the creaturely limit on understanding which parables as sermon illustrations cannot fully overcome. So why not accept the unity of vv 33-34 and maintain the contextual distinction between hearing and understanding?

We have no compelling reason not to think that Jesus sometimes told parables to mystify a general audience, and that he explained them in private to his disciples. But it would be gratuitous to suppose that all his parables carried that purpose. Certainly Mark does not suppose so (see 12:12). And it ought to be clear from the rest of his gospel that he does not restrict Jesus to parabolic speech on all the occasions when outsiders formed part of the audience. H.-W. Kuhn (*Ältere Sammlungen* 134) argues that the lack of "in" with "parables" and a verb of speaking reflects pre-Marcan tradition, because Marcan redaction in 3:23; 4:2; 12:1 puts "in" with "parables" and verbs of speaking. But here alone does a contrastive "apart from parables" follow. Mark drops the usual ἐν probably to avoid the locative impression that the contrast with χωρίς might leave.

The possibility that "speaking the word" (ἐλάλει . . . τὸν λόγον) echoes an early Christian formula (Acts 4:29, 31; 8:25; 11:19; 13:46; 14:25; 16:6, 32; Phil 1:14; Heb 13:7; John 12:48; 15:3; cf. Mark 2:2; 8:32) does not favor Mark's use of tradition in v 33, for he is just as likely to have used such a formula in his own composition as was an earlier traditioner. Neither here nor in vv 2-20 does "the word" include the explanations of the parables, for it is associated only with the parables over against their explanations. John 6:60; 8:43 (cf. 16:12; 1 Cor 3:2; Heb 5:12-13; 12:20) do not make good cross-references; for they speak of inability to hear the word, whereas Mark 4:33 speaks of ability to do so. Unlike Mark, Arr. *Epict. Diss.* 2.24.11-14 equates ability to hear with ability to understand.

To say that hearing is less than understanding is not to make the clause, "according as they were able to hear," into a negative assessment of the huge crowd. The negative assessment came earlier with respect to their being outsiders. The emphasis lies on the abundance of Jesus' parables, on the exclusivity of his parabolic speech, and on his private explanations. Mark tucks the ability of the crowd to listen into a subordinate clause that only implies a closure of Jesus' present parabolic speech. But this implied closure is enough to prepare Mark's audience for the transition to a new, non-parabolic pericope.

The rarity of ἐπιλύω, "explain," elsewhere in the NT (only at Acts 19:39, and there in quite a different sense; 2 Pet 1:20) means that the word has no value for the question whether v 34 is Marcan or pre-Marcan. H. Anderson (141) correctly notes that v 34b does not deny Jesus' speaking in parables to the disciples; it only says that he added explanations for them. J. M. Robinson (*Problem* 25, 46) notes for ἐπέλυεν the connotation of resolving, as in resolving a riddle. Mark's translations of Aramaic words (5:41; 15:22, 34) show that he knows Aramaic. Therefore the equivalence of ἐπέλυεν to פשׁר (cf. the equivalence of μυστήριον to רז and of παραβολή to משׁל) does not rule out his composition of vv 33-34 (as thought by H.-J. Klauck, *Allegorie* 255-56). Against the view that Mark makes everything said by Jesus during his ministry into something indirect and veiled (so C. E. B. Cranfield 171-72) stands the word "such," which limits "many parables" to the kind reported in this pericope. The similar view that v 33 does not link up with vv 11-12, but describes God's word as unfathomable despite Jesus' parables (so J. Ernst 146), wrongly implies an unfathomability of Jesus' non-parabolic speech and requires a divorce of v 33 from v 34, according to which parables need explanation rather than giving it.

JESUS' AUTHORITY OVER THE WIND AND SEA

Mark 4:35-41 (Matt 8:23-27; Luke 8:22-25)

The story of Jesus' stilling a storm starts a series of three successive miracle stories. The others are about the exorcism of Legion and the cure of Jairus's daughter along with the healing of the woman with a chronic flow of blood (5:1-20, 21-43). Historical chronology and topography seem to have determined the order of these stories: the first takes place on the sea, the second on the other side from Galilee, and the third back on the Galilean side after the return trip. By happy coincidence (it is hard to prove redactional manipulation), the stories also seem to progress from Jesus' stilling the stormy sea, which represents the threat of death; to his exorcising the unclean spirits called Legion, who made their victim dwell in the realm of death (the tombs) and self-destructively lacerate himself; to Jesus' conquering death itself in Jairus's daughter, whose case, surrounding as it does that of the woman, may make the woman's chronic flow of blood represent the impurity of death. The story of the storm at sea begins with departure in a boat (vv 35-36). The storm comes next (v 37), then the rousing of Jesus from sleep (v 38), his stilling the storm (v 39), and his asking the disciples why they are scared rather than trustful (v 40). The story closes on the note of their awestruck fear — at Jesus, for the storm no longer threatens (v 41).

4:35-36 *(Matt 8:18, 23; Luke 8:22-23)* "And he says to them [complete with αὐτοῖς — contrast vv 26, 30]" signals a new start. "To them" means "to his own disciples," the ones most recently mentioned in v 34b. "On that day, when evening came" typifies Mark's duality of expression. As often, the second member adds specificity to the first (cf. F. Neirynck, *Duality* 45-53, 94-96). The dual expression links the following story with the day of parables, and the reference to evening prepares for Jesus' sleeping (v 38). Mark may even intend the delay of the sea-crossing till evening to put one last accent on the fulness of Jesus' parabolic teaching: it took up the whole day (see also the comments on vv 1-2, 33-34). The historical present tense of λέγει, "he says," highlights the authority of his words, "Let us go through to the other side." Next, their effect comes into view. The disciples leave the crowd (cf. 1:18, 20; 10:28-29) and take along Jesus "as he was, in the boat." The references to the disciples, the crowd, and Jesus' being in the boat add further links with vv 1-34, particularly with vv 1, 33-34. But he is the only one who is already in the boat (v 1); and since he is the object of "take along," he can belong neither to the "they" who are the subject of that verb nor to the "they" who leave the crowd. So it is only the disciples who leave the crowd, the huge one of which they have formed a part till now (v 1). Since only Jesus is already in the boat and since the disciples have been part of the crowd till now, Mark must want his audience to think of the private explanations referred to in vv 10-20, 34 as following the disciples' present separation from the crowd. This separation underscores the disciples' belonging to Jesus' new family (see the comments on 3:33-34 for Mark's apologetic point in this emphasis). That they "take him along" once they get in the boat anticipates their crewing while he sleeps (v 38; contrast 5:40; 9:2; 10:32; 14:33). The substitution of "leaving the crowd" for the usual verb of embarkation (4:1; 5:18; 6:45; 8:10, 13) and the historical present tense of "take him along" emphasize the effect of Jesus' exhortation as seen in the disciples' obedience.

"And other boats were with him" means that Jesus' disciples include more than the Twelve, just as v 10 has already indicated ("the ones around him with the Twelve"). Jesus' sowing the word has yielded too abundant a harvest for one boat to hold them all. Emphasis on this point comes from the chiasm of (a) "as he was"; (b) "in the boat"; (b') "and other boats"; (a') "were with him," and especially from the forward position of "other boats." That the rest of the story loses sight of the other boats only shows to what length Mark goes to introduce them here as a pointer to Jesus' magnetism (cf. the comments on 1:16-20; 2:13-17; 3:13; also Mark's emphasis on the power of Jesus to attract crowds in general). Since "to them" (v 35a) has referred to Jesus' "own disciples" whom he privileged with explanations of his parables (v 34b) and since those disciples included "the ones around him" as well as "the Twelve" (v 10), his exhortation to go with him to the other side has included more disciples than the Twelve. All of them have left the huge crowd. Because Jesus will still the storm, the narrative will quickly concentrate on his boat. Presumably the Twelve are in it, the rest of his disciples in the other boats. The rest may reappear in 5:16, however; and it is hard not to think that Mark means them to make it through the storm with Jesus.

4:37-38 *(Matt 8:24-25; Luke 8:23-24)* The historical present tense of γίνεται, "takes place," dramatizes the power of the threat about to be described (cf. 2:15; M. Reiser, *Syntax und Stil* 89, 97). Several other data likewise magnify the threat: (1) the choice of λαῖλαψ, "gale"; (2) the additions of μεγάλη, "great," and ἀνέμου, "of wind," which apart from emphasis on the power of the threat are superfluous; (3) the statement that the waves were breaking over into the boat; (4) the chiasm of verb–subject–subject–verb in the statements about the gale and the waves; and (5) the further statement that as a result "the boat was already being filled." "Already" sharpens the point of emphasis, and the non-mention of any sailorly effort by the disciples to bail out the water and ride out the storm leaves the impression that they are utterly helpless. Meanwhile, Jesus sleeps the sleep of utter calm. Mark is not interested in Jesus' being tired, but in his having nothing to fear from a sea storm, which ancients deeply feared for its threat to life. The emphatic αὐτός, "he himself," contrasts the calmness of his sleep with the raging of the sea. Since he will not call on God to still the storm but will still it himself, we would do wrong to interpret his sleep as one of trust in God (cf. Lev 26:3-9; Job 11:13-20; Pss 3:6[5]; 4:9[8]; Prov 3:21-26). He trusts in his own abilities as God's Son. By placing Jesus in the elevated afterdeck, where he finds a headrest (cf. Verg. *Aen.* 4.554, 560; BAGD s.v. προσκεφάλαιον), Mark explains how Jesus can sleep: he lies sheltered from the waves that are beating into the lower part of the boat. If it is true that normally he would be steering on the elevated afterdeck (R. Kratz, *Rettungswunder* 210-14), the sleeping dramatizes his divine self-confidence. The historical present tense of ἐγείρουσιν, "they arouse," and of λέγουσιν, "they say," stresses the contrastive fear of the disciples. "Teacher" reflects Jesus' having taught them for the whole day (vv 1-2) and implies the authority of his words, an authority that even the wind and sea will recognize. The construction οὐ plus the indicative implies that the disciples do not doubt that Jesus cares: "You care that we are perishing, don't you?" (against H. C. Waetjen [*Reordering of Power* 112], who imagines that they infer a lack of care from his falling asleep and failing to man the tiller from the afterdeck). But they show no faith that his care can translate into his saving them from destruction (cf. v 40).

4:39 *(Matt 8:26; Luke 8:24)* The simplex ἐγείρουσιν, "they arouse," of v 38 now gains a perfective διά, with the result διεγερθείς (hapax in Mark), perhaps to imply Jesus' rising to his full height (J. A. Kleist 199), certainly to add intensity of one sort or another. A mighty act of power is in the offing. At this point the questions in v 40 would seem appropriate. That is to say, the disciples' frantic rousing of Jesus would naturally lead to his asking, "Why are you scared? Don't you have faith yet?" By the same token, his calming the storm, by being delayed, would naturally lead to the disciples' awestruck response (v 41; so the order in Matt 8:25-26). As it is, we have an a-b-a'-b' pattern in vv 38bc, 39, 40, and 41, respectively. The unnaturally forward position of Jesus' rebuking the wind and commanding the sea that this pattern produces gives those actions great prominence and thereby emphasizes his powerful words. Further emphasis accrues from the distinguishing of the rebuke to the wind and the command to the sea, the doubling of the command to the sea ("be silent" and "be muzzled"), the asyndeton between the commands, and another a-b-a'-b' pattern in (a) the rebuke to the wind; (b) the commands to the sea; (a') the abatement of the wind; and (b') the calming of the sea. The emphasis in the command to silence (σιώπα — present imperative; cf. notes on 1:3) and the ongoing effectiveness of the command to be muzzled (πεφίμωσο — perfect imperative) look forward to a calm that lasts long enough for completion of the voyage.

Jesus' rebuking the wind, which has caused the threatening waves, looks like his rebuking unclean spirits (cf. the exorcistic use of ἐπιτιμάω in 1:25; 3:12; 9:25; and the rebuke of Peter as "Satan" in 8:33; see esp. O. Böcher, *Christus Exorcista* 22-24). Similarly, Jesus' telling the sea, "Be muzzled," recalls his muzzling the the unclean spirit in 1:25 (in conjunction with a rebuke, as here). On the other hand, ἐπιτιμάω can hardly carry an exorcistic connotation in 8:30, 32; 10:13, 48, and the assumption that ancient people attributed storms to malevolent demons may lack substance. The usual cross-references to Rev 16:5; *Jub.* 2:2; *1 Enoch* 60:16; 61:10; 66:1-2; 69:22; *2 Enoch* 19:4 do not hit the mark of associating sea storms with malevolent demons; for in those passages the angels of the wind and water do God's bidding (cf. Rev 7:1-3; *CAD* s.v. *imḫulla*), and in *1 Enoch* 101:4-7 God himself sends the sea storm (cf. also Exod 15:10; Josh 24:7; Pss 29:3-9; 77:17-20[16-19]; 104:3-4; Jonah 1:4; Job 26:12 [the last only if we translate with "stirs up"]). For comparable materials also outside the Jewish and Christian spheres, see the citations by K. Kertelge, *Wunder* 96-97; W. Fiedler, *Antiker Wetterzauber* 1-45; B. Blackburn, *Theios Anēr* 44-45, 193-95; but on tracking down those citations one is struck by the slimness of evidence for demons' causing storms (cf. F. Pfister's discussion of magic for controlling the weather rather than of demons as causing bad weather [in *RAC* 2. 175 and *PWSup* 4. 334]). Not even the cross-reference to *PGM* III. 226-28 hits the mark; for there the sea is parallel to the gods of Olympus as well as to the most eminent demons, and these demons are not necessarily bad. In fact, they appear to be good. Jesus' personification of the wind and sea need not demonize them any more than his personification of the barren fig tree (11:14) will demonize it. The fact that despite his shutting up demons in Mark 1:25, 34; 3:12, the verb σιωπάω never occurs in those passages does not encourage a demonic understanding of his silencing the sea. Hence, we should not think of him as exorcising demons of the wind and sea, but should think instead of language that emphasizes his power by echoing not only the accounts of exorcisms but also OT passages concerning God's rebuking and stilling the sea (Job 26:11-12 [translating with "stills" rather than with "stirs up," which would disturb the synomymous parallelism]; Pss 65:8[7]; 66:6; 106:9; 107:29-30; Nah 1:4 [cf. 2 Macc 9:8; 1QH 6:23-27] plus many more passages dealing in general with God's control over the sea; cf. the calling on the gods to still the storm in Jonah 1:5-6 with Jesus' stilling the present storm; also the attribution to Pythagoras of the god-like power to lull violent gales and hailstorms and to still the waves of rivers and seas in order that his companions might enjoy an easy crossing [Iambl. *VP* 135]).

The abatement of the wind (v 39b) reverses the gale of wind (v 37) and stems from Jesus' rebuking the wind (v 39a). In parallel fashion, the coming of a calm (v 39b) reverses the beating of waves into the boat (v 37) and stems from his silencing, or muzzling, the sea (v 39a). References to the wind remain constant (vv 37, 39a, 39b), but Mark shifts from waves (v 37) to sea (v 39b) to calm (v 39b). The greatness of the calm (cf. the greatness of the branches in v 32) cancels out the greatness of the gale (v 37) and thereby magnifies the effective authority of Jesus' word, now demonstrated in the world of nature as it has been demonstrated in the world of parables. The assonance of γαλήνη μεγάλη and the parallelism between καὶ ἐγένετο γαλήνη μεγάλη, "and a great calm came to pass," and καὶ γίνεται λαῖλαψ μεγάλη, "and a great gale comes to pass" (v 37), add to the note of calm. Despite rejecting the notion that Jesus is portrayed as exorcising a particular storm-demon, we might think that he is portrayed as quelling the powers of chaos in general. The sea represented those powers in ancient near eastern thought (for summaries, see B. W. Anderson in *IDB* 4. 808-10; O. Eissfeldt, *Kleine Schriften* 2. 258-62; 3. 256-64; R. Kratz, *Rettungswunder* 14-106).

4:40-41 *(Matt 8:26-27; Luke 8:25)* "And he said to them" shifts the address from the wind and sea to the disciples. Jesus' questions, "Why are you scared? Don't you have faith yet?" put him in a good light: in his presence the disciples have no reason to be scared, and he has done so many marvels that by this time they ought to have faith. Their being faithlessly scared of the wind and waves now changes to a reverential fear of Jesus (cf. 5:15, 33; 9:32; 10:32; 11:18; 16:8; also 6:20; 9:15). The switch from δειλοί, "scared," to ἐφοβήθησαν, "feared," signals this change. The cognate accusative φόβον, "fear," emphasizes it. And the addition of μέγαν, "great," makes the disciples' reverential fear match the greatness of the calm that reversed the great gale of wind. The great fear comes to speech. But whereas the disciples' being scared of the storm prompted them to speak to Jesus, their being afraid of him prompts them to speak to one another. What they say takes the form of a question: "Who then is this one, [seeing] that both [or 'even'] the wind and the sea are obeying him?" (cf. 1:27; 2:12; 7:37). The question magnifies the figure of Jesus: he looms too large for the disciples' comprehension. The ὅτι-clause ("[seeing] that . . .") puts the emphasis on his authority rather than on their ignorance. The inferential ἄρα, "then," makes their question arise out of the obedience of the wind and sea rather than out of any mistaken or deficient view concerning Jesus. The next story will answer their question by identifying him as "Son of the Most High God" (5:7) — an answer shouted with "a great voice" that will match the disciples' "great fear." The pairing of "the wind and the sea" in obedience to Jesus' word matches the pairing of "the wind and . . . the sea" as objects of his rebuke and silencing (v 39); and the obedience of the wind and the sea parallels the obedience of unclean spirits to his teaching (1:27). "Both . . . and" (or "even . . . and)" and the forward position of "the wind and the sea" emphasize the marvel of their obedience. For Mark, the key point is that the man who will later be crucified is the man who without prayer to God or adjuration in God's name successfully commands the wind and the sea. He is a divine man who represents the one true God.

NOTES

See L. Schenke (*Wundererzählungen* 1, n. 1) for a brief list of different theories regarding a pre-Marcan collection of miracle stories, or perhaps two such collections, beginning with the present story; also for references to further literature. The reasons given for these theories sometimes agree with another view, however. It is currently popular to say, for example, that the motif of crossing the Sea of Galilee betrays the hand of a pre-Marcan collector-redactor who used the motif to tie together originally independent stories. But Mark himself may have done so. And since Jesus ministered in Galilee and some of his closest disciples were fishers, it is reasonable to think that he really did cross the Sea of Galilee with them and that these stories occur together because the events narrated in them were historically interconnected by sea-crossings (cf. H. Kruze in *NTS* 30 [1984] 510-13). D.-A. Koch (*Bedeutung* 34-39), F. Annen (*Heil* 209-14), and J.-M. van Cangh (in *RTL* 3 [1972] 76-85 and in *L'Évangile selon Marc* 324-25) have criticized in detail the theories especially of H.-W. Kuhn (*Ältere Sammlungen* 191-213) and P. J. Achtemeier (in *Int* 16 [1962] 169-76 and in *JBL* 89 [1970] 265-91; 91 [1972] 198-21).

A similar theory of R. Pesch (1. 278-79) also deserves criticism, some of which applies to the other theories as well. He posits a pre-Marcan collection of miracle stories, concentrically arranged, that reaches beyond the three stories in 4:35–5:43:

a) Summary (3:7-12)
   b) Stilling the storm (4:35-41)
      c) Healing the Gergasene demoniac (5:1-20)
         d) Healing the flow of blood and raising Jairus's daughter (5:21-43)
      c') Feeding the five thousand (6:32-44)
   b') Walking on the water (6:45-51)
a') Summary (6:53-56)

But we have seen reasons to doubt that 3:7-12 originally introduced materials beginning not till 4:35 (see the notes on 3:7-12). Furthermore, c and c' (the healing of the Gergasene demoniac and the feeding of the five thousand) do not correspond to each other in content. b and b' correspond to each other better, but not quite so well as might appear at first glance; for the contrary wind in 6:45-51 does not pose the threat to life that the storm in 4:35-41 poses. And one wants to know why Mark would awkwardly break up an artistically arranged collection of miracle stories. For example, why would he intrude the choosing of the Twelve (3:13-19) right after the introductory summary despite their not playing a role till their mission (6:6b-12)? They are mentioned in 4:10 only in passing, perhaps only as an afterthought; and Jesus' choosing them would come nicely just before his sending them out. If Mark wants to give them time to spend with Jesus before they represent him, why does Mark not put the choosing of the Twelve earlier, where it would not interrupt the collection? After all, he put the call of Simon, Andrew, James, and John very early (1:16-20). Why does he not delay the introductory summary till after the section on parables (4:1-34), just before the first story in the supposed collection? It would fit there quite well. And why does he not delay the rejection of Jesus at Nazareth (6:1-6a), the mission of the Twelve (6:6b-13), and the death of John the Baptizer (6:14-29) till after the supposed collection? There they would lead nicely into the conflict with the Pharisees and some of the scribes from Jerusalem (7:1-23). Just as the notion of an earlier collection fails to explain why Mark awkwardly inserts other materials, so also the form critical notion of his stringing together originally isolated units of tradition leaves unanswered the question why he fails to sew together similar units and why he jams together dissimilar units. We do better to think that the crazy quilt is due to the untidiness of historical chronology (recollected by Peter — see pp. 1026-45) than to authorial mismanagement.

The miracles in 4:35-41; 5:21-43 are not unique in featuring the element of faith. The healing of the paralytic featured the faith of the four who brought him (2:5); and even earlier the leper expressed faith (though the word itself is not used) when he said, "If you will, you are able to cleanse me" (1:40; cf. 1:30b, 32; 3:10). Moreover, Jesus stills the storm despite his disciples' lack of faith (4:40), whereas the woman with the flow of blood has faith (5:34). Jairus needs an exhortation to faith (5:36), and an exorcistic story in which faith plays no role whatever interrupts the other stories (5:1-20). The unity of 4:35-41; 5:21-43 as a Marcan or pre-Marcan cluster centering around faith therefore stands in doubt.

Making the miracle stories in this section of Mark represent Jesus' encouraging the church to patient endurance of sickness, death, demonic oppression, and "natural" disasters (so H. J. Held in *Kirche* 86-87) underestimates the mainly Christological point of the stories and fails to note that in them Jesus negates those evils rather than enabling his disciples to endure them patiently. To say that in these stories the miracle itself is the main point, for no teaching accompanies the miracles, is to give the Christological emphasis its due (so K. Kertelge, *Wunder* 90). But a contrast with earlier miracle stories is out of order; for some of them, too, were unaccompanied by teaching (1:29-34, 40-44; also 3:7-12); and the teaching that did accompany the others had a Christological point (1:21-28; 2:1-12; 3:1-6). To think that the following of the present miracle stories with the story of unbelief at Nazareth (6:1-6a) is intended to show the inadequacy of miracles as prompters to faith (so C. H. Talbert, *Reading Luke* 95) mistakes the meaning of 6:1-6a, which is to show the unreasonableness of unbelief in the face of Jesus' miracles.

O. Betz (in *Studies in the NT and Early Christian Literature* 235-37) interprets the sea-crossing by Jesus and the disciples in terms of Israel's crossing the Reed Sea under Moses' leadership (Exodus 14). But there the danger came from enemies. Here it comes from a storm. There the wind enabled a crossing. Here it threatens a crossing. There the crossing was by foot. Here it is by boat. There the waters engulfed enemies. Here it engulfs no one (though boats beside Jesus's have come along). These differences are too pronounced for the parallel to stand.

Taking Jesus along in a voyage across the Sea of Galilee hardly symbolizes Christian missionaries' preaching him to the nations of the world (so E. Hilgert in *Oikonomia* 52-54), for it is the storm and Jesus' stilling of it that offer the main point of the story. It may be true that a private miracle like this one has the purpose of magnifying the person of Jesus before his disciples, whereas he performed healings and exorcisms in public to demonstrate the coming of God's rule. But Mark puts the public healings and exorcisms to the same Christological use that the private miracles have had from the beginning. See H. van der Loos, *Miracles* 641-44, for a summary of materials concerning the domination of natural forces by outstanding human beings (though H. Baarlink [*Anfängliches Evangelium* 109-10] is probably correct to deny that early Christians segregated "nature-miracles" from other miracles). According to Philostr. *VA* 4.13, people regarded Apollonius of Tyana as "stronger than a storm" (cf. Apollonius's describing the sea as having "submitted itself to the ship" despite the stormy season, presumably because of his presence on board [ibid. 4.15]). *PGM* I. 120; V. 137; XXIX. 1-10 speak of deities who control and still the stormy wind and sea. But the phraseology in Mark echoes the OT with respect to God's domination of these forces. The citation by G. Theissen (*Miracle Stories* 140-41) of *PGM* VII. 320-23 is inappropriate, because there the petitioner is commanding birds, earth, air, sea, wind, demons, and human beings other than himself to fall silent in order that he may consult an oracle undisturbed. Since Jesus' stilling of the storm is not described as an exorcism (see the foregoing comments), we can hardly suppose that he rebukes the disciples for failure to exercise the exorcistic authority which he gave them earlier and which they have exercised in the meantime (3:15; 6:7, 13) and will later try and fail to exercise (9:14-29; N.B. the dissimilarity in the present lack of an attempt — against C. D. Marshall, *Faith* 216-17).

W. H. Kelber (*Kingdom* 49-50; *Mark's Story* 30-31) identifies the main point of Mark as the disciples' failure; their fear as fear of the rebuke implicit in Jesus' questions; and their own question, "Who then is this . . . ?" as one of ignorance concerning Jesus' identity and of mistaking the sea-crossing for a sea-miracle (cf. R. M. Fowler, *Loaves and*

Fishes 102). Well, if Mark does not want his audience to repeat the mistake, he botches the job of negating the miraculous element. The disciples' question is not one of ignorance, for its continuation identifies Jesus as the successful commander of wind and sea. And their fear relates more naturally to their own following question than to his preceding questions; thus, the fear consists of reverential awe before his power rather than of shock at his implicit rebuke. Besides, fear is not a normal reaction to rebuke; and the interrogative character of the rebuke softens it considerably (as in 8:17-21). Failure on the part of the disciples falls far short of forming the main point of the story, Mark's redaction or no. Kelber (*Kingdom* 48-49) also supposes that this story was originally independent from the scene in vv 1-34. He then deduces that "to them" in v 35a originally referred to a general audience, not to the disciples mentioned in v 34b. But even apart from the possibility that v 35a, including "to them," stems from Mark, to think that Jesus exhorted a general audience to sail with him across the Sea of Galilee, or that at a pre-Marcan stage he was portrayed as doing so, strains the imagination.

According to M. A. Tolbert (*Sowing the Gospel* 101, 166), Jesus' having explained "all things" to the disciples (v 34) makes their present fear ironical. But those things had to do with the parables, none of which represented an ability of his such as would enable him to still a storm. So the explanations can hardly have prepared them for this miracle.

See the comments on 1:32-33 for ὀψίας γενομένης, "when evening came." The phrase probably implies an overnight voyage that lands Jesus and his disciples on the opposite shore the next morning (cf. 5:1). But since Mark uses the phrase often and does not stress darkness here, or even mention it, the suggestion that the phrase alludes to the powers of darkness which equate with the stormy powers of chaos and that the phrase therefore prepares for an epiphany (J. Ernst 149; R. Pesch 1. 269) seems ill-advised. Besides, Jesus makes no appearance to his disciples (contrast 6:48-50). Counting the evening with the foregoing day (v 35) does not conform to the Jewish practice of counting evening as the start of a new day, but see the notes on 14:12 that Jews as well as Gentiles could count an evening with the preceding day (see also 15:42 and cf. S. J. De Vries in *IDB* 1. 783). Or does "evening" (ὀψίας) mean "late in the afternoon, toward sunset" rather than "after sunset, toward dark" (cf. BAGD s.v. ὄψιος 2)? D.-A. Koch (*Bedeutung* 95, n. 18) argues that Mark deduces "when evening came" from Jesus' sleeping later in the story (cf. B. M. F. van Iersel and A. J. M. Linmans [in *Miscellanea Neotestamentica* 2. 18-19], who take all of v 35 and some of v 36 as Mark's fabrication). The argument presupposes that Mark is composing without the benefit of tradition or historical reminiscence at this point. Marcanisms do not rule out those possibilities, however.

According to R. Pesch (1. 266), Mark wants his readers to think that Jesus gave private explanations from his boat to disciples in the other boats. But until they embarked, the disciples were part of the huge crowd; and once they embarked, they started crossing the lake. To translate μετ᾽ αὐτοῦ "with it" (i.e. with Jesus' boat) rather than "with him" does not fit Mark's Christological emphasis. E. Lohmeyer (90) thinks that Mark shows himself a landlubber by using διέλθωμεν, "let us go through" (v 35), which elsewhere refers often but not exclusively to land-travel or fording streams. More likely, the prefix δι- anticipates going "through" the wind and waves of the sea storm (cf. 1 Cor 10:1). The simplex form of the verb occurs regularly enough for sea voyages, and the meaning of the prefix does not favor land over sea. Acts 18:27 offers a use of the complex form for a sea voyage; and at 6:53 Mark will prefix διά to περάσαντες, "having crossed," with reference to a sea voyage.

Since only the disciples "leave the crowd" (see the foregoing comments), we should not make out of that phrase a theologically significant reference to Jesus' withdrawal from the crowds. On the contrary, the reference to "other boats" that were "with him" runs in the direction of his attracting a large number of people as disciples. The v.l. ἀφίουσιν τὸν ὄχλον καί, "they leave the crowd and," probably stems from a desire to make him as well as his disciples leave the crowd, as though "let us go" implied that he as well as his disciples was with the crowd. In that case, however, "as he was, in the boat" would make nonsense (against C. E. B. Cranfield [173], who suggests that the better attested participle is a stylistic correction of parataxis in the v.l.).

G. Wohlenberg (144-45) takes "ἐν the boat" with "they take along," understands ἐν as meaning "into" rather than "in," and imports Jesus' tiredness to interpret "as he was" (v 36). Several times in Matthew, the verb "take along" (παραλαμβάνω) governs a prepositional phrase of destination; but the preposition is always εἰς, the proper equivalent of "into," never ἐν (4:5, 8; 27:27). Mark, on the other hand, never puts a prepositional phrase of destination with this verb. The far greater usualness of the meaning "in" for ἐν favors construal with "as he was," and Jesus' not sleeping till v 38 leaves "as he was" meaningless in its own sentence unless we construe "in the boat" with "as we was." 4 Kgdms 7:7 LXX; Luc. *Asin.* 24 also support the latter construal. The aorist tense of ἀφέντες, "having left," allows and even favors that the disciples take Jesus along right after they leave the crowd, not as they leave the crowd (cf. 1:18, 20; 7:8; 8:13; 12:12; 13:34; 14:50; 15:37). Thus, "take along" has to do with "let us go through to the other side," not with "having left the crowd."

J. Wellhausen (2. Aufl., 36-37) and his followers take a view similar to Wohlenberg's, but say that Mark inserts "as he was" to link the following story with vv 1-34 for the first time (cf. esp. v 1). But the foregoing comments have shown that the various elements of vv 35-36 fit nicely with each other as well as with vv 1-2, 10. Therefore we are free to see a greater amount of composition by Mark, and the question whether or not he bases his composition on a historical connection rests on more general considerations.

See R. Kratz, *Rettungswunder* 204-7, for a survey of reasons suggested for Mark's mentioning "other boats" (v 36). Ps 107:23-30, which provides the most pertinent background for our story, may have triggered the mention (cf. esp. the LXX [106:23] with Mark's πλοῖα), but not by way of fulfilment of the OT (against D. E. Nineham 148). Mark uses the OT rather by way of analogy (A. Suhl, *Funktion*), and differences from Ps 107:23-30 rule out a literary origin there of the present story (see R. Glöckner, *Neutestamentliche Wundergeschichten* 61-62). L. Schenke (*Wundererzählungen* 31-32) argues that since elsewhere it takes only one boat to hold the disciples and Jesus (5:1-2; 6:31-32; 8:13-14), the other boats mentioned here do not hold a larger circle of disciples. But only in chap. 4 does Mark mention "the ones around him" as well as "the Twelve" (v 10). Schenke (op. cit. 77-78) also thinks that the boat full of disciples stands for the church, the storm for trial and persecution, the sleeping of Jesus for a delay of the Second Coming, and the calming of the storm for deliverance at the Second Coming. Mark's stress on Jesus' being in the boat damages this view (contrast the snatching away of Jacob in *T. Naph.* 6:1-10, where despite some phraseological similarity in the description of the wind [λαῖλαψ ἀνέμου μεγάλου, "a gale of great wind"] an allegorical presentation of Israelite history further distances the passage from Mark 4:35-41). The portrayal of the disciples as not yet *having* faith does not fit Christians' *losing* faith because of a delay in the Second Coming. And to a symbol of the Second Coming we expect a reaction of joyful celebration, not of fearful awe such as Mark describes.

The definite article with προσκεφάλαιον may be generic (reflecting the Aramaic emphatic state) or deictic (so E. C. Maloney, *Semitic Interference* 109). Either way, there is no need to identify the headrest, pillow, or cushion as the only one aboard. On the other hand, Mark's pointing it out with the definite article would fit a purpose of dignifying Jesus. Both the distinction between the stern and τὸ προσκεφάλαιον and the usual meaning "pillow, cushion" for the latter disfavor that Jesus uses the stern itself, or the elevated deck which characterizes it, as the headrest. More likely, "in (ἐν) the stern on (ἐπί) the headrest" means that he is sleeping beneath the elevated deck of the stern, there·protected from the elements and out of the crew's way, and on a sandbag ordinarily used for ballast when not stored there (S. Wachsmann, *Excavations* 111-12; cf. F. Neirynck, *Duality* 45-53, 94-96, on the frequency in Mark of increasingly specific temporal and local statements).

R. Pesch (1. 271) thinks that only a large ship such as sailed the Mediterranean would have a stern, that a Galilean fishing boat would not, and that the story of Jonah, who went to sleep on a large ship sailing the Mediterranean, has deeply influenced the present story. There may be some influence in the sequence of wind–water–boat (Jonah 1:4; Mark 4:37), in the reference to perishing (Jonah 1:6; Mark 4:38), in the use of κοπάζω, "abate," and in the idiom "feared a great fear" (Jonah 1:10, 16; Mark 4:41; cf. L. Goppelt, *Typos* 72-73 [English]). But all four of these features arise naturally under the circumstances; and the idiom "feared a great fear" occurs elsewhere, too (see 1 Macc 10:8; cf. Ps 53:6[5]; Isa 8:12; Ezek 27:28). Furthermore, Jesus goes to sleep up in the stern, not down in the hold as Jonah did. The Lord sends the storm in Jonah, but not here. Jonah 1:4 LXX has πνεῦμα for "wind" and κλύδων μέγας, "a great billow," where Mark has λαῖλαψ μεγάλη ἀνέμου, "a great gale of wind" (cf. Jer 32:32 LXX, but without ἀνέμου). The LXX does not have Mark's γαλήνη, "calm"; nor does the MT have a corresponding Hebrew word. The disciples do not battle the storm as the sailors battled one in Jonah. The captain approaches Jonah, whereas the disciples arouse Jesus. Jonah's fleeing the presence of the Lord ill suits a comparison with Jesus. Jonah's being thrown overboard to abate the storm contrasts with Jesus' speaking the storm down. And Jesus claims to be greater than Jonah only in Q (Matt 12:41 par. Luke 11:32), not in Mark. Indeed, Jonah's name never appears in Mark. Despite the possibility of some phraseological influence, then, it seems doubtful that the story of Jonah lies at the base of the present story. Cf. Str-B 1. 452 for the rabbinic story of a boy's praying a sea storm still. Though "stern" may refer simply to the hind end of a fishing boat, the present boat needs to be large enough to hold thirteen. Therefore it is not unreasonable to think of a stern in the sense of an elevated afterdeck (see *Views of the Biblical World* 5. 86 for the wide variety of boats and ships used in NT times; D. Sperber, *Nautica Talmudica* 31, for the probability of fairly sizeable vessels on the Sea of Galilee; and S. Wachsmann, *Excavations* 40-42, 55, 111-13, 119-20, 133, on the new archeological evidence that vessels large enough to hold thirteen and feature an elevated afterdeck did indeed ply these waters). Regarding sudden storms on the Sea of Galilee, see W. L. Lane 175 and other literature cited there. With the disciples' arousing Jesus, cf. OT passages cited by R. Glöckner (*Neutestamentliche Wundergeschichten* 61-62) concerning suppliants' arousing God to save them from distress (Pss 7:7[6]; 10:12-13; 44:24-27[23-26] et passim).

Failure to note the implied affirmative answer to the question in v 38c leads to a mistaken interpretation of the question as accusatory (see, e.g., D.-A. Koch, *Bedeutung* 96; cf. the more moderate assessment by R. Glöckner [*Neutestamentliche Wundergeschichten* 69-71], who relates the question to the OT way of getting God's help in a crisis). Hence, there is no reason to regard the question as a redactional addition designed by Mark to criticize the disciples and those in his church whom they represent for holding a "divine man" Christology. Jesus' questions in v 40 criticize the disciples for *not* having believed that he could and would act as the Son of God by rescuing them, for thinking that the storm had become too overpowering for his abilities (cf. v 37; against L. Schenke, *Wundererzählungen* 82-85).

It is also argued that Mark replaces a form critically demanded request for help by fabricating the faithless question in v 38c, and that he follows up by fabricating Jesus' reproachful questions in v 40, which interrupt an original connection between the calming of the storm (v 39) and the disciples' awestruck response (v 41). Thus, Mark changes a miracle story regarding Jesus into a story of unbelief regarding the disciples (J. Gnilka 1. 193-94; L. Schenke, *Wundererzählungen* 37-44, 82-93; cf. B. M. F. van Iersel and A. J. M. Linmans in *Miscellanea Neotestamentica* 2. 18-23, but with an acceptance and repositioning of v 40ab in pre-Marcan tradition). Form criticism describes what we usually find, but what we usually find does not justify our supposing that the unusual was once the usual; for traditioners and redactors are just as likely to conform the unusual to the usual (as does the par. Matt 8:25). Here, the disciples' question in v 38c stems just as naturally from the description of the storm as a request for help would have done, perhaps more naturally, for the waves are beating into the boat and it is filling up — too late for help, it seems. The disciples and Jesus are already perishing. And it is not his reproachful questions in v 40 so much as his commands in v 39 which are interruptive (see the foregoing comments). We would expect a fabricator of vv 38c, 40 to keep the fabrications together, and for emphasis to insert both of them before v 39 (see Matt 8:25-26). The next-to-last position of v 40 brings no emphasis such as a fabricator-inserter would want, i.e. neither the initial emphasis of a forward position, which Jesus' words of command have, nor the final emphasis of a last position, which the awestruck response of the disciples have. Schenke (op. cit. 41) correctly observes that "not yet" in v 40 demands a context larger than this single story. But since the story might well have enjoyed such a context prior to Mark's writing, the observation does not make a strong argument for regarding v 40 as his fabrication to transform a miracle story into a story concerning failure of discipleship. Even though we were to grant fabrication and insertion into their present positions of vv 38c, 40 we would have to say that the overall effect of the story is more doxological of Jesus than critical of the disciples.

In v 40 we might favor the v.l. οὕτως; πῶς οὐκ, ". . . in this way? How is it that . . . not?" over οὔπω, "not yet," on the ground that the latter softens the rebuke by implying the disciples' coming to faith later, and also on the supposition of assimilation to οὔπω in 8:17, 21 (J. Gnilka 1. 196). But since the verb which goes with οὔπω differs in 8:17, 21, that passage will more naturally offer evidence for a Marcan or dominical liking of "not yet" (see also 11:2; 13:7) than a basis for present scribal assimilation. Furthermore, "in this way" and "how?" might soften the rebuke as much as or more than "not yet" does (L. Schenke, *Wundererzählungen* 35-37). Whether or not Mark adds a reference to the faith which the disciples do not yet have, the context determines that this faith be faith in Jesus' power to work a miracle of deliverance. For throughout his gospel, Mark plays up the miracles of Jesus. He does not play them down or devalue them. See E. C. Maloney, *Semitic Interference* 142-44, against taking τί in the exclamatory sense of the Aramaic מָה, "Why, . . . !" (against M. Black, *Aramaic Approach* 121-23). But see Black, op. cit. 71-72, on the possibility that in v 41 ὅτι goes back to an Aramaic דְּ, more naturally translated ᾧ, "whom," which would make a typically Semitic redundancy with αὐτῷ, "him." A. T. Robertson (*Grammar* 699) thinks differently that "the ὅτι is almost equal to ὥστε ['so that,' indicating result]." The attempt of R. Pesch (1. 269, n. 3) to set out the original story in rhythmic, tricolic strophes fails to carry conviction. The third lines do not correspond to each other in style or in contents (a ὥστε-clause regarding the filling of the boat, a direct quotation from the disciples, a direct quotation from Jesus, a καί-clause regarding fear, and a ὅτι-clause regarding the obedience of wind and sea). And putting the disciples' fear with the abatement of the wind and the coming of calm rather than with the disciples' speaking to one another is at least questionable (see R. A. Guelich 1. 262 against earlier, similar attempts by E. Lohmeyer [89] and G. Schille [in *ZNW* 56 (1965) 32]).

JESUS' DOUBLE VICTORY OVER LEGION

5:1-20 (Matt 8:28-34; Luke 8:26-39)

The story of the Gergasene demoniac divides into several parts: (1) Jesus' arrival in the region of the Gergasenes (v 1); (2) a demoniac's confronting him, with emphasis on the past condition of the demoniac (vv 2-5); (3) repetition of the demoniac's confronting him, but with emphasis on the present contest between Jesus and the unclean spirits inhabiting the demoniac (vv 6-10); (4) Jesus' victory over the unclean spirits (vv 11-13); (5) the response of the people in the region (vv 14-17); and (6) proclamation by the ex-demoniac and its doxological effect with regard to Jesus (vv 18-20).

5:1 *(Matt 8:28; Luke 8:26)* "And they came into [εἰς] the other side of the sea" points up Jesus' success in keeping the disciples from perishing (4:35-41, esp. 38). "Into [εἰς] the region of the Gergasenes" refers to a region on the east side of the Sea of Galilee (see the notes on v 1 for discussion of the vv.ll.). The two successive εἰς-phrases typify Marcan duality (cf. esp. 1:39; 11:1, 11). As usual, the second member gives greater specificity to the first (F. Neirynck, *Duality* 45-53, 94-96).

5:2-5 *(Matt 8:28; Luke 8:27, 29)* "And when he came out of the boat" narrows attention down to Jesus in preparation for the following confrontation, in which the disciples at first play no role (cf. also vv 18, 21, which mention only Jesus, though v 31 will make evident that the disciples have been with him all along and v 16 will have cast them as eyewitnesses and narrators). "A man with an unclean spirit came from the tombs to meet him" presents another challenge to Jesus after that of the storm at sea. If it is textually original, εὐθύς, "immediately" (omitted by B W it sy^{s,p}), stresses the confrontation of powers. The use of ὑπήντησεν, "came to meet," which occurs only here in Mark, prepares for the greater detail of v 6, which will mention seeing Jesus from a distance, running to him, and doing obeisance before him. "Unclean spirit" occurs often in Mark (eleven times). Here it links up with the ritual uncleanness of tombs just as it will later link up with the ritual uncleanness of pigs (vv 11-13). But both linkages reflect the underlying Jewish milieu in which the story was originally told, not the interests of Mark or of his primarily Gentile audience, who ate meals in necropoles and considered pigs ritually clean to the extent of offering them in sacrifice as well as eating them (E. S. Johnson, Jr., in an unpublished paper read at the SBL meeting, November 1989, in Anaheim, California; cf. R. Glöckner [*Neutestamentliche Wundergeschichten* 98-99], who goes too far, however, in denying that ritual purity plays any role). According to word order, some emphasis falls on the demoniac's dwelling in the tombs and thus makes the ensuing contest one of Jesus versus the power of death. By indicating not only that the man comes from the tombs on this occasion but also that he has been living there, the clause "who had his dwelling in the tombs" confirms the nature of the contest.

The inability of anyone to bind the demoniac stresses the power of the unclean spirit. "Not even with a chain," a phrase that takes a prominent first position, intensifies the emphasis. A series of Greek negatives — οὐδέ, "not even"; οὐκέτι, "no longer"; and οὐδείς, "no one" (bis) — heaps further emphasis on the spirit's power. The second of the negatives implies increasing strength on the part of the demoniac: not even the short-lived successes of past efforts to chain him are possible any more. The details concerning past efforts show how overpowering he is and give the reason (διά plus the accusative) behind the "no longer." Those efforts took place "many times." The forward position of πολλάκις, "many times," stresses the point. The mention of both fetters (for the feet) and chains (for the hands), also in an emphatic forward position, indicates the extent of the efforts to subdue the demoniac. But his having pulled apart the chains and smashed to pieces the fetters rivets attention on the failure of these many and extensive efforts. The chiasm which puts τὰς ἁλύσεις, "the chains," after its infinitive and τὰς πέδας, "the fetters," before its infinitive underlines the failure; and a string of infinitives in the perfect tense indicates and likewise underlines that the efforts, having failed, are over and done with (v 4). "And no one was strong enough to subdue him" (cf. 3:27; 9:18 and contrast the description of Jesus as the one stronger than John the Baptizer [1:7]) formally pronounces the verdict of failure and repeats in slightly different phraseology the introductory statement, "And no one was able to bind him" (v 3b). This inclusion wraps up the emphasis on failure (cf. B. Blackburn, *Theios Anēr* 202-3). Thus Mark sets the stage in a way that will make Jesus' exorcism uniquely masterful (cf. the comments on 9:18; 14:37).

A second mention of the tombs brings attention back to the power of death. "In the mountains" adds the note of danger; for in the ancient world mountains did not connote refuge from the pressures of civilization, but exposure to perils of the wild (see, e.g., Ps 121:1 where, despite modern sentiment to the contrary, the traveler most likely calls for the Lord's protection from those perils rather than looking to the mountains as the source of the Lord's protection). The demoniac's yelling evinces his torment. His lacerating himself with stones points up the life-destroying aim of the spirit that possesses him. That this behavior goes on "constantly" shows how unrelentingly the spirit plies its death-dealing trade. The addition of "night and day" sharpens this point, typifies Marcan duality (F. Neirynck, *Duality* 45-53, 94-96), and, as elsewhere, reflects a Jewish method of reckoning twenty-four hour days from sunset to sunset (cf. 4:27). The forward position of the adverbial expressions concerning time and place and the use of a periphrastic verbal construction heap emphasis on the malevolent control that the spirit exercises over its victim (on emphasis in the periphrastic see S. E. Porter, *Verbal Aspect* 480).

5:6-10 *(Matt 8:29; Luke 8:28-31)* Having detailed the unclean spirit's mastery so as to make Jesus' exorcism the more impressive once it occurs, Mark now details the demoniac's approach, already mentioned in v 2. Again as often in Marcan duality, the second mention adds specificity (cf. the comments on v 1). Mark wants to show the spirit's recognition of superior power in the person of Jesus. "Seeing Jesus from a distance" (cf. 9:20; 11:13; 15:40) shows the far-reaching range of his powerful presence. The demoniac runs. He does not run from Jesus to escape. He runs toward Jesus to get rid of him. The running shows

desperation in the face of Jesus' superior power. The doing of obeisance shows
recognition of Jesus' divine majesty (cf. Jas 2:19). The loudness of voice and the
historical present tense of λέγει, "he says," emphasize the strength of the shout,
"Why are you interfering with me, Jesus Son of God Most High? I adjure you
by God that you not torment me." Bookwise, the shout answers the disciples'
question in 4:41: "Who then is this one . . . ?" (cf. 1:24; 3:11). Storywise, the
shout represents the unclean spirit's attempt to resist exorcism; for the torment
will consist of Jesus' saying, or of the exorcistic *effect* of his saying, "Come out,
you unclean spirit, from the man." Specifically, though the parr. Luke 8:31; Matt
8:29 seem to take the torment as punishment in hell (cf. Luke 16:23; Rev 14:11;
20:10), the unclean spirits' outcries which accompany the paroxysm during expulsion in Mark 1:26; 9:26 favor that here, too, the torment refers to pain that the
unclean spirit as well as the demoniac would feel at the moment of expulsion (cf.
Rev 9:5; 18:7, 10, 15 for torment in this world). A concession by Jesus will
eliminate the usual paroxysm and therefore the tormented outcry as well (vv
10-13).

Further details of the present outcry reveal in ascending order of strength
the means used in the spirit's attempt to ward off Jesus: (1) the question why
Jesus is interfering (see the notes on 1:23-24); (2) the use of his name and title
to seize control over him (see the comments and again the notes on 1:23-24); and
(3) the adjuration in the name of none less than God. For Mark, of course, the
spirit's identification of Jesus as God's Son holds central interest (cf. 1:1 and the
comments on that verse). The verb of adjuration (ὁρκίζω) usually occurs in
Hellenistic formulas of exorcism (see BAGD s.v. for references) and suits the
paganism of the demoniac and of the territory (contrast the Jewish ἐπιτιμάω,
"rebuke," in 1:25 plus comments and notes ad loc.). Here the unclean spirit tries,
so to speak, to exorcise Jesus out of exorcising it, and in the attempt uses the
most potent name possible. Ironically, since Jesus is the Son of the very God by
whom the unclean spirit adjures him, the attempt fails. That the spirit describes
God as "Most High" reflects the polytheism of the demoniac and of the pagan
territory in which the story takes place (cf. esp. Acts 16:17; further references in
BAGD s.v. ὕψιστος 2 — though "Son of the Most High" in 4QpsDan Aᵃ
[= 4Q243] shows the possibility of Palestinian rather than extra-Palestinian Hellenistic background [see J. A. Fitzmyer, *Wandering Aramean* 106, against
F. Hahn, *Titles* 291-93]). That Jesus has been telling the spirit to come out and
that it is still resisting shows how difficult a case he is dealing with. But the
greater the difficulty, the larger the success.

In v 8, γάρ, "for," implies that Jesus' command to come out preceded the
demoniac's self-defensive question and adjuration (contrast 1:23-25) and therefore
that ἔλεγεν means "he had been saying" (as in 5:28; 6:18; among others, see
M. Zerwick, *Biblical Greek* §290, against J. A. Kleist [200], who translates ἔλεγεν,
"he was *about* to say"). Because the self-defensive maneuvers followed the
command to come out, no command to shut up preceded the command to come
out (again contrast 1:23-25; also 1:34; 3:11-12). No delayed command to shut up
now follows, for the failure of the command to come out has made it evident that

something more than a command to shut up is needed. That Mark advances the demoniac's question and adjuration out of chronological order (if we take ἔλεγεν in v 8 as having the force of a pluperfect) puts great weight on the strength of the demonical self-defense. Mark's purpose is to magnify Jesus' ultimate victory. If Mark wanted merely to camouflage the failure of the command to come out, he would probably have delayed the command till v 13, if not have omitted it altogether. Its placement in v 8 does not camouflage or even deemphasize the failure so much as it calls attention to the failure by giving first mention to the self-defense and making Jesus' command the reason for the self-defense rather than the overcoming of it. The something that is needed beyond the usual command to shut up is the knowledge of the unclean spirit's name, which will expose Jesus' mistake in addressing one unclean spirit when he issued the command to come out, whereupon the spirits (plural, as they will turn out to be) seized a temporary advantage through using their accurate knowledge of Jesus' name and title (contrast Gen 32:30[29]). The failure of Jesus' command to come out was due, then, not to his ignorance of the demonical name as such; for neither here nor elsewhere does he use demonical names in exorcism, as exorcism normally requires (see, e.g., *T. Sol.* 2:1; 3:6; 4:3-4; 5:1, 6-7 et passim; *b. Meʿil.* 17b; A. Deissmann, *LAE* 260-61; C. Bonner in *HTR* 36 [1943] 44-47). His power needs no such trick of the trade; rather, the failure was due to his commanding a single unclean spirit to come out when in fact the victim needed to be dispossessed of a large number of unclean spirits.

Jesus now forces the revelation of the demonical name. That in answer to his inquiry the spirits reveal their name despite endangering themselves by so doing shows submission to the authority of a superior. Ellipsis of the verb in both Jesus' question and their answer lends vigor to the dialogue and thus emphasis to its promising outcome. The historical present tense of λέγει, "he [the demoniac] says," also emphasizes the spirits' identification of themselves: "Legion [is] my name, because we are many" (for possession by more than one demon, see 16:9; Matt 12:45 par. Luke 11:26; Luke 8:2; cf. *b. Ber.* 51a; and Hor. *Carm.* 1.3.30 if "febrium . . . cohors" refers to a cohort [one tenth of a legion] of fever demons). Πολλοί, "many," takes an emphatic forward position. Here we find the reason why no one has been able to bind or tame the demoniac — he has the strength of over six thousand unclean spirits (see the following notes) — and therefore why this is turning out to be a case more difficult than those that Jesus has dealt with before. Mark wants to impress on his audience how many unclean spirits Jesus is about to exorcise. The adverbial πολλά, "much, urgently" (see the notes on 1:45), exalts the figure of Jesus by portraying the demoniac as reduced from bold adjuration to groveling supplication. Where is the untameable wild man of the earlier verses? Now that Legion have been forced to reveal their name, they know that exorcism is certain and imminent. "Not send them out of the region" implies their resignation to Jesus' throwing them out of the man. The chiasm which puts αὐτόν, "him," after its verb and αὐτά, "them," before its verb (contrast some of the vv.ll.) stresses this resignation. At best the spirits can hope that Jesus will let them stay in home territory rather than banishing them, say, to the wilderness or to ruins, which are dangerous to human beings because the demons wandering and lurking in such places lack human hosts and would sorely like to have one (cf. Matt 12:43 par. Luke 11:24; Tob 8:3; also Isa 13:21; 34:14; Bar 4:35), or — worse yet — to the underworld of the sea (H. Herter in *RJV* 1 [1950] 116). Jesus is in complete control of their fate, and they know that he is.

5:11-13 *(Matt 8:30-32; Luke 8:32-33)* In the entire story δέ, "but," occurs only here (though another adversative will occur in v 19). It contrasts the favorable possibility presented by the herd of pigs on the mountain with the unfavorable possibility of being sent out of the region. "The mountain" relates back to "the mountains" in v 5 and forward to "the steep slope" in v 13. The herd of pigs suit the paganism of the region. According to Roman custom they were doubtless used for sacrifices and meals in the necropolis where the demoniac resided (see E. S. Johnson, Jr., in an unpublished paper read at the SBL meeting, November 1989, Anaheim, California). The large size of the herd accommodates the large number of the spirits. Their plea now turns desperate (πολλά, "much"). Thus Jesus' superiority stands out. The plea also turns positive (contrast v 10) and, as often in Marcan duality, more specific: "Send us into the pigs that into them we may enter" (cf. v 10 and the comments on v 1). The chiasm that puts "into the pigs" after its verb and "into them" before its verb emphasizes the herd of pigs as the unclean spirits' desired new host. Ordinarily, spirits would not want animals as hosts, though against their will an exorcist might send them into animals (R. Pesch, *Besessene* 37-38, n. 82). But here the spirits think they will be lucky if they gain a new host at all, even of this kind, and do not have to leave the neighborhood of the tombs, where they feel at home (cf. v 10; Matt 12:43-44a par. Luke 11:24). Not only does Jesus have power to cast them out. He also has authority to tell them where they may go next — and they acknowledge that he does. His permission displays an exercise of that authority and stands in place of a renewed command to come out. So cowed are the spirits now that such a command is no longer needed.

"Coming out" marks the success of the exorcism. But this success will go beyond exorcism. Neuter plural subjects like τὰ πνεύματα τὰ ἀκάθαρτα, "the unclean spirits," usually take a singular verb. The plural of εἰσῆλθον, "entered," therefore stresses the large number of the unclean spirits whom Jesus allows to enter the pigs. For the pigs, the specification "about two thousand," which far exceeds the number of 100-150 in a herd of normal size and even the number of 300 or more in an extraordinarily large herd (Varro *Rust.* 2.4.22), makes this emphasis explicit. (In a later addition to the story we would expect "about six thousand" to correspond to the number in a Roman legion.) The rushing down a steep slope into the sea and drowning there give visible evidence that the spirits have come out of the man and fulfilled their urge to destroy life (cf. v 5; 9:22; Rev 9:5). A switch from the aorist tense of εἰσῆλθον and ὥρμησεν, "rushed," to the imperfect tense in ἐπνίγοντο, "were drowning," draws out the drowning for prolonged attention. But since the purpose of the spirits in asking that Jesus send them into the pigs was to stay in the region, the drowning of the pigs spells disaster to the spirits' hope of staying there. Unwittingly, they bring homelessness on themselves (contrast the freedom to return in Luke 11:24). Since they have inhabited the pigs and Mark writes nothing about their leaving them, the spirits must go into the water with them — a fearsome fate for the spirits, for in *T. Sol.* 5:11 a demon pleads with Solomon: "Do not condemn me to water" (see also *T. Sol.* 11:6). They would have preferred wandering in the wilderness or lurking in ruins.

5:14-17 *(Matt 8:33-34; Luke 8:34-37)* The fleeing of the herdsmen shows them awestruck at the display of Jesus' power. Their announcing the event in the city agrees with the Roman practice of locating necropoles right outside cities and stems from wonderment. The announcement in the hamlets, too, shows the extent of the herdsmen's wonderment. The populace respond in kind. "They came [ἦλθον — aorist indicative] to see [ἰδεῖν — another aorist, but only an infinitive] what had happened." But "they come [ἔρχονται — present indicative] to Jesus and see [θεωροῦσιν — another present indicative] the one being demonized. . . ." The doubling of coming and seeing, the switch to the historical present tense, and the escalation from an infinitive to another main verb emphasize the awe-inspiring presence of Jesus and the saving effects of the exorcism he has performed. So strong is this emphasis that the historical present tense causes the substantive participle, which acts as a direct object, to go into the present tense (τὸν δαιμονι-ζόμενον, "the one being demonized") and keeps it in the present tense even after the main verb has switched to the aorist (v 16). Not till v 18 will the participle settle back into the normal aorist (ὁ δαιμονισθείς, "the one having been de-monized"). The saving effects of the exorcism are (1) the sitting of the ex-de-moniac, in contrast with his former breaking loose from fetters and chains; (2) his being clothed, in contrast with his former nakedness (probably implied by his lacerating himself with stones); and (3) his sanity, in contrast with his former incessant yelling and other wild behavior (cf. Jesus' calming the sea in 4:35-41). Mark does not tell where the ex-demoniac got his clothes. The effect is all. "The one who had had Legion" gives one last reminder of the magnitude of this exorcism. "And they feared" indicates the people's standing in reverential awe of Jesus, as his disciples did at 4:41, not yet in anger over loss of the pigs or in fear of further loss; for the plea that he leave does not come till after the following narration, which will include the episode concerning the pigs (cf. Ps 65:8).

To confirm to readers the reliability of the story, Mark next mentions the narration of the event to the people who have come. Just as this narration comes on top of the earlier announcement (v 14), so the narrators come on top of the herdsmen who made the earlier announcement but who, having been on the mountainside with their pigs rather than on the shore where the demoniac con-fronted Jesus (v 2), do not know the details of the exorcism that Jesus' companions know ("how it happened to the demoniac and concerning the pigs"). Apparently, then, these additional reporters are "the Twelve," who have come in the same boat with Jesus, plus "the ones around Jesus," who have come in "other boats with him" (cf. vv 10, 35-36). But Mark calls them "the ones who had seen" to stress the reliability of their story. Again as usual in Marcan duality, the present narration adds specificity to the earlier announcement (see the comments on v 1).

Separate mention of the demoniac and of the pigs emphasizes the double victory of Jesus over Legion. The emphasis now lies, not on "what" (τί) has happened (as in v 14), but on "how" (πῶς) it has happened, i.e. on the details that Mark has included to highlight the display of Jesus' power (cf. A. T. Robertson, *Grammar* 1032). "Concerning the pigs" gives the reason for the plea that Jesus "go away from their borders." It is unclear whether "they" refers to the herdsmen, to their fellow countrymen, or to all of them together — probably the last possibility. In any case, their reason is not only economic. It is also religious in that the pigs were used for sacrifice. Mark's interest does not lie in fear of further loss, however, but on the people's fear of Jesus himself; for he wants to erase the notion of a Jesus crucified out of weakness. This desire shows itself in the infinitive παρα-καλεῖν, "to beseech." As the unclean spirits besought Jesus not to send them away (ἀποστείλῃ — v 10), so now these people beseech Jesus himself to go away (ἀπελθεῖν). This twist underscores his authority: whether sending away or going away, he can only be besought, not ordered about.

5:18-20 *(Luke 8:37-38)* The reference to Jesus' getting into the boat passes over anything that he might have said to the people. Attention shifts to the ex-demoniac, who beseeches him "that he might be with him." The aspiration to be with Jesus matches the very purpose for which he chose the Twelve according to 3:14, ἵνα ὦσιν μετ' αὐτοῦ, "that they might be with him." But here μετ' αὐτοῦ moves ahead of the verb for emphasis on Jesus: the ex-demoniac wants to be with him, his great and powerful deliverer, rather than with his compatriots. The desire to be with him, emphasized by the historical present tense of "beseeches," contrasts sharply with his own earlier attempt to ward off Jesus as well as with his compatriots' request that Jesus leave, and thus shows the completeness of Jesus' success in calming this stormy man. Jesus exercises his authority again by not allowing the ex-demoniac to be with him. The strong adversative ἀλλά, "rather," and the historical present tense of λέγει, "he says," stress the authority of the contrary command to go home (contrast the tombs in vv 2-3, 5, but cf. 2:11) and report to his family how many things the Lord has done for him and how much he had mercy on him. The adding of "your family" (τοὺς σούς) to "your house" typifies Marcan duality. The ex-demoniac's family have not come with the others who have come to see for themselves. "How many things" may refer to the details of his new state of being seated, clothed, and sane (v 15). What Jesus has done for him, the Lord has done (see 13:20 for another use, outside OT quotations, of κύριος for God). *Jesus* implies that he is the Lord's agent; but since 1:2-3 applied to Jesus and John the Baptist an OT passage that speaks of the Lord and his messenger, *Mark* probably implies here that Jesus has acted as the Lord (cf. 2:28; 12:37 in addition to 5:20). The perfect tense of πεποίηκεν, "has done," brings out the completeness and permanence of Jesus' action. "And how much he had mercy" specifies the character of the things the Lord Jesus has done for the man (cf. Mark's penchant for such duality and M. Reiser, *Syntax und Stil* 134-36, on this kind of paratactic "and").

Literarily, the man's going away (ἀπῆλθεν) from Jesus matches the people's request that Jesus go away (ἀπελθεῖν) from their borders (v 17). The man's beginning to preach contrasts with his beginning to beseech Jesus to be with him (v 18). Mark shifts from ἀπάγγειλον for an informal report, such as Jesus commanded that the man give to his family and such as the herdsmen had already given (v 14; cf. 6:30), to κηρύσσειν for a formal, gospel-like proclamation (cf. the proclamations by John the Baptizer, Jesus, an ex-leper, and the disciples in 1:4, 7, 14, 38, 39, 45; 3:14; 6:12; 13:10; 14:9). "In the Decapolis" expands the field of the ex-demoniac's proclamation beyond his home and even beyond the region of the Gergasenes, whose people already know by having come and seen and heard, to the much larger territory of the ten cities referred to by the designation "the Decapolis" (cf. 7:31). This expansion serves Mark's purpose of showing the powerful effect of Jesus' action. Exemplary evangelism is not the point; rather, evangelism serves the Christological point that Jesus' act of power inspired the ex-demoniac to exceed by far the commission that Jesus gave him. "How many things Jesus had done for him" now makes an editorial identification of Jesus with the Lord, who in Jesus' own words had done exactly that (ὅσα plus a form of ποιέω and the dative of advantage in both vv 19 and 20). Highlighting this identification is the chiasm of verb–indirect object–subject (ἐποίησεν αὐτῷ ὁ Ἰησοῦς, "Jesus had done for him") as compared with subject–indirect object–verb (ὁ κύριός σοι πεποίηκεν, "the Lord has done for you"). "And all marveled" clinches the Christological point regarding Jesus' greatness rather than making a missionary point regarding Gentile evangelism. Mark omits any telling of the family at home, not necessarily to imply failure to do so, but because the marveling of all in the Decapolis makes a private audience at home not worth mentioning even if it did occur. The forward position of πάντες, "all," underscores the universality of admiration heaped on Jesus.

NOTES

R. Pesch (1. 279-82, 292-93) thinks that the present position of this story points to Gentile evangelism as a result of preceding Jewish rejection in 4:1-34. But we have seen that 4:1-34 and the "other boats" in 4:35-36 count for good success, not rejection, in Jesus' ministry among the Jews. Therefore the present story may owe its position to the actualities of topography and chronology. The many vivid details, given from the standpoint of external observation, may derive from eyewitness reporting by a disciple and from descriptions of the demoniac's earlier behavior by locals. Mark writes up these details in a way that furthers his own ends, however.

In v 1 the v.l. "Gadarenes" (A C f¹³ Majority Text syᵖ·ʰ) is probably due to parallel influence from Matt 8:28. But to decide between "Gerasenes" (ℵ* B D latt sa) and "Gergasenes" (ℵ² L Δ Θ f¹ 28 33 565 700 892 1241 1424 al syˢ bo) is much more difficult. The argument of T. Baarda (in *Neotestamentica et Semitica* 181-88) that "Gergasenes" arose out of a conjecture by Origen deserves respect (cf. M.-J. Lagrange in *RB* 4 [1895] 512-22), but itself depends on a conjecture that the similar but differently spelled OT "Girgashites" influenced Origen (*Joh.* 6 §§208-11). The possibility remains that Origen was working with earlier tradition (cf. F. G. Lang [in *ZDPV* 94 (1978) 145-46, n. 4], who posits an original "Gergasenes," changed in the West to the better known "Gerasenes," which was then "corrected" in the East to "Gadarenes"; contrast W. M. Christie [*Palestine Calling* 78], who accepts "Gerasenes" as original but regards it as a contraction of "Gergasenes").

The present commentary rests hesitantly on the v.l. "Gergasenes." In v 14 the definite article with "city" most naturally refers back to the city implied in v 1. But Gerasa lies about thirty miles southeast of the nearest point on the southeastern shore of the Sea of Galilee (and even Gadara lies about five miles southeast), i.e. too far away for the city folks' arrival at lakeside an apparently very short while after Jesus performed the exorcism there. Yet modern Kursi, which is associable with ancient Gergasa (N.B. the consonantal similarity in that both begin with a guttural, proceed with *l,* and tail off with *s*), has a location on the east shore of the lake. Not far away, a steep slope such as the story refers to leads down toward the lake (though it does not drop off into it — but Mark does not say that the pigs fell from a cliff directly into the sea; cf. G. Dalman, *SSW* 176-79). And recent excavations have uncovered at least one nearby cave, which could have been used for a tomb as caves often were (Mark does not describe the tombs as cut out of rock [contrast 15:46]), and a fifth century church quite possibly commemorating the occurrence there of the exorcism (D. Urman in *CNI* 22 [1971] 176-77; J.-B. Livio in *BTS* 152 [1973] 6-16; V. Tsaferis in *IEJ* 22 [1972] 276-77; cf. W. M. Christie [*Palestine Calling* 79-80], who reports having found in 1893 both a number of ancient caves evidently used as tombs and also a modern bedouin cemetery in front of the caves, which were subsequently obliterated by the falling in of part of the hillside — though M.-J. Lagrange [in *RB* 4 (1895) 519-20] denies any evidence of burials). It is easier to believe that Mark or, more likely, a pre-Marcan traditioner knew the topography and correctly mentioned the Gergasenes than that later scribes, scattered about the Roman Empire, knew the topography and corrected a false mention of the Gerasenes by Mark, or even that Origen first corrected it and influenced others to do so. This likelihood increases with acceptance of the Petrine origin of Mark's materials (see pp. 1026-45). Origen fails to mention manuscript support for "Gergasenes," but does mention that in Matt 8:28 a few manuscripts read "Gadarenes." His purpose is probably not to contrast fewness with nullity, however, but to contrast fewness with preponderance, i.e. with many manuscripts supporting "Gergasenes." Apart from the topographical and archeological features of Gergasa that favor the originality of "Gergasenes," the total unimportance and little knownness of Gergasa make it difficult to see why strong and early support developed for this reading if it is not original; but in several ways it is easy to see how and why a shift to "Gerasenes" and, beginning with Matthew, "Gadarenes" may have occurred (though J. Monson has suggested in a private communication to the present writer that Matthew refers to people from Garada on a basaltic plateau above Kursi [Josephus *Ant.* 13.13.5 §375; idem *J.W.* 1 §90] "with a switch [in spelling] something like *Gabara* [Josephus's usage] = *Araba* [Talmudic usage] in central Lower Galilee"): (1) Gerasa and Gadara were much larger and better known (see E. Schürer, G. Vermes, F. Millar, and M. Black, *History* 2. 132-36, 149-55). (2) The reference in v 20 to the ex-demoniac's preaching in the Decapolis might naturally shift attention to those other cities, both of which belonged to the Decapolis, whereas Gergasa did not. (3) A shift to Gerasa might have come about or been helped along by the ease of omitting the second g in Gergasenes (cf. E. F. F. Bishop [*Jesus of Palestine* 134], who cites an Arabic parallel). (4) A shift to Gerasa might also have come about or been helped along through association of Gerasa with גָּרַשׁ, "drive out, cast out," which tallies with the exorcistic content of the story. Finally, (5) Jesus tells the ex-demoniac to "go" (ὕπαγε) home, but he "went away" (ἀπῆλθεν) and preached in the Decapolis. "Away" (ἀπ-) plus the reference to the Decapolis seems to mean that he left "the region of the . . .-enes." But then that region would have to be of the Gergasenes; for along with other cities, Gerasa and Gadara *are* the Decapolis whereas Gergasa is not (though it is located in the territory of the Decapolitan city of Hippus).

That this story is set probably in the region of the Gergasenes favors that the sea voyage does not derive from Mark's redaction apart from tradition; for a sea voyage provides the most probable way of Jesus' going to that region, and that region seems an unlikely one to have been fabricated as an object of Jesus' visit. Furthermore, the "they" of "they came" in v 1 seems traditional rather than redactional; for it is unlikely on the one hand that Jesus sailed alone (against the v.l. "he came"), and it is natural on the other hand that in v 2 the narrative should narrow down to him for his confrontation with the demoniac (cf. 1:21; 8:22; 11:15, 27). In view of v 16, it is probably untrue to say that those who come in v 1 play no role in vv 2-20 (cf. the comments on v 16; also the comments and notes on 4:35-36). The presence of Marcan locutions in vv 1-2 need not imply the absence of tradition. The objection that a voyage across the Sea of Galilee would have taken only two hours or so whereas the voyage in 4:35-41 started in the evening and the story in 5:1-20 takes place during daylight, leaving a several hours' gap indicative of an artificial connection, does not consider possibilities such as the storm's prolonging the voyage and the boats' lying at anchor till daybreak.

According to L. Schenke (*Wundererzählungen* 174), Mark thinks that the Sea of Galilee sits in the middle of the Decapolis (7:31), that the region of the Gerasenes is identical with the Decapolis, and that therefore the region of the Gerasenes can include the east shore of the sea, despite the distance of Gerasa itself, without posing a problem. But in v 20 "went away" implies that "in the Decapolis" represents a wider region than that of the Gerasenes or, if we adopt the v.l. "Gergasenes," a different region from that of the Gergasenes; and in 7:31 "into the midst of the borders of Decapolis" will not act as an adjective modifying "the sea of Galilee," but will form the last prepositional phrase in a string of prepositional phrases that act as adverbs modifying "he went."

See E. C. Maloney, *Semitic Interference* 131-35, and M. Reiser, *Syntax und Stil* 20-21, for opposite answers to the question whether ἄνθρωπος, "a man" (v 2), represents Semitic interference for τις, "someone." To suppose that ἄνθρωπος without further description means a Jew (so J. D. M. Derrett in *JSNT* 3 [1979] 6, 16, n. 26) is to neglect the neutrality of the word, the predominance of Gentiles to the east of Galilee, and pointers to Gentileness in the present story (the calling of God "Most High," pig-herding, preaching in the Decapolis — the combination of which does not create a necessity but does establish a probability favoring a non-Jew).

Among others, R. Pesch (1. 284) thinks that this story originally lacked anything about pigs, that the exorcism took place at Gerasa, and that a transfer of the story to seaside occurred when the episode about the pigs was added. But the archeologically favored proximity of tombs to the steep slope and sea supports a location of the exorcism there. The large number of the unclean spirits favors an original connection of the exorcism with the herd of pigs. And separating the episode about the pigs from the story of the exorcism makes it difficult to explain the origin of that episode. To explain its origin by appeal to an Assyrian incantational text in which a demon is supposed to leave a demoniac and enter a pig (R. C. Thompson, *Devils and Evil Spirits* 2. 13-27 [tablet N]; idem, *Semitic Magic* 208-9; J. F. Craghan in *CBQ* 30 [1968] 531) labors under several wide differences: (1) the Assyrian incantational text dates from about seven hundred years earlier than Mark and the material in it from much earlier yet (according to Thompson himself, *Devils and Spirits* 2. xi), to say nothing of geographical distance; (2) the Assyrian demon is forced into a pig, but Legion asks to be sent into pigs; and (3) Legion destroys the pigs, but a human being kills the Assyrian pig, which is only a suckling, and dismembers it and places the pieces one by one on the various bodily parts of a bedridden sick man before the demon departs from the sick man (contrast the lack of bodily contact between Mark's demoniac and the pigs). Furthermore, (4) the Assyrian text does not say that the demon enters the slain, dismembered pig; and precisely because the pig is no longer living, we may well doubt that the demon does so.

J. Jeremias (*Jesus' Promise* 30-31, n. 5) thinks that someone inserted the episode about the pigs "only . . . because the swineherds witnessed the expulsion of the demon (v. 14)." But he does not explain the long jump from the swineherds' seeing what happened to the demoniac to the fabrication of their pigs' being possessed and plunged into the sea. And the reference to "the herdsmen" (v 14), which Jeremias takes to be traditional, depends on the supposedly inserted episode concerning the pigs. The foregoing considerations likewise militate against denying that tradition lies behind vv 16-17, i.e. against attributing vv 16-17 (and 21a) to Mark's wanting to get Jesus back across the lake (so, e.g., R. H. Lightfoot, *History and Interpretation* 88-90). Other considerations, noted below, will militate against treating vv 18-20 as a non-traditional Marcan or pre-Marcan construct designed for the motif of a broken messianic secret.

To reveal the plurality of the unclean spirits before v 9 would spoil the dramatic buildup of the story. Therefore we should not think that the author of v 2, which speaks of an unclean spirit in the singular, does not know about Legion. Nor should we think that the demoniac's meeting Jesus on shore in v 2 contradicts his seeing Jesus from a distance and running to do him obeisance in v 6 (so, e.g., C. H. Cave in *NTS* 11 [1964-65] 94); for Mark chooses ὑπήντησεν, "came to meet," because its meaning leaves room for those later details. See the note on 1:23-24 concerning "a man with an unclean spirit." For tombs (cave-like rooms naturally or artificially formed in rock [cf. Matt 27:60 and what is still to be found near modern Kursi], or small room-like structures [cf. Luke 11:47]) as dwellings for the poor and outcast, see Ps 67:7 LXX; Isa 65:4 (cf. Job 30:5-6; Heb 11:38). The regular leaving of food for the dead would have supplied the demoniac with ample sustenance (E. S. Johnson, Jr., in an unpublished paper read at the SBL meeting, November 1989, Anaheim, California). With tombs as the haunts of demons, cf. *b. Ber.* 3b; *b. Šabb.* 67a; *b. Giṭ.* 70a; *b. Sanh.* 65b. M. Reiser (*Syntax und Stil* 128-30) notes that the paratactic καί in v 3b, where we might have expected a relative pronoun, is Greek as well as Semitic in style. Here, the preceding ὅς-clause would make a ὅν-clause awkward. As it is, the καί-clause gives independent weight to the inability of anyone to bind the demoniac.

Since gravesites were regularly visited and meals often eaten there, the people of the city and hamlets near the present necropolis naturally wanted to subdue the demoniac. Rabbinic literature lists four characteristics of madness: (1) running about at night; (2) staying overnight at burial places; (3) tearing apart one's clothes; and (4) destroying what one has been given (Str-B 1. 491-92). The behavior of the present demoniac matches the first two characteristics but exceeds the third if v 15 implies former nakedness rather than torn clothing, and exceeds the fourth in that he destroyed restraints rather than mere gifts. Devotees of a false god might voluntarily lacerate themselves to achieve an effect *on* the deity (see, e.g., 1 Kgs 18:28), but here self-laceration seems to denote an involuntary effect *of* the unclean spirit on its victim.

The story may be influenced by the language of Isa 65:1-7, 11 LXX, which has διὰ παντός, "always" (so also Mark); τοῖς δαιμονίοις, "to the demons" (cf. forms of δαιμονί-ζομαι in Mark); ἐν τοῖς μνήμασιν, "in the tombs" (so also Mark), and references to pigs, mountains, and an attempt to keep others at a distance. But against derivation of Mark's story as such, or even of these details in it, from the LXX of Isaiah, (1) it is an unclean spirit that tries to keep Jesus at a distance to avoid exorcism, but in Isaiah it is Jews who out of a holier-than-thou attitude try to keep others at a distance; (2) Mark writes of a herd of pigs, Isaiah of pig's flesh; (3) Mark describes demonic possession, Isaiah heathen worship; (4) Mark's mountain provides pasture for pigs, Isaiah's mountains places of worship for pagans; (5) Mark uses μνημείων for tombs (v 2) before switching to the Septuagintal word; (6) Mark repeatedly speaks of an "unclean spirit" and "unclean spirits" rather than of "a demon" or "demons," as in the LXX of Isaiah; and (7) the victim in Mark has a dwelling in the tombs, whereas pagan worshippers only sleep overnight in them according to Isaiah (though we may understand Mark to mean that the yelling and self-laceration took place in the tombs during the night and in the mountains during the day). Cf. R. Glöckner, *Neutestamentliche Wundergeschichten* 99-101. The difference between the two Greek words for tombs may be due to simple stylistic variation (cf. 15:46 vv.ll.; 16:2 vv.ll.) or to the difference between Mark's using the one word when writing with his own preferred diction (v 2) and the other word when writing under the influence of the LXX of Isaiah, which perhaps has superficially affected the wording of the tradition (vv 3, 5). In either case, we do not need to posit separate sources to explain this difference. Since in v 2 the tombs have no function, this verse does not represent early tradition to which vv 3-5 have been added. Rather, Mark's mentioning the tombs in v 2 anticipates their traditional mention in vv 3, 5, where they function as the habitat of the demoniac. F. C. Synge (in *ExpTim* 92 [1980-81] 330) thinks that the material in vv 3-5 between the two occurrences of "in the tombs" represents a pre-Marcan insertion which led to repetition of the phrase. But the description therein of the demoniac's untameability (cf. Judg 14:6; 16:9, 12; Jer 2:20) is of the same character as the immediately following description of his yelling and self-laceration and therefore seems to be of one piece with it.

Doing obeisance to Jesus shows deference to him, but shouting, "Why are you interfering with me, . . . ?" (which is even closer to 1 Kgs 17:18 than was Mark 1:24), and adjuring him do not show deference. If it is inadmissible to interpret the shout and adjuration by the obeisance, it is likewise inadmissible to interpret the obeisance by the shout and adjuration, as though the obeisance is a part of the self-defense, perhaps even a trick designed to make Jesus relax his exorcistic urge. On the contrary, the deity to which the obeisance points highlights the need and futility of the self-defensive maneuvers. See J. Schneider in *TDNT* 5. 462-63, n. 7, against taking "Jesus, Son of God Most High" with the following adjuration; *PGM* I. 262-347 for adjurations of deities that they treat the adjurer kindly; and S. Eitrem, *Some Notes* 24-25, on the use of βασανίζω, "torment," in exorcistic texts. With the comment that the demon is neither Jewish nor pagan, J. Wellhausen (2. Aufl., 38-39) resists seeing paganism behind "God Most High." But he makes no allowance for the suiting of a demon's language to the character and environment of the demoniac. The pigs and population of the present territory leave little room for doubt. The suitability of "God Most High" to this setting makes doubtful that Mark has substituted "Son of God Most High" for an earlier, non-filial title (as thought by J. Zmijewski in *SNTU* A/12. 5-34).

The reasons given in the comments for the absence of a command to shut up eliminate the need to suggest less convincing reasons, e.g., that the privacy of the setting makes a command to silence unnecessary (but the pigherders are within range — v 14) or that the subsequent conversation between Jesus and Legion would make inappropriate an earlier command to shut up (but such a command would be no more inappropriate than the earlier command to come out — against E. Lemcio in *NTS* 32 [1986] 204, n. 37; T. A. Burkill, *Myterious Revelation* 89-90). Some commentators think that the command to come out (v 8) did not originally belong to the story, that Mark or someone before him inserted the command out of conviction that a story of exorcism requires it, and that the original narrator would have disagreed on the ground that a demon would not have been able to resist such a command even for a moment (see, e.g., E. Haenchen 192-93). But if Mark or another inserter of the command could think such resistance possible, so also could the original narrator. It is hard to understand the comment of J. Gnilka (1. 205) that insertion of the command to come out overlooks the irony that the unclean spirit has already been reduced to a helpless "exorcist." The success or failure of the spirit's adjuration of Jesus still hangs in the balance; and use of the name of God Most High in the adjuration and Jesus' need to learn the spirit's name indicate that the balance is tipping in the spirit's favor. The citation of 6:52 by C. E. B. Cranfield (177-78) to support the view that Mark inserts v 8 rests on failure to notice that 6:52 describes a state of affairs existing at the time of the preceding event rather than narrating an event that happened prior to the time of the preceding event (as 5:8 does).

With an appeal to v 28 it might be argued that the imperfect of ἔλεγεν in v 8 denotes that Jesus was speaking simultaneously with the demoniac (v 7). But the participles "having heard" and "having come" in v 27 favor that in v 28 the speaking will occur prior to, not simultaneously with, the touching. It overinterprets the imperfect tense of ἔλεγεν in v 8, however, to treat it as iterative, as though Jesus vainly issues command after command that the spirit come out.

If Jesus' previously commanding unclean spirits to shut up when they shouted out his divine sonship (3:11-12; cf. 1:24-25, 34) were designed to keep it secret, we would not expect such a command to be missing here in v 9. For there is nothing about Gentile territory that makes maintenance of the secret unnecessary. Though Gentiles might not join in a Jewish messianic revolt, they would likely misunderstand messiahship as entailing such a revolt. Moreover, the Jewish disciples of Jesus, both the Twelve and apparently those in other boats as well, are with him and he has not yet revealed to them the necessity of his death and resurrection, which according to the dominant theory of the secret have to be revealed before the secret can out. Therefore we should forget about such a secret, treat the earlier commands to silence as attacks on the self-defensive maneuvers of the spirits, and account for the present lack of a command to silence as due to Jesus' need to find out the spirit's name since a command to come out has not worked. See *PGM* I. 162-63 for asking a demon to divulge its name; *PGM* IV. 3037-39; XIII. 243-44 for an exorcist's getting a demon to speak; *ANET* 29-31 or H. Gressmann, *Altorientalische Texte* 77-79, for a demon's addressing an exorcist; Acts 19:13-16 for a demon's doing so in self-defense; and for other comparable materials, *Jub.* 10:1-9; *b. Pesaḥ.* 112b-113a; *b. Giṭ.* 68a; *b. B. Bat.* 73a; *b. B. Šabb.* 67a; Luc. *Philops.* 10, 12, 16, 31; Philostr. *VA* 3.38; 4.20.

We should not think that the demoniac is appealing to pity by noting how many unclean spirits inhabit him. The spirit itself identifies itself as Legion. See O. Bauernfeind, *Worte* 36-37, for treating "Legion" as a proper name, not merely as an indication of number. "Legion [is] my name" would have to be jettisoned for the latter view to stand. J. Jeremias (*Jesus' Promise* 30-31, n. 5; idem, *NT Theology* 1. 86-87) conjectures that since the Aramaic behind "Legion" (לְגִיוֹנָא) could also mean "legionary" (Str-B 2. 9), the unclean spirit refuses to divulge its name and describes itself instead as one of a large company, but that Mark understands a plurality of unclean spirits. The correlation with a large herd of pigs favors Mark's understanding, however. To avoid this correlation one may also conjecture an earlier version of the story lacking the episode concerning the pigs (cf. the notes on v 1), but the necessity of making a second conjecture weakens the first one. And we are still left with the irrelevance of a reference to many unclean spirits if they are not inhabiting the demoniac. Unclean spirits outside the demoniac play no part in the story, not even by way of standing ready to help their compatriot in the demoniac; and the numerousness of legionaries does not explain why a single one would bear the name "Legionary."

Since the text explicitly associates Legion with numerousness, we have no reason to think of a covert reference to the occupation of Palestine by Roman legions. Such a reference would more likely have fit Jewish territory, anyway. One could conjecture, of course, that the event did take place in Jewish territory but that the story came to circulate without indication of place and only later gained an unhistorical pagan location. But a house of conjectures is no sturdier than a house of cards. Even more conjectural is the suggestion of G. Theissen (*Miracle Stories* 89 [n. 21], 255 [n. 58]) that the unclean spirits are spirits of the dead — hence, the tombs — more specifically, of fighters who fell in battle resisting the Romans. P. Winter (*Trial* 180-81) goes so far as to suggest, quite oppositely, that the pigs represent the tenth Roman legion, which was stationed in 70-135 C.E. near the site of the story and whose emblem was a wild boar (cf. T. Reinach [in *REJ*

47 (1903) 177], who notes the Roman practice of sacrificing pigs), and that the drowning of the pigs may represent the drowning of some Roman soldiers who took a swim. But the date is probably too late, and a wild boar is not the same as herded pigs. O. Betz (in *Studies in the NT* 238-39) draws parallels with the imprisonment of demons in Sheol during the coming age (1QH 3:17-18) and with the drowning of the Egyptians in the Reed Sea (Exodus 14; Ps 107:11; cf. Isa 43:16-17), sees an underlying wordplay between שׁדִים, "demons," and זֵדִים, "insolent ones," and interprets the story as meaning that the real enemy of Israel is not Rome, but Satan and his demons. But the Egyptians were human beings, not demons; and זֵדִים matches no word in Mark's text.

Now that Legion have revealed their plurality, it may seem puzzling to read the singular in v 10, "he [or 'it'] was beseeching," as in v 12. It does not explain the singular to conjecture an original meaning, "legionary," in v 9; for v 10 goes right on to state that the beseeching consisted in a plea not to send "them" out of the region. Does the singular illustrate the rule that in Greek a neuter plural subject (here, an implied τὰ πνεύματα τὰ ἀκάθαρτα) may take a singular verb? But the adjective that has just described Legion — πολλοί, "many" — is masculine (v 9). Furthermore, in v 12 the same verb takes the plural; and in v 13 the same neuter plural subject takes a plural verb.

The puzzle clears up when we pay attention to gender. In v 2 ἄνθρωπος, "man," establishes a masculine reference to the demoniac; for πνεῦμα, "spirit," is neuter. This reference clearly carries through v 7a (cf. ὅς, αὐτόν [ter], κράζων, κατακόπτων ἑαυτόν, ἰδών, κράξας — all unambiguously masculine). The first person pronoun that occurs three times in v 7 therefore refers to the demoniac. But the demoniac is so dominated by the unclean spirit (as it is called till the revelation of its plurality) that one can scent the spirit as well as hear the man in the question and adjuration of v 7. And true to scent, in v 8 Jesus speaks to the man (for there is no indication of a shift from the man who shouted — κράξας, masculine — in v 7), yet tells the "unclean spirit" (τὸ πνεῦμα τὸ ἀκάθαρτον, neuter) to come out. Jesus continues to speak to the man in v 9, for αὐτόν is masculine, not neuter. But he asks for the name of the spirit; the name of the man would not provide useful information. Since Jesus asks the man, it is the man who answers. Since Jesus asks for the name of the spirit, the man answers *as* the spirit, at first in the singular ("Legion [is] *my* name") because it is the man who is answering, then in the plural ("because *we* are many") since he is answering as the spirit who is really more than one spirit. But the plural adjective πολλοί, "many," is masculine because the man is acting as the spirits' mouthpiece and because they are personal (cf. the masculine τόν modifying λεγιῶνα, which is properly feminine, in v 15; also the masculine participles modifying πνεῦμα in 3:11; 9:20, 25-26). Verse 10 simply repeats the pattern of a singular verb for the man's speaking, followed by a plural reference to the spirits in the words that represent them. In v 11 the mention of the herd of pigs raises the prospect of the spirits' being dispersed on coming out of the man. This prospect makes it appropriate that the spirits themselves should speak as a plurality capable of dispersion: "*they* besought" (v 12). But the man is still acting as their mouthpiece; so after the pattern of v 9 the accompanying plural participle λέγοντες, "saying," is masculine. Finally, their going out of the man takes away his function as their mouthpiece; hence, the plural participle that describes their going out — ἐξελθόντα — is neuter in agreement with its noun πνεύματα, "spirits," which is the subject of the plural verb εἰσῆλθον, "entered" (v 13; cf. 3:11).

T. Sol. 5:1-13; 13:1-17 are sometimes cited as parallels to vv 7-10. But there, demons at first refuse to give Solomon their names and instead ask who Solomon their opponent is, whereas here the unclean spirits exhibit their knowledge of Jesus' name and title. V. Taylor (282) correctly notes that in v 10 ἵνα μή is epexegetic rather than telic. But the phrase was telic rather than epexegetic in 3:9. J. Ernst (156) thinks it unnatural that Legion should not want to be sent out of the region and deduces that a natural meaning — viz., that Roman legions did not want to leave Palestine — underlies the unnatural one. But the portrayal of demons as territorial has the support of Matt 12:43-44a par. Luke 11:24; and we may find it more natural to imagine that the soldiers who made up Roman legions would have liked to go home, or at least move to a more desirable part of the empire, not stay in Palestine. G. Schwarz (in *NTS* 22 [1975-76] 214-15) supposes that χώρας (v 10) derives from mistaking םוהת, "abyss" (so Luke 8:31b), for םוחת, "region." But he has to explain the change from "into" to "out of" as following on the supposed confusion, whereas "into the abyss" would more likely have forestalled it. See G. Dalman, *Words* 65, for criticism of a similar earlier suggestion.

For πρός as indicating presence and proximity (v 11), see 2:2; 5:11; 6:3; 9:19; 11:4; 14:49, 54; and E. C. Maloney, *Semitic Interference* 55-57, on the position of μεγάλη, "large." M. Zerwick (*Biblical Greek* §252) thinks that the aorist tense of παρεκάλεσαν (v 12) indicates successful pleading, whereas the imperfect tense of παρεκάλει in v 10 indicated only an attempted plea. F. Annen (*Heil* 56) attributes the aorist to tradition. Πέμψον, "send" (hapax in Mark), probably belongs to the tradition; for in v 10, which was editorial, Mark preferred the synonym ἀποστείλῃ. Or the shift from ἀποστείλῃ (v 10) to πέμψον (v 12) may be a stylistic variation suited to the shift from "out of the region" to "into the pigs." When exorcised, demons may vent their anger with some mischief (Josephus *Ant.* 8.2.5 §§46-48; Philostr. *VA* 4.20; *Acts Pet.* 11). But here the demons have themselves asked to be sent into the pigs for the purpose of staying in the region. Therefore the drowning of the herd looks like the demons' destroying their new habitat more completely than they were able to destroy their old one, the man. Perhaps we are meant to think that a human being has at least some resistance or divine protection, as in Rev 9:5.

The plea in v 12 is no more particular than the one in v 10; and the one in v 10 is not necessarily iterative, for verbs of speaking often take the imperfect of extended rather than iterative action and πολλά, "much," may refer to urgency rather than to repetition. Therefore the switch from the imperfect of παρακαλέω (v 10) to the aorist of that verb (v 12) may be explained by the addition to the latter of λέγοντες, "saying." By indicating extended action, this present participle eliminates the need for the imperfect of the verb (a point missed by J. A. Kleist [200-201] and M. Zerwick [*Biblical Greek* §272], who give different explanations). With the demons' plea cf. again *ANET* 29-31 or H. Gressmann, *Altorientalische Texte* 77-79, where a demon meekly addresses a god of exorcism after the failure of a first exorcist, even says that the god has come in peace, calls itself the god's servant, volunteers to leave, and asks only that the god celebrate a feast day with it and the prince of the city; and see *b. Pesaḥ.* 112b for the granting of a concession to a demon. Taking the ἵνα in v 12 as imperatival increases redundancy with the preceding clause by making the ἵνα-clause as well as the preceding clause a request (against H. G. Meecham in *JTS* os 43 [1942] 180; V. Taylor 282). It is therefore better to take the ἵνα in its more usual telic sense. The redundancy that remains does not imply a combining of different sources or a redactional addition to tradition (though the possibility remains). To pick an example at random, the redundancy in a passage such as Rev 2:5 (μετανόησον . . . εἰ δὲ μὴ . . . ἐὰν μὴ μετανοήσῃς, "repent . . . but if not . . . if you don't repent") carries no such implications.

Against pagan practices, pig-keeping is prohibited in *m. B. Qam.* 7:7, as is the eating of pork in Lev 11:7; Deut 14:8 (cf. Isa 65:4; 66:17; Str-B 1. 492-93). The influence of the spirits on the pigs is highlighted by the fact that on their own, pigs do not stay together; yet they plunge as a herd into the sea (J. D. M. Derrett in *JSNT* 3 [1979] 5-6). They can swim; but so also can other animals and human beings, who may nevertheless drown. Therefore the pigs' drowning does not require any further demonic activity. Because of their revulsion against pigs, a Jewish audience would find humorous satisfaction in the drowning of the herd as well as in the self-banishment of the unclean spirits.

The combination of vv 10 and 12 implies that the unclean spirits will have to leave the region (whether to wander hostless or to find a new host in territory foreign to them is left uncertain) if Jesus does not allow them to enter the pigs. Therefore the drowning of the pigs implies in turn either that the spirits have to leave the region even though Jesus does allow them to enter the pigs (for the drowning takes away the spirits' new hosts in the region) or, more probably, that they leave the region by going into the sea with the pigs (see the foregoing comments; cf. Luke 8:31; *Lev Rab.* 24.3; *PGM* IV. 1245-46; O. Weinreich, *Religionsgeschichtliche Studien* 13-15, esp. n. 22; O. Böcher, *Christus Exorcista* 22-24; F. Annen, *Heil* 140-41, 153, 157, 161; J. Teixidor in *Sumer* 18 [1962] 55, on the sea as a proper place of demons — though these demons' resistance against exorcism from a landlubber prevents our identifying them with water-demons [on which see T. Hopfner, *Griechisch-ägyptischer Offenbarungszauber* 1 §§210, 225, 270] returning to their own element). We would make a mistake, then, to suppose that the spirits think far ahead, as though by plan they trick Jesus into letting them enter the pigs in order that they might destroy the pigs and thereby make the Gergasenes pressure him into leaving because of the loss (so O. Bauernfeind [*Worte* 34-56], who adds that Jesus finally outsmarts the spirits by unexpectedly leaving the ex-demoniac as a permanent witness in the region). But the double use of παρακαλέω, "beseech," especially with πολλά, "much," favors a plea of desperation over trickery. The spirits hardly think ahead, certainly not so far ahead as the interpretation says. Rather, they are portrayed as stupid in carrying out their purpose of destroying life (cf. a demon's threat to kill its host in Philostr. *VA* 3.38), because the destruction robs them of their new hosts. This stupidity is a foil that enhances the cleverness of Jesus (cf. R. Bultmann, *HST* 210-11).

A Roman legion normally consists of about 6000 footmen, 120 horsemen, and a number of auxiliaries. If the unclean spirits number so many yet crowd into the demoniac, the disparity between their number and the only 2000 or so pigs poses no problem: the pigs will offer a less crowded condition. On the other hand, "legion" is capable of loose usage (see Latin dictionaries s.v. *legio*); and τέλος can refer both to a battalion of 2048 and, it would appear, to a legion (LSJ s.v. τέλος 10). Therefore "about 2000" pigs may correspond to a battalion of 2048 spirits loosely called "Legion" (cf. J. Jeremias, *Jesus' Promise* 30-31, n. 5). J. Carmignac (in *ASTI* 7 [1968-69] 67) suggests that "about two thousand" arose by a misvocalization of כאלפים as dual, כְּאַלְפַּיִם, rather than plural, כַּאֲלָפִים, "in groups"; but this suggestion loosens the link with "Legion." Because of the episode concerning the pigs, M. Dibelius (*From Tradition to Gospel* 89, 101) suggests that a story about a Jewish exorcist has been transferred to Jesus (see also T. Reinach in *REJ* 47 [1903] 172-78). But Jesus was a Jew.

J. D. M. Derrett (in *JSNT* 3 [1979] 6-7) reports that it takes four times as many people to keep pigs as it takes to keep sheep; so for a herd of about two thousand pigs we are meant to think of quite a few herders. Against J. D. Kingsbury (*Christology of Mark's Gospel* 18-19), it is no problem that the herdsmen do not take part in the action till v 14. Why should their presence be mentioned earlier rather than assumed from the reference to a herd of pigs (v 11)? "There" defines the mountain where the pigs were feeding as close to the location of Jesus' encounter with the demoniac. Furthermore, the demoniac's shout is "loud." So the herdsmen's hearing and seeing what happened so as to tell others coheres with the earlier part of the story. From this standpoint we have no reason to regard the episode about the herdsmen or, more broadly, about the herd and the herdsmen as a later addition to the story.

Cf. 6:36 and esp. 6:56 for hamlets with cities (and towns). The man's being clothed may imply a prior lewdness as well as relate to the earlier habit of gashing his bare skin (so R. Pesch 1. 292). M. Reiser (*Syntax und Stil* 158-60) detects emphatic asyndeton between "sitting" and "clothed and sane" (v 15), but perhaps the text simply means that the man was sitting in a clothed and sane state, so that "and" would not have been appropriate anyway. Since v 9 used λεγιών as a proper noun, we should treat it the same way in v 15 and regard its τόν as anaphoric: "the [aforementioned] Legion" (cf. the anaphoric use of the definite article with previously mentioned proper names in passages such as 1:4-6, 9-14; 6:14-20, 21-22; 15:1-15, 40-47; 16:1 v.l.). For ἤρξαντο, "began," see the notes on 1:45.

"And concerning the pigs" in v 16 does not argue for later addition of the episode in vv 11-13, for this phrase does not make an addition to v 16. It merely follows the order of the narrative: (1) episode concerning the demoniac; (2) episode concerning the pigs. Nor is there anything awkward about Mark's putting "about [περί] the pigs" with "narrated," for he often uses περί-phrases with verbs of speaking, hearing, and writing (1:30; 5:27; 7:6, 17 v.l., 25; 8:30; 10:10; 14:21). Hence, we should avoid attaching "about the pigs" to "it had happened," which *would* be awkward. The only awkwardness comes in the paralleling of a πῶς-clause and a περί-phrase, but that is due to Mark's desire to emphasize the "how" (πῶς) of the exorcism rather than his or an earlier traditioner's addition of the pigs. To take but one other example, Rev 2:2 follows up "I know" with nouns as direct objects and then switches to an epexegetic "that"-clause; yet nobody infers a redactional addition or a combining of different sources. "Narrated" requires an indication of subject matter (cf. 9:9), but εἶδον, here in the form οἱ ἰδόντες, "the ones who saw," may occur absolutely (as in 2:12; 4:12; 6:38; 10:14; 12:15; 15:32). Therefore, both the πῶς-clause and the περί-phrase belong to "narrated," neither one to "saw." Apart from Mark's Christological aim, "concerning the pigs" (v 16) favors that anger over loss and fear of further loss cause the Gergasenes to ask that Jesus leave; for elsewhere his undamaging mighty acts attract people rather than provoking them to get rid of him. Except for loss of the pigs, moreover, the Gergasenes' past efforts at taming the demoniac would predispose them to welcome Jesus as the ridder of this danger. Cf. Acts 16:16-24; 19:23-27.

J. W. Bowman (144-45) argues from the presence of many Gentiles in Galilee and Judea that the present observers are Jews living among Gentiles. This conclusion does not follow; and the references to "the region of the Gergasenes" (v 1) and to "the Decapolis" (v 20), the episode concerning the pigs, and the request that Jesus leave seem to imply Gentiles (cf. the notes on v 2).

Historically, we may suppose that the ex-demoniac fears lest the Gergasenes' asking Jesus to leave will translate into a rejection of him, too, and that Jesus sends him to his family because they will "have to take him in" (Robert Frost). If so, the commission to announce to them (ἀπάγγειλον αὐτοῖς) how many things "the Lord" has done for him does not have an evangelistic purpose, but a purpose of reintegrating him into his family (J. Gnilka 1. 206; cf. the non-evangelistic use of ἀπήγγειλαν in v 14). But Mark's main interest lies in the wider proclamation throughout the Decapolis of what "Jesus" has done. In relation to πεποίηκεν, ὅσα is an accusative of direct object ("how many things [the Lord] has done"; cf. 3:8); in relation to ἠλέησεν, an adverbial accusative ("how much [the Lord] has had mercy"), though ὡς, "how," would have been stylistically better. C. E. B. Cranfield (181-82) notes that since ἐλεέω is not used in the perfect active so far as we know, the perfect of the parallel πεποίηκεν probably gives the aorist ἠλέησεν the force of a perfect: completion of action and permanence of result. The chiasm that puts σοι at the extremes of σοι πεποίηκεν καὶ ἠλέησεν σοι, "for you he has done and he has had mercy on you," stresses personal benefit. The text does not indicate a reason for Jesus' refusing to let the ex-demoniac be with him. Suggestions range from Jesus' not wanting an ex-demoniac or a born pagan in his company to his wanting to leave a witness in the region. Or he may think it premature to start gathering in the Gentiles (cf. 7:27). But it is probably best to say that he refuses the ex-demoniac's request because being "with" Jesus belongs as a privilege only to the Twelve (3:14). The view of W. Wrede (*Messianic Secret* 141) that

Jesus refuses out of fear that the man might betray the messianic secret and sends him to his family where the secret may be guarded (cf. esp. 8:26) rests on an oversight: people of the region already know in detail what has happened (vv 14-16), though the man's family still need to be informed. That is to say, v 19 contains no attempt to guard a secret; quite the reverse, it contains a command designed to make sure that everyone in the region, including the man's absent family, knows (cf. the criticism by R. A. Guelich 1. 285-86 of the view that sees a connotation of secrecy in the man's "house"). Thus is spoiled any parallel with 1:44-45a; 7:36, where commands *not* to tell are happily violated.

M. A. Tolbert (*Sowing the Gospel* 166-68) thinks that Jesus does not allow the ex-demoniac to be with him because as good soil the ex-demoniac does not need the nurture of the farmer (= Jesus) to bear much fruit (cf. 4:26-29): "for the former demoniac 'to be with' Jesus would only slow the harvest [of evangelism in the Decapolis], ..." But we have seen that the ignorance of the "man" in 4:26-29 ruled out an identification of him with Jesus. That passage does not teach against a delay of harvest. On the contrary, it sets out intermediate stages of growth necessary to take place prior to harvest. And the fruit that was harvested represented true and full discipleship more likely than it represented the making of more disciples.

Against attempts to include friends and fellow heathen in general in τοὺς σούς (so, e.g., E. Lohmeyer 98), "into your house" prelimits τοὺς σούς to the ex-demoniac's family (v 19). Εἰς, "into," favors the meaning "your house" over "your household" for οἶκόν σου. So also does the fact that elsewhere in Mark οἶκος always means "house" (twelve times). Since parataxis characterizes Mark's writing, the presence of καί, "and," instead of δέ, "but," at the start of v 20 does not argue strongly in favor of a wider meaning for τοὺς σούς. On two counts there is no breaking of a messianic secret: (1) Jesus has issued a command to tell some people; (2) he has not issued a prohibition against telling others. Thus what the ex-demoniac does exceeds rather than breaks Jesus' command. An adversative δέ would have tended to make the audience think mistakenly of his breaking it. Cf. the comments and notes on 1:45; 7:36. We should also note that the identity of Jesus as the Messiah does not come into view (cf. C. F. D. Moule in *Jesus und Paulus* 243), nor does even his identity as "Son of God Most High" (against ibid.), but only what he has done. The request that he leave the region and his doing so make it unnecessary that he command silence to keep from being thronged to death. In fact, the opposite problem leads to a contrary command.

R. H. Lightfoot (*History and Interpretation* 89-90) suggests that churches in the Decapolis adopted and Gentilized this story to explain how the Christian mission started there. But if it did not begin thus, we are left with the problem of explaining how and why those churches adopted and Gentilized *this* particular story. Moreover, though the story breathes the atmosphere of paganism (most emphasized by F. Annen, *Heil* passim), even as supposedly Gentilized the story does not make explicit that the demoniac was a Gentile or help form a block of narratives set in Gentile territory; so symbolism of Gentile evangelism seems to be out of view (cf. D.-A. Koch, *Bedeutung* 78-80; W. Schmithals 265ff.). Yet again, the marveling of everybody in the Decapolis (v 20) does not amount to conversion and therefore does not portray the desired effect of later evangelism among the Gentiles. As noted in the comments, marveling makes a Christological rather than evangelistic point (against Z. Kato, *Völkermission* 56-59). On the Decapolis, see E. Schürer, G. Vermes, and F. Millar, *History* 2. 125-58; H. Bietenhard in *ZDPV* 79 (1963) 24-58; and see the note on v 43 concerning the question of a messianic secret here.

F. Annen (*Heil* 162-90) thinks that since pigs and nakedness represent paganism, Hellenistic Jewish Christians used this story to argue against Judaizers in the church that Jesus himself had freed a pagan from his uncleanness. But the story does not relate the pigs to the demoniac, and we can only infer from the man's being clothed at the end that he was naked when lacerating himself under the influence of Legion. Yet an inference hardly makes the main point of a story. Similarly, according to R. H. Lightfoot (*History and Interpretation* 88-90), vv 18-20 symbolize that Gentile converts to Christianity should not become proselytes to Judaism, but should remain among their own people to bear witness to what Israel's God has done for them through Jesus (cf. Rom 15:9-12). But being with Jesus hardly represents being a Gentile Christian proselyte to Judaism, as this view requires; and once again the closing statement that "all marveled" gives the episode — and indeed the whole story — a Christological rather than an anti-Judaistic or Gentile evangelistic bent (also against W. H. Kelber [*Kingdom* 50-52 and *Mark's Story* 31-32], who thinks that Mark shifts the emphasis from "Jesus' breaking of demonic power" to "his breaking of the Gentile barrier"). The foregoing destruction of the pigs caters to a Judaistic rather than a Gentile attitude. See J. Ernst 157 against inferring that v 19 reflects Jewish Christian prejudice against Gentile Christians.

In the comments we have noted the repetitiveness that characterizes the narrative (see also R. Pesch 1. 282-83; idem, *Besessene* 14). This characteristic has several possible explanations. It may derive (1) from the use of repetition in oral communication, i.e. from its use in the oral tradition (cf. W. H. Kelber, *Oral and Written Gospel* 64-70); (2) from pre-Marcan redaction of oral or written tradition; (3) from Mark's intertwining more than one version of the story; or (4) from his redaction of oral or written tradition. The first and last possibilities tend to make the middle two otiose. The pre-Papian tradition that Mark draws on Peter's preaching (Eus. H.E. 3.39.15) favors the first possibility. Mark's penchant for duality and the characteristically Marcan emphases evident in the repetitions favor his redaction. But a mixture of oral repetition and Mark's redaction is likewise possible. To follow Pesch (*Besessene* 48; cf. idem in *EcumRev* 23 [1976] 371-74) in tracing this story through five stages, each having a different point, requires much imagination and runs the danger of too hastily giving up the attempt to find coherence in the story as we presently have it. F. Annen (*Heil* 39-74) makes a detailed attempt to separate redaction from tradition and also provides much information on the history of interpretation (11-19, 77-101, 111-32) and on stories of exorcism outside as well as inside the Bible (115-27). Mark would not have allowed the story to close with marveling by all (v 20) if he had redacted the story to denigrate miracles (as thought by L. Schenke, *Wundererzählungen* 193-95).

THE POWER OF JESUS THAT SAVES FROM DEATH

5:21-43 (Matt 9:18-26; Luke 8:40-56)

The intertwined stories of Jairus's daughter and the woman with a flow of blood subdivide as follows: Jesus' crossing the sea and a crowd's gathering to him (v 21); Jairus's coming and request (vv 22-23); Jesus' going with Jairus (v 24); the touching of Jesus' garment by the woman with a flow of blood (vv 25-28); the healing of the woman (v 29); Jesus' question (v 30); the disciples' remark (v 31); Jesus' conversation with the woman (vv 32-34); the report of the death of Jairus's daughter (v 35); Jesus' encouragement (v 36); entry into Jairus's house (vv 37-40a); entry into the room where Jairus's daughter lies (v 40b); the healing of the girl (vv 41-42a); astonishment (v 42b); commands to secrecy and to give the girl something to eat (v 43).

5:21 *(Luke 8:40)* "And after Jesus had crossed in the boat again to the

other side" builds on 4:35; 5:1 and means that he has sailed back to the west or
northwest side of the Sea of Galilee (contrast "the other side of the Jordan" as
Transjordan, to the east). Though the disciples will take part in the story (see vv
31, 37-38), Mark focuses on Jesus and leaves to be inferred their accompanying
him (cf. the comments and notes on v 2). The gathering of a large crowd to him
(cf. 4:1 recalls attention to his magnetism and thus counteracts the Gergasenes'
having asked him to quit their borders (v 17). "And he was beside the sea"
probably implies magnetism so great that a large crowd gathers before he can go
inland. Incidentally, the statement provides a starting point for the journey that
he is about to take with a synagogue ruler. Matters will not change very much if
we treat the crowd rather than Jesus as the subject of "was beside the sea."

5:22-23 *(Matt 9:18; Luke 8:41-42)* "One of the synagogue rulers, by name
Jairus" may derive from historical memory because the man became a disciple
well known in the Church and perhaps because his name can be read not only as
יָאִיר, "he will enlighten" (Num 32:41; Judg 10:3-4; Esth 2:5), but also as יָעִיר,
"he will arouse, awaken" (1 Chr 20:5; see BAGD s.v. Ἰάϊρος) and thus taken as
a foregleam of Jesus' raising Jairus's daughter (R. Pesch in *BZ* nf 14 [1970]
252-56). But the Semitic reading will have been limited to the tradition, for the
Mark who elsewhere has to translate Aramaic expressions for his Gentile audience
can hardly intend that audience to understand such a meaning here. And even at
the level of early Semitic tradition there is the difficulty that Jesus, not Jairus,
does the awakening. Since Jairus holds a position of leadership, his coming as a
suppliant makes for a flattering portrait of Jesus. The historical present tense of
ἔρχεται, "comes," and of πίπτει, "falls," dramatizes the desperation of Jairus (cf.
1:40 and esp. 7:25) and thereby highlights the greatness of the miracle that Jesus
is about to perform. Jairus's seeing Jesus parallels the demoniac's seeing Jesus,
which took place just before an act of obeisance similar to the present act of
suppliance (v 6; cf. 6:49, 50; 9:20; 12:28). The shift from προσεκύνησεν αὐτῷ,
"did obeisance to him" (v 6), to πίπτει πρὸς τοὺς πόδας αὐτοῦ, "falls at his feet,"
exhibits the shift from obeisance to suppliance.

Jairus's beseeching Jesus displays urgency in the very meaning of παρακαλεῖ, "beseeches" (cf. 1:40; 5:10, 12, 17, 18; 6:56; 7:32; 8:22; Acts 9:38), in its
historical present tense (so א A C L 28 33 565 892 1241 *pc* bo, almost all other
texts having the imperfect), in the addition of a characteristically Marcan adverbial
πολλά, "much" (see the notes on 1:45 and, against a necessarily iterative meaning,
the notes on 5:10), and in the alliterative piling up of words beginning with π
(see G. Lüderitz in *Markus-Philologie* 180). The beseeching offers another link
with the story of the demoniac, where Mark repeatedly portrayed Jesus as the
object of such action (vv 10, 12, 17, 18). The kind of beseeching here in view
highlights the power and authority of Jesus. "My dear daughter is at the point of
death" tells the reason for Jairus's plea. The diminutive form and first position of
τὸ θυγάτριον μου, "my little daughter," reflect loving concern for the daughter.
"Come in order that you may lay [your] hands on her" identifies the plea itself
(cf. 6:5; 7:32; 8:23, 25; 16:18; 4 Kgdms 5:11 LXX; 1QapGen 20:22, 29; also
Mark 1:31, 41; 6:2; 9:27; 10:16). The abruptness of the construction ἵνα ἐλθών

(on which see the following notes) heightens the sense of urgency. "In order that she may be saved and live" (i.e. get well and enjoy a normal lifespan) both gives the purpose for the requested coming and laying on of hands and exhibits the synagogue ruler's belief in the supernatural power of Jesus. Death has come so close that deliverance will bring life (cf. the psalmists' portraying illness as death [in Ps 30:3-4(2-3), for example] and the inscriptional evidence gathered by F. V. Filson in *BAR* 4. 336-37 on the use of σῴζω, "save," for health and welfare). Since Mark might have used ἰαθῇ, "be cured," or θεραπευθῇ, "be healed," he may intend σωθῇ καὶ ζήσῃ, "be saved and live," to carry overtones of a larger salvation that includes eternal life (cf. 3:4; 5:28, 34; 6:56; 8:35; 9:43, 45; 10:17, 26, 30, 52; 13:13, 20; 15:30, 31; also 16:16).

5:24 *(Matt 9:18; Luke 8:42)* "And he [Jesus] went away with him [Jairus]" shows Jesus' intention to save and give life (cf. 2 Kgs 4:30; Acts 9:39). "And a great crowd was following him" reemphasizes Jesus' magnetism (cf. v 21 and esp. 3:7). Their crushing him intensifies the emphasis and prepares for vv 27, 31. At 3:9 θλίβω, "crush," occurred in its simplex form because there was only the danger of crushing. Here, the verb gains a perfective preposition, συν-, which heightens the thought to one of actual crushing. Since ὄχλος πολύς refers back to the large crowd in v 21, we would expect an anaphoric definite article to produce "*the* large crowd." The lack of such an article puts emphasis on the large crowd as such, i.e. on their numerousness.

5:25-34 *(Matt 9:20-22; Luke 8:43-48)* Now begins another story sand-wiched between the introduction and the conclusion of the story concerning Jairus's daughter. We have no right to deny the possibility that the one happened during the course of the other. It is the stuff of life that events are often intertwined. We can speak confidently about a Marcan technique of sandwiching — i.e. of his artificially moving one story into the middle of another — only if special reasons incline us to think so. Those reasons will have to arise out of textual details. Unless they do, we may assume traditional or historical interconnection. Under that assumption it is still possible to think that Mark wants his readers to see an anticipation of Jesus' delivering Jairus's daughter from death in his delivering the woman from her malady, or that Mark interprets the woman's deliverance as a deliverance from death similar to the deliverance of Jairus's daughter. At the very least, the interruption of the story concerning the daughter by the story concerning the woman heightens tension with respect to the daughter's fate; for the daughter is at the point of death.

5:25-28 *(Matt 9:20-21; Luke 8:43-44)* The sentence which forms vv 25-27 starts by referring to a woman and proceeds with a strikingly long series of participial phrases. The first five are attributive, describing her. The last two are circumstantial, telling what she does in relation to the main verb. Only then do we read the main verb and its object. The placement of the subject first ("a woman"), far ahead of its verb ("touched"), switches attention from Jairus and his daughter. The serializing of the first five participles magnifies the prior hope-lessness of the woman's condition to highlight the power of Jesus in the miracle of healing that he will perform on her. So also does the renewed alliterative use of π: πολλὰ παθοῦσα ὑπὸ πολλῶν ἰατρῶν καὶ δαπανήσασα τὰ παρ' αὐτῆς (so G. Lüderitz in *Markus-Philologie* 179; cf. v 23). The long time that the woman has suffered from the flow of blood (twelve years); the high degree of her suffering at the hands of many physicians (we may take πολλά as adverbial, "much [in degree]" — see the notes on 1:45 — or as a direct object, "many things," and we should note both the emphatic forward position of πολλά and the double emphasis and wordplay in πολλά . . . πολλῶν, "much . . . many"); her spending not just a large proportion or even most of her financial resources, but *all* of them (and if only rich people could afford doctors [cf. G. Theissen, *Miracle Stories* 237], this would come to a large amount); her being benefited in no way (μηδέν being adverbial and positionally emphatic); her coming rather into a worse condition (emphasized both by the doubly and strongly adversative ἀλλὰ μᾶλλον, "but rather," and by the forward position of εἰς τὸ χεῖρον, "into a worse condition") — these descriptions detail the wretchedness of the woman (see B. Blackburn, *Theios Anēr* 202-3, on the motif of others' failure; and F. W. Danker, *Benefactor* 94-95, for a sick person that everyone has given up on).

"Hearing about Jesus" shines a ray of hope and again highlights the reputation that he has built up. "Coming in the crowd" shows the woman's determination. The asyndeton that characterizes the relation of each of these two participles to what precedes it emphasizes Jesus' reputation and the woman's determination (cf. M. Reiser, *Syntax und Stil* 158-60). "From behind" prepares for Jesus' turning and asking who touched him (v 30). Mark makes nothing of any reticence due to her uncleanness (Lev 15:19-33; Ezek 36:17; *m. Zabim* 5:1, 6) or to her being a woman in a society dominated by males, though these factors may have been at work. "Touched his garment" shows her faith and the greatness of Jesus' power inasmuch as that power radiates even through his clothing. The woman does not have to touch his body, nor does he have to lay his hands on her (cf. v 23; 3:10; 6:56 and contrast the conjuration in *PGM* XXIIa. 2-9 that is thought necessary to cure a flow of blood). Verse 28 makes this point explicit: "for she had been saying, 'If I touch even [or 'only' — A. T. Robertson, *Grammar* 208] his garments, I will be saved.' " Indeed, v 28 emphasizes the point; for an author's writing omnisciently of a subject's inner thoughts signals an emphasis. "She had been saying" means "she had been saying in herself" (so Matt 9:21), i.e. thinking (cf. Gen 20:11; 26:9; Num 24:11). It would be easier to touch Jesus' garments and keep her secret than to touch his body and keep her secret. Or so she thought. Σωθήσομαι, "saved," means delivered from her flow of blood, but may carry overtones for Mark and his audience of salvation from sin and all its effects (cf. the comments on v 23).

5:29 *(Luke 8:44)* The drying up of the woman's fountain of blood exhibits Jesus' power. The immediacy with which it happens magnifies that power even more, especially in view of the twelve years of worse-than-useless treatment by many physicians (see also the comments on 1:42, whose phraseology is similar). The shift from ῥύσει, "flow" (v 25), to πηγή, "fountain," and the further description of the malady as a μάστιγος, "whip, scourge, affliction," emphasize the severity of her condition and thus magnify Jesus' power yet again (cf. 3:10).

Knowing in her body that healing has occurred means that the woman feels the
flow of blood stop. The effect leaves no doubt about Jesus' power. The perfect
tense of ἴαται means that she is healed for good. His power eliminates relapses.

5:30 *(Luke 8:45-46)* Jesus' "knowing in himself [cf. John 6:61; 11:38] the
from-him power, having gone out" (so a literal translation) adds supernatural
knowledge to supernatural power (see 2:8 with comments; cf. 6:2, 14). The
immediacy of his knowing, the omniscience with which Mark writes about it, the
mention of Jesus' name, and its forward position all show the supernaturalness
of Jesus' knowledge to be another point of emphasis. The crowd's following him
(v 24) may help determine his turning. But since he turns "*in* the crowd" (as the
woman came "*in* the crowd"; cf. the crowd's pressing him — vv 24, 31), the
turning indicates his knowledge that the woman came "from behind" (v 27). The
asyndeton with which "turning" is attached to the preceding emphasizes this
knowledge (again cf. M. Reiser, *Syntax und Stil* 158-60). "Who touched me, [i.e.
my] garments?" further indicates Jesus' knowledge of the means by which the
woman has tapped his healing power. But Mark writes in ways that emphasize
Jesus' supernatural power as well as his supernatural knowledge: (1) he makes
the power itself the direct object of Jesus' knowledge; (2) he puts ἐξ αὐτοῦ, "from
him," in the attributive position, where it adjectivally describes the power as
Jesus's in its origin rather than adverbially modifying its having gone out; and
(3) he uses a mere participle ἐξελθοῦσαν, "having gone out," instead of a ὅτι-clause
with a finite verb, "that . . . had gone out," and delays the participle so as to let
the emphasis rest again on Jesus as the origin of the power rather than on the
coming out of the power (see also the following notes on v 30). The text gives
no indication that God controls the power going out. Nor does Jesus' knowing
that the power has gone out imply that he willed it to go out because he could
tell that someone had touched him with faith. The aorist tense of ἐξελθοῦσαν,
"having gone out," probably indicates that the power went out just before he
perceived that it had gone out. So also does the "immediately" which modifies
his perception following the miracle. Thus Mark portrays Jesus as so charged
with power that it will go out from him even apart from his will or God's
intervention (cf. Luke 5:17; 6:19). We should not think of the power as an attribute
that enables Jesus to work this miracle, then. "The power" *is* the miracle, an act
of power going out from Jesus. In the plural, δύναμις is the word normally
translated "miracles"; but Mark also uses the singular for a miracle (again see
6:5; 9:39). His choosing the word that means an act of power rather than σημεῖον,
"sign," τέρας, "wonder," or θαῦμα, "marvel," makes the apologetic point that Jesus
will not go to the cross out of weakness (cf. S. Schulz [*Stunde* 64, 66], who
observes that Mark's attention to Jesus' power drives out other themes that we
might expect, e.g., thankful joy on the part of the healed).

5:31-34 *(Matt 9:22; Luke 8:45-48)* The disciples' uncomprehending remark, "You see the crowd pressing you and you are saying, 'Who touched me?' "
provides a foil that makes Jesus' supernatural knowledge stand out in bold relief.
He does not bother to respond. (Nor does Mark editorialize on the disciples'
ignorance, so that we need not think that he is attacking them, only that he is

exalting Jesus.) Instead, Jesus looks around to see the woman who has touched him (cf. περιεβλέπετο in v 32 with βλέπεις in v 31). He knows she is there. Since Mark knows that the person who has touched Jesus is a woman, the substantive participle naturally goes into the feminine gender (τὴν τοῦτο ποιήσασαν, "the woman who had done this"). But since Mark pays special attention to Jesus' supernatural knowledge throughout the passage, the feminine gender may indicate that Jesus also knows the sex of the healed person.

After a long string of καί's beginning in v 21, the adversative δέ, "but," introducing v 33 and the forward position of ἡ . . . γυνή, "the woman" — again far ahead of its verbs because of intervening participles (cf. v 25) — set the woman and her reactions emphatically opposite Jesus' question and searching look around (cf. M. Zerwick, *Untersuchungen* 17). Her reactions of fear and trembling bear witness to his supernatural power, which she knows by "what had happened to her," and to his supernatural knowledge, which he has made evident both in his question, "Who touched me?" and in his looking around to see the woman who has touched him. The repetitiousness of the reference to her knowing (cf. 29), the asyndeton with which Mark introduces her knowing, and the omniscience with which he writes about it call special attention to this witness. Her coming and falling before Jesus (cf. 3:11; 7:25) suits his majesty. Her telling him "all the truth" repeats, in effect, the story of his healing her and emphasizes the actuality of the powerful deed. J. A. Kleist (203) points out that the crescendo with which each colon surpasses its predecessor in length and importance heightens the effect:

a) ἦλθεν, "she came,"
b) καὶ προσέπεσεν αὐτῷ, "and she fell before him,"
c) καὶ εἶπεν αὐτῷ πᾶσαν τὴν ἀλήθειαν, "and she told him all the truth."

"All" indicates that every detail bears repetition as a witness to Jesus' power and knowledge. If the woman was afraid to confess her ritual impurity, she now overcomes that fear; but again Mark makes nothing of her having been ritually impure.

Another adversative δέ, "but," emphatically contrasts Jesus' encouraging words to the woman with her fearful reaction to his earlier question and looking around. His address, "Daughter," ties in with the story of Jairus's daughter (vv 23, 35), which frames the present story, and portrays Jesus as addressing the woman from a position of authority (cf. Ruth 2:8; 3:10; Ps 45:11[10]). She is a member of his new family (cf. 2:5; 3:31-35). "Your faith has saved you" (cf. 10:52; also 2:5; 5:36; 9:23-24) adds his authority to what she already "knew in her body" (cf. v 29). The statement also complements her belief in his power and shows that it was not her touch as such that saved her, but her touching him with faith (as the crowd that pressed him had not been doing). Cf. 2:5; 4:40; 10:52; 11:22. The perfect tense of σέσωκεν, "has saved," corresponds to the perfect tense of ἴαται, "was healed," in v 29. As there, it stresses the completeness and permanence of the cure (again cf. the comments on v 23). So also does the sixfold repetition of the s-sound in ἡ πίστις σου σέσωκέν σε (see J. A. Kleist 203-4 on the soothing as well as hissing use of this sound). "Go in peace [i.e. with well-being instead of further trouble] and be well from your affliction [μάστιγος; cf. v 29 with comments]" looks to the future and both effects and assures an ongoing condition of health (cf. 1:44; 2:11; 5:19; 10:52 for the command to go; and Judg 18:6; 1 Sam 1:17; 29:7 et passim for future well-being). The asyndeton at the beginning of "go in peace" adds emphasis. Thus the double command is far from being an appendage awkwardly redundant of a past cure.

5:35 *(Luke 8:49)* A number of items underscore the seeming hopelessness in the news that Jairus's daughter has died: (1) the asyndetic abruptness with which v 35 begins; (2) the interruption of Jesus "while he was still speaking" (cf. 14:43); (3) the historical present tense of ἔρχονται, "people come"; (4) the question, "Why do you still trouble the teacher?" (5) the repetition of ἔτι, "still"; and (6) the placement of the subject ἡ θυγάτηρ σου, "your daughter," before its verb (unusual for Mark — see M. Reiser, *Syntax und Stil* 98). There seems to be no doubt; the news comes straight from the house of the synagogue ruler himself, as emphasized by the ellipsis of "the house" and consequent attention to "the synagogue ruler." The ellipsis (or should we say the substitution of "the synagogue ruler" for "the house"?) is so striking that at first sight it seems as though the ruler has gone back home rather than that he is accompanying Jesus. But the second person singular of σου in ἡ θυγάτηρ σου, "your daughter," and of σκύλλεις, "do you trouble," makes Jairus the addressee — present, not absent. The hope-lessness underlying the question, "Why do you still trouble the teacher?" (cf. John 11:21, 32), stands out against the foil of the woman's faith in vv 25-34.

5:36 *(Luke 8:50)* Since the report and the question are addressed to Jairus, when Jesus hears them he *over*hears them (παρακούσας — so ℵ* B L W Δ 892* pc e; see B. M. Metzger, *Textual Commentary* ad loc., on the dropping of παρ-in other textual traditions). But because Jesus brushes aside the report and the question, he not only overhears the word; he also *ignores* it, not so much the announcement of the daughter's death (for he says to believe rather than fear), but the question urging that Jairus not trouble him any more (see Matt 18:17, the LXX, MM, and BAGD s.v. παρακούω for this meaning; cf. the dropping of παρα-in Luke 8:50 because the bringing in of ἀπεκρίθη, "answered," implies that Jesus did *not* ignore the word). "Being spoken" is not tautologous after "the word," but indicates that Jesus was ignoring the word at the time it was being spoken. "Being spoken" also parallels "while he was still speaking" (v 35a) and forestalls confu-sion of this word with "the word" used absolutely for the gospel (cf. the comments on 1:45). The historical present tense of λέγει, "says," and the present tense of the imperative verbs φοβοῦ and πίστευε emphasize Jesus' commands: the first one negative, "Don't fear"; the second one positive, "Only believe" (cf. 9:23-24, the notes on 1:3, and the comments on 5:36; contrast the unemphatic present imper-atival subjunctive of φοβέομαι in Matt 1:20; 10:26; Luke 12:4, 5; Rev 14:7). An adversative δέ, "but," contrasts this encouragement with the bad news that has just arrived. The same power that cured the woman suffering a flow of blood will take care of Jairus's daughter. The woman's faith in Jesus' power saved her.

Jairus's faith in that same power will save his daughter. The woman's com-
mendable fear followed her healing and consisted of reverential awe. The fear
prohibited to Jairus would consist of prior unbelief that Jesus will work a miracle.
Asyndeton stresses the command to believe (M. Reiser, *Syntax und Stil* 142).
"Only" stresses that Jesus is *able* to do all that is needed and that he *will* do it.
He is in charge. He knows what to do. Therefore believing entails no risk on
Jairus's part. Jesus puts himself at risk by telling Jairus to believe. But that is no
risk at all, since Jesus — crucified though he will be — is God's Son (1:1, 11 et
passim).

5:37-40a *(Matt 9:23-24; Luke 8:51-53)* Jesus' not allowing anyone except
Peter, James, and John to follow along with him excludes the large crowd and
the rest of the disciples and prepares for the semi-privacy of the coming miracle.
The exception of the inner trio provides the miracle with a requisite number of
discipular witnesses in addition to the parents (cf. Deut 19:15). A miracle so
stupendous as raising the dead benefits from such a number of witnesses (cf.
Jesus' taking these same three disciples up the Mount of Transfiguration [9:2]
and deep into Gethsemane [14:33]).

Jesus and the three now enter the house of the synagogue ruler. The present
historical tense of ἔρχονται, "come," and of θεωρεῖ, "sees," emphasizes the uproar
of people weeping and wailing. So also do the heaping up of terms for mourning
("uproar and [people] weeping and wailing"), the adverbial πολλά, "much," and
the alliterations with θ, κ, λ, and ρ in καὶ θεωρεῖ θόρυβον καὶ κλαίοντας καὶ
ἀλαλάζοντας πολλά (cf. G. Lüderitz in *Markus-Philologie* 178, n. 38). This
mourning dramatizes the woeful power of death in order that Jesus' greater power
may stand out all the more. The switch from the plural "come" to the singular
"sees" prepares for Jesus' confrontation with the mourners. Unless ἔρχονται εἰς
in v 38 means "come to" instead of "come into," εἰσελθών, "having entered"
(v 39), probably repeats the item of entry to prepare for Jesus' throwing the
mourners out. The historical present tense of λέγει, "says," emphasizes the needlessness of the uproarious weeping and wailing (cf. Acts 20:10). To Jesus, Jairus's
daughter is not a daughter, but τὸ παιδίον, "the little child" (cf. 7:25, 28, 30). It
is tempting to understand Jesus' statements as straightforward: "the little child
has not died [she is alive], but is sleeping [and will wake up]." The mourners do
understand Jesus thus and think of an absurdly ignorant misdiagnosis. But Jesus
has not yet seen the girl so as to be in a position for making any kind of diagnosis.
He does not elsewhere correct wrong medical diagnoses. And Mark does not call
attention to any supernatural knowledge (contrast v 30; 2:8 and comments ad
loc.). (The further argument that raising the girl from sleep would not constitute
a miracle, and thus neither Mark nor pre-Marcan traditioners would have preserved the story, does not hold up; for the story would still tell of a healing that
occurs at the point of death [cf. v 23; H. van der Loos, *Miracles* 569-70]). In
agreement with Matt 9:18; Luke 8:42, 49, 52-53, then, we should understand that
Jesus' determination to raise the girl from death and his confidence of success
lead him to deny death with respect to its present, apparent irreversibility and to
hint at his raising the girl by using the euphemism of sleep, not as usual for its

unhappy similarities to the effects of death — proneness, unconsciousness, and inactivity — but unusually for its happy similarity to the short duration of this particular death and for the happy similarity between awaking someone from sleep and the miracle of raising the girl that he is about to perform (cf. Dan 12:2). It is in this prospective sense that the statement, "The little child has not died," contradicts the report in v 35: "Your daughter has died." The placement of the subject before its verb parallels v 35 and intensifies the contradiction (see the Greek text and the comments on v 35), and the strength of the adversative ἀλλά, "but," underlines sleep as opposed to death. When Jesus says that the little child is only sleeping, the mourners laugh him to scorn. They fail to understand the happy euphemism. But their view of the child's death will prove wrong, his correct.

5:40b *(Matt 9:25; Luke 8:54)* The emphatic αὐτός, "he himself," calls attention to Jesus' authority in throwing out all the mourners (cf. Acts 9:40). The historical present tense of παραλαμβάνει, "takes along," stresses his further exercise of authority in causing "the little child's father and mother and the ones with him [i.e. Peter, James, and John — v 37; cf. 3:14]" to accompany him. The historical present tense of εἰσπορεύεται, "goes in" (i.e. goes into the room where the child is lying), makes vivid his confrontation with the power of death; and the adversative δέ, "but," at the start of v 40b sets the whole of his action in opposition to the mourners' scornful laughter (cf. M. Zerwick, *Untersuchungen* 17).

5:41-42a *(Matt 9:25; Luke 8:54-55)* Because the child has died, Jesus grasps her hand, apparently to raise her, instead of laying his hands on her to heal her as Jairus requested he do when she was still alive (v 23; cf. Jesus' grasping the hand of Peter's mother-in-law to raise her in 1:31). The action conveys his life-giving power (cf. 9:27, too, and the comments on 1:30-31), and this without the corporal manipulations required for raising the dead in 1 Kgs 17:17-24; 2 Kgs 4:29-37; and perhaps Acts 20:9-12 (but cf. Luke 7:11-17; John 11:38-44; and esp. Acts 9:36-42; also Matt 11:5 par. Luke 7:22) and without any of the wide variety of manipulations commonly practiced in Hellenistic magic. The historical present tense of λέγει, "he says," emphasizes Jesus' equally powerful words, all the more impressive by virtue of quotation in their original Aramaic form, "Talitha koum," the translation of which, "Little girl, to you I say, arise," recalls Jesus' words to the paralytic, "To you I say, arise" (2:11). That the translation includes "to you I say" even though "Talitha koum" means only, "Little girl, arise," heightens the possibility of influence from those earlier words. In the Greek translation of what Jesus says *to* Jairus' daughter, the more affectionate κοράσιον, "little girl," occurs instead of the more objective παιδίον, "little child," which occurred in his speaking *about* her (v 39). The interruptiveness of "to you I say" calls attention to the miracle-working power of Jesus' command, "Arise" (again cf. 2:11; also Luke 7:14). The emphatic forward position of "to you" implies that this command carries enough power to raise even the dead (cf. *b. Taʿan.* 2a plus other rabbinic references in Str-B 1. 523). Mark gives the translation as a contrast with magical formulas so esoteric and nonsensical that they mock would-be translators (for examples, see almost any page of *PGM;* cf. also Philostr. *VA* 4.45; *PGM* XIII. 278-82). Jesus does not need to use such formulas. Plain, understandable words suffice, just as a simple, everyday gesture suffices. To westerners, however, the easternness of the Aramaic phrase connotes great power (G. Theissen, *Miracle Stories* 254-55; cf. 148-50). Nonetheless, translation of a phrase spoken by Jesus in the language that he regularly spoke strips away all magic (see Or. *Cels.* 5.45), with the result that in its nakedness the power is sheer (against Theissen and many others; see also the comments and notes on 7:33-35). The present tense of the imperative ἔγειρε, "arise," emphasizes this power (cf. the comments on 3:3).

"Immediately" goes on to show that Jesus' gesture and word generate so much power that they need no time to take effect (cf. esp. v 29; also 1:42; 2:12; 7:35; 10:52; F. W. Danker, *Benefactor* 187, 189; contrast 2 Kgs 4:32-37). The girl's standing up and walking around proves the point (cf. 2:9-12; 9:27; also 1:31; 3:5). "For she was twelve years old" keeps readers from falsely taking the earlier diminutives — θυγάτριον, "little daughter" (v 23), παιδίον, "little child" (vv 39, 40 [bis], 41), and κοράσιον, "little girl" (vv 41, 42) — as indicating an infant too young to walk. Thus, the diminutives have probably connoted endearment (with the exception of παιδίον, which may be taken as a faded diminutive). Walking around recalls again the healing of the paralytic (2:9).

Though Mark has said that Jesus grasped the hand of the girl, he does not say that Jesus raises her (contrast 1:31; 9:27). We may be meant to infer that he does, but the omission allows attention to rest on her standing up and walking around. The switch from ἔγειρε, "arise," to ἀνέστη, "stood up," is probably due to Mark's explanation that the girl is quite old enough to stand up and walk around by herself. Since ἀνίστημι will appear for Jesus' resurrection in the passion predictions (8:31; 9:31; 10:34), but ἐγείρω for the same event in 14:28; 16:6-7, it would be hard to say that Mark shifts from ἔγειρε (so Jesus' command) to ἀνέστη (so the editorial comment) to prefigure the resurrection of Jesus. We might just as well say that Mark uses both verbs to accomplish that purpose. In 9:27 ἀνέστη will again occur, but for the standing up of a demon-possessed boy after Jesus has grasped his hand and raised him. Mark may simply use synonyms to avoid monotony as he has used θυγάτριον, θυγάτηρ, παιδίον, and κοράσιον for the girl; ἔρχομαι εἰς, εἰσέρχομαι, and εἰσπορεύομαι for entry; ἐκπλήσσω, ἐξίστημι, θαμβέω, φοβέομαι, and θαυμάζω for awestruck reactions to Jesus' mighty deeds; λέγω, διαστέλλομαι, ἐπιτιμάω, and παραγγέλλω for commanding, and so on. Whatever the reason for the shift from ἔγειρε to ἀνέστη (and a better one than those thus far discussed will arise in connection with v 42b), it is likely that the power which Jesus displays to make the girl stand up and walk after dying prefigures the power by which he himself will stand up after being dead for three days (see also the comments on 9:26-27).

5:42b *(Luke 8:56a)* The idiomatic expression, "And they were astonished with great astonishment," recalls a similarly idiomatic expression at the close of the story about Jesus' calming the storm: "And they feared a great fear" (4:41). As there, the use of cognates plus the adjective "great" is emphatic (on the construction, see E. C. Maloney, *Semitic Interference* 185-89). Here it emphasizes the magnitude of the astonishment and thus of the miracle that caused it (for a textually distant but verbally close parallel, see Gen 27:33 LXX). It appears that for the girl's standing up in v 42a Mark used ἀνίστημι to get a wordplay here in v 42b with ἐξίστημι and its cognate ἔκστασις for the witnesses' "standing outside themselves," i.e. "being astonished" (not "frightened," which would disagree with v 36 — against E. Lohmeyer 107-8). The story about the healing of the paralytic may also be influencing Mark's phraseology again (cf. 2:12; also 6:51; 16:8). If Mark writes εὐθύς, "immediately," between the verb and its cognate noun, the immediacy of the astonishment matches the immediacy of the girl's standing up and walking and thus enhances the miracle all the more. Εὐθύς, "immediately," has good support in ℵ B C L Δ 33 892 cop[bo] eth, but the support lacks broad distribution in different textual families. The position of εὐθύς between ἐξέστησαν and ἐκστάσει may favor authenticity on the ground of its awkwardness. On the other hand, we might expect Mark to have written καὶ εὐθὺς ἐξέστησαν as a parallel to καὶ εὐθὺς ἀνέστη; for he usually puts εὐθύς after καί in a situation such as the present one. We might then regard the present position of εὐθύς as a sign of awkward interpolation by a scribe. But on the other side again, what keeps us from thinking that Mark has had an afterthought or that his amanuensis has fallen behind but is catching up by means of a late insertion and that the awkward position of εὐθύς will lead to later scribal omission?

5:43 *(Matt 9:26; Luke 8:56b)* Since the preceding story ended with Jesus' command to report at home how many things the Lord had done (v 19), and with a proclamation throughout the Decapolis (v 20), the present command not to let anyone know what has happened must not derive from Mark's redaction. Otherwise, he would hardly have allowed the earlier proclamation to stand. The two commands come to him as traditional data. We need to ask why Jesus issues such apparently contradictory commands. They are not contradictory in fact, however. The command that the ex-demoniac should report to his family at home agrees very nicely with the family privacy that characterizes the miracle performed on Jairus's daughter. No inconsistency appears, then, between Jesus' command to the ex-demoniac and his command to the intimates in Jairus's house. The present command is usually judged Christological rather than historical, or redactional rather than traditional, because of the impossibility of keeping secret the raising of the girl. People will see her alive; so the command belongs to the artificially imposed messianic secret. But no such impossibility attaches to the command if its purpose is not to keep the raising permanently secret, but to keep it secret only long enough to allow a getaway by Jesus. Several factors favor the latter alternative: (1) The command to give the girl something to eat does not aim at proving that she has come back to life, for her standing up and walking around have already provided such proof. One might say that the command aims at provision of the nourishment that will enable her to continue standing up and walking around, but her parents would soon enough provide her with such nourishment without having to be told to do so. Rather, Jesus wants them to feed her before the outsiders discover her alive; for the command to give her something to eat is put in conjunction with the command not to let anyone know what has happened.

He wants to delay the discovery so as to get away from the large crowd that have been crushing him (5:24, 31). (2) The very next verse (6:1) indicates that Jesus does in fact make a getaway ("and he went out from there") with his disciples following ("and his disciples follow him"). The crowd that followed him to Jairus's house and the mourners there are notably absent (contrast 5:24, 31, 38-40). Furthermore, the division in 6:1 between "he went out from there" (i.e. from Jairus's house) and "he goes into his home town" implies Jesus' leaving before the crowd discover that he has raised the dead. Mark puts some weight on the point also by using the finite verb "went out" rather than a mere participle, such as we find in 1:29, 45; 3:6; 5:2, 13; 6:12, 24, 34, 54; 7:31; 9:30; 11:12; 16:8, and this despite the immediately following finite form of the same verb in the simplex. (3) Jesus repeatedly tries to get away from crowds that threaten to mob him because of his miracles (1:35-37, 45; 2:13; 3:7-12, 13, 20; 4:10 [with 1], 34 [again with 1], 35-36; 6:30-33, 45-46; 7:17, 24, 31; 8:10; 9:25 [with 28], 30; 10:1 [with 10]). (4) The stupendousness of raising the dead magnifies the threat and therefore makes the purpose of getting away from the crowd perfectly plausible — historically, literarily, or any other way one chooses to look at it. Cf. C. F. D. Moule in *Jesus und Paulus* 243; H. C. Kee, *Community* 95; but contrast W. L. Lane (198-99), who thinks that Jesus holds back because of unbelief on the part of those who laughed at him.

Mark's last emphasis, then, falls on Jesus' taking measures to avoid being thronged to death. This emphasis bears witness to the stupendousness of the miracle. The adverbial πολλά, "much, strictly," highlights the danger and thus the miracle. The use of a second verb of speaking (εἶπεν, "said") doubles the emphasis.

NOTES

See K. Kertelge, *Wunder* 110-14, for lists of dictional and conceptual similarities between the two stories in vv 21-43, and between them and earlier miracle stories. He thinks of a pre-Marcan collector who edited the stories so as to produce these similarities. An answer to the question whether or not Mark writes v 21 on the basis of tradition depends on an answer to the same question with regard to 4:35-36; 5:1-20, on which see the foregoing comments and notes ad loc. For the tracing of both tradition and redaction in v 21, see G. Rochais, *Les récits* 45-46. But his opinion that the first half of the verse originally concluded the preceding story of exorcism mistakes 8:10, 13 as conclusions rather than as introductions and overlooks Mark's habit of starting pericopes with topographical statements.

In relation to vv 1, 17-20, "the other side" in v 21 means the west side of Galilee. One might think that originally, i.e. apart from the present context, the expression referred to the east side (so K. L. Schmidt, *Rahmen* 145-46). But the Jewishness of the following material ("one of the synagogue rulers," "Talitha koum," etc.) disfavors territory dominated by Gentiles. That v 22 looks much like introductions to miracle stories at 1:40; 2:3 does not imply that Mark makes up v 21 apart from tradition — unless we insist on rejecting the topographical notes in the introductions to all other miracle stories in Mark (see 1:21-23; 2:1-2; 3:1; 5:1-2; 6:32-35; 7:24-25, 31; 8:22; 9:14; 10:46).

C. P. Thiede (in *Bib* 65 [1984] 550-52, 557) suggests that in v 21 we should omit εἰς τὸ πέραν, "to the other side," with P[45] (c) f because 7Q5, which he takes to represent Mark 6:53, omits "to the land" in connection with the same verb διαπεράω, "cross over." The earliness of 7Q5 favors this view if 7Q5 does represent Mark 6:53 (but see the notes on 6:52-53). So also does the omission of "to the land" in Mark 6:45 P[45vid] W f^1 q sy[s] and the lack of "to the land" in the parr. Matt 9:1; Luke 8:40, for the likelihood of parallel influence on Mark 5:21 P[45] (c) f is lessened by larger differences in Luke 8:40 and by the fact that Matt 9:1 leads into an entirely different story. The appearance of "to the other side" in 4:35; 5:1; 6:45 v.l.; 8:13 may be taken with equal validity to favor the originality of the phrase in the tradition or in Mark's redaction at 5:21, or to favor that these other occurrences prompted scribal insertion in 5:21. Similarly, the omission of "to the other side" may here be taken as due to scribal offense-taking at the pleonastic combination of cognates in διαπεράσαντος . . . εἰς τὸ πέραν, and in 6:45 P[45] al as due to the same with respect to the overstuffed combination εἰς τὸ πέραν πρὸς Βηθσαϊδάν, "to the other side to Bethsaida," both of which combinations may exhibit Mark's penchant for duality (F. Neirynck, *Duality* 45-53, 94-96); or the presence of "to the other side" may be taken as a scribal gloss engendered by the cognate participle in 5:21, the overfulness in the present v.l. and in 6:45 v.l. being a sign of scribal insertion. But the overfulness has on its side that διαπερᾶν εἰς τὸ πέραν is a literal translation of the Aramaic עֲבַר לְעֵיבַר (cf. *Tg. Ps.-J.* Deut 30:13, noted by G. Rochais [*Les récits* 43], who also argues strongly for omitting ἐν τῷ πλοίῳ, "in the boat," with P[45] D Θ f^1 28 565 700 *pc* it sy[s] [ibid. 39-43]; but see B. M. Metzger, *Textual Commentary* ad loc.). Putting πάλιν, "again," right before συνήχθη, "gathered," with P[45] א* D 565 700 it sy[p] conforms to Mark's usually putting πάλιν right before or after the verb it modifies. This placement shifts "again" from the sea-crossing to the gathering of the crowd (cf. 2:2; 4:1; D. B. Peabody, *Mark as Composer* 126-30).

Elsewhere in Mark συνάγομαι (it always occurs in the passive) takes a πρός-phrase rather than an ἐπί-phrase (4:1; 6:30; 7:1), even where enemies gather and we might expect ἐπί in the sense "against" (7:1), which characterizes συνάγομαι ἐπί in the NT outside Mark. But the other Marcan passages use the historical present; here we have an aorist. Does Mark prefer different prepositions with different tenses? The lack of any prepositional phrase with συνήχθησαν in 2:2 makes it non-exceptional. See 5:24; 6:34; 8:1; 9:14; 12:37 for ὄχλος πολύς, "a large crowd," and the concordance for numerous other occurrences of ὄχλος without πολύς.

"Of the synagogue rulers" (v 22) may imply a plurality of rulers in a local synagogue, a plurality of local synagogues each having one ruler, or — as favored by the lack of reference to a local synagogue or to local synagogues — rulers as a general class (cf. 6:15; 8:28; 9:37, 42; 12:28; 13:1; 14:66; also 9:17) but only one per synagogue (see, e.g., Luke 13:14). P. Parker (in *JBL* 100 [1981] 396 and in *New Synoptic Studies* 73) overlooks the last possibility in his attack on Mark's accuracy. W. Schrage (in *TDNT* 7. 844-47) sets out evidence for one ruler per synagogue (cf. B. Lifshitz in *RB* 67 [1960] 58-64); but Acts 13:15; 14:2 D favor that at least some synagogues had more than one, for the contexts do not favor attendance at the synagogue of rulers from other, unmentioned synagogues. Synagogue rulers had charge of synagogue buildings and of the worship services held there.

G. Rochais (*Les récits* 56-57) thinks that in v 22 ὀνόματι, "by name," may be a scribal gloss since this use of the dative appears nowhere else in Mark (cf. the omission of "by name, Jairus" in D it and the defense of this omission by J. K. Elliott in *NT Textual Criticism* 53-54). But 2:14; 10:46; 14:32; 15:7, 21, 43 (to take some representative examples) display a wide variety of grammatical constructions in the introduction of names. It should arouse no suspicion, then, if yet another construction should appear in the authentic text of 5:22. See fuller discussions in B. M. Metzger, *Textual Commentary* ad loc.; J. Gnilka 1. 211.

In v 23 it is hard to decide whether the v.l. παρεκάλει, "was beseeching," arose by assimilation to the same form in vv 10, 18, or whether the v.l. παρακαλεῖ, "beseeches," arose by assimilation to the historical present tense of other verbs in the preceding verse. Since in vv 10, 18 παρεκάλει is followed by a ἵνα of purpose-cum-indirect discourse (so also in 6:56; 7:32; 8:22; cf. the infinitive of purpose-cum-indirect discourse in 5:17) and since in v 12 παρεκάλεσαν, "they besought," is followed by a participle of λέγω, "saying," to introduce direct discourse, it appears that v 23 begins with direct discourse (παρακαλεῖ followed by a participle of λέγω and a recitative ὅτι), wobbles toward purpose-cum-indirect discourse (a ἵνα dependent on παρακαλεῖ plus the subjunctive in ἐπιθῇς, "might lay [hands] on"), but falls back into direct discourse (the second person of ἐπιθῇς, "you," instead of the expected third person, "he"). Perhaps anticipation of a ἵνα of purpose in the last clause of v 23 leads to the fall-back into direct discourse — but the first ἵνα has already been written and is allowed to stand. If indecision lies at the root of this textual phenomenon, we should neither treat the first ἵνα as imperatival (as is usually done — see BAGD s.v. ἵνα III2) nor supply παρακαλῶ or θέλω before it (H. B. Swete 101-2). For the purpose of translation we may regard ἐλθών as having the force of an imperative finite verb (cf. the Semitic imperatival participle), with the result that the preceding as well as following ἵνα is telic: "Come in order that. . . ."

Θυγάτριον (v 23) is usually regarded as a faded diminutive, for v 35 follows up with the normal form of the noun. But the normal form occurs in the words of others who bear news of the daughter's death. On the father's lips the diminutive carries a note of endearment (cf. 7:25) and therefore undermines the suggestion of W. Grundmann (7. Aufl., 150) that Jairus is concerned about losing his position as synagogue ruler if his daughter dies and people interpret her death as God's judgment. With ἐσχάτως ἔχει, "is at the point of death," cf. the Latin in extremis esse and the several Marcan occurrences of κακῶς ἔχω, "be ill" (1:32, 34; 2:17; 6:55; also 16:18). See W. Wagner in ZNW 6 (1905) 211-12 on "save" in the sense "heal." E. Lohmeyer (100-101) thinks that because it does not reappear in the latter part of the story about the girl, the verb "save" does not carry a larger meaning than "cure" as it does in the story about the woman, where it appears twice (vv 28, 34). But after three occurrences in the intertwined stories, the larger meaning might have established itself well enough; and the visible details of the girl's being raised take the place of "save," whose generality suits the invisibility of the woman's cure. M. Black (Aramaic Approach 71, n. 1) thinks that "be saved and live," which he describes as a combination impossible in Aramaic, goes back to the single Aramaic verb איח (see 3:4; 8:35; 13:20; 15:30 for the saving of life, and esp. 3:4 for the saving of life even when the whole body is not threatened). The use of "save" in vv 23, 34 does not favor the view that the two stories were drawn together partly because of their sharing this word, for it is just as likely that the sharing of this word stems from an original connection between the stories (see the last notes on this pericope).

In v 25 οὖσα, "being," indicates an ongoing condition; and ἐν tells the condition "in" which the woman was (BAGD s.v. εἰμί III4) or which she had (sociative ἐν, "with," like the Hebrew בְּ; cf. 1:23 with comments). For another instance of ῥύσει αἵματος, "flow of blood," see Lev 15:25 LXX (also M. J. Selvidge, Woman 47-48, on the difference of this diction from the Greek diction normally used for menstruation). It is hard to tell whether Mark means an overfrequent and heavy menstrual flow, a continuous light one, or another kind of blood loss (see H. van der Loos, Miracles 509-10; also R. Meyer and F. Hauck in TDNT 3. 419-32 on the resultant ritual uncleanness and Josephus J.W. 6.9.3 §§426-27; m. Zabim 5:1, 6). M.-J. Lagrange (140) notes the middle eastern custom of calling in as many physicians as possible, the high cost of doing so, and the deleterious effects of their often contradictory prescriptions. But Mark is not attacking the custom, or even physicianly incompetence as such (as thought by E. Lohmeyer 101), but is setting up a foil to Jesus' success. See O. Weinreich, *Antike Heilungswunder* 195-97; R. and M. Hengel in *Medicus Viator* 332-34; and B. Blackburn, *Theios Anēr* 202-3, for ancient references to physicians' failures, and esp. 2 Chr 16:12; Job 13:4; Tob 2:10; Sir 10:10; Philo *De sacr. A. et C.* 70; *m. Qidd.* 4:14 (but contrast Sir 38:1-15). With τὰ παρ' αὐτῆς, "her possessions" (v 26), cf. οἱ παρ' αὐτοῦ, "his family" (3:21). C. F. D. Moule (*Idiom-Book* 51-52) suggests that τὰ παρ' αὐτῆς, which literally means "the things from beside her," emphasizes "the disastrous movement away of all her small [Why not large?] savings." The doubly adversative "but rather" toward the end of v 26 may keep Mark from writing δέ, "but," instead of καί, "and" (but in an adversative sense), before the preceding phrase. M. Reiser (*Syntax und Stil* 113-15) cites other, non-Semitic examples of an adversative καί introducing a negative statement.

That Mark elsewhere combines a περί-phrase with ἀκούω, "hear about . . ." (7:25), but never makes τά, "the things," a direct object of ἀκούω, favors the v.l. without τά in v 27. א* B C* Δ *pc* probably insert τά to give ἀκούσασα a direct object (cf. Luke 22:37; 24:19, 27; Acts 1:3; 18:25; Phil 2:20) and to provide τὰ παρ' αὐτῆς (v 25) with a parallel. The shift from the singular "garment" (v 27) to the plural "garments" (v 28) may be due to the difference between the one garment that the woman touches and the garments any of which she hopes to touch, whereas Jesus does not know which one she touches (hence the plural again in v 30).

For patients' touching the healer, his clothes, or something else closely associated with his body, see also 3:10; 6:56; Luke 6:19; Acts 5:15; 19:12; and O. Weinreich, *Antike Heilungswunder* 63-66, 175-78 (cf. E. Yamauchi in *TynBul* 34 [1983] 179). The story in 2 Kgs 13:20-21 shows that healing through contact with Jesus' clothing does not necessarily imply a Hellenistic magical origin of the story concerning the woman (see H. K. Nielsen in *Probleme der Forschung* 81-87; cf. D. Daube, *NTRJ* 234-35). J. Ernst (161) asks whether she has heard about the *Kontaktwundern* mentioned in 3:10 (see the comments in the present commentary ad loc., esp. on μάστιξ). A Jewish origin probably betrays itself in "the fountain of her blood," which comes from Lev 12:7 LXX (= MT), and in the reference to her "body," which comes from Lev 15:19 LXX (somewhat against a reference to "flesh" in the MT). See Str-B 1. 594-95; K. Kertelge, *Wunder* 117-18, for the possibility that Jesus acts as a new Moses in stopping the flow of blood (v 29); but J. Gnilka (1. 214-15) argues that the rabbinic tradition regarding Moses is too late (c. 150 C.E.) and too exceptional. We might add that in the rabbinic tradition Moses himself does not perform a miracle of such stoppage, as Jesus does. Since elsewhere Mark uses θεραπεύω, "heal," we might attribute its synonym ἴαται to his source (v 29). But since he never uses θεραπεύω in the perfect tense (which elsewhere in the NT characterizes only the participial form of the verb), he may simply prefer its synonym for that tense.

It is true, of course, that Greek participles modifying direct objects of verbs of perception act like finite verbs for the nouns they modify (see, e.g., BDF §416). Nonetheless, in v 30 the stress falls on the direct object ("the power") rather than on the action in the participle ("going out"). G. Vermes (*Jesus the Jew* 75) draws a parallel between Jesus and Hanina ben Dosa, who senses the efficacy of his prayer for healing by the fluency of his prayer. But the means of healing differ radically, and Jesus senses that a healing has taken place only after it has done so. To observe that he does not know who touched him is not to disprove the supernaturalness of his knowledge that an act of power has gone out. Knowledge does not have to be all-encompassing to be supernatural, and the supernaturalness of the act of power rubs off on the knowledge of its going out (against E. Schweizer 117 et al.). Nothing implies that the crowd consists of sick people who are touching Jesus to be healed by him, or that he asks who touched him not because he does not know who did but because he wants to shift the woman's faith from his clothes to his person. For he does not correct her faith, but commends it. Besides, she touched his clothes because they were *his*. Without his question (v 30) the miracle would not have become known. But because the crowd did not see the miracle take place, they do not express admiration. The woman's fear, trembling, prostration, and telling of all the truth therefore replace the usual expression of admiration by onlookers.

See M. Reiser (*Syntax und Stil* 116-17) on the adversative καί in the middle of v 31. The initial καί is also adversative. W. L. Lane (193) thinks that the disciples are impatient because of the dire condition of Jairus's daughter. The omission of τῶν ἱματίων, "the [my] garments," may be an example of ellipsis (cf. v 30). If so, we should translate v 31, "Who touched my [garments]?" Otherwise, the omission supports that in v 30 τῶν ἱματίων was appositive to μου: "Who touched me, [i.e.] my garments?" (cf. the placement of μου before ἥψατο, "touched," and the delay of τῶν ἱματίων till afterward). The shorter version of the question may clarify that the ultimate source of the healing power was Jesus, not his garments.

According to A. T. Robertson (*Grammar* 838), the imperfect περιεβλέπετο (v 32) is ingressive ("began to look around") or means that Jesus kept looking around till the woman came forward. "Fear and trembling" (v 33) is a stereotyped combination (see 1 Cor 2:3; 2 Cor 7:15; Eph 6:5; Phil 2:12; Exod 15:16 LXX; Deut 2:25 LXX; 11:25 LXX; Dan 5:19 Theod; Jdt 2:28; 15:2; 4 Macc 4:10). W. Grundmann (7. Aufl., 151) thinks that the woman fears the consequences of possibly having made Jesus unclean and therefore unfit to enter the house of the synagogue ruler. But "knowing what had happened to her" gives quite a different reason for her fear, a reason that runs in the opposite direction from thinking of what might have happened to Jesus and that qualifies her fear as awe in the face of a miracle (cf. 4:41; 5:15; 9:6; 16:8). Disregarding the text opens the door to unfalsifiable, unverifiable suggestions, such as that the woman fears discovery, fears a misinterpretation of her action as designed to transfer her illness to Jesus or to entice him, or fears an angry reaction from him, perhaps to the extent of his reversing the miracle. The external evidence for substituting αἰτίαν αὐτῆς, "her case," in place of ἀλήθειαν, "truth," is so slim (W *f*¹³ [l] 28 sa^mss) that we should probably reject the substitution as due to parallel influence from Luke 8:47 rather than taking Luke 8:47, where the grammatical construction differs widely, as evidence for αἰτίαν αὐτῆς in Mark's original text. On the other hand, Mark's penchant for Latinisms favors this v.l.; for αἰτία seems to be used in the sense of *causa* (BDF §5[3b]).

The terminological link between Jairus's daughter and Jesus' addressing the woman as daughter (v 34) may just as likely originate in Jesus' mind as in the mind of a storyteller or redactor and therefore does not argue for insertion of the one story in the other. Since the text mentions no prayer to God on the part of the woman but does say that she expects to be healed if she touches Jesus' clothing, "your faith" means faith in Jesus, not faith in God (as also in v 36; 10:52, where similar situations obtain — against F. Hahn in *Glaube im NT* 50). Jesus does not correct her saying to herself that if she would touch even his garments she would be saved (v 28); rather, he characterizes her speaking thus as faith and repeats her own verb of salvation. The parallel between going in peace and being well from affliction recalls the Septuagintal translation of שׁלום, "peace," with ὑγιής, "well," and ὑγιαίνω, "be well," a number of times (see U. Luck in *TDNT* 8. 310-11) and may combine a Hellenistic blessing with a Jewish one (V. K. Robbins in *NTS* 33 [1987] 510). The prepositions εἰς, "into, in," and ἀπό, "from," before "peace" and "your affliction" make a happy contrast.

See W. Thissen, *Erzählung* 154-55, on the relation between faith and miracles; G. von Rad and W. Foerster in *TDNT* 2. 400-420 on "peace," which does not connote peace of mind but may carry overtones of a larger salvation just as the verb "save" may do (C. J. Hemer in *Medicine and the Bible* 53-54; H. K. Nielsen, *Heilung* 71-74); and *Gos. Nic.* 7; Eus. *H.E.* 7.18.1-4 for early traditions concerning the woman. W. Foerster (in *TDNT* 7. 990) argues that since "save" always refers to saving the whole person yet here Jesus heals only one part of the woman's body, the verb must include more than physical deliverance. Though the conclusion is possibly correct (cf. the foregoing comments), the weakness of Foerster's argument lies in overlooking that the malfunction of only part of the woman's body affects her whole person, so that an exclusively physical deliverance could retain the holistic meaning of "save."

Since "nothing in the incident [concerning the woman] . . . indicates that the miracle either impressed the crowds or persuaded them of anything," argues T. J. Geddert (*Watchwords* 48-50), there is no support for "the notion that Jesus is publicly displaying his mighty miracles/δυνάμεις for their value in verifying his claims" (cf. similar downgradings of miracles in 6:2, 5, 14; 9:39). The present case presents the unusual case of an involuntary miracle, of course. But we need to ask how miracles function for Mark and his audience, who know the source and extent of Jesus' power (N.B. the editorialness of the introductory phrases in v 30). On this point Geddert (op. cit. 50-52) unfortunately disregards John the Baptizer's designation of Jesus as the Stronger One (1:7), Jesus' enduement with the Spirit (1:10), and the definition of the unforgivable sin as attributing Jesus' exorcisms to an unclean spirit rather than to the Holy Spirit (3:22-30) and appeals instead to the failure of miracles to induce adherence to Jesus in his lifetime, but only amazement, wonder, and perhaps even praise. But if belief in Jesus is not limited to those who followed him around all the time, then many of the ones amazed at his miracles will count as believers, drawn to faith by those miracles.

On the ground that although Mark likes the indefinite third person plural such as ἔρχονται, "people come," represents, nowhere else does he use this verb in the present tense without a preceding καί, "and," W. Hendriks (in *L'Évangile selon Marc* 45-46) argues that tradition underlies v 35a (cf. Luke 8:49). Without prejudice to the question of tradition, however, the absence of καί in v 35a is better explained by Mark's desire to intensify the badness of the news with abruptness. We might consider the possibility that "from [the house] of the synagogue ruler" does not qualify "come," but "they, people" (cf. M. Zerwick, *Biblical Greek* §80, on the absolute use of ἀπό- and ἐκ-phrases). Then the verb would not be indefinite (but see E. C. Maloney, *Semitic Interference* 137). The aorist ἀπέθανεν, where Luke 8:49 has the perfect tense (but see Luke 8:52-53), stresses the occurrence of death (cf. 3:21; G. Rochais, *Le récits* 61).

On the stereotyped command, "Fear not!" (v 36), see G. Wanke and H. Balz in *TDNT* 9. 203, 212. It is hard to tell whether μή with the present imperative φοβοῦ implies that as a result of the bad news Jairus has started to fear and should stop, or that he should not start fearing now that he has heard it. Again, the link between the stories in the motif of faith could have arisen in the mind and mouth of Jesus as easily during interlocking events as at a later date in storytelling or redacting.

The text of v 37 would more naturally read αὐτῷ συνακολουθῆσαι for accompanying Jesus (cf. 14:51). But since the inner trio of apostles belong to the Twelve whom Jesus chose to be μετ' αὐτοῦ, "with him" (3:14; cf. 5:18; 14:33), Mark writes μετ' αὐτοῦ συνακολουθῆσαι. It is admittedly a matter of judgment, but the mention of Peter, James, and John as a trio occurs too infrequently (three times) to be ascribed to Mark's redactional interest, which would likely have taken advantage of other opportunities to introduce them (cf. J. Ernst in *Begegnung mit dem Wort* 47). Perhaps in anticipation of the definite article with "brother," Mark writes only one definite article to cover the trio (cf. his omitting the definite article with names accompanied by "the brother" or something similar in 1:16, 19; 3:17-18; 10:46, though fairly well supported vv.ll. add the definite article). He writes the one definite article to point back to 1:16-20. Jesus' accepting the designation "the Christ" before the entire band of his disciples (8:27-30) will show that the present exclusion of all of them except Peter, James, and John has nothing to do with a messianic secret. For this reason, too, the introduction of the trio should not be ascribed to Mark's redaction. On the ground that "the ones with him" in v 40 is a technical term in the tradition for the entire band of the Twelve (cf. 3:14), not just for the inner trio (cf. 14:33), it might be thought that Mark constructs and inserts v 37. But 1:36, which referred to the ones with Simon, and 2:25, which referred to the ones with David, show that "the ones with him" is *not* a technical term in the tradition for the entire band of the Twelve. Verse 37 does not come too early by anticipation of v 40 (as thought by G. Schmahl, *Zwölf* 128-31; W. Schmithals 286 et al.), for Mark distinguishes between entry into the house (v 38) and entry into the girl's room (v 40). If then only Peter, James, and John will enter the house with Jesus and the parents, Mark must mention the exclusion of others in v 37. 1 Kgs 17:19-24; 2 Kgs 4:32-37 (cf. Acts 9:36-43) do not provide background at this point; for in those passages Elijah does not take the mother with him, and Elisha shuts out another mother and his servant Gehazi, whereas Jesus takes along both the parents and the inner trio of his disciples (against E. Wendling, *Entstehung* 48). Contrast the apparently complete privacy in 7:33; 8:23. As will become apparent in the notes on "Talitha koum" (v 41), the present semi-privacy has nothing to do with the secrecy of rites and incantations. "The brother of James" may distinguish the John referred to here from John the Baptizer. The last mention of either one occurred at 3:16-17, where the same phrase appeared and kept the audience from thinking of this John as Peter's brother.

G. Rochais (*Les récits* 62-63) argues that Jesus has to get rid of a second crowd in vv 38-40 because Mark inserted the story of the woman, in which another crowd played a necessary role. But however many or few were following Jesus to Jairus's house, the presence there of weepers and wailers causes no difficulty. It is exactly what we would expect in that culture. Besides, it may exaggerate to call the weepers and wailers a "crowd." Mark does not (contrast Matt 9:23). Are the weepers and wailers professional mourners? Κλαίοντας and ἀλαλάζοντας, "weeping" and "wailing," are masculine in gender, but men as well as women hire themselves out as professional mourners (G. Stählin in *TDNT* 3. 838, 843). On the other hand, the recency of the girl's death and Jairus's erstwhile absence tend toward the mourners' consisting of family and perhaps friends, and toward the mourning as emotional rather than solely ceremonial (cf. John 11:33). By contrast, Matthew adds flutists and a crowd because in his version the girl has been dead from the start and plenty of time has elapsed for flutists to be hired and a crowd to gather (in part, cf. M.-J. Lagrange 143).

To say with B. Witherington III (*Women* 73-74) that in Jesus' presence, death *is* sleep, not *like* sleep, is to play with words (v 39). Sleep is still a metaphor. Jesus' raising the dead simply adds to the suitability of the metaphor. J. Gnilka (1. 217) says that sleep is not a euphemism for death, but an indication that Jesus will raise the girl from death. For how can sleep represent death right after death is denied? But if death is denied, we have to ask, how can sleep indicate a coming resuscitation from death? If then we soften the denial of death to mean that the girl's death, like sleep, will not last very long (cf. *Gen. Rab.* 96 [60c]), the euphemistic use of sleep for death creeps back in. It has been suggested that we have here a development in the direction of a catachesis which instructs Christians how to respond to death: do not fear, only believe, because death is mere sleep (cf. 1 Thess 4:13-14). The lack of an eschatological frame of reference, however, and the Christological emphasis in the astonishment at v 42 tend away from this suggestion.

Καταγελάω (v 40) means "laugh down," hence, "laugh to scorn." The mourners do not laugh Jesus to scorn because of any claim on his part that he will raise the dead. In their understanding he has just denied that the girl is dead. On ridicule as a motif in miracle stories, see O. Weinreich, *Antike Heilungswunder* 87-88; B. Blackburn, *Theios Anēr* 205. "Of the child" may come right after "the father" rather than after "and the mother" because the father is the only one to have fetched Jesus. Differently, P. Joüon (*Grammaire* §129a and *L'Évangile* 240) discovers a Hebrraism in the coming of the genitive right after the first of compounded governing nouns. By the same token, however, "of it" (i.e. of the young child) should have followed "and the mother." After entering the house (v 38), going into "where the child was" (v 40) implies, as we might guess on other grounds, that the synagogue ruler and his family do not live in a one-room house. A. Oepke (in *TDNT* 1. 784) suggests that Jesus takes the parents and the inner trio of disciples into the child's room to maintain Jewish standards of propriety, for the child is a girl. But for that purpose he does not need to take any disciples, and Luke 7:36-50; John 4:4-30 portray Jesus as careless of such standards (cf. Acts 9:40).

On "Talitha koum" (v 41), see H. P. Rüger in *Markus-Philologie* 82; M. Wilcox in *Logia* 469-76; idem in *ANRW* II 25/2. 1000-1002. W. S. Vorster (in *Neot* 14 [1981] 68) observes that Mark uses and translates foreign (i.e. Aramaic) words and phrases to put across his narrative point of view — here, for emphasis on the power of Jesus' word to raise even the dead. In only one other instance does the Aramaic plus translation have to do with a miracle (7:34), whereas in a number of other instances it has nothing to do with miracles (see 3:17; 7:11; 14:36; and esp. 15:22, 34, where we read the same formula ὅ ἐστιν μεθερμηνευόμενον, "which is translated," i.e. "which means when translated") — a point that weakens the suggestion that the Aramaic originally lacked a translation, that the following command to silence originally referred to keeping the Aramaic secret as a foreign magical formula (ῥῆσις βαρβαρική), and that Mark added a translation with the result that it is now the miracle itself which needs to be kept secret (J. Gnilka 1. 211-12; cf. 10:46, where Mark makes the Aramaic appositional to its preceding translation; 11:9-10, where "hosanna" lacks a translation because it has changed from an easily translatable prayer into a hardly translatable exclamation).

See O. Weinreich, *Antike Heilungswunder* 171-74; H. van der Loos, *Miracles* 558-64; B. Blackburn, *Theios Anēr* 192-93, for ancient extra-biblical accounts of raising the dead. Since it is only natural that the unburied corpse should be at home, we should not see a significant parallel in Elijah's raising a widow's son at home (1 Kgs 17:17-24) or in Elisha's raising the Shunamite's son at home (2 Kgs 4:17-37). Furthermore, Jesus does not pray and stretch himself out on the child repeatedly, as Elijah and Elisha did. Nor is the child said to breathe again (1 Kgs 17:22 MT) or cry out (3 Kgdms 17:22 LXX) or grow warm, sneeze, and open her eyes (2 Kgs 4:34-35).

The correlation between the child's age of twelve years (v 42) and the woman's suffering for twelve years (v 25) is not the sort of link likely to have been fabricated, for it probably carries no theological meaning. We should not see in the correlation an allusion to the choice of the twelve apostles. Mark leaves such an allusion unclear. Two periods of time so disparate in kind hardly relate to each other, much less to Jesus' making a selection from among his followers. We are justified only in seeing an interesting coincidence in historical data. N. Turner (*Grammatical Insights* 65-66) thinks that "for she was twelve years old" explains why Jesus used *talitha* ("tender lamb") and the sexless *koum* rather than the feminine *koumi*. But this view requires a textually unsupported repositioning of the "for"-clause, and Mark surely does not assume that the audience for whom he has to translate Aramaic would recognize the sexlessness of *koum*, would expect the feminine *koumi*, and would understand another meaning of *talitha*.

According to H. J. Ebeling (*Messiasgeheimnis* 131-35), a historically impossible command to silence has the literary-theological purpose of portraying Jesus as a holy man: he does not seek glorification (v 43). With appeals to 1:44; 7:32-37; 8:22-26; 9:25 (cf. Acts 9:40), T. W. Manson (in *Studies in the Gospels* 212) thinks that since the raising of Jairus's daughter cannot be kept secret, the method of raising her is to be kept secret. But as in 1:44; 9:24, 27, the ordinariness of the healing gesture and the plainness of the healing word leave nothing in the method worthy of being kept secret. In 7:32-37 it will be the crowd who are told to keep the secret even though Jesus has performed the healing apart from them; and they will break the command to secrecy, not by telling the method, of which they are apparently ignorant, but by telling the fact. In 8:22-26 there will be no command to secrecy, only a command to go home rather than into town. The similarity in the diction of 5:43 to that of 7:24; 9:30 does not imply Mark's fabrication of these passages, for the similarity may reflect dictional preferences in tradition or Mark's dictional preferences in redacting tradition.

See J. H. Moulton and W. F. Howard, *Accidence and Word-Formation* 450, on the Semitism of "said" in the sense "commanded" plus an infinitive. We may presume that Jesus sees the girl's need for nourishment, as he will see the need of the four thousand for nourishment (8:2-3). But Mark omits her eating (contrast Luke 24:41-43) and even the carrying out of the command to give her food. Hence, there is no second proof (after her standing up and walking around) of coming back to life, no need to suppose that vv 42 and 43 or parts of them originally appeared in a different order, and no reason to imagine that a pre-Marcan collector of miracle stories added the command to give her food in anticipation of and preparation for the command to give the five thousand food (6:37; against P. J. Achtemeier in *JBL* 89 [1970] 279-81). It is equally possible that Jesus was as solicitous of the girl's need as he was of the crowd's need.

D. O. Via (*Ethics* 110-11) writes that in vv 21-43 Jesus turns the dead sexuality of the woman, whose flow of blood made her ritually unfit for intercourse, into a restored sexuality as new as that of the girl, who is just now marriageable (cf. M. J. Selvidge in *JBL* 103 [1984] 619-23; F. Kermode, *Genesis of Secrecy* 131-33). The correspondence between the twelve years of dead sexuality and the twelve years of age is supposed to support this view. But Mark relates the twelve years of blood-flow to the woman's suffering at the hands of physicians and spending all her resources without avail, not to ritual unfitness for intercourse; and he relates the girl's twelve years of age to her ability to get up and walk, not to marriageability. Furthermore, the girl's being called a "little child" and a "little girl" and the rabbis' regarding a girl as marriageable not till the age of twelve and one half years (Str-B 2. 10) tend away from Via's interpretation.

E. Lohmeyer (104) says that not as the story of the woman, the story of the girl lacks Hellenistic traits (indirect discourse, periods, very many participles) and has Semitic traits instead (much parataxis, Semitisms in vv 22 [εἷς for τις] and 42 [ἐξέστησαν . . . ἐκστάσει μεγάλῃ], and in v 41). G. Rochais (*Les récits* 58) would seem to add ἵνα ἐλθών (v 23), corresponding to the Aramaic די אתה ו (cf. 16:1; Luke 7:3; 12:36). P. J. Achtemeier (31 and in *JBL* 89 [1970] 276-79) concludes that the stories were not reduced to writing by the same person. These scholars overestimate the stylistic differences between the stories. The story of the woman has several examples of indirect discourse in vv 27, 29, 30, 33 (bis), but the story of the girl also has several examples in vv 36, 43 (bis). The story of the woman has three periods in vv 25-27, 30, 33, but the story of the girl has two in vv 36, 40 — and with the same construction: subject + participle(s) + verb. To be sure, the series of participles appearing between the subject and the verb in vv 25-27 seems endless; but the construction of the period is not at all unique, and 14:67; 15:43 provide other examples of Mark's stringing participles together. The story of the woman has fifteen participles, the story of the girl nearly as many: fourteen. The two stories exhibit almost the same incidence of parataxis: an average of just below 1.5 per verse. The two Semitisms in the story of the girl are matched by two Semitisms in the story of the woman (ἐν in the sociative sense of בְּ — v 25 [see E. C. Maloney, *Semitic Interference* 181-82]; "go in peace" — v 34 [see BAGD s.v. εἰρήνη 2]). The story of the woman does not contain transliterated Aramaic, as the story of the girl does; but the story of the girl is stylistically more Hellenistic in having two genitive absolutes (vv 21, 35).

In favor of a secondary dovetailing of the two stories, L. Schenke (*Wundererzählungen* 199) argues that the seven successive participial phrases in vv 25-27 betray Mark's hand in turning originally finite verbs into participles to indicate what was happening in the meantime, i.e. during the first part of the story concerning Jairus's daughter (cf. E. Lohmeyer 101). If Mark does make such a change, however, he probably purposes to highlight the hopelessness of the woman's condition by creating a string of participles; for only the last of the seven ("coming in the crowd from behind") describes what was happening in the meantime. All the rest reach back across the twelve preceding years, and a merely literary interlude is served by participles no better than by finite verbs. The point, then, has extremely little to do with the meantime; and even if it had everything to do with the meantime, the participial phrases might do this job precisely because something *was* happening in the meantime. True, neither story absolutely requires the other; but that fact only allows the possibility of original independence. It does not favor such independence. Under the theory of secondary dovetailing, J. R. Edwards (in *NovT* 31 [1989] 203-5) says that Mark purposes the woman's story to show what kind of faith Jairus needs to exercise.

If we were to omit vv 24-34, "while he was still speaking" (v 35a) would carry on directly from v 23, which contains the words of Jairus. "He" would then refer to Jairus, whereas in the present text of Mark Jesus is still speaking (v 34), so that a shift to Jairus is required in the further part of v 35 ("your daughter has died"). This shift seems at first to argue for an original reference to Jairus's still speaking, which would produce a smoother text by eliminating the shift; and if originally Jairus was still speaking, the story of the woman intruded later. But if Jairus were still speaking prior to the intrusion, the story would lack any statement that Jesus journeyed from the seashore to Jairus's house (v 24 being considered a redactional introduction to insertion of the story about the woman [for even a traditional v 24a would spoil the direct connection between vv 23 and 35a], and v 38 having to do with entering the house, not with journeying to it). Furthermore, there would be no need to reintroduce Jairus as the synagogue ruler while he was still speaking. As it is, ἀπὸ τοῦ ἀρχισυναγώγου, "from [the house] of the synagogue ruler," reintroduces Jairus to make the shift from Jesus to him as the one about to be addressed. Leaving "the house" to be supplied makes the shift clearer by putting the stress on Jairus himself.

One might suppose that intrusion of the story about the woman led to a reintroduction of Jairus, that originally v 35a read, "While he was still speaking, people come saying,. . . ." But even this supposition is left with the unlikelihood that the daughter has died so shortly after her father's departure from home that news of her death reaches him almost as soon as he reaches Jesus with his plea. It is much easier to believe that her death occurred a while later and that the news of it catches up with her father after Jesus has started to go with him to his house, during the course of which journey Jesus is speaking by now. The delay caused by the story of the woman adds to the tension (Will Jesus reach Jairus's daughter in time to keep her from dying?), but it does not create that tension. For the tension arises already both in Jairus's statement that his daughter is at the point of death and in the request that Jesus come, a request implying distance (v 23). Even without the story of the woman, Jesus would seem not to have arrived in time.

The appeal to 6:12-30; 14:1-11 (cf. John 12:1-8) does not favor Mark's inserting the story of the woman to gain some passage of time (so E. von Dobschütz in *ZNW* 27 [1928] 195-96), because in 6:12-30 the story of John the Baptizer's death will effect a delay in the narrative of the disciples' mission but not a delay in the mission itself (for otherwise Herod would not be said to have thought of John's rising from the dead) and in 14:1-11 the danger of an uproar, not the anointing of Jesus, will delay his arrest and execution. In contrast with John 11:1-21, Mark does not make anything of the present delay, which seems very slight (E. Lohmeyer 101).

Though ἀπὸ τοῦ ἀρχισυναγώγου might mean "some people from [the house] of the synagogue ruler" (so M. Black, *Aramaic Approach* 107-8), such a meaning founders on the rarity of this usage for the subject of a verb in Hellenistic Greek, on its absence in the

QL, proto-Mishnaic Hebrew, and Biblical and Middle Aramaic, on the greater naturalness of taking an ἀπό-phrase as adverbial when it occurs with ἔρχονται, "come," and on Mark's fondness for the indefinite third person plural, "they, people," which here eliminates any need to treat the ἀπό-phrase unusually as the subject (E. C. Maloney, *Semitic Interference* 134-37).

The remention of the crowd in v 24 (cf. v 21) is sometimes regarded as artificial (Why do they press Jesus?) and as designed to introduce an interpolation, i.e. the story about the woman. But the crowd's pressing Jesus provides a necessary backdrop to her working through them to touch him surreptitiously; so rementioning them does not at all look artificial. Failure to write that they were following Jesus might lead an audience to think that he and his disciples proceeded alone with Jairus (cf. the statement of C. E. B. Cranfield [182], apparently building on V. Taylor [289], that "in view of Mark's restraint with regard to connecting-links, the preparation for *vv.* 25-34 in *v.* 24 and the backward link in *v.* 35 must be taken seriously" [Taylor: as "historical, and not merely literary"]). We might then shift the charge of artificiality to v 21, since on the surface the crowd have no function there except to highlight Jesus' magnetism. But, as noted above, it would be more artificial to have the news of the daughter's death trailing Jairus so closely that he could not finish his plea before that news arrived. If then there really was an interval during which the healing of the woman took place, Mark's mentioning the gathering of a crowd at seaside in v 21 strikes one as entirely natural in that the gathering provides a reason why Jairus should seek Jesus there; and it saves Mark from the awkwardness of having to backtrack in v 24 to the gathering of a crowd when it is not their gathering that now needs to be noted, but their following Jesus in a way that provides a necessary backdrop to the woman's actions. The probability of an interval allowing more time for the death of Jairus's daughter works against the view of J. Sundwall (*Zusammensetzung* 34) that originally the story of the woman followed that of the girl, the references to twelve years toward the close of the first story and toward the start of the second then acting as a hinge.

Some commentators regard v 28 ("for she was saying, 'If I would touch even his garments, I will be delivered'") and v 34a ("but he said to her, 'Daughter, your faith has saved you'") as Mark's redactional fabrications inserted to cancel out an original notion that by itself touching Jesus' garments brought healing. In other words, Mark corrects magic with faith. Because the disciples' comment in v 31 ("you see the crowd pressing you and you are saying, 'Who touched me?'") lays the groundwork for distinguishing the touch of faith from ordinary touching, that verse, too, has been attributed to Mark's program of correcting magic with faith. But the editorial character of "for she was saying" (v 28; cf. v 8) does not imply that the following expression of faith has no foundation in the tradition, and injecting faith does not get rid of touching Jesus' garments for a cure. To get rid of that, Mark would need to eliminate the touching altogether. And the woman would not have touched Jesus' garments had she not believed in that means of healing — unless an earlier version had it that she touched his garments without thought of healing, perhaps accidentally, yet healing came to her anyway. But then her "coming in the crowd from behind" lacks significant purpose (v 27), Jesus' looking around to see the one who had "done this" loses much of its meaning (v 32), and her telling him "all the truth" turns vapid (v 33). Better to think that from the start faith was wedded to touch.

Since the disciples do not ask Jesus a question in v 31, it is no problem that he does not respond to their remark but looks around to see the woman. Drawing her out makes the best comment on their remark, anyway. See esp. L. Schenke, *Wundererzählungen* 196-216, for the foregoing arguments that are here opposed.

Still on the side of original independence but with a different twist, J. Gnilka (1. 209-13) inclines to treat v 24a as traditional and the genitive absolute in v 35a as redactional. Thus he gains a traditional statement concerning Jesus' journey and some needed delay for the death of the girl; but he loses a smooth, direct connection between vv 23 and 35a. Indeed, the coming of people from the ruler's house appears very abruptly under this view. Gnilka's observation (1. 212, n. 15) that the historical present tense prevails in the story of the girl, but past tenses in the story of the woman, does not imply different sources and therefore an original independence of the stories; for Mark himself likes to use the historical present tense, which in the story of the girl sounds a note of urgency (N.B. the switch to past tenses once Jesus pronounces the word of healing — vv 42-43), whereas the story of the woman needs no such note. Rather, the past tenses in the story of the woman heighten the tension by slowing down the narrative at the very point where an audience wants it to move faster for the girl's sake. Redaction rather than original independence therefore makes a better explanation of the difference in tenses.

Yet again, to argue for original independence H. Anderson (151) asks whether it is "historically probable that the same Jesus who forbids any of the crowd to follow him (verses 37-38) should have allowed the crowd and what transpired in its midst (5:24-34) to impede his progress to Jairus' home, especially in light of the extreme urgency of Jairus' plea about his daughter." But the question rests on the doubtful presupposition that it was to avoid a slow-down in the healing that Jesus allowed very few to enter with him into Jairus's home (and this for the same purpose that he threw out the weepers and wailers). More probably, the privacy relates to the command to silence and its purpose. The appearance of the theme of faith in both stories (vv 34a, 36) does not make a good argument in favor of their late redactional union, for it could just as well be that Jesus had faith on his mind in v 36 because of a chronologically preceding v 34a as that Mark or an earlier traditioner fabricated one or both references to faith to unite the stories. That Mark elsewhere may intertwine materials (3:22-30; 6:14-29; 11:15-19; 14:1-11, 53, 72) does not imply that he does so here; besides, the historicity of intertwinedness may be defended in other passages, too.

The stories have points of contact beyond that of faith — viz., salvation (vv 23, 28, 34), belief (vv 34, 36), fear (vv 33, 36), the number twelve (vv 25, 42), "daughter" (vv 34, 35), and healing by physical contact (vv 27-31, 41) — some of which have already been commented on. The number of these contacts and the superficiality of some of them (e.g., the woman takes the initiative in touching Jesus' garments, but he does the seizing of the girl's hand) may suggest equally well that similarities brought together originally independent stories, that bringing together originally independent stories caused them to be assimilated to each other, and that interdependent occurrence of the stories underlies the similarities in historical fact, in redactional assimilation, or in both. At the textual level, an element of impurity binds these stories together no more than it binds them to the preceding story of the demoniac. The woman's flow of blood is presented as an affliction from which she is saved, not as an impurity from which she is cleansed (contrast 1:40-44). Nor is it presented as a source of possible contamination for others — the crowd, the disciples, Jesus. The corpse of the girl likewise fails to be presented as a source of contamination or an object of cleansing. We have already seen that though the spirits which possessed the demoniac were described as unclean (but as elsewhere in Mark and therefore not as forging a distinctive link with a supposed element of impurity in the present stories), nothing was made of what Jews regard to be the impurity of pigs — as would need to have been done for Mark's Gentile audience (see 7:2-4); for Gentiles regard pigs as pure, worthy of sacrificial offering as well as of eating. At most, then, the element of impurity can have bound these stories together in a pre-Marcan Jewish stage. J. Schmid (114) attributes the vividness of the present narrative to Peter's report of intertwined events (so also K. L. Schmidt, *Rahmen* 148).

JESUS' ASTONISHING MIRACLES
AS INVALIDATION OF UNBELIEF

6:1-6a (Matt 13:53-58; Luke 4:16-30)

The story of a visit by Jesus to his home town starts with his going there and the disciples' following him (v 1). Next, Mark reports Jesus' teaching in the local synagogue and the astonished and offended reaction of the townspeople (vv 2-3), then Jesus' aphoristic response to their reaction (v 4). Finally, Mark explains the fewness of the miracles that Jesus works in his home town as due to the townspeople's unbelief (vv 5-6a). Thus the placement of the story here makes for a contrast with the belief of Jairus and of the woman with a flow of blood (5:21-43, esp. 23, 28, 34, 36). Mark makes the unbelief as well as the belief serve his purpose of magnifying Jesus' miracles, however.

6:1 *(Matt 13:53-54; Luke 4:16)* "And he went out," followed shortly by a reference to the synagogue, recalls Jesus' statement that he "went out" for the very purpose of preaching from one place to another (1:38-39, followed by a reference to synagogues; see also 1:45 with comments). "From there" means from Jairus's house (5:21-43). "And he comes to his home town" brings Jesus to Nazareth (cf. 1:9, 24). The singular of "synagogue" in v 2 will show that πατρίδα means "home town" rather than "home country" (cf. BAGD s.v. πατρίς 2). Mark refers to "the home town" instead of calling it by its name, "Nazareth of Galilee" (1:9), to prepare for v 4 and create sympathy for Jesus, not to avoid tarnishing the place-names "Nazareth" and "Galilee" (as thought by K. E. Dewey in *The Passion in Mark* 99, n. 12). The town that should have taken pride in its native son (N.B. the cognateness of πατρίδα to πατήρ, "father") took offense instead. Since the disciples will play no part in the story, the statement, "His disciples follow him," prepares for the summoning and sending of the Twelve (vv 6b-13), whom Jesus chose to be "with him" (3:14), and thereby emphasizes his magnetism and authority. The historical present tense of ἔρχεται, "comes," and of ἀκολουθοῦσιν, "follow," intensifies the emphasis.

6:2-3 *(Matt 13:54-57; Luke 4:16-21)* "And when the Sabbath had come" (cf. 16:1) leads to Jesus' teaching in the synagogue. As can be told from the reaction of the audience, the teaching adds another emphasis on his authority (cf. esp. 1:21-22, 27). Mark describes the reaction as one of astonishment (ἐξεπλήσσοντο, "they were being knocked out" in a metaphorical sense — cf. 1:22; 7:37; 10:26; 11:18). That he pays no attention to the content of Jesus' teaching, only to its effect, and that the townspeople will take offense at Jesus show the strength of Mark's desire to stress Jesus' authority: even offended astonishment serves the emphasis. That the astonishment was going on (imperfect tense) as the people were listening (ἀκούοντες, a present participle) brings it into the closest possible connection with Jesus' teaching. Since Mark does not otherwise distinguish among the townspeople, "many" means "all" (as often in Semitic speech) to emphasize that the all are many rather than to imply many but not all. The forward position of πολλοί, "many," intensifies this emphasis, which magnifies yet more the striking authority of Jesus' teaching.

The astonishment of the townspeople now finds expression in four questions which Mark attributes to taking offense at Jesus. The first two questions deal with Jesus' activities, and each one features a contemptuous οὗτος, "this guy": "From where [does] this guy [have] these things? And what [is] the wisdom given to this guy and the miracles such as are taking place through his hands?" The third question deals with Jesus' occupation and part of his family background and features another contemptuous οὗτος: "This guy is the carpenter, isn't he, the son of Mary and brother of James and Joses and Jude and Simon?" The fourth question deals with the rest of his family background: "And his sisters are here with us, aren't they?" Asyndeton divides the questions dealing with his occupation and family background from those dealing with his activities, and parataxis connects the questions within each pair. Though 4:41 showed that οὗτος need not be contemptuous, the attribution of the present questions to offense-taking supports a contemptuous usage here (cf. 2:7).

"From where [does] this guy [have] these things?" asks where Jesus got his wisdom and miracles and prepares for the upcoming reference to his being a local carpenter whose occupation and family background will sharpen the point of this first question (contrast the question "who?" in 2:7; 4:41, where Jesus' occupation and family background are not in view). "These things" is prospective, for the next question specifies the things as Jesus' wisdom and miracles. Asking about the source and character of Jesus' wisdom and miracles and describing the wisdom as "given" and the miracles as taking place "through his hands" accepts the wisdom and miracles as undeniable but stops short of attributing them to Jesus himself. He is only the recipient of wisdom, his hands only an instrument used by miracles (contrast 5:30; Acts 7:22a; and cf. the suggestion of M.-J. Lagrange [148] that "given" alludes to Jesus' never having undertaken rabbinic studies). The ellipsis of verbs, the alliteration with τ, the assonance of the vowels and diphthongs in various forms of οὗτος, and the chiasm in (a) πόθεν τούτῳ (b) ταῦτα; (b′) καὶ τίς ἡ σοφία ἡ δοθεῖσα (a′) τούτῳ; highlight the astonishment caused by Jesus' wisdom and miracles. By falling outside the chiasm, the miracles in the second question gain an importance of their own which prepares for vv 5-6a (cf. the comments on vv 13, 14). They do not make a separate question, however; for that would require another interrogative (τίνες). The meaning of τοιαῦται, "such as," stresses the remarkableness of the miracles; and the position of διὰ τῶν χειρῶν αὐτοῦ, "through his hands," before γινόμεναι, "are taking place," stresses the instrumentality of Jesus' hands in preparation for v 5.

Since ancient Greeks considered manual labor degrading, Mark's Hellenistic audience might respond with contempt to the identification of Jesus as a carpenter, as Celsus will do a little later (Or. Cels. 6.36). But Palestinian Jews do not despise manual labor (Str-B 2. 10-11). Mark hardly wants to portray Jesus in a poor light. And the definite article with "carpenter" points to the offense of Jesus' being well known to the townspeople rather than to any offense in his being a carpenter, for which we would expect an anarthrous noun.

We should likewise reject a slurring use of "the son of Mary" to imply bastardy (for which use see E. Stauffer [in Neotestamentica et Semitica 119-28], who misinterprets the vv.ll. as motivated by Christological offense at an implication of bastardy rather than by Hellenistic offense at manual labor, and then wrongly brings in other passages, both inside and outside the NT, that really do imply bastardy). Not only is the evidence unconvincing that in itself "the son of Mary" carries such an implication (rather, the implication that Jesus' father no longer lives in Nazareth, probably because he has died; see H. K. McArthur in *NovT* 15 [1973] 38-58, esp. 45-46, against the oft-repeated statement that it is insulting to call a man the son of his mother rather than of his father), but also a number of factors militate against the implication of bastardy and favor the connotation of familiarity instead: (1) the parallel between this designation and Jesus' being the well known carpenter; (2) the additional parallel with his being the brother of three men whose names the townspeople know; (3) the closeness of this second parallel in that one definite article modifies both "son" and "brother," a closeness so striking that some of the textual tradition eliminates it by inserting a second "the"; and (4) yet another parallel with Jesus' sisters living among the townspeople. Hence, "from where?" indicates a puzzlement that grows out of familiarity with him and his family, not a suspicion that grows out of knowing something unsavory about the circumstances of his birth.

The audience of Mark's book know the answer to the question of origin: Jesus got these things from the Holy Spirit, who descended into him at his baptism (1:9-10). Inclusion of the question reminds Mark's audience of this fact. A question of character now grows out of the question of origin; for uncertain origin implies uncertain character: "What [are] the wisdom that has been given to this one and the miracles such as are happening through his hands?" (cf. v 14). As does the question of origin, the question of character indicates suspicion. Mark's audience also know the answer to this question: Jesus' wisdom and miracles are of the good character to be expected from the one whom God addressed as his beloved and well-pleasing Son (1:11; cf. the increasing association of wisdom with deity in Judaism of the NT era — literature cited in BAGD s.v. σοφία). Again, inclusion of the question is a reminder that God so addressed Jesus. The townspeople cannot deny the phenomena of Jesus' remarkable wisdom and stupendous miracles (cf. the sequence teaching-exorcism in 1:21-28). They can only wonder where these phenomena come from and what they represent (cf. the charge in 3:20-29 that Jesus casts out demons by their ruler). In addition to exorcisms, Mark intends the miracles and wisdom to verify the authority of Jesus' teaching (again cf. 1:21-28). The people are not referring to miracles that Jesus has performed elsewhere and that they have heard about. "Miracles" refers to the few miracles performed in Nazareth according to v 5b. Τοιαῦται, "such as," is based on αὗται, meaning "these (near at hand)," not "those (at a distance)" (see 4:33; 7:13; 9:37; 10:14; 13:19 for the consistently near rather than distant meaning of τοιοῦτος). "Through his hands" clinches this forward reference, since Mark will write in v 5b that Jesus performs miracles in his home town by laying his hands on a few sick people (cf. 1:30-31; 5:22-23 for the conveyance of healing power through Jesus' touch). The connotation "in person" which "through his hands" conveys (see MM s.v. χείρ; J. H. Moulton and W. F. Howard, *Accidence and*

Word-Formation 462) points up that the miracles take place directly, not through prayer or the use of external means. "Such as" magnifies the impressiveness of these miracles over against their fewness. It takes only a few to excite astonishment. Since then the astonished questions refer forward to the few but impressive miracles performed in Nazareth, the exception that Jesus makes in performing them (v 5b) belongs to the original form of the story so long as the questions belong to it (cf. C. D. Marshall, *Faith* 194-95).

The townspeople's third and fourth questions, "This guy is the carpenter, isn't he, the son of Mary and brother of James and Joses and Jude and Simon? And his sisters are here with us, aren't they?" (v 3), demand an affirmative answer (so οὐκ with indicative verbs). They also raise the issue of identity and suggest a possible origin of Jesus' wisdom and power — viz., his family — that the townspeople cannot entertain because it is so patently absurd (cf. Or. *Cels.* 1.28). For Mark, identifying Jesus as the carpenter misses his identity as the one stronger than John the Baptizer (1:7). Identifying him as Mary's son misses his identity as God's Son (1:1, 11; 3:11; 5:7; 9:7; 12:6; 13:32; 14:61-62; 15:39). Identifying him as the brother of James, Joses, Jude, and Simon misses his identity as the one whom another Simon (plus his brother Andrew) and another James (plus his brother John) dropped everything to follow (1:16-20). And saying that his sisters are there misses his having just recently healed the woman with the flow of blood and raised Jairus's daughter. All in all, the third and fourth questions miss the point that Jesus has a new family of mothers, brothers, and sisters, over whom he presides (3:31-35). The imperfect tense of ἐσκανδαλίζοντο in the clause, "And they were taking offense at him," parallels the imperfect tense of ἐξεπλήσσοντο in the clause, "And many [or 'all'] were being astonished," and spoils astonishment at his words and deeds with unbelief in his person. Furthermore, Mark portrays their unbelief as a trap (cf. the literal meaning of σκανδαλίζω). He is writing his book to rescue people from that trap by identifying the true origin of Jesus' wisdom and power, which may then counteract the scandal of the Crucifixion (cf. Matt 11:6 par. Luke 7:23).

6:4 *(Matt 13:57; Luke 4:23-27)* The aphorism that Jesus uses in response, "A prophet is not dishonored except in his home town and among his relatives and in his house," portrays the townspeople's unbelief as due to prejudice. For Mark, prejudice against Jesus because of his crucifixion is just as baseless as prejudice against him because of familiarity with him and his family. There seem to be a narrowing down and a climactic order in the progression from home town (fellow townspeople) to relatives (extended family) to house (immediate family living in the same building; cf. Gen 12:1 and see the concordance s.v. ἀτιμάζω, ἀτιμία, ἄτιμος, and ἀτιμόω that the *alpha*-privitive carries the force of "dis[honored]," not merely of "un[honored]" or "without [honor]"; also Isa 53:3 LXX and O. J. F. Seitz in *SE VII* 457).

6:5-6a *(Matt 13:58; Luke 4:28-30)* The following of the absolute statement, "Jesus was not able to do there even one miracle," with the qualifying clause, "except that by laying his hands on a few sick people he healed [them]," does not imply that a tradition of Jesus' having worked no miracles at all in

Nazareth embarrasses Mark so much that he conjures up a few miracles to give Jesus better press. Otherwise, the question concerning "miracles such as are happening through his hands" (v 2) becomes awkward, perhaps nonsensical, since "such as" and the present tense of γινόμεναι imply miracles that are happening under the very noses of the Nazarenes just as his wisdom shows itself in the teaching they are hearing on this very Sabbath as he speaks in their synagogue. Furthermore, the construction οὐδεμίαν . . . εἰ μή, "not one . . . except," will recur in v 8 and 10:18, where the exceptions that the disciples may take a staff and that God is good seem not to originate with Mark (cf. 9:8). Rather, Jesus' healing power has elsewhere demonstrated itself so profusely that the present working of only a few miracles hardly counts. In a backhanded way, then, Mark turns the fewness of miracles here into a testimony concerning the multitude of miracles that Jesus has performed elsewhere. Furthermore, the forward position of ὀλίγοις ἀρρώστοις, "a few sick people," emphasizes the exceptions that give this testimony. "And he was marveling on account of their unbelief" rules out lack of power as the reason for Jesus' inability. The imperfect tense of ἐθαύμαζεν appears to make his marveling concurrent with the townspeople's astonishment (ἐξεπλήσσοντο, also imperfect — v 2), with their taking offense (ἐσκανδαλίζοντο, also imperfect — v 3), and with his inability (οὐκ ἐδύνατο, also imperfect — v 5). The editorial statement that Jesus is marveling on account of the townspeople's unbelief shows that Mark does not want his audience to take the aphorism in v 4 as a valid excuse for the unbelief.

On the ground that familiarity breeds dishonor, Jesus understands his fellow townspeople's taking offense at him. But because of their astonishment at his wisdom and miracles, he marvels at their unbelief. Recognizing the chiastic pattern of (a) the townspeople's astonishment (v 2), (b) their taking offense (v 3), (b′) Jesus' explaining their offense-taking as an example of the truism that familiarity breeds dishonor (v 4), and (a′) his marveling at their unbelief in that it contradicts their astonishment (vv 5-6a) keeps us from wrongly thinking that he should not marvel that the truism works. He marvels rather that it works even in conjunction with astonishment. Here lies the main point: not unbelief itself, but the invalidation of unbelief by Jesus' astonishing words and deeds. Mark's stating this point as a narrator omniscient of Jesus' inner thoughts adds emphasis to the invalidation.

NOTES

The threat of death tied together the stories of Jesus' stilling the storm, casting out Legion, and raising the daughter of Jairus. But it did so only in a loose way, because the terminology of death was prominent solely in the story of Jairus's daughter and was completely absent from the story of the woman with a flow of blood. Only the interconnection of the stories of the woman and the daughter prompted us to see the motif of death in the story of the woman. The demoniac dwelt among the tombs, and Legion appeared to have been bent on destroying him; but other aspects of that story vied for attention and got more of it. The disciples feared that they were perishing in the storm, but Mark emphasized Jesus' authority over the wind and sea more than he emphasized the rescue of the disciples from death. Geography and chronology appeared to play a more determinative role than any thematic consideration in the ordering of materials. So also in chaps. 6ff. Mark continues to put together disparate materials (though he makes thematic connections where he can) according to a scheme of topographical and chronological progression.

K. L. Schmidt (*Rahmen* 153) tries to make vv 1-6 the high point of 3:7–6:13 with respect to Jesus' rejection in Galilee. On the contrary, Mark has been emphasizing Jesus' successes (see also vv 6b-13) and makes the best he can of the present rejection. Unaccountably, Schmidt thinks that if vv 1-6 form a high point, the statement in v 1 that Jesus "went out from there" loses its connection with Jairus's house in 5:35-43.

Some remarks by B. Mayer (in *BZ* nf 22 [1978] 188-89) illustrate the uncertainty of distinguishing between tradition and redaction in v 1a and elsewhere in Mark. Though Mark likes ἐξέρχομαι and ἐκεῖθεν, Mayer argues, elsewhere he uses a participle and only one finite verb with ἐκεῖθεν (7:24; 9:30; 10:1); therefore ἐξῆλθεν ἐκεῖθεν καὶ ἔρχεται, "he went out from there and goes" (v 1a), derives from tradition. Likewise, since Mark nowhere else uses πατρίς, "home town" (vv 1, 4), it derives from tradition. But for special emphasis may not a redactor vary his usual construction (cf. the comments on 5:43)? May he not borrow a term like πατρίς from tradition (v 4) and use it in redactional composition as well (v 1)? Yes, he may. But "may" is not "does"; and even demonstrable Marcanisms would not kill the possibility of using favorite locutions to pass on traditional items of information (see also C. E. B. Cranfield 192 and H. Anderson 158 for opposing views). Since Mark likes to use the historical present tense, "comes" (ἔρχεται) looks Marcan in style but again may rest on tradition; so it is impossible to tell which verb rests on tradition, which one arises out of redaction, or whether both verbs are traditional or redactional.

J. Gnilka (1. 228) thinks that Mark replaces a traditional "Nazareth" with τὴν πατρίδα αὐτοῦ, which can mean "his home country" as well as "his home town," to conform to the secondary insertion of v 4, which has τῇ πατρίδι αὐτοῦ. We will see reasons to deny a secondary insertion of v 4, but it remains probable that Mark writes the more ambiguous term to prepare for its occurrence in v 4 as well as to create sympathy for Jesus (see the foregoing comments). B. Mayer (in *BZ* nf 22 [1978] 188-89) thinks that Mark inserts "and his disciples follow him" (v 1b) to indicate that the disciples will share Jesus' fate of rejection. But the noting of their many successes in the very next pericope (vv 6b-13; see esp. vv 12-13) makes this interpretation unlikely. Matt 13:53 and Luke 4:16 omit the disciples' following Jesus, probably not because Matthew and Luke know pre-Marcan tradition lacking it, but because in contrast with Mark the disciples play no role in the following Matthean and Lucan pericopes. Since Jesus chose the Twelve to be with him (3:13-19), their presence should not surprise us; and since Mark's audience need to know that the Twelve are available to be summoned and sent (6:6b-13), neither should their mention surprise us or strike us as awkward (cf. 2:23; 3:7, 9; 4:10, 34, 35-41; 5:1, 16, 31).

See the notes on 1:45 for the pleonastic use of ἤρξατο, "he began" (v 2); and 1:34 (with comments); 10:45; 14:24 on the anarthrous use of πολλοί, "many," with the meaning "all." The best textual tradition favors πολλοὶ ἀκούοντες, "many, hearing" (see B. M. Metzger, *Textual Commentary* ad loc.). Addition of the definite article in some texts has the apparent purpose of changing the all who are many into the majority but not all so as to leave room for a minority whose belief Jesus rewards with a few miracles (v 5b). But Mark will not say that Jesus performs a few miracles for a few believers; rather, that he performs only a few miracles because the Nazarenes do not believe. Mark does not mention any exceptions to the lack of belief as he does mention exceptions to the lack of miracles. Changing the present participle to the aorist in some texts conforms to the more usual tense of an introductory circumstantial participle, but loses emphasis on the concurrence of listening and astonishment.

B. Mayer (in *BZ* nf 22 [1978] 190-91) notes that ἀκούω, "hear," is lacking in other passages where διδάσκω/διδαχή, "teach/teaching," and ἐκπλήσσω, "astonish," occur (1:22; 11:18b). He concludes that in v 2 ἀκούοντες comes from tradition and originally referred (as we can tell by subtracting Jesus' teaching and the audience's astonishment as Mark's additions) to hearing that Jesus has come to Nazareth (cf. 2:1; 3:21; 6:55; 7:25). But ἀκούω will occur in 11:18a, though in a slightly different connection; and the Nazarenes' hearing that Jesus has come to town would leave occasionless their questions about the source of his wisdom, which looks traditional because it is not characteristically Marcan.

R. A. Guelich (1. 308) correctly describes as groundless the interpretations of ἐξε- πλήσσοντο, "were astonished" (v 2), as all the Nazarenes' initially favorable response that later turns unfavorable and as a favorable response by many whom a minority then sway against Jesus. For the four questions that immediately follow define the astonishment in terms of taking offense at him. There is no progression from favor to disfavor. Disfavor reigns from the start. Yet neither does Guelich's equating the astonishment with incredulity (cf. 10:26) quite pass inspection. True, Jesus will marvel at his fellow townspeople's unbelief. But that is an unbelief in his person, whereas their astonishment is not at all incredulous of his wisdom and miracles.

For the connection between teaching and wisdom, see Job 33:33; Prov 4:11; Wis 6:9; Sir 4:23-24; 9:17-18; 11QPs^a 18:5-7 (cited by B. Mayer in *BZ* nf 22 [1978] 191-92). Since the first question in v 2 concerns the origin of Jesus' wisdom and miracles, we are not dealing with the Jewish belief that the origin of the Messiah himself will be unknown (John 7:27; Justin *Dial.* 8.4; *b. Sanh.* 97a). See B. M. Metzger, *Textual Commentary* ad loc., on the text critical question regarding καὶ αἱ δυνάμεις . . . γινόμεναι, "and the miracles . . . taking place" (v 2). Mayer (op. cit. 192-93) favors the v.l. with ἵνα and γίνωνται as difficult in its ambiguity: Is ἵνα ecbatic or epexegetic? But external support for this v.l. is comparatively weak (C* D K [Θ 700] *al* it sy^h), and Mayer wrongly denies the most usual telic meaning of ἵνα, which would here produce an easy and therefore suspect v.l.: "And what [is] the wisdom that has been given to this one in order that even miracles such as these might take place through his hands?"

The position of τοιαῦται, "such as these," after αἱ δυνάμεις, "the miracles," stands against the suggestion of G. Wohlenberg (170) that we should read an exclamation: "And such miracles are taking place . . . !" E. Grässer (in *NTS* 16 [1969-70] 13) refers τοιαῦται to miracles recently narrated in Mark's text rather than currently performed in the presence of the townspeople. But the parallel with the wisdom that they hear Jesus utter in their presence and the upcoming editorial reference to a few miracles that he performs in their town militate against Mark's committing the blunder of confusing the townspeople with the audience of his gospel.

With a cross-reference to 11:28, 30, J. Dupont (*Études* 338-39) attributes the double question in v 2 to Mark's style. So also in v 3. Perhaps so, but duality of form does not imply absence of tradition. For the attribution of wisdom and power as a pair to Christ, see 1 Cor 1:24 (cf. Luke 24:19; Acts 7:22b); to the Messiah, Isa 11:2; *Pss. Sol.* 17:22-23 (see further K. Berger in *ZTK* 71 [1974] 1-30); to God, Job 12:13. Even for Mark and his audience, however, the references to Jesus' wisdom and miracles doubtfully allude to Isa 11:1-3, according to which "the Spirit of wisdom . . . and of strength" will rest on the messianic "branch" (נצר; cf. "Nazareth"). Mark mentions neither "Nazareth" nor "the Spirit" (against O. Betz, *Jesus. Der Messias Israels* 301-17). The reference to Jesus' miracles uses δύναμις in the plural (and in the singular only with respect to his inability to perform a miracle), whereas the LXX uses ἰσχύς and both the MT and the LXX use the singular. W. L. Lane (201, n. 4), C. E. B. Cranfield (193), and others think that "through his hands" does not refer to healing by touch, but reflects Semitic synecdochic use for the whole person's activity (cf. BAGD s.v. χείρ 1). But the regular use of Jesus' hands to heal (see 1:41; 5:23 [plural, as here]; 7:32; 8:23 [plural], 25 [plural]; cf. 10:16 [plural]) combines with a literalistic reference to his hands in v 5b to militate against such a figurative interpretation. J. A. Kleist (205) cites Soph. *El.* 1350; Hes. *Th.* 718 for non-Semitic literalistic usage.

In v 3 τέκτων probably means "carpenter, wood-worker, builder" (BAGD s.v.), but other meanings have been adopted — in particular, "stonemason" and "metalworker" (see H. Höpfl in *Bib* 4 [1923] 41-55; C. C. McCown in *Studies in Early Christianity* 173-89; and, for the possibility that Jesus worked as a carpenter in nearby Sepphoris, R. A. Batey in *NTS* 30 [1984] 249-58). C. E. B. Cranfield (194-95) and R. E. Brown (*Birth* 537-39) effectively defend the v.l. "the carpenter, the son of Mary" over against the v.l. "the carpenter's son and Mary's," for a defense of which see H. K. McArthur in *NovT* 15 (1973) 47-52; J. K. Elliott in *NT Textual Criticism* 54-55. "The son of Mary" does not hint at the Virgin Birth; for the townspeople who use the designation do not believe in Jesus, and Mark does not include in his book anything else about the Virgin Birth. J. M. Robinson (*Problem* 81, n. 1.) suggests that Mark omits Jesus' father Joseph to gain an allusion to Jesus' divine sonship. But the omission of Joseph in a passage where the matter of Jesus' sonship does not come up even though his mother plays a role — i.e. in 3:31-35 — undermines the suggestion. D. Dormeyer (in *Vom Urchristentum zu Jesus* 131-34) suggests that Mary substitutes for Joseph to indicate that Davidic genealogy, as represented by Joseph, no longer counts — rather, family relations in the kingdom of God, as represented by Mary (contrast the absence of "father" with the presence of "mother" in 3:32-35). But this suggestion is undermined by Mary's standing outside the circle of Jesus' new family in 3:31 and by the parallel between her saying that he had gone berserk (3:21) and the scribes' saying that he had Beelzebul (3:22, 30). That Jesus' brothers all have patriarchal names (Jacob, Joseph, Judah, and Simeon according to their OT spellings) suggests a pious family. His sisters remain anonymous, perhaps because they are unmarried. Their description as "here with us" compensates for their anonymity; it does not imply that Jesus' mother and brothers are living elsewhere. Ἐσκανδαλίζοντο ἐν αὐτῷ is probably a Semitism in which ἐν corresponds to בְּ (cf. Matt 11:6 par. Luke 7:23; Matt 13:57; 26:31, 33; Sir 9:5; 23:8). Therefore Paul's non-Semitic uses of the verb and its cognate noun (1 Cor 1:23; 8:13; 2 Cor 11:29) seem not to feed into the present passage (against E. Wendling [*Entstehung* 56], whose other evidences of Pauline influence seem equally weak).

By subtracting vv 3c-6 as Mark's additions, P. J. Achtemeier (28) thinks to restore an originally favorable implication to the questions in vv 2b-3b. But the questions referring to Jesus' trade, mother, and siblings (v 3ab) carry an unfavorable implication even without vv 3c-6; and the questions "from where?" and "what?" (v 2b) point in the same direction (see the foregoing comments). Not as here, 1:27-28 (to which Achtemeier appeals) provides an explicitly favorable answer to the question "what?" Therefore it seems that Mark's reference to astonishment in v 2b puts the best possible interpretation on following disparaging questions rather than that he adds material which turns admiring questions into disparaging ones. In general, commentators create a false problem by treating astonishment and disparagement as contradictory. The two reactions are quite agreeable with each other, for everybody knows that evil often puts on a good show (cf. 2 Cor 11:12-15). See the comments on 2:27 against the view that "and he was saying to them" (v 4) implies an interpolation.

POxy. 1. 6; *Gos. Thom.* 31 look like edited versions of the saying most originally preserved in Mark 6:4, except for Luke's retaining the probably original introduction, "Truly I say to you" (4:24). "A prophet is not" (*POxy.* 1. 6) matches Mark. "No prophet is" (*Gos. Thom.* 31) may match the stylistic improvement, "no prophet is," in Luke 4:24 (K. Beyer, *Semitische Syntax* 1/1. 131; but see J. D. Crossan, *In Fragments* 283). As in Luke, more importantly, the adjective "acceptable" simplifies the statement by getting rid of the last two of the three negatives in οὐκ ἔστιν προφήτης ἄτιμος εἰ μή, "A prophet is *not* *dis*honored if *not"* (so Mark; but see E. C. Maloney, *Semitic Interference* 92-99, against Semitic interference in Mark). Cf. the different riddance of two of the three negatives in John 4:44, which also replaces "his" with "his own" and advances the reference to home for emphasis: προφήτης ἐν τῇ ἰδίᾳ πατρίδι τιμὴν οὐκ ἔχει, "A prophet in his own home country does not have honor." The prolix "in his home town (πατρίδι) and among (ἐν) his relatives and in his house" (so Mark) shortens to "in his home town and in his house" in Matt 13:57, and shortens further to "in his home town" in Luke 4:24; John 4:44. By keeping only one prepositional phrase, *Gos. Thom.* 31; *POxy.* 1. 6 likewise represent the end of a shortening, simplifying process; but *Gos. Thom.* 31 makes the single remaining phrase more specific by substituting "village" for πατρίδι, which can carry the broad meaning "home country" as well as the narrow meaning "home town." This substitution betrays knowledge that the saying has its original setting in the narrative about Jesus' visiting his home town of Nazareth. Therefore we should reject both the theory that v 4 comes into the episode by interpolation and the argument that *Gos. Thom.* 31; *POxy.* 1. 6 show the saying to have originally existed outside a narrative setting (see also W. Schrage, *Verhältnis* 75-77).

The argument of M. Smith (*Jesus the Magician* 15) that v 4 interrupts the original transition from offense-taking (v 3b) to its consequence in Jesus' inability to perform miracles (v 5a) overlooks that the aphorism on a dishonored prophet (v 4) follows the offense-taking just as appropriately as the inability to perform miracles would follow it. The argument of E. Grässer (in *NTS* 16 [1969-70] 6) that an aphorism dealing with prophets contradicts Jesus' coming as a teacher and miracle-worker (v 2) neglects that prophets teach (see esp. Jer 32:33) and work miracles (cf. esp. Elijah and Elisha). Yet again, the addition in the extra-canonical documents of the statement that a physician does not perform healings (ποιεῖ θεραπείας) on those who know him betrays knowledge that the saying has its original setting in the episode at Nazareth, where Jesus "was not able to perform (ποιῆσαι) even one miracle, except that by laying his hands on a few sick people he healed (ἐθεράπευσεν) them" (Mark 6:5). Because of its offensiveness, Matthew changes this statement and Luke omits it. But in *POxy.* 1. 6; *Gos. Thom.* 31 its reference to the performance of a few healings triggers a revisionary expansion of Luke 4:23: "Physician, heal yourself." The expansion borrows phraseology from the omitted narrative, links it with the Lucan saying about a physician, and revises that saying in accordance with the narrative about Jesus' not performing healings. The result is a parallel to the first member of the saying. The purpose for constructing such a parallel is assimilation to the two-memberedness of the surrounding sayings, which exhibit a penchant for expansion such as appears throughout this non-canonical book (here, see *Gos. Thom.* 29, 30, 32; similarly the context of *POxy.* 1. 6 — E. Haenchen in *Die Bibel und wir* 160, n. 10). So we have additional evidence that the extra-canonical version stands at the end of a redactional line, not at its beginning (see also W. Schrage, *Verhältnis* 76-77, on the Gnostic generalization in *Gos. Thom.* 31).

It is easier to see the extra-canonical second half of the saying as growing out of the canonical narrative, with some help from the saying in Luke 4:23, than to see it as a pre-canonical basis for canonical expansion into an ideal narrative scene. Such composition would be more complicatedly inventive than the developmental process outlined here. It is hard to accept, for example, that the ones who know the physician in the extra-canonical sources turn into Jesus' relatives in Mark (so R. Bultmann, *HST* 31) or into his immediate family in Mark (so J. D. Crossan, *In Fragments* 284). Similarly, the massiveness of the preserved tradition of Jesus as a healer and the minimalness of the tradition which portrays him as a prophet makes it hard to accept the argument of Crossan (op. cit. 285) that "the tradition was more interested in Jesus as a literal prophet than as a metaphorical (or literal) physician," with the result that "it was almost inevitable that the second stich of the saying ["no physician heals the ones who know him" — *Gos. Thom.* 31] fell away [in the canonical gospels]." Moreover, it is hard to think that a Christian writer would want to fabricate an ideal scene of unbelief embarrassing to the Christian view of Jesus as an all-powerful miracle-worker — as shown by Mark's taking care to note exceptions and attributing their fewness to unbelief, by Matthew's omitting Jesus' inability, and by Luke's and John's eliminating the entire statement — and it is hard to think that if a Christian writer did improbably fabricate an ideal scene of unbelief such a writer would not have made Jesus perform many miracles in the locale so as to magnify the guilt of the unbelievers. The same argument militates against Mark's fabricating this scene out of Q (W. Schenk in *ZNW* 70 [1979] 150-52).

Arguments favoring historicity include (1) the unlikelihood that a Christian would fabricate the reference to Jesus as "the carpenter, the son of Mary" (see the vv.ll., the synoptic parallels; Luke 3:23; John 1:45; 6:42, all of which state things differently); (2) the realism in the naming of Jesus' brothers and in the mention of his sisters; (3) the unlikelihood that the names of Jesus' brothers would interest Mark's probably Roman audience; (4) the unlikelihood that a Christian would fabricate the slighting reference to men who will become prominent in the church, i.e. to Jesus' brothers, particularly James; (5-6) the double unlikelihood that Christians, who believe in Jesus as the Christ and Son of God, would portray him as merely a prophet and then make him out to be a largely failed prophet at that, one who cannot perform very many miracles in his home town; and (7) the unlikelihood that Christians, who believe in Jesus' supernatural knowledge, would portray him as marveling at the Nazarenes' unbelief. See L. Oberlinner, *Historische Überlieferung* 345-50, against seeing in this pericope a polemic against the early church in Jerusalem, led by Jesus' brother James.

J. Ernst (170) implies that Jesus could have spoken the saying in v 4, because doing so does not require thinking of himself as a prophet any more (we might add) than the saying in 2:17 required thinking of himself as a physician. True, Jesus may be speaking only analogically. But his activities of healing and preaching (and preaching not just expositorily of the OT) make it easy to believe that he *does* think of himself as a prophet and a physician, and therefore all the easier to accept the authenticity of these sayings. See BAGD s.v. προφήτης 3 for NT references and secondary literature on prophetic Christology; and R. Pesch 1. 320; F. G. Downing, *Christ and the Cynics* 128 §165b, for a convenient summary of extra-biblical parallels. C. E. B. Cranfield (196) notes that because these parallels are not couched in terms of "a prophet," we should designate Jesus' saying an aphorism, not a proverb. Its prophetic character probably grows out of the OT history of rejected prophets (cf. O. H. Steck, *Israel und das gewaltsame Geschick der Propheten* 213-14).

It is commonly held that Mark adds "and among his relatives and in his house" to recall the disbelief in Jesus by his family at 3:20-21, 31-35. The strength of this position lies in the tension between 6:2-3 and 6:4: only the townspeople *as distinct from* Jesus' mother, brothers, and sisters fail to give him his prophetic due in vv 2-3, whereas v 4 includes his immediate family among those who fail to do so. (Therefore it is doubtful that in v 4 Mark adds Jesus' family from vv 2-3.) But the passage in chap. 3 identified οἱ παρ' αὐτοῦ (v 21) as including only his immediate family (vv 31-32); so this position does not account for an addition of the wider circle of relatives in 6:4, especially since Mark likes dual expressions whereas an addition of two phrases produces a triple expression. And if Jesus' immediate family really did try to seize him because they thought he had gone berserk (it is very hard to think that Christians would fabricate a story containing even the suggestion of insanity in him), then he himself has as much reason as Mark does to construct an aphorism that alludes to them as well as to his fellow townspeople. The wider circle of his relatives will then form the link between the townspeople, who both speak about his immediate family and include among themselves that wider circle, and his immediate family, to whom the wider circle are related.

M.-J. Lagrange (149) notes that Jesus can speak of a prophet's not being dishonored *except* among his own without contradicting the Ger(g)asenes' rejection of him because he went into their region as an unknown (5:1-20). But his reputation precedes him to Nazareth. R. P. Meye (*Jesus and the Twelve* 58-59) suggests that Jesus does not mean the term "prophet" to apply to himself, only the part of the saying that mentions dishonor to do so. But "prophet" is the only part of the saying unparalleled in other sayings about dishonor. Hence, we are not dealing with a proverb whose reference to a prophet would have to be kept even in application to a non-prophet.

An exception is not a contradiction; so v 5b contradicts v 5a no more than v 8b will contradict v 8a and no more than 8:14b will contradict 8:14a. R. P. Martin (*Mark* 173) follows J. Weiss (*Schriften* 1. 125) in the view that Mark discriminates between miracles and acts of healing that are not to be reckoned as miracles in the strict sense. But "except" implies that the healings *are* miracles. Weiss' interpretation would seem to require at the start of v 5b a stronger disjunction, an adversative δέ or an ἀλλά, "but," rather than εἰ μή, "except." T. A. Burkill (*Mysterious Revelation* 139-40) suggests that Mark adds v 5b to allow for the conversion of some Jews in the apostolic age. But for that, Jesus' Galilean successes outside Nazareth would more than suffice. Those same successes would also eliminate any need to add exceptive miracles in Nazareth for the purpose of answering the question how the gospel can be true if the Jewish people rejected it (against D. E. Nineham 163-64).

Since Mark does not attribute miracles to psychological suggestion, he does not mean that unbelief makes miracles psychologically impossible, much less that Jesus tries and fails to perform more miracles at Nazareth. Rather, Jesus refuses "because it would have contradicted the essence of his mission to satisfy a thirst for sensationalism" in the face of crass unbelief (L. Goppelt, *Theology of the NT* 1. 148; cf. J. Schmid 118). But it overdoes the point to say that Mark connects faith in Jesus' miracles (v 2) with unbelief (v 6), as though Mark attacks faith in Jesus' miracles as inimical to belief in his person (M. E. Boring, *Truly Human/Truly Divine* 18). The text says that unbelief makes him unable to work more than a few miracles, not that the townspeople's recognizing the miracles that he has worked makes him unable to do more. According to J. Ernst (170), v 5b means that not even unbelief can keep Jesus from working miracles. K. Beyer (*Semitische Syntax* 1/1. 114) argues against Semitic style by saying that v 5b adds two exceptions, not one exception; i.e. it limits the miracles to healings and it limits the healings to a few. But whether or not Mark writes Semitically, a non-Semitic phrase may idiomatically render a Semitic tradition.

Verses 4-5 find their unity in individually close ties with the foregoing and following verses. Verse 4 delivers a wry comment on the foregoing questions, and v 5 makes sense of the secondary reference to miracles in v 2 (a point that undermines the view of H. J. Held [in *Kirche* 87] that the references in v 2b to wisdom and miracles have no referents in the present narrative [but note Jesus' teaching in v 2a as well as his miracles in v 5] and therefore summarily conclude everything from 1:14 onward). Finally, v 6a wraps together the questions and the fewness of miracles in a package of unbelief (against D.-A. Koch [*Bedeutung* 147-55], who sees disunity; also K. L. Schmidt [*Rahmen* 155-56] and others). To say that ἐσκανδαλίζοντο in the sense of damnation overestimates "the comparatively insignificant guilt of the people of Nazareth (despising a prophet)" (E. Grässer in *NTS* 16 [1969-70] 16; cf. G. Stählin in *TDNT* 7. 340-57) either fails to draw a connection between despising a prophet and disbelief or underestimates the guilt of disbelief. Besides, ἐσκανδαλίζοντο does not necessarily imply damnation (see 14:27, 29; 16:7). Disbelief may forestall miracles, but miracles do not always require faith (see, e.g., 3:1-6; 4:35-41;

6:35-44). Hence, the few miracles that Jesus does perform need not imply that some do believe despite the unbelief of most (against W. Grundmann [7. Aufl.] 122). The townspeople do not disbelieve in Jesus' ability to work miracles, moreover; they disbelieve in his person as a legitimate prophet (vv 2-4; against W. G. Kümmel [*Theology of the NT* 63-64], whose argument that the synoptics do not elsewhere make Jesus the object of faith skates past the personal objections in vv 2-4). Other passages having to do with faith and lack of faith in his ability to work miracles are therefore irrelevant to vv 5-6a. So also is the suggestion of A. Fridrichsen (*Problem* 79-80) that Jesus cannot perform miracles because the townspeople rob him of opportunity by failing to bring their sick. See D. O. Via, *Ethics* 177-79, against F. Belo's Marxist interpretation.

THE EXTENSION OF JESUS' AUTHORITY THROUGH THE APOSTLES

6:6b-29 *(Matt 9:35; 10:1, 7-11, 14; 14:1-12; Luke 3:19-20; 9:1-9; cf. Luke 10:1-12; John 1:19-21)*

In the course of his itineration Jesus now commissions the Twelve (vv 6b-7), tells them what to take and what not to take for their travels (vv 8-9), and instructs them on staying in homes and leaving the places they visit (vv 10-11). The Twelve carry out the commission by preaching, casting out demons, and healing the sick (vv 12-13). The resultant enhancement of Jesus' reputation causes the people and Herod to identify him variously (vv 14-16; cf. 4:41, where the disciples asked the question of Jesus' identity). Herod's reason for identifying Jesus with John the Baptizer is then spelled out in a narrative flashback (vv 17-29). The flashback subdivides into Herod's arrest and imprisonment of John (vv 17-20) and the beheading of John (vv 21-29).

6:6b-7 *(Matt 9:35; 10:1; Luke 9:1-2)* Verse 6b provides a general occasion for vv 7-11 and probably implies that the events in vv 12-13 take place while Jesus itinerates. The imperfect tense of περιῆγεν, "he was going around," does not correspond to the imperfect verbs in vv 2, 3, 5, 6a, but is due to the linear character of the action in and of itself. The contrast between the attributive position of κύκλῳ, "in a circle," in 3:34; 6:36 and its present predicate position favors construing it with "he was going around" (cf. Rom 15:19) rather than with "the towns" (against C. F. D. Moule, *Idiom-Book* 109-10). But either way, "the towns" means towns around Jesus' home town of Nazareth. "Teaching" points to the same activity that he has engaged in there. Again Mark gives no indication of what Jesus was teaching. What counts is the authority that he exercises in teaching (see v 2 with comments and esp. 1:22, 27). The present historical tense of προσ-καλεῖται in the statement, "And he summons the Twelve," stresses his further exercise of authority in summoning the apostles from among the larger group of disciples (cf. 3:13-15 with comments). Summoning the Twelve does not imply that they have not been with him, only that he brings them close to send them out with authority. Sending them as his qualified representatives (so the conno-tation of ἀποστέλλειν) carries this emphasis forward yet another step (again cf.

3:13-15 with comments). The present tense of ἀποστέλλειν is iterative with respect to his sending one pair of apostles after another (so also in 3:14). "Two by two" supplies mutual protection, conforms to the law of two or three witnesses (Deut 19:15; cf. Num 35:30; Deut 17:6; 2 Cor 13:1; 1 Tim 5:19), and indicates a sufficient testimony (cf. 11:1; 14:13; and many further references cited by J. Jeremias in *NT Essays* 136-43). The authority which Jesus gives over the unclean spirits represents his own authority, so great that he has enough to share (cf. 1:27; 3:13-15; also 16:17). The imperfect tense of ἐδίδου, "was giving," may indicate that he repeats the action of giving authority with the dispatch of each pair; or it may simply imply that the giving takes an oral form, for verbs of speaking often take the imperfect (cf. ἔλεγεν in v 10). The view that the imperfect implies a continued exercise of Jesus' authority in the work of Christian mission-aries at Mark's time (so E. Best, *Following Jesus* 196, n. 11) mistakes a possible implication of the perfect tense for that of the imperfect. Despite the purpose of Jesus' choosing the Twelve "to preach" (3:14), Mark delays preaching till v 12 to let all the emphasis fall on Jesus' using the Twelve to extend his authority in the most dramatic way possible, i.e. by exorcising unclean spirits. For the same purpose, healing forms part of the mission despite the absence of healing from the commission (v 13; contrast *Gos. Thom.* 14).

6:8-9 *(Matt 10:9-10; Luke 9:3)* "And he gave them orders" (καὶ παρήγ-γειλεν αὐτοῖς) again calls attention to Jesus' exercising authority over the Twelve. The verb occurs elsewhere in Mark only at 8:6. But the main emphasis falls on the authority that Jesus *shares* with the Twelve and exercises *through* them. Because of it, people are to give them board and room and listen to them — and woe to those who do not! Thus, the Twelve will not need a number of provisions ordinarily taken and will not need to move from house to house within a locality. Mark mentions only those orders which highlight the shared, extended authority of Jesus (contrast the much fuller texts in Matthew and Luke, including a doubtless original note of eschatological urgency that is missing in Mark; see comparisons of the parallels by F. Hahn, *Mission* 42-46; H. K. Nielsen, *Heilung* 82-85). The Twelve are to take "not one thing for the road, except a staff only: no bread, no bag, no small change in the belt. Rather, [he gave orders that they be] shod with sandals. 'And you shouldn't put on two tunics'" (cf. Gen 32:11[10]; Exod 12:11; contrast Josh 9:3-6). The forward position of μηδέν, "not one thing," and the present tense of the subjunctive verb αἴρωσιν, "take," stress the prohibition and therefore the sharing and extension of Jesus' authority (see S. E. Porter, *Verbal Aspect* 326, on the present subjunctive). The strength of the adversative ἀλλά, "rather," and the vigor of the following ellipsis stress the requirement of sandals.

6:10-11 *(Matt 10:11, 14; Luke 9:4-5)* "And he was saying to them" inter-rupts Jesus' words, but does not necessarily imply the insertion of material from another setting (see the comments on 2:27). The appearance of a similar command not introduced by such a formula yet following similar prohibitions in Luke 10:4-5, usually regarded as reflecting Q, argues against taking "and he was saying to them" as a sign of insertion. The introductory formula merely sets off the following instructions on staying in homes and leaving places that the disciples will visit from the preceding instructions about provisions for travel. Moreover, the editorial interruption turns attention back to Jesus' authoritative speaking. Mark is not interested in Jesus' words for the sake of the historical occasion on which they were uttered, or even for the possible application of their content to the state of affairs that obtains at the time of writing, so much as he is interested in the authority with which Jesus speaks, whatever he says. If the contents happen to heighten the aura of authority, so much the better. The instruction to stay in one house till leaving a locality highlights the authority of Jesus with which he invests the Twelve: with it they should stay as long as they want (contrast *Did.* 11:4-5; also *b. 'Arak.* 16b, where the question concerns how long a man and his wife should stay in a lodging where they are mistreated). The instruction to leave any place that does not welcome them or listen to them (contrast 9:37) and to shake off the dust under their feet "for a testimony against them [i.e. against the people of that place]" likewise highlights this authority: resistance is dangerous. In line with Jesus' investing the Twelve with his authority, their "going out from there" in vv 10-11 (bis) parallels Jesus' "going out from there" (v 1; see also 7:24; 10:1).

   6:12-13 *(Matt 10:7-8; Luke 9:6)* The disciples "went out" just as Jesus "went out," and they "preached" just as he "preached" (cf. v 1 with v 30; also 1:38-39, 45; 3:15; 5:20; 7:36; 13:10; 14:9). Their message of repentance matches his message of repentance (1:14-15; cf. 1:4). Even the emphatic present tense of their non-indicative μετανοῶσιν, "might repent," matches that of the same non-indicative verb in his message (1:15; again see S. E. Porter, *Verbal Aspect* 326, on the emphasis in a non-indicative present tense). They cast out demons as he has cast out demons — and in accordance with his having chosen them "to have authority to cast out demons" (3:15, whence derives the order of mention, first preaching and then casting out demons; cf. 6:7). In fact, they cast out "many" demons just as he has cast out "many" demons (1:34; cf. 1:39, too). The imperfect tense of ἐξέβαλλον, "were casting out," highlights the repeated success of the Twelve in extending Jesus' authority over the demons. And the Twelve heal sick people — again the imperfect tense of ἐθεράπευον, "were healing," highlights repeated success — just as he has done in his home town (v 5, the statement there and the one here both using forms of ἄρρωστος, "sick," and θεραπεύω). Two differences favor that Mark is using tradition, however, not making up the therapeutic activities of the Twelve out of the story of Jesus at Nazareth: (1) there Jesus laid his hands on the sick, here the Twelve anoint them with olive oil (i.e. rub olive oil on them); (2) there he healed only "a few," here the Twelve heal "many." Thus, through the twelve apostles' preaching of repentance, exorcising of many demons, and healing of many sick people, Mark shows how Jesus uses the Twelve to extend the scope and impact of his authority over human behavior, over the demonic world, and over disease (cf. D. L. Dungan, *Sayings* 50). In fact, the healing of "many" after the healing at Nazareth of only "a few" shows that the effectiveness of Jesus' authority has bounced back to normal (cf. 1:34; 3:10), no longer strapped in the least by people's bewildering unbelief (cf. vv 5-6a). The fact that neither 3:13-15 nor 6:7 has prepared for these healings makes them come as a surprising and therefore emphatic display of Jesus' power, extended through the Twelve. Adding to the emphasis on this display is the chiasm in (a) καὶ δαιμόνια πολλά, "and many demons," (b) ἐξέβαλλον, "they were casting out," (b') καὶ ἤλειφον ἐλαίῳ, "and they were anointing with oil," (a') πολλοὺς ἀρρώστους, "many sick people." The placement of δαιμόνια and ἀρρώστους at the extremes of this chiasm stresses the objects in which is displayed the power of Jesus. The falling of καὶ ἐθεράπευον, "and they were healing [them]," outside the chiasm gives the healings an importance of their own (cf. the comments on vv 2, 14). The prediction of Jesus that he would make the first disciples "fishers of human beings" (1:17) has come true, as indicated also by his sending the Twelve in pairs, which corresponds to the two pairs of brothers in the pericope where Jesus made his prediction (1:16-20; cf. G. Schmahl, *Zwölf* 114-16). Thus Jesus' power not only to perform exorcisms and miracles, in this case through the Twelve, but also to predict the future, in this case also to determine the future, is on its way to becoming an important apologetic theme in Mark.

6:14-16 *(Matt 14:1-12; Luke 9:7-9)* An allusion in these verses to John the Baptizer's martyrdom combines with an omission of it in 1:14 to necessitate a flashback that narrates it in vv 17-29. Mark does not purpose merely to give information about John or to fill the interval of the Twelve's mission (which cannot be filled by an event of earlier date, anyway); rather, he wants to play up the miraculous power of Jesus by showing how it causes Herod Antipas, son of Herod the Great and ruler of Galilee and Perea (4 B.C.E.–39 C.E.), to think that John has come back from the dead in the person of Jesus and that John's being raised has enabled him to work wonders which outstrip anything he did prior to his execution (cf. John 10:41). The sandwiching of this subsection between statements regarding the miraculous ministry of the Twelve (vv 12-13, 30) draws a parallel between the marvelous power of Jesus and the Twelve's exercising that same power (cf. the comments on 6:6b-13).

The statement, "And the king, Herod, heard," lacks a direct object referring to Jesus and his activities or to the Twelve and their activities. Instead, we read a series of following clauses governed by γάρ, "for" (see the grammatical discussion, with references to earlier literature, by H. W. Hoehner, *Herod Antipas* 186-87). Mark is interested not so much in *what* Herod hears as in *why* he hears. He hears because Jesus' reputation has become well known and because people are making religiously heroic identifications of Jesus. The loose, exaggerated use of "the king" for a man whom Augustus has refused to make a king and instead has made a mere tetrarch (see the following notes) and Mark's emphasizing "the king," to which "Herod" is only an appositive, prepare for Herod's promise of up to half his kingdom (v 22). Ὄνομα includes not only the name of Jesus but also his reputation as a miracle-worker (see the last clause of v 14). That αὐτοῦ, "his," refers to the Jesus of vv 6b-11 shows that Mark thinks of Jesus' reputation as enhanced by the mission of the Twelve in the intervening vv 12-13. The predicate adjective φανερόν, "well known, manifest," and the emphatic first position that it holds in its clause reinforce this enhancement.

The opinion that in the person of Jesus God has raised John the Baptizer from the dead shows the length to which some have had to go to explain Jesus' miracles without becoming his disciples: "and because of this [John's supposedly having been raised from the dead] the miracles are at work in him." Putting it this way grants again the undeniability of the miracles but stops short of attributing them to Jesus' own power. The chiasm which in the Greek text puts "John the Baptizer" before its verb and "the miracles" after its verb emphasizes Jesus (mistaken for John) as the locale where miracles are at work. The falling of ἐν αὐτῷ, "in him," outside the chiasm gives special importance to Jesus as this locale (cf. the comments on vv 2, 13). The opinion of others (set off by an adversative δέ, "but" — so also for the remaining opinions) that Jesus is Elijah (emphasized by the forward position of Ἠλίας, "Elijah") does not entail belief in a resuscitation; for according to 2 Kgs 2:1-12 Elijah went up to heaven without dying. But it does show that these people believe that Elijah has returned from heaven to earth (in accordance with the prophecy in Mal 3:23[4:5], though Mark does not mention the passage, because his point consists again in the lengths to which people have had to go in order to explain Jesus' miracles without becoming his disciples). The opinion of yet others that Jesus is "a prophet like one of the prophets" (emphasized by the ellipsis of ἐστιν, "he is") entails belief neither in a resuscitation nor in a return from heaven, but in a similarity of divine empowerment between Jesus and the OT prophets (cf. esp. Luke 7:16; 24:19). After the excursion into various opinions among the people, the participle ἀκούσας returns to Herod's hearing (cf. v 14a; also 3:8 for a similar hearing), implies his hearing the various identifications of Jesus, and leads into a quotation of the identification adopted by Herod, viz., that Jesus is John, whom God has raised. But instead of the general phrase "from the dead," as in the opinion of some of the people, Herod specifically refers to his having had John beheaded. The casus pendens "[he] whom I beheaded" plus the resumptive demonstrative pronoun οὗτος, "this one [i.e. John]," which contrasts with ἐγώ, "I," betrays and emphasizes the alarm that Herod feels. It also prepares for the story of John's beheading.

   6:17-20 *(Matt 14:3-5; Luke 3:19-20)* The conjunction γάρ, "for," makes the whole of the following story an extended footnote which tells what has led up to Herod's thinking that Jesus is John come back to life. That is to say, the flashback to the beheading serves Mark's emphasis on the power of Jesus, which so amazes people that it gives rise to this as well as other identifications of him. Αὐτός, "he himself," points forward to Herod and distinguishes him from John, to whom οὗτος, "this one," referred at the close of v 16 (cf. M. Reiser, *Syntax und Stil* 15; E. C. Maloney, *Semitic Interference* 113-16, against an Aramaism here). Ἀποστείλας, "sending," indicates that Herod had his subordinates arrest John by tying him up and putting him in prison. Herodias, the former wife of Herod's brother Philip, supplied the motive for Herod's taking action against John. John's condemnation of Herod for having married her supplied the reason for her resentment of John. Her wanting to kill him, which δέ, "but," contrasts with Herod's mere imprisonment of him (cf. M. Zerwick, *Untersuchungen* 16-17), shows the extent of her resentment and prepares for his beheading, which gives Mark reason to include the story as a way of stressing the opinion that Jesus works so powerfully that even the king who had John beheaded thinks that Jesus is this same John risen. Herodias's inability to have John killed grew out of Herod's fearing John because of his knowledge that John was a righteous and holy man (cf. 11:18, 32). Doubtless Mark wants this description to rub off on Jesus, with whom Herod and some of the people (and Mark himself, though in a different way) associate John (cf. Acts 3:14). Herod's keeping John safe from Herodias's murderous design, his being at a loss what to do with John after hearing him much (i.e. his having become convinced from John's own mouth and at length that he ought to release him, yet not wanting to displease Herodias), and his liking to hear John speak (cf. 12:37b) all add weight to this favorable description of John as a righteous and holy man. More weight is added to it through the parallelism of the imperfect tense which characterizes all the main verbs in vv 18-20 (except for the direct quotation within v 18) and makes concurrent the actions indicated by them. Yet more weight is added through the chiasm of (a) ἀκούσας, "having heard," (b) αὐτοῦ, "him," (c) πολλά . . . , "much . . . ," (c′) ἡδέως, "gladly," (b′) αὐτοῦ, "him," (a′) ἤκουεν, "he was hearing."

6:21-29 *(Matt 19:6-12)* Mention of "an opportune day," of Herod's hosting a birthday banquet for himself, and of courtiers, top ranking military officers, and leading Galilean provincials (cf. Rev 6:15; H. W. Hoehner, *Herod Antipas* 102, n. 3, 119-20, n. 3) calls attention to the significance of John's beheading: it involved the high and mighty (cf. Mark's emphasis on Herod as "the king" in v 14 with comments; also vv 22, 25, 26, 27). The entrance of Herodias's daughter and her dancing, pleasing Herod and his guests, and then going out to consult her mother imply a stag party. Mark is not interested in any lewdness of the dance — he does not mention lewdness — but in the uniqueness of a princess' doing what only harlots and heterae normally do. This uniqueness, the resultant expansiveness of Herod's offer (v 22b) and oath (v 23) to give the girl whatever she wants, up to half his kingdom, and Mark's emphasizing the offer with asyndeton or δέ, "but," before "the king said" (see the vv.ll. in v 22) and emphasizing the oath with πολλά, "much, vehemently" (if we are to accept the word with P[45] D Θ 565 700 it as a characteristically Marcan adverbial use — see the note on 1:45), all imply the greater importance of John the Baptizer, for whose head the girl's mother prompted her to ask in preference to anything else, and therefore the greater importance of Jesus himself, whom Herod later equated with John (vv 14-16). Another δέ in v 24b emphasizes the point.

The immediacy and haste (or eagerness) with which the girl carried out her mother's instruction, the promptness and unmistakability which she wanted in the delivery of John's head ("at once . . . on a platter"), and the immediacy with which her request was granted again emphasize the greater importance of John and therefore of Jesus. The forward position of περίλυπος, "very sorrowful," and the comment that only Herod's oath, sworn in the presence of his guests, made him grant the girl's request emphasize his extreme sorrow. That sorrow, in turn, recalls the righteousness and holiness of John and indirectly of Jesus (see the comments on v 20). Ἀποστείλας, "sending" (v 27), echoes v 17 and again indicates the carrying out of an order by an underling, here an executioner. The beheading in the prison takes us back to vv 16-17 ("whom I had beheaded . . . in prison") to recall the occasion for this flashback, i.e. Herod's startled identification of Jesus as John raised from the dead. The grisly details of the executioner's bringing John's head on a platter and giving it to the girl and of her giving it to her mother, plus the reverential details that John's disciples heard, came, took his corpse, and put it in a tomb, all emphasize the unmistakable reality of John's death. This unmistakable reality makes Herod's identification of Jesus with John all the more striking: what mighty powers must be at work in Jesus to push the king into identifying him with a man whose head the king himself had seen delivered on a platter to his own dining room, and then to his wife's dining room, and whose corpse had been interred in a different location!

NOTES

Some have thought that the statement concerning Jesus' itineration (v 6b) goes with the preceding pericope (vv 1-6a) to indicate the result of rejection at home (see, e.g., J. D. Crossan in *NovT* 15 [1973] 105). But although the home town of Jesus provides a point of reference for his going around in a circle, Mark likes to start new pericopes with topographical movement; the following of Jesus' topographical movement with a summons matches the introduction of a new pericope, also featuring the Twelve, in 3:13; and his teaching starts what seems to be an internal parallel with the Twelve's preaching (v 12; cf. people's "hearing them" in v 11), later equated with teaching (v 30). These same phenomena also militate against splitting off v 6b as a discrete summary (so R. A. Guelich 1. 313-14). Elsewhere ἤρξατο, "he began," does not tend to occur in the first clause or two of a pericope (see the concordance s.v. ἄρχω); and in 1:16a; 3:13a statements of topographical movement follow a summary and introduce a call or summons whereas here the supposed summary (v 6b) is rather the statement of topographical movement that introduces a summons. The argument that v 6b must be a summary because a rejection precedes it (vv 1-6a) just as rejections preceded earlier summaries (1:14a; 3:1-6) neglects that John's having been given over (1:14a) had to do with Jesus' coming after John (1:7), not with John's being rejected as Jesus was rejected. Moreover, John's having been given over did not precede a summary, as the rejection of Jesus in 3:1-6 preceded the summary in 3:7-12, but formed a constituent part of the summary by introducing it.

According to V. Taylor (298), the position of vv 1-6a suggests that the period of preaching in synagogues is ending. But Mark has mentioned synagogues so irregularly (1:21, 23, 29, 39; 3:1) and the last mention occurred so far back in the text (3:1) that we can scarcely feel confident in treating the present mention as pivotal. J. Dupont (*Études* 344-49) draws a parallel between the progression from the Twelve to Jesus' family in 3:13-19, 20-35 and the chiastic progression from Jesus' family to the Twelve in 6:1-6, 7-13. The parallel breaks down on the failure of Jesus' family to play an active role in 6:1-6 as they do in 3:20-35. The townspeople only refer to them in 6:3.

The mission of the seventy-two in Luke 10:1-12 supports the historicity of the present mission of the Twelve if the mission of the seventy-two represents an independent, variant report (in Q, it is usually thought) of the mission of the Twelve. This argument loses some of its force if the mission of the seventy-two belongs to a different occasion, though one could still argue that apart from a historical basis, traditions of more than one mission of Jesus' disciples would probably have failed to arise. Christian fabrication of the missions would probably have resulted in the disciples' preaching about Jesus, as they do not. Since the Twelve do not engage in a common mission after the Resurrection, but stay in Jerusalem for the most part (Acts 8:1), the notion that later missionizing has been read back into Jesus' lifetime not only lacks evidence. It goes against the evidence (cf. C. K. Barrett, *Signs* 31-32). That the text does not tell where Jesus sends the Twelve poses no problem to the historicity of the mission. The Galilean setting is evident enough, and the particulars of locations within this setting would not provide anything of theological interest. The implication that the Twelve possess more than Jesus allows them to take makes another poor argument against the historicity of the instructions. In Josephus *Ant.* 17.5.7 §136 even a slave wears two tunics, and not for the special purpose of hiding a secret message, for which a patch sewn on the inner tunic serves (against M.-J. Lagrange 153), but apparently because of the slave's journey, as here in Mark. Copper coins do not have very much value. And bread with a knapsack in which to carry it hardly requires wealth. Because the copper coins, if allowed, would be "for the belt," πήραν means "a traveler's bag" for bread, not "a begger's bag" for money (as thought by A. Deissmann [*LAE* 108-10], against whose view see W. Michaelis in *TDNT* 6. 119-21). J. J. O'Rourke (in *JBL* 85 [1966] 350) puts forward evidence that εἰς means "for" rather than "in" (v 8 [bis]).

It is often thought that Mark fabricates the narrative framework of the orders that Jesus gives to the Twelve (see, e.g., J. Gnilka [1. 236-38], who attributes vv 6b-7, 12-13 to Mark's redaction). But those orders could hardly have existed in the tradition outside a narrative framework. What sense would it make to read, "Take nothing for [the] road except a staff only [and so on]," without knowing who is being addressed and what is the occasion? As elsewhere, then, we may assume that Mark writes up the narrative framework in his own style, but on the basis of tradition (cf. B. Rigaux in *Der historische Jesus und der kerygmatische Christus* 468-86). Naturally, his style may intrude itself less into Jesus' words.

The Twelve have been with Jesus long enough to represent him. They have heard him preach and teach and have seen him cast out demons. The necessity of spending time with him before going out to represent him — a necessity explicitly stated in 3:13-15 — undermines the suggestion that the commission in 6:8-11 originally followed the choice of the Twelve in 3:13-15. In favor of the suggestion, E. Best (*Following Jesus* 193-95) argues that the strangeness of Jesus' choosing the Twelve to be with him only to say that he immediately sends them away causes Mark to separate their mission from their choice. But that same strangeness would equally cause an earlier traditioner to keep the choice and the mission apart.

See the notes on 1:45 for the use of ἤρξατο, "he began" (v 7), and E. C. Maloney, *Semitic Interference* 152-54, on the repetitive distributive δύο δύο, "two by two," as a Semitism that is truly un-Greek (against a widespread opinion to the contrary). "Two by two" may correspond to later church practice (cf., for example, the pairings in Acts of Peter and John, Paul and Barnabas, Barnabas and Mark, Paul and Silas), but the church may have gotten its practice from Jesus' sending the Twelve in pairs (cf. Luke 10:1 P[75] B L et al.). See C. E. B. Cranfield (198-99) against V. Taylor's casting doubt on the historicity of Jesus' giving the Twelve authority over unclean spirits. Παρήγγειλεν αὐτοῖς ἵνα, "he gave them orders that" (v 8), may be Marcan despite occurrence of the verb only once elsewhere. Mark likes to use verbs of command and other verbs of speaking with ἵνα (3:9; 5:43; 7:36; 8:30; 9:9, 18; 10:48; 13:34; so G. Schmahl, *Zwölf* 70).

A staff counts as an exception necessary for steadying oneself and fending off wild animals (and possibly bandits). Sandals and one tunic do not count as exceptions, however, because you wear them as necessary items of clothing rather than carrying them as you would carry bread, bag, and small change. Yet putting on an extra tunic would count as carrying rather than wearing. Short distances between Galilean towns make unnecessary the taking of bread for roadside nourishment, of a bag in which to carry the bread, and of an extra tunic for warmth while sleeping outdoors between towns and cities. Hospitality in the towns will provide bread and bed and thus eliminate the need of small change for purchasing bread and staying at inns (cf. Acts 9:30; 16:15, 40; 17:5-7; 18:1-3). That the distinction between necessaries and unnecessaries runs throughout this instruction makes an allusion to Moses' staff unlikely as well as unnecessary (against J. D. M. Derrett, *Jesus's Audience* 181-86).

Matt 10:10; Luke 9:3 prohibit the taking of a staff, and Matt 10:10; Luke 10:4 prohibit the taking of sandals; so some have thought that the longer distances of later, extra-Palestinian missionary travel have led Mark or a traditioner before him to allow a staff and sandals (see, e.g., H. K. Nielsen, *Heilung* 82-85). But the rocky and often precipitous paths from village to village in Galilee make a staff and sandals necessary for protecting the feet and whole person (thus the pathos of David's going barefoot in 2 Sam 15:30), whereas paved and relatively level Roman roads leading from city to city outside Palestine allow for increased rigorism, evoked by the mercenariness which the instructions in Matthew and Luke try to curtail and which reflects later Christian experience, the Galilean mission being too short for mercenariness to become a problem (see R. H. Gundry, *Matthew* 186-88). Mark's allowing a staff and sandals does not presuppose an original prohibition of both in Q any more than prohibiting two tunics presupposes an original prohibition of one tunic in Q. (Matt 10:10; Luke 9:3 prohibit two tunics just as Mark does.) The allowance of a staff is stated as an exception (εἰ μή) because a staff is carried just as bread, bag, and small change — all prohibited — are carried. Sandals are not allowed as an exception; they are commanded (παρήγγειλεν is still governing) adversatively (ἀλλά), i.e. in opposition to the prohibition of bread, bag, and small change rather than in opposition to a prohibition of sandals in Q. Ordinarily, the wearing of sandals is assumed. But so also is the taking of bread (8:14), of a bag (Luke 22:36), of money (John 4:8; 12:6), and perhaps of two tunics (otherwise, why the prohibition? — cf. Luke 3:11 and again Josephus *Ant.* 17.5.7 §136 in the context of a journey, though Polyaenus 4.14 cites the wearing of two tunics as a sign of effeminacy). The wearing of sandals cannot be assumed in the face of Jesus' prohibiting these other items, ordinarily taken even though they are not absolutely necessary. Some have said that Jesus allows sandals, but prohibits shoes (ὑποδήματα — Matt 10:10; Luke 10:4). This attempt at harmonization comes to grief on the meaning of ὑποδήματα as "things underneath that are tied" — i.e. σανδάλια, "sandals," with which ὑποδήματα is used indiscriminately in the LXX and Josephus (J. H. Thayer, *Lexicon* s.v. σανδάλιον) — and on Mark's use of the cognate participle ὑποδεδεμένους, "tied underneath," with σανδάλια.

Χαλκόν means copper money, i.e. small change, much less valuable than the gold and silver coveted by later Christian mercenaries attacked in Matthew and (indirectly) in Luke. Ὑποδεδεμένους is a participle put into the accusative apparently to act as a predicate adjective after an implied αὐτοὺς εἶναι (or πορεύεσθαι): "rather, [he gave orders that they be (or 'go')] shod with sandals" (cf. this construction with that in 1:6). Then Mark switches to direct discourse: "and you should not put on two tunics." The roughness of the shifts looks more like his writing up of oral tradition than like his redaction of an earlier written source. Other examples of switching from indirect to direct discourse (see BDF §470[2]; A. T. Robertson, *Grammar* 442-43; J. A. Kleist 206) subvert the argument that the present switch implies the use of two sources. B* 33 *pc* substitute the imperative ἐνδύσασθε for the subjunctive of prohibition. B² 892 *pc* substitute the infinitive ἐνδύσασθαι to avoid the switch to direct discourse.

Historical reasons suggested for the prohibitions in vv 8-9 include the following: (1) the eschatological need for haste; (2) the evangelistic need to make the message believable, i.e. not subject to the suspicion of preacherly mercinariness; (3) the didactic need to exemplify the trust of the pious poor in God's provision (cf. Matt 6:25-34 par. Luke

12:22-32; L. Schottroff and W. Stegemann, *Jesus von Nazareth* 62-69); (4) the sacredness
of the mission in analogy to the sacredness of the temple, where one was not to enter with
staff, sandal, wallet, or dust on the feet (*m. Ber.* 9:5; see T. W. Manson, *Sayings* 181);
(5) the ideal of asceticism on the part of wandering radicals who outdo even the Cynics
in this respect (G. Theissen, *Sociology* 8-16); (6) the desire to carry out the typology of
the Passover, which Israelites were to eat with loins girded, sandals on feet, and staff in
hand before going into the wilderness, where God fed them (Exod 12:11; see U. W. Mauser,
Christ in the Wilderness 133-34); (7) the practice of hospitality toward travelers, especially
among coreligionists (cf. Josephus *J.W.* 2.8.4 §§124-27).

But none of these suggestions entirely satisfy. The prohibited items would hardly
slow down the Twelve. A bag of bread, some copper coins, and a second tunic for warmth
would hardly give the impression of mercinariness. If allowed, such limited items might
be God's provision for the pious poor. The prohibition of bread and a second tunic have
no analogy in regulations of propriety for the temple and therefore cast doubt on any such
analogy with respect to the other prohibitions. The temporal circumscription of the mission
— indeed, its apparent brevity — disfavors an ideal of asceticism. So also does the implication that Jesus and the Twelve normally take bread, a bag, small change, and a second
tunic — an implication confirmed by outright pronouncements in 8:14; Luke 22:36; John
4:8; 12:6 (cf. M. Hengel, *Charismatic Leader* 27-35). Evangelizing Galilee does not look
like eating the Passover; Galilee does not look like the wilderness where God fed the
Israelites; and the prohibitions of bread, bag, small change, and a second tunic have no
counterpart in the Passover, which featured bread, or in the Exodus, which featured the
taking of bread (Exod 12:34, 39) and of far more than small change and a second tunic,
viz., the gold and silver jewelry of the Egyptians and their clothes (Exod 12:35-36). The
practice of hospitality toward travelers, especially among coreligionists, seems to presuppose a network of Jesus' followers able to provide hospitality for the Twelve. The presupposition may or may not be justified; but, more seriously, such a provision would explain
how the Twelve can manage without the prohibited items but not why they should have
to. So we are left with a question mark. Cynic philosophers wear only one garment and
carry only a staff and (what Jesus prohibits) a bag (Diog. Laert. 6.13, 22 [where even in
this context the bag is for food], 23; Luc. *Peregr.* 15, 24; Arr. *Epict. Diss.* 3.22.10, 50).

Since "house" is described as a place to "stay," not as a place to preach or worship,
and since it is the locality (τόπος, "place"), not the house, that may not welcome a pair of
the Twelve or listen to them, we would do wrong to think that the house reflects household
evangelism and house-churches in early Christianity (cf. G. B. Caird in *ExpTim* 81 [1969-
70] 40-43 on the collective response of a locality rather than varying individual responses
within it). Staying in a house as long as you are in a locality does not imply a more or
less lengthy stay such as might reflect early Christian practice. Έως, "until," plus the
subjunctive leaves the length of stay indeterminate; and *Did.* 11:4-5 shows Christianity
slightly later than Mark going in the direction of short, not long, stays for itinerant preachers
(cf. the allowance of bread in *Did.* 11:4-5 for longer journeys such as later take place
outside Palestine). Mark shifts from the singular ὃς ἂν τόπος μὴ δέξηται, "whatever place
does not receive," to the plural μηδὲ ἀκούσωσιν, "neither do they hear" (v 11). But the shift
does not imply that he interpolates the plural expression; for "place" collectivizes the people
living in a town, and it comes as naturally to an author as to an interpolator to switch from
a collective singular to a plural. We will note better reasons for the theory of interpolation.
One might think that listening implies the meaning "synagogue" for "place." But would
the Twelve be invited to preach in synagogues? And have not people listened to Jesus
outside synagogues, too?

The imperative force of "shake out" probably rubs off somewhat on "going out"
(cf. C. F. D. Moule, *Idiom-Book* 179-80). According to Neh 5:13; Acts 18:6a (cf. 13:51),

"shake out" has to do with clothes, not with shoes (contrast Luke 10:11: "wipe off" with reference to the feet). "The dust under your feet" therefore means the dust that used to be under your feet but that you kicked up when walking, with the result that it settled in your clothes (against H. J. Cadbury in *Beginnings of Christianity* 5. 270). According to those same passages, shaking it out does not constitute a last call to repentance ("for a witness to them"); it delivers a symbolic prophecy of judgment ("for a witness against them"). As in the OT, delivering the prophecy not only makes known what will happen. It also causes and thereby insures the happening; for God's word will not return to him void, but will accomplish what he pleases (Isa 55:11; see esp. 2 Kgs 13:14-19, where the fulfilment of a prophecy is strictly limited to the extent to which it is symbolically acted out; also Rev 10:1-4, where not writing a prophecy causes and thereby insures non-occurrence). Neh 5:13; Acts 18:6a disfavor replacing a prophecy of judgment with a riddance of ritual uncleanness (Str-B 1. 571) or with a protestation of innocence by the preachers; but Acts 18:6b favors that such a protestation may go along with the prophecy of judgment. Since v 10 neither says nor implies anything about household evangelism and since v 11 neither says nor implies anything about length of stay, we have no right to contrast settled evangelism that takes more than a day in v 10 with whirlwind evangelism by evangelists who according to v 11 preach only once in a town. Neh 5:13; Acts 13:51; 18:6 associate the shaking out of dust with far longer stays. W. L. Lane (208, n. 35) thinks that because shaking out dust would be comprehensible in a Semitic milieu, "for a testimony against them" must be Mark's cultural translation in a non-Semitic milieu. But the phrase is not a cultural translation in 1:44; 13:9.

The suggestion that the ἵνα following ἐκήρυξαν, "preached" (v 12), is telic ("in order that") has little to commend it. Mark likes to use an epexegetic ἵνα, "that," after verbs of speaking (see the note on v 8). Jesus' preaching included the nearness of God's rule and belief in this good news as well as repentance (1:15; cf. Matt 10:7 par. Luke 9:2). Mark limits the preaching of the Twelve to repentance, perhaps because that is the only theme common to the preaching of Jesus and John the Baptizer (1:4) and because an identification of Jesus as John is coming up next (6:14-16). Some have suggested that Mark adds anointing with oil (v 13) from church practice. But it is just as likely that church practice originates here, and Mark does not say that the Twelve anointed the sick with oil "in the name of the Lord" and prayed over them, as Jas 5:14 prescribes for church practice. On the use of oil, see also Luke 10:34; Isa 1:6 and other references to primary literature in R. Herzog, *Wunderheilungen* nos. 19 (pp. 16-17), 79 (pp. 43-45); O. Böcher, *Dämonen-furcht* 216-17; idem, *Christus Exorcista* 151-52; H. Schlier in *TDNT* 1. 230-31; 2. 472-73; H. van der Loos, *Miracles* 311-12; J. Hempel, *Heilung* 238-41). The usual NT distinction between exorcisms and healings favors taking v 13a and v 13b as complementary rather than synonymous. Therefore, anointing with oil does not form part of an exorcistic ritual. Oil is widely used as a soothing medicament, but the miraculous power which Jesus has imparted to his disciples speeds up its effectiveness here. He heals with his word, his touch, and his spittle. The disciples' use of oil, a substance foreign to themselves, shows that it is only through his power that they heal. Cyr. H. *Catech.* 20.3 dates from a later period, features exorcised oil, not oil for exorcism, and has to do with a protective charm at baptism, not with healing from a sickness. Against a Marcan criticism of miraculous healing, see 1:44-45 and H. K. Nielsen, *Heilung* 110-24, esp. 110-12.

R. Laufen (*Doppelüberlieferungen* 298-99) thinks that Mark depends on a shortened source, for he would not omit the disciples' preaching of God's rule (cf. Matt 10:7; Luke 9:2; 10:9, 11), as Jesus preached it (Mark 1:14-15). But Mark is showing the extension of *Jesus'* authority; so he may well omit the preaching of *God's* rule as putting the accent in the wrong place for the point he wants to make. If Luke 10:1-20 represents Q, more or less, we might surmise that Mark knows this form of the tradition (though not necessarily

Q itself). But usually unanswerable questions arise. Does Mark omit the harvest-saying, or does the Q-tradition or Luke add it? So also with regard to the saying about sheep and wolves. Does Mark add "not one thing for the road" to stress Jesus' power to determine the conduct of his disciples? But the phrase seems necessary for the exception of a staff, in whose originality we have seen reason to believe. Does Mark add the prohibition of bread, or does the Q-tradition or Luke omit it — and in either case, why? And so on. Luke's "purse" looks redactional, his greeting of "peace" primitive. But does Mark omit the greeting or not know it? So also with regard to the saying about the laborer worthy of his wages. Does Mark's "place" (cf. Luke 10:2) substitute for "city," or vice versa for an urban audience? Does he add "neither hear you" (v 11) in anticipation of the preaching of the Twelve (v 12) and in accord with his penchant for duality and his emphasis on hearing (see chap. 4, for example; also 6:20; 7:14; 9:7; 12:37)? Probably yes. But does he add "for a witness against them"? Only if the same phrase in 1:44; 13:9 is redactional (but see the comments ad loc.). More generally, however, the narrative setting of Luke 10:1-20, the difficulty in making sense of Luke 10:2-12 apart from a narrative setting, and the difference from the narrative setting in Mark 6:6b-13 call in question the supposition that Luke 10:1-20 represents Q and that Mark draws on Q.

W. L. Lane (210) writes of a "new section" that consists of 6:14–8:30 and "focuses upon a period during which Jesus was frequently in retirement beyond the borders of Galilee." In fact, however, there is no indication of movement from Galilee till 7:24; and only three pericopes (7:24-30, 31-37; 8:27-30) give indication of settings outside Galilee. Furthermore, there appears to be no more retirement in this section than in earlier passages such as 1:35, 45; 2:1; 3:7, 13, 20; 4:10, 34, 35-36; 5:1; and almost all the audiences in 6:14–8:30 are larger than the circle of disciples.

On the ground that news about Jesus would have reached Herod's ears long before now, K. L. Schmidt (*Rahmen* 172-73) guesses that vv 14-16 originally belonged with Jesus' entering Capernaum (2:1; see H. W. Hoehner, *Herod Antipas* 191-97, for a full discussion). C. R. Kazmierski (*Jesus, the Son of God* 23) thinks that Mark inserts vv 14-29 at this point to imply that the Twelve preach the same gospel that John the Baptizer as well as Jesus preached (1:1-15). Admittedly, the Twelve's preaching of repentance (v 12) leads smoothly into a pericope featuring John, because he preached the baptism of repentance (1:4), and may therefore have led Mark to limit the preaching of the Twelve to repentance (see the notes on v 12). But John's preaching gets no mention here. This omission and the strongly Christological introduction in vv 14-16 point to another purpose for the insertion. For the same reasons we should reject the opinion of J. R. Edwards in *NovT* 31 (1989) 205-6 that Mark inserts the story of John's martyrdom to warn that preachers of the Christian gospel may likewise suffer martyrdom (cf. M. A. Tolbert [*Sowing the Gospel* 197-98], whose drawing of a parallel between John's martyrdom and the persecution that causes temporary believers to apostatize suffers also from the failure of John to apostatize under persecution). The suggestion of R. M. Fowler (*Loaves and Fishes* 114-21) that Mark designs vv 14-29 to contrast Herod's kingship with that of Jesus suffers from the failure of Jesus' kingship to appear in the pericope — or to have appeared earlier in Mark, for that matter. It will not appear till 15:2, and then not as a feature of Marcan Christology (see the comments and notes ad loc. et passim). The question of Jesus' identity in vv 14-16 prepares for the question of his identity in 8:27-30 (so E. Schweizer 133; N. R. Petersen, *Literary Criticism* 59-60), but this preparation does not explain why Mark includes the beheading of John in vv 17-29 and why he inserts the whole of vv 14-29 at this point. Schweizer (134) thinks that Mark inserts vv 14-29 here to show the world's increasing blindness to God's revelation (cf. the assignment by W. Schmithals [313] of v 15 to a Marcan messianic secret). Granted, vv 14-16 contain false identifications of Jesus. But what favorable identifications! So the accent falls, not on their falsity, but on what prompted them, i.e. on the miracles that are at work in Jesus. E. Best (*Following Jesus* 192-94) thinks that Mark inserts vv 14-29 because they do not show Jesus acting apart from the Twelve during the mission on which he sent them. But why then does Mark insert anything at all? Why does he not skip from the mission of the Twelve (vv 12-13) directly to their regrouping with Jesus (v 30; cf. the suggestion of M.-J. Lagrange [165] that Mark does not know what Jesus did during the mission because Peter, Mark's informant, was not with Jesus then)?

The story of Jesus' death and burial may color the story of John's death and burial, or vice versa, in the use of κρατέω, "seize" (v 17; cf. 14:46), in the delay of execution because of fear on the part of officialdom (v 20; cf. 11:18, 32; 12:12; 14:2), in the similarity between εὐκαίρου, "opportune" (v 21), and εὐκαίρως, "opportunely" (14:11), and in the phraseology concerning burial (v 29; cf. 15:45-46). But it is unlikely that Mark inserts the pericope as a preview of Jesus' death, burial, and resurrection; for Herod's view that God has raised John from the dead is mistaken, predictions of Jesus' passion and resurrection have not yet started to appear in Mark, and the later parallel between John and Jesus in 9:11-13 will not spell out the elements of death, burial, and resurrection. Moreover, κρατέω is very common for seizing (see the lexicons and concordances). Mark mentions an imprisonment of John but not of Jesus, and a laying of hands on Jesus but not on John. Putting a corpse in a tomb would be a natural way to describe anybody's interment. And Mark makes no attempt to include in his account of John's interment items such as a request for the corpse, its being wrapped in a shroud, and the tomb's being hewn out of rock — items which will appear in 15:42-47 and at least some of which are likely to have characterized John's interment. Mark's mentioning that John's *disciples* inter John contrasts with his mentioning that Joseph, whom he will *not* call a disciple, inters Jesus (15:42-47), the disciples having fled (14:52).

E. Lohmeyer (117-18) argues that the sequencing of scenes in vv 17-29, the large number of motifs and characters, the roundedness of the composition, the high proportion of non-Marcan expressions, the absence of the historical present tense as opposed to numerous instances of the aorist and imperfect tenses, and the free use of participles and of the genitive absolute betray a pre-Marcan narrative written in cultivated style though going back to an Aramaic source and displaying a popular character. But we should not underestimate the extent to which Mark uses his own compositional technique in taking over tradition (whether written or oral). Tradition may supply the scenes, motifs, characters, and locutions that occur seldom if ever elsewhere in his gospel (though he is as capable of a hapax legomenon as an earlier traditioner or Jesus himself was); but we should not expect to find the historical present in a flashback. For by definition and relation to surrounding historical narrative, a flashback takes a kind of pluperfect standpoint. Γάρ-clauses, such as those in vv 17a, 18, 20a appear often in Mark (see the concordance s.v.). The profusion of parataxis in vv 19, 20b-22a, 25-29 is characteristic of this gospel (see the concordance s.v. καί, "and"). The proleptic αὐτός, "himself" (v 17), will occur twice more in 12:36, 37. Ἀποστέλλω, "send," which occurs in the form of a characteristically Marcan aorist circumstantial participle at v 17, looks Marcan in 3:14, 31; 5:10; 6:7; 8:26; 11:1, 3; 12:13; 14:13. So also does each of the following: the imperfect of θέλω, "wish" (vv 19, 26), in 3:13; 6:48; 7:24; 9:30; the imperfect of δύναμαι, "be able" (v 19), in 4:33; 5:3; 6:5; 7:24; the imperfect of φοβέομαι, "fear" (v 20), in 9:32; 10:32; 11:18, 32; 12:12; 16:8; the circumstantial participle of οἶδα, "know," modifying the subject (v 20) in 12:15, 28 v.l.; the aorist circumstantial participle of ἀκούω, "hear" (vv 20, 29), in 2:17; 3:21; 5:27, 36; 6:16, 29; 7:25; 10:41, 47; 12:28; 14:11; 15:35 (cf. 3:8; 6:2); the adverbial πολλά, "much" (vv 20, 23), in passages listed in the notes on 1:45; hearing someone "gladly" (v 20) in 12:37; the duality in a notation of time (v 21) at 1:21, 32, 35; 2:20; 4:35; 5:5; 10:30; 11:2, 14; 13:11, 24; 14:1, 3, 12, 25, 30, 43; 15:42; 16:2; the aorist participle of γίνομαι, "become," in a temporal genitive absolute (v 21) at 1:32 (followed by ὅτε, as here); 4:35; 6:2, 35, 47; 14:17; 15:33, 42 (with a second temporal note, as here); 16:1; the aorist participle of εἰσέρχομαι, "go in," in a genitive absolute (v 22) in 9:28; the aorist circumstantial participle of ἐξέρχομαι, "go out" (v 24), in 1:29, 45; 3:6; 5:13; 6:12, 34; 7:31; 9:30; 16:8; the substantive participle of βαπτίζω, "baptize," for John (v 24; contrast v 25) in 1:4; 6:14; the aorist circumstantial participle of εἰσέρχομαι (v 25) in 1:21; 2:1; 5:39; 7:24, 25; 11:15; 15:43; 16:5; εὐθύς, "immediately" (vv 25, 27), in passages too numerous to list; μετά, "with," following εὐθύς (v 25) in 3:6 (cf. 4:16; 6:50); the aorist circumstantial participle of γίνομαι (v 26) in 9:33; the aorist circumstantial participle of ἀπέρχομαι, "go away" (v 27), in 7:30; 14:39 (not to list very.many passages where Mark seems to be responsible for non-participial forms of εἰς-, ἐξ-, and ἀπέρχομαι); and the aorist of τίθημι, "put," plus ἐν μνημείῳ, "in a tomb" (v 29), for interment (15:46).

In view of Jesus' later identification of John with Elijah (9:13), it is often suggested that Herod and Herodias are patterned after Ahab and Jezebel, enemies of Elijah in 1 Kings. It is likewise suggested that the story in Mark, especially those features of it that differ from Josephus Ant. 18.5.1-2 §§109-12, 116-19, has drawn on the canonically enshrined and extracanonically developed story of Esther, beginning with the banquet of Ahasuerus, including the presentation of Vashti's severed head on a platter, and extending to the king's taking pleasure in the girl Esther and promising her half his kingdom (above all, see R. Aus [Water into Wine 39-74], who appeals not only to the MT and LXX but also to Josephan, targumic, and rabbinic materials on Esther; also R. Pesch 1. 339 with references to earlier literature). The dates of some of the comparable materials, particularly the targumic and rabbinic ones, are questionably pre-Marcan, however; and the parallels are sometimes highly selective within those materials and often forced. Ahab did not imprison Elijah, preserve him, or gladly hear him, for example; nor did Jezebel succeed in getting Elijah killed. Herod's perplexity consists in being caught between his own respect for John and Herodias's wanting to kill him, whereas in rabbinic tradition the perplexity of Ahasuerus arises out of Vashti's refusal to parade her beauty before his banqueters. The classes of banqueters are parallel only if Mark 6:21 omits a couple of classes in Esth 1:3 and a strained equation is made between one or two other classes. Esther does not dance to the pleasure of Ahasuerus as Herodias's daughter dances to the pleasure of Herod, and thus Ahasuerus's offer to give Esther up to half his kingdom grows out of a completely different circumstance from that out of which grows the similar offer by Herod. Thus also, the beheading of John grows out of a completely different circumstance from that out of which grows the beheading of Vashti; and apart from their beheadings and the presentation of their heads on platters, John and Vashti play dissimilar roles. Details such as Herod's liking to hear John and the burial of John's corpse by his disciples do not seem explicable by borrowing from the stories of Elijah and Esther. Nor do these and other details likely derive from motifs in Hellenistic fairy tales. Kings often had a court sage, soothsayer, or prophet; but they did not imprison him out of malice only to consult him out of respect (against C. Bonner in HTR 37 [1944] 41-44; contrast the terror and venality of Felix in relation to Paul in Acts 24:24-26). Motifs that we find also in Hdt. 9.108-13; Liv. 39.43.1-5; Plut. Arat. 17; Dio Cass. 65.15; Josephus Ant. 18.5.1 §115 do not establish the character of a fairy tale, for such motifs may reflect the actualities of ancient court life (H. Windisch in ZNW 18 [1917] 73-81).

The lack of a moralistic tone in Mark favors history over legend. Josephus puts the execution of John at Machaerus in Perea; and archeological discoveries of a prison as well as a palace there, and of two dining rooms (triclinia), one large and one small, fit John's imprisonment, Herod's banquet, and the separateness of Herod and Herodias during the banquet, presumably because the men were eating in the large dining room, the women in the small one (V. Corbo and S. Loffreda in SBFLA 31 [1981] 257-86, pls. 26, 29-34; F. Manns in SBFLA 31 [1981] 287-90; B. Schwank in NTS 29 [1983] 434; R. Riesner in

BK 39 [1984] 176). The apparent lack of separate dining rooms in the Herodian palaces at Masada, the Herodion, and Jericho makes this undesigned coincidence all the more impressive as evidence for historicity. The objection that "the number of guests described here (end of vs. 21) . . . is only conceivable at the Herodian Palace in Tiberias, the capital of Galilee" (E. Schweizer 132) does not hold water. As a matter of fact, Mark writes nothing about a large number or about the location. But more to the point, it is inconceivable that Herod would not "be surrounded by his courtiers" even at Machaerus (C. E. B. Cranfield 211), to say nothing of the possibility of a special trip by them to celebrate Herod's birthday (cf. v 21: "for his courtiers [et al.]") — a possibility not at all unthinkable in view of Herod's giving a luxurious feast for Artabanus and Vittelius on a bridge in the middle of the Euphrates River (Josephus *Ant.* 18.4.5 §102; cf. Dio Cass. 59.17.5; esp. against the opinion of P. Parker [in *JBL* 100 (1981) 397-98] that Mark must not know that Machaerus is c. 100 miles from Galilee). Josephus (*Ant.* 18.4.6 §106) remarks on Philip's having gone about with only a few select companions, as though it was unusual; so we may assume that Herod did otherwise. On John's being under Herod's jurisdiction, see T. W. Manson, *Servant-Messiah* 40-41 (with R. H. Gundry, *Matthew* 42, on the redactional character of "Judea" in Matt 3:1); on other historical questions, H. W. Hoehner (*Herod Antipas* 110-71), who argues strongly, for example, that Herodias's first husband may well have borne the name Philip (v 17) as well as the name Herod (Josephus *Ant.* 18.5.4 §136; see esp. pp. 131-36 in Hoehner). We are not bound to understand the dancing of Herodias's daughter as sensual (ibid. 156-57), though such dancing may not have violated the standards of behavior in Herod's household.

The position of W. Schenk (in *NTS* 29 [1983] 453-83) that John's ministry lasted till c. 35 C.E. crumbles under massive evidence, not only in Marcan tradition but also in Q, John, and Acts, that at least by the middle of Jesus' ministry John belonged to the past (Mark 1:14 parr.; 9:11-13 par.; 11:30 parr.; Luke 7:18-35 par.; 11:1; 16:16 par.; John 5:31-35; 10:40-41; Acts 1:5, 22; 10:37; 11:16; 13:24-25; 19:4; cf. John 3:23-24). Even in the fourth gospel, where the ministries of the two men overlap, John has faded into the past by chap. 5. Schenk thinks that vv 17-29 are a Marcan construct designed to supplement vv 14-16 and therefore not drawn from special tradition. But what evidence do we have that Mark writes so inventively elsewhere that we could believe in his writing thus here? C. Saulnier (in *RB* 91 [1984] 362-76) puts the Josephan chronology on which Schenk relies in considerable doubt.

The suggestion that at the base of vv 17-29 lay only a short tradition corresponding to Jewish martyrology, later enriched with the popular motif of a vengeful woman (see J. Gnilka 1. 245-46; idem in *Orientierung an Jesus* 85-86), suffers from the absence of physical torture, brave endurance, eloquent statements of fidelity, prayer, and divine vindication, all of which characterize such martyrology. Even John's defending the Law does not match what we usually find in Jewish martyrology of the period, for he suffers martyrdom for exposing someone else's wrongdoing, not for adhering to the Law himself (contrast the late Jewish martyrology cited in D. Dormeyer, *Passion* 43).

A large number of considerations suggest that in vv 14b-15 Mark draws on the tradition behind 8:28 to explain why Herod says that Jesus is John raised from the dead: (1) Editorial γάρ-clauses characterize Mark (and here γάρ, "for," is best taken as governing all the intervening clauses [vv 14b-15], just as γάρ in v 17 makes the whole of the story concerning John's beheading an explanation of Herod's adopting the identification of Jesus with John). (2) The structure of the present γάρ-clause — predicate adjective + γάρ + a form of γίνομαι, "become" — matches the structure of an apparently editorial statement in 9:6. (3) Φανερόν, "well known," has occurred in an apparently editorial statement at 3:12 (contrast the apparently traditional character of 4:22). (4) The καί, "and," before ἔλεγον, "they were saying," in v 14 appears to replace a traditional δέ, "but," in 8:28, because the present insertion is made at a cost of the original setting, in which a question and its answer were put over against each other. (5) In v 14 ἔλεγον appears to replace a traditional εἶπαν αὐτῷ λέγοντες, "they spoke to him, saying" for the sake of a parallel with introductions to the second and third identifications, where Mark inserts ἔλεγον twice again for a stylistic improvement which does not surpass even his abilities. (6) The shift from "the [disciples] said" (8:28) to "they [some people in general] were saying" agrees with the frequency in Mark of indefinite third person plural verbs (and with the frequency in Mark of this particular verb in the imperfect tense — though this is less significant, because many authors like to use the imperfect in verbs of speaking). (7) Mark seems to transform the short answer "John the Baptist" (8:28) into a complete statement, "John the Baptizer has been raised from the dead," because insertion has caused a loss of the traditional question (8:27b). (8) The substantive participial phrase ὁ βαπτίζων, "the Baptizer," looks like Mark's revision of a traditional nominal phrase τὸν βαπτιστήν, "the Baptist," at 8:28 (so also 6:25) in agreement with an editorial preference at 1:4 (so also 6:24 — all according to the most probably original vv.ll.). (9) "Has been raised from the dead" looks like an addition to the tradition for the purpose of assimilating it to the following story of John's death. (10) "And because of this the miracles are at work in him" looks like an addition to the tradition for the purpose of assimilating it to the foregoing references to Jesus' and the disciples' miracles, in particular, to the phraseology of v 2, "and the miracles such as were taking place through his hands," except that there the accent fell on miraculous effects because the character of the miracles was at issue, whereas it falls here on miraculous abilities because Jesus' personal identity is at issue (the theory of mistranslated Aramaic becoming unnecessary — against G. Dalman, *Words* 201; cf. R. H. Gundry, *Matthew* 285-86; R. Pesch 1. 333). (11) The first δέ, "but," in v 15 looks like a refinement of the first καί, "and," in 8:28 for the purpose of contrasting the first two identifications. (12) The short answer "Elijah" appears to give way to the complete statement, "He's Elijah," to match the earlier redactional complete statement and again to compensate for loss of the traditional question (see the seventh point above). (13) A similar change takes place in the third identification and for the same reason, as can be seen in the shift from a short answer, "[He is] one of the prophets" (8:28), to the long answer, "[He is] a prophet like one of the prophets." (14) "A prophet like one of the prophets" appears to change a traditional identification of Jesus with "one of the prophets" (8:28) into a mere comparison, perhaps because the OT predicted the return of no prophet except Elijah, already named (Mal 3:23[4:5]). Appealing to 9:37-39, 41; 13:6, 13, some would add (15) that ὄνομα, "name" (v 14), counts as a Marcanism. But one may defend the traditional character of ὄνομα in the cross-references, and they do not carry the present connotation of "reputation" (BAGD s.v. IV). Nonetheless, even a traditional use of ὄνομα in the cross-references may have triggered a redactional usage here, signaled as redactional by the different connotation.

A borrowing of vv 14b-15 from the tradition behind 8:28 would undercut the suggestion of J. Ernst (179) that before their incorporation into Mark, vv 14-16 represented an attempt by the followers of John to vindicate him as risen from the dead in Jesus; and if for a contextual reason Mark adds a reference to John's being raised from the dead (see the foregoing discussion), we need neither the suggestion of D. E. Aune (in *ANRW* II 23/2. 1541-42) that originally Jesus was thought to be using for miracles the demon that John was accused of having before his death (cf. Matt 11:18 par. Luke 7:33) nor the suggestion of C. H. Kraeling (in *JBL* 59 [1940] 147-57) that Jesus was thought to call up John's own spirit as giving him great power because John had been wrongfully killed. The parallel with identifications where there is no question of a demon or of the spirit of a wrongfully killed person also disfavors these suggestions and makes Kraeling's distinction between John's being raised (as some people say) and Jesus' being a raised John (as they do not quite say) look too subtle. The Marcan redaction suggested and outlined above answers to a detailed comparison of vv 14b-15 and 8:28 better than does a hypothesized redaction in the opposite direction, i.e. a taking over in vv 14b-15 of the tradition behind 8:28 without changing it significantly, but then abbreviating it at 8:28. The details of the opinion that John has been raised from the dead and that miracles are at work in Jesus would not have so much point in 8:27-30 as they do here; and "one of the prophets" does not merely abbreviate "a prophet like one of the prophets." It conveys a different meaning.

If then the tradition behind 8:28 did not explicitly mention John's being raised, the historicity of Herod's hearing about Jesus and thinking that he is John stands on firmer ground (cf. the possibility that the Herodians who plotted with the Pharisees against Jesus in 3:6 informed Herod about him [cf. also 12:13; Luke 8:3; Acts 13:1; H. W. Hoehner, *Herod Antipas* 120-21, 303-6]). For an only inferred raising of John is unlikely to have put in Mark's mind the idea of making Herod himself, not just some people in general, think that John has been raised from the dead. Other cross-references that are sometimes used to argue for Mark's fabrication of Herod's identifying Jesus with John (1:27; 4:41; 6:2-3, 52; 8:14-21; 14:61-62) often do not even pose the possibility of a special identity for Jesus. Far from posing that possibility in 6:2-3, for example, the townspeople of Nazareth think that he is nobody special at all (see also 1:27; 6:52; 8:14-21). The traditional character of the remaining cross-references is defensible.

D. Catchpole (in *Jesus and the Politics of His Day* 327) considers several items inimical to the historicity of vv 14-16: (1) the explaining of Jesus' activities only on the supposition that he is someone who has been raised from the dead; (2) Herod's anticipating the Christian scheme whereby this individual raising brings apocalyptic eschatology into the present; (3) Herod's regarding John, whom he executed, as raised in Jesus; and (4) Herod's seeing continuity between a miracle-worker (Jesus) and a non-worker of miracles (John). But it would be harder to do so for a Christian suffering no guilty conscience over John's death and rating Jesus far superior to John to see continuity than it would be for Herod, who does suffer such a conscience and does not rate Jesus above John. We need not assume that Herod knew about any overlapping of John's and Jesus' ministries. Belief that someone has been raised from the dead to haunt your conscience need not have anything to do with apocalyptic eschatology (cf. raisings from the dead in the OT that carried no eschatological overtones). And belief that Jesus is someone raised from the dead is only one of several explanations offered here.

It is hard to verify or falsify the suggestion that John's disciples identified Jesus with John because they wanted to believe that God had raised their martyred master from the dead. The later existence of disciples of John as distinct from disciples of Jesus (Acts 18:24–19:7) and the portrayal of John in the fourth gospel as ministering concurrently with Jesus (John 3:22–4:2) lessen the likelihood of that suggestion (cf. Jesus' identifying John with Elijah in Mark 9:11-13 and the view of J. A. T. Robinson [*Twelve NT Studies* 28-52] that John may well have identified Jesus with Elijah, certainly not himself with Elijah). The opinion that Elijah has returned in Jesus suggests a belief or hope that the last days have arrived, for God is to send Elijah just before the Day of the Lord (Mal 3:23-24[4:5-6]). But the opinion that Jesus is "*a prophet*," as distinct from "*the* [Mosaic eschatological] prophet" (John 1:21, 25; 6:14; 7:40, 52 P[66]; Acts 3:22-23; 4QTestim 5-8; 1QS 9:10-11; cf. Mark 9:7 parr. with Deut 18:15), does not suggest such a belief or hope; nor does the supposed raising of one person, John, as distinct from the resurrection of many. Since Herod adopts the identification of Jesus with John rather than with Elijah, we might then be guilty of overinterpretation to make Herod think that a raised John portends eschatological judgment against his illegitimate marriage to Herodias. R. Pesch (1. 333-35) takes the view that an equation of John with Elijah enables some people to think that Jesus is John, since in accordance with Rev 11:3-12; *Apoc. Elijah* 35:7-21 they expect Elijah not only to return in the end time but also to perform miracles, suffer martyrdom, and be raised from the dead. From this point of view U. Wilckens (*Resurrection* 108-9) concludes that Mark's purpose is to portray Jesus instead of Elijah-John as the martyr who was raised from the dead. But nowhere do we find an identification of John with a martyred and raised Elijah. J. A. T. Robinson (*Twelve NT Studies* 28-52) notes John's denial that he is even a returned Elijah (John 1:21, 25) and the lack of evidence that others identify him as such until Jesus does so (Mark 9:13; cf. Matt 11:14 with comments in R. H. Gundry, *Matthew* 211). Furthermore, the late dates of Rev 11:3-12; *Apoc. Elijah* 35:7-21 (and the latter may depend on the former) weaken the presupposition that already by Jesus' time or, at the latest, by Mark's time, some people expect Elijah not only to come back but also to die and be raised.

Jesus' identification with John is helped by their being almost the same age. J. Gnilka (1. 247) infers from this identification and from the later identification of John with Elijah (9:11-13) that John performed miracles as Jesus and Elijah did. But though we *might* set down "John did not one sign" (John 10:41) to an anti-Baptist polemic in the fourth gospel, the synoptists' favorable portrayal of John plus their failure to report any miracles performed by him makes the inference doubtful. Moreover, "because of this" (v 14) attributes the miracles to John's having been raised from the dead and therefore implies a recognition that he had not performed miracles before. To say that δυνάμεις refers to divine powers that raised John from the dead rather than to divine powers that show themselves in his miracles (so W. Grundmann [7. Aufl.] 171) is to misread the text as though it says that the δυνάμεις have caused the raising of John. As it is, διὰ τοῦτο, "because of this," makes the raising cause the δυνάμεις. Though we have no other evidence that a person raised from the dead was thought to have miraculous powers, it is as easy to suppose that Herod inferred thus as it is to suppose that anyone else did.

The Mark who quotes and alludes to the OT comparatively seldom and assumes his audience's ignorance of Semitic words can hardly expect the Gentiles who make up the bulk of that audience to detect in his calling Herod a king an allusion to King Ahab with his wife Jezebel (against P. Carrington 132-33). Because of Luke 13:31, V. Taylor (307-8) thinks that vv 14-16 present Herod as less hostile than he actually was. But this opinion rests on the presupposition that the passages deal with the same moment or, if with different moments, that Herod's attitude did not develop. Furthermore, Mark says nothing about Herod's attitude toward Jesus, only something about his opinion of Jesus' identity; and given Herod's regarding Jesus merely as a curiosity in Luke 23:8-12 (whose tradition has probably led to redaction of Mark 6:14-16 in Luke 9:9 — against the view of R. Glover [in *NTS* 11 (1964-65) 99] that Luke 9:9 rests on better information), we do not know whether the Pharisees correctly represent Herod as wanting to kill Jesus in Luke 13:31 (cf. H. W. Hoehner, *Herod Antipas* 219-20). On Herod as tetrarch rather than as king, see Matt 14:1; Luke 3:19; 9:7; Acts 13:1; Josephus *Ant.* 17.8.1 §188; 17.9.4 §§224-27; 17.11.4 §318; idem *J.W.* 2.2.3 §§20-22; 2.6.3 §§93-95 (but see idem *Ant.* 17.9.5 §238 for his having been earlier "called to the kingdom [or 'to the kingship']" by his father Herod the Great). His later request, at Herodias's urging, for the title "king" led Augustus to depose and exile him (Josephus *Ant.* 18.7.1-2 §§240-56; idem *J.W.* 2.9.6 §§181-83).

V. Taylor (308) suggests that καί before ἔλεγον in v 14 may have the force of ὅτι, "because." But a causal relation between the two clauses on either side of this καί would seem to run in the opposite direction if there is such a relation at all; i.e. the various identifications are made because Jesus' reputation has become well known instead of his becoming well known because the various identifications are made. More probably, the reputation and the identifications stand on an equal footing as reasons for Herod's hearing. See B. M. Metzger, *Textual Commentary* ad loc.; F. Neirynck in *ETL* 65 (1989) 110-18 for ἔλεγον, "people were saying," instead of ἔλεγεν, "he [Herod] was saying," which probably arose by assimilation to the singular of ἤκουσεν, "he heard," earlier in the verse and by assimilation to ἔλεγεν in v 16. Luke 9:7 favors ἔλεγον, whereas Matt 14:2 skips to ἔλεγεν in Mark 6:16 (R. H. Gundry, *Matthew* 285). The remention of Herod's "having heard" in v 16 also implies that in v 15 the identification of Jesus with John is made by others than Herod (against the view of P. J. Achtemeier [in *JBL* 89 (1970) 269-70] that in vv 14 and 15-16 Mark records a doublet from tradition and that a later copyist changed -εν to -ον in v 14 to get rid of the repetition). We could take ἐγήγερται (and ἠγέρθη in v 16) deponently ("has risen"), but the divine passive is more probable ("has been raised [by God]"). Only people who do not know that John baptized Jesus and that John and Jesus ministered concurrently (but those events did not take place in Galilee, where the present events are taking place — see 1:9-15 parr.; John 1:35–4:3) can think that Jesus is John raised from the dead.

On belief in the return of Elijah, see the literature cited in BAGD s.v. Ἡλίας. We should not understand εἷς (v 15) as indefinite, because the parallels with John and Elijah show the question to be one of personal identity ("one of the prophets") rather than of vocational identity ("a prophet"). On the use of εἷς, see E. C. Maloney, *Semitic Interference* 126-31. C. Perrot (in *De la Tôrah au Messie* 417-23) uses the pairing of Elijah with Moses in Mal 3:22-23(4:4-5); Mark 9:5 and elsewhere to argue that the pre-Marcan tradition here referred to the first prophet Moses. But for such a reference we would expect "*the* prophet" (again see John 1:21, 25; 6:14; 7:40, 52 P⁶⁶; Acts 3:22-23; 4QTestim 5-8; 1QS 9:10-11 and cf. Mark 9:7 parr. with Deut 18:15), if not Moses' name; and because the greater specificity of "the prophet" would make for a closer parallel with "John the Baptizer" and "Elijah," it is hard to think that an original "the prophet" was changed to "one of the prophets" (8:28) or to "a prophet like one of the prophets" (v 15).

Because "hearing" (v 16) forms an inclusion with "heard" (v 14a), some commentators deny that Herod heard the intervening identifications of Jesus (vv 14c-15) and say that he heard only about Jesus' reputation for performing miraculous deeds (v 14b). But it is not Jesus' own miraculous deeds that immediately precede (see vv 12-13); so the reputation of Jesus which Mark introduces with γάρ, "for," to explain why Herod heard looks forward to the identifications just as his hearing in v 16 looks backward to them.

According to E. Schweizer (133), the delay of Herod's opinion till v 16 shows that Mark is disinterested in Herod's uneasy conscience. But "whom I beheaded" and references to Herod's fearing John, knowing him to be a righteous and holy man, suffering perplexity, hearing John gladly, and becoming very sorrowful at the request for his head (vv 20, 26) all show that Mark has not lost interest in Herod's uneasy conscience, which helps Mark exhibit the length to which people must go to explain the miracles at work in Jesus.

Some commentators say that Herod adopts the identification of Jesus with John only ironically: "Not another Baptist!" So long as this interpretation hides in the historical recesses of Herod's mind or of a hypothetical, differently worded tradition prior to Mark, we have no way of verifying or falsifying it. But it sits uneasily on the wording of Mark's text, in particular, on Herod's adding a reference to the beheading of John and on his adding it with the emphasis of a casus pendens plus a resumptive demonstrative pronoun. This emphasis and the parallel identifications in vv 14b-15 disfavor punctuating Herod's statement as a question.

Since Herod had married Herodias, John did not accuse him of adultery; rather, of breaking the law against marrying your brother's wife (Lev 18:16; 20:21; see A. Finkel, *Pharisees* 49-50, on a violation of the law of levirate marriage [Deut 25:5] according to Slavonic Josephus, and D. Lührmann 116 on the allowance of marriage to your brother's wife in Greek and Roman law). "Because he married her" defines "because of Herodias the wife of Philip his brother" (v 17). "For John was saying to Herod" then makes John's rebuke, "It is not lawful for you to have the wife of your brother" (v 18), the reason for Herod's imprisonment of John. Herodias's wanting to kill John shows her unsatisfied with his imprisonment. Herod's fear of John keeps her from carrying out her wish, however, and derives from his knowing that John is a righteous and holy man (cf. Josephus *Ant.* 18.5.1 §117). But Herod's "having sent" to seize John combines both with Herod's not having gone to hear him before imprisoning him and with John's not having gone to rebuke Herod before being imprisoned to make an inconcinnity out of John's speaking directly "to Herod" (cf. "you" and "your" — v 18) prior to imprisonment. The text does not even contain any indication that John fulminated to the public against Herod's marrying Herodias. It seems therefore that Mark has advanced what John said directly to Herod after imprisonment. If so, John's private rebuke lay behind his beheading rather than behind his imprisonment.

Why then *did* Herod imprison John? Josephus (*Ant.* 18.5.2 §118) answers that Herod feared the development of a revolt among John's followers. Under the assumption that historical tradition underlies Mark's account; we can then trace a progression from Herod's imprisoning John out of political fear to his keeping John safe out of religious fear once he came into direct contact with John. At the expense of inconcinnity, Mark advances the private rebuke to play up John's being "a righteous and holy man"; for this suits Mark's apology for the crucifixion of Jesus, whose association with John makes readers think of him, too, as a righteous and holy man (cf. the view of M. S. Enslin [in *ZNW* 66 (1975) 13-14] that Christians changed the reason for John's imprisonment and execution to avoid even an indirect association with the sedition that Herod feared would develop around John — but why then did Christians not change the far more damaging reason stated for Jesus' crucifixion, viz., that he was king of the Jews?). The suitability to Mark's apology and the many Marcan traits in the compositional style of the pericope favor his making the advance instead of an earlier traditioner's having made it. W. L. Knox (*Sources* 1. 50-51) casts doubt on the Josephan version of John's martyrdom by asking why Herod would think that John's moralistic preaching might lead to a rebellion. But Herod does not fear the development of a rebellion out of John's moralistic preaching, according to Josephus; rather, out of John's turning his influence over the masses from a moral end to a seditious one. More than one ruler has been known to fear the same development with respect to popular religious leaders.

See K. Berger, *Gesetzesauslegung* 165-66, on the combination of "righteous" (i.e. loving fellow human beings) and "holy" (i.e. loving God — v 20). Matt 11:2 par. Luke 7:18 suggest that Herod did not put John in solitary confinement. R. Aus (*Water into Wine* 40) suggests wordplay in an underlying Aramaic that had נטר for Herod's preservation of John as well as for Herodias's grudge against John, and מטרתא for the prison in which Herod preserved John. Likewise, J. Carmignac (in *ASTI* 7 [1968-69] 71) suggests wordplay in an underlying Hebrew (or Aramaic, we might add): שמר for the preservation of John, שמע for Herod's hearing him, and שמם for Herod's perplexity. It is questionable, however, that שמם, "to be desolated, appalled," can underlie Mark's ἠπόρει, "he was at a loss." Ἀπορέω never stands for שמם in the LXX, and Herod's hearing John gladly would not fit well with appalment. Nor does Herod's hearing John gladly contrast with Herod's perplexity, for this perplexity arises from the conflict between respect for John and Herodias's wanting to kill him (against F. Field, *Notes* 29-30). Hence, the καί after ἠπόρει is not adversative; and C. Bonner (in *HTR* 37 [1944] 41-44) loses his argument for translating πολλὰ ἠπόρει, "he was wont to raise many questions." We might still adopt his translation of ἠπόρει, however (cf. LSJ s.v. ἀπορέω I2). If so, Mark's using πολλά as an adverb ("very, much") far more often than as a direct object ("many") would favor translating the whole phrase, "he was very wont to raise questions." However ἠπόρει is to be translated, we might better take πολλά with ἀκούσας αυτοῦ, "having heard him much"; for the adverbial πολλά follows its verb or verbal (as in 1:45; 4:2; 5:10, 23, 38, 43; 6:23, 34; 15:3) almost twice as often as it precedes its verb or verbal (as in 3:12; 5:26; 8:31;

9:12, 26; cf. 12:27). Furthermore, hearing John "gladly" would then take off on hearing him "much" (cf. Mark's penchant for duality); and much hearing would complement Mark's using the adverbial πολλά almost always with verbs of speaking (1:45; 3:12; 4:2; 5:10, 23, 38, 43; 6:23, 34; 15:3). The v.l. which replaces ἠπόρει, "was at a loss," with ἐποίει, "was doing," has inferior though not inconsiderable external support, requires the less likely treatment of πολλά as a direct object (for ποιέω is transitive), and produces a meaning strange to the context ("he was doing many things," presumably things that he had heard John tell him to do — but what are they, for Herod neither stops living with his brother's wife nor releases John?). The possibility that "he was doing many things" is a Semitism which means "he was hearing John often" (BDF §414[5]; J. H. Moulton and W. F. Howard, *Accidence and Word-Formation* 445-46) has in its favor that a linguistically sensitive Greek copyist would be tempted to change it but not to produce it; yet Mark's preference for the adverbial πολλά, his placement of πολλά predominantly after its verb or verbal, and the better quality of the external support for ἠπόρει remain stumblingblocks to the originality of ἐποίει and a Semitic understanding of it (see also B. M. Metzger, *Textual Commentary* ad loc.).

In v 21, the "when"-clause concerning a birthday may define "opportune" (εὐκαίρου) in relation to Herod's making a banquet. But to call a birthday opportune for giving a banquet elicits no more than a yawn. Herodias's wanting to have John killed (v 19), her carrying out that desire (vv 24-28), and the use of "opportunely" for another murderous design (14:11) favor that Mark is describing Herod's birthday as opportune for Herodias's having John killed.

The comments on v 22 lean hesitantly on the v.l. θυγατρὸς αὐτῆς τῆς Ἡρωδιάδος in A C K W (*omit* τῆς) Θ Π f¹³ 28 33 892 1009 Majority Text (remainder) it[a,d,ff2,i,l,q,r2] vg sy[h] rather than on the v.l. θυγατρὸς αὐτοῦ Ἡρωδιάδος in ℵ B D L Δ 565, because the latter v.l., which means that the daughter was Herod's, disagrees with her being the daughter of Herodias according to v 24 except under the unlikely supposition that Herod and Herodias already had a daughter old enough to dance (*pace* W. Schenk in *NTS* 29 [1983] 467-68) or that she belonged to Herod as well as to Herodias because Herodias brought her into Herod's household (Josephus [*Ant.* 18.5.4 §136] mentioning a Salome who was Herodias's daughter by her first husband and who was, according to Justin *Dial.* 49, the present dancer [see R. Aus, *Water into Wine* 49, on her age as probably twelve years or slightly more; cf. 5:41-42 for another κοράσιον, "girl," twelve years old]). It looks as though a copyist recognized neither a redundant Aramaism that anticipates the name of the daughter's mother ("her daughter, [i.e.] Herodias's") nor a quasi-demonstrative use of αὐτῆς ("the daughter of that [aforementioned] Herodias" — see E. C. Maloney, *Semitic Interference* 113-16) and therefore switched to the masculine pronoun and omitted τῆς, perhaps under the supposition that Herod would hardly have sworn to give as much as half his kingdom to anyone's daughter but his own. The copyist then thought either that the daughter had the same name that Herod's new wife had (Ἡρωδιάδος as appositive to θυγατρός) or, more awkwardly because of the absence of "and," that the daughter was Herodias's as well as Herod's (Ἡρωδιάδος as a genitive of relationship, like αὐτοῦ: "his daughter, Herodias's"). M. Black (*Aramaic Approach* 97) notes that αὐτοῦ is the easier and therefore inferior v.l. in that it probably makes the girl bear her mother's name and have Herod as her father at the same time. J. K. Elliott (in *NT Textual Criticism* 55-56) supports the v.l. with αὐτῆς on the ground that it represents a parenthetical explanation characteristic of Mark's style (cf. 1:2-3; 2:10, 16, 21; 6:14-15; 7:2, 3-4, 19, 26; 8:14; 12:12a; 13:14; 14:36). The omission of αὐτῆς in f¹ it[aur,b,c,f] syr[s,p,pal] cop[sa,bo] goth arm eth geo Diatessaron[a,p] leaves θυγατρὸς τῆς Ἡρωδιάδος, "the daughter of Herodias," and also appears to have come from failure to understand the redundant Aramaism or the quasi-demonstrative (against B. M. Metzger, *Textual Commentary* ad loc.).

E. P. Gould (113) treats ἤρεσεν impersonally ("it pleased") to avoid duplicating the subject of the genitive absolute ("she," i.e. "the daughter" — v 22). But such duplication abounds in κοινή Greek, and this verb normally has a personal subject. Though BAGD pronounce the active and middle voices of αἰτέω interchangeable, the use of this verb in 10:35, 38; 11:24; 15:6, 8, 43 lends support to the interpretation that sees in the shift from active (vv 22-23) to middle (vv 24-25) a shift from simple asking to asking in a business-like way (cf. J. H. Moulton, *Prolegomena* 160-61). The differences between ὅ τι ἐάν, "whatever," the recitative ὅτι plus ἐάν, "if," and the recitative ὅτι plus ὅ ἐάν, "whatever" (v 23 vv.ll.), do not materially alter the meaning of Herod's oath. With the offer of up to half his kingdom, cf. Esth 5:3, 6; 7:2 (also 9:12; 1 Kgs 13:8; Luke 19:8). E. Schweizer (134) finely comments, "This petty prince, ruling by the grace of Rome, could not give away one handsbreadth of his territory." Is Herod drunk? Probably so (cf. Esth 1:1-12; Liv. 39.43.1-5), but Mark does not mention drunkenness; for it would frivolize the offer and oath and thereby weaken his point that John is more important than half of Herod's kingdom.

The going out of the daughter to ask her mother what to request (v 24) shows that the dance was not planned with a view to John's beheading. According to M.-J. Lagrange (161), μετὰ σπουδῆς means "with eagerness," since εὐθύς, "immediately," already carries the idea of haste (v 25). But Mark likes to use dual temporal expressions (F. Neirynck, *Duality* 45-53, 94-96). Besides, "with haste" is not quite synonymous with "immediately"; for one can do something slowly even though doing it right after something else. Historically, immediacy and haste may have been designed to insure John's beheading before Herod sobered up and retracted his offer and oath. Correspondingly, the adverbial πολλά, "much" (v 23), and the plural of ὅρκους, "oaths" (v 26), may imply a drunkenness that made Herod repeat himself vociferously. But N. Turner (*Syntax* 26) cites a number of passages where the plural apparently refers to the words of a single statement; Mark may use τοὺς ὅρκους as a plural of category for assonance with τοὺς ἀνακειμένους; and near eastern hyperbole and face-saving may suffice to account for what happened.

N. Turner (*Syntax* 349-50) also argues from Hebrew word order that the phrase beginning "because of" modifies "becoming very sorrowful" rather than "did not want" (v 26). The hendiadys in "because of the oath and the ones reclining at table with him," meaning "because of the oath that he had sworn in the presence of his table guests," implies that only the prospect of losing face, not conscientiousness as well, led Herod to grant the girl's request (cf. J. D. M. Derrett, *Jesus's Audience* 339-56, and the possibility of taking the "because of"-phrase with "becoming very sorrowful" and thus of separating the oath from Herod's not wanting to deny the girl). Beheading is sanctioned in *m. Sanh.* 7:1. J. Carmignac (in *ASTI* 7 [1968-69] 71) detects an underlying wordplay between קערה, "platter," and נערה, "girl." For John's disciples, see 2:18; Matt 11:2 par. Luke 7:18; Luke 11:2; John 1:35, 37; 3:25; 4:1; Acts 19:1-7.

THE POWER OF JESUS TO FEED FIVE THOUSAND MALES WITH FIVE LOAVES AND TWO FISH

6:30-44 (Matt 14:13-21; Luke 9:10-17; John 6:1-15; cf. Mark 8:1-9; Matt 15:32-38)

The story of the feeding of the five thousand starts with Jesus' taking the apostles to a deserted place to get a little rest after their Galilean mission (vv 30-34). This part of the story breaks down into the apostles' coming together to Jesus and reporting on their activities during the mission (v 30), his telling them to come with him for a little rest (v 31a), the reason they need to go to a deserted place for a rest (v 31b), their going away by boat (v 32), people's seeing them go and beating them to their destination on foot (v 33), and Jesus' compassionate teaching of the people when he arrives (v 34). Then comes the feeding itself (vv 35-44), which breaks down into a dialogue between Jesus and the disciples on the feeding (vv 35-38) and his multiplying bread and fish so as to accomplish the feeding (vv 39-44).

6:30 *(Luke 9:10a)* "And the apostles come together to Jesus" marks the completion of their mission, summarized in vv 12-13. The historical present tense of συνάγονται, "come together," signals an exit from the flashback in vv 17-29. The designation οἱ ἀπόστολοι, "the apostles," harks back to ἀποστέλλειν in v 7, reminds readers of the authority with which Jesus sent the Twelve (cf. 3:14-15; 6:7), and avoids using "disciples" for Jesus' followers right after its use in v 29 for John's followers. The summary of the apostles' report to Jesus does not identify their message as one of repentance and their deeds as those of exorcism and healing, as vv 12-13 did, but plays on the magnitude of their accomplishments (πάντα ὅσα ἐποίησαν καὶ ὅσα ἐδίδαξαν, "all things, [i.e.] how many things they had done and how many things they had taught") to highlight the extension of Jesus' power through their ministry (cf. 3:28; 11:24; 12:44 for the doubly emphatic combination πάντα ὅσα; 3:8; 5:20 for ὅσα ἐποίησαν; and ἀπήγγειλαν, "reported," in v 30 with παρήγγειλεν, "ordered," in v 8). The putting of their deeds before their teaching (contrast vv 12-13; Rom 15:18) stresses the side of their mission that most apparently extended Jesus' power (cf. the sole mention of exorcisms in v 8; also 2 Cor 12:12, which has a polemical context). The switch from preaching (v 12) to teaching (v 30) implies that he shared with them his didactic authority, too (cf. v 6b).

6:31-33 *(Matt 14:13; Luke 9:10b-11; John 6:1-4)* The historical present tense of λέγει, "he says," stresses the authority with which Jesus commands the apostles: δεῦτε ὑμεῖς αὐτοί . . . , "Hither! You yourselves. . . ." Δεῦτε echoes his sovereign call of Simon and Andrew (1:17). But instead of ὀπίσω μου, "after me," as in that passage, we read ὑμεῖς αὐτοί, an extremely forceful direct address. It might be paraphrased, "I mean *you*." By highlighting the apostles, it stresses the degree to which Jesus' power has been extended: to such a degree that the apostles are exhausted. The statements that "the people who were coming and going were many" and that the apostles "did not even have time to eat" (cf. 3:20) do not tell why they need a little rest so much as they tell why the apostles need to go with Jesus to a deserted place (cf. 1:35, 45). The Galilean mission has caused the need for rest. The present traffic of people is causing the need for privacy if the rest is to be gotten. The huge amount of the traffic revives emphasis on Jesus' magnetism, shown now through the thronging of people to the apostles, whom he empowered, as well as to him. Presumably, teaching and healing and exorcising keep the apostles and Jesus from eating; but Mark does not say so. For the moment he lets the emphasis fall exclusively on the magnetism. Not having time to eat contrasts with the subsequent feeding of the five thousand. But the disciples will not eat food even then; instead, they will serve it and gather up the remaining fragments. So the emphasis on magnetism as shown in not being able to eat will continue throughout the story (cf. the linear character of the imperfect εὐκαίρουν, "they were having time [not even to eat]").

The repetition of phraseology from Jesus' command in the statement that he and the apostles go away "to a deserted place alone" provides backdrop for another, upcoming display of his magnetism. "In the boat" recalls the boat that they used earlier (4:1, 35-41; 5:1-2, 18, 21), prepares for the contrastive travel of the people "on foot," and sets the stage for the story of Jesus' walking on the sea (vv 45-52). The repetition of "many" to describe those who "saw them [the apostles and Jesus] going and recognized [them] and ran there together on foot from all the cities and arrived ahead of them" identifies the crowd with the "many" who were coming and going (cf. v 33 with v 31) and redoubles the emphasis on Jesus' power of attracting people (cf. vv 54-55). "From all the cities" exhibits the comprehensively wide range of that power. "Ran" shows its intensity as well as explaining how it is that the people arrive earlier than Jesus and the apostles. "Together" links with "from all the cities" to imply that as the "many" who saw the apostles and Jesus leave run along, more people join them. As a result, when Jesus comes out of the boat, he will see "a large crowd" (v 34). Such is his own and now also his apostles' magnetism despite the usual desertedness of the place.

6:34 *(Matt 14:14; Luke 9:11b; John 6:5a)* Ἐξελθών recalls Mark's use of the same verb for Jesus' "coming out" of the boat in 5:1-2 (see also 6:54) and therefore undermines the hypothesis that Mark has returned to a source which he stopped using in 5:43 and which originally referred to an exit from Jairus's house (so P. J. Achtemeier in *JBL* 89 [1970] 281; R. Pesch 1. 346-47). Moreover, it seems unlikely that either a historical Jesus or a pre-Marcan redactional one would have fed five thousand people on Jairus's front lawn. Mark now calls the many people whom Jesus sees waiting for him "a large crowd" to carry forward his emphasis on the greatness of Jesus' attractive power (cf. 5:21 with comments and notes on the combination πολὺν ὄχλον). As a narrator omniscient of Jesus' inner feelings, Mark uses this omniscience to put across a point of view sympathetic to Jesus and therefore contributive to an apology for the Crucifixion: Jesus is a man of compassion. His compassion on the crowd grows out of their being "like sheep not having a shepherd," not out of their hunger and lack of food (as in 8:2), and leads him to teach them. Thus, by teaching them he shepherds them; and his feeding them will come in response to the disciples' wanting privacy to eat their five loaves and two fish rather than in response to any dire physical need on the part of the crowd. As the activity of teaching connotes authority (1:21-22, 27), so the figure of a shepherd connotes authority (see Num 27:15-23, which puts forward Joshua, whose Hebrew name becomes Jesus in Greek, as leader of God's people in order that they "may not be like sheep not having a shepherd"; cf. also Mark 14:27; Matt 9:36; 1 Kgs 22:17; 2 Chr 18:16; Jer 31:10; Ezek 34:5, 8; Zech 10:2; 13:7; Jdt 11:19; *2 Apoc. Bar.* 77:16). The adverbial πολλά, "much" (not "many things" as a direct object), typifies Mark's style (see the notes on 1:45) and stresses Jesus' didactic authority by indicating that he holds the crowd under his sway till late in the day (see 4:2 with 4:35, as well as 6:35).

6:35-38 *(Matt 14:15-17; Luke 9:12-13; John 6:5b-9)* The anarthrousness of ὥρα, "hour," in both its occurrences brings out the muchness and lateness of the hour rather than its particularity. Since ὀψία, "late," means before or after sundown (see BAGD s.v. 2 and Mark 15:42 for late afternoon before sundown), to say that an hour is "much" (πολλῆς/-ή — contrast 11:11) probably means that it is mid-to-late afternoon (see also the following notes). Thus the Jews' main mealtime at the end of the afternoon is fast approaching, and the narrative will proceed from there to evening (v 47) and finally to the fourth watch of the night (v 48). Now begins a dialogue between Jesus and the disciples on the feeding of the people. Mark uses δέ, "but," much less than he uses καί, "and"; but here he twice intersperses δέ to stress Jesus' answers to the disciples. The doubling of the reference to mid-to-late afternoon, the doubling of the emphasis on this temporal reference with a repetition of ἤδη, "already," the intensification of this double emphasis with a forward placement of ἤδη in both of its occurrences and with an ellipsis of the verb in the second temporal reference, the description of the place as deserted, and the emphasis on this description through the forward placement of ἔρημος, "deserted," all give the disciples' following suggestion a large amount of reasonableness. The asyndeton with which the disciples introduce their suggestion at the start of v 36 puts the reasonableness on exhibit. This reasonableness will make the power of Jesus stand out in bold relief when he feeds the crowd in a way that defies reason. The suggestion itself, "Dismiss them," implies his authority over the crowd. "In order that they may go away into the surrounding hamlets and towns and buy for themselves something to eat" prepares for the contrastive reclining on green grass and being served food by the disciples right there. Jesus' answering command, "You give them [something] to eat," sounds unreasonable. Its unreasonableness will again make his power stand out in bold relief when he multiplies bread and fish enough and to spare for the disciples to carry out the command. The emphatic ὑμεῖς, "you," puts the disciples in their proper role of continuing to minister for Jesus (cf. vv 6b-13, 30) and contrasts with "for themselves": the disciples want the crowd to buy their own food, but Jesus tells the disciples to give the crowd the food that they — the disciples — have on hand and hope to eat in privacy if Jesus will only dismiss the crowd according to their suggestion (cf. v 31 with v 36).

The historical present tense of "they say" (v 37) underscores the disciples' subservience: far from reacting against Jesus' command by mocking it as unworkable or by underestimating his power (so their question is often misunderstood), they ingenuously ask whether he means for them to go away and buy two hundred denarii worth of bread and give it to the crowd to eat (contrast the tone of Num 11:13, 21-22; 2 Kgs 4:43). They assume that the food in their lunchbox is not enough to feed the crowd but that two hundred denarii worth of bread would be enough; and they stand ready to do Jesus' bidding even though it entails going away to the surrounding hamlets and towns, spending their own money there, buying bread as they suggested that the crowd do, and bringing it back to feed the crowd. So strong a hold does Jesus have on the disciples! The historical present tense of λέγει, "he says" (v 38), and the asyndeton that introduces "see" after "go" (both verbs in the emphatic present tense of the imperative — cf. the notes on 1:3) underscore the authority of his command to go see how many loaves of bread they have, i.e. how many they have on hand without going to buy more. Likewise, the historical present tense of λέγουσιν, "they say," reflects that authority by highlighting their obedience to the command. But it also stresses the smallness of the number of loaves, and additionally of the fish, to magnify the coming miracle of multiplication.

6:39-44 *(Matt 14:18-21; Luke 9:14-17; John 6:10-13)* The narrative of the actual multiplication starts with another emphasis on Jesus' authority: ἐπέταξεν αὐτοῖς means that Jesus ordered the disciples. "To cause all [the people] to recline" indicates that the disciples are to carry out his will on the crowd. "Group by group" implies the large size of the crowd; they have to be divided up. "The green grass" on which the disciples are to make them recline will provide a suitable cushion such as is used for reclining at formal meals, like the one about to be served with Jesus acting as host and his disciples as waiters. "All" indicates that despite the large size of the crowd, his coming miracle will fail to feed not a single one of them. Nobody stands outside the sphere of his power no matter how small the supply of food he has to work with. The carrying out of his order reemphasizes the large size of the crowd by repeating the reference to division into groups. This reemphasis plays up in advance the stupendousness of the miracle. Mark shifts from συμπόσια, which means groups of people eating together, to πρασιαί, which means garden plots, to portray the groups metaphorically as planted in rows, like row crops in a garden, so as to be served easily. The addition "by hundreds and by fifties" may reflect the division of Israel into groups of thousands, hundreds, fifties, and tens (Exod 18:21, 25; cf. Num 31:14; 1QS 2:21; 1QSa 1:14-15, 27-2:1; 1QM 4:1–5:16; CD 13:1; H. Braun, *Qumran* 1. 67-68), but minus the groups of thousands and tens, because when multiplied together the remaining numbers, fifty and one hundred, come to five thousand, the very number Jesus is about to feed. Moreover, subtracting the OT groups of thousands and tens makes κατὰ ἑκατὸν καὶ κατὰ πεντήκοντα refer most naturally, not to discrete groups of hundreds and fifties, but to one large rectangle filled with rows of people. Longways, each row has one hundred people; sideways, fifty. The abundance of alliteration with π and with the gutterals χ and κ and of assonance with the vowels α, ο, and ω puts greatest possible weight on the impressively large size of the crowd and therefore on the impressively large amount of power exhibited in the miracle: . . . πάντας συμπόσια συμπόσια ἐπὶ τῷ χλωρῷ χόρτῳ. καὶ ἀνέπεσαν πρασιαὶ πρασιαὶ κατὰ ἑκατὸν καὶ κατὰ πεντήκοντα.

The miracle itself starts with Jesus' taking the five loaves and the two fish. The meaning of εὐλόγησεν is disputable. The substitution of εὐχαριστήσας, "having given thanks," in the corresponding location at 8:6 and the parallel between thanksgiving and blessing in 8:6-7; 14:22-23 favor that εὐλόγησεν means praising God for the bread and fish, not calling down God's gracious power on the bread and fish. "Looking up to heaven" then implies that God is the object of praise, not the source of power. The asyndeton with which "looking up to heaven" is introduced stresses this gesture and the resultant implication that only he who from heaven was pronounced God's Son (1:11; cf. 9:7) could possibly have performed the miracle to follow. The prefixing of κατ- to -έκλασεν, hapax in the NT except for Luke's parallel, keeps the mention of bread-breaking from being understood as a mere formula that refers primarily to the start of a meal. Instead, the prefix emphasizes multiplication of the bread by describing its breaking as a breaking *down,* a snapping apart of the loaves into pieces. Jesus was giving the pieces to his disciples in order that they might set the pieces before the crowd. The present tense of the subjunctive in παρατιθῶσιν, "might set before," emphasizes the largeness of the task and therefore of the miracle (see S. E. Porter, *Verbal Aspect* 326, on the emphasis in a present subjunctive; also the notes on 1:3). Jesus divides up the two fish for all. Leaving the emphasis on "for all" are the chiasm of τοὺς δύο ἰχθύας ἐμέρισεν, "the two fish he divided," in relation to κατέκλασεν τοὺς ἄρτους, "he broke down the loaves," and the omission of giving the fish to the disciples that they might present the fish to the crowd. As a preliminary result of the multiplication, "all ate and were filled" — no exceptions, no half empty stomachs (cf. Deut 8:10). The addition of being filled to eating and the parataxis that gives equal weight to being filled (Mark could have written, "All ate *until* they were filled" — cf. 6:10; J. A. Kleist 138) stress the completeness of the miracle. As a final result of the multiplication, "they [the disciples — see 8:19] picked up fragments, twelve baskets' fulnesses, and [some] of the fish" (cf. Ruth 2:14; 2 Kgs 4:44; 2 Chr 31:10; Ath. *Deipn.* 1.13a; Cic. *Top.* 5.25; *b. Ber.* 52b). These leftovers provide the disciples with a basketful apiece. But for now Mark does not write anything about the disciples' eating the leftovers. Instead, he indicates the immediate departure of the disciples (v 45) and saves their eating the leftovers till 7:2 (see the comments and notes ad loc.). Here, then, all attention focuses on the superabundance produced by Jesus' power.

Apart from the disciples' bearing witness to this superabundance by picking up the leftovers, their role is kept in the shadows. They are only the indirect objects of Jesus' command to make everybody recline (v 39) and the indirect objects of his giving the bread in order that they might set the loaves before the crowd (v 41). Mark does not bother to write that the disciples actually make everybody recline or actually set the bread before the crowd (contrast 8:6). He does not bother to mention them even as the indirect objects and intermediaries in the distribution of the fish. The spotlight concentrates on Jesus and his miraculous actions. Since there is no indication that the crowd knows that a miracle has taken place (cf. 2 Kgs 4:42-44), Mark omits the standard statement of admiration by onlookers. Instead, his closing statement stresses the magnitude of the miracle by noting that those who have eaten are five thousand males. For emphasis he has saved this information till last. Ἄνδρες, "males," excludes women and children; and the form of the statement excludes them not only from the number of males but also from the eaters: "the ones having eaten the loaves were five thousand males" (without a following "apart from wives and children," as in Matt 14:21), not "five thousand males ate the loaves" (leaving open the possibility that wives and children ate, too). See also the comments on 8:1-9.

NOTES

Among many others, A.-M. Denis (in *SE IV/1* 171-79) thinks that the motif of bread unites the pericopes in 6:30–8:26. But bread is missing from 7:31-37; 8:10-12, 22-26 (see the further discussion and objections in Q. Quesnell, *Mind of Mark* 10, 13, 68-70). W. L. Lane (224) discusses whether to treat 6:30-44 as a single pericope or to divide the passage into two pericopes, 6:30-34 and 6:35-44, or 6:30-33 and 6:34-44, or 6:30-31 and 6:32-44. It is best to regard the passage as a single pericope because of the identity between those who come and go (vv 31-32), those who run along the shoreline and arrive at Jesus' destination ahead of him (v 33), and the five thousand whom Jesus feeds (vv 34-44; see the comments on vv 31-33). Furthermore, it seems wrong to divide the command to go (v 31) from the actual going (v 32); equally wrong to divide the arrival of the crowd (v 33) from Jesus' seeing them when he gets out of the boat (v 34); and again wrong (though less so) to divide his having compassion on them and teaching them (v 34) from his feeding them (vv 35-44).

The usual assumption that 6:30-44 and 8:1-9 are a doublet for a single feeding will probably lead to the conclusion that elements in 6:30-37 such as Jesus' teaching, the disciples' taking the initiative, and "deserted place" rather than "wilderness" come from Mark's redaction rather than from pre-Marcan tradition (cf. the argument of R. A. Martin in *SBL 1987 Seminar Papers* 322, 324-25 that only 8:1-9 exhibits translation Greek, though the greater popularity of the feeding of the five thousand — it is narrated more often than the feeding of the four thousand — may have led to more Graecizing, so that it does not necessarily follow that the feeding of the five thousand evolved from that of the four thousand; also S. E. Porter, *Verbal Aspect* 160-61; R. L. Mowery in *CRBR 1988* 235-37 on the unreliability of Martin's method). See the notes on 8:1-9 in favor of two feedings, however. Because of diction, a γάρ-clause in v 31b, and the positioning of subjects after their verbs in vv 30, 31b, 33a, most scholars say that vv 30-33 are heavily indebted to Mark's composition (see, e.g., H. Anderson 170-71). To say so, however, does not imply the absence of underlying tradition. A Galilean mission on the part of the Twelve would naturally have concluded with a regathering to Jesus (v 30). Earlier withdrawals, such as we found in 1:35, 45, might establish a traditional or historical pattern of which 6:31-32 is a part as easily as they might establish a textual basis for redactional fabrication in 6:31-32. And to say that all these passages are redactionally fabricated is to substitute hypothesis for argument so far as 6:31 is individually concerned. Besides, the passages attribute different purposes to the withdrawals: for prayer (1:35), for avoidance of city-crowds (1:45), for rest (6:31). These differences favor discrete traditions. In view of the fishing occupation of some of Jesus' disciples, the use of a boat (v 32) might be traditional and ultimately historical as easily as redactional.

In v 30 the apostles gather to Jesus. In v 32 he and they go away together. In v 34 he gets out of the boat. In v 35 they approach him. These are natural progressions in narrative. They do not give a good basis for positing different sources or for separating redaction from tradition. In particular, the narrative leaves the apostles' getting out of the boat to be inferred and focuses on Jesus' getting out of the boat. This focus prepares for the main burden of the statement, i.e. his compassion on seeing the crowd. Insofar as ἀπόστολοι (v 30) harks back to ἀποστέλλειν (v 7), "apostles" carries a functional meaning. But by the time Mark writes, the term has become titular, too. We might say that the function has justified the title (H. B. Swete 128).

In δεῦτε, "hither!" and the motif of rest E. Wendling (*Entstehung* 64) and W. Egger (*Frohbotschaft* 126-27) see evidence that v 31 draws on the dominical saying recorded in Matt 11:28(-29). But Matt 11:28(-29) looks like a Matthean composition that postdates Mark (R. H. Gundry, *Matthew* 218-19). Besides, it seems improbable that Mark would apply to a rest *from* the work of discipleship a dominical invitation to the rest consisting *in* discipleship. R. M. Fowler (*Loaves and Fishes* 77-78) thinks that just as in 3:20 the crowd were unable to eat, so also here in v 31 it is the ones coming and going that have no opportunity to eat. The interpretation is faulty at both ends. The crowd's inability to eat would not have led very well into the relatives' thinking that Jesus had gone berserk (3:21), and the comers' and goers' lack of opportunity to eat would not give good reason for Jesus and the apostles to depart for privacy and rest. If Mark's Jesus feeds the people because their large number and their coming and going keeps them from eating, as Fowler thinks, the feeding should take place before Jesus and the apostles seek privacy.

The difference between the Lord's giving food according to agricultural seasons and the apostles' and Jesus' not having opportunity to eat makes an allusion to Ps 103:27 LXX unlikely. The verb ἀναπαύσασθε, "rest," may allude to the cognate noun ἀναπαύσεως in Ps 22:2 LXX, since in the further part of the present passage Mark will imply that Jesus takes the role of a shepherd (v 34; cf. Ps 23:1), since the crowd will lie down on green grass (v 39; cf. Ps 23:2), since Jesus will feed them (vv 41-42; cf. Ps 23:1, 5), since the whole episode takes place beside the waters of the sea (vv 32-33, 45; cf. Ps 23:2), and since messianic expectation features the figure of shepherding (Jer 23:4; Ezek 34:23; *Pss. Sol.* 17:40; CD 13:9; *Midr. Ps.* 29 §1 [W. G. Braude 1. 380]; cf. D. C. Allison, Jr., in *IBS* 5 [1983] 134). But in Psalm 23 "rest" describes drinking water. Because of the crowd, moreover, Jesus will not succeed in giving the disciples rest. Mark will not compare Jesus to a shepherd outright, but the crowd to sheep without a shepherd. Even in an implied comparison of Jesus to a shepherd, he would be such only to the crowd, not to his disciples, who, far from resting, will work in serving food to the crowd and in gathering the leftovers. The disciples, not Jesus, will be the ones to make the crowd lie down on green grass. And the Sea of Galilee does not correspond very closely to the still waters beside which a shepherd leads his sheep. Jesus does not lead the crowd beside the Sea of Galilee anyway, nor is it said or implied that they drink from it (contrast Ps 23:3a). Therefore allusions to Psalm 23 are subject to doubt.

Similarly, Mark gives no indication that the disciples eat along with the crowd. On the contrary, the disciples will not eat till after a sea-crossing in 7:2 (again see the comments and notes ad loc.); and Jesus will say in 8:19-20 that he broke the loaves "for the five thousand" and (later) "for the four thousand." Therefore Mark is not portraying an anticipation of the Lord's Supper or of the messianic banquet, which would require that the disciples share in the food here and now (contrast Matt 14:20; R. H. Gundry, *Matthew* 294). The ἔρημος τόπος, "deserted place," differs from the ἐρημία, "wilderness," in 8:4 and has farms and towns in the surrounding region (v 36). Therefore we should not suppose that the typology of God's people gathered in the wilderness as in olden times is hovering in the background (against U. W. Mauser, *Christ in the Wilderness* 104-5). The combination ἔρημος τόπος occurs in the LXX only at Jer 13:24 (Cod. A); 40(33):12 (except for Cod. A); Dan 4:25, and nowhere at all for the wilderness of the Exodus.

The putting of πολλοί after the first two verbs in v 33 seems to mark a transition: the ones who saw the apostles and Jesus going and recognized them are "many," as in v 31; but the ones who in the next part of v 33 "were running together from *all* the cities" include others as well. In v 33, is "many" the subject of "saw" as well as of "recognized," or only of "recognized"? If only of "recognized," εἶδον would be a characteristically Marcan indefinite third person plural verb: "people saw" (V. Taylor 33). But then "many" would seem to imply that some of those who saw failed to recognize. Such an implication would run counter to Mark's emphasis on magnetism. Hence, "many" probably describes the people who saw as well as those who recognized, just as in v 31 "many" described the people who were coming as well as those who were going.

Luke 9:10-11 puts the feeding of the five thousand at Bethsaida, whereas in Mark no move toward Bethsaida is made till after the feeding (v 45). Even then, a storm will foil the move (v 53); and arrival in Bethsaida will not occur till after the feeding of the four thousand and a number of other events (8:22). But "a city called Bethsaida" in Luke can hardly represent an alternative traditional or historical site of the feeding of the five thousand, for Bethsaida is not "a deserted place" from which Jesus might "dismiss the crowd in order that going into the surrounding towns and hamlets they might get lodging and find provisions of food" (Luke 9:12). Omission of the feeding of the four thousand and repositioning of the material between Mark 8:1-9 and Mark 8:22 have apparently led Luke to bring together the feeding of the five thousand and Bethsaida. John 6:1-21 follows suit, but without mentioning Bethsaida.

Since Mark does not say that the apostles and Jesus sail across the sea or go to the other side (contrast 4:35; 5:1, 21; 6:45, 53; 8:13), we should presume that they sail from one point to another on the same side — the western, in view of the just-finished Galilean mission. Thus, crossing the Jordan River so as to arrive at Bethsaida on the eastern side (so Luke 9:10; John 6:1) does not enter Mark's picture and therefore poses no roadblock against the crowd's arriving ahead of the apostles and Jesus. By putting the feeding in Bethsaida, Luke and John force themselves to reverse the order of arrival (Luke 9:11; John 6:2-5). This reversal counts against supposing that there was another Bethsaida, on the west side of the lake (for the eastern one, see Josephus *J.W.* 2.9.1 §168; 3.10.7 §515; Plin. *HN* 5.15).

We might ask how the crowd know Jesus' goal so as to reach it ahead of him and the apostles. But if he and the apostles were sailing off shore, more or less parallel with it and within view, the crowd do not know Jesus' goal. Their running together "there," i.e. "to the deserted place," simply means that they are already there when he decides to put in at that spot, not that they know ahead of time his decision to put in there.

For another Marcan use of προέρχομαι, "come beforehand" (v 33), see 14:35. Both here and there, part of the textual tradition has a form of the more common προσέρχομαι, "come to" (see B. M. Metzger, *Textual Commentary* ad loc., for discussion). Since the people who go by foot arrive earlier than Jesus and the apostles, it is more likely that Jesus and the apostles have to sail the long way around some land that juts into the sea while the people take a straight route across the land to a destination on the same side of the sea than that the people have to run the long way around a curving shoreline while Jesus and the apostles sail straight across the water.

The juxtaposing of teaching and feeding makes the feeding symbolize the teaching (so E. Best, *Gospel as Story* 49, 63) no more than the juxtaposing of teaching and exorcism in 1:21-28 made the exorcism symbolize the teaching. Likewise, the juxtaposing of teaching and feeding deemphasizes the miracle of feeding no more than the juxtaposing of teaching and exorcism in 1:21-28 deemphasized the miracle of exorcism. The exercise of authority in teaching and the exercise of power in miracle and exorcism supplement each other, but the one is neither symbolized nor deemphasized by the other. Concerning Mark's pleonastic use of ἤρξατο, "he began," see the notes on 1:45.

Dion. Hal. *Ant. Rom.* 2.54.4 uses πολλή, "much," with ὥρα, "hour," for a point of time either on the way toward nightfall or at nightfall — the context does not allow us to say for sure. But Polyb. 5.8.3-8 uses the expression for a point of time that leaves enough light for setting up camp and looting the houses and towns in the vicinity — hence, mid-to-late afternoon. Similarly, the use in Josephus *Ant.* 8.4.4-5 §§118-22 requires that enough daytime be left for a royal address of some length and for the offering of thousands of sacrifices.

S. Masuda (in *NTS* 28 [1982] 192-93) notes occurrences of "hour" in Mark's narrative of Jesus' last week in Jerusalem (11:11; 13:11, 32; 14:35, 37, 41; 15:25, 33, 34) and infers that the use of "hour" in v 35 alludes to the Eucharist and the Passion. But this is to read Mark backwards. None of the later passages describes the hour as "much." A number of them have nothing to do with the hour of Jesus' Passion (11:11; 13:11, 32; 14:35); and Mark sets the Lord's Supper in the "evening" (14:17), not at a certain "hour." In fact, the contrast between "when [the] hour had already become much" — i.e. mid-to-late afternoon — and "when it had become evening" (14:17) militates against an allusion to the Lord's Supper. It is the temporal note concerning the disciples' rowing against a contrary wind (6:47), not the temporal note concerning the feeding of the five thousand, which corresponds to the temporal note concerning the Lord's Supper.

Here, the disciples need to eat (v 31b); so they take the initiative (vv 35-36). In 8:1-3, the crowd will need to eat; so Jesus will take the initiative. Most loaves are disk-shaped, seven inches or more in diameter and about one-half inch thick (A. van Selms in *ISBE* [2nd ed.] 1. 542). The disciples figure that 200 denarii would buy enough loaves for the crowd. The disciples' treasury may have that much money, or they may have in mind to collect money from the crowd to accomplish the errand. According to *m. Pe'a* 8:7, 200 denarii worth of bread would amount to 2400 loaves, i.e. approximately half a loaf or a half-day's ration for each of 5000 men — enough in view of the farms and towns nearby on the west side of the lake (cf. 1 Sam 2:36; Jer 37:21; Cic. *Verr.* 3.81; Ath. *Deipn.* 3.20), but not enough for a crowd of 5000 on the more desolate east side of the lake, where they would have to travel farther to find food (John 6:7 with John 6:1, 16-17, 22-25; cf. J. Jeremias, *Jerusalem* 123; L. Schottroff and W. Stegemann, *Jesus von Nazareth* 58; A. Ben-David, *Talmudische Ökonomie* 1. 300-305).

The evidence that 200 denarii would buy a half day's ration for each of 5000 men shows that the question in v 37b is not pessimistic — unless the disciples do not have 200 denarii; but their question presupposes possession of that amount of money, and Jesus does not excoriate them for lack of faith. "Deserted place" does not disagree with the presence of hamlets and towns in the surrounding region, for to reach the hamlets and towns the crowd or the disciples would have to "go away" from the deserted place (vv 36-37). The shift from the deliberative subjunctive ἀγοράσωμεν, "should we buy?" to the future indicative δώσομεν, "shall we give?" means that if the disciples *were* to buy bread they would *indeed* be in a position to give the crowd something to eat (BDF §369[3]; S. E. Porter, *Verbal Aspect* 415-16).

According to J. Carmignac (in *ASTI* 7 [1968-69] 71), underlying v 38 is a wordplay between להם, "to them," לחם, "bread," לכם, "to you" (= Mark's "do you have"), and לכו, "go." R. M. Fowler (*Loaves and Fishes* 114-19) discovers in the disciples' possession of 200 denarii and five loaves and two fish a disobedience against Jesus' instructions in vv 8-9. But those instructions pertained to the mission on which he sent them, and implied that when traveling with him they did take money and food. In 8:14-21 he will rebuke them, not for bringing a loaf, but for thinking that bringing only one is insufficient. The mention of two fish militates against our seeing in this passage either a translation of the Lord's Supper into a miracle story or a transfer to Jesus of Elisha's miracle of multiplying bread (2 Kgs 4:42-44; cf. 1 Kgs 17:7-16) or even an allusion to one or both of those events (and thus is lost a link which is sometimes used to support a relation with the Elisha-like raising of Jairus's daughter in a hypothetical pre-Marcan collection of miracle stories). That the bread is slightly more prominent than the fish does not imply that Mark or a pre-Marcan tradition has deemphasized the fish in favor of an allusion to eucharistic bread. It is due merely to the fact that bread is a staple, fish a condiment (cf. *b. Ber.* 44a). On the other hand, remention of the fish in the gathering of leftovers (v 42) damages the eucharistic interpretation. The use of fish as a condiment on bread motivates a late but pre-Marcan addition of fish to the story (so U. H. J. Körtner in *ZNW* 75 [1984] 32) no more than this use favors the originality of fish in the story. In the absence of clearly eucharistic or eschatological features, the lack of wine tends away from interpreting the event either as an anticipation of the Lord's Supper or as an anticipation of the messianic banquet (contrast the addition of drinking Jesus' blood in John 6:52-59). The suggestion of S. Masuda (in *NTS* 28 [1982] 195) that the proper meaning of συμπόσια, "drinking party," alludes to the Lord's Supper suffers from the dryness of the present meal. Mark gives no hint of an allusion to the manna in the wilderness (contrast John 6:30-51), and it is stretching a point to appeal to Wis 19:11-12 for a parallel between the fish in the feeding of the five thousand and the quails that "came up from the sea" in the wilderness (cf. *2 Apoc. Bar.* 29:3-8).

The shift from ἀνακλῖναι (v 39) to ἀνέπεσαν (v 40) for reclining is probably due to the shift from a causative meaning, according to which Jesus orders the disciples to make all the people recline, to a simple statement that the people do recline. Apparently Mark prefers the shift to a different verb over a finely tuned shift from the causative active voice of ἀνακλίνω to the deponent passive voice of the same verb (to which, however, a good part of the textual tradition conforms ἀνακλῖναι through failure to note its causative force — see B. M. Metzger, *Textual Commentary* ad loc.; R. H. Gundry, *Matthew* 293-94). Green grass implies springtime (cf. the reference to Passover in John 6:4), though grass may stay green in sheltered and well watered spots on into early summer. We should not overinterpret the green grass as symbolic of the Passover or of apocalyptic fertility. Mark gives us no reason to think of more than a suitable cushion on which to recline. Likewise, in connection with πρασιαί, we should not think of plots in a garden of flowers and imagine that brightly colored clothes called forth the image (so, e.g., B. W. Bacon, *Gospel of Mark* 300). To the contrary, see MM s.v. πρασιά and the references in LSJ s.v. πρασιά for plots in a garden of vegetables or fruit (cf. Str-B 2. 13).

A. G. Hebert (in *SE II/1* 70) objects to a rectangle of 100 × 50 with the argument that in v 40 κατά is distributive, indicating larger groups of 100 each and smaller groups of 50 each (just the sizes common to early local churches, he adds; cf. H. Montefiore in *NTS* 8 [1961-62] 137). But a rectangular understanding does not neglect the distributive use of κατά: longways, each row makes a group of 100; sideways, each row makes a group of 50. And the rectangular understanding has the advantage of agreement with the figure of rows in a garden, πρασιαί corresponding to שורות in the Talmud: "the disciples were arranged in rows like [the vines in] the vineyard" (*y. Ber.* 4 §1 end, cited by I. Abrahams [*Studies* 2. 210-11], who does not think the rectangular understanding necessary, however; see fuller citations in Str-B 2. 13).

Those who interpret 6:30-44 eucharistically set great store by the collocation of λαμβάνω, "take," εὐλογέω, "bless," κλάω, "break," and δίδωμι, "give," in v 41 and 14:22 (also in 8:6 except for εὐχαριστέω, "give thanks," instead of εὐλογέω [but cf. 8:7; 14:23]). The actions expressed by these verbs are the normal actions of the host at a meal, however (see G. H. Boobyer in *JTS* ns 3 [1952] 161-71, esp. 162-63); and if Mark or a pre-Marcan redactor were concerned to call attention to a parallel between the passages, we might expect that person not to include "looking up into heaven" in v 41 despite its absence from 14:22, not to use a finite form of εὐλογέω in v 41 but a participial form as in 14:22, not to switch from εὐλογέω in v 41 to εὐχαριστέω in 8:6 and back to εὐλογέω in 14:22, not to prefix κατά to κλάω in v 41 but not in 14:22 or 8:6, and not to express the direct object of the breaking in v 41 but not in 14:22. (The occurrence of "taking" at the beginning of a sentence in v 41, but in the middle of one at 14:22, is argumentatively insignificant; for the mid-position will grow out of a circumstance irrelevant to the comparison, viz., that Jesus will institute the Lord's Supper during the eating of another meal.)

B. M. F. van Iersel (in *NovT* 7 [1964] 167-69) argues that just because the collocated verbs express a host's normal actions, the collocation would be unnecessary apart from a eucharistic allusion. But a eucharistic allusion does not provide the only possible reason for collocation. The portrayal of Jesus as host at a miraculous meal rather than at a eucharistic one offers just as good a reason. Not that a miraculous meal could not represent a eucharistic one; but the miraculous element suffices, a eucharistic element being unneeded to explain the collocation. Since no miracle of multiplication will occur at the institution of the Lord's Supper, the present such miracle does not favor a eucharistic allusion. Van Iersel's argument that the non-eucharistic texts John 11:41; Rom 14:6; 1 Cor 10:30; 1 Tim 4:3-4 do not collocate the actions to the same extent that Mark 6:41 and 14:22 do overlooks that those extra-Marcan texts are not narratives of a host's actions. When we come across non-eucharistic narratives in Acts 27:35; Xen. *An.* 7.3.22, collocations of similar extent do confront us. Van Iersel tries to avoid this damaging evidence by noting the absence of giving in Acts 27:35 (contrast Mark 6:41; 14:22; cf. the absence of blessing in Xen. *An.* 7.3.22). We might equally well note the absence of looking up to heaven in Mark 14:22 (contrast 6:41). Furthermore, van Iersel fails to appreciate the reason for the absence of giving in Acts 27:35, i.e. Paul's acting as an encouraging example rather than as a host, and the fundamental difference between giving to the disciples in order that they may serve others in v 41 and giving to the disciples in order that they may eat in 14:22. Though further reflection has led van Iersel (*Reading Mark* 110) to retract his eucharistic interpretation, J.-M. van Cangh (*La multiplication* 82-83, 100 and in *L'Évangile selon Marc* 330) tries to salvage the argument from collocation by attributing the collocation in Acts 27:35 to recollection of the Lord's Supper (Luke 22:19). But his admission that Acts 27:35 does not describe a eucharistic celebration evacuates this attribution of argumentative value. On the other hand, B. Reicke (in *TZ* 4 [1948] 401-10; cf. Q. Quesnell, *Mind of Mark* 203-4) defends a eucharistic connotation in Acts 27:35 by noting contextual references to salvation, no loss of life, not even the perishing of one hair from the head, the number of diners, and the disposal of uneaten grain (Acts 27:22, 34, 37-38). But apart from the questionability of these parallels with the present feeding (e.g., "grain" differs from "loaves"), none of them has a parallel in accounts of the institution of the Lord's Supper. Against the eucharistic interpretation see also J. Roloff, *Kerygma* 237-41; R. M. Fowler, *Loaves and Fishes* 137-47.

Looking up to heaven in prayer (v 41) is seldom mentioned in Jewish sources (Str-B 2. 246-47). But Jesus' portrayal of a toll collector as not wanting to lift his eyes to heaven in prayer (Luke 18:13) implies that at least Jesus considers such a gesture normal; and according to John 11:41-42, he himself lifts his eyes upward in prayer (see also Josephus *Ant.* 11.5.6 §162; *1 Enoch* 13:5; *b. Yebam.* 105b; *Gen. Rab.* 33.3 on Gen 8:1; and the LXX of Deut 4:19 and esp. of Job 22:26 but not of Gen 15:5; 2 Macc 7:28, where looking up into heaven has to do only with the heavenly bodies). No prayer will accompany the gesture in Mark 7:34, which will therefore portray Jesus as drawing on divine power if not asking for it. Since blessing means praising God (see the foregoing comments), the attachment of αὐτά, "them [fish]," to εὐλογήσας in 8:7 will probably mean praising God for the fish rather than infusing the fish with divine power (similarly at Luke 9:16 in comparison with Luke 22:17, 19; also 1 Cor 10:16, where for several reasons "the cup of blessing which we bless" means the cup for which we give thanks: (1) the associated texts of 1 Cor 10:30; 11:24 speak of giving thanks; (2) *we* do not infuse the cup with power; (3) Samuel can bless a sacrifice in 1 Sam 9:13 only because God's power flows through him as a prophet; and (4) it is only when *God* blesses bread that it becomes abundant [Exod 23:25; against R. H. Gundry, *Matthew* 528]). Normally, an accusative following εὐλογέω indicates the object of blessing, not the subject for which blessing is offered (therefore the weakly supported omission of αὐτά [v.l. ταῦτα] in 8:7). Verse 41 says that Jesus divides up the two fish for all, but not that he sets them before the crowd (contrast John 6:11, where he himself distributes the loaves as well as the fish). Presumably, the division of the fish corresponds to the breaking of the loaves; and Mark means his audience to infer that the disciples set the fish before the crowd just as they set the bread before the crowd. "Fragments" means "uneaten broken pieces," not "fallen crumbs" (C. S. Mann 303). As an Oriental host, Jesus provides more than necessary (E. F. F. Bishop, *Jesus of Palestine* 142). Did the disciples not need to pass out the leftover fragments, or did the five thousand leave them on the ground? See D. Daube (*NTRJ* 37), who also suggests that people discarded pieces of bread which they had used for spoons and forks. But here the bread *is* the food, fish only the condiment. One does not use bread to eat bread. 8:19-20 undermines the view of Bishop (loc. cit.) that "fragments, twelve baskets' fullnesses" (so a literal translation) means enough pieces to fill twelve baskets rather than twelve baskets filled with pieces.

Because of its supposed awkwardness, καὶ ἀπὸ τῶν ἰχθύων, "and [some] of the fish" (v 43), is widely regarded as an addition to the original story. But the phrase is good Hellenistic Greek (E. C. Maloney, *Semitic Interference* 134-37); and the lack of parallelism with κλάσματα, "fragments" (accusative of direct object), is due to the fact that the fish were not subject to the action of the cognate verb κατέκλασεν, "he broke down," in v 41. The grammatical constructions in vv 38, 41 give no reason to suspect addition of fish to the story at those points. No ground is left for positing a later addition, then (cf. B. D. Chilton in *JTS* ns 34 [1983] 594-95 against the view of R. M. Fowler, *Loaves and Fishes* 53-54, that Mark invents and inserts the fish throughout), or for thinking that the fish are deemphasized in favor of a eucharistic allusion in the leftover fragments of bread. The bread of the Lord's Supper is not notable for being left over at all, let alone in abundance.

W. H. Kelber (*Kingdom* 56-57; *Mark's Story* 36) thinks that Mark's Jesus shows the disciples how to feed the Jewish Christian church once he has gone, i.e. in the absence of him as the great shepherd (cf. 14:27). But the variety of ways in which Mark emphasizes the large size of the crowd (see esp. vv 34, 39-40, 42-44) favors that the intermediary role of the disciples contributes to that emphasis — the crowd is so large that Jesus needs helpers — rather than symbolizing their making up for his absence at a later date. Mark's closing the pericope with a notation of the immense number of males fed shows that he does not omit the standard statement of admiration by onlookers to deemphasize the miraculous element in favor of fulfilment of manna-typology, allusion to the Lord's Supper, or anticipation of the messianic banquet (against A. Schweitzer [*Quest* 376-80], who suggests that originally there was no reference to eating to the full, but only to the eating of fragments having an eschatological sacramental significance). Only by keeping in mind the hand-to-mouth existence of most people in first century Palestine can we appreciate the stupendousness of feeding so many to the full, with an excess (cf. Ezek 34:23; John 10:1-30). This miracle far exceeds that of Elisha, who fed one hundred men with twenty loaves — one loaf per five men (2 Kgs 4:42-44, which also mentions leftovers). Five loaves for five thousand males comes to one loaf per one thousand males. The parallel drawn by D. Daube [*Appeasement* 32-33] between eating, satisfaction, and leftovers in vv 42-43 and Ruth 2:14 as eschatologically and messianically interpreted in *b. Šabb.* 113 suffers from Mark's numerical emphasis, which has no counterpart in those passages, not to detail the other rabbinic interpretations which compete with the one selected by Daube for comparison). See the notes on 8:8 concerning the different Greek words for "baskets" there and here.

J. M. Bassler (in *JR* 66 [1986] 162) admits that only ideal, informed readers would catch parallels with the later institution of the Lord's Supper, but affirms that the implied readers, though they do not understand the significance of the bread any more than the disciples do in v 52, will understand by recollection when they read about the institution in 14:22-25. But as confirmed in 8:13-21, the failure to understand in 6:52 will consist in failure to see a miracle in the feedings here and in 8:1-9, not in failure to remember the feedings as such, much less in failure to see a symbolic meaning in them. And we have repeatedly discovered reasons to reject a eucharistic interpretation of 6:30-44.

J. W. Bowman (155) thinks that the feeding of the five thousand contrasts with Herod's banquet (v 21). But there, no emphasis whatever fell on eating. The banquet was only the framework of a story. Here, feeding is of the essence. R. M. Fowler (*Loaves and Fishes* 85-86) supports a contrast with Herod's banquet by drawing a parallel between the triplet of Herod's guests (courtiers, military officers, and leading provincials — v 21) and the triplet of Jesus' guests (groups, garden plots [or rows], and 100 × 50 — vv 39-40). But the parallel breaks down at a crucial point: v 21 distinguishes three classes of guests; vv 39-40 use three synonymous ways of describing the arrangement of one class of guests ("males" — v 44). The exclusion of women and children reflects the numbering only of males (for soldiery) in Israel, a numbering that we have seen to underlie the arrangement by hundreds and fifties (cf. Exod 18:21, 25 with Numbers 1–3, 26). The notion of an eschatological army does not enter the picture, however. Jesus had the five thousand males reclined to eat, not mustered to fight. Thus the emphasis stays on the magnitude of the miracle (cf. H. Montefiore [in *NTS* 8 (1961-62) 135-41], who correctly sees no militarism in Mark but at the underlying historical level detects a messianic rebellion in the making and prevented by Jesus [cf. John 6:15]).

Inclusion of admiration for Jesus' stilling a storm (4:41), of fright at his sea-walking (6:49-50), and of amazement at the abatement of wind when he got in a boat (6:51) favors that here Mark does not omit such a statement of admiration to depress the miraculous element. Jesus does not perform this miracle in a way that would enable the five thousand to observe it. He neither gestures nor speaks to multiply the loaves and fish (contrast the usualness of miracle-effecting gestures and words). Not even the small number of loaves and fish is apparent to the five thousand. If then they do not know that a miracle has occurred, they can hardly express admiration. Then also they cannot have received an epiphany (against H. Baarlink, *Anfängliches Evangelium* 133), and their failure to express admiration hardly symbolizes failure to understand divine revelation (as thought by E. Schweizer 140). It is the disciples who know the small number of loaves and fish and therefore should have detected a miracle despite the absence of a multiplying gesture or word. Their failure to do so will come in both as an explanation, for explanation, and for criticism (v 52; 8:13-21). Meanwhile, if the miracle constitutes an epiphany to the disciples, the epiphany has failed.

It is unhelpful to distinguish between miracles of healing that people ask for and unrequested nature-miracles the means of which are unclear and the proof of which is emphasized. 3:1-6 presented a miracle of healing that nobody asked for. 4:35-41 presented a nature-miracle that the disciples desperately roused Jesus to perform. Apart from speaking a word of healing or instruction, the means of some healing miracles remain unclear (2:1-11; 3:1-6; 10:46-52). And stories of healing miracles regularly include proof (1:29-31, 39-44; 2:1-11; 3:1-6; 5:21-43; 7:31-37; 8:22-26; 10:46-52).

Parallels sometimes cited do not pass inspection on a closer look. Neither Philostr. *VA* 4.25 nor Or. *Cels.* 1.68 has to do with real food. Luc. *Philops.* 35 does not present a miracle of multiplying a small amount of food. Nor does *PGM* I. 103-15, in which it is a demon that provides out of thin air not only an abundance of food but also banqueting rooms and waiters in the person of other demons. See also the notes on 8:1-4.

JESUS' AMAZING FEAT OF WALKING ON THE SEA

6:45-52 (Matt 14:22-23; John 6:16-21; cf. Mark 4:35-41; Matt 8:23-27; Luke 8:22-25)

The story of Jesus' walking on the sea starts with the departure of the disciples, the dismissal of the crowd, and Jesus' going away to pray (vv 45-46). The main part of the story consists of his appearance to the disciples at sea (vv 47-50). This part subdivides into the distance between the boat, which the disciples are rowing, and Jesus, who is on land (v 47), his coming to the disciples as they are rowing against a contrary wind (v 48), their terror (vv 49-50a), and his reassuring self-identification (v 50b). Finally, Mark notes Jesus' getting into the boat, the dying down of the wind, and the amazement of the disciples (vv 51-52).

6:45-46 *(Matt 14:22-23a; John 6:16-17a)* The strong verb ἠνάγκασεν, "compelled," emphasizes the separation of the disciples from Jesus by implying that they get into a boat and go ahead of him against their will. "Immediately," the doubling of topographical references ("to the other side, to Bethsaida"), and the distance indicated by those references add to this emphasis. The separation gains yet further emphasis from "he himself" (αὐτός) as distinct from the disciples: "while he himself dismisses the crowd" (cf. v 36; 8:3, 9). This multiple emphasis on separation will enhance the reunion to follow. The historical present tense of "dismisses" suits the use of ἕως in the sense "while." Jesus' "taking leave" of the crowd complements his sending them away: he, too, will leave. His going away to the mountain to pray (cf. 1:35; 3:13; 9:2) sets the stage for the next part of the story: from his vantage point on the mountain he will see the disciples at sea; and his praying puts him in contact with God, as whose Son he will reveal himself to his disciples by walking on the sea (cf. Luke 3:21; 9:28; perhaps also Deut 33:2; Judg 5:4-5; Hab 3:3). As in 1:35, Jesus' praying may recommend him as a godly person, not a criminal worthy of crucifixion; but there is no indication that he prays for power to work miracles. According to Mark, that power already resides in Jesus.

6:47-50 *(Matt 14:23b-31; John 6:17b-20)* The reference to evening indicates passage of time since the feeding of the five thousand in mid-to-late-afternoon (see v 35 with comments and notes). Several contrasts illuminate the meaning of vv 47-48: (1) The contrast between evening, by which time the boat is already in the middle of the sea, and the fourth watch of the night, which is the last, stresses the force of the contrary wind by indicating that the disciples have rowed nearly all night without making much headway (and even with the result of being blown backward, as it will apparently turn out). Failure, not danger, is in view (contrast 4:35-41). Mark's choice of βασανιζομένους (literally, "being tormented" or "tormenting themselves [i.e. 'straining']") to describe the disciples' ordeal adds to this emphasis. But the greater the force of the wind, the clearer the implication of Jesus' divine sonship when the wind dies down. (2) The boat contrasts with Jesus, referred to emphatically with αὐτὸς μόνος, "he himself alone." (3) "In the middle of the sea" and "on the land" contrast with each other.

These second and third contrasts accentuate the plight of the disciples: they and Jesus are in different places, and without him they are helpless.

Mark probably intends Jesus' seeing the disciples at sea to imply supernatural vision (as in Philostr. *VA* 5.30; 8.26). Mention of a mountain has provided a natural vantage point; but the fourth watch of the night (c. 3:00 A.M.–6:00 A.M.) and the mistaking of Jesus for a ghost imply darkness. "He comes to them walking on the sea" certainly carries an emphasis on his supernatural power — supernatural to the point of divine, since only a divine being can walk on water (Job 9:8; 38:16; Ps 77:20[19]; Sir 24:5-6 [where "in (ἐν) the earth" shows that "in (ἐν) the waves of the sea" means among but on top of the waves]; *Odes Sol.* 39:10; cf. 2 Macc 5:21 and R. Kratz, *Rettungswunder* 109-13; R. Reitzenstein, *Hellenistische Wundererzählungen* 125, for passages in extra-biblical Greek and Latin literature). The historical present tense of ἔρχεται, "comes," sharpens the point; and the statement that "he was wanting to pass by them" sharpens it even further, for "passing by" (παρέρχομαι) indicates a parade of divinity such as characterized OT theophanies (see Exod 33:19, 22; 34:5-6; 2 Kgdms 23:3-4 LXX; 1 Kgs 19:11; Job 9:8, 11, esp. in the LXX; Amos 7:8; 8:2; Dan 12:1 LXX; Gen 32:32 LXX [if τὸ εἶδος, "the form, appearance," is subject rather than object]; E. Lohmeyer, *Urchristliche Mystik* 57-79). The otherwise unnecessary ἤθελεν, "he was wanting," stresses Jesus' intention of parading as a divine being and prepares for the disciples' mistaking him for a ghost — a misidentification that his desire will have to overcome. The disciples' seeing him carries forward the theme of theophany (and perhaps reverses Job's complaint that if God were to pass by him he would not see God — Job 9:11). Underscoring Jesus' ability to do what only a divine being can do are an adversative δέ, "but," another reference to Jesus' walking on the sea, the placement of ἐπὶ τῆς θαλάσσης, "on the sea," before περιπατοῦντα, "walking" (v 49; contrast v 48), the disciples' thinking that Jesus is a ghost, the placement of φάντασμα, "ghost," before ἐστιν, "is," and the disciples' screaming. Mark's taking the role of an omniscient narrator to expose their inner thoughts shows what stress he puts on the point. The clause, "for all saw him and were terrified" (ἐταράχθησαν), leaves no room for doubt: the theophany is so overpowering that everyone in the boat falls under its sway. Thus "the ones seeing" (v 49) turns out to be descriptive of "all" (v 50) rather than restrictive to some. The interruptiveness and redundancy of the "for"-clause lend it emphasis; and the forward positions of πάντες, "all," and αὐτόν, "him," stress that nobody missed seeing him and that it was truly he whom they saw.

As in the theophanies of Exodus 33–34 and 1 Kings 19, this theophany includes divine speech. Several features in the introduction to Jesus' divine speech lay great stress on it: (1) the adversative δέ, "but"; (2) the immediacy of the speaking; (3) the unusualness of μετ' αὐτῶν, "with them," with a verb of speaking (only here in Mark); (4) the doubling of the finite verbal reference to the speaking (again only here in Mark): "but immediately he spoke with them, and he says to them" (cf. M. Reiser, *Syntax und Stil* 132-33); and (5) the switch from the aorist ἐλάλησεν, "he spoke," to the historical present tense of λέγει, "he says." Μετ' αὐτῶν, "with them," may simply avoid a duplication of αὐτοῖς, "to them"; but in view of Mark's using the latter elsewhere when he needs an indirect object with λαλέω and in view of the assuring tone of Jesus' following words, Mark may wish to anticipate and emphasize that tone by his choice of a preposition that indicates fellowship. The commands, "Cheer up!" and "Stop being afraid," frame Jesus' corrective self-identification, "It is I." This self-identification literally means "I am" (ἐγώ εἰμι). Though it usually means nothing more than a colloquial "it's me," the theophanic features of the story and the divine self-identification in the theophany at Mount Sinai, "And Yahweh passed by before him [Moses] and proclaimed, 'Yahweh, Yahweh, a God merciful and gracious . . .'" (Exod 34:6), suggest a divine "I am" associated in the tradition with the title Yahweh (cf. Exod 3:14; John 8:58; also Deut 32:39; Isa 41:2-14; 43:1-13; 44:1-5; 46:4; 48:12; 51:9-16; P. B. Harner, "*I Am*" 34-35; W. Berg, *Rezeption* 157-262; H. Zimmermann in *BZ* nf 4 [1960] 54-69, 266-76) and giving a delayed answer to the disciples' question on another stormy night at sea: "Who then is this?" (4:41). It is another question whether Mark's original readers understood, or were expected to understand, this association. The asyndeton which introduces both "I am" and "Don't be afraid" emphasizes Jesus' cheerful self-identification and prohibition. Likewise emphatic is the present tense in μὴ φοβεῖσθε, "Don't be afraid" (see the comments on 5:36).

6:51-52 *(Matt 14:32-33; John 6:21)* Since Jesus has already demonstrated his power over the sea by walking on it and since the wind is posing only difficulty, not danger (see v 48), there is no need for him to rebuke the wind or silence the sea (contrast 4:39). Now his mere presence is enough: the wind dies down when he goes up to his disciples into the boat. The distance indicated in v 47 ("the boat was in the middle of the sea, and he alone on the land") has closed up. The disciples' amazement serves to emphasize his divine presence, now seen in the abatement of the wind (cf. 4:39; Ps 107:28-29). The emphasis on this new evidence of his divine presence gets much reinforcement from Mark's writing that the disciples are amazed λίαν, "very," and ἐκ περισσοῦ, "exceedingly," and that they bottle up their amazement ἐν ἑαυτοῖς, "in themselves," so overawed are they (cf. 2:8; 4:17; 5:30; and possibly 9:50 for the private, inner meaning of the reflexive pronoun with ἐν). The forward positions of these expressions — they all appear before the verb (see the Greek text) — lends them great weight. To take the abatement of the wind as natural rather than supernatural does justice neither to the amazement nor to the parallelism: just as the water provided firm footing for Jesus' walking part way across the sea, so the wind dies down to provide him easy boating the rest of the way (cf. Philostr. *VA* 4.13, 15; 7.10, 41; 8.15; Iambl. *VP* 135).

Mark goes on to state that the disciples "did not understand on the basis of the loaves, but their heart was hardened." The two clauses of the statement are synonymous: hardheartedness equals failure to understand because of the loaves; i.e. the loaves should have caused understanding (so according to the v.l. ἀλλ᾽ ἦν, "but . . . was," supported by ℵ B L Δ Θ 33 892 1241 1424 *al* sy^hmg co). The meaning of each clause is that non-recognition of a miracle in the feeding of the five thousand (see the comments and notes on vv 41-44) has led to the disciples' amazement at the abating of the wind (cf. 3:5 and esp. 8:14-21 with comments; also 4:12; 7:14 and for the causal meaning of ἐπί + the dative, sometimes with a temporal connotation, too, 1:22; 3:5; 9:37, 39; 10:22, 24; 11:18; 12:17; 13:6 as well as passages outside Mark; cf. J. P. Heil, *Jesus Walking* 6 [n. 13], 74 [n. 108]). (Alternatively and under the v.l. ἦν γάρ, "for . . . was," supported by A D W *f*[1,13] Majority Text lat sy, the second clause supplies a reason for the first: hardheartedness caused failure to understand because of the loaves, which failure has led to amazement at the abating of the wind.) These clauses do not hold up the disciples, their amazement, or even their ignorance and hardheartedness for criticism so much as they protect the feeding miracle by forestalling an inference that it may not have occurred if the disciples are now amazed at the abatement of the wind. Conversely, an understanding that Jesus fed the five thousand miraculously would have kept the disciples from amazement at the abating of the wind when he got into the boat. That the disciples have with them in the boat twelve baskets full of leftovers from the feeding (cf. 6:43 with 7:2, and contrast 8:14) sharpens the point. Also sharpening it are the strength of the adversative ἀλλ', "but," and the advancement of αὐτῶν, "their," not by way of emphasizing the owners of the heart, but by way of letting final attention rest on a heart that is hardened (cf. 7:19, 35; 12:15, 37; 14:40, 65; 15:19 for similar exceptions to the norm of post-position for this and other genitive pronouns).

NOTES

The old suggestion that in accordance with Eus. *H.E.* 3.39.15, transposing the third person plural to the first person plural takes us back to Peter's reminiscences works especially well in this story. Nevertheless, Mark's habit of inserting γάρ-clauses should exempt vv 50a, 52 from this suggestion, to say nothing of other Marcan touches. Despite these touches, it is hard to imagine that a story like this was ever told without indications of place and time (cf. K. L. Schmidt, *Rahmen* 193). H. Ritt (in *BZ* 23 [1979] 71-84) argues that Mark's commentary on the feeding of the five thousand (v 52) would immediately follow the feeding if the topographical and temporal connection between it and the walking on the sea were not traditional (cf. John 6).

The discrepancy between starting for Bethsaida and arriving at Gennesaret leads P. J. Achtemeier (in *JBL* 89 [1970] 284) to believe that the feeding of the five thousand and the walking on the sea were originally separate from each other. Similarly and for several reasons, L. Schenke (*Wundererzählungen* 238-39) attributes the connection of walking on the sea with feeding the five thousand to Mark's redaction: (1) because v 45 relates to v 31, which was redactional; (2) because v 44 closes off the feeding; (3) because its being already late in v 35 disagrees with its being still daytime in vv 45-46 (cf. v 47); and (4) because v 52 betrays a theological reason for putting the two stories side by side. But starting for Bethsaida (or for Gennesaret, as Achtemeier thinks it originally read) looks like the start of a new pericope, not the end of the feeding, for which v 44 already provides an appropriate conclusion; and going to Bethsaida in v 45 does not relate very well to the search for privacy in v 31, for a town is not "a deserted place" such as Jesus seeks for privacy (cf. 1:35, 45). A notation of the number fed (v 44) does not forestall a traditional continuance of the narrative. We saw that the "much hour" of v 35 allows the daylight necessary to vv 45-46 (see the comments and notes on v 35). And v 52 provides a theological deduction from a traditional juxtaposition of the stories as easily as it provides a theological reason for redactional juxtaposition.

"To the other side" does not disagree with "toward Bethsaida," for the Galilean mission of the Twelve (cf. the Nazareth-setting of vv 1-6a with the lack of a topographical shift in vv 6b-13, 30) couples with Mark's avoidance of "to the other side" in vv 31-33 to show that the feeding of the five thousand took place on the west side of the lake — and Bethsaida is on the east side, just to the east of where the Jordan River empties into the lake (see also the notes on vv 32-33, 53). The duality of the topographical expression typifies Mark's style (cf. esp. 5:1; F. Neirynck, *Duality* 45-53, 94-96), but does not imply that he makes up topography (on the location of Bethsaida, see B. Pixner in *BA* 48 [1985] 207-16; on the name, H. P. Rüger in *Markus-Philologie* 76; and C. C. McCown in *JPOS* 10 [1930] 32-58 against positing a second Bethsaida on the west side of the lake, its being unlikely anyway that two towns on the same lake would have the same name). Presumably the "deserted place" where Jesus fed the five thousand (v 32) lies somewhere southwest of Capernaum and therefore at a distance from Bethsaida that makes sailing across the lake advantageous.

In v 45 P[45vid] W f[1] q sy[s] omit εἰς τὸ πέραν, "to the other side," and one might regard it as an interpolation due to influence on a scribe from Matt 14:22 (cf. L. Vaganay in *RB* 49 [1940] 5-32). But the difficulty that the disciples and Jesus will arrive on the same side in Gennesaret (v 53) rather than on the other side in Bethsaida (v 45) offers a plausible reason for scribal omission, and the weight of external evidence favors inclusion. Furthermore, omission would combine with v 53 to leave the impression that the feeding of the five thousand took place on the east side; yet, as noted above, the preceding context favors the west side as the location of the feeding (see the notes on vv 32-33 against accepting a Lucan and Johannine location on the east side). It is not quite correct to argue for the omission that Mark uses εἰς τὸ πέραν only for unspecified or general destinations, and other expressions for specific ones (see 5:1; 6:32; 8:10).

J.-M. van Cangh (in *L'Évangile selon Marc* 329-30) thinks that Mark omits "to the other side" from v 32, introduces Bethsaida into v 45, and thus somewhat retroactively shifts the feeding of the five thousand from the east side of the lake to the west side to distinguish a feeding of Jews from a later feeding of Gentiles (8:1-9). But to think that "to the other side" originally stood in v 32 makes the following pedestrian travel to Jesus' landing site and the arrival ahead of him unlikely because of the distance. Moreover, the nearness of hamlets and towns in v 36 is less suitable to the sparsely populated east side than to the more thickly populated west side.

Among others, W. L. Lane (234-35) thinks that Jesus abruptly compels the disciples to leave lest they add "fuel to the fire" of a messianic uprising "by revealing to the people the miraculous character of the evening meal" (cf. esp. C. H. Dodd, *Historical Tradition* 212-16). Perhaps so at the historical level; but since Mark does not suggest a messianic uprising, or even messianic excitement, he aims in a different direction. Furthermore, the only gospel that mentions such excitement and an uprising in the making has the people already cognizant of the miraculous sign (see John 6:14-15). Their lack of cognizance in the synoptics and the lack of compulsion in John raise a doubt whether the compulsion represents a trace of messianic uprising even at the historical level. The foregoing comments take note of a contextual reason for mentioning the compulsion, i.e. emphasis on separation to play up the remarkable reunion to follow. Again at the historical level, it is only natural that the disciples would resist sailing across the lake without Jesus. P. Lapide (in *Conc* 138 [1980] 37-39) suggests that the disciples do not want to leave Jesus in danger from Herod Antipas (cf. esp. 6:14-29; Luke 13:31-32) by going outside his territory to Bethsaida while Jesus remains in it.

It is possible that v 46 refers to Jesus' taking leave of the disciples; but his forcing the disciples to embark and go ahead in v 45a seems to have put them temporarily out of the picture, and his dismissing the crowd in v 45b seems to determine the referent of αὐτοῖς, "them," in the immediately following phrase regarding farewell (so Matt 14:23). There is no implication that the disciples would stand in the way of Jesus' dismissing the crowd, only perhaps that his forcing the disciples to proceed across the lake will make the crowd more willing to leave and certainly that it will enable him to pray alone on the mountain once he has dismissed the crowd. "Taking leave" of the crowd does not disagree with dismissing them, but simply implies that Jesus does not stay here any longer than they do. Hence, we have no positive reason to infer that originally Jesus dismissed the disciples instead of the crowd (so L. Schenke, *Wundererzählungen* 239-40, following T. Snoy in *ETL* 44 [1968] 232-33). Jesus' having pitied the crowd, taught them, and fed them make appropriate the connotation of close relationship that leave-taking tends to have (see concordances and lexica s.v. ἀποτάσσομαι). To ascribe the mountain to a Marcan or pre-Marcan messianic secret (so, e.g., J. Schreiber, *Theologie des Vertrauens* 164-67) betrays more influence from W. Wrede than from Mark, who relates the mountain solely to the business of prayer.

For the boat, cf. v 32. Whether or not Mark writes πάλαι, "already," in v 47 just after ἦν, "was" (so P⁴⁵ D *f*¹ 28 *pc* it vg^mss), this v.l. correctly captures his emphases on the separation between Jesus and the disciples and on the disciples' rowing without success from evening onward (see B. M. Metzger, *Textual Commentary* ad loc., for a text critical evaluation). J. Gnilka (1. 268) correctly notes that the many different uses of βασανίζω, "torment," keep it from a necessarily eschatological connotation in v 48. Jews and Greeks divide the night into three watches, Romans into four; so Mark is using Roman reckoning by referring to the fourth watch (BAGD s.v. φυλακή 4). The contrast with "on the land" and the disciples' terror and amazement rule out the meaning "by the sea" for ἐπὶ τῆς θαλάσσης (as in Exod 14:2 LXX; John 21:1; cf. other passages cited in BAGD s.v. ἐπί II1aγ). The suggestion that the use of "sea" rather than "lake" heightens the thought of separation between Jesus and the disciples runs aground on the occurrence of "sea" also in 4:35-41, where he is in the boat with them (against H. Ritt in *BZ* 23 [1979] 77). The similarities between this passage and 4:35-41 have suggested to some that the present one spun off from the other. Those similarities include particulars of phraseology with regard to the onset of evening, going "to the other side," and leaving or dismissing the crowd, not just the generalities of a voyage, sea, wind, and following calm. But walking on the sea marks a fundamental difference from sleeping in the boat, and borrowing of phraseology and motifs does not imply compositional spin-off.

W. N. Brown (*Indian and Christian Miracles* 3-29, 53-71) hypothesizes that the present story is borrowed from India. Unfortunately for this hypothesis, however, the Buddha is never said to walk on water, only to fly across it or to disappear on one side and reappear on the other (cf. Iambl. *VP* 91, 136; L. Bieler, ΘΕΙΟΣ ΑΝΗΡ 1. 94-97). Nor does wading through miraculously shallow water, as in the Indian tradition, correspond to Jesus' walking on the sea. For a representative defense of OT rather than Greco-Roman background, see B. Blackburn, *Theios Anēr* 145-52.

Against a theophanic passing by, T. Snoy (in *L'Évangile selon Marc* 360-61) contrasts the lack of restraint in Jesus' showing himself to the disciples with the careful restraint in God's letting Moses see only his back (Exod 33:23) and revealing himself to Elijah only in a still small voice (1 Kgs 19:12-14). Yet no blaze of glory blinds the disciples; and God does not show himself to them directly, but through his Son, as similarly through his archangel Michael in Dan 12:1 LXX. Snoy's view that Jesus wants to pass by seen but unrecognized in accordance with Mark's theory of a messianic secret (cf. C. H. Turner in *JTS* os 28 [1926-27] 355-57) overestimates the theory and mistakenly rests on prooftexts that have to do with Jesus' avoiding crowds (1:43-45; 7:24, 36; 9:30) rather than, as here, his disciples. See W. Berg, *Rezeption* 103-44. Berg (331-33) notes that the disciples' fear does not arise from recognition of a theophany; rather, from mistaking Jesus for a ghost. Nighttime contributes to the mistake (cf. the LXX of Job 20:8; 33:15 Cod. A; Wis 17:3-4, 14-15; Luke 24:36-43 with 24:29; and Str-B 1. 691 with particular references to nighttime apparitions at sea). Fear arising from recognition is set in daytime (Dan 10:4–11:1; Tob 12:15-22; *Apoc. Abr.* 9:1–10:3). Jesus corrects the disciples' mistake by identifying himself verbally; only then does the theophany fulfil his wish (ἤθελεν — v 48).

J. M. Bassler (in *JR* 66 [1986] 170) argues that the theophanic connotation of passing by would mystify the original audience of Mark and that the evangelist deliberately uses mystifying language to set them up for deliverance from incomprehension through the later message of the Cross. But that later message will not clarify the point of passing by, and the supernatural act of walking on the sea is enough to connote a theophanic parade whether or not the audience know comparable passages in the OT. H. Fleddermann (in *CBQ* 45 [1983] 391-92) thinks that Amos 7:8; 8:2 establish that a theophanic passing by connotes rescue. But passing by did not connote a rescue of Moses in Exodus 33–34, and Amos does not deal with a rescue so much as with the cancellation of a disaster which would otherwise have occurred. Moreover, Jesus is not being portrayed as one who may bring disaster as God was portrayed in Amos.

God's passing by implies the momentariness of theophany (see O. Betz and W. Grimm, *Wesen und Wirklichkeit* 83), but not necessarily his leaving the scene once he has passed by. Instead, he may stay on the scene for prolonged speech (as in the passages following Exod 33:19, 22; 34:5-6; 1 Kgs 19:11); and it may be the human beings who leave (Exod 34:29; 1 Kgs 19:19). Therefore Luke 24:28 does not provide a good parallel (against D. E. Nineham 184), and we need not suppose that the disciples' terror changes Jesus' intention to pass by, as though getting into the boat interrupts or negates passing by. It merely ends the theophanic parade. Much less do we need to suppose that an interruption or negation implies an original version of the story devoid of Jesus' getting into the boat (and of the contrary wind which as a consequence dies down — so K. Kertelge, *Wunder* 146; D.-A. Koch, *Bedeutung* 104-7; but Koch argues well against E. Lohmeyer's separation of two originally independent stories that the windy part of the story presupposes the theophanic part). Nor does ἤθελεν imply an interruption or negation of theophany, as though Jesus wants to pass by but does not, or cannot, because of the disciples' terror. Mark uses this verb over three times more often for attained or attainable desire (1:40, 41; 3:13; 6:22, 25, 26; 8:34; 9:13, 30, 35; 10:43, 44, 51; 12:38; 14:7, 12, 36 [by filling in an ellipsis]; 15:9, 12) than he does for unattained or unattainable desire (6:19; 7:24; 8:35; 10:35, 36; 14:36). Thus we have reason to infer that Jesus does indeed pass by before getting in the boat. See T. Snoy in *L'Évangile selon Marc* 348-49 that ἤθελεν, "he was wanting," is not equivalent to the weaker ἔμελλεν, "he was about to" (so H. Riesenfeld, *Zum Gebrauch von ΘΕΛΩ* 13-14; cf. C. H. Turner in *JTS* os 28 [1927] 356-57; H. G. Meecham in *ExpTim* 47 [1935-36] 284-85). The presence of a direct object with παρελθεῖν puts a difficulty in the way of the meaning "to approach," which this verb may have when used absolutely.

The contrary wind makes the theophany unintelligible no more than the wind, earthquake, fire, smoke, cloud, and trumpet-blast make the cited OT theophanies unintelligible; nor does seeing Jesus and being terrified conflict with seeing him and thinking he is a ghost. To the contrary, see γάρ, "for," in v 50a (against R. Bultmann, *HST* 216). The chiastic structure of the story — (a) rowing against a contrary wind; (b) being terrified at a theophany; (b') being assured; (a') amazement at the abatement of the wind — favors its integrity (cf. W. Schmithals 332). Mark switches from ἐμβαίνω, "embark" (v 45), to ἀναβαίνω, "go up" (v 51), because the center of gravity has shifted from the boat to the disciples: Jesus goes up *to them* into the boat, but they merely embarked into an *empty* boat. See J. O'Callaghan in *SPap* 11 (1972) 89, n. 12, for the possibility that 7Q15 represents v 48 (though cf. the following notes on vv 52-53); and 1 Sam 28:3-25 for seeing a ghost.

Symbolic interpretations — e.g., that the contrary wind represents persecution and that Jesus' coming to the disciples around the fourth watch of the night represents the Second Coming (A. E. J. Rawlinson 88) — lack textual and contextual support. For a detailed criticism of the eschatological interpretation, see E. Best, *Following Jesus* 232; but his own view that the story symbolizes the risen Jesus' coming to his people whenever they are in need puts the accent on help for continuance of the voyage, whereas the narrative accents theophany and says nothing about any help (the abatement of the wind being a sign of his divinity, not the result of any word or action) or about continuance of the voyage (v 53 belonging to the next pericope and merely setting the stage for the next event).

Though the wind subsides, as in 4:39, Jesus does not rescue the disciples. The narrative carries not even a hint of mortal danger. The wind is only "contrary" to the direction in which the disciples are headed; no waves threaten to engulf them; and Jesus neither does nor says anything to effect a rescue (contrast 4:37-39). Therefore it goes beyond the text to speak of a pre-Marcan redactor's making an original story of epiphany into a story of rescue (so, e.g., L. Schenke, *Wundererzählungen* 243-44; cf. R. Bultmann, *HST* 216). That Jesus starts from a mountain conforms to the theophany on Mount Sinai (cf. Deut 33:2; Judg 5:4-5; Hab 3:3), but does not imply that in an earlier version of the present story he appeared to his disciples only on the mountain. God himself moved from the mountain down to the tabernacle.

W. Berg (*Rezeption* 328-29) tries to wring an emphasis on mortal danger out of the widespread use of "in the middle of the sea" where such danger is in view (Exod 14:29; 15:8; Neh 9:11 et passim). In fact, however, some of the passages he cites do not apply. For example, Ezek 26:12 speaks of throwing stones, timber, and dust into the middle of the sea — no danger to human life here — and other passages offer different phraseology to denote mortal danger. Those passages that properly apply do not stress danger so much as the marvel of God's making the land dry where the water had stood deepest. In Mark, the middle of the sea merely stresses the separation of the disciples and Jesus by contrast with his location on the land. V. Taylor (328) minimizes the force of "middle" (contrast Matt 14:24; John 6:19), apparently to keep the disciples close enough to shore for a naturalistic explanation (e.g., wading near the shore) for what Mark takes as a miracle.

In view of the wind's dying down, J. M. Bassler (in *JR* 66 [1986] 163-67) thinks that Mark's audience expect him to mention the disciples' incomprehension of Jesus' stilling the storm (4:35-41), not of his feeding the five thousand. But the feeding immediately precedes, and Jesus' taking no action to calm the wind contrasts with his having taken action to still the storm; so Mark's audience do not expect a different reference. The suggestion that the disciples do not understand because Jesus' passion has not yet occurred (so P. J. Achtemeier 112) puts in place of Mark's own explanation (viz., hardheartedness) an item which has yet to appear in Mark's text and which, when it does start appearing, prompts new incomprehension rather than clearing up old incomprehension (see 8:31-33). Nor does Mark ever come round to portraying Jesus' passion as an enlightenment, not even in 9:9, which mentions his resurrection rather than his passion as the signal of freedom to tell about the Transfiguration. According to F. J. Matera (in *Bib* 70 [1989] 163-71), the disciples are portrayed as not understanding that the feeding of the five thousand showed Jesus to be the messianic shepherd after the pattern of Ezek 34:11, 23. But Mark cannot and would not expect his audience of Gentiles, to whom he must and does explain Jewish customs (7:2-4), to understand the disciples' ignorance thus. M. Boucher (*Mysterious Parable* 73-74) suggests that if the disciples had penetrated the allusion in the feeding of the five thousand to an eschatological exodus of salvation, complete with new manna, they would not have been confounded at the demonstration of power and glory in Jesus' walking on the sea. True, because the forthright demonstration is easier to understand than a symbolic allusion would be. But failure to understand the harder-to-understand feeding of the five thousand does not explain failure to understand the easier-to-understand walking on the sea; so the suggestion does not explain Mark's γάρ-clause (v 52). Before, amazement has been evoked by miracles understood as such (2:12; 5:42). Here, the miracle would still have been understood as such but would not have evoked amazement had an earlier miracle been so understood (cf. 16:8). See C. Spicq, *Notes* 1. 367-71, on θαρσεῖτε, "cheer up."

W. Berg (*Rezeption* 2, 323) notes that the motifs which make up the story as a whole — walking on the water, parading by in theophany, fright, etc. — occur together nowhere in the OT or other ancient literature. He also notes the absence of true parallels with the crossing of the Reed Sea (12-14), draws the necessary distinction between walking on the sea and walking through it (35, 76-84), collects parallels from ancient extra-biblical literature for walking on water (37-39, 54-76, 85-102), and argues contextually for walking on the sea here, as opposed to walking along it (43-53). In extra-biblical literature, walking on water does not constitute a miracle of legitimation, only seldom a miracle of salvation, and even then not of salvation from the waters of death, but represents a supernatural capability inherent in divine beings and granted to demigods. So also here, we might add, the rowers' discipleship keeps them from needing Jesus to perform a miracle of self-legitimation. We have seen that the contrary wind thwarts their rowing but does not threaten their lives; so neither do they need a miracle of salvation. Rather, walking on the sea comes naturally to the one whom Mark portrays as the Son of God. That the story did not originate as a story about an appearance by the resurrected Jesus, see C. H. Dodd in *Studies in the Gospels* 23-24; R. H. Fuller, *Formation* 162-63; A. R. C. Leaney in *SE* V/2. 101-13.

J. O'Callaghan (in *Supplement* to *JBL* 91/2 [1972] 1-10) identifies 7Q5 (DJD 3, pl. 30) with vv 52-53. For the strongest defense of this identification and for references to other discussions, see C. P. Thiede in *Bib* 65 (1984) 538-59; idem, *Die älteste Evangelien-Handschrift?* For criticisms of Theide's arguments, see H.-U. Rosenbaum in *BZ* nf 31 (1987) 189-205. Most of the erstwhile discussion is beside the point, however; for even critics of O'Callaghan's identification have allowed more similarity between the two texts than actually exists. In line 2 of 7Q5 a *nu* needs to follow the *omega* to produce the masculine genitive plural of the third person pronoun — i.e. αὐτῶν, "their" — if Mark 6:52-53 is to be represented. Instead, an *iota*-adscript follows the *omega*, producing the masculine or neuter dative singular of the definite article — i.e. τῷ, "the" (cf. 7Q15) — as can be seen by comparison with the *iota* of καί, "and," in line 3 of 7Q5. There is no physical evidence such as damage to the fiber of the papyrus or stain remaining after the flaking off of ink to suggest that the *iota*-adscript really forms the initial vertical stroke of a *nu;* and the next ink mark, curving as it does, looks quite unlike the initial upstroke of an *eta* (for Mark's ἡ, "the") such as we find in both lines 4 and 5. As can be seen from the spacing of *nu* and *eta* in line 4, the amount of space before the next ink mark in line 2 does not allow for the finishing out of the *iota*-adscript as a *nu* before the start of an *eta;* and the formation of the *nu* in line 4 shows that we should not treat the curve of the next ink mark as the juncture between the diagonal and second vertical strokes of a *nu.* In line 3, an *iota* should follow the *tau* for Mark's διαπεράσαντες, "having crossed over," spelled with an initial *tau* instead of an initial *delta.* But the vertical stroke following the *tau* does not appear to have the leftward curve at its bottom that both the *iota*-adscript in line 2 and the *iota* of καί in line 3 have. 7Q5 gives us only two readable words, then: τῷ and καί. The dative singular form of the first of these prohibits an identification with Mark 6:52-53. Words meaning "the" and "and" would not suffice to identify the manuscript, anyway. And since the only other manuscripts that were discovered in Cave 7 and can be identified with certainty represent the LXX of Exodus and the Epistle of Jeremiah, neither one of which has to have come from Christian copying, we have no reason to suspect that 7Q5 represents a Christian text such as Mark (for nearly all the foregoing points, credit belongs to G. Fee, who hopes to publish a full treatment).

AN OVERFLOW OF HEALING POWER

6:53-56 (Matt 14:34-36; John 6:22-25)

In this short pericope Mark reports the rest of Jesus' and the disciples' voyage (v 53), people's bringing their sick to Jesus (vv 54-55), and his going to places where sick people touch the fringe of his garment and are healed (v 56). "And having crossed over to the land" indicates the completion — thanks to Jesus' intervention — of the voyage begun in v 45. "To Gennesaret" identifies the point to which he and the disciples come after crossing over. Gennesaret is a plain southwest of Capernaum off the northwest shore of the Sea of Galilee (Josephus *J.W.* 3.10.7-8 §§506-21; cf. *Tg. Onq.* Num 34:11; G. Dalman, *SSW* 128, 130). Since Jesus instructed his disciples to go ahead to the city of Bethsaida on the other side (v 45) and since that city lies on the northeast side of the sea, Mark apparently wants his readers to assume that as a result of the contrary wind, the actual landing site turns out to be different from the one originally intended (cf. the apparent distinction between πρός, "toward," for the intended landing site in v 45 and εἰς, "to," for the actual landing site in v 53; also 8:22). If Mark knows that Bethsaida is a town and Gennesaret a plain (cf. vv 54-56), he probably knows enough about Palestinian topography to avoid the false implication that the town is located on the plain. The unexplained shift from Bethsaida to Gennesaret favors a different landing site over a more specifically defined one, for a plain is less specific than a city. The reference to beaching (προσορμίσθησαν — see E. F. F. Bishop, *Jesus of Palestine* 146, for this meaning in preference to mooring) may derive from the boat language of a fisherman like Peter (cf. pp. 1026-45 on the Petrine background of this gospel), but it suits Mark's contrast between the middle of the sea and the landing site.

   Both Jesus and the disciples get out of the boat (cf. 5:2); but now that the narrative has moved away from the mission of the Twelve, the people's recognition focuses on Jesus (contrast v 33). The immediacy of the recognition and the people's running around the region (cf. v 33; 5:6) and bringing around their sick punctuate his magnetism and known power to heal (cf. 5:21ff.). The addition of both ὅλην, "whole," and ἐκείνην, "that," to τὴν χώραν, "the region," intensify this punctuation. "On pallets" shows that this power is a match even for serious illnesses. The forward position of the corresponding Greek phrase ἐπὶ τοῖς κραβάτοις sharpens the point. "The whole region" (cf. esp. 1:28), "where they heard he was," and "wherever he entered into towns or into cities or into hamlets" — these expressions show how far Jesus' reputation has spread and how widely his healing power continues to work. In particular, though Semitic repetition may be partly at work here (M. Black, *Aramaic Approach* 115), the doubling of περι-, "around," and the quadrupling of εἰς, "into," and the collocating of the three terms κώμας, "towns"; πολεῖς, "cities"; and ἀγρούς, "hamlets" — which elsewhere in Mark occur only singly or in pairs (1:33, 45; 5:14; 6:6, 33, 36) — heighten the effect of Mark's summary. Jesus goes into one town, city, and hamlet after another and there occur healings of the sick who have been put in the market places. He is so full of healing power that the healings occur without his saying a word or performing a gesture. The putting of the sick ἐν ταῖς ἀγοραῖς, "in the market places" (cf. Hdt. 1.197), suggests numerous healings in serial fashion. The positioning of the phrase ahead of its verb reinforces the point. So many are those who need healing and so many are the localities where they have been brought that they can only implore Jesus to come close enough for them to touch his garment as he hurries through. Just the fringe of it will do, as emphasized again by the forward position of κἂν τοῦ κρασπέδου τοῦ ἱματίου αὐτοῦ and by the ascensive use of καί in κἂν, "even the fringe of his garment" (cf. b. Taʻan. 23b). Many sick people touched Jesus for healing according to 3:10, and the woman with the flow of blood touched only his garment with equally good effect according to 5:24b-34 (cf. 3:10); but here the mere fringe of it suffices both in spite of and because of the large numbers of people to be healed. Jesus' power is equal to their needs: "and as many as touched it were delivered" (ἐσῴζοντο, as in 5:28, 34 — see the comments ad loc.). The clustering of verbs in the imperfect tense — περιέδραμον, ἤκουον, εἰσεπορεύετο, παρεκάλουν, and ἐσῴζοντο, "people were running around," "they were hearing," "he was entering," "they were beseeching," and "they were being saved" — and the iterative force of the aorist ἥψαντο, "touched," with ἄν reinforce the magnitude and extent of his healing ministry: these things take place time after time in place after place. Ὅσοι, "as many as," rules out any power failures.

NOTES

T. Snoy (in ETL 44 [1968] 205-41) thinks that originally v 53 followed v 44, Mark having sandwiched vv 45-52 between them. But the transition from v 44 to v 53 would have been extremely abrupt. The two verbs in v 42 have the crowd as their subject. It is only by forward reference to 8:19-20 that we can identify the subject in v 43 as the disciples. Even then it excludes Jesus. Verse 44 goes back to the crowd as subject. Yet with no indication of a shift in subject, Snoy's theory makes the "they" of v 53 refer to Jesus and the disciples.

The diction of vv 32-34, 36 seems to have influenced the diction of vv 53-56 with respect to coming out of the boat, recognition on the part of people, their running, and the mention of cities, towns, and hamlets. In addition, "having crossed over" seems to echo 5:21; "that whole region," 1:28 (cf. also the use of περι- as a prefix in both passages); "on pallets," 2:1-12; "bringing the sick," 1:32 (the addition of "around" being due to parallelism with "running around"); and sick people's touching Jesus or his clothing to be saved from their sickness, 3:10; 5:27-31 (cf. Acts 5:15-16; 19:11-12; Philostr. VA 4.1; 8.24; H. D. Betz, Lukian 145-46). But the absence of exorcisms and of teaching, which are prominent elsewhere in Mark, and the discrepancy between setting out for Bethsaida (v 45) and arriving at Gennesaret combine with the failure of "Gennesaret," προσωρμίσθησαν, "beached," ἀσθενοῦντας, "sick," and ὅσοι ἄν plus the aorist indicative to appear elsewhere in Mark to favor that Mark is using tradition rather than composing out of whole cloth. If "to the land" belongs in his original text (see the notes on vv 52-53), word order favors that the phrase goes with "having crossed over," whereas "to Gennesaret" goes with "they came" (contrast Matt 14:34). Thus it is unlikely that "to the land . . . to Gennesaret" represents Marcan duality. The dense population of the Plain of Gennesaret suits the subject matter of vv 53-56. "That region" seems to identify Gennesaret and thereby rule out the view of M.-J. Lagrange (177) that "Gennesaret" (as distinct from "Gennesar") refers to a town. The people of the region are the indefinite third person plural subjects of main verbs in vv 55-56. "Recognizing him" (v 54) rules out the disciples as subjects of those verbs.

The view of P. J. Achtemeier (in *JBL* 89 [1970] 285-86) that Mark composes vv 53-56 to displace 8:22-26, which used to follow Jesus' walking on the sea, falls into the trap of making Mark create a glaring discrepancy between Gennesaret and Bethsaida. The further explanation that Mark omits exorcisms because the immediately preceding stories included no exorcism, in contrast with the preceding context of 1:32-34; 3:7-12, overlooks the lack of exorcism between 1:32-34 and 3:7-12. So apart from adherence to tradition, Mark is likely to have included exorcisms here just as he did in 3:7-12.

After reaching the middle of the sea in an easterly direction (v 47) the disciples headed back west and now arrive with Jesus at Gennesaret. In Mark's only other use of διαπεράω, i.e. at 5:21, the word referred to a return trip. The addition of the seemingly otiose ἐπὶ τὴν γῆν . . . καὶ προσωρμίσθησαν, "to the land . . . and they beached," as well as the striking appearance of "to Gennesaret" instead of the expected "to Bethsaida" suggest that Mark is going out of the way to make his audience understand "having crossed to the other side" from the later standpoint of the middle of the sea, with which coming to land and beaching make a strong contrast, rather than from the earlier standpoint of the western shore. And the contrariness of the wind (v 48) suggests that before Jesus rejoined them and the wind died down, the disciples were blown too far off their eastward course to make continuance toward Bethsaida practicable or desirable. Otherwise, such continuance would follow abatement of the wind, as in 4:35, 39; 5:1. Hence, "having crossed to the other side" took its starting point in the middle of the sea. Despite the many goings back and forth across the Sea of Galilee, Mark uses the added expressions only here. Their uniqueness supports the suggested connotations, for the mere borrowing of tradition would not explain the otiosity of the added expressions. Πάλιν, "again," which described the return crossing at 5:21, does not recur here, because the disciples did not reach the other side originally intended. The omission again supports the suggested connotations. The perspectival shift to the middle of the sea then allows the contrariness of the wind to suggest a reversal of the original easterly direction. The discrepancy between setting out for Bethsaida (v 45) and arriving at Gennesaret (v 53) is so glaring that to regard either location as a redactional intrusion is to make the redactor almost unbelievably inept. More likely, both locations are traditional, and the added expressions are designed to resolve the discrepancy (cf. the story told by G. Dalman [*SSW* 175-76] that on April 6, 1908, he and his party set sail for Bethsaida from the eastern shore below Hippus but were driven by a strong east wind to Capernaum).

J. Konings (in *L'Évangile selon Marc* 149) asks why Jesus stilled the storm if the disciples and he do not continue crossing the sea in the original direction. The question rests on overlooking that Jesus did *not* still the storm. Since the abatement of the wind is unenacted, there is no implication that he intended to continue crossing the sea in the original direction. D. E. Nineham (186) objects: Mark does not say that the contrary wind caused a change of direction, and a voyage from near Capernaum to Gennesaret scarcely counts as crossing the sea. But voyaging to the middle of the sea and back again covers enough water to count as a crossing, especially since the landing place Gennesaret differs from the deserted place of embarkation even though both lie on the west side; and the mention of Gennesaret instead of Bethsaida indicates a change of direction clearly enough.

The notion that Mark wants his audience to understand the landing at Gennesaret as the result of disobedience by the disciples (J. Schreiber, *Theologie des Vertrauens* 96-97) sits uneasily with the preceding emphasis on their amazement (vv 52-53) and with the following emphasis on Jesus' successes in Gennesaret. Above all, however, Mark gives credit to the disciples for making a yeomanly effort to reach Bethsaida, and blames their failure on the contrary wind (v 48). These considerations undermine the symbolic interpretation which sees the aborted voyage to Bethsaida as a failure of Jewish disciples to carry out a mission to Gentiles, the following material as Jesus' educating the disciples for a later mission to Gentiles in Bethsaida (8:13-22a), and the healing in two stages at Bethsaida (8:22b-26) as representing his two attempts to engage the disciples in a mission to Gentiles (E. S. Malbon, *Narrative Space* 28-29, 41-42). Another problem in this interpretation is that the disciples engage in no mission once they do arrive in Bethsaida. W. H. Kelber's version of the interpretation (*Kingdom* 57; *Mark's Story* 36-37) puts the mission to Gentiles in Gennesaret. But the disciples are equally inactive here, and Gennesaret is a Jewish region in which Pharisees and scribes from Jerusalem quickly pop up (7:1). For that matter, Bethsaida is not associated with Gentiles, either (see abundant evidence in the notes on 7:24, 31). Against the view of E. Schweizer (143) that Mark probably portrays miracle-mania in vv 54-56, see K. Kertelge, *Wunder* 36; J. Gnilka 1. 273. The favorable portrayal of the woman who touched Jesus' clothing for healing (see esp. 5:34) stands against an unfavorable portrayal here. The Greek word translated "fringe" (κράσπεδον) may equally well mean the tassel required by Moses (Num 15:38-39; Deut 22:12; Matt 9:20; 23:5). R. P. Booth (*Jesus and the Laws of Purity* 31-32) advocates this meaning as Mark's way of forestalling a false inference from 7:1-23 that Jesus does not keep the Law. But since Mark has to explain to his audience Jewish laws of purity (see 7:2-4), we can hardly suppose that he expects them to understand a subtly apologetic allusion to the law of the tassel.

JESUS' DOMINANCE OVER PHARISEES AND SCRIBES AND HIS AUTHORITY OVER THE OLD TESTAMENT LAW

7:1-23 (Matt 15:1-20)

In this pericope much material goes to make two brief but emphatic points: (1) Jesus powerfully puts down the Pharisees and some of the scribes from Jerusalem on a question of cultic purity (vv 1-13); (2) he authoritatively pronounces all foods clean despite cultic laws to the contrary (vv 14-23). The first main section starts with a question by Pharisees and scribes (vv 1-5) and ends with Jesus' answer (vv 6-13). His answer falls into two subsections, the first centering on a quotation of Isa 29:13 (vv 6-8), the second centering on quotations of Exod 20:12 (= Deut 5:16) and Exod 21:17 and supporting a charge leveled by Jesus in the first subsection (vv 9-13). The second main section starts with his telling the crowd what is and is not unclean (vv 14-15) and ends with his answering the disciples' question about the meaning of his statement (vv 17-23). More particularly, the denial of defilement from without in v 18b repeats the denial in v 15a and gets a physical explanation in the causal ὅτι-clause of v 19a. Likewise, the affirmation of defilement from within in v 20 repeats the affirmation in v 15b and gets a moral explanation in the γάρ-clause of vv 21-22, followed by a summarizing statement in v 23.

Given the importance of cultic purity and food laws in first century Judaism and given their off-putting effect on Gentiles, we might infer that Mark wants to assure his Gentile audience that belief in Jesus does not require the adoption of Jewish practice in these matters. Jesus' going to Gentile territory and performing an exorcism and a healing in the next two pericopes (7:24-30, 31-37) might seem to favor such an inference. But would Mark's audience need assurance if they know so little about these matters that he has to insert a lengthy explanation of them (vv 3-4)? If not, here and in the following pericopes the main accent falls on Jesus' power and authority. Whenever Mark bothers to give the content of Jesus' teaching (as he does once in a while — usually he notes only its stunning effect), it is not so much for instruction in the subject matter as to highlight Jesus' power and authority in upsetting prevailing opinion and practice.

7:1-5 *(Matt 15:1-2)* The historical present tense of συνάγονται (cf. 4:1; 6:30) emphasizes the drawing power of Jesus in that "the Pharisees and some of the scribes gather together to him." The scribes are a professional class, theologians; most of the Pharisees are laymen. "Coming from Jerusalem" implies a setting in Gennesaret (cf. 6:53) and indicates how far the report of the mighty acts that Jesus has performed there has spread, and into what important circles (see the comments and notes on 3:22 for further interpretation). "Some of the scribes" implies the existence of a larger number of them than those who come from Jerusalem. "Some of his disciples" corresponds to "some of the scribes" and likewise implies the existence of a larger number of them than those whom the Pharisees and scribes see eating with defiled hands. Since the rest of the passage displays no defensiveness, but goes on the attack against the accusing questioners, the addition of "some of" to "the disciples" probably does not play down the number to reduce the offense of eating with defiled hands. On the contrary, this offense is underscored by several means: (1) the hyperbaton which advances "some of the disciples" into the main clause; (2) the forward position of κοιναῖς χερσίν, "with defiled hands," in the remainder of the subordinate clause; (3) the addition of an explanation, "this is [= i.e.] with unwashed [hands]"; and (4) the historical present tense of "are eating."

The disciples are eating "the loaves." The anaphoric definite article refers back to the five loaves broken by Jesus and eaten by the five thousand (6:35-44). On that occasion the disciples picked up twelve baskets full of leftovers but were not said to have eaten any of the leftovers. The anaphoric definite article with the singular, "the loaf" (meaning "the bread" [τὸν ἄρτον]), in v 5 will favor that tradition underlies v 2 and that the tradition had an anarthrous singular (ἄρτον, "bread"; cf. 3:20 and the arthrous plural following up the anarthrous plurals in 8:4-6). Otherwise v 5 would have the plural just as v 2 does, especially since the definite article in v 5 points back to the bread mentioned in v 2. Mark changes the traditional singular to a plural and adds the definite article to indicate that the disciples are eating the leftovers of the earlier loaves. That the disciples are eating but not Jesus agrees with the number of baskets full of leftovers, i.e. twelve, one for each of the Twelve but none for him.

That the Pharisees and some of the scribes see some of the disciples eating indicates that some of the disciples have finally found opportunity to eat (contrast 6:31) and calls forth a parenthetical explanation of contrasting Pharisaic-Jewish cultic practice (vv 3-4; cf. 2:18a and *POxy.* 840. 2, on which see J. Jeremias, *Unknown Sayings* 47-60). Mark designs the explanation for the benefit of his predominantly Gentile audience, for Jews do not need such an explanation (cf. its complete omission in Matthew, written for Jews). Within the explanation Mark designs the hyperbole "all the Jews" to highlight Jesus' iconoclastic power (see the following notes on the extent of the hyperbole and cf. similarly expansive statements at 1:5, 33, 39; 6:33, cited by S. Westerholm, *Jesus and Scribal Authority* 73-74). Having the same design are the forward positions of "the Pharisees and all the Jews," the interruption of the first main clause by the first "except"-clause, the forward position of "with a fist" within the first "except"-clause, the interruption of the second main clause with another "except"-clause (under the assumption that "[coming] from [the] market place" starts the second main clause [see the following notes]), and the forward position of "many other things" in the third main clause (see the Greek word order for all of these).

The length of the parenthesis leads Mark to leave incomplete the sentence interrupted at the end of v 2, to start a new sentence with καί, "and," at the beginning of v 5, and to mention again "the Pharisees and the scribes" as the compound subject of that sentence. There is no need to repeat the refinement "some" with "scribes" in the introduction to the question why Jesus' disciples "do not walk [i.e. do not behave] according to the tradition of the elders [i.e. according to the legal comments or case decisions of teachers past or present or both — cf. Josephus *Ant.* 13.10.6 §297; 13.16.2 §408; *m. Pe'a* 2:6; *m. 'Ed.* 8:7; *m. 'Abot* 1:1; *b. Nid.* 45a et passim; E. P. Sanders, *Jewish Law* 108-30], but eat bread with defiled hands." Nor is there need to repeat the refinement "some" with "disciples." The historical present tense of "asks" puts weight on the question, while the strength of the adversative ἀλλά, "but," and the forward position of κοιναῖς χερσῖν, "with defiled hands," sharpen its point. In and of itself, the question might look innocent. But the earlier accusation by scribes from Jerusalem that Jesus has Beelzebul (3:22) has prepared the ground for an accusatory question. So also have Jesus' earlier, antagonistic encounters with the Pharisees (2:15–3:6; cf. *m. 'Ed.* 5:6). Mark's present explanation of Pharisaic and Jewish practice hints at an accusatory tone. And Jesus' counter accusation that his questioners are hypocrites will leave no doubt about that tone, for which people's beseeching him that they might touch even the fringe of his garment for healing has provided a foil in 6:53-56.

7:6-13 *(Matt 15:3-9)* An adversative δέ, "but," puts Jesus' counter accusation over against the accusatory question of the Pharisees and scribes. The counter accusation displays a chiastic pattern: (a) an OT-based description (vv 6-7) leading into (b) a charge (v 8), and (b') a charge (v 9) growing out of (a') an OT-based description (vv 10-13). A quotation of Isa 29:13 (cf. *PEger.* 2. 3) is introduced with the sarcastic statement, "Beautifully did Isaiah prophesy about you the hypocrites, as it is written," and followed by the application, "Leaving the commandment of God, you hold to the tradition of human beings." Emphasizing the sarcasm are the forward position of καλῶς, "beautifully," and the addition of "the hypocrites" to "you." At the start of the quotation כִּי, "because," drops out because the quotation will halt before the main clause (cf. the LXX, though it picks up the causal idea in the following διὰ τοῦτο, "because of this"). The people's drawing near to God with their mouth (so Isa 29:13) also drops out to focus on their honoring God with their lips while their heart is far from him. This focus prepares for a further discussion of honoring in vv 9-12, that of honoring one's father and mother. The interrelationship between the two forms of honoring suggests that the connection between vv 6-8 and vv 9-13 is original.

In comparison with the MT and the LXX, οὗτος ὁ λαός, "this people," advances not only for a closer parallel with the forward position of the subject in the next clause but also for a sarcastic accent. In the same comparison and for the same sarcastic purpose, οὗτος moves ahead of ὁ λαός within the phrase. Against the MT and the LXX, "their" falls away from "lips" to stress the hypocrisy of lip-service as such; and με, "me," moves ahead of τιμᾷ, "honors," perhaps for another sarcastic accent. Again in disagreement with the MT and the LXX, the third person plural of "honor" gives way to the third person singular. The resultant τιμᾷ links aurally with τίμα in v 10; and the charge of lip-service blankets the people, considered as a single unit. "But their heart is far from me" corresponds to the MT yet agrees with the LXX in using an adversative δέ, "but," for וְ and especially in using the adverb πόρρω, "far," with the active verb ἀπέχει, "is . . . from," where the MT uses a predicate adjective with an implied copulative verb (R. H. Gundry, *Use of the OT* 15, n. 8). The position of πόρρω before ἀπέχει stresses distance. Μάτην δὲ σέβονταί με, "but worthlessly do they worship me," agrees with the LXX in again putting an adversative δέ for וְ and with the LXX against the MT ("and their fear of me is") by reading וְתֹהוּ, "and worthlessness" (cf. Isa 41:29), instead of וַתְּהִי, "and . . . is." Since וְ and יְ are often confused, a different Hebrew text may underlie the LXX and Mark. In any case, "worthlessly" fits "you hypocrites" in Mark's introduction and takes an emphatic first position.

The use of a predicate phrase, "they worship me," for the Massoretic nominal phrase, "their fear of me," and of σέβονται, "they worship," instead of the expected φοβοῦνται, "they fear," for יִרְאָתָם , "their fear," shows close contact with the LXX. The plural possessive "their" has led Mark to switch from the third person singular in "honors" to the third person plural in "worship." "Teaching [as] teachings commandments of human beings" agrees with the LXX against the MT ("a commandment of human beings [that is] taught"), except that Mark advances "teachings" and omits "and" to make a double accusative (the LXX: "teaching commandments of human beings and teachings"). The omission of "and" agrees with the MT against the LXX. The double accusative, the advancement of "teachings," and in common with the LXX the double translation of מְלֻמָּדָה, "taught," with the cognates διδάσκοντες, "teaching," and διδασκαλίας, "[as] teachings," all highlight the didactic activity of the elders whose tradition the Pharisees and scribes follow. The advancement of "teachings" and the omission of "and" also leave "commandments of human beings" to stand at the end of the quotation in stark contrast with "the commandment of God" and in parallel with "the tradition of human beings," both in the next verse (cf. "the tradition of the elders" in vv 3, 5). Adoption of the Septuagintal plural "commandments" (reading מצות as a plural rather than as a singular in the construct state) disagrees with the singular "commandment" in the MT, but suits the plurality of extrabiblical purity-laws exampled in vv 3-4.

In Isaiah, "this people" refers to the whole nation. According to Mark's context, "this people" refers to the Pharisees and scribes, not to the Jewish nation, not even to the crowd who will appear in v 14; for the Pharisees and scribes are the ones teaching the commandments of human beings who are their elders and whose commandments make up "the tradition." The changes in the wording of the quotation suit this shift of referent. It is often said that only the LXX suits the context in Mark and that since we can hardly believe that Jesus used the LXX, especially in dialogue with scribes from Jerusalem, the quotation is not authentically dominical. The LXX is supposed to be suitable in two respects: (1) it presents a complete statement at this point; (2) teaching the commandments of human beings (so the LXX) corresponds to the Pharisees' and scribes' attempt to impose the tradition of the elders. The MT is supposed to be unsuitable in that it presents an incomplete statement at this point and portrays the people as fearing the Lord only because their leaders tell them to do so. But since the LXX has turned up in manuscripts dating from the NT era and discovered as far south in Palestine as Qumran, since Bar Kokhba wrote some of his letters in the Greek language, since Greek has turned up on ossuaries discovered in Jerusalem (cf. R. H. Gundry in *JBL* 83 [1964] 404-8), and since one or more probably Greek-speaking synagogues existed in first century Jerusalem (Acts 6:9; M. Hengel, *Between Jesus and Paul* 1-29), we should not dismiss the possibility of Jesus' using the LXX even in dialogue with scribes from Jerusalem. On the other hand, we must also consider the possibility of a Hebrew textual tradition closer to the LXX than is the MT (cf. R. H. Gundry, *Use of the OT* 14-16, and p. 22 in the present commentary). But most importantly, the MT probably does not mean that the people fear the Lord only because their leaders tell them to do so. Rather, the prophets, seers, wise men, and sages (vv 10, 14) teach a message devoid of sin and judgment, with the result that the people's behavior belies their worship (see esp. vv 15-16, 20-21, 24; cf. Isa 1:2-20). Thus the humanly taught fear of God is misleading *in substance* just as is the tradition of the elders (cf. R. T. France, *Jesus and the OT* 248-250). The MT is good enough to make the point. If Mark can sharpen the point with some use of the LXX, so much the better. And if the LXX can transform an incomplete statement into a complete one, so also can Jesus, especially in view of his needing only those words which in their Isaianic context are subordinate (cf. the separation of geographical terms that are objective in Isa 8:23 MT [and vocative in the LXX], so that they become either absolute or part of a compound subject along with "the people" in the un-Septuagintal quotation at Matt 4:15-16).

Verses 9-13 will substantiate the charge in v 8 of leaving God's commandment for the sake of human tradition. Moreover, "the commandment of God" in v 8 anticipates the same phrase in v 9 (cf. v 13). Yet "you hold fast the tradition" (v 8) echoes vv 3-5; "of men" (v 8) echoes v 7; and "the commandment" (v 8) echoes "the commandments" in v 7, though with a shift from the plural (as also in v 9) with a view toward the single commandment of honoring one's parents (vv 10-13). Hence, v 8 acts as a hinge that draws an inference from the preceding and looks forward to the following. The asyndeton with which the verse starts, the contrast between "having left" (ἀφέντες) and "you hold fast" (κρατεῖτε), the replacement of "of the elders" (vv 3, 5) with "of human beings," and the resultant contrast between "the tradition of human beings" and "the commandment of God" intensify the charge.

The hinge-like function of v 8 implies that the introduction to v 9, "and he was saying to them," does not mark a topical gap, but emphasizes the following substantiation: "Beautifully do you set aside the commandment of God in order that you may establish your tradition!" (cf. T. Levi 16:2 and the comments on 2:27 concerning καὶ ἔλεγεν αὐτοῖς). By meaning and by grammatical weight as a main verb, "set aside" sharpens the accusatory participle "having left" (v 8). Earlier, the deferential attribution of the tradition to the elders (vv 3, 5) changed into a slurring attribution of the tradition to human beings as opposed to God (v 8). Now the tradition simply attaches to Jesus' questioners ("your tradition") with regard to their having received it, holding to it, and establishing it (στήσητε, "you cause to stand"; cf. v 13: ἧ παρεδώκατε, "which you have handed on"). As in v 8, the commandment of God in the OT and extrabiblical human tradition stand in opposition to each other. Here in v 9 τὴν παράδοσιν ὑμῶν, "your tradition," takes an emphatic position before its verb to become the butt of Jesus' criticism. The correspondence between Isaiah's prophecy and the hypocrisy of the Pharisees and scribes makes his prophecy beautiful in its accuracy. Here in v 9, then, the earlier sarcasm turns to irony: setting aside the commandment of God for the sake of tradition has sparked the invention of a legal device — Corban — beautiful in its piety, which in accordance with the nature of irony means the opposite: *ugly* in its *im*piety. The first position of καλῶς, "beautifully," emphasizes this irony and parallels the first position of καλῶς in v 6. The parallelism adds further emphasis.

The conjunction γάρ, "for," introduces an explanation of the beauty with which the Pharisees and scribes piously set aside God's commandment. The commandment that Jesus refers to has two prongs, the second one a sanction, and occurs in Moses' statements, "Honor your father and your mother" (Exod 20:12 = Deut 5:16) and "Let the one who reviles [for the Hebrew 'curses'] father or mother surely die" (Exod 21:17; cf. Lev 20:9; Deut 27:16; Ezek 22:7; Prov 20:9a LXX; *m. Sanh.* 7:4, 8). The present tense of the imperative verbs τίμα, "honor," and τελευτάτω, "let . . . die," carries emphasis (contrast the unemphatic aorist imperative of the former verb in 1 Pet 2:17; cf. the notes on 1:3). An adversative δέ, "but," introduces a legal device which stands as an example of reviling your father and mother instead of honoring them. The emphatic ὑμεῖς, "you," stands in contrast with Moses. What "you say" nullifies what "Moses said." Since what "Moses said" is God's commandment, what "you say" nullifies God's commandment and makes the beauty of legal piety ironic rather than admirable. "Corban," a Hebrew or Aramaic word that Mark translates with δῶϱον, "gift" (cf. Lev 2:1, 4, 12-13 LXX), refers to the legal device of declaring something that one owns as destined to be given in offering to God (whether or not the declaration is ever carried out or is even intended to be carried out). The declaration has the purpose and effect of keeping the declarer from letting others such as his parents use the item to meet their needs in the meantime (cf. Prov 28:24; 1 Tim 5:4; and see *b. Qidd.* 31b on honoring as providing with physical necessities).

The anarthrous ἄνθϱωπος, "man," in the clause, "if a man should say to his father or mother," stands in place of a possible τις or indefinite εἷς, "someone," and links up with ἐντάλματα ἀνθϱώπων, "commandments of men ['of human beings']" (v 7), and τὴν παϱάδοσιν τῶν ἀνθϱώπων, "the tradition of men ['of human beings']" (v 8). After "you say" at the start of v 11, we expect something like "he is not allowed" at the head of v 12. Instead, a new sentence starts before the old one finishes: "You do not allow." The anacoluthon created by this direct address heightens the accusatory tone of Jesus' charge. The emphatic position of οὐδέν, "anything," in the new sentence, "You no longer allow him to do anything for his father or mother," stresses the completeness of "nullifying the word of God by means of your tradition which you have handed on." These latter phrases extend the charges already leveled. Not only do the Pharisees and scribes leave God's commandment *to hold fast* the tradition of human beings (v 8) and set aside the commandment of God to establish the tradition that has now become their own (v 9). They have also *handed* it *on* as tradition (τῇ παϱαδόσει ὑμῶν ᾗ παϱεδώκατε — v 13; see F. Neirynck, *Duality* 76-81, for similarly emphatic cognate constructions). The intensification of the charge and its magnification in the final, sweeping statement, "And many such similar things you do," drive the Pharisees and scribes from the field. Jesus has vanquished them. They are not heard from again in the story. The redundancy in παϱόμοια, "similar," plus τοιαῦτα, "such," with πολλά, "many things," and the position of this accusative of direct object before its verb strengthen the force of the final, sweeping statement.

7:14-15 *(Matt 15:10-11)* Since Jesus has not previously summoned the crowd (with the possible exception of 3:23; but see the comments ad loc.; also 8:34), the crowd is incidental to the summons and "again" simply emphasizes the authority that he repeatedly exercises in summoning people to himself, no matter how many they are (see 3:13 and 7:31 with comments; also 3:23; 6:7 for earlier summons by Jesus and 6:45 for an earlier contrastive dismissal of a crowd by him). The command to listen echoes a similar command in 4:3 (cf. 4:9, 23, 24; 9:7). There, however, it had no object; and it took the present tense of the imperative for an emphasis consonant with the long time that Jesus spent telling parables (see 4:33-35). Here the command takes the aorist tense, normal for the imperative, and has the object μου, "me," to stress the authority inherent in Jesus' person, an authority that qualifies him to change the OT itself (cf. 9:7). Πάντες indicates that this authority holds for "all" despite their being so many as to form a crowd. The further command to understand echoes the pairing of hearing and understanding in 4:12 (cf. 8:17-18), doubles the emphasis on Jesus' didactic authority, and gives advance notice of the puzzling character of what he will now say. In view of OT food laws (see Leviticus 11; Deut 14:3-20; cf. Dan 1:5, 8-16; Esth 14:17; Tob 1:10-12; Jdt 10:5; 11:12; 12:1-2; 1 Macc 1:62-63; 2 Macc 6:5, 7, 18-28; 7:1-2, 42), it is puzzling that Jesus should say, "There is nothing from outside a man going into him which is able to defile him," or in better English, "There is nothing which is able to defile a man by going into him from outside." His further statement, "Rather, the things going out from a man are the things that defile a man," is also puzzling in that he does not identify the defiling things that go out from a man. (Again take "man" in the sense of "human being, person.") Both statements are puzzling yet again in that defilement may be taken as cultic, moral, or both. And in view of Johanan ben Zakkai's insistence on the practice of cultic purity despite the inability of external things to defile or purify a person (*Num. Rab.* 19.8), it is puzzling not only whether οὐδέν . . . ἀλλά is comparative ("not so much as") or absolute ("nothing . . . but"), but also, if it is absolute, whether the denial of defilement from without necessarily entails the giving up of cultic rules.

Since the Pharisees and scribes have not asked about unclean foods, but about unclean hands (see vv 1-5), Jesus' saying marks a progression from the question *how* to eat to the question *what* to eat. The progression is natural (therefore we need not imagine that Mark has sewn together materials which originated in different settings — see the following notes) and entails shifting from a question about the oral law of the elders to a question about the written law of the OT. Jesus' forensic power took care of the first question. His didactic authority will take care of the second, which he himself raises. Isaiah's distinction between lips and heart (v 6) may prompt Jesus to introduce the question of food laws for the purpose of denying defilement from without in favor of affirming defilement from within, i.e. for the purpose of redefining defilement as moral rather than cultic (again see the following notes and cf. D. Daube, *NTRJ* 142-43). The use of Isaiah's word "heart" in vv 19, 21 agrees with this possibility. The presence of δύναται, "is able," in v 15a and its absence from v 15b (cf. v 18) combine with the strength of the adversative ἀλλά, "rather," to highlight the difference between inability to defile and actuality of defilement (against the view of N. J. McEleney [in *CBQ* 34 (1972) 450] that "is able to defile" means scarcely more than "does defile").

7:17-23 *(Matt 15:12-20)* Jesus' entering εἰς οἶκον ἀπὸ τοῦ ὄχλου, "into a house away from the crowd," may suggest that the scene has moved back to Capernaum and the home there of Simon Peter and Andrew (cf. 1:29 with 2:1; also 3:20; 9:33). Their home would provide a natural setting for the disciples' inquiry about Jesus' statement in v 15. But 7:24 cannot refer to that home; in view of 9:33 we can hardly think that 9:28 does so; and in view of 10:1 we can hardly think that 10:10 does so. Moreover, we have read nothing that takes Jesus away from Gennesaret (6:53; contrast 7:24). Mark calls the statement in v 15 "the parable" because παραβολή has come to refer not only to comparative statements but also to puzzling ones (cf. the notes on 3:23). We have already identified the puzzles in v 15. The historical present tense of λέγει, "he says," emphasizes the authority with which Jesus utters the following words.

Those words begin with the question, "Are you thus also without understanding?" (cf. v 14; 4:12-13, 40; 6:52; 8:17, 21). "Thus also" asks whether by
way of their inquiry (οὕτως literally means "in this [way]") the disciples have put
themselves in a class with the crowd of v 14; and ὑμεῖς, "you," emphasizes the
comparison with the crowd (cf. 13:29). The next question indicates that the
disciples do know that nothing entering from outside a man is able to defile him
(οὐ plus the indicative νοεῖτε, "You know, don't you, . . . ?"). The next question
also turns quickly into a didactic statement ("because it does not enter his heart
but passes out into the latrine"), the following editorial phrase interprets the
statement as an abrogation of all food laws, and the final three statements replace
food laws. Thus the lack of understanding implied in the first question arises out
of the disciples' failure to solve the puzzles of the saying in v 15 according to
what they already know; and Mark's accent falls, not on the disciples' lack of
understanding, but on the greatness of Jesus' authority in entirely abrogating an
important and well-known Jewish practice in favor of another standard, i.e.
avoidance of moral defilement from within. Αὐτοῦ, "his," advances, not to emphasize the owner of the heart, but to let a final stress rest on the heart as such
(cf. the comments on 6:52). Repetition and assonance in εἰς τὴν καρδίαν . . . εἰς
τὴν κοιλίαν, a strongly adversative ἀλλ᾽, "but," and the following ellipsis of a
second "it goes" accent the difference between the heart and the stomach. In the
OT, defecation does not defile the defecator. (Deut 23:13-15[12-14] does not say
otherwise, but speaks of nakedness; and according to Ezek 4:12-15 human dung
defiles the food it is used to cook, not the defecator.) Mark 7:18b-19b grows out
of the non-defiling character of defecation in the OT. Therefore Jesus is turning
the law inside out in two ways: (1) by denying defilement through ingestion;
(2) by affirming defilement through excretion. But just as ingested food does not
defile the eater, so also defecated food does not defile the defecator. Hence, the
defiling emissions will be different from defecated food.

At the beginning of v 20, ἔλεγεν δέ, "but he was saying," indicates a return
to Jesus' words after the phrase "cleansing all foods" and favors that that phrase
is to be considered editorial. Δέ also marks a shift from denial of defilement from
without to affirmation of defilement from within. Since καὶ ἔλεγεν (αὐτοῖς) is not
followed by a recitative ὅτι in 4:9, 26, 30; 5:30; 8:24; 12:35, 38; 14:36, we might
consider the possibility that in v 20 ἔλεγεν δέ is followed by a ὅτι of indirect
discourse. More likely, however, the ὅτι is recitative and thereby emphasizes
Jesus' authority in setting up a new law of purity.

The introduction to the list of vices stresses their origin from within by
means of casus pendens plus a resumptive demonstrative pronoun ("What goes
out from a man — *that* defiles a man" [v 20]) and by means of a further, dual
reference to origin from within ("for [1] from within [2] out of the heart of men"
[v 21a]). The duality of this further reference and the forward position that it
enjoys in its own clause add to the emphasis on interior origin. The switch from
"man" to "men" shows the singular and the Greek definite articles to be generic.
It is possible that "evil designs," the only item in the Greek text of the vice-list
to have a definite article, stands as a general heading over the vices, or at least

over those also mentioned in the plural (which come first), to stress their inner origin (cf. Prov 6:18 LXX). Favoring the possibility is the placement of this item alone before the verb. The plural of the first six nouns after "evil designs" underlines the practice of evil, the doing of evil deeds. In this section of the list the obvious similarities between "fornications" and "adulteries," between "thefts" and "covetings," and between "murders" and "malicious acts" suggest the following scheme: (a) fornication; (b) thefts; (c) murders; (a′) adulteries; (b′) covetings; (c′) malicious acts (πονηρίαι — see BAGD s.v. πονηρία). Likewise, the not-so-obvious similarities between the vices mentioned in the singular, which make up the rest of the list and have to do with defects of character more than with concrete acts, suggest the following scheme: (a) deceit (or treachery); (b) licentiousness; (c) an evil eye (i.e. stinginess [see references in R. H. Gundry, *Matthew* 113]; alternatively, envy [see BAGD s.v. ὀφθαλμός 1], though a pagan or former pagan might take the expression to mean a malevolent glance that casts a spell); (a′) slandering; (b′) insolence; (c′) senselessness (of a moral sort). According to this scheme, slander is a kind of deceit or treachery; insolence the framework of licentiousness (i.e. *open* debauchery); and stinginess a form of senselessness. Otherwise, this part of the list, or the whole list, seems to lack organization apart from the division between plural and singular nouns (though the Ten Commandments may determine the order of murders–adulteries, thefts occurring just before them here, as in Jer 7:9, and the prohibition of theft occurring just after the prohibitions of murder and adultery in the Ten Commandments and Mark 10:19; cf. the different order murder–theft–adultery in Hos 4:2). A summarizing statement begins with asyndeton and thus gives final emphasis to the inner origin and defiling effect of the vices featured in the new law of purity that Jesus has set up: "All these evil things go out from within and defile a man." Πονηρά, "evil things," echoes πονηρίαι, "malicious acts," and ὀφθαλμὸς πονηρός, "an evil eye." The modification of πονηρά by πάντα, "all," as well as by ταῦτα, "these," the forward positions of the modifiers, and the placement of the whole phrase and of ἔσωθεν, "from within," ahead of ἐκπορεύεται, "go out," intensify the emphasis. "Go out" and "defile a man" also echo the introduction to the list (v 20). The resultant inclusion intensifies yet again the emphasis on inner origin and defiling effect.

In vv 6-13 Jesus equated the Mosaic law with God's Word and scolded the Pharisees for nullifying God's Word with their tradition. Now Jesus himself is nullifying God's Word with regard to food. But it is the prerogative of Jesus as God's Son to change the Law. Such a change does not count as human tradition, for Jesus' word is divine. In view of the editorial phrase, "cleansing [i.e. 'declaring clean'] all foods," Mark's point is exactly this: Jesus has authority to change the commandments because he is divine and the elders are not (cf. S. Schulz, *Stunde* 82-83; also J. H. Neyrey in *Semeia* 35 [1986] 91-128; J. J. Pilch in *BTB* 11 [1981] 111-12; W. Paschen, *Rein und Unrein* 186-87).

NOTES

See A. Pangritz (in *Texte & Kontexte* 24 [December 1984] 28-46) for criticism of F. Belo's materialistic attempt to make vv 1-23 an attack on idealism. Jesus does not deny the difference between purity and impurity, but redefines it. D. E. Nineham (188) turns things upside down in saying that Mark seems to put vv 1-23 here as "a reminder that this ministry . . . was to be brought to an ignominious end." There can be no reminder, because Mark has yet to mention an ignominious end; and when he does come to narrate it, he will do all he can to take away the ignominy. His purpose here is to trumpet abroad the polemical and legal triumphs of Jesus. E. S. Malbon ("The Narrative Context of Mark 7:1-23," a paper read at the SBL conference in Chicago, December 1984) thinks that the Galilean setting out of doors gives Jesus, a Galilean and outdoorsman, an advantage over the scribes from Jerusalem, who are indoorsmen far from their base of power. But Mark's first emphasis on the overpowering authority of Jesus found him indoors — in a synagogue, the haunt of scribes (1:21-28) — and Mark will yet emphasize that authority as exercised in the temple at Jerusalem (most of chaps. 11–12). And what of the non-scribal Pharisees in the present passage? They are not indoorsmen, and probably not Jerusalemites, either.

In v 1 R. A. Cole (118) thinks of hendiadys: "the Pharisaic scribes." But for that meaning we would expect either "the scribes of the Pharisees" (as an echo of 2:16) or "some of" to precede "the Pharisees" and "the scribes" rather than to come between them; and the repetition of "the" with "scribes" stands somewhat in the way (cf. 2:18). E. P. Gould (125) thinks that "some of" implies that the scribes are not so well represented as the Pharisees, but the same phrase at 2:6 carried no comparative implication. According to A. J. Hultgren (*Jesus and His Adversaries* 118), "some of the disciples" represents Gentile Christians in Mark's day who do not practice handrinsing, as distinguished from other disciples who do practice it and thus represent Jewish Christians in Mark's day who continue the practice. But the implication that other disciples are eating with rinsed hands is unnecessary — and unlikely, since practicers would hardly eat with non-practicers. The more likely implication is that other disciples are not eating at all. Besides, the practicers are Jewish. "Coming from Jerusalem" probably modifies only "some of the scribes"; for otherwise Mark would be implying that although only some of the scribes living in Jerusalem come, all the Pharisees living there come (G. Wohlenberg 200). Furthermore, the scribes of 3:22 were mentioned without the Pharisees and described as having come down from Jerusalem. Here, Galilean Pharisees may have called scribes from Jerusalem to help them against Jesus; for the wisdom of Jerusalemites was well known (*Lam. Rab.* 1.1 §4).

See C. E. B. Cranfield (231) against eliminating a full stop at the end of v 1. To eliminate it would make the cultic practices of the γάϱ-statement in vv 3-4 the reason for gathering together in v 1 rather than the reason for asking the question in v 5. But the cultic practices make a better reason for asking the question than for gathering together.

"Seeing" does not favor an official inspection or a purposed action by Jewish authorities, but neither does it disallow such an inspection or action (against J. Ernst 202; again see the comments and notes on 3:22). Hyperbaton occurs more often in Aramaic than in Greek, the present subject matter favors an Aramaic background, and Mark's frequent translations of Aramaic show his acquaintance with it. Therefore hyperbaton is more likely in v 2 than is a combination of "seeing someone doing something" (cf. 1:10) and "seeing that someone is doing something" (cf. 2:16; C. E. B. Cranfield 231; M. Black, *Aramaic Approach* 53-54).

There is no disparity between the picking up of fragments in 6:43 and the eating of the loaves in 7:2; for loaves are not eaten whole, but only after being broken into fragments. Nor does the back reference to the loaves with which Jesus fed the five thousand encourage a eucharistic interpretation (Q. Quesnell, *Mind of Mark* 221-29). That interpretation requires the disciples to have eaten along with the five thousand, i.e. in conjunction with Jesus' taking bread, blessing it, breaking it, and giving it to the disciples, as at the institution of the Lord's Supper. Furthermore, Mark's account of the institution will use the anarthrous singular "bread" (ἄρτον — 14:22) rather than the arthrous plural (7:2) or the arthrous singular (7:5). Nor does the question about the loaves link up with the failure to understand on the basis of the loaves in 6:52; 7:17-18; 8:4, 14-21. For there it is the disciples who do not understand. Here it is the Pharisees and some of the scribes from Jerusalem who ask a question; and as indicated by Jesus' responses, they ask an accusatory question whereas the disciples do not.

A back reference to the loaves with which Jesus fed the five thousand eliminates any need to interpret the definite article with "loaves" in v 2 (and presumably with "bread" or "food" in v 5) as meaning "their" (so E. C. Maloney, *Semitic Interference* 109), to describe the singular in v 5 (cf. 3:20; 6:8; 7:27; 8:14; 14:22) as more Semitic than the plural in v 2 (so J. Wellhausen [1. Aufl.] 56-57), or to posit a generalizing switch in meaning from "loaves" to "food" (cf. R. P. Booth, *Jesus and the Laws of Purity* 121-22). To eat bread (ἄρτον, singular) is to eat food in general (BAGD s.v. ἄρτος 2; M. Ottossohn in *TDOT* 1. 237); but bread is a staple, and the plural ἄρτους in v 2 suggests loaves of bread in particular (cf. 2:26; 6:37, 38, 41 [bis], 44, 52; 8:4, 5, 6, 14, 16, 17, 19). It might be argued that since Mark uses "some of" with "the disciples" nowhere else, v 2 looks traditional. But "some of the scribes" in v 1 may affect Mark's composition in v 2. Besides the arthrous singular ἄρτον in v 5, what does favor that tradition underlies v 2 is the explanation, "this is [= i.e.] unrinsed [hands]"; for apart from tradition Mark "would probably have directly substituted ἀνίπτοις for κοιναῖς" (Booth, op. cit. 35; also 156-73 for the pre-Jesuanic consideration of hands apart from the rest of the body as susceptible to defilement, and ibid. 121; M. Smith, *Tannaitic Parallels* 31-32, on "defiled" as an assumption of defilement because handrinsing has not insured purity; cf. esp. *b. Šabb.* 14a).

To a Gentile ignorant of Jewish language concerning cultic purity, κοιναῖς would mean "common" as opposed to "private." Hence, Mark explains with ἀνίπτοις, "unrinsed." His usual introduction to such an explanation, "which is" (3:17; 7:11, 34; 12:42; 15:16, 42), gives way to "this is" in order that the demonstrative pronoun may highlight Jewish practice as different from that of the Gentiles for whom he writes. The proper cultic synonym for κοιναῖς is ἀκαθάρτοις, "impure" (cf. v 19c; Acts 10:14, 28, 11:8); but Mark is more interested in explaining the *reason* for defilement (failure to rinse) than in a simple definition of κοιναῖς as *meaning* defilement.

It is commonly stated that at the time of Mark very few Jews practiced handrinsing and the other cultic rules mentioned by him in vv 3-4. For example, some of the Pharisees called *haberim* are singled out as a minority who banded together in small associations to maintain cultic purity among themselves. It is also said that not till after 70 C.E. was there a move to generalize those rules among the Jews. But not very much documentary evidence about the matter has survived from the time of Mark and before. Besides his statement, which points to an early general practice, Jdt 12:7 speaks of immersion prior to morning prayer and of staying in a tent till the evening meal, apparently to preserve purity, which would eliminate the need for handrinsing just before the meal (cf. Mark 7:4). Similarly, *Sib. Or.* 3:591-92 says that the Jews "are always sanctifying their skin [some MSS read 'hands']" at dawn for prayer. *Sib. Or.* 4:165-66 speaks of immersion and prayer, and *Ep. Arist.* 305-6 of a "custom of all the Jews [cf. Mark's 'all the Jews' — v 3] to wash hands while praying" (cf. Lev 15:11; Pss 24:3-4; 26:6; Isa 1:15-16a [metaphorical usage depending on a physical practice]). Though Christian and dating probably from late in the first century, John 2:1-10 contains earlier tradition and reflects Jewish practice; so the water of purification contained in stone vessels and mentioned in John 2:6 must serve the Jewish practice of handrinsing, apparently on the part of a general crowd at a wedding, since the immersion pools in which persons and vessels were purified could have hardly any drawn water (*m. 'Ed.* 1:3; cf. *m. Miqw.* 1:1–6:11). *M. Yad.* 1:1–2:4 talks of handrinsing without stating its purpose, *m. 'Ed.* 5:6 seems to put rejection of handrinsing in the category of heresy, and *m. Ḥag.* 2:5-6 mentions immersion before eating. From a later date *Num. Rab.* 20.21 tells of a shopkeeper's recognizing Jewish customers by their handrinsing (cf. *b. Šabb.* 14b, 62b; *y. Šabb.* 1, 3d, 40 and other rabbinic literature cited in Str-B 1. 695-704; 4/2. 627).

In none of these passages does handrinsing appear as an innovation or as the hallmark of a minority of Jews; rather, it is assumed to be traditional and general. In the earliest Jewish sources handrinsing is not associated with eating; rather, with praying. Jdt 12:7 seems to imply an association with eating, however (see the preceding paragraph here); and the setting of a wedding in John 2:6 favors an association with eating over one with praying. Since pagans commonly rinsed their hands or dipped their right hand in water before entering a temple, praying, and sacrificing (see E. P. Sanders, *Jewish Law* 39-41, 262-63), the Jewish association with praying may stem from pagan influence without negating a more distinctively Jewish association with eating. Because of Jewish food laws and the use of hands for eating, it would be only natural that among Jews handrinsing should be associated with eating. The weakness of early literary evidence for this association (a weakness used negatively toward Mark [ibid.]) may therefore run parallel to a similar weakness with respect to the related practice of immersion in pools, about which Sanders writes: "Archeology shows that purifying water in a miqveh by connecting it with another pool is much earlier than the earliest literary evidence. It also reveals that stone vessels were not subject to impurity and that making them was a substantial industry. Literature does not even hint at the second fact, and it points somewhat weakly to the first" (ibid. 243; see 214-27 for details).

R. P. Booth (*Jesus and the Laws of Purity* 185-86) talks about "a remarkable uniformity of evidence, both before and after Jesus' time, that hands were rinsed to remove impurity," but Booth draws back on the ground that handrinsing would seem useless apart from preceding immersion to purify the whole body — yet "we have no cause to think . . . that the questioning Pharisees believed the disciples to have immersed that day." That is an argument from silence, however; and at Luke 11:38, as Booth admits (op. cit. 245, n. 123), a Pharisee's astonishment that Jesus, who was neither a priest nor a Pharisee nor one of the *haberim,* had not immersed himself points in the direction of a general practice of immersion by lay Jews. Furthermore, the archeological evidence referred to above supports an early such practice; and we should not let later mishnaic discussions of different grades of defilement lead us to expect too much from our earlier literary sources. In view of *t. Ber.* 5:13, 27 (cited by E. P. Sanders, *Jewish Law* 228-30, for lack of uniformity after 70 C.E.; cf. *m. Para* 10:5, too), we may suppose greater uniformity in Mark's time than later. Hence, the extent of his hyperbole "all the Jews" may itself have been subject to hyperbole in modern scholarship.

Other opinions limit the cultic washings specified by Mark not only to Pharisaic associates (*haberim* — Booth, op. cit. 190-203), but also to priests prior to partaking of sacrifices in the temple (cf. Lev 22:1-16) or to the Pharisees in general (J. Neusner, *Rabbinic Traditions* 3. 288; idem, *From Politics to Piety* 83-86; idem, *Judaism* 70; J. Bowker, *Jesus and the Pharisees* 38-40). The hypothesis that Jews of the Diaspora followed these practices more closely and more generally than Palestinian Jews did (see, e.g., E. P. Sanders, *Jewish Law* 39-41, 228-36, 262-63) may seem to get support from Jdt 12:7; *Sib. Or.* 3:591-94; *Ep. Arist.* 305-6. But the setting of Jdt 12:7 looks Palestinian (Booth, op. cit. 159-60); and though living among Gentiles might have driven some Jews to extremes in the practice of cultic purity, considerations of convenience are more likely to have led most of them to laxer practice. Whatever his personal identity, the author of Mark knows enough to translate Aramaic expressions a number of times, to explain "Preparation" as the day before the Sabbath (15:42), and so on. Right in this passage he uses κοιναῖς Jewishly, mentions "the tradition of the elders" in characteristically Jewish fashion, and accurately refers to the Jewish practice of immersion. Therefore he probably knows what he is talking about also when describing the Jewish practice of handrinsing before eating.

By referring to Jews in the third person, Mark adopts either the ethnic standpoint of his Gentile audience or the theological standpoint of Christians for whom "there is neither Jew nor Greek" (Gal 3:28a). The post-Jesuanic temporal standpoint and the possibly Christian theological standpoint make the disciples under review non-exceptions to the hyperbolic description. J. W. Bowman (161) doubts that Gentiles would be interested in the long explanation provided by vv 3-4, and so thinks that it is addressed to Jewish Christians to let them revel in their violations of Jewish practices that they formerly followed. But Jewish Christians would need no explanation of such practices.

Rinsing hands πυγμῇ probably means rinsing hands that are cupped in a fist-like fashion, but with fingers held slightly apart to allow full coverage with the least possible amount of water — alternatively, with a fistful of water (see BAGD s.v πυγμή 1 for these and other views; S. M. Reynolds in *JBL* 85 [1966] 87-88 against the view of Str B 2. 13-14 that the v.l. πυκνά is correct; M. Hengel in *ZNW* 60 [1969] 182-98 for a possible Latinism, rebutted by Reynolds in *ZNW* 62 [1971] 295-296; and T. C. Skeat in *JTS* ns 41 [1990] 525-27 for a highly imaginative conjecture that makes πυγμῇ an early scribal error; cf. Exod 30:17-21; Lev 15:11; Deut 21:6; 1QS 5:13-14; *m. Yad.* 1:1-2; *b. Ber.* 60b; *b. Soṭa* 4b; *b. Šabb.* 62b). Some have interpreted καὶ ἀπ' ἀγορᾶς ἐὰν μὴ βαπτίσωνται οὐκ ἐσθίουσιν as meaning, "And they do not eat [anything] from the market place unless they immerse [it]," with the result that v 3 refers to the cleansing of hands, v 4a to the cleansing of food, and v 4b to the cleansing of utensils (see E. F. F. Bishop in *ExpTim* 61 [1949-50] 219 and the literature cited in W. L. Lane 243, n. 5; also M. Reiser, *Syntax und Stil* 18-19; E. C. Maloney, *Semitic Interference* 136-37, against the necessity of Semitic interference). For this meaning, however, we would expect the active voice: βαπτίσωσιν. As it is, the middle voice of βαπτίσωνται looks reflexive: "they immerse themselves." If βαπτίσωνται thus expresses something about the persons of those who eat, "from the market place" probably does so, too (BAGD s.v. ἀγορά). Then the construction is pregnant: "[coming] from [the] market place, they . . ." (cf. ibid. s.v. ἀπό I5; BDF §209[4]; and the v.l. ὅταν ἔλθωσιν, "whenever they come," in D W *pc* it vg^mss). But the suggestion of J. Lambrecht (in *ETL* 53 [1977] 43, n. 58) that we supply "bringing with them food" makes the construction overly pregnant.

Though the v.l. ῥαντίσωνται, "they sprinkle themselves," enjoys the impressive support of א B *pc* sa, we should give the nod to βαπτίσωνται, partly because it conforms to the Jewish practice of self-immersion (contrast Jesus' failure to immerse himself according to Luke 11:37-38; see R. P. Booth, *Jesus and the Laws of Purity* 23-24) and partly because the strangeness of this practice to Gentiles might prompt a scribal change to the more easily understandable ῥαντίσωνται. The possibility that ῥαντίσωνται refers to sprinkling the water of the ashes of the red heifer (Num 19:17-19) suffers from impracticability: the ashes are kept at Jerusalem and used not till the third day after defilement. Practicers of such a rule would have to stay away from market places or starve to death. On the other hand, self-immersion goes beyond handrinsing, which takes away only lesser impurity than what might be contracted in the market place (ibid. 200-202).

"Immersions" of cups, pitchers, and copper kettles (and of dining couches if we follow the v.l. of A D W Θ *f*^1,13 Majority Text latt sy^p,h sa^mss Or; cf. the immersion of beds and mattresses in *m. Miqw.* 7:6-7) make up Mark's other examples of tradition. See B. M.

Metzger, *Textual Commentary* ad loc., for discussion of text critical questions; and T. A. Burkill, *New Light* 104-8; J. Gnilka 1. 277 against regarding vv 3-4 as a late gloss. Since evidence is lacking that Christians disputed among themselves or with Jews any more over the practices listed in addition to handrinsing than over handrinsing itself, i.e. not at all, we can scarcely say that Mark adds the further practices to increase the relevance of Jesus' reply.

R. A. Guelich (1. 363) adduces several arguments for ascribing the parenthetical explanation in vv 3-4 to a pre-Marcan redactor rather than to Mark himself. (1) Only here in Mark does "the Jews" occur as a collective designation. (But hapaxes count neither for nor against this or that redactor [or tradition], for one is as likely as another to use a hapax [see p. 21]; and "the Jews" in the oft-repeated phrase "the king of the Jews" looks like a collective designation [15:2, 9, 12, 18, 26].) (2) Ellipsis does not characterize Mark's style. (But the kind of ellipsis that occurs in v 4a does not characterize anybody's style and therefore again counts neither for nor against this or that redactor [or tradition].) (3) The parenthetical explanation centers on the tradition of the elders, whereas Mark's interest lies in the question of defiled hands. (It is a mistake, however, to pit the elders' tradition against the question of defiled hands; for this question grows out of that tradition, and in the parenthetical explanation the question of defiled hands enjoys pride of place, the reference to the tradition of the elders occurring in a subsequent participial phrase and the references to other practices all having to do with immersions that parallel handrinsing.) Though coming from the same author who is responsible for the parenthetical explanation, "this is" (v 2) would not argue strongly for a pre-Marcan redactor; for Mark had reason to switch from his more usual "which is" (see the foregoing notes).

The argument that the aiming of the accusatory question at disciples rather than at Jesus betrays an origin of the material in the primitive church, represented by the disciples, not in his life, does not hold water. For later fabrication would probably have appealed to Jesus' own practice, and the Pharisees' and scribes' assumption that as a teacher Jesus is responsible for the conduct of his disciples agrees with rabbinic standards (D. Daube in *NTS* 19 [1972-73] 1-16, esp. 4-8). Nobody in a non-observant milieu would think to fabricate a dispute with Jesus on handrinsing (against C. E. Carlston, *Parables* 164-65); and as noted before, evidence is lacking even for a dispute between the Palestinian church and non-Christian Jews on handrinsing (against R. Bultmann, *HST* 18).

According to D. R. Schwartz (in *NTS* 32 [1986] 153-59), Jesus probably does not castigate the Pharisees for overemphasizing external purity, but participates in Pharisaic criticism of that overemphasis on the part of priests. This opinion flies in the face of Jesus' addressing his criticism to Pharisees and scribes. See the notes on 2:17, the comments on 2:27, and the notes on 4:1-34 concerning the formulas that introduce his statements in vv 6, 9, 14, 18, 20. These formulas do not necessarily betray the compositing of originally independent materials. The presence of a Greek theatre in Sepphoris, near Nazareth, enhances the possibility of Jesus' using ὑποκριτῶν for "stage actors" (i.e. "hypocrites") primarily concerned about their public image instead of true piety (A. Stock in *BTB* 16 [1985] 3-7; R. A. Batey, *Jesus & the Forgotten City* 83-103; cf. *Pss. Sol.* 4:6, which contains a possibly Pharisaic charge of hypocrisy in others). J. Gnilka (1. 282) states that in biblical Greek hypocrisy has to do with objective discrepancy, not with subjective pretense (cf. N. Turner, *Christian Words* 219-20). But the OT alliance of evil with deceit (see U. Wilckens in *TDNT* 8. 565-66) and the NT distinction between false profession and true (see, e.g., Matt 6:1-17; 7:21-23; 13:24-30, 36-43, 47-50; 22:11-14; 25:1-13) may prompt the biblical use of ὑποκριτής, "actor," in the pejorative sense of "hypocrite." To the extent that acting on stage lies in the background, hypocrisy includes subjective pretense as well as objective discrepancy. "Teaching [as] teachings commandments of human beings" (v 7) looks similar to Col 2:22, "according to the commandments and teachings of human beings" (with a generic Greek article before "human beings"), and to Titus 1:14, "Jewish myths and commandments of human beings who turn away from the truth." But Col 2:22; Titus 1:14 may depend on Mark or a pre-Marcan tradition as easily as vice versa, or both sides may depend on Isa 29:13 LXX. In fact, the order commandments–teachings and the "and" connecting those two nouns in Col 2:22 match Isa 29:13 LXX rather than Mark 7:7; and the "commandments of human beings" in Mark 7:7 matches Isa 29:13 LXX rather than "teachings of human beings" in Col 2:22.

According to E. Wendling (*Entstehung* 89-90), καλῶς in v 6 is serious, dull, detractive from καλῶς in v 9, and therefore inauthentic. On the contrary, the first καλῶς delivers a sarcastic barb which shades nicely into the ironic καλῶς that follows. For two reasons, J. D. Crossan (*Four Other Gospels* 83-85) thinks that Mark inserts the accusation of Isa 29:13 in direct dependence on *PEger.* 2: (1) since Matt 15:7; Acts 28:25 reflect Mark 7:6 in the unusual introduction, "Beautifully did Isaiah prophesy about you," Mark must take the introduction from *PEger.* 2; (2) except for following *PEger.* 2, no very obvious reason induces Mark to omit "draws near with their mouth," whereas *PEger.* 2 omits it because of having just used "mouth" in Jesus' protest, "Why do you call me with your mouth 'Master'?" But (1) does not logically follow, for *PEger.* 2 might just as easily reflect the NT. As for (2), we have already seen that the omission focuses the remainder on the theme of honor for a link with vv 9-13; and in *PEger.* 2, "with your mouth" may come from Isa 29:13 just as "Why do you call me . . . 'Master'?" may come from Luke 6:46. That is to say, *PEger.* 2 may be composited of OT and NT passages. According to R. P. Booth (*Jesus and the Laws of Purity* 40), the omission of the people's coming near with their mouth may indicate Mark's or the church's unwillingness to admit that the Israelites come near to God in their supplications. This suggestion leaves the question why Mark or the church is not equally unwilling to admit that the Israelites honor God with their lips. It also misses the shift of referent from the nation to the Pharisees and scribes.

M.-E. Boismard (in *L'Évangile selon Marc* 93-96) thinks that vv 9-13 are added to the primitive text of Mark under the influence of Matt 15:3-6. But see R. H. Gundry, *Matthew* 303-5, for evidence of Matthew's redacting Mark. According to J. Wellhausen (2. Aufl., 54), vv 9-13 form a parallel with vv 6-8, not a continuation of them. The opinion is only partly true. A formula introduces Jesus' words in vv 6 and 9, but "he said to them" yields to "and he was saying to them." In both passages the accusation starts with "beautifully," but sarcasm yields to irony (missed by treating Jesus' words in v 9 as a question). An OT quotation forms the centerpiece of each accusation, but the introductory formula "as it stands written" plus a recitative ὅτι yields to "for Moses said" for an antithetic parallel with "but you say." Apart from "beautifully," the first verse of vv 9-13 parallels the last verse of vv 6-8 far more closely than it parallels the first verse of vv 6-8. Even so, holding fast the tradition of human beings yields to establishing your tradition. And most importantly, vv 9-13 substantiate the accusation leveled in vv 6-8. So vv 9-13 mark a progression rather than presenting a carbon copy.

To say that in and of itself Jesus' condemnation of the Pharisees and scribes implies the end-time apostasy (so K. Berger, *Gesetzesauslegung* 1. 489-90) smacks of overinterpretation. For καλῶς, "beautifully," cf. 12:28, 32. The use of "tradition" and "hold fast" in the editorial vv 3-4 does not prove the redactional fabrication of v 8, where the terms reappear. Mark may write vv 3-4 with the tradition behind v 8 in mind (see also R. P. Booth, *Jesus and the Laws of Purity* 40-41). It is unclear why E. Schweizer (146) should think that the second "beautifully" (v 8) and the shift from "the tradition of the elders" (vv 3, 5) to "your tradition" (v 9) imply the later addition of vv 9-13. Speakers and writers often repeat themselves with twists of phraseology and meaning. In v 10 the quotation of Exod 20:12 (= Deut 5:16) is entirely Septuagintal, but in agreement with the MT as well, and the quotation of Exod 21:17 basically Septuagintal (see R. H. Gundry, *Use of the OT*

12-16, and again p. 22 in the present commentary for a caveat against drawing diachronic inferences from use of the LXX). Since "the tradition of human beings" occurs in the singular (v 8), it is very doubtful that in the same sentence the singular of "the command-ment of God" contrasts the unity of God's commandment with the multiplicity of "com-mandments of human beings" (v 7), or that Jesus is attacking the Pharisees' counting 613 commandments in the OT law, or that he is pointing to the commandment to love God (Deut 6:5) as all-inclusive. On the contrary, he selects another commandment in v 10 and elsewhere avoids concentrating on a single commandment by adding love of neighbor to love of God (12:28-31). See B. M. Metzger, *Textual Commentary* ad loc., on the vv.ll. στήσητε, "establish," and τηρήσητε, "keep," in v 9. "Establish" makes a better internal contrast with "set aside" in the same sentence. "Keep" makes a better external parallel with "hold fast" in the preceding sentence. A better internal contrast probably weighs more than a better external parallel. In v 11, ὅ is an accusative of reference: "with regard to whatever of mine you might be benefited by."

See M. Black, *Aramaic Approach* 107, for a Semitic indefinite use of ἄνθρωπος, "a man, human being," in v 11, and M. Reiser, *Syntax und Stil* 20-21, against a necessarily Semitic element. It is sometimes argued that Jesus' comments on Corban do not pit oral tradition against scripture, but scripture against scripture, i.e. the written law on vows against the written law on parents. The argument is simplistic. Jesus is attacking the oral traditioners' misuse of the written law on vows in making it nullify the written law on parents (see T. W. Manson, *Teaching* 315-19). But the claim is then made that the makers of the oral tradition agree with Jesus (*m. Ned.* 3:2; 9:1; cf. Str B 1. 706). They agree with him to the extent of saying that no vow should be taken that works to the detriment of parents, and even to the extent of annulling such a vow at the request of the vower. But so far as we can tell, they insist on keeping the vow, even though wrongly made, if the vower fails to request an annulment (*m. Ned.* 9:1; Philo *Hypoth.* 7:3-5 §358; cf. Num 30:3[2]; Deut 23:22-24[21-23]). Jesus condemns such insistence and thereby implies that any vow which would void God's Word must itself be voided (B. Witherington III, *Women* 12-13; see S. Westerholm, *Jesus and Scribal Authority* 76-78; A. I. Baumgarten in *JANESCU* 16-17 [1984-85] 5-17 for the view that before 70 C.E. Pharisees would not have released the son in Jesus' example from the Corban-vow, that leniency in such cases came later). Jesus' demand that would-be disciples "hate" their parents (Matt 10:37 par. Luke 14:26) may look like the rabbinic argument that a vow to God overrides a duty to parents. But Jesus is talking about a vow made for the purpose of depriving parents self-servingly, whereas following him even at the expense of parents has a different, self-denying purpose.

R. Pesch (1. 370) suggests that the scribes' having come from Jerusalem (v 1) may determine the choice of Corban, a gift that might benefit the temple there (cf. Matt 27:6), to represent the nullifying of God's commandment. On Corban, see esp. J. D. M. Derrett, *Studies* 1. 112-17; J. A. Fitzmyer, *Essays* 93-100; idem in *Jésus aux origines de la chris-tologie* 89-90; G. Vermes in *Essays in Honour of Yigael Yadin* 364-66; M. Wilcox in *ANRW* II 25/2. 1002-4; H. P. Rüger in *Markus-Philologie* 80-81; H. Hübner, *Gesetz* 147-51; E. P. Sanders, *Jewish Law* 54-57; other literature in BAGD s.v.; cf. Ezek 20:28; 40:43; CD 6:15-16; 9:1; 16:14-15; Josephus *Ant* 4.4.4 §73; idem, *Ag.Ap.* 1.22 §167; *m. Ned.* 1:1-2. See E. J. Goodspeed, *Problems* 60-62, on the possibility of reading the indicative ὠφελήθης in a contrary-to-fact condition with ἐάν, "you would have benefited," rather than the subjunctive ὠφεληθῇς, "you might be benefited." Because Philo (*Hypoth.* 7.3-5 §358) makes Corban apply within a family but *m. Ned.* 3:2 does not, Sanders (op. cit. 56-57) hypothesizes that just as with respect to handrinsing so also with respect to Corban, Mark reflects Judaism in the Diaspora, not in Palestine. But this argument overlooks the afore-mentioned apparent requirement in the Mishnah that Corban apply even within a family unless an annulment is requested. One would hardly expect greater distance from the temple to produce greater strictness in the application of a regulation dealing with the temple; and on the whole, Judaism of the Diaspora looks less strict than Palestinian Judaism. Philo (*Spec.* 3.1 §7) equates what Moses said with God's Word (cf. vv 9-10, 13). If the clause, "which you have handed down" (v 13), extends the charges (see the comments), there is no redundancy in it and no need for the conjectural emendation παρελάβετε, "you have received," which *would* be redundant (cf. v 4).

The v.l. πάντα, which produces the meaning "all the crowd" (v 14), lacks the weight of external evidence favoring πάλιν, "again." It also seems to stem from the observation that Jesus has not summoned a crowd before (cf. the foregoing comments). This observation favors that Mark is writing v 14 on the basis of tradition. The main words in this verse appear often in Mark, but may do so because of pre-Marcan tradition concerning Jesus' deeds and words. We do not know enough to deny the authenticity of this tradition. 2 Sam 20:16; Isa 6:9; 1 Macc 2:65 suggest that Jesus may well have solicited attention with a call to hear and understand. Nor do we know enough to deny a Jesuanic practice of saying something to a crowd and explaining it in private to disciples (vv 14-15 and 17-23, respectively; cf. D. Daube, *NTRJ* 141-50, and, esp. in view of the word "parable" [v 17], Mark 4:10 in context and with comments and notes ad loc.). No historical difficulty attaches to the practice, and there is nothing messianic about the present saying (v 15) and its explanation (vv 18-23). Even if there were, no historical difficulty would necessarily attach to it. To be sure, W. Wrede (*Messianic Secret* 139-40) sees a historical difficulty in the non-mention of a crowd till v 14 and concludes that Mark unhistorically drags them in to prepare for the motif of secrecy in vv 17-23. But public pronouncements to the Pharisees and scribes suffice for such preparation (vv 1-13), and it is no more unlikely from the historical standpoint that a crowd have been present than that the disciples are often present though unmentioned till they become significant in the narrative (see, e.g., the non-mention of the disciples between 1:35-38 and 2:15-17, though nobody denies the implication that they were with Jesus; likewise between 2:23-28 and 3:7-12; and within the single pericope 3:20-35 the crowd of disciples do not appear till v 32, in 4:1-34 not till v 10, et passim). A number of passages make unacceptable the presupposition that a crowd have not been standing around listening to the present dispute (2:1-12; 3:1-6; 6:54-56; 10:1-12; 11:15-18, 27-33; 12:1-37).

J. D. Crossan (*In Fragments* 253-55) avers that because the second person in *Gos. Thom.* 14c matches that in Q (Matt 23:25-26 par. Luke 11:38-40), we should prefer *Gos. Thom.* 14c rather than Mark 7:15 as original (cf. J. D. G. Dunn in *À cause de l'Évangile* 263-64). But Q has to do with immersion, not with handrinsing or avoidance of defiling foods, and therefore does not relate to v 15. Furthermore, the second person in *Gos. Thom.* 14c need not relate to Q, but may derive from assimilation to materials in 14ab with which 14c has been thrown together. In other words, Q provides no foundation on which to build a comparison favoring the originality of *Gos. Thom.* 14c over that of Mark 7:15. Cf. R. P. Booth, *Jesus and the Laws of Purity* 23-25, 227, n. 4; and see W. Schrage, *Verhältnis* 55-57, for the dependence of *Gos. Thom.* 14c on Matt 5:11, whose "into the mouth" reflects Matthew's favorite diction (R. H. Gundry, *Matthew* 307-8) and probably affects Acts 11:8 (cf. idem in *The Four Gospels 1992*) rather than going back with Acts 11:8 to a more original phraseology than Mark's (so Crossan, loc. cit.).

The argument of J. D. G. Dunn (in *À cause de l'Évangile* 263-64) that Matt 15:11 comes closer to the original than does Mark 7:15 rests largely on what he thinks to be an a priori likelihood that here and elsewhere Matthew's parallels to Mark reflect oral traditions as well as Mark. But before we presume that Matthew actually does reflect those traditions, we need to test whether Matthew's differences from Mark fall into patterns adequately explicable as redaction of Mark according to characteristically Matthean diction, style, and theology rather than as a mixture of such redaction and oral traditions identifiable because they interrupt those patterns. If so, we have no need to count on Matthew's use of oral traditions no matter how many of them were floating around. The more consistent the patterns, the less likely the intrusion of oral traditions. See R. H. Gundry, *Matthew* passim, for evidence of largely consistent patterns.

The definite article with ἄνθρωπος (ter in v 15) is generic ("a man, human being") and rules out a Semitic use of ἄνθρωπος for the indefinite τις ("someone"; see E. C. Maloney, *Semitic Interference* 131-34). Many commentators remark the importance of v 15 for ethics: not outward action, but the disposition of the heart makes a person morally clean or unclean. Makes a *person* morally clean or unclean — yes; but we must guard against overinterpreting v 15 to mean that dispositions determine the moral character of all actions, as though a right disposition would launder murder (to take an extreme case). Dispositions generate actions corresponding to them — that is the correct point to make.

By appeal to the Semitic "not . . . but" for relative degree ("Defilement from outside is less important to avoid than defilement from within"), the attempt is constantly made to avoid in v 15 an absolute denial of defilement from without (cf. H. Kruse in *VT* 4 [1954] 385-400). Relative degree would put Jesus in the camp of the OT prophets (cf. Isa 1:1-17; 58:1-14; Jer 7:21-31; Hos 6:4-6; Amos 5:21-27). B. F. Meyer (*Aims* 149) argues for relative degree by citing Jesus' polemics against ritual without morality. But the supportive citations are not persuasive. Verses 10-13 do not mean that taking a vow which will deprive one's parents is only relatively wrong. Matt 5:34 prohibits oaths absolutely (μὴ . . . ὅλως, "not . . . at all"), not relatively. Matt 23:16-22 attacks sophistry in oath-taking, but does not compare oath-taking with moral matters. Matt 23:23 makes the comparison that Meyer's argument needs, but the language of conserving ritual ("and not to forsake those things") contrasts with the disjunctive language of Mark 7:15 ("nothing . . . ; rather, . . ."; cf. the statement of H. Räisänen [in *JSNT* 16 (1982) 94, n. 41] that "the sweeping οὐδέν ['nothing'] and the strengthening δύναται ['is able']" stand in the way of interpreting Mark 7:15 only in terms of relative degree). Matt 23:25-26 does not deal with ritual practice, and the parallel Luke 11:39-41 abrogates rules of ritual cleanness (R. H. Gundry, *Matthew* 464-66).

To Meyer's citations, R. P. Booth (*Jesus and the Laws of Purity* 102-3) adds Jesus' telling the leper to observe the ritual law of cleansing (1:44) and Jesus' acknowledgement of the Sabbath commandment (2:27; 3:4). But even Booth recognizes that in all probability Jesus wanted to insure the ex-leper's reentry into normal social life, not to take a theological position on ritual law (ibid. 234, n. 131). And in 2:27; 3:4 Jesus did not describe the Sabbath as less important than human benefit, but as meant for it — hence, he and his disciples broke the Sabbath to fulfil its purpose. The argumentative appeal to the "unlawful" action of David (2:26) shows that Jesus recognized his disciples' action as breaking the Sabbath (cf. "Lord also of the Sabbath" in 2:28). His touching a leper (1:41) apparently flouted Lev 13:45-46. (On the other hand, though touching a corpse brings defilement [cf. Mark 5:41], the Law does not prohibit it.) So Jesus' behavior and comments have accorded with an absolute disjunction in v 15 better than with a comparative statement. Accenting the second member of sayings like this one (so J. Jeremias, *NT Theology* 1. 18-19) does not decide in favor of the comparative interpretation; for an absolute disjunction may include emphasis on the second member, here on the danger of defilement from within. Extended from food laws to handrinsing, v 15 exculpates the disciples of all wrongdoing only under the absolute interpretation, because the relative interpretation would tag them with venial sin. It seems doubtful that Jesus would defend them so weakly. Therefore we need not separate off vv 17-23 as giving v 15 an absolute meaning that it did not originally have. Neither its original meaning nor its authenticity depends on our doing so.

Against the radical surgery of accepting v 15a but not v 15b as authentic (or vice versa, we might add), J. D. G. Dunn (in *À cause de l'Évangile* 255, n. 13) notes that "a typical Jewish *mashal* would have balancing clauses." W. Schmithals (343) reasons that if v 15a refers to ingested food, v 15b must refer to defecated food (cf. M. Boucher, *Mysterious Parable* 64-68). Verse 15b as well as v 15a refers, then, to cultic defilement. But that meaning does not merely disagree with the OT; it also makes no point beyond that of replacing an avoidable cultic defilement (eating unclean foods) with an unavoidable cultic defilement (defecating). We should therefore take v 15b as a statement about moral defilement. Such a statement does not force us to take v 15a similarly, for the denial of cultic defilement from without may spark the affirmation of moral defilement from within not by way of logical necessity but by way of verbal and conceptual association. We have already seen this kind of progression in the shift from how to eat to what to eat. (The view that unclean food defiles a person differs from the view that the person's unclean hands defile the food, unclean hands having defiled a person even before the eating of the food.) Treating v 15a as well as v 15b in terms of moral defilement would break the association of v 15a with the earlier cultic question of eating with defiled hands. Denial of cultic defilement from without leaves room for cultic defilement from within (as from some kinds of bodily discharges — so the OT) and for moral defilement both from without and from within. Affirmation of moral defilement from within leaves room for moral defilement from without and for cultic defilement both from without and (if we disregard the preceding denial) from within. But Jesus is making only certain points, not providing a comprehensive treatment. Verses 17-23 elaborate the denial of cultic defilement from without and the affirmation of moral defilement from within and therefore do not offer an interpretation imposed on v 15 but one so natural that it is just as likely to have stemmed from Jesus as from the Gentile Hellenistic church.

It is an additional question whether vv 17-23 stem from Hellenism for other reasons, such as the physical rationale in v 19 and the vice-list in vv 21-22 (for Hellenistic parallels see F. G. Downing, *Christ and the Cynics* 129-30 §160). As explained in the foregoing comments, the physical rationale rests on a failure of the OT to regard defecated food as defiling. There is no reason to introduce Hellenistic thinking about bodily processes (as does R. P. Booth, *Jesus and the Laws of Purity* 72-73). A Hellenistic origin would probably betray itself in a contrast between soul and body. The contrast between heart and stomach looks more Jewish than Hellenistic and takes off on the earlier, Isaianic contrast between heart and lips (v 6). In response to V. Taylor (346-47), C. E. B. Cranfield (241-43) has shown that the listed vices need not derive from Hellenism through Paul, but may come from the OT, Mark naturally using terms that appear in the LXX.

We might add that even Hellenistic influence on Mark through Paul would not rule out Mark's use of dominical tradition. It would only require that he assimilate that tradition to a possibly more Hellenistic set of vices in Paul (cf. Rom 1:29-31; 1 Cor 6:9-10; Gal 5:19-21; Eph 5:3; Col 3:5, 8; 1 Tim 1:9-10; 2 Tim 3:2-5; also Wis 14:25-26; Philo *Conf.* 24 §117; idem *Heres* 35 §173; *3 Apoc. Bar.* 4:17; 8:5; 13:4). On the other hand again, the present list differs from contemporary vice-lists, both pagan and Jewish, in stressing sins against fellow human beings, not sins against God, the gods, one's nation, or the social order (M.-J. Lagrange 191). Paul's lists include items of the latter sort (hatred of God, idolatry, drunkenness, carousings, etc.). So it may be best to think that the list in Mark represents Jesus' teaching and reflects his emphasis on loving one's neighbor as the way to love God, and that Paul's lists derive from dominical tradition but show other influence as well. The vice-list in 1QS 4:9-11 provides evidence for the possibility that a first century Jew like Jesus might draw up a list such as the one Mark records.

Hellenistic Jewish literature provides little support for the view that the denial of cultic defilement and affirmation of moral defilement in vv 17-23 (and in v 15) derive from Christianized Hellenistic Judaism. Philo (*Spec.* 3 §§208-9) depreciates but does not reject laws of cultic purity. In fact, he probably does not even depreciate them, but allegorizes them. In *Migr.* 16 §§89-93 he positively warns against laxity toward cultic laws (cf. *Praem.* 1 §§2-6). Variant readings would weaken an anti-cultic implication in Pseudo-Phocylides *Sentences* 228; but even the usual reading, "Purifications of the soul, not of the body, are cleansings," depreciates rather than rejects cultic purification. The language of 1QS 2:25b-3:12; 5:13-14 is just as strong, yet emanates from a community noted for emphasis on cultic purity (cf. *y. Ter.* 8:3-4; *y. 'Abod. Zar.* 2:3). *Ep. Arist.* 234 offers a relative depreciation, not an absolute rejection; for the question has to do with "the *highest* form of glory."

The view of J. D. Crossan (*In Fragments* 250-55; *Four Other Gospels* 85) that Mark composes the dialogue in vv 17-23 around the traditional aphorism in v 15 stumbles over the participial phrase in v 19c. Its distance from the subject which it apparently modifies ("he" in v 18a) favors that Mark is working with tradition in vv 17-23 as well as in v 15. Free composition would probably have produced less awkwardness.

"Parable" in v 17 may have led to scribal interpolation of v 16 from 4:23. The external support for v 16 does not weigh enough to ascribe the verse to Mark. The absence of a Matthean parallel to v 16 also weighs against its originality in Mark, especially since Matthew does take over the same expression in 13:9 (par. Mark 4:9; see also Matt 11:15; 13:43). The view that "parable" does not accurately describe v 15, but stresses the disciples' ignorance (so H. Anderson 187), falsely treats v 15 as straightforward in meaning.

The two questions in v 18 may betray Mark's love of duality, which says nothing for or against the presence of underlying tradition, however. R. P. Booth (*Jesus and the Laws of Purity* 49) rejects the first question as Mark's redactional emphasis on the disciples' dullness and accepts the second question as authentic because of its greater mildness (but see the foregoing comments on v 18). P. Sigal (in *PEGLBS* 2 [1982] 79) asks why Jesus says that food does not go into the heart when nobody believes or says that it does (cf. Q. Quesnell, *Mind of Mark* 94). But Jesus does not imply that anybody believes or says so; rather, he is building on a point obvious to all ("You know, don't you, . . . ?").

G. Vermes (*Jesus the Jew* 29; cf. M. Black, *Aramaic Approach* 217-18; J. D. M. Derrett, *Studies* 1. 176-83; B. J. Malina in *Forum* 4 [3, 1988] 22-25) thinks (1) that in v 19 "food" was metaphorical in Aramaic for "excrement"; (2) that a possible Aramaic euphemism for the latrine — viz., דּוּכָא, "the place" — may have invited a pun on the verb דְּכָא, "be clean"; (3) that the function of cleansing belonged originally to the latrine; (4) that the original form of the saying may have run, ". . . it does not go into his heart but into his stomach, and so goes out into the place [the latrine], where all food [excrement] is cleansed away"; (5) that therefore Jesus did not repeal food laws; and (6) that Mark twisted the saying to justify Gentile Christian abandonment of those laws. But this reconstruction, the similar reading in sy^s, and the other vv.ll. all smack of attempts to improve Mark's syntax, which precisely because of its disjointedness looks original.

R. P. Booth (*Jesus and the Laws of Purity* 72-73) argues that a Jew speaking to a Jewish audience would not argue that defecation can rid a man of cultic defilement contracted from food. But Jesus does not talk about getting rid of cultic defilement; he denies the contraction of such defilement in the first place. According to J. M. Bassler (in *JR* 66 [1986] 170), Mark uses Jesus' voiding of God's Word (i.e. the food laws) to make credible the disciples' incomprehension and thus to deliver the audience of the gospel from that same incomprehension later on. But nothing is revealed later on that will explain the voidance any more than what the audience of the gospel already know — viz., that Jesus is God's Son — explains it. M. B. Riddle (in H. A. W. Meyer's *Critical and Exegetical Handbook* 95) objects that if καθαρίζων, "cleansing," in v 19c modifies -ει, "he," in v 18a, the vv.ll. would not have arisen, the word would bear an unusual sense, and the editorialness of the interpretation would be unique in Mark. But the distance of καθαρίζων from -ει and the intervention of verbs with a different subject suffice to engender the vv.ll. J. A. Kleist (209) notes that in Eur. *IT* a participle in line 23 modifies the subject of λέγει as far back as line 16, with an intervening direct quotation, just as in Mark. "Cleansing" in the sense "pronouncing clean" is not unusual (BAGD s.v. καθαρίζω 2a). And in this very pericope we find an editorial interpretation at vv 2-4, plus an editorial aside in 2:10b and perhaps in 13:14b. W. Paschen (*Rein und Unrein* 181) says that against v 19c, v 19ab denies defilement through food without affirming the cleanness of all foods. But since only eaten foods are in view, v 19c draws a correct deduction. As in the OT, βλασφημία may mean blasphemy of God rather than slandering of human beings; but slandering fits the humanly interpersonal sins that make up the rest of the list in vv 21-22.

For several reasons R. A. Guelich (1. 378-79) doubts that v 19c comes from Mark: (1) Mark shows more interest in what defiles than in food laws such as v 19c abrogates. (2) Βρώματα is hapax in Mark for "foods." (3) Normally Mark introduces parenthetical comments with a conjunction. Presumably Guelich has in mind the conjunction γάρ, "for." But γάρ-clauses give a reason for the preceding, whereas v 19c offers a theological description — and we have no right to limit Mark's parenthetical comments to reason-giving. Hapaxes have no value in decisions of source (see the notes on vv 3-4 and p. 21). And it is wrong to pit defilement and food laws against each other, for according to the OT unclean foods are defiling.

L. Cope (in *New Synoptic Studies* 153-56) uses what he takes to be the jumbledness of vv 1-23 and the tight-knittedness of Matthew's parallel to argue for Matthean priority. But improvement of a jumbled version is at least as easy to accept as the jumbling of a tightly knitted version. Under the view of Marcan priority, many different diachronic analyses of vv 1-23 have been offered, e.g., that vv 5, 15 are original, all the others being pre-Marcan or Marcan additions; that vv 1 (or 1-2), 5, 15 are original; that vv 1-2, 5-7 (or 5-8) are original; that vv 1-2, 5, 9-10a, 11-13a are original (for a survey, see J. Lambrecht in *ETL* 53 [1977] 29-39, 80-82). These differences of opinion symptomize some fundamental problems with such analyses and the principles on which they are based (see pp. 17-24).

Let us take R. P. Booth, *Jesus and the Laws of Purity,* as an example. He distinguishes five subjects in vv 1-23 — (1) handrinsing; (2) hypocrisy; (3) infringement of God's law by adherence to tradition; (4) defilement by eating; (5) defilement by evil designs — and argues that a single unit of tradition would not contain so many. But the hypocrisy is incidental to the infringement, which stands in Mark's text as an answer to the question of handrinsing. The two kinds of defilement exist for their contrast with each other. Otherwise, the only noteworthy shift occurs in the transition from how to eat (with defiled hands or not) to what to eat (impure food or not); but despite a narrative break (v 14), even Booth holds these two subjects together in what he considers to be the original core.

Booth argues that since handrinsing does not infringe a commandment of God, the materials about human tradition that does infringe it (vv 6-8, 9-13) did not originally answer the question about handrinsing. Hence, too, Mark has inserted into the question a reference to tradition to link the question verbally with those materials. But as an answer to the question, they do not require that handrinsing infringe a commandment of God as Corban infringes it, only that handrinsing and Corban both belong to human tradition and that human tradition lacks authority. The answer presupposes the questioners' classification of handrinsing as human tradition and progressively describes human tradition as competing with God's commandment (vv 6-8) and as occasionally even contradicting it (vv 9-13) — reasons enough to reject the authority of human tradition. Booth's ridding the question of a reference to human tradition creates what he calls a "dialectic gap" between the question and vv 6-8, 9-13; but his reasoning threatens to turn viciously circular: vv 6-8, 9-13 do not answer the question in v 5 because the question originally lacked a reference to human tradition; the question originally lacked a reference to human tradition because vv 6-8,

9-13 do not answer the question in v 5. He cannot break out of the circle by assigning handrinsing to the custom of the *haberim* rather than to the elders' tradition; for he himself has the *haberim* urging Jesus and his disciples to adopt this custom as a religious rule. Besides, why should the higher standard of the *haberim* not help make up the elders' tradition? This tradition includes many different practices and opinions. To answer the question, Jesus does not have to mention eating with defiled hands (nor does he mention it in v 15 any more than in vv 6-8, 9-13), for the question itself appeals to the underlying issue of the elders' tradition (cf. S. Westerholm, *Jesus and Scribal Authority* 74).

Actually, a dialectic gap between vv 5 and 15, which Booth unites as the original core, exceeds the one that he sees between vv 5 and 6-8, 9-13. For to fill the gap between the question of how to eat and the saying on what to eat, he has to trace a progression mostly unexpressed in the text: (1) from defilement of the hands after one has immersed one's whole body for general cultic purification (2) to defilement of liquid with which the defiled hands have come in contact (3) to defilement of otherwise pure food that has come in contact with the defiled liquid (4) to defilement of the whole person through eating the defiled food. This progression makes sense, but it is more straightforward to interpret v 15 as referring to food thought to be defiling because it has been prohibited, not because it has been contaminated. In agreement with the shift in audience (v 14), such an interpretation would make v 15 a non-answer to v 5. The prohibition of certain foods is not mentioned explicitly; but neither is the defiling of allowable foods, either by contact with something unclean or by non-kosher preparation. Of course, the saying in v 15 may cover food that defiles for any possible reason — prohibition, non-kosher preparation, contact with uncleanness. But even exclusively under the progression traced by Booth, the shift from defiled hands to defiling food puts at least as much distance between v 15 and v 5 as between the intervening verses and v 5.

Strangely, Booth does not allow progression from the particular to the general in vv 5-13 (i.e. from handrinsing to human tradition), but does allow the reverse progression in v 15 (i.e. from defilement in general to defiling food in particular). He not only allows it; he strains for it by dropping "going into him" from the original version and thereby spoiling the parallel with "going out of the man" and forcing a change from ἔξωθεν, "from outside," to ἔξω, "outside" (again in the original version). It overinterprets "going into him" to argue against its authenticity that it urges Jews to violate OT food laws despite the fact that not even Paul does so (1 Cor 7:17-20). There is no urging. Including the phrase, v 15 only treats those laws as indifferent, as Paul does (1 Cor 9:19-23). With respect to Corban, Booth accepts the possibility of a line of tradition from Jesus through Stephen and his circle to Paul. The immediate literary context in vv 17-23 favors such a line also with respect to "going into him."

D. Lührmann (in *WD* 16 [1981] 85-86) thinks that later parts of this pericope reflect the extra-Palestinian Christian question of eating meat sacrificed to idols. This opinion rests on failure to appreciate the distinction between that question (as in 1 Corinthians 8–10) and the question of eating kinds of food that would bring ritual defilement in the non-idolatrous setting of Jewish Palestine (as in Acts 10:9-16; 11:4-10). E. Wendling (*Entstehung* 91-92) sees Pauline influence on vv 1-23. The editorial v 19c might well reflect Rom 14:20b, but the evidence is not entirely convincing with respect to the de-claredly dominical material in our passage. For example, Paul uses ἀκυρόω, "nullify," in Gal 3:17; but there the Law is the subject of possible nullification, not the object of nullification as in Mark 7:13. Paul uses ἀσύνετος, "without understanding," in Rom 1:21, 31, but of the heathen (contrast Mark 7:18), and in Rom 10:19, but in a Septuagintal quotation. Besides, whatever truer parallels may exist might stem from the influence of pre-Marcan dominical tradition on Paul. But H. Anderson (181-82) argues against authenticity that Paul's letters give evidence of extra-Palestinian discussion of questions concerning law and tradition and that we have no clear evidence from Jesus' time or earlier of Jews' practicing cultic cleansing before they ate food. But we have found just such evidence (see the notes on vv 3-4). And even if we had not, where is similar evidence from the time between Jesus and Mark? And why should extra-Palestinian discussion disfavor, much less rule out, Palestinian discussion? The long explanation in vv 3-4 shows that at least this particular issue is not a live one for Mark's intended audience; otherwise they would already understand it. Lührmann (op. cit. 79) thinks that in v 2 the defining of κοιναῖς, "common, defiled," with ἀνίπτοις, "unrinsed," rather than with the cultic term ἀκαθάρτοις, "unclean," banalizes the problem. But Mark merely wants to make the cultic term that he does use — viz., κοιναῖς — understandable to Gentiles, and to do so he proceeds to the reason for impurity (failure to rinse the hands) rather than contenting himself with a mere synonym. H. Räisänen (in *Logia* 480-82) notes that "I know and am persuaded in the Lord Jesus" (Rom 14:14) is not the language of allusion to Jesus' sayings (as in 1 Cor 7:10, 25; 9:14; 14:37; 1 Thess 4:15), but of subjective conviction (as in Rom 8:38; 15:14; Gal 5:10; Phil 1:25; 2:24; 2 Thess 3:4; 2 Tim 1:12). Yes, but not for the reason that the dominical saying in Mark 7:15 does not hover in the background (as Räisänen thinks; cf. his *Torah and Christ* 209-41); rather, for the reason that Paul goes beyond the dominical saying about objective cleanness and uncleanness to his own statement about subjective cleanness and uncleanness. Therefore the conclusion does not follow that Paul is ignorant of the saying later enshrined in Mark 7:15.

On the authenticity of vv 14-23, E. P. Sanders (*Jesus and Judaism* 325) writes: "Here the great *fact* is that Jesus' followers did not know that he had directly opposed the law, and in particular they did not know him to have opposed the laws governing *Sabbath, food, and purity.*" Citing Romans 14, Sanders goes on to state that neither the Roman Christians nor Paul had a dominical tradition which clarified the proper stance toward the Law on these points. Yet to provide our standards for measuring dominical tradition, we should hardly look to Paul, who rarely cites dominical tradition on any point, or to the Roman Christians, about whose knowledge of dominical tradition we know nothing at all. Mark, our earliest gospel, offers a more reliable standard; and it says that Jesus abrogated laws of food and purity and violated the Sabbath. The known fact is, not that his followers did not know such a tradition, but that some of them kept those laws and some of them did not. The rest is conjecture. That it will take a later vision to convince Peter of his not needing to keep food laws (Acts 10–11) matches his other disagreements with the plain meaning of Jesus' words (Mark 8:31-33; 14:26-31). But we should note that here in Mark he may be one of those eating with defiled hands (which differs from eating prohibited foods) and that he will eat with sinners till James's men appear on the scene (Gal 2:11-16). Only the taking of a sceptical view concerning authenticity in general, and that on more theoretical grounds, leads to a denial of authenticity here. J. Gnilka (1. 286-87) notes that not all parts of the church fully and immediately took over Jesus' teaching on marriage and divorce and his practice of open table fellowship, either, and that the legalistically looser circle of early Christians centering around Stephen may have represented Jesus more faithfully on cultic questions than other early Christians did (cf. M. Hengel, *Between Jesus and Paul* 40-44, 54-58; E. Larsson in *NTS* 33 [1987] 205-25, esp. 207-8, 214-15, 223). The appeal to open table fellowship is particularly important, for eating with sinners entails the probability of eating unclean foods and nobody disputes that Jesus did eat with sinners, yet the early church disputed over table fellowship with them (Gal 2:11-16, "sinners" applying to Gentile as well as Jewish flouters of the law). So why should Peter's and others' failure to accept Jesus' teaching on food laws undermine the authenticity of that teaching any more than their failure to follow his teaching and example in regard to eating with sinners undermines authenticity? And if Jesus can raise the Mosaic law on divorce to the higher level of permanence in marriage (Mark 10:2-12 parr.), why should he not raise the Mosaic law on clean foods to the higher level of a clean heart?

H. Räisänen (*Torah and Christ* 210-11) objects that Jesus' eating with Jewish sinners is not the same as Peter's eating with Gentile sinners. But this distinction makes no difference, for eating with either kind of sinner entails the probability of eating unclean foods. Räisänen (op. cit. 242-301) also rejects the appeal to a legalistically looser circle of early Christians centered around Stephen and representing Jesus more faithfully on cultic questions than other early Christians did. He argues, for example, that Stephen was concerned with the temple, but Paul with circumcision (ibid. 300). True, but laissez faire attitudes toward the temple and circumcision (and toward food laws) may easily be of a piece; so it remains realistically possible — and all we need at this point is a realistic possibility — that Paul's laissez faire attitude toward food laws, and thus his insistence on open table fellowship, stems from Jesus' teaching as preserved on all such matters in Stephen's circle.

The argument that the relative interpretation makes v 15 ambiguous enough to account for disputes in the early church suffers two faults: (1) the pressure of Jewish law, tradition, and society makes ambiguity unnecessary to account for Christian disputes on matters concerning which Jesus spoke plainly; (2) the absolute interpretation also leaves ambiguity: Is Jesus denying moral, cultic, or both moral and cultic defilement from outside? Is he affirming moral, cultic, or both moral and cultic defilement from inside? Whatever their sense, do the denial and affirmation add up to an imperative or to a matter of indifference? Are the things that come out of a person bodily discharges, thoughts, words, or acts? Except for v 19c, whose editorial character rules it out of our question concerning what Jesus said, vv 18-23 give a perfectly clear answer only to the last question. See W. G. Kümmel in *Das Wort und die Wörter* 35-46; S. Westerholm, *Jesus and Scribal Authority* 80-82, in favor of authenticity; H. Räisänen in *JSNT* 16 (1982) 86-88; idem in *Logia* 477-84; idem, *Torah and Christ* 209-301, against it. Räisänen's attack rests explicitly but mistakenly on the supposition that the meaning of v 15 is clear. Westerholm's defense, seeking as it does to explain why the early church argued over table fellowship and eating meat sacrificed to idols, generalizes the meaning of v 15 by divorcing the saying in it from an original connection with food laws. We have seen the unnecessity of this explanation, and especially in a cultically sensitive culture such as the first-century Jewish one it would be hard to imagine a non-dietary meaning of the statement that nothing entering from outside can defile a person. So why posit an original independence of v 15 from its present dietary setting?

JESUS' EXORCISING A DEMON AT A DISTANCE AND WITHOUT COMMAND

7:24-30 (Matt 15:21-28)

As often in Mark, this pericope starts with an indication of topographical movement (v 24a). Next comes Jesus' unsuccessful attempt to stay incognito by entering a house (v 24bc). Mark then tells of a Syrophoenician woman's coming to Jesus as a result of hearing about him (vv 25-26a). Her request that Jesus cast a demon out of her daughter and the ensuing dialogue with Jesus make up the main part of the story (vv 26b-29), which closes with her finding the child delivered from the demon (v 30).

7:24-26a *(Matt 15:21-25a)* An adversative δέ, "but," signals a topographical shift "from there," i.e. from the house mentioned in v 17 (cf. 8:30 with 8:28),
to a completely different region. We need not go so far back as 6:53 for Gennesaret
or imagine an unknown referent in differently arranged and perhaps unextant
pre-Marcan tradition (cf. the use of ἐκεῖθεν for exit from a house in 6:1, 10; 9:30;
10:1 and from a locality in 6:11, but never from a region); and the comment of
W. Schmithals (351) that one travels from house to house or from region to region
but not from house to region does not take sufficient account of Mark's going
right on to say that Jesus enters a house in the region. Ἀναστάς indicates that
Jesus "stood up" from a seated position that he had taken to instruct his disciples
in the house of v 17 (cf. 9:28 and 9:35 with 10:1; also 4:1; 12:41; 13:3). His going
away "into the region of Tyre" prepares for an encounter with a Gentile woman.
His not being able to escape notice even though he enters another house in order
that no one might recognize him (cf. v 17; 2:1-2; 3:7-8, 20; 6:30-33; 9:30) exhibits
his power of attraction, a favorite theme of Mark (cf. esp. 1:45). That Mark calls
on his narrator's omniscience to identify Jesus' wish to escape notice betrays how
much Mark wants to underscore this power of attraction. The emphatic position
of οὐδένα, "no one," sharpens the contrast between Jesus' desire to stay incognito
and his inability to do so. Widespread reports of his mighty acts make him unable.
The καί which introduces the statement concerning his inability is adversative:
"but." A much stronger adversative, ἀλλ', "rather," introduces an incident that
results from his failure to stay incognito and thereby adds emphasis to that failure.

"Immediately a woman, hearing about him": "immediately" points up that
Jesus has elsewhere exercised his power so effectively and startlingly that even
in this foreign region his presence excites an instant report. Εὐθὺς ἀκούσασα,
"immediately hearing," precedes γυνή, "a woman," which it modifies. This emphatic position accentuates the point (cf. 3:7-8; 5:27). "About him" appears to
mean "about his presence in the house" rather than "about the miracles and
exorcisms that he has been performing elsewhere," for those activities became
known in the Tyrian region some time ago (see 3:8). The clause concerning the
unclean spirit possessed by the woman's little daughter provides a reason for the
woman's coming and prepares for her request. The asyndetic relation of "coming"
to "having heard" gives the narrative a staccato-like quality that puts an emphasis
on Jesus' magnetism (against regarding the two participles as mere Semitic auxiliaries — cf. M. Black, *Aramaic Approach* 125-26). The woman's falling at Jesus'
feet suits not only her desperation but also his dignity (cf. 5:22, also in the context
of a daughter's need). An adversative δέ, "but," sets off Mark's parenthetic
description of her as "a Greek [with regard to culture, including religion as well
as language and other matters], a Syrophoenician by descent." This description
prepares for the coming dialogue, which depends on her daughter's non-Jewishness: neither culturally nor lineally is she Jewish. Mark may also design the
description to capture the interest of his mainly Gentile audience, who will take
great encouragement from the outcome of the story.

7:26b-30 *(Matt 15:25b-28)* Perhaps through influence of the tradition he
is using, Mark has described the daughter's condition in accordance with Jewish

concern for cultic purity: she has "an unclean spirit" (v 25; cf. the probably Semitic ἧς . . . αὐτῆς, "whose . . . her," redundant in Greek but not in Aramaic or Hebrew, where a simple pronoun resumes the relative pronoun because the latter — ד in Aramaic, אשר in Hebrew — is indeclinable [cf. 1:7; E. C. Maloney, *Semitic Interference* 116-18]). In the woman's indirectly quoted request for an exorcism, Mark switches to an expression that he regularly uses with "cast out," as here: "the demon" (so also vv 29, 30). The placement of this direct object before its verb (see the Greek text) carries a note of desperation, and the anaphoric definite article points back to "an unclean spirit." Emphasis falls on πρῶτον, "first," in Jesus' reply, "Let the children [i.e. my Jewish disciples] be satisfied first [i.e. be fully taught]." "First" implies that the woman's daughter may receive the salvific benefits of God's kingdom at a later date. But the next clause, "for it is not good [or 'beautiful' in the sense of 'fitting' — καλόν] to take the bread of the children [i.e. the time and effort needed to teach my disciples] and cast it to the little dogs [i.e. to Gentile children like the woman's daughter]," makes the delay so indefinite that in effect Jesus is denying the woman's request (see O. Michel in *TDNT* 3. 1101-2; Str B 1. 724-26 for the pejorative use of "dogs"). In a word, "first" stresses postponement, not promise. The assonance of the two infinitives λαβεῖν and βαλεῖν and the chiasm of putting the one infinitive first ("to take the bread of the children") and the other one last ("and [it] to the little dogs to cast" — so the Greek word order) emphasize the contrast between Jesus' disciples and Gentile children. The diminutive κυναρίοις, "to the little dogs," is chosen for its suitability to Gentile children, represented by the woman's daughter. The diminutive would ill suit the woman herself, grown mother that she is (cf. the following comments and notes on the crowd of diminutives in this pericope and on the figurative use of "children" for Jesus' disciples and of "little dogs" for Gentile children).

Mark does not engage in the speculation that Jesus is half-joking, testing the woman's faith, or deciding on the scope of his mission. In only one other passage will Mark say that Jesus does not want to be known, i.e. in 9:30–31: καὶ οὐκ ἤθελεν ἵνα τις γνοῖ. There, Mark will give Jesus' teaching the disciples about his coming death and resurrection as the reason why he does not want to be known. The parallelism of phraseology with 7:24 (οὐδένα ἤθελεν γνῶναι) suggests that Jesus wants privacy to teach his disciples here, too. Mark's omitting to identify the reason underlying Jesus' desire shows that for the moment he is not interested in it, but only in the fame of Jesus that makes privacy impossible. But if the underlying reason is the same as that in 9:30-31, taking the bread from the little children and throwing it to the little dogs means depriving the disciples of the attention that teaching them demands and giving it instead to the woman's daughter and other Gentile children in her train. Verse 27 does not contrast the whole Jewish nation and all Gentiles, then, but the Jewish disciples of Jesus and Gentile children. (We should not let Matthew's application to salvation-history determine Mark's or Jesus' meaning [cf. R. H. Gundry, *Matthew* 309-17, esp. on the redactional origin of Matt 15:24].) Also favoring a contrast between teaching the disciples and meeting the needs of Gentile children is the fact that granting the woman's request would deprive the Jewish nation of nothing — Jesus is not even in their land — but would deprive the disciples of private teaching (W. Grundmann [7. Aufl.] 199; cf. the view of K. Tagawa [*Miracles et Évangile* 116-21] that the disciples would be deprived of their rest).

In three ways the contrast between teaching the disciples and meeting the needs of Gentile children spoils the often supposed contrast between evangelism of Jews and evangelism of Gentiles: (1) unevangelized Jews are outside the picture; (2) adult Gentiles are outside the picture; (3) at issue is teaching versus exorcism, not evangelism in one arena versus evangelism in another arena. One might argue that Mark omits Jesus' teaching the disciples to *make* the following episode fit a contrast between evangelism of Jews and evangelism of Gentiles. But the phraseological parallel with 9:30-31 favors that Mark interrelates the passages yet makes the omission simply because Jesus does not gain privacy to teach his disciples here as he will in 9:30-31 (cf. 9:28-29). Historically, it is just as likely that Jesus contrasts filling the needs of his disciples with filling the needs of a Gentile child (and others of her like that would follow) as that he contrasts filling the needs of Jews in general with filling the needs of Gentiles in general. Mark's emphasis falls on exorcism, however, not on the identity of the children as opposed to little dogs.

The woman's first directly quoted word consists of her address to Jesus as "Lord." Though the Greek word χύριε may carry little more than the force of the English word "sir," the woman's evident belief in Jesus' supernatural power favors a higher meaning; and apart from the historical question of what she means by the word, Mark probably reads out of χύριε the kind of divine lordship that accords with Christian belief about Jesus (cf. 1:3; 2:28; 5:19[?]; 9:24; 11:3; 12:36-37; 13:35; T. A. Burkill, *New Light* 63, 89). Accordingly, he accents Jesus' lordship by introducing it with a compound formula, ἡ δὲ ἀπεκρίθη καὶ λέγει αὐτῷ, "but she answered and says to him." Just as the adversative δέ in v 24 highlighted Jesus' going into Gentile territory, so the adversative δέ in v 28 highlights Gentile acknowledgment of his lordship. The second part of the introductory formula features a vivid historical present tense, which is more than usually striking in that it stands parallel with an aorist verb following a pair of verbs in the imperfect tense (ἠρώτα, "she was asking" — v 26; ἔλεγεν, "he was saying" — v 27; cf. the aorist εἶπεν, "he said," in v 29; M. Zerwick, *Untersuchungen* 73; M. Reiser, *Syntax und Stil* 132-33). Ordinarily the verb of answering occurs in a participial form, the verb of saying in the indicative mood (or vice versa). Here we have the only instance in Mark where these verbs occur together in the indicative mood — a further sign of emphasis on the following address "Lord." Turning the dialogue into a duel of wits, the woman rebuts Jesus' answer with the counter observation that "even the little dogs under the table eat from the little children's little crumbs" (cf. Philostr. *VA* 1.19; *Jos. Asen.* 10:13; 13:8). The ascensive καί, "even," and the position of the whole subject-phrase before its verb sharpen the point of the counter observation. It does not portray little children as deliberately throwing little crumbs to pet dogs (contrast v 27 where, however, it is not little children who do the throwing), but as eating so messily (as little children do) that little crumbs fall to the floor by accident. In v 27, the connotation of τέκνα/-ων, which literally means "born ones, [Scottish] bairns" (we would expect the much more usual υἱοί/-ῶν, "sons," if Jesus were referring to Jews in general), emphasized the disciples' Jewish lineage and Jesus' parental-like duty to feed them first (cf. Mark's using the diminutive θυγάτριον, "little daughter," in the sympathetic description at v 25 and then changing to non-diminutive forms in vv 26, 29; similarly in 5:23, 35). The switch in v 28 to the less familial but diminutive παιδίων, "little children's" (see also v 30), correlates with letting the little dogs eat the little children's little crumbs. Both κυνάρια and ψιχίων are diminutive for "little dogs" and "little crumbs" (on κυνάρια see R. H. Gundry, *Matthew* 314-16, esp. for the possibilities of an underlying Aramaic גּוּרָא, "puppy," or כַּלְבָּא, "dog," the latter capable of a diminutive form [GKC §86g, esp. n. 1], though the dialogue probably takes place in Greek; also J. D. M. Derrett [*Studies* 1. 151, n. 4], who strongly defends a true diminutive by citing Pl. *Euthphr.* 298DE; Xen. *Cyr.* 8.4.20; Arr. *Epict. Diss.* 4.1.111 [cf. Ar. *Ach.* 542; Xen. *Oec.* 13.8]). Δαιμόνιον occurs often elsewhere in Mark and outside Mark, and here Mark associates it with non-diminutive forms of "daughter" (vv 26, 29) as well as with the diminutive παιδίον (v 30); so its diminutive form is insignificant. Though the meaning of diminutives often faded, their concentration in the present passages looks intended for effect.

Jesus' admiration of the woman's cleverness in conceiving that a little Gentile "dog" might enjoy a little "crumb" of his mighty power at the same time that some little Jewish "children" are enjoying a full portion leads him to respond, "On account of this saying, go; the demon has gone out of your daughter." He borrows the woman's indirectly quoted expression "the demon" and, strikingly, does not go with her to confront the demon and speak a word of exorcism. (Presumably he is trying to husband his time for teaching the disciples, for after vv 1-23 it is hard to think that he is avoiding the cultic defilement of a Gentile house.) Rather, he tells her to go and announces the demon's departure as having happened. The asyndeton with which the announcement begins (we expect "because" or "for") and the perfect tense of ἐξελήλυθεν, "has gone out," emphasize his power in accomplishing the exorcism at a distance and the supernatural knowledge displayed in his announcing the exorcism (cf. 2:8; Iambl. *VP* 142). We might think that the exorcism took place when the woman exercised faith. But nowhere does Mark's text identify the moment of faith or even mention faith — only cleverness in pressing the request (contrast the parallel Matt 15:28; also Mark 2:5; 5:34; 9:24; 10:52). Therefore the final emphasis falls on the evidence that the demon has indeed gone out: "And going away to her house, she found the little child cast on a bed and the demon gone out." So great is Jesus' power that he has not needed to pronounce a word of exorcism in the presence of the demon. To underscore that power, "cast on a bed" gives proof of the demon's exit (cf. 1:26; 9:26); and "the demon gone out" (v 30) echoes the announcement, "The demon has gone out . . ." (v 29), to underscore Jesus' supernatural knowledge.

NOTES

W. Grundmann (esp. 2. Aufl., 152-53) suggests that "bread" links together the pericopes in 6:35–7:30 (cf. 6:41, 52; 7:2, 27). But the intrusion of 6:53-56, a pericope which does not mention bread and which, apart from the possible exception of 6:53, is not necessary to a transition from 6:52 to 7:1, breaks the supposed linkage. 1 Kgs 17:8-24 does not provide the source of the present story, or even an object of allusion. There we read of a widow in Sidonian territory, her son, illness, death, and a raising from the dead by repeated physical contact and prayer; here, of a woman in Tyrian territory, her daughter, demon-possession, and a wordless exorcism at a distance.

In the history of the early church, the forsaking of OT food laws by Jewish Christians opened the door to mass evangelism of Gentiles; for Jewish Christians could then mingle freely with Gentiles, eat their food, and not require them to change their eating habits, a requirement that would have sharply reduced the number of Gentile converts (cf. Acts 10:1–11:18; also 11:19-26 with Gal 2:11-14, esp. in view of the Petrine origin of Mark's material — see pp. 1026-45). Similarly, Mark has recorded Jesus' declaring all foods clean (vv 1-23) and now records Jesus' going into Gentile territory and saving the daughter of a Gentile woman from demonic possession.

Since Jews live in the Tyrian region, we cannot say whether Jesus enters a cultically pure Jewish house or violates laws of cultic purity by entering a Gentile house. Mark associates the entry with a desire for privacy, not with cultic violation. And neither here nor in several following pericopes, also set outside Galilee (vv 31-37; 8:1-9, 22-26), does Jesus or Mark make note of faith on the part of Gentiles. Nor does Jesus preach or teach, and Mark does nothing to soften Jesus' grudgingness in the present pericope or add even so much as a miracle or an exorcism to Jesus' passage through Sidon (v 31). It is also extremely doubtful whether we should count the setting of 8:22-26 — viz., Bethsaida — as predominantly Gentile. Over against the pagan cities of Tyre, Sidon, and Sodom, Bethsaida is ranged with Chorazin and Capernaum as a center of Jesus' Jewish ministry (Matt 11:20-24 par. Luke 10:12-15). Indeed, three of his twelve closest disciples come from there (John 1:44); and popularly it belongs to Galilee (see John 1:43-44; 12:21; Ptol. *Geog.* 5.16.4; and the interchange of Gaulanitis [the proper territory of Bethsaida] and Galilee in Josephus *Ant.* 18.1.1 §4; 18.1.6 §23). Jesus aims to go there during his Galilean ministry (Mark 6:45), or does go there with his disciples, crowds following (Luke 9:10; cf. the comments and notes on Mark 6:45, 53). Probably, then, we should not imagine a preview here of the conversion of Gentiles in the church age, i.e. of the history of salvation according to the principle "to the Jew first, also to the Greek" (as in Acts 3:26; 13:46; Rom 1:16; 2:9-10; 9:1–11:36; 15:8-9; Eph 1:1-13; 2:11-22). W. Schmithals (353) adds that since many people from around Tyre and Sidon have already benefited from Jesus' ministry (3:8), no emphasis falls now on the Gentile mission, which Mark's church no longer debates but presupposes. We have already seen that Jesus does not oppose the Jewish nation to Gentiles, but opposes his disciples to Gentile children.

Whatever the amount of Jesus' subsequent activity in Galilee, Mark's giving no reason for the departure to Tyrian territory probably means that the adversative δέ, "but," is not meant to ring down the curtain on Jesus' Galilean ministry. In view of the popular placement of Bethsaida in Galilee, the miracle yet to be narrated as occurring in Bethsaida (8:22-26) will probably count as a continuation of the Galilean ministry. At least Mark makes no negative point of closure here, only the positive point of an especially notable incursion into the completely different region of Tyre (against D. E. Nineham 197).

P. J. Achtemeier (26-27 and in *JBL* 89 [1970] 287-88) thinks that to justify the mission of the church to Gentiles, Mark has shifted the story from a Galilean setting; i.e. originally a foreigner came to Jesus in Galilee, but now Mark makes Jesus go to foreign territory, where a native comes to him. Achtemeier argues that several inconcinnities favor this view: Why should Mark identify the woman as Syrophoenician when Jesus is in Syrophoenicia? (But Jews live there, too, just as Gentiles live in Galilee [A. Alt, *Where Jesus Worked* 25-29]; and for clarity the coming dialogue depends on the audience's knowledge that the woman is not Jewish [cf. G. Theissen, *Miracle Stories* 126]). Why should Jesus say that the children have to be fed first when he has already fed them? (But the feeding in view is his private teaching of the disciples concerning his death and resurrection. Even under a broader view of feeding the children as feeding the whole Jewish nation, Jesus' having fed the five thousand would not necessarily mean that he has completed his Jewish ministry; and an original setting in Galilee would not give a different answer to Achtemeier's question unless the incident were dated prior to the feeding of the five thousand — a possibility also for the Syrophoenician setting — or unless the referents of "the little children" and "the little dogs" were shifted from Jews and Gentiles.) Since Jesus has come to Syrophoenicia, why should the woman not expect him to deliver her daughter? (Answer: because he has gone into a house for privacy [v 24].) "House" implies an area with which Jesus is familiar and where he is known. (Why, given the law of hospitality even to strangers, a law presumed by Jesus himself in 6:10; Matt 10:12-14 par. Luke 10:5-7; Luke 9:4? Besides, according to 3:8 Jesus is known around Tyre and Sidon.) For privacy Jesus goes to uninhabited areas, not into houses (1:45). (But Jesus has become so well known in Galilee that he cannot find privacy even in uninhabited areas [cf. the argument of R. A. Guelich (1. 384) against interpreting Jesus' entry into the present house in terms of a messianic secret]; so it is historically quite conceivable that he seeks privacy in a house on foreign soil.) Achtemeier concludes that pre-Marcan tradition originally located the house in the village of 8:26 and that therefore Jesus wanted to avoid being mobbed because of his having healed the blind man (8:22-26). (But the grounds for this conclusion are now seen to be weak.)

Similarly, R. Pesch (1. 391) relates the taking of bread (v 27) to the taking of bread at the feedings of the five thousand and four thousand (6:41; 8:6), and the children's being filled (v 27) to the crowds' being filled at those feedings (6:42; 8:4, 8) to argue that along with the feedings, the present story portrays the banquet of salvation as for Gentiles in addition to Jews. But "to take bread" is a stereotyped phrase (for non-eschatological and non-eucharistic usage, see 8:14 par. Matt 16:5; Luke 6:4; 24:30; John 21:13; Acts 27:35; cf. *b. Ber.* 51ab); and the present story gives no indication that the little dogs are "filled," only the children. Little crumbs hardly provide the sort of meal that is filling.

Again similarly, T. A. Burkill (*New Light* 88) says that Mark makes Jesus visit the regions listed in 3:7-8 to anticipate and authenticate the world-wide mission of the church. But both during his present journey and also during his coming passage through Transjordan and visit to Judea and Jerusalem (chaps. 10ff.), Jesus fails to visit Idumea, mentioned in 3:8, and does not engage in evangelism. Though the disciples will make an appearance at a later point in the present journey (8:2, 10), their non-mention till then puts another question mark against regarding Jesus' departure to Tyrian territory as an anticipation of the church's going out on a world-wide mission (contrast 1:38: "let *us* go elsewhere [with respect to Galilean territory] . . . in order that I may preach there, too"; also contrast 4:33; 5:1; 6:6b-13, 45). Burkill argues well, however, that the feeding of the children first does not refer to the feeding of the five thousand; for Mark did not describe the five thousand as Jews, and v 27a seems to mean that the children are still being fed whereas the five thousand were filled some time ago. Nor does the dogs' eating of the children's crumbs (v 28) look forward to the feeding of the four thousand (8:1-9); for the four thousand will not eat the fragments left over from the earlier feeding, and the apparent simultaneity of the children's and dogs' eating disagrees with the sequentiality of the feedings (ibid. 82-83).

For recent attempts to separate between tradition and redaction, see esp. J. Ernst

210; J. Gnilka 1. 289-91; D.-A. Koch, *Bedeutung* 85-92; L. Schenke, *Wundererzählungen*
254-67. The results are inconclusive and sometimes contradictory. In v 24a, it is said, Mark
may construct the reference to Tyre out of 3:8 — but after so long? And why not an
immediate carry-over of "and Sidon" from 3:8, as in the v.l. here at 7:24a, rather than a
later reference to Sidon that reflects a journey so circuitous as to have been scarcely
fabricated by a redactor (v 31)? If Mark has constructed the reference to Tyre out of tradition
behind "a Syrophoenician" in v 26a, as others think, he would probably have included
Sidon in the same breath, as at 3:8 and in the present v.l. Though v 24b represents his
interests, it looks fabricated only if we assume that Jesus did not on occasion seek privacy
— an unjustifiable assumption. The action and the dialogue depend on each other; so we
should not regard one as original and the other as added.

For the Marcan or pre-Marcan redactional insertion of "first" in v 27a, or of v 27a
as a whole, some have argued that the adverb relativizes the absolute refusal in v 27b and
that in v 28 the woman replies only to the absolute refusal. The argument is simplistic.
"First" stresses a postponement that under the circumstances amounts to a refusal. The
γάρ-clause in v 27b does not compete with feeding the children first, but provides a
rationale for it. (One might think that Mark's penchant for γάρ-clauses would have
prompted the assignment of v 27b to his redaction rather than using it as a yardstick to
measure v 27a.) And several features of the woman's reply seem to counter the word "first"
in Jesus' refusal by implying that the dogs eat *while,* not *after,* the children are being filled:
(1) the dogs' being under the table (cf. Hom. *Il.* 22.69; Judg 1:7); (2) their eating "the little
crumbs" (contrast "the bread" in v 27b); (3) the diminutive form κυνάρια for pet dogs or
puppies that might be expected to lap up crumbs as children drop them; (4) the present
tense of "eat," which, though probably gnomic, may also indicate concurrent action.
L. Schenke (*Wundererzählungen* 256) denies that the difference between children and dogs
suits the children's temporal priority. But why not? Moderns may feed their dogs before
their children, but ancients hardly did so — and the diminutive κυνάρια and the position
of the dogs under the table show that in view are not street-roaming scavengers, which
would not be fed at all, but pets, which are fed after the children eat.

Those who take the feeding of the five thousand (6:35-44) as symbolic of filling
the Jews with the bread of salvation and the feeding of the four thousand (8:1-9) as filling
the Gentiles with it can hardly take v 27a as correlatively redactional; for v 27a implies
that the Jews have *not* yet been filled whereas 6:42 has said that the five thousand,
supposedly representing the Jews, *have* been filled (cf. Burkill's comments, cited above).
Of course, the idea of Jews first, then Gentiles, might have traveled from authentic Jesuanic
tradition to Paul as easily as from Paul into inauthentic Jesuanic tradition. Or both Jesus
and Paul may have independently expressed the idea — it derives from their common
Jewish heritage (see Isa 2:2-4; 11:10; 19:19-25; 25:5-8; 42:1-9; 45:14-17, 20-25; 49:1-7;
51:4-5; 55:1-5; 56:6-8; 60:1-3; 66:18-24; Mic 4:1-5; Zeph 3:8-10; Zech 8:20-23; 9:9-10;
14:1-21; non-canonical texts in J. Jeremias, *Jesus' Promise* 61).

According to C. E. Carlston (*Parables* 168), 9:30 goes against "standing up" as the
meaning of ἀναστάς in 7:24; and the best reading connects ἐκεῖθεν with ἀναστάς in the
sense "went up from there." On the contrary, the connection of ἐκεῖθεν with a form of
-έρχομαι in 9:30 favors connecting ἐκεῖθεν with ἀπῆλθεν in 7:24 despite the intervention
of ἀναστάς, which therefore keeps its normal meaning. T. A. Burkill (*New Light* 67-69)
notes the absence of any indication that Jesus leaves Galilee because his ministry there
has failed, or because he fears for his life.

In connection with a city, like Tyre, "boundaries" does not mean city-limits, but
surrounding region (cf. esp. 5:17 with 5:14; Matt 2:16; Josephus *Ant.* 6.9.5 §191). Εἰς
might mean "up to," but Matt 15:21 correctly takes it in the more natural sense of entrance
(R. H. Gundry, *Matthew* 310; cf. Jesus' going "through Sidon" according to v 31). Εὐθύς,

"immediately," probably modifies ἀκούσασα, "having heard," because of their standing side by side and because of the intervention of an adjectival clause regarding the woman before other verbal possibilities come into view (ἐλθοῦσα, "coming," and προσέπεσεν, "fell"). Elsewhere it is hard to know whether εὐθύς modifies the participle, the main verb, or the whole statement (1:10, 18, 29; 2:8, 12; 5:30; 6:27, 54-55; 8:10; 9:15, 24; 11:2; 14:45; 15:1). At 1:43; 9:20, however, Mark seems to put the participle before εὐθύς to make εὐθύς modify the main verb. At 6:25 he puts εὐθύς after the participle to range it alongside two other adverbial expressions modifying the participle.

H. Anderson (189) inclines to prefer the v.l. which adds "and Sidon" (v 24) on the supposition that it was later omitted to conform with v 31. But since v 31 will refer to Sidon itself rather than to the region of Sidon, it is more likely that in v 24a Mark does not include Sidon with Tyre in referring to the region, and that the undisputed reading in v 31, "the region of Tyre," echoes the original reading without Sidon in v 24a. "And Sidon" appears to derive by parallel influence from Matt 15:21, then, perhaps also from the stereotypical pairing of Tyre and Sidon in canonical and non-canonical passages too numerous to list here.

Sometimes Jesus finds privacy in a house (7:17ff.; 9:28, 33; 10:10) or elsewhere (4:10ff., 34; 6:45; 8:27 with 8:34; 9:30; 10:32e et passim in the passion narrative). At other times he does not find privacy in a house (1:29ff.; 2:1ff., 15; 3:20; 7:24ff.) or elsewhere (1:35ff., 45; 6:31ff.). This mixture of success and failure speaks for historicity, because redaction would probably have produced a more consistent result and less variety of place, whereas we have not only houses but also uninhabited areas, mountains, roads, boats, and non-Galilean regions.

T. A. Burkill (*New Light* 72, n. 2) suggests that v 26a exegetically paraphrases an original Aramaic that meant "Aramean woman." The purpose of the paraphrase would be to make clear the woman's paganism as well as her non-Jewish birth. Building on the conjectural emendation ἡ δὲ γυνὴ ἦν χῆρα Φοινίκισσα, "Now the woman was a widow, a Phoenician" (see P.-L. Couchoud in *JTS* os 34 [1933] 120-21), G. Schwarz (in *NTS* 30 [1984] 626-28) suggests an original Aramaic כְּנַעֲנִיפָא, which could be taken both as "Canaanitess" (so Matthew) and as "Phoenician" (so Mark). These suggestions can hardly be proved or disproved, but "Canaanitess" easily falls into the category of Matthew's habitual conforming of Mark to OT language. The v.l. χῆρα (sy[s,c]) may stem from a mistaken scribal correlation with 1 Kgs 17:8-24.

R. Pesch (1. 388) thinks that "a Syrophoenician by descent" is designed to keep "a Greek" from being understood as a Hellenistic Jewess. Perhaps so, but "a Greek" seems to represent a Gentile clearly enough (cf. Acts 17:12). Therefore the addition of "a Syrophoenician by descent" is more likely designed to keep Mark's audience from thinking that "a Greek" includes Greek descent as well as Greek culture. The inclusion of Greek descent in the usual meaning of Ἑλληνίς makes the qualification necessary (cf. esp. Luc. *Deor. Conc.* 4, where Greek and Syrophoenician descents are contrasted). To put it the other way around, "a Syrophoenician by descent" would be contradictory if the woman were Greek by descent as well as by culture. The meaning, half-Greek by descent and half-Syrophoenician by descent (again cf. Lucian loc. cit.), would seem to require at least a καί, "and," between the two designations. It is anachronistic to exclude religion from a cultural description like "Greek." Cultural Greekness may imply that the woman belongs to high society (again cf. Acts 17:12; also G. Theissen in *ZNW* 75 [1984] 211-13). The better economic circumstances possibly reflected in the use of κλίνην, "bed" (v 30; cf. 4:21; 7:4), rather than κραββατόν, "pallet" (2:4, 9, 11, 12; 6:55), tend toward this possibility. The woman's belonging both to high society and to the Gentile population that economically and politically domineered the Jewish population of the region (for the latter, see ibid. 202-25) would make her acceptance of the designation "little dogs," whether for

herself or for her daughter, all the more remarkable. E. Lohmeyer's discussion (146) is
marred by failure to recognize a lineal, not just geographical and political, meaning in
"Syrophoenician" (for the lineal, see Lucian loc. cit.; Juv. *Sat.* 8.159; Eunap. *VS* §496 [pp.
522-24 in the LCL edition] — all in context). "Syro-" distinguishes the Phoenicia belonging
to the province of Syria from Libophoenicia around Carthage, North Africa (BAGD s.v.
Συροφοινίκισσα). "By descent" steers "Syrophoenician" away from any connotation of
immorality (as R. A. Guelich [1. 385] correctly observes).

   We should avoid overinterpreting the imperfect tense of ἠρώτα in v 26b as meaning
that the woman "kept asking"; for even apart from iterativeness the linearity of most speech
often causes verbs of speaking to take the imperfect, and the settings of the only other
Marcan occurrences of this verb — both of them in the imperfect — do not favor iter-
ativenes (4:10; 8:5; so also the imperfect of ἐπερωτάω in Mark). Perhaps Jesus' eating at
table prompted his answer in v 27. This answer may rest on a maxim which he applies to
the woman's request (see J. D. M. Derrett in *NovT* 15 [1973] 172; cf. *Tg. Neof.* Exod
22:30). Thus the diminutive "little dogs" and the position of the dogs under the table would
have a domestic origin unrelated to the question of Jews and Gentiles. On the other hand,
the maxim may have already alluded to the economic deprivation of the Jewish population
by the Gentile population, especially by Tyrians (cf. G. Theissen in *ZNW* 75 [1984] 214-17).
By determining who gets the food, Jesus takes the role of a father — but only by implication, not with any theological thrust.

   Some commentators think that Jesus opposes the equating of Jewish and Gentile
privileges, not the substitution of Gentile privilege for Jewish privilege (so, e.g., C. E.
Carlston, *Parables* 170). But whatever the privileges, "to take the bread of the children
and throw [it] to the little dogs" surely indicates substitution, unless we suppose that the
children are expected to get down on the floor and fight for their food on equal terms with
the little dogs. Then we would expect different phraseology.

   Though Mark highlights the woman's addressing Jesus as "Lord" (v 28), the typi-
cality of this address among Gentiles favors an origin in the earliest tradition. The suggestion of B. E. Thiering (in *NovT* 12 [1970] 2) that κυνάρια, "little dogs," is a pun on κοινός,
"defiled," both referring to Gentiles (cf. Acts 10:14), encounters some difficulty in the
absence of κοινός from the present pericope, in the distance of v 27 from v 5, and in the
application of κοινός to Jewish hands in the preceding pericope, whereas κυνάρια refers to
Gentiles here. Furthermore, Jesus' denial of cultic defilement in vv 1-23 ill suits his using
the category here to describe Gentiles.

   It draws gratuitous inferences to reason that the going out of power from Jesus (5:30)
implied that he has limited power, with the result that he now wants to conserve his power
for Jews (so E. Haenchen 273-74). "First" (v 27) might make nonsense to the woman only
if Jesus were speaking about the history of salvation: Jews before Gentiles. But he is
probably speaking only about the present occasion of his need to teach his disciples in
private, and according to what sounds like a proverb at that. Even if he were speaking
about the history of salvation, his use elsewhere of cryptic language shows that we should
not make understandability to the woman a criterion of authenticity. His response, "On
account of this saying . . . ," hints not only at surprise that she did understand but also at
admiration of her cleverness.

   It generalizes too sweepingly to argue that the favorable attitude elsewhere displayed
by Jesus toward women and Gentiles rules out the authenticity of v 27, of the continued
dialogue dependent on it in vv 28-29a, and of all or the latter half of v 24, in particular,
the desire for privacy. Verse 27 has nothing to do with his attitude toward women in general,
and probably not with his attitude toward Gentiles in general — rather, with his desire to
teach the disciples, a desire that has at least temporarily taken him away from ministering
even to the Jews. Nor would a salvation-historical understanding of v 27 imply harshness

toward Gentiles in general, only a conviction that the time of their salvation is not ripe (see esp. L. Goppelt, *Jesus, Paul, and Judaism* 53-55). Without vv 24, 27-29a we would expect Jesus to go to the woman's house for performance of the exorcism. That he does not go favors the originality of these verses, for only they provide a reason for his not going, viz., desire for privacy.

In v 28 the v.l. ναί, "yes," probably represents parallel influence from Matthew (cf. 2 Cor 1:20; Phlm 20; Rev 22:20). See R. H. Gundry, *Matthew* 315, on Matthew's reason for adding the word. According to J. A. Kleist (209-10), καί before τὰ κυνάρια in v 28 may mean either "but" or "and." But its position and the cleverness of the woman's retort favor the ascensive meaning, "even." This meaning shows that the woman is arguing cleverly, not humbly acquiescing to whatever Jesus grants (against H. Anderson 191; W. Schmithals 354-55). "Eat from" is a Hebraism (see, e.g., Gen 2:16, 17).

To say that the woman acknowledges Jesus as giver of the bread of life at the messianic banquet (see J. Jeremias, *Eucharistic Words* 234) does not fit the domesticity of the scene — little dogs and little children. We might think of the crumbs as pieces of bread used for wiping the hands and tossed by little children to their favorite puppies (so J. D. M. Derrett, *Studies* 1. 151-52; cf. J. Jeremias, *Parables* 184). But where is the evidence that crumbs were so used? On the contrary, see *b. Ber.* 52b, which speaks of wiping the hands with a napkin and laying it on the table or on a cushion, and of gathering crumbs at least the size of an olive but leaving the rest. Crumbs in this size-range are not large enough to use as napkins. Besides, little children do not usually wipe their hands. Hence, the woman probably means crumbs dropped by accident.

A. R. C. Leaney (in *JTS* ns 25 [1974] 490) denies that the woman's argument is gnomic; rather, he says, she is appealing to the fact that fringe groups have all along been benefiting from Jesus' ministry. Perhaps so, but a gnomic retort would fit the proverbial sound of Jesus' foregoing remark. And is it likely that the woman is so well acquainted with the sociology of Jesus' ministry that she can instantaneously use it as an argument? See L. Marcel, *La sagesse africaine* 32-34, for the possibility that the woman is trading proverbs with Jesus.

Some have seen in v 28 an allusion to Judg 1:7: seventy captured kings, having had their thumbs and big toes cut off, gathered scraps under Adoni-Bezek's table. W. Storch (in *BZ* nf 14 [1970] 256-57) detects an argument that if even a cruel captor like Adoni-Bezek had mercy enough to let his captives eat the same food as his own children ate, Jesus should, too, so to speak. J. D. M. Derrett (*Studies* 1. 155) detects a warning that Jesus not treat the woman cruelly, as Adoni-Bezek did his captives and was punished by having *his* thumbs and big toes cut off. Historically, however, it is not easy to think that a Syrophoenician woman would know Judg 1:7. Literarily, the disparity between mutilated kings and little dogs poses a problem. Contextually, Judg 1:7 emphasizes cruelty, not mercy (against Storch); and Mark 7:28 presents eating crumbs under the table as a gift of mercy, not as a sentence of cruelty (against Derrett). Verdict: no allusion to Judg 1:7.

We should not infer a notice of the woman's faith from Jesus' command, "Go" (v 29). At 2:11 the command was probably due to the faith of the four men who brought the paralytic, not to his faith (see 2:4-5 with comments); and the Gergasene demoniac certainly did not exercise faith, yet Jesus told him, "Go" (5:19).

According to V. Taylor (348, 351), since Mark notes the exorcism as having occurred but does not describe the occurrence itself, his emphasis falls only on Jesus' supernatural knowledge, not on exorcism at a distance as well. To the contrary, "on account of this saying" (v 29) demands a causal connection between the dialogue and the exorcism — hence, exorcism at a distance but, because of the distance, no exorcistic command by Jesus or description of the demon's exit by Mark. To say that because the story does not describe the exit of the demon the point lies in the dialogue (vv 27-28) is to disregard the climax of the story, which describes the woman's finding her daughter delivered (v 30). Exorcism at a distance hardly symbolizes the salvation of "far-off" Gentiles; for they are "brought near," whereas the present Gentile patient stays at a distance (contrast Eph 2:13). See Matt 8:5-13 par. Luke 7:1-10 and John 4:46-54 for examples of Jesus' healing at a distance (cf. O. Weinreich, *Antike Heilungswunder* 8); Philostr. *VA* 3.38 for exorcism at a distance, but with the use of a hare by the patient's husband; *b. Ber.* 34b for healing at a distance, but in answer to prayer. That the present exorcism takes place at a distance, in the girl's home, and apart from a crowd of witnesses explains why we do not read that bystanders express their amazement. Hence, we have no reason to infer from the absence of such an expression that Mark's interest lies in the breaking down of the barrier between Jews and Gentiles rather than in the exorcism as such (against E. Schweizer 152-53).

THE STUPENDOUS HEALING OF A DEAF MUTE

7:31-37 *(Matt 15:29-31)*

A notation of Jesus' traveling to a new location opens the story of his healing a deaf and dumb man (v 31). Next comes the bringing of the man and the request for healing (v 32), followed by Jesus' use of means for healing (vv 33-34) and the healing itself (v 35). The story closes with a publication of the healing (v 36) and people's astonishment (v 37).

   7:31-32 *(Matt 15:29-30)* Just as in v 14 "again" related only to the action of summoning, not to the crowd as well (see the comments ad loc.), so also "again" here relates only to Jesus' "going out" (ἐξελθών — cf. v 24; also 1:35-38; 2:13; 6:1; 8:27; 9:30), not to the region of Tyre as well; for so far as the Gospel of Mark is concerned, Jesus has not entered and left that region before. "Through Sidon to the Sea of Galilee between the borders of Decapolis" indicates a looping north and then east and south to another region dominated by Gentiles, as in the preceding story (cf. the notes on 5:20 concerning Decapolis). But in contrast with the preceding story, where identification of a woman as Greek and Syrophoenician had the purpose of making the following dialogue understandable, Mark does not identify anyone in this narrative as Gentile. The same observation will hold for the feeding of the four thousand (8:1-9). Mark never identifies regions as Jewish or Gentile and hardly expects his audience to do so. They are probably unac- quainted with the populational character of most of the regions he mentions: Galilee, Gennesaret, Dalmanutha, Decapolis, Transjordan, Judea, Idumea (not to list the names of cities and towns). Besides, the populations were mixed throughout these regions — in different proportions, to be sure, but mixed. So it outruns the text to think that Mark is setting forth a dominical anticipation of world-wide evangelism. "To the Sea of Galilee" indicates the end of this journey and implies that Mark sets both the healing of the deaf mute and the following feeding of the four thousand on the east shore of the sea. In agreement, 8:10 tells of Jesus' getting into a boat. "Between the borders of Decapolis" gives the most natural meaning of ἀνὰ μέσον plus the following genitive and indicates, not the location of the Sea of Galilee, but the region through which Jesus traveled to arrive there. In agreement, the Damascene part of Decapolis bordered on the region of Sidon; and the parts of Decapolis which centered in Hippus and perhaps Gadara lead to the east shore of the Sea of Galilee (F. G. Lang in *ZDPV* 94 [1978] 147-54; E. Schürer, G. Vermes, F. Millar, and M. Black, *History* 2. 130-36; M. Avi-Yonah, *Holy Land* 169-70, 174). The proclamation of the Gergasene demoniac in Decapolis (5:20) has prepared for Jesus' excursion into this region. Since its people have heard of him, they bring a deaf mute for hand-laying. So often has Jesus used this gesture to heal people that here it stands for the desired healing itself. The historical present tense of φέρουσιν, "they bring," and of παρακαλοῦσιν, "they implore" (cf. 5:23), stresses the helpless plight of the deaf mute and the urgency with which the people who bring him ask Jesus to lay his hand on him. The sorrier the plight and the greater the urgency, the more powerful an effect on the audience when they learn of the healing.

7:33-35 Most likely, Jesus' "taking him aside from the crowd" implies that the people who brought the deaf mute *are* the crowd (see the following notes). The implication of a large number casts a sidelong glance at Jesus' magnetism. The privacy does not prepare for the command to silence (v 36); for he will address that command, not to the man, but "to them," i.e. to the crowd who have brought the man. It appears rather that Jesus feels the need for privacy to work a particularly difficult miracle (cf. 5:40; 8:23 and the extremity of amazement noted here in 7:37). Favoring this view are the extraordinary means he uses on this occasion, viz., sticking his fingers in the man's ears, spitting on his own fingers, applying the saliva to the man's tongue, looking up to heaven, and groaning — all in addition to the usual word of healing. This procedure is turning out to be much more complex than the simple laying on of a hand that the people have asked for (v 32).

Sticking fingers into the ears mimics and thereby aids the opening of the ears to hear (cf. the metaphorical use of fingers for power — Exod 8:19; Ps 8:3; Luke 11:20 and other materials cited by J. M. Hull, *Hellenistic Magic* 82-83; Str-B 2. 15). Spitting, as though getting rid of something in your mouth that keeps you from talking plainly, mimics and thereby — along with application of saliva from Jesus' well-functioning tongue to the man's bonded tongue — aids the loosening of the bond (cf. Luke 13:16). Furthermore, physical contact transfers healing power (see the comments and notes on 1:31); and saliva is curative, especially that of a great or divine man (see the following notes). Mark does not mention any compassion or prayer on Jesus' part (contrast 6:34; 8:2; 9:29 with 9:14-18; Luke 18:13; John 11:32-42; 17:1; Rom 8:26; Exod 2:23-24; 6:5; Ps 123:1; Tob 3:1); so it is doubtful that we should think of either one in connection with the heavenward look and groan. A groan requires the vigorous exhalation of breath, which has life-force (cf. C. D. Buck, *Dictionary* 1131 [16.39]). Therefore the magical papyri sometimes prescribe a groan to endue the words of a spell with the power of accomplishment (*PGM* IV. 1406, 2492; VII. 766-79; XIII. 945-46; A. Dieterich, *Abraxas* 202, ll. 15-16; idem, *Eine Mithrasliturgie* 6, 64; T. Hopfner, *Griechisch-ägyptischer Offenbarungszauber* 1. 484-87 §780; cf. Mark 8:12 with comments; John 20:22; *PGM* IV. 1405-6, 2492, 3081-84; Luc.

Philops. 12; Acts of Xanthippa and Polyxena 5). Here, then, the groan has the purpose of enduing the command to be opened with the power of accomplishment. A Hellenistic audience would respond to Mark's text with this understanding. If not a gesture of prayer, the heavenward look at least indicates the heavenly source and therefore the supernatural character of this power (cf. 6:41 with comments and notes). Modern "faith-healers," too, will often groan with a heavenward look in the act of healing.

The looking up to heaven and groaning and the retention of the Aramaic word ἐφφαθά argue that Mark details the unusually complex means to highlight the difficulty of the miracle. Even Jesus has to take special measures to perform this one. And well he might, for without some extra exertion the deaf mute might not hear Jesus' word, the hearing of which will be at once necessary to and constitutive of the healing. Again, however, the greater the difficulty, the greater the exhibition of healing power. At 5:41, too, the remembrance of an Aramaic word called attention to the extraordinary difficulty of a healing, or rather of a raising. The Aramaic word is not a secretive, nonsensical, and difficult-to-pronounce word of magic like the elaborate and numerous abracadabras regularly packed into Hellenistic and Roman incantations (dating mostly from a later period — see H. C. Kee, *Medicine* 95-121). Nor is it even a meaningful foreign word of magic embedded in and sometimes translated into a regularly spoken language (as in *PGM* XXXVI. 315), for Jesus spoke Aramaic regularly. Nevertheless, the original audience of Mark spoke Greek regularly and Mark writes his book in Greek; so for them the Aramaic word connotes the power that a magical word would be thought to have. Elsewhere Mark uses other Aramaic words to make other emphases. The present context of a miracle determines the emphasis on power (cf. the comments and notes on 5:41). Mark adds to this emphasis by putting the introductory verb λέγει into the present tense, "he says," and by translating ἐφφαθά with a Greek verb strengthened by a perfective preposition, διανοίχθητι, "be completely opened." The Aramaic and its translation provide a curative word for the man's deaf ears to complement the curative saliva applied to his mute tongue. Yet Jesus addresses the word, not to the man's ears, but to the man himself. "To him" is singular; so also is the command to be opened: ἐφφαθά . . . διανοίχθητι. The whole man is concentrated in his ears, and to heal a deaf mute is so stupendous that claimed instances are extremely rare in antiquity (R. Pesch [1. 397], citing only R. Herzog, *Wunderheilungen* no. 44 [though the text uses ἄφωνος, "mute," alone, not κωφός, "deaf," as well] and *b. Ḥag.* 3a).

"Immediately" emphasizes that despite the difficulty, Jesus' power is so overwhelming that it requires no delay to effect the opening of the man's ears. Mark now refers to them as αἱ ἀκοαί, literally "the hearings," to stress the restoration of their function, whereas in v 33 he needed only to refer to them as τὰ ὦτα, "the ears," outwardly visible organs into which Jesus stuck his fingers. The advancement of αὐτοῦ, "his," adds to this stress rather than emphasizing the owner of "the hearings" (cf. the comments on 6:52). Likewise, Jesus' power works an immediate loosening of "the bond" of the man's tongue with the result that "he was speaking plainly" rather than "with difficulty" (as in v 32; cf. F. W.

Danker, *Benefactor* 189). Or perhaps we should accept εὐθύς before ἐλύθη with P⁴⁵ᵛⁱᵈ ℵ (L εὐθέως) D 892 syrᵖᵃˡᵐˢ (eth), because Mark elsewhere prefers the spelling εὐθύς and because the awkwardness of associating immediacy with the loosening of the bonded tongue but not with the opening of the ears makes this reading more difficult and therefore more likely original. If we were to reject the notion of immediacy altogether with B D 33 itᵃ,ᵇ,ᵈ,ff2,i,q,r1 copᵇᵒ, the main point — viz., the effectiveness of Jesus' power — would remain (see B. M. Metzger, *Textual Commentary* ad loc.). For this point Mark needs only to state *that* the man was speaking plainly. What he said is irrelevant; so Mark omits it.

7:36-37 *(Matt 15:31)* It would not make sense to order the man alone to say nothing about his healing, for his plain speech has already betrayed the miracle. Mark does not say why Jesus "ordered that they [i.e. the crowd, who now hear the man speaking plainly] should tell no one." Presumably Jesus does not want to be troubled any further (cf. v 24). Mark's interest lies rather in the stupendousness of the miracle, which causes the crowd, "however much he was ordering them," to "proclaim" the miracle "all the more" (μᾶλλον περισσότερον, literally "rather [in an adversative comparative sense] more abundantly" — a pleonastic emphasis; cf. 1:44-45; 5:20 for the thought and 5:26; 9:42; 10:48; 14:31 v.l.; 15:11 for the use of μᾶλλον in an adversative comparative sense). An adversative δέ, "but," and an emphatic αὐτοί, "they," set the crowd's reaction over against Jesus' order. Emphasis on the stupendousness of the miracle reaches a climax in the crowd's second reaction: "and they were extremely abundantly astonished [cf. 1:22; 2:12; 5:42; 6:2, 51; 10:26; 11:18], saying, 'He has done all things well [cf. Gen 1:31; Sir 39:16], and he makes the deaf and dumb to hear and speak' " (v 37). Nearly everything in this verse is emphatic: (1) the forward position and strong meaning of ὑπερπερισσῶς, "extremely abundantly" (N.B. esp. the echo of περισσότερον in the preceding verse, but with an intensifiying ὑπερ-, "extremely," now added); (2) the strong meaning and imperfect tense of ἐξεπλήσσοντο, which denotes a state of astonishment; (3) the first position of καλῶς, "well, beautifully"; (4) the universal plural of πάντα, "all things," despite the reference to only one miracle; (5) the placement of πάντα before the verb πεποίηκεν, "he has done," whose object it is; (6) the perfect tense of πεποίηκεν, which indicates a finished job of healing (cf. 5:19); (7) the present tense of ποιεῖ, "he makes," which causes this miracle to typify Jesus' miraculous activity as a whole; (8) the advancing of τοὺς κωφούς, "the deaf," away from its infinitive ἀκούειν, "to hear," to a position ahead of the main verb ποιεῖ; (9) the plural of τοὺς κωφούς and of τοὺς ἀλάλους, which makes the healing of the one deaf mute in this story an example of many such healings (cf. Isa 29:18-19; 32:3-4; 35:5-6; Wis 10:21; Matt 11:4-5 par. Luke 7:22; Mark 3:8; 5:20; but not *Gen. Rab.* 95.1; *Midr. Ps.* 146 §§4-5 [W. G. Braude, *Midrash on Psalms* 2. 367], which have to do with healings at the resurrection); and (10) the cognatic assonance and wordplay of ἀλάλους λαλεῖν, literally "the unspeaking to speak."

NOTES

Besides F. G. Lang in *ZDPV* 94 (1978) 152-54; see D. Baly, *Geographical Companion* 120, for possible routes indicated by v 31. Lang thinks that Mark makes up the circuitous journey to portray Jesus as the pioneer of Gentile evangelism (op. cit. 154-60); but in the comments and notes on vv 24-30, 31-37, we have already seen reasons to doubt such a portrayal. We will see more. The possible routes, realistic as they are, make needless the conjecture of J. Wellhausen (2. Aufl., 57-58), followed by H. Bietenhard in *ZDPV* 79 (1963) 54, that בֵּית צַיְדָא, "Bethsaida," was misheard as צַיְדֹן, "Sidon." Though the conjecture is put forward to solve a supposed but unreal topographical difficulty, it suffers from a linguistic difficulty of its own, viz., the unlikelihood that at one and the same time בֵּית would have dropped out and the vowels in צַיְדָא would have undergone a complete change. Wellhausen points to the dropping of Βηθαρ- in Josephus *Ant.* 17.10.6 §277 as compared with idem *J.W.* 2.4.2 §59, but it is unaccompanied by any other change similar to the one required for Wellhausen's conjecture here. The mention of Sidon seems to represent tradition (see the following notes), which may mention that city because it marks the northernmost reach of Jesus' journey, twenty miles north of Tyre. Of course, the accompanying mention of Tyre and the long standing association of Sidon with Tyre may add to this reason for mentioning Sidon. "Going out from the borders of Tyre" rules out the explanation sometimes given that Tyrian territory includes Sidon. Mark adds "of Galilee" to "the Sea" to avoid confusion with the Mediterranean Sea, along whose coast lie Tyre and Sidon (so also 1:16, but there because Mark was referring to the Sea of Galilee for the first time). It is as unlikely in pre-Marcan tradition as it is in Mark that the topographical movement indicated by v 31 ended the preceding pericope, where this movement would have no point (against W. Marxsen, *Mark* 69-70).

It is often said that the heightened use of means in 7:31-37 tends toward Hellenistic magical practices and grows out of the Gentile setting of the story. If so, we would need to add that even this heightened use is still a far cry from the wordy formulas and silly concoctions typical of Hellenistic magic. Furthermore, we should not underestimate the amount of magic used by Jews, including pious ones (see Tob 6:1–11:15, which antedates the NT); and Jesus' heightened use of means again in 8:22-26 will have as Jewish a setting as Galilee if we are to judge by Matt 11:21 par. Luke 10:13; Luke 9:10; John 1:44; 12:21 (cf. another heightened use of means right in Jerusalem, hardly a Gentile setting, according to John 9:1-7; also 5:25-34; 6:14 and the comments and notes on Mark 6:45, 53). To a certain extent, Christian theologians might want to see accommodation to prevailing culture at the same time that they put Jesus' miracles in a class by themselves. The often cited cross-reference Exod 8:15(19) is only marginally appropriate. In that passage "the finger of God" is singular and wholly metaphorical (either for God's power or for Moses' staff). Here, the plural shows that the mention of Jesus' fingers literally has to do with his sticking two of them in the man's ears, one finger per ear. The resultant transfer of healing power is not metaphorical.

The similarities between 7:31-37 and 8:22-26 suggest to L. Schenke (*Wundererzählungen* 273-80; cf. W. Grundmann [2. Aufl.] 164) that the two stories therein stood alongside each other in the tradition, but in reverse order after the pattern of Isa 35:5-6 (so also others before Schenke). To support such an order, he argues that since 7:37 has no parallel in 8:22-26 and refers to "all things" that Jesus has done, the acclamation in 7:37 originally covered both stories by coming at the end of the second story. Mark separated the stories and reversed their order to put them where, at the expense of the miraculous, they might carry symbolic meanings, the healing of the deaf mute symbolizing the opening of ears to hear Jesus' teaching in 7:1-30, the healing of the blind man symbolizing the opening of the disciples' mental eyes to see the true character of Jesus' messiahship. But there is no teaching within the present story or in its immediate context (vv 27-29 having the character of repartee and making the subsequent exorcism arise out of grudging concession rather than out of positive teaching), even though Mark might have followed up with a teaching of the four thousand (8:1-9) after the pattern of Jesus' teaching the five thousand (6:34). Moreover, a mere pair of stories would still leave a hyperbole in the "all" of the acclamation and in the plurality of healings of deaf and dumb people. Under Schenke's hypothesis and in view of specific references in the acclamation to making the deaf and dumb to hear and speak, the lack of a similarly specific reference to Jesus' making the blind to see poses a problem unless Mark omits the reference because of his reversing the order of the stories. But we may doubt the likelihood of an originally tripartite specification: it would overstuff v 37b. The likely reason for the absence of an acclamation in 8:22-26 is that there the miracle will occur clear outside town, within eyeshot but at such a distance that apparently the townspeople will not be watching. Here the crowd are within earshot as well as eyeshot.

With others, R. Pesch (1. 399) says that this story symbolizes Jesus' saving the Gentiles: he opens their ears to hear the gospel and loosens their tongue to preach it. Strange, then, that Jesus does not preach the gospel to the mute after healing him, and even stranger that it is the crowd, not the man, who preach — but not the gospel or to the mute.

It is hard to imagine that a redactor would make up the circuitous route and functionally useless reference to Sidon. No convincing reason is forthcoming to tell why, if he wants to portray Jesus as a minister to unevangelized Gentiles, he does not retain the prior setting in Tyrian territory or establish a new setting in Sidon rather than through-passing it in favor of a return to the Sea of Galilee, Jesus' old haunt, and in favor of a route that takes him between the borders of Decapolis, where an ex-demoniac has already preached (5:20). The prolixity of ἀνὰ μέσον τῶν ὁρίων Δεκαπόλεως, literally "up [the] middle of the borders of Decapolis," seems designed to distinguish this penetration of Decapolis from Jesus' having grazed it in 5:1 (see the comments and notes ad loc. regarding the topographical vv.ll. and the implication of "he went away" in 5:20).

According to many commentators, however, Mark incorrectly puts the Sea of Galilee in the middle of Decapolis. But why should we think that he does? ᾿Ανὰ μέσον plus the genitive regularly means "between, into the middle of something" as well as stationary location within it (BAGD s.v. ἀνά 1a). In Matt 13:25 darnels were not in the midst of the wheat before the sower sowed them; hence, ἀνὰ μέσον τοῦ σίτου does not modify the darnels, but the sowing (cf. "in his field," a similarly adverbial phrase in v 24). So also here, ἀνὰ μέσον τῶν ὁρίων Δεκαπόλεως need not be an adjectival phrase modifying the Sea of Galilee, as though the Sea of Galilee were in the middle of Decapolis. It is not, and Mark has already shown his knowledge that it is not by putting the Decapolis primarily at a distance from the shore of the Sea of Galilee (a just-delivered demoniac dwelling near the shore has to "go away" to preach in the Decapolis; see 5:1, 18-20 with comments and notes). The phrase in question modifies Jesus' going (ἦλθεν) and thus makes the last in a series of adverbial phrases, all topographical. Moreover, this last one completes an a-b-a'-b' pattern: just as the point of origin ("the borders of Tyre") is followed by the locality through which Jesus set out ("Sidon"), so the destination ("the Sea of Galilee") is followed by the locality through which Jesus arrives ("the borders of Decapolis"; see 10:1; 11:1 for further examples of listing an ultimate destination before an intermediate one). To the contrary, Z. Kato (Völkermission 45-46, 84) cites 5:1; 11:11 for a Marcan habit of putting forward a general destination and then specifying the destination more closely, which would mean here that the middle of the borders of Decapolis specifies the part of the Sea of Galilee to which Jesus came. But in both of those cross-references the specifying phrase starts with the same preposition εἰς, "to," with which the general phrase started, whereas here Mark follows up an εἰς-phrase with an ἀνὰ μέσον-phrase. For the specification of a part of the Sea of Galilee we would have expected him to follow the pattern of 5:1; 11:11 by using εἰς τὸ μέσον, for which see 3:3 par.; 14:60 (without τό); Luke 4:35; 5:19; John 20:19, 26. Since Decapolis is a region, "the borders of Decapolis" means the region which is Decapolis rather than the region which surrounds it (cf. 10:1, where "the borders of Judea" means the region which is Judea, not the region surrounding it; contrast the region surrounding Tyre in 7:24 [with the notes ad loc.], 31).

In an unpublished paper, D. W. Chapman adds several more reasons to deny that Mark is trying to locate the Sea of Galilee physically in the middle of Decapolis. These reasons are worth paraphrasing in full (though Chapman's own view that Mark locates the Sea of Galilee *culturally* in the middle of Decapolis is to be rejected for the reasons already stated here): First, Mark is very sparing in providing larger geographic settings for places, towns, cities, etc. In his entire gospel the only locale that he places in a larger geographic context is Nazareth ("of Galilee" — 1:9). Second, Mark would hardly have waited seven chapters and by-passed at least eight opportunities (in 1:16; 2:13; 3:7; 4:1; 5:1, 21; 6:45, 53) to locate the Sea of Galilee, the single most important geographic feature in his book, in the middle of Decapolis. Third, such a location would require Mark to believe that the Sea of Galilee is not in Galilee! Yet Mark appears to have been the first writer to refer to the body of water in question as "the Sea of Galilee." Under the view opposed, why did he not call it "the Sea of Decapolis"? Fourth, 1:16, 21, 28-29 imply a location of Capernaum beside the Sea of Galilee and at the same time in the region of Galilee. Thus Mark presents the sea and the region of the same name as at least bordering each other.

In v 32 μογιλάλον literally means "speaking with difficulty" and refers to the inarticulate grunts of a deaf mute. Because of its infrequency and a probable allusion to Isa 35:5-6 in v 37b (cf. also the probable allusion to Isa 35:5-6 in Matt 11:5 par. Luke 7:22), the word is usually thought to echo Isa 35:6 LXX, where it stands for אִלֵּם. On the other hand, Mark may choose the word also to set the stage for his reference to "the bond" which makes it difficult for the man to use his tongue (v 35b) and to prepare for the man's speaking ὀρθῶς, "plainly," upon healing (v 35c).

Φέρουσιν and παρακαλοῦσιν are characteristically Marcan indefinite third person plural verbs: "people bring" and "people implore" (v 32). But Mark goes on to mention "the crowd" (v 33), those who disobey Jesus' command (v 36), and those who are astonished (v 37). Are they all the same? Or does a small group who bring the deaf mute differ from the crowd and disobey Jesus by proclaiming the miracle to the crowd, the crowd then being astonished by the proclamation? Or does a small group bring the deaf mute, a large group ("the crowd") proclaim the miracle, and yet others hear and marvel? Or should we distinguish only those who hear and marvel, all the others being the same? Jesus takes aside only the deaf mute; so even if the people who brought him differ from the crowd, they are in no better position than the crowd is to proclaim what Jesus has done. But the fact that Jesus' taking the deaf mute away from the crowd immediately follows people's bringing him to Jesus favors that those people are the crowd. The fact that the people whom Jesus commands but who disobey are referred to with a mere pronoun favors that they are the crowd, last-mentioned. The facts that Mark signals no change of subject between vv 36 and 37 and that he does not even provide an audience for the proclamation in v 36 favor that those who are astonished are the same as those who make proclamation. They are all the same.

According to D. Traktellis (*Authority and Passion* 45), Jesus uses the therapeutic technique of touch because the deaf mute understands the language of touch but not that of sounded words. We should not accept this explanation, however, because Jesus speaks the word ἐφφαθά to the man and Mark translates it. On other occasions, moreover, Jesus has used touch to heal people who were not deaf; and he has healed people who could hear without speaking to them (1:31; 5:25-29; 6:5).

For the medicinal and magical use of spittle, the following references to primary literature are representative: John 9:6; Plin. *HN* 28.2, 6-7 §§8, 30-31, 35-39; Luc. *Nec.* 7; Petr. *Sat.* 131; Tac. *Hist.* 4.81-82; 6.18; Suet. *Vesp.* 7; Dio Cass. 66.8; *b. Šabb.* 108b; *Deut. Rab.* 5.15; *Acts Phil.* 82. For discussion, see J. Preuss, *Biblical and Talmudic Medicine* 85-86, 277, 531; A. Jirku, *Materielen* 61-65; L. Blau, *Das altjüdische Zauberwesen* 162; J. J. Hess in *ZAW* 35 (1915) 130-31; Str-B 1. 216-17; 2. 15-16; E. Lesky in *RAC* 2. 433-46; S. Eitrem, *Some Notes* 56-60; E. E. Evans-Pritchard, *Nuer Religion* 171-72; O. Böcher, *Dämonenfurcht* 218-20; idem, *Exorcista* 102; J. M. Hull, *Magic* 76-78; D. Smith in *Trin-Journ* ns 6 (1985) 151-56; E. Yamauchi in *Gospel Perspectives* 6. 137-40. Magic and medicine are often mixed up, but Yamauchi (ibid.) and H. C. Kee (*Miracle* 75-76) downplay the magical use in favor of the medicinal use (cf. animals' licking their wounds and dogs and snakes licking well the patients at the shrine of Aesculapius in Epidaurus — R. Herzog, *Wunderheilungen* nos. 20, 26; Ar. *Plut.* §§690, 733-47; Kee, op. cit. 83-87). Though the bulk of the magical materials, particularly those in *PGM*, postdates the NT, enough from the first century and earlier has survived to show the amount of continuity necessary to the interpretations offered here (cf. S. R. Garrett in *Religion, Science, and Magic* 162, n. 19, and other literature cited there). The healings performed by Jesus carry out the OT and later Jewish motif of Yahweh as a healer (so Kee, *Medicine* 125) and signal the arrival of God's rule. We would overdraw the evidence and even contradict much of it to classify Jesus as a magician (cf. Kee in *Religion, Science, and Magic* 121-41). Nonetheless, the absence from the OT of exorcisms such as he has performed and the pervasiveness of Hellenistic culture in first century Palestine as well as in the provenance of Mark (wherever it was written in the Roman Empire) assure that Jesus' miraculous activities and their methods bear a relation to that culture similar enough to make them understandable in it. There is no need to ascribe them to later Hellenization of the tradition. The evidence cited above falsifies the denial by Kee (ibid. 138) that the magical and medical use of spittle is missing from the Hellenistic and Roman periods, and his interpretation of Jesus' use of spittle here and in 8:22-26 as a flouting of Jewish laws of purity (ibid. 136-38) rests on a passage according to which spittle defiles only when the spitter is already defiled for another reason (Lev 15:8) and on another passage in which spittle has to do with shame, not with impurity (Num 12:14).

The verb "touched" in v 33 and the immediately preceding mention of Jesus' fingers favor that he spits on his own fingers and applies the saliva to the deaf mute's tongue (cf. the v.l. in P45 W 0131 sy^s Ephraem and the Arabic Diatessaron 21:3, according to which Jesus spits on his fingers before sticking them in the mute's ears; see P.-L. Couchoud in *JTS* os 35 [1934] 12 for a defense of this v.l.). Since we have no reason to suppose that the mute's tongue is hanging out of his mouth, it hardly seems probable that Jesus spits directly on it (contrast his spitting directly into a blind man's eyes at 8:23). And since no demon is mentioned, it seems improbable that Jesus spits on the ground to indicate or force the exit of a demon. The application of spittle to the deaf mute's tongue also tends against an apotropaic connotation. In Gal 4:14 the prefix ἐξ-, "out," may point up such a connotation, differing from that in the present passage and 8:23, where we read only the simplex πτύσας, "having spit." The view that Jesus sticks his fingers into the mute's ears and puts saliva on his tongue to generate faith miscarries on the failure of Mark to mention faith. The means have to do with Jesus' working the miracle, not with the mute's believing for a miracle.

J. M. Hull (*Hellenistic Magic* 84) thinks that Jesus' groaning forces out a dumb demon by sympathetic magic. But the groaning at 8:12 and in magical spells is not a means of exorcism; hence, the groaning probably does not imply demonic possession and exorcism here. Likewise, it is not quite correct to say that Jesus groans to work himself up for performance of a miracle. Groaning is part of the performance itself. On groaning and other uses of the breath in healing, prayer, and the like, see O. Böcher, *Dämonenfurcht* 220-24; idem, *Christus Exorcista* 102-4.

According to G. Mussies in *NTS* 30 (1980) 425-29, a word of healing has been kept in its original language because it worked only in that language, i.e. because the very sound of it carried power and because a demon who understood only Aramaic was causing the deafmuteness. Except for 5:41, then, why no Aramaic in stories of healing and exorcisms elsewhere in Mark? Perhaps because the healings here and in 5:41 are unusually difficult.

Besides the literature cited in BAGD s.v. ἐφφαθά with particular reference to the alternatives Aramaic versus Hebrew and questions of gender and number, see S. Morag in *JSS* 17 (1972) 198-202; H. P. Rüger in *Markus-Philologie* 79; M. Wilcox in *ANRW* II 25/2. 998-99; F. L. Horton in *ZNW* 77 (1986) 101-8. Since Aramaic has a longer history in the region of Decapolis than Greek has, we cannot infer from ἐφφαθά, if it is Aramaic, that the deaf mute is Jewish. Jews do live in Decapolis, however (E. Schürer, G. Vermes. F. Millar, and M. Black, *History* 2. 125-58). Either Mark writes as an omniscient narrator by revealing what Jesus said in private, or the healed man reported what Jesus had said, or the word was heard at a little distance just as the physical manipulations were observed at a little distance. The notion that αὐτῷ carries a double meaning, that Jesus commanded the heaven as well as the man to be opened (so H. C. Waetjen, *Reordering of Power* 136, with reference to a summoning of God's rule), stumbles over Mark's subsequently reporting that the man's ears were opened but not that the heaven was opened (contrast 1:10). With the use of ἀκοαί for "ears," including emphasis on their function of hearing (v 35), cf. 2 Macc 15:39; Luke 7:1; Acts 17:20; Heb 5:11; *Barn.* 10:12.

A. Deissmann (*LAE* 304-7) and others (e.g., S. Eitrem and H. Herter in *RAC* 2. 382-84) suggest that the noun "bond" in v 35 implies demonic possession as the cause of the deafmuteness, in accordance with the expression "whom Satan has bound" in Luke 13:16 (cf. "a spirit of infirmity" in Luke 13:11) and with the use of the verb "bind" in Hellenistic magical spells dealing with physical maladies and demons. This suggestion suffers from a failure of the present passage to contain any reference to a demon, a spirit, or Satan (contrast Luke 13:11, 16; Acts 20:22; Rev 20:2) and from the absence of any indication of hostility, resistance, or characteristically violent exit on the part of a demon (contrast 9:17, 25-26). In and of itself binding does not imply the demonic (see, e.g., Matt 16:19; 18:18; Rom 7:2; 1 Cor 7:27, 39; Str-B 1. 738-47). These considerations also militate against the views of J. M. Hull (*Hellenistic Magic* 68-69, 83) that the difficulty of this case lies in the inability of a deaf and dumb demon inhabiting the mute to reveal its identity or hear an exorcistic command and that Jesus sticks his fingers in the mute's ears to open an exit for the demon. Hull may be correct, however, in relating the v.l. μογγιλάλον, "speaking hoarsely," to a scribal demonic interpretation.

It modernizes the story by dulling its miraculous edge to suggest with V. Taylor (355) that the patient reads Jesus' lips or hears him faintly because he is not completely deaf. Since Mark emphasizes the plainness of the man's speech and says nothing about its content, the miracle does not symbolize the loosing of the disciples' tongues in 8:27-29 to confess Jesus as the Christ (so W. Schmithals 357) or, more generally, the speaking of orthodox doctrine in the church (so J. Ernst 216). We have no evidence that in Mark ὀρθῶς connotes orthodox doctrine. The contrast with difficulty of speech (v 32) prescribes a connotation of manner instead of content. Someone born a deaf mute has never heard a language spoken and therefore has not learned the motor skills necessary to speaking a language. We might then infer from the immediacy of the man's plain speaking that he has not been a deaf mute from birth (cf. the inclination of H. van der Loos [*Miracles* 524-25] to posit hysterical deafmutedness). The inference may underinterpret the miracle, however. J. A. Kleist (147-50) remarks the modal use of ἐλάλει for ability to speak. Throughout vv 32, 33, 35, 37 Mark maintains the order deafness–muteness, which represents cause and effect.

The imperfect tense of διεστέλλετο, "he was ordering," contrasts with the aorist tense of διεστείλατο, "he ordered," but does not have to indicate repeated commands that are repeatedly violated. Mark uses the singular ὅσον, "however much," not the plural ὅσα, "however many times"; so as often in verbs of speaking, the imperfect probably represents extended rather than iterative action. According to 5:19-20, Jesus had commanded the ex-demoniac of the Gergasene country to go home and tell his family about his deliverance; but the man exceeded Jesus' command by going away and making a proclamation in Decapolis. It should come as no surprise, then, that Jesus here tries to avoid another general publication. He has learned his lesson. The suggestion that it was traditional to keep the means of healing secret fails to note that traditional commands to keep magical formulas secret are addressed to the user. Here, Jesus would be the user. Moreover, the suggestion does not fit his ordering the crowd rather than the man not to tell anybody. Thus G. Theissen, *Miracle Stories* 150, is forced to think that the present command to silence was originally addressed only to the man. Nor is there any indication that Jesus wants only the means of healing to be kept secret. On the contrary, vv 36b-37 indicate that he has in view the healing itself. The crowd's astonishment at the healing probably does not suggest a lack of expectation and therefore their having brought the deaf mute for blessing rather than for healing (cf. W. L. Lane 266); for the requested laying on of Jesus' hand has previously had to do with physical healing, not with spiritual blessing (5:23; 6:5; also 8:23, 25; cf. 1:31, 41; 5:41).

The command not to tell anyone does not fit the theory of a messianic secret or secret of the miracles. Jesus addresses his command to the crowd. What is known to a crowd is not a secret. Why would Mark, if interested in a messianic secret or secret of miracles, water down the privacy of the healing (v 33) by doubling the public knowledge of it, as he would be doing through a redactional fabrication of v 36 and an insertion of this verse before v 37 which, if traditinal, already requires a public knowledge of the healing? Moreover, the command and the disobeying of it in v 36 do not interrupt an original connection between vv 35 and 37 and thereby prove a redactional insertion of v 36; for without the command and disobedience to it the transition from a healing performed apart from the crowd to their astonishment at it becomes very abrupt. Lest we think that Mark inserts the command and disobedience to it for the purpose of alleviating this abruptness, let us ask whether he makes Jesus impose a secret on the crowd rather than on the healed man because tradition has it that the crowd is astonished at the healing. No, because it would fit a secret far better for Mark to make Jesus impose it on the healed man (cf. 1:44a; 5:43; 8:26; 9:8) and then to have him betray it out of joy instead of having the crowd betray it out of astonishment (cf. 1:43-45; 5:19-20). So tradition underlies v 36, too. These considerations are even more devastating of the theory that Mark fabricates the privacy in v 33a as well as the command in v 36.

Because Mark makes Jesus' miracles signs of messiahship and of divine sonship, L. S. Hay (in *JAAR* 35 [1967] 20-21) theorizes that an original command to keep the healing a secret has expanded into a messianic secret. But in the context of Mark, the presence of a crowd clamps the command not to tell closer to the theme of explosively favorable reaction than to that of secrecy; and we cannot assume that prior to Mark, Christians told isolated stories of Jesus' miracles without portraying him as the Christ and Son of God.

Without a second τούς in v 37b (so ℵ B L Δ 33 892 1241), "deaf" and "dumb" describe the same group, as is appropriate after the healing of a man who was both deaf and dumb; and the καί before τοὺς κωφούς means "and." The delay of καὶ ἀλάλους, "and dumb," the distinction and separation between ἀκούειν and λαλεῖν, "to hear" and "to speak," and a consequent misinterpretation of the καί before τοὺς κωφούς as meaning "both" probably led to insertion of a second τούς (so A D Θ 0131 *f*1,13 Majority Text), which

makes "the deaf" and "the dumb" refer to different groups. V. Taylor (356) suggests that
the plural of the deaf and dumb whom Jesus has healed implies an earlier group of stories
concerning such healings. A pre-Marcan collection of miracle stories is not hard to imagine,
but one specializing in healings of the deaf and dumb seems doubtful. Better, then, to think
of hyperbole.

D. E. Nineham (202) argues that "dumb" (ἀλάλους, literally "unspeaking" — v 37)
implies that prior to the miracle the man was not able to speak at all and that therefore
"plainly" (v 35) was later added to the story. But at its start, "with difficulty" (μογι-) gives
the only indication of the malady of the tongue; "plainly" provides a proper contrast; and
the shift from μογι- to the more usual α-privitive with λάλους (cf. 9:17, 25) probably stems
from the desire for a clearer wordplay with λαλεῖν. Moreover, speaking "with difficulty"
does not contradict dumbness if Mark is referring to the inarticulate grunts of a deaf mute
(cf. the preceding notes on μογιλάλον).

According to H. Räisänen (Messiasgeheimnis 71-74), the acclamation in v 37 implies against vv 33a, 36 that the healing took place in the presence of the crowd. Not
necessarily, for we can just as easily infer that the crowd who brought the deaf mute now
hear the results of the healing, perhaps even at a distance if it is not too great. Therefore
the redaction critical conclusions drawn by Räisänen do not follow. They have their own
problems anyway, such as that Mark nowhere else imposes a secret on a crowd.

W. L. Lane (287) thinks that just as the healing of the blind man in 8:22-26 will
anticipate the disciples' insight into Jesus' identity in 8:27-30, the healing of the deaf mute
in 7:31-37 anticipates the confession of Jesus as the Christ in 8:27-30 (see also G. Minette
de Tillesse, Le secret messianique 61). But we will see reasons to deny anticipation in
8:22-26; and the distance of 7:31-37 from 8:27-30, the acclaiming rather than confessing
of Jesus in 7:37, and the acclaiming of him by onlookers rather than by the former deaf
mute himself cast doubt on anticipation in 7:31-37. Furthermore, 7:37 has nothing about
Jesus' identity, as 8:27-30 will; and the false identifications of him in 8:28 will come from
the likes of the people who acclaim him in 7:37.

THE POWER OF JESUS TO FEED FOUR THOUSAND PEOPLE
WITH SEVEN LOAVES AND A FEW SMALL FISH

8:1-9 (Matt 15:32-38; cf. Mark 6:32-44; Matt 14:13-21; Luke 9:10b-17; John 1:1-15)

In the story of Jesus' feeding the four thousand Mark first identifies the occasion
and need (vv 1-3). Then he details the way in which Jesus fills the need (vv 4-7).
The story closes with an emphasis on the superabundance of the miracle and
Jesus' dismissal of the crowd (vv 8-9).

8:1-3 (Matt 15:32) "In those days," combined with the later statement that
after feeding the four thousand Jesus sails to Dalmanutha (v 10), indicates that
this story takes place during his time on the eastern shore of the Sea of Galilee
(cf. 7:31 and, for analogous implications, 1:9; 13:17, 24). "Again" may imply
that at a time subsequent to the healing of the deaf mute (7:31-37) a crowd forms
in addition to the one present on that occasion. But Mark describes the crowd as
"large" (πολλοῦ). The last time he so described a crowd was in the pericope about
feeding the five thousand (6:34), and the present pericope corresponds in content

to that one. More probably, then, "again" harks back to the large crowd of five thousand. The genitive absolute πολλοῦ ὄχλου ὄντος καὶ μὴ ἐχόντων τί φάγωσιν may be taken causally or temporally: "because [or 'when'] there was a large crowd and they did not have anything to eat." Mark may want his audience to think of the same crowd that witnessed Jesus' healing of the deaf mute (7:31-37), especially since the present crowd's already having stayed with Jesus three days makes the introductory phrase "in those days" a natural link identifying the crowd in this story with the one in the preceding story. Such an identification would favor a causal understanding of the genitive absolute (though by definition an absolute construction does not itself indicate any relation to the rest of the sentence). Mark's describing the crowd as large revives his emphasis on Jesus' magnetism and prepares for the miracle of feeding "about four thousand" (v 9). The asyndeton with which v 1 begins calls attention to the magnetism.

"Summoning the disciples" implies the authority of Jesus (cf. the comments on 3:13). The historical present tense of λέγει, "he says," lends weight first to the compassion that he says he has for the crowd. This emphasis puts across a point of view favorable toward him and therefore conducive to an apology for the Cross (cf. the comments on 6:34). The historical present tense of λέγει lends weight also to the crowd's having stayed with him already for three days and not having anything to eat. Here his magnetism is powerfully reflected. Not only does a fulness of description emphasize his sway over the crowd. So also certain nuances of the text emphasize his ability to keep the crowd despite harsh circumstances: (1) the forward position of ἤδη ἡμέραι τρεῖς, "already three days"; (2) the nominative absoluteness of that phrase, whereas we would have expected an ordinary accusative of duration (cf. the somewhat different vv.ll. in B and D it); (3) the vivid present tense of προσμένουσίν μοι, "they are staying with me"; (4) the apparent implication of the parallelism between the present tense of προσμένουσιν and that of ἔχουσιν that the crowd have stayed with Jesus three days even though they have had nothing to eat for the whole time (rather than that they have just now run out of food); (5) the repetitiveness of including his notice that they have nothing to eat, after Mark has offered the same information in v 1; (6) the addition of the note, "And some of them have come from afar"; (7) the putting of this note in an independent clause, which not only emphasizes Jesus' drawing power even at a distance but also keeps the long distance journey of some from turning into a mere cause of fainting on the return trip; and (8) the forward position of ἀπὸ μακρόθεν, "from afar." "If I should dismiss them" implies Jesus' authority over the crowd (cf. 6:36 where, however, the disciples positively suggest that Jesus should dismiss the crowd.)

8:4-7 *(Matt 15:33-36)* Mark does not put forward the disciples' question, "From where will anyone be able to satisfy these people with food here in the desert?" to criticize them for forgetting the feeding of the five thousand. The question elicits no rebuke from Jesus, and v 19 will show that the disciples remember in detail the feeding of the five thousand; so we should not read forgetfulness, much less impertinence, into the question. Rather, by defining the locale more closely, the question magnifies the miracle which Jesus is about to perform. Before, reasonably nearby hamlets and towns offered the possibility of buying enough bread (so the disciples' suggestion in 6:36-37). Now, the people are not merely at "a deserted spot" (ἔρημον τόπον) in otherwise populated territory (so 6:31-32, 35); they are "on a wilderness" (ἐπ᾽ ἐρημίας). No hamlets or towns lie in easy reach, for the whole territory is unpopulated. The plight is more desperate than before also because it is not merely mid-to-late afternoon after a partial day's teaching (as in 6:35 — see the comments ad loc.); rather, the people have already stayed with Jesus for three days without food. The emphatic positions of τούτους, "these people," and ὧδε, "here," call special attention to the difficulty he faces in meeting their need. But by replacing an expected "give to eat" (cf. 6.37b; also 5:43; 6:37a; 8:1, 2), "satisfy with bread" anticipates the miracle of "satisfying" the large crowd with more than enough bread (v 8).

As in 6:38, Jesus asks how many loaves the disciples have. The answer "seven" differs from the five loaves and two fish earlier on hand (though "a few small fish" will be mentioned shortly). Highlighting this difference is δέ, "but," in the introduction to the answer. Mark usually writes καί, "and," as in the corresponding introduction at 6:38b. The difference, in turn, stresses this second miracle of feeding as a new outburst of Jesus' creative energy (cf. the comments on v 8). The historical present tense of παραγγέλλει, "he orders," underscores his exercise of authority over the crowd by making them recline on the ground (cf. 6:39, which mentioned green grass and the intermediary role of the disciples, however, and used the verb ἐπέταξεν, whose meaning of imposing a certain arrangement by way of command better suited the organizing of the presumably Jewish crowd into hundreds and fifties like the judicial groupings of Moses' Israel [Exod 18:25] — but Jesus does not treat the present Decapolitan crowd, presumably made up mostly if not exclusively of Gentiles, like Israel of old). This time, after taking the bread he "gives thanks" for it rather than saying a "blessing" (6:41). As a blessing is distinctively Semitic, this shift, too, may suit the present crowd of Gentiles; but since saying a blessing over the fish will shortly come into the story, we may be dealing with simple variety of expression (cf. 6:41 with comments and notes ad loc.). The asyndeton between taking the bread and giving thanks speeds the narrative toward Jesus' performance of a miracle. Again he uses the disciples to set the food before the crowd; and again the present tense of the subjunctive παρατιθῶσιν, "might set before," emphasizes the largeness of the task and therefore of the miracle (see S. E. Porter, *Verbal Aspect* 326, on the emphasis in a present subjunctive). Mark reserves the fish for separate treatment, describes them as few and small (ἰχθύδια, diminutive — contrast 6:38, 41-42), and gives them a blessing distinct from the thanksgiving for the loaves — all to stress Jesus' power in multiplying so little to the satisfaction of so many. (Hence, we should not think that Mark depresses the fish in an attempt to assimilate the story to the Lord's Supper, in which fish play no part at all.)

8:8-9 *(Matt 15:37-38)* Mark magnifies Jesus' miracle by indicating that the crowd not only eat, but eat to the full; that they (the disciples according to v 20) take up seven baskets of leftover fragments; and that they (the crowd) number "about four thousand." The approximation and the failure to specify males (contrast 6:44) suit the indefiniteness in the number of small fish. As in v 5, δέ, "but," highlights the difference from the earlier five thousand (contrast καί in 6:44) and thereby completes the emphasis on this second miracle of feeding as a new outburst of Jesus' creative energy (cf. the comments on v 5). Mark's last statement emphasizes Jesus' authority over the crowd: "And he dismissed them" (cf. v 3). Since Mark likes to start pericopes with the notation of a topographical shift, v 10, which will contain such a notation, belongs to the next pericope (cf. J. Gnilka 1. 301). See the comments on 6:30-44 for other observations relevant to 8:1-9 but unrepeated here.

NOTES

See Q. Quesnell, *Mind of Mark* 28-36; J. Konings in *L'Évangile selon Marc* 147-77; W. Egger, *Frohbotschaft* 123, n. 12; R. M. Fowler, *Loaves and Fishes* 5-31, against theories of a pre-Marcan collection and of two pre-Marcan cycles reflected in 6:30–8:26 — theories associated especially with L. E. Keck, K. Kertelge, H.-W. Kuhn, P. J. Achtemeier, and R. Pesch). The differences which distance the relevant stories from each other and which critics consequently cite against two pre-Marcan cycles count also against two cycles parallelistically constructed by Mark himself — as follows, for example:

6:30-44	Feeding a large crowd	8:1-9
6:45-56	Crossing the Sea of Galilee	8:10
7:1-23	Conflict with Pharisees	8:11-12
7:24-30	Conversation about bread	8:13-21
7:31-37	Healing with the application of spittle and laying on of hands	8:22-26

Here are two examples of differences cited by critics: (1) the sea-crossing in 6:45-56 includes the story of Jesus' walking on the water and introduces a general ministry of healing on the other side, but 8:10 barely mentions a sea-crossing; (2) the conversation about bread in 7:24-30 occurs within a story about exorcism, but in 8:13-21 within the story of another sea-crossing. Such differences break down a supposed cyclical parallelism even though the feedings correspond to each other, and the methods of healing the deaf mute and the blind man likewise. According to E. C. Maloney (*Semitic Interference* 162-65), the temporal nominative absolute in v 2 does not characterize Hellenistic Greek and may therefore derive from a Hebrew or Aramaic substratum or from the narrator's own Hebrew or Aramaic style (against C. E. B. Cranfield 255 et al.). Whatever its derivation, by construction and position the temporal reference is emphatic. J. Gnilka (1. 302) cites Gen 40:13; Josh 1:11 for a biblical motif, possibly present here, that after three days God's help arrives. But Gen 40:13 does not speak of God's help; rather, of Pharaoh's action in restoring his butler. And in Gen 40:19 the same three days have to do with the opposite of help, i.e. with Pharaoh's having his baker executed. The three days in Josh 1:11 are part of a command the rest of which says to prepare sufficient food — quite different from the miraculous supply of food after three days that we have in the feeding of the four thousand. Hos 6:2 would provide better support, but there the third day is grammatically tied to the time of God's help whereas here the three days are grammatically tied to the duration of human distress. An allusion to Jesus' resurrection after three days (so H. C. Waetjen, *Reordering of Power* 138-39) has against it that predictions of that event do not start till v 31 and that a crowd's spending three days with Jesus does not correspond very well to his spending three days in a tomb.

M. Reiser (*Syntax und Stil* 113-15) denies the necessarily Semitic character of an adversative καί introducing a negative statement in v 2. But the καί is not adversative: not having anything to eat does not stand against staying three days with Jesus, but sides with it to help form the two-pronged reason for his compassion. See E. C. Maloney (*Semitic Interference* 109-11) against regarding the anarthrousness of οἶκον, "home" (v 3), as a Semitism.

Jesus had compassion on the five thousand, too, but not because they had stayed with him a long time without food; rather, because they were like Israel of old, i.e. "like sheep without a shepherd" (6:34), a description appropriate to a Jewish crowd (cf. Num 27:17; 1 Kgs 22:17 et passim). Such a description would not suit the present Decapolitan crowd so well. The earlier compassion led to Jesus' teaching. Not so here, because the present compassion relates to physical hunger rather than to lack of good leadership. Distance characterizes Gentiles in Josh 9:6, 9 (plus a stay of three days in v 16, as in Mark, but not without bread, not as in Mark); Tob 13:11; Isa 5:26; 39:3; Acts 2:39; 22:21; Eph 2:12-13; rabbinic passages cited in Str-B 3. 585-86; but not in the sometimes-cited Isa 43:6; 49:12; 57:19; 60:4, 9; Jer 30:10; Zech 6:15, which refer to Jewish exiles. Those characterizations of Gentiles as distant have led to interpreting "from afar" (v 3) as symbolic of the Gentileness of the crowd, and perhaps of the Gergasene demoniac as well (5:6). But the use of "from afar" in 11:13; 14:54; 15:40, where it can have nothing to do with Gentileness, undermines this interpretation. So also might the limitation of the characterization to "some" of the crowd undermine it; i.e. one could argue that this limitation destroys a general characterization of the crowd as Gentile. Back on the other side, one could argue that the limitation makes the characterization irrelevant apart from a reference to Gentileness. But at 7:26 Mark showed himself capable of mentioning Gentileness explicitly and emphatically, yet he does not exercise that capability here. Nor did he mention explicitly and emphatically the Jewishness of the five thousand. On the other hand, he does mention explicitly and emphatically — and twice over — the large size of the present crowd (vv 1, 9), as he did even more often with respect to the five thousand (6:31, 33, 34, 44). We do better, then, to see in "from afar" a characateristically Marcan allusion to Jesus' magnetism. Confirmation will come from 8:14-21, which will stress big numbers rather than ethnic origins. The already noted Jewish coloration of the earlier feeding and the Gentile coloration of the present feeding belong to pre-Marcan tradition, not to Mark's interests.

Each of the seven loaves generates a basketful of leftovers in addition to the quantity consumed by the four thousand. Under the hypothesis that the feeding of the four thousand grows out of the feeding of the five thousand, it may further be hypothesized that the seven loaves arise by adding the five and two of the loaves and fish in the feeding of the five thousand. The two having been used, the fish in the feeding of the four thousand are now kept for their traditionality and for parallelism with the earlier feeding but are reduced to an appendage and turned into a vague "few," perhaps because fish play no part in the Lord's Supper whereas the loaves *are* thought to suggest the Lord's Supper. In addition to the doubtfulness of the eucharistic interpretation, however, the suggested numerical development needs some apparent motivation, one that accounts for the switch from five thousand to four thousand as well as from five loaves and two fish to seven loaves and a few fish. Otherwise, why would anyone add five of one item on the menu and two of another item to get seven of the first, and then reduce the number fed?

The numbers in the feedings are therefore subjected to a variety of symbolic interpretations, most often distributed between the larger Jewish and Gentile interpretations of the feedings. Thus, the five of the loaves and the five in five thousand are associated with the five books of the Law; the four in four thousand with the four winds (cf. 13:27), with the four corners of the earth (cf. Rev 7:1), or with the four points of the compass; the seven loaves and the seven basketfuls of leftovers with the seven deacons (Acts 6:3), with the seven Noahic commandments given for the whole human race according to Jewish interpretation of Gen 9:4-7 (Str-B 3. 36-38), with the seven heathen nations in Canaan (Deut 7:1; Acts 13:19), with the seven in the seventy peoples of the world according to Jewish reckoning, with the seven in the seventy missioners of Luke 10:1-20, with the LXX, or with the general notion of completeness; the twelve baskets of leftovers with the twelve tribes of Israel or with the twelve disciples. But not only have we seen reasons to doubt the Jewish and Gentile interpretations of the two feedings. After Jesus' declaring all foods clean (7:19), he hardly feeds people with the Law. The qualification ὡς, "about, approximately," with "four thousand" tends away from a symbolic meaning; for at the level of symbolism there is no need for approximations. Are deacons, missioners, and heathen nations meant to be eaten, as are the seven loaves? The seven deacons were Hellenistic Jews, not Gentiles. One would think that the twelve tribes or the twelve disciples might be symbolized by the number of thousands making up the crowd, not by the number of basketfuls left over by the crowd. Subtle symbolisms do not elsewhere characterize Mark; and the two fish and few fish seem to resist symbolic interpretations. The indeterminate number of fish in the feeding of the four thousand suggests that none of the numbers carry symbolism; otherwise, those fish, too, would have been assigned a number.

In the notes on 6:41 we have seen reasons to doubt allusion to the Lord's Supper in the predicates "bless" and "give thanks." But we also need to note the refinement of the proposed allusion by some who theorize that whereas εὐλογέω represents Jewish blessing of the bread in 6:41; 14:22 par., εὐχαριστέω represents Gentile thanksgiving for the bread in 8:6, agreeing with Hellenistic tradition of the Lord's Supper in 1 Cor 11:24; Luke 22:19. This theory is spoiled by the use of εὐλογέω in the Gentile setting of 8:7, and of εὐχαριστέω in the Jewish setting of 14:23 par. J.-M. van Cangh (La multiplication 105-9 and in L'Évangile selon Marc 340) resorts to suggesting that the Jewish Hellenistic church added εὐλογήσας αὐτά in 8:7. Thus argument turns into circular reasoning. S. Masuda (in NTS 28 [1982] 201-3) uses the reversal in 14:22-23 of the order εὐχαριστέω–εὐλογέω in 8:6-7 to argue that both verbs connote the Lord's Supper. Then what would count as not connoting it?

In favor of a pre-Marcan assimilation to the Lord's Supper, H. Patsch (in ZNW 62 [1971] 217) argues that the absolute use of εὐχαριστέω, "give thanks," is limited in the gospels to the Lord's Supper and feeding miracles, and — so far as thanksgiving at table is concerned — is limited to the NT. But none of the synoptic accounts of the feeding of the five thousand contains that verb; and it occurs in Acts 27:35 with reference to bread about to be eaten, but without reference to the Lord's Supper. Granted, that passage adds the indirect object "to God"; but frequent occurrences of the verb without an indirect object yet without reference to the Lord's Supper make it difficult to think that the lack of an indirect object in the present passage points to the Lord's Supper. See Rom 1:21; 1 Cor 1:14 ℵ* B 1739 sa^ms bo^pt Cl Origen Chrysostom^1/2 John-Damascus; 10:30; 14:17; 2 Cor 1:11; Eph 1:16; 5:20; 1 Thess 5:18 (cf. also the concordance s.v. εὐχαριστία). Some of these other passages tell what thanks is given for, but "taking the seven loaves" does as much in Mark 8:6. 1 Cor 10:30 offers another instance of thanksgiving at table without an indirect object yet without reference to the Lord's Supper. See Rom 14:6 for thanksgiving to God at ordinary meals (cf. 1 Tim 4:3-4).

For three reasons, some think that Mark or someone before him inserted v 7, dealing with fish, to harmonize this story with that of the five thousand: (1) the disciples do not say that they have any fish (v 5; contrast 6:38); (2) the fish are not mentioned with the loaves in the performance of the miracle (v 6; contrast 6:41); and (3) the fish are missing from the gathering of leftovers (v 8; contrast 6:43). R. M. Fowler (Loaves and Fishes 53-54, 87) identifies Mark as the inserter and adds that Mark harmonizes the stories in this way to heighten the disciples' forgetfulness in vv 17-21. But a harmonizer would tend to follow the pattern of 6:38, 41, 43 by making the disciples say that they have some fish, by mentioning the fish with the loaves in the performance of the miracle, and by including leftovers of the fish. Mark's not following the pattern set in chap. 6 favors that he disentangles the fish from the bread in the tradition, where they were intertwined, and treats the fish separately to highlight the power of Jesus by stressing the fewness and the smallness of the fish (see the foregoing comments). Diminutive meanings of diminutive forms may fade; but Mark seems to like diminutive forms for their diminutive meanings (cf. the comments and notes on 7:24-30), and the shift from the non-diminutive ἰχθύς in chap. 6 to the present diminutive ἰχθύδιον joins with the description of the fish as few and with the separateness of their mention to favor a truly diminutive meaning. Fowler's position that Mark rewrites tradition in the feeding of the four thousand but composes the feeding of the five thousand after the pattern of the other feeding leaves one wondering why despite the absence of fish from the tradition behind the feeding of the four thousand he fabricated the fish in his composition of the earlier feeding and thus led himself to insert them into the tradition that he now rewrites. For signs of Marcan composition of 8:7, see the literature cited ibid. 199, n. 18, 200-201, n. 32. But B. Chilton (in *JTS* ns 34 [1983] 594) warns, "Fowler concludes rather unreflectively that Marcan composition immediately implies Marcan invention. This is simply to confuse a judgment of style with a judgment of history. . . ." S. Masuda (in *NTS* 28 [1982] 196-98) conveniently gathers together characteristically Marcan dual and other expressions throughout the pericope.

Juv. *Sat.* 3.14; 6.542 associates the kind of baskets mentioned in 6:43 (κοφίνων) with Jews. That association does not imply, however, that the kind of baskets referred to in 8:8 (σπυρίδας) are not also used by Jews, i.e. are limited to Gentiles. On the contrary, Christian Jews used one of the latter for an escape of Paul, a Christian Jew (Acts 9:25). See Q. Quesnell, *Mind of Mark* 229-31, n. 56, on different possible meanings of the underlying Greek words κόφινος and σπυρίς. Or does Mark's penchant for duality make them synonyms? F. J. A. Hort (in *JTS* os 10 [1909] 567-71) gives evidence that there are no grounds for defining a σπυρίς as larger than a κόφινος; rather, both kinds of baskets come in a variety of sizes. Κόφινος represents a stiff wicker basket, σπυρός a flexible mat-basket used especially for fish and other edibles.

It is puzzling why L. Schenke (*Wundererzählungen* 303-6) should argue that Mark devalues the miraculous element in this story by having Jesus withdraw from a crowd of miracle-seekers in vv 9b-10 and refuse to give a sign in vv 11-12, and by exposing the failure of miracles to produce faith and understanding in vv 13-21. The crowd do not ask for a miracle, Jesus takes the initiative to perform one (vv 2-3), and Mark does nothing to erase that initiative. It is the Pharisees, not the crowd, who will ask for a sign — and a sign from heaven, not a miracle by Jesus (see the comments on vv 11-12). He will remind the disciples that his miracles have been more than adequate rather than blaming their lack of faith and understanding on any inadequacies in the miracles.

Mark presents the miracles of feeding as distinct events, separated in time and differing in details, such as west side of the Sea of Galilee versus east side, a deserted place close to hamlets and towns versus a wilderness, initiative-taking by the disciples versus initiative-taking by Jesus, five loaves versus seven, two fish versus a few, five thousand versus four thousand (see esp. 8:19-20). But the weight of recognized scholarship comes down on the side of viewing the two accounts as variants of a single event (Q. Quesnell, *Mind of Mark* 36-38). From there on, opinions differ wildly: 6:30-44 represents the earlier version. No, 8:1-9 represents the earlier version. A plague on both your houses, for both versions mix early and late elements. A pre-Marcan traditioner divided the original event. No, Mark did. Whoever it was, he did so to portray the salvation of Gentiles after the salvation of Jews. No, to portray the Lord's Supper for Gentiles as well as for Jews. No, the difference between Jews and Gentiles has nothing to do with the division of the original event; the division has the purpose of making the disciples look all the more stupid when later they forget two miracles of feeding instead of only one.

Arguments for treating one or the other version as secondary balance each other fairly evenly, and sometimes draw contradictorily on the same phenomena of the text. Jesus' taking the initiative is supposed to rest on a secondary Christological heightening in 8:1-9; so also his expressing compassion himself rather than having it attributed to him editorially. But the supposed artificiality of his feeling compassion for the crowd because they lack a good leader rather than because they lack food — this and the similarly supposed unlikelihood of having so much happen in a day as happens in 6:30-44 are thought to betray the secondariness of that passage. On the other hand again, the crowd's staying with Jesus for three days without food is thought to make 8:1-9 look fabricated. Mark's tendency to blackball the disciples gives the sharpness of their question in 6:37 a secondary cast. No, the greater mildness of their question in 8:4 exhibits a general tendency in the tradition to whitewash them. At 6:36 the talk of buying food in nearby hamlets and towns looks contrived to some, but to others the presence of thousands in a wilderness looks contrived at 8:4. In 8:7 the separateness of the fish seems odd to some, but to others the feeding of more people with less food and a greater number of basketfuls left over makes 6:30-44 look like a secondary heightening of the miracle. Does the length of 6:30-44 represent the detailedness of pre-polished tradition or accretions to tradition? Does the abbreviatedness of 8:1-9 represent early spareness or later polishing? Of course, each side draws up lists of Marcanisms to argue for the secondariness of one or the other version, or of parts thereof, and of non-Marcanisms to argue for originality.

But Mark may impose his style on tradition in greater as well as lesser degrees, and the other arguments fight each other to a standoff or grow pale on close scrutiny. For example, in 6:30-44 the disciples take the initiative only with respect to asking that Jesus dismiss the crowd. He takes the initiative to feed the crowd on the spot, as he does in 8:1-9. A voyage short enough to be followed on land, some teaching, and a miracle do not overstock a single day in 6:30-44. We might expect a redactor to put the numerically more impressive miracle in a climatic second position rather than first. This expectation holds not only under the theory that the second feeding represents the bringing of salvation or of the Lord's Supper to Gentiles (for in the church they outnumber Jews by the time of Mark), but also under the theory that Mark doubles the story to make the disciples' forgetfulness all the more inexcusable (for a more impressive second feeding would better add to their inexcusability). The lack of nearby hamlets and towns where provisions might be bought suits the three days' stay and sparsely populated east shore in 8:1-9, whereas the dense population on the west shore suits the nearness of hamlets and towns and the shorter stay in 6:30-33. And so on.

We may therefore need to reexamine the main reasons for supposing an originally single event instead of the two events that Mark narrates. Those reasons are the close and obvious similarities between the narratives and the psychological unlikelihood that the disciples would forget an earlier feeding so quickly as to ask their question at 8:4 instead of requesting a repetition of the earlier feeding. Already noted differences in detail counterbalance some and perhaps all of the similarities, however; and similar events invite similar language to narrate them, especially when they represent something so customary as a meal. Moreover, we must take account of a tendency to assimilate traditions to each other, even to amalgamate them with each other. We have already observed amalgamation in Luke's and John's parallels to these very feeding miracles (see the notes on 6:30-44). Assimilations are evident in Matt 14:13-21; 15:32-39, and full scale amalgamations of other incidents in Matt 8:28-34; 9:27-31; 20:29-34 (R. H. Gundry, *Matthew* ad loc.). The possibility of doubling is not to be denied, yet opposite tendencies are not only possible but also clearly at work in the materials closest to Mark, i.e. in the later gospels. In the absence of materials earlier than Mark and pointing to original singularity in the feeding miracle, the evidence of later assimilation and amalgamation damages the hypothesis of pre-Marcan or Marcan doubling. In principle, we should accept the possibility of more than one feeding as much as we accept the possibility of more than one exorcism, more than one healing of the blind, etc.

It might be countered that Mark's penchant for duality drives us to the hypothesis that he doubles the miracle of feeding. But generally recognized duality in Mark consists of restating the same item of information, often with greater specificity. 8:19-21 looks back on the feedings as different events, however; and the narrative of the second feeding exhibits less specificity than that of the first. The sea stories in 4:35-41; 6:45-52 and the healings in 7:31-37; 8:22-26 hardly come by way of a duality-hungry Mark dividing originally single incidents; therefore the sea stories and those healings do not support such a hypothesis for the feeding stories. The basic character of the differences between stilling a storm and walking on the sea and between deaf-muteness and blindness favor that whatever similarities between the pairs may be due to editing represent the assimilation of different stories to each other rather than the production of pairs out of originally single stories.

We turn, then, to the psychological argument for doubling. It depends on the historicity of the disciples' question in 8:4 if the second feeding is historical. But the second feeding as a whole might be historical and their question in particular, unhistorical, or at least verbally assimilated toward 6:37b without thought of the psychological problem so created. No powerful argument would be left for the doubling hypothesis. Nonetheless, the psychological problem may not prove intractable even on the historical level.

For help, we first take up a similar problem in two passages often related to the present one. At 6:51-52 Mark editorialized that lack of insight into the feeding of the five thousand made the disciples very amazed at Jesus' walking on the sea and at the abatement of a contrary wind when he got into their boat. Given the connotations of theophany in that episode, we may say that the disciples had not deduced from Jesus' having fed the five thousand that he is God's Son, who might be expected to demonstrate his deity by walking on the sea and for whose deity the wind stops opposing the boat into which he gets to continue his crossing. Such a failure of deduction is not psychologically inconceivable; and since it has nothing to do with failure of memory, 6:52 does not favor forgetfulness in 8:4 (against W. Wrede, *Messianic Secret* 104).

In 8:13-21, particularly in v 16, we may paraphrase the disciples as reasoning, "He is warning us against the leaven of the Pharisees and against that of Herod because we do not have enough (leavened) bread of our own and might have to purchase some from Pharasaic and Herodian vendors." Jesus' response will score the disciples for not deducing from the abundance of leftovers at the two feedings that unavailability of bread from acceptable sources would pose no problem when he is around: he can multiply the disciples' one loaf more than sufficiently. But since they were thinking along a different line because of his warning, the failure of deduction is not psychologically inconceivable. Furthermore, 8:13-21 will not portray them as having forgotten the feeding of the five thousand. So we can hardly treat the disciples' question in v 4 as reflecting forgetfulness. Rather, they did not recognize the feeding as a miracle (see the notes on 6:42-44 and the comments on 6:51-52).

What immediately strikes one about the disciples' question at v 4 is the contrast with 6:51-52; 8:13-21 in that the question elicits no editorial or dominical criticism. We should also note that one feeding would have justified Jesus' criticism in 8:13-21 well enough, just as the one feeding that had thus far taken place justified Mark's criticism in 6:51-52 well enough. But in the present passage, far from criticizing the disciples himself or yielding the page to an editorial criticism by Mark, Jesus answers their question, "From where . . . ?" by asking them for their own loaves. This difference puts a barrier in the way of interpreting the present passage by means of the other ones. Failure of deduction is in view no more than is forgetfulness. Therefore we have two possible reasons for saying that Mark or someone before him doubled a single feeding to make the disciples look twice as ignorant. Such a purpose would probably have led to a highlighting of ignorance within the story. (We have already seen reasons to doubt a redactional emphasis on Gentile evangelism that would provide the motive for doubling a single feeding.)

Under normal circumstances we do not find the disciples suggesting miracles. They are, after all, Jesus' disciples; he, their master. Not even when a storm threatened their very lives did they expect or ask him to deliver them with a miracle (cf. 4:38 with 4:40-41). Nor have they been in the habit of suggesting that he perform for others miracles of the sort they have seen him perform before. At the feeding of the five thousand, the disciples took the initiative in broaching the need of the crowd to eat. Here, Jesus does. Furthermore, the crowd have been with him three days, without food it seems; and he has done nothing to alleviate their hunger. Under these circumstances it is not psychologically inconceivable that the disciples should stay in character, that they should hang back from suggesting what Jesus has failed to announce or do. It would be historically improbable and theologically and therefore redactionally inappropriate for them to do otherwise. And it is psychologically quite conceivable that their present question should echo the earlier one, only suited to the new setting of a wilderness in which there are no hamlets or towns nearby. The psychological argument for doubling fails, then. For Mark, moreover, the question, "From where . . . ?" (v 4), is Christologically threatening in that it could raise a doubt in the minds of his audience whether the miracle of feeding the five thousand occurred inasmuch as that feeding did not seem miraculous to the disciples. In this respect, then, Mark can hardly be held responsible for the question; and to the extent that the question is part and parcel of the feeding narrative, he can hardly be held responsible for a doubling of the feeding. See the notes on 6:30-44 for observations relevant to 8:1-9 but unrepeated here.

THE POWER OF JESUS' DENYING THE REQUEST FOR A SIGN

8:10-12 (Matt 12:38-39; 15:39–16:4b; Luke 11:16, 29; 12:54-56)

The pericope on Jesus' denying the request for a sign opens with a topographical shift (v 10), proceeds with the request (v 11), and closes with his refusal (v 12). The immediacy of his getting in the boat and leaving with the disciples after feeding the four thousand makes a deliberate contrast with his forcing the disciples to get in the boat and leave while he stayed to dismiss the crowd and go up the mountain and pray immediately after the feeding of the five thousand (6:45-46). He arrives in the district of Dalmanutha. The Pharisees' coming out and disputing with him by way of seeking a sign from heaven sets up a test. Past Marcan portrayals of the Pharisees (2:16, 24; 3:6; 7:1, 3, 5), the challenge in their present question, and future challenges of the same sort (10:2; 12:15; cf. Matt 19:3; 22:18, 35; Luke 10:25) make this test a contest with the Pharisees. The use in adjacent phrases of the complex συζητεῖν, "to dispute," and of its simplex form ζητοῦντες, "seeking," makes a wordplay that emphasizes the contest. So also does the asyndetic relation of the participial phrases "seeking from him a sign from heaven, testing him." As a result of this emphasis, Jesus' triumph will appear the greater. Since the scribes' accusation in 3:22, 30 that he gets his power from Beelzebul, an unclean spirit, had to do with exorcisms, not with miracles, "a sign from heaven" does not have to mean a miracle. Furthermore, σημεῖον, "sign," will not mean "miracle" in 13:4; it will carry that meaning only possibly in 13:22, and then only in conjunction with "wonders" in the stereotyped phrase "signs and wonders." Mark uses δύναμις for "miracle" (6:2, 5, 14; 9:39; cf. 5:30). Yet again, no one is present who needs a miracle performed. For these reasons it appears that the Pharisees are not asking Jesus to produce another miracle, more spectacular, of his own making. Rather, they are asking him to persuade God to show approval of him with a different kind of display, one that resists attribution to satanic power, magic, or any other source besides God himself (cf. the contrast in 11:30-32 between "from heaven" [for 'from God'] and "from human beings"). Exactly what kind they leave open (but cf. 15:32; Exod 4:8-9; 1 Sam 2:34; 10:1-13; 2 Kgs 20:8-11; 2 Chr 32:24; Isa 7:10-17; 38:7-8; 2 Macc 2 :21; *b. B. Meṣ.* 59b; *b. Sanh.* 98a; other rabbinic literature cited by A. Schlatter, *Matthäus* 413-15; Str-B 1. 127-28, 640-41; and K. H. Rengstorf in *TDNT* 7. 234-36; and the argument of J. Gibson in *JSNT* 38 [1990] 42-47 for "apocalyptic phenomena which embody or signal the onset of aid and comfort for God's elect and/or the wrath that God was expected to let loose against his enemies and those who threaten his people," in which case Jesus will reject such triumphalism [ibid. 54-55]).

Jesus' groaning differs somewhat from that in 7:34. There he looked up to heaven as he groaned in a mighty effort to work a particularly difficult miracle. Here he does not look up to heaven, for to do so would have ill suited the refusal of a sign from heaven. Besides, the Pharisees have not asked him to work a particularly difficult miracle, and God himself would be the one to give a sign "from heaven" (cf. the probably divine passive in δοθήσεται, "will be given," as also at 4:25; 6:2; 13:11). Thus, in the request παρ' αὐτοῦ means "from him" as the one who would ask God to show a sign rather than "from him" as the one who would himself work a sign. Τῷ πνεύματι αὐτοῦ, "in his spirit," replaces looking up to heaven. Since "spirit" connotes power (see the comments on 1:7-8; E. Sjöberg in *TDNT* 6. 362-67, 369 et passim; E. Schweizer in *TDNT* 6. 397-98, 439-42 et passim), "groaning in his spirit" indicates that Jesus is audibly giving force to his following pronouncement, the power of which will shut down the Pharisees' attempt to embarrass him (cf. the clairvoyant power of his spirit in 2:8 — as here, in conflict with his enemies; also Rom 8:26; 2 Macc 6:30; Sus 22 Theod; Philo *Jos.* 32 §187; *Mart. Pol.* 9:2; *Mart. Con.* 5:1 for groaning to give force to a statement rather than to work a miracle). The intensifying prefix ἀνα-, "deeply," strengthens the thought of Jesus' giving force to his pronouncement (cf. the comments on 7:34). The historical present tense of λέγει, "he says," emphasizes the pronouncement itself, which starts with the rhetorical question, "Why does this generation seek a sign?" The question receives no answer, however, because the emphasis falls on Jesus' assertion that God will not give a sign to this generation. "I say to you," the Hebraism ἀμήν, "truly," which introduces it, and the Hebraistically idiomatic, archaic, and solemn form of the denial, "If to this generation a sign will be given!" strengthen the assertion. The forward position of "to this generation" pinpoints those whose request is denied. Again, since Mark likes to start pericopes with a topographical shift, v 13, which contains such a notation, belongs to the next pericope (cf. the final comment on vv 8-9).

NOTES

K. L. Schmidt (*Rahmen* 203) regards v 11 rather than v 10 as the original introduction to this pericope. But ordinarily Mark uses ὅρια, "boundaries" (5:17; 7:24, 31; 10:1), whereas μέρη, "parts, district," makes its only appearance in v 10 (cf. B. M. Metzger, *Textual Commentary* ad loc., on the vv.ll.). The singularity of this appearance combines with the difference of μέρη from the more usual ὅρια to undermine a denial of tradition in v 10. Our uncertainty over the topographical referent of "Dalmanutha" (see the literature cited in BAGD s.v.; W. L. Lane 271, n. 6) positively favors tradition — and not only tradition, also historicity. For who would insert a regional name of opaque reference? Never mind modern doubts about topographical accuracy at some points in Mark. When the evangelist or a traditioner before him identifies other regions by name, the referent is at least recognizable from other sources. Presumably Dalmanutha was somewhat recognizable at one time, but not so much as to have made its way into extant literature, and therefore probably not so much as to have come to mind for the fabrication of an inauthentic itinerary. Inasmuch as the well known Magdala could have provided the Mag- of Magadan in the parallel Matt 15:39 and the Dal- in Mark's Dalmanutha, both Magadan and Dalmanutha may be considered variants of Magdala, situated on the west shore of the Sea of Galilee and on the south side of the Plain of Gennesaret.

Likewise and despite much opinion to the contrary, there is no general need to attribute travel by boat to Mark's redaction. We read about such travel often in Mark; but Jesus, his fishermen, and other disciples might naturally and often have set sail in a ministry centered on the northwest shore of the Sea of Galilee. More particularly, on the other hand, H. Kruze (in *NTS* 30 [1984] 520) casts doubt on the present boat trip by asking whether Mark has forgotten that Jesus came by land to the Decapolitan east shore of Galilee and that no boat would be available in this "wilderness" (cf. v 4). In fact, however, we do not know enough to deny the availability of a boat in this place. One person's historical imagination may supply a boat in a number of ways (e.g., by way of a fishing vessel working the east side of the lake though based on the west side) as validly as another person's historical imagination may keep all boats away. On the side of Kruze, J. Gnilka (1. 302, 305) argues that a possibility of the crowd's fainting on their way home exposes the unoriginality of the boat trip by betraying a landlocked location. But if the four thousand came from east of the lake, as they probably did since Jesus came from that direction (7:31), their going home by land does not contradict Jesus' sailing with his disciples in the opposite direction.

W. H. Kelber (*Kingdom* 61) says that the lack of διαπεράζω, "cross over," and πέραν, "the other side," indicates a side trip along the east shore, which will make the voyage in v 13 a lake-crossing from east to west in contradiction of arrival at Bethsaida to the northeast (v 22). (This view rests on a supposed rearrangement of pre-Marcan materials rather than on final Marcan redaction; see E. S. Malbon in *JBL* 103 [1984] 370-72 for analysis and criticism of this point.) But the lack of those terms is probably due to their needlessness in view of the recency and specificity of Mark's identifying the Decapolitan

shore of Galilee (7:31), in view of the temporal linkage of the intervening incident with
that locale (8:1), and in view of the specifying of Dalmanutha as the destination (8:10). A
similar specifying of destination characterized 5:1, but Mark used πέραν because his
audience would have had to go all the way back to 2:1 for the last specifically named
whereabouts of Jesus. In 6:32-33, on the other hand, the lack of specificity for both starting
point and destination and the lack of διαπεράζω and πέραν combined with each other and
with the crowd's running along shore to imply a side trip, which then suited a projected
crossing to Bethsaida (6:45). We may therefore take the present voyage as a crossing from
east to west, which suits the above-mentioned possibility that Dalmanutha is a variant of
Magdala. The later crossing to Bethsaida then becomes unproblematic.

See the notes on 1:45 concerning Mark's use of ἤρξατο, "began." John 6:30 contains
a request for a sign after the feeding of the five thousand. Deut 18:18-22 deals with the
testing of a prophet. But the word "sign" does not occur in that passage; and the test
consists in fulfilment of prophetic predictions, which do not enter the picture here. The
word does appear in Deut 13:2-5, a passage concerning the capital punishment of prophets
who lead Israel into idolatry. But nobody has accused Jesus of teaching idolatry; so it is
doubtful that the Pharisees are trying to elicit a sign in order that they may level a capital
charge against him if he fails.

One might discount "from heaven" as an interpretative expansion since it does not
occur in any version of Jesus' sign-saying. Though still outside the words of Jesus, it does
occur in a different context at Luke 11:16, however; and an expansion is not necessarily
false for being interpretative. In this case, Jesus' prior miracles and exorcisms and the
scribes' firsthand observation and acknowledgment of them (again see 2:1-12; 3:1-6, 22,
28-30) make it probable that "sign" means a special act of God rather than another deed
of Jesus. "From heaven" militates both against the view that Jesus has already given a sign
to Jews in the feeding of the five thousand and to the Gentiles in the feeding of the four
thousand (so Z. Kato, *Völkermission* 102) and against the view that since the scribes have
condemned Jesus' exorcisms as demonic (3:22, 28-30), they are asking for scriptural proof
(so K. Grayston in *ExpTim* 88 [1976-77] 15).

Testing Jesus puts the Pharisees on the side of Satan (1:12-13). R. P. Martin (*Mark*
168-69) thinks "testing" too weak a translation of πειράζοντες; he prefers the connotation
of enticement to sin. But 1:12-13 did not define Satan's temptation of Jesus as enticement
to sin; and the Pharisees' "seeking from him a sign from heaven" and Jesus' "groaning
deeply in his spirit" connote a contest of prophetic legitimation, not of messianic morality.
"The Pharisees challenge Jesus on the supposition that he will either accede and fail to
produce the sign, or refuse and lose his popularity with the people" (M. Boucher, *Mysterious Parable* 76; see J. D. Kingsbury in *NTS* 36 [1990] 54-55 on this as the first direct
challenge to Jesus on a matter related to his own actions).

One might think that in v 12 Jesus groans out of sorrow or exasperation; but the
legitimizing character of the test, the reference to Jesus' spirit, and the emphatic features
noted in the comments argue for the stronger meaning, viz., groaning as gathering and
concentrating inner power to make a pronouncement prophetically heavy with judgment
(cf. the use of ἀναστενάζω in Hdt. 1.86; 6.80; Sus 22 Theod; 2 Macc 6:30 to give a
pronouncement force — against the opinion of J. B. Gibson in *BT* 38 [1987] 122-25 that
in these passages the verb connotes dismay, a likely possibility only in Sus 22 Theod).
The very speaking of the prophetic word contributes to its fulfilment (L. Dürr, *Wertung*).
Cross-references to 1:41; 3:5; 6:41 for Jesus' "pneumatic excitement" (R. Pesch 1. 408)
are ill-advised. Other emotions appear in those passages. But see Ezek 21:11-12 LXX;
John 11:33, 38; 13:21; *Gos. Barth.* 1:22.

P45 W omit λέγω ὑμῖν, "I say to you" (cf. the omission of ὑμῖν alone by B L 892
pc). The agreement of the omission with formulas of solemn denial in the OT and in

rabbinic literature may argue equally well for the originality of this v.l. (so G. W. Buchanan in *HTR* 58 [1965] 325, n. 28) and for secondary assimilation of the longer reading to those formulas. The thinness of external evidence for omission and the regularity of the Jesuanic formula ἀμὴν λέγω ὑμῖν favor the longer reading. Yet scribes might have been so used to Jesus' formula that they added it to an originally shorter reading.

On sign-seeking, cf. 1 Cor 1:22; and see R. H. Gundry, *Matthew* 243, for an argument that the exception to Jesus' refusal — viz., "the sign of Jonah" — was given to a different audience on a different occasion. Others think that Q adds the exception out of a sentiment that the absolute denial is too harsh, or out of seeing an opportunity to insert an allusion to Jesus' death and resurrection. Still others think that Mark drops the exception, either as unintelligible (assuming the version known to him did not refer to Jesus' death and resurrection) or as contradicting Mark's aversion to Jesus' legitimizing himself to outsiders (see the discussion in J. S. Kloppenborg, *Formation* 128-30). But the miracle stories in 2:1-12; 3:1-6 demonstrate most emphatically that Mark is not adverse to including material in which Jesus legitimizes himself to outsiders, i.e. to scribes and (as here) to Pharisees. Mark's identifying the unpardonable sin with the scribes' attribution of Jesus' exorcisms to an unclean spirit (3:28-30) makes the same point (cf. Matt 12:28 par. Luke 11:20). Dropping the exception as unintelligible remains possible, though even if late and even if wrong, the reference to Jesus' death and resurrection (seen at least in Matt 12:40) shows that sense can be made of the exception. One might also think that Mark or someone before him dropped the exception to imply that Jesus' past miracles and exorcisms obviate any need for a sign from heaven, or to rivet attention solely on the strength of Jesus' pronouncement against the Pharisees. The Hebrew idiom that puts "if" at the start of a solemn denial calls down a curse on the speaker if the speaker does such and such a thing (see esp. Gen 14:23; Num 5:19-22; 14:11, 22-23; 32:11; Deut 1:35; 1 Kgs 3:14; 2 Kgs 6:31; Pss 7:4-6[3-5]; 95:11; Heb 3:11; 4:3, 5; and BAGD s.v. εἰ IV; W. L. Lane 276, n. 21, 278; P. Joüon, *Grammaire* §165d, n. 3).

"This generation" does not always carry a pejorative connotation (see, e.g., 13:30). In 8:38; 9:19, added adjectives will give it such a connotation. Here, the context strikes a pejorative note (cf. Gen 7:1; Ps 95:10). R. Pesch (1. 408) thinks that out of conviction that the end-time apostasy is occurring, Jesus condemns the whole of his generation despite the limitation to Pharisees of the request for a sign (cf. Deut 32:5, 20; Ps 95:10; *Jub.* 23:14, 16), also that he refuses a sign because he considers his preaching of repentance an eschatological sign. But the requested sign is to be "from heaven," preaching repentance does not qualify, and refusing a request does not imply its prior granting.

Others think that the disparity between "the Pharisees" in particular and "this generation" in general is due to Mark's redactional importation of the Pharisees as Jesus' chief opponents. But because they really are his chief opponents (cf. the role of Paul, a Pharisee, in leading a persecution of the primitive church), their appearing on the scene and testing Jesus with a request for a sign from heaven does not at all seem unlikely. He may simply regard them as representative of "this generation."

Of course, a sizable body of opinion denies that the Pharisees really are Jesus' chief opponents (for a survey, see E. P. Sanders, *Jesus and Judaism* 287-92). But the vast amount of circular reasoning required to hold this opinion — i.e. the necessity of attributing to redaction the appearance of Pharisees as Jesus' opponents on numerous occasions and in all strata of synoptic tradition: Mark, Q, and specially Matthean and Lucan materials — speaks ill of the opinion. To say that early Christians turned the Pharisees into Jesus' opponents only after they started opposing the early Christians' preaching of him does not ring true to the breadth of the materials casting them in the role of his opponents. The political role of the chief priests in Jesus' death in no way rules out prior theological opposition to him on the part of the Pharisees.

But the Pharisees may not *represent* "this generation." They may *be* "this generation." Context often defines this expression more or less narrowly. In 8:38 the description
"sinful and adulterous" will exclude disciples who are unashamed of Jesus and his words.
In 9:19 the description "unbelieving" will include only the disciples who have failed to
cast out a demon. In Matt 11:16-19 par. Luke 7:31-35 "this generation" of children in the
marketplace excludes the children of wisdom (cf. the probable inclusion of scribes alone
in "this generation" at Luke 11:50-51, and of scribes and Pharisees alone at Matt 23:36).
In Mark 8:12, therefore, "this generation" that "seeks a sign" may include only the
Pharisees. Even under the supposition that Luke 11:29 represents the very same saying
that we have in Mark 8:12, Luke's interest in crowds would put a question mark against
the originality of that referent (and Luke 11:37 says that while Jesus was speaking, "a
Pharisee" invited him to dinner).

᾿Εξῆλθον (v 11) echoes ἦλθεν (v 10), but this compositional touch does not require
a non-traditional origin of the Pharisees. "Come out" often leaves the point of origin more
or less vague (see 3:21; 4:3; 14:48 for good examples). Though traditional controversy
stories normally carry direct quotations of opponents' objections, v 11 gives only an indirect
quotation. But 3:2, 4; 10:2 also lack direct quotation, and the present Pharisees do not
lodge an objection so much as they make a request (again cf. 10:2). So indirect quotation
does not imply non-traditionality.

According to B. H. Branscomb (139), Jesus refuses to give a sign because he knows
that he cannot perform a miracle at will and because he does not want to tempt God by
trying to do so for a mere demonstration. This interpretation confuses a sign from heaven
with a miracle performed by Jesus. Of course, one might suggest that he is unsure of God's
working a sign on his behalf (presumably in answer to prayer — cf. 1 Kgs 18:20-38). The
suggestion remains unprovable, however, and has against it the confidence of Jesus in his
abilities and in his closeness to God as seen everywhere else. Without calling in question
Jesus' confidence or closeness to God, H. C. Kee (*Medicine* 80) writes that Jesus presents
himself as a miracle-worker only to meet the needs of the sick and demon-possessed, and
that he will not act to corroborate his own authority. H. Anderson (199-200) writes similarly
about Mark's way of presenting him. Again, however, a sign from heaven does not equate
with a miracle performed by Jesus; and 2:1-12; 3:1-6, 28-30 have shown that he does act
to corroborate his own authority and that Mark likes to present him as acting thus.

Mark's topographical distancing of the Pharisees' request for a sign from the feeding
of the four thousand makes it doubtful that he portrays the Pharisees as like the disciples
in not understanding the feeding (against R. A. Edwards, *Sign of Jonah* 77). But the request
for a sign does look illegitimate after the feeding of the four thousand and other miracles
preceding, and Jesus' damning refusal prepares for the damning questions that he will put
to the disciples in the following pericope.

Mark's noting the deep groan that precedes Jesus' present refusal puts an accent on
the verbal putdown of the Pharisees rather than on a theological criticism of their request.
L. Schenke (*Wundererzählungen* 305-6) transmutes vv 10-12 into what he envisions to be
the state of Mark's church, i.e. a state of suffering. According to this view, the church is
meant to read these verses as a warning against seeking an apocalyptic miracle of deliverance at the Second Coming. Why then will Mark go on to write a whole chapter of promises
concerning the Second Coming, of exhortations to watch for it, and of predictions concerning events that will finally signal its nearness (13:1-37)? E. Haenchen (285) goes the
furthest in arguing that the denial of a sign shows the tradition of miracles to be a late
intruder into Jesuanic tradition. Yet again, however, a sign from heaven does not equate
with a miracle performed by Jesus; and the facts remain that our earliest gospel carries the
most emphasis on miracles as powerful, that Q (which may antedate Mark) carries the
same emphasis (Matt 11:4-6 par. Luke 7:22-23; Matt 11:20-24 par. Luke 10:13-15), and

that the later gospels do not strengthen that emphasis, which is proper to the meaning of the term, but weaken it in favor of miracles as didactic (so Matthew), merciful (so Luke), and symbolic (so John). Moreover, the NT books written even before Mark — viz., Paul's epistles — show miracles as acts of power to have been part and parcel of Christianity at its earliest documented stage (Rom 15:19; 1 Cor 2:4-5; 12:10, 28-29; 2 Cor 6:7; 12:12; Gal 3:5; 1 Thess 1:5).

J. Jeremias (*NT Theology* 1. 72, n. 2) argues that since belief in Jesus' resurrection obviated the need for a sign in the early church, the demand for a sign must be authentic. We might add that the danger of casting doubt on the reality of his miracles would probably have checked an early Christian fabrication of this episode. Semitisms offer additional support for historicity. They do not insure it, but they do point to a provenance where authentic information about Jesus was most likely to have been remembered — and there are plenty of Semitisms in vv 11-12. R. Pesch (1. 409) lists them: ἐξῆλθον for יָצָא; the pleonastic ἤρξαντο; σημεῖον with the meaning of אוֹת; "heaven" for "God"; the asyndetic relation of the "seeking" and "testing"; τῷ πνεύματι for בְּרוּחַ; τί for מָה; the word order ἡ γενεὰ αὕτη for הַדּר הַזֶּה; ἀμήν; "if" at the start of a solemn denial; and "will be given" for "God will give." Though τί naturally means "why?" in its present Greek context (cf. E. C. Maloney, *Semitic Interference* 142-44), the abundance of Semitisms favors that τί rests on an exclamatory מָה, "how!" (cf. M. Black, *Aramaic Approach* 123; BDF §300[2]; GKC §148).

THE SUPERADEQUACY OF JESUS' MIRACULOUS POWER

8:13-21 *(Matt 16:4c-12; Luke 12:1)*

A topographical shift signals the start of a new pericope (v 13). Then Mark notes the disciples' forgetting to take enough bread (v 14) and Jesus' warning against the leaven of the Pharisees and against that of Herod (v 15). Rounding off the pericope are the disciples' misunderstanding (v 16) and Jesus' reminding them of the leftovers at his feedings of the five thousand and four thousand (vv 17-21).

8:13 *(Matt 16:4c)* "Leaving them" refers to Jesus' leaving the Pharisees and finalizes his denying their request for a sign from heaven (cf. vv 11-12). Here we have the only instance in Mark of Jesus' leaving anyone (though 4:36 comes close). Therefore "again" goes with "embarking," not with "leaving" (cf. B. M. Metzger, *Textual Commentary* ad loc.), and relates to Jesus' getting in a boat as recently as the start of the preceding pericope (v 10). The asyndeton between "leaving" and "again embarking" stresses his judgmentally quick departure from the sign-seeking generation of Pharisees. "The other side" to which he goes away will turn out to be the northeastern shore of the Sea of Galilee, where Bethsaida is located, across the water from Dalmanutha if Dalmanutha is a variant of Magdala (cf. v 22; 6:45; 8:10 with notes; and R. H. Gundry, *Matthew* 322).

8:14 *(Matt 16:5)* The statement that the disciples have forgotten to take loaves of bread gives the information necessary to understand their reasoning in v 16. The plural "loaves" allows for an exception in the follow-up: "and except for one loaf they did not have [any loaves] with themselves in the boat." The doubling of the reference to lack of bread makes the emphasis on the disciples' needing more bread a foil against which Jesus will remind them of his power as seen in the large amounts of leftovers when he fed the five thousand and four thousand (cf. the comments on 6:35-37; 8:1-4 for similar emphases on need that have the same purpose). Having but one loaf with themselves in the boat — not enough to satisfy them all (cf. the comments on 6:37) — contrasts with their having had five loaves and seven loaves, to say nothing of fish, on the earlier occasions (cf. vv 19-20).

8:15 *(Matt 16:6)* The choice of διεστέλλετο, "he was ordering," stresses Jesus' authority. Mark does not clearly indicate that the disciples' taking only one loaf of bread makes Jesus reflect on his immediately preceding dispute with the Pharisees. But Jesus' ordering the disciples to beware of the leaven of the Pharisees might derive by natural progression from bread to the leaven that makes bread rise, and from the Pharisees' sign-seeking to leaven as a common metaphor of evil. The warning against the leaven of Herod might have a similar derivation if Dalmanutha, where the dispute with the Pharisees took place, is a variant of Magdala, located in the tetrarchy of Herod Antipas near his capital Tiberias (see the comments on v 10). The asyndeton between ὁρᾶτε, "look out," and βλέπετε, "watch out" — both in the emphatic present tense of the imperative (cf. the notes on 1:3) — highlights the warning (cf. 5:39). So also does the duality of these commands (cf. J. Dupont, *Études* 429, n. 147, on the possibility that Mark adds an un-Semitic βλέπετε, but also the notes on 12:38 for the possibility of a Semitic substratum).

8:16 *(Matt 16:7)* Since the reasoning of the disciples contrasts with Jesus' foregoing warning, the καί that opens v 16 may be adversative ("but"). Ὅτι may be epexegetic ("about the fact that"), indirectly interrogative ("why"), or — if we read a direct quotation with the v.l. ἔχομεν, "we have" — directly interrogative ("why?") or recitative (equivalent to quotation marks) rather than causal ("because"). Therefore it is again uncertain whether the disciples think Jesus' warning to be prompted by his dispute with the Pharisees. Nevertheless, the arrangement of statements in vv 15-16 strengthens the possibilities that Mark thinks the warning prompted thus and that he portrays the disciples as thinking so. Their reasoning seems to imply the misunderstanding that Jesus does not want them to buy additional loaves from the Pharisees and the supporters of Herod (though Jesus speaks only of Herod himself), as the rabbis might say to beware of the leaven or meat of the Samaritans (H. Windisch in *TDNT* 2. 906; cf. Str-B 1. 541-42). But what stands out is Mark's leaving these possibilities unclear and omitting an interpretation of the two kinds of leaven that Jesus warns against (contrast the synoptic parallels). The unclarity and omission show what little concern Mark has for the derivation and character of the disciples' dullness and for the meaning of Jesus' warning. Mark's emphasis falls instead on Jesus' miraculous power. This third reference to the lack of bread (the first two references occurred in the editorial introduction of v 14) again highlights the need which provides a foil for Jesus' coming reminders of his twice-proved power to supply more than enough bread. The forward position of ἄρτους, "loaves," stresses the contrast between a plurality of loaves and the single loaf that the disciples have (so also in v 17).

8:17-21 *(Matt 16:8-12)* Since Jesus can hardly have failed to hear his disciples reasoning with one another in the close quarters of the boat, Mark probably does not intend γνούς, "knowing," to imply supernatural knowledge (cf. 6:38; 15:45; contrast 2:6-8, where scribes reasoned "in their hearts" and where Mark strengthened γνούς with the perfective ἐπι-, added "in his spirit," and emphasized the introduction to Jesus' clairvoyant statement with "immediately"; also 9:33-35). Γνούς merely provides the immediate occasion for Jesus' questions, which Mark emphasizes with the historical present tense of λέγει, "he says." The questions gain even greater emphasis from their occurring together and asyndetically in a long series. The criticism of the disciples has the purpose of underlining the superadequate power that Jesus displayed in feeding the five thousand and four thousand. "Why do you reason about the fact that you do not have loaves of bread?" implies that the lack should not have disturbed them. "Don't you yet understand or comprehend?" (cf. v 21; 4:13, 40; 6:52; 7:18; 9:18-19) strengthens the implication. "Not yet" carries a further implication that the doubling of the miracle of feeding should by now have caused the disciples to understand. "Do you have your heart hardened?" bears some resemblance to Isa 6:10 (cf. Mark 3:5; 6:52) and implies that only the dullest sensibilities could have failed to detect the miraculous element in the feedings of the five thousand and four thousand (see the comments on 6:52) and consequently have failed to apply to the present need the magnitude of Jesus' miraculous power as displayed on those occasions (for the heart as an organ of thought, reason, and understanding in biblical anthropology, see nearby examples in 2:6, 8; 7:21; 11:23). The first position of πεπωρωμένην, "hardened," puts great weight on the notion of dullness. "Having eyes you see, don't you, and having ears you hear, don't you?" borrows from Jer 5:21; Ezek 12:2, anticipates the healing of the blind man (vv 22-26), and recollects the healing of the deaf mute (7:31-37). The forward positions of ὀφθαλμούς, "eyes," and ὦτα, "ears," stress the ability to see and hear.

The disciples correctly answer the next two questions: "You remember, don't you, when I broke the five loaves for the five thousand how many baskets full of fragments you picked up?" and "[You remember, don't you,] when [I broke] the seven [loaves] for the four thousand how many baskets' fulnesses of fragments you picked up?" The construction οὐ with an indicative verb in a question expects an affirmative answer and gets one with μνημονεύετε in the present context, because the correct answers of the disciples show that they do indeed remember. The identical construction in the parallel question about seeing and hearing indicates that they remember because they do indeed see and hear — they saw and heard what Jesus did and said when he fed the two multitudes. But seeing, hearing, and remembering have not added up to comprehending that Jesus performed miracles of feeding that eliminate any need for concern over failure to bring enough bread for the present boat trip — hence, the question, "Don't you yet comprehend?" (cf. v 17 and the lack of perception despite seeing and the lack of understanding despite hearing in 4:12). Again, the critical tone highlights past displays of Jesus' power that should be keeping the disciples from concern.

The introduction to this last question gets only a normal imperfect verb:

ἔλεγεν, "he was saying" (cf. M. Zerwick, *Biblical Greek* §272). But twice Mark emphasizes the correct answers of the disciples with the historical present tense in λέγουσιν, "they say," not to flatter the disciples but to accent the superadequacy of Jesus' miraculous power. Twelve baskets of leftovers! Seven baskets of leftovers! Even the wording of the questions carries this accent. The placement of the direct object τοὺς πέντε ἄρτους, "the five loaves," before its verb stresses the fewness of the loaves that Jesus multiplied so abundantly (perhaps also with respect to the seven loaves, but ellipses leave some uncertainty). The adding of πλήρεις, "full," in a surprising position after πόσους κοφίνους κλασμάτων, "how many baskets of fragments?" points to superadequacy. So also does the even more surprising switch in v 20 from the adjective πλήρεις to the noun πληρώματα, "fulnesses," its escalation to a direct object, and its advancement ahead of the reference to fragments. The asyndeton that precedes the introduction to the disciples' first answer (v 19b — before "they say"), the absence of an introduction to Jesus' second question, the further asyndeton that precedes his second question (v 20a — before ὅτε, "when"), and the ellipses in this second question of "You remember, don't you," "I broke," and "loaves" lay yet more emphasis on the disparity between initial fewness and the abundance of leftovers. And, generally speaking, Jesus' questions and the disciples' answers lay more emphasis on the surpluses than on the feedings as such: his power is more than enough for any emergency. The unemphasized lack of understanding in v 21 serves, then, as a foil that thrusts into greater prominence the superadequacy of Jesus' miraculous power and protects the second feeding as well as the first from the inference that they may not have occurred since Jesus' warning has made the disciples concerned over their having only one loaf (again see the comments on 6:51-52).

NOTES

"Again" (v 14) cannot relate back to 6:45 as well as to 8:10, for Jesus did not embark in 6:45 as he does in 8:10, 14. To explain the disciples' not taking bread, P. Carrington (166) appeals to Labrador boatmen who take no homemade bread on fishing trips because it goes sour from damp atmosphere and inferior leaven. Why then the disciples' concern over not having taken more than one loaf? Why the taking of even one? For damp atmosphere the Sea of Galilee does not match the waters off the coast of Labrador, and a short trip across a lake does not match a long session of fishing.

In v 14 the doubling of the reference to lack of bread despite a third reference following in v 16 shows that the emphasis falls on the loaves that the disciples need but do not have rather than on the one loaf that they do have. Therefore we should avoid both the view that the one loaf is a redactional insertion and the interpretation that it symbolizes Jesus — an interpretation that does not link up very well with the following references to leaven or to the recollections of the leftovers at Jesus' miracles of feeding, the accounts of which were geared to miracle-working power rather than to eucharistic symbolism. Moreover, Jesus' use of bread to symbolize his body has yet to come in 14:22 and therefore would not likely prompt those hearing Mark for the first time to think of a symbolic meaning here. Perhaps it would if they were already acquainted with the Words of Institution — but only perhaps, and given the possibility that Mark writes for unbelievers we cannot be sure that he assumes any knowledge of the Words of Institution (cf. pp. 1022-26).

The probably Semitic construction with εἰ μή, "except," in v 14b further undermines the view that the exception of one loaf is a redactional insertion (cf. K. Beyer, *Semitische Syntax* 1/1. 104-5, with a caveat by E. C. Maloney, *Semitic Interference* 92-97).

It is mystifying why the framework of the disciples' forgetting to take enough bread for a lake-crossing should be thought unsuitable for Jesus' warning against the leaven of the Pharisees and against that of Herod (so R. Pesch 1. 412). As already noted, Jesus has just encountered the Pharisees, quite possibly near Herod's capital (see the foregoing comments, H. W. Hoehner, *Herod Antipas* 91-100, and a map s.v. "Tiberias" and "Magdala" [for Dalmanutha]); and apart from Passover, bread implies leaven. Jewish and Christian figurative use of leaven for the permeating power of corruption, including the evil disposition of human beings (see 1 Cor 5:6; Gal 5:9, and H. Windisch in *TDNT* 2. 905-6 for further references to primary and secondary literature), and the indication in Luke 23:8 that Herod will want to see a sign just as the Pharisees ask for a sign here in Mark (vv 10-12; cf. his interest in Jesus' miracles at 6:14) suggest that Jesus is using leaven as a figure for sign-seeking, which in its unreasonable demand for absolute proof betrays unwillingness to believe (cf. H. Windisch in *TDNT* 2. 902-6).

That the saying in v 15 probably stood in Q or L (cf. Luke 12:1 and discussions by I. H. Marshall and J. A. Fitzmyer in their commentaries ad loc.) cancels any probability that Mark fabricated it on the basis of 3:6; 6:14-29; 12:13. Neither leaven nor warnings using ὁρᾶτε, "look!" or βλέπετε, "watch out!" occur in those passages. 3:6; 12:13 mention Herodians, not Herod (again as here); and 6:14-29 does not link Herod with the Pharisees (as here). These dissimilarities also weaken the hypothesis that Mark added "and the leaven of Herod" to "the leaven of the Pharisees." If Jesus did not speak similar warnings on different occasions, it is more probable that an addition of the interpretation "which is hypocrisy" led to omission of "and the leaven of Herod" in the tradition taken over at Luke 12:1. R. Pesch (1. 413, n. 3) argues strongly that the naming of Herod not only represents tradition, but also favors authenticity. For at the time and place of Mark and of pre-Marcan tradition there was no reason to warn against Herod — only at Jesus' time and place — as shown by the deletions of Herod in Matt 16:6 par. Luke 12:1 as compared with Mark 8:15 and by similar deletions in Matt 12:14 par. Luke 6:11 as compared with Mark 3:6 and in Luke 20:20 as compared with Mark 12:13.

According to a common opinion, the saying in v 15, though traditional, did not originally belong to the present context. It occurs in a different context at Luke 12:1. There is no natural transition from v 14 to v 15, or from v 15 to v 16. Verse 15 alludes back to vv 11-12, but v 16 carries on from v 14 rather than from v 15. And the topic of leaven, broached in v 15, drops out of sight thereafter. So run the arguments in favor of this opinion.

But whether Luke 12:1 derives from Q or L, or even from Mark, the saying may have been detached from a narrative context as easily as a narrative context fabricated for it; and we should not rule out the possibility of Jesus' issuing such a warning more than once. There *is* a natural transition from v 14 to v 15 in that the topic of bread leads naturally to that of leaven, and from v 15 to v 16 in that the topic of leaven leads naturally to a reconsideration of the topic of bread. If a redactor could associate leaven with bread so as to insert v 15, Jesus too could associate leaven with bread so as to respond in the manner of v 15. R. M. Fowler (*Loaves and Fishes* 110) correctly notes that what discontinuity does exist between vv 15 and 16 does not stem from the jamming together of different traditions (or, we might add, from the difference between tradition and redaction), but from the differing thoughts of various characters in the story (cf. G. Ziener in *TTZ* 67 [1958] 247-48). Contrary to an argument favoring the original independence of the saying in v 15, v 16 does not carry on very well from v 14; for the reasoning in v 16 seems to require something more substantial than common forgetfulness to take enough bread. Verse 15 provides just that: a warning whose metaphorical language links up with the forgotten bread to create a conundrum that sparks the disciples' reasoning. The alluding of v 15 back to vv 11-12 could argue for the authenticity of Mark's narrative setting just as well as for the original independence of v 15 from vv 13-14, 16-21. C. E. B. Cranfield (259-60) argues that it is not Mark's habit to insert sayings into the body of a narrative, but to append them at the end. To the extent that Mark adds sayings at all, the argument probably holds up. And the disappearance of leaven after v 15 gives possible reason for a pre-Lucan or Lucan detachment of the saying in that verse from its narrative context, represented by Mark, and also for pre-Lucan or Lucan and Matthean additions of interpretation (leaven as hypocrisy in Luke 12:1, as teaching in Matt 16:12). It is at least as likely that the disciples' concern over bread caused Jesus to veer away from explaining the figure of leaven in favor of removing their concern as that he disregarded their concern in favor of an explanation of the figure.

Again according to a common opinion, Mark fabricated vv 13-14, 16-21 out of bits and pieces from past episodes and according to his own theological interest in the disciples' ignorance prior to the Crucifixion and Resurrection. These verses, it is alleged, cannot have circulated apart from the feeding miracles. They carry no independent point. Against this argument, in circles where the feeding miracles were known the present material may have circulated independently to the extent of making the point that Christians must never doubt the adequacy of Jesus' power. The presupposition in one story of knowledge to be gotten from other stories does not foreclose the possibility of independent circulation. Many stories presuppose such knowledge: who Jesus was, where he lived, when he lived, etc. But independent circulation is a form critical canon that does not always work. As most form critics have recognized, many materials in the passion narrative depend on other materials without making themselves suspect as to traditionality. The narrative of Jesus' temptation in 1:12-13 depends on the story of his baptism in 1:9-11 (see the comments and notes ad loc.); yet we do not deduce Mark's fabrication of the temptation narrative, for we have Q-based versions in Matt 4:1-11; Luke 4:1-13. If traditions may have circulated together, a tradition underlying Mark 8:13-21 may have circulated with the stories of the feedings. A Petrine origin of Mark's traditions (see pp. 1026-45) would also make unnecessary the supposition of discrete traditions always circulating independently. When Peter told stories, presumably he often interconnected them in the telling just as they were interconnected in his experience and memory. Even apart from an immediately Petrine origin of Mark's traditions, the original disciples' telling of stories about Jesus very probably included interconnections that passed on into the tradition. We should allow as much weight to the possibility that originally interconnected traditions broke apart as we do to the possibility that originally unconnected traditions came together.

Other arguments are adduced for Mark's fabrication of vv 13-14, 16-21. For each one, a counter argument is available. (1) The reference to one loaf in v 14 takes no obvious effect later in the passage. Not so! The reference provides a basis for the possibility of a miraculous multiplication, a possibility raised in later references to the miraculous multiplications that Jesus has already performed. (2) The editorial comment in 6:52 shows that the key diction and concern of 8:13-21 is Marcan. But in 6:52 Mark may have anticipated traditional diction that he was going to use in 8:13-21; Jesus may have been concerned over the disciples' ignorance before Mark was; and though the Greek wording differs slightly, 10:5 supports a Jesuanic use of hardheartedness. (3) Verse 21 rings back to v 17b. But traditioners, and indeed Jesus himself, must have been capable of inclusive repetition. Even *Ringkomposition* by Mark does not imply lack of tradition to work with: the thought could be traditional, the repetition Marcan (cf. the comments and notes on 4:12-13).

It seems somewhat unlikely that Mark would think up the disciples' forgetting to take loaves of bread. If he were thinking up the one loaf after the analogy of the five loaves and seven loaves, we might expect him to say simply that "they [the disciples] had (only) one loaf with themselves in the boat" and that "they reasoned with one another about the fact that they have (only) one loaf." We might also expect him to have included a fish and to have used a number of expressions different from those that he has in fact used: (1) οὐ, "not" (as in 6:52), instead of οὔπω, "not yet" (vv 17, 21; also in dominical sayings at 4:40; 11:2; 13:7); (2) the phraseology of Isa 6:9-10 (as in 4:12) instead of that of Jer 5:21; Ezek 12:2 plus memory (v 18, the addition of memory being unnecessary to the questions in vv 19-20); (3) πληρώματα, "fulnesses," for the leftovers of the five thousand (as in 6:43) instead of πλήρεις, "full" (v 19); and (4) περισσεύματα, "surpluses," for the leftovers of the four thousand (as in v 8) instead of πληρώματα (v 20).

In the absence of Mark's sources, no argument can be made for or against his creativity from the Marcan hapax legomena ἐπελάθοντο, "they had forgotten" (v 14), and μνημονεύετε, "you remember" (v 18; though a cognate noun occurs in a dominical saying at 14:9). But διελογίζοντο, "they were reasoning" (v 16; also v 17), occurs in other dominical sayings (2:8; 9:33; cf. 7:21) as well as in editorial patches (2:6, 8; 11:31), νοεῖτε, "you understand" (v 17), in another dominical saying (7:18) as well as in a probably editorial patch (13:14), and συνίετε, "you comprehend" (vv 17, 21), in other dominical sayings (4:12; 7:14) as well as in an editorial patch (6:52). We may cast the suspicion of Marcan or pre-Marcan creativity on these other dominical sayings, too; but then argument gives way to ever-increasing hypothesis accompanied by ever-widening circles of reasoning.

These observations do not prove the traditional origin of vv 13-14, 16-21; but they do show that these verses — even vv 17b-18 (which E. Schweizer [160-61] takes to be a Marcan insertion) — do not slavishly imitate other passages or depend on diction clearly exclusive to Mark's editing. To this extent the theory of Marcan fabrication lacks support. And again we need to remind ourselves that traits of Marcan composition — e.g., frequent parataxis (vv 13, 14, 15, 16, 17, 18, 20, 21), asyndetic participles (v 13), duality (vv 14, 15, 15-16, 17, 19-20), and the historical present tense (vv 17, 19, 20) — do not disprove the use of tradition. More positively, the lack of a miracle performed to feed the disciples with their one loaf favors slightly Mark's use of tradition. For he delights in taking over miracle stories and might therefore be expected to fabricate a miracle story here if he were thinking up the entire pericope, or the entire pericope but for v 15 (cf. the use of this passage by H. Räisänen [*Messias-Geheimnis* 122-25] to argue that Mark agrees with the theology of glory represented by the miracles).

E. Stauffer (in *The New Testament Age* 2. 507-8) interprets the leavens of the Pharisees and of Herod as their secret service apparatus consisting of observers, hearing posts, Sabbath-watchers, and liquidation commissars. But leaven represents danger of corruption more naturally than danger of persecution. This observation likewise militates against the view of T. A. Burkill (*New Light* 56-57) that "Herod" refers anachronistically to Herod Agrippa II, who is supposed to have suppressed the eschatological ardor of later Christians, rather than to Herod Antipas, who is out of the picture by the time Mark writes. One may also doubt the presupposition underlying this view, viz., that Mark is writing about recent church history. To explain the leavens, J. Gnilka (1. 310-11) parallels the Pharisees' unbelief in 3:6 and Herod's misidentification of Jesus in 6:14-16. The parallel is somewhat skewed, however, in that 6:14-16 puts the accent on Jesus' miracles, belief in which caused Herod to misidentify Jesus with a man whom Herod admired and whose life he wanted to save, viz., John the Baptizer (contrast the Pharisees' plotting against Jesus' life in 3:6).

In support of the disciples' taking the warning of Jesus literally rather than metaphorically, W. L. Lane (281, n. 39) notes that "leaven" sometimes means "leavened bread" (rabbinic references in Str-B 1. 729). He also notes that taking the leaven as Jewish nationalistic, political messianism has no foundation in the text (281, n. 38). According to

A. Negōiṭā and C. Daniel (in *NovT* 9 [1967] 306-14, Jesus says אֲמִירָה, "speech, word," but his disciples mistake it for the similarly pronounced חֲמִירָא, "leaven." The identification of the leaven as teaching in Matt 16:12 might seem to support this hypothesis. But since that verse is redactional, the linkage of the two Aramaic words need not go back any farther than Matthew's writing, and then by wordplay, not by mistake. His frequent insertions of teaching eliminate any need to see such a linkage even at the redactional level, however (cf. R. H. Gundry, *Matthew* 643, s.v. διδασκ-/διδαχ-). The total absence of teaching here in Mark and the different identification of the leaven as hypocrisy in Luke 12:1 do more than eliminate a need; they positively undermine a confusion of Aramaic homonyms by the disciples. The admission that אֲמִירָה could mean "teaching" only by extension ("par extension" — Negōiṭā and Daniel, op. cit. 311) further undermines the hypothesis, and the argument that Mark omits teaching because he assumes his audience's knowledge of the homonyms (ibid. 312) overlooks his having to translate Aramaic expressions time and again (see F. Neirynck, *Duality* 106-7, for references).

In v 16 διελογίζοντο refers to a reasoned discussion or argument. So W. L. Lane (280) suggests that "the disciples interpreted Jesus' words as an indirect reproach for their failure to bring provisions" and that as a result they "began quarreling concerning whose responsibility it was to procure bread." But though the connotation of quarreling will approach διαλογίζομαι in 9:33, Mark will switch to διαλέγομαι in 9:34 for that connotation, the stated content of the discussion will spell out its connotation as quarrelsomeness, and διαλογίζομαι occurs without that connotation in 2:6, 8 (bis); 11:31. Nonetheless, the attachment of πρὸς ἀλλήλους, "with one another," to the one verb here in 8:16 and to the other verb at 9:34 and in the vicinity of the first verb tends toward Lane's suggestion.

If we read ἔχουσιν, "they have," with P45 B f1 28 565 700 pc k co (cf. εἶχαν D it), ὅτι may be epexegetic ("about the fact that"), causal ("because"), or indirectly interrogative ("why"). If we read ἔχομεν, "we have," with א A C L Θ f13 Majority Text vg syp.h bomss, the resultant direct quotation leaves the possibilities that ὅτι is recitative (equivalent to quotation marks), directly interrogative ("why?"), or causal with ellipsis ("[He has given us this warning] because we do not have loaves of bread"). 2:6-7 shows that following διαλογίζομαι a direct quotation does not need to be introduced with a recitative ὅτι (see also 11:31, the only other Marcan passage where a direct quotation follows διαλογίζομαι, but with the help of λέγοντες, "saying" [cf. the v.l. λέγοντες here], rather than with the help of a recitative ὅτι). On the other hand, the ὅτι in v 17 will not be capable of being taken as recitative, for a direct quotation will not follow it ("you have," not "we have"). The indirectness in v 17 and the interrogative character of τί in that verse also disfavor an almost immediately following second interrogative in ὅτι. Likewise on the disfavorable side, a causal ὅτι in v 17 would leave an ambiguity: Does the ὅτι-clause identify the cause of the reasoning as such, or the cause underlying its choice of subject matter? The most natural understanding, then, treats the ὅτι in v 17 as epexegetic. Since this ὅτι echoes the one in v 16, we have a parallelistic reason to treat the one in v 16 as epexegetic, too. The comparative weakness of the v.l. ἔχομεν gives further help to this conclusion by leaving only the causal and epexegetic possibilities to compete with each other in the arena of ἔχουσιν.

Just as the plural "loaves" in v 14 allowed for an exception of one loaf in the follow-up, so also in v 16 the same plural allows for the already stated exception. Thus no numerical contradiction exists that would provide footing to distinguish between tradition and redaction or to interpret the one loaf symbolically for avoidance of a numerical contradiction and for an allusion to the eucharistic body of Jesus (against J. Mánek in *NovT* 7 [1964] 13).

Though a question may be harshly critical, as in 9:19, the questions in vv 17-21 breathe a softer tone in the contrast between the mere fact of the disciples' seeing and hearing without understanding and Jesus' stated purpose in 4:11b-12 that non-disciples not understand when they see and hear and that therefore they stay unconverted and unforgiven (cf. the notes on the questions in 4:40). The vv.ll. with πῶς, "how is it that?" (v 21), seem to stem from a desire to soften even further Jesus' reproach of the disciples (cf. B. M. Metzger, *Textual Commentary* ad loc. Mark 4:40). In v 18 ἔχοντες may idiomatically translate the Hebrew text of Jer 5:21 or reflect the LXX of Ezek 12:2. Reflection of Ezek 12:2 LXX would entail both a shift from a relative pronoun plus a finite verb to a participle and an omission of "to see" (so the MT as well as the LXX). Because Jesus is addressing his disciples, the third person of the OT texts changes to the second person. In the OT texts the phraseology occurs in declarative sentences and therefore denies seeing and hearing. Jesus' using the phraseology in an interrogative sentence that implies an affirmative answer shifts the meaning with the result that the participles are not concessive ("Though you have eyes, you do not see . . . ," as in a declarative sentence), but causal ("Since you have eyes, you see, don't you . . . ?"). Of course, it is possible to treat v 18a (as well as the preceding clause or two) as declarative rather than interrogative. But doing so would spoil the parallelism of a series of questions that begins with "Why are you reasoning . . . ?" and vv 19-20 simply have to be taken as positive indications of the disciples' remembrance, based on what they saw and heard at the feedings. M. A. Beavis (*Mark's Audience* 90-91) correctly sees an allusion to Isa 6:10a but incorrectly denies any allusion to Jer 5:21 or Ezek 12:2. Close phraseological similarity falsifies the denial. Since the disciples, though dull, do see and hear, cross-references to spiritual blindness and deafness in *POxy.* 1. 11-22; W. Scott, *Hermetica* 2. 182, are not quite on target.

The disciples are like the non-disciples of 4:11b-12 in seeing and hearing yet not understanding. But the disciples did not understand in 4:10, 13, either. Because they heard correctly, however, Jesus illuminated the kingdomly meaning of the parables by giving explanations to the disciples (see 4:11b, 14-25, esp. 24-25, with comments and notes). So also here he illuminates the miraculous character of the feedings by calling the disciples' attention to the greater amounts of leftovers as compared with the starting amounts of bread and fish. The issue of Jesus' identity does not come into the picture; so we have no reason to relate the present pericope to 8:27-30 (against S. Brown in *JBL* 92 [1973] 62-63). Nor does the issue of feeding Gentiles come into the picture, as though the disciples wilfully neglected to take extra loaves which Jesus could use to feed the Gentiles (against J. B. Gibson in *JSNT* 27 [1986] 32-36; cf. D. Senior in *BTB* 12 [1982] 67-69). He has already fed the supposedly Gentile four thousand (vv 1-9) and is now heading for the Jewish town of Bethsaida (v 22). At least it is so classified in Matt 11:20-21 par. Luke 10:13-15. Nor does the significance of miracles as signs that God's kingdom is advancing come into the picture (against T. J. Geddert, *Watchwords* 61-71). Simply and only in view are the miraculous character of the feedings and the disciples' imperception of it.

K. P. Donfried (in *Kirche* 101-3) thinks that Mark makes Jesus rebuke the disciples for failure to understand that the bread in the feeding miracles represents Jesus' body in accordance with the Lord's Supper. But Mark has not yet allowed the disciples to hear even the passion predictions, much less the Words of Institution. Surely he does not expect the disciples to know those predictions and words in advance! His audience are no better off, for they too have not yet come across those predictions and words. The interpretation therefore fails to make Mark a credible author.

A. J. Jewell (in *LQHR* 35 [1966] 117-20) hypothesizes that Mark knows Paul's version of the Words of Institution (1 Cor 11:23-25), constructs the present question, "You remember, don't you, . . . ?" (v 18c), out of the repeated command, "Do this in remembrance of me" (1 Cor 11:24, 25), with the result that he will omit the command in 14:22-25, and thereby displays a eucharistic understanding of the feeding miracles. But it is Luke 22:19-20 that will show close contact with 1 Cor 11:23-25. Mark 14:22-25 will not, even in respects other than remembrance.

There is no need to think that Jesus' reference to "breaking bread" carries overtones of the Lord's Supper or of early Christians' fellowship meals (against R. Pesch 1. 414-15, citing Acts 2:46; 20:7; 1 Cor 10:6). The expression occurs often in connection with ordinary meals (see the notes on 6:41), and Jesus uses it here simply because he broke the bread but did not himself serve it to the five thousand and four thousand. The disciples did that. The emphasis on the superadequacy of Jesus' miraculous power tends away from a eucharistic interpretation (sometimes combined with a carry-over of Jewish and Gentile evangelistic symbolism in the feeding miracles). Cross-references to Luke 12:22-32; Matt 6:25-34 are not entirely appropriate; for those passages teach trust in God's daily providence, but here Jesus calls attention to his miraculous ability to multiply bread in emergencies.

The ratio in one loaf for twelve disciples would make for an easier miracle than that required by the ratios in five loaves for five thousand men and seven loaves for four thousand. But Jesus does not ask about the amounts of food available over against the numbers of people who needed it ("How many loaves did you have when I fed . . . ?"), but about the amounts of leftovers. Even if Mark is the first to divide one miraculous feeding in two, or to bring two miraculous feedings into proximity (but see the comments and notes on vv 1-9), tradition may underlie vv 19-20, which would then have to imply only a redactional doubling.

Why does Jesus remind the disciples of the five loaves and seven loaves if the one loaf symbolizes the unity at table of Jews and Gentiles in the church (as thought by W. H. Kelber, *Kingdom* 61-62; idem, *Mark's Story* 40-41; A. Stock, *Call* 127)? To say that the disciples are on the verge of siding with the Pharisees and Herodians in opposing the inclusion of Gentiles despite 7:1-23 (so Kelber) lacks textual support. 7:1-23 may have carried implications for such inclusion, but it made nothing of them and stressed instead the opposition of Pharisaic tradition to the OT. Absent when the Syrophoenician woman confronted Jesus in 7:31-37, the Pharisees are not portrayed as opposing the inclusion of Gentiles. Herodians would not oppose it, but the text does not even mention them — rather, Herod, a Gentile!

According to D.-A. Koch (*Bedeutung* 110-12), Mark wants to show that nature-miracles, such as the feedings, cannot bring a clear understanding of Jesus. Only the Crucifixion and Resurrection can bring that. But Jesus' questions blame the dullness of the disciples, not any inferiority of nature-miracles. In fact, he stresses the superadequacy of the feedings; and the Crucifixion and Resurrection will not make possible in a way thus far impossible an understanding of the point at issue, viz., that Jesus can feed the twelve disciples with one loaf.

JESUS' HEALING A DIFFICULT CASE OF BLINDNESS

8:22-26

The story of Jesus' healing a blind man at Bethsaida opens with a topographical shift (v 22a; cf. v 13) and the bringing of the man to Jesus (v 22b). The healing occupies the main part of the story (vv 23-25) and subdivides into two stages: (1) partial healing, with the result of unclear vision (vv 23-24); (2) complete healing, with the result of clear vision (v 25). Finally, Jesus sends the man home (v 26).

8:22 The historical present tense of ἔρχονται, "they come," shows Mark's eagerness to narrate Jesus' performance of a difficult miracle in Bethsaida, where Jesus and the disciples arrive at long last (cf. 6:45, 53). For the first time in a while, Mark puts the verb indicating a topographical shift in the plural (as in 6:53), because Jesus and the disciples have been in dialogue with each other in a boat (though the disciples have accompanied him also when Mark has used the singular — see 7:17, 24, 31; 8:10, 13). As in 7:32, the present historical tense of φέρουσιν, "they bring," and of παρακαλοῦσιν, "they entreat," emphasizes the blind man's need for sight. "They" means "people," probably the same as τοὺς ἀνθρώπους, "the people," to be seen by the blind man after his healing (v 24, where the definite article will look anaphoric). Since the blind man cannot see Jesus' whereabouts, "in order that he might touch him" means "in order that Jesus might touch the blind man to heal him" (cf. 1:41; 7:32-33; and the rest of the present pericope), not "in order that the blind man might touch Jesus to receive healing" (cf. 3:10; 5:27, 28, 30, 31; 6:56 [bis]).

8:23-24 The blind man cannot see to follow; so Jesus must take hold of his hand to lead him outside the village of Bethsaida. Mark's calling Bethsaida a "village" (κώμη) instead of a "city" (πόλις — see the following notes) links this pericope with the next, which has its setting among the "villages" of Philip's Caesarea (v 27). As in 7:33 Jesus took the deaf mute aside from the crowd because he wanted privacy to work a difficult miracle the power of which Mark was concerned to emphasize, so here Jesus takes the blind man outside the village for the same reason. At 7:33 Mark used ἀπολαβόμενος for the taking aside. Now the prefix changes to ἐπι- because Jesus must lay hold *on* the blind man's hand to lead him aside. Again at 7:33, Jesus spat on his own fingers and touched the deaf mute's tongue. Now Jesus spits directly into the blind man's eyes because they are exposed as the deaf mute's tongue was not; then he lays his hands on the blind man (i.e. on his eyes, as v 25 will make plain). The asyndeton between spitting and hand-laying emphasizes these means of working a miracle (concerning which see the comments and notes on 7:33).

Jesus now asks whether the blind man sees anything (see A. T. Robertson, *Grammar* 916, on the use of εἰ to introduce a direct question). By virtue of its forward position τι, "anything," gets some emphasis. Jesus detects or suspects that sight has not fully returned; he is not taken by surprise. Since the man has been blind and since he is about to say that he sees, ἀναβλέψας probably means "receiving sight" (as in 10:51, 52 of another blind man [see E. S. Johnson in *NTS* 25 [1978-79] 376-77) instead of "looking up" (as in 6:41; 7:34; 16:4). "I see the people" is qualified by a subordinate clause indicating lack of visual clarity: "in that [or 'because' — epexegetic or causal ὅτι] like trees I see [the people] walking around." "Like trees" describes "the people," not "I," and "walking around" describes "the people," not "trees" or "I." At the distance to which Jesus has withdrawn the patient outside Bethsaida (v 23a), the people who are walking around in the village look so indistinct that the patient compares them to a forest or a clump of trees whose many branches and leaves make them hard to distinguish from one another (esp. when they are waving in the wind, as perhaps implied by the people's milling about). The hyperbaton evident in the advance of "the people" into the main clause stresses "the people" as an answer to Jesus' question, "Do you see anything?" Thus the emphasis falls on the degree of success that the miraculous cure has thus far attained rather than on the residual unclarity of vision. In the subordinate clause the first position of ὡς δένδρα, "like trees," combines with the difference in gender between δένδρα and περιπατοῦντας, "walking around," to limit the comparison to people and trees as such and thereby exclude a nonsensical implication that trees walk around. There is an alternative understanding of the comparison, viz., that though the objects of sight look like trees, their walking around means that they must be human beings. But it makes the analogy primarily one of shape (the torsos and limbs of the people being compared to the trunks and limbs of trees) rather than one of indistinctness. To that extent it misses the contextual point.

8:25 "Then" (εἶτα) forcefully identifies a second stage. "Again he laid [his] hands on his eyes" is unique. Nowhere else does Jesus have to apply his hands more than once for a complete healing. The present double application — the plural "hands" implies both hands, one for each eye — implies greater than usual difficulty in effecting a cure and thereby magnifies the cure once Jesus has effected it. We should speak of a second miracle, then, corresponding to the second application of his hands. This time there is no need for further saliva; the man's eyes are still moist from the first application. Mark switches from ὄμματα, "eyes" (v 23), to the synonymous ὀφθαλμούς, perhaps for catchword association with v 18. The statements, "And he opened his eyelids wide, and he was restored, and he was seeing all things distinctly," carefully set out three steps (cf. *Acts Pet.* 20). The measured pace of the narrative prolongs attention on the fulness and clarity of vision that Jesus effects and thereby on the power that enables him as God's Son to effect it. The prefixes in διέβλεψεν and ἐνέβλεπεν sharpen the emphasis on fulness and clarity (contrast the simplex of βλέπω in vv 23, 24); they do not imply a straining to see (cf. 10:21, 27; 14:67). Ἀπεκατέστη, "was restored," probably implies that the man was not born blind (cf. his ability to recognize human beings and compare them to trees); but even if he was, the emphasis lies on present rather than past ability to see clearly. The addition of τηλαυγῶς, "distinctly," emphasizes vision good enough to see clearly even at a distance; the adverb literally means "far-shining-ly." And ἅπαντα, "all things," stresses completeness: not only can the ex-blind man see the people in the village clearly, but nothing at all remains unclear. The switch from aorist to imperfect in ἐνέβλεπεν indicates ongoing clarity of vision.

8:26 Jesus' sending the man home and telling him not even to go into the village seem to imply that the man does not live in the village, at least not in this village, but that people brought him to Jesus from elsewhere. On the other hand, since village is public and home private, perhaps the text means that people of the village brought a local blind man to Jesus from the village square, where he had been begging, and that Jesus tells him not to go back to the village (understood as a public square), but to go home (understood as a private residence within the village; cf. the way in which a person living in town may be said to go to town). The ambiguity of the text on this point shows to what extent emphasis falls on the aim of Jesus' sending and command rather than on the meaning of his command.

We would make a mistake to identify secrecy as the aim of Jesus' sending the ex-blind man home with the command not even to go into the village. Mark is quite capable of writing a command to secrecy after a private miracle (see 5:43; apparently 1:44, too, since no bystanders were mentioned). He is even capable of writing a command that a crowd keep a miracle secret (7:36). Yet no command to secrecy appears here. For such a command we would expect καὶ διεστείλατο αὐτῷ (πολλὰ) ἵνα μηδενὶ λέγῃ or . . . ἵνα μηδεὶς γνοῖ τοῦτο, "and he ordered him (much) that he should speak to no one" or ". . . that no one should know this" (cf. 5:43; 7:36; 8:30; 9:9). Going home, not into the village, does not imply going home instead of telling the villagers that he can now see (cf. the vv.ll.). It implies going home instead of begging from the villagers. They had presumably picked up the blind man off the street where he was begging (cf. 10:52 with 10:46). It might be objected that Mark has not described the man as a beggar. But a blind man's begging goes without saying (see John 9:1 with 9:8). The explicit mention of blind Bartimaeus's begging will be due only to the need of explaining why he is sitting alongside the road that Jesus is traveling (10:46). The villagers' bringing the present blind man to Jesus implied his begging, probably in their market place. Why else would they have brought him? If it were his family that brought him, we would have been told so (cf. 1:30; 3:21, 31; 5:22-23, 40; 7:24; 9:17); and those he is enabled to see in the distance would hardly be identified as τοὺς ἀνθρώπους, "the people" (v 24).

At 2:11-12 the command to go home had nothing to do with secrecy; rather, going home was to demonstrate a miracle — and it was to be a public demonstration at that (as in 8:26 the going home is to be within eyeshot of the people in the village). Nor at 5:19 did the command to go home have anything to do with secrecy. A crowd was present, and Jesus followed up with a further command in opposition to secrecy, a command to tell family members about the exorcism that had been worked on the teller. In 7:29-30 going home had nothing to do with secrecy, but stemmed from assurance that an exorcism had indeed occurred. Quite similarly, in 1:44 the command, "Go show yourself to the priest and offer for your cleansing the things that Moses prescribed," had the purpose of "a testimony to them" (the preceding command to say nothing to anyone having had the purpose of hurrying up the testimony — see the comments ad loc.). In 5:34 "go in peace" formed part of a declaration of healing, a crowd was present, and the going had the purpose of showing that a miracle had taken place. And in 10:52 the command to go will have nothing to do with secrecy — the healing of blind Bartimaeus will have taken place in the midst of a large crowd — but will imply that he does not have to sit begging at roadside anymore. Thus, 8:26 imposes no secrecy concerning the miracle or the means by which Jesus has effected it, much less a messianic secret (for his identity as the Christ has not entered the picture). Rather, this verse carries a demonstration of healing: the man can now see to go home without needing people to take him there as he did need them to bring him to Jesus (v 22). The prohibition of going into the village does not add secrecy, but clinches the demonstration of a miracle by stressing that the ex-blind man has no more need to take up his old occupation of begging in the village. The duality of v 26, the meaning and first position of μηδέ, "not even," and the placement of εἰς τὴν κώμην, "into the village," emphasize this demonstration (cf. BDF §445[2]).

NOTES

For a synoptic comparison of 7:31-37 and 8:22-26, see R. M. Fowler, *Loaves and Fishes* 105-6. He attributes the similarities between these passages to pre-Marcan composition by the same person and thinks that Mark uses the stories to frame and highlight the disciples' metaphorical deafness and blindness in the intervening pericopes (ibid. 105-12). Unfortunately for this view, the disciples were not deaf and blind (see vv 18-20 with comments and notes) and were not subject to any criticism at all in vv 10-12. Similarities between the passages admit of different and perhaps complementary explanations: (1) Jesus' re-use of technique; (2) pre-Marcan assimilation; and (3) Marcan assimilation. Deep differences between the stories, beginning with the difference between deaf muteness and blindness, disfavor the theory of a doublet. See the notes on 7:31-37 concerning the theory that that passage and this one were once paired in reverse order. See those same notes on the question of Hellenistic influence. What J. Jeremias (*NT Theology* 1. 89-90) regards as later patterning (exclusion of the public, physical manipulations, etc.) may equally well be regarded as primitivity.

The story may appear here because in the tradition Jesus performed the healing at this point on his way northward (cf. v 27). Alternatively, we may think of catchword associations (see the verbal parallels discussed above) lacking theological depth. This may be the only miracle that Mark describes as occurring in stages, but in 5:1-20 he described an exorcism as occurring only after a first effort had failed. The emphasis on difficulty magnified the greatness of Jesus' power once he did succeed. So here, too, as shown by the heightened use of means. (To think that prolongation of a miracle because of its difficulty degrades Jesus' power is to betray an ignorance of stories concerning heroic deeds and to think too abstractly, the logical extreme of which is the unbiblical denial that anything can be thought to require effort on God's part.)

E. S. Johnson (in *NTS* 25 [1978-79] 370-83) argues that Matthew omits this story, not because Jesus at first fails to heal the blind man completely, but because a representation of the disciples as blind disagrees with Matthew's portrayal of the disciples as knowledgeable. Matthew does portray them as knowledgeable, but instead of omitting this story he amalgamates it with another one (see R. H. Gundry, *Matthew* 178, 405-6, on Matt 9:27-31; 20:29-34). According to H. C. Kee (*Community* 57-58), Mark uses vv 22-26 to teach that understanding does not arise out of available evidence, but comes by revelatory insight. The dichotomy is false, and Mark writes up the miracle to make evidence available.

See J. Preuss, *Biblical and Talmudic Medicine* 270-79; O. Weinreich, *Antike Heilungswunder* 189-94; B. Blackburn, *Theios Anēr* 191, on the healing of blindness in general. According to a very popular interpretation of vv 22-26, the two stages in the present healing symbolize two stages in the disciples' gaining insight into the identity of Jesus: (1) they gain insight into his messiahship but still lack the clarity of vision that would make them understand the necessity of his passion and resurrection (vv 27-33); (2) they ultimately gain insight into the necessity of his passion and resurrection as the Son of man and Son of God. In favor of this interpretation are adduced (1) the fact that this is his only miracle to be described by Mark as taking place in stages; (2) the placement of this miracle between 8:13-21, which features the disciples' ignorance, and 8:27-9:1, which features their insight into Jesus' messiahship, but an insight lacking further insight into the necessity of his passion and resurrection; (3) the common use of blindness as a figure for ignorance and of sight as a figure for understanding (see references in H.-J. Klauck, *Allegorie* 348); (4) parallels between the present story and the immediately fore-going and following pericopes: privacy in vv 23 and 27; the use of ἐπερωτάω, "ask," in vv 23 and 27, 29, of βλέπω, "see," in vv 23, 24 and 18, of ὀφθαλμούς, "eyes," in vv 25, 18, of ἄνθρωποι, "people," in vv 24 and 27; and the command in v 26 not to go into the village vis-à-vis the command to secrecy in v 30.

Against the foregoing arguments, the healing is only semiprivate in that people bring the blind man to Jesus and plead for his healing; and healing occurs within eyeshot of the people. What degree of privacy there is highlights the difficulty of the healing, whereas the privacy in v 27 will be incidental to Jesus' traveling with his disciples on the road. The exorcism in 5:1-20, as we have noted, required a second effort by Jesus. Ἐπερωτάω is too common in Mark (where it appears twenty-five times) to carry parallelistic significance here. The disciples "see" (βλέπω) already in v 18. They do not need sight *as* understanding. They need understanding *as well as* sight. The use of ὄμματα for eyes in v 23, i.e. before its synonym ὀφθαλμούς in v 25, runs at cross-purpose to a parallel with ὀφθαλμούς in v 18. ῎Ανθρωποι, "people," are the objects of unclear seeing in v 24, but the subjects who falsely opine in v 27; and for parallelistic significance here in vv 24 and 27, this plural noun occurs too often elsewhere in Mark (see 1:17; 3:28; 7:7, 8, 21; 8:33; 10:27; 11:2, 30, 32; 12:14; 14:41). The command not to go into the village does not equate with the command to secrecy (see the foregoing comments).

The healing can hardly symbolize a breakthrough to recognition of Jesus' mess-iahship (for a recent presentation of this view, see F. J. Matera in *Bib* 70 [1989] 163-71); for just as the false opinions concerning Jesus' identity in v 28 will date at least as far back as 6:14-16, so in 8:27–9:1 Peter's confession will represent what the disciples have been thinking for some time, i.e. prior to their display of ignorance in vv 13-21 and perhaps since their calls, beginning in 1:16-20 (cf. also 3:13-19; 6:7-13, 30-31). Even otherwise, nothing happens to the disciples between 8:13-21 and 8:27–9:1 that would "heal" their intellectual blindness so as to bring about a first recognition of Jesus as the Christ in correspondence to the blind man's initial recovery of sight. And if Jesus' teaching about the Passion and Resurrection is supposed to correspond to the second stage of the blind man's healing, he should also teach regarding his messiahship before Peter confesses it. But he does not. To get around this difficulty by extending the first stage of the disciples' intellectual healing backward into the first part of Jesus' ministry clashes with the disciples' ignorance in vv 13-21 and confronts the same difficulty that he did not teach his messiahship. Anyway, healing of blindness may display his power or represent conversion as easily as symbolizing Christological education. Unclear vision in the first stage of the blind man's healing can hardly represent seeing without understanding, for even with unclear vision the healed man understands that he is seeing human beings, not trees.

In the second stage of the miracle, which is supposed to symbolize Jesus' making the disciples see the necessity of his passion and resurrection, he wastes no time in making the blind man see clearly. But the first and only indication that the disciples see the necessity of Jesus' passion and resurrection comes not till 14:27-31, and then only by implication. In the meantime, they display ignorance of this necessity despite his repeated teaching concerning it (vv 31-33; 9:9-13, 31-37; 10:32-45). Even after their implied understanding in 14:27-31, one of them will betray him (14:43-45), the rest will flee (14:50), and one of the rest will deny him three times (14:66-72). The insight of the centurion at the cross (15:39) cannot count as the second stage of the disciples' intellectual healing; for he differs from them in personal identity. And since all the Marcan miracles have heretofore provided support for the disciples' Christological belief rather than symbolizing their pilgrimage to such belief (so, too, with respect to future Marcan miracles), we should reject the symbolic interpretation of the present miracle.

F. G. Lang (in *ZTK* 74 [1977] 7) suggests a variation on the symbolic interpretation, viz., that the first stage of the blind man's healing represents Peter's speaking *for* the disciples in his confession that Jesus is the Christ (v 29) and that the second stage represents God's speaking *to* several disciples in identifying Jesus as his Son (9:7). But Jesus is the chief actor in both stages of the healing, whereas in both of these two future identifications of him he will remain primarily passive.

E. Dinkler (in *The Future of Our Religious Past* 178) doubts the authenticity of Bethsaida because of the pervasive parallel between v 22 and 7:31-32. But why should the data of tradition not be worked up orally or scribally in parallelistic style where possible? Under the supposition that vv 22-26 did not originally belong with vv 13-21, the shift from the plural in "they come" (v 22a) to the singular in "to him" (v 22b) is said to give the whole clause, "And they come into Bethsaida," the look of a redactional addition, or at least to give the plural in "they come" the look of a changed singular. Against these alternatives, K. L. Schmidt (*Rahmen* 207-8) argues for the possibility that the v.l. "he comes" (ℵ* A *f*[1] sy[s,p,h]) represents Mark's original text: this singular verb is to be preferred as the more difficult reading in that the preceding story puts Jesus and his disciples together. But Jesus was the subject of "was saying" in the last verse of the preceding story; so the present singular reading is no more difficult than the plural — less so, in fact, since it harmonizes with "to him."

One might think that Mark introduces Bethsaida here to make up for the failure to reach Bethsaida in 6:53 (cf. 6:45). But because of the topographical difficulty caused by that failure (landing in Gennesaret on the same side of the lake as the one from which the disciples started to cross the lake), we would rather expect Mark to have written "Bethsaida" instead of "Gennesaret" in 6:53 and thus to have enhanced the preceding miracle. The view of P. J. Achtemeier (in *JBL* 89 [1970] 285-86) that the present story followed the sea-walking story (6:45-52) in a pre-Marcan cycle of miracle stories carries the liability of making Mark undermine the miracles of sea-walking and sudden calm by keeping Jesus and the disciples from reaching his stated goal of Bethsaida (cf. 6:45 with 6:53 and the comments and notes ad loc.).

"To him" presupposes an earlier mention of Jesus just as much as "they come" presupposes an earlier mention of him and the disciples. It is therefore impossible to tell whether we are dealing with traditions interconnected before Mark or with traditions interconnected by Mark. The shift from "they" who come (i.e. Jesus and his disciples) to "they" who bring the blind man is more striking than the shift from "they come" to "to him." But the indefinite third person plural, which "they bring" represents, characterizes Mark's writing. We have no convincing reason in the shift from plural to singular, then, to think that he adds Bethsaida.

But another argument comes forward in favor of Mark's adding Bethsaida, viz., that vv 23, 26 speak of a "village" (κώμη), whereas decades before Mark wrote his book, Philip had raised the status of Bethsaida from that of a village to that of a city (Josephus *Ant.* 18.2.1 §28; idem *J.W.* 2.9.1 §168; 3.10.7 §515; Luke 9:10; John 1:44). This argument is reversible, however: since the longer Bethsaida had been a city the less likely anyone would have added its name to a story taking place in a mere village, the present association of Bethsaida with a village probably dates from a time so early that the memory of Bethsaida's original status was still lingering. We may consider other factors, too: (1) the Petrine source of Marcan tradition as early Galilean and reflective of Bethsaida's original status (cf. pp. 1026-45); (2) the possibility of a visit by Jesus and his disciples to the old fishing village ("Bethsaida" means "house of fishing" or "fisher's house") rather than to the new city that Philip built on higher ground (cf. the fishing occupation of several disciples of Jesus and their going "into the villages of Philip's Caesarea" but not into Philip's Caesarea itself — v 27); (3) the possible implication from the lack of coins minted in Bethsaida that its legal status as a village continued despite Philip's upgrading it to a city in respect of fortifications and population (Josephus *Ant.* 18.2.1 §28; cf. Josephus's comment on the large size of Galilean villages — *J.W.* 3.3.2 §43; also A. H. M. Jones, *Cities* 282, 465, n. 76; A. N. Sherwin-White, *Roman Society* 129-31; and, in general, C. Kopp, *Holy Places* 180-86). J. Gnilka (1. 313) doubts that Mark bothered himself with legal niceties, but we are speaking of pre-Marcan tradition (cf. K. L. Schmidt, *Rahmen* 208-10).

Jesus' healing in private does not indicate his turning from crowds to teach the disciples (as thought by J. Roloff, *Kerygma* 129-31), for he will continue his commerce with the crowds (see 8:34–9:1; 10:1-9, 17-22; 11:18, 27-12:41). J. Gnilka (1. 314) thinks that the story merely details the procedure of the healing rather than emphasizing the difficulty of the case and the consequent greatness of the miracle. But the detailing needs a motive, which emphasis on difficulty and greatness provides. This emphasis need not imply that blindness as such poses greater difficulty than other maladies, only that this particular case poses greater than usual difficulty. For the use of spittle in healing, see the notes on 7:33; and for the use of spittle specifically in the healing of blindness, J. Preuss, *Biblical and Talmudic Medicine* 277. J. K. Howard (in *SJT* 37 [1984] 165) suggests that Jesus uses saliva to clean dirt and dried secretions from the patient's eyelids. What then did Jesus clean with saliva from the deaf mute's tongue (7:33)? Jesus' healing the blind man corresponds to God's promising sight to the blind (Ps 146:8; Isa 29:18; 35:5).

M. Zerwick (*Untersuchungen* 62) suggests that in v 24 the imperfect of ἔλεγεν, "he was saying," connotes hesitancy. But elsewhere Mark uses the imperfect of this verb nearly four dozen times without such a connotation (see the concordance s.v. λέγω). R. M. Fowler (*Loaves and Fishes* 111) draws a parallel between the two verbs for seeing in v 24, βλέπω and ὁράω, and the same two verbs in v 15. He then deduces that the blind man obeys Jesus' command to see in v 15 as the disciples did not in vv 16-21. But the use in vv 23-25 of other verbs of seeing — ἀναβλέπω, διαβλέπω, and ἐμβλέπω — as well as of βλέπω and ὁράω confuses a parallel with βλέπω and ὁράω in v 15. Besides, in v 24 the matching pair occur in reverse order and for unclear vision. The reverse order calls in question the parallel, and the unclear vision would make a strange indication of obedience to Christ's command.

Since a man born blind or blinded so long as to have more or less forgotten how to interpret visual images would sustain as much difficulty interpreting visual images of trees as interpreting those of human beings, the comparison of human beings to trees does not tell us anything about such a difficulty. He may have no difficulty at all in interpreting visual images, only in seeing them clearly. Thus medical discussions such as those by W. J. P. Boyd in *SE VII* 83-85; J. K. Howard in *SJT* 37 (1984) 163-70; G. Walker in *ExpTim* 87 (1975-76) 23; and H. van der Loos, *Miracles* 420, n. 2, lose their relevance. The comparison of human beings to trees has suggested lens distortion that causes objects to appear bigger than they are. But then so also would trees appear bigger, and relative sizes would remain the same. Final healing corrects unclarity, not misproportion.

E. F. F. Bishop (*Jesus of Palestine* 151) writes of "men and women who can be seen almost enveloped in the brushwood they are carrying for the fire, so that they do resemble 'trees walking.'" But did they all shed their brushwood in the next moment so as to clarify the patient's vision? The often cited parallel in R. Herzog, *Wunderheilungen* no. 18 (= *SIG* 3. 1168, ll. 120-23), does not make the grade. The blind man at Epidaurus at first sees the trees in the sanctuary, but only during a dream-vision or upon waking from one. He does not see human beings as though they are trees, nor does he see trees because they are large objects that partiality of healing limits him to seeing. Neither trees nor human beings are walking about, and no improvement in clarity of vision is needed or provided. See J. Wellhausen (2. Aufl.) 62; W. C. Allen in *ExpTim* 13 (1901-2) 330; M. Black,

Aramaic Approach 53-54; and G. M. Lee in *NovT* 20 (1978) 74 on various possibilities that in v 24 ὅτι mistranslates epexegetically or causatively a relative pronominal ךְ in underlying Aramaic, or that a translator missed such a ךְ. The danger in these possibilities is a nonsensical implication that trees walk.

Lexicons list "see clearly" as well as "open wide the eyes" for definition of διαβλέπω (v 25), but we may question the suitability of "see clearly" here and elsewhere (see H. Almquist, *Plutarch und das NT* 55-56; E. Roos in *Eranos* 51 [1953] 155-57). Here, three synonyms in a row — "saw clearly" (διέβλεψεν), "was restored" (ἀπεκατέστη), and "was seeing clearly" (ἐνέβλεπεν) — would seem excessive even though the imperfect tense of the third verb advances the thought to continued seeing. More likely is a progression from opening the eyes wide (perhaps as a result of Jesus' prying the eyelids farther apart) to restoration of capability and finally to exercise of that capability. In Arist. *Insomn.* 462A διαβλέπω cannot mean clear sight, because darkness prevents seeing even when the eyes are wide open. In Plut. *Mor.* 973F διαβλέπω means opening the eyes wide after drugged sleep; in Luc. *Mer. Cond.* 22, after waking up early in the morning (despite the LCL translation by A. M. Harmon). In Plut. *Alex.* 14.2, Diogenes has been lying in the sun. Presumably his eyes have been closed or half-closed, but he opens them wide when Alexander approaches and shades him from the sun. Dion. Com. 2.13 uses διαβλέπω for the wide-eyed vision necessary for a general to see all that is happening on a battlefield. Phld. *Vol. Rhet.* 19.7 has to do with an owl's widely opened eyes, glowing in the dark. The meaning in Pl. *Phd.* 86D is probably that of opening the eyes wide as a characteristic facial expression. In the part of *PLond.* 418. 19 where διαβλέπω occurs, mutilation of the papyrus and obscurity of language forestall a clear interpretation (so the editor F. G. Kenyon, *Greek Papyri* 2. 302). In Luke 6:42 par. Matt 7:5 par. *POxy.* 1. 26, διαβλέπω could mean the opening of an eye wide after removal of a wooden beam that caused it to be squintedly closed.

Often ἐμβλέπω occurs in passages that include rational insight, but Acts 1:11 is enough to show that such insight attaches to the word only by context. Its basic meaning is "look intently, gaze, stare." W. L. Lane (285, n. 51) sees a progression from looking up (ἀναβλέψας) to opening the eyes wide (διέβλεψεν) and getting a clear view of everything (ἐνέβλεπεν). But this interpretation suffers from the separation of the second and third verbs from the first verb, and from the intervention between the second and third verbs of ἀπεκατέστη, "was restored," which Lane does not take into account. Nor does he take into account βλέπω and ὁρῶ in the man's own words, which come between the first and second verbs that Lane does deal with.

R. Bultmann (*HST* 213) thinks that because of correspondence with 2:11; 5:19, Jesus' sending the ex-blind man home (v 26a) marks the original ending of the story. But in neither 2:11 nor 5:19 did the command to go home end the story. According to S. Eitrem (*Some Notes* 58-59), Jesus sends the ex-blind man home to avoid evil spirits in the crowded village. But the story has not attributed the blindness to demonic influence, and evil spirits lurk in lonely places more than in crowded villages. Since the blind man lived at home prior to his healing, his home can hardly represent a house church which he ought to join rather than going back to non-Christian associations represented by the village, which he is not supposed to enter (against E. Best, *Following Jesus* 139, n. 20). The argument of B. M. Metzger (*Textual Commentary* ad loc.) for the commonly accepted reading in v 26b μηδὲ εἰς τὴν κώμην εἰσέλθῃς is stronger than arguments for other readings by C. H. Turner (in *JTS* os 26 [1924-25] 18), J. K. Elliott (in *NT Textual Criticism* 58), and J. M. Ross (in *NovT* 29 [1987] 97-99). The v.l. μή, "not," in ℵ* W stems from uneasiness with the emphatic force of μηδέ, "not even" (against J. I. Miller in *NovT* 28 [1986] 97-103).

We hear no acclamation at the close of vv 22-26, because Jesus has performed the miracle outside the village, within eyeshot of the people in it but at a distance that keeps them from telling immediately whether a miracle has occurred. The falseness of the identifications of Jesus in v 28 will destroy the parallel seen by R. H. Lightfoot (*History and Interpretation* 90-91) between v 24 and that verse. Here, partial sight compares human beings to trees but does not falsely identify them as trees. The breakdown of this parallel spoils the parallelistic structure that Lightfoot sees throughout the rest of vv 23-26 and vv 27-30, i.e. between vv 23 and 27, vv 25 and 29, and vv 26 and 30.

JESUS' POWER TO PREDICT HIS OWN FATE
AND THAT OF OTHERS

8:27–9:1 (Matt 16:13-28; Luke 9:18-27; John 6:67-71; 12:25)

A confession of Jesus as the Christ takes up the first section of this pericope (8:27-30), which subdivides into the notation of a topographical shift (v 27a), Jesus' asking who people say he is (v 27b), the disciples' answer (v 28), Jesus' asking the disciples who they say he is (v 29a), Peter's answer (v 29b), and Jesus' command to tell no one (v 30). The next section contains Jesus' teaching about himself (8:31-33) and subdivides into the necessity of his passion and resurrection (vv 31), his outspokenness (v 32a), Peter's rebuking him (v 32b), and his rebuking Peter (v 33). The last section deals with discipleship (8:34–9:1). First, Jesus issues a summons to self-sacrifice (8:34), then a rationale for it (8:35-38), and finally a promise (9:1).

Most outstandingly, this pericope is loaded with predictions. The initial section sets the stage for the first of Jesus' several predictions concerning his own fate. That prediction leads to predictions of others' losing life by wanting to save it, saving it by losing it, incurring future shame by being ashamed now, and not dying till seeing the rule of God. This outburst of predictive energy will carry through the rest of the the gospel and add an important element to Mark's apology for the Cross (cf. prediction and fulfilment already in 1:17 and 6:7-13, 30).

8:27-28 *(Matt 16:13-14; Luke 9:18-19)* Jesus went out of Bethsaida (cf. vv 22-26). Though ἐξῆλθεν, "went out," is singular, Mark adds Jesus' disciples because of their importance in the following dialogue (cf. 1:36; 3:31a for two earlier examples of this grammatical phenomenon — also the genitive absolute at 10:46). "Into the villages of Philip's Caesarea" strikes an odd expression. We would have expected "the region of Philip's Caesarea" after the pattern of 5:1, 17; 7:24, 31; 8:10. In fact, Matthew changes the wording to read "into the region [τὰ μέρη — literally, 'the parts'] of Philip's Caesarea"; and here in Mark the texts of D and the Old Latin simply omit the reference to villages. Luke makes a substitution for the whole expression. Mark is apparently referring to villages in the vicinity of the Caesarea built by Herod Philip about twenty-five miles north of the Sea of Galilee, as distinguished from Caesarea on the Mediterranean coast and to the south. The mention of villages links this pericope with the preceding one, which had its setting in a village (vv 22-26); but the awkwardness of the expression as a whole, the unexpectedness of the reference to Philip's Caesarea, and its lying in the opposite direction from Jerusalem, to which the following materials point, argue for the historicity for the topographical setting.

"On the road" takes a forward position to emphasize that the following dialogue does not take place in a village and thus to prepare for Peter's taking Jesus aside and especially for Jesus' references to following behind him (vv 33, 34; cf. 10:32-34). Ἐπηρώτα, "he was asking," forges a verbal link with ἐπηρώτα in v 23. The unnecessary repetition of "his disciples" (the simple pronoun "them" would have sufficed — cf. "him" in v 23) sets the stage for a distinction between the disciples and others (cf. the comments on v 29). Ἐπερωτάω usually gets no help in Mark (see 5:9; 7:5; 8:23, 29; 9:16, 21, 28, 33; 10:2, 17; 12:28; 13:3; 15:2; exceptions at 8:27; 9:11; 12:18; 14:60; 15:4). Here, however, "saying to them" adds further stage-setting for a distinction between the disciples and others, about whose opinion Jesus asks first: "Whom do the people (οἱ ἄνθρωποι) say I am?" "The people" echoes v 24 and just possibly refers by context to those who brought the blind man (v 22) and whom he saw on receiving sight. If so, the definite article is anaphoric (as in v 24; cf. also v 33). The advancement of με, "I," away from its infinitive εἶναι, "am," and ahead of the verb λέγουσιν, "say," stresses the figure of Jesus.

"But they spoke to him, saying" parallels the introduction to Jesus' question. The adversative δέ, "but," distinguishes the disciples from the people about whose opinion Jesus has asked them. The distinction prepares for a different opinion on the part of the disciples (v 29). א* B C*vid pc read ὅτι before Ἰωάννην, "John." To the rest of the textual tradition, it probably seems unnecessary after λέγοντες, "saying," and potentially confusing in advance of the ὅτι before εἷς τῶν προφητῶν, "one of the prophets" — potentially confusing because it might seem to set up a parallel between the first two opinions and the third opinion. It does not set up such a parallel, however. Though both ὅτι's are recitative, the first one introduces Mark's direct quotation of the disciples' answer, the second one the disciples' direct quotation of the people's third opinion (their first and second opinions having been quoted indirectly by the disciples). From the context of Jesus' question we may easily fill in the ellipses in the disciples' answer: "[Some say you to be] John the Baptist, and others [say you to be] Elijah, but others [say, 'He is] one of the prophets.'" The accusatives Ἰωάννην τὸν βαπτιστήν and Ἠλίαν parallel the accusative subject με of the infinitive εἶναι in Jesus' foregoing question (also in his following question — v 29). Therefore the same infinitive is implied in the disciples' response. The recitative ὅτι in v 28a favors another ὅτι of the same kind in v 28b. The resultant switch to direct discourse, a switch highlighted by another δέ, entails a switch from second person ("you are") to third ("he is" — cf. 6:14-15), since the people quoted directly were not speaking to Jesus as the disciples are speaking to him when they quote the people indirectly. An epexegetic ὅτι, "that," would carry on the implied second person. The use of ellipsis despite the switch from indirect to direct discourse gives to the people's identifications of Jesus the appearance of a list.

The same three popular identifications of Jesus appeared in the same order in 6:14-15 (cf. John 1:19-23). There, the implication of a resurrection of John the

Baptizer was spelled out; and "a prophet like (ὡς) one of the prophets" implied the opinion that Jesus is another in the line of prophets. Here, the lack of "a prophet like" and the resultant closer parallel with John and Elijah seem to imply the opinion that Jesus is another returned prophet (cf. H. Braun, *Qumran* 1. 68, against an identification of Jesus as the eschatological prophet spoken of in 1QS 9:10-11; 4QTestim 5-8). None of the popular identifications rise to the height of Jesus' true person and work.

8:29-30 *(Matt 16:15-20; Luke 9:20-21; John 6:67-71)* The emphatic αὐτός, "he himself," suggests that Jesus stands apart from the just-mentioned popular identifications of him. They are wrong. Again ἐπηρώτα, "was asking," recalls the preceding pericope (cf. the comments on v 27). The strong ὑμεῖς, "you," distinguishes the disciples from "the people" mentioned in v 27. Hence, δέ is adversative: "but." Again με, "I," advances ahead of the verb and away from its infinitive to emphasize the figure of Jesus. In introducing Peter's answer to Jesus' question who the disciples say he is, Mark uses asyndeton, adds "answering," and uses the historical present tense in "he says" (in all three respects contrast v 28a) to stress the following confession: "You are the Christ." We can see the importance that Mark attaches to this confession in his having incorporated "Christ" into the very first phrase of his gospel (1:1; see also 9:41; 14:61-62). Here, the definite article makes a slight contrast with 1:1; 9:41 and brings out the titular meaning, "the Anointed One" (cf. 14:61-62). Mark wants to establish this office of Jesus before citing the prediction of Jesus' passion and resurrection.

The first section of the pericope ends with a command so stern that Mark writes ἐπετίμησεν, "he rebuked." He uses this verb nine times throughout his book, but only in 3:12; 10:48 and the present passage does ἵνα follow it. We may doubt that 10:48 influences the usage before us, for Mark has yet to write that verse. Besides, at 10:48 the verb will not have Jesus as its subject, as it does here. But at 3:12 the verb did have him as its subject. Furthermore, 3:12 followed a declaration that he is the Son of God, just as 8:30 follows a declaration that he is the Christ (cf. the combination of "Jesus," "Christ," and "Son of God" in 1:1); and at 3:12 the rebuke consisted of a stern command not to make him known as God's Son, just as at 8:30 the rebuke consists in a stern command to be telling no one about his being the Christ. Hence, our understanding of 8:30 should follow the lead of 3:12. There, ἐπιτιμάω stressed the gravity of a command that Jesus issued in order that crowds might not throng him even more dangerously than they were already doing. So also here, the phraseology stresses the gravity of a command that he issues in order that crowds might not throng him. But this time his ultimate purpose is not to avoid being crushed to death, but to gain privacy for predicting his passion and resurrection (vv 31-33; 9:14-15, 25, and esp. 30-31; 10:32-34). The crowds have been bothersome and dangerous enough even under their views that he is John the Baptist, Elijah, or one of the prophets (see not only 3:7-12, but also 1:35-37, 45; 2:1-2; 3:20; 4:1; 6:31-33; 7:24; 9:9, 25, 30). What would they do if they believed him to be the Christ, God's Son? In 3:12 ἵνα seemed to indicate not only, and perhaps not mainly, the content of the rebuke (epexegetic ἵνα), but its purpose and result (telic and ecbatic in combination for achieved purpose). So also here.

Despite their belief in the messiahship of Jesus, the disciples will obey his command by not telling anyone for the rest of the gospel. He does not have to overcome them as he had to overcome the unclean spirits; so the emphatic locution at the start of 3:12 — viz., the forwardly positioned adverbial πολλά, "much," plus the iteratively imperfect ἐπετίμα, "he was [repeatedly] rebuking" (cf. 3:11) — is here toned down to an unenhanced aorist. On the other hand, Mark wants the last accent in this part of the pericope to fall on the effectiveness of Jesus' rebuke. So strongly does Mark want this accent for its demonstration of Jesus' authority that he does not even say whether Jesus accepts the designation "the Christ." We have to infer that he does from his command not to tell, just as we will have to infer from the next section that he radically modifies the usual Jewish expectations of the Christ by predicting his passion and resurrection. The shift from "the Christ" to "the Son of man" is what makes the modification an inference on our part rather than an outright statement on Mark's or Jesus' part.

8:31-32a *(Matt 16:21; Luke 9:22)* Jesus' further words require a new introduction, because they carry no rebuke such as the preceding words were described as carrying (v 30). Hence, the new introduction need not imply the importing of an originally detached tradition or a Marcan fabrication. Nonetheless, the new introduction sports a characteristically Marcan pleonastic καὶ ἤρξατο, "and he began" (see the notes on 1:45). In view of the authority which Jesus' teaching connotes in Mark (see esp. 1:21-28) and in view of the following prediction of his passion and resurrection (the first of several such predictions — see esp. 9:30-32; 10:32-34, but also 9:9, 12; 14:8, 17-25, 41-42), "to teach them" shows that Mark is emphasizing the predictive power of Jesus (cf. "he was teaching" in 9:31). A probably recitative ὅτι (see the following notes) intensifies this emphasis. The didactic forecasting helps take the sting out of Jesus' passion (cf. John 2:18-19 and forecasting the circumstances of one's own death as indicative of divine power in the Greco-Roman world — see, e.g., Philo *Mos.* 2.51 §§290-91; Suet. *Dom.* 15.3; Iambl. *VP* 136; D. E. Aune, *Prophecy* 178; A. B. Kolenkow in *ANRW* II 23/2. 1494; and, more generally, B. Blackburn, *Theios Anēr* 15-23, 76-77 et passim).

That Jesus' fate "is necessary" makes it a matter of God's plan as well as of Jesus' foreknowledge (cf. 9:11; 13:7, 10). Now *all* the sting is removed. Neither Aramaic nor Hebrew has a construction corresponding to δεῖ plus an infinitive. The Greek construction does occur, however, for Semitic statements concerning what will happen or ought to happen (cf. the MT, LXX, and Theod of Lev 5:17; 2 Kgs [4 Kgdms] 4:13-14; Isa 30:29; Dan 2:28, 45). Hence, Mark's use of the construction does not imply a lack of underlying Semitic tradition (cf. W. J. Bennett, Jr., in *NovT* 17 [1975] 119). He uses it for its apologetic value in stressing the necessity of Jesus' passion and resurrection: they will happen on good purpose.

The shift from "the Christ" (v 29) to "the Son of man" (cf. esp. 9:9, 12, 31; 10:33) is probably due to Jesus' liking the latter phrase for oblique reference to himself (see the notes on 2:10), perhaps due also to the strangeness of suffering to the prevailing notions of messiahship (but cf. the context of suffering around Dan 7:13, which provides background for his use of "the Son of man"). Apart from these possible reasons, which are easily attributable to Jesus, there seems to be no redactional reason for Mark to have made the shift. Indeed, the emphasis on authority and lordship in the preceding two references to Jesus as the Son of man (2:10, 28) and Mark's special interest in Jesus' authority and lordship would probably have inclined Mark away from making a redactional shift that would bring "the Son of man" into association with suffering.

Though "the Son of man" favors an underlying Semitic, Jesuanic tradition, some have thought that πολλὰ παθεῖν, "to suffer much," cannot be naturally retroverted into Aramaic or Hebrew. Yet it occurs often in Hellenistic Greek (see, e.g., Hom. *Od.* 5.223; Hdt. 9.37; Plut. *Per.* 34; Josephus *Ant.* 13.9.3 §268; 13.15.5 §403; Matt 27:19; *Barn.* 7:11) and twice elsewhere in Mark (5:26 [editorial]; 9:12; cf. the notes on 1:45 concerning Mark's predilection for the adverbial πολλά, which is therefore to be preferred here over a πολλά of direct object, "many things"). So Mark may insert the phrase to excite sympathy by characterizing the Son of man's being rejected and killed as much suffering. On the other hand, *Tg. Ket.* Prov 26:10 offers a possible Aramaic substratum (סגי חייש). The same or a similar Hebrew or Aramaic phrase seems to underlie *As. Mos.* 3:11, whose extant Latin is generally agreed to rest on a Semitic substratum. Therefore πολλὰ παθεῖν in Mark 8:31 may likewise rest on a Semitic substratum, one that goes back to Jesus himself. Though the word order here and in 5:26; 9:12 occurs in some of the Hellenistic texts, it also corresponds to the word order in the targumic text (see D. Meyer in *ZNW* 55 [1964] 132). The forward position of "much" emphasizes intensity of suffering. The supposed chronological problem that suffering should follow rejection disappears if much suffering includes both rejection and killing (cf. H. F. Bayer, *Jesus' Predictions* 180). But chronology is not on Mark's mind. He puts πολλὰ παθεῖν in its forward position to stress the pathos that will make his audience react with sympathy rather than disgust at Jesus' coming crucifixion. Ἀποδοκιμασθῆναι, "to be rejected," is sometimes regarded as a non-Jesuanic Christian borrowing from Ps 117:22 LXX, as in Mark 12:10 (cf. Acts 4:11; 1 Pet 2:4, 7). But ἀπεδοκίμασαν (so the LXX) corresponds nicely to מָאֲסוּ (Ps 118:22 MT); so it is gratuitous to deny that Jesus used the psalmic passage and that his use led to later Christian use.

Just as the apparent lack of a redactional reason for the shift from "the Christ" to "the Son of man" favored Mark's drawing on tradition, so also the contrast between the first position of the elders here and the first position of the chief priests wherever Mark mentions these classes and the scribes in editorial statements (11:27; 14:43, 53; 15:11 — the only other Marcan passages where the three classes appear together) and his failure to mention crucifixion as the mode of Jesus' death speak in favor of Mark's drawing on tradition, indeed on authentic tradition (so also in 9:31; 10:34). The occurrence of "crucify" and "cross" no fewer than ten times in the passion-and-resurrection narrative (15:13, 14, 15, 20, 21, 24, 25, 27, 30; 16:6) and the summons to cross-taking in the immediate context here (8:34) — a summons that might well have induced an inventive Mark to specify crucifixion as the mode of Jesus' death — strengthen the argument for tradition and authenticity instead of fabrication. The same argument obtains with

respect to ἀναστῆναι, "to rise up" (so also 9:9-10, 31; 10:34). For in the passion-
and-resurrection narrative and in the tradition cited earlier than Mark in 1 Cor
15:4, only the different verb ἐγείρω will occur in the passive for Jesus' resurrection
(see 14:28; 16:6; also many passages in later but sometimes pre-Marcan parts of
the NT, esp. Rom 6:4; 1 Cor 15:12, 13, 14, 16, 17, and 20 with 15 and with
1 Thess 1:10). Were Mark or someone before him fabricating the predictions out
of the narrative or out of earlier tradition that fed into it, we would expect him
to use the verb that is going to appear in the narrative. (It would be Procrustean
to maintain the inauthenticity of the predictions by attributing ἀναστῆναι to a
pre-Marcan but inauthentic tradition that did *not* feed into the narrative.) And if
Mark or someone before him were using ἀναστῆναι in fabricated predictions to
stress Jesus' power and authority (N. Perrin in *Christology and a Modern Pilgrimage* 26-27, et al.) we would expect the same verb to replace ἐγείρω in the
passion-and-resurrection narrative.

For a number of reasons the same argument obtains yet again with respect
to "after three days" (μετὰ τρεῖς ἡμέρας), whose forward position apologetically
stresses the quickness with which Jesus will rise after being killed (see also 9:31;
10:34): (1) neither Mark nor the tradition that he adopts will bother to note when
the Resurrection occurs, only when the tomb is discovered empty (16:1-7; cf.
M. J. Harris, *Raised Immortal* 12). (2) The apparent discrepancy between "after
three days" (cf. Matt 27:63 with Matt 12:40) and the discovery of Jesus' tomb as
empty already on the Sunday morning following the preceding Friday on which
he was killed makes Marcan or pre-Marcan fabrication unlikely. (3) By showing
that others noticed and eliminated the apparent discrepancy, the shift to "on the
third day" (τῇ τρίτῃ ἡμέρᾳ or τῇ ἡμέρᾳ τῇ τρίτῃ) in Matt 16:21; 17:23; 20:19; Luke
9:22; 18:33; 24:7, 46; Acts 10:40 v.l. and already before Mark in 1 Cor 15:4
favors that Mark is following authentic tradition; for if he is not, he or someone
before him was thoughtless in creating the apparent discrepancy. (The lack of ἐν
in these other passages disfavors influence from Hos 6:2 MT LXX.) (4) That
building a temple "through three days" (διὰ τριῶν ἡμερῶν — 14:58) equates with
building it "in three days" (ἐν τρισὶν ἡμέραις — 15:29) exhibits a variation in
phraseology which shows that Mark could have avoided the apparent discrepancy
if authentic tradition were not influencing him. (5) The lack of theological elaboration, such as "according to the scriptures," "for our sins," "from the dead," etc.
(1 Cor 6:14; 15:3, 20, 23; Luke 24:25-27; Acts 2:32-33; 5:31), and of reference
to Jesus' heavenly exaltation, such as we read in early Christian preaching and
teaching (Acts 2:32-33; 5:31; 10:40-43; Rom 8:34; Eph 1:20-22; Heb 10:12; 1 Pet
3:22; Rev 3:21; 22:1), speaks yet further against Marcan or pre-Marcan fabrication
(Harris, op. cit. 67). Theological elaboration began earlier than Mark; so a fabrication would likely include it. (One might think that the scheme of death and
resurrection reflects later Christian development of the exaltation-motif, but the
presence of the scheme in pre-Pauline tradition [1 Cor 15:3-5] undermines such
thinking and preserves the argument that lack of reference to Jesus' heavenly
exaltation speaks against Marcan or pre-Marcan fabrication.)

Mark's point comes out in the comment καὶ παρρησίᾳ τὸν λόγον ἐλάλει, "and he was speaking the word outspokenly." The phraseological closeness to 2:2b (καὶ ἐλάλει αὐτοῖς τὸν λόγον) tags the comment as probably editorial. The addition of παρρησίᾳ, its placement in first position after the conjunction, and the advance of τὸν λόγον to second position, ahead of the verb, put great weight on the point that Jesus really did teach the disciples beforehand about his passion and resurrection. Mark's audience can be absolutely sure that Jesus was not taken by surprise, that those events happened by design.

EXCURSUS ON THE CLASSES OF THE SANHEDRIN WITH REFERENCE TO JESUS' PASSION

The great Sanhedrin in Jerusalem was the Jewish supreme council. According to Mark, it consisted of three classes: the chief priests, the scribes, and the elders. Throughout the latter half of Mark these classes appear variously with reference to Jesus' passion. The variety with which they appear might be set down to different traditions, deliberate redaction, or a combination thereof. In any case, a rationale does seem to govern the variety (against J. D. Kingsbury [in *NTS* 36 (1990) 42-65], who thinks that Mark presents the Jewish leaders as a united front against Jesus without distinguishing their roles).

Chief priests–scribes–elders probably represents a descending order of officialness and influence. Mention of all three classes suits the first passion prediction in 8:31, especially the reference in it to Jesus' being rejected. But the elders appear first (and in that position here alone) because of the Pharisees' and scribes' recent appeal to the elders (7:3, 5). In 10:33 the elders drop out to leave the chief priests in first place, since they will take the lead in dealing with the Gentiles, of which this passion prediction speaks (cf. 15:3, 10, 11). It is also the only passion prediction to speak of Jerusalem; so on Jesus' arrival in Jerusalem 11:18 naturally repeats "the chief priests and the scribes" from 10:33 in relating that they were seeking how they might destroy him. In 11:27 the elders reappear, but in third position now that the leading position of the chief priests has been established. The reappearance of the elders lends a wholeness to the Sanhedrin (cf. 14:53, 55). This wholeness suits the nature of 11:27-33 as a grand jury proceeding in which they challenge Jesus' authority to cleanse the temple (again cf. 7:3, 5, where the elders represent authority). The proceeding will eventuate in his arrest (see 14:43, the only other passage where all three classes occur in this order).

To echo 11:18, where the chief priests and the scribes were seeking how to destroy Jesus, "the chief priests and the scribes" reappears in 14:1, where these two classes "were seeking how they might kill [him] after seizing him with cunning." In 14:10 the chief priests appear alone because they have charge of the temple money with which to strike a bargain with Judas Iscariot. In 14:43 the order chief priests–scribes–elders echoes 11:27 because Jesus is being arrested as the outcome of the grand jury proceeding in 11:27-33. Its being the first hearing in his trial makes appropriate at 14:53 the mention of each of the three classes, beginning with the chief priests, to whom Judas bargained to give Jesus over. The addition of "all" and the advance to second position of the elders, who are mentioned least often, emphasize the wholeness of the Sanhedrin for this official proceeding. Likewise in 14:55, which picks up the thought of 14:53 after a short digression to Peter in 14:54, we read of "the chief priests and the whole Sanhedrin."

For the continuation and completion of the Sanhedrin's deliberation after dawn, 15:1 echoes the order in 14:53 at the start of their deliberation, but with a subordination of the elders and scribes and an omission of the definite article from the latter ("with the elders and scribes"), because the chief priests on account of their position are about to act alone in dealing with the Roman governor Pilate. And so they do, and are mentioned without reference to the other classes, in 15:3, 10, 11. In 15:11 they use the crowd to influence Pilate. Finally, in 15:31 the scribes reappear alongside the chief priests to echo 10:33-34, where these two classes were paired and where ἐμπαίζω, "mock," occurred, though there for what the Gentiles were going to do, here for what the chief priests and scribes do in imitation of the Gentiles to whom they have given Jesus over (cf. 15:20). But 15:31 subordinates the scribes ("with the scribes"), because the chief priests have been acting alone in dealing with Pilate, a Gentile.

8:32b-33 (Matt 16:22-23) Peter's reaction now confirms that Jesus really did teach the disciples beforehand about his passion and resurrection. By taking Jesus aside (προσλαβόμενος — literally, "taking [Jesus] to [another place]" as distinct from ἀπολαβόμενος αὐτόν, "taking him away," in 7:33 and ἐπιλαβόμενος, "taking hold on," in 8:23), Peter for the moment stops being a disciple; for disciples follow behind their teacher at a little distance (see esp. 1:17-18, 20; 2:14; 6:1, 31; 8:34; 10:21, 28, 32, 52). Peter compounds his error by rebuking Jesus; for only Jesus has the authority to rebuke his disciples, not they him (see v 30). Mark's omitting to indicate what Peter says in rebuking Jesus shows that for Mark the center of gravity does not lie in what Peter's words might reveal about his motive (as, for example, that he takes Jesus aside so as not to embarrass him before the other disciples) or about his opinion (as, for example, that the Christ is destined for rulership, not for passion and resurrection). It lies rather in the outspokenness of Jesus' prediction, as indicated by the reaction of Peter, an outspokenness that adds to the apologetic force of the prediction. Contrastively, Matt 16:22b and sy⁵ c k here in Mark make up for Mark's omission. The pleonastic use of ἤρξατο, "he began," echoes v 31 (again see the notes on 1:45).

Jesus' turning and seeing his disciples points up that they are following behind him, as disciples do, but that Peter is not among them and therefore is not acting as a disciple. An adversative δέ, "but," highlights this contrast and the following rebuke of Peter. Jesus' rebuking him shows who really has the authority to engage in rebuke. Especially after the aorist ἐπετίμησεν, "he rebuked," the jarring historical present tense of λέγει, "he says," and its coordinated finite rather than conjunctive participial form underline the importance of the rebuke: "Get behind me, Satan, because you are not thinking the things of God; rather, [you are thinking] the things of human beings." Jesus tells Peter to go back (ὕπαγε ὀπίσω) to his position among the disciples, where he belongs, following after Jesus (cf. 2 Kgs [4 Kgdms] 9:19), not taking him aside by walking ahead of him or at least beside him. The outspokenness with which Jesus predicted his passion and resurrection justifies this rebuke of Peter. The scriptural and therefore divine necessity of Jesus' passion and resurrection (see δεῖ in v 31) justifies the shocking epithet, "Satan." By itself the epithet means either that Peter is acting like Satan, a tempter (cf. 1:13), or that Satan is inhabiting and using him to tempt Jesus (cf. 3:22, 30 with 3:23, 26; also 1QS 3:17-23; 4:9-11). But Satan does not think human things, as Peter does; and the epithet looks similar to a nickname — yet nicknames deal in analogy (as does "Peter," Simon's new name meaning "stone" [cf. 3:16 and see C. C. Caragounis, *Peter and the Rock*]), not in identification. So the epithet merely compares Peter with Satan. Merely? The comparison is so damaging that it frighteningly highlights the seriousness of allowing oneself to be scandalized by Jesus' passion.

Context dictates that "the things of God" be the divinely necessitated suffering, rejection, killing, and resurrection of the Son of man. To think them is to take their side (so the meaning of φρονεῖς τά). Because of the epithet "Satan" we expect to read about "the things of Satan" by way of contrast; instead, we read about "the things of human beings," which context dictates be an expectation that leaves no room for passion and resurrection on the part of the Christ. The strength of the adversative ἀλλά, "rather," and the vigor of the following ellipsis of φρονεῖς underscore the contrast between the things of God and the things of human beings. Those who identify Jesus with John the Baptist, with Elijah, with one of the prophets (vv 27-28) do not join Peter in confessing Jesus as the Christ. But he shares their notion of the Christ's glory first, last, and always. Only by getting behind Jesus in the position of a follower can one think the things of God, i.e. take sides with Jesus' prediction of his fate. Throughout these verses Peter's failure to think the things of God makes a foil that sets off the accuracy of Jesus' prediction.

8:34-38 *(Matt 16:24-27; Luke 9:23-26; John 12:25; cf. Matt 10:32-33, 38-39; Luke 12:8-9; 14:27; 17:33)* That the disciples accompany the summoned crowd shows that in v 33 Jesus did not turn around and look at the disciples to rebuke Peter for their benefit. We have no reason to think that they even heard what he said to Peter. On the contrary, Peter's taking him aside indicates a private conversation apart from the disciples. The turning around and seeing them ("seeing" is better than "looking at" for ἰδών) was to differentiate Peter from the disciples. Jesus' summoning the crowd along with his disciples exemplifies his authority (see the comments on 3:13). The presence of a crowd revives emphasis on his magnetism. This emphasis overpowers any sense of need that Mark might feel to indicate where the crowd comes from. The summoning of the crowd shows that the subsequent sayings do not tell disciples how to continue following Jesus.

Instead, they tell non-disciples how to start following him. The sayings do not get the emphasis that Mark gave to accepting rather than rejecting Jesus' passion and resurrection. He introduced that emphasis with two verbs of speaking, the strong verb ἐπετίμησεν, "rebuked," and the vivid historical present λέγει, "says." The sayings at hand get only a colorless εἶπεν, "said." In Mark, discipleship plays second fiddle to Christology. The command to follow interests Mark mainly as a contribution to his apology for the Cross, in particular, as an indication of Jesus' ability to predict his followers' as well as his own fate and as a warning not to be ashamed of his fate, but to be so unashamed as to risk sharing it.

The sayings are bound together by catchwords, similarities of grammatical structure, and connections of thought. In vv 34 and 35 εἰ τις θέλει, "if anyone wants," and ὅς . . . ἐὰν θέλῃ, "whoever would want," correspond to each other. Each saying in vv 35-38 starts with γάρ, "for." The repeated γάρ makes each of these sayings a reason to obey the command in v 34, but the reasons build one on another till they reach a climax in a saying on the last judgment. Ὃς γὰρ ἐάν, "for whoever," in the first reason (v 35) corresponds to the same phrase in the fourth reason (v 38). Repeated references to τὴν ψυχὴν αὐτοῦ, "his life," and to saving or gaining it and losing or forfeiting it link the first three reasons together (vv 35-37). The middle two reasons (vv 36 and 37) take an interrogative form, both starting with τί γάρ, "For in what way . . . ? For what . . . ?" and are flanked by futuristic statements of warning-cum-promise (v 35) and sheer warning (v 38). The commercial language of the two questions grows out of the commercial language of the warning-cum-promise, and the topic of shame in the sheer warning grows out of the topic of shame in the second question. Though set apart by an introductory formula, 9:1 corresponds to 8:38 by way of following up a warning with a promise (cf. the warning-cum-promise in v 35) and by virtue of the similarity between the coming of the Son of man in the glory of his Father with the holy angels (8:38) and seeing that the rule of God has come with power (9:1). Overall, we see chiasm in (a) . . . τις . . . (8:34); (b) ὃς γάρ . . . ἐμοῦ . . . (8:35); (c) τί γάρ . . . ἄνθρωπον . . . τὴν ψυχὴν αὐτοῦ (8:36); (c′) τί γάρ . . . ἄνθρωπος . . . τῆς ψυχῆς αὐτοῦ (8:37); (b′) ὃς γάρ . . . με . . . ἐμούς . . . (8:38); (a′) . . . τινες . . . (9:1; C. Coulot, *Jésus et le disciple* 47).

If we may suppose that Mark knows a pre-Q form of the saying in v 34 much like that in Luke 14:27 (see R. H. Gundry, *Matthew* 200-201, on redactional changes in Matt 10:38), contextual sense is made of the following treatment by Mark. The shift from negative ("not . . . cannot . . ." — Luke 14:27) to positive ("let him . . .") makes the saying into a command congruent with Jesus' command to Peter in the preceding verse and with Jesus' summoning the crowd in v 34a. The shift from "whoever does" to "if anyone wants to" calls for a voluntary decision suitable to the crowd of non-followers. Jesus' summons is a call to start following. Once again to link up with his preceding command to Peter, "behind me" advances with its infinitive "to follow"; but for added emphasis on the proper position of a disciple, it comes ahead of the infinitive (see the Greek word order in contrast with v 33b, where "behind me" follows its verb). The infinitive of "follow" (so P[45] C* D W Θ 0214 f[1] Majority Text lat sa[mss]) may replace "comes" to emphasize yet further that proper position in contrast with Peter's having taken Jesus aside and perhaps in reminiscence of 1:18. The redundancy in the resultant phrase (following would by itself imply a position behind Jesus; cf. the non-redundant πορεύομαι ὀπίσω in the LXX for הלך אחרי [H. Seesemann in *TDNT* 5. 290] as well as the non-redundant ἔρχεται ὀπίσω μου in Luke 14:27) would put enormous weight on the proper position of a disciple and prompt a non-redundant parallelistic v.l. in א A B C² K L Γ f¹³ 33 892 1241 *al* aur c (k) l bo. Perhaps we should favor the non-redundant v.l. "to come," however, since its presence in the parallels (Matt 16:24 and, with a slight modification, Luke 9:23) may reflect Mark's original text as easily as its presence in some Marcan texts may stem from scribal assimilation to the other synoptics — also since "to follow" may have come about through assimilation to "let him follow" later in the saying. The addition of "let him deny himself" may represent an idiomatic Greek translation of Aramaic behind "hate . . . his own life" (μισεῖ . . . τὴν ψυχὴν ἑαυτοῦ — Luke 14:26; K.-G. Reploh, *Lehrer* 126-27) to prepare for losing one's life in vv 35-37. Thus self-denial means putting one's very life at risk, not psychological selfless-ness, renunciation of family ties, possessions, etc., or asceticism (this last possi-bility being set forth by J. D. M. Derrett in *Alternative Approaches to NT Study* 61-67). There is no need to conjecture a traditional saying, "If anyone wants to follow me, let him deny himself," which Mark blends with the pre-Q tradition represented in Luke 14:27. Contextually oriented redaction of the pre-Q tradition is enough to explain the wording of Mark 8:34. E. Best (*Following Jesus* 34) argues for the independent traditionality of self-denial on the ground that 14:30, 31, 72 contain the verb "deny." But there it refers to Peter's denying Jesus, a far cry from self-denial.

The disciple's cross finally comes in, but with a change of "carry" (βαστάζει) to "take" (ἀράτω) to make cross-taking part of the conversion that Jesus urges on the crowd of non-followers, as opposed to cross-bearing as synonymous with coming behind Jesus in a linear sense (so Luke 14:27). This change links up with the change of a warning into a command. "And let him follow me" progresses to the linear sense of discipleship subsequent to conversion and replaces "cannot be my disciple" for inclusion with the initial "if"-clause. Something of a chiasm results: (a) "If anyone wants to follow behind me," (b) "let him deny himself," (b′) "and let him take up his cross," (a′) "and let him follow me." Wanting to follow and following correspond to each other, as do self-denial and cross-taking. The closing command to follow is not redundant, however; for actual following goes farther than wanting to follow, and a command exceeds a condition.

Self-denial, taking one's cross, and following Jesus all exalt him. He has not predicted that he will be killed by crucifixion, nor will he make such a prediction between now and his passion. The crowd to whom he speaks do not know that he will be killed at all. (Similar things could be said about the context of this saying in Q.) Therefore, "let him take up his cross and follow me" does not mean following Jesus with one's own cross to Jesus' crucifixion. It means no more than exposing oneself to shame and ridicule by following him wherever he goes. But what a powerful metaphor of exposing oneself to shame and ridicule!

For only criminals are condemned to take crosses. Not only has Jesus not said that he has taken a cross, or that he will take one; and not only does he say only that his followers are to take one. But also he will not take his cross even in the passion narrative. Simon of Cyrene will take it (see 15:21-22; contrast John 19:17, where Jesus' carrying his own cross contributes to John's wholesale program of putting Jesus firmly in charge of his own fate). Yet further, Jesus does not speak of his disciples' being *nailed* to crosses, only of their *taking* crosses, i.e. of picking up the horizontal beam. In the Roman world condemned people might be forced to pick up that part of a cross at the beginning of their journey to the place of execution. On the way, others hurl insults at them, spit on them, and make sport of them (cf. the warning against shame in v 38). Though in vv 35-37 death becomes a subsequent possibility, cross-taking means only subjecting yourself to shame, to "the howling, hostile mob" (J. Jeremias, *NT Theology* 1. 242). Since the text refers to a literal following behind Jesus at this very time, prior to his passion (see 10:21, 28, 32, 52; cf. 9:38; 11:9; 1 Kgs 19:20; *t. Pesaḥ.* 1:27; *Midr. Deut.* 31:14 et passim — cited by K. Grobel in *JBL* 60 [1941] 397), taking one's cross can hardly have a literal meaning. Not only has Jesus not taken a cross. Those who follow him from this point on will have taken crosses no more than those who earlier started following him took crosses. Nor *can* they take crosses in a literal sense; for no Roman court of law has condemned them to death by crucifixion (cf. J. C. O'Neill in *Suffering and Martyrdom in the NT* 11-12). Losing one's life will not come into the picture till the sayings in vv 35-37, and there the means of death will remain unspecified.

If we may again suppose that Mark knows a pre-Q form of the saying in v 35, a form much like that in Matt 10:39; Luke 17:33 (cf. John 12:25; W. Rebell in *NTS* 35 [1989] 203-9), contextual sense is made of the following treatment by Mark. He inserts γάρ, a favorite conjunction meaning "for," to make this saying a reason for the command to which he has attached it. If Matthew's ὁ εὑρών, "the one finding," echoes pre-Q tradition behind Mark, the shift to ὅς . . . ἐάν, "whoever," suits Mark's transforming the saying from one about continuance in discipleship to one about deciding whether or not to become a disciple. But Luke 17:33 also has ὅς ἐάν, and both Mark and Luke follow up with a finite verb plus an infinitive and put the object of the infinitive before it. So Mark may use a tradition more like Luke 17:33 than like Matt 10:39 (see R. H. Gundry, *Matthew* 201, for possible redactions by Matthew). Mark replaces "seeks to preserve" (so Luke) or "finding" (so Matthew) with "wants to save" for a link with the "wants to follow," which he inserted in v 34. Again his purpose is to transform the saying from one about continuance in discipleship to one about deciding whether or not to become a disciple. This same replacement shifts the meaning from disciples' preserving or finding their life during the endtime distress (so Matt 10:39; Luke 17:33) to non-disciples' saving their life by not accepting the risk entailed in becoming disciples in the first place (as in the redactional changes at v 34). The adversative δέ, "but," occurs also in Luke but not in Matthew and highlights the antithetic parallelism. In comparison with Luke but not Matthew, Mark supplies "his life" in the second stich for parallelism with the first stich. "For my sake and the gospel's" anchors the saying in the good news that Jesus embodies and preaches (1:15). The substitution of "will save" (σώσει) for "will find" (εὑρήσει — so Matthew) or for "will keep alive" (ζῳογονήσει — so Luke) makes an inclusion with "to save" (σῶσαι) in the first stich (cf. the inclusion using different forms of ἀκολουθέω in v 34) and shifts the meaning from the result of disciples' continuing in discipleship to the result of non-disciples' becoming disciples.

The indicative mood of θέλει in v 34 made for a strong condition: "if anyone really does want to follow behind me." The subjunctive mood of the parallel θέλῃ in v 35 makes for a weak condition: "for whoever would want to save his life." The first condition is to be encouraged — but not the second, for it will lead to its opposite, i.e. to losing your life, trifling it away (see A. Oepke in *TDNT* 1. 394-95 on the underlying Semitic expression אָבַד נַפְשׁוֹ). The verb θέλει/-ῃ, "wants/would want," puts the choice between following behind Jesus and saving your life in terms of desire. But the desire to follow must translate into obedience to the commands to deny yourself, take up your cross, and follow behind Jesus. On the other hand, the mere wishing to save your present life is enough to make you lose it in the age to come, whether or not you succeed in saving it now. The indicative mood appears again on the positive side: "but whoever will lose [ἀπολέσει — 'will in fact lose,' not just 'would want' or 'or be willing to lose'] his life . . . will save it." "For my sake" makes a Christological emphasis attractive to Mark. The collocation of Jesus' sake and the gospel's sake (cf. 10:29; 13:9-10; and 14:6-9, which also has the phrase "the whole world," as does the present passage) shows that the gospel is on its way from being "the gospel of God" (1:15) to being "the gospel of Jesus Christ, Son of God" (1:1). See B. M. Metzger, *Textual Commentary* ad loc., for the retention of "my sake." Jesus does not command his hearers to lose their lives, or even to want to do so; only to deny themselves, take up their crosses, and follow behind him. But if some followers do lose their lives for the sake of Jesus and the gospel, they will save them for the world to come; so they need not worry. Wanting to save your life now has the opposite effect in the world to come and betrays lack of willingness to become a disciple. Emphasizing this maxim is the chiasm of (a) wanting to save your life; (b) losing it; (b') losing your life; and (a') saving it.

The rhetorical question, "For in what way [adverbial τί] does gaining the whole world and forfeiting his life profit a man?" evokes an answer too obvious to be stated except by a commentator: "In no way at all" (cf. *Sentences of Menander* 843: "Nothing is more valuable than [your] life" [Jaekel, p. 81]). So also with regard to the rhetorical question, "For what [τί of direct object] would a man give [as] an exchange for his life?" Implied answer: "Everything he could, even the whole world if he had it." But he cannot — hence the subjunctive mood of δοῖ, "would give." Ψυχή carries alternating connotations of present life and eternal life. Saving your present life results in losing your eternal life. Losing your present life for the sake of Jesus and the gospel results in saving your eternal life. Gaining the whole world is not worth losing your present life, much less your eternal life. And nothing will buy back even your present life, much less your eternal life, once you lose it.

In the declaration that concludes the call to self-sacrificial discipleship, the subjunctive mood reappears lest any encouragement be given to the possibility warned against: "For whoever would be ashamed (ἐπαισχυνθῇ) of me and my words in this adulterous and sinful generation, also the Son of man will be ashamed of him whenever he comes in the glory of his Father with the holy angels" (v 38). If we may yet again suppose that Mark knows a pre-Q form of the saying in v 38, a form much like that in Matt 10:32-33 par. Luke 12:8-9, contextual sense is made of the following treatment by Mark. He omits the confessional half of the saying (Matt 10:32 par. Luke 12:8), because his concern does not have to do with the need of disciples to confess Jesus before non-disciples, but with the need that non-disciples not allow shame to keep them from becoming disciples in the first place. Γάρ, "for," replaces δέ, "but" (Matt 10:33 par. Luke 12:9), because omission of the confessional half has led to loss of the original antithetic parallel between confessing and denying. Rationale replaces parallelism. Mark's ὅς . . . ἐάν, "whoever," plus an aorist subjunctive verb carries over from pre-Q tradition or slightly modifies pre-Q's ὅς plus a future indicative verb (cf. Matt 10:33 with Luke 12:8 and see H. Fleddermann in *SBL 1987 Seminar Papers* 609-10). "Is ashamed of me" replaces "denies me" because of Mark's transforming this half of the saying from one concerning a disciple who denies Jesus to one concerning a non-disciple who is ashamed to become a disciple (cf. the same transformation in preceding sayings). Mark adds "and my words" (cf. 8:35; 10:29). This addition interprets being ashamed of Jesus as being scandalized by his recently spoken prediction of the Passion and Resurrection (v 31). It also sets up a parallel between "me and my words" (v 38) and "me and the gospel" (v 35). Of course, the present audience have not heard the prediction of Jesus' passion and resurrection; but though taking up your cross may cause shame to come on you, the words he has spoken to the crowd (vv 34-37) are not themselves possible objects of shame, as are the words predicting his passion and resurrection. The inconcinnity of a different audience is due to Mark's importing the saying into a new context, with the result that at this point we should interpret his text literally rather than historically. The addition of "my" changes "the word" in the sense of "the saying" (v 32) to "the words" that make up the saying (see also 10:24; 13:31). The emphatic possessive adjective ἐμούς, "my," modifying "words," stresses Jesus as predictor of his own fate (cf. Mark's general emphasis on the authority of Jesus' teaching, starting in 1:21-28). "In this adulterous and sinful generation" replaces "in front of people" because of the shift from a special, formal occasion on which a disciple has to confess or deny Jesus before onlookers (probably before a human tribunal in synagogue or court) to an informal occasion on which a non-disciple has to decide whether to become a disciple in the midst of people whose wickedness will lead them to abuse him in everyday life if he does become a disciple (cf. the comments on taking up your cross — v 34). The description "adulterous and sinful" highlights this newly envisioned occasion (cf. 9:19; Isa 57:3; Jer 3:1–4:2; 13:27; Ezekiel 16, 23; Hosea 1–3; 5:3-4; Luke 9:41; 11:29; Matt 12:39, 45; 16:4; 17:17; Acts 2:40; Phil 2:15; Jas 4:4). Casus pendens carries over from the pre-Q tradition and highlights the danger of being ashamed of Jesus and his words.

"The Son of man" probably reflects the pre-Q form known to Mark and implied for this half of the saying by Luke 12:8 but omitted in Luke 12:9 either for literary reasons or to alleviate the apparent discrepancy with the forgivableness of speaking a word against the Son of man (Luke 12:10; cf. P. Vielhauer, *Aufsätze* 101-2; H. Fleddermann in *SBL 1987 Seminar Papers* 610-12). The position of the phrase before the verb of which it is the subject sets up a parallel with the first half of the saying, where the subjective relative pronoun naturally preceded its verb. "Will be ashamed of him" replaces "will deny him" for parallelism with an earlier, similar change. The reason for the earlier change requires that "will be ashamed of him" mean "will disown him." Pre-Q's "the Son of man" and "before the angels of God" (cf. Luke 12:9) remind Mark of sayings that he will use in 13:26-27. These sayings describe the Son of man's coming with much power (cf. 9:1) and glory (cf. 10:37) and sending out angels. A reference to God as Father of the Son will follow several verses later (13:32). Mark borrows this phraseology to shift from the last assize of disciples to the judgment that will fall on non-disciples at the Son of man's coming (cf. G. R. Beasley-Murray in *RevExp* 75 [1978] 565-72). The shift results in a warning to non-disciples lest they allow shame over Jesus and his words to keep them from becoming disciples. Heightening this warning is the overall parallelism between the two halves of the saying ("whoever" — "the Son of man"; "is ashamed of" — "will be ashamed of"; "me and my words" — "him"; "in this adulterous and sinful generation" — "when he comes . . ."). "In the glory" contrasts with and compensates for shame over Jesus and his words. "Of his Father" (contrast 10:37) shows that God is not ashamed of his Son even though others may be. Inserting "of his Father" establishes this point at the linguistically odd expense of making the Son of man the Son of God. But this linguistic oddity well suits Mark's emphasis on Jesus as God's Son (see 1:1 with comments) and prepares for God's pronouncement of Jesus as his beloved Son in 9:7 (J. Schlosser, *Le Dieu de Jésus* 125). The angels shift roles. They were assessors at the last assize (or, less likely, a periphrasis for God — Luke 12:8). Now they are warriors accompanying the Son of man on his coming invasion of the world (cf. 2 Thess 1:7). This shift suits his own shift in roles from witness in court to commander on campaign. "The Son of man" also recalls v 31, but how different the destinies predicted! There, much suffering, rejection by the Sanhedrin, and being killed. Here, coming, glorification by the Father, and an angelic army in escort. The resurrection that Jesus also predicted in v 31 makes possible a transition from that immediate destiny to this ultimate one. The glory of his ultimate destiny will reverse the scandal of his being rejected and killed.

In summary of vv 34-38, why should you deny yourself, take up your cross, and follow Jesus? (1) Because you will save your life for eternity even though you lose it now. Here is a savings account with better returns than you ever dreamed of (v 35). (2) Because your life is much more valuable than the whole world; so do not be gulled into making a foolish deal (v 36). (3) Because once you have lost your life, there is no buying it back, no matter how much you offer. The opportunity to invest in futures is now; do not let it slip by (v 37). (4) Because when the tables are turned on this hostile world, when the glorious Son of man

comes with the approval of God his Father and with the holy angels as his army,
you will want to be on his side, not on the world's side.

9:1 *(Matt 16:28; Luke 9:27)* The reference in 8:38 to the Son of man's
glorious coming leads Mark to introduce a saying that refers to the powerful
coming of God's rule (cf. the parallel in 11:9-10 between "the one coming in the
name of the Lord" and "the coming rule of our father David"). "And he was
saying to them" attaches this saying to the preceding material — thus "to them"
means "to the crowd with the disciples" (cf. v 34) — yet sets the statement apart
for a special emphasis that relates to the following pericope (cf. the comments
on 2:27). Jesus himself adds emphasis with "truly I say to you." He goes on to
predict "that there are some of those standing here such as will not taste death
till they see God's rule [as] having come with power," i.e. till they see that God
has powerfully imposed his rule (see Heb 2:9; 4 Ezra 6:26; Str-B 1. 751-52 for
the Semitic expression "taste death"; A. T. Robertson, *Grammar* 1040-42, on
participles modifying objects of verbs of perception as having a realistic force;
and cf. 13:26 and, for not dying till such-and-such happens, John 21:18-23; *Jub.*
16:16; *2 Apoc. Bar.* 48:30; 76:1-2; 4 Ezra 6:25-26; 14:9). Along with its fulfilment, this prediction will demonstrate Jesus' ability to forecast the future; and by
taking place before fulfilment of his earlier prediction concerning passion and
resurrection, the fulfilment of this prediction will lend credence to the earlier one.
From now on, Mark will capitalize on Jesus' predictive power whenever he can
to counteract the scandal of the Crucifixion. The literary device of inclusion in
the two predictions at 8:31 and 9:1 sets this emphasis going. *See the comments
and notes on 9:2-8 for further discussion of 9:1.*

NOTES

Against dividing off 8:27–10:52 as a section of private ecclesiastical teaching, we should
note that in 8:34–9:1 Jesus speaks to a crowd as well as to his disciples, that the dialogue
in 9:14-27 takes place in a crowd, that in 10:1-9 he teaches crowds, that in 10:13-16 he
addresses his disciples with others present, that in 10:17-22 he gives salvific instruction
to a non-disciple, and that 9:2-8, 14-27; 10:13-16, 46-52 offer narratives as well as
teachings. Speaking to crowds and outsiders will continue in 11:15–12:40; 14:3-9, 12-31;
and private teaching, much of it just as open to the description "ecclesiastical," is to be
found outside 8:27–10:52 in 4:10-20; 7:17-23; 8:13-21; 11:20-25; 12:41-44; 13:1-37;
14:3-9, 12-31. In 9:28-29; 10:10-12, 23-31 private instruction of the disciples will follow
public discourse; but no private instruction follows the public discourse in 8:34–9:1 (the
Transfiguration being an event, not a lecture), and private instruction has followed public
discourse already in 4:10-20; 7:17-23. Hence, 8:27–10:52 does not prove itself distinctive.
See also the notes on 10:1ff.

It is often noted that 8:27–10:52 contains three predictions by Jesus of his coming
passion and resurrection (8:31; 9:31; 10:32-34), each followed by indications of the
disciples' failure to understand (8:32-33; 9:32; 10:35), which are followed in turn by
corrective instructions on discipleship (8:34–9:1, 33-37; 10:36-45). But there is three times
more material outside these passages in 8:27–10:52; so they can hardly determine the
whole character of this part of Mark. The amount of extra material would diminish if we
added to the repetitive scheme a fourth element, viz., indications of Jesus' supernaturalness

(9:2-8, 38-41; 10:46-52; so P. J. Achtemeier 33). But Jesus' supernaturalness is scarcely the point of 9:38-41. Even otherwise, the remaining amount of extra material would continue to spoil the scheme of three predictions each followed by similar kinds of material. Also spoiling this scheme is 9:9-13. There we read another prediction by Jesus of his passion and resurrection, but he makes it backhandedly and mentions his resurrection before his passion. The disciples who hear this prediction include only Peter, James, and John; their ignorance relates only to the resurrection; and no corrective instruction on discipleship follows. Predictions of Jesus' passion spill over into the further part of Mark, too (14:8, 17-25, 41-42); portents of his passion have already appeared (3:6, 21; 6:4, 17-29); and the disciples have already betrayed their ignorance (4:13, 40; 6:52; 7:18; 8:13-21). So yet again 8:27–10:52 proves undistinctive.

See E. Dinkler (in *The Future of Our Religious Past* 177) and H. F. Bayer (*Jesus' Predictions* 154) against putting v 27a with the preceding pericope. Mark likes to start pericopes with a topographical shift. It is puzzling why E. Best (*Following Jesus* 20) should think that the impreciseness and peculiarity of "to the towns of Philip's Caesarea" should point to Marcan redaction. Redaction would more likely produce a simple, precise place-name. If Mark were having to make up the topography, we would probably be reading "Galilee" (cf. ibid. 22, n. 8). The further argument that a story used for confessional and catechetical purposes would not likely preserve topographical information underestimates the power of tradition and overestimates our knowledge of the way primitive Christians used this story. Nor does the occurrence of "his disciples" in the topographical statement despite a recurrence of the phrase in the very next statement prove that Mark has made up the topography. Though the duality of the occurrences may be due to Mark — the first one designed to prepare for a dialogue by putting the disciples with Jesus, the second designed to prepare for a distinction between the disciples and others (see the foregoing comments) — the possibility is not foreclosed that Mark is redacting tradition in regard to both the topography and the dialogue.

To argue that Jesus would not ask the disciples about Jewish opinion when they were traveling outside Jewish territory falsely assumes that stepping outside Jewish territory shuts down Jesus' interest in and the disciples' knowledge of Jewish opinion. The Jewish-ness of the following references to "John the Baptist," "Elijah," "one of the prophets," and "the Christ" seems unlikely to have prompted Mark to think up a Gentile setting (contrast the Gentile centurion's identification of Jesus as "God's Son" rather than as "the Christ" — 15:39). Since with the exception of 7:24 Marcan passages on secrecy occur in non-Gentile settings and since in the Gentile setting of 5:1-20 Jesus commands publication, not secrecy (5:19), the argument of W. Schmithals (387) collapses that Mark thinks up the villages of Philip's Caesarea to link the messianic secret with non-Jewish territory. In actuality, "the villages of Philip's Caesarea" makes a very Jewish locution (see the LXX of Num 21:32; 32:42; Josh 10:39 and many, many further examples listed in Hatch and Redpath s.v. κώμη; cf. G. Dalman, *SSW* 195-207; also against the conjecture of J. Carmignac [in *ASTI* 7 (1968) 82] that בקצוות, "into the borders," has been misread as בקריות, "into the villages"). On Philip's Caesarea, see E. Schürer, G. Vermes, F. Millar, and M. Black, *History* 2. 169-71; A. N. Sherwin-White, *Roman Society* 127-31; A. H. M. Jones, *Cities* 277, n. 67, 283-84, n. 76.

Many interpreters take the occurrence of "way" (ὁδός) in v 27 as the first in a series in which this word represents the way of discipleship through following Jesus to the Cross (see, e.g., E. Best, *Following Jesus* 15-18; W. H. Kelber, *Kingdom* 67-85, esp. 67-70). At 8:27; 9:33-34; 10:32 the word occurs in association with predictions of the Passion and Resurrection, at 10:17 in association with refusal to follow Jesus, and at 10:46, 52 in the story of Bartimaeus's healing, taken to be symbolic of conversion to discipleship. "The way of [the] Lord" in 1:2-3 is supposed to have prepared for this later symbolic use (not to list theological uses of "way" in the NT outside Mark). But in 1:2-3 the way of the Lord did not lead toward the Cross; for if carried out to completion, preparing that way by baptism, repentance, and confession of sins would have ended in wholesale acceptance of Jesus rather than in his passion and resurrection. "Way" occurred at 2:23 in connection with a journey by Jesus and his disciples (against the statement of J. Schreiber [*Theologie des Vertrauens* 190-91] that prior to 8:27 Mark does not portray Jesus as on a journey), but with reference to Sabbath-breaking, not to the Passion and Resurrection; again at 4:4, 15, but with regard to unresponsive hearers of the word, the reverse of discipleship; again at 6:8, but in connection with the disciples' powerfully successful mission, not their cross-taking; and yet again at 8:3, but for the way home on which the four thousand might faint for hunger. These earlier uses do not encourage a sudden switch to the way of the Cross.

Even discounting earlier uses as traditional (but occurrences in 9:33; 10:46 as well as later occurrences in 11:8; 12:14 will lay equal claim on traditionality), to interpret "the way" in 8:27 and following passages as the way of the Cross runs into a ditch. Here in 8:27 "the way" occurs *before* the first passion prediction. It is not even Mark's device for moving Jesus from Galilee toward Jerusalem for the Crucifixion, for Jesus has not yet started south toward Jerusalem. On the contrary, he is traveling north from Bethsaida (v 22), away from Jerusalem, through the towns of Philip's Caesarea. "The way" is simply the road on which an event takes place as Jesus and others travel between localities, whatever the direction or destination of their travel. He predicts his passion in 9:9-13, but "way" does not appear in that passage (to say nothing of its non-appearance with the Passion predictions in 14:8, 17-25, because there his having arrived in Jerusalem forestalls references to the way). In 9:33-34 Jesus associates "the way" with the disciples' dispute over greatness, not with his coming passion; and he corrects them with the example of a little child, not with the example of his passion. In 10:32 "the way" occurs in closer association with a crowd of pilgrims than with the twelve disciples (see the comments ad loc.). In the story of blind Bartimaeus "the way" first appears as his place of begging (v 46) — hardly the right theological meaning — so that his following Jesus "on the way" (v 52) suits a demonstration of Bartimaeus's healing better than it suits a symbol of discipleship through cross-taking.

The use of "way" does not stop after the story of Bartimaeus. At the Triumphal Procession, crowds spread their garments and straw on "the way" into Jerusalem (11:8). Here we have the way of honor and acclamation, not of crucifixion. And "the way of God" that Jesus teaches according to 12:14 does not include his crucifixion, for the expression refers to his public teaching, from which his crucifixion is absent. The twelve disciples break down at the end of their journey with Jesus. One of them betrays him. The rest forsake him and flee for their lives. One of the rest also denies him three times. And before arriving in Jerusalem they betray ignorance of the purpose for which he is going there. Some way of discipleship! Since Mark is at pains to point out the disciples' ignorance as a foil to Jesus' predictive power, and the breakdowns as fulfilments of predictions by Jesus, we can scarcely imagine that he wants "the way" to represent the way of discipleship. More often than not, we should translate ὁδός with "road" to avoid unintended theological connotations associated with "way."

D. Catchpole (in *Jesus and the Politics of His Day* 327-28) argues against the historicity of vv 27-30 that the Jesus who preaches about God's rule would not ask for opinions about himself. But Jesus' taking on himself a kingdom-bringing role that exceeds all expectations — he even forgives sins (2:1-12) — makes his asking for opinions about himself compatible with his preaching of God's rule. The argument that Jesus would not ask his disciples for Jewish opinion equally well known to him (so R. Bultmann, *HST* 257) assumes that a leader has as much close contact with the general populace as his followers have. The history of politics teaches better. The yet further argument that Jesus would not violate rabbinic custom by questioning his disciples on a point of information strikes a humorous note when it comes from those who in other respects deny a rabbinic relation between Jesus and his disciples with respect to the handing down of tradition, which would enhance the historicity of Mark and the other gospels. The sober points to make, however, are that Jesus is a rabbi with a difference, and more than a rabbi, and that he asks not to be taught by the information received but to teach his informants with respect to it (cf. 3:4; 4:13; 6:38; 7:18-19; 8:17-21; 9:33; 12:24, 35-37; R. P. Casey in *The Background of the NT and Its Eschatology* 58-60; E. Dinkler in *The Future of Our Religious Past* 178-79). It is uncertain why J. Ernst (235) thinks a roadway to the towns of Philip's Caesarea an extremely unsuitable locale. Jesus' constant itineration must have had him talking theology often in settings like this.

We should be wary of reading a bad connotation into the generic use of οἱ ἄνθρωποι, "the people" (v 27), unless the context favors such a connotation. Not only does the present context fail to do so (there is no contrast with God or his Son, only with the disciples, who are also human beings). See the foregoing comments on the possibility that οἱ ἄνθρωποι is not even generic, but refers to the "they" who brought the blind man (v 22) and whom he saw when healed: τοὺς ἀνθρώπους (v 24).

G. Theissen (*Miracle Stories* 170-71) argues that the switch from accusatives of indirect discourse to a nominative of direct discourse within the directly quoted answer of the disciples (v 28) shows that Mark is transforming the direct discourse of the tradition reflected in 6:15 into indirect discourse, but lapsing back in the end to the traditional direct discourse. More likely, Mark simply avoids the doubling up of direct quotations without intermission; i.e. he avoids making the first part of the direct quotation of the disciples' answer another direct quotation by them of the people's opinions. The possibility of abbreviation as compared with 6:15 might indicate that Mark is here writing up tradition in view of the tradition that he wrote up in 6:15, not necessarily that he repeats in abbreviated form the same tradition that he used earlier. More probably, he writes up present tradition in an elliptical form because of the surrounding infinitive constructions, not because of earlier use (see the foregoing comments; also the notes on 6:14-16 that there Mark borrowed from the tradition behind the present passage, not vice versa).

It is reasoning in a circle to argue that by showing Mark's tendency to make events provoke the question of Jesus' identity, passages such as 1:27; 4:41; 6:2; 14:61; 15:2 support Marcan fabrication in 8:27-30 (so D. Catchpole in *Jesus and the Politics of His Day* 327-28). Those passages, too, may depend on pre-Marcan and historical traditions; and given the phenomenon of first century Christianity, we might find it odd if events did not provoke questions of Jesus' identity. It is likewise reasoning in a circle to argue that statements about Jesus' identity in 1:11, 24; 3:11; 14:61-62; 15:2, 39 support Marcan fabrication particularly in Peter's confession (ibid.). The more Christian fabrication is required to describe all these passages as inauthentic, the more difficult it is to explain how and why Christianity started. Questions of historicity require a framework of discussion larger than literary details. For sample defenses of the general authenticity of vv 27-31, see V. Taylor 374-75; H. Baarlink, *Anfängliches Evangelium* 211-14; of inauthenticity, R. Bultmann, *HST* 257-59; M. Horstmann, *Studien* 12-18.

M. E. Boring (*Sayings* 199) supposes that "one of the prophets" does not mean an old prophet returned, but a prophet as such, and hypothesizes that Mark is rejecting a portrayal of Jesus as prophet because he (Mark) objects to the claims of Q to represent sayings of the risen Jesus channeled through Christian prophets. But not only does "one of the prophets" probably mean an old prophet returned. Denying that Jesus was a prophet would not forestall his speaking through Christian prophets. A prophet channels the word of the Lord, not the word of another prophet. Conversely, it would be strange for Q to portray Jesus as a prophet to justify his speaking through Christian prophets after Easter. Besides, we may doubt that Boring has succeeded in rescuing the hypothesis that sayings of the risen Jesus, channeled though Christian prophets, were backdated to the earthly Jesus (in *NTS* 29 [1983] 104-11; on the contrary, see D. Hill in *NTS* 20 [1973-74] 262-74; J. D. G. Dunn in *NTS* 24 [1977-78] 175-98; D. E. Aune, *Prophecy* 233-45).

Gen. Rab. 13.7 associates Honi the Circle-Drawer with Elijah because both men made others serve God. The association of Jesus with Elijah does not betray its reason. G. Vermes (*Jesus the Jew* 89-90, 95) toys with the possibility of the historical rather than eschatological Elijah, but inclines toward the eschatological Elijah, not as a forerunner, but as an agent of Israel's final restoration.

H. F. Bayer (*Jesus' Predictions* 157) argues for the historicity of Peter's confessing Jesus as the Christ that a churchly confession would probably have been put on the lips of all the disciples, not just Peter's. According to the authors of *Peter in the NT* 65-66, the crucifixion of Jesus as a would-be king of the Jews favors the possibility that some of his followers may have thought him the Christ (cf. the possibly independent traditions in John 1:41; 6:67-69). Since Jesus has not been anointed with oil for his ministry, Peter must mean "the Christ," i.e. "the Anointed One," in the figurative sense of the one designated by God, or endued with the Spirit of God, to bring about God's rule. For a royal connotation, Peter may link Jesus' preaching of God's rule with Jewish expectation of a new Davidic king acting as God's vicegerent.

J. Gnilka (2. 15) argues that since "Christ" or "Messiah" does not occur absolutely in Jewish literature till later (first in *2 Apoc. Bar.* 29:3; 30:1; cf. 4 Ezra 7:26-29; 12:32), the present absolute use may represent Christian tradition put on Peter's lips. But what makes Peter less likely than the author of Second Baruch or anyone else to have been first in using the title absolutely? Nothing demands that a non-Christian Jew have been first. Besides, long before Mark and even longer before Second Baruch, Dan 9:25-26 used "messiah" absolutely, though anarthrously and in v 25 with a following appositive. CD 20:1 also used "messiah" absolutely, though anarthrously, if "from Aaron and from Israel" goes with "arise," as favored by the contrast with the construct state, "messiah *of* . . . ," in CD 7:21a; 12.23; 13:20; 14:19 (so the translation of C. Rabin, *Zadokite Documents* 36; cf. I. Abrahams, *Studies* 1. 136-38). 1QSa 2:12 may present a pre-Christian absolute use that is arthrous. In Mark, "Son of God" holds more importance than does "Christ" (see 1:1, 11; 3:11; 5:7; 9:7; 14:61; 15:39; cf. 1:24; 12:6), which is so insufficient that it requires augmenting in 1:11; 14:61; 15:32. Therefore we would expect Marcan fabrication at least to include "Son of God" in Peter's confession, perhaps even to have "Son of God" alone. For literature on χριστός, see BAGD s.v.

Peter's rebuking Jesus implies that Peter has a non-Christian, Jewish idea of messiahship. E. Dinkler (in *The Future of Our Religious Past* 172-76) argues that such a non-Christian idea makes it easier to accept the historicity of Peter's confession. Even had Peter meant "the Christ" in a Christian sense, however, we would not be forced to deny historicity; for it is conceivable that a prediction of Jesus' passion and resurrection might have revised Peter's prior idea of messiahship (and the criterion of dissimilarity is useless for making negative judgments). Dinkler weakens his own argument for the historicity of Peter's confession by denying the historicity of vv 30-32, i.e. of the command to silence, the prediction of the Passion and Resurrection, and Peter's rebuke of Jesus. The result of this denial is to turn Jesus' rebuke of Peter into a rejection of Peter's confession (as though to say, "It is satanic of you to call me the Christ"), a rejection due to thinking Jewishly of messiahship (ibid. 186-89; cf. F. Hahn, *Titles* 223-28; C. Breytenbach, *Nachfolge* 207-19; cf. W. H. Kelber, *Mark's Story* 46-49; C. Myers, *Binding the Strong Man* 244). This theory requires the unhistoricity of 14:61-62 (but see the notes ad loc.) and has against it the absence from Q of any polemic against the title "Christ" and the use of "Christ" for Jesus already in the earliest books of the NT but without indication of any dispute over its appropriateness and with the development from title to personal name already in place (see the concordance s.v. Χριστός in Galatians and 1 Thessalonians). M. D. Hooker (in *NTS* 17 [1970-71] 48) asks why the early church would have remembered and repeated such a story, what needs in the early church the story would have met, and how it came to be so drastically altered as to take on a diametrically opposed meaning (cf. O. Betz in *NovT* 6 [1963] 20-48 in favor of Jesus' messianic consciousness).

For several reasons, Peter's confession rings true to the Christology of Mark's text: (1) Mark puts "Christ" in the superscript at 1:1 and (2) includes sayings that use "Christ" favorably at 9:41; 14:61-62. (3) That no further qualification is needed to make the use of "Christ" favorable at 9:41 shows Mark's acceptance of the term as a correct identification of Jesus. (4) "The Christ" contrasts with incorrect identifications in 6:14-16; 8:28. (5) Jesus' questions in vv 27, 29a set the stage for a correct identification by Peter. (6) The command in v 30 not to speak to anyone about Jesus implies the truth of Peter's confession, for its falsehood would demand that Jesus reject it in the disciples' hearing rather than insist that they keep it from the ears of others. (7) Mark never refers negatively to false messianism of a Jewish nationalistic sort that might tar Peter's confession (H. Räisänen, *Messias-Geheimnis* 104-5). (8) Jesus calls Peter "Satan" for having rejected the prediction of the Passion and Resurrection, not for having confessed him as the Christ. The prediction of the Passion and Resurrection implies, however, that Peter's confession needs supplementation. Though Mark does not indicate that Peter misunderstood Jesus' messiahship by hoping for Jewish nationalistic glory, Peter's rebuking Jesus because of the prediction (vv 31-32), Jesus' returning a rebuke (v 33), and what we know of Jewish messianism during the period (see, e.g., *Psalms of Solomon* 17–18; 4QMess ar; John 6:15; Acts 1:6) seem to imply such a misunderstanding (cf. J.-B. Frey in *Bib* 14 [1933] 133-49; against J. Ernst [in *Petrus und Papst* 2. 29 and in *Cath* 32 [1978] 62], who draws an unlikely distinction between eschatological enthusiasm and nationalistic messianism).

According to L. S. Hay (in *JAAR* 35 [1967] 21-22), 9:30-31 will show that the command to secrecy in 8:30 has to do with Jesus' passion and resurrection, predicted in 8:31, not with his Christhood, confessed in 8:29. But 9:30 will have to do with the wanting of his whereabouts to be kept unknown in order that he may have privacy to teach the disciples about his coming passion and resurrection (9:31). That teaching will not include a command to keep the Passion and Resurrection secret. Moreover, a command to secrecy relates to the foregoing more naturally than to the following (1:44; 5:43; 7:36; 9:9), and especially so in 8:30 because "concerning him" seems to mean "concerning Jesus as the Christ" (cf. 8:29) and because the formula "and he began to teach" dissociates the following prediction of passion and resurrection (8:31) from the command to secrecy (8:30).

Mark's habit of using "he began" as an auxiliary — he will even use it again at 10:32 to introduce another prediction of passion and resurrection despite earlier such predictions in 8:31; 9:9, 12, 31 — forestalls our treating it as the signpost of a new *main* section beginning in v 31. The almost immediate re-use of the expression for Peter's rebuke in v 32b also militates against such a treatment. R. P. Martin (*Mark* 188-89) notes that the auxiliary use forestalls a contradiction of earlier allusions to Jesus' passion and resurrection. Even otherwise, the first explicit teaching of those events appears here. "Teach" signals a new pericope only subsidiarily to topographical notations (1:21-22; 2:13; 4:1-2; 6:1-2, 6b, 34; 9:30-31; 10:1; 12:35), which signal new pericopes also apart from "teach" (passim). Verse 31 carries no topographical note. Therefore "to teach" does not signal a new pericope or a new, originally separate tradition (against U. Luz in *ZNW* 56 [1965] 21-22, n. 60). In 4:1-2 Mark used "teach" (bis) and "teaching" for parables concerning the mystery of God's rule. Therefore we cannot agree with H. Riesenfeld (in *Neutestamentliche Studien für Rudolf Bultmann* 160-62) that in 8:31 "teach" gains specific content for the first time and thereby demonstrates a thrust toward discipleship in this part of Mark. We will see that the materials on discipleship stand in the service of Christology, not of ecclesiology. M. Zerwick (*Untersuchungen* 139) suggests that in v 31 ὅτι may be epexegetic rather than recitative. But an undoubtedly recitative ὅτι in another passion-and-resurrection prediction at 10:33 and a probably recitative ὅτι in yet another one at 9:31 favor the same kind here. So also does the occurrence of "the Son of man" elsewhere in Mark almost exclusively in directly quoted statements of Jesus (the single exception occurring at 9:9).

"The many afflictions of the righteous" (Ps 34:20[19]; πολλαὶ αἱ θλίψεις τῶν δικαίων in Ps 33:20 LXX; 4 Macc 18:15) does not come close enough to Jesus' "suffer much" (πολλὰ παθεῖν) to make an allusion likely. The probably adverbial use of πολλά distances the two passages from each other at the point where they might seem closest; and though the interchange of θλῖψις and its cognate θλίβω with πάσχω and its cognate πάθημα in 2 Cor 1:4-7; 2 Thess 1:4-7 opens the possibility of taking Mark's παθεῖν as a non-Septuagintal allusion to רעות in Ps 34:20 MT, nowhere in the LXX does πάθημα translate this frequently used Hebrew word (against L. Ruppert, *Jesus als der leidende Gerechte?* 65-66). Likewise, "and after three days" (καὶ μετὰ τρεῖς ἡμέρας) improbably echoes Hos 6:2 MT LXX; for there we read "after [מן and μετά] two days . . . on [ב and ἐν] the third day." This difference militates against a derivation of ἀναστῆναι, "to rise up," from ἀναστησόμεθα, "we will rise up," in Hos 6:2 LXX. The underlying קום occurs for resurrection also in Isa 26:19, where the LXX puts the deponent middle ἀναστήσονται and the passive ἐγερθήσονται in parallel. The persecution of the righteous in passages such as Wis 2:10-20; 5:1-7; *1 Enoch* 103:9-15 provides at most only a broad background.

On the other hand, the explicit quotation of Ps 118:22-23 in Mark 12:10-11 with parabolic reference to Jesus' being killed (so also in Acts 4:11; 1 Pet 2:4, 7) makes probable that "to be rejected" (ἀποδοκιμασθῆναι) here alludes to that OT passage (cf. esp. Ps 117:22 LXX, but not Isa 53:3, where the LXX does not have Mark's verb and the Hebrew חדל connotes forsakenness rather than rejection). This allusion, the explicit appeals to Scripture in Mark 9:12; 14:21, and the use of δεῖ at 9:11 in a paraphrastic quotation of Mal 3:23(4:5) show that δεῖ refers to scriptural necessity (cf. Luke 24:26 with 24:27; John 20:9; Acts 3:21 et passim — see W. Grundmann in *TDNT* 2. 22-23), not to general apocalyptic necessity (Rev 1:1; 4:1) or to a particular apocalyptic law that suffering precedes glory, and not merely to the pattern of rejection suffered by prophets (cf. 1 Thess 2:15), except as that pattern may represent Scripture itself. Scripture is God's Word. What is written there must happen. It still takes supernatural insight to know that one's own fate will fulfil what is written there, however; and for the moment Mark apologetically rests with necessity as such and with Jesus' prescient application of it to his own case.

The apocalyptic use of δεῖ in Mark 13:10; Dan 2:28 LXX Theod, 45 Theod does not have to do with suffering; and in Mark 13:7 it has to do with wars, not with the suffering of persecution and martyrdom issuing in glory. Therefore we should see apocalyptic necessity neither in Mark 8:31 nor in pre-Marcan tradition. "The Son of man" is not enough to salvage the apocalyptic interpretation, for that expression occurs often without apocalyptic significance (against M. Horstmann, *Studien* 24-26). The route from δεῖ through the rejected stone in Ps 118:22 to the stone in Dan 2:34-35, 44-45, then to the one like a Son of man in Dan 7:13 and finally back to the rejected Son of man in Mark 8:31 (so K. Snodgrass, *Parable* 101), seems more circuitous than probable. W. J. Bennett, Jr. (in *NovT* 17 [1975] 113-29), argues against H. E. Tödt (*Son of Man* 164-70), who supports scriptural necessity, that since מאס, "reject," occurs too often to favor a particular allusion to Ps 118:22, δεῖ refers generally to God's will. The undoubtedly particular allusions to Ps 118:22 in Mark 12:10; Acts 4:11; 1 Pet 2:4, 7 undermine this argument. According to B. L. Mack (*Myth* 244), δεῖ refers to a necessity caused by Jesus' prediction itself. But a necessity growing out of the prediction makes strange the occurrence of δεῖ within the prediction.

J. D. Kingsbury (*Christology of Mark's Gospel* 94-97, 157-79) notes that "the Son of man" does not correct "the Christ," for "the Son of man" does not address the issue of Jesus' identity. Nowhere in Mark does Jesus say, "I am the Son of man," or does anyone else say, "You are [or 'He is'] the Son of man" (contrast such statements using "the Christ" and "the Son of God," esp. the statement in 14:61-62). Jesus uses "the Son of man" to refer to himself, but in and of itself the phrase tells nothing more about him than that he is a human being. His portraying himself as suffering may supplement "the Christ," which does not connote suffering, or may even correct notions of politically or otherwise grandiose Christhood (cf. Pss 18:2-51[1-50]; 78:65-72; Isa 9:5-6[6-7]; 11:1-10; Amos 9:11-12; *Pss. Sol.* 17:21-44). These possibilities have as much or more plausibility than the hypothesis that two originally independent traditions — one of Jesus as the Christ and the other of Jesus as the Son of man — have come together here. Cf. the unity of Christhood and a self-referential "the Son of man" in 14:61-62, though there the Son of man is exalted rather than suffering. To the extent that "the Son of man" relates to Dan 7:13, and unless the "one like a Son of man" in that text collectivizes the suffering people of God (but even then the phrase connects with their coming exaltation, not with their present suffering), Jesus means that he must suffer *despite* rather than *because of* his being "the one like a son of man"; for Daniel portrays the one like a son of man as given dominion (G. Vos, *Self-Disclosure* 236-37), and the Son of man who will suffer according to Jesus' prediction certainly does not differ from Jesus himself (cf. E. Schweizer 167 and the notes on 2:10). R. A. Horsley (in *NovT* 27 [1985] 334-48) denies that a monolithic, widespread Zealotic messianism provides a foil for Jesus' suffering. The Zealots may not come into existence till the Jewish war of 66-73 C.E.

The elders are laymen. The chief priests consist of the ruling high priest, ex-high priests, members of high priestly families, and their high-ranking priestly friends. The scribes are theologians. See the literature cited in BADG s.v. ἀρχιερεύς. The view that regards "to be killed" as a redactional fabrication designed to link Jesus' passion with the killing of the OT prophets (Acts 3:15; 7:52; Rom 11:3; 1 Thess 2:15; N. Perrin in *Christology and a Modern Pilgrimage* 26) sits uncomfortably alongside Mark's dismissing the identification of Jesus as one of the prophets (v 28). Likewise, the view that looks on "to be killed," not as a sign of authenticity (as in the foregoing comments), but as a fabrication conditioned by the Jewish authorities' inability to crucify Jesus (so R. McKinnis in *NovT* 18 [1976] 95) does not take account of 10:33-34, where the prediction that "they will kill [the Son of man]" will follow the prediction that the Jewish authorities "will give him over to the Gentiles," who do have the ability to crucify him. "After three days" would seem to mean "on the fourth day." But the NT outside Mark has "on the third day," and Mark's account has Jesus risen on the third day (counting the day of death and that of resurrection). Therefore, some regard the phraseology as loose, "three" meaning "a few" because Hebrew and Aramaic do not have an exact equivalent for "a few" (so, e.g., J. Jeremias in *Tradition und Glaube* 226-27, with appeal to J. B. Bauer in *Bib* 39 [1958] 354-58). But what about the plural of מְעַט? The plural of אֶחָד (Hebrew) and of חַד (Aramaic) can also mean "a few"; and מִסְפָּר, too. Yet again, the simple plural "days" can mean "a few days." And the passages usually listed for a loose sense of "three days" can just as easily carry the strict sense (for references exemplifying all these expressions, see Jeremias loc. cit.; Bauer loc. cit.; R. H. Gundry, *Matthew* 245; and F. Field, *Notes* 11-13; H. W. Hoehner in *BSac* 131 [1974] 247-49 for "after three days" as meaning "on the third day"). We do better, then, to rely on the Jewish method of reckoning part of a twenty-four hour day for the whole. This method results in counting part of Friday, all of Saturday, and part of Sunday as three days, after which Jesus rises up. For the Jewish method, see Gen 42:17-18; 1 Sam 30:1, 12-13; 2 Chr 10:5, 12; Esth 4:16–5:1; G. Delling in *TDNT* 2. 949-50; and for the third-day motif, see esp. *Gen. Rab.* 91.7 on 42:17; *Midr. Pss.* on Ps 22 §5 (with quotations of Exod

15:22; Josh 2:16; 2 Kgs 20:5; Hos 6:2; Jonah 2:2, 11; Esth 4:16); *Esth. Rab.* 9.2 on 5:1 (with quotations of Gen 22:4; 42:17; Hos 6:2; Jonah 2:1); W. L. Craig in *Gospel Perspectives* 2. 176 (against such a motif as a theological datum in the NT period).

As we have seen, later as well as earlier books of the NT use ἐγείρω in the passive. So also do later parts of Mark. Ἀνίστημι corresponds to קום in the OT, and both Greek verbs occur in the LXX for resurrection (Isa 26:19; Ezek 38:14; Dan 12:2; 2 Macc 7:9, 14). Therefore we have scant reason to treat ἀνίστημι as a Hellenistic substitute for ἐγείρω. On the other hand, the difference between the Son of man's rising up in v 31 without reference to God's action and God's causing the seed of David to rise up in 2 Sam 7:12 makes doubtful that Jesus draws קום-ἀνίστημι from that OT text (against D. E. Aune in *NovT* 11 [1969] 23-24). J. Jeremias (in *Tradition und Glaube* 228-29) thinks that a loose sense of "after three days" allows an allusion to "on the third day" in Hos 6:2. But not only is the loose sense doubtful (see the foregoing criticism). The synonymous parallelism in Hos 6:2 between "on the third day" and "after *two* days" rules out synonymity in "after *three* days."

H. Conzelmann (in *Int* 24 [1970] 184-85) denies that Jesus' prediction is designed to remove the offense of a cross ("as if the passion were annulled by the resurrection"), and affirms the opposite: the passion is a necessary condition for the glory. One may not dispute this last statement, but neither resurrection as apology nor Jesus' predictive power as apology implies annulment of the passion as such, only annulment of its shame and reversal of its deadly outcome. We will see that Mark writes up his account of the passion and resurrection in an apologetic way.

If Jesus predicted his passion and resurrection once, why not more than once? He spoke more than once about God's rule, the law of love, etc. In principle we have no reason to assume that the different predictions go back to a single original prediction, and therefore no reason for confidence in our ability to detect redactional changes, whether through multiplication or otherwise, of a single original tradition. Differences in wording, in topographical and chronological setting, and in literary context may point to originally multiple predictions, particularly in view of the failure of the predictions to betray a clearly traceable genealogy of development from singularity to multiplicity. Similarity in the structure of 8:31; 9:31; 10:33-34 is as easily due to sameness of subject matter as to multiplication of a single tradition. The statistical argument of R. A. Martin (in *SBL 1987 Seminar Papers* 322, 324-25, 327) that only 8:31 shows evidence of translation Greek is skewed by his inclusion of 8:32–9:1 with 8:31 and by the brevity of the compared passages 9:30-32; 10:32-34. Furthermore, equally authentic traditions may undergo different degrees of Graecizing.

Predictions of the Passion without the Resurrection (9:12 [but see 9:9-10]; 14:8, 17-25, 41-42; Luke 17:25) do not argue strongly for an earlier, more original prediction lacking the Resurrection (and therefore referring to suffering but not necessarily to death); for the contextual associations of those predictions of the Passion — the comparable fate of John the Baptist, an anointing symbolic of Jesus' burial, bread and wine as symbolic of violent death, betrayal by Judas, and the Second Coming by way of contrast — these associations make predictions of the Resurrection unneeded and unsuitable. It also seems very unlikely that Jesus would predict the abortive end of his mission and leave it at that. What would be his purpose? To discourage his disciples?

The view that Jesus predicted only his suffering, all the rest being added by Christians, also appeals to "the complete helplessness of the disciples on Good Friday and their stubborn doubt despite the appearances of the resurrected One," both phenomena being incomprehensible if the disciples had heard "the detailed announcement of his suffering found in vs. 31" (E. Schweizer 166). These phenomena also undergird the view that Jesus' predictions are entirely inauthentic. Those who themselves doubt the bodily resurrection of Jesus and his ability to predict both it and his prior death do not occupy a strong position from which to argue that the disciples could not have harbored the same doubt. In fact, both because of messianic expectations antithetic to passion and resurrection and because of appearances of the resurrected one, it may have been easier to doubt before Easter than it has been since Easter. We have already noted that differences between the predictions and Mark's account of the Passion and Resurrection favor the authenticity of the predictions.

That "suffer much" occurs often outside Mark (see the comments on v 31 for references) debilitates the argument that the frequency of the phrase in Mark (5:26; 8:31; 9:12) favors Marcan fabrication (against W. Schmithals in *Theologia Crucis —Signum Crucis* 417). At the same time, the indirectness of the quotation in 8:31 allows a measure of Hellenistic paraphrase (see O. J. F. Seitz in *SE VII* 452-55). Some have thought that "to suffer much" betrays unoriginality by appearing too early: rejection should precede it. But roughness may signal authenticity instead of interpolation, suffering much may include rejection as well as being killed, and the present text of Mark offers an a-b-b'-a' construction that looks traditional, i.e. active infinitives sandwiching a pair of passive ones. The further argument that the redactional use of "kill" in 14:1 favors Marcan fabrication in the present passage (Schmithals, op. cit. 418, n. 6) overlooks the possibility that traditional passion predictions will influence Mark's diction in 14:1 and that borrowing "crucify" from the passion narrative would not fit the subjects of 14:1, viz., the Sanhedrin. It will be the Romans, not the Sanhedrin, who crucify Jesus.

E. Haenchen (361, n. 1) argues that since in 14:36 Jesus will consider the possibility of not being killed, the prior predictions that he will be killed are inauthentic. On the contrary, the emotional turmoil of Jesus in 14:36 depends on a conviction that he will be killed. The unlikelihood that Christians would make up an uncomplimentary story in which he suffers such turmoil and has second thoughts combines with that dependence on prior conviction to favor the authenticity of the predictions.

Q includes no sayings that predict the Passion and Resurrection of the Son of man. But such prediction would ill suit a document whose largely non-narrative character forestalls an account of fulfilment. Whatever reason kept Q from narrating Jesus' passion and resurrection also kept Q from recording predictions thereof. We may draw inferences negative toward the authenticity of the predictions no more than we do toward the authenticity of the passion-and-resurrection narrative. See O. J. F. Seitz in *SE VII* 458-65 for the theme of rejection in Q, a theme that supports the Marcan tradition of passion predictions; also J. Jeremias, *NT Theology* 1. 282-83, for Marcan allusions that support those predictions.

The philosophical presupposition that rules out supernatural prescience and bodily resurrection would dictate one or more of the following possibilities if one does not reject the authenticity of Jesus' predictions in toto: (1) recognizing the seriousness of the Jewish leaders' opposition to him, Jesus applies to himself the OT and intertestamental tradition that Israel rejects and kills the prophets and other righteous sufferers but that God will vindicate them. (2) Jesus' sense of divine commission to restore Israel and his failure to do so lead him to believe that he must die to save Israel from judgment (at the hands of the Romans in their crushing of a nationalistic revolt) and thereby make Israel's restoration possible after all (cf. N. T. Wright in *SBL 1985 Seminar Papers* 75-95). (3) Jesus believes that God's rule is soon to break forth in fulness and that the period of preceding woes has started or is about to start, and he draws the conclusion that he and his disciples will lose their lives in the end-time woes but will enjoy the resurrection of martyrs in the immediately following triumph of God's rule (D. C. Allison, Jr., *End* 137-38; C. K. Barrett, *Jesus and the Gospel Tradition* 49-53).

These possibilities suffer certain inadequacies. The tradition of rejected and vindicated prophets and other righteous sufferers does not include the forecasting of their own deaths and vindication through quick resurrection, as here. The notion of an individual's vicariously dying to save Israel from a disastrous revolt has no precedent. The relation of the prediction to the confession of Jesus' messiahship, the use of "the Son of man" in the prediction itself, the concentration of the prediction on the Son of man's individual passion and resurrection, the extreme quickness of his predicted resurrection (surely the end-time woes are expected to last longer than three days), the relating of the disciples' possible martyrdom to Jesus rather than to the end-time (vv 34-38), the difference in phraseology (to say the least) between Jesus' "rising" and the disciples' "saving their lives" (v 35), and the failure of a general resurrection to be mentioned in the prediction or in the context all pose further question marks. The generality of Allison's cross-references to Isa 57:13; 61:1-3; 63:17; 65:13-14; 66:5-16 evacuates them of significant support for the third possibility. Barrett's cross-reference to Mark 10:35-40 allows but does not require that James and John will die at roughly the same time that Jesus will die. The passage might also mean that they will suffer his fate eventually if not soon. Did he also expect his disciples to rise with him after three days? It seems doubtful. To ease the problem we might eliminate the three days as inauthentic, but the foregoing arguments favoring their authenticity block this retreat. Barrett also cites Jesus' command to watch with him in Gethsemane (14:34, 37-38) as an indication that Jesus expects the disciples to die, too. But why then command only three of them to watch? Does he expect only three, these three, to die with him? He commands the rest only to sit while he prays (14:32); and he prays for the passing of the hour and cup only from him, not from any others as well (14:35-36, 39).

Whether Mark or others before him added details to make the predictions conform more closely to the actuality or tradition of the Passion and Resurrection is another question. The above-noted differences between the predictions and the narrative tend against this possibility as well as against later fabrication of the predictions in toto. Relaxation of an antisupernaturalistic presupposition would, of course, pave the way to prescience on Jesus' part, as opposed to his deducing the future and Christians' adding details ex eventu. Mark would certainly object to a naturalistic explanation of Jesus' predictions. In their supernatural character lies Mark's apologetic point.

Παρρησία (v 32) does not demand a large audience. It demands outspokenness to whatever size of audience one has (cf. H. Schlier in *TDNT* 5. 873-74 on its use in the private sphere). Contrast the veiled allusion to Jesus' death in 2:19-20; also earlier hints in 3:6; 6:1-6a; 1:14 with 6:14-29 (cf. the contrast between παρρησία and veiled language in John 11:11-14). Jesus' outspokenness concerning his passion and resurrection does not contrast with his command not to speak to anyone about him as the Christ (v 30), for he limits his outspokenness to the disciples and does not command them to tell others about his passion and resurrection — nor do they till later, outside Mark's book, when they also proclaim him as the Christ. He does not talk outspokenly because he is a righteous man who has nothing to hide (so R. Pesch 2. 53-54), but because he is a divine man who can clearly forecast his own fate. Though "the word" often means the good news preached and taught by Jesus in Mark, it more naturally refers here to the saying in which Jesus has predicted his own fate. For this usage, also Marcan, see 5:36; 7:29; 10:22; 11:29; 12:13; 14:39; and esp. 9:10, because it refers to a saying on the Son of man's resurrection.

The middle voice of προσλαμβάνω commonly refers to a taking aside (see, e.g., Acts 17:5; 18:26; 27:33, 36; 28:2; Rom 14:1, 3; 15:7 [bis]; Phlm 12, 17 as well as Mark 8:32). R. Pesch (2. 47) distinguishes between the use of ἐπιτιμάω for scolding in v 32 and its use for enjoining in v 30. We should rather stress what these two uses have in common, i.e. severity of tone. Thus the difference in applications of the word offers little support for distinguishing between occasions or sources. Pesch also compares Peter's rebuking Jesus for predicting the Passion and Resurrection with *Gen. Rab.* 56 on 22:7, where Sammael (a satanic figure) rebukes (גער = ἐπιτιμάω) Abraham to dissuade him from sacrificing Isaac (op. cit. 54). But Jesus has not said that he will sacrifice himself, as though Peter could dissuade him. Dissuasion would have to be directed to the elders, chief priests, and scribes. In killing Jesus, moreover, they will have no intention like Abraham's of offering a sacrifice to God. Therefore Peter rebukes Jesus, not to dissuade him, but to protest Jesus' prediction as such. Since Jesus' turning and seeing the other disciples highlights the contrast between their proper position at a little distance behind him and Peter's improper position ahead of or alongside him, Peter does not represent the other disciples in receiving Jesus' rebuke (against E. Best, *Following Jesus* 24-25).

U. B. Müller (in *ZNW* 64 [1973] 167) thinks that inspired by Peter's sleeping in Gethsemane (14:32-42), denying Jesus three times (14:66-72), and suffering Paul's rebuke (Gal 2:11-21), a Christian might have fabricated Jesus' rebuke of Peter. But to the extent that those other materials may be considered authentic, so also may the present rebuke. It is unclear why U. Luz (in *ZNW* 56 [1965] 21, n. 60) should think that the vulgar Greek of ὕπαγε and φρονεῖς τά argues against a Semitic substratum. Though not often, ὑπάγω does occur in the LXX for הלך; and the LXX of 1 Maccabees, written originally in Hebrew, uses φρονεῖν τά at 10:20. Ὕπαγε means to go away (cf. C. H. Turner in *JTS* os 29 [1927-28] 287-88), but this meaning does not imply that Peter is to leave Jesus entirely. For that meaning Mark would write εἰς τὰ ὀπίσω, which refers to the things behind the one spoken to or about (see, e.g., John 6:66; 18:6; 20:14; and the LXX of Pss 6:11 א A; 9:4; 49:17), rather than ὀπίσω μου, which means behind the speaker (cf. Isa 38:17 LXX). The latter phrase referred to discipleship in 1:17, 20, and is about to do so again in 8:34. Hence, it does so here in 8:33, too. The little distance at which disciples followed behind their teachers (see the notes on 1:17) suits ὕπαγε; and Jesus uses this verb instead of δεῦτε, "hither!" (1:17), or an imperative form of ἀπέρχομαι, "come away" (1:20), or of ἀκολουθέω, "follow" (8:33), because Peter has taken a position in front of or alongside him, a position Peter has to leave if he is to get behind him. Jesus addresses Peter as Satan, but only to put Peter back in a position where he will no longer have to address him as Satan. N.B. the absence of ὀπίσω μου, except in a v.l., from Matt 4:10, where Jesus told Satan himself to leave: ὕπαγε, Σατανᾶ. Here, ὀπίσω μου triggers in the very next verse a call to follow after Jesus — ὀπίσω μου yet again, but with ἀκολουθεῖν instead of ὑπάγειν because the crowd and the disciples are not in front of him or beside him, as Peter is (against C. H. Dodd [in *JTS* ns 5 (1954) 246], who, following J. Wellhausen, has to treat μου as intrusive). Jesus' command that Peter "go behind him" ill suits a play on Peter's name as meaning "stone" in the sense of a stumbling block lying on Jesus' path to the Cross (so B. A. E. Osborne [in *NovT* 15 (1973) 187-90], who also uses post-NT rabbinic texts to draw associations between a stone as a stumbling block, Satan, and the evil inclination in human beings). A stone cannot "go" anywhere. Only if the epithet "Satan" meant that Satan is inhabiting and using Peter (but see the foregoing comments) would it imply Jesus' over-coming satanic force with a rebuke much as he overcomes demonic force with a rebuke (1:25; 9:25; cf. 3:12; 4:39).

The argument of B. A. E. Osborne (op. cit. 188) that the causal ὅτι in v 33 demands an equation of the things of human beings with the things of Satan presupposes that the ὅτι-clause gives the reason behind the epithet "Satan." It does not. It gives the reason behind the command to go behind Jesus. J. Gnilka (2. 13) attributes "but the things of the people" to redactional addition because Satan's things would make the proper contrast with God's things. But God and human beings make as proper a contrast as do God and Satan, and no problem attaches to Satan's siding with the false notions of the people. One might even suspect that he spawns those notions. It seems unlikely that the saying originally told what Peter is *not* thinking without telling what he *is* thinking. The link between "of the people" (τῶν ἀνθρώπων — v 33) and "the people" (οἱ ἄνθρωποι — v 27) looks more subtle than Mark or someone before him is likely to have fabricated. Better to imagine the inspiration of the moment for Jesus himself. Both expressions occur on his lips. The difference between the verbs "think" and "give back" drives a wedge between their respective objects "the things of God . . . the things of the people" on the one hand (v 33) and "the things of Caesar . . . the things of God" on the other hand (12:17). If anything, the interests of the people and the interests of Caesar would stand opposed to each other, as will Caesar's interests and God's.

The scatteredness of the Q-parallels to 8:34–9:1 in Matt 10:33, 38-39; Luke 12:9; 14:27; 17:33 (cf. John 12:24-26) might be due to the disengagement of sayings from their original narrative settings (if not to Jesus' repeating himself). This possibility would still allow redactional changes in the wording and in principle has no less likelihood than that Mark or someone before him collected the sayings from hither and yon and set them in this narrative. Characteristically Marcan language in the seams at 8:34a; 9:1a and characteristically Marcan use of γάϱ, "for," in vv 35, 36, 37, 38 could prove no more than Mark's redaction of unified material. But again in principle, Marcan or pre-Marcan collection of scattered sayings remains a possibility. Suggestions range from the pre-Marcan independence of each saying through pre-Marcan combining of various ones of them to Mark's own collection of them all. What goes beyond principle and makes it probable that the sayings in 8:34–9:1 were not entirely united at the beginning is that the differences between Mark's version and the putative version of Q are explicable as due to Mark's assimilating the sayings to a single new context (see the foregoing comments and, for an argument that he drew on a pre-Q collection, R. A. Piper, *Wisdom* 193-202).

E. Best (*Gospel as Story* 87) suggests that Mark sandwiches the sayings on discipleship between the prediction of Jesus' death and resurrection and the Transfiguration to insure that the sayings are understood in the light of the prediction and the Transfiguration. It would be hard to deny that the content of the sayings relates to the prediction of Jesus' death and resurrection. But Mark's purpose is to warn against being scandalized by the Cross. Although the command at the Transfiguration to hear Jesus (9:7) may hark back on a literary level to the sayings about discipleship (but also to the prediction of the Passion and Resurrection), a main emphasis will fall on the uniqueness of Jesus' glory and authority, not on a prospect of the disciples' sharing his glory and authority (hence the weakness of the suggestion by R. Laufen [*Doppelüberlieferungen* 340-41] that Mark adds 9:1-8 to encourage cross-taking).

It is also said that to interpret discipleship as suffering prior to glorification, Mark repeatedly holds back Jesus' teaching on discipleship till after Jesus predicts his passion and resurrection (so not only vv 34-38 in relation to vv 31-33, but also 9:33-50 in relation to 9:30-32 and 10:35-45 in relation to 10:32-34) and that Mark weaves this teaching into Jesus' journey to the Cross to portray him as literally showing the way in addition to teaching it (see, e.g., A. Stock, *Call* 140-41, 146). These features of the text may sometimes rest on traditional or even historical connections, however, rather than on Marcan manipulations. In any case, if Mark were primarily concerned to teach such a view of discipleship, he might have made Jesus here predict his crucifixion and in the passion narrative take his cross as a model for the disciples' cross-taking. He might also have provided vv 34b-38 with a more emphatic introduction in v 34a (see the foregoing comments) and delayed the disciples' mission, which included teaching as well as preaching, exorcism, and miraculous healing (6:7-13, 30; cf. 1:17c), till after Jesus had taught them the true meaning of discipleship. But Mark's accent does not fall on discipleship so much as on Jesus' power of prediction (the pericope comes to a climax in 9:1) and on being unashamed of him.

M. E. Boring (*Sayings* 200) takes "the crowd" in v 34 as Mark's addition to include the church in Jesus' audience. But Mark's redaction shows that he has an even wider audience in view: the crowd represent non-Christians, summoned to Christian discipleship. We cannot be sure of the historicity of the crowd. As Boring says, they are inappropriate to the preceding context. But in a near eastern setting are they ever very far away from a figure like Jesus (cf. M.-J. Lagrange 221)? A summons to discipleship is as appropriate to them as to the wider audience of Mark, and "the villages of Philip's Caesarea" could easily produce them (cf. v 27). Strangers provoke curiosity, a famous stranger like Jesus even more curiosity. The different setting of the saying in Luke 14:27 mentions "many crowds" (v 25). Not so in Matt 10:38, but Matthew has probably moved the saying into Jesus' private commissioning of the Twelve (R. H. Gundry, *Matthew* 200). On balance it seems more likely that in his characteristically dualistic fashion Mark adds "with his disciples" to a tradition of "the crowd" because of Peter's having taken Jesus aside from the other disciples (cf. 4:10). Mark's frequent use of "summon" (προσκαλέω) does not imply that he makes up the crowd any more than he makes up the disciples, whose mention he may add but whose presence is surely traditional and historical.

G. Schwarz (in *NovT* 17 [1975] 109-12) supposes an Aramaic נכר, "ignore, treat as a stranger," underlying ἀπαρνησάσθω in v 34, and hypothesizes an original meaning, "let him consider himself a stranger (i.e. a non-Jew)," which gave way to "let him deny himself." But it is a question whether the Aramaic verb can connote ignoring either in the sense of treating as a non-Jew or in the sense of denying. Schwarz cites no passages for such connotations.

For Mark's starting to develop the motif of discipleship, U. Luz (in *The Messianic Secret* 84) argues that from here through 10:52 "the verb *akolouthein* ('to follow') is hardly ever . . . used in the simple sense of 'go after someone' but always in the pregnant sense of 'be a disciple of' (8:34; 9:38[?]; 10:21, 28, 32, 52), whereas previously this was never the case (3:7; 5:24; 6:1(?), cf. 11:9; 14:13, 54) — except for the actual 'sayings about discipleship'." But 9:38 falsifies this argument, for "follow *us*" would imply discipleship to the disciples as well as to Jesus; and 10:32, 52 doubtfully refer to disciples (see the comments ad loc.). On the other hand, though it appears before 8:27–10:52, the statement in 6:1 that "his [Jesus'] disciples follow him" would come under the motif of discipleship far more naturally than 9:38; 10:32, 52 do. And why should a motif of discipleship stop at 10:52? Only because occurrences of "follow" in 11:9; 14:13, 54 would not fit? In view of taking up one's cross, we might think that Mark would carry the motif of discipleship — if he is responsible for it — above all right into the passion narrative. Even though we were to disregard those features of v 34 which resist attribution to Jesus' crucifixion (see the foregoing comments), he would be at most implying his coming crucifixion, not predicting it outright. In an inauthentic saying we would expect a bold, clear indication of an exemplary death by crucifixion; and we would not expect churchly fabrication of a saying whose demand for a literal following can no longer be met and therefore might seem to rule out the possibility of any further salvation. Only by spiritualizing, in which Mark does *not* engage, can the demand still be met. See J. Schneider in *TDNT* 7. 578-79 for different views of cross-taking.

The argument against authenticity that the pre-passion association of crosses with criminals makes the metaphor of cross-taking (-carrying in Q) too harsh till after Jesus' crucifixion (E. Schweizer 175-76) underestimates Jesus' daring, evident throughout his speech. One thinks of his parables of the good Samaritan and of the Pharisee and toll collector, not to mention many other examples. Even after Jesus' crucifixion, moreover, the foolishness of preaching the Cross (1 Cor 1:18) makes doubtful that Christians would insert cross-taking into a saying or make up a whole saying to feature it. The similar argument that prior to the Crucifixion an audience would not have understood the metaphor of cross-taking (D. E. Nineham 230) underestimates familiarity with the procedure of crucifixion. Many in Jesus' audience may have participated in hurling abuses at a condemned criminal who had just taken his cross (cf. the numerous references in Josephus to crucifixions in Palestine of the NT era — *Ant.* 12.5.4 §256; 13.14.2 §380; 17.10.10 §295; *J.W.* 2.5.2 §75; 2.12.6 §241; 2.14.9 §§306-8; 5.11.1 §§449-51), and A. Schlatter (*Matthäus*

350-51) suggests that the willingness of Jewish rebels to risk crucifixion by the Romans underlies Jesus' saying.

The view of M. P. Green (in *BSac* 140 [1983] 117) that cross-taking means submission to the rule of the authority formerly rebelled against runs into the problem that cross-taking starts the punishment for *lack* of submission. J. C. O'Neill (in *Suffering and Martyrdom in the NT* 12-16) suggests that taking a cross alludes to Isaac's carrying the wood on which he was to be sacrificed (Gen 22:6). But the OT story puts no emphasis on Isaac's taking or carrying the wood. Abraham takes it, lays it on Isaac, and finally lays it on an altar. The text has Isaac only mentioning the wood. Nor does following *behind* Jesus correspond to Isaac's going *together* with his father. Again, Abraham's purpose of sacrificing his son on the wood finds no match in the purpose of Jesus, who will himself be killed. We may also doubt that Jesus would expect a disciple's cross to trigger thoughts of the wood that Abraham laid on Isaac. If Matthew fabricated the saying in Matt 11:29 (so R. H. Gundry, *Matthew* 218-20), it does not provide a more original, cross-less form of the saying in Mark 8:34 par. (cf. the view of G. Schwarz in *NTS* 33 [1987] 255-65 that the underlying Aramaic meant to take up wood, i.e. a yoke).

It goes too far to say that in vv 35-37 ψυχή means "self" instead of "life" (so D. R. Fletcher in *Int* 18 [1964] 157-58). Except in a modern sense, you do not save or lose yourself except by saving or losing your life. Therefore we should retain a play on temporal versus eternal life. At the same time it is true that the meaning "soul" for ψυχή and for the underlying נפש interrelates the meanings "life" and "self."

Jesus' command in 1:17 puts a question mark against the claim that in 8:35 he makes his first unequivocal demand for absolute allegiance to his own person, not just to his message (so W. L. Lane 308). Some take "for my sake" to be a pre-Marcan addition. But why should the Jesus who commands people to follow him not be capable of saying "for my sake"? If he foresees suffering for himself, it seems unlikely that he does not foresee suffering for his followers because of him. On the other hand, the lack of "for my sake" in Luke 17:33; John 12:25 argues against its originality in this particular saying. That Luke keeps the phrase at 9:24 (his proper parallel to Mark 8:35), uses phrases with ἕνεκεν at 4:18; 6:22; 18:29; 21:12, and elsewhere never drops such a phrase favors that Q-Luke 17:33 lacks it and that Matt 10:39 adds it. On the other hand, the absence of "his life" from Luke 17:33 favors that "for my sake" has been dropped by Luke as part of a larger omission. The absence of "for my sake" from John 12:25 seems due to replacement by a characteristically Johannine "in this world." Ἕνεκεν, "for the sake of," occurs nowhere in the Johannine corpus. See the notes on 10:29 and esp. 14:9 for the authenticity of "and the gospel's" and against a reference to angelic preaching of the gospel at the close of the age. Cf. R. Laufen, *Doppelüberlieferungen* 326-29; and for an argument that Mark adds "and the gospel," T. Söding, *Glaube* 204, n. 16. See R. H. Gundry, *Matthew* 201, 339, that the verb "find" in the parallels Matt 10:39; 16:25 represents Matthean redaction, not the original wording of the saying. That "find" makes a more exact antonym of "lose" than does "save" works against the originality of "find" by making a change less likely. Elsewhere, moreover, Jesus shows a predilection for "save" but not for "find" in talking about personal fate (see esp. 3:4 par., where he links "save" and "life" [ψυχή] as here, but also 5:34 par.; 10:52 par.; 13:13 parr., 20 par.; Luke 7:50; 17:19; 19:10).

L. E. Keck (in *NTS* 12 [1965-66] 357-58) thinks that Mark adds "and the gospel's" to bring the command to cross-taking over into the church age and relate it to the risk of being a Christian. But since Mark has Jesus preaching the gospel (1:15) and keeps the sake of Jesus and that of the gospel distinct (he does not write, "for the sake of the gospel concerning me"), it seems better to say that the gospel is what Jesus has been preaching. Nonetheless, Keck rightly criticizes W. Marxsen's treatment of καί as epexegetic, producing the unnatural "for the sake of me, even the gospel." Cf. *Tg. Isa* 53:1 for an Aramaic equivalent of "gospel" used absolutely, as here.

With v 35, cf. Josephus *J.W.* 1.18.3 §357. Lacking Jesus' paradoxical language is the statement in *'Abot R. Nat.* B 35 that keeping the Torah will result in keeping your life and that losing the Torah will result in losing your life. J. B. Bauer (in *Neutestamentliche Aufsätze* 7-10) and W. A. Beardslee (in *JAAR* 47 [1979] 61) draw a parallel between the language of this verse and that of a general urging his soldiers to bravery in battle (see, e.g., Hom. *Il.* 5.529-32; 15.561-64; Xen. *An.* 3.1.43; 3.2.39; idem *Cyr.* 3.3.45; 4.1.5; Isoc. *Arch.* 107; Dion. Hal. *Ant. Rom.* 6.9; 9.9; Polyb. 3.63; Curtius 4.14.25; 5.9.26; Sall. *Cat.* 58.15-17; Hor. *Carm.* 3.2.14; Cic. *Tusc.* 2.54; the Syriac *Sayings of the Wise Menander* 56 [P. Riessler, *Altjüdisches Schrifttum* 1054]). But a general argues that courage in combat leads to a victory that will cut losses and thereby better the chance of saving your present life, whereas Jesus says that if you want to save your present life you are guaranteed to lose eternal life. And according to a general, fearful fleeing leads to a defeat that will increase losses and thereby worsen the chance of saving your present life, whereas Jesus says that if you actually lose your present life you can be sure of saving your eternal life. Jesus does not talk about exercising courage so as to avoid death now, but about courage to die now so as to live afterward. If his saying bears any relation to the typical pep talk of a general to his soldiers, then, he has thoroughly transmuted the logic. The strength of the language about losing life and the contrast with saving life resist the attempt of W. Rebell (in *NTS* 35 [1989] 210-13) to do away with the possibility of martyrdom.

The differences between vv 36-37 and Phil 3:7-8 disfavor Pauline influence (see E. Wendling, *Entstehung* 112). Nor does Josephus *J.W.* 1.18.3 §355 make an entirely happy parallel, because the Josephan passage compares ruling the whole world with the loss of many others' lives, not with the loss of one's own life. But cf. Psalm 49; Sir 11:18-19; Matt 6:19-21; Luke 12:13-21, 33-34; 2 *Apoc. Bar.* 51:7-16, esp. 15. R. Bultmann (*HST* 97) also points to the folkloristic theme that life itself is the highest good. Gaining the whole world (v 36) does not mean winning it to Christ through evangelism, and probably does not mean winning its approval. The commercial language favors coming to own the whole world — the ultimate of earthly wealth.

The Aramaism ὁμολογέω ἐν (see BAGD s.v. ὁμολογέω 4) in Matt 10:32 par. Luke 12:8 favors that another active verb parallelistically characterized the next saying. If so, we should not treat "will be denied" in Luke 12:9 as a divine passive indicating the unoriginality of "the Son of man" in Mark 8:38. Rather, both the confessional saying and the one about denial originally had "the Son of man" with an active verb (W. G. Kümmel in *Jesus und der Menschensohn* 215-16); and Luke 12:9 does not mean that God will deny the denier of Jesus, but that the Son of man will do so. See the foregoing comments on v 38 for the reason Luke switches to the passive voice. The suggestion that he switches to effect a smooth transition to the passive verbs in his next verse (so R. H. Gundry, *Matthew* 214) fails to take account that because the passive verbs in 12:10 are impersonal, from the verbal standpoint a single shift from personal active to impersonal passive would have made a smoother transition than does a double shift from personal active to personal passive and then to impersonal passive. The substantival participle at the start of Luke 12:9 seems to abbreviate an original full-scale relative clause (so Luke 12:10 and Matt 10:33 as well as 10:32 — against ibid. 198).

J. Jeremias (*NT Theology* 1. 7, n. 2) thinks that "is ashamed of" and "deny" came about through confusion of חפר and כפר in pre-Marcan Aramaic tradition. But in the LXX αἰσχύνομαι and its complex and cognate forms represent חפר so very seldom in comparison with other Greek words that such a confusion seems unlikely. One could think alternatively that Mark, who gives evidence of knowing Aramaic, was helped by the similarity between the Aramaic words to make a switch in Greek words corresponding to them. B. Lindars

(*Jesus, Son of Man* 51-53) recognizes that so long as confession and denial stayed paired, "confess" would have forestalled confusion of the Aramaic words by implying the proper antonym "deny." To maintain Jeremias's view, therefore, Lindars delays confusion till someone separated confession and denial. But we have seen that Mark himself seems to have performed the separation for a redactional reason. So no intervening Aramaic stage is left during which a confusion is likely to have occurred.

Again it is overdoing things to equate "me" and "my words" by making the καί between them epexegetic: "even." The definite article before ἐμοὺς λόγους (producing in literal translation "the my words") puts a wide roadblock in the way of an epexegetic καί, and the notion that Jesus and his words are equated because only in them is he still present in the church (so M. Horstmann, *Studien* 43-44) mistakes the passage as ecclesiastical. It is a call to conversion, not to perseverance. To be sure, in Rom 1:16; 2 Tim 1:8, 12 ἐπαισχύνομαι will spell out the possibility of being ashamed of the gospel, but with respect to not preaching it, whereas here the possibility of shame has to do with not denying yourself, taking up your cross, and following Jesus — in short, with unconversion.

P[45vid] W k sa Tert omit λόγους, "words," probably because of homoioteleuton (so B. M. Metzger, *Textual Commentary* ad loc.). The argument for the v.l. that its meaning "my [followers]" comes close to 9:37; Matt 10:40; 25:40, 45; Luke 10:16 overlooks the greater closeness of "me and the gospel" in 8:35; 10:29 to the better attested reading "me and my words." The comments have noted a contextual emphasis in the possessive adjective ἐμούς, "my"; hence, J. M. Ross (in *NovT* 25 [1983] 62-63) is wrong to argue from the lack of contextual emphasis to the originality of omitting λόγους.

Some have argued that since Mark uses "adulterous" nowhere else and "sinful" nowhere else as an adjective, the phrase "in this adulterous and sinful generation" crept in before Mark. But a double description of "generation" was becoming widespread and variegated: "crooked and perverted," "unbelieving and perverted," "evil and adulterous," "adulterous and faithless" (Phil 2:15; Luke 9:41; Matt 12:39; 16:4; 17:17; *Tg. Isa* 57:3). Mark likes dual expressions, as in his immediately preceding insertion "me and my words." His double description appears nowhere else in the NT. And the OT provides ample background for the association of adultery and sin. So there is no convincing reason not to hold Mark responsible for inserting the phrase.

By using "the Son of man" in v 38, Jesus cloaks a very large claim in the modesty of an indirect third person reference to himself (cf. 2 Cor 12:2-5). Not only does it favor authenticity that the phrase never occurs in a Christian confession or other kind of statement that would identify who Jesus is (against the argument of B. L. Mack, *Myth* 71, n. 14, that the language of confession [in Q] is mystifying if the saying is read as authentic). It also favors authenticity that the church would not likely produce a saying, whether through modification of an already existing one or through creation ex nihilo, that might be understood as some modern scholars do in fact understand it to distinguish the Son of man from Jesus and give ultimate authority to the Son of man rather than to Jesus (against which distinction see H. Fleddermann in *SBL 1987 Seminar Papers* 613-16). If "the Son of man" in Luke 12:8 implies that "the Son of man" originally stood in tradition behind Luke 12:9 (see the foregoing comments), then O. J. F. Seitz (in *SE VI* 490-93) is wrong to argue that a messianic secret leads Mark to fabricate the saying in v 38 as a way of leaving it uncertain whether Jesus is the Son of man. See the comments and notes on 2:10 for further details, and D. C. Allison, Jr., *End* 134, for a summary of arguments against regarding "sentences of holy law," like this one, as necessarily inauthentic (cf. also Fleddermann, op. cit. 612-13). Underneath this saying and others like it rests the lex talionis. See also the notes on 13:26 against the argument that the absence of "glory" and "angels" from 14:62 disfavors the authenticity of 8:38; 13:26; and R. Leivestad in *Glaube und Gerechtigkeit* 95-108 against interpreting the glory of the Son of man's father as the pristine glory of Adam.

VISUAL AND AUDITORY EVIDENCE THAT JESUS IS GOD'S SON

9:2-13 *(Matt 17:1-13; Luke 9:28-36)*

This pericope divides in two: (1) the transfiguration of Jesus (vv 2-8) and (2) the conversation between him and three of his disciples on the way down the mountain where they have seen him transfigured (vv 9-13). The Transfiguration subdivides into Jesus' taking Peter, James, and John up a high mountain (v 2), a change in Jesus' appearance (v 3), an appearance of Elijah with Moses and their talking with Jesus (v 4), a suggestion by Peter (vv 5-6), a cloud and a voice from heaven (v 7), and a seeing of Jesus alone (v 8). The conversation subdivides into a command to secrecy (vv 9-10) and a discussion about Elijah (vv 11-13).

9:2-4 *(Matt 17:1-3; Luke 9:28-31)* As usual, a topographical shift marks the start of a new pericope. But the unusually specific indication of time, "and after six days," ties the following story of Jesus' transfiguration to the preceding prediction (9:1) as a fulfilment of it. This fulfilment demonstrates his predictive power and thereby supports the reliability of his having predicted death and resurrection for himself (v 31). The high point of the story will be reached in the Father's declaration that Jesus is his beloved Son and in his consequent command to hear Jesus (v 7), i.e. listen to Jesus' prediction of the Passion and Resurrection, his summons to cross-taking and the predictive reasons supporting the summons, and his prediction that some of the audience will see God's rule as having come in power (8:31–9:1; cf. 4:9, 23 for Jesus' own commands to hear what he has said). For these words help take away the scandal of the Crucifixion by putting the death of Jesus in God's predetermined plan, known and told ahead of time by Jesus himself and including the suffering of his disciples and compensatory glory to follow. Closing references to his passion and resurrection (vv 9-12) will clamp the pericope yet more tightly to the preceding one, with its initial prediction of those events.

The present historical tense of παραλαμβάνει, "takes along," emphasizes that Jesus' taking along Peter, James, and John (cf. 5:37; 14:33; and to a lesser extent 13:3) fulfils that part of the prediction in 9:1 which referred to "some of the ones standing here." The historical present tense of ἀναφέρει, "he takes them up," and the reference to "a high mountain" start not only an emphasis original to the story on the splendor and revelation of Jesus' divine sonship but also an editorial emphasis on the fulfilment of that part of the prediction in v 1 which dealt with seeing that God's rule has come with power, for mountains symbolize power and dominion (cf. Dan 2:35, 44-45; Matt 28:16-18; Rev 17:9-10; and many other passages, biblical and extrabiblical, cited by W. Foerster in *TDNT* 5. 476-78, 480-81). The description of the mountain as "high" (contrast 3:13; 6:46; 11:1; 13:3; 14:26) adds to these emphases and makes it appropriate that Jesus should take only the three closest of his disciples. The great height of the mountain also makes it a suburb of heaven where deceased righteous heroes may speak with Jesus, and God to the three disciples. "Privately, alone" makes a dual expression typical of Mark. Its duality puts weight on the imminent fulfilment of the limiting

phrase in Jesus' prediction, "some of the ones standing there". "Privately" (κατ'
ἰδίαν) modifies the verb and therefore refers to a private taking away from the
crowd that Jesus summoned in 8:34. "Alone" (μόνους) modifies Peter, James, and
John and therefore stresses separation from the other disciples, also mentioned in
8:34 (cf. 9:9).

"And he was transfigured" displays a divine passive, which means that God
transfigured Jesus (cf. the Father's voice in v 7). Thus the Transfiguration looks
forward to the coming of the Son of man "in the glory of his Father" (8:38). The
glistening of Jesus' garments defines his transfiguration. The unusual first position
of the subject τὰ ἱμάτια αὐτοῦ, "his garments," emphasizes their visual indication
of Jesus' divine sonship (cf. the auditory indication in v 7). So also does the pair
of expressions following the participle "glistening," viz., "exceedingly white, such
[garments] as a launderer on the earth is not able thus to whiten." In particular,
this emphasis is carried by λίαν, "exceedingly," οἷα, "such [garments] as," ἐπὶ
τῆς γῆς, "on the earth," and οὕτως, "thus, in this way," the position of the subject
γναφεύς, "launderer," before its verb, the duality (not to say redundancy) of οἷα
. . . οὕτως, and the position of οὕτως before its infinitive. E. F. F. Bishop (*Jesus
of Palestine* 56) points out that since "a launderer" needs no modifier, ἐπὶ τῆς γῆς
may modify "to whiten" with reference to bleaching clothes and thus may mean
"on the ground" rather than "on the earth." The word order may seem to be
contrary; but if we adopt this syntax, the forward position of ἐπὶ τῆς γῆς will
emphasize that divine whiteness exceeds what can be attained by bleaching on
the ground. So also οὕτως, "in this way," will refer back to ἐπὶ τῆς γῆς as the
method of bleaching, fill up the position that that phrase would occupy if it were
not thrust into an emphatic forward position, and therefore make no redundancy
with οἷα. On examination, then, the syntax suggested by Bishop offers some
interpretative advantages (cf. G. D. Reynolds [in *BT* 4 (1953) 42], who appeals
to the oriental practice of bleaching clothes on the ground and argues that "no
launderer on earth" would require τις before γναφεύς and probably ἐν τῇ γῇ instead
of ἐπὶ τῆς γῆς). "Before them" yet again brings us back to the fulfilment of "some
of the ones standing here." Mark's Hellenistic audience would understand the
Transfiguration as indicative of Jesus' divinity (see the Hellenistic literature cited
by J. Behm in *TDNT* 4. 757).

Though apocalyptic literature describes angels and departed righteous
people as arrayed in glistening white garments, Mark does not so describe Elijah
and Moses. They are here, not as competitors with Jesus — only he is said to be
arrayed in glistening white garments — but as foils to highlight that he alone is
God's beloved Son to be heard. The appearance of Elijah gives an eschatological
signal to the three disciples, however; for Elijah is to come back before the Day
of the Lord according to Mal 3:23-24(4:5-6) (cf. vv 11-13 here in Mark). Despite
Moses' coming before Elijah in the OT, Mark mentions Elijah first to highlight
this signal (cf. the order Elijah–Moses in the most reliable MSS of the LXX at
Mal 3:22-24) and perhaps also to link Elijah's not having died with Jesus' prediction concerning some who will "not taste death. . . ." Moses comes in secondarily ("with Moses"). But why Elijah and Moses? Why not others? Apparently

because these two are the only OT figures to have seen a theophany on a mountain (D. Baly in *ExpTim* 82 [1970-71] 83). But a major difference is that the Transfiguration reveals Jesus, not God. Even God will figure in the narrative only to exalt Jesus (v 7). But Jesus is revealed as divine; so we are back to theophany after all.

Elijah and Moses appear to the disciples but are talking with Jesus, not to the disciples. "Talking with Jesus" does not reveal what Elijah and Moses say to him. Rather, it prepares for Peter's wanting to make three tabernacles in order that he and his fellow disciples may keep listening to what Elijah and Moses are saying to Jesus. "Talking with Jesus" also prepares for God's command that the three disciples listen to Jesus instead; for Jesus, not Elijah and Moses, represents the rule of God. Since glory connotes power (as shown by the three disciples' terror in v 6b; cf. the parallelism of "glory" and "power" in 8:38–9:1; 13:26; also 2 Pet 1:16-18), the divine glory seen in the transfigured Jesus shows that on this occasion some of those who heard the prediction in 9:1 now see God's rule as having come in power even before the Son of man's coming in the glory of his Father with the holy angels (8:38). God's rule has become visible in the transfigured Jesus, the glory of whose glistening garments represents the power of that rule (contrast the suffering of the Son of man — 8:31-32a).

9:5-6 *(Matt 17:4, 6; Luke 9:32-33, 34b)* Strictly speaking, Peter does not answer a question, for no one has asked him one (contrast 8:29, which the present phraseology echoes). But he is responding to what he and his fellow disciples have seen and heard; in that sense ἀποκριθείς is more than a meaningless appendage (see v 6a; 11:14; 12:35; 14:40, 48). The present historical tense of λέγει, "says," emphasizes the statement of Peter that shows his and his fellow disciples' terror. This terror, in turn, adds to the emphasis on their seeing that God's rule has come in power before their very eyes — and thus on the fulfilment of Jesus' prediction in 9:1. Despite Matthew's and Luke's substitutions of "Lord" and "Master," Peter's addressing Jesus as "Rabbi" looks honorific, as in 11:21 (where Peter will again address Jesus) and 14:45 (though treacherously spoken by Judas Iscariot; cf. also 4:38; 10:51). If so, it does not signal a retreat from Peter's confessing Jesus as "the Christ" (8:29). Nor does Mark seem to regard it as a retreat; for his criticism in v 6 relates to the suggestion concerning tabernacles more naturally than to this address, which probably comes to Mark in the tradition and does not capture his interest one way or the other. Though "Rabbi" means "my great one," which would contribute to Mark's Christological emphasis, he does not translate it, as he does a number of other Semitic expressions (3:17; 5:41; 7:11, 34; 15:22, 34; cf. 10:46; 14:36). Presumably, he knows his Gentile audience to be already familiar with it (D. Lührmann 156; see J.-B. Frey, *Corpus Inscriptionum Judaicarum* 1 §§568, 611, for inscriptions discovered in Salerno and Venosa, Italy, and containing "Rabbi").

The occurrence of "here" in the statement, "It's good we're here," makes a verbal link with "here" in the prediction at 9:1 and thereby furthers the interpretation of that prediction as now fulfilled. The forward positions of καλόν, "good," and ὧδε, "here," emphasize the link and fulfilment; and though apart from the prediction at 9:1 Peter's statement would probably mean that the three disciples' presence is good for the purpose of making three tabernacles, in the context of that prediction his statement probably reflects on the prediction: the three disciples' presence is good because they are seeing the rule of God as having come in power just as Jesus predicted that some who heard his prediction would do. "We" then excludes Jesus, Moses, and Elijah and distinguishes Peter, James, and John from the rest who heard Jesus' prediction but are not present. Likewise in the suggestion of making three tabernacles, "we" means only Peter, James, and John; for Peter is hardly suggesting that Jesus, Moses, and Elijah join in constructing the tabernacles, and no one else is around. The limitation to three tabernacles — one each for Jesus, Moses, and Elijah and therefore none for the three disciples — and the emphatic forward positions of σοί, Μωϋσεῖ, and Ἠλίᾳ show that Peter has in mind places of honor, as though Moses and Elijah share the Father's glory with Jesus (cf. 8:38). The falling back to the OT order of Moses before Elijah suits the OT association of "tabernacle" with Moses. Since Peter's suggestion overexalts Moses and Elijah, more of whose words Peter and his fellow disciples want to hear, Mark designs his editorial comment, "for he [Peter] did not know what [or 'how'] he should answer" (cf. 14:40), to keep the audience of the gospel from overlooking Peter's error (against the view of T. E. Boomershine in *Semeia* 39 [1987] 57-58 that Peter's suggestion sounds no more than a humorous note of stupidity). "For they were terrified" gives the reason for the error, brings the other two disciples into it (Peter has acted as their spokesman; cf. 8:29), and emphasizes the overpowering glory of God's rule that they are seeing in fulfilment of 9:1 (cf. 2 Pet 1:16-18 and the eschatological associations of tabernacles as outlined by I. Abrahams, *Studies* 2. 51-55, and H. Riesenfeld, *Jésus transfiguré* 29-53). Strengthening this emphasis are the infelicity of a second γάρ-clause following immediately on another one (so also in 11:18), the perfective preposition in ἔκφοβοι, "terrified," the emphatic position of this adjective, and the uneasy fit between it and Peter's happy "it's good we're here" (contrast somewhat the simple statement ἐφοβοῦντο γάρ, "for they were afraid," in 16:8; but that verse, the present one, and 4:41; 5:15, 33; 9:32; 10:32 all portray a fear appropriate in response to manifestations of deity — D. Catchpole in *JTSA* 18 [1977] 6-10).

9:7-8 *(Matt 17:5, 7-8; Luke 9:34a, 35-36a)* The cloud signals God's presence (cf. Exod 16:10; 19:9; 24:15-16; 33:1; 40:34-38; Num 9:15-22; 1 Kgs 8:10-11; Isa 4:5; 2 Macc 2:8; and further literature cited by D. Daube, *NTRJ* 30-32). The overshadowing (cf. Exod 24:15 ἄλλος) corrects Peter's suggestion of making three tabernacles, and by correcting it confirms that he had in mind honorific tabernacles rather than ordinary shelters. The location on a high mountain and Exod 40:34-38 LXX favor that ἐπισκιάζουσα includes complete envelopment, not just shade overhead (cf. Num 14:14; Ps 105:39; Isa 4:5). That the voice comes out of the cloud (cf. Exod 24:15; 33:9-11; Num 11:24-25; 12:5-6; Deut 31:15-16) might seem to imply that the three disciples are not in it because it has enveloped only Jesus, Moses, and Elijah. But Exod 24:15-18 tells of God's speaking to Moses out of a cloud even though Moses has been in it for a long while. Therefore despite the doubtfulness of an allusion to Exodus (see the following notes), linguistic usage in Exodus makes it better to assume that the present cloud envelops the disciples as well as Jesus, Moses, and Elijah. In it, the disciples can no longer see Jesus, Moses, and Elijah; but they hear God's voice. The disciples' looking around implies that the cloud has lifted. They look around to see Moses and Elijah yet see "no one (οὐδένα); rather, [they see] Jesus alone with themselves." As emphasized by the forward position of οὐδένα, Moses and Elijah are no longer to be seen. Their speaking with Jesus has been replaced with God's voice because they left under cover of the cloud (cf. Acts 1:9; 1 Thess 4:17; Rev 10:1; 11:12). "Alone" has a narrower referent than in v 2, but it makes an inclusion with the earlier occurrence.

The voice of God declares the divine and beloved sonship of Jesus, as at his baptism (1:11; cf. the comments ad loc.). But this time the voice comes out of the cloud, not out of heaven, perhaps because the high mountain already juts up into heaven (but see 2 Pet 1:18, which does not describe the mountain as high, however); and the voice addresses the disciples, not Jesus. Correspondingly, "you are" changes to "this is." The declaration of Jesus as God's beloved Son counteracts taking offense at his predicted passion and at the consequent command to take up one's cross and follow him (8:31-38). The tradition in 2 Pet 1:17-18 that "on the holy mountain" God said, "This is my beloved Son, in whom I am well pleased," suggests that Mark has replaced an "in whom"-clause with an echo of 4:3, 9, 23, 24; 7:14 in the command to hear Jesus (cf. 11:14; 12:37; and Mark's emphasis, beginning in 1:21-28, on Jesus as an authoritative teacher; see R. J. Bauckham, *Jude, 2 Peter* 209-10, on the probable independence of 2 Pet 1:17-18 from Matt 17:5). Adding emphasis to the declaration of Jesus as God's beloved Son and to the command, "Hear him," are (1) the parallelistic structure of καὶ ἐγένετο νεφέλη . . . , καὶ ἐγένετο φωνή . . . , "and there came a cloud . . . , and there came a voice . . ."; (2) the assonance of νεφέλη and φωνή; and (3) the absence of a transitional λέγουσα, "saying" (as also in 1:11). Asyndeton puts further emphasis on the command to hear Jesus. We may doubt the often suggested allusion to Deut 18:15: "Him you shall hear" (cf. *Clem. Hom.* 3.53). Mark's word order and imperative mood agree with his own 7:14, but differ from the word order and indicative mood in both the LXX and the MT of Deut 18:15. The command to hear Jesus contrasts with the three disciples' interest in hearing Elijah and Moses talk with him (v 5: "it's good that we [three disciples] are here") and in the present context refers most particularly to his coming command not to relate what they have seen till after the Resurrection (v 9), for the three disciples have already heard his recent prediction of the Passion and Resurrection and his summons to cross-taking and the predictive reasons supporting the summons (8:31–9:1). The disciples' looking around and no longer seeing anyone but Jesus alone with themselves gets rid of any possible ambiguity concerning the one declared to be the beloved Son of God, but it also reinforces the point that the disciples should pay attention solely to Jesus because, as they have seen, God's rule has come with power in him, not in Moses and Elijah, to whom Mark has attributed no transfiguration. Intensifying this point are (1) the suddenness (ἐξάπινα) with which the disciples look around and see no one except Jesus; (2) the indirect middle voice of περιβλεψάμενοι, which emphasizes that the disciples themselves look around (A. T. Robertson, *Grammar* 809); (3) the double negativity, side-by-side placement, assonance, and forward position of οὐκέτι οὐδένα, "no longer anyone"; (4) the echo of ἴδωσιν, "they see" (v 1), in εἶδον, "they saw" (v 8; cf. vv 4, 9); (5) the strength of the adversative ἀλλά, "rather"; and (6) the vigor of the ellipsis of "they see" in the ἀλλά-clause, which therefore centers attention on the remaining "Jesus alone with themselves." The Transfiguration has anticipated the coming glory of the Son of man, which will also be seen (14:62), and has revealed the power of God's rule that has already arrived.

9:9-10 *(Matt 17:9; Luke 9:36b)* During the descent down the mountain Jesus' ordering the three disciples to relate the things that they have seen to no one till after he has risen from the dead parallels a similar command in 8:30 (cf. also 5:43; 7:36). As usual, he commands silence to avoid the danger of being mobbed (cf. esp. vv 15, 25 and see the comments on 8:30). After the Resurrection, that danger will have passed. Here, moreover, a premature publicizing of the Transfiguration would counteract both the teaching that the Son of man must suffer and the general summons to cross-taking (8:31-38). As in apocalyptic, prior secrecy makes the present telling more delightful to the literary audience (cf. Dan 8:26; 12:4; H. J. Ebeling, *Messiasgeheimnis* 200-201; T. L. Donaldson, *Jesus on the Mountain* 137). The forward position of μηδενί, "to no one" (cf. 16:8), emphasizes prior secrecy.

Postponing till after Jesus' resurrection the publication of his transfiguration also fits into Mark's apology for the Cross. Then, telling about the Transfiguration can have its desired effect of helping to counteract the scandal of the Crucifixion. Transfiguration will team up with resurrection — both of them fulfilments of predictions by Jesus — to deal a double blow against any perceived shame in the manner of his death. Thus the postponement neither deemphasizes the Transfiguration on account of its apocalyptic overtones (see 8:38; chap. 13 to the contrary) nor favors a theology of suffering as opposed to a theology of glory. Vice versa! For Jesus does not command secrecy till after the Son of man has been killed, but till after the Son of man has risen. Attention focuses on his resurrection from the dead, not on his death, as shown especially by the addition of ἐκ νεκρῶν, "from [the] dead," in a forward position (so also in v 10; cf. 12:25, 26 as to word order, but contrast 6:14, 16 in that respect). If the Cross alone reveals who Jesus really is, why tell about his transfiguration at all, even after his resurrection? To do so is to subvert the supposed theology of suffering, for the Transfiguration is reported as an event of glory that preceded suffering. According to the principle "no crown without a cross," a theology of suffering needs the glorious event itself, not just the telling of it, to follow the Crucifixion. Thus the retrojection of an appearance by the risen Jesus into his earthly life (cf. the following notes) would undermine the very theology of suffering that some of those who suppose such a retrojection think to be the reason for it.

The taking of only the three disciples closest to Jesus has minimized the risk of premature publication yet conforms to the law of two or three witnesses and, above all, satisfies the terms required for fulfilment of Jesus' prediction in v 1. Εἶδον, "had seen," echoes ἴδωσιν, "see," in v 1 (cf. ὤφθη αὐτοῖς, "was seen by them" or "appeared to them," in v 4 and εἶδον in v 8) and reinforces that the intervening verses have narrated a fulfilment of that prediction. The forward position of ἃ εἶδον, "the things that they had seen" (for the placement of the direct object before its verb, see 16:8 again), underlines this fulfilment and the three disciples' witnessing it. Since in 15:39 seeing an event will include hearing what was spoken at the time, "the things that they had seen" includes the declaration of Jesus' divine sonship and the command to hear him. The indirect discourse in v 9 may seem to make "the Son of man" purely titular. But even though the phrase refers to oneself in direct discourse, it is modestly third person and therefore can come over into indirect discourse without a shift in meaning or connotation (cf. the comments and notes on 2:10). As in 8:32, Mark uses τὸν λόγον, "the saying." His stress falls on the effect of Jesus' command: the three disciples "kept the saying [i.e. they observed the command not to relate to anyone what they had seen], though they were discussing among themselves (πρὸς ἑαυτοὺς συζητοῦντες) what the rising from the dead is." Jesus' word, which the forward position of τὸν λόγον stresses, takes effect and thereby shows his power. The forward position of πρὸς ἑαυτούς in relation to συζητοῦντες also stresses this effectiveness. As such, rising from the dead would not be meaningless to first century Jews. But the definite article is anaphoric: "*the* rising from the dead" refers back to *the Son of man's* rising from the dead. Verses 11-13 will bring out that the disciples are discussing his resurrection in relation to the expected coming of Elijah (against M. A. Tolbert [*Sowing the Gospel* 207-8], who argues that of all the disciples Peter, James, and John should have known the meaning of resurrection because of Jesus' having raised the daughter of Jairus [5:22-24, 35-43] and because of the appearance of Elijah with Moses [9:4] — as though Jesus were referring to resurrection in general and as though Elijah had died and both he and Moses had already been resurrected).

9:11-13 *(Matt 17:10-13)* Λέγοντες, "saying," enables us to take the following ὅτι as interrogative, "why?" (cf. the comments on ἐπηρώτα in 8:27; M. Black, *Aramaic Approach* 119-21). The disciples ask why the scribes say it is necessary for Elijah to come first, i.e. to come before the Day of the Lord and therefore in the disciples' view — since resurrection is associated with that day — before the Son of man's resurrection. This question grows out of scribal teaching based on the statement in Mal 3:23-24(4:5-6) that God will send Elijah before the Day of the Lord, out of Jesus' recent mention of the scribes in his first prediction of the Passion and Resurrection (8:31), out of Elijah's appearance on the Mount of Transfiguration (cf. esp. his having been mentioned first and chiefly in v 4), and out of the immediately foregoing mention of the Son of man's resurrection from the dead (vv 9-10). Stressing Elijah over against the Son of man is the placement of Ἠλίαν, "Elijah," in a position not merely ahead of the infinitive of which it is the subject but even ahead of the main verb. The forward positions of Elijah's name also in vv 12-13 carry the same emphasis.

An adversative δέ, "but," sets Jesus' answer opposite the disciples' question. He does not answer their "why?" by saying, "Because it is thus written by Malachi the prophet," but vaults over scribal opinion by giving his own deeper and fuller reason: Elijah must go beyond Malachi's prophecy to restore all things. Malachi prophesied only that Elijah would come before the Day of the Lord and "turn the heart of fathers to children, and the heart of children to their fathers" (3:24[4:6]). "Restores all things" enlarges Malachi's prophecy to include everything needed for the consummation. So Jesus affirms on the one hand indeed (μέν) that Elijah is going to effect a universal restoration, but denies on the other hand that this will take place before the passion of the Son of man (the καί before πῶς having an adversative meaning, "yet," which Semitically complements μέν where δέ would offer a better Greek complement). To stress the denial Jesus asks his own question, a leading one that builds on his preceding statement: "Yet how [can it be that] it is written against the Son of man in order that he may suffer much [cf. 8:31] and be treated with contempt [if in fact Elijah, having come beforehand, restores all things]?" For the meaning "concerning" with the verb of writing, περί is used elsewhere (14:21; Matt 4:6; 11:10; 26:24; Luke 7:27; 24:44 et passim). Here and in the next verse, then, ἐπί probably means "against," as for example in 3:24, 25, 26; 10:11; 13:8 (bis), 12; 14:48, and signals the following references to suffering. Likewise, when Mark elsewhere uses "it is written" to introduce a formal quotation of the OT, ἵνα does not follow; rather, ὅτι or nothing corresponding (1:2; 7:6; 11:17; 14:27). Here in v 12, then, ἵνα introduces the purpose of OT passion predictions, as in 14:49; John 20:31; 1 Cor 9:15; 2 Cor 2:3, 9; 1 John 1:4; 2:1; 5:13, rather than introducing their content or, after a break, answering a question limited to the preceding words (Question: "And how is it written about the Son of man?" Answer: "That he should suffer much and be treated with contempt" — so M. D. Hooker, *Son of Man* 131). "The Scripture foretells and by foretelling determines the issue" (H. B. Swete 194). The falling of emphasis on Elijah's restoration of all things, not on his coming first (only a participial phrase; contrast the disciples' question, which dealt solely with coming first), points up the implication that an earlier restoration of all things would leave no room for the Son of man's maltreatment, especially a maltreatment so severe as to be emphasized by the forwardly positioned πολλά, "much." Jesus leaves his question unanswered to spotlight the implication that a restoration of all things by Elijah has not yet occurred and will not occur till after the Son of man has suffered. Otherwise, Scripture would be broken (cf. Justin *Dial.* 49).

The disciples' question grew in part out of Jesus' reference to the Resurrection. Jesus' counter question has shifted their attention to the Passion. Though the Passion implies that Elijah's restoration of all things will come only later, however, the counter question has not made clear whether the Resurrection will take place before or after that restoration (cf. Str-B 3. 9; 4/2. 785, 787-88 for later rabbinic speculations that Elijah will appear directly before the Day of the Lord, one day beforehand, or three days beforehand). This unclarity does not matter to Mark, however. It is enough for him that Jesus has power to predict his own death even against the seeming implication of the scribes' scripturally based expectation concerning Elijah.

"Nevertheless I say to you" contrasts what the scribes say with what Jesus is now going to say; i.e. it contrasts Elijah's having already come with his having yet to come. His having already come does not refer to his appearance on the Mount of Transfiguration, for Jesus goes on to say what can refer only to the earlier fate of John the Baptist: "and they did against him [αὐτῷ — dative of disadvantage; contrast the much more frequent dative of advantage with ποιέω] as many things as they wanted [ἤθελον, which occurred several times in the story of John's martyrdom for the wishes of Herod, Herodias, and Herodias's daughter (6:19, 22, 25, 26); cf. its later use for the wishes of those who will cry out for Jesus' crucifixion (15:9, 12; also Dan 8:4; 11:3, 36; 2 Macc 7:16; CD 4:11; *Jub.* 2:29; *Acts Thom.* 32, always in a bad sense)], just as it is written against him." The καί, "both," right before Elijah's name indicates that he as well as the Son of man has come (cf. Matt 11:7-11 par. Luke 7:24-28) and that despite the failure of John to restore all things, he did fulfil that part of Malachi's prophecy which concerns Elijah's coming (cf. 2 Kgs 1:8 with Mark 1:6 and the comments ad loc.). Thus not only does John's maltreatment explain why he did not restore all things. But also the scripturalness of Elijah's maltreatment parallels and supports John's maltreatment, which in turn parallels and supports the scripturalness of the Son of man's coming maltreatment and so contributes to Mark's apology for the Cross.

The present tense and indicative mood of ἀποκαθιστάνει, "restores," rule out a past accomplishment of the predicted restoration (against *Gos. Thom.* 51). John the Baptist is not at the time engaged in restoring all things, for he has suffered martyrdom (6:14-29). Nor did he restore all things prior to martyrdom; otherwise, the Son of man would not have to suffer. Therefore we should take the present tense as futuristic (cf. Matt 17:11 and the LXX of Mal 3:24[4:6]). The perfect tense of ἐλήλυθεν links up with the completion of John's ministry through martyrdom and consequently has nothing to do with a similar perfect tense in v 1, as though Elijah came on the Mount of Transfiguration to fulfil the visible coming of God's rule. Apparently Jesus looks forward to a yet further coming of Elijah before the end (cf. *Seder 'Olam Rabbah*). But Mark is not interested in that implication (contrast Matt 17:11). He is interested, rather, in God's plan that both Elijah-John the Baptist and Jesus the Son of man suffer first. Since neither Malachi nor any other OT prophet speaks about maltreatment of the coming Elijah, perhaps the clause "according as (καθώς) it is written about him" refers to the written record of the historical Elijah's maltreatment, considered a pattern for the maltreatment of Elijah returned as John. Of course, 1 Kgs 19:2, 10 speaks only about an attempt to take Elijah's life (cf. Rom 11:2-3; *1 Enoch* 89:52). The attempt proved unsuccessful, whereas John has been killed (hence Matthew's omission of the scriptural appeal). But the very wording of the statement that "they did as many things as they wanted" to the returned Elijah seems to carry the implication that what the enemies of Elijah wanted but failed to do in the OT the enemies of John have succeeded in doing. Adding emphasis to God's plan as revealed in and determined by the Scripture is the concentric structure of vv 12c-13: (a) "Yet how [can it be that] it is written . . . ?"; (b) "in order that he may suffer much . . ."; (c) "Nevertheless I say to you . . ."; (b′) "and they did against him . . ."; (a′) "just as it is written . . ." (C. Myers, *Binding the Strong Man* 253). The central statement that Elijah has come (c) answers to the statement which sets up this concentric structure by declaring that Elijah does come first to restore all things (v 12b). The strength of the ἀλλά, "nevertheless," which introduces the central statement calls special attention to the authority of Jesus' teaching ("I say to you"; cf. esp. 1:21-28).

NOTES

According to N. Perrin (*Rediscovering* 200-201 and in *NovT* 11 [1969] 67-70), Mark composes 9:1 according to the form of 13:30, according to the content of 8:38, and for the purpose of promising a reward to those who face persecution and possible martyrdom (8:34-38). But similarities of form and content may derive from Jesus' habits of speaking as easily as from Mark's imitation of his sources, and the promise of seeing the consummation of God's rule before dying hardly comforts those who face the prospect of losing their lives for the sake of Jesus and the gospel. For Mark's fabrication of the saying, Perrin argues that seeing God's rule as having come in power parallels seeing the Son of man's coming in power (13:26), yet Matthew and Luke do not have this phraseology except when drawing on Mark. Well, then, do we reject the authenticity of all Jesus' sayings represented in the Marcan tradition but not outside it? The use of a characteristically Marcan ἕως (9:1) instead of the non-Marcan μέχρι (13:30) carries no implication for the saying as a whole; for the meaning ("until") is no different and a good number of other Jesuanic sayings contain ἕως (6:10, 23; 9:19 [bis]; 12:36; 13:19, 27; 14:25, 32, 34; not to list Q-sayings in Luke and Matthew).

Features of 9:1 that tend toward its authenticity include the characteristically Jesuanic asseveration, "Truly I say to you" (cf. J. Jeremias, *NT Theology* 1. 35-36; B. D. Chilton, *Galilean Rabbi* 202), the particularity of the group identified as "some of the ones standing here," the Semitic character of the expression "taste death," the characteristically Jesuanic theme of God's rule, and the characteristically Jesuanic way of describing that rule as "coming" (see, e.g., the Lord's Prayer). Unless the authenticity of 13:26 is rejected, the similarity between "in power" (9:1) and "with much power" (13:26) also tends toward the authenticity of 9:1. The prediction that God's rule will have come before all the contemporaries of Jesus have died contradicts his professed ignorance of end-time chronology (13:32) no more than does the prediction that "this generation will not pass away till all these things take place" (13:30). He professes ignorance of the exact time ("the day and the hour"), but affirms knowledge of the generation that includes his hearers. He does not teach the imminence of the end in a strict sense (i.e. that it may come at any moment), but the unexpectedness of the end for those who pay no heed to premonitory signs. Thus fails the argument that because of weakened imminence, 9:1 betrays a late derivation from 13:30 (so G. R. Beasley-Murray, *Jesus and the Kingdom of God* 187-93 with references to earlier literature). Only by isolating 13:30 from its context could one sustain this argument. But then "all these things" would have no referent. Luke 17:20-21 probably refers to the coming of God's rule through the present ministry of Jesus (cf. Luke 11:20) without denying signs in the end-time (cf. Luke 21:25-33).

The following discussion of 9:1 makes several points: (1) By itself, the grammatical structure of the prediction in 9:1 does not require interpretation in terms of the consummation. (2) The content of the prediction does favor an original reference to the consummation, however. (3) Mark's date of writing probably allows retention of the original reference. (4) His take-over of end-time phraseology favors such retention. (5) But his arrangement of materials and redaction of the transfiguration narrative favor that he presents the Transfiguration as a preliminary fulfilment.

Does 9:1 imply that the "some" will die after seeing that God's rule has come in power (cf. Luke 2:26)? Not necessarily, because Matt 10:23 does not imply that the disciples will finish the cities of Israel after the Son of man comes. On the contrary! Matt 5:18 may or may not imply that one iota or tittle will pass away from the Law after all things are fulfilled, but probably does not in view of foregoing and following statements upholding the permanence of the Law. Matt 5:26 par. Luke 12:59 does imply that you will go out of debtors' prison if you pay the last farthing; but it is not at all certain — in fact, it looks doubtful — that you will meet the condition. Matt 13:39 par. Luke 13:35 probably means that Jerusalem will eventually see Jesus and say, "Blessed. . . ." But Mark 13:30 par. Matt 24:34 par. Luke 21:32 can hardly imply that this generation will pass away after all things take place. On the other side again, Mark 14:25 par. Matt 26:29 par. Luke 22:18 certainly means that Jesus will drink wine after the period of his abstinence. The Passover-saying in Luke 22:16 carries a similar meaning. Luke 22:34 differs slightly in having οὐ plus a future indicative verb in the first clause, but the construction is basically equivalent to οὐ μή plus an aorist subjunctive verb. This verse implies that the cock will crow after Peter's three denials. Taking into account all the other synoptic sayings of Jesus that have οὐ μή plus an aorist subjunctive verb (or an equivalent) followed by ἕως ἄν (or an equivalent) plus an aorist subjunctive verb, then, we have to say that the grammatical construction itself leaves unanswered the question whether what will not happen until another event takes place will then happen, or whether even the other event will ever take place. Sometimes the meanings of the words that are poured into the grammatical construction make the matter clear in one way, sometimes in the opposite way, sometimes not at all. Hence, the grammatical construction in 9:1 does not determine that those who will see God's rule as having come in power will die afterwards; and the words themselves do not demand that understanding.

Does 9:1 necessarily imply that the others who are standing there will die before the privileged "some" will see that God's rule has come in power? Only Matt 5:18 has anything comparable to the implied distinction in Mark 9:1 between the some and the others who are standing in Jesus' audience. The reference in Matt 5:18 to "one iota and one tittle" of the Law implies many other iotas and tittles in the Law. The saying certainly does not imply that those other iotas and tittles will pass away from the Law before all things take place. Whether they as well as one iota and one tittle will pass away after all things take place remains grammatically possible (though theologically improbable, as noted above, because of foregoing and following statements upholding the permanence of the Law). Hence, the grammatical structure of Mark 9:1 does not imply that the others who are standing there will die before the privileged some see that God's rule has come in power. The others might live beyond its coming in power without seeing that it has so come. Jesus' prediction does imply that they will die, however; for not dying at a later date would imply the contradiction that they will live up to the consummation and thus that they, too, will live to see God's rule as having come in power.

Was the prediction in 9:1 made up to assure Christians that even though some of their original number had died, the full coming of God's rule would not be delayed past the deaths of all those who heard Jesus? If Mark writes at a time when none of Jesus' hearers are still living, we cannot imagine that he would fabricate the prediction with reference to the consummation; for all possibility of fulfilment would already have passed, and fabrication of the saying could therefore only make the problem of delay intolerable. It is obvious to say that only some in a group of people will still be living at the time of an event in the more or less distant future. Consequently, the emphasis does not fall on remaining alive, but on seeing God's rule as a result of having remained alive. This emphasis exacerbates the problem of delay yet further. The same things are to be said against the suggestion that a Christian prophet fabricated the prediction after all Jesus' hearers had died but before Mark wrote.

From the standpoint of possible fulfilment, on the other hand, we could conceive that Mark or a Christian prophet made up the prediction if some of Jesus' hearers were still living. The earlier the date of the gospel, the greater the possibility that they were. But the earlier the date of the gospel, the less likely a problem of delay serious enough to prompt a fabrication of the prediction. The theory of a pre-Marcan fabrication by a Christian prophet suffers even more severely from this argumentative dilemma. Moreover, if Mark sees a fulfilment in the Transfiguration, he is unlikely to have made up the prediction in language that relates better to the Son of man's coming at the consummation.

We have reason to deny, however, that Jesus is predicting a coming of God's rule before the consummation, after which people who have not seen it will live on and then die, still before the consummation. The Son of man's coming in 8:38 sets a consummative tone for the coming of God's rule in 9:1. The dual reference in 13:26 to coming in power and glory supports a conceptual (if not historically chronological) connection between the sayings in 8:38 and 9:1, and therefore a common reference to the consummation. To be sure, "the rule of God" (9:1) differs in phraseology and meaning from "the Son of man" (8:38). But the shared verbal expression "come in . . . ," the similarity of the elements in which the Son of man and God's rule come — viz., "glory" and "power" — and the combination of these elements in 13:26 point to different ways of describing the same event.

Also favoring this understanding is Jesus' saying in 13:30 that his generation will not pass away till all the things which he has been predicting have taken place. He has been predicting the events of the consummation, which reach their climax in the Son of man's coming with much power and glory. The Son of man's coming before Jesus' generation passes away simply universalizes for a whole generation what Jesus says in 9:1 to a particular audience standing in front of him. Of course, 13:30 does not mean that nobody will die before all things take place (on the contrary, see 13:7-8 and esp. 13:12, 20), only that no more than an ordinary lifespan will elapse before they do. To explain the deaths of the others in Jesus' audience as due to widespread martyrdom during the great tribulation, thought to be inaugurated by Jesus' passion (so J. Jeremias, *NT Theology* 1. 137), requires an originally different audience that included only disciples. The present audience is mixed (8:34). Chapter 13 will set out disastrous, recognizable events as preceding the Son of man's coming. But they did not precede Jesus' transfiguration, resurrection, ascension, or sending of the Spirit at Pentecost (the events usually identified as the fulfilment of 9:1 if the consummation is not). Therefore neither Jesus' transfiguration nor his resurrection or ascension or sending of the Spirit can qualify as the Son of man's coming; and if his coming equates with the coming of God's rule in power, neither can they qualify as the coming of God's rule in power. Mark's spending a large portion of his papyrus on chap. 13 favors that in agreement with Jesus' reference to the consummation, he sees the final fulfilment of 9:1 as outstanding yet still possible (a Marcan position that favors, in turn, an early date of writing, before the passing away of all Jesus' audience).

Not only does the program of events leading to the consummation rule out a satisfactory fulfilment of 9:1 in Jesus' transfiguration, resurrection, ascension, or sending of the Spirit. So also does the pointlessness of saying that some will not taste death until they see an event only a week or, at most, some months away. They would not expect to die before then anyhow. This consideration may influence Mark (for whom historical perspective increases the pointlessness) not to dismiss the consummative meaning but to retain it in phraseology and in placement beside 8:38.

The narratives of the Transfiguration, Resurrection, Ascension, and Pentecost do not mention a coming of God's rule in power (on the contrary, see Acts 1:6-8 so far as Pentecost is concerned) or a related coming of the Son of man. The Transfiguration, to take the closest example, focuses on the identification of Jesus as God's beloved Son who must be heard. Yet we have seen in the comments that Mark redacts the narrative to make the event at least a preliminary fulfilment of the prediction in 9:1. Delay of the final, fully satisfying fulfilment may imply God's merciful extension of salvific history because of Israel's unbelief and the need to evangelize Gentiles. But Mark's point differs. He introduces the Transfiguration as a stopgap-fulfilment to support Jesus' prowess at prediction.

On the supposition that v 1 originally referred to the full imposition of God's rule in the end-time, the some who will not die till they see that event will not die afterwards, either. For by elsewhere affirming the doctrine of resurrection (12:18-27), Jesus implies the banishment of death at the full imposition of God's rule and thus the not dying of those who live up to its full imposition. On the same supposition, those who stand outside the charmed circle will die before the event; for the full imposition of God's rule will not be unseen by anyone alive at the time. These two conditions — viz., that some will not die before the event and that others will — combine with the authenticity of the saying to imply that Jesus thought of God's rule as fully coming after an interval long enough either for old age to take its toll of death on part of his audience or — more likely, in view of chap. 13 — for the messianic woes to do so. Unless Mark wrote his gospel at a date later than most people think, i.e. later than the 70s, a full imposition of God's rule could still have met these two conditions exactly. One might argue that the failure of Jesus' prediction to reach a fully satisfying fulfilment in the stated period justifies unbelief. Mark would probably argue back that the occurrence of a preliminary fulfilment in the stated period calls for belief in a final fulfilment yet to come.

W. L. Lane (312) suggests that "taste death" alludes to the possibility of losing one's life for the sake of Jesus and the gospel in v 35 and that the promised seeing then compensates for martyrdom. But the seeing comes *before* the tasting of death and therefore can hardly compensate for it. From the standpoint of Mark's making the Transfiguration a preliminary fulfilment of 9:1, one could say that the seeing will steel for martyrdom those who see. But from the standpoint of the originally intended sense of 9:1, seeing God's rule as having come in power would seem to forestall the possibility of martyrdom; i.e. God's powerful rule would presumably have eliminated martyrdom.

B. D. Chilton (*God in Strength* 268-69) suggests that those who will not taste death are angelic figures like Moses and Elijah, whom Jewish traditions around the time of the NT regarded as immortal. But in his narrative of the Transfiguration Mark does not even mention, much less highlight, any immortality or angelic brightness of Moses and Elijah; nor does he draw any parallel between them and the transfigured Jesus. A. L. Moore (*Parousia* 127, n. 4) suggests that the prediction in 9:1 may rest on selectivity rather than on longevity. But for selectivity we would expect the shorter statement: "Truly I say to you that some are standing here such as will see the rule of God [as] having come in power." John 6:64 with 6:60, 66-67 shows that τινες in Mark 9:1 does not necessarily point to few as opposed to many, or even to a minority as opposed to the majority. The similarities with 8:38; 13:26-27 and the emphasis on power weigh in favor of seeing as literal observation and against seeing as understanding a past event in a way that replaces a previous way of understanding it.

'Εληλυθυῖαν, "having come," may seem puzzling at first. Why not simply ". . . until they see the rule of God"? But the participle allows the addition of "in power." So the emphasis falls on the power in which God's rule will be seen to have come, not on the coming as such. The perfect tense of the participle gives the double sense of completed arrival and ongoing presence, almost as though to say, ". . . until they see God's rule *established* in power." Completed arrival may imply occurrence in the immediate past as easily as in the recent or distant past. Hence, it does not necessarily follow that some of Jesus' hearers will live long enough to come to the recognition that God's rule arrived during his ministry (so C. H. Dodd, *Parables* 53-54, n. 1; cf. N. Perrin, *Kingdom* 67-68, against Dodd's later, more expansive view that finds the fulfilment of v 1 also in Jesus' resurrection, Pentecost, the church, and a transhistorical consummation). Use of the perfect tense for the coming of God's rule recalls the perfect tense in 1:15 for the drawing near of God's rule. One could suppose that 1:15 stemmed from Marcan or pre-Marcan fabrication or that it represented (whether by quotation or summary) what Jesus actually preached. So the cases for authenticity and inauthenticity are evenly balanced with respect to the perfect tense. If Mark borrowed "in the glory" from 13:26-27 and added it to 8:38 (see the comments on 8:38), he may likewise have borrowed "having come in power" from 13:26-27 (cf. 14:62) and added it to 9:1. If so, the reference to power does not pose a problem to his presenting the Transfiguration as a fulfilment of Jesus' prediction in 9:1. Instead, power sets the tone for the Transfiguration. But as we have seen, the placement of 9:1 alongside 8:38 sets for 9:1 a consummative tone that makes the Transfiguration only a preliminary fulfilment. Thus, "having come in power" may reflect the original wording and represent, with 13:26, a certain habit of locution on Jesus' part. An original reference to power in 9:1 may have helped lead Mark to borrow from 13:26-27 in 8:38 (again see the comments ad loc.)

M. A. Tolbert (*Sowing the Gospel* 206-7) sees a fulfilment of v 1 in v 7. Thus the kingdom of God comes in power, not through the image of transfiguration, but through hearing the word of Jesus. But v 1 contains a promise of seeing (cf. vv 2 ["and he was transfigured before them"], 4 ["and there appeared to them . . ."], 8 ["and suddenly looking around they saw . . ."], 9 ["the things that they had seen"]), not of hearing. The disciples, all of them, have long since heard the word of Jesus (see esp. 3:31–4:20, 33-34) — they have even preached it (6:12) — whereas 9:1 looks to the future. This forward look rules out a back reference to his summons to suffering discipleship (against Tolbert, loc. cit.); and v 7 will present a *command* to hear Jesus, not a *hearing* of him.

"In power" occurs in Rom 1:4 with regard to Jesus' being designated God's Son according to the Spirit of holiness by resurrection from the dead. But the presence of the phrase also at Mark 9:1 does not imply that Jesus' prediction reached fulfilment in the Resurrection. Placement of the prediction right after a reference to the Son of man's coming in glory and placement of the Transfiguration right after that reference associate the Transfiguration with the coming in glory rather than with the Resurrection. When the Resurrection is broached in vv 9-13, it turns out to be a chronological boundary and puzzle, not a parallel to the Transfiguration. Nor, despite opportunities, will Mark tailor the story of the empty tomb to that of the Transfiguration. At 16:5 a young man clothed in a white robe will be sitting in the tomb, but he will not be Jesus. The young man's attire will not glisten, as Jesus' does, nor will it be exceedingly white, as Jesus' becomes; and his robe (στολή) will differ in designation from Jesus' garments (ἱμάτια).

Overall, E. Wendling (*Entstehung* 111) suggests influence on 9:1 from 1 Thess 4:15-16 and 1 Cor 4:20. But the phraseology of 1 Thess 4:15-16 is dissimilar; and despite the early date of 1 Thessalonians, Paul's discussing the fate of those who have died reflects a later standpoint than that reflected in the exclusive attention given to the living at Mark 9:1. The phraseology of 1 Cor 4:20 ("for not in word [is] the rule of God, but in power") does come close to that of Mark 9:1. But Paul probably refers to the present rule of God as shown in the miracle-working that accompanies Christian evangelism (cf. Gal 3:5) and thus betrays once again a standpoint later than that of Mark 9:1. Perhaps Paul picks up and reapplies this dominical saying (against the argument of A. M. Ambrozic, *Hidden Kingdom* 205-6 — an argument that runs counter to the criterion of dissimilarity — that "in power" is not authentic because no other text in the OT, intertestamental Jewish literature, or the NT describes God's rule as coming in power; perhaps Ambrozic has overlooked *Tg. Isa* 40:9-10 as well as 1 Cor 4:20).

F. G. Lang (in *ZTK* 74 [1977] 6) sees in 9:2-29 a double scene corresponding to a double scene in 10:1-31. The correspondence is not convincing, however. For example, the Pharisees' testing Jesus on divorce (10:2) does not correspond very closely to the scribes' disputing with his disciples over a failed exorcism (9:14). Not only does the subject matter differ greatly, but also the antagonists are different.

M. Horstmann (*Studien* 57-58), J. Lambrecht (in *BTB* 3 [1973] 266), and others think that Mark inserted the Transfiguration between the prediction in v 1 and the problem of Elijah in vv 11-13. Thus the question in v 11 originally posed the following problem: the necessity of Elijah's coming before the arrival of God's rule seems to forestall the soon arrival that Jesus has predicted for that rule. Verses 12-13 then solved the problem by saying that Elijah has already come. Against this reconstruction, the emphasis in vv 12-13 falls, not on Elijah's coming, but on his restoration of all things, which has not yet taken place (see the comments on vv 11-13); and from Jesus' standpoint Elijah has plenty of time to come before all Jesus' audience taste death.

The Transfiguration has often been treated as a backdated story that originally told about an appearance of the risen Jesus. F. Watson (in *JSNT* 24 [1985] 55) argues for this view that elsewhere in the NT God gives honor and glory to Jesus only after the Resurrection (Heb 2:9; 1 Pet 1:21; 1 Tim 3:16) and that the backdating of a miraculous catch of fish and of Peter's swimming, both having occurred after the Resurrection (John 21:1-8), to an earlier time (Luke 5:1-11 and Matt 14:28-31 [with a change to Peter's walking on water]) support a similar backdating here (cf. R. Bultmann [*HST* 259, n. 2], who asserts that Jesus' receiving honor and glory in 2 Pet 1:16-18 can refer only to the Resurrection or Ascension). But the paradigmatic backdatings do not rest on firm or generally accepted ground; and if the honoring and glorifying of Jesus seem appropriate enough to a time before his Resurrection to prompt backdating, they may have belonged to that period from the start (cf. R. J. Bauckham, *Jude, 2 Peter* 210-11; R. H. Stein in *JBL* 95 [1976] 88-89). In v 15 we will discover an indication that Jesus' garments continue to glisten after he descends the mountain. But this afterglow will hardly support the hypothesis that the Transfiguration was originally an appearance of the risen Jesus, for none of the early accounts of his appearances — not even Rev 1:12-16, which features his apparel — describe his garments as glistening and exceedingly white. Since a delay in the telling of a story does not imply that hearers will think of it as having just taken place, it is unconvincing to say that the command to keep quiet about the Transfiguration till after the Resurrection (v 9) is a device to explain why people used to regard the Transfiguration as having followed the Resurrection. The notion that a backdated appearance of the risen Jesus anticipatively substitutes for an appearance after he has risen (so, e.g., N. Perrin, *Resurrection* 24) rests on a disputable supposition that Mark ends his gospel without the latter kind of appearance. It also suffers from similarities between the Transfiguration and the Son of man's coming in glory over against dissimilarities that divide the Transfiguration from the Resurrection.

The lack of luminosity in our earliest account of an appearance by the risen Jesus on a mountain, i.e. in Matt 28:16-20, and unluminous earthly appearances of the risen Jesus in Luke-Acts and John cast doubt on the view of J. M. Robinson (*Problem* 29-31 and in *JBL* 101 [1982] 9) that the luminosity of the Transfiguration brands it as originally — and therefore pre-Johanninely, pre-Lucanly, pre-Mattheanly, and even pre-Marcanly — a luminous appearance of the risen Jesus on the Gnostic trajectory which progressively includes the luminous appearances to Stephen, Saul of Tarsus, and John the Seer and other such appearances related in Gnostic literature (cf. C. E. Carlston in *JBL* 80 [1961] 234-36). We may have evidence for a trajectory of increasing luminosity, a luminosity that starts in heaven and descends to earth (cf. the earthly locale of luminous appearances in Rev 1:9ff. and later literature), but not for an additional trajectory of decreasing luminosity. Rather, Matthew, Luke-Acts, and John represent appearances that are unluminous because Jesus' heavenly session is yet to begin and because their primitivity leaves them unaffected by a later luminizing that will eventually include even earthly appearances. That Matthew lacks an ascension of Jesus yet has him appear on earth after his resurrection shows that ascension is not a precondition of earthly appearances. Conversely, that John alludes to an ascension of Jesus (20:17) yet afterward has him appear unluminously on earth (20:19-23, 26-29; 21:1-23) shows that ascension does not preclude later earthly appearances, even those of an unluminous sort. Paul's listing the appearance to him alongside appearances to others (1 Cor 15:5-8) says nothing one way or another about the locale and look of Jesus on those occasions. The parallelism has to do with appearances as such. We have no right to read more than that into the text, much less to argue from eisegesis. Therefore we should not speak of Mark's transferring luminosity, and with it authority, from the exalted risen Jesus to the earthly Jesus before the latter's death and resurrection. He is building up the earthly Jesus to foster faith in the risen Jesus. These two Jesuses do not compete with each other in Mark's Christology.

The non-Gnostic Apocalypse of Peter, which some have thought to support the tracing of the Transfiguration back to an appearance of the risen Jesus, does not even mention the Resurrection, but combines the Mount of Transfiguration and what happened there with the Mount of Olives and the discourse that Jesus gave there before his passion and resurrection. Or if we take the position that in this Apocalypse of Peter the closing ascension presupposes Jesus' passion and resurrection, the postdating of the discourse favors a similar postdating of the Transfiguration, which then turns out to have originally referred to an event before the Passion and Resurrection (R. H. Stein in *JBL* 95 [1976] 87-88).

Pistis Sophia describes what some have taken to be the Transfiguration and locates it after the Resurrection. But equation with the Transfiguration is doubtful; for the setting is on the Mount of Olives, all the disciples are present, Jesus is bathed in light and caught up to heaven, an earthquake occurs, and he descends back to earth and relates his journey. If the Transfiguration has contributed to the story, so also has the Mount of Olives of the Olivet Discourse as well as an appearance of the risen Jesus. In any case, transference of the Transfiguration to the risen, exalted Jesus is more likely than is transference to the earthly Jesus, especially in a gnosticizing atmosphere that devalues the earthly Jesus in favor of the heavenly one.

J. D. Crossan (*Four Other Gospels* 165-74 and *Cross* 347-51) thinks that Mark not only backdates an appearance of the risen Jesus, but does so by using and redacting the story of Jesus' resurrection in *Gos. Pet.* 9:35-36; 10:38-42, i.e. by making the two men from heaven into Elijah with Moses, by transmuting the reaching to heaven of the men's heads and the overpassing of heaven by Jesus' head into Jesus' taking Peter, James, and John up a high mountain, by taking over the shining light and heavenly voice, and by adding characteristically Marcan themes — all for the purpose of making the period from the Resurrection to the Second Coming one of suffering rather than glory. Of course, Mark might just as easily add his emphases to material from another quarter. The apocryphal story looks wild with late material of an exaggerative sort: in addition to the tremendous heights, even the elders are keeping watch with the soldiers, the watchers actually see the risen Jesus being helped out of the tomb, the cross follows under its own locomotion, the voice asks whether Jesus has preached to the dead, yet the answer comes from the cross, not from Jesus. If Mark tamed this material, he belongs in a circus (cf. the fantastic exaggerations in the Acts of John 90-91 and the not-so-exaggerated but NT-dependent Acts of Peter 20). See R. E. Brown in *NTS* 33 (1987) 321-43; S. E. Schaeffer in *SBL 1991 Seminar Papers* 499-507 for general arguments against giving priority to the Gospel of Peter.

Good reasons exist for denying a backdated appearance. Elsewhere, all stories concerning appearances of the risen Jesus begin with his absence and proceed to his speaking, and sometimes to his acting, to make himself known. Not so here. Elsewhere we find no tradition that the risen Jesus appeared at one time to Peter, James, and John, other disciples being absent. The apparently traditional character of Peter, James, and John at 5:37; 14:33 (see the comments and notes on 5:37) and the singling out of Peter at 16:7 militate against supposing that Mark has transformed an appearance to Peter alone (cf. 1 Cor 15:5; Luke 24:34) into an appearance to the three. The switch from the singular of Peter's not knowing (v 6a) to the plural of the three disciples' being afraid (v 6b) hardly supports the hypothesis that the Transfiguration was originally an appearance of the risen Jesus to Peter alone. Both halves of v 6 come from Mark. Elsewhere, too, he stresses ignorance as well as fear (see, e.g., v 10; 6:52a; 9:32; 10:32) and switches back and forth between writing about the three disciples and singling out Peter (cf. R. H. Stein in *JBL* 95 [1976] 92-93 and see the comments on v 6 for a contextual explanation of the present switch from singular to plural). Elsewhere in the NT, ὤφθη refers to appearances of the risen Jesus. Here it not only fails to refer to an appearance of Jesus. It refers on the contrary to the appearing of Elijah with Moses (against T. J. Weeden, *Traditions in Conflict* 118-24, esp. 119). In appearances of the risen Jesus, we find nothing analogous to the appearance of Elijah with Moses in conversation with Jesus. Angels appear in stories of the empty tomb, but not alongside the risen Jesus, much less talking with him. Nor do we find anything analogous to Peter's suggestion, the cloud, or divine voice that identifies Jesus as God's beloved Son. For the theory, we would expect to find points of analogy that might offer opportunity for Mark's or an earlier traditioner's redaction. They are missing. On the whole question, see esp. C. H. Dodd in *Studies in the New Testament* 25; C. E. Carlston in *JBL* 80 (1961) 233-40; R. H. Stein in *JBL* 95 (1976) 79-96; J. E. Alsup, *Post-Resurrection Appearance Stories* 141-44.

If the Transfiguration is not a backdated and redacted appearance of the risen Jesus, one may think of a legendary development or of an authentic vision (cf. C. Rowland, *Open Heaven* 366-68). Naturally, philosophical presuppositions with regard to the supernatural will affect historical critical judgments on a point like this. From the historical critical standpoint, C. E. Carlston (in *JBL* 80 [1961] 233-40) reasons that the Transfiguration would have forestalled the three disciples' cowardice during the Passion (cf. esp. Peter's denials) just as appearances of the risen Jesus destroyed their cowardice afterward. This reasoning calls in question the historicity of the Transfiguration but does not require the backdating of an appearance of the risen Jesus, as Carlston thinks it does (cf. R. H. Stein in *JBL* 95 [1976] 86). Applied elsewhere, the reasoning would likewise call in question the historicity of Jesus' miracles and exorcisms. Yet whatever moderns may think of the historicity of those miracles and exorcisms, it is quite evident that the primitive church believed in their historicity and that therefore the first disciples and Jesus himself most probably believed that he performed such deeds. (The NT trajectory does not go from less to more of miracles and exorcisms as such, i.e. as acts of raw power, in Jesus' ministry, but from more to less: [1] miracles and exorcisms as such [Mark; cf. Paul's appeal to miracles as powerful confirmation of the gospel]; [2] miracles and exorcisms as didactic occasions [Matthew]; [3] miracles and exorcisms as acts of humanitarianism [Luke]; [4] miracles as theological signs and works, with a dropping of exorcisms except for the grand exorcism of Satan from the world [John].) If the disciples showed cowardice during Jesus' Passion despite their conviction that they had often seen him perform miracles and exorcisms, showing cowardice despite a similar conviction with regard to the Transfiguration poses no insurmountable obstacle.

It does not follow from the change in Luke 9:28 to "approximately eight days after" that Luke knows "after six days" (v 2) to be an untraditional addition by Mark (against E. L. Schnellbächer in *ZNW* 71 [1980] 252). The phrase in Mark takes its starting point from the time when Peter confessed Jesus as the Christ and Jesus predicted his passion and resurrection, issued a summons to discipleship, and supported his summons with further predictions, including one that God's rule would soon be seen as having come in power (8:27–9:1). Mark has probably inserted some of that material, however (see the comments and notes ad loc.). So the Transfiguration may originally have answered, not to the prediction concerning God's rule, but to Peter's confession and Jesus' prediction of the Passion and Resurrection: at the Transfiguration God owns Jesus as his beloved Son the Christ even though Jesus must suffer and rise (E. Best, *Following Jesus* 55). Against this reconstruction, one could suppose that the inserted material did not include the prediction concerning God's rule (cf. the editorial break in 9:1a), i.e. that the Transfiguration may originally have stood after the prediction (9:1) even though that prediction did not originally stand after the call to discipleship (8:34-38).

Though "after two days" may leave some ambiguity in 14:1, the occurrence of Jesus' crucifixion on Friday (15:25 with 15:42) and the announcement of his resurrection on Sunday (16:1-2 with 16:6) clearly give the meaning "on the third day" (1 Cor 15:4; Matt 16:21; 17:23; 20:19; Luke 9:22; 18:33; 24:7, 46) to the phrase "after three days" (8:31; 9:31; 10:34). Therefore "after six days" probably means "on the sixth day." For the same reason, "after two days" will probably mean "on the second day." Thus we should not accept the argument that a chronological ambiguity as to whether "after six days" means on the sixth day or on the seventh supports a forward allusion to Jesus' passion because of similar ambiguity in the chronology of Passion Week (so E. L. Schnellbächer in *ZNW* 71 [1980] 252-57).

To make "after six days" the day of crucifixion or of resurrection, i.e. the seventh day of Passion Week according to Mark's chronology, J. Schreiber, *Theologie des Vertrauens* 119-20, and H. Weinacht, *Menschenwerdung* 53-55, mistake and underestimate his interest in noting small transitions, represented by evenings and mornings (11:11, 19, 20; 14:17; 15:1, 25, 33, 34, 42; 16:2), for an interest in counting seven days of Passion Week (11:12; 14:1, 12, 58; 15:29, 42; 16:1, 2; cf. W. H. Kelber, *Kingdom* 77-78). D. Dormeyer (*Passion* 66) is not content to reason that if "after three days" in predictions of the Resurrection means "on the third day," then "after six days" in 9:2 means "on the sixth day." He goes on to reason that since the sixth day of the week is the Day of Preparation (15:42), the Transfiguration prepares for but does not bring about the consummation of God's rule (cf. J. M. Nützel, *Verklärungserzählung* 240-41). But "after six days" does not mean on the sixth day of the week any more than "after three days" means on the third day of the week. In fact the third day, when Jesus rose, will turn out to be the first day of the week. N. Perrin (in *Christology and a Modern Pilgrimage* 27-28) draws a theological as well as phraseological parallel between the occurrence of the Transfiguration, representing the Second Coming, after six days and the occurrence of the Resurrection after three days. But the parallel provides no rationale for "after six days." Why not "after seven days" — or, better yet, "after three days" to match the Resurrection? And why not suppose a theological as well as phraseological parallel with the Passover and Unleavened Bread "after two days" (14:1)? See E. Best, *Following Jesus* 59-60, n. 7; R. H. Stein in *JBL* 95 (1976) 82-83 for criticism of other symbolic interpretations of the six days, esp. that of F. R. McCurley in *JBL* 93 (1974) 67-81. Until Mark comes to the passion narrative, he usually leaves the day of an event unspecified. Further favoring the traditionality of "after six days," then, are the unusualness of its specificity and the insignificance of six days over against equally good or better possibilities for relating the Transfiguration to Jesus' immediately foregoing prediction. Not only might a creative redactor have chosen another number. More likely such a redactor would have used a general expression, say, "in those days," "after [some] days," or "after these things" (as in 1:9; 2:1; 8:1; 16:12, 16 et passim outside Mark).

To say that Mark inserted Peter, James, and John leaves the question, Who then did see the Transfiguration as originally reported? If no one, then what was the use of the story? If all the disciples, why the narrowing down to these three despite the presence of all at Peter's confession? If it be answered that Mark narrows down the observers to these three because he has inserted an originally unconnected prediction that only some will not taste death till they see God's rule as having come in power, then we need to remind ourselves that since Jesus is still addressing "the crowd with his disciples" (8:34) the disciples do not need to be narrowed down to satisfy the condition in the prediction. All the disciples would count as some of those standing there. The omission of the definite article before John's name in v 2 is text critically well supported, but may be due to a scribe's pairing of James and John as brothers. On the other hand, Mark may pair them thus and a later scribe or scribes insert the definite article for a parallel with the definite articles accompanying the other personal names.

R. Pesch (in *Jesus und der Menschensohn* 175) sees similarities between Jesus' transfiguration and the translation of Enoch according to *1 Enoch* 71-72. It is hard to see anything but differences: (1) Alone, Enoch passes out of sight into heaven and stays there; but with three others, Jesus ascends no higher than a mountain and afterwards descends. (2) Jesus is transfigured, and his clothes glisten; but Enoch's body merely relaxes, and his spirit is transformed. (3) Enoch sees angels and heavenly secrets, but departed human beings speak with Jesus. (4) Enoch falls down to worship God, but God says to listen to Jesus. (5) God speaks to Enoch but confers no title on him (see E. Isaac in *OT Pseude-pigrapha* 1. 50, n. s), whereas God does not speak to Jesus but announces to others that Jesus is his beloved Son. (6) God promises that the righteous will have eternal dwelling places with Enoch, but Peter suggests the construction of tabernacles too few to accommodate the disciples and is rebuffed even for that small suggestion.

Since in Mark's chronology Peter confessed Jesus as the Christ and Jesus both predicted the Passion and Resurrection, summoned people to discipleship, and predicted the seeing of God's rule all on the same occasion (8:27–9:1), we might take the Transfiguration as confirming one or more of those statements. For the audience of Mark it confirms all of them. But from the standpoint of the principals in the story, a confirmation of Peter's confession and of Jesus' prediction of the Passion and Resurrection would recommend the presence of all the disciples at the Transfiguration; for Peter spoke on behalf of them all, and Jesus taught his passion and resurrection to all of them. For confirmation of his summons to discipleship, the crowd need to have seen the Transfiguration; for he addressed the summons to them (8:34). The prediction of seeing God's rule is left. It fits, for the three disciples correspond to "some of the ones standing here." For Mark, then, the Transfiguration confirms, i.e. fulfills, the prediction of 9:1. Confirmation of Peter's confession and of Jesus' passion-and-resurrection prediction and summons to discipleship comes by indirection.

E. Wendling (*Entstehung* 138) considers the possibility of some general influence from 2 Corinthians 3–4 on the Transfiguration (see esp. 3:18; 4:6). But perhaps pre-Marcan tradition of the Transfiguration exercised influence on Paul. More probably, he draws only on the OT; for he writes about the transfiguration of Christians, not about that of Christ. Mark writes about Jesus' garments and glistening whiteness, Paul about the face of Christ and shining light. And Paul's key word "glory" appears only in Jesus' prediction (v 1), not in Mark's narrative of the Transfiguration (vv 2-8).

Verses 2-3 lack distinctive allusions to Exodus 24 and 34. Tellingly, for example, Mark does not describe Jesus' face as shining in the manner of Moses' face. The significance of this omission and of the absence of other allusions that might have been made increases in view of Moses' role in the following part of Mark's narrative. Besides omissions we have differences. They include Moses' going up the mountain before a period of six days versus Jesus' going up the mountain after a period of six days; Moses' taking Aaron, Nadab, Abihu, seventy elders, and Joshua, and then only Joshua, versus Jesus' taking three companions; the shining of Moses' face versus the shining of Jesus' garments; Moses' talking with God versus departed human beings' talking with Jesus; God's talking to Moses but not to Joshua or to Moses' other companions versus God's talking to Jesus' companions but not to Jesus himself; and a crowd's subsequently running to Jesus (vv 15, 25) versus Aaron's and the Israelites' fearing to approach Moses. The appearance of Elijah with Moses has no counterpart in the Sinai-narrative, and ancient Jewish literature does not limit God's mountainous and cloud-cloaked revelations to Sinai. Thus whatever Matthew and Luke may do to conform the Transfiguration to the Sinai-narrative in Exodus, v 2 seems not to allude to it, much less grow out of it (H.-J. Steichele, *Der leidende Sohn Gottes* 173-81; against J. M. Nützel, *Verklärungserzählung* 161).

According to W. L. Lane (320), "it is particularly significant that the correlation of the cloud and the voice is limited to the exodus accounts of the Pentateuch" (see also *Jub.* 1:2-3, however). But God spoke to Ezekiel out of a cloud in Babylonia (see esp. Ezek 1:1-4 with 2:1), and in the land of Uz God spoke to Job out of a whirlwind (Job 38:1), which *T. Job* 42:1-3 interprets as including a cloud. So an allusion to Exodus still rests on shaky ground.

The glistening white garments of v 3 do not match the clear pavement of sapphires in Exod 24:10. Not only do the materials differ; but also the garments belong to Jesus, the pavement to the God of Israel. Nor does Peter's misbegotten suggestion of making three tabernacles on the high mountain (v 5) match God's command, carried out, to build a single tabernacle on flat land at the base of Mount Sinai. Nor does Moses' drawing near by himself to God (Exod 24:2) match the disciples' seeing Jesus alone after the departure of Moses and Elijah (against B. D. Chilton in *NTS* 27 [1980-81] 120). Yet again, an allusion to Exodus rests on shaky ground.

J. M. Nützel (*Verklärungserzählung* 154) suggests that the genitive absolute καταβαινόντων αὐτῶν ἐκ τοῦ ὄρους, "as they [Jesus and the three disciples] were descending from the mountain," alludes to Exod 34:29b LXX: καταβαίνοντος . . . αὐτοῦ ἐκ τοῦ ὄρους, "as he [Moses] was descending from the mountain." But an allusion would probably have contained a reference only to Jesus, the accompaniment of the disciples being understood (as often in Mark — see 1:39 with 1:38; 2:1, 13 with 2:15-16; 2:23a with 2:23b-24; 3:1, 7, 20 with 3:34-35; 4:1 with 4:10 et passim). Mark's ἐκ is text critically suspect (supported by B D Ψ 33 *pc*, against ἀπό in ℵ A C L W Θ *f*¹,¹³ Majority Text). And ἐκ τοῦ ὄρους is the natural complement of εἰς ὄρους ὑψηλόν, "to a high mountain," in v 2, the present definite article being added anaphorically (cf. 3:13; 6:46; 13:3, 14; 14:26; Exod 24:12-13 LXX). Still yet again, an allusion to Exodus rests on shaky ground.

B. D. Chilton (in *NTS* 27 [1980-81] 122, n. 17) supports a parallel between Jesus and Moses by appealing to Josephus *Ant.* 4.8.48 §326. There, Moses is said to disappear (ἀφανίζεται) while bidding farewell to Eleazar and Joshua ('Ιησοῦν); and disappearance equates with translation, as shown by Josephus's use of disappearance (ἀφανεῖς) to describe Enoch and Elijah in translation (*Ant.* 9.2.2 §28). But translation does not equate with transfiguration. Jesus neither says farewell nor disappears. Quite oppositely, Mark's accent falls on the disciples' seeing Jesus transfigured right in front of them (ἔμπροσθεν αὐτῶν) and on the appearing — i.e. the being seen (ὤφθη) — of Elijah with Moses (vv 2-4). When Moses and Elijah disappear, the accent falls all the more on seeing Jesus (v 8). Besides, if a parallel did exist between Jesus' transfiguration and Moses' translation, the location of Moses' translation on Mount Abaris opposite Jericho (so Josephus *Ant.* 4.8.48 §325) would distance it from the theophany that he saw on Mount Sinai. Thus fails the attempt to use Josephus's account of Moses' translation as evidence that Jesus' transfiguration consists in a Christologically literary reinterpretation of the theophany on Mount Sinai. In turn, the attempt to use such a reinterpretation for evading historical and psychological questions in respect to the present form of the narrative (ibid. 122) is foredoomed (see also idem, *Profiles* 83-85).

There appears to be no allusion to Ezek 20:40; 40:2 (cf. 17:22-23) in v 2 (against W. Zimmerli in *Donum Gentilicium* 8, n. 1). The high mountain in Ezekiel refers to Mount Zion, where the temple is located and sacrifices are offered. The Transfiguration has nothing to do with the temple and its sacrifices.

We should probably translate ἐγένετο στίλβοντα with "became glistening," not with "were glistening" (cf. S. E. Porter [*Verbal Aspect* 491], who makes στίλβοντα modify λευκὰ λίαν so as to produce "glistening exceedingly white"). J. A. Ziesler (in *ExpTim* 81 [1969-70] 265-66) argues that Jesus himself is transfigured, not merely his garments. In favor of this position one could argue that glistening white garments are worn not only by God and by angels, but also by righteous human beings who have been changed into heavenly beings (*1 Enoch* 14:20; 62:15-16; *2 Enoch* 22:8-10; *Mart. Isa.* 9:9; cf. the white garments in Dan 7:9; Mark 16:5; Matt 28:3b; John 20:12; Acts 1:10; Rev 3:4-5, 18; 4:4; 6:11; 7:9, 13; 19:14; *Apoc. Abr.* 13:14) and that therefore the transfiguration of Jesus refers to a change in the appearance of him himself (cf. Matt 17:2; 28:3a; Luke 9:29; Exod 34:29-35; Ezek 1:26-28; Dan 7:9; 12:3; Rev 1:14, 16; 10:1; *1 Enoch* 38:4; 50:1; 104:2; *2 Enoch* 1:5; 4 Ezra 7:97; *2 Apoc. Bar.* 51:3, 5, 10, 12; Philo *Mos.* 2.14 §70; *Bib. Ant.* 12:1; 19:16; Eunap. *VS* pp. 364-65 of the LCL edition). But since Mark does not describe any shining of Jesus' face (contrast Matt 17:2; Luke 9:29), the Transfiguration seems limited to the garments. Thus, the "and" which introduces a description of Jesus' garments introduces a definition of the Transfiguration. This characteristically Marcan parataxis does not require a separate item of information, just as "Robert looks formal, he's wearing a tuxedo" may mean only that Robert is wearing formal attire, not also that the exposed parts of his body look formal.

Nothing in the text implies that Jesus possesses a glory hidden at other times by his clothes and flesh. On the contrary, the divine passive in v 2 and the emphasis on the glistening of his garments point to a glory bestowed from without. Hence, J. Behm (in *TDNT* 4. 757) and B. Blackburn (*Theios Anēr* 117-24) correctly deny that the Transfiguration derives from a Hellenistic milieu (as thought by D. Georgi, *Opponents* 172-73; M. Smith, *Clement* 225-26). In the same vein, H. C. Kee (in *Understanding the Sacred Text* 135-52) denies a Hellenistic story of epiphany by appealing to the shining of the righteous, especially those who have suffered, at their resurrection and glorification in Jewish apocalyptic. He also appeals to the Semitic "Rabbi" in v 5 and to the use of "the son of God" for a Jewish king but not for a Hellenistic divine man (cf. M. Hengel, *Son of God* 23-41, though see ibid. 30 and esp. P. Bureth, *Les Titulatures impériales* 23-25, for an exception in the case of rulers). H.-J. Steichele (*Der leidende Sohn Gottes* 186) adds appeals to the Jewishness of mountain-theology, of cloud-theology, and of Moses and Elijah. We might further add the Hebraistic use of ἀποκριθείς, "answering," in the sense of "speaking up" (BAGD s.v. 2) and the Semitic use of μίαν, "one," in v 5 (E. C. Maloney, *Semitic Interference* 156-59).

The views of J. A. McGuckin (*Transfiguration* 5-97 and in *CR* 69 [1984] 271-79) that Mark removes an original analogy between Jesus and Moses, transforms two pre-Marcan angels into Elijah with Moses, and so on, seem backward. Instead, Matthew adds an analogy to Moses; and Luke adds "his [Jesus'] exodus" and changes Moses and Elijah into two anonymous men like those at the empty tomb (Luke 24:4) and ascension (Acts 1:9-11). U. W. Mauser (*Christ in the Wilderness* 114-18) says that Moses and Elijah figure in the Transfiguration because they were preeminently men of the wilderness, like Jesus. But his being baptized and tempted in the wilderness and feeding the four thousand there hardly suffice to qualify him as preeminently a man of the wilderness, and no allusion to the wilderness crops up in the story of the Transfiguration. M. E. Thrall (in *NTS* 16

[1969-70] 306) and M. Pamment (in *ExpTim* 92 [1980-81] 338) think that Moses and Elijah are paired because both were rejected by Israel and vindicated by God, as Jesus will be. But where else in the synoptic tradition do Moses and the OT Elijah appear as rejected and vindicated? Acts 7:17-43; Heb 11:23-29; Rev 11:3-10; and the literature cited by J. Jeremias in *TDNT* 2. 940 are too late to weigh heavily in favor of their calling to mind rejection and vindication. Synoptic tradition portrays Moses as the revered lawgiver and Elijah as the expected restorer.

       J. Jeremias (in *TDNT* 2. 938-39) notes that Jewish tradition usually pairs Enoch and Elijah because they are the only two in the OT to have escaped death by being translated instead (cf. the primary literature cited by G. Lohfink, *Himmelfahrt* 68-69). He then hypothesizes that the substituting of Moses for Enoch reflects a weaker, extra-canonical Jewish tradition according to which Moses, too, escaped death by being translated instead (cf. ibid.). Underlying this hypothesis is the supposition that escaping death by being translated instead provides the rationale for the present pairing and appearance of Moses and Elijah. But transfiguration does not equate with translation, and foregoing and following predictions of Jesus' death make incongruent a choice of Moses and Elijah on the ground that they did not die. Better a choice of figures whose violent deaths could prefigure the killing of Jesus. One might defuse this criticism by denying that predictions of Jesus' death originally framed the Transfiguration. But not only does settling on a rationale for the present pairing and appearance of Moses and Elijah then become more uncertain. It remains problematic to the rationale of escaping death by being translated instead that no allusion is made to translations of Moses and Elijah. They are not even described as transfigured.

       Since Mark does not describe Elijah and Moses as transfigured human beings who were translated to heaven, cross-reference to the OT and later Jewish literature concerning their translations and transfigurations are relevant neither to pre-Marcan tradition concerning the Transfiguration nor to Mark's version of it. Though he has Elijah appearing in the person of John the Baptist and therefore as forerunner of the Christ (cf. vv 11-13 with 1:2-6), he does not portray Moses thus; so neither does a cross-reference to Rev 11:3-13 bear on Mark's purpose. That passage and the later Jewish literature postdate Mark, anyway. Though they may draw on pre-Marcan Jewish tradition relevant to pre-Marcan dominical tradition (cf. the notes on 1:1-8), appeal to dominical tradition earlier than Mark lengthens the chronological distance from extant comparable literature; and we might expect a forerunning role for Moses in pre-Marcan dominical tradition to have left some trace in Mark. The precedence of Elijah-like miracles over a Moses-like miracle in Rev 11:5-6 may qualify as such a trace, only outside Mark. But miracle-working is not reflected in Mark's account of the Transfiguration, his mentioning Elijah first is explicable by vv 11-13, "Elijah *with* Moses" differs from an "Elijah *and* Moses" that might have reflected dependence on a tradition like Rev 11:3-13, and the lapse back to "Moses and Elijah" disfavors such dependence. Neither the Law nor messianic prophecy comes into the Transfiguration; so Moses and Elijah do not stand for the Law and the Prophets, respectively. Besides, Elijah was not a writing prophet and delivered no messianic prophecy. Nor do Moses and Elijah appear with Jesus as those whose past sufferings look forward to his; for neither one of them was killed, as Jesus has predicted he will be killed; and the Transfiguration looks forward to his final glory (8:38), not to his intermediate suffering.

       J. M. Nützel (*Verklärungserzählung* 105-6) appeals to a purportedly synonymous use of σύν, "with," and καί, "and," in the LXX and in Mark 4:10; 8:34; Luke 7:6; 8:1 (cf. W. Grundmann in *TDNT* 7. 768-69) and denies that in v 4 σύν subordinates Moses to Elijah. But Mark does use σύν for subordination. At 4:10 it subordinates "the Twelve" to "the ones around Jesus" for contrast with "those outsiders" (4:11). At 8:34 it subordinates "the disciples" to "the crowd" because Jesus' call to follow behind him is addressed to the crowd — "if *anyone* wants to follow behind me" — not to his disciples, who are already following behind him (cf. 8:33). Similar things could be said concerning Luke 7:6; 8:1, and concerning μετά plus the genitive, "with," in Mark 1:29; 15:1, 31.

Speaking with heavenly beings in *Apoc. Zeph.* 8:1–9:5 implies belonging to their realm (so R. Pesch 2. 74). But there the scene is set in heaven, as the Transfiguration is not; Moses and Elijah speak with Jesus, not he with them; and the apocalyptic passage emphasizes speaking a heavenly language, of which we hear nothing in Mark. We must also remind ourselves that Mark does not mention the heavenliness of Moses and Elijah. As noted in the comments, their speaking with Jesus prepares for the command to hear him instead.

See G. Dalman, *Words* 331-40; R. H. Gundry, *Matthew* 458, 601, on dating the use of "Rabbi" for a teacher. Here, however, the address may have a wider meaning, something like "Sir" but more honorific. "Good" does not mean enjoyable or advantageous to the three disciples. That meaning would require the dative of advantage ἡμῖν to produce "it is good for us to be here" (so 9:42; 14:21). As it is, the accusative ἡμᾶς produces "it is good [that] we are here." Assignment of Peter's suggestion to a Marcan program of making the disciples look ignorant leaves the rest of the story vapid. Mark's editorial statement in v 6 actually excuses Peter by explaining his nonplus as due to terror. This excuse serves to heighten the impressiveness of the Transfiguration (see C. R. Kazmierski, *Jesus, the Son of God* 120-26).

On the supposition that the Transfiguration occurs around the time of the Festival of Tabernacles, when nationalistic feelings run high among Jews, R. P. Martin (*Mark* 129-30) interprets Peter's suggestion as a Zealotic call to lead God's people against their enemies (so Elijah) and to freedom (so Moses). Since minor Jewish revolts occurred earlier, it would be a merely semantic quibble to note that the Zealots may not have come into being till the war of 66-74 C.E. More seriously, however, Elijah neither led Israel against her enemies nor issued a call to arms against them. Making tabernacles on a mountain would look more pacifistic than militaristic. And the suggestion to make them can scarcely have anything to do with the Festival of Tabernacles; for apart from the possibility of two persons per tabernacle, such a connection would require six tabernacles rather than three (cf. M. Smith, *Jesus the Magician* 20; J. A. Ziesler in *ExpTim* 81 [1969-70] 264 — the latter against H. Riesenfeld, *Jésus transfiguré* 146-205). Nor are the three tabernacles of Peter's suggestion to be equated with eternal tabernacles like those in Luke 16:9 (cf. *1 Enoch* 39:3-4, 7-8; *T. Abr.* 20:4; John 14:2; Zech 2:11 LXX — so C. Breytenbach, *Nachfolge* 243); for again Peter would have suggested the making of three more to include himself, James, and John. To exempt the three disciples on the ground that Peter is wanting to make paradisic tabernacles for heavenly beings (so M. E. Thrall in *NTS* 16 [1969-70] 309) entails the unlikelihood that he thinks of himself and his colleagues, or is portrayed as doing so, as adept in heavenly architecture. And does he consider the materials available on a high mountain suitable for paradisic tabernacles? Besides, this view overlooks the lack of emphasis on Moses' and Elijah's heavenliness. 2 Cor 5:1-4 speaks of an eternal building, not of an eternal tabernacle, and reserves "tabernacle" for what is earthly. The inclusion of tabernacles for Moses and Elijah and the isolation of a mountaintop rule out an allusion to the OT tent of meeting (Exod 33:7-11; so O. Betz and W. Grimm, *Wesen und Wirklichkeit* 88), to the OT tabernacle, or to God's tabernacling eternally with his people (Rev 7:15; 21:1-3; and the LXX of Ezek 37:27; 43:7, 9; Joel 3:21; Zech 2:10; 8:3, 8). Besides, tabernacles for human beings differ from a tabernacle for God (cf. Exod 24:16 Aq).

If Peter's mistake consisted in failure to recognize the temporariness of the Transfiguration (ibid. 87-88), we would not expect him to suggest the making of tabernacles; for they often connote temporariness rather than permanence (Isa 38:12; 2 Cor 5:1, 4; 2 Pet

1:12). Tabernacles are usually thought of as tents (cf. the OT tabernacle). But the present circumstance of a high mountain probably dictates shelters made of leafy branches, as were those constructed for the Festival of Tabernacles (Lev 23:33-36, 39-43; Neh 8:13-18; Zech 14:16-19), or shelters made of stones (I. Abrahams, *Studies* 2. 50). The differences in material and appearance do not affect Peter's purpose of honoring Moses and Elijah equally with Jesus.

C. H. Turner (in *JTS* os 29 [1927-28] 3) defends the v.l. θέλεις, "do you want" (D W Θ f^{13} 28 543 565 b ff^2 i), before ποιήσωμεν, "we should make" (v 5; cf. 10:36, 51; 14:12; 15:9). But this v.l. looks like an attempt to get rid of an offensive instance of parataxis (though W 28 retain the καί, "and," before ποιήσωμεν, apparently out of respect for the original reading) and to relieve Peter of some blame by transforming his enthusiastic but badly mistaken suggestion into a question regarding Jesus' wish. The vv.ll. in v 6 that put another word in place of ἀποκριθῇ, "he should answer," seem to take exception at the lack of a preceding question. The phrase ἀποκριθείς . . . λέγει, "answering . . . [Peter] says," in v 5 was so stereotypical that it resisted a substitution for ἀποκριθείς.

B. D. Chilton (in *NTS* 27 [1980-81] 120) leaves the misimpression that Peter's not knowing how to answer represents stupefaction before the disclosure of Jesus' divine sonship. The voice that discloses it speaks only after Peter's nonplus, however; and Mark identifies ignorance due to terror as the reason for the misbegotten suggestion concerning tabernacles (v 6). Therefore neither should we think of ignorance concerning Jesus' coming passion or concerning the temporariness of Moses' and Elijah's visit. The uneasiness of fit between the terror of Peter, James, and John and Peter's happy statement, "It's good we're here," makes difficult an ascription of both these elements to the same source (say, to Mark's creativity) and favors instead that Mark adds the γάρ-clause concerning terror (v 6b). Mark's prefixing of ἐκ in 9:15; 12:17; 14:31, 33; 16:5, 6 to intensify the meaning of the following word combines with his consistent use of φόβος and φοβέομαι for fear (see the concordance s.v.) to disfavor the translation of ἔκφοβοι with "excited" (against J. A. Kleist, *Memoirs* 45, 102).

Against the argument of M. Horstmann (*Studien* 83) that v 7 is redactional because it interrupts vv 6 and 8, suddenly looking around follows on the disciples' terror no better than it does on God's speaking to them out of a cloud. In fact, the sudden looking around favors a preceding cloud-cover and has no discernible reason apart from it. Contrast the singular number of the cloud of God's presence with the plural of the clouds in which the Son of man will come (13:26; 14:62).

The word order καὶ ἐγένετο φωνή, "and there came a voice," in v 7b differs from the word order καὶ φωνὴ ἐγένετο, "and a voice came," in 1:11. Influence from the word order of καὶ ἐγένετο νεφέλη, "and there came a cloud," in v 7a makes the difference. Conversely, the lack of a participle to go with καὶ ἐγένετο φωνή disfavors taking the participle ἐπισκιάζουσα periphrastically with ἐγένετο, "was overshadowing," rather than with νεφέλη, "a cloud overshadowing" (cf. S. E. Porter, *Verbal Aspect* 491). The contrary argument that Mark is not interested in the origin of the cloud (J. M. Nützel, *Verklärungs-erzählung* 141) rests on the mistaken assumption that a non-periphrastic ἐγένετο would turn attention to the question of origin. It does not. Simple occurrence is in view.

The parallelistic structure of v 7 need not signal that the second occurrence of καὶ ἐγένετο betrays a Marcan insertion (against J. Zmijewski in *SNTU* A/12. 28-30). Nor do the Transfiguration and the appearance of Elijah the forerunner make superfluous the declaration that Jesus is the messianic Son of God (as thought ibid.). Elijah does not appear as a forerunner in vv 4-8. He was not thought to be the forerunner of the Messiah, anyway (see the notes on vv 11-13). And both the appearance of so august a figure as Elijah (and of Moses, too, though he is thought to be a Marcan import — ibid.) and Peter's using "Rabbi" to address Jesus make the filial declaration climactic rather than superfluous.

The view that "my beloved Son" (v 7) does not merely surpass but corrects "Rabbi" (v 5; so J. Schreiber, *Theologie des Vertrauens* 114) has against it that two later occurrences of "Rabbi" have nothing following in their pericopes that could correct them (see 11:21; 14:45). Furthermore, terror would prompt high Christology, not low Christology (cf. v 6). U. B. Müller (in *ZNW* 64 [1973] 180) infers from the command to hear Jesus that the disciples are to pay no attention to Peter's confession of Jesus as the Christ (8:29) and that therefore the Transfiguration does not confirm the confession. Against this inference, the nearer possibility is that the disciples are to hear Jesus rather than paying attention to what Moses and Elijah said when speaking with him. Mark's using the Transfiguration as an apology for the Cross turns upside down the thesis of Müller that Mark's redaction transforms a traditional scene of enthronement (here Müller builds on an earlier thesis of P. Vielhauer) into an occasion for Jesus' teaching about the Passion (ibid. 159-93). Similarly, Mark's failure to show interest elsewhere in the session of Christ makes it unlikely that he presents the Transfiguration as proleptic of Jesus' present state (so M. E. Thrall in *NTS* 16 [1969-70] 305-17). Ps 110:1 will not be interpreted in 12:35-37 with reference to sitting on God's right hand; and 14:62 will refer to seeing the Son of man seated there at the start of his future coming, not to his present state. The similarity of v 8 to Exod 2:12 LXX is fortuitous. There is no substantial reason to detect an allusion.

According to K. L. Schmidt (*Rahmen* 225-27), vv 9-10 belong to the Transfiguration and v 11 starts a new pericope. But v 11 gives no indication of a topographical shift such as Mark likes for starting a new pericope. From that standpoint v 9 makes a better start. But the present tense of the participle καταβαινόντων, "descending," a reference to the mountain, and the inclusion that descending the mountain makes with ascending the mountain in v 2 favor a continuation of the pericope. Not till arrival on completion of the descent does a new pericope start (v 14).

The identifying of Marcan locutions (διεστείλατο, "he ordered"; τὸν λόγον, "the word"; πρὸς ἑαυτούς, "to themselves"; συζητοῦντες, "discussing") and of the Marcan theme of secrecy (E. Best, *Following Jesus* 62-63; M. Horstmann, *Studien* 72-74) demands Mark's fabrication neither of the whole of vv 9-10 nor of their framework. He might use his preferred diction in writing up tradition; and in the absence of his sources we can hardly be confident of what distinguishes his diction and theology from theirs, anyway. Nor is all the diction in vv 9-10 distinctively Marcan even by confident standards (cf. H. F. Bayer, *Jesus' Predictions* 166-69, against taking 9:9b as Mark's fabrication).

On the supposition that nothing like the Transfiguration happened to Jesus during his lifetime, some have thought that Mark or an earlier traditioner made up the command to silence and the disciples' obeying it (vv 9-10) to explain an absence of the Transfiguration from the earliest stage of dominical tradition. But permission to tell about the Transfiguration as soon as Jesus rises from the dead would provide an explanation only till the Resurrection. Thus vv 9-10 would provide no explanation for an absence of the Transfiguration from dominical tradition in the period just following the Resurrection. Yet that is the stage for which an explanation is needed according to this view. Incidentally, we do not take other commands to secrecy as indicating that the pericopes in which they stand used to narrate appearances of the risen Jesus.

Jesus' descending the mountain to go toward his death does not imply that the fulfilment of 9:1 will paradoxically come in his death rather than in apocalyptic events represented by the Transfiguration (so H. Anderson 227). Mark maintains apocalyptic expectation in 8:38 and throughout chap. 13. R. P. Martin (*Mark* 171-72) suggests that the disciples would expect Jesus to be translated to heaven, as were Elijah and Moses (cf. U. B. Müller in ZNW 64 [1973] 182-93). Perhaps so, but the belief that Moses died in accordance with the OT predominates over the belief that he was translated (J. Jeremias in *TDNT* 2. 939, n. 92; 4. 854-55). On the other hand, the pairing of Elijah with Moses instead of Enoch, the only other OT person usually thought to have been translated, may imply the background of a minority opinion that Moses did not die, but was translated (ibid. 2. 938-39; cf. Rev 11:3-12). Even then, however, the suggestion of building tabernacles seems to be based on an expectation that Jesus was *not* going to be translated; and insofar as the command to hear him may look forward as well as backward, it would rule out such an expectation.

Commanding the disciples not to tell anyone differs from the heathen's not hearing till they are told, for "anyone" includes Jews as well as the heathen. Therefore the command to silence does not allude to Isa 52:15–53:1 (against O. Betz in *Das Evangelium und die Evangelien* 74). Nor does the text of the command to secrecy give any reason to discover a deep theological meaning to the effect that only the Cross and the Resurrection will enable people to understand Jesus truly. On the contrary, the three disciples are not to tell even the other disciples about the Transfiguration; yet Jesus himself has already taught the others as well as the three about his death and resurrection (8:31).

According to S. Kim (*"Son of Man"* 1), the secret is that "the Son of man" is "the Son of God." But Jesus tells the disciples not to relate "the things that they have seen," and nowhere among those things are "the Son of man" and "the Son of God" equated. God has identified Jesus as his Son, of course; but demons have so identified Jesus long ago in Mark — and in public settings (3:11; 5:7 with 5:14, 16; cf. 1:24). Prior to the Resurrection, moreover, both Jesus himself and the centurion at the cross will declare the divine sonship of Jesus (14:61-62; 15:39). So unless he disregards his own command to secrecy and Mark does, too, the secret cannot consist in an equation even between Jesus as a person and the Son of God, much less in an equation between titles.

The command not to tell about the Transfiguration is not inconsistent with Jesus' telling a general audience about the Son of man's coming in glory (8:38), as thought by W. Wrede (*Messianic Secret* 67). The one is an accomplished event, the other only an unfulfilled prophecy; the one witnessed by disciples, the other only predicted by Jesus. From this point of view, then, it is unnecessary to appeal critically to an original independence of 9:9 from the occasion of 8:38 (so R. H. Stein, *Proper Methodology* 79). Wrede correctly disputes, however, that inability to understand the Transfiguration till after the Resurrection underlies the command to silence: "If the meaning of the Transfiguration was to be discerned only later, then it seems more or less harmless if people heard about it earlier" (loc. cit.).

T. A. Burkill (*Mysterious Revelation* 216) asks why — apart from Mark's philosophy of history — the Transfiguration should be kept secret from the other disciples now that they know Jesus to be the Christ. But the command to secrecy is general. Though included, the other disciples are not particularly in view. So the question is inappropriate (cf. K.-G. Reploh [*Lehrer* 114], who thinks that Jesus is commanding silence on the part of all the disciples, not just the three; and see 1:44; 5:43; 7:24, 36; 8:30; 13:32; 16:8 that μηδενί, "to no one" [9:9], need not have particular reference to the rest of the Twelve).

J. Gnilka (2. 26-27) contrasts the literal seeing of the Transfiguration (v 9) with seeing God's future rule as existential participation in it (v 1). This contrast neglects the element of existential participation in seeing the Transfiguration, and the literalness of seeing God's future rule. Gnilka (2. 40-41) also thinks that Jesus' resurrection marks the end of preceding commands to silence as well as of the command in v 9. To an extent, yes — e.g., with reference to 8:30 — but Jesus' commanding demons to be silent had the purpose and effect of defeating them and carried no implication that after his resurrection they could resume their unwanted shouting of his divine sonship.

M. Horstmann (*Studien* 128-34) argues that the motifs of fear and silence after the Resurrection in 16:1-8 make a double messianic secret in which the paradox of Jesus as the suffering Son of God characterizes the gospel after the Resurrection (and until the

Second Coming) as well as before it. But after the Resurrection in 16:1-8 there is no command not to tell; and the not telling in 16:8 grows out of fear, not out of obedience to any command, as it does in 9:10 (see H.-T. Wrege, *Gestalt* 167; E. Lemcio in *NTS* 32 [1986] 196; and, for a general caution against making 9:9 the key to Mark's theology, H. Räisänen, *Messias-Geheimnis* 111-17).

In none of the other predictions of Jesus' resurrection does "from [the] dead" occur. Here it makes up for the lack of an immediately preceding reference to his coming death. The command to silence, which includes a reference to the Resurrection, issues in a failure of understanding (v 10). It therefore reverses the text to say that the disciples' failure to understand issues in the command to silence. Nor does Peter's not knowing how to answer earlier in v 6 prompt the command to silence, for a similar command in 8:30 followed upon a correct answer (see 1:1; 9:41; 14:61-62 for the correctness of the answer).

Dan 10:1 Theod does not support our taking τὸν λόγον as "the matter" of the Transfiguration, i.e. as "the things that they [the disciples] have seen" (vv 9-10; so M. Sabbé in *La Venue du Messie* 69). Though Dan 10:1 Theod associates τὸν λόγον with a vision, the phrase does not refer to "the matter" of the vision as such, but to "the word" of the glorious being who speaks to Daniel in the vision (see v 10, also vv 9, 15, 19, 20ff.). So also with regard to Dan 12:8 LXX (cited ibid.). In Mark, Jesus has spoken since the close of the Transfiguration; so τὸν λόγον means "the word, the saying" here, too.

J. Schreiber (*Theologie des Vertrauens* 111-12) appeals to the use of κρατέω for violent seizure in 3:21; 6:17; 12:12; 14:1, 44, 46, 49, 51 to argue that in v 10 the disciples mistreat Jesus' word and therefore Jesus himself. But the verb carries non-violent and sometimes beneficial meanings in 1:31; 5:41; 7:3, 4, 8; 9:27. Cf. Dan 5:12 Theod for an association of κρατέω with things that have been kept secret. In Mark 9:10 the translation which takes πρὸς ἑαυτούς with the preceding rather than the following and then takes ἐκράτησαν as a characteristically Marcan Latinism — "and they kept the matter to themselves [i.e. in their memory — *(memoria) tenere*], though they were discussing what the rising from the dead is" — suffers from a number of liabilities: (1) earlier occurrences of κρατέω in the sense of observance (7:3, 4, 8); (2) Mark's never using κρατέω elsewhere in the sense of keeping something in the memory; (3) the probability that keeping in memory would here take the imperfect rather than aorist tense (G. Wohlenberg 246); (4) the frequency of λόγος in the sense of a saying (5:36; 7:29; 8:32; 10:22; 11:29; 12:13; 14:39); (5) Mark's never using λόγος elsewhere in the sense of a matter; (6) the use of συζητέω, "discuss," with πρός in 1:27; 9:14, 16; and (7) Mark's never using κρατέω elsewhere with πρός. The passages that H. B. Swete (192) cites for κρατέω as keeping in memory (7:3, 4, 8; 2 Thess 2:15; Rev 2:14ff.) have to do rather with putting into practice.

B. M. F. van Iersel (*Reading Mark* 138-39) asks why the disciples' ignorance of the Resurrection was not noted after 8:31, where Jesus first predicted his resurrection, and answers that the Transfiguration has anticipated the Resurrection. But an anticipation of the Resurrection should make it more understandable, not less understandable, than the mere prediction of it. The correct answer is that the disciples are not ignorant of the Resurrection as such, but do not understand how the resurrection of Jesus relates to the prior coming of Elijah according to scribal doctrine. Elijah's appearance at the Transfiguration has created this puzzle for them.

For literature on Elijah's return (vv 11-13), see J. Jeremias in *TDNT* 2. 928-41. Mal 3:23-24(4:5-6) says that God will send Elijah before the Day of the Lord, not that God will send him ahead of the Messiah. Nor does any other pre-Christian text say that Elijah will be forerunner of the Messiah (see the discussion among M. M. Faierstein in *JBL* 100 [1981] 75-86; D. C. Allison, Jr., in *JBL* 103 [1984] 256-58; and J. A. Fitzmyer in *JBL* 104 [1985] 295-96). Even here the disciples stop short of quoting the scribes as saying that Elijah must come before the Messiah (against the argument that the present reference to scribal doctrine implies a first-century Jewish belief in Elijah as the Messiah's forerunner). "Come first" leaves room for the disciples' own application of scribal doctrine to Jesus' mention of the Resurrection. The disciples appear to assume that the Son of man's resurrection will accompany or trigger the resurrection of others and thus occur on arrival of the Day of the Lord after Elijah's return (a point overlooked by J. Marcus [in *ZNW* 80 (1989) 42-43, n. 2] in arguing that the disciples cannot be struggling with the expectation of Elijah's coming before the Son of man's resurrection, but must be struggling with an expectation of Elijah's coming before an event that has already taken place). Given the eschatological nature of that day, the disciples would make this assumption quite naturally. Its naturalness leaves no good reason to suppose a radical break between vv 10 and 11 such as would justify the theory that vv 11-13 stem from a different tradition. Likewise, to imagine that because resurrection is the topic of vv 9-10, but Elijah of vv 11-13, Mark has inserted vv 11-13 (cf. H. Anderson 227; J. Schmid 173 et al.) leaves "first" without a pre-Marcan referent that is still discernable. One wonders whether there is a better possibility than the Son of man's resurrection and therefore whether the topical difference between vv 9-10 and 11-13 does not represent dialogical progression rather than redactional amalgamation. Malachi's "Day of the Lord" provides a possible and indeed likely underlying referent for "first," but why do the disciples even think of that day if not because Jesus has just mentioned his resurrection? M. Black (in *SJT* 39 [1986] 9-12) proposes that vv 9-13 represent an authentic didactic pesher on Mal 3:23-24(4:5-6); Isa 53:3 (but see the following notes against the use of Isa 53:3).

Saying that "to come first" and "having come first" in vv 11-12 mean coming before the coming of the Son of man in 8:38, or before seeing that God's rule has come with power in v 1, depends on dropping the intervening material as a late insertion. But the immediately following reference in v 12 to the Son of man's passion favors an original connection with the Son of man's resurrection in v 10. This connection then supports the originality of Mark's contextual meaning, i.e. "coming first" as coming before the Son of man's resurrection.

For הָשִׁיב, "will turn" (Mal 3:24 MT), Mark's ἀποκαθιστάνει, "restores," agrees with the LXX in diction but not in form (cf. Sir 48:10). Though this amount of agreement with the LXX may tempt some to deny that Jesus made the affirmation, the astonishing universality of the role assigned to Elijah — a role that surpasses even the expansions in *m. Sota* 9:15; *m. B. Meṣ.* 1:8; 2:8; 3:4-5; *m. ʿEd.* 8:7; and later rabbinic literature cited by J. Jeremias in *TDNT* 2. 928-34 — makes it unlikely that a Christian, jealous of Jesus' role, would have made up the affirmation, much less have put it on Jesus' lips (cf. the observation by R. T. France [*Jesus and the OT* 250-51] that expansions of Elijah's role "in the purely Semitic milieu of Ecclesiasticus and the Mishnah" undercut an inference of inauthenticity from present contact with the LXX).

M. E. Thrall (in *NTS* 16 [1969-70] 307-8) correctly criticizes the view of H. Baltensweiler (*Verklärung* 76-82) that Elijah is put forward as a peaceful restorer to counteract a political concept of Jesus' messiahship. As a matter of fact, nothing is said about peaceful versus violent means of restoration. J. D. M. Derrett (*Law* 360) propounds that Elijah's restoration of all things entails his own suffering. But the suffering of John the Baptist, whom Jesus identifies as Elijah, did not effect the restoration of all things; for then the Son of man would not have to suffer at a later date.

P. J. Heawood (in *ExpTim* 64 [1952-53] 239) and J. Wellhausen (2. Aufl., 70) make a sceptical question out of the middle of v 12: "Coming first, does Elijah indeed restore all things?" This question then gets a negative answer in the following "and how?"-question, which appeals to the scriptural necessity that the Son of man suffer. J. Marcus (in *ZNW* 80 [1989] 46-63) adopts this interrogative interpretation, proceeds to treat the two clauses as a case of scriptural contradiction, sees a resolution growing out of the scriptural suffering of the Son of man to the effect that Elijah is not coming first to restore all things, but has already come and suffered. But militating against this interpretation is the declarative thrust of μέν, "indeed, it's true," which even in a question would assume an affirmative answer in the mind of the questioner (LSJ s.v. AI3). Jesus' failing to say that Elijah-John restored all things when he came and saying on the contrary that people did against him as many things as they wanted to do and that the Son of man has yet to suffer make a timeless interpretation of "restores" nonsensical and require a future fulfilment of the restoration.

See M. Reiser, *Syntax und Stil* 112-13, on the combination καὶ πῶς, "and how?" (v 12), which introduces a question about the Son of man's suffering. There is no need to consider this question an interpolation. The foregoing comments have shown how it contributes to the flow of thought. Admittedly, the question interrupts the contrast between Elijah's restoring all things and his suffering maltreatment. But this sort of awkwardness may signal originality rather than interpolation. Matthew and Luke often make omissions and rearrange Mark's materials to produce a smoother text. For this very purpose, in fact, Matt 17:11-12 shifts and rephrases the "and how?"-question. Since the easier text is more likely later, we should not think that Matthew is falling back on pre-Marcan tradition. Unless we lapse into circular reasoning by regarding as non-dominical other occurrences of πῶς, "how?" in reference to Scripture (2:26; 12:26, 35-36), the present such occurrence does not need to be so regarded. Though πῶς may be exclamatory (see, e.g., 10:23, 24), its interrogative meaning when used elsewhere in reference to Scripture subverts an exclamatory meaning in reference to Scripture here.

See the comments and notes on 2:10 for "the Son of man," and on 8:31 for "suffer much." Ἐξουδενηθῇ, "be treated with contempt," is a non-Septuagintal alternative to ἀποδοκιμασθῆναι, "to be rejected," in allusion to Ps 118:22 (so Acts 4:11, too; again cf. Mark 8:31). O. J. F. Seitz (in *SE VII* 453-54) notes that the LXX uses ἐξουδενέω and ἀποδοκιμάζω with about equal frequency for מאס, the verb in Ps 118:22. The Son of man's suffering and being treated with contempt is not presented as atoning. For this reason 1QS 5:6; 9:3-5; 1QH 5:3-6 do not make good parallels — also because in those passages it is not the suffering of the elect but their righteous conduct that atones for sin (cf. H. Braun, *Qumran* 1. 69). For the first of these reasons we should also favor an allusion to Ps 118:22 over an allusion to Isa 53:3.

R. T. France (*Jesus and the OT* 123-24) argues nevertheless that the general theme of suffering and being treated with contempt favors Isa 53:3; that nothing in Mark 9:12 suggests Ps 118:22; that elsewhere Mark uses the Septuagintal ἀποδοκιμάζω, not ἐξουδενέω, in citing Ps 118:22 (Mark 12:10 [cf. 8:31]); that 1 Pet 2:7 does likewise; and that even though ἐξουδενέω does not appear in Isa 53:3 LXX (but see Aq Sym Theod), elsewhere the LXX often uses it for the verb בזה of Isa 53:3. Against these arguments, however, not only do we have no evidence that ἐξουδενέω represented Isa 53:3 in any pre-Christian text or in the NT, but also Acts 4:11 definitely displays a use of this verb in the citing of Ps 118:22. Furthermore, nowhere else does Mark contain a citation of Isa 53:3, but it does contain both an allusion to and a quotation of Ps 118:22 in 8:31 and 12:10. Yet again, the possibility that an absolute use suits ἐξουδενέω better than it suits ἀποδοκιμάζω (cf. 1 Cor 1:28; 6:4; 2 Cor 10:10, for example) may account for the present switch in verbs.

These latter considerations militate also against an allusion to Ps 88:39 (σύ . . . ἐξουδένωσας . . . τὸν χριστόν σου, "you have treated your anointed one with contempt"). The possibility of such an allusion suffers the additional liability that in the psalm Yahweh is the subject whereas in the passion predictions it is sinners who do this sort of thing to the Son of man. One can find the Son of man's suffering in the context of Dan 7:13 by regarding "the one like a Son of man" as collective for persecuted Israel (cf. Ps 80:15-18). But Jesus uses "the Son of man" as an individualistic self-reference. The scripturalness of

Jesus' suffering therefore rests, not necessarily or exclusively on an OT passage or passages where "the Son of man" occurs, but on whatever OT passage or passages Jesus sees as predicting his own suffering (with the diffuse use of "it is written," cf. 1:2-3; John 7:38; Gal 4:22 and comparable Jewish material cited and discussed by J. Marcus in ZNW 80 [1989] 44-45). J. Bowker (Religious Imagination 149-58 and in JTS ns 28 [1977] 19-35) theorizes that "it is written" points to OT passages where "Son of man" connotes mortality. Though the theory would sit comfortably here and in other passion predictions, it stretches to the breaking point when Bowker is forced by his theory to say that in 2:10, 27 Jesus has authority on earth to forgive sins and exercise dominion over the Sabbath despite his mortality. Nothing in the contexts surrounding those verses suggests tension between mortality on the one hand and authority and dominion on the other.

The parallel between πῶς γέγραπται ἐπὶ τὸν υἱὸν τοῦ ἀνθρώπου, "how [can it be that] it is written against the Son of man . . . ?" (v 12), and καθὼς γέγραπται ἐπὶ αὐτόν, "according as it is written against him [Elijah]" (v 13), has several possible explanations: (1) both phrases derive from Jesus; (2) one or the other derives from Jesus and its counterpart is added; (3) both are added. That Jesus rooted in Scripture the parallel between his fate and John's is as likely as that a later Christian did so — perhaps more likely, for a later Christian's jealousy of the unique value of Jesus' death would tend toward breaking down the parallel rather than supporting it with Scripture. If there is no need to regard the πῶς-clause in v 12 as an addition (see the foregoing notes), that clause does not argue for regarding the καθὼς-clause in v 13 as an addition.

It is no argument for addition of the καθὼς-clause in v 13 that the OT does not predict maltreatment of the coming Elijah. Not only are historical narratives like 1 Kings 19 often interpreted as typologically predictive, but also no other pre-Marcan document predicts that the coming Elijah will be maltreated. We may hypothesize that v 13 refers to a lost writing such as might underlie Rev 11:1-13 (cf. Apoc. Elijah 4:7-19; 5:32; J. Jeremias in TDNT 2. 939-41). But the evidence for such a writing is indirect and questionable, appearing only in Christian literature. Moreover, the evangelists regularly use γέγραπται for the OT; and Rev 11:1-13 talks of two forerunners, not of one as in Mark 9:11-13 (cf. the notes on v 4; W. Wink, John the Baptist 14, n. 2; H.-J. Steichele, Der leidende Sohn Gottes 105, n. 234). A general reference to the violent fate of the OT prophets does not quite satisfy the demand of the final phrase ἐπ᾽ αὐτόν, "against him."

According to Steichele (op. cit. 107), the suffering of the forerunner shows that the suffering of Jesus should not pose a stumbling block. But Wink (op. cit. 15-16) points out that a suffering Elijah scandalizes Jewish expectation of a successfully restorative Elijah just as a suffering Christ scandalizes Jewish messianic expectation. According to W. H. Kelber (Kingdom 76), vv 11-13 argue against the scribal objection that John's violent death contradicts his fulfilling the role of Elijah as the eschatological restorer. The argument is that the Son of man's death will vindicate John's death, which in turn has prepared for the Son of man's death. This interpretation founders on the fact that it is Jesus, not the scribes, who affirms that Elijah restores all things. Perhaps the disciples never did think of John the Baptist as the returned Elijah because, unlike Elijah, John performed no miracles. Certainly his violent death has more recently kept the disciples from identifying him with Elijah. The failure of Elijah and Moses to appear as forerunners of the Messiah in pre-Christian Jewish literature does not deter the Transfiguration from prefiguring the Second Coming (as thought by P. Vielhauer, Aufsätze 207-8). Pre-Christian Jewish beliefs in Elijah's coming before the Day of the Lord and in a Mosaic eschatological prophet play into a prefigurement of the Second Coming well enough.

THE SUPERPOWER OF JESUS
IN A SPECIALLY DIFFICULT EXORCISM

9:14-29 (Matt 17:14-21; Luke 9:37-43a; 17:6)

The story of Jesus' casting out a mute spirit starts with Jesus' and a crowd's meeting each other (vv 14-18), peaks in the exorcism itself (vv 19-27), and tails off in a conversation between Jesus and the disciples (vv 28-29). In the first section he and the three disciples accompanying him see a crowd (v 14). The crowd greet him (v 15). He asks why they are arguing with the disciples who have not been with him (v 16). The answer comes from the father of a demoniac (vv 17-18). In the second section Jesus voices his exasperation and commands the son to be brought (v 19). People bring the son (v 20a), and the spirit convulses him (v 20b). In answer to Jesus' inquiry the father describes his son's state (vv 21-22). Jesus and the father have an exchange on the question of Jesus' ability (vv 23-24), and the exorcism follows (vv 25-27). In the last section, the disciples ask Jesus about their inability to cast out the spirit (v 28), and Jesus answers (v 29).

9:14-15 *(Matt 17:14; Luke 9:37)* On descending from the Mount of Transfiguration Jesus, Peter, James, and John come toward the remaining disciples and see a crowd around them. The large size of the crowd contributes to the impressiveness of the impact that Jesus will make on them. Mark specially mentions scribes as part of the crowd because they are leading the crowd in disputation with the disciples. We should probably include the rest of the crowd with the scribes in the disputation; for Jesus will ask the crowd why they are disputing with the disciples (cf. v 16 with v 15), and the plural συζητοῦντας, "disputing," may modify the collective singular ὄχλον, "crowd," as well as the plural γραμματεῖς, "scribes," just as the same singular noun takes plural participles and verbs in v 15 (J. A. Kleist 123-24). The reason behind the disputation will turn out to be the disciples' inability to exorcise a spirit. This inability makes a foil against which Jesus' ability to perform the exorcism will stand out in powerful contrast. The crowd and the scribes will not be able to point at any inability on *his* part!

The crowd are amazed (ἐξεθαμβήθησαν) at the sight of Jesus (cf. Iambl. *VP* 36; H. D. Betz, *Lukian* 159-60). Their amazement amounts to more than surprise that he has suddenly appeared on the scene. In 1:27; 10:24, 32 it is the simplex form of the verb (θαμβέω) that refers to the awe with which Jesus' teaching or action strikes people. But here we read the compound form having the perfective ἐκ-, which elsewhere will connote awe so extreme as to cause emotional distress, bodily tremors, and psychological bewilderment. The contexts of these other occurrences will identify reasons for such extreme awe: the prospect of imminent, violent death in 14:33-34 and the seeing of a seated young man, robed in white, instead of the supine corpse of Jesus, wrapped in a shroud, at 16:5-8 (cf. 15:46). What then does the present context identify as the reason for the extreme awe of the large crowd who see Jesus at the base of the mountain? What else than the glistening white garments of his transfiguration? Mark has not indicated that they have dimmed (nor will he; so one wonders whether he intends his audience to assume a transfiguration that continues right to the Crucifixion and thereby counteracts its shame (cf. the durative force of ἐληλυθυῖαν, "having come," in v 1). And something so striking as the heavenly whiteness of Jesus' garments seems required to account for a word so strong as ἐξεθαμβήθησαν. The extremity of the circumstances leading to later use of this word support this judgment. The immediacy (εὐθύς) of the crowd's extreme awe, the inclusion of "all" of them — large crowd though they are — and the placement of "all the crowd" before both the circumstantial participial phrase and the verb emphasize the impact which the sight of Jesus makes on the crowd. Further emphasis on this impact accrues from their hailing Jesus and from their running to him to hail him (cf. 6:54-55; 10:17 for the running). If the imperfect tense of ἠσπάζοντο carries an iterative meaning — i.e. they were hailing Jesus one after another — yet further emphasis accrues to the impact that Jesus' appearance makes on the crowd; but perhaps we have here only the imperfect into which verbs of speaking often go because of the linear character of speech (M. Zerwick, *Biblical Greek* §272).

9:16-18 *(Matt 17:14-15a, 16; Luke 9:38-40)* Since συζητέω, "dispute," takes περί, "concerning," for the subject matter of the dispute, we should treat τί as an adverb ("*Why* are you disputing with them [the disciples]?" rather than as a direct object ("*What* are you disputing with them?"). The reported failure of the disciples will provide the reason behind the dispute. The answer of "one from the crowd" (cf. 14:18 for εἷς ἐκ . . .) includes the honorific address διδάσκαλε, "Teacher." This address calls to mind the authority with which Jesus teaches, as demonstrated in his casting out demons (1:21-28). Strikingly, the answer also alludes to the answerer's having brought his son to Jesus, though Jesus was not present at the time. Thus attention focuses on Jesus as the one whom the answerer hoped and expected to be present for the deliverance of his son, who has "a mute spirit," i.e. one that keeps him from speaking during seizures (cf. Luc. *Philops.* 16). The ability to speak between seizures will eliminate the need to mention a restoration of speech in v 27, as was done in 7:35. Meanwhile, however, the coming descriptions of the demoniac's seizures do not include the usual shrieking and adjurations (contrast 1:23-25; 3:11; 5:6-10). Though the spirit will let out a shriek toward the end of the story, that shriek will signal the end of the spirit's dominion over the son. This dominion goes beyond the causing of dumbness, however. The spirit seizes the son, dashes him to the ground, and makes him foam at the mouth, grind his teeth, and stiffen up. Ὅπου ἐάν, "wherever" (or "when-ever"; see BAGD s.v. ὅπου 1δ), indicates that the dominion is so complete that the spirit can strike him down at will. The pronominal redundancy and chiasm of (a) αὐτόν, "him," (b) καταλάβῃ, "it seizes," (b′) ῥήσσει, "it dashes [to the ground]," (a′) αὐτόν, "him," enhance the point. The details of the spirit's hold over the son — they will come up progressively throughout the story — make Jesus' exorcism all the more impressive in its display of superior power. The inability of the disciples, whom the father asked to exorcise the spirit in Jesus' absence, has the same effect and, like the details of the spirit's hold over the son, will come in for renewed attention (cf. 5:26). The forward position of αὐτό, "it," emphasizes that the disciples were no match for the spirit. Οὐκ ἴσχυσαν indicates a lack of strength on their part and makes a foil to Jesus as the stronger one whose coming John the Baptizer predicted in 1:7 (E. Wendling, *Entstehung* 228; cf. the comments on 5:4; 14:37). The ellipsis of "to cast it out" (cf. the filling in of this ellipsis by D W Θ 565 a b sa) leaves the emphasis on lack of strength per se so as to underscore the coming display of Jesus' strength.

9:19-20 *(Matt 17:17; Luke 9:41-42a)* Ἀποκριθείς, "answering," may be stereotypically unemphatic, but an adversative δέ, "but," and the present historical tense of λέγει, "he says," underscore Jesus' following, exasperated rebuke of his generation. He rebukes them for unbelief. Mark probably wants his own audience to take a warning against unbelief in Jesus, unbelief caused by the scandal of the Crucifixion. Jesus himself may have in mind a lack of faith in him, for his outburst relates to a matter that figures prominently among his activities — exorcism. The rebuke is wide-ranging. The father's later plea, "Help my unbelief" (v 23), seems to include him in the unbelieving generation. So also does Jesus' answering "them" although the father has just been speaking to him. The father represents the crowd, as Mark has carefully prepared us to infer by calling him "one from the crowd." Thus the unbelieving generation takes in the father and the crowd. But it does not take in the disciples; for they stand opposite the crowd in the foregoing dispute, and Jesus will not mention unbelief on their part when they ask him why they failed at exorcising the spirit. The very disputatiousness of the scribes and of the rest of the crowd casts them in the role of unbelievers (see esp. 8:11; 12:28) and therefore casts their opponents in the dispute, i.e. the disciples, in the role of believers (cf. S. E. Dowd [*Prayer* 117, n. 109], who infers from v 15 that in running toward Jesus the crowd left the nine disciples, who do not reenter the picture till his entering a house in v 28). It looks as though Jesus is condemning the crowd, including the father and the scribes in it, for making the disciples' failure a reason to dispute the power of Jesus himself, whom the disciples represent and whose shared exorcistic ability they have demonstrated in the past (6:13). "O" dignifies Jesus' speech with an elevated style that lends it gravity (J. A. L. Lee in *NovT* 27 [1985] 16-18). The questions, "How long shall I be with you?" and "How long shall I put up with you?" exhibit considerable emotion as well as pointing up the gravity of unbelief. "Bring him to me" shows Jesus' determination to expose the baselessness of unbelief.

Naturally for Mark, the crowd carry out Jesus' command. Though ἰδών, "seeing," is masculine and might therefore seem to modify the demoniac or Jesus, its nominative case requires that it modify the neuter subject τὸ πνεῦμα, "the spirit" (see v 26 and cf. the notes on 5:7-8 concerning the masculine as bringing out the personality of spirits). On seeing Jesus, then, the spirit convulses the demoniac in a demonstration of power designed to intimidate Jesus and, so far as Mark is concerned, to heighten the effect when Jesus demonstrates the superiority of his power. The immediacy of the convulsion strengthens this effect. So also does addition of the details that the demoniac falls on the ground and rolls around foaming at the mouth (cf. Luc. *Philops.* 16). What the father has described achieves a vivid demonstration on the spot. In agreement with the spirit's causing dumbness, there is no verbal attempt to ward off Jesus (contrast 1:24; 5:7).

9:21-22 *(Matt 17:15b)* Not content with the already vivid details concerning the spirit's power over the demoniac (contrast the sparsity of detail in Matthew and Luke), Mark now includes a dialogue between Jesus and the father that adds yet further details. They will make a successful exorcism look all the more impressive. In answer to Jesus' inquiry, "How long a time is it since this happened to him?" the father not only supplies the information, "From childhood," which makes the possession nearly lifelong and therefore harder to break (cf. 5:25-26; Hippoc. *Morb. Sacr.* 11), but he also expatiates on the many times that the spirit has cast the demoniac both into fire and into waters to destroy him (cf. 1:24; Philostr. *VA* 3.38). An adversative δέ, "but," highlights this answer; and the forward positions of πολλάκις, "often," εἰς πῦρ, "into fire," and αὐτόν, "him," and the combination καί . . . καί, "both . . . and," heighten one's sense of the spirit's power and therefore of the superpower that Jesus is about to exercise. "Nevertheless, if you are able — anything, help us by having compassion on us" raises a question concerning Jesus' ability (contrast 1:40) at the same time that it makes an appeal for his help. The question and the appeal are heightened by the strength of the adversative ἀλλ᾽, "nevertheless," by the forward position of τι, "anything," and by the aposiopesis of omitting the supplementary infinitive ποιεῖν, "to do," of which τι would have been the direct object. The question of Jesus' ability stems from the failure of the disciples: if their ability derives from his, their failure seems to imply the inadequacy of his ability. Since the father has a stake in the welfare of his son, the father includes himself as a possible co-beneficiary of Jesus' help.

9:23-24 An adversative δέ, "but," shifts attention to the answer of Jesus: "With respect to your phrase, 'If you are able,' all things [are] able [to be done] for the person who believes" (cf. 5:36; 6:5-6a; 10:27, 52; 11:22-24; 14:36). This answer neatly shifts the focus from Jesus' ability, about which there should be no question, to the belief of a petitioner — the father in this case or, in other cases, any petitioner. The dropping of τι, "anything," from the aposiopetic εἰ δύνῃ, "if you are able" (contrast the presence and emphatic forward position of τι in v 22), allows the emphasis to fall now on πάντα, "all things." Πάντα includes the particularly difficult exorcism at hand. The cognates δύνῃ, "you are able," and δυνατά, "able [to be done]," make a wordplay that is missed if we translate δυνατά with "possible." The ellipses of "are" and "to be done" concentrate attention on this wordplay. Since the phrase ἐκ παιδιόθεν, "from childhood," implied that the son is grown (v 21), the editorial designation of the son as τοῦ παιδίου, "the child" (v 24), either puts him at the upper limit of childhood or, in conjunction with mention of the father, reflects back on the earlier spells of demonic possession that characterized the son's childhood. Mark emphasizes the father's saying, "I believe, help my unbelief," by describing it as a shout (κράξας), by noting its immediacy upon Jesus' raising the question of belief (εὐθύς), and by commencing the introductory formula with asyndeton. The purpose of this emphasis is to portray Jesus as worthy of belief. Apparently the father brought his son with faith in Jesus' ability to exorcise the spirit; but the failure of the disciples, who represent Jesus, crushed his faith in Jesus' ability — hence, the rebuke — and now his faith revives, but accompanied by some vestigial unbelief (cf. Luc. *Philops.* 16; also R. Herzog, *Wunderheilungen* nos. 9, 13, for initial faith, and nos. 3, 4, 35-37, and [though less relevant] 61, for unbelief giving way to faith). The asyndeton before βοήθει, "help," and the present tense of this imperative verb (contrast the ordinary aorist imperative of the same verb in v 22; cf. the notes on 1:3) stress the need for Jesus' help in getting rid of unbelief that lingers because the disciples' recent failure has raised the spectre of failure on Jesus' part, too.

9:25-27 *(Matt 17:18; Luke 9:42b)* As in 7:33-35 Jesus wanted privacy to perform the very difficult healing of a deaf mute (see the comments ad loc.), so here he wants privacy to perform the very difficult exorcism of a spirit that causes deafness and muteness. But the crowd "is running together to him." This statement harks back to a similar statement in v 15 that the crowd were running toward Jesus and greeting him as they arrived, and indicates both that the intervening material has had its setting in the first part of the crowd's running toward Jesus (προστρέχοντες) and that they are still running but coming close enough to be congealing together around him (ἐπισυντρέχει). Thus he cannot gain so much privacy as before. At least he can try to exorcise the spirit before any more of the crowd arrive, however; so he rebukes the spirit, which now gains the description "unclean" to indicate its meriting the rebuke. Ἐπετίμησεν, "he rebuked," refers to the exorcistic command itself (see the comments on 1:25). But Mark's interest does not go to Jesus' wanting as much privacy as possible for an especially difficult exorcism; rather, to Jesus' magnetism. So he puts the verb of running in the historical present tense and in the singular number. This switch from past indicative and plural verbal expressions (see v 15) emphasizes that Jesus' magnetism exercises itself wholesale. An adversative δέ, "but," intensifies the emphasis.

Addressing the spirit as deaf as well as dumb heightens the difficulty of the exorcism which Jesus is performing and may carry some irony in that a deaf spirit should not be able to hear his command to come out — but he *makes* it hear. One might almost say that he heals the spirit's deafness to exorcise the spirit. We should not make very much of this possibility, however; for Mark and Jesus may mean only that the spirit causes dumbness and deafness even though it itself can speak and hear (cf. its shouting when it comes out and the initial refusal of a spirit to speak according to Plut. *Mor.* 438B; Paris MS 2316, both discussed by C. Bonner in *HTR* 36 [1943] 43-44 [see also *T. Sol.* 5:1-2; 7:3; 13:1-2 and the comments on Mark 5:8], though W. Schenk [in *ZNW* 63 (1972) 86] thinks that enabling the spirit to hear will also enable it to shout in demonstration of the exorcism [v 26a]). The doubly descriptive address exhibits Jesus' knowledge of the spirit and therefore his power over it (cf. the comments on 5:6-10). Ἐπιτάσσω, "command," indicates the authority of his words (cf. esp. 1:27; *PGM* I. 253-55; VII. 331-33; but also Luke 10:17; *PGM* XIII. 744). Ἐγώ, "I," highlights the authority of his person in giving a command to come out and sets him in contrast with the failed disciples. "And never again enter into him" raises Jesus' power to the level of permanency (cf. Josephus Ant. 8.2.5 §§45, 47; Philostr. *VA* 4.20; *PGM* IV. 1244 and contrast the repetitiveness of the demoniac's earlier seizures; also Matt 12:43-45 par. Luke 11:24-26).

The spirit's shouting, convulsing the son severely, and leaving him resting on the ground so limp as to look dead give auditory and visible evidence of exit (cf. 1:25-26 with comments; Josephus *Ant.* 8.2.5 §47). The assonance of κράξας, "shouting," and σπαράξας, "convulsing," lend weight to the first two items of evidence; and πολλά, "severely" (perhaps "repeatedly"), stresses the unmistakability of the convulsion as evidence of successful exorcism. But Mark devotes most attention to the evidence of the son's looking dead, which leads "the many" (which probably means all the crowd [see BAGD s.v. πολύς I2aβ] and at least means a large number of them) to say in character with Jesus' description of them as an unbelieving generation that the son has in fact died. Hardly the deliverance the father asked for — rather, a defeat for Jesus and a victory for the spirit by way of fulfilling its purpose to destroy the son (cf. v 22a)! But no, Jesus seizes the son's hand and raises him with the result that he stands up — alive. A marvelous victory for Jesus and defeat of the spirit after all! Not only has the demon gone for good. Jesus' action of grasping and raising the son has restored the son's strength (cf. 1:31; 5:41-42; also 2:11-12, but without physical contact). Because of his seeming to have died, ἀνέστη, "he rose," probably looks forward to Jesus' rising from the dead in accordance with his recent prediction (8:31 — ἀναστῆναι) and allusion (9:9 — ἐκ νεκρῶν ἀναστῇ) and in accordance with the prediction that he is going to make in the very next pericope (9:31 — ἀναστήσεται; see the comments on 5:41-42, where the phraseology is remarkably similar; also those on 7:31-37 concerning the difficulty of healing a deaf mute, a difficulty considered as great as that of raising the dead). Another adversative δέ, "but," highlights Jesus' victory over the spirit.

9:28-29 *(Matt 17:19-20)* The house that Jesus now enters is not Peter's; for that is located in Capernaum (2:1-2), yet in the next two pericopes Jesus and his disciples will leave the present house and go to Capernaum (vv 30, 33). Nor does Jesus' entering a house start a new pericope; for Mark notes it with a mere genitive absolute (contrast 3:20 and passages where additional expressions signal the beginning of a new pericope — 1:29; 2:1; 7:24; 9:33). Rather, the entry marks a shift within the pericope (as in 7:17; 10:10; cf. 7:30). The subject matter of vv 28-29 confirms this judgment. The placement of the subject before its predicate (οἱ μαθηταὶ αὐτοῦ κατ᾽ ἰδίαν ἐπηρώτων αὐτόν, "his disciples were asking him privately") turns attention from the father to the disciples as Jesus' interlocutors (see M. Zerwick [*Untersuchungen* 91], who contrasts 4:10; 7:17; 13:3 but goes too far in saying that the present word order emphasizes the disciples as those who had failed — on the contrary, see 10:10, where the same word order will merely turn attention from the Pharisees [10:2] to the disciples as Jesus' interlocutors). The disciples' asking him in private why they could not cast out the spirit does recollect their failure, however, and once again makes out of it a foil to magnify his ability to accomplish the exorcism. His answer, "This kind [of spirit] is able to come out by no means except by prayer," is puzzling at first because he did not pray when he exorcised the spirit. But in accordance with the question of the disciples' failure he is telling what *they* must do: for an exorcism as difficult as this one they must pray. Jesus' power as the Son of God is so great that in performing the exorcism he did not need to pray. So the statement stands last as the final part of a foil consisting in the disciples' inability and failure. The forward positions of τοῦτο τὸ γένος, "this kind," and ἐν οὐδενί, "by no means," magnify the foil and thereby the ability and success of Jesus.

NOTES

Several doublets appear in 9:14-29. They have been used to distinguish both between two originally different stories and between tradition and Marcan or pre-Marcan redaction. The crowd run to Jesus twice (vv 15 and 25). But we noted in the comments that the running in v 25 progresses beyond the running in v 15. Furthermore, running is only a participle in v 15, but is a main verb in v 25; and the present tense of both forms indicates a continuous running, not two successive runnings. The double mention of it looks like Mark's love of emphatic duality, in this case to make a characteristic emphasis on Jesus' magnetism. The comment of H. Anderson (229) that in vv 14, 17 the crowd are already gathered, but in v 25 only in the process of gathering, is partly correct but misleading. The crowd's running toward Jesus in v 15 shows that in v 14 they were gathered around the disciples, and the present tense of the participle that describes the crowd's running toward Jesus shows that in vv 17 and 25 not all of them have yet gathered around Jesus.

Both v 17 and vv 19-20 speak of the son's being brought to Jesus. But v 17 would hardly stand in a story where Jesus was present at the time of bringing. His initial absence makes v 17 entirely compatible with vv 19-20. Also, the father brings his son in v 17; but in vv 19-20 Jesus commands the crowd to bring the son, and they do (N.B. the plural in φέρετε and ἤνεγκαν).

Both vv 17-18 and vv 20-22 describe the son's possession. (Verse 26 does not count; for it gives evidence of exorcism, not of possession.) But vv 20-22 confirm and elaborate vv 17-18 (cf. L. Schenke, *Wundererzählungen* 317, and again Mark's love of emphatic duality). These descriptions do not point to an earlier division between a story of epilepsy as demonic possession and a story of deafmuteness as illness, for deafmuteness is attributed to the spirit, not to the son (ibid. 318). It could be argued back that demonic possession accounted for epilepsy in one earlier story and for deafmuteness in another, and that the common element of demonic possession helped bring the stories together. But minimizing the differences between two earlier stories weakens the argument for positing two earlier stories, i.e. the argument from perceived contrasts in the present text. Moreover, the lack of an outcry by the spirit and the lack of dialogue between it and Jesus exhibit a basic rather than superimposed interrelation between the deafmuteness and the demonic possession.

There are two requests for exorcism (vv 18 and 22). But the first occurs only in a flashback, and the father directed it to the disciples. The second occurs as part of current action in the story, and the father directs it to Jesus. Had the disciples not failed, the second request would not be needed. The two requests do not compete with each other, then.

Finally, unbelief appears twice, first in v 19 to describe a generation and again in vv 23-24 with respect to the demoniac's father. But if the father belongs to the generation described as unbelieving, he is ipso facto unbelieving. That he is "one from the crowd" (v 17) shows that he does belong to this generation and that his individual unbelief exemplifies their collective unbelief.

In v 14 K.-G. Reploh (*Lehrer* 220) prefers the v.l. ἐλθών . . . εἶδεν, "coming . . . he saw" (A C D Θ 067ᵛⁱᵈ f¹,¹³ Majority Text lat syᵖ,ʰ bo), over ἐλθόντες . . . εἶδον, "coming . . . they saw" (א B L W Δ Ψ 892 pc k sa), because the singular allows "the disciples" to retain its normal reference to the Twelve whereas the plural forces an unusual reference to the nine disciples, i.e. to those besides Peter, James, and John. By indicating that Jesus came to the disciples by himself, not with the three, the singular would imply that the story of the exorcism used to be independent from the story of the Transfiguration and therefore that Mark inserted the story of the exorcism here. But the external support for the plural outweighs, though it does not outnumber, that for the singular. Moreover, the singular looks like the easier, smoother, and therefore inferior reading — a move to retain Jesus as the subject from vv 12-13 and to prepare for a reference to Jesus alone in v 15 — and perhaps to make "the disciples" retain its normal reference. But 8:33; 16:7 show that even after the choice of the Twelve (3:13-19), "the disciples" does not always include all the Twelve. So also does 14:32 with 14:43 unless it is implied that Judas Iscariot went to Gethsemane with Jesus and slipped away while Jesus was praying (but see John 13:30). Since the passages in which these cross-references occur display no tension between "the disciples" and the one or more who are excepted, the argument fails that here the singular poses the more difficult and therefore superior reading (against L. Schenke, *Wundererzählungen* 328). The cross-references also scotch the claim that even the plural reference to the disciples implies that originally Jesus approached them by himself, the story of the exorcism being independent from the story of the Transfiguration (H. Anderson 229-30).

Many have argued that in the villages of Philip's Caesarea (cf. 8:27) Jesus would not likely find either scribes or a crowd of people knowing about his past miracles and exorcisms. To lessen this problem, V. Taylor (397) adopts a suggestion that the anarthrousness of "scribes" points to merely local clergy, because elsewhere Mark always writes the definite article with "scribes." More to the point, even Mark's narrative does not necessarily locate the present story close to Philip's Caesarea. It does locate Peter's confession of Jesus as the Christ there. But the Transfiguration has intervened, it occurred on a high mountain, Mark used the mountain itself as a topographical marker rather than locating it by means of another topographical reference, and he will not locate the house of v 28. "He [Jesus] brings them up a high mountain" (v 2) may therefore have indicated a move from the neighborhood of Philip's Caesarea instead of a mountain climb within the neighborhood. In fact, "going along through Galilee" after exit from a house (v 30 with v 28) will probably imply a Galilean location of the house; for other occurrences of παραπορεύομαι indicate travel within an area already entered, not travel by which entrance is made (2:23 with 2:21; 11:20 with 11:19; 15:29 with 15:22; cf. the possibility that "into waters" [9:22] refers to a location beside the Sea of Galilee). If the house will have a Galilean location, so also may the Mount of Transfiguration. Thus no problem adheres to the presence of a crowd and of scribes below the mountain (unless one disputes the presence of scribes even in Galilee — but see the notes on 2:16). Besides, if on form critical grounds we deny the originality of the narrative sequence by positing that Mark inserted the Transfiguration (but see the notes on 9:2-13), those same grounds will call in question the originality of a pre-Marcan coupling of Peter's confession and the present exorcism. As to the lack of a definite article with "scribes," it is probably due to simple parallelism with the anarthrous ὄχλον, "crowd," and to the incorporation of scribes into the crowd.

E. Haenchen (31-32) thinks that originally the crowd were disputing with the disciples and that the theme of disputation led to introduction of the scribes. Oppositely, J. Gnilka (2. 44-46) sees Mark's redaction in the references to a large crowd and the disputation. Such scholarly disagreement illustrates the uncertainty which attends efforts to separate tradition and redaction in the absence of sources and independent parallels.

Similar uncertainty attends the inferring of different sources and the distinguishing between tradition and redaction on the grounds that the scribes drop out after their initial mention in v 14, that the disciples play a role only in vv 14-19, 28-29, and that the father switches from a subordinate role in vv 14-19 to a leading one in vv 21-24. Scribes would naturally make up the disputants in the crowd; and since the disputation stops when Jesus arrives on the scene and the dialogue between him and the father starts, there is no need to mention the scribes again. The disciples are not active in vv 14-19 — a large crowd surrounds them, scribes dispute with them, and the father refers to them in a flashback — and they merely ask a question in vv 28-29. The father begins to play a leading role already in vv 14-19: he speaks out of the crowd, describes the condition of his son, and reports the failure of the disciples. For representative attempts to distinguish between tradition and redaction, see E. Best, *Following Jesus* 66-72; J. Gnilka 2. 44-46; K. Kertelge, *Wunder* 174-79; D.-A. Koch, *Bedeutung* 114-26; K.-G. Reploh, *Lehrer* 211-21; W. Schenk in *ZNW* 63 (1972) 76-94; L. Schenke, *Wundererzählungen* 314-49; W. Schmithals 407-8; P. J. Achtemeier in *CBQ* 37 (1975) 471-91.

D.-A. Koch (*Bedeutung* 123) thinks that the ignorance of the disciples' disputation in v 10 casts a bad light on them in vv 14, 16, where further disputation takes place (the verb συζητέω occurring in all these verses). But vv 14, 16 do not say that the disciples were disputing with the scribes, or even that the scribes and the disciples were disputing with one another (cf. the phraseology of v 10). Rather, only the scribes are said to have been disputing. So no blame falls on the disciples in this respect.

T. L. Budesheim (in *ZNW* 62 [1971] 206-7) observes that in v 14 Mark does not identify the topic of dispute, and concludes that instead he stresses the fact of a dispute to set up a parallel with disputes between Jesus and the scribes. Mark goes on to quote Jesus' asking the reason behind the dispute and the father's answering with a report of the disciples' failure to exorcise the deafmute spirit (vv 16-18). But we still do not know what the scribes were saying. In this respect the dispute looks unlike the disputes of the scribes with Jesus, where Mark does tell what the scribes said (2:6-7, 16, 18[?], 24; 3:22, 30; 10:2; 11:27-28, 31-33; 12:13-14, 16, 18-23, 28, 32-33, including disputes with the Pharisees). So Mark refuses to quote what the scribes say here, not to set up a parallel, but to concentrate attention on the reason behind the dispute, which provides the setting for Jesus' exorcism. The disciples play only supporting roles.

The command that Peter, James, and John not tell anyone what they have seen (v 9) and the prediction that only some of the crowd will see God's rule as having come in power (v 1) might seem to forestall the crowd's seeing the heavenly whiteness of Jesus' garments. But seeing this afterglow contradicts neither a prohibition of narrating the story (διηγήσωνται) nor a prediction that only some would see God's rule as having come in power. The crowd did not see the Transfiguration in process, and the disciples do not tell them the story of it. H. B. Swete (195) objects to the crowd's seeing an afterglow that the same phenomenon in Moses' case had an effect opposite from the crowd's running to Jesus. But Mark did not build his version of the Transfiguration on the story of Moses (see the comments and notes on vv 2-8); and the three disciples found the Transfiguration attractive, not repelling (v 5).

E. Best (*Following Jesus* 66-68) argues for the general traditionality of vv 16-19 that the disciples fail to act rather than failing to understand, that Mark likes δύναμαι for "be able" whereas ἰσχύω occurs here, and that "generation" characterizes Q rather than Mark. On the other hand, since the disciples, not the crowd, have failed at this exorcism, Best thinks it inappropriate that Jesus should upbraid the crowd for unbelief (v 19). He therefore suggests that in an earlier form of the story Jesus upbraided the scribes (cf. v 19 with v 14). But the scribes have failed at this exorcism no more than the crowd has, and Best correctly sees that the upbraiding does not conform to Jesus' way of rebuking the disciples. See the foregoing comments on the rationale for this upbraiding of the crowd, and on the crowd as including the scribes and the father.

R. Pesch (2. 84) eliminates "to the disciples" and "around them" from v 14 and "to you" from v 17b and substitutes "to them" for "to your disciples" in v 18c to get references to the scribes at vv 14c, 16b, 18c, and 19a in a supposedly original form of the story which dealt with a failure of the *scribes* to perform the exorcism (cf. W. Schenk in *ZNW* 63 [1972] 79-80). But these emendations are worse than the disease of pronominal ambiguity which they are supposed to cure. In fact, the narrative makes the antecedents of the pronouns reasonably clear; and it seems doubtful that any Christian would have shifted a failure of Jesus' enemies, the scribes, over to Jesus' disciples (see esp. R. Tannehill in *JR* 57 [1977] 386-405 against the notion of T. J. Weeden [*Traditions in Conflict* passim] that Mark portrays the disciples as ecclesiastical opponents).

Some argue that the greater likelihood of Jesus' addressing a question to the disciples favors our understanding him to be asking them, not the crowd and the scribes among them, why they were disputing with the crowd and the scribes (v 16). J. Gnilka (2. 45) proceeds to see a break between vv 16 and 17 on the ground that one from the crowd answers a question that Jesus asked his disciples (v 17). But the fact that one from the crowd answers him favors that Jesus asked the crowd and the scribes among them why they were disputing with the disciples; and vv 14-15 have already shown that he asked his question of the crowd and the scribes among them, not of the disciples. The disputation was with the disciples, it was the crowd who ran and hailed Jesus, and he asked them why they were disputing with the disciples. See E. C. Maloney, *Semitic Interference* 126-31, on the Semitism εἷς, "one," for τις, "someone."

According to G. Minette de Tillesse (*Le secret messianique* 94), v 17 represents the primitive start of the story and vv 14-16 come from Mark; for v 17 does not contain an answer to the question in v 16. Jesus asks the scribes why they are disputing with his disciples, but the father — hardly a scribe — answers. On the one hand, however, would Mark have fabricated a question that is not answered? On the other hand, does not the father's flashback give the reason for the disputation? Jesus questions the crowd, but the father speaks up to him because as a member of the crowd his involvement in the reason for the disputation exceeds that of other members of the crowd, even the scribes. What could be more natural? Since ἀποκρίνομαι can carry the Hebraistic meaning "speak up" (BAGD s.v. 2), which would alleviate an apparent discrepancy between vv 16 and 17, we have no need to separate them in their origin. The very Hebraism supports their belonging together from the start.

Does a wordplay between ירק and חרק underlie the reference in v 18 to foaming and grinding (so J. Carmignac in *ASTI* 7 [1968] 71)? Probably not, for ירק seems limited to spitting. Ξηραίνεται is usually translated "he becomes stiff." Less likely translations are "he becomes thinner" (i.e. his health is deteriorating — G. Theissen, *Miracle Stories* 52) and "he is exhausted" (C. E. B. Cranfield 301). "He becomes thinner" corresponds to the basic meaning of ξηραίνω, "wither," but would describe what happens over a period of time, whereas the father is describing what happens during individual seizures (cf. the parallel expressions "he foams at the mouth and grinds his teeth").

The statement of H. J. Held (in *Kirche* 90-91) that v 18 identifies the point of the story as the disciples' inability rather than as Jesus' ability puts things in reverse. The many details that stress the difficulty of the exorcism would blunt a point of the disciples' inability by making excuses for it. On the other hand, these same details sharpen the point of Jesus' ability. So the disciples' inability provides a foil for his ability. 2 Kgs 4:29-31 provides a similar foil in the contrast between the inability of a servant and the ability of his master to perform a miracle. In view of the ability of Jesus' disciples to perform miracles and exorcisms on all other known occasions, however (3:14-15; 6:7, 13), we should not press the present contrast beyond the point of this specially difficult exorcism.

The compassionate tone of Isa 40:11; 46:4 differs so radically from the exasperated tone of Mark 9:19 that we should not imagine a relation between the passages (against H. E. Tödt, *Son of Man* 179). In arguing that the "unbelieving generation" can be neither the crowd (because they have not had opportunity to believe or disbelieve) nor the scribes (because they play no more role in the story), E. Lohmeyer (186) neglects the role already played by the crowd and scribes in disputing with the disciples. In the further part of v 19 M. Dibelius (*From Tradition to Gospel* 278) detects the mythological motif of a divine being who temporarily appears on earth in human guise and then goes back to heaven. Against this view, R. Pesch (2. 90) puts forward Jewish prophetic and sapiential traditions in Num 11:11ff.; 14:27; Deut 32:5, 20; 1 Kgs 19:4; Prov 1:20ff.; Isa 6:11; 46:4; 65:2; Jer 5:21-22; 15:18; Ezek 12:2; *1 Enoch* 42:1-3. But though these traditions provide background for the question, "How long will I put up with you?" they do not satisfy the implication of coming absence in the preceding question, "How long will I be with you?" The sole exception, *1 Enoch* 42:1-3, tends toward Dibelius's view by speaking of wisdom's return to heaven. The predictions of Jesus' coming violent death (8:31; 9:12 et passim) make that view otiose, however, by providing another basis for the implication of his coming absence. The view that Mark inserts v 19 because the question "how long?" implies the typically Marcan answer, "Till the Son of man's death and resurrection" (cf. 8:31; 9:9-13; D.-A. Koch, *Bedeutung* 122), stumbles over the regularly open-ended meaning of this question (see esp. Ps 89:47[46], but also 1 Sam 1:14; 16:1; 2 Sam 2:26; 1 Kgs 18:21; Job 19:2; Pss 4:3[2]; 6:4[3]; 13:2-3[1-2]; 62:4[3]; 74:10; 79:5; 80:5[4]; 82:2; 94:3; Prov 1:22; Jer 4:14, 21; 12:4; 23:26; 31:22, listed by R. Pesch 2. 90).

A radically different interpretation of vv 19-20 identifies the disciples as those whom Jesus calls an unbelieving generation; for since the father has just mentioned the disciples in v 18b, "them" in v 19a naturally refers to the disciples rather than to the crowd. Furthermore, unbelief on the disciples' part makes a better reason for their failure at exorcism than does unbelief on the part of the crowd, because the father's bringing his son to Jesus shows that he had faith, which Jesus would hardly fail to honor even though the crowd disbelieved (cf. R. H. Gundry, *Matthew* 350; W. L. Lane 332). But against this interpretation, general disbelief made Jesus unable to perform very many miracles in Nazareth (6:1-6a); so the disbelief of the present crowd might well have contributed to the disciples' inability to cast out the deafmute spirit. And, as noted above, when the disciples ask Jesus why they could not exorcise it, he does not mention unbelief on their part, but prayerlessness (vv 28-29). We are not at liberty to equate prayerlessness with unbelief or to read into the passage a connection between them, e.g., that prayerlessness causes unbelief. Jesus himself does not draw such a connection. Passages such as Acts 9:40; 28:8; Jas 5:15 link prayer with healing, not with exorcism; and Mark 11:24 makes believing a condition of successful praying, not praying a means of achieving or exercising faith (as would be the case here; cf. the non-mention of prayer as a means by which the disciples successfully performed exorcisms in 6:13 — and this non-mention despite a mention of anointing with oil as the means of healing [against W. Schenk in *ZNW* 63 (1972) 77-78]). Since Jesus' rebuke constitutes an answer (ἀποκριθείς) even though the disciples have said nothing to him, he seems to be addressing the crowd, one of whose number has just spoken to him (v 17; again see BAGD s.v. ἀποκρίνομαι for the Hebraistic meaning "speak up"). Besides, "generation" seems too broad a term to apply only to a few disciples, especially when a large crowd is present. Jesus will point out the unbelief of the one who speaks up out of the crowd, and that one will come to believe and will ask for help to overcome his unbelief (vv 23-24). Unbelief belongs on the side of the crowd, then, not on the side of the disciples.

According to M.-J. Lagrange (240), the masculine ἰδών, "seeing," does not modify the neuter τὸ πνεῦμα, "the spirit," ad sensum (v 20). Rather, along with πεσών, "falling," it modifies the demoniac; and the whole clause, "the spirit immediately convulsed him," makes an anacoluthic interruption. But since the masculine participles in v 26a cannot describe the demoniac but have to describe the neuter τὸ . . . πνεῦμα in v 25, the masculine ἰδών probably modifies the same neuter noun in v 20.

Because the Greek word for a corpse — viz., πτῶμα — means "that which has fallen," E. S. Malbon (*Narrative Space* 79-81) finds a connotation of death in the demoniac's falling on the ground (v 20). But it is methodologically wrong to depend on an etymological meaning; and here, rolling around and foaming at the mouth keep falling on the ground from connoting death. For the connotation of death, falling on the ground should rather have attached to becoming stiff (v 18) or to becoming, as it were, dead (v 26). Furthermore, πτῶμα does not appear in this passage.

E. Best (*Following Jesus* 68-69) argues that the unbelief of the father does not explain the inability of the disciples and that therefore we should consider vv 22b-23 an addition to the story. This argument not only overlooks the explanation in 6:5-6a of Jesus' inability by the Nazarenes' unbelief. It also overlooks that the father's unbelief in vv 22b-23 coheres with the unbelief of the crowd (v 19), and does so especially because he is a member of the crowd (v 17).

Several have suggested that Mark or a pre-Marcan redactor added vv 22b-23, vv 21-24, or vv 28-29, or both vv 22b-23 and vv 28-29 or vv 21-24 and vv 28-29, to explain failures at exorcism in the life of the church and to restore success by urging faith, prayer, or both. But we have no evidence from the NT period that the church was suffering failures at exorcism (on the contrary, see Mark 16:17-18, 20; Rom 15:19; 1 Cor 2:4-5; 4:19-20; 12:10, 28-29; 2 Cor 6:7[?]; 12:12; Gal 3:5; 1 Thess 1:5; 2 Thess 1:11 with 2:9; 2 Tim 1:7-8[?]; Heb 2:4; Jas 5:14-15; Rev 11:6; and the stories of exorcisms and miracles in Acts). Lack of faith on the part of the father would not represent lack of faith on the part of the church. That would require lack of faith on the part of the disciples, but the disciples are not portrayed as lacking faith. Mark's having used the Nazarenes' unbelief to explain Jesus' inability to work very many miracles in Nazareth (6:5-6a) does not favor Mark's presently inserting a dialogue on faith and unbelief to explain churchly inability, for the Nazarenes do not correspond to the church. As for prayer, in the church period a more likely explanation of failure at exorcism would be lack of *enough* prayer, not lack of *any* prayer (as here); and a more likely remedy would be more prayer, not prayer as such. Even if not, "this kind" would provide an explanation and remedy only with respect to a deafmute spirit. One cannot be sure, but it seems unlikely that a Christian would have incorporated such a narrow restriction in a fabricated saying of Jesus. Churchly failure at exorcism (if there was such) would probably have included a broad variety of possessions.

Since faith can belong to the original version of a miracle story (see 5:36 and cf. 2:5; 5:34; 10:52), the presence of faith in the present story of an exorcism should not prompt a theory of interpolation. The material on faith and prayer in 11:20-25 will derive from tradition, will not relate to exorcism (or healing), and therefore will fail to support a Marcan interpolation here. The agreement of Matthew and Luke in omitting vv 21-24 does not prove that they knew a pre-Marcan tradition lacking the material in these verses. If Matthew had known such a tradition he would probably have not felt compelled to make up for his omission by the addition of similar material on faith later on in his version (Matt 17:20). Furthermore, his redaction of the first part of the story gave him reason to omit vv 21-24; and throughout, Luke seems to show secondary influence from Matthew (R. H. Gundry, *Matthew* 351-53).

Contemporary commentators use vv 22-24 to argue that in Mark this exorcism does not stress Jesus' power, but teaches a lesson of faith (see, e.g., H. J. Held in *Kirche* 90-91). But to see in these verses a lesson of faith is to stop in midstream. This lesson teaches Jesus' worthiness to be the object of faith; and it is learned by "one from the crowd" (v 17), not by the disciples (vv 23-24). Nor does the one who learns it turn into a disciple by following Jesus. Christology, not discipleship, is on exhibit.

The plural number of "waters" (v 22) may be Semitic (E. Klostermann 91), though some have suggested that it represents a multiplicity of occasions. O. Böcher (*Christus Exorcista* 22-24) thinks that the waters into which the spirit throws the boy are a demonic element. But the parallel throwing of the boy into the fire favors a more ordinary meaning, i.e. that seizures make him fall into fire and waters according as he is near one or the other at the time (cf. J. Ernst [268], who conjectures nearness to the Sea of Galilee and notes the constant burning of fire in homes). This ordinary meaning also takes away any reason to diagnose pyromania and hydromania, which do not agree with being thrown into fire and waters, anyway. Cf. Philostr. *VA* 3.38. J. Wilkinson (in *ExpTim* 79 [1967] 39-42) gives a medical analysis in terms of epilepsy, yet identifies epilepsy, not as a disease, but as a symptom admitting of more than one cause, not excluding demonic possession. See also E. Yamauchi in *Gospel Perspectives* 6. 129-31; P. J. Achtemeier in *CBQ* 37 (1975) 481, n. 35; and, for the other side, G. Petzke in *NTS* 22 (1975-76) 189-90.

In v 23 J. Carmignac (in *ASTI* 7 [1968-69] 67-68 and in *The NT Age* 1. 83-84) traces τό, usually taken as a referential accusative introducing a quotation (cf. BDF §267[1]; B. M. Metzger, *Textual Commentary* ad loc.), back to a Hebrew exclamatory ה, "Ah!" confused by a Greek translator with the Hebrew definite article. He rules out an Aramaic exclamatory ה on the ground that Aramaic non-use of ה as a definite article would have forestalled confusion. Besides the doubtfulness of favoring Hebrew over Aramaic in Jesus' words, we may wonder whether an exclamatory ה would be likely to introduce a fragmentary quotation about to be negated. Carmignac's cross-references, Num 17:28(13) and Job 6:13, do not seem to support the possibility.

Again in v 23 the grammatically possible translation, "[All] things [are] able [to be done] *by* the one who believes," would imply that the disciples failed because of unbelief and would therefore require that Jesus have criticized them for unbelief in v 19. But we have seen reasons to doubt that understanding of v 19. And here his addressing the father rather than the disciples, his taking up the father's question regarding Jesus' ability, and the father's immediately following response, "I believe; help my unbelief," favor that Jesus means, "All things [are] able [to be done] *for* the one who believes." The father's response also undermines an identification of "the one who believes" with Jesus, as though he is about to present himself as an example of faith (cf. the notes on 11:22-24). For if it is Jesus' faith that will win the exorcism, the father's affirming belief yet asking Jesus to help his unbelief becomes irrelevant. Nevertheless, P. J. Achtemeier (in *CBQ* 37 [1975] 480) notes the absence of any indication that the father's faith "ultimately rose above its ambiguity" and concludes that vv 23-24 contrast the insufficient faith of the father with the effective faith of Jesus. We should conclude, rather, that faith is not the point of the story. Otherwise we would have been told unambiguously either that Jesus exercised faith enough to be effective, or that the father attained it — also against C. D. Marshall (*Faith* 118-20), who holds that Jesus stands as a man of faith over against the faithless disciples and father (but the father has affirmed his faith and Jesus will not attribute the disciples' failure to unbelief, nor were they included among the unbelieving generation — see the foregoing comments). According to C. E. B. Cranfield (302-3), context favors the meaning that a person of faith will not set any limit on what Jesus or God can do. But that meaning is limited to the context. The text itself says that there is nothing that cannot be done for a person of faith, and the point of the story lies in Jesus' power as highlighted by the disciples' weakness. The modern notion of faith as a psychologically beneficial agent of healing is out of the picture (R. and M. Hengel in *Medicus Viator* 351).

See A. Oepke in *TDNT* 5. 637 on the upper age-limits of παῖς (fourteen years) and παιδίον (six years). The double shouting of Bartimaeus in 10:47-48 will arise out of no inspiring word of Jesus or direct inspiration of the Holy Spirit and therefore disfavors the view of E. Lohmeyer (188-89) and W. Grundmann (7. Aufl., 255) that the father in the

present story shouts as a result of such inspiration (v 24). His shouting indicates desperation, as does also the shouting of the spirit at exit (v 26). M. Zerwick (*Untersuchungen*
62) suggests that the imperfect tense of ἔλεγεν, "he was saying" (v 24), connotes hesitation
on the father's part. But hesitation does not agree with the forcefulness indicated by κράξας,
"shouting," or with the immediacy indicated by εὐθύς; and Mark uses the imperfect of
λέγω nearly four dozen times without a connotation of hesitancy (see the concordance s.v.).

    S. E. Dowd (*Prayer* 111-14) interprets the second half of the father's shout as a
request that Jesus help his unbelief by healing the son. In view of Jesus' preceding statement
that all things are able to be done for the person who believes, however, the father is more
probably asking Jesus to help his unbelief in order that he (the father) may believe for the
healing of his son. According to C. D. Marshall (*Faith* 121), who appeals to a durative
force in the present imperative βοήθει (v 24) as opposed to the aorist imperative βοήθησον
(v 22), "help my unbelief" displays recognition "that faith can only continue to exist by
dint of divine aid. . . . Faith is not a secure possession attained once for all, ..." But the
Father is not asking for sustenance of faith; rather, for transformation of vestigial unbelief
into faith. The switch to a present tense of the imperative in v 24 may be prompted by
close association with the present indicative of πιστεύω, "I believe," and is emphatic rather
than durative, anyway (S. E. Porter, *Verbal Aspect* 326). If we were to see durative force
in the present imperative, that force would have to do with the time it takes to transform
vestigial unbelief into faith, not with sustenance of faith.

    H. D. Betz (in *Semeia* 11 [1978] 79-80) says that with the father's declaration of
faith and request that Jesus help his unbelief, the miracle story "flips over" into a conversion
story. Betz even speaks of the father's membership in the group of disciples. But faith for
a miracle does not equate with conversion to discipleship. Otherwise we would have to
regard the four who brought the paralytic, the woman with the flow of blood, and blind
Bartimaeus as converted disciples even before the occurrence of healing; for they all had
faith for healing (2:5; 5:34; 10:52). Besides, the present father must have had faith earlier;
for he brought his son for exorcism.

    R. Pesch (2. 93) thinks that v 25a means a renewed running to Jesus which the
father's shout motivates. To support this view, Pesch supposes that the conversation
between Jesus and the father is meant to be taken as a private one, apart from the crowd
(cf. 7:33; 8:23). But there is no indication of a pulling apart from the crowd (as there is
in the cross-references), and the father answered Jesus from out of the crowd. The phraseological similarity to v 15 and the linearity of the action in both v 15 and v 25 favor a
continued running motivated by Jesus' original appearance on the scene. For the lack of
a definite article with "crowd" in v 25 despite an apparent back reference to vv 14-15, cf.
3:32 with 3:30, and 5:24 with 5:21. Perhaps the wideness of the gap between 9:14-15 and
9:25 or the continued running of those members of the crowd who have not yet arrived
leads Mark to avoid an anaphoric definite article. M. Zerwick (*Biblical Greek* §34) classifies the use of the arthrous nominative for a vocative in τὸ ἄλαλον καὶ κωφὸν πνεῦμα,
"you mute and deaf spirit" (v 25), as a Semitism.

    Jesus' performing the exorcism while the crowd are still running together forestalls
an acclamation. See K. Tagawa, *Miracles et Évangile* 92-94, on the optionality of including
acclamations in miracle stories. R. Pesch (2. 94) nicely comments that the crowd's saying,
"He [the son] has died," parodies the acclamation which often appears at this point in
similar stories, e.g., in 1:27; 2:12.

    As in vv 28-29, Mark writes repeatedly about Jesus' going into a house with the
disciples and their asking him a question in private. But this repetitiveness could belong
to the tradition, indeed to the actuality of what happened in the life of Jesus with his
disciples, as easily as to Mark's redaction. Staying in homes during itineration and engaging
in private dialogue are exactly what we would expect. No validity attaches to the argument

of L. Schenke (*Wundererzählungen* 330-31) that the lack of contextual preparation for entry into a house proves its secondariness. The itinerant character of Jesus' ministry as a whole prepares for such entry. Since even in the second half of Mark Jesus ministers in public (10:1-9, 17-22, 46-52 et passim) and since even in the first half he has dealt with his disciples in private (1:16-20, 29-31, 35-38; 3:13-19; 4:10-20, 34, 35-41; 6:6b-11, 45-52; 7:17-23; 8:14-21), we can hardly think that Mark has embarked on a program of creating private settings now that Jesus has started to predict his passion and resurrection. In the absence of evidence that Jesus and the disciples always camped out and seldom or never engaged in private dialogue, then, no reason comes from this quarter to treat vv 28-29 as Mark's addition.

Nor does the acclamation with which stories of miracles and exorcisms often end favor that Mark has added the private dialogue in vv 28-29 to replace an original acclamation. For such an acclamation would play into his Christological emphasis, he often includes acclamations (1:27-28; 2:12; 4:41; 5:14-16, 20; 7:36-37), and disagreement with a stereotypical form as likely points to a pre-stereotyped version as to an imposition that postdates stereotyping. Luke 9:43 shows that acclamation can be a secondary stereotyping. Nor does v 29 oppose v 23 (as thought, e.g., by H. Aichinger in *Probleme der Forschung* 127; K.-G. Reploh, *Lehrer* 213) so as to support the theory that vv 28-29 have been added. Verse 23 implies lack of faith on the father's part; v 29 implies lack of prayer on the disciples' part. Lack of prayer caused their failure, an actual one. The father's lack of faith only threatened to forestall a successful exorcism by Jesus.

Since Jesus has not presented himself as an example of faith (see the notes on v 23) and since he appears to be advising prayer for a specially difficult exorcism, not prayer in general or even prayer for ordinary exorcisms, it is inappropriate to cross-reference his non-exorcistic praying — the only kind he is said to have practiced (as in 1:35; 6:46; 14:32-42). In fact, one of his exorcisms (1:21-28) was narrated before the first mention of his praying (1:35; against S. E. Dowd [*Prayer* 119], who thinks that he is portrayed as drawing his power from prayer). Similarly, the disciples have earlier enjoyed considerable success in exorcism — without prayer, it would seem (6:13; cf. 3:15; 6:7). Hence, "this kind" refers to a class of demons requiring prayer if the disciples are to cast them out, not to all demons as requiring prayer if the disciples are to cast them out (as would seem to be required for the interpretation of H. C. Kee [in *Protocol of the Twelfth Colloquy* of The Center for Hermeneutical Studies in Hellenistic and Modern Culture* 28] that prayer is urged to avoid the charge of magic). More particularly, "this kind" means demons causing deafness and dumbness as different from those causing other symptoms easier to deal with. Is Jesus saying that exorcism of this class needs prayer *rather than* a command to come out? Against this view, Jesus did issue such a command. But then he did not pray for the exorcism; so his procedure already differed from what he commands the disciples to do. Or is Jesus saying that this class needs special prayer *in addition to* a command to come out?

Besides variations in the described symptoms of demonic possession, see Luke 13:11; *PGM* CXIV. 1-14 for indications that demons afflict their victims in various ways. The latter passage even refers to mute demons (cf. *1 Enoch* 8, 69; *PGM* IV. 3037-46; XCIV. 39-60; against K.-G. Reploh [*Lehrer* 213-14], who denies such distinctions). Thus, "this kind" (v 29) does not mean the kind of demon that resists exorcism by Christians at the time of Mark's writing, as though the demons in Jesus' day were easier prey (so ibid.). The anachronism of reading that kind back into Jesus' day would only blur such a distinction anyway.

What Jesus says in v 29 about the spirit, "is able to come out," may be an Aramaism for "is able to be cast out" (cf. M. Zerwick, *Biblical Greek* §1, n. 2, on an Aramaic tendency to avoid the passive). Str-B (1. 760; 4/1. 528-29) note that in Judaism, recitation of the

Shema (Deut 6:4-6) and of Psalms 3 and 91 was considered a powerful antidote to evil spirits. But the Shema is not a prayer; Psalms 3 and 91 are prayers for protection, not for exorcism; and the cited rabbinic literature postdates the NT by too much to provide firm footing for an interpretation of v 29. On the v.l. that adds "and fasting" to v 29, see B. M. Metzger, *Textual Commentary* ad loc.; and on fasting as a means of exorcism, O. Böcher, *Dämonenfurcht* 273-84. *Clem. Hom.* 9.23 prescribes the laying on of hands as well as prayer for exorcism and healing.

On the assumption that this story circulated independently, D. E. Nineham (242) asks why Mark has put it here and answers that Mark may have done so to bring Jesus back to work among people and to draw a parallel between the disciples' failure at exorcism and their earlier failure to understand the truth about Jesus. But why put Jesus back to the work of exorcising demons if, as many think, Mark now wants to concentrate on Jesus' teaching the disciples in private? The drawing of a parallel between their two kinds of failure would provide a basis for such teaching, but Mark has written up the story in a way that uses their present failure as a foil for Jesus' success in a specially difficult exorcism, not as the occasion for a didactic thrust.

More specifically along the didactic line of interpretation, contemporary commentators often use vv 28-29 to argue that in Mark this exorcism does not stress Jesus' supernatural power, but teaches prayer as a necessary means of effective discipleship (see, e.g., E. Best, *Gospel as Story* 87). If the necessity of prayer formed the main point, however, the purpose of the pericope would lie in the direction of making disciples into more successful exorcists, not in teaching them piety. But the necessity of prayer does not form the main point. Rather (and as mentioned in the foregoing comments), it is the last part of a foil which exhibits the supernatural power of Jesus, who even in this specially difficult case needs only to speak an authoritative word, in contrast with the weakness of the disciples, who have to pray. This way of interpreting vv 28-29 agrees with the Christologically emphatic points that pervade the earlier bulk of the pericope: the crowd's amazement at the sight of Jesus, his magnetism, the detailing of the demoniac's symptoms to enhance the exorcism once it occurs, the highlighting of the question concerning Jesus' ability over against the disciples' proved inability, and the detailing of evidence that the spirit has gone out once Jesus commands it to do so.

JESUS' ABILITY TO PREDICT HIS DEATH AND RESURRECTION

9:30-32 (Matt 17:22-23; Luke 9:43b-45)

This short pericope starts with Jesus' and the disciples' going through Galilee (v 30), comes to its main subject matter in another prediction by him concerning his death and resurrection (v 31), and closes with the disciples' ignorance and fear (v 32). "And going out from there" means going out from the house mentioned in v 28. "They" refers to Jesus, who had entered that house, and his disciples, who had conversed with him there (vv 28-29). "Were going along through Galilee" implies an avoidance of ministry along the way and provides the setting for Jesus' prediction; it does not carry overtones of a march to Jerusalem, for he and his disciples will shortly come to their home base, Capernaum (v 33). His not wanting anyone to know means that he and his disciples are traveling incognito (cf. 5:43 and esp. 7:24). Mark identifies the reason for this kind of traveling as Jesus' teaching the disciples about his approaching death and resurrection. He gave his first such prediction in a similarly private setting, "on the road" (8:27-32a) with the crowd absent or at a distance (cf. 8:34). The historical implication is that Jesus wanted to redefine his messiahship in a way that the disciples needed to accept but that the general Jewish populace was sure to reject. They were all looking for political dominance. He was taking the role of a sufferer. But Mark is writing for Gentiles. They do not entertain nationalistic messianism; so he is not concerned to correct it, as Jesus was. In fact, Mark does not set the passion prediction over against such messianism. Nor did he mention such messianism as the reason why Peter raised an objection in 8:32, nor will he relate the disciples' personal ambition in 9:33-34 to nationalistic messianism. It will become evident from 10:35-40 that such ambition does arise out of that kind of messianism, but even there nationalistic messianism will provide only the framework of personal ambition through association with the Messiah. It will not provide a foil for Jesus' passion. Mark, then, is uninterested in the passion prediction as a correction. In his gospel not even the disciples come to accept this prediction or the others as corrective of nationalistic messianism. Instead, he is interested in the prediction as a prediction; for as such it carries great apologetic value in defanging the crucifixion of Jesus.

By comparison with 8:31 the auxiliary ἤρξατο, "he began," yields to γάρ, "for," which makes the prediction a reason for Jesus' wanting privacy. The element of teaching carries over, but as a finite verb, not as an infinitive (see the comments on 8:31 for Mark's emphasis on Jesus' authority). The addition of "and he was saying to them" makes the following ὅτι recitative rather than epexegetic (as it was in 8:31; cf. 4:2; 11:17; also 12:35) and in parallel with "he was teaching his disciples" puts a dual emphasis on Jesus' predictive power as exhibited in the direct quotation introduced by ὅτι. The element of necessity drops out, "the Son of man" carries over, and suffering much also drops out. The two omissions let emphasis fall on the futuristic present tense of "is being given over," which stresses certainty of fulfilment. Though Mark usually puts subjects after finite verbs, the position of "the Son of man" in 8:31, where the phrase appeared before the infinitive whose subject it was, leads here to the reverse order. There results a wordplay between "the Son of man" at the start of the clause and "hands of men" at its end. Being given over "into hands of men" replaces rejection by the elders, chief priests, and scribes and introduces the element of betrayal from within the ranks of Jesus' disciples. The seeming unlikelihood of such betrayal enhances the apologetic value of the prediction. "Into hands of men" connotes oppressive and violent treatment (cf. 14:41, 46; Lev 26:25; Deut 1:27; 2 Sam 24:14; 2 Kgs 21:14; Job 9:22-24; 16:11; Ps 106:41; Jer 26:24 MT; 26:24 LXX; Dan 7:25; 11:11; Zech 11:6; 1 Macc 4:30; Jdt 6:10; Sir 2:18; Acts 21:11; 28:17) and thereby marks an advance on mere rejection. The anarthrousness of the nouns highlights the quality of violence; and "men" does not merely generalize the elders, chief priests, and scribes. It stresses the mercilessness of human beings in contrast with God's mercy (again see 2 Sam 24:14; Sir 2:18). Killing carries over, but changes from the passive voice to the active for additional stress on merciless violence. The passive is retained, however, in a second, participial reference to killing. That there is no need for this second reference shows the extent to which stress continues to fall on merciless violence. This stress contributes to Mark's apology: despite appearances Jesus will die, not as a criminal, but at the hands of criminals. The climactic reference to resurrection after three days stays. The forward position of μετὰ τρεῖς ἡμέρας, "after three days," stresses the quickness with which Jesus will rise. The future tense of both "they will kill" and "he will rise" favors a futuristic present tense in "the Son of man is being given over" and once again highlights Jesus' power of prediction (cf. fuller comments on 8:31).

Mark uses the disciples' failure to understand Jesus' prediction as a contrast to Jesus' foreknowledge, and their fearing to ask him what he meant as an indication of his awesomeness (cf. esp. 10:32; 12:34). Verse 32b may imply that they are afraid to ask Jesus even though they do not want to remain ignorant (M. Reiser, *Syntax und Stil* 115-16). Perhaps they are afraid because they do not understand what Jesus expects them to understand. But Mark cares nothing for these possibilities. Otherwise he would state them as matters of fact. Instead, his emphasis falls on ignorance and fear as such, because they provide foils that make Jesus' foreknowledge and awesomeness stand out. The adversative δέ, "but," at the very start of v 32 and the ongoingness of the disciples' ignorance and fear, as indicated by the imperfect tense of ἠγνόουν and ἐφοβοῦντο, strengthen these emphases. Since ἠγνόουν does not require a direct object (see, e.g., 1 Cor 14:38; 1 Tim 1:13; Heb 5:2; 2 Pet 2:12 in the NT), its present direct object τὸ ῥῆμα, "the word," concentrates attention on Jesus' prediction (see 14:72 for the only other Marcan instance of τὸ ῥῆμα, there also in reference to a prediction by Jesus). And since ἐπερωτάω, "ask," is followed by its direct object twenty-three times elsewhere in Mark, the precedence of its present direct object αὐτόν, "him," sharpens the disciples' awe at Jesus (see 12:34 for the only other Marcan instance of ἐπερωτάω preceded by its direct object, there also to sharpen a sense of awe at Jesus).

NOTES

According to R. Pesch (2. 99), κακεῖθεν ἐξελθόντες, "and coming out from there" (v 30), referred in a pre-Marcan passion account to exit from the region of Philip's Caesarea (8:27), not from the house mentioned in 9:28. But wherever else Mark uses ἐκεῖθεν with ἔρχομαι or a compound thereof, exit from a house is meant (see 6:1 with 5:38-39; 6:10; 7:24 with 7:17; 10:1 with 9:33). Only in 6:11 does ἐκεῖθεν not refer to exit from a house, but there the verbal is ἐκπορευόμενοι, "going out," not a form of ἔρχομαι, as here.

Against secret teaching as the reason for traveling incognito, as Mark writes in vv 30-31, E. Haenchen (322-23) argues that Jesus will not travel incognito after leaving Galilee (see 10:1-2, 17, 32, 46; 11:8-10) and concludes that Jesus wants to avoid a renewal of his Galilean ministry and go consciously and deliberately (and without delay, adds J. Gnilka [2. 53]) to his passion and resurrection in Jerusalem. But Mark, too, knows that traveling incognito is unnecessary to a private passion prediction (see 10:32). It is one way of gaining privacy, however, just as taking the Twelve aside is another way of doing so (as in 10:32). And Jesus is not hurrying to Jerusalem. He is headed to Capernaum, where he will go "in the house," sit down, call the Twelve, and give a large amount of teaching (10:33-50; also against J. Schmid [177], who says that Jesus enters Galilee "only to traverse it"). When he does head toward Jerusalem, we read of no attempt to keep people from knowing. Instead, crowds come to him and travel with him; and he teaches them "as was his custom" (10:1).

Failure to recognize that Jesus is not yet headed to Jerusalem also underlies the view that Mark artificially distributes the passion-and-resurrection predictions throughout the journey to Jerusalem as a commentary "revealing the significance of the accompanying events" (D. E. Nineham 248). In fact, only the prediction in 10:32-34 is given during the journey to Jerusalem; and Mark will specially note this peculiarity of that prediction by starting his introduction, "Now they were on the road going up to Jerusalem," in contrast with going out to the villages of Philip's Caesarea (8:27), going down a mountain (9:9), and going along through Galilee (9:30) to Capernaum (9:31) for the other predictions.

The imperfect tense of ἐδίδασκεν, "he was teaching," and ἔλεγεν, "he was saying," is common in verbs of speaking (M. Zerwick, *Biblical Greek* §272) and therefore carries no special nuance such as repetition of this prediction several times during the journey. See H. F. Bayer, *Jesus' Predictions* 169-71, against the view that Semitisms and 14:41 show v 31a to have once circulated independently from v 31b (cf. J. Jeremias, *NT Theology* 1. 281-82). The real and alleged Semitisms consist of (1) "the Son of man"; (2) the futuristic present tense of "is being given over" as resting on an Aramaic participle; (3) a divine passive (which we will find wanting); (4) the following of παραδίδοται, "is being given over," by εἰς, "into" (= ‏ב‎), rather than by a simple dative (as in classical Greek; see R. Kearns, *Traditionsgefüge* 42-43); (5) the expression "into hands of . . ." (though the plural probably represents a Graecization of the usual Semitic singular, as in most of the passages cited in the comments ad loc. — cf. the MT with the LXX; also ibid.); and (6) an underlying wordplay on "the Son of man" and "the sons of men" (which we will also find wanting). 14:41 would limit the original version of the saying to the Son of man's being given over into the hands of men. But the occasion of Jesus' betrayal will favor truncation there of a full passion-and-resurrection prediction rather than expansion here of a short prediction limited to being given over. "After three days" favors tradition instead of expansion in v 31b (see the comments on 8:31). And the use of "stand up" for resurrection and the correspondence of the participle "having been killed" to an Aramaic participle behind "is being given over" display Semitisms in v 31b as well as in v 31a.

W. Schmithals (in *Theologia Crucis — Signum Crucis* 419) posits that being given over into hands of men comes by anticipation from the passion narrative (14:41), where it stems from the oldest confessional tradition (Rom 4:25; 8:32; 1 Cor 11:23; Gal 2:20; Eph 5:2), and that Mark replaces "the hands of sinners" (14:41) with "hands of men" to make a wordplay with "the Son of man" (cf. 2:27-28; 8:33; 14:21; Matt 9:6, 8; Luke 24:7). But the confessional tradition is just as likely to have stemmed from the passion narrative — more likely, in fact; for the explicit references to God as giving Jesus over (Rom 8:32) and to Jesus' giving himself over (Gal 2:20; Eph 5:2) exhibit theological development. Moreover, a play on "the Son of man . . . [the sons of] men" would be more likely in Jesus' Semitic speech, where the presence of "the sons of" would make the wordplay apparent, than in Mark's Greek, where ellipsis swallows a wordplay (against G. Strecker [in *Int* 22 (1968) 434], whose appeal to Matt 9:8 mistakes a redactional echo of "the men" in Matt 8:27 for a redactional wordplay, limited to Greek, with the "the Son of man" in Matt 9:6 — see R. H. Gundry, *Matthew* 165; H. F. Bayer, *Jesus' Predictions* 170, n. 131). Nothing favors that Jesus used only once the phraseology of being given into people's hands.

J. Jeremias (*NT Theology* 1. 282) classifies v 31 as a ‏משל‎, a riddle, because "the son of man" might be understood either as a title ("the Son of man") or generically ("a man") and the underlying Aramaic contained a wordplay with "the sons of men." But it is doubtful that the phrase had attained the status of a recognizable title by Jesus' time or that his use of it had yet made it recognizably titular. Under the assumption that the Greek for "men" idiomatically represents "the sons of men" in the underlying Aramaic, Jeremias also sees a wordplay between "the Son of man" and "the sons of men." But to argue that such a wordplay makes v 31 more original than the otherwise similar 14:41 ("behold, the Son of man is being given over into the hands *of sinners*") depends on the unwarranted assumption that these two sayings (and perhaps all the passion-and-resurrection predictions) stem from a single saying in the pre-Marcan tradition. Even more basically, we should question whether the Greek for "men" idiomatically represents the Aramaic for "the sons of men." The bulkiness of "into the hands of the sons of men" makes such phraseology unlikely. The lack of "the son(s) of" in the phraseology of 2 Sam 24:14; Sir 2:18 ("into [the] hand of man" and "into hands of men," respectively) supports this opinion.

J. Schaberg (in *NTS* 31 [1985] 208-22) and C. C. Caragounis (*Son of Man* 199) see in this passion-and-resurrection prediction an allusion to Dan 7:25 because of the reference to "one like a son of man" in Dan 7:13, because of the expression "will be given [LXX: παραδοθήσεται] into his hand [LXX: 'hands']" in Dan 7:25 itself, because of the Danielic addition "for a time, times, and half a time," and because of the upcoming reference to resurrection in Dan 12:2. Against this view, even if we identify the "they" who are "given into his hand" in Dan 7:25 with "the one like a son of man" in Dan 7:13, the "men" into whose hands Jesus will be delivered do not correspond to "the king" into whose hand "the holy ones of the Most High" are delivered in Dan 7:25; and "after three days" differs from "for a time, times, and half a time" in Dan 7:25. The latter phrase refers to a duration of three and a half years, the former to a point of time after three days. The latter phrase also refers to a period of oppression, the former to a moment of vindication. Apart from "being given into hand(s) of," a locution much too common to link passages by itself, Mark 9:31 does not come close enough to Zech 11:6 to justify an allusion to that OT passage (as thought by W. Grimm, *Verkündigung* 219-22).

Against treating the present tense of παραδίδοται, "is being given over" (9:31), as progressive rather than futuristic in conjunction with the future tense of following parallel verbs, Mark used παρέδωκεν to help identify Judas Iscariot (3:19) but has written nothing as yet to make his audience think that Judas's betrayal is already in motion. To the contrary, see 14:10-11 and cf. the possibility that the present tense of the verb here in 9:31 rests on an Aramaic participle referring to an event soon to happen. It is popular to treat παραδίδοται as a divine passive meaning that God will give Jesus over into the hands of men just as in Isa 53:6, 12 LXX the Lord gives his servant over to suffering and death (cf. Rom 8:32 and the divine and scriptural necessity of Jesus' death according to Mark 8:31; 9:12; 14:21, 27, 36, 39, 41, 49). But Jesus' prediction contains nothing of the vicariousness that dominates the suffering in Isaiah 53, and no version of Isaiah 53 uses the expression "into hands of. . . ." Moreover, the prior use of παραδίδωμι for what Judas Iscariot will do and the coming and repeated uses of this verb both by Mark (in editorial statements) and by Jesus himself (in his sayings) for Judas's giving Jesus over to the Jewish authorities and their crowd (10:33b; 14:10, 11, 18, 21, 41, 42, 44) disfavor a divine passive in Jesus' intention as well as in Mark's. Furthermore, 10:33c will use the same verb of the Jewish authorities' giving the Son of man over to the Gentiles, 15:1 the same verb of their giving Jesus over to Pilate, and 15:15 the same verb of Pilate's giving Jesus over to the soldiers who will crucify him. Thus "hands of men" includes the hands of the Jewish Sanhedrin, of the Gentile governor, and of his soldiers. "Of men" does not favor a divine passive by way of contrast (as thought by M. D. Hooker, *Son of Man* 135); for when God — or for that matter anyone else — gives so-and-so into the hands of someone else, God does so out of anger or animosity (see the cross-references listed in the comments). Indeed, the incompatibility of this regularly antagonistic connotation with Jesus' sense of God's protagonism toward him argues strongly against a divine passive here.

To redeem a divine passive in παραδίδοται, K. Stock (*Boten* 158) uses the portrayal of Jesus' betrayer as the one "through whom" (δι' οὗ) he is given over (14:21) to argue that Judas will act as the agent of God. But "through whom" may point to the originator of an action as well as to someone else's agent (BAGD s.v. διά AIII2b; M. Zerwick, *Biblical Greek* §113). Admittedly, the use for an originator appears less often than that for an agent; and the reference to Scripture in 14:21 might favor that God will use Judas as an agent. But Jesus' use of the active voice in his preceding prediction, "One of you will give me over" (14:18), will favor Judas as originator of an action that merely accords with Scripture (καθὼς γέγραπται, "according as it is written" — 14:21). The use of παραδίδωμι for the actions of the Jewish authorities and Pilate, who do not even come close to being portrayed as God's agents, favors this judgment. The following up of the passive with an active referring to human action in 10:33; 14:41-42 likewise undermines a divine passive. See also the comments on 1:14 against a divine passive.

D. J. Moo (*OT* 92-97) canvasses various positions on the question whether παραδίδοται in v 31 derives from Isaiah 53 LXX. He favors at least some general influence from Isaiah 53. P. Hoffmann (in *Orientierung an Jesus* 187-88) sees in "hands of men" an allusion to thinking "the things of men" in 8:33. But there, "the things of men" meant not wanting Jesus to be killed and arose out of loyalty to him. Here, on the contrary, "hands of men" will carry out a desire to kill him and will arise out of rejecting him. To argue for the original unity of v 31 and against supposing a later addition of "and having been killed, after three days he will rise," G. Scholz (in *LingBib* 57 [1985] 87) notes the chiastic order of (a) being given over, (b) killing, (b') being killed, and (a') rising. The future of ἀνίστημι occurs regularly in the middle voice without special nuance or emphasis. Hence, to interpret the middle voice of ἀναστήσεται as meaning "he must rise" (so H. F. Bayer, *Jesus' Predictions* 209-10) lacks justification.

The attempt to trace the disciples' ignorance (v 32) to an ambiguity in the Aramaic אזדקיף, which can refer either to crucifixion or to exaltation (so M. Black in *ZNW* 60 [1969] 7 with dependence on G. Kittel in *ZNW* 35 [1936] 282-85), founders on the difficulty that in Mark, where the ignorance is mentioned, Jesus distinguishes between his being killed and his rising. Since the near context does not mention persecution, we should not infer that the disciples are afraid to suffer as Jesus' disciples (so J. Gnilka 2. 54). Besides, that object of fear would not reflect ignorance or forestall inquiry.

THE EXPLOSIVE FORCE OF JESUS' TEACHING

9:33-50 (Matt 5:13; 10:40, 42; 18:1-9; Luke 9:46-50; 14:34-35; 17:1-2; John 13:20)

This long pericope, consisting mainly of Jesus' sayings, is set in Capernaum. The first subsection grows out of a dispute over greatness (vv 33-37), the second out of a rivalrous confrontation (vv 38-50). It is commonly thought that the pericope "consists of a group of sayings which appear to have been built up primarily through catchword-association" (W. L. Lane 338). The catchwords are "if" (vv 35, 42, 43, 45, 47, 49), "who(ever)" (vv 37 [bis], 39, 40, 41, 42), "one of" (vv 37, 42), "children" and "little ones" (vv 37, 42), "name" (vv 37, 38, 39, 41), "cause to stumble" (vv 42, 43, 45, 47), "(it is) good" (vv 42, 43, 45, 47, 50), "be

thrown into" (vv 42, 45, 47), "fire" (vv 44, 48, 49), and "salt" (vv 49, 50). As the
references to parallels in the other gospels show, some of the sayings that appear
together in vv 33-50 appear elsewhere in different, scattered settings. But how
do we decide whether catchword-association attracted originally separate sayings
to each other, or whether it reflects the thinking of a speaker on a single occasion,
the breaking up of original unity being a secondary development? A large amount
of conceptual unrelatedness may incline us to judge the catchword-associations
superficial and therefore secondary. Even superficial associations by way of
catchwords may characterize stream-of-consciousness speaking on a single occasion, however (cf. P. Carrington 205). If beneath such associations, others of a
deep conceptual sort are to be found, they will still not decide the issue, because
a speaker's thinking may well carry over from one occasion to another. We shall,
in fact, discover both catchword and conceptual associations in vv 33-50. We may
ascribe the conceptual ones to a redactional activity that went beyond superficial
catchwords, or we may suppose that Jesus thought and therefore spoke and acted
similarly on different occasions. In the end, then, we should doubt our ability to
decide with great certainty whether any, some, or all of these sayings and incidents
originally belonged together.

9:33-34 *(Matt 18:1; Luke 9:46)* Jesus' and the disciples' going to Capernaum marks the beginning of a new pericope and shows that we are not yet
dealing, and have not been dealing, with a journey to Jerusalem; for Capernaum
is the base of Jesus' Galilean ministry. "In the house" may refer to Peter's home
there (cf. 2:1-2; 7:17 with comments). Agreeing with this possibility is the prominence given to the phrase by its forward position (see the Greek word order,
which may display chiasm in the relation of the locative phrases to their verb and
verbal, respectively). Jesus' asking the disciples, "What were you arguing about
on the road?" implies that he gave his preceding passion-and-resurrection prediction (vv 30-32) "on the road" just as he had given his first one "on the road" (cf.
8:27 with 8:31; see also 10:32-34). An adversative δέ, "but," introduces the
disciples' silence by way of contrast with an answer-demanding question (cf. 3:4).
Presumably they keep silent out of sheepishness over having discussed with one
another who is the greatest (in their own number, we are certainly meant to
understand from Jesus' following remarks; cf. 10:35-45). But Mark is not interested in the reason behind the disciples' silence; so he leaves the reason unidentified and switches from διελογίζεσθε, which emphasizes the reasoning element
in argument, to διελέχθησαν, which emphasizes the verbal element in argument.
To signal the switch he prefixes πρὸς ἀλλήλους, "with one another," and then he
quotes the very words of the question over which the disciples had been arguing:
"Who [is] the greatest?" For Mark it is enough that their silence will enable Jesus
to show his supernatural knowledge of the argument (cf. 2:8) just as he showed
supernatural knowledge of his coming death and resurrection. Such knowledge
turns into an apologetic weapon that Mark increasingly wields against the scandal
of the Cross: Jesus is aware of all that is taking place and that is yet to take place.

9:35-37 *(Matt 10:40; 18:2-5; 23:11; Luke 9:47-48; John 13:20)* Jesus'
sitting puts him in the authoritative posture of a teacher (see the comments on

4:1-2). Ἐφώνησεν does not connote the loudness of a shout, but in view of the setting inside a house the certain degree of loudness that this verb does connote (cf. 1:26 [with added emphasis]; 10:49; 14:30, 68, 72 [bis]; 15:35) displays the vigor with which Jesus exercises authority over his disciples. Mark writes "the Twelve," which distinguishes the small group of apostles from the large group of disciples (see the notes on 3:14, 16), to provide a numerical framework for the upcoming contrast between first and last, i.e. between first and twelfth. The present historical tense of λέγει, "he says," emphasizes the following words, whose appropriateness to the Twelve's unconfessed topic of argument and whose accuracy of prediction in that none of the Twelve will take precedence over the others during their lifetimes will display Jesus' supernatural knowledge: "If anyone wishes to be first, he will be last of all" (cf. "the first ones of Galilee" in 6:21 and esp. 10:43-44 for verbal parallels; also the comments and notes on 10:43-44 for a futuristic rather than imperative future in Mark's meaning, though perhaps vice versa in Jesus' meaning). The position of πρῶτος, "first," before εἶναι, "to be," emphasizes firstness. The chiastic positions of ἔσχατος, "last," and διάκονος, "servant," strengthen the contrast between firstness and lastness, or servanthood. Πάντων, "of all" (bis), universalizes the contrast; and the coming of πάντων before ἔσχατος and again before διάκονος intensifies that universalism. More specifically, "first" and "last" have to do with rank; and "of all" means the taking of a servant's role, also a matter of rank, not merely in relation to Jesus, but also in relation to one another. Presumably the child whom Jesus takes, causes to stand in the midst of the Twelve, and hugs to himself lives in the house where they are. A saying interprets this object lesson: "Whoever receives one of such children [as I have hugged this one] on the ground of my name [for this child represents others likewise acceptable to me] receives me [inasmuch as I have received the child]; and whoever receives me does not receive me; rather, [he receives] the one who sent me [for I am that one's messenger]." Twice, the forward position of ἐμέ, "me," stresses the receiving of Jesus. A third forward position of ἐμέ but this time following οὐκ, "not," plus the strongly adversative ἀλλά, "rather," and the ellipsis of "he receives" in the ἀλλά-clause stresses the sender of Jesus as the one received. Thus this subsection of the pericope reaches a preliminary climax in the receiving of Jesus by the receiving of a child, and an ultimate climax in the receiving of God by the receiving of Jesus. "Not . . . rather" is an emphatic way of saying "not . . . so much as."

The lone child that Jesus hugs is the representive "one" of children such as are to be received on the ground of Jesus' name. Since Jesus is sitting (v 35), he does not have to bend down to hug the child, whose standing posture enables Jesus to reach out and envelop the child in his embrace. Just as by sitting he took the authoritative posture of a teacher, so he makes the child take the reverential posture of standing, as befits one who will turn out to represent all children who believe in Jesus (see v 42, where "these" with "little ones who believe in me" will point back to "such children" as the present one represents; also 10:13-16, where children will come to Jesus and possess God's kingdom). "In the midst of them [the Twelve]" visually indicates that a believing child belongs in the circle of Jesus' disciples. Hugging visually represents his reception, and reception means acceptance into his new family (cf. 3:31-35). The forward position of ἐν τῶν τοιούτων παιδίων, "one of such children," emphasizes reception of even a lone child who believes in Jesus. "On the ground of (ἐπί) my name" specifies the basis of that acceptance, viz., his own reception of such a child (again cf. v 42; 10:13-16; and the comments and notes on 13:6). Receiving even a lone child on this basis equates with receiving Jesus. This equation, highlighted both by a switch from the aorist subjunctive δέξηται for the receiving of a child to the present subjunctive δέχηται for the receiving of Jesus (S. E. Porter, *Verbal Aspect* 326) and by a further equation of receiving Jesus with receiving God who sent him, stresses the necessity that adult believers not pursue greatness. If they do pursue it, they will shut out child-believers and therefore Jesus himself and God. Thus Jesus turns the question of greatness inside out: he shifts attention from greatness among the Twelve to their reception of children, which shows humility in contrast with the self-exalting pride that caused them to argue with one another which of them was the greatest. The "all" whom the Twelve are to serve may not include people in general, for the passage deals with intramural rivalry among disciples. But the "all" who bear Jesus' name do include children. He is concerned about relations among those who believe in him. Mark's point graduates from Jesus' supernatural knowledge of the question over which the Twelve had been arguing to the explosive force of Jesus' prediction that contrary to the societal norms of trying to be first and of denigrating children, believing adults will take the last place of a servant who receives even children who believe (see 1 Tim 4:12; J. Jeremias, *NT Theology* 1. 227, n. 2, on children's lowliness in society).

9:38-42 *(Matt 10:42; 18:6; Luke 9:49-50; 17:1-2)* Just as the Twelve's receiving and serving child-believers will counteract pretensions to grandeur, so the Twelve's letting the independent exorcist carry on his ministry apart from themselves will counteract those same pretensions. In fact, this subsection on the independent exorcist comes full circle in its summary of mutuality in the community of believers: allowance of the independent exorcist (vv 39-40), hospitality to the Twelve (v 41), and, once again, regard for believing children (v 42).

The asyndeton with which the subsection opens befits the abruptness of John's dismissing the independent exorcist as unauthorized and the contrast between the Twelve's forbidding that exorcist and the foregoing motif of reception. The address, "Teacher," calls to mind Jesus' authority (cf. the comments on his seated position in v 35). The reference to his name in John's remark, "We saw someone casting out demons in your name," suggests that Jesus' foregoing statement about receiving one of such children on the ground of his name (v 37) triggers John's remark. (This suggestion is as good as that which makes the association between vv 33-37 and vv 38-41 secondary, as though the references to Jesus' name attracted two originally separate items of tradition to each other.) That the name of Jesus effects exorcisms even when used by an independent highlights Jesus' power.

Mark may intend some irony in the Twelve's telling the independent exorcist to stop doing what they themselves have recently tried and failed to do (cf. vv

14-29; Num 11:26-29). We might take ἐκωλύομεν as a conative imperfect ("and we tried to prevent him"), but it may merely represent the linear imperfect often used in verbs of speaking ("and we were forbidding him" — cf. M. Zerwick, *Biblical Greek* §272). The plural of the first person pronoun in the clause, "because he was not following us," is at first surprising, perhaps shocking: we would have expected a reference to following Jesus (or to following Jesus *alone,* though the limitation of "we" to the Twelve favors a similar limitation of "us"). But Jesus does not correct John's "us." Instead, he will confirm and expand it to include himself (vv 40-41) in correlation with his preceding identification of himself with his disciples, even those who are children (see v 37 again). Nevertheless, he does not want the Twelve to think that his preceding concentration on them and on the exemplary child rules out others' bearing his name, too. So he commands, "Stop forbidding him, for there is no one who will do a miracle on the ground of my name [ἐπὶ τῷ ὀνόματί μου, as in v 37] and be able quickly [i.e. soon afterward] to speak evil of me." Δέ, "but," sets Jesus as an opponent of forbidding over against John as a zealot of forbidding.

Here, evangelistic ministry constitutes the setting; for exorcisms and miracles performed during itineration ("he was not following us") look like the accompaniments of Jesus' and the disciples' public proclamations (see 6:6b-13 for the disciples, et passim for Jesus), not like communal exercises designed to build up the faithful. "There is no one who" (cf. 7:15; 10:29) makes a stronger negation than the simpler, usual, and expected "no one" (so 2:21, 22; 3:27; 5:3, 4; 10:18; 11:2; 12:34; 13:32). Jesus means that using his name to work a miracle (which he adds to exorcisms to broaden the scope of his remark) and turning around to slander the owner of that name cannot go together. Either the name will not be effective (but for this meaning Jesus would probably have reversed the order of miracle-working and slander and made the inability go with miracle-working rather than with slander), or a person who thinks so much of the name as to use it in working a miracle will not slander its owner (cf. 2 Macc 4:1; Acts 19:9 for the use of κακολογέω in the sense of slander). Ταχύ, "quickly," leaves open the possibility of later apostasy (E. Schweizer 195).

Another γάρ-clause gives a second reason to stop forbidding the independent exorcist: "for he who is not against us is for us" (v 40). The chiastic word order of (a) verb, (b) prepositional phrase, (b′) prepositional phrase, and (a′) verb puts emphasis on the forwardly positioned prepositional phrase ὑπὲρ ἡμῶν, "for us." Jesus does not say that the person who is for them is not against them. If there were no doubt that the independent exorcist was for them, the Twelve would probably not have told him to stop. But his not following them made them doubt or deny that he was for them, even though his use of Jesus' name showed that he was not against them, either. Jesus' saying eliminates the supposed limbo: since he is not against us (he uses my name and, as I have just said, no one will do a miracle on the ground of my name and be able soon after to speak evil of me), he is for us; so stop forbidding him.

A third γάρ-clause gives yet another reason for not forbidding the independent exorcist and introduces the first of a pair of "whoever"-sayings: "for whoever

gives you a cup of water to drink in name that you are Christ's [i.e. 'under the
category that you belong to Christ' — BAGD s.v. ὄνομα II; cf. 1 Cor 3:23 with
1 Cor 1:12] — truly I say to you that he will by no means lose his reward" (v 41).
That is to say, minimal hospitality given to the Twelve because they belong to
Christ (general humanitarianism is not in view) suffices to insure entrance into
God's kingdom; for such hospitality gives evidence of faith in the gospel they
preach. Well, if even minimal hospitality brings such insurance, then following
Jesus and the Twelve must not be required; so stop forbidding the independent
exorcist because he is not following us. The status of the "whoever"-clause as a
nominative absolute lends weight to the minimal hospitality described therein.
Χριστοῦ, "Christ's," harks back to the confession of Peter (8:29), implies Jesus'
acceptance of it, and casts the giving of a cup of water in the mold of a Christological confession that is acted out. The forward position of Χριστοῦ underscores
the Christologically confessional character of the act.

A second "whoever"-saying gives the negative side of the third reason for
not forbidding the independent exorcist (the γάρ in v 41 carrying over to v 42,
too): "and whoever causes one of these little ones who believe in me to stumble
[contrast vv 37a, 41a], it would be better for him rather if an upper millstone were
laid around his neck and he be cast [βέβληται, the perfect tense indicating
completed action with continuing result] into the sea." Again the status of the
"whoever"-clause as a nominative absolute lends weight, this time to the danger
of causing a stumbling. "One of these little ones who believe in me" alludes to
the children represented by the child that Jesus caused to stand in the midst of
the Twelve (vv 36-37). "Causes . . . to stumble" means "makes to sin," as the
disciples are liable to make believing children do if they strive for greatness rather
than receiving and serving all, even children, in the community of believers (cf.
Rom 14:13; 1 Cor 8:9 and see the following notes on the nature of the sin).
Ὀνικός, translated "upper," literally means "having to do with a donkey" and
here describes the upper millstone so heavy that it has to be turned by donkey-
power. Such a stone, laid around the neck, kills all hope of the corpse's rising to
the surface and floating to shore for burial (cf. Rev 18:21 and see J. D. M. Derrett
[in ZNW 76 (1985) 284 and in DownRev 103 (1985) 218-22], who probably goes
too far in detecting both an allusion to a donkey's burial, i.e. to no burial at all
[Jer 22:9 with 36:30], and to prevention of pollution of the Holy Land by the
corpse's floating to shore). People of the Bible look with horror on any kind of
death that precludes burial (J. B. Payne in ISBE [2nd ed.] 1. 556). The unrealism
of having your head shoved through the center hole of an upper millstone with
the result that you are wearing the millstone like a collar (cf. the change of Mark's
περίκειται, "is laid around," to κρεμασθῇ, "be hung" [presumably with a rope], in
Matt 18:6) intensifies the sense of horror. So also does the non-Jewishness of
execution by drowning. Such a fate contrasts with the reward promised in v 41.
Furthermore, Jesus describes this fate as καλόν, "better." The forward position of
καλόν and the lack of an answer to the question, Better than what? concentrate
emphasis on the description. Whatever it is that makes drowning with an upper
millstone around your neck better must be horrible beyond description. The

indicative mood of ἐστιν, περίκειται, and βέβληται — "is," "is being laid," and "has been cast," respectively in literal translation — add that whatever it is must be horrible *in fact*. By implication Jesus is warning of eternal judgment (cf. the explicit references in vv 43-49). Thus the certainty of eternal judgment for causing a stumbling balances the certainty of eternal life for offering hospitality (i.e. giving a cup of water in token of believing the gospel) so as to provide a twofold reason to stop forbidding the independent exorcist.

In summary, the independent exorcist is not to be hindered, (1) because suspecting fellow believers outside one's close circle underestimates the number of people loyal to Jesus (v 39b); (2) because a sense of rivalry makes believers fail to recognize their friends (v 40); and (3) because receiving a messenger of the gospel brings salvation to a quondam unbeliever (v 41), whereas causing even a child who believes in Jesus to sin brings judgment on the believer who causes the sin (v 42).

9:43-48 *(Matt 18:8-9)* Now comes a series of three sayings beginning καὶ ἐὰν σκανδαλίζῃ plus a part of the body as subject: "and if your hand [successively, 'your foot' and 'your eye'] should cause you to stumble" (cf. Job 31:1; Prov 6:17-18; 23:33; 27:20). Again sinning is in view, but sinning caused from within by a member of one's own body, not from without by critics such as the Twelve. And again eternal judgment is in view, but this time for self-made sinners, not for those who cause others to sin. Jesus warns the Twelve against self-induced sinning, not only to keep them from it, but also by deflating them to keep them from forbidding the independent exorcist and from rejecting children: insiders and grownups like the Twelve have their own danger to avoid. The switch from the aorist subjunctive σκανδαλίσῃ (v 42) to the present subjunctive σκανδαλίζῃ (vv 43, 45, 47) accentuates the warning (S. E. Porter, *Verbal Aspect* 326; cf. the notes on 1:3).

With some exceptions the sayings exhibit a parallelism that further accentuates their warning tone. Take, for example, the three occurrences of καλόν ἐστιν, "better it is," as already in v 42 and again with καλόν thrust into an emphatic forward position but now with the added emphasis of asyndeton. So also with regard to the continuation "to enter into . . . than to. . . ." Some differences turn up, however. In the first saying σκανδαλίζῃ σε, "should cause you to stumble," comes before its subject ἡ χείρ σου, "your hand," but this establishing of sin as the main concern allows the subjects ὁ πούς σου and ὁ ὀφθαλμός σου, "your foot" and "your eye," to precede the second and third occurrences of σκανδαλίζῃ σε for emphasis on the bodily members that might lead a disciple to sin. "Cut it off," which suits a hand and a foot (cf. Deut 25:11-12), yields to "throw [= gouge] it out," which suits an eye. In the second half of the third saying the pronoun σέ, "you," comes forward for emphasis. The emphatic position of κυλλόν, "maimed," is exchanged for an unemphatic position in the parallel χωλόν, "lame," only to return in the further parallel μονόφθαλμον, "one-eyed." "To go into life," which occurs in the first two sayings and in the first one contrasts with "to go *away* into Gehenna," becomes "to go into the kingdom of God" and thereby shows the futuristic side of God's kingdom in the teaching of Jesus. "To go away into

Gehenna" becomes "to be cast into Gehenna" (so the second and third sayings)
and thus relates all three sayings to being "cast into the sea" (v 42) and interprets
the earlier expression as a figure of eternal judgment. The first saying ends with
the horrifying phrase "into unquenchable fire." The second saying has nothing at
this point. But the third saying has the even fuller and therefore more horrifying
compound clause, "where 'their worm does not die and the fire is not quenched'
[a quotation of Isa 66:24; cf. esp. LXX^A]." The maggots that constantly feed on
garbage in the Valley of Hinnom (= Gehenna) and the fires that constantly burn
there stand for the eternal torment of sinners. The shift from Isaiah's conjunction
"for" to "where" is determined by a difference in the preceding context, in
particular, by "Gehenna." The shift from Isaiah's predictive future tense to the
futuristic present tense adds vividness to the warning. Alternatively, J. A. Kleist
(216) speaks of "the full force of the negative universal present." The deletion of
"their" from "fire" lessens attention on the punished in favor of attention on the
punishment — naturally, since "the men who have transgressed against me
[Yahweh]," to whom "their" refers in Isaiah, do not appear in Mark, where Jesus
has been using the singular "you." "Their" might refer to the two eyes, the two
feet, and the two hands in the preceding context; but probably not, because it is
"you" who have those pairs, not the pairs as such, that will be thrown into
Gehenna. Thus "their" is only a relic from Isaiah's text (cf. B. D. Chilton, *Galilean
Rabbi* 101-7).

In the biblical period, maiming sometimes substitutes for capital punishment. Furthermore, by preserving life, maiming counts as more merciful punishment. By the same token, maiming the body if necessary to enter God's kingdom
shows self-mercy in comparison with keeping one's body whole at the cost of
going to hell (cf. *Tg. Ps.-J.* Gen 38:25). So great are the glories of his kingdom
and the miseries of hell! But self-mutilation is prohibited in Judaism (beginning
in the OT — see Deut 14:1; cf. 1 Kgs 18:28; Zech 13:6). By contradicting this
prohibition, Jesus' advocacy of whatever self-mutilation might be necessary to
enter God's kingdom raises the glories of the kingdom and the miseries of hell
to almost unimaginable degrees, with the unfortunate result that a commentator
such as R. Pesch timidly sees the disagreement with Jewish prohibition of self-
mutilation as evidence that Jesus does not intend his words to be taken literally
(cf. E. Best, *Following Jesus* 85). Pesch alleviates the severity of Jesus' words
also by introducing the consideration that God makes a person new in the kingdom
(presumably meaning that God will restore lost hands, feet, and eyes at the
resurrection). But this consideration would be pertinent only under the provision
that Jesus really does advocate self-mutilation as possibly necessary. It is more
natural to take him literally not only with respect to self-mutilation (cf. Josephus
Life 34 §§169-78; idem *J.W.* 2.21.10 §§642-44; *m. Nid.* 2:1; *b. Nid.* 13b; Ael. *VH*
13.24; Val. Max. 6.5.3; J. D. M. Derrett, *Jesus's Audience* 201-4) but also with
respect to having a mutilated body in God's kingdom. Better that than a whole
body in hell, Jesus seems to be saying (cf. the scars of crucifixion evident on his
resurrected body — John 20:27; Rev 5:6). The asyndeton which three times
introduces "better it is" and the emphatic position of καλόν, "better," before ἐστιν,

"it is," sharpen the point. Above all, Jesus is accentuating the need to maintain discipleship by avoiding sins that would subvert it.

9:49-50 *(Matt 5:13; Luke 14:34-35)* "For everyone will be salted with fire" makes a reason for obeying the commands in vv 43-48 (against K. Stock, *Boten* 127) and indicates that fire represents judgment, as it did in those verses. Since the reason relates backward to ways of avoiding the fire of Gehenna, "everyone" may mean everyone who fails to avoid this fire (so ibid.) rather than everyone without exception. On the other hand, the emphatic forward position of πᾶς, "everyone," favors an unlimited meaning, which is more natural anyway; and Jesus switches from the figure of the fire that burns garbage in the Valley of Hinnom to a double figure in which the figure of fire is compared with the figure of salt. So he probably means that fire will fall on everyone without exception, as when salt is sprinkled indiscriminately, in order that true believers might pass the test of fire (cf. 1 Cor 3:12-15) and apostates suffer the just-mentioned judgment of eternal fire and decay. Because of similarity between the actions of sprinkling and throwing, the expression "will be salted with fire" comes close to the expression "to throw fire on the earth" in Luke 12:49 (cf. baptism in the Holy Spirit and fire — Matt 3:11 par. Luke 3:16). Strikingly, a reference to "peace" follows closely in Luke 12:49 just as a reference to "peace" follows here in Mark 9:50. In both passages fire stands for judgment, and peace has to do with interpersonal relations. This conjunction of fire and peace in two passages otherwise quite different from each other favors that the sayings on fire and peace belonged together from the very first and that their conjunction derives from Jesus himself. The passive voice of "will be salted" probably implies God's action. The position of πυρί, "with fire," before ἁλισθήσεται, "will be salted," emphasizes the figurativeness and frightfulness of being salted with fire.

The verb "will be salted" served the figure of fire, standing for judgment, and suggested the noun "salt." The noun now becomes its own figure of speech, standing quite differently for peace. This difference causes Jesus to introduce the new figure with the statement, "Salt is good [unlike the horrible fire of judgment]" (cf. *Sop.* 15.8). The adjective καλόν, "good," forges a link with the sayings in vv 42, 43, 45, 47, in each of which καλόν occurred. As in those verses, its forward position is emphatic. So also is the asyndeton with which the affirmation begins, as in vv 43, 45, 47. Salt is good when it stands for good relations among believers in Jesus. Asyndeton stresses the command, "Have salt among yourselves." "And be at peace among one another" parallelistically defines this command and thus forms an inclusion with the dispute at the start of the pericope (vv 33-34; cf. the salt which, because of its preservative power, stands for the perpetuity of a covenantal relationship — Exod 30:35; Lev 2:13; Num 18:19; Ezra 4:14; 2 Chr 13:5; Ezek 43:24; *Jub.* 21:11 — and perhaps specifically for a meal of covenantal friendship). "But if the salt should become saltless" refers to the possibilities that sodium chloride will dissolve away from impure salt, that unscrupulous dealers will adulterate salt with cheaper ingredients, and that gypsum will mask the taste of salt (see E. P. Deatrick in *BA* [1962] 44-45; C. E. Carlston, *Parables* 174-78). These possibilities stand, in turn, for the breakdown of peaceful relations among believers, as in the Twelve's arguing which of them is the greatest and in their forbidding the independent exorcist. "With what will you season it?" points up the impossibility of believers' finding peace outside their community and therefore the necessity of keeping the peace that is to be found within it. An adversative δέ, "but," and the forward positions of τὸ ἅλας, "the salt," ἄναλον, "saltless," and αὐτό, "it," stress the impossibility and the necessity. Without peace within the community, hostility from without will lead believers to apostatize. So stop arguing with one another who is the greatest, serve all, including even children, and stop forbidding the independent exorcist. To avoid causing sin, be at peace in your own circle, with him, and with all who make up the body politic of God's kingdom. All that counts is allegiance to Jesus, not greatness, adulthood, or following "us."

Such allegiance and Jesus' teaching that the one who is not against us is for us, that minimal hospitality for the name of Christ insures reward, that causing even a child-believer to sin will bring worse than imaginable judgment, that it is worth mutilating oneself, if necessary, to enter God's kingdom — such allegiance and teaching add to the point which Mark wants to put across in the pericope: the point is not discipleship and communal life, but explosive force. Jesus teaches with an authority that shatters norms and in combination with his power to predict the Passion and Resurrection helps counteract the scandal of the Crucifixion.

NOTES

Though connections exist between the various didactic statements contained in vv 33-50, a catechist would probably have tightened those connections or chosen more uniform materials (J. Gnilka 2. 67 against R. Bultmann, *HST* 149-50). D. Wenham (in *JSNT* 14 [1982] 113-18) uses certain agreements between Matthew and Luke against Mark in vv 33-42 parr. to argue against Marcan priority, but see R. H. Gundry, *Matthew* 201-3, 235-36, 358-62, 403, 459, for another view. Writing on vv 33-37, V. K. Robbins (in *SBL 1982 Seminar Papers* 421-23) gives examples of chreiai in which a demonstrative action is later expanded with an explanatory saying, and he concludes that v 37 represents just such an expansion. Originally, then, Jesus addressed the question of greatness only by setting a child in the midst of the disciples. But the saying in v 35 has already addressed the question of greatness. So Robbins deletes that saying, too, from the original chreia, not to detail other deletions with regard to the question itself and its occasion. We may think of these possibilities (though the exemplary parallels do not support the further deletions), but in the absence of pre-Marcan literary remains we may not speak confidently. Words and actions may accompany each other from the start (cf. the institution of the Lord's Supper; Acts 21:10-11; and many actions-cum-words on the part of OT prophets).

D. E. Nineham (251-52) thinks that entry into Capernaum (v 33) disagrees with the secrecy of the journey though Galilee (v 30). But wanting to avoid crowds along the way does not imply wanting to avoid them at one's destination. And even if otherwise, Jesus does avoid them during this visit to Capernaum. He enters "the house" (see 2:1; cf. 7:17) and converses there only with the Twelve (contrast 2:2-12; also 7:24). Only on his leaving Capernaum and arriving in Judea do crowds reappear (10:1).

E. S. Malbon (*Narrative Space* 192, n. 29) argues that v 33 does not refer to Peter's house in Capernaum, (1) because ἐν τῇ οἰκίᾳ differs from ἐν οἴκῳ in 2:1, which did refer to Peter's house; (2) because "his" does not modify the noun as it did in 2:15 (cf. 6:4; 14:3); and (3) because Jesus' family do not make an appearance, as they did in 3:20-21. But the definite article in 9:33 may be anaphoric, referring back to Peter's house. At 1:27 οἰκία occurred for Peter's house, and a perusal of Marcan passages containing οἰκία and οἶκος turns up no distinction in meaning or usage; so the occurrence of the one word in 2:1 and of the other in 9:33 makes no difference. The house in 2:15 is probably Levi's, not Jesus' or Peter's, and the word is οἰκία, not οἶκος as Malbon's argument demands. A coming of Jesus' family to Peter's house in 3:20-21 would not require that all references to Peter's house include their coming. In fact, the indubitable references in 1:29; 2:1 do not include it. Besides, 7:17 and especially 9:28 with 9:30, 33a suggest that entering εἰς οἶκον in 3:20 did not mean entering Peter's house, but entering an unspecified house.

The quite untheological use of "on the road" in 8:3, the fact that the road mentioned in 8:27 was heading into the villages of Philip's Caesarea, not to Jerusalem, and the fact that the road mentioned in 9:33b was heading into Capernaum (cf. v 30, 33a), not to Jerusalem, make it doubtful that "on the road" in 9:33a is a Marcan construct bearing the theological freight of a reference to Jesus' passion-road to Jerusalem (cf. the notes on 8:27). The question who is the greatest (v 34) lends to the verbs διελογίζεσθε and διελέχθησαν (vv 33-34) the connotation of argument. Otherwise they might refer only to reasoning and discussion. Questions of rank loomed large in Jewish society. Jesus' closest followers might have expected to occupy positions of honor and authority in the coming kingdom of God (cf. 10:35-40 par.), but the present dispute seems to deal with current rank (cf. 1QSa; 1QS 2:19-25; 5:20-24; 6:3-6, 8-13; Str-B 1. 249-50, 774; 4/2. 1131-32, 1138-43). If the question of greatness were Mark's construct based on 10:43 (see, e.g., J. D. Crossan, *In Fragments* 289), he would likely have brought the element of greatness from 10:43 into Jesus' answer, too (9:35b; cf. the comments on 10:43-44).

A form of καθίζω occurs for Jesus' sitting in v 35 and 12:41, whereas forms of the synonym κάθημαι occur in 4:1; 13:3. R. Pesch (2. 104) suggests that the former are historical reminiscences going back to a pre-Marcan passion narrative and that the latter are Christological references alluding to the posture of a teacher. He supports his suggestion by noting the use of λέγει, "says," rather than διδάσκει, "teaches," in 9:35. But after sitting down and watching the crowd in 12:41, Jesus will summon the disciples and give them what can only be described as teaching, introduced with the asseverative, "truly I say to you" (12:43; cf. the didactic tone established in 12:14, 35, 38); and 13:5 has λέγειν instead of διδάσκειν where Pesch's argument would require διδάσκειν even though a great amount of teaching follows (cf. 10:46; 12:36; 14:62; 16:5 for non-didactic uses of κάθημαι in Pesch's putative pre-Marcan passion narrative, and 11:2, 7; 14:32 for similar uses of καθίζω in the same). That Jesus teaches even when Mark does not use "teach" or "teaching" in introductory formulas (see 7:14-15, 17-23; 8:34–9:1, 11-13, 33-50 et passim) does not imply the insignificance of those terms when he does use them. By the same token, the fact that Jesus often teaches without Mark's mention of sitting does not imply that where Mark does mention it the authoritative posture of a teacher is not in view. Otherwise why mention it at all (against E. Best, *Disciples and Discipleship* 39-40)?

Because Mark uses προσκαλέομαι, "summon," editorially more often than φωνέω, "call," Best (loc. cit.) argues that tradition underlies v 35a, where ἐφώνησεν occurs. The argument presupposes and requires the synonymity of the two verbs. But they are not quite synonymous. Unlike προσκαλέομαι, φωνέω connotes a certain loudness of voice (though not a shout — see the foregoing comments). Therefore the comparative infrequency of φωνέω may be due to the infrequency of circumstances in which any loudness is needed rather than to Mark's writing προσκαλέομαι except when under traditional influence to write φωνέω.

"He called" does not disagree with the presence of the disciples and thus indicate a difference in origin between vv 33-34 and v 35a; for despite a certain loudness of voice, the called may be situated close to the caller (as in 10:49; Luke 8:8, 54; John 2:9; 10:3; 12:17; 13:13; 18:33; cf. Mark 8:34; 10:42). Just as the decease of Jairus's daughter made appropriate Jesus' calling her with a certain loudness of voice even though both he and she were in the same house (Luke 8:54), so Jesus' sitting down makes appropriate his calling the Twelve with a certain loudness of voice even though both he and they are in the same house.

On the ground that the pronominal references in vv 33-34 to the disciples of vv 30-32 sit awkwardly alongside "the Twelve" of v 35a, Best (op. cit. 140-43, also 39-40) doubts that the same person wrote both vv 33-34 and v 35a. He goes on to assign vv 33-34 to Mark and v 35a to tradition. But the foregoing comments give a rationale for the transition from the disciples to the Twelve, and Mark seems to show his own interest in the Twelve at 3:14, 16; 4:10; 6:7; 10:32; 11:11; 14:10, 17, 20, 43. Since the historical present tense of λέγω in the third person occurs in Mark seventy-two times, καὶ λέγει αὐτοῖς, "and he says to them," hardly favors a pre-Marcan source over Mark's composition (against Best, op. cit. 39-40). Nonetheless, we have reason to believe that though Mark composes vv 33-35a together, historical tradition contributes to his composition. Independent support of the importance of Capernaum in Jesus' ministry comes from Matt 8:5; 11:23; Luke 4:23; 7:1; 10:15; John 2:12; 6:17, 24-25, 59. There is every probability that he conversed with his disciples in homes (cf. the notes on v 28). See R. H. Gundry, *Matthew* 359-60, on Matthew's redactional reason for omitting Mark 9:35. Luke does not omit it, however (see Luke 9:48c against Gundry, loc. cit.).

Under the view that Mark writes 9:35b in anticipation of 10:43-44, J. Ernst (275) suggests that Mark allows the contrast between first and last in 10:31 to modify the wording borrowed from 10:43-44 (cf. W. Schmithals 428-29; H. Fleddermann in *CBQ* 43 [1981] 60). But 9:35b and 10:31 may display a Jesuanic predilection for the contrast, and 10:43-44 a modification according to situational needs. Furthermore, since 9:35b like 10:43-44 reverses roles only among disciples whereas 10:31 will reverse the roles of non-disciples vis-à-vis disciples, it is unlikely that in 9:35b Mark borrows "last" by anticipation from 10:31. Again under the view that Mark anticipatively borrows 9:35b from 10:44, one could say that he changes a "whoever"-clause into an "if anyone"-clause after the pattern of 8:34. But if 8:34 represents tradition, so also may the wording of 9:35b. Then the wording of 10:44 will represent another tradition, perhaps another saying, or assimilation to "whoever"-clauses in other sayings of Jesus (for Mark alone, see 3:29, 35; 8:35 [bis], 38; 9:37, 41, 42; 10:11, 15, 43; 11:23).

Behind διάκονος, "servant," and παιδίον, "child," M. Black (*Aramaic Approach* 218-23 and in *ExpTim* 59 [1947-48] 14-16) detects a wordplay on the Aramaic טליא, which can mean either. But R. Le Déaut (in *Bib* 49 [1968] 393-94) and H. Fleddermann (in *CBQ* 43 [1981] 64, n. 35) have cautioned that διάκονος would be unusual for טליא. An original disunity of vv 35 and 36 would also destroy the wordplay.

J. Gnilka (2. 25) suggests that Mark created v 36 under the influence of 10:16. It is as hard to verify this suggestion as to falsify it. The obvious similarities between the passages are matched by dissimilarities: Jesus' taking a child versus others' bringing children, one child versus more than one, Jesus' making the one child an exemplary passive object of being received versus his making children exemplary active subjects of receiving ("whoever does not receive the rule of God as a child [receives it]" — 10:15), and so forth.

Though vv 36-37 do not present the child as itself an example of unconcern over rank, as we might expect from vv 33-34, this omission does not divorce vv 36-37 and vv 33-35 from each other; for receiving a child provides an example of unconcern over rank. All interpretations of v 36 that point to a childlike virtue worthy of imitation — innocence, trustfulness, etc. — fail to consider that v 37 goes on to make a child the object of reception, not of imitation. Children occupy last place in the social hierarchy; so some have interpreted Jesus' taking a child and standing it in the midst of the Twelve as making the child a visual representation of being last of all, interpreted by being a servant of all, so as to be first. But his hugging the child goes beyond what is needed for such an object lesson and favors that he is not making the child an example of being last of all so much as he is making himself an example of being last of all, servant of all, by receiving into his arms even a child. It is the servant, not the child, who occupies last position; and it takes a servant to receive a child. Indeed, to receive a child *is* to serve the child inasmuch as reception entails the services of a hospitable welcome. Of course, to defend the originality of Jesus' making the child an example of being last of all, one may posit a later addition of the hugging and of the saying on reception. But 10:13-16 favors the originality of Jesus' treating children who believe as acceptable.

Citing *b. Meg.* 13a, R. Pesch (2. 107) interprets vv 36-37 as teaching charitable reception of poor and helpless children, orphans in particular, and as making Jesus an example of what it means to be a servant even of such children when he takes and hugs one (see also Str-B 1. 774; K.-G. Reploh, *Lehrer* 143-44). But taking and hugging a child fall short of the charity necessary to care for orphans, i.e. of taking them into one's household, feeding them, and providing them shelter, and can scarcely represent it without further indication (again see *b. Meg.* 13a). Furthermore, nothing in the present passage suggests that the child is a poor and helpless orphan. On the contrary, "one of such children" implies the presence of other children, just as "many such parables" referred to parables spoken on the occasion of 4:33, just as "such miracles" referred to miracles taking place on the occasion of 6:2, just as "such [children]" will refer to the children brought to Jesus on the occasion of 10:14, et passim. "Such children" (τῶν τοιούτων παιδίων) does not distinguish a certain kind of children, such as orphans, from other children any more than "such parables" distinguishes a certain kind of parables from others, any more than "such miracles" distinguishes a certain kind of miracles from others. "Such children" means the children at hand (so also in 10:14) just as "such miracles" means the miracles at hand, and so on. Unless the house where Jesus and the disciples are staying is an orphanage, then, "one of such children" means one of the household children attendant on Jesus as his believing admirers (cf. v 42) rather than an orphan as distinguished from other, unorphaned children; and receiving means treating as a believer. If receiving means that rather than giving charity to orphans, the parallel with receiving Jesus stands firm and v 37a and v 37b need not be broken apart as expressing essentially different ideas (cf. 6:11 for the use of δέχομαι, "receive," in parallel with ἀκούω, "hear"; 10:15 for the use δέχομαι in the receiving of God's rule; and, above all because of a certain similarity to the present passage, Luke 2:28, where Simeon "receives" the baby Jesus into his arms in recognition of Jesus' being the Savior).

Verse 37b has a parallel with a different context in Matt 10:40. But that parallel is the result of Matthew's conflating Mark 9:37b and the saying behind Luke 10:16 (R. H. Gundry, *Matthew* 201); so we should not infer the originality of the context of Matt 10:40 — on the contrary, see Matt 18:5 — nor should we follow H. Fleddermann (in *CBQ* 43 [1981] 62-63) in seeing the content of a Q-saying represented by Matt 10:40 and redaction represented by Mark 9:37, for example, by a shift to "whoever"-clauses. Such clauses are more Semitic than Greek (though they are not un-Greek — see K. Beyer, *Semitische Syntax* 1/1. 166-67) and therefore less likely to have resulted from redaction. By the same token, we should not follow J. Gnilka (2. 55) when he uses Matt 10:40 to argue that in v 37 Mark has shifted from adults' receiving adults to adults' receiving children (cf. W. Schmithals 429-30; J. D. Crossan, *In Fragments* 109).

In vv 38-39 the parallelism between ἐν, "in (by means of)," and ἐπί, "on (the basis of)," causes the means and ground of exorcism to merge in Jesus' name. In v 37, however, ἐπί needs to be interpreted in terms of parallelism within the saying where it occurs. There, receiving God ("the one who sent me," as Jesus calls God) by receiving Jesus implies that the name of Jesus is one with the child being received just as Jesus is one with God who is being received. Thus there is no parallel with using Jesus' name as a means of exorcism. Only by using a false parallel of the latter sort can D. O. Via (*Ethics* 87-88) support a tension between receiving a child with whom Jesus has not united his name (and who therefore is not a believer) and "one of these little ones who believe in me" (v 42; cf. "because you are Christ's" — v 41). To see influence of the early church in references to Jesus' name is to imply that he did not accept Peter's identifying him as the Christ, or that Peter did not make that identification in the first place. Otherwise we have no need to deny such language on the part of Jesus, and churchly language of this sort will have derived from his language.

Just as in 3:14-15 ἀποστέλλω connoted Jesus' sending the Twelve with authority derived from him, so in 9:37 it connotes God's sending Jesus with authority derived from him. See K. H. Rengstorf in *TDNT* 1. 413-20; Str-B 1. 590; 2. 167 for the principle that "the sent one is like the sender," and M. Zerwick, *Biblical Greek* §445, for οὐκ . . . ἀλλά in the sense "not . . . so much as." Another example of this meaning occurs in John 12:44, but Mark 2:17 seems to have presented an absolute disjunction.

It is commonly thought that Mark interpolated vv 38-40 or 38-41, because these verses break a good connection between v 37 and v 41 or v 42. But an earlier juxtaposition of "one of such children" (v 37) and "you" (v 41), or of "one of such children" (v 37) and "one of these little ones" (v 42), would have been jarring. At the same time, the connection between vv 37 and 41 is otherwise weaker than that between vv 37 and 42 (E. Best, *Following Jesus* 81-82; also for other arguments). One wonders whether the similarity between Jesus' name as the basis for receiving a child and Jesus' name as the basis for not forbidding an exorcist does not connect vv 37 and 38-39 at least as well as the similarity between receiving a child "on the basis of" (ἐπί) Jesus' name and giving disciples a cup of water "in name that" (ἐν ὀνόματι ὅτι) they are Christ's would connect vv 37 and 41, or at least as well as the similarity between receiving a child and not causing a little one to stumble would connect vv 37 and 42. It stretches our general impression of Mark's uncreativity (which does not rule out a large amount of compositional activity in writing up available data, however) to say that he has transformed James' and John's asking whether Jesus wants them to call down fire from heaven on Samaritans (Luke 9:52-54) into John's announcement that the disciples have forbidden an independent exorcist to use Jesus' name. The wideness of the differences is too obvious to detail.

The uniqueness of John's playing a solo role favors the historicity of the story in vv 38-40. S. Eitrem (*Some Notes* 4-5) thinks it probable that the independent exorcist used Jesus' name as one among many names (v 38). Perhaps so, but we may hesitate to attribute to an apparently Jewish exorcist in first century Palestine the syncretism that caused pagan exorcists to draw magical names from a variety of sources. Hence, Eitrem's further speculations that Jesus exercised leniency out of common sense, out of pity for the possessed, out of recognition that his name worked ex opere operato, or out of desire to mobilize as much support as he could to defeat Satan in behalf of God's rule also become doubtful.

The contrast between the independent exorcist's successful use of Jesus' name and the unsuccessful use of Jesus' name by Sceva's seven sons (Acts 19:13-17; cf. Acts 8:9-24; 13:6-11) disfavors leniency without regard to the allegiance mentioned in v 40. It also disfavors Christian fabrication of a story which portrays a non-follower's use of Jesus' name as successful. The additional contrast with Matt 7:22, where as a result of Christian redaction we read of false prophets who have cast out demons in Jesus' name (cf. R. H. Gundry, *Matthew* 131-32; I. H. Marshall, *Luke* 563), likewise disfavors Christian fabrication of a story which portrays a non-follower as using Jesus' name not only successfully but also with Jesus' approval. Nor would we expect Christians to make up a story in which the Twelve appear in the bad light of intolerance over against a tolerant Jesus (see pp. 1-15 against the view of T. J. Weeden [*Traditions in Conflict* passim] and others that Mark treats the Twelve as ecclesiastical enemies). We might also hesitate, then, to separate v 40 from vv 38-39 either in pre-Marcan tradition or in the life of Jesus.

The counter argument that Jesus' name would not have been used in exorcism during his lifetime has some strength, but is considerably weakened by the immediacy with which his name begins to be used after his lifetime not only in exorcism but also in miracle-working and prayer and, above all, in the preaching of eternal salvation. The counter argument may also underestimate the impact that he made on his contemporaries while he was still ministering. Is it too much to suppose that the disciples used his name after his lifetime because they had used it on their Galilean mission during his lifetime? Is it too much to suppose that they saw the independent exorcist when they were apart from Jesus on that mission? "Because he was not following us" (v 38) hardly reflects a later setting in which church leaders are followed (so, e.g., H. Anderson 236; cf. H. J. Held in *Kirche* 91-92), for "follow" is not so used in Acts–Revelation. Not even Acts 13:43 represents such a technical usage.

To interpret the independent exorcist as anachronistically representing non-Christians who sympathize with persecuted Christians reads a backdrop of persecution into the story. But the text of the story gives no evidence of such a backdrop; and the foregoing and following verses speak positively about receiving the disciples and giving them a cup of water, not negatively about their being rejected and pursued. Moreover, the phrase "in name that (ὅτι) you are Christ's" (v 41, literally translated) will give a reason that could motivate only a fellow disciple to give a cup of water.

Κακολογέω does not carry a strong enough meaning to support the argument that κακολογῆσαί με, "to speak evil of me" (v 39), reflects a churchly rather than a Jesuanic locution and setting (against E. Best, *Following Jesus* 82-83). In 1 Cor 12:3 Paul uses the much stronger language of anathema (contrast BAGD and LSJ s.v. κακολογέω). See Best, op. cit. 84, against the view that identifies the independent exorcist with Paul. The difference between telling about an exorcism and performing exorcisms in Jesus' name blunts the argument of D. E. Nineham (194) that Jesus' ordering the Gergasene ex-demoniac to go tell his family how great things the Lord had done for him (5:19) would have forestalled the disciples' forbidding the independent exorcist.

P. Fiebig (*Wundergeschichten* 35-36) cites the use of Jesus' name in a miracle that a non-Christian Jew intended to perform but did not. Josephus (*Ant.* 8.2.5 §§46-47) writes about the use of Solomon's name in an exorcism. Solomon was an earthly figure, and it was his earthy wisdom concerning roots that contributed to the exorcism; so exorcism in the name of Jesus does not necessarily imply a heavenly Christology and therefore a suitably late date (against E. Haenchen 327).

J. K. Elliott (in *NT Textual Criticism* 57-58) argues that in v 38 Marcan duality favors the v.l. "who does not follow us, and we forbade him, because he does not follow us." But the external evidence favoring this v.l. looks inferior (A K Π *pler*); and Marcan duality normally features different and more specific wording in the second member, and that without interruption, whereas "and we forbade him" interrupts here and "does not follow us" is simply repetitive. Therefore we are dealing with conflation (cf. B. M. Metzger, *Textual Commentary* ad loc.).

In v 39, according to W. Schmithals (431), Mark takes "stop forbidding him" from the source behind 10:14, where the command has greater suitability because of the immediate presence of the ones not to be forbidden. But the verb is often used distantly (see Luke 6:29; 11:52; 23:2; Acts 11:17; 1 Cor 14:39 et passim). See K. Beyer, *Semitische Syntax* 1/1. 213, on the Semitic construction in v 39. In v 40, according to H. Fleddermann in *CBQ* 43 (1981) 65-66, Mark redacts Q (= Matt 12:30 par. Luke 11:23) by reversing "the one not being with me is against me" (with consequent loss of not gathering and scattering), by expanding it to include disciples ("us"), and by weakening the bond from personal attachment ("with") to general support ("for") — all for adaptation to the story of the independent exorcist. But we need other evidence to support a Marcan boldness that would lead to a reversal of Jesus' meaning. Here, the reversal would be so complete that historical probability lies on the side of his having made related statements differing according to the needs of separate occasions or — better — that Matt 12:30 and Luke 11:23 do not represent Q, but represent Matthew's characteristically bold redaction and the secondary influence of Matthew on Luke (R. H. Gundry, *Matthew* 235-36).

K.-G. Reploh (*Lehrer* 149-50) and R. Bultmann (*HST* 24-25) argue that v 40 did not originally go with v 39, because v 39 has already given a reason for v 38 and because "us" in v 40 does not fit "me" in v 39 but does fit the persecution of Mark's church ("against us"). Persecution is not in view, however. The independent exorcist certainly does not represent persecutors, either originally or in his Marcan setting. There is no law against supporting a statement with more than one reason. (Verse 41 will give yet another reason.) Mark may insert γάρ, "for," into sayings that stood side by side from the start but without that conjunction. And though "us" in v 40 differs from "me" in v 39, it harks back to "us" in v 38; so one could equally well argue that v 40 originally went with v 38 and that Mark or someone before him inserted v 39.

More specifically on the pronouns, in v 39 Jesus used "you" (plural) to address the disciples and "me" to discuss the use of his name in exorcism. He switches to "us" in v 40 because John has said that the independent exorcist was not following "us" (v 38). In v 41 Jesus will return to "you" (plural) to make possible a description of the disciples as belonging to him ("you are Christ's").

That Jesus had to be told about the independent exorcist excluded Jesus from the "we" who saw that exorcist. That the "we" who saw him excluded Jesus favors that the "us" whom the exorcist was not following did not include Jesus. That the independent exorcist was not following at the time the disciples saw him (N.B. the imperfect tense of ἠκολούθει) confirms that "us" as well as "we" excluded Jesus. This exclusion poses no problems, however, to Jesus' including himself now that the disciples are present with him in v 40. Moreover, a statement in Cic. *Lig.* 33 similar to the one in v 40 suggests that Jesus draws on a proverb (H. Baltensweiler in *TZ* 40 [1984] 130-36). If so, "us" loses some of its specificity and the distinction between "us" as the disciples and "us" as the disciples plus Jesus is dulled. Though these multiple considerations do not prove the original unity of the sayings in vv 39-41, they do show that there is no need to see in the pronominal changes any evidence favoring different origins (against J. Gnilka 2. 59 et al.). The alliteration, assonance, and paronomasia seen by M. Black (*Aramaic Approach* 169-71) in the Aramaic possibly underlying vv 39ff. tend against theories of heavy redaction, creation, and interpolation by Mark.

Verse 41 does not merely give an example of someone "for us" (v 40; so H. Fleddermann in *CBQ* 43 [1981] 66). The independent exorcist has already provided that. Moreover, γάρ, "for," makes v 41 ratiocinative, not exemplary; and "because you are Christ's" and the following asseveration would be otiose in an example. For giving a cup of water as minimal hospitality, see Prov 25:21; L. Goppelt in *TDNT* 6. 159. Giving a cup of water probably implies that the one given the drink is a traveling preacher (cf. Matt 10:42, whose context adds the element of persecution — R. H. Gundry, *Matthew* 202-3).

G. Wohlenberg (259) follows the v.l. ἐν (τῷ) ὀνόματί μου, "in my name" (א* C³ D Θ W *f*¹³ Majority Text latt sy^hmg), and suggests that Mark interpretatively adds "because you are Christ's." But this v.l. looks easier and therefore inferior. On the ground that "because you are Christ's" contradicts Jesus' rebuke of Peter's confession of Jesus as the

Christ, H. C. Waetjen (*Reordering of Power* 160-61) conjecturally emends the text to read "for whoever will give you a cup of water to drink in my name." But 8:30 defines the rebuke as a prohibition of telling anyone that Jesus is the Christ, not as a denial that he is; and the rebuke in 8:33 has to do with the Passion, not with christhood (cf. 1:1; 14:61-62; and the notes on 8:27-33 that even prior to Mark the rebuke in 8:33 did not relate to Peter's confession).

A back reference to Peter's confession does not require Marcan redaction here; for if in Jesus' life Peter has already confessed him as the Christ, Jesus may refer to himself as such. The argument that the anarthrousness of Χριστοῦ (v 41) betrays late, churchly use of Χριστός as a personal name rather than as a title (its original use) has some force but overlooks the possibility that the anarthrousness is due to the notion of possession in the genitive case rather than to a non-titular, personal use of Χριστός. For in the very similar passage 1 Cor 1:12-13, Χριστοῦ occurs anarthrously as a possessive genitive, but the arthrousness of the immediately following ὁ Χριστός (and this despite the anarthrousness of the parallel Παῦλος) shows the tenuousness of denying the titular sense in the preceding anarthrous occurrence (cf. the switch from arthrousness in 1 Cor 15:23 to anarthrousness in 2 Cor 10:7). Besides, it is as easy to imagine that late personal use of Χριστός led to the dropping of an original definite article as it is to imagine late Christian fabrication of the whole phrase "in name that you are Christ's." The very awkwardness and Semitic archaism of the phrase militates against late Christian fabrication (J. Schmid 279) and for Matthew's smoothing it out (Matt 10:42) rather than depending on an earlier version (R. H. Gundry, *Matthew* 202-3). The comparable Pauline passages display none of this awkwardness and archaism (cf. also Rom 8:9). The putting of a parenthetical phrase such as "truly I say to you" between a relative clause and a main clause (so v 41) corresponds to Semitic style (K. Beyer, *Semitische Syntax* 1/1. 193).

The parallel in Luke 17:1-2 (cf. Matt 18:6-7, too) is usually traced to Q and regarded as more original than Mark 9:42. But among other features of Luke's version, its nature as a periodic sentence makes this judgment doubtful. The probably Semitic character of Mark's casus pendens resumed by an unemphatic personal pronoun (E. C. Maloney, *Semitic Interference* 86-90, 99-104) and his probably Semitic use of the positive for the comparative in καλόν (see the following notes) increase the doubt. Luke's lack of "who believe in me" might be taken as favorable toward omitting the phrase in Mark (cf. the vv.ll., which omit only εἰς ἐμέ, "in me," however, just as the presence of the phrase in Matthew is often taken as the source of a scribal insertion in Mark. The external support for the phrase is strong, however; and apart from the possibility of a shorter version in Q, the length of Luke's periodic sentence and the lack of a contextual referent for "these" may have led to omission of the phrase. Its inclusion in Mark will forge a link with 8:29, as did "Christ" in 9:41. Its rejection (cf. Acts 2:44; 19:18; Eph 1:19; 2 Thess 1:10) will dull the edge of questions concerning historicity (cf. the notes on v 41).

W. Schmithals (432-33) thinks that in v 42 Mark uses part of the Q-saying and saves the rest of it for use in 14:21 ("woe to . . . through whom," as in Luke 17:1). It is equally possible that Q amalgamated two similarly worded sayings or that Jesus spoke similarly on more than one occasion. 14:21 will deal with the betrayer Judas Iscariot, yet he is never portrayed as a cause of stumbling. On the contrary, it is Jesus who in the passion narrative will be portrayed as such (14:27, 29 par.). Therefore it is unlikely that in "woe to . . . through whom" we have anything more than a locution that Jesus used more than once. But does Mark 9:42 come from Q or a pre-Q tradition, a specifying adaptation to the Marcan context occurring in the process (βέβληται replacing ἔρριπται to go with βληθῆναι in vv 45, 47, for example — see H. Fleddermann in *CBQ* 43 [1981] 67-69)? Or was Q's version separated from a pre-Marcan but Marcan-like context and generalized?

K. L. Schmidt (*Rahmen* 234) includes the independent exorcist as well as the children in "these little ones who believe in me" (v 42). But like "such as these" (τοιούτων) in v 37, "these" (τούτων) more naturally limits the referent to children who are present, one of whom Jesus took and hugged in vv 36-37. This limitation also militates against inclusion of all believers in the church (so T. Söding, *Glaube* 287-90; W. Schmithals 433 et al.). One may treat "these" as a merely Semitic way of individualizing the members of a group (cf. M. Black, *Aramaic Approach* 96), but the singling out of a child in vv 36-37 favors a stronger meaning.

If v 42 were divorced from its present context, we could interpret "these little ones who believe in me" as an epithet hurled at Jesus' disciples to characterize them as simpletons and to dissuade them from faith in him (so J. Jeremias, *NT Theology* 1. 111; cf. M. J. Borg, *Conflict* 204). But the present context favors a reference to children. Also favoring such a reference are Jesus' reception of children according to 10:13-16 parr. and the present combination of an address to the disciples with the demonstrative pronoun "these," which distinguishes "the little ones" from the disciples. Only if this saying was originally addressed to non-disciples would the epithetic interpretation work (cf. J. Ernst 281). But nowhere else in the NT are non-disciples said to be the cause of stumbling; yet professing disciples, or Christians, are said to be such (vv 43, 45, 47 parr.; Matt 13:41; 16:23; 17:27; Rom 14:13, 21; 16:17; 1 Cor 8:13 [bis]; 1 John 2:10; cf. Rev 2:14).

What sorts of sins are represented in vv 42-43, 45, 47 by stumbling? Though stumbling may represent a wide variety of sins (see 4:17 for apostasy, 6:3 for unbelief, and 14:27, 29 for cowardice, to take only other Marcan examples) and though hand, foot, and eye may likewise and individually engage in a wide variety of sins (the hand in theft and violence, for example, the foot in consorting with the wicked and running to do evil, the eye in covetousness and stinginess — see the concordance and Justin *1 Apol.* 15.2; *Sentences of Sextus* 13), the collocation of stumbling because of hand, foot, and eye and also of causing little ones to stumble makes a striking parallel with *b. Nid.* 13b, which speaks against adultery with the hand (masturbation) and with the foot (adultery in the normal sense, with the penis, euphemistically called a foot) and against playing with children (one interpretation of which is pederasty). According to this same rabbinic passage, moreover, it is good that the offender's stomach be split so that he not go down to the pit of destruction (cf. Jesus' similar statements, beginning with "it is good"); and the earlier *m. Nid.* 2:1, a quotation of which begins *b. Nid.* 13a, prescribes cutting off the hand of a masturbater (cf. Jesus' commands to cut off an offending hand or foot). Jesus may therefore build on a Jewish tradition that condemned pederasty and prescribed cutting off the hand of a masturbater and the penis of an adulterer. If so, the whole of vv 42-48 deals with sexual sins. The rabbinic material contains no reference to a lustful eye. Whether such a reference has failed to survive or whether Jesus adds it would be hard to tell. To maintain parallelism with having two hands over against being maimed and to enable a continuation of this parallelism with having two eyes over against being one-eyed, he speaks of having two feet over against being lame. Thus is lost the euphemism of a foot for the penis. A reference to adultery is not necessarily lost, however; for the foot may lead a man into the house of another man's wife as well as into the house of a harlot (cf. Prov 5:1-20; 6:20-35; against W. Denning in *NTS* 36 [1990] 130-41, esp. 138, though in most respects Denning's investigation of the rabbinic parallel deserves praise). Of course, it takes two feet to walk into a house of adultery or harlotry; and a lustful look normally engages both eyes. But Jesus commands the cutting off of one foot and the gouging out of one eye both to maintain parallelism with the cutting off of the one hand used in masturbation (as also in *m. Nid.* 2:1; *b. Nid.* 13ab) and to set up the contrasts between going to hell with a pair and entering life in God's kingdom though only one of a pair remains. Without at least one foot a person could not even limp into the kingdom. Without at least one eye a person could not see to enter the kingdom at all. It is another question whether Mark's audience of Gentiles undersood Jesus' warnings in terms limited to sexual behavior, or whether Mark intended them to do so. He is interested in the explosive force of Jesus' teaching, not in its ethical content.

With metaphorical language, v 42 comes close to poetic justice in that just as in the offense a stone causes stumbling, so in the punishment a stone causes sinking (cf. Prov 26:27; also Exod 15:4-5; *Jub.* 4:31-32). J. A. Kleist (147-50) notes the modal use of the indicative in ἐστιν, "would be." This indicative and the use of the positive for the comparative in καλόν rest on a Semitic substratum (cf. Acts 20:35; Gal 4:27; M. Black, *Aramaic Approach* 117; E. C. Maloney, *Semitic Interference* 192-96; P. Joüon, *Grammaire* 141g, n. 6). This use is generally recognized for vv 43, 45, 47; but the use of μᾶλλον, "rather," in the context of a comparative at 5:26; 7:36, to take only Marcan examples (cf. 14:31), favors the positive for the comparative also in v 42, where καλόν and μᾶλλον both occur. The meaning of μᾶλλον implies that the as yet undescribed fate of the person who causes stumbling is so bad as to make being cast into the sea with a heavy millstone around the neck comparatively good. For execution by drowning, see Plut. *Mor.* 257D; Polyb. 2.60.8; Suet. *Aug.* 67; Diod. Sic. 14.112; 16:35; Josephus *Ant.* 14.15.10 §450; idem *Ag.Ap.* 1.34 §306-8.

The absence of a persecutor in the text or context spoils the attempt of B. M. F. van Iersel (*Reading Mark* 135-36 and in *NedTTs* 24 [1980] 26-27 and in *Fructus Centesimus* 335-38) to avoid self-mutilation in Mark 9:43, 45, 47. He interprets those verses to mean that disciples should not recant even though a persecutor should maim them. That it is your hand, foot, or eye rather than a persecutor that makes you stumble into sin, that it is you, not a persecutor, who does the mutilation to yourself, and that the mutilation is commanded also undermine this view (contrast 2 Maccabees 7, cited by van Iersel).

H. Koester (in *HTR* 71 [1978] 151-53) uses Quint. *Inst.* 8.3.75 to argue against literal mutilation by anyone and for church discipline instead (cf. J. I. H. McDonald in *Studia Biblica 1978 II* 174-75). But in Quintilian's comparison between our executing even criminals related to us by blood and physicians' amputating mortified limbs, the amputation is not self-performed as in 9:43-48. Moreover, Koester's interpretation forces him to treat entering into life, or into God's kingdom, as "a hyperbolic transgression of the parameters of the parable"; and B. M. F. van Iersel (in *Fructus Centesimus* 334-35) points out that Paul does not speak of expulsion when using the metaphor of a body for the Church, but uses the completely different metaphor of a leavened lump of dough when speaking of expulsion from the Church (see 1 Cor 5:6-8). Self-mutilation likewise militates against drawing parallels with Xen. *Mem.* 1.2.51-55 and related Socratic tradition (contrast esp. Pl. *Symp.* 205E) and then interpreting the amputations as figurative of forsaking house, brothers, sisters, mother, father, children, or fields for the sake of Christ and the gospel (10:29; so H. Hommel in *ZNW* 57 [1966] 1-23). If the command in Col 3:5, "Therefore kill [your] members [that are] on the earth," derives from Mark 9:43, 45, 47, it veers from Jesus' literalism by defining "members" (μέλη) as "fornication, uncleanness, [etc.]."

Mark's use of σε, "you," for the subject of infinitives in vv 43, 45, 47 might be considered the Graecization of a Semitic σοι, "for you," represented in Matt 18:8-9 (so J. Gnilka 2. 65 with appeal to K. Beyer, *Semitische Syntax* 1/1. 80 n.). But Matthew's σοι may echo the σοι that is determined by συμφέρει, "it is advantageous," in Matt 5:29-30 rather than by Semitic syntax. The irony that the eyesight which keeps you from literal stumbling leads you into moral stumbling does not have so much bite as in Matt 5:29-30; for here "eye" comes last (v 47), there it comes first.

J. Gnilka (2. 63) thinks that the double form in Matt 5:29-30 (eye–hand) is more original than the triple form in Mark 9:43-48 (hand–foot–eye). On the contrary, Matthew advances the eye to first position to link it with lust and adultery in the preceding verse. It is then enough for him to retain the hand, omit the foot, and later — in 18:8-9 — make up for the omission by combining the hand and the foot in a single saying so as to form a pair of sayings with addition of the eye-saying and thus to confirm that the double form is due to his redaction.

On Gehenna, see J. Jeremias in *TDNT* 1. 657-58; H. P. Rüger in *Markus-Philologie* 77; C. Milikowsky in *NTS* 34 (1988) 238-41; and other literature cited in BAGD s.v. γέενα. To Milikowsky's distinction between Gehenna for disembodied souls, beginning right after death, and Gehenna for bodies and souls, beginning not till the Resurrection and Last Judgment, should be added the possibility of living right up to the Last Judgment and therefore not needing resurrection. Did Mark or someone before him add "into the unquenchable fire" (v 43) to explain "into Gehenna" to Gentile readers? Such an explanation might have come from v 48, which in turn may have been drawn from Isa 66:24 LXX and added to explain "into Gehenna" in v 47. Since the LXX merely mirrors the MT of Isa 66:24, however, v 48 may depend directly on the MT. *Tg. Isa* 66:24 provides another possible source, especially since a reference to Gehenna occurs there, as here. One could equally well theorize that the reference to fire in v 49 presupposes similar references in vv 43, 48 in an originally connected series, that the references in vv 43, 48 attracted v 49 from an originally independent station, or that references to fire were added to vv 43, 48 for assimilation to v 49 whether or not the sayings were originally connected. "Of fire" in Matt 18:6 shows that Matthew found "into the unquenchable fire" in the text of Mark 9:43 that he used.

J. M. Ross (in *NovT* 25 [1983] 63-64) argues for the originality of vv 44, 46 (A D Θ *f*¹³ Majority Text lat sy^{p,h} Bas) that there was no reason to insert them, whereas omission would eliminate redundancy. But there *was* a reason to insert them: insertion made for a more complete parallelism in sayings that are otherwise so closely parallel that final references to fire and Gehenna in vv 43, 45 almost cry out for the follow-up which is attached to the final reference to Gehenna in v 47. Therefore the weightier external evidence favoring omission of vv 44, 46 (ℵ B C L W Δ Ψ 0274 *f*¹ 28 565 892 *pc* k sy^s co) deserves the nod.

In Isa 66:24 "their" refers to transgressors. It loses that referent in Mark 9:48 and either lacks an antecedent or refers to the two hands, the two feet, and the two eyes that are thrown into Gehenna. According to K. Bornhäuser, *Gebeine* 13, 23, the worm's not dying and the fire's not being quenched mean that nothing of the corpse is left over for resurrection and participation in eternal life — in a word, annihilation. But these expressions seem more likely to mean that the worm and the fire feed forever on the body of the damned. The conjunction of fire and worms with weeping in pain forever in Jdt 16:17 supports this opinion (cf. Sir 7:17). Death and resurrection do not come into the picture. Jesus speaks of those living at the time of the consummation, who will therefore go directly into God's kingdom or be thrown directly into Gehenna.

W. W. Fields (in *GTJ* 6 [1985] 299-304) suggests that "will be salted" goes back to the Hebrew and Aramaic מלח, which means to be destroyed as well as to be salted (see also P. Parker in *New Synoptic Studies* 71-72). But Judg 9:45, the first cross-reference cited for this view, speaks of sowing a city with salt after its destruction, not by way of destroying it, and therefore does not favor the suggestion. The second cross-reference, Isa 51:6, uses מלח for destruction by dispersal in the manner of smoke, which does come close to the destruction by fire in Mark. But since everyone will be salted with fire yet not everyone destroyed by fire (cf. the foregoing comments), this suggestion lacks conviction.

If Jesus referred to the fiery destruction of Sodom and Gomorrah in Lot's time (see Matt 10:15 par. Luke 10:12; Matt 11:23-24; Luke 17:28-32; and commentaries ad loc.), the present association of salt and fire may derive from the turning of Lot's wife into a pillar of salt (cf. Luke 17:32 ["Remember Lot's wife"] with Gen 19:24-26). Fire and brimstone rained down like sprinkled salt (see J. Jeremias, *Unknown Sayings* 78). Or the association of salt and fire in both Lev 2:11-16 and Ezek 43:24 may have suggested their present association. Yet those passages do not deal with judgment. At the level of diction Lev 2:13a LXX remains a possibility of influence on Jesus' saying, however. Common to them are the words "every" and "will be salted" (contrast the MT: "you shall salt") and the placement of the dative of means before the verb. A personal reference will have replaced "gift of your sacrifice," and "with fire" will have replaced "with salt."

J. D. M. Derrett (*Studies* 1. 25-29) interrelates v 49 with vv 43-48 by noting that both salt and fire were used in amputations, the latter for cauterization, the former as a disinfectant. But the text speaks of being salted *by means of* fire, which is not the same as the use of salt *and* fire. Furthermore, the universality of "everyone" in v 49 disagrees with the conditionality of the "if"-clauses and their subjunctive mood in vv 43-48 (see B. M. F. van Iersel in *Fructus Centesimus* 334 for further criticism of Derrett's view). The universality of "everyone" also disagrees with salt as symbolizing the preservation of sufferers in Gehenna that they may forever burn without being burned up, that worms may forever eat on them without eating them up (M.-J. Lagrange 254). Jesus' disciples will escape such a fate yet are included in the prediction that everyone will be salted with fire.

The interpretation of fire as purifying and of salt as standing for persecution (cf. Num 31:22-23; Prov 27:21; Isa 48:10; 1 Cor 3:10-15; 1 Pet 1:6-7; 4:12; Rev 3:18) has no contextual support. The restriction of v 49 to true disciples (so W. L. Lane 349; F. Hauck in *TDNT* 1. 229 et al.) yet again runs into difficulty with the universality of "everyone." D. C. Allison, Jr. (*End* 124-28), thinks that the universal "everyone" includes Jesus: he, too, will suffer the eschatological woes. But Jesus is the thrower of fire onto the earth, not one on whom it falls (Luke 12:49). It is being baptized and drinking that represent his own suffering (see Luke 12:50 [N.B. the adversative δέ, "but"]; Mark 10:38-39 and contrast the synonymity in Ps 11:6). Moreover, as the Son of man who will come from heaven at the close of the messianic woes, he will be absent during them (see esp. Luke 17:22-23 parr.). One could suppose that he considers his coming death as the start of the messianic woes. But his prediction that he will rise after three days blocks that avenue. At least by present context, then, fire means future judgment. If Jesus portrays himself as the Son of man who will come as judge, he does not count as a true exception to the universal "everyone" who will be salted with fire, i.e. judged. The judge stands in a class by himself. He is not subject to judgment. See R. Pesch (2. 116-18) on the interpretation of salt and fire as the preparation of food and thereby as a symbol of new birth or persecution; also on other interpretations (so, too, H. Anderson 239). Of course, if we disengage v 49 from its present context (cf. V. Taylor [413], who discounts γάρ, "for," as a compiler's addition), almost any guess is as good as another.

Attempts to distinguish between tradition and redaction in v 50 — e.g., to assign "salt is good" and "be at peace with one another" to redaction (see, e.g., H.-J. Klauck, *Allegorie* 280-86; J. Gnilka 2. 63) — depend on guesswork more than on data. According to G. Bertram (in *TDNT* 4. 837, n. 42), v 50 does not set out the possibility that salt may lose its saltiness, but denies that it can (cf. *b. Bek.* 8b) and thereby denies that God's rule can lose its power. The contrast between "salt is good" and "if the salt should become saltless" — a contrast indicated by the adversative δέ, "but," which introduces the clause on becoming saltless — stands against this interpretation. So also does Matt 5:13. The lack of a substitute for salt does not imply the indestructibility of salt, as Bertram argues.

G. Schwarz (*Jesus und Judas* 41-42) suggests that salt becomes saltless when it is not broken up so as to be used for seasoning, that its being broken up stands for Jesus' death, and that the use for seasoning stands for redemption. As a whole, then, the saying figuratively expresses the necessity that Jesus die if redemption is to be purchased. Nothing in the immediate context favors a figurative allusion to his redemptive death, however. Within the saying there is no reference to the breaking up of salt. Becoming salt*less* (the

Greek contains an α-privitive) hardly equates with the failure of salt to be broken up. And only with great difficulty would the breaking up of salt have stood for Jesus' death and seasoning for redemption, anyway. The association of salt with seasoning (ἀρτύσετε) disfavors the suggestion of L. Köhler (*Kleiner Lichter* 73-76) that the salt which becomes saltless consists in slabs of salt which enhance burning in ovens but eventually have to be replaced because the heat has changed their chemical composition. On salt, see the rabbinic passages cited in Str-B 2. 21-23.

W. L. Lane (349-50) interprets good salt as "allegiance to Christ and the gospel," which allegiance then generates peace among Christian believers: "Have salt in yourselves, *then* you will be able to maintain peace with one another" (cf. BDF §442[2]; D. E. Nineham 257; E. Best, *Following Jesus* 88). But since allegiance to Christ and the gospel came up quite far back in the passage (vv 38-41), it is simpler to give the καί in v 50 its usual meaning "and" rather than "then." The result is synonymous parallelism in which the prosaic second clause interprets the figurative first clause. Καί then has the force of "i.e."; and ἐν ἑαυτοῖς does not mean "in yourselves," but "among yourselves," in agreement with the parallel ἐν ἀλλήλοις, "among one another" (cf. esp. 10:43-44; 1 Thess 5:13 and see M. Lattke in *ZNW* 75 [1984] 44-59). The delay of ἅλα, "salt," so as to make both clauses start with a verb plus an ἐν-phrase favors this synonymous interpretation. To have salt, then, means to share salt as in peaceful fellowship at table.

Citing as a parallel the first part of *Derek Ereṣ Zuṭa*, W. Nauck (in *ST* 6 [1953] 166-70) interprets the command to have salt among yourselves as a command to exercise intelligence. But the rabbinic passage is not hortatory, nor is it entirely clear in that passage that salt does represent intelligence; and the Marcan context does not support a figure for intelligence. So both the parallel and the interpretation are questionable.

The possibility of a wordplay between מלכות, "kingdom," and מלח, "salt," tends toward an original unity of the sayings in vv 47-50. But the outgrowing interpretations of F. C. Grant (*Earliest Gospel* 116) that "have salt ἐν yourselves" means to control yourselves and of J. A. Baird (*Justice* 176) that it means to have God's rule in yourselves lack the specificity required by the following command to be at peace among yourselves. Matt 5:9; Rom 12:18; Heb 12:14 do not offer very good cross-references; for they command the pursuit of peace with all people (cf. Col 4:5-6, which couples salt with gracious speech in answering "each one" of "the outsiders"), whereas here Jesus commands peace among his disciples, as Paul commands peace among Christians in 2 Cor 13:11; 1 Thess 5:13. These latter two passages may echo dominical tradition, though some would infer Pauline influence on Mark (see, e.g., E. Wendling, *Entstehung* 111).

JESUS' DEMONSTRATION THAT DIVORCE IS WRONG
AND REMARRIAGE ADULTERY

10:1-12 (Matt 19:1-12; Luke 9:51; 16:18; cf. Matt 5:31-32)

The account of Jesus' pronouncements on divorce and remarriage starts with his going to Judea (v 1) and the Pharisees' asking him about divorce (v 2). It continues with his answering by means of a question of his own regarding the Mosaic Law (v 3), the Pharisees' answer (v 4), and his response to it (vv 5-9). Finally, the disciples ask him about the foregoing dialogue (v 10), and he condemns divorce and remarriage both by a man (v 11) and by a woman (v 12).

10:1 *(Matt 19:1-2; Luke 9:51)* "From there" means from the house in

Capernaum mentioned in 9:33. "Having stood up" reverses the seated position that Jesus took in 9:35 (cf. 7:24 with comments). The present historical tense of ἔρχεται, "he comes," emphasizes his entrance "into the borders of Judea and Transjordan" (cf. 3:8 for the substantive use of πέραν τοῦ Ἰορδάνου), probably as the beginning of the fulfilment of his predictions that he will undergo his passion at the hands of the Jewish authorities, close to whom this move now brings him (8:31; 9:31; 10:33). Mark lumps Judea and Transjordan together. Even though he will have Jesus approach Jerusalem from the direction of Transjordan (vv 32, 46; 11:1, 11; see G. Dalman, *SSW* 233-39, on Galilean pilgrims' usually avoiding the direct route through Samaria), he mentions Judea first because the events of the Passion will take place there (cf. his putting the ultimate goal Jerusalem first in 11:1 and then working backward through Bethphage and Bethany — also 7:31, and see 1:5; 13:14 for his knowledge that Jerusalem is located in Judea). Both the present historical tense of συμπορεύονται, "travels together," and the adverb πάλιν, "again," highlight the powerful attraction of crowds to Jesus. Only here in Mark do we read of crowds in the plural. Perhaps the doubling of place names leads to the plural, crowds coming together in both Judea and Transjordan. In any case, emphasis falls on the hugeness of the number of people whom Jesus attracts. Mark uses -πορεύονται probably because the crowds are traveling to Jerusalem for the Passover Festival as Jesus is. Where he is stationary, a crowd "comes together" (συνέρχεται — 3:20), "gathers together" (συνάγεται — 4:1), or "runs together" (ἐπισυντρέχει — 9:25). "Again" relates most recently to 9:25; but single crowds, too, have repeatedly flocked to him earlier in Mark. His teaching the present crowds calls attention to his authority. To underline that authority Mark repeats "again," writes that Jesus has been in the habit of teaching crowds, puts the clause concerning this habit in a forward position, and omits the content of the teaching. Διδάσκω occurred as recently as 9:31 for his teaching the disciples, and in 6:34 most recently for his teaching a crowd; but see also 1:21, 22; 2:13; 4:1, 2; 6:2, 6; 8:31; 11:17; 12:14, 35; 14:49 — a list of references that amply justifies Mark's editorial comment.

10:2-9 *(Matt 19:3-8; cf. Matt 5:31)* The approach of the Pharisees distinguishes them from the crowds, since Jesus is already teaching the crowds, and therefore also distinguishes his remarks to the Pharisees from whatever he was teaching the crowds. The Pharisees ask him whether it is lawful for a husband to divorce his wife. According to Mark, who writes with authorial omniscience, they design their question to test Jesus (cf. 7:5 and esp. 8:11; 12:13-15); but Mark does not specify the difficulty which makes the question testing. It is enough for him that Jesus will pass the test over the effort of the Pharisees to confound him.

To highlight the back-and-forth of ensuing dialogue, vv 3, 4, 5 each open with an adversative δέ, "but." Jesus begins to outfox the Pharisees by asking a question of his own — "What did Moses command you?" — their answer to which will offer a base for his answer to follow. Ὑμῖν, "you," pinpoints the Pharisees (so also in v 5). They had asked indefinitely about "a husband." Since Jesus might have used ἡμῖν, "us," or used no pronoun whatever, ὑμῖν also distances the Pharisees from Jesus in preparation for his attributing hardheartedness to them and making his own pronouncement in opposition to the Pharisaically held command of Moses. The forward position of ὑμῖν emphasizes this specificity and distance. In the Pharisees' reply, "Moses permitted to write a certificate of divorce and to divorce," they shift from Jesus' verb of command to a verb of permission, avoid his pointed and distancing "you" by omission of a corresponding "us," take phraseology directly from Deut 24:1 (cf. Deut 24:3, too), advance "a certificate of divorce" ahead of "to write" (see the Greek text of Mark), omit "for her" and the giving of the certificate into the wife's hand, substitute divorcing for sending away from the house, and omit the direct object "her" — all in contrast with the LXX as well as with the MT and all for emphasis on divorce as a husbandly privilege (see Mur 19 [DJD 2. 104-9] for a certificate of divorce, and Mur 115. 3-4 [DJD 2. 243-54] for ἀπολύω in the sense of divorce, as here).

Jesus does not deny the statutory force of Moses' words. Far from doing so, he corrects the Pharisees' description of those words as a permission by calling them "this command." But he also shows his supernatural knowledge of Moses' purpose in writing the command, i.e. "for the purpose of [inciting] the hardness of your heart." The forward position of πρὸς τὴν σκληροκαρδίαν ὑμῶν highlights this knowledge and puts the Pharisees, who will help kill him, in a bad light as the objects of judgment (cf. Jesus' purpose of judging outsiders by telling parables — 4:11b-12; also Rom 5:20; 7:13). "But from [the] beginning of creation," also in an emphatic forward position (see 13:19 for the same phrase), paraphrases Gen 1:1 and signals the fundamental nature of Jesus' pronouncement that will confirm the judgmental purpose of Moses' command. An adversative δέ, "but," and the change of "in the beginning God created . . ." (Gen 1:1) to "from [the] beginning of creation" indicate that despite Moses' command, God has always disapproved divorce.

"Male and female he made them" comes from Gen 1:27 in agreement with the LXX (cf. Gen 5:1-2). The emphatic forward position of "male and female" prepares for the becoming one flesh of the two. Jesus assumes that the Pharisees know the OT context well enough to avoid misidentifying "he" as Moses instead of God. "On account of this a man shall leave his father and mother, and the two shall be one flesh" comes from Gen 2:24, again in agreement with the LXX (cf. Eph 5:31; 1 Cor 7:10-17). But Mark has omitted the intervening clause, "and he shall cleave to his wife," if we are to follow the reading of א B Ψ 892* *l*48 sys goth. The weight (though not volume) of this external evidence and the possibility of assimilation to the fuller forms in Genesis, in Matthew, or in both of them favor omission of the clause over its inclusion, as in other textual traditions of Mark. Thus, just as in quoting Deut 24:1 Jesus skipped an intervening member ("and he gives [a certificate of divorce] into her hand"), so also he skips an intervening member here (see R. H. Gundry, *Use of the OT* 16-17; idem, *Matthew* 378-79). The omission of "and he shall cleave to his wife" would raise the possibility that in v 7 of Mark's text ἄνθρωπος, "man," and αὐτοῦ, "his," are generic, including both the male and the female of v 6, with the result that "the two" in v 8 refers directly to man as male and female and with the further result that the "man" who in v 9 is not to separate what God has yoked together may be either male or female, either husband or wife, as in vv 11-12 (see esp. B. Hemelsoet in *Miscellanea Neotestamentica* 2. 52-55). But since the Pharisees have raised a question only about a husband's divorcing his wife, since ἄνθρωπος merely reflects the LXX (for שׁיאִ), and since a clear reference to a woman's divorcing her husband will not appear till Jesus gets alone with his disciples in a house (v 12), even without v 7b ἄνθρωπος and αὐτοῦ in v 7a mean a man as distinct from a woman (just as in the LXX) more naturally than they mean a human being as either a man or a woman.

Furthermore, good arguments favor inclusion of v 7b. The external support is widespread (D W Θ *f*¹³ Majority Text lat syᵖ'ʰ co [A C L N Δ *f*¹ *al:* τῇ γυναικί]). Without "and he shall cleave to his wife" in v 7b, "the two" in v 8a would nonsensically refer to "his father and mother" in v 7a rather than to "he" and "his wife" in v 7b, or would awkwardly jump behind "his father and mother" and pluralize the singular ἄνθρωπος earlier in v 7a, or would jump farther back — and therefore even more awkwardly — to "male and female" in v 6. One might use this nonsensicalness or awkwardness to argue for the omission of v 7b, since difficult readings are more likely to be changed than easier ones. But here the possibility of homoioteleuton cancels out that argument: a scribe might easily have skipped from the "and" that starts v 7b to the "and" that starts v 8a. Against divorce, inclusion of a man's cleaving to his wife would contribute to the argument from oneness. Non liquet on the text critical question.

Though "this command" refers to Deut 24:1, it lends an imperatival force to the future tense of "shall leave," "shall cleave" (if text critically accepted), and "shall be" in Jesus' counter quotations of Gen 1:27; 2:24. "And so no longer are they two; rather, [they are] one flesh" draws a deduction from these imperatively future quotations and pinpoints the part of them that Jesus makes the basis of his following inference: "What therefore God has yoked together [by commanding male and female to become one flesh in marriage, the leaving of father and mother implying marriage rather than a casual liaison] let not a man [with particular reference to such a man as will leave his father and mother and become one flesh in marriage with a female] separate" (cf. Mal 2:15-16). The strength of the adversative ἀλλά, "rather," the following ellipsis of "they are," and the abstract neuter ὅ, "what," instead of the generic masculine οὕς, "those whom" (cf. αὐτούς, "them," in v 6), stress becoming one flesh. "A man," mere creature that he is, stands in contrast with "God," great creator that he is. The forward positions of ὁ θεός, "God," and ἄνθρωπος, "a man," stress this contrast. The present tense in the imperative μὴ χωριζέτω, "let not . . . separate," stresses Jesus' prohibition (contrast the unemphatic aorist infinitive of this verb in 1 Cor 7:10; cf. the notes on 1:3). The Mosaic law made provision only for a man to divorce his wife, not for a wife to divorce her husband.

Gen 1:27 did not deal with marriage and divorce, but with fruitfulness, i.e. with propagation of the human race so as to fill the earth, subdue it, and rule over other creatures in it (see Gen 1:28). In Gen 2:24, "for this cause" did not refer to God's making the first human beings "male and female," but to God's making Eve out of Adam's rib. The reason for a man's leaving his father and mother, cleaving to his wife, and becoming one flesh with her was not sexual, then. It had to do with Eve's origin in Adam: since woman came from man, man should unite himself with woman to recapture their original unity. Becoming one flesh referred to what happens in sexual union, and still refers to that in Jesus' use. But Genesis did not present this sexual union as recapturing the unity of an original androgynous human being; for Genesis did not portray Adam as bisexual before God made Eve from one of Adam's ribs, and the use of a rib fails to connote the division of a bisexual being into two beings of different sexes. Nor does Jesus' saying that "they are no longer two, but one flesh" imply the recapture of an original androgynous unity; for he has dated the separateness of male and female to the very beginning: "from [the] beginning of creation, male and female he made them" (against D. Daube, *NTRJ* 71-83; idem, *Appeasement* 17-19). Jesus goes beyond Genesis, however, by making a man's and a woman's becoming one flesh the reason why the man should not divorce the woman. Jesus does not limit himself, then, to the way in which the quoted statements were intended to be taken. They were unrelated and distant from each other, and neither of them dealt with the topic of divorce. But Jesus clamps them together and draws an inference concerning that topic, an inference so powerful in its effect that the Pharisees vanish from the story.

10:10-12 *(Matt 19:9; Luke 16:18; cf. Matt 5:32)* The word order in v 10 emphasizes the topographical shift to a house, the shift in Jesus' interlocutors from the Pharisees (v 2) to the disciples (cf. the generous use of δέ, "but," to indicate shifts in speakers at vv 3, 4, 5; also 9:28 with 9:14 and, except for word order, 7:17 with 7:5, 14; 4:10 with 4:1-2 [but without reference to a house]), and the topic of the disciples' question. In the absence of a verb of motion, εἰς, "into," implies a going from the crowds and from the Pharisees into a house. "Again" may refer to the implied entry into a house (cf. 9:33 for the most recent entry into a house), or it may compare the disciples' inquiry (ἐπηρώτων) with the Pharisees' inquiry (ἐπηρώτων — v 2). The former possibility is favored by Mark's using "again" about twice as often in statements of motion as in references to speaking, and never in references to speaking where "again" could possibly apply to motion (against P. Ellingworth [in *JSNT* 5 (1979) 63-66], who neglects the implication of motion in εἰς). "Concerning this" harks back to the dialogue between the Pharisees and Jesus. The disciples' inquiry highlights the unexpectedness of what Jesus has said to the Pharisees. Mark's omitting to particularize the point of the disciples' inquiry concentrates attention on this unexpectedness as such.

The present historical tense of λέγει, "he says," stresses Jesus' authoritative pronouncement, "Whoever divorces his wife and marries another [woman] commits adultery against her; and if she, after divorcing her husband, marries another [man], she commits adultery" (cf. the prohibition of adultery in the Decalogue). If translated "against her," as above, ἐπ' αὐτήν means against the divorced wife. She is still his spouse. God's ordinance, evident since creation, makes divorce an instrument of sin instead of a way to avoid it. Divorce leads to adultery through another marriage; it does not free from adultery in another marriage.

The forwardly positioned αὐτή, "she," shifts attention from the man who might divorce his wife to the woman who might divorce him and refers to the same woman whom he might divorce, not to the woman whom he might next marry; for the woman whom he might next marry came into the picture, not in her own right, but only as the accessory necessary to Jesus' charging the man with adultery. There is no "against him" to match "against her"; but it goes without saying in a male chauvinistic society that if a man commits adultery against his wife by divorcing her and marrying another woman, a woman commits adultery against her husband by divorcing him and marrying another man (cf. Rom 7:2-3; Sir 23:22-23).

Verses 11-12 deserve closer treatment, however; for Matt 5:32; Luke 16:18 give representations of a parallel version in Q. (We may discount Matt 19:9 as based on Mark 10:11.) The indefinite relative pronominal construction in Mark (ὃς ἂν ἀπολύσῃ, "whoever divorces") looks closer to the original than does the substantive participle strengthened by πᾶς in Matthew and Luke (πᾶς ὁ ἀπολύων, "every [man] divorcing"); for though the substantive participle could go back to Hebrew, it can hardly go back to Aramaic, which Jesus is more likely to have been speaking and which is compatible with the relative pronominal construction (see K. Beyer, *Semitische Syntax* 1/1. 142, 196-99, n. 5). This judgment is strengthened by Matthew's apparent retention of the relative pronominal construction in the second saying, where Mark will lack it. The difference between ἄλλην (Mark) and ἑτέραν (Luke), both of which mean "another [woman]," is insignificant, as is that between μοιχᾶται (Mark) and μοιχεύει (Luke) for committing adultery. Mark adds "against her"; for the phrase does not appear in Q, it spoils the parallelism, and "commits adultery" is enough to condemn the man who has divorced and remarried. The addition has the purpose of heightening the explosive force of Jesus' pronouncement. In the Greco-Roman world of Mark's audience as well as in the Jewish world of Jesus' audience, a man is thought to commit adultery against the husband of a woman with whom he commits adultery, but not against his own wife (see F. Hauck in *TDNT* 4. 730-33). Jesus upsets this norm.

Unlike Jewish women, Gentile women in Mark's audience can divorce their husbands (J. Wettstein 1. 602-3; R. Leonhard in PW 5. 1241-45; T. Thalheim in PW 5. 2011-13, though see M. McDonnell in *American Journal of Ancient History* 8 [1983] 54-80 for some qualification with respect to Roman women). To apply the second saying to them, he transforms the woman who in Q is divorced by her husband into a woman who divorces her husband. The shift of the woman from object to subject causes ὃς ἐάν (so Q according to Matthew, for Luke's substantive participle again looks unoriginal) to become ἐὰν αὐτή, "if she"; and the shift from passive voice to active voice forces a change of the adverbial prepositional phrase "from a husband" into the participle's object, "her husband." It also forces the addition of ἄλλον, "another [man]," which parallels ἄλλην in v 11, to be the object of "should marry." Thus, the original parallelism of grammatical structure breaks down; and the second saying becomes less Semitic in style (K. Beyer, *Semitische Syntax* 1/1. 145). The application to women would suit, but not require, a generic interpretation of ἄνθρωπος (bis) and αὐτοῦ in vv 7, 9. But even with the omission of v 7b, as we have already seen, only by reading v 12 first would one be drawn to such an interpretation. Though Mark has revised the saying for application to Gentile women, the revision serves his larger purpose of emphasizing the explosive force of Jesus' pronouncements. For Gentiles do not consider a woman who divorces her husband and marries another man an adulteress.

Mark allows the reversal of Moses' law regulating divorce (cf. 2:23-28; 7:14-23) to stand last in the pericope as an example of his teaching, astonishing in its radicality, astonishing in its argument, astonishing in its authority. As the power of Jesus' miracles recedes from view, his pronunciatory power comes forward in ever more detail. In chaps. 8–9 he upset expectations by pronouncing that the Son of man must be killed and rise after three days, that one must lose life to save it, that Elijah has already come, that anyone who wants to be first will be last, that entering God's kingdom with a maimed body is better than going to hell with a whole body. Now in chap. 10 he upsets a norm by calling the remarriage of a divorced person adultery, and will continue to upset one norm after another by blessing children, by describing wealth as a disadvantage impossible for anyone but God to overcome, and by advocating a life of voluntary servitude. Even on his way to crucifixion, *especially* on his way to crucifixion, Mark's Jesus dumbfounds disciples and silences enemies with the explosive force of his pronouncements.

NOTES

See the notes on 8:27 that chap. 10 does not belong to a section on private ecclesiastical teaching. But a number of scholars have hypothesized a pre-Marcan catechism or a collection of dialogues and disputations behind at least large portions of chap. 10, e.g., behind vv 2-9 on marriage, behind vv 13-16 on children, behind vv 17-22 on possessions, and behind vv 35-40 on rank, to which Mark has added the instructions in vv 10-12, 23-27, the dialogue in vv 28-31, and the prediction of passion and resurrection in vv 32-34 plus the further instructions in vv 41-45. Opinions differ on details, even to the extent of omitting from the pre-Marcan source vv 13-16 and of including in it much of vv 35-40. Those who hypothesize a pre-Marcan catechism or collection agree, however, on its purpose to teach proper conduct in a Christian community and on Mark's redactional enhancement of that purpose. See R. Busemann, *Jüngergemeinde;* D. O. Via, *Ethics;* R. Pesch 2. 128-30; H.-W. Kuhn, *Ältere Sammlungen* 36-38, 146-91; E. Best, *Disciples and Discipleship* 80-83, 87-88; and K.-G. Reploh, *Lehrer* 173-210 (differently).

The text puts some roadblocks in the way of this hypothesis, however. Verses 2-9 start with a test question that comes from outside the community, viz., from the Pharisees. In vv 10-12 the disciples register no protest, disagreement, or even surprise (contrast Matt 19:10), as might be expected against the background of an ecclesiastical dispute. Though the topic of children in vv 13-16 follows naturally on the topic of marriage in vv 2-12, one might correctly counter that the question in vv 2-12 has to do with divorce more than with marriage. But the real roadblock to the ecclesiastical hypothesis consists in the fact that vv 13-16 deal with the question of Jesus' receiving children and with the necessity of the disciples' receiving God's rule as a child receives it, not with the question of the disciples' receiving children as in 9:36-37 and a putative ecclesiastical setting. Receiving

God's rule as a child receives it points to conversion, not to life in the Christian community. Similarly, vv 17-22 have to do with possessions in relation to conversion, not in relation to Christian communal life. Verses 35-40 come closest to discussing life in the Christian community. But although Jesus speaks so as to affect it, the question has to do with rank in the consummation, not at the present time. It seems better, then, to stick by Mark's usual emphasis, i.e. the norm-shattering authority with which Jesus teaches (see the foregoing comments; also W. Weiss, *"Eine neue Lehre in Vollmacht"* 31-32, against a pre-Marcan collection).

Why did Mark introduce a pericope on divorce at this point? If not because it happened to belong to an earlier collection (and even then we would have to ask why he introduced the collection as a whole at this point), perhaps because the pericope had a traditional association with the last part of Jesus' ministry in Judea and Transjordan. Because of its theological insignificance, Transjordan has the look of tradition. Additionally, to prepare for the soon coming materials that detail the physical and polemic force with which Jesus will take over the temple and argue down his opponents right in Jerusalem, Mark may now be gathering materials that demonstrate the verbal force of Jesus' pronouncements.

K. L. Schmidt (*Rahmen* 238) doubts that v 1 finishes the preceding pericope or starts the following one. He suggests instead that v 1 forms a summarizing bridge between Jesus' ministries in Galilee and in Jerusalem, and concludes that "from there" refers neither to the house nor to Capernaum in 9:33 (but, presumably, to Galilee as a whole [cf. 1:14]). A summarizing bridge — yes. But prior to the passion narrative Mark regularly starts pericopes with topographical movement, as here, and elsewhere always uses "from there" (ἐκεῖθεν) in relation to preceding entrance into a house (6:1 with 5:38-39; 6:10-11; 7:24 with 7:17; 9:30 with 9:28). In one of these instances, ἐκεῖθεν is accompanied by ἀναστάς, "standing up," a form of ἔρχομαι, "go," and εἰς τὰ ὅρια plus a genitive, "into the boundaries of," as here (see 7:24).

R. Busemann (*Jüngergemeinde* 102-3) separates v 1 from vv 2-9 because Mark's Jesus does not teach Pharisees. But linking v 1 with vv 2-9 does not make him teach Pharisees; it only makes him carry on a dialogue with them after or during his teaching of the crowds. In comparison with v 1, the "approaching" of the Pharisees in v 2 is not strong enough to provide the usual topographical shift.

See B. M. Metzger, *Textual Commentary* ad loc., on the text critical question regarding "and" between "Judea" and "Transjordan." Both the omission of "and" and the substitution with "through" seem to stem from failure to recognize Mark's reason for putting Judea before Transjordan (on which see the foregoing comments). Matt 19:1 may be taken as bearing early witness to an original lack of "and" in Mark, but may equally well be taken as contributing to a scribal omission of "and" in Mark. The redactional stretching of Judean boundaries in Matt 3:1, 5; 19:1 (see R. H. Gundry, *Matthew* 42, 45, 375-76) favors the latter possibility. The v.l. "through" erases the topographical difficulty. But easier readings are inferior, as is the external evidence for this one. The distinction between Judea and Tansjordan at 3:7-8 spoils the view of F. G. Lang (in *ZDPV* 94 [1978] 145-46, n. 4) that the καί in question is explicative: "into the borders of Judea, i.e. Transjordan."

The argument that Mark's fondness for indefinite third person plural verbs favors the omission of "approaching, Pharisees" with D it sy[s] (sa[mss]) overlooks that the omission would not leave ἐπηρώτων indefinite. The "they" who "were asking" would be the "crowds" of v 1. Elsewhere Mark does not mention a crowd or crowds first and then use a third person plural verb that could be taken as indefinite. Here, the external support for omission is comparatively weak; and the omission might even stem from knowledge that the Pharisees do not question the lawfulness of divorce as such. That they test Jesus also at

8:11; 12:15 with 12:13 favors their present inclusion. P. Ellingworth (in *JSNT* 5 [1979] 63-66) argues for omission that it would allow the disciples to question Jesus "again" in v 10. This argument, too, overlooks that omission of the Pharisees in v 2 would make the crowds the questioners.

Many Galilean pilgrims would be traveling the roads to Jerusalem. But traveling together "to him" (πρὸς αὐτόν) and prior emphasis on Jesus' attracting crowds in the places where he goes favor his attracting pilgrims from Judea and Transjordan in v 1 (cf. 3:7-8). It will therefore be likely that the large crowd in 10:46 comes from Jericho rather than from Galilee.

We have massive evidence that Matthew used Mark, little that he had narrative traditions parallel to yet more original than Mark. Elsewhere he assimilates Mark and Q to rabbinic disputes. Therefore it is more likely that in Matt 19:3 he assimilates Mark 10:2 to the rabbinic dispute over allowable grounds for divorce than that he preserves an original tradition of the Pharisees' question about the legality of divorce and that Mark has christianized the question (R. H. Gundry, *Matthew* 90-91, 377, 650 s.v. "Rabbinic language").

It is commonly thought, however, that although Matthew does not preserve the original tradition of the Pharisees' question, either Mark has christianized it and Matthew rejudaized it, or that Mark has made it up from a Christian standpoint and Matthew judaized it. Because Jews do not dispute the legality of divorce as such, but only its proper grounds (*m. Giṭ.* 9:10), Mark is supposed to have manipulated or fabricated the question so as to prepare for Jesus' denying the legality of divorce and to put the Pharisees in a bad light, i.e. in the role of his testers (cf. the notes on 8:10-12 for πειράζοντες as testing and as putting the testers on Satan's side — 1:12-13). But though the Pharisees are sometimes put in a worse than historical light, particularly by Matthew, there remains too much evidence of their antipathy toward Jesus for us to deny the possibility of their asking him a question that would justify Mark's phrase "testing him." So the issue boils down to whether Mark's version of the question is conceivable in a Jewish milieu.

J. D. Crossan (*In Fragments* 209-10) defends the possible Jewishness of the question by arguing that "if Jesus could be asked whether he accepted the Roman law on tribute in 12:13-17, he could also be asked whether he accepted the Jewish law on divorce in 10:2-9." But since he was a Jew, his acceptance of Jewish law is a less likely question to be asked than one about his acceptance of a Roman law. Others defend the possible Jewishness of the question by suggesting that the Pharisees were trying to lure Jesus into saying something on divorce that would get him in trouble with Herod Antipas and Herodias. They support their suggestion with appeals to Herod's having imprisoned John the Baptizer for criticizing his marriage to Herodias, to Jesus' having now moved (v 1) into the territory where Herod had imprisoned John, to Herodias's having requested and received the head of John because of his criticism, and to the possibility that since a Jewish woman could not divorce her husband, v 12 alludes to Herodias's having divorced her first husband to marry Herod. The evidence favoring this suggestion is not so clear as first appears. Josephus (*Ant.* 18.5.4 §136) uses διαστᾶσα (from διΐστημι, "separate") for Herodias's action. On the one hand, it may mean desertion. On the other hand, it may include divorce; for Josephus uses another compound of ἵστημι — viz., ἀφίστηι — for Salome's divorcing Costobar (*Ant.* 15.7.10 §§259-60), the cognate noun ἀποστάσιον occurs for divorce in Deut 24:1 LXX; Mark 10:4; and elsewhere, a woman often divorced her husband simply by leaving him (G. D. Fee, *1 Cor* 293-94), and a large number of Greek words for separation are used for divorce (see the following notes on v 9). John the Baptizer did not criticize the marriage of Herod to Herodias because it violated OT law concerning divorce, but because it violated OT law against a man's taking his brother's wife (cf. 6:17 with Lev 18:16; 20:21).

Nevertheless, John's example might prompt Pharisees to try luring Jesus into a statement on the related matter of divorce, a statement that would get him in trouble with

Herod and Herodias. This possibility receives no support from a woman's divorcing her husband and marrying another man in v 12, however. For the parallels in Matt 5:32b; Luke 16:18b represent a more original version (Q's) in which a woman does not divorce her husband (see the foregoing comments). So the possibility of a lure in view of John's fate remains just that, a possibility — no more. But no less, either; so we should not rule out an asking of the question by Pharisees.

Alternatively — and the greater the number of realistic possibilities, the less reason to rule out an asking of the question by Pharisees — they may ask simply out of knowledge that Jesus has made variously heretical statements (see, e.g., 2:5, 17, 27-28; 7:6-15). His future embroilment in further theological issues supports this possibility (10:17-22; 11:27-33; 12:13-17, 18-27, 28-34, 35-37). Even apart from his past statements and future embroilment, CD 4:21; 11QTemple 57:17-19 raise the possibility that other Jews whom the Pharisees consider heretical deny the lawfulness of divorce, so that Jesus might well be tested on the question of divorce. The similarity between Mark 10:6 and CD 4:21 in quoting Gen 1:27 to prove the permanency of marriage supports this possibility. CD 4:21 condemns as whoredom the taking of two wives "in their [masculine] lifetime." This condemnation may take in polygamy. But polygamy is unlikely to be primarily in view, and perhaps not at all; for it will come up for separate prohibition in regard to "the prince" (5:2; see G. Vermes, *Post-Biblical Jewish Studies* 50-56). The condemnation in 4:21 certainly takes in divorce, either by disallowing it or by redefining it as not carrying the right to remarry (cf. 1 Cor 7:10-11 under the view that χωρισθῆναι/-ῇ includes divorce in addition to desertion, or divorce by means of desertion, as favored by Mark 10:9; contrast the essential formula in an orthodox bill of divorce, "Lo, you are free to marry any man" [*m. Giṭ.* 9:1-3], no such right needing to be stated for the man). See J. A. Fitzmyer (in *H. L. Ginsberg Volume* 109-10); J. de Waard, *Comparative Study* 34, n. 1, that CD 13:17-19 has nothing to do with divorce, much less allows it. 11QTemple 57:17-19 forbids divorce: "and he shall not take in addition to her another wife, for she alone shall be with him all the days of her life; and if she dies, he shall take for himself another [wife]." Again, polygamy is unlikely to be primarily in view, and perhaps not at all; for it has already come up for separate prohibition in regard to "a king" (56:18-19). In view of the preceding "alone," the last part of 57:17-19 means that only if the wife dies shall another be taken. This exclusivity, seen also in the condemnatory reference to two wives in CD 4:21, fails to appear in Eccl 9:9, which therefore does not support a weak interpretation of 11QTemple 57:17-19 and CD 4:21 (against B. Vawter in *CBQ* 39 [1977] 532-34). Since CD 4:21 delivers a general condemnation of divorce, we should think of its prohibition to a king in 11QTemple 57:17-19 as specific rather than exclusive. Under the Pharisaic and usual supposition that by definition divorce entails the right of remarriage, it is therefore quite conceivable that Pharisees tested Jesus on the legality of divorce. There is no need to think that Mark makes up or christianizes their question. Its limitation to the right of a man to divorce his wife corresponds to a Jewish milieu, and the contrast between this narrowness and Mark's broadening of v 12 to include Gentile women who divorce their husbands disfavors his manipulation or fabrication of the question in v 2 (cf. S. Westerholm, *Jesus and Scribal Authority* 120).

To bring Deut 24:1 into the discussion, according to E. Haenchen (338-39), Mark has to make Jesus ask a question (v 3) that clumsily allows a correct response by the Pharisees (v 4). On the contrary, the question is not clumsy; for the narrative has not yet made clear what positions Jesus and the Pharisees will take. The question simply allows the Pharisees to state their position Mosaically in order that Jesus may counter it if necessary. His purpose in asking what Moses commanded is not to put the Pharisees in the embarrassing position of having to admit that Moses only permitted divorce. For Jesus himself will call Deut 24:1 "this command" (v 5). Thus it is wrong to argue that he does not directly defy the Law in that Moses did not command divorce (so E. P. Sanders, *Jesus and Judaism* 256-57). According to Jesus, Moses did command it. Jesus' own pronouncement will not rest on treating Deut 24:1 as a permission, but on treating it as a command judgmentally designed to incite the Pharisees to divorce their wives against God's ordinance. E. Schweizer (203) correctly contrasts Jesus' concern for God's will with the concern of the Pharisees for their rights, but wrongly correlates this contrast with the contrast between Jesus' talk of command and the Pharisees' talk of permission. Their talk of permission does betray a concern for rights; but Jesus denies that God's will is to be found in the command which he has asked about, and the command is Moses's, to which God's will stands in contrast.

Πρός (v 5) hardly indicates that Moses wrote Deut 24:1 "against" hardheartedness; for an emphasis on curbing hardheartedness would weaken the immediately following contrast with God's will. Moreover, Moses did allow men to divorce their wives, did not impose the requirement of giving the woman a certificate of divorce but presupposed its being given as customary, and prohibited remarriage to the same woman after she had been remarried and divorced a second time or widowed, not to protect her from male whims, but to protect her first husband from being defiled by her (cf. her defilement by a second marriage with Jesus' equating divorce-cum-remarriage with adultery — vv 11-12). Finally, the interpretation of πρός as meaning "against" rests on a humanitarian understanding of hardheartedness as inconsiderateness toward the wife, whereas biblical usage favors stubborn disobedience to God (see J. Behm in *TDNT* 3. 613-14 for references).

Perhaps, then, πρός means "with regard to" (cf. 2 Cor 5:10) and indicates a concessive view of Deut 24:1 (see E. Schwyzer and A. Debrunner, *Griechische Grammatik* 2. 509-12, on the wide range of meanings possible for πρός). But this meaning of πρός is unusual, and "this command" seems too strong for a concession. It does not pass muster to interpret Jesus' pronouncement as distinguishing God's secondary will from his primary will and to cite Ezek 20:25 in support (so J. Gnilka 2. 72; D. Daube in *JJS* 10 [1959] 1-13; K. Berger, *Gesetzesauslegung* 1. 20-22, 268-69, 540-43). Ezek 20:25 describes statutes as "not good," not because they represent God's second best, but because he uses them to incite sin and judgment. Here, Jesus' pronouncements do not improve on Moses' command. They reverse it.

In contrast with the referential meaning of πρός, the telic meaning (sometimes weakened to or combined with an ecbatic meaning) is common. Here it carries a boldness that agrees with Jesus' calling Deut 24:1 "this command" instead of a mere permission, as the Pharisees described it. But we must specify Moses' purpose in relation to the Pharisees' hardheartedness. He did not purpose to *expose* it (as thought by H. Greeven in *NTS* 15 [1968-69] 377-78; W. Weiss, *"Eine neue Lehre in Vollmacht"* 184-85). It is Jesus who does that — right here. Moses purposed to *incite* hardheartedness (cf. the use of πρὸς τὴν ἐλεημοσύνην in Acts 3:10 for the purpose of inciting alms). If πρός meant "with regard to," the Pharisees' hardheartedness would precede Moses' command as its cause and would refer to their desire for divorce. The precedence would have to be logical rather than chronological, and the reference prescient. The telic meaning more simply as well as more forcefully makes the Pharisees' hardheartedness follow Moses' command as its result and refer to the very act of divorce (cf. the concrete rather than psychological meaning of hardheartedness in the OT — B. S. Childs, *Exodus* 170-75; G. von Rad, *OT Theology* 2. 151-55).

M.-J. Lagrange (258) and E. S. Fiorenza (*In Memory of Her* 143) interpret "the hardness of your heart" broadly to mean the unwillingness of past as well as present Jewish men to accept God's will that they not divorce their wives. But Jesus is addressing the Pharisees; so they are in view at least specially and probably exclusively. We should not assume that Jesus is speaking historically or social scientifically.

According to K. Berger (*Gesetzesauslegung* 1. 508), only the LXX of Deut 24:1 lends itself to description as "this command," only "the two" of Gen 2:24 LXX links with the "male and female" of Gen 1:27, and only the ἄνθρωπος of Gen 2:24 LXX (for אִישׁ in the MT) allows both omission of "and he shall cleave to his wife" and a generic reference to the male and female of Gen 1:27. Even so, the high degree of Hellenization in first century Palestine — and Jesus grew up only several miles from the Hellenistic city of Sepphoris while it was under construction (Did Joseph and he ply their trade there [cf. R. A. Batey, *Jesus & the Forgotten City* 65-82]?) — makes Jesuanic use of the LXX a realistic possibility. After all, fragments of the LXX dating from the NT era have been found in Palestine. "And he shall cleave to his wife" shows, moreover, that in the LXX itself ἄνθρωπος is not generic but refers to a man, a male; and Jesus' argument does not require a generic interpretation of ἄνθρωπος. Ἀνήρ would work as well, i.e. would allow omission of v 7b (if it is to be text critically omitted), would refer to the male of v 6, and would allow the female of v 6 to be brought back into the picture as one of "the two" of v 8 (see E. C. Maloney, *Semitic Interference* 131-35, against treating ἄνθρωπος as a Semitic equivalent of τις, "someone"). Not even the Septuagintal reference to "the two" is necessary to Jesus' argument. "They" would refer as easily to "male and female"; and Jesus' argument rests on oneness after marriage, not on twoness beforehand. Prior twoness is only a foil to emphasize the subsequent oneness. Furthermore, the pre-NT distinctiveness of "the two" to the LXX stands in doubt. *Jub.* 3:7 supports the MT in omitting the phrase. But the Samaritan Pentateuch, Samaritan Targum, Targum Pseudo-Jonathan, Targum Neofiti I, OT Peshitta, Latin Vulgate, and Philo support inclusion (R. H. Gundry, *Use of the OT* 16-17); and some Hebrew manuscripts of the OT among the Dead Sea Scrolls have shown that Septuagintal variations from the MT often rest on a different Hebrew text. So Jesus' argument may rest, not on the LXX, but on a Hebrew text or on an exegetical tradition that informed both the LXX and other textual traditions.

It is also doubtful that the LXX of Deut 24:1 really does lend itself to description as a command. To say that it does depends on treating the future indicative verbs γράψει, δώσει, and ἐξαποστελεῖ as imperatival: "he shall write," "he shall give," and "he shall send [her] away." But the future indicative is often equivalent to an aorist subjunctive, especially when they occur in parallel clauses; and here we have reasons to choose this possibility: (1) The καί, "and," before γράψει does not normally introduce the apodosis that an imperatival future would demand; but it would make a natural continuation of the protasis begun with the second ἐάν, "if," plus the aorist subjunctive εὕρῃ, "he should find." (2) The lack of a second ἐάν before ἀπελθοῦσα γένηται ἀνδρὶ ἑτέρῳ, "going away she should become another man's" (v 2; contrast the repetition of ἐάν in v 1) favors that the second ἐάν in v 1 is continuing to govern the construction after the string of future indicative verbs. (3) The switch back to an aorist subjunctive in ἀποθάνῃ, "should die," in v 3 favors that the protasis is continuing. (4) The lack of a καί at the head of v 4 favors that not till this point does the apodosis begin. Probably, then, the preceding verbs in the LXX do not command divorce and do not provide the basis of "command" in Mark's text.

The similarity between CD 4:21 and Mark 10:6 leads J. de Waard (*Comparative Study* 30-34) to translate Mark's ἀπό . . . ἀρχῆς κτίσεως, "according to [the] principle of creation," in agreement with CD's ויסוד הבריאה, "and [the] foundation of the creation." But Mark's ἀπό is temporal, meaning "from the time of, since" (cf. 13:19), not "according to," and therefore does not allow the translation "principle" for ἀρχῆς. We should probably take the second genitive in ἀπό . . . ἀρχῆς κτίσεως as one of apposition: "since [the] beginning, i.e. since creation." "He made them," also in v 6, does not necessarily imply that ἄνθρωπος means both male and female in v 7 (so B. Hemelsoet in *Miscellanea Neotestamentica* 1. 54). It is just as possible that because God made male and female, a male human being is to leave his parents for the purpose of taking to wife a female human being. According to K. J. Thomas (in *NTS* 24 [1977-78] 87), *Gen. Rab.* 18.5 contains an interpretation of Gen 2:24, quoted in v 7, as prohibiting divorce and of Deut 24:1, alluded to in v 4, as lifting the prohibition for Jews (see also *y. Qidd.* 1.1; cf. M. R. Lehman in *ZAW* 72 [1960] 264-66). If then this tradition dates back to Jesus' time, he may be using Gen 1:27 to show that Jews, too, fall under the stricture of Gen 2:24, that Deut 24:1 does not release them from it. On the other hand, the rabbinical passage may mean that Gentiles do not limit the right of divorce to men (so H. Freedman and M. Simon, *Midrash Rabbah* 1. 145, nn. 1-3). Against modern tendency to the contrary, we should probably avoid reading more than sexual union into becoming one flesh (v 8). In 1 Cor 6:16-17 becoming one flesh refers to becoming one body with a prostitute as opposed to becoming one Spirit with the Lord, and in Eph 5:28-31 a man's becoming one flesh with his wife equates with loving his own body. See R. H. Gundry, *Sōma* 62-64.

According to D. O. Via (*Ethics* 103-5) Mark grounds the indissolubility of marriage in realized eschatology. But Jesus' argument goes back to creation, not forward to the end. So Via reasons that Jesus' argument goes back to creation to show that the last things will be like the first things (*Endzeit = Urzeit;* see *Barn.* 6:13b). Yet 12:25 will present a denial by Jesus that marriage survives the resurrection; in other words, the last things will *not* be like the first so far as marriage is concerned. Via is then driven to describe the relation between eschatologically permanent marriage and eschatologically discontinued marriage as "paradoxical." It seems better to think that Jesus is arguing on principle concerning marriage up to the resurrection (cf. the cautious comments of E. P. Sanders, *Jesus and Judaism* 256-59). Via may start off on the wrong foot by inferring that in the beginning there was no hardness of heart and that therefore the time of hardheartedness has passed: Jesus is speaking in the eschaton, when "the original vitality of the first time" is recovered for believers. But he is speaking to Pharisees about their present hardheartedness and is pronouncing on marriage in general, not on marriage among his disciples.

A. J. Hultgren (*Jesus and His Adversaries* 120-21) argues that v 9 did not originally follow vv 7-8, because vv 7-8 need no follow-up, because yoking (v 9) presents a view of marriage less binding than becoming one flesh does (vv 7-8), and because antithetic parallelism such as we find in v 9 characterizes wisdom and legal sayings but not conclusions of exegetical arguments (as here). He goes on to trace v 9 to the Hellenistic church, because according to K. Beyer (*Semitische Syntax* 1/1. 167-68) the introduction of the saying with a relative pronoun in the accusative is Greek, not Semitic; because yoking is a figure for marriage in Hellenistic culture (Xen. *Oec.* 7.30; Josephus *Ant.* 6.13.8 §309), but not in un-Hellenistic Jewish literature; and because χωρίζω occurs for divorce in Hellenistic literature (including Josephus *Ant.* 15.7.10 §259; 1 Cor 7:10, 11, 15; see further BAGD s.v.), but not in the LXX or elsewhere in the gospels.

The heavy hellenization of Palestine vitiates much of Hultgren's argumentation (cf. the present commentary, p. 22). If Josephus, a Palestinian Jew of the first century, can compare marriage to yoking and use χωρίζω for divorce, nothing forestalls Jesus from doing so, too. Later Jewish rabbis will often use the same comparison (D. Daube, *NTRJ* 73). The LXX uses so many terms for divorce (ἀπολύω, ἀποστέλλω, βιβλίον ἀποστασίου, ἐκβάλλω, ἐξαποστέλλω, and possibly ἄφεσις, ἀφίστημι, and ἀφίημι — ibid. 369) that the use of χωρίζω should not seem to violate Semitic terminology. That terminology has not narrowed down to technical language (cf. the use of still other terms by Philo and Josephus — ibid. 370-72). Beyer says only that introduction with a relative pronoun in the accusative is less frequent in Semitic than in Greek; and in the very passage cited by Hultgren, Beyer offers two examples of this construction in the Hebrew OT — Gen 41:55 and Prov 3:12 — with a corresponding translation in the LXX. Comparing the one flesh of sexual union with being yoked together weakens the marital bond not at all, as shown by the continuation of v 9: ". . . let not a man separate." Verses 7-8 do not provide a complete argument, for it is not self-evident that the creation of male and female and their becoming one flesh imply a prohibition of divorce. Jesus' interlocutors know and believe Gen 1:27; 2:24 but have not drawn his inference from those passages (cf. J. de Waard, *Comparative Study* 33-34). "Therefore" makes v 9 an exegetical deduction, one that is necessitated by the interlocutors' having failed to draw Jesus' inference. Even though we were to follow J. Sundwall (*Zusammensetzung* 63) in omitting "therefore" from an earlier version of v 9, Jesus may have adopted a wisdom saying and added the conjunction for the purpose of drawing an inference from the OT. Antithetic parallelism also characterized the inference drawn from the OT at 7:8, to which Hultgren (144, n. 98) therefore has to give the same dismissive treatment that he gives here to v 9.

Unidentified houses are mentioned not only in 10:10 (εἰς τὴν οἰκίαν πάλιν), but also in 2:1 (ἐν οἴκῳ ἐστίν); 3:20 (ἔρχεται εἰς οἶκον); 7:17 (εἰσῆλθεν εἰς οἶκον); 7:24 (εἰσελθὼν εἰς οἰκίαν); 9:28 (εἰσελθόντος αὐτοῦ εἰς οἶκον); 9:33 (ἐν τῇ οἰκίᾳ γενόμενος). There is no apparent distinction between οἰκία and οἶκος. Mark favors the anarthrous construction in prepositional phrases. The two arthrous constructions in 9:33; 10:10 cannot refer anaphorically to the last mentioned house in 9:29; for topographical shifts have occurred between 9:29 and 9:33, and between 9:33 and 10:10. The definite article at 9:33 may have pointed to Peter's and Andrew's home in Capernaum (see the notes ad loc. and 1:29). The definite article at 10:10 can hardly do so, however; for Jesus is far away in Judea or Transjordan. Perhaps it refers back to the last time the disciples made inquiry from Jesus in a house (9:28), even though the house is different. The definite article is then anaphoric so far as being in a house is concerned. It is as though Mark has written so often of entry into various houses that by the time he reaches 9:33 and 10:10, any house that Jesus enters merits a definite article even though the house is not otherwise identified (cf. E. C. Maloney, *Semitic Interference* 104-9, against a reflection of the emphatic state in Aramaic). The notes on 9:28-29 discuss the likelihood that Jesus often talked to his disciples in private homes. It is as likely that the sayings in vv 11-12 lost their narrative framework on incorporation into Q as that Mark made up a narrative framework to incorporate them here. Though the home privacy of the pronouncements to the disciples in vv 10-12 keeps us from considering vv 1-9 a pure story of controversy (contrast the absence of private pronouncements in 2:1–3:6), the phrase "testing him" in v 2 shows that the private pronouncements have not obliterated the element of controversy and Jesus' victory over his opponents.

Verses 11-12 assume that remarriage follows divorce. Jesus does not address the question whether divorce would be allowable if remarriage did not follow (cf. 1 Cor 7:10-11; Matt 19:10-12). Verses 5-9 condemned divorce. Verses 11-12 condemn remarriage as well. Since remarriage usually follows divorce, the two condemnations form a natural progression that derives from a primary historical association more easily than from secondary redactional combination. It is quite unlikely that the topic of remarriage would have arisen apart from the topic of divorce.

Without v 9, vv 11-12 do not necessarily condemn divorce, only divorce-cum-remarriage. To the extent that divorce is wrong according to vv 11-12, it is wrong only in its probably leading to remarriage, which would count as adultery. So argues D. O. Via (*Ethics* 112-14). But why would remarriage count as adultery if divorce is not wrong in and of itself, as in v 9? Verses 11-12 require the undergirding provided by v 9.

We might translate ἐπ᾽ αὐτήν in v 11, "with her." If so, the husband who divorces his first wife commits adultery with his second wife. But elsewhere Mark's Jesus does not use ἐπί in the sense "with"; yet several times the preposition means "against" (see 3:24, 25, 26; 9:12 [with comments ad loc.]; 13:8 [bis], 12; 14:48). Therefore we should keep the traditional understanding that Jesus is speaking about adultery that a husband commits against his first wife even though he has divorced her so as to marry a second wife. N. Turner (in *BT* 7 [1956] 151-52) objects that elsewhere in Mark ἐπί means "against" only in connection with physical violence, which would not fit here. But the meaning "against" does not require a connection with physical violence (see, e.g., 1 Cor 7:36; 2 Cor 1:23; 10:2); and were Turner's point nevertheless granted, it would still not be so problematic as Mark's using ἐπί for "with" nowhere else. Probably too convoluted and insufficient is Turner's combining the use of χρεμετίζω ἐπί plus an accusative, "neigh after" (as a figure of committing adultery with), in Jer 5:8 LXX with the substitution of Mark's verb μοιχάομαι, "commit adultery," plus an accusative in an allusion to Jer 5:8 at *Pss. Sol.* 8:10. Not even the influence of Jer 5:8 LXX caused *Pss. Sol.* 8:10 to use ἐπί with μοιχάομαι.

The comments on vv 11-12 have assumed that "and marries another [woman] commits adultery" in Luke 16:18a reflects Q more accurately than "makes her to commit adultery" in Matt 5:32a reflects Q. J. D. Crossan (*In Fragments* 211-12) argues to the contrary that Matthew's version reflects an earlier Jewish milieu in which a husband had the right to divorce his wife, whereas Luke's version reflects a later Gentile milieu in which the husband himself becomes an adulterer by marrying another woman after divorcing his wife. In other words, both Matt 5:32a and Matt 5:32b reflect the masculinity of Jewish law; but Luke 16:18a reflects the mutuality of Greco-Roman law, and only Luke 16:18b the masculinity of Jewish law (cf. B. Vawter in *CBQ* 39 [1977] 530-31).

Against Crossan's view, in Luke 16:18a it is only the husband who divorces his wife, as in Jewish law; and under Greco-Roman law a husband's remarrying another woman would count as adultery no more than it would under Jewish law. According to Luke 16:18a, a husband who divorces his wife and marries another woman commits adultery; and according to Luke 16:18b her new husband, if she remarries, also commits adultery whether or not he is marrying for the first time. According to Matt 5:32a, a husband who divorces his wife makes her commit adultery in a remarriage; and according to Matt 5:32b in agreement with Luke 16:18b, the next man to marry her also commits adultery whether or not he is marrying for the first time. Matthew's version implies that a husband should not divorce his wife lest he cause the adultery of his former wife and her next husband. On the one hand, then, Mark 10:11 agrees with Luke 16:18a against Matt 5:32a yet antedates the writing of Luke 16:18a. On the other hand, Matt 5:32a exhibits Matthew's predilection for ποιέω (he writes this word nineteen times in pericopes where parallel synoptic pericopes lack it, and another nineteen times in pericopes unique to his gospel). It also exhibits his assimilation of the saying to a contextual emphasis on treating people well (passim in Matt 5:21-48; also 6:14-15; 7:1-5, 12) — here by demanding that a husband treat his wife well by not forcing her, given the economic circumstances of women, into an adulterous remarriage. Therefore we should regard Luke 16:18a rather than Matt 5:32a as closer to Q even apart from Matthew's exceptive phrase (which Crossan freely concedes to be redactional).

H. Anderson (244) finds legalities affecting remarriage in vv 11-12, presupposes Jesus' disinterest in or opposition to legalities, and therefore doubts the Jesuanic character of these verses, at least in their present form. The presence of the same material in Q, whose version is no less legal, puts an initial question mark against Anderson's reasoning. Verses 5b-9 in Mark were also no less legal: there Jesus used hardheartedness, divine example, and divine precept to abrogate Deut 24:1 (cf. D. Daube, *NTRJ* 76-79). Then he drew his own legal conclusion. J. Gnilka (2. 70) argues that from the very start the lack of sanction makes inappropriate a description of Jesus' pronouncements as legal. But not even Deut 24:1-4 contained sanctions, yet Jesus described it as a command. Gnilka correctly calls attention, however, to many examples of sayings that begin with a conditional relative clause (in 3:29, 35; 4:25; 8:35 et passim), a form that suits the Jesuanic origin of vv 11-12 (though v 12 has undergone some un-Semitic redaction — see the foregoing comments and K. Beyer, *Semitische Syntax* 1/1. 145, 267).

The absoluteness of v 11 prohibits attaching the condition that Jesus means to outlaw only arbitrary divorce such as *m. Yebam.* 14:1 allows (against S. van Tilborg, *Jewish Leaders* 118-19). E. Haenchen (338) thinks that vv 11-12 weaken Jesus' view of marriage as indissoluble by saying that only remarriage, not just divorce, counts as adultery (cf. W. Weiss, *"Eine neue Lehre in Vollmacht"* 195-96). But since by itself divorce entails no sexual union with another, how could divorce count as adultery even under the strongest view of marriage as indissoluble?

That it is "the two" who become one flesh (v 8) tended toward monogamy. That a man's marrying "another woman" after divorcing his first wife constitutes adultery (v 11) presupposes and requires monogamy; for if polygamous relationships were legitimate, nothing would be wrong with remarriage to another woman, either. But Jesus is not addressing the question of polygamy; so we are left with an implication (cf. D. Daube, *NTRJ* 75).

J. N. Birdsall (in *Gospel Traditions in the Second Century* 15-16) favors the v.l. that puts the woman's divorcement of the man before his divorcement of her (W [l *pc* sy^s] in vv 11-12) and appeals to the same order in 1 Cor 7:10-11 and to Herodias's divorcement of her first husband to marry his brother Herod Antipas. But it was Herod's marrying his brother's wife, not any action of Herodias, which drew fire from John the Baptizer (6:18); and we have no reason to think that Jesus differed from John in being exercised over an action of Herodias rather than of Herod. As to the order in 1 Cor 7:10-11, Paul probably reverses the Jesuanic order because more Corinthian women than men were divorcing their mates (cf. 1 Cor 11:2-16).

To gain an allusion in v 12 to Herodias's deserting her first husband, one might decide for the v.l. ἐξέλθη ἀπὸ τοῦ ἀνδρός, "goes out from the husband," in D (Θ) *f*¹³ (28) 565 (700) it. But the rest of the external evidence, weightier as well as more voluminous, favors ἀπολύσασα (or ἀπολύσῃ) τὸν ἄνδρα αὐτῆς, "divorcing (or, 'divorces') her husband." Furthermore, the v.l. has an easy explanation: in view of the Pharisees' asking only about a man's right to divorce his wife (v 2), a woman's divorcing her husband has been changed to a woman's going out from her husband because he has divorced her (not because she is deserting him, as the v.l. is usually understood). D. Daube (*NTRJ* 366-68) argues that ἀπολύσασα arose by influence from v 11 and the rest of the synoptic tradition on divorce and from Greco-Roman women's divorcing, not just deserting, their husbands. This argument overlooks that these factors stand as good a chance of having influenced Mark as of having influenced copyists of his book. Ironically, H. Greeven (in *NTS* 15 [1968-69] 384, n. 1) regards ἀπολύσασα, which for Daube means divorce rather than desertion, as so ambiguous that scribes substituted ἐξέλθη to tilt the meaning toward desertion rather than divorce. But the active voice of ἀπολύσασα plus an accusative object, as here, leaves no ambiguity. For desertion we would expect the middle voice. The argument of R. W. Herron, Jr. (in *JETS* 25 [1982] 278), that ἐξέλθη κτλ. is favored by its similarity to 1 Cor 7:10-11 overlooks that χωρίζομαι, the verb which Paul uses for the woman, is elsewhere used for divorce. In fact, it is used for divorce right here in Mark 10:9.

A Jewish woman may take legal action with a view to inducing her husband to divorce her, but she cannot divorce him (see Josephus *Ant.* 15.7.10 §§259-60 with 18.9.6 §§353-62; *m. Yebam.* 14:1; Str-B 1. 318-19; J. D. M. Derrett, *Law* 381-83, 386-88; B. Witherington III, *Women* 5; I. Abrahams, *Studies* 1. 66-72; Z. W. Falk in *The Jewish People in the First Century* 1. 517-18; and E. Schweizer in *EvT* 42 [1982] 294-97; H. Weder in *EvT* 43 [1983] 175-78; against B. Brooten in *EvT* 42 [1982] 65-80; also E. Bammel in *ZNW* 61 [1970] 95-101; idem in *HTR* 51 [1958] 102, n. 12). The fifth century B.C.E. papyri from the eclectic Jewish military colony in Elephantine, Egypt, are chronologically, culturally, and geographically too far removed from the Jewry of first century Palestine to contradict Josephus and the rabbis on this matter.

JESUS' ELEVATION OF CHILDREN TO MEMBERSHIP IN GOD'S KINGDOM

10:13-16 (Matt 18:3; 19:13-15; Luke 18:15-17)

The bringing of little children to Jesus and the disciples' rebuking them (v 13) set the stage for his teaching (vv 14-15) and action (v 16). His teaching subdivides into a command (v 14) and a warning (v 15), both directed to his disciples.

10:13 *(Matt 19:13; Luke 18:15)* The third person plural of προσέφερον is indefinite ("people"; cf. the "crowds" of v 1). In view of the disciples' rebuke and Jesus' having to command them to stop forbidding the children from coming to him, the imperfect tense of προσέφερον is probably conative ("were trying to bring"). "Children" is reminiscent of "the child" and of "the children" represented by the child in 9:36-37 (forms of παιδίον throughout). But there Jesus took the initiative with respect to one child for the purpose of making that one an object lesson. Here, others bring more than one child to him "in order that he might touch them." It is parents, presumably, who are bringing their children for a touch of blessing (cf. v 16), not of healing (as often elsewhere). But Mark's interest does not lie in those who bring the children; so he does not identify them. Nor does he identify those whom the disciples rebuke. Are they the people who bring the children, the children themselves, or both? Nor does Mark tell why the disciples rebuked whomever they rebuked. His interest lies solely in Jesus' response.

10:14 *(Matt 19:14; Luke 18:16)* Just as the introduction of the disciples' rebuke opened with an adversative δέ, "but," for contrast with the bringing of children, so also the introduction to Jesus' response opens with an adversative δέ for contrast with the rebuke. His seeing what is happening shows that the disciples have succeeded in keeping the children away from him. The disciples' taking it on themselves to engage in rebuke makes him indignant. In mentioning this indignation, Mark writes as an omniscient narrator: he knows the inner feelings of Jesus. Here, he means his audience to see in Jesus' indignation an outburst that will upset the traditional denigration of children: "Let the children come to me. Stop forbidding them, for of the [children] such as these is the kingdom of God." Μὴ κωλύετε αὐτά, "stop forbidding them," recalls μὴ κωλύετε αὐτόν, "stop forbidding him [the independent exorcist]," in 9:38-40, a passage right alongside the earlier one on children (9:33-37). Asyndeton sharpens the present prohibition. The forward position of τῶν . . . τοιούτων, "of the [children] such as these" (again see 9:37), gives it great weight. Its genitive case is possessive (cf. a child's receiving God's kingdom and thus having it in possession in the very next verse). The belonging of God's kingdom to the children such as were coming to Jesus — we may infer from their coming that they belong to the class of little ones who believe in Jesus (9:42) and therefore deserve reception on the ground of his name (9:37) — makes nonsense, and worse, of the disciples' attempt to forbid their coming. It is astonishing not merely that Jesus wants these children to come, but that he even assigns God's kingdom to them.

10:15 *(Matt 18:3; Luke 18:17)* The warning of Jesus in v 15 begins with a solemn asseveration: "Truly I say to you." Making a child's behavior the model for adult behavior — on pain of non-entrance into God's kingdom — needs the personal authority of Jesus himself to back it up. Asyndeton at the start of the asseveration and the omission of ὅτι, "that," afterward sharpen the warning (cf. M. Reiser, *Syntax und Stil* 148). In 9:37 Jesus spoke of a grownup's receiving one of such children — a matter of community among believers. Here he warns against not receiving God's kingdom as a child receives it — a question of conversion. Earlier the child was object, other believers subject. Now the child is subject, God's kingdom object. Earlier Jesus used a child to warn his disciples against striving for greatness. Now he warns them against keeping children from coming to him; for children's reception of God's kingdom provides the model that adult non-disciples must follow if they, like the children who are receiving God's kingdom, are to enter it. To receive God's kingdom means to submit to his endtime rule (cf. E. P. Sanders, *Jesus and Judaism* 141-42). "As a child" alludes to the non-resistance of the children who are coming to Jesus. "Whoever does not receive" gives "kingdom" the dynamic meaning "rule" and implies that God's rule has arrived, making itself available for reception (in Mark, cf. esp. 1:15). "Will by no means enter into it" gives "kingdom" a spatial meaning, too, and implies futurity (in Mark, see esp. 9:47; 10:23; 14:25), which leaves open the question of entrance and thus allows Jesus to issue a warning.

10:16 *(Matt 19:15)* Jesus' hugging the children goes beyond touching them, for which they were brought in v 13, and thereby dramatizes his approval of their coming to him. It also echoes 9:36-37. But there he was dramatizing the way disciples ought to accept a child who already bears his name. Here he is dramatizing his own approval of children as newcomers to him. Blessing the children one after another (κατευλόγει is an iterative imperfect or, if accented κατευλογεῖ, an iterative historical present) means speaking a blessing while laying hands on them and therefore after hugging them (N.B. the difference in tense between the aorist participle ἐναγκαλισάμενος and the present participle τιθείς). Does the prefix κατ- imply that blessing, the gift of salvation, flows through his hands "down" on the children? Whether or not, the complex form of the verb stresses Jesus' authority to elevate even children to the heirship of God's kingdom.

If Mark or someone before him were arranging different materials without regard for chronology, we would expect him to put this pericope on letting little children come to Jesus beside the one on receiving a little child on the ground of Jesus' name (9:33-37). For the similarity between these two pericopes outweighs the supposition that Mark or someone before him puts the present pericope right after the one on divorce because children come naturally out of marriage, which Jesus has defended against divorce. Nothing in the text suggests an editorial integration of the subject matters in vv 1-12 and 13-16; and if something had suggested such an integration, we would still expect Mark or a predecessor to have combined 9:33-37 as well as 10:1-12 with 10:13-16.

NOTES

Entry into a house at v 10 and exit at v 17 put vv 13-16 in the house. Those who bring children to Jesus might then be parents in the household, though neighbors, too, may be bringing theirs. The masculine gender of αὐτοῖς forestalls our thinking of mothers alone as those who bring their children, though a generic masculine might include mothers. These historical possibilities do not take account of the redactional possibility that Mark or someone before him has inserted vv 13-16 between vv 10-12 and 17, or that he or someone before him has constructed the whole framework of entry and exit. Nevertheless, the likelihood that an episode in which people bring children to Jesus really did take place in a house is at least as great as the possibility of a redactionally fabricated house.

J. Sauer (in *ZNW* 72 [1981] 27-50) infers from traits of healing stories — bringing a patient to Jesus, his touching the patient or laying on of hands, etc. (cf. esp. 8:22b-26) — that the present story originally dealt with the question whether children are legitimate subjects for miraculous healing in the church. We need evidence that the NT church debated such a question. Προσέφερον (v 13) does not necessarily mean carrying and therefore does not necessarily imply that the παιδία are children too young to walk. Though Luke 18:15 changes Mark's παιδία to τὰ βρέφη, "the infants" (see J. A. Fitzmyer, *Luke* 1193), and though the παιδία in Gen 17:12 LXX; Luke 1:59 were only eight days old, the παιδίον in Mark 5:39-42 was twelve years old and capable of walking. To distinguish between older children and younger ones and then to suppose that the former bring the latter (so W. L. Lane 359; cf. E. Lohmeyer 203) overrefines the passage. "Stop forbidding them" does not support the overrefinement; for Jesus prohibits forbidding the *coming* of children to him (cf. the preceding command), not forbidding the *bringing* of them to him.

The addition of ἐπιτιμήσας, "rebuking," in v 14 by W Θ *f*[1,13] 28 565 *pc* sy[s,hmg] looks attractive as a possibly Marcan way of countering the disciples' rebuke of the children with Jesus' rebuke of the disciples. Is it better to suppose that scribes omitted the word as overloading the sentence, or that they added it under the influence of ἐπετίμησαν in v 13? External evidence strongly favors omission.

Κωλύω, used in v 14 for the disciples' forbidding the children, occurs also in baptismal contexts at Matt 3:14; Acts 8:36; 10:47; 11:17. But baptism does not come into the present passage (cf. E. Best, *Disciples and Discipleship* 92-94; P. K. Jewett, *Infant Baptism* 55-59; K. Aland, *Did the Early Church Baptize Infants?* 95-99; G. R. Beasley-Murray, *Baptism* 320-29; J. Jeremias, *Infant Baptism* 48-55; O. Cullmann, *Baptism* 25-26, 72-80). The suggestion that "stop forbidding them" is a redactional insertion from 9:39 rests on the claim that there "stop forbidding him" fit better, presumably because of the match-up with "we were forbidding him" in 9:38 and because of the present switch from rebuking (v 13) to forbidding (v 14). But this switch may be due to the intervening verb of permission (ἄφετε), for which a verb of forbidding makes a better antonym than a second verb of rebuke would make.

J. D. Crossan (*In Fragments* 315-18) thinks that Mark draws on Mark 9:36-39 to create the remainder of vv 13-14, 16, too. But it stretches our imagination to think that now Mark reverses the order of 9:36-37 and 9:38-39 (as the theory requires), transforms a disciple's report to Jesus into Mark's own report to the audience of his gospel, adds the elements of touching, rebuking, blessing, and laying on of hands, fails to give a reason for the forbiddance despite his giving one before, switches from one child to an indeterminate number of them, adds Jesus' anger, omits his making a child stand in the midst, and replaces his receiving a child with a command that the disciples allow children to come to him. A redactional take-over would probably not have produced so many dissimilarities. The similarities among them seem to stem, then, from the common figuring of a child and children in two incidents and from attitudes expressed more than once by Jesus and the disciples toward children and outsiders.

Jesus' command to let the children come to him (he does not say to let others bring the children to him) favors a reference to the children themselves in "them" whom the disciples rebuked (against the v.l. οἱ δὲ μαθηταὶ ἐπετίμων τοῖς προσφέρουσιν, "and the disciples were rebuking the ones bringing [the children]" — so A D W [Θ *f*¹,¹³] Majority Text lat sy Bas, apparently in an attempt to get rid of the ambiguity, perhaps to relieve the disciples of blame for "picking on" children). Are the disciples trying to avoid a delay in Jesus' progress toward Jerusalem when they forbid the children to come to him (cf. v 48)? The request of James and John to sit on the right and left of Jesus in his glory (v 35) and the Triumphal Procession (11:1-11) would fit an eagerness to arrive in Jerusalem. But the editorial statement that Jesus' followers are afraid at his going to Jerusalem (10:32) shows that Mark himself aims in a different direction; and, historically speaking, cultural denigration of children suffices to explain the disciples' forbidding them. See H. Anderson 245 for other views. The view of J. D. M. Derrett (*Studies* 4. 121) that the disciples were trying to shield Jesus from being treated as a source of magical power apart from faith flatters the disciples and thereby disagrees with the generally unflattering portrayal of them elsewhere in Mark.

G. Klein (*Ärgernisse* 68-69) denies the authenticity of vv 13-14 on the ground that "come to me" reflects the language of Christian faith. Do we then deny the authenticity of "follow me" and similar expressions? If so, how do we explain Jesus' gathering of disciples? The children can hardly be a figure of speech for adult disciples in v 14 when it is the adult disciples whom Jesus angrily tells to stop forbidding the children. Likewise, the child in v 15 can hardly be a figure of speech for an adult disciple when the child will provide a pattern of action for an adult's becoming a disciple. The τοι-, "such as," in τῶν . . . τοιούτων (v 14) calls attention to the children's having come to Jesus, just as in 2 Cor 12:3 the τοι- in τὸν τοιοῦτον ἄνθρωπον, "the man such as this," calls attention to the man's being "in Christ" (v 2). Again, therefore, Jesus is not speaking of adults who are like children, who have a childlike quality or childlike qualities. The -ούτων, "these," in τοιούτων restricts the referent to the children at hand (cf. 9:37; G. R. Beasley-Murray, *Baptism* 326-27). When τοιοῦτοι includes others similar but not at hand, further expressions so indicate (as with the addition of "many" in 4:33 and of "many similar" in 7:13, for example). See the comments on 9:37 and E. Best, *Disciples and Discipleship* 91, that τοιούτων is not equivalent to a simple τούτων, "these" (cf. 6:2; 9:37; 13:19 as well as 4:33; 7:13).

If Jesus spoke v 15 on a different occasion, his reference to a child's receiving God's kingdom still favors the possessive interpretation of the genitive τῶν . . . τοιούτων in v 14 (cf. BAGD s.v. εἰμί IV1). A qualitative genitive to the effect that God's kingdom has the characteristics of children would not make very good sense; and for the meaning that God's kingdom consists in such children we would expect οἱ γὰρ τοιοῦτοι εἰσὶν ἡ βασιλεία τοῦ θεοῦ, "for the [children] such as these are the kingdom of God" (cf. Exod 19:6; 1 Pet 2:9; Rev 1:6; 5:10; 20:6). The saying in v 14 does not deny that God's kingdom belongs to adults who become Jesus' disciples. Much else in his teaching indicates that it does. Here, then, he means that it belongs to the children who have come to him as well as to adults who have become his disciples. See A. Oepke in *TDNT* 5. 646-47; J. Jeremias, *NT Theology* 1. 225, on the low status of children in Judaism of the NT era.

E. Lohmeyer (203) provides a rationale for v 14: since according to 9:1 a few but only a few adults will live to see God's kingdom as having come in power, the last generation will consist mainly of present children, who therefore should not be denied Jesus' attention and blessing. This rationale neglects the force of τῶν τοι-, "the . . . such as," in τῶν τοιούτων. As already noted, these elements in the phrase point up the children's being at hand because they have come to Jesus, not their being children, for which τούτων, "these," would have been enough and an anarthrous παιδίων, "children," better (cf. also the notes on 9:36-37).

Citing the innocence of children in Jonah 4:11 and possibly in Sir 30:1-13, the intermixture of favorable with unfavorable remarks about children in rabbinic literature (Str-B 1. 607, 773-74, 780-81, 786; 2. 423, 528-29; 4/1. 468-69), and the revelation to "babies" (νηπίοις) in Q (Matt 11:25 par. Luke 10:21), A. M. Ambrozic (*Hidden Kingdom* 151-52) interprets ὡς παιδίον as follows: "like a disciple of the wise who admits his lack of wisdom as he asks to be instructed, the follower of Jesus must admit that he is unwise in matters of the kingdom, and that his only way into the kingdom consists in his acceptance of its mystery. . . ." But the present passage says nothing about instruction: neither those who bring children nor the children themselves ask for it (contrast Mark 4:10-11); Jesus gives none (contrast 4:13ff.); and receiving the kingdom itself differs from receiving instruction about it. Furthermore, the babies in Q differ from the children here; for babies cannot "come" to Jesus, therefore would not be "forbidden" to do so, and are in no position to "receive" God's kingdom. "Babies" is figurative in Q, for literal babies cannot understand revelation. Here, "children" is literal.

For a number of reasons v 15 is usually thought to have been an originally independent saying, redactionally inserted here because of the catchword παιδίον/-α, "child/-ren": (1) v 14 brings the episode to a natural conclusion; or, if v 16 belongs to the original, vv 13-14, 16 do not need v 15. (2) The parallel in Matt 19:13-15 omits Mark 10:15. (3) By representing the saying in a different version and context, Matt 18:3 demonstrates its original independence. (4) So also does the different version and context in John 3:3, 5. (5) The superfluousness of Mark 10:15 is shown by the omission of Mark 10:16 in Luke 18:15-17 when Mark 10:15 is taken over. (6) Mark 10:15 is worse than superfluous; it interrupts the progression from vv 13-14 to v 16 if v 16 belongs to the original. (7) In vv 13-14, 16 children play a major role; v 15 makes a child only the point of a comparison. (8) In v 14 God's kingdom belongs to children who come to Jesus; in v 15 a child receives it. (9) Verse 14c gives a promise; v 15 a warning. (10) "Truly I say to you" demarcates v 15. (11) The plural reference to children in vv 13-14 yields to the singular reference to a child in v 15 only to revive in v 16.

On principle we should allow the possibility of an insertion of v 15, but the theory of insertion is less certain than usually thought. Catchwords lead to twists and turns in original speaking as well as to secondary association in later redaction. Verse 14 does not bring the episode to a natural conclusion, for the purpose of bringing the children to Jesus — viz., "that he might touch them" — remains unfulfilled. Economy and logical progression of a lock-step sort do not characterize oral communication, but superfluousness does. Matt 19:13-15 omits Mark 10:15 because Mark 10:15 has already appeared in Matt 18:3, where it had the characteristics to be expected of Matthean redaction (R. H. Gundry, *Matthew* 360, 384). Such a redaction leaves no need to posit an independent tradition behind Matt 18:3 (cf. R. Bultmann, *HST* 32). If John 3:3, 5 is related to Mark 10:15 at all, great uncertainty attends the character of that relation. One could think, for example, of a saying related in thought but spoken on a different occasion, or of an entirely post-Marcan development of the saying in Mark 10:15 rather than of a development starting before Mark with a detached or differently contextualized version of the saying. Luke 18:15-17 omits Mark 10:16, probably not because Mark 10:15 is felt to make it superfluous (again the purpose of touching remains unfulfilled), but because Luke dislikes Jesus' hugging children (he omits it also at Luke 9:47; contrast Mark 9:36 and cf. similar omissions in Matt 18:2; 19:15, which may have exercised a secondary influence on Luke [R. H. Gundry, *Matthew* 360]). We can hardly assume that no saying which starts with "truly I say to you" was remembered in its original context, or that no such saying was originally spoken alongside another saying not so introduced. With regard to form critical rules that would dictate otherwise on these matters, we have only to open our ears to speeches, lectures, sermons, homilies, and ordinary conversation to learn that in the real world those rules do not necessarily apply.

Verse 15 certainly makes a different point from that in v 14; but since sayings originally spoken in succession usually make related rather than synonymous points, the question is whether the shifts in meaning and expression are reasonably conceivable. A shift from the coming of children to Jesus to their making a good example of receiving God's kingdom seems quite conceivable. Better than conceivable, it forms a nice progression. For since the kingdom centers on Jesus and his ministry, receiving the kingdom fits coming to him (cf. J. A. Ziesler in *JTS* ns 33 [1982] 557). The switch from the plural "children" (v 14) to the singular "child" (v 15) is due to the singular of ὅς ἄν, "whoever" (v 15), which reflects the individuality of receiving the kingdom. It would sound unnatural to compare an individual adult's reception of the kingdom to the reception of it by children as a class. The disciples' forbidding the children to come to Jesus makes the shift from promise to warning appropriate. In fact, however, there is no real shift of this sort at all; for the statement that "of the [children] such as these is the kingdom of God" neither addresses the children nor holds them up as examples to be followed by the addressees. Jesus is addressing the disciples, and they have already come to him. Otherwise they would not be called disciples. Jesus speaks to them about children who likewise come to him. So the statement gives his reason for commanding the disciples to let the children come to him, i.e. to stop forbidding them. The shift from command to warning is entirely natural.

The contextual links between vv 14 and 15 consist in three parallels: (1) between coming to Jesus and receiving God's kingdom; (2) between possessing God's kingdom and entering it; and (3) between the cause-and-effect of coming to Jesus so as to possess God's kingdom and the cause-and-effect of receiving God's kingdom so as to enter it. Furthermore, the warning directed to adults in v 15 reverses the disciples' rebuking of children in v 13: stop forbidding the children; rather, let them come in order that Jesus' hugging and blessing them may warn of exclusion from the kingdom any adult who has yet to follow their example. Verse 16 then highlights not only Jesus' accepting the children who come to him, but also his making them an example necessary to follow. Hugging, blessing, and laying hands on them go beyond the mere touching for which the children were brought and thereby dramatize their possession of God's kingdom and assure their entry into it.

When v 15 is nevertheless considered an insertion, it is often thought that in v 14c τῶν . . . τοιούτων, "of the [children] such as these," has replaced an original τούτων or αὐτῶν, "of these" or "of them," to go with ὡς, "as," in v 15. An insertion of v 15 does not demand such a replacement, however; for τῶν . . . τοιούτων may simply emphasize the children at hand as having come to Jesus. Some critics go so far as to consider the whole of v 14c, "for of the [children] such as these is the kingdom of God," a fabrication added to go with v 15 (see, e.g., R. Busemann, *Jüngergemeinde* 122-24; cf. Mark's penchant for γάρ-clauses). But the motif of God's kingdom characterizes the teaching of Jesus; and it seems unlikely that the early church would assign God's kingdom to children. The assignment is so surprising that Jesus makes a more likely author.

Even if divested of its present context, the child in v 15 is not a figure of speech for an adult disciple. Making the child a point of comparison requires a literal meaning, as in vv 13-14, 16; and v 15 is as devoid of the element of instruction without vv 13-14, 16 as it is with those verses (contrast the mention of revelation in Matt 11:25 par. Luke 10:21, where babies are a figure of speech for adult disciples). A mistaken treatment of the child in v 15 as figurative leads Busemann (op. cit. 121-24) to reason that the contrast with literal children in vv 13-14, 16 may favor a redactional insertion of ὡς παιδίον, "as a child," by Mark.

J. D. M. Derrett (in *NovT* 25 [1983] 1-18) reasons that since Jews regard a child as too young to receive the yoke of God's kingdom, Jesus cannot base his comparison on a child's receiving the kingdom. Derrett goes on to interpret a child's receiving it as a child's receiving now the promise of a future inheritance. Thus, v 15 amplifies what it means in v 14 that the kingdom belongs to children such as these; the hug in v 16 signifies co-inheritance with Jesus; and the blessing, with laying on of hands, plays on Gen 48:1-20 to say that he, like Jacob, "refused to recognize seniority." This OT text provides general background for blessing, with laying on of hands; but to tease out of it a refusal to recognize seniority overlooks that in Mark children stand in contrast with adults whereas in Genesis Jacob was dealing with two boys (Ephraim and Manasseh), and that in Mark the question is not one of seniority in the kingdom, not even one of who enters first, but one of entering or not. Inheritance fitly combines the kingdom's belonging to the children now and their entering it in the future; but receiving the kingdom interprets coming to Jesus, not inheriting the kingdom. This inheritance is the outcome rather than the interpretation of receiving the kingdom by coming to him. Hugging the children represents accepting the children — but as co-heirs of the kingdom? Jesus appears to act in God's behalf as conveyer rather than co-heir of the kingdom. The youthfulness of children would prevent Jesus from making them an example of receiving the kingdom by taking on the yoke of the Law, but not from making them an example of receiving the kingdom by coming to him — in faith, if we may take a cue from 9:42.

To interpret receiving the kingdom as willing acceptance of Jesus' instruction concerning it, A. M. Ambrozic (*Hidden Kingdom* 143ff.) appeals to the giving and receiving of wisdom, knowledge, instruction, etc., in wisdom literature. By way of expanding our earlier observation, however, receiving the kingdom itself differs from receiving wisdom, knowledge, and instruction about it. Mark 4:10 spoke of giving "the mystery" of the kingdom, not of giving the kingdom itself. In Mark 4:13ff. the disciples received explanation of parables concerning the kingdom; they did not receive the kingdom itself. According to Matt 11:25 par. Luke 10:21, God "has revealed" things to babies, but Mark 10:15 carries no trace of the language of revelation, explanation, or mystery.

Modesty, innocence, dependence, trustfulness, simplicity, and freshness have all been suggested as the point of comparison in receiving God's kingdom as a child receives it (cf. D. O. Via, *Ethics* 129-31). But apart from the factual questionableness and overpsychologizing modernity of these suggestions, Jesus' having already made a child his Exhibit A-1 of objective lowliness in society (9:33-37) favors that receiving God's kingdom as a child receives it means submitting to God's rule. What else can a weak and helpless child do? See G. Dalman, *Words* 124-25 (also J. I. H. McDonald in *SE VI* 328-32, except that he draws overly detailed parallels with Jewish theological education of children), and cf. the frequent use of simplex and compound forms of δέχομαι in the LXX for קבל. Since δέχομαι does not elsewhere connote receiving a gift of grace, but acceptance as opposed to rejection, we should not infer from the verb that the kingdom comes as a gift of God's grace — however true the message of grace may be on other grounds.

The suggestion that we take παιδίον as a direct object ("whoever does not receive God's rule as [one receives/I receive] a child" — so W. K. L. Clarke, *NT Problems* 37-38) is beset by a number of weaknesses: (1) The denigration of children in first century Judaism cripples the suggested comparison between receiving a child and receiving God's rule (contrast the comparisons between God's rule and a treasure and very valuable pearl [Matt 13:44-46]). (2) The disciples' forbidding children to come to Jesus probably illustrates this denigration and certainly erects a contextual barrier against the suggested comparison, which would seem to demand that the disciples have been forbidding Jesus to receive children. (3) To supply "receives God's rule" after "as a child" is more natural than supplying "one receives" or "I receive" between "as" and "a child," because "receives

God's rule" simply echoes the preceding clause whereas "one receives" or "I receive" would entail more of a shift from "whoever receives." (4) Whether or not v 15 represents the same saying that is represented in Matt 18:3; John 3:3, 5, these cross-references favor taking the child as subject rather than object. (5) So also does the immediately preceding statement that God's kingdom belongs to children who come to Jesus (Mark 10:14). The first, third, and fourth weaknesses apply even under the supposition that v 15 originally had no association with the present context.

F. A. Schilling (in *ExpTim* 77 [1965-66] 56-58) considers ὡς παιδίον an adjectival phrase describing God's kingdom as being "like a child," i.e. small. To receive it as such, then, is to accept it both in and despite its present smallness. The parable of the mustard seed (4:30-32) is supposed to favor this interpretation. That parable included the compensating factor of the kingdom's ultimate largeness, however; and accepting the kingdom in and despite its small beginning would invite, perhaps require, an inclusion of its ultimate largeness to encourage such acceptance. Unfortunately for the view in question, the present saying does not include the compensating factor.

According to D. O. Via (*Ethics* 131), receiving the kingdom and entering it occur simultaneously in the present as well as in the future; for both of the Greek verbs for receiving and entering appear in the aorist subjunctive. On the contrary, the two clauses in which these verbs occur are not parallel. One is the subject of the other; and one is a relative conditional clause whereas the other, by contrast, is a strong negation of the future. Hence, and with a more accurate inclusion of the negatives, present refusal to receive the kingdom as a child receives it is followed by future failure to enter it. To avoid a spatial implication in entering the kingdom, J. Marcus (in *JBL* 107 [1988] 672-74) disregards this temporal distinction and similarly confuses entering the kingdom with receiving it.

G. Klein (*Ärgernisse* 68) argues against the authenticity of v 15 (a) that Jesus did not split God's kingdom between the present and the future, as v 15 does, and (b) that Jesus spoke of the kingdom's coming, not of people's entering it. These arguments are not arguments in the true sense, but Procrustean beds. The former would demand rejecting the authenticity either of all sayings regarding the present kingdom or of all those regarding the future kingdom, whereas the tension between already and not yet seems characteristic of Jesus (see, e.g., G. R. Beasley-Murray, *Jesus and the Kingdom of God* passim). Where is the evidence that he spoke of the kingdom's coming but not of people's entering it? Elsewhere, entering God's kingdom has to do with the last day, not with the present (see H. Windisch in *ZNW* 27 [1928] 163-92; against V. Taylor 423-24).

According to W. L. Lane (361), Jesus' attitude toward children contrasts with the pagan practice of exposing infants. But Jesus is reacting to Jewish men who would not think of exposing infants; and since a child who accepts God's rule must be older than an infant, not even Mark's original Gentile audience are likely to have thought of the suggested contrast.

J. Jeremias (*Infant Baptism* 49) describes the Jewish practice of taking children to elders, i.e. scribes, for blessing right after the Day of Atonement. Here in Mark we are on the other side of the calendar from the Day of Atonement, however. We might surmise that this incident is chronologicaly displaced; but a surmise lacks certainty, and Jesus' hugging the children as well as blessing them goes beyond what scribes did on the Day of Atonement. Hence, we cannot infer with any confidence that the disciples are resisting a treatment of Jesus as no more than a scribe (so ibid.).

Though the doubling of participles in v 16 looks Marcan, it does not follow that Mark has added "hugging them" after the pattern of 9:36. The consistent omissions by Matthew and Luke of Jesus' hugging children suggest that it offended early Christian sensibilities regarding his dignity. Therefore we are dealing with a characteristic gesture of Jesus more likely than with a Marcan addition.

THE POWER OF JESUS TO SHATTER THE ECONOMICS OF SALVATION

10:17-31 (Matt 19:16-30; Luke 18:18-30)

The first main part of this pericope on wealth consists of a dialogue between Jesus and a rich man (vv 17-22); the second main part of a dialogue between Jesus and his disciples (vv 23-27); and the third main part of a dialogue between Jesus and Peter (vv 28-31). Each of the first two main parts has a concentric structure, the central item of each relating to the first and fifth items just as they relate to each other (cf. F. Manns, *Essais* 52-53; C. Coulot, *Jésus et le disciple* 98-99). In the first main part, (a) a rich man approaches Jesus with a question (v 17); (b) Jesus answers with the demands of the Law (vv 18-19); (c) the man responds by citing his obedience to those demands (v 20); (b') Jesus answers with his own demands (v 21); (a') the man departs with unwillingness to obey these demands (v 22). In the second main part, (a) Jesus looks around at the disciples and remarks how difficultly those who have means will enter God's kingdom (v 23); (b) the disciples are amazed (v 24a); (c) Jesus remarks how difficult it is for a rich person to enter God's kingdom (vv 24b-25); (b') the disciples ask a question out of extreme astonishment (v 26); (a') Jesus looks intently at the disciples and remarks that only God can save a rich person (v 27). The third main part has an a-b-a'-b' structure: Peter notes his own and his fellow disciples' (a) leaving all and (b) following Jesus (v 28; cf. *Ap. Jas.* 4:1), and Jesus responds with two promissory predictions (a') concerning what those who have left all will receive (vv 29-30) and (b') the final last position of those who refuse to follow him and the final first position of those who do follow him (v 31).

10:17 *(Matt 19:16; Luke 18:18)* "And as Jesus was going out to a road" harks back to his having entered a house (v 10) and implies that his blessing the children (vv 13-16) took place in the house. The running of "one" to Jesus again exhibits Jesus' magnetism, all the more so since προσδραμών, "running to," takes an emphatic forward position (cf. esp. 6:33; 9:15, 25). The man's kneeling exceeds the reverence shown to an ordinary teacher and thereby highlights for Mark's audience the divine sonship of Jesus (cf. 1:1 with comments and notes; also 1:40; 5:22). The address "Good Teacher" shows recognition not only of Jesus' didactic authority but also of his moral virtue (a point not to be lost on those who might draw an opposite inference from his having died by the means used to execute criminals). The unusualness of such an address in the Jewish sphere emphasizes these characteristics of Jesus and will prompt his later question, "Why do you call me good?" Meanwhile, the question of the man, "What should I do in order that I might inherit eternal life?" seeks an authoritative answer.

10:18-19 *(Matt 19:17-19; Luke 18:19-20)* The adversative δέ, "but," prepares for an unexpected question in return: "Why do you call *me* good? [The word order puts emphasis on με, 'me.'] No one [is] good except one, [i.e.] God (εἰ μὴ εἷς ὁ θεός)." The recurrences of δέ in vv 20, 21, 22, 24 (bis), 26 will continue to highlight the liveliness of response and counterresponse. No one would be surprised to hear that God is good. But neither Jew nor Greek would say that God alone is good. Jesus says so, however. Again Mark means his audience to see the explosiveness of Jesus' pronouncements. That God alone is good lays the groundwork for the inadequacy of keeping commandments, even *God's* commandments (vv 19-21). Since in 2:1-12 some scribes asked, "Who is able to forgive sins except one, [i.e.] God (εἰ μὴ εἷς ὁ θεός)?" and Jesus proceeded to heal a paralytic for proof of his own divine prerogative to forgive sins, here he borrows those scribes' phraseology and proceeds to answer the present question for proof of his divine possession of goodness (cf. his self-references to divine sonship [13:32; 14:62 with 14:61 and passages outside Mark, such as Matt 11:27; Luke 10:22] as well as others' references to it in Mark [1:1, 11; 3:11; 5:7; 9:7; 14:61; 15:39, not to list many such references outside Mark]). The demonstration of Jesus' divine possession of goodness lays the groundwork for following him as the only way to inherit eternal life, have treasure in heaven, enter God's kingdom (v 21). Asyndeton and word order put emphasis on τὰς ἐντολάς, "the commandments," in Jesus' statement, "The commandments you know." He does not say, "Keep the commandments to inherit eternal life." He will, in fact, deny that keeping them brings eternal life (v 21). "The commandments you know," the following quotation of some of them, and the man's claim to have kept the ones quoted set the stage for that denial. Jesus starts quoting the second table of the Decalogue: "You shouldn't commit adultery, you shouldn't murder, you shouldn't steal, you shouldn't bear false witness." Then he substitutes a variant of the prohibition of stealing, "You shouldn't defraud," in place of the next prohibition, the one against coveting. Thus is left room for the man to affirm his keeping of all the commandments quoted (its being easier to keep from defrauding than to keep from coveting — cf. Rom 7:7-11). Perhaps Jesus also wants to make special application to the about-to-be-revealed wealthiness of the man (the wealthy not needing to covet, but liking to defraud — cf. D. E. Nineham 274). Finally, Jesus doubles back to the last commandment of the first table, "Honor your father and mother," to take up the only other commandment dealing with interpersonal relations, on which he is concentrating because of the damage done to them by wealth (cf. his selection of the commandment concerning parents to argue against the Pharisees' tradition on an economic matter [7:8-13]). As in 7:10 (see the comments ad loc.), the present tense of the imperative τίμα, "honor," carries some emphasis, here in contrast with the unemphatic aorist subjunctive of prohibition used in the preceding verbs, and thus prepares for the following reference to youth. The approach to the prohibition of coveting, the substitute for it, and the reversal of direction make that prohibition conspicuous by its absence and therefore, as the story unfolds, conspicuous in its applicability to the man.

10:20-21 *(Matt 19:20-21; Luke 18:21-22)* By failure to catch the implication that Jesus' goodness derives from his divine sonship, the man misunderstandingly drops "good" from "teacher." "All these things I have guarded against since my youth" breathes a sigh of relief that he has done everything necessary to inherit eternal life (cf. 2:17; Pr Man 8; 4 Ezra 3:36). The forward position of ταῦτα πάντα, "all these things," heightens the sense of relief. "Since my youth" implies the present adulthood of the man, probably takes as its starting point his having become fully obligated to keep the commandments at thirteen years of age (cf. *m. Nid.* 5:6), and adds to his relief in that no youthful transgressions of the quoted commandments stand between him and eternal life.

The mention of Jesus' name helps another δέ, "but," shift attention back to him. A perfective ἐμ- escalates the meaning of -βλέψας from "looking at" to "looking intently at." The intensity of Jesus' looking at the man and the recency of Jesus' having hugged children in physical demonstration of receiving them (v 16; 9:36) provide a frame of reference so concrete that ἠγάπησεν probably refers to Jesus' putting his arm around the man, patting him, or doing some other such thing in physical demonstration that he "loved" him (cf. Luke 7:47 with 7:38, 44-46; Plut. *Per.* 1.1; Xen. *Cyr.* 7.5.50; *Gos. Barth.* 4:71 et passim in the resurrection narrative of the Bartholomew tradition). This demonstration of love exhibits Jesus' divine goodness. "One thing is lacking so far as you are concerned" (cf. Ps 22[23]:1 LXX) does not mean that the man's past obediences need the addition of one more thing, but that the man is lacking in the one and only thing necessary (cf. the exclusive "one" in v 18; also Luke 10:42; against H. Ridderbos, *Coming* 293). Jesus upsets the notion that keeping the commandments brings eternal life. Ἕν, "one thing," gets emphasis from its forward position and contrasts with ταῦτα πάντα, "all these things," which the man has kept since his youth. Σε is an accusative of reference ("so far as you are concerned") likewise emphatically positioned before the verb. Ὑστερεῖ, "is lacking," makes a wordplay with μὴ ἀποστερήσῃς, "You shouldn't defraud." This wordplay points up that the man's failure to go sell however many things he has and give to the poor, as Jesus now tells him to do, will amount to a covetousness that defrauds the poor by stealing from them what belongs to them. Double asyndeton drives home the necessity of carrying out Jesus' commands to go and sell. The forward position of ὅσα ἔχεις, "however many things you have," underlines the amazing comprehensiveness of the second command. "Then [translating καί inferentially — M. Reiser, *Syntax und Stil* 120-21] you will have treasure in heaven" (cf. Str-B 1. 429-31) provides a motive for obedience which outweighs that comprehensiveness, however. Since the rich man has asked about eternal life (v 17), "treasure in heaven" means eternal life, not a reward above and beyond eternal life (see S. Légasse, *L'appel* 57-61). Jesus shifts to this figure of speech for a contrast with his questioner's earthly possessions. "And hither! Follow me" (cf. 1:17, 20; 2:14) implies that charity as such will suffice to inherit eternal life no more than keeping Decalogic commandments does. The only charity that counts is what comes as the price of discipleship, emphasized by the present tense of the imperative ἀκολούθει, "follow" (cf. the comments on 2:14). But what charity! The rabbis forbade selling all your property lest you be reduced to poverty and dependence on others (*m. ʿArak* 8:4; *b. Ketub.* 50a). Jesus sovereignly reverses the prohibition (but cf. *b. Taʿan.* 24a).

10:22 *(Matt 19:22; Luke 18:23)* The man's frowning describes a change of outward appearance because of Jesus' command. His being saddened describes his inward emotion as he went away from Jesus. "However many things you have" (v 21) did not tell how many things he had. They might have been few.

"For he had many acquisitions" at once reveals his wealth, however, and also gives the reason for his reaction and sets the stage for Jesus' iconoclastic teaching on wealth as a detriment to entering God's kingdom. The periphrastic construction ἦν . . . ἔχων, (literally) "was having," stresses the man's many acquisitions to highlight the revolutionariness of that teaching; and the very word for acquisitions, κτήματα (cognate to κτάομαι, "acquire"), contrasts with selling and alludes to the unmentioned covetousness (πλεονεξία, the desire "to have more") which not only keeps the man from selling but also, it would appear, prompted him to make many acquisitions in the first place. Saving till now the secret of the man's many acquisitions has made the audience of Mark share Jesus' love for the rich man — a love the sharing of which an earlier revelation might have forestalled (R. Tannehill in *ANRW* II 25/2. 1808-9) — again to increase the impact of Jesus' iconoclastic teaching.

10:23-24a *(Matt 19:23; Luke 18:24)* Now that the rich man has left, Jesus looks around (περιβλεψάμενος, which links with ἐμβλέψας, "looking at," in vv 21 and 27), sees his disciples, who by implication have been watching, and addresses an astonishing observation to them. Mark stresses the observation with the historical present tense of λέγει, "says," because of his interest in the iconoclastic force of Jesus' teaching. Against the view that wealth combined with piety is a sign of God's favor (Deut 28:1-14; Job 1:10; 42:10; Prov 10:22), Jesus says, "How difficultly will the ones having means enter into the kingdom of God!" The remark arises out of the gloomy, sorrowful departure of the rich man, who had "many acquisitions." "Means" (χρήματα, cognate to χράομαι, "make use of") replaces "acquisitions," however, for reference to the money that would come from the sale of acquisitions but that a covetous man would find difficult to give to the poor even though he had sold his acquisitions (see lexicons on the use of χρήματα for money; Acts 4:37 for such a use in respect of money gotten by selling; Acts 2:45; 5:1 for the use of κτήματα in respect of acquisitions that are sold; and again Acts 4:37 for the cognate κτήτορες, "acquisitors"). "Many" modified "acquisitions" in v 22, but drops out here, not because Jesus is saying that even a small amount of money hinders entrance into God's kingdom, but because "means" does not need "many" to connote wealth. "A man of means" is ipso facto a rich man (hence, πλούσιον, "a rich [person]," in v 25). Though the expressions are essentially synonymous, inheriting eternal life (v 17; cf. v 30) and having treasure in heaven (v 21) give way to entering God's kingdom (vv 23, 24, 25) in preparation for the impossibility of a camel's going through the eye of a needle (v 25). The forward positions of "the ones having means" and "into the kingdom of God" (see the Greek text; so also in vv 24-25 for the latter phrase) highlight the explosiveness of what Jesus has said. The disciples' amazement underlines this explosiveness. The plural in "at his words" includes both the saying addressed to the rich man (v 21; called "the word" in v 22) and the saying just now addressed to the disciples (cf. 8:33; 13:31 for similar plurals referring to Jesus' sayings; contrast 5:36; 7:29; 8:32; 9:10; 10:22; 11:29; 12:13; 14:39 for the singular of "word" in reference to one saying — apart from the singular of "word" elsewhere in the sense of the gospel).

10:24b-25 *(Matt 19:24; Luke 18:25)* "Again" prepares for an amplification of Jesus' teaching. "Answering" indicates a response to the disciples' amazement, since they have asked no question. Once more the historical present tense of λέγει, "he says," underlines the iconoclastic force of his words. "Children" (τέκνα), which did not appear in the initial saying (v 23b), implies that in his amplification Jesus takes the authoritative role of a father to explain something which his disciples, childish in their failure to understand, have not grasped. Or perhaps this address simply shows affection (cf. 2:5). It certainly adds emphasis to the following words. The exclamatory "how!" echoes v 23b, and a switch from the future tense in v 23b to the present tense transforms a prediction into a maxim. The statement that it is difficult to enter into the kingdom of God widens the initial statement in v 23b by omitting the reference to those who have means (with the grammatical results that the verb of entering turns into the impersonal verb of being, plus an infinitive, and that the adverb "difficultly" turns into the predicate adjective "difficult"). At least so it seems to many modern commentators and ancient scribes, the latter of whom filled in the gap left by the omission. But a number of factors call in question a deliberate widening in v 24b and favor a casual ellipsis designed to be filled from the preceding and succeeding verses: (1) "again"; (2) "answering"; (3) the repetitions of "how difficult!" and of entering the kingdom; and (4) the asyndeton which at the start of v 25 not only emphasizes that a camel goes through a needle's eye more easily than a rich person into the kingdom, but also clamps that saying as tightly as possible to the difficulty of entering the kingdom. But even though v 24b were to refer to a general difficulty in entering the kingdom, a rich person has special difficulty. So Jesus goes on to say that it is easier for a camel to go through the eye of a needle than for a rich person to enter into the kingdom of God. Later rabbis will talk about the impossibility of an elephant's going through the eye of a needle (Str-B 1. 828). But elephants are not seen in Palestine. Jesus speaks instead about a camel, because the common Palestinian use of camels as beasts of burden better suits the comparison to a person whose wealth prevents entrance into the kingdom just as a camel's burdens keep it from going through narrow openings and add to the impossibility of going through a needle's eye (E. Lohse in *Glaube und Eschatologie* 161-63). Since a camel cannot go through a needle's eye but it is "easier" for a rich person to enter God's kingdom, with humorously ironic hyperbole the entrance of a rich person into the kingdom turns out to be, not nearly impossible, not even fully impossible, but more than impossible. The forward positions of "easier," "a camel through the eye of a needle," and "a rich [person] into the kingdom of God" (see the Greek text) highlight this more-than-impossible.

10:26-27 *(Matt 19:25-26; Luke 18:26)* The explosiveness of Jesus' teaching comes forward again, and even more prominently, in the disciples' astonishment. It surpasses their earlier amazement in that Mark writes περισσῶς ἐξεπλήσσοντο, "were exceedingly astonished," plus a question of bewilderment, instead of a simple ἐθαμβοῦντο, "were amazed," without an adverb and without a following question (so v 24a). This escalation is due to Jesus' intervening equation of difficulty with more than impossibility. The disciples direct their question "to themselves," which probably means "to one another" (πρὸς ἑαυτούς — cf. 1:27; 9:10, 33; 11:31; 12:7; 14:4; 16:3; also πρὸς ἀλλήλους here in 10:26 M* k syᵖ geo; and contrast the easier and therefore suspect v.l. πρὸς αὐτόν, "to him," in א B C Δ Ψ 892 co). "Who then can be saved?" means, "If a pious person whose wealth is a sign of God's favor will not be saved, what hope of deliverance from hellfire does someone without that sign have?" Alternatively, from v 25 we are meant to supply πλούσιος with τίς: "What [rich person]?" Jesus' looking intently at the disciples matches his earlier looking intently at the rich man (v 21). But instead of a loving gesture such as he gave the rich man, he speaks the most astounding word of all: "With human beings, [this is] impossible; but [this is] not [impossible] with God, for all things [are] possible with God." Asyndeton emphasizes the gaze; and the gaze, the historical present tense of "he says," ellipses of the subject in the first two clauses of Jesus' saying, ellipses of the verb in all three clauses, ellipsis of the predicate adjective in the second clause, the strength of the adversative ἀλλ᾽, "but," with which the second clause opens, the antithetic parallelism of the first two clauses, the addition of a γάρ-clause, the chiastic word order of this clause in relation to the first two, its contrastive inclusion of the subject "all things," and the emphatic forward position of this subject — all these phenomena emphasize the explosiveness of Jesus' teaching that wealth makes salvation so humanly more than impossible that only the Almighty can bring it about (see references in R. H. Gundry, *Matthew* 390, on the allusion to Gen 18:14; also Mark 9:23 and esp. 14:36).

10:28-31 *(Matt 19:27-30; Luke 18:28-30)* The asyndeta with which v 28 and v 29 open follow up the asyndeton in v 27 to give the impression of a brisk exchange between Jesus and his disciples. Here, Peter speaks for them. Their having left all and followed Jesus contrasts with the rich man's sad departure at being told to sell all, give to the poor, and follow him. The emphatic ἡμεῖς, "we," brings out the contrast. Ἠκολουθήκαμεν σοι, "followed you," contrasts with the rich man's having gone away (v 22). The perfect tense of ἠκολουθήκαμεν stresses the completeness of the disciples' commitment, which has led to their present status as followers (against M. Black, *Aramaic Approach* 129-30). For Mark, Peter's statement carries factual truth and demonstrates the power of Jesus' magnetism (cf. 1:18, 20). Nor does Jesus criticize Peter for a sense of self-achievement. Rather, he issues two predictions of present and future rewards.

"Truly I say to you" adds solemnity to the first prediction. Omission of the ὅτι, "that," which is expected to follow, adds force (M. Reiser, *Syntax und Stil* 148). The universal negative in the words, "There is no one who has left . . . but that he will receive . . . ," makes the prediction more emphatic than the expected "you who have left . . . will receive . . ." would have been. The list of things left defines "all things" in Peter's statement. "House" leads to those with whom one has lived in it. Jesus lists them by class in ascending order of closeness to the one who leaves, viz., siblings, parents, and children. Because children have not reached sexual maturity, they do not need distinction as to sex. The order "brothers . . . sisters . . . mother . . . father" makes a chiastic pattern as to sex (cf. 3:35 up through "mother"). One is likely to have more than one brother and sister (hence the plurals), but not more than one father and mother (hence the singulars). The omission of "wife" suits Jesus' having taught the indissolubility of marriage (vv 1-12; cf. Peter's taking his wife on journeys — 1 Cor 9:5). Similarly, the use of τέκνα instead of παιδία avoids the shirking of fatherly responsibility for small children (cf. 9:36-37; 10:13-16, where παιδίον/-α occurs; see J. A. Wilde in *SBL 1978 Seminar Papers* 2. 63). "Farms" complements "houses" to finish out the mention of family property at the two extremes of the list. It may also be that the order of the list reflects increasing value in a rural society: brothers being of least value to a man because they compete for the family inheritance; sisters of more value because they can be married off at a profit, though they drain family resources beforehand; the mother of even greater value because of her labors on behalf of the family; the father of truly great value, because from him comes the inheritance; and farms of most value because they constitute the land that makes possible the family's existence from one generation to the next. By using "or" in v 29 Jesus is not promising a reward for less than full sacrifice. That meaning would fit neither his demand to sell everything and follow him (v 21; cf. v 28) nor Peter's statement that the disciples had left "all things" (v 28); and for that meaning we would expect "or" in v 30, too, in order that single rewards might match single sacrifices tit for tat (if you leave your house, you will gain other houses; but if you leave your brothers, you will gain other brothers, and so on). Furthermore, one can hardly leave father but not mother, children but not home, and so on (T. E. Schmidt, *Hostility* 115). The purpose of "or," then, is not to set out alternatives for people unwilling to leave all, but to make allowance for those people whose all does not include every item on the list — people, say, whose mother has died, who have no children, and so on. The switch to "and" in v 30 heaps all the rewards on top of each other so that en masse they outweigh the listed sacrifices, however many or few they have had to be. Those without mothers or children to leave, for example, will get such among fellow believers.

"On account of me" harks back to Jesus' calls to follow him (1:16-20 [including the leaving of a father]; 2:14; 8:34). "On account of the gospel" harks back to Jesus' preaching the gospel of God (1:14-15). Together, these phrases echo his calling on people to save their life by losing it, as he says, "on account of me and the gospel" (8:35; cf. also 13:9-10). He does not set out an ascetic ideal of poverty. Poverty serves evangelism, not private sanctification. For the present time of persecutions (διωγμῶν — literally, "pursuits"; cf. 4:17), Jesus promises a hundredfold reward of houses, brothers, sisters, mothers, children, and farms. If they have to flee from their pursuers to as many as a hundred different places, they will find a hundred different houses and families and farms through the hospitality of their fellow believers (cf. 3:31-35; John 19:26; Acts 2:44-45; 4:32-37 [including "a field" in v 37]; Rom 16:1b, 13; Gal 4:19; 1 Tim 5:1; Phlm 10; and the early Christian phenomenon of house-churches; also 2 Sam 24:3 par. 1 Chr 21:3 for a hundredfold). They are already enjoying such hospitality as they travel about with Jesus. The order of the first list repeats itself in the second; but "father" drops out, perhaps in view of God's fatherhood over Jesus' disciples.

Disciples have only one true father (cf. 11:25; Matt 23:9; differently, 1 Cor 4:15; Phlm 10). Alternatively, the omission of "father" may reflect the death of Joseph, Jesus' foster father (cf. 3:31-35). Best of all, Jesus predicts "in the coming age eternal life" (which the rich man wanted to inherit — v 17). "This time" and "the coming age" derive from Jewish eschatological terminology (H. Sasse in *TDNT* 1. 204-7). The many who are now first but will then be last are those who do not heed Jesus' call to leave all and follow him. Those who are now last but will be first are those who do leave all, whether or not they have had many possessions, and follow Jesus. Final lastness means exclusion from God's kingdom. Final firstness means admission into it. An adversative δέ, "but," contrasts final lastness with the destiny detailed in v 30 and about to be summarized as final firstness. The pericope ends, not on the minatory note of a judgmental prediction (v 31a), but on the encouraging note of a promissory prediction (v 31b; cf. 9:35; Luke 14:9-11; contrast the reverse order and consequent minatory emphasis in Matt 20:16; Luke 13:30).

NOTES

J. Jeremias (*Unknown Sayings* 44-47) defends the version of this story found in *Gos. Naz.* 16, but see J. D. Crossan (*In Fragments* 222-26) to the contrary. W. Egger (*Nachfolge* 179-84) surveys various deconstructions that aim to account for tensions in vv 17-31. The present comments and notes seek to show that the tensions are more imaginary than real, that the interconnections and progressions are more original than redactional. Jesus' party-going right after a call to follow him (2:14-17; cf. Matt 11:19 par. Luke 7:34; John 2:1-11) and his banquet-giving (6:35-44 parr.; 8:1-9 par.) scotch the theory that vv 17-31 deal with the question how it is possible for some to be ascetics (so ibid. 98-107). F. Manns (*Essais* 53-54) and C. Coulet (*Jésus et le disciple* 100) see concentric structure in the whole of the passage, not just within each of its main parts. Some of the correspondences between supposedly matching items are purely formal and highly selective, however. For example, the introduction in v 17a consists of a narrative statement, the conclusion in v 31 of a Jesuanic saying. Life eternal appears alone in v 17b but as the last in a list of items in v 30. Honoring your father and mother appears as the last of half a dozen commandments in v 19, leaving mother or father (N.B. the change in order and the shift from "and" to "or") in the middle of a list of things left for the sake of Jesus and the gospel in v 29b. Ἔφη, "he said," appears in vv 20 and 29; but the speakers differ (the rich man and Jesus) and their statements present a contrast rather than a correspondence (keeping the commandments without result of eternal life and receiving eternal life [among other things] for having left all to follow Jesus).

The lack of a definite article in εἰς ὁδόν (v 17) points to a road as such (as in 6:8 par. Matt 10:10 [but not Luke 9:3]; Matt 10:5). The road to Jerusalem has not yet appeared on Mark's verbal map (see 2:23; 8:27 with 9:33-34) and will not till 10:32, where the definite article will accompany it (as also in 10:46, 52; 11:8). The present indefiniteness favors tradition over redaction (cf. E. Lohmeyer 207, n. 1), though definiteness would not prove redaction, nor does it elsewhere. The denial by K. L. Schmidt (*Rahmen* 241-42) that going out to a road relates to going into the house at v 10 is dogmatic and unappreciative of narrative continuity.

See E. C. Maloney, *Semitic Interference* 126-31, on the Semitic use of εἷς, "one," for τις, "someone" (v 17). The rich man does not ask Jesus to grant a request. He asks only a question of information. Therefore just as his running shows Jesus' magnetism, so his kneeling shows extraordinary reverence toward Jesus, not earnest entreaty (contrast 1:40; 5:22-23; and despite the ending of this story in unconversion, cf. the comment of K. Berger [*Gesetzesauslegung* 1. 429] that kneeling characterizes stories of conversion). Though the address "Good Teacher" does not appear in contemporary Jewish literature, a rabbinic occurrence dating from the fourth century (*b. Taʿan.* 24b) shows its suitability to a Jewish milieu. And though E. Lohmeyer (208, n. 2) points to Greek use of "good" in direct address, he does not example the combination "good teacher" in a non-Jewish milieu.

W. L. Lane (365) draws a contrast between the rich man's thinking that he must do something to inherit eternal life (v 17) and Jesus' having spoken of receiving God's kingdom as a child receives it (v 15). This contrast founders on Jesus' telling the rich man to do more than he has already done. The similarity between receiving the kingdom and inheriting eternal life also militates against the suggested contrast and favors that the obedience which Jesus demands is evidential *of* repentance and faith, not meritorious *as* repentance and faith (cf. 1:15). See S. Légasse, *L'appel* 27, n. 28, for parallels to inheriting eternal life.

E. C. Maloney (*Semitic Interference* 142-44) refutes the suggestion of M. Black (*Aramaic Approach* 122-23) that τί is a Semitism meaning, "Can it be that . . . ?" (v 18). For the authenticity of v 18, it is often noted that the doctrine of Jesus' sinlessness (John 8:46; 2 Cor 5:21; Heb 7:26; 1 Pet 2:22) would have kept early Christians from making up a statement that could easily be taken to imply his sinfulness. The observation of L. Cope (in *New Synoptic Studies* 153) that text critical evidence in the parallel Matt 19:17 betrays the early church's preference for Mark's text over the Christologically safer text of Matthew might seem to weaken this argument, and Cope himself uses his observation to argue against Marcan priority. But scribes seem to have conformed Matthew to Mark because of the abrupt shift from the neuter τί ἀγαθόν . . . περὶ τοῦ ἀγαθοῦ, "what good thing . . . concerning the good thing," to the masculine gender in Matthew's original εἷς ἐστιν ὁ ἀγαθός, "One is the good [one]." The canonical authority of Mark overcame whatever Christological offense might have otherwise kept scribes from assimilating Matthew to Mark for a grammatico-stylistic reason. Cope's attempt to ground the priority of Matthew's original in a reference to the Torah (ὁ νόμος, "the Law"), not to Jesus, comes to grief in the LXX of the very passages which his prooftext *m. ʾAbot* 6:3 plays upon, viz., Prov 3:35; 4:2, 4; 28:10. The LXX uses the neuter δῶρον . . . ἀγαθόν, "a good gift" (4:2), and ἀγαθά, "good things" (28:10). It does not describe ὁ νόμος as ἀγαθός. A reference to the Torah in the statement of Matthew's Jesus would almost certainly have stuck to the neuter. The masculine ὁ νόμος is nowhere in sight, and the neuter τί ἀγαθόν . . . περὶ τοῦ ἀγαθοῦ already leans toward and perhaps refers to the Torah.

B. B. Warfield (*Christology and Criticism* 104-5) argues that a contrast between Jesus and God entails an illegitimate stress on με, "me" (v 18). The position of με before the verb does put stress on it, however; and the indubitable contrast between Jesus and God in 2:7, which also carried the phrase "except one, [i.e.] God," favors that contrast here as well. See the foregoing comments on Jesus' drawing the contrast to highlight his proceeding to exercise a divine prerogative. To say that he merely rejects flattery and avoids self-righteousness in favor of keeping the commandments (so D. E. Nineham 270; T. A. Burkill, *New Light* 132, n. 8, for example) is to miss the implication that he possesses the goodness of God. Or to say with K. Berger (*Gesetzesauslegung* 1. 399) that because God alone is good, Jesus can do nothing else but point to God's commandments is to neglect that Jesus does do something else, something astonishingly self-promoting: he tells the rich man that keeping God's' commandments will not bring him eternal life, but that carrying out Jesus' commands will — and it is the *one* thing that will. To foist on Jesus' own words the interpretation that as a human being he has yet to grow into goodness (cf. Heb 4:15;

5:8) attributes to him a developmental self-analysis. See V. Taylor 426-27 for a survey of interpretations.

For references to the goodness of human beings as well as of God, see W. Grundmann in *TDNT* 1. 12-16; E. Lohmeyer 209, nn. 1-2; V. Taylor 426; C. E. B. Cranfield 326. Even after we discount redaction, it is clear that on other occasions Jesus describes some human beings as good (Matt 12:35 par. Luke 6:45; Matt 25:21 par. Luke 19:17; Matt 5:45; 7:15-19; 22:10; 25:23; Luke 8:15). Here, then, he must be using "good" in a sense that would qualify a person to inherit eternal life, i.e. in a sense appropriate only to God. K. Berger (*Gesetzesauslegung* 1. 398-99, n. 1) denies the definition of goodness as kindness in favor of goodness as uprightness, seen in the Decalogic commandments immediately quoted. But because Mark will shortly refer to Jesus' love (v 21) and because throughout biblical and extra-biblical literature goodness includes kindness as well as uprightness, we do well not to restrict the meaning here.

An allusion to Deut 6:4 is unlikely in εἰ μὴ εἷς ὁ θεός, which says that God alone is good, not that he alone is God (contrast the phraseology in 12:29, which quotes Deut 6:4). By the same token, εἷς is probably not a divine title, "One." Even more distant are the thought and wording of Exod 20:2-3, which teaches exclusivity of worship, not the exclusivity of God's goodness. See also the notes on 2:7.

Philo *Mut.* 1 §7 does not really contradict the statement in the comments that neither Jew nor Greek would say that God alone is good. Writing in an epistemological vein, Philo affirms exclusivity in the sense that God's goodness is inapprehensible, noetically as well as empirically. Speaking of conduct, Jesus affirms exclusivity in the sense that God's goodness is unattainable. The different frames of reference keep the statements from intersecting. The further statement of Philo in *Somn.* 1. 23 §149, often cited with the former one, does not affirm the exclusivity of God as good.

R. Busemann (*Jüngergemeinde* 91) asks what relation the list of commandments in v 19 has to the goodness of God alone in v 18. None, we may answer; for Jesus has stopped responding to the address "Good Teacher" and started responding to the question, "What should I do to inherit eternal life?" The pattern is a-b-a'-b'.

By saying, "You know the commandments," and quoting some of the Decalogue, Jesus rejects the question, "What should I do . . . ?" just as by asking, "Why do you call me good? [And so on]," he rejects the address "Good Teacher." So states E. Lohmeyer (209-10). We have seen, however, that Jesus does not reject the address "Good Teacher"; and the loving gaze that he gives the man after the man's affirmation of obedience does not favor his rejecting the question of what the man must do. Nor does Jesus' going on to tell him the one thing he must do. It distorts the picture to note that unlike a typical rabbi, Jesus does not interpret some commandments but merely quotes them (E. Schweizer 211-12: "absence of all legalistic pedantry"). The one thing necessary differs from and goes far beyond the commandments merely quoted.

It is not true to say that only the commandments of the second table are mentioned because it is by a man's obedience to them that his obedience to those of the first table must be outwardly demonstrated (C. E. B. Cranfield 328). Not worshiping other gods, not practicing idolatry, not taking the Lord's name in vain, and keeping the Sabbath need no demonstration beyond themselves. Nor can obedience to the second table demonstrate obedience to the first table, for non-murderers may practice idolatry, non-adulterers may break the Sabbath, and so on. Moreover, the command to honor your father and mother belongs to the first table, though it shares the social dimensions of the later commandments. The suggestion that Jesus doubles back to the command to honor your father and mother because its promise of a long life on earth links up with the rich man's question about inheriting eternal life is weakened by the difference between long life now and eternal life hereafter.

For arguments favoring the prohibition of adultery before murder (as in A W Θ f[13] 157 *pm* lat Cl Majority Text) rather than vice versa (as in B א[corr] C Δ Ψ *pc* sy[s] co[sa,bo]), see R. H. Gundry, *Use of the OT* 17-19; idem, *Matthew* 386). Adultery comes before murder also in Luke 18:20 (which seems to reflect Mark's original text, since Luke agrees with Mark in the subjunctive of prohibition — contrast Matt 19:18) and in Rom 13:9; Jas 2:11; Exod 20:13-14 (some Hebrew MSS, LXX[B,Luc[75]]); Deut 5:17-18 (some Hebrew MSS, LXX[B]); Nash Papyrus; Philo *Decal.* 24-25 §§121-34; 32 §§168-70; Tert. *Pudic.* 5; Theoph. *Autol.* 2.35; 3.9; Clem. *Strom.* 6.146-47. Later assimilation to the usual OT order of murder before adultery seems more likely than later divergence from it; and Rom 13:9; Jas 2:11 may reflect the dominical order in Mark's original text (cf. the characteristically dominical emphasis on loving one's neighbor in both epistolary contexts). If we nevertheless favor murder before adultery as the original order, the possibility arises that Jesus starts with the most serious injury, works downward, and ends on a positive commandment. The omission of μὴ ἀποστερήσῃς, "You shouldn't defraud," in B* K W Δ Ψ f[1,13] 28 700 1010 *al* sy[s] lr Cl and by Matthew and Luke is probably due to scribes' and the other synoptists' purging from the list of commandments the one commandment not found in the Decalogue. Later insertion of such a commandment seems less likely.

According to R. Busemann (*Jüngergemeinde* 94-95), Mark inserts "you shouldn't defraud" to guard against breaking the command, "Honor your father and mother," when giving up everything to follow Jesus: duty to parents persists, as shown in 7:8-13 by his criticizing the use of Corban to defraud parents. The absence of "defraud" from 7:8-13 makes the connection between defrauding here and the misuse of Corban there so subtle, however, that we do better to ascribe it to the mind of Jesus than to Mark's redaction. And it is easier to see "you shouldn't defraud" as leading via Corban to "honor your father and mother" than to see it as holding in check the commands of Jesus to sell all, give to the poor, and follow him. Those commands do not come up till two verses later, and a concern to hold them in check with regard to filial duty would probably have caused Mark to qualify the leaving of mother and father in vv 29-30, too.

With the prohibition of defrauding (v 19), cf. Exod 21:10 LXX; Lev 19:13 with 19:11[ἄλλος in the Hexapla]; Deut 24:14 LXX[A,F]; Sir 4:1 LXX. Could it be that the last of these cross-references has supplied the subjunctive of prohibition, which distinguishes Mark's version of the quoted commandments from all other versions (except those of Jas 2:10 and of Luke, who follows Mark)? Does Jas 2:10 reflect Marcan or pre-Marcan tradition in this respect? Since Jas 2:10-11 clearly quotes the Decalogue but uses the subjunctive of prohibition, it is wrong to make that subjunctive into an argument that Jesus does not quote from but only alludes to the Decalogue. G. L. Archer and G. Chirichigno (*OT Quotations* 21) suggest Jesus' use of a textual tradition like that of Deut 24:14 LXX[A,F]. It is generally recognized, however, that LXX[A] and its followers often betray influence from the NT (cf. R. H. Gundry, *Use of the OT* 166, n. 3).

The middle voice of ἐφυλαξάμην may be deponent: "I have kept" (v 20; BAGD s.v. φυλάσσω 2b). But by disagreeing with the feminine gender of τὰς ἐντολάς, "the command-ments," the neuter phrase ταῦτα πάντα favors the normal meaning of this verb in the middle: "I have guarded against all these things [i.e. the things prohibited *in* the commandments]." Because the rich man asked what he should do to inherit eternal life even though he had a clear conscience, W. Harrington (160) interprets his claim to have kept the command-ments as an indication of remaining dissatisfaction (cf. v 20 with v 17). But for this meaning, "I have guarded against *these* things" would have sufficed. "I have guarded against *all* these things *since my youth*" says more and thereby favors a shift from dissatis-faction to relief, perhaps even to a newly won confidence.

S. T. Lachs (*Rabbinic Commentary* 331) theorizes that in v 21 ἠγάπησεν, "loved," mistranslates רחם according to its Hebrew meaning instead of its intended Aramaic meaning, "pitied." This theory appeals to a false dichotomy between Hebrew and Aramaic meanings. Furthermore, pity would not become appropriate till the middle or end of v 22. Love becomes appropriate as early as v 21, however.

E. Lohmeyer (208-9) notes that the rich man's question contained an ambiguity: Was he asking what *in* the Torah he should do, or what *beyond* it he should do? Verse 21 answers with what he should do beyond it. W. Harnisch (in *Festschrift für Ernst Fuchs* 171-76) goes on to say that selling all, giving to the poor, and following Jesus contrast as non-achievements with the achievements of keeping the Torah. But this contrast imposes on the words of Jesus a too Pauline opposition of faith to works. How is the avoidance of adultery, for example, more an achievement than is the selling of all and giving to the poor? How is the doing of good less an achievement than is the avoidance of sin?

On four grounds, R. Busemann (*Jüngergemeinde* 98-99) argues that "And hither! Follow me" is a late addition to v 21: (1) Jesus' having already answered the man's question; (2) the awkwardness of a copulative καί, "and," after a clause introduced with an ecbatic καί, "then"; (3) the suitability of the man's sorrowful response to the commands to sell all and give to the poor as against the unsuitability of such a response to the command to follow Jesus; (4) the redactional character of the similar v 28. This last argument is circular: v 28 may come from tradition. The man's leaving (ἀπῆλθεν) constitutes a response to the command to follow, and this response is as suitably negative as is his sorrow in relation to the commands to sell and give. If there is any awkwardness at all, it belongs to the ecbatic καί; and it is awkward because the promise of having treasure in heaven advances from the expected last position of an ecbatic clause to stand contrastively beside selling all and giving to the poor. The command to follow Jesus comes afterward, not because it is redactional, but because its coming one step earlier would have damaged the contrast. In view of Jesus' other calls to follow him (1:17, 20; 2:14; 8:34), including one with the rationale of saving your life (ψυχήν — 8:34 with 8:35-37), the commands to sell all and give to the poor do not by themselves tell the man what he must do to inherit eternal life.

Because the promise "and you will have treasure in heaven" interrupts a series of imperatives and represents a common Jewish and Christian theme, C. Coulot (*Jésus et le disciple* 118-19) considers the promise a redactional addition. But agreement with Jewish and Christian themes provides no basis for denial of authenticity. Matt 6:19-21 par. Luke 12:33-34, cited by Coulot (cf. Luke 16:9), provides an independent basis in Q for the affirmation of authenticity. And we should hardly expect a series of three successive imperatives to proceed further without interruption. Since "and" does not appear between the first two imperatives, the "and" which introduces the third imperative leads one to expect an interruption before any further imperative. Without the promise, conversely, we would expect "go, sell . . . , give . . . , and hither, follow me," not "go, sell . . . , *and give* . . . , and hither, follow me."

T. E. Schmidt (*Hostility* 111) discusses reasons not to limit Jesus' commands to the rich man at hand: (1) the similarity of v 21 to 1:16-20; 2:14; 8:34; (2) the application of v 21 to the disciples in vv 28-30; and (3) the absence of any reference in v 22 to the rich man's loving his possessions. Yet his crestfallen departure and Mark's editorial comment, "for he had many possessions," imply a love of possessions; and Jesus' not making the same demand of everybody, not even of the apostles, suggests that his demands differed from one person to another. Though Simon and Andrew, James and John, and Levi left all to follow Jesus (v 28), they did not have to sell all their possessions and give to the poor (1:16-20; 2:14). Not only does Jesus' command to sell all contradict the rabbinic prohibition of selling all (see the foregoing comments). His command to give the proceeds to the poor and follow him contradicts the requirement at Qumran that you put your wealth in a treasury common to the sect which you are joining (J. W. Bowman 214). J. Carmignac (in *ASTI* 7

[1968-69] 71) thinks that underlying v 22 is a wordplay between וַיָּשָׁב and וַיֵּשָׂם for going away and grieving. But שׁוּם, "estimate," would not produce Mark's λυπούμενος, "grieving"; and though שָׁמַם, "be astonished," would come closer (but not close enough, for in the LXX λυπέω never stands for it), Carmignac's assonant form would not represent that verb.

To some, the shift from κτήματα (v 22) to χρήματα (v 23) seems to indicate different origins for vv 17-22 and vv 23-27. But one can detect a rationale for the shift. As explained in the foregoing comments, κτήματα means "acquisitions" and therefore contrasts with selling. Χρήματα means "means" and refers especially to money, e.g., money gotten by selling (Acts 4:37). It is natural, then, that κτήματα should occur in Mark 10:22 for the many acquisitions which Jesus has told the rich man to sell and give to the poor, and that χρήματα should occur in v 23 for the means, the money, which comes from the sale of κτήματα but is hard to give up.

R. Busemann (*Jüngergemeinde* 208-9) thinks vv 17-22 go easier on the rich man than vv 23-27 do. But "how difficultly!" and "how difficult!" in vv 23-27 stem from the same love of Jesus for the man that vv 17-22 note; and the man is just as lost according to vv 17-22, where despite Jesus' loving him he leaves downcast and sorrowing at Jesus' demand, as he is lost according to vv 23-27. In fact, "all things are possible with God" leaves the door of salvation open at least as wide in vv 23-27 as does the possibility in vv 17-22 that the rich man will do what is lacking despite his sorrow at having to do so.

Against treating vv 23-27 as originally independent from vv 17-22, C. E. B. Cranfield (325) notes that vv 17-22 seem incomplete without some comment by Jesus on the rich man's sorrowful departure — a strange ending if an ending it is. Of course, to overcome this objection one might dismiss vv 22, which tells of the rich man's sorrowful departure, as a transitional addition that spoils the original climax of the apothegm in v 21 (so W. Harnisch [in *Festschrift für Ernst Fuchs* 162-63, 171-74], except that he hesitates to dismiss v 22a along with v 22b — but he must do so to overcome the objection). Conversely, the dialogue in vv 23-27 needs material such as we find in vv 17-22 to prompt it. We can hardly imagine Jesus' exclaiming out of the blue — or his being made to do so — that the wealthy find it humanly more than impossible to enter the kingdom of God; and it is hard to imagine material more likely than that in vv 17-22 to have prompted the exclamation and dialogue.

If Mark were in the habit of fabricating houses and other places of privacy for Jesus to teach his disciples, we would have expected him to do so in v 23. By the standards of those who think that he does so elsewhere, his failure to do so here disfavors redaction. The occurrence of expressions in vv 23-27 that appear elsewhere in Mark a significant number of times — περιβλεψάμενος, "looking around"; ἐθαμβοῦντο, "were amazed"; ἐξεπλήσσοντο, "were astonished"; πρὸς ἑαυτούς, "to themselves" — does not imply that Mark has pieced together these verses from different sources, much less created them out of nothing (cf. J. Schlosser, *Le règne* 541-69, for example). They may have appeared significantly often in the tradition, or Mark may have borrowed a few traditional occurrences and multiplied them, or have inserted all the expressions — but into originally unified tradition. Schlosser (loc. cit.) argues that the general sayings in vv 24, 26-27 originally went together without reference to rich people. But the present framework of reference to the rich gives a sharper point to the force of Jesus' exclamation in v 24, to the extreme of the disciples' astonishment in v 26, and to the emphasis on human impossibility in v 27.

J. Schmid (192) argues for the redactional character of v 24 that v 25 links better with v 23, since v 24 generalizes the difficulty of entering the kingdom whereas vv 23 and 25 specify the difficulty only of a rich person in entering it. In support of this argument he cites Matthew's and Luke's omission of v 24, the inversion of vv 24 and 25 in D it (against whose originality see E. Best, *Disciples and Discipleship* 20-21), and the vv.ll. which insert references to the rich in v 24. But we have seen reasons to doubt a generalization in v 24; and the editorial manipulations of v 24 in Matthew, Luke, and Marcan vv.ll. argue for the traditional as well as textual originality of v 24. That is to say, the more difficult is more likely to be original in tradition history as well as in textual history.

Under the generalizing view of v 24, R. Busemann (*Jüngergemeinde* 58) thinks that the difficulty of entering the kingdom disagrees with the promise of salvation in vv 28-31. But if God is able to save even the rich, as stated in v 27, he is all the more able to save others as well. If v 24 were designed to soften the impossibility of a rich person's entering God's kingdom to a mere difficulty (so L. Schottroff and W. Stegemann, *Jesus von Nazareth* 35), we would probably see in the verse an explicit reference to the rich. As it is, such a reference is at most implied and perhaps totally absent.

N. Walter (in *ZNW* 53 [1962] 209-12) puts a break between v 24a and v 24b to explain why v 24b essentially repeats v 23 and why v 26a essentially repeats the disciples' amazement in v 24a. But "again" and "answering" in v 24b indicate a continuation rather than a new start, and "were exceedingly astonished" in v 26a intensifies rather than repeats the earlier amazement. It is puzzling why the disciples' amazement in v 24a should be thought to necessitate the repetition in v 24b of "how difficult . . . !" from v 23b (so E. Schweizer 209). Their even greater astonishment in v 26 does not bring another repetition, but leads to a new saying (v 27) just as their amazement in v 24a could have led directly to the new saying in v 25.

The change from the plural of "they who have means" (v 23) to the singular of "a rich [person]" (v 25) is due to the comparison with a camel and is thus so natural that we dare not use it to assign separate origins to the sayings in which they occur. The eleventh century Byzantine exegete Theophylact suggested that "The Eye of the Needle" is the name of a small gate in Jerusalem. With much dependence on Islamic sources R. Köbert (in *Bib* 53 [1972] 229-33) has revived the interpretation of κάμηλος, "camel," as κάμιλος, "rope, ship's towline" (more recently, see F. Gignac in *To Touch the Text* 44). The stress on human impossibility in v 27 and the rabbinic parallels featuring an elephant militate against these and similar suggestions and favor another large animal, i.e. a camel (see T. Zahn, *Matthäus* 598-99, n. 71). The figure of a camel loaded with burdens suits a rich man loaded with wealth so well that the theory of an earlier version of v 25 unlimited to the rich looks doubtful.

The sheer impossibility of a camel's going through the eye of a needle does not disagree with the mere difficulty of a rich person's entering the kingdom of God. The exclamatory πῶς, "how!" shows that the difficulty is not mere, and the severity of a difficulty may make the difficulty equal to an impossibility. This lack of necessary disagreement takes away a reason to think of vv 24, 26-27 as secondary. A disagreement would require the secondariness of v 23, too, though few take that position.

K.-G. Reploh (*Lehrer* 192-201) asks why the disciples should be astounded as though they themselves are rich and despairing of entry into the kingdom (vv 24, 26). He then reasons that their astoundment is artificially constructed to make them represent rich people in Mark's church. That the disciples are not rich but have left all to follow Jesus (v 28) is supposed to support the artificiality of the construction. Elsewhere in Mark, however, the verbs of astoundment that Mark uses here — θαμβέομαι and ἐκπλήσσομαι — carry no connotation of despair (see 1:22, 27; 6:2; 7:37; 10:32; 11:18, with a possible exception in 10:32). Because of its perfective prefix, ἐκθαμβέομαι would be the verb which might carry that connotation (9:15; 14:33; 16:5, 6). There is no reason why the disciples cannot be astounded over the fate of others whose wealth would seem to indicate God's favor.

To allow Marcan composition of the introduction in vv 26a, 27a is not to imply that the sayings in vv 26b, 27bc stem from an independent tradition. Perhaps they do, but it is equally possible that these sayings occurred together in pre-Marcan tradition, even that

Jesus was remembered to have spoken them on the same occasion, and that Mark has written up the introductions according to his own manner and purpose. It may be that "to be saved" intrudes technical Christian terminology into the disciples' question (v 26b). But the disciples, and then early Christians, may have learned this terminology from Jesus (cf. 8:35; also Luke 19:10 with I. H. Marshall, *Luke* 698-99). Allusive quotation of the OT in v 27c gives no reason to deny authenticity. It is likely that Jesus used the OT.

Verses 26-27 do not teach salvation by God's grace so much as salvation by God's power. God's power would not save the rich man despite his failure to sell all, give to the poor, and follow Jesus. It would enable him to obey these commands. In such respects W. C. van Unnik (in *Verborum Veritas* 30-36) offers a partial corrective to F. G. Lang (in *Rechtfertigung* 329-35) as well as a stock of extra-biblical parallels to v 27. See also S. E. Dowd, *Prayer* 69-94, for background on the issue whether anything is impossible with God, and the foregoing comments in the present commentary for indications that v 27 is anything but a lame climax (against K.-G. Reploh, *Lehrer* 192).

Verses 23-27 do not deal with rich disciples, but with rich non-disciples. Jesus addresses his disciples but speaks of the rich as outside their midst (cf. vv 17-22). Therefore the contrast with vv 28-31 is not one between rich and poor in the church, but between rich non-disciples and poor disciples in the world — and between their respective loss and gain, as in 8:34-38.

Verses 28-31 are often regarded as unoriginal to the present context. Perhaps so, but appreciation of the contrast between the disciples and the rich man might lead to a different estimate, one that recognizes a single historical episode. The asyndeton with which v 28 opens does not favor insertion of an originally independent tradition. It is one in a series of asyndeta (see the foregoing comments).

More formidable are reasons put forward by E. Best (*Disciples and Discipleship* 17-18; *Following Jesus* 112-13) to consider vv 28-31 originally independent and partly unhistorical: (1) These verses do not speak of wealth, as do the preceding verses. (2) The preceding verses carry no promise of earthly reward, as these verses do. (3) Peter would not have shown astoundment in vv 24, 26 if he had left all, as v 28 makes him claim to have done. (4) "The historical Peter had not at his call (1:16-18) left house and wife (1:28-31), and may even have continued to possess a boat (3:9; 4:1, 36) and a net (Mt 17:24-27), and so he could not have said 'we have left all.'" (5) "If the saying of vv. 29f. had originally been addressed [sic] to Peter it would surely have contained a reference to 'ships' rather than 'fields.'"

But why should vv 28-31 speak of wealth when Peter and his fellow disciples were not wealthy to begin with? Yet the rich man's sorrowful departure because Jesus had told him to divest himself of his wealth and Jesus' sayings on the difficulty of the wealthy in entering the kingdom might easily have prompted a non-wealthy disciple to point to himself and his fellows by way of contrast (also against the assertion of J. Schmid [190] that Peter's remark in v 28 is psychologically improbable). Verses 28-31 carry a promise of earthly reward because the disciples have in fact left all to follow Jesus and therefore need the families and resources of sedentary believers to carry on an itinerant ministry. The rich man's failure to sell all, give to the poor, and follow Jesus made it appropriate that such a promise not appear in vv 17-27.

Having left all to follow Jesus does not preclude astoundment that wealth makes entry into the kingdom humanly impossible; for people consider wealth combined with piety, as in the case of the rich man, a sign of God's favor, and Jesus does not call all believers to follow him (in the literal sense) as disciples ("learners," who to learn from Jesus have to go around with him and who include more than the Twelve). It is non-following believers who provide new houses, families, and farms for itinerant believers who have forsaken such. These sedentary believers will hardly be barred from the kingdom (cf. 3:13-14 with 3:9; 3:32-35; 4:10; 6:7-11). Only later will "follow" and "disciple" lose their literal reference to itinerant pupils and evangelists so as to include all believers (cf. M. Hengel, *Charismatic Leader* 61-63). The historical Peter may not have sold his property and goods, but he has left them — and that is all he claims to have done. The plural of "you" (ὑμῖν) in "truly I say to you" and the generality of "there is no one who" (v 29) make a reference to "farms" appropriate. Only a limited address to Peter, Andrew, James, John, and a few other fishers would make "ships" (better: "boats") more appropriate. There are more farmers than fishers.

See the notes on 1:45 for the pleonastic use of ἤρξατο, "began." The "and" between "left" and "followed" is telic: "we left all things for the purpose of following you" (M. Reiser, *Syntax und Stil* 130-31). The combination of leaving and following occurred in a narrative statement at 1:18. We need not deduce that Mark fabricates Peter's statement in v 28, however; for a tradition behind v 28 may have influenced the composition of 1:18. Or that narrative statement may have been traditional rather than editorial, for Peter may have told the story of his call in words that he used also in reminding Jesus of that event. J. Ernst (in *Begegnung mit dem Wort* 53) goes so far as to argue that Peter's statement is original and historical precisely because of its agreement with the call story, though Ernst's opinion that vv 29-30 arise out of later Christian fabrication leaves one wondering why Peter's statement was preserved in the tradition if not because of its evoking a dominical saying such as vv 29-30 provide. Conversely, it is hard to think of a more likely evocation of vv 29-30 than v 28 provides.

One also wonders why vv 29-30 would have followed v 21 more naturally than they follow v 28 (so H. Anderson 248). Verse 21 spoke of selling all and giving to the poor. Verses 29-30 speak of leaving all, as v 28 does. R. L. Lindsey (*Hebrew Translation* 47-49) argues for the priority of Luke 18:29 in that the definition of "house" as "household" by what he considers to be Luke's redactional addition of "or wife or brothers or parents or children" makes for an easier understanding than "house" as a physical structure corresponding to "farms," as in Mark. But "or" sets out an alternative, not a definition; so "house" remains a physical structure in Luke. Even otherwise, a greater ease would disfavor Luke's version. The more difficult version is likely prior.

E. S. Fiorenza (*In Memory of Her* 145-46) argues that to limit wandering charismatics to men, Luke 18:29 adds "wife" to the list of those left. The absence of "wife" in the similar list at Mark 10:29 then implies that originally women as well as men left house, family, and farms to follow Jesus. The presence of "wife" among those to be "hated" for the sake of discipleship in Luke 14:26 undermines this argument, however. Some have regarded "wife" in Luke 14:26 as redactional; but its presence looks more original than its absence in the parallel Matt 10:37; and Luke 14:20, which also looks more original than its parallel in Matt 22:6, favors the originality of "wife" in Luke 14:26 (R. H. Gundry, *Matthew* 200, 435). Luke 8:1-3; 23:49 mention women as followers of Jesus, but as material supporters, not as charismatics (cf. Mark 15:40-41, esp. διηκόνουν, "were serving"). "Wives" fails to appear among the things received in v 30, not to avoid hundredfold polygamy, but because "wife" did not appear among the things left in v 29.

There is no need to give ἀγρούς the meaning "region" instead of "farms" for an allusion to charismatic preachers who wander from the region of their upbringing. That meaning would violate the family orientation of the preceding items. And in what sense would "regions" be a reward? See the foregoing comments on the climax to which "farms" brings the lists in vv 29-30.

K. Stock (in *Bib* 62 [1981] 581) thinks that "on account of the gospel" means "because that person has believed the gospel," not "because that person has preached the gospel." But since Jesus is speaking only about the one who has heeded his call to follow him for the purpose of learning and evangelism, not about believers in general, we should probably include the preached gospel. If Jesus preached "the gospel of God," i.e. the good news that "God's rule has come near" (1:14-15), and if he called some people to follow him (1:17, 20; 2:14; 8:34; cf. 3:13-15), we should not reject out of hand the authenticity of "on account of me" or of "on account of the gospel" (v 29). Similarly, if he foresaw his own sufferings, we should not deny tout court his foreseeing and predicting the persecutions of his followers. "With persecutions" (v 30) is not out of place. It defines the situation in which a hundredfold new resources are needed. See the notes on 8:35; 14:9 for further discussion.

The duality of "now, in this time" typifies Mark (F. Neirynck, *Duality* 45-53, 94-96) and may favor his insertion of "now" (cf. its lacking a counterpart in the contrastive "coming age" and its absence from Luke 18:30; Mark 10:30 D *pc* a q sy^s). "Time" (καιρῷ) is a Hellenistic equivalent for the more Jewish "age" (αἰῶνι). "This time" may therefore represent Mark's Hellenization of an original "this age" as opposed to "the coming age." Or is it that since Jesus does not elsewhere contrast the two ages (except in redactional touches — so J. Schmid 196 with respect to Luke 16:8; 20:34-35; Matt 12:32; 13:39, 40, 49; 24:3; 28:20), Mark has inserted the whole contrast, and perhaps also repeated the list of v 29 between the elements of the contrast? If repetition of the list goes to Mark's account, Jesus' promise may have been exclusively eschatological in its original version. Yet the currency of the contrast between two ages leaves possible that Jesus as well as later Christians used it (cf. the Aramaic background discussed by K. Beyer, *Semitische Syntax* 1/1. 119-20; M. McNamara, *Targum and Testament* 133-35; and the notes on 4:13-20, which defend the authenticity of that passage, including "the age" in v 19).

Jesus' and his disciples' repeatedly going into houses and the repeated scribal and Pharisaic criticisms of Jesus and his disciples — including the coming of scribes from Jerusalem, the lying in wait to catch him in a chargeable offense, and a plot against his life (2:1–3:6 passim; 3:22; 7:1-5; 8:11, 15; 9:14; 10:2, not to list later passages, others that mention entering a house, or the passion predictions) — show that the hospitality and persecutions of which Jesus speaks have already started. To Mark and his audience, "now, in the present time" begins with Jesus' time; for Jesus is speaking yet is absent at the time of Mark's writing and their hearing the gospel read (2:20; against B. M. F. van Iersel in *NedTTs* 24 [1980] 20). P. J. Achtemeier (49-50) cites vv 29-30 as an example of Jesus' predicting something fulfilled only after Mark's narrative comes to an end. But since Jesus speaks of what is already happening (contrast *T. Job* 4:6-7), the accent does not fall on the then and now of his prediction and its fulfilment. At least it does not do so till he speaks of eternal life in the coming age and of final lastness and firstness. Chap. 13 will differ in this respect. To argue that the promise of present earthly reward disagrees with Jesus' teaching elsewhere (so J. Schmid [196], who cites Matt 6:4, 6, 17) puts too much meaning into the word "reward." Jesus is promising a provision for need more than a prize for service. Is "with persecutions" inserted to keep insincere people from following Jesus for earthly rewards (E. Best, *Following Jesus* 114), or to debunk pretentiousness with an ironic joke (R. C. Tannehill, *Sword* 43-44)? Or does it merely provide the reason why his followers have to flee from house to house, from family to family, from farm to farm? The unemphatic position of the phrase favors this last possibility.

Because repetitiveness characterizes oral communication, the repetitiveness of the list in v 30 does not favor literary fabrication by Mark. The duality of Marcan style does not go to the elaborate length that characterizes this list; and Matthew's and Luke's omission of the list comes from redaction (see the commentaries), not from a more original pre-Marcan tradition. Jesus' statements in 3:33-35 differ enough from the list in 10:30 to reduce to a suggestion the argument that those statements helped Mark fabricate this list, but they resemble it well enough to suit its dominical authenticity (cf. D. O. Via, *Ethics* 143).

Peter's verb "followed" does not recur in Jesus' response. But "on account of me" amounts to the same thing and therefore takes away any reason to treat the non-recurrence as evidence that Mark has artificially constructed the dialogue (against R. Cameron, *Sayings Traditions* 74-77). One might argue more convincingly that recurrence would suit artificial construction better than a shift in phraseology does. 2 Sam 24:3 and its parallel 1 Chr 21:3 show that "a hundredfold" need not carry distinctively eschatological overtones, especially when referring to people, as there and here; nor was the expression eschatological in 4:8, 20 (see the comments and notes ad loc.). Hence, it offers no basis to regard the following list as eschatological (so D. O. Via, *Ethics* 144-45) or to regard it as a secondary uneschatological addition (so Cameron, loc. cit.). Even if "a hundredfold" had been eschatological in 4:8, 20, the present references to people and property would not be equivalent to the eschatological fruitfulness there. By disjoining "house" from the next-listed family members, "or" prevented our taking οἰκίαν in v 29 as a "household." Parallelism then requires that neither should οἰκίας be taken thus in v 30.

J. R. Donahue (*Theology and Setting* 43) suggests that antipatriarchalism in Mark's church keeps "fathers' from the list of receipts in v 30. The suggestion makes one wonder why Mark retains the double emphasis on honoring fathers as well as mothers in 7:9-13 and 10:19. D. O. Via (*Ethics* 143) answers that antipatriarchalism in Mark's church leaves room for natural family relations apart from the church. But "houses" and "farms" show that persecuted disciples find new families, not in the church qua church, but in the families of fellow believers hospitable to them.

Does v 31 represent a floating tradition, originally detached but later inserted here and in the parallel Matt 19:30 as well as in Mark 9:35; Matt 20:16; Luke 13:30 (cf. *POxy.* 654. 3; *Gos. Thom.* 4; 1 Cor. 4:9)? Or did Jesus himself apply the dictum variously? Or did it stray from original settings in Mark 9:35 and especially 10:31, only to surface in Luke 13:30 and Matt 20:16; *POxy.* 654. 3; *Gos. Thom.* 4? H. Anderson (252) thinks that v 31 probably attacks a sense of self-achievement in v 28. But the immediately favorable response of Jesus to v 28 in vv 29-30 undermines this view.

According R. Pesch (2. 135), the references to "first" and "last" in Mark 10:31 form an inclusion with like references in 9:35b so as to clamp together the whole complex of community instructions sandwiched between the second and third passion-and-resurrection predictions. There is a phraseological similarity, but 10:31 uses "first" and "last" for future entrance and non-entrance into the kingdom of God whereas 9:35b used "first" and "last" for present rank among the disciples. Despite having "first" without "last," 10:44 will provide a closer parallel to 9:35b. We have already seen, moreover, that by and large chap. 10 does not have to do with life in the Christian community, but with life in society at large (vv 1-12) and with conversion (vv 13-16, 17-31).

JESUS' ABILITY TO PREDICT HIS OWN DESTINY

10:32-34 (Matt 20:17-19; Luke 18:31-34)

This pericope is set on the road to Jerusalem. Jesus' going there and its effect introduce the pericope (v 32a-d). His third complete prediction of the Passion and Resurrection finishes it out (vv 32e-34; cf. 8:31; 9:31; also 9:9, 12 for a similar but fragmented prediction).

10:32a-d *(Matt 20:17)* Since v 17 has already put Jesus on the road and since v 23 has already put the disciples with him, a reference in v 32 to the disciples' being on the road with Jesus at their head would strike Mark's audience as otiose. It therefore seems unlikely. The introductory δέ, "but," supports this judgment; for δέ occurs comparatively seldom in Mark (less than half as often per page than in Matthew and Luke) and usually, perhaps always, to indicate some sort of contrast. Here, a reference to people in general who were going up to Jerusalem on the road would make a natural contrast with Jesus and the disciples, recently said to be on the road. Mark's penchant for the indefinite third person plural supports this judgment. That Jesus is going on ahead adds further support; for προάγω implies some distance (see esp. 6:45; 16:7, but also 11:9; 14:28), yet ordinarily the disciples follow at only a little distance (see the comments on 1:17) and Mark is about to mention those who follow at so little a distance that for a private communication Jesus is able to take along the Twelve — from among those followers, it seems. Because of a continuative καί, "and," those who "were amazed" equate with the road-travelers ahead of whom Jesus goes at some distance, not with those following less distantly.

Another adversative δέ draws another contrast, this time between the people in general, to whom Mark has just referred, and those who are now described as following Jesus. Supporting this contrast is the already noted distinction between following, which implies little distance, and Jesus' going on ahead of the people in general, which implies greater distance. Also supporting this contrast is the distinction between amazement, attributed to the people in general, and fear, attributed to the followers.

We may question whether ἀκολουθοῦντες, "following," is circumstantial or substantive. Elsewhere in Mark, the definite article plus δέ and a participle always and obviously presents a circumstantial construction. Here that would work out to the meaning, "but some, [while] following, were afraid" (cf. 1:45; 5:40 v.l.; 6:24 v.l., 27 v.l., 37, 49; 8:33; 9:19; 10:3, 20 v.l., 22, 50; 12:3 v.l., 14 v.l., 15; 14:11, 52; 15:2; BAGD s.v. ὁ I2). But the attributive construction is possible (see, e.g., Luke 20:35: οἱ δὲ καταξιωθέντες τοῦ αἰῶνος ἐκείνου τυχεῖ, "but the ones counted worthy to attain that age"); and Mark will use οἱ ἀκολουθοῦντες as a substantive very shortly in 11:9, where parallelism with οἱ προάγοντες, "the ones going on ahead," insures that οἱ ἀκολουθοῦντες means "the ones following." The usage in 11:9 may reveal Mark's intention in 10:32. The facts that οἱ ἀκολουθοῦντες occurs in Mark only in these two locations, that the contrastive προάγω occurs in both of them, and that ὁδός does, too (cf. 11:8), favor this possibility.

"On the road" implies open country. "Going up to Jerusalem" anticipates Jesus' saying in v 33 (cf. 11:1, 11, 15, 27; contrast 3:22). His "going ahead of them" shows him pressing toward the fate which he has predicted for himself. People in general are amazed at his going on ahead of them; and the ones following him are afraid at having to go on ahead with him. The followers are not afraid because they understand him to be heading toward his passion, and themselves with him into danger (cf. 3:22; 7:1 as well as the passion predictions). Not even the Twelve understand that (see 8:32-33; 9:9-10, 32-34; 10:35-45); and when Mark writes elsewhere that people are afraid and Jesus is in view, as here, they are not afraid of danger so much as they are afraid of a display of Jesus' supernatural power, as in his performing a miracle, exorcising a demon, swaying a crowd, predicting the future, rising from the dead (9:41; 5:15, 33; 6:50; 9:32; 11:18; 16:8). So here the fear of some bathes Jesus' push toward Jerusalem in a supernatural aura (see R. Otto, *Idea* 162-63, and cf. the inexplicable darkness at Jesus' crucifixion, the superhuman loudness of his last outcry, and the rending of the veil of the temple from top to bottom in 15:33-39). The followers are afraid, just as the people in general are amazed, because they do *not* understand his onrush. The ignorance out of which grow amazement and fear highlights his supernatural knowledge and determined confrontation of the fate awaiting him in Jerusalem. Since "the things that are going to happen to him" (v 32e) are sure and soon (so the double connotation of τὰ μέλλοντα), the manner of his travel matches and signifies certainty and soonness.

10:32e-34 *(Matt 10:17-19; Luke 18:31-34)* As compared with his introductions to the other passion-and-resurrection predictions (8:31; 9:31), Mark adds "and having taken along again the Twelve" because others are following and Jesus reserves these predictions for his disciples. One might presume that "the ones following" are his disciples, since discipleship entails following. But elsewhere Mark writes "his disciples" when he refers to Jesus' followers in the religious sense; and in 11:9, his only other use of ἀκολουθέω as a substantive participle, "the ones following" will clearly not mean "the disciples," but will simply distinguish people at the back from those at the front of the train that accompanies Jesus toward Jerusalem (11:9). To anticipate James and John plus "the ten" (vv 35, 41), Mark here writes that Jesus took along "the Twelve" rather than that he took along "his disciples." Jesus has not taken along the Twelve on any earlier occasion; so Mark puts "again" before "the Twelve," not before "having taken along." As a result, "again" harks back to any sort of action in which Jesus deals with the Twelve (see 9:35 for the most recent one). As an adverb, of course, "again" modifies the participle, but with respect only to the object of the action rather than to the action-cum-object (see R. Busemann, *Jüngergemeinde* 135, for the alternative view that Mark alludes to Jesus' taking along three of the Twelve up the Mount of Transfiguration — 9:2 [cf. 14:33]; also the notes on 3:14, 16 for the distinction between the Twelve and the disciples). Except for 7:4 (where παρέλαβον has the special connotation of receiving traditions from the past), Mark uses παραλαμβάνω everywhere else for a taking along that separates some who are taken from others who are left (see 4:36; 5:40; 9:2; 14:33). Here, then, the taking along separates the Twelve from a larger group of followers (cf. 2:15; 3:7; 5:24; 11:9; 15:41 for followers different from the Twelve).

The pleonastic "he began" comes over from 8:31 (cf. the notes on 1:45). The elements of amazement and fear lead to the omission of teaching (contrast 8:31; 9:31). What is needed is not a lesson, but assurance. "To say" comes over from 9:31, but changed to an infinitive because of "he began." But "to them" (αὐτοῖς) intervenes to come closer to its antecedent ("the Twelve") and to make room for addition of "the things that were going to happen to him." This addition lends greater weight to Jesus' power of prediction by pointing to the nearness and certainty of fulfilment. The wordplay in ἀναβαίνοντες . . . συμβαίνειν . . . ἀναβαίνομεν, "going up . . . to go together [i.e. to happen] . . . we are going up," adds still further weight; and as if that were not enough, the following increase in amount of detail will raise the emphasis on Jesus' predictive power to the nth degree. The forward position of αὐτῷ, "to him," stresses his power to predict even his own fate, especially with regard to the Passion, since "to happen to him" excludes actions of his own doing, i.e. going up to Jerusalem and rising. The carry-over of "say" from 9:31 makes ὅτι recitative, as there (see the comments ad loc. and the notes on 8:31).

"Behold!" adds a note of drama missing in the earlier predictions but suitable to the nearness and certainty of Jesus' passion and resurrection. "We are going up to Jerusalem," also missing in the earlier predictions, brings out that nearness and certainty (cf. Jesus' going on ahead and the amazement and fear in v 32), justifies the exclamatory "behold!" and with it calls more attention to Jesus' ability to predict his own fate. "The Son of man" carries over from 8:31; 9:12, 31. Its forward position helps draw a distinction between Jesus and the others whom he included in "we." As in 9:31, the Son of man's suffering much (so 8:31; 9:12) drops out, here in anticipation of the following details concerning that suffering. "Will be given over" echoes 9:31 instead of 8:31 ("to be rejected") or 9:12 ("be treated with contempt"). But the tense shifts from present to future because the combination of "are going up" with the earlier "is being given over" would require an awkward shift from the progressive present to a futuristic present (see the comments on 1:14 and the notes on 9:31 against a divine passive in "is being given over"). "Into the hands of men" (9:31) drops out in favor of a more detailed reference to the chief priests and the scribes. These two groups come in this order from 8:31 to link up with Jerusalem, their base of power (on the omission of the elders, see the excursus following the comments on 8:31-32a).

The power of Jesus to predict even the details of his passion comes to full flower in the following pentateuch of clauses, which have no parallels in 8:31; 9:12, 31: (1) "and they [the chief priests and the scribes] will condemn him to death" (cf. 14:64); (2) "and they will give him over to the Gentiles" (cf. 15:1); (3) "and they [the Gentiles] will mock him" (cf. 15:20; also 15:31 for the chief priests' and scribes' mocking him); (4) "and they will spit on him" (cf. 15:19; also 14:65 for spitting on Jesus by some members of the Sanhedrin); (5) "and they will flog (μαστιγώσουσιν) him" (cf. φραγελλώσας, "having scourged," in 15:15). "And they will kill [him], and after three days he will rise" repeats 9:31 except that "him" in the preceding clause leads to ellipsis here and except that "having been killed" drops out after the pattern of 8:31, which is different from 9:31 and 10:34 only in having infinitives rather than finite verbs. The added details in 10:33-34 have loaded the prediction with so much emphasis on maltreatment that a second reference to being killed would be otiose. The details gain in impressiveness from the assonance of five successive verbs ending in -ουσιν, "they"; from the framing of these verbs by two other verbs ending in -εται, "he"; from the alternation of αὐτόν, "him," plus a dative of indirect object after both κατακρινοῦσιν, "they will condemn," and παραδώσουσιν, "they will give over," with αὐτῷ, "him," after both ἐμπαίξουσιν, "they will mock," and ἐμπτύσουσιν, "they will spit on"; and from the further assonance of these last-mentioned verbs' starting both with ἐμπ-. As in 8:31; 9:31, the forward position of "after three days" calls special attention to the quickness with which Jesus will rise.

NOTES

Several factors in v 32 lead S. E. Porter (*Verbal Aspect* 459, 480) to construe ἦσαν with ἀναβαίνοντες for an emphatic periphrastic imperfect, "was going up": (1) the starting of a pericope with v 32; (2) the indubitable periphrastic imperfect ἦν προάγων, "was going ahead," in the very next clause of the verse; and (3) the simple imperfect verbs just following. For this construal, however, we might expect ἐν τῇ ὁδῷ, "on the road," to follow rather than precede ἀναβαίνοντες (cf. 10:52, the only other Marcan passage where ἐν τῇ ὁδῷ modifies a verb of physical motion). The intervention of the prepositional phrase between ἦσαν and ἀναβαίνοντες calls in question a parallel with ἦν προάγων and the following simple imperfects and looks instead like 1:13, where a similar intervening phrase damaged the possibility of a periphrastic imperfect in ἦν . . . πειραζόμενος, "was being tempted" (see the comments ad loc.).

As remarked above, 11:8-9 will offer another conjunction of "road," "going on ahead," and "following." There, the contrast between the ones who go on ahead and those who follow will show that following refers only to a position in the back of a procession, not to discipleship as well. As a result, "the road" will carry no theological freight. Accordingly, "the road" has a purely mundane meaning here, too. Confirmation comes from the traveling on the road of people who, unlike the followers, do not even try to keep up with Jesus (cf. the notes on 1:2-3; 8:27; 10:52). See 15:40-41 for the presence of women among the followers referred to in v 32. The masculine gender of οἱ . . . ἀκολουθοῦντες forestalls a limitation to women, however.

There are possibilities of identifying the third person plurals in v 32a-d other than the identifications made in the foregoing comments. For example, the road-travelers who are amazed and the ones who are afraid as they follow are one and the same group, consisting of disciples. They are amazed because Jesus has told them that he will suffer and die at the hands of the Jewish authorities, who reside in Jerusalem. They are afraid because of his having said that anyone who wants to follow him must take up his or her own cross (8:34). Weaknesses in this view include disregard of the second adversative δέ, "but," and of the difference between amazement and fear.

With an appeal to v 50, E. Best (*Disciples and Discipleship* 147) thinks that the δέ in οἱ δὲ ἀκολουθοῦντες (v 32) may be continuative, "and." But the δέ in v 50 will *not* be continuative. It will set Bartimaeus as subject of the next action over against the people who have just called him. Mark uses καί so often and δέ so relatively seldom that δέ almost certainly denotes a shift in subjects (also against R. P. Meye [*Jesus and the Twelve* 162-63], whose Marcan cross-references in support of a continuative δέ in the middle of v 32 are better understood as indicating contrasts of various sorts). To equate those who are amazed with those who fear, R. Busemann (*Jüngergemeinde* 131-32) cites the ascription of amazement and astonishment to the same group of people in vv 24, 26. But not only does the second adversative δέ in v 32 stand in the way of this equation. There is no indication of a shift in the earlier verses, and being astonished (ἐκπλήσσομαι) related more closely to being amazed (θαμβέομαι) than being afraid does. To equate the followers who are amazed not only with those who are afraid but also with the Twelve (so both Meye, loc. cit., and Büsemann, loc. cit.) makes "taking along the Twelve" awkward, for under this interpretation Mark has already described the Twelve as following and Jesus as going on ahead of them. In saying that Mark writes v 32a to direct Jesus' teaching to all disciples, not just to the Twelve, E. Best (*Following Jesus* 120) overlooks that the taking along of the Twelve limits to them the address of vv 33-34.

According to yet another interpretation, the road-travelers and amazed ones are disciples, but the ones following and fearing are people in general. But Mark would not likely describe people in general as following Jesus if he meant to distinguish them from disciples who regularly follow Jesus. The suggestion of W. Wrede (*Messianic Secret* 276-78) and G. Zuntz (in *Markus-Philologie* 215) that we omit "and they were amazed" from v 32 not only lacks external support. It also misses the link with amazement in v 24. Wrede alternatively suggests the omission of fear. See E. Best, *Disciples and Discipleship* 144, on other conjectural emendations.

Jesus goes on ahead of his disciples in 14:28; 16:7, too. But not only do the destinations differ — there, Galilee; here, Jerusalem — but also people here follow him within sight. There, none of his disciples will see him till they arrive in Galilee. It will not do to say that some are afraid because they know *what* is going to happen in Jerusalem though they do not know *why* it will happen (so W. Schmithals in *Theologia Crucis — Signum Crucis* 423). If vv 35-45 are any guide, the fearful do not even know *what* will happen. But their ignorance is not explicitly stated, as it is one way or another in 8:32b-33; 9:10, 32; and here ignorance is implied before the passion-and-resurrection prediction is quoted, whereas those passages reverse the order (against H. Räisänen, *"Messias-Geheimnis"* 127-28).

R. McKinnis (in *NovT* 18 [1976] 81-87) uses the striking parallelism in vv 33-34 to argue for a hymnic origin. But heavy parataxis disfavors such an origin (contrast the relative lack of parataxis in the possibly hymnic Phil 2:5-11; Col 1:15-20; 1 Tim 3:16). This same parataxis points to pre-Marcan Semitic tradition, and to that extent tends toward dominical authenticity. "To the Gentiles" sounds Jewish (cf. Acts 3:13), therefore pre-Marcan (for Mark writes with a Gentile audience in mind — 7:2-4), and again possibly authentic.

The order of events in the passion narrative will be as follows: delivery to the chief priests, scribes, and elders (14:43-46; cf. 14:10) – condemnation to death (14:64) – spitting (14:65) – delivery to the Gentiles (15:1) – scourging (15:15) – again spitting (15:19) – mockery (15:20) – crucifixion (15:27) – mockery (15:31) – death (15:37). The order in 10:33 differs in large measure. Delivery to the chief priests and scribes (the elders being omitted) and condemnation to death come first and killing, naturally, comes last, as in the passion narrative. But spitting is delayed till later than both of its occurrences in the passion narrative. This delay moves delivery to the Gentiles up a notch. Scourging is much delayed, till the next to last position; and the diction changes from scourging (φραγελλόω, a Latin loanword with respect to a punishment inflicted on slaves and provincials after a capital sentence) to flogging (μαστιγόω, as in John 19:1, but usually in reference to a lesser punishment such as would be inflicted by synagogues — Deut 25:2-3; Matt 10:17). Mockery comes before both spitting and flogging, whereas it will follow both spitting and scourging in the passion narrative even though two instances of it will occur there.

These differences do not destroy the position that Mark or someone before him drew these details from the tradition of Jesus' passion. One could think of haphazard borrowing plus arrangement according to a logical order, e.g., general mockery followed by a partic-ular example of it in spitting, and flogging as a prelude to killing, or progressively more terrible suffering (F. Hahn, *Titles* 37). One could also think that the deletion of the elders anticipates 11:18; 14:1; 15:31 (cf. the deletion of the scribes, too, in 15:3, 10-11). Neverthe-less, the elders appear with the chief priests and scribes not only in the account of Jesus' being delivered to the Jewish authorities (14:43), but also in 8:31; 11:27; 14:53; 15:1; and we would have expected scourging instead of flogging for more terrible suffering or a prelude to killing. So borrowing from the passion tradition might have been expected to follow it a little more closely in this and other respects. At least one's confidence that such borrowing occurred should undergo some erosion. The logical order in the passion prediction might derive from a genuine prediction, which we would expect to follow such an order, more easily than from rearrangement of events in the passion narrative.

According to R. Busemann (*Jüngergemeinde* 143-44), Mark rearranges items so as to make mockery a summarizing action. Then he selects as examples spitting and scourging because they will bring to a close Jesus' hearings before the Sanhedrin and Pilate, respectively. But why should Mark reach back to the spitting of the Jewish Sanhedrin after he has shifted from them to the Gentiles? Furthermore, spitting is only one of a number of actions with which Jesus' hearing before the Sanhedrin will close (see 14:65 for covering his face, cuffing him, taunting him to prophesy, and slapping him as well — all mentioned after spitting); and spitting will be as much a part of the end of Jesus' hearing before Pilate as a part of the end of Jesus' hearing before the Sanhedrin (15:19). Busemann cites 15:20, 31 as summaries whose similarities to 10:33-34 favor Mark's redaction of the latter. But 15:20 will speak of undressing and dressing Jesus and hark back to clothing him in purple, crowning him with thorns, greeting him as a king, striking him, spitting on him, and doing obeisance to him; and 15:31-32 will quote the very words of the chief priests and scribes and compare what they say with the equally specific words of passers-by. Narrative detail, not general summary!

Since the chief priests and the scribes will give the Son of man over to the Gentiles and since the Gentiles will kill him, the chief priests' and scribes' condemning him to death amounts to the same thing as the Sanhedrin's condemning him to be worthy of death in 14:64 (against the distinction drawn by R. McKinnis in *NovT* 18 [1976] 90-91). Jesus has called for cross-taking in following him (8:34). His present prediction of delivery to the Gentiles invites a reference to crucifixion, a Gentile mode of capital punishment. And in the passion narrative "crucify" will occur for what the Gentiles do (15:13, 14, 15, 20, 24, 25, 27; 16:6), but "kill" for what the Jewish authorities seek to do (14:1). Even so, in the present text we read "kill" instead of "crucify" for what the Gentiles will do. The more general verb favors the authenticity of the prediction, for a fabrication of the prediction after the fact would likely have led to the use of "crucify." The argument of N. Perrin (in *Christology and a Modern Pilgrimage* 26) that "kill" comes from later Christian vocabulary not only overlooks these details. It also overlooks that the passion predictions in Mark do not display an explicitly prophetic Christology like that displayed in the passages cited by Perrin for support, i.e. in Acts 3:14-23; 7:52; 1 Thess 2:15 (cf. Rom 11:3).

Some try to counter the argument that prediction ex eventu would have had "they will crucify" rather than "they will kill" by saying that the contrast with "he will rise" determines the choice of killing. But rising does not make a better contrast to killing. For that we would expect "he will be made alive." In reality, crucifixion would have made a better complement to rising, because both actions feature upward motion. Hence, we are supported in our expectation that a prediction ex eventu would have spoken specifically of crucifixion.

Attempts to maintain the authenticity of the prediction by giving it a naturalistic explanation — e.g., by attributing it to Jesus' meditation on Isa 50:6; Ps 22:8(7) — achieve only partial success. He may have meditated on those passages and predictively applied them to himself. But such self-application does not necessarily follow from meditation and, more importantly, the supernatural element remains if the prediction came true in detail — unless we are to think of a fulfilment purely by chance. C. E. B. Cranfield (334-35) estimates the details as readily foreseeable. But the progression from Jewish to Gentile hands, from a capital sentence at the hands of the Sanhedrin through mockery, including spitting as well as flogging, to execution at the hands of the Gentiles, is not so usual and therefore not quite so easy to foresee as this estimate makes it out to be. Isa 50:6

LXX uses the nouns μάστιγας, "lashes" (as suffered in a flogging), and ἐμπτυσμάτων, "spittings," cognate to two of Jesus' verbs; but the order is the reverse, and nothing in the passion prediction corresponds to ῥαπίσματα, "slaps," which comes between the other two nouns in Isa 50:6 LXX. This omission is the more remarkable in that ῥαπίσματα will appear in the dative at Mark 14:65. Jesus' verb ἐμπαίξουσιν, "they will mock," does not appear in Ps 21:8 LXX. Though W. Wrede (*Messianic Secret* 84) does not believe in a detailed supernatural prediction, he clearly sees that Mark's point is no other. See R. Pesch, in *Jesus und der Menschensohn* 180, for a long list of OT passages dealing with mockery, torture, and capital condemnation of the righteous; and J. Carmignac in *ASTI* 7 (1968-69) 71 for the possibility of an underlying Hebrew (or Aramaic, we might add) wordplay in וְשִׂחֲקוּ בוֹ וְיָרְקוּ בוֹ, "and they will mock him and spit on him." Such a wordplay would suit the authenticity of this passion-and-resurrection prediction.

The Sanhedrin are predicted to condemn Jesus to death and give him over to the Gentiles; and it is the Gentiles who are predicted to do the dirty work of mockery, spitting, scourging, and killing. The exclusion of the Jewish people at large and the distribution of blameworthy actions among Jewish authorities and Gentiles make inappropriate any talk of anti-Jewish sentiment.

R. McKinnis (in *NovT* 18 [1976] 97-98) thinks that "after three days" means three days after Jesus' being given over, not three days after his being killed. This interpretation does not solve any chronological problem, however; for the Thursday night of betrayal will already be Friday by Jewish reckoning. Even a reckoning of the night of betrayal as Thursday would not provide enough days for a long understanding of "after three days"; and "after three days" has appeared in 8:31 without a contextual reference to being given over, and has appeared at 9:31 in immediate grammatical connection with being killed, the giving over appearing separately. See also the comments and notes on 8:31; 9:31.

JESUS' POWER TO PREDICT THE DESTINY OF HIS DISCIPLES

Mark 10:35-45 (Matt 20:20-28; Luke 22:24-27)

This pericope falls into two halves: a dialogue (vv 35-40) and a monologue (vv 41-45). The dialogue also subdivides into two halves: a request by James and John (vv 35-37) and Jesus' answer (vv 38-40). In the request, James and John speak first (v 35), then Jesus (v 36), then James and John again (v 37). In the answer, Jesus speaks first (v 38), then James and John (v 39a), then Jesus again (vv 39b-40). In response to the other disciples' indignation at James and John (v 41), Jesus monologizes on servanthood (vv 42-45).

10:35-37 *(Matt 20:20-21)* As usually, this pericope starts with movement. The historical present tense of προσπορεύονται for James' and John's coming to Jesus with a request for privileged seats "on his right and left in his glory" underscores their ignorance of his approaching passion and helps signal the start of a new pericope. The parallel with Peter's protest after the first passion-and-resurrection prediction and with the disciples' arguing after the second one which of them was the greatest favors that James and John make their request out of such ignorance rather than out of an understanding of Jesus' death and a looking beyond it to his resurrection and their eternal life. As in those earlier passages, Mark is using discipular ignorance as a foil against which to bring out Jesus' predictive power, which helps erase the scandal of the Cross. "The sons of Zebedee" recalls 1:19-20; 3:17 and forestalls a confusion of this James with James the son of Alphaeus, also one of the Twelve (3:18).

"Teacher" implies Jesus' authority. "We want that you should do for us whatever we ask you [to do for us]" is unintendedly humorous in its request for a signed blank check (cf. 6:22-23). The forward position of ὃ ἐὰν αἰτήσωμεν σε, "whatever we ask you," highlights this humor. What James and John "want" recalls Jesus' prediction to the Twelve that if anyone "wants" to be first, he will be last of all and servant of all (9:35; see also Jesus' use of this verb in the same connection at 10:43-44). In view of that prediction, James and John do not volunteer to say what they want. But Jesus refuses to sign a blank check and asks what they want. An adversative δέ, "but" (the first of several indicating dialogic shifts; see also vv 37, 38, 39 [bis]), and the dropping of "that" (ἵνα) before "I should do for you" sharpens his question (so also v 51; 14:12; 15:9, 12; contrast the presence of ἵνα with θέλω, "I want," in 6:25; 9:30 as well as in 10:35; cf. M. Reiser, *Syntax und Stil* 149-50). Not only does their reference to his glory stem from their having heard him speak of the Son of man's coming "in the glory of his Father" (8:38; cf. 13:26), from their having seen the Transfiguration (9:2-8), and from their having identified him with the Son of man and transmuted the Father's glory into his glory. Their reference to his glory also betrays ignorance of his approaching passion despite the predictions of it in 8:31; 9:12, 31; 10:33-34 (see 8:32 and esp. 9:32 for this ignorance); and their asking to be seated, as they say, "one on your right and one on your left in your glory" (cf. Matt 19:28 par. Luke 22:28-30) shows ignorance of the necessity that they take up their crosses and follow Jesus (see 8:34-38 and cf. the irony that two bandits, "one on [his] right and one on his left," will be crucified rather than seated in glory with him [15:27]). The forward position of εἷς σου ἐκ δεξιῶν καὶ εἷς ἐξ ἀριστερῶν, "one on your right and one on your left," stresses this ignorance. By contrast, Jesus knows his own destiny and that of James and John, too.

10:38-40 *(Matt 20:22-23)* Jesus' answer once again displays his supernatural knowledge. "You don't understand what you're asking for" sets their ignorance as a foil against which that knowledge stands out. The switch from an active form of αἰτέω, which refers to simple asking (v 35), to a middle form, which escalates the asking to pleading or to a business proposition (J. H. Moulton, *Prolegomena* 160-61), makes James' and John's ignorance even more pathetic so as to increase the effectiveness of the foil. Jesus' question, "Are you able to drink the cup that I am drinking or to be baptized with the baptism that I am being baptized with?" (cf. 14:23, 24, 36), implies that contrary to their expectation they must drink the bitter dregs of suffering and feel a flood of woe overwhelming them if they would hope to share in his later glory (again cf. 14:23-24). In particular, "are you able" implies a fate that is foreboding and a danger that they may recant (cf. Peter's denials). Moreover, it implies that Jesus is able to endure such a fate (so the emphasis in 14:32-42) and that he foreknows his endurance as well as the fate itself. The present tense of the verbs is futuristic, again emphasizing certainty and nearness in the fulfilment of his passion prediction (cf.

the present tense of "is being given over" in 9:31). Carrying the same emphasis is the chiasm of (a) infinitive, (b) object (including an adjectival clause), (b′) object (again including an adjectival clause), and (a′) infinitive (see the Greek text).

James' and John's answer, "We are able," receives no criticism. It simply provides Jesus an opportunity to display foreknowledge of their fate and endurance as well as of his own: "The cup that I am drinking you will drink; and the baptism that I am being baptized with, you will be baptized with." The forward positions of the objects and their adjectival clauses keep the emphasis on Jesus' passion as the pattern for James' and John's passion and thereby on Jesus' passion as the primary subject matter. Again the present tense of Jesus' drinking and being baptized is futuristic, emphasizing the certainty and nearness of fulfilment. Δέ, "but," introduces a contrastive statement in which sitting on Jesus' right or left enjoys a prominent forward position that links up with James' and John's request. The translation, "But to sit on my right or left is not mine to give; rather, [it will be given] to those for whom it has been prepared," would favor that Mark is using tradition; for his emphases on Jesus' authority and foreknowledge would prevent such an admission on the part of a Jesus whose words Mark was making up. On the other hand, ἀλλ', "rather," may carry the force of "except" (as in 4:22; 6:9; 9:8) with the result that Jesus' authority and foreknowledge are better preserved: ". . . is not mine to give except [that it is mine to give] to those for whom it has been prepared [with the implication that it has not been prepared for James and John]" (cf. M. Black, *Aramaic Approach* 113-14; J. A. Kleist 218). Mark's characteristic emphases favor this translation, though Jesus himself may have meant the other (and even with "except," he appears to disclaim having the ultimate authority of the one who prepared the seats of highest honor for others besides James and John, for in all probability the passive obliquely refers to God as the preparer — cf. Matt 20:23 ["prepared by my Father"]; 22:4, 8; 25:34; Luke 2:31; 14:17; 1 Cor 2:9; Heb 11:16; 1 Pet 1:5; Rev 12:6; 21:2; and for Jesus as the preparer, John 14:2-3). Under either translation, the strength of ἀλλ' as an adversative and the following ellipsis of a subject and verb concentrate attention on "those for whom it has been prepared."

The switch from ἐξ ἀριστερῶν (v 37) to ἐξ εὐωνύμων (v 40) is not due to use of different traditions. Both phrases mean "on the left," but the second one literally means "on the well named," i.e. "on the lucky side," which by euphemistic inversion means just the opposite: "on the unlucky side." The switch is due to Jesus' intervening prediction of James' and John's unlucky sharing of his suffering and death. The euphemism will reappear in 15:27, again to connote bad luck. As compared with 10:37, "one" drops out in 10:40, but because of a switch in verbal constructions and because of an exchange of "and" for "or" between "right" and "left," not because of different traditions. The chiasm in the order of (a) sitting on Jesus' right and left, (b) cup and baptism, (b′) cup and baptism, and (a′) sitting on his right and left (vv 37-40) stresses Jesus' foreknowledge and again disfavors a use of different traditions; for such chiasm is unlikely to have come about by the adding of foreign material.

10:41-45 *(Matt 20:24-28; Luke 22:24-27)* This final episode in the pericope leads from the earlier prediction of Jesus' death to an interpretation of his death. The interpretation will contradict any notion that he died the death of a hapless criminal. The indignation of the ten against James and John, whose request they have heard, sets the stage and may imply that they share James' and John's ambition and ignorance. Mark repeats the names of James and John to make it clear that the ten are indignant at them for what they requested, not at Jesus for what he has answered.

"Summoning them" probably means Jesus' summoning the ten, since James and John are presumably still with him as a result of the preceding dialogue. The "them" to whom he speaks may include all twelve apostles, however, if by virtue of his summons the ten join up with James and John. The summoning and the historical present tense of λέγει, "he says," emphasize Jesus' authority. More particularly, λέγει emphasizes the authority of his following statements.

"You know" contrasts with "you do not know" in v 38 and points to the Twelve's knowing something true of society at large which unbeknown to them does not hold true among themselves. Ironically, then, even what they "know" highlights their ignorance, which in turn highlights the superior knowledge of Jesus. Οἱ δοκοῦντες ἄρχειν τῶν ἐθνῶν does not mean "the ones seeming to rule the Gentiles," for those who rule the Gentiles really do rule them — they do not merely seem to — and "their great ones" in the synonymously parallel next stich are truly great. No δοκοῦντες is present in that stich even to suggest a false appearance of greatness. In the first stich, then, δοκοῦντες connotes recognition based on fact: "the ones recognized to be ruling the Gentiles" (cf. the translation "the distinguished rulers" — so J. A. Kleist [218], who appropriately cites Eur. *Tro.* 613). Even in Gal 2:2, 6, 9, sometimes cited to support false appearance, Paul may be disregarding the importance of appearance rather than denying its truthfulness.

"Their great ones" recalls the disciples' disputing which of them was "the greatest" (9:34) and forecasts "whoever wants to be great" (10:43). The presence of "their" with "great ones" and the fact that the Jews have no king of their own favor the translation "Gentiles" over "nations" for ἐθνῶν. On the other hand, "their" may distinguish "the nations," including the Jews, from the Twelve; for though the Jews have no king of their own, foreign kings rule over them. The prefix κατα- in κατακυριεύουσιν, "wield lordship," and κατεξουσιάζουσιν, "wield authority," may be taken as perfective, stressing dominance but not necessarily tyranny (K. W. Clark in *Studies in NT Language and Text* 100-105 = idem, *Gentile Bias* 207-12) or as connotative of opposition, "against." Usage elsewhere tends strongly toward conquest by violence (see Hatch and Redpath and BAGD s.v.; cf. Jas 2:6 and the dropping of κατα-, apparently for amelioration [cf. "benefactors"], in Luke 22:25). Even human domination of the earth in the LXX of Gen 1:28; 9:1, 7 needs to be read according to an ancient conception of warring with nature, not according to a modern conception of embracing nature. According to Jer 3:14 LXX, the Lord will restoratively dominate Israel, but he must conquer them because of their present rebelliousness. It appears, then, that κατα- does connote opposition. In the present passage this connotation sharpens the contrast with beneficial service (vv 43-45).

Now Jesus shatters generally recognized norms by using present non-rule among the Twelve to predict their future servanthood and slavery despite the possibility of their wishing for greatness and firstness. That possibility makes his prediction unlikely of fulfilment and therefore impressive in fulfilment. Under scrutiny is the Twelve's relation to one another, not to society at large, much less to God. The element of greatness, present in 10:43b but not in 9:35, would fit the context of 9:35 more closely than it fits the present context, because in 9:33-34 the disciples themselves were arguing which of them was the greatest whereas in 10:42 it is Jesus who mentions "the great ones," and not with respect to the Twelve but only by way of comparison with rulers of the Gentiles. This greater closeness of 10:43b to 9:33-34 than to 10:42 disfavors that 9:35 was taken from 10:43b-44; for otherwise, especially because of the dispute over greatness in 9:33-34, the element of greatness would probably have gone over from 10:43b to 9:35. The greater closeness to 9:33-34 also suggests that in his answer at 10:43b Jesus reflects back on the incident recounted in 9:33ff.

If Jesus does reflect back, we may trace certain developments from 9:35 to 10:43-44. He adds 10:43a ("but [δέ] it is not thus among you") to state a present fact which contrasts with 10:42b (against J. A. Kleist [147-50], who treats οὐχ . . . ἐστιν as modal, "ought not to be"; but cf. C. Myers, *Binding the Strong Man* 279, where the correct rejection of an imperatival sense is marred by interpretation in terms of dry sarcasm — as though some of the Twelve were ruling the others). Addition of the strong adversative ἀλλ', "rather," highlights the prediction that follows. "Whoever would wish" (N.B. the subjunctive) replaces "if anyone wishes" (N.B. the indicative), because the ten disciples *might* entertain an ambition like that of James and John (cf. the indignation of the ten [10:41] and James' and John's "we wish" and Jesus' "what do you wish . . . ?" [10:35-36]), whereas in chap. 9 all the Twelve were *actually* engaged in a dispute over who was greatest. Μέγας, "great," keeps the emphatic forward position that its counterpart πρῶτος, "first," had in 9:35. The counterpartness of πρῶτος in 9:35 and the parallel with πρῶτος here in 10:44 escalate the meaning of μέγας from "great" to "greatest" (cf. the use of the comparative μείζων with the meaning "greatest" in 9:34). Γενέσθαι, "to become," replaces εἶναι, "to be," which is reserved for 10:44. "Among you" is added to accommodate 10:43a. "Will be" comes from 9:35. As there and in accordance with "you will drink" and "you will be baptized" in 10:39, it is a predictive future (so also in v 44). An imperatival future would not make so good a parallel with "it is" in v 43a (contrast the absence of "it is" and the imperative of γινέσθω, "let him become," in Luke 22:26, which may represent the intended meaning of Jesus). What Mark's Jesus offers, then (and despite the usual, unscrutinous understanding), is prediction, not command. "Your" replaces "of all" to link with "among you" (bis). "Last" drops out because the replacement of "first" with "great" has destroyed the original contrast between first and last. Διάκονος, "servant," advances from its final position in 9:35 and replaces ἔσχατος, "last," for a contrast with the occupants of thrones (10:37, 40, 42).

For parallelistic emphasis, 10:44 is added. "And whoever would wish" repeats a part of 10:43b. "Among you" comes down, too, but before the infinitive to stress the contrast with Gentiles. "To be first" finally comes over from 9:35, but with a reversal of word order (9:35 had "first to be") because "among you" has taken an emphatic forward position that leaves only the last position in the clause for a further emphasis. Ἔσται πάντων, "will be of all," comes over from 9:35, but δοῦλος, "slave," replaces ἔσχατος, "last," for a parallel with διάκονος, which has already come over from 9:35 (cf. Rom 15:25; 16:1; 1 Cor 9:19-23; 16:15; 2 Cor 4:5; Col 1:7, 25; b. Qidd. 32b; see E. Best, *Following Jesus* 125-26; K. Stock, *Boten* 140, on the approximate equivalence of διάκονος, which connotes the personal character of service, and δοῦλος, which connotes its obligatory character; also Pl. *Grg.* 518A for the connotation of ignobility in both words). Greatness is not achieved in vv 43-44, then. It is only wanted. Being a servant and a slave will not give a new definition of greatness or provide a new avenue to it. It will deny greatness. The overall chiasm of (a) μέγας, "great," (b) γενέσθαι, "to become," (c) ἐν ὑμῖν, "among you," and (c') ἐν ὑμῖν, "among you," (b') εἶναι, "to be," (a') πρῶτος, "first," dramatizes this prediction.

The Son of man provides a model, which because of his authority is also a reason, for this sort of behavior on the part of the Twelve. The καί before γάρ means "even" and puts the servanthood of "the Son of man" (which takes a prominent forward position to go with καί) over against the dominion of "the one like a son of man" in Dan 7:13-14 (cf. *1 Enoch* 45:3-4; 46:4-5; 48:1–49:4; 61:8-9; 62:1-9; 63:11 and see the notes on 2:10). Mark makes nothing of this contrast, however, and can hardly expect his Gentile audience to detect it. The strength of the adversative ἀλλά, "rather," the following ellipsis of a second "has come," and the addition of "and to give his life [as a] ransom in substitution for many" (cf. 14:24) put huge emphasis on serving as opposed to being served and as more important than coming. In saying that his serving goes to the extent of giving his life as a ransom in substitution for many, Jesus interprets his approaching death as supremely self-sacrificial for the saving of many others' lives. Thus the Marcan apologetics of miraculous ability, of didactic authority, and of predictive power metamorphose into an apologetic of beneficial service. The Cross will not bring shame to its victim, but salvation to his followers.

NOTES

R. Laufen (*Doppelüberlieferungen* 123) cites a number of differences between vv 35-40 and 41-45 to prove that the two passages did not belong together in earlier tradition or historical actuality: (1) Verses 35-40 deal with the end, vv 41-45 with the present age. But the indignation of the ten leads naturally from a comment about the end to a comment about the present age. Furthermore, already in vv 35-40 Jesus' answer to James and John introduces the present age in the form of their suffering and martyrdom; and in vv 41-50 the future tense, used in vv 35-40 to predict events that will happen during the present age, reappears for similar predictions. (2) Verses 35-40 criticize a desire to exercise power, vv 41-45 the actual exercise of power. In fact, however, neither passage contains any criticism. Not even "you don't know what you're asking for" contains a criticism; for Jesus uses his observation only to ask a question to whose answer by James and John he pays respect, indeed, whose answer he affirms. Besides, the actual use of power by some people makes a good basis for comments on the potential use of power by others. (3) Luke 22:24-27 provides another form and setting for vv 42b-45a. Yes, but Mark's may be at least traditional, perhaps historical as well, and Luke's not. In fact, a perusal of secondary literature turns up a large body of opinion that denies the originality of Luke's form and setting (see, e.g., E. Trocmé, *Passion* 31, 69; J. A. Fitzmyer, *Luke* 1411-16; G. Schneider, *Lukas* 449-50). (4) Verses 35-40 are basically narrative, vv 41-45 a sequence of sayings. But sayings may grow out of narrative because they did in fact have historical settings open to narration. Moreover, the difference between vv 35-40 and 41-45 is easily over-stated; for the words of Jesus and of James and John, to whom he responds, make up about as much of vv 35-40, proportionately speaking, as Jesus' words make up of vv 41-45. And his words in vv 41-45 are introduced with a narrative statement that carries forward the story line in vv 35-40. (5) Verses 41-42a look Marcan and therefore indicate the importation of originally independent material in vv 42b-45. But it is only natural that a writer's own diction and style intrude more into traditional narrative transitions than into traditional non-narrative materials connected by those transitions. To recognize Marcanisms in "hear-ing," "began" (used auxiliarly), "to be indignant," and "summoning" is not to prove that Mark had no traditional transition on which to impose some of his favorite locutions (cf. J. Gnilka [2. 99], who suggests the following pre-Marcan transition: "and Jesus says to them [his disciples]"); and frequent occurrence in Mark may derive from frequent occur-rence in pre-Marcan tradition as well as from Mark's redaction. Some have described "the ten" as a Marcanism on the ground that Mark likes "the Twelve" and here subtracts James and John. But Mark uses "the ten" nowhere else even though it would have made especially good sense in 14:17, where we read "the Twelve" despite Jesus' having sent two of the disciples to prepare the Passover (14:13). Though Mark uses "the ten" nowhere else, even where we expect it, he does use ἄλλος, "other," very often (twenty-two times). Since he might have written "the other disciples," then, "the ten" is as likely traditional as redac-tional. (6) To be understood, vv 42b-45 do not require a dispute such as vv 35-40 provide. True, but a dispute gives vv 42b-45 sharper focus and greater reason for being. It is hard to think of a better historical occasion for Jesus' comments on greatness than indignation aroused by others' request for superior honors. Cf. V. Taylor 442-43.

The facts that Jesus has taken along the Twelve in v 32 and that the ten plus James and John will still be with him in v 41 may make προσπορεύονται, "go to" (v 35), seem too strong (R. Busemann, *Jüngergemeinde* 146-47). But Mark uses this strong verb, which is hapax in the NT, to link up with συμπορεύονται, "go together" (v 1), and with ἐκπορευο-μένου, "going out" (v 17), in reference to the journey to Jerusalem (cf. vv 32-33). The verb also helps him signal the start of a new pericope. James and John might have spoken up from their positions among the Twelve. The nature of their request makes it more appro-priate, however, that as a pair they approach Jesus from behind even though the ten are in earshot. Presumably, they have all been trailing behind him (cf. v 32).

E. Best (*Following Jesus* 123) argues for the traditionality of James and John: "indeed had Mark introduced them there would have been no need to identify them as the sons of Zebedee since this had already been made clear twice (1.19; 3.17)." We need not doubt traditionality, but the argument is weak. One could equally well say that just as Zebedee was mentioned in 3:17 to distinguish his son James from James the son of Alphaeus (3:18), so in 10:35 Zebedee is mentioned to distinguish James from the James who is among the ten (10:41). Because of the dual nature of the request, John comes in, not merely as James' brother (as in 1:19; 3:17), but as also a son of Zebedee. See J. W. Wenham, *Easter Enigma* 34-35, for the view that James and John are Jesus' cousins.

In v 36, the "me" after "what do you want?" points toward the supplementary infinitive "to do," which never appears, however, and yields to the clause, "I should do for you." We might presume that the first mention of James in 1:19; 3:17; 10:35 implies

his being older than John, that in his capacity as the older brother James would want to
sit on Jesus' right, the place of higher honor, and that as the younger brother John would
want to sit on Jesus' left (cf. 2 Sam 16:6; Josephus *Ant.* 6.11.9 §235; 1 Kgs 2:19; Ps 110:1;
1 Esdr 4:29; Sir 12:12; Acts 7:55-56; Rom 8:34; Str-B 1. 835-36). But in John 13:23-25
the beloved disciple — traditionally identified as John, who is otherwise strangely missing
in the fourth gospel — reclines on Jesus' right; and James and John may be asking for
confirmation of positions which they currently take at meals of Jesus with his disciples
(W. L. Lane 379, n. 77). The request of James and John seems to rest on Jesus' promise
that the Twelve "will sit on thrones judging the Twelve tribes of Israel" (Matt 19:28 par.
Luke 22:30). Apparently James and John expect Jesus as the Christ to reestablish the
Davidic kingdom when he arrives in the once royal city of Jerusalem, or — more likely,
in view of the reference to glory — when he comes as the Son of man "in the glory of his
Father with the holy angels" (8:38; cf. 13:26). The ignorance which Mark attributes to the
disciples makes it useless to ask whether or how they interrelate that coming from heaven
and the present coming to Jerusalem from Galilee. Though the requested positions may
grow out of meal practice, *sitting* in glory rules out a reference to *reclining* at the messianic
banquet (cf. 14:25 with 14:18); and "glory" does not link up very well with a banquet
(against J. Jeremias, *Eucharistic Words* 205). The suggestion that James and John want to
replace Moses and Elijah (cf. 9:4; J. Ernst 307) suffers from the failure of Moses and Elijah
to have sat on Jesus' right and left. The suggestion that James and John allude to Ps 110:1
and that Jesus subsequently alludes to Ps 110:2 (cf. the use of κατακυριεύω, "wield lordship," in v 42 with the same in Ps 109:2 LXX; so C. Myers, *Binding the Strong Man* 279)
suffers from the limitation of Ps 110:1 to sitting on the right, whereas James and John ask
to sit on the left as well as right, and from the reference of the psalm to a Jewish king's
ruling from Zion, whereas Jesus refers to Gentile rulers. See E. C. Maloney, *Semitic
Interference* 156-59, on the Semitism εἷς . . . εἷς, "one . . . one."

Some have argued that Jesus' asking whether James and John are able to share his fate
implies that if they are, and if they do share it, he will give them seats on his right and left.
Since the statement that he has no authority to decide who sits on his right and left then
disagrees with this implication, the conclusion is drawn that the question and succeeding
dialogue (vv 38-39) represent an originally independent tradition or a prophecy after the event
of James' and John's suffering and martyrdom. But the assumed implication of the question
is unnecessary, and the denial of authority (if such it is — see the foregoing comments) does
not square with any other dominical occasion. "Are you able . . . ?" may better imply that
whether or not Jesus can or will seat James and John on his right and left, their request takes
no account of the prior fate which they will have to share with him. The statement about his
not having authority then takes up the slack left by the delay in answering their question, as
indicated by the adversative δέ, "but," in v 40. J. Gnilka (2. 99) correctly notes that vv 38-39
are neither viable nor sensible as an isolated unit. One could suppose that they derive from a
lost setting, but the present setting looks good enough. Without these verses, none of the
episode is likely to have been remembered; for Jesus' deferring to God in v 40 would not
hold very much appeal, and a simple refusal of the request would carry no interest.

The independence of the reference to Jesus' baptism in Luke 12:50 does not prove
the original independence of Mark 10:38-39. Luke 12:50 may have split off from its original
context. Luke 12:49-53 (and perhaps an even wider context) looks like a miscellaneous
collection of sayings with different origins (J. A. Fitzmyer, *Luke* 994; S. Légasse in *NTS*
20 [1973-74] 164). The absence of the cup from Luke 12:50 combines with the absence
from Mark 10:38-39 of an exclamation about being distressed to give the impression of
two different sayings.

J. A. T. Robinson (*Twelve NT Studies* 160) and W. Barclay (*Introduction to John
and the Acts of the Apostles* 38-39) deny the futuristic force of the present tense in "I am

drinking" and "I am being baptized" (v 38). But as late as 14:32-42 the cup will have yet
to be drunk; and at 9:31 the similar present tense in "is being given over" looked to the
future, for Jesus had yet to be given over into the hands of men (see 14:41-42 with
14:43-47). He still has yet to be given over.

According to V. Howard (in *CBQ* 39 [1977] 520), the answer, "We are able," shows
that James and John do know what they are asking for; and Jesus confirms that they do
(". . . you will drink . . . you will be baptized"). Howard goes on to deduce that vv 38b-39,
where also Jesus remarks their ignorance, originally belonged to a different context. But
James' and John's answer relates to Jesus' questioning their ability, not to his remarking
their ignorance. His remarking their ignorance relates back to their initial request.

The frequent use of drinking a cup for undergoing divine judgment need not make
us think that the cup of Jesus, James, and John connotes divine judgment (as thought, e.g.,
by L. Goppelt [in *TDNT* 6. 149-53] and A. Feuillet [in *RB* 74 (1967) 371-72, 377-82], who
give references to primary literature; see also the discussion by G. Delling in *NovT* 2 [1957]
92-115). For a metaphorical cup may alternatively contain the sufferings of martyrdom
(*Mart. Isa.* 5:13 — the point stands whether or not we see Christian influence there; *Mart.
Pol.* 14:2), sexual rejection accompanied by physical drubbing (Plaut. *Cas.* 933), the tears
of a pious woman (*Bib. Ant.* 50:6), or even human consolation (Jer 16:7) and blessings
from God (Pss 16:5; 23:5; 116:13; cf. Str-B 1. 836-37). Since context defines the contents
of a metaphorical cup, Jesus' cup is defined by the passion predictions, especially by the
immediately foregoing one in vv 33-34. Those predictions mention suffering only at human
hands. As we would expect from Jesus' call to take up your cross and follow him (8:34),
James' and John's cup is the same as that of Jesus (again cf. *Mart. Pol.* 14:2; also rabbinic
literature appropriately cited in Str-B 1. 838 on drinking from the same cup as sharing the
same fate). So also with the metaphorical baptism that Jesus shares with James and John.
It is set in the context of human conflict at Luke 12:50; and although overwhelming waters
signify divine judgment in Genesis 6–8; Isa 30:27-28; Jonah 2:3-6(2-5), they signify
suffering at the hands of fellow human beings in 2 Sam 22:5; Pss 18:4; 42:7; 69:1-2, 14-15
(cf. Isa 43:2). Josephus (*J.W.* 4.33 §137) even uses the verb "baptize" for such suffering.
So also does Ps 68:3 Aq Sym, and Job 9:31 Aq uses "baptize" for divinely caused but
non-judgmental suffering. Moses' tasting the cup of death in *Tg. Neof.* Deut 32:1 (see R. Le
Déaut in *Bib* 43 [1962] 82-86) differs from Mark 10:38-39 in having the verb "taste" and
the noun "death" and in restricting the metaphor to death itself — a natural one in old age
(so also the cup of death for Abraham in *T. Abr.* 16A) — as opposed to persecutory suffering
issuing in a violent, premature death (cf. *Tg. Neof.* Gen 40:23; *Frg. Tg.* Gen 40:23 for the
verb "taste" with the noun "death" and for a restriction of the metaphor to death itself).
Since divine judgment is not in view, we should avoid supposing that Jesus plays on the
baptism of repentance as an escape from divine judgment (so W. L. Lane 380-81; cf. the
view of M. G. Kline [in *WTJ* 27 (1965) 131-39] that baptism is a water ordeal). For Greek
and Latin parallels to the cup and baptism, see J. Wettstein 1. 457.

Acts 12:2 mentions James' martyrdom, Rev 1:9 John's suffering (see F.-M. Braun,
Jean le Théologien 1. 375-88, on the unreliability of traditions that make John a martyr,
too; shorter treatments in V. Taylor 442; R. Schnackenburg, *John* 1. 86-88, with references
to older literature). Since a cup and baptism do not have to include death and since between
themselves James and John endured both suffering and violent death, Jesus' prediction
does not require the martyrdom of John as well as of James. A late, non-violent death of
John makes it difficult to think of a late Christian prophecy read back onto Jesus' lips,
however; for a Christian prophet would probably have taken care to distinguish John's
suffering from James' martyrdom and would have hesitated to venture a genuine prediction
of John's martyrdom. E. P. Sanders (*Jesus and Judaism* 147) gives further arguments for
the authenticity of vv 38-39.

A Christian fabrication of vv 38-39 after the pattern of, or for an allusion to, the rite of baptism and the eucharistic cup creates problems. So also does a sacramental interpretation of vv 38-39 regarded as a traditional unit. "Are you able?" then makes nonsense, for it requires no great ability to drink the cup of the Eucharist or to undergo baptism in water. Under the sacramental interpretation baptism should come first, the cup second; for baptism is a rite of initiation. But Mark has the reverse order. Nor is it easy to identify Christian baptism in water with the baptism of Jesus in water; for his lies in the past yet the baptism of which he speaks lies in the future, or is at least in process toward the future. Eucharistic symbolism might lead to a metaphorical cup of suffering; but Christian baptismal symbolism might lead to a metaphorical baptism of suffering only under the influence of Paul's interpretation of baptism, and then only under the non-resurrection half of it (Rom 6:1-11). 1 Cor 10:21 has no bearing on the present text (against E. Wendling, *Entstehung* 134-35). There, baptism is missing. Here, Jesus does not speak of eating at table or of demons. He questions the ability to endure. Paul questions a possibility of consistency.

To say that though John did not die a martyr as James did he did die with Christ in accordance with Gal 2:19; Rom 6:1-11; 7:4, 6 (cf. K.-G. Reploh, *Lehrer* 161-62) attributes too much Pauline theology to Mark and again neglects the question of discipular endurance in the question, "Are you able?" This element is alien to co-crucifixion with Christ, in which his suffering and death count as the already accomplished suffering and death of Christians, and this by faith at conversion, not by endurance following conversion. Concerning the view that vv 38-39 relate to the messianic woes, see the notes on 9:49; and J. Gnilka 2. 101 against the notion that the present passage polemicizes against hegemonic claims by bishops in Jerusalem. Gnilka (2. 99) identifies vv 35-38 as the oldest version of the story, a biographical apothegm. But then the story ends strangely with a question — and not with one about Jesus, but with a question about the ability of disciples. Whether or not vv 39-40 originally belonged to vv 35-38 (for a defense of the unity of vv 35-40 against form critical fragmentation, see J. Muddiman in *The Glory of Christ in the NT* 55-56), the low Christology of v 40 disfavors Christian fabrication.

Because "not mine to give" may suggest that the giving belongs to another, or to others, J. Muddiman (op. cit. 56-58) translates v 40, "The authority to grant places on my right and left does not belong to me, but to those who have been prepared [*sc.* by God] to do so," and then interprets the prepared ones as the executioners who seated two bandits on crosses at Jesus' right and left in the Crucifixion (15:24-27). Thus Jesus defines his glory (10:37) as his death on a cross. But not only does this interpretation of glory disagree with the meaning of "glory" in its two other Marcan occurrences, both of them Jesuanic (8:38; 13:26); and not only is crucifixion never portrayed in Mark or elsewhere in the gospel tradition as being seated (though the use of a small wooden peg, called the *sedile* or seat, to support victims of crucifixion would have justified such a portrayal). The singular of the verb ἡτοίμασται, "it has been prepared," rules out the executioners. They have not been prepared. It is the sitting on Jesus' right and left that has been prepared. Thus οἷς, "for whom," must refer to those who will sit, not to those who will seat them. Muddiman might avoid this problem by revising his translation as follows: "But the sitting on my right and left is not mine to give; rather, [the sitting on my right and left is theirs to give] for whom it [the act of giving] has been prepared." But this translation would entail an awkward shift in implied subjects from the articular infinitive τό . . . καθίσαι, "to sit," previously used as a subject, to the anarthrous infinitive δοῦναι, "to give," previously used only as a predicate nominative (literally, "my to-give," a verbal noun modified by a possessive adjective). Moreover, preparation of the sitting itself makes more sense than would a preparation of the giving of seats. Muddiman dismisses too quickly the translation (not *mis*translation — see the foregoing comments) according to which *Jesus* gives seats to those for whom the sitting has been prepared. Under the traditional translation, a divine passive answers to the suggestion in "not mine to give" that the giving belongs to another. This answer leaves Muddiman's translation without reason.

See the notes on 1:45 for Mark's use of ἤρξαντο, "they [the ten] began," plus an infinitve (v 41). Since in the view of W. Schmithals (463) vv 42-45 presuppose that the ten have not heard vv 35-40, he hypothesizes that originally v 42 followed v 40, Mark later composing v 41 as a transition. Jesus' summoning the ten in v 42 might appear at first to support this hypothesis. But on second thought, the earshot implied in summoning puts the ten close enough also to have heard the dialogue between Jesus and James and John. Nothing else in vv 42-45 presupposes that the ten have not heard.

Though J. Ernst (308) admits that the reaction of the ten is historically possible because it is psychologically understandable, he thinks it superfluous after Jesus' rebuke of James and John. But not only is history full of superfluities. Jesus has not rebuked James and John. Even if he had, his rebuke would not likely have satisfied the ten, especially if they have been entertaining similar ambitions or have had such ambitions sparked by James' and John's request to Jesus.

The references to the ten and James and John make it doubtful that in v 42 "them" refers to the large crowd who will surface in v 46, as though they are the same as the ones going up to Jerusalem in v 32 (cf. R. Busemann, *Jüngergemeinde* 152). Those pilgrims lie too far back in the context, anyway; and the large crowd of v 46 will originate in Jericho. E. Arens (*ΗΛΘΟΝ-Sayings* 120) thinks that in v 42 Mark adds δοκοῦντες for irony, Matt 20:35 preserving the original wording. But Matthew probably drops δοκοῦντες to tighten the parallelism, as he often does (R. H. Gundry, *Matthew* 403). T. W. Manson (*Teaching* 313-15) correctly argues that factuality of rule subverts the translation "the ones seeming" for οἱ δοκοῦντες, but the argument equally subverts his translation "the ones aspiring." E. Stauffer (in *The NT Age* 505-6) translates with "the ones seeming" and infers that though the Caesar is called *princeps,* "leader," he treats people as though he is a *dominus,* "master"; i.e. Rome is a pseudo-republic. Perhaps we are also to detect an allusion to Sejanus or Pilate. But this suggestion turns Jesus' wording topsy-turvy by making it describe apparent non-rule as genuine rule, whereas if it deals with mere appearance at all, it describes apparent rule as genuine non-rule. There is no good reason to distinguish in v 42 between great and not-so-great rulers (against E. Klostermann 108). Synonymous parallelism suffices.

Nor is there good reason to see in vv 42-45 a Marcan reinterpretation of the martyrdom in vv 38-39 as daily service, a dying to self (cf. E. Best, *Following Jesus* 125); for the daily service in vv 42-45 goes to the extent of martyrdom (v 45). Since v 31 reversed the order of non-disciples and disciples but vv 43-44, like 9:35, reverse roles only among disciples, these later verses probably do not illustrate v 31. An illustrative purpose, moreover, would probably have borrowed "last" to stand over against "first" (as in v 31; 9:35). Instead, we read "slave." H. Fleddermann (in *CBQ* 43 [1981] 60) and J. D. Crossan (*In Fragments* 289) argue that the phrase "and servant of all" in 9:35 betrays borrowing from 10:42-44, i.e. the reverse of what is argued in the foregoing comments. But since "slave," not "servant," stands over against "first" in 10:44, a borrowing in 9:35 would likely have put "slave" instead of "servant" to stand with "last" over against "first." As E. Best (*Disciples and Discipleship* 149) finely notes, vv 43-44 do not necessarily imply that any Christian should exercise authority. Whoever wishes to do so will be a servant and a slave, and a person in that position does not exercise authority. Jesus' words apply to interrelations among the twelve apostles: none of them will rule the others. By the time of Mark's writing, this prediction has proved true. We should not detect an escalation from "servant" to "slave" or from a reference to the Twelve in "of you" to a reference to all people in "of all." The repetition of "among you" shows that "slave of all" means "slave of you all" in parallel with "servants of you." Otherwise we have the disjunction of being a slave of all society but being first only among the Twelve.

A number of questions have arisen with regard to the saying in v 45: Is the first part, "for even the Son of man has not come to be served; rather, [he has come] to serve," authentic? Is the remainder, "and to give his life [as] a ransom in substitution for many," authentic? Does the saying lie here in its original setting? Does it allude to a passage or two in Isaiah? For a general discussion, see A. Feuillet in *RSPT* 51 (1967) 365-402.

Against the authenticity of the first half it is argued that καὶ γάρ, "for even," is Hellenistic. (Καὶ γάρ does not mean "for also," for then it would carry the false implication that someone else or others have come to serve and give their lives as a ransom.) But apart from the increasingly attractive possibility that Jesus often spoke Greek, a Hellenistic feature might represent a translational locution just as well as it might represent a non-Semitic and therefore non-Jesuanic origin. "The Son of man" strikes a Semitic note (contrast the Hellenized version "[the] man Christ Jesus" in 1 Tim 2:5), which increases the likelihood of Jesuanic origin (cf. the notes on 2:10). To be sure, Luke 22:27b has "I" (ἐγώ) instead of "the Son of man." But if Luke 22:27b is brought in as a parallel tradition, support for the authenticity of this half of the saying doubles. Furthermore, a Hellenizing of the Semitic expression "the Son of man" is more likely than a Semitizing of the Hellenistic ἐγώ (cf. P. Stuhlmacher, *Reconciliation* 20-23; against C. Colpe in *TDNT* 8. 448; H. E. Tödt, *Son of Man* 207-8, 211; J. Jeremias in *ZNW* 58 [1967] 166-69). Sayings in which Jesus states in the third person that "the Son of man has come" occur very rarely — elsewhere only in Matt 11:19 par. Luke 7:34 and Luke 19:10 — just often enough to support the authenticity of v 45a (par. Matt 20:28a). But sayings in which Jesus states in the first person, "I have come" (ἦλθον or ἐλήλυθα), occur much more often in the synoptics (Mark 1:38; 2:17 par. Luke 5:32; Matt 5:17 [bis]; 9:13; 10:34 [bis; cf. Luke 12:51] par. Luke 12:49; Matt 10:35); and in the fourth gospel they multiply like rabbits (John 5:43; 7:28; 8:14 [bis], 42; 9:39; 10:10; 12:27, 46, 47; 15:22; 16:28 [bis]; 18:37). This strong tendency to move away from the third person to the first puts a heavy burden of proof on anyone who would argue that the absence of "the Son of man" from Luke 22:27 undermines the Semitic argument for the authenticity of Mark 10:45a. The typically Semitic negative-positive parallelism of "has not come to be served; rather, [he has come] to serve" adds weight to this argument. Though these counter arguments suffice, the implication of other possibilities deserves notice: if differences in phraseology may indicate that originally (i.e. in Jesus' speech) Mark 10:45 followed on Luke 22:27 rather than that Luke 22:27 presents a parallel to Mark 10:45a (I. H. Marshall, *Luke* 813-14) or if those differences and the difference in settings favor the repetition of similar teaching on different occasions (S. H. T. Page in *Gospel Perspectives* 1. 148-53), then the absence of "the Son of man" from Luke 22:27b does not undermine the Semitic argument for the authenticity of Mark 10:45a.

Against the authenticity of v 45a it has further been argued that the aorist tense in οὐκ ἦλθεν, "has not come," implies the pastness of Jesus' ministry. But the aorist does not require the pastness of his whole ministry. How else but with an aorist could he have referred to that part of his ministry that had elapsed thus far? So long as he had a sense of divine commission — and it would take diehard scepticism to deny that he did — ἦλθεν refers to his appearance on the public scene no matter how much or little of that commission remained to be carried out (cf. 12:6; also passages where Jesus has portrayed himself as sent by God [9:37 par. Luke 9:48; Matt 10:40 par. Luke 10:16; Matt 15:24; Luke 4:43 et passim in John] and the argument of J. Jeremias [in *ZNW* 58 (1967) 166-67] that "has not come" means "does not intend"). Apparently Mark sees no incongruity in οὐκ ἦλθεν; for he will narrate the rest of Jesus' ministry but does not change the aorist (ibid. 141-43). The connotation of appearance on the public scene casts doubt on the generalizing interpretation that a son of man (i.e. a human being) such as Jesus is obligated to serve others (so P. M. Casey in *JSNT* 29 [1987] 42-43).

The rarity of διακονέω in the LXX does not argue against the authenticity of v 45a.

If the verb appeared often in the LXX we would probably hear the argument that v 45a derives from Hellenistic Jewish Christianity, not from Jesus. J. A. Emerton (in *JTS* ns 11 [1960] 334-35) argues against the authenticity of v 45a that in the passive (ithpᵉel) עבד, which corresponds to διακονέω, "serve," means "be done, be made, become," not "be served," as required by διακονηθῆναι, "to be served." But the aforementioned contrast with Dan 7:14 may mean that we should think of the different Aramaic verb פלח, "work for, serve," which occurs there. The LXX and Theodotion never use διακονέω for פלח, but their using no fewer than four other Greek verbs for only ten instances of this Aramaic one exhibits a variety that opens the door to διακονέω. As pointed out by D. R. A. Hare (*Son of Man Tradition* 203-4), however, Dan 7:14 has to do with the forced service of those who have been subjugated, a connotation foreign to Mark 10:45. We should therefore adopt the suggestion of P. Stuhlmacher (*Reconciliation* 21) and G. Schwarz (*Jesus und Judas* 73) that διακονηθῆναι/-ῆσαι represents the Aramaic verb שמש in Dan 7:10. This verb connotes willing service such as Mark 10:45 requires. In fact, the old Syriac versions of Mark 10:45 use this verb.

Against the authenticity of v 45b a number of arguments are put forward. Nowhere else does Jesus interpret his death. More specifically, in no other saying does he attach a salvific significance to the death of "the Son of man." The notion of a ransom appears neither elsewhere in his synoptic teaching nor in the rest of the NT where a dominical origin might have resulted in its preservation (see, e.g., Rom 5:8; Gal 1:4; 2:20; Eph 5:2, 25; John 10:11, 15, 17-18; 15:13; 1 John 3:16). This notion and the phraseology used to express it show later Christian influence. The inimitability of the Son of man's giving his life in substitution for many sets v 45b apart from his imitable serving in v 45a. And Luke 22:27 has no parallel to Mark 10:45b though it does to Mark 10:45a.

But we have noted that Luke 22:27 may not be parallel to Mark 10:45 and that the passages in which they occur may have to do with different occasions. Even apart from those possibilities, the questions, "For who [is] greater [τίς γὰρ μείζων], the one reclining or the one serving? [It is] the one reclining, [is it] not?" (Luke 22:27a), are not to be considered a tradition that Mark omits because of his advancing the rest of the material to a new setting not at table. Those questions are better explained by Lucan redaction, influenced by the new setting of the Last Supper into which Luke has transposed the material and by his redaction in v 24 ("as to who of them seems to be greatest [τὸ τίς αὐτῶν δοκεῖ εἶναι μείζων]"; cf. J. A. Fitzmyer, *Luke* 1412; D. E. Smith in *JBL* 106 [1987] 613-38, esp. 620, 623, 628-29, 630-32). Semitisms in Mark 10:45b as well as in 10:45a support the hypothesis that Luke 22:27 is part of a later Hellenistic version transposed to the Last Supper. The further Semitisms in v 45b are three in number: (1) the use of τὴν ψυχὴν αὐτοῦ as a reflexive, "himself," including the larger meaning, "his life" (cf. 1 Macc 2:50; Sir 29:15; Jer 45:5; *Mek.* Exod 12:1, all with "give," as here; contrast the Hellenized version ἑαυτόν, "himself," in 1 Tim 2:6 [cf. 1 Macc 6:44] and giving the body as a basically synonymous but different Greek expression in Thuc. 2.43.2 and 2 Macc 7:37, which combines it with the Semitic expression); (2) the use of "in substitution for many" (ἀντὶ πολλῶν) for the beneficiaries (cf. Isa 53:11-12 for the linguistic point whether or not there is an allusion to that passage; see E. C. Maloney, *Semitic Interference* 139-42, on the Semitic use of "many" for "all"; and contrast the Hellenized version ὑπὲρ πάντων, "on behalf of all," in 1 Tim 2:6, where ἀντί shifts to ἀντίλυτρον because of Hellenization; also contrast the ὑπέρ and περί with πολλῶν in Mark 14:24 par. Matt 26:28); and probably though not necessarily (3) the paratactic "and" used epexegetically to mean "*by* giving his life . . ." (and thus ruling out a reference to Jesus' pre-passion ministry; cf. J. Jeremias, *Abba* 216-29; E. Lohse, *Märtyrer und Gottesknecht* 117-22; J. Roloff in *NTS* 19 [1972-73] 38-64; H. Patsch, *Abendmahl* 170-80). These Semitisms demand a pre-Marcan origin. But in the tradition v 45b could hardly have existed by itself; so the chances of its authenticity are enhanced by the arguments already canvassed for the authenticity of v 45a, with which v 45b was one in the tradition. It seems unlikely that a saying dealing simply with service and set in a pericope dealing only with service should have been given a soteriological twist without dominical support, especially since indisputably Christian formulations concerning Jesus' death do not use the vocabulary of service. But the table-setting of the Last Supper might easily have prompted Luke to make a transposition and led him further to put exclusive emphasis on serving. Διακονέω refers primarily and often to the serving of food at table. An exclusive emphasis on serving needs only the omission of self-giving as a ransom in substitution for many, an omission aided and abetted by the recently quoted Words of Institution, which make the reference otiose (Luke 22:19-20, longer text). The exclusive emphasis on serving typifies the ethical motif that cuts a wide swath throughout Luke-Acts. Luke's omission of James' and John's request and of Jesus' answer (Mark 10:35-40), Luke's putting of the disciples' contention over which of them was the greatest after the institution of the Lord's Supper rather than before it, where vying for places of honor would find its natural occasion (see Mark 12:39; Luke 14:7-11), and the inconcinnity of Jesus' portraying himself as serving when he has just acted as host give the impression that Luke has indeed tacked material from Mark 10:41-45 onto his tradition concerning the Last Supper. Jesus' washing the disciples' feet according to John 13:4-17 does not offer much help to rescue the traditionality of Luke's placement of this material. For διακονέω does not occur in that passage; and though the word is not limited to food-serving (as shown, for example, by the epexegetic "and to give his life . . ." right here in Mark 10:45b), the setting at table, the immediate precedence of eating a meal, and the immediate subsequence of a reference to eating and drinking at Jesus' table in his kingdom (Luke 22:30) make διακονέω in Luke 22:27 connote, not feet-washing, but food-serving even more than usually. The inconcinnity with acting as host remains.

The suitability of an original connection between v 45a and v 45b does not depend on the possibility of imitating Jesus by performing the same service that he performed, but on the possibility of imitating him by performing service as such. "To give his life . . ." specifies the kind of service he will perform. It need not imply that the Twelve will perform the same kind. 1 Pet 2:21-24 likewise makes Jesus' salvific death an example to be followed non-salvifically (cf. John 12:23-26, where salvifically fruitful death shades into service, and John 13:1-20, where the salvific symbolism of feet-washing shades into following Jesus' example of service in feet-washing — S. H. T. Page in *Gospel Perspectives* 1. 139-40; cf. G. Vos, *Self-Disclosure* 281-82).

We should not disallow out of hand the possibility of Jesus' coming to believe and teach that his death will carry salvific value. If he does so at all, it is no sign of inauthenticity that v 45b represents his first such interpretation — one had to be first — or even that it represents his only such interpretation. But it is not his only such interpretation, for also in the various versions of the Words of Institution he gives his death salvific value — though not (except for πολλῶν, "many") with any of the diction in v 45, a fact that disfavors Christian fabrication of v 45 on the basis of the Words of Institution (Mark 14:24; Matt 26:28; Luke 22:19-20; 1 Cor 11:24-25). That these salvific interpretations do not appear till after several non-interpretative predictions of the Son of man's death (8:31; 9:12, 31; 10:33-34; cf. 2:20) exhibits a reserve which favors authenticity. Also favoring it are the link by way of "the Son of man" with those earlier predictions and the absence of "the Son of man" from indisputably Christian formulations concerning Jesus' death. If he saw his death as of a piece with his preceding ministry, as he probably did, it makes sense that he should graduate from predicting the fact of his death to indicating its value. If he did not indicate its value to be salvific, we have to wonder how the first disciples came to believe and proclaim it so — not as a martyr's death, needed again and again and valuable only for Israel and only for her fate in the present world (2 Macc 7:37-38 with 8:2-7;

4 Macc 6:26-30; 9:21-25; 17:20-22, 18:4; cf. Exod 32:30-32 and see R. S. McConnell, *Law and Prophecy* 185; C. Maurer in *ZTK* 50 [1953] 20-24 against S. K. Williams [*Jesus' Death* 217-20, 224-25], who traces vicariousness to 4 Maccabees rather than to Jesus or the OT), but valuable for "many" in the broadest sense and for all eternity. The Maccabean martyrs died as righteous men for adherence to the Law; but Jesus neither describes the Son of man as righteous nor makes him die for adherence to the Law.

It is untrue that the rest of the NT does not make the notion of a ransom part of Jesus' salvific work. The word used here, λύτρον, does not appear elsewhere; but the closely related words ἀντίλυτρον, ἀπολύτρωσις, and λυτρόω appear in this connection at Rom 3:24-25; 1 Cor 1:30; Eph 1:7; Col 1:14; 1 Tim 2:6; Titus 2:14; Heb 9:15; and in 1 Cor 6:20; 7:23 "you have been bought with a price" explains the notion of ransom. A similar explanation appears in Gal 3:13; 4:5. The notion of Jesus' giving himself for others appears also in Gal 1:4; 2:20; Eph 5:2, 25. Slight differences in wording — not only in the terminology of ransom, but also in the use of παραδίδωμι instead of δίδωμι for giving at Gal 2:20; Eph 5:2, 25, the use of the Greek reflexive pronoun instead of the Semitism τὴν ψυχὴν αὐτοῦ (whose authenticity is indirectly supported by John 10:11, 15, 17-18; 15:13; 1 John 3:16), and the similar avoidance in the non-Marcan passages of the Semitisms "in substitution for many" and (to reach back into Mark 10:45a) "the Son of man" — again favor authenticity. For Christian fabrication would likely have reflected the later vocabulary. Of course, one could say that v 45b reflects an earlier stage of a Christian fabrication than passages elsewhere in the NT do. But then an argument reduces to a hypothesis; for an earlier stage can only be hypothesized, and it would increase the chance of authenticity and decrease the chance of fabrication. Earlier than Galatians, 1 Corinthians, and Romans is getting pretty early. The possibility that passages elsewhere in the NT derive from authentic dominical tradition looks better and better.

Against the authenticity of v 45b, M. Smith (*Clement* 202) nevertheless argues that Jesus' speaking of betrayal and setting guards at Gethsemane (14:32, 34; cf. Luke 22:40) show that he did not intend to give his life a ransom in substitution for many. But his deliberately going into a situation where betrayal will become easy justifies the phraseology of giving his life a ransom in substitution for many. He will tell most of his disciples simply to sit, not to stay awake; and though he will tell Peter, James, and John to stay awake (14:34, 37-38), he will make no attempt to escape even when Judas Iscariot is still distant and an escape would seem possible (see 14:41 with comments and notes).

The reduction of v 45 to the putatively original statement, "A man may give [in the sense of 'risk'] his life for many" (so B. Lindars, *Jesus, Son of Man* 76-81), unnecessarily demands that "the Son of man" be generic as well as self-referential (see again the notes on 2:10), wrongly cuts v 45 from its context by eliminating the motif of service (What motif better than service can we suggest even for the saying as pared down by Lindars?), disregards the earlier passion predictions by weakening the giving of life to the risking of life, and misreads the rest of the NT by treating the notion of ransom as a later addition. The fact that v 45a may have a parallel in Luke 22:27 and v 45b in 1 Tim 2:6 does not prove a combination of two originally independent sayings in v 45 as a whole (so B. Lindars in *ExpTim* 93 [1981-82] 292-95), for Luke 23:27 and 1 Tim 2:6 might just as conceivably represent the fragmentation of an original unity. Moreover, neither v 45b nor 1 Tim 2:6 is so much as a clause; and correspondence between "the Son of man" in Mark 10:45a and "[the] man Christ Jesus" in 1 Tim 2:5 gives representation to both halves of Mark 10:45 in 1 Tim 2:5-6 (cf. J. Jeremias, *Abba* 225-26).

By word order and sense, ἀντὶ πολλῶν, "in substitution for many," goes with λύτρον, "ransom," not with δοῦναι, "to give." Ἀντί makes the Son of man's death a ransom that takes the place of many, i.e. that substitutes for their death and thereby gives them eternal life (see R. E. Davies in *TynBul* 21 [1970] 72-81 on ἀντί). A. Schenker (in *La Pâque du*

Christ 75-90) denies the implication of a substitutionary death by noting that λύτρον means a sum of money, a price of ransom, and that 1 Sam 26:21; 2 Kings 1:13-14; Pss 72:14; 116:15 portray human life as precious, valuable. The OT passages do not help interpret Mark 10:45, however; for in all of them the preciousness of human life leads to its preservation, not to death for its value in payment. Since the price of ransom in substitution for many consists in the Son of man's giving his life, substitutionary death is hard to avoid.

Substitutionary death for "many" appears in Isaiah 53 (see esp. vv 11-12), and Luke 22:37 favors that Jesus saw his death in the light of that passage (see S. H. T. Page in *Gospel Perspectives* 1. 145-47 for further evidence). But even if he did, it does not necessarily follow that Mark 10:45 alludes to Isaiah 53; or it may follow that the allusion is severely limited to the phrase "in substitution for many." Isaiah speaks of a "servant" (עבד in the MT, παῖς in the LXX), Jesus of "the Son of man." Though the servant's death benefits many, he serves Yahweh; but the Son of man serves the many themselves. Neither the Marcan verb διακονέω nor its cognates appear in Isaiah 53 LXX, and they seldom appear elsewhere in the LXX. Jesus' expression "has come . . . to serve and to give his life [as] a ransom" stresses the Son of man's voluntariness; but in Isa 53:10 the shift from third person references to Yahweh ("Yahweh has caused the iniquity of us all to fall on him. . . . Yahweh was pleased to crush him" — vv 6, 10) to the second person ("if *you* would make his life a guilt offering, . . ."; cf. the LXX) deliberately avoids a possible misunderstanding in what would have been the more natural phraseology, viz., "if *he* would make his life/himself [נפשׁו then doubling as a reflexive] a guilt offering, . . ." (cf. the conjectural emendations designed to get rid of the second person). The possible misunderstanding would consist in thinking that the servant of Yahweh makes his own life a guilt offering, but the preceding context would still favor that "he" refers to Yahweh as the subject. It is different in Isa 53:12, where the Servant of Yahweh "poured out his life to death"; but "to death" distances that expression from Mark 10:45, and Isa 53:12 LXX reads the passive: παρεδόθη εἰς θάνατον ἡ ψυχὴ αὐτοῦ, "his life was given over to death." Similarly, the phraseological differences between *making* life something (תשׂים . . . נפשׁו — Isa 53:10; the LXX has the soul seeing) and *pouring out* life (נפשׁו . . . הערה — Isa 53:12) on the one hand and, on the other hand, *giving* life (δοῦναι τὴν ψυχὴν αὐτοῦ — Mark 10:45) calls in question a Jesuanic allusion to Isaiah 53 in the expression "his life." Doubt increases with observation that unlike Isaiah's expressions, Jesus' expression occurs commonly among Jews for the deaths of martyrs and among Greek-users for the deaths of soldiers (F. Büchsel in *TDNT* 2. 166). "A ransom" (Mark 10:45) is not the same as "a guilt offering" (Isa 53:10), as shown by the facts that the LXX never translates אשׁם with λύτρον or any of its cognates and that none of the Hebrew words represented elsewhere in the LXX by λύτρον and its cognates appear in Isaiah 53. This linguistic phenomenon demonstrates a material difference between a ransom and a guilt offering (against critics of C. K. Barrett [in *NT Essays* 4-7; cf. idem, *NT Essays* 20-26; M. D. Hooker, *Jesus and the Servant* 45-78], who not only noted this phenomenon but also anticipated his critics by arguing that a merely linguistic difference does not satisfy the demands of the phenomenon). Isaiah interprets the death of Yahweh's Servant as providing a vicarious atonement for sins. Isaiah's vocabulary is rich and repetitive in references to them. Vicarious atonement may stand in the wings of Mark 10:45, but it does not come on stage. Sins go entirely unmentioned. To mention vicarious atonement for sins would go beyond what is needed to illustrate the motif of service in the Son of man's giving his life as a ransom in substitution for many. These many material and linguistic differences outweigh the grammatical observation of J. Jeremias (*NT Theology* 1. 292, n. 3) that only in Isa 53:10 and Mark 10:45 is taking or giving a life further defined by a predicative accusative. We would have to assess the matter differently had the verbs and predicative accusatives matched up. As it is, only the accusatives of direct object match up.

Do the decisive words and concepts come, then, not from Isaiah 53, but from Isa 43:3-4, 25, and the parallelistically negative-positive structure plus the doing away with sins from Isa 43:22-25 (W. Grimm, *Verkündigung* 231-77; P. Stuhlmacher, *Reconciliation* 22-25; see also G. Schwarz [*Jesus und Judas* 74-75], who adds the wicked as the ransom for the righteous in Prov 21:18)? If so, Jesus is saying in effect that he will take the place of certain Gentile nations as the ransom for Israel in order that those Gentile nations might also be ransomed. Prima facie, such a replacement seems unlikely. Nowhere else does Jesus play a role expected of Gentile nations. The voluntariness of the Son of man's serving and giving his life clashes with Yahweh's giving Egypt, Ethiopia, and Seba (and possibly Edom and Leummites as well, depending on the translation of Isa 43:4). These nations do not serve, as the Son of man does; and we can be sure that they do not willingly accept their role as ransom. Though that role will entail loss of life if the ransom consists in Yahweh's allowing Cambyses to conquer them in payment for Cyrus's having permitted Israel to return from exile or if in line with later Jewish thought Yahweh will cast the heathen into Gehenna in place of Israel (Grimm, op. cit. 242-47), the only life mentioned by Isaiah is Israel's (נַפְשְׁךָ, "your life" — v 4), not that of the ransom as in Mark 10:45. Moreover, the loss of life in conquest occurs on both sides and is incidental to the conquest as such. Of lesser argumentative weight (lesser because Jesus' λύτρον, "price of ransom," may represent an alternative translation of כפר), λύτρον does not occur in the LXX of Isa 43:3-4, which has ἄλλαγμα, "price of exchange." Likewise, to translate תחת the LXX uses ὑπέρ, "in behalf of" (tris), not Jesus' ἀντί, "in substitution for." In view of his using "the Son of man" in earlier passion predictions, the possibility is slim that Isaiah's אדם, "humankind" or "Edom," underlies "the Son of man" in Mark 10:45. Moreover, אדם is an object, whereas "the Son of man" is a subject. "Many" does not appear in Isa 43:3-4. One could think of an association of this passage with Isa 53:11-12, where "many" does occur; but the wide difference between the heathen and Yahweh's Servant makes the association unlikely. This wide difference also makes unlikely a correspondence between the ransom in Isa 43:3-4 and the guilt offering in Isa 53:10.

Since the contents of Isa 43:22-24 bear no material similarity to Mark 10:45, the structural similarity of negative-positive parallelism hardly makes Jesus depend on that passage. And whereas Isa 43:25 speaks of Yahweh's doing away with Israel's sins, Jesus does not speak of doing away with anyone's sins. To doubt an allusion to passages in Isaiah is not to weaken the case for the authenticity of Mark 10:45, for use of the OT does not favor authenticity. In fact, some scholars consider use of the OT a sign of inauthenticity (though that inference does not follow, either).

A ransom does not pay for pardon from guilt. It pays for release from slavery (as correctly noted by D. Seeley [in *SBL 1989 Seminar Papers* 547], whose drawing of a parallel with the Greco-Roman tradition of philosophers' lives and noble deaths as a service to others is weakened not only by the lack of ransom-terminology in that tradition but also by the Semitisms in Jesus' saying). Jesus does not spell out the kind of slavery he has in mind, however; nor does he indicate to whom the ransom is paid (but see H. Ridderbos, *Coming* 167-68, for inferences). The "we" whose sins the Servant of the Lord bears in Isa 53:4-6 are "my people" (v 8); so the "many" whom the Servant justifies and whose sin he bears in vv 11-12 may be limited to Israel or the majority thereof. The "many nations" in 52:14-15 will then be others, who look on aghast. The doubtfulness of Jesus' alluding to Isaiah leaves an open question whether his "many" is similarly limited. Even with an allusion, Isaiah's usage would not necessarily determine Jesus' usage (cf. Rom 5:19). Lack of the definite article differentiates "many" from "the many" who constitute the elect in the QL, though even the arthrous expression may carry a broader meaning (cf. S. K. Williams in *JBL* 102 [1983] 492; see J. Jeremias in *TDNT* 6. 538-39).

Verse 45 does not portray Jesus as "great" and "first" by virtue of his service; for in vv 43-44 those adjectives only describe whoever among the Twelve wants to be so, and Jesus proceeds to deny greatness and firstness. To an extent it is correct of M. Hengel (*Studies* 37) to argue that since 10:45 brings to a climax the primarily didactic section 9:30–10:45 and that since the similar 14:24 will bring to a climax the account of the Lord's Supper, the vicarious death of Jesus has importance in Mark. Yet we need to recognize that in the overall scheme of Mark this doctrine serves, not itself, but an apology for the Cross (see the foregoing comments on v 45).

THE MERCY OF DAVID'S SON IN RESTORING SIGHT TO BARTIMAEUS

10:46-52 (Matt 9:27-31; 20:29-34; Luke 18:35-43)

An arrival in Jericho opens this story (v 46a). Then Mark introduces Bartimaeus (v 46b) and relates this blind beggar's request (vv 47-48), Jesus' calling for him (v 49), his coming (v 50), and the dialogue that takes place when he comes (vv 51-52a). The healing of Bartimaeus and his following Jesus cap the story (v 52b).

10:46 *(Matt 9:27; 20:29-30; Luke 18:35)* "And they come into Jericho" not only sets the stage for a healing of Bartimaeus on the road leading out of the city. It also marks Jesus' progress toward Jerusalem, along the road to which lies Jericho (cf. v 32 and 11:1). The historical present tense of ἔρχονται, "they come," heightens the sense that the fulfilment of Jesus' passion-and-resurrection predictions is about to take place. Mark is playing up Jesus' power to predict the destiny that awaits him in Jerusalem. Since Jesus took the Twelve aside in v 32e, "they" seems limited to Jesus and the Twelve (see also vv 35, 41). On the way out from Jericho, however, the disciples (a larger body than the Twelve) and a crowd are present, too. Despite the historical circumstance that pilgrims are streaming to Jerusalem for the Passover, Mark's past emphasis on Jesus' magnetism favors that his description of the crowd as "considerable" (ἱκανοῦ) is designed to recall that magnetism. The position of the complex subject "the son of Timaeus, [i.e.] Bartimaeus, a blind beggar" before its verb draws attention to the patient. Contrary to Mark's usual practice of putting an Aramaic expression first and then translating it (see 3:17; 5:41; 7:11, 34; 14:36; cf. 12:42; 15:16, 42), the half-translation "the son of Timaeus" precedes the Aramaic "Bartimaeus," to prepare for the rather similar "Son of David, Jesus" in Bartimaeus's request (cf. v 47; H. B. Swete 242-43) and thus gives no impression of being a translation at all (cf. B. L. Mack, *Myth* 296-97, n. 2). The blindness of Bartimaeus sets the stage for a miracle of healing, his begging sets the stage for a request that will procure the miracle, and his "sitting on the edge of the road" (παρά plus the accusative, as in 4:4, 15) sets the stage for a contrastive "following Jesus on the road" (ἐν plus the dative — v 52).

10:47-48 *(Matt 9:27; 20:30-31; Luke 18:36-39)* In the report that Bartimaeus heard, "It's Jesus the Nazarene," the designation of Jesus as "the Nazarene" distinguishes him from other men bearing the name "Jesus" and identifies him in a Judean setting as the famous miracle-worker from a Galilean town (cf. 1:9, 24; 14:67; 16:6). The forward position of "Jesus the Nazarene" (see the Greek text) plays up his fame. The statement that Bartimaeus "began to shout and to say" stresses the loudness and insistence of the following plea. His putting the honorific title "Son of David" before the personal name "Jesus" (contrast Matt 1:20) suits a plea for mercy (which will turn out to be a request for healing, not for alms — see v 51). "Many" may mean "all," but Mark's other uses of πολύς in the plural (and there are quite a number of them) do not strongly favor this meaning. In any case, "many" stresses the considerable size of the crowd. The lack of an anaphoric definite article with "many" weakens the view that the many who rebuke Bartimaeus in v 48 are the very same many in substitution for whom the Son of man gives his life in v 45 (as thought by D. O. Via, *Ethics* 159). Nevertheless, the verbal echo heightens the emphasis on a considerable number of people. Their scolding attempt to silence Bartimaeus makes him shout all the more and calls to mind the disciples' scolding the children who came to Jesus (10:13). An adversative δέ, "but," and the wordplay between πολλῷ, "the more" (literally, "by much") and the earlier πολλοί, "many," highlight Bartimaeus's renewed plea for mercy. In it, Jesus' personal name drops out but the honorific title "Son of David" stays.

10:49-50 *(Matt 9:28; 20:32; Luke 18:40)* Jesus' standing still and telling the scolders to call Bartimaeus overturns their supposed authority in favor of Jesus' true authority (cf. 10:14) and implies that because of the considerable crowd, he hears but does not see Bartimaeus. The historical present tense in the statement, "And they call the blind [man]," and the repetition of the verb φωνέω, "call," stress the capitulation of the many to Jesus' authority. Their telling Bartimaeus to be cheerful promises something good (cf. 6:50; C. Spicq, *Notes* 1. 367-71) and issues in his flinging away his cloak. Their telling him to get up issues in his jumping up. (Both commands carry the emphasis of the present tense [see the notes on 1:3; cf. the comments on 3:3; 6:50].) And their telling him that Jesus is calling him issues in his going to Jesus. In other words, his actions carry out, and even exceed, their words. Jesus has told *them* to call Bartimaeus. But they tell Bartimaeus that *Jesus* is calling him. Thus they play the role of Jesus' agents to carry out his will despite their earlier rebuke of Bartimaeus. How quickly Jesus' exercise of authority turns things about. The rat-a-tat-tat of asyndeton between commands to Bartimaeus and between his flinging away his cloak and jumping up dramatizes this turnabout, the latter part of which is set off by ὁ δέ, "but he."

10:51-52 *(Matt 9:28-31; 20:32-34; Luke 18:40-43)* Jesus' answer is really a question that responds to Bartimaeus's actions: "What do you want [that] I should do for you?" (cf. v 36 for the phraseology). The question asks whether Bartimaeus wants money (he is begging) or something else. By causing a certain abruptness, the omission of ἵνα, "that," emphasizes θέλεις, "do you want" (see the comments on v 36). The forward position of σοι, "for you," and an adversative δέ, "but," center attention on Bartimaeus as a possible beneficiary of Jesus' power. Mark now refers to Bartimaeus as "the blind [man]" to rivet attention on the malady that Jesus' power will cure. "Rabbouni," a heightened form of "Rabbi," reflects tradition. Mark may keep this form and leave it an untranslated foreign word from the East to crown Jesus with a numinous quality. "That I may see again" reflects an epexegetic ἵνα after ellipsis of θέλω, "I want" (cf. 6:25; 9:30; 10:35). Alternatively, an imperatival ἵνα would yield "let me see again." The name of Jesus is brought forward to distinguish him from Bartimaeus. Jesus' command that Bartimaeus "go" (ὕπαγε) represents a linguistic habit of Jesus in the performance of miracles (cf. 1:44; 2:11; 5:19, 34; 7:29) and implies, "You don't have to sit on the edge of the road begging any more" (cf. the comments on 8:26). Similarly, "your faith has saved you" repeats 5:34 (cf. 2:5; Luke 7:50; 17:19) and is redolent of a salvation larger than deliverance from blindness (cf. v 26; 8:35; John 9). Asyndeton emphasizes this salvation, and "immediately" emphasizes the effectiveness of Jesus' power in restoring Bartimaeus's sight. "And he began to follow [ἠκολούθει — an inceptive imperfect] him on the road" contrasts with Jesus' command to go. But the contrast does no damage to Jesus' authority; rather, it enhances his magnetism and demonstrates his power to perform a remarkable miracle (cf. 7:36). For Bartimaeus could not be following Jesus unless he were seeing again. We should note well the progression in the compound sentence, "And immediately he saw again and began to follow him on the road." The contrast between following Jesus on the road and the earlier "sitting on the edge of the road" (v 46) points up the miracle. It also recalls "the ones following" Jesus "on the road going up to Jerusalem" in v 32 and anticipates "the ones following" on that same road in 11:8-9. Just as in those passages the road and following carry only mundane meanings, not the connotation of discipleship on the way to the Cross (see the notes on 1:2-3; 8:27 as well as the comments and notes on 10:32), so also here the road and following carry only mundane meanings. Elsewhere, too, the road clearly carries a theologically freightless meaning (2:23; 6:8; 8:3, 27; 9:33, 34; 10:17). The present road is only the hinge on which swings the miracle-highlighting contrast with sitting and begging. The considerable crowd that are on the road do not qualify as disciples (v 46). Disciples follow Jesus full time and at his command (1:17-18, 20; 2:14; 10:21) or invitation (8:34; cf. 6:1; 10:28; 14:54). But he has told Bartimaeus to do just the opposite: "go." So Bartimaeus's following falls into the category of occasional following, a kind of following less than that required of disciples though it may characterize a wider circle of believers along with the masses (2:15b [if the reference is to the toll collectors and sinners rather than to the disciples in 2:15a]; 3:7; 5:24; 9:38; 10:32; 11:9; 15:41). We must remember that Jesus did not require all believers to become disciples. Bartimaeus, of course, has not been privy to any of Jesus' passion predictions and knows nothing even of Jesus' call to cross-taking. As a whole, then, the latter half of v 52 highlights Jesus' powers of healing and attraction. Bartimaeus's following Jesus serves these emphases rather than teaching discipleship (cf. J. D. Kingsbury, *Christology of Mark's Gospel* 104-5; idem, *Conflict in Mark* 134, n. 3; J. Roloff, *Kerygma* 125-26).

NOTES

P. J. Farla (*Jezus' Oordeel* 5-32, 511-12) thinks that vv 46-52 combine a miracle-story and the story of a call to discipleship (cf. J. R. Butts in *Early Jewish and Christian Exegesis* 217-18 and M. G. Steinhauser [in *ExpTim* 94 (1982-83) 204-6], who emphasizes call at the expense of miracle; also J. Dupont in *RAT* 8 [1984] 165-81; H. D. Betz in *Semeia* 11 [1978] 72ff., 115ff.; P. J. Achtemeier in *Semeia* 11 [1978] 115-45; C. D. Marshall, *Faith* 142-43). The miraculous element is obvious; but the personal name of Bartimaeus, his throwing away his garment, and his following Jesus are supposed to represent the call story. Sometimes, however, miracle-stories include personal names (1:29-31; 5:22-24, 35-43; John 11:1-44; Acts 9:36-43; and perhaps Acts 20:7-12; cf. Luke 8:2); and call-stories do not always include personal names (Mark 10:17-22, esp. 21, parr.; Luke 9:59-60). Even under the uncertain supposition that Bartimaeus has been using his garment to collect alms (cf. Judg 8:25 for collection but not for begging), his flinging it away is not presented as leaving an occupation or giving up a possession to follow Jesus, but as getting rid of something that would impede his jumping up and coming to Jesus for a cure — and following Jesus has to await the cure. In Exod 22:25-26(26-27); Deut 24:12-13 the cloak is not a tool of occupation; and as a possession it is inalienable, not the disposable sort of possession that Jesus' disciples have to give up (against Steinhauser, loc.cit.). The verb for calling is not the καλέω of call-stories, but φωνέω. Jesus does not call Bartimaeus directly, as in call-stories. The call has the purpose of inquiring what Bartimaeus wants, not of commanding that he follow. And Jesus' commanding that he go instead of follow makes it highly unlikely that the miracle-story to which the command belongs would ever have been combined with a call-story containing a diametrically opposed command.

These same textual phenomena undermine the theory of A. J. Droge (in *SBL 1983 Seminar Papers* 252) that vv 46-52 represent an attempt to transpose a call-story into a miracle-story. His argument that we do not discover in vv 46-52 the scheme of a miracle-story — problem, solution, and proof — does not hold up. Begging alongside the road because of blindness and yelling for mercy present a problem. Calling the blind beggar, asking what he wants done for him, and restoring his sight provide a solution. And following Jesus on the road proves that Bartimaeus can see again. The popularity of the symbolic interpretation should not blind us to the regular features of a miracle-story that appear in this pericope.

It is correct that this story pays more attention to Bartimaeus than to Jesus, details their confrontation, and devotes little space to the healing proper (so K. Kertelge, *Wunder* 179). These phenomena highlight the faith of Bartimaeus, which takes a prominent forward position in v 52a; but the highlighting of his faith serves to exalt the miraculous deed of Jesus ("What do you want [that] I should do [ποιήσω] for you?" — v 51). The immediacy and evidence of the healing bring the story to a climax on the note of Jesus' power. Even — no, especially — the transformation from sitting alongside the road to following on the road strikes that note.

More particularly, Mark neither amplifies the blindness of Bartimaeus nor mentions a healing gesture nor quotes a healing word (or so it is said) nor closes with an acclamation of Jesus. Many interpreters put these omissions together with Bartimaeus's faith and following and deduce that Mark or someone before him has transformed a miracle-story into a story of faith and discipleship, a story that Mark or someone before him may have put here to cap a whole section on discipleship (8:27–10:52). But in a style characteristic of miracle-stories, Bartimaeus's blindness *is* amplified with the addition that he was begging on the edge of the road. Blindness would have required no amplification, however. Mention it and the need is starkly apparent. Few miracle-stories tell how long the person in need has been victimized or give a medical report revealing the cause of the malady.

8:22-26 mentioned blindness without amplification, but was no story of faith and discipleship. Neither was 3:1-6, though Jesus did not gesture to heal the man with a withered hand. Here, there *is* a healing word — "Go, your faith has saved you" (v 52) — for only after the utterance of this statement does Bartimaeus gain sight (contrast 5:25-34). In other words, the statement about faith is subordinate to the statement about healing. True, Luke 18:42 replaces "go" with "see again," but not because a healing word is absent; rather, because the difference between Jesus' command to go and the actuality of the ex-blind man's following him is jarring. The healing gesture in Matt 9:29; 20:34 derives from Matthew's combining this story with the one in Mark 8:22-26, not from a sense of lack in the present story; and Matt 9:29 changes the indicative statement about faith in Mark 10:52 to an imperative statement to gain correspondence with the force of the imported gesture of healing, again not from a sense of lack in the present story (see R. H. Gundry, *Matthew* 178, 406). Not all miracle-stories originally ended in the acclamation of Jesus (see the notes on 8:26; 9:14-27, 28-29); so Bartimaeus's following him on the road does not necessarily replace such an acclamation. The absence of an acclamation allows a smooth transition to continuation of the journey toward Jerusalem in which this story was set from the beginning (cf. the notes below). Bartimaeus's following Jesus, we have already seen, serves Mark's usual emphases on Jesus' powers of healing and attraction; and we have long since noted reasons not to recognize a whole section on discipleship in 8:27–10:52 (see pp. 440-41).

Nor does this healing of blindness join with the healing of blindness in 8:22-26 to form an inclusion, everything in between being a kind of healing of blindness, i.e. an opening of the disciples' eyes to the full dimensions of Jesus' messiahship and of their own discipleship (cf. E. Best, *Gospel as Story* 62; R. P. Meye, *Jesus and the Twelve* 77-80). A. Stock (*Call* 113, 135-36, 146-48) argues for this view from the isolation of these two miracle-stories — they do not occur in blocks of similar stories and thus they carry symbolic as well as literal meaning. But much of the material between them — viz., 8:32-33; 9:6, 10-11, 18, 27, 32, 33-34, 38-45; 10:10, 13-14, 24-26, 35-38 — betrays just the opposite of a symbolic healing. That is to say, the disciples' eyes remain closed. Moreover, an intervening miracle-story appears in 9:14-29. It, too, stands apart from other miracle-stories and thereby spoils the supposed uniqueness of the other two in standing so. Moreover again, its point lies in the miracle of an exorcism, not in faith for discipleship (see the comments and notes ad loc.). We may even doubt the isolation of 8:22-26. It stands right beside a sizeable section on miracles (7:24–8:21) if the discussion of the feedings of the five thousand and four thousand (8:13-21) qualifies as belonging to that section. We have also seen from time to time that between 8:22-26 and 10:46-52 passages often taken as referring to discipleship teach Christology or conversion instead. The only reference to the disciples' blindness (8:18) comes prior to and apart from the first passion prediction (8:31) and therefore scarcely symbolizes their blindness to the Cross (against J. Ernst 312-13; see also the notes on 8:22-26 against a symbolic interpretation).

E. P. Sanders (*Jesus and Judaism* 123) identifies vv 46b, 47, 51-52 as the oldest stratum of this story. If only that much, however, we might expect a reference in v 52b to Bartimaeus's getting up (cf. 1:31; 2:12; 5:42; 9:27; and his sitting in 10:46b). As it is, the command to go and his following instead fit his already having gotten up in a supposedly later insertion (vv 49-50). See E. Best, *Following Jesus* 140, against attribution of more or less vv 47-49 to Mark.

There is no reason to suspect the location of the story at Jericho, and the story of Zaccheus (Luke 19:1-10) independently supports the tradition of Jesus' journeying through that city. Given the traditionality of this location, questions concerning the reason for Mark's placing the story here (Is it awkwardly placed? If so, why? Does it close out a section of Mark's book, or introduce another one, or link two sections?) become inappropriate. Mark puts the story here because the tradition put it at this time and place, and the tradition looks trustworthy.

According to E. S. Johnson, Jr. (in CBQ 40 [1978] 192), "and his disciples and a large crowd" (v 46b) would make more sense if it were the subject of coming into Jericho (v 46a). But no, others need to accompany Jesus on the way out in order that they may rebuke Bartimaeus, and then call him (vv 48-49). Since Mark's statement that "they come into Jericho" puts Jesus and the Twelve inside the city (cf. vv 35, 41), we can hardly think that the subsequent miracle originally took place before entrance (so J. Gnilka 2. 108). Luke 18:35 puts it before entrance to set up a parallel between Jesus' "drawing near to Jericho" and the statement in 19:11 that he spoke the parable of the minas "because he was near Jerusalem" (cf. 19:28); so Luke's placement does not represent an independent or pre-Marcan tradition. Yet ὁδός does not suit a street in the city. It refers instead to a road outside the city (cf. esp. Luke 14:21, 23; Matt 22:7-10; see also the concordance). The sitting of Bartimaeus on the edge of the road during Jesus' exit therefore favors a location just outside Jericho along the road from that city to Jerusalem. Therefore again, if either of the statements including Jericho is redactional, the one about entering must be. But it would be too abrupt for the traditional story to start with a reference to leaving Jericho. The omission of entry into Jericho causes Matt 20:29-34 to start that way, but Matthew has made preparations which forestall abruptness: he "has already indicated the start of Jesus' ascent from Jericho to Jerusalem by adding 'being about to' in v 17 [see the v.l.] and putting 'on the road' a bit later in the same verse. So now the ascent continues" (R. H. Gundry, *Matthew* 404; also 400). It is not that Marcan mention of Jesus' entry gives Bartimaeus time to hear about him before he exits (so R. Busemann, *Jüngergemeinde* 162-63), for Bartimaeus hears that it is Jesus only as Jesus is going out of Jericho (vv 46-47). Rather, the teller of the traditional story needs to put Jesus in Jericho before pulling him out (cf. W. Schmithals 472). From the start, then, the story seems to have been set in the framework of a journey through Jericho to Jerusalem. Jesus' not stopping in Jericho so far as the story is concerned creates no problem, for only what happens after passing through is narrated (cf. 11:11b-12 for another instance of two different movements connected by a shared locale where nothing is recorded to have happened, and 7:31 for a somewhat similar use of Sidon). So long as Jericho lies on the route to Jerusalem and so long as ὁδός does not carry theological freight (see the comments on v 52), Mark has no reason to move a miracle originally located inside Jericho to the road outside it.

Citing the switch from the plural "they," as in Matt 20:29, to the singular "he," as in Luke 18:35, D. Peabody (in *Colloquy on NT Studies* 114-15) says that in v 46 Mark conflates Matthew and Luke in regard to entering Jericho (as in Luke) and in regard to exiting Jericho (as in Matthew). But why then does Mark combine Matthew's plural with Luke's entry, and Luke's singular with Matthew's exit? Some try to harmonize entry and exit by saying that Mark and Matthew refer to exit from old Jericho, Luke to entry into new Jericho (see Josephus *J.W.* 4.8.3 §459; H. van der Loos, *Miracles* 423). But we do not know that the old site of Jericho continued to be inhabited by people or called by the name "Jericho."

We might attribute the disciples and the large crowd to Mark (so J. Roloff, *Kerygma* 122); but in the tradition the disciples regularly accompany Jesus, elsewhere Mark uses πολύς, not ἱκανός, to describe a crowd as large (4:1; 5:21, 24; 6:34; 8:1; 9:14; 12:37), and as noted in another connection others need to be available in order that Jesus may tell them to call Bartimaeus (as well as that they may first try to silence him — but some redaction critics take the attempt as an addition). Since Mark elsewhere uses πολύς to describe a crowd as large, its plural πολλοί, "many," which describes those who rebuke Bartimaeus (v 48), will most naturally refer to the crowd rather than to the disciples (contrast the clarity with which the disciples are identified as rebukers in 10:13). Since no shift will occur, these same πολλοί will most naturally be the ones whom Jesus tells to call Bartimaeus and who will do so in v 49. The ambiguity in referents is much less than it is sometimes taken to be, and not nearly so much as to justify redaction critical judgments. Jesus' using the disciples in 6:41; 8:6 to distribute food at the miraculous feedings differs so much from his command to call Bartimaeus that those passages do not support his using the disciples to call Bartimaeus here (against a suggestion by J. Ernst 314-15).

"*They* come (ἔρχονται) into Jericho," but "*he* goes out (ἐκπορευομένου αὐτοῦ) from Jericho." This difference might seem to draw a redactional boundary between coming and going and to make "his disciples and a large crowd" look like a redactional addition. But it need be no more than a narrowing down in preparation for Jesus' performing the subsequent miracle. This sort of narrowing down appears often (1:21, 38-39; 4:10; 5:1-2, 21 with 31 and 37; 6:32-34 et passim; for the opposite development, see 2:23; 6:1, 6b-7). See the following excursus on the Secret Gospel of Mark against treating the shift from plural to singular as a sign that *SGM* 1 has dropped out between vv 46a and 46b.

Ἐκεῖθεν, "from there," might well substitute for the second mention of Jericho in v 46. But the second mention combines with the contrast between εἰς, "into," and ἀπό, "from," to stress the uninterruptedness of the narrative so far as Jericho is concerned. Ἐκεῖθεν occurs in Mark's narratives only after something has been described as occurring in the place referred to (6:1; 7:24; 10:1; cf. 6:10, 11). The disciples play no role in this story, but their mention prepares for Jesus' sending two of them on an errand in 11:1-7. See R. Pesch 2. 323 for the suggestion that Jesus and the others arrive in Jericho on the Friday before Passover, spend the Sabbath there, leave for Jerusalem on Palm Sunday, and arrive later that day.

The parallel with "Son of David, Jesus" undercuts the suggestion that "son of Timaeus" precedes "Bartimaeus" as a result of pre- or post-Marcan interpolation. One would expect a glossator to interpolate the phrase at the usual place, after the name. The parallel with "Son of David, Jesus" also weakens the argument that "the son of Timaeus" does not come from Mark (so E. Best, *Following Jesus* 141). Though Mark usually writes ὅ ἐστιν (μεθερμηνευόμενον), "which is (translated)" (3:17; 5:41; 7:11, 34; 12:42; 15:16, 22, 34, 42), here the desire for parallelism may take over. Besides, though "the son" translates the Aramaic "Bar-" without Mark's audience being told so, "-timaeus" translates nothing, but simply repeats the Greek "of Timaeus." Though "-timaeus" presumably goes back to the Aramaic טִימַי (probably from טְמָא, "be unclean" — see Str-B 2. 25), its having a good Greek meaning ("honored, prized") and common usage as a Greek proper name (Τιμαῖος — see LSJ s.v.; W. Pape and G. E. Benseler, *Wörterbuch* 2. 15261) makes a translation of this part of the Aramaic unnecessary for Mark's Greek-speaking audience — in fact, potentially confusing to them. Clarity wins out over correctness. See H. P. Rüger in *Markus-Philologie* 75-76.

Matthew's and Luke's omissions of Bartimaeus's name do not prove its unoriginality to the story (cf. K. Kertelge, *Wunder* 179-80). The omissions derive from Matthew's doubling the blind man and from secondary Matthean influence on Luke (R. H. Gundry, *Matthew* 177). See the foregoing notes that miracle stories sometimes include personal names (cf. also E. Best, *Disciples and Discipleship* 45-46). Since Bartimaeus is otherwise unknown, it lacks substance to conjecture that an anonymous blind man whom Jesus healed came to be identified with a well known Christian named Bartimaeus who lived in Jericho (so D. E. Nineham 285). More likely, the personal name reflects a date prior to stereotypical anonymizing such as occurs in the later synoptics (cf. E. P. Sanders, *Tendencies* 168-73).

M. A. Tolbert (*Sowing the Gospel* 189-92) argues that because Mark mentioned the names of the Twelve (3:16-19), mention of Bartimaeus's name makes him an ideal disciple and thus argues for unhistoricity. But why this name? Where did it come from if not from historical data (N.B. the Aramaic, which makes derivation from Plato's Timaeus [cf. ibid.

189, n. 21] doubtful)? And would not Tolbert's argument require the idealistic dehistoricizing of Levi (2:14), Jairus (5:22), the Marys and Salome (15:40, 47; 16:1), Joseph of Arimathea (15:43), and possibly others whose names are mentioned?

W. Grundmann (7. Aufl., 297) seems to favor the v.l. ὁ with τυφλός, "the [well known] blind [man]." The inclusion of Bartimaeus's name supports this v.l.; but the qualitative weakness of A C Θ $f^{1,13}$ Majority Text sy[h], which support it, as compared with א B D L W Δ Ψ 892* 1241 1424 pc co Or, which omit it, suggests later insertion, probably under the influence of the ὁ which modifies υἱός, "the son." Apparently Bartimaeus is sitting just outside Jericho on the edge of the road to Jerusalem because throngs of Passover pilgrims who have to pass that way provide him with an excellent opportunity to beg alms successfully. The religious fervor of this season makes the pilgrims more than usually prone to give a blind man alms. R. McKinnis (in *NovT* 18 [1976] 84) draws a theological as well as linguistic parallel with the parabolic falling of a seed "on the edge of the road" in 4:4, 15. But Bartimaeus's faith and healing disagree with Satan's snatching away the seed of the word. Moreover, Jesus does not teach Bartimaeus; yet the sown seed represented the taught word.

"The Nazarene" (v 47) did not appear to carry the derogatory connotation of "an outsider" in 1:9, 24, nor will it in 16:6; so we may doubt that it is more than topographical in 10:47 and 14:67. The adversative δέ, "but," in v 48b will disjoin the renewed shouting from the initial shouting as well as from the intervening rebuke. This disjunction prohibits taking ἤρξατο, "he began" (v 47), as more than Mark's usual auxiliary (against E. Best [*Following Jesus* 140], who thinks that the verb telegraphs repeated shoutings; see the notes on 1:45). The further occurrences of δέ in vv 50, 51 will add the contrastive vigor of further shifts. Bartimaeus uses an OT-like plea to God for mercy, but redirects it to Jesus (see also Matt 15:22; Luke 17:13) just as Jesus parabolically redirects it to Abraham (Luke 16:24). Cf. the LXX of Pss 6:3; 9:14; 24:16; 30:10; 40:5, 11; 50:3; 85:3, 15-16; 108:26; 122:3; the MT of Ps 4:2(1); Josephus *Ant.* 9.4.4 §64; and non-Jewish parallels in BAGD s.v. ἐλεέω; J. A. Kleist 219.

The Jewish tradition that portrays Solomon as an expert in exorcism does not explain why Bartimaeus should call Jesus "Son of David" in a plea for the mercy of a healing. Bartimaeus's blindness is not blamed on a demon (contrast Matt 12:22). Nor does the Davidic sonship of Solomon figure in the pre-Christian Jewish tradition of his expertise in exorcism, nor the Davidic sonship of Jesus in Mark's other miracle stories (or elsewhere in the gospels except for Matt 12:23). Except for *T. Sol.* 20:1, "Son of David" never occurs as an address. In the exception, the address does not introduce a request either for a healing or for an exorcism; and its phraseology may show influence from the NT (D. C. Duling in *HTR* 68 [1975] 248-49). Wherever "son of David" occurs for Solomon in the Bible and outside it, Solomon's name accompanies the phrase (with the exception of Eccl 1:1, where we read instead the description "the preacher, . . . king in Jerusalem"). "Son of David" also describes Absalom (2 Sam 13:1), Joseph the husband of Mary (Matt 1:20), and the messianic king (Mark 12:35 parr.; Matt 1:1; 12:23; 21:9, 15; *Pss. Sol.* 17:21 with 17:32; and much rabbinic material postdating the NT — Str-B 1. 525; see J. A. Fitzmyer, *Essays* 115-21, for related expressions and cf. 2 Sam 7:12-16; Psalm 89 on Davidic kings). So "Son of David, Jesus" would scarcely call Solomon to mind (cf. Duling, op. cit. 235-52, for primary and secondary literature, and B. D. Chilton in *JSNT* 14 [1982] 92-96 for an attempt to rehabilitate the Solomonic interpretation, an attempt that glosses over the just-mentioned differences).

The Jewish nationalistic overtones of "Son of David" are lost in the individuality of Bartimaeus's plea (K. Kertelge, *Wunder* 181). Why then does he call Jesus "Son of David"? Isaiah predicted healing, including the healing of blindness, in the coming salvation (29:18; 35:5-6; 61:1 LXX). God will perform this healing according to Isa 35:4 with

35:5-6. Yahweh's servant or prophet proclaims it in Isa 61:1 LXX. But in Ezek 34:23-24 Yahweh uses Yahweh's servant David the prince, presumably a son (i.e. a descendant) of David, to shepherd the people (cf. Jer 23:1-6); and according to Ezek 34:4, 16 this shepherding includes healing (cf. D. E. Aune in *NovT* 11 [1969] 30). Though Jewish literature of the NT era shows no expectation that the Davidic Messiah will heal people, then, perhaps the´actuality of Jesus' ministry and reputation as a healer leads via these OT passages to his being called "Son of David" in a plea for the mercy of a healing.

It has been suggested that the crowd try to silence Bartimaeus because they expect Jesus to set up the messianic kingdom on arrival in Jerusalem, and they do not want Jesus to delay for the performance of a healing miracle. Jerusalem lies only eighteen miles up the road. At the opposite extreme, it is said that the crowd object to Bartimaeus's calling Jesus "Son of David," because the title carries a political overtone disagreeable with Jesus' teaching. But when did they gain such good understanding? Jesus told unclean spirits to stop calling him "the Holy One of God" (1:24-25) and "the Son of God" (3:11-12; cf. 5:7), because they were trying to gain control over him by magical use of those titles, not because he wanted to keep his divine sonship secret (see the comments and notes ad loc.). In using "Son of David," Bartimaeus is pleading for mercy, not trying to use magic. From that standpoint, then, Jesus has no need to silence him. After Peter confessed Jesus as the Christ, on the other hand, Jesus told his disciples not to speak to anyone about him, i.e. about his identity as the Christ (8:29b-30). Though "Son of David" does not necessarily connote the Christ, it may do so (see the foregoing notes). Hence, we might think that Jesus would try to silence Bartimaeus. But the disciples were not to speak in the first place, whereas Bartimaeus has already spoken, indeed shouted, in earshot of a large crowd. Too late for a command like the one in 8:30. This circumstance makes it unnecessary to say that Jesus does not give such a command because "Son of David" inadequately represents him anyway (12:35-37; so A. M. Ambrozic, *Hidden Kingdom* 43; J. D. Kingsbury, *Christology of Mark's Gospel* 113).

The distance separating vv 47-48 from 15:39 makes it improbable that "Son of David" here prepares for "Son of God" there (so J. Ernst [314], who suggests a background like Rom 1:3, where Davidic descent and divine sonship stand cheek by jowl). The intervention of a discussion about Davidic sonship and another title — viz., "the Christ" — increases the improbability (12:35-37). "Son of David" does not come into the present text by way of Marcan or pre-Marcan redaction to tie the story to the Triumphal Procession, for 11:10 will eulogize "the coming kingdom of our father David," not Jesus as the Son of David. Nor is "Son of David" a Marcanism. If Mark were making a substitution for an original "Son of God" to maintain a messianic secret of Jesus' divine sonship, we would almost certainly find the address "Teacher" (see the concordance s.v. διδάσκαλος in Mark). Nor does the succession "Jesus the Nazarene"–"Son of David, Jesus"–"Son of David"– "Rabbouni" (vv 47-48, 51) offer solid ground for redaction critical distinctions. A personal name and indication of topographical origin naturally come first. The dropping of topographical origin and adding of an exalted title follows naturally in a shouted appeal. The dropping of the personal name occurs naturally in a repetition of the shouted appeal. And a respectful but more personal address ("Rabbouni" means "my great one") naturally appears in a close confrontation (against R. Busemann, *Jüngergemeinde* 167; L. Schenke, *Wundererzählungen* 358-59; E. S. Johnson, Jr., in *CBQ* 40 [1978] 195, among others).

Verse 48 does not interrupt the story (as thought by Busemann loc. cit.). Its content — the attempt to silence Bartimaeus and his shouting all the more — heightens dramatic tension and supplies ingredients necessary to what follows. For without v 48 much of vv 49-50 would lose its basis. The command to call Bartimaeus (as opposed to an immediate confrontation with Jesus), the telling of Bartimaeus to cheer up and get up because Jesus is calling him, his throwing away his garment, and his jumping up would turn histrionic without the unsuccessful attempt to silence him. Therefore we should not regard v 48 as a redactional addition or think that the twofoldness of Bartimaeus's address and plea to Jesus represents different redactional levels.

The large size of the crowd makes their being both around Bartimaeus and with Jesus a non-problem (against E. Best, *Following Jesus* 141). Telling Bartimaeus to quiet down has nothing to do with a Marcan or pre-Marcan messianic secret; for whatever that secret is (if it is even correct to speak of one), only Jesus imposes it because among human beings only he knows it. Here, it is the considerable crowd who tell Bartimaeus to quiet down — and without indication that he should do so because he is breaking a secret of Jesus' true identity (contrast 1:24-25; 3:11; 8:29-30). Rather, the rebuke poses an obstacle that magnifies Bartimaeus's faith, which in turn magnifies Jesus' miracle (cf. W. Wrede, *Messianic Secret* 279-80). It is no inconcinnity that the crowd first try to silence Bartimaeus and then encourage him. It only reflects the effect of Jesus' command that they call Bartimaeus (against Busemann loc. cit.). Though it does not necessarily favor the use of tradition, the fact that the verb for calling in the sense of summoning, φωνέω, differs from the usual Marcan verb of that meaning, προσκαλέομαι, at least leaves no reason to suspect redaction.

Bartimaeus may have been wearing his cloak over his shoulders, sitting on it as he begged, or using it to receive alms as it lay spread out on his lap or in front of him (cf. the v.l. ἐπιβαλών, "throwing [putting] on," which implies that he has not been wearing his cloak — 565 sy⁵). Ἀποβαλών, "flinging away," favors none of these possibilities over the others. Unlike ἀποτίθημι and ἀπεκδύω, this verb does not appear in probable allusions to disrobing for baptism; so an allusion to that practice is unlikely — all the more unlikely because nothing in the story corresponds even remotely to putting on a new garment after baptism (see Rom 13:12; Eph 4:22-25; Col 3:8-10, 12; Heb 12:1; Jas 1:21; 1 Pet 2:1).

Though flinging away his garment and jumping up indicate joyful response to the command, "Cheer up!" it goes beyond the text to say that Bartimaeus acts as he does to run to Jesus (so E. Lohmeyer [226], whose closest cross-reference [Luc. *Catapl.* 15, "eine genaue Parallele"] contains no reference to a garment or to running). Mark knows the verb "run" (5:6; 6:33, 55; 9:15, 25; 10:17; 15:36), but uses the colorless "came" (ἦλθεν). Nothing is said about others' leading Bartimaeus to Jesus, but his not seeing again till after Jesus pronounces a healing word keeps us from saying that sight has already returned. The mechanics by which Bartimaeus came to Jesus would not sharpen Mark's point; so Mark omits them. Attempts to make up for this omission — by saying, for example, that others led Bartimaeus or that, being only functionally blind, he could see a little — are vain.

The similarity of the question, "What do you want [that] I should do for you?" (v 51), to v 36 does not create overtones of Jesus' authority to grant any request whatever; for it turned out that ultimately, if not immediately, he did not have authority to grant the earlier request (v 40; against J. Gnilka 2. 111). But the legitimate request of Bartimaeus may contrast with the illegitimate request of James and John (V. K. Robbins in *JBL* 92 [1973] 239). "Rabbouni," it is often said, implies that Bartimaeus is becoming a disciple of Jesus (see, e.g., D. O. Via, *Ethics* 162; P. J. Achtemeier in *Semeia* 11 [1978] 124). The translation of "Rabbouni" by "Teacher" in John 20:16 might seem to support such an implication. But in view of Mark's using the address "Teacher" (διδάσκαλε) ten times elsewhere in his gospel, we would expect him to use it here, too, if he meant to indicate that Bartimaeus is attaching himself as a disciple to Jesus as a teacher. Furthermore, rabbinic literature uses "Rabbouni" in addresses to God but not in addresses to human beings; and the Targums use it only occasionally with regard to human beings. Thus extra-biblical usage supports a meaning even more respectful than that which would characterize a disciple's address to his teacher. See G. Mussies in *NTS* 30 (1984) 424; also M. Black, *Aramaic Approach* 23-24, 44-46; S. Schulz in *Abraham unser Vater* 432-33; P. Kahle,

Cairo Geniza 204; idem, *Masoreten des Westens* 2. 1; H. P. Rüger in *Markus-Philologie* 81; and other literature cited in BAGD s.v. ῥαββουνί.

Ἀναβλέπω may mean to receive sight for the first time (John 9:11, 15, 18 with 9:1-2) as well as to regain the ability to see ("see again") and therefore does not have to imply that Bartimaeus was once able to see. But restoration of sight is favored by the omission of any indication that Bartimaeus was born blind. Such a birth would have been worth mentioning to enhance the miracle (cf. John 9:1-2). See 1:41-42; 2:11-12; 7:29-30 against the view that the reference to restored sight in v 52b is redundant after the reference to salvation in v 52a (so, e.g., E. Best, *Following Jesus* 139; E. S. Johnson, Jr., in *CBQ* 40 [1978] 198). If "your faith has saved you" implied earlier healing (as in 5:34 with 5:28-29), Bartimaeus would not have just now asked for healing. An allusion to Isa 42:18 is doubtful. There, the command, "Look, you blind, that you may see," links with a command that the deaf hear; and both commands have to do with the same people, i.e. those who "have seen many things but do not observe them," whose "ears are open but no one hears" (v 20; cf. 6:9-10). Hence, Isa 42:18 relates more closely to Mark 4:12; 8:18 than to a miracle story. E. Best (*Disciples and Discipleship* 4) goes too far in saying that Jesus permits Bartimaeus to follow him. There is no request. There is no granting of a request.

EXCURSUS ON THE SECRET GOSPEL OF MARK

M. Smith *(Clement)* has published and discussed what he argues to be an authentic letter written to one Theodore by Clement of Alexandria *(flor.* 180-200 C.E.). Theodore wants to know whether all the materials in a Carpocratian version of Mark are truly present in a secret version of Mark (from here on referred to as *SGM* for the Secret Gospel of Mark) used in the church at Alexandria, Egypt. The Carpocratians are a Gnostic sect reputed to engage in sexual immorality (see F. F. Bruce, *"Secret" Gospel* 16-18, for the accuracy of this reputation). According to the putative letter of Clement, Mark wrote a public gospel, probably canonical Mark, during Peter's stay in Rome, but after Peter's martyrdom took his own notes and Peter's to Alexandria, where he wrote an expanded, secret gospel *(SGM).* The letter goes on to quote two sections of *SGM,* the first *(SGM* 1) a story of Jesus' raising from the dead a rich young man who then pleads to be with Jesus, keeps Jesus in his house for six days, receives a command from him, comes to Jesus in the evening wearing a linen cloth on his naked body, and throughout that night listens to Jesus teach the mystery of God's kingdom. The letter locates this section between Mark 10:34 and 35 and denies that it includes the Carpocratian phrase "naked [man] with naked [man]" and other, unquoted Carpocratian materials that Theodore has asked about. The second, shorter section *(SGM* 2) is said to follow Mark 10:46a and to record Jesus' non-welcome in Jericho of the rich young man's sister and mother plus Salome.

Questions have been raised about the authenticity of Clement's letter; and Smith's interpretation of the putative letter, including a dating of canonical Mark after *SGM,* has received extensive review (see the bibliography in *Protocol of the Center for Hermeneutical Studies in Hellenistic and Modern Culture,* Colloquy

18, pp. 72-73, and the whole of Colloquy 18 itself). We need therefore to scrutinize two more recent attempts to make canonical Mark postdate *SGM,* one by H. Koester, another by J. D. Crossan (a further attempt by H.-M. Schenke [in *SecCent* 4 (1984) 65-82] being left aside as largely dependent on Koester's work, though with some revision; see also M. Meyer in *Semeia* 49 [1990] 129-53 with criticism by J. D. Crossan in the same issue, pp. 161-65). Koester (in *Colloquy on NT Studies* 35-57 and in *Gospel Traditions in the Second Century* 34-36) argues not only that *SGM* predates canonical Mark, but also that a proto-Mark predates even *SGM* and that Matthew and Luke redacted different versions of proto-Mark, Luke the original version, Matthew a longer version containing the material that we find in Mark 6:45–8:26. Thus we should speak of Matthew's great addition rather than of Luke's great omission, and even then only in terms of Matthew's fidelity to his source. *SGM* represents a less thorough redaction of proto-Mark in its longer version. The Carpocratians then redacted *SGM. Canonical Mark came through another, later redaction of *SGM,* mainly by way of omitting the story of the rich young man whom Jesus raised from the dead and the sequel to that story in Jesus' non-welcome of the women. Carpocratian use of *SGM* prompted these omissions. Finally, canonical Mark was expanded by the various additions of the short ending, the long ending, and the Freer Logion. For the lateness of canonical Mark and its non-use by Matthew and Luke, Koester argues from the failure of canonical Mark to be certainly quoted till the second half of the first century; from the non-appearance of canonical Mark in the papyri till the mid-third century; from textual instability at the end of canonical Mark; from Luke's apparent non-inclusion of Mark 6:45–8:26 as against Matthew's including all of it except Mark 8:22-26; from sentences and small pericopes in canonical Mark which have no parallels in Matthew and Luke; from apparent remnants in canonical Mark of an expansion of proto-Mark in *SGM,* i.e. from remnants of the story about the rich young man; from canonical Marcan phrases and terms that differ from Matthew and Luke; and from other links connecting canonical Mark to *SGM* but distinguishing it from Matthew and Luke.

D. Peabody (in *Colloquy on NT Studies* 87-132) has criticized Koester's arguments from the standpoint of Mark's dependence on Matthew and Luke, i.e. from the standpoint of the Griesbach or two-gospel hypothesis. The arguments also need criticism from the standpoint of the Mark-Q hypothesis plus Luke's use of Matthew as a subsidiary source. Though several pieces of evidence that Luke used Matthew as a subsidiary source will surface in the following discussion, limitation of space does not allow a full detailing of such evidence (but see R. H. Gundry, *Matthew* 650, s.v. "Luke's being influenced by Matthew"; idem in *The Four Gospels 1992*). Thus many of the criticisms will leave Luke out of account and concentrate on Mark and Matthew.

Koester's theory requires a very late date for canonical Mark. Carpocrates flourished during Hadrian's reign (117-138 C.E.); so according to the theory, canonical Mark has to postdate the time within or after this period that the Carpocratians began to use *SGM* for their own purposes. That canonical Mark is not certainly quoted till the second half of the first century and not represented in the papyri till the mid-third century does not necessitate or favor such a late date, however. These phenomena are just as well explained by Mark's rough style (which Papias's elder felt obliged to defend [Eus. *H.E.* 3.39.15]) and comparative brevity (which made Mark a poor relative of Matthew, Luke, and John). Nor does the later, known textual evolution of canonical Mark necessitate or favor an earlier, unknown textual evolution; for canonical Mark may provide the starting point of textual evolution as easily as lie along its path, especially since the abruptness of the ending at 16:8 (if that verse does mark the original ending of the gospel) or the loss of the original ending (if at first the gospel went beyond 16:8) explains the subsequent textual evolution so adequately that no recourse to a tradition of earlier textual evolution is needed. So far as the earlier material in Mark 6:54–8:26 is concerned, it is just as easy to think that its repetitiveness, to which Koester himself points, led Luke to omit it as to think that a revised version of a proto-Mark added it to an original version of proto-Mark. The word-statistics offered to support such an addition are unimpressive.

Koester seems to step on firmer ground when he comes to sentences, small pericopes, and various remnants of *SGM* which appear in canonical Mark but have no parallels in Matthew and Luke. But these largely omissive agreements of Matthew and Luke against canonical Mark are better explained as redactions of canonical Mark. For however one explains the agreements of Matthew and Luke against canonical Mark, these agreements fall into patterns that we can trace elsewhere in Matthew, most of the time without Luke's agreement against Mark and often in Q-materials and materials peculiar to Matthew as well. So unless proto-Mark exercised so overpowering an influence on Matthew that he redacted Q and materials peculiar to his gospel in servile imitation of an already revised proto-Mark, his and Luke's dependence on successive versions of a proto-Mark does not provide an explanation of all the phenomena that require explanation. By casting our net more widely than Koester has done, we shall see how Matthean redaction of canonical Mark better explains all those phenomena. To follow the order of Koester's discussion will make for easier comparison with his treatment.

Both Matthew and Luke omit the saying about the humanitarian purpose of the Sabbath (Mark 2:27a) but reproduce the one about the Son of man's lordship over the Sabbath (Mark 2:27b), and do so in a word order that disagrees with Mark but not with each other. But Matthew constantly pares down non-Christological materials and expands Christological materials, and does so without Luke's agreement against Mark (see, e.g., the unique expansions in Matt 3:14-15; 11:28-30; the unique omissions in 9:1-8, omissions that let Jesus' authority to forgive sins stand out the more; and in 21:9 the unique addressing of hosanna to Jesus as the Son of David). On the other hand, Luke elsewhere adds rather than subtracts humanitarianism (see, e.g., Luke 7:11-17; 13:10-17; 17:11-19). So we do better to think that here Matthew is redacting canonical Mark and influencing Luke than to think that Matthew and Luke depend on different versions of a proto-Mark that happen to agree at this point.

Mark's parable of the growing seed (4:26-29) is neither omitted by Matthew as well as Luke, as Koester argues to support dependence on proto-Mark, nor in the strict sense is it replaced by the parable of the tares (Matt 13:24-30). Rather, Matthew uses the parable of the growing seed to help create the parable of the tares, which is his conflation of the parables of the sower and of the growing seed plus a reminiscence of John the Baptist's preaching (cf. Matt 3:12). The reason for this conflation is simple: "by itself" and "how, he does not know" in the parable of the growing seed do not fit Matthew's stressing human responsibility and the necessity of understanding, or knowledge, for true discipleship (13:13-15 et passim); so his concern over the mixed multitude in the professing church of his day takes over to produce a new parable.

In the pericope about the great commandments (Mark 12:28-34; Matt 22:34-40; Luke 10:25-28), Matthew and Luke agree against Mark in omitting the Shema, the scribe's compliment of Jesus, and the repetition of the commandments. On the other hand, Luke's "lawyer" agrees with canonical Mark's "scribe" against Matthew's "Pharisees"; and Luke agrees with canonical Mark against Matthew also in having the scribe, or lawyer, recite the commandments and in having Jesus compliment him. Matthew omits the Shema to arrive as quickly as possible at the commandments. His battle against antinomianism often leads him to stress commandments, as in the Q-section at 5:17-20, but without the agreement of Luke 16:16-17, and as in his unique form of the Great Commission (28:18-20). Furthermore, he is more interested in trinitarianism, again as in his unique form of the Great Commission, than in the monotheism of "Hear, O Israel, the Lord our God is one Lord"; and he cuts the story short to leave the stress on obeying the whole of the Law, not just part of it (again as in 5:17-20 but not the present Lucan parallel) and to put the Pharisees, whom he has characteristically imported into the passage, in a bad light (as often elsewhere in his gospel, including both Q-passages and unique passages in chaps. 3, 5, 23, and 27). Should we expect the evangelist who constructs a sevenfold woe against the scribes and Pharisees (chap. 23) to take over a scribe's complimenting Jesus and Jesus' reciprocal compliment even though this evangelist's copy of Mark had both compliments? Hardly!

Koester argues that *SGM* 2 provides an original link between Mark 10:46a and b, the expurgation of which link produced an awkward text in canonical Mark. The link consists in an incident that happens in Jericho, whereas canonical Mark mentions entrance into Jericho only to have Jesus leave without having done anything there. But since the healing of blind Bartimaeus takes place on the road from Jericho, the mention of arrival in Jericho looks suitable, especially if Jesus and the Twelve spent the Sabbath there, having arrived on Friday and leaving on Palm Sunday morning so as to arrive in Jerusalem late that Sunday afternoon. Besides, this is not the only passage in which Mark has Jesus going somewhere but not doing anything while there. In 7:31 he goes to Sidon and the Sea of Galilee, and in 11:11b to Bethany; but Mark associates no incident with either of these visits — and we do not hypothesize an expurgation of earlier materials (see also the comments and esp. the notes on 10:46). To double the blind man, Matthew omits Bartimaeus's name. Luke's concurrence with the omission shows Matthean influence, because he writes of only one blind man and therefore has no reason to omit the name (R. H. Gundry, *Matthew* 176-77). Recourse to a proto-Mark is otiose.

Mark's "the gospel of God" (1:15) drops out of Matt 4:17 because of the following substitute regarding repentance and the nearness of the kingdom. This substitute has the purpose of drawing Jesus and John the Baptist together as co-preachers of repentance and the kingdom (cf. Matt 3:1-2 with 4:17 and Matthew's correlating Jesus and John the Baptist in a number of places — ibid. 649, s.v. "John the Baptist parallel Jesus"). Concerning Mark 8:35 and Matt 16:25, Matthew omits "and the gospel" to concentrate attention on Jesus, as often, and to make "on account of me" correspond exactly to Matt 5:11; 10:18, 39. Luke's agreeing with the omission despite his lacking parallels to the phrase "on account of me" in Matthew's earlier passages argues for Matthew's influencing him here. In Matt 19:29 as compared with Mark 10:29, Matthew's exchanging "the gospel" for "my name" is to be expected since he inserts ὄνομα, "name," five times in shared pericopes and uses the word five more times in unique pericopes.

In Mark 1:21-28 it is easier to think that the story, complete with the reference to "a new teaching with authority" (v 27), is meant by Mark to illustrate Jesus' "teaching as one having authority" (v 22), the repetitiveness in v 27 being designed to keep Mark's audience from missing the illustrative connection, than to see a post-Matthean addition in v 27. Luke does *not* agree with Matthew's omission of "a new teaching with authority" (see Luke 4:36); and Matthew's omission is part of a far larger omission of the whole story, which he omits in favor of an editorial emphasis on Jesus' didactic authority in the Sermon on the Mount (Matt 7:28-29 par. Mark 1:22).

Jesus' teaching a crowd by the sea in Mark 2:13 may seem "entirely gratuitous between the story of the healing of the paralytic (Mk 2:1-12) and the account of the call of Levi (Mk 2:14)" (so Koester), but it does not follow that the lack of this teaching in Matt 9:9; Luke 5:27 implies its redactional addition in a later version of Mark. Again, Matthew's omission is part of a larger omission; for Matthew omits the entirety of Mark 2:13, not just Jesus' teaching a crowd by the sea, and Matthew does so because he has inserted "the crowds" into the immediately preceding verse (contrast Matt 9:8 with Mark 2:12; Luke 5:26) and will yet introduce other elements of Mark 2:13 into Matt 13:1-2 to compensate for the present omission (R. H. Gundry, *Matthew* 165-66, 251-52). Compensations for earlier omissions are a regular feature of his style (ibid. 649, s.v. "Compensation"). Luke 5:27 disagrees with Matthew in taking over part of Mark 2:13 and omits the rest of it without having Matthew's reasons for omission. All in all, then, the evidence does not point to Matthean and Lucan dependence on a proto-Mark, but to Matthean and Lucan dependence on canonical Mark and subsidiary, partial dependence of Luke on Matthew.

At Matt 13:1 "was sitting" replaces Jesus' teaching in Mark 4:1-2 because as yet no audience has appeared. Nevertheless, sitting — the posture of a Jewish teacher — connotes didactic authority, indirectly reflects Jesus' teaching in Mark's version, and thus eliminates the need to posit a proto-Mark that lacked the element of teaching. "Beside the sea" appears in Matthew as well as in canonical Mark; so its absence from Luke 8:4 cannot argue for a proto-Mark lacking it. Furthermore, Luke's agreement with canonical Mark's singular "a crowd" against Matthew's plural "crowds" argues for dependence on canonical Mark rather than for co-dependence with Matthew on a proto-Mark; and Jesus' teaching while seated in a boat at Luke 5:1-3, which has no other synoptic parallel, suggests that Luke does not really agree with Matthew against Mark in this respect. That is to say, Luke 8:4 drops Jesus' teaching while seated in a boat beside the sea because Luke 5:1-3 has already included this element, not because Luke 8:4 depends with Matt 13:1 on a proto-Mark. Matt 13:1 and Luke 8:4 have different reasons to omit the teaching in Mark 4:1-2. The teaching in Mark 6:30 looks like an original correlary to the proclamation in Mark 6:12, not like a redactional addition to a proto-Mark. Yet again, the omission of the teaching just after Matt 14:12 and in Luke 9:10a hardly counts as an agreement against Mark 6:30 that would argue in favor of common dependence on a proto-Mark; for Luke takes over the rest of Mark 6:30 but Matthew omits the entirety of Mark 6:30-31 except for transmuting Mark 6:30 into an announcement by the disciples of John the Baptist that John has been executed (ibid. 289).

Matt 16:21 exchanges διδάσκειν, "to teach," in Mark 8:31 for δεικνύειν, "to show," to keep the former for public teaching and the latter for private instruction (cf. the private audiences in Matt 4:8; 8:4). In Luke 9:22 εἰπών, "saying," disagrees with Matthew as much as with Mark and therefore does not support common dependence of Matthew and Luke on a proto-Mark (cf. Luke 24:7). Matt 17:22 and Luke 9:43 do agree in not saying that Jesus "was teaching," against Mark 9:31; but the unique command in Luke 9:44a, "You — put these words in your ears," looks like compensation for an omission rather than like co-dependence with Matthew on a proto-Mark that lacked Jesus' teaching here. Against such co-dependence, we have the agreement of Luke 9:43b-45 with Mark 9:30-32 against Matt 17:22-23 in having "his disciples," the disciples' failure to understand Jesus' prediction of the Passion and Resurrection, and the disciples' fearing to ask him about it, all of which Matthew lacks. The agreement of Luke 18:33 with Mark 10:34 in ἀναστήσεται, "will rise up" (see also Luke 24:7), over against ἐγερθήσεται, "will be raised," in Matt 20:19 favors that the earlier agreement of Matt 16:21 with Luke 9:22 in having ἐγερθῆναι instead of the ἀναστῆναι of Mark 8:31 came by way of conforming canonical Mark's verb to other traditions (see 1 Cor 15:4 for an example earlier than Mark), including Mark's own account of the Passion (14:28) and Resurrection (16:6), not from a proto-Mark having the other verb, especially since Matthew writes the other verb eleven times where synoptic parallels lack it and eight more times in pericopes peculiar to his gospel. The agreement of Matt 16:21; 20:19 and Luke 9:22; 18:33 in "on the third day" (see also Matt 17:23; Luke 24:7) against "after three days" in Mark 8:31; 10:34 (see also 9:31) is explained much more easily and economically as an elimination of the apparent discrepancy between "after three days" and the discovery of the empty tomb on the Sunday morning following the Friday of Jesus' death (see the comments on 8:31) than as co-dependence on a proto-Mark. How unlikely that canonical Mark would change an original, easy, and widespread "on the third day" (again see esp. 1 Cor 15:4) to a problematic "after three days"! Both Matt 16:21-22 and Luke 9:20 lack the plainness of Jesus' speech that Mark 8:32 mentions. But Matthew omits it because it makes Peter's obtuseness inexcusable. This omission lightens the onus on Peter. As is well known, Matthew often ameliorates or erases the misunderstanding of disciples. Here, Luke goes even further by erasing also Peter's rebuke of Jesus and Jesus' counter rebuke. No need to hypothesize a proto-Mark to account for these developments.

Matt 19:2 omits Jesus' teaching in Mark 10:1 because Matthew has just devoted to Jesus' instructions the whole of his chap. 18, about the latter three quarters of it unparalleled in Mark. Now Matthew wants authentication of those instructions (cf. the sequence of instructions and miracles in chaps. 5–7 and 8–9); so he substitutes ἐθεράπευσεν, "he healed," a favorite of his, which he inserts ten times into paralleled pericopes. The same substitution of healing for teaching takes place in Matt 14:14 despite the underlying agreement of Luke 9:11 ("he was speaking to them about the kingdom of God") with Mark 6:34 ("he began to teach them much"). The fact that Luke 9:11 also agrees with Matt 14:14 in the mention of healing favors a drawing on Matthew as well as on canonical Mark, but co-dependence with Matthew on a proto-Mark that mentioned only the healing would not explain Luke's underlying agreement with Mark on Jesus' verbal ministry. The absence of a Lucan parallel to Mark 10:1; Matt 19:2 deprives Koester of a possible argument from agreement against Mark at that point.

In Mark 6:34, Jesus' compassion leads to a comparison of the crowd with shepherdless sheep and a statement about his teaching. But Matthew has already used this comparison in 9:36 and has devoted most of chap. 13 to parables. He did mention the healing as well as teaching ministry of Jesus in 9:35, however. So in 14:14 (parallel to Mark 6:34) Matthew omits the already used comparison of the crowd to shepherdless sheep and exchanges teaching for healing (cf. 19:2 with Mark 10:1). Luke's similarity to Matthew in these respects, along with agreements of Matthew and Luke against Mark earlier in the passage, suggests subsidiary influence of Matthew on Luke; for a comparison between the crowds and shepherdless sheep failed to appear in Luke's parallel to Matthew 9:36, i.e. in Luke 8:1. Hence, Luke does not have Matthew's reason to omit the comparison here and seems to have no reason of his own. Similarly, the lack of a reference to Jesus' healing people in Luke's parallel to Matthew 9:35 — again in Luke 8:1 — takes away the association which in Matthew triggers the exchange of teaching for healing. That Jesus' speaking about the kingdom of God in Luke 9:11 looks much more like Jesus' teaching in Mark 6:34 than like his healing in Matt 14:14 disfavors Matthean and Lucan use of a proto-Mark which lacked teaching at this point.

Matt 21:13 subtracts Jesus' teaching from Mark 11:17 to emphasize the following quotations of the OT (which Matthew likes more than any of the other evangelists do) and to make those quotations entirely accusatory, not at all didactic (cf. Matthew's intensifying the guilt of Jewish leaders throughout his gospel and esp. in this its last part). That Luke 19:46 agrees with Matthew's subtraction of Jesus' teaching favors Matthean influence, for elsewhere Luke does not exhibit so much as Matthew does the tendencies which have led to the present subtraction. Matt 22:41 subtracts Jesus' teaching from Mark 12:35 because Matthew has shifted the audience from a large crowd (cf. Mark 12:38), for whom teaching is appropriate, to Pharisees, for whom in view of his ubiquitous anti-Pharisaic tendency a confrontal question designed to embarrass is more appropriate: "What seems correct *to you?*" (Matt 21:42). Luke 20:41 joins Matthew in subtraction of Jesus' teaching, and for the similar reason that Luke has turned the scribes into the addressees (cf. Luke 20:39 and contrast "How come *the scribes* say . . . ?" in Mark 12:35 with the question to the scribes in Luke 20:41, "How come *they* [people in general] say . . . ?"). But Luke's retention of the scribes, though in another capacity, shows that he is working with Mark as well as with Matthew rather than drawing independently from Matthew on a proto-Mark; for the scribes make no appearance at all in Matthew's version. The agreement of Matt 23:1-2 with Luke 20:45 in subtracting "the teaching" of Jesus from Mark 12:38 derives from the immediately foregoing circumstances that we have just noted for the passages. Similarly, Matt 23:1-2 subtracts "the teaching" from Mark 12:38 to prepare for substitution of a description of and woes to the scribes and Pharisees (Matt 23:2-36) instead of a warning against them (Mark 12:38b-40). Furthermore, Matthew will compensate for the subtraction by introducing designations of Jesus as "teacher" and "instructor" in 23:8, 10; and the substitution in Matt 23:1 of ἐλάλησεν, "talked," which Luke 20:45 does not share, displays a favorite verb of Matthew, one that he inserts into paralleled pericopes thirteen times and uses once in a pericope peculiar to his gospel. The added participle λέγων, "saying," contrasts with finite forms of λέγω in Mark 12:38; Luke 20:45 and occurs as an insertion sixty-one times in Matthew, as part of unique pericopes twenty-three times — thus Matthean redaction, not dependence on a proto-Mark.

In Mark 4:11-12 Koester claims to detect an awkwardness that betrays earlier textual evolution. The awkwardness consists in a disparity between the plural of "parables" and the singular of "mystery," which appears also in *SGM* 1, and in the giving of the mystery itself as opposed to the gift of knowing the mysteries in Matt 13:11; Luke 8:10. Of course, *SGM* 1 may echo Mark 4:11-12 rather than 4:11-12 echo a proto-Mark; and the parables are not the mystery itself in 4:11-12. They are the means by which the mystery is communicated to insiders and obscured from outsiders. To be *given* the mystery is not awkward if by definition "mystery" includes revelation, i.e. if a mystery is a secret revealed to insiders. Nor does the singular of "mystery" in 4:11 betray any awkwardness. It matches the singular of "kingdom": the kingdom (singular) is a mystery (singular). Matt 13:11 pluralizes "mystery" out of the thought that different parables exhibit different facets of the kingdom (so also *Gos. Thom.* 62, in likely dependence on Matthew). In accordance with this thought, Matthew multiplies the parables of the kingdom (chap. 13). The correlation of the one mystery with the one gospel in Eph 6:19 has little if any bearing on Mark 4:11; for here exists, as we have just seen, a correlation between the one mystery and the one kingdom. And as is well known, Matthew repeatedly adds the element of knowledge, or understanding, to Mark, and usually does so without agreement from Luke (see R. H. Gundry,

Matthew 650 s.v. "Understanding"). The present addition does not need to echo a proto-Mark, then; and the unusual agreement of Luke against Mark may arise by subsidiary influence from Matthew. Koester would have to show that in every passage where Matthew has knowledge and understanding and canonical Mark does not, canonical Mark has denuded the text of *SGM* and that most of the time Luke has independently and at corresponding locations done the same thing to an original proto-Mark. Otherwise, it is easier to think that Matt 13:11 adds knowing as Matthew does elsewhere.

In 20:22-23 Matthew omits the baptism consisting in Jesus' death (Mark 10:38-39; cf. Luke 12:50) so as not to detract from his earlier portrayal of Jesus' baptism in water as a proper example for would-be disciples to follow. In Matt 3:13 Jesus comes "to the Jordan . . . to be baptized." Both expressions are peculiar to Matthew and highlight that Jesus had his own baptism in mind when going to the Jordan. The point is reinforced by Matthew's inserting 3:14-15, also peculiar to his gospel. There, Jesus insists on being baptized, against John the Baptist's objection, and calls baptism "the fulfilment of all righteousness," i.e. the doing of what is right. As a result, *"This* is [instead of 'You are'] my beloved Son, in whom I am well pleased" sets forth Jesus as a proper example to be followed in baptism (cf. 28:19). That is the only baptism of Jesus which Matthew is interested in. Romans 6:1ff. presupposes that Jesus' death is a figurative baptism making believers' baptism a participation in his death.

Matt 17:14-21 omits most of Mark 9:14b-16 because the subject matter of the argument between the scribes and the disciples lacks specificity and because the crowd's amazement at seeing Jesus lacks a readily apparent reason. Matt 17:14-21 also omits Mark 9:21, 22b-24 and parts of Mark 9:25-27, 28 because Matthew has delayed the demonic element for later mention. Perhaps he also objects to the questioning of Jesus' ability and to the halting faith of the father (cf. Matthew's unique criticisms of "little faith" in 8:26; 14:31; 16:8; 17:20). Jesus' seeing the crowd running together in Mark drops out because of Jesus' and the disciples' coming to the crowd at the beginning of the story (Matt 17:14). In Matthew the demon exits without so much as a whimper (contrast Mark) so as to highlight the authority of Jesus (cf. Matt 28:18). Koester's own noting of the possible magical associations of Mark's (ἐκ)θαμβέομαι provides a possible reason for Matthew's and Luke's omission. It is gratuitous to think that deafmuteness and epilepsy in Mark 9:25-27 exclude each other. Matt 17:14-21 replaces "having a mute spirit" with "because he is epileptic and suffers badly" to unify the statement with the epileptic symptoms which he sees in Mark's following descriptions. Such literary unification, seen also in the frequent tightening up of parallelism, characterizes Matthew's style. Since the terminology of death and resurrection recalls the terminology in which Jesus' death and resurrection are described (as Koester himself notes), the inference of a relation to *SGM* is again gratuitous (for further details and on Luke's agreements with Matthew against Mark, see R. H. Gundry, *Matthew* 348-53).

Matt 20:17-19 omits the amazement and fear of the disciples as Jesus presses toward Jerusalem for martyrdom (Mark 10:32). Luke 18:31-34 makes the same

omission. Matthew makes it because in his gospel Jesus' disciples *do* understand his coming passion. In Matt 17:23, after the second complete passion-and-
resurrection prediction, the clause "and they were exceedingly grieved" replaced
"but they did not understand the saying, and feared to ask him" (Mark 9:32).
Their grief showed understanding — hence, the present omission. Luke's agreement in the omission shows subsidiary influence from Matthew, for Luke 18:34
uniquely adds a threefold statement of the disciples' ignorance, which apart from
such influence should have caused Luke to retain the amazement and fear in
Mark. Contrary to Koester's assertion, amazement at Jesus' going ahead makes
good sense in the context of canonical Mark, where Jesuanic events are characteristically portrayed as numinous. In Mark 16:8, for example, we expect some
joy and delight (as in Matt 28:8). Instead, we read of fear and trembling. Even
Jesus' death by crucifixion is a numinous event, witnessed as such by a Roman
centurion (Mark 15:37-39).

In its story of the youth whom Jesus raised, *SGM* seems to conflate νεανίσκος, "young man," in Matt 19:16-22, the look of love in Mark 10:17-22, and
πλούσιος, "rich," in Luke 18:18-23. At least it is just as easy, if not easier, to think
so as it is to posit a late redactor of Mark and equate him with the author of *SGM*.
As usual, Matthew's omitting the disciples' amazement at Jesus' teaching about
wealth (cf. Matt 19:23 with Mark 10:23-24) protects the doctrine of understanding
and knowledge as necessary ingredients of true discipleship. Calling in a late
redactor to make an addition to canonical Mark overlooks a Matthean trait that
is much more widespread than the passages Koester makes the bases of his
argument.

With regard to Mark 14:51-52, Koester considers it a remnant of the story
concerning the young man whom Jesus raised in *SGM,* a story which *SGM* added
to a proto-Mark but which was expurgated, except for this remnant, by the
orthodox canonical Mark at an even later date. But why was the remnant of the
story not expurgated along with its previous part? Koester needs to answer this
question, but a convincing answer is made more difficult by the fact that the
enigmatic character of Mark 14:51-52 left by itself would have provided a strong
motive for deleting it at the same time that the raising of the young man was
supposedly deleted (a point missed by H.-M. Schenke [in *SecCent* 4 (1984) 77]
when he weakly answers "the necessary and difficult question" by saying that the
expurgator "no longer saw the connection between the two passages"). It is easier
to view Mark 14:51-52 as a foregleam of Jesus' resurrection (see the comments
ad loc.), to explain Matthew's and Luke's omissions of it as due to its irrelevance
to their purposes, and to regard the additions in *SGM* as expansions of the sort
we find everywhere in apocryphal literature.

In the passages discussed by Koester we have seen evidences of Matthew's
subsidiary influence on Luke, detectable because the point on which Luke agrees
with Matthew against Mark suits Matthew's interests and style but not Luke's.
This special phenomenon within the general phenomenon of Matthew's and
Luke's agreements against Mark can be seen in a number of other passages not
germane to Koester's discussion and not supportive of his thesis. Matthew's

redaction of Mark and subsidiary influence on Luke therefore offer an explanation more comprehensive and less top-heavy than Koester's. Every other textual phenomenon to which Koester appeals can likewise be treated more adequately than by his theory.

J. D. Crossan (*Four Other Gospels* 106-20) also treats canonical Mark as a revision of *SGM,* but he goes on to argue that *SGM* 1 and 2 do not simply disappear from canonical Mark. Rather, they appear as dismembered elements scattered elsewhere in canonical Mark. The redactor, considered to be the same person as the one who redacted *SGM,* scatters these elements to offset Carpocratian corruption of his own *SGM* 1 and 2.

The general argument for this theory is that the dismembered elements do not fit the contexts to which they have been scattered and that Matthew, Luke, and modern students have consequently found it difficult to interpret these elements. More particularly, Crossan argues that since *SGM* reads "*he* comes into Jericho" in Mark 10:46a, "*they* come into Jericho" looks like a pluralization by canonical Mark. In the first place, however, the singular of Jesus' coming into Jericho in Clement's quotation of v 46a may be influenced by the singular of Jesus' going out of Jericho (v 46b) or by the singular of his drawing near to Jericho in Luke 18:35 (cf. M. Smith, *Clement* 368-69, for Matthean and Lucan contaminations of Clement's quotations of Mark 10:17-31) rather than by a hypothetical singular of Jesus' coming into Jericho in *SGM.* Moreover, a singular reading in *SGM* would say nothing about the chronological relation between *SGM* and canonical Mark. Had *SGM* come earlier, canonical Mark's deletion of *SGM* 2 would not have favored a switch to the plural; for the deletion would give no cause for such a switch. Without *SGM* 2, on the contrary, the singular of Jesus' exit follows even more closely on the plural of his and the disciples' entrance. On the other hand, a plural reading of v 46a in *SGM* would be no easier than the plural reading in canonical Mark. More difficult, rather; for though both have Jesus speaking to the Twelve in vv 41-45, in *SGM* 2 the Twelve disappear and the young man (whose presence might justify the plural) is mentioned only obliquely whereas in canonical Mark v 46a directly mentions the disciples right alongside Jesus.

Secondly and more importantly, the third person plural in v 46a fits the third and first person plurals in vv 32-33 ("they were going up to Jerusalem. . . . we are going up to Jerusalem") so nicely that even though Clement were following *SGM* in reading the singular, it seems more likely that in v 46a the third person plural, referring to Jesus and the Twelve, represents the original reading, changed to the singular by *SGM* to avoid awkwardness and confusion with *SGM*'s immediately following third person plural that refers entirely differently to the sister and mother of the young man plus Salome. Third person plurals with verbs of topographical movement in 11:1, 12a, 20, 27 further favor the originality of the same in 10:46a. The ease with which the shift to the singular in 10:46b can be explained (it prepares for Jesus' confrontation with Bartimaeus — see the notes ad loc.) makes that shift a nonargument for omission of *SGM* 2 by canonical Mark.

Now we need to recognize that the position of *SGM* 2 presents exactly the kind of contextual problem for the greater earliness of *SGM* that Crossan tries to establish and use for his theory that dismembered elements of *SGM* are scattered throughout a later canonical Mark. Not only does *SGM*'s plural reference to the young man's sister and mother plus Salome jar against the immediately preceding and probably original plural reference to Jesus and the Twelve. But also the key statement in *SGM* 2, "and Jesus did not receive them," does not fit the immediate context. If the women had not received Jesus, *SGM* 2 would have provided the reason for his leaving Jericho in v 46b. But the nonreception is the other way around.

We can explain the key statement only on distant contextual and extra-Marcan grounds or by recourse to an abridgement of *SGM* 2. For example, a combination of Mark 15:40 and its parallel Matt 27:56 could make Salome the mother of James and John, who in Mark have recently asked for places of high honor and whose mother did the asking according to Matt 20:20. Her asking may prompt Jesus' non-reception; or, in reverse, his non-reception constitutes or confirms his denial of her request. Recourse to an abridgement of *SGM* 2, the missing part of which would theoretically provide the contextual point of Jesus' turning a cold shoulder to the women is a counsel of despair, however. Clement's putative letter says that *SGM* 2 adds "only" what is then quoted. Hence, Crossan is forced to consider *SGM* 2 expurgated even before canonical Mark is supposed to have expurgated it further. Not only does the necessity of adding an earlier expurgation threaten to bring down the hypothesis under its own weight, but also Jesus' non-reception of the women requires nothing more to understand the statement. We may want to know why he does not receive them, but in and of itself the statement carries a complete meaning. The supposition of an earlier expurgation of unknown additional material therefore grows out of the exigency of a theory, not out of the evidence at hand.

Crossan next thinks that canonical Mark transfers "Bethany" from *SGM* 1 to 11:1, 11, 12; 14:3, and "house" from *SGM* 1 to 14:3. The awkward position of "Bethany" in 11:1 (contrast Luke 19:28-29; Matt 21:1) is supposed to support this transfer. But the awkwardness — if there is any — begins with the first position of Jerusalem! Actually, Mark will work backward quite logically and topographically from the destination Jerusalem through Bethphage, an intermediate point, to Bethany, the closest point (see the comments on 11:1). It is hard to think that 11:11, 12; 14:3 originally had no name for the place where Jesus and the Twelve stayed outside Jerusalem. It is also hard to think that if these texts originally had no place-name, canonical Mark inserts it repeatedly rather than transferring it once. If the house in 14:3 will come from *SGM* 2, where will its owner Simon the leper come from? He does not appear in *SGM* 2. Are we to suppose that only Simon belonged to 14:3 from the start? If so, in what capacity besides owner of the house? And where besides his house did the anointing in 14:3 take place?

Canonical Mark is also supposed to transfer "'Son of David, have mercy on me.' But the disciples rebuked her" from *SGM* 1 to 10:47-48. Crossan argues this point from the awkwardness of the word order in 10:47: "Son of David, Jesus, have mercy on me." Since the request for sight will come only after a later question from Jesus in v 51, Bartimaeus originally shouted only "Jesus!" in the earlier, secret version of v 47. But this theory succeeds only in creating questions. What precedent is there for an address with the mere "Jesus"? Why would canonical Mark break up "Son of David" and "have mercy on me" and make them straddle "Jesus" rather than adding them as a unit after "Jesus" so as to produce a more normal word order (as in Luke 18:38; see the comments on vv 47-48 concerning a possible reason for the placement of "Son of David" before "Jesus")? Why does "Jesus" not disappear, as in v 48? In its specifying of the request for sight, v 51 will go beyond the cry for mercy in vv 47-48; hence, no redundancy will favor a later addition of that cry.

Yet again, Crossan thinks that canonical Mark transfers "rolled the stone from the door of the tomb" from *SGM* 1 to 16:3. But then we would expect canonical Mark to retain *Jesus'* rolling the stone from the door of the tomb, as in *SGM* 1. We would expect so especially because of the women's question in 16:3, "*Who* will roll the stone from the tomb for us?" Crossan takes the absence of this question in Matt 28:1; Luke 24:2 as evidence of addition in Mark 16:3. But the absence in Matthew does not reflect the text of Mark used by Matthew. Rather, the question "drops out because [Matthew's] inserting the sealing of the stone and the guarding of the tomb [see 27:62-66, unique to Matthew] makes their [the women's] question senseless. Nobody would dare unseal the stone and roll it away for them. Because of the guard, nobody could" (R. H. Gundry, *Matthew* 586). And the question is not really absent in Luke 24:2. Rather, it is tucked into the comment that they "found the stone rolled away from the tomb," which chiastically conflates "from . . . the tomb" and "looking up they see that the stone is rolled away" in Mark 16:3 and 4, respectively. Within the text of Mark itself, the rolling of a stone to the door of the tomb in 15:46 prepares for and thus favors the originality of the question in 16:3. Transfer of the question from *SGM* 1 to 16:3 would probably have resulted only in a simple reference to the stone's having been rolled away, as in 16:4, not in the women's questioning who will roll it away; for in *SGM* 1 rolling away the stone is not presented as a problem.

Supposedly, canonical Mark transfers Jesus' going into the tomb, where the young man was, from *SGM* 1 to 16:5 and transforms it into the women's going into the tomb of Jesus and seeing a young man. Luke 24:4 puts two men in the tomb — but for a redactional reason that Crossan himself notes in his references to Luke 9:30; Acts 1:10; so this difference from canonical Mark does not support a different text in an earlier version. Likewise unsupportive are the angel of the Lord and the happening of everything outside the tomb in Matt 28:2; for these differences from Mark are clearly redactional (R. H. Gundry, *Matthew* 586-87). Crossan offers no possible reason for the putative transfer in canonical Mark. Without the women's going into the tomb of Jesus and seeing a young man, what would we suppose *SGM* had at this point that is not Lucan or Matthean redaction? What else did the women do, see, hear? These questions are pressing; for they deal in part with the very heart of the story, not with an unessential possible add-on.

Canonical Mark is further supposed to transfer "he raised him [by] grasping the [= his] hand" from *SGM* 1 to 1:31; 5:41; 9:27. Said to support this theory is the absence of the clause from Matt 8:15 par. Luke 4:39; Matt 17:18 par. Luke 9:42, though it is present in Matt 9:25 par. Luke 8:54. But the facts are different. There is no absence of the clause from Matt 8:15 par. Luke 4:39. Rather, Matt 8:15 changes the verb from active to passive (as in 9:25 vis-à-vis Mark 5:41) and the participle from "grasping" to "touching." Luke 4:39 changes grasping the hand to rebuking the fever, and raising to standing up. The absence in Matt 17:18 is part of a far larger omission-cum-summary of Mark 9:26b-27 (see ibid. 351 for characteristically Matthean redaction). The same thing has happened in Luke 9:42-43, but with characteristically Lucan redaction. Even otherwise, if Matthew and Luke draw from canonical Mark rather than from *SGM* (so Crossan, *Four Other Gospels* 115, 119-20), then the absence of the clause would be irrelevant to the question of the relation between canonical Mark and *SGM;* for the absence would be due to the influence of canonical Mark, not to the influence of *SGM.* On the other hand, if the absence were due to influence from *SGM*, why retention of the clause in Matt 9:25 par. Luke 8:54 (as recognized by Crossan) and in Matt 8:15 par. Luke 4:39 (as just recognized by us)? Or if Matthew and Luke draw from both canonical Mark and *SGM*, then agreement with one or the other has no argumentative value; for nothing is falsifiable — and therefore nothing verifiable — when disagreement with the one can always be explained by dependence on the other. Further questions arise: What would motivate canonical Mark to retain and scatter the particular clause at issue but not others in *SGM?* What would motivate him not only to retain it, but also to repeat it? What gesture or other means of healing is supposed instead of grasping and raising in a *SGM* earlier than canonical Mark? Is there good evidence for a more original gesture or other means?

In one respect Crossan disagrees with the foregoing criticisms by positing that when canonical Mark transfers the clause in question to 9:27, he also shifts other elements of *SGM* 1 by adding "since childhood" to 9:21 and the boy's becoming "as if dead, so that many were saying, 'He has died' " to 9:26. The absence of these elements in Matt 17:18 par. Luke 9:42 is cited in support; but we have already referred to an easier explanation, i.e. characteristically Matthean and Lucan redaction of canonical Mark. If canonical Mark has transferred the notion of youth from *SGM* 2 to 9:21, instead of ἐκ παιδιόθεν, "since childhood," in 9:21 we might expect ἐκ/ἀπὸ νεότητος, "since youth," to correspond to ὁ νεανίσκος, "the young man," in *SGM* 1. One also wonders whether the appearance of having died in 9:26 reflects very well the actuality of having died and the entombment that we read about in *SGM* 1. Furthermore, it would seem more likely that if canonical Mark were in the business of dismembering *SGM* 1 and scattering elements of it, he would have put the young man's being raised from the dead in another story of healing rather than in the story of exorcism which 9:14-27 presents.

Next, canonical Mark is supposed to shift "the young man, gazing at him [Jesus], loved him . . . he was rich" from *SGM* 1 to 10:17-22, but with a change to "from my youth" and with a reversal that makes Jesus love the young man (see the comments on 10:21 for the probably physical connotation of loving as putting an arm around, patting, or such like). The transfer is also supposed to prompt addition of the young man's crestfallenness and sorrowful departure because of his having many acquisitions. But the rich man in 10:17-22 is not said to be young. He looks back on his youth. One could think that canonical Mark transforms the young man of *SGM* 1 into an adult to counter a Carpocratian pederastic interpretation of *SGM* 1, but to change the young man's loving Jesus to Jesus' loving an adult male would only expose the story to a different kind of homosexual interpretation — and a more highly charged one at that, because Jesus himself would become the initiator of homosexual love. It is hard to think that canonical Mark would blunder so badly against his own intention.

Canonical Mark is supposed to transfer "he [the young man] began to beseech him [Jesus] that he might be with him" from *SGM* 1 to 5:18. Matt 8:34 omits the statement, and Luke 8:38 rephrases it. But the plea in Mark 5:18 leads naturally into Jesus' refusal and commissioning of an ex-demoniac to go proclaim what the Lord has done for him (5:19). Without the plea, the commission would be abrupt. Therefore an earlier absence of the plea seems unlikely. Other differences between *SGM* 1 and 5:1-20 increase the unlikelihood of a transfer: raising the dead versus casting out demons and Jesus' allowance of the plea to be with him versus his refusal of the plea. One could explain this last difference as stemming from canonical Mark's desire to guard against Carpocratian homosexual interpretation, but then his blunder in making Jesus love the rich man in 10:21 stands out all the more. And what would canonical Mark do with Jesus' choosing the twelve apostles "in order that they might be with him" (3:14)? The absence of the plea to be with Jesus in Matt 8:34 belongs to a far larger redactional omission by Matthew (R. H. Gundry, *Matthew* 161) and therefore does not support an absence of the plea in an earlier version of Mark 5:18. Neither does the rephrasing of the plea in Luke 8:38 support absence; it only favors that Luke's copy of Mark had the plea.

Canonical Mark is supposed to transfer "they came into the house" from *SGM* 1 at least to 3:20 (if not also to 1:29; 2:15) to set up a rhythm of calling or visiting. Since a house appears to be forced on 3:20, as shown by the absence of 3:20-21 from Matthew and Luke, an earlier version of Mark must have lacked this addition from *SGM* 1. So runs Crossan's argument. But the coming together of a crowd is said to keep Jesus and the Twelve from being able to eat. Why then should it seem forced that Jesus goes into a house, apparently to eat? The frequency of Mark's references to Jesus' going into a house (see the concordance s.v. οἰκία and οἶκος; cf. esp. 2:1-2) support the originality of such an entry in 3:20. It is easily probable that Matthew and Luke omit Mark 3:20-21 because of the offensive charge that Jesus has gone berserk. Besides, Matthew immediately follows up the names of the Twelve (10:2-4 par. Mark 3:16-19) with their commission (10:5-42), which does not appear in Mark till much later (6:7-11). This clamping together of items separated in Mark makes it easy to omit what immediately follows the names of the Twelve in Mark, i.e. Mark 3:20-21. Luke finds it easy to do the same thing for the similar reason that he follows up the names of the Twelve (6:14-16) with the Sermon on the Plain, accompanied by healings (6:17-49). And in all probability, offense at the charge in Mark 3:20-21 that Jesus has gone berserk again plays a part.

Canonical Mark is supposed to transfer "after six days" from *SGM* 1 to 9:2. The unoriginality of the phrase in 9:2 is betrayed, argues Crossan, by its unclarity, which is betrayed in turn by "approximately eight days" in the parallel Luke 9:28. But "*approximately* (ὡσεί) eight days" does not clarify anything. And Matt 17:1 retains "after six days"; so Matthew seems to think Mark's phrase clear. "After six days" obviously means that six days after Jesus made the preceding statements, the Transfiguration occurred. The question whether the six days include or exclude the days of the statements and of the Transfiguration has no bearing on the relation between canonical Mark and *SGM*, for the same sort of question attaches to the phrase in *SGM* 1: Does it include or exclude the days of coming to the young man's house and of Jesus' commanding him?

To avoid homosexuality, says Crossan, canonical Mark transfers "when evening arrived the young man comes to him wearing a linen cloth on his naked [body]" from *SGM* 1 to 14:51-52, where its awkwardness is shown by its absence from Matt 26:56 par. Luke 22:53. By contrast, the statement makes a quite natural reference in *SGM* 1 to a nude nocturnal baptism. For the sake of argument, let us grant that NT references to "taking off" and "putting on" (Gal 3:27; Eph 4:20-24; Col 3:8-14) reflect the practice of disrobing before baptism and re-robing after baptism rather than that those references generated the practice; and let us grant that for ritual reasons early Christian baptism was performed at night, though Acts 16:33 offers quite a different reason for the only NT example of nocturnal baptism, and Hippolytus (*Trad. Ap.* 21) mentions baptism at dawn, not at night, and writes as late as the early third century. Even granting these debatable assumptions, we have to ask why *SGM* 1 says not a syllable about baptism (Where is the water?) or about disrobing and re-robing (Where is the new garment?). We should note that against all synoptic evidence to the contrary, the baptismal hypothesis requires that Jesus himself baptize the young man (see also John 4:2, though some take it as a historically false qualification of 3:22; 4:1). We also need to know why canonical Mark would choose the flight of the disciples as the event to which to transfer a young man's wearing a linen cloth on his naked body. To adopt Crossan's theory, one has to suppose not only such a transfer, but also Mark's fabrication of the young man's following with Jesus, of his being seized by Jesus' captors, and of his fleeing naked — none of which is suggested by *SGM* 1 or, except for the fleeing, by the context in canonical Mark. There, in canonical Mark, the young man's wearing a linen cloth on his naked body prepares naturally for his fleeing naked out of the grasp of his would-be captors, just as his fleeing and that of the disciples lead naturally into Jesus' being taken away by himself. The larger significance of the incident may not be immediately transparent, but the contextual meaning of the narrative as such is crystal clear. It is in *SGM* 1, not in 14:51-52, that contextual meaning as well as larger significance becomes clouded. What is actually said in *SGM* 1 leaves entirely unclear even a superficial connection between wearing a linen cloth on a naked body and anything else in the context. If, as Koester says, *SGM* had Jesus teaching the mystery of God's kingdom in chaps. 4 and 10 alike, then Jesus' teaching the young man "the mystery of God's kingdom" can hardly count as catechism leading to nude baptism; for according to chap. 4, Jesus teaches this very mystery to a huge crowd that includes outsiders. Never mind that he teaches it in such a way as to obscure it from the outsiders. Baptismal catechsim is not even addressed to outsiders. Nor does the mystery of God's kingdom as taught in chap. 4 include moral instructions such as characterize baptismal catechism. Matthew and Luke omit 14:51-52 probably because they plan to replace "the young man" of Mark 16:1-8, who parallels the one in 14:51-52, perhaps also because the incident does not suit their redactional purposes or because its significance would escape their audiences.

Against the theory that Mark 10:13-45, including *SGM*, represents a lection used at the nude nocturnal baptism of catechumens (cf. M. Smith, *Clement* 167-88), E. Best (*Disciples and Discipleship* 83-86) cogently argues that the monotheistic confession in v 18 is nowhere else associated with Christian baptism. Nor is the Decalogue, partly quoted in v 19, till a post-Marcan date (cf. *Did.* 2:1-3). Christian baptism has never required prior riddance of all one's worldly goods (v 21; cf. vv 28, 23-27). The rich man who goes away downcast because he has many worldly goods (v 22) makes a strange example for baptizees. And the details of the passion-and-resurrection prediction (vv 33-34) are otiose in a baptismal confession.

We may add to Best's arguments. The passion-and-resurrection prediction defines in advance Jesus' baptism, not as a rite — he has already undergone the rite of baptism (1:9-11) — but as his suffering, to be shared by James and John (see 10:35-40, which gives no hint that James and John have yet to undergo the rite — to the contrary, see John 1:29-42). One could argue that Jesus' prediction of suffering interprets the rite; but even in Rom 6:1-23, where Paul relates baptism to participation with Christ in his death, burial, and resurrection, the point has to do with morality, not with suffering. In *SGM,* morever, Jesus relates his baptism of suffering to James and John, not to the young man with a linen cloth on his naked body. And σινδών, "a linen cloth," though used occasionally in non-canonical Christian literature for baptismal garb, had a wide variety of uses and so far as we can tell never turned into a technical term for baptismal garb. More seriously, since the young man comes to Jesus already wearing a σινδών, the baptismal hypothesis must treat it as the garment taken off before baptism to symbolize renunciation of the old life, not as the baptismal garment put on after baptism to symbolize new life in Christ. If in disagreement with Crossan one retains the originality of 14:51-52 as well as *SGM* 1, the baptismal hypothesis raises the question, Why is the young man still wearing the old garment in 14:51-52? Leaving the old garment in the clutches of Jesus' captors hardly represents baptism, a voluntary act, as though the baptism occurs symbolically in 14:51-52 rather than literally in *SGM* 1; for 14:27-31 has pre-interpreted the flight from Jesus' captors as scandalous. One may find a new garment of baptism in the στολή of the young man in Jesus' empty tomb (16:5; cf. R. Scroggs and K. I. Groff in *JBL* 92 [1973] 531-48, though H. Fleddermann [in *CBQ* 41 (1979) 415] pertinently notes that the baptismal motif of dying and rising with Christ, as in Rom 6:1-11, occurs nowhere in Mark, not even in 10:38-39). One may even identify that young man with the young men of *SGM* and 14:51-52 (but not with the rich man who turns back from discipleship in 10:17-22; for he looks back on his youth, whereas only Matt 19:20, omitting that look, turns him into a downcast young man for a contrast with the children who have just received Jesus' blessing — cf. also Matthew's insertion of children who praise Jesus in the temple [21:15-16]). It is certainly better not to equate the σινδών and the στολή; for στολή connotes a long formal robe such as scribes like to wear (12:38-39), whereas the earlier mentioned σινδών appears to be a mere piece of cloth, easily abandoned, or at most a scanty tunic, easily slipped out of. But στολή, like σινδών, though used occasionally in non-canonical Christian literature for baptismal garb, had a wide variety of uses and so far as we can tell never turned into a technical term for baptismal garb. And why the use for new life in Christ of a word whose only other occurrence in Mark has characterized the pompous and rapacious scribes? Why no young man's reaffirmation of the Cross between scandalous flight and announcement of the Resurrection (against the theory of M. Meyer [in *Semeia* 49 [1990] 145-47] that 16:1-8 presents a reaffirmation of baptismal loyalties after a forsaking of them in 14:51-52)?

An identification of the young men in *SGM,* Mark 14:51-52, and Mark 16:1-8 as one and the same young man in successive stages of Christian initiation might give the baptismal hypothesis some much needed help. But standing against such an identification is the lack of an anaphoric definite article after the initial mention of a young man. Instead, the second mention is accompanied by an indefinite τις (14:51), and the third mention is simply anarthrous (16:5). Yet in every comparable situation Mark starts with an indefinite expression and thereafter uses the anaphoric definite article: so with reference to the paralytic (2:3, 4, 5, 9, 10), the man with the withered hand (3:1, 3, 5), the Gergasene demoniac (5:2, 8 [cf. 15, 16, 18]), the woman with a constant flow of blood (5:25, 33), the synagogue-ruler (5:22, 35, 36), the Syrophoenician woman (7:25, 26), the blind man of Bethsaida (8:22, 23), the father of the boy with a mute spirit (9:17, 21, 24), the blind beggar (10:46, 49, 51), the inquiring scribe (12:28, 32), the widow with two mites (12:42, 43 [cf. 44]), and the servant girl (14:66, 69). The case of the synagogue-ruler has special pertinence, because the second and third references to him carry the anaphoric definite article even though the story of the woman with a constant flow of blood has intervened, as in the discontinuous mentions of a young man.

Canonical Mark is supposed to transfer "the mystery of the kingdom of God" from *SGM* 1 to 4:11 to situate Jesus' teaching, not in secret ritual (as in *SGM* 1, capitalized on by the Carpocratians — cf. Iren. *Haer.* 1.25.5), but in publicly spoken parable (4:1-2). But though Jesus teaches the mystery of God's kingdom through publicly spoken parable, even in canonical Mark — indeed, emphatically in canonical Mark — his explaining the parabolic mystery of God's kingdom takes place only in private with the disciples (see 4:10, 13-20, 33-34; cf. other Marcan passages concerning the disciples' private audiences with Jesus). In 4:11, therefore, "the mystery of the kingdom of God" is not at all problematic, but right at home. It does not need to be regarded as a foreign body intruded from *SGM* 1 (see also J. Marcus, *Mystery* 86-87, n. 41). Changes in Matthew and Luke derive from a desire to stress the culpability of outsiders and the element of understanding (an ideal trait of disciples that Matthew often emphasizes).

Finally, canonical Mark is supposed to transfer "and from there, arising, he returned to Transjordan" from *SGM* 1 to 10:1a, where the strangeness of the conjunction "the borders of Judea and Transjordan" betrays the transfer (cf. the omission in Luke 9:51 and the revision "the borders of Judea beyond the Jordan" in Matt 19:1). But why should canonical Mark think that he needs to preserve an unessential piece of topographical information, especially when according to Crossan's theory he lets far more essential elements of the story disappear entirely — viz., the woman who is sister to the young man, her prostrating herself before Jesus, Jesus' anger, and the loud shout from the tomb? Why does canonical Mark not omit the entire story if he finds it objectionable? If out of respect for tradition he preserves any of the story by scattering it in bits and pieces, why does his respect for tradition not lead him to preserve some more essential bits and pieces than a topographical detail that is more problematic in *SGM* 1 than it is in 10:1? For presumably *SGM* referred to Judea at 10:1a. Otherwise, a transfer of Transjordan from *SGM* 1 to 10:1a would not have produced the supposedly strange conjunction. *SGM* 1 makes Jesus leave Judea after having done a number of things there (10:1b-34) and head away from Jerusalem to Transjordan even though both editorial and Jesuanic statements have just announced that he and those with him are going up to Jerusalem (10:32-33). In canonical Mark, Jesus does nothing in Judea before he arrives in Transjordan, with the result that canonical Mark merely works backward from ultimate destination to intermediate destination, as in 11:1, to highlight the region and city where Jesus' passion-and-resurrection predictions will be fulfilled (see the comments and notes on 10:1; 11:1).

Others have shown in detail that *SGM* is largely a confused pastiche of phrases gathered from elsewhere in Mark and the other canonical gospels (see, e.g., F. F. Bruce, *"Secret" Gospel* 11-13; D. Schmidt in *Protocol of the Center for Hermeneutical Studies in Hellenistic and Modern Culture*, Colloquy 18, pp. 41-43). Despite Clement's supporting the Marcan authenticity of *SGM*, then, and despite the efforts of some present-day scholars to date *SGM* before canonical Mark and the other gospels, we should regard *SGM* as apocryphal non-Marcan additions to canonical Mark, additions which postdate the other gospels, too, and which the Carpocratians supplemented for their own purposes (see Bruce, op. cit. 12-13, for other examples of Clement's credulity).

To break new ground, we may note that Jesus' commanding the young man in *SGM* 1 hardly means his commanding him to come in the evening wearing a linen cloth on his naked body; for the lack of any reference to baptism makes sartorial preparation for baptism an unlikely meaning, and the lack of any reference to or hint of sexual relations makes sartorial preparation for homosexual intercourse an equally unlikely meaning. Jesus is not said to be wearing a linen cloth on *his* naked body, and the text of *SGM* says nothing to suggest that the young man exposed his nakedness by taking off the linen cloth that he was wearing. On the contrary: "for Jesus was teaching him the mystery of the kingdom of God." The conjunction γάρ, "for," and the imperfect tense of ἐδίδασκε, "was teaching," define the activity of "that night" didactically rather than sexually or baptismally.

Only if Clement's denial is false that "naked [man] with naked [man]" and "the other things about which you [Theodore] wrote" occur in *SGM* should we allow a homosexual meaning in *SGM*. Yet Clement of Alexandria writes as one who knows "word for word" (κατὰ λέξιν) "the very words" of *SGM*, which was written in Alexandria, left to the church in Alexandria, and "most carefully guarded" there, being read to initiates into the great mysteries. Clement's instruction to deny that Mark wrote *SGM* even though in Clement's belief Mark really did write it by way of expanding the original version (in our terms, canonical Mark) seems designed to keep Carpocratians from passing off their objectionable additions to *SGM*, such as "naked [man] with naked [man]," as having Marcan authority.

To discover what Jesus commanded the young man, let us step back to the preceding clause, "for he was rich." It explains why the young man has a house despite his youth. It also echoes descriptions of the rich adult man in vv 22, 25 ("for he had many acquisitions. . . . a rich [man]"; cf. Luke 18:23: "for he was exceedingly rich") and recollects Jesus' commands that the adult rich man go sell all that he has, give to the poor, and come follow him (v 21). Since, then, in *SGM* 1 "and after six days Jesus commanded him" immediately follows "for he was rich," and since the verb of command (ἐπέταξεν) has no direct object (contrast the infinitival and clausal direct objects in 6:27, 39; 9:25), the commands to the rich adult man are meant to fill the ellipsis in *SGM* 1 (cf. 1:27, where an ellipsis after this same verb is to be filled with an earliér command in 1:25). Like the rich adult man in 10:17-31, then, the rich young man in *SGM* is also commanded to go sell all that he has, give to the poor, and come follow Jesus. Instead of inserting the story of the rich young man right after the story of the rich adult man the author of *SGM* delays it till after the passion-and-resurrection prediction in 10:32-34 so as to put Jesus on the road to Jerusalem through Jericho, where *SGM* will set the sequel as a second insertion. *SGM* borrows the youth of the rich man from Matt 19:16-22; and his youth reminds *SGM* of the young man in Mark 14:51-52, from where *SGM* now borrows the wearing of a linen cloth on a naked body. By wearing only that much when he comes to Jesus, the young man demonstrates his obedience: during the balance of the day, i.e. between the time of Jesus' command and the evening, the rich young man disposed of his wealth and now has nothing left but the linen cloth, only what a corpse needs (cf. 15:46). Thus he has qualified himself to follow Jesus. As a result, Jesus can teach him the mystery of God's kingdom. The linen cloth on a naked body represents dispossession, then, not baptisal or homosexual ritual; and *SGM* 1 offers a counterbalance to the rich adult man who left downcast and did not return having dispossessed himself. This contrast links up with the growing ideal of poverty in Alexandrian Christianity. The growth of this ideal causes an adverse reaction in Clem. *Q.d.s.* 11. Nonetheless, Clement's letter to Theodore betrays an attraction to the secrecy of *SGM*.

Anticipating the contrast between the two rich men is the young one's gazing at Jesus and loving him right after being raised. The wording ἐμβλέψας αὐτῷ ἠγάπησεν αὐτόν exactly matches v 21a. But in *SGM* the rich young man already begins to exhibit the difference between himself and the rich adult man by doing to Jesus what Jesus unsuccessfully did to the earlier rich man. (The use of ἠγάπησεν for the young man's loving Jesus carries homosexual overtones no more than Jesus' loving the rich adult man did.) Confirming the parallel between the two rich men is the description in *SGM* 2 of the young one as him "whom Jesus loved," just as Jesus had loved the adult one — only the verb has changed to the imperfect tense (ἠγάπα), presumably because of the linear character of the young man's following Jesus, who loves him because he is following (cf. John 11:5, 36; 13:23; 19:26; 21:2, 7, 20). His request to be with Jesus is being fulfilled. Since in *SGM* 1 Jesus seems to have given the same commands to the rich young man that he gave to the rich adult man, perhaps *SGM* 2 implies that the young man's sister and mother, accompanied by Salome, have in mind to ask for him a place of high honor such as Salome, understood as the mother of James and John, asked for them.

JESUS PROVED AS PREDICTOR AND ACCLAIMED
AS THE COMING ONE

11:1-10 (Matt 21:1-9; Luke 19:28-40; John 12:12-19)

The story of the Triumphal Procession begins with a prediction that Jesus gives in his instructions on getting a colt (vv 1-3), proceeds with the fulfilment of that prediction (vv 4-6), and reaches its goal in Jesus' sitting on the colt to much acclaim (vv 7-10).

11:1-3 *(Matt 21:1-5; Luke 19:28-31; John 12:12)* The historical present tense of ἐγγίζουσιν, "they draw near," and the mention of Jerusalem before Bethphage, Bethany, and the Mount of Olives even though Jerusalem lies beyond them emphasize Jerusalem as the place where Jesus' passion-and-resurrection predictions will be fulfilled. As a result of mentioning the place of fulfilment first, Mark has to work backward to Bethphage, probably situated on the west slope of the Mount of Olives just across the Kidron Valley to the east of Jerusalem, to Bethany, situated lower down on the south slope of the Mount of Olives and farther east from Jerusalem. Pilgrims coming from Jericho would go through or past the villages in the reverse order. The awkwardness of two successive but unappositional phrases beginning with εἰς, "to," shows how very intent Mark is to make Jerusalem the center of attention because it will become the place of fulfilment (cf. his having lived in Jerusalem [Acts 12:12] and therefore writing from the standpoint of a Jerusalemite; see 7:31; 10:1 for other instances of his mentioning an ultimate destination before an intermediate one). Πρὸς τὸ ὄρος τῶν ἐλαιῶν, "at the Mount of Olives," gives the location of both Bethphage and Bethany.

The present historical tense of ἀποστέλλει, "he sends," and of λέγει, "he says," likewise emphasizes another prediction of Jesus which the two disciples whom he sends will discover to come to pass (cf. 6:7; 14:13). ᾽Αποστέλλει connotes that he sends the disciples with his authority. "The village opposite you," to which he sends them, seems to be Bethany; for the band have come only *near* to Bethphage and Bethany, and coming from Jericho they would go past Bethany before Bethphage. Moreover, Bethany's lying farther off the Roman road leading into Jerusalem gives more meaning to "opposite you" than the phrase would carry in a description of Bethphage. Jesus would have little need to send the disciples to Bethphage, for his whole band are to pass right by it on the way to Jerusalem. Apparently they have arrived at a fork in the road, the left fork leading to Bethany on a side road, the right fork leading past Bethphage on the main, Roman road to Jerusalem.

The command to go fetch a colt contains a prediction, and the prediction contains a number of details whose fulfilments will aid Mark's emphasis on Jesus' predictive power: (1) the disciples' finding a male colt; (2) the immediacy of finding him as they are entering the village (N.B.: not merely right after they have entered it); (3) the colt's being tied; (4) no one's ever having sat on him before; and (5) the possibility that someone will say, "Why are you doing this?" What Jesus tells the disciples to say in response carries a promise that he will return the colt ("and immediately he sends him again here") and makes him the master of the unbroken colt ("his master has need"). The forward position of ὁ κύριος αὐτοῦ, "his master" (contrast the later position of the subject in 2:17), and the connotation of authority in this second ἀποστέλλει, "he sends" (cf. v 1), stress Jesus' mastery over the colt. Though χρείαν takes an objective genitive, which would here yield, "need of him [the colt]," elsewhere Mark's genitives depending on χρείαν follow the verb ἔχω, "have," which as here is preceded by χρείαν (2:17; 14:63). Moreover, Mark's genitives usually follow their governing nouns. Here, the genitive αὐτοῦ follows ὁ κύριος, precedes both χρείαν and ἔχει, and therefore goes with ὁ κύριος to produce "his master." So Jesus is exercising a lordly prerogative by requisitioning the colt as a means of transportation. The abruptness of the command, "Loosen him and bring [him]," emphasizes this exercise. Πάλιν ὧδε, "again here" or (more idiomatically) "back here," makes its clause part of the disciples' response, i.e. a promise that Jesus will shortly return the colt even though he is the colt's master. For although "here" might equally well point to the place of Jesus' speaking, "again" requires a return to the place of the colt's origin (cf. B. M. Metzger, *Textual Commentary* 109). Mark will not narrate the return of the colt, because he has no interest in the fulfilment of a promise made by disciples. Narrating such a fulfilment would weaken the climax of the story with an anticlimax. "Immediately," the forward position of αὐτόν, "him [the colt]," and the use of the present tense in "he sends" with the futuristic meaning, "he will send," make up for the lack of such a narrative by intensifying the promise of a return. That no one has yet sat on the colt will bring honor to Jesus as the first one to sit on him (cf. Num 19:2; Deut 21:3; 1 Sam 6:7; 2 Sam 6:3; Zech 9:9 LXX; Luke 23:53; the stories of the Virgin Birth [an unused womb]; *m. Sanh.* 2:5; Hom. *Il.* 6.94; Hor. *Epod.* 9.22; Ov. *Met.* 3.10-11; Verg. *Geor.* 4.540). Great emphasis falls on this honor: to "no one" is added "of human beings" to universalize the negation; and the emphatic second negative, "not yet," comes forward to stand between "no one" and "of human beings" (see the Greek text). In view of Jesus' having done what others cannot do (see esp. 1:27-28; 2:7; 4:41; 5:3-5, 15; 6:48-52), is there an implication that he will sit on the unbroken colt with such mastery as to eliminate the need of breaking him (but see the following notes on the possibility that unriddenness does not equate with unbrokenness)?

11:4-6 *(Matt 21:6; Luke 19:32-34a)* On going away the disciples find a colt tied, just as Jesus said they would. The question, "What are you doing [by] loosing the colt?" also fulfils what he said might happen. The historical present tense in "they loose him [the colt]" emphasizes their obedience to Jesus' instruction and anticipates the present participle "loosing" to indicate action going on at the time of the question. The sharpening of a chronologically general "immediately" (v 2) to a locally specific "by a door outside on the street" to indicate just how soon it is that the disciples find the colt (i.e. as they enter using the street), the transformation of a possibility of asking ("and if someone should say to you" — v 3) into the actuality of asking, the multiplication of a singular "someone" (v 3) into the plural "some of the ones standing there" all magnify the fulfilment of Jesus' prediction. The failure of Mark to remention the colt's not yet having been sat on (cf. v 2) argues for the use of tradition, for we would have expected a repetition if Mark or someone before him were fabricating these details in the interest of an emphasis on prediction and fulfilment. "And they [the two disciples] spoke to them [those who asked what they were doing] according as Jesus had said" shows Jesus' lordship over the disciples as well as over the colt (cf. 14:16; 16:7). "And they allowed them" shows his lordship also over those who asked, since the disciples are loosing the colt because Jesus the colt's master has need.

11:7-10 *(Matt 21:7-9; Luke 19:35-38; John 12:13-18)* The historical present tense in the statement, "And they bring the colt to Jesus," stresses Jesus' lordship over the disciples. Their not riding the colt saves the colt for first use by Jesus. Those who put their garments on the colt seem to be the two disciples, since Mark gives no hint of a shift in subjects and since the garments of more than two would exceed what could be used on a single colt. These considerations outweigh Mark's acknowledged habit of using an indefinite third person plural, which would here yield, "And people throw their garments on him [the colt]." "And he sat on him" indicates the purpose of throwing garments on the colt: it is to give Jesus honor by making a saddle that he can sit on (cf. 2 Kgs 9:12-13). Ordinary pilgrims are on foot. Jesus takes the seated position of a dignitary (C. Schneider in *TDNT* 3. 441-43). Matt 21:4-5 quotes Zech 9:9, which stresses the meekness of a king who comes into Jerusalem on a colt, the foal of a donkey (cf. the claimed intention of Mephibosheth to ride on a donkey in accompanying King David as a "servant" to him [2 Sam 19:27(26)], and contrast the mule ridden by a king or royal claimant [2 Sam 18:9; 1 Kgs 1:33-48]). But Mark is interested in Jesus' dignity, not in his meekness, in Jesus' divine sonship, not in his kingship; so he does not quote Zech 9:9. He does not even make clear that the colt is a humble young donkey rather than a young horse, a steed fitter for the sort of figure Jesus cuts in this gospel (cf. Rev 19:11; *m. Sanh.* 2:5; and the words of King Shapur to Samuel in *b. Sanh.* 98a). In fact, though in Palestinian and Egyptian Greek πῶλος might mean a donkey colt, it would do so by translation of a Hebrew word carrying that meaning or by contextual qualification (as, e.g., in BGU 373. 7, where ὄνον, "donkey," immediately precedes and qualifies πῶλον μιϰρόν, "little colt"; *PLille* 8. 8-9, where ϰαὶ ὄνους θηλείας β, "and two female donkeys," determines that the immediately following ϰαὶ πώλους β means "and two donkey foals"; and *Geopon.* 16.21.6, where τοὺς τῶν ὄνων πώλους, "the colts of the donkeys," contrasts with the absolute use of πῶλος for horses' colts in 16.1.8-13). Otherwise and in the Roman setting of Mark and his audience, πῶλος means a young male horse (cf. BAGD s.v. πῶλος). The historical present tense of ἐπιβάλλουσιν, "they throw on," accentuates the honorific gesture of making a saddle out of garments.

Further honor accrues to Jesus in the spreading of garments in the road (again cf. 2 Kgs 9:12-13, but also Plut. *Cat. Min.* 12.1 764C; *Acts Pil.* 1:2; Str-B 1. 844-45), in the large number of people who do so, in the cutting of straw from the fields by others (the spreading of this straw in the road to be inferred from the previously mentioned spreading of garments in the road), in the retinue of "the ones going ahead and the ones following" (cf. 1 Kgs 1:38-40 [though with David's mule rather than with what Mark's audience would take to be a young male horse]; Josephus *Ant.* 11.8.5 §§329-39; and the funeral processions described in Josephus *J.W.* 1.33.9 §§671-73; idem *Ant.* 7.1.6 §§40-41), and in their shouting an acclamation (cf. 1 Kgs 1:38-40; Josephus *Ant.* 16.2.1 §§12-15; idem *J.W.* 1.33.9 §670). Emphasizing this further honor are the forward positions of πολλοί, "many," and τὰ ἱμάτια αὐτῶν, "their garments," of ἄλλοι, "others," and στιβάδας, "straw," and the adversative δέ, "but," which distinguishes ἄλλοι as additional to πολλοί for a crowd of honorers that is very large indeed. Though Mark does not tell the mileage to Jerusalem (it is about two miles), the paving of the road from a point farther away than Bethphage and Bethany makes for a "red carpet" the astoundingness of whose length magnifies the VIP that Jesus is. Here, 2 Kgs 9:12-13 provides somewhat of a contrast by making garments the pavement of a mere staircase or the top thereof (also contrast the shorter distances in the passages cited in Str-B 1. 844-45). The doubling of the pavement with straw as well as with garments despite the fact that since Jesus is sitting on the colt instead of walking on foot he does not need any pavement at all adds to the astoundingness of its length. The crowd's accompanying him before and behind replaces his leading the people (10:32) now that he has paused to procure the colt and is sitting on him in the midst of the crowd, part of whom have proceeded forward in the meantime. (We may call them a "crowd" even though Mark does not use the word, for he speaks of them as "many" plus "others" [cf. "crowd" and "multitude" in the parr.].) The part of the crowd that goes before Jesus does so not to lead him but to lay the honorific pavement.

What the crowd shout glorifies Jesus by applying an OT blessing to him (Ps 118:25-26), by using a non-Septuagintal "Hosanna!" acclaiming him and the kingdom coming with him rather than a petitionary translation, "Save now," addressing God (cf. 2 Sam 14:4; 2 Kgs 6:26), by inserting into the quotation an association between Jesus as the one who comes in the name of the Lord and the coming kingdom "of our father David," by citing the repetition of "Hosanna!" with "in the highest [places]" added to make heaven itself ring with angelic acclamation for the coming of Jesus as God's means of bringing the kingdom, just as the earth is ringing with such acclamation (cf. Ps 148:1), and by chiastically putting "Hosanna!" at the extremes of what is shouted.

NOTES

R. H. Lightfoot (*Gospel Message* 45, n. *) suggests that to stress the present visit to Jerusalem, Mark omits earlier visits such as are described in John (passim) and seem to be implied in Matt 23:37 par. Luke 13:34, probably also in Mark 14:49 parr. and possibly in Mark 14:3 parr. More precisely, we might add, Mark is writing an apology for Jesus' crucifixion. To include earlier visits would detract from the visit that brings this apology to a climax.

The order Jerusalem–Bethphage–Bethany (v 1) does not betray topographical ignorance, for the succeeding narrative shows knowledge that Jerusalem is Jesus' destination, not an intermediate point on the way to it. See K. W. Clark in *IDB* 1. 396 for different suggested sites of Bethphage (Clark wrongly uses Mark 11:1 to locate the village southeast of Bethany) and G. Dalman, *SSW* 252-54; Str-B 1. 839-40; V. Eppstein in *ZNW* 55 (1964) 48-49 on Bethphage as the outermost limit of Greater Jerusalem. Since Bethphage will not reappear in this story or later, we have no reason to consider it a preparatory redactional insertion. Bethany will reappear later, however (vv 11, 12; 14:3); so Mark may insert it here by way of preparation, but perhaps also by way of identifying "the village opposite you" (v 2). Jerusalem and the Mount of Olives will also reappear (vv 11, 15, 27; 15:41 and 13:3; 14:26, respectively); so Mark may insert them, too, by way of preparation (cf. 10:32, 33).

The twoness and anonymity of the disciples sent to fetch the colt and the characteristically Jesuanic ὑπάγετε, "go," support the authenticity of vv 1-7. The reference to "a new colt" in Zech 9:9 LXX is sometimes thought to underlie and therefore deauthenticate Mark's "colt on which not even one of human beings has yet sat." But then we would have expected "a new colt" in Mark's text. Though he and his Hellenistic audience would read a larger meaning than "master" into κύριος, the lesser meaning satisfies the historical demands of the story; so κύριος does not argue for late fabrication of the finding of the colt.

E. A. Judge (in *New Documents Illustrating Early Christianity . . . published in 1976,* pp. 36-45, esp. 43) notes that ὁ κύριος αὐτοῦ (v 3) does not portray Jesus as the colt's true owner, still less as God, but as an unspecified yet legitimate claimant, the master of the colt for this occasion of need (cf. Roman requisitioning). With Jesus' requisitioning the colt, cf. Num 16:15; 1 Sam 8:16. J. D. M. Derrett (*Studies* 2. 167-77) speaks of a public pool of animals for requisitioning and borrowing and notes that disciples of rabbis sometimes carry out requisitioning in their masters' interests. If Jesus has Zech 9:9 in mind, however, he is acting more as a king than as a rabbi (though, as we will see, his kingship does not represent Marcan Christology). Requisitioning an animal from a public pool would eliminate any need to think of his having made a prior arrangement. But he is only now arriving in the vicinity of Jerusalem; so prior arrangement is unlikely anyway. It would undermine Mark's theme of prediction and fulfilment.

E. Haenchen (376) argues that Jesus would not choose an unbroken colt. Such a colt would be too difficult to ride. But the symbolic importance of unriddenness (see the foregoing comments) may outweigh the practical importance of docility. A leading of the mother alongside the colt might pacify him. On the possibility that a historical tradition underlies the mention of his mother in Matt 21:1-7, see E. F. F. Bishop, *Jesus of Palestine* 212; R. H. Gundry, *Use of the OT* 197-99; idem, *Matthew* 409; A. Frenz in *NovT* 13 (1971) 259-60; J. D. M. Derrett, *Studies* 2. 181 (though others see a misinterpretation of Zech 9:9 and J. Carmignac [in *ASTI* 7 (1968-69) 83-84] conjectures that the female donkey arose by partial dittography of ומצאתם, "and you will find," plus confusion of מ and ןו to produce אתון, "female donkey"). Furthermore, Derrett (op. cit. 2. 172-73) notes that the colt is not described as unbroken, only as unridden, and suggests that he may have been used to carrying non-human loads and therefore already docile enough to carry Jesus. For Mark, however, these possibilities may be ill-conceived. In view of Jesus' having done what other human beings cannot do (see esp. 1:27-28; 2:7; 4:41; 5:3-5, 15; 6:48-52), part of the point may lie in his mastering the colt.

V. Taylor (455) argues that since Mark uses κύριος, "master," for Jesus nowhere else, in v 3 it does not refer to Jesus, but to another man as owner of the colt. And since Jesus sends a message, not to the owner, but to anyone (τις) who challenges the disciples, the owner must be with Jesus. The owner rather than Jesus becomes the one who sends the colt back again. But κύριος does refer to Jesus in 1:3 with 1:7 and in 12:36. Moreover, an owner besides Jesus does not show up with him once the colt is brought; Jesus, not an owner besides him, turns out to need the colt; and it seems unlikely that an owner who lives in a village not yet reached by Jesus would already be with him, or would have known the time of his arrival so as to go out and meet him. The v.l. "and immediately he will send him [the colt] here" (so G W Ψ f¹ 700 *al* lat) makes the last clause in v 3 a prediction by Jesus to the disciples instead of a promise by the disciples to anyone who might challenge their loosing the colt. A prediction would suit Mark's emphasis, but the shift from present tense to future and the omission of "again" look like a scribal attempt to make the text easier (cf. Taylor [454], who speaks of the false scribal assumption that the clause describes the effect of Jesus' message). A shift in the opposite direction seems unlikely. Since Jesus seems to have in mind an outworking of Zech 9:9 (cf. *b. Sanh.* 98), making the disciples promise his return of the colt may be meant as an assurance that "he is righteous" (so Zech 9:9; cf. Num 16:15). But the lack of an allusion to or quotation of Zech 9:9 keeps this point from coming out in Mark's narrative.

Though πρὸς τὴν θύραν, "at the door" (v 4), occurred in narrative statements at 1:33; 2:2, those statements may have rested on tradition. Even if not, the better textual tradition in 11:4 (B L W Δ Θ Ψ f¹³ 565 892 Or^pt) lacks the definite article contained in 1:33; 2:2 (and in 11:4 א A C D f¹ Majority Text); and the resultant anarthrous phrase occurs in a direct quotation. These differences cast some doubt on the argument that Mark has made up v 4. The evidence concerning ἔξω, "outside" (also in v 4), is mixed. Elsewhere in Mark the word occurs in both narrative statements and direct and indirect quotations. Its frequency (ten times in Mark) favors neither redaction nor traditionality.

To describe the finding of the colt in vv 1-7 and the finding of the upper room in 14:12-16 as finding legends entails a Christological and ultimately philosophical judgment that rejects Jesus' predictive ability in favor of a folkloristic motif (cf. 1 Sam 10:1-13). Of course, a folkloristic motif may arise out of real life experiences; and such experiences are no less real for engendering and matching a folkloristic motif. Though often cited as a parallel, Ael. Arist. *Or.* 49.45 contrasts with the present story of finding in that the searcher is not told where the objects of his search are to be found; rather, the owner of those objects is told to keep them for the searcher — more a story of providence than of finding.

At the textual level, the parallel with rabbis' riding donkeys, disciples following behind (cf. G. Kittel in *TDNT* 1. 213), is weakened not only by Mark's not specifying a donkey colt and thereby leaving πῶλον to be understood as a young male horse (see the foregoing comments) but also by the crowd and their preceding as well as following Jesus. The Palestinian setting and the probability of Jesus' intending to carry out Zech 9:9 favor a donkey colt in the event itself, however. So at the historical level, the rabbinic parallel creeps back in.

On the grounds that an emphasis on Jesus' prediction and its fulfilment would be anticlimatic after the much more important passion predictions and that in vv 4ff. the repetition of phraseology occurring first in vv 2-3 differs from the summarizing statement of fulfilment at 14:16a, occurring in the comparable passage 14:13-16, J. D. Crossan (in *SBL 1972 Proceedings* 1. 22-24 and in *BR* 17 [1972] 35-37) denies the present emphasis on fulfilment of Jesus' prediction and hypothesizes that the repetition in vv 4ff. replaces an original quotation of Zech 9:9 with an emphasis on the disciples' obedience. But a summarizing statement is not the only way to emphasize fulfilment of prediction, and the comments have noted that vv 4ff. do not repeat the phraseology of vv 2-3 so much as they add to it — the disciples find a colt tied *"to a door on the street,"* not just "immediately"; they loose him and are challenged by *"some of the ones standing there,"* not only by "someone"; the challengers ask what they are doing by *"loosing the colt,"* not merely, "Why are you doing this?"; the disciples bring the colt *"to Jesus and they put their garments on him* [the colt] *and he sat on him"* (italics for additions); plus the paving of the road and so on — all for the purpose of magnifying the fulfilment of Jesus' prediction. Small predictions and fulfilments cooperate rather than compete with the fulfilment of the passion predictions (besides 14:12-16, see also predictions plus fulfilments of the disciples' flight [14:27, 50], Peter's denials [14:30, 66-72], betrayal by one of the Twelve [14:18, 20-21, 43-46], and — though without fulfilment in the present text of Mark — Jesus' going ahead of the disciples into Galilee and their seeing him there [14:28; 16:7]). The disciples obey Jesus in vv 4ff. — yes; but only the fulfilment of his prediction makes it possible for them to do so (as in 14:12-16, too).

The observation of T. A. Mohr (*Markus- und Johannespassion* 56) that at the festivals of Tabernacles and Dedication palm branches were carried, not strewn, is irrelevant in Mark; for Mark writes nothing about branches of any kind, much less about palm branches (contrast Matt 21:8; John 12:13; 2 Macc 10:6-7; *m. Sukk.* 3-4; *Tg. Esth II* 3:8). Especially because of its association with "fields," στιβάδας carries its usual meaning of straw, grass, reeds, and suchlike. Furthermore, the branches in Matt 21:8 and the palm branches in John 12:13 may represent late assimilation of the story to a custom practiced at the festivals of Tabernacles and Dedication (cf. R. H. Gundry, *Matthew* 410). If so, the strongest argument for dating the Triumphal Procession at those festivals rather than at Passover collapses (for a discussion of possible dates and the primary and secondary literature pertaining to the question, see B. A. Mastin in *NTS* 16 [1969-70] 76-82). To argue against authenticity by saying that a colt would have eaten the straw — therefore the colt, too, is unhistorical — entails questionable assumptions that a rider could not have kept the colt's head up and that a fabricator of the straw would have suffered from naivety about the eating habits of colts. The objection that a crowd would not have paved a road with their garments and straw for about two miles presumes too much knowledge of crowd behavior. The passages cited in Str-B 1. 844-45 (cf. S. T. Lachs, *Rabbinic Commentary*

344-45) deal in shorter distances, but distances long enough to keep us from rejecting out of hand the longer distance in the Triumphal Procession.

It would not make good sense to identify those who garmented the road with those who went ahead, and those who strawed it with those who followed; for the strawing would have had no purpose behind Jesus. To limit the acclaimers to "the little band with Jesus" (so A. Stock, *Call* 160) and suggest that they may have "unostentatiously dropped their garments in front of the ass . . . , while only a few quietly murmured 'Hosanna' " (so E. P. Sanders, *Jesus and Judaism* 306), may lessen the problem of Sanhedric and Roman inaction against a messianic demonstration, but it violates the wording and spirit of the text. Those who paved the road can hardly differ from those who acclaimed Jesus, yet vv 8-9 say that the pavers were "many" plus "others" and that the foregoers and followers "were shouting." "Hosanna!" is much more likely to have been shouted than murmured, anyway. To the extent that you scale down the paving and acclamation you create another problem: Why was the event remembered as significant enough to be handed down and dressed up in the tradition?

The first syllable of "Hosanna!" in both its Hebrew and Aramaic forms (הוֹשִׁיעָה and הוֹשַׁע) corresponds to the second syllable in the original form of Jesus' name יְהוֹשׁוּעַ. The עַשׁ- of "Hosanna" in its Aramaic form corresponds fairly closely to שׁוּעַ- in both the original form of Jesus' name and its late form יֵשׁוּעַ (cf. T. A. Mohr, *Markus- und Johannespassion* 59). This wordplay favors the acclamation of Jesus over an acclamation of God, also over praise of God for Jesus and for the kingdom coming with him (contrast Luke 19:37; *Did.* 10:6; but cf. Matt 21:9). The Semitic character of the wordplay pushes back the date of the tradition at this point. On the Aramaic form and for a pre-Jesuanic turning of "hosanna" from a petition to an acclamation, see J. A. Fitzmyer in *Tradition and Interpretation in the NT* 110-18; R. H. Gundry, *Use of the OT* 41-43. Though "in the highest [places]" points to heaven, Jesus may be acclaimed by angels up there as easily as God is acclaimed by human beings on earth (cf. Ps 148:7-14 with 148:1-6).

Originally, Ps 118:26a may have welcomed an ordinary pilgrim, but the shift from the third person singular in v 26a to the second person plural in v 26b favors a welcome of the Davidic king in v 26a (quoted in Mark 11:9) and of his people or troops in v 26b (unquoted in Mark 11:9-10). A messianic interpretation was given the passage in rabbinic and targumic literature (Str-B 1. 849-50; J. Jeremias, *Eucharistic Words* 257-62). The sitting of Jesus on a heretofore unridden colt, the paving of the road in front of Jesus, and the welcome to the coming kingdom of David give the welcome to Jesus a Davidic messianic overtone. Yet it probably goes too far to think that in and of itself ὁ ἐρχόμενος, "the one coming," has become a messianic title; for the context seems to cast a messianic light on the phrase rather than the phrase a messianic light on its context (cf. Matt 11:3 par. Luke 7:19; Matt 23:39 par. Luke 13:35; Matt 3:11; John 1:15, 27; 6:14; 11:27; 19:4; Heb 10:37; Dan 7:13; Mal 3:1, 23[4:5]). See Str-B 1. 845-49 on the use of Psalms 112–118 at Jewish festivals. At the Triumphal Procession the ones going ahead may have shouted the first hosanna and blessing, and the ones following may have antiphonally shouted the second blessing and hosanna. Or one group may have shouted the hosannas and the other the blessings (cf. J. A. Sanders in *Early Jewish and Christian Exegesis* 181-85 on antiphony in Psalm 118 and in early Jewish interpretation of it).

Both here and in Ps 118:26a we might construe "in [the] name of [the] Lord" with "blessed." Favoring this construal in Ps 118:26a are the origination of the blessing "from the house of the Lord" in the parallel stich Ps 118:26b and the instruction in Num 6:22-26 that priests are to bless Israelites by saying, "The Lord bless you. . . ." Thus "in [the] name of [the] Lord" would refer to priestly authority to pronounce the Lord's blessing. Mark's omission of Ps 118:26b, the prominence of Jesus in Mark and possibly of a Davidic king in Ps 118, and the word order in both texts tend, however, toward construing "in [the] name of [the] Lord" with "the one coming." Then "in [the] name of [the] Lord" would mean "with authority to act on behalf of the Lord."

If an OT prophet can speak of the kingdom of the daughter of Jerusalem as coming and can put it in parallel with Yahweh's reigning on Mount Zion (Micah 4:7-8), if Jesus and the Pharisees can speak of God's kingdom as coming (Matt 6:10 par. Luke 11:2; Luke 17:20a), we have no good reason to deny the Jewishness and therefore the authenticity of the crowd's speaking of David's kingdom as coming, especially since according to Jewish thought God's kingdom will come in the form of David's kingdom. The argument that Jews would speak only of a coming *again* or *re*establishing of David's kingdom (so E. Lohmeyer 231-32) wrongly presumes a Jewish locution so stereotyped as to resist variation. Here, the description of David's kingdom as coming grows quite naturally out of the description of Jesus as coming. To describe David's kingdom as coming again or reestablished would spoil the parallelism.

Against the argument that "our father David" is un-Jewish according to *b. Ber.* 16b and therefore inauthentic, see Acts 4:25 and the contrary rabbinic evidence cited in Str-B 2. 26. The vagueness of the appeal to tannaitic authority in *b. Ber.* 16b (no names are cited), the less limited use of "father" in the immediately following period of the contrary evidence, and the very early date of Acts 4:25 (which is more Jewish than Christian) diminish the argumentative value of *b. Ber.* 16b. Luke, who writes for Gentiles, would hardly omit the phrase because of un-Jewishness. He omits it, rather, to make Jesus "the king" (cf. Luke 23:2, 3, 37, 38; Acts 17:7) and to make room for a borrowing from the nativity story: "in heaven peace, and glory in highest [places]" (cf. Luke 19:38 with Luke 2:14). Matthew transmutes "the coming kingdom of our father David" into "the Son of David" and advances its position to emphasize the Son-of-David Christology which characterizes his gospel (R. H. Gundry, *Matthew* 411). Therefore neither Luke nor Matthew gives evidence of considering "the coming kingdom of our father David" un-Jewish. A Christian formulation would probably have produced "the coming kingdom of the Son of David," on the order of "the kingdom of the Son of man" (so redactional passages in Matt 13:41; 16:28; 20:21; 25:31 with 25:34, 40; cf. Eph 5:5; Col 1:13; 2 Tim 4:1; Heb 1:8; Rev 11:15), or simply "the Son of David" (as in Matt 21:9) or "the king" (as in Luke 19:38) or "the king of Israel" (as in John 12:43). That in contrast with the crowds of the later gospels the crowd in Mark at most imply the Davidic kingship of Jesus exhibits a reserve that favors historically authentic tradition. Bartimaeus's calling Jesus "Son of David" on the way out of Jericho (10:47-48) could have triggered the crowd's reference to David's kingdom and their associating Jesus with it (cf. 12:35-37 and the later designations of Jesus as "the king of the Jews" [15:2, 9, 12, 18, 26] and "the king of Israel" [15:32]).

W. H. Kelber (*Kingdom* 94) argues for Marcan composition of vv 9-10 that "the Hosanna-frame . . . is reminiscent of the *euangelion*-frame in 1:14-15 [which he also takes to be composed by Mark]." But vv 9-10 do not exhibit a hosanna-frame so much as they exhibit chiasm ([a] "Hosanna! [b] Blessed. . . . [b'] Blessed. . . . [a'] Hosanna . . . !"), which does not characterize 1:14-15. Besides, framing and chiasm occur too commonly in a variety of materials to prove composition by Mark; and in 1:14-15 the frame is split between an editorial statement and a direct quotation, whereas in 11:9-10 the entire chiasm falls inside a direct quotation. That the blessing on the coming kingdom grows out of the preceding citation of Ps 118:25-26 need not point to Mark's composition. The crowd might just as easily be responsible. Kelber's treatment of "the coming kingdom of our father David" as a "wrong confession" that Mark puts on the lips of the acclaimers to expose its inadequacy depends largely on misinterpreting Bartimaeus's "Son of David" as evidence of Christological blindness (ibid. 94-97). Jesus' stopping to heal Bartimaeus and citing his faith did not seem critical of "Son of David." Quite the opposite! See also the comments and notes on 12:35-37.

Mark stresses Jesus' prediction, its fulfilment, and the acclamation of Jesus. One gets the impression, however, that it is not so much Jesus' messiahship as his divine sonship that occupies Mark. Certainly he accepts the messiahship. But it is another question whether the Triumphal Procession carries a messianic meaning for Jesus and the crowd — perhaps for neither of them, perhaps for Jesus but not for the crowd, perhaps for the crowd but not for Jesus, perhaps for both of them.

Since the crowd do not call Jesus "the Son of David" (as in Matt 21:9) or "the king" (as in Luke 19:38) or "the king of Israel" (as in John 12:13), one might think that they regard him only as a prophet who has been announcing the coming of God's kingdom, which they interpret as coming in the form of David's kingdom. But why then their acclaim of Jesus? A prophet is not a proper or likely object of acclaim. John the Baptizer was not acclaimed, and Elijah prepares *beforehand* (Mal 3:23[4:5]; cf. Mal 3:1; Mark 1:2-3 parr.; 9:11-13 par.; Matt 11:20 par. Luke 7:27). Why do the crowd set up a parallel between Jesus as coming and the kingdom of David as coming? By associating a coming Jesus with a coming kingdom of David they seem to think they are about to install Jesus as a Davidic king (though they may not have Zech 9:9 in mind, as Jesus does; for otherwise they would probably hail him as already their king, as in that OT text). His sitting while they walk and their paving the road before him link up with a more-than-prophetic, more-than-Elijahic messianic understanding.

Why then do the Jewish and Roman authorities not take action to stop the demonstration because of the political dangers it poses? We do not know, but plenty of possible answers present themselves. The demonstration may be over and done with before the authorities can stop it. An absence of their own from the crowd may make them unaware of the character of the demonstration, perhaps of the demonstration as such. The procession may halt before entrance into Jerusalem (cf. v 11 and see V. Mariadasan, *Le triomphe messianique* 1-56, esp. 17-18). By the time the authorities find out about the demonstration, the crowd may have dispersed of their own accord and thus made clear that they were not mounting an armed rebellion with Jesus at their head (cf. his cleansing the temple the next day rather than attacking the Romans, and the suggestion of C. F. D. Moule [86-87 and in *Jesus und Paulus* 248-49] that Jesus deliberately leads the procession into the temple, next door to the Roman garrison, to avoid a messianic uprising). The crowd accompanying him may not stand out among crowds of other pilgrims streaming into Jerusalem at the same time, all of them singing and shouting in a celebrative mood (cf. W. Harrington 176). Most of these possibilities can easily supplement each other. Though some defenders of the historicity of the story think it necessary to scale down or eliminate its messianism, the question why the authorities do not act to stop the procession in mid-course is not so damning as to cast serious doubt on historicity. Lack of historical imagination can distort critical judgment as badly as historical credulity can distort it.

The non-quotation of Zech 9:9 in Mark 11:1-10 supports the historicity of the Triumphal Procession, for derivation of the story from Zech 9:9 would probably have left quoted phrases, perhaps quoted statements as well. But we find none. This absence contrasts with later imposition of Zech 9:9 on the story (Matt 21:4-5; John 12:15; Clem. *Paed.* 1.5.15; cf. A. Suhl, *Funktion* 57-58). Similarly, the differences between being tied to a vine in Gen 49:10-11 and at a door outside on the street in Mark 11:4 and between the ruler's binding his colt in Gen 49:10-11 and Jesus' commanding the disciples to loose a colt in Mark 11:2 militate against derivation from Gen 49:10-11 (cf. C.-P. März, "*Siehe*" 139-40). Only much later do we find an imposition of Gen 49:10-11 on the story (Justin *1 Apol.* 32; Clem. *Paed.* 1.5.15). Hence, we should deny an association of the statement, "Blessed [is] the one coming in [the] name of [the] Lord," which derives from Ps 118:26, with the phrase "until Shiloh comes" (or whatever other translation is to be given Gen 49:10) and reject the conjectural emendation of Mark's ἐπὶ τοῦ ἀμφόδου, "on the street," to ἐπὶ τῆς ἀμπέλου, "on the vine" (so P.-L. Couchoud in *JTS* os 34 [1933] 126; E. Lohmeyer 230, n. 4). "At a door outside on the street" does not contradict itself, and its pleonasm typifies Mark's style.

David's fleeing Jerusalem by way of the Mount of Olives and weeping along with those who accompanied him differ so radically from the Triumphal Procession that we can hardly use 2 Sam 15:30 for background to Mark 11:1-10. It would be a tour de force to postulate that the Triumphal Procession is meant to reverse David's flight. Nor does Zech 14:4-5 provide any better background. It has to do with the capture of Jerusalem by the Gentile nations and the Lord's splitting the Mount of Olives to provide passage for a remnant of the Jerusalemites to escape — a far cry from anything in Mark 11:1-10. *Tg. Ket.* Cant 8:5 associates the resurrection with the Mount of Olives, and *Pesiq. R.* 115a associates the Shekinah with it. But Mark 11:1-10 does not even come close to the resurrection or the Shekinah. Hence, we should avoid using those passages either to interpret the Triumphal Procession or to explain the origin of the story concerning it (against E. Lohmeyer 229).

The Triumphal Procession will not come up at Jesus' trial, not because the incident did not take place or lacked messianic character, but because no armed rebellion came about. C. E. B. Cranfield (353) complains that Mark 11:11 makes "an incredibly quiet ending to a messianic demonstration." Quiet — yes, but not incredibly so; for the unarmed crowd are in no position to mount a rebellion, and Jesus has shown no desire to lead one. The *Jerusalemites'* calling Jesus "the prophet" in Matt 21:11 does not denude the *pilgrims'* acclamation of its messianic character, especially not in view of Matt 21:9, where the pilgrims call him "the Son of David." Besides, "the prophet" as well as "the Son of David" is redactional in origin (see R. H. Gundry, *Matthew* 411). The disciples' ignorance in John 12:16a is likewise redactional, nor can it mean even in Johannine terms that the disciples were ignorant of Jesus' messiahship; for they have known of that ever since John 1:41. Rather, they do not recognize till later that "these things were written about him" in the OT, as John explicitly indicates in 12:16b (see also vv 14-15). Hence, these parallels offer no argument against the messianic character of the Triumphal Procession.

Though Jesus does not speak messianically on this occasion, he does act messianically by carrying out Zech 9:9, to which Mark 11:1-10 has similarities despite a lack of quotational fragments or blocks (cf. *Gen. Rab.* 75.6). Backed up by his spectacularly impressive Galilean ministry, this action suffices to prompt a nearly messianic acclamation. Now that Jesus is about to die, and anticipates it, he has no reason to keep his messiahship hidden from the crowd. He will not keep it hidden from the Sanhedrin, either (14:61-62). They may fear a messianic revolt, but he knows better and would not accept a draft. Once in their clutches, he will not be able to lead a revolt anyway. Those who reject historicity at these points will need to do so on grounds other than historical incoherence.

Some of the passages often cited as parallel to Mark 11:7-10 are not entirely appropriate. Entering a citadel within Jerusalem to celebrate victory over enemies that have been holding the citadel (1 Macc 13:51) does not come very close to Mark 11:7-10. Nor does thanksgiving for the recapture and rededication of the temple (2 Macc 10:6-7). In neither of those celebrations does anyone play a role like the one Jesus plays in the Triumphal Procession. Josephus *J.W.* 2.13.5 §§261-63 par. idem *Ant.* 20.8.6 §§167-72 describes no procession from the Mount of Olives to Jerusalem, only a planned attack on Jerusalem by a false prophet who wanted to be king and said that at his command the walls of Jerusalem would fall down and provide entrance for the attack. Josephus *J.W.* 2.17.8-9 §§433-48 describes an entry, but no procession.

Among others, J. Gnilka (2. 114) argues for disunity of the pericope that in vv 8ff. the colt plays no more role. This argument limps. Now that disciples have fetched the colt and saddled it with their garments and now that Jesus is sitting on it, there is no need to mention it in the description of the procession. The difference between using garments for a saddle (v 7) and using them for a pavement (v 8) points to a difference between the disciples who have fetched the colt and the "many" who pave the road, not necessarily to an additional difference in origin between vv 2-7 and 8-11. The difference between κύριος as "master" in v 3 and κύριος as "Lord" in v 9 is due to shifts in speakers (from Jesus to the crowd) and in referents (from Jesus as master of the colt to the Lord in whose name Jesus comes). These shifts neither necessitate nor favor an additional shift from one source to another (cf. the shift in the reference of κύριος from Jesus in Rom 10:9, 12, 13 to God in Rom 11:2-3 — Rom 10:16 going either way and the passage as a whole hardly lending itself to source critical division). Other, more complicated source critical divisions of the pericope betray even greater insensitivity to narrative progression (see, e.g., the analyses of W. Schenk [*Passionsbericht* 166-75] and H. Patsch [in *ZTK* 68 (1971) 1-26], who see fused together two originally independent stories).

The interconnections of 11:1-10 with 10:46-52 lack depth and significance (against D. Catchpole in *Jesus and the Politics of His Day* 319-34; cf. J. Dupont in *RAT* 8 [1984] 166). "The road" in which many strew their garments is simply a continuation of the road going up to Jerusalem through Jericho (10:32, 46, 52). Bartimaeus called Jesus "the Son of David" (10:47-48), but the crowd do not. Instead, they refer to "our father David" (11:10); and theirs is an acclamation, whereas Bartimaeus's is a plea. He throws away his garment as useless (10:50), but they use their garments to pave the road (11:8). Jesus' pronouncement of salvation by faith (10:52) and his coming in the name of the Lord (11:9) do not match each other. Not as in 11:9, there is no acclamation of Jesus in 10:52; and not as in 10:52, following Jesus complements preceding him in 11:9.

Though 10:46-52 enjoys no privileged relation to 11:1-10, Jesus' preceding ministry, of which 10:46-52 forms a part, fits to a certain extent the pattern of victory followed by acclamation in triumphal procession into a city, especially a capital city, and into a temple there (cf. 1 Macc 5:52-53; Josephus *Ant.* 12.8.5 §§348-49; 13.11.1 §§304-6). Mark's Roman audience would think of Roman triumphal processions. Jesus' conquests of demons, disease, and death lead naturally to acclamation. But Mark stops short of taking the whole procession into Jerusalem and the temple (hence the present substitution of "Triumphal Procession" for the traditional "Triumphal Entry"; see the comments on v 11). The messianic overtones of the acclamation do not relate to Peter's confession of Jesus' messiahship in 8:27-30, because that confession was made in private, was commanded to be kept secret, and is therefore incapable of providing either a historical or a redactional basis for the public acclamation in 11:9-10.

A STRONG CURSE BY JESUS

11:11-14 (Matt 21:10-11, 17-19)

This pericope begins with Jesus' entering Jerusalem and then leaving it to go back to Bethany (v 11). Next, he hungers on the way back out from Bethany (v 12) but finds nothing except leaves on a fig tree to which he goes for food (v 13). Finally, he curses the fig tree (v 14).

11:11 *(Matt 21:10-11, 17)* Mark likes to start pericopes with indications of topographical movement. The two main verbs in v 11 give just such indications, but in v 12 a similar indication is subordinated in a genitive absolute to Jesus' hunger. The contrast in v 11 between εἰσῆλθεν εἰς, "he went into," and ἐξῆλθεν, "he went out of," recalls similar contrasts in 5:1-2; 10:46. Both of those started new pericopes. Now the focus of attention narrows down to Jesus; only he is said to enter Jerusalem and the temple (cf. Ps 24:7-10). All these factors add up to the conclusion that v 11 starts a new pericope rather than finishing off the previous one. Jesus' sitting on a colt and a crowd's acclamation of him brought the previous pericope to a climax outside Jerusalem. Now Mark narrates an uneventful entry by a private pilgrim, not a triumphal entry by a crowd-accompanied celebrity (cf. Luke 19:37-39 with 19:41, 45; John 12:12-19; contrast Matt 21:10, 14-17; and see V. Mariadasan, *Le triomphe messianique* 1-56, esp. 1-15). The statement that Jesus went into Jerusalem has only the purpose of setting the stage for departure to Bethany, and "into the temple and having looked around at all things" sets the stage for cleansing the temple back in Jerusalem the next day.

The asyndetic succession of two phrases beginning with εἰς, one with Jerusalem as its object ("into Jerusalem into the temple"), recalls the asyndetic succession of two phrases beginning with εἰς, one with Jerusalem as its object, at the start of the foregoing pericope (v 1). "Looking around at all things" signals Jesus' irritation (cf. 3:5, 34; 5:32; 10:23); for "all things" will turn out to be, or at least to include, the commercial traffic going on in the temple and passing through it (see vv 15-16). The lateness of the hour, emphasized by the forward position of ὀψίας ἤδη, "late already," tells why Jesus puts a stop to that traffic not till the next day. His going out "with the Twelve" to stay overnight in Bethany is a reminder of his prediction to them that in Jerusalem he will suffer and be killed (10:32-33). The mention of the Twelve has the purpose of recalling that prediction, the only one of the passion predictions to name Jerusalem and be directed to "the Twelve." The threat posed by Jerusalem makes Jesus cautious. He does not stay there overnight (cf. his praying for release from the fate that awaits him — 14:35-36, 39).

11:12-14 *(Matt 21:18-19)* The next day's exit from Bethany sets things moving again toward the cleansing of the temple. Jesus' getting hungry, seeing a leafy fig tree at a distance, coming to find, if possible, something on it that he might eat, finding nothing but leaves, and responding with the curse, "Never again may anyone eat fruit from you," set the stage for a fulfilment of the curse. The fulfilment will have taken place within twenty-four hours (cf. Mark's emphasis on Jesus' predictions and their fulfilments). "And his disciples were listening" prepares for Peter's remembering (v 21) and leaves no room for doubting the fulfilment once it has occurred. The linear character of ἤκουον, "were listening," contrasts with the simple aorist of εἶπεν, "he said," to emphasize that the disciples really did hear what they later see to have come to pass. Though "his disciples" may include more than the Twelve, and often does, here the phrase appears to describe only the Twelve (cf. v 11) as those who learn by listening ("disciple" meaning "learner").

"He hungered" tells why the fig tree caught Jesus' eye. "At a distance" tells why he did not immediately notice that the tree had nothing he could eat. "Having leaves" supplies the reason why despite the distance he went to the tree hoping he might find something to eat. This reason rules out the possibility of finding figs that had not ripened the last fall but had stayed on the tree through the winter and had now ripened. Not only is this phenomenon at best rare (cf. Arr. *Epict. Diss.* 3.24.86-87; Marc. Aurel. 11.33), but also "the presence of such figs . . . would in no way be signalled by the presence of such leaves as the Markan story indicates" (W. R. Telford, *Barren Temple* 4). Mark does not say that Jesus went to the tree in hope of finding "figs" or "fruit," i.e. ripe figs. Of course not. It was not the season for them, not even for the early figs that grow on the old wood of the tree and ripen in June, much less for the summer figs that grow on the new wood and ripen August–October. Jesus could hope to find only buds which form just before and as the tree leafs and for whose presence leaves might therefore excite a realistic hope. Εἰ, "if," plus the future indicative in εὑρήσει, "will find," and the illative ἄρα, "then," stress the realism of his hope. At maturity early figs are "very good" (Jer 24:2, 3, 5), but buds are of marginal edibility. People do eat them, however; and according to *m. Šeb.* 4:7, one may eat bread with them in the field (cf. Jesus' being out-of-doors) "after they have begun to glisten," i.e. after they have begun to mature, turning rosy. M.-J. Lagrange (293) denies their edibility as early as Passover; but B. W. Bacon (in *DCG* 1. 593) reports having found on March 1st olive-sized buds on a tree not even yet in leaf, and "boys sometimes nibble these buds" (see also W. M. Christie, *Palestine Calling* 118-20; E. F. F. Bishop, *Jesus of Palestine* 217; P. Carrington 237; and the observation of Lagrange himself [loc.cit.] that leaves appear as early as the end of March, especially on the east side of the Mount of Olives — in agreement with Christie [loc. cit.], who notes that the trees reach full leaf in a week). Mark's use of "something" rather than "figs" or "fruit" for what Jesus hoped to find fits the circumstances exactly. Indeed, the forward positions of τι, "something," and of ὁ . . . καιρός, "the season," stress that he did not hope to find "figs" or "fruit." His finding "nothing but leaves" fits the circumstance that the buds fall off before the real fruit appears (Christie, loc. cit.). Οὐδέν, "nothing" — also emphasized by its forward position and consequent separation from εἰ μὴ φύλλα, "but leaves" — prepares for a wordplay with μηδείς, "no one," in v 14. How then does the unseasonableness of *figs* explain why Jesus did not find *buds?* It does not, and the nonsense of thinking that it does shows that the γάρ-clause, "for the season was not of figs," takes two steps backward to explain why Jesus went to find "something" instead of "figs" or "fruit." Possibly in 12:12 and certainly in 16:4, too, γάρ-clauses will rationalize an item two steps back in the text (W. J. Cotter in *CBQ* 48 [1968] 62-66). The shoving of nothing-but-leaves ahead of the γάρ-clause puts a great amount of emphasis on Jesus' not finding anything to satisfy his hunger. This emphasis will make the audience of Mark sympathetic to Jesus' cursing the fig tree. "And answering" makes the curse a response to his not finding anything but leaves (cf. the comments on 9:5, 6; 12:35; 14:40, 48). "No longer forever" indicates the strength of the curse. The forward position of these words and of the phrase "from you" intensifies its strength. "May no one eat fruit" adds yet further strength in that the fig tree is not to bear fruit to maturity even though Jesus had not expected to find mature fruit. His expectation was reasonable; so the curse is appropriate. No buds now? Well, then, no fruit in June — or ever afterwards. The double negative of "no longer. . . . no one" (cf. 2:2; 5:3; 7:12; 9:8; 12:34; 14:25; 15:5) and the slight archaism in the optative of φάγοι, "may . . . eat," lend further weight to the curse (cf. J. A. L. Lee in *NovT* 27 [1985] 13-15). But the leaves of the tree make fulfilment of the curse unlikely, especially fulfilment before twenty-four hours have passed. All the more will such a fulfilment exhibit the power of Jesus' words (see vv 19-25).

NOTES

See the excursus on the chronology of Mark 11 just following the notes on vv 27-33. This excursus includes an examination of symbolic and eschatological interpretations of the fig tree. A. E. Harvey *(Jesus and the Constraints of History* 120-21) argues for the historicity of the Triumphal Entry (sic) from the oddity — indeed, the scandal — that Jesus enters Jerusalem ostentatiously on a colt rather than humbly on foot, as presupposed in *m. Ḥag.* 1:1; *b. Ḥag.* 6a and implied by *m. Ber.* 9:5. But v 11 does not say that Jesus entered Jerusalem and the temple on a colt. Surely he did not enter the temple on a colt. Since then both "into Jerusalem" and "into the temple" modify "he entered" without so much as an "and" between them, why should we think that he entered Jerusalem on a colt, either? His sending rather than riding the colt back (v 3) is easier to understand, in fact, if he dismounted before entry.

Jesus' looking around at "all things" in the temple need not include the sanctuary proper (ναός), for Mark's word (ἱερόν) may refer more generally to the precincts of the temple. In view of v 17 ("My house shall be called a house of prayer for all the nations"), Jesus may have been inspecting the temple to determine its fitness for praying on the part of all the nations (J. D. M. Derrett in *DownRev* 95 [1977] 79-88). On the other hand, unfitness for their praying may have struck him unexpectedly when he looked around. E. von Dobschütz (in *ZNW* 27 [1928] 197) says that Jesus did not cleanse the temple precipitously, but only after a night of reflection. Perhaps so, but nothing in the text speaks of reflection; and it is dangerous to psychoanalyze Jesus. Perhaps he fumed all night. He might have cleansed the temple immediately had evening not already fallen.

Since Jesus curses the fig tree on exit from Bethany, not from Bethphage (v 1), the curse is unrelated to the meaning of Bethphage, viz., "house of unripe figs." Hunger supplies the motive for Jesus' going a distance to find something edible. But the curse stems not merely from disappointment in failing to satisfy the hunger. A sense of wasted effort exacerbates the disappointment to the extent of eliciting a curse.

Some object that Jesus would not have hungered just after eating breakfast at the home of his hosts. But we do not know that he had eaten breakfast. In fact, eating early in the morning was not customary (E. F. F. Bishop, *Jesus of Palestine* 217). Maybe this was to be a first eating at the normal hour in mid-morning. Jesus may have left Bethany a little late, for Mark does not write "early in the morning" (πρωΐ), as he will do in v 20. Other possibilities exist (see W. R. Telford, *Barren Temple* 7-8; R. A. Cole 176). Because Jesus will take action, attention concentrates on his hunger whether or not the disciples are hungry. Since Mark denies hunger on the part of the disciples no more than he affirms it, there is no disparity with Jesus' hunger to provide an argument against the historicity of the cursing that stems from his hunger.

J. C. Meagher *(Clumsy Construction* 65-66) criticizes Mark for dulling the climactic "nothing but leaves" with an earlier, trivial mention of leaves. This criticism undervalues the reason for an earlier mention, viz., the need to explain why Jesus went to the fig tree despite its distance — not a trivial point. It also misses the emphasis in the second mention:

"*nothing* but leaves." If anything, the progression from leaves to nothing but leaves adds to a sense of climax.

To support the hypothesis that in v 13c "for it was not the season of figs" is a gloss, M. Trautmann (*Zeichenhafte Handlungen* 341-45) argues that Matthew would not have omitted the explanation, because he treats the story as only a miracle, not as a symbol. On the contrary, Matthew treats the story as a symbol and omits the explanation to leave the Jewish hierarchy in Jerusalem, whom he makes the fig tree represent, without excuse. He highlights their guilt regularly (R. H. Gundry, *Matthew* 415-17).

K. Romaniuk (in *ZNW* 66 [1975] 275-78) punctuates v 13c as a question: "For (γάρ) was it not the season of figs?" Since it is the Passover season in Mark yet that season is not the season of figs, this punctuation requires a supposition that in pre-Marcan tradition the story was set in the summer or fall. But γάρ-clauses seem to characterize the latest level of Mark's text; so the necessity of resorting to pre-Marcan tradition casts doubt on the interrogative punctuation. Furthermore, under this punctuation γάρ cannot take its usual meaning "for," because its being the season of figs does not explain why the tree has nothing but leaves. It would not even explain why the tree has leaves, for leaves appear long before the figs ripen.

The fig tree's being in leaf and Jesus' hoping to find on it something edible though immature rule out the season of Rededication (December). Its not being the season of figs rules out also the season of Tabernacles (September–October). The season of Passover meets all these qualifications and fits the chronology of Mark 11–16 (see esp. 14:1-2, 12-16).

A large number of hypotheses rest on the mistaken supposition that the story does not make horticultural sense. According to these hypotheses, the text of the story has suffered miscopying, glosses have crept in, the seasonal setting has undergone a redactional change, the story developed around a misunderstood statement of Jesus, arose as an aetiological legend explaining a naturally withered fig tree, derived midrashically, haggadically from the OT, transmuted the parable of Luke 13:6-9 into a supposedly historical event, or used horticultural nonsense to signal symbolism (for a critical survey, see W. R. Telford, *Barren Temple* 1-38). The issue of historicity eventually devolves on the philosophical question of miracles, for horticultural and various kinds of critical reasons to deny historicity dissolve in the test tube.

W. L. Lane (400-401) thinks it "important to stress . . . that neither his [Jesus'] hunger nor his disappointment in the failure to find fruit [sic — rather, 'something'] is cited as the ground of the pronouncement in verse 14 [the curse]." But what other meaning should we attach to ἀποκριθείς? The tree has "spoken" to Jesus by failing to provide anything but inedible leaves. He "answers" with a curse. The use of ἀποκριθείς for his response to a tree is too striking to be discounted as meaninglessly stereotyped. Cf. the comments on 9:5.

We should guard against allowing modern sympathy toward plant life and unsympathy toward cursing to influence our estimate of what Jesus meek and mild could or would not do. His making the cursing and withering of the fig tree represent the power of faith (vv 22-23) will cast doubt on interpretations that would absolve him of cursing an innocent plant out of displeasure.

J. Jeremias (*NT Theology* 1. 87-88, 132) and H.-W. Bartsch (in *ZNW* 53 [1962] 258) think that Mark's optative φάγοι, which expresses a wish, mistranslates an Aramaic imperfect, which carried a prophetic prediction, as in Matt 21:19. But an Aramaic imperfect may express a wish. The interest of Mark in Jesus' predictive ability would probably prevent the change of a prediction into a wish. Matt 21:19 does not carry a prophetic prediction so much as a prohibition (μηκέτι ἐκ τοῦ καρποῦ γένηται εἰς τὸν αἰῶνα, "never again should fruit come from you"; except in B L, note the absence of οὐ μή for strong negation of the future). The very speaking of a prophetic prediction would contribute to fulfilment (L. Dürr, *Wertung*), this prediction — if it were a prediction — would convey a dire message, and Jesus would be speaking it in response to finding nothing but leaves where he had hoped to find something edible. The difference between such a power-packed, disappointment-induced prophecy of woe and an imprecatory wish seems negligible.

Extension of the predictive interpretation to mean that no one will ever again eat fruit from the fig tree because the end will come before the fruit is ripe, i.e. before about eight weeks have gone by, discounts the implication in other dominical sayings of a significant interval prior to the end and forgets that the end will bring unparalleled fruit-fulness. To say that no one will ever again eat fruit from the fig tree means that Jesus will die before its fruit ripens (so R. P. Martin, *Mark* 134) is to neglect the universality of "no one." To say that no one will eat fruit from the fig tree *until* the end is to deny the force of "never again." Εἰς τὸν αἰῶνα does not mean "up to but not including the age to come" (see BAG s.v. αἰών 1b against R. H. Hiers in *JBL* 87 [1968] 397-98). That meaning would require something like the phraseology in 14:25 (οὐκέτι οὐ μή . . . ἕως . . . ὅταν, "no longer by any means . . . until . . . when"; similarly, Luke 22:18; Matt 26:29; see H.-W. Bartsch in *ZNW* 53 [1962] 259 on the Aramaisms in οὐκέτι εἰς τὸν αἰῶνα, "never again" or, literally, "no longer for the age [i.e. forever]," and in "from you" with "eat").

THE AWE-INSPIRING TEACHING OF JESUS AT HIS CLEANSING OF THE TEMPLE

11:15-18 (Matt 21:12-16; Luke 19:45-48; John 2:13-22)

In this short pericope Jesus reenters Jerusalem and the temple (v 15a; cf. v 11), cleanses the temple (vv 15b-16), and teaches (v 17). The crowd's astonishment at his teaching then causes the chief priests and scribes to fearfully plot his destruction (v 18).

In the statement, "And they come into Jerusalem," the historical present tense of ἔρχονται highlights Jerusalem as the place where Jesus' passion-and-res-urrection predictions will reach fulfilment (cf. the comments on 10:33, 46; 11:1, 11, the more modest aorist for entrance into Jerusalem at 11:11a probably being due to lack of time for anything more than looking around before leaving for the night). His "entering into the temple" implies that what he is about to do arises from what he saw when he looked around after "he entered . . . into the temple" late on the previous day (v 11). What he now does consists in a ferocious exercise of authority and power: throwing out the sellers and buyers, overturning the moneychangers' tables and the dovesellers' seats, not allowing anyone to carry a vessel through the temple, and teaching the sellers, buyers, and moneychangers with the use of OT texts, " 'My house shall be called a house of prayer for all the nations' [Isa 56:7], but you have made it 'a den of bandits' [Jer 7:11]." The chiastic pattern of (a) beginning to throw out (b) the sellers and buyers and (b') the tables and seats (a') overturning (see the Greek word order) dramatizes the cleansing. The further chiastic pattern in the statement, "My house [a] a house of prayer [b] will be called . . . , but you [b'] have made it [a'] a den of bandits," likewise adds force to Jesus' teaching, as do the strong ὑμεῖς plus an adversative δέ, "but you," and the associated shift from a future passive verb to a perfect active one. The succession of phrases featuring the temple — "into the temple," "in the temple," and "through the temple" — help tie together the first part of the pericope. As "into the temple" prepared for cleansing, so "in the temple" and "through the temple," which relate to the activities of the merchants and vessel-carriers, highlight the need for cleansing. Mark's use of ἐδίδασκεν, "he was teaching," alongside ἔλεγεν, "he was saying" (see also 4:2; 9:31; 12:35, 38), puts the emphasis on Jesus' exercise of authority in what he says as well as in what he does. Increasing this emphasis is the very awkwardness of Mark's dual verbal expression (contrast Matt 21:13; Luke 19:46-47). The relation of the present pericope to the cursing of the fig tree is one of parallelism in the verbal exercise of authority, then. The condemnatory teaching recalls the cursing. The use of the imperfect tense in οὐκ ἤφιεν . . . ἐδίδασκεν . . . ἔλεγεν after the aorist in ἤρξαντο ἐκβάλλειν . . . κατέστρεψεν means that Jesus was not allowing anyone to carry vessels through the temple and was teaching and speaking simultaneously with his beginning to throw out the sellers and buyers and with his overturning the tables of the dovesellers (so also the implication of the present tense in λέγων, "saying," at Luke 19:46 and probably of the historical present tense of λέγει, "he says," at Matt 21:13; see M. Zerwick, *Biblical Greek* §§275-76 — against the objection that after throwing out the traffickers addressed in v 17 Jesus could not have gathered an audience including them). The awkwardness of saying that "he was teaching" while throwing out traffickers and overturning tables shows the extent to which Mark goes to stress Jesus' exercise of didactic authority. Οὐ plus the indicative mood of γέγραπται in the question, "It's written, isn't it?" implies that it *is* written. Jesus is speaking and does not identify God as the speaker in the OT quotation (contrast 7:6-7 in relation to 7:8-9; 12:26, 36-37). Moreover, he has taken it on himself to cleanse the temple and will refuse to say that anyone, even God, gave him authority to cleanse it (vv 27-33). Yet again, though 14:58 par.; 15:29 par.; and John 2:19 differ with respect to who might destroy the temple, they agree that Jesus is the builder. In 11:17, therefore, "my house" probably means Jesus' house and carries this meaning for him as well as for Mark and his audience (cf. Matt 16:18).

The chief priests and the scribes are not the traffickers, but the hierarchs in charge of the temple (on the absence of the elders, see the excursus on the classes of the Sanhedrin right after the comments on 8:31-32a). Just as the disciples heard when Jesus cursed the fig tree (v 14), so now the chief priests and the scribes hear him condemn the traffickers (v 18). As they hear they plot how to destroy him. Mark says nothing about their meeting together to plot against him *after* they have heard (cf. 14:1-2; contrast 14:53, 55; and N.B. that in 12:12 the chief priests, scribes, and elders will seek to seize him *before* leaving him). Likewise they fear Jesus as they observe the crowd's astonishment. So strong is the effect of his teaching that hearing, plotting, and fearing run simultaneously with each other and with the crowd's being astonished. Seeking to destroy him sets going the fulfilment of his passion predictions (8:31; 9:12, 31; 10:33-34) and thus begins to revive emphasis on his predictive power. The prompting of the plot by fear of him confirms the strength of his exercise of authority (cf. 4:41; 5:15, 33; 6:20; 9:32; 10:32; 16:8). So also does the reason for fear of him, viz., that "all the crowd were astonished at his teaching" (πᾶς . . . ὁ ὄχλος ἐξεπλήσσετο ἐπὶ τῇ διδαχῇ αὐτοῦ). This statement recalls 1:22: "And they were astonished at his teaching [καὶ ἐξεπλήσσοντο ἐπὶ τῇ διδαχῇ αὐτοῦ], for he was teaching them as having authority and not as the scribes" (see also 1:27; 6:2). It also prepares for the hierarchs' fear of the crowd themselves — because of the crowd's being in awe and support of Jesus (11:32; 12:12, 37; 14:1-2) — and for the hierarchs' attempt to destroy his hold on the crowd (11:27-33). The infelicity of stringing together two γάρ-clauses in succession and the parallelism further created by the imperfect tense in both ἐφοβοῦντο, "they were fearing," and ἐξεπλήσσετο, "were astonished" (cf. a similar parallelism in v 32), put great weight on his power over both the hierarchs and the crowd. By attaching "all" to "the crowd" and putting the phrase before its verb (whereas a subject normally follows its verb in this gospel), Mark displays the effect of Jesus' didactic authority at its highest power (so also 2:13; 4:1; 9:15).

And so we have reached Mark's main point: the awe-inspiring power of Jesus' teaching, backed up as it is by his strong actions. He strikes fear even in the hearts of the hierarchs who are trying to destroy him. In fact, they are trying to destroy him *because* they fear him, *because* he has a powerful hold on the crowd. He will be crucified, then, not because of any weakness in him. Quite oppositely, because of his power! Furthermore, the power for which he will be crucified is a power that he exerts for the benefit of all the nations, Gentiles as well as Jews. He uses his power for the sake of Mark's audience, that is to say, and at great cost to himself. So for his crucifixion Jesus deserves honor and worship, not scorn and ridicule.

NOTES

The transliteration Ἰερουσαλήμ is close to ירושלם, "Jerusalem." The more distant transliteration Ἰεροσόλυμα arises by way of assimilation to Greek city-names beginning with ἱερ- to designate their bearers as locations of a temple (ἱερόν). Here (v 15) and elsewhere Mark uses the more distant transliteration to accommodate his Gentile audience and to designate Jerusalem as the location of the Jewish temple, for which he normally uses τὸ ἱερόν (nine times, including v 15, with only three exceptions in ὁ ναός for the sanctuary proper; D. Lührmann 187-88). But since Mark started using the more distant transliteration early on (see 3:8, 22; 7:1; 10:32, 33 for occurrences prior to Jesus' arrival in Jerusalem), since its first occurrence had to do with admirers of Jesus, and since Mark did not use τὸ ἱερόν till 11:11, we would go too far to say that the more distant transliteration has anticipated or connoted the cleansing of the temple and the controversies that are about to take place there.

See the excursus on the chronology of Mark 11 just following the notes on vv 27-33. This excursus includes an examination of symbolic and eschatological interpretations of the temple-cleansing vis-à-vis the cursing and withering of the fig tree. Since no ritual cleansing of the temple takes place — rather, a stopping of commercial traffic — we might consider speaking of disruption (cf. M. J. Borg, *Conflict* 171, 345, n. 42). But to speak of cleansing has become traditional; and in a non-ritual sense, cleansing describes Jesus' action well. Furthermore, disruption might seem to imply an intention to stop sacrificial worship. Not so. Stopping commercial traffic in the temple would only limit such traffic to markets outside the temple, and sacrificial worship would go on. By no means could pilgrims exchange their money and buy ritually clean animals and doves solely at the temple. Not till John 2:15 do we read that Jesus drove out sacrificial animals; so J. D. M. Derrett (in *DownRev* 95 [1977] 83-84) suggests that they were located elsewhere, only business deals for their purchase being made in the temple. He has to admit, however, that doves must have been sold there. See the further discussion below.

V. Taylor (461-62) and J. A. T. Robinson (in *Jesus and the Politics of His Day* 455-60) detail some reasons to reject Mark's late date for the temple-cleansing in favor of an early date, such as that in John 2:17-22 (cf. H. W. Hoehner, *Chronological Aspects* 38-43). Resisting these reasons is John's habit of antedating. He antedates the Ascension, the giving of the Spirit, the claims and recognition of Jesus to be the Christ and God's Son, the very existence of Jesus, etc.

The sellers sell sacrificial animals guaranteed to be clean to pilgrims who live too far away to bring their own and to locals who do not want to risk having their own animals declared unclean by priestly inspectors. The moneychangers give acceptable Tyrian currency for other currencies in order that worshipers may pay the temple tax and buy the sacrificial animals (*m. Šeqal.* 1:3; 4:7-8; 5:3-5 et passim). Doves are sold to worshipers who cannot afford animals (Lev 1:14; 5:7, 11; 12:6, 8; 14:22, 30; 15:14, 29; Luke 2:24). See J. Jeremias, *Jerusalem* 48-49, on rabbinic evidence for these activities. In part, the mishnaic materials discussed by V. Eppstein (in *ZNW* 55 [1964] 43-46, 56) and J. Liver (in *HTR* 56 [1963] 173-98) and summarized by W. L. Lane (405) relate to the temple tax, due two weeks before Passover, and to that extent should not determine our understanding of what is happening at Passover. J. Carmignac (in *ASTI* 7 [1968-69] 71) detects an underlying wordplay in שׁוּלחנות השׁוּלחנים, "the tables of the moneychangers."

That in cleansing the temple Jesus acts as a prophet, not as the Messiah, may or may not be true; for contemporary Judaism does not expect an eschatological prophet to cleanse and restore the temple (E. P. Sanders, *Jesus and Judaism* 89-90). In the OT, moreover, it was kings, not prophets, who cleansed and restored the temple (2 Kgs 12:2-17[1-16]; 23:1-7; cf. J. Jeremias, *Jesus als Weltvollender* 41-44); and the Messiah is a king who will "purge Jerusalem," where the temple is located (*Pss. Sol.* 17:30; see D. Runnells in *Spirit Within Structure* 15-37; N. Q. Hamilton in *JBL* 83 [1964] 370-72; cf. T. A. Mohr, *Markus- und Johannespassion* 96-98, for emphasis on covenantal renewal in cleansings of the temple). J. Roloff (*Kerygma* 94-95) argues that in vv 27-33 Jesus' appeal to the baptism of John, who was "truly a prophet" (v 32), demands an essential parallel that makes the temple-cleansing a prophetic act similar to John's baptism. Not necessarily. One could think, for example, of an argument from the less to the greater: if baptism by a prophet had God's authority behind it, much more does temple-cleansing by the messianic king. But if Jesus does act as a prophet rather than as the messianic king, no inferences are to be drawn damaging to his messiahship or consciousness thereof. On various occasions he acts and speaks also as a sage, God's Son, a healer, an exorcist, an apocalyptic figure. To act and speak as one of these is not to deny the other roles.

With καὶ οὐκ ἤφιεν, "and he was not allowing" (v 16), cf. esp. 1:34. Several possibilities exist for the carrying of vessels through the temple. (1) The general context of the temple makes one think of vessels used in cultic worship (so the meaning of σκεῦος a little more than a third of the time in the LXX). (2) The more specific context of selling, buying, and moneychanging suggests vessels used to carry money (so J. M. Ford in *Bib* 57 [1976] 249-53, with references to rabbinic literature). (3) Giving the fullest possible force to διά, "through" — first prefixed to the verb "carry" and then governing "the temple" — suggests vessels used to carry, not cultic materials or money from one point to another within the temple, but water by way of a short cut across the temple precincts when going between Ophel and the eastern suburbs of Jerusalem (so J. Jeremias, *NT Theology* 1. 145). One might broaden this third view to include the carrying of various sorts of merchandise.

The only other occurrence of σκεῦος in Mark has to do with ordinary vessels in a private home (3:27), and nearly two-thirds of occurrences in the LXX are non-cultic. Though the cultic interpretation may correspond to Jesus' intention and though Mark writes in awareness that his audience know little of Jewish cultic practice (see 7:2-4), he does not describe any of the commercial traffic as cultic. So although we know from other sources the cultic purpose of at least some of the commercial traffic, that purpose does not determine the meaning of Mark's text.

Whether or not it was cultic vessels that Jesus prohibited from being carried through the temple, the narrow prohibitive character of his action goes in the opposite direction from the broad allowance in Zech 14:20-21, according to which even common pots and pans will be so holy as to be used for sacrificial meat. Neither is Jesus retaining for sacred use common vessels that people brought into the temple with the intention of taking them out, as though the prohibition of carrying them through the temple means that people may bring them in but not take them out (C. Roth, *NovT* 4 [1960] 177-78); for Zech 14:20-21 does not indicate that the cooking pots of Jerusalem and Judah may not be taken from the temple once they have been brought in for boiling the sacrifices. If the further statement in Zechariah that "there will no longer be a trader in the house of Yahweh of hosts" means that traders will no longer be needed because "every cooking pot in Jerusalem and in Judah will be holy," then Jesus is not fulfilling Zech 14:20-21; for he is prohibiting the carrying of vessels through the temple. If the statement means that "there will no longer be a Canaanite in the house of Yahweh of hosts" because cultically impure people will be kept out, Jesus is still not fulfilling Zech 14:20-21; for he does or says nothing to keep out foreigners. Elsewhere, moreover, he disdains laws of cultic purity (1:41; 2:15-17; 5:25-34; 7:1-23). John 2:16 does not provide convincing evidence to the contrary, for there an allusion to Zech 14:21 is questionable (the LXX does not support it) and possibly redactional (to contrast the trade in sacrificial animals, which only John among the evangelists says that Jesus drives out, with the Baptist's designation of Jesus as "the Lamb of God that takes away the sin of the world" — so John 1:29, 36, again uniquely).

Nor does Mal 3:1 apply; for in Matt 11:10 par. Luke 7:27 Jesus applies that OT passage to John the Baptist, not to himself (cf. Mark 1:2); nor does he quote Mal 3:1 here, and his inspection of the temple on the previous day disagrees with the suddenness of coming in Mal 3:1 (W. M. Watty in *ExpTim* 93 [1981-82] 236). Josephus *Ag.Ap.* 2.8 §106 does not apply, either; for it has to do with a prohibition of carrying vessels into the holy place rather than with a prohibition of carrying vessels through the precincts of the temple. So also Jesus' prohibition of carrying vessels *through* the temple contrasts somewhat with the rabbinic prohibition of *entering* the temple mount with certain things (*m. Ber.* 9:5; *b. Ber.* 54a; 62b). The rabbinic passages which mention that prohibition also prohibit using the temple mount as a shortcut. This prohibition comes close to one understanding of Jesus' prohibition. His prohibition of carrying vessels through the temple need not contradict the rabbinic prohibition of taking a shortcut through the temple. It may rather include the activity for which a shortcut was being taken. With the violence of Jesus' action, cf. Num 25:6-12; Neh 13:8; Ps 106:28-31; Sir 45:23-24; 1 Macc 1:23-26; 2:54.

See R. H. Gundry, *Use of the OT* 19, on the OT texts which Jesus quotes in v 17. That the narrative in vv 15-16 moves to a saying in v 17 gives no ground to think that the saying comes out of thin air or from a separate tradition. The saying could hardly have circulated by itself, narratives often move to a climax in a saying, and explanatory words regularly accompany unusual gestures like Jesus' cleansing the temple (M. J. Borg, *Conflict* 173; cf. the comment of W. Schmithals [494] that without v 17 the narrative loses its crowning conclusion). "And he was teaching and he was saying to them" displays the interest of Mark in Jesus' exercise of didactic authority, but this fact does not undermine the originality of v 17. The tradition may have had only "he was saying" or "he said" (cf. the comments on 2:27). CD 9:5 (אין כתוב כי, "is it not written that") provides a Semitic substratum for Jesus' οὐ γέγραπται ὅτι (cf. also John 10:34). Editorial statements in Mark 1:35; 6:46 exhibit an interest in his praying. But no editorial statements exhibit a like interest in the praying of others; so we lack grounds for supposing that such an interest prompted Mark or someone before him to fabricate and ascribe to Jesus a saying about prayer by all nations. The meaning of Isa 56:7 MT, ". . . for all the peoples," suits Jesus' purpose; so Mark's agreement with the LXX in ". . . for all the nations" does not argue against authenticity. The argument that "the use of Isa. 56.7 with its reference to the Gentiles could only have become part of the pericope after the beginning of the Gentile mission" (E. Best, *Following Jesus* 217) overlooks that Gentiles missionized by Christians did not go to the temple in Jerusalem to pray, but that Gentiles converted to Judaism did. "All the nations" must include Gentiles but need not exclude Jews (cf. R. H. Gundry, *Matthew* 595-96).

To be *called* a house of prayer is to *be* a house of prayer (BAGD s.v. καλέω 1aδ; cf. Luke 19:45). J. Wellhausen (90) suggests that we should translate v 17 "by [not 'for'] all the nations" because Jesus, unlike Isa 56:7, stresses prayer rather than universality. G. D. Kilpatrick (in *Studies in the Gospels* 157) demurs, citing the infrequency of the dative of agent in the NT, but still avoids universality by translating v 17 with "in the eyes of all the nations." If Isaiah can speak universalistically, however (cf. 1 Kgs 8:41-43; Zech 14:16; Mal 1:11), why not Jesus as well, especially if he is borrowing from Isaiah (cf. Matt 8:11 par. Luke 13:29)? Moreover, the dative conforms to ל, "for," in the MT. Redactional reasons cause the omission of "for all the nations" in Matt 21:13; Luke 19:46 (see R. H. Gundry, *Matthew* 412-13; idem, *Use of the OT* 19-20, n. 5). There is no need to appeal to an oral tradition lacking the phrase and thereby indicating Mark's addition of it.

The emphatic ὑμεῖς, "you," makes a contrast with μου, "my," not with "all the nations." "Den of bandits" contrasts with "house of prayer." Emphasizing this contrast is the position of οἶκος προσευχῆς, "house of prayer," before κληθήσεται, "shall be called." The commercial traffic in the temple is limited to the outer court, but Mark makes no distinction between the outer court and the rest of the temple. So although Jesus clears the outer court to enable all the nations to use it as well as the rest of the temple, Mark is content with the holistic significance of Jesus' action (with this synecdochic use of τὸ ἱερόν, "the temple," for the outer court, cf. the reverse synecdochic use of τὸ ἱερόν in Acts 21:28 for the inner court).

The quotation of Jer 7:11 compares the traffickers' takeover to bandits' taking over a cave for refuge. Not as in Jer 7:11, however, the emphasis falls on take-over rather than on refuge. This emphasis and Jesus' throwing out the buyers as well as the sellers and moneychangers (contrast Luke 19:45) makes unnecessary both a close comparison of the sellers and moneychangers to bandits and an equation of the bandits with revolutionary Zealots, later called by the same term (see BAGD s.v. λῃστής 2). Even in Jer 7:11 the comparison to bandits goes fairly far afield to include oppression of aliens, orphans, and widows, idolatry, adultery, and perjury in addition to the more bandit-like crimes of theft and murder. In current usage λῃστῶν, "of bandits" (so also Jer 7:11 LXX), carries the very connotation of violence that the corresponding פרצים carries in Jer 7:11 MT. Ezek 18:10-18 proves that such violence can include swindling (see the following and F. Field, *Notes* 15).

It is often claimed that the sellers and moneychangers in the temple did not swindle pilgrims with exorbitantly high prices and rates of exchange. But even I. Abrahams, often cited for that claim, admits occasional abuses such as Jesus is attacking (*Studies* 1. 87); and the evidence for those abuses falsifies the short shrift usually given them (beginning with *m. Ker.* 1:7, see the many passages cited by C. A. Evans in *SBL 1989 Seminar Papers* 522-39; idem in *CBQ* 51 [1989] 256-64, with dependence on J. Jeremias, *Jerusalem* 49, 96-99, 195-98). Much of that evidence relates to the Jewish hierarchs, but the sellers and moneychangers work under their aegis. Naturally, then, it is "the chief priests and the scribes" who seek how to destroy Jesus (v 18), and "the chief priests and the scribes and the elders" who will challenge his authority to do "these things" (vv 27-28). The rapacity of the sellers and moneychangers heightens the outrage of their commercializing a house of prayer and contributes to the crowd's implied sympathy toward Jesus' counteraction and their stated admiration of his counterteaching. Heightening the rapacity, in turn, is its perpetration right within the temple-turned-den. Usually, as in Jer 7:11, bandits do their work outside and retreat to their den for refuge.

The distinction between the bandit-like traffickers and the chief priests and scribes does not imply an identification of the bandits with the Zealots in the first Jewish revolt, for the hierarchs will show up on the side of the traffickers (vv 27-33) whereas the Zealots and the hierarchs will fight against each other (Josephus *J.W.* 4.3.1ff. §§121ff.). M. J. Borg (*Conflict* 171-77) thinks that the temple is a den of bandits in that it is a center of resistance to foreign rule, bandits being rebels against Roman rule; and that the temple is a center of such resistance because it is the center of Israel's holiness. Thus Jesus wants to open the temple for unholy foreigners. But it is a long jump from merchants in the temple to a military establishment there. Not till a third of a century later will the temple turn into a center of violent resistance against the Romans.

It goes slightly too far to say that Mark understands Isa 56:7; Jer 7:11 as directed against the chief priests and the scribes, not just against the traffickers in the temple (so H. Anderson 266). Mark does not say that the chief priests and the scribes plot against Jesus because they perceive that he has addressed them, too (contrast 12:12), but because they fear Jesus on account of the crowd's astonishment at his teaching the traffickers. The politico-commercial reality of the hierarchs' sponsoring the traffickers lies just below the surface of the text.

According to V. Eppstein (in *ZNW* 55 [1964] 42-58), the high priest Caiaphas has recently introduced commerce into the outer court of the temple to compete with four markets run by the Sanhedrin on the Mount of Olives (for which markets see *y. Ta'an.* 4:5). But then it is strange that the Sanhedrin should react by seeking to destroy Jesus and by challenging his authority (vv 18, 27-28). They should rather applaud his action. So Eppstein (op. cit. 57) is forced to say that the gospel tradition errs in having the chief priests question Jesus' authority. One would have thought that the chief priests took Caiaphas's side and that Eppstein should have spoken of error in respect to the Sanhedrin exclusive of the priestly hierarchs who control the temple. In any event, it is a weakness in his theory that he has to deny the attribution to the Sanhedrin of the challenge to Jesus' authority. See also C. A. Evans in *CBQ* 51 (1989) 265-67 for some speculativeness in Eppstein's theory, and the rest of ibid. 237-70 plus M. D. Hooker in *BJRL* 70 (1988) 7-19 for a defense of cleansing the temple as Jesus' purpose (against E. P. Sanders, *Jesus and Judaism* 61-76), though Evans' appeal to a Marcan attack on the temple lacks validity (see the following comments and notes on Mark 13-15).

In v 18 it is usually thought that the second γάϱ-clause gives the reason for the first one just as the first one gives the reason for the preceding statement (cf. 6:17-18; 9:6). In other words, just as the hierarchs seek to destroy Jesus because they fear him, so they fear him because of his hold on the crowd. The later shift from fearing Jesus (11:18) to fearing the crowd (11:32; 12:12; 14:1-2) favors this view. But we should at least mention the possibility that the two γάϱ-clauses give two independent reasons for the hierarchs' seeking to destroy him: (1) their fear of him because he has stopped the temple traffic, over which they have heretofore had control; (2) the popularity of Jesus with the crowd, over whom the hierarchs have likewise had control till now (see 8:35-39; 9:39-41 for other γάϱ-clauses probably in coordinate rather than subordinate relation to each other).

Those who deny historicity argue that one man could not have stopped the commercial traffic, that the disciples are not said to have helped Jesus, that stopping the traffic would have caused Jesus' arrest by the temple police or by the Roman garrison stationed next door at the Fortress of Antonia and patrolling the rooftops around the temple, and that stopping the traffic would also have come up as a charge against Jesus at his trial. Those who defend historicity are prone to posit exaggeration in Mark's narrative and to scale down the historical fact to a more or less symbolic protest confined, say, to pushing away a pair or two of sellers and buyers and to overturning a table or two and a chair or two, not enough to draw the immediate attention of police, soldiers, or Sanhedrin and not too difficult for one man to do. Not only does this scale-down go against Mark's text and emphasis on Jesus' power, however. One wonders whether the scale-down is necessary.

Why will Jesus' stopping the temple traffic not come up against him at his trial? Because it will have already come up against him in public debate, and he will have embarrassed those who challenged his authority (vv 27-33). Because the charge that he said he would destroy the temple and build another one in three days will overshadow his having cleansed the temple (14:57-58; 15:29). Because cleansing the temple and appealing to Scripture in the process do not constitute a crime, but an act of piety. He takes nothing, burns or destroys no records of indebtedness, does nothing revolutionary (N. Q. Hamiton in *JBL* 83 [1964] 371).

Why does Jesus' stopping the temple traffic not get him arrested on the spot? Because the crowd stand in admiration (v 18c)? Because the Sanhedrin fear him on account of the crowd's admiring him (v 18b)? Because disturbing the crowd by arresting him might incite a riot (14:1-2)? Because the Roman garrison could not care less whether the commercial traffic stops so long as the crowd are not incited to riot (contrast Acts 21:30-36 and see the statements of Josephus in *J.W.* 2.12.1 §224 that Roman soldiers patrolled the rooftops to prevent violent revolution [νεωτεϱίζοι] by a multitude). The passages usually cited for intervention always entail an uproar, armed rebellion, or pillaging on the part of hundreds or thousands of people. Often the interventions lack the speed required here for the antihistorical argument and sometimes have nothing to do with the temple, but with events hither and yon (see Josephus *J.W.* 1.33.2-3 §§648-55; 2.1.2-3 §§4-13; 2.4.2 §§57-59; 2.4.3 §§60-65; 2.13.5 §§261-63; idem *Ant.* 17.6.2-23 §§149-63; 17.9.3 §§213-18; 17.6.5 §§173-77; 17.10.7 §§278-84; 20.5.1 §§97-99; 20.8.6 §§169-72; Acts 21:30-36, 38). By contrast, Jesus acts alone in cleansing the temple, the crowd do not riot, and to all appearances Jesus accomplishes his purpose quickly.

Can Jesus have stopped the temple traffic without the help of his disciples? In modern times charismatic personalities have been known to do similar feats, sometimes to have had a similar effect even without effort (see, e.g., C. G. Finney, *Memoirs* 183-84; G. Le Bon, *Crowd* 133-59, esp. 151-55). In assessing historical possibilities we should not neglect the awe in which holy men like Jesus were and are held. Whatever moderns may think of stories concerning miracles and exorcisms performed by him, it is certain that he gained the reputation of a charismatic with supernatural powers. That is all that is necessary for this occasion. The presence of an admiring crowd can only have added political force to the charismatic actions he took against the temple traffic.

E. Haenchen (384) objects that the crowd would not have supported these actions because the temple traffic served their needs. But not only is there considerable evidence that they were charged exorbitantly high prices (see the foregoing notes), but also markets outside the temple served their needs well enough. Though one should allow for typically near eastern exaggeration, i.e. for a hyperbole in narrative form, the reasons for thinking of such in the present narrative lack conviction. According to the criterion of dissimilarity, the dissimilarity of Jesus' cleansing the temple to his other actions supports authenticity (M. Trautmann, *Zeichenhafte Handlungen* 116-18; against the objection of E. Haenchen [*Gott und Mensch* 97] that elsewhere Jesus does not take violent action). If Luke uses Mark's version (as is commonly thought), the shorter version of the temple-cleansing in Luke 19:45-46 does not show Mark's version to be an expanded *chreia* (against R. F. Hock and E. N. O'Neill, *Chreia* 1. 41).

THE STARTLING FULFILMENT OF JESUS' CURSE AND HIS STARTLING ANSWERS

11:19-25 (Matt 5:23; 6:5, 14-15; 21:19-22)

This pericope starts with Jesus' going outside Jerusalem when it becomes late (v 19) and proceeds with the sighting of the cursed fig tree in a withered state (v 20). Then come Peter's startled remark (v 21) and Jesus' startling comments on faith and cursing (vv 22-23), on faith and prayer (v 24), and on prayer and forgiveness (v 25).

11:19-21 *(Matt 21:19-20)* Again since Mark likes to start pericopes with indications of topographical movement and since he subordinates the indication of topographical movement in v 20 to seeing the fig tree withered, the main-clausal indication in v 19 of Jesus' departure from Jerusalem starts a new pericope (cf. the comments on v 11). Mark not only mentions Jesus' going outside Jerusalem, as is necessary for passing by the fig tree the next morning. He also makes it habitual with ὅταν plus an augmented tense (ἐγένετο) and with the imperfect tense of ἐξεπορεύοντο: "and whenever it became late, they would go out of the city" (cf. Luke 21:37). According to W. L. Lane (403, n. 34), "the particle ὅταν in Mark usually means 'when' and not 'whenever.'" But Mark's only other use of it with an augmented tense was clearly iterative and, as here, was followed by the imperfect tense: "and the unclean spirits, whenever they were seeing him, were falling before him and shouting, . . ." (3:11; cf. 11:25, where the action will again be iterative ["whenever you stand praying"] despite an unaugmented tense). J. H. Moulton (*Prolegomena* 248) complains that an iterative meaning in 11:19 "produces an awkward sequence" (cf. the adoption of the v.l. ὅτε, "when," for a single action by F. Field, *Notes* 35). Not so. The iterative meaning builds on an earlier exit from Jerusalem at eventide (v 11). Two such exits establish a pattern of movement to be assumed by the audience on future occasions till Mark gives different information (cf. 13:1-3; 14:12-16, 17).

The iterative meaning has caused Mark not only to forsake his usual genitive absolute ὀψίας γενομένης, "when evening came" (1:32; 4:35; 6:47; 14:17; 15:42), but also to exchange ὀψία for the adverb ὀψέ, "late," which prepares for the contrastive adverb πρωΐ, "early" (v 20); to exchange ἐξέρχομαι, "go out," which he never uses in the imperfect tense, for the imperfect ἐξεπορεύοντο, "they were going out," which prepares for παραπορευόμενοι, "going along" (v 20), and which he always uses for linear action of one kind or another (cf. 1:5; 6:11; 7:15, 19,

20, 21, 23; 10:17, 46; 13:1); and to exchange ἐκ, "out from," which denotes motion, for ἔξω, "outside," which denotes position (even when followed by a genitive object and construed with a verb of motion, with which it stresses the positional result of the motion — see 5:10; 8:23; 12:8). Like ὀψίας in the usual genitive absolute, ὀψέ takes a forward position to stress lateness. The exchange of "into Bethany" (v 11) for "outside the city" prepares for the open country in v 20 and fits Mark's purpose in citing the habitualness of exit from the city by Jesus and the Twelve, i.e. to explain why the chief priests and scribes do not seize Jesus in the city at night while his admiring crowd are sleeping. The first night that he and the Twelve later spend there the hierarchs will in fact seize him (see 14:17, 30, 37, 40, 41 with 14:43ff.; 15:1).

Since v 19 builds on v 11, the designation of Jesus and the Twelve as the subjects of going out in v 11 eliminates the need for a similar designation here. Otherwise, v 19 would read quite ambiguously (cf. the v.l. ἐξεπορεύετο, "*he* would go out," which seems to stem from forgetfulness of v 11 because of the chief priests, scribes, and crowd in v 18). Jesus' and the Twelve's seeing the fig tree already withered as they go along in the morning relates back to the Twelve's having heard him curse the fig tree (v 14c). "From [the] roots" implies a process that took place over the space of the intervening day, that contrasts with the much more usual wilting of leaves to avoid as much as possible direct exposure to sunlight and consequent loss of moisture, and that therefore struck first at the very source of the tree's life (cf. Hos 9:16 LXX; also Job 18:16; 31:12; Ezek 17:9; Plut. *Pomp.* 21; idem *Crass.* 11.7). Jesus' word is so powerful that the tree has no prospect of revival. Even the roots have dried up despite the soil's shielding them from the sun and surrounding them with moisture from the spring rains of the Passover season. Since the roots lie underground, invisible to the observers, Mark is writing as an omniscient narrator to emphasize the power of Jesus' curse. Peter remembers the curse (cf. 14:72) and speaks to Jesus (presumably on behalf of the Twelve, as in 8:29, considering the plural of "you" in 11:22-25; cf. 9:5). The historical present tense of λέγει, "says," emphasizes the fulfilment of Jesus' word as noted by Peter: "Rabbi [an honorific address, kept in the Aramaic for greater impressiveness — cf. 9:5 again], look! The fig tree that you cursed is withered!" The perfect tense of ἐξήρανται, "is withered," stresses the completion and permanence of the effect produced by Jesus' word; and "which you cursed" gives credit to his word. "The fig tree is withered" would have sufficed were not the emphasis falling on the power with which Jesus spoke the previous day. The absence of "from [the] roots" from Peter's remark confirms that Mark writes the phrase out of authorial omniscience to emphasize the fulfilment of Jesus' curse.

11:22-25 (*Matt 6:14-15; 21:21-22*) The present historical tense of λέγει, "says," emphasizes the startling statement of Jesus that follows. Mark is not so interested in the doctrines of faith, prayer, and forgiveness as in the power with which Jesus startles his listeners in commenting on these topics (as stated outright in v 18b; cf. the series of Jesus' teachings that upset standard views in chaps. 9–10). What could be more startling than his backing up a command to have faith in God with an "amen"-declaration that whoever does not doubt in his heart but believes that what he is saying is happening will indeed see his words come to pass — even a curse against the Mount of Olives ("this mountain") that it be taken up and thrown into the sea (the Dead Sea, visible from the Mount of Olives) — just as Jesus' words cursing the fig tree have come to pass? Doubly startling, since ancient people believe that mountains reach down to the very foundations of the earth (cf. the overturning of mountains at their "roots" in Job 28:9 with the conjunction of roots and mountain-removal in Mark 11:20-23)! Triply startling, in that the rabbis speak of uprooting mountains and moving them close together so that they knock and grind against each other, as in a mountain range (*b. Sanh.* 24a; *b. Soṭa* 9b); but Jesus speaks of a removal so complete that the mountain disappears in the depths of the sea! Asyndeton makes this "amen"-declaration so quadruply startling that a v.l. γάρ, "for," was inserted; and anacoluthon (a ὅς-clause dropped and picked up with αὐτῷ) makes the declaration quintuply startling. The futuristic present tense of γίνεται, underlined by the strength of the preceding adversative ἀλλά, "but," carries a note of certainty ("is as sure to happen as though it were already happening"; cf. A. T. Robertson, *Grammar* 880: "is starting to take place"; also N. M. Watson in *ExpTim* 77 [1966] 282-85 on the possibility of an underlying Aramaic participle used for the future tense). This note makes the declaration yet more startling (cf. 5:36; 9:23-24). And what could be more startling than Jesus' backing up the "amen"-declaration with the further declaration that "all things whatever that you ask for in prayer believe that you have received and they will be yours"? The present tense of the imperative πιστεύετε, "believe," carries weight (see the notes on 1:3 and the comments on 1:15). "On account of this I say to you" implies an argument from the less to the greater: if believing in God guarantees the effectiveness of a curse, believing in God to the extent of "such certitude that it [the favorable answer to a prayer request] is assumed to have been realised even before the request was made" (C. D. Marshall, *Faith* 171; cf. the "prophetic perfect" in Hebrew) much more guarantees the effectiveness of a prayer request. "All things whatever" is even more startling than a mountain's being taken up and thrown into the sea, and a forward position puts emphasis on the objective clause beginning with the phrase. "All things" would have been startling enough. The addition of "whatever" adds to the startlingness. And what could be more startling than Jesus' telling those who have anything against anyone to exercise forgiveness as they stand praying, rather than to pray for vindication and retribution, and to exercise forgiveness "in order that also your Father in heaven might forgive you your trespasses"? His forgiving you requires your forgiving others even though they are in the wrong! The requirement of forgiveness takes an emphatic present tense of the imperative in ἀφίετε (again cf. the notes on 1:3; contrast the unemphatic aorist imperative of this verb in Matt 6:12 par. Luke 11:4; Luke 17:3; 23:34).

NOTES

See the excursus on the chronology of Mark 11 just following the notes on vv 27-33. This excursus includes an examination of symbolic and eschatological interpretations of the withering of the fig tree. According to a suggestion of P. Carrington (240-41), since v 19 indicates that Jesus and the disciples habitually left Jerusalem in the evening and since v 20 lacks a reference to the next day, πρωΐ (v 20) may refer to a morning some days later and thereby both sharpen the point of Peter's remembering (v 21) and break down, or at least weaken, the chronology of three days that vv 12, 19-20 are otherwise supposed to present. This suggestion requires antedating the Triumphal Procession before Palm Sunday, and hence before the preceding Sabbath. If not, "the Passover and Unleavened Bread" would come sooner than "after two days" and thereby contradict 14:1. But in the absence of any indication that a day or two or several have intervened, πρωΐ more naturally means the next morning, just as "they come again into Jerusalem" (v 27) will give the impression of the next visit to that city.

The disciples see the fig tree withered, and Peter remembers the curse. But Mark does not say that the rest of the disciples have forgotten; so we have no right to read the motif of ignorance out of vv 20-21. Carrington's cross-references to Pss 37:3-4, 35-36; 90:6 (loc. cit.) suffer from featuring the wrong kind of tree (the green bay), or from featuring grass rather than any kind of tree, and from attributing witheredness to being cut down (not as here).

"It is Peter who interprets Jesus' words to the fig tree," notes S. E. Dowd (*Faith* 58), who then goes on to say that Mark interprets those words as a prayer by following up with Jesus' response on faith and prayer (so also ibid. 119-20). But Jesus' addressing the fig tree and its then withering justify Peter's interpretation at the expense of Dowd's. For Mark as for Jesus, prayer would have entailed an address to God. Addressing a mountain likewise rules out the description of v 23 as a prayer (against ibid. 64). The parallelism with v 24, which does speak of prayer, is more verbal than conceptual at that point.

Against historicity it is argued that this is the only destructive miracle said to have been performed by Jesus. Because the drowning of the pigs in 5:1-20 happened only incidentally to the exorcism of Legion, that story does not parallel the present one, where destruction forms the main point. In 4:39; 11:23, however, Jesus addresses impersonal objects for the purpose of doing away with them. Furthermore, he inherits a long tradition of destructive, punitive miracles (see Exod 7:14–12:30; 1 Kgs 13:1-5; 2 Kgs 1:4, 10, 12; 2:23-24; 5:27; Bel 23-27; cf. Acts 5:1-11; 13:6-12) and repeatedly pronounces woes on human beings, the very pronunciation of prophetic words like woes contributing to their fulfilment. Therefore his pronouncing a curse on a fig tree should come as no surprise. Besides, the fact that the fig tree belongs neither to the realm of human being nor to the animal kingdom but to the kingdom of plants makes the search for parallels and analogies unnecessary and the argument from any lack of parallels and analogies unconvincing. We possess no stories in which Jesus heals plants, nor do we know that his healing human beings would necessarily carry over to plants in need of healing. Thus the uniqueness of the present miracle makes a double edged argument: in accordance with the criterion of dissimilarity it could argue for authenticity rather than for fabrication.

But, it is countered, the destructiveness of this miracle is not unique. The miracle looks suspiciously like the destructive miracles which the apocryphal gospels make Jesus perform. To mention those miracles is only to highlight the uniqueness of the present miracle, however. They are destructive of human life, not of plant life. Jesus is said to have performed them as a boy, not as an adult. And the wide temporal gap between Mark, or pre-Marcan tradition, and the apocryphal gospels puts in serious doubt any lineage that would link the cursing of the fig tree with the destructive miracles narrated in the apocryphal gospels. The failure of the later canonical gospels to provide additional stories of destructive miracles makes the gap deep as well as wide.

Why does the fig tree wither from the roots (v 20) despite Jesus' having cursed it only with permanent unfruitfulness (v 14)? Because withering from the roots insures such unfruitfulness. A mere wilting of the leaves would have left open the possibility of revival and future fruitfulness. There is complementarity between unfruitfulness and withering, then; not disparity.

With v 22, cf. John 14:1 (but not Iambl. *VP* 138-39, which has to do with a disposition to believe anything that might lead to the divine, with God's ability to do anything without regard to the curse or prayer of a human being). "Whoever . . . believes" (v 23) and "believe that you have received" (v 24) undermine the interpretation of ἔχετε πίστιν θεοῦ as indicative with a subjective genitive, "You have God's faithfulness," rather than imperative with an objective genitive, "Have faith in God" (v 22; cf. Acts 3:16; Rom 3:22, 26; Gal 2:16 [bis]; 3:22; Eph 3:12; Phil 1:27; 3:9; Col 2:12; 2 Thess 2:13; Rev 14:12, some of whose objective genitives are disputed, though probably with insufficient reason; and Mark 10:27; 14:36 for differently worded Jesuanic expressions of confidence in God's omnipotence; see S. E. Dowd, *Prayer* 59-63, for fuller discussion). The view that combines a subjective genitive with an imperative (to paraphrase, "just as God has confidence that what God says will come to pass, so you have confidence that what you say will come to pass" [so H. C. Waetjen, *Reordering of Power* 184-85]) has against it the references to praying and asking and the combination of believing with receiving (v 24), all of which favor a belief in God's power and willingness to accomplish your curse and answer your prayer. And though God declares God's word reliable in order that others may have confidence in it (Isa 55:10-11), where else is God said to have confidence in that word? See the comments on 1:1 against Waetjen's argument that elsewhere Mark never uses an objective genitive. The Semitic cast of the present objective genitive and the Jewish rather than Christian tone of having faith in God (see J. Jeremias, *NT Theology* 1. 161-62) tend away from regarding the command in v 22 as a redactionally created summary of the following sayings.

According to J. Roloff (*Kerygma* 167-68), the command originally meant to have faith in God despite the eschatological judgment to come, which the withering of the fig tree represents. The command then substitutes for an interpretation of the withering such as the disciples wanted Jesus to give them. But v 21 recorded an exclamation, not a request for interpretation; and the weaknesses of symbolic interpretations will be exposed in the excursus on the chronology of Mark 11.

See S. E. Dowd, *Prayer* 96-103, for background on faith in God as faith in God's power. The suggestion of M. Black (*Aramaic Approach* 90-91) that we take v 22 as a conditional imperative, "if you have faith in God" (so the v.l. in ℵ D Θ *f*[13] 28 *al*), stumbles over the shift from the second person plural "you" in v 22 to the third person singular "whoever" in v 23 (see further arguments in B. M. Metzger, *Textual Commentary* ad loc.). C. A. Wanamaker (in *Studia Biblica 1978 II* 331) uses this change to argue for an original independence of v 23 from v 22, created redactionally to link the following with the preceding. But the second person plural appears also in the first clause of v 23 ("Amen I say to you"), which typifies Jesus' style of speech. The absence of this clause in Luke 17:6 would argue for its redactional addition only if we were dealing with two versions of the same saying (but see the following discussion). By modulating the shift from second person plural to third person singular, the clause makes vv 22 and 23 suit each other so well that we do not need to suppose an original independence of v 23. For other examples of the shift from second person plural to third person singular, both in addresses to the disciples and in addresses to outsiders, see 4:24-25; 7:14-15, 18-19; 9:39-42; 10:5-8, 14-15, 18, 29-30, 42-45. Not by a long way can all these be attributed to secondary combinations. The further argument of Wanamaker that having faith in God and believing that what you are saying is happening differ so markedly as to point to different origins — this argument overlooks the periphrases for God's name in the passive voice of "be lifted up" and "be thrown" and in the impersonality of the expression "it will be for him." These periphrases bring v 23 very close to having faith in God.

The saying about mountain-moving has something of a differently situated parallel in Matt 17:20 par. Luke 17:6 as well as a proper parallel in Matt 21:21. Matt 17:20 conflates its proper parallel Mark 9:29 with Mark 11:23 (R. H. Gundry, *Matthew* 352-53); so Luke 17:6 provides a better basis of comparison (and comes very close to the Q-saying as reconstructed by J. Zmijewski in *Begegnung mit dem Wort* 86-89). Luke 17:6 does not have the clause, "Amen I say to you" (Mark 11:23). The main differences remaining may be set out as a series of oppositions between Mark 11:23 and Luke 17:6, respectively: "whoever" versus "if you"; a mountain versus a sycamine tree; being lifted up and thrown versus being uprooted and planted; not doubting in one's heart but believing that what one is saying is coming to pass versus having faith like a mustard seed; "it ['what he is saying'] will be for him" versus "it [the sycamine tree] would have obeyed you"; and the order speaking–believing versus the order believing–speaking.

The number and width of these differences favor that on an earlier occasion Jesus used a nearby sycamine tree to speak about a beneficial use of faith and that on the present occasion he uses the Mount of Olives, over which he and his disciples are going along, to speak of a destructive use of faith (in line with the immediately preceding cursing and withering of the fig tree). Planting connotes a beneficial act and therefore suggests a planting in the fresh water Sea of Galilee, where even the notoriously thirsty sycamine tree can find plenty to drink (contrast Matthew's redaction in Matt 15:13; 17:20; see *m. B. Bat.* 2:11 and other rabbinic literature cited in Str-B 2. 234 on the deep- and wide-rooted search for water by the sycamine tree). Throwing connotes a destructive act (cf. its frequent use in relation to eternal punishment) and therefore suggests the tearing loose of one of what ancient people thought to be pillars that support the sky and hold in position the disc of the earth over subterranean waters, a tearing loose and throwing of stability itself into the watery depths of instability itself (cf. esp. Job 9:5-6). Mark 11:23 and Luke 17:6 move in opposite directions.

The Semitisms "amen," "whoever . . . his . . . for him" (i.e. casus pendens resumed by an unemphatic pronoun; see E. C. Maloney, *Semitic Interference* 86-90, 99-104), "be lifted up and be thrown" (passive periphrases for the divine name, as already noted), and "it will be for him" (an impersonal periphrasis for the divine name, again as already noted; see J. Jeremias, *NT Theology* 1. 10) make it likely that v 23 represents a different saying from that in Luke 17:6, not a saying redacted at a later Greek stage from a saying like that in Luke 17:6. We might consider the possibility of a Marcan redactional intrusion in "and does not doubt in his heart but believes that what he is saying is happening" (so, e.g., F. Hahn in *ZNW* 76 [1985] 153). V. Taylor (466-67) suspects that the preceding command to have faith in God (v 22) has caused "if you have faith like a grain of mustard" (Luke 17:6) to drop out and be replaced by the intrusion. But 1 Cor 13:2 relates "all faith" to removing mountains and seems to depend on a pre-Marcan version of Mark 11:23. Since "*all* faith" easily summarizes "and does not doubt in his heart but believes that what he says is happening," but stands opposed to faith *as small as a grain of mustard,* the comparatively very early date of 1 Cor 13:2 favors the originality of the middle part of Mark 11:23. It takes much more faith to remove a mountain than to replant a tree (cf. the foregoing note on the ancient conception of mountains). Only the conflation in Matt 17:20 eliminates this difference. Though not generally considered so early as 1 Cor 13:2, Jas 1:6-7 provides an even closer parallel to the middle part of Mark 11:23, and therefore support for its originality. Of course, we could think that 1 Cor 13:2; Jas 1:6-7 represent a pre-Marcan intrusion into the saying and that Mark 11:23 takes over this intrusion along with the rest. But then we are unnecessarily hypothesizing two pre-epistolary versions, one lacking the intrusion and the other having it. Apply Occam's razor and settle for a single version always having had the part about not doubting but believing. The great frequency of οὐ or μή (alone or in a compound) plus ἀλλά, "not . . . but," in reported sayings of Jesus supports the authenticity as well as the traditionality of that part (against J. D. Crossan, *In Fragments* 157-58, in dependence on F. Neirynck, *Duality* 90-94; see the concordance). (Why ἀμήν before λέγω ὑμῖν and ὅτι after it should be judged characteristically Marcan additions [so Crossan, loc. cit.] is mystifying [again see the concordance].) If the command in v 22 to have faith in God is discounted as redactional, omission of the middle part of v 23 ("and does not doubt" through "is happening") would leave a promise in the original version that whoever merely tells a mountain to be lifted up and thrown into the sea — faith or no faith, discipleship or no discipleship — will see his or her words come to pass. Jesus' call to faith and discipleship makes unlikely such an unqualified promise.

Doubting may carry the weak meaning of leaving a matter undecided; so F. C. Synge (in *ExpTim* 89 [1977-78] 203-5) is correct to note the inadequacy of "doubt" as a translation of διακρίνω, "discriminate," which here means to decide that mountain-moving is impossible. But "discriminate" does not at all spell out the present meaning, and "doubt" may carry the strong meaning of disbelief; so it is better to retain the translation "doubt" despite its inadequacy. Not doubting in the heart defines faith as such rather than describing an unusually large amount of faith.

We should not think of mountain-moving as a distinctively eschatological thaumaturgic ability. Jesus relates mountain-moving to faith, not to the times; and comparable rabbinic usage does not deal in eschatology. W. R. Telford (*Barren Temple* 115-16) uses *y. Taʻan.* 4.5 to argue differently; but though in this passage R. Akiba hails Bar Kokhba as the Messiah, R. Yohanan contradicts this identification and it is he, not R. Akiba, who says that Bar Kokhba's soldiers can uproot cedar trees. Thus we have no reason to think that this ability has taken on an eschatological cast. Nor should we introduce the rabbinic description of acute interpreters of the law as uprooters of mountains (Str-B 1. 759), for the element of faith establishes a non-legalistic framework for Jesus' saying (see Telford, op. cit. 110-16, for discussion of rabbinic sayings concerning the moving of mountains and the uprooting of trees).

Because of the command to have faith in God, the passive voice in "be lifted up and be thrown into the sea" means, "May God lift you up and throw you into the sea" (cf. the many OT passages cited by C. D. Marshall, *Faith* 166, nn. 2-3, though God's causing mountains to shake, break apart, and sink into the sea as the result of an earthquake, to smoke as the result of lightning-caused forest fires, to melt as an erosive effect of a rainstorm, and — metaphorically — to flatten out for safe and easy travel by returning exiles does not quite match lifting up a mountain and throwing it into the sea; and in particular the difference from metaphorically flattening a mountain as an eschatological activity of God [Isa 40:4; 49:11] undermines the eschatological interpretation of lifting up a mountain and throwing it into the sea [against Marshall, op. cit. 166]). Elsewhere Jesus does not speak of his own believing (cf. the notes on 9:23); so we have no reason to think of an implication that faith made his cursing of the fig tree effective. Because of the proverbial use of mountain-moving for doing something extremely difficult, v 23 provides a natural complement to the startling fulfilment of Jesus' curse. The addition of being lifted up and thrown into the sea makes the mountain-moving a destructive act. Its destructiveness makes the speaking to the mountain a curse, as much a curse as Jesus' speaking to the fig tree that no one should ever again eat fruit from it. The element of faith comes into this mountain-cursing because in themselves the disciples, unlike Jesus, lack the power to speak a mountain into the sea.

Jesus does not speak generically about a mountain or mountains, as in a proverb, but about "this mountain," i.e. the Mount of Olives, over which he and his disciples are currently going along and on which the now withered fig tree is located (cf. John 4:20-21, where "this mountain" [bis] refers to Mount Gerizim, at the foot of which Jesus and the woman of Samaria are conversing, and Zech 4:7, where a mountain stands for a particular difficulty; contrast 1 Cor 13:2, where it is unclear whether removing mountains is literal or figurative). As the demonstrative "this" destroys attempts to make "mountain" a proverbial figure of speech for difficulties in general but makes a literal reference to the Mount of Olives as a particular example of difficulty, so "the sea" can refer to the Dead Sea because on a clear day it is visible, though barely so, from the Mount of Olives. Since the Dead Sea is distant, the difference in phraseology between "this mountain" (here) and "the sea" (too far away to be modified even with "that") fits the present setting exactly. The conjunction of all these factors makes unlikely a bringing together of materials from originally different settings, for then we would have to suppose a redactor too clever by half.

The unlikelihood of originally different settings makes otiose the hypothesis that Mark or someone before him created vv 21-22a to link vv 22b-23 with the cursing and withering of the fig tree. With regard to the theory that Mark or someone before him fabricated not only vv 21-22a but also v 22b, and did so with the help of "if you have faith" in a Q-saying (Matt 17:20 par. Luke 17:6), we have to remind ourselves that the Q-saying goes back to an earlier time and different place and therefore that in Mark 11:22 Jesus himself could have drawn from it.

Though the present setting of v 23 looks original, the settings of vv 24 and 25 do not. The freewheeling character of oral discourse allows for a switch in subject matter from cursing to prayer as easily as textual redaction does, but it seems unlikely that Jesus (or an oral traditioner) would begin two sayings in succession with "I say to you." In v 24, "on account of this" looks like the replacement of an original "amen," as occurs in v 23, for a rationalistic but secondary linkage between the two sayings. The phrase is missing in the parallels Matt 21:22; John 16:23-24 (cf. John 14:13-14; 15:7, 16). In v 24 "you pray for and," which with "you ask for" makes a hendiadys for asking in prayer, looks like an addition by Mark to slake his thirst for duality and to link v 24 with "house of prayer" in v 17. This addition then attracts v 25, where praying is a traditional part of the saying. But it is *not* a good argument for this position that Matt 21:22 lacks "you pray for and," for Matthew does not omit it but changes it to the phrase "in prayer." Nor does the lack of the verb "pray" in the Johannine parallels make a good argument, for "pray" appears nowhere else in John, either, or in 1–3 John or Revelation. Matt 7:7 par. Luke 11:9 ("Ask and you will receive . . .") looks like a streamlined version of Mark 11:24 (cf. also Matt 18:19; Eph 3:20; 1 John 3:22; 5:14-15; Jas 1:5-7; Sir 7:10). The different synoptic settings agree with importation of the saying here.

Conversely, in both vv 23 and 24 "I say to you" looks traditional; for apart from the traditionality of each occurrence, a redactor would not likely create the awkwardness of having two successive sayings start with the same clause. Moreover, the traditionality of each occurrence helps explain the secondary attraction of the sayings to each other. For the same reason the element of believing looks traditional in both sayings. We have already seen reason to accept in v 23 the traditionality of not doubting but believing. The lack of "believe" in the Johannine parallels does not prove its untraditionality in v 24, for John reserves this verb for Christologically oriented belief (even when God, Moses, and Scripture are in view — against F. Hahn in *ZNW* 76 [1985] 162). Yet again the attraction of the sayings to each other implies the traditionality of "it will be for him" and "it will be for you." A redactor would not likely create the awkwardness of having two successive sayings end with the same idiom, already an awkward one in Greek because of its Semitic origin. If with J. D. Crossan (*In Fragments* 95-96, 157-58) we assign to Mark's redaction "Amen I say to you," "and doesn't doubt in his heart but believes that what he is saying is happening" in v 23, and in v 24 not only "you pray for and" but also "believe that" and

"and it will be for you," the question arises, What is left to attract these sayings to each other?

The meaning of v 24 is either conditional ("*if* you believe . . . , it will be for you") or consecutive ("believe . . . ; *then* it will be for you"). But the parataxis in "believe that you have received, *and* it will be for you," though not unknown in non-Semitic Greek (M. Reiser, *Syntax und Stil* 120-21), looks as though it rests on a Semitic substratum, especially since ἔσται ὑμῖν, "it will be for you," represents another Semitism (see the notes on v 23 concerning the impersonal periphrasis for the divine name in "it will be for him"). These probable Semitisms favor the authenticity of v 24 and disfavor that it was redactionally pieced together from sayings represented in Matt 5:23; 6:5, 14-15. Except for the Semitism in "it will be for you," it would be natural to take the singular verb ἔσται, "will be," as having its implied subject in the neuter plural πάντα ὅσα, "all things whatever," referred to in translation by "they," and to take the dative ὑμῖν as possessive, "yours."

The idea that originally the saying in v 24 had to do with the final renewal of the world (F. Hahn in *ZNW* 76 [1985] 166-67) does not suit the open-endedness of "all things whatever." The notion that the end-time renewal of the world will come for the asking also strikes a doubtful note. Because of Mark's liking for the present tense, J. K. Elliott (in *NT Textual Criticism* 59) regards the v.l. λαμβάνετε, "you are receiving" (A f^{13} Majority Text), in v 24 as original. But Mark likes to use the *historical* present, and this present tense is not historical. It also looks like an assimilation to the present tense of γίνεται, "is happening," in v 23. J. Ernst (332) considers Matt 21:22 more original than Mark 11:24, and Matt 6:14 more original than Mark 11:25; but see R. H. Gundry, *Matthew* 109-110, 418, for characteristically Matthean redaction.

The saying in v 25 seems most obviously imported from an originally different setting. It shares with the preceding only the element of prayer, and that only with v 24, where prayer was redactionally imported. Furthermore, the scattering of the parallels in widely different locations (Matt 5:23; 6:5, 14-15; 16:19; 18:18; Luke 6:37; John 20:23; cf. *1 Clem.* 13:2; Pol. *Phil.* 2:3; 6:2) again suits the importation of a floating saying. For standing in prayer, see also 1 Kgs 8:14, 22; Neh 9:4; Ps 134:1; Luke 18:11, 13; Matt 6:5; Str-B 2. 28; and for forgiving others as a prequisite to praying for one's own forgiveness, see not only Matt 6:12 par. Luke 11:4, but also Sir 28:2-12 (cf. Luke 17:3-4; Matt 5:23-24; 18:15-35; Eph 4:32; Col 3:12-13). S. E. Dowd (*Prayer* 124-26) notes that to interpret the command to forgive as excluding imprecatory prayer such as Jesus' cursing of the fig tree might encourage would be to imply an unlikely criticism of the cursing. Likewise, v 25 says that mutual forgiveness in the church is a precondition, not for effective prayer, but for God's forgiveness. On this last point, however, we might think either that "praying" refers back to praying for "all things whatever" (v 24) and by implication adds to faith as a condition of successful prayer a further condition, viz., God's forgiveness of the petitioners' trespasses — or, less likely because of the preceding prayer for "all things whatever," that "praying" in v 25 implies praying for God's forgiveness.

Unless we see a church catechism lying behind every set of Jesus' sayings addressed to the disciples with the plural "you," this pronoun does not prove that a church catechism lies behind vv 22-25. See H.-W. Kuhn, *Ältere Sammlungen* 39-43, for a survey and rejection of past work on the possibility that a pre-Marcan collection underlies not only these several verses but also large parts of 11:15–12:40. Ὁ πατὴρ ὑμῶν ὁ ἐν τοῖς οὐρανοῖς, "your Father in heaven" (v 25), looks Matthean (for it or an equivalent thereof occurs often in Matthew), but Luke 11:13 (ὁ πατὴρ ὁ ἐξ οὐρανοῦ, "the Father from heaven") par. Matt 7:11 shows its presence in Q and thereby supports its Jesuanic origin despite redactional multiplication in Matthew.

JESUS' OUTWITTING ALL THREE CLASSES OF THE SANHEDRIN

11:27–12:12 (Matt 21:23-27, 33-46; Luke 20:1-19)

The pericope on Jesus' authority to cleanse the temple falls into two halves, a dialogue between the Sanhedrin and Jesus (11:27-33) and a parable spoken by him to and about them (12:1-12). The first half opens with his and the disciples' return to Jerusalem (v 27a) and the Sanhedrin's questioning that authority (vv 27b-28). The middle part consists of his counter question concerning John's baptism (vv 29-30) and the Sanhedrin's intramural discussion of the dilemma posed them by Jesus' counter question (vv 31-32). Finally comes their weak answer (v 33a) and his strong refusal to answer (v 33b). In the second half, an editorial introduction (v 1a) leads to Jesus' parable of the tenant farmers (vv 1b-11), which subdivides into a man's establishing a vineyard, leasing it out, and leaving (v 1b-g), his sending of slaves to collect rent and their suffering various fates (vv 2-5), his sending his son and the son's fate (vv 6-8), the fate of the tenant farmers (v 9), and a citation from the OT (vv 10-11). Finally, the Sanhedrin retire because they fear the crowd more than they want to arrest Jesus for having exposed them with his parable (v 12). The question about Jesus' authority (11:27) and his refusal to answer (11:33) form an inclusion that frames the first half. "In parables" (12:1) and "the parable" (12:12) form an inclusion that frames the second half. And the Sanhedrin's coming (ἔρχονται — 11:27) and going away (ἀπῆλθον — 12:12) form an inclusion that frames the entire pericope. This last inclusion and the absence in 12:1 of any topographical movement such as Mark regularly notes at the start of pericopes disfavor a treatment of 11:27-33 and 12:1-12 as separate pericopes (see M. Y.-H. Lee, *Jesus und die jüdische Autorität* 65-74).

This confrontation starts a series of verbal victories that Jesus wins over his opponents, the last of whom turns into an admirer (see also 12:13-17, 18-27, 28-34). Having cleared the field of his opponents and won over one of them, Jesus will expose to a large crowd his opponents' ignorance (12:35-37) and their dangerousness and doom (12:38-40). Having earned the admiration of the crowd, he will display to the disciples his insight (12:41-44) and foresight (13:1-37). With this preparation, Mark's audience will take the following passion of Jesus as a backlash against his having defeated opponents dangerous to society as well as to himself, not as a penalty deserved by him for any danger that he posed to society.

11:27-28 *(Matt 21:23; Luke 20:1-2)* The historical present tense of ἔρχον-ται in the statement, "And they come again into Jerusalem," rivets attention on the city where Jesus' passion-and-resurrection predictions will be fulfilled (cf. the comments on 10:33, 46; 11:1, 15). More exactly, "again" marks the third entry into Jerusalem (cf. vv 11, 15). "They" is not indefinite, but refers to Jesus and his disciples (working backward, see vv 22, 21, and esp. v 19 in relation to vv 15a, 11-12). The statement that "as he [Jesus] was walking around in the temple the chief priests and the scribes and the elders come to him" presents another historical present tense in a second ἔρχονται, "come." This tense stresses the immediately following contest of authorities, the Sanhedrin's authority versus Jesus' authority. The forward position of ἐν τῷ ἱερῷ, "in the temple," shifts attention from Jerusalem to the temple and recalls the temple-cleansing, because the Sanhedrin are going to challenge Jesus' authority to have performed that action. That he will outwit all three classes of the Sanhedrin in meeting this challenge adds to the impressiveness of his verbal victory (cf. the excursus on the classes of the Sanhedrin just following the comments on 8:31-32a). Physical confrontation leads to verbal confrontation: "By what authority are you doing these things?" (cf. Acts 4:7). "What" (ποίᾳ) centers attention on the nature of the authority. One can think of prophetic, priestly, royal, and messianic possibilities (see M. Y.-H. Lee, *Jesus und die jüdische Autorität* 106-10, on the personal rather than abstract character of authority in Jewish thought). The pointing to things at hand with "these" combines with the present tense of "are doing" to indicate that Jesus continues to have stopped the commercial traffic in the temple. The plural number of ταῦτα, "these things," refers to the stoppages of selling, buying, money-changing, and transport; and the placement of this direct object ahead of its verb contains a barb, as if to say "of all things *these* things" (so also in the next question). "Or who gave this authority to you that you should be doing these things?" implies that in stopping the traffic Jesus has usurped the Sanhedrin's authority over the temple; for they have controlled that traffic — indeed, sponsored it. "Or who" shifts attention to the source of his authority, if he has any. The forward position of σοι, "to you," contains another barb, as if to say "of all people to *you*"; and the combination ταύτην . . . ταῦτα, "this [authority] . . . these things," separated only by a conjunction, makes a wordplay that sharpens this second question. The two questions are not designed to elicit information, however; for the Sanhedrin do not need to be told that Jesus lacks the kind of authority that rabbinic ordination confers, and they would not dream of suggesting that he got authority from God. They design their questions to embarrass Jesus, to leave him defenseless, to expose him as an imposter. He will counter question in kind and succeed where they fail.

11:29-32 *(Matt 21:24-26; Luke 20:3-6)* An adversative δέ, "but," plus the name of Jesus switches attention to him for an introduction of his counter question. Though it may mean no more than τινα, "a certain," the word ἕνα, "one," can carry emphasis (cf. E. C. Maloney, *Semitic Interference* 126-31). Here it contrasts the oneness of Jesus' question with the twoness of the questions asked him by the Sanhedrin. They have failed to embarrass him with two. He now succeeds in embarrassing them with one. In conjunction with ἐπερωτήσω, "I will ask," ἕνα λόγον means "one word" in the sense of "one question" (contrast the absence of "one" from "word" in Jer 38:14 MT [45:14 LXX]). The command "and answer me" and the promise "and I will tell you . . ." give a double example of parataxis, a phenomenon common in Mark, probably because of a strongly Aramaic substratum of tradition (cf. the characteristically Jewish substitution of "heaven" for "God" in the upcoming question). Jesus means, "If you answer me, then I will tell you by what authority I am doing these things" (cf. Matt 21:24). "By what authority . . ." alludes to the first of the two questions asked him (so also in v 33).

As shown especially by its repetition, the command to answer portrays him as taking charge. In striking contrast with the preceding double parataxis, the staccato-like question-cum-demand, "The baptism of John — from heaven was [it] or from human beings? Answer me," gives emphasis to his taking charge. The forward position of "the baptism of John" calls attention to a new subject. The alternatives "from heaven" and "from human beings" allude to the second question that the Sanhedrin asked Jesus. The placement of "from heaven" before "was" and thus away from the alternative "from human beings" hints at the correct but self-damaging answer that the Sanhedrin ought to give. So pointed is the dilemma posed by these alternatives, so insistent Jesus' demand for an answer — he now repeats the demand — that the Sanhedrin fall into disarray: they reason to themselves (i.e. among themselves in face-to-face consultation — see A. T. Robertson, *Grammar* 613), "If we should say, 'From heaven,' he will say, 'Why then didn't you believe him?' [cf. John's fulfilling scribal expectation according to 9:11-13]. But [if] we should say, 'From human beings — ' " (cf. John 3:27; Acts 5:38-39). The strength of the adversative ἀλλά, "but," and the following, striking ellipsis of ἐάν, "if," underline the danger of saying, "From human beings"; and Mark eagerly points out the quailing of the Sanhedrin before that possible answer: "they were fearing the crowd" (cf. 11:18; 12:12 and N.B. the implication that the crowd are listening). The anacoluthon and asyndeton in this editorial accusation, the intrusiveness of the accusation, the consequent transformation of the Sanhedrin's following rationale from a directly quoted apodosis into a further editorial remark, and the parallelism created by the imperfect tense of both ἐφοβοῦντο, "they were fearing," and εἶχον, "were holding," all give the accusation a highly dramatic effect. In his further editorial remark, the evangelist identifies the reason behind the Sanhedrin's fearing the crowd, viz., "all were holding John that he had really been a prophet." The forward position of ἅπαντες, "all," the hyperbaton by which "John," the proper subject of the "that"-clause, advances to become the direct object in the preceding clause, the use of ὄντως, "really," and the putting of ὄντως ahead of ὅτι, "that," which introduces the clause to which ὄντως belongs — these features of Mark's text stress the recognition of John's witness to Jesus by all except the Sanhedrin (cf. 1:5; 9:13; Matt 21:23, Luke 7:30, 33). So also the position of ἐξ οὐρανοῦ, "from heaven," before ἦν ἢ ἐξ ἀνθρώπων; "was it, or from human beings?" implies the truth of the answer, "From heaven," and therefore the truth of John's testimony. And what did John testify concerning Jesus? That one stronger than John was coming (1:7-8). Here he is, showing himself stronger than the Sanhedrin, too.

11:33 *(Matt 21:27; Luke 20:8)* The historical present tense of λέγουσιν, "they say," stresses the embarrassment evident in the Sanhedrin's answer, "We don't know." By the same token, the matching present historical tense of λέγω, "I say," plus the emphatic ἐγώ, "I," stresses Jesus' authority in refusing to answer them. To keep this refusal absolute, Mark avoids writing an ἀποκριθείς for Jesus' answering that would correspond to ἀποκριθέντες for the Sanhedrin's answering. On the other hand, "neither" implies that the Sanhedrin's answer was so weak that it did not qualify as a genuine answer to Jesus' question. Thus the dialogue ends with his overpowering them in theological debate (cf. the comments on 2:1–3:6). His not needing to answer their questions — he said that he *would* answer them if they answered his question, but they did not — proves him victorious. They lose face (a serious loss in near eastern culture). The shame to which he puts the very ones who will get him crucified cancels the shame of his crucifixion.

12:1a *(Matt 21:33a; Luke 20:9a)* For ἤρξατο, "he began," see the notes on 1:45. Though Jesus began to "speak to them in parables," only one parable follows. The reference to other parables, too, lets Mark's audience know that the polemic power of Jesus' parables exceeds the space available to record them in detail (see also the comments on 4:33-34; cf. John 20:30). Αὐτοῖς, "to them," takes a forward position to stress his addressing the parables to the Sanhedrin (cf. 11:27; 12:12) and thus to stress his overpowering the Sanhedrin with the parables (again see 12:12) just as he overpowered them in debate (see 11:33 with comments).

12:1b-g *(Matt 21:33b-g; Luke 20:9b-d)* The representative parable of the tenant farmers starts with phraseology borrowed largely from Isa 5:1-2: "A man *planted a vineyard and put a fence around* [it] *and dug a vat* [under the winepress] *and built a tower* and leased it [the vineyard] out to farmers and went on a journey" (italics for borrowed phraseology). In the absence of contrary evidence, this borrowing gives a clue to two parts of the parable's meaning: (1) the vineyard stands for the Jewish people ("the house of Israel and the men of Judah" according to Isa 5:7; cf. the emphatic forward position of Mark's ἀμπελῶνα, "vineyard," in contrast with the word order in Isa 5:2 MT LXX, Matthew, and Luke); (2) the man who plants the vineyard represents God ("Yahweh of hosts" — Isa 5:7; cf. the position of ἄνθρωπος, "a man," before its verb). To leave room for the rejected stone (λίθον) that becomes head of a corner (v 10 and Ps 118:22), Jesus omits the digging up and removal of stones (Isa 5:2). Isaiah stressed that the vineyard failed to bear good grapes despite the planter's lavishing a capital investment on it, i.e. that the people have failed to live righteously despite Yahweh's good treatment of them (5:3-4). Jesus shifts the emphasis by omitting the vine which is planted in the vineyard and expected to produce good grapes but bears sour ones instead (Isa 5:2) and by bringing in a new element, the tenant farmers, to stand for the Sanhedrin. The man's leasing the vineyard to tenant farmers and going away stands for God's putting his people under the charge of leaders such as the Sanhedrin. Thus the large capital investment in the vineyard now gives the reason why the man will repeatedly try to get something back for his investment, and even take the risk of sending his one, beloved son. No longer does the productivity of the vine stand in the center; rather, the behavior of those in charge of the vineyard.

12:2-5 *(Matt 21:34-36; Luke 20:10-12)* Jesus' having used phraseology from Isa 5:1-2 makes it likely that "some of the fruits" which the tenant farmers are supposed to pay as their rental fee stands for justice and righteousness (so Isa 5:7-12; cf. Hos 10:12-13; Amos 6:12; Matt 3:8, 10; 7:16-20; 12:33; Luke 3:8-9; 6:43-44; Rom 6:22; Gal 5:22-23; Eph 5:9; Phil 1:11; Heb 12:11; Jas 3:17-18; rabbinic quotations by F. Hauck in *TDNT* 3. 614-15, n. 4). Hence, the slaves whom the man sends (and whom Jesus puts into the parable as another element not found in Isaiah 5) probably represent prophets like Isaiah who tried to collect rent for God by calling his people to justice and righteousness (see Luke 7:33-35; 11:31-32 and esp. 6:23; 11:47-51; 13:34-35 all with parr.; Acts 7:52; 1 Thess 2:15; Heb 11:32-38; cf. the designation of OT prophets as the Lord's servants, i.e. slaves — 2 Kgs 9:7; 17:13, 23; 21:10; 24:2; Ezra 9:11; Jer 7:25; 25:4; 26:5; 29:19; 35:15; 44:4; Ezek 38:17; Dan 9:6, 10; Amos 3:7; Zech 1:6; 1QpHab 2:9; 7:5; the use of Jesus' verb ἀποστέλλω, "send," in the LXX of 4 Kgdms 17:13; 2 Chr 36:15-16; Jer 7:25; 25:4; 33:5; 42:15 for the Lord's sending [שׁלח] his prophets; and O. H. Steck, *Israel und das gewaltsame Geschick der Propheten* 73-74, 214-15). But emphasis does not fall on the fruits or on what they represent. It falls rather on the farmers and the slaves. Though "them" would have sufficed for back-references to "farmers" in v 1, "the farmers" appears twice in v 2 to put onus on the Sanhedrin, whom the farmers represent. The forward placement of the second back-reference, occurring as it does in connection with the owner's purpose to receive some fruits of the vineyard, increases the onus. So also does a contrastive chiasm in (a) the first slave's being sent off (b) to take some of the fruits over against (b') his being taken and (a') sent off empty (M. A. Tolbert, *Sowing the Gospel* 235-36). The fates inflicted by the farmers on the slaves illustrate rejections suffered by the OT prophets. The fates of the individually mentioned slaves also show increasing maltreatment: the first slave gets only a good beating (cf. 13:9) and an empty-handed send-off, but the second slave gets more dangerously hit on the head and shamefully disgraced. To let the accent fall on disgrace as such, Jesus does not define the means by which it is inflicted. Again we should note that disgrace, loss of face, counts as serious in near eastern culture (cf. the comments on 11:33 and D. Daube, *NTRJ* 301-3). Worst of all, the third slave gets killed (cf. *Vit. Proph.* 3:2, 18; 6:2; and the biblical and rabbinic literature cited in Str-B 1. 940-43; 3. 747, to which add Neh 9:26, 30; Heb 11:32-35). A progressive narrowing down of the verbal expressions which describe these crimes — from three (the first slave is taken, beaten, and sent away empty), to two (the second slave is hit on the head and disgraced), and finally to one (the third slave is killed) — highlights the increase in maltreatment (cf. H. Weder, *Gleichnisse Jesu* 148). The forward positions of κἀκεῖνον, "and that one" (v 4), ἄλλον, "another" (v 5), and the second κἀκεῖνον (v 5) highlight the victims of maltreatment. The addition of "many others," some of whom the tenant farmers beat and some of whom they kill — again the maltreatment goes from bad to worse — heaps further guilt on the tenant farmers (and through them on the Sanhedrin). In the middle of v 5 the ellipsis of "he sent" gives prominence to "many others." Also giving it prominence are the added combination οὓς μέν . . . οὓς δέ, "some . . . but others" (see the notes on 4:4 concerning μέν . . . δέ), and the failure of the associated δέροντες, "beating," and ἀποκτέννοντες, "killing," to have anything that they might modify. The prominence of "many others" stresses the inexcusability of the tenant farmers, i.e. of the Sanhedrin. The unrealism of a man's sending many other slaves after maltreatment and murder of the first three intensifies guilt and confirms an allusion to the OT prophets.

12:6-8 *(Matt 21:37-39; Luke 20:13-15a)* After a long string of καί's, two sudden cases of asyndeton in v 6a and v 6b emphasize the owner's having one more representative to send and his actually sending that one as last and despite the crimes committed on the many slaves he has sent before. The variant readings in the textual tradition show the force of these asyndeta. Jesus' audience expect the owner to send another slave and are surprised to hear instead that the owner sends his beloved son. But before learning that he has one more representative to send they were surprised already that he had sent so many slaves. By no means did they expect him to send another one. At that point, then (even in an originally shorter version of the parable conforming to the rhetorical law of three — see the following notes), the audience did not expect the owner to send anyone at all, but to go himself. So the first surprise came in his delaying to go himself and sending yet another. That up till now the audience have not even known of the existence of his son adds to the second surprise, that of sending a son rather than a slave. The son stands for Jesus (see 1:11 parr.; 13:32 par.; 14:61-62 parr.; Matt 11:25-27 par. Luke 10:21-22 for Jesus' self-consciousness of divine sonship; cf. 4QFlor 1:11; 1QSa 2:11-12 for pre-Christian use of "Son of God" in a messianic sense). Ἔτι ἕνα, "still one," indicates that the owner has run out of slaves. They are all injured or dead. Placement of ἔτι ἕνα before the verb delays appositional identification of the one remaining representative. This delay adds yet again to the surprise at a son rather than a slave. The absence of a definite article and of "his" concentrates attention on the son as such: that a father would risk a son adds pathos to surprise. Ἀγαπητόν, "beloved," deepens the pathos and echoes the statements of God the Father at Jesus' baptism (1:11) and transfiguration (9:7). The use of ἀγαπητός for יחיד, "only," in the LXX of Gen 22:2, 12, 16; Judg 11:34 Cod. A; Jer 6:26; Amos 8:10; Zech 12:10 adds the connotation of uniqueness to the primary meaning of belovedness (cf. the similarity between יחיד and ידיד, "beloved," also translated with ἀγαπητός in the LXX of the Psalms; and see the comments on 1:11). These elements of surprise and pathos help demonstrate the strength of God's demand on the Sanhedrin, whom the tenant farmers represent. The owner's saying that the tenant farmers will respect his son deepens the pathos yet further, sets the stage for their attempt to seize ownership of the vineyard by killing the sole heir (who therefore *has* to be an only son for the rest of the parable to work), and heightens the guilt incurred for the murder. Ἔσχατον, "last," suits the eschatological dimension of Jesus' ministry: he is God's last messenger.

"Those," an adversative δέ, "but," and another repetition of "the farmers" put the farmers at a contrary distance to stress the wickedness of their plot. This distance is emphasized by the pre-verbal positions of "those (the) farmers" and "to one another" (as πρὸς αὐτούς, [literally] "to themselves," ought to be translated in view of the following "let us"; see the word order of the Greek text). The asyndeton between "This is the heir" and "Hither! Let us kill him" and the present tense of the subjunctive ἀποκτείνωμεν, "let us kill," heighten the stress on wickedness (see S. E. Porter, *Verbal Aspect* 326, on the emphatic character of a present subjunctive). The law allows the son to act on behalf of his father by way of evicting the tenant farmers, by taking legal action against them for their failure to pay rent and for their crimes against his father's slaves, and by reclaiming the vineyard. On the other hand, the tenant farmers will be able to lay their own legal claim to the vineyard if they kill the son and the owner has died. Not that killing the son would legalize their claim, only that it would make possible a legal claim by right of possession. They would not think that by killing the son the inheritance will be theirs unless they also think that the owner has died. The very words "heir" and "inheritance" arise out of a mistaken deduction that the coming of the son signals the owner's death and the son's purpose to claim the vineyard (cf. the audience's aforementioned expectation that the owner will come himself rather than sending another slave, let alone his own only, beloved son). The mistakenness of the tenant farmers' deduction plus knowledge of that mistakenness — the audiences of Jesus and Mark know what the farmers do not know, viz., that the owner has *sent* the son — injects irony into the parable. The forward position of ἡμῶν, "ours," deepens the irony. How delusive the happy prospect which the farmers imagine for themselves!

The killing of the son by the tenant farmers may have been suggested by the bloodshed in Isa 5:7 as well as by Jesus' premonition of his own violent death (cf. 8:31; 9:12, 31; 10:33-34; 14:8, 21, 22-28, 32-42). Highlighting this crime is chiasm in (a) the owner's sending his son and (b) saying that the farmers will respect a son and of (b') their speaking murderously about the son and (a') now killing him (cf. H. Weder, *Gleichnisse Jesu* 154). Throwing the son out of the vineyard after killing him shows how utterly the farmers reject him: they do not even give his corpse a decent burial (cf. 1 Sam 17:44, 46; 2 Sam 21:1-14; 1 Kgs 14:11; 21:24; Isa 14:19-20; Jer 7:33; 16:4 and the seeming shamefulness of Jesus' crucifixion). Ἔξω, "outside," implies resistance to the son's exercise of authority within the vineyard, i.e. the Sanhedrin's resisting Jesus' exercise of authority among the Jewish people, particularly in driving the sellers and buyers out of the temple (see 11:15-18 with 11:27-33). The outrageousness and incredibility of the farmers' behavior heap all the more blame on the Sanhedrin.

12:9-12 *(Matt 21:40-46; Luke 20:15b-19)* The tension that has been mounting with each increase in the seriousness of the tenant farmers' crimes has reached the breaking point. So Jesus switches to a question: "What then will the owner of the vineyard do?" The question borrows phraseology from Isa 5:4-5 and the form of a rhetorical question from Isa 5:4, and draws Jesus' and Mark's audiences into the logic and justice of the owner's final, judgmental action (cf. the apologetic thrust of the question in Isa 5:4 and the ancient near eastern obligation of a family to seek blood vengeance for the killing of one of their own). The striking shift from one aorist indicative verb after another throughout vv 1-8 to verbs in the future tense suggests that we have in the owner's coming and destroying the farmers (not his destroying the vineyard, as in Isa 5:5-6) an anticipatory parallel to Jesus' predicting in chap. 13 the destruction of the temple, which will entail the destruction of the Sanhedrin centered there. Just as in Isa 5:7 the vineyard belongs to Yahweh, κύριος in the LXX, so the ἄνθρωπος, "man" in the sense of "human being" (v 1), has turned into the κύριος, "owner" — or, interpretatively speaking, "the Lord" (also κύριος) — to stress the man's right to destroy the farmers.

Since the story might have stopped with destruction, the owner's giving the vineyard to others has its own significance (cf. *Sipre* Deut 32:9 §312 [134b], cited in Str-B 1. 874m; Matt 8:11-12 par. Luke 13:28-29; Rom 11:17-24). It represents a transfer of leadership from the Sanhedrin to Jesus and his disciples. For elsewhere Jesus speaks of the Twelve as joining him in judging the twelve tribes of Israel (Matt 19:28 par. Luke 22:28-30; cf. the combination of "shepherds" and "David" in Jer 23:4-6), and right here he goes on to cite Ps 118:22-23 with respect to a stone which the builders rejected (very possibly the king of Israel, subject to messianic interpretation), but which the Lord has made "head of a corner." The anarthrousness of λίθον, "stone," and of κεφαλὴν γωνίας, "head of a corner," and casus pendens plus a resumptive οὗτος, "this," emphasize the shift from rejection to headship. This figure of speech implies a building the rest of which will be made up of Jesus' disciples just as he and they are "the others" to whom God gives the vineyard. Becoming "head of a corner" makes a wordplay with "hit on the head" (v 4) and compensates especially for that maltreatment of one of the slaves. In Mark's context, which may be historical as well as literary, the builders represent the Sanhedrin (so also Acts 4:11). The crowd's having quoted Ps 118:25-26 at the Triumphal Procession (11:10) and Jesus' having used the verb "reject" (ἀποδοκιμάζω) in his first passion prediction (8:31) may have led him to Ps 118:22-23, or led him *back* to it if he had it in mind as early as the first passion prediction. Furthermore, the building (ᾠκοδόμησεν) of the tower (v 1) may have helped lead him to the builders (οἱ οἰκοδομοῦντες) in the psalm; and the owner — i.e. lord — of the vineyard may have helped lead him to the Lord of the building. The figure of a vineyard has changed to the figure of a building (cf. Jer 1:10; 24:6; 1QS 8:5; 1 Cor 3:9; Col 2:7), but the second figure extends the meaning of the first. Behind the Greek text the Hebrew אבן, "stone," plays on הבן, "the son." (Both א and ה are gutturals, בן being the same in both words.)

In Ps 118:23, "this" (זאת, feminine) refers to the rejected stone's having become head of a corner. For this referent, Greek requires the neuter τοῦτο. Mark's overly literal, Septuaginal, and feminine αὕτη refers to the head itself (κεφαλήν, feminine) and thus sharpens the Christological point of the quotation. The marvel of the Lord's making the rejected stone head of a corner agrees with Jesus' having predicted that he will rise from the dead three days after being killed (8:31; 9:31; 10:33-34) and gets emphasis from the forward position of "from the Lord" (see the Greek text). But since giving the vineyard to others linked up with Jesus' and the Twelve's judging the twelve tribes of Israel, becoming head of a corner refers to rulership following resurrection, not to resurrection itself. The figurative language, directed as it is to the Sanhedrin, again agrees with the limitation of his plain predictions to the disciples. "You've read even this scripture, haven't you?" sarcastically puts down the Sanhedrin, especially the scriptural experts, or scribes, among them (cf. v 26; 2:25). In fact, the scribes were sometimes called "builders" (see the following notes). Οὐδὲ τὴν γραφὴν ταύτην, "even this scripture, haven't you?" holds a prominent forward position and implies that the Sanhedrin have indeed read even this scripture — it forms part of the oft-sung Hallel, and οὐ plus an indicative verb in a question implies an affirmative answer — and that they should therefore expect the Lord to thwart their seeking to destroy Jesus (cf. D. Daube, *NTRJ* 432-36, on reading but not understanding the OT). Though the "others" who get the vineyard are plural and "head of a corner" is singular, the disciples have already represented Jesus (6:7-13), will do so again after his resurrection (13:10; 14:9), and as just noted will share in his rule over Israel.

The predictive power of Jesus comes out in the Sanhedrin's seeking to seize him (cf. 11:18): fulfilment of the parable and of his passion predictions is on the verge. The forward position of αὐτόν, "him," underscores this point. The Sanhedrin's fearing the crowd contrasts with their seeking to seize Jesus, tells why they do not seize him on the spot, and recalls the strength of his hold on the crowd. The use of καί, "and," instead of the expected adversative δέ or ἀλλά, "but," to introduce the fear adds emphasis to his hold on the crowd (cf. M. Reiser, *Syntax und Stil* 105-7, 115-16; BDF §442[1]). Mark's writing as an omniscient narrator when he says that the Sanhedrin fear the crowd shows where his editorial emphasis lies. In 11:18 the imperfect tense of ἐφοβοῦντο told of the Sanhedrin's ongoing fear of Jesus because the crowd were amazed at his teaching. Here the aorist of ἐφοβήθησαν tells of the Sanhedrin's taking fright at the crowd because "they knew that he had spoken the parable with reference to them [the Sanhedrin]" (cf. J. A. Kleist 223; also C. F. D. Moule, *Idiom-Book* 53, for the suggestion that πρὸς αὐτούς means "against them"). But was it the *Sanhedrin* who knew that Jesus had spoken the parable regarding themselves? Or was it the *crowd* who knew that he had spoken it regarding the Sanhedrin? The Sanhedrin's fear of the crowd would find stronger justification in the crowd's recognizing that Jesus told the parable to attack the Sanhedrin. The switch in subjects from the Sanhedrin to the crowd and back to the Sanhedrin would then correspond to the rhythm of main clauses, a subordinate clause, and another main clause. Otherwise, "for they [the Sanhedrin] knew that he had spoken the parable with reference to them" tells why they are seeking to seize him in the first place (see 11:13; 16:4 for other instances where a γάρ-clause gives the reason for something two steps back). Apparently the Sanhedrin fear a turning of the crowd against them as a result of the parable. "And leaving him they went away" (cf. 1:20; 8:13 for the phraseology) lets the last accent fall on the Sanhedrin's quitting the field defeated by Jesus' hold on the crowd and by his parable, particularly by those elements in it to which the omniscient narrator has just given emphasis (cf. 11:8-10, 18, 32-33; 12:17, 28, 34, 37 for a string of similar emphases in this part of Mark). These are the things that Mark underlines to exhibit Jesus' strength even in the events leading immediately to the Crucifixion.

NOTES

It is often said that in 11:27–13:37 Mark overloads the third day of Passion Week (counting from Palm Sunday). Perhaps he has collected episodes from various times and places, but it is hard to prove. The episodes fit the occasion. One dialogue may engender another, especially in a public setting. And who is to say that they could not have taken place in one day? It takes about six minutes to read the whole passage aloud, and the episodes consist almost entirely of dialogue and soliloquy capable of being spoken in short bursts, not of narrative about other activities requiring a long time. The fact that the episodes lack temporal links to each other is double-edged. It may signal a collection of originally unrelated episodes, but it may also mean that occurrence on the same day left no need for temporal links. The logical progression of the episodes may adequately imply a chronological progression. The absence of Mark's favorite "immediately" is insignificant; for he rarely uses it with verbs of speaking, and then only in situations of emergency (1:30; 6:50; 9:24), whereas 11:27–13:37 consists almost entirely of talk, none of it in emergency.

See O. Schwankl, *Sadduzäerfrage* 434-38; J.-G. Mudiso Mbâ Mundla, *Jesus und die Führer Israels* 299-302; H.-W. Kuhn, *Ältere Sammlungen* 39-43; J. Gnilka 2. 172 that Mark 11–12 does not incorporate a pre-Marcan collection of controversy stories (against M. Albertz, *Streitgespräche* 16-36, summarized by M. J. Cook, *Mark's Treatment* 31-34). For one thing, the pericopes in these chapters are diverse in form and content. Verses 15-17 tell what Jesus did that created a controversy but do not include the controversy itself. In vv 27-33 his authority to do what he has done is questioned, and he refuses to answer. On his own initiative he tells parables in 12:1-12. His enemies pose a dilemma to him in 12:13-17, and he avoids its horns; in 12:18-27 a puzzle, and he solves it. In 12:28-34 a questioner turns into an admirer. In 12:35-37 Jesus poses a puzzle which nobody solves; and in 12:38-40 he issues a warning. This variety within progression has the look of real life rather than of purely literary compilation. To a large extent the principle of selection would cause such a compilation to look samey and lack progression.

We might consider the possibility of a parallel between 2:1–3:6 and 11:27–12:37, in particular of parallels between the scribes' challenging the authority of Jesus to forgive sins (2:1-12) and the Sanhedrin's (including the scribes') challenging his authority to cleanse the temple (11:27–12:12), between the Pharisaic scribes' asking why Jesus eats with sinners and toll collectors (2:13-17) and Pharisees' and Herodians' asking whether it is permissible to pay a poll tax to Caesar (12:13-17), between the Baptist disciples' and the Pharisees' asking why Jesus' disciples do not fast (2:18-22) and the Sadducees' asking about the resurrection (12:18-27), between the Pharisees' accusing Jesus' disciples of breaking the Sabbath (2:23-28) and a scribe's asking what is the most important commandment (12:28-34), and between the Pharisees' plotting against Jesus for his healing on the Sabbath (3:1-6) and Jesus' asking whose son is the Christ (12:35-37). But beyond the element of authority shared by the first pair and the references to taxation in the second pair (though only by implication in the first member), the parallels lack substance. Furthermore, the parable in 12:1-12 has to be amalgamated with the challenge to Jesus' authority in 11:27-33; and the friendliness of the scribe in the last part of 12:28-34 subverts a parallel with 2:23-28, where the Pharisees start an observation that ends in a plot to destroy Jesus (3:6).

According to J. R. Donahue (*Are You the Christ?* 118-20), Mark imports the present challenge to Jesus' authority from earlier in his ministry, where the references to that authority and to John the Baptizer were more at home and where "these things" did not refer to the temple-cleansing; and Mark did so to make the episode fit into an anti-temple motif running through the last part of his gospel. But this theory wrongly takes the cleansing of the temple to have been an attack on it and fails to recognize that "teacher" and "rabbi," whose presence in this part of Mark is noted by Donahue himself (see 11:21; 12:14, 19, 32), connote Jesus' authority, particularly in terms of Mark's Christology (see esp. 1:21-22, 27). The theory also fails to recognize that in Jerusalem of all places the issue of Jesus' authority is at home. Here reside his chief competitors, the Jewish authorities. John the

Baptizer preached nearby, and not very long ago "all the Judean region and all the Jerusalemites were going out and were being baptized by him" (1:5). So a reference to him is not out of place in Jerusalem (cf. 6:14-16; 8:28; Matt 11:12-13 par. Luke 16:16 for the remembrance of John).

Whether or not Jesus assumed the role of a prophet in cleansing the temple, the Sanhedrin may regard him as a possibly false prophet. They certainly regard him as a rebel against their authority (cf. *m. Sanh.* 1:5; 11:1, 5). The ἵνα in v 28 may be telic (". . . gave you this authority *in order that* you should do these things"), ecbatic (". . . gave you this authority *with the result that* you do these things"), both telic and ecbatic for achieved purpose, or epexegetic (". . . gave you this authority, *i.e.* [authority] to do these things"). An underlying Aramaic ᶜ might also be telic, ecbatic, both telic and ecbatic, or epexegetic. The ecbatic meaning fits the passage most naturally, however, and thereby favors an underlying ᶜ, because ἵνα does not normally carry that meaning.

"These things" could hardly be mistaken for a reference to Jesus' walking around in the temple; for he needed no authority to do that, and the plural of "these things" disagrees with the singularity of walking around in the temple whereas the cleansing of the temple entailed the several actions of expulsion, overturning, and prohibition (vv 15-16; see the comments ad loc.). Against treating "these things" as a reference to Jesus' teaching (v 17), the verb of doing (ποιέω bis — v 28) refers more naturally to the actions which made up the temple-cleansing than to teaching; Jesus has taught in synagogues before (1:21-22; 6:2; Luke 4:16-32; cf. Mark 1:39); and whatever the response to the content of his earlier teaching, nobody has yet challenged his authority to teach (cf. J.-G. Mudiso Mbâ Mundla, *Jesus und die Führer Israels* 15). Inclusion of Jesus' so-called Triumphal Entry in "these things" overlooks that Jesus entered Jerusalem privately, not publicly and therefore not triumphally (see the comments v 11). To say that "these things" originally referred to his baptismal activity, reported in John 3:22, 26 (R. Bultmann, *HST* 20, n. 1), leaves out of account the fourth evangelist's program of Christianizing Jesus, the antedating of Christian baptism as a part of that program, and the unlikelihood that Jesus would imply the heavenly origin of John's baptism if the Sanhedrin were asking about another baptismal activity — his own — which might seem rivalrous to John's (see John 3:25-30). For a general reference to Jesus' ministry, W. Weiss (*"Eine neue Lehre in Vollmacht"* 144-45) appeals to such a reference in "these things" at 6:2b (cf. M. Y.-H. Lee, *Jesus und die jüdische Autorität* 111-16). But there the expression referred specifically to Jesus' wisdom and miracles, immediately mentioned. It is hard to know why the repetition of "these things" (see vv 28 [bis], 29, 33) should be thought to favor a general reference over a specific one (so Weiss, loc. cit.). The parallel with John's baptism does not favor a general reference (as thought ibid. 157-60 in connection with a hypothesis that this episode had its origin in a conflict between Christians and Baptists), because that baptism could not be more specific. And it is unconvincing to argue from the fact that in none of Mark's controversy stories have preceding actions of Jesus or the disciples been referenced by "these things" (so ibid. 144-45, n. 145); for in the very first of those stories "these things" referred to what his opponents had just thought (2:8), and there is no essential difference between the present use of the demonstrative pronoun for what he has done and the use in 2:24 of the relative pronoun (ὅ) for what the disciples were doing. Context determines the referent of any pronoun.

We would have to overlook the redactional character of "signs" throughout the Fourth Gospel to accept the theory of T. A. Mohr (*Markus- und Johannespassion* 100-108) that Mark puts questions concerning authority, which Jesus refuses to answer, in place of an earlier demand for a sign, which Jesus granted (John 2:18-22). See A. W. Argyle (in *ExpTim* 80 [1968-69] 343) and H. Kosmala (in *ASTI* 5 [1966-67] 97-100) for words of caution against seeing in the challenge to Jesus' authority a contrast between ordained rabbis and ordinary teachers of the Jewish law, i.e. the scribes (so D. Daube, *NTRJ* 205-23; idem in *JTS* os 39 [1938] 45-59). The Sanhedrin are not asking Jesus what rabbi ordained him; for as noted in the comments the Sanhedrin already know that Jesus is not ordained. They are only trying to embarrass him. So he does not appeal to the prophet John because prophetic authority weighs more than rabbinic authority. Nor does he claim that his authority, like John's, comes from God. Nor did the testimony of John to Jesus, which lies in the background, say that the Stronger One would get his authority from God. Jesus uses John only to impale the Sanhedrin on the horns of an embarrassing dilemma, and then refuses to answer the question put to him. Hence, attempts to milk Christology out of this passage — in particular, a primitive Christology in which Jesus stands alongside John rather than over him — mistake a forensic ploy for a Christological implication. The whole dialogue has to do with nothing deeper than saving and losing face. This lack of Christology makes an argument for historicity even more compelling than one from a primitive Christology.

The questions of the Sanhedrin (v 28) presume that Jesus has usurped their authority. Since it is only human, his counter question (v 30) escalates the dialogue to the level of divine authority versus merely human authority. To to sure, the counter question has to do with John's baptism, not with Jesus' cleansing the temple. But the Sanhedrin themselves recognize John's witness to Jesus ("he will say, 'Why then didn't you believe him?'" — v 31), and in chap. 1 the only words of John that Mark quotes consist of a testimony to the coming Stronger One (see 1:7-8). Therefore, divine authority for John's baptism spells divine authority for his witness to Jesus, which in turn spells divine authority for Jesus' cleansing the temple.

B. F. Meyer (*Aims* 122) interprets "the baptism of John" (v 30) to mean that John witnessed people's self-baptism, not that he baptized them. This interpretation is contradicted by John's title "the Baptizer," by the emphatic ἐγώ, active voice, and direct object in his statement, "I have baptized you," by the parallel between his baptizing people in water and the Stronger One's baptizing people in the Holy Spirit (the latter hardly a self-baptism merely witnessed by the Stronger One), and by the passive voice and ὑπό of agent instead of the reflexive middle in the phrase "baptized by John" (see 1:4, 5, 8, 9 et passim and esp. Luke 7:29, where "the baptism of John" is construed with the passive participle "having been baptized"). 1:1-11, especially 1:1, did not make John's baptism the basis of Jesus' authority (against W. Grundmann [2. Aufl.] 236-37); for there ἀρχή referred to a temporal beginning, not to a theological foundation (see the comments on 1:1). Nor does the possibility that John's baptism was from heaven parallel the Spirit's descending from heaven on the newly baptized Jesus. For baptism and the Spirit differ. So also do the verbal forms that go with them: "descending" in 1:10, "was" in 11:30. And John's baptism included the baptisms of many more people than Jesus, none of which other baptisms involved a descent of the Spirit.

J. Jeremias (*NT Theology* 1. 55-56) thinks of an implication that Jesus' authority rests on what happened to him when John baptized him, i.e. on the descent of the Spirit into him and on the words of the Father to him. But does Jesus expect the Sanhedrin to know about those things? And if he had them in mind, why does he ask a general question about the authority of John's baptism instead of appealing to what happened to himself alone?

S. Kim (in an article to appear in *ANRW* II 26/1; cf. idem in *Tradition and Interpretation in the NT* 134-35) goes beyond Jeremias to say that the baptismal assurance of Jesus' divine sonship implies his having acted as the Son of God in cleansing the temple. From there Kim goes on to interpret the cleansing as symbolic of coming destruction because Jesus' saving death will outmode the sacrifices and because he will build a new community to outmode the temple where those sacrifices are offered. Not only do the criticisms of Jeremias's view apply here, too. In the excursus on the chronology of Mark 11 we will see that a symbolic view of the temple-cleansing cannot be sustained. In chap. 13 Jesus will give an apocalyptic rather than soteriological and ecclesiological rationale for the destruction of the temple. The soteriological rationale looks more Johannine than Jesuanic (see John 1:29, 36; 2:15a, 18-20, all distinctive of John).

The observations that in rabbinic debate counter questions are integrally tied to the topic of the original question and that they bring the argument to closure (Str-B 1. 861-62; G. S. Shae in *NovT* 16 [1974] 13-14) would not bear on the present pericope even if they were entirely accurate. (They are not.) Jesus is challenged by the whole Sanhedrin, not only by the scribes (or rabbis) among them. They design their questions to embarrass him into silence, not to draw him into theological debate; and he returns the favor. Nor is his question about John's baptism integrally tied to the topic of his own authority.

Διελογίζοντο πρὸς ἑαυτούς (v 31) probably indicates reasoning to themselves collectively, not reasoning against one another in argument (for which διελέγοντο would have been more appropriate — see 9:34) or reasoning privately (for which ἐν ἑαυτοῖς, "in themselves," or ἐν ταῖς καρδίαις αὐτῶν, "in their hearts," would have been more appropriate — see 2:6, 8). To treat εἴπωμεν as hortatory, "let us say" (v 32), would make nonsense of Mark's immediately following editorial comments and of the Sanhedrin's answer, "We don't know" (v 33). To treat εἴπωμεν as deliberative, "should we say?" would make sense but would neglect the probability of Semitic influence in an ellipsis of ἐάν, "if" (K. Beyer, *Semitische Syntax* 1/1. 96-97). E. C. Maloney (*Semitic Interference* 92) argues that "the ellipsis of ἐάν in Mk 11:32 . . . is equally at home in Greek," but his argument fails because in the supportive citations of Arr. *Epict. Diss.* 1.18.23; 4.1.10 but not in Mark or Semitic examples the ellipses include the verb as well as the conditional conjunction. We might translate the last clause of v 31, "Why then didn't you believe it [αὐτῷ as neuter and as referring to τὸ βάπτισμα, 'the baptism']?" But the follow-up, "for they were all holding John that he had really been a prophet," favors a masculine reference to John. To construe ὄντως with εἶχον, "they were really holding," rather than with ἦν, "had really been" (v 32), puts Mark's accent in the wrong place; for in a variety of ways he is stressing the strength of John as a prophet, not the strength with which the crowd were holding him as a prophet. If John was strong, Jesus is stronger yet.

The absence of "the Son of man" from vv 27-33 contrasts with the prominence of "the Son of man" in earlier disputes over Jesus' authority (2:1-12, 23-28, esp. 2:10, 28). This contrast resists an interpretation of vv 27-33 in terms of the Son of man's authority (against A. J. Hultgren, *Jesus and His Adversaries* 71, 74). J. R. Donahue (*Are You the Christ?* 119-20) tries to explain the absence of a Christological title by means of a messianic secret imposed "most severely" on the whole section 11:1–12:44. But in 2:1-12, 23-28 Mark allowed Jesus to use "the Son of man" in public debate with his enemies; so a messianic secret does not explain the absence of "the Son of man" in a similar situation here.

According to E. Haenchen (394-95), an historically inauthentic messianic secret keeps Mark from letting Jesus reveal the source of his authority. Against such a rationale, however, we should note that the cleansing of the temple carried a weaker implication of messiahship than did sitting on a donkey and accepting an acclamation explicitly associated with David's kingdom. Yet Mark did not hide the stronger implication. In asking why Jesus does not answer that God gave him authority, Haenchen correctly perceives that claiming authority from God does not necessarily imply messiahship — for example, prophets too get their authority from God — but mistakenly treats the Sanhedrin's questions as a sincere inquiry rather than joining Jesus in recognition of the questioners' design to embarrass him, not to get information from him. The same mistake underlies the interpretation of V. Eppstein (in *ZNW* 55 [1964] 57) that the hierarchs of the temple are asking Jesus whether

the Sanhedrin or the Pharisees have authorized Jesus to act as he has done. This interpretation also requires excluding the Sanhedrin and the Pharisees from those who challenge his
authority ("the chief priests and the scribes and the elders," according to v 27). Otherwise
they of all people would know the answer to the question.

According to F. C. Synge (in *ExpTim* 92 [1980-81] 331), the repetition of "from
men" (vv 30, 32) implies that Mark has intruded everything from after the first occurrence
of that phrase through its second occurrence. "The law of the intruded middle" which
informs this position creates problems for itself, however, in that three other phrases are
also repeated: "by what authority I do these things" (vv 29, 33), "answer me" (vv 29, 30),
and "from heaven" (vv 30, 31). Consistent application of the supposed law would create
contradictions.

Failure to see in v 30 Jesus' use of a debating trick, not his implying an answer to
the question asked him, dogs the argument of R. Bultmann (*HST* 20) that Jesus' question
brings his counterattack to a successful conclusion, as though the heavenly origin of John's
baptism implies the heavenly origin of Jesus' authority. Thus vv 31-32 would "derive from
a Hellenist (perhaps from Mark himself)." In response to Bultmann we may concede that
an argument from analogy ("Just as the Baptist received his authority from God and not
from human beings, so also do I") does not transgress the bounds of possibility. Indeed,
rabbis argue thus. But we must note that in Jesus' self-defense this kind of argument would
carry little weight, for any imposter could make the same claim by drawing the same
analogy. Since Jesus does not say or imply that God passed authority to him through John
or mention his baptism by John, the claim would not even require an imposter to have
been baptized by John. Nor would mention of Jesus' baptism by John have helped an
argument from analogy. How would the heavenly origin of a baptism that John administered
to many people support the authority of Jesus alone? His baptism by John did not confer
such authority, nor would it have been accepted as doing so. Otherwise every Tom, Dick,
and Harry baptized by John could have claimed similar authority and been acknowledged
as possessing it. Not John's baptism of Jesus — rather, his testimony to Jesus as the
Stronger One is what supports Jesus' authority to cleanse the temple, exactly as implied
in vv 31-32.

Beyond weaknesses in an analogical argument, the context apart from vv 31-32
makes unlikely the originality of such an argument and favors that from the start Jesus
was trying to impale the Sanhedrin on the horns of an embarrassing dilemma. Twice he
demands that they answer his question, whereas a closing counter question would imply
its own answer (contrast the lack of a demand to answer in 2:19, 25-26; 3:4; Luke 13:15;
14:3, 5, and even where an answer does follow — 10:3; 12:16; Matt 17:25; *POxy.* 840.
2). The demand that his addressees answer with one of two opposing possibilities suits a
dilemma. To close the argument, a counter question would need to imply only one possible
answer, at least only one possible answer in the frame of thought shared by Jesus and his
audience. But here that requires adding hypothesis on hypothesis by way of shifting from
the Sanhedrin to a general audience on whom Jesus could count to agree with him that
John's baptism was from heaven — a shift necessitated solely by supposing the unoriginality of vv 31-32. This hypothesis necessitates yet another, viz., that since only the
Sanhedrin are likely to have challenged Jesus' authority to cleanse the temple, the original
antecedent of "these things" did not refer to the cleansing. His two demands that the
Sanhedrin answer him are then dismissed as overly severe as well as inimical to a closing
counter question. Too many hypotheses are being stacked on top of each other.

Furthermore, historical probability favors a challenge to Jesus' authority by the
Sanhedrin; for they oppose him whereas the general populace adulate him and are therefore
unlikely to be challenging his authority. And the disputatious tone of vv 28-29 as well as
of vv 31-32 shows that he is answering a challenge to his authority, not an innocent inquiry

such as the general populace would make. Since he enjoys cordial relations with John and John's disciples (see esp. Matt 11:2-11 par. Luke 7:18-28; contrast later tension between Christians and Baptists as reflected in John 3:25-26), the disputatious tone of vv 28-29 also undermines the hypothetical shift of Jesus' original audience from the Sanhedrin to disciples of John (against G. S. Shae in *NovT* 16 [1974] 18). Even without Jesus' two demands for an answer, each of the questions asked of him carries a disputatious tone.

As with Jesus' counter question in v 30, his questions in 2:19, 25-26; 3:4; 10:3; 12:16; Luke 13:15; 14:3; Matt 17:25; *POxy.* 840. 2 — many of them counter questions, too — do not bring closure, but are followed up by further words or actions on his part. Luke 14:5 does bring closure, but with a question which unlike Mark 11:30 has only one possible answer yet, as in Mark 11:33, makes Jesus' critics unable to answer back. These passages favor the originality of the follow-up to his present counter question.

Also favoring the originality of this follow-up is the appearance of the chiastic pattern — (a) initial question; (b) counter question; (b') answer to counter question; (a') answer to initial question — in 10:2-9; 12:14-17; and rabbinic passages cited by Str-B 1. 861-62 as well as in Mark 11:27-33. In some of the rabbinic passages the dialogue proceeds even further, and in Mark 11:27-33 we read refusals to answer rather than answers. The underlying scheme shines through quite clearly, however, and puts an apocopation of the present pericope in serious doubt. The scheme definitely falsifies the argument that rabbinic counter questions bring arguments to closure. Not a single one of the counter questions cited ibidem does so (cf. D. Daube, *NTRJ* 151-57). The probable Semitism in the ellipsis of ἐάν before εἴπωμεν in v 32 ("[if] we should say" — see the foregoing notes) favors an early date which in turn favors a presumption that vv 31-32 are original.

A comparison of the MT and the LXX at Gen 15:6; Exod 4:1, 5, 8, 9; 14:31; 19:9; Num 14:11; Deut 9:23; 28:66; 2 Chr 32:15; Jer 40:14(47:14 in the LXX) et passim suffices to falsify Bultmann's argument that in v 31 ἐπιστεύσατε, "did you [not] believe," betrays the hand of a Hellenist. The Septuagintal version of those passages corresponds in meaning to the Hebrew, and to Mark in both meaning and construction (πιστεύω plus a dative). Against Bultmann, see also J.-G. Mudiso Mbâ Mundla, *Jesus und die Führer Israels* 10-11.

Bultmann does not ascribe v 33 to the supposedly later hand of a Hellenist such as Mark. If that verse is considered original (though it is not by some who follow Bultmann on vv 31-32), we may add that the Sanhedrin do not need to say, "We don't know," unless they detect that Jesus is posing an embarrassing dilemma; and in the face of their refusal to answer his question he needs to affirm the heavenly origin of John's baptism — if he is to make an argument from analogy — rather than responding tit for tat with his own refusal to answer.

G. S. Shae (in *NovT* 16 [1974] 11-12) reasons that since "from heaven . . . or from human beings?" is necessary to the story, this question of Jesus and the Sanhedrin's "who?" to which it corresponds, belonged to the original form of the story. On the other hand he reasons that since Jesus's "I will tell you by what authority" is unnecessary, this promise and the Sanhedrin's "by what authority?" to which it corresponds, did not belong to the original form. Beneath this reasoning lies a mistaken assumption that what is unnecessary is also unoriginal. Favoring the originality of the unnecessary elements in the present story, however, are the synthetic parallelism formed by the Sanhedrin's two questions, and the a-b-a'-b' pattern created by Jesus' responses. Such phenomena do not likely stem from accretion. The probability that an Aramaic בְּ underlies the instrumental ἐν, "by," in the question and responses whose originality is dismissed by Shae joins the typically Semitic parallelism to argue for an early date — and an early date tends towards originality. Cf. the Semitic arguments for the originality of the second question and response: (1) the frequency of the locution "give authority" in the LXX and Josephus; (2) the Palestinian Jewishness of asking about the transfer of personal authority; and (3) the reflection of an ecbatic Aramaic ‎ב‎ in the probably but unusually ecbatic ἵνα of v 28 (see also C. Marucci in *ZTK* 108 [1986] 293-94). A. J. Hultgren (*Jesus and His Adversaries* 69-70) sets out these arguments but like Shae neglects a probable Semitism in denying originality to the first question and response. Shae fails to note that in the second question, for whose originality he argues, the demonstrative pronoun in "this authority" refers back to the authority mentioned in the first question and thereby implies the originality of the first question. Hultgren quietly drops the demonstrative in yet another hypothesis necessitated only by the exigency of an earlier one.

Contrary to much current opinion, the Sanhedrin's reasoning that if they answer, "From heaven," Jesus will ask them why they did not believe John does not sound like a later Christian fabrication. To later Christians, jealous of Jesus' uniqueness and wary of the Baptist sect, believing John would seem rivalrous to believing Jesus. H. Anderson (269) assigns not only the high estimate of John in vv 31-33 to later Christians, but also the rejection of John to the later Jews with whom those Christians were locked in controversy. But only the Sanhedrin have disbelieved John; and those who hold him to have been really a prophet consist of the wider Jewish populace. It is historically certain that they do (Josephus *Ant.* 18.5.2 §§116-19). Moreover, Jesus himself has advertised John as a prophet, more than a prophet, the Lord's messenger, the greatest among those born of women, and the hinge of history (Matt 11:9-15 par. Luke 7:26-28; 16:16). So there is no good reason to look to later controversy between Christians and Jews.

EXCURSUS ON THE CHRONOLOGY OF MARK 11

The chronology of Mark 11 has come under criticism. It is said that originally Jesus rode into Jerusalem, cleansed the temple, and had his authority to cleanse it challenged — all on the same day (not to speak of further dialogues taking place on the third day — see the notes on 11:27-33). Mark, then, has torn these events apart and distributed them among three days by delaying the temple-cleansing one day, by inserting the cursing of the fig tree between the Triumphal Procession and the temple-cleansing, by delaying the challenge to Jesus' authority yet another day, and by inserting the withering of the fig tree between the temple-cleansing and the challenge to Jesus' authority. To use the cursing and the withering of the fig tree as dividers at the beginnings of the second and third days, Mark may also have broken up an original unity of cursing and withering by delaying the withering one day. According to this theory, Mark double-sandwiched the cursing and the withering after the Triumphal Procession and the challenge to Jesus' authority, respectively, to single-sandwich the temple-cleansing between the cursing and the withering. The single sandwich exhibits the purpose behind his procedure, i.e. to make the cursing and the withering interpret the temple-cleansing, and vice versa, as symbolizing the coming destruction of the temple because of religious fruitlessness (above all, see W. R. Telford, *Barren Temple;* alternatively but similarly, judgment on the Jewish nation or hierarchy because of their religious fruitlessness).

Arguments for the foregoing theory are multiple: (1) evidence of the symbolic meaning of fig trees in Mark's Jewish and Christian milieu; (2) the naturalness of uninterrupted progression from Triumphal Procession through temple-cleansing to challenge of authority, and of the same from cursing to withering; (3) the absence of the cursing and withering of the fig tree from Luke's and John's accounts of the Triumphal Procession, temple-cleansing, and challenge to Jesus' authority; (4) the anticlimaticness of merely looking around the temple after a triumphal procession; (5) the provincialism implied in looking around like a country bumpkin seeing big city lights for the first time; (6) the concentration of Marcanisms in v 11, which delays the temple-cleansing; (7) the awkwardness in v 14 of the statement that "the disciples were listening," an awkwardness which betrays that Mark inserts the statement to delay the withering by a day; (8) the likelihood that the Jewish hierarchy would have challenged Jesus' authority immediately, not waited till the next day (cf. Matt 21:14-16; John 2:18); (9) the presence of Marcanisms in vv 18-20, 27, which delay the challenge; (10) the distance of "these things" in the challenge (v 28 bis) from its natural antecedent, viz., the several stoppages that made up the cleansing of the temple some verses and one day earlier (vv 15-17); and (11) Mark's habit of sandwiching originally independent traditions (1:23-26 between 1:21-22 and 1:27; 3:22-30 between 3:20-21 and 3:31-35; 5:25-34 between 5:21-24 and 5:35-43; 6:14-29 between 6:6b-13 and 6:30-31; 14:3-9 between 14:1-2 and 14:10-11; 14:54, 66-72 with 14:53, 55-65).

How well do these arguments hold up? To be sure, literal fruitlessness often represents religious fruitlessness; and fig trees and figs often appear in pronouncements of judgment, especially in those having to do with Israel. Both the OT and the post-canonical literature of early Judaism contain these metaphors. But Mark 7:2-4 contradicts the argumentative presupposition that Mark's audience were steeped in Jewish lore and that he played on their knowledge of it. That passage shows his audience to be deficient in their knowledge of it and that he wrote with an awareness of their deficiency. Hence, he could not and probably would not count on the mere juxtaposition of fig tree and temple to create a metaphorical association between the two. In the OT, moreover, symbolic actions of the prophets arose out of intention to communicate a message and did not entail the miraculous. But Jesus' cursing the fig tree and its withering arise out of hunger and disappointment and do entail a miracle.

Yet again, the supposed parallels in the OT and later Jewish lore to the cursing and withering of the fig tree leave something to be desired. In those parallels, generally speaking, the fig tree does not represent the temple, but Israel. Even with respect to Israel (if one allows that the temple stands for Israel), the use of figs and fig trees does not correspond very closely to Mark's story. Take, for example, the six passages regarded by W. R. Telford (*Barren Temple* 142-56) as primary for OT background. In Jer 8:13 the lack of figs on the tree is the result of judgment, in Mark the reason for judgment (according to the symbolic interpretation). In Isa 28:3-4 eating a first-ripe fig represents destruction, whereas in Mark there are not even any buds to be eaten, much less first-ripe figs; and withering rather than eating is supposed to represent destruction. Not as with Jesus' finding nothing but leaves, God delightedly finds first-ripe figs in Hos 9:10.

Thus in Hos 9:16 the judgment of a dried up root and inability to bear fruit does not stem from fruitlessness. In Mic 7:1 God does not find the early figs that he craves; they represent the godly person, not the temple; and the time is fall, at the close of the late harvest, not spring, prior to the early harvest (as in Mark). In Joel 1:7, 12 locusts have ruined the fig trees by stripping them of leaves and bark. Their white branches exposed to the sun, the fig trees waste away from the top down rather than from the roots up, as in Mark. Other OT passages, such as Isa 34:4; Jer 11:16-17; 24:1-10; 29:17; Ezekiel 17; Hos 2:14[12]; Amos 4:9; Nah 3:12; Hab 3:17; Ps 105:33 require no comment, nor do passages in post-canonical Jewish literature.

The parable in Luke 13:6-9 provides only a slim base for a symbolic action derived, it is sometimes suggested, by way of early Christian transmutation of the parable into a deed. For immediate cursing and withering, as in Mark, do not derive easily from giving another year of opportunity, cultivation, and fertilization, and then destroying the tree only if·need be, as in the parable. Nor do cursing and withering derive easily from chopping down, as in the parable (cf. W. R. Telford, *Barren Temple* 233-38; M. Trautmann, *Zeichenhafte Handlungen* 328-30; and see J. A. T. Robinson in *Jesus and the Politics of His Day* 460 for the view that in Luke 13:6-9 Jesus reflects on his cleansing the temple at an earlier, Johannine date).

Not only do the details of comparable passages differ from those in Mark. The text of Mark itself fails to support a symbolic interpretation. Only a failure to have borne fruit, i.e. figs, could well represent religious fruitlessness. But Mark carefully avoids saying that Jesus went to find fruit and failed to find any (see the foregoing comments); and Jesus equally carefully avoids saying that the curse of future inability to bear fruit corresponds to past failure to bear fruit. Furthermore, if Mark's explanation, "for it was not the season of figs," were nonsensically to give the reason for Jesus' not finding fruit (as required by the symbolic interpretation) rather than the reason for his going to find something other than fruit (viz., edible buds), Mark would be excusing the fruitlessness of the tree and entirely vitiating the supposed symbolism of deserved judgment. Far from signalling a symbolic meaning, horticultural nonsense would make theological nonsense, too. Mark's excusing the fig tree would likewise vitiate both the addition to the symbolic interpretation that "nothing but leaves" represents hypocrisy, the unusual symbolic interpretation according to which συκῆ, "fig tree," somewhat homophonously represents the sicarrii (revolutionary assassins in the first Jewish revolt — so C. Daniel in *Numen* 13 [1966] 97-102), and the eschatological interpretation according to which the fig tree should have miraculously borne fruit out of season because the age of salvation had dawned (cf. the view of J. D. M. Derrett [in *HeyJ* 14 (1973) 249-65] that vv 11-14 present a midrash on Genesis 3 with respect to messianic fruitfulness). W. R. Telford attaches the eschatological interpretation to the usual symbolic one by writing, "Although it was not the season for figs, the fig-tree in the Messianic Age should have rendered to its rightful owner its fruit, . . ." (*Barren Temple* 196). Unfortunately, Mark's γάρ, which makes the unseasonability of figs a reason, contradicts Telford's "although," which makes their unseasonability a concession. The eschatological interpretation requires Jesus (or whoever was responsible for the story) to have believed, not merely that the messianic age of year-round fruitfulness was about to begin (so R. H. Hiers in *JBL* 87 [1968] 395), but that it had already begun. Did Jesus really think that all trees and vines were now bearing fruit in the manner expected for the messianic age? Was he blind?

P. J. Achtemeier (23-25) offers a slightly different combination of the symbolic and eschatological interpretations: "the season was not of figs" means that it was not time for the consummation in the temple. Rather, the temple and its cult were facing destruction, symbolized by the temple-cleansing sandwiched between the cursing and the withering of the fig tree, which also symbolize the destruction of the temple and its cult. Jesus replaces the temple; faith and prayer (vv 22-25) replace the cult. But such symbolism puts incredible demands on Mark's audience and imports foreign bodies into the text and context. How would the audience know that the fig season had anything to do with the consummation in the temple? That Jesus' cleansing the temple aimed toward replacing it? That clearing space for prayer in the temple aimed toward replacing the cult rather than reviving it? One might have thought that the audience would find it easier to deduce that clearing space for prayer in the temple aimed toward reestablishment rather than destruction.

The eschatological use of καιρός, "season," in 1:15 does not give an advance eschatological connotation to καιρός in 11:13. The horticultural terminology surrounding the latter occurrence differs widely from the eschatological terminology surrounding the former occurrence, not to mention the textual distance separating the two occurrences; and in 11:13 καιρός is the key word *giving* an explanation (a horticultural one) rather than the key word *needing* an explanation (an eschatological one). The opinion that the use of καιρός in these passages contrasts unseasonability in Jerusalem, where God's kingdom is unfulfilled, with seasonability in Galilee, where God's kingdom has been fulfilled (so W. H. Kelber, *Kingdom* 99-100), neglects not only the lack of horticulture in 1:15 and the lack of eschatology in 11:13, but also the difference that in 1:15 seasonability demands repentance and faith whereas in 11:13 unseasonability — if as in this and other eschatological and symbolic interpretations it is wrongly construed with Jesus' finding nothing but leaves — justifies the lack of fruit.

Since the cursing and withering of the fig tree do not represent judgment on the temple, they do not interpret the cleansing of the temple as a preview of such judgment. Confirmation of this point comes from both redaction and tradition (as distinguished by those who hold to judgmental symbolism) in the pericope on the cleansing itself. The redaction emphasizes Jesus' teaching, the Sanhedrin's fearing him, and the crowd's astonishment at his teaching — all Christological emphases, not judgmental ones. The OT quotations in v 17 have been differently assigned to redaction and to tradition, but in either case they call attention to making the temple a den of bandits instead of a house of prayer for all the nations. This abuse of the temple justifies Jesus' actions but does not define the purpose behind them, for such abuse might engender a literally reformative purpose as easily as a symbolically destructive one. According to D. Juel (*Messiah and Temple* 133-34), on the contrary, "a den of bandits" ill suits commercial traffic in the temple but well suits the destruction of the temple predicted in the Jeremianic context surrounding the phrase; so destruction is the point of v 17 and of the whole pericope. But it is strange exegesis to make determinative what is *not* quoted against what *is* quoted. In vv 15b-16, commonly regarded as traditional, Jesus' doing nothing against the temple itself but attacking only a certain use of it signifies reformation more naturally than destruction. His later prediction of destruction will concern the very stones and buildings of the temple (13:1-2) and, unlike the cleansing, will have its matrix in the end-time woes (13:3-37).

Even without v 17, it is difficult to see in Jesus' stoppage of commercial traffic a sign of coming destruction that will put an end to the sacral function of the temple; for "if Jesus had wished to oppose the sacral function of the temple, he would have passed through the court of the gentiles to make his protest where the sacrifices were actually offered" (N. Q. Hamilton in *JBL* 83 [1964] 372). At the least we would expect a pronouncement of judgment, as in 13:1-2, 14-20. Without a pronouncement of judgment, stopping the traffic looks reformative. John 2:19 may seem to put a judgmental word here; but John's habit of antedating, combining, and expanding dominical traditions casts doubt on a historical association of that saying with this event. Even more to the point, the wording of John 2:19, "*You* destroy this temple, and in three days I will raise it" (or "*If* you . . . I will"; see C. H. Dodd, *Interpretation* 302, n. 1), carries not a syllable of judgment, but a promise, speaks of destruction by the Jews, not by their enemies at God's behest, much less by Jesus, and evokes an interpretation in terms of his body, not in terms of the temple building (John 2:21). The judgmental part of the saying referred to in Mark 14:58, "I will destroy this man-made temple" (cf. 15:29), carries the label of false witness against Jesus (14:57); and Mark 14:58; 15:29; John 2:19 all use ὁ ναός, which refers to the sanctuary proper, rather than τὸ ἱερόν, which refers to the whole complex of the temple, including outlying buildings and courts. Stopping the commercial traffic in the outermost court does not stop the sacrificial worship in the innermost court; for people can still buy their sacrifices in markets on the Mount of Olives or, if they live close enough, bring their own. So there is no stoppage of sacrifices from which stoppage could be elicited a sign of coming destruction. Besides, Mark says nothing about the cult of sacrifices. His Jesus does not drive out sacrificial animals, as in John. They are not even mentioned. Only doves are mentioned, and that only to describe their sellers. Nor does Mark indicate that the selling, buying, moneychanging, and vessel-carrying had anything to do with the sacrificial cult (contrast the detailed explanation of Jewish cultic practice in 7:2-4). These activities appear to be a solely commercial encroachment on space that should be devoted to prayer. In the Greco-Roman world temples, including the one in Jerusalem, served as banks for general purposes (see N. Q. Hamilton in *JBL* 83 [1964] 365-70). Therefore Mark's audience would have no reason to associate the cleansing of the temple with a stoppage of the sacrifices, nor could he assume that they would make such an association. In fact, foregoing and succeeding passages should *keep* them from making the association. Although 2:23–3:6 and 7:1-23 show that Jesus abrogated the laws of Sabbath and diet, in 1:44 he commanded a healed leper to offer for his cleansing "the things that Moses commanded"; and in 14:12-16 he will command two of his disciples to prepare the Passover, which includes a sacrifice (see esp. v 12). In view of these commands, Mark cannot have hoped that his audience would interpret the temple-cleansing as aiming at a stoppage of the sacrifices. Jesus himself cannot have hoped both to stop the offering of sacrifices and several days later to eat a sacrificial meal with his disciples. He must have purposed, then, to restore commercial space to its proper use for prayer. That purpose shines through Mark's text, but Mark himself accents the psychological impact of Jesus' actions.

Peter's remembrance and remark in v 21 do not display ignorance of a symbolically judgmental meaning in the cursing and withering of the fig tree (against J. Ernst in *Begegnung mit dem Wort* 53-54). Jesus neither corrects a misunderstanding nor deepens a superficial understanding, but answers at the level of the supernatural. Thus Peter's remembrance and remark appear in a positive light. The parable of the vineyard in 12:1-11 will not cast a judgmental shadow backward on the cleansing of the temple. For the vineyard would represent the temple in such an interpretation, yet the vineyard is not destroyed. It is not even put to different use, but given to others. Nor will the prediction in 13:1-2 of the destruction of the temple cast a judgmental shadow backward on the cleansing of the temple. Nine pericopes intervene, and Mark works no miracle for Hezekiahs. Moreover, the destruction predicted in 13:1-2 will not be attributed to any evil, much less to evil perpetrated in the temple. Hence, the destruction will not look judgmental, but eschatologically necessary and therefore irrelevant to the temple-cleansing (13:7). For similar reasons, the rending of the veil of the temple in 15:38 fares even worse as a retroactive interpretation of the temple-cleansing. As in 14:58; 15:29, moreover, 15:38 will use ὁ ναός, referring to the sanctuary proper, not τὸ ἱερόν, referring to the whole complex as in chap. 11. The future tense in "shall be called" (v 17) need not add an eschatological interpretation to a symbolically destructive act by implying that Jesus wants to institute the expected worship of God by Gentiles in the messianic age (Isa 2:2-4; Mic 4:1-2; Zech 14:16). After all, Gentile proselytes have long been coming to the temple for worship (see, e.g., 1 Kgs 8:41-43 par. 2 Chr 6:32-33; Acts 2:11; 8:26-27). Jesus is reclaiming old space, not creating new space; and the emphasis falls on the contrast between "a house of prayer" and "a den of bandits," not on "all the nations." Just as the cursing and withering of the fig tree fail to lend a symbolic-cum-eschatological interpretation to the cleansing of the temple, then, so also cleansing of the temple fails to lend that kind of interpretation to the cursing and withering of the fig tree.

Now we need to examine vv 22-25 for their significance in the interpretation of the cursing and withering of the fig tree. To the credit of W. R. Telford (*Barren Temple* 49-59), he recognizes the seriousness of the problem posed by these verses, viz., that they make the cursing and withering of the fig tree teach the power of faith rather than symbolizing the destruction of the temple. He labors desperately to turn back this lesson of faith. The very desperation of his labor exposes the weakness of the symbolic interpretation if the attempt at turning back fails.

First, Telford gets rid of v 26 on text critical grounds. Almost everyone does. But then Telford argues redactionally from the non-Marcan character of v 25 that that verse did not belong to Mark's original text either, but was added by combining elements from Matt 5:23-24; 6:5, 7, 14-15, as shown by Matthew's omission of Mark 11:25 in Matt 21:18-22. Contrary to Telford, however, Matthew often omits what he has used before; and an anticipatory use of Mark 11:25 in the Sermon on the Mount typifies Matthean redaction (see R. H. Gundry, *Matthew* 85-86, 103, 109-10, on Matthew's division and distribution of Mark 11:25). One also wonders why the non-Marcan character of v 25 should not point to pre-Marcan tradition rather than to post-Marcan scribal addition. If in Telford's view Marcanisms betray Marcan redaction and non-Marcanisms betray post-Marcan redaction, he has set up the rules in a way that unfairly precludes traditionality: "Heads I win, tails you lose." On the contrary, the lack of text critical evidence that Mark ever circulated without v 25 argues for pre-Marcan tradition (see S. E. Dowd, *Prayer* 40-43; C. D. Marshall, *Faith* 172-74, where it is noted that "your Father in heaven" [v 25] prepares for "from heaven" [v 30] and [though less likely because of circuitousness and a difference in hamartiological diction] that "forgive your trespasses" [v 25] prepares for "the baptism of John" [v 30] by way of John's having preached "the baptism of repentance for forgiveness of sins" [1:4]; see also C. A. Wanamaker in *Studia Biblica 1978 II* 329-37 against the attempt to rid Mark's text of v 25 by H. F. D. Sparks in *Studies in the Gospels* 244-46).

Telford admits that the evidence for a post-Marcan addition of v 24 is "less compelling" than for that of v 25, but he still thinks it "a reasonable possibility." If unconvinced with respect to v 25, then, we may proceed to his treatment of vv 22-23. He regards these verses as original to Mark's text and added by him to the cursing and withering of the fig tree. But Mark adds them, he says, not to teach a lesson of faith so much as to interpret "this mountain" as the temple mount and to predict that the temple will be thrown into the sea, so to speak, just as the story of the fig tree symbolically portrayed the withering of the temple, so to speak, and just as 13:1-2 will predict in plain language the destruction of the temple.

We should note well that Telford's interpretation of vv 22-23 depends on the absence of vv 24-25 from the original text of Mark, for vv 24-25 — and especially the less easily jettisoned v 24 — make vv 22-23 teach the power of faith rather than the destruction of the temple. But aside from that dependence, to interpret vv 22-23 of the destruction of the temple fails to distinguish between the temple and the mountain on which it stands, fails to recognize the implication in 13:2 that the temple mount will remain as the site of the tumbled down stones of the temple, fails to prove that the destruction of the temple is taught to happen as the result of the disciples' exercising faith (a thought completely foreign, indeed contradictory, to other passages that certainly do deal with the destruction of the temple), fails to take account that nowhere else does Mark use "mountain" for the site of the temple, and fails to note that since Jesus and the disciples have not yet arrived in Jerusalem (see v 27) but are traversing the Mount of Olives, "this mountain" more likely refers to the Mount of Olives than to the temple mount, for which "*that* mountain" would be more appropriate from the standpoint of the Mount of Olives. Telford (*Barren Temple* 112) cites *b. B. Bat.* 3b-4a for an application of uprooting mountains to tearing down the temple. But in that passage the dictum on uprooting mountains has to do with royal prerogatives in general, the application to Herod's tearing down the temple coming only later, incidentally, and without any reference to the temple mount or any wordplay between uprooted mountains and the temple mount (see also S. E. Dowd, *Prayer* 72-75, against identifying "this mountain" with the temple mount).

C. D. Marshall (*Faith* 168-69) follows Telford, among others, in identifying "this mountain" with the temple mount, but to avoid making the disciples' faith determine the destruction of the temple Marshall makes the temple mount figurative of "the unbelieving temple system as such." But since the disciples can hardly destroy that system with a word of faith, Telford then has to interpret the lifting up of this mountain and casting it into the sea not as destruction but as the disciples' ability "to overcome the massive weight of such institutionalized opposition." Thus an expression that connotes destruction is reduced to one that connotes resistance. Marshall argues that because being lifted up and thrown into the sea differs from the fate of the Mount of Olives in Zech 14:4, "this mountain" must mean the temple mount. But the difference need show only that Jesus is not drawing on Zech 14:4. The further attempt of Marshall to make being thrown into the sea a symbol of judgment on the unbelieving temple system depends on appeals to 5:13; 9:42. But in 5:13 pigs rushed into the sea because Jesus permitted Legion to enter them. There was no judgmental throwing of the pigs or demons into the sea. And in 9:42 being thrown into the sea would be better than judgment and therefore is not equivalent to it.

To say alternatively with D. Juel (*Messiah and Temple* 135-36), S. E. Dowd (*Prayer* 37-55), C. D. Marshall (*Faith* 163-72), and others that vv 22-25 were imported to contrast the church (i.e. the Christian community) as a house of prayer for all the nations with the temple, which should have been what the church is but had turned into a den of bandits, misses the points of emphasis in those verses, viz., faith and forgiveness, not prayer. In fact, vv 22-23 do not even mention prayer. To say again alternatively that vv 22-25 were imported to make lack of faith on the part of Jews in general the reason for the destruction of the temple as portrayed symbolically in vv 11-21 overlooks that in vv 22-25 Jesus addresses his disciples and talks neither to nor about the Jews in general; that vv 22-24 center on faith, not on lack of faith; that the kind of faith on which they center has to do with performing mighty deeds and getting what you pray and ask for, not with accepting the advent of God's rule and the role of Jesus in it so as to avoid a destruction of the temple; and that v 25 speaks about forgiveness, not about lack of faith. Therefore vv 22-25 also fail to support the symbolic interpretation of Jesus' hunger as a longing for Israel to believe him, or in him; and the overall argument fails that Mark has unhistorically sandwiched the cursing of the fig tree between the Triumphal Procession and the temple-cleansing, and the withering of the fig tree between the temple-cleansing and the challenge to Jesus' authority. What of the other arguments for this view?

Topically, the Triumphal Procession, temple-cleansing, and challenge to Jesus' authority fit together. So also do the cursing and withering of the fig tree. But topical fit does not demand uninterrupted chronology. In the absence of convincing reasons to accept a symbolic interpretation of the cursing and withering of the fig tree and of the temple-cleansing, a redactional unification of originally separated materials seems more likely than a redactional breakup of originally unitary materials. Matthew, in fact, does exactly that — he unifies the materials that are separated in Mark, and he does so in a manner and for a purpose characteristic of his redactional practices elsewhere (R. H. Gundry, *Matthew* 412-18). That in Luke and John the cursing of the fig tree does not come between the Triumphal Procession and the temple-cleansing, or the withering of the fig tree between the temple-cleansing and the challenge to Jesus' authority, does not prove an original connection between the Triumphal Procession, the temple-cleansing, and the challenge to Jesus' authority (as thought by J. Jeremias, *Eucharistic Words* 90-91). For Luke and John do not narrate the cursing and withering of the fig tree elsewhere, either; and in John the temple-cleansing and the challenge to Jesus' authority lie miles apart from the Triumphal Procession (in chaps. 2 and 12, respectively). If Jesus started from Jericho in the morning (cf. 10:46b), he would have arrived in Jerusalem not till late in the day, too late for cleansing the temple. The merchants and moneychangers would already be closing shop. Enough time would have remained only for looking around. So Mark's chronology has historical probability on its side. Perhaps the fig trees in Luke 13:6-9 and John 1:50 lead the third and fourth evangelists to omit the cursing and withering of Mark's fig tree.

As usually in Mark, the topographical movement in v 11 starts a new pericope; so Jesus' looking around in the temple does not bring the Triumphal Procession to an anticlimax, but prepares for cleansing the temple on the next day and in the same pericope. Similarities to v 1 do not prove differently that v 11 completes an inclusion which makes v 11 an end rather than a beginning. To be sure, both verses have "into Jerusalem" immediately followed by another "into"-phrase, and a reference to "Bethany" preceded by "into." But "they" is the subject in v 1, "he" in v 11. The verbs and their tenses differ: "draw near" in v 1, "entered" in v 11. And "Bethphage" (v 1) is missing from v 11. The new start in v 11 insures that the enseatment of Jesus and the acclamation by the crowd brought the Triumphal Procession to a climactic ending (see the comments on v 11).

Looking around does not cast Jesus in the role of a wide-eyed provincial. Rather, he looks around as the Son of God to see what needs doing, just as he looked around "with anger" at the Pharisees (3:5), just as he looked around at his disciples to pronounce them his family in rejection of his close relatives (3:34), just as he looked around to unmask the woman who had touched him (5:32), just as he looked around to warn his disciples how difficult it is for a rich person to enter God's kingdom (10:23). His looking around is imperial, stern. Only the looking around of disciples might carry a connotation of naivety or awe (9:8).

In some respects v 11 comes closer to vv 15, 19, 27; 13:1 than to 11:1, but again differences in number and phraseology forestall simplistic redaction critical judgments. If Jesus and the Twelve really did commute between Bethany and Jerusalem during Holy Week — and there is nothing inherently doubtful about their doing so — the wording of the narratives will naturally exhibit similarities. The presence of so-called Marcanisms, such as the asyndetic pairing of prepositional phrases, the Hellenistic spelling of "Jerusalem" (see the Greek text), and the references to Jesus' "looking around," "all things," the onset of evening, and "the Twelve," does not disprove underlying tradition. As usual, in fact, frequency in Mark might mean frequency in pre-Marcan tradition, or Marcan phrasing of tradition, or Marcan additions to tradition as easily as wholesale Marcan fabrication of nontraditional linkage. For example, the use of "the Twelve" may arise by compositional allusion to 10:32-34 (see the comments); but the Twelve's accompanying Jesus is inherently likely and traditional, though the tradition may not have used that expression. J. Wellhausen (2. Aufl., 89) argues that the contrast between the absence of "again" from v 15 and its presence in v 27 shows that Mark has constructed v 11 in anticipation of vv 15, 19 (cf. also 2:1 with 1:21; 2:13 with 1:16; et passim). In v 27, however, "again" is more likely, or at least just as likely, a Marcanism the absence of which in v 15 therefore says nothing one way or the other about the issue of tradition versus redaction in v 11 (see C.-P. März, "Siehe" 26-27; L. Schenke, Studien 29-31; W. R. Telford, Barren Temple 45-46; T. A. Mohr, Markus- und Johannespassion 64-69; and E. Best, Disciples and Discipleship 149, n. 94, for different positions). In the absence of pre-Marcan materials, we are in the dark. Hence, the so-called Marcanisms in v 11 do not prove that Mark has constructed the verse to create an unhistorical chronology for the sake of a supposed symbolism.

"And the disciples were listening" may well be a redactional statement, but not for the purpose of postponing the withering of the fig tree against a traditional immediacy of withering. Instead, the purpose is to give assurance that even though Jesus was not addressing his disciples, he really did curse the fig tree. They heard him curse it. Thus no one should think to explain away the later-noticed witheredness of the tree in any way but as a fulfilment.

Mark himself gives the reason why the chief priests and the scribes do not challenge Jesus' authority immediately: "for they feared him, for all the crowd were astonished at his teaching" (v 18). They must not say or do anything to challenge Jesus on the spot lest the admiring crowd leap to his defense. The care and cunning of the Jewish authorities vis-à-vis the crowd on one side and the riot-conscious Romans on the other side has the ring of truth (cf. Josephus J.W. 2.17.6 §426; 2.17.9 §441) and runs right through the passion narrative (cf. v 32; 12:12, 34b; 14:1-2, 10-11, 43-44, 49). To the contrary, D. E. Nineham (305) thinks fear of Jesus' popularity a strange reason for wanting to destroy him, a more natural reason for not daring to arrest him, as in 12:12; 14:1-2. But this line of thinking is specious, for fearing your enemy because of his popularity might easily make you want to destroy him. His popularity would survive at most in people's memory, and he himself could no longer capitalize on his popularity at your expense.

To accept the substance of v 18 as historical, we need not deny Mark's composing the verse in his own style and with his own emphases (cf. the notes on so-called Marcanisms). He likes γάρ-clauses. Here, two of them occur in succession. Ζητέω, "seek," and πῶς, "how," will occur together with reference to Jesus' passion also in 14:1, 11, and ζητέω alone with the same reference in 12:12; 14:55. See also 3:6 for αὐτὸν ἀπολέσωσιν, "they might destroy him." However much of Mark's redaction goes into v 18, the purpose is not chronological, to postpone the challenge to Jesus' authority, but Christological, to emphasize the Jewish authorities' fear of Jesus and the crowd's admiration of him. Similar considerations apply to the linkages in vv 19-20, 27. If incidents such as the Triumphal Procession, the temple-cleansing, and the challenge to Jesus' authority were interconnected in the tradition and possibly in historical actuality (and the challenge to Jesus' authority must have been traditionally and historically interconnected with *some* exercise of authority), we have no reason in principle to deny that historically intervening incidents might have made their way into the tradition at the same time. The very early pre-Papian tradition that Mark got his information from Peter (Eus. *H.E.* 3.39.15) supports this possibility (see pp. 1026-45).

"These things" in v 28 (bis) refers to the stoppages that made up the temple-cleansing, not to Jesus' healing or teaching or walking around in the temple, for which he would need no "authority" (so correctly W. R. Telford, *Barren Temple* 48, against *POxy.* 840. 2). But does occurrence of the cleansing on the previous day make "these things" so awkward and inappropriate that we must deduce an originally same-day challenge to Jesus' authority? Not only do the cleansing and "these things" stand close to each other in the text. They are also topographically near. Most of all, "these things" are at hand the day after the cleansing because the commercial traffic in the temple is still at a halt (N.B. the present tense of ποιεῖς, "are you doing"). That is the implication, which rebuts the charge of awkwardness (cf. R. H. Hiers in *JBL* 90 [1971] 84).

Mark's sandwiches vary in their chronological relations and implications. The narrative of John the Baptist's death (6:14-29) pretends to be no more than a flashback (see esp. v 16). Peter's denials (14:66-72) surely occurred during Jesus' trial (see esp. v 54). Mark leaves it vague when the anointing of Jesus took place (14:3-9; contrast "while he was in Bethany" [v 3] with the specific indications of time in vv 1, 12). Nothing prevents the exorcism in 1:23-26 from having taken place during Jesus' teaching in the synagogue, or the healing of the woman with a constant flow of blood during his journey to Jairus's house (5:25-34). Given this mixture of evidence, we have no reason to deduce from the double sandwich in chap. 11 that Mark has fabricated an unhistorical chronology. The credit for that belongs to Matthew.

L. Schenke (*Studien* 29-31) says not only that Mark has fabricated an unhistorical chronology of three days in chap. 11, but also that this chronology starts an unhistorical chronology of Holy Week in its entirety. Why then does the marking of progression in days lapse at several points after chap. 11? Even within chap. 11, "late," "evening," and "early, in the morning" stress times of day more than a succession of days. The end of Tuesday will not be indicated. Wednesday will remain silent. 14:3 will be curiously ambiguous. The day in 14:12 will relate to a festival, not to the week of passion. And 16:1 will start a new week, not cap an old one (cf. W. R. Telford, *Barren Temple* 41-42).

R. H. Lightfoot (*History and Interpretation* 81; *Gospel Message* 61) argues that since the immediately impending crisis of Jesus' death sounds no alarm in chaps. 12–13, Mark must be inserting these chapters and thereby breaking up an original connection between chaps. 11 and 14–16. But Jesus does sound an alarm in 12:6-11. The questions subsequently asked him do not lend themselves to answering with predictions of his passion and resurrection. The anointing of him, Judas Iscariot's bargain to betray him, and the Last Supper in chap. 14 do not follow up the Triumphal Procession, the cursing and withering of the fig tree, and the temple-cleansing in chap. 11 any more naturally than they follow up the dialogues and soliloquies in chaps. 12–13. One could argue, in fact, that Jesus' confrontations with his enemies, withdrawal from the temple, prediction of its destruction, and outline of the course of the age till he comes in triumph set the stage for the Passion more appropriately and completely than would the events in chap. 11 by themselves. The fear of Jesus that reduces the Sanhedrin to plotting how to destroy him rather than arresting him on the spot (11:18) prepares for their trying to discredit him before his admirers as well as it prepares for his betrayal (14:1). Therefore the reminder of that plot in 14:1 does not demonstrate insertion of the intervening material. It simply picks up the story line after a long section of talk. An intermediate reminder of the plot at 12:12 keeps the story line alive in the midst of the talk.

T. A. Mohr (*Markus- und Johannespassion* 110-13) refines Lightfoot's theory in such a way that Mark inserts 12:1–14:11 to create a section that includes chap. 11 and centers around the old temple of the Jews, which the new temple consisting of the church is to replace. But Mark 11–13 contains little or no ecclesiology. It deals almost exclusively in Christology and uses the temple only as a showcase for Jesus' various powers. We will see reasons to reject the view that the church stands under the figure of a new temple.

J. Schmid (215) thinks the parable interruptive of the sequence of conflicts and surprising in its attack on the Sanhedrin, and concludes that Mark has inserted the parable. But Jesus is not attacking. He is counterattacking. The Sanhedrin's attacking his authority makes it entirely natural that he should counterattack. As a counterattack, the parable does not interrupt a sequence of conflicts so much as it brings closure to the first conflict, which otherwise ended in Jesus' refusal to answer a question. That refusal marked a victory for him, but it also left a question unanswered. Hence, the link in 12:1a between the questioning of his authority and the present parable concerning his authority — and fate — does not look artificial (against L. Schenke, *Studien* 32-34).

H.-W. Kuhn (*Ältere Sammlungen* 42) thinks that Mark puts 12:1-12 here to make Jesus give an indirect answer to the question he refused to answer directly in 11:27-33, i.e. the question, "Who gave you this authority . . . ?" (11:28). The indirect answer: God, whose only and beloved Son I am (cf. 12:6). But Jesus himself may have given such an answer. Its indirectness favors that the connection with the challenge to his authority is both original and Jesuanic.

K. Snodgrass (*Parable* 55-71) argues for the greater originality of Matthew's version and, because of agreements between Matthew and Luke against Mark, for the presence of the parable in Q. But those agreements, like similar ones found elsewhere, may derive from secondary influence of Matthew on Luke (see R. H. Gundry, *Matthew* 424-32; idem in *The Four Gospels 1992*); and it is more probable that Matthew smooths out the roughness in Mark 12:5b and creates an allusion to the former and latter prophets than that Mark adds v 5b to compensate for his earlier scaling down of the plurality represented in Matthew (see Gundry, *Matthew* 424-32, for simpler explanations of a Matthean redactional sort; also J. S. Sibinga in *NovT* 26 [1984] 383-84).

See B. Dehandschutter (in *L'Évangile selon Marc* 203-19) that *Gos. Thom.* 65 adapts Luke's version and that Mark's stands closest to the original (cf. K. Snodgrass in *NTS* 20 [1974-75] 142-44; idem, *Parable* 52-54; W. Schrage, *Verhältnis* 137-45; A. Lindemann in *ZNW* 71 [1980] 236-37; H. Weder, *Gleichnisse Jesu* 152-53; C. L. Blomberg in *Gospel Perspectives* 5. 189-90). On the principle that the more difficult version is likely to be the more original because traditioners and redactors tend to make things easier for their audiences, the greater plausibility of *Gos. Thom.* 65 stands against its greater originality, not for it (as thought by J. D. Crossan, *Four Other Gospels* 53-62). More specifically, H. Koester (in *The NT and Gnosis* 199-200) sees in *Gos. Thom.* 65 an original climactic series of three. More likely, *Gos. Thom.* 65 conforms the whole parable to the rhetorical law of three by retaining two of the slaves plus the son and trimming the rest. Against the argument that a Gnostic editor deleted all references to salvation-history in the more original canonical versions of the parable, Koester cites *Gos. Thom.* 52 (op. cit. 203, n. 24). But that passage makes the disciples say, "Twenty-four prophets spoke in Israel, and all of them spoke in [reference to] you," only to have Jesus turn aside their salvation-historical statement with the retort, "You have omitted the one living in your presence and have spoken about the dead."

Among others, W. L. Lane (415, n. 1) and M. Y.-H. Lee (*Jesus und die jüdische Autorität* 22-23, n. 6, 159) think that ἐν παραβολαῖς means "parabolically," as in 3:23, rather than "in more than one parable." But the fact that in 3:23 the phrase referred to more than one parable — i.e. to the parables of Satan's casting out Satan, of a kingdom divided against itself, of a house divided against itself, of Satan's rising up against himself, and of the house of a strong man — and likewise in 4:1 to the parables of the seeds, the lamp, etc., favors a present reference to more than one parable, only one of which Mark records in detail (cf. 4:10, where the disciples ask Jesus about "the parables" despite his having spoken only one parable and despite his proceeding to give an explanation of only one; also 4:33, where Mark refers to many parables that he leaves otherwise unrecorded). These other passages and the characteristically Marcan pleonastic use of ἤρξατο, "he began," here in 12:1 make doubtful an allusion to Ps 77:2 LXX (ἐν παραβολαῖς; contrast the singular במשל in the MT [78:2]).

The use of ἄνθρωπος, "a man," in the sense of τις, "someone," is Semitic (E. C. Maloney, *Semitic Interference* 131-34, somewhat against M. Reiser, *Syntax und Stil* 20-21). For textual comparisons with Isa 5:1-2, see R. H. Gundry, *Use of the OT* 43-44; and idem, *Matthew* 425, for further details about the fence, the tower, etc.; also for literature on the realism of the parable and against overinterpreting the absence of the landlord and the tenant farmers' contrary behavior. There is nothing to indicate whether the owner was a foreigner living abroad (for the various possibilities, see K. Snodgrass, *Parable* 31-34, and esp. J. Drury in *JTS* ns 24 [1973] 373). Jesus' omissions of the digging and of the vine in Isa 5:2 and his changing προλήνιον, "vat (in front of a winepress)" (LXX), to ὑπολήνιον, "vat (under a winepress)," throw difficulties in the way of the suggestion by P. C. Beentjes (in *Bib* 63 [1982] 519-20) that Mark inverts the Isaianic order. Similarly, his failure to invert the Septuagintal order of building and tower throws a difficulty in the way of Beentjes's similar suggestion that Mark inverts the Septuagintal order of verbs and their direct objects (or vice versa). It seems rather that after putting the direct object "vineyard" first for emphasis, he simply reverts to the normal order verb–direct object. Why D. E. Nineham (311) should call the Isaianic phraseology in Mark "no doubt the work of the Evangelist, or one of his predecessors" is mystifying unless Jesus did not know or use the OT and unless the Septuagintal cast of some of the borrowed phraseology cannot have arisen by Hellenistic rewording of the original parable (but see C. E. Carlston, *Parables* 179, n. 4, for the possibility of such rewording, and C. A. Evans in *BZ* nf 28 [1984] 82-86 for non-Septuagintal, Hebrew features, esp. Mark's keeping verbs in the third person rather than switching to the first person of the LXX, and using ὑπολήνιον rather than προλήνιον for the vat).

Several factors may have combined to prompt a parable based on Isa 5:1-2: (1) the widespread Jewish interpretation of the tower in Isa 5:2 as the temple and of the vat as the altar (*Tg. Isa* 5:2, 5; *t. Meʿil.* 1:16; *t. Sukk.* 3:15; cf. *1 Enoch* 89:56, 66b-67, 73; *Barn.* 16:1-2, 4-5); (2) Jesus' having cleansed the temple just yesterday; (3) his having just now been challenged concerning his authority to do so; and (4) his standing at this moment in the temple. His audience, also familiar with the interpretation of Isa 5:1-2 in terms of temple and altar, would then have understood the tenant farmers as the hierarchs ensconced in the temple, i.e. as the Sanhedrin who meet there nearly every day (B. D. Chilton, *Galilean Rabbi* 111-14).

Since the tenant farmers represent the Sanhedrin, ensconced in the temple, we might think that the vineyard represents the temple, not the Jewish people as a whole. But such a limitation would go against Isaiah's and others' portrayal of Israel as a vineyard or vine, against the widespread Jewish interpretation of the tower as the temple, and against Jesus' prediction that the temple will be destroyed (13:1-2). Whereas the vineyard will be given to others, only the tenant farmers will be destroyed. Furthermore, the authority of the Sanhedrin is not limited to the temple; and the fruits of the vineyard represent the conduct of all the people more naturally than they represent the liturgy of the temple. For portrayals of Israel as a vineyard or vine, see the references cited by J. Behm in *TDNT* 1. 342, to which add Isa 27:2-6; Jer 12:10; Ezek 17:5-10; also O. H. Steck, *Israel und das gewaltsame Geschick der Propheten* 270-71, n. 7.

A. Cornette (in *FV* 84 [1985] 42-48) adds that the fence represents the Law. Since the Pharisees will not help kill Jesus, Cornette also limits the tenant farmers to the Sadducees and makes the Pharisees those to whom the owner gives the vineyard after destroying the wicked tenants. But in rabbinic literature a fence represents the oral law (see, e.g., *m. ʾAbot* 1:1), which Jesus rejects (7:8-13). And though the Pharisees are not mentioned during the trial and crucifixion of Jesus, they have consistently opposed him, even to the point of plotting his death (3:6). He has opposed them and warned against them (see esp. 8:15), and they will shortly join in an attempt to trip Jesus up (12:13). Some candidates for the new tenants!

Three considerations undermine an interpretation of the vineyard as Israel's election and the tenant farmers as her stiff-neckedness (so R. Pesch 2. 220): (1) the frequent use of a vineyard or a vine for the Jewish people themselves; (2) Jesus' drawing on Isaiah 5, where the vineyard is so identified; and (3) his comparing the leading disciples to farmworkers (Matt 9:37-38 par. Luke 10:2; John 4:35-38; cf. 1 Cor 3:6-9). That comparison makes probable a similar comparison of the Jewish leaders to farmers (cf. his comparing the latter to builders in Mark 12:10).

In v 2 τῷ καιρῷ hardly means "at the time agreed on," "at the appropriate time" (so J. D. M. Derrett, *Law* 296), or "the fifth year after planting" (cf. Lev 19:23-25). In association with taking fruit from the vineyard, in the absence of any reference to Lev 19:23-25, and in the neighborhood of "season of figs" (11:13), the phrase simply means "at harvest time" (cf. Ps 1:3 LXX). Ἀπὸ τῶν καρπῶν does not have to be considered a Semitism for "some of the fruits" (see E. C. Maloney, *Semitic Interference* 137, against M. Black,

Aramaic Approach 108), though J. Carmignac (in *ASTI* 7 [1968-69] 71) notes the possibility of an underlying wordplay in מפני הכורמים מפרי הכרם, "from the farmers from the fruits of the vineyard." The plural of "fruits" multiplies the produce of the vineyard to include not only grapes but also olives, figs, melons, gourds, cucumbers, and other vegetables and grains, as was not unusual for vineyards in those days (J. F. Ross in *IDB* 4. 785). The word "fruits" itself disfavors payment in money gotten from the sale of the fruits, also payment in raisins or in wine made from the grapes of the vineyard (for the latter of which we would expect ἐκ τοῦ γενήματος τῆς ἀμπέλου, "the product of the vine" — 14:25). Derrett (op. cit. 296-97) supposes that the slaves and son would take shares of the crops and market them there and then, i.e. before returning to the owner. This supposition does not sit easily with the owner's sending slaves that *he*, not they, might receive some of the fruits. The prophets were sent to the whole of the Jewish people, not just to the hierarchs; but as the prophets held the hierarchs peculiarly responsible to insure justice and righteousness among the whole of the people, so the slaves in Jesus' parable go to the tenant farmers to receive fruits from the whole of the vineyard. For empty-handedness, see Gen 31:42; Deut 15:13; Ruth 1:21; Job 22:9; Jer 14:3; Jdt 1:11; Sir 29:9, esp. in the LXX.

Since in v 4 κεφαλιόω, which after the analogy of γναθόω, "hit on the cheek," presumably means "hit on the head," occurs only here, F. C. Burkitt (in *AJT* 15 [1911] 175) conjectures a paleographical blunder for ἐκολάφισαν, "they buffeted" (cf. 14:65). But the analogy with γναθόω seems stronger than a conjectural emendation. We would expect the textual tradition to preserve an original reading as well as a blunder, and a blunder would likely exchange an uncommon word for a common one rather than vice versa. See the literature cited in BAGD s.v. κεφαλιόω. Against an allusion to John the Baptizer's beheading in the hitting of the second slave on the head (so J. D. Crossan in *JBL* 90 [1971] 452; W. J. Bennett, Jr., in *NovT* 17 [1975] 13; W. H. Kelber, *Oral and Written Gospel* 63-64, 112), hitting on the head differs from beheading (cf. 6:27); and such an allusion would require the death of the second slave to correspond to John's death — yet death does not come into the parable till the mission of the following slave.

M. Hengel (in *ZNW* 59 [1968] 8) argues that since in Matt 22:3-4 a parabolic reference to OT prophets derives from redaction of a more original version lacking that reference (cf. Luke 14:17), in Mark 12:2-5 the parabolic reference to OT prophets likewise derives from redaction. Possibly, but not necessarily. Elsewhere Jesus refers to the sending of the OT prophets (Matt 23:37 par. Luke 13:34), and his borrowing from Isa 5:1-2 casts the parable in an OT mold that favors another such reference here.

There are several reasons to regard "and many others, beating some [of them] and killing others [of them]" as a post-Jesuanic addition: (1) By conforming to the rhetorical law of three, the trio of individually mentioned slaves seem to bring closure to the part of the parable dealing with slaves. (2) The killing of the third slave brings the maltreatment of the slaves to a climax which makes the beating and killing of others anticlimactic. (3) The lack of anything which δέροντες, "beating," and ἀποκτέννοντες, "killing," might modify gives the impression that someone added the second half of v 5, left ἀπέστειλεν, "he sent," to be supplied, and disregarded or forgot that this intervening ellipsis and the sameness of meaning in "killed" and "killing" keep the participles from modifying "they" in "they killed." (4) The combination μέν . . . δέ has no Semitic equivalent and seems necessary to the participial phrases, i.e. seems not to have been imposed on them, yet a large number of Semitisms and the wordplay between הבן and אבן favor an originally Semitic version of the parable (see M. Hengel in *ZNW* 59 [1968] 7-8, n. 31; M. Y.-H. Lee, *Jesus und die jüdische Autorität* 80, for over a dozen possible Semitisms, though several of them are found also in un-Semitic Greek).

Some consider the whole of v 5 secondary because the sending and killing of the third slave as well as the sending and killing of further slaves seems to spoil the climax in the sending and killing of the son yet satisfies the rhetorical law of three. But no, v 5 heightens the tension by magnifying the risk in sending the son. The climax does not suffer, but gains also for the reason that one would never dream of the tenant farmers' daring to kill an only, beloved son as though he were another slave. And Jesus is as likely as a later redactor to have satisfied the rhetorical law of three (cf. H. Weder, *Gleichnisse Jesu* 148, n. 6). J. Swetnam (in *Bib* 65 [1984] 414; 66 [1985] 137) sees progress in the revelation of Jesus' divine sonship to Jesus himself (1:11), to a select group of apostles (9:7), and now to Jesus' enemies (12:6). In view of the parabolic nature of the present passage, however, the last of these revelations will be better served by 14:61-62.

The emphatic forward position of ἕνα, "one," and the consequent separation from its noun υἱόν, "son," argue against treating it as a Semitic indefinite use of "one" for "a." Whether an underlying חד meant "one" or "a" we cannot be certain. But if ἀγαπητόν rests on יחיד, "only," as often in the LXX, an underlying Aramaic may have meant "an only son." Is ἀγαπητόν then added in last position by assimilation to the baptismal and trans-figurational voices, or simply by linguistic habit based on the LXX, the association with those voices subsequently arising only in the story line of the whole gospel (cf. the suggestion of M. Hengel [in *ZNW* 59 (1968) 30, n. 96] that ἀγαπητόν interprets ἕνα)? If the voices represented experiences of Jesus about which he spoke to his disciples, in the parable he himself may echo the phraseology of those voices. Since the beloved one in Isa 5:1 is portrayed as a bridegroom in relation to his bride (represented by the vineyard), the use of ἀγαπητός in the LXX for דוד, "beloved," may not influence Mark 12:6, where ἀγαπητός quite differently describes a son in relation to his father.

Limiting the original as distinct from Marcan referent of the owner's son to the expected eschatological prophet, or to John the Baptizer, does not pay due to Jesus' talking about himself as God's Son in a uniquely privileged sense (above all, see Matt 11:27 par. Luke 10:22). The stress in the parable on the son's heirship puts him in a different class from that of the slaves, who represent prophets. R. Pesch (2. 218) cites the LXX of Exod 10:3; Lev 26:41; 4 Kgdms 22:19; 2 Chr 7:14; 12:7, 12; 34:27; 36:12 for the use of ἐντρέπομαι in the sense of showing respect to God and God's messengers, and infers a reference to the eschatological prophet from the present use of this verb. But those passages included priests and scribes as well as prophets and differ from the present passage by including respect for God, whereas the parable speaks of respect for the owner's son but not for the owner, who represents God. The eschatological implication of ἔσχατον, "last," favors no Christology — prophetic, royal, filial, or any other — above another. Because of word position and (except for "again" back in v 4a) the lack of earlier adverbs indicating before and after, we should probably understand ἔσχατον as an adjective modifying αὐτόν, "him [as] last," rather than as an adverb modifying ἀπέστειλεν, "he sent . . . lastly."

The contrast between the owner's slaves and son cannot be "fully explained from the dramatic climax of the parable," with the result that "nothing [Christological] can be made of the distinction" (as thought by J. D. G. Dunn, *Jesus and the Spirit* 36); for Jesus might have skipped directly from the sending of the slaves to the coming of the owner. The tenant farmers' maltreatment of the slaves would quite well enough have justified the owner's coming; so we cannot afford to discount the Christological implication of the son's being sent and then murdered.

For the legal situation of the owner, the son, and the tenant farmers, see the summaries in W. L. Lane 418, n. 13; R. Pesch 2. 217-18; K. Snodgrass, *Parable* 36-38; and more detailed discussions in J. D. M. Derrett, *Law* 286-312; M. Hengel in *ZNW* 59 (1968) 25-29; and E. Bammel in *RIDA* 3/6 (1959) 11-17. C. E. Carlston (*Parables* 184-85) criticizes these legal discussions on the grounds that the law does not allow the tenant farmers to acquire intestate land by murder, that their deducing the death of the owner does not arise out of the parable itself, and that "*defensible* conduct [on the part of the tenant farmers] would have put Jesus' hearers on the side of the tenants — and thus robbed the parable of any point!" (cf. J. A. T. Robinson in *NTS* 21 [1974-75] 448). But the legal discussions do not contest the illegality of the murder. They only explain how the inheritance might become the tenant farmers' if they get away with the murder. The murder keeps Jesus' hearers on the side of the owner. As we have already seen, the tenant farmers' deduction that the owner has died arises out of the wording of the parable in v 7. Under any view of the legalities involved, the tenant farmers' killing the heir to make the vineyard their own implies the death of the heir's father. If they are thinking that the father has not died but has abandoned the vineyard or is about to do so (as thought by Derrett, *Law* 305-6), talk of the heir and his inheritance would lose its appropriateness. And the law of blood vengeance would keep the tenant farmers from thinking that they could get away with killing the son if his father were still alive. But Carlston and E. Haenchen (398, n. 8) are correct to stress that the message of the parable is not to be discovered in legal and other realistic background. Unrealisms offer surer clues. Some of the legal discussions also read into the parable matters that do not affect its point.

The wording of vv 7-8 recalls Gen 37:20, 24 (see esp. the LXX). Yet though Joseph was beloved (Gen 37:3-4), unlike the son in Jesus' parable he was not an only son. Moreover, Joseph was not killed, but only thrown into a pit, whereas the son in the parable is killed and thrown out of the vineyard but not into a pit. Despite allusions to the story of Joseph in *T. Dan* 1:4-9; *T. Gad* 1:4–5:11; *T. Jos.* 1:1–20:6; *T. Benj.* 2:1–3:7, then, a similar allusion by Jesus or a redactor of his parable remains uncertain — though still possible, since NT use of the OT often strays from the OT meaning and context.

To make the point that the tenant farmers pollute the vineyard, according to J. D. M. Derrett (in *JTS* ns 25 [1974] 431), Mark insists on the remarkable and improbable killing of the son inside it. But the text stresses throwing him outside, not killing him inside. K. Snodgrass (*Parable* 60-61) thinks that originally, as in Matthew and Luke, before killing the son the tenant farmers threw him outside the vineyard to keep its produce ritually clean and saleable, and that to introduce a desecration of the corpse Mark may have reversed the order and brought the killing inside the vineyard. But in Matthew and Luke the throwing out relates to inheritance, not to the produce of the vineyard; i.e. the son is ejected from his inheritance. The normality of expulsion before killing may not at all favor the originality of that order. It may rather have influenced Matthew and Luke to change Mark's order because of its abnormality. The progression of leading Jesus away, going out, and coming to Golgotha in Matt 27:31-33 (par. Luke 23:26, 32-33) favors a secondary switching of Mark's order to conform to what happens in the passion story (cf. Heb 13:12-13), but a secondary switching in forgetfulness that the vineyard represents Israel, not Jerusalem.

Far from betraying the hand of a redactor, the outrageousness of the tenant farmers' crimes and the incredibility of the owner's repeatedly sacrificing the life and limb of his slaves, and then even of his one, beloved son, bear the stamp of Jesus' parabolic style. They also stand in the tradition of God's sending one prophet after another at the expense of their lives and limbs because of Israel's rebelliousness. Elsewhere in his parables Jesus uses unrealism (three measures of flour for one lump of dough, for example) and draws on prophetic themes (God's kingdom, for example; cf. H. Weder, *Gleichnisse Jesu* 155, n. 41).

E. Lohmeyer (244) lists but does not explain several other unrealisms: (1) a tower instead of a watchman's hut; (2) payment in grapes (and other produce, we should add), which would perish in transport to the distant owner; (3) the immediacy with which the vineyard bears fruit, τῷ καιρῷ meaning "at the season [of harvest]" (v 2), as though three years were not required for the vines to start producing (cf. M.-J. Lagrange 306) and as though Lev 19:23-25 did not forbid eating fruits till the fifth year after planting; and (4) the owner's planting a vineyard only to go away for a long time or permanently. The tower comes from Isa 5:2. The frequently figurative use of fruit for works overcomes the unrealism of payment in quickly perishable produce. An initial period of bearing no fruit and of the owner's presence would not contribute to the purpose of the parable.

That the owner will take it on himself to destroy the tenant farmers, as though he were a king with an army at his command (cf. Matt 22:7; Cic. *Att.* 5.21; 6.1), shows parable tending toward interpretation in terms of God as the king of the universe who uses the armies of nations to accomplish his purposes. C. E. Carlston (*Parables* 184, n. 32) criticizes the Ciceronic parallel by noting the contrasts between the justice of the owner's cause and the injustice of Brutus's cause, and between the owner's delaying to destroy the tenant farmers and Brutus's wasting no time to use cavalry for collecting a debt. But these contrasts make it less problematic, not more problematic, that the owner should finally yet justly act like Brutus!

J. D. Crossan (*Four Other Gospels* 61) thinks he detects a seam between vv 8 and 9 in the shifts from third person to second, from past tense to future, and from the son to a stone. But the shift to second person does not occur till v 10a and does not last. Verses 10-11 go back to the past tense, and the wordplay underlying "the son" and "a stone" (הבן and אבן) favors a seamless substratum; for otherwise we would have to make both the unlikely supposition that a subtle wordplay was added to a parable which had already reached closure and the further supposition that a Semitic wordplay was followed by assimilation to the LXX.

The question, "What then will the owner of the vineyard do?" (v 9a), "is so general that it must have been connected with its answer from the first" (C. E. Carlston, *Parables* 180). The assertion that the motif of destroying the tenant farmers and giving the vineyard to others has parallels in the primitive church but not in Jesus' teaching (ibid.) not only rejects Matt 8:11 par. Luke 13:28-29 without argument (ibid., n. 13) but also fails to take account of Matt 19:28 par. Luke 22:29-30 (noted above). D. E. Nineham (312) uses Luke 17:9 as evidence that Jesus does not ordinarily answer questions to which his parables lead and argues that the answer in Mark 12:9b may therefore come from a redactor. Luke 17:9 does not supply the needed evidence, however, because it records a rhetorical question containing an answer within itself, as does also Matt 18:12 par. Luke 15:4. In Matt 21:31; Luke 7:42-43; 10:36, on the other hand, Jesus' audiences answer questions to which his parables lead. Matt 21:31 may be redactional, however (see R. H. Gundry, *Matthew* 421-24); and in Luke 18:8 Jesus himself answers such a question, as here in Mark 12:9b. There are no further such questions to consider; so Jesus' other parables fail to provide the amount and kind of evidence needed for Nineham's argument.

On God's coming for judgment, see J. Schneider in *TDNT* 2. 667, 670-71; H. D. Preuss in *TDOT* 2. 34-38; on judgment as destruction, A. Oepke in *TDNT* 1. 395-97; B. Otzen in *TDOT* 1. 20-22. If OT prophets could predict the Babylonian destruction of Jerusalem and of the Jewish authorities based there, we should not regard the coming Roman destruction as evidence of inauthenticity in Jesus' similar prediction. Luke 13:6-9 seems to threaten judgment on Israel, not alone on the Jewish authorities, and therefore provides only a partial parallel. But the limitation to Jerusalem and the temple in 13:2 parr.; Matt 23:37-39 par. Luke 13:34-35; Luke 19:41-44 comes very close.

Δώσει, "he will give," probably drops the prefix of ἐξέδετο, "he leased out" (literally, "he gave out" — v 1), for economy of expression. If so, giving means leasing out. The "others" to whom the owner will give the vineyard cannot represent Gentile Christians (and so need not reflect the later influx of Gentiles into the church); for just as the tenant farmers represented leadership (the Sanhedrin), so also must the others represent leadership (Jesus and the Twelve; cf. the foregoing comments). For the same reason, the others do not represent the whole church, Jewish as well as Gentile Christians. Since Gentiles do not come into the picture, "to others" does not give evidence that Mark inserts this parable to interpret the Sanhedrin's rejection of Jesus in the light of the Gentile mission (against R. H. Stein, *Proper Methodology* 207-8).

Limitation of the others to Jesus and the Twelve in accordance with Matt 19:28 par. Luke 22:29-30 eliminates any need to say with C. E. Carlston (*Parables* 185) that although the vineyard at first represents Israel, by the end of the parable it is the tenant farmers who represent Israel. The vineyard represents Israel all the way through; only the leadership shifts. Against a limitation to leaders even in the first part of the parable, Carlston (op. cit. 189) objects that in the OT all the people, not just a few leaders, maltreated the prophets and that nothing in the parable suggests such a limitation. But since the borrowing from Isaiah 5 suggests that the vineyard represents the Jewish people, the importation of tenant farmers does suggest that they represent only the leaders of the Jewish people. And though in the OT and Jewish tradition all the people often rejected the message of the prophets, it was their leaders who maltreated them (so the stories of Elijah and his fellow prophets [1 Kgs 18:1-15; 19:1-14], of Micaiah [1 Kgs 22:26-27], of Amos [*Vit. Proph.* 7:1-2]; of Isaiah [*Vit. Proph.* 1:1; Heb 11:37]; of Micah [*Vit. Proph.* 6:1]; of Zechariah the son of Jehoiada [2 Chr 24:19-22; *Vit. Proph.* 23:1], of Uriah [Jer 26:20-23], of Jeremiah [Jer 20:1-18; 26:8-15; 32:1-5; 37:11–38:13], and of Ezekiel [*Vit. Proph.* 3:2]; cf. the limitation to Jewish leaders and Jerusalem in Matt 23:29-32 par. Luke 11:46-47; Matt 23:37-39 par. Luke 13:34-35).

The amount of allegory contained in a parable does not determine whether or not Jesus spoke the parable in its present form or at all. We know how much allegory he used only from the earliest versions of his parables as we have them. Denying authenticity to the present parable because it has a more than usual amount of allegory, or revising it so as to reduce the amount, is Procrustean. Granted that some of Jesus' parables contain no allegory whatever. But it does not follow that others cannot contain allegory, even much of it. Parables include a number of subspecies, and a speaker may easily use more than one of them. Jesus did, quite apart from the question of allegory. Take his use of parabolic maxims as well as of parabolic stories, for example (cf. the notes on 3:23; G. B. Caird, *Language* 160-67; J. J. Vincent in *SE I* 85-88).

The killing of some of the owner's slaves corresponds to the fate of some of the OT prophets, but the beating, head injury, and disgrace inflicted on the other slaves do not correspond to the prophets' known fates (though see Heb 11:32-38). Nor did the Sanhedrin kill Jesus to get any kind of inheritance. Nor was his corpse thrown out of anywhere and left unburied. These differences show that the parable is not entirely allegorical.

Nowhere else does Mark use "the Scripture" in the singular, and the occurrences of its plural form in 12:24; 14:49 do not introduce a direct quotation such as follows here. We have no reason, then, to regard "the Scripture" as evidence that Mark or an earlier redactor has added the quotation in vv 10-11 (cf. E. Best, *Following Jesus* 219). One may suppose that the question, "You've read . . . , haven't you?" (v 10), has been redactionally assimilated to 2:25; 12:26 (so H.-J. Klauck, *Allegorie* 287); but it is more likely that all three passages provide evidence of a characteristically Jesuanic locution, one that supports the originality of the following quotation of Ps 118:22-23. The probable allusion to that OT passage in the expression "and to be rejected" at 8:31 par. Luke 9:22; Luke 17:25, the underlying wordplay between בֵן, "the son," in the narrative and אֶבֶן, "stone," in the quotation, the leaving of room for the rejected stone through omitting in v 1 the digging up and removal of stones, mentioned in Isa 5:2, and the wordplay, already prepared for in v 4, between "hit on the head" and "head of a corner" all likewise support originality (on the wordplay, see esp. K. Snodgrass, *Parable* 113-18). J. Gnilka's feeling forced to back-date an addition of the quotation to a pre-Marcan and possibly Semitic redaction — and this despite the presently Septuagintal form of the quotation — testifies to the force of these arguments. (Two other arguments sometimes given for originality — viz., the familiarity of Psalm 118 as one of the oft-sung Hallel psalms and the rabbinic practice of sometimes ending a parable with an OT quotation — would equally well suit a redactional addition.)

For a later addition of vv 10-11 J. R. Donahue (*Are You the Christ?* 124) argues that those verses carry the theme of vindication whereas vv 1-9 do not. But the destruction of the tenant farmers and the giving of the vineyard to others do vindicate the son post mortem, and we can hardly expect the story to include a resurrection of the son. What we have instead of resurrection is a shift from הבן to אבן. This shift makes possible a further vindication of the son, now a stone, a vindication that reverses his former fate. In the Semitic original the subtlety of the shift makes for a smooth transition which favors that vv 10-11 belonged to vv 1-9 from the start.

That a change from killing to vindication would come as naturally to Jesus as to a later redactor is shown by Jesus' many promises of vindication and reward to those who follow him at great cost, and by his including resurrection alongside passion in the predictions of his own destiny (see the comments and notes on 8:31 for their authenticity). C. E. Carlston (*Parables* 182, n. 24) objects that Jesus is said to predict his resurrection only to the disciples, not to his enemies. But the figurativeness of the present allusion to his vindication and its reference to his coming rulership, not to his resurrection (see the foregoing comments), make up for that difference.

Carlston (op. cit. 180-81) argues for later addition of vv 10-11 also on the ground that the wrath of the Sanhedrin in v 12 springs from the parable in vv 1-9, not from the OT quotation in vv 10-11. This ground is slippery. In vv 10-11 Jesus slurs the Sanhedrin as missing the meaning of Ps 118:22-23 and as being the builders who stupidly rejected the headstone of the corner. So in their ignorance and behavior those builders are one with the preceding tenant farmers.

For textual comparisons between vv 10-11 and Ps 118(117):22-23, see R. H. Gundry, *Use of the OT* 20. None of the agreements between Mark and the LXX against the MT is necessary to Jesus' use of the quotation; so from the textual standpoint, too, we need not consider the quotation a redactional addition. If Jesus did not quote the LXX, the Hebrew or Aramaic underwent assimilation to the LXX in passage to Greek. Later Greek-speaking use of Ps 118:22-23 may have contributed to such assimilation (cf. Acts 4:11; Eph 2:20; 1 Pet 2:7; *Barn.* 6:4; Justin *Dial.* 36.1). This use does not disfavor Jesus' ending the parable with a quotation of Ps 118:22-23, for Christian quotations of the OT may have followed his lead as easily as prompting a false imputation of the OT quotation to him (cf. H. Riesenfeld, *Gospel Tradition* 168-69).

C. A. Evans (in *BZ* nf 28 [1984] 85) suggests a link between the rejected and sacrificed child in *Tg. Ket.* Ps 118:22, 27 and the murdered son in the parable of Mark 12:1-9. But not only does Mark 12:10 use "stone" instead of "child" in quoting Ps 118:22 and reflect the LXX rather than the Targum (and who knows the date of the Targum?); but also "child" differs from "son," the similarity between הבן and אבן favors an audiovisual wordplay between "the son" and "stone" over a conceptual step from "son" to "child," and a murder differs from a sacrifice. The wordplay אבן–הבן appears to have been common (see Exod 28:9-10; Josh 4:6-9, 20-21; 1 Kgs 18:31; Lam 4:1-2; Isa 54:11-13; Zech 9:16 with 9:13; and K. Snodgrass, *Parable* 63, 113-18, for targumic and rabbinic literature and the Palestinian Syriac Lectionary as well). In Ps 118:22 the builders have no definable referent, but CD 4:19-20; 8:12 with 8:3 and rabbinic literature (see Str-B 1. 876; 3. 379) identify them with scribes and students of the Law. Acts 4:11 identifies the builders with the Sanhedrin. The contrast between the explicitness of this identification and its implicitness in Mark 12:10 favors that a Jesuanic implication was later drawn out (cf. H. F. Bayer, *Jesus' Predictions* 103-4). 1 Corinthians 3:10-15 portrays Christian leaders as builders (cf. Rom 15:20; 2 Cor 10:8; 12:19; 13:10).

J. Jeremias (*Eucharistic Words* 256-62) has shown that Ps 118:25-26 was messian-ically interpreted by Jesus' time. Perhaps therefore Ps 118:22-23 was also interpreted thus. See Str-B 1. 875-76 for the rabbis' identifying the rejected stone that became head of a corner with Abraham, David, and the Messiah. "Of a corner" may seem to favor a cornerstone of the foundation; but since an apex also forms a corner, a capstone makes an equally good possibility. If no building goes on between the rejection of the stone and its becoming "head of a corner," then it may be a cornerstone. But if the stone is rejected till the last moment of building, it can be only a capstone; for a cornerstone has to be laid first (so *T. Sol.* 22:7–23:4). "Head" favors the topmost position that a head occupies in a body; i.e. it favors a capstone which by definition stands at the apex of the building. For discussions of both definitions, see J. Jeremias in *TDNT* 4. 274-75; idem in *ZNW* 29 (1930) 264-80; F. F. Bruce in *ExpTim* 84 (1972-73) 232; H. F. Bayer, *Jesus' Predictions* 107-8; J. R. Donahue, *Are You the Christ?* 126-27, n. 1. F. Field (*Notes* 15) and BDF §138(2) assert that despite agreement in gender and number, "this" does not refer in v 11 to "head of a corner"; but they offer no argument beyond the underlying Hebrew, which does not determine Greek grammar.

At 4:12-13 Jesus told parables to obscure truth from outsiders. But there the truth would have enlightened them concerning the nature of God's rule. Here, the parable condemns the Sanhedrin; so Jesus wants them to understand. It is also possible that by now he is ready to disclose to unbelievers more of the truth concerning himself. More particularly, though his divine sonship comes out only obliquely because of the figurative-ness of the parable (cf. I. H. Marshall in *Int* 21 [1967] 97-98), Jesus takes no pains to conceal his divine sonship (cf. his soon admitting before the Sanhedrin to his messiahship and divine sonship — 14:61-62). At the same time, we have no indication that the Sanhe-drin understand that the parable teaches his divine sonship, only that the parable attacks them. In fact, the later question of the high priest on behalf of the Sanhedrin, "Are you the Christ, the Son of the Blessed One" (14:61), will imply that they do not now understand the parable to teach his divine sonship or, at most, that they only suspect it to do so (against J. Coutts [in *Studia Biblica II* 41-42], who thinks that 12:12 teaches the Sanhedrin's understanding of Jesus' death and resurrection). If a secret is preserved, then, it is not preserved on purpose (contrast 4:12-13), but by the accident of the Sanhedrin's stupidity — and only to be broken before them two days hence. Even this observation does not conform to Mark's emphasis, however. He emphasizes what the Sanhedrin do understand, not what they do not understand. And he does not disparage what they do understand as deficient, much less as false. So it is exegetically inappropriate to defend a messianic secret (better: a Son-of-God secret) by importing obduracy to describe their understanding or by distinguishing between superficial knowledge and true insight.

Historically, Galilean pilgrims admiring of Jesus, a fellow Galilean, made up "the crowd"; and the Sanhedrin feared that this crowd might rise up in violent defense of Jesus should the Sanhedrin arrest him. W. L. Lane (420-21) thinks that the echo of 11:18-19 in 12:12 may imply the end of the third day in Jerusalem. But 12:12 echoes only 11:18, which does not indicate the end of the second day; and 11:19 seemed to distance the end of the second day somewhat from the events recorded in 11:18.

JESUS' MARVELOUS ESCAPE FROM THE HORNS OF A DILEMMA

12:13-17 (Matt 22:15-22; Luke 20:20-26)

In this pericope on paying tax to Caesar, Mark first exposes a plot to trip up Jesus in his speaking (v 13) and then cites the question designed to trip him up (v 14). In the second half of the pericope Mark exhibits Jesus' seeing through the plot (v 15ab), cites his answer (vv 15c-17b), and notes the admiration he earned for it (v 17c). His answer subdivides into a request to see a denarius (v 15c), the bringing of a denarius (v 16a), his question concerning it (v 16bc), the answer to his question (v 16d), and his comment (v 17ab).

12:13-14 *(Matt 22:15-17; Luke 20:20-22)* Coming as it does on the heels of the statement, "And leaving him, they went away" (v 12d), "they send" means a sending by the just-mentioned Sanhedrin (see 11:27 with 12:1, 12); so we should not think of an indefinite third person plural. The use of ἀποστέλλουσιν for sending echoes vv 2, 3, 4, 5, 6 and thereby implies that those who are sent by the Sanhedrin will represent them much as the slaves and the son represented the owner of the vineyard in the parable of those verses. The historical present tense of ἀπο-στέλλουσιν and the omniscience with which Mark writes stress the purpose of the Sanhedrin to trap Jesus into saying something that the Pharisees, some of whom they send, could use to kill his popularity with the crowd (whose opinion the Pharisees are in a position to influence) or something that the Herodians, some of whom they also send, could take to their Roman sponsors in accusation that he is subverting Caesar's government (see 3:6 for an identical combination of Pharisees and Herodians, whose plot there makes them natural emissaries of the Sanhedrin here; cf. 8:15). The placement of αὐτόν, "him," before ἀγρεύσωσιν, "they might trap," thrusts Jesus forward as the object of this plot (cf. the forward position of αὐτόν in v 12a). The further historical present tense in "they say" stresses the attempt to trap Jesus. This attempt begins with fulsome flattery. The Pharisees and Herodians address Jesus respectfully: "Teacher." They contrast their knowledge of him ("we know") with their ignorance concerning John's baptism ("we don't know" — 11:33; cf. the possible wordplay in Greek between ἐξουσία, "authority" in the sense of "being lawful," in 11:27-33 passim, and ἔξεστιν, "be lawful," in 12:14). They describe Jesus as truthful and impartial, and his teaching as "on [the basis of] truth" (see also v 32, but there sincerely; cf. 1QapGen 2:5-7, 10, 18, 22). They identify his teaching as "the way of God" (i.e. the way that God commands people to live — see W. Michaelis in *TDNT* 5. 87). The length of this preamble and its chiastic structure in (a) "Teacher," (b) "true," (c) "you don't give a rap for anyone's favor," (c') "rank doesn't impress you," (b') "on [the basis of] truth," and (a') "you teach" emphasize their flattery (see J. D. Crossan, *Four Other Gospels* 81, for the chiasm; R. Funk, *Jesus as Precursor* 82, for the translations in c and c'). So also do the placement of "true" before "you are," the strong adversative ἀλλ', "rather," reintroducing Jesus' truthfulness as the climatic element, and the placement of "on [the basis of] truth" and then "the way of God" before "you teach" (see the Greek text). The greater the flattery, the greater Jesus' ability to see through it. Ironically, the length of the preamble and its chiastic structure also hint at the truthfulness of the flattery.

The proneness of that unegalitarian society to fawn on eminent people makes all the more remarkable Jesus' teaching God's way truthfully rather than seeking favor or showing favoritism (J. Ernst 345). Since the showing of favoritism is usually expressed with a combination of πρόσωπον and λαμβάνω or θαυμάζω, "take (or 'wonder at') a face" (so the par. Luke 20:21, for example; see W. Weiss, *"Eine neue Lehre in Vollmacht"* 208, for further references and cf. the Hebrew פנים נשא, "lift up a face"), the use of οὐ . . . βλέπεις εἰς πρόσωπον, "you don't look into a face," produces a double reference to not gazing at sidelong facial images stamped on Roman coins but prohibited by the Mosaic law as well as to not showing favoritism. This flattery makes Jesus an extraordinarily scrupulous Jew; for in frequent use of such coins, most Jews gazed often at those images. The addition of ἀνθρώπων, "of human beings," prepares for a contrast between God and Caesar, a mere human being despite the stamping of his image on coins and despite the inscription proclaiming him son of a deified former Caesar.

Together with "the way of God," the wording of the double question, "Is it lawful to give tax to Caesar or not? Should we give, or shouldn't we give?" establishes a legal frame of reference in which it is hoped that Jesus will advocate either a practice illegal according to Roman law or one displeasing to the crowd, with whom Jesus is so popular that the Sanhedrin have not dared to arrest him (v 12). The asyndeta before the first question and between it and the second question add force to both questions. The greater their force, the greater Jesus' ability in escaping the dilemma they pose. The Herodians could accuse him of subverting Roman authority if he declares paying tax illegal because of the requirement that it be paid in Roman coins stamped with a Mosaically prohibited image of Caesar and with a legend proclaiming his supposedly divine ancestry. Since the Pharisees pay tax, they could join in this accusation, but not so enthusiastically, for their own influence on the crowd is at risk whereas the Herodians, owing their elevated status to the Herods, care little for what the crowd think of them and aim only to please the Roman sponsors of the Herods. The Pharisees' payment of tax to Caesar leaves them — and much more the Herodians — in no position to disagree with a defense of paying it. But should Jesus mount such a defense, they — and especially the Pharisees, since they have much influence on the Jewish masses — might cause him to lose his popularity with the crowd so that they might arrest him without fear of the crowd's rising up on his behalf.

12:15-17 (*Matt 22:18-22; Luke 20:23-26*) "But he, knowing their hypocrisy" points up Jesus' power to see through the ruse. The advancement of αὐτῶν, "their," does not emphasize those characterized by hypocrisy, but lets the final accent in the phrase rest on hypocrisy as such (cf. the comments on 6:52). "Why do you test me?" (cf. 8:11; 10:2) exposes the ruse for what it is. Jesus' seeing through it and exposing it transform into demonstrated fact the preceding flattery of him as true and uncaring of others' approval and rank. The adversative δέ, "but," is the first in a series that set him against his opponents. He commands them to bring him a denarius. Highlighting this question-cum-command is the chiastic structure of (a) "Why" (b) "me" (c) "do you test?" (c') "Bring" (b') "to me" (a') "a denarius in order that I may see [it]" (so the word order of the Greek text). "In order that I may see [it]" exposes as flattery the description of him as so pious that he never gazes at facial images stamped on Roman coins. The clause also prepares for a further question about the image and inscription visible on the denarius and shows that Jesus knows beforehand what argument he is going to make out of them. (But it is excessive to say with C. H. Giblin [in *CBQ* 33 (1971) 526] that this clause means, "Jesus sees beyond what they will see.") The Pharisees and Herodians bring a denarius. The historical present tense in "he says" emphasizes the immediately following question, "Whose [are] this image and inscription?" because it displays Jesus' ability to outwit his enemies, here by forcing them to answer, "[It is] Caesar's." Ellipsis of "are" in the question and of "it is" in the answer sharpen the point that Jesus is making. At this juncture it is usually said that because using the coin of a ruler amounts to acknowledging his authority, the Pharisees and Herodians impale *themselves* on one horn of the dilemma: they give concrete evidence of acknowledging in practice that Caesar has a right to tax them and that he owns the coin. But people use a coin for its value in exchange whether or not they acknowledge the sovereignty of the ruler whose image and superscription is stamped on the coin (cf. J. D. M. Derrett, *Law* 321), and the coin does not belong to him because his image and superscription appear on its face. It belongs to the person who earned it or otherwise gained it. Therefore Jesus' command, "The things of Caesar give back to Caesar," is no more logically compelling than his argument from Exod 3:6 will be exegetically compelling (v 26). In Jesus' universe of discourse, what counts as argumentatively persuasive is not logical validity, exegetical accuracy, or the like, but cleverness, wordplay, oneupmanship. So the shift from Caesar's image and inscription on the coin to Caesar's things, i.e. to the coin itself and others like it, entails a leap of imagination the *artistry* of which is convincing that the payment of tax is giving back to Caesar what belongs to him (cf. the comments on vv 26-27). The forward position of "the things of Caesar" brings this part of Jesus' command close to his opponents' answer, "Caesar's." This closeness makes the imaginative leap obvious. But one imaginative leap leads to another; so giving back to Caesar his things leads to giving back the things of God to God. Thus Jesus ends by seizing both horns of the dilemma.

But what are "the things of God"? For Jesus they are the divine necessity of his suffering, rejection, and being killed (see 8:33 with 8:31); and right after mentioning them he called on the crowd to deny themselves, take up their crosses, and follow him at the possible cost of their lives (8:34-38). For his audiences there and here, then, "the things of God" consist in the divine obligation to follow Jesus thus. "Give" (δίδωμι) has become "give back" (ἀποδίδωμι) to emphasize the obligatory character of the command to pay tax and follow Jesus.

Not since 11:33 has the name of Jesus appeared. Its mention in the introduction to his command lends gravity to the command. Now a tailpiece highlights the amazing ability that he has to defeat his enemies in verbal combat: "and they were marveling at him." Even those who have come to trap him in his speech succumb to admiration of his person. Thus, after repeated use of the adversative δέ, "but," Mark switches back to a continuative καί, "and." No more need for contrast! Since even the would-be trappers of Jesus succumb, Mark uses a perfective ἐξ- with -εθαύμαζον to magnify their marveling (contrast the simplex form of the verb in 5:20; 6:6; 15:5, 44 and the v.l. here in v 17).

NOTES

D. Daube (*NTRJ* 158-69) thinks that the sequence of the questions asked Jesus in 12:13-17, 18-27, 28-34, 35-37 corresponds to four kinds of questions dealing with a point of OT law, a possibly ridiculous belief, a matter of conduct, and an apparent contradiction in the OT apart from the Law, and asked during the Passover liturgy by a wise son, a wicked son, a son of simple piety, and the head of the family (cf. the Passover setting in Mark and the possibility that early Jewish Christians told these stories on Passover eve). Weakening this theory are its leaving high and dry both the question of Jesus' authority (11:27-33), his parable concerning the tenant farmers (12:1-12), his warning against the scribes (12:38-40), his teaching the disciples about giving (12:41-44), and his answering their question about the future (13:1-37). Moreover, the Pharisees and Herodians who ask a legal question do not correspond to the wise son who asks that kind of question in the Passover liturgy, nor does the destructive purpose behind their question correspond to the edificatory purpose behind the question asked by the wise son at Passover. In general, the questions in that liturgy deal with the meaning of Passover, whereas the questions in Mark 12:13-37 fly in four different directions, none of them leading to the Passover (cf. J. Gnilka 2. 172). And Jesus has a family of disciples, but none of them correspond to sons (see 3:31-35). For further criticism of Daube's hypothesis, see J.-G. Mudiso Mbâ Mundla, *Jesus und die Führer Israels* 303-5; also 61-63 for the historicity of the story in 12:13-17, and p. 46 for Semitisms in it.

The preservation of this story but not its "ekthaumaturgic" use by Mark (see v 17b) may owe something to Jesus' addressing a question of practical importance among Christians and to its offering evidence contrary to accusations of their disloyalty to Rome. Against positing an original association of the story with the controversies in 2:1–3:6 (so, among others, M. J. Cook [*Mark's Treatment* 40-41], who sees a direct continuation) are differences in form, the contrast between the Galilean setting of 2:1–3:6 and the Judean setting of 12:13-17, and the suitability of those respective settings to the contents of the stories, e.g., the greater danger in Judea of being charged with sedition if Jesus gives an impolitic answer to the question of paying tax (F. F. Bruce in *Jesus and the Politics of His Day* 250).

J. Lambrecht (*Redaktion* 53, n. 1) suggests influence from Q, as represented in Luke 11:53–12:1, on vv 13, 15. But it is doubtful that Luke 11:53-54 represents Q, and Luke 12:1 may come from L instead of Q. Each passage has Pharisees, but Mark has Herodians as well and Luke, scribes. Though in both passages Jesus' enemies design to trap him in his speech, the diction in Mark 12:13 does not match the diction in Luke 11:54; and Jesus' calling the Pharisees and some of the scribes "hypocrites" in 7:6 (cf. 7:1) leaves no need to explain the "hypocrisy" of the Pharisees and Herodians as secondarily influenced by the "hypocrisy" underlying Luke 12:1. Rather, Mark 7:16; 12:13; Luke 12:1 support one another's authenticity in respect to Jesus' use of "hypocrites" and "hypocrisy."

Since the Sanhedrin did not withdraw in 11:33, their sending others in 12:13 would fail to link with that verse if 12:1-12 were dropped out as a Marcan insertion. This failure does not prove the untraditionality of 12:13, however; for 12:1-12 may be occupying its original place (see the notes ad loc.), and 12:13 does link with the Sanhedrin's withdrawal in 12:12. Even if 12:1-12 does not occupy its original setting, the Sanhedrin's sending others may have related to a context as different from 11:27-33 as from 12:1-12, or to no context at all (the story having circulated independently).

Because of 3:6, according to A. J. Hultgren (*Jesus and His Adversaries* 153), Mark has to reintroduce the Pharisees and Herodians in 12:13; but the weight of the passion tradition, in which others engineer Jesus' death, keeps Mark from letting the Pharisees and Herodians carry out their earlier plot to destroy Jesus. This line of thought is not compelling. The difference between destroying Jesus (3:6) and catching him in a statement (12:13) would tend either to keep Mark from importing the Pharisees and Herodians here or to argue that importation would have resulted in use of the same verb or of a synonym. Importation is also likely to have resulted in displacement of the Sanhedrin, i.e. in the Pharisees' and Herodians' coming on their own initiative, as will the Sadducess (v 18) and a scribe (v 28), rather than being sent by the Sanhedrin, who also came on their own initiative (11:27).

"Some of" suggests that the Pharisees and Herodians are not at home in Jerusalem as they would be in Galilee. This suggestion gains support from the presence of "some of" the scribes in Galilee (2:6, 16) plus Mark's description of those scribes as "having come down from Jerusalem" (3:22; see also 7:1, 5). (The scribes in 1:22 were spoken about but not said to be present.) Mark seems to have distinguished between scribes who resided in Galilee and others who resided in Jerusalem but went down to Galilee. Similarly, he may here distinguish between Pharisees and Herodians who reside in Galilee but have come up to Jerusalem for Passover and others who have not. An allusion to 3:6 and 8:15 would favor that because those who have come up from Galilee had earlier conspired against Jesus, the Sanhedrin sends them.

In sending some of the Pharisees and Herodians the Sanhedrin purpose to trap Jesus (v 13). But it is the Pharisees and Herodians who attempt the entrapment by going and asking him about paying tax (v 14). To make this distinction, however, tends to neglect the Pharisees' and Herodians' asking on behalf of the Sanhedrin. We could take λόγῳ as an instrumental dative referring to the question that the Pharisees and Herodians ask Jesus ("in order that they might catch him by means of [their own] word") instead of a dative of respect referring to his answer ("in order that they might catch him with regard to [his own] word").

Concerning the Herodians (v 13), see the notes on 3:6. Their presence in Jerusalem makes good sense for Passover season, but especially good sense if Herod Antipas has come (so Luke 23:7). Judas the Galilean led a revolt over taxation earlier in the first century (Acts 5:37; Josephus *Ant.* 18.1.1 §§1-10, 23-25; idem *J.W.* 2.8.1 §§117-18; 2.17.8 §§433-40). This revolt and the Herodians' dependence on Rome for privileged positions show why the Herodians would have accused Jesus of subversion had he taught against paying tax to Caesar. M. Hengel, who traces the Zealots back to Judas the Galilean, suggests that the Pharisees and Herodians suspected Jesus of being a Zealot (*Zealots* 194).

Against the statement of W. R. Farmer (*Synoptic Problem* 263) that "there is no obvious explanation for Matthew's changing the order of Mark's phrasing . . ." in Mark 12:14, see R. H. Gundry, *Matthew* 441-42. Farmer's statement serves the theory that Mark conflated Matthew and Luke. A. J. Hultgren (*Jesus and His Adversaries* 42-44) defends the independence of the short version in *Gos. Thom.* 100 by arguing that although the descriptions in Mark 12:14 of Jesus as a true teacher and as teaching the way of God "would lend themselves readily to the Gnostic pericope," they do not appear in *Gos. Thom.* 100. But Hultgren overlooks that in *Gos. Thom.* 100 the acknowledgedly key command, "and give to me what is mine," has led to a shift in the questioners from opponents to disciples, i.e. to Gnostics, to whom alone that command can be suitably addressed. This shift has led in turn to omission of the purpose to trap Jesus; and that omission has led, again in turn, to a further omission of the flattery designed to help trap him. So also there is no longer an entrapping question, only the statement, "Caesar's agents demand taxes from us," and no longer a counterentrapment by Jesus. The descriptions of him which might seem to appeal to Gnostics drop out, then, because they belong to hostile flattery and because that flattery and everything related to it is inimical to the Gnostic addition to Jesus' saying. See also W. Schrage, *Verhältnis* 189-92; R. M. Grant and D. N. Freedman, *Secret Sayings* 189.

F. F. Bruce (in *Jesus and the Politics of His Day* 257) thinks that "the disproportionately lengthy preamble to the [Pharisees' and Herodians'] question was scarcely framed with the simple purpose of flattering Jesus." If so, we would have to disagree with Mark's reference to "their hypocrisy." But the length of the preamble and Jesus' counter question, "Why do you tempt me?" tend to favor that reference. Against equating the description of Jesus as a true teacher with "the teacher of righteousness," or "the right teacher," in QL, see H. Braun, *Qumran* 1. 71. On the other side, see J. Morgenstern, *Some Significant Antecedents* 1-7.

The γάρ-clause in v 14 (literally, "for you don't look into people's face") probably does not stem from Mark himself. He likes to insert γάρ-clauses, but as editorial comments. This one is not editorial. And though Mark uses Semitic locutions in his own composition, the Semitic character of not looking into people's face (see Lev 19:15; Deut 10:17; 28:50; 2 Kgs 3:14 et passim) tends toward traditionality. Jesus' not looking into people's face, i.e. not paying attention to their appearance or being impressed by a good appearance, provides the reason why he is true and does not court anyone. With "the way of God" (v 14), cf. Deut 8:6; 10:12-13; Job 23:11; Ps 1:6; 27:11; 119:15; Jer 21:8; Matt 7:14; 21:32; Acts 18:25, 26; *Did.* 1:1-2; also Acts 9:2; 19:9, 23; 24:14, 22; contrast Gen 6:12; Matt 7:13.

Though there is some uncertainty (J. D. M. Derrett, *Law* 329), κῆνσον (v 14) probably means a census-based poll and land tax. The Greek word comes on loan from the Latin *census*, and such a tax was imposed on Judea, Samaria, and Idumea, but not on Galilee, in 6 C.E. (Josephus *Ant.* 18.1.1 §§1-4; Acts 5:37). Thus, though the question, "Should we give or not give?" does not fall appropriately from any Galilean Pharisees and Herodians sent by the Sanhedrin, the Judean residence of the Sanhedrin makes the question suitable, as though they seek outside judgment — Jesus is a Galilean — on an internal issue. The tax has to be paid in Roman coinage, not in Jewish coinage devoid of Tiberius's image and of an ascription of deity to the deceased Augustus (F. F. Bruce in *Jesus and the Politics of His Day* 258; E. Stauffer, *Christ and the Caesars* 114-20, 124).

So early as the first century there may be little evidence of Jewish objection to using coins stamped with Tiberius's image and with an ascription of deity to Augustus (so W. L. Lane 423-24 with references to more detailed discussions). But the wording in v 14 ("Is it *lawful* to give tax to Caesar or not?") shows that Jesus is being tempted to make such an objection, and the preceding flattery attempts to put him in the class of Jews who scrupulously avoid gazing at coins stamped with Caesar's image and superscription (cf. *b. Pesah.* 104a; *y. 'Abod. Zar.* 3:1; H. Loewe, *"Render Unto Caesar"* 79-96). "Is it lawful . . . ?" puts forward a theoretical question. "Should we . . . ?" puts forward a practical question.

Ὑπόκρισιν (v 15) means "hypocrisy" in the sense of stage-acting (see the notes on 7:6). Here it refers to acting as though desirous of knowing the true answer to a serious question, but in fact wanting to entice Jesus into a self-damaging statement. The v.l. ὑποκριταί, "hypocrites" (so P[45] N W Θ *f*[1,13] 28 33 565 *al* q sy[h**]), seems to be prompted by a combination of ὑπόκρισιν earlier in the verse and of parallel influence from Matt 22:18.

See the notes on 8:10-12 for πειράζετε (v 15) as testing or contesting, not enticement to sin, and for testing Jesus as putting testers on the side of Satan (1:12-13). J. D. Crossan (*Four Other Gospels* 21) thinks that πειράζετε, "do you test" (v 15a), could come from ἐπείραζον, "they were testing," in *PEger.* 2. 44, and that vv 15b-16a could come by way of rephrasing *PEger.* 2. 50-54. He argues for the greater originality of the non-canonical fragment that its "Teacher Jesus" leads smoothly to "Teacher" (after "mouth") and that its "mouth" connects smoothly with "lips." This argument falls short. According to textual criticism, smoothness in a variant reading usually spells secondariness, and Matthew and Luke commonly smooth out Mark. So smoothness does not necessarily indicate originality. Furthermore, an important reason for believing in Q rather than in the Griesbach hypothesis is the unlikelihood of Luke's disintegrating sayings that appear integrated in Matthew; and when not drawing on Q, Luke and especially Matthew tend to integrate Marcan and other non-Q materials rather than disintegrating them. Mark, too, tends toward integration, as in the present string of stories, in 2:1–3:6 et passim. Yet the greater originality of *PEger.* 2 would imply the distintegration of its contents in the canonical gospels. More likely, then, *PEger.* 2 represents a post-canonical style of writing evident also in the Secret Gospel of Mark and Mark 16:9-20 (to name but two examples). That is the style of a pastiche, here by putting together parts of Mark 7:6-13 par.; 12:1-12 par.; John 3:2 (cf. E. Stauffer, *Christ and the Caesars* 112-14).

See B. Schwank in *Anfänge der Theologie* 62-63; H. StJ. Hart in *Jesus and the Politics of His Day* 241-48; F. W. Madden, *History of Jewish Coinage* 247; E. Stauffer, *Christ and the Caesars* 124-27; M. Bünker in *Wer ist unser Gott?* 162-63 on the denarius that Jesus asks to see. "Bring me a denarius" may imply that out of piety he never carries a denarius (so ibid. 167), that on this occasion he happens not to be carrying one, or that apart from his own practice he wants to put his opponents in an embarrassing position. Though it is beside the point to decide between these possibilities, Jesus has probably seen a denarius before. Otherwise he might not know what it is on the coin that he can use against his opponents. To an extent K. Wengst (*Pax Romana* 59-61) is correct to say that in not taking a denarius but making his opponents bring a denarius of their own, Jesus means, "It's your problem." But Wengst goes far beyond the text in adding that Jesus also means, "It's not a problem for my disciples and me, because we have escaped taxation by not earning any income. Give all Caesar's coins back to him, not just what he requires by way of tax. Then come follow me in money-free discipleship, and you will no longer face the problem, either" (similarly E. Schillebeeckx, *Christ* 584: "[Jesus and his disciples] have dropped out of the monetary system"). Not only does the text fail to say these things. It is also doubtful that Jesus and his disciples could escape a tax, especially a poll tax, by appeal to their living off charity in the course of itinerant ministry (cf. Matt 17:24-27). Moreover, giving back to Caesar all his things, i.e. all coins having his image and inscription on them, would still leave all the imageless coins used by Jews for everyday transactions.

Historically, having in the temple of the one true God, who prohibits images, a coin stamped with an image of Tiberius and with a blasphemous ascription of deity to Augustus may sharpen Jesus' argument and the Pharisees' and Herodians' embarrassment (cf. M. Bünker in *Wer is unser Gott?* 168 and J. Gnilka 2. 152-53, though Gnilka regards as unhistorical the setting in the temple [11:27; 14:49]). But Mark makes nothing of this point, perhaps because the majority of Jews use such coins without compunction. E. Lohmeyer (252) objects that since the Pharisees and Herodians have to *bring* the coin, they do not have it on their persons. More likely, they bring it *because* they have it on their person (cf. 9:17, 19-20 par.; Matt 14:17-18; John 2:6-8; 20:27; 21:10; Acts 4:34, 37; 5:2; contrast being *sent* or going *away* in Mark 6:27; 11:2, 7 to bring something not immediately at hand).

The inner logic of this pericope has not run its course by the end of v 16 (against

G. Petzke in *Jesus Christus in Historie und Theologie* 231-34); for the final word belongs to Jesus, and the Pharisees' and Herodians' answer, "Caesar's," does not tell whether using the denarius to pay tax counts as repayment of a debt or as participation in idolatry. Verse 17 cannot be discarded so easily. E. Stauffer (in *The NT Age* 504-5) thinks that Jesus speaks realistically, not theologically, i.e. that he does not defend Caesar's right to tax (as Paul does in Rom 13:1-7 with a doctrine of divine ordination), but only refuses to resist the practice of Caesar to tax (cf. *b. Pesaḥ.* 112b). This view pays insufficient attention to the possessive "of Caesar" and to the parallel with giving back the things of God to God — surely a matter of obligation, not just of non-resistance to raw power (cf. I. Abrahams, *Studies* 1. 62-65; also B. Schwank in *Anfänge der Theologie* 62-63 for the probability that a Greek inscription Καίσαρος, "Caesar's," on the coin prompted the dialogue in vv 16-17 to take place in Greek).

A. J. Hultgren (*Jesus and His Adversaries* 77-78) sees the original point of the story (constructed as he thinks by the primitive Palestinian church) to be that because the last days have arrived, giving the things of God to God is more important than giving the things of Caesar to Caesar. Unfortunately for this view, the story contains not even a remnant of eschatology or of an evaluative comparison between giving to Caesar and giving to God. In an antinomy the emphasis may fall on the second member, but Jesus puts forward giving to Caesar and giving to God as harmonious.

It is true, of course, that eschatology overarches all Jesus' teaching. But eschatology does not cancel ethics. Therefore we need not make giving back to Caesar ironic instead of ethical. Several other features of the text prohibit us from doing so: (1) the emphasis on obligation through the addition of ἀπο-, "back"; (2) the possessive genitive behind "whose?" and "Caesar's"; and (3) the forward position of τὰ Καίσαρος, "the things of Caesar."

It probably goes too far to say that by distinguishing sharply between Caesar and God (v 17), Jesus tacitly protests against the idolatrous claims on the coin (so W. L. Lane 424). The sharp distinction has to do with differences of ownership, not with differences between an image and the divine Spirit, or between polytheism and monotheism. It is likewise doubtful that in Jesus' saying we should take the καί as adversative (". . . *but* the things of God to God" — cf. C. Myers, *Binding the Strong Man* 311-12, where Jesus is said to be setting out a choice between opposites), for nothing in the pericope indicates that Jesus wants to point up a conflict of interests between Caesar and God. For that we have to go elsewhere. C. F. D. Moule (97) thinks that Jesus would have won just by saying to give back Caesar's things to Caesar, but that he seized the opportunity to add a penetrating remark on giving back God's things to God. Perhaps so, but an answer limited to Caesar's things would probably have made Jesus appear disloyal to God and to that extent — a significant one — Jesus would have lost.

According to Jesus' original meaning, says J. D. M. Derrett (*Law* 335-36), you should obey the commands of Caesar and thereby obey the commands of God (so Eccl 8:2). Only if Caesar commands something contrary to God's law should obedience to the king's command cease. But Jesus says nothing to the effect that you obey God by means of obeying Caesar. Derrett also argues that just as the things of God include more than tithes and oblations, the things of Caesar include more than his coins. Perhaps so, but only under the proviso that Caesar's coins are specially in view and that tithes and oblations may not be in view at all (see the foregoing comments).

S. G. F. Brandon (*Jesus and the Zealots* 345-49) thinks the Zealots would have agreed with v 17 because in their thinking, Palestine and all its resources belonged to God, not to Caesar. But apart from a possible anachronism of speaking about Zealots so early as Jesus' lifetime (M. Smith in *HTR* 64 [1971] 1-19; M. Borg in *JTS* ns 22 [1971] 504-12; R. A. Horsley and J. S. Hanson, *Bandits* 197-98, 217-23; R. A. Horsley in *NovT* 28 [1986]

159-92; yet see M. Hengel, *Zealots* passim, esp. xi-xvii, 76-145, 330ff.), his asking for a coin with Caesar's image and making a point of its belonging to Caesar forces Brandon to say that Mark reverses the true intention of Jesus, which was to condemn paying tax to Caesar as an act of disloyalty to God. Furthermore, to assume the truth of the charge in Luke 23:2 that Jesus forbade paying tribute to Caesar is to neglect that in Luke 20:20-26 Jesus teaches just the opposite.

C. H. Giblin (in *CBQ* 33 [1971] 516-26) and others argue that since Caesar's things have to do with his image on the denarius, God's things have to do with God's image on human beings. Thus, to give back to God the things of God means to give ourselves back to God. But Jesus does not refer to God's image. In the absence of such a reference it is more probable that Caesar's image contrasts with the prohibition of making an image of God than that Caesar's image parallels the image of God in which human beings were made. Nowhere else does Jesus talk of that image of God. And a parallel between Caesar's image and God's would necessitate a like parallel between Caesar's inscription and God's. To his credit, Giblin sees this necessity and cites Prov 7:3; Jer 31:33; Isa 44:5. But Prov 7:3 speaks about a son's writing on his own heart the commandments of his human father, not about God's having written God's commandments on the hearts of human beings the way God created human beings in God's image. At Jer 31:33 God is the writer and God's law what is written, but the writing has not yet occurred and will not occur till the last days; so this inscription would not provide the synonymous parallelism with God's image in which God created human beings at the beginning. The same chronological problem plagues the citation of Isa 44:5. There, moreover, the inscription, "[Belonging] to the Lord," does not indicate obedience to God's law or commandments. The Lord will not write the inscription as God created human beings in his image. ידו may mean "with his hand" rather than "on his hand" and thus not refer to an inscription on a human being. Only part of the Septuagintal tradition (Codd. B *L C* [in *O* sub asterisk) contains a reference to the hand; and that part means "with his hand" (an instrumental dative), not "on his hand" (which would require the accusative). For his apologetic purpose Mark might have used Jesus' innocence of seditious teaching on taxes. Instead, he uses the marveling of those who have tried to trap Jesus. See J. O'Callaghan in *SPap* 11 (1972) 83-89 for the view that 7Q7 may represent v 17. The fragment is too small for firm identification, which therefore depends mainly on a judgment concerning the associated 7Q5 (see the notes on 6:52-53).

JESUS' EXPOSÉ OF THE SADDUCEES' IGNORANCE

12:18-27 (Matt 22:23-33; Luke 20:27-40)

Another example of Jesus' conquests in debate opens with a question from Sadducees that aims against the doctrine of resurrection (vv 18-23; N.B. the inclusion formed by two occurrences of "resurrection," one in v 18 and another in v 23). The question breaks down into the Sadducees' approach (v 18), their quoting the Mosaic law (v 19), their describing a special case of resurrection (vv 20-22), and their trying to make the doctrine of resurrection look unscriptural by showing the incompatibility of the Mosaic law with the case of resurrection that they have described (v 23). The reply of Jesus (vv 24-27; N.B. both the mention of his name to signal that the second half of the pericope is starting and the inclusion formed by the two occurrences of "you are deceived" in vv 24 and 27) subdivides in two: (1) a charge that the Sadducees are ignorant (vv 24-25) and (2) a scriptural proof of resurrection (vv 26-27). The charge consists of a counter question (v 24) and a statement (v 25). The scriptural proof likewise consists of a counter question (v 26) and a statement (v 27).

12:18-23 *(Matt 22:23-28; Luke 20:27-33)* The present historical tense of "come" stresses the Sadducees' attempt to overpower Jesus in debate now that the Pharisees and Herodianṣ have failed to trap him. "Who say there is no resurrection" explains something about the Sadducees that Gentile readers need to know if they are to understand the following story (cf. Acts 23:8; Josephus *J.W.* 2.8.11-14 §§154-66; idem *Ant.* 18.1.3-5 §§12-22; *m. Sanh.* 10:1; *m. 'Abot.* 1:7; *'Abot R. Nat.* [recension A] 5, [recension B] 10; R. Meyer in *TDNT* 7. 46-47). The Sadducees' saying there is no resurrection denies the predictions of Jesus that he will rise from the dead (8:31; 9:9, 31; 10:34). The Christological stakes are high, then; and Jesus' resurrection will add an eventful refutation to the present discoursive refutation. But he has predicted his resurrection only to the disciples. So only Jesus, the disciples, and Mark's audience can understand the issue Christologically (but see 9:10). The irony that the Sadducees cannot do so piles another kind of ignorance, a Christological kind, on top of their ignorance of the Scriptures and of God's power (v 24).

Ἐπηρώτων, "they were asking," is imperfect, as verbs of speaking often are. The address "Teacher" echoes v 14. Immediately, "Moses" comes forward to set up a possible conflict between Jesus as teacher and Moses as legislator. The Sadducees appear to accept only the Pentateuch as authoritative (see the following notes); so they quote the law of levirate marriage out of Deut 25:5 with some help from Gen 38:8 (see R. H. Gundry, *Use of the OT* 45; G. L. Archer and G. C. Chirichigno, *OT Quotations* §107, for textual comparisons; cf. Ruth 4:5, 10). Before the quotation, ὅτι is recitative. The intrusion of ἵνα between the protasis and the apodosis of the quotation works a surprising shift from direct to indirect discourse. This anacoluthon highlights the imperatival force of the subjunctive verbs following ἵνα. Thus: "Moses wrote to us, 'If anyone's brother should die and leave behind a wife and [parataxis for 'but'] not leave a child' — [he wrote] that (ἵνα) his brother should take the wife and raise up offspring for his brother" (see BDF §470[1] on the imperatival force, though BDF §470[3] ought to list Mark 12:19 also for shifting from direct to indirect discourse; cf. 11:31-32). By wordplay ἀναστήσῃ in the quotation relates the law of levirate marriage to the issue of resurrection because this verb can refer to raising up the dead as well as to raising up offspring (i.e. begetting, not rearing, offspring) for a deceased brother. The case of the seven brothers (seven for completeness) all of whom successively had the same wife because each died childless and left the wife widowed till she herself finally died — this case looks contrived. For the sake of argument, however, and despite men's avoidance of marriage to women whose past several husbands have died (*b. Yebam.* 64b; *t. Šabb.* 15:8) and despite possible current abeyance of the law of levirate marriage, the Sadducees present this case as sober fact. Emphasizing the purported factuality are asyndeton at the start of v 20 and the forward positions of ἑπτὰ ἀδελφοί, "seven brothers," ὁ πρῶτος, "the first" (the eldest), ὁ δεύτερος, "the second" (the next eldest), ὁ τρίτος, "the third" (the third eldest), οἱ ἑπτά, "the seven" (in descending order of age), and ἡ γυνή, "the wife" (vv 20-22). Again at the start of v 23 asyndeton and the forward position of "in the resurrection" emphasize the purported problem (see Ach. Tat. 1.12.2-3; 8.12.1-3 for another example of fast-moving emphasis gained by asyndeton). "Whenever they rise" does not pose a redundancy after "in the resurrection," but narrows the focus down to the resurrection of the seven brothers and one woman — thus a definite rather than indefinite "they." The Sadducees might have stopped with asking whose wife the woman will be (cf. *b. Šabb.* 30b for Gamaliel's statement that women are destined to give birth every day, like a hen). But they want to make the supposed unscripturalness of resurrection as obvious as possible; so they add "for the seven had her [as] wife." That is to say, resurrection would make shambles of the Mosaic law by giving to the woman *at one and the same time* the seven husbands that the Law had required her to have *one after another* during her mortal life. A man might practice polygamy, but a woman? In the resurrection? Out of the question!

12:24-27 *(Matt 22:29-33; Luke 20:34-40)* Asyndeton at the start of v 24 underscores the accusatory question that Jesus is about to ask. The construction οὐ plus an indicative verb in that question, "Because of this you're deceived, aren't you, not understanding the Scriptures or the power of God?" implies the answer, "Yes, you are deceived." "Because of this" refers to the story of the seven brothers as evidence of this deception. The plural of "Scriptures" contrasts with the singular of "this scripture" in v 10, where Jesus was referring to a single passage, and may imply the whole OT in contrast with the Pentateuch, which alone the Sadduceees accept as Scripture, just as the following reference to "angels in heaven" will imply his disapproval of the Sadducees' denying the existence of angels (Acts 23:8). Jesus' reference to "the power of God" (v 24) suggests that he has in mind the reference in the early Jewish prayer גבורות, "Powers [of God]" (second of the Eighteen Benedictions), to God's raising the dead.

In v 25 Jesus borrows the Sadducees' own expression, ὅταν . . . ἀναστῶσιν, "whenever they rise," but inserts γάρ, "for," to introduce support for his charge of ignorance and ἐκ νεκρῶν, "from among dead [people]," to prepare for the raising of the dead (v 26) and for the denial that God is a God of dead people (v 27). The forward position of ἐκ νεκρῶν emphasizes that God will transform the seven brothers and their wife from dead people into living people (again see v 27). A comparison of the resurrected with heavenly angels in the non-practice of men's marrying and of women's being given in marriage particularizes the Sadducees' ignorance of God's power: they fail to understand that God can change conditions of life — and that God will change them, with the result that levirate marriage in present life will pose no difficulty for resurrected life. The futuristic present tense in "they neither marry nor are given in marriage" and in "are like angels in heaven" makes the conditions of resurrected life so certain to prevail in time to come that they can be spoken of as already in force. The strong adversative ἀλλ᾽, "rather," underlines the change to angelic likeness. An appeal to "the Book of Moses at the [passage concerning the burning] bush" particularizes the Sadducees' ignorance of the Scriptures. Jesus appeals to a passage whose authority even they accept, the words "Book" and "Moses" connoting that authority. The chiastic ordering in vv 25-26 of the particulars concerning the two kinds of ignorance with which Jesus charged the Sadducees in v 24 gives his charge added force. An adversative δέ, "but," and "concerning the dead [people] that they are being raised" broaden the scope of Jesus' answer from the seven brothers and their wife, who he has just said neither marry nor are given in marriage whenever they rise from among dead people, to include in the resurrection the dead people from among whom the seven brothers and their wife arise (N.B. the anaphoric definite article pointing back to the previously and anarthrously mentioned dead people). Another futuristic present tense in "concerning the dead [people] that they are being raised" makes the resurrection of these dead people just as certain as that of the seven brothers and their wife, i.e. as certain as though it were already taking place. The forward position of these phrases emphasizes the certain resurrection of the dead people. "You've read, haven't you?" (again οὐκ plus an indicative verb) implies that the Sadducees have indeed read Exod 3:6 and should therefore know better than to deny the resurrection (cf. Mark 2:25; 12:10; D. Daube, *NTRJ* 432-36).

The switch from ἀναστῶσιν, "rise" (v 25; cf. Mark 12:18, 23), to ἐγείρονται, "are being raised" (v 26), produces a divine passive meaning, "God is raising." This meaning leads appropriately to an OT quotation about God, and from there to God's being the God of living people. In this respect, "how God spoke to him [Moses]" helps the divine passive; but πῶς, "how," also stresses the divine source of what was said to Moses (cf. A. T. Robertson, *Grammar* 1032).

From the standpoint of grammatical historical exegesis the inference, "He is not a God of dead people but of living people," does not follow from "I [am] the God of Abraham and the God of Isaac and the God of Jacob"; for from that standpoint God was only stating that at the time of speaking God was the God whom Abraham, Isaac, and Jacob had worshipped during their mortal lifetimes — no implication of afterlife, much less of bodily resurrection, favored or even suggested. Rather, the argument is scripturally artistic by way of drawing a surprising inference never before thought of. "Concerning the dead" includes the patriarchs among those who are presently dead. Therefore the statement that God "is not a God of dead people but of living people" means that presently dead people will have to come back to life by virtue of resurrection. In speaking to Moses, God alluded to past patriarchal history. Since the Sadducees have raised a question about resurrection, Jesus transfers God's statement to a new temporal frame, viz., the future. Just as that statement, when pointed backward, demands past physical life for Abraham, Isaac, and Jacob even though they are now dead, so also the statement, when pointed forward, demands future physical life for Abraham, Isaac, and Jacob even though they are now dead. Though corresponding to the Hebrew of Exod 3:6, the ellipsis of "am" between "I" and "the God of . . ." (contrast Matthew and the LXX) crisps the argument. The anarthrousness of θεός, "a God," νεκρῶν, "of dead [people]," and ζώντων, "of living [people]," universalizes and principles the argument (cf. the representative role of the patriarchs,

as noted by O. Schwankl, *Sadduzäerfrage* 405). And another strong adversative
ἀλλά, "rather," underlines the description of God as a God of living people, not
of dead people.

Modern exegetes would brand the transfer of Exod 3:6 from past to future
as highhanded violation of the originally intended meaning. But in first century
Palestinian Judaism, as remarked before, an argument's consisting of grammatical
historical exegesis would have lacked cogency, just as in another two thousand
years different techniques of interpretation (psychological, sociological,
economic, rhetorical, and structural posing possibilities that grow out of the
present, to say nothing of unpredictable possibilities) may cause grammatical
historical exegesis to lose its cogency. What counted then was ingenuity at playing
with words by such means as transferring them to new frames of reference where
they could be made to say new things, as indeed at the popular level may still
count for more than does grammatical historical exegesis.

Jesus grounds the resurrection in the nature of God, not in the nature of
human being, and emphasizes that grounding by introducing his declaration with
asyndeton. "You are much deceived" gives an outright affirmative answer to the
question with which he began in v 24, "You're deceived, aren't you, . . . ?" and
thus completes the inclusion with a powerful putdown of the Sadducees. The
addition of "much" and its placement before the verb makes the answer stronger
than the question, and another asyndeton gives such force to the putdown that
variant readings have developed to soften its impact.

NOTES

See O. Schwankl, *Sadduzäerfrage* 11-62, for the history of the exegesis of this pericope
and ibid. 501-87 for its basic historicity. J. Jeremias (*NT Theology* 1. 184, n. 3) argues for
the historicity of vv 18-25 from their lacking both a supportive reference to Jesus' resurrection and a comparison between those to be resurrected in the future and the already
resurrected Jesus. This argument fails, however; for prior to his death Jesus could not refer
or be made to refer to his resurrection except by way of prediction, yet until fulfilment a
prediction does not count as evidence. According to A. J. Hultgren (*Jesus and His Adversaries* 124), vv 18-25 deal with a question that Christians asked about those of their number
whose spouses had died and who had remarried. But neither the Sadducees nor Jesus
indicates that the legitimacy of such people's remarriage in the present age stands in
question; and the law of levirate marriage points to a Jewish milieu such as Jesus's, whereas
we have no other evidence that Jewish Christians made levirate marriage either a practice
or a point of argument. At most, then, we may attribute the preservation of the story to
Christians' asking whose wife a remarried woman will be at the resurrection.

D. E. Nineham (318-20) suggests that because of similarity this story was pre-
Marcanly paired with the preceding one or that Mark paired the two stories to get a
succession of Pharisees (v 13) and Sadducees (v 18). But the Pharisees were accompanied
by the Herodians and, more importantly, we have no evidence from elsewhere of a Marcan
interest in pairing Pharisees and Sadducees. The latter appear only here in Mark. As for
similarity, the topics of tax and resurrection are unrelated, and posing a dilemma and
presenting a puzzle differ from each other. Also, using an object lesson in a dialogue differs
from using Scripture in a soliloquy.

Since Mark says that the Sadducees deny the resurrection yet Dan 12:1-2 clearly teaches it and Isa 26:19; Ezek 37:1-14; and possibly Job 19:25-27 at least imply it (cf. 2 Macc 7:9, 14; 12:43), we may infer that the Sadducees do not accept the full authority of the OT outside the Pentateuch. This inference agrees with the limitation to the Pentateuch of their and Jesus' arguments. Apparently because angels and demons do not appear in the Pentateuch, the Sadducees also deny the existence of angels and demons, the angel of the Lord not being a true exception, but the Lord's alter ego (Acts 23:8). For further description of the Sadducees, see the literature cited in BAGD s.v. Σαδδουκαῖος; also W. L. Lane 426-27 and additional literature cited there.

Under the view that the "us" to whom Moses wrote (v 19) refers to the Sadducees, O. Schwankl (*Sadduzäerfrage* 338) notes their self-consciousness and claim to be the true fulfillers of the Torah or, if Christian redaction is to be seen here, the separation of Christianity, represented by Jesus, from Judaism, represented by the Sadducees. But "us" could easily refer to all Jews, Jesus included; so we should not build very much on it.

On the one hand, the Sadducees may be adapting the story in Tobit about a Sarah who had seven successive husbands killed by a jealous demon before the marriages could be consummated (3:8, 15; 6:13; 7:11). The Sadducees may even have wrung their appeal to the law of levirate marriage out of the emphasis in Tobit on taking wives "from among their [Jewish] brothers" (4:12; cf. 6:9-12; 7:12-13). On the other hand, the Sadducees may be adapting the story in 2 Macc 7:1-41 of a mother and her seven sons, all eight of whom will be resurrected in compensation for their martyrdoms (so O. Schwankl, *Sadduzäerfrage* 347-52). The rhetorical law of three leads the Sadducees to list the first three brothers, and then to lump together the remaining ones. Contrast seven women's wanting to marry one man in Isa 4:1.

In v 23, א B C D L W Δ Ψ 33 892 *pc* c r¹ k sy^p co lack ὅταν ἀναστῶσιν, "whenever they rise." But in its favor, it must have seemed redundant after ἐν τῇ ἀναστάσει, "in the resurrection." Scribes would therefore have wanted to prune it away, but hardly to have inserted it; and "the pleonasm [more particularly, the duality] is in accord with Mark's style (cf. 13.19f.)" (B. M. Metzger, *Textual Commentary* ad loc.). Matthew and Luke also omit it because of its seeming redundancy; as a result, parallelistic influence strengthens the stylistic reason for scribal omission in Mark.

Since Pharisees would say that in the resurrection the wife will belong to her first husband, the Sadducees try to close that door by adding "for the seven had her [as] wife." J. G. Janzen (in *JSNT* 23 [1985] 43-58) interprets the Sadducees as meaning that if in an ideal number of attempts (seven) progeny was not raised up for a dead man by the means that God provided in the Mosaic law, what gives reason to hope that God will raise up the dead man himself as *not* provided in the Mosaic law? But this interpretation mistakes an attempted reductio ad absurdum for a profound theological argument. The Sadducees are not arguing from lack of evidence for a resurrection. They are posing a problem of marriage if there is a resurrection.

H. Anderson (278) distinguishes between answers to a characteristically Pharisaic question regarding the mode of resurrection (vv 24-25) and to a characteristically Sadducean question regarding the fact of resurrection (vv 26-27). But 1 Cor 15:35 shows that a modal question about resurrection can be used to deny the fact of resurrection. It is therefore gratuitous to bring Pharisees into the picture (cf. the observation of J. D. Kingsbury [in *NTS* 36 (1990) 45] that Mark does not portray the Sadducees as ridiculing the Pharisees, but as opposing Jesus).

In v 24 διὰ τοῦτο, "because of this," is easily as usually retrospective. When prospective, according to BAGD s.v. οὗτος 1bβ, it is followed by a ὅτι-clause, a ἵνα-clause, an infinitive phrase, or a noun — in other words, by a substantival expression of one sort or another, as to be expected for the appositional definition of a pronoun like τοῦτο. In

Mark 12:24 we might dare to think of a substantival participle; but that would produce (in expanded translation) "you who don't know the Scriptures or the power of God," which would have to act as the subject of "are deceived" and thus leave τοῦτο undefined. Therefore τοῦτο must look backward, leaving the participles to be taken much more naturally as circumstantial.

A merely temporal circumstance ("while . . .") would be jejune, however; and a concession ("although . . .") would nonsensically imply that *ignorance* of the Scriptures and of God's power should have kept the Sadducees from being deceived. By contrast, a causal circumstance makes good sense: "You're deceived, aren't you, because . . . ?" But if the circumstantial participle is causal yet does not define "because of this," Jesus must be speaking of two causes underlying two senses of being deceived: (1) the cause of being deceived as a charge; (2) the cause of being deceived as a state of mind. The charge finds its cause in the Sadducees' story of the seven brothers: this story prompts Jesus' charge. The state of mind finds its cause in the Sadducees' ignorance of the Scriptures and of God's power: this ignorance prompted their telling of the story.

C. K. Barrett (*Holy Spirit* 74-75) suggests that in v 24 Jesus originally spoke in the plural of "the Powers of God," meaning the second of the Eighteen Benedictions itself, not to the power of God referred to in it. But the follow-up in v 25 seems to describe what God's power will do at the resurrection, not quote the second benediction; and the use of the singular in 14:62 favors the originality of the singular here. Probably, then, Jesus used the singular because he was referring to only one of the powers mentioned in the second benediction. His recollection of this benediction may have turned his mind to the first benediction, which addresses God as "God of Abraham, God of Isaac, God of Jacob" and may therefore have turned his mind further to the similar phraseology in Exod 3:6. Or did Jesus think first of Exod 3:6 and then proceed through the first benediction to the second? For primary texts, see Str-B 4. 211, 215; cf. D. Daube, *Appeasement* 6-8.

According to B. Witherington III (*Women* 32-35), Jesus denies the contraction of new marriages after the resurrection, not the eternality of present marriages. The comparison with angels has to do, then, with immortality, as in Luke 20:36, not with unmarriedness. But if levirate marriage is not discontinued, the Sadducees' puzzle remains and Jesus has not really answered them. If levirate marriage *is* discontinued, however, so also are other marriages; for Jesus does not distinguish in his answer between levirate marriage and other marriages. Luke 20:36 need not compare the immortality of resurrected people with the immortality of angels to teach the eternality of present marriages. It may rather make the comparison to give the reason why no marriage at all will be needed. The Sadducees' case had to do with procreation in this life; so Jesus appeals to the lack of need for procreation in the next life. See O. Schwankl, *Sadduzäerfrage* 366-75, for different answers to the question why Jesus denies that the institution of marriage will endure on into the resurrected state.

E. S. Fiorenza (*In Memory of Her* 143-45) correctly points out that in v 25 Jesus does not teach the asexuality and sexual undifferentiation of resurrected people, but she errs in asserting that he teaches the abolition of patriarchal marriage. "They neither marry nor are given in marriage but are like angels in heaven" denies marriage as such, not a particular kind of marriage. Furthermore, the historical fact of patriarchal marriage leaves the Sadducees' question intact even under a denial of its continuation after the resurrection, indeed, even under a denial of its present validity. (By dismissing v 26a, "but concerning the dead that they are raised," as secondary but saying nothing about v 25a, "for whenever they are raised from among dead [people]," Fiorenza leaves it unclear whether she thinks Jesus is speaking in the mode of consistent eschatology or in that of realized eschatology.) A denial of patriarchalism in marriage rather than of marriage as such would require Jesus to deny being given in marriage, as women presently are, but would not require him to deny marrying. It would also require him not to compare the resurrected with angels, for angels are known for non-marriage, not for egalitarian or matriarchal marriage.

See Str-B 1. 887-90 on Jewish belief that at the resurrection present relations will resume, though we lack an explicit reference to marriage. Outside Sadducean circles, Jews consider angels immortal and therefore as not needing to procreate and therefore again as not marrying or being given in marriage. *1 Enoch* 104:4, 6; *2 Apoc. Bar.* 51:10 compare the perfected righteous with angels, though not in respect to non-marriage (cf. the standing of the righteous before God with the angelic hosts in 1QH 3:21-23; 6:13; 11:13; 1QS 4:22; 11:8).

The adversative δέ, "but," which introduces the scriptural argument for resurrection (vv 26-27) hinders the attempt of O. Schwankl (*Sadduzäerfrage* 365) to make the argument from God's power (v 25) spill over into the scriptural argument. Thus it is also hard to accept the causal interpretation that Schwankl gives to Jesus' initial question (v 24), i.e. the interpretation that the Sadducees do not understand God's power because they do not understand the Scriptures. If one were to adopt a causal interpretation, the reverse would do as well: the Sadducees do not understand the Scriptures (N.B. Jesus' mentioning them first) because they do not understand God's power.

J.-G. Mudiso Mbâ Mundla (*Jesus und die Führer Israels* 80) thinks to support a gnomic use of the present tense in ἐγείρονται, "they are raised" (v 26), with an identical use by Paul in 1 Cor 15:15-16, 29, 32, 35, 42-44. But Paul's use, like that of Jesus, is futuristic (cf. the intermingled future tense in 1 Cor 15:22-29, 37, 49-52, 54). The switch from the active voice in ἀναστῶσιν, "rise" (v 25), to the divine passive in ἐγείρονται, "are raised" (v 26), makes a good transition to statements about God (see the foregoing comments), matches other switches from τέκνον, "child" (v 19), to σπέρμα, "seed" (vv 19, 20, 21, 22), and from ἀφῆκεν, "left" (v 20), to καταλιπών, "having left" (v 21), and back to ἀφῆκαν (v 22; O. Schwankl, *Sadduzäerfrage* 307), and therefore does not support the theory that vv 26-27 were added later. The necessity of throwing out "not knowing the Scriptures" as secondary in v 24 if vv 26-27 are taken as secondary weakens the case for the second-ariness of vv 26-27. If "not knowing the Scriptures" were secondarily inserted in antici-pation of the addition of vv 26-27, we would expect "Scripture" instead of "Scriptures"; for vv 26-27 quote only one OT passage. As it is, the plural seems not only to anticipate that passage, but also to slur the Sadducees' rejection of all parts of the OT except the Pentateuch. In other words, "not knowing the Scriptures" seems at one with vv 18-25 and therefore demanding of the integrity of vv 26-27 (cf. the preparation for "the Scriptures" by the Sadducees' "Moses wrote" [ἔγραψεν, cognate to γράφας, "Scriptures"], and also for "the Book of Moses").

No argument against integrity can be gotten from a Septuagintal cast of the OT quotation in v 26, either. For Mark agrees with the MT *against* the LXX in the ellipsis of "am." Except for LXX[A,Luc(75)], Mark also disagrees with the LXX as well as with the MT in writing "the" with each occurrence of "God" (though see R. H. Gundry, *Use of the OT* 21, for a different textual criticism at this point). D. M. Cohn-Sherbok (in *JSNT* 11 [1981] 67) points out that verbs left to be supplied in the Hebrew OT do not always take the present tense. But to conclude to the deficiency of Jesus' argument is wrong, for his argument does not rest on a missing present tense (see the foregoing comments).

R. Bultmann (*HST* 26) admits that though in his view vv 26-27 are an addition, they were not originally independent; for they would have a place only in debate. If not originally in the present debate, where else? His answer: in the church, or perhaps between the church and the Sadducees. But it is cynical to say that vv 26-27 betray churchly origin by their "thoroughgoing Rabbinic character" and that "the Sadducees figure as the opponents [only] because it was traditional for them to deny the resurrection" — cynical because it is just as likely that Jesus ran into the Sadducees as that the church did and because he is as likely as later followers of him to have answered a rabbinically styled question in something of a rabbinic manner. Cohn-Sherbok (op. cit. 64-73) notes differences between Jesus' argumentation and rabbinic rules of argument, also between his argument and the argument of Gamaliel (in *b. Sanh.* 90b) that since the patriarchs did not inherit the land of Israel, God must raise them to keep his promise that they will inherit it. Since Jesus was not a trained rabbi, Cohn-Sherbok uses these differences as evidence of authenticity.

F. G. Downing (in *JSNT* 15 [1982] 42-50) argues that Philo (*Abr.* 10-11 §§50-55) comes close to interpreting Exod 3:6 as Jesus does, i.e. as meaning that God has related himself to mortal human beings so closely that awkward and inescapable questions arise about mortality as such. But in Philo a contrast between perishability and imperishability does not arise out of or give rise to a *question* about resurrection, or even about immortality, but arises out of concern to maintain a high view of virtues. They are the theme, the perishability of human beings a given. F. Dreyfus (in *RB* 66 [1959] 213-24), followed among others by E. E. Ellis (in *Mikra* 701) and O. Schwankl (*Sadduzäerfrage* 384-96), can point to covenantal associations of "the God of Abraham and the God of Isaac and the God of Jacob," but cannot show that God's faithfulness to God's covenant with those patriarchs demands their resurrection. For God did not promise them resurrection.

J. G. Janzen (in *JSNT* 23 [1985] 43-58) interprets Jesus as meaning that the God of Abraham, Isaac, and Jacob is the God of the living in that the stories of those patriarchs tell of sterility issuing in birth just as the Sadducees' story, which grows out of a patriarchal narrative in Genesis 38, starts with sterility and ends in resurrection (cf. Rom 4:18-25; Heb 11:11-12). But Jesus compares the resurrected with angels, not with babies, and appeals to a part of the Pentateuch notable for the merciless killing of babies, not for their miraculous births. Baby Moses is an exception in respect to killing, but his birth is still no miracle of reversed sterility.

According to A. J. Hultgren (*Jesus and His Adversaries* 126), vv 26-27 show that "the doctrine of the resurrection of the dead has been [Hellenistically] swallowed up by the doctrine of the immortality of the soul." But then it is strange that v 26 speaks of "the dead" as being "raised" — terminology more appropriate to bodily resurrection than to the immortality of the soul. Therefore Hultgren (op. cit. 129-30) tries to work out a synthesis by saying that a Hellenistic Jewish Christian used the immortality of the soul as an apology for the resurrection of the body: since the dead (v 26) are living already as immortal souls (v 27), they will gain new bodies at the last day. But none of Hultgren's primary sources use the immortality of the soul to *argue* for resurrection of the body (though, of course, Josephus [*J.W.* 2.8.14 §163; *Ant.* 18.1.3 §14] makes the Pharisees *combine* the two). 4 Macc 7:18-19 denies that Abraham, Isaac, and Jacob died; and according to 4 Macc 16:24-25, those who have died for God are presently living to him. Hultgren uses both of those passages to support his view (op. cit. 128-29), but neither one of them fits the description of the patriarchs and other deceased people as "the dead" (v 26).

Nor should we attribute to Jesus himself a "more spiritual view of the resurrection" that would "help to overcome the obstacle which the resurrection, more crudely conceived, presented to Greeks" (W. Harrington 189). The language of rising and being raised from among the dead befits what only Greek-thinking people would call crude. It does not befit airier views of resurrection. The comparison with angels has to do with unmarriedness, not with non-physicality. Even in *1 Enoch* 104:4, 6 the comparison with angels has to do with joy and companionship (and with kaleidoscopic beauty in *2 Apoc. Bar.* 51:10) even though *1 Enoch* 15:1-7 has emphasized the proper spirituality of angels (cf. Tob 12:19). See R. H. Gundry, *Sōma* 161-83.

It is not enough to say that Jesus plays on Jewish belief that the patriarchs and martyrs are even now living to God (4 Macc 7:19; 16:25). If they are already living to God without having been resurrected, where lies the necessity of a future resurrection?

Jesus would be saying nothing to answer the Sadducees' question. Moreover, his phrase "concerning the dead" undermines any belief or argument that the patriarchs are presently alive (that the dead lack an active relation to God, see Pss 6:6[5]; 30:10b[9b]; 88:11-13[10-12]; 115:17; Isa 38:18-19). This phrase also favors a futuristic present tense in "they are raised," meaning "they will be raised," and a similarly futuristic reference in his statement that God "is not a God of dead people but of living people," meaning "of people who will be resurrected to life" rather than "of people who even though they have died are still living." Much less should we think that Mark has added vv 26-27 to replace physical resurrection in the future with a non-physical life that has already begun for the deceased. Matthew's insertion of "am" into the quotation of Exod 3:6 changes Jesus' argument (see R. H. Gundry, *Matthew* 446). For its style, cf. Mark 2:25-26.

Verse 26 may seem to start awkwardly, but in fact its phraseology contributes to the chiastic structure of Jesus' answer. In relation to God's power he has told how people will live *whenever* (ὅταν) they rise from the dead. Now he shows from the Scriptures *that* (ὅτι) the dead are being raised. The step back from a description of life following the resurrection to an argument that dead people are as good as already being raised makes "but concerning the dead that they are being raised" a natural, almost necessary, transition. "But concerning the resurrection of the dead" would have been smoother; but putting the dead in their own initial phrase signals a chiastic shift from the resurrected, and putting the raising of the dead in a separate "that"-clause emphasizes the certainty of their being raised.

Without the mention and description of the Sadducees in v 18 and without the appeal to Exod 3:6 in v 26, the question put to Jesus might seem not to call the resurrection in question Sadducee-like, but Pharisee-like to ask him something about marriage ("Whose wife . . . ?"). Differently, vv 26-27 refute an attack on resurrection such as the Sadducees would make (cf. E. Schweizer 247). But why should Jesus' answer start so harshly in v 24 unless already before vv 26-27 Sadducees are trying to embarrass him over his belief in the resurrection? H. Anderson (276) cogently argues that since according to v 18 the Sadducees deny the factuality of resurrection and since according to vv 26-27 Jesus affirms its factuality, vv 19-23 do not raise a question about the manner of resurrection, v 25 did not originally conclude the pericope, and vv 26-27 probably formed an integral part of the original story. At first the pericope in vv 18-27 seems to stop cold. But Mark will tuck his comment on this pericope (that Jesus answered the Sadducees καλῶς, "well") into his introduction to the next one (v 28).

A SCRIBE'S COMING TO RECOGNIZE
THE TRUTH OF JESUS' TEACHING

12:28-34 *(Matt 22:34-40; cf. Luke 10:25-27)*

Jesus' dialogue with a scribe is the first of a pair of pericopes dealing with scribes (see also vv 35-40). The two pericopes go from good (Jesus commends a scribe) to bad (Jesus condemns the scribes). In the present pericope a scribe asks Jesus to identify the most important commandment (v 28). Jesus obliges, but goes beyond the question by identifying the next most important commandment, too (vv 29-31). The scribe praises Jesus' answer (vv 32-33), and Jesus pronounces him not far from God's kingdom (v 34ab). The pericope closes with an editorial notation that nobody dared to question Jesus any more (v 34c).

12:28 *(Matt 22:34-36; Luke 10:25)* As sometimes elsewhere, εἷς carries the sense of τις, an indefinite "one." Thus "one of the scribes" means "a scribe" (E. C. Maloney, *Semitic Interference* 126-31). This scribe's having heard the Sadducees and Jesus debate with each other (see vv 18-27, but not vv 13-17, for there some Pharisees and Herodians tried to trap Jesus in his speech rather than debating him) gives Mark opportunity to advertise Jesus' forensic victory: "seeing ('knowing' — v.l.) that he [Jesus] had answered them [the Sadducees] well." Enhancing this advertisement are (1) the asyndeton with which the participial construction begins; (2) the fact that it begins thus despite its being the third successive participial construction in the verse and despite the starting of the second one also with asyndeton; (3) the forward position of καλῶς, "well," in the ὅτι-clause introduced by the third participle; and (4) the omniscience with which Mark writes about the reason behind the scribe's question. Καλῶς probably comes to Mark in anticipation of the tradition in v 32. By itself the phrase "them debating" might refer to the Sadducees debating among themselves over Jesus' preceding answer to their question on resurrection. But the immediately following reference to his answering them "well" seems to indicate that the debate took place between the Sadducees and Jesus.

We have no good reason to think that the scribe approaches Jesus any less antagonistically than did the Pharisees or the Sadducees. His seeing that Jesus has answered the Sadducees well may indicate a desire to do a better job than they of dragging Jesus into a theological quagmire. Mark uses the same verb to introduce the scribe's question that he used to introduce the Sadducees' antagonistic question (viz., ἐπερωτάω, "ask, question" — cf. v 18; also for ἔρχονται . . . πρός, "come to," which parallels προσελθών, "having come to," in the present verse). The phraseology also recalls that of 10:2, where Pharisees were said to "test" Jesus with a question. And the scribe's later declaration that Jesus has taught truly and Jesus' responsive description of him as not far from God's kingdom may imply final capitulation rather than initial good will. In fact, the initial failure of the scribe to address Jesus respectfully and the final clause of the pericope, "And no one was daring to question him any more" (v 12c), show that with his question the scribe is daring to challenge Jesus antagonistically.

The question, "What commandment is first of all?" will allow Jesus to display, not his cleverness in overcoming a dilemma (as in vv 13-17) or in using a part of Scripture to defend a doctrine that does not seem to be taught there (as in vv 18-27), but his ability to identify the most important part of God's law. The separation of ποία, "what?" from its noun ἐντολή, "commandment" (contrast Matt 22:36), puts some weight on the difficulty of identifying the commandment. The anarthrousness of πρώτη, "first" (so also in v 29), stresses the quality of firstness (see M. Zerwick, *Biblical Greek* §179, against C. F. D. Moule, *Idiom-Book* 113, 207; cf. the anarthrousness of δευτέρα, "second," in v 31).

12:29-31 *(Matt 22:37-40; Luke 10:26-27)* Asyndeton stresses the forcefulness of Jesus' answer, which starts with a quotation of Deut 6:4-5. He will go on to quote also an earlier passage in the Pentateuch (Lev 19:18), but to emphasize the first rank of the commandment in Deut 6:4-5 he quotes these texts against normal practice in reverse order. Basically, Mark follows the LXX of Deut 6:4-5.

Between the second and third tones the intrusion of a non-Septuagintal as well as non-Massoretic phrase καὶ ἐξ ὅλης τῆς διανοίας σου, "and with your whole mind," produces four tones instead of the original three. The new one probably comes from reading the third Hebrew tone as מַדֲּעֲךָ, "your mind," before reading it with the LXX as מְאֹדְךָ, "your strength" (A. Finkel, *Pharisees* 174); and it may have the particular purpose of relating the command to love God to the intellectual activity that characterizes a scribe such as Jesus' questioner (cf. the similar comment on τῆς συνέσεως in v 33; and R. H. Gundry, *Use of the OT* 22-24, on text critical problems here and in the OT). Similarly, Jesus' going beyond the scribe's question by identifying the second most important commandment, "You shall love your neighbor as yourself" (Lev 19:18), seems to rest on a word-association of the second commandment with the first, for only in these texts of the Pentateuch (plus Deut 11:1, based on Deut 6:5, and Lev 19:34, based on Lev 19:18) does וְאָהַבְתָּ occur as a jussive: "and you shall love." We would expect an imperative (see W. Diezinger in *NovT* 20 [1978] 81-83). Addition of the second commandment may also have the purpose of stressing that the scribe must not stop at thinking lovingly about God but must go on to act lovingly toward his neighbor. Asyndeton and the anarthrousness of δευτέρα, "second," stress the quality of being second most important. "There is no other commandment greater than these" clamps the first and second commandments together so tightly that the scribe will not be able to rest on an abstract fulfilment of the first command-ment. Another asyndeton stresses the supreme greatness of these two command-ments.

12:32-33 *(cf. Luke 10:25-27)* Mark used the adverb καλῶς, "well," to describe Jesus' answering the question of the Sadducees (v 28). Now the scribe himself uses the same adverb to describe Jesus' answering his question. The placement of the adverb first, even before the address to Jesus, underlines the description. The abruptness of the question — it did not start with a respectful address (again see v 28) — now gives way to the respectful address διδάσκαλε, "Teacher." Jesus has proved his didactic superiority. The combination καλῶς, διδάσκαλε produces an exclamation, "Well (said), Teacher!" which adds more weight to that superiority. The exclamation makes the following sentence start with asyndeton: "On [the basis] of truth you have spoken." The asyndeton and the forward position of "on [the basis of] truth" highlight the truthfulness of Jesus' speech. The scribe is echoing the phraseology of the Pharisees in v 14. But they were flattering Jesus in an attempt to trip him up. By now Jesus has so over-powered the tricky Pharisees, the blundering Sadducees, and the inquiring scribe that the phraseology has lost every tinge of flattery and carries the tones of total assent and pure admiration — so total and pure that the scribe paraphrases what Jesus has just said.

The paraphrase omits "Hear, Israel, the Lord our God . . . Lord," keeps "(he) is one," and adds "there is no other besides him" from Deut 4:35 (cf. Exod 8:6[10]; Deut 4:39; 2 Sam 7:22; 1 Kings 8:60; 2 Kgs 19:19; 2 Chr 33:13; Isa 37:20; 45:21). Together, the omission and addition bring out more clearly the connection between monotheism and undivided love. The omission leads to a substitution of "him" for "the Lord your God" in the first commandment. The paraphrase also turns the imperatival future tense of "love" into an articular infinitive to make undivided love the subject of the added predicate, "is much more than all whole burnt offerings and sacrifices." This addition, perhaps prompted by the setting in the temple, substitutes for "there is no other commandment greater than these" and displays the scribe's understanding what other commandments (i.e. commandments to offer sacrifices) might wrongly vie with the two most important ones. "Soul" and "mind" collapse into "understanding" (συνέσεως) to recapture the three tones and chime in with the scribe's display of understanding. Συνέσεως may again play on the distinctively scribal activity of thinking about the meaning of the OT law (cf. the comment on διανοίας in v 30). The forward position of περισσότερον, "much more," shows the scribe's further understanding that Jesus' expression "no greater" rules out the existence of *equally* important commandments as well as ruling out the existence of *more* important commandments. Omission of "your" from "heart," "understanding," etc., suits the scribe's addressing Jesus, whom it would be entirely inappropriate for him to instruct.

12:34 *(Matt 22:46; Luke 10:28; 20:40)* Ἰδὼν ὅτι . . .-ως ἀπεκρίθη, "seeing that he answered . . .-ly," forms an inclusion with the same phraseology in v 28 (a point in favor of reading ἰδών in v 28 rather than the v.l. εἰδώς, "knowing"). The present editorializing that in Jesus' view the scribe has answered νουνεχῶς, "in a manner that showed he had a mind," amounts to a description of the scribe as now obedient to at least part of the foremost commandment, viz., to love God ἐξ ὅλης τῆς διανοίας σου, "with your whole mind" (cf. ἐξ ὅλης τῆς συνέσεως, "with the whole understanding," in v 33). The forward position of νουνεχῶς stresses this point. From the primacy of love the scribe has correctly deduced the inferiority of sacrifices in the temple (M.-J. Lagrange 324). Jesus' statement, "You are not far from the kingdom of God" (cf. *Gos. Thom.* 82), supports Mark's editorial estimate. Since the scribe started out antagonistic to Jesus (see the comments on v 28), the statement means that the scribe is *not now* far from God's kingdom. But Mark puts the final accent, not on the scribe's loving God with his mind, but on the effect of Jesus' answer: "And no one was daring to question him any more." The assonance and forward positions of οὐδεὶς οὐκέτι, "no one any more," highlight his forensic victory. "Any more" and the imperfect tense of ἐτόλμα, "was daring," make the victory both permanent and inclusive of his earlier answers, too. The initiative will shift to Jesus now that he has passed every test. After all, even one of his enemies' own experts — a scribe — has confessed the truth of his teaching. See the comments on 8:32 that ἐπερωτάω, preceded by its direct object as here, sharpens a sense of awe before Jesus.

NOTES

According to J. H. Ropes (*Synoptic Gospels* 27), Mark uses this story to portray Jesus as an orthodox Jew, undeserving of crucifixion (cf. H.-W. Kuhn in *Tradition und Glaube* 302-4). True, but insufficient. Verse 34b interprets the double καλῶς, "well" (vv 28, 32), not merely in terms of Jesus' orthodoxy, but in terms of his ability to outwit opponents in theological repartee. He is *superior* in his orthodoxy.

Many have followed G. Bornkamm (*Geschichte und Glaube* 1. 37-45) in the opinion that the inquiry after the most important commandment, the emphasis on monotheism, the Septuagintal cast of the OT quotations in vv 29-33, and the rationalism of διάνοια, "mind," σύνεσις, "understanding," and νουνεχῶς, "thoughtfully," point to a Hellenistic Jewish Christian origin of this pericope in the Diaspora. But whether or not the rabbinic distinction between heavy and light commandments dates from quite so early as the NT (see O. H. Lehmann in *SE I* 558), the distinction shows that a question concerning the most important commandment might come up in Palestinian Judaism (see also the distinction in *m. Ḥag.* 1:8 between essential and unessential rules in the Law). Besides, we dare not overdraw the distinction between Palestinian Judaism and its counterpart in the Diaspora. We now know that Palestine was more Hellenized than previously thought. Jesus, for example, grew up about an hour's walk by Roman road from the Hellenistic city of Sepphoris and only ten minutes' walk from full view of that city. He may even have worked on its reconstruction during his young manhood (R. A. Batey in *NTS* 30 [1984] 249-58; idem, *Jesus & the Forgotten City* 65-82). On the other hand, Paul calls himself a Hebraist though he came from Tarsus, far away from Palestine, and often quotes the LXX as well as making his own translation of the Hebrew OT (Acts 9:11, 30; 11:25; 21:39; 22:3; Phil 3:5). The LXX was known and used even in Palestine (see p. 22).

To account for the Septuagintal traits of the present OT quotations, we might just as easily think of assimilation to the LXX in the transmitting of Jesuanic tradition as of initial use of the LXX in a wholesale fabrication of the story by Hellenistic Jewish Christians living outside Palestine. In some respects, moreover, the quotations disagree with the LXX as well as with the MT; and if Deut 4:35 LXX^A is influenced by the NT in reading ἄλλος, "other" (cf. R. H. Gundry, *Use of the OT* 166, n. 3), that word in Mark 12:32 agrees with the MT against the LXX. The probability that the third Hebrew tone of the Shema has been read in two different ways, one of them non-Septuagintal and typical of rabbinic interpretation by analogy of words (see the foregoing comments on v 30), argues for un-Greek origin. So also does the probability of Jesus' using typically rabbinic word-association to couple Lev 19:18 with Deut 6:4-5 (see the foregoing comments on v 31).

K. Berger (*Gesetzesauslegung* 192) argues that the association of Deut 4:35 with Deut 6:4-5 could have been made only on the basis of the LXX; for only it has "the Lord your God" in Deut 4:35 to correspond with "the Lord our God" in Deut 6:4-5. But that part of Deut 4:35 does not appear in Mark 12:32; so the association seems to depend instead on correspondence between the being of only one God (Deut 6:4-5) and the being of no other God besides (Deut 4:35), which are not distinctively Septuagintal. Greek and Hellenistic Jewish writings associate piety toward God (or the gods) and justice to fellow human beings; but the language of those writings tends strongly toward that of moral philosophy, especially toward Stoic language of that sort (R. H. Fuller in *Essays on the Love Commandment* 50); and not even Hellenistic Jewish literature ever quotes Deut 6:4-5 and Lev 19:18 in tandem. The closest parallel, *T. Iss.* 5:2b ("love the Lord and your neighbor"), does not quote these two commandments explicitly, much less put them forward as the first and second commandments in importance (see also *T. Iss.* 7:6; *T. Dan* 5:3; *T. Benj.* 3:3-5; *Jub.* 36:3-7; Philo *Spec.* 2.15 §63; idem *Decal.* 22 §§108-10; idem *Abr.* 37 §208; idem *Virt.* 8 §47; 18 §95; and further literature cited and discussed by K. Berger, *Gesetzesauslegung* 143-68). We also always have to keep in mind the possibility of Christian influence on, if not Christian composition of, the Testaments of the Twelve Patriarchs. Nor does rabbinic literature couple the two love-commandments and make them the most important. Even NT writers eliminate the first of them in favor of the second and make the second incorporate all other commandments rather than outrank them (Rom 13:9; Gal 5:14; Jas 2:8; cf. *b. Šabb.* 31a and the equalizing of the first two commandments in Matt 22:39). So if Luke 10:27; *Did.* 1:2; and later Christian literature echo Jesus' teaching, the distinctiveness of the coupling and of the first and second ranking of these commandments favors authenticity.

Monotheism and the subordination of sacrificial worship appear already in the OT. The events of the Seleucid and Maccabean periods plus current domination by Rome make resistance to polytheism a continuing concern in Palestinian Judaism as well as in the Diaspora (see 1QH 7:32 and 10:9, "there is none beside you," just as in the supposedly Hellenistic Jewish Christian, extra-Palestinian Mark 12:32); and a subordination of sacrificial worship excellently suits the general tenor of Jesus' teaching (cf., for example, Matt 23:23 par. Luke 11:42), as Matthew well saw and consequently inserted quotations of Hos 6:6 in Matt 9:12; 12:7 (R. H. Gundry, *Matthew* 168, 224). 1 Sam 15:22; Ps 40:7-9[6-8]; 50:7-15; 51:17-19[15-17]; Prov 15:8; 21:3; Isa 1:10-17; Jer 6:16-20; 7:1-26; 11:15; Hos 6:6; Amos 4:4-5; 5:4-27; Mic 6:6-8; 1QS 9:3-5; and rabbinic literature cited in Str-B 1. 499-500 prove that subordination of sacrificial worship is not limited to the Diaspora (cf. Prov 16:6; and, on the Hellenistic side, see Prov 16:7 LXX; Dan 3:38-40 LXX Theod; *Ep. Arist.* 234; *Sib. Or.* 4:24-30; and, for an extreme Christian view postdating the NT, *Barn.* 2:7-8, but not *Bib. Ant.* 22:5-6, as shown by 22:7-9).

Being not far from God's kingdom relates to Jesus' eschatological talk of entering and not entering God's kingdom (9:47; 10:15, 23, 24, 25 et passim) and therefore does not count as post-Jesuanic de-eschatologizing of the kingdom (cf. K. Kertelge in *À cause de l'Évangile* 320-21). (It is another question whether Jesus spoke of entering the kingdom now as well as later.) A. M. Ambrozic (*Hidden Kingdom* 177-81) uses the contrast between the favorable portrayal of the scribe in this pericope and the unfavorable portrayal of scribes elsewhere in Mark to argue for authenticity. The contrast in Luke 10:25-37 between Jesus' leaving open the definition of "your neighbor" and a restrictive Jewish definition (Str-B 1. 353-57) also argues for authenticity (cf. P. Perkins, *Love Commands* 21-22; J. Piper, *Love Your Enemies* 92-94).

R. H. Fuller (in *Essays on the Love Commandment* 46) calls v 28 "painfully overloaded" and describes the overload as "a sure sign of redactional expansion." It does not follow, however, that Mark has forced the story into an unoriginal setting. Emphasis does not imply intrusion.

K. Berger (*Gesetzesauslegung* 188-89) insists that in v 28, ποία means "what kind of?" not merely "what?" as τίς does. But "what kind of?" asks for a description. Yet Jesus answers by identifying a commandment, not by describing one. Taking ποία in the sense "what kind of?" and then relating it to the rabbinic distinction between heavy and light commandments also overinterprets the word. For as a matter of course the "first commandment of all" belongs to the heavy sort; so asking for its classification would have no purpose. See Str-B 1. 249, 900-905 on the distinction.

Since πάντων, "of all" (v 28), does not agree in gender with ἐντολή, "commandment," the interpretation has arisen that "first of all" does not mean "foremost of all the commandments," but "the commandment that is more important than everything else, whether other commandments or not." But Jesus' stating that there is no other *commandment* greater than the two he has quoted (v 31) shows that πάντων occurs ad sensum, perhaps stereotypically, to intensify the superlative "first," just as in v 33 πάντων modifies the implied feminine noun θυσιῶν, "sacrifices," as well as the neuter ὁλοκαυτωμάτων, "whole burnt offerings," and just as in Thuc. 4.52 §3 πάντων modifies the implied feminine noun πόλεσι, "cities," despite feminine articles and pronouns modifying and referencing this same noun elsewhere in the immediate context (cf. Matt 22:36; V. Taylor 485-86; BDF §164[1]; A. T. Robertson, *Grammar* 410).

"First" means "most important" without regard to reasons for greatest importance (cf. "last of all" [9:35] and "slave of all" [10:44]). The scribe may be asking which of the 613 commandments counted in the Law by the rabbis is most important. See W. Grundmann in *TDNT* 4. 535-36 on the rabbinic count and its date.

Recitation of the Shema, which begins with Deut 6:4-5, plays a very large part in Jewish piety (see L. Jacobs in *EncJud* 14. 1370). So from that standpoint it comes naturally to Jesus that he should start his answer with those verses. It is unlikely that in v 29 an ἐστιν is implied between the first κύριος and ὁ θεὸς ἡμῶν to produce "[The] Lord [is] our God" or, taking κύριος as a predicate nominative in emphatic first position and as anarthrous for emphasis on the quality of lordship, "Our God [is] Lord." (Then κύριος εἷς ἐστιν would mean, "One Lord is he" or "[The] Lord is one.") For ellipsis of the verb would normally occur in the second rather than first clause in order that the first might give a clue to the second. Hence, we have only one clause in which κύριος is subject, ὁ θεὸς ἡμῶν appositive, and κύριος εἷς predicate nominative with ἐστιν. We might expect κύριος to be arthrous and the order of κύριος εἷς to be reversed; but except for supplying ἐστιν at the end of the clause, the LXX, which Mark follows, is simply reflecting the Hebrew of Deut 6:4. The supplying of ἐστιν at the end of the clause puts κύριος εἷς in an emphatic position: *"one Lord."*

The Hebrew of Deut 6:4 may be translated, "The Lord our God [is] one Lord," "The Lord our God — the Lord [is] one," "The Lord [is] our God; the Lord [is] one," or "The Lord [is] our God, the Lord alone." The first three translations stress the undividedness of the Lord, the last the exclusivity of Israel's relation to the Lord. None of the translations demand monotheism, but there can be no doubt that in NT times monotheism characterized Jewish understanding of the text (see v 32 in the present pericope, for example). And most of the OT passages listed in the comments on v 32 favor monotheism at a date much earlier than the NT.

Adherence to many gods results in divided loyalty. But adherence to one God in exclusion of other gods entails a demand for undivided loyalty (cf. the way in which the Shema has apparently influenced the presentation of the first commandment of the Decalogue, "You shall have no other gods before me," in Josephus *Ant.* 3.5.5 §91). Hence, the pronouncement that "the Lord our God is one Lord [not many lords]" leads to the command to love God with "all" one's heart, soul, and strength. In fact, the paratactic "and" before "you shall love" means "therefore" (cf. M. Reiser, *Syntax und Stil* 123-26). "Heart" connotes thoughts and feelings. "Soul" connotes physical and psychological energy and life itself, possibly to the point of martyrdom in the understanding that developed among Jews after the Maccabean martyrs died. "Strength" connotes physical and material capabilities, including property and other forms of wealth (F. Stolz in *TDOT* 1. 861-67; C. Westermann in *TDOT* 2. 71-96). Though "mind" may show Hellenistic influence (yet see 1QS 1:11-12), one needs to ask why such influence intruded here (cf. the answer suggested above, viz., that the intellectual activity which makes a scribe a scribe must not stop at analyzing God according to the OT law, but must progress to loving God accordingly). Assigning heart and soul to one's personal existence, and mind and strength to one's powers (so R. Pesch 2. 240), illegitimately severs the heart and soul from one's powers and the mind and strength from one's personal existence. One's powers include the heart's thinking and feeling and the soul's life-force. One's personal existence includes the mind's reasoning and the bodily strength which enables the accumulation and management of property and other wealth. "As yourself" in the command to love your neighbor means "in the same way that you care for your own needs." Loving yourself is a given and point of comparison, not a command. "It is the attitude of the natural man which must be overcome" in the very loving of your neighbor (R. Bultmann, *Jesus* 116).

K. Berger (*Gesetzesauslegung* 178-79) argues that since the LXX always uses καρδία or διάνοια but more often καρδία and never both in the same passage for לבב, the presence of both here in Mark shows the Hebrew text not to stand behind Mark; i.e. Mark's text rests on a Hellenistic base. But against the presupposition of this argument, i.e. that καρδία and διάνοια offer a double translation of לבב, why does διάνοια come after ψυχή, "soul," rather than after καρδία? Berger (op. cit. 69-70) answers that the frequency of the pair "heart and soul" caused resistance to the intrusion of "mind" after "heart" (cf. Deut 6:6 LXX; Josh 22:5; 1 Kgs 2:4; 8:48; 2 Kgs 23:3; 2 Chr 6:38; 34:31; Jer 32:41). But no one has protected the pair of heart and soul in Mark 12:33; and Deut 6:5 does not really have that pair anyway — rather, a triplet of heart, soul, and strength, as in 2 Kgs 23:25 (cf. 1QS 1:11-12). So it seems more likely that a second translation of לבב would have intruded after "heart" if it were going to intrude at all. Otherwise, we might expect it to be tacked on after the entire triplet, as in Luke 10:27. Put as it is ahead of "strength," it looks like a play on the third Hebrew tone (see the foregoing comments). Even under Berger's analysis of the textual phenomenon, it follows only that the Hebrew text does not underlie the redactional stage at which "mind" was added. It does not follow that the Hebrew text did not underlie a more original version of the story or that Jesus did not quote the Hebrew text in the event itself. Since Mark twice writes the synonym ἰσχύος, "strength," where the LXX (except for ἄλλος in the Hexapla) has δυνάμεως, "power," V. P. Furnish (*Love Command* 29-30) errs in saying that at v 30 Mark substitutes διανοίας, "mind," for δυνάμεως and then at v 32 interprets διανοίας with συνέσεως, "understanding," to stress the moral law at the expense of the ceremonial.

In importance, the commandments that Jesus cites are first and second in comparison with each other. But together they outrank all other commandments. The attempt of Furnish (op. cit. 26-27) to erase the distinction between the first and second commandments ("It [the second] is, simply, the second of two mentioned as together comprising the chief commandment . . .") neglects that if "first" means "foremost in importance" (so vv 28, 29), parallelism demands that "second" mean "second most important." Jesus maintains this distinction by referring to the two commandments as "these" rather than amalgamating them into "this" (v 31). Though too quick to detect post-Jesuanic Hellenization, K. Kertelge (in *À cause de l'Évangile* 306-7, 317-19) correctly argues against merging the first commandment into the second and against deducing the inauthenticity of Jesus' adding the second most important commandment from the scribe's asking only for the commandment of first importance. J. Gnilka (2. 163) likewise argues cogently against lopping off vv 31-34 or vv 32-34 to find a more original version of the story.

On καλῶς as an exclamation in v 32, see BAGD s.v. 4c; V. Taylor 488; and esp. G. Wohlenberg 320, where a number of possibilities are canvassed. 1QapGen 2:5-7, 10, 18, 22 shows that the scribe's description of Jesus' speech as truthful need not be attributed to post-Jesuanic Hellenistic influence. According to J.-G. Mudiso Mbâ Mundla (*Jesus und die Führer Israels* 139), the scribe omits God's name out of reverence for it. But in reciting the Shema twice daily the scribe would have pronounced אלהים, "God," and in substitution for יהוה, "Yahweh," he would have pronounced אדני, "Lord" (cf. the notes on v 36). So Jesus' having just pronounced those names has more likely made it superfluous for the scribe to repeat them.

To say that loving God and your neighbor is "much more than" offering sacrifices is not to displace the sacrifices with love, but to superordinate love to them. In the OT and rabbinic literature, too, the superordination of love or other virtues does not displace the sacrifices or other commandments (*b. Sukk.* 49b). The love-commandments still belong within the sphere of the Law. All in all, then, we should not think of a Hellenistic Jewish or Hellenistic Jewish Christian rejection of the sacrificial cult (see D. J. Moo in *JSNT* 20 [1984] 6-11; W. Schmithals 540-42; Mudiso Mbâ Mundla, op. cit. 199-203).

Saying that the scribe weakens Jesus' statement by shifting from μείζων, "greater," to περισσότερον, "much more," and from "all" to "all burnt offerings and sacrifices" (so ibid. 203-4, 213; cf. K. Berger, *Gesetzesauslegung* 256-57) does the scribe an injustice. Jesus' compliment gives him better press (v 34). Both adjectives are comparative. Neither one overmatches the other in meaning. And "all burnt offerings and sacrifices" limits the earlier "all" (which was the scribe's own!) no more than Jesus's "another commandment" did (vv 28, 31). Rather, it selects an example of what a lesser light than Jesus might have falsely identified as the most important commandment.

G. Murray (in *DownRev* 102 [1984] 271-75) thinks that Jesus' commendation of the scribe in v 34 comes unneeded and therefore inappropriately after material having to do with a friendly question. But the question was antagonistic (see the comments on v 28); and even if it had been friendly, a commendation would have corresponded to it in tone and therefore capped the conversation quite appropriately.

Wis 6:17-20 does not make a good parallel to Mark 12:34, for becoming a king through desire for wisdom differs radically from showing by a sensible answer that you are not far from God's kingdom. Nor does the Passover Haggadah, which speaks of him "who does not know how to ask," make a good parallel (as thought by D. Daube, *NTRJ* 166-68); for not *daring* to ask and therefore not asking (so v 34) differs radically from not knowing *how* to ask and therefore receiving instruction. A full discussion of the relation between vv 28-34 and Luke 10:25-29 belongs in commentaries on Luke, because the best possibility is that Luke or his source reworks Mark or a pre-Marcan tradition (cf. J. Kiilunen, *Doppelgebot*).

JESUS' EXPOSÉ OF THE SCRIBES

12:35-40 (Matt 22:41–23:36; Luke 20:40-47)

Now Jesus turns interrogator by asking a question about the scribes' designation of the Christ (v 35; cf. his turning interrogator in 3:4 after repeated challenges by his enemies, as here, though there he addressed them whereas here he asks about them). He follows with a quotation from David (v 36) and challenges their designation with a question (v 37a). Mark then inserts a note concerning Jesus' hold on the crowd (v 37b), and a denunciation of the scribes closes out the pericope (vv 38-40).

12:35-37 *(Matt 22:41-46; Luke 20:41-44)* Since Jesus has already answered the scribe in v 34ab and since Mark's statement that "nobody was daring to question him any more" has intervened in v 34c, Jesus' "answering" does not mean that he answers the scribe, but that he responds to the lack of further questions by asking his own question about the scribes (cf. the comments on 9:5-6; 11:14; 14:40, 48). The question and its answer will be the first of three monologues (vv 35b-37b, 38b-40, 43b-44) following several dialogues. "Teaching" revives the contrast between Jesus' teaching with authority and the scribes' teaching without it (cf. 1:21-22, 27), for he is about to attack them. The redundancy of "teaching" after "was saying" exhibits Mark's desire to revive this contrast. He has not mentioned a departure from the temple since Jesus' return to it in 11:27; so "in the temple" implies that Jesus has stayed there since then. This topographical note signals a new pericope, though for a change no movement is involved.

"How come the scribes say that Christ is 'Son of David'?" (cf. 9:11-13) presupposes not only general scribal agreement on this designation of the expected Christ, but also the lack of this designation in the OT. (In extant literature, it appears first in *Pss. Sol.* 17:21.) On the basis of this absence Jesus is challenging the scriptural accuracy of the scribal designation. The position of the predicate nominative υἱὸς Δαυίδ, "Son of David," before ἐστιν, "is" (or at least of υἱός before ἐστιν — see the v.l.), stresses the designation to intensify the challenge. Similarly, αὐτὸς Δαυίδ, "David himself," and the asyndeton with which Jesus' quotation of David begins sets David's designation of the Christ in emphatic contrast with the scribes' designation. "In the Holy Spirit," which indicates the divine inspiration of a scriptural statement by David (cf. 2 Sam 23:1-2; Acts 1:16; 4:25; 28:25; 2 Tim 3:16; Heb 3:7; 10:15; 11QPsᵃ col. 27, ll. 3-4; also Mark 13:11), contrasts with the question, "How come the scribes say . . . ?" This further contrast puts the scribal designation of the Christ as "Son of David" in a poor light.

Jesus quotes David's statement in Ps 110:1. It is hard to tell whether Jesus and the scribes agree on the messianic meaning of Psalm 110 (i.e. on David's meaning that God [the first-mentioned κύριος, "Lord"] addresses the Christ [the next-mentioned κύριος]) as well as on the Davidic authorship of Psalm 110 (so the MT LXX), or whether Jesus exhibits exegetical brilliance by being the first to interpret the psalm in this way (as he showed his exegetical brilliance by interpreting Exod 3:6 of the resurrection — see vv 26-27 with the comments ad loc.). The absence of a messianic interpretation of Psalm 110 in Jewish literature written earlier than the first half of the third century favors his being the first, though some have hypothesized that Christian use of the psalm temporarily drove out an earlier Jewish messianic interpretation (Str-B 4/1. 452-65). Except for omission of ὁ, "the," before κύριος, "Lord" (perhaps to let emphasis fall on τῷ κυρίῳ μου, "to my Lord"), the Greek text of the quotation follows the LXX, which corresponds closely to the Hebrew text. A seeming exception to this correspondence — viz., ὑποκάτω, "under" — comes from Ps 8:7 LXX, which also corresponds to the Hebrew text of another psalm traditionally ascribed to David. The further quotation of what the Lord said to David's Lord, "Sit at my right [hand] till I put your enemies under your feet," spells out the lordship of the Christ and provides a necessary complement to "[the] Lord said to my Lord."

An emphasis on David's calling the Christ "my Lord" comes out in the repetition of αὐτὸς Δαυίδ, "David himself" (cf. v 37a with v 36a), in the switch from the ordinary aorist εἶπεν, "said" (v 36a), to the vivid historical present λέγει, "says" (v 37a), in the qualitative thrust of the anarthrous κύριον, "Lord," in the statement as a whole, "David himself says him [to be] Lord," and in the asyndeton which introduces it. The heavily emphasized designation of the Christ as Lord now leads to the challenging question, "So whence (καὶ πόθεν) is he his son?" This question asks for the source of the designation "Son of David." In view of Jesus' noting the divine inspiration of David and citing of Ps 110:1, the question asks for an inspired scriptural source. There is none. So the scribes stand exposed: they pass for experts in Scripture, but their designation of the Christ does not even come from it. The placement of αὐτοῦ, "his," before ἐστιν υἱός, "is he son," does not emphasize whose son the Christ is not, but makes emphasis fall on the refusal of the OT to use the word "son" for the relationship of the Christ to David (cf. the comments on 6:52) and therefore on the contrast between David's calling the Christ "my Lord" and the absence from the OT of "Son of David" for the Christ (see J. Marcus in *NovT* 31 [1989] 135-36 for the emphatic position of αὐτοῦ). Also highlighting this contrast is the chiastic structure of vv 35-37: (a) "And answering, Jesus was saying [while] teaching in the temple"; (b) "How come the scribes say that the Christ is 'Son of David' "; (c) "David himself said in the Holy Spirit, 'The Lord said to my Lord, . . .' "; (c′) "David himself says him [to be] 'Lord' "; (b′) "So from where [do the scribes get it that the Christ] is his 'son'?"; (a′) "And the large crowd was listening to him gladly." The powerful effect of Jesus' exposing the scribes comes out in the editorial comment about his grip on the crowd, which Mark characteristically describes as πολύς, "large" (cf. 4:1; 8:1; 5:21, 24; 6:34; 8:1; 9:14), and whose listening he describes with ἡδέως, "gladly," to emphasize the extent and power of that grip (cf. 6:20). The placements of the subject ὁ πολὺς ὄχλος, "the large crowd," before its verb (against the usual Marcan order of verb–subject) and of the adverb ἡδέως last add weight to this emphasis.

12:38-40 *(Matt 23:1-36; Luke 20:45-47)* "And in his teaching he was saying" (cf. 1:22, 27; 11:18; and esp. 4:2) does not serve to separate vv 38-40 from vv 35-37, as though Mark were starting a new pericope. Rather, it serves to tie vv 38-40 to vv 35-37 by recalling v 35a: "And responding, Jesus was saying as he taught in the temple, . . ." (cf. the comments on 2:27 with regard to ἔλεγεν, "was saying"). The immediately foregoing intrusion of Mark's editorial remark about Jesus' grip on the crowd necessitates this connecting link. Mark does not want his audience to think that the pericope which started in v 35 ended with v 37. Instead, he wants vv 38-40 to cap Jesus' exposé of what the scribes *say* with Jesuanic teaching which authoritatively denounces what those same scribes *do*. The forward position of "in his teaching" highlights Jesus' authority.

The denunciation starts with a warning against the scribes (βλέπετε, "watch out" — an imperative in the emphatic present tense; cf. the notes on 1:3) and peaks in a prediction of judgment on them. The description of their liking to walk around in long robes, liking greetings in the market places, and liking chief seats in the synagogues and chief couches at banquets (cf. Luke 14:7-11) teams up with the designation of the scribes as "the ones devouring the houses of widows and praying a long time for show." They pray aloud, as was the custom, and in public (cf. Matt 6:5). We might think that the description and the designation add to the crowd's previous enjoyment in listening to Jesus because they resonate to his exposé of these parading scribes. But since the crowd are those who fawningly greet the scribes and otherwise pay them honor and admiration, the denunciation must shock the crowd.

The forward position of ἐν στολαῖς, "in long robes," emphasizes the scribes' ostentation. Walking around in such robes and being greeted in the market places make a pair, because scribes are greeted as they walk around in the market places. Seats and couches make another pair, because both are "first," meaning "chief."

Οἱ κατεσθίοντες . . . προσευχόμενοι, "the ones devouring . . . praying," starts a new sentence with asyndeton and casus pendens, the latter resumed by οὗτοι, "these" (cf. E. C. Maloney, *Semitic Interference* 88). These literary devices make the scribes' devouring of widows' houses and praying a long time to make themselves look good stand out in reprehensibility. So also do the forward positions of προφάσει, "by way of pretext," and μακρά, "a long time," in description of the scribes' praying. Jesus' final pronouncement, "These will receive very harsh judgment," closes out the denunciation with a forceful prediction (cf. Jas 3:1; Wis 6:6). Asyndeton intensifies its force.

NOTES

H. Anderson (283) suggests that before Mark wrote, the material in vv 35-44 had been attached to that in 11:27–12:34 on the basis of the catchwords "scribe(s)" (vv 28, 32, 35, 38) and "widow(s)" (vv 40, 42, 43). But it would be only natural for Jesus to speak of the scribes after one of them had asked him a question ("not far from the kingdom of God" still being outside the kingdom) and for Jesus to take notice of a widow after mentioning widows in his warning against the scribes. That is to say, catchwords may suggest a historical association as easily as a redactional one.

Jesus' taking the initiative in v 35 does not count against historicity. It would be surprising if someone like Jesus did not take the initiative at times. J. Gnilka (2. 169) suggests that λέγουσιν used to be indefinite ("people say"), Mark having inserted "the scribes." But Mark's penchant for the indefinite makes it unlikely that he would have gotten rid of it by such an insertion. P. M. Casey (in *ExpTim* 96 [1984-85] 236) argues against authenticity on the grounds that "the Christ" occurs here in a manner undocumented in Judaism of the period and generally absent from Jesus' other teaching, but characteristic of the early church. But on what ground should we prefer innovation by the early church to innovation by Jesus? His cautious acceptance of the designation in 8:29-30 and similar use of it himself in 9:41; 13:21; Luke 24:26, 46 weakens part of Casey's argument; for rejecting the authenticity of some or all of those passages, too, makes the argument circular.

Though the anarthrousness of υἱὸς Δαυίδ emphasizes the quality of Davidic sonship (so also in Matt 1:1, 20; 15:22; *Pss. Sol.* 17:21), the use of the phrase elsewhere with the definite article (Matt 12:23; 21:9, 15) shows that we should not distinguish sharply between a description ("a son of David") and a title ("Son of David"; cf. the variation between arthrous and anarthrous occurrences of "Son of God" throughout Mark and elsewhere). Because of contrast with the directly quoted designation "Lord," the present discussion puts quotation marks around "Son of David."

See E. C. Maloney, *Semitic Interference* 113-16, for translating αὐτός in vv 36, 37 "himself," or possibly "the aforesaid," rather than like a prepositive Aramaic pronoun, "he," anticipating the following noun, "David" (against M. Black, *Aramaic Approach* 117). It is unlikely that ἐν τῷ πνεύματι τῷ ἁγίῳ, "in the Holy Spirit," implies the Holy Spirit's catching David up to heaven to overhear what God will say to the Christ (cf. Rev 4:1 and the futurity, as Jesus speaks, of the Christ's exaltation to God's right hand). For this implication we would expect the apocalyptic formula ἐν πνεύματι, "in Spirit," and a subsequent mention of vision or audition (cf. Ezek 11:24 LXX; 37:1 LXX; Rev 1:10; 4:2; 17:3; 21:10; F. Neugebauer in *NTS* 21 [1974-75] 89; and Matt 22:43 with comments in R. H. Gundry, *Matthew* 451).

The play on the double κύριος, "Lord," in v 36 and Ps 109:1 LXX does not reflect a similar play in the MT, which reads יהוה and then אדני. But by Jesus' time אדני was probably substituted for יהוה, and a play on two occurrences of the Aramaic מרא is possible (J. A. Fitzmyer, *Wandering Aramean* 90). See H. Stegemann in *Qumrân* 195-217 that though Jewish manuscripts of the LXX had archaic and square Hebrew characters for the tetragrammaton and Christians were the first to introduce κύριος into the written text of the LXX, the Jews were *reading* κύριος by the time of Jesus (see also the notes on 1:3).

The appearance of "the son of man" in Psalm 8 may lead Jesus to bring "under your feet" from that psalm into his quotation of Ps 110:1 (see 14:62 for Jesus' using "the Son of man" with phraseology borrowed from Ps 110:1 and Dan 7:13; and B. M. Metzger, *Textual Commentary* ad loc., on the v.l. ὑποπόδιον, "footstool," which probably represents assimilation to Ps 109:1 LXX). But "Son of man" itself plays no part here. If then it is illegitimate to read "Son of man" backward into the present passage, where it does not occur, from 14:61-62, where "Lord" will not occur, it is also illegitimate to read "Son of God" from 14:61-62 and other passages, beginning with 1:1, into the present passage. For neither does "Son of God" occur here (against J. D. Kingsbury [*Christology of Mark's Gospel* 112-13], according to whom the present passage teaches that the Christ is David's Lord because he is also and primarily the Son of God). Cf. Luke 20:43; Acts 2:34; 1 Cor 15:25-26; Heb 1:13; 2:8; 10:13. On various understandings of Psalm 110, including the messianic one, see D. M. Hay, *Glory* 27-33.

"Son of David" naturally indicates physical or legal descent from David (cf. Matt 1:1, 6-17; Luke 3:23-31; John 7:42; Rom 1:3; 2 Tim 2:8; Rev 22:16). Some have suggested that it connotes political likeness as well and that Jesus assigns Son-of-David Christology to the scribes without overtly embracing it himself because he wants to avoid its political connotation. But his quoting the command, "Sit at my right [hand] till I put your enemies under your feet," tends toward political messianism. So we can hardly think that avoidance of such messianism is on his mind.

Some have thought to resolve a scriptural antinomy between Davidic sonship and lordship over David by assigning Davidic sonship to Jesus' earthly life, and lordship over David to Jesus' subsequent session at the Lord's right hand (see, e.g., D. Juel, *Messianic Exegesis* 144). But the scribes have not ascribed Davidic sonship to Jesus, for they do not identify him with the Christ; Jesus does not apply Ps 110:1 to himself, for he speaks about the Christ solely in the third person; and only Ps 110:1 is quoted, not 2 Sam 7:14 or another passage on Davidic sonship, too, as would be required for the resolution of a scriptural antinomy (see M. de Jonge in *Intertextuality in Biblical Writings* 96, n. 11, where it is noted that the scribes, not the OT, are quoted for "Son of David"). According to v 37, moreover, Jesus is using Ps 110:1 only for David's calling the Christ "my Lord," not for the session at the Lord's right hand; and nothing here indicates that the Lord's right hand means a heavenly exaltation like Jesus's. In all these respects, contrast 14:62 (as well as other uses of Ps 110:1 in the NT).

The Christ's Davidic sonship does not cease: once David's son, always his son. Since then session at the Lord's right hand does not supersede Davidic sonship, the Christ may be David's Son and David's Lord at the same time before the session, too. Revelation of lordship may follow (so the possible implication of "until" — v 36; cf. "you will see" in 14:62), but lordship itself need not wait. Not only the absence of a second, apparently contradictory OT quotation supporting the Christ's Davidic sonship but also the facts that "Lord" as well as "Son of David" applies to "Christ" in *Pss. Sol.* 17:21, 32; 18:7 and that the passage in which these verses are located represents scribal Christology undermine the interpretation of Mark 12:35-37 as setting forth a material antinomy between Davidic sonship and lordship over David and as affirming both sides of the antinomy. The scribes would have agreed, yet Jesus is opposing them. "There would indeed be nothing remarkable in the fact that a son should attain to a higher rank than his father, and for the scribes it would not in the least be strange that the Messiah should be greater than David" (G. Dalman, *Words* 285-86). But Jesus does not ask a question about superior greatness; rather, about the scribes' *calling* the Christ "Son of David" over against David's *calling* him "my Lord." And if Jesus meant to use antinomy for the addition of lordship over David to Davidic sonship, he would be asking how the Christ can be David's Lord if he is David's son — as in Matt 22:45 with wording just opposite that in Mark. As noted by S. H. Smith (in *NovT* 31 [1989] 113), 11:10 implied that the Jews are David's sons ("our father David"). The Jewishness of the Christ may now combine with that implication to sharpen the point that nowhere does the OT call him "Son of David."

See H. Braun, *Qumran* 1. 72-73, for criticism of the notion that Jesus denies the Christ's Davidic sonship to foster a high priestly Christology; J. A. Fitzmyer, *Essays* 115-21, on the historical development of Davidic messianism; and ibid. 123; R. H. Gundry, *Matthew* 452; R. E. Brown, *Birth* 505-12; idem, *Virginal Conception* 55-56, n. 87; D. Juel, *Messianic Exegesis* 143, on the unlikelihood that the historical Jesus is denying the Davidic descent of the Christ (against C. Burger, *Jesus als Davidssohn* 42-71 [among others]). None of Jesus' other statements contain such a denial. He did not even reject or correct the designation "Son of David" in Bartimaeus's address to him (10:47, 48). His trial and crucifixion as the King of the Jews and the readiness of his disciples to confess him as the Christ become difficult to explain if he denied the requisite descent from David. Other parts of the NT affirm his Davidic descent. And in view of the nearly total exclusion of "Son of David" from the Christological vocabulary of the primitive church, how would we explain Christian belief in Jesus' Davidic descent if he were denying the necessity of such descent or if he were known not to have descended from David?

Supposing that vv 35-37 were fabricated by a limited circle of Christians who against mainline Christology denied Jesus' Davidic descent or the necessity of it only betrays weakness in the unhistorical estimate of vv 35-37. No other evidence supports the existence of such a circle (see R. E. Brown, *John* 2. 329-30, against adducing John 7:42 as evidence). The argument against historicity that "if . . . Jesus himself had uttered these words, it is difficult to understand how the Church so soon came to prize and proclaim his own Davidic descent" (D. E. Nineham 330) overlooks the distinction between Davidic descent and the term "Son of David." Apart from Matthew, who tries to make the gospel appealing to Jews, no NT writer or Christian uses "Son of David" for Jesus. In view of Christian belief in his Davidic descent, how do we explain this nearly total exclusion of "Son of David" from the Christological vocabulary of the primitive church except by appeal to historicity? Jesus' questions (vv 35, 37) inoculated most of his followers against the term. See also R. P. Gagg in *TZ* 7 (1951) 20-22; E. Lövestam in *SEÅ* 27 (1962) 81-82.

It is doubtful that we should compare a denial of the Christ's Davidic sonship with non-Davidic messiahs in Judaism of the period. In QL the "messiah of Aaron," i.e. the priestly messiah, does not obliterate the "messiah of Israel," i.e. the Davidic messiah. The existence of a pre-Christian Son-of-man Christology lacks convincing evidence. Military success rather than Christological reflection seems to have caused Rabbi Akiba to proclaim the non-Davidid Bar Kokhba the Messiah. Or do we know that Bar Kokhba was not a Davidid? See E. Schürer, G. Vermes, and F. Millar, *History* 1. 543-52, esp. 543, n. 130, for a survey and references to primary materials.

As used elsewhere in the NT, πόθεν does not mean "from what standpoint?" or "in what way?" It asks for source: "from where?" The contrast between "How come the scribes say . . . ?" and "David himself said in the Holy Spirit," i.e. between uninspired and inspired utterances, supports a limitation of πόθεν to the question of source. Even when expressing surprise or negation, πόθεν asks for source. Take, for example, some passages cited for surprise or negation in LSJ s.v. 4 and for the meanings "why, in what way?" by BAGD s.v. 3: Soph. *Phil.* 1159 (lyr.) means, "Where will my means of living come from?" Eur. *Phoen.* 1620 means, "From where could I get my livelihood?" Idem *Alc.* 781 means,

"Where would you have gotten such knowledge?" Ar. *Vesp.* 1145 and idem *Ran.* 1455 mean, "Where did you get that idea?" Dem. 18.47 means, "From where could these things originate?" Dem. 24.157 means, "What could be the source of such a desire?" Jer 15:18 LXX means, "Where will my healing come from?" Plut. *Mor.* 526F means, "Where would I get the time?" Luke 1:43 means, "What has caused this to happen to me?" John 1:48 means, "What is the source of your knowledge?" John 6:5 means, "Where can we buy bread to bring here?" Likewise, Marks 12:37 means, "Where does the designation 'Son of David' come from?" with the contextually implied answer, "Not from anyone speaking in the Holy Spirit!" The immediately following warning against the scribes (vv 38-40) reinforces the negative implication of Jesus' question; but the switch from πόθεν to πῶς, "how?" or "how come?" in Matt 22:45; Luke 20:44 alters his argument. In Pl. *Phdr.* 269D the coordinate use of πῶς and πόθεν makes a double question having two different concerns.

We might object that so long as the *idea* conveyed by "Son of David" occurs in the OT, as it does, non-occurrence of the phrase as such does not matter. The objection betrays a conceptualistic preoccupation that lapses into overinterpretation. Just as Jesus' use of Exod 3:6 and his association of Deut 6:4-5 with Lev 19:18 were linguistically clever rather than conceptually compelling, so also is his present use of Ps 110:1 (see vv 26, 29-30, and the אבן-בן wordplay underlying his use of Ps 118:22-23 in Mark 12:10-11). As often in contemporary Jewish use of Scripture, the argument is formal, not material.

Those commentators are correct who see in πόθεν a question to be answered negatively rather than perspectively, but they err in thinking that Jesus asks about descent. "Lord" contrasts with "Son of David" neither in respect to descent nor in respect to kind of messiahship, but in respect to verbal appearance in the OT versus verbal non-appearance there. Jesus is asking about terminology. Justification for his terminological question comes from the notable fact that not only is "Son of David" missing in the OT despite prophecies of a Davidic messiah but that also in the Davidic covenant, out of which sprang those prophecies, the Lord uses "seed" for David's royal descendants but "son" for their relationship to the Lord (2 Sam 7:11-16; cf. Rom 1:3-4). In the NT, only Matthew unites "Christ," "Son of David," and Davidic descent (1:1-17). We must conclude, then, that debates over whether Jesus is denying the Christ's Davidic sonship, and if so whether in the sense of ancestry, political likeness, or both, or whether he is adding lordship over David to Davidic descent, and if so whether in equal or greater measure, concurrently or sequentially, are beside Jesus' point even though these debates are of historical importance to us (see G. Schneider in *Bib* 53 [1972] 66-81 for a survey). Jesus is exposing the scribes, not answering Christological questions.

That Jesus does not answer Christological questions or refer to himself favors authenticity. Christian fabrication or heavy redaction would improbably have left Christological ambiguities and a failure of implication that Jesus is the Christ such as we find here (see esp. M. Gourges, *À la droite de Dieu* 140-43, and contrast the Christological clarity and forthrightness of Acts 2:34-36; 5:31; 10:42-43; Rom 1:2-4, cited by V. Taylor 493).

Because of their concentric structure, J. D. Crossan (*In Fragments* 262-66) regards vv 35b-37b as a redactional creation by Mark himself. More particularly, Crossan analyzes the concentric structure as follows: (a) ". . . is 'Son of David'?" (v 35b); (b) "David himself said . . ." (v 36a); (c) "the Lord said to my Lord . . ." (v 36b); (b′) "David himself says . . ." (v 37a); (a′) ". . . is he his son?" (v 37b). Then Crossan supports his position by noting that Mark likes double questions and inclusions such as (a) and (a′) represent (cf. F. Neirynck, *Duality* 125-26, 131-33). But artistic composition does not imply lack of traditional data, for artists often use raw materials given to them rather than spinning material out of their own heads. Nor does Mark have a monopoly on double questions and inclusions. Jesus, too, may have used them. As to the concentric structure, we should not divide v 36, as Crossan does; for v 37a corresponds to the whole of v 36. Thus vv 35b-37b display chiasm rather than a concentric structure (though Crossan describes as chiastic the concentric structure that he sees).

Since in *Barn.* 12:10-11 Barnabas speaks the argument of Mark 12:35b-37b, Crossan (op. cit. 265) deduces that Mark redactionally puts the argument on Jesus' lips. Rather, Barnabas makes a redactional shift in the other direction to assimilate this argument of Jesus into a longer argument that he — Barnabas — is making out of various parts of the OT. Barnabas also transfers Jesus' argument from its NT setting to the OT as a further assimilation to that longer argument.

The crowd's hearing (v 37c) probably refers only to their hearing Jesus ask about the scribes' calling the Christ "Son of David" (vv 35-37b). Jesus did not direct his remarks in preceding pericopes to the crowd. E. S. Malbon (in *NovT* 28 [1986] 115) thinks it ominous that the crowd hears Jesus gladly, because Herod Antipas heard John the Baptizer gladly (6:20) yet had him beheaded (6:27) just as a crowd will arrest Jesus (14:43) and yell for his crucifixion (15:8-15). We might add that the crowd will act under impulse from the Jewish authorities just as Herod acted under impulse from Herodias and her daughter. But Mark counterbalanced John's fate with Herod's admiration, and he is again counter-balancing Jesus' fate with the crowd's admiration. So we would do wrong to stress ominousness.

In vv 38-40, does Mark excerpt tradition from Q or take over an independent tradition that also made its way into Q and attach it to vv 35-37? Do yet other possibilities exist? To answer these questions we must compare vv 38-40 with Luke 11:43, which represents Q. (We may ignore Matt 23:6-7 almost entirely, because it conflates Mark 12:38-40 and Q.) In Mark, the addressees are a crowd; in Q-Luke, the Pharisees. In Mark, Jesus issues a warning to watch out; in Q-Luke, a woe. In Mark he describes the scribes; in Q-Luke, the Pharisees in distinction from "the lawyers," who are the same as the scribes (Luke 11:45). In Mark he speaks of liking (θέλω), in Q-Luke of loving (ἀγαπάω; in Matthew, φιλέω). Walking around in long robes, as in Mark, has no counterpart in Q-Luke. In both Mark and Q-Luke Jesus mentions greetings in the market places and chief seats in the synagogues — but in reverse order, and in Q-Luke he mentions only one chief seat. In Mark he mentions chief couches at banquets, the devouring of widows' houses, long pretentious praying, and very harsh judgment to come, none of which appear in Q-Luke.

Three main explanations of these phenomena present themselves: (1) Mark (or his source) changed and supplemented an originally single tradition; (2) Luke deleted items from this tradition and made other changes, too; and (3) Jesus referred to greetings in the market places and chief seats in the synagogues both when speaking to others about the scribes and when speaking to the Pharisees about themselves, but reversed the order and made a slight shift in number on these different occasions as well as saying other things when he spoke about the scribes. So far as we can tell, it is not like Mark (or his source) to have made so many changes and additions as required in the first explanation. Nor is Luke likely to have made so many changes and deletions. In particular, Luke's interest in the poor and in widows (the twelve occurrences of χήρα, "widow," in Luke-Acts account for nearly half its occurrences in the NT) makes it unlikely that he would have omitted the devouring of widows' houses. His interest in meals, of which he also writes very much in Luke-Acts, makes it unlikely that he would omit the chief couches at banquets. And the woe in Q-Luke makes it unlikely that he would have omitted the very harsh judgment to come (see Luke 6:24-26; 10:13-15; 11:47-51; 17:1-2; 21:23-24 for his retention of judgmental pronouncements following woes). In fact, every one of the items missing in Luke would have undergirded the initial woe and therefore adds to the unlikelihood of omission. The explanation that Jesus spoke of greetings in the market places and of chief seats in the synagogues on more than one occasion is the simplest and most understandable.

The argument that the warning is less appropriate than the woe and therefore betrays a redactional importation of vv 38-40 underestimates the appropriateness of the warning. In relation to Mark's context, the warning harks back to Jesus' asking how come the scribes say "the Christ is 'Son of David' " (v 35), and a warning suits the pretensions of the scribes and their devouring of widows' houses. The scribes are dangerous because their pretensions bring them an influence that masks their evil activities.

One could hypothesize that Mark changes Pharisees into scribes to suit the scribes in vv 35-37 and invents the devouring of widows' houses to suit the widow's mite in vv 41-44; but without better evidence than we have that vv 38-40 really do parallel Luke 11:43, such a hypothesis would be gratuitous as well as disagreeable with Mark's apparent lack of inventiveness elsewhere. C. A. Evans (in *SBL 1989 Seminar Papers* 538) suggests that the setting of the temple favors a Marcan reference to Sadducean rather than Pharisaic scribes (cf. J. Jeremias, *Jerusalem* 231-32). But Mark's only sectarian identification of scribes has them belonging to the Pharisaic sect (2:16), and twice he ranges scribes alongside Pharisees (7:1, 5); so doubt plagues the suggestion. On the other hand, one could argue that Mark's writing about "the scribes of the Pharisees" and distinguishing the scribes and the Pharisees show an awareness that not all scribes are Pharisees. Even this considera-tion does not favor Sadducean scribes, however; for Mark never identifies any scribes as Sadducean, nor does he ever associate scribes and Sadducees. The use of φιλέω, "love," in Luke 20:46 (the true Lucan parallel to Mark) echoes Q-Luke 11:43 or derives by secondary influence from Matthew (R. H. Gundry, *Matthew* 457) rather than implying Mark's omission of the verb. Why would he omit it when retention would allow θέλω, "like," to take a lone infinitive as its direct object and φιλέω, the following nouns (a perfectly acceptable construction)? Matthew's agreement with Luke 11:43 in putting the seats before the greetings supports that Q had this order rather than the reverse, as in Mark and Luke 20:46. Luke's inconsistency in writing the singular of "seat" in 11:43 but its plural in 20:46 (and in 14:7) favors that Q had the singular. Matthew probably assimilates the singular in Q to the plural in Mark. Luke's further inconsistency in having robes at 20:46 but not at 11:43 combines with their absence from Matthew to favor that Q did not have them. Matthew's writing "couch" in the singular looks like the effect of Q's singular of "seat," and his plural of "seat" like the effect of the same in Mark. In other words, to make greetings introduce his unique addition of being called "Rabbi," Matthew delays Q's pair of "seat" and "greetings" by putting Mark's last item, "couches," first. But the singular of Q's "seat" shifts to "couch" now that "couch" replaces "seat" in first position. Then working back up Mark's list, Matthew adopts "seats" and "greetings." The plural of "seats" contrasts with its singular in Q and thereby shows that Matthew is not switching to Q, but working back up Mark's list after adopting its last item to be his first.

H. Fleddermann (in *CBQ* 44 [1982] 60) argues that Mark's τῶν θελόντων, "who like," works well with the infinitival object περιπατεῖν, "to walk around," but not with the nominal objects ἀσπασμούς, πρωτοκαθεδρίας, and πρωτοκλισίας, "greetings," "chief seats," and "chief couches." At most this argument favors an insertion of the nominal objects from a pre-Q tradition (and then we would have to suppose that Luke omits the chief couches at banquets despite his liking of meal-scenes). In fact, however, θέλω takes nominal objects fairly often; so the shift to them from an infinitival object is no more jarring that a shift in English from a gerund as object (and a gerund often makes the best translation of a Greek infinitive) to nominal objects: "who like walking around in long robes, and saluta-tions in the market places, etc."

If Mark and Q rest on different occasions, Fleddermann's further arguments for the greater originality of Q do not apply, either. Even if they did, their weaknesses would be apparent. Q's putting the greetings last seems no more climactic than Mark's putting the chief seats and the chief couches after the greetings — indeed, less so — and climactic order might come from redaction, anyway. The singular of "the chief seat" in Q is no more plausible than Mark's plural — again less so, for the chief seat in the synagogues is distributed not only among multiple synagogues (just as the chief couches are distributed among multiple banquets) but also throughout the row of seats located up front and facing the rest of the congregation, so that the occupiers of this row enjoy much visibility (cf. *t. Meg.* 3:21). Q-Luke 11:43 pairs up the chief seat and the greetings because synagogues, where the chief seat is located, and market places, where the greetings are given, complement each other.

The frequency in Mark of βλέπετε, "watch out," and of the scribes' role as Jesus' main opponents may reflect tradition rather than redaction. Since he is addressing a crowd in Mark, a warning against the scribes is just as appropriate as the woe in Q, where he is addressing the Pharisees. J. Dupont (*Études* 429, n. 147) argues from the absence of βλέπε/-ετε ἀπό, "watch out against, beware of," in the LXX that the expression is Hellenistic. If so and unless Jesus is speaking Greek, the authenticity of the warning stands in doubt. But the possibility that Jesus is speaking Greek or borrowing Greek usage while speaking Aramaic looks more realistic now than it used to (see p. 22 here). Even apart from this possibility, ראה, "see," can denote warning (as, e.g., in 2 Kgs 10:23 with פן, "see lest" = "beware that . . . not"; cf. W. Michaelis in *TDNT* 5. 325; *Tg. Onq.* Exod 10:10 [using the synonymous חזה). The addition of מן, "from," might produce the meaning, "learn from," as in Judg 7:17; but מן can also be used pregnantly for turning away, as in Ps 28:1: "Do not be deaf [turning away] from me, lest you be silent [turning away] from me" (ἀπό occurring twice in the LXX). Since we have only one extra-NT example of βλέπε/-ετε ἀπό, and that unlike the present expression in having a direct object between the verb and the prepositional phrase (καὶ σὺ βλέπε σατὸν ἀπὸ τῶν Ἰουδαίων, "and you, watch out for yourself against the Jews" — BGU IV, 1079. 24-25 [41 C.E.]), the possibility of a Semitic substratum meaning to watch out for and turn away from is not out of the question (cf. J. Wellhausen, *Einleitung* [1. Aufl.] 32).

The progression from a warning against the scribes to a prediction of coming judgment on them is so natural, almost predictable itself, that one should not use the difference between warning and prediction to argue for an original independence of vv 38-39 and v 40. We find the same progression in Jude, to take an example hardly suspected of original disunity (cf. 2 Peter 2; Rev 2:14-16). Though vv 38-39 describe the scribes as pretentious and v 40 describes them as avaricious, v 40 also describes them as pretentious; so one cannot draw a contrast that could prove original disunity. Even though v 40 did not share with vv 38-39 the description of them as pretentious, a progression from pretense to avarice would not be unsuitable and therefore would not count against integrity. Verse 40 starts a new sentence with a different construction (see the comments and following notes); but unless we believe in no more than one sentence and kind of construction per unit of tradition, neither does this phenomenon count against integrity. In fact, apart from a backward reference to the scribes in vv 38-39, the devourers and prayers of v 40 have no identification. This vagueness causes H. Anderson (285) to identify them as moneyed priests in contrast with poor scribes. Not only does this identification lack textual support. The devouring of widows' houses in v 40 provides the only activity posing a danger that gives point to the warning against scribes in vv 38-39. Divorce the devourers from the scribes and the warning against the scribes sounds as vague as does the reference to devourers and those who pray a long time.

When a scribe walks through a market place, people rise to greet him with "Father," "Teacher," "Rabbi"; and in a crowd he is given the honor of being greeted first. It is considered good style to have a scribe and his disciples at one's banquet. The scribe is given a more honorable couch than the elderly, even than the host's parents (see W. L. Lane 439-41; J. Jeremias, *Jerusalem* 111-16; and the primary literature cited by them).

Lack of explanation by Mark makes it doubtful that the scribes' long robes are a specially Jewish religious costume, such as the טלית (Str-B 2. 31-33, but see K. H. Rengstorf in *Abraham unser Vater* 392-93) or a garment reserved for wearing to the synagogue on Sabbath days (so ibid. 394-403; see 7:3-4; 14:12; 15:42-43 for Mark's habit of explaining Jewish religious customs). Furthermore, rabbinic literature does not make it clear that the טלית was originally a religious garment or that the scribes were concerned to wear such a garment or make others join in wearing it; and though στολή, "long robe," is transliterated into the Hebrew and Aramaic of rabbinic literature, the transliteration never parallels טלית (ibid. 392-93). We also lack evidence that special clothing was worn to synagogues on the Sabbath so early as the first century (cf. CD 11:3; *Jub.* 31:1 for the possibility of newly washed clothes). H. Fleddermann (in *CBQ* 44 [1982] 55) argues further that since long robes do not appear in Q but synagogues do, the connection between them is unoriginal and the explanation of the one by the other, incorrect. But this argument fails if Mark 12:38-40 rests on an occasion different from the occasion in Q. On the other hand, that walking around in long robes stands closer in the text to market places than to synagogues points away from a practice specially associated with attending synagogues on the Sabbath. One could say, of course, that to display their piety the scribes wear religious garments in market places as well as in synagogues. But the Mosaic law requires tassels on the hem of regular robes (Num 15:38-39; Deut 22:12); so it is simpler to say that Jesus is referring to regular robes decorated for religious show with longer-than-usual tassels (Matt 23:5). Nothing requires such robes to be expensive; so we do not have to think only of wealthy scribes employed by the chief priests and distinguished by their robes from other, mostly poor scribes (against B. Witherington III, *Women* 16-17). This discussion has only historical interest, however; for the text of Mark shows no interest in anything but ostentation. At this point the ostentation is not even religious.

Οἰκίας, "houses" (v 40), may carry the larger sense of "possessions, property, estates" (O. Michel in *TDNT* 5. 131; E. Lohmeyer 264, n. 3). According to J. D. M. Derrett (*Studies* 1. 118-26), Jesus charges the scribes with taking financial advantage of widows' estates over which they have gained trusteeship by publicizing their piety. The Jewish evidence cited for this sort of practice dates from long after Jesus, however (*b. Giṭ.* 52b; Maimonides, *Mishneh Torah* 13.5.10.6-7). Furthermore, Jesus mentions the praying after the devouring, as though the scribes pray a long time while or after they devour widows' estates, not beforehand. H. Fleddermann (in *CBQ* 44 [1982] 61) also objects that Mark would have explained a recondite Jewish law of trusteeship. Derrett's view makes προφάσει the true reason for the scribes' praying a long time, but the word much more often refers to a falsely alleged reason. More likely, then, is the view of J. Jeremias (*Jerusalem* 114) that scribes, who were not to accept wages for their teaching, sponged off the hospitality of widows (cf. Jesus' and the disciples' living off charity from women of means, though none of these women are said to be widows — 15:40-41; Luke 8:1-3; 10:38-42; see I. Abrahams, *Studies* 1. 79-81; and, more generally as early cross-references, Isa 1:17, 23; 10:2; *Pss. Sol.* 4:1-25; *As. Mos.* 7:6). In any case, there were widows aplenty to be taken advantage of; for adolescent girls were often married off to men a number of years their senior.

Some have taken the long prayers as prayers for widows in exchange for their charity. But H. Fleddermann (in *CBQ* 44 [1982] 61-66) associates the long prayers with the temple cult and supposes that the scribes use the cult as a pretext for urging widows to deplete their financial resources. But however closely Mark may link the scribes to the priests, it is the priests, not the scribes, who get money given by widows to support the temple cult; yet it is the scribes, not the priests, who devour widows' houses. Moreover, it is the scribes, not the priests, who pray a long time; yet it is the priests, not the scribes, who officiate in the cult. It would be unnatural for praying to indicate that aspect of the temple cult at which the priests officiate, i.e. the offering of sacrifices. In 11:17 prayer referred to what all the nations are meant to do at the temple, to prayer in the usual, restricted sense of the word. And "for a long time" would make a very unnatural way of describing the temple cult as "constantly repeated, never-ending" (ibid. 66). This unnaturalness makes Fledder-mann revert immediately to phraseology reminiscent of the text itself: "the perverted long prayers of the scribes" (ibid.)

Not only does the meaning of the phraseology resist an interpretation that makes praying a long time the falsely alleged reason for devouring widows' houses. So also does the syntax of the phraseology. Subordination of the praying to the devouring would be required to make the one a falsely alleged reason for the other. But they are coordinated. If they were closely related as well, this coordination would make praying the falsely alleged reason and devouring the true reason for doing something else, just as in Thuc. 3.86.4 (cited ibid. 62) a treaty is a falsely alleged reason and prevention of import and control of Sicily are the real reasons for the Athenians' sending ships. But Mark's text does not reveal anything else for which devouring and praying might be the real and pretextual reasons, respectively. Since "pretext" raises the question, Pretext for what? and since the context provides no answer, we are forced back to the more general translation of προφάσει, "for show," which fits vv 38-39 and "for a long time" perfectly. A single definite article clamps together the coordinated participles "devouring" and "praying," then, not to contrast them as true and falsely alleged reasons, much less as goal and means, but as incompatibles. "Much speaking" describes the praying of Gentiles in Matt 6:7 and therefore does not provide a good parallel to the long prayers of scribes.

Some have thought that the nominative of οἱ κατεσθίοντες . . . προσευχόμενοι, "the ones devouring . . . praying" (v 40), agrees ad sensum with the genitive of τῶν γραμματέων, "the scribes" (v 38), to produce an appositive (cf. the relative clause in Luke 20:47). But 3:35; 6:16; 12:10; 13:11, 13 show that for this sort of thing Mark favors a resumptive οὗτος, "this," whose antecedent does not finish out the preceding sentence but begins the new sentence of which οὗτος is a part (see 7:20, too). Instead of treating περισσότερον as elative ("very harsh" — v 40), we might treat it as truly comparative ("more harshly than if they [the scribes] devoured widows' houses but prayed only a short time").

JESUS' UPSETTING POPULAR OPINION ON THE SIZE OF GIFTS

12:41-44 (Luke 21:1-4)

The true godliness of a widow now contrasts with the pretended righteousness of the scribes "who devour widows' houses" (v 40). The story of the "widow's mite" starts with Jesus' observing the giving of monetary offerings in the temple (v 41). A widow's gift forms the core of the story (v 42). But the main point comes in the strikingness of Jesus' comment concerning the relative values of the various gifts he has observed (vv 43-44).

12:41-42 *(Luke 21:1-2)* His enemies vanquished, Jesus stops walking around in the temple, takes a seat opposite the treasury (cf. John 8:20), and watches "how the crowd throws money into the treasury." "How" probably has to do with differing amounts. Many rich people put in a great deal (πολλά, an adverbial accusative telling the extent to which they throw coins into the boxes, i.e. "much," not an accusative of direct object; for the neuter gender disagrees with the masculine gender of χαλκόν, "money" — cf. the note on 1:45 for Mark's liking of the adverbial πολλά). The wordplay between πολλοί, "many," and πολλά and the forward position and assonance of πολλοὶ πλούσιοι, "many rich [people]," heighten a contrast with the next-mentioned one poor widow. Though μία, "one," which helps describe her, may mean no more than τις, "a certain," the contrast between "rich" and "poor" favors a corresponding contrast between "many" and "one." (N.B. that Luke 21:1-2 omits "many" in changing μία to τινα.) The poverty of the widow will naturally be taken as due to a scribal devouring of her estate (v 40). The delay of πτωχή, producing "one widow, a poor [one]," emphasizes the poverty. The two λεπτά that she throws in are the smallest coins in circulation and worth only ⅛ cent apiece; i.e. they amount to no more than a quadrans (the smallest Roman coin, worth ¹⁄₁₄₄ of a denarius before Nero's devaluation of the denarius, ¹⁄₆₄ of a denarius after his devaluation, a denarius being the daily wage of a manual laborer in Matt 20:1-16). In defining two lepta as "a quadrans" (cf. S. Krauss, *Griechische und lateinische Lehnwörter* 2. 500), Mark uses a Latin loan word to make sure his Roman audience do not miss the seeming smallness of the gift, which will make Jesus' comment the more startling in its power to upset popularly held opinion (cf. pp. 1041-45 on the Roman provenance of Mark).

12:43-44 *(Luke 21:3-4)* Jesus' "summoning his disciples" shows him exercising authority over them. "Truly I say to you" highlights the accuracy of his following estimate (cf. *1 Enoch* 98:1, 4, 6; 99:6; 103:1-23; 104:1; cf. K. Berger, *Amen-Worte* 48-49). As earlier in Mark, Jesus upsets popularly held opinion, here the opinion that the rich have obviously given more than the poor widow has given. On the contrary, according to Jesus, "this poor widow has thrown [money] into the treasury to a greater extent [πλεῖον — an adverbial accusative like πολλά in v 41] than all those who have been throwing [money into the treasury]." "All" emphasizes that the extent of her giving surpasses not only the average giving of the crowd, but also the heavy giving of the rich, even the heaviest of their giving, so that she realizes the aristocratic virtue of generosity for public benefit, here for support of the temple-cult (G. Theissen in *NTS* 35 [1989] 351). Increasing this emphasis are Mark's forward placement of ἡ χήρα αὕτη, "this widow," his addition of ἡ πτωχή, "the poor [one]," and his advancement of πλεῖον πάντων, "to a greater extent than all," ahead of ἔβαλεν, "threw," and away from τῶν βαλλόντων, "those who have been throwing," with which πάντων is grammatically construed. The alliteration with π in vv 41 (πολλοὶ πλούσιοι . . . πολλά) and 43 (πτωχὴ πλεῖον πάντων) increases the emphasis yet more (cf. G. Lüderitz in *Markus-Philologie* 180).

The explanation, "For they all out of their surplus threw [into the treasury], but this [poor widow] out of her lack threw [into the treasury] absolutely everything she had (πάντα ὅσα εἶχεν), her whole livelihood," rationalizes Jesus' estimate of the gifts. Stressing the contrast with the widow's oneness and poverty are the forward placement of "all" and "out of their surplus," the demonstrative αὕτη, "this [widow]," where a simple ἡ, "she," would have sufficed, an adversative δέ, "but," the forward placement and sheer length of "out of her lack absolutely everything she had," and the addition of an appositive "her whole livelihood" even though the main verb has intervened. Since the widow had two lepta, she could have thrown in one and kept the other for herself. But she did not. She gave not only out of poverty, in contrast with those who gave out of abundance (cf. 2 Cor 8:13-14). She gave all that she had. The purpose of this emphasis is not to teach a doctrine of giving, however, but to exhibit the power of Jesus to revolutionize the usual view of things (cf. the comments on chaps. 9–10, in particular, the last, summarizing paragraph [before the small print] on 10:10-12). Allowing all the attention to concentrate on this point is the remarkable lack of any contrast between ostentatious giving and unostentatious giving (and this despite the ostentation in vv 38-40; also contrast Matt 6:1-4), of any reference to freedom from covetousness and anxiety, trust in God, or love for God on the widow's part, and of any exhortation to follow her example. Jesus does not even commend the poor widow, much less condemn the rich.

NOTES

The inner connection seen by T. E. Schmidt (*Hostility* 116) between vv 41-44 and vv 38-40 is marred somewhat in that although the widow in vv 41-44 corresponds to the widows in vv 38-40, the rich people in vv 41-44 do not correspond very closely to the scribes in vv 38-40. Scribes are usually poor, and vv 38-40 do not portray them as rich. Nor do vv 41-44 portray the rich as ostentatious in their giving, as the scribes are in other activities according to vv 38-40.

According to E. Best (*Temptation* 88, n. 1), juxtaposing a commendation of the widow's gift to the temple and a prediction that the temple will be destroyed (13:2) tells the audience of Mark to keep up ordinary duties of morality and Christian mission despite persecution. This interpretation is strained. Jesus evaluates the true worth of the widow's and others' gifts but says nothing that would enjoin gift-giving or commend the widow's giving her whole livelihood (as would be required for Christians, too, if the pericope were to make her giving exemplary in contrast with that of the rich). And though giving her whole livelihood could conceivably stand for Christian mission, such giving can hardly represent ordinary duties of morality. The giving of a whole livelihood is extraordinary.

Quite differently, A. G. Wright (in *CBQ* 44 [1982] 256-65) says that Jesus *laments* the widow's giving her whole livelihood: "her contribution was totally misguided, thanks to the encouragement of official religion" (263). For this interpretation Wright cites (1) Jesus' saying nothing commendatory about the widow's action; (2) his not issuing an exhortation to imitate it; (3) the commonness of his observation that how little you have left counts more than how much you give (cf. Xen. *Mem.* 1.33.3; Arist. *Eth. Nic.* 4.1.19; Josephus *Ant.* 6.7.4 §149; Str-B 2. 45-46; S. T. Lachs, *Rabbinic Commentary* 375-76); (4) the absence from the observation of any contrast between human and divine evaluations; (5) the absence of any indication that the disciples had difficulty comprehending Jesus' observation; (6) his putting human needs above the Sabbath and Corban (2:23–3:5; 7:10-13); (7) the immediately preceding context of scribes' devouring the houses of widows; and (8) the immediately following context of Jesus' predicting the destruction of the temple.

But the comparison in which Jesus says that the widow has given to a greater extent than all the others have given makes his observation no more lamentful than commendatory. The absence of an exhortation to imitate the widow's action proves only that the story is not parenetic. Though other sages may often say that the proportion of your gift counts more than its amount, popular opinion does not say so; and Jesus is not speaking to fellow sages who might agree with him. Furthermore, he does not merely contrast large proportion with small, but giving all of a subsistence with giving some of a surplus. The absence of a contrast between human and divine evaluations is irrelevant; for Jesus is giving his own evaluation to an audience whom it might surprise. "Truly I say to you" assures them of its truth despite popular opinion to the contrary. Their expressing no difficulty of understanding is neutral with respect to whether Jesus laments or commends the widow's action or does neither, for his evaluation of her gift remains the same in any case. Nothing indicates that she is giving under scribal influence; and the money goes to the temple, not to a scribe. So neither directly nor indirectly is a scribe devouring her house (though as mentioned in the comments her poverty may be taken as due to such scribal activity). Total giving of a voluntary sort differs fundamentally from subjection to others' unscrupulosity and overinterpretation of the Law, as in the matters of Sabbath and Corban. If predicting the destruction of the temple implies wastefulness at all, it implies the wastefulness of others' gifts as well as the widow's. Yet the story hinges on the difference between the extent of their giving and that of hers; and nothing indicates that worship in the temple has meanwhile lost its validity. On the contrary, the temple is to be a house of prayer for all the nations (11:17a); and its future desecration evokes horror (13:14).

D. Lührmann (212) thinks that behind this story lies competition between church and synagogue for widows. But as the widow in the story is poor, so most widows were poor — and therefore financially burdensome (for the church, see esp. Acts 6:1; 1 Tim 5:3-16; Jas 1:27). It is hard, then, to imagine a competition for them. Elsewhere we have no evidence of such a competition.

Contrasting a "clearly more original" version in Luke 21:1-4, W. R. Farmer (*Synoptic Problem* 269) considers the threefold repetition of "treasury" (vv 41, 43) and the interpretative gloss, "which is a quadrans" (v 42), signs of expansion in Mark. But Luke and Matthew regularly streamline Mark's narrative while adding much teaching of Jesus (cf. I. H. Marshall, *Luke* 750-52). See Str-B 2. 33-37 against treating Jesus' sitting opposite the treasury as prohibited and therefore unhistorical. J. Gnilka (2. 176) thinks that observation of the gifts would have been easier if Jesus were closer than opposite the treasury, notes that only the second mention of the treasury in v 41 is necessary, sees the similarity between Jesus' sitting opposite the treasury in v 41 and his sitting opposite the temple in 13:3, and concludes that Mark fabricates Jesus' sitting opposite the treasury. On the other hand, the posture and locale of Jesus may derive from tradition in both v 41 and 13:3, or from tradition in v 41 and from redaction in 13:3 or vice versa, as well as from redaction in both verses (cf. the note on 9:35 regarding κάθημαι and καθίζω). Observation of the gifts may be a non-problem (see the following notes). Do we expect Jesus to be standing right next to the receptacles for close observation of the gifts?

That people throw money into the treasury may seem to favor "treasury-receptacle" over "treasury-hall" as the meaning of γαζοφυλάκιον. But *m. Šeqal.* 5:6 uses נתן, which is more or less equivalent to Mark's βάλλω, "throw," for giving into the treasury-hall. Since there were thirteen trumpet-shaped receptacles, the singular number and arthrousness of "the treasury" point to the hall where these receptacles were located. The non-use of γαζοφυλάκιον elsewhere for a receptacle supports this interpretation (Str-B 2. 37-45; cf. Neh 12:44; 2 Esdr 22:44; Josephus *Ant.* 19.6.1 §294; idem *J.W.* 5.5.2 §200; *m. Šeqal.* 6:5).

E. Haenchen (432-33) denies historicity on the ground that the smallness of the openings into the trumpet-shaped receptacles in the treasury and Jesus' sitting "opposite the treasury" would not have allowed observation of the amounts of money given. But an exchange between offerer and priest, for which Str-B 2. 39-40 argues strongly, might have made observation possible, perhaps easily so. Though ἐθεώρει means observation by seeing, this verb does not rule out the hearing of words spoken between offerer and priest, words that indicated the amount of gifts (see 5:38; Luke 24:37-39; John 4:19 et passim against V. Taylor 496). The manner in which coins were thrown in may have allowed observation even without such an exchange and even at some distance.

A woman might be recognized as a widow by her attire. See Str-B 2. 45, supported by the Soncino edition of the Babylonian Talmud, that *b. B. Bat.* 10b does not prohibit a gift any smaller than she gave; and R. Pesch 2. 262 that Mark may use λεπτά either for Greek coins circulating in Palestine or as a Greek equivalent of פרוטות; also against the argument that λεπτά betrays unhistoricity (so E. Lohmeyer 266). Since coins circulated far and wide, the Latin loanword "quadrans" does not by itself prove that Mark wrote in Rome or for a Roman reading audience (see esp. H. J. Cadbury, *Making of Luke-Acts* 89, n. 15). But Mark uses many other Latinisms (see pp. 1043-45), and this loanword suits a Roman locale and audience particularly well (cf. W. M. Ramsay in *ExpTim* 10 [1898-99] 232, 336 over against F. Blass in *ExpTim* 10 [1898-99] 185-86, 286-87). Where else would an author feel the need to translate two lepta into a quadrans? Matt 5:26 mentions the quadrans, and Matthew was hardly written in or for Rome; but deliberately translating another coin into the quadrans (so Mark) differs from a merely independent mention of the quadrans. Mark's translation typifies his love of duality, including ὅ ἐστιν, "which is" (3:17; 5:41; 7:11, 34; 12:42; 15:16, 22, 34, 42; cf. 7:2).

Mark often writes of Jesus' summoning people, but he may have traditional support for writing thus in v 43. There is no reason to prefer the statement that originally Jesus addressed bystanders (J. Gnilka 2. 176) over Mark's statement that Jesus summoned the disciples. E. Lohmeyer (266) asks whether v 43 means that the widow gave to a greater extent than anyone else did, or whether she gave to a greater extent than all the others put together did? The adverbial πλεῖον and the reference in v 44 to the rich people's surplus, which they hardly held in common, favor the individualistic understanding.

One might ask how Jesus knows that the two lepta given by the widow represent everything she had. His supernatural knowledge comes to mind, but Mark makes no point of it (contrast 2:8 and Mark's repeated emphasis on Jesus' predictive ability). The question therefore goes abegging in favor of an emphasis on Jesus' ability to revolutionize standard opinions. In attributing "her whole livelihood" to a redactor who did not bother with the question how the widow would survive on leaving the temple, E. Haenchen (433) fails to consider that Jesus may not have bothered with that question. He seems not to have bothered with it when he called people to forsake all and follow him (see esp. 10:21, but also 1:16-20; 2:13-14; 3:13-14; 8:34-37; 10:23-31; Luke 12:14-15; 14:33 et passim). Verse 44 presents a γάρ-sentence, and Mark likes the conjunction. It appears in a number of his editorial statements. This sentence is not editorial, however; so the most that can be said with any likelihood is that Mark inserts a favorite conjunction into a traditional saying.

JESUS' ABILITY TO PREDICT THE FATES OF THE TEMPLE, OF THE WORLD, AND OF THE ELECT AND HIS COMING AS THE SON OF MAN

13:1-37 (Matt 24:1-36, 42; 25:13-15; Luke 12:38, 40; 17:23-24, 37b; 19:12-13; 21:5-33)

The Olivet Discourse (chap. 13) starts with a dialogue (vv 1-4) that shades into a long monologue (vv 5-37). The dialogue breaks down into an exclamation by one of the disciples (v 1), a responsively menacing prediction by Jesus (v 2), and a consequent inquiry by Peter, James, John, and Andrew (vv 3-4). After its narrative introduction (v 5a), the monologue breaks down into two main sections. The first (vv 5b-23) centers on what precedes the coming of the Son of man and is marked off by chiastic inclusion. The section starts in vv 5b-6 with (a) βλέπετε, "watch," and (b) a reference to deceivers who will use Christ's name and ends in vv 21-23 with (b′) a reference to false christs heralded by false prophets and (a′) βλέπετε plus a summarizing statement. The second section (vv 24-37) centers on the coming of the Son of man and is marked off at its start by a strongly adversative ἀλλά, "but," and a temporal shift, "in those days after that tribulation," and closes with a widening of Jesus' address to include everyone (v 37). Similar commands and the shared use of λέγω (in different forms, but both of them in the first person singular), ὑμῖν, and πᾶς (again in different forms, but both of them plural) help vv 23 and 37 demarcate the end of each section: (1) "But you — watch out. I've told you all things beforehand" (v 23). (2) "But what I tell you, I tell all, 'Keep awake'" (v 37). ("Truly I tell you" in v 30 stands apart as stereotyped and as similar only in "I tell you.")

The first main section breaks down further: vv 5b-13 center on what precedes the coming of the Son of man but does not signal its nearness (see esp. vv 7b, 8b), and vv 14-23 on what precedes it but does signal its nearness (see esp. vv 14, 19-20). Both of the main sections break down (even further, so far as the first one is concerned) into a series of commands accompanied by explanations of the circumstances evoking them. The commands are to watch out against deception (vv 5b-6), not to be alarmed at cosmic upheavals (vv 7-8), to watch yourselves when people give you over to trial and death (vv 9-13), to flee to the mountains on seeing the abomination of desolation (vv 14-20), not to believe false prophets' heraldry of false christs (vv 21-23), to understand the general nearness of the Son of man's coming once an unequaled tribulation has started with the abomination of desolation (vv 24-31), and to watch, stay awake, and be alert in view of the impossibility of knowing the exact time of the Son of man's coming (vv 32-37). Signaling the beginnings of these subsections are a sudden command to watch out in βλέπετε (v 5b), an adversative clause in ὅταν δέ plus ἀκούσητε, "but whenever you hear" (v 7), another βλέπετε plus another δέ (v 9), another ὅταν δέ but this time followed by ἴδητε, "but whenever you see" (v 14), καὶ τότε ἐάν plus τις ὑμῖν εἴπῃ, "if anyone should say to you" (v 21), ἀλλά plus the temporal phrases "in those days after that tribulation" (v 24, where, as already noted, this locution signals a major break as well as a new subsection), and περὶ δὲ τῆς ἡμέρας ἐκείνης ἢ τῆς ὥρας, "but concerning that day or hour" (v 32; cf. 12:26 for another Jesuanic use of περὶ δέ to recapture a topic for further delineation).

Unlike ὅταν δέ in vv 7, 14, καὶ ὅταν in v 11 does not signal the start of a new subsection, for δέ indicates a shift but καί a continuation, here of the subject matter in vv 9-10. In fact, v 11 defines watching yourselves in vv 9-10 as not worrying beforehand what to say when you are given over to trial in the course of evangelism; and vv 12-13 add detail about being given over to trial, the hatred that generates it, and the salvation that compensates for martyrdom. Furthermore, ἄγωσιν, "they lead," which follows ὅταν in v 11, falls outside the complementary relation of hearing and seeing as indicated by ἀκούσητε and ἴδητε in vv 7, 14. The use of ἄν in crasis plus an aorist subjunctive verb puts v 21 in parallel with vv 7a, 14. But a continuative καί replaces the earlier adversative δέ because vv 21-23 pick up and carry forward a theme begun in vv 5b-6, perhaps also because an adversative δέ would follow awkwardly after the stronger adversative ἀλλά that precedes in v 20b. Ὅταν, "whenever" (vv 7a, 14), changes to τότε ἐάν, "then if" (v 21), to suit "those days" and "the days" in vv 17, 19, 20. In vv 26, 27 καὶ τότε is followed by future indicative verbs. Therefore those two instances make their own pair within a subsection rather than paralleling καὶ τότε plus a crastic ἄν and an aorist subjunctive verb at the beginning of a subsection in v 21. In vv 13b, 15a, 15b, 17, 18, 23, 28, 31, 37, δέ makes sense only as indicating shifts within a subsection, not as starting new subsections. The same observation applies to ἀλλά in v 20b and ὅταν in v 28b. In v 28a the command to learn the parable of the fig tree does not introduce a new section or subsection (though it does introduce a new unit within a subsection), because the parable gets its meaning entirely from vv 24-27. In vv 14, 15, 16, 18 the commands to understand, not to come down from the roof or enter the house or turn back, and to pray support the command to flee. They do not constitute further subsections.

In all subsections of the first main section and apart from introductory subordinate clauses in vv 7, 14, 21, commands precede the explanations of the circumstances evoking them. But in both subsections of the second main section, explanations (vv 24-27, 32) precede the commands (vv 28-31, 33-37). This double reversal of order puts huge emphasis on the high point, i.e. on the coming of the Son of man, around which each of these subsections revolves. The devotion of two subsections to his coming and the sheer length of each subsection add to this emphasis.

One prediction after another makes up the explanations of the commands. So chap. 13 greatly enhances Mark's portrayal of Jesus as a predictor. Not all that he here predicts has happened by the time Mark writes, however. In fact, because of disputed questions concerning date and concerning the meaning of particular predictions, it is debatable how much has happened. But certainly enough has happened — e.g., persecutions and world-wide evangelism — to give confidence in the fulfilment of whatever remains. Besides, Mark has already told about Jesus' prediction that two fishers of fish would become fishers of human beings (1:16-18) and about its fulfilment (6:6b-13, 30-31), about his prediction that some standing in his audience would not die till they saw God's rule as having come in power (9:1) and its fulfilment (9:2-8), and about his prediction that the disciples would find a colt (11:2-3) and its fulfilment (11:4-6). Mark has also recorded the predictions of Jesus' passion and resurrection (8:31; 9:9, 12, 31; 10:32-34), whose fulfilment he will yet narrate (chaps. 14–16). And further predictions plus their fulfilments are going to crowd into the remainder of Mark's text: concerning an encounter with a man carrying a water jar and the provision of an upstairs room (14:13-15), betrayal by one of the Twelve (14:17-21, 10-11, 43-45), desertion by all the disciples (14:27, 50), and denials by Peter (14:30, 66-72). Let Mark's audience combine these predictions and fulfilments with the many stories already narrated about Jesus' exorcisms, healings, and authoritative teaching and they will know that Jesus is a fully reliable character. But not only will they know that what he predicted has already or will surely come to pass. What he predicted in chap. 13 is — climactically — that as the Son of man he will come in clouds with much power and glory. So this negation of the scandal of the Cross, though it will occur in the real world beyond the time of Mark's writing the gospel and his audience's hearing it read, occurs in the world of Mark's text not merely before their time but even prior to the Cross. Thus he insulates the following passion narrative against deductions damaging to Jesus. The length of Jesus' monologue in 13:5-37 (the longest in Mark), its uninterruptedness (unique in Mark), and its coming just before the passion narrative and thus delaying it for a long time thicken that insulation.

13:1-4 *(Matt 24:1-3; Luke 21:5-7)* "And as he goes out from the temple" signals the end of the section that began at 11:27 and consisted of stories set in the temple (12:35). It also offers a basis for the following exclamation by one of Jesus' disciples, "Teacher, look — what magnificent stones and what magnificent buildings!" and for Jesus' following prediction of the destruction of the *temple* (contrast 11:19, where even though Jesus has just cleansed the temple Mark writes that "they [Jesus and the disciples] were going outside the *city*"). "Stones" refers to the Herodian masonry, admirable for its massive dimensions and handsome style. The plural "buildings" includes surrounding structures along with the sanctuary proper, all of which make up the temple complex. Putting great emphasis on the magnificance of the stones and buildings are the historical present tense of the introductory λέγει, "says," the injunction to look, and the duality and verblessness of the exclamation. This emphasis makes Jesus' menacing prediction the more striking. Grammatically, βλέπεις ταύτας τὰς μεγάλας οἰκοδομάς may be taken as a question ("Do you see these large buildings?") or as a declaration ("You're looking at these large buildings"), and interpretatively as unstressed (equivalent to a gesture, a mere acknowledgement) or as stressed (with the implication that the anonymous disciple will not be able to look at the buildings after their destruction or, in view of it, should not look at them with admiration even now — see C. E. B. Cranfield 391-92). Regardless of stress or lack thereof, after the disciple's exclamation concerning the magnificence of the stones and buildings and beginning with ἴδε, "look," a question whether he sees them seems inappropriate. Of course he sees them; otherwise he would not have broken out in exclamation over them and told Jesus to look. By contrast, a declaration complements the exclamation; for a declaration that the disciple is looking balances the injunction that Jesus look (ἴδε is an exclamatory imperative). We expect an adversative to connect the following prediction to the declaration: "You're looking at these large buildings, but (δέ or ἀλλά) a stone will by no means be left here on a stone that will by no means be torn down." Instead, the asyndetic lack of an adversative brings on the prediction with a jolt that fits and intensifies the direness of the prediction (cf. Jer 26:18; Mic 3:12; Josephus *J.W.* 6.5.3 §§300-309; *b. Yoma* 39b). The description of the buildings as "large" makes the prediction of their razing more remarkable (cf. Hag 2:15; Luke 19:44; Josephus *J.W.* 7.1.1 §§1-3; and Jesus' having quoted in Mark 11:17 a passage from Jer 7:11 that leads right into a prediction of the destruction of Solomon's temple). "Here" (ὧδε) pinpoints the prediction in a way that makes its meaning unmistakable and that will make its fulfilment equally so. And the doubling of the strongly negative construction οὐ μή plus an aorist subjunctive verb ("will by no means . . .") emphasizes the certainty of destruction.

Jesus' sitting on the Mount of Olives indicates a shift from the site of the temple to a point "opposite the temple" (cf. 12:41 for the phraseology) on his way to Bethany (cf. 14:3; also 11:11, 19). Mention of the temple completes a chiasm in vv 1-3 of (a) "temple," (b) "stones," (c) "buildings," (c') "buildings," (b') "a stone on a stone," and (a') "temple." This chiasm highlights the stupendousness of Jesus' prediction. "Were asking him privately" implies that a larger audience heard him predict the destruction of the temple. Mark may list the names of the private inquirers — Peter, James, John, and Andrew — to assure readers of the reliability of the tradition that Jesus made the further predictions which will now follow. "When will these things be?" asks about the time of the destruction of the temple. "And what [will be] the sign when (ὅταν) all these things are about to be consummated?" (cf. Dan 12:7 LXX) asks for a forewarning signal (cf. the ὅταν-clauses also in vv 7, 14, 28-29 concerning the time to expect the end and the time not to expect it). Clarity and comprehensiveness will enhance the apologetic value of Jesus' predictions and their fulfilment. No Delphic vapor here! The addition of πάντα, "all," to ταῦτα, "these things," accentuates the comprehensiveness of the fulfilment which will surely come about.

For a number of reasons, "all these things" does not refer to the events predicted in vv 5b-27: (1) Since Jesus has yet to speak of those events, the disciples have yet to learn of them and therefore cannot ask about them or be said to ask about them. (2) Since Mark has yet to write about these events, his audience have yet to learn of them and therefore he cannot expect his audience to understand them as the referent. (3) To Mark himself, though he knows what he is going to write next, a "sign" for "all these things" would make nonsense if "all" comprehended the events predicted in vv 5b-27; for those events begin with ones which according to vv 5b-13 neither constitute the end nor even signal it and therefore neither deserve to be signaled themselves nor as a matter of fact are given a sign to signal them. Nor do these preliminary events signal the later events predicted in vv 14-27; they only start before those later events (cf. vv 7-8). (4) The presence of a possible antecedent in v 2 combines with the just-mentioned nonsense to prohibit a prospective ταῦτα . . . πάντα, "all these things that you are about to speak of." (5) A prospective understanding would imply without evidence the disciples' prescience that Jesus was going to predict many more events. (6) "Opposite the temple" favors a back-reference to his prediction of destruction for the temple, whereas the following verses will say nothing more about that destruction. Therefore, the plural of "these things" and the addition of "all" do not link the just-predicted destruction of the temple to the yet-to-be-predicted coming of the Son of man and its precursors. Rather, they highlight the wonder of Jesus' predicting destruction for the multiple buildings that made up the temple complex and the tearing down of the many stones that went into those buildings: each tearing down of a huge stone, each razing of a large building, is a distinct event to be viewed as the astounding fulfilment of an unlikely prediction. The complex infinitive συντελεῖσθαι, "to be brought to completion *together*," makes the point emphatic; and the delay of πάντα, "all," till the end of the question gives the emphasis a final touch.

13:5-8 *(Matt 24:4-8; Luke 21:8-11)* Jesus opens his response with a warning: "Watch out [βλέπετε, an imperative in the emphatic present tense — cf. vv 9, 23, 33 and the notes on 1:3] lest anyone deceive you." The position of the direct object ὑμᾶς before its verb carries something of the sense "you of all people!" Asyndeton at the start of the reason for this warning — "Many will come on [the basis of] my name saying, 'It's me,' and will deceive many" — stresses the seriousness of the danger of deception. The same emphasis is served by the double use of "many," by the position of the subject πολλοί, "many," before its verb, and by the position of the direct object πολλούς, "many," before its verb. We would expect that the greater the number of charlatans coming on the basis of Jesus' name, the fewer the number of people taken in by their competing and therefore mutually contradictory claims. But the deception will be so clever as to produce the opposite effect: an increase in the number of deceived people with each increase in the number of deceivers. Ἐπὶ τῷ ὀνόματί μου, "on [the basis of] my name," favors that ἐγώ εἰμι keeps its idiomatic meaning, "It's me," as in 6:50; 14:62, rather than taking on the theological meaning, "I AM" (the divine title of Exod 3:14; cf. John 8:58). But does "my name" refer to the personal name "Jesus" or to another, titular name that Jesus has? The rising up of "false christs" (vv 21-22), Peter's confession of Jesus as "the Christ" (8:29), and Jesus' associating "name" with "Christ" (9:41) and saying, "I am" (ἐγώ εἰμι, as here), in answer to the question, "Are you the Christ?" (14:61-62; cf. Matt 24:5; John 4:25-26), provide reasons aplenty to understand the deceivers as coming on the basis of Jesus' titular name "the Christ," i.e. as coming and saying that they are the Christ just as he came and said that he was the Christ (cf. other passages where ἐπὶ τῷ ὀνόματί μου refers to a similar use of his name as the basis for a duplication of his actions — 9:37, 39; see also Luke 24:47 with 24:46; Acts 2:38; 4:17-18 with 4:10; 5:28, 40; Matt 24:5; John 4:25-26; and esp. 3 Kgdms 20:8 LXX, where ἐπὶ τῷ ὀνόματι describes Jezebel's writing letters as though she were Ahab himself; J. Gibson in *JSNT* 38 [1990] 48-49).

Already Jesus is ignoring the four disciples' question by predicting events that will *not* signal the immediate destruction of the temple. In fact, he will continue to ignore both its destruction and the time of its destruction in favor of detailed predictions concerning other events (see the comments on vv 14-20). He is using the question of the four disciples as a platform from which to speak on a variety of topics dealing with the future. His purpose is to prepare the disciples to avoid danger. Mark's purpose differs: he wants to exhibit the predictive power of Jesus in full flower. Jesus wants the disciples to avoid not only the danger of being deceived by false christs, but also the danger of being deceived by disastrous events. An adversative δέ, "but," marks the shift from the one danger to the other. Disciples should not be alarmed (θροεῖσθε, another imperative in the emphatic present tense; again cf. the notes on 1:3) when they hear the noise of battles at hand and the reports of battles too far away for their noise to be heard (cf. 2 Thess 2:2). A wordplay between the cognates ἀκούσητε, "hear," and ἀκοάς, "reports," highlights these international disasters. Mark's interest lies in Jesus' ability to predict them despite the Pax Romana. Jesus wants to assure his disciples that these disasters belong to God's plan (δεῖ, "are necessary") and that they will *signal* the end (i.e. the end of the present evil age) no more than the appearance of false christs will *constitute* the end. Mark's interest lies in Jesus' ability to foretell God's plan, its necessities and the pace of its outworking. Jesus wants to steel his disciples against the disasters of conflict between nations and kingdoms, of widespread earthquakes, and of famines. He calls these disasters the "beginning of birthpangs" to keep the disciples from the alarm of thinking that the disasters have brought the end. Asyndeton emphasizes the necessity, which means the strong certainty, of international conflicts. Asyndeta likewise emphasize the coming occurrence of widespread earthquakes and famines. The forward position of ἀρχὴ ὠδίνων, "beginning of birthpangs," and the ellipsis of "are" join yet another instance of asyndeton to emphasize that the disasters will not signal the end. Again, the interest of Mark lies in Jesus' power to give detailed predictions of the disasters; so for Mark the asyndeta, wordplay, and word order emphasize that power.

13:9-13 *(Matt 24:9-14; Luke 12:11-12; 21:12-19)* An adversative δέ and emphatic ὑμεῖς, producing "but you," turn the disciples' attention from the cosmic events just described to their own persons. Another βλέπετε (cf. v 5) conveys another warning. The preceding warning had to do with the danger of deception. This one has to do with the danger of persecution, which Jesus goes on to describe. "Watch yourselves!" commands precaution — but to what purpose? To avoid persecution (cf. Matt 10:23)? Yet the following description of persecution leaves no doubt that the disciples will suffer it. So "watch yourselves" must mean to take precaution lest persecution cause you to disown Christ (cf. 2 John 8). Evangelism would then be thwarted, yet the very purpose of God in allowing you to be persecuted is that you should bear witness to the good news before people and among nations that would otherwise not hear it (cf. the rest of v 9 and v 10). The command in v 11 not to worry ahead of time what to say in court will confirm this understanding of the warning to watch yourselves (cf. T. J. Geddert [*Watch-*

words 86-87], who overinterprets βλέπετε, however, as "calling for discipleship," whereas precautionary watching satisfies the demand of the text and 4:12 shows that βλέπω does not imply discernment in Mark). The present tense in the imperative of μὴ προμεριμνᾶτε, "don't worry ahead of time," carries emphasis (contrast the unemphatic aorist subjunctive of prohibition in this verb at Matt 6:31 par., 34 par.; 10:19; and yet again cf. the notes on 1:3).

Asyndeton emphasizes the first item of persecution: "people will give you over to tribunals and to synagogues." "Tribunals" (συνέδρια, "sanhedrins") includes lesser, local Jewish courts as well as the Great Sanhedrin, or Supreme Court, in Jerusalem. "Synagogues" presupposes the disciplinary aspect of life in Jewish assemblies. Asyndeton also emphasizes the second item, "you will be beaten," which defines the discipline to be meted out on the disciples (cf. 12:3, 5). The placement of "before governors and kings" ahead of "you will stand on account of me for a witness to them" stresses what seems unlikely, viz., that nobodies like the disciples will bear witness to the high and mighty.

What seems even more unlikely is that "among all the nations the good news must first be preached." The forward positions of "among all the nations" and "first" (see the Greek text) stress the point of unlikelihood. "First" means "before the end" (cf. v 7). Paul's epistles and the Book of Acts let us know that by the time Mark writes his gospel, the disciples of Jesus have indeed undergone the experiences predicted by him. So also his prediction of prior evangelization of all nations has already achieved fulfilment (Rom 1:5, 8-17; 11:11-36; 15:14-21, 26; Eph 2:11–3:21; Col 1:6, 23, 27; 1 Tim 3:16). These fulfilments, all the more impressive because of their unlikelihood, contribute to Mark's apologetic emphasis on the predictive ability of Jesus. The prediction of international evangelism implies that we are to understand the governors and kings as Gentiles, and the Jewish local courts and synagogues as including those scattered throughout the Diaspora as well as those located in Palestine (cf. E. Lohse in *TDNT* 7. 866-67). The couching of the prediction in terms of necessity (δεῖ — v 10; cf. v 7) stresses the certainty of world-wide evangelism. Thus, "[the] beginning of birthpangs" (v 8d) is not limited to the first part of a short period before the end, but covers the entirety of the period during which Jesus' disciples bear witness, suffer persecution, and stand in danger of deception, however long or short that period may turn out to be.

The participle παραδιδόντες, "giving over" (v 11), echoes the initial prediction of persecution, παραδώσουσιν ὑμᾶς, "they will give you over" (v 9), and identifies the settings in which the disciples are not to be anxious beforehand as to what they should say. Those settings — Jewish tribunals and synagogues and Gentile courts of governors and kings — could easily overawe nobodies like Jesus' disciples. The command, "But whatever is given you in that hour, speak this, for you are not the ones speaking, but the Holy Spirit [is speaking]" (cf. 12:36), implies a continuing fulfilment of John the Baptizer's prediction that Jesus would baptize his followers "in [the] Holy Spirit" (1:8; cf. the comments ad loc. on the beginning of that fulfilment in Jesus' ministry). The Holy Spirit's speaking confirms what we would have thought anyway, viz., that "whatever is given you" contains a divine passive. The strongly adversative ἀλλ᾽, "but," and casus pendens plus a resumptive τοῦτο, "this," put emphasis on whatever the Holy Spirit gives the disciples to say (cf. Exod 4:12; Jer 1:9). The un-Semitic character of this construction shows the emphasis to be Greek redactional (cf. E. C. Maloney, *Semitic Interference* 86-90, 126-31).

The theme of giving over unites vv 9-13 by reappearing for a third time in v 12: "And brother will give over [παραδώσει] brother to death, and father [will give over] child [to death], and children will rise up against parents and will kill them [or 'have them killed' — cf. 14:55]." A man's giving his brother over to death echoes *Tg. Neb.* Mic 7:2, and children's rising up against their parents compresses Mic 7:6 (see R. H. Gundry, *Use of the OT* 33; contrast the full form in Matt 10:35; cf. Isa 19:2; Zech 13:3; 4 Ezra 6:24; *1 Enoch* 99:5; 100:2; *b. Sanh.* 97a, though H.-H. Schroeder [*Eltern und Kinder* 134] doubts that the Enochian passages allude to Mic 7:6 and that the use of Mic 7:6 had become common by Jesus' time). Micah deals with a general breakdown in family life; but Mark's context makes discipleship to Jesus, not a general breakdown, the reason for betrayals of disciples by members of their own families. This prediction gives greater specificity to the indefinite "they" in the first prediction of giving over (v 9). The greater the specificity, the more astonishing is Jesus' power of prediction. Because the family forms the most stable and fundamental unit of society, betraying the members of one's own family shows the extreme either of desire to escape persecution oneself, or of hatred toward the gospel, or of both. Even persecution so severe as this will not signal the end, however.

"And you will be hated by all" (v 13a; for "all," cf. Mic 7:6 LXX, though limited there to the men of the household) gives a broader prediction which is nevertheless impressive, because early Christians are in fact beginning to suffer general ostracism by the time Mark writes (cf. Matt 5:11; John 15:18-20; Heb 10:32-34; 1 Pet 2:12 et passim; 1 John 3:13). The durative force of the periphrastic future ἔσεσθε μισούμενοι (literally, "you will be being hated"; A. T. Robertson, *Grammar* 889) prepares for enduring to the end. "On account of my name" (cf. v 9) alludes to the disciples' confessing Jesus as the Christ and using his name in exorcism and performance of miracles (cf. 9:37, 38, 39, 41; 13:6; 1 Pet 4:14; Pol. *Phil.* 8:2; Tac. *Ann.* 15.44; Justin *1 Apol.* 4; Tert. *Apol.* 2) and indicates that the hatred will represent something different from ordinary anti-Jewish sentiment, the prediction of which would be unremarkable.

The promise of salvation to the one who endures to the end (v 13b) again alludes to Micah 7, this time to v 7 (see both the MT and the LXX), and probably also to Dan 12:12-13 MT Theod (R. H. Gundry, *Use of the OT* 47). An adversative δέ, "but," contrasts this salvation with hatred by all. Casus pendens in "the one enduring to [the] end" combines with the resumptive οὗτος, "this one," to emphasize endurance. The anarthrousness of τέλος, "end," contrasts with the arthrousness of τὸ τέλος, which in v 7 referred to the end of the present age. Hence, Jesus is not now referring to the end of the present age, but to one's own end in case of martyrdom, and is buttressing his disciples against this possibility by giving assurance of eternal salvation (cf. 8:35; 10:26; Rev. 2:10; also BAGD s.v. τέλος 1dγ; V. Taylor 510 for a variety of non-eschatological uses of εἰς τέλος — against R. H. Gundry, *Matthew* 193-94). Endurance then means loyalty to the point of martyrdom and proves genuineness of discipleship. Jesus says nothing about the one who recants to avoid martyrdom, but the implication is unhappy. "Will be saved" contains a divine passive: God will grant eternal salvation to the martyr.

13:14-20 *(Matt 24:15-22; Luke 21:20-24)* Jesus' earlier warning, "But you — watch yourselves!" (v 9a), now broadens out to include a severer danger than he has thus far described. "But when you see the abomination of desolation standing where he ought not [to stand]" signals that Jesus is now going beyond the mere "beginning of birthpangs" (mentioned in v 8) to events that will immediately precede the end (cf. v 7 with vv 19-20, 24-31). An adversative δέ, "but," contrasts the passivity of enduring normal persecution with the activity of taking flight on sight of the abomination of desolation. This abomination refers to a sacrilege that causes people to desert the temple. "Where he ought not [to stand]" (v 14a) may at first seem vague, but the reference to the temple at the beginning of Mark 13, the immediately following reference to Judea (v 14b), and the present allusion to Daniel, where references to "the sanctuary" and "sacrifice" point to the temple, make the meaning clear: of all places, the abomination should not be standing in the precincts of the temple. The horror of religious abomination takes precedence over mundane topography (cf. Matt 24:15; M.-J. Lagrange 341). The masculine gender of ἑστηκότα, "standing," disagrees with the neuter gender of τὸ βδέλυγμα, "the abomination," but agrees with the masculine participles in Daniel's Hebrew text (see R. H. Gundry, *Use of the OT* 47-49) and thereby implies that the abomination is personal, say, the image of a god or of a deified ruler (so the usual meaning of Daniel's שִׁקּוּץ, perhaps in conjunction with an altar (cf. 1 Macc 1:54, 59; 6:7; 2 Thess 2:3-4; Rev 13:8, 14-15; Josephus *Ant.* 18.3.1 §§55-59; 18.8.2-9 §§261-309; idem *J.W.* 2.9.2 §§169-71; 6.6.1 §316). That Jesus speaks so direly about the desecration of the temple shows him to be a good Jew and exhibits the same concern for the temple that led him to cleanse it (11:15-19).

Since Jesus first predicted the destruction of the temple (v 2) and since Dan 9:26-27, the original passage to speak of abomination in connection with desolation, speaks also of destruction, some have thought that "the abomination of desolation" connotes desolation through destruction as well as through desertion. But Dan 11:31 and especially Dan 12:11, to whose phraseology Mark 13:14 comes closest (for details, see R. H. Gundry, *Use of the OT* 47-48), speak only of stopping the regular sacrifices and setting up a profanatory object — they say nothing about the destruction of the temple — and Dan 9:26-27 appears to put the abomination of desolation before the destruction. Furthermore, 1 Macc 1:54 indicates that Antiochus Epiphanes, to whom Daniel's prophecy first applied, desecrated the temple, not that he destroyed it. The gates were burned, the buildings ransacked, the priests' chambers torn down, and the whole site abandoned — but the sanctuary and surrounding courts were not destroyed so as to require rebuilding (1 Macc 2:12; 4:36-51; see also Josephus *Ant.* 12.5.4 §§248-53). Even an effective siege or a military takeover stopping short of destruction would make it too late to flee in accord with Jesus' immediately following command. Much more would destruction such as Jesus predicted ("a stone will not be left on a stone that will not be torn down" — v 2). And despite his prediction of destruction, he says nothing more about it and never answers the question concerning the time when it will occur and the sign that it is about to do so (v 4). Instead, he makes the abomination itself a sign, but not of the soon destruction of the temple — rather, of a far more important event, an event the four disciples did not even have in mind when they asked their question — the coming of the Son of man plus the unequaled tribulation immediately preceding it. Therefore, only an abomination which causes worshipers to forsake the temple and which portends their coming persecution for failure to worship the abomination — only that and nothing more satisfies the wording of Mark's text. (Since no emphasis falls on the destruction of the temple, it seems doubtful that Mark wrote after the destruction, i.e. after 70 C.E., right at the time, or shortly before when the destruction might have been anticipated with horror — see the following notes and pp. 1041-45). For the moment, all the emphasis falls on danger to life and limb. And though Jesus implies the specificity of the abomination by his talk of seeing it and fleeing, the danger that it portends seems to affect everyone in its vicinity, not just his disciples. But since he is addressing his disciples, he commands those of them who will be in Judea to flee (cf. Gen 19:17).

The parenthetical clause, "Let the reader understand" (cf. Dan 9:23, 25; Rev 13:9, 18; 17:9), may represent Mark's command that the reader of his gospel understand the meaning of the abomination — in particular, the personalizing implication of the grammatically irregular masculine participle (cf. D. Daube, *NTRJ* 425-37) — or may represent Jesus' command that the reader of Daniel understand the expression in terms of Jesus' teaching (cf. *Barn.* 4:5-6). Mark may think the expression obscure to his readers unacquainted with Daniel. Jesus may think the expression obscure to readers of Daniel used to thinking that Antiochus Epiphanes perpetrated the abomination already in Maccabean times (again cf. 1 Macc 1:54). The repeated use of Daniel throughout the Olivet Discourse favors a dominical allusion to Dan 12:9-10, just before Daniel's final mention of the abomination of desolation: "And he said, 'Go, Daniel, for [these] words are sealed up till the end-time . . . and none of the wicked will understand, but those who have insight will understand'" (cf. 1QS 3:13; 9:18). But the imperative third person singular disagrees with the interrogative indicative second person plural that elsewhere in Mark characterizes Jesus' other references to reading the OT. Not as in v 14, moreover, those references are explicit in their citations ("what David did . . . at [the passage about] Abiathar" — 2:25-26; "this Scripture" — 12:10; "in the Book of Moses at [the passage about] the thorn-bush" — 12:26). And Mark's breaking into the words of Jesus with an indubitably editorial insertion at the end of 2:10 (cf. also 3:30; 7:11, 19) favors a similar insertion here (differently from Matthew — see R. H. Gundry, *Matthew* 481, where the interpretation of Mark needs revision; also D. Daube, *NTRJ* 24-25). Such an insertion would fit Mark's emphasis on the predictive power of Jesus. In fact, since under normal circumstances "the reader" would not mean a private reader, but a public reader to whom an audience is listening (cf. Rev 1:3), the command to understand may imply that the public reader should understand the masculine participle so as not to shift to the grammatically regular but predictively inferior neuter gender (see H. A. Guy in *ExpTim* 65 [1953-54] 30, where it is suggested that the command originally stood in the margin, put there perhaps by Mark himself on noticing that public readers tended to use the neuter or otherwise correct the masculine; also E. Best in *IBS* 11 [1989] 124-32).

As elsewhere in the NT, the urgency of a command to flee dictates that the verb be put into the present tense of the imperative (besides the parr., cf. Matt 2:13; 10:23; 1 Cor 6:18; 10:14; 1 Tim 6:11; 2 Tim 2:22; contrast the unemphatic aorist in other non-indicative forms of φεύγω at Matt 3:7 par. Luke 3:7; Matt 23:33; Acts 27:30). Only disciples in Judea are to flee. Others will be preaching elsewhere among all the nations (v 10; cf. v 37 for Jesus' addressing "all" through the four mentioned in v 3). "Then" starts a series of τότε's (vv 14, 21, 26, 27) and stresses the need to flee neither earlier nor later, but at that very time. The mountains to which the Judean disciples are to flee will be the mountains of Judea, the Judean wilderness, long a hideout for refugees and others (2 Samuel 23–24; Ezek 7:16; 1 Macc 2:28; Josephus *J.W.* 5.10.1 §§420-23; and, though not necessarily with reference to the mountains of Judea, Gen 14:10; 19:17, 19; 1 Kgs 22:17; Jer 16:16; Nah 3:18; Heb 11:38).

The rest of the passage (vv 15-20) seems limited to Judea. Certainly the command that the man of leisure ("who is on the housetop") not lose time by coming down and entering his house to take something out (cf. 6:8) labors under this limitation, with special reference to Jerusalem, the chief city of Judea. So also for the prohibition against a field hand's going back to get his cloak, the woe to women whose pregnancy and nursing will hamper or preclude speedy escape (cf. Josephus *Ant.* 14.13.7-8 §§352-58), and the command to pray against wintertime, whose heavy rains in Judea would make flight difficult or impossible because of flooding roads and wadis (Rev 12:13-17, esp. 12:15-16; Josephus *J.W.* 4.7.5 §§433-36; cf. 4.4.5 §§286-87). Instead or also, cold and lack of shelter may be in view (cf. *Tanḥ.* 156b; *Midr. Qoh.* 1:14, cited by Str-B 1. 952). Even the prediction of an incomparably extreme tribulation, so extreme that it will confirm that things have progressed beyond the "beginning of birthpangs," so extreme that Judean disciples should pray that it not happen in wintertime, and so extreme that the Lord will shorten it to avoid total loss of life — in particular, to save the lives of the elect (cf. Gen 18:22-23) — even this prediction seems to stay within the boundaries of Judea. A series of adversative δέ's in vv 15 (bis), 17, 18 distinguish the various possibilities for the elect living in Judea; and the strongly adversative ἀλλά in v 20 emphasizes the shortening for their sake. For Mark himself, who probably writes his gospel far away from Judea for people living likewise far away from Judea (see pp. 1041-45), Jesus' instructions meet no practical need. Rather, they show his ability to predict the future in detail; they help form Mark's apology for the Cross.

13:21-23 *(Matt 24:23-28; Luke 17:23-24, 37b)* Jesus now gives another warning against deception, deception that if successful would keep his disciples in Judea from fleeing to the mountains for safety. The last time, he warned against being deceived by those who will come claiming to be the Christ and against being alarmed by warfare and its effects so as to think that the end has come (vv 5-8). At this point in the text, however, the abomination of desolation is standing where he ought not to stand and unequaled tribulation has set in; so the end *is* near, as implied by καὶ τότε, "and then" (cf. 2 Thess 2:8). Such circumstances heighten the danger of deception. This danger comes now not so much from the false christs as from their false prophets, whose proclamations, "Look — here [is] the Christ! Look — there [is the Christ]!" will further the danger of deception. Ellipses of "is" and of "is the Christ" and asyndeton before the second ἴδε, "look," stress the danger; and the present tense of the imperative πιστεύετε with μή makes Jesus' warning more emphatic: "Don't ever believe [him]" (cf. the comments on 1:15; A. T. Robertson, *Grammar* 851-54, esp. 853-54; and see C. D. Marshall, *Faith* 148-49, for a contrast with 1:15 — a contrast curtailed somewhat, however, by a lack in the Olivet Discourse of the kingdom-terminology that characterized 1:15).

The next statement gives a reason for the emphatic warning: "For false christs [the ones heralded as 'here' or 'there'] and false prophets [the heralds] will arise; and they will give signs and wonders to deceive, if possible, the elect." The verb of deception, πλανάω, has gained a perfective preposition, ἀπό-, to heighten the degree of danger (contrast the simplex form of the verb in vv 5b-6). The same heightening is to be seen in Jesus' giving to the false christs false prophets to act as their heralds and to back up the heraldry with signs and wonders (cf. the beast and the false prophet in Rev 13:1-18; 16:13; 19:20; 20:10). Since now, in contrast with vv 5-6, the false christs are *being* proclaimed rather than proclaiming themselves, the giving of signs and wonders is probably limited to the false prophets (again cf. the passages in Revelation). The giving of signs and wonders is characteristically prophetic rather than messianic, anyway (N.B. its absence in vv 5b-6, where false prophets did not appear). "If possible, the elect" at once gives a final emphasis to the danger of deception and an indication that the elect will not succumb.

Ὑμεῖς δέ, "but you," emphatically distinguishes the elect from those who will succumb to deception (cf. v 9). Βλέπετε, "watch out," repeats the warning in vv 5 and 9. Because the warning is general, however (cf. πάντα, "all things," in the following clause), the verb gets no object, whether a clause ("lest anyone deceive you" — v 5) or a reflexive pronoun ("yourselves" — v 9). "I have told you all things beforehand" gives the reason why the watchful elect will escape deception: to be forewarned is to be forearmed. For Mark, the statement fits perfectly and prominently into his emphasis on Jesus' predictive power. This emphasis gains from asyndeton at the start of the statement, from the perfect tense of προείρηκα, "have told . . . beforehand," and from the comprehensiveness of πάντα (meaning all things that the disciples need to watch out for).

13:24-27 *(Matt 24:29-31; Luke 21:25-28)* The succession of phrases, "but in those days after that tribulation [cf. v 19] . . . and then . . . and then" (vv 24, 26, 27; cf. v 21), displays Jesus' knowledge of God's timetable. The darkening of the sun, the failure of the moon to give its light, and the shower of falling stars display Jesus' knowledge of the final details and provide a black curtain against which the glory of the Son of man's coming shines out all the more. Since Jesus is the Son of man (8:38; 10:45; 14:62), the details in the description of the Son of man's coming contribute to the awesomeness of Jesus that Mark likes to emphasize: (1) people in general will see Jesus' coming (ὄψονται is an indefinite third person plural; cf. 9:1 for the motif of seeing); (2) he will come "in clouds," a divine mode of transport (9:7; 14:62; Dan 7:13; also Rev. 1:7; 10:1; 14:14-16; Exod 34:5; Lev 16:2; Num 11:25; Pss 18:12-13[11-12]; 97:2; Isa 19:1; Nah 1:3 et passim [cf. the comments on 9:7]); (3) he will come with much power (cf. the coming of God's rule "in power" — 9:l); (4) he will come with glory (cf. 8:38; 10:37; Ps 8:6[5]); (5) he will send angels (cf. 8:38) and gather his elect from the four winds (i.e. from all directions — cf. 1 Chr 9:24 LXX; *CPR* 115. 6 [cited in A. Deissmann, *Bible Studies* 248]), from the extremity of earth to the extremity of sky (cf. Zech 2:10[6]; Deut 13:8[7]; 30:4; Jer 12:12; *1 Enoch* 57:2; Philo *Cher.* 29 §99; idem *Migr.* 32 §181).

The Son of man will have angels at his disposal, the elect belong to him (despite the omission of αὐτοῦ, "his," in D L W Ψ *f*¹ 28 565 892 *pc* it Or^lat), and they will number so many that the angels will have to go to the farthest horizons of earth and sky to gather them all. Since according to v 20 the Lord chose the elect, their belonging to the Son of man in v 27 makes the Son of man the Son of God and thus heir to the elect. This is the Jesus of the future. His coming will need no heralding, "Look — here [is] the Christ! Look — there!" It will herald itself in the heavens and across the expanse of the earth. Only false christs will appear in a corner and need heralds to advertise their whereabouts. The periphrastic future, "will be falling" (ἔσονται . . . πίπτοντες; contrast πεσοῦνται, "will fall," in Isa 34:4 LXX; Matt 24:29), implies a shower of meteorites that continues for some time (cf. A. T. Robertson, *Grammar* 889; also medieval Samaritan literature in which events such as those described in v 24 do not take place in a cataclysm of one day, but over a period of months — see J. Macdonald, *Theology of the Samaritans* 372-73). The extension of the shower of meteorites adds to the unmistakability of the event of the Son of man's coming. The insertion of "out of the heaven" into the phraseology of Isa 34:4 sets up a parallel with "in the heavens" in the next clause (for "of the heavens" in the MT, omitted by the LXX). This parallel creates a double emphasis on the sky-wideness of the public stage on which the Son of man will appear. The assonance and inclusion created by the similar verbal endings of σκοτισθήσεται, "will be darkened," and σαλευθήσονται, "will be shaken," add dramatic effect. The gathering of the elect from everywhere will further eliminate the need for invitations to come and see. The strongly adversative ἀλλά, "but" (v 24), lays weight on the contrast between the deceptive, private way in which false christs will come and the overpowering, open way in which the Son of man will come. Though this prediction of Jesus cannot count as a fulfilled one, it points forward to an ultimate reversal of the Crucifixion; and, as noted before, Mark's recording the fulfilments of many other predictions made by Jesus gives reason to believe that this grandest of all will also reach fulfilment.

13:28-31 *(Matt 24:32-35; Luke 21:29-33)* An assurance that the Son of man will come strengthens Mark's stress on the predictive ability of Jesus. The parabolic use of a fig tree and the emphatic position of ἀπό . . . τῆς συκῆς, "from the fig tree," probably derive in part from the recent incident of the already leafed and subsequently withered fig tree, for Mark narrated that incident not very far back (11:12-14, 20-25); partly from the quotation in v 25 of Isa 34:4, for that OT passage goes on to speak of a leaf that withers from the fig tree; and partly from the place where Jesus is speaking, the Mount of Olives, for figs as well as olives grow there (again see 11:12-14, 20-25). The command to learn the following parable, taken from the fig tree, anticipates the closing command to understand the point of the parable. Thus the two commands form an inclusion. The order of words in the Greek text of v 28b accentuates "already," "tender," and "near." The resultant emphasis on nearness anticipates Jesus' interpretation of the parable. In that interpretation, which is also a parenetic application, the emphatic ὑμεῖς, "you," after οὕτως καί, "thus also," recalls vv 9a, 11d, 23a (cf. 7:18, too); ὅταν ἴδητε, "when you see," recalls v 14a; and ταῦτα, "these things," recalls v 4a. But on the disciples' lips "these things" in v 4a could refer only to the destructions of buildings and the tear-downs of stones, whereas in the meantime Jesus has predicted other things and ignored those destructions and tear-downs. Furthermore, he has denied that the first ones of these other things will signal the end (v 7). Therefore "these things" in v 29 must refer to the things that *will* signal the end, i.e. the later ones of these other things predicted from v 14 onward ("but when you see . . . , then"), yet exclusive of the things predicted in vv 24-27, toward which they point. Γινόμενα, "happening," assumes certainty of fulfilment.

Despite the indicative of γινώσκετε in v 28, γινώσκετε in v 29 is probably imperative ("know" as a command to understand, a command that matches the introductory command to learn) rather than another indicative; for in v 14 indubitable imperatives followed ὅταν ἴδητε, "when you see." Moreover, we would expect the indicative to occur in the future tense ("you will know") rather than in the present tense ("you know," which would almost have to be taken as awkwardly futuristic to make good sense); and the strong assurance in the next saying favors a command over a statement of fact. The present tense of the imperative γινώσκετε is linear, like the present participle γινόμενα — the recognition is to accompany the happenings over a span of time — and makes something of a wordplay with the present tense of the indicative γινώσκετε. Once again, "near" carries emphasis by virtue of Greek word order. The addition of the figurative expression, "at [the] doors," lends further emphasis to the nearness of the Son of man's coming when the predictions are seen to be taking place. The matching consonants in θέρος, "summer," and θύραις, "doors," make a wordplay that sharpens the emphasis. In the last two sayings, the emphasis expands to include not only the nearness of Jesus' coming once the abomination of desolation takes place and the unequaled tribulation sets in, but also the certainty of the fulfilments of all his predictions. Asyndeton, "truly I say to you," οὐ μή plus the aorist subjunctive, "will by no means," and the addition of "all" to "these things" intensify the emphasis. Since the addition of "all" fortified but did not expand the referent of "these things" in v 4, since v 30 continues on from v 29 with no disjunction, and since an adversative δέ, "but," and a switch from "these" (ταῦτα) to "that" (ἐκείνης) favor a new topic in v 32, the addition of "all" to "these things" in v 30 seems not to expand the referent, i.e. seems not to include the Son of man's coming (cf. the non-inclusion of his coming in the "all things" of v 23, as shown by contextual position, by the completed and therefore non-prospective action of the perfect tense in προείρηκα ὑμῖν, "I have told you beforehand," and by the immediately preceding command to watch out against deception). Rather, the addition of "all" fortifies the reference of "these things" to the premonitory events described in vv 14-23, just as "these things" in v 29 referred to those same events. ("That day or hour" will then refer to the event so signaled, i.e. to the coming of the Son of Man.)

That "this generation will not pass away till all these things happen" (cf. Dan 12:7) also intensifies the emphasis on nearness in that Jesus identifies his contemporaries as those who will see all these things coming to pass. The final accent falls on certainty: "Heaven and earth will pass away, but my words will by no means pass away." This phraseology is suggested by the mention of earth and heaven in v 27 and by the immediately preceding denial in v 30: "This generation will by no means pass away till . . ." (cf. also the plural of Jesus' "words" in the vicinity of "this generation" at 8:38). The parallelism of phraseology suggests that "my words" does not refer to the statement, "Truly I say to you that this generation will by no means pass away till all these things happen," but that like that statement it refers to the foregoing predictions of "all these things." Mark can hardly be happier with this tradition, for it emphasizes what he want to emphasize — Jesus' predictive power. The asyndeton with which v 31 begins heightens this emphasis.

13:32-37 *(Matt 24:36, 42-51; 25:13-30; Luke 12:35-46; 19:12-27)* Jesus has predicted what will signal the general nearness of his coming and has stressed the certainty of fulfilment. He now denies that anyone except the Father knows the exact time ("that day or hour") of his coming, apparently because the Lord has cut off the foregoing days of unprecedented tribulation and has not revealed how many of them he has cut off (cf. v 20). Δέ, "but," marks this shift in thought. Suddenly "day," which has repeatedly appeared in the plural (see vv 17, 19, 20 [bis], 24), appears in the singular; and the even narrower term "hour" is added. Because of its coupling with "hour," "day" does not carry an eschatological connotation, as in "the Day of the Lord." Nor does "hour," as in "the hour of the trial" (Rev 3:10). Rather, "day" represents the smallest unit of time on the calendar, and "hour" the smallest unit of time in a day (hence Paul's having to use the adjective ἄτομος, "indivisible," in a temporal sense [so also Arist. *Ph.* 236a] plus a figure of speech, "twinkling of an eye," to express an even smaller unit — 1 Cor 15:52; cf. "a *half* hour" in a durative sense at Rev 8:1 and outside the NT; also Rev 9:15). The pairing of these terms therefore confirms the distinction between the general nearness of Jesus' coming, known by the occurrence of premonitory events, and the exact time, unknown to all but the Father. That Mark does not exclude Jesus' ignorance of the exact time bears tribute to Mark's respect for tradition. His emphasis on Jesus' predictive power might have kept him from including that ignorance. On the other hand, uncertainty regarding the exact time works in favor of watchfulness, which helps the emphasis on Jesus' predictive power by inducing an expectation of fulfilment. The asyndeton with which βλέ-πετε, "watch out," and ἀγρυπνεῖτε, "stay alert," are each introduced underscores these two commands. Nowhere else in the NT does βλέπω carry the connotation of eager expectation of the Second Coming. Heb 10:25 comes closest to this connotation, but in reality means only "see." Yet βλέπω often connotes wariness against danger, as already in vv 5, 9, 23. Here too, then, in view of your ignorance concerning the exact time of the Son of man's coming, you should be wary lest "coming suddenly he should find you sleeping." This wariness requires alertness, staying awake. Thus, v 33a rests on v 33b and builds up to v 36. "For you do not know when the time is" (cf. *b. Sanh.* 97a) narrows the focus of v 32, which included everybody except the Father, down to the disciples. As a result, καιρός, "time" — rare in its proper sense of a determined time — seems to summarize in a single word the dual expression in v 32, "that day or hour," rather than referring to a prolonged "season." The Lord and Father has determined the time (cf. vv 20, 32).

The parable of a man who leaves his house to go on a journey and then comes back hints at Jesus' departure and coming back. The purpose of the journey goes unexplained in order that the meaning of the parable may appear elsewhere. The failure of the departing man to indicate when he will return leaves the time of return uncertain, as demanded by the meaning of the parable. The euphony of three successive words beginning with *alpha* (ἄνθρωπος ἀπόδημος ἄφεις; cf. also the euphonious endings -ος, -ος, -εις) and shortly thereafter of three occurrences of αὐτοῦ framing three other words containing ου (δούς, δούλοις, and ἐξουσίαν) paves a smooth path to the climax: "and commanded the doorkeeper that he should stay awake." The abrupt loss of euphony sharpens the command (cf. G. Lüderitz in *Markus-Philologie* 180; and on the notorious sleepiness of slaves, *b. Qidd.* 49b). "Having left his house" domesticates "away on a journey" so as to prepare for authorization of the household slaves. "To each his task (ἔργον)" at once defines the authorization and individualizes it in preparation for mention of the one slave the command to whom will form the point of the parable. "And he commanded the doorkeeper that he should stay awake" makes that point by completing the process of increasing specification and by recalling the Son of man's being "at [the] doors," which may have suggested this parable (cf. v 29). But the command does not define the task of the doorkeeper, which is to open the door when the master comes knocking. Rather, it speaks of readiness to perform that task. The parabolic strain caused by the shift from task to readiness underlines the importance of readiness. Syntax underlines it a second time; for up to the command that the doorkeeper stay awake, mere circumstantial participles have told what the man away on a journey did. Now we read a main clause containing the first finite verb expressed in the parable, "he commanded." Apart from the following subordinate clause, which gives the substance of the command, this is the only finite verb expressed anywhere in the parable, "it is" having been left unexpressed before "away on a journey." This ellipsis and asyndeton gave the parable an emphatically abrupt start. Placement of the indirect objects "to his slaves," "to each," and "to the doorkeeper" before the direct objects "authority," "his task," and "that he should watch" directs attention last of all to the command to stay awake, and thereby puts even further emphasis on it, as does also the presesnt tense of the subjunctive γρηγορῇ, "he should watch" (see S. E. Porter, *Verbal Aspect* 326, and contrast the non-indicative aorist forms of this verb in Mark 14:37 par. Matt 26:40; 1 Pet 5:8; Rev 3:3). The very awkwardness of linking the giving of the command to the two circumstantial participles with another "and," as though a third circumstantial participle were coming up whereas it turns out to be a main clause instead, rivets attention on the command.

Jesus' command that the disciples "therefore stay awake" grows out of the house-owner's command to the doorkeeper and cuts short any continuation of the story (When did the house-owner return? Was the doorkeeper awake at the time? What reward or punishment did he receive?) and thereby puts exclusive emphasis on the house-owner's command. Jesus' corresponding command also leads to another mention of the disciples' ignorance ("for you do not know when" — cf. v 35 with v 33), but with insertion of "the master (κύριος, 'Lord') of the house is coming," which derives from the parable but now refers to the Son of man, and with substitution of the four Roman watches of the night — "whether evening, midnight, cockcrowing, or early morning" — in place of "time." This substitution confirms the restricted meaning of καιρός in v 33. The repetition and paronomasia of οὐκ οἴδατε γὰρ πότε ὁ κύριος (v 35) as compared with οὐκ οἴδατε γὰρ πότε ὁ καιρός (v 33) enhance the uncertainty which calls for wakefulness. That Jesus speaks of the night watches even though he has mentioned the "day" of his coming creates an inconcinnity. But the inconcinnity of this shift, which is only somewhat eased by an intervening "hour" and "time," brings out the figurative meaning of the night watches and the emphasis that they lay on incalculability. Since travelers do not usually arrive home at night, how incalculable must be the day of the Son of man's coming to be compared to arrival during one of the night watches! To the elements of nearness (v 30), certainty (v 31), and incalculability (vv 33-35), Jesus now adds the element of suddenness to warn against sleeping, a figure for carelessness in professed discipleship (for suddenness, cf. Luke 21:34; 1 Thess 5:3; and for the danger of sleeping, cf. Rom 13:11; 1 Thess 5:6; but not Matt 25:5, for there the wise virgins as well as the foolish fall asleep). The final command to stay awake widens to include "all." Jesus has been speaking in private to four of his disciples (v 3), and the house-owner's slaves stand appropriately for Jesus' disciples, not for all humanity. Hence, "all" means all disciples. The absence of a qualifying "of you" prevents limitation to the Twelve. Jesus' purpose in the command to stay awake is to insure the disciples' alertness. Because of Mark's emphasis on Jesus' predictive ability, however, the command gains another purpose, that of assuring Mark's audience that the prediction of Jesus' future coming will certainly take place. Parenesis serves Christology.

Three-step parallelism characterizes these last verses and highlights the need to watch and therewith the predictive ability of Jesus. "Stay awake, therefore" (v 35a) harks back to "Watch out, be alert" (v 33a); "for you do not know when (πότε) the master of the house is coming, whether . . ." (v 35b) harks back to "for you do not know when (πότε) the time is" (v 33b; for πότε see also v 4, and N.B. that the push for parallelism is so strong that in vv 35-36 the "for"-clause is brought in despite its intruding between "watch" and "lest . . ."); and "lest coming suddenly he find you sleeping" (v 36) harks back to "[it is] like a man away on a journey . . . and he commanded the doorkeeper that he should stay awake" (v 34). Verse 37 then clinches the point of readiness by repeating and expanding the leading command in each of the parallel sections.

NOTES

R. Pesch (*Naherwartungen* 19-47) surveys studies of chap. 13 during the period 1954-68. D. Wenham (in *TSFBul* 71 [1975] 6-15; 72 [1975] 1-9) brings the survey more up to date. On earlier studies, see G. R. Beasley-Murray, *Jesus and the Future*. E. Haenchen (459-61, n. 23) criticizes the views of E. Trocmé (*Formation* 215-29) that chap. 13 brought the original version of Mark to a close and climax, and of W. Marxsen (*Mark* 151-206) that chap. 13 illustrates Mark's orientation to an imminent coming of the Son of man, to take place in Galilee. The view of J. Lambrecht (in *Bib* 47 [1966] 321-60) that in chap. 13 Mark uses a developed form of Q rests on an underestimation of Matthew's redactional activity and raises the question, Why does Mark not use much more of Q here and elsewhere? Against the view of D. Wenham (*Rediscovery*) that all three synoptists know a pre-synoptic eschatological discourse and that Mark abbreviates it, see R. Bauckham in *ExpTim* 96 (1984-85) 346; F. W. Burnett in *CBQ* 48 (1986) 351-53. It is another question whether Mark alone knows an eschatological discourse and uses it in its entirety.

J. Jeremias (*Eucharistic Words* 90-93) argues that since the fourth gospel has no counterpart to the Olivet Discourse, though it does have counterparts to most other items from the Triumphal Procession onward, Mark has inserted the discourse. Others argue for an insertion of the discourse that 14:1 follows on 12:44 more smoothly than on 13:37 (see, e.g., P. J. Achtemeier 115). The fourth evangelist's emphasis on realized eschatology weakens the first argument, however; for he might have omitted the discourse because of its opposite emphasis on futuristic eschatology. Or he may have transmuted the Olivet Discourse into the Upper Room Discourse (in particular, John 14–16; cf. the shared themes of persecution by the synagogue, hatred from the world, martyrdom, birthpangs, prayer, endurance-abiding, the ministry of the Holy Spirit in the disciples, Jesus' coming and gathering his own, his relation as Son to God his Father, etc.). The announcement in Mark 14:1 that the Passover was going to arrive after two days follows on the story of a widow's mite no more smoothly than on the Olivet Discourse. In either case, there is a noticeable shift. What needs to be said, however, is that Jesus' exit from the temple and proceeding to the Mount of Olives in the introduction to the discourse (13:1, 3) provides a smooth transition from the story of the widow's mite and thereby prepares for a new beginning in 14:1. One may attribute this introduction to Mark's redaction; but then the argument for insertion of the discourse becomes viciously circular, for even the presence of Marcanisms (e.g., the genitive absolutes in vv 1, 3, where by classical standards dative and accusative participles should modify αὐτῷ and αὐτόν [cf. 5:2; 9:9], the use of ἐκπορεύομαι, "go out," in a genitive absolute [cf. 10:17, 46; see also 6:11; 11:19], the historical present tense of λέγει, "says," κατ' ἰδίαν, "privately," etc.; see J. Gnilka 2. 182; R. Pesch, *Naherwartungen* 96-98) — if we could prove them to be Marcanisms and not locutions characteristic of pre-Marcan tradition — could not disprove the traditionality of Jesus' exiting the temple, of a disciple's remarking its magnificence, of Jesus' predicting its destruction, of his location on Olivet, and of the question about the time and sign of destruction, none of which represent Mark's known interests.

If Mark had felt free to place the Olivet Discourse wherever he wanted, he might have placed it after Jesus' resurrection — say, at a farewell meeting with the disciples in Galilee (cf. 14:28; 16:7). That placement would have suited exceedingly well both the forward-looking character of the discourse and the falling of the fulfilments of Jesus' predictions, including those that have taken place between his resurrection and Mark's writing, outside the narrative. Traditionality does not negate the insulative use of the present placement, however; for Mark might have omitted the discourse or moved it to a position where it would not insulate the passion narrative from deductions damaging to Jesus (see the foregoing comments).

The interpretation of chap. 13 as joining chaps. 14–16 to form a double conclusion of Mark's book — in the passion of the Christian community and in the passion of Jesus, respectively — mistakes the meaning of chap. 13 (against N. Perrin and D. C. Duling, *NT* 239-42, 252). Only vv 9-13 deal with the passion of the Christian community. Otherwise we read about general distress, the danger of deceit, and the coming of the Son of man, which coming is *not* described as a vindication of persecuted Christians or as a judgment on their persecutors.

Scepticism that Jesus taught eschatology outside chap. 13 will naturally lead to scepticism that he spoke the material in chap. 13. But if he taught eschatology elsewhere, there is no reason in principle why he should not have spoken the present material. Its length poses no problem. About eschatology as about any other topic Jesus is almost bound to have spoken at different lengths on different occasions; and premonition that he was soon to be killed makes it both understandable and appropriate that he should have spoken here at considerable length, just as Mark records.

Chapter 13 is occasionally likened to farewell discourses such as we find in Genesis 49; Deuteronomy 33; Joshua 23–24; 1 Samuel 12; 1 Kgs 2:1-9; 1 Chronicles 28–29; John 13–16; Acts 20:17-38; 2 Timothy; 2 Peter; Tob 14:3-11; 1 Macc 2:49-70; and the various testaments of Adam, Abraham, Isaac, Jacob, the twelve patriarchs, Moses, and Job. A certain similarity does exist in the common concern of the soon-to-die speakers over the future of their addressees, but more striking are the differences. Elsewhere the speakers deliberately take the initiative, here Jesus only responds to an exclamation and a question. Elsewhere the imminence of the speakers' deaths prompts the discourse, and they or the narrators refer to the approach of death. Not so here. Elsewhere the speakers reflect on the past and sometimes give a blessing. Jesus does neither. Not only does he look exclusively to the future. He looks to his own future and speaks of his coming. This is not a farewell discourse, then. It is a prediction of home-coming. These differences support authenticity by undermining the view according to which the literary genre of farewell discourse had so much force that such a discourse was put on Jesus' lips without his having spoken it. In some ways his words spoken at the Last Supper and on the way to Gethsemane will come closer to a farewell discourse (14:17-31 passim).

Though chap. 13 contains some material that appears also in apocalyptic literature, too many features of such literature are missing from the chapter to allow an apocalyptic classification, either. Jesus does not report having seen a vision. No angel plays the role of an interpreter. Nor does Jesus grant or interpret a vision to the disciples. There is no survey of history to show the outworking of God's plan from past to present, no division of history into epochs, no numerical calculations of time, no revelation of astronomical and similar secrets, no heavenly settings, no exaggerated figures, no monstrosities, no bestial terrors, no demonic onslaughts, no cries for vengeance against persecutors, no last great battle or war, no slaughter of persecutors, no replacement of pagan empires with the kingdom of God on earth, no restoration of the temple, no resurrection, not even of martyrs, no last judgment, no blissful reward for the righteous, no final punishment of the wicked.

On the positive side, there are far more commands than an apocalyptic vision would contain; and the commands relate so closely to the predictions that we cannot subtract the commands to expose an original apocalypse. E. Brandenberger *(Markus 13)* is one who tries; but after his subtraction of vv 5b-6, 9-13, 21-23 as Marcan insertions, commands remain in vv 7, 14, 15, 16, 18, 28, 29, 33, 35, 37. Nor does the character of these remaining commands differ from that of the commands in the subtracted verses. To put it the other way around, the latter commands are no less "apocalyptic" than those in the supposed pre-Marcan written apocalypse. Taken together, the commands provide the basic structure of the discourse. Without them there is no discourse at all.

D. E. Aune *(Prophecy* 186-87, 399-400, n. 93, followed by V. K. Robbins, *Jesus the Teacher* 178-79) thinks that Mark has constructed chap. 13, and especially its intro-ductory verses, after the Greco-Roman patterns of a peripatetic dialogue, a dialogue at a temple, and a question-cum-oracular response (cf. Varro *Rust.;* Cebes of Thebes; Plut. *De def. or.;* idem *De E apud Delphos;* Florus *Vergilius orator an poeta;* Numenius). Aune himself puts his finger on a weak spot in this hypothesis, viz., that Mark 13 does not have the give-and-take of dialectic whereas the Greco-Roman dialogues, though sometimes containing long speeches, do contain such give-and-take. Furthermore, the four disciples' question arises out of a prediction by Jesus, which in turn arose out of a disciple's exclamation, quite unlike coming to a Greco-Roman oracle with a premeditated question. And again differently, Jesus is at some distance from the temple when he answers the four disciples' unpremeditated question. Whatever Greco-Roman peripatetic and temple dia-logues may have been artificially constructed were so constructed because people really did engage in such dialogues. We must leave room, then, for historical tradition as well as for artificial construction. In the present case, the need to posit a mixture of peripatetic dialogue, temple dialogue, and consultation of an oracle (plus farewell speech and apoc-alypse, according to Robbins, loc. cit.) overloads the hypothesis of artificial construction by Mark. Where else do we find such a mixture? Varro's *Res Rusticae* starts out like a farewell speech (1.1.1ff.) and develops into a temple dialogue (1.2.1-1.69.4), but the temple dialogue is only a flashback to a completely different occasion. Earlier in Mark, Jesus has several times sat to teach after moving about (4:1, after moving from house to seaside; 9:35, after traveling through Galilee; 12:41, after moving to a point opposite the treasury in the temple); and a host of references can be cited for his carrying on dialogue, such as it is, while moving about, sometimes with stationary dialogue or teaching in the wake (2:23-28; 6:53–7:16 with 7:17-23; 8:10-12, 13-21, 27-9:1, 9-13, 30-32 with 33-50; 10:1-9 with 10-12, 17-31, 32-45; 11:19-25; 14:17-21, 26-31). The whole section 11:27–12:44 consists of peripatetic dialogue in the temple (see esp. 11:27b). So why single out chap. 13 for Greco-Roman comparisons? What we have is Jewish realism: visitation at the temple during Passover, going back and forth between Bethany and Jerusalem, an admiring comment on the magnificence of the temple as seen from Mount Olivet, and a responsive question about a disturbing prediction.

It is presently popular to posit that Mark created chap. 13 by gathering isolated sayings of Jesus and clusters thereof and welding them together with the help of sayings of Christian prophets, references to historical events, and OT allusions. One wonders why Jesus could not have alluded to the OT as easily as Mark is supposed to have done, why apart from predictions of persecution and gospel-preaching (both of which Jesus is likely to have foreseen, and the latter to have commanded — cf. 6:7-11) historical events are so poorly served by the supposed references to them (see the following notes), and why Christian prophets are needed for what Jesus said according to this gospel, our earliest preserved tradition of his words and deeds — except for the earlier 1 Thess 4:15-17, which however attributes to him words of very similar import; 1 Cor 7:10-11, which does not bear directly on eschatology (but see vv 26, 29-31); 11:23-26, which climaxes in a reference to Jesus' coming, just as in Mark 13. Both the close interrelation between commands and predictions and the logic of the progression from one topic to another also argue against taking chap. 13 as a redactional pistache of originally isolated materials. The topics that Jesus discusses would have had little meaning in an earlier isolation from each other. The absence of editorial intrusions, such as "and he was saying to them" (contrast chap. 4, for example), suits and illustrates this interdependence.

Among others, H. Anderson (290) argues that because elsewhere Jesus does not string together OT allusions or set out an apocalyptic timetable, Mark has done so here. But the argument is double-edged, for elsewhere in his writing neither does Mark string together OT allusions or set out an apocalyptic timetable. The argument also exaggerates the use of OT phraseology (there is much, but for the most part too little to speak of stringing together). It pays too little attention to the frequency with which Jesus uses OT phraseology elsewhere (see R. H. Gundry, *Use of the OT* passim). And the argument fails to take sufficient account of the great differences between the Olivet Discourse and typical apocalyptic (including the difference that the discourse delays expectation till future time — which we will see cannot have arrived when or before Mark writes, because the wording of the text does not correspond well enough to the events of 66-70 C.E. — whereas typical apocalyptic urges expectation at the present time). What we have, then, is neither a farewell discourse nor a Christianly redacted Jewish apocalypse nor a Greco-Roman peripatetic or temple dialogue or oracular response nor a collection of Jesuanic sayings pieced together with Christian prophetic, historical, and apocalyptic additions and OT allusions. Chapter 13 consists of a private eschatological discourse spoken by the earthly Jesus.

The refusal to give a sign in 8:11-12 differs so much from the present passage that that refusal does not endanger the authenticity of the present passage. There, Jesus was responding to Pharisees who were testing him with respect to the validity of his ministry. Here he is responding to disciples who have asked a believing question with respect to the time when a prediction of his will reach fulfilment. Even so and furthermore, he does not give the disciples a sign such as they seek any more than he gave the Pharisees a sign such as they sought. Instead, he gives his disciples a sign (the abomination of desolation and unequaled tribulation following it) such as will alert them to an event that they did not even ask about (the Son of man's coming). Redaction would almost certainly have assimilated the disciples' question and Jesus' answer to each other (as in Matthew, where the question is assimilated to the answer, and in Luke, where the answer is assimilated to the question).

The already noted absence from Mark 13 of many prominent features of Jewish apocalyptic likewise resists the argument that by inserting signs Mark 13 apocalypticizes the signless eschatology of Jesus' authentic teaching, represented by Luke 17:20-37. The latter passage means that the coming of God's rule does not require careful scrutiny to be seen. It will be unmistakably visible whether or not signs will herald its coming. That they will, see Luke 21:28. Only neglect of them will cause surprise (cf. Luke 12:49-56; Matt 16:2-3; Rev 3:3; H. Ridderbos, *Coming* 472-76; G. R. Beasley-Murray, *Jesus and the Future* 172-83). Paul or a Paulinist seems also to have thought that observance of signs does not contradict watching for the Day of the Lord or its coming with unexpected suddenness on the wicked (cf. 2 Thess 2:1-4 with 1 Thess 5:1-11; R. H. Gundry in *NTS* 33 [1987] 175, n. 26). Matt 24:26-28, 37-41 puts Q-Luke 17:22-23 alongside signs without any sense of contradiction. In the Book of Revelation the soon coming of Christ lives compatibly alongside events that must take place beforehand (cf. 22:20 with chaps. 4-18). Even if we were to say that by the time the Book of Revelation was written all those preceding events that look like predictions had already occurred, it would remain true — and therefore argumentatively cogent — that at the textual level the precedence of signs does not contradict the soon coming of Christ.

From the disparity between destruction in the disciples' question and profanation in Jesus' answer, many have concluded to a prophecy after the event (see, e.g., F. W. Beare in *Christian History and Interpretation* 172-73). On the contrary, such a prophecy would have reiterated the destruction initially predicted in v 2 and would have set out the chronology and sign for which the disciples asked; for the chronology and precursive events would have been available to a historian posing as a prophet.

The failure of this discourse to return to the destruction of the temple after the preceding, brief prediction in v 2, the failure of it to answer the four disciples' questions in v 3 concerning the time and sign of the destruction, and the failure even of v 2 to say anything about the destruction of Jerusalem all make it unlikely that the discourse reflects the destruction of Jerusalem and the temple in 70 C.E. or strives to cool down a resultant overheated expectation of a near end of the age. Nor does the instruction to flee on seeing the abomination of desolation (v 14) or the strong denial that this generation will pass away before the occurrence of "all these things" (vv 30-31) or the repeated exhortations to watch (vv 33-37) turn down the thermostat. Quite the contrary!

On the other hand, to make the commands to watchfulness define Mark's overall purpose as one of saying, "The events of 66-70 C.E. have signaled, or are signaling, the nearness of the end; so be ready for the Son of man's coming at any moment," leaves the rest of the gospel largely irrelevant and overlooks the failure of the discourse to correspond very closely to the events of 66-70 C.E. Notably, the coming of many in Christ's name (v 6) does not fit the first Jewish revolt against Rome (see the following notes). The hearing of wars and reports thereof and the fighting of nations and kingdoms against each other do not give a good description of the Romans' suppressing a revolt by a single one of their subject peoples. The Jews were not a kingdom, and the terminology ranges too widely. B. Reicke (in *New Synoptic Studies* 222) correctly speaks of Jesus' "worldwide perspective" which "is not compatible with the local revolt of the Zealots." Cannibalism, pestilence, internecine conflict, the burning of the temple, fulfilment of prophecy — at least some of these striking features of the first Jewish revolt against Rome and its suppression we would expect a so-called prophecy after the event to include (see Josephus *J.W.* 5.1.1-5 §§1-38; 5.10.2-5 §§424-45; 5.13.1 §§527-33; 6.3.1-6.5.3 §§177-309; 7.1.1 §1; and cf. the attachment of a statement concerning fulfilment to a prophecy in Acts 11:28).

Against the argument that non-mention of the burning of the temple disproves a prophecy after the event, S. G. F. Brandon (*Jesus and the Zealots* 235, n. 2) notes that the temple was razed along with the whole of Jerusalem (Josephus *J.W.* 7.1.1 §§1-3). But since fire destroyed the temple before the razing occurred, we would still expect a mention of the burning. N. Walter (in *ZNW* 57 [1966] 41-42) counters that Mark may omit the burning because he is interested only in the final result: razing. On the contrary, Mark shows interest in much else that will precede the razing: false christs, false prophets, warfare, persecution, profanation of the temple, etc.

Regardless of the historicity or unhistoricity of Christians' fleeing from Jerusalem to Pella prior to the destruction of the temple in 70 C.E. (Eus. *H.E.* 3.5.2-3; Epiph. *Haer.* 29.7; 30.2; idem *De mens. et pond.* 15; *Clem. Recogn.* 1.39 (1.37 sy); *Asc. Isa.* 4:1-14, esp. 13), the command to flee into the mountains (v 14) disagrees with such a flight. For Pella lay at the base of low-lying foothills in the Transjordan valley, not in mountainous terrain; and "into the mountains" hardly means "through the mountains to a refuge in a valley on the other side of the Jordan River." It does not follow that since Jerusalem is situated in the mountains, fleeing to the mountains must imply another mountain range, such as the Transjordanian range. To stay in Pella would be to stop short of that range, and it makes better sense to think of fleeing into mountains immediately surrounding a city (cf. esp. Ezek 7:15-16, but also 1 Macc 2:28; 2 Macc 5:27; and, though not necessarily for refuge, Ps 121:1-8). Jesus' command carries no indication of flight from Judea rather than flight within Judea (E. S. Malbon, *Narrative Space* 88).

According to Eus. *H.E.* 3.5.2-3, moreover, the Christians of Jerusalem fled quite a while before the Romans set up what many suppose to have been "the abomination of desolation," i.e. before the Romans entered the precincts of the temple, erected military standards there, and offered sacrifices to the images of Caesar affixed to those standards (Josephus *J.W.* 6.6.1 §316). Nor should we think of another, later flight of Christians at the time the Romans captured the temple and offered pagan sacrifices in its courts. By that time it was too late to flee. Several months earlier the Romans had surrounded Jerusalem with a continuous wall studded with thirteen guard towers, each manned day and night by sentries. Earlier yet, those Jews who sneaked out of Jerusalem to find food in the immediate environs were caught and crucified. After the Romans captured the temple, offered pagan sacrifices, and burned the temple, escape continued to prove impossible, as shown by the later request of the rebel leaders Simon and John that they and their families be granted safe passage through the blockading wall (Titus refused the request) and as shown by vain attempts to escape through and hide in underground passages (Josephus *J.W.* 5.11.1 §§446-51; 5.12.1-3 §§499-512; 6.2.8 §§157-63; 6.6.1-3 §§316, 323, 351; 6.7.3 §§370-73; 6.8.4-5 §§396-98, 401-2; 6.9.4 §§429-33; 7.2.2 §§26-29). To say that people outside Jerusalem might flee even though people caught inside during the siege could not flee overlooks that the Romans had controlled the Judean countryside for some time prior to their desecration and destruction of the temple; and the Romans continued to control it. Furthermore, it is wrong to exclude Jerusalemites from "the ones in Judea" (v 14). Jerusalem belongs to Judea; and as vv 15-16 make clear, the broader term merely includes those Jerusalemites working in the fields outside the city as well as those lounging on housetops within it. Conversely, the addressing of those who are lounging on housetops as well as those who are working in the fields shows that "Judea" includes Jerusalem; for most of the housetops are located there.

The Zealots made the temple their fortress, chose a hayseed to officiate as high priest, plundered the vessels, wine, and oil of the temple, interrupted the sacrifices, and shed human blood in the temple (Josephus *J.W.* 4.3.7-10 §§151-192; 5.13.6 §§562-66; 6.2.1 §§93-110; cf. 1QpHab 11:17–12:10). But none of these crimes against the temple caused it to be deserted (to the contrary, for example, see Josephus *J.W.* 4.3.11-14 §§193-223); so the reference to "the abomination of desolation" does not reflect them, either (against S. Sowers in *TZ* 26 [1970] 317-19; see also the possibility that Josephus accuses the Zealots falsely [M. Hengel, *Zealots* 185-86, 209-10, 217-24]).

It represents a counsel of despair to say that Mark means chap. 13 to reflect the Jewish war but that through ignorance he misrepresents it. The disagreements between his text and the historical events are too many and too radical. The events did not take place in a corner. Many Jews deserted to the Romans. Much communication passed from Jews in Palestine to Jews of the Diaspora, including the many who lived in Rome, a likely locale for the writing of Mark. The war lasted for years — plenty of time for circulation of news concerning it — and, as still evident on the Arch of Titus, the Romans publicized their victory by parading booty and captives into Rome. This triumphal procession even included huge pictorial representations of events in the war (Josephus *J.W.* 7.5.3-6 §§121-57). Whether writing just before, right at, or just after 70 C.E., Mark is not liable to have suffered from very much ignorance of what went on. From beginning to end, then, the events and circumstances of the Jewish war disagree with the text of Mark too widely to allow that text to reflect those events and circumstances.

Not only does failure of correspondence do away with the interpretation of vv 14-23 according to events in the first century. So also do the repeated indications earlier in vv 7, 8, 10 that other events have to take place before the unprecedented tribulation. If Mark were writing at the time of the abomination of desolation or just afterward, there would be no point in stressing the precedence of those events. They would already have taken place. The final stage would already have started. Furthermore, to say that Mark emphasized the Second Coming instead of the destruction of the temple because that destruction had already happened whereas the Second Coming had not makes him inconsistent and inopportunistic. Under the view that he wrote prophecy after the event, he emphasized other events that had already happened: the appearance of deceivers, wars, persecution, etc. Why not the destruction of the temple, too — indeed *especially,* since the disciples asked about it? And why did Mark miss a golden opportunity to play up a prediction the fulfilment of which enhances Jesus' reputation as an accurate predictor of the future?

See R. Pesch, *Naherwartungen* 74-77, for a survey of outlines suggested for chap. 13. At first sight vv 5b-23 seem concentric: (a) watch — deceivers (vv 5b-6); (b) when you hear — wars (vv 7-8); (c) watch — persecution (vv 9-13); (b') when you see — abomination of desolation (vv 14-20); (a') watch — false christs and false prophets (vv 21-23). Under a high estimate of Mark's redactional activity it could be said that such a structure would make persecution central in reflection of the church's present experience. What we truly have is not concentricity, however, so much as alternation with progress. Things build up toward a goal rather than revolving around a center. Unlike the deceivers at the beginning, the false christs toward the end will have false prophets. By contrast with the command not to be alarmed at wars, the command to flee at sight of the abomination of desolation shows a much worsened state of affairs. Persecution, then, is but an early one of increasingly dangerous tests of the disciples' mettle. In fact, the abomination of desolation will pose a general danger greater than the persecution of disciples alone. Thaumaturgic false prophets touting false christs will pose the greatest danger of all: "deceiving, if possible, the elect." These tests lead up to a lengthy double climax in the coming of the Son of man (vv 24-31, 32-37).

The attempt to make vv 14-20 the center of the whole discourse likewise fails, and thereby also the attempt to make the destruction of the temple in 70 C.E. and related events the referential lodestar of the discourse. Not only does the wording of vv 14-20 lack correspondence to those events; but again the discourse builds up to a lengthy double climax in the Son of man's coming. It does not revolve around the destruction of the temple. The destruction is not even mentioned, much less described accurately or fully; and the subsections surrounding vv 14-20 do not correspond to each other closely enough to establish a concentric structure. For example, the immediately following command not to believe false prophets' heraldry of false christs does not correspond to the immediately preceding command to watch yourselves when people give you over to trial and death; rather, it develops a command in the very first subsection (vv 5b-6).

The attempt of F. G. Lang (in *ZTK* 74 [1977] 5, n. 3) to make vv 14-23 the center of *all* chap. 13, not just of the discourse in vv 5b-37, likewise fails. Though both vv 1-4 and vv 32-37 deal with the question of time, so also does every other section in his outline (see vv 5-8, 9-13, 14-23, 24-27, 28-31). Furthermore, to attain the proposed concentric structure, disparate topics have to be lumped together in single sections: cosmic disasters (vv 7-8) with deceivers (vv 5-6), false prophets and false christs (vv 21-23) with the threat of physical death (vv 14-20). Again as before, the buildup to a lengthy double climax in the Son of man's coming spoils the concentric outline.

The attempt to establish alternating series of warnings (vv 5b-6, 9-13, 21-23) and instructions (vv 7-8, 14-20, 24-37) likewise fails. The warnings contain an instruction not to worry beforehand but to speak whatever is given you; and the instructions contain warnings not to be alarmed, not to come down from the roof, not to enter the house, not to turn back, not to be found sleeping. There is no fundamental distinction between watching out against deceit and refusing to be alarmed, between watching yourselves when being given over and fleeing when seeing the abomination of desolation, and so on, that would make the first in each pair a warning and the second quite differently an instruction.

V. K. Robbins (*Jesus the Teacher* 43-45) suggests that 13:1-2 (where Jesus comes out of the temple and announces its destruction) inverts 1:14-15 (where Jesus came into Galilee and announced the coming of God's rule), and that 13:3-4 (where the first four disciples evoke from Jesus a discourse about a future when he will no longer be with them) inverts 1:16-20 (where he summoned these same four to follow him). But differences in diction undermine deliberate inversion (e.g., ἦλθεν versus ἐκπορευομένου for travel, κηρύσσων versus εἶπεν for speaking, etc.); the absence of Jesus does not play so major a role in chap. 13 as following him does in 1:16-20; and in 13:10 world-wide evangelism seems to carry out rather than invert fishing for human beings in 1:17.

J. Gnilka (2. 181) notes that the prediction of destruction for the temple could hardly have stood alone in pre-Marcan tradition. Then he contrasts the lone anonymous disciple in vv 1-2 with the four named disciples in vv 3-4 and concludes that the prediction stood with the lone disciple's exclamation as an apothegm, but apart from the following question of the four and Jesus' long answer. Supposedly, then, Mark transformed εἷς, "someone," into a disciple (cf. 10:17), added "Teacher" to suit the transformation, and inserted vv 1-2 with the help of an introductory genitive absolute, which he created for linkage with the preceding context. Under this reconstruction, however, the question of the four named disciples becomes occasionless or inauthentic (and if inauthentic, the following discourse occasionless); and Jesus still makes his prediction of destruction while he is in or near the temple. Only the contrast between the lone anonymous disciple and the four named disciples poses a stumblingblock to the integrity of the passage. Not much of a stumbling-block, however; for the contrast may be due, not to insertion, but to the lone disciple's falling outside the charmed circle of those four disciples who alone among the Twelve are named by Mark apart from the apostolic list in 3:16-19. For obvious reasons, the exception in Judas Iscariot does not weaken this possibility. (The highly uncertain identification of "James the little" [15:40] with "James the [son] of Alphaeus" [3:18] would provide another exception, but not one evident in Mark's text; for the descriptive phrases differ.) Though εἷς may mean "one" in the sense of τις, "someone" (E. C. Maloney, *Semitic Interference* 126-31), the mention by name of four disciples in the immediate context favors the sense of "a single one."

Disciples take the initiative in speaking to Jesus at 1:30, 37; 6:35; 9:11, 28, 38; 10:10, 35; 11:21; 14:12; so there is no reason to doubt the traditionality or authenticity of vv 1-2 on the ground that in first century Jewish culture a disciple would not have taken the initiative represented by the exclamation over the temple. The address, "Teacher," need not be considered a result of Mark's redaction. It was the natural way for a disciple to address his master, and Mark's interest in Jesus as a teacher may grow out of tradition as easily as it might add to tradition. The argument that a disciple would not have remarked the magnificence of the temple after spending several days around it and making several trips to and from it (so R. Pesch, *Naherwartungen* 85) is untrue to human nature. Even one who resides permanently in magnificent surroundings will often remark their magni-ficence (cf. G. R. Beasley-Murray's personal anecdote [*Commentary on Mark Thirteen* 19-21], the likes of which we can all duplicate many times over). On Herod the Great's beautification of the temple, see Josephus *Ant.* 15.11.3 §§391-402; idem *J.W.* 5.5.1-6 §§184-226; *b. Sukk.* 51b; B. Mazar in *Jerusalem Revealed* 25-40, esp. 25-32; J. F. Strange in *ANRW* II 19/1. 650-54.

T. E. Geddert (*Watchwords* 86) interprets βλέπεις as seeing with discernment and thereby forces himself to take the verb as part of a question whether Jesus' questioner sees through the magnificence of the temple to its present corruption and future destruction. Unfortunately for this view, βλέπω occurred in 4:12 for seeing without discernment (as completely overlooked in the discussion of that passage ibid. 82). This fact also undermines Geddert's interpretations of the verb elsewhere in Mark, especially elsewhere in chap. 13 and most especially in 13:33, which he interprets as "a call to see the kingdom established in the passion of Jesus" even though chap. 13 breathes not a syllable about that topic but deals with the Second Coming instead (see the following notes against the correlation of v 35 with the passion narrative).

Jesus predicts the destruction of the temple in a discourse that comes just before the passion narrative, which also mentions that destruction (14:58; 15:29; cf. 15:38) and in which he is crucified at the instigation of the temple authorities. But for several reasons there is no implication that the destruction will take place in consequence of the Crucifixion: (1) 13:1-2 deals with the whole complex of temple buildings (τὸ ἱερόν), whereas 14:58; 15:29, 39 deal with the sanctuary alone (ὁ ναός); (2) the rest of chap. 13 shows no interest in the destruction of the temple; (3) by representing as false the testimony that Jesus said he would destroy the temple, 14:58 and 15:29 disengage that testimony from the truly reported prediction in 13:1-2 that the temple will be destroyed, but not that Jesus will destroy it; (4) chap. 13 contains nothing about his rebuilding the temple, as do 14:58; 15:29; and (5) 14:59-64 indicates that because of disagreements among the witnesses against Jesus, he was condemned for a completely different statement made only then before the Sanhedrin. In sum, the passages do not correspond closely enough to justify an implication that his crucifixion issues in the destruction of the temple. The further argument that 13:2 uses the passive of καταλύω, "be torn down," but the later verses its active, "tear down" — with Jesus as the subject — overlooks the possibilities that he is the hidden subject in the passive or, better, that his being the stated subject of the active makes false the testimony reported in the later verses.

The difference between ναός, "sanctuary" (14:58), and ἱερόν, "temple," between λίθοι, "stones," and οἰκοδομαί, "buildings" (13:1-2), also undermines the view that Mark has created 13:2c out of 14:58 (against R. Pesch, Naherwartungen 87-93). Elsewhere in Mark, with the exception of Peter's declaration at 14:31, οὐ μή plus an aorist subjunctive for strong negation of the future occurs only on the lips of Jesus, as here, and therefore does not demonstrate redactional creativity. Nor would it even though some occurrences were to be found in editorial seams. M. J. Borg (Conflict 177-80) appeals to Luke 19:44 as well as to the present parallel Luke 21:6 in favor of the authenticity of Mark 13:2 (cf. J. Dupont, Études 440).

R. Pesch (Naherwartungen 95-96) thinks that because Jesus predicts destruction without warning of it, not as in OT prophecies of the destruction of Jerusalem, the prediction has been read onto his lips after and out of the event itself. The parallel with those OT prophecies is not entirely apt, however; for Jesus' prediction does not include a destruction of Jerusalem (contrast, e.g., Jer 7:4, 12, 14, 34; 26:6, 18; Mic 3:12). Even more to the point, he is addressing a disciple. The OT prophets were addressing apostates. A disciple needs only to be told. Apostates need also to be warned, for their repentance may save the day.

The shift in location between vv 2 and 3 does not necessarily indicate originally independent sources or occasions, or fabrication on Mark's part. It is historically realistic to think of stages in one of Jesus' habitual commutes from Jerusalem to Bethany. His sitting opposite the temple implies opposition to it no more than his sitting opposite the treasury implied opposition to the treasury (cf. v 3 with 12:41, both of which use κατέναντι). Nor does the Mount of Olives appear to stand for "the eschatological counter mountain" (W. H. Kelber, Kingdom 112) where God's rule will be established to replace the temple and its mount. In that day Yahweh's feet "will stand" on the Mount of Olives (Zech 14:4), but

Jesus "sits" on it. We have already seen that recent pericopes do not describe a Jesuanic mission against the temple.

The contrast between Jesus' sitting on the Mount of Olives in v 3 and the standing of Yahweh's feet on the same mountain in Zech 14:4 precludes an allusion here to the passage there. The splitting of the mountain in Zech 14:4 further distances the passages from each other. Nor will Jesus' command to flee (Mark 13:14) allude to the flight in Zech 14:5; for he will command a flight into the mountains, but Zechariah spoke of a flight through the valley created by the splitting of Olivet and then onward to the other side of the mountains.

Since a large crowd participated in the Triumphal Procession on the Mount of Olives (11:1-10), this mountain hardly counts in the present passage as a mystic mount of secret revelation. Only in 4:34 does κατ' ἰδίαν, "privately," describe Jesus' teaching. In 9:22 it describes an ascent up a mountain where three disciples see him transfigured, but he does not teach them there. In 7:33 it describes withdrawal from a crowd to perform a miracle, in 6:31, 32 a retreat for rest, and in 9:28; 13:3 the disciples' asking Jesus a question rather than his teaching them.

Mark assumes that his audience will understand Peter, James, John, and Andrew to have been in the larger audience who heard what Jesus said to the unnamed disciple in v 2. When a verb comes first and there follows a compound subject with its first member in the singular, the verb commonly agrees in number with that first member (so, e.g., in 1:36; 1 Tim 1:20; Lev 25:54 LXX; see G. D. Kilpatrick in *NovT* 27 [1985] 382; I. Soisalon-Soininen in *De Septuaginta* 116). Therefore the singular number of ἐπηρώτα, "was asking," does not imply that Mark has added to an originally lone Andrew the names of Peter, James, and John, or to an originally lone Peter the names of James, John, and Andrew. For those who consider earlier references to Peter, James, and John redactional (5:37; 9:2; but see the notes on 5:37), the presence of Andrew in v 3 looks traditional and the other names redactional. Oppositely, E. Lohmeyer (267-68) suggests that the placement of Andrew last, against 1:16-17, betrays an original limitation to the inner circle of Peter, James, and John, to whom Andrew has been redactionally added. These theories are unnecessary. The order of names reflects their order in the apostolic list (3:16-19), because that list is more recent than the account of their call (1:16-20). The absence of Andrew from 5:37; 9:2; 14:33, which also mention only Peter, James, and John, makes it doubtful both that Mark would have added Andrew to a traditional mention of the three and that he would have added the three to a traditional mention of Andrew. If Mark were writing entirely on his own, we should probably be reading a characteristically Marcan reference to "the Twelve" or to "the disciples."

W. Harrington (200) suggests that Jesus' addressing Peter, James, John, and Andrew emphasizes the importance of the discourse, these disciples having followed Jesus longer than the other disciples have followed him. But the ordering of their names according to the apostolic list in 3:16-19 rather than according to the account of their starting to follow him in 1:16-20 casts doubt on the suggestion. It is easier to think that Mark reflects tradition and that the tradition mirrors an event in which these four apostles made inquiry together because of their closeness to each other as two pairs of brothers who had shared the trade of fishing and started following Jesus at the same time.

The statement, "What I say to you I say to all" (v 37a), shows that the limitation of the eschatological address to four disciples has nothing to do with a motif of secrecy. Nor do they take the initiative in asking their question, for their question arises out of what Jesus has just predicted. OT predictions of the destruction of the temple do not usually entail the end of history. Dan 9:24-27 makes the only exception. We would err, then, to say that the disciples could not think of the destruction except in connection with the end of history.

K. Grayston (in *BJRL* 56 [1974] 374) claims that elsewhere Mark uses ταῦτα, "these things," as a true plural, not as a collective. But though ταῦτα may refer to different things (usually of the same sort, however, as for example in 7:23 [various vices]; 10:20 [various commandments]; 11:28 [various actions in cleansing the temple]; 13:8 [various disasters]), it also refers to different instances of the very same thing (as in 2:8 [identical reasoning on the part of various scribes]; 8:7 [a few small fish]). So no problem attaches to interpreting ταῦτα as solely a reference to the destructions of buildings and the tear-downs of stones in the temple complex (see the foregoing comments on v 4 and cf. the alternative suggestion of G. R. Beasley-Murray [*Commentary on Mark Thirteen* 27] that the plural implies a series of events in which destruction forms the climax).

The listing of four disciples by name in v 3 probably triggers in v 5 the distinguishing of Jesus with an adversative δέ, "but," and a remention of his name (cf. v 2). Thus the remention need not signal the introduction of fresh tradition. The pleonastic use of ἤρξατο, "began," may add some weight to the distinguishing of Jesus from the four (see the notes on 1:45), but it overinterprets δέ to say that Mark uses it because Jesus does not answer the disciples' question directly (rather, at all) and that therefore δέ links up with the length of the following monologue to give ἤρξατο more than auxiliary force (so J. Lambrecht, *Redaktion* 92-93). Δέ often appears in the introduction to a perfectly straightforward answer (examples could be multiplied indefinitely, but for a sampling in the present neighborhood see 10:4, 37, 39a, 51b; 11:6; 12:16c; 14:62, 64, 68, 70, 71), and δέ occurs very often to indicate a simple shift in speakers (10:1-9, 17-22, 23-27 et passim).

On βλέπετε, "watch out," in vv 5b, 9, 23, 33, see the notes covering 12:38. L. Gaston (*No Stone on Another* 14, 52-53) accepts the v.l. γάρ, "for," in vv 6a, 7b, 9b. Though he argues that the other synoptists read this conjunction in Mark, it reads so smoothly and logically that no scribe is liable to have omitted it. The jarring effect of asyndeton might well have led Matthew and Luke to insert it, moreover (Luke perhaps under subsidiary influence from Matthew). In Mark, then, the v.l. arises by parallelistic influence from the other synoptics and perhaps also from textually unassailable occurrences of γάρ in the surrounding context (vv 8, 11, 19, 22, 33, 35).

The deceivers, disasters, and persecutions of vv 5b-13 look like signs that signal the end in Jewish eschatology. Not so here: "but the end is not yet. . . . These things [are the] *beginning* of birthpangs. . . . And among all the nations the good news must first be preached" (vv 7, 8, 10). But it is gratuitous to deny that Jesus could have transferred these events out of the realm of eschatological signs. Though the NT shows accommodation to the delay of the end, the remarkable lack of soul-searching over its delay is better explained by attributing the transferral to Jesus than by attributing it to the early church. A churchly accomplishment of the transfer would probably have arisen out of such soul-searching, which in turn would probably have left stronger traces in the NT.

To say that according to v 8d the end will already be starting with the predicted disasters disregards the opposite thrust in the preceding verse: "but the end is not yet" (cf. vv 10, 14, too). Rather, these disasters will be a beginning that does *not* signal the end. Much worse will be the disasters that do signal it (vv 14-23). Mark and his audience may well have related recent and current wars, earthquakes, and famines to Jesus' predictions; but those events need not have prompted the predictions. OT and Jewish eschatology provides a more likely source (J. Schmid 235).

"On [the basis of] my name" does not differ in meaning from "in my name" (see 9:37, 38, 39, 41). The opinion that Mark adds "on [the basis of] my name" to "I am," or vice versa, neglects that by itself neither phrase gives enough information to make very much sense. Apart from "on [the basis of] my name," "I am" does not tell who the deceivers will claim to be. Apart from "I am," "on [the basis of] my name" does not tell the use to which the deceivers will put the name. Will they use it in a claim to act *on behalf of* the

Christ or to act *as* the Christ? But together, the phrases tell in favor of the latter possibility. Far from competing with each other, then, the phrases complement each other and prepare for the reference in vv 21-22 to "false christs." That reference will confirm the understanding of v 6 that we have reached.

L. Gaston (*No Stone on Another* 14) sees in v 6 a confusion of false prophets who will come on the basis of Christ's name to represent him, and false christs who will say, "I am," claiming to *be* Christ. But a false prophet would probably *speak* on the basis of Christ's name (Matt 7:22; Deut 18:18-20; Jer 14:14-15 et passim), whereas a false Christ would probably *come* on the basis of Christ's name, as here (see esp. Matt 24:5, but also Mark 11:9 parr.; Matt 23:39 par. Luke 13:35). T. J. Weeden (*Traditions in Conflict* 77-81) goes considerably beyond the text in imagining that pneumatic excitement causes the deceivers in vv 6, 21-22 to burst out in a plenipotential "I am [the Christ]," but he correctly rejects an identification of the deceivers with Jewish messianic pretenders. Elsewhere, "on [the basis of] my name" (ἐπὶ τῷ ὀνόματί μου) always modifies actions of people on Jesus' side (a point overlooked by J. Gibson in *JSNT* 38 [1990] 48-49). Therefore the deceivers must arise within the Christian community. They can hardly be false christs who will arise in the non-Christian sector of the Jewish community. It is no argument for non-Christian claimants that they will deceive "many" rather than "many *of you*" (so ibid.); for since the warning to beware implies that disciples might be deceived, the many who will be deceived may come from their ranks (cf. v 37: "but what I say to you [four disciples] I say to all [my disciples]").

Furthermore, in neither the Christian community nor the non-Christian sector of the Jewish community do we hear of messianic claimants between Jesus' time and Mark's. Certain leaders of the Jewish revolt against Rome (66-73 C.E.) did act like kings according to Josephus *J.W.* 2.17.8-9 §§433-48; 4.9.3-8 §§503-44. But not only does their belonging to the unbelieving Jewish community disqualify them from being the referents of vv 6, 21-22. Also, Josephus nowhere calls those leaders christs or writes that they claimed to be the Christ, as in v 6, or had false prophets heralding them as the Christ and performing signs and wonders to support such heraldry, as in vv 21-22. To be sure, false prophets promised miraculous signs and divine deliverance; pretension to kingship might equate with pretension to Christhood; and Josephus *J.W.* 6.6.4 §§312-13 says that the Jewish war was prompted mostly by a sacred written oracle of the Jews, apparently a messianic prophecy, according to which someone from their country should at about that time rule the world. It is uncertain, however, whether this oracle was referred to a future messianic king or was applied to the pretenders to kingship either by the pretenders themselves or by their followers. Pretension to kingship does not have to entail pretension to Christhood. And though false prophets promised miraculous deliverance by God, their notorious and disastrous failure to make good on those promises stands in sharp contrast with the actuality of the signs and wonders predicted by Jesus (Josephus *J.W.* 2.13.4-5 §§258-63; 6.5.2 §§285-87; idem *Ant.* 20.8.6, 10 §§167-72, 188; cf. idem *J.W.* 7.11.1 §§437-41). A Christian writer would have delighted in the failure rather than attributing actual signs and wonders to prophets considered false at least by Christians and known by everyone to have failed. One might think that to spare the Jewish nation in Roman eyes, Josephus suppresses the messianic claims of the pretenders. But he does not suppress their treasonable, kingly actions or a good deal else that his Roman audience would find reprehensible. He even describes Menahem "as indeed a king" (οἷα δὴ βασιλεύς) and says that Menahem was wearing royal robes at the time of his murder (*J.W.* 2.17.8-9 §§434-48). Since messianic claims would offend Romans only insofar as those claims entail royal claims competitive with Caesar's (cf. Luke 23:1-4, 13-16; John 18:28–19:16), Josephus's failure to suppress the royal claims leaves the absence of messianic claims unexplained. One may then resort to supposing that he does not believe in the coming of the Christ and for this reason suppresses messianic claims by leaders of the Jewish revolt. But he does not believe in their kingship, either; yet he does not suppress their royal claims. Quite possibly, then, messianic claims are missing because those leaders made none; nor may their followers have accorded them messianic status. The same things can be said about bandits (whether or not we call them Zealots) who led lesser Jewish uprisings prior to Jesus' ministry (Acts 5:36-37; Josephus *J.W.* 2.4.1-3 §§56-65; idem *Ant.* 17.10.5-8 §§271-85; Tac. *Hist.* 5.9). But these bandits are irrelevant, anyway; for neither could Jesus be referring in a prediction to historical figures who preceded him nor would anyone putting a supposed prediction on his lips make him do so (against R. A. Horsley and J. S. Hanson, *Bandits* 88-134). The hybrid view of E. Haenchen (438-40) that recent and present Jewish leaders who have turned out to be false are prompting fear and expectation that similarly false leaders will arise in the church suffers again from lack of firm evidence that the Jewish leaders claimed Christhood or were proclaimed to be the Christ.

The failure of the rest of the NT to refer to false christs leaves without foundation the view that vv 5b-6 arose by redactional imitation of vv 21-22 for the purpose of applying future deception in the final tribulation to recent and present deception in church life (see the notes on vv 21-22 for criticism of the reverse hypothesis, which makes vv 5b-6 generative of vv 21-22). More particularly and with the barely possible exception of Simon Magus (Acts 8:8-24; Justin *1 Apol.* 26.1-3; Iren. *Haer.* 1.23.1), we have no evidence that between Jesus and Mark anyone, let alone "many," arose in the church to claim christhood. The thought seems to be that many imposters will take advantage of Jesus' absence, the original disciples' forgetfulness, and new disciples' never having known Jesus (cf. E. Lohmeyer 278).

See R. H. Gundry, *Use of the OT* 46-56; L. Hartman, *Prophecy Interpreted* passim; R. T. France, *Jesus and the OT* 254-57, on probable and possible borrowing from Dan 11:44 in Mark 13:7, from Dan 2:28 in Mark 13:7 (cf. Rev 1:1), from Isa 19:2; 2 Chr 15:6 in Mark 13:8, from Dan 12:12-13 in Mark 13:13, from Dan 9:27; 11:31; 12:11 in Mark 13:14, from Dan 12:10 in Mark 13:14, from Exod 9:18; 10:14; 11:6; Joel 2:2; Dan 12:1 in Mark 13:19 (cf. Exod 9:24; 10:6; Deut 4:32; Jer 30:7; Joel 2:2; Rev 7:14; 16:18; 1 Macc 9:27; 1QM 1:9-14; *Jub.* 16:8; *As. Mos.* 8:1; Josephus *J.W.* Proem 1, 4 §§1, 12; 5.10.5 §442; 6.9.4 §429; Pl. *Resp.* 6 492E), from Deut 13:2-4(1-3) in Mark 13:22, from Isa 13:10; 34:4 in Mark 13:24, from Dan 7:13; Zech 12:10 in Mark 13:26, from Deut 13:8(7); 30:4; Isa 27:13; Jer 12:12; Zech 2:10(6) in Mark 13:27, and from Dan 12:7 in Mark 13:30. To that list add Dan 2:45; 9:26 for the wars mentioned in Mark 13:7; and Jer 50:41–51:6(27:41–28:6 LXX) for some of the significant diction in Mark 13:7-8, 14-20 (detailed in J. Lambrecht, *Redaktion* 108). Textual affinities with the MT, LXX, Theod, OT Pesh, and Targums are very mixed. On the question whether use of the LXX betrays redaction or inauthenticity, see p. 22. As noted in the comments, Mark 13:13 grows out of Mic 7:7. An allusion to Dan 12:1, 12-13 MT or Theod (see R. H. Gundry, *Use of the OT* 47) is to be doubted; for that passage deals with survival (so also 2 Esdr 6:25; 7:27), whereas Mark 13:13 deals with martyrdom. The thought of Hab 2:3 also differs. See Lambrecht, op. cit. 138-40. Because elsewhere in chap. 13 allusions concentrate on Dan 7:13; 11:40–12:13, Lambrecht (op. cit. 105) casts some doubt on the allusion to Dan 2:28 in Mark 13:7. But we do not reject the allusion to Dan 7:13 because other allusions to its immediate context are lacking (so also concerning the allusions to Dan 2:45; 9:26, 27; and scattered OT passages outside Daniel).

In vv 7, 10 necessity does not mean certainty of occurrence due to prophecy, whether scriptural or oral. Scripture is not cited, and necessity forms part of the oral prophecy rather than growing out of it. Necessity means certainty of occurrence due to inclusion in God's plan. It does not matter whether God is pleased or displeased with what will happen. Presumably the necessary wars of v 7 will displease God, and the necessary preaching in v 10 will please God.

With ἀκοὰς πολέμων, "reports of battles," cf. ταῖς τοῦ πολέμου φήμαις, "the news of battles," in Josephus *J.W.* 2.10.1 §187. Hearing about battles does not reflect the spatial distance of Mark's audience from the Jewish revolt that began in 66 C.E. and took place in Palestine (so J. Gnilka 2. 187); for the addressees hear the noise of battles directly as well as hearing reports of battles (see the foregoing comments). Hearing battles requires that they be within earshot just as hearing reports requires that the reports be within earshot, and reports of battles would be unnecessary if those battles were within earshot. Therefore the wordplay between ἀκούσητε and ἀκοάς does not destroy the distinction between hearing the noise of battles and hearing reports of battles (as thought by J. Lambrecht, *Redaktion* 105). 1 Kgdms 2:24 LXX; Dan 11:44 LXX Theod imply too much distance for direct hearing. Chronology does not enter the picture, as though heard battles are going on and reported battles are only in the offing.

Both the distinction between battles close enough to hear and those too distant to hear and the command not to be alarmed show that v 7 does not warn against putting hope in a Jewish messianic rebellion against Rome (against W. Grundmann [7. Aufl.] 353-54). You are not alarmed at what you have put your hope in. Nations' rising against each other makes a reason for alarm, not for keeping calm. Likewise, nations' rising against each other constitutes the occurrence of battles rather than providing a reason for their occurrence. In v 8, therefore, γάρ makes nations' rising against each other the reason why the end is not yet: battles will delay the end. For the idea of an appointed end, see Dan 8:19; 11:27, 35; 12:4, 9, 12-13; Hab 2:3; 2 Esdr 6:25; 9:1-6; *2 Apoc. Bar.* 83:1-23.

The mention of earthquakes between international warfare and famines keeps famines from being taken as the natural result of war; and κατὰ τόπους, "from place to place," describes the earthquakes in a way that disfavors the rumbling of the earth under the feet of marching armies and their chariot wheels (as in the Septuagintal use of σεισμός at Jer 10:22; 29:3[47:3 MT]; Nah 3:2). So both the earthquakes and the famines are acts of God. On the frightfulness of earthquakes, see Sen. *QNat.* 6.

For birthpangs as a metaphor of painful events and for a period of such events preceding the messianic kingdom, see Isa 13:8; 26:17-18; 66:7-9; Jer 4:31; 6:24; 13:21; 22:23; 49:22; 50:43; Hos 13:13; Mic 4:9-10; John 16:20-22; 1 Thess 5:3; 2 Thess 2:1-12; Revelation 4–19; 1QH 3; 1QM; *1 Enoch* 99:1–100:6; *Sib. Or.* 2:153-73; 3:538, 635-51; *Jub.* 23:11-25; 2 Esdr 4:51–5:13; 6:17-24; 13:29-32; 15:1–16:78; *2 Apoc. Bar.* 27:1-15; 48:31-41; 70:1-10; *Apoc. Ezra* 3:11-15; *b. Sanh.* 97a, 98ab; *b. Šabb.* 118a; *b. Ketub.* 111a; *Gen. Rab.* 42.4; and other rabbinic literature cited in Str-B 4/2. 977-86. D. C. Allison, Jr. (*End* 5-25), discusses differences of opinion among the Jews as to whether there is to be a period of such events, and if so, when it starts, how long it lasts, and who suffers during it (cf. E. P. Sanders, *Jesus and Judaism* 124). Jesus' addition of "beginning" divides this period.

Still in v 8, "these things" do not include the coming of deceivers (vv 5b-6); for their coming will not bring pain like birthpangs, and in v 7 an adversative δέ, "but," began a new prediction of events that *will* bring such pain. Nothing in the immediate context suggests the birth of a new age. Even the later description of the Son of man's coming (vv 24-27) stops short of mentioning a new age. Nor do birthpangs signal the end of the disciples' disgrace, as giving birth ends the disgrace of a childless woman (so A. Schlatter, *Matthäus* 699); for Jesus has yet to predict persecution, and another adversative δέ (v 9) will mark the shift to persecution as a new prediction different from that of birthpangs.

The plural in "birthpangs" disagrees with the singular in "the travail of the Messiah," used by rabbis for the disasters out of which the messianic age will be born (Str-B 1. 950). Moreover, Jesus speaks about "the beginning" of birthpangs, does not describe them as "of the Messiah," and (as just noted) does not speak about the consequent birth of a messianic age (cf. G. R. Beasley-Murray, *Commentary on Mark Thirteen* 37). Jesus either revises rabbinic usage, disregards it, or does not know it. Or it had yet to appear.

Against the view that in the end Mark rejects the disciples by making them represent false messianism, a Christology of glory rather than of suffering, vv 9-13 promise as well as demand a positive role for them during the period of the church. Many think that since vv 9-13 occur in different contexts at Matt 10:17-22; Luke 12:11-12, Mark has put these verses in their present context. More probably, Matthew has transferred them from their Marcan context (the earliest we know of and quite possibly the original and historical context) to make the Galilean mission of the Twelve preview the present mission of the church (cf. R. H. Gundry, *Matthew* 180-81, 191-93, 203). Nor does Luke 12:11-12 seem to rest in an original context (see the commentaries ad loc.). Minor agreements between Matt 10:19 and Luke 12:11 (in the omission of προ-, "beforehand," and in πῶς ἤ, "how or") are best explained by secondary influence of Matthew on Luke; for the omission of προ- suits Matt 6:31, 34 but not the parallels Luke 12:29, 32, and Matthew likes πῶς and ἤ (ibid. 192, 644 s.v. ἤ, 647 s.v. πῶς; Gundry in *The Four Gospels 1992*).

Some have doubted the integrity of the sayings in vv 9-13 and suggested that Mark binds them together because of the catchword παραδίδωμι, "give over" (vv 9, 11, 12, the occurrence in v 11 possibly being an addition of his). The parallel in Matt 10:17-22 does not support this doubt and suggestion, however; for that passage incorporates the whole of Mark 13:9-13, including each occurrence of παραδίδωμι. The parallel in Matt 24:9-14 lacks most of Mark 13:9-13 because of the transfer to Matt 10:17-22. The fragmentariness of the parallel in Luke 12:11-12 might support the disintegrity of Mark 13:9-13; but there Luke substitutes for παραδίδωμι a favorite of his: εἰσφέρω, "bring in" (see the concordance s.v.). His context differs also from that of Matt 10:17-22. It is easy to see that Luke has gathered together disparate materials in his chap. 12. He has a contextually redactional reason to split off that part of a larger whole which can be made to contrast with the immediately preceding word against the Son of man and blasphemy against the Holy Spirit (Luke 12:10).

There is a certain parallelism *within* each of the verses 9, 11a, and 12, i.e. between "you will be beaten" and "you will stand" (v 9), between "what you should say" and "say this" (v 11a), and between "will give over," "will rise up against," and "will cause to be killed" (v 12). But there is no parallelism *between* these verses; so we have no good reason to say that vv 10, 11b, 13 disturb a poetic structure which characterized them in a pre-Marcan source. Nor did vv 5b-8 display a parallelism that would support an underlying poetic structure here (against E. Lohmeyer 269-70).

In v 9 the omission of βλέπετε δὲ ὑμεῖς ἑαυτούς by D W Θ f¹ 28 565 700 it sy^s is probably due to scribal difficulty with ἑαυτούς as an object of βλέπετε, "But you — watch yourselves!" Jesus does not mean that his disciples should observe themselves spectatorially, however. He means that they should observe themselves precautiously.

"Give over" (παραδίδωμι) runs like a red thread from the imprisonment of John the Baptizer (1:14) through the betrayal, arrest, trial, and crucifixion of Jesus (3:19; 9:31; 10:33 [bis]; 14:10, 11, 18, 21, 41, 42, 44; 15:1, 10, 15) to the persecution of the disciples (13:9, 11, 12; cf. the further connections drawn by R. H. Lightfoot [*Gospel Message* 51-55] between chap. 13 and the Passion, connections that tend away from treating chap. 13 as an originally shorter, independent apocalypse, for some of them belong to the warp and woof of the chapter). On the other hand, chap. 13 contains no references or allusions to the Passion.

In vv 9-10 J. Lambrecht (*Redaktion* 126) detects chiasm: (a) "on account of me," (b) "for a witness," (c) "to them," (c') "and to all the nations," (b') "first must be preached," (a') "the good news" (so the Greek word order). But the supposedly corresponding elements do not match up grammatically. Rather, a prepositional phrase stands against the subject of an infinitive, another prepositional phrase against a verbal phrase, and an indirect object against a prepositional phrase (in which we will see, moreover, that the preposition probably does not carry the same meaning as an indirect object — rather, "*among* all the nations").

"People [an indefinite 'they'] will give you over *to* tribunals" makes better sense than "people will give you over *in* tribunals." But "*in* synagogues you will be beaten" makes better sense than "*into* synagogues you will be beaten." Thus, construing the phrase about synagogues with beating would force a shift in the meaning of εἰς. Furthermore, by this construal a meaningless emphasis, demanded by forward position, would fall on synagogues as the place of beatings (contrast the meaning*ful* emphasis in the forward positions of kings and governors and, in v 10, of all the nations). Therefore we should construe καὶ εἰς συναγωγάς with the foregoing: "and people will give you over to tribunals and to synagogues." This construal suits Mark's penchant for duality (cf. the doubling of εἰς-phrases in 1:39) and use of εἰς-phrases elsewhere for impersonal indirect objects of παραδίδωμι (9:31; 14:41 — "is being given over to the *hands* of men/sinners"; 13:12 — "will give over to *death*" [with a telic or ecbatic nuance]) over against his use of a simple dative for personal indirect objects (10:33 — ". . . to the *chief priests* [et al.] . . . to the *Gentiles*"; 14:10 — "to *them* [the chief priests]"; 15:1 — "to *Pilate*"). The construal also avoids an immediate shift in the meaning of εἰς and produces an asyndetic introduction to "you will be beaten." This introduction then parallels the asyndetic introduction of "people will give you over." Luke 21:12 also construes synagogues with giving over. Matt 10:17 construes them with beating, but changes εἰς to ἐν to avoid an immediate shift in the meaning of εἰς and adds "their" to "synagogues" for a characteristically antisynagogical emphasis suitable to the forward position of "in their synagogues" under his construal.

R. Pesch (2. 284) follows C. H. Turner (in *JTS* os 26 [1924-25] 19) in construing "and in tribunals and in synagogues" with "you will be beaten." This construal produces an attractive parallel with "and before governors and kings you will stand . . ." and saves "you will be beaten" from the orphanage of not having a prepositional phrase attached to it. But now "they will give you over" suffers the same orphanage in disagreement with the construal of εἰς-phrases meaning "to . . . ," not "in . . . ," with παραδίδωμι, "give over," in 9:31; 13:12; 14:41. And in 13:11 the use of "lead" in connection with the giving over of the disciples favors that 13:9 refers to people's giving them over to tribunals and synagogues by leading them there.

Construing the tribunals with the giving over and the synagogues with the beating would provide the giving over and the beating with a prepositional phrase each. It would also produce a chiastic order of (a) predicate, (b) prepositional phrase, (b′) prepositional phrase, and (a′) predicate. The aforementioned shift in the meaning of εἰς stands in the way, however. The Semitic practice of repeating a preposition before every noun in a series which it governs (M. Black, *Aramaic Approach* 114-15) also argues against breaking apart the present εἰς-phrases. When coupled with tribunals, synagogues make better sense as places to which people will give over the disciples than as places in which they will be beaten. And the chiastic destruction of the asyndetic introduction of "you will be beaten" disagrees with the asyndetic character of this passage at several other points. For a description of the disciplinary beating imposed by Jewish tribunals and synagogues and for references to primary literature, beginning with Deut 25:1-3; 2 Cor 11:24, see C. Schneider in *TDNT* 4. 516, 518-19; D. R. A. Hare, *Theme* 43-46.

The phraseology of v 9 does not correspond closely enough to that of Mic 3:2-3, 9 LXX to justify a double meaning of δαρήσεσθε, "you will be flayed" as well as "you will be beaten" (against F. W. Danker in *NovT* 10 [1968] 162-63). In Mic 1:1-7 it is none less than the Lord God who bears witness to the whole earth against Samaria and Jerusalem; and the Lord God does so in the land, not out among the nations, and by bringing judgment more than by speaking (in both respects, contrast Mark 13:9). In Mic 3:8 the prophet is filled with the Spirit of Yahweh to expose the sin of Israel, but Micah is not on trial as the disciples are on trial in Mark 13:11. Consequently, parallels are unlikely. Likewise, in Mic 2:2 it is a man (גבר) whose house is wrongfully seized, but in Mark 12:40 it was widows whose houses the scribes devoured; so no parallel existed there that could support similar parallels between Micah and Mark 13:9, 11.

At 1:44 and 6:11 the witness consisted in the offering of sacrifices and a symbolic gesture, respectively. In 13:9, however, standing fails to make very obvious sense as a witness. Therefore the speaking of whatever the Holy Spirit gives you during your hour in court (v 11) defines the witness in v 9 as spoken (cf. BAGD s.v. μαρτύριον 1). But are the addressees of this spoken witness supposed to benefit or suffer from it? Both purposes appear in earlier, similar passages. At 1:44 εἰς μαρτύριον αὐτοῖς meant "for a witness *to* them." At 6:11 it meant "for a witness *against* them." Here in 13:9 the immediately following reference to preaching the good news among all the nations (v 10) favors that the Holy Spirit will prompt the disciples to speak an evangelistic witness to Gentile governors and kings rather than an accusatory witness against Jewish persecutors or against the Gentile governors and kings themselves. Even apart from preaching the good news among all the nations, bearing an accusatory witness against Jewish persecutors would make poor sense. For the disciples' complaining to Gentile governors and kings about persecution from unbelieving Jews would have no eschatological significance, and there is not the slightest hint that the Gentile governors and kings would rectify injustices perpetrated on the disciples by Jewish persecutors. Moreover, standing before those governors and kings is for Jesus' sake and does nothing to release the church for a mission to the Gentiles (against R. P. Martin, *Mark* 223); for rejection by Jews suffices for such a release (see esp. Matt 21:42-43; Acts 28:17-31). Bearing an accusatory witness against the Gentile governors and kings themselves would make even poorer sense, for they would not have heard the good news before and therefore would not yet have had opportunity to reject it and persecute its preachers.

One may combine the evangelistic and accusatory interpretations by saying that if the governors and kings reject the witness borne to them before the end, it will turn into a witness against them at the last judgment. But at the last judgment the disciples will not be standing before governors and kings. Governors and kings will be standing before the Lord, and the text says nothing about such a shift. The failure of attempts to make αὐτοῖς mean "against them" deflates the view that preaching the good news in v 10 grows out of a mistakenly evangelistic understanding of the witness in v 9 (cf. the comments and notes on 1:44; 6:11).

Concerning the authenticity of "on account of me" (v 9), see the notes on 8:35; 10:29; and concerning the authenticity of preaching the good news among all the Gentiles (v 10), see the notes and comments on 1:14-15; 8:35; 10:29; and, esp. concerning the use and authenticity of the noun εὐαγγέλιον, "good news," the notes on 14:9 and R. H. Gundry *Matthew* 480-81, 596. In the first instance, the good news will feature the arrival of God's rule (1:14-15). But insofar as Jesus has predicted his death and resurrection (8:31; 9:9, 12, 31; 10:33-34) and coming in glory (8:38; cf. 13:24-27; 14:62) and has interpreted his death as a ransom for many (10:45; cf. 14:22-25), the good news of God's rule now incorporates those elements, too (cf. 1:1: "the good news of [in the sense of 'concerning'] Jesus Christ"). By now Jesus has preached and taught so much that as a term "the good news" is understandable without further qualification.

If Jesus foresaw his rejection at the hands of the Jewish authorities ensconced in the temple at Jerusalem (so the passion predictions and the Words of Institution), it puts no strain on credibility to say that he replaced the OT prophetic expectation of all the nations' streaming to the temple there (cf. esp. Isa 2:2-4; Mic 4:1-5) with a mission that would take the messianic salvation to all the nations (cf. his condemnation of the Jewish nation, esp. their leaders, and his allusions to the salvation of Gentiles — Mark 11:15-17; 12:1-9 parr.; Luke 10:12-15 par.; 11:31-32 par.; 13:28-29 par.). Premonition of his death and resurrection would naturally make him leave this mission to the disciples. That he did anticipate a period of international evangelism following his death and resurrection would solve the problem that he portrays God's rule as eschatological yet gives ethical teaching often unmotivated by an imminent end and, indeed, often assuming a continuation of present conditions. It is hard to deny the authenticity of either side of his teaching: that among disciples God's rule has taken effect, and that it has not yet taken effect in the world at large.

The early church did not disagree among themselves over the evangelism of Gentiles, but only over the status of believing Gentiles and relations between them and Jews in the church. Therefore the disagreement does not subvert the authenticity of Jesus' reference to the evangelism of Gentiles. S. G. Wilson (*Gentiles* 27-28) counters this argument by citing three factors: (1) a considerable lapse of time between Jesus' resurrection and the start of the Gentile mission; (2) a carrying out of that mission almost entirely by Hellenistic preachers, such as Paul and Barnabas, not by the original disciples who were supposed to have heard Jesus' words; and (3) the possibility that the questionable status of Gentile converts rested on a more fundamental conviction that Gentiles will not participate in salvation till the consummation. Even Judaism did not make Gentiles wait till the consummation, however, but welcomed them as proselytes in the present age; and Philip and Peter started very quickly to evangelize Gentiles (Acts 8:26-40; 10:1-40). The concentration in Acts on the Gentile mission of Paul and Barnabas does not imply that the original disciples were not similarly engaged.

To be sure, we read about a division of labor whereby Paul and Barnabas were to go to the Gentiles, and James, Cephas (Peter), and John to the Jews (Gal 2:9). But the agreement of these three pillars shows their support of the Gentile mission (see also Acts 15:6-21), as does also Cephas's eating with Gentile converts in the church at Antioch. Only later did he withdraw from table fellowship with them (Gal 2:11-14) — a progression exactly opposite from initial resistance to Gentile evangelism, followed by acceptance of it (cf. the redactional and therefore late origin of Matt 10:5b, 23; 15:24 — R. H. Gundry, *Matthew* 183-85, 194-95, 312-13; against the view that Mark 13:10 corrects pre-Matt 10:5b, 23 [so H. Schürmann in *BZ* nf 3 (1959) 87; J. Lambrecht in *Bib* 47 (1966) 336-37]). Even the division of labor seems to have broken down, for Peter addresses 1 Peter to Gentiles scattered about Asia Minor (1 Pet 1:1, 14, 18; 2:9-10; 4:3). This point carries weight even under the supposition that 1 Peter derives from a Petrine school rather than from Peter himself. And apart from the possibility of preaching only to Jews in synagogues, churches, and other gatherings — an unlikely possibility, because large numbers of Gentile proselytes and God-fearers attended synagogue and because Gentiles and Jews intermingled in churches and other gatherings — 1 Cor 9:5-6 implies that "the remaining apostles [besides Paul] and the brothers of the Lord and Cephas" went around on a mission similar to that of Paul and Barnabas. Even the Judaizers wanted to win Gentiles (see esp. Gal 6:13). We may also consider it a historical possibility, though a much disputed one, that the Apostle Thomas evangelized Southern India (K. S. Latourette, *History of the Expansion of Christianity* 1. 107-8). In retrospect, the absence of debate over the Gentile mission as such and the limitation of debate to the status of Gentiles in the church and to relations between them and Jewish believers positively supports the Jesuanic origin of that mission, for otherwise the debate would probably have started with the question of evangelizing Gentiles versus waiting for them to stream in at the consummation. That the good news had been preached among all nations by the time Mark wrote, i.e. within a generation (see the NT epistolary references cited in the comments on v 10), overturns the argument that expecting the end in one's own generation contradicts a mission among all the nations and therefore rules out its Jesuanic origin. Of course, "among all the nations" and similar phraseology in the NT epistles must be understood in terms of the Roman Empire, as would go without saying in the settings of Jesus and Mark.

Whether authentic or not, does v 10 break into the passage by way of insertion? In favor of this possibility it is argued that v 11 carries on from v 9b: "they will give you over . . . , and whenever they lead you, giving [you] over, . . ." But the preaching of the good news in v 10 carries on from v 9b just as well; for this preaching gives the reason why the disciples will be hauled to court. Why else, if not for evangelistic activity, will they stand before governors and kings (see H. Ridderbos, *Coming* 485-86)? That is to say, preaching among all the nations follows very naturally on bearing witness to the governors and kings who rule those nations. "And whenever people lead you, giving [you] over" then circles back to people's giving the disciples over to Jewish tribunals and synagogues and to the disciples' being beaten and standing before governors and kings. One might say that this introductory clause of v 11 was added because of the insertion of v 10. But then we would have expected only a repetition of giving over. The addition of leading and its superordination to giving over favor an expansion of the initial thought following a similar expansion of the scope of witness to include evangelization among all the nations.

Heavy redaction by Matthew (see R. H. Gundry, *Matthew* 191-94, 478-80) vitiates the argument that Matt 24:14 represents the original position of the saying in Mark 13:10, which Mark has shifted to amplify the meaning of "on account of me" (13:9; so R. P. Martin, *Mark* 223). Both conceptually and positionally, moreover, gospel-preaching in v 10 relates to "for a witness to them" better than to "on account of me." The saying in v 10 may drop out after Luke 21:13 because Luke considers his expansion in v 13 an adequate substitute, because he plans to put the saying in a climactic position at 24:47-48, because as elsewhere in his first volume he wants to avoid the noun "gospel," and because he thinks of the period before the siege of Jerusalem and does not consider the nations evangelized as yet. In other words, he need not know an earlier version of the Olivet Discourse lacking Mark 13:10. One might also say that Mark added "for a witness to them" to the end of v 9 as well as inserted v 10. But the occurrence of the same phrase in 1:44; 6:11 suggests a characteristically Jesuanic locution, or at least a traditional one. There is no reason why Jesus could not have seen in persecution a means of furthering the gospel. Μαρτύριον denotes the contentual message of a witness, not the activity of bearing witness.

Taking a cue from W Θ *pc*, the ancient versions, and Matt 10:18, G. D. Kilpatrick (in *JTS* ns 9 [1958] 81-86 and in *Studies in the Gospels* 145-58) attaches καὶ εἰς πάντα τὰ ἔθνη to the foregoing: "you will stand on account of me for the purpose of a witness to them and among all the nations." But this construal creates an extremely awkward shift from a telic εἰς with μαρτύριον, "for [the purpose of] a witness," to a locative εἰς with πάντα τὰ ἔθνη, "among all the nations," and a similarly awkward parallel between the dative pronoun αὐτοῖς, "to them," and the prepositional phrase εἰς πάντα τὰ ἔθνη. The last position of this same prepositional phrase in 1:44; 6:11 disfavors putting it next to last, as in Kilpatrick's construal (against it, see also A. Farrer in *JTS* ns 7 [1956] 75-79; C. F. D. Moule in *JTS* ns 7 [1956] 281; R. P. Martin, *Mark* 223-24; I. F. Church, *Study* 149-51; C. E. B. Cranfield 398-99; J. Lambrecht, *Redaktion* 133-35). As noted by Cranfield, the use of "preach" elsewhere in Mark for human preaching undermines a reference here to an apocalyptic proclamation from heaven, as in Rev 14:6-7. Nor does the present passage introduce an angel to make proclamation, as does Rev 14:6-7. At best, then, it is gratuitous to suppose that alone or originally the saying in Mark 13:10 referred to an apocalyptic proclamation from heaven (see also the notes on 14:9).

The closed setting of governors' and kings' courts makes "witness" (μαρτύριον) appropriate. Likewise, the expansion "among all the nations" makes appropriate a shift to public proclamation (κηρυχθῆναι, "to be preached"). "All the nations" does not define "to them"; for "to them" refers back to "governors and kings," and "all the nations" far outruns "governors and kings" in meaning. "All the nations" may include the Jews, but it empha- sizes the Gentiles (cf. 11:17; Z. Kato, *Völkermission* 149-50). The causal use of the paratactic καί at the start of v 10 (". . . for a witness to them, *because* the good news must first be preached among all the nations") is typically Semitic (though not necessarily so — see M. Reiser, *Syntax und Stil* 126-28).

According to R. Kühschelm (*Jüngerverfolgung* 168-70), "first" implies a long period of evangelization and therefore favors the translation "to all the nations" instead of "among all the nations," which would allow a short period. Yet "first" denotes order, not duration; and if the disciples will already be among all the nations, a witness to those nations would take no more time for travel.

Since κηρύσσω, "preach," elsewhere takes a dative of indirect object (Luke 4:18; Acts 8:5; 10:42; 1 Cor 9:27; 1 Pet 3:19), we should take εἰς πάντα τὰ ἔθνη locatively: "among all the nations," not "to all the nations" (cf. the locative ἐν in the parallel Matt 24:14 and the use of εἰς for ἐν with κηρύσσω in Luke 4:44). Because of ὅπου ἐάν, "wherever," the similar-meaning phrase εἰς ὅλον τὸν κόσμον will bear a locative sense in 14:9 ("wherever the good news is preached in the whole world" — cf. the locative ἐν in the parallel Matt 26:13; also Matt 3:1; 4:23; 11:1; Acts 9:20; 20:25; 2 Cor 1:19; Gal 2:2; Col 1:23; 1 Tim 3:16) and will thereby confirm the locative sense here (and in 1 Thess 2:9, we might add). This sense allows but does not require a limitation of the preaching to Jews living in the Diaspora. On the other hand, comparable passages do not support such a limitation. Many of them disfavor or exclude it, in fact (see esp. Matt 24:14; Acts 20:25; 2 Cor 1:19; Gal 2:2; Col 1:23; 1 Thess 2:9; 1 Tim 3:16). The whole of the location, whatever that location, provides the audience.

"Among all the nations" bursts the boundaries that would limit the governors and kings to local Palestinian rulers, such as Pontius Pilate and Herod Antipas and — at a later date and under the supposition of a prophecy after the event — Felix, Festus, and Herod Agrippa (cf. Acts 12, 23, 26). Again apart from the mention of all the nations in v 10, the plural of both "governors" and "kings" also tends away from a limitation to Palestine. In particular, Judea had only one governor at a time; no other Palestinian territories had governors; and Jesus does not seem to be speaking of successive governors and kings, but of governors and kings ruling at the same time in various territories. Cf. 4:32; 11:17; 14:9; 15:39.

"And the good news must first be preached among all the nations" makes essentially the same point as "the end is not yet" (v 7) and "these things [are the] beginning of birthpangs" (v 8). That this point has been made twice before, and very recently, should keep Mark's audience not only from misunderstanding "first" to mean "above all" (a non-temporal sense unexampled elsewhere in the synoptics), but also from misunderstanding it to mean "before you are given over to tribunals and synagogues, beaten, and made to stand before governors and kings" (cf. v 9). Besides, "must" is too strong for the mere point that preaching will precede persecution; and that point is itself suspect, for the wording demands not just that preaching precede persecution, but that all the nations be evangelized first — yet persecution started long before all the nations were evangelized. L. Gaston (*No Stone on Another* 20) seems to think that Mark should have written "before the end" if that is what he meant in v 10. But variety of expression dictates otherwise, and the presence of the statement in v 7 that "the end is not yet" interprets "first" in advance and as meaning "before the end" without repeating "the end" (see BAGD s.v. πρῶτος 2a for the meaning "first" in the sense of "earlier"). It is not merely that the good news must be preached before the end, but that all the nations must first have it preached among them. Though the good news must be preached among all the nations before the end comes, the text does not say that the end will come as soon as all the nations have heard the good news. The fact that Jesus' disciples have already gone out preaching (6:7-13, 30; cf. 1:17; 3:14) shows that their preaching in the future (13:10) is not predicated on a correction of the wrong messianic expectations which they have vented since their earlier preaching (cf.

8:32-33; 10:35-37; against N. R. Petersen in *Neot* 18 [1984] 45-49; idem in *Int* 34 [1980] 163-66).

Contrary to the view that v 11 comes from a source different from that of v 9b, v 11 does not make sense without v 9b; for v 11 does not tell why or to whom people lead you when they give you over. To whatever extent Luke 12:11-12 may reflect Q, mention of "the synagogues and the rulerships and the authorities" in Luke 12:11-12, which otherwise parallels v 11, also favors that v 11 comes from the same source as does v 9b, which similarly mentions tribunals, synagogues, governors, and kings. See G. R. Beasley-Murray (*Commentary on Mark Thirteen* 47) against the view that Luke 21:15 is more original than Mark 13:11.

Much as in Jesus' case, Jewish persecutors may give the disciples over to Gentile governors and kings (cf. 10:33; 15:1). But the text does not say so; hence, J. Lambrecht (*Redaktion* 131) stands on weak ground to limit the leading and giving over in v 11a to Jews' leading and giving the disciples over to Gentile governors and kings. The newness of "lead" (the verb is not to be found in v 9b) may rather mark a progression from people's giving the disciples over to Jewish tribunals and synagogues to those tribunals' and synagogues' leading them to Gentile governors and kings. Then "giving [you] over" would draw a parallel with the earlier giving over to the Jewish tribunals and synagogues. Otherwise, "giving [you] over" regresses to that earlier giving over.

Lambrecht (loc. cit.) uses the mention of the Holy Spirit to deny that "whatever is given you" contains a divine passive (v 11). Since the Holy Spirit is God's Spirit, however, the argument seems not to hold up. Lambrecht also sees an emphasis on the gratuitous character of what the disciples are to say. But the combination "whatever . . . this" somewhat differently emphasizes its not having been rehearsed. Repeated emphasis on the non-eschatological character of the events predicted in vv 5b-13 precludes an interpretation of "that hour" (v 11) as the last hour of history. The clause, "whenever they lead you, giving [you] over," defines "that hour" as the hour of being given over to Jewish tribunals and synagogues and of standing before governors and kings (cf. v 9).

The presence of γάρ, "for," in the last clause of v 11 does not suffice to characterize the whole clause as composed by Mark. Others, too, use γάρ; and he may add it to traditional material. The apparent traditionality of his other references to the Holy Spirit makes it unlikely that he composes a clause which highlights the Holy Spirit (see 1:8 and esp. — because of the doubled definite article in the Greek text — 3:29; 12:36; cf. 1:10, 12; Luke 12:12). The γάρ-clause is not repetitious of the preceding clause (as is sometimes thought); for the preceding clause uses a passive and issues a command whereas the γάρ-clause gives the reason for the command by interpreting the passive as divine. The occurrence of ἀλλά, "but," in the γάρ-clause marks the second occurrence of ἀλλά in v 11. But this fact favors that Mark has added the γάρ-clause no more than the second ἀλλά in 2:17 and 14:36 favors that he has made similar additions there. In each passage, the second ἀλλά gives parallelistic emphasis.

To J. Jervell (in *God's Christ and His People* 95) the presence in Matt 10:19a par. Luke 12:11 of "how or" (πῶς ἤ) before "what" (τί) suggests speaking in tongues, and the description in Matt 10:20 of the Spirit as "speaking in you" confirms the suggestion. But for that meaning an explicit reference to tongues is needed. By no means do all those whom the Spirit fills speak in tongues (see Acts 4:8, 31; 6:3, 5, 10; 7:55-56; 13:9-10 et passim), and "how" includes more possibilities than speaking in tongues. Indeed, the omission of "how or" in Matt 10:19b par. Luke 12:12 leaves the impression of synonymity with "what." Besides, Mark 13:11 shares neither "how or" nor "speaking in you," which Matthew adds by way of redaction (R. H. Gundry, *Matthew* 192-93, 644 s.v. ἤ, 647 s.v. πῶς); and in a number of passages the description of the Spirit as in a person has nothing to do with speaking in tongues (see John 14:17; Rom 8:11; 1 Cor 6:19 et passim).

R. Hamerton-Kelly (*God the Father* 66-67) suggests that Jesus' own experience prompted the prediction of family betrayals in v 12 (cf. 3:20-21, 31-35 parr.; Matt 5:11-12 par. Luke 6:22-23; Matt 10:37 par. Luke 14:26; Matt 24:9; John 15:18-21). It is a delicate question whether v 12 is secondary to Matt 10:35-36 par. Luke 12:52-53. The allusion in v 12 to *Tg. Neb.* Mic 7:2 favors a negative answer, but see R. H. Gundry, *Use of the OT* 78-79.

For the authenticity of the reference to Jesus' name (v 13a), see the notes on 9:37, 41. W. L. Lane (460, n. 58) suggests that the salvation promised in v 13b means vindication, as in Job 13:16 LXX; Phil 1:19, 28. But these cross-references are better interpreted of physical deliverance. On the other hand, not only does the anarthrousness of τέλος stand in the way of interpreting Mk 13:13b in terms of physical survival till the eschatological end (see the foregoing comments). The usage of ὑπομένω favors religious loyalty over physical survival (see the lexicons s.v.). If τέλος were referring to the end of the age, Jesus might be promising salvation from persecution as well as or instead of salvation from judgment. If τέλος refers to martyrdom, however, persecution has done its worst and Jesus is promising salvation from judgment instead of salvation from persecution.

Suffering and dying for something or someone appears also in 2 Macc 6:28; 7:9, 11, 23; 8:21; 13:14; 14:38; 4 Macc 1:8, 10; 6:22, 27, 30; 9:6-7, 29-30; 10:10; 11:20; 13:9; 16:19, 25. See K. Beyer, *Semitische Syntax* 1/1. 211, on the Semitic character of the conditional participle used as subject of the main clause (meaning in v 13b, "but if anyone endures to [the] end"), though the resumptive "this one" Graecizes the further part of the sentence (ibid. 217, n. 1; E. C. Maloney, *Semitic Interference* 126-31). The usual meanings of εἰς, "into, to, till," and the placement of εἰς τέλος before the resumptive οὗτος favor "till the end," going with "the one who endures," rather than "at the end," going with "this one will be saved."

It has been suggested that v 14 comes from a Christian prophet in anticipation of the setting up of Caligula's image in the temple (40 C.E.; cf. T. W. Manson, *Sayings* 328-31, where v 14 is treated as a revision of pre-Luke 21:20-24). The imperial order to have it set up was never carried out, however; so it is questionable that such a prophecy would have been preserved (Josephus *J.W.* 2.10.1, 3-5 §§184-87, 192-203; idem *Ant.* 18.8.2-9 §§261-309; Philo *Legat.* 29-43 §§184-338; Tac. *Hist.* 5.9). Mark is sometimes made responsible for introducing "when you see" (v 14) to match "when you hear" (v 7). But a traditioner or Jesus himself might just as easily have made this match. To say similarly that Mark is responsible for introducing "where he ought not [to stand]" in place of an originally clearer expression (so J. Gnilka 2. 193) raises the question why Mark would make a clear expression unclear, for in textual criticism we regard the more difficult as earlier. T. J. Geddert (*Watchwords* 207, 218-20, 237) answers that Mark is deliberately ambiguous because he wants to leave it open whether the events of the Jewish war are leading immediately to the end. But why then does he retain the command to flee when seeing the abomination of desolation, and the parable according to whose interpretation "you know that he [the Son of man] is near, at [the] doors, when you see these things coming to pass" (vv 28-29)? Apparently Mark considers both "the abomination of desolation" and "standing where he ought not [to stand]" clear enough.

More strongly than Geddert, N. Walter says in *ZNW* 57 (1966) 42-45 that because the end did not come in 70 C.E., Mark redacts his source so as to disconnect the end from the events of that year. The redaction takes the form of "where he ought not [to stand]," which Walter interprets as an indefinite reference to some mysterious location of the Antichrist. Against this interpretation, "ought not" demands a specific location known for its sacrosanctity; the mention of Judea points to the temple as that location; and we have already seen that the disagreement of much else in chap. 13 with the events of 66-70 C.E. militates against Mark's writing at a later date, which would have allowed him to iron out the disagreement. "The holy place" (Matt 24:15) correctly interprets "where he ought not [to stand]" as a reference to the temple. We should not think that because Mark's Christianity has desacralized the temple, he changes "the holy place" to "where he ought not [to stand]." Matthew's phrase is redactional (R. H. Gundry, *Matthew* 482), and "where he ought not [to stand]" implies the sacrosanctity of the temple, not its desacralization.

See D. Daube, *NTRJ* 418-22, on the possibility that Mark's masculine accusative singular participle ἑστηκότα, "standing," interprets personally the grammatically flawed definite article in הַשִּׁקּוּץ מְשׁוֹמֵם at Dan 11:31. Formally, we may treat the participle ἑστηκότα as a neuter accusative plural and make it describe "the abomination" and "the desolation," the first of which is neuter (τὸ βδέλυγμα; cf. J. A. Kleist 225; W. C. van Unnik in *Miscellanea Neotestamentica* 1. 107). But this construal is unlikely; for instead of "*and* desolation" we read "*of* desolation," which makes a single unit with "the abomination." Thus, the participle should have taken the form of a neuter accusative singular (ἑστηκός). Furthermore, though an abomination may stand, a desolation does not. For another personalization of a neuter noun, see the v.l. αὐτόν, "him," referring to τὸ πτῶμα αὐτοῦ, "his corpse," in 6:29 ℵ W *pc*.

Unless βωμός, "altar" (so 1 Macc 1:54), lies hidden behind Mark's text, the personalization of the abomination of desolation disfavors an altar as the referent. B. W. Bacon (*Gospel of Mark* 133) thinks that Mark has personalized the abomination under Pauline influence (cf. 2 Thess 2:3-12). Apart from the question whether Paul wrote 2 Thessalonians, however, the difference between the abomination's "standing," as does the image of a person, human or divine (cf. Rev 13:14-15), and the lawless one's "sitting," as does the person himself — say, a king on his throne — distances the passages from each other and suggests that Paul has carried a traditional personalization even further (cf. R. H. Gundry in *NTS* 33 [1987] 171: "an image stands even though it portrays its subject in a seated position; but a person receiving worship would sit" — also Str-B 1. 951 for the rabbinic development of an altar into an image and Gundry, op. cit. 174-75, n. 26, for material defending the Pauline authorship of 2 Thessalonians). The mention of false Christs in the plural (v 22; cf. "many" in v 6) shows that the abomination of desolation hardly represents a developed doctrine of one Antichrist (for which see 2 Thess 2:3-12; Rev 13:1-18) or even of a main Antichrist (1 John 2:18-23; 4:1-3).

R. Pesch (*Naherwartungen* 143) argues that predominant Septuagintal usage favors the inclusion of destruction in the meaning of ἐρημώσεως (v 14). He admits that its meaning does not include destruction in the LXX of Lev 26:34-35; 1 Esdr 1:55. But elsewhere, too, the word means the desertion caused by destruction, not the destruction itself — and destruction is not the only cause of desertion. It just happens to be the most frequent cause. See the LXX of 2 Chr 30:7; 36:21; Jdt 8:22; Ps 72:19; Jer 4:7; 7:34; 22:5; 32:18; 51:6, 22; Dan 8:13; 9:18 (also Dan 8:13 Theod; 9:2 Theod) as well as the previously cited Dan 9:27; 11:31; 12:11; 1 Macc 1:54. Saying that "desolation" means "destruction" and that it takes place long enough after erection of the abomination to make flight possible in the meantime (thus, "the abomination *leading to* destruction" — cf. J. Lambrecht, *Redaktion* 150-51) would not bring v 14 into conformity with the events of 70 C.E., for Josephus explicitly states that the temple was burning up at the time the Romans were offering sacrifices in its court to their military standards (*J.W.* 6.6.1 §316). The Hebrew of Dan 9:27; 11:31; 12:11 probably means an abomination that causes horror. But horror causes desertion — hence, the transition to desolation. See D. Ford, *Abomination of Desolation* 144-92, for a survey of positions on the abomination.

Private reading seems to be in view at 2:25; 12:10, 26. But the plural there contrasts with the singular in 13:14, and the present singular of reading contrasts with the plural of seeing and fleeing. These contrasts favor an address to the one who reads Mark to others. Only by accepting that Mark depends on an earlier, non-dominical apocalypse can we take seriously the conjecture that commanding the reader to understand derives from such an apocalypse. Since no text critical evidence casts doubt on the command, ascribing it to a post-Marcan glossator entails even greater conjecture.

The command to understand does not identify what is to be understood. Possible identifications in addition to those discussed in the comments include understanding the Danielic source of "the abomination of desolation" and understanding the referent of the abomination. This latter possibility is often related to the theory that deliberate vagueness cloaks an anti-Roman meaning lest discovery of such a meaning by Roman officialdom lead to persecution of the church. Earlier in Mark, however, the verb here used for understanding (νοέω) had to do with understanding Jesus' power to upset laws of purity (7:18) and to multiply bread (8:17). Most likely, then, the present usage has to do with understanding his power to predict the abomination. See D. Daube, *NTRJ* 422-24, on the possibility but not probability that "let the reader understand" does not break in parenthetically, but finishes out the sentence beginning, "But whenever you see. . . ." Under this construal, "then let the ones in Judea" would start a new sentence.

Because 1 Macc 2:28; 2 Macc 5:27 have to do with fleeing to organize resistance, not with fleeing to escape persecution, J. Lambrecht (*Redaktion* 155-56, n. 2) objects that they do not make good parallels with v 14. But 1 Macc 2:28 speaks about zeal for the Law and maintaining the covenant, not about organizing resistance; and the immediately following vv 29-38 speak of flight from persecution. Organized resistance came only later in reaction to the persecutors' attacking fugitives on the Sabbath and the fugitives' offering no defense (vv 39-48). It is not just that the Maccabees and their followers decided to fight back on the Sabbath. They did not fight back even on other days of the week till they heard about the Sabbath massacre of other fugitives. Initially, they — like those others — fled into the mountains for a safe haven in which to keep the Law. Similarly, 2 Macc 5:27 speaks of flight into the mountains to avoid pollution, not to organize resistance. The objection of E. Lohmeyer (276 and *Ergänzungsheft* 17) that Judeans outside Jerusalem could hardly flee into the mountains because they would already be in them neglects that the mountains of Judea, traditionally used for refuge, need not include all towns and fields outside Jerusalem but within Judea. On the contrary, see Jesus' reference to "the one in the field" (v 15; see also 15:21; Jer 32:6-15).

Though "when you see" implies the immediate proximity of the abomination, the "you" who see it do not have to be coterminous with "the ones in Judea" who flee. There is a change from second person to third. The third person plural in reference to those who should flee may include the second person plural in address to those who see; but physical barriers may keep "the one on the housetop," whom the third person plural certainly includes, from seeing the abomination even though the housetopper lives in Jerusalem, and distance as well as physical barriers will obviously keep "the one in the field," whom the third person plural also includes, from seeing the abomination. We only have to suppose that those who see spread the news (against E. Lohmeyer [loc. cit.], who creates unnecessary difficulties). There is no need to interpret "see" (ἴδητε) as eschatological perception rather than as physical seeing (against W. H. Kelber, *Kingdom* 120).

We could exclude Jerusalemites from "the ones in Judea" by supposing that "the one on the housetop" and "the one in the field" live in Judean towns outside Jerusalem. But the text does not demand such an exclusion, and the commanded suddenness of flight — there is to be not even a descent from the housetop or a return to the edge of a field where a garment was left at the start of work (cf. Verg. *Geor.* 1.299) — favors inclusion of Jerusalem and her immediate environs; indeed, favors a concentration on Jerusalem and her immediate environs. Farther away, suddenness so extreme would not be needed.

The appearance of vv 15-16 in a different context at Luke 17:31 seems at first to support a theory of different sources. But the context of Luke 17:31 does not tell where to flee. It does not even command flight. Yet the prohibitions of coming down from the rooftop and of returning from the field presuppose such a command. So Mark 13, which does command flight and tells where to flee, looks to have the original context (whether or not Luke 17:22-37 represents only Q [which then may have lost the original context and gathered eschatological sayings from a variety of sources] or represents Q plus insertions from Mark 13 [and perhaps subsidiarily from Matthew]). The woe to pregnant women and nursing mothers attaches to the commands concerning men of leisure and field hands just as well as it attaches to the general command to flee. In fact, the reference to women nicely balances out the reference to men.

The attempt to correlate the flooding of the Jordan in Josephus *J.W.* 4.7.5 §§433-36 (cf. also 4.4.5 §§286-87) with the flight of the woman to the wilderness in Rev 12:6, 15-16 (cf. *Mart. Isa.* 4:13; *Clem. Recogn.* 1.39 [sy 1.37]) — a flight that succeeded despite the dragon's casting out of his mouth a river to carry her away — and then to use this correlation in favor of interpreting Mark 13:14 as a reference to Christians' fleeing from Jerusalem across the Jordan River to Pella fails on at least two counts: (1) Pella is not wilderness, but belongs to the Decapolis, and a main road runs through Pella; (2) behind Rev 12:6, 15-16 lies the wilderness of Sinai and the exodus of Israel through the Reed Sea, not any wilderness in Transjordan or a flight of Christians across the Jordan to Pella. Epiphanius (*Haer.* 29.7; 30.2; *De mens. et pond.* 15) puts such a flight just before the Roman siege of Jerusalem. He writes later than Eusebius, however, and does not specify a date. In some possible contrast, Eusebius says that a flight of Christians from Jerusalem to Pella occurred before the war (*H.E.* 3.5.3). Whether his statement means before the start of the war in 66 C.E. or before the southern offensive in the spring of 68 C.E., he does not relate the flight to Mark 13:14 parr.; and Josephus's description of the siege of Jerusalem makes it unlikely in the extreme that Christians could have fled the city just before its capture (see the foregoing notes). Even under the supposition that they did take successful flight at that late date, their fleeing to Pella would still disagree with fleeing into the mountains. A city located on a main road in foothills does not qualify as a mountainous hiding place. See J. Verheyden in *ETL* 66 (1990) 368-84 for arguments and literature for and against the historicity of a Christian flight to Pella. Naturally, unhistoricity would further undermine any interpretation of Mark 13:14 parr. in terms of such a flight.

Some eminent Jerusalemites fled after the Roman Cestius's ill-fated attempt to capture the inner city and temple and before the later siege by Titus. But they deserted to Cestius, and he had done nothing that answers to "the abomination of desolation standing where he ought not [to stand]"; so even though there were evidence that Judean Christians fled to the mountains during this interval, their flight would still not conform to v 14 (see Josephus *J.W.* 2.19.4-2.20.1 §§527-56; also 4.6.3 §§377-79; 4.7.1, 3 §§397, 410; cf. Luke 21:20-21). So also in respect to desertions that occurred later but still prior to the destruction of Jerusalem and the temple (Josephus *J.W.* 5.10.1 §§420-23; 6.2.2-3 §§113-18). Desertion to the Romans does not equate with flight to the mountains.

By interpreting the place where the abomination ought not to stand as the land of Palestine apart from the temple, Jerusalem, and Judea, one might evade the difficulty that once the Romans stepped into the sacred precincts of the temple, erected their idolatrous military standards, and offered sacrifices to them it was too late for flight. Thus, those in Judea, which includes Jerusalem, might flee to the mountains prior to the siege of Jerusalem and desecration of the temple, i.e. during the Roman campaign in northern Palestine, where the Romans first erected their standards. But resisting this interpretation are: (1) the source of "the abomination of desolation" in Daniel, which refers explicitly to "the city," "the sanctuary," and "the continual burnt offering"; (2) the equally explicit reference to "the temple of God" in the comparable passage 2 Thess 2:4; (3) the greater enormity of temple-desecration as compared with desecration of northern Palestine; (4) the inability of "the ones in Judea" to "see" the abomination if it stood in northern Palestine; (5) the implication in the command not even to come down from the roof that the streets of Jerusalem will already be clogged because the standing of the abomination right in Jerusalem has caused a panic; and (6) doubtfulness that an event at the distance of several days' journey would necessitate a flight so sudden that one should not even come down to take anything out of his house or turn back to take his cloak from the edge of a field.

Only by treating the abomination as an invader approaching Jerusalem could we suppose that Judeans outside the city would think (except for Jesus' command) to flee into the city. But we have just seen reasons to locate the abomination in the temple. Thus, danger will radiate from within the city, not toward her from without. Moreover, the mention of "the one on the housetop" before "the one in the field" suggests that news of the abomination will spread outward from the city, whereas news of an approaching invader would move in the opposite direction and reach a field hand first. The temptation will not be to flee into Jerusalem for the protection of her walls, then, but to stay there in expectation of her deliverance (against J. Wellhausen [2. Aufl.] 103).

See M. Ambrozic (*Hidden Kingdom* 227) against the interpretation of W. Marxsen (*Mark* 182-89) that v 14 commands flight to the mountains of Galilee, there to await the coming of the Son of man. Galilee goes unmentioned in vv 14-27. Since the Romans took over that territory in the first part of their campaign to crush the Jewish rebellion, refuge could hardly be found there. Nor was it a traditional place of refuge, as were the mountains of the Judean wilderness. And why bother to write a book like Mark's if the Son of man is about to come?

To put the mountains in Galilee and then make Judea represent Judaism, the Galilean mountains Christianity, and the command to flee a command to leave Judaism and join the international church (H. Giesen in *SNTU* A/8 [1983] 37 in development of a suggestion by R. Pesch, *Naherwartungen* 145-47; cf. W. H. Kelber, *Kingdom* 121) not only misplaces the mountains in Galilee. It also calls for similarly symbolic interpretations of wintertime, of the woeful difficulties possibly to be experienced by pregnant women and nursing mothers, etc.

One can suppose from a comparison with Matt 24:17-18; Luke 17:31 that the sayings in Mark 13:15-16 stood in Q and that to stress urgency and create symmetry, Mark inserts μηδὲ εἰσελθάτω, "neither enter," and adds ἆραι τὸ ἱμάτιον αὐτοῦ, "to take his cloak" (J. Lambrecht, *Redaktion* 157-59). Mark is not known for redactional symmetry, however; and he does not write in and for a historical situation requiring a stress on urgency. It rather looks as though Luke (1) prefixes "on that day" for linkage with "day" in Luke 17:29, 30; (2) changes "the one on the housetop" to "who will be on the housetop" for linkage with "will be" in Luke 17:30; (3) inserts "and his vessels (σκεύη) in the house" to balance the man on the housetop, to provide in advance some things for him to take if he should descend, and possibly to make up for having put "his own court" and "his possessions (ὑπάρχοντα)" in 11:21 for "into the house" and "his vessels" in Mark 3:27; (4) omits "neither enter" in conjunction with Matthew and possibly under subsidiary influence from Matthew to tighten up the parallelism between the two sayings, the second of which has nothing corresponding (Matthew often tightens up traditional parallelisms, and the correspondence of "neither enter" to the building of staircases on the exterior of Palestinian houses favors the originality of the phrase); (5) puts "them" in place of Mark's "anything out of his house" to refer back to "his vessels in the house," just inserted; (6) joins Matthew in replacing εἰς with ἐν for "in the field" (it is unlikely that Mark would do the opposite for the meaning "in"); (7) inserts "likewise" as a literary flourish; and (8) omits "to take his cloak" for ease of transition to Lot's wife, whose looking "back" (εἰς τὰ ὀπίσω — Gen 19:26 LXX; so also Mark) is not said to have a cloak in view. That all Luke's differences can be explained as redactions of Mark (with some possible but unnecessary subsidiary influence from Matthew) casts doubt on the presence of these sayings in Q.

In v 15 we should perhaps favor the v.l. which omits δέ, "but" (B 1424 *al* c). The omission is more awkward, and therefore liable to change, but asyndetically emphatic. Perhaps we should likewise favor the v.l. τι ἆραι (B K L Ψ 892 *pc*). It has a more awkward but emphatic word order. Some have thought that Jesus does not prohibit coming down from the housetop, but only doing so for the purpose of entering to take something out of the house. G. R. Beasley-Murray (*Commentary on Mark Thirteen* 73-74) even supposes that Jesus commands descending an outer staircase instead of an inner one. But "neither enter to take" implies that the prohibited descent would be by way of an outer staircase. Moreover, the man in the field is hardly allowed to turn back at all, not even for a purpose other than taking his cloak; and Josephus speaks of jumping from roof to roof (*Ant.* 13.5.3 §140). So Jesus is probably prohibiting descent as well as entry.

The flat roofs of houses provided a place for eating, conversation, sleeping, prayer, study of the Law, drying fruits and vegetables, and other activities (Josh 2:6; 1 Sam 9:25-26, esp. in the LXX; Isa 22:1; Acts 10:9, 20; Str-B 1. 952). Since the man in the field is not wearing his cloak, he must be working (against the argument that since Simon of Cyrene will be coming from the field at 9:00 A.M., when nobody quits work [15:21, 25], the present man in the field has to be working no more than Simon will be working). The contrast between him and the man on the housetop therefore favors that the housetopper is taking his leisure. A man of leisure might want to grab some valuables unnecessary to subsistence but dear to a person of means. The cloak, on the other hand, was a necessity. Since working men used it as a cover at night, it had to be returned by nightfall if anyone took it as security (Exod 22:25-26[26-27]; Deut 24:12-13). That even a cloak should be left behind by a field hand shows the urgency of flight once the abomination of desolation is seen. Repetition of the αι-sound in the woe of v 17 may also stress this urgency (cf. G. Lüderitz in *Markus-Philologie* 176). Jesus told his disciples not to get disturbed ahead of time (v 7a), but now he says to take the quickest possible action at the time. The γάρ, "for," of v 19 indicates that the prediction of unprecedented tribulation is designed to reinforce the necessity of speedy escape. The context of flight and the association with nursing mothers shows that the woe to pregnant women does not imply the danger of monstrous and untimely births, as in the apocalypse of 4 Ezra 5:8; 6:21. See *Tanh.* 55a parr. (cited by Str-B 1. 952) for expectant and nursing mothers as most in need of help.

The "it" whose happening in winter is to be prayed against (v 18) probably refers back to the abomination of desolation, which starts the days of tribulation and thereby necessitates a sudden flight. The mention of winter does not imply that the tribulation will end before summer, but only that winter would make a bad time to flee from the onset of tribulation, however long the tribulation might last. E. Schweizer (273) identifies lack of provisions in the fields as the main danger in wintertime. But the mountains to which the refugees are told to flee do not have fields in which to forage, at least not fields in the sense of farmlands. The much-wanted rainfall late in the summer when Caligula was seeking to have his image erected in the Jewish temple has no bearing on v 18, for here the rain may fall unwantedly in the winter (against W. Grundmann [7. Aufl.] 359; see Josephus *Ant.* 18.8.6 §§284-86).

The argument that the difference between the third person plural in "let them flee" (v 14) and the second person plural in "(you) pray" (v 18) betrays a difference in sources (so J. Gnilka 2. 193) neglects that the command to flee starts with a second person plural: "when you see." One might also say that whether or not they will find themselves in Judea at the time, all disciples are to pray that the abomination of desolation not be set up during winter. At least their fellow disciples who do find themselves there may benefit from those prayers.

A look at 12:29-30 should dispose of the argument that the use of "God" in v 19 and of "Lord" in v 20 betrays a difference in sources (so J. Gnilka 2. 193). The alternation and combination of these two divine names often occurs elsewhere, too. That they may imply different sources behind the Pentateuch says nothing about source criticism here, because the alternation and combination belonged to what for first century Jews formed the seamless robe of the Pentateuch and as such shaped their own usage. "God" suits the reference to creation (cf. Gen 1:1), and "Lord" suits the salvific act of cutting off the days of tribulation.

The tautology in "since [the] creation that God created" looks Semitic, as does οἵα . . . τοιαύτη, "such as . . . such as" (where we would put only one "such as"), earlier in v 19. Οἵα agrees with Dan 12:1 MT Theod, τοιαύτη with Exod 9:18 MT LXX (cf. E. C. Maloney, *Semitic Interference* 116-18). For similarly Semitic tautologies, see 2:19; 4:30; 7:13; 11:28; 12:14, 23; 13:20. These tautologies are sometimes attributed to Mark, but their Semitic character makes them equally attributable to earlier traditioners and to Jesus (cf. other Semitisms, noted below, in vv 19-20). The tautological οἵα . . . τοιαύτη emphasizes severity of tribulation. "From [the] beginning of creation" recalls the same dominical phrase in 10:6 (cf. the notes ad loc.). The tautological second reference to creation increases emphasis on unprecedentedness of severity. The double negative οὐ μή plus a subjunctive verb for strong negation of the future emphasizes unrepeatability of severity. The tautologically double reference to the Lord's cutting off the days of tribulation (v 20) underlines the Lord's regard for the elect, who might otherwise perish with the rest of humanity. The tautological reference to God's electing the elect emphasizes their election itself.

It is sometimes thought that ἕως τοῦ νῦν, "until now" (v 19), betrays Mark's conviction that he and his audience are living in the time of the unprecedented tribulation which immediately precedes the Son of man's coming (see, e.g., R. Pesch, *Naherwartungen* 151-53). The phrase does represent its speaker's standpoint (see the LXX of Gen 15:16; 18:12; 32:5; 46:34; 47:3 Cod. A; Deut 12:9; 3 Kgdms 3:2; 2 Esdr 5:16; Ezek 4:14). But Jesus, not Mark, is the speaker; and if an end-minded Mark were putting his own words on Jesus' lips, he would hardly have gone on to write that a tribulation so severe as this "will by no means take place" in the future, either. A conviction that the last tribulation had already started would make those words nonsensical. Only a gap stretching forward from the speaker to that tribulation makes them sensible. Jesus' standpoint supplies such a gap.

As the anarthrous use of κύριος, "Lord," is Semitic, so also is οὐκ . . . πᾶσα σάρξ, "not all flesh," meaning "no human beings at all" (v 20; cf. Gen 9:11). H. Giesen (in *SNTU* A/8 [1983] 38) thinks that at least on the redactional level, the world-wide mission of v 10 makes "all flesh" refer to all human beings throughout the world. But v 20 speaks of "the days" of the unprecedented tribulation, the purview concerning which has been limited to Judea from v 14 onward. It may be better, then, to interpret "all flesh" as meaning "all human beings throughout Judea" and to regard the world-wide tribulation in the Book of Revelation as the later development of a local tribulation described by Jesus. In connection with Revelation, world-wide means as wide as the Roman Empire (cf. the notes on v 10).

Since "all flesh" is threatened, the unprecedented tribulation does not consist of persecution; for persecution would threaten only the elect. Here, then, "saved" (ἐσώθη) means physical survival, not eternal salvation (contrast v 13). "On account of the elect" implies that the Lord will shorten the unprecedented tribulation to preserve some elect for the gathering that will take place when the Son of man comes (v 27). The designation of disciples as "the elect" (i.e. God's "chosen ones" [cf. v 22]) stresses the difference between disciples and non-disciples, a difference that will come out with awful clarity at the end. The language of election occurs in apocalyptic literature; but it occurs elsewhere, too. In fact, it originates in the OT outside apocalyptic. So we dare not use it to describe Mark

13 holistically as an apocalypse. Cf. Luke 18:7; Matt 22:14 as well as the NT epistles and Rev 17:14.

The aorist tense of ἐκολόβωσεν, "has cut off," probably corresponds to a prophetic perfect in Hebrew: the shortening of the tribulation is as good as already done. We should not think that the Lord will shorten the individual days, but that he will lop off a number of days from the total that have been planned for the tribulation. Dan 8:14 mentions "2,300 evenings [and] mornings," Dan 12:11 "1,290 days," Dan 12:12 "1,335 days," but Rev 11:3; 12:6 only "1,260 days" (cf. Dan 7:25; 12:7; 1 Cor 7:29; Rev 11:2; 13:5; and the cancellation of the seven thunders in Rev 10:1-7; but not Rev 12:7, which concerns the quite different phenomenon of darkening the sun, moon, and stars a third of the time that they are supposed to shine). The cutting short of those days of tribulation does not compare with the cutting short of the rainy season in *1 Enoch* 80:2; for the cutting short of the tribulation is to save the elect (cf. *Barn.* 4:3), the cutting short of the rainy season to judge sinners with poor crops (cf. the similarly judgmental *Apoc. Abr.* 29:13). There is no cutting short in 4 Ezra 4:26; *2 Apoc. Bar.* 20:1; 54:1; 83:1, only a hastening to the end. G. Delling (in *TDNT* 3. 823-24) says that the cutting short in Mark means a diminution "of the purpose and power of the oppressors." The direct object "the days" resists this non-temporal interpretation, however.

Though vv 21-23 join vv 5b-6 to make an inclusion, it is one of a fully synonymous sort. C. Breytenbach (*Nachfolge* 309) correctly notes that vv 5b-6 belonged to the beginning of birthpangs whereas vv 21-23 belong to the unequaled tribulation that will follow, starting with the abomination of desolation. (Again note that if the abomination is associated with the destruction of the temple, the activities of the false prophets have to postdate 70 C.E. and therefore cannot be equated with the activities of false prophets earlier than the destruction.) Furthermore, the signs and wonders of vv 21-23 did not appear in vv 5b-6. Nor did the false prophets; and vv 5b-6 mentioned the successful deception of many, perhaps false disciples, whereas vv 21-23 mention the near but unsuccessful deception of the elect, i.e. true disciples.

E. Lohmeyer (277) argues that because a number of false christs cannot appear after the one and only Antichrist of v 14 has appeared, vv 21-23 did not originally belong here. But v 14 did not speak of the Antichrist — rather, of the abomination of desolation — and the image of a god or deified ruler does not necessarily equate with the Antichrist. Even though v 14 had spoken of the Antichrist, according to vv 15-20 he would appear to bring tribulation on all flesh rather than posing and being posed as the Christ with signs and wonders, as in vv 21-23. This difference, recognized by Lohmeyer, would allow the Antichrist and false christs to coexist outside and inside the church, respectively, rather than putting the Antichrist inside Judea and false christs and false prophets outside Judea (so Lohmeyer). We have no indication, then, that vv 21-23 have left behind the Judean limitation imposed by v 14. Not till vv 24-25 will Jesus' language lift this limitation.

Despite common use of "the elect," v 22 would not follow well on v 20; for the rising up of false christs and false prophets does not grow out of the cutting short of the unprecedented tribulation or provide a reason for the cutting short. Danger to life and limb, not danger of deception, provides such a reason. Verse 21 gives the needed transition from the one danger to the other and therefore should not be treated as an interruptive addition (against J. Schmid 240).

"And then" (v 21) does not favor insertion of new material over transition within old material (see 1 Cor 4:5; Gal 6:4; 2 Thess 2:8; also 1 Cor 13:12 [bis]; Gal 4:8). Nor does the command to watch out and the assertion that Jesus has foretold everything favor that v 23 marks the end of an insertion. The command and assertion may just as well mark the end of premonitory events in a discourse that from the start proceeded from such events to the coming of the Son of man.

That Luke's parallel to v 21 appears in a different context (Luke 17:23) does not require Luke to be following a different tradition, for he might have moved the saying. But Matthew writes the saying twice. His first version (Matt 24:23) closely parallels Mark. His second version (Matt 24:26) closely parallels Luke, often agreeing with Luke against Mark. Matt 24:26 and Luke 17:23 agree against Mark 13:21 in writing "they" instead of "anyone"; in putting "to you" after the verb of speaking instead of before it; in writing ἰδού, "behold," instead of ἴδε, "look" (bis); in putting "in the wilderness" (Matthew) or "there" (Luke) before "in the inner rooms" (Matthew) or "here" (Luke) as opposed to Mark's order "here . . . there"; in having two commands instead of one; in having -ελθητε, "should go," instead of πιστεύετε, "believe," in the first command; and in sharing the sayings about lightning and vultures in the following non-Marcan section (Matt 24:27-28; Luke 17:24-37, esp. 24 and 37).

These agreements and Matthew's inclusion of two versions show that the saying was present in Q as well as in Mark. Matt 24:23 relies on Mark 13:21. Matt 24:26 and Luke 17:23 rely on Q. We should not assume the originality of the Q-context, however; Mark's context may be original (see the notes on vv 14-20). It would take too long to examine every possible interrelationship between the various versions of the saying. What follows seems best supported by the textual data:

The occurrence of "and if anyone to you should say" in the otherwise quite different Mark 11:3 as well as in 13:21 (cf. 7:11, too) suggests a dominical locution. The use of "if . . . should say" in Matt 24:26 favors both the originality of this construction and its appearance in Q. In Luke 17:23, "and they will say" (καὶ ἐροῦσιν) represents Luke's assimilation to the future tense in Luke 17:22, 24 and especially to Luke 17:21: "neither will they say" (οὐδὲ ἐροῦσιν). Since Matthew has no parallel to Luke 17:20-21 (nor does Mark), we may presume that that passage did not appear in Q. But if it did, we would only have to say that Q rather than Luke assimilated the one saying to the other. The third person plural in Matt 24:26 refers to the false christs and false prophets just mentioned in the Marcan tradition that Matthew has taken over; so Q may have had the third person singular, pluralized by Luke and Matthew for different contextual reasons. Mark's penchant for the indefinite third person plural, such as we find in Luke 17:23, makes unlikely his changing an original "they [people] will say." His disinterest in "then" (τότε; he uses it only six times, always in Jesus' words) makes similarly unlikely that he inserts it here for secondary linkage with "those days" of unprecedented tribulation and with other occurrences of "then" in vv 14, 26, 27. Q or Luke may omit it because of detachment from the original context. In a secondary smoothing out of word order, Q seems to have repositioned "to you" after the verb of speaking. Since elsewhere Mark uses ἰδού about as often as he uses ἴδε (seven times and nine times, respectively), since elsewhere Matthew and Luke always replace Mark's ἴδε with ἰδού or omit or otherwise change Mark's ἴδε (see the synoptic parallels to Mark 2:24; 3:34; 11:21; 13:1; 15:4, 35; 16:6), since Luke never uses ἴδε, and since both Matthew and Luke use ἰδού very often (62 times in Matthew, 57 in Luke, 23 in Acts), Mark's ἴδε looks traditional rather than redactional. Luke 17:21 has the words and the word order "here . . . there," just as Mark does. Yet Mark has no parallel to Luke 17:21; so "here . . . there" looks like a dominical locution (see J. Carmignac in *ASTI* 7 [1968-69] 71-72 for the possibility of an underlying Semitic wordplay). The order in Luke 17:23, "there . . . here," may then be attributed to secondary chiasm; i.e. Luke 17:23 reverses the order for chiasm with v 21. The chiasm provides a variety the need for which was felt when the sayings in Luke 17:20-21 and 22-37 were first set alongside each other. Matthew seems not to have liked "here" and "there" in either order. First he writes "here . . . here" (24:23; cf. his using "here" [ὧδε] six other times where synoptic parallels lack it). Then, drawing on Matt 11:7-9; 6:6, he substitutes "in the wilderness he is . . . in the inner rooms" (24:26; see R. H. Gundry, *Matthew* 485). "The Christ" drops out of Q because the new context in

Q has no false christs and because the immediately preceding and following sayings speak about "the Son of man" (see Matt 24:27; Luke 17:22, 24). In Matthew, moreover, the contrast between "the Christ" and "false christs" has already been drawn. The "or" in Matt 24:23; Luke 17:21, 23 looks like redactional riddance of asyndeton. That Matthew's version of Q (Matt 24:26) does not have "or" supports the originality of its absence in Mark. Because Q does not speak of deception, an original "don't believe" yields both to "don't go away," which matches "there," and to "nor pursue after," which matches "here" (Luke 17:23). Matt 24:26 advances "don't go," changes "away" to "out" for further correspondence with 11:7-9 ("What did you go out into the wilderness to see?" [tris]), and switches back to not believing (as in v 23 and Mark) because of Matthew's having adopted the Marcan material on deception (v 24).

Some have suggested that "don't believe" does not mean to disbelieve the one who reports the Christ's whereabouts, but to disbelieve the false christs themselves. The false christs have yet to be mentioned in v 21, however; so it is better to make the already mentioned "anyone" who reports that the Christ is here or there the object of disbelief. It is also unconvincing to suggest that in vv 21-22 Mark composes a doublet of vv 5-6 to transform an originally apocalyptic prediction into a description of his own church at the time of writing. This suggestion neglects the lack of evidence that false christs and false prophets were threatening to deceive the church with signs and wonders. In fact, nowhere else in the NT do we read of false christs. The consequent suggestion that Mark means the false christs to be taken not as false christs, strictly speaking, but as false teachers succeeds only in exposing the weakness of any contemporizing interpretation. Cross-references to 1 John 2:18; 4:3 offer no help, for they portray *anti*christs who make Christological denials whereas the *false* Christs make and receive Christological affirmations (against H. Anderson 297).

"False christs" need not be a redactional insertion in v 22 if "in my name" was not a redactional insertion in v 6 (see the notes ad loc., also on Jesus' absence as giving opportunity to imposters). An equation of the false christs with the false prophets would violate the differences between vv 21-22 and 5-6 (see the foregoing comments). False prophets figured in the first Jewish revolt (Josephus *J.W.* 2.13.4-5 §§258-63; 6.5.2 §§285-87; 7.11.1 §§437-41; idem *Ant.* 20.5.1 §§97-99; 20.8.6, 10 §§167-72, 188; cf. 18.4.1 §§85-87); but false prophethood does not entail false messiahship, and the false prophets arise after the abomination of desolation in the Olivet Discourse whereas they arose beforehand in the Jewish war if the abomination is associated with the destruction of the temple. We also lack firm evidence that between Jesus and Mark anyone claimed messiahship or was proclaimed as the Christ (cf. the notes on v 6). Therefore the prediction in vv 21-22 that false christs will arise does not look like a prophecy after the event. Acts 5:36-37; Josephus *J.W.* 2.4.1-3 §§56-65; 2.13.4-5 §§258-63; idem *Ant.* 17.10.5-8 §§271-85; 20.5.1 §§97-99; Tac. *Hist.* 5.9 are irrelevant, because they refer to events which took place at least partly even before Jesus spoke, much more and entirely before Mark wrote.

According to R. Pesch (*Naherwartungen* 113-15), Mark composes and inserts v 21 to say that the events of 70 C.E. are leading to the appearance of false christs and false prophets, not necessarily to the coming of the Son of man. But in v 21 "then" refers to "those days" of unprecedented tribulation which the abomination triggers, just as in v 14 "then" meant "when you see the abomination . . ." and just as in v 26 "then" will mean "in those days after that tribulation" when "the sun will be darkened. . . ." Since vv 21-22 refer to the same period of time that vv 18-20 referred to and since vv 24-27 will refer to what happens after that period, the appearance of false christs and false prophets in vv 21-22 does not delay the coming of the Son of man beyond the cutting off of the tribulation. Pesch's appeal to similar constructions in v 5b; 7:11; 11:3 and to supposedly Marcan diction in v 21 assumes what is questionable, viz., that those passages and that diction derive from Mark rather than from tradition.

Alone, v 21 might refer to conflicting or at least different localizations of one and the same Christ. But since it can equally well refer to different localizations of competing christs and since the γάǫ, "for," with which v 22 begins exhibits such a reference, there is no need to draw a contrast with the false christs in v 22 and ascribe the two verses to different sources. Again alone, the localizations in v 21 may be taken equally well as mistaken opinions or as misleading announcements; but γάǫ points to misleading announcements unless it can otherwise be proved that vv 21 and 22 had different origins (against E. Lohmeyer 278). Γάǫ is not linguistically harsh (as supposed by J. Schmid 240); for it simply gives the reason why you should not believe, i.e. the falsity of the christs whose locations are published.

The switch from the second person plural "you" to the third person plural "the elect" does not indicate that vv 21 and 22 have different origins. Similar shifts occur often where we would not dream of different origins. In Rom 8:27, to take but one example, Paul switches to the third person "saints" after repeatedly using the first person "we." Then he switches back to "we" only to return again to the third person in "the ones who love God," "the ones who are called . . . ," "the ones whom he foreknew," and so on, including a switch from "us" to "the elect" (vv 28ff.). The theological reasons for the third person references are obvious. Here in Mark 13:22 "the elect" highlights the salvation of Jesus' addressees (cf. vv 20, 27; D. Daube, *NTRJ* 196-201).

It may be objected that v 22 does not relate well to vv 14-20 because the flight in vv 14-20 did not allow leisure for the rise of false prophets in v 22. In fact, however, times of crisis breed all sorts of charlatans, as in the Jewish war of 66-73 C.E. Similarly, "the warning against people who proclaim that 'Christ is here' or 'there' need not be taken as a denial of Christ's nearness, but on the contrary may be seen as a warning against those who exploit the fact of his nearness to point people to false Christs" (D. Wenham in *Christ the Lord* 131).

"False christs" interprets the "many" in v 6 who come on the basis of Christ's name and say, "I am." "False prophets" interprets the "anyone" in v 21 who announces the Christ's whereabouts. The rising up of false christs and false prophets may echo the rising up of nations and kingdoms against each other in v 8. The giving of signs and wonders may echo Deut 13:2-3(1-2), especially according to the Targums *Neofiti 1* and *Pseudo-Jonathan*, which differ from the MT and LXX in describing the prophets as false. "To deceive" echoes Mark 13:6. "The elect" echoes v 20 and anticipates v 27. But Jesus may have formulated the saying thus. For one and the same speaker may echo and interpret his own words and draw from other materials as well; and Jesus, if speaking in Aramaic, is more likely than Mark, writing in Greek, to have borrowed from targumic tradition. Mark likes γάǫ-clauses but does not monopolize them; so he might have inserted γάǫ rather than making up the saying in v 22. The same judgment applies to the parenthetic "if possible." Furthermore, though Mark likes parentheses (see V. Taylor 50 with reference to and in correction of C. H. Turner in *JTS* os 26 [1924-25] 145-56), elsewhere they occur primarily and perhaps exclusively in editorial remarks whereas the present parenthetic clause belongs to Jesus, who elsewhere shows fondness for "possible" (9:23; 10:27; 14:35, 36).

It is not quite correct to say that in 2 Thess 2:9 the man of lawlessness performs his own signs and wonders (so J. Schmid 240). Rather, his coming is "with" (ἐν) them. Who will perform them is left open. Since it is false prophets who will give signs and wonders and deceive people (Deut 13:2-3, 6[1-2, 5]; Jer 23:13, 32; Ezek 13:10; Mic 3:5; cf. Mark's avoidance of "signs and wonders" in reference to Jesus), one might think that Mark adds "false christs" to link vv 21-22 with vv 5b-6, especially if he made up those earlier verses. But if he did not, the linkage looks original and it is taken for granted that the false prophets perform the signs and wonders on behalf of the false christs. It can be taken for granted because of the absence of signs and wonders from vv 5b-6, which speak about false claimants to Christ's name but not about false prophets, and because of the appropriateness of signs and wonders to the false prophets in v 22. One might distinguish the present false christs and their prophets as non-Christian Jews from professedly Christian deceivers in vv 5b-6; but those earlier verses set the tone for vv 21-22, and in vv 21-22 the limitation of the attempted deception to "the elect" makes it highly probable that the false christs and their prophets profess membership among the elect. We should also note the absence of any indication that the false christs and their prophets will foment insurrection against Rome. An allusion to the royal pretenders and prophets active in the Jewish revolt would lead us to expect such an indication. And against much current eisegesis, the text breathes not a word to the effect that the false christs and their prophets will try to lead the elect away from suffering for Christ and the gospel. See G. R. Beasley-Murray, *Commentary on Mark Thirteen* 83-85, for Jewish belief in the initial hiddenness of the Christ and against any contact with the wilderness of the Exodus, but neither in vv 21-22 nor in vv 5b-6 does Mark's text mention hiddenness or a wilderness. For those, see Matt 24:26.

Citing 2 Cor 13:2; 1 Thess 3:4, E. Wendling (*Entstehung* 159) sees Pauline influence in "I've told you all things beforehand" (v 23b). But 2 Cor 13:2 has nothing to do with eschatology, and Paul may draw the probably eschatological subject matter in 1 Thess 3:4 from dominical tradition (cf. 1 Thess 4:15-17). We would have to assign v 23 to redaction only on the presuppositions that Jesus could or would not tell his disciples to watch out and that he could or would not summarize his predictions up to this point and echo his own and his disciples' phraseology in so doing (cf. vv 4, 5b). See the foregoing notes on the switching of persons.

"In those days" (v 24) typifies OT language, often as here with reference to the future, including the eschatological future (see, e.g., Jer 3:16, 18; 31:29; 33:15-16; Joel 3:2[2:29]; 4[3]:1; Zech 8:23; and J. Macdonald, *Theology of the Samaritans* 372, for Samaritan usage). But non-futuristic, non-eschatological usage — such as the refrain in Judges, "In those days there was no king in Israel . . ." — reminds us that the phrase gets its meaning solely from its context. Since Mark likes dual expressions, especially in temporal notes (see also 1:21, 32, 35; 2:20; 4:35; 5:5; 6:21; 10:30; 11:2, 14; 13:11; 14:1, 3, 12, 25, 30, 43; 15:42; 16:2; cf. the duality of geographical expressions at the end of 13:27), we might consider the possibility that for linkage with "in those days" in v 17, with "those days" in v 19, and with "the days" in v 20 he has added "in those days" (cf. 1:9; 2:20; 4:35; 8:1), or that for greater precision as well as for linkage with "tribulation" in v 19 he has added "after that tribulation." Since "those days will be tribulation" (v 19), "in those days" may seem to put the following events within the unprecedented tribulation rather than "after that tribulation." But "the days" of that tribulation have been cut off (v 20) and μετά plus the accusative ("after . . .") implies no temporal gap in its other Marcan occurrences (1:14; 8:31; 9:2, 31; 10:34; 14:1, 28, 70); so the end will come within those days, cutting off the rest of them and putting the tribulation in the past.

In the OT phraseology of vv 24-25, which describes the undoing of the fourth day of creation (Gen 1:14-19), "the sun" and "the moon" parallel each other as the primary luminaries. "The stars" and "the powers in the heavens" parallel each other as the most numerous luminaries. Being darkened causes no light to be given, and falling out of the heaven is caused by being shaken. Thus, the subjects of the verbs display the structure a-a'-b-b'; but the verbs display the structure a-b-b'-a' by putting the divine passive in the first and last clauses and the active voice in the intervening lines. "Out of the heaven" (an adverbial phrase) tells from where the stars will fall because the powers that are "in the heavens" (an adjectival phrase) will be shaken. Not coming from the OT, "out of the heaven" takes the singular that is characteristic of the Greek word οὐρανός. Coming from Isa 34:4, "in the heavens" takes the plural that is characteristic of the corresponding Hebrew word שׁמים.

"The powers in the heavens" (v 24; cf. 6:14) are synonymous with "the stars" (cf. ancient belief in the stars as powerful heavenly beings whose motions in the sky determine the course of earthly events, a belief that lay at the base of astrology; see BAGD s.v. δύναμις 6; also the targumic texts cited in Str-B 1. 956, but not Billerbeck's own comment). For further comments, see L. Hartman, *Prophecy Interpreted* 156-57; R. H. Gundry, *Matthew* 487). The celestial disasters are often taken to indicate the final birthpangs out of which will come a new creation (contrast the "beginning of birthpangs" in v 8), but Jesus neither repeats the figure nor speaks of a new creation. Are the powers of the heavens shaken because the more powerful Son of man comes through their territory during his descent (so W. Grundmann [7. Aufl.] 362)?

It is tempting to say that celestial disasters provide God's answer to the signs and wonders performed by false prophets, for up through v 20 Jesus has spoken of nothing that is recognizably supernatural (cf. D. E. Nineham 356). But one wonders whether on this interpretation modernly strict standards of the supernatural are illegitimately excluding events predicted in the earlier verses. Even more doubtfully should we take the celestial disasters as the sign requested in v 4; for these disasters do not presage the destruction of the temple (yet the disciples asked for a sign that would do so), and they accompany the Son of man's coming after the tribulation rather than preceding it during the tribulation. Similarly, because in v 26 τότε means "then" in the sense of "at that time," not "then" in the sense of "next," the celestial disasters do not count as signs that the Son of man is about to come, but as events that take place as he comes. Only vv 14-23 encompass the signs of his coming. It is likewise questionable whether the celestial disasters are meant to be taken as figurative of earthly disasters. OT usage, which favors the figurative, does not determine NT usage; and the coming of the Son of man in clouds is almost surely meant to be taken literally (see esp. Acts 1:9-11; 1 Thess 4:15-17). The argument for figurativeness that in v 27 the world is still intact (so R. Pesch, *Naherwartungen* 172) overlooks the celestial rather than earthly locale of the chaos in vv 24-25. Besides the OT allusions noted in the comments on the celestial disasters, cf. Ezek 32:7-8; Joel 2:10; 3:3-4(2:30-31); 4(3):15; Amos 8:9; Zeph 1:15; Hag 2:6, 21; Rev 6:12-13; *1 Enoch* 80:4-8; 102:2; 4 Ezra 5:4; *As. Mos.* 10:5; *Sib. Or.* 3:796-806. J. Lambrecht (*Redaktion* 174) casts doubt on an allusive quotation of Isa 13:10; 34:4 and decides instead for Joel 2:10-11; 3:3-4(2:30-31); 4(3):15, but Jesus' phraseology comes much closer to Isaiah's than to Joel's (see R. H. Gundry, *Use of the OT* 51-52).

Who are those that will see the Son of man coming? One might identify them with the sun, moon, stars, and heavenly powers, regarded as angelic beings. But the contrast with supposed private revelations of the Christ — revelations directed to human beings — and the frequency in Mark of the indefinite third person plural ("they" in the general sense of "people") favor an identification with human beings. Jesus' later statement to the Sanhedrin that they will see the Son of man coming (14:62) also favors this identification. The present switch from the definite third person plural reference to the heavenly powers in v 25 to an indefinite third person plural reference to human beings in v 26 need not indicate a secondary insertion of vv 24-25 or a collocation of materials deriving from originally independent sources; for since the sun, moon, stars, and heavenly powers are not normally said to see, in and of itself the language of seeing indicates a switch in subjects, a switch clear enough to satisfy the demands of continuous speech. Furthermore, an indefinite third person plural often follows a definite third person plural, contextual factors being left to spell the difference between them. A difference in sources can explain very few instances of this phenomenon (see 1:22 with 1:21; 1:30 with 1:29 [?]; 1:32 with 1:31; 2:3 with 2:2; 2:18b with 2:18a; 3:21b with 3:21a; 6:14 with 6:13; 6:55-56 with 6:54; 8:22b with 8:22a; 10:13 with 10:10-12; 14:12 with 14:10-11).

See the notes on 2:10 concerning "the Son of man," whose mention here links up with other phraseology to produce an allusive quotation of Dan 7:13. Strangely, A. J. B. Higgins (*Jesus and the Son of Man* 66) argues against the authenticity of v 26 that it "gives no hint . . . of some sort of relationship between this figure [the Son of man] and Jesus." One would rather have expected that an identification of the Son of man with Jesus might be used as an argument against authenticity. Because of increasingly explicit Christology in early Christianity, the absence of such an identification, or at least the lack of explicitness, argues for authenticity. The connection of the man-like figure in Daniel with the rule of God on earth harmonizes with Jesus' preaching the coming of that rule through his own ministry on the one hand and with his using Danielic phraseology concerning himself on the other hand. The Palestinian sky does not regularly feature clouds; so their appearance easily becomes symbolic in Daniel, here, and elsewhere (G. R. Beasley-Murray, *Commentary on Mark Thirteen* 89). In combatting polytheism, Dan 7:13 would not be introducing a second deity alongside the Ancient of Days in the man-like figure who comes "with the clouds of heaven." Abraham traveled on a cloud (*T. Abr.* 8:3 [Recension B]; 10:1 [Recension A]). The church will be caught up "in clouds" (1 Thess 4:17). And the two witnesses will ascend "in a cloud" (Rev 11:12). Therefore clouds do not imply the deity of those transported by them. Nevertheless, they remain a mode of transport used by God for himself and for those whom he wishes to honor with his own mode of transport. Since the Son of man has already come in the person of Jesus (10:45), his future coming will be a coming again (cf. 8:38; 14:62; Heb 9:28; and the observation of J. Lambrecht [*Redaktion* 181] that because Hebrew and Aramaic do not have a composite word, בוֹא and אָתָא can mean "come again" as well as "come"). We are therefore justified in speaking of the *Second* Coming or *Return* of Christ.

F. Flückiger (in *TZ* 26 [1970] 400) errs in arguing that the Son of man's sending angels to gather the elect rules out a descent to the earth. The descent is vertical to one locality, the sending horizontal to the extremities of the earth and heaven. R. T. France (*Jesus and the OT* 227-39) thinks that Jesus portrays himself as the Son of man ascending to God in heaven so as to exercise his authority in the destruction of Jerusalem and gather the elect through evangelism of the nations (cf. M. Casey, *Son of Man* 172-77). But angels gather the elect, whereas human beings evangelize the nations. That Dan 7:13, which underlies Mark 13:26, does not describe an ascent to heaven (as in *Midr. Pss.* on Psalm 2 §9 [Braude 1. 40-41]), but a descent to earth (as in *Gen. Rab.* 13.11 on Gen 2:6; *Num. Rab.* 13.4 on Num 7:13), see the notes on 14:62. The shaking of the heavenly powers does not favor ascent over descent in Mark, for those powers may shake in terror whatever the direction of the Son of man as he passes through their territory. Since he will come not till after the tribulation, which follows the church age, and since his coming compares with the coming of a man to his servants (vv 34-36), ascent to heaven would mismatch the wider context, too.

Except for seeing a tradition behind the Son of man's coming in v 26 (cf. 14:62; Rev 1:7), J. Lambrecht (*Redaktion* 191-92) considers vv 24-27 a Marcan fabrication. To rebut his arguments, however, Semitic tradition may be assimilated to the LXX; and in some important respects the allusions to the OT are quite un-Septuagintal (see R. H. Gundry, *Use of the OT* 51-55; also the considerations on p. 22 of the present commentary). There is no good reason to doubt that Jesus used OT phraseology. And he himself may have referred back to the tribulation that he had described and to the elect whom he had already mentioned, and may have borrowed phraseology from his earlier sayings. None of these counter arguments prove authenticity or disprove Marcan or earlier redaction, but they do expose weaknesses in the denial of dominical tradition.

Predictions of the Son of man's passion and resurrection and of his heavenly session and return nowhere appear in one and the same dominical saying. This separation favors the authenticity of these predictions; for Christian fabrication would probably have led to their combination according to the overall scheme of his passion, resurrection, heavenly session, and return. Whereas Christians tend to think according to this grand scheme (so John 14-16 [under the assumption that the Upper Room Discourse is heavily redacted]; Acts 3:12-26; Col 3:1-4; 1 Thess 4:14-17; Heb 9:23-28; 1 Pet 5:1-4; and the Book of Revelation), Jesus appears to have given separate predictions according to the needs of particular historical occasions.

Against Jesus' having spoken of the Second Coming in particular or at all, M. J. Borg (*Conflict* 221-22) thinks it (1) psychologically unlikely that Jesus conceived of his removal from earth to heaven in preparation for a return and (2) pedagogically unlikely that he taught about his return when not even his closest disciples understood his first having to die and rise from the dead. But if he predicted his death and resurrection, no psychological difficulty adheres to his conceiving of a removal to heaven and a return to earth. Already in the OT, Elijah is said to have been bodily removed to heaven and destined to return (2 Kgs 2:1-12a; Mal 4:5(3:23); cf. Mark 9:2-8 parr.); and we know that Jesus was acquainted with the OT traditions concerning Elijah (Mark 8:28 parr.; 9:11-13 par.; Luke 4:25-26; 9:54). Furthermore, if Jesus wanted to teach the disciples about a return of his, he could hardly have waited till they understood the necessity of his death and resurrection. The lack of such understanding made it all the more needful to teach them about his return — lest his removal make them lose faith that God would ever establish the kingdom through Jesus.

Attempts to trace the doctrine of the Second Coming to early Christian exegetical work on Ps 110:1 and Dan 7:13, interpreted at first in terms of Jesus' exaltation to heaven (cf. *1 Enoch* 70-71) but reinterpreted through Zech 12:10-11 with the result that ascent turned into descent (so N. Perrin, *Rediscovering* 173-85), or to early Christian hesitation to believe that Jesus' death and resurrection exhausted the meaning of messianic salvation in the ongoing history of the church (so J. A. T. Robinson, *Jesus and His Coming* 140-59) do not reckon sufficiently with the lack of any similar doctrine in Jewish literature of the period. The closest possible parallel, 4 Ezra 13:3-7, falls short; for there "that man flew with the clouds of heaven," but he "came up out of the heart of the sea" and "flew up" on a mountain, not from heaven to earth, as in the Second Coming, and not after a period of absence. Whatever it is, the return of the Anointed One with glory in *2 Apoc. Bar.* 30:1-2 follows the messianic kingdom on earth. The absence of any Jewish teaching that the Messiah would descend in clouds or would come a second time at the end of the present age after coming earlier, makes unlikely that the original Christians, being Jewish, would have thought to interpret the OT or church history in such a way. Far more likely that they would have thought of God rather than the Messiah as bringing the end, as in much Jewish eschatology (cf. G. R. Beasley-Murray, *Jesus and the Kingdom of God* 20-62).

M. J. Borg (in *The Glory of Christ in the NT* 215-16) argues that the Easter event triggered belief that the end was at hand because resurrection will occur then according to Jewish belief. But again, why a coming from heaven in clouds? And the eschatological resurrection was thought to include all the righteous dead, and possibly the wicked dead as well, not a lone individual as the first fruits of a more numerous resurrection to come and not the Messiah as that lone individual (not even in 4 Ezra 7:26-44).

In both 8:38 and 13:26 the Son of man comes "in (ἐν) . . ." and then "with (μετά). . . ." (Two successive occurrences of the same preposition are naturally out of the question.) "In" has to do with surrounding circumstance. "With" introduces either personal or impersonal accompaniment. Thus, just as "power" shifts from "in" (9:1) to "with" (13:26), so "glory" shifts from "in" (8:38) to "with" (13:26) to allow the introduction of "clouds" after "in" — this for the sake of an allusion to Dan 7:13. But *in* clouds disagrees somewhat with Dan 7:13 MT ("*with* clouds"), Theod ("*with* the clouds"), and LXX ("*on* [ἐπί] the clouds"; so also Matt 24:30). The text might have read "in much power and glory

with clouds" or "with clouds in much power and glory," but the order in 8:38 "in . . . with"
and the desire to introduce "clouds" before "much power and glory" give us the present
reading. The resultant "in clouds" emphasizes the Son of man's dignity in that the earlier
position gives prominence to the clouds as a divine mode of transport. Yahweh came "in"
a cloud at the theophanies in Exod 19:9; 34:5; Num 11:25 (cf. the interchange of עַם,
"with," and בְּ, "in," at Dan 2:43; 5:30 in comparison with Dan 7:2). The plural of "clouds"
supports an allusion to Dan 7:13 despite the use of "in." The correspondence between
"with the holy angels" (8:38) and "with much power" (13:27) favors that "much power"
(δυνάμεως πολλῆς) means a large army of angels (cf. the sending of angels in the next
clause, and the LXX of 2 Chr 24:24; Ezek 38:15). In 14:62, which will also speak about
the Son of man's coming, power will turn into a divine title ("the Power"); and the influence
of 8:38 having waned, "in clouds" will change to "with the clouds of the heaven" for a
closer and more extensive allusion to Dan 7:13 MT Theod.

As evidence for the inauthenticity of 13:26, A. J. B. Higgins (*Jesus and the Son of
Man* 62-65) cites the use of "power" as a Jewish periphrasis for "God" in 14:62 over
against its normal use in 13:26, also the absence of "glory" and "angels" from 14:62 over
against their presence in 13:26. But Jesus is capable of using "power" in ways other than
as a periphrasis for "God" (see 9:1; 12:24 par.; 13:25 parr.; Matt 11:21 par. Luke 10:13;
Luke 10:19; and the notes on 14:62 for the view that there "the Power" represents a
reporter's reverential substitute for the tetragrammaton, which Jesus used —
blasphemously in the judgment of the Sanhedrin), and the absence of "glory" and "angels"
from 14:62 does not argue for the inauthenticity of 13:26 so much as it exhibits closer
adherence to Dan 7:13 (so also with respect to Mark 8:38).

With the gathering of the elect, cf. Exod 19:17; Ps 50:5; Isa 11:11-12; 27:12-13;
43:6; 56:8; Jer 23:3; 29:14; 31:8; 32:37; Ezek 11:17; 20:34, 41; 28:25; 34:13; 36:24; 37:9;
39:27-28; Zech 2:10(6); 9:14; 10:6-12; Tob 14:7; 1 Cor 15:52; 1 Thess 4:16; 2 Thess 2:1;
Rev 11:15-19; 14:14-16; 2 Esdr 6:23; *Pss. Sol.* 11:1; 17:28; *Shemoneh Esreh* 10. Jesus
does not mention resurrection; so presumably he means the elect who survive the tribulation
(contrast v 13b according to the foregoing comments). Nor does he speak of an upward
gathering or tell to what place the elect are gathered. Attention focuses on his power and
glory, not on the fate of the martyrs or the destination of the elect. In these respects, contrast
1 Thess 4:15-17; and see J. Lambrecht, *Redaktion* 186-88; R. H. Gundry in *NTS* 33 (1987)
166, 174, n. 25.

In v 27 we expect "from [one] extremity of the earth to the [other] extremity of the
earth," as in Deut 13:8 MT LXX, or "from [one] extremity of the heaven to the [other]
extremity of the heaven," as in Deut 4:32 MT; 30:4 LXX; Ps 19:7 MT LXX (18:7). By
including both the extremity of earth and the extremity of heaven (i.e. of the sky), Jesus
puts all possible emphasis on universality. The OT use of the combination "from . . . to"
for earthly origin (even when references to heaven follow) negates the interpretation of
J. A. Kleist (226) that in Mark 13:27 "from [the] extremity of earth" indicates earthly origin
and "to [the] extremity of heaven" indicates heavenly destination (cf. G. R. Beasley-Murray, *Commentary on Mark Thirteen* 92, against the view that the one phrase refers to the
highest point on earth, i.e. Jerusalem, and the other to the highest point in heaven; also
against the view that Jesus refers to the horizon as the line where earth and sky meet). And
against the suggestion of H. J. Holtzmann (*Die Synoptiker–Die Apostelgeschichte* 262)
that from a Palestinian standpoint "[the] extremity of [the] earth" means the farthest east,
where one sees the extremity of the earth, and "[the] extremity of [the] heaven" means the
farthest west, where one sees the sky dipping down into the Mediterranean Sea, we have
to ask why then Jesus did not say "[the] extremity of [the] sea" instead of "[the] extremity
of [the] heaven"?

J. Gnilka (2. 203) argues that nowhere in the tradition of Jesus' parables do we find anything comparable to the command to learn (v 28a). But Gnilka himself thinks that the command to stay alert (ἀγρυπνεῖτε — v 33) may be the original introduction to the following parable (2. 208). The structure of a command to learn a parable plus the parable itself does not differ very much from the structure of a command plus a parable supportive of the command. Given the parenetic point inherent to these two parables (and to much else throughout chap. 13), there is nothing out of place in the introductory commands; and it would take something out of place, something awkward in relation to the following parables, to justify treating the introductory commands as Marcan insertions designed to tie the parables to their contexts. Without the first of these commands (v 28a) the first parable would not even specify a fig tree. Yet this specification is needed, for only a fig tree satisfies the horticultural demands of the parable.

We might have expected a plural: "the branches." For a fig tree has more than one branch, and elsewhere in the NT κλάδος always takes the plural. But since "the fig tree" is generically singular, so also is "its branch." It makes little difference whether we treat ἐκφύῃ as present active ("puts forth [leaves]") or as second aorist passive ("[leaves] are put forth"; cf. Josephus Ant. 2.5.5 §83). The latter treatment produces a parallel with the second aorist of γένηται, the other verb in the clause, and a chiastic pattern of (a) subject; (b) verb; (b′) verb; and (a′) subject. In Palestine the almond tree blossoms early in what we call the spring. Most other trees — carob, olive, oak, terebinth — are evergreen. The fig tree sheds its leaves for the winter, however, and blossoms just before the onset of summer. This behavior makes its blossoming the best harbinger of summer (cf. Cant 2:11-13). The summer is bound to come soon after the fig tree blossoms; so the mere possibility of the Son of man's coming at any time (imminence without certainty) would not meet the demands of the parable. Only a certainly soon coming meets it.

Since "already" (ἤδη) occurs elsewhere in Mark seven times outside the words of Jesus and only once on his lips and since the parable does not demand this adverb here in v 28, Mark may have added it for emphasis on nearness. We might have expected "already" to go with the nearness of summer: "you know that the summer is already near." But "near" needs no help in its own, final clause; so "already" introduces nearness at the very start of the parable. In effect, the meaning is that as soon as the tree leafs, you know that summer is near.

Ancient Jews spoke of only two seasons: winter and summer. Since summer is harvesttime and fruits are gathered in harvest, "the summer is near" makes the parable of the fig tree follow nicely on the gathering of the elect in v 27 (cf. 2 Sam 16:1-2; Isa 16:9; 28:4; Jer 8:20; 40:10, 12; 48:32; Matt 3:12 par. Luke 3:17; Matt 12:30 par. Luke 11:23; Matt 6:26; 13:30; 25:24, 26; Luke 12:17-18; John 4:35-36). On the other hand, since Jesus uses θέρος, "summer," we should not allegorize the parable in terms of that gathering, as would be suggested by θερισμός, "harvest," often used figuratively for salvific and judgmental gatherings (see F. Hauck in TDNT 3. 132-33). The passages cited by R. Pesch (Naherwartungen 179, n. 772) for a figurative use of "summer," too, do not survive scrutiny. Amos 8:1-3 comes closest to surviving, but it features the fruit of summer rather than summer itself. Isa 28:4 is pre-summer in orientation, and Jer 51:33; Joel 4(3):13 do not even use the word "summer."

It is unnecessary to suggest that in v 29 καί, "also," may go with its whole clause rather than with ὑμεῖς, "you [plural]," alone (so G. R. Beasley-Murray, Commentary on Mark Thirteen 95); for this second person plural pronoun does not really jar against the second person plural verbal endings in v 28. Rather, it emphasizes the addressees in order that they may take seriously the climactic command which it helps to introduce. Earlier occurrences of ὑμεῖς have likewise followed second person plural references and made similar emphases (see vv 9a, 11d, 23a). Hence, "thus also," which also introduces v 29, does not draw a comparison between "you disciples in particular" (v 29) and "you people in general" (v 28; against J. Lambrecht, *Redaktion* 197). Both from the start of the discourse and from the start of the parable, Jesus has been addressing disciples (N.B. esp. μάθετε, "learn," cognate to μαθητής, "disciple"). "Thus also you" draws an analogy between the disciples' knowing without effort that the summer is near and their more important knowing by obedience to Jesus' command that the Son of man is near. In 7:18 "thus also you" differed radically in that the second person pronoun contrasted with a preceding third person reference to "the crowd." It fails to carry conviction to assume that in the clause, "when you see these things happening" (13:28), Mark but not Jesus can have echoed and anticipated similar expressions in 13:4, 14 (cf. v 7), 30 (against R. Pesch, *Naherwartungen* 179-80; J. Gnilka 2. 203-4).

In a number of OT passages the Day of the Lord is said to be near (Isa 13:6; Jer 31:16; Ezek 30:3; Joel 1:15; 2:1; Obad 15; Zeph 1:7, 14; cf. Jer 31:16 LXX). But in Mark 13:29 it is the Son of man who will be near when the events of vv 14-23 are taking place. Furthermore, his nearness will bring hope; for he will gather his elect when he comes. But the nearness of the Day of the Lord threatens judgment on the wicked, not just deliverance for the elect; yet judgment goes completely unmentioned here. As shown both by the wording of v 30 and by the seasonal referent in the parable of the fig tree, nearness is not limited to spatial nearness; nor does it mean suddenness (for which see v 36). Spatial nearness at the doors stands for the temporal nearness of the Son of man's coming, and that event will take place soon after premonitory signs. We cannot wiggle out of the non-fulfilment of v 30 by saying that his coming is only capable of happening at any moment once the signs have appeared, as though nearness allows the possibility of a delay, or that his coming will take place quickly once it starts, though it need not start for a long time.

The budding of the fig tree carries a happy connotation, argues J. Dupont (*Études* 484-96, esp. 487); yet in the context of chap. 13 and with the application in v 29 the budding represents the calamities which will signal the nearness of the Son of man's coming. Hence, neither the present context nor the present application of the parable is original. Against this argument, the budding carries a happy connotation only because it promises that fruit is soon to come. In that respect the present context and application suit the parable very well, for the foretold calamities promise that the Son of man is soon to come and send his angels to gather the elect. Like Dupont's argument, however, this counter argument says too much. The parable deals only in the chronology of events, not in their character. Since the argument transgresses this boundary, no characterological counter argument is needed.

As shown by Acts 5:9; Jas 5:9; Rev 3:20, each of which may be influenced by dominical tradition, "at [the] doors" requires a person to be near in v 29. (L. Gaston [*No Stone on Another* 37] cites Acts 5:9 for an impersonal subject, but "the feet" that are "at the door" do not belong to a robot — rather, to "the ones who buried your [Sapphira's] husband.") Events do not come through doors, persons do. The Son of man, whose coming vv 24-27 have just described, meets this requirement. But it rules out an impersonal referent to the end as near (cf. v 7b), though the coming of the Son of man does mark the end. The required personal referent also rules out an underlying wordplay between קיץ, "summer," and קץ, "end," as in Amos 8:2. Such a wordplay is possible only in Hebrew, not in Aramaic (though *Tg. Neb.* Jer 8:20 uses קצא, "end," for קיץ in Jer 8:20 MT), much less in Greek. Like the summer, the end could be near; but being an event, the end can be at the doors no more than the summer, a season, is at the doors. Yet again, the personal referent required by this figure rules out an earlier meaning of the parable to the effect that in the earthly ministry of Jesus the rule of God was near. The passages usually cited for such an earlier meaning contradict it instead. Though Jesus initially announced the nearness of God's rule (Mark 1:15 par.; cf. Matt 10:7 par. Luke 10:9, 11) and later implies the futurity of its arrival (see, e.g., Luke 11:3; Mark 14:25 par.), at least in his ministerial deeds that rule is more than near — it has already arrived according to what he says in Matt 12:28 par. Luke 11:20 (see G. E. Ladd, *Presence of the Future* 138-45, on ἔφθασεν as indicating arrival, not just nearness; also Matt 11:2-6 par. Luke 7:18-23 and the comments on Mark 1:15). Similarly, Matt 16:2-3 par. Luke 12:54-56 criticizes failure to discern a time that has already arrived. Yet according to the parable of the fig tree, the summer has not yet arrived, but is only near. The statement in Luke's version of the parable that God's rule is near (see Luke 21:31) does not support an earlier meaning such as we are questioning; for this version represents later redaction, and according to this version God's rule stays in the eschatological future rather than arriving in the earthly ministry of Jesus.

To achieve an impersonal reference to God's rule as near, we would have to treat "at [the] doors" as a redactional addition that came with a shift from God's rule to the Son of man. The dropping of this phrase in Luke 21:31 demonstrates this necessity. We could then hypothesize that the phrase originally stood in the parable of the doorkeeper (vv 34-36). But it is hard to tell where the phrase would fit in that parable; for being at the doors portrays nearness, as in the parable of the fig tree, much more naturally than it portrays suddenness, as in the parable of the doorkeeper (v 36). Better to think that being at the doors in the parable of the fig tree suggested the doorkeeper in the later parable. Only an insistence that Jesus did not, could not, predict his return would require the dropping of "at [the] doors" from the original version of the parable concerning the fig tree (and on that question, see the foregoing notes).

Insofar as the abomination of desolation is personal (see v 14 with comments and notes), W. L. Lane (478-79) could defend his view that that abomination is near, at the doors. But insofar as the abomination is probably the image of a god or deified ruler, it is unnatural to speak of it as near, at the doors. Besides, the Son of man provides a much closer as well as more natural antecedent; and Lane again runs into the problem of impersonality by including the tribulation, whose description continues on through v 20, along with the abomination. If what will be near really did include the tribulation, beginning with the abomination, then "these things" that signal its nearness would have to refer to the events predicted in vv 5b-13 as starting beforehand. Yet vv 7-8 treat those events as non-premonitory, whereas vv 14-20 describe the events distinctive of the tribulation as premonitory of the Son of man's coming just as v 29 treats "these things" as premonitory of someone's coming through the doors right away.

L. Gaston (*No Stone on Another* 34) thinks that in searching for an antecedent to "these things" of v 29 it is wrong to skip over vv 24-27. But since being near, at the doors, implies the coming which vv 24-27 have described, the things that signal its nearness find their antecedent necessarily and naturally in earlier verses. Isa 46:13 displays a temporal use of nearness in the MT as well as in the LXX; and θύρα, "door," takes the singular everywhere else in Mark, always outside dominical sayings (see 1:33; 2:2; 11:4; 15:46). Therefore, the present plural may well be authentically dominical. A redactional insertion would probably have taken the usual non-dominical singular. F. Blass, A. Debrunner, and F. Rehkopf (*Grammatik* §141.4) speak of a formal plural for a single door; but it is particularly in relation to a large structure, such as city walls, the temple complex, and prisons, that we read the plural (John 20:19, 26; Acts 5:19, 23; 16:26, 27; 21:30), and this even in the Hebrew Bible (1 Kgs 7:5; Ps 24:7, 9; Prov 1:21; 8:3, 34; Cant 7:14[13]; Isa 3:26; 13:2; Jer 1:15; Ezek 42:4, 11, 12; Mic 5:5[6]; cf. the alternation between singular and plural in the LXX of Exod 40:5-6; Lev 1:3, 5; 4:4, 7; 17:4, 5 et passim). That it is the wide world which the Son of man is about to enter therefore makes the plural appropriate (cf. Mic 5:6). There is no need, then, to assign either the temporal use of nearness or the plural of "doors" to a Hellenistic source (against J. Jeremias in *TDNT* 3. 173-74, esp. n. 8). Even though it could be proved that the temporal and the plural were exclusively Hellenistic, the conclusion would not follow that Mark has added the phrase (so R. Pesch, *Naher-wartungen* 180). For Jesus grew up in Hellenized Galilee, Jas 5:9 uses the expression chronologically, and the overall contents of James show its author to be no more Hellenistic than Jesus is likely to have been.

H.-J. Klauck (*Allegorie* 316-25) ascribes to redaction the verb of knowing (γι-νώσκετε), even in its first occurrence (v 28), plus much else (esp. in v 29). Originally, then, the parable said only, "When its branch becomes tender and puts forth leaves, the summer is near." But Matt 16:2-3 par. Luke 12:54-56 supports that Jesus wanted his audiences to understand eschatological chronology; and if he wanted people to understand the eschato-logical chronology of his first coming, the presumption is that he wanted at least his disciples to understand the eschatological chronology of his return. The rest of Mark 13 does not make sense apart from such a concern. To eliminate it, therefore, we should have to deny the authenticity of the rest of Mark 13 as well. But allowing authenticity takes away the fundamental reason to strip eschatological knowledge from the meaning of the parable.

At 8:12, 38; 9:19, context tars "this generation" with evil connotations. So here in 13:30 "this generation" may likewise refer to the wicked — deceivers and deceived, haters and persecutors — mentioned earlier in the discourse. A connotation of evil would not evacuate the chronological meaning of "this generation" as Jesus' contemporaries, however.

Though v 4 supports the synonymity of "these things" and "all these things," the referents of these expressions in vv 29-30 (viz., the premonitory events described in vv 14-23) differ from their referents in v 4 (viz., the destructions of the buildings and the tear-downs of the stones that make up the temple complex; see the comments ad loc.). We now know that "all these things" did not take place before Jesus' contemporaries passed away. Not even the exclusion of the Son of man's coming from "all these things" relieves this problem of non-fulfilment, for some of the things remaining after this exclusion — in particular, the abomination of desolation, the unprecedented tribulation triggered by it, and the rising up of false christs with false prophets — were supposed to signal the soon coming of the Son of man, in fact, his coming sooner than originally planned, since the Lord has cut short those days (v 20). But even if the events in and around 70 C.E. had corresponded well to those predicted in vv 5b-23 or 14-23 (we have seen that they did not), the Son of man still did not come soon, certainly not in the generally and widely visible way predicted (against H. Giesen in *SNTU* A/8 [1983] 18-69). On the other hand, neither was Nineveh destroyed in forty days to fulfil the Lord's message through Jonah; and that prediction was stated just as unconditionally as the present prediction of Jesus and with even greater chronological precision. Biblical prophecy often undergoes change, often by way of delayed fulfilment (cf. Luke 13:6-9 for a Jesuanic, parabolic representation of God's delaying judgment after deciding to impose it immediately). Apparently Mark wrote before this delay extended so far as to make Jesus' saying problematic (cf. the foregoing notes on 9:1 among the notes on 9:2-8; also Isaiah 38; Jer 18:7-10; Ezek 18:24-29; 2 Pet 3:1-9; the implications of Matt 18:21-35; Acts 21:10-14; 27:21-31; and D. Ford, *Abomination of Desolation* 74-76, 98-100, n. 72).

Against a change by way of delay, D. Carson (in *EBC* 8. 491) argues that the NT presents the Second Coming as "qualitatively unlike all other divine visitations" and that v 22 seems to mean that God will hasten the end, not postpone it. Well, hastening the end spells change; so apparently the NT does *not* present the Second Coming as qualitatively different, at least not so far as changeability is concerned. And to argue from hastening against postponement is to overlook that only the unprecedented tribulation is said to be shortened. Meanwhile, the period leading up to that tribulation (see vv 5b-13) might be extended by more than the tribulation is shortened.

Carson's further attempt to make the tribulation cover the whole of the church age (ibid. 495, 507) runs afoul of numerous indications that the tribulation forms only its closing period: "But not yet [is] the end. . . . These things [are] the beginning of birthpangs. . . . And among all the nations the good news must first be preached. . . . But when you see the abomination of desolation . . . then let the ones in Judea flee. . . . But woe . . . in those days. . . . For those days will be tribulation such as has not happened since the beginning of creation . . . to the present and will by no means happen. . . . But in those days, after that tribulation. . . ." Moreover, "will by no means happen" (v 19) seems to mean that no tribulation equal to the unprecedented closing one will happen between the time of Jesus' speaking and the coming of the Son of man; for it goes without saying that no such tribulation will happen after his coming. Hence, the unequaled tribulation does not occupy the whole of the church age.

E. E. Ellis (*Luke* 246-47) seeks an out through interpreting "the last generation" in 1QpHab 2:7; 7:2 as including several lifetimes. Then he draws the conclusion that "this generation" of Jesus means the last phase in redemptive history however long that phase may last. But 1QpHab 2:7; 7:2 do not require several lifetimes. Even if they did, the jump from several lifetimes to what has thus far become more than nineteen centuries of several lifetimes apiece may strain a tendon. Furthermore, leaving the generation open-ended minimizes and probably nullifies the meaning of "this." The emphatic negation, "will by no means pass away" (οὐ μή plus the subjunctive), turns vapid. *Of course* this generation would not pass away if by definition if could extend out indefinitely!

W. Pannenberg (*Jesus —God and Man* 226) thinks that Jesus' prophecy of the Second Coming was fulfilled in the way other prophecies have been fulfilled, i.e. "in such a way that the original sense of the prophecy is revised by an event that corresponds to it but nonetheless has a more or less different character than could be known from the prophecy alone." Thus the eschatological event of Jesus' resurrection fulfilled in his own generation the prediction of the Second Coming. Fulfilments of this sort are generally recognized, however; yet Jesus' resurrection did not count for the Second Coming in early Christian recognition. To appeal on the contrary to the fourth gospel, one must conjure up a late editor for the tacking of futuristic eschatology onto that gospel. The necessity of such a conjuration neutralizes any argument that might have been gotten therefrom. See M. Künzi, *Naherwartungslogion Markus 9,1 par* 213-24, for a history of the interpretations of v 30. Many of them do not merit comment here.

The phraseology of v 30 differs too much from that of 9:1 to justify the opinion of R. Pesch (*Naherwartungen* 181-87) and others that Mark constructs v 30 after the pattern of 9:1. The only large exception to this difference — viz., "truly I say to you" — does not favor redaction over tradition (see B. D. Chilton in *ZNW* 69 [1978] 203-11 on the debate over ἀμήν, "truly"). J. Lambrecht (*Redaktion* 203-11) thinks that the saying in v 30 is also patterned after a saying in Q represented better by Matt 5:18 than by Luke 16:17, plus some influence from a saying in Q represented better by Matt 23:36 than by Luke 11:51. But see R. H. Gundry, *Matthew* 79-80, 472, for Matt 5:18 as deriving from a saying in Q better represented by Luke 16:17 and redacted by Matthew in anticipation of Matt 24:34 par. Mark 13:30, and for Matt 23:36 as less original than Luke 11:51, particularly where similar to Mark 13:30. The width of the differences between Mark 13:30 and Luke 11:51 leaves too little room for the hypothesis that "Mark 13:30 represents the form the Q saying [Luke 11:51] took when it was repeated apart from its context and became an isolated saying" (G. R. Beasley-Murray, *Jesus and the Kingdom of God* 334).

To treat the saying in v 30 as originally independent would be to make it nonsensical for lack of an antecedent to "all these things." To treat it as a saying of the ascended Jesus through a Christian prophet creates the same problem unless it is thought that the saying was designed from the start for insertion into the present material. But then a new problem emerges, that of imagining how the present material was being communicated in a manner (orally? scribally?) and setting (church? scriptorium?) that fostered, or at least allowed, interjection by a Christian prophet. Solutions to this problem may be forthcoming, but it seems more economical to attribute the saying to the earthly Jesus and assign it to this eschatological discourse.

With v 31, cf. Pss 102:26-28(25-27); Isa 40:6-8; 51:6; 54:10; 55:11; Dan 6:13 Theod; 1 Pet 1:24-25; Rev 22:6. J. A. Kleist (226) suggests that we take the future "will pass away" as modal: "may pass away" (cf. 3:28). The position that the saying in v 31 circulated independently at a pre-Marcan stage of the tradition and came into its Marcan context by virtue of the linking verb παρέρχομαι, "pass away," which occurs once in v 30 and twice in v 31 — this position assumes without evidence that such a development is more likely than that from the start Jesus linked the sayings by means of παρέρχομαι or its Semitic equivalent (presumably עבר; cf. the originality of linking words throughout 1 John). We should resist the view of J. Schmid (243) and others that v 31 contains a general statement of wide application. By itself, "my words" could indeed apply to Jesus' whole teaching equally well as to his presently preceding words alone (cf. E. Schweizer 282). But "my words" belongs to an asseveration, and the strength of this asseveration favors a narrow application to words hard to credit, as in the present context. So also with respect to vv 32 and 33-37, which Schmid generalizes along with v 31.

With respect to the hypothesis that the saying in v 31 is patterned after a Q-saying preserved in Matt 5:18 (see J. Lambrecht, *Redaktion* 211-23, esp. 223; E. Schweizer 279), see the foregoing notes on v 30. In addition, the sovereignty which Jesus exercises over the OT law, even to the point of annulling it in Mark 7:14-23, deflates the argument that Mark 13:31 gives us an ecclesiastical transfer of a Jesuanic statement regarding the OT law to Jesus' own words.

According to D. E. Nineham (358-59), vv 28-37 present the Second Coming as only a sign pointing to the end, which is completely indeterminate (v 32), whereas vv 24-27 presented the Second Coming as the end itself, to which some earlier events will point. We have seen that "these things" whose occurrence signals nearness in v 29 do not include the just-described coming of the Son of man. But even if they did, the end would not be completely indeterminate; for his coming — complete with celestial disasters, clouds, much power and glory, and a world-wide gathering of the elect by angels — would advertise the nearness of the end with unmistakable clarity, comprehensiveness, and force. The error comes in making the end the subject of nearness in v 29. As we have seen, "at [the] doors" requires the Son of man to be the subject. Thus, his coming *is* the end, not a sign pointing to it; and "these things" do not include his coming, but only what the disciples see from v 14 ("But when you see the abomination of desolation . . .") through v 23 ("But you — watch out [βλέπετε]. I have told you all things beforehand"). We might note the difference between what will be seen by the disciples, addressed as "you," and what will be seen by people in general (the indefinite "they" of v 26). The disciples will see the events of the unprecedented tribulation. People in general will see the Son of man's coming.

See the comments for the point that vv 32-37 make only the exact time of the Second Coming indeterminate. It is hard to understand why C. E. B. Cranfield (in *SJT* 35 [1982] 503-4) should think that ignorance of the exact time would reduce to "bathos" a knowledge of general nearness in v 30. Knowledge of general nearness remains important even though one does not know the exact time. Moreover, vv 14-23 (with the opening phrases of vv 24, 26, 27) and vv 28-29 demand a knowledge at least of general nearness. See G. R. Beasley-Murray, *Commentary on Mark Thirteen* 107-8, for a good discussion of "that day or hour" as a reference to exact time.

The suggestion that vv 32-37 provide Jesus' original answer to v 4 does not pass muster, for v 4 asks when the temple will be destroyed but vv 32-37 speak about the coming of the housemaster and of staying awake for it (cf. the comments on v 4). Alone, v 32 might be taken as an answer to v 4, or more properly as a declaration by Jesus that he is unable to tell the disciples when the destruction of the temple will occur or what sign will portend it. But "that day or hour" suits the Son of man's coming better than it suits the destruction of the temple. A person arrives during an hour of the day; but the dismantling, stone by stone, of a huge complex of buildings (ἱερόν, not ναός) takes much more than an hour, or even a whole day. According to R. Pesch (*Naherwartungen* 177), on the other hand, Mark does not let Jesus answer the question about the time of destruction because for Mark the destruction already lies in the past. From the standpoint of Mark's emphasis on Jesus' predictive ability, however, all the more reason to let Jesus tell when the temple will be destroyed; for pastness of fulfilment would demonstrate chronological accuracy of prediction.

Emphasis on Jesus' predictive ability also militates against the theory that in v 32 Mark adds "nor the Son" or that he constructs the whole saying to make Jesus ignorant as well as all others except the Father and thus to excuse the delay of the Second Coming. One may attribute the phrase or the whole saying to a pre-Marcan Christian who did not share that emphasis, but even that attribution seems unlikely. The standard argument against it holds up: attribution of ignorance to the Son runs against the grain of increasingly high Christological assertions in the NT church (cf. the omission of the entire saying after Luke 21:33, of Jesus from the circle of the eschatologically ignorant in Acts 1:7, and the explanation of delay by appeal to God's longsuffering rather than to Jesus' ignorance of the time in 2 Pet 3:1-9); and at an early date, prior to the highest Christological assertions, there was no need to attribute ignorance to Jesus, for his generation did not die out for some decades (J. D. G. Dunn, *Jesus and the Spirit* 34-35).

The framework of a filial relation to God, which elsewhere entails knowledge rather than ignorance (Matt 11:25-27 par. Luke 10:21-22; John 5:20; 15:15), lessens the chance of Christian fabrication (R. H. Gundry, *Matthew* 492). E. Haenchen (452) defends that chance by appealing to the limitation of Jesus' ignorance to the exact time and by appealing to the acceptability of subordinationist Christology in the NT church (1 Cor 15:28; John 14:28). The first appeal weakens the argument for authenticity — we should add that the limitation to exact time helps protect Mark's emphasis on the predictive ability of Jesus — but it does not demolish that argument. (And questions of historicity deal in probabilities.) The second appeal contains some truth but does not quite make the needed point. For acceptable though subordinationist Christology was, the attribution of ignorance to the disciples did not require a similar attribution to Jesus. The implication that on other matters Jesus knows more than the angels in heaven does not argue for Christian fabrication (as thought by R. Leivestad, *Jesus in His Own Perspective* 112), for Jesus has regularly spoken and acted with greater-than-angelic knowledge and authority (see, e.g., 2:5-11).

But some will say that ignorance was attributed to Jesus to put down apocalyptic enthusiasm — and what stronger argument against such enthusiasm than to say that not even the Son knows the exact time? In the NT church, however, we know of no apocalyptic enthusiasm so great that it elsewhere evoked a denial of Jesus' knowledge. Despite its strongly realized eschatology and subordinationist Christology, the fourth gospel magnifies Jesus' knowledge rather than lessening it; and in Mark 13 the repeated commands to watch out and stay alert and awake undermine a Marcan attack on apocalyptic enthusiasm.

One might take a view like W. H. Kelber's (*Kingdom* 124-28; *Mark's Story* 69-70) that Mark does not kill apocalyptic expectation of the Son of man's coming, but in view of his failure to come in 70 C.E. saves that expectation by divorcing his coming from the destruction of the temple and by postponing his coming (but not beyond the lifetime of Jesus' contemporaries — hence as the very next and eschatological event, everything preliminary having already taken place; cf. B. S. Crawford in *JBL* 101 [1982] 243). But we have seen that the predictions of premonitory events ill correspond to the actualities of the destruction and associated events. In normal prophecy after the event, the correspondence is close.

With v 32, cf. not only Dan 12:13 LXX but also Zech 14:7; *Pss. Sol.* 17:23; *2 Apoc. Bar.* 21:8; 1QM 1:4-13. See R. H. Gundry, *Matthew* 492, on the authenticity and Christology of the saying. Because its emphasis on ignorance of exact time does not contradict knowledge of general nearness once the abomination of desolation is seen, we have no need to regard v 32 as inserted from another, more original context; and to treat v 32 as originally independent from any context would be to make it nonsensical for lack of an antecedent to "that day or hour." *What* day or hour? R. Pesch (2. 310) makes the valid point that since ignorance of exact time serves the exhortation to watchfulness, it does not excuse delay in the Son of man's coming. Excusing the delay would require a larger chronology than "that day or hour." By the same token, v 32 would mount an ineffective attack on apocalyptic enthusiasm. In modern times such enthusiasm sometimes goes so far as to set a day and hour; but in ancient times it was content to say that the end would come soon (cf. Luke 19:11; 2 Thess 2:1-12), whereas v 32 denies knowledge only of the day or hour.

The occurrence of "day" and "hour" in a parable at Matt 24:50 par. Luke 12:46 (cf. "day" in Matt 24:42 and "hour" in Matt 24:44 par. Luke 12:39, 40) offers no solid reason to say that Mark has imported "hour" from that parable (perhaps parallel, or partly parallel, to the parable in Mark 13:34-36) and added it to "day" in v 32. For that other combination of "day" and "hour" (see also Matt 25:13; John 16:25-26) may join with the present one to imply that Jesus liked the word-pair well enough to use it more than once. The absence of the word-pair from Mark 13:34-36 as opposed to its presence in Matt 24:50 par. Luke 12:46 does not prove that Mark has shifted "hour" to v 32 (and then dropped "day" from v 35 and substituted the four watches of the night), for Mark's parable of the doorkeeper differs so much from Q's parable of the burglar that Mark himself is unlikely to have used, or even to have known, the parable of the burglar (but see the following notes on the better possibility of such usage by Jesus). The use of "that" with "day" corresponds to the use of "those" with "days" in vv 17, 19, 24; 1:9; 8:1 and to "that day" in 2:20; 4:35; 14:25 (with some possible help from the use of "that day" for the Day of the Lord in the OT, though by no means was "that day" used exclusively for the Day of the Lord).

The use of "that" with "hour" in 13:11 and the meaning of "or" in the phrase "that day or hour" (τῆς ἡμέρας ἐκείνης ἢ τῆς ὥρας) favor that "that" modifies "hour" as well as "day" (cf. Matt 10:14). To have repeated "that" ("that day or that hour") would have distinguished "day" and "hour" too much. The inevitable question, How does "that hour" differ from "that day"? would have diverted attention from the simple meaning of exact time. Thus, the absence of "that" from "hour" gives no handle to the hypothesis that Mark or someone before him added "or hour" to an original "that day."

By tying "day or hour" to the recently described Second Coming, "that" disfavors an additional reference to Jesus' passion (against T. J. Geddert, *Watchwords* 107-9, with appeals to 2:20; 14:41). Besides, the passion narrative will portray Jesus as chronologically cognizant concerning his passion, and that to a high degree of exactitude; yet v 32 denies exact knowledge to the Son. Hence again, "that day or hour" does not refer to the Passion as well as to the Second Coming.

It is sometimes said that because v 26 and 8:38 have mentioned "the Son of man" as coming, v 32 also means "the Son of man" in mentioning "the Son," or that an original "Son of man" has been apocopated. But v 26 lies far back — a whole parable and several sayings intervene — 8:38 even farther back; and in v 32 mention of "the Father" in the phrase immediately following "neither the Son" implies that we should understand "the Son" as God's, not man's. Indeed, anticipation of the reference to God in "the Father" causes "of God" to be omitted; for in referring to himself as "the Son" in relation to "the

Father," Jesus does not need to include "of God" (cf. 1:11; 9:7). Even in the fourth gospel, Jesus never uses "the Son of God" alongside a reference to God as his Father (contrast John 5:25 with 5:26, and note that in 5:27 "Son of man" is spelled out in full). John 10:35-38 provides only an apparent exception, because Jesus quotes himself as having said, "I am [the] Son of God," but only outside this quotation does he refer to God as his Father. In Mark 8:38 Jesus spoke of God as the Father of the Son of man, but to do so he spelled out "the Son of man" in full, as in John 5:27 but not in Mark 13:32.

For Jesus to have said "my Father" would have distinguished Jesus from "the Son." As it is, the absence of "my" allows Jesus to speak of himself in the third person, which parallels the third person references to "no one" and "the angels." The mention of angels along with the Father and the Son in 13:32 as in 8:38 does not support an interpretation of "the Son" as "the Son of man," for there the angels accompanied the Son of man. Here they do not know "that day or hour." Not only do their functions differ completely. As an argument their presence in 13:32 is neutralized by the absence from 8:38 of anything corresponding to the universally negative "no one" featured in 13:32 and referring in the first instance to human beings. For angelic ignorance, as in v 32, see also 1 Pet 1:12; Eph 3:9-10; 4 Ezra 4:52; Str-B 2. 47.

Support for these observations comes from Matt 11:27 par. Luke 10:22, whose additional similarity in having the very phrase "except the Father" that we find in Mark 13:22 strengthens the support. Since in Matt 11:27 par. Luke 10:22 "all things" that "have been given over" (παρεδόθη) by the Father to Jesus consist of the things that the Father *has* revealed to "infants" (a figure for Jesus' disciples), that passage does not contain a material contradiction of the withholding of other information in Mark 13:32. Therefore that passage should not be pitted against the originality of "neither the Son" in Mark 13:32. See R. H. Gundry, *Matthew* 215-18, esp. 218, on the Semitisms which favor an early date for Matt 11:27 par. Luke 10:22 and thus heighten the probability of its authenticity, and against treating that passage generically of a father who teaches his son a trade — a treatment that would distance the passage from Mark 13:32. To say nothing of Jesus' own Hellenism, the Semitisms and non-generic use of "the Father" and "the Son" undermine the position that "the Son" (without "of God") cannot go back to Jesus but can have arisen only in later Hellenistic Christianity. The prominence in QL of special knowledge, including personal knowledge (1QH 12:11), vitiates the old argument of E. Norden (*Agnostos Theos* 277-308) and W. Bousset (*Kyrios Christos* 83-89) that the special personal knowledge of the Father and Son in Matt 11:27 par. Luke 10:22 can likewise have derived only from later Hellenistic Christianity.

Editorially, the divine sonship of Jesus has been known since the very start of Mark's gospel (1:1). In the story told by Mark, that sonship came forward almost as quickly in the shouts of unclean spirits, people besides Jesus being present (3:11; 5:27; cf. 1:24). Even if we were to discount the shouts of these spirits because he told them not to make him known (3:12; cf. 1:25 — though context requires a prohibition of any *further* publication, and no prohibition at all attaches to 5:27), at 8:38 he made known his divine sonship to a crowd as well as to his disciples; at 9:7 the Father made it known to Peter, James, and John (cf. 12:6); here in 13:32 Jesus makes it known to those same three plus Andrew; and in 14:61-62 Jesus will make it known to the Sanhedrin. Therefore we have every reason *not* to believe that Mark keeps Jesus' divine sonship secret till the Roman centurion proclaims it at the foot of the cross (15:39), as though Mark wants his audience to associate that sonship with suffering rather than with glory. J. D. Kingsbury (*Christology of Mark's Gospel* 19) argues in response that by associating the reference to Jesus' divine sonship in 13:32 with events that will follow the Passion, Mark keeps the sonship secret till 15:39. But this argument not only disregards the just-listed editorial and narratological revelations. It also fails to take seriously that already in 13:32, i.e. that in speaking to four of the disciples prior to 15:39, Jesus refers to himself as the Son of the Father (cf. Kingsbury's own rejection of a reference in 13:32 to "the Son of man" [ibid.]).

Only if we were to isolate the command that disciples stay awake for the Son of man's coming (vv 33-37) would that command disagree with earlier indications that other events must take place first. Given its position following those indications, and especially following the parable of the fig tree, staying awake for the Son of man's coming applies only to the immediately preceding yet still future period of unequaled tribulation. Paul's post-Jesuanic ethicizing of the command backdates it through application to present time (1 Thess 5:1-11; 1 Cor 16:13) and comes close to backdating the tribulation itself (Rom 13:11-14; 1 Cor 7:25-31; but see 2 Thess 2:3-4).

Because Mark likes γάϱ-clauses, we might hypothesize that he constructs "for (γάϱ) you don't know when the time is" (v 33b) as a redactional connection between vv 32 and 34 (so J. Gnilka 2. 208). Perhaps so, but we cannot be sure. As noted before, Mark is not the only one to use γάϱ-clauses; Jesus is capable of repeating himself (as v 33b repeats v 32); and Mark may insert γάϱ when writing up traditional material. Here, the real question boils down to whether or not the following parable originally related to uncertainty about the exact time of the Second Coming. If so, we have little reason to call v 33b (or v 33a) redactional. If not, we have considerable reason to do so. But the coming of a man suits the coming of the Son of man better than it would suit the coming of the kingdom (cf. a man's going away to *receive* a kingdom and then returning — Luke 19:12). Therefore we should not attribute to the parable an original reference to the coming of the kingdom in Jesus' earthly ministry.

As a whole, the parable and the foregoing and succeeding sayings, i.e. vv 32-37, look primarily like a digest and amalgam of earlier traditions that later made their way into Matt 24:42-51 par. Luke 12:36-46 (cf. Matt 25:14-30 par. Luke 19:12-27). Denial of knowledge concerning the day or hour (Mark 13:32) shortens pre-Matt 24:50 par. pre-Luke 12:46a (see also Matt 24:43-44 par. Luke 12:39-40). Βλέπετε, "watch out" (Mark 13:33a), echoes Mark 13:5, 9, 23. The immediately following ἀγϱυπνεῖτε prepares for the following parable by telling what watching out requires, i.e. alertness. "For you do not know when the time is" (v 33b) repeats the thought of v 32 just as the same thought is repeated in pre-Luke 12:39-40 and 12:46a. In phraseology, "[it is] like (ὡς) a man . . ." (v 34) adapts pre-Luke 12:36: "And you, [be] like (ὅμοιοι) men. . . ." In substance, the man in v 34 is the master rather than the menservants of pre-Luke 12:36. His going away on a journey differs from the master's evening out at a local wedding feast in pre-Luke 12:36, but agrees with and originates in another master's being away far and long enough to require the transfer of domestic rule to a steward in pre-Luke 12:42-46. Reference to "his house" comes from the intervening parable in pre-Luke 12:39, however. The giving of authority to his slaves combines the plurality of slaves held responsible in pre-Luke 12:37-38 and the transfer of domestic rule in pre-Luke 12:42. It is the background of pre-Luke 12:42 that causes the superfluous and unusual use of "authority" in the sense of delegated responsibility. "His work" would have sufficed. A narrowing down to the responsibility of the doorkeeper to stay awake (γϱηγοϱῇ) derives from the combination of two elements: (1) the staying awake of the menservants in pre-Luke 12:36(-37) to open the door immediately when their master comes knocking and (2) the singleness of the steward to whom the other master transfers domestic rule in pre-Luke 12:42. The combination of multiple slaves and one doorkeeper allows a further combination of working, which comes from the task of distributing food to the household in pre-Luke 12:42 (but see also Luke 19:12-27), and staying awake. The command that the disciples stay awake combines the parabolic element of staying awake with the command to the disciples that they be ready in pre-Luke 12:40a. It also harks back to the command in Mark 13:33a, but with a new verb (γϱηγοϱεῖτε) drawn from this other material. "For you do not know when the master of the house is coming" (v 35b) again echoes "because at an hour that you don't suppose, the Son of man is coming" (pre-Luke 12:40b) plus "the master of that slave will come on a day that he [the slave] doesn't expect and in an hour that he doesn't know" (pre-Luke 12:46a). "Whether evening or midnight or cock-crowing or early morning" (the rest of v 35b) fills out "and if in the second and if in the third watch" (pre-Luke 12:38) and substitutes Roman watches for Jewish ones (cf. the adoption of Roman watches in b. Ber. 3b). Jews divided the night into three watches (Judg 7:19; Jub. 49:10, 12; BAGD s.v. φυλακή 4; S. Krauss, Talmudische Archäologie 2. 420), the Romans into four (cf. Acts 12:4; BAGD loc. cit.; Krauss, loc. cit.). Since the master is attending a wedding feast for at least the evening of the first Jewish watch, only the remaining two watches are relevant in pre-Luke 12:36-38. But since the master is away on a journey in Mark 13:34-35, none of the watches may be excluded. Being away on a journey broadens the geographical purview of the parable so as to make the Roman division fitting (though we might consider the possibility that for a Roman reading audience Mark switched from the Jewish division to the Roman — cf. 6:48). "Lest coming suddenly he find you sleeping" (v 36) adapts pre-Luke 12:39: "if the house-master had known at what hour the thief was coming, he wouldn't have let his house be dug through." Finally, "but what I say to you I say to all, 'Stay awake' " (v 37) adapts pre-Luke 12:41: "But Peter said, 'Lord, are you speaking this parable to us or also to all?' " (cf. D. Wenham, Rediscovery 57-62). In this last instance we must bear in mind the possibility that Luke 12:41 does not represent pre-Marcan tradition (see the discussion and references to other literature in I. H. Marshall, Luke 533, 539-40), but the apparent use throughout vv 32-37 of material from pre-Luke 12:36-46 tends toward the pre-Marcan traditionality of this piece, too.

The just-outlined skipping back and forth combines with freedom of adaptation to give the impression of a speaker who spontaneously draws on various elements in previous remarks. One might argue that a Christian redactor, not Jesus as speaker, lengthened the evening in town to a journey out of town for correspondence with experienced delay of the Second Coming. But a journey out of town occurs already in Luke 12:42-46 (and see J. A. Fitzmyer, Luke 987; I. H. Marshall, Luke 533-34, 542, for cautions against dismissing as secondary the element of delay). One might also argue that a Christian redactor but not Jesus would have failed to think, when changing a wedding feast in town to a journey out of town, that the man away on a journey could not enter town at night, the gates being closed. But Matt 2:9-11; Luke 2:8-20; 11:5-6 destroy this argument. By no means did everybody live in a walled town or city; and the question of historicity in Matt 2:9-11; Luke 2:8-20 has nothing to do with the issue; for like Luke 11:5-6, Mark 13:34 is parabolic. Yet again, one might argue for a Christian redactor instead of Jesus from the unrealism of the command that the doorkeeper stay awake for the whole time of a journey by his master, and from the unrealistic limitation to the night watches, whereas a man away on a journey is just as likely, or more likely, to return in daytime. But unrealism characterizes a number of Jesus' parables, indeed enhances their points. Here and quite apart from the possibility of his building the present parable on other, earlier ones, these unrealisms enhance both the need for constancy in the disciples' readiness and the possibility of the Son of man's returning at an unexpected moment (cf. the familiar phrase, "like a thief in the night," based on the saying in Matt 24:43 par. Luke 12:39, in 1 Thess 5:2, 4b; 2 Pet 3:10a; Rev 3:3b; 16:5a). We should also note that unrealism already characterizes the parable in Luke 12:36-38: in real life all the slaves in a household do not need to stay awake to open the door when the master comes knocking late at night. How many handles does the door have? In this respect, Mark 13:34 looks more realistic, not less so. Limitation of space prohibits a discussion of D. Wenham's view (Rediscovery 15-49) that Mark at first reflects the parable of the talents in Matt 25:13-30; but see R. H. Gundry, Matthew 502-10, for Matthean redaction that would undermine that view.

Several dual expressions crop up in vv 33-35: "watch out" and "be alert"; "away on a journey" and "having left his house"; "having given to his slaves authority" and "to each his work"; "when the master of the house is coming" and "whether evening or midnight or cock-crowing or early morning." Since duality characterizes Mark's writing, we might put some of these expressions to his account, e.g., "watch out" (because of its earlier occurrences), "having left his house" (because of Mark's liking to use circumstantial participial phrases), "having given his slaves authority" (again because of Mark's liking to use circumstantial participial phrases, but also because this phrase seems to echo 3:15; 6:7 and because in the parable the slaves have nothing to do, much less anything to do that requires authority), and "whether evening . . ." (because of correspondence between the four Roman watches and other Roman or Latin features of Mark). The matter is not so easy to decide, however; for "watch out" might represent a thematic thread original to the discourse, "his house" seems to rest on pre-Luke 12:39, "having given his slaves authority" seems to rest on pre-Luke 12:37-38, 42, and the night watches seem to rest on pre-Luke 12:38. A penchant for duality characterizes Semitic speech in general, not just Mark's speech.

J. Lambrecht (*Redaktion* 242-43) defends the v.l. that includes "and pray" after "be alert" (v 33) on the grounds (1) that only B D *pc* a c k omit "and pray"; (2) that Mark may have inserted "and pray" in 14:38 as well as here; (3) that δεόμενοι, "requesting," in Luke 21:36 presupposes "and pray" here; and (4) that Mark inserted prayer in 11:17, 24. But B and D and their supporters make a strong combination in view of their frequent disagreement. The large amount of parallelistic influence that affected the early textual history of the synoptics makes it easier to think of influence from 14:38 on 13:33a. The standing of 14:38 in the body of its pericope tends toward the traditional rather than the redactional. Δέομαι is a favorite word of Luke — fifteen of its twenty-two occurrences in the NT belong to Luke-Acts — and it typifies his redactional interest in prayer. The absence of prayer in the parallel Matt 24:42; 25:13 supports its absence from Mark 13:33 and its redactional insertion in Luke 21:36. On the opposite side, prayer may belong to the tradition behind Mark 11:17, 24. With ὡς ἄνθρωπος, "[it (i.e. the situation) is] as if a man" (v 34), cf. 4:26 (also 4:31). Ἄνθρωπος may carry the meaning of τις, "someone," as in 4:26; 7:11; 12:1; but the attached adjective ἀπόδημος, "away on a journey," allows the usual meaning, "a man" (E. C. Maloney, *Semitic Interference* 131-34; M. Reiser, *Syntax und Stil* 20, n. 31; see R. Kühner and B. Gerth, *Ausführliche Grammatik* §405b2[a] on ἀπόδημος).

Since elsewhere in the synoptics ἀποδημέω means taking a long journey (see 12:1 parr.; Matt 25:14, 15; Luke 15:13; cf. ἐκδημέω in 2 Cor 5:6, 8, 9), we should not minimize the length of the journey indicated by ἀπόδημος in Mark 13:34, as though the authenticity of the parable depends on the master's return before one whole night has passed and as though authenticity must be preserved at any cost. It goes too far to make "his house" stand for the church or a local house-church. The owner only leaves the house; it plays no distinct role in the parable. Nor did Jesus, for whom the owner stands, leave a house-church. Likewise, "the doorkeeper" and "the slaves" do not represent a church leader and lay people, respectively. The doorkeeper does not lead the other slaves. Their receiving authority contradicts his representing a leader of others in the church; and if such a representation were meant, his being commanded to stay awake would contradict the command that "all" stay awake (v 37) by concentrating that command on church leaders (against P. S. Minear, *Commands of Christ* 152-57; also J. R. Donahue, *Gospel in Parable* 58-60, where all the slaves, not just the doorkeeper, are portrayed as authoritative ministers).

Against the suggestion that Mark inserts "to each his task" in v 34 to counteract apocalyptically incited quitting of work, see the discussion of 2 Thess 3:6-12 by R. Russell in *NTS* 34 (1988) 105-19. Furthermore, "to each his task" only builds up to the task of the doorkeeper (see the comments on increasing specificity). The tasks remain entirely undefined. Even the task of the doorkeeper remains undefined. Only from the application in vv 35-37 can we infer that he is to open the door when the master comes knocking. Otherwise we might suppose that he is to keep it locked against intruders, open it for his fellow slaves, etc. A definition of the task would detract from the emphasis on watchfulness. Hence, we should not import from 9:35; 10:41-45 the definition in terms of service to one another, or from 13:10 the definition in terms of world-wide evangelism.

If the giving of authority to the slaves, to each his task, merely prepares for the command that the doorkeeper stay awake, there is no need to say that the parable "breaks down" unless all the slaves are supposed to stay awake (as thought by C. E. Carlston, *Parables* 198). The shift from the singular command in v 34 to the plural command in v 35 signals the shift from parable to application. Consequently, the plural command does not imply that all the slaves in the parable were to stay awake with the doorkeeper. Waiting outside the door for someone to come out of his house in daytime makes Prov 8:34 an inappropriate cross-reference for v 34, where the doorkeeper is told to stay awake inside for his master's return home at nighttime. The bride's being in bed when her beloved knocks and his having left by the time she gets up and goes to the door make Cant 5:2-6 another inappropriate cross-reference. Just as "a man" changed to "the owner (κύριος) of the vineyard" once the man had planted the vineyard (Mark 12:1, 9), so "a man" changes to "the master (κύριος) of the house" once the man has acted as master by giving his servants authority to run the house while he is away (13:34, 35). These progressions are as likely on the lips of Jesus as in the pen of Mark.

Jesus' finding the disciples asleep after telling them to stay awake in Gethsemane does not imply that Mark has redacted 13:34-36 in anticipation of 14:32-42. It is just as likely that in reminiscence of 13:34-36 Jesus told the disciples to stay awake, but that they fell asleep "because their eyes were being weighed down" (14:40b). C. B. Cousar (in *Int* 24 [1970] 333) uses the commands to stay awake for prayer in 14:32-42 to define staying awake in 13:33-37 similarly rather than in the sense of apocalyptic withdrawal. E. Best (*Following Jesus* 153) defines staying awake as preparedness to suffer a cross, again as in Gethsemane (see also T. J. Geddert, *Watchwords* 89-107). But the present context calls for expectancy, not prayer, much less preparedness to suffer a cross, to which the return of the master would not at all correspond. Underlining the call for expectancy is repeated emphasis on an uncertain time of return, and the ministry of Paul (to take but one of many possible examples in the history of the church) proves that expectancy need not lead to apocalyptic withdrawal. The call for expectancy likewise negates the interpretation of staying awake as an ascetic defense against demons, who flourish at night and induce sleep (so O. Böcher, *Christus Exorcista* 126-28, 131; idem, *Dämonenfurcht* 296-98; idem, *Mächte* 48-49). The context does not point to demonic activity.

R. H. Lightfoot (*Gospel Message* 53) draws parallels between the night watches of v 35 and the time schedule of Jesus' passion and uses those parallels to establish Jesus' passion as a model for the disciples' taking their own crosses. Verbally, "early" (πρωΐ) does appear in both 13:35 and 15:1; and the narrative statements that a cock crowed twice (14:68, 72) match cockcrowing as the name of a night watch (13:35). But one wonders whether if Mark had meant to associate the night watch "evening" with the evening of the Last Supper he would not have repeated the adverb ὀψέ in 14:17 (so 13:35) instead of switching to the substantival adjective ὀψίας (though cf. 11:11 with 11:19). Above all, "today, this night" (14:30) is too general to match "midnight" (13:35). Had Mark wanted a parallel here, he would only have had to say that it was midnight when Jesus went to Gethsemane. As it is, "today, this night" is associated with Peter's denials and defined as the time before the second cockcrowing, which turns out to include some time before the first cockcrowing as well. In other words, "today, this night" and the cockcrowings are intermeshed, not distinguished as a parallel with 13:35 would require. Furthermore, the taking of Jesus to Pilate makes "early" refer in 15:1 to morning, not to the last watch of the night as in 13:35. Consequently, the two cockcrowings appear to encompass the last watch ("early" in 13:35) as well as all or some of the next-to-last one ("cockcrowing" in 13:35). Thus the suggestion of T. J. Geddert (*Watchwords* 133; see also 94-103, 282-83, n. 51) that "Mark refrained from speaking of 'the midnight hour' in the Gethsemane account even though in his scheme of things he must have thought of it as such" because "he may not have wanted to 'over-identify' with the midnight hour lest readers mistake the Gethsemane experience itself, and not the whole passion, for 'The Hour' of eschatological fulfilment" — this suggestion, already desperately over-subtle, falls short of solving the problems that plague the parallels drawn by Lightfoot.

E. Lövestam (*Spiritual Wakefulness* 84-91) and E. Best (*Following Jesus* 153) reasons that since people do not travel at night, the watches of the night represent the present evil age, which lulls Christians to sleep. But Luke 11:5-6 proves the possibility of travel at night in Jesus' parables; and here nighttime serves the point of unexpectedness, i.e. incalculability. Listing the night watches does not allude to a delay in the Second Coming (against J. Gnilka 2. 210). Such an allusion would require a reference to years, as in a reference that could have been made to the house-owner's staying away for years or for a long time.

"To all" (v 37a) does not necessarily betray a redactional inclusion of the whole church; for if Jesus was speaking to only four of his disciples, as vv 3-5a indicate, he might himself have broadened the application of his command to wakefulness to include all other disciples, too. Again the repetitiveness of the commands to watch out, stay alert, and stay awake are as easily Jesuanic as Marcan or intermediarily redactional. Since Jesus is speaking during the week of Passover, the command that all stay awake may be triggered by the need to stay awake till late on Passover eve (*m. Pesaḥ.* 10:8; *b. Pesaḥ.* 109a, 120b; *t. Pesaḥ* 10:9; so W. Grundmann [7 Aufl.] 366; cf. D. Daube, *NTRJ* 332-35). On the other hand, uncertainty concerning the night watch during which the master will return from a journey (v 35), inclusion of night watches past midnight (v 35), ignorance concerning the day or hour of the Son of man's coming (v 32), and uncertainty concerning the season of the year when escape from the abomination of desolation will have to be made (v 18) all distance the Second Coming from any necessary connection with the Passover.

In v 37 ὅ, "what," refers forward to γρηγορεῖτε, "stay awake." The plural v.l. ἅ, "the things which" (A [W] *f*[1],13 Majority Text q sy[h]), refers backward to vv 33-36, and perhaps to the earlier parts of the discourse as well, and thereby leaves γρηγορεῖτε hanging. To an extent it is true that "I say to all" (v 37) contrasts with "privately" (v 3; see the comments ad loc.). But the more immediate contrast is with "I say to you" (v 37); and "privately" modified the question of Peter, James, John, and Andrew, not Jesus' response. "I say to you" helps form a verbal inclusion with "tell us" in v 4, but Jesus has not told them what they asked to know. W. Grundmann (7. Aufl., 367) detects no proper conclusion to the discourse and reasons that the immediate lead into the passion narrative equates Jesus' passion with the start of the eschatological woes described in chap. 13. But the generalization in 13:37 provides a well-rounded conclusion to the discourse, and an equation between Jesus' passion and the start of the eschatological woes would contradict their delay till the abomination of desolation (see esp. vv 7-8, 14, 18-19).

FURTHER PREDICTIONS AND THE START OF FULFILMENT

14:1-11 (Matt 26:1-16; Luke 7:36-50; 22:1-6; John 12:1-8)

The double reference in vv 1-2 and 10-11 to the chief priests' plot to kill Jesus makes an inclusion that defines vv 1-11 as a pericope. On exhibit is the predictive power of Jesus in that the details of his passion predictions are beginning to be fulfilled. Mark is also showing that Jesus did not suffer the disgrace of burial without prior anointing. The pericope subdivides into the chief priests' and scribes' plotting to kill Jesus (vv 1-2), the perfuming of his head by a woman in Bethany (vv 3-9), and Judas Iscariot's striking a bargain to give him over to the chief priests (vv 10-11). The middle section consists of the perfuming itself (v 3), some observers' criticism of it (vv 4-5), and Jesus' defending the woman who did it (vv 6-9).

14:1-2 *(Matt 26:1-5; Luke 22:1-2)* Δέ, "but," signals a new temporal setting that contrasts with the last one. Since "after three days" refers to the day after next (in particular to Easter Sunday after Good Friday — cf. 8:31; 9:31; 10:34 with 15:42; 16:1-2), "the Passover and Unleavened Bread were after two days" means that the Passover and Unleavened Bread were to come the next day. Since Jesus died on Friday (15:42), which came right after the Passover-first day of Unleavened Bread (14:12), Thursday is the Passover-first day of Unleavened Bread. The day from whose standpoint v 1a is written must then be Wednesday. Thus the narrative has moved beyond the discovery of the fig tree withered, the polemics in Jerusalem, and the Olivet Discourse on Tuesday (11:20–13:37), which followed the cursing of the fig tree and the cleansing of the temple on Monday (11:12-19), which in turn followed the Triumphal Procession at the end of a day's walk from Jericho on Sunday, Saturday the Sabbath having been spent resting in Jericho (10:46–11:11).

The reference to Passover and Unleavened Bread as coming after two days prepares for "not in the festal assembly" (v 2). "And the chief priests and the scribes were seeking how by seizing him with cunning they might kill [him]" (cf. Exod 21:14 and R. H. Gundry, *Use of the OT* 56) recalls 11:18 ("and the chief priests and the scribes . . . were seeking how they might destroy him") and 12:12 ("and they [the chief priests and the scribes and the elders — 11:27] were seeking to seize him") and carries forward the beginning of the fulfilment of Jesus' passion predictions in 8:31 (". . . to be rejected by the elders and the chief priests and the scribes and to be killed"); 9:31 ("and they will kill him"); and especially 10:33 ("and the Son of man will be given over to the chief priests and the scribes, and they will condemn him to death . . . and they will kill [him]"; cf. 12:7-8). The similarities in phraseology favor a deliberate attempt to highlight Jesus' predictive power by showing how the predictions are starting to take place. The forward placement of αὐτόν, "him," and ἐν δόλῳ, "with cunning," not only favors construal with κρατήσαντες, "by seizing," rather than with ἀποκτείνωσιν, "they might kill." It also gives emphasis to the cunning with which they were seeking to seize Jesus. The present tense of the subjunctive ἀποκτείνωσιν (contrast the non-indicative aorist verbs in 8:31; 11:18, 27; 12:12) emphasizes their murderous intent (cf. S. E. Porter, *Verbal Aspect* 326).

"For they were saying" introduces the reason for cunning (again cf. 12:12), not the reason for seizing and killing Jesus. This resolve on cunning casts the Sanhedrin in a bad light and will find its opportunity in Judas Iscariot's offer (vv 10-11). "They" probably refers to the chief priests and scribes, whom Mark has just mentioned, not to people in general; for people in general would have no reason to say, "Not in the festal assembly, lest a riot of the people will be" (cf. 11:8-10), or to refer to themselves as "the people" (τοῦ λαοῦ). The indicative mood of ἔσται with μήποτε, having the force of "otherwise there will be . . . and we don't want that!" (cf. Heb 3:12), underscores the certainty of the people's rioting on Jesus' behalf if he is arrested in their midst (cf. 11:32). This certainty reminds us of Mark's stress on Jesus' hold over the masses. The ellipsis in "not in the festal assembly" (a full statement would read, "Let us not seize him in the festal assembly") sharpens the element of cunning in avoidance of a riot.

14:3-5 *(Matt 26:6-9; Luke 7:36-39; John 12:1-6)* Jesus' presence in Bethany recalls previous indications that he is staying overnight in that town and going back and forth to Jerusalem (11:11-12, 19-20, 27; 13:1-3). This is the first and only time we read about the house of Simon the leper, however; and we cannot tell whether Jesus stays there regularly or is eating there only as a guest at meal. Nor do we learn from Mark anything more about Simon. "The leper" distinguishes this Simon from Simon Peter, whose house in Capernaum Jesus visited (1:29; cf. 2:1; 9:33). The designation also distinguishes this Simon from Simon the Cananaean (3:18), from Simon the brother of Jesus (whose residence in Nazareth would forestall a confusion with the present Simon, however — see 6:3), and from Simon of Cyrene (who has yet to be mentioned in 15:21).

The asyndetic addition in v 3 of a second genitive absolute having Jesus as the subject right after the opening genitive absolute, which has already had him as the subject, calls attention to the unusualness of the woman's pouring perfume on Jesus' head "while he was reclining [at meal]." Ordinarily, people would have anointed themselves before going out (Matt 6:17); or a host might anoint them on entry into his house (Luke 7:46). Details concerning the perfume that the woman has — its being contained in an alabaster flask, made with unadulterated nard, and costing much — enhance the honor paid to Jesus and give apparent justification to the criticism that the woman wastes the perfume when she breaks the flask and pours out the perfume. Nard holds "the foremost possible rank among perfumes" (Plin. *HN* 12.25.42; cf. 13.2.18). Asyndeton introduces the breaking of the flask and thereby punctuates the unexpected lavishness of the outpouring. In the first place, pouring out the perfume exceeds smearing a bit of it (see Polyb. 26.1.13 for an excellent illustration of this point). In the second place, breaking the flask makes it henceforth unusable and therefore dramatizes the completeness of the outpouring: not a drop is held back.

Though δέ, "but," sets those who become indignant over against the woman, Mark leaves it indefinite who growl at the woman after becoming indignant and saying to one another, "For what purpose has this waste of perfume taken place?

For this perfume could have been sold for over three hundred denarii [over a full year's wages for a fully employed manual laborer according to Matt 20:1-16; Tac. *Ann.* 1.17; Tob 5:14; rabbinic passages in Str-B 1. 831] and given to the poor." Matthew attributes these reactions to the disciples, Luke to "the Pharisee" (later addressed as "Simon"), and John to Judas Iscariot. Mark's omitting to identify the woman's critics shows a lack of interest in blackballing the disciples. He concentrates instead on the woman's act and the meaning that Jesus will give it. The attachment of "over" to "three hundred denarii" makes the perfume indeterminately high priced (contrast John 12:5 and cf. the statement of Plin. [*HN* 13.3.20] that the cost of luxurious perfume "exceeds four hundred denarii per pound" [the lower prices listed in 12.26.43-44 having to do with nard-leaves prior to mixture with oil to produce perfume]). Not only does noting the high cost of the perfume give apparent justification of the criticism. So also does mentioning the possibility of charitable use.

14:6-9 *(Matt 26:10-13; Luke 7:40-50; John 12:7-8)* Δέ, "but," sets Jesus as the woman's defender over against her critics. For Mark, Jesus' answer does two things: (1) it adds yet another passion prediction to strengthen the portrayal of Jesus as able to foretell his own fate; (2) it adds another prediction of different content, too, that "wherever the gospel is preached in the whole world" the woman's work "will be talked about in memory of her." By the time Mark writes, of course, both predictions have come to pass so as to confirm his apology for the Cross. The concurrence of the further passion prediction and the Sanhedrin's plot to kill Jesus suggests his supernatural knowledge of that plot (cf. vv 30, 41-42) and forecasts the speedy fulfilment of his prediction. Ἄφετε αὐτήν, "leave her [alone]," recalls 10:14. "Why are you causing her troubles?" refers to the critics' growling at her. The forward position of αὐτῇ, "her," suggests that she is the last person at whom they should be growling; and the forward position of κόπους, "troubles," suggests that troubles are the last things they should be causing her. "A good work" contradicts their description, "this waste" (ἀπώλεια, usually translated "destruction"), and establishes a contrast with the dastardly plot of the Sanhedrin and the coming equally dastardly offer of Judas Iscariot to give Jesus over to them. The forward position of καλὸν ἔργον, "a good work," and the cognateness of ἔργον to ἠργάσατο, "worked," provide an emphasis that intensifies the contradiction and contrast. "In me" (ἐν ἐμοί) contrasts with the critics' reference to "the poor." Though a Semitism (see the following notes), the preposition ἐν highlights in Greek the close association of the good work with Jesus' very body. The quick, asyndetic succession of a command, question, and declaration (v 6) gives this first part of Jesus' response a powerful thrust. "For you always have the poor with you" builds up to the passion prediction in the following statement: "and whenever you want you are able to do well for them, but me you do not always have." Whether or not the language struck the woman's critics as a passion prediction, earlier predictions of the Passion will have inclined Mark's audience to understand the language so. In the statement about the poor (v 7a), the adverb "always" receives the most emphasis, the direct object "the poor" the next most emphasis (see the Greek word order). In Jesus' statement about himself (v 7c), the direct object "me" receives the most emphasis, the adverbial phrase "not always" the next most emphasis. This reversal pinpoints the coming absence of Jesus; and an adversative δέ, "but," highlights the reversal. But the statement might be understood as referring to an absence due simply to his itineration elsewhere, especially in Galilee. So the next statements, "She has done what she could (ἔσχεν [meaning that what 'she had' she used]); she has anticipated perfuming (μυρίσαι) my body for the preparation for burial" (v 8), insure that Jesus is making a passion prediction. His being in the prime of life rules out an implication of normal death. The indirectness of the prediction — burial only implies death — suits the presence of the woman and perhaps of others in addition to the Twelve (cf. 2:20). It appears that only the Twelve have heard explicit passion predictions (8:31; 9:31; 10:32-34), and Jesus' statements need not imply that the woman had in mind the meaning that he gives to her deed. The fact that she perfumed only the head of Jesus, whereas he speaks of his body, favors that she did *not* have in mind a preparation for burial (cf. also the different diction in 16:1, where women "have bought aromatics [ἀρώματα] in order that they might anoint [ἀλείψωσιν] him"). Since Jews ordinarily use cheap oil for corpses (see the comments on 16:1), his funereal interpretation of the expensive perfume gives him dignity in burial so as to erase the shame of what turns out to be crucifixion.

Emphasizing Jesus' prediction are (1) the asyndeton with which both v 8a and v 8b begins; (2) the wordplay which began with παρέχετε, "cause" (v 6), continued with ἔχετε, "have" (v 7 bis), and now climaxes in ἔσχεν, "could" (v 8); (3) the repetition of ποιέω, "do" (vv 7, 8; see also v 9); and (4) the silence of Jesus as well as of Mark with regard to the woman's motive (contrast Luke and apparently John, where the foregoing story of Jesus' raising Lazarus from the dead, the special role played in that story by Mary, and a following back-reference to the raising of Lazarus [John 12:9-11] seem to imply that Mary anointed Jesus out of thankfulness for his raising of her brother Lazarus). Again, all attention in Mark focuses on the woman's act and the predictive interpretation that Jesus gives it. Anticipatory preparation adds a detail that has not appeared in earlier passion predictions — viz., that Jesus' corpse will not be prepared in the usual manner between death and burial — and thus enhances his foresight. "But truly I say to you" and the absence of a following ὅτι, "that," emphasize his additional prediction that alongside the gospel itself, what the woman has done will be talked about throughout the whole world (cf. *Midr. Qoh.* 7:1 with John 12:3b) with the result that she will be remembered (see M. Reiser, *Syntax und Stil* 148, on the omission of ὅτι). Δέ, "but," which occurs with the ἀμήν-formula only here in the gospels, draws a contrast between the modesty and the world-wide discussion of her good work. "Whole" makes the prediction of such discussion unlikely of fulfilment and therefore the fulfilment more impressive.

14:10-11 *(Matt 26:14-16; Luke 22:3-6)* The description of Judas Iscariot as "the one of the Twelve" harks back to the mention in 3:19 of Judas as one of that chosen number. Thus the definite article before "one" is probably anaphoric. Adding emphasis to Judas's name and description and therefore to the perfidy that he is about to exhibit is the forward placement of his name and description.

Similarly, his going away to the chief priests "in order that he might give him over to them" presents the reverse of discipleship by contrast with his having gone away to Jesus among those chosen "in order that they might be with him" (3:13-14; N.B. the use of ἀπῆλθεν/-ον πρός, "went away to," both there and here, and cf. 14:17). The present going away also begins to fill out the description in 3:19, "who also gave him over," and to narrate the fulfilment of Jesus' predictions that he will be given over (9:31; 10:33; see also 14:18, 21, 41-44) as well as to indicate the way out of the chief priests' and scribes' recently noted predicament (14:1-2; see S. M. Smith in *NTS* 35 [1989] 175-78, 181). This way out causes the chief priests such joy that they promise to give Judas money (on their being mentioned alone at this point, see the excursus on the classes of the Sanhedrin just following the comments on 8:31-32a). Δέ, "but," sets them off from Judas to distinguish the two parties in the bargain; and the indefinite amount of money that they promise for his dastardly deed contrasts with the over three hundred denarii devoted to perfuming Jesus' body in preparation for burial. The Sanhedrin's seeking how to seize Jesus with cunning now yields to Judas's seeking how to give Jesus over conveniently. Jesus' predictions are indeed starting to be fulfilled. The non-attribution of any reason or motive — neither disgruntlement with the wasteful anointing and with Jesus' defense of it nor the desire for money (which is only promised, not demanded) — makes the accent fall on this beginning of fulfilment (so H.-J. Klauck, *Judas* 49) and on the perfidy of Judas's offer and effort (so L. Schenke, *Studien* 136).

NOTES

According to G. W. E. Nickelsburg (in *HTR* 73 [1980] 153-94), Mark 14–15 belongs to a genre of stories concerning persecution and vindication, the vindication of Jesus originally having occurred in 15:38-39, not in 16:1-8 (see also Genesis 37ff.; Ahikar; Esther; Daniel 3, 6; Susanna; Wisdom 2, 4–5; 3 Maccabees; 2 Maccabees 7). In addition to the motif of righteous suffering, the typological components of provocation (Mark 11:15-18), conspiracy (11:18; 12:12-13; 14:1-2), trial and accusation (14:53-64), reaction (14:63), etc., are supposed to associate Mark's passion narrative with this genre. For the provocation, however, Nickelsburg has to reach far back before chaps. 14–15. (Even under the supposition that Mark has not inserted 14:3-9 in its present position, the substitution of that passage for 11:15-18 by J. B. Green [*Death of Jesus* 171] neglects that the anointing of Jesus is not said to have provoked Judas, let alone the chief priests and the scribes; that it is they, not he, who needs provoking since they rather than he want to kill Jesus; and that they are provoked to plot Jesus' death already before the anointing.) Further problems are created by Mark's order of episodes (as compared with the rest of the supposed genre) and by the necessity of treating some of the components in Mark as ironic (e.g., investiture and acclamation). To designate 14:62 and 15:29-32 as Jesus' decision (another component in the supposed genre) is also problematic. If the typological components were to help us understand how the story of his passion and resurrection took shape, they would still fail to help us make historical critical judgments; for real life as well as fiction often follows the scheme detected by Nickelsburg in stories of persecution and vindication. As to the motif of righteous suffering, we should note the absence from Mark of faithfulness to the Torah, of details concerning Jesus' physical suffering, of composure on his part (to the contrary, see 14:32-39; 15:34), of an example set by him in his suffering (see D. J. Moo, *OT* 293-96; H.-J. Steichele, *Der leidende Sohn Gottes* 259, n. 241; M. Hengel, *Atonement* 40-41; E. Best, *Temptation* xlvii-xlix; D. Juel, *Messianic Exegesis* 102-3).

The main phenomena put forward in favor of a pre-Marcan passion narrative — viz., that most of the materials in chaps. 14–15 could not have circulated independently from one another but are interdependent for their meaning, that Matthew and Luke do not redact Mark's passion narrative so freely as they have redacted earlier materials in Mark, and that even John follows Mark's passion narrative or a similar one fairly closely though differing widely from earlier materials in Mark — are as explicable by historical interdependence of the events narrated (whether or not a narrative of them predated Mark) as by written or oral interdependence in a pre-Marcan passion narrative. And Matthew and Luke may follow Mark's passion narrative fairly closely, not because a pre-Marcan passion narrative known to them inhibits their redactional tendencies, but because the materials in Mark's passion narrative are more interdependent than are the earlier materials in Mark. If John knows and uses Mark, he may follow Mark's passion narrative fairly closely for the same reason. Otherwise we are back to the possibility of historical interdependence for the events themselves. And in all three cases, we have also to consider the possibility of authorial fatigue: Matthew, Luke, and John may have simply grown tired of redacting Mark so much as they did before. These considerations apply whatever the suggested context of a pre-Marcan passion narrative: preaching, catechism, martyrology, liturgy (in particular, the Lord's Supper — see J. Green, *Death of Jesus* 175-215).

W. H. Kelber (*Oral and Written Gospel* 184-99) roundly criticizes theories of a written pre-Marcan passion narrative but wrongly pits orality and Jesus' death against each other. After all, Paul makes the Cross the essence of the oral gospel (1 Cor 1:18; 15:1ff. et passim; for criticism from the standpoint of up-to-date oral studies, see T. P. Haverly, "Reversals in Mark's Passion Narrative and the Characterization of Peter" [unpublished paper for the SBL meeting in Anaheim, CA, November 1989] 1-7). As elsewhere in Mark (except for those few passages that are comparable with pre-Q tradition), the impossibility of telling whether style and substance derive from Mark, from tradition, or from both Mark and tradition foredooms attempts to discover a pre-Marcan passion narrative (for surveys of the attempts, see D. Juel, *Messiah and Temple* 1-39; E. Linnemann, *Studien* 110-15; G. Schneider in *BZ* 16 [1972] 222-44; J. Ernst in *TGl* 70 [1980] 160-80; D. Dormeyer, *Passion* 4-23; T. A. Mohr, *Markus- und Johannespassion* 14-35; W. Schenk in *EvE* 36 [1984] 527-43; M. L. Soards in *BB* 11 [1985] 144-69; J. R. Donahue in *The Passion in Mark* 8-16; idem, *Are You the Christ?* 5-30; B. L. Mack, *Myth* 249-68). If Mark derives his information from Peter (Eus. *H.E.* 3.39.15), we may need to look no farther than Peter's telling what he saw and heard. At the same time, the apologetic concerns which drive the rest of Mark's gospel (take, e.g., the emphasis on Jesus as a great predictor) drive the passion narrative, too, whether we assign those concerns to tradition or to redaction. So the passion narrative does not stand apart (cf. Haverly, op. cit. 8-11).

Mark has not mentioned the evening of Tuesday (contrast 11:11, 19; 14:17), probably because Jesus' exit from the temple after a long day during which he went into Jerusalem, commented on the withered fig tree along the way, had one confrontation after another, warned against the scribes, commended a widow, left the temple, sat on the Mount of Olives, and delivered a lengthy discourse all make it obvious that he went to Bethany for the night (cf. v 3: "and while he was in Bethany"). Verse 1 then offers a fresh start. On the chronology of Passion Week and Easter, see esp. R. Pesch 2. 323-28; L. Schenke, *Studien* 27-36. Attempts to trace a deliberately constructed week of passion run into problems. Against starting such a week on Sunday, as weeks do start, that day is not specified in 11:1-11; and the next Sunday, which *is* specified (16:2), is then left hanging. Against starting the week on Monday and including the following Sunday, weeks do not start on Monday and end on Sunday; and Monday is not specified in 11:12, where we read only of the day after the Triumphal Procession, entry into Jerusalem, and exit to Bethany. The events of the Passion and Resurrection span eight days, not seven.

On πάσχα, "Passover," see H. P. Rüger in *Markus-Philologie* 81. In v 1, "Passover" refers to the festival by that name. In v 12a it will refer to the Passover sacrifice, in vv 12b, 14, 16 to the Passover meal, including the sacrifice. If in Exod 23:15; 34:18; Lev 23:6; 2 Chr 35:17 the LXX can use the arthrous neuter plural of ἄζυμος for הַמַּצּוֹת, "the unleavened [loaves of] bread," a Semitic tradition may underlie Mark's similar Greek (against L. Schenke, *Studien* 21-22). For brevity, Mark does not put "the Festival of" before "Unleavened Bread" (see Exod 12:17 MT; Josephus *Ant.* 3.10.5 §250 for similar examples of abbreviation; contrast Exod 23:15; 34:18; Lev 23:6; 2 Chr 35:17; 1 Esdr 1:17; Luke 22:1 et passim). For the association of Unleavened Bread with Passover, including the requirement that unleavened bread be eaten on Passover as well as during the seven following days of Unleavened Bread, see Exod 12:17-20; Lev 23:5-6; 2 Chr 35:17; 1 Esdr 1:17; Josephus *Ant.* 3.10.5 §249. In v 12 this association will turn into an equation of Passover with the first day of Unleavened Bread (see R. H. Gundry, *Matthew* 524, for a rationale and other references, to which add — besides Matt 26:17 parr. — Luke 22:1; Josephus *Ant.* 11.4.8 §§109-10; 14.2.1 §21; idem *J.W.* 2.1.3 §10; Str-B 2. 812-15; G. Amadon in *ATR* 27 [1945] 109-15). There is no need to suppose that πρώτῃ ἡμέρᾳ τῶν ἀζύμων, "on [the] first day of Unleavened Bread" (v 12), will misread an original πρὸ τῶν ἡμερῶν τῶν ἀζύμων, "before the days of Unleavened Bread." Only in Acts 12:3; 20:6 do we read *"the days* of Unleavened Bread."

T. A. Mohr (*Markus- und Johannespassion* 120-22) distinguishes between tradition and redaction in vv 1-2. As usual, our lack of Mark's source makes the distinction uncertain. Mohr also argues from the Sanhedrin's earlier seeking to arrest and destroy Jesus (11:18; 12:12; cf. 3:6) that the traditional element in vv 1-2 must have started a pre-Marcan passion narrative in which the present seeking was not redundant as it is in the larger context of Mark's gospel. The argument fails, however, because repetition may indicate an ongoing effort by the Sanhedrin rather than the juxtaposing of different traditions by Mark. Apart from the confrontations in chaps. 11–12, the Sanhedrin's present seeking to arrest and kill Jesus lacks motivation; i.e. vv 1-2 depend on a prior context.

The description of some scribes who appeared in Galilee as having come from Jerusalem (3:22; 7:1), the inclusion of the scribes among those who make up the whole Sanhedrin (15:1), and the inclusion of the elders with the chief priests and scribes (8:31; 11:27; 14:43, 53; 15:1) should keep us from assigning the chief priests to Jerusalem and the scribes to Galilee (against the tendency of J. Gnilka 2. 219). E. Haenchen (461-62) questions whether the chief priests and the scribes are the Sanhedrin (v 1). But though one might doubt that they are the whole of that body, surely they represent it (cf. v 55; 15:1); and their seeking to arrest and kill Jesus favors that they are indeed the whole (see the excursus just following the comments on 8:31-32). Seeking how they might kill him is not equivalent to a formal decision to do so, but it may presuppose such a decision (cf. Matt 26:4; John 11:53, 57). The question of historicity does not revolve around Mark's non-mention of a formal decision, however; and it lacks even a sober historical imagination to object that he could not know about the Sanhedrin's plot. Word gets around. The Sanhedrin were a large body of seventy-one members. Some of them may even have become Christians (John 3:1-21; 7:50-52; 19:38-42; Acts 6:7; 15:5 — against L. Schenke, *Studien* 13-15). See V. Taylor 528 against the notion that in v 2 "they were saying" means that others than the Sanhedrin were speaking.

Again in v 2, C. E. B. Cranfield (414) fills an ellipsis by adding κρατήσωμεν αὐτόν: "[let us] not [seize him]. . . ." Jesus has come to Jerusalem along with other pilgrims (10:1, 32, 46; 11:1-10); so the Sanhedrin cannot think of seizing him before the festival to avoid an uproar (the people to riot have already arrived) or after the festival (the man to be seized can be counted on to have left with his fellow pilgrims; cf. Josephus *J.W.* 2.1.3 §§10-13; idem *Ant.* 17.9.3 §§213-18; *b. Pesaḥ.* 80a for pilgrims' usually returning home after staying in Jerusalem for the week of Passover-Unleavened Bread). Hence, μὴ ἐν τῇ ἑορτῇ needs to be understood locally, "not in the festal assembly" (cf. Pss 73:4 LXX; 117:27 LXX; Luke 22:6; John 2:23; 7:10-11; Plot. *Enn.* 6.6.12) rather than temporally, "not during the festival" (see J. Jeremias, *Eucharistic Words* 71-73). The reference to cunning supports the local understanding, for otherwise we would read a purely temporal statement: "and the chief priests and the scribes were seeking *when* they might arrest and kill him" (cf. the omission of ἐν δόλῳ, "with cunning," in D a i r[1], apparently under a temporal understanding of ἐν τῇ ἑορτῇ).

The preceding reference to Passover and Unleavened Bread does not favor a temporal understanding over a local one, for Passover and Unleavened Bread entail assembly as well as calendar; nor does a non-historical evaluation of vv 1-2 subvert the arguments for a local understanding, for those arguments would grow out of the situation even though it were fictional (against L. Schenke, *Studien* 48-49). To support a pre-Marcan temporal understanding, T. A. Mohr (*Markus- und Johannespassion* 124) has to suppose that Mark adds ἐν δόλῳ. Since *killing* Jesus in the festal assembly would hardly be considered even to be rejected, Schenke (op. cit. 43-44) argues for the temporal understanding that though the Sanhedrin decided not to kill Jesus during the festival but apart from the assembly, they might well have *considered* the possibility of killing him during the festival. On the contrary, the placement of αὐτὸν ἐν δόλῳ before κρατήσαντες even though ἀποκτείνωσιν follows as the main verb favors that the cunning on which they decide has to do with *arresting* Jesus outside the festal assembly, not with killing him before or after the festival. A public execution of Jesus still risks an uproar, but not one that could succeed in making him its leader. The Sanhedrin do not fear an uproar over the death of Jesus, but one that might thwart their effort to put him to death. The literal meaning of εὐκαίρως, "at a good time," may seem at first to support a temporal understanding of μὴ ἐν τῇ ἑορτῇ. But in 6:31 the cognate εὐκαίρουν had to do with absence of crowds, just as in the local understanding at 14:2; so 6:31 turns out to support the local rather than the temporal. This local understanding spoils the argument that vv 1-2 imply more than two days' time till the Passover and therefore a position prior to chap. 11 in a pre-Marcan passion account lacking chaps. 11-13 (against Mohr, op. cit. 124).

In v 2 the people stand over against their leaders the Sanhedrin (BAGD s.v. λαός 1cα). In editorial comments of similar content, Mark writes about "the crowd" (11:18, 32; 12:12), but here the leaders themselves are speaking. Their use of τοῦ λαοῦ for "the people" may connote the people of God, as often in the LXX (cf. the preceding references to Passover and Unleavened Bread); but it goes farther than warranted to say that the leaders act in behalf of God's people (cf. J. Gnilka 2. 220). After all, the leaders hold back for fear that the people will disown their action to the extent of rioting against it. Only by overlooking the earlier statements which point to fear of acting against the crowd's high estimation of Jesus (11:18; 12:12; cf. 11:32) and Mark's repeated emphasis on Jesus' magnetic power over crowds (1:27-28, 37 et passim) could we reduce the Sanhedrin's present fear from one of an uproar in Jesus' behalf to one of mere tumult over a sensational execution, a tumult that would disturb the festival and thus profane it (so L. Schenke, *Studien* 61-62). Of course, if the unusual use of "people" rather than the editorially frequent "crowd" points away from redaction to tradition, we might posit a pre-Marcan reference to fear of tumult over a sensational execution. But we would still have to ask why Jesus' execution should cause a sensation if not for his popularity. In John 11:47-57 Jesus has yet to arrive in Jerusalem, and the Sanhedrin express concern over universal belief in him rather than over an uproar in the festal assembly. Despite these differences, that passage and the present one may imply the fear of a messianic revolt if the Sanhedrin leave Jesus alone. In the Johannine passage a reference to Roman reprisal makes such an inference clear, or at least likely. Schenke (op. cit. 64-65) argues that since the Sanhedrin will arrest and kill Jesus during the festival (14:43-47) and that since an uproar of the crowd will occur (15:6-14), Mark is here building up to a demonstration that the Sanhedrin are not in control of the events (cf. C. Maurer in *Redaktion und Theologie des Passionsberichtes nach den Synoptikern* 122). But the Sanhedrin will cunningly arrest Jesus at night in the Garden of Gethsemane and during the festival, not in the festal assembly or before or after the festival; and they will use the crowd to achieve the end of killing Jesus (15:11). So Mark does not engage in such a demonstration. With the plotting against Jesus' life, cf. esp. Pss 10:7-10; 35:20; 37:32; 52:4-6(2-4); 71:10-11.

We should note in particular the verbal correspondences that help make vv 1-2 and 10-11 an inclusion: "the chief priests and the scribes"–"the chief priests"; "were seeking"–"was seeking"; "how"–"how"; "with cunning"–"conveniently." See E. Best, *Disciples and Discipleship* 151-53, for a basis in tradition. The failure of Judas to criticize the good work narrated in vv 3-9 and the failure of vv 10-11 to ascribe Judas's offer of betrayal to unease with the good work may seem to favor that Mark has inserted the story of vv 3-9 into an unoriginal setting. On the contrary, the absence of Judas's motive focuses all attention on fulfilment as such, the fulfilment of Jesus' passion predictions, and therefore may derive from Mark's interest in that theme at least as easily as from a pre-Marcan independence of vv 3-9 and 10-11 from each other. Against insertion of vv 3-9, R. Pesch (2. 337) argues that if v 10 had originally followed on the heels of vv 1-2, the chief priests would not have been mentioned again in v 10 (the scribes of vv 1-2 dropping off for shorthand; cf. v 55; 15:3, 10, 11, 31 on the tendency to designate the chief priests alone because of their leadership in the Sanhedrin). This argument is not airtight, however; for one could think that Mark rementions the chief priests because he has inserted vv 3-9. On the other hand, the earlier dating of the incident in John 12:1 does not provide an airtight argument for Marcan insertion. For there, once Jesus enters Jerusalem he does not commute back and forth to Bethany; hence, John finds it easier to antedate the anointing of Jesus than to break up his stay in Jerusalem. See E. Lohmeyer 292 for parallels between vv 3-8 and 10:13-16, but they seem relatively insignificant.

It is very much disputed whether one or two incidents underlie vv 3-9 and the parallels in Luke and John. (Matthew depends on Mark alone.) The many differences among the narratives suggest separate incidents: (1) Bethany during Passion Week versus an unspecified but apparently Galilean locale prior to Passion Week and even prior to Jesus' long journey to Jerusalem in Luke 9:51ff.; (2) a leper versus a Pharisee; (3) an unobjectionable woman versus a sinful woman; (4) perfuming the head of Jesus versus a tearful wetting, drying, kissing, and anointing of his feet; (5) a breaking of the flask and consequently exhaustive use of the perfume versus no breaking of the flask and therefore a not necessarily exhaustive use of the perfume; (6) a plurality of critics versus a single unbeliever; (7) angry, vocal criticism of the woman for wasting perfume that could have brought over three hundred denarii for charitable use versus disdainful, silent unbelief in the prophethood of Jesus; and (8) his defending the woman on the grounds that the poor will stay but he will not, that the perfuming has prepared his body for burial, and that world-wide talk of the woman's good work will guarantee a remembrance of her versus Jesus' defending himself with a parable on forgiveness and love and then pronouncing the woman's sins forgiven. These differences characterize Mark-Matthew versus Luke. John is hybrid, agreeing with Mark-Matthew on Bethany and with Luke on the feet rather than the head, but presents further differences: a time six days before the Passover, an identification of the woman as Mary the sister of Lazarus and Martha, a wiping away of the perfume rather than of tears, an identification of the critic as Judas Iscariot, and a definitely inexhaustive use of perfume that allows the remainder to be kept. See B. Witherington III, *Women* 110-14.

But against a theory of two different incidents we have the unlikelihood of so many and so often unusual coincidences as the following: (1) the location in a house; (2) the belonging of the house to a man named Simon; (3) the occasion of a meal; (4) the timing of the central action in the course of reclining at the meal; (5) the appearance of a woman as doer of the action; (6) her putting perfume on Jesus; (7) the *mention* of an alabaster flask as containing the perfume (since perfume was commonly kept in alabaster flasks [Plin. *HN* 13.3.19; I. Ben-Dor in *QDAP* 11 (1944) 101-2], it is not the alabaster flask as such which merits notation); (8) a following objection; and (9) a defensive response by Jesus.

We might suppose that prior to the writing of the gospels, especially in the oral tradition, details concerning one incident were transferred to the other incident. On the other hand, it is more economical to think of redaction at the canonical level so long as the redaction agrees with the sort of redaction we can recognize elsewhere on a firmer base. The distinguishing of redaction from tradition depends a great deal on Luke's treatment of tradition and on whether John reflects the synoptics, pre-synoptic tradition, or independent tradition; but the heavy concentration of Semitisms that run throughout the story in Mark combines with several peculiarly Jewish features lying below the surface to favor the integrity, originality, and historicity of Mark's account. Though the task of spelling out the details of Lucan and Johannine redaction does not belong in a commentary on Mark, we might allude to the likelihood of Luke's redacting Mark with the help of additional material (cf. the possibility of his adding the parable of the two debtors with his adding the parable of the good Samaritan in 10:25-37 [contrast the parr.]) to introduce as he does elsewhere prophetic Christology (most recently in 7:16, which is unique to Luke), the free forgiveness of sinners (cf., for example, the even more recently mentioned friendship of Jesus with them in 7:36), and a contrast between contrite sinners and self-righteous Pharisees (as again uniquely in the preceding pericope at 7:30). We might also allude to the likelihood of John's characteristically redacting the synoptics or pre-synoptic tradition to symbolize the death of Jesus through the Satanic incitement of Judas Iscariot (cf. 6:70-71; 13:26-27; also the antedating habit of John and again his finding it easier to antedate the anointing than to break up Jesus' stay in Jerusalem with a commute to Bethany otherwise uncharacteristic of John's passion narrative — against J. F. Coakley in *JBL* 107 [1988] 242-43).

Here are the possible, probable, and certain Semitisms: (1) the more Aramaic than Greek abundance of asyndeta in vv 3 (tris), 6 (bis), 8 (bis); (2) the more Aramaic than Greek periphrastic construction in ἦσαν . . . ἀγανακτοῦντες, "were being indignant" (v 4); (3) πρὸς ἑαυτούς, "to one another" (v 4), which in normal Greek would denote the persons against whom indignation is directed whereas here it stands for the Aramaic ethical dative; (4) εἰς τί, "for what purpose?" (v 4), and τί, "why?" (v 6), which correspond to Semitic idiomatic use of the interrogative pronoun to express indignation; (5) the generic definite article with "poor" (vv 5, 7), corresponding to the emphatic state of Aramaic nouns; (6) ἠργάσατο ἐν ἐμοί, "she has worked in me" (v 6), reflecting the Hebrew and Aramaic use of בְּ, "in," plus a person with a verb of doing where Greek normally uses εἰς plus the accusative or a simple dative; (7) the antithetic parallelism in ἔχετε . . . , οὐ ἔχετε, "you have . . . , you do not have" (v 7); (8) in that parallelism the futuristic use of the present tense — most apparent in the negative phrase, which looks forward to Jesus' absence — corresponding to Aramaic more probably than to usage indigenous to Greek; (9) ὃ ἔσχεν, "what she had" in the sense "what she could" (v 8), for which Mark elsewhere uses δύναμαι and ἰσχύω but which corresponds to the Aramaic אַת לה; (10) the making of the adverbial thought of anticipation into the main verb (v 8), as often in Hebrew and Aramaic; (11) the ἀμήν-formula (v 9; but see the notes on 13:10 that the εἰς in κηρυχθῇ τὸ εὐαγγέλιον εἰς ὅλον τὸν κόσμον, "the gospel is preached in the whole world," does not carry the meaning of the Aramaic ל, "to"); (12) the καί (best omitted in English translation) at the start of the apodosis in v 9 (see E. C. Maloney, *Semitic Interference* 72-73); and (13) the avoidance of God's name by way of the phrase "in memory of her" (see the following notes on v 9; also for the point that the passive verbs in v 9 are not Semitic divine passives; but otherwise see J. Jeremias, *Abba* 107-9, 115-16, for all but the thirteenth Semitism).

Lying below the surface are some peculiarly Jewish features: (1) the description of Simon as a leper with a house in Bethany, east of Jerusalem (v 3), a description that links up with the spotting of a place for lepers east of Jerusalem according to 11QTemple 46:16-18 (cf. Y. Yadin, *Temple Scroll* 1. 304-5; idem in *BAR* 10/5 [1984] 46); (2) the concern of some onlookers for almsgiving, one of the three pillars of Jewish piety (Tob 12:8) and one that receives special attention at Passovertide (v 5; John 13:29; *m. Pesaḥ.* 9:11–10:1; J. Jeremias, *Eucharistic Words* 54; W. L. Lane 493); (3) the possible recollection of the pun in Eccl 7:1, "A good name is better than good ointment," as triggering Jesus' description of the perfuming as "a good work" (v 6; J. D. M. Derrett, *Studies* 1. xii, n. 1); (4) the allusion to Deut 15:11 in v 7 (see R. H. Gundry, *Use of the OT* 56); (5) the distinction between almsgiving and works of love, the superiority of works of love over almsgiving, and the importance of burying the dead as the last possible work of love to be done for a person (vv 6-8; for details, see J. Jeremias, *Abba* 109-15); and (6) the remembering in heaven of what is spoken on earth (for details, see the following notes on v 9).

These peculiarly Jewish features and the Semitisms number so many and pervade Mark's version so thoroughly as to make their attribution to redaction (whether Marcan or pre-Marcan) unlikely as well as unnecessary. Also supporting integrity, originality, and historicity are the occurrence of κόπος, "trouble," with παρέχω, "cause," in non-Marcan dominical sayings at Luke 11:7; 18:5 as well as in Mark 14:6, and the references to doing something on earth so that someone will be remembered in non-Marcan dominical sayings at 1 Cor 11:24, 25; Luke 22:19 as well as in Mark 14:9 (see the balanced discussion in I. H. Marshall, *Last Supper* 51-53). V. K. Robbins (in *The Passion in Mark* 36) suggests that Mark knows the remembrance in 1 Cor 11:25, 26 and transfers it to Mark 14:9. But the difference between remembrance of Jesus and remembrance of the woman makes the suggestion doubtful. Indeed, redaction by any Christian would probably have made Jesus rather than the woman the object of remembrance in v 9 (also against L. Schenke [*Studien* 81-82], who fails to see that vv 6-8 as well as v 9 deal more heavily with the woman and her work than with Jesus and his burial).

The duality of two successive prepositional phrases, asyndetically juxtaposed and using the same preposition (v 3; cf. 1:39; 5:1; 11:1, 11), and the duality of two successive genitive absolutes, also asyndetically juxtaposed (v 3; cf. 6:22; 8:1; 14:18, though without asyndeton or repetition of the substantive), could tend toward Marcan composition (though they would not tell whether Mark is merely passing on tradition in his own style or fabricating untraditional material). With ἀγανακτοῦντες, "becoming indignant," cf. 10:14, 41. The γάρ-clause in v 5a suits Marcan composition. With the presence and coming absence of Jesus (v 7), cf. 2:19-20. Σῶμα (v 8) will occur in the account of Jesus' burial (15:43, 45 v.l.; cf. 14:22); and the topographical use of ὅλον, "whole" (v 9), appears also in 1:28, 33, 39; 6:55; 15:33.

It is often argued that the un-Greekness of putting two genitive absolutes in succession and with the same subject shows that Mark or an earlier traditioner added one of them. It is then argued that since only the one concerning reclining at meal helps an understanding of the story, the one concerning Bethany and the house of Simon the leper must count as the addition. But Mark's love of duality makes it possible that he is responsible for both of the genitive absolutes. On the other hand, we have already noted a reason to believe that tradition contributes Simon the leper; and not only does the similarity between Mark's description of Simon as a leper with a house in Bethany, east of Jerusalem, and the spotting of a place for lepers east of Jerusalem according to 11QTemple 46:16-18 disfavor redaction and favor the traditionality (and indeed the historicity) of both the location of the house and the description of Simon. So also does the fact that Simon's leprosy plays no part in the story. Instead, it raises unanswered questions: Was he still alive? Still a leper? A recovered leper? A miraculously healed leper? What was Jesus doing in a leper's house? (On such questions, see J. Neusner, *Idea of Purity* 60-61.) Similarly, D. Lührmann (232) points out that Jesus' reclining at meal does not help an understanding of the story in Mark, but only in Luke, where the meal-setting prepares for Jesus' reference to what the host should have done by way of anointing Jesus his guest. Hence, the meal-setting as well as the locale in Simon's house rests on tradition. On the probable redactionality of Luke's description of Simon as a Pharisee, see R. Holst in *JBL* 95 (1976) 438-39, also on the probability that Luke drops the location in Bethany; and see M. Black, *Aramaic Approach* 9, against the theory of a mistranslation behind "the leper."

"Having" and "breaking" do not stand in an asyndetic relation to each other in v 3, for "breaking" starts a new sentence of which "poured" is the main verb, "came" having been the main verb of the sentence to which "having" belonged. Since in Luke the question is one of Jesus' prophetic clairvoyance, not of wasting very expensive perfume, Luke speaks simply of μύρον, which then takes the normal meaning of perfume made with myrrh, coming from southern Arabia and northern Somaliland (see esp. Ath. *Deipn.* 15.688C et seqq.; also G. W. van Beek in *BA* 23 [1960] 70-95). But Mark speaks of pure nard, imported perhaps all the way from the Far East. Thus, μύρον takes the unusual meaning of exotic and very expensive perfume made with the leaves of the nard plant, the most desirable variety of which grows in India, though other varieties grow in Syria, Tarsus, Gaul, and Crete (Plin. *HN* 12.26.42-46; Ath. *Deipn.* 15.688E; Hor. *Carm.* 2.11). The unusualness of this meaning is supported by the failure of W. H. Schoff (in *JAOS* 43 [1923] 222) to find any other western reference to the funereal use of nard (cf. the primary and secondary literature cited in BAGD s.v. νάρδος).

For the possibilities that πιστικῆς means "pure" in the sense of "unadulterated" (as an extension of the meaning "faithful, trustworthy"), or "drinkable, liquid" (as though derived from πίνω, "drink"), or "made from spicatum" or "mixed with the oil of the pistachio nut" or "made from piçita" (as though derived from the name of a plant), see BAGD s.v. πιστικός. Differences in spelling make unlikely an etymological or transcriptional derivation from πίνω, spicatum, and piçita. Since the pistachio nut provides oil with which nard leaves and other aromatic solids are mixed to produce perfume (Plin. *HN* 12.46.100-102) and since πιστικῆς might transliterate the Aramaic for that nut, viz., פיסתקא, the meaning "mixed with the oil of the pistachio nut" offers a better possibility (M. Black, *Aramaic Approach* 223-25). Nevertheless, for that meaning we would expect the use of πιστάκιον, "pistachio nut." Therefore since nard was often adulterated and unadulterated nard highly valued (Plin. *HN* 12.26.43; 13.2.16), the extended meaning "unadulterated" seems best.

To explain the breaking of the flask, E. Renan (*Life of Jesus* 259) appeals to a near eastern custom of breaking a vessel that has been "employed in the entertainment of a stranger of distinction." Renan has observed the custom, but does not cite any evidence that it dates back to NT times. D. G. Linder (in *ZNW* 4 [1903] 179-81) appeals to the ancient custom of anointing a corpse, breaking the flask from which the ointment came, and putting the broken flask in the coffin of the corpse. In both of these customs, however, breaking follows outpouring whereas the aorist tense of Mark's συντρίψασα more naturally indicates the reverse order. Furthermore, the breaking and outpouring lead directly to the criticism of waste, preparation for burial not entering the picture till much later; and in an allusion to the ancient custom we might have expected a use of λήκυθος rather than ἀλάβαστρον for the broken flask (cf. ληκέω, "burst asunder," and the diction of the primary evidence cited by Linder).

It is sometimes said or implied that breaking a flask at its neck was usual and necessary for pouring out the perfume. Not so. If the perfume was poured in through the neck for storage, it could be poured out without breaking the neck. The woman needed only to remove the stopper or untie the piece of cloth that covered the mouth of the flask (see I. Ben-Dor in *QDAP* 11 [1944] 93-112, esp. 101 and pls. XXII-XXIII). As said in the comments, therefore, breaking the flask dramatizes the outpouring of all the contents by making the flask henceforth unusable. The subsequent criticism that the perfume might have been sold for the very high price of three hundred denarii also implies a complete outpouring.

Again because in Luke the question is not one of wasting very expensive perfume, Luke omits the breaking of the flask and thereby leaves the impression that the woman used from the flask only what she needed to anoint Jesus' feet, just as a host might use a portion of olive oil to anoint the head of his guest (cf. Luke 7:46). Omission of the breaking leads Luke to substitute the usual and conservative smearing (ἤλειψεν; cf. W. Michaelis in *TDNT* 4. 800, n. 2) for the extravagant pouring. The late date (c. 300 C.E.) and demonic orientation of the tradition in *b. Sanh.* 101a leaves it questionable whether the there-mentioned scruple against anointing directly from a flask rather than smearing with the hand has any bearing on Jesus' funereal interpretation (so D. Daube, *NTRJ* 315) or on Luke's substitution of smearing for pouring.

In Luke, moreover, the feet of Jesus substitute for his head. The head was a usual object of anointing (Exod 29:7; 1 Sam 10:1; 2 Kgs 9:3, 6; Ps 23:5; 133:2; 141:5; Eccl 9:8; Matt 6:17; Luke 7:46; Ath. *Deipn.* 15.691B,F, 692A,B,C; Hor. *Carm.* 2.11; Ov. *Ars Am.* 3.443; Tib. 2.2.7; 3.3.63; Polyb. 26.1.13), but the sinful woman would hardly shed her tears on Jesus' head, wipe it, and kiss it (see the passages cited by J. F. Oakley in *JBL* 107 [1988] 246-48 for the unusual anointing of feet). Since not only kings were anointed on the head (1 Sam 10:1; 2 Kgs 9:3, 6), but also priests (Exod 29:7; Ps 133:2), rabbis (*b. Ketub.* 17b), and ordinary people (Ps 23:5; 141:5; Eccl 9:8; Matt 6:17; Luke 7:46; and the just-cited passages in Athenaeus, Horace, Ovid, Albius Tibullus, and Polybius), the application of perfume to Jesus' head rather than to his feet does not necessarily connote kingship. Furthermore, plain olive oil rather than perfume seems to have been used for anointing to kingship (see the LXX of 1 Kgdms 10:1; 16:1, 13; 3 Kgdms 1:39; 4 Kgdms 9:3, 6). Anointing by an uncommissioned woman, in contrast with anointing by a prophet, would hardly be recognized as a royal anointing. The verb that is cognate to the royal title χριστός, "anointed one," and that is used for royal anointings in the LXX at 1 Kgdms 10:1; 16:3, 12, 13; 3 Kgdms 1:39; 4 Kgdms 9:3, 6 — viz., χρίω — is not used here. And Jesus interprets the pouring of perfume on his head in terms of burial, not in terms of accession to kingship.

J. F. Coakley (in *JBL* 107 [1988] 248) argues for the priority of the anointing of Jesus' feet that the unusualness and extravagance of such an anointing might have been regularized to the anointing of Jesus' head, that "if the woman's act followed the normal practice of hospitality [as in anointing the head], it would have been performed before, not during, the meal," and that rubbing perfume on the feet (so John 12:3) evokes an interpretation in terms of anointing the body for burial more naturally than does the pouring of perfume on the head. But even under the view that in John 19:38-40 the packing of Jesus' body with no less than approximately one hundred pounds of myrrh and aloes is not an anointing (ibid. 253), such a packing betrays John's penchant for heightening (cf. his Christology) and thus favors a shift by him from the normal anointing of the head to the unusual and extravagant anointing of the feet rather than a regularization by Mark (also against the suggestion that Mark wants to avoid an implication of high living and decadence — ibid. 255). The use of very expensive perfume shows that the woman's act does not follow the normal practice of hospitality, nor do we have any indication that she acts as hostess or in behalf of a host or hostess; so it does not follow that she would have performed her act as customarily before the meal. There is no reason why rubbing the feet with perfume should evoke an interpretation in terms of anointing the body for burial more naturally than would the pouring of perfume on the head. It is the use of perfume, not its place of application on the body, which evokes the said interpretation.

J. K. Elliott (in *ExpTim* 85 [1973-74] 105-7) distorts the materials cited in Str-B 1. 427-28 to say that people ordinarily anointed the feet but not the head. His description of Matt 6:17 as "not relevant here" is unjustified, for Jesus is talking about anointing the head to avoid being noticed as fasting — hence, about an anointing so usual as to be unremarkable (cf. Eccl 9:8: "let not your head lack oil"). One of Elliott's proof-texts for anointing the head as an anointing for kingship — viz., Ps 133:2 — refers to a priestly anointing instead ("running down on Aaron's beard"), and he simply ignores the many other passages that make anointing the head a practice usually having nothing to do with kingship. Thus there is scant reason for supposing that to avoid Roman suspicion of insurrectionism, Mark separates a royal anointing from a royal procession (cf. John 12:1-19) and gives the anointing a funereal meaning.

Because the woman poured the contents of her flask from above Jesus' head down on it, R. Zwick (*Montage* 337) interprets the outpouring as the anointing of Jesus with the power of the Holy Spirit to undergo the Passion. But perfume does not represent the Holy Spirit. Olive oil does. The vocabulary of anointing does not appear in vv 3-9, and in 1:10 (cited by Zwick for support) neither the vocabulary of outpouring nor that of anointing appears. Instead, the Holy Spirit appears as a dove, descending "into" Jesus, not on his head.

O. Betz (in *Das Evangelium und die Evangelien* 72-74) detects a wordplay related to מָשְׁחַת, "destruction," in Isa 52:14 (where the context requires destruction in the sense of disfigurement). The wordplay entails מָשַׁח, "anoint," שַׁחַת in the sense "grave" as well as in the sense "destroy," and an extension of מָשְׁחַת to mean "laying [someone] in a grave, burial" as well as "destruction." Thus are tied together in the story the elements of anointing, destruction of the perfume, and Jesus' coming burial. In fact, however, anointing is not mentioned in Mark (or Matthew) — only pouring and perfuming. Luke, who does mention anointing (but with the use of ἀλείφω, not χρίω), writes nothing about destruction or burial. John mentions anointing and burial, but not destruction. And the extension of מָשְׁחַת to mean burial is questionable.

Since in 9:38; 10:13 Mark notes that it is the disciples who try to prevent an action (see also Luke 9:54) yet in v 4 he mentions neither the disciples nor an attempt at prevention, the "certain ones" (τινες) who criticize the woman's action seem not to include the disciples (contrast Matthew and John). Followed by a direct quotation, being indignant πρὸς ἑαυτούς means expressing indignation by speaking to one another in criticism of the woman's deed. See the comments and notes on 1:43 for "were growling" as a translation of ἐνεβριμῶντο (v 5).

Since v 7 distinguishes Jesus from the poor, he is hardly portrayed as the poor man par excellence and the woman's good work is hardly put forward as an act of charity to the poor. The contrast between "always" and "not always" adds to the distinction between Jesus and the poor rather than defining it as though he belongs in the category of the poor except for not being always present (against W. L. Lane 493-94; J. Ernst 401; F. W. Danker in *JBL* 85 [1966] 467-72 et al.). That you always have the poor with you (v 7a) is a matter of fact that engenders the desire to give alms (v 7b), not a matter of fate that discourages the desire (cf. S. Krauss, *Talmudische Archäologie* 63-74; A. Cronbach in *HUCA* 18 [1944] 131-39).

The "whenever"-clause in v 7b is usually considered an insertion because it interrupts the parallelism between always having the poor and not always having Jesus (cf. Matthew's and John's omission of the clause). The insertion is then explained as designed to forestall a wrong inference that alms no longer need to be given (see, e.g., E. Schweizer 289). But "whenever you *wish*, you are *able* to do well for them" does not make almsgiving a continuing *obligation*; and the omission in Matthew and John probably represents, not a more original form of the saying, but a redactional denial that doing well to the poor is a matter of desire rather than of obligation (cf. Matt 6:1-4) and a redactional tightening of parallelism (as Matthew often engages in). The absence of the "whenever"-clause from John 12:8 may also show Matthean influence (though, of course, many would say that John does not know the synoptics; all the same, cf. the omission of the central part of Zech 9:9 in John 12:15, an even larger omission than in Matt 21:5).

Some have argued oppositely that by making alms a matter of desire, the "whenever"-clause betrays its character as an insertion designed to relax the obligation of charity (see, e.g., E. Lohmeyer 294). But the clause relaxes the obligation no more than does Jesus' telling the critics to leave the woman alone and not cause her trouble for having failed to sell the perfume and give to the poor (vv 4-6). She has wished to perfume him instead of giving to them. Allowable! Suitability in this respect to vv 4-6 supports the originality of the "whenever"-clause. So Mark's looser parallelism, in which the "whenever"-clause interrupts, may well represent the original form. In fact, this clause is the only one in v 7 that links the verse with v 6: doing well for the poor corresponds to working a good work in Jesus. Furthermore, the clause links with v 5 in that the weakness of "whenever you want you are able" (N.B. the use of the subjunctive rather than of the indicative in ὅταν θέλητε) calls in question the actuality of the critics' self-proclaimed concern for the poor. So unless v 7 in its entirety is considered an insertion between vv 6 and 8, the "whenever"-clause again looks original.

Against an insertion of the entirety of v 7, ἐποίησεν, "she did," in v 8a harks back to ποιῆσαι, "to do," in v 7b. (This link lends further support to the originality of the "whenever"-clause.) Also resisting an insertion of the entirety of v 7 is the characteristically Jewish distinction that it provides between almsgiving and works of love, the latter being superior and burying the dead being the most important work of love (see the foregoing discussion of Semitisms). Of course, one could suppose that a Jewish Christian redactor inserted v 7 to make the distinction; but its naturalness makes the supposition gratuitous.

Against an underlying distinction between almsgiving and works of love, C.-P. März (in *SNTU* A/6-7 [1981-82] 97) argues that good works include more than works of love, that it is giving a public funeral that counts for a work of love, and that v 7 points to Jesus' presence but not to the superiority of a work of love. But v 7 points to his coming absence, not to his current presence, and does so to say that the good work of perfuming his body overrides the obligation to give alms. That giving a public funeral counts as a work of love does not imply that perfuming a body in preparation for burial does not count as another such work. And that good works include more than works of love does not exclude the perfuming from the subcategory of works of love.

L. Schenke (*Studien* 108-9) relegates v 5 as well as v 7 to a secondary status because they both deal with alms such as might have been given had the perfume been sold, whereas vv 6 and 8 deal with the character of the perfuming. But we have already noted links between v 7 and vv 6, 8; and the perfuming loses much of its character as a work of love if the foil of almsgiving is withdrawn. J. A. L. Lee (in *NovT* 27 [1985] 11-13) describes the use of εὖ, "well," with ποιῆσαι, "to do," as slightly archaic (by NT times the synonymous καλῶς would usually appear instead of εὖ) and therefore dignifying of Jesus' spoken style.

K. Kertelge (in *The Interpretation of Mark* 81) posits an eschatological point in the oldest version of the story, which ended, he thinks, with the saying, "You always have the poor with you, but me you don't always have"; i.e. "the tradition spoke originally of the irreplaceable significance of Jesus' presence." This interpretation misconstrues the wording even of the hypothetically shortened saying to which it appeals; for that wording mentions Jesus' coming absence, not his current presence as in other sayings that talk about the nearness or arrival of God's rule in the ministry of Jesus (see, e.g., Matt 11:2-6 par. Luke 7:18-23; Matt 12:28 par. Luke 11:20). Here, Jesus' presence is only implied; and the mention of his coming absence does not carry an eschatological message, but a defense of the woman's good work. Nor should the comment of R. Bultmann (*HST* 263) that vv 8-9 give the story a new point and thereby dull the original point in vv 6-7 go unchallenged. Verses 8-9 *sharpen* the point of vv 6-7 by explaining the kind of good work the woman has performed (cf. D. Daube, *NTRJ* 315-16), by revealing the reason for Jesus' coming absence, and by compensating for criticism of the woman's good work with the promise of favorable talk about it.

V. Taylor (532) and C.-P. März (in *SNTU* A/6-7 [1981-82] 98) correctly reject an allusion to 12:44 in 14:8a. There, a widow gave all her livelihood. Here, the woman may have more than the over three hundred denarii that it took to buy the perfume. One might supply both ποιῆσαι εὖ between ὃ ἔσχεν and ἐποίησεν, and εὖ to ἐποίησεν: "what she had [for the purpose of doing well] she did [well with]." Luke's making the story into one of forgiveness and love might easily lead to dismissal of a traditional reference to burial (cf. J. Delobel in *ETL* 42 [1966] 415-75; against the position of R. Holst in *JBL* 95 [1976] 444-45 that Luke would not have omitted a reference to burial).

Because stories of this kind usually end in a single saying of Jesus and because v 8 exhibits foresight that his body will not be anointed in the usual manner between death and burial, D. E. Nineham (375) considers v 8, and presumably v 9, too, a later addition. The form critical rule might be used to lop off v 7 as well, however; and in any case stories tend to be rounded off by omission as well as expanded by addition. The question of Jesus' foresight boils down to a judgment whether here and elsewhere the textual data suffice to overturn an antisupernaturalistic presumption. It would be inaccurate to say that the text makes Jesus foresee for himself a criminal's death that will prevent an anointing of his corpse. It is lack of time that will prevent the anointing of his corpse prior to burial. His burial will be quite unlike that of a criminal. And women will come as soon as possible after the burial to anoint his corpse (15:42–16:1).

On the ground that the present woman did not intend to anticipate Jesus' burial, B. L. Mack (*Myth* 202) describes the anticipatory interpretation of her deed as a piece of "rhetorical chicanery." This description smacks of modernism. Jewish religious literature around the time of the NT contains much that strikes moderns as rhetorical chicanery but that ancients would have appreciated; and D. Daube (*NTRJ* 313) notes that "the Rabbis were quite familar with acts of this sort — acts with immediate legal or religious effect though, in reality, an essential element is yet to come." Besides, to defend the woman's deed by giving it an interpretation that she did not intend does not count as chicanery even by modern standards; for the deed is defensible quite apart from her intention.

According to J. K. Elliott (in *ExpTim* 85 [1973-74] 106-7), the lack of reason to bring aromatics for anointing in 16:1 now that Jesus has already been prepared for burial in 14:8 betrays the inauthenticity of the funereal interpretation. But the women of 16:1 will hardly have regarded the perfuming of Jesus' head as sufficient even though they knew that interpretation. (If absent from the meal in Simon the leper's house, they may have neither heard the interpretation nor heard about it.) Furthermore, the two Semitisms in 14:8 (ὃ ἔσχεν and προέλαβεν μυρίσαι) favor an early date for the saying and thus tend toward authenticity. Elsewhere they do not characterize Mark's style (see the foregoing notes).

R. P. Martin (*Mark* 202) defends the authenticity of the funereal interpretation on the ground that since the women of 16:1 will come to anoint Jesus' body as though it has not already been prepared for burial, this interpretation cannot be considered a prophecy of the Passion after the event of the Passion. But insofar as those women may not regard the perfuming of his head as sufficient or may not know his interpretation of the perfuming, this argument for authenticity fares no better than the one for inauthenticity — and the Semitisms make it unnecessary.

L. Schenke (*Studien* 110-18) says that Mark plays down Jesus' foreknowledge of his own burial by ascribing equal foresight to the woman and thereby making her an example of accepting the way of the Cross. But Mark writes only about Jesus' funereal interpretation of her good work, not about any correspondingly prescient intention on her part. For Schenke's interpretation, such an intention needs to have been mentioned editorially by Mark in v 3, and may also need to have been exhibited in a change from the perfuming of Jesus' head (which does not correspond entirely well to a funereal intention) into an anointing of his body (as in Jesus' transmutative interpretation — v 8). From the use of "body" D. Daube (in *ATR* 32 [1950] 188) infers that the perfume ran down all over Jesus when it was poured on his head. Not so, for he was reclining (v 3).

The juxtaposition of preaching the gospel (v 9) with preparation for burial (v 8) starts to make Jesus' death part of the gospel (cf. vv 22-25 in contrast with 1:14-15; 13:10). The absolute use of "the gospel" is often thought Hellenistic and thence used to argue against the authenticity of v 9. The argument should proceed in the opposite direction: the Semitic character and dominical frequency of the ἀμήν-formula and the Jewishness of remembering in heaven what is spoken on earth (see the following notes) favor that as a Hellenistic Jew, Jesus developed the Isaianic use of the verbal cognate (בָּשַׂר — Isa 40:9; 41:27; 52:7; 60:6; 61:1) into the absolute noun and used the noun in this saying and others (cf. 1:15; 8:35; 10:29; 13:10 and see R. H. Gundry, *Matthew* 61 [with 41-44], 339, 394, for the redactionality of omissions in the other synoptics). On the question whether Jesus foresaw world-wide preaching during an interim before a second coming, see the notes on 13:10.

Mark 14:14 shows that ὅπου ἐάν plus the subjunctive (as here in v 9 behind "wherever the gospel is preached in the whole world") does not necessarily carry an iterative meaning that would exclude a single proclamation of the gospel by an angel at age-end, as in Rev 14:6-7 (so J. Jeremias, *Abba* 117-20; idem, *Jesus' Promise* 22-23). On the other hand, a gospel proclaimed by an angel at the end of the age is very unlikely to include the story of the woman's good work. Nothing like it appears in Rev 14:6-7. And the absence from Mark of references to an angel, to his flying in midheaven and shouting loudly to make himself heard world-wide, and to the world's last chance for salvation requires that Mark have laundered an earlier statement like that in Rev 14:6-7 to an unlikely extent (cf. F. Hahn, *Mission* 71-72).

The spatial meaning of "in the whole world" favors that ὅπου ἐάν means "wherever," not "whenever," just as in vv 13-14 "follow" and "enter" will favor "wherever." The argument of J. Jeremias (in *ZNW* 44 [1952-53] 106) that "whole" implies a single occasion of preaching neglects the possibility of a constative aorist in κηρυχθῇ, "is preached [from one occasion to another]." The more usual meaning of ὅπου ἐάν, "wherever," leads one to understand the aorist in this way; and ὅπου ἐάν in 9:18 does not at all have to be understood as meaning "whenever" (see BAGD s.v. καταλαμβάνω 1b; ὅπου 1aδ), much less in 6:55, 56. The temporal translation in Mark 14:9 sy[s] does not determine Mark's meaning. It is also doubtful that Rev 14:6-7, which Jeremias cites, really does support his punctiliar interpretation of Mark 14:9. The eternal gospel shouted in that passage from midheaven by a flying angel may well represent the message that Christians are to preach world-wide during the last part of the present age. A. L. Moore (*Parousia* 204) argues that whether local or temporal, ὅπου ἐάν is at least indefinite and therefore cannot point to a definite time at the end of the age. But the use of the similarly but questionably indefinite ὅταν, "whenever," in 8:38; 12:23, 25; 13:14, 28, 29 for definite times at the end of the age undermines this argument.

A non-angelic interpretation of "is preached" rules out a divine passive, though even an angelic interpretation would leave some doubt. Avoidance of God's name may be achieved by putting a verb in the passive or by substituting an angelic subject, but the angelic subject needs no protection by the passive. Such protection would only lessen the angel's role of protecting God's name (cf. in the Book of Revelation the frequent mention of angels who speak for God). Since the woman's good work will be talked about wherever the gospel is preached, the talk will take place on earth, not in heaven. Hence, "will be talked about" is certainly not a divine passive.

"In the whole world" applies then to talk of the woman's good work as well as to preaching of the gospel. But will the whole world consequently remember the woman? It is hard to be sure, but perhaps not, at least not in Jesus' originally intended meaning. For though there is much about human remembering in the OT and Jewish literature of the intertestamental and NT periods, Acts 10:4, 31; Gen 30:22; Exod 28:12; 30:16; Lev 24:7; Num 10:9-10; Pss 25:6-7; 37 title LXX; 69 title LXX; Isa 23:18 LXX; Jer 15:15; Mal 3:16; Tob 12:12; Sir 45:9, 11; 50:16; CD 20:18-20; *1 Enoch* 98:6-8; 99:3; 103:1-4; 104:1; *T. Job* 40:4 speak of hearing, seeing, remembering, and recording in heaven or before God what is said, sounded, prayed, or otherwise done on earth. It may be, then, that God and the angels will remember the woman because they will hear the talk which takes place on earth concerning her good work. This remembrance would look forward to the last judgment and bode well for the woman. One might argue to the contrary that v 9 does not identify God and the angels as those who will remember the woman (cf. D. Jones in *JTS* ns 6 [1955] 183-91; W. Schottroff, *"Gedenken"* 265-70, 306-13; A. R. Millard in *Apostolic History and the Gospel* 245-47 [much of these discussions having to do with a similar question about 1 Cor 11:25]). But neither does it identify earthlings as those who will remember her (contrast Exod 12:14; 13:8-9, which do identify earthlings as rememberers); and though many of the cross-references identify God and the angels as the rememberers, some of those passages do not, yet they indubitably have them in mind (see Exod 36:14 LXX; Ps 37 title LXX; Isa 66:3; Hos 14:8 LXX; Sir 45:9, 11; cf. D. W. A. Gregg in *TynBul* 30 [1979] 165-68; idem, *Anamnesis* 17-18, on the closeness of the Hebrew as well as Septuagintal text of Sir 45:9 to Luke 22:19; 1 Cor 11:25). It is less certain whether Mark's audience understood the woman to be remembered in heaven or whether he himself intended the statement to be so understood, but the predominance of heavenly memory in religious literature (see J. Jeremias, *Abba* 117-20; idem, *Eucharistic Words* 244-49) suggests that they did. Even if ὅπου ἐάν were iterative, it would militate against heavenly remembrance of the woman no more than the repeated almsgiving of Cornelius, the repeated conversations of Yahweh-fearers, and so on militate against heavenly remembrance of those people for their deeds (see the cross-references cited above). To posit that the original form of v 9 lacked a reference to preaching the gospel in the whole world is to remove the occasion of talk about her deed. B. L. Mack (*Myth* 312) does not hit the target in appealing to v 9 for his statement that "to 'preach' the gospel is not to proclaim the kerygma for Mark, but to make the stories about Jesus memorable." Verse 9 does not say that Jesus or the stories about him will be remembered, but that the woman will be remembered. On memory, see J. Reumann, *Supper of the Lord* 26-34.

Saying that "memory of her" defines the good work of the woman as her remembering Jesus' death (αὐτῆς as a subjective genitive — so J. H. Greenlee in *ExpTim* 71 [1959-60] 245; cf. M. R. Mansfield, *"Spirit and Gospel"* 126) forgets that her good work looks forward to his death (and then only in his interpretation of the work without her intending it so), not backward to his death; and if she performed the work in memory of his death, she remembered his death not only anachronistically before he died but also, and again anachronistically, before her work was talked about as a consequence of gospel-preaching in the whole world. The telic or ecbatic εἰς makes memory a purpose or result of the talk; hence, the memory must follow rather than precede the talk.

Comments to the effect that the woman's anonymity makes her more an example than an object of remembrance (see, e.g., J. Ernst 402) overlook that others can no longer do what she did (i.e. prepare Jesus' body for burial) and that her good work ("what this [woman] has done") rightfully captures the interest that otherwise might have gone to her name. It goes well beyond the text to transmute Jesus' interpretation of her deed as an anticipative preparation of his body for burial into an exemplary acceptance of the Cross as the way of salvation and discipleship (against L. Schenke, *Studien* 148-50).

See E. C. Maloney, *Semitic Interference* 126-31, that with "of the Twelve," "one" retains a numerical force rather than weakening in Semitic fashion to the meaning of an indefinite pronoun (v 10). Considered alone, the use of the definite article before "one of the Twelve" may offer a Semitism (cf. Gen 42:32 MT LXX) or normal Greek (see the papyri cited in BAGD s.v. εἰς 1aβ; against F. Field [*Notes* 38-39], who thinks that ὁ εἰς has to mean "the first," which is absurd, and that "he who was one of the Twelve" would require ὁ ὢν κτλ. and therefore that Mark did not write the definite article [Why then a scribal insertion that only makes an absurdity, if such it is?]). But the contrast in Gen 42:32 between "the one" who is not with Jacob and "the youngest" who is with Jacob has no counterpart in Mark 14:10, and neither Semitic nor normal Greek explains the absence of the definite article before "one of the Twelve" in 14:20, 43. Despite the argument of V. Taylor (534) that Mark seldom uses cross-references, his using "Iscariot" with "Judas" only here and in 3:19 favors that the definite article points back to that passage (see the foregoing comments). In 14:20 the definite article drops off along with "Judas Iscariot" because Jesus wants to answer somewhat indefinitely the question who will betray him. "Judas" reappears in 14:43, but neither "Iscariot" nor the definite article before "one of the Twelve" does so, because Mark is more concerned there to draw a parallel between "one" and the likewise anarthrous "crowd with swords and clubs" than to reflect 3:19. Cf. K. Stock, *Boten* 150-54; G. Schmahl, *Zwölf* 98-100; and the notes in the present commentary on 3:14, 16.

J. Gnilka (2. 229) seems to infer that because Mark does not reveal the reason for Judas's departure, "went away" does not relate to the house of Simon the leper. On the contrary, that house provides the contextual point of departure; and the non-revelation of Judas's reason for departure only shows the strength of Mark's desire to stress that Jesus' passion predictions are starting to be fulfilled. Mark does not say that Judas Iscariot returned after going to the chief priests, but he will indicate in v 43 that Judas came from them. Therefore, argues W. Vogler (*Judas Iskarioth* 46-47), the going away from Jesus in v 10 must originally have followed the eating with him in vv 17-21. But the same kind of reasoning would nonsensically require that because Mark will not speak of Judas's going to the chief priests either during the meal, on the way to Gethsemane, or after entering Gethsemane, the coming from them in v 43 must originally have preceded the eating with Jesus in vv 17-21. Mark is interested only in the fulfilment of Jesus' prediction of being given over to the chief priests and therefore leaves it to be inferred from Judas's seeking how to give him over conveniently and from Jesus' going with the Twelve to eat the Last Supper that Judas has come back from the chief priests, and to be inferred from Judas's coming from the chief priests to arrest Jesus that Judas has meanwhile gone back to them.

Mark does not say that Judas wanted or purposed to get money for giving Jesus over to the chief priests (contrast Matt 26:15). The promise to give Judas money seems to have arisen out of their own joy, not out of his desire or demand. Nor does Mark say that unease with the episode in vv 3-9 made Judas offer to give Jesus over (cf. the absence of the episode between the Sanhedrin's plot and the arrangement for betrayal in Luke 22:1-6, and see H. B. Swete [326-27] for refinement of the possibilities of unease: [1] despair on Judas's part because of Jesus' coming death; [2] resentment of the financial waste, defended by Jesus; and [3] a conviction that Jesus knows about Judas's pilfering or treacherous intentions [cf. John 12:4-8, which, however, does not relate this incident to Judas's betrayal of Jesus — contrast John 13:2, 27-30]). Nor does Mark say what the chief priests heard (v 11). He expects his audience to fill this ellipsis from the general tenor of the passage: they heard Judas's offer to give Jesus over to them.

T. A. Mohr (*Markus- und Johannespassion* 148) errs in saying that according to v 10 Judas has already betrayed Jesus by going to the chief priests and that according to v 11 he has yet to betray him. To betray Jesus *is* to give him over (παραδίδωμι); so Judas can hardly intend to give Jesus over to the chief priests on an occasion when Jesus is not even present. To ask *what* Judas betrayed, then, is inappropriate. He will give over a person, not reveal a secret or anything of that sort. It has been clear for a long time that Jesus will be the object of betrayal (see 3:19). See J. Carmignac in *ASTI* 7 (1968-69) 72 for the possibility of an underlying wordplay in וישמעווישמחו, "and they [the chief priests] heard and rejoiced" (cf. Luke 1:58). "Conveniently" shows that Judas *is* seeking to fulfil the condition, "not in the festal assembly" (against L. Schenke, *Studien* 120-21). This back-reference to vv 1-2 is much more natural than a forward reference to the divinely appointed "hour" of Jesus' passion would be (cf. v 41). God will not frustrate Judas's effort to give Jesus over apart from the festal assembly. On the contrary, Judas will give him over in the privacy of Gethsemane, far from the madding crowd.

JESUS' PRESCIENCE CONCERNING PREPARATIONS FOR THE PASSOVER

14:12-16 (Matt 26:17-19; Luke 22:7-13)

Preparations for the Passover open with the disciples' asking Jesus where he wants them to make such preparations (v 12). His sending two of them and giving instructions to those two form the bulk of the pericope (vv 13-15). The instructions consist of two pairs of commands ("go . . . follow" and "say . . . prepare"), each pair bisected by two predictions ("and a man will meet you . . . and he himself [another man, a housemaster] will show you . . ."). The carrying out of Jesus' commands and the fulfilment of his predictions close out the pericope (v 16).

14:12 *(Matt 26:17; Luke 22:7)* "And on the first day of Unleavened Bread" harks back to v 1, "and the Passover and Unleavened Bread were after two days," and thus indicates a temporal progression to Thursday (see the notes on v 1). "The first day" replaces the earlier reference to the Passover in order that "the Passover" may occur in the next clause as a sacrifice rather than as a festival (contrast v 1). "Unleavened Bread" then includes the day of Passover as well as the further week of festival. "When they were sacrificing the Passover" gives an explanation helpful to Mark's Gentile audience unacquainted with the Jewish Passover (cf. esp. 7:2-4). "They" refers to Jews in general. The Passover is sacrificed in late afternoon. If it is already late afternoon, the imperfect tense of ἔθυον describes the sacrifices as already taking place. If it is earlier in the afternoon, the imperfect tense describes what habitually happened ("when they sacrificed the Passover year by year"). The historical present tense of λέγουσιν, "say," stresses the disciples' portrayal of Jesus as a good Jewish teacher who *wants* them to prepare the Passover. Similarly, though he will include the disciples (see vv 15-16), the second person singular of φάγῃς, "that you may eat," portrays him as a good Jewish teacher who wants his disciples to prepare for *him* to eat the Passover. The omission of ἵνα, "that," after θέλεις, "do you want," sharpens the disciples' question in a way that emphasizes this favorable portrayal (contrast 10:35 and see the comments on 10:36).

14:13-15 *(Matt 26:18; Luke 22:8-12)* The historical present tense of ἀποστέλλει and λέγει in the statement, "And he sends two of his disciples and says to them, 'Go into the city . . . ,'" confirms Jesus' desire to eat the Passover. It also emphasizes the predictions interspersed among his commands, for in this part of his gospel Mark is constantly exhibiting the predictive power of Jesus. The extensive parallelism of phraseology with 11:1-2 increases this emphasis by reminding Mark's audience of an earlier incident in which obedience to Jesus' commands likewise exhibited that power. The first prediction is full of details, and all the more impressive for them. A man will meet the two disciples. The fact that he will meet them rather than they him makes the prediction unlikely in prospect and again impressive in fulfilment. For it would be remarkable enough if Jesus knew that the two were going to meet a man by virtue of their approaching him at Jesus' instructions. But his knowing that a man is going to meet them by virtue of his approaching them — what a testimony to Jesus' prescience! Not only will a man meet the two disciples, but also he will be carrying a jar of water. The unusualness of a man's carrying a jar of water — what a woman would do in those days, for a man would normally carry water in a skin — adds to the impressiveness of the prediction and may imply that the man is a domestic servant. Because of Mark's stress on Jesus' predictive power, we would err to think that Mark wants his audience to think of prearrangements on Jesus' part either here or in the following (against R. H. Gundry, *Matthew* 525). Besides, prearrangements would not agree very well with a number of elements in the story: (1) the disciples' happening at the moment to have taken the initiative by means of their question (prearrangements would have required a time of meeting set beforehand by Jesus); (2) the generality of Jesus' instruction to go into the city (Jerusalem is big and thronged with tens of thousands of pilgrims as well as with permanent residents, so that prearrangements would have demanded a particular place of meeting, also set beforehand by Jesus); (3) the open-ended "wherever" of the command to follow when the man enters a house (prearrangements would likely have led to a more restrictively stated address — cf. 6:10; 14:9); and (4) the question to be relayed from "the teacher" to "the housemaster," i.e. "Where is my guest room where I may eat the Passover with my disciples?" (prearrangements would probably have eliminated any need for the question or would have led to a different question, e.g., "Where is the guest room where my disciples may prepare the Passover?"). Now it becomes apparent why Jesus sent two of his disciples: he wanted to undergird his relayed question with sufficient testimony (cf. 6:7; Num 35:30; Deut 17:6; 19:15; Matt 18:16; Luke 10:1; John 8:17; 2 Cor 13:1; 1 Tim 5:19; Heb 10:28).

Asyndeton sharpens the command to follow the man carrying a jar of water and may thereby highlight the absurdity of the command. Or so it seems until Jesus' prediction comes to pass! It stays unknown whether the housemaster is expected to recognize "the teacher" as Jesus, or whether he is expected to provide a room for Jesus without knowing his identity as he would provide one out of respect for any teacher. Though the definite article may act as a weak possessive, with the result "our teacher" in v 14, "the teacher" appeared in 5:35 without this or a similar meaning. So we should probably think of a titular meaning that highlights Jesus' authority (cf. esp. 1:21-22, 27). "My guest room" implies that as the teacher Jesus has authority to commandeer the room. The forward position of ὁ διδάσκαλος, "the teacher," emphasizes his authority. "My disciples" implies his didactic success as well as authority. The forward position of τὸ πάσχα μετὰ τῶν μαθητῶν μου, "the Passover with my disciples," emphasizes this success as well as his desire to eat the Passover as a good Jewish teacher should. The second prediction is as remarkably detailed as the first: the room that the housemaster will show the disciples (αὐτός emphatically distinguishes him from the man carrying the jar of water) will be upstairs, large, furnished (or paved or paneled — ἐστρωμένον), prepared. Such details, the asyndeton between them, and the redundancy of "prepared" again make Jesus' prediction the more impressive. That the housemaster will neither refuse nor hesitate to show the room makes the prediction and Jesus' authority more impressive yet. Since the room is already prepared, "and there prepare for us" has to do with preparing the Passover meal, as in vv 12, 16 (cf. Isa 21:5). The forward position of ἐκεῖ, "there," underlines the locative element in the prediction which will be fulfilled in the disciples' obedience to Jesus' instructions.

14:16 *(Matt 26:19; Luke 22:13)* "And the disciples went out" implies that the two have been staying with Jesus in Bethany, perhaps in the house of Simon the leper (cf. v 3). "And they went into the city" means entrance into Jerusalem in accordance with Jesus' command (v 13). "And they found just as he had said" indicates the fulfilment of both his predictions, details and all (for other occurrences of εὑρίσκω for finding Jesus' statements or predictions to have come true, see 7:30; 11:2, 4). "And they prepared the Passover" shows the two disciples obedient to his command and sets the stage for the Last Supper.

NOTES

Secondary literature on the Last Supper seems endless. G. R. Beasley-Murray (*Jesus and the Kingdom of God* 258-73) and I. H. Marshall *(Last Supper)* offer fairly up-to-date summaries and evaluations of the more important and recent of such literature. Pride of place belongs to J. Jeremias, *Eucharistic Words;* H. Schürmann, *Jesu ureigener Tod;* idem, *Abendmahlsbericht;* idem, *Paschamahlbericht;* idem, *Einsetzungsbericht;* idem, *Jesu Ab-*

schiedsrede; idem, *Traditionsgeschichtliche Untersuchungen* 159-97; H. Patsch, *Abend-mahl;* R. Pesch, *Abendmahl;* P. Neuenzeit, *Herrenmahl;* J. Wanke, *Beobachtungen.*

The equation of Passover with the first day of Unleavened Bread (v 12) does not contradict v 1, for that verse can as easily mean that Passover and Unleavened Bread were to arrive together after two days as it can mean that they were to arrive in succession after two days. V. K. Robbins (in *The Passion in Mark* 26-28), who nevertheless sees a contradiction, also gives Mark's equation of Passover with the first day of Unleavened Bread a symbolic interpretation: "the leaven of the Pharisees and the leaven of Herod [8:15] are thoroughly removed when Jesus eats with disciples in the setting of betrayal and death." That leaven is supposed to be a lust for the miraculous, which Mark is correcting with a theology of the Cross. But since v 12 says that Jews in general slaughtered the Passover on the first day of Unleavened Bread, Mark has not given the removal of leaven even so much as a generally Christian connotation, much less the particular connotation of a theology of the Cross as opposed to a theology of miracles. The phraseology of vv 1, 12 merely sets the stage for a festival of more than one day; or it prepares for the bread of the Lord's Supper without emphasizing its unleavenedness (cf. v 22).

The statement that Jews in general slaughtered the Passover on the first Day of Unleavened Bread also militates against the theory that because NT accounts of the Last Supper fail to mention meat, Jesus must have celebrated the Passover a day early without a Passover sacrifice (see, e.g., E. Stauffer, *Jesus and His Story* 93-95). Besides, Mark omits meat, not because Jesus celebrates the Passover earlier than the slaughter of the Passover sacrifices, but because Mark's interest lies in Jesus' predictions of betrayal and death, which predictions involve a dish of sauce, bread, and a cup of wine, rather than in the Passover as such, where meat is prominent (see the comments on vv 17-25). Nor do other accounts of the Last Supper show interest in the Passover as such. Only if it meant "during the [Passover] festival" could μὴ ἐν τῇ ἑορτῇ (v 2) argue against the arrest of Jesus on Passover night and therefore against Mark's identification of the Last Supper with a Passover meal. But the phrase meant "not in the festal assembly" (see the notes on v 2), and even under the temporal translation one could think that Judas Iscariot's offer enabled the Sanhedrin to arrest Jesus during the Passover festival without inciting the riot which they had feared. Some have argued from the non-paschal character of the Last Supper in John 13:1ff. that Mark makes the supper into a Passover meal in order that the institution of the Lord's Supper during that meal might be seen to obliterate it with a new ritual (see, e.g., B. W. Bacon, *Beginnings* xxviii-xxx, 195-98; idem, *Gospel of Mark* 172-76). More likely, however, a Johannine interpretation of Jesus' death as the true Passover sacrifice caused a shift of his death from the afternoon after Passover evening to the afternoon before Passover evening, and thus a deletion of the Passover element from the Last Supper.

With the dual indication of time in v 12, cf. the passages discussed and listed by F. Neirynck, *Duality* 45-53, 94-96; and see the notes on v 1 and R. H. Gundry, *Matthew* 524, for placement of the Passover sacrifice on the first day of Unleavened Bread. As shown by the evidence there discussed, this placement does not favor insertion of vv 12-16 from an independent source or a confusion of the Aramaic קְמִי, "before" (in an original "on the day before the Unleavened Bread"), with קַמָּאה, "first." The practice of removing leaven a day earlier than the start of the week-long Festival of Unleavened Bread causes that day, i.e. Passover, to be called the first day of Unleavened Bread (cf. J. C. Rylaarsdam in *IDB* 3. 663-64; Str-B 2. 812-15; and esp. *m. Pesah.* 1:1-4).

It is sometimes thought that by putting the Passover sacrifice, which in NT times took place in late afternoon, on the first day of Unleavened Bread, Mark uses a non-Jewish method of calculating days from midnight to midnight or from sunrise to sunrise rather than from sunset to sunset, that his use of such a non-Jewish method produces an inaccurate placement of the time of sacrifice on the Day of Passover-first day of Unleavened Bread rather than in the last part of the preceding day, and that the inaccuracy of this placement disproves Mark's Jewishness and therefore his identification with John Mark of Jerusalem (P. Parker in *JBL* 100 [1981] 396). But apart from a deliberate accommodation by Mark to his Gentile audience, already in Lev 23:27, 32 the day preceding the Day of Atonement is reckoned to include the evening between that day and the Day of Atonement. Therefore a Jew might well view the Passover sacrifice and the Passover meal as belonging to the afternoon and evening of the same day. In fact, Josephus, who was a first century Jew, does exactly so in *J.W.* 2.1.3 §10, where the Passover sacrifices are lumped together with an equation of the Festivals of Unleavened Bread and Passover. The sacrificing of the Passover originally between sunset and total darkness (Lev 23:5; Num 9:3, 5, 11; Deut 16:6) may have aided this view. By NT times the number of Passover sacrifices had grown so large that the late afternoon had to be used. This development and that of removing all leaven the evening and morning before the afternoon of Passover sacrifice (*m. Pesaḥ.* 1-3) may have aided the putting of Passover sacrifice and Passover meal on the same day of sunrise to sunrise. Besides, we have an abundance of evidence that Jews calculated days from sunrise to sunrise as well as from sunset to sunset, and did so concurrently (see H. W. Hoehner in *BSac* 131 [1974] 249-59; R. T. Beckwith in *EvQ* 43 [1971] 221-27; cf. J. Morgenstern in *AJSL* 36 [1920] 176-79, n. 1; idem in *HUCA* 10 [1935] 15-28; idem, *Some Significant Antecedents* 8-15).

See R. Pesch 2. 347-48 that the switch from "the Twelve" (v 10) to "the disciples" (vv 12, 13, 14) and then back to "the Twelve" (v 17) does not prove that vv 12-16 originate in a source different from the one that lies behind the foregoing and following verses. In vv 10-11 "of the Twelve" complemented "one." In vv 12-16 "the disciples" suits "the teacher" (v 14) but most naturally refers to the Twelve since it is the Twelve whom Jesus has paired up in the past just as he now commissions two of the disciples (cf. 6:7; also 1:16-20; 10:35; 11:1). In v 17 "the Twelve" will prepare for "one of you" (v 18), i.e. "one of the Twelve" (v 20). The suitability of the terms to their immediate contexts smacks of compositional technique rather than of a difference in sources. The further argument that the lack in John of anything corresponding to vv 12-16 proves an origination of these verses in a different source (so J. Jeremias, *Eucharistic Words* 90, 92-93) neglects an evident reason for redactional omission by John, viz., his changing the Passover meal to a pre-Passover meal so as to have Jesus die as the true Passover sacrifice at the very time such a sacrifice was supposed to be offered (John 13:1; 18:28; 19:14, 36 with Exod 12:46). Nor do the phraseological similarities between vv 12-16 and 11:1-6 prove a different origin, for Mark may be writing up this part of a continuous tradition in a way that recollects the earlier passage. According to K. Stock (*Boten* 154-56), Mark will switch from "the disciples" in vv 12, 13, 14 to "the Twelve" in v 17 because vv 12-16 have relevance to all disciples but vv 17-21, which concern betrayal by an intimate, will have particular relevance only to the apostles. Actually, however, vv 12-16 are even more restricted in relevance than vv 17-21 will be; for vv 12-16 relate in particular to only the two disciples whom Jesus sends to prepare the Passover. It is vv 22-25 that will gain wider relevance by narrating the institution of the Lord's Supper. But by then Mark will have switched to "the Twelve," and he will not reintroduce "the disciples."

H. Schürmann (*Paschamahlbericht* 121-22) argues that since the finding of a foal was inherently more necessary to the Triumphal Procession in 11:1-10 than is the finding of a room in Jerusalem to the eating of the Passover in 14:12-16, Mark must have modeled 14:12-16 after 11:1-10. This argument does not survive scrutiny. In 11:1-10 there was no dependence on Gen 49:10-11 or Zech 9:9 so as to have required a foal (see the notes ad loc.). An older animal would have done well enough. For that matter, Jesus might have stridden rather than ridden toward Jerusalem to the acclamation of crowds. The foal was unnecessary, but the Passover meal cannot be eaten outside Jerusalem. Because Jesus has been staying in Bethany, then, a room has to be found in Jerusalem.

To prove the secondariness of the question where to prepare the Passover, L. Schenke (*Studien* 163-66) cites several inconcinnities in vv 12-16: (1) the question gets no answer; (2) all the disciples ask the question, but only two of them go away to prepare the meal; (3) the disciples take the initiative in asking the question, but Jesus takes the initiative in sending the two; (4) their question stresses preparation, but his instructions stress location; and (5) the question refers only to Jesus' eating, whereas the instructions include the disciples' eating in accordance with the character of the Passover as a communal meal. But the question *does* get an answer: wherever (ὅπου ἐάν) the man with the jar of water enters — more particularly, in the guest room — there prepare the Passover meal. No inconcinnity attaches to Jesus' sending two of his disciples, especially since he has earlier paired them up to do his bidding (6:7; 11:1; cf. 1:16-20; 10:35; Luke 7:18; 10:1; Matt 10:2-4; 18:16, 19-20; 26:37). In 11:2 he took the initiative in sending two of his disciples because they could not have imagined that he was going to ride in a Triumphal Procession. Here, they know perfectly well that he has come to celebrate the Passover and therefore ask him where he wants them to prepare it. The question itself gives the truly important initiative to him: his desire will govern their action. Their initiative lies only in asking what he wants. He takes the initiative in speaking only if we have already cut off their question from his speaking; otherwise, his speaking arises in response to their question. Both their question and his response put the element of location in first place, followed by the element of preparation. And the very fact that they ask where *they* should make preparations shows that they mean to eat with him, just as he takes them to mean in vv 14 ("where I may eat the Passover with my disciples") and 15 ("and there prepare for us"). The further theory of Schenke (op. cit. 192) that the main point of vv 13-16a originally lay in the location of the Last Supper requires the location not merely to have been described as a guest room in the house of an unnamed host, but to have been identified as the guest room in so-and-so's house. Of that we have no trace, however.

All in all, then, neither the placement of the Passover sacrifice on the first day of Unleavened Bread (v 12) nor the switch from "the disciples" (v 12) to "the Twelve" (v 17) nor the lack of a Johannine parallel to vv 12-16 nor phraseological similarities to 11:1-6 in 14:12-16 provide strong evidence for a pre-Marcan narrative lacking vv 12-16. Nor will the mention of the Twelve in v 17 after two of the disciples have been sent ahead provide such evidence (see the notes ad loc.). And if not, the attempt to make the Last Supper a non-Passover meal through deletion of vv 12-16 suffers.

According to V. K. Robbins (in *The Passion in Mark* 26), "when the disciples ask Jesus if they should go away to prepare the passover, they are mimicking their action in the Feeding of the Four Thousand when they asked Jesus if they should go away to buy food for the crowd (6:37)." But no, for here they ask on their own initiative *where* he wants them to prepare. There, they asked *whether* they should buy food; and their question came in response to Jesus' command that they feed the crowd. Preparations for Passover include not only the finding of a suitable room but also the setting of the table, which presupposes the sacrificing and roasting of a lamb and the getting of wine, unleavened bread, and condiments (Str-B 4/1. 41-54). The stress on location in the Upper Room makes the getting of provisions in the city and sacrificing of a lamb at the temple a presupposition rather than a part of the preparation. The suggestion that for Mark πάσχα, "Passover," resonates with πάσχω, "suffer," in regard to Jesus' suffering (cf. 8:31; 9:12; and the references gathered by J. Jeremias in *TDNT* 5. 903, n. 62) is interesting but ill-founded, because Mark correlates the death of Jesus with the bread and cup of wine, not with the meat from a Passover sacrifice (contrast 1 Cor 5:7; John 1:29, 36; 19:36 with Exod 12:8-10, 46; Rev 5:6 with 15:3).

"Going away" (v 12) presupposes not only that Jesus and the Twelve are lodging in Bethany, but also that they must offer the Passover sacrifice in Jerusalem, the only legitimate place to do so (J. Jeremias, *Eucharistic Words* 42-43). "Prepare" has no direct object, whereas it does have one in v 16. But neither does it have one in v 15 or in the parallels at Luke 22:9, 12 or in the unparalleled passages Luke 9:52; 12:47. In other words, the verb is used intransitively as well as transitively; and an explicit mention of the Passover as the direct object of "prepare" in v 12, as in v 16, would have overloaded a single sentence with three occurrences of "the Passover." So L. Schenke (*Studien* 164-65) has no good reason to regard the lack of a direct object as evidence that in v 12 "prepare" is secondary.

See K. L. McKay (in *NovT* 27 [1985] 213) on the combination of present and aorist imperatives in ὑπάγετε, "go," and ἀκολουθήσατε, "follow" (v 13). Ὕδατος may be taken as a descriptive genitive with κεράμιον ("water-jar") rather than a genitive of content ("jar of water"). If descriptive, the jar may be empty. But why describe the jar as a water-jar if it is empty? Why not κεράμιον without ὕδατος? The man's going home favors that his jar is filled with water. If it is, he seems to be a domestic servant bringing a supply of water to the household rather than a water-seller going home after selling the contents of his jar (see J. Jeremias, *Jerusalem* 8, for the possibility of a water-seller).

L. Johnson (in *ExpTim* 77 [1965-66] 157-58) argues for an identification of the housemaster (v 14) with John Mark that "one of the Twelve" (v 20) will imply the presence of more persons than the Twelve. But D. G. Rogers (in *ExpTim* 77 [1965-66] 214) correctly objects that "one of the Twelve" will simply add horror and pathos to the prediction of betrayal. See G. Dalman, *Jesus-Jeshua* 107-8; Str-B 1. 988-89; D. Daube, *NTRJ* 128, n. 1; S. Safrai in *The Jewish People in the First Century* 2. 903-4 on not taking rent from pilgrims for their use of a room to celebrate the Passover. "My guest room" (v 14) does not imply that Jesus has previously used the room; for in Mark Jesus has been staying in Bethany, not in Jerusalem. One might think of earlier visits to Jerusalem, such as the fourth gospel records; but that gospel gives no indication that a house-master in Jerusalem reserved a room for Jesus on such visits; and Jesus' visiting Mary, Martha, and Lazarus in Bethany suggests otherwise (John 11:1-46; 12:1-8). If ἐστρωμένον means "furnished," then carpets, cushions, and table are probably in view.

For the possibility of an underlying wordplay in וַיֵּצְאוּ וַיִּמְצְאוּ, "and they went out and found," see J. Carmignac in *ASTI* 7 (1968-69) 72. With the two disciples' finding just as Jesus had said (v 16), cf. 1 Sam 10:1-16 (esp. in the LXX [1 Kgdms 10:1-16] because of diction that Mark shares: ἀπέρχομαι, "go away," εὑρίσκω, "find," and ἀπαντάω, "meet"). The sign-character of that passage has no counterpart in Mark, however. With the predicted meeting of someone, cf. 1 Kgs 17:8-16; 2 Kgs 1:3-4. Against any attempt to depress the predictive element in favor of the imperative element, v 16 shows that Mark likes them both, because they support his Christology of Jesus as the prescient and authoritative Son of God: "and they found just as he had told them [fulfilled prediction] and prepared the Passover [fulfilled command]" (cf. the alternation of commands and predictions in vv 13-15 and the discussion in T. A. Mohr, *Markus- und Johannespassion* 154).

THE PRESCIENCE OF JESUS CONCERNING HIS BETRAYAL, VIOLENT DEATH, AND ULTIMATE VICTORY

14:17-25 (Matt 26:20-29; Luke 22:14-23)

Mark's account of the Last Supper divides in two: (1) Jesus' prediction that one of the Twelve will give him over (vv 17-21); (2) the predictions of his violent death and ultimate victory in the Words of Institution (vv 22-25). The first part subdivides into his coming to the guest room (v 17), the first prediction proper (v 18), the vexed protestations of the disciples (v 19), a repetition of the prediction with an added detail and some scriptural support plus a woe to the one who gives him over (vv 20-21). The second part subdivides into Jesus' actions and words concerning bread (v 22), his actions concerning a cup and the disciples' drinking from it (v 23), and his words concerning the cup (vv 24-25).

14:17-18 *(Matt 26:20-21; Luke 22:14)* "And when evening came" sets the proper time for a Passover meal as opposed to the usual late meal, eaten toward the end of the afternoon (J. Jeremias, *Eucharistic Words* 44-46). The singular in "he comes" echoes the earlier portrayal of Jesus as a good Jewish teacher who wants to eat the Passover (see v 12 with comments), and the historical present tense highlights that portrayal. "With the Twelve" echoes "with my disciples" in Jesus' instructions (v 14; cf. also 11:11). The shift from "my disciples" to "the Twelve" prepares for his prediction that one of those closest to him will betray him. "And as they were reclining [at table]" reflects the formal character of the Passover meal, sitting being the posture at ordinary meals. Though Mark does not explain to his Gentile audience the Jewish historical background, reclining also symbolized God's setting Israel free at the time of the Exodus; for slaves did not enjoy the luxury of reclining at formal meals (ibid. 48-49), and at the first Passover the Israelites may have stood to eat (as implied in Exod 12:11, perhaps, by eating with girded loins, shoes on feet, and staff in hand). "And eating" prepares for Jesus' coming reference to one who is eating with him (v 18c) and for Mark's coming introduction to the Words of Institution (v 22). "Truly I say to you" stresses the reliability of Jesus' shocking prediction, "One of you will give me over" — shocking because although he has spoken before of being given over (9:31; 10:33-34), he has not till now identified the betrayer as one of his disciples, much less as one of the Twelve closest to him. In a phrase borrowed from Ps 41:10(9), Jesus heightens the pathos by adding that the betrayer will be one "who is eating with me" (or "who eats with me" — i.e. regularly as well as right now; cf. Jn 13:18; Obad 7; 1QH 5:23-24). Placement of the subject "one of you" before the verb "will give me over" and of the appositive "who is eating with me" after the verb heightens the pathos yet more by putting intimacy both first and last. To feel this pathos we should recall that in ancient near eastern culture, eating with someone connotes an almost sacred trust of friendship. For Mark, there is not only pathos, but also astonishing accuracy of detail in Jesus' unlikely prediction that one of his most trusted intimates is going to betray him. Such predictive power strengthens Mark's apology for the Cross.

14:19-21 *(Matt 26:22-25; Luke 22:21-23)* Both the asyndeton with which Mark introduces the disciples' grief and question (and which causes enough stylistic offense to produce the vv.ll. καί, "and," and οἱ δέ, "but they" — cf. M. Reiser, *Syntax und Stil* 155-56) and the grief itself and the question which expresses it emphasize the shocking unlikelihood of Jesus' prediction — again all the more impressive in fulfilment because of its unlikelihood. The same emphasis comes out in the phrase "one by one," which forms part of Mark's introduction; in the negative answer implied by the question, "Not I, [is it]?" (cf. 4:21), in the emotion-laden verblessness of this question, and in Jesus' likewise verbless an-swer, "One of the Twelve [again a reference to one of the disciples closest to him — cf. vv 10, 43], the one dipping with me into the one bowl [a paraphrase of the earlier allusion to Ps 41:10(9), but with a heightening of intimacy from eating together to dipping together into one and the same bowl]." An adversative δέ, "but," in the introduction to Jesus' answer sets it as a prediction to be fulfilled over against the disciples' contradictory question. By describing the false-friendly action of dipping as the betrayer's own, the middle voice of ἐμβαπτόμενος (the active voice is used in the parr. Matt 26:23; John 13:26 [bis]) characterizes him as perfidious. The lack of a direct object for dipping as well as for eating concentrates attention on the element of intimacy (so L. Schenke, *Studien* 234-35). The repetition of "one" with "bowl" (see the notes on the text critical question) highlights the intimacy. And the ignorance displayed in the apostles' question, though not a blameworthy ignorance (contrast 6:52; 8:16-21), creates a foil against which Jesus' prescience stands out in marked contrast.

A causal ὅτι (v 21) introduces Scripture as the reason for the giving over of Jesus; i.e. the OT assigns to him the fate of going away in this manner (καθώς, "according as," which also in 1:2; 4:33; 9:13; 11:6; 14:16; 15:8; 16:27 includes manner as well as fact). Presumably he has in mind Ps 41:10(9), whose phrase-ology he has just used. A scriptural reason also fits nicely into Mark's apology for the Cross. The verb changes from ἀναβαίνομεν, "we are going up" (10:33), to ὑπάγει, "[the Son of man] is going [away]," because Jesus is no longer ascend-ing the road to Jerusalem with the Twelve, but is going from them to his enemies as a result of being given over. The underlying idea of going links the two sayings, however. Jesus' statement in 14:7, "But me you do not always have [with your-selves]," also contributes to the choice of "is going away"; for otherwise we would expect the recency of "will give me over" in v 18 and the parallel with "is being given over" in v 21b to produce "is being given over" here in v 21a. Thus, the present pericope links up with the one in vv 1-11 and by defining the Son of man's coming in chap. 13 as a return links up with that pericope as well.

By pinpointing the betrayer, not the one to be given over, as the true criminal, the woe to "that man through whom the Son of man is being given over" exonerates Jesus of any guilt that Mark's audience may have attached to Jesus because of the Crucifixion. "That man" puts the betrayer at a critical distance. So also does μέν . . . δέ, "on the one hand . . . on the other," which in view of its relative rarity in Hellenistic Greek may apologetically dignify the language of Jesus (so J. A. L. Lee in *NovT* 27 [1985] 1-8). The construction μέν . . . δέ also draws "the Son of man" forward in v 21a (and in the echoing latter part of v 21b) for a contrast with "that man." "Good for him if he hadn't come into existence — that man" (cf. 9:42; *1 Enoch* 38:2; *m. Ḥag.* 2:1; *b. Ber.* 17a; *Exod. Rab.* 40[96d], cited in Str-B 1. 989-90) exposes the enormity of the betrayer's guilt by headlining the horror of his judgment, worse than the Son of man's fate. A number of elements add to the exposé: (1) contrastive wordplay between "the Son of man" and "that man"; (2) asyndeton; (3) ellipsis of "it would have been"; (4) substitution of the stronger οὐκ instead of the weaker, expected μή for "not"; (5) pleonastic repetition of "that man"; and (6) placement of the second "that man" in the climactically last position (if to be repeated at all, we would expect "for that man" instead of "for him" after "good"). The futuristic use of the present tense in "is going" and "is being given over" highlights the predictive element in the woe: so sure is Jesus to be going to those to whom he is being given over that the fulfilment is as good as in process right now.

14:22-25 *(Matt 26:26-29; Luke 22:15-20; 1 Cor 11:23-26)* Recent research favors the long text of Luke 22:15-20 (see esp. vv 19-20; B. M. Metzger, *Textual Commentary* ad loc.; H. Schürmann, *Traditionsgeschichtliche Untersuchungen* 159-97). The large-scale agreement of Luke's long text with 1 Cor 11:23-26 favors that Luke depends either on 1 Cor 11:23-26 or on the same earlier tradition which Paul quotes in that passage. Since Luke 22:15-18 contains introductory material missing in 1 Cor 11:23-26 but understandably omitted by Paul as unuseful to his non-narrative purpose of correcting abuses in the Corinthian church, the pre-Pauline tradition probably included that introductory material and Luke depends on that tradition rather than on 1 Cor 11:23-26. Supporting this judgment are (1) the presence in Luke 22:19 of "is given," which neither 1 Cor 11:24 nor Mark 14:22 par. Matt 26:26 has; (2) the presence in Luke 22:20 of "which is poured out for you," which 1 Cor 11:25 does not have and for which Mark 14:25 probably does not provide the source, because otherwise Luke is likely also to have followed Mark's immediately preceding and parallelistically more satisfying "this is my blood of the covenant" (cf. "this is my body") rather than writing the elliptical and unparallel "this cup [is] the new covenant in my blood"; and (3) the probable echo in 1 Cor 11:26 (". . . you proclaim the Lord's death till he comes") of the tradition behind Luke 22:18 (about Jesus' not drinking "till the kingdom of God comes"), which therefore does not have to derive from Mark 14:25 par. Matt 26:29 and whose reference to coming (ἔλθῃ, as in 1 Cor 11:26 but not Mark and Matthew) and whose forward position, contrasting with its last position in Mark and Matthew, favor that it does not derive from the other synoptics.

Since Paul wrote 1 Corinthians around 51 C.E., the tradition which he quotes in 1 Cor 11:23 and which Luke quotes in Luke 22:15-20 dates from even earlier. The earliness of this tradition opens up the possibility that Mark redacts the same tradition. If such a redaction turns out to fit the concerns which he displays in the surrounding context, especially his concern to emphasize Jesus' ability to predict his own fate, then we will have evidence favoring that Mark redacts the pre-Pauline, pre-Lucan tradition. Thus, Jesus' statement of strong desire to eat the Passover with the apostles before he suffers (Luke 22:15) drops out because the statement emphasizes his desire rather than his predictive ability. This omission leaves without cue his statement that he will not eat the Passover till it is fulfilled in the kingdom of God (Luke 22:16); so despite its consisting of a prediction, this statement drops out, too. Because Jesus' initial taking of the cup, giving thanks, and telling the apostles to take it and distribute it among themselves contains no element of prediction (Luke 22:17), Mark omits it as well. Jesus' statement that he will not drink from the fruit of the vine till the kingdom of God comes (Luke

22:18) consists of another prediction that has lost its cue, then; but its predictive character and promise of Jesus' ultimate victory keep Mark from omitting it. Instead, he delays it for climactic attachment to the cup of the Lord's Supper. No longer does it attach to an earlier cup of the Passover meal (contrast Mark 14:24-25 with Luke 22:17-18, and cf. the placement of the cup of the Lord's Supper after the Passover meal in 1 Cor 11:25; Luke 22:20).

Now Mark comes to the institution of the Lord's Supper, which provides plenty of grist for his predictive mill. "And as they were eating" echoes v 18 minus its reference to reclining, which needs no repetition, to provide an introduction suitable to Jesus' following actions and words. The participial phrases, "having taken bread, having blessed," deal with the necessary but unpredictive preliminaries as briskly as possible (cf. 6:41; 8:6). The asyndeton between them (so also Luke 22:19 but not 1 Cor 11:23-24; Matt 26:26) quickens the headlong rush toward Jesus' breaking the bread, giving a piece to each of the Twelve, and saying, "Take, this is my body" (again cf. 6:41; 8:6). It is easier to think that Paul and Luke change εὐλογήσας, "having blessed" (so Mark), to εὐχαριστήσας, "having given thanks" — or, better, that they and Mark provide alternative Greek translations of a Semitic tradition — than to think that Mark changes εὐχαριστήσας to εὐλογήσας; for the latter is not quite at home in Greek when meaning to bless in the sense of praising God, a sense derived from the Septuagintal use of εὐλογέω for ברך, "bless" (see H. W. Beyer in *TDNT* 2. 754-63) and favored here by the parallel with εὐχαριστήσας, which regularly means to give thanks (cf. Mark 14:23; also 6:41 with 8:6, and 8:6 with 8:7 and the usual Jewish prayer of thanksgiving: "Blessed are you, O Lord our God, king of the world, who bring forth bread from the earth"). The command to take derives from the command to take the Passover cup (Luke 22:17). Neither 1 Cor 11:24 nor Luke 22:19 has a command to take the bread. Mark inserts it to make up for his omission of the command to take the Passover cup. But because "this" immediately follows in the bread-word ("this is my body"), he writes an objectless "take" rather than "take this," as in Luke 22:17. Everywhere else in the context, too, an object follows "take" (Mark 14:22, 23 parr.; 1 Cor 11:23). The anomaly that in Mark 14:22 the command to take lacks an object confirms that Mark has inserted the command into an unoriginal context that resists the original object "this." Reapplied to the bread of the Lord's Supper, the command begins to draw the Twelve into the action in a way that brings out Judas Iscariot's perfidy, stressed by Mark as an apologetic foil to Jesus' innocence of wrongdoing. The command also compensates in advance for Mark's upcoming omission of the command, "Do this in remembrance of me."

Taken together, Jesus' breaking the bread, giving a piece of it to each of the Twelve, telling them to take it, and saying that it represents his body make yet another passion prediction, this one taking the form of an object lesson acted out and accompanied by interpretation (above all, cf. the predictions of Ezekiel, starting in chap. 4 of his book). "Because" or "for" might easily have joined the predictively interpretative statement, "This is my body," to the command, "Take." Instead, asyndeton gives the statement an emphasis that highlights its predictive character. At this point, then, Mark does not tamper with the tradition.

Since Jesus is reclining in the body with his disciples, "this is" must mean "this represents" (but G. B. Caird [*Language* 101-2] correctly warns against "mere" symbolism, for "many symbols, such as a kiss, a handshake and the presentation of a latchkey, are a means, even the means, of conveying what they represent"; for a more realistic interpretation see J. Schmid 259-63). Presumably, the original Semitic left "is" to be supplied (cf. Luke 22:20). The use of "body" (σῶμα) instead of "flesh" (contrast John 6:51-58; and see H. Schürmann, *Einsetzungsbericht* 18-19, 107-10, 141-43, against the originality of "flesh") does not derive from the original distance of the bread-word, spoken during the Passover meal, from the cup-word, spoken afterwards, as though they carry discrete meanings. The repetitions of "this," of an implied or expressed "is," of a predicate nominative ("my body" and "the new covenant in my blood" or, as revised by Mark, "my blood of the covenant"), and of an interpretative participial phrase ("being given for you" [Luke 22:19, corresponding to a futuristic Aramaic or Hebrew participle and Graecized by omission of the participle in 1 Cor 11:24] and "being poured out for many/you" [Mark 14:24 parr., again corresponding to a futuristic Aramaic participle and this time completely omitted in 1 Cor 11:25]) — these repetitions show that Jesus intended the bread-word and the cup-word to be taken in conjunction with each other, as indeed Mark takes them by bringing them together (so also Matthew; 1 Cor 10:16-17; *Did.* 9:1-5; Justin *1 Apol.* 66.3 et al.). The pairing of "flesh" and "blood" would have connoted a living union of the two, as in Lev 17:11, 14 (cf. Job 6:4 LXX and the *concealment* of Jesus' death behind the pairing of flesh and blood in John 6:51-58).

By itself σῶμα does not mean the whole person or the person as such (R. H. Gundry, *Sōma*), however. We may also doubt that its Hebrew and Aramaic equivalents — גף, גויה, גופה, גוף, and גופא — ever mean the person apart from bodily presence, as required by the interpretation that Jesus is here assuring the Twelve of his coming personal presence at table with them even though he will be absent in the body. But σῶμα, גויה, and גופה may mean "body" in the sense of "corpse" (see the lexicons and references therein, esp. 1 Sam 31:10, 12 MT with 1 Kgdms 31:10, 12 LXX; 1 Chr 10:12 MT with LXX for the translation of גויה and גופה by σῶμα in this sense). So the context of the passion narrative and the conjunction with shed blood recommend the translation, "This is my corpse." Supporting this translation are the surrounding uses of σῶμα in reference to Jesus' burial, for he was not buried alive (14:8; 15:43, 45 v.l.). In v 22 τοῦτο, "this," takes its neuter gender from the subsequent predicate nominative σῶμα despite the masculine gender of the antecedent ἄρτον, "bread." Thus, though Hebrew and Aramaic have no neuter, the emphasis in the Greek text falls on the predictive symbolism to which σῶμα gives expression; and a parallel develops with τοῦτο in v 24, where the neuter gender happens to agree with the antecedent ποτήριον, "cup," as well as with the predicate nominative αἷμα, "blood."

"Being given for you" (so Luke 22:19, though the more Semitic "for many" in the cup-word at Mark 14:24 suggests that this latter phrase occurred in the original tradition of the bread-word) drops out as superfluous after Mark's insertion of a command to take the bread when Jesus gave it. The command, "Keep doing this for my remembrance" (1 Cor 11:24; Luke 22:19), also drops out, but because Mark is interested in apologetic prediction rather than in its opposite, i.e. liturgical remembrance. "And the cup likewise after dining, saying" (Luke 22:20; so also 1 Cor 11:25 except for "likewise also") changes to "and having taken the cup, having given thanks, he gave [it] to them . . . and he said to them" for parallelism with the similar expressions that led up to the bread-word. This parallelism emphasizes the twofoldness, and therefore the clarity, of the acted and spoken passion prediction (cf. 6:41; 8:6 once more, noting that the present switch from "blessing" [v 22] to "giving thanks" [v 23] matches the progression from 6:41 to 8:6 but reverses the order in 8:6-7; for the asyndeton, see the comments on 14:22). Instead of inserting an unparalleled command to take the cup as he inserted an unparalleled command to take the bread, or a command to drink from it (as in Matt 26:26 and by implication in the command, "Keep on doing this . . . ," in 1 Cor 11:24; Luke 22:19; cf. the command to eat in Matt 26:26; Mark 14:22 v.l.; 1 Cor 11:24 v.l.), Mark now inserts an unparalleled statement that "they all drank from it." Narrative obliterates liturgy. As insured by πάντες, "all," which occupies an emphatic final position and probably refers to the Twelve exclusive of Jesus, this narrative statement exposes the perfidy of the betrayer, one of the Twelve (cf. esp. vv 17, 18, 20). He even drank the cup of the Lord and did so only a short while before betraying him. Perfidy on the part of an intimate, not criminality on the part of Jesus, put Jesus on a cross. So intent is Mark to make this point that he inserts the disciples' drinking from the cup ahead of Jesus' interpretation of the cup. This insertion causes an addition of "to them" to "he said," because "he gave [it] to them" no longer precedes immediately, as it did in v 22.

"This cup [is] the new covenant in my blood" (1 Cor 11:25; Luke 22:20; cf. Jer 31:31) changes to "this is my blood of the covenant" (cf. Exod 24:8, esp. in the OT Peshitta and Targums Pseudo-Jonathan and Onqelos; also Heb 9:20) for emphasis on Jesus' blood rather than on the new covenant that it will establish. For it is in Jesus' shed blood that Mark finds a passion prediction. This change makes unnecessary the question whether Mark's wording can be retroverted into Aramaic. "Of the covenant" and "being poured out for many" (cf. Isa 53:12 MT) indicate the sacrificial character of Jesus' approaching death, its violence and atoning value for others — an indication of divine approval and salvific benefit (and the latter for more than the Twelve, indeed for Mark's audience, too, if they will believe) in opposition to human condemnation and shameful crucifixion (cf. the comments and notes on 10:38-39 and esp. 10:45). By omitting the references to the covenant and to outpouring on behalf of many Mark could have tightened the parallel with the bread-word, from which he did drop "being given for you [or, more likely, 'for many']" (cf. his tightening of parallelism at the start of v 23). Why does he not make such omissions? Because he has in mind to add the prediction of abstinence till the drinking anew in God's kingdom and because the covenant, by including many, describes the blood in a way that provides the subjects of that kingdom. In other words, Mark keeps the description of the blood because this description helps him attach the climactic, vindicative prediction of v 25 in an understandable way. Before attaching that prediction, however, he omits the command, "Keep doing this, as often as you drink [the cup], for my remembrance" (1 Cor 11:25, presuming that the reference in v 26 to "the death of the Lord" indicates a shift from tradition to comment). As in the omission at v 22 of a similar command, this omission derives from Mark's interest in apologetic prediction rather than in liturgical remembrance. Though Paul's version antedates Luke's, one could say that Luke's lacking the second command to keep doing this represents a more original pre-Pauline tradition. Even so, however, the reason for omission still stands with regard to the first such command (and see I. H. Marshall, *Last Supper* 51-53, for a sympathetic evaluation of arguments favoring the traditionality of both commands and the authenticity of the tradition, to which arguments can now be added that "the one real argument against the authenticity of the saying," i.e. "its absence from Mark," is not real at all; for a redactional concern to exalt prediction over liturgy explains the absence).

By having put the narrative statement, "And they all drank from it," before the cup-word, Mark has enabled himself now to attach without interruption Jesus' prediction of abstinence till the drinking anew in God's kingdom: "Truly I say to you that by no means will I any more drink of the product of the vine till that day when I drink it anew in the kingdom of God" (v 25). At its original position in Luke 22:18, this saying provided a rationale for Jesus' command to take a Passover cup and distribute it. But Mark 14:24 contained no command to take the cup of the Lord's Supper; so the new, subsequent position of the saying on abstinence leaves no need for a rationale. All the emphasis can rest on the predictive character of the saying. Hence, Mark asyndetically omits γάρ, "for," which Luke 22:18 keeps and whose originality is supported by paralleled occurrences of λέγω γὰρ ὑμῖν, "for I say to you," in Luke 3:8; 10:24 as well as by unique occurrences in Luke 14:24; 22:16, 37. On the other hand, Mark keeps ἀμήν, "truly," which Luke characteristically omits.

"By no means will I any more drink" (οὐκέτι οὐ μή plus an aorist subjunctive) implies that Jesus will soon die (cf. v 30) — thus another passion prediction, an indirect one. It also implies that he has drunk on this occasion, just as his statement that he will by no means eat the Passover any more (Luke 22:16) supports his immediately preceding statement that he has strongly desired to eat this Passover before he suffers (Luke 22:15; cf. the exclusion of present occasions at Luke 1:48; 5:10; 12:52; 22:69 in ἀπὸ τοῦ νῦν, "from now on," the alternative to Mark's οὐκέτι in Luke 22:18). Non-drinking on this present occasion would probably require "I am no more drinking" (οὐκέτι plus a present indicative as, e.g., in 7:12; 10:18). Yet in Mark the preceding Institution of the Lord's Supper both lacks and seems to exclude that Jesus ate or drank with the Twelve, for "he gave to them and said, 'You take'" (cf. also the inappropriateness of eating and drinking his own body and blood, even symbolically, and the contrast between wine of bloodshed in the cup-word and wine of celebration in the present saying). Because it says nothing about eating, then, but implies that Jesus has just drunk with the Twelve and also because it speaks of his drinking anew in the kingdom of God but omits any reference to his resurrection even though he has just referred to his death, this final prediction in Mark's order of sayings is confirmed to be displaced (cf. I. H. Marshall, *Last Supper* 53-56; P. J. Achtemeier 100; J. Schlosser, *Le règne* 374-75). In Luke 22:18 Jesus makes the prediction earlier, in conjunction with eating the food as well as drinking the wine of the Passover meal, the cup of the Lord's Supper being instituted not till after that meal (cf. vv 15-17, 20a; 1 Cor 11:25a). So apparently Jesus ate and drank with the Twelve at the Passover meal but abstained from the wine with which he afterwards instituted one half of the Lord's Supper, and probably also from that portion of bread with which he instituted the other half of the Lord's Supper during the Passover meal. For an apologetic climax, however, Mark has delayed till now the prediction originally made before the Institution; i.e. he has delayed the prediction of an abstinence that ends in celebration. The betrayed one will celebrate victory in the coming kingdom. This is the final note that Mark wants to strike in the pericope.

"Until that day when I drink it anew in the kingdom of God" replaces "until the kingdom of God comes" (Luke 22:18), whose originality is supported by the parallel "until it [the Passover] is fulfilled in the kingdom of God" (Luke 22:16), by numerous other instances of Luke's ἕως οὗ, "until [the time in which]," in dominical sayings (see the concordance), by Paul's ἄχρι οὗ ἔλθῃ, "until he comes," by the absence of Mark's "until that day when" from all other dominical sayings, and by the absence of pleonastic demonstratives from biblical and contemporaneous Hebrew and Aramaic and the presence of almost perfect parallels to Marcan usage of demonstratives in the Hellenistic author Epictetus (E. C. Maloney, *Semitic Interference* 124-26). "That day" of kingdom-come echoes "that day" of the Son of man's coming (13:32; N.B. that even the Semitic ἐκείνης, which τῆς makes superfluous, carries over; cf. also the occurrences of Mark's ὅταν, "when," in 13:4, 7, 11, 14, and esp. 28, 29). By emphasizing Jesus' drinking rather than the kingdom's coming, Mark highlights the vindication of Jesus in a celebration of final victory. That Jesus does not say he will drink *with his disciples,* but only that *he* will drink (contrast Matt 26:29), centers attention on this vindication. The position of καινόν, "(a)new," after πίνω, "I drink," rather than after αὐτό, "it," favors the adverbial translation, "when I drink it anew," over the adjectival translation, "when I drink it [as] new [wine]" (against B. Buetebela [in *RAT* 8 (1984) 12-16], whose appeal to 1:27; 2:21-22 is vitiated by the position of the adjective after its nouns in those passages). Conversely, the direct object αὐτό seems to take its position before the verb, not for emphasis (as though wine were taking precedence over some other beverage), but to separate it from καινόν, with which it might otherwise be construed (cf. H. Schürmann, *Paschamahlbericht* 21, n. 103). To underscore the element of prediction, Mark has transferred newness from the present covenant (1 Cor 11:25; Luke 22:20) to the future drinking. Thus, the assumption that in vv 22-25 Mark redacts a pre-Lucan and even pre-Pauline tradition unlocks the door to an interpretation that suits his preceding emphases on Jesus' power of prediction and on Judas's perfidy. Nor is Mark by any means finished with these emphases (see the comments on vv 26-31, 43-52).

NOTES

On the ground that vv 17-21 fail to note a fulfilment of the predictions which Jesus makes in these verses, L. Schenke (*Studien* 212-13) denies that they point up Jesus' prescience; rather, they point up the willingness with which he accepts his God-given role of suffering. But there is not a word of willingness in these verses — at best resignation to a fate in accordance with Scripture (v 21a), at worst retaliation against the betrayer (v 21bc). For willingness, we have to wait till v 36c; and it would be anachronistic to bring fulfilment into the narrative at the present juncture. The fulfilment will come soon enough, and appropriately, in vv 43-47.

The writer of Ps 41:10(9) complains about a friend who used to eat with him and no more does so, but has joined his enemies in speaking against him, not in betraying him. But Jesus speaks about a betrayer who is presently eating with him. Therefore vv 17-21 were hardly created out of Ps 41:10(9) (T. A. Mohr, *Markus- und Johannespassion* 178).

"Evening" (ὀψία) can include late afternoon before sunset as well as twilight after sunset; for though a day ends at sunset according to the reckoning used for the Sabbath, it is still Friday in 15:42 despite the fact that "it has already become evening." One might think that in 15:42 Mark will follow another reckoning, according to which a day extends past sunset to midnight or dawn; but his use there of sabbatarian terms for Friday — viz., παρασκευή, "Preparation," and προσάββατον, "Pre-Sabbath" — will favor that here he uses the sabbatarian method of reckoning. In 1:32, then, "when the sun had set" seems to have qualified "when evening came" in a way that precluded an otherwise possible reference to late afternoon before sunset. Here in 14:17, however, the unqualified "evening" may carry such a reference (so also 4:35; 6:47 [N.B. the temporal advance in 6:48]; 11:11 as well as 15:42).

For Mark's use of "the Twelve," see the notes on 3:14, 16. Jesus' having sent two disciples into the city to prepare the Passover (vv 12-16) would seem to have left only ten of the Twelve to accompany him to Jerusalem, yet "he comes with the Twelve" (v 17). We might think that the two did not belong to the Twelve. But 6:7 said that Jesus sent out the Twelve two by two; so the two who prepared the Passover probably did belong to the Twelve. Apart from the possibility of loose usage in that "the Twelve" has become stereotyped (cf. the appearance of the risen Christ "to the Twelve" despite Judas Iscariot's prior apostasy — 1 Cor 15:5) and in that all the Twelve will recline at the Passover meal with Jesus, we may infer that the two returned to Bethany after making preparations just as we may infer that Judas rejoined the Twelve after going to the chief priests and that he will leave before coming to Gethsemane for the arrest of Jesus (cf. the notes on vv 10-11). It is just as gratuitous to say that the two waited at the guest room as to say that they rejoined the others. Since Jesus' prediction contained no indication that he knew the street address of the room, but only the way the two would find it, Mark's audience may more naturally assume that the two rejoined the others to lead them there. E. Best (*Disciples and Discipleship* 153-54) points out that a reference to "the disciples" in v 17 might easily be mistaken for a reference to only the two disciples of v 16 and that neither "the apostles" nor "the ten" would conform to Mark's habit of speech.

Though reclining (ἀνακειμένων) does not prove this meal to be Passover (for diners recline at other meals throughout the gospels), this posture certainly suits the Passover. See 2:15 for the synonymity of ἀνάκειμαι and κατάκειμαι (used recently in 14:3); and T. A. Mohr (*Markus- und Johannespassion* 169-70), E. Best (*Disciples and Discipleship* 152, n. 106), and L. Schenke (*Studien* 203-9) for stylistic arguments for and against the traditionality of v 18a. Lost in these arguments are the possibilities that frequently occurring stylistic traits may derive from tradition rather than from Mark and, perhaps more likely, that Mark writes up tradition partly in his own style. We need not consider the omission in Matt 26:21 of "the one eating with me" a sign that the phrase is a gloss on Mark 14:18

(C. E. B. Cranfield 423), for Matthew had reasons to omit the phrase (R. H. Gundry, *Matthew* 526).

See the notes on 1:45 for the pleonastic use of ἤρξαντο, "they began" (v 19), and T. A. Mohr, *Markus- und Johannespassion* 172, on the Septuagintal-cum-Hebraistic and traditional character of εἰς, "into" (v 20; cf. J. J. O'Rourke in *JBL* 85 [1966] 351). By interpreting λυπεῖσθαι as disagreement with Jesus' prediction of betrayal by one of the Twelve, L. Schenke (*Studien* 227) tries to wring out of v 19 a characteristically Marcan portrayal of the disciples as ignorant. The cross-references that he cites for such an interpretation are unconvincing, however. John 21:17 more naturally refers to Peter's grief that Jesus should question his love a third time (cf. Peter's weeping on denying him three times — Mark 14:72 parr.). In 2 Cor 2:1-2, 4, 5 "many tears" defines λυπέω in terms of sorrow rather than disagreement. And in 2 Cor 7:9 the contrast with rejoicing defines λυπέω in this same, normal sense of sorrow.

The question μήτι ἐγώ; suggests a possibility only to negate it: "Not I, [is it]?" (v 19). Cross-references commonly cited to support a more or less positive rather than negative μήτι ("Perhaps I, [is it]?") are unconvincing. To say that in Matt 12:23 the crowds mean, "Is this perhaps (μήτι) the Son of David?" overlooks that in Matt 16:14, 17 only the disciples regard Jesus as the Messiah, the people in general regarding him as John the Baptist, Elijah, Jeremiah, or one of the prophets. To be sure, the very form of a question raises the possibility that Jesus is the Son of David, but it is a possibility which μήτι negates. If in Matt 26:22 the eleven may use μήτι according to its normal meaning ("I am not [the betrayer], am I?"), so also may Judas Iscariot in Matt 26:25; for the construction and wording are the same. Jesus' response, "You said [it]," agrees with the possibility raised by Judas's question but disagrees with the negative answer implied by μήτι, just as "you said [it]" gives mixed responses also in Matt 26:64; 27:11. Not even the most promising cross-reference, John 4:29, needs to mean, "Is this perhaps the Christ?" for in John 4:39 the Samaritans attribute their faith in Jesus to the woman's saying that he told her everything she had done, not to a suggestion of hers that he might be the Christ. She negatived the possibility; her fellow Samaritans accepted it as a fact. In *Herm. Man.* 4.4.1 μήτι most naturally carries a negative implication: "If a wife . . . or again a husband should fall asleep [= die] and one of them [= the survivor] should marry, the one marrying doesn't sin, does s/he?" The immediately following answer confirms the negative implication. In Ps.-Callisth. 2.14.9 v.l. the possibility is broached and supported that a purported messenger of Alexander is in truth Alexander himself (μήτι σὺ ὁ Ἀλέξανδρος; "You aren't Alexander, are you?") only to have it dismissed.

"Not I, [is it]?" is psychologically and historically impossible, argues T. A. Mohr (*Markus- und Johannespassion* 179-80), because eleven of the Twelve disciples would know they are not betrayers of Jesus; hence, the question reflects self-examination at early Christian celebrations of the Lord's Supper. On the contrary, Jesus uses the future tense: "will give me over." The eleven know what they have not done in the past, but they do not know what they will do in the future. Peter will thrice deny Jesus despite present protestations to the contrary. And the eucharistic self-examination commanded in 1 Cor 11:27-32 grows out of a situation (abuse of the Lord's Supper) quite different from the betrayal of Jesus.

According to V. K. Robbins (in *The Passion in Mark* 31), the position of "not I, [is it]?" between references to the betrayer emphasizes the possibility of betrayal by anyone who enters discipleship (v 19). But "one of you" (v 18) and "one of the Twelve" (v 20) tend in the opposite direction by narrowing down Jesus' prediction rather than expanding betrayal to include a phenomenon that will later plague the life of the church under persecution (cf. E. C. Maloney, *Semitic Interference* 154, on the mixture of Semitic and Hellenistic idiom in εἷς κατὰ εἷς, "one by one").

Some consider the saying in v 20 a variant of the saying in v 18b. But the saying in v 20 could not stand by itself, for its lack of a predicate makes it senseless apart from the saying in v 18b. Someone has built it on the foundation of the earlier saying, and that someone might as well be Jesus as a redactor. On the other hand, "one of the Twelve" sounds as though Jesus is talking to someone else about the Twelve, in particular about one of them, rather than to the Twelve about one of themselves; so we might contemplate the possibility that Mark, prompted by the preceding "one of you," adds "one of the Twelve" to a traditional "the one dipping with me into the bowl." Elsewhere in the synoptics Jesus sometimes uses the third person to speak about his audience as a whole or in part (see, e.g., 3:31-35; 8:34–9:1), but he never uses "the Twelve" either in addressing them or in speaking about them to others (contrast John 6:70). In the phrase "one of the Twelve," εἷς retains its numerical force; it does not represent the Semitic indefinite use of "one" (see E. C. Maloney, *Semitic Interference* 127-31).

Since v 17 has said that Jesus is eating with the Twelve, the mention of the Twelve after the plural address "you" does not imply that he is hosting a larger number of diners than the Twelve (against G. Wohlenberg 348). Nor does Sir 31:14, despite some phraseological similarity, make a good parallel to Mark 14:20. That verse has to do with greed, this one with intimacy. Since Jesus chose the Twelve to be "with him" (3:14), since they are all eating with him (v 18), and since eating with him entails dipping with him into the one bowl, the switch from "the one eating with me" (v 18) to "the one dipping with me into the one bowl" does not single out the betrayer as Judas Iscariot any more than the switch from "one of you" (also in v 18) to "one of the Twelve" does. After all, no one has asked Jesus to single out the betrayer. Each one has only asked whether he himself is the betrayer, and has implied a negative answer to his own question. Historically, if "the one dipping with me into the one bowl" had singled out Judas as the betrayer, the other disciples would have interfered; and Mark would probably have noted the interference, for it would have enhanced his portrayal of Jesus as the one whose predictions come true no matter what his disciples do or say to the contrary. Thus the present tense of "dipping" is not futuristic, and v 20 intensifies the pathos of v 18 and the unlikelihood of fulfilment rather than identifying the betrayer more closely.

The suggestion that dipping with Jesus into the one bowl signifies a rejection of Jesus' leadership (so F. C. Fensham in *RevQ* 5 [1964-66] 259-61) illegitimately gives "with me" a bad connotation (to the contrary, see v 18 and 3:14 again). The cross-references used to support this suggestion, viz., 1QS 6:4-5; 1QSa 2:17-22, prohibit anyone's extending his hand over the bread and wine before the messianic priest does so at the start of a meal. But by now Jesus and the Twelve are in the midst of their meal. If they are eating the first course of a Passover meal, as favored by context, the bowl contains a sauce of stewed fruit and bitter herbs. We should probably accept the v.l. "one" before "bowl" (so B C* Θ 565). Its failure to appear in the parallel Matt 26:23 may be equally well explained as evidence for its unoriginality in Mark or as the parallelistic reason for its omission in the remaining texts of Mark. Why then might Matthew have omitted it and Marcan scribes followed suit? Because to write another "one" after "one of the Twelve" seemed to overload Jesus' answer, especially after two other instances of "one" in the immediately preceding verse and yet another one in the verse before that, or because the writing of the numeral ΕΙΣ, "one," as only the second word after the preposition ΕΙΣ, "into," seemed confusing or tasteless.

The foregoing comments established the sensibility of a causal ὅτι at the start of v 21. Thereby falls the argument that the saying in v 21 must have originally followed a verb of speaking, producing an epexegetic or recitative ὅτι, in a different context. On the supposition that "the 'woe-oracle' in Mk 14:21 is unique; there is no other like it in the biblical tradition," V. K. Robbins (in *The Passion in Mark* 32-34) argues that originally the saying started with the woe and that Mark violated the usual order of "woe to . . . ,

because/for . . . ," plus a pronouncement of judgment, by prefixing the "because"-clause
to link the woe-oracle with the foregoing prediction of betrayal. Against this argument,
however, v 21 is not unique; for Luke 17:1-2, which occurs in a different context and has
nothing to do with Jesus' betrayal, exhibits the same order of crime, woe, and judgment,
plus a similar grammatical independence of the crime from the woe as well as of the
judgment from the woe, a similar introduction of the woe by an adversative conjunction
(πλήν in Luke 17:1), a similar asyndeton in the introduction of judgment; and a similar
backhanded description of the judgment by way of unfavorable contrast with another fate
already horrible enough. These similarities do not offer evidence that the saying in Mark
14:21 has been assimilated to the one in Luke 17:1-2. They offer evidence of a Jesuanic
locution. In Mark 14:21 the adversative δέ, "but," with "woe" shows that the foregoing
"because"-clause depends on the prediction of crime in v 20, not on the following woe.
Once again, then, we should not take the ὅτι as epexegetic or recitative rather than causal;
for direct discourse started without a recitative ὅτι in v 20 and continues without interruption in v 21. A full stop is to be put, not at the close of v 20, but after "concerning him"
at the close of v 21a; and the whole of vv 20-21a sets out the crime for which the following
woe is pronounced, and does so, just as in Luke 17:1-2, without an *initial* "because" or
"for" such as introduces the crime when the crime follows the woe (see references listed
by Robbins, op. cit. 32, n. 29). As elsewhere and normally, the ὅτι-clause looks backward,
giving a scriptural reason for the already predicted betrayal by an intimate. Invariably,
other Marcan ὅτι-clauses that carry a causal meaning follow a main clause.

    In defense of the authenticity of v 21, S. Kim (*"Son of Man"* 45-46) pertinently
asks why Jesus should be forbidden to refer to the OT, why he should not use the
passio-iusti motif, why similarity to 9:31 should work against authenticity unless 9:31 be
shown inauthentic; and Kim notes that the double wordplay between "Son of man" and
"that man," resting as it does on a Semitic expression used for Jesus almost entirely by
himself, favors authenticity. In arguing that v 21 is wholly a fabrication of Mark, on the
other hand, J. D. Crossan (*In Fragments* 146-47) overlooks the likelihood — or, to put it
cautiously, the possibility — that similarities to other dominical sayings point to authentically dominical locutions and concerns. B. Lindars (*Jesus, Son of Man* 74-76) thinks that
the double occurrence of "the Son of man" indicates that v 21 derives from sayings
originally independent of each other. But it is unlikely that such sayings would have been
so amenable to combination with μέν . . . δέ, perhaps also unlikely that more than one
saying would have played on "the Son of man . . . that man." Rather, the double occurrence
is designed to highlight this wordplay. The shift from "me" (vv 18, 20) to "the Son of
man" (v 21 bis) matches an identical shift in 8:27, 29, 31, the last verse of which contains
a passion prediction, as here (cf. "the Son of man" in yet other such predictions at 9:9, 12,
31; 10:33-34; see the comments and notes on 2:10-11; 8:31).

    "Goes" (ὑπάγει) here means "goes to those to whom that woeful man gives over
the Son of man" (N.B. the parallelism between going and being given over). It would
overinterpret "goes" to say that it means going to death, though that, of course, will be the
outcome of being given over to the Sanhedrin. A. Schlatter (*Matthäus* 740) notes the use
of אצל for departure through death; but the infrequency of this use and the failure of the
LXX ever to translate אצל by ὑπάγω leave the field open to the contextual meaning of
Jesus' going to his enemies as a result of betrayal. The use of ὑπάγω in John 7:33; 8:14,
21-22; 13:3 et passim for Jesus' going to the Father progresses far beyond the usage in
Mark 14:21, though it may originate here, and refers to Jesus' heavenly destination rather
than to his death, though he will pass through death on his way to that destination.

    R. Pesch (in *Jesus und der Menschensohn* 181-82) denies a futuristic present tense
in "is going" and says instead that the action has already started. We should resist this
interpretation, however; for "is being given over" parallels "is going" yet is already shown

to be a futuristic present tense by "will give me over" in v 18. The parallel with "is being given over" combines with its passive voice to weaken the suggestion that "is going away" brings out the voluntariness of Jesus in his passion. Moreover, ὑπάγω occurs elsewhere in Mark almost exclusively in commands, which connote the opposite of voluntariness (1:44; 2:9, 11; 5:19, 34; 6:38; 7:29; 8:33; 10:21, 52; 11:2; 14:13). The appeal of H. E. Tödt (*Son of Man* 187-88, 199) to ἄγωμεν, "let us go," in vv 41-42 fails to help the voluntaristic interpretation, because there the verb will be framed by "the Son of man is being given over into the hands of sinners" and "the one giving me over has come near." What we have is necessity, not voluntariness (cf. vv 33-36, 39).

The disparity between being given over and voluntariness causes L. Schenke (*Studien* 241-71) to hypothesize an original independence of v 21b from v 21a and to treat v 21b as traditional but v 21a as Mark's redactional fabrication. The non-voluntariness of ὑπάγει loosens the mainspring of this hypothesis, however. Mark is unlikely to have fabricated a Jewish-sounding "Son of man"-saying in writing for an audience to whose ignorance of Jewish ways and words he elsewhere shows great sensitivity. Ὑπάγω occurs in the reported words of Jesus far more often than in editorial seams (see the concordance). Καθὼς γέγραπται, "according as it is written," does go to Mark's account in 1:2. But in 9:13 Jesus is reported to have used this same phrase with regard to John the Baptist's passion, and in 9:12; 14:27, 49 Jesus is reported to have related his own passion to Scripture (cf. 7:6; 11:17). So only by a circular reasoning that would deny the authenticity also of those passages could we use 1:2 against the authenticity of 14:21a.

J. Bowker (*Religious Imagination* 149-69) uses "according as it is written concerning him" (v 21) to argue that the statement, "The Son of man goes," rests on OT, targumic, and rabbinic usage in which "son of man" means "man as mortal, born to die" (cf. P. M. Casey [in *JSNT* 29 (1987) 40-42], who additionally thinks of "that man" as referring to betrayers as a class). But we have seen that "goes" (ὑπάγει) does not mean "dies," and such a background would both fail to explain and make it more difficult to explain the glorious and powerful connotations of "the Son of man" in 2:10, 28; 8:38; 13:26-27; 14:52 et passim. See K. Beyer (*Semitische Syntax* 1/1. 80, n. 1) and E. C. Maloney (*Semitic Interference* 124-26) on the questionability of a Semitism in ἐκεῖνος, "that," and ibid. 192-96 against a Semitic use of the positive degree for the comparative in καλόν, "good." See also the comments on 1:14 and the notes on 9:31 against a divine passive in "is being given over." "Good for him if he hadn't come into existence — that man" shows that οὐαί, "woe," carries its usual meaning "alas." The woe bewails judgment, then, rather than pronouncing or describing it. Taken strictly, the implied judgment might be less frightful than eternal damnation but more frightful than never having come into existence. One wonders what besides eternal damnation would be more frightful, however. In 3:28 Jesus spoke of the possibility that any sin or blasphemy might be forgiven. Here, he indicates that in the case of the betrayer this possibility will not be actualized. So the sayings contradict each other not in the least (against J. Gnilka 2. 238). Cf. God's avenging the deaths of martyrs in 2 Macc 7:17, 19.

Did. 9:1-4 puts the cup before the bread, but *Did.* 9:5 puts eating before drinking. Does this phenomenon reflect the originality of the earlier cup of Passover and a confusion of that cup with the later cup of the Lord's Supper? If Mark omits the earlier cup because he is adopting only those elements of the Institution which contribute to his portrayal of Jesus as the great predictor, we need not suppose that the order bread–wine reflects Essene practice (against D. Flusser in *Immanuel* 2 [1973] 23-27); but see J. Groh in *CTM* 41 (1970) 279-95 for other parallels between the Last Supper and the supper described in 1QS 6:4-6; 1QSa 2:17-22, which he regards as a Passover meal rather than a messianic banquet, even an anticipatory one.

The taking of the cup "after dining" (1 Cor 11:25; Luke 22:20) does not imply that

Jesus took the bread before dining and therefore does not contradict Mark's statement that Jesus took the bread "while they were eating" (v 22; so also v 18). Though it does not prove the specific setting of a Passover meal, Paul's starting his citation of the eucharistic tradition with a narrative statement ("on the night that he [the Lord Jesus] was given over" — 1 Cor 11:23) and doing so despite his writing an epistle rather than a gospel support the traditionality and historicity of the synoptic setting at Jesus' last Passovertide and casts doubt on the supposition that the tradition of the Last Supper ever circulated independently of the passion narrative. D. E. Nineham (384) suggests that Gentiles might understand εὐλογήσας (v 22) as blessing in the sense of consecration rather than of praise to God. Not likely, however; for praiseful blessing predominates in secular Greek (BAGD s.v. εὐλογέω 1), and the parallel with εὐχαριστήσας, "having given thanks" (v 23), would immediately turn an audience back to this predominant meaning. Cf. the comments on 6:41 concerning the synonymity of blessing and giving thanks. The former expression is Jewish and the latter, Greek; but see the notes on 8:6-7 against inferring too much from this distinction.

Breaking the bread does not symbolize a violent death, but describes the normal way of giving each diner a piece (N.B. the absence of "being broken" in the best textual tradition of 1 Cor 11:24b). E. Schweizer (300) argues that "since the breaking of bread signified the beginning of the meal, it is not possible that the meal had begun earlier [in v 17]"; hence, "vss. 22-25 were at one time handed down independently, without any connection to vss. 17-21" (cf. the repetition of "while they were eating" — vv 18, 22). This argument takes several wrong turns. So far as we can tell from the earliest available though admittedly post-NT Jewish evidence, (1) bread played no part at all in the first course of the Passover; and (2) the main course started with wine, not with bread (see G. J. Bahr in *NovT* 12 [1970] 188-98). (3) Verse 22 simply backs up to tell what Jesus did and said with respect to bread and a cup (vv 22-25) in addition to what he said with respect to the betrayer (vv 17-21). The order is not necessarily chronological. The prediction of betrayal by one of the Twelve comes first as a logical lead into the eucharistic prediction of death. (4) The repetition of "while they were eating" merely connects the two predictions to the same occasion. In and of itself the repetition of an expression does not imply insertion of originally independent material. Only if insertion is established on other grounds should we speak of a Marcan sandwich.

The point concerning repetition of the eating deserves expansion. H. Anderson (310-11) and D. E. Nineham (378-79) argue that we would not read "and while they were eating" in v 22 if this verse had originally been preceded by another subsection containing the same phrase, as in v 18. But Mark may deliberately repeat the phrase to signal the start of a new subsection that tradition has already associated with the same meal and therefore with the preceding subsection. The different order of the two subsections vv 17-21 and 22-25 in Luke 22:14-20 and 22:21-23 does not have to imply an original absence of Mark 14:17-21 before 14:22-25, and may derive instead from Luke's rearranging the subsections to prepare for the addition of further materials dealing with other topics and possibly brought together after the pattern of a Hellenistic symposium.

R. Pesch (2. 348) thinks that the repetition of the eating marks a progression from hors d'ouvres to the Passover meal, the Passover liturgy having intervened. But again it is more likely that the repetition directs attention back to the earlier stage-setting because something new is going to grow out of the same eating that has already produced the table-talk in vv 18b-21. Though defended by C. H. Turner (in *JTS* os 29 [1927-28] 10) and his followers, the parallelistic v.l. in v 22 k looks secondary; for scribes would not likely have broken up the parallelism, and assimilation to Matthew (in the usually accepted Marcan reading) would likely have been more thoroughgoing.

Exod 16:15 LXX (οὗτος ὁ ἄρτος, "this [is] the bread") differs too much from Mark 14:22 (τοῦτό ἐστιν τὸ σῶμά μου, "this is my body") to provide a good parallel. So also does

Jos. Asen. 16:14. Some have explained the neuter gender of Jesus' τοῦτο as a reference to the actions of taking, blessing, breaking, and giving rather than to the neuter σῶμα, which the masculine ἄρτος represents (see, e.g., D. W. A. Gregg, *Anamnesis* 12-13; W. F. Orr and J. A. Walther, *1 Corinthians* 271-72; cf. B. L. Mack, *Myth* 118-19, for a list of various possibilities). But those actions as such can hardly represent Jesus' body. J. Morgenstern (*Some Significant Antecedents* 13-14) takes the choice of ἄρτον instead of ἄζυμον to mean that Jesus and the disciples were eating leavened instead of unleavened bread. On the contrary, Mark's putting the Passover sacrifices on the first day of Unleavened Bread and the Last Supper on the evening of the same day shows that at least for him ἄρτον may be ἄζυμον. So also Josephus describes the bread of presence as unleavened and uses ἄρτος for it (*Ant.* 3.6.6 §§142-43; 3.10.7 §256; cf. the LXX of Exod 25:30; 40:23; Lev 24:7; Num 4:7; 3 Kgdms 7:48; 2 Chr 4:19; 13:11; also Mark 2:26; Heb 9:2). The sacrificial meat of the Passover meal might seem to have represented Jesus' body given for many better than bread does. Then we would expect an equation with his flesh rather than with his body, however; and he seems to have intended an eating and drinking more frequent than the economics of a meat dish would allow. At least the first disciples understood him so. For this reason the Passover meat does not merit any mention, not because the meal is not Passover (cf. the statement of W. H. Kelber [*Mark's Story* 74]: "Jesus drastically recasts the traditional Passover in view of his death"). Against the originality of "body," J. Jeremias (*Eucharistic Words* 200) argues that nowhere else does the underlying Semitic word complement "blood." But we are not dealing with a complementary relation; rather, with a parallel in which "body" and "blood" each refers to Jesus' death, and would do so even though the other term did not appear in the pericope.

"And they all drank from it" (v 23) implies a common cup. As can be told from its placement before the cup-word and from the absence of a command to take the cup, the statement that they all drank from the cup corresponds to the command to take the bread. A command to take the cup would have produced a fourth instance of λαμβάνω, "take," in two successive verses. According to rabbinic literature, each Passover celebrant had his own cup. Either individual cups were not yet in vogue at Jesus' time, or he and his disciples did not follow the custom of using individual cups, or for this particular drinking Jesus passed his cup around, or each of the Twelve poured from Jesus' cup into his own cup (cf. Str-B 4. 58-61). The statement that "they all drank from it [the cup]" would tend against this last possibility as a historical one only if the statement were historical instead of redactional (but see the comments on v 23b). If the statement alludes to the perfidy of Judas Iscariot, we have no need to deduce that some Christians objected to drinking from a common cup or ate only bread at the Lord's Supper. Nor does the emphasis on "all" imply community with Christ (as in 1 Cor 10:1-4, 16-17; cf. *Did.* 9:4; so T. A. Mohr, *Markus- und Johannespassion* 192-93), for then the statement that they all drank would follow the cup-word. As it is, the statement says that all to whom Jesus gave the cup drank from it (thus the perfidy of Judas Iscariot), not that all to whom Jesus said, "This is my blood . . . ," drank from the cup (as though they all shared in his blood by drinking).

With v 24, cf. *m. Pesah.* 10:6; and on allusions to and textual comparisons with Exod 24:8; Isa 53:12; Jer 31:31, see R. H. Gundry, *Use of the OT* 57-59; on the unnecessary retroversion of τὸ αἷμά μου τῆς διαθήκης, "my blood of the covenant," into Aramaic or Hebrew, ibid. 58, n. 3; G. Dalman, *Jesus-Jeshua* 160-61; J. A. Emerton in *JTS* ns 6 (1955) 238-40; 15 (1964) 58-59; H. Gottlieb in *ST* 14 (1960) 115-18; J.-E. David in *Bib* 48 (1967) 291-92; R. H. Fuller, *Mission* 69-70; J. Jeremias, *Eucharistic Words* 193-95; E. C. Maloney, *Semitic Interference* 57-62; on "covenant," J. Reumann, *Supper of the Lord* 34-41. The association of the covenant with bloodshed implies a new covenant (cf. 1 Cor 11:25; 2 Cor 3:6; Luke 22:20; Heb 8:8-12; 9:11–10:31; and, though without reference to bloodshed, Jer 31:31). This covenantal connection does not rule out atonement, however (cf. H. Ritt in *BZ* ns 31 [1987] 168); for Jews and Jewish Christians regard all bloody sacrifices, including covenantal ones, as atoning (see esp. Matt 26:28; Heb 9:11-22; *Tgs. Onq.* and *Yer. I* Exod 24:7-8 against D. Seeley in *SBL 1989 Seminar Papers* 547-48). The outpouring of blood implies violent death (cf. Matt 23:35 par. Luke 11:50; Acts 22:20; Rom 3:15 [= Isa 59:7]; Rev 16:6), which alone can have atoning value (cf. Heb 9:22). The present participle ἐκχυννόμενον, "being poured out," may rest on an Aramaic or Hebrew participle pointing to an event in the near future (Jeremias, op. cit. 178-79). "Many" echoes 10:45, offers a Semitic substitute for "all," and describes "all" as "many" rather than delimiting "many" as fewer than "all." Because of its anarthrousness, "many" probably refers to all Israel (as apparently in Isa 53:12) or to all human beings (as in 1 Tim 2:6) rather than to an elect remnant (cf. E. C. Maloney, *Semitic Interference* 139-42; W. Pigulla in *MTZ* 23 [1972] 72-82; J. B. Bauer in *BLit* 53 [1980] 137-38; C. Schedl in *BLit* 54 [1981] 226-28; F. Werner in *BLit* 54 [1981] 228-30).

One might argue that the disagreement in Luke 22:20 between the nominative case of ἐκχυννόμενον, "being poured out," and the dative case of αἵματι, "blood," shows the originality either of the absence of "being poured out for many," as in 1 Cor 11:25, or of Mark's version of the cup-word, in which the nominative case of the participle agrees with that of αἷμα. But since a container as well as its contents can be poured out (see, e.g., Rev 16:1, 2, 3, 4, 8, 10, 12, 17; 2 Kgdms 20:10 LXX), Luke's version means that the cup is poured out. Thus the nominative case of ἐκχυννόμενον agrees with that of τοῦτο τὸ ποτήριον, "this cup." Mark's change to "this is my blood" then shifts the referent of "being poured out" from the cup to the blood, and the second half of the cup-word in Luke is seen to be less parallel with that of the bread-word (where διδόμενον, "being given," agrees with σῶμα, "body" — Luke 22:19) than usually thought, just as the first halves of each saying in both Luke and 1 Corinthians 11 are already well recognized to be less than very parallel. The tendency would be to make the sayings more rather than less parallel, and the phraseology of pouring out blood had become so stereotyped (see Hatch and Redpath s.v. ἐκχεῖν) that a shift from the cup that is being poured out to blood that is being poured out is easily imaginable, but not the opposite shift. Luke's wording may refer to the pouring out of Jesus' cup into the cups of the apostles or to its being poured out as they drink straight from it. The cup represents the new covenant in that the pouring out of the cup represents the action of shedding the sacrificial blood with which the covenant is being inaugurated. The wine is only implied. In Mark's wording the cup represents the blood itself, and again the wine is only implied.

If the phraseology of "this is my blood of the covenant" arises out of Mark's redaction (see the foregoing comments), the objection falls that no Jew would drink blood or ask his disciples to drink it, even symbolically. The original Lucan-Pauline phraseology does not equate the cup with blood or even have the blood being poured out. Whether or not the wine was blood-like red, its liquidity would have sufficed to represent Jesus' blood. In fact, however, the cup-word does not even mention wine; so the wine's representation of Jesus' blood lies beneath the surface, where closeness in color as well as in liquidity becomes unimportant (cf. H. Patsch, *Abendmahl* 49).

According to M. Smith (*Jesus the Magician* 122-23), the Lord's Supper is a magical rite of eating the body and drinking the blood of a god who is identified with a magician. But in contrast with the Demotic magical papyrus to which Smith appeals (*PDM* XV. 1-20, where the wine of a mixed potion is equated with the blood of Osiris so as to inflame the female drinker with love for the male mixer — with love like that of Isis for Osiris), the institution of the Lord's Supper says nothing about the inflaming of love for God or for Jesus his representative. Smith's further appeal to the command in the Upper Room Discourse of John 13–16 that the disciples love one another overlooks that Jesus does not institute the Lord's Supper in that passage (nor does he speak of love in the precursive substitute for the Lord's Supper at John 6:22-59) and that in the Upper Room Discourse more emphasis falls on the disciples' loving one another and on God's and Jesus' loving them than on their loving Jesus and God and on God's loving Jesus, as would be expected from the papyrus, where drinking wine represents drinking the blood of Osiris so as to inflame both Isis and the devotee of Osiris with love for Osiris. At the same time, this papyrus does show how natural is the comparison of blood to wine. Even here we see a difference, however; for as we have just noted, the cup-word of Jesus does not so much as mention wine. And originally "the product of the vine" belonged to a Passover cup, not to the cup of the Lord (see the comments on v 25).

Since Mark has moved the saying in v 25 from its original earlier position, the attempt of D. Daube (*NTRJ* 330-31) to correlate the saying with the fourth and last cup of the Passover liturgy fails (see rather G. J. Bahr in *NovT* 12 [1970] 200-202). E. Linnemann (in *Jésus aux origenes de la christologie* 105-6) correctly notes that v 25 mentions neither the coming nor the nearness of God's kingdom, nor does it put an interval between the death of Jesus and his drinking anew. But the more original parallel Luke 22:18 does mention the coming of the kingdom. One could understand that Jesus will drink anew when he rises from the dead, that his resurrection will coincide with the coming of the kingdom, and therefore that he will not drink till his death and resurrection. But the apparent shortness of the time till he dies and the stated speed with which he will rise ("after three days" — 8:31; 9:31; 10:34) then make the prediction of abstinence jejune, and for this meaning we would expect an explicit reference to his resurrection. B. S. Crawford (in *JBL* 101 [1982] 240) suggests that the prediction came from a Christian prophet. Even apart from the overall weakness of the hypothesis that sayings of Christian prophets speaking in the name of the exalted Jesus were transferred to the earthly Jesus, however, the present prediction of abstinence and especially the adverb οὐκέτι, "any more," are not likely to have been spoken as from a Jesus already separated by exaltation from table fellowship with his disciples.

We might debate whether the prediction in v 25 stresses abstinence more than it stresses drinking anew in the kingdom of God. Since abstinence occupies the main clause but drinking takes the climactic last position, we should probably settle for a complementary relation which stresses neither side over the other. By the same token, the saying is as much a prediction of victory as one of abstinence, and vice versa. We need not think of a Nazirite vow (against M. Wojciechowski in *Bib* 65 [1984] 94-96); for at least by the time of the NT such a vow included more than abstinence from wine, most prominently of all the practice of not cutting the hair (see esp. Num 6:1-21; Judg 13:5, 7; 14:8-9; 16:15-31; 1 Sam 1:11 MT in contrast with 1 Kgdms 1:11 LXX; Acts 18:18); and others abstained from wine without becoming Nazirites so far as we can tell (Jer 35:1-11; Luke 1:15b). Furthermore, in Luke 22:15-16 Jesus does not speak of total fasting, but of not eating the food of Passover; so parallelism favors that his abstinence from the fruit of the vine will have to do only with Passover wine. And why? Because of his coming absence. If he were to be present, he would certainly eat and drink the Passover with his disciples, as he will when he comes back to transform the Passover meal into the messianic banquet. He does not use the formula of an oath, and the context makes his language read more like a bittersweet prediction than like a vow (cf. J. A. Ziesler in *Colloquium* 5 [1972] 12-14 with D. Palmer in *Colloquium* 5 [1973] 38-41; also 1 Sam 14:24; Mark 9:1 parr.; Luke 2:26; John 21:23; Acts 23:12, 14, 21 [but contrast the oath-language here with its absence from Mark 14:25 — against ibid.]; *Jub.* 16:16). Concerning the implication of an intermediate period, cf. the notes on 13:10.

Contextual and redactional considerations favor that the reason Mark attaches the saying in v 25 where he does is to counterbalance the imminent passion of Jesus with his ultimate victory, not to correct an overrealized eschatology that inflates the present at the expense of the future (so L. Schenke, *Studien* 335-37; P. J. Achtemeier 100). Jesus puts off final salvation, the full establishment of God's rule (v 25); and even the salvific significance of the Lord's Supper looks forward to the death of Jesus on the morrow. Therefore, the old Palestinian targumic tradition that relates to Exod 12:42 and speaks of four nights when Yahweh delivers his people, including the Passover night when he is expected to bring them final salvation, does not provide a very good parallel. See J. Jeremias, *Eucharistic Words* 183; B. Buetebela in *RAT* 8 (1984) 10-11 on the Semitism "drink from" plus the liquid drunk (though "drink from" plus the container of the liquid, as in v 23, is natural Greek). BDF §§164, 169 makes this Semitism probable rather than certain. For the messianic banquet, see Matt 8:11-12 par. Luke 13:28-29; Matt 22:1-10; Luke 14:15-24; 22:28-30; Rev 2:17; 19:9; Isa 25:6; 1QSa; 4QpPs 37; *1 Enoch* 62:14; *2 Apoc. Bar.* 29:4-8; Str-B 1. 992; 4. 1154-65.

A CONTEST OF PREDICTIVE ABILITY
JESUS VERSUS PETER AND THE TWELVE

14:26-31 (Matt 26:30-35; Luke 22:31-34; John 13:36-38)

The Passover meal had to end before midnight or 2 A.M. (J. Jeremias, *Eucharistic Words* 46, n. 6); so Jesus and the Twelve now leave the guest room for the Mount of Olives (v 26). He predicts their deserting him and his going ahead of them to Galilee after the Resurrection (vv 27-28). Peter counterpredicts his loyalty to Jesus (v 29), but Jesus counters in turn by predicting Peter's denials of him (v 30). Then Peter, joined by the rest of the Twelve, counters a second time by predicting that Jesus' counterprediction will by no means and under no circumstances come to pass (v 31). Thus the pericope revolves around competing predictions whose speedy fulfilments and nonfulfilments will fortify Mark's apology for the Crucifixion. An alternation of καί, "and," and δέ, "but," in the introductions to the contestants' predictions (see vv 27a, 29a, 30a, 31a, 31c) sets a competitive tone (cf. M. Zerwick, *Untersuchungen* 15).

14:26-28 *(Matt 26:30-32)* As often in Mark, a new pericope starts with topographical movement: Jesus and the Twelve go out to the Mount of Olives after hymn-singing, as was possibly traditional to do at the close of the Passover meal (*m. Pesaḥ* 10:5-7). The present historical tense of λέγει, "says," highlights Jesus' double prediction, "All of you will be tripped up, because it is written, 'I will strike the shepherd and the sheep will be scattered.' But after I have been raised, I will go ahead of you into Galilee." By contrast with the "all" who drank from the eucharistic cup (v 23) and by contradiction of Peter's coming prediction of loyalty (v 29; cf. v 31), the "all" of those who Jesus predicts will be tripped up increases the unlikelihood that his present prediction will be fulfilled and therefore enhances the impressiveness of fulfilment when it does occur (v 50). To be tripped up is to fall into sin because of some baneful influence. Again the OT gives warrant, but more explicitly than at vv 18, 21, in support of the apologetic point that the Passion and its effect on the disciples will agree with Scripture. The quotation comes from Zech 13:7 (see R. H. Gundry, *Use of the*

OT 25-28, for textual comparisons). The MT and the LXX read the command, "Strike." Jesus' quotation reads the prediction, "I will strike." This shift keeps the quotation from implying that his enemies will obediently and therefore blamelessly carry out the command of God. The unidentification of the striker also keeps God from blame. The emphasis thus falls on prediction as such and therefore on the agreement between Jesus' imminent fate and the ancient sacred text. The striking of the shepherd stands for Jesus' passion. The sheep's being scattered defines the disciples' being tripped up. The figurative language suits their forsaking Jesus by fleeing (v 50). The strongly adversative ἀλλά, "nevertheless," sets Jesus' going ahead of them to Galilee after his resurrection over against his being struck at Jerusalem, and sets their regrouping in Galilee over against their being scattered at Jerusalem. But he does not say explicitly that the disciples will regroup in Galilee. Such a regrouping is only implied by his preceding them there. So the emphasis stays on Jesus' predicting his own earlier arrival as the resurrrected one. The disciples will not leave him in a grave when they go back to Galilee. He will arrive before they do (see also the comments on 16:7).

14:29-31 *(Matt 26:33-35; Luke 22:31-34; John 13:36-38)* Of the Twelve, Peter is the one most likely to falsify Jesus' prediction that all the disciples will be tripped up, will be scattered. He has shown his loyalty to Jesus by confessing him to be the Christ (8:29), by taking him aside and rebuking him for predicting the Passion (8:32), and by joining the rest of the disciples in asking, "Not I, [is it]?" (14:19). His loyalty rises to the present occasion with the counterprediction, "Even if all will be tripped up, yet I [will] not [be tripped up]," meaning, "Your 'all' will not include me!" The indicative mood in the protasis of this conditional sentence suggests that Peter thinks the tripping up of his fellow disciples quite possible (contrast v 31). Emphasizing the confidence of his self-exclusion are the ascensive καί, "even," the forward placement of πάντες, "all," and — in the apodosis — the strongly adversative ἀλλ', "yet," the ellipsis of the verb, and in the absence of a verbal ending the strong ἐγώ, "I," contrasting as it does with πάντες. The historical present tense of λέγει, "says," highlights Jesus' next prediction as it did the last one (cf. v 27). "Truly I say to you" sets the certainty of its fulfilment opposite Peter's counterprediction. The emphatic σύ, "you," underlines that the one most likely to falsify Jesus' first prediction will fulfil a second prediction as well. "Today" dramatizes this fulfilment by bringing it close at hand and thus displays the acuteness of Jesus' predictive ability. The successive expressions "this night," "before the cock crows twice," and "thrice" sharpen this acuteness with the addition of increasingly specific and therefore astonishing detail, the fulfilment of which will immeasurably heighten the impressiveness of Jesus' predictive ability. The asyndeta with which the temporal terms are strung together and the forward positions and triplicity of those terms add to the heightening. Furthermore, the one most unlikely to desert Jesus will not merely desert him. He will even deny him! By matching the triplicity of the temporal terms, the triplicity of the denials magnifies the detailedness of the prediction. So also does the forward position of τρίς, "thrice." Delaying the key statement "you will deny me thrice" till the end of the prediction creates suspense; and prediction of a threefold denial as well as of desertion adds to the unlikelihood that will enhance fulfilment. The forward position of με, "me," stresses the object of denial, the most unlikely object imagineable considering Peter's past and present relations to Jesus. Similar but larger increases in the unlikelihood and therefore greater impressiveness of fulfilment accrue from Peter's adding a second counterprediction, strengthened by the adverb ἐκπερισσῶς, "vehemently" (cf 6:51), by the imperfect tense of ἐλάλει, "kept on saying," by the addition of dying with Jesus if necessary, by the escalation from οὐκ, "not" (v 29), to οὐ μή, "by no means" (v 31), by use of the future indicative instead of the more frequent and expected aorist subjunctive with οὐ μή, and by all the disciples' joining Peter in his counterpredictions. Not as in the protasis of his first counterprediction, the subjunctive mood in the protasis of his second one suggests that he thinks the necessity of his suffering with Jesus a remoter possibility than that of his fellow disciples' being tripped up (contrast v 29). That the following apodoses both use the future indicative makes for equally strong counterpredictions of his own loyalty. Just as the first counterprediction echoed Jesus' first verb σκανδαλίζομαι, "be tripped up," so now the second echoes Jesus' second verb ἀπαρνέομαι, "deny." The "all" that identifies those who counterpredict loyalty at the end of the pericope contrasts with the "all" that in Jesus' initial prediction identified those who will be tripped up (v 27). Who will win this contest of predictive ability? But Mark has already said so much about Jesus' abilities that we know in advance. No contest!

NOTES

Skipping from v 26 to v 32 produces an uninterrupted narrative and therefore suggests that Mark inserted vv 27-31, perhaps out of chronological sequence, since Luke 22:31-34; John 13:36-38 locate the prediction of Peter's denials during the Last Supper rather than afterwards, as here (so W. L. Lane 510 and many others). For this view it is also argued that the dialogue would have taken place more naturally at table than on the way from the Upper Room to Gethsemane. But there is no problem in Jesus' and the disciples' speaking on the way. It has often happened so (1:16-20; 2:23-28; 8:14-21, 27–9:1, 9-13, 30-32; 10:1-9 with 10:10; 10:17-31, 32-45; 11:20-25; 13:1-37). Omission of something that took place between the beginning and the end of a walk or journey will naturally leave a smooth transition, because beginning and end complement each other; but their complementarity does not favor the omission. And Luke and John may have transferred the prediction of Peter's denials to the Last Supper as part of their larger program of expanding the table-talk after the pattern of a Greco-Roman symposium.

   Because the rabbinic tradition cited in Str-B 4. 76 is of late date, one may question whether ὑμνήσαντες, "having hymned," refers to singing the little Hallel (Psalms 114–18 or 115–18; cf. E. Linnemann, *Studien* 86). Tending in favor of that tradition for the NT period, however, are the Septuagintal use of ὑμνέω and cognates in the Book of Psalms and Philo's description of the Passover as celebrated "with prayers and hymns" (*Spec.* 2.27 §148). Though Mark's audience of Gentiles might think of a Christian hymn, Septuagintal usage shows that they might think equally well of the Jewish Psalms. See J. Jeremias, *Eucharistic Words* 256-62, for Jewish eschatological and messianic interpretation of the Hallel; and H. Gese, *Essays* 122, n. 5, versus Str-B 1. 839-40 on the enlargement of the boundary of Jerusalem to accommodate all the pilgrims who needed to stay in the city through Passover night (cf. also J. Jeremias,

Jerusalem 61-62, 101; S. Safrai in *The Jewish People in the First Century* 2. 903-4). L. Schenke (*Studien* 354-56) detects competition between going out to the Mount of Olives (v 26) and going into Gethsemane (v 32) and uses the competition to argue against an original connection of vv 27-31 to vv 32-42. Such a connection would have made vv 27-31 include a prediction of the disciples' sleeping in the garden; and Jesus will occupy center stage in vv 32-42, whereas the disciples occupy it in vv 27-31. These arguments do not hold up, however. Gethsemane will simply specify a site on the Mount of Olives. A prediction of the disciples' sleeping would make no sense prior to the context of Jesus' agony and prayer. Besides, the disciples' fleeing from Gethsemane (v 50) will relate back to the prediction on the Mount of Olives that they would be scattered. And Jesus the predictor is as central to vv 27-31 as Jesus the prayer will be to vv 32-42.

Jesus' equation of being scattered with being tripped up, i.e. led into sin, implies that the disciples should follow Jesus to their own deaths (see D. Seeley in *SBL 1989 Seminar Papers* 547-48 on the tradition of imitating the noble death of a martyr). T. A. Mohr (*Markus- und Johannespassion* 222-23) thinks that vv 27, 29-30 are designed to overcome the scandal of their contrary behavior, i.e. their disloyalty to Jesus. But for that, a citation of the OT would more likely have followed the statement in v 50 that they fled from the scene of his arrest. As it is, the citation of Zech 13:7 supports a prediction of Jesus. The suggestion of J. Christensen (in *ST* 10 [1957] 33-39) that the scattering of the sheep alludes to Ezek 12:14-15 founders on the explicitness of Jesus' quoting Zech 13:7 instead, on the nonuse of sheep as a metaphor in Ezek 12:14-15, and on the contrast between the exile of the prince along with his people in Ezek 12:1-16 and the striking of the shepherd over against the scattering of the sheep in Mark 14:27. Against the background of the passion predictions, "I will strike" (v 27) connotes striking dead (as, e.g., in Acts 7:24 with Exod 2:12-14 LXX; also Acts 12:23), though striking does not always lead to death (see the concordance and lexica). According to R. T. France (*Jesus and the OT* 107-8), the change from the imperative, "Strike" (Zech 13:7 MT LXX), to the indicative, "I will strike," is "a necessary grammatical adaptation to the New Testament context, caused by the abbreviation of the quotation to exclude the mention of the sword of Yahweh, which would render the imperative meaningless." But the "I" of the indicative is identified in Mark's context no more than the "you" of the imperative would be identified had Mark followed the MT and LXX; so the shift is not due to the omission of Yahweh's sword. The unidentification of the "I" likewise spoils the interpretation according to which the shift from "you" to "I" is said to teach that Yahweh will strike the shepherd with judgment which would otherwise fall on the sheep (E. Best, *Temptation* 157-58; idem, *Gospel as Story* 69).

Switching from the "I" who strikes the shepherd (v 27b) to the "I" who rises and goes ahead to Galilee (v 28) may seem abrupt (so H. Anderson in *The Use of the OT in the New and Other Essays* 291). But it is evident from the institution of the Lord's Supper and from the passion predictions, starting in 8:31, that Jesus is the one to be struck. If he were the striker, who would be the shepherd? Not Peter, because in the developing dialogue he has yet to be distinguished from the rest of the Twelve (see v 29); nor has he been portrayed as a shepherd, as Jesus has (6:34), nor will anything happen to Peter that will cause the rest to be scattered. Furthermore, by signaling the end of the OT quotation, the strongly adversative ἀλλά, "but, however," clears the field for a new "I." The old one was not identified, anyway. The dispute whether Zech 13:7 portrays the deserved striking of an evil shepherd or the undeserved striking of a good shepherd need not detain us; for OT meaning does not always determine NT application, and in Jesus' use of the text the reason for striking does not enter the picture.

Likewise, it matters not with regard to being scattered whether Zechariah's parataxis veils a telic clause, but Mark's an ecbatic one. L. Schenke (*Studien* 387-88) says that here "scattered" means "shepherdless" rather than implying separation from one another. But it is hard to think that the disciples fled from Gethsemane in a body (v 50). That Peter subsequently followed Jesus at a distance and went into the high priest's courtyard (vv 54, 66-72) isolates at least him from the rest, as therefore the rest are presumably isolated from each other (though 16:7 may imply that by Easter the disciples have regrouped without Peter as well as without Judas Iscariot). Some have thought that all the disciples' being tripped up reflects the belief of Jesus in the onset of the eschatological tribulation (see, e.g., J. Jeremias, *Central Message* 49-50). But Jesus relates the tripping up to his own death, not to the eschatological tribulation; nor does he relate his own death to the eschatological tribulation (cf. the notes on v 35). Furthermore, the verb for tripping up, σκανδαλίζω, and its cognate noun σκάνδαλον occur nowhere in the NT for a phenomenon of the eschatological tribulation. Matthew does insert the verb at 24:10 of his gospel, but that verse stands in the middle of a section devoted to the noneschatological characteristics of the church age (R. H. Gundry, *Matthew* 475-81). And the noun occurs in Matt 13:41 for false disciples that will be weeded out at the end, after the tribulation, but that have been in the church from the start, before the tribulation (ibid. 273). Cf. 4:16-17 for being tripped up by persecution.

B. Lindars (*NT Apologetic* 129-30) ascribes "artificiality" to v 28 because of "the plain and unadorned way in which Jesus is represented as saying μετὰ τὸ ἐγερθῆναί με ['after I have been raised'] as if there were nothing unusual or unexpected about it all." On the contrary, Jesus has repeatedly said that he would rise after being put to death, just as here (8:31; 9:9, 12, 31; 10:33-34). Better then to speak of traditionality than of artificiality (cf. the comments on 8:31 for the traditionality of the passion-and-resurrection predictions). Lindars (op. cit. 130-32) also thinks that Zech 13:7 was originally applied to the Crucifixion, only later to the flight of the disciples. More likely, however, Jesus' using Zech 13:7 secondarily for his death as well as primarily for their flight led early Christians to apply to Jesus other passages in the last part of Zechariah (esp. 9:9; 11:13; 12:10; see Matt 21:5; 27:9; John 12:15; 19:37; Rev 1:7).

Ἐγερθῆναι may be deponent, "have risen," rather than passive, "have been raised" (cf. 2:12 with 2:9, 11; 4:27; 6:14, 16; 12:26; 13:8, 22; 14:42; 16:6). Alternation with ἀνίστημι, "rise up," and its cognate noun for resurrection in 8:31; 9:9, 10, 32; 10:34; 12:18, 23-26 would favor the deponent meaning but for the fact that even ἀνίστημι and its cognate noun may encompass an act of power performed on the person who rises up, as in 5:41-42; 9:27; 12:18, 23-26 (see also Rom 4:24; 6:4; 1 Cor 15:12-19, 52; cf. 3:26 with 13:8 for a synonymity of the two verbs apart from the doctrine of resurrection). Contextual factors favor a true passive of ἐγείρω in 16:7 (see the comments ad loc.), and here in chap. 14 the smiting of the shepherd by someone else likewise favors that Jesus is to be raised by someone else. Ἐγείρω and ἀνίστημι each occur both in narrative statements and in Jesus' sayings; so we lack a method of assigning one verb to tradition and the other to redaction.

R. H. Stein (*Proper Methodology* 156) detects Mark's diction not only in ἐγερθῆναι but also in προάξω, "I will go ahead," and Γαλιλαίαν, "Galilee." To be sure, these words occur elsewhere in Mark and except for ἐγερθῆναι almost always in narrative. But Mark may draw on tradition for narrative as well as for sayings just as he may use his own diction in sayings as well as in narrative. The construction μετά, "after," plus an articular infinitive occurred in narrative at 1:14; but even under the supposition that Mark fabricated that verse, in 14:28 he may impose the same construction on a traditional saying. For that matter, a single occurrence in 1:14 does not establish a feature of his style; and frequent use of the construction elsewhere in the NT raises the possibility of traditional use (see Luke 12:5; 22:20; Acts 1:3; 7:4; 10:41; 15:13; 19:21; 20:1; 1 Cor 11:25; Heb 10:15, 26, not to list occurrences outside the NT). As often, then, we lack firm ground on which to distinguish Mark's redaction from tradition.

Προάγω, "go ahead," did not connote a shepherd's leading his sheep in 6:45 (where

the disciples preceded Jesus); 10:32 (where Jesus preceded a crowd of non-disciples —
see the comments ad loc.); 11:9 (where some of a crowd preceded Jesus), nor will it do
so in 16:7 (where the disciples will be predicted to see Jesus not till they arrive in Galilee,
to which he will have preceded them; see also Matt 14:22; 21:31 for examples of a transitive
use that does not entail leading — against C. F. Evans in *JTS* ns 5 [1954] 3-18). Nor does
this verb seem to have been used of shepherding. John 10:4, which does have to do with
shepherding, uses different phraseology that clearly expresses presence: ἔμπροσθεν αὐτῶν
πορεύεται, "he goes in front of them" (cf. Mark 2:12; 9:2 et passim for the notion of
presence in ἔμπροσθεν). Here in 14:28, then, προάξω does not continue the shepherding
metaphor of v 27b and mean that the risen Jesus will lead the apostles back to Galilee.
No, he will precede them there.

It is misleading to set the temporal and spatial meanings of προάγω against each
other; for to go somewhere earlier than others do requires spatial precedence, and to go
ahead of them in space entails an earlier arrival (cf. Matt 2:9 with 2:11). The only question
is how far ahead and how much earlier. And unless we are to think of the toll collectors
and prostitutes who go ahead into God's kingdom as a united body of people (Matt 21:31),
M. Wilcox (in *NTS* 17 [1970-71] 428) is incorrect to infer that Jesus' going ahead of the
disciples presupposes their not being scattered, as though the quotation of Zech 13:7 did
not originally precede the going ahead.

The destination Galilee carries no theological freight. Where else would we expect
Galileans like Jesus and his disciples to go after a pilgrimage to Jerusalem? Nowhere does
Mark describe Galilee as Gentile territory (for that description, see Matt 4:12-16; on the
contrary, cf. Mark 1:14 with 1:21, 39; 15:41 with the Jewish names included therein), and
Galilee appears nowhere else in Mark as the starting point of an evangelistic mission among
Gentiles. Those who came to Jesus in Galilee from Idumea, Transjordan, and the region
of Tyre were not described as Gentile, even though the regions from which they came were
Gentile; nor were the four thousand whom he fed on the other side of the Sea of Galilee
described as Gentile (3:8; 8:1-10; contrast 7:26; 13:10). He did not preach in the Decapolis,
nor were the demoniac and those to whom Jesus preached in that region described as
Gentile (5:1-20). Nor were the deaf mute and his fellow Decapolitans so described (7:31-
37). Even if they were Gentiles, or included Gentiles, Mark made no point of the fact; and
he described Jesus' excursion into the borders of Tyre and Sidon as an attempt to avoid
ministry, not as the genesis of an evangelistic mission to Gentiles (7:24). Similarly, Jesus
did not evangelize the villages of Philip's Caesarea (8:27ff.), and he gave no indication
that the evangelism among all nations in which his disciples were to engage would have
its start in Galilee (13:10; 14:9). Tending against even an implication of that sort is his
calling the temple in Jerusalem "a house of prayer for all the nations" (11:17) and his
speaking about evangelism among all the nations in plain rather than geographically coded
language (again see 13:10; 14:9) and not till the discourse that he delivered on the Mount
of Olives, far away from Galilee, in a Judean setting that is physically and verbally more
Jewish, not less Jewish, than earlier settings (10:1; 11:1, 11-12, 15, 19, 27; 12:35, 41;
13:1-3, 14; 14:1-3 et passim). And neither 14:28 nor 16:7 hints at any kind of evangelistic
mission, either the start of a new one or a renewal of the old one which took place in
Galilee (1:14ff.; 6:12-13). Both 14:28 and 16:7 mention only a seeing of Jesus there. Hence,
we should reject the interpretation according to which going ahead to Galilee does not
have to do with physical geography but symbolizes Jesus' prompting the disciples to take
up the task of evangelism, especially evangelism of the Gentiles (so G. H. Boobyer in
BJRL 35 [1952-53] 334-48; C. F. Evans in *JTS* ns 5 [1954] 3-18; idem, *Resurrection* 81;
M. Karnetski in *ZNW* 52 [1961] 252-57; J. Schreiber, *Theologie des Vertrauens* 172-84;
E. Best, *Temptation* 173-77; J.-M. van Cangh in *RB* 79 [1972] 67-75; T. A. Mohr, *Markus-
und Johannespassion* 215-18).

Luke 22:31-34 lacks a prediction of the tripping up and scattering of all the disciples, though it does carry a prediction of Peter's denials. Whether Luke is drawing on non-Marcan tradition, redacting Mark, or doing a bit of both, the command that Peter strengthen his brothers when he has turned again seems to echo their having been tripped up; and the tenor of Luke 22:31-34 fits Luke's program of portraying the disciples and (in Acts) the early Christians as sympathetically as possible. Therefore the absence of a prediction that all the disciples will be tripped up and scattered does not look original (against J. D. Crossan in *SBL 1972 Proceedings* 1. 40).

Alone, the prediction of Peter's denials would not provide a satisfactory definition of being tripped up, for the parallelism both of passive voice and of plural number favors that in the first instance being scattered defines being tripped up (against M. Ruhland [*Markuspassion* 14], who drops the Zechariah-quotation from pre-Marcan tradition). The unparallel active voice and singular reference to Peter make the prediction that he will deny Jesus a less suitable definition of being tripped up, but one that is added in view of Peter's counterprediction that he will not be tripped up, i.e. scattered, with the rest. Without the striking of the shepherd and the scattering of the sheep, it would be unclear why the disciples will be tripped up and what form their being tripped up will take. Without Jesus' going ahead of the disciples into Galilee after he is raised, the Passion in the quotation, "I will strike the shepherd," would be deprived of the Resurrection. But against such a deprivation stands the fact that the Resurrection has regularly accompanied the Passion in earlier predictions of this sort (8:31; 9:9, 12, 31; 10:33-34; 14:22-25). Thus, to say that the tradition originally skipped from v 27a to v 29 is to sunder what was from the start a cohesive unit.

H. Anderson (315) and J. D. Crossan (in *SBL 1972 Proceedings* 1. 40-43) argue on the contrary that Peter's first counterprediction (v 30) takes no account of Jesus' going ahead into Galilee or even of the striking of the shepherd and of the sheep's being scattered (vv 27a-28), but only of all the disciples' being tripped up. But of course not, because Peter's counterprediction that he will not be tripped up exempts him from the scattering which defines being tripped up and which is caused by the striking, and exempts him also from having to catch up with Jesus in Galilee. He will not have left Jesus, or so he says. The correspondence of 16:7 to the resurrected Jesus' going into Galilee ahead of the disciples in 14:28 does not prove that 14:28 was fabricated out of 16:7; for even under the supposition that Mark will there add "as he told you" and perhaps also "there you will see him," that verse may presuppose the present one (cf. the switch from the future tense in "I will go ahead" to the present tense in "he is going ahead," which may then indicate that what Jesus now predicts will be approaching or receiving fulfilment then). Nor does the allusion in John 16:32 to Zech 13:7, quoted in Mark 14:27b, prove an independent circulation of Zech 13:7 in the early church; for the Johannine allusion occurs in the same temporal and topographical setting and with the same referent to the disciples' being scattered that we find in Mark.

Crossan argues further that subtraction of vv 27b-28 reveals an earlier concentric structure in vv 27a, 29-31: (a) the tripping up of all; (b) Peter's protestation; (c) the prediction of his denials; (b') his reiterated protestation; (a') protestation by all (cf. M. Ruhland, *Markuspassion* 15-16). But it is a mistake to separate vv 27b-28 from v 27a. They make up a single sentence and should be read as a unit. Therefore vv 27b-28 belong to the tripping up of all (a). In v 31, moreover, "likewise" shows that the protestation by all (a') is of a piece with Peter's reiterated protestation (b'), just as the tripping up of all (a) does not differentiate between Peter and the rest. Not counting the introduction in v 26, then, there are only four subdivisions, in two pairs; and the prediction of Peter's denials (c) does not occupy a central position (cf. the foregoing, initial comments on vv 26-31).

To support a Marcan Christology of Davidic kingship, J. R. Donahue (in *The Passion in Mark* 76) draws a parallel between Peter's protestation of loyalty to Jesus (v 29) and Ittai's protestation of loyalty to David (2 Sam 15:19-21). But the parallel breaks down; for Peter will prove disloyal, whereas Ittai proved loyal.

Since we do not know whether "today, this night" (v 30) was spoken before or after midnight, no inference can be drawn concerning various methods of calculating days. Before midnight, the methods of calculating days from sunrise to sunrise and from sunset to sunset would allow "today" to include "this night"; but the calculation of a day from midnight to midnight would be ruled out, because then Peter would be denying Jesus the next day. If Jesus spoke the prediction after midnight, all three methods of calculation would satisfy the wording.

J. D. M. Derrett (*Making of Mark* 2. 243) suggests that Peter's first counterprediction sounded to Jesus like the crowing of a cock, the Semitic word for a cock being the same as that for a heroic man such as Peter was proclaiming himself to be (גְּבַר; cf. just such a wordplay in *b. Yoma* 20b). For the realism, literalness, and textual originality of two cockcrowings, see D. Brady in *JSNT* 4 (1979) 42-57 (cf. H. Kosmala in *ASTI* 2 [1963] 118-19). We are not to regard one of them as a watch of the night called "the cockcrowing" (midnight–3 A.M.). Brady incorporates the cockcrowings into the biblical theme of lower creatures' rebuking human beings; but neither will the cock speak, as Balaam's ass did, nor will Peter's denials contrast as unnatural with the cockcrowings as natural in accordance with Isa 1:3; Jer 8:7 et passim. Derrett (in *NTS* 29 [1983] 142-44) gives evidence that "denial . . . is not complete until done thrice," and argues that the vv.ll. which have only one cockcrowing represent scribal attempts to lighten Peter's blameworthiness: he did not persist in denials against the warning of a first cockcrowing (against the attempt of J. W. Wenham [in *NTS* 25 (1978-79) 523-25] to establish the textual originality of only one cockcrowing).

R. M. Fowler (*Loaves and Fishes* 134-38) finds the Marcan point of vv 26-31 in the disciples' failure to understand that Jesus will have to suffer and die. Not so, for they have not denied that one of themselves will betray him, but have individually questioned that they are the one; and now they do not deny that Jesus the shepherd will be struck, but predict that they will not be tripped up when he is struck. In particular, Peter's "even though it is necessary that I die with you" (v 31a) militates against ignorance concerning Jesus' suffering and death. The argument that this Petrine clause corresponds to nothing in the preceding part of the pericope and therefore enters by way of redactional addition (so M. Ruhland, *Markuspassion* 22) rests on a mistaken omission of the Zecharian "I will strike . . ."-quotation from pre-Marcan tradition (see the foregoing notes on v 27).

All the Twelve cannot have spoken as Peter did, simply because Jesus had not predicted that anyone but Peter was going to deny him. So argues T. A. Mohr (*Markus- und Johannespassion* 218-19), who then reasons that because v 31b says that all the Twelve did speak as Peter spoke, Mark must have fabricated v 31b. This reasoning is fallacious, for the prediction of Peter's denials grows out of the prediction that all the Twelve will be tripped up. So the rest of the Twelve will naturally have supposed that by predicting their being tripped up as well as Peter's, Jesus means that they will deny him as well as be scattered just as he meant that Peter will deny him as well as be scattered. It might be argued that v 27 defines being tripped up as being scattered, not as denying Jesus. Yes, but when Peter protests that though all the rest should be tripped up, i.e. scattered, Jesus adds denial to the definition; and perhaps excepting the details of three times before the cock crows twice, the rest of the Twelve would naturally assume that the addition applies to them just as the original definition did. Being scattered from Jesus and denying him do not contradict each other.

L. Schenke (*Studien* 424) regards vv 27-31 as a redactional fabrication by Mark to identify non-acceptance of the Cross with being tripped up, giving up the faith, non-discipleship. But Jesus' prediction that he will go ahead of the disciples into Galilee does not treat them as future apostates, at least not unless apostasy is weakened to mean a temporary lapse. Only by isolating the prediction of being tripped up both from its immediate context and from the larger contexts of the disciples' coming world-wide mission (13:9-13) and of early Christian traditions that the resurrected Jesus appeared to them (see esp. 1 Cor 15:5, 7) could σκανδαλισθήσεσθε, "you will be tripped up," describe a final, permanent apostasy. Moreover, Peter and the rest of the disciples accept dying with Christ, and do so explicitly and vehemently. They take the correct view but will lack the courage to act on it. These verses set out competing predictions of personal behavior. They do not criticize false theology. Similarly, the constant emphasis that Mark has been putting on Jesus' predictive ability throughout vv 12-31 upsets the view of Schenke (op. cit. 342-47) that Mark has sewn together originally isolated traditions regarding the finding of a room for the Passover meal (vv 12aβ, 13-16a), a woe-saying (v 21b), and a cultic memory (vv 22-24) and redacted these traditions to correct the Christology of Jesus as a divine man. The truth is more nearly the opposite. See J. Gnilka 2. 251 against the hypothesis that vv 27-31 come from tradition out of which vv 66-72 were later fabricated. His making the prediction of Peter's denials secondary to vv 66-72 is to be resisted, however. The argument that the prediction would not have circulated apart from the denials is beside the point; for from the start the prediction and the denials may have circulated together, neither side fabricated out of the other.

The Fayyum Fragment, which parallels Mark 14:26-31 (for a photograph as well as a transcription of the text of the fragment, see J. Finegan, *Hidden Records* 210-11), lacks the hymning, the Mount of Olives, the pronoun referring to Jesus' disciples, and his name, which appears in both Mark's and Matthew's introductions to his first prediction. The fragment agrees with Matthew against Mark by including "in this night" in the first prediction, but disagrees with Matthew by putting the phrase before "you will be tripped up" rather than later, and agrees with Mark against Matthew in lacking "in me" after "you will be tripped up." The fragment agrees with Mark against Matthew also in putting "the sheep" before "will be scattered" and in lacking "of the flock." The lack of Jesus' further prediction that after being raised he will go ahead of the disciples to Galilee disagrees with both Mark and Matthew. So also does the lack of a pronominal reference to Jesus in the introduction to Peter's counterprediction. The use of "even" (καί) with "if" (εἰ) agrees with Mark against Matthew, but the order of the two words is the reverse of Mark's. The lack of "will be tripped up" after "all" in Peter's counterprediction disagrees with both Mark and Matthew, but the lack of "yet" (ἀλλ') agrees with Matthew against Mark (though Matthew has the similarly adversative δέ in οὐδέποτε, "but not at any time [i.e. 'never']"). The fragment lacks Mark's and Matthew's "truly I say to you" and the following reference to "this night," though Mark's "today" may have been included in the badly damaged final line of the fragment. The lack of ἤ after πρίν, "before," agrees with Matthew against Mark; but the inclusion of "twice" agrees with Mark against Matthew, though in a slightly different word order. Besides these comparisons, we may note different grammatical constructions in the fragment: a prepositional articular infinitive phrase for going out, the use of ὡς before "he [Jesus] said," another prepositional articular infinitive phrase for what is written in Scripture, a genitive absolute for the introduction to Peter's counterprediction, a different spelling of the Greek word for "cock," and a different word for crowing.

Under the hypothesis that Matthew redacted Mark (see R. H. Gundry, *Matthew* 529-31, for details), the agreements of the Fayyum Fragment with Matthew against Mark favor a dependence on Matthew rather than on pre-Matthean tradition. It would remain possible that the agreements with Mark against Matthew stem from additional dependence on pre-Marcan tradition rather than on Mark, but additional dependence on Mark rather than on pre-Marcan tradition would parallel the other dependence on Matthew and avoid a positing of dependence on tradition known only through Mark when Mark is all that is needed to explain the agreements with Mark against Matthew — and Mark was surely available during the last part of the third century (the probable date of the fragment). The disagreements with both Mark and Matthew look condensive and otherwise stylistic. They may also give evidence of reliance on memory as opposed to direct use of Mark and Matthew. Therefore the omission of Jesus' prediction of going ahead to Galilee — and it is only one of a number of omissions, though the largest of them — need not imply a pre-Marcan tradition lacking that prediction. A desire to underscore Peter's denials might easily have led to this omission.

THE FLOWERING OF FULFILMENT FOR JESUS' PREDICTIONS

14:32-52 *(Matt 26:36-56; Luke 22:39-53; John 12:27; 17:1–18:11; Heb 5:7)*

Jesus and his disciples now go to Gethsemane, where he tells them to sit while he prays (v 32). Then he takes along Peter, James, and John, expresses his sorrow, and tells them to stay and keep awake (vv 33-34). His prayer comes next (vv 35-36), then his finding the three disciples asleep, reproaching Peter, and commanding all three to keep awake and pray (vv 37-38). He prays again (v 39), only to find the three disciples asleep a second time (v 40) and a third time (vv 41-42). Then Judas Iscariot comes to Gethsemane with an armed crowd (v 43). Jesus' arrest takes place (vv 44-47) with Judas's identifying kiss (vv 44-45), the seizing of Jesus (v 46), and a bystander's swordplay (v 47). Jesus gives an oral response to his arrest by force of arms (vv 48-49), his disciples forsake him and flee (v 50), and a young man who kept on following with him barely escapes when seized (vv 51-52).

14:32 *(Matt 26:36; Luke 22:39-40; John 18:1)* The unusually high concentration of verbs in the historical present tense — "come" (v 32), "says" (v 32), "takes along" (v 33), "says" (v 34), "comes" (v 37), "finds" (v 37), "says" (v 37), "comes" (v 41), "says" (v 41), "arrives" (v 43), and "says" (v 45) — displays the excitement of Mark over Jesus' entrance into the Passion; for with that entrance the fulfilments of the passion predictions start coming to full flower. None of the verbs in the historical present tense introduces his praying (contrast the normal imperfect tense in vv 35-36, 39, which does introduce his praying). Mark is not very interested in the praying as such. He is interested, rather, in Jesus' being given over to the Jewish authorities and in the disciples' failure of loyalty, both in fulfilment of Jesus' predictions. So all the verbs in the historical present tense deal with Jesus' and the disciples' coming to the parcel where Judas will give Jesus over and where the disciples' loyalty will start to break down, and with the initial breakdown itself and Jesus' initial passion. Thus Mark writes, "And they *come* to a parcel whose name [is] Gethsemane, and he *says* to his disciples, 'Sit here till I've prayed.'"

14:33-34 *(Matt 26:37-38)* The historical present tense in the statement, "And he takes along Peter and James and John with him," emphasizes Jesus' seeking the help of his three closest disciples (contrast his seeking complete

solitude for prayer in 1:35; 6:46; Luke 5:16) and carries on the dramatic buildup
to the initial breakdown of even their loyalty. This breakdown will lead to their
forsaking him and fleeing — i.e. to their being tripped up, scattered — just as
Jesus predicted would happen (v 27). Similarly, the historical present tense in "he
says" emphasizes the expressions concerning his alarm (ἐκθαμβεῖσθαι) and dismay
(ἀδημονεῖν) — "My soul is very sad, to [the point of] death" — which start his
predicted suffering (cf. 15:34; Luke 12:50; Heb 5:7). The duality of alarm and
dismay makes the same emphasis. The historical present tense in "he says" also
emphasizes his command, "Stay here and keep awake," which even the three
closest disciples will fail to obey as their loyalty starts to break down. The
perfective περι- in περίλυπος, "very sad," and the first position of this predicate
adjective intensify the element of sadness. Mark uses his authorial omniscience
of Jesus' inner feelings to excite sympathy for him. The asyndeton which introduces "stay here and keep awake" adds further emphasis to that command (whose
relation to the preceding statement of sadness is illative). As usually in the NT,
the present tense of the imperative γρηγορεῖτε gives even greater emphasis to the
command "keep awake" (S. E. Porter, *Verbal Aspect* 354-55; see 1 Pet 5:8 for an
unemphatic aorist imperative of this verb). Just as in 13:33-37 keeping awake
had to do with watching for Jesus' coming, so here it has to do with watching for
Judas's coming, as can be told from Jesus' telling the disciples in v 41 to sleep
on when for the third and last time he returns, this time to watch in his own behalf
for Judas's coming since they have fallen asleep on each of the previous occasions.
They were to have watched on his behalf in order that he might give himself
entirely to praying through his emotional distress. As v 42 will indicate, he wants
to know when Judas draws near in order that he may go to meet Judas.

14:35-36 *(Matt 26:39; Luke 22:41-44; John 12:27)* "And going forward"
prepares for Jesus' return to find the three disciples asleep. "A little" allows them
to see before they fall asleep what he does and to hear what he prays (even private
prayer usually being said aloud in that culture). The imperfect tense of ἔπιπτεν in
the statement that "he was falling on the ground and praying that if it is possible
the hour might pass away from him" may be iterative and imply that Jesus falls
on the ground two more times in vv 39-42, rather than indicative of prolonged
or repeated falling on the ground during the first prayer. If so, the imperfect tense
of προσηύχετο, "he was praying," and of ἔλεγεν, "he was saying," may likewise
be iterative and prospective as well as indicative of continuous action in progress
(as imperfect verbs of speaking often are; contrast the aorist of these verbs in
v 39). Of course, we may disregard Jesus' further praying and say that Mark puts
Jesus' falling on the ground into the imperfect tense for the sake of parallelism
with the verbs of speaking, for the purpose of implying prolonged or repeated
falling on the ground during the first prayer, or for a dramatization of the falling
"as taking place under the eyes of the narrator" (H. B. Swete 343; cf. A. T.
Robertson, *Grammar* 883). But these possibilities seem less likely in view of
Mark's omitting any later falling on the ground and his only implying a third
prayer. It looks as though he wants the imperfect in vv 35-36 to cover the second
and third prayers in order that he may stress other matters in the rest of the episode.

Jesus' falling on the ground and praying that if possible he may be spared "the hour," which will turn out to be "the hour" of his "being is given over into the hands of sinners" (v 41), exhibits foreknowledge of his betrayal. His saying, "Abba, Father, all things [are] possible for you. Take this cup away from me," exhibits foreknowledge of his death, which likewise serves Mark's apologetic purpose (see 10:38-39 and esp. 14:23-24 for the cup as a figure of death). Not even kneeling is the normal posture for prayer. Standing is (11:25; Luke 18:11, 13; Matt 6:5 et passim). So falling on the ground displays panic (cf. 5:22 par.; Luke 5:12; Matt 17:6; 18:26, 29 et passim; R. Feldmeier, *Krisis* 163-65). "This" describes "the cup" as near (contrast the nonsense of "this" with "the hour" because indirect discourse took a distant standpoint, whereas Mark has now switched to direct discourse). The nearness of the cup causes Jesus' panic. The panic, in turn, dramatizes his foreknowledge of betrayal and death and together with the asyndeton which introduces "take this cup away from me" excites further sympathy for him. (The relation of the request to the preceding theologoumenon is again illative.) "But [I request] not what I want, but [I request] what you [want]" shows that his crucifixion will be God's will. That God *can* take away the cup — an ability emphasized by the ellipsis of "are" between "all things" and "possible for you" — shows all the more that Jesus' crucifixion will be God's will (cf. S. E. Dowd, *Prayer* 151-58, where emphasis wrongly falls on an insoluble problem of theodicy, however, as though Jesus' resurrection and second coming did not take care of the problem — see also 8:35-37; 10:29-31). Both the strength of the adversative ἀλλά, "but," its repetition, and the further ellipses in "but [I request] not what I want, but [I request] what you [want]" underscore the admirableness of Jesus' subordinating his will to that of his Father.

14:37-38 *(Matt 26:40-41; Luke 22:45-46)* Three occurrences of the historical present tense in the statement, "And he comes and finds them sleeping [cf. 13:36] and says to Peter," again emphasize Jesus' seeking the help of his three closest disciples (cf. the comments on v 33) — he interrupts his praying to see whether according to his instruction they have stayed nearby and kept awake — and highlight the breakdown of loyalty that he has predicted and that he goes on to speak of: "Simon, you are sleeping! You weren't strong enough (οὐκ ἴσχυσας) to keep awake for one hour!" The Greek text may be punctuated so as to produce questions; but in a question οὐκ plus the indicative would imply that Simon *was* strong enough to keep awake for one hour. Jesus and Mark want to stress Simon's weakness, however (see v 38b), in contrast with his protestation of loyalty even to the extreme of dying with Jesus (vv 29, 31a), in fulfilment of Jesus' prediction of Simon's coming denials of him (v 30), and in contrast with Jesus' own strength to keep awake even without angelic or other help (contrast Luke 22:43 and see the comments on Mark 5:4; 9:18; M. Dibelius in *Redaktion und Theologie des Passionsberichtes nach den Synoptikern* 68; P. Dschulnigg, *Sprache* 404). The duality of sleeping and not being strong enough to keep awake for one hour heightens the stress on Simon's weakness. The singling out of Simon shows that Jesus has in mind not only the coming breakdown in all the disciples' loyalty when they forsake him and flee, but also and particularly the breakdown in

Simon's loyalty when he denies Jesus three times. This breakdown as well as the other starts here. Even the number of times that Simon falls asleep previews the number of times he will deny Jesus (cf. M. Ruhland, *Markuspassion* 50-56). The command to all three disciples, "Keep awake, and pray that you not enter into [i.e. 'succumb to'] temptation," contains imperative verbs emphatic, as often, by virtue of their present tense (γρηγορεῖτε . . . προσεύχεσθε — cf. S. E. Porter, *Verbal Aspect* 354-55, and contrast the unemphatic aorist imperatives of these verbs in 1 Pet 5:8 [again] and Jas 5:14) and will serve to show the truth of Jesus' statement that "the spirit [is] eager but the flesh [is] weak" when they fall asleep two more times (cf. the shift from Peter to all the disciples in v 31). Asyndeton and ellipses add emphasis to this statement (we expect "*for* the spirit *is* eager but the flesh *is* weak"). So also does alliteration (πνεῦμα πρόθυμον; cf. the preceding πειρασμόν, whose ρ and whole ultima also anticipate πρόθυμον, and the following προσηύξατο), and the construction μέν . . . δέ gives the statement dignity (see the notes on 4:4). Since in that culture people prayed with their eyes open, the command to pray does not work against the command to keep awake, as it would if the three disciples were to close their eyes in prayer.

14:39-42 *(Matt 26:42-46)* Mark's referring to Jesus' second prayer but not quoting it (contrast Matthew) shows his comparative disinterest in the prayer as such. Fortifying this impression is the skipping of even a reference to Jesus' third prayer (again contrast Matthew; in Mark we can only infer a third prayer from Jesus' coming back to the disciples a third time). Instead of quoting the second prayer, Mark goes directly to Jesus' finding the disciples asleep again and stresses the fleshly weakness of the disciples by writing that "their eyes were weighed down" and that, presumably out of embarrassment, "they did not know what they should answer him" (cf. 9:6, 32). The advancement of αὐτῶν, "their," does not emphasize the owners of the eyes, but lets a final stress rest on eyes that are weighed down (cf. the comments on 6:52). By contrast, Jesus looks strong. He has kept awake. To counter the scandal of the Cross, Mark wants a strong Son of God, strong in flesh as well as in spirit (cf. the designation of Jesus as "the stronger one" [1:7: ὁ ἰσχυρότερος, cognate to the present ἴσχυσας] and the double emphasis on the loudness of his shout from the Cross [15:34, 37]). The historical present tense of Jesus' coming the third time and speaking to the three disciples (cf. the three denials that Peter is about to make) headlines the following announcement that Jesus' prediction concerning betrayal is verging on fulfilment.

As shown by vv.ll. which supply τὸ τέλος as the subject, ἀπέχει is difficult primarily because its subject is not identified, at least not immediately. All interpretations labor under this difficulty. Most probably, the concluding statement in the present series of statements supplies the subject: "the one giving me over" (v 42). The delay in identification creates suspense, and the suspense joins other elements in the passage to dramatize the fulfilment of Jesus' prediction that he would be betrayed. He himself announces the fulfilment. But what does ἀπέχει mean? One could think that its frequent use for full payment and the Sanhedrin's promise to give Judas Iscariot money (vv 10-11) favor the translation, "He [the one giving me over] is receiving [his payment] in full." But for that meaning we expect a direct object, as in Matt 6:2, 5, 16; Luke 6:24; Phil 4:18; Phlm 15; and extra-NT passages cited by BAGD s.v., in secondary literature referred to there, and by W. Barclay in *The NT in Historical and Contemporary Perspective* 75-77 (the Leiden papyrus cited by J. de Zwaan in *The Expositor* 6th Series, 12 [1905] 470-71, n. 1, leaving the door open to an absolute use in the sense of full payment — but only slightly open, because the commercial context includes a list of items paid for; indeed, U. Wilcken, *Urkunden der Ptolemäerzeit* 1. 406, provides a revised edition of this papyrus that differs from C. Leeman's original edition in giving ἀπέχω a direct object); and it would be passing strange for the Sanhedrin to pay Judas in full on the verge of his giving Jesus over to them rather than earlier, at the striking of the bargain (cf. Matt 26:15 with 27:3-5 in contrast to Mark 14:10-11), or later, on delivery (cf. Luke 22:3-6 with Acts 1:18). Failing a direct object, ἀπέχω means "be distant." It has already meant this in its only other Marcan occurrence (7:6). Such a meaning at this point balances the last in the present series of statements ("behold, the one giving me over has drawn near" — v 42) and contributes to a progression in the series: (1) The three disciples are to sleep on because the betrayer is still distant. (2) But the hour of betrayal has struck and he is already leading the arresters toward Gethsemane. (3) Finally, he comes close; so it is time to get up and meet him and them (cf. A. Bornemann in *TSK* 16 [1843] 104-6). Now we see why Jesus does not identify the subject of ἀπέχει immediately. He expects the three disciples to hear what he is saying to them on this third return just as he expected them to hear what he said previously on returning and finding them asleep. But they could hardly go back to sleep, as they previously did and as now he exasperatedly tells them to do again, if they were to know that it is the betrayer who is in the distance. Of course, we might expect an adverb or an adverbial phrase to modify ἀπέχει, as one usually does when this verb means "be distant" (see, e.g., 7:6 par.; Luke 7:6; 15:20; 24:13, but in these passages [and in the papyri cited for this meaning by MM s.v.] only to indicate degrees of distance, as is unnecessary to do in Mark 14:41). Yet the absolute use of ἀπέχει is determined by and parallel to the absolute use of its counterpart ἤγγικεν, "has drawn near," which also takes an adverbial expression much of the time elsewhere (11:1 parrs.; Matt 15:8; Luke 7:12; 10:9 et passim).

Since "the hour has come" and since "the Son of man is being given over into the hands of sinners," the betrayal that Jesus predicted is already in motion as Judas leads "the sinners" to the place where they can seize Jesus apart from the festal assembly (cf. vv 1-2). Jesus sees them in the distance; so there is no need for the three disciples to watch any more. Καθεύδετε τὸ λοιπὸν καὶ ἀναπαύεσθε needs to be taken, then, as an exasperated command, "Sleep for the remainder [of the time till the betrayer has drawn near] and rest," rather than as a disappointed question, "Are you sleeping on and resting?" or as an accusation, "You're sleeping on and resting." The present tense of the imperative verbs underlines Jesus' exasperation (cf. the notes on 1:3). "The Son of man is being given over into the hands" recollects the very phraseology of the passion prediction in 9:31 and reemphasizes the violence that will be done to Jesus (see the comments on 9:31). Replacing "of men" (so 9:31) with "of sinners" highlights the injustice that he will suffer. "Behold" highlights it yet more. Overall, triple asyndeton — before "he is distant," before "the hour has come," and before "behold, the Son of man is being given over . . ." — gives a staccato-like emphasis to this fulfilment of Jesus' prediction concerning betrayal and to his announcement that the fulfilment is now in motion.

"Rouse yourselves, let's go" (cf. John 14:31) ends the three disciples' sleep, because "the one giving me [Jesus] over has drawn near." The remainder of time (τὸ λοιπόν) has run out. No more leisure to sleep. The fulfilment of Jesus' prediction presses on, as emphasized again by triple asyndeton, another "behold," and the position of ὁ παραδιδούς με, "the one giving me over," before ἤγγικεν, "has drawn near." Having withstood sleep, Jesus now goes bravely to meet his fate. He does not say ὑπάγωμεν, "let's go away," i.e. "let's get out of here before Judas and the sinners who want to abduct me arrive," but ἄγωμεν, "let's go," i.e. "let's go to meet Judas and the sinners into whose hands he is giving me over" (cf. the notes on 1:3 for emphasis in the present tense; also the comments on 3:3 for emphasis in the present imperative ἐγείρεσθε, "raise yourself").

14:43 *(Matt 26:47; Luke 22:47a; John 18:2-3)* "And immediately" stresses the speed with which Jesus' prediction proceeds to final fulfilment. "While he is still speaking" (cf. 5:35) reinforces this speed by indicating that Judas comes right as Jesus is saying to the three disciples, "Behold, he who gives me over has drawn near." No longer is the betrayer distant (contrast v 41). Just as Mark introduced Jesus' and the disciples' coming to the place of betrayal with a historical present tense (ἔρχονται, "they come" — v 32), so now he introduces Judas's arrival with another historical present tense (παραγίνεται, "arrives") to emphasize the fulfilment of Jesus' prediction that is taking place. The identification of Judas as "one of the Twelve" yet again helps Mark portray the Crucifixion as stemming from an act of perfidy rather than from a pursuit of justice (cf. vv 10, 20). Stressing this perfidy is the addition that with Judas, who should have been with Jesus (see esp. 3:14), arrives a crowd "with swords and clubs" and "from the chief priests and the scribes and the elders." This description — intensified as it is by the framing of "the crowd" between two μετά-phrases ("with . . . with . . ."), by the duality of the weapons with which the crowd arrives, and by the listing of all three classes of the Sanhedrin from whom they come — presents the Crucifixion as stemming from hellbent animosity. One is tempted to translate ὄχλος with "gang" instead of "crowd" (see A. Finkel, *Pharisees* 60-61, on the brutality of the chief priests and their agents).

14:44-47 *(Matt 26:48-54; Luke 22:47b-51; John 18:4-11)* Mark's editorial explanation that "the one giving him [Jesus] over [cf. v 42] had given them [the crowd] a signal" intensifies Judas's perfidy by exposing how carefully planned it was. An adversative δέ, "but," highlights this perfidy by distinguishing Judas's having given them a signal from his mere arrival with them in company. His designation as "the one giving him [Jesus] over" rather than by the simple personal pronoun "he," which would have sufficed, highlights his perfidy yet more. The signal, "Whomever I kiss — he it is," and the casus pendens plus the resumptive personal pronoun with which it is explained (see E. C. Maloney, *Semitic Inter-*

ference 86-90) deepen the perfidy with a show of affectionate homage designed to mask his betrayal of Jesus (cf. Prov 27:6 under the translation of נעתרות by "treacherous"). "Seize him and lead [him] away securely" exposes the show as a charade. The present tense of the imperative ἀπάγετε, "lead away," highlights the fulfilment of Jesus' predictions that one of the Twelve would give him over (vv 18, 20) and that the Son of man would be given over into the hands of men (9:31), to the chief priests and the scribes (10:33; cf. S. E. Porter, *Verbal Aspect* 354-55). Judas has already arrived at Gethsemane (παραγίνεται — v 43); so "coming" (ἐλθών) refers to his coming to Jesus. For another emphasis on the speed with which the fulfilment of Jesus' prediction is occurring, Mark adds "immediately coming to him" (εὐθὺς προσελθὼν αὐτῷ). The asyndetic relation of these participial phrases and their striking redundancy in the repetition of (-)ελθών intensify this emphasis. Judas's address, "Rabbi" — strengthened by a historical present tense in the introductory "he says" — deepens the perfidy yet further with an honorific title (cf. Ps 41:7a[6a]). Mark's adding κατα- to the verb of kissing (cf. v 45 with v 44) apparently implies a kiss "down" on a lower part of the body, as on the hand or feet, rather than on the face (cf. Luke 7:38, 45; Xen. *Mem.* 2.6.33; *y. Qidd.* 1:7; A. Wünsche, *Der Kuss* 28-32, 39-40; M. Dibelius, *Botschaft und Geschichte* 1. 275-76; and the greater likelihood of Judas's feigning humility). Otherwise, κατα- is perfective of prolonged kissing, as perhaps in Luke 15:20; Acts 20:37, adding yet another accent on his perfidy (cf. Prov 27:6 under the translation of נעתרות by "profuse"). Henceforward Judas disappears from the story. Mark is uninterested in the betrayer's fate. He is interested only in the fulfilment of Jesus' prediction of betrayal (contrast Matt 27:3-10; Acts 1:15-20; and even John 18:5b). Οἱ δέ, "but they," switches the focus back to the crowd. Mark needs only to say that they "seized" Jesus in accordance with Judas's instructions (the leading away, also in accordance with those instructions, will take place in v 53), but first of all Mark adds that they "laid hands on him." The addition indicates again the fulfilment of Jesus' prediction that he would be "given over into the hands of men" (9:31) and carries to completion the more recent statement that "the Son of man is being given over into the hands of sinners" (14:41; cf. G. Lüderitz in *Markus-Philologie* 177 on the emphatic repetitiousness of v 46). As usual, fulfilment of Jesus' predictions subtracts scandal from the Cross.

An adversative δέ, "but," shifts attention to a bystander's drawing his sword and lopping off the ear of a slave belonging to the high priest. The classical Greek expression εἷς . . . τις, "a certain one" (cf. BDF §247[2]), makes the number of the swordsman singular and his identity indefinite. Matthew, Luke, and John will identify him as a disciple. John will go so far as to identify him as Simon Peter (cf. the appeal of M.-J. Lagrange [394] to Soph. *OT* 118 that εἷς . . . τις implies a close acquaintance, but nothing in the Sophoclean line or context supports such an implication). Traditionally, it has been thought that the synoptists withheld Peter's name to keep him from recrimination and that John revealed the name because by the time the fourth gospel was written Peter had died and therefore all possibility of recrimination had died with him. (Some modern scholars think differently that the naming of Simon Peter belongs to a general program of debunking him in John's gospel, but such a program is disputed.) In one way or another, Matthew, Luke, and John all follow up with Jesus' rejection of swordplay on his behalf (and Luke with his healing of the ear, too). Not so Mark. Here, in fact, Jesus' responding to the incident by noting that the crowd have come "with swords" implies that the swordsman is not a disciple at all, but one of the crowd who is brandishing his sword as Jesus is being arrested. To identify the swordsman in Mark as a disciple makes Jesus' response inappropriate, because sword-wielding by a disciple would undermine Jesus' description of his arresters as the ones who have swords. Mark, too, has described the crowd, but not the disciples, as having swords (v 43). And we would not expect him to refer to a disciple as "a certain one of the bystanders," for in several further references to bystanders never is the reference to Jesus' disciples (see 14:69, 70; 15:35, 39). We would rather expect Mark to refer to a disciple as "one of his disciples" (13:1; cf. 11:1; 14:13; perhaps as "one of the Twelve" except for the use of this phrase elsewhere only for Judas Iscariot — 14:10, 20, 43). Added to Jesus' failure in Mark to say or do anything about the swordplay, the failure of the arresters to take action against the swordsman confirms that the swordsman belongs to the crowd of arresters. The lopping off of an ear is not a disciple's act of defending Jesus, then, but an accident in which one member of the crowd injures another member of the crowd (cf. Ps 37:14-15). The mereness of lopping off an ear fits an accident to a comrade at least as well as it fits a deliberate attack on Jesus' arresters. Perhaps Mark intends his audience to see some grim humor, perhaps a foregleam of the coming reversal of Jesus' arrest and passion (chap. 16), especially in view of the injured slave's belonging to none other than the high priest, who is about to take the lead in condemning Jesus to death, and in view of the disgrace of having an ear cut off (Lev 21:18; Josephus *Ant.* 14.13.10 §366; idem *J.W.* 1.13.9 §§269-70; *t. Para* 3:8; *PTebt.* 3. 793).

14:48-49 *(Matt 26:55-56b; Luke 22:52-53)* Jesus responds (ἀποκριθείς — cf. the comments and notes on 9:5; 11:14; 12:35; 14:40), not by correcting swordplay on his behalf, but by speaking to the crowd of swordsmen and clubsmen to whom Judas has identified Jesus. His question, "As against a bandit have you come out with swords and clubs to take me with [you]?" might be re-punctuated as an indignant declaration followed by equally indignant asyndeton; but either way, the question foreshadows the crucifixion of two bandits with him (15:27) and exposes the injustice of his arrest by indirectly and ironically calling to mind his beneficial healings and exorcisms instead of banditry. The forward position of ὡς ἐπὶ λῃστήν, "as against a bandit," emphasizes the foreshadow and irony. The shift from "seize" (forms of κρατέω in vv 44, 46; see also v 49) to "take . . . with" (συλλαβεῖν — v 48) suits the arresters' coming out, for now they will have to take Jesus with themselves back to the Sanhedrin. His sarcastic observation, "Day by day [as opposed to the nighttime raids of a bandit and his being arrested at night] I was with you in the temple, [I] teaching, and you didn't seize me," refers in its Marcan context to the last week of his public ministry (11:15-18; 12:12, 14, 35) and exposes the discrepancy between their launching against him a kind of military expedition, as though he were a bandit to catch whom they have had to arm themselves and come out into the countryside, and Judas's having just called him "Rabbi." The forward position of "day by day" emphasizes this discrepancy. By implying face-to-face closeness and therefore easy apprehensibility, so also does πρὸς ὑμᾶς, "with you" or (more literally) "toward you" (cf. esp. 2 John 12). "But [this has happened] in order that the Scriptures should be fulfilled" recalls at least Zech 13:7, which Jesus quoted in v 27, perhaps also Exod 24:8; Isa 53:12; Pss 22:2, 8-9, 19(1, 7-8, 18); 41:10(9); 69:22(21); 109:25; Lam 2:15 (cf. Mark 14:18, 24; 15:14, 29, 34, 36; also Pss 37:14; 71:11 with Mark 14:41, 44, 46), and teaches that despite and through the injustice God is achieving his purpose of salvation. A strongly adversative ἀλλά, "but," and the ellipsis of "this has happened" accentuate the fulfilment of the Scriptures.

14:50-52 *(Matt 26:56c)* "And leaving him, they all fled" (contrast 1:18, 20; 2:14; 3:13-14; 10:28 et passim) marks the fulfilment of Jesus' prediction that the disciples would "all be tripped up" and "scattered" (v 27). "All" in the fulfilment not only matches "all" in the prediction. It also contrasts with the "all" who protested their loyalty (v 31; cf. v 29) and drank the cup representing Jesus' covenantal blood (v 23). Because Mark does not write "the disciples," narrative syntax requires that the "all" who left Jesus and fled refer to the foregoing crowd who have just come to seize him and who will shortly seize a young man following with him; but narrative sense requires that it refer instead and in fact to the disciples, last mentioned in vv 32-42 except for the description of Judas in v 43. This violation of syntax exhibits Mark's eagerness to spell out the fulfilment of Jesus' prediction. So also does the use of "all" despite exclusion of Judas, whom Mark included in Jesus' prediction (cf. vv 17-20 with vv 26-27), and despite exclusion of the anonymous young man who will follow with Jesus for a little after the eleven have fled. Mark's omitting to tell what motivated them to flee leaves only Jesus' earlier prediction as an explanation.

Forward position shifts attention to "a certain young man" who now makes a cameo appearance in the gospel. He has often been identified with John Mark, who, it is suggested, leaves his signature with the appearance. But even under a historically true identification of the young man with John Mark, textual anonymity (contrast the supplying of personal names for other cameo figures in 5:22; 6:14, 17, 19, 21, 22; 10:46; 15:2, 4, 5, 6, 9, 11, 12 14, 15, 21, 40-41, 43, 47; 16:1; cf. 6:3) makes it doubtful that Mark wants to reveal his authorship or imply the trustworthiness of his gospel as coming from a participant in one of the events narrated therein. How could he expect his audience to infer that the unidentified young man wrote the gospel? Or if somehow he could expect them to do so, how could he further expect them to equate the young man with himself (John Mark) rather than with someone else as author (cf. the lack of widespread tradition in the early church that the young man was John Mark — as noted by J. Weiss, *Das älteste Evangelium* 405-7)? Only an unwarranted assumption that the first audience knew more about the incident than the story itself reveals can save the theory of a Marcan signature. It seems instead that the story of the young man takes off on the motif of the disciples' flight, and more especially (as we are about to see) that it anticipates the resurrection of Jesus. The very refusal of Mark to answer the obvious questions — Who was the young man? Where did he come from? What motivated him to follow? Why was he wearing a linen cloth on his naked body, and only that much? — concentrates attention on this preview.

The imperfect tense of -ηκολούθει, "was following" (there is no need to take the verb conatively, "was trying to follow"), indicates that the young man is not fleeing with the eleven. We might think on the contrary that he had been following to Gethsemane rather than now following from Gethsemane; for though the crowd have seized Jesus, their leading him away has yet to be mentioned in v 53. But they appear to seize the young man *as* he is following, whereas Jesus has been in Gethsemane for some time before they even arrive on the scene; and the prefix συν-, "with," prepares for a contrast with Peter's following "from afar" as Jesus is being led away. This contrast works better if the young man and Peter are following more or less concurrently. So a second violation of narrative syntax — the mention of a young man's following with Jesus before it is said that the crowd led Jesus away — exhibits Mark's eagerness to anticipate Jesus' resurrection.

And how is that? The young man's having on a linen cloth anticipates the linen cloth in which Jesus will be buried (15:46). The repetition of "linen cloth" within both 14:51-52 and 15:46 and the anarthrousness of the first occurrence and arthrousness of the second in each passage underscore this anticipation. The young man's nakedness, except for the linen cloth, may anticipate the soldiers' dividing Jesus' garments among themselves (cf. 15:24 with 15:21; also nakedness as precursive to resurrection in 1 Cor 15:37; 2 Cor 5:3; *1 Clem.* 24:1-5). The crowd's seizing the young man (κρατοῦσιν αὐτόν) parallels their having seized Jesus (ἐκράτησαν αὐτόν — v 46; cf. v 49). Here, the historical present tense calls special attention to the parallel. As earlier but vice versa, narrative syntax requires that the "they" who seize the young man be the eleven who have just left Jesus and fled, but narrative sense requires that it refer instead and in fact to the penultimately mentioned crowd who have seized Jesus. This third violation of syntax exhibits Mark's eagerness to establish the parallel that will anticipate Jesus' resurrection. Although the young man's fleeing comes close to the disciples' fleeing, they left *Jesus* (ἀφέντες αὐτόν), whereas the young man leaves behind his *linen cloth* (καταλιπὼν τὴν σινδόνα). Leaving it behind anticipates Jesus' resurrection, portrayed as a leaving behind of his linen burial cloth. To be sure, Mark will write nothing about Jesus' abandoning the linen burial cloth in the empty tomb, but presumably only because none of Jesus' enemies will be there to clutch the cloth when he leaves it behind (and J. Knox [in *The Joy of Study* 27-30] notes the lack of a back reference to 14:3-8 in 16:1-8 [and in 15:46-47, we might add], though 16:1-8 obviously relates to 14:3-8). On the other hand, Mark will call the angel in the empty tomb "a young man" (16:5-7; see the comments ad loc. that there the designation refers to an angel, not to a human being) to recollectively associate the present young man with Jesus' resurrection. Though neither young man is Jesus himself, together they represent him in his death, burial, and resurrection. Or should we say that the present young man is the same as the angelic young man, so that one and the same young man represents Jesus in his death, burial, and resurrection? The exchange of a linen cloth for a white robe will highlight the Resurrection (cf. the parallel between περιβεβλημένος in 14:51 and περιβεβλημένον in 16:5), for whiteness suits resurrected life (see, e.g., Rev 7:9 with 7:14-17 and 21:1-4; also 19:14). The present emphasis on nakedness prepares for this exchange. And just as the young man flees the scene of Jesus' arrest, so the women who discover the emptiness of Jesus' tomb will flee the scene of his resurrection. In accordance with his predictions (8:31; 9:9 with 9:12; 9:31; 10:33-34) and intimations (9:38; 13:24-37; 14:25, 62), then, this episode anticipates the reversal of his crucifixion and burial by virtue of his resurrection. An adversative δέ, "but," calls attention to the young man's successful escape.

NOTES

Against an apologetic understanding of vv 32-52, H. Conzelmann (in *Int* 24 [1970] 189) cites Jesus' hesitation, the necessity of his achieving obedience, and the lying of the Cross outside his control. But an apologetic understanding is served, not disserved, by his hesitation; for by making a foil against which his willingness as the Son of God to obey his Father stands out the more, death on a cross turns into the will of God and turns Jesus into a moral hero rather than a criminal. Furthermore, his foregoing predictions of betrayal and flight turn the present episode into an apologetic fulfilment, especially since the pericope ends on the notes of betrayal and flight. And again, his strength to keep awake and pray, the description of his arresters as "sinners," his bravery in going to meet both them and his betrayer, the details of their weaponry and of his betrayer's perfidy, the upbraiding of Jesus' arresters for a military expedition, as though he were a bandit hiding in the wilds and apprehensible only by surprise when they would have had only to seize him in the temple during any of the days he had taught there as the rabbi whom the betrayer has just addressed him as being, and Jesus' citing of the Scriptures as fulfilled all make for a powerful apologetic thrust.

This thrust likewise obstructs the interpretation of T. A. Mohr (*Markus- und Johannespassion* 236) that in vv 32-42 Mark takes aim against a Jewish Christian downplaying of the Crucifixion and thereby of cross-bearing on the part of disciples. Mark is writing an apology for the Crucifixion over against the shamefulness with which crucifixion was regarded throughout the Greco-Roman world, not a theology of discipular suffering as opposed to a Jewish Christian theology of discipular glory. Mohr (op. cit. 232) also argues that because vv 32-42 are Christologically embarrassing in their attention to Jesus' grief-caused panic, Christians must have preserved the traditional material in these verses for their parenetic value ("keep awake and pray . . ."). The argument may or may not hold true for a pre-Marcan stage of the tradition, but in their present form these verses are far more apologetic than parenetic. Among attempts to separate redaction from tradition might be mentioned those of G. Schneider in *ZNW* 63 (1972) 188-209; W. Mohr in *ZNW* 64 (1973) 194-208; and E. Best, *Following Jesus* 147-50, though we have repeatedly noted basic difficulties that usually make such attempts unsatisfying (cf. W. H. Kelber in *The Passion in Mark* 41-42).

Supporting the historicity of the episode narrated in vv 32-42 are (1) the multiplicity of traditions referring to it (see esp. Heb 5:7-8, since Luke as well as Matthew may depend entirely on Mark, and even John 12:23, 27; 14:30-31; 18:1, 11 on the synoptics); (2) the Christologically offensive strength of language used to describe Jesus' distress (though a desire to excite sympathy for him weakens this argument somewhat); (3) the earliness of the tradition as implied by the Aramaic "Abba"; (4) Jesus' asking for immunity from betrayal and death instead praying for strength to endure them (as would be expected had the episode been generated out of earlier martyrological stories); and (5) the absence from his praying of OT phraseology such as Christians might have put on his lips (though the presence of such phraseology would not argue against historicity; for Jesus, too, used the OT). (6) He proceeded only a little distance away from the three disciples; so before going to sleep they may easily have heard what he prayed, or the loudness of his outcries (Heb 5:7) may have awakened them to hear what he was praying (J. D. G. Dunn, *Jesus and the Spirit* 17-20). The opinion of E. Lohse (*History* 63-64) that this conjecture does not represent "a convincing explanation" misconstrues argumentative requirements. All that is needed for the anti-historical objection to fall (i.e. for the failure of the objection that nobody could have heard what Jesus prayed) is a single realistic possibility, and Lohse does not even try to prove unrealism in these plural possibilities. F. C. Burkitt (in *JTS* os 17 [1916] 296) and B. Saunderson (in *Bib* 70 [1989] 224-33) discuss the further possibility that the young man wearing a linen cloth may have heard Jesus' prayers. For the usually audible speaking of private as well as public prayers, see *t. Ber.* 2:13; and cf. the mistaking of inaudible prayer for drunkenness in 1 Sam 1:13 and the instruction in Matt 6:6 that you enter a storeroom and lock the door before praying, probably to prevent others' hearing as well as seeing, though the emphasis falls there on seeing.

There is no need to think that the episode in Gethsemane did not originally intervene between the Last Supper and Jesus' arrest. For the reference to Gethsemane is hardly fabricated, and the story of Jesus' praying there needs the narrative framework provided by the Last Supper and his arrest. It seems likely, then, that the story circulated with them from the start rather than being inserted between them at a later date. Nor should Luke's parallel be used to argue for the originality of only one prayer in Gethsemane. To be sure, Luke does not write "again," "saying the same word," or "the third time" (so Mark 14:39, 41). Yet the statement in Luke 22:44 that after praying once and being strengthened by an angel (so Luke 22:41-43) Jesus fell into a state of agony and prayed more earnestly refers to further praying. Nor again do we need to think that in accordance with the law of three as applied to prayer, Mark has added "and he [Jesus] comes the third time" (v 41) and that therefore the tradition included only two departures, prayers, and returns to the disciples. Jesus may have followed this law just as Daniel is said to have followed it in his general practice of praying (Dan 6:11, 14[10, 13]) and just as the psalmist and Paul testify that they followed it in praying for relief from particular distresses, much as here (Ps 55:18[17]; 2 Cor 12:8). If Mark were intent on making Jesus go away and pray three times, not just a traditional once or twice, why are a third departure and prayer entirely unmentioned instead of mentioned explicitly, as in Matt 26:44? For Mark mentions a third coming to the disciples but only implies a third departure and praying (against H. Anderson 317-18; K. G. Kuhn in *Redaktion und Theologie des Passionsberichtes nach den Synoptikern* 81-111; J. W. Holleran, *Synoptic Gethsemane* 144; see the foregoing comments that for the sake of Jesus' third confrontation with the sleeping disciples Mark suppresses the third praying; also R. Feldmeier, *Krisis* 70-112, for the integrity of vv 32-42 and F. Neirynck, *Evangelica* 133-41, on Marcan duality as undermining Kuhn's theory of separate sources). Since Jesus has told only Peter, James, and John to keep awake and pray, it is only they to whom he speaks about sleeping on, resting, and then rousing themselves and going with him in vv 41-42 (cf. vv 33-34, 37-38). The other disciples do not come back into the picture till v 50, as signaled by "all," which contrasts with the three. There is no difficulty, then, in knowing what disciples are in view throughout vv 37-42. The coming together of the three and of the rest by the time of the flight in v 50 goes unmentioned simply because it lacks significance and can easily be inferred from the "all" in that verse (against E. Linnemann, *Studien* 11, et al.).

In v 32 Jesus tells his disciples to sit while he prays. "Here" indicates that to pray he will go farther into Gethsemane. Thus will Judas Iscariot gain opportunity to go fetch the crowd of Jesus' arresters (contrast John 13:18-30). In vv 33-34 Jesus tells Peter, James, and John, whom he has taken farther in, to stay *and keep awake*. Another "here" indicates that to pray he will go yet farther into Gethsemane. Then in v 38 he tells the three *to pray* as well as to keep awake. His omitting to put the rest of the disciples under obligation to keep awake and pray militates against the suggestion that he hoped for God's salvific intervention during the Passover celebration and that in accordance with a regarding of the celebration as ended when deep sleep overpowered the celebrants he feared lest the disciples' going into such a sleep would kill the chance of this intervention before it took place (so D. Daube, *NTRJ* 332-35; D. E. H. Whiteley in *SE I* 111-12; cf. *m. Pesaḥ* 10:8; *b. Pesaḥ* 120b; Str-B 1. 969-70). It would have been just as dangerous for the rest of the disciples to go into a deep sleep as for the three to do so (A. Feuillet, *L'agonie* 216-17). Furthermore, though *m. Pesaḥ* 10:8 allows resumption of the Passover meal if celebrants only doze instead of sleeping deeply, by the time Jesus and the disciples reach Gethsemane there is no question of resuming their Passover meal. And even though we could trace back to the first century the distinction of a fifth century rabbi between dozing as sleeping lightly enough to give a confused answer when spoken to and deep sleep as sleeping to the extent of inability to answer at all (Daube, op. cit. 334), a problem would remain. For in vv 37-39 the disciples do not answer Jesus confusedly. They do not answer him at all, just as in vv 40 and 41-42.

The progression from "sit here" through "stay here and keep awake" to "keep awake and pray" also undermines both the theory of a dittographical buildup in the history of the tradition from one prayer to two prayers and finally to three, and the theory of an amalgamation of different sources. One could suppose a tradition-historical or redactional buildup after the pattern of synthetic parallelism; but the law of parsimony favors the simpler explanation that Jesus did not care whether the rest of the disciples kept awake but wanted his three closest ones, the only ones he is said to have renamed (3:16-17), to help him by keeping awake with him, and told them when they fell asleep to keep awake by praying.

Mark does not even translate "Gethsemane" from Semitic to Greek (contrast 15:22); so symbolic interpretations of it are out of place. As a matter of fact, it means "oil-press [for olives]" (see BAGD s.v. Γεθσημανί and the literature cited there); and the parcel so named is located on the lower, Kidron side of Mount Olivet (John 18:1-2; cf. J. Jeremias, *Jerusalem* 6-7). So the mention of Gethsemane in v 32 does not compete with the mention of the Mount of Olives in v 26 or provide evidence that the episode in Gethsemane did not originally belong to the passion narrative. "Gethsemane" specifies the spot on the Mount of Olives where the following episode took place. For similar specifications, see 1:14 with 1:16; 1:21; 5:1; 6:45, 53; 7:24, 31; 8:13 with 8:22; 9:9 and 9:14 with 9:28; 9:30 with 9:33; 10:1 with 10:10; 11:11, 15, 27; 14:3; 15:20b with 15:22. W. H. Kelber (in *ZNW* 63 [1972] 174) underrates John 18:1-2 in saying that apart from Mark 14:26, 32 parr. we do not know Gethsemane to be located on the Mount of Olives and that therefore Mark may have put it there fictively. "Across the brook Kidron" is equivalent to the Mount of Olives; and in other respects, too, John 18:1-2 gives evidence of resting on complementary tradition.

J. W. Holleran (*Synoptic Gethsemane* 107-10) argues further that use of "the disciples" in v 32 combines with non-use of that designation henceforward in the passion narrative to support an original independence of the present episode. A simpler explanation suffices: "the disciples" does not appear henceforward in the passion narrative because the disciples themselves play no role in it. They flee in v 50, where to show the fulfilment of v 27 Mark uses "all" instead of "the disciples." Only Peter plays a role, and he is naturally referred to by name (14:66-72). When after the Passion the disciples come back in view, once again we read "the disciples" (16:7).

Gen 22:5 is often cited as a cross-reference to Mark 14:32ff. (see esp. J. Grassi in *JAAR* 50 [1982] 449-58), but the wide extent of differences that divide these passages casts doubt on a deliberate allusion. Abraham leaves his young men a distance from Mount Moriah, but Jesus takes all his disciples right into Gethsemane. Abraham goes farther for the purpose of worship, Jesus for the purpose of prayer. Abraham takes Isaac along to offer him as a sacrifice; but Jesus takes Peter, James, and John along to keep awake with him. Isaac goes as far as Abraham does, but the three disciples are told to stay while Jesus goes forward a little farther. Similar and sometimes greater differences between the present passage and Exod 24:2, 14; Lev 16:17; 1 Kgs 19:1-8 spoil those cross-references, too.

To support a Marcan Christology of Davidic kingship, J. R. Donahue (in *The Passion in Mark* 76) draws a parallel between the three disciples' accompanying Jesus into Gethsemane and the accompaniment of David into exile by his three commanders Joab, Abishai, and Ittai (2 Sam 15:19-24). But Peter, James, and John are listed together as accompanying Jesus whereas David's three commanders are not listed together as accompanying him; so the parallel breaks down.

See the comments and notes on 5:37 for the traditionality of Peter, James, and John; also C. R. Kazmierski, *Jesus, the Son of God* 153; J. Ernst in *Begegnung mit dem Wort* 55-56). Paul's naming James the brother of the Lord along with Cephas (Peter) and John as the pillar apostles (Gal 2:9; cf. Gal 1:19) favors the traditionality of an inner trio that originally included James the brother of John, now martyred (Acts 12:2). E. Best (*Following Jesus* 147) argues that because only Peter plays a further part, Mark must have added James and John. But by the same token the tradition must have had only Peter accompanying Jesus up the Mount of Transfiguration (9:2-8) — not a likely possibility. Furthermore, the leading role of Peter (1:16-20, 29-30, 36; 3:16; 8:29, 32-33; 11:21; 13:3; not to list extra-Marcan references) and his having just portrayed himself as more loyal to Jesus than the other disciples are (14:29, 31a) make it historically as well as literarily natural for Jesus to have addressed him individually in the presence of others (as at 8:33 and esp. 14:30).

W. L. Lane (515) suggests that Jesus took along Peter because Peter had boisterously avowed loyalty to him in vv 29, 31, and James and John because they had confidently affirmed their ability to drink his cup and undergo his baptism (10:38-39a). But even before Peter's avowals and James' and John's affirmation, Jesus took along these three, and did so apparently because he favored them (5:37; 9:2). Here he does not want to expose their bravado. He wants their help. His not getting it does not represent the motif of the righteous sufferer's abandonment by his family and friends, for falling asleep in the privacy of Gethsemane because of heavy eyelids hardly amounts to the deliberate avoidance and public renunciation of which righteous sufferers complain (Pss 31:12[11]; 38:12[11]; 88:9, 19[8, 18]).

A. Feuillet (*L'agonie* 217-18) suggests that Peter, James, and John are said to see Jesus' abasement just as they saw his glory at the Transfiguration. But here no emphasis whatever falls on their seeing what happened (contrast "before them . . . appeared to them . . . they saw . . ." in 9:2, 4, 8). In fact, Jesus' going a little farther than the three and their falling asleep would undermine such an emphasis. Moreover, it is probably the Crucifixion rather than Gethsemane that stands over against the Transfiguration — yet the three did not see the Crucifixion — and we must remind ourselves of those already noted elements that make vv 32-42 enhance, not abase, the figure of Jesus.

E. W. Stegemann (in *TZ* 42 [1986] 366-74) thinks that Peter, James, and John are featured here and in the earlier passages as coming martyrs, like Jesus, back to all of whose deaths Mark's audience can look by the time he writes his gospel. But an early martyrdom of John is highly questionable (see the notes on 10:38-39). A date of writing prior to the Jewish revolt of 66-74 C.E. (see pp. 1041-45) calls in question the presupposition that Mark was written before Peter's martyrdom, occurring in the period 64-67 C.E.; and allusions to martyrdoms of Peter, James, and John are by no means clear in their accompanying Jesus into Jairus's house to witness a raising from the dead (5:37-42), in their accompanying Jesus up a high mountain to witness the Transfiguration (9:2-8), or in their accompanying him into Gethsemane to keep watch for him.

See the comments on 9:15 for the connotation of ἐκθαμβεῖσθαι, "to be amazed" (here with alarm; cf. Ps 31:23[22]; 116:11). With Jesus' praying also out of dismay, cf. Ps 61:3(2). According to T. Söding (in *BZ* nf 31 [1987] 85-86), Jesus' coming face-to-face with the fact that God his Father will give him over into the hands of sinners causes a panic of grief. But see the notes on 1:14 against assigning to God the giving over of Jesus. Nonetheless, more than fear of death as such is at work in Jesus. He is alarmed, dismayed, and deeply grieved that one of the Twelve will betray him, that the rest will forsake him, that his leading disciple will deny him three times, that he will be given over into the hands of sinners, and all of these before daybreak.

The element of deep grief militates against the view that Jesus fears his own apostasy in the eschatological temptation (and see the following notes on v 38 that we should not define πειρασμός as the eschatological temptation; against T. A. Burkill, *New Light* 68). Alarm and dismay would fit with fear, but grief does not fit so well; and fear of apostasy would probably have evoked, not a request for immunity, but one for steadfastness, as in Luke 21:36 (which should not be understood in terms of exemption, because κατισχύσητε, "prevail," then loses its force; see also Mark 13:13b). Even apart from eschatology we would expect a prayer for steadfastness rather than for immunity.

See R. H. Gundry, *Use of the OT* 59, on the borrowing in v 34 of phraseology from Pss 42:6, 12(5, 11); 43:5; Jonah 4:9 (cf. Judg 16:16; 1 Kgs 19:4; Sir 37:2; 51:6; 1QH 8:32). Because ἕως θανάτου, "to [the point of] death," occurs often in the LXX, D. J. Moo (*OT* 240-41) doubts an allusion to Jonah 4:9. The phrase even occurs with λυπή in Sir 37:2 LXX. But Jesus' known interest in Jonah (see Matt 12:39-41 par. Luke 11:29-30, 32) plus the connection of this phrase with extreme grief in Jonah 4:9 LXX makes probable an allusion to that passage in Mark 14:34, where we see the same connection. For the juxtaposition of different OT texts, as here, see 1:2-3; 10:6-8; 11:17; 12:19, 29-33; 13:24-26; 14:62 (not to list many examples outside Mark). That the phraseology in Jonah 4:9 has to do with a death-wish (Jonah 4:3, 8; cf. Num 11:14-15) does not demand a death-wish here, for OT meaning does not determine NT meaning. Jonah became so angry (MT) or grieved (LXX) over the death of a gourd that he too wanted to die (cf. Judg 16:16); but Jesus becomes so grief-panicked over the prospect of his own death that he is about to die before being given over to his enemies (G. Dautzenberg, *Sein Leben* 127-30). His subsequent prayer to have the cup of death taken from him will show that he does not want death (cf. R. Feldmeier, *Krisis* 150-51; A. Feuillet, *L'agonie* 80-82). It is gratuitous to distinguish between an immediate death in Gethsemane and a death subsequent to his betrayal and then to think that he wants the first instead of the second (so J. Héring in *RHPR* 39 [1959] 99-101; idem in *Neotestamentica et Patristica* 65-69; D. Daube in *NovT* 5 [1962] 98). If he wanted to die at all, he might have welcomed his cup.

Association with the participle of motion, "going forward," rather than with the verb of speaking, "was praying," makes μικρόν an adverb of space, "a little distance," rather than of time, "a little while" (v 35). The association of falling on the ground with praying keeps the falling from connoting death in accordance with the etymological meaning of the Greek word for a corpse, i.e. πτῶμα, "that which has fallen" (against E. S. Malbon, *Narrative Space* 79-81; see further argumentation in the notes on 9:20). G. Szarek (in *SBL 1976 Seminar Papers* 113) compares Jesus' falling on the ground in v 35 with the falling of seeds on the ground and bearing fruit abundantly in 4:8, and his being given over throughout the passion narrative with the giving over by the fruit in 4:29. Out of these comparisons Szarek deduces that just as the seeds fall on the ground and die and in a sense die again in the harvesting of the fruit that they produce, so also Jesus falls on the ground and dies emotionally so as to make possible his physical death on the Cross. This deduction rests on an illegitimate importation of the Pauline and Johannine idea that out of the death of a seed comes fruitful life (1 Cor 15:36; John 12:24). Moreover, fruit was the subject of giving over in 4:29, but Jesus is just the opposite — the object — of giving over in the passion narrative. He is praying, Szarek goes on to argue (114-16), for deliverance from doubt that his death will be useful (cf. 15:34). But the hour and the cup have to do with betrayal and death, respectively (vv 23-24, 41), whereas Szarek's interpretation requires the hour and the cup to represent "his present anguish."

"And he was praying . . . and he was saying" (vv 35-36) parallels the coordination of verbs of speaking in 1:14-15; 6:50; 7:28; 8:33; 10:47; 14:61 (cf. M. Reiser, *Syntax und Stil* 132-33, on the question of a Semitism). But only in 14:35-36 does an indirect quotation separate the coordinated verbs; so we can hardly use the coordination to argue that the intervening material (the indirectly quoted prayer) is of Mark's fabrication. The use of "hour" elsewhere in Mark disfavors an eschatological connotation here. Most instances are obviously uneschatological (6:35 [bis]; 11:11; 13:11; 15:25, 33 [bis], 34). Paired with "that day," the hour in 13:22 refers to the exact time of the Son of man's coming (cf. Rev 3:3), not to an eschatological period. In 14:37 "one hour" refers mundanely to the length of time that Peter was unable to keep awake. And the hour that has come in 14:41 is characterized by the Son of man's being given over into the hands of sinners. Therefore, the hour which in 14:35 Jesus prays might pass away from him but which in accordance with God's will comes anyway does not carry eschatological freight. It does not even cover the whole of Jesus' passion and glorification, as in the Gospel of John (see esp. 12:23, 27; 13:1; 17:1, where, not as here, the hour is described as Jesus's), but refers simply and solely to the hour of betrayal (contrast the eschatological hour of divine judgment on the enemies of Jesus and his people esp. in Rev 3:10; 14:7, 15).

The meaning of the cup does not equate with the meaning of the hour, then, but marks a progression from betrayal to death. Likewise, "all things [are] possible for you" corrects "if it is possible" (cf. a similar correction in 9:22-23; N.B. that in 13:22 "if possible" calls in question, not the ability of God, as here, but the ability of false prophets). Hence, neither a supposed synonymity nor the difference between indirect discourse and direct discourse in vv 35b and 36, respectively, argues effectively for different underlying traditions. At most, one could effectively argue that Mark has fabricated the ἵνα-clause of v 35 in anticipation of and preparation for the traditional themes of divine possibility and the hour of betrayal in vv 36, 37, 41b (cf. L. Schenke, *Studien* 494-507; T. Söding in *BZ* nf 31 [1987] 81, point 4, et al., but without avowing the traditionality of v 41b; also A. Feuillet, *L'agonie* 65). Schenke (op. cit. 500) distinguishes between the possibility that God's will might accommodate the passing away of the hour from Jesus (v 35) and the possibility that arises out of God's power to do anything (v 36). This distinction is tenuous; for "if possible" might relate to God's power as easily as to his will, and what God wills conditions his power to do anything.

P. M. Beernaert (in *L'Évangile selon Marc* 241-67) makes v 36 the discrete center-point of a concentrically structured section made up of vv 17-52. But to treat the verse thus is to overlook both that it carries forward in direct discourse what has already begun with indirect discourse in v 35 and that the statement in v 39, "And again having gone away, he prayed the same thing (λόγον, 'word')," robs v 36 of centrality. J. D. G. Dunn (*Jesus and the Spirit* 18) treats v 36 as coming from an independent tradition because "this cup" is not integral to the passage as is "the hour" (cf. vv 37, 41). But the passage as a whole is integral to the Last Supper (preceding) and to the arrest (following), and "this cup" harks back to the cup-word at the Last Supper (vv 23-24). So v 36 looks to be at home right where it is. Nor does "Abba" suggest an original independence of v 36 from v 35, for indirect discourse suffices to explain the absence of "Abba" from v 35 just as direct discourse suffices to explain its presence in v 36. Almost certainly Mark writes the Aramaic "Abba" in v 36 because of its common use in Greek-speaking Christianity, where the translation "Father" was immediately provided without a formula of translation (see Rom 8:15; Gal 4:6, and contrast the formulas of translation in Mark 3:17; 5:41; 7:11, 34; 15:22, 34 with the absence thereof here and in 10:46, which was probably influenced by anticipation of 10:47 — see the comments ad loc.). As shown by 5:41, the definite article with πατήρ, "Father," overliterally translates the emphatic state of "Abba." On occurrences of "Abba" outside the NT, see H. P. Rüger in *Markus-Philologie* 73-74 and, more generally and with references to secondary literature, J. Schlosser, *Le Dieu de Jésus* 136, 179-209; G. Schelbert in *Mélanges Dominique Barthélemy* 395-447; J. Barr in *JTS* ns 39 (1988) 28-47. On the possibility of all things with God, see 10:27.

Linked with the address of God as Father, the symbol of the cup implies that Jesus as Son is at table with God, who as Father acts as host, passing or taking the cup (cf. Ps 23:5). "This" applied to Jesus' "cup" also in 14:23-24; but there the disciples were to drink it. Here, only Jesus is to drink it; and in 10:38-39 two of the disciples were destined to join him in drinking his cup. Since he is now speaking to God, however, not to anyone to whom he has earlier spoken about the cup, Mark or an earlier traditioner may have added "this" to make a narrative connection with the earlier passages, especially with the more recent one.

Drinking a cup often symbolizes the suffering of divine punishment (Pss 11:6; 75:9[8]; Isa 51:17, 22; Jer 25:15; 49:12; 51:7; Lam 4:21-22; Ezek 23:31-34; Hab 2:15-16; Zech 12:2; Rev 14:10; 16:19; 17:4 with 18:6; *Pss. Sol.* 8:13-14; 1QpHab 11:14-15; R. Feldmeier, *Krisis* 176-85). Isa 51:17-23 says that the cup of God's wrath has been taken away, yet Jer 49:12 speaks of those "whose judgment was not to drink the cup [i.e. who, like Jesus, did not deserve to drink it]" but who "will certainly drink [as Jesus must]." Therefore, suggests W. L. Lane (517), Jesus suspects that he will have to drink his cup even though he has done nothing to deserve it, prays that it might be taken away from him, and recognizes that it consists in the vicarious suffering of a punishment deserved by others. To be sure, he has said that he will give his life in substitution for many (Mark 10:45), that his body will be given for many (Luke 22:19; 1 Cor 11:24), and that the cup, or his blood, will be poured out for many (Luke 22:20; Mark 14:24; cf. the addition of "for the forgiveness of sins" in Matt 26:28). But a metaphorical cup does not always contain divine punishment (see the notes on 10:38), and Jesus has said that James and John will drink his cup (10:39b). So unless we assign to them as well as to Jesus the vicarious suffering of punishment deserved by others, as such the figure of Jesus' cup does not imply that kind of suffering. In 10:45 and the Words of Institution, where the vicarious aspect of his suffering does come forward, that aspect is unshared by others such as James and John.

M. Black (*Aramaic Approach* 298 and in *ExpTim* 59 [1947-48] 195) notes that the OT never uses a cup to represent suffering and death but that such a usage does appear in rabbinic literature and in *Frg. Tg.* Gen 40:32 (F). The judgments portrayed as a cup in the OT often entailed death, however; and in any case the cup-word in Mark 14:23-24 has made clear the meaning of a violent death. This meaning and the reference of "the hour" to Jesus' betrayal foreclose the possibility that he is praying for deliverance from a premature death in Gethsemane, prior to his betrayal and the laying of violent hands on him. They also foreclose the possibility that "this cup" is "a vivid expression of his experience of satanic temptation" to avoid the Cross (R. P. Martin, *Mark* 204-5). The cup *is* the Cross, not a temptation to avoid it.

One might fill two of the ellipses in v 36 with a verb in the future tense: "but not what I want [will take place]; rather, what you [want will take place]." The future tense would suit Mark's portrayal of Jesus as a predictor; but had he so intended here, Mark would probably have supplied the verb to make such a portrayal explicit. The preceding imperative would favor that we supply another imperative, "let . . . take place" (bis; cf. γενηθήτω in Matt 26:42), except for the fact that Mark writes the negative οὐ instead of μή, which the imperative would require. E. Lohmeyer (316) correctly notes this fact, but unwittingly brings back the imperative by filling the ellipses as follows: "but [it is not to be asked] what I want, but [it is to be asked] what you [want]." A better reading would be: "but [I request, αἰτοῦμαι] not what I want; rather, [I request] what you [want]" (cf. 6:22, 23, 24, 25; 10:35, 38; 11:24; 15:6, 8, 43).

The disjunction of what Jesus wants and what the Father wants spoils the view of C. A. Blaising (in *JETS* 22 [1979] 333-43) that as in Isa 51:21-23 the cup is taken away only after it has been drunk, so Jesus prays in conjunction with the Father's wish that the cup may be taken away *after* he has drunk it, and likewise that the hour may pass away from him *after* he has entered it, i.e. that the Father may "not abandon him forever to the desolation of wrath and judgment for sin" (ibid. 342). Blaising appeals to Jesus' saying elsewhere that he came not to do his own will but the Father's, as though Jesus means merely that the initiative belongs to the Father (John 5:30; 6:38-40). Jesus does ascribe initiative to the Father, but doing the Father's will rather than his own implies the theoretical possibility of disobedience (cf. John 7:17; 9:31). Furthermore, though Blaising's interpretation relieves the tension between Jesus' prayers and passion predictions, it does not relieve the tension between his prayers and predictions of the Resurrection. Had he lost confidence in God's will to raise him from the dead even though he had not lost confidence in God's will to see him suffer and die? Ps 40:9(8) (cf. Ps. 143:10) speaks about the doing of God's will (though doing it and its taking place differ, and the psalmist's delight to do it contrasts with Jesus' dread of undergoing it — cf. Heb 5:7-8). The coming to pass of God's will in the Lord's Prayer according to Matt 6:10b does not provide the source for submitting to it in the present prayer; rather, the present prayer lies behind Matt 6:10b (cf. the absence in Luke 11:2 of a request that God's will come to pass).

See D. Daube in *SE I* 539-45 on Jesus' following a Jewish pattern of accepting death in love: (1) acknowledgment ("all things [are] possible for you"); (2) wish ("take this cup from me"); (3) surrender ("but [I request] not what I want; rather, [I request] what you [want]"). A foregoing note has shown the unnecessariness of Daube's argument that because of the traditionality of this pattern the disciples would not have had to *hear* what Jesus said to *know* what he said. The language of the prayer characterizes his speech so completely that we may find easier to believe that he himself spoke it than that the disciples imitated it in conjunction with putting a Jewishly patterned prayer on his lips (with "Abba, Father," cf. Matt 11:25 par. Luke 10:21; Matt 6:9 par. Luke 11:2; with "all things [are] possible for you," cf. Mark 10:27 parr.; with "but [I request] not what I want; rather, [I request] what you [want]," cf. Mark 3:35 [not to appeal to Matthean fabrications in Matt 6:10b; 7:21; 18:14; 21:31]).

According to C. K. Barrett (*Jesus and the Gospel Tradition* 46-52), Jesus prays not merely that he escape death, but that God's kingdom may come if possible without Jesus' having to die. Jesus says nothing about the coming of the kingdom, however; and it is only Matthew's redaction of the Lord's Prayer which links that event with the coming to pass of God's will, and in the sense of realized eschatology rather than in the futuristic sense required by Barrett's suggestion (see Matt 6:10 with R. H. Gundry, *Matthew* 106-7). Barrett argues that Jesus would probably have tried to escape had he not thought that doing so might keep the kingdom from coming. But if he wanted the kingdom to come, he wanted God's will to be done in other respects, too; so the same reticence to make an escape would have obtained. See ibid. 533 and R. Feldmeier, *Krisis* 39-49, 133-39, for the historicity of Jesus' prayer and against the collocation of scattered pre-Johannine materials, as suggested by R. E. Brown, *NT Essays* 192-98.

One might think that Satan is attacking a weak spot in the three disciples, i.e. their flesh, their physical need for sleep (K. G. Kuhn in *The Scrolls and the NT* 94-113); but Mark does not mention Satan (contrast 1:13), and temptation comes from human quarters, too (8:11; 10:2). So we can say at least that no emphasis falls on Satanic activity. O. Böcher (*Mächte* 48) goes far beyond the text of v 37 in describing the sleep of the three disciples as induced by demons. *M. Yoma* 1:4 offers the simple observation that eating food induces sleep. The disciples have just eaten a full and abnormally large meal. The hour is late. And Jesus did not pinpoint the time of his betrayal as this very night. So no dread is likely to have kept the disciples awake. Since Jesus regularly addresses Peter as Simon (see also Matt 16:17; 17:25; Luke 22:31 [bis]; John 1:42; 21:15, 16, 17), since the only exception deals with Peter's denials (Luke 22:34), and since in Mark Jesus never addresses Simon as "Peter," we can hardly say that Jesus here reverts to "Simon" because the fallings asleep and the denials which they portend make inappropriate the new name that Jesus gave him in recognition of his apostleship (3:14, 16; so H. B. Swete 325). "Simon" is simply traditional (E. Best, *Following Jesus* 157, n. 17; J. Ernst in *Begegnung mit dem Wort* 55-56). M. Black (in *Biblical Studies: Essays in Honor of W. Barclay*) suggests that "one hour" means "one moment," a sense unusual in Greek but idiomatic in Aramaic and Syriac. Perhaps so, but "till I have prayed" (v 32), the meanings of μείνατε and γρηγορεῖτε, "stay" and "keep awake," and the linearity of the imperfect ἔπιπτεν and προσηύχετο, "was falling" and "was praying," suggest a longer time of praying than "one moment" would allow.

To argue that v 38a is a late insertion, L. Schenke (*Studien* 512-16) uses the switch from second person singular in v 37 to second person plural in v 38a, the repetition of keeping awake in v 38a vis-à-vis v 37, the asyndeton between v 38a and v 38b, and the sensibility of skipping from v 37 to v 38b ("You weren't strong enough to keep awake for one hour. The spirit [is] eager, but the flesh [is] weak"). But by carrying on the theme of wakefulness already begun in v 37, the command in v 38a, "Keep awake, and pray that you not enter into temptation," follows up v 37 even better than v 38b does. Without v 38a, moreover, Jesus uncharacteristically limits himself to mere observations. And if asyndeton has rhetorical value, as it does here, we dare not draw source critical conclusions from it. Since all three disciples have been sleeping, the switch from second person singular in v 37 to second person plural in v 38a does not need to indicate a jump from one source to another. The rest of the episode would entail that switch even if v 38a were treated as a redactional insertion.

Schenke (loc. cit.) also sees a contradiction between Jesus' observation, "You were not strong enough to keep awake for one hour" (v 37b), and his command, "Keep awake . . ." (v 37a). Jesus would not command the three to do what not even Peter was strong enough to do. One wonders about the truth of this presupposition. Its truth granted, however, the seeing of a contradiction depends on overlooking the prayer that you not enter into temptation. Contextually, not entering temptation means not going to sleep again. Answered prayer would make up for fleshly weakness, would counteract the physical need for sleep. Thus, praying not to succumb has the purpose of keeping awake so as to provide Jesus with the help that he failed to get when the three disciples fell asleep.

Nor are there any other convincing reasons to think that in v 38 as a whole Mark has inserted an originally independent saying or that the saying originally dealt with the great tribulation expected to wind up the present age (cf. 13:14-23), here called a πειρασμός ("test, trial, temptation"), and possibly thought by Jesus to have already started with his own persecution and to include that of the disciples with him. The use of πειρασμός in Matt 6:13 par. Luke 11:4 need not refer to that tribulation. In fact, the anarthrousness of this noun both here and there militates against such a particular reference and contrasts with the arthrousness of the noun in Rev 3:10, where to carry that reference the noun needs the help not only of the definite article but also of "the hour" and of "coming on the whole world to test the ones dwelling on the earth." Nowhere else among Jesus' sayings or in the rest of the NT does πειρασμός refer to eschatological tribulation; and the only other NT collocation of πειρασμός, flesh, and weakness (Gal 4:13-14) has to do with conversion, not with perseverance. Of course, γρηγορεῖτε, "keep awake," recalls 13:35, 37, where the same command has already appeared; and "he comes and finds them sleeping" (14:37 and, similarly, 14:40) recalls 13:36: "lest coming suddenly he find you sleeping." But that passage had to do with the Son of man's coming "in clouds and with much power and glory" (13:26), whereas this passage has to do with the coming of Judas Iscariot. Furthermore, the present passage has to do with keeping awake by praying not to succumb to πειρασμός, whereas the earlier passage had to do with keeping awake so as not to be caught by surprise. Nor was keeping awake set in the context of imminent betrayal (N.B. the distance of 13:35, 37 from 13:9, 11, 12, and the use in 13:9 of a different predicate, βλέπετε ἑαυτούς, "watch out for yourselves," instead of γρηγορεῖτε, "keep awake" [so 14:34, 37, 38]); nor was praying set in the context of keeping awake (N.B. the distance of 13:18 from 13:35, 37). These differences also weaken the basis of the hypothesis that Mark or someone before him fabricated the disciples' sleep to exemplify, overliteralistically, the sleep against which Jesus warned in chap. 13. At least in the present passage we should resist the temptation to treat wakefulness and sleep solely, or even primarily or at all, as symbols of spiritual alertness and dullness. In the only other NT collocation of keeping awake and praying (Col 4:2-4), keeping awake carries a purely literal meaning: "Spend much time in prayer [by] keeping awake in it. . . ."

Nowhere in Mark or throughout the rest of the NT is γρηγορέω, "keep awake," followed by a telic ἵνα-clause. Yet commonly in Mark an epexegetic ἵνα, often followed by μή, "not" (sometimes in a compound), as here in 14:38, introduces the content of what is said, written, wanted, or granted (3:9, 12; 5:10, 18, 43; 6:8, 12, 25; 7:26, 32, 36; 8:22, 30; 9:9, 12, 30; 10:35, 37, 48, 51; 12:19; 13:18, 34; 14:12, 35). Two of these introductions follow προσεύχομαι, "pray," and one of these two includes a following μή, again as here in 14:38 (13:18; 14:35). Therefore the present ἵνα-clause does not attach to the verb γρηγορεῖτε to give the purpose of keeping awake and praying. Rather, it attaches solely to the verb προσεύχεσθε, which immediately precedes it, to give the content of the praying. The disciples are to pray that they not succumb to πειρασμός, i.e. that they not fall asleep again. Thus we do not have to suppose the oddity of a ἵνα that is telic in relation to γρηγορεῖτε as well as epexegetic in relation to προσεύχεσθε. Nor need we suppose that because not succumbing to πειρασμός is the purpose of keeping awake, πειρασμός must differ from falling asleep and get its meaning from an originally different context or at least from earlier pericopes in Mark. Jesus has not taken the three with him to prepare them for their own gruelling experience in the future, but to give him help in his own emotional struggle at present. Both their all being tripped up, i.e. scattered, when as the shepherd he is struck (v 27) and Peter's denying him thrice before daybreak (v 30) are foregone conclusions. Jesus has predicted those events. They are certain to take place. He would not now be telling them to keep awake and pray for the purpose of falsifying his predictions (against T. Söding in BZ nf 31 [1987] 93). If Mark had added "and pray" to the command "keep awake" (so E. Best, Following Jesus 151), he would probably have made the same addition in 13:33-37 (as in a parallelistic v.l. at 13:33). But he did not. The suggestion of A. Loisy (L'évangile Marc 415) and J. Héring (in Neotestamentica et Patristica 64-65) that originally Jesus said to pray that he not succumb to temptation finds some support in the extremity of his distress. But since this suggestion flies in the face of "you not enter" and since Jesus started by telling the three disciples merely to stay where he left them and keep awake, it is more probable that he now tells them to pray that they not succumb again to the temptation of going to sleep.

To go into temptation would be not merely to confront it but also to succumb to it, like falling into temptation at 1 Tim 6:19. Not to go into temptation means to overcome it (cf. the provision of a way out of it in order that one may bear it — 1 Cor 10:13; similarly, 2 Pet 2:9; *b. Ber.* 60b). See R. H. Gundry, *Use of the OT* 59-60, on the borrowing of phraseology from Ps 51:14 MT in v 38, and idem, *Sōma* 111-12, against a reference to the Holy Spirit and for a reference to the human spirit in both passages. The human spirit of Jesus was mentioned in 2:8; 8:12.

Against Pauline influence on vv 35-38 (so E. Wendling, *Entstehung* 171), Paul opposes the flesh as lusting after sin to the Holy Spirit as bringing forth righteousness (see esp. Gal 5:16-24) whereas Jesus makes the human spirit as resolute and the flesh as physically weak antagonistic to each other; and it was the weakness of Paul's flesh, not of the Galatians' own flesh, that posed a πειρασμός to them (Gal 4:13-14; contrast the weakness of the three disciples' own flesh). The eagerness in 2 Cor 8:11-18 is not associated with the spirit, as in Mark 14:38, and is not opposed by any weakness of the flesh; nor is the eagerness thwarted. Nor does the praying and keeping awake in Col 4:2-3 aim against one's own succumbing to temptation, as here, but toward evangelistic success on the part of another. If a relation exists between these Pauline passages and the passage in Mark, the differences are easier to explain as adaptations of Jesuanic material to the life of the church than as adaptations of churchly material to the life of Jesus. For further discussion, see E. Lohse, *History* 59-61.

In v 39 Mark avoids prolixity of direct discourse by writing that in his second prayer Jesus spoke "the same word" as before (cf. similar avoidances at 1:20; 3:31; 5:33; 11:6; 14:70; 15:8; M. Zerwick, *Untersuchungen* 31). A switch from the imperfect tense of praying (προσηύχετο — v 35; cf. the similarly linear present tense in v 38) to the constative aorist (προσηύξατο — v 39) suits this summarizing phrase. J. W. Holleran (*Synoptic Gethsemane* 46) presumes too much in denying that "say the same word" means praying to the same effect as in vv 35-36 rather than repeating the very words that were quoted indirectly and directly in those verses.

According to E. Best (*Following Jesus* 151), Mark inserts a reference to the three disciples' eyes (v 40) to make the point that sleeping leads to not seeing (cf. 8:22-26). Mark's wording puts the matter almost the other way around, however: having heavy eyelids leads to sleeping. Though having heavy eyelids comes close to not seeing, the issue is not one of sight but of staying awake. The explanation that the three had heavy eyelids is designed neither to exonerate the disciples nor to criticize them, but simply to provide a foil against which Jesus' strength stands out.

E. Best (*Following Jesus* 150-51) supports a redactional emphasis on discipleship by treating vv 38, 40bc as Mark's insertions and by claiming a lack of resolution so far as the outcome of Jesus' prayers is concerned (cf. T. Söding in *BZ* nf 31 [1987] 83-84). But in the notes on v 38 we have seen the weakness in regarding that verse as an insertion by Mark, and the explanation in v 40b of why Jesus found the three disciples sleeping ("for their eyes were weighed down") points to fatigue of body ("the flesh is weak"; cf. the blameless terror at 9:6) rather than to failure of discipleship. Hence, their not knowing what to answer him in v 40c does not arise out of failure to understand the necessity that Jesus die (as thought by W. H. Kelber, *Mark's Story* 76; idem in *The Passion in Mark* and in *ZNW* 63 [1972] 166-87, esp. 179-80; A. Feuillet in *NTS* 22 [1975-76] 415). It is Jesus, not the disciples, who questions the necessity of his death (contrast 8:32), which by now they have accepted (14:31). They have even accepted the possibility of their own dying with him (again 14:31). And it is not a question of understanding, as in 6:52-53, but of embarrassment. A resolution is reached, not only in "but [I request] not what I want; rather,

[I request] what you [want]" (v 36), but also in "the hour has come . . ." (vv 41-42). Even a lack of resolution would not have left discipleship to capture the spotlight, for Jesus' last words to the three disciples point to his foreknowledge in that he indicates the coming to pass of his predictions of betrayal and passion.

D. Daube (*NTRJ* 332-35; cf. J. W. Holleran, *Synoptic Gethsemane* 46-49) compares the three disciples' not knowing what they might answer Jesus (v 40) with a fifth century rabbinic opinion that a man is dozing but not sleeping if when addressed he answers, but not sensibly (cf. the foregoing note on going to sleep as ending the Passover celebration). This opinion postdates Jesus by nearly four hundred years, however; and the three disciples do not answer unsensibly. They do not answer at all. In fact, they are not even addressed, and fail to answer only in the sense of not responding verbally to a circumstance (as also in 9:5; 11:14; 12:35; 14:48).

Jesus' coming a third time ruins the suggestion that his return symbolizes the Second Coming (so R. S. Barbour in *NTS* 16 [1969-70] 236). Mark does not believe in three second comings. The three discoveries of the disciples asleep correspond to the three denials of Peter, but not to the three passion predictions in 8:31; 9:31; and 10:33-34 or to the three notations of the hours of crucifixion in 15:25, 33, 34-37 (as thought by W. H. Kelber in *The Passion in Mark* 53). For Mark does not number the predictions or the notations as he does number the discoveries and the denials; and if we ourselves bother to number the passion predictions, they turn out to exceed three (see also 9:12 with 9:9; 14:8, 22-24).

On the asyndeta in vv 41-42, see M. Reiser, *Syntax und Stil* 139-41; and on the possibility of an underlying Hebrew (or Aramaic, we might add) wordplay in נומו ונוחו, "sleep and rest," see J. Carmignac in *ASTI* 7 (1968-69) 72. For τὸ λοιπόν in v 41, we might consider "therefore" instead of "for the remainder"; but Jesus has said nothing just preceding on which the illative meaning could fasten, whereas the chronologically adverbial meaning suits the linearity of the commands to keep on sleeping and resting. For surveys of meanings proposed for ἀπέχει (v 41), see C. E. B. Cranfield 435-36; W. L. Lane 514, n. 75; R. Pesch 2. 393-94; J. W. Holleran, *Synoptic Gethsemane* 52-56; K. W. Müller in *ZNW* 77 (1986) 83-94. Little or no evidence supports the suggested translation, "It [your sleeping and resting] is enough" (see esp. J. de Zwaan in *The Expositor* 6th Series, 12 [1905] 461-64). The suggestion that Judas is receiving Jesus as Philemon receives Onesimus (Phlm 15-16; so G. H. Boobyer in *NTS* 2 [1955-56] 44-48) stumbles against Philemon's receiving Onesimus as one receives a full payment of what rightfully belongs to him (though no longer as a slave, but as a beloved brother) and against explicit indications that Judas does not receive Jesus as one receives a full payment but that just oppositely he gives Jesus over to others. Judas's giving Jesus over to others also contrasts with Philemon's receiving Onesimus "forever" (which holds true whether or not Philemon will do more than Paul says by freeing Onesimus — Phlm 21). M. Black (*Aramaic Approach* 225-26), followed by R. Le Déaut (in *Bib* 49 [1968] 392), hypothesizes that ἀπέχει translates דחיק, "[The end and the hour] are pressing," as though it were רחיק, "[The end and the hour] are distant." But this hypothesis demands the originality of the v.l. in D c q, whereas that v.l. has little external support and from the internal standpoint probably originates in a combination of desire to clarify the subject of ἀπέχει and parallel influence from Luke 22:37. For Jesus to say that "he [God] is distant" (cf. 15:34; R. Feldmeier, *Krisis* 209-15) disagrees with the affectionate tone of Jesus' immediately preceding prayers and does not complement the later statement that the betrayer "has drawn near" (v 42) so well as does an identification with the betrayer whose present distance allows opportunity for further sleep and rest.

We need not consider Jesus portrayed as thinking one moment that Judas is distant and as surprised the next moment that Judas has drawn near, so that Jesus has to arouse the three disciples right after telling them to sleep on and take their rest. Such a portrayal would disagree with the knowledge which Jesus exhibits in every other respect of his passion, and a statement that Judas is distant would seem to depend on similar knowledge. We might want a narrative transition between Jesus' statements, "He is distant" and "The hour has come" — say, a narrative transition to the effect that the three disciples did sleep on and take their rest, that Judas drew near, and that Jesus renewed his speaking to the three disciples. But all interpretations of the passage labor under the absence of a narrative transition, if not between ἀπέχει and the coming of the hour, then between the command to sleep on and take rest and ἀπέχει. Under the interpretation, "He is distant," a narrative transition fails to appear in order that pride of place may go to Jesus' own announcement of fulfilment: "The hour has come. Behold, the Son of man is being given over. . . ." So great is Mark's concern to emphasize this announcement that he sacrifices narrative and leaves it to be inferred from Jesus' final announcement, "Behold, the one giving me over has drawn near," that the three disciples had indeed slept on and taken their rest and that in the meantime the once distant betrayer had drawn near.

K. W. Müller (in *ZNW* 77 [1986] 94-100) parses ἀπέχει as a third person singular imperfect active indicative of ἀποχέω, "pour out," and interprets Jesus to mean that God has poured out God's wrath into the cup which Jesus had prayed that God might take away from him but which Jesus will shortly have to drink in his death. The imperfect tense would indicate linear action in past time, however ("was pouring out"); and such action would seem to be without point here. Furthermore, why should God not be mentioned as subject of the verb? "Into the cup" would seem to be required, too; for without it the pouring out would more naturally be understood as from a cup or other container (cf., for example, Rev 16:1-21). And it would seem more natural for Jesus to say that God has filled a cup (cf. Rev 17:4) than to say that God has poured out into it (for a cup as itself being poured out, cf. the notes on 14:24), or for Jesus to say that he now has to drink it (as in 10:38; cf. 14:23 parr.; 1 Cor 10:21; 11:26, 27, 28; Rev 14:10 et passim outside the NT) than to say that God has poured out into it (as though it were empty back in 10:38 and even as recently as 14:36).

For the meaning that the hour "has passed away" (so M. Ruhland, *Markuspassion* 24-26) we should have had παρῆλθεν instead of ἦλθεν (cf. v 35; 6:48; 13:30, 31 [bis]). Since Mark usually puts a verb before its subject, no emphasis is to be detected in the forward positions of ἦλθεν, "has come," and παραδίδοται, "is being given over" (v 41; against J. W. Holleran, *Synoptic Gethsemane* 57). The notes on v 35 have shown that neither the hour nor its coming in v 41 is eschatological. Its coming is merely chronological just as the betrayer's drawing near is merely topographical (v 42); so no separation between sources or between tradition and redaction is to be based on a supposed distinction between eschatology and topography (against E. Best, *Following Jesus* 149-50; L. Schenke, *Studien* 465-71). According to 13:11, the disciples will have their hour in court when people give them over to the authorities. W. H. Kelber (in *The Passion in Mark* 44) says that this parallel with the hour of the Son of man's being given over into the hands of sinners (14:41) casts the passion of Jesus in an eschatological light. But no, for 13:11 falls into the pre-eschatological section of chap. 13. Not till 13:14 does the great tribulation to end all tribulations start. An uneschatological parallel remains, however, between the giving over and leading of the disciples and Jesus to the authorities.

Even under the view that God is the one who is giving the Son of man over into the hands of sinners in v 41 (yet see the notes on 1:14; 9:31 against a divine passive here and elsewhere), we should not distinguish between a soteriological giving over in v 41 and a historical one in v 42. Not a syllable of salvation is to be found in v 41; and the present tense of being given over, juxtaposed as it is with that of Judas's being distant and with the hour's having come, makes v 41 just as historical in tenor as is v 42, where the participle of giving over occurs likewise in the present tense. The notion that the switch from a divine passive ("is being given over" — v 41) to a profane active ("the one giving me over" — v 42) reflects a difference between sources or between tradition and redaction (so Schenke, op. cit. 465-71) assumes what needs to be proved, i.e. that the passive is divine. It is simpler to say that the one who gives Jesus over in v 42 — viz., Judas Iscariot — identifies the one by whom Jesus is being given over in v 41 and that the passive occurs in v 41 not to imply divine action but to accommodate the phrase "into the hands of sinner," which an active voice would make very awkward, almost impossible (cf. 9:31; 10:33; and again the notes on 1:14; 9:31; also the shift from passive to active in 10:33 without discernible reason why being given over to the chief priests and scribes should be done by God but the giving over to the Gentiles should not be done by God). As consistently elsewhere, the passive takes "the Son of man" as its subject (9:31; 10:33; 14:21, 41); and the active takes "Jesus" or a pronoun referring to him as its direct object (10:33; 14:10, 11, 18, 42, 44; 15:1 [with an ellipsis to be filled in from the preceding occurrence of "Jesus"], 10, 15). Two instances of the latter construction occur in dominical sayings (10:33; 14:18). The first of these includes a switch from the former construction to the latter construction; and the second of these uses "me," to be called "the Son of man" three verses later, just as 14:42 uses "me," having been called "the Son of man" one verse earlier. So the switch from "the Son of man" to "me" again provides no solid basis for distinguishing between sources or between tradition and redaction. "Sinners" may refer to Gentiles, impious Jews, or both. It is possible that Jesus turned this epithet, which pious Jews applied to Gentiles and impious fellow Jews, against those who so used it. See BAGD, s.v. ἁμαρτωλός, and cf. the comments and notes on 9:31.

T. A. Mohr (*Markus- und Johannespassion* 237) argues that since "rouse yourselves" (ἐγείρεσθε — v 42) corresponds to the earlier "sit" (καθίσατε — v 32) and that since Jesus directed the earlier command to all the disciples, he directs this later command also to them. But for a counterpart to sitting we would expect standing up (ἀνίστημι), as in 2:14 and 9:35 with 10:1 (cf. 7:17 with 7:24; 10:46 with 10:50; 14:60). Rousing yourself is the counterpart to a prone position, as in the three disciples' sleeping (see 1:30 with 1:31; 2:4 with 2:11-12; 4:38a with 4:38b-39; 5:39 with 5:41; 9:20 and 9:26 with 9:27; cf. 15:46 with 16:6). In commands, ἐγείρω has taken the active voice at 2:9, 11; 3:3; 5:41; 10:49. Probably because the three disciples are sleeping, the voice changes in v 42 to the middle: "rouse yourselves" (ἐγείρεσθε; see E. C. Maloney, *Semitic Interference* 81, for a probable lexical Semitism). M. R. Mansfield (*"Spirit and Gospel"* 127-29) sees an intimation that the disciples will be raised from their stupor through an encounter with the resurrected Jesus (ἐγείρεσθε), who will lead them (ἄγωμεν) in triumph over all their foes. But the text says nothing about Jesus' having been raised, and "let's go" does not connote triumph (though it may carry the connotation of setting out to meet an advancing enemy — see C. H. Dodd, *Interpretation* 406-7).

W. H. Kelber (in *The Passion in Mark* 45-46) imputes an eschatological connotation to Jesus' being given over, because the announcement that the one giving him over "has drawn near" (v 42) uses the very same verbal form (ἤγγικεν) which in its only other Marcan occurrence Jesus used for the kingdom of God (1:15) and because from now on Jesus will be portrayed as the king of the Jews. But for this parallel to work well, Jesus should have drawn near to the betrayer just as the kingdom of God had drawn near to the Jews. And it is more than a little doubtful that Jesus' kingship over the Jews represents the kingdom of God. For in answer to Pilate's question, "Are *you* [σύ in forward position] the king of the Jews?" (15:2a), Jesus rejects the title as a self-designation and stresses instead that it comes from Pilate, not from anything Jesus or his disciples have said: *"You* [σύ again in forward position] are saying ['the king of the Jews']" (15:32b). This answer contrasts sharply with his "I am" plus supportive claims when asked whether he is the Christ, the Son of the Blessed One (14:61-62). In speaking to others, too, Pilate calls Jesus the king of the Jews (15:9) and quotes the crowd incited by the chief priests as also calling him the king of the Jews (15:12). Pilate's soldiers and whoever wrote the inscription of the charge against Jesus call him the king of the Jews (15:18, 26), and the chief priests and scribes call him the king of Israel (15:32). Not very reliable commentators on Jesus' office, these. To be sure, the chief priests and scribes will speak the truth in also calling Jesus "the Christ" (15:32); but Mark's audience know that they do only because of previous indications stemming from Mark, Peter, and Jesus himself (1:1; 8:29; 9:41; 14:61-62). No similar indications are forthcoming for Jesus' kingship over the Jews. Not even in the request of James and John to sit on Jesus' right and left or in the Triumphal Procession toward Jerusalem does Mark or anyone in the narrative portray Jesus as the king of the Jews — or as the king in God's kingdom, either (contrast Mark 10:37 with Matt 20:21, and Mark 11:1-10 with Matt 21:1-9; Luke 19:28-38; John 12:12-19). For Mark, the king in the kingdom of God remains God, not Jesus (contrast also Matt 2:2; 13:41, 43; 16:28; 20:21; 25:31, 34, 40; John 1:49; 18:36; Eph 5:5; Col 1:13; 2 Tim 4:1, 18; Heb 1:8; 2 Pet 1:11; Rev 3:21; 11:15; 17:14; 19:12, 16). One could appeal to irony: Jesus is the king of the Jews despite disbelief that such a sufferer could be their king (so Kelber). But irony is notoriously hard to prove, and in this case "the king of the Jews" never occurs against the background of a disbelief that would create an atmosphere favorable to irony. For all that we can tell, Pilate will really believe Jesus to be the king of the Jews so far as the crowd are concerned. The soldiers will appear to believe likewise. Disbelief will enter the picture not till the final occurrence of "king" at 15:32, and then only on the part of the chief priests and scribes, not on that of the crowd, and only in conjunction with and second to "the Christ" and modified by "of Israel" rather than "of the Jews" — and, like all the references to "the king of the Jews," quite apart from "the kingdom of God." The absence of a Jesuanic claim to kingship and of a discipular ascription of kingship to him — an absence the more striking in that among Jews kingship often went along with Christhood, which Jesus did claim and which his disciples did ascribe to him — shrinks the relevance to Mark of Greco-Roman traditions concerning a suffering, dying king (against V. K. Robbins, *Jesus the Teacher* 187-91). At most, Mark's original audience might have read the passion narrative in the light of those traditions; but the text of Mark itself does not put that audience in very good company if they did so. Jesus himself may have accepted "the Christ" but not "the king of the Jews" because "the Christ" can carry a non-royal meaning (as in its use for patriarchs, priests, and prophets) whereas "the king of the Jews" cannot (cf. F. Hesse and M. de Jonge in *TDNT* 9. 493-521). In general, the foregoing notes argue against F. J. Matera, *Kingship* passim.

To support a Marcan Christology of Davidic kingship, J. R. Donahue (in *The Passion in Mark* 76) draws a parallel between Judas's betrayal of Jesus and Ahithophel's betrayal of David (2 Sam 15:12, 31; 16:20–17:4). But these betrayals took such different forms — Judas gives Jesus in person over into the hands of sinners, whereas Ahithophel advised David's enemy in David's absence — that the parallel proves argumentatively worthless. Mark leaves no evidence that he had it in mind.

We may ask where the narrator (Mark or someone before him) got his information about Jesus' arrest (vv 43-52), or whether he deduced or made up certain elements in the episode, if not the whole episode. But E. Lohmeyer (321) errs in saying that the descriptions of the kiss as a signal, of the swordsman as a bystander, and of his victim as the high priest's slave represent the standpoint of someone in the crowd that accompanied Judas Iscariot. Nor in other respects does the narrator take an opposite standpoint on Jesus' side. Rather, the narrator looks at both sides from a transcendent standpoint of omniscience.

L. Schenke (*Studien* 126) considers v 43 traditional because it lacks "Iscariot" after "Judas" and "the" before "one of the Twelve" (contrast the presence of both in v 10). Doubtless "Judas" is traditional, but Mark may leave out a traditional "Iscariot" because the fuller designation has occurred very recently in his text. And he may again add "one of the Twelve" to stress perfidy, but this time without an initial "the" (as also without it in v 20) because the recency of its having pointed back to 3:19 has eliminated the need for a further anaphoric use. If Mark adds "one of the Twelve" to stress the perfidy of Judas Iscariot and uses this stress to promote an apology for the Cross, the designation provides no evidence that Mark is starting to copy a passion narrative that began with Jesus' arrest (against the argument for such a view that foregoing occurrences of the designation in vv 10, 20 would have kept Mark from using it here if he were writing freely). Appeal to early Christian summaries in Acts 2:23; 7:52; 13:28 does not succeed, either; for though they allude to Jesus' delivery to the Gentiles, they do not mention his arrest (and Acts 10:38 does not even mention his delivery to the Gentiles). The further argument that from this point onward John's passion narrative starts running closely parallel to Mark's (John 18:2ff.) neglects earlier close parallels in John 13:21-38; 18:1 and significant differences in John 18:12-14, 19-24.

B. L. Mack (*Myth* 292-93) sees irony in the Sanhedrin's sending a crowd to arrest Jesus and in the ensuing tumult of swordplay over against the Sanhedrin's having feared a tumult should they arrest him in the presence of a crowd. But vv 1-2 used "people," not "crowd" (as in v 43); and the swordplay of a single bystander hardly rises to the level of "a tumult of the people." "Crowd" (ὄχλος) does not connote an official body; so the crowd that arrives with Judas Iscariot probably does not consist of the Levites who had responsibility to police the temple (contrast Luke 22:52, where the crowd of Luke 22:47 melds into the chief priests, captains of the temple, and elders). The coming from the chief priests, scribes, and elders and the particular mention of the high priest's slave may then imply that personal servants of the Sanhedrists made up the crowd (against E. Haenchen 498; cf. John 18:3, 12, which mention a Roman cohort alongside the servants; also J. Blinzler, *Prozess* 126-28, for an auxiliary police force at the disposal of the Sanhedrin). With their weapons, cf. *m. Šabb.* 6:4; *b. Pesaḥ.* 57a; *t. Menaḥ.* 13:21; Josephus *Ant.* 18.3.2 §61; idem *J.W.* 2.9.4 §176). F. Field (*Notes* 76-77) suggests that μαχαιρῶν (v 43) means "knives" rather than "swords" (cf. the use of this Greek word for a butcher's knife by Dion. Hal. *Ant. Rom.* 11.37.5-6), but the suggestion misses the irony of going on a military expedition as against a bandit (v 48). On the classes of the Sanhedrin with reference to Jesus' passion, see the excursus just following the comments on 8:31-32a.

See R. H. Gundry, *Matthew* 537, on Judas's need to identify Jesus in an ostensibly peaceful way, as by a kiss (vv 44-45), against the historical objections of B. W. Bacon in *HibJ* 19 (1920-21) 476-93, esp. 485-86. To the understanding that Judas designed the signal of a kiss to mask his betrayal of Jesus, E. Schweizer (317) objects that Judas's moving in with an armed crowd made obvious what he was doing. But why then a kiss at all instead of a gesture by hand or a verbal identification? Might not Judas have hoped that a kiss would dissociate his action from the crowd's bearing of arms (cf. 2 Sam 15:5 and esp. 20:8-10)? One could of course deny the pertinence of the question by suggesting that Mark or someone before him fabricated the kiss to deepen Judas's perfidy. The suggestion is incapable of proof, however; and the Semitism "Rabbi" with which the kiss is associated in v 45 favors an early date and, to that extent, authenticity. The kiss drops out of John 18:2-11, not on traditional grounds, but as part of a redactional transfer of initiative to Jesus. M. Aberbach (in *Essays presented to Chief Rabbi Israel Brodie on the occasion of his seventieth Birthday* 13-14) notes that a disciple is not permitted to greet his master first, since to do so would imply equality and hence insult the master. Thus Judas insults Jesus at the same time that he masks the betrayal with a kiss. G. Schwarz (*Jesus und Judas* 28-29) argues that betrayal and a kiss are psychologically incompatible. This argument neglects the element of perfidy.

The swordsman's antic (v 47), Jesus' response to arrest (vv 48-50), and the escape of the young man (vv 51-52) are scarcely to be regarded as Marcan or pre-Marcan additions of originally independent traditions; for none of these items could have stood well by itself (against V. Taylor 557). On the supposition that the swordsman in v 47 belongs to Jesus' party, E. Linnemann (*Studien* 41) lists several difficulties in the narrative of Jesus' arrest. The arresters would surely have fought back, for example; and the content of Jesus' response in v 48 identifies the addressees as his arresters (cf. v 43), yet the bystanders who supplied the swordsman are the most recent possible antecedent of "them" whom he addresses. These difficulties disappear when the swordsman is correctly identified as one of the crowd who came to arrest Jesus. An argument for historicity also disappears, i.e. that the church would not have made up an incident uncomplimentary to the disciples in that one of their number lopped off the ear of the high priest's servant. That argument would be weak even if the swordsman were a disciple, however; for Mark's account, our earliest, contains no criticism of the swordplay which might even be read in a complimentary light. It is a question for commentaries on the other gospels why the swordsman there turns into a disciple.

As throughout the rest of chap. 14, the singular of ἀρχιερεύς in v 47 refers to the high priest ruling at the time, whereas the plural in v 43 referred to the chief priests who made up part of the Sanhedrin. The violence in v 47 seems pointless after the arrest in v 46 (H. Anderson 323). For that very reason, however, the reverse order in Luke 22:49-54a; John 18:10-12 looks like a secondary smoothing out of the narrative. On the other hand, this smoothing out comes at the cost of separating the arrest from the signal which prompts it. The diminutive ὠτάριον may refer to an outer ear of the high priest's slave (BAGD s.v.) or to his earlobe (BDF §111[3]). Under the first possibility the use of the non-diminutive οὖς in 4:9, 23; 7:33; 8:18 will have included the inner ear; under the second possibility, the whole of the outer ear. Some discussions of the lopping off of the ear are marred not only by a presupposition that Mark means the swordsman to be taken as a disciple of Jesus but also by a sacral interpretation of *PTebt.* 3. 793 (col. 11, l. 3–col. 12, l. 4; M. Rostovtzeff in *ZNW* 33 [1934] 196-99; D. Daube in *JTS* ns 11 [1960] 59-62; E. Lohmeyer 322; G. W. H. Lampe in *Jesus and the Politics of His Day* 343-45). The foregoing comments have argued against the presupposition, and in *PTebt.* 3. 793 the mere location of a house across the street from a shrine does not make the man who lives in the house a priest who loses his fitness for service at the shrine by having his ear cut off. In fact, the man is said to be a desert guard ([ὁ ἐρημο]φύλαξ). On the other hand, the cutting off of Hyrcanus's ears to disqualify him from any further service as high priest (Lev 21:18; Josephus *Ant.* 14.13.10 §366; idem *J.W.* 1.13.9 §§269-70) may suggest that the shameful actions of the present high priest should have disqualified him. Under the supposition that he had more than one slave, the definite article with "slave" might make this slave specially represent the high priest in disqualification (cf. the view of B. T. Viviano in *RB* 96 [1989] 71-80 that the slave is no lowly domestic, but the chief assistant or deputy of the high priest — though this view labors against the meaning and connotation of δοῦλον, "slave").

E. Linnemann (*Studien* 41) sees a difficulty in that v 48 seems to presuppose that Jesus has not yet been arrested, yet he was arrested in v 46. But v 48 presupposes no such thing; rather, it says that the crowd have come out and that they intend to take him with them back to the Sanhedrin. No anachronism here, then; for they can have already arrested him without having yet taken him back. At first blush, the response of Jesus to his arrest (v 48) would seem to follow the arrest itself (v 46) more naturally than it follows the intervening episode concerning the swordsman (v 47; E. Lohmeyer 321). A second look reveals, however, that the episode sets the stage for Jesus' response by dramatizing the arms-bearing about which he tweaks his arresters. He responds, in fact, more to the arms-bearing with which the arrest is carried out than to the arrest as such. E. Schweizer (318) thinks it unmeaningful that Jesus should be quoted as saying to the armed crowd who have come to arrest him that he had been with them while he was teaching in the temple, yet they had not seized him. Then Schweizer deduces that Jesus spoke thus on another occasion and to the Sanhedrin rather than to the crowd. But the crowd represent the Sanhedrin, who have sent them; and we need not deny that this crowd as well as their senders were listening in the temple as Jesus was teaching there, or deny that had the Sanhedrin dared they would have used the same crowd to arrest Jesus there.

With the imperious tone of Jesus in vv 48-49, cf. that of the brothers about to be martyred in 2 Maccabees 7. In Mark 14:49a, "with you" disfavors the construing of "I was" with the delayed "teaching" to form a periphrastic construction, for "I was teaching with you in the temple" does not give so good a sense as "I was with you in the temple, [I] teaching" (cf. the comments on 1:13). Therefore, we should not appeal to a periphrastic construction to argue that Mark fabricated v 49a. Nor does he elsewhere use καθ' ἡμέραν, "day by day"; and a daily teaching in the temple might seem to imply tradition in view of Mark's mentioning only two days of teaching there (11:12–12:40). Yet the distributive κατά appears with other objects at 6:40; 13:8; 14:19; 15:6, and Mark has spelled out the progression from one day to the next during Jesus' time of teaching in the temple (see 11:12 with 11:15-18, and 11:19-20 with 11:27–12:40). Furthermore, the editorial introduction in 12:35, "teaching in the temple," matches the present phraseology except for word order (see also Mark's emphasis from 1:21-22 forward on Jesus' teaching). The use of πρός, "with," with εἰμί, "am," is more often editorial or narrative (4:1; 5:11 [barring a periphrastic verbal construction]; 6:3) than dominical (9:19), as is also the use of κρατέω, "seize" (elsewhere dominical only at 7:8, over against thirteen editorial and narrative uses, for which see esp. 7:3-4). And the paratactic καί connecting the clauses of these two verbs and meaning "but" typifies Mark's use of parataxis. Hence, the wording and very possibly the substance of v 49a appear to have come from him. So strong is his apologetic desire to expose Jesus' arresters, then, that he uses "day by day" for only two days of teaching in the temple (contrast his normal use of the distributive κατά in passages already listed). His other uses of the distributive κατά, the distributively temporal character of one of them (in 15:6), and his failure to use κατά plus the accusative in a non-distributively temporal way militate against translating καθ' ἡμέραν merely "during day" (so A. W. Argyle in ExpTim 63 [1951-52] 354), though the better distributive translation still creates a contrast with the nighttime raids of a bandit and with Jesus' being arrested at night. If the substance as well as wording of v 49a comes from Mark, the daily teaching in the temple does not support the early visits of Jesus to the temple and Jerusalem of which the Gospel of John speaks.

In v 49b ἀλλ', "but," slightly favors that the subsequent ἵνα-clause concerning fulfilment of the Scriptures represents Jesus' words rather than an editorial comment. If he referred to Scriptures elsewhere (cf. esp. the non-specific references in 9:12, 13; 14:21; also 1 Cor 15:3-4), he may have referred to them here, too. It is better to fill in an ellipsis ("but [this has happened] in order that the Scriptures should be fulfilled") than to reject a normally telic ἵνα in favor of an abnormally imperatival ἵνα ("but let the Scriptures be fulfilled"; cf. the notes on 5:23). Only in v 49b does fulfilment of the OT come into Mark, and even then without quotation of a particular passage. Elsewhere things are said to happen in accordance with the OT (1:2; 9:12-13; 14:21) and because of the OT (14:27). Mark emphasizes Jesus' predictions and narrates their fulfilments rather than quoting the OT as fulfilled (see A. Suhl, Funktion).

L. Schenke (Studien 360) does not consider v 50 emphatic enough to count as a fulfilment of Jesus' prediction that the disciples will be tripped up and scattered (v 28). But the use of πάντες, "all," in both passages gainsays this opinion. Verse 50 does not describe a flight all the way to Galilee; for Peter will soon enter the high priest's courtyard (v 54), and as late as 16:7 the disciples will need a command to go to Galilee (D. Catchpole in JTSA 18 [1977] 5). That "all" forsook Jesus and fled implies that Peter, James, John and the rest of the Twelve (except for Judas) have come back in view since vv 33-42. The flight of all the disciples explains why Jesus alone was arrested. Though the bargain for betrayal and the signal of a kiss have made clear that the crowd came to arrest Jesus, not the disciples, the seizing of the young man in vv 51-52 suggests that if the disciples had not all fled, they too would have been arrested. It normally happens in persecution that leaders, like Jesus, are targeted first and mainly, however. E. Schweizer (316) thinks that the flight of all the disciples in v 50 would fit better right after the arrest of Jesus in vv 43-47, for they would not linger during Jesus' response. But Mark need not mean that they lingered. Narratively, it is easier for him to mention Jesus' response to arrest right after the arrest itself and to save mention of the flight for a lead into the escape of the young man (vv 51-52). Because the psalmist in Pss 31:12(11); 38:12(11); 88:9, 19(8, 18) has fallen ill, his friends and family have forsaken him out of loathing and his enemies have taken advantage of his incapacitation (cf. Sir 37:2). But Jesus' situation differs. He has not fallen sick. His disciples flee out of fear for their own fate. And his enemies take advantage of finding him apart from a festal assembly. So the psalmic motif of a forsaken and attacked righteous sufferer is doubtfully at play (and N.B. the repeated confession of sin in Ps 38:3, 4, 5, 18). Mark is writing up historical tradition, not spinning wholecloth out of the OT. Nor was anyone before him spinning wholecloth out of the OT. See R. Feldmeier, *Krisis* 161-62, for other arguments. J. B. Tyson (in *The Messianic Secret* 37) argues that the disciples would not have fled had Jesus really predicted to them his death and resurrection. But foreknowledge of a danger or disaster need not keep one from trying to avoid it. On the contrary, such foreknowledge may have the opposite effect (cf. 13:14-16).

According to M. Ruhland (*Markuspassion* 43-44), the flight of the disciples originally fulfilled the eschatological flight commanded in 13:14 (cf. 14:38); and the nakedness of the fleeing young man paralleled 13:16. But the worker in the field of 13:16 is to flee without retrieving his overgarment. He will not flee naked, for he will have been wearing his undergarment while working in the field. Moreover, the eschatological flight is to take place "when you see the abomination of desolation standing where he ought not [to stand]"; but nobody has yet seen that abomination.

Against interpreting vv 51-52 as representative of Jesus' arrest, death, burial, and resurrection, M. Gourges (in *NTS* 27 [1980-81] 675) notes that Jesus was arrested but not the young man and that Jesus did not even try to escape whereas the young man both tried and succeeded. But the young man was seized, i.e. arrested, just as Jesus was seized, i.e. arrested (cf. vv 44, 46, 48, 51, esp. 46b and 51b); and the escape of the young man does not contradict the death of Jesus so much as it anticipates his resurrection. By symbolizing his burial in a linen cloth, the wearing of a linen cloth by the young man actually implies Jesus' death.

F. Kermode (*Genesis of Secrecy* 55-64) and H. Fleddermann (in *CBQ* 41 [1979] 412-18) represent a common interpretation of the young man in their saying that he is a figure of desertion, a typical deserter whose flight from persecution represents the universal flight of the disciples and their rejection of the Cross. This interpretation is considerably weakened by the facts that the young man was continuing to follow with Jesus after the disciples had all fled, that the young man fled only when seized whereas the disciples fled before they could be seized, and that the disciples are said to have deserted Jesus when they fled (ἀφέντες αὐτόν) but the young man is not said to have deserted him when he fled. He is said instead to have deserted his linen cloth (καταλιπὼν τὴν σινδόνα). Besides, since the disciples are said to have deserted Jesus, there is no need to manufacture a fictive figure of desertion. The disciples themselves represent it. And the details of the young man's linen cloth and nakedness do not link up with the flight of the disciples.

Deprived of his garment, according to Gen 39:12-13, Joseph fled seduction. Naked, according to Amos 2:16, even courageous heroes will flee battle. Without his linen cloth and completely naked, the present young man flees arrest. The differences between what is fled weaken the argument that the shared element of naked flight shows vv 51-52 to have been fabricated out of one or both of the OT passages. Unlike the present young man, Joseph is not said to have fled naked (though *T. Jos.* 8:3 deduces that he did), nor is Joseph used as a type elsewhere in Mark. A linen cloth plays no part either in the story of Joseph or in Amos 2:16. The present young man has not been a courageous hero like the גבורים of Amos 2:16. And the LXX of Amos 2:16 uses διώξεται, "will be pursued," whereas Mark

14:52 uses ἔφυγεν, "fled" (see also A. Vanhoye in *Bib* 52 [1971] 401-6 against C. G. Montefiore, *Synoptic Gospels* 1. 349-50; H. Waetjen in *ASTI* 4 [1965] 117-20).

Taking a historical standpoint, W. L. Lane (527) infers from the expensiveness of linen that the young man wearing it belonged to a wealthy family, and from the absence of any other clothing that he had dressed hastily to accompany Jesus. On the basis of these inferences Lane goes on to suggest an equation of the young man with John Mark. In support of this suggestion we might add that according to Acts 12:12-13 the house of John Mark's mother had room enough to hold a sizeable number of disciples (ἱκανοί) and had a maid to open the door (παιδίσκη). L. Johnson (in *ExpTim* 77 [1965-66] 158) surmises that as a young man whose father had died, John Mark hosted the Last Supper, stayed at home, went to bed, got up in anxiety, went to Gethsemane, and arrived just in time to see Jesus' arrest. G. Robinson (*NT Detection* 69) surmises that Judas Iscariot had brought the arresters to John Mark's house after the departure of Jesus and, not finding Jesus, went to Gethsemane in hope of finding him there, and that John Mark had awakened and trailed after them as a result of their arrival at and departure from his house. Though conjectural, varying in probability, and non-contributory to Mark's point, such suggestions should not be lightly dismissed (yet see the notes on 15:46 against regarding linen as a particularly expensive material). They also expose the weakness of M.-J. Lagrange's argument (396-97) that the Last Supper could not have taken place at the young man's house because he is dressed in a night garment. Lagrange's own suggestion remains possible, however. It is that the young man lived in a house on the property of Gethsemane and got up to see what was happening. Following with Jesus to Gethsemane would forestall this possibility; but the young man follows with Jesus from Gethsemane, after Jesus' arrest and the flight of the eleven. In this respect, the earlier suggestions need modification: the following with Jesus should not be referred to John Mark's going to Gethsemane. The text says nothing about that. Papias's statement that Mark "neither heard the Lord nor followed him" (Eus. *H.E.* 3.39.15) may militate against an identification of the young man with John Mark; but the statement may merely show that Papias failed to equate the young man with John Mark or may merely mean that John Mark did not follow Jesus as a full-time auditor of Jesus' teaching.

R. Pesch (2. 402) says that as in 5:37, συνηκολούθει indicates a non-religious following. True, but in 5:37 the three who followed with Jesus into Jairus's house — Peter, James, and John — followed him religiously, too; and the non-compounded ἀκολουθέω occurs for non-religious following in 2:15; 3:7; 5:24; 11:9; 14:13, 54. So the difference between the compounded and non-compounded forms of this verb does not lie in a distinction between non-religious and religious following, but in the distinction between simple following and following so closely as to be with Jesus in contrast to the distance of others. Whether the present young man followed Jesus religiously as well as physically remains unknown, then. The singular αὐτῷ can hardly mean that he followed Jesus with the crowd; for Mark has not used "crowd" since v 43, and in the meantime he has twice referred to the crowd with the plural αὐτοῖς, "them" (vv 44, 48). So the young man was following close to Jesus, not following along with the crowd as they were following Jesus. They were not following him anyway, but had come to arrest him and lead him off (vv 44, 48-49, 53).

Because the linen cloth was on his naked body, the young man fled stark naked when leaving the linen cloth in the clutches of his would-be captors. Omission of "on [his] naked [body]" with W *f*¹ c k sy^s sa^mss would allow him to flee naked of an outer linen cloth but still wearing an undergarment (χιτών). Though favored by V. Taylor (561-62), the omissive v.l. looks like an attempt to avoid stark nakedness; and external support for omission lacks sufficient weight. For further discussion of vv 51-52, including refutation of their baptismal interpretation, see the excursus on the Secret Gospel of Mark just following the notes on 10:46-52.

THE FULFILMENTS OF JESUS' PREDICTIONS OF HIS REJECTION BY THE SANHEDRIN AND OF PETER'S DENIALS

14:53-72 (Matt 26:57-75; Luke 22:54-71; John 18:12-27)

This pericope is often regarded as two pericopes, the first having to do with the Sanhedrin's trying Jesus (vv 53-65), the second with Peter's denying him (vv 66-72). It is better, however, to see a single pericope in which Mark introduces both events (vv 53-54) and then narrates in succession the trial of Jesus before the Sanhedrin (vv 55-65) and the synchronous denials of Jesus by Peter (vv 66-72). Thus the denials do not appear to be a sidelight to Jesus' trial. On the contrary, they carry just as much weight, and do so to emphasize the exact fulfilment of his prediction of them. By putting his trial alongside Peter's denials and giving them a common introduction, moreover, Mark makes the trial a similar fulfilment of Jesus' passion predictions. The whole, then, turns into a double apologetic appeal to Jesus' predictive power.

The introduction (vv 53-54) subdivides into the taking of Jesus to the high priest (v 53a), the gathering of the Sanhedrin (v 53b), and Peter's following (v 54). Mark is now in a position to take up both Jesus' trial before the Sanhedrin and Peter's denials. The trial subdivides into the seeking of admissible testimony against Jesus (v 55), the failure of the search (vv 56-59), the high priest's interrogation of Jesus (vv 60-62), the Sanhedrin's condemnation of Jesus (vv 63-65), and the abuse of him (v 65). The denials subdivide into the first (vv 66-68a), the second (vv 68b-70a), and the third (vv 70b-72).

Ordinarily Mark uses the adversative δέ, "but," sparingly and puts the subjects of his verbs after them. Not so in vv 53-72, however. Both action and dialogue shift back and forth so often that to emphasize the shifts in actors and speakers Mark uses the adversative δέ in vv 55a, 61a, 62a, 63a, 64c, 68a, 70a, 71 and puts subjects before verbs in vv 54a, 55a, 56a, 56b, 57, 60a (but not οὗτοι, "these," in v 60b, because the demonstrative force of this pronoun regularly causes it to precede a verb of which it is the subject), 61a, 61b, 62a, 63a, 64c, 65b, 68b (ἀλέκτωρ, "a cock"), 69 (ἡ παιδίσκη, "the maid," but not οὗτος, "this [man]"), 70a, 70b, 71a, 72a. These two ways of emphasizing shifts in actors and speakers coincide in vv 55a, 61a, 62a, 63a, 64c, 68a, 70a, 71a.

14:53-54 *(Matt 26:57-58; Luke 22:54-55; John 12:12-16, 18)* The leading away of Jesus corresponds to Judas Iscariot's instructions in v 44. Forms of ἀπάγω, "lead away," occur both here and there (cf. 15:16). The replacement of "securely" (v 44) with "to the high priest" prepares for the high priest's courtyard in the next verse and for his presiding role in vv 55-64. The coming together of "the chief priests and the elders and the scribes" (cf. 15:1 for the same order) corresponds to Jesus' passion predictions (8:31; 10:33). The historical present tense of "come together" underlines this correspondence; and by indicating the full body of the Sanhedrin, made up of representatives from these three classes, "all" stresses the completeness with which those predictions are being fulfilled (cf. v 55). Peter's following Jesus "from afar" contrasts with the young man's following "with" (συν-) Jesus (v 51) and thus preserves the fulfilment of Jesus' prediction that all his disciples would be scattered (see v 50 with v 27). The forward position of ὁ Πέτρος ἀπὸ μακρόθεν, "Peter from afar," enhances the contrast — and thus the preservation — by emphasizing that the distance at which Peter follows avoids a contradiction of his having fled. Though his flight has put him at a distance, however, Peter's following shows a determination to die with Jesus if necessary (cf. v 31) and therefore points up the unlikelihood of a fulfilment of Jesus' prediction that Peter will deny him three times this very night (v 30). Mark does not mention the stopping and turning around that following at a distance required of a fleeing Peter; for to have mentioned them would have detracted from the flight which fulfilled a prediction of Jesus, and the inference comes easily. That Peter "followed him as far as inside, [i.e.] into the courtyard of the high priest, and was sitting down with the servants and was warming himself [facing] toward the light [of the fire]" does not merely complete Mark's preparations for the story of Peter's denials. It supports with further details the already implied unlikelihood that Jesus' prediction of those denials will reach fulfilment. In particular, Mark's doubling his notice of the length to which Peter follows Jesus ("as far as inside" and "into the courtyard of the high priest"), putting these notices in an asyndetic relation to each other, and mentioning the company of the servants of the high priest (perhaps also of other Sanhedrists) and Peter's risking identification in the firelight heighten the unlikelihood by detailing those actions of Peter that seem to augur a fulfilment of his prediction rather than Jesus's. But the greater the unlikelihood that Jesus will win the contest of predictive ability, the greater the impressiveness of his victory.

14:55-59 *(Matt 26:59-61)* Mark mentions the chief priests again, but omits listing the elders and the scribes (cf. v 53). Instead, he summarizes with "the whole Sanhedrin" (cf. 15:1 and "all" in 14:53) to stress once more the completeness with which Jesus' passion predictions are coming to fulfilment (see the comments and notes on v 53). The forward position of "the chief priests and the whole Sanhedrin" enhances this stress. The Sanhedrin's seeking testimony against Jesus in order that they might put him to death (cf. the phraseology of Ps 36:32 LXX) also fulfils these passion predictions. The iterative imperfect of ἐζήτουν, "were seeking" (BDF §327), emphasizes the fulfilment. At the same time, this statement creates sympathy for Jesus in that the Sanhedrin are so bent on his death that they have hauled him to trial before finding testimony against him. Their finding no testimony because false witnesses are contradicting one another implies that the Sanhedrin are seeking true testimony, but their failure to find such testimony serves Mark's apologetic purpose of showing that Jesus does not deserve condemnation. The iterative imperfect of οὐχ ηὕρισκον, "were not finding," and of ἐψευδομαρτύρουν, "were testifying falsely," emphasize his innocence. That the bearing of false witness breaks the commandment, "You should not bear false witness" (10:19), makes his innocence stand out in bold relief. "Many" narrows down from "the whole Sanhedrin." The large number of false witnesses also emphasizes the Sanhedrin's failure to find true testimony, for the agreement of only two witnesses would have sufficed to establish the truth of an accusation

(Num 35:30; Deut 17:6; 19:15; 11QTemple 61:6-7; Josephus *Ant.* 4.8.15 §219). The forward positions of πολλοί, "many," ἴσαι, "equal [i.e. in agreement with each other]," and αἱ μαρτυρίαι, "the testimonies," put even further emphasis on this failure. "Some" narrows down from "many" just as "many" narrowed down from "the whole Sanhedrin"; and the forward position of τινες, "some," turns attention to the false testimony that these some spoke against Jesus: "We ourselves heard him saying, 'I myself will destroy this handmade temple and in three days will build another one, not handmade' " (cf. 15:29). Mark's audience know from 13:1-2 that Jesus made quite a different prediction about the temple and that these witnesses were not in Jesus' audience though they may have seen and heard him act and speak in behalf of the temple to make it into a divinely intended house of prayer for all the nations (11:15-17). To emphasize the falsity of the witnesses' claim to have heard Jesus make the prediction which they attribute to him, Mark writes an emphatic ἡμεῖς, "we ourselves," before "heard him saying." To emphasize the false elements in the purported prediction, he writes an emphatic ἐγώ, "I myself," before "will destroy the temple" (in 13:2 Jesus did not portray himself as destroyer of the temple), places "this the handmade" (τοῦτον τὸν χειροποίητον) after "the temple" (in 13:2 he did not disparage the temple thus), and places "in three days" at the head of the next clause and "another [temple] not handmade" in chiastic position before "[I myself] will build" (none of which corresponds even remotely to Jesus' prediction in 13:2). Similarly, the forward position of οὐδὲ οὕτως ἴσα, "not even thus equal," stresses the disagreement that exposed the falsity of the witnesses' testimony. They did not agree with each other even when restricted in number ("some" as opposed to "many") and testifying on the same point (what Jesus said about the temple as opposed to multiple accusations by the many). Whether or not Mark wants his audience to think that the false witnesses had seen and heard Jesus act and speak in behalf of the temple, Mark probably means his audience to infer that Jesus' having reformatively cleansed the temple gave the lie in advance to any testimony which would attribute to him a determination to destroy and replace it.

14:60-62 *(Matt 26:62-64; Luke 22:67-70; John 12:19-21)* The focus narrows down yet again, this time from the some who bore false witness to the high priest who is chairing the session. His standing up parallels their standing up and thereby puts him, like them, in a prosecutorial role. "In the midst" provides an audience for his following address to the rest of the Sanhedrin (vv 63-64). But first he asks Jesus, "You're making no answer, are you? What [is it that] these [witnesses] are testifying against you?" (see also v 40 for ἀποκρίνομαι plus an accusative of direct object; cf. 15:4, 5). The forward position of σου, "you," accentuates Jesus as the accused. Mark doubles Jesus' refusal to answer — "but he kept silent, and he made no answer" — to emphasize Jesus' strength in withstanding the attempt to browbeat him into an admission of guilt. With regard to ἀποκρίνομαι, "answer," M. Zerwick (*Biblical Greek* §229) says that the passive deponent is usual in Hellenistic Greek and that therefore the middle voice adds a note of solemnity. If so, the solemnity in the middle voice of ἀπεκρίνατο (v 61a) reinforces the emphasis on Jesus' strength in withstanding the high priest's attempt (contrast 15:5 and see the comments ad loc.). Perhaps Jesus' refusal to answer also shows an acceptance of his passion as the Father's will (cf. vv 36, 39).

To another question from the high priest, "Are you the Christ, the Son of the Blessed One?" Jesus does make answer; for though he is no criminal, he *is* the Christ and God's Son. Mark emphasizes the question of Jesus' christhood and divine sonship by introducing it with asyndeton (startling enough to cause its elimination in some of the textual tradition), by escalating the aorist ἐπηρώτησεν plus the participle λέγων ("asked . . . saying" — v 60) to the imperfect ἐπηρώτα plus the coordinate clause καὶ λέγει αὐτῷ ("was asking . . . and he says to them" — v 61b), by using the historical present tense in λέγει even though pairing λέγει with a preceding imperfect tense in ἐπηρώτα, and by using the unnecessary σύ, "you" (contrast its absence in v 70). Σύ may carry a note of contempt: "you of all people" (E. Lohmeyer 328). Jesus' affirmation, "I am" (cf. 1 Tim 6:13), feeds into Mark's writing this gospel to argue for Jesus' christhood and divine sonship despite the scandal of the Cross.

"And you will see the Son of man sitting at the right [hand] of the Power and coming with the clouds of heaven" exhibits the ongoing ability of Jesus to predict his own destiny — this time in respect of what will happen to him after the Crucifixion and Resurrection — right as his passion predictions are in a process of fulfilment that insures to Mark's audience the fulfilment of this further prediction. It also feeds into Mark's portraying Jesus as a figure who shares the power and glory of God himself, the appearance of a crucifixion to the contrary notwithstanding (cf. 13:26). The second person plural of ὄψεσθε, "you will see," directs Jesus' answer broadly to the whole Sanhedrin rather than narrowly to the interrogating high priest (cf. "they will see" in 13:26). The rest of the phraseology comes from Ps 110(109):1; Dan 7:13; but "sitting at the right [hand] of the Power" intervenes between "the Son of man" and "coming with the clouds of heaven" for emphasis on Jesus' exalted position (contrast 13:26), and within the intervening phrase ἐκ δεξιῶν, "at the right [hand]," jumps ahead of καθήμενον, "sitting," and away from the dependent τῆς δυνάμεως, "the Power," to stress with chiasm the Son of man's position as the highest and most favorable one possible. By comparison, the Sanhedrin have no power. So heavy is this stress that "power" no longer represents a surrounding circumstance (9:1) or a large angelic army (13:26) — much less, in the plural, astral deities (13:26) — but the very person of God. As such a representation, "Power" jumps back from the Son of man's "coming in clouds with much power and glory" (13:26), gains a definite article, substitutes for an expected "God" in the preceding reference to heavenly session (cf. Acts 2:34-35 with 2:36; Rom 8:34; Eph 1:20 with 1:17; Col 3:1; Heb 10:12; 12:2; Mark 16:19; contrast Luke 22:69), loses "much" to accommodate the new titular usage, and leaves "glory" unattended and unmentioned but allows "the clouds" to regain the Danielic addition "of heaven" (see R. H. Gundry, *Use of the OT* 60-61; M. Black in *SJT* 39 [1986] 12-17). Now that "with" no longer governs "much power and glory" (13:26), it takes the place of "in" with "the clouds of heaven" (so also Dan 7:13 MT Theod). Jesus' prediction refers to a single, literal seeing of the Son of man at the last day. Heaven will open and he will be visible sitting at the right hand of the Power. "Sitting" does not mean "taking a seat," but "in a seated position." Then leaving that position but still in full view, the Son of man will come with the clouds of heaven. (Matthew and Luke prolong the seeing and the sitting, respectively.) Sitting at the right hand of the Power and coming with the clouds of heaven, the Son of man will not as now be subject to judgment by the Sanhedrin. The Power in heaven will vindicate him.

14:63-65 *(Matt 26:65-68; John 12:22-24)* Δέ, "but," shifts attention to the high priest (contrast vv 61, 62). His tearing the undergarments that he is wearing (τοὺς χιτῶνας αὐτοῦ), where we expect him to tear only his outer garments (τὰ ἱμάτια αὐτοῦ — see Matt 26:65; Acts 14:14; 16:22; and the LXX of Gen 37:29, 34; 44:13; Lev 10:6; 13:45; Josh 7:6; Judg 11:35 et passim), and the historical present tense of λέγει, "says," intensify both the question, "Why do we still have need of witnesses?" and the declaration, "You have heard blasphemy" (yet Mark's audience know better, for in 1:11; 9:7 none other than God the Father has called Jesus his beloved Son), and also the further question, "How does it appear to you?" The intensification in tearing down to the bare skin and in the historical present tense stresses the high degree of fulfilment reached by the prediction of Jesus that the Sanhedrin would reject and condemn him. The forward positions of ἔτι, "still," and χρείαν, "need," serve the high priest's implication that the Sanhedrin no longer lack the evidence which they have been seeking. The forward position of ὑμῖν, "to you," is designed to evoke a response from the Sanhedrin. And respond they do. The "all" who came together with the high priest in v 53 now join in condemning Jesus as liable to the death penalty. As in v 53, "all" emphasizes the completeness with which Jesus' passion predictions are being fulfilled, especially the one which said that the chief priests and scribes would "condemn him to death" (10:33). The fact that the "all" who condemn him includes Joseph of Arimathea (cf. βουλευτής, "councilor," in 15:43 with συμβούλιον, "counsel," in 15:1) even though Joseph enjoys a good reputation, lives in expectation of God's kingdom, will dare to ask Pilate for Jesus' corpse, and will give it a proper burial — this fact shows to what length Mark is going to emphasize completeness of fulfilment. The forward position of ἔνοχον, "liable," emphasizes what the Sanhedrin think to be Jesus' liability. Liability to the death penalty leaves room for the Roman trial and crucifixion of Jesus (cf. 10:33-34; 15:1, 15; E. Bickermann in *RHR* 112 [1935] 180-83). Execution for blasphemy would have been carried out by stoning (Lev 24:10-16; Josephus *Ant.* 4.8.6 §202; Philo *Mos.* 2.37 §202; *m. Sanh.* 7:4; cf. Num 15:30-31 with 15:32-36).

Again the action narrows down to "some" (cf. v 57). These members of the Sanhedrin spit on Jesus, cover his face, cuff him, and tell him to prophesy. Mark reveals neither the purpose for which they cover Jesus' face nor what they challenge him to prophesy (contrast the question, "Who is the one who hit you?" in some vv.ll., Matthew, and Luke). It is their actions as such that interest Mark, because those actions fulfil the passion predictions. In particular, the challenge to prophesy highlights finely and ironically the fulfilment of Jesus' prophecy that they would reject him. The action narrows down yet further to "the servants" (οἱ ὑπηρέται). To evoke sympathy for Jesus, the statement that they "received him with slaps" (a Latinism for "treated him to blows" — see C. F. D. Moule, *Idiom-Book* 192) puts αὐτόν, "him," before the verb and ῥαπίσμασιν, "with slaps," even before αὐτόν. The statement also seems to imply that at the close of the Sanhedrin's deliberation Jesus was brought "below" to "the courtyard," where the servants (ὑπηρέται) were sitting the last time Mark wrote about them (cf. vv 54 and 66, and see the following notes on v 65). Since Peter was then sitting with them, their mention here makes a fitting lead into the story of his denials (vv 66-72). Why does Mark go into such extensive detail on the condemnation and abuse of Jesus? The answer is clear: the greater the detail, the greater the impressiveness of the fulfilment of Jesus' predictions that he would be rejected by the Sanhedrin (8:31; 9:12) and condemned to death and mocked and spit upon (9:31; 10:33-34; cf. 15:19). And the interweaving of Jesus' trial and Peter's denials (see also vv 53-54) brings out the double fulfilment of Jesus' predictions of his own condemnation to death by the Sanhedrin and of Peter's denials. By framing the challenge that Jesus prophesy, these two fulfilments ironically show him to be the prophet that the Sanhedrin think he is not.

14:66-68a *(Matt 26:69-70; Luke 22:56-57; John 18:17)* "And while Peter was below in the courtyard" harks back to v 54 and moves the narrative backward to pick up what Peter was doing during Jesus' trial before the Sanhedrin. The historical present tense of ἔρχεται, "comes," and of λέγει, "says," headlines this shift to the fulfilment of Jesus' prediction that Peter would deny him three times (v 30). The action has now narrowed down to "one (μία) of the maids of the high priest." That it is a mere maid whose comment prompts Peter's first denial (and his second, too — vv 69-70a) contrasts his babbling weakness with the quiet strength of Jesus, who resisted pressure from a personage no less imposing than the high priest. It also makes more impressive the fulfilment of Jesus' prediction, for Peter is not liable to deny Jesus under pressure from a mere maid. Mark's mentioning that the maid belongs to the high priest supports these contrastive points. "Seeing (ἰδοῦσα) Peter warming himself" harks back to v 54, where Mark called the fire τὸ φῶς, "the light," to prepare for the maid's seeing Peter despite nighttime. Her "staring (ἐμβλέψασα) at him" may be due to dimness of light. It may also be meant to parallel her master's standing up just before speaking to Jesus (v 60). The doubling and intensification of the maid's observation of Peter, the asyndeton between "seeing . . ." and "staring . . . ," and the historical present tense of λέγει, "she says," build up to her "were" to emphasize that not only had Peter been with Jesus (as Jesus appointed him to be — 3:14) but also that Jesus is a Nazarene (cf. 1:9, 24; 10:47; 16:6) and thus opposed to and despised by the Jerusalemites with whom Peter is sitting. Peter's first denial takes the form of feigned ignorance, emphatic in its doubling and in its incorrect use of "neither . . . nor" with synonymous verbs: "I neither know nor understand what you are saying." Once more Mark emphasizes "you" by using σύ in addition to the second person singular verbal ending (again contrast v 70). He also puts σύ ahead of τί, "what," for a contrast with the maid's καὶ σύ, "you, too." Perhaps Peter means to cast aspersion on the maid's Judean accent as incomprehensible — a denial of Jesus that seeks a linguistic way of escape.

14:68b-70a *(Matt 26:71-72; Luke 22:58; John 18:25)* Peter exits into the forecourt to escape the pressure. But Jesus' prediction will catch up with him. The text critical question whether Mark wrote, "And the cock crowed," is finely balanced as to external evidence (see the *UBSGNT* ad loc.) and internal criteria (see B. Metzger, *Textual Commentary* ad loc., regarding the possibilities of copyists' adding the words to correspond to v 30 and to enable Peter to count the next cockcrowing as the second one and, on the other hand, of copyists' assimilating Mark to the omissions in the other gospels, perhaps to avoid the question why Peter does not repent on hearing the cock crow the first time). If the statement belongs in Mark, the evangelist himself — true to his emphasis elsewhere on Jesus' predictive power — writes it to stress exactness and completeness in the fulfilment of Jesus' prediction at v 30: ". . . before the cock crows twice. . . ." In fact, since Peter will hear the cock crow the second time in v 72, there is no reason to think that he does not hear the cock crow the first time in v 68. But so sure is Jesus' prediction to be fulfilled that the first cockcrow fails to warn Peter off from the second and third denials (C. Maurer in *Redaktion und Theologie des Passionsberichtes nach den Synoptikern* 122). Nor does his exit rid him of the maid. Rather, "seeing him she began again to speak" — yet this time not to him or to those with whom he had been sitting to warm himself at the fire, but to the bystanders outside in the forecourt, where he has gone (and apparently the maid, too). For not only does their standing distinguish them from the sitters in the courtyard, but also they will shortly address Peter where he is. The maid's comment shifts slightly from the being of Peter, too, with Jesus (v 67) to his belonging to the band of Jesus' disciples: "This [man] is [one] of them." The forward position of ἐξ αὐτῶν, "of them," underscores this belonging. Peter hears what she says to the bystanders, and the "again" of her second comment is matched by the "again" of his second denial. Two down, one to go — Mark is counting.

14:70b-72 *(Matt 26:73-75; Luke 22:59-62; John 18:26-27)* "And after a little [while]" shows that the fulfilment of Jesus' prediction is hastening toward completion. "Again" marks the third and final test of predictive accuracy and does not imply that the bystanders to whom the maid spoke the last time and who now speak to Peter have spoken to him before, but only that he is addressed in this third test as he was in the first one. The bystanders administer the third test by saying to Peter, "Truly you are [one] of them." The meaning and first position of ἀληθῶς, "truly," and again the forward position of ἐξ αὐτῶν, "of them," reinforce the test by emphasizing the bystanders' conviction that the maid was correct in identifying Peter as one of Jesus' disciples. "For you, too [like them], are a Galilean" continues the reinforcement by giving the reason for their conviction (and probably alludes to a difference in accent — so Matt 26:73; cf. Acts 2:7; *b. ʿErub.* 53b; *b. Meg.* 24b). The forward position of Γαλιλαῖος, "Galilean," sharpens the geographic point. Non-use of σύ, "you," in the bystanders' two statements confirms an emphasis in preceding instances of this and other nominative personal pronouns (v 58 — ἡμεῖς, "we," and ἐγώ, "I"; v 61 — σύ; v 62 — ἐγώ; v 67 — σύ; v 68 — σύ). Peter's starting to curse and swear corresponds to the reinforcement of the third test and leaves no doubt that Jesus' prediction of Peter's denials has reached fulfilment — all the more so in that ἀναθεματίζειν apparently implies Jesus as the object of Peter's cursing (there is no reflexive pronoun here; see G. Bornkamm, *Geschichte und Glaube* 1. 34; idem, *Jesus of Nazareth* 211-12, n. 20; H. Merkel in *The Trial of Jesus* 66-71; G. W. H. Lampe in *BJRL* 55 [1973] 354; J. D. M. Derrett in *NTS* 21 [1974-75] 551, esp. n. 9). Peter's oath-taking, which differs from his cursing, strengthens the denial, "I do not know this man that you are talking about." Whereas the first denial was private and evasive and the second one still evasive but public, the third is direct and public as well as stronger (D. Daube in *Theology* 72 [1969] 293). At first Peter only denied knowing *what* the maid was talking about (οὔτε οἶδα . . . τί λέγεις — v 68). Now he denies knowing *whom* the bystanders are talking about (οὐκ οἶδα . . . ὃν λέγετε); and distantly, perhaps disparagingly, he calls Jesus τὸν ἄνθρωπον τοῦτον, "this man," a far cry both from Jesus' synchronous confession of himself as "the Christ, the Son of the Blessed One" (vv 61-62) and from Peter's own, earlier confession of Jesus as "the Christ" (8:29; against M. Ruhland [*Markuspassion* 10], who sees no relation between the contents of Peter's denials and Jesus' confession). The introduction of each denial with an adversative δέ, "but," has combined with the use of a mere καί, "and," to introduce the statements to and about Peter. Thus the denials stand out distinctly so as to highlight their fulfilment of Jesus' prediction that Peter would deny him three times. We would expect especially the second statement by the maid to have been introduced by an adversative δέ (M. Zerwick, *Untersuchungen* 15). To compensate for non-use of δέ, however, the subject ἡ παιδίσκη, "the maid," moved forward (v 69), as does οἱ παρεστῶτες, "the bystanders," though not so far forward (v 70).

"And immediately" dramatizes the fulfilment of a sole remaining detail in Jesus' prediction: the cockcrow. "A second time" notes the exactitude of its fulfilment, for Jesus said, "Before the cock crows twice, thrice you will deny me." The forward positions of "immediately" and "a second time" accentuate the drama and exactitude of fulfilment. After writing that Peter remembered the prediction (cf. 11:21), Mark requotes it and calls it τὸ ῥῆμα, "the word," which in its only other Marcan occurrence referred to another prediction by Jesus (9:32). The use of "the word" as well as of "how Jesus had said to him" puts double emphasis on the prediction about to be requoted. The very awkwardness of this combination adds to the emphasis. So also does the use of ὡς, "how," instead of ὅ, "which" (so the v.l.), plus a recitative ὅτι, prepared for by ὡς, which points back to the contest of predictive ability in vv 27-31 (see J. N. Birdsall in *NovT* 2 [1958] 272-75 on the use of ὡς to recall a situation as well as to introduce the words spoken therein; and T. Muraoka in *NovT* 7 [1964] 60-63 on a similar Septuagintal usage). Peter's remembering not only gives Mark an opportunity to requote Jesus' prediction; it also provides a basis for Peter's emotional reaction. "Today" and "this night" drop out in the requotation (contrast v 30) to let emphasis concentrate on the numerical aspects of the prediction and its fulfilment. For the same reason Mark delays δίς, "twice," in order that it may chiastically stand alongside τρίς, "thrice," and retains the perfective ἀπ- before -αρνήσῃ (so v 31, but not vv 68, 69) to include all three denials. Peter's weeping dramatizes the fulfilment with pathos. We do not know for sure what ἐπιβαλών means. If it means "putting [his cloak] over [his head]," why the omission of "his cloak" (to say nothing of "his head"; cf. 11:7)? If it means "beginning" (plus a finite verb where English would put an infinitive), why does Mark not use his favorite ἤρξατο, instead (as in D Θ 565 latt sy^{s,p,h} co^{sa} goth arm geo)? If it means "thinking [it] over," why the omission of τὸν νοῦν or τὴν διάνοιαν or a following dative, such as occur elsewhere with this meaning, and why the redundancy with "remembered" earlier in v 72 (see BAGD s.v. ἐπιβάλλω for references)? If it means "going outside," why not the use of ἐξελθών, which occurs in the synoptic parallels and comes from a verb that Mark uses thirty-nine times? Perhaps it is best to say that the expression means something like our colloquial "pushing on" (cf. 4:37) in the non-spatial (i.e. metaphorical) sense of "proceeding," as in *PTebt.* 50. 12; Diog. Laert. 6.27. Thus a good translation would be: "and he proceeded to weep." By adding the agony of defeat in this contest of predictive ability that Peter has lost to Jesus (see vv 27-31 with comments), the pathos of Peter's weeping underlines the fulfilment of Jesus' prediction. Weeping over its fulfilment has replaced the bravado that characterized unbelief in its fulfilment. All in all, as noted by E. Lohmeyer (332-33), the absence of information on Peter's purpose in going to the high priest's courtyard, on the reason for the maid's presence, on the way she knew that Peter had been with Jesus, on what the bystanders did when Peter was unmasked, and on his departure (unless ἐπιβαλών refers to it) and the absence of any condemnation of Peter and of his restoration leave all possible emphasis on fulfilment.

NOTES

Too limited is the choice between the possibilities (1) that vv 53 and 54 formed the traditional introductions to the Sanhedric trial and Peter's denials, respectively, vv 55 and 66 having arisen by way of Marcan composition (except for "one of the maids of the high priest"), and (2) vice versa. Mark may have composed both pairs of verses on the basis of tradition. Moreover, though the story of the trial might easily have circulated without the story of Peter's denials, the story of his denials could hardly have circulated apart from the story of the trial. For the story of the trial provides the only probable framework that could make the story of the denials meaningful with respect to their location, the presence of those who challenged Peter, the absence of Jesus, the cock's crowing before the end of Passover night, and the contrast between Peter's denials and Jesus' confession. So the two stories are likely to have been told together in pre-Marcan tradition (cf. the storytelling device of digression and resumption that C. A. Evans [in *JBL* 101 (1982) 248-49] finds in extra-NT literature where no one would detect a piecing together from different sources).

According to R. E. Brown (*John* 795-96), the omission in Luke 22:66-71 of a Sanhedric sentence condemning Jesus (cf. Luke 18:31-33; Acts 13:28) favors that Mark exaggerates in narrating a formal trial at the conclusion of which the Sanhedrin passes a condemnatory verdict. But Luke omits the verdict to stress Jesus' innocence. Throughout Luke-Acts, redactional emphasis falls on the innocence of Jesus and his followers (see F. J. Matera in *ETL* 65 [1989] 43-59 for Luke 22:66-71 as Luke's redaction of Mark without another source). More broadly, Luke 22:54-71 appears to smooth out the narrative by proceeding directly to the denials from Peter's following Jesus at a distance into the high priest's house. But the desire to maintain narrative continuity couples with this maneuver to postpone the Sanhedric trial till daytime, the abuse of Jesus staying in its original position between the now reversed denials and trial. That in Luke the abuse lacks the occasion of Jesus' condemnation and is consequently inflicted by his arresters rather than by some of the Sanhedrin, who have not yet convened, and that the personal pronouns in Luke 22:63-65 should refer by narrative syntax to Peter but in fact refer to Jesus substantiate Luke's reversal.

Against the view that Luke depends on more reliable non-Marcan tradition, we should note a number of items with respect to Luke 22:63-65: (1) 'Ανήρ, "man," occurs 27 times in Luke and 100 times in Acts, but only 4 times in Mark and 8 times in Matthew. (2) Συνέχω, "hold in custody," occurs 6 times in Luke and 3 times in Acts, but not at all in Mark and only once in Matthew. (3) Δέρω, "beat," occurs 5 times in Luke and 3 times in Acts, but only 3 times in Mark and once in Matthew. (4) Ἕτερος, "other," occurs 33 times in Luke and 17 times in Acts, but not at all in Mark and only 10 times in Matthew. (5) Except for δέρω, Luke often inserts the foregoing words into Marcan tradition (cf. the concordance with a synopsis, the references being too numerous to cite even when occurrences in passages unique to Luke are discounted as possibly attributable to Lucan tradition rather than to redaction). (6) The plural of ἕτερος occurs with a corresponding πολύς, "much, many," in 4 passages that give a clear impression of coming from Luke's hand (Luke 3:18; 8:3; Acts 2:40; 15:35). (7) Ἐπερωτάω, "ask," is inserted into Marcan material in Luke 6:9; 18:40; 20:21 (and Luke 8:9 changes the ἠρώτων of Mark 4:10 to ἐπηρώτων). (8) Ἐνέπαιζον, "were mocking," might easily come from the passion prediction in Luke 18:32 parr. and anticipate the same word in Luke 23:11. (9) "Prophesy: who is he that hit you?" may represent the subsidiary influence of Matthew on Luke (see R. H. Gundry in *The Four Gospels 1992* for numerous other examples of such influence, which would also take away any argument from the shorter text of Mark 14:65 — but see the following notes ad loc. against that text). (10) It falls in line with Luke's heavy redactional emphasis on Jesus' innocence (see, e.g., Luke 23:4, 13-16, 20, 22, 24-26, 40-41, 47) that Luke's statement concerning the mockers, "Blaspheming, they were speaking against him," anticipates *and replaces* the charge that Jesus blasphemed. (11) Though it is argued that Mark 14:55-64 gives no ground for the implication of Mark 14:65 that Jesus claims to be a prophet (for the Christ is no prophet), this argument cuts in the opposite direction, too (for in Luke the testing of Jesus' prophetic ability does not prepare for the trial concerning his christhood); and it overlooks that in Mark, Jesus' prophesying his session at the right hand of the Power and coming with the clouds of heaven does prepare for the test of his prophetic ability, whereas in Luke the test has nothing to prompt it. (12) Nor is there anything wrong with the position of the remaining abuse in Mark 14:65, for the condemnation of Jesus has provided the rationale, and therefore the occasion, for that abuse. (13) There is no need to save the dignity of all the Sanhedrin by denying that any of them would have abused Jesus in the fashion described and by shifting a supposedly earlier referent of "some" to a different set of people; for Acts 22:30–23:10, a passage whose historicity is supported by Paul's having to apologize for an unscriptural insult against the high priest, shows the Sanhedrists, and even the high priest himself, capable of abusive behavior. From the standpoint of religious culture, moreover, such behavior is to be expected: "had the elders not struck Jesus or at least spat on him (we are told they did both), they could not have cleared themselves from implications of condoning the (apparently) outrageous behavior which every pious Jew must abhor" (J. D. M. Derrett, *Oriental Lawyer* 19-20; cf. *b. Mo'ed Qat.* 16a).

Therefore, the different order in Luke 22:54-71 provides no evidence for an original independence of the episodes concerning the trial, the abuse, and the denials, and hence no support for Mark's having advanced the trial from daytime to nighttime so as to sandwich the Sanhedric trial between Peter's entrance into the high priest's courtyard and the denials, or to sandwich the denials between the Sanhedric trial and the Sanhedric consultation. Nor then does the different order in Luke 22:54-71 provide evidence that Mark has transposed the Sanhedric trial and Peter's denials to make them take place synchronously and thus, perhaps by way of attacking Jewish Christianity based in Jerusalem and associated with Peter, to set the denials in sorry contrast with Jesus' confession. This contrast belongs to the tradition, and it is historically just as likely that the Sanhedric trial and Peter's denials took place synchronously as that the denials and the abuse took place synchronously (as in Luke 22:54-71).

To the extent that the Sanhedric trial of Jesus violated almost every judicial regulation known from the Mishnah and to the extent that mishnaic judicial regulations were in force at the time of Jesus, his trial is exposed as unjust or Mark's report of it is exposed as tendentious. It is much debated to what extent those regulations were already in force, however (for a survey of the debate, see D. Juel, *Messiah and Temple* 59-64). Broadly, they exhibit a concern to protect the rights of accused people. The whole book of Susannah (see esp. vv 44-59) and 11QTemple 61:9 prove the existence of such a concern by Jesus' time and therefore favor that the mishnaic judicial regulations enshrine tradition early enough to provide background for the Sanhedric trial of Jesus. Even in capital cases, nonetheless, *b. Sanh.* 46a allows irregularities for emergencies and protection of the Torah. Since we have no reason to doubt such an allowance in Jesus' time and have every reason to believe that the Sanhedrin treated Jesus' case as an emergency fraught with great danger to the Torah, the mishnaic judicial regulations do not compete with the irregularities in Jesus' trial so as to require either a later dating of those regulations or a de-historicizing of that trial. Mark does not explain the irregularities to his Gentile audience. Therefore it seems unlikely that he has fabricated them to make the Sanhedrin look malicious and Jesus maltreated. One could suggest that a Christian before Mark fabricated the irregularities for a Jewish audience who required no explanation. But not only would such a suggestion require the conjecture of a pre-Marcan fabricator. A pre-Marcan date would also decrease the chance of fabrication, and a Christian is unlikely to have fabricated details the falsity of which might easily be recognized and exposed in an early Jewish setting.

Mark has the Sanhedrin meeting in the high priest's house, whereas *m. Sanh.* 11:2 puts their meeting place in the "Chamber of Hewn Stone." Yet an irregular meeting place is not necessarily an illegal one, and Mark does not present the meeting place as illegal. In fact, he mentions the high priest's house only in the introduction to Peter's denials, not in his introduction to Jesus' trial. Against *m. Sanh.* 4:1, the trial takes place on Passover eve. But we know that it does only from earlier Marcan passages; and since Mark does not mention the fact here, neither he nor his tradition is likely to be fabricating an anti-Sanhedric point. He implies that the Sanhedric trial takes place and reaches a capital verdict at night, as *m. Sanh.* 4:1 prohibits. In fact, however, the implication appears only in the materials about Peter's denials and Jesus' delivery to Pilate; so Mark is hardly making a point of nocturnal injustice. According to *m. Sanh.* 4:5, witnesses are to be warned and carefully examined regarding their testimony. But Mark has no reason to mention such a warning. His silence does not imply that there was none. And the Sanhedrin's finding of disagreement in the testimony which they heard against Jesus and consequently throwing out that testimony implies careful examination. Jesus' trial starts with prosecutorial testimony and never comes round to favorable testimony, though *m. Sanh.* 4:1 requires that capital cases start with reasons for acquittal. Mark merely stresses the falsity of the testimony against Jesus and thus its Sanhedrically acknowledged inadmissibility, however, not its being the first and only kind of testimony given. Against *m. Sanh.* 4:1, the Sanhedrin do not wait a day to pass a capital verdict. But Mark neither notes the failure to wait (N.B. the absence of his favorite adverb εὐθύς, "immediately") nor makes a point of illegality.

According to *m. Sanh.* 7:5, a capital verdict cannot be passed against a blasphemer unless the blasphemy has included a pronunciation of the divine name, i.e. of the tetragrammaton (יהוה, YHWH, "Yahweh"). But though Jesus is quoted with a substitute for the tetragrammaton, Mark does not point out any technical violation of the standard by which blasphemy is to be judged. We would have expected not only Mark but also a pre-Marcan Christian who had in mind a legally informed Jewish audience to have done a better job of highlighting illegalities fabricated for the purpose of making the Sanhedrin look malicious and Jesus maltreated.

Against finding a tradition historical background in the suffering of the righteous man in Wis 2:12-20; 5:1-7 (so, among others, J. R. Donahue in *The Passion in Mark* 65-66), the Sanhedrin have sent out to arrest Jesus rather than lying in wait for him (Wis 2:12). They do not detest him because his conduct is strangely holy and accusatorily standoffish (Wis 2:15-16). In answer to a question, he confesses that he is the Christ, the Son of the Blessed One; but he does not boast that God is his Father on the ground and in the sense that God is the Father of righteous people in general (Wis 2:16). He is abused to punish him for having spoken what is judged blasphemous, but not insulted and tortured to test his tolerance and patience (Wis 2:19). He is condemned as liable to the death penalty for having blasphemed, but not condemned to a shameful death for the purpose of testing whether God will protect him from it (Wis 2:20; N.B.: the episode in Mark 15:33-37 will not represent the purpose of Jesus' present condemnation). He refuses to defend himself against false witnesses, but he does not stand confident before God at the last judgment to face his persecutors, who will stand there fearful for their crimes; nor does he say or imply that they will be subject to unfavorable judgment and he to favorable. On the contrary, he says that they will see him sitting at God's right hand and coming with clouds — not subject to judgment at all (against Wis 5:1). Neither he nor Mark portrays his persecutors as shaking with fear and amazement over his vindication at the last judgment (Wis 5:2). Nor is it said that they will acknowledge his being counted among the sons of God, i.e. among the saints, at the last judgment; rather, a Roman centurion will call him God's Son at the Crucifixion (contrast Mark 15:39 with Wis 5:5).

J. Ernst (439) summarizes the different tradition and redaction critical analyses of vv 53-65 by E. Linnemann, *Studien* 127-35, and W. Schenk, *Passionsbericht* 229-43. See also D. Dormeyer, *Passion* 149-50, 157-74; T. A. Mohr (*Markus- und Johannespassion* 252-75). On the other side, O. Betz (in *ANRW* II 25/1. 620-32) argues for unity and historicity. In support of the theory that the Sanhedrin convened only in the morning, as at 15:1, and that having two accounts of Jesus' Sanhedric trial made Mark think of two sessions and therefore led him to put one of them at night, V. Taylor (565, 646) cites Mark's mistaken distinction between two feedings of multitudes (6:35-44; 8:1-9) and the lack of a reference to nighttime in 14:53-65. D. E. Nineham (407) goes on to suggest that vv 55-59 and 61b-64 offer alternative accounts, along with 15:1, of a single morning session. The notes on 8:1-9 have called in question the mistakenness of the distinction between two feedings; but even otherwise, 15:1 will not present another trial leading to a redundant condemnation, but only a consultation growing out of the earlier condemnation and eventuating in Jesus' delivery to Pilate. "Warming himself [facing] toward the light" and especially the use of "light" for "fire" (v 54) *does* imply nighttime for 14:53-65 (see A. N. Sherwin-White, *Roman Society* 44-46, for the possibility of a trial at night). On the other hand, the body of the Sanhedric trial in Luke 22:66b-71 and even that of the Roman trial in Mark 15:1b-15 contain no indications of daytime. The suggestion of a doublet in vv 55-59 and 61b-64 requires that to keep the accusation concerning the temple from competing with the one concerning blasphemy, Mark transforms the first of these two into a false accusation unacceptable to the Sanhedrin. We will discuss reasons to doubt such a transformation, however, and also reasons to trust the historicity of both accusations (reasons such as the un-Marcan portrayal of the Sanhedrin as concerned for truth and the Semitism "through [a literal translation of διά] three days," on the one hand, and the Semitisms "the Blessed One" and "the Power," on the other hand). Since the Sanhedrin hardly condemned Jesus under both accusations, the historicity of both favors the reliability of Mark's account as we have it.

J. R. Donahue (*Are You the Christ?* 211) suggests that Mark writes up vv 53, 55-65 because his community "had undergone trials before Jewish officials," and "one of Mark's purposes in picturing Jesus as being tried is to encourage his community in these trials and to give them a theology for understanding their situation." But Mark's audience were Gentiles (2:18; 5:41; 7:2-4 et passim), who would not have undergone trial before Jewish officials. The many and peculiarly Jewish features of Jesus' trial before the Sanhedrin — such as talk about a temple made with human hands versus another one not so made, the use of "the Christ," "the Blessed One," "the Son of man," "the Power," and the tearing of undergarments on hearing blasphemy — would inhibit an easy application to Christians standing trial before Gentile officials. It is often argued that similarities between 15:2-5 and 14:55-64 show Mark or someone before him to have fabricated 14:55-64 after the pattern and in anticipation of 15:2-5, perhaps (if it was Mark himself) to shift blame from Pilate to the Sanhedrin; for a fabrication in the reverse would have offended Mark's Roman audience, or at least Roman officialdom, whereas he wanted to please them (see, e.g., G. Braumann in *ZNW* 52 [1961] 273-78). But beside reasons to trust the historicity of vv 55-64, close inspection turns up more numerous and substantial dissimilarities than similarities between 15:2-5 and 14:55-64, respectively: (1) "king of the Jews" versus "the Christ, the Son of the Blessed One"; (2) "You are saying ['king of the Jews']" versus "I am [the Christ, the Son of the Blessed One]"; (3) the precedence of a specific question concerning Jesus' office over unspecified multiple accusations versus the reverse order (with a consequent absence from 14:61 of the "no longer" which we read in 15:5); (4) the lack of a specific accusation that Jesus refuses to answer versus the specific accusation concerning the temple and his refusal to answer it; (5) wonderment on Pilate's part versus a successful attempt to draw out Jesus on the high priest's part; and, including Jesus' trial before Pilate (15:6-15), (6) an attempt by Pilate to release Jesus versus an outburst by the high priest against Jesus; and (7) Pilate's succumbing to popular pressure despite a conviction of Jesus' innocence versus the Sanhedrin's reaching a verdict of capital guilt. It is only natural that if Jesus did not defend himself before the Sanhedrin, he would not do so before Pilate, either; and it is only natural that two silences of Jesus should be described in the same phraseology.

One could imagine that a purpose of pleasing the Romans led Mark to make changes by turning "the king of the Jews," which would fall naturally from the lips of a Roman such as Pilate, into "the Christ, the Son of the Blessed One," which would suit a Jewish setting such as the Sanhedrin represents; by turning Jesus' avoidance of a politically seditious claim for himself into a Christian-like confession of his christhood and divine sonship; by replacing Pilate's wonderment and attempt to release Jesus with the high priest's attempt to draw out Jesus and outburst against him; etc. But to the degree that dissimilarities between the passages are recognized, the similarities between them become argumentatively less valuable for establishing a fabrication of one out of the other. And some of the dissimilarities are not so amenable to explanation by a Marcan tendency to please the Romans. For example, how would it please them for Mark to introduce into the Sanhedric trial the specific accusation that Jesus said he would destroy the temple only to build another one in three days? The characterization of the accusations as false would have spoiled any pleasure the Romans might have gotten from the testimony that he had said he would destroy the present temple; and they would have taken displeasure in the very thought of Jesus' building another temple, no matter how long it took, much more if no

longer than three days. Besides, Pilate's having been relieved of his post by the time Mark
wrote (Josephus *Ant.* 18.4.2 §§88-89) makes questionable whether Mark would have tried
to please them by shifting blame from Pilate to the Sanhedrin (or would have succeeded
if he did try). Josephus tried to please the Romans and gave Pilate fairer treatment than
Philo afforded him, but Josephus did not cover up Pilate's blunders (*Ant.* 18.3.1-2 §§55-62;
J.W. 2.9.2-4 §§169-77; cf. *Ant* 18.4.1-2 §§85-89; contrast Philo *Legat.* 38 §§299-303).

The historicity of Jesus' trial before the Sanhedrin is supported by the portrayal of
them as so concerned for truth that they rejected testimony which except for its contradic-
toriness would have served their purpose of putting Jesus to death (contrast Matt 26:59).
This portrayal is antithetical to the bad light in which the Sanhedrin otherwise appear (C. K.
Barrett, *Jesus and the Gospel Tradition* 57). Concerning the question, How could a
Christian have found out what happened at a Sanhedric trial of Jesus, the Sanhedrin, large
as it was, must have had its share of talkers. After the trial, they may have talked about it
despite their antagonism to Jesus, more likely because of it. And some Sanhedrists may
have later converted to the church and reported on the trial (cf. John 12:42; Acts 6:7; 15:5).
Right during it, Peter was sitting with the servants of the Sanhedrin (v 54; cf. vv 66-72),
the very servants who shortly joined their masters in abusing Jesus (v 65). It is not unlikely
that word about the trial circulated then and there. The lack of emphasis on illegal procedure
in the trial also supports historicity, for a Christian fabricator would probably have emphasized illegalities (R. Kempthorne in *SE VII* 284-85).

R. Pesch (2. 425) argues that the high priest's anonymity supports an early date and
provenance in Jerusalem for the tradition concerning Jesus' Sanhedric trial. For only then
and there could the identity of the high priest have been presupposed as well as known.
This argument is not entirely convincing, however; for the story does not require that the
high priest's name be known (cf. D. Lührmann in *NTS* 27 [1980-81] 470, n. 7). From other
sources, of course, we know his name to have been Caiaphas (Matt 26:57; John 11:49;
18:13-14, 24, 28; Josephus *Ant.* 18.2.2 §35; 18.4.3 §95). On his house, see C. Kopp, *Holy
Places* 352-57; M. Broshi in *Jerusalem Revealed* 57-58; N. Avigad, *Discovering Jerusalem*
95-139.

The supposed inconcinnity between the singular and the plural of ἀρχιερεύς within
v 53 (and throughout the rest of the chapter) is no real inconcinnity. The singular refers to
the ruling high priest, the plural to other chief priests; and all the chief priests who come
together include the ruling high priest, to whom Jesus' arresters take him, just as the chief
priests who sent them in v 43 included the ruling high priest whose slave had his ear lopped
off in v 47 (cf. Acts 22:30–23:5). The difference between singular and plural does not
provide a reliable basis, then, for distinguishing between traditions or between tradition
and redaction. Nor does the difference in v 53 between the tenses of "led away" and "come
together" offer such a basis. Mark likes to use the present tense for past events, but he
may have transformed a past tense in the tradition into the present tense as easily as he
may have fabricated a brand new statement using the present tense (to mention only two
of several possibilities — against T. A. Mohr, *Markus- und Johannespassion* 254).

For the Great Sanhedrin, the supreme court of seventy-one members, see *m. Sanh.*
1:6; W. L. Lane 530-32; for various views of it, H. Mantel in *EncJud* 14. 836-39; S. Westerholm, *Jesus and Scribal Authority* 40-42; and on the order of the three classes making
up the Sanhedrin, see the excursus just following the comments on 8:31-32a. Perhaps after
the pattern of the Great Sanhedrin, the synagogue at Alexandria had seventy-one elders
(*t. Sukk.* 4:6). The suggestion that a quorum of twenty-three members would satisfy the
demands of "all the chief priests and the elders and the scribes" (v 53) and of "the whole
Sanhedrin" (v 55; so Lane 531; R. Pesch 2. 417, 426 et al.) flies in the face of linguistic
probability (for a mere quorum, "all" and "whole" would likely have been avoided), in the
face of Mark's emphasizing the completeness with which Jesus' passion predictions are

being fulfilled, in the face of the rule that a false prophet be tried by the court of seventy-one (*m. Sanh.* 1:5; cf. Mark 14:65), and in the face of the analogy in Josephus *J.W.* 2.20.5 §§570-71, where it is said that in Galilee all members of a Galilean court of seventy-one should hear capital cases. Though it may be easier to imagine the assembly of a mere quorum in the middle of the night, we are in no position to deny the historicity of full attendance. For since 11:18, the Sanhedrin have been seeking how to destroy Jesus (see also 11:27; 12:12, 13, 18; 14:1-2, 10-11, 43). Are any of them likely to have missed the opportunity that Judas has now provided? It is doubtful that the number twenty-three represents a quorum of the Great Sanhedrin in Jerusalem anyway; rather, the number of judges in lower courts (*m. Sanh.* 1:1, 4; S. Safrai in *The Jewish People in the First Century* 1. 392, 397-98).

The *consulting* together of the wicked against the righteous in passages such as Ps 31:14; 71:10 does not quite match the *coming* together of the Sanhedrin in Mark 14:53. The one had the purpose of hatching a plot. The other has the purpose of conducting a trial. And Peter's *following* from a distance in v 54 contrasts with the *standing* at a distance of the psalmist's loved ones, friends, and relatives in Ps 38:12(11). Moreover, this psalmist repeatedly confesses his sins (vv 3, 4, 5, 18). Therefore, the present episode in Jesus' passion is not modeled after the ostracism of a supposedly righteous sufferer in Psalm 38 or after the plottings against truly righteous sufferers in Psalms 31, 47 (cf. the notes on v 50). K. Schubert (in *Jesus and the Politics of His Day* 394) suggests that Peter followed Jesus at a distance to see him manifested triumphantly as Lord and Christ (cf. 8:29, 32). Perhaps so, but one wonders whether Peter would have fled prior to following at a distance if he entertained such an expectation at this juncture. Much more recently than his confession of Jesus' christhood and rebuke of Jesus for predicting the Passion, Peter has seemed to accept that prediction by expressing willingness to die with Jesus, if necessary (v 31). And his denials of Jesus will not breathe an air of confidence in Jesus' triumph. On the use of φῶς for the light of a fire, see BAGD s.v. 1bα; MM s.v. "Warming himself" implies a fire, but Mark uses πρὸς τὸ φῶς, "[facing] toward the light," for reasons explained in the foregoing comments. Those reasons and the generality of the usage to which they here lead eliminate the need to suppose a mistranslation of the Hebrew אוּר as אוֹר, "light," rather than as אוּר, "flame, fire" (so G. W. Buchanan in *ExpTim* 68 [1956] 27).

Do "all" (v 53) and "the whole" (v 55) turn what would otherwise be a mere hearing into a full-fledged trial? Only if we eliminate the already terminated testimonies against Jesus, the accusation that he has spoken blasphemy, and the condemnation of him as liable to the death penalty (14:55-64). Since in 1:32 "all" modified both "the sick" and "the demon-possessed" (for Mark hardly meant to say that people brought to Jesus all the sick but not all the demon-possessed), so in 14:53 "all" modifies not only "the chief priests" but also "the elders" and "the scribes." In v 55, then, "the chief priests" do not stand apart from "the whole Sanhedrin," which would then consist only of the elders and the scribes (cf. E. P. Sanders, *Jesus and Judaism* 311); rather, "the whole Sanhedrin" avoids a re-listing of the elders and the scribes once a mention of the chief priests has recalled the list in v 53. To draw a modern academic analogy, "the teachers of chemistry and the whole faculty" would not imply that the teachers of chemistry lack membership in the faculty. Cf. Acts 22:30 with 23:1.

The repetition of phraseology from v 56a in v 57 and from v 56b in v 59 has suggested to some that vv 55-56 and vv 57-59 may represent different versions of the same tradition. Several factors favor progression in one and the same tradition, however: (1) the narrowing down from "the whole" (v 55) to "many" (v 56), even further to "some" (v 57), and finally to "the high priest" (v 60; cf. similar narrowings down from "all" [v 64] through "some" [v 65a] and "the servants" [v 65b] to "one of the maids of the high priest" [v 66], and earlier from "the disciples" [v 32] to "Peter and James and John" [v 33] to "Peter" [v 37]); (2) the narrowing down from many unspecified testimonies (v 56) to a single specified testimony (vv 57-59), which seems to give an example of the many; (3) the seeking for a single admissible testimony already in v 55; and (4) the implication of "not even thus" in v 59 that the single specified testimony, apparently the last one, came closer to admissibility than the many other unspecified testimonies. One may ascribe these progressions to redaction of different versions that lacked them. But to recognize the progressions is to leave no reason for denying that Mark wrote up a unified tradition in a way that brings them out, or that they belonged to a unified tradition before Mark incorporated it, or that the progressions rest on historical actuality.

L. Schenke (*Der gekreuzigte Christus* 27) detects an inconcinnity in vv 55b-56: it is the second clause of v 56 indicating that the testmonies disagreed with one another which tells why the Sanhedrin failed to find testimony useful for passing a capital sentence against Jesus, whereas that reason should have come from the γάϱ-clause in v 56a: "for many were giving false testimony against him." One has to read the text piecemeal to detect such an inconcinnity, however. Γάϱ is naturally taken to govern the second clause, too. Falsity does tell why the Sanhedrin could not use the testimonies for their purpose. And disagreement among the testimonies does not tell why the Sanhedrin failed to find useful testimony so much as it gives evidence for the falsity of the testimonies which they heard.

In Jewish courts, antagonistic witnesses themselves acted as prosecutors. Like all false testimony, that which is given against Jesus violates the Decalogue (Exod 20:16; Deut 5:20). It would also come close to some of the psalms concerning righteous sufferers (Ps 27:12; 31:19[18]; 35:11; 109:2; cf. Matt 5:11) except for the fact that those psalms offer nothing like the present rejection of false testimony by the very enemies of Jesus. The ϰαί in v 56 is adversative ("but"; so E. C. Maloney, *Semitic Interference* 70); for the disagreement in the testimonies does not oppose the bearing of false witness, but exposes it. Hence, the ϰαί is ecbatic ("with the result that"). To say that "false" and "not in agreement" do not suit each other (so L. Schenke, *Der gekreuzigte Christus* 37) or that "not in agreement" softens "false" (so J. R. Donahue, *Are You the Christ?* 77; idem in *The Passion in Mark* 67) is to miss the ecbasis veiled by the parataxis (cf. E. Best *Following Jesus* 221-22, n. 12). Jesus' use of ἀνίστημι for the standing up of prosecutorial witnesses (Matt 12:41 par. Luke 11:32), the same use in Sus 34, and a similar use of םוּק, "stands up," in 11QTemple 61:7 show that the present such usage (Mark 14:57) need not depend on Ps 26:21 LXX; 34:11 LXX (cf. 108:2-5 LXX).

Despite its puzzling character, says J. D. G. Dunn (*Unity* 324), Jesus' word about the temple (v 58) was preserved because the first Jewish Christians thought that he would return quickly to make the cleansed temple center of the messianic kingdom. But the temple that Jesus cleansed is the temple that he is said to have predicted he would destroy, not the other temple that he is said to have predicted he would build in three days; and the temple that he cleansed was still standing and continued to stand for several decades. Apart from a mistaken attribution to Mark of anti-Jewish Christian bias, it is also unlikely that he would have ascribed to false witnesses a saying treasured by the first Jewish Christians.

J. Jeremias (in *Tradition und Glaube* 221-29) treats the wording of v 58b as a more or less accurate recollection of an enigmatic dominical saying and discovers a temporal outline of catastrophe, three days of tribulation, and the building of a new temple. But the saying does not associate the three days with tribulation; and even when taken as imprecise, a period so short as three days does not allow enough time for the events of the tribulation as described in 13:14-23. One could deny that Jesus stands behind that description; but whatever he expected by way of eschatological tribulation, it seems unlikely to fit into three days. Not only does his traveling toward Jerusalem for three days straight in Luke 13:33 militate against regarding the third day as an eschatological turning point; so also does Luke 13:32 (to which Jeremias appeals), for Jesus' coming to an end on the third day will not mark such a turning point. His resurrection will, yet it follows by another three days. The scheme of three days in Luke 13:32-33 rests on the precise amount of time it took to travel from Galilee to Jerusalem (and Luke devotes a massive amount of attention to Jesus' journey from the one to the other), not on an imprecise amount of time thought to contain the eschatological tribulation (and see the notes on 8:31; R. H. Gundry, *Matthew* 245, against taking three days as imprecise).

Nowhere in Jewish literature is the Messiah portrayed as destroyer of the temple. But already in the OT, God is portrayed as destroyer of the temple (and before that also of the tabernacle — Jer 7:12-15; 26:4-6, 9). He is similarly portrayed in the intertestamental period (*1 Enoch* 90:28-29 — see M. Black, *Book of Enoch* 20, on a date prior to 165 B.C.E. for *1 Enoch* 83-90). Very probably, then, saying that Jesus predicted he would destroy the temple entails a charge that he arrogated to himself a divine role. And since the relevant Jewish literature deals with actual destruction, we need not join P. Joüon (*Grammaire* §113l, n. 3) in treating "I will destroy" as modal for Jesus' ability to destroy the temple rather than as predictive of destruction by him. Matt 26:61 does not represent a modal interpretation of Mark 14:58 so much as it represents a deliberate change (on which see R. H. Gundry, *Matthew* 542).

Nowhere in Jewish literature certainly written before Mark is the Messiah portrayed as builder of the temple. In fact, 4QFlor 1:1-13 passes over a golden opportunity to include such a portrayal. For 2 Sam 7:13 portrays David's seed, whom God calls God's son (cf. Mark 14:61-62) and whom 4QFlor 1:1-13 identifies as the end-time "Shoot of David" (= the Messiah), as builder of God's house (= the temple); but 4QFlor 1:1-13 identifies the builder with someone besides the messianic figure. It does not follow that this preference for another builder (we will shortly discover who it is) implies rejection of an already existing tradition that the Messiah will build the temple (as suggested in passing by D. Juel, *Messiah and Temple* 179). For reaction against an already existing tradition does not always provide the generative force behind the development of a new tradition; and in the case before us, earlier and contemporary evidence of an already existing counter tradition is lacking. Because the pre-Marcan comments on 2 Sam 7:11-14 in 4QFlor 1-2, on Gen 49:10 in 4QPBless 3-4, and on Isa 11:1-4 in 4QpIsaᵃ equate the figure of a branch with the Davidic Messiah, it is inferred that before Mark the Branch who builds the temple in Zech 6:12 must have been understood as the Messiah (ibid. 189-90). But the evidence is only inferential; and we could reason contrariwise that because the Messiah was not at first expected to build the temple, there was hesitation to equate the temple-building Branch in Zech 6:12 with the Messiah. We should also note that in Mark 14:61b πάλιν, "again," need not indicate a question on the same topic as before, i.e. a new version of the question about the alleged temple-saying, as though the destruction and building of the temple relate now to messiahship and divine sonship. Another question is in view, but not necessarily another one on the same topic as before (cf. 7:14, where πάλιν includes the summoning but not the crowd, who have not been summoned before; 14:69, where πάλιν will include the maid's speaking but not the bystanders, to whom she has not spoken before; and 14:70b, where πάλιν includes the speaking to Peter, who has been addressed before, but not the bystanders, who have not spoken to him before). In later Jewish literature the Messiah is only seldom portrayed as builder of the temple (*Lev. Rab.* 9.6 on Lev 7:11-12 par. *Num. Rab.* 13.2 on Num 7:12 par. *Midr. Cant.* 4:16 §1; *Tg. Isa* 53:5; *Tg. Neb.* Zech 6:12). These portrayals may easily stem from a longing for restoration of the temple and of the Davidic kingdom because the Romans destroyed the temple and the Jewish state in 70 C.E. and turned Jerusalem into a Roman colony in 135 C.E.

In Jewish literature written certainly before 70 C.E. and probably before the dates of Mark's writing and Jesus' trial, God is portrayed as builder of the temple (Exod 15:17;

1 Enoch 90:28-29; *Jub.* 1:17; 11QTemple 29:8-10; 4QFlor 1:3, 6 [N.B.: God instead of
the Davidic Messiah — cf. the foregoing discussion]). God continues to be portrayed as
builder of the temple in later Jewish literature, and this portrayal predominates as well as
antedates the portrayal of the Messiah as builder of the temple (see *Sib. Or.* 5:420-33
[shortly after 70 C.E. — J. J. Collins in *The OT Pseudepigrapha* 1. 390] and in rabbinic
literature, esp. *Midr. Ps.* 90:17 §19 [Braude 2. 99], which draws a contrast between the
indestructible temple that God will build and the now destroyed temple that the hands of
flesh and blood built, plus numerous other passages cited in Str-B 1. 1004-5[*b*] and the
Mekilta of R. Ishmael 3 §10 [cited by J. Goldin, *Song at the Sea* 235-39]). Probably, then,
saying that Jesus predicted his building of the temple entails a charge that he arrogated to
himself another divine role. Strengthening this probability is the fact that whereas "handmade" comes to mean "made by human beings," "not handmade" comes to mean "made
by God" (see, e.g., Acts 7:47-50; 17:24, according to which God does not dwell in
handmade structures such as pagan temples or the house that Solomon built for God, but
inhabits what God's own hand has made, i.e. the entire universe, so that "not handmade"
means "made by God's hand rather than by human hands"; similarly, "handmade circumcision" as circumcision performed by human hands [Eph 2:11] in contrast with "circumcision not made with hands" as circumcision performed by God in Christ [Col 2:11-15:
N.B. esp. "the working of God"]).

Saying that Jesus predicted both his destruction of the temple and his building of
another one brings to virtual certainty the entailment of a charge that he arrogated to himself
divine roles. Such a charge fits the attempt of the Sanhedrin to convict Jesus of a capital
offense (cf. 2:6-7); but if Christians believed that Jesus was destroyer of the temple and
builder of another one, none of them would have described as false a testimony that he
predicted his destruction of the one and building of the other. See D. R. A. Hare, *Theme*
26-28, that merely predicting a destruction of the temple (but not by oneself) was probably
not considered a capital offense. In the OT period, Uriah the son of Shemaiah did lose his
life for such a prediction; but Micah of Moresheth did not, nor did Jeremiah (Jeremiah
26). By the first century the possibility of capital punishment had dropped out of Jeremiah's
story (Josephus *Ant.* 10.6.2 §§89-95), and for over seven years just prior to the destruction
of Jerusalem and the temple in 70 C.E. Jesus the son of Ananus predicted that destruction
without suffering execution (Josephus *J.W.* 6.5.3 §§300-309).

The use of "temple, sanctuary" instead of "house" or "kingdom" disfavors an
identification of the new temple with the messianic kingdom of David in accordance with
2 Sam 7:16 (so F. Flückiger in *TZ* 26 [1970] 405). Moreover, God is the maker of David's
house according to 2 Sam 7:11, whereas Jesus is the builder of another temple according
to Mark 14:58. David's house is his dynasty; and his son is the builder of Yahweh's house,
the temple in Jerusalem. Much more commonly, "another temple not handmade" is interpreted as a metaphorical allusion to the Christian community. Nothing in the context of
Mark 14:58 hints at this community, however. The use of ἄλλον, which often means
"another of the same kind," instead of ἕτερον, which sometimes means "another of a
different kind" (cf. J. B. Lightfoot, *Galatians* 76), tends toward a new temple of the same
kind, i.e. a literal building, rather than a new temple of a different kind, i.e. the Christian
community. More decisively, neither Mark nor a Christian before him is likely to have
offered a metaphorical allusion to the Christian community only to characterize as false
the testimony carrying the allusion (against the many efforts of D. Juel [*Messiah and
Temple* 117-39] to find some positive Marcan use of the temple-charge — he constantly
has to posit "a deeper level" of meaning). Christians are portrayed as God's temple in
1 Cor 3:16-17; 6:19; 2 Cor 6:16; Eph 2:21; 1 Pet 2:4-8; Rev 3:12, but never as a temple
not made with hands. The description of the church as "a spiritual house" in 1 Pet 2:5 is
not equivalent to "another [temple] not handmade," for a spiritual house is not a house

made by God (the meaning of "not handmade"), but a house inhabited by God's Spirit, just as "a spiritual person" is one that is inhabited and informed by God's Spirit (to take from 1 Cor 2:6-16 but one of many possible Pauline examples; cf. Eph 2:22). Furthermore, the figure of God's temple carries an individualistic rather than communal meaning almost certainly in 1 Cor 6:19 (R. H. Gundry, *Sōma* 76-78) and probably in 1 Cor 3:16 (if 1 Cor 6:19 provides Paul's own commentary on 1 Cor 3:16, as favored not only by a shared use of ναός, "temple, sanctuary," but also by a shared reference to God's Spirit and a similarity between God's contextual actions of ruination [φθείρει] in 1 Cor 3:17 and abolishment [καταργήσει] in 1 Cor 6:13) and in 2 Cor 6:16 (for separation from idols relates to individual conduct more naturally than to communal behavior — not to discuss the question whether 2 Cor 6:16 belongs to a non-Pauline interpolation). The only certainly communal uses of the figure occur, then, exclusively in later NT literature. Among them, 1 Pet 2:4-8 uses terms other than ναός (the word used in Mark 14:58). Rev 3:12 refers to eschatological incorporation into God and the Lamb (cf. Rev 21:22), not to the present Christian community. Eph 2:21 is left alone.

So far as earlier, Jewish literature is concerned, QL compares the community of God's elect to a temple (1QS 5:5-7; 8:4-10; 9:3-6; CD 3:18–4:10; cf. 1QpHab 12:3-4), but uses "house" (בית), which does not match ναός, and reserves "sanctuary" (מקדש), which does match it, for the temple in Jerusalem. Nor is God said to build the house-community. The seeming exception, CD 3:19, quotes 1 Sam 2:35 with reference to God's building the Zadokite priesthood, not the community as a whole.

It is wrong to cite the raising of Israel on the third day in Hos 6:2 to support a building of the church in three days (as does S. Kim, *"Son of Man"* 79-80); for Hos 6:2 has to do with restoration from apostasy, not with the formation of a new community, and uses the metaphor of healing a wound, not that of building a temple. Neither was the temple in Jerusalem destroyed by Jesus when he died. For it continued to stand for forty years, and Christians continued to worship there. The rending of its veil at Jesus' death did not meet the standard of destruction demanded by καταλύσω in Mark 14:58 and by "a stone will by no means be left here on a stone that will not be torn down (καταλυθῇ)" in 13:2; and the direction of the rending from top to bottom indicates an act of God, not of Jesus. Even though the rending were to portend the destruction of the temple, then, the prediction that Jesus will destroy the temple could not be in view. To say that the rending of the veil signifies the destruction of the temple by Jesus' death in the sense that "the old religious order [of the temple] comes to an end" (D. Juel, *Messiah and Temple* 206) again runs up against the truly Jesuanic prediction in 13:2, for there the temple will be destroyed in the sense that not one of its stones will be left on another.

Nor did Jesus build the Christian community three days after he died, certainly not in Mark, where his disciples were not to see him risen till they arrived in Galilee yet another three days' journey from where they were three days after his death (16:7). They lived as a community long before his resurrection after three days; for already at 3:14 he chose the apostles "that they might be with him," and Mark says nothing else about Jesus' resurrection that could qualify as building the Christian community. Nor does "in (διά) three days" in 14:58 refer to an indeterminately short interval so as to allow more time for Jesus to build the Christian community in the period following his resurrection; for then we would read at least the indeterminate δι' ἡμερῶν, "after [a number of] days," of 2:1, if not δι' ἐτῶν, "after [a number of] years" (cf. Acts 24:17; again see the notes on 8:31 and R. H. Gundry, *Matthew* 245, against an indeterminate meaning of three days). Nor did Jesus build the Christian community three days (whether or not indeterminate) after the destruction of the temple in 70 C.E., for the Christian community had long since been established by that time.

Nor should we think that if "another [temple] not made with hands" stood for the

Christian community, it would describe that community as a spiritual temple in contrast with the physical temple in Jerusalem. The Christian community is a physical reality. Because the Holy Spirit inhabits the body of every individual believer (1 Cor 6:19), the same Spirit inhabits the physical reality of the Christian community as a whole (Eph 2:22). "Not made with hands" often describes a physical reality. The heaven and the earth, made by God's hand rather than by human hands (Acts 7:47-50; 17:24), consist of the physical universe (as even in Philo *Spec.* 1 §67). The house not made with hands, eternal in the heavens, is more substantial, not less substantial, than the present body, just as a solid building is more substantial than a tent-house; and having such a building in the eschatological body contrasts with the nakedness of disembodiment (2 Cor 5:1-4). Circumcision that is not handmade is not spiritual, non-physical, but consists in stripping off "the body of the flesh [a less spiritual phrase being hard to imagine], in the circumcision of Christ [apparently a figure of speech for the Crucifixion]," and relates to baptism (a physical rite) and the resurrection of Christ from the dead (Col 2:11-12; cf. the physical uncircumcision of Gentiles, mentioned in Col 2:13, and the handmade circumcision in the flesh of Jews, mentioned in Eph 2:11). The greater and more perfect tabernacle not made with hands is described as heavenly and more substantial because constructed by God, not as spiritual and less substantial than the earthly tabernacle, which human beings constructed (Heb 9:1–10:18).

Nor need we consider the contrast between a handmade temple and one that is not handmade a late intrusion from the Hellenistic church into the false testimony at Mark 14:58. To be sure, the contrast may at first look Hellenistic; but the absence of this contrast from all the parallels does not support a late intrusion, for redactional reasons to omit the contrast are apparent (see the following notes and R. H. Gundry, *Matthew* 542-43). And we have positive reasons to allow its originality. Hellenism had swept over Jewish Palestine to a far greater extent than thought in earlier modern scholarship (M. Hengel, *Judaism and Hellenism*). Though later in date, the rabbinic tradition which contrasts the manmade temple in Jerusalem and the eschatological temple made by God (*Midr. Ps.* 90:17 §19 [Braude 2. 99]) proves non-Christian Jews capable of drawing such a contrast. The description "handmade" appears already in the OT, where its application to idols might well have stimulated Jesus' enemies to charge that he blasphemed the temple in Jerusalem by describing it as idols are described (see, e.g., Lev 26:1 LXX; Ps 155:4 MT; Isa 16:12 LXX; 19:1 LXX; 31:7 MT LXX; 46:6 LXX; Wis 13:10; cf. Philo *Legat.* 36 §290; *Bib. Ant.* 22:5-6). The use of "handmade" to describe temples that house idols provides a similar possible stimulus for charging that Jesus blasphemed the temple by relegating it to a heathen status (cf. Acts 17:24). On the other side, the very first chapter of the Bible speaks about the making of heaven and earth without the instrumentality of human hands. And not only have we seen that NT usage disfavors a contrast between physical and non-physical structures, but also the temporality of the contrast between the present temple and a future one reflects Jewish eschatological thought rather than Platonic Hellenistic thought (as is found in Philo *Mos.* 2 §18, where the manmade temple of material substance is said to be patterned after an immaterial form in the mind, and in idem *Immut.* 25, where the soul provides a pattern for the work of human hands — neither of which ideas parallels a contrast between man-made and God-made temples).

The prophecy of destruction for the temple in Jeremiah 26 not only contains nothing like the accusation that Jesus said he himself would destroy the temple and in three days build another; but also the testimony is presented as true that Jeremiah had said the things which he was accused of saying, whereas the testimony is presented as false that Jesus said the things which he is accused of having said. Against a vaticinium ex eventu E. P. Sanders (*Jesus and Judaism* 73-74) correctly argues, "After the temple was in fact destroyed . . . the Christians would not have composed a threat by Jesus that he would destroy it, nor would they have turned an existing prophecy that the temple would be destroyed into such a threat." But according to Sanders (op. cit. 71-73), early Christians did not want to admit that Jesus had spoken against the temple; and this reluctance led them (or Mark) to describe as false the testimony that he had done so (cf. the statement of J. R. Donahue [in *The Passion in Mark* 70] that "Jesus is tried and put to death for his opposition to the Temple," a statement at odds with Mark's indication that Jesus was condemned for saying, "I am . . . ," right on the spot, not for having said, "I myself will destroy . . . ," some time earlier). Why then was the prediction in 13:2 allowed to stand as a true word of Jesus? And why such reluctance when for the early Christians, and especially for the Gentile audience of Mark (whether Christian or non-Christian), the temple was either losing its significance or never had any? Better for early Christians to admit that Jesus had spoken against an outmoded temple (and in time a temple whose destruction fulfilled and vindicated his prediction of the event) than to admit that he had spoken what the supreme court of the Jews regarded as blasphemy, surely a more embarrassing accusation.

Nevertheless, Sanders thinks that Jesus predicted the destruction of the temple and its nearly immediate replacement in the new age (op. cit. 73). What we require, however, is an explanation why Mark accepts the prediction of destruction as a true word of Jesus but does not so accept a prediction that Jesus himself would destroy it and build another in three days. One could say that Mark does not accept the latter because it did not come to pass — i.e. Jesus did not himself destroy the temple and build another one in three days — but does accept the prediction of destruction as such because it remained to be fulfilled (cf. D. C. Allison, Jr., *End* 152). But then Mark need only delete the unfulfilled and unfulfillable features of the prediction and thus bring it into harmony with 13:2 without having to save Jesus' credibility by uncharacteristically crediting the Sanhedrin with so much concern for truth that they rejected conflicting testimony. As it is, the lack of harmony with 13:2 supports the traditionality, indeed the authenticity, of 14:58 as false testimony.

The Sanhedrin did not find the testimony that they were seeking, because the many who were testifying against Jesus were testifying falsely. The falsity of their testimony was exposed by their disagreement with one another. Not even the some who now testify that Jesus spoke against the temple can agree with each other. Mark's audience know their testimony to be false because the wording of the dominical prediction that the witnesses report disagrees with the wording of the dominical prediction that Mark reported in 13:2. But the Sanhedrin know the testimony to be false only (and again) because the witnesses disagree with each other. Just how they disagree with each other Mark does not say. Nor did he say in regard to the many unquoted witnesses. He is interested only in the fact of disagreement as an indication of the falsity which leads the Sanhedrin to throw out all the testimony (on cross-examination to expose falsity, see Sus 44–59; 11QTemple 61:9; *m. Mak.* 1:5; *m. Sanh.* 4:5; 5:1-3; D. Daube, *NTRJ* 230). The disagreement of the some need not consist in the wording of the prediction that they quote, though the differences in wording between Mark 14:58; Matt 26:61; and Acts 6:14, and especially right within Mark between 14:58 and 15:29, suggest such a possibility. The disagreement may have to do with the setting of the prediction: when, where, and to whom Jesus spoke it (see again Sus 44–59; *m. Sanh.* 5:1, 3). If with the setting, the testimony will be doubly false: (1) from the standpoint of the Sanhedrin, false to the circumstances of the prediction; (2) from the standpoint of Mark's audience, false to the wording of 13:2.

It has been suggested that the disagreement among the false witnesses consists in the difference between separate predictions which Jesus is testified to have made: (1) that he would destroy the temple and (2) that he would build another temple in three days (J. A. Kleist, *Memoirs* 135, 173-74; R. Pesch 2. 433). But the second claim depends for its meaning on the first, and "not even thus" (v 59) implies that the two claims make up a single unit over which the witnesses disagree (N.B. the collective "we" [v 58] and the singular of "testimony" [v 59] and of "what?" [v 60]). For quotations of separate predictions, moreover, we would have expected "one said, . . . ; and another said,. . . ." To state that "the falseness of the suborned witnesses lies in their malicious purpose" (W. Harrington 229) contradicts Mark's finding the falsity in their disagreement with one another and foists on his text a description of them as suborned. To say that their falsity consists in a misinterpretation of Jesus' prediction (as in taking "another [temple] not handmade" architecturally rather than communally, according to one suggestion) misconstrues the witnesses' role. They are to report, others to interpret. The testimony has to do with what Jesus said, not with what he meant. Nor does "false" mean that Jesus said nothing at all like what the witnesses are testifying; for the destruction in 14:58 resembles that in 13:2, and the three days in 14:58 resemble the three days in 8:31; 9:31; 10:34.

Do other passages offer possible bases for the present false testimony? We could treat the saying in John 2:19 as authentic and find the falsity of the present testimony in the changing of a conditional command, "(You) destroy this temple," into a threatening prediction, "I myself will destroy this temple," in the adding of a pejorative "handmade" to "this temple" and a contrastive "not handmade" to "another [temple]," and thus in misrepresenting Jesus' words as referring to the temple-building in Jerusalem (as in John 2:20 on the part of his audience) rather than to his own body (as in John 2:21 on the part of the evangelist). Yet John 2:19 bears the marks of Johannine redaction, as we would expect in a gospel that redacts the words of Jesus so heavily as the fourth one does. That is to say, John 2:19 (1) draws on the synoptics or on pre-synoptic tradition; (2) transfers the saying from the mouth of Jesus' accusers to his own mouth (cf. the transfer of the accusation "the king of the Jews" to his own mouth in John 18:36-37; also the reverse transfer of a saying of Jesus in Mark 12:9 to his enemies' mouth in Matt 21:41); (3) changes the predictive "I myself will destroy" to the imperative "(you) destroy" (using λύω, which occurs often in Johannine literature, instead of καταλύω, which never occurs there — see the concordance); (4) keeps "this" with "temple" because John has Jesus speaking in the temple; (5) drops "handmade" because the handmade temple will not be the temple that Jesus will raise in John's further revision of the saying; (6) Graecizes the Semitism διά with ἐν before "three days" (so also Mark 15:29; see J. Jeremias in *Tradition und Glaube* 220-21 for the underlying בְּ, "in" [Ezra 10:8, 9 MT = 1 Esdr 9:4, 5 LXX: ἐν] or "after [the course of]" [Gen 7:4; Exod 19:15; 2 Sam 13:23; Amos 4:4]); (7) advances "I will build" and replaces it with "I will raise" to initiate a characteristically Johannine enigmatic allusion to Jesus' resurrection; and (8) replaces "another one not handmade" with "it," i.e. "the temple of his body" (as John 2:21 goes on to explain), to complete the allusion. Overall, this revision typifies John's portrayal of Jesus as the divine Word who naturally to his deity takes charge of his death and resurrection. For example, no one takes his life from him; he lays it down of his own accord, as he has authority to do; and he is not raised by the Father, but himself takes up his life again (John 10:17-18). So also here, John makes Jesus command his enemies to destroy the temple of his body (cf. Jesus' insistence on getting arrested in John 18:2-11, his denial in John 19:11 that Pilate has any authority to exercise over him, and the deliberate bowing of his head and giving over of his Spirit in John 19:30); and he makes Jesus raise the temple of his own body.

(Jeremias's distinction between a temporal "in" and a temporal "after" for בְּ does not stand up; for the passages cited to support "after" could just as well be cited to support "in." For example, "*after* seven more days I will send rain on the earth" [Gen 7:4] could just as well read "*in* seven more days I will send rain on the earth," since in this and the other passages "after" would envision an interval following the stated period no more than "in" would envision an occurrence before the end of the stated period. Thus, whereas Mark 14:58; Matt 26:61 have "through (διά) three days," Mark 15:29; John 2:18 have "in [ἐν] three days"; and Mark 8:31; 9:31; 10:34 have "after [μετά, presumably resting on בְּ] three days" whereas their synoptic parallels have the simple dative ["on"] plus a singularized "the third day" [cf. Luke 13:32-33]. The indeterminate amount of time in view at Mark 2:1; Acts 24:17 makes "after" sound better than "in" for διά in those passages.)

Or we might treat Acts 6:14 as indirectly conveying what Jesus really said. There, Stephen is quoted to the effect that "Jesus the Nazarene — this one will destroy this place and change the customs which Moses gave over to us." Perhaps Stephen was borrowing from Jesus, and Luke omits the false testimony quoted in Mark 14:58 in favor of a true version that found its way into Stephen's preaching. But no, Luke characterizes as false witnesses those who quoted Stephen thus (Acts 6:13); and the words of Stephen against the temple that Luke himself quotes contain nothing about Jesus' destroying it and building another (see Acts 7:44-50). So it looks as though Luke transfers the present false witnesses and their testimony to the story of Stephen (so J. D. Crossan, *In Fragments* 310) or omits them here in anticipation of their presence there. "Place" (a Lucanism — see the concordance s.v. τόπος and esp. Acts 6:13; 7:49; 21:29 [bis]) then substitutes for "temple." "Handmade" drops out because the building in three days of another temple, not handmade, gives way to the charge that Stephen spoke of Jesus' changing the Mosaic customs. This charge, too, represents Luke's favorite diction (see the concordance s.v. ἔθος, Μωϋσῆς, παραδίδωμι, and esp. Luke 1:9; 2:42; Acts 15:1; 16:21; 21:21; 26:3; 28:17); and the priority of the corresponding part of Mark 14:58 receives support from the Semitism that it contains in διὰ τριῶν ἡμερῶν (cf. S. Arai in *NTS* 34 [1988] 397-410, esp. 398-99).

Well, then, we might treat Mark 15:29 as offering an earlier and more accurate version of what Jesus said: "the one destroying the temple and building [it] in three days." But the longer passage within which 15:29 appears (i.e. 15:29-32) simply rehearses in order the rejected false accusation brought against him with regard to the temple (15:29; cf. 14:57-58), his capitally judged confession to be the Christ (15:32; cf. 14:61-62), and the title "the king of the Jews," avoided by him in answer to Pilate (15:2), used for him by the Jews according to Pilate (15:12; cf. 15:9, 18, 26), and changed by the chief priests and scribes to "the king of Israel" to suit the shift to their Jewish lips from the Gentile lips of Pilate (15:32). "This" drops out because the indirectness of the quotation in 15:29 makes the pronoun inappropriate away from the temple, whereas "this" in the direct quotation of 14:58 appropriately implies that the words were spoken in the temple. The dropping of "this" leads to the dropping of "handmade," too (as in Matt 26:61; John 2:19; Acts 6:14). Supporting the naturalness of this further omission is the character of 15:29 as mockery, which requires only an allusion, whereas a formal accusation requires a full and exact quotation (cf. *m. Sanh.* 7:5). Thus, "another [temple] not handmade" drops out altogether (cf. the omission in 15:32 of the Jewish expression "the Son of the Blessed [One]," which accompanied "the Christ" in 14:61). Again the Graecizing of διά with ἐν for ל favors the priority — and indeed the earliness and authenticity — of the version quoted in 14:58.

Certain problems beset our tracing the false testimony in 14:58 back to 13:2. There, Jesus predicted the destruction of τὸ ἱερόν, "the temple" in the sense of the sanctuary plus related surrounding structures; but here in 14:58 he is accused of having said he would destroy τὸν ναόν, "the temple" in the sense of the sanctuary alone (see D. Juel, *Messiah and Temple* 127-28, that in 11:11, 15, 16, 27; 12:35; 14:49 as well as in 13:2 τὸ ἱερόν unquestionably refers to the whole complex of buildings, whereas in 15:38 ναός unquestionably refers to the sanctuary alone, against the contention of J. R. Donahue [*Are You the Christ?* 104-5] that ναός and ἱερόν differ not in meaning but only in traditionality and redactionality, respectively). The prediction in 13:2 says nothing about Jesus' building another sanctuary in three days; and he spoke that prediction in private to a single disciple (13:1-2), several others listening in but limited to disciples (13:3-4; see also 12:43 and the addressing of commands to watch elsewhere in the NT only to Christians — against including non-disciples in the "all" of 13:37), so that even though the witnesses in chap.

14 tell a falsehood in claiming to have heard him, it becomes a question how they could have known about the prediction. Yet the common use of καταλύω, "destroy," and the cognateness of οἰκοδομάς, "buildings" (13:2), and οἰκοδομήσω, "I will build" (14:58), favor a derivation of the false testimony from the true saying; and the problems besetting this derivation are not insuperable. In fact, they are of the sort that suits Mark's describing the present testimony as false. The sanctuary is included in the temple-complex; so 14:58 does not contradict 13:2. The building of another temple in three days favors an additional derivation from the resurrection predictions, in which μετά, "after," provides another Graecization besides ἐν for ‫ל‬ (8:31; 9:31; 10:34). This additional derivation is favored also by the probability that reference to an indeterminately short period of time (as opposed to the period of three days specified in the resurrection predictions) would have produced δι' ἡμερῶν, "through days," as in 2:1 (cf. Acts 24:17, and yet again see the notes on Mark 8:31 and R. H. Gundry, *Matthew* 245, against an indefinite interpretation of the three days). Thus, the false testimony seems to have mingle-mangled the predictions of destruction for the temple and of Jesus' resurrection. If so, the false witnesses distorted the predictions by making him arrogate to himself the roles of divine destroyer and divine builder of the temple, by a narrowing of focus to the most sacred of the buildings, and by adding a pejorative "handmade" to describe the present sanctuary and a favorable "not handmade" to describe the future sanctuary in a way that reflects badly on the present one.

From a historical standpoint it seems unlikely that a Christian would have mingle-mangled Jesus' predictions of destruction for the temple and of his own resurrection so as to produce a false testimony against Jesus. In view of Judas Iscariot's dealings with the Sanhedrin, however, it is quite conceivable that some members of that body learned of those predictions and, not having heard Jesus speak them yet wanting to accuse him of a capital offense, did give false testimony by mingle-mangling them. This possibility saves us from having to deny the privacy of the settings in which Jesus is said to have predicted the destruction of the temple and his resurrection. If accepted as historical at all, the predictions of resurrection are generally agreed to have a suitable setting in the private audience of his disciples. The suitability of a like setting for his prediction of destruction for the temple is sometimes denied (see, e.g., E. P. Sanders, *Jesus and Judaism* 71), but apart from the need to give the false witnesses knowledge of this prediction it is hard to understand why. The prediction does not carry the threatening tone and penitential demand that characterized the predictions of destruction brought against the temple by prophets such as Jeremiah, Micah, and Uriah when they preached in public (Jer 7:1-15; 26:1-15, 20; and the whole of Micah in relation to Mic 3:12). We have already noted that in no way does the discourse following the prediction in 13:2 elaborate the destruction of the temple.

J. R. Donahue (*Are You the Christ?* 77-84, 103-38) thinks that the recurrence of disagreement in v 59 as compared with v 56 signals an insertion by Mark of a saying in v 58 that he redacted in part out of bias against the temple. But we have often noted reasons to question that repetitions indicate Marcan insertions of intervening material. Earlier comments and notes have discovered no bias against the temple. And Mark's redacting an oracle about the temple according to such a bias would have worked at cross-purpose with his casting the pall of falsehood over it.

J. D. Crossan (*In Fragments* 309-12) sees the saying in v 58 as a teaching of the false prophets in chap. 13 — i.e. a teaching that the destruction of the temple and the Second Coming coincide (or that Jesus is going to come right away now that the temple is destroyed, or is certain to be destroyed, at a time of writing around 70 C.E.) and that Jesus will build the eschatological community immediately afterwards — a teaching which Mark opposes by describing as false the witnesses who put it on the lips of Jesus (cf. D. Lührmann in *NTS* 27 [1980-81] 466-69). Not only does this view err in attributing an indefinite meaning to "in three days" and a communal meaning to "another [temple]." It also lacks evidence in the saying or its immediate context to support either an association of the destruction of the temple with the Second Coming or an equation of the false witnesses with the false prophets (and in 15:29 of the mockers with the false prophets). The suggestion of W. L. Lane (528, n. 108) that copyists added "handmade" and "not handmade" to Mark's text lacks text critical support.

Gos. Thom. 71 ("Jesus said, 'I will destroy [this] house, and no one will be able to [re]build it'") is best understood as a gnostic revision of Mark 14:58: (1) the saying is made truly Jesuanic so as to serve gnostic teaching; (2) "handmade temple" is exchanged for "house" to get a word easily understood as a metaphor of the physical body (cf. 2 Cor 5:1) or of the material world; (3) for a characteristically gnostic denial of physical resurrection or of a new material world, the building of another temple in three days is replaced by the inability of anyone to rebuild the house; (4) alternatively (but less likely because of the exchange of "temple" for "house"), the inability to rebuild serves gnostic anticultism (D. E. Aune, Prophecy 173). The suggestion of J. D. Crossan (In Fragments 307-8) that Gos. Thom. 71 makes sense when read as referring to the Jewish temple and may therefore represent the most primitive version of the saying fails to explain why a truly reported prediction by Jesus that he will destroy that temple (surely an increasingly welcome thought to the increasingly Gentile church) should give way to a false testimony that he said so, or why the inability of anyone to rebuild the Jewish temple (again a welcome thought) should give way to Jesus' building another temple in three days (which as we have seen cannot refer to the building of the Christian community).

According to L. Schenke (Der gekreuzigte Christus 27), v 60 connects better with v 56 than with vv 57-59. But wherein lies the better connection? The truth is opposite; for the singular of τί, "what?" fits the singular of ἡ μαρτυρία αὐτῶν, "their testimony," in v 59 better than it fits the plural of αἱ μαρτυρίαι, "the testimonies," in v 56. Just as one arises out of (ἀνίστημι with ἐκ — 9:9, 10; 12:25), so the high priest arises into (ἀνίστημι with εἰς; see J. J. O'Rourke in JBL 85 [1966] 351 on εἰς with verbs of motion).

According to Gen. Rab. 82.8 on Gen 35:17, arising in a trial may indicate the taking of an adversarial role or the shortening of a trial and making of concessions. The question of dating rabbinic traditions aside, both of these possibilities can fit the present occasion; for the high priest can be thought to take an adversarial role because the prosecutorial witnesses have failed, or because of their failure he may be thought ready to close the trial by making concessions — till Jesus utters what the high priest considers blasphemy. In view of the Sanhedrin's repeatedly emphasized antipathy toward Jesus and the parallel between the high priest's standing up and the prosecutorial witnesses' having done likewise, the possibility of taking an adversarial role seems much more likely.

T. A. Mohr (Markus- und Johannespassion 255) thinks that disagreement among the prosecutorial witnesses makes the high priest's questions senseless and therefore literarily preparatory for Jesus' silence in v 61a rather than historically authentic. But one could argue in the reverse that the disagreement makes perfect sense of the high priest's questions: he asks them because the witnesses have not agreed with each other. Agreement would have lessened, if not eliminated, the need for questioning Jesus. His silence has strengthened the suspicion of guilt despite disagreement among the witnesses.

A strictly literal translation in vv 60-61, "Are you answering nothing? . . . and he was answering nothing," sounds as though "nothing" refers to the accusation leveled against Jesus. It refers rather to what he might say in self-defense, but does not (cf. 9:6; 14:40). To take τί as an adverbial accusative, "Why?" (see M. Black, Aramaic Approach 119, but with reference to the v.l. ὅτι), does not make so good a sense as does taking it to be an accusative of direct object: "What [is it that]?" The high priest is asking about the content of the testimony, not about the motivation behind it. The meaning scarcely shifts if we treat τί as an accusative of general reference in a single question: "You're making no answer, are you, with respect to what these [witnesses] are testifying against you?" Mark's love of duality favors two questions over one, however (cf. the twin declarations immediately following in v 61a; see 8:17-18 for more than two questions in succession); and an accusative of general reference would seem harsh (cf. C. E. B. Cranfield 442).

Jesus' silence does not correspond to or grow out of silence on the part of righteous sufferers in Pss 38:14-16(13-15); 39:10(9); for he remains silent because the evident falsity of the testimony against him makes an answer unnecessary, whereas the psalmists remain silent out of penitence for their own sins. They are suffering, but they are not righteous. Only Isa 53:7 corresponds to Jesus' case, but Mark makes nothing of the correspondence. Not even the phraseology carries over. Justin (*Dial.* 102-3) treats Jesus' silence as a fulfilment of Ps 22:16(15). But Mark does not borrow from that OT passage, either; and it refers to a dry tongue, not to a silent one. Jesus the son of Ananus was silent under interrogation, but not in the face of a false charge; and he lived later than Jesus of Nazareth (Josephus *J.W.* 6.5.3 §305).

"Again" does not prove a suture at the start of v 61a (against B. Lindars, *Jesus, Son of Man* 110-12), unless after asking one question interrogators never ask another one. If they never do, we will have to posit a remarkable number of sutures, with or without "again," at 14:69 (with 14:66-67); 15:4 (with 15:2); 15:12, 14 (with 15:9), too, and in earlier passages at 8:20, 21 (with 8:19, where some would see wholesale composition by Mark); 8:29 (with 8:27); 12:16 (with 12:15), to say nothing about all sorts of other literature. Since "I am" follows a question more naturally than it follows a statement, we should reject an ironic translation of v 61b: "You are the Christ, the Son of the Blessed One" (entertained by M. A. Beavis in *CBQ* 49 [1987] 583-84). Though making up the main part of a question, the Greek words underlying "Are you the Christ . . . ?" match those of Peter's confession, "You are the Christ" (σὺ εἶ ὁ χριστός — 8:29). But not only are the contextual differences between the passages "even greater" than the structural parallels that Beavis sees between them (see ibid. 586 for those differences). On close examination the structural parallels themselves — (1) setting; (2) first question and conflicting reports; (3) second question and confession; (4) Son of man-saying; and (5) condemnation — also break down. In Jesus' trial, the conflicting reports are not given in answer to a question; and when the first question is asked, it is met with silence. The Son of man-saying is part of a confession in Jesus' trial, but not in the earlier passage. And we do not have a condemnation in the earlier passage, but the rebuke of a rebuke.

The question of the high priest does not come out of the blue, but not because a kingly connotation of "the Christ, the Son of the Blessed One" links onto an implication that Jesus assumed a kingly prerogative in cleansing the temple (cf. his being condemned and crucified in chap. 15 as the would-be king of the Jews; so J. T. Townsend, "The Tradition behind Mark's Passion Narrative" 22-24 [unpublished paper for the SBL meeting in Anaheim, CA, November 1989]). For the charge before the Sanhedrin has been that Jesus assumed the divine prerogatives of destroying the temple and building another, not a kingly prerogative in cleansing the temple. The inadmissibility of the testimony against Jesus and his refusal to answer an acknowledgedly false accusation motivate the high priest's question. The mention of a new temple in that accusation may well have led the high priest to think of the messianic age and thus of the Messiah himself whether or not the Messiah was thought to build a new temple. So then the high priest's use of "the Christ" could have led him to use "the Son of the Blessed One." For divine sonship was attributed to the Davidic kings in 2 Sam 7:14 and Ps 2:7. The first of these two passages is given a pre-Christian Jewish messianic interpretation in 4QFlor 1:10-12. "The Son of God" in 4QpsDan A[a] = 4Q243 may offer another pre-Christian Jewish use for the Messiah. And the parable of the wicked tenant farmers, directed as it was to the Sanhedrin, drew an analogy between a vineyard owner and his son, on the one hand, and God and Jesus on the other hand (12:1-11; cf. Matt 11:27 par. Luke 10:22; J. D. Kingsbury, *Christology of Mark's Gospel* 118-19, 150-51). Moreover, Judas Iscariot may have told the Sanhedrin that Jesus had accepted a messianic designation from the disciples (C. E. B. Cranfield 443). So there is no good reason to suppose only that a Christian put the question of the high priest on his lips.

For Jews, "the Christ" did not connote divine nature; and insofar as "the Son of the Blessed One," like "the Son of God" for which it substitutes, stands in a non-restrictive appositional relation to "the Christ," the filial phrase connotes divine appointment rather than divine nature. There is no historical theological difficulty, then, in supposing that the high priest really did ask Jesus the quoted question (see the wide-ranging discussion and the primary and secondary literature cited by M. Hengel, *Son of God* 21-56; also H. Baarlink, *Anfängliches Evangelium* 214-19). Under a purely appointive view of divine sonship, this second questioning by the high priest lowers the stakes from Jesus' arrogating to himself the divine activities of temple-destroying and temple-building to his claiming for himself the high but still only human office of Messiah. Then the high priest asks his question more out of frustration at failure to catch Jesus in one capital offense than out of determination to catch him in another such offense — and Jesus' answer does the high priest an unexpected favor by providing another such offense. On the other hand, the testimony that Jesus had arrogated to himself the divine activities of temple-destroying and temple-building may have put the high priest in mind of something more than appointive divine sonship. If so, "the Son of the Blessed One" restrictively heightens "the Christ." There is no lowering of stakes, and the continued interrogation bespeaks the high priest's determination. Similarly and perhaps more likely than either of these possibilities, however, though by itself a messianic claim may not have been thought a capital offense, the rabbinic tradition that Bar Kokhba was slain because he did not pass the test of smell after he claimed messiahship (*b. Sanh.* 93b; cf. the following notes on v 65) suggests the possibility that to find a capital charge against Jesus the high priest had in mind to put him to a test if he claimed messiahship — but that the high priest unexpectedly heard blasphemy instead, so that what might have been a messianic test in the covering of Jesus' face, cuffing him, and challenging him to prophesy turns into a repudiation of blasphemy (cf. A. Kirschenbaum, *Self Incrimination* 138-39, on Jesus' statement as the crime itself, not as the confession of a crime). Much more important for Mark than the high priest's state of mind, however, is that the Gentile audience of this gospel will almost certainly hear overtones of divine nature in "the Son of the Blessed One"; and Mark's sensitivity to his audience's cultural milieu (see esp. 7:2-4), his constant emphasis on Jesus' divine powers but lack of any emphasis on Jesus' prophethood (which appears only indirectly in the traditional 6:4), and the high Christology that has already developed in the church (see esp. Rom 1:3-4; 9:5; 2 Cor 8:9; Phil 2:5-11) make it likely that Mark intends his Gentile audience to hear those overtones.

That in v 61b Mark uses "the Son of the Blessed One," which appears only here in his gospel, instead of "(the) Son of God," which appears in 3:11; 5:7; 15:39 and above all in the superscription composed by him at 1:1 (as well as elsewhere in early Christian literature), favors his use of primitive and therefore likely authentic tradition. For "the Blessed One" substitutes for "God" in a reverential way characteristic of Jews but uncharacteristic of Christians and probably arose by abbreviation of the common rabbinic expression "the Holy One, blessed [is] he" (G. Dalman, *Words* 200; Str-B 2. 51). Or the rabbinic expression represents an expansion of "the Blessed One." *1 Enoch* 77:2 provides some probably pre-Christian Jewish evidence for "the Blessed One" and thus turns back the argument for inauthenticity that vv 61-62 reflect a Christology of the church. Appeals to the opinion of J. Klausner (*Jesus of Nazareth* 342) that "the Blessed One" represents a clumsy and therefore inauthentic attempt at Jewish usage (so, e.g., B. Lindars, *Jesus, Son of Man* 212; D. E. Nineham 407; J. R. Donahue, *Are You the Christ?* 90, n. 1) neglect not only *1 Enoch* 77:2 but also *m. Ber.* 7:3; *b. Ber.* 50a (Str-B 2. 51). D. Lührmann (in *NTS* 27 [1980-81] 471, n. 32) says that τοῦ εὐλογητοῦ, "of the Blessed [One]," would go back to הברוך, which never occurs for God (with only the possible exception of the place-name Kaphar ha-Baruk, which may appear in Mur 43 2 [DJD 2. 159-60] in the form הברך). But the alternation between the simple adjective ἀγαπητός, "beloved," and the synonymous perfect passive participle (i.e. verbal adjective) ἠγαπημένος in Mark 1:11 parr.; 9:7 parr. as compared with Eph 1:6, and in Rom 1:7; Eph 5:1 as compared with Rom 9:25; Col 3:12, makes it possible that τοῦ εὐλογητοῦ goes back to the passive participle המברך, which does occur for God in the rabbinic literature cited above. There, the expression is not used absolutely to substitute for God's name, as in Mark 14:61. But the one probably pre-Christian occurrence of a corresponding expression in *1 Enoch* 77:2 does example an absolute use in substitution for God's name; and the rabbinic occurrences represent a substantival use of the participle in apposition to God's name. The counter appeal of D. Juel (*Messiah and Temple* 78-79) to H. Danby's translation "who is to be blessed" overlooks that this translation would work well in Mark 14:61 ("the Son of the One who is to be blessed"). As for the theory that Mark is imitating Jewish style, where else can it be demonstrated that he does so rather than following Jewish Christian tradition? His frequent translations of Jewish terms and explanations of Jewish customs tend in the opposite direction. You do not imitate only to explain. Granted, periphrases such as "the Blessed One" and "the Power" might rest on early but inauthentic Jewish Christian tradition (so C. R. Kazmierski, *Jesus, the Son of God* 167-69). Nonetheless, early Jewish Christianness tends toward authenticity; and historical criticism deals in probabilities. An exclusively later application to Jesus of exalted titles such as "the Christ, the Son of the Blessed One" seems improbable. His crucifixion would have forestalled it. Not even his resurrection would have prompted it; for the Jews did not expect the Christ to rise from the dead, and they contemplated the return of Elijah and the coming back to life of Jeremiah or one of the other prophets without exalting them to messianic status or divine sonship. Jesus must have laid claim to the titles before his crucifixion and had those claims justified by his resurrection (see R. H. Gundry in *CSR* 20 [1990] 183-84).

Parallel influence of Matthew on scribes explains the weakly supported insertion of "you have said that" before "I am" in v 62 (Θ *f*¹³ 565 700 *pc* Or; cf. Matt 26:64: "you have said"). Subsidiary influence of Matthew on the original text of Luke explains "you say that I am" in Luke 22:70 (see R. H. Gundry in *The Four Gospels* 1992). So we need not adopt the Marcan v.l. to explain either the v.l. itself or the text of Luke 22:70. The argument that no Christian scribe would have changed an unequivocal "I am" to "you have said that I am" (so J. D. G. Dunn in *The Messianic Secret* 127-28) underestimates the parallel influence of Matthew on scribes (see É. Massaux, *Influence*) and neglects that Matthew changed Mark in that very way because he wanted to keep Jesus from answering under oath in violation of Matt 5:33-37, a passage unique to Matthew's gospel (R. H. Gundry, *Matthew* 544).

The combination of "I am" (v 62a) with "Are you . . . ?" (v 61b) argues against taking "I am" as a divine title (cf. Exod 3:14) and thus as a claim to deity (see R. Pesch 2. 437-38, n. 35, for literature pro and con). The similar view that "I am" is a revelational formula, as at 6:50; 13:6, does not fare much better; for the revelation depends entirely on context, in particular, on the speaker's identity. In and of itself "I am" reveals nothing. Hence, a nobody like the man born blind uses the expression just as Jesus does (John 9:9). Following the question, "Are you the Christ, the Son of the Blessed One?" the answer "I am" is taken as elliptical much more naturally than as absolute. Filling in the ellipsis we would read, "I am [the Christ, the Son of the Blessed One]," a reading that does not conform to the I AM of God in the OT (for fuller criticism see D. R. Catchpole, *Trial* 132-35).

"I am" is a confession, "you will see . . ." a prediction. It is more likely that ὄψεσθε, "you will see" (v 62b), echoes ὄψονται, "they will see," in 13:26 than that it alludes to Zech 12:10; for John 19:37 and Rev 1:7, which do allude to Zech 12:10, include the key element of piercing, not present here (cf. F. Borsch in *NTS* 14 [1967-68] 566). K. Brower (in *JSNT* 6 [1980] 39) finds the fulfilment of Jesus' prediction in the darkness and veil-rending at Jesus' crucifixion. But not only does hanging on a cross between two bandits disagree with sitting at the right hand of the Power and coming with the clouds of heaven. Also, the darkness will not be attributed to clouds; and a Roman centurion rather than the Sanhedrin will see the rending of the veil. Though a seat at God's right hand does not refer to heavenly session in Ps 110:1, it refers to heavenly session throughout the NT, including Mark 14:62. Otherwise we would have to suppose that the Son of man will sit at God's right hand somewhere on earth (but where?) and then to go heaven with the clouds thereof (but why then ἐρχόμενον, "coming," instead of ὑπάγοντα, "going," as in v 21; John 7:33; 8:14, 21-22; 13:3 et passim)?

Jesus jumps from his present interrogation to his heavenly session and second coming. While the Sanhedrin were still considering his case, it would have been premature to mention his intervening death and resurrection (against N. Perrin [in *The Passion in Mark* 92-94], who disregards the omission by alleging that Jesus incorporates his crucifixion, burial, and resurrection in his sitting at the right hand of the Power and coming with the clouds of heaven). H. Giesen (in *SNTU* A/8 [1983] 45) argues that since "you will see" has two objects, "sitting" and "coming," these two must relate to each other as one action, not as two different actions, and therefore must refer to heavenly session but not to the Second Coming. The basis of this argument is unsound. "You will see" has only one object, "the Son of man." "Sitting" and "coming" modify that object and may easily refer to successive actions on the Son of man's part. But according to J. A. T. Robinson (*Jesus and His Coming* 51), Jesus does not distinguish between sitting and coming as successive actions, one in heaven, the other to earth; they are parallel, referring differently to one and the same heavenly exaltation. They are successive rather than synonymous elsewhere in the NT, however; and parataxis may veil relationships different from synonymity. Take subsequence, for example, a relationship that parataxis may introduce in synthetic parallelism (see, e.g., Ps 51:15[13]). Even if coming as well as sitting referred to exaltation, the Son of man's coming to receive exaltation would still need to precede his sitting to enjoy it; yet v 62 presents the reverse order. For the meaning of descent rather than ascent in both Dan 7:13 and Jesus' use of that passage, see the notes on 13:26; R. H. Gundry, *Use of the OT* 232-33; idem, *Matthew* 546; G. R. Beasley-Murray, *Commentary on Mark Thirteen* 91; idem, *Jesus and the Kingdom of God* 300-301; idem in *RevExp* 75 (1978) 576-77 (where emphasis falls on the theophanic character of Dan 7:13 and on the OT theophanic pattern of God's coming from heaven to earth for judgment and salvation, as in Dan 7:21-22); idem in *CBQ* 45 (1983) 44-58; idem in *L'Apocalypse johannique* 425-26; M. Casey, *Son of Man* 178-84; and other literature cited by R. Pesch 2. 439, n. 41. For ascent, see J. A. T. Robinson, *Jesus and His Coming* 43-51; M. D. Hooker, *Son of Man* 167-71; and J. Schaberg in *Apocalyptic and the NT* 69-94, where pre-Marcan tradition is said to have indicated a sitting in the chariot of Merkabah mysticism and then a coming to heaven in that chariot — but if so, God, at whose right hand the Son of man is sitting in the chariot, would also have to ascend from earth to heaven; and this implication seems unlikely.

Though 9:12; 10:45; 14:24 may favor that in the back of his mind Jesus was thinking of the exaltation of the Servant of Yahweh following that servant's suffering in Isa 52:13–53:12, the present phraseology echoes other OT passages. Notably, Isa 52:13–53:12 does not speak of sitting at God's right hand, as Mark 14:62 does, much less of coming with clouds. Nor do the thrones and crowns of *1 Enoch* 108:12; *Asc. Isa.* 9:25; *T. Job* 41:4; *Apoc. Elijah* 1:8 measure up to a seat at God's right hand.

The combination of sitting at God's right hand and coming with the clouds of heaven does not appear in non-dominical NT materials and therefore seems unlikely to have a Christian origin here. Nor is "the Son of man" elsewhere associated with sitting at God's right hand; so Christian fabrication again seems unlikely. Whatever its date, the Jewish midrashic combination of Ps 110:7 and Dan 7:13 with regard to the Messiah, once in connection with divine sonship (as per Ps 2:7; cf. Mark 1:11; 9:7) just as here in Mark 14:61-62, exposes the weakness of arguing that the present combination of those passages must have arisen out of churchly Christology (see *Midr. Pss.* 2:7 §9; cf. 18:36 §29 [Braude 1. 40-41, 259-61]; E. Lövestam in *SEÅ* 26 [1961] 97-99). These Jewish midrashic combinations take away any need to suppose with O. J. F. Seitz (in *SE VI* 478-88) that the synonymously parallel combination of "the man of your right hand" and "the Son of man whom you made strong for yourself" in Ps 80:18(17) acted as a catalyst by drawing to itself first the sitting at God's right hand in Ps 110:1 and then the one like a Son of man who comes with the clouds of heaven in Dan 7:13 (with the result that the order of sitting and coming reflects successive stages in Christian midrashic development rather than successive activities of the Son of man). Nowhere do the NT and Jewish midrashic passages make recognizable use of Ps 80:18(17).

M. Horstmann (*Studien* 20) and J. Gnilka (in *Der Prozess gegen Jesus* 17) consider "and you will see the Son of man sitting on [the] right [hand] of the Power and coming with the clouds of heaven" a Marcan addition to "I am." But "the Son of man" characterizes Jesus' speech, not that of the church (see the notes on 2:10); and we have here the same blend of modest self-reference in the third person and personally high claims that characterizes a number of other sayings in which Jesus uses "the Son of man" (see 2:10, 28; 8:38; 13:26 and, so far as his resurrection is concerned, 8:31; 9:9, 31; 10:33-34; cf. the same sort of blend in 2 Cor 12:1-5). "The Power" does not substitute for "God" elsewhere in the NT even though the allusion to Ps 110:1 in "sitting on the right [hand] of . . ." appears very often (Mark 12:36 parr.; Acts 2:34-35; Rom 8:34; Eph 1:20; Col 3:1; Heb 1:3, 13; 8:1; 10:12; 12:2; Mark 16:19). Yet the substitution of "the Power" for "God" typifies Jewish reverential usage and thereby favors that Mark is drawing on primitive tradition (cf. the notes on "the Blessed One" in v 61b and see G. Dalman, *Words* 200-202; Str-B 1. 1006; J. R. Harris in *ExpTim* 32 [1920-21] 375; G. Scholem, *Jewish Gnosticism* 67-69; A. M. Goldberg in *BZ* nf 8 [1964] 284-93 [where it is noted that the rabbinic combination "the mouth of the Power" appears to grow out of an earlier absolute use of "the Power"]; and esp. *b. Šabb.* 87a; *b. Sota* 37a par. *'Abot R. Nat.* 35; Eus. *H.E.* 2.23.13 for absolute usage, as here; cf. a similar Samaritan usage in Acts 8:10, a probably Jewish heretical usage, in the plural, at *m. Sanh.* 4:5, and a non-Jewish use of μεγάλη δύναμις τοῦ ἀθανάτου θεοῦ, "Great Power of the Immortal God," as a divine title for the god Μήν, "Men" [*New Documents* 3. 31-32]). Jesus is just as likely to have used OT phraseology as Mark is (cf. E. E. Ellis in *CTR* 3 [1989] 348-49), and Mark is unlikely to have created a chronological problem by putting on Jesus' lips a prediction about the Sanhedrin which failed to reach fulfilment in their lifetimes. This failure implies not only the traditionality and probable authenticity of the prediction, but also Mark's fitting the prediction into his apology under an implicit expansion of "you" to include the successors of Jesus' Sanhedric contemporaries (cf. an analogous expansion in 13:37). The notes on 13:30-31 apply also to the chronological observation that the Sanhedrists died without seeing the Son of man sitting at the right hand of the Power and coming with the clouds of heaven. The wording of 13:30-31 disallows a posthumous seeing of those sights in 14:62.

To regard the "you" in "you will see" as Mark's audience would allow him to have composed the saying without creating a problem of unfulfillability (cf. N. Perrin in *The Passion in Mark* 92), but the context favors an address by Jesus to the Sanhedrin. "And" links "you will see . . ." to "I am," which answers the high priest's question. And Mark's writing "they" in the similar saying at 13:26 ("and then they [people] will see the Son of man coming in clouds . . .") when he might have addressed his audience with a "you" (cf. the constant use of "you" for the disciples, the original ones and all others, throughout 13:5b-37 [again see esp. v 37]) favors that the "you" who will see the Son of man in 14:62 are *not* Mark's audience.

G. Vermes (*Jesus the Jew* 147-49, 183-84) considers "I am" as well as the rest of v 62 a Christian fabrication, because elsewhere Jesus shows reticence toward christhood and in the synoptic parallels to v 62 avoids a straightforward "I am." But we have already noted non-historical, non-traditional reasons for the parallel wordings; and the circumstance of Jesus' trial eliminates any further need for him to buy time with reticence (C. F. D. Moule in *Jesus und Paulus* 248-49: "it is perfectly clear that there is no possibility now of his leading a rebellion"). Moreover, we need to qualify Jesus' earlier reticence. He neither denied nor avoided his christhood when Peter confessed it, but only told the disciples not to speak about him (8:30) and in speaking to them later referred to himself as "Christ" (9:41). (It would be reasoning in a circle to discount this later reference as secondary [cf. the notes ad loc.].) The command to secrecy in 9:9 was temporally conditioned. The commands in 1:34; 3:12 had to do with the technique of exorcism and the danger of being crushed to death. Passages such as 1:43-44; 5:43; 7:36; 8:26 had to do with the publicizing of Jesus' healings, not with his identity as the Christ and Son of God. See the notes ad loc.

B. Lindars (in *JSNT* 23 [1985] 40) opposes the authenticity of v 62 on the ground that the context and the allusion to Dan 7:13 contradict the indefinite meaning which characterized Jesus' use of "the Son of man" for a particular example (Jesus himself) of a class (human beings). But apart from the questionability of such a use, why cannot "the Son of man" in v 62 mean "a human being, in particular, me" just as in Dan 7:13 "one like a son of man" means "someone who looked like a human being as opposed to the beasts that previously appeared"? See G. R. Beasley-Murray in *RevExp* 75 (1978) 572-74 for criticisms of anti-historical arguments by H. E. Tödt, *Son of Man* 36-37; also D. R. Catchpole, *Trial* 136-40, for similar criticisms.

The argument of some that Jesus does not command the high priest and Sanhedrin to keep his messiahship-divine sonship secret because he does not need to — they do not believe in it (so E. Lemcio in *NTS* 32 [1986] 204, n. 37; J. D. Kingsbury, *Christology of Mark's Gospel* 121) — fails to explain why Jesus not only affirms it rather than remaining silent (as in vv 60-61) or avoiding an answer (as in 15:2; cf. Matt 26:64; Luke 22:67-68) but also strengthens his affirmative answer by adding an even more exalted claim. Under the theory of a messianic or Son-of-God secret, does unbelief eliminate the need for secrecy? It did not in 4:11-13 (for the outsiders were unbelievers) or in 5:43 (for the weepers and wailers had incredulously laughed at Jesus). If Jesus commanded others not to tell unbelievers, why does he himself tell unbelievers? To overturn grandiose christhood and divine sonship by asserting that he is the Christ, the Son of the Blessed One, insofar as he is the righteous sufferer? No, for he talks of heavenly session and theophanic return rather than of suffering.

Nor does "the Son of man" correctively replace "the Christ, the Son of the Blessed One." Jesus has just accepted the latter two designations. "The Son of man" does not even correctively subtract grandiosity from "the Christ, the Son of the Blessed One." Heavenly exaltation and theophanic coming *add* grandiosity (cf. the rejection of corrective interpretations by D. Juel, *Messiah and Temple* 85-94). "The Son of man" is a self-reference which despite its third person and association with Dan 7:13 never rose to the level of a NT Christological title (see the notes on 2:10). Here, Dan 7:13 is quoted allusively but without emphasis, which falls rather on the Son of man's future position and coming (M. de Jonge in *Jésus aux origenes de la christologie* 174). We might have expected "me" in correspondence with "I"; but 8:38 has already offered a shift from the first person pronoun to the third person of the self-referential "Son of man"; and the allusive quotation of Dan 7:13, which speaks of "one like a son of man," makes the shift even more appropriate than in 8:38, which also described the Son of man's coming, but without using the phraseology of Dan 7:13. The shift from first person to third in 8:38 shows that the same shift need not signal a redactional addition in the rest of 14:62 (as thought by L. Schenke, *Der gekreuzigte Christus* 37-38), for such an addition is out of the question in 8:38.

We would overinterpret the shift from "the Christ, the Son of the Blessed One" to "the Son of man" to say that it indicates a reversal of roles, as follows: inasmuch as "the Son of man" connotes judgmental authority (cf. Dan 7:13-14), when he comes he will judge his judges. In Dan 7:13-14, on the contrary, "one like a son of man" is given "dominion, glory, and a kingdom," but not the function of judgment. Instead, "the Ancient of Days" acts as the judge (Dan 7:22; cf. Wis 5:2, where the righteous sufferer will not function as judge, but be judged favorably; *T. Benj.* 10:6, where Enoch, Seth, Abraham, Isaac, and Jacob do not become judges, nor are they said to have suffered innocently, or at all; *1 Enoch* 62:3, 5, where the Son of man comes to inflict judgment but is not said to have suffered innocently, or at all). And Mark 14:65 says nothing about judgment by anyone (contrast *1 Enoch* 62:3, 5; *2 Macc* 7:34-38; *4 Macc* 10:21; 12:18). In view is the vindication of Jesus, not the judgment of the Sanhedrin. Moreover, the same shift from "the Christ" to "the Son of man" occurred in 8:29-31, but with a reversal in roles just opposite the one suggested for 14:65; i.e. from non-suffering christhood (cf. 8:32) to the suffering of the Son of man. The present shift in roles arises, then, not from the shift in terminology but from the phraseology of "sitting at [the] right [hand] of the Power and coming with the clouds of heaven." See A. J. B. Higgins in *Promise and Fulfilment* 138-39 against seeing a priestly Christology in v 62. To interpret Jesus as meaning that the Sanhedrin will see the true Israel vindicated (so C. F. D. Moule in *NT und Kirche* 424) is to make several mistakes. Elsewhere Jesus uses "the Son of man" individualistically of himself, not collectively of the true Israel. It is his identity and destiny that are at issue before the Sanhedrin, not the identity and destiny of the true Israel. Jesus would have to be too early a Paulinist to say that the true Israel will sit at God's right hand (Eph 1:3; 2:6; Phil 3:20; Col 3:1-4). And the true Israel's coming in the clouds of heaven would differ from and probably disagree with the gathering of the elect right after the coming of the Son of man according to 13:24-27.

Despite the usual meaning of χιτών, "undergarment," BAGD (s.v.) consider the plural χιτώνας a general reference to clothes. Yet χιτώνας in 6:9 seems to have meant undergarments; for if they had been pieces of clothing in general, the prohibition against putting on two of them would have been tantamount to a prohibition against wearing an undergarment and an outer garment at the same time. Much more likely is a prohibition against putting on more than one undergarment (cf. E. F. F. Bishop [*Jesus of Palestine* 247], who reports that it is still a practice among Palestinians to layer their clothing in cold weather — and it was cold enough for Peter and the servants of the Sanhedrin to be warming themselves at a fire). Did the high priest open up or take off his outer garment to tear his undergarments? Favoring so is Josephus's statement that on one occasion the chief priests had bare chests for having torn their vestments (ἐσθήτων — *J.W.* 2.15.4 §322; similarly, *b. Mo'ed Qat.* 25a; Ov. *Her.* 6.27). Out of many other examples of tearing one's garments to express horror, see Gen 37:29; 44:13; Judg 11:35; 2 Kgs 6:30; 11:14; 18:37; 19:1; Esth 4:1; Jdt 14:19; Acts 14:14; Josephus *J.W.* 2.15.2 §316; *m. Sanh.* 7:5; Ov. *Her.* 12.153; 15.122; idem *Fast.* 4.448 (cf. 2 Macc 4:38). Lev 10:6; 21:10 prohibit priests from tearing their vestments, but only with regard to mourning the dead; and Ezek 42:14; 44:19 prohibit the wearing of priestly vestments even so far away from the sanctuary as the outer court of the temple. Since the Sanhedrin are meeting in the high priest's house, then, the clothes that he tears do not consist of his vestments.

W. Schmithals (664-65) thinks that Jewish persecution of Christians for proclaiming Jesus as the Christ defines the present charge of blasphemy in terms of Jesus' messianic claim (cf. E. Haenchen 514; J. R. Donahue, *Are You the Christ?* 96-97). This view stumbles over the failure of any passage in the NT to associate such persecution with a charge that Christians are blaspheming when they make such a proclamation. In 1 Cor 4:13; 1 Pet 4:4; Rev 2:8 non-Christians are said to blaspheme Christians; and the only passages in which Christians are said to have blasphemed — viz., Acts 6:11, 13; 26:11 — do not say that they blasphemed by proclaiming Jesus as the Christ, but only that Stephen blasphemed Moses, God, the temple, and the Law and that Paul "was forcing them [Christians] to blaspheme." Acts 26:11 does not say that Christians blasphemed at all, for the Christian standpoint of the speaker (Paul, referring to what he had done before becoming a Christian) favors a conative imperfect in ἠνάγκαζον, "I was trying to force [them to blaspheme]" (N. Turner, *Grammatical Insights* 86-87). As to Jesus, the Sanhedrin is unlikely to have considered a claim to messiahship blasphemous, at least not capitally so. On the one hand, Jewish messianic expectation was too diverse to have provided a foundation firm enough for laying capital charge against a messianic claimant. On the other hand, the purely human character of the expected messiah, or messiahs, would have made it very difficult to justify the charging of a messianic claimant with capital blasphemy. For these same reasons and to the extent that "the Son of the Blessed One" may have meant no more than "the Christ" (but see the foregoing notes on v 61 and the treatment of "the Son of the Blessed One" as restrictive by J. Marcus in *NovT* 31 [1989] 125-41), a claim to divine sonship would provide an unlikely basis for the charge of capital blasphemy.

W. Schmithals (loc. cit.) and before him W. Wrede (*Messianic Secret* 74-75) correctly note that since for Mark divine sonship entails deity, he would consider Jesus' claim to divine sonship blasphemous to the Sanhedrin even though they, innocent of such an entailment, would not. But the just-mentioned failure of the NT to associate Jewish persecution of Christians with a charge that they are blaspheming by proclaiming Jesus as the Christ holds also for proclaiming him as the Son of God and therefore makes improbable any Marcan (or pre-Marcan) fabrication of a similar charge with respect to Jesus' self-proclamation. Furthermore, as noted by J. C. Doudna, *Greek* 19, the use of the genitive βλασφημίας, "blasphemy," after ἠκούσατε, "you have heard," betrays a lack of Marcan interest in the content of the blasphemy; for in accordance with classical Greek, the papyri use an accusative after ἀκούω for the content of what is heard (and a genitive for the person heard, and a genitive or an accusative for a sound or voice heard).

H. Anderson (330) thinks that since Jesus respectfully substituted "the Power" for God's name, Mark probably presents the charge of blasphemy as false. But his failing to describe this charge as false contrasts with his repeated descriptions of the preceding testimonies as false (vv 56-59), and he would probably have explained to his Gentile audience the Jewish requirement that capitally punishable blasphemy include a pronunciation of the tetragrammaton (*m. Sanh.* 7:5; cf. Mark 7:3-4 for an explanation of this sort). For other understandings of Jesus' supposed blasphemy, see D. R. Catchpole, *Trial* 126-48; idem in *TynBul* 16 (1965) 10-18.

Our attention better goes to the just-cited passage *m. Sanh.* 7:5. It says that a blasphemer is not liable, i.e. cannot be condemned to death, unless the blasphemy has included a pronunciation of the tetragrammaton (so also Lev 24:16 LXX ["but let (the one) naming the name of 'Lord' (MT: יהוה) die by death"]; Philo *Mos.* 2.37 §§203-4; 2.38 §§206-8; *b. Ker.* 7b; cf. *m. Yoma* 3:8; 6:2; *m. Soṭa* 7:6 for a limitation in *m. Sanh.* 7:5 to the tetragrammaton, i.e. for an exclusion of other divine names; and see Mark 2:7 for a supposed blasphemy of God that did not include a pronunciation of the tetragrammaton and that therefore did not draw a capital charge). Yet when giving testimony during a trial, witnesses to capital blasphemy use a substitute for the tetragrammaton. Only in closing does the chief witness pronounce the tetragrammaton in quoting the blasphemy. Before the chief witness quotes it with the tetragrammaton, however, the court is cleared of observers. Only the judges, the witnesses, and the accused remain. On hearing the chief witness pronounce the tetragrammaton, the judges stand up and tear their garments. Of the reasons listed in Str-B 1. 1007 for tearing one's garments, only the hearing of the tetragrammaton has a legal setting (D. Juel, *Messiah and Temple* 97). In view of the mishnaic regulation that witnesses to capital blasphemy use a substitute for the tetragrammaton so long as an audience of non-jurists are present, then, how would we expect Jesus' blasphemy — if it did include a pronunciation of the tetragrammaton — to be quoted by witnesses, in his case by the judges themselves, to non-jurists? Why, of course, with a substitute for the tetragrammaton just as in Mark's text. Thus Jesus did pronounce the tetragrammaton. It is the right hand of יהוה, "YHWH," concerning which Ps 110:1 speaks; so Jesus must have said, "I am, and you will see the Son of man sitting at [the] right [hand] of Yahweh . . . ," and the Sanhedrists who later reported to non-jurists what Jesus had said used "the Power" as a substitute for Jesus's "Yahweh" (cf. the substitution of "God" for "Lord" [κύριος — Greek for the tetragrammaton] in quotations of Ps 110:1 at Acts 2:34-35 with 2:36; Rom 8:34; Eph 1:20 with 1:17; Col 3:1; Heb 1:13 with 1:1; 10:12; Mark 16:19 and the substitution of rhetorical flourishes at Luke 22:69; Heb 1:3; 8:1; 12:2; also the paucity of occurrences of the tetragrammaton in QL and the use of four dots and of archaic Hebrew characters for it also in QL and even in pre-Christian manuscripts of the LXX, where we might have expected ὁ κύριος, "the Lord" [for details see H. Stegemann in *Qumrân* 195-96, 200-202]).

But though capitally punishable blasphemy requires a pronunciation of the tetragrammaton, such blasphemy consists not merely in pronouncing it, but also in dishonoring it. In the first place, "blasphemy" means "slander." Secondly, blaspheming the name Yahweh stands in parallel with cursing God in Lev 24:15b-16. The whole passage Lev 24:10-16 provides the basis for the requirement in *m. Sanh.* 7:5 that capital blasphemy include a pronunciation of the tetragrammaton, and the mishnaic passage uses the piel of גדף as a synonym for the verbs of cursing קלל and נקב in the levitical passage. Thirdly, the parallel between blaspheming and cursing persists even when pronouncing the tetragrammaton in blasphemy is thought to differ from and go beyond cursing God, taken now as cursing the gods without pronouncing the tetragrammaton (so *b. Ker.* 7ab; Philo *Mos.* 2.37-38 §§196-208; and probably Lev 24:15b-16 LXX if δέ is adversative, as in Philo *Mos.* 2.37 §203; cf. Josephus *Ant.* 4.8.10 §207; idem *Ag.Ap.* 2.33 §237; *b. Ker.* 7ab). Fourthly, the connotation of the English word "curse" would unduly restrict the meaning of the corresponding Hebrew words and therefore of the parallel blasphemy. In Isa 37:6, for example, an Assyrian is said to have cursed God merely by saying that Yahweh the God of the Jews would not deliver Jerusalem from the Assyrians. Far from speaking against Yahweh, the Assyrian has even claimed that Yahweh sent the Assyrians and is with them (Isa 36:4-21). In the Jewish view, however, to associate Yahweh with idolatrous heathen is to curse Yahweh, to dishonor the tetragrammaton pronounced in the blasphemy (cf. Philo *Mos.* 2.38 §§206, 208 [according to which blasphemy of the tetragrammaton may consist merely in uttering it "unseasonably" (ἀκαίρως, ἀκαιρευόμενοι)] and the parallel in Josephus *Ag.Ap.* 2.33 §237 between blaspheming and ridiculing [χλευάζειν]). Elsewhere in Mark, fifthly, blasphemy always consists in dishonoring someone by verbal robbery: in 2:7 by verbally robbing God of the prerogative to forgive sins, in 3:28-30 by verbally robbing the Holy Spirit of enabling Jesus to perform exorcisms, in 7:22 by verbally robbing other people of their rights to property and dignity (as may be inferred from the sandwiching of blasphemy between envy and arrogance), and in 15:29 by verbally robbing Jesus of his supposedly claimed power to destroy the temple and build another one in three days.

So what does Jesus say that in the judgment of the Sanhedrin dishonors the tetragrammaton pronounced by him? We may best think that the high priest and rest of the Sanhedrin judge Jesus to have verbally robbed God of incommensurateness and unity by escalating himself to a superhuman level, by portraying himself as destined to sit at God's right hand and come with the clouds of heaven (cf. Dan 7:13 LXX, according to which one like a Son of man comes, not *to* the Ancient of Days, but *as* an ancient of days — noted by W. Bousset, *Religion* 264-65; F. F. Bruce, *NT Development* 81, though the parallel is weakened by the anarthrousness of "ancient of days" in the LXX [contrast Theod]). Support for this view comes from R. Jose's asking R. Akiba how long he will "profane the Shekinah" by interpreting the thrones of Dan 7:9 as set one for the Holy One, blessed be he, and one for David (*b. Sanh.* 38b). Profaning the Shekinah sounds very much like blaspheming the tetragrammaton (but N.B. that R. Akiba does not pronounce the tetragrammaton). (One might suppose that Jesus does not portray himself, but someone else, as sitting at God's right hand when he refers to "the Son of man"; but even so, if R. Jose could charge R. Akiba with profaning the Shekinah for putting a third party [David] on a throne beside God's throne, presumably the high priest could charge Jesus with blasphemy for putting a third party [the Son of man] at God's right hand.) R. Jose and R. Akiba flourished in the generation immediately following what Christians call the apostolic age, and these rabbis' dialogue forms part of a discussion concerning "all the passages which the *Minim* have taken [as grounds] for their heresy" (Soncino translation). If one grants the reliability of this talmudic tradition, the early date of the dialogue and its reference to heretics, such as Christians were considered to be, suggest that R. Akiba was refuting a placement of Jesus beside God with a placement of David beside God (it only sharpens the point if David stands for the Messiah yet to come) and that R. Jose sees in this refutation an offense to God's honor ironically similar to the one for which Jesus was condemned. Rabbinic opinions on the point continued to differ in afteryears (see the discussion in D. R. Catchpole, *Trial* 140-41). But the opinion expressed first by R. Jose shows that a body so bent on doing away with Jesus as were the Sanhedrin could easily find blasphemy of the tetragrammaton in Jesus' putting himself beside God.

In *m. Sanh.* 7:5 all the judges are to stand and tear their garments when hearing the tetragrammaton pronounced in a report of blasphemy. Here, the high priest is already standing; and only he is said to tear his garments when hearing what he tells his fellow judges is blasphemy. But the situations differ. In *m. Sanh.* 7:5 previous testimony has prepared all the judges to stand and tear their garments when the chief witness pronounces the tetragrammaton. In Mark the chief priest has stood up earlier to play a role like that of the prosecutorial witnesses, Jesus' statement comes as a surprise, and the high priest has to coach the other judges into regarding it as blasphemous. Whether they tore their garments on agreement with the judgment of the high priest Mark does not say, for his interest proceeds to the condemnation of Jesus by all of them. The moment for tearing of garments may have passed by the time the other judges reached that agreement.

The collocation of capital blasphemy and clothes-rending in *m. Sanh.* 7:5 as well as in Mark favors not only that at least on this point the Mishnah reflects early Sanhedric jurisprudence and early formalization of the Sanhedrin as a judicial body (against the view that either the mishnaic passage represents a later idealization of the Sanhedrin and its jurisprudence or the obliteration of the Sadducean sect by the destruction of Jerusalem and the temple in 70 C.E. led to a jurisprudence that better protected the rights of accused people), but also that Mark's account of Jesus' trial rests on trustworthy information (against the view that a Christian fabrication of the dialogue between the high priest and Jesus, and perhaps of the whole Sanhedric trial of Jesus, makes the mishnaic passage irrelevant, since Christians would neither know nor care about a Sanhedric requirement that capital blasphemy include a pronunciation of the tetragrammaton, but only about putting in Jesus' mouth words that satisfy the requirement of a Christian confession). For though Christians might have fabricated an account so defamatory of the Sanhedrin, Christians are unlikely to have fabricated — or even to have been able to fabricate — an account corresponding so subtly to a later idealization of Sanhedric jurisprudence in cases of capital blasphemy. Two differences make the correspondence subtle: (1) the difference between Jesus' not being brought to trial for capital blasphemy but supposedly uttering it on the spot and the Mishnah's dealing with cases in which the accused is brought to trial for a capital blasphemy previously uttered; (2) the difference between avoiding the tetragrammaton in a report following Jesus' trial and avoiding the tetragrammaton in all but the final testimony during a trial. This double subtlety would require not only that a Christian fabricator have known Sanhedric jurisprudence for cases of capital blasphemy and not only that such a fabricator have taken care to keep the Sanhedrin from violating their own jurisprudence in such cases (in itself an unlikely care in view of the well-known violations of Sanhedric jurisprudence in other respects when Mark and the Mishnah are compared), but also the double subtlety would require that a Christian fabricator buried the correspondence between the conduct of Jesus' trial as to capital blasphemy and a normal condemnation for capital blasphemy beneath the surface of the story, and did so by making Jesus speak blasphemy on the spot rather than earlier and by making him speak in the words of a reporter concerned to avoid pronouncing the tetragrammaton in the presence of non-jurists rather than by quoting the very words that Jesus spoke, including the tetragrammaton. Cf. the pre-Jesuanic date of naming the name (i.e. the tetragrammaton) in blasphemy at Lev 24:16 LXX.

J. Ernst (438) regards the threefoldness of the high priest's actions in vv 60, 61, and 63 as artificial. But the threefoldness is not noted, and the actions progress naturally from asking Jesus a question about the testimony brought against him through asking him a question about his office to an outburst against him, the first question prompted by accusations made against him, the second by his refusal to answer the first, and the outburst by his answer to the second. Artificiality?

See the notes on 1:45 concerning the pleonastic use of ἤρξατο, "began," with infinitive phrases (v 65). The forward position of αὐτοῦ, "his," which we might expect to have followed πρόσωπον, "face," contributes to parallelism between the present infinitive phrases by maintaining the placement of a personal pronoun right after each infinitive. See D. J. Moo, OT 142, n. 2: J. Blinzler, Prozess 164-66; and above all F. Neirynck in ETL 63 (1987) 5-47 against omitting "and to cover his face" (so D a sy^s bo^{mss}; R. H. Gundry in RevQ 2 [1960] 559-67) and on other text critical questions concerning v 65 and its synoptic parallels. Matt 26:67-68 omits the covering, not because it was absent from the original text of Mark 14:65, but because Matthew wants an allusion to Isa 50:6 (R. H. Gundry, Matthew 547). That Matt 26:67-68 mentions Jesus' face but not the covering, and Luke 22:63-64 the covering but not his face, favors that the original text of Mark 14:65 mentioned both. Apparently Mark's omitting to tell the purpose for which Jesus' face was covered led to scribal omission of that element. Or Matthew's omission of the covering may have led to scribal omission in Mark of the face as well as of the covering. Or both of these factors may have been at work.

D. E. Nineham (408) says that almost every word of v 65 could have come from the LXX of Isa 50:6; 53:3-5; Mic 4:14; 1 Kgs (3 Kgdms) 22:24. But the contrasts are so manifold that derivation from those OT passages seems unlikely. In Isa 50:6 the speaker gives his cheeks to slaps; in Mark 14:65 the servants receive Jesus with slaps, and his cheeks are not mentioned. In Isa 50:6 the face is not covered, but spit upon (cf. Num 12:14; Deut 25:9; Job 30:10); in Mark 14:65 Jesus' face is covered, but not said to be spit upon. In Isa 53:3-5 LXX the face of the Lord's Servant is turned away (and in Isa 53:3-5 MT people hide their own face from the Servant of Yahweh); in Mark 14:65 some of the Sanhedrin cover Jesus' face. In Isa 53:3-5 the Servant of Yahweh is caused pain, wounded, bruised, and chastened by God; in Mark 14:65 Jesus is cuffed by some of the Sanhedrin.

In Mic 4:14 LXX the cheek of the tribes (MT: the judge) of Israel is struck with a rod; in Mark 14:65 Jesus is hit with clenched fists as well as slapped with open palms, and again his cheek is not mentioned. In 1 Kgs 22:24 the false prophet Zedekiah tries to shut up the true prophet Micaiah by striking Micaiah on the cheek and asking how the Spirit of Yahweh passed from him (Zedekiah) to speak to Micaiah; in Mark 14:65 Jesus is cuffed, but his cheek is not mentioned and he is told to prophesy. Further undermining a derivation of v 65 from the LXX is the possibility of an underlying Semitic wordplay in ויסתירו ויסטו(ר) for the covering and slapping of Jesus' face (so J. Carmignac in *ASTI* 7 [1968-69] 72); but this possibility is weakened by the failure of (περι)καλύπτω to occur in the LXX for סתר, "cover."

Though Luke 22:64 says that the abusers of Jesus covered him for the purpose of challenging him to prophesy, i.e. to divine, who was hitting him (so also Matt 26:67-68 with mention of the face but not of the covering), O. Böcher (*Mächte* 49; *Dämonenfurcht* 298-306) advocates that they covered the face of Jesus to protect themselves from his evil eye. But the cross-references cited by Böcher provide scant support for this interpretation. Haman is not yet condemned when they cover his face in Esth 7:8 (cf. 7:9), and by his own action he has fallen on a couch. So there was no reason to fear retaliation from an evil eye, especially not if covering his face is metaphorical for a dead faint, as suggested by his falling on a couch and by the comparable Arabic expression cited by G. Gerleman (*Esther* 123-24; cf. Esth 7:6). The covering of people for stoning in *m. Sanh.* 6:3 has to do with modesty, not with protection from the victim's evil eye, and seems not to include the face. W. Schenk (*Passionsbericht* 240) suggests that the abusers of Jesus challenge him to prophesy again about the temple (cf. vv 57-58 and the presence of τινες both there and here). But the "some" who abuse him are not necessarily the "some" who gave false testimony concerning such a prophecy, and the Sanhedrin's rejection of that false testimony makes it unlikely that the challenge to prophesy takes off on the testimony. In 15:29 it will be others whose blasphemy of Jesus takes off on it (cf. 15:31-32). Jesus' prediction that the Sanhedrists will see the Son of man sitting on the right hand of the Power and coming with the clouds of heaven establishes a more likely runway. He has just made that prediction, and the Sanhedrin have judged it capitally blasphemous. So now they abuse him as a false prophet (cf. D. Hill, *NT Prophecy* 52).

The suggestion of O. Betz (in *ANRW* II 25/1. 637-39) that the covering of Jesus' face and challenge that he prophesy allude to Isa 11:3-4 — in particular, to "he will not judge by the sight of his eyes" — struggles against the differences between legal decisions (Isa 11:3-4) and prophesying (Mark 14:65) and between justful disregard of appearances (Isa 11:3-4) and inability to see (Mark 14:65). *B. Sanh.* 93b; *Midr. Isa.* 11:3-4; *Pesiq. R.* 38:1; and *Yal. Šimoni* 2:125 tell of an expectation based on Isa 11:3-4 that the Messiah will be able to judge by scent. But again, Jesus is challenged to prophesy, not to judge; and though we may surmise that the testing of Bar Kokhba according to his ability to smell entailed a partial covering of his face, we are not told that it did. Moreover, the covering of Jesus' face "all around" (περι-; see A. T. Robertson, *Grammar* 617; BAGD s.v. περι-καλύπτω) would seem to eliminate a test of judgment by scent. Such a test might entail the covering of the eyes and ears ("he will neither judge by the sight of his eyes nor decide by the hearing of his ears" — Isa 11:3), but not the covering of his nose as required by περικαλύπτειν (v 65). See D. L. Miller in *JBL* 90 (1971) 309-13 on the game of blind man's buff played with Jesus; also W. C. van Unnik, *Sparsa Collecta* 3-5.

For several reasons the Sanhedrin's abuse of Jesus seems to have taken place where they were meeting: (1) 14:65 mentions no disassembly or translocation, and (2) 15:1 says nothing about a reassembly. (3) Yet 14:66, 68b take care to identify different locations for Peter's denials. On the other hand, the servants are in the courtyard of the high priest (14:54). So under the lack of any indication that they are called into the meeting-place of the Sanhedrin, Mark seems to use the Latinism "received (ἔλαβον) him with slaps" to imply that the Sanhedrin dismiss Jesus into the hands of their servants. Prudence dictates that the Sanhedrin consult with each other in Jesus' absence. At 15:1, then, δήσαντες will best be understood causatively: the Sanhedrin will have their servants bind Jesus before delivering him to Pilate themselves.

Among others, K. E. Dewey (in *The Passion in Mark* 96-114) tries to distinguish between tradition and redaction in vv 53-54, 66-72. G. Klein (*Rekonstruktion* 49-98), E. Linnemann (*Studien* 70-108), and B. L. Mack (*Myth* 305-6) attack the historicity of Peter's denials (Mack with a list of Marcan and Petrine features that might equally well be cited in favor of historicity, since we have no way of distinguishing the historical from the Marcan and Petrine). R. Pesch (in *NT und Kirche* 42-52, 58-62) defends it. See the notes on 15:16 for the meaning of αὐλή as "courtyard," not "residence, palace." E. C. Maloney (*Semitic Interference* 126-31) regards μία, "one," in v 66 as equivalent to the indefinite τις, "a certain one," and therefore indicative of Semitic interference. But the narrowing down of the narrative from the whole Sanhedrin (vv 53, 55) to some of them and their servants (v 65) and now to a maid may favor the retention of some numerical force in μία.

Apparently in reference to *m. Šebu.* 8:3, 6, E. Schweizer (332) says that "I neither know nor understand what you're saying" (v 68) resembles the phraseology of a rabbinic oath. If so, the reference to cursing and oath-taking in v 71 becomes redundant. But the mishnaic passage does not give such phraseology the status of an oath. To make an oath, an "Amen" is required in answer to "I adjure you."

Several translations alternative to "I neither know nor understand what you're saying" have been offered for οὔτε οἶδα οὔτε ἐπίσταμαι σὺ τί λέγεις: (1) "I neither know [him], nor do I understand what you're saying"; (2) "I neither know nor understand [what you're saying]. What are you saying?" (3) "I neither know nor am acquainted [with him]. What are you saying?" (cf. C. E. B. Cranfield 446-47). In all these translations, "what you're saying" is equivalent to "what you mean." The expression of the direct object in v 71 ("I do not know *this man* with reference to whom you speak") militates against the alternative translations, for all of them require an ellipsis of the direct object. The supposition of a mistranslated Aramaic in v 68 that really meant "I am neither a companion of (ידע for personal intimacy) nor do I know at all (חכם for recognition, general knowledge) him of whom (ד, which could be taken to mean 'what,' as τι in Mark's Greek text) you speak" (C. C. Torrey, *Our Translated Gospels* 16-17; M. Black, *Aramaic Approach* 79-80) makes the denial in v 71 unnaturally repetitious in its wording; and it is no more "curious" for Peter to say that he does not know or understand what the maid has said than it is for the unpaid guardian and the borrower in *m. Šebu.* 8:3, 6 to say to the owner of a missing ox, "I don't know what you're saying" (cf. W. J. P. Boyd in *ExpTim* 67 [1955-56] 341).

J. A. Kleist (229) takes the maid in v 69 to be different from the one in v 66; but the definite article ἡ is surely anaphoric, and πάλιν more naturally means "again" (as very often elsewhere in Mark) than "in turn." Whether the maid followed Peter into the forecourt to pester him or to return to a doorkeeping post is a matter of speculation. She may have gone into the forecourt before Peter and seen him when he arrived, probably not knowing she would be there; for she speaks to the bystanders about him as though he has just shown up. See the comments on v 69 for indications that she is no longer in the courtyard.

W. L. Lane (541, n. 151) suggests that the imperfect tense of ἠρνεῖτο (v 70a) points to repeated denials. But more than one denial in the second round would spoil the overall number of three denials, one for each round; and verbs of speaking often take the imperfect tense to express the linearity of a single utterance rather than the iterativeness of multiple utterances. The verb of denial occurred in the aorist tense at v 68, but accompanied by a present participle, which took care of linearity. Here, the imperfect tense may make up for the lack of that participle.

O. F. J. Seitz (in *SE I* 516-19) thinks of ἀναθεματίζειν (v 71) in terms of Peter's binding himself under oath to tell the truth, posits an underlying חלילה לי plus a מִן-phrase, and cites Acts 23:12, 21; 2 Sam 23:17 par. 1 Chr 11:19 for support. But in none of these cross-references do we find oathful self-binding to tell the truth, and their contexts make crystal clear what other sorts of actions people bind themselves to perform. The same observations apply to all other OT occurrences of the Hebrew expression (Gen 18:25; 44:7, 17; Josh 22:29; 24:16; 1 Sam 2:30; 12:23; 14:45; 20:2, 9; 22:15; 24:7[6]; 26:11; 2 Sam 20:20; 1 Kgs 21:3; Job 34:10). The sole possible exception in Job 27:5 does have to do with speaking the truth, but only insofar as a justification of Job's friends would contradict his integrity in other respects; and again the context clarifies the point.

R. Pesch (in *NT und Kirche* 51) sees parallels between Peter's three denials and Jesus' three passion predictions (8:31; 9:31; 10:33-34), the three attempts of the Sanhedrin to arrest and destroy Jesus (11:18; 12:12; 14:1-2), Jesus' three entries into Jerusalem (11:11, 15, 27), his threefold praying and the threefold sleeping of Peter, James, and John in Gethsemane (14:32-42), the threefold dialogue concerning Jesus and Barabbas (15:6-15), and the framing of Jesus' crucifixion with the third, sixth, and ninth hours of the day (15:25, 33-34). Only the parallel with the praying and sleeping in Gethsemane is valid, however; for they are numbered as the denials are numbered, but Mark numbers none of the other threesomes. All the others but for the dialogue are scattered from each other, and the framing of Jesus' crucifixion with the third, sixth, and ninth hours produces only two segments of time.

Against the view that Mark is drawing a parallel between three interrogations of Peter and the three interrogations which persecuted Christians have had to undergo (Plin. *Ep.* 10.96.3; *Mart. Pol.* 9–10; so G. W. H. Lampe in *BJRL* 55 [1973] 352-53), Peter is *not* interrogated before his second denial (rather, the maid speaks about him to the bystanders). Pliny's interrogative method belongs to him alone. Polycarp's interrogator addresses him six times, not three. Nothing indicates that Peter's life is in danger; and the maid's comment, "This [man] is [one] of them" (v 69), simply draws out the implication of καί, "too," in the challenge, "You, too, were with the Nazarene Jesus" (v 67), that Peter is not the only one who has been with Jesus. So neither is there any need to suppose that later persecution of Christians for being members of the church has intruded into the maid's comment (ibid. 350-51).

G. Vermes (*Jesus the Jew* 46-48) argues that "Galilean" connotes rebellion. But such a connotation makes no sense in the present passage. For how would the bystanders have known that Peter is a rebel? His peaceful presence in the high priest's courtyard speaks otherwise. Nor would Peter's being a rebel cause the bystanders to deduce that he belongs to the band of Jesus' disciples; for that band have neither rebelled against Roman rule nor been slandered as rebels, nor has Jesus been accused of rebellion. Barabbas will take the role of rebel (15:7). The strength of Peter's reaction need not indicate an accusation that he is a rebel, for the repetition and reinforcement of the observation that he is one of Jesus' disciples sufficiently accounts for the strength of reaction. See 1:9 for the non-political, geographical background of "Galilean."

In v 70 C. E. B. Cranfield (447) accepts the v.l. καὶ ἡ λαλία σου ὁμοιάζει, "and your speech is like [a Galilean's]" (A Θ *f*¹³ Majority Text q sy^{p.h} bo^{pt}), on the grounds that ὁμοιάζει militates against an assimilation to Matt 26:73, which lacks this verb, and that the presence of ὁμοιάζει in Cod. D of Matt 26:73 supports the presence of this verb in Matthew's copy of Mark. But since Matthew likes words with ὁμ- (he inserts them eight times in shared material and uses them another eight times in unique passages — R. H. Gundry, *Matthew* 646) and since a Marcan "and your speech is like [a Galilean's]" would have carried a meaning easy to understand, Matthew is unlikely to have rejected the Marcan v.l. if he had found it in his manuscript of Mark.

According to K. E. Dewey (in *The Passion in Mark* 101), Mark leaves the direct object of Peter's cursing deliberately ambiguous to imply that in view of 8:38 Peter's cursing of Jesus amounts to a cursing of himself, too (v 71). Unfortunately for this view, 8:38 does not use the vocabulary of cursing to describe being ashamed of Jesus and his words or to describe being punished for such shame. It is not entirely convincing to compare Peter's denial, "I do not know this man that you're talking about," with the disciplinary statement, "I've never known you" (*b. Mo'ed Qat.* 16a). The wording does not occur exclusively in disciplinary statements (see Str-B 1. 469). Peter speaks *about* Jesus, not *to* him as in the disciplinary use. To effect a thirty days' separation, the disciplinary use treats an acquaintance of the speaker *as though* the speaker has never known him; but to escape identification as one of Jesus' disciples, Peter denies knowing Jesus *at all*.

If "and the cock crowed" does not belong in the original text of v 68, notes D. E. Nineham (409), v 72 implies that Peter heard only the second crowing, the one that made him remember, the first one going unmentioned because he did not hear it. But see B. M. Metzger, *Textual Commentary* ad loc., on the probability of parallel influence in the omission, and J. D. M. Derrett, *Studies* 4. 129-31; D. Brady in *JSNT* 4 (1979) 42-57 for internal evidence favoring the longer texts in both v 68 and v 72 (esp. against J. W. Wenham in *NTS* 25 [1978-79] 523-25). The longer texts are favored also by better external evidence.

K. E. Dewey (in *The Passion in Mark* 103) suggests that Matt 26:75b and Luke 22:62 agree against Mark in the statement, "And going outside, he [Peter] wept bitterly," because they base themselves on pre-Marcan tradition, and that Mark omits the exit because v 68b has already put Peter outside and omits the bitterness of the weeping to downplay any notion of repentance. But it is easier to posit (1) subsidiary influence of Matthew on Luke (cf. R. H. Gundry, *Matthew* 551; idem in *The Four Gospels 1992*); (2) Matthew's having changed the difficult ἐπιβαλών to ἐξελθών, "going out" (a favorite of his, for he inserts nominative participles of ἐξέρχομαι ten times in paralleled pericopes and uses them four times in peculiarly Matthean pericopes); and (3) his having prepared for this change by locating Peter "outside" in the courtyard (Matt 26:29) rather than "down" in it (Mark 14:66) for the first denial and by transferring him as far as "the gate" (Matt 26:71) instead of "the forecourt" (Mark 14:68) for the second and third denials. That Luke does not prepare for Peter's exit as Matthew does favors subsidiary influence from Matthew in the exit itself.

D. E. Nineham (399-400) suggests that the story of Peter's denials is designed to encourage Christians who have not stood fast under persecution (cf. T. A. Burkill in *Christianity, Judaism and Other Greco-Roman Cults* 1. 67-73). But the absence of any restoration — the episode does not even end with Peter's weeping in repentance, but with his weeping in remembrance of Jesus' prediction of the denials — makes the story *dis*couraging. And even 16:7 will present neither repentance nor restoration so much as an indication that Jesus' predictions, not Peter's, have and will come to pass (cf. 14:26-31).

Nor does Mark incorporate Peter's denials to expose a continuing ignorance of the necessity that Jesus die and that his disciples follow him in the suffering of persecution. Though at a distance, Peter was the only one of the Twelve to follow Jesus into the lion's den (so to speak). He wants to save his neck, but not because he fails to recognize the necessity of Jesus' death; rather, because he expects Jesus to die but against his boast lacks the courage to die with him (contrast v 31). Nor should we impose a penitential interpretation on Peter's weeping. As just noted, he weeps in remembrance of Jesus' prediction of the denials, not in repentance of them. So even the weeping contributes to the theme of fulfilment.

THE FULFILMENT OF JESUS' PREDICTION THAT HE WOULD BE GIVEN OVER TO THE GENTILES AND FLOGGED

15:1-15 (Matt 27:1-2, 11-26; Luke 23:1-5, 17-25; John 18:28-40; 19:16a)

Jesus' Roman trial starts with his being delivered to Pilate (v 1). The rest comes in pairs: Pilate's questioning whether Jesus is the king of the Jews (v 2a) and Jesus' answer (v 2b); the chief priests' accusing Jesus (v 3) and his refusal to answer (vv 4-5); an explanation concerning the custom of releasing a prisoner (v 6) and an identification of the prisoner Barabbas (v 7); the crowd's request for release of a prisoner (v 8) and Pilate's asking if they want him to release Jesus (vv 9-10); the chief priests' inciting the crowd to ask for the release of Barabbas (v 11) and Pilate's asking what then they want done with Jesus (v 12); the crowd's yelling for Jesus' crucifixion (v 13) and Pilate's asking what crime Jesus has committed (v 14a); the crowd's yelling all the more for Jesus' crucifixion (v 14b) and Pilate's releasing Barabbas and giving Jesus over for crucifixion (v 15).

15:1 *(Matt 27:1-2; Luke 23:1; John 18:28)* "And immediately" hurries the story line to the next point of emphasis, viz., the fulfilment of Jesus' prediction that "the chief priests and the scribes . . . will give him over to the Gentiles" (10:33). With increasing specificity, "in the morning" takes the narrative beyond the Sanhedric trial of Jesus, Peter's denials, and the cockcrowings, all of which occurred at night, to a consultation of the Sanhedrin. The forward position of συμβούλιον, "consultation," puts emphasis on the activity that will bring Jesus' prediction to fulfilment. The chief priests will deal with Pilate (vv 3, 10) and the crowd (v 11), but so strong is Mark's desire to emphasize the completeness with which Jesus' prediction is coming to fulfilment that after "the chief priests" Mark adds "with the elders and scribes, even [or 'i.e.' — καί] the whole Sanhedrin" (cf. 14:53, 55, 64). The lumping together of the elders and scribes under a single definite article in a subordinate prepositional phrase (contrast 14:53) and the redundancy of the reference to the whole Sanhedrin reveal the cost that he is willing to pay for this emphasis. The preverbal placement of these subjective phrases and of the participial phrases modifying them adds to the emphasis on completeness of fulfilment. Inclusion of the elders even goes beyond Jesus' prediction in 10:33. Mark does not spell out the topic of the Sanhedrin's consultation, but only its outcome; for that is what fulfils Jesus' prediction. The consultation issues in the binding of Jesus, which starts a parallel with Barabbas, who also was bound (v 7; cf. v 6: δέσμιον, "prisoner, bound person," cognate to δέω, "bind"), and prepares for a contrast with Barabbas's release (ἀπολύω, "loosen away"; vv 6-15). The asyndeton with which Mark introduces the binding of Jesus dramatizes this beginning of fulfilment. Whereas in Gethsemane Jesus was only seized and "led away" (ἀπήγαγον — 14:53; cf. 14:44), here the binding causes Mark to use the stronger verb ἀπήνεγκαν, "they brought [him] away" (cf. vv 16, 20b with v 22). (Φέρω is often so strong that it means "carry," not just "bring" or "take.") "And they gave him over to Pilate" uses the same verb (παραδίδωμι) that Jesus used in predicting that the Sanhedrin would give him over to the Gentiles

(10:33; see further 15:15-16). The seemingly interminable delay till we read that the Sanhedrin took Jesus away and gave him over to Pilate adds suspense to Mark's playing up the fulfilment of Jesus' prediction, and Mark's complete silence on the Sanhedrin's reason for giving Jesus over to Pilate rather than stoning Jesus themselves focuses all possible attention on that fulfilment.

15:2-5 *(Matt 27:11-14; Luke 23:2-5; John 18:29-38)* Pilate's question to Jesus, "Are you yourself the king of the Jews?" (v 2), parallels the high priest's question, "Are you yourself the Christ, the Son of the Blessed One?" (14:61), anticipates the inscription on Jesus' cross (15:26; cf. 15:9, 12, 18, 32), and implies that to portray him as an insurrectionist the Sanhedrin convert what they judged was his blasphemous claim to be the Christ (14:61-64) into a treasonous charge that he claims to be the king of the Jews (cf. their equating "the Christ" and "the king of Israel" in 15:32; also John 1:49; 12:13) and perhaps that from a Gentile standpoint and derogatorily Pilate turns "the king of Israel" into "the king of the Jews" (though Jews may use "the king of the Jews" in addressing Gentiles — Josephus *J.W.* 1.14.4 §282; idem *Ant.* 14.3.1 §36; 15.10.5 §373; 15.11.4 §409; 16.9.3 §291; 16.10.2 §311). Pilate would care nothing about blasphemy of the divine name, specifically the tetragrammaton, but would care a lot about any threat to Caesar's authority (cf. Acts 18:12-16; 23:28-29). Mark is so taken up with the fulfilment of Jesus' prediction that the Sanhedrin would give him over to the Gentiles, however, that he omits the charge implied by Pilate's question.

An adversative δέ, "but," signals a switch in subjects at the start of v 2a, as also in vv 4, 5, 6, 7, 9, 11, 12, 13, 14a, 14b, 15, usually in conjunction with an advance of the subject to stand before the verb (though in v 8 καί, "and," will create a sense of continuity between "the crowd," just following, and the "them" which in v 6 will have anticipated the crowd). Jesus' answer, "You yourself are speaking," simultaneously admits "the king of the Jews" as a given designation (hence the clause in Pilate's later statement to the crowd, "whom you call the king of the Jews" [v 12], and the inscription on the cross, "The King of the Jews" [v 26]) and rejects the phrase as a self-designation (hence Pilate's following motions toward releasing Jesus instead of executing him as an insurrectionist). In the introduction to Jesus' answer, the historical present tense of λέγει, "he says," stresses his following admission of "the king of the Jews" as a given designation but rejection of it as a self-designation; and the emphatic σύ, "you yourself," in the answer itself counteracts the emphatic σύ in Pilate's question so as to eliminate all suspicion of insurrectionism.

The chief priests now come forward by themselves (cf. 14:10; 15:10-11) to accuse Jesus "much." We should take πολλά as a characteristically Marcan adverbial accusative (see the note on 1:45), not as an accusative of direct object, "of many things" (see J. H. Moulton and W. F. Howard, *Accidence and Word-Formation* 446). This vigor of accusation makes the imperfect tense of κατηγόρουν, "were accusing," merely linear (as imperfect verbs of speaking often are) rather than iterative (as though the chief priests were lodging one accusation after another) and gives the reason for Pilate's question and exclamation, "You're making no answer, are you? Look, how much they're accusing you!" "Again" indicates that the question is Pilate's second (cf. v 2). This one repeats verbatim the high priest's first question in 14:60. But there the question dealt with Jesus' not answering those who bore false witness against him before the chief priests. Here the question deals with his not answering the chief priests who charge him before Pilate. Because of parallelism with the adverbial πολλά, we should take πόσα as also adverbial, "how much," rather than as objective, "how many things." Thus Pilate shows himself in agreement with Mark on the vigor with which the chief priests press the implied charge that Jesus claims to be the king of the Jews. Other charges are not in view (as would be so under an objective understanding of the accusatives); rather, the necessity of pressing this one charge because Jesus has refused to confess that he is the king of the Jews though he did confess before the Sanhedrin that he is the Christ, the Son of the Blessed One (14:61-62). Verses 3-5 do not stand in tension with v 2, then. They carry the matter forward. "But no longer did Jesus answer with respect to anything" echoes a clause in 14:61 except that Mark adds ἔτι to οὐκ, producing "no longer," because here Jesus has answered Pilate's first question (v 2). For emphasis Mark also advances οὐδέν, "in no way" (another adverbial accusative), ahead of the verb; and the passive ἀπεκρίθη replaces the middle ἀπεκρίνατο for "answer," perhaps because less solemnity attaches to political interrogation by Pilate than to theological interrogation by the high priest (see the comments on 14:61). The reason that Jesus now refuses to answer is that the chief priests are pressing a charge to which he has already responded. There is no tension between his present silence and his having answered, then; for the one presupposes the other. The addition that Pilate "marveled" at Jesus' no longer making answer exhibits an apologetic point, i.e. the strength of Jesus in withstanding efforts to elicit from him an admission of guilt (cf. the comments on 14:60-62). Furthermore, his silence will make the question of Pilate to the crowd all the more impressive; for if Pilate sees no crime in him despite his refusal to defend himself, how flimsy must be the case against him (cf. vv 9, 12, and esp. 14a; also Acts 25:16).

15:6-7 *(Matt 27:15-16; Luke 23:19; John 18:39a, 40b)* A short explanation now comes in to make possible an understanding of the next episode. The explanation divides into the general, "Now at each festival he used to release to them one prisoner, [the one] whom they asked for [παρῃτοῦντο, imperfect to correspond to the habitual imperfect of ἀπέλυεν, 'he used to release'], " and the specific, "Now the [man] called Barabbas was bound [cf. the binding of Jesus in v 1] with the insurrectionists who had committed murder in the insurrection." Does the distributive κατά . . . ἑορτήν mean "at each and every festival during the year" or only "at each celebration of this festival [the Passover]"? Probably the latter, since Mark's gospel knows only the Passover (so John 18:39). In either case, a forward position gives emphasis to κατά . . . ἑορτήν. "He" refers to Pilate, of course. In anticipation of vv 8-15, "to them" means the crowd. Ἕνα may mean "a"; but the release of a single prisoner from among a number of prisoners and, in the present story, the release of Jesus or Barabbas but not both of them favor the proper meaning of ἕνα, "one." In fact, this meaning prepares for the release of Jesus or Barabbas but not both.

Since "Barabbas" was a common surname (see *b. Ber.* 18b; H. P. Rüger in *Markus-Philologie* 74; BAGD s.v. Βαραββᾶς), "the one called (ὁ λεγόμενος) Barabbas" does not imply a nickname (contrast the phraseology of Mark in 3:16a-17) or carry a slur ("the so-called 'Son of Abba' [i.e. 'Son of the Father']" in contrast with Jesus, who recently and truly addressed God as his "Abba, Father" [14:36]). Elsewhere Mark's translations of Aramaic expressions show that he does not presume a knowledge of Aramaic on the part of his audience; yet a slur would require them to understand the Aramaic Βαρ- as meaning "Son of" without Mark's telling them so ("Abba" already having been translated at 14:36, though without explicit indication of translation). Ὁ λεγόμενος does not have to carry a slur (see, e.g., Matt 1:16) and usually does not (see a concordance s.v. λέγω). But neither is it likely that ὁ λεγόμενος refers merely to the bearing of a name (contrast the phraseology for that in 5:22; 14:32). Rather, Mark is setting up another parallel with Jesus, whom Pilate will say the crowd "call" (λέγετε) the king of the Jews (v 12; cf. the comments on v 1). "Bound" implies the imprisonment of Barabbas (cf. 6:17). His being bound "with the insurrectionists who had committed murder in the insurrection" makes him an insurrectionist and murderer (cf. the synonymity of being with Jesus and being one of his coterie in 14:67, 69, 70; also Luke 23:19, 25; John 18:40; Acts 3:14). The placement of ἐν τῇ στάσει, "in the insurrection," and φόνον, "murder," before the verb calls attention to the criminality of Barabbas and his fellow prisoners. Against this foil Jesus' innocence stands out in bold relief: Barabbas deserves to be bound and crucified; Jesus does not. Mark avoids obscuring this apologetic contrast with details concerning the insurrection, about which we know nothing more even from other sources.

15:8-10 *(Matt 27:17-19; John 18:39b)* "And going up" describes "the crowd," but not the same crowd that came to arrest Jesus in Gethsemane (14:43); for they would not need stirring up to ask for Barabbas's release and Jesus' crucifixion (15:11-14). And because they came from the Sanhedrin to arrest Jesus, it would not make sense for Mark to say that the Sanhedrin gave Jesus over to Pilate out of envy, as though Jesus were popular among his arresters! No, this is the crowd whom Mark has described as gladly hearing Jesus and as feared by the Sanhedrin (11:18, 32; 12:12, 37; 14:1-2, 48-49). They appear not to have a particular prisoner in mind when they go up and request the customary release. For even though Mark has introduced Barabbas, he avoids mentioning him as the object of the crowd's request (see the following notes for further reasons to deny that the crowd had in mind the release of Barabbas). Nor do they appear to have in mind the release of Jesus, for Mark gives no indication that they even know as yet of Jesus' standing trial before Pilate or of the Sanhedrin's having condemned Jesus as liable to the death penalty. And Mark avoids making Jesus the object of the crowd's request just as he avoids making Barabbas such an object. Pilate is the one who insinuates Jesus into their request; and he does not give them a choice between Jesus and Barabbas (the chief priests will be the ones to insinuate Barabbas into the crowd's request), but answers with a question whether they want him to release to them the king of the Jews. It is a test question which implies not only the Sanhedrin's charge that Jesus claims to be the king of the

Jews, but also the Sanhedrin's warning that a large number of Jews, represented now by the very crowd that asks Pilate to release a prisoner, regard Jesus as their king. The omission of ἵνα, "that," after θέλετε, "do you want," sharpens the question (see the comments on 10:36). Pilate might have said "your king," but that would have prejudged their attitude toward Jesus' putative claim of kingship over them. "Of the Jews" better preserves the testing character of Pilate's question. He asks it, Mark explains, because he knows that the chief priests have given Jesus over to him on account of envy, i.e. envy of Jesus' hold on the crowd. Before, his hold on the crowd made the chief priests and their fellow Sanhedrists fear both him and the crowd and thus draw back from arresting him in the festal assembly (see esp. 11:18, 32; 12:12; 14:1-2). Now that they have given him over to Pilate in consequence of a secret arrest and trial, it becomes appropriate to speak of their envy instead of their fear. "On account of envy" revives the apology that Mark has often made out of Jesus' magnetism (cf. Phil 1:15; *1 Clem.* 5:2, 4-5). The forward placement of the phrase puts emphasis on this apology. "Had given him over" points once again to the fulfilment of Jesus' prediction in 10:33. And as in 15:3, Mark singles out the chief priests as the masterminds (cf. 14:10). If justified by the crowd's answering Pilate's question in the affirmative, the envy of the chief priests will support their implied warning to him that a large number of Jews regard Jesus as their king.

15:11-12 *(Matt 27:20-22a; Luke 23:18, 20; John 18:40)* The chief priests do not share Mark's authorial omniscience concerning Pilate's knowledge of their envy; so they mistakenly suppose that he will grant a request by the crowd for Jesus' release rather than regarding such a request as justification of their warning and therefore as warrant for having Jesus crucified. Because of this supposition they stir up the crowd in order that Pilate might release Barabbas instead of Jesus. That is to say, the chief priests successfully use the popularity of a freedom-fighter with the crowd to combat the popularity that Jesus has had with them, and by asking Pilate to follow the festive custom of releasing one prisoner of their choice this very crowd have given the chief priests an opportunity to manipulate them so. Thus the preceding identification of Barabbas comes into play and accomplishes Mark's purpose of making a foil against which the injustice of Jesus' crucifixion may stand out. Emphasizing this foil are μᾶλλον, "rather," and the placement of the direct object τὸν Βαραββᾶν, "the [aforementioned] Barabbas," before its verb. At the chief priest's incitement, we may infer, the crowd lodge a request for Barabbas's release. But to emphasize the fulfilment of Jesus' predictions that the chief priests would reject him (8:31; 9:12, 31; 10:33), Mark omits the crowd's request and leaves only the purpose of the chief priests' incitement of them (thus a telic rather than epexegetic ἵνα in contrast with 5:18, 23; 6:56; 7:26, 32; 8:22; 9:18 and esp. 6:25; 10:35, 37, 51; 14:12).

"Again" (v 12) makes the answer of Pilate his second to the crowd (cf. v 9). "What then do you want I should do with respect to him whom you call the king of the Jews?" confirms the implication of his first answer that the chief priests have warned him of a large following ready to rebel against Caesar and make Jesus their king. This second answer also betrays puzzlement over what the crowd desire for Jesus if they regard him as their king yet want Pilate to release Barabbas instead of Jesus — and the custom is to release only one prisoner (v 6). What better fate than release? The omission of ἵνα, "that," after θέλετε, "do you want," again sharpens the question (cf. v 9 and the comments on 10:35).

15:13-14 *(Matt 27:22b-23; Luke 23:21-23)* "But again they yelled" implies that the crowd's previous request for Pilate to release Barabbas took the form of yelling (cf. ἀνέσεισαν, "stirred up," in v 11; also the use of "again" with "taking along the Twelve" in 10:32 because Jesus had taken along the Twelve in earlier episodes even though different verbs expressed his doing so), not that they have previously yelled for Jesus' crucifixion as now they do (for similar limitations on the meaning of "again," see 7:31, where Jesus goes out again, but not for a second time from the Tyrian region; and 14:70b, where Peter is again spoken to, but not for a second time by those who now speak to him). Though Pilate is in the right to follow a custom of releasing to the crowd a prisoner of their choice and though the crowd are in the right to make their choice known by acclamation (R. Pesch 2. 466), Mark's having mentioned the chief priests' envy of Jesus and incitement of the crowd turns the yelling into a feature of Jesus' trial that smacks of a "kangaroo court" and contrasts both with the crowd's mild-mannered asking in v 8 and with their yelling, "Hosanna! Blessed [is] the one coming in [the] name of [the] Lord," at the Triumphal Procession less than a week earlier (cf. 11:9 with 10:1, 46). Enhancing these contrasts is a shift from indirect quotations of the crowd (vv 8, 11) to direct quotations of them (vv 13, 14). "Crucify him" brings into view the horrid method of Jesus' execution that causes Mark to write his gospel as an apology. And it adds to the flavor of a kangaroo court that the crowd should yell for Roman imposition of such a fate on a fellow Jew. Jesus himself gave the lie to the chief priests' implication that he claimed kingship (v 2). By yelling for his crucifixion the crowd now give the lie to the chief priests' implication that the crowd call Jesus their king. Disabused of suspicion both that Jesus wants to lead an insurrection and that the crowd want him to lead one, Pilate asks, "Why, what bad thing [κακόν, 'crime'] has he done?" (cf. 3:4; Juv. 6.219-24). In contrast with the committing of murder by Barabbas and his fellow insurrectionists (v 7), Jesus has done nothing bad to which the crowd can point; so they only repeat their demand for his crucifixion instead of answering Pilate's question. Thus is exposed a miscarriage of justice. The addition of "vehemently" (περισσῶς) to the final yelling strengthens this exposé.

15:15 *(Matt 27:24-26; Luke 23:24-25; John 19:16a)* The miscarriage of justice shows up again in Pilate's "wanting to do the thing satisfactory to the crowd" despite his knowing that the chief priests have incited them out of envy (v 10) and in his releasing Barabbas, the very one who deserves crucifixion for insurrection and murder (v 7). The forward positions of τῷ ὄχλῳ, "to the crowd," and τὸ ἱκανόν, "the thing satisfactory," emphasize this miscarriage. The statement that Pilate "gave Jesus over [to the soldiers — see vv 16-27], having had him flogged, in order that he might be crucified" completes the miscarriage of justice so far as the Roman trial is concerned. Jesus goes to his execution without even the formality of a verdict, false though a verdict of guilty would have been (contrast 14:64 and N.B. that the Sanhedrin's passing of a verdict does not apply to Jesus' Roman trial). Mark uses παρέδωκεν, "gave over," to show completion of the fulfilment of Jesus' prediction that the Sanhedrin would "give him over to the Gentiles" (10:33). The Sanhedrin have already given him over to Pilate (v 1). Pilate's now giving him over to the soldiers (to be understood as Gentile soldiers, it goes without Mark's saying) fulfils the plural of "to the Gentiles" in Jesus' prediction and by means of inclusion (the account begins and ends with a giving over of Jesus) emphasizes that fulfilment. Though strictly speaking the Sanhedrin gave Jesus over only to Pilate and Pilate rather than the Sanhedrin now gives him over to the soldiers, the latter delivery stems from the former and therefore counts as completing the fulfilment of 10:33. The flogging of Jesus (φραγελλώσας, from the Latin *flagello*) fulfils the detail of Jesus' prediction that the Gentiles would whip him (μαστιγώσουσιν — 10:34). The switch to a Latinism is probably due to the Semitic character of the dominical saying on the one hand and the Roman setting of the present episode, about which Mark is writing in his own words, probably for a Roman audience (cf. the immediately foregoing and following Latinisms in τὸ ἱκανὸν ποιῆσαι, "to satisfy," and πραιτώριον, "praetorium" [vv 15a, 16a], possibly also in τιθέντες τὰ γόνατα, "kneeling" [v 19]).

NOTES

From here on in Mark, temporal notices occur in 15:1, 25, 33, 34, 42; 16:1. But against treating these notices as a means of signaling new pericopes, for the most part Mark has used topographical movement rather than temporal progression to introduce new pericopes. Moreover, because the temporal notices in 15:25, 33, 34 appear in the middle of related material, not at the beginning, they can hardly signal new pericopes. Each of the other temporal notices is accompanied by topographical movement, which as usual does signal a new pericope.

    D. Patte (*Structural Exegesis* 64-66) notes several structural oppositions in vv 1-15, and J. Gnilka (2. 296-97) surveys various assignments of material to tradition and redaction. We might think that in v 1 πρωΐ does not mean morning, but means the last watch of the night, preceded by the watch called "cockcrowing" (as in 13:35; cf. the cockcrowings in 14:68, 72). Apart from mention of night watches, however, when Mark refers πρωΐ to the hours just before dawn he adds qualifications to that effect (see 1:35; 16:2; contrast 11:20). On the historical realism of Pilate's hearing Jesus' case early after sunrise, see Sen. *De ira* 2.7.3; Macrob. *Sat.* 1.3; and further references and discussion in A. N. Sherwin-White, *Roman Society* 45. A v.l. substitutes preparing consultation for making consultation. The par. Matt 27:1 substitutes taking consultation for making consultation (cf. Matt 12:14; 22:15; 27:7; 28:12), though a v.l. there makes the opposite substitution. The text of Mark 3:6 varied between giving consultation and making it. The freedom with which these substitutions are made militates against the drawing of meaningful distinctions, as for example between the give-and-take of discussion and agreement on a plan. Συμβούλιον can mean "council" (as to the councilors or their meeting) as well as "consultation." Here, however, the making of a council would require the Sanhedrin to have adjourned at night and to have reconvened in the morning; and without saying a word about what transpired in the council per se, the statement would skip from the reconvening to Jesus' being bound and delivered to Pilate. "Having made consultation" (a Latinism from *consilium capere* — BDF §5[3b]) does not refer back to the trial held at night (as thought by F. J. Matera,

Kingship 9, et al.), for a consultation does not easily equate with a trial (3:6). Furthermore, a back reference to the trial held at night would require that "immediately in the morning" unnaturally exclude the next-mentioned consultation; and the trial issued in the Sanhedrin's mocking of Jesus (14:65) whereas the consultation issues in their binding him and delivering him to Pilate (cf. R. H. Gundry, *Matthew* 552). That the consultation preceded the delivery of Jesus to Pilate does not require the consultation to have occurred during the night, for the delivery need not have been the very first event to have occurred in the morning (against G. Schneider in *NovT* 12 [1970] 27-28).

During the night, the Sanhedrin reached a verdict that Jesus was liable to the death penalty for blasphemy (14:64). His consequent mockery supports their reaching this verdict, though not necessarily their adjourning the meeting (14:65). So the consultation in the morning (15:1) must deal with the tactical question of how to proceed in view of the probability that the people would riot in Jesus' behalf should the Sanhedrin have him publicly stoned for blasphemy (14:1-2; cf. 11:18, 32; 12:12, 34b; 14:10-11, 48-49a) and possibly in view of Pilate's presence in town and of Roman denial to the Sanhedrin of executionary authority except in cases where a Gentile had entered the temple farther than the outer court (though in contrast with John 18:31b such questions do not concern Mark; see E. Lohse in *TDNT* 7. 865-66; P. Winter, *Trial* 12-20, 97-130; A. N. Sherwin-White, *Roman Society* 32-43; J. Blinzler, *Prozess* 229-44; D. R. Catchpole in *The Trial of Jesus* 59-63; A. Strobel, *Stunde* 21-45; E. Schürer, G. Vermes, F. Millar, and M. Black, *History* 2. 218-23; J. Gnilka and K. Müller in *Der Prozess gegen Jesus* 28-31 and 41-83, respectively, on the question of the Sanhedrin's holding authority to execute criminals). Since a desire to emphasize the fulfilment of Jesus' prediction that the Sanhedrin would give him over to the Gentiles motivates the omission of every other possible reason for his delivery to Pilate, we have no need for the explanation of S. G. F. Brandon (in *SE II* 37-38) that Mark makes the omission to allow his fabrication of the insurrectionist Barabbas — this to apologize for Jesus' crucifixion as an insurrectionist by heaping blame on the Sanhedrin rather than on Jesus. Even under Brandon's hypothesis, why would an explanation of Sanhedric incompetence to execute Jesus have kept Mark from fabricating an episode in which the Sanhedrin stir up the crowd to ask for a true insurrectionist?

The decision to give Jesus over to Pilate made advisable a reformulation of the charge against Jesus (see the foregoing comments), but Mark leaves the matter to inference because he is writing with apologetic concerns. See the notes on 14:65 that the Sanhedrin did not adjourn after reaching their verdict at night. As 14:66 took up the narrative concerning Peter that had broken off with 14:54, so 15:1 takes up the narrative concerning Jesus that broke off with 14:65 (cf. John 18:14, 19, 28; also 18:18, 25). Because Peter's denials have intervened and Mark wants to emphasize the completeness with which Jesus' prediction of delivery by the Sanhedrin to the Gentiles is reaching fulfilment, Mark relists the classes of the Sanhedrin in 15:1 (cf. 14:53, 55 and the excursus just following the comments on 8:31-32). The relisting need not imply the start of an originally independent tradition, then, or of a tradition from which 14:53, 55-65 derived. Since the Sanhedrin reached a verdict of capital guilt at night (14:64) and since they did not even adjourn and reconvene, much less convene during the daytime, adjourn before nightfall, and reconvene on the next day, the consultation in the morning neither complies with nor was intended to comply with the regulation in *m. Sanh.* 4:1 that a verdict of capital guilt should be delayed a day.

Opposing the supposition that 15:1 represents an originally independent and perhaps more original version of Jesus' Sanhedric trial are the failures of the text to say anything about the Sanhedrin's convening, about the presence of Jesus, about the bringing of a specific charge against him, about the testifying of witnesses, about an interrogation, about a verdict (cf. the notes on 14:53-72 with a cross-reference to Luke 22:54-71). These failures far outweigh the claimed failure of 15:1 to presuppose what transpired during the night. In fact, what transpired during the night explains these failures. The terminology of consultation instead of trial also presupposes what transpired during the night.

The delivery of Jesus to Pilate is a surprising and therefore doubtfully historical outcome of the Sanhedrin's capital verdict only if they have lost their fear of the people who admire Jesus, only if Mark or someone earlier has made up the crowd's admiration of Jesus, or only if the Sanhedrin have the authority to carry out capital punishment in a case of blasphemy — all undemonstrable possibilities. Pilate, his office, and the reason for his presence in Jerusalem would be known in a Palestinian milieu where the tradition behind 15:1-15 first circulated. So Mark merely follows tradition in omitting to identify Pilate as the prefect of Judea and to say that he had come to Jerusalem in case the influx and excitement of many Passover pilgrims should ignite riot and insurrection (cf. Luke 13:1). A Roman audience may well have known who Pilate was, anyway; for in 36 C.E. he was sent back to Rome. Josephus (*J.W.* 2.9.2 §169), Philo (*Legat.* 38 §299), and Tacitus (*Ann.* 15.44) anachronistically call him a procurator; but a Palestinian inscription shows him to have been a prefect (the usual referent of ἡγεμών, "governor," a functional term which Matt 27:2 applies to him; J. Vardaman in *JBL* 81 [1962] 70-71; E. Schürer, G. Vermes, and F. Millar, *History* 1. 358). For further information about him, see Josephus *Ant.* 18.3.1-3 §§55-64; 18.4.1-2 §§85-89; 18.6.5 §177; idem *J.W.* 2.9.2-4 §§169-77; Philo *Legat.* 38 §§299-305; and on events in Rome entailing the fall from power of his friend Sejanus in 31 C.E., events that could have made the usually resolute Pilate pliable in the hands of the present crowd, see H. W. Hoehner in *New Dimensions in NT Study* 115-26, esp. 121-25 (against the argument that Pilate's present pliability undermines the historicity of Mark's account). Though opposed by J.-P. Lémonon (*Pilate et le gouvernement de la Judée* 273-79), this possibility favors a late date for the trial and death of Jesus and gets support from Pilate's stopping to issue coins offensive to Jews early in 32 C.E. (E. Bammel in *JJS* 2 [1951] 108-10; cf. Philo *Legat.* 24 §§159-61). In 26 C.E., long before Sejanus's fall and Jesus' trial and death (even under an early dating), Pilate had already yielded to popular Jewish pressure (Josephus *Ant.* 18.3.1 §§55-59; idem *J.W.* 2.9.2-3 §§169-74); so the fall of Sejanus is not needed for the historicity of Pilate's present yielding. More generally on the proneness of Roman judges to yield before popular clamor, see E. Bickermann in *RHR* 112 (1935) 208-10; A. Strobel, *Stunde* 124-27; and the whole of *Les villes libres de l'Orient gréco-romain et l'envoi au supplice par acclamations populaires* by J. Colin.

Without v 2, the narrative of Jesus' trial before Pilate does not even imply a particular charge against Jesus; so the material in the verse seems original to the narrative. But it is sometimes thought that Pilate's question whether Jesus is the king of the Jews and Jesus' answer (v 2) originally followed the chief priests' accusations, Pilate's interrogation, and Jesus' refusal to answer (vv 3-5, "no longer" having to be considered an addition to v 5 on reversal of the original order) or originally followed the chief priests' accusations (v 3), the rest being added by Mark (D. Dormeyer, *Sinn* 285-90; H.-J. Steichele, *Der leidende Sohn Gottes* 226). But the vigor of the chief priests' accusations seems due to Pilate's inability to elicit a confession from Jesus that he is the king of the Jews. An original delay would have avoided a repetition of Pilate's name in successive clauses (cf. v 1) only to produce a repeated reference to the chief priests in successive clauses (vv 1 and 3). To make the repetition of Pilate's name work in favor of rearrangement, then, a reference to the chief priests has to be excised from the tradition behind v 1. Yet who did present Jesus to Pilate if not the chief priests?

E. Lohmeyer (335) uses too fine a filter in commenting that at most Pilate can have said, "Have you *called* yourself the king of the Jews and *acted* thus?" but not "*Are* you yourself the king of the Jews?" As in 14:61, the question of being this or that carries within itself the question of corresponding self-identification and activity. It is puzzling why D. R. Catchpole (in *Jesus and the Politics of His Day* 328) should deny the historicity of Pilate's question because its terminology "aligns Jesus with Jewish kings in general (see Josephus, *BJ* 1:282; *AJ* 14:36; 15:373f, 409; 16:291, 311, for example)." Such an alignment on Pilate's part makes historical sense: if Jesus was charged with claiming to be the king of the Jews, Pilate would naturally think of him in terms of those others.

A. Stock (*Call* 160) argues that since the portrayal of Jesus as king starts right where he looks least like the traditionally expected Messiah, he must have been crucified as a messianic king; otherwise, this portrayal would not have attached to the Passion. Verse 32 supports this argument, but we should bear in mind that the portrayal does not stem from Mark, the disciples of Jesus, or Jesus himself, but from the chief priests as echoed by Pilate. The question, "Are you yourself the king of the Jews?" (v 2), is no more ironic than was the question, "Are you yourself the Christ . . . ?" (14:61). The phraseology is parallel (σὺ εἶ . . . ;).

M. Zerwick (*Untersuchungen* 65) uses parallelism with the aorist of εἶπεν, "he [Jesus] said" (14:62), to argue against emphasis in the historical present of λέγει, "he [Jesus] says" (15:2). Yet Mark may want to emphasize Jesus' accepting "the king of the Jews" as a given designation but rejecting it as a self-designation. Moreover, at 14:61 a historical present of λέγει introduced the question of Jesus' christhood and divine sonship, to which he said, "I am." So an emphasis was already established.

"You yourself are speaking" has been interpreted as an affirmative answer, rather like the emphatic colloquialism, "You said it!" or at least as an affirmative answer guarded by the qualification that more needs saying to keep the questioner from mis-perceptions. Here, for example, Jesus might be implying that though he is the king of the Jews, he is not the insurrectionist that Pilate has in mind. Even when qualified in this way, however, the emphatic σύ, "you yourself," tends to become vapid (cf. the comments on 14:70; N. Turner, *Grammatical Insights* 72-75). The contrast with Jesus' straightforward "I am" at 14:62 in answer to a very similar question that could have carried equally military-political overtones disrecommends any sort of affirmative mean-ing here in 15:2. If Pilate had understood such a meaning, both historically and narra-tivally he would be expected to regard it as a challenge to Caesar's authority. Further-more, Pilate says to the crowd that *they* call Jesus the king of the Jews (so the superior textual tradition in v 12) rather than that Jesus claims the title for himself.

In Matt 26:25 "you yourself have spoken" avoids telling Judas that he is the betrayer. Outside the words under dispute, Matthew gives no indication of Jesus' knowing who of the Twelve will betray him (on the contrary, see Matt 26:50a construed as a question); and even under a supposition that Jesus did know, to tip Judas off that Jesus knows of Judas's bargain to betray him (Matt 26:14-16) would run the risk of Judas's backing down and frustrating the fulfilment of Jesus' prediction (Matt 26:21). In Matt 26:64 "you yourself have spoken" avoids the terms of an oath under which Matthew's Jesus would otherwise have answered in contradiction of his own, uniquely Matthean prohibition of oath-taking (see Matt 5:33-37; and in Matt 26:64 N.B. the following πλήν, most naturally taken as an adversative, "nevertheless," introducing what Jesus does affirm not under oath [the rejec-tion of this meaning by M. E. Thrall (*Greek Particles* 71-72) springs from a failure to see that Matthew keeps Jesus from answering under oath]). "You yourself are saying that I am" in Luke 22:70 is shown to avoid an affirmative answer by the parallel "but if I should say to you [that I am the Christ], you would by no means believe; and if I should ask [you a question], you would by no means answer" (Luke 22:67-68). In John 18:34, "Are you yourself saying this on your own initiative or have others spoken to you about me?" avoids an affirmative answer to Pilate's question, "Are you yourself the king of the Jews?" Jesus' further answer, "My kingdom is not of this world [and so on]" (v 36), explicitly denies kingship over the Jews; for to be their king would be to have a kingdom of this world. When Pilate then asks whether Jesus is not then a king, Jesus' answer, "You yourself are saying that I am a king" (v 37), accepts the title as a given designation but rejects it as a self-designation. For himself, Jesus goes on to claim instead that he has come into the world to bear witness to the truth. Pilate's persistence in calling Jesus the king of the Jews (v 39) offers an example of characteristically Johannine irony, which grows out of people's failure to understand the truth that stands before them in plain view (cf. v 38; 19:3). Even D. R. Catchpole (in *NTS* 17 [1970-71] 213-27), who argues against evasiveness in all these passages, recognizes a certain evasiveness in comparable rabbinic passages (but see I. Abrahams, *Studies* 2. 1-3, for denial of an affirmative answer in these passages).

T. A. Mohr (*Markus- und Johannespassion* 286) argues that the parallel with πόσα in v 4 makes πολλά objective rather than adverbial in v 3. But surely Mark's penchant for the adverbial πολλά and its coming first in this passage favor arguing in reverse that the parallel with πολλά in v 3 makes πόσα adverbial rather than objective in v 4. Even this argument needs refinement, however; for κατηγόρουν, "were accusing," already has an object of the person in the genitive αὐτοῦ, "him," so that πολλά would have to be an accusative of general reference, "concerning many things," if it were not an adverbial accusative of degree. But nowhere else in the NT does κατηγορέω take an accusative of general reference. And since everywhere else in his gospel Mark uses ἴδε only as an exclamatory imperative, "look!" (2:24; 3:34; 11:21; 13:1, 21; 15:35; 16:6), we should resist the temptation to treat it here in 15:4 as a transitive imperative, taking as its object either the whole of the πόσα-clause or πόσα alone (the latter of which possibilities would seem to require the relative pronoun ἅ, "that," after πόσα as well as the taking of πόσα objectively, "how many things," instead of adverbially, "how much").

As in 14:61, Jesus' silence (v 5) is reminiscent of Isa 53:7. He may be consciously playing the role of Yahweh's Servant in that passage (cf. his possible though disputable allusions to Isaiah 53 in Mark 9:12; 10:45; 14:24), but Mark makes nothing of the parallel. The phraseology of neither the MT nor the LXX comes over. Nor does Pilate's marveling at the silence of Jesus reflect Isa 52:13-15; for there the astonishment is unrelated to the silence of Yahweh's Servant in Isa 53:7, and it is kings rather than the servant who are silent. Though in Mark 5:20 θαυμάζω, "marvel," describes the reaction of people to an exorcism, in 6:6 it describes Jesus' reaction to the unbelief of his fellow townspeople and in 15:44 Pilate's reaction to the quickness of Jesus' death. So this verb gives us insufficient reason to infer that the silence of Jesus gives Pilate an overawing sense of Jesus' divine power.

Against L. Schenke (*Der gekreuzigte Christus* 47-51), Pilate's marveling at Jesus' silence is not left dangling by an abrupt transition to the episode concerning Barabbas so much as that episode fills a gap which would otherwise be left after Pilate's marveling. The necessity of explaining the paschal privilege and Barabbas's imprisonment would cause as much abruptness in an independent version and in other settings as in the present context. Against hypothesizing that to heighten the guilt of Jewish officialdom the episode has driven out an earlier condemnation of Jesus by Pilate, the episode is bound to the rest of the pericope by the chief priests' machinations against Jesus, by his designation "the king of the Jews," by Pilate's acting as judge, by his reluctance to condemn Jesus, and by Pilate's expedience; and the episode is unlikely to have circulated independently, for it makes sense only in the framework of Jesus' Roman trial (cf. V. Taylor 577; J. Ernst 452).

D. E. Nineham (416) finds it difficult that the dialogue between Pilate and the crowd seems to presuppose his having to release either Jesus or Barabbas and execute the other one (cf. "rather" in v 11); yet Pilate has not condemned Jesus by the close of vv 2-5, so that he could release both Jesus and Barabbas. Yes, he could release both; but he does not want to release a true insurrectionist such as Barabbas is. So he tries to play on Jesus' popularity, of which he knows the Sanhedrin are envious. T. A. Mohr (*Markus- und Johannespassion* 292) finds it difficult that the crowd would not have known whom Pilate meant by "the king of the Jews." The difficulty is only apparent. Mark is writing for an audience who know from v 2 that "the king of the Jews" refers to Jesus. He does not need to inform them of the means by which the crowd learned the referent of this phrase. And it is hard to imagine how under the circumstance of a typically Roman open-air trial in a public place with Jesus present (cf. John 18:28-29, 33, 38b; 19:1, 4, 5, 9, 13) they could have failed to learn very quickly that Pilate was judging Jesus' case and alluding to the charge against Jesus in using "the king of the Jews." Mohr's describing the question of Pilate, "Why, what bad thing has he done?" (v 14), as redactional because it makes no sense after the exchange between Pilate and Jesus and after the chief priests' accusation (vv 2-3; ibid. 294) wrongly presupposes that Pilate had come to accept the accusation despite Jesus' refusal to accept "the king of the Jews" as a self-designation (on the contrary, see v 10).

The explanation concerning a custom of releasing one prisoner every Passover (v 6) suits the Gentile and probably Roman audience for whom Mark writes. They would be unfamiliar with the custom (cf. esp. 7:3-4). On the other hand, the definite articles in "the one called Barabbas," "the insurrectionists," and "the insurrection" (v 7) imply an audience familiar with the insurrection and its principals. The audience that needs the foregoing explanation would probably be unfamiliar with them, however. Not even the first century Jewish historian Josephus mentions an insurrection led by Barabbas shortly before Jesus' crucifixion, though Josephus does mention other uprisings in the first two-thirds of the first century (*Ant.* 18.1.1 §§4-10; see R. A. Horsley and J. S. Hanson, *Bandits* passim; D. M. Rhoads, *Israel in Revolution* 47-93, but also the notes on 13:5b-6 against a messianic element). Hence, the definite articles probably belong to a version of the episode told earlier in a Jewish milieu where the insurrection and its principals were well known. If so, the definite article in "the one called Barabbas" need not imply a knowledge on Mark's part that Barabbas had "Jesus" as his primary name (Matt 27:16, 17; so A. E. J. Rawlinson 227-29), though it is conceivable that Mark drops a traditional "Jesus" from before "the one called Barabbas" because he wants to avoid tarnishing the name of Jesus of Nazareth with Barabbas's insurrectionism and murder, or because he wants to avoid a possible confusion of two Jesuses (but contrast Matthew's putting "Jesus" and "Barabbas" side by side *following* "called," and "Jesus the Barabbas" and "Jesus the one called Christ" on either side of "or"). See Luke 22:47 for phraseology like that in Mark 15:7 yet without any known additional name that might have dropped out of an initial position: "the one called Judas" (cf. also Matt 9:9; John 9:11; and, for the putting of a personal name before "the one called," and a title or nickname after it, Matt 1:16; 4:18; 10:2; 27:22).

The failure of Josephus to mention Barabbas's insurrection weakens the argument that despite popular pressure Pilate would not have released an insurrectionist like Barabbas. He was too minor an insurrectionist for Josephus to have known or mentioned and, it would appear, too minor for Pilate not to release and thereby risk the Jews' undercutting his position before the emperor in Rome (as in Philo *Legat.* 38 §§301-5; Josephus *Ant.* 18.4.1-2 §§85-89; cf. the earlier note on the falling from power of Pilate's friend Sejanus). Similarly, the failure of Josephus to mention Barabbas's insurrection gives no more reason to doubt its historicity than does Josephus's apparent failure to mention a comparable incident mentioned in Luke 13:1 (cf. I. H. Marshall, *Luke* 553; J. A. Fitzmyer, *Luke* 1006-7). As just noted, first century Palestine was rife with minor uprisings that anticipated the major revolt starting in 66 C.E. We cannot expect Josephus to have mentioned them all (cf. the arguments of J. Gnilka in *Der Prozess gegen Jesus* 18-19 that the episode concerning Barabbas must belong to the oldest tradition because his name does not function etiologically, but only instances a much-used personal name, and because the crowd functions as required for the carrying out of Roman justice, as in Josephus *J.W.* 2.9.4 §§175-77; 2.14.8 §§301-4 [though the latter passage involves only the chief priests and leading laymen, not a crowd]). If Barabbas's insurrection had occurred recently, as seems implied by his being still in prison rather than already executed, the chief priests may have tried to implicate Jesus in the insurrection by charging that he claimed to be the king of the Jews and warning that he had gained a following (cf. C. K. Barrett, *Jesus and the Gospel Tradition* 60). Or Barabbas's insurrection may have inspired them to try exciting Pilate's fear of another insurrection led by Jesus.

Accepting the historicity of the name "Jesus Barabbas," A. E. J. Rawlinson (227-29) thinks that the crowd asked for the release of Jesus Barabbas but that Pilate mistook them to be asking for the release of Jesus of Nazareth and therefore offered to release Jesus of Nazareth. In return for the crowd's supporting the request of the chief priests for Jesus' crucifixion, the chief priests then supported the crowd's request for the release of Jesus Barabbas. But Pilate does not at first *offer* to release Jesus; rather, he asks the crowd whether they *want* him to release Jesus (v 9). He is testing whether in accordance with the implied warning of the chief priests the crowd really do regard Jesus as their king.

Apart from v 6, its synoptic parallels in Matt 27:15; Luke 23:17 v.l., and John 18:39, we have no evidence for the releasing of a prisoner each Passover. In particular, the silence of Josephus is notable. Yet the custom of releasing a prisoner every Passover suits this festival in that the Jews are celebrating their release from Egyptian bondage (cf. *m. Pesaḥ.* 8:6, whatever the promise there of release from prison may mean). E. Bammel (in *Jesus and the Politics of His Day* 427-28) comments that the Roman prefects, "whose office was in the succession of the Hasmonean kings," adopted the custom from the Hasmonean kings and that because of this Jewish derivation Josephus does not mention the custom as a privilege accorded the Jews by the Romans (cf. John 18:39: "you have a custom [ὑμῖν as a dative of possession] that I should release one to you at the Passover"; also the middle voice of παρῃτοῦντο and αἰτεῖσθαι in Mark 15:6, 8 to indicate the crowd's asking for themselves). Occasional releases of prisoners in other settings, sometimes temporary and sometimes by acclamation of a crowd, do not entirely explain the custom to which Mark refers, then; but they do explain how it could be that in the administration of Palestine the Romans adopted a Jewish custom similar except for its regularity to those occasional releases. Again cf. *m. Pesaḥ.* 8:6; but also Josephus *Ant.* 20.9.3, 5 §§208-10, 215; Liv. 5.13.8; *PFlor.* 61. 59-65, cited by A. Deissmann, *LAE* 269, n. 1; the Ephesian inscription cited ibid. 269; *Digest* 48.16; and a wide variety of Babylonian, Assyrian, Greek, seemingly Roman, and perhaps other materials cited by R. L. Merritt in *JBL* 104 (1985) 57-68. Merritt sees the custom of releasing prisoners at religious and other festivals as prompting Mark to fabricate the episode concerning Barabbas. The custom could just as well support the traditionality and historicity of the episode. It would be easier to think of *abolitio,* the acquittal of a prisoner not yet condemned, than of *indulgentia,* the pardon of a condemned prisoner. For further discussion, see C. B. Cheval in *JBL* 60 (1941) 273-78; J. Blinzler, *Prozess* 301-3, 317-20; J.-P. Lémonon, *Pilate et le gouvernement de la Judée* 191-95.

An occasional practice of releasing prisoners was enough to make understandable the release of Barabbas instead of Jesus; so fabrication of a yearly custom seems improbable. For shifting blame from the Romans to the Jews (as Mark or someone before him is often thought to have done), an occasional practice would have worked even better than a yearly custom; for an occasional practice would have portrayed the Jews as so bloodthirsty that they asked for the release of Barabbas instead of Jesus even though it was not customary to release a prisoner every Passover. The anarthrousness of ἑορτήν, "festival," and the habitual imperfect tense of ἀπέλυεν, "used to release," of παρῃτοῦντο, "used to ask for," and of ἐποίει, "used to do," militate against a non-distributive use of κατά (cf. Josephus *J.W.* 1.11.6 §229), as though Pilate was going to release a prisoner only at the present festival. The commonness of "Barabbas" as a surname (see the comments on v 7) under-mines the theory that originally Barabbas was none other than Jesus himself, given "Barab-bas" as a title meaning "Son of the Father" or "Teacher" (so H. A. Rigg in *JBL* 64 [1945] 417-56; H. Z. Maccoby in *NTS* 16 [1969-70] 55-60; S. L. Davies in *NTS* 27 [1980-81] 260-62). This theory supposes that to include the crowd with the chief priests as guilty of Jesus' death, Christians fabricated a second Jesus Barabbas, for whose release the crowd yelled rather than for the release of Jesus Barabbas of Nazareth (as historically). One wonders, then, why Mark impugns the crowd only here and portrays them as Jesus' admirers everywhere else (for further criticisms, see C. S. Mann 637-39).

The crowd's "going up" (ἀναβάς — v 8) implies that the trial was being held at an elevated place. Perhaps no more is meant than that a crowd of pilgrims went up to Jerusalem from their encampments in the valleys bounding the city (cf. 10:32). But the Fortress of Antonia and Herod's Palace, in either of which Pilate may have been residing, were located in heights of the city; so even from within it the crowd would have had to go up. J. Colin (*Les villes libres* 14-15) favors the v.l. ἀναβοήσας, "crying out" (א² A C W Θ Ψ *f*¹,¹³ Majority Text sy bo^ms), because of its technical use for acclamations at trials. But it is that use plus possible scribal ignorance of and puzzlement over the appropriateness of "going up" that would have made easy an exchange of ἀναβάς for ἀναβοήσας. The homophony of the two words can be cited for an exchange in either direction. See G. S. Sloyan, *Jesus On Trial* 34-35, and other literature cited there on the Fortress of Antonia versus Herod's Palace. The palace seems more likely, on which see R. M. Mackowski, *Jerusalem* 102-11. Since the crowd appear not to have Jesus in mind when they go up to ask Pilate for the customary release of a prisoner (see the foregoing comments), we have no need to explain how they knew that Jesus was standing trial before Pilate. They did not know, but on arrival they learned. The intransitive use of αἰτέω, "ask," is so well established (see, e.g., Matt 7:7, 8 par. Luke 11:9, 10; Jas 4:3) that G. M. Lee (in *NovT* 20 [1978] 74) has no firm basis for his suggestion that "to ask according as he was in the habit of doing for them" (αἰτεῖσθαι καθὼς ἐποίει αὐτοῖς) includes a mistranslation of the Aramaic הוֹא ד, "that which," as though it were הוֹך ד, "as."

"Because of envy" subverts the interpretation which imputes to God the chief priests' giving Jesus over to Pilate (as well as all other instances of Jesus' being given over). F. J. Matera (*Kingship* 18) thinks that Mark inserts v 10 "to shift the onus of guilt from the crowd to the priests." But v 10 provides only a reason for Pilate's question: the chief priests' envy of Jesus caused Pilate to ask the crowd whether they wanted him to release Jesus. The crowd have asked for the release of a prisoner, but have not yet done anything blameworthy. It is v 11 alone that shifts the onus of guilt from the crowd to the chief priests — or better: *forestalls* putting an onus of guilt on the crowd — by attributing to incitement by the chief priests the crowd's request for a release of Barabbas instead of Jesus.

E. Schweizer (337) thinks that the last position in v 10 of οἱ ἀρχιερεῖς, "the chief priests," combines with its first position in v 11 to stress the guilt of the chief priests. But Mark normally delays a subject till after its predicate and advances the subject when using an adversative δέ to indicate a shift in the subjects of main clauses; so no such emphasis is to be seen here. We should not think that v 11 starts with οἵτινες καί, "who also" (so Θ 565 700; J. K. Elliott in *NT Textual Criticism* 59). Like the omission of "the chief priests" by B 1 *pc* sy^s bo at the close of v 10, this v.l. tries to avoid two successive mentions of the chief priests.

In v 12, the text critically debatable θέλετε, "do you want," probably echoes v 9 in Mark's original text rather than entering by parallel influence from that verse in later copying. It would be easy for later copyists to simplify the construction, ". . . do you wish [that] I should do," by omission, which produces the smoother question, "What then shall [or 'should'] I do . . . ?" (cf. B. M. Metzger, *Textual Commentary* ad loc.; R. H. Gundry,

Matthew 563). The variant omission of ὃν λέγετε, "with respect to him whom you call" (again see Metzger, *Textual Commentary* ad loc.), may stem from scribal desire to make Pilate recognize a kingship of Jesus over the Jews that Christian copyists believe in (cf. Matt 27:22, 37; Luke 23:38; John 18:39; 19:15, 19-22) but that the original text of Mark puts only in the mouth of the crowd as quoted by Pilate.

Nor is there irony in Pilate's calling Jesus the king of the Jews (for he only alludes to the implied charge of the Sanhedrin that Jesus claims to be such [v 9] and to the implied warning by the Sanhedrin that the crowd call him such [v 12]) or in Pilate's alluding to the implied charge and the warning (for Pilate takes them seriously) or in the crowd's rejecting what Mark regards as Jesus' kingship over the Jews (for nowhere does Mark himself present Jesus as the king of the Jews or quote the disciples as so confessing or proclaiming him or Jesus as so presenting himself — see the notes on 14:42). We might find irony in the belying of the Sanhedrin's implied warning that Jesus has gained a following for his claim to Jewish kingship by the very crowd who according to the warning were his followers, and this belying at the incitement of the Sanhedrists themselves. We might find irony also in the crowd's asking for the release of the real insurrectionist Barabbas instead of Jesus, the insurrectionary charge against whom they themselves have proved indubitably false by twice yelling for his crucifixion. But since Mark leaves only implied both the charge that Jesus has claimed to be the king of the Jews and the warning that in his kingly pretension he has gained a crowd of adherents, we have no reason to believe in Marcan irony (contrast the explicit quotation of Jesus' passion predictions as a basis for irony in the challenge that he prophesy at the very time those predictions are being fulfilled, in part by the challenge itself — 14:65).

The necessity of stirring up the crowd to ask for Barabbas's release instead of Jesus' disfavors the view that the crowd had in mind from the very start to ask for Barabbas's release, for stirring up seems stronger than encouragement to pursue an original purpose. And if the crowd have all along purposed to ask for Barabbas's release, the reference to the chief priests' envy is left high and dry. One has to stray far from the immediate context to discover a reason for their envy unless this crowd consists of people who but for the chief priests' incitement would have asked Pilate to release Jesus. Mark puts Barabbas's identification (v 7) just before the crowd's going up to ask for the release of a prisoner (v 8) rather than just before the chief priests' inciting them to ask for the release of Barabbas (v 11), not to imply that from the start the crowd had in mind to ask for his release, but to allow the chief priests' envy (v 10) to set the stage for their stirring up the crowd. Mark's having inserted an explanation concerning the custom of releasing one prisoner (v 6) encourages him to add an identification of Barabbas right afterward. The result is an a-b-a'-b' structure: (a) custom (v 6); (b) Barabbas (v 7); (a') custom (vv 8-10); (b') Barabbas (vv 11-15). The introduction of Barabbas in v 7 creates suspense till his role in Jesus' trial is activated in vv 11-15.

One could imagine that the chief priests argue to the crowd that asking for Jesus' release might bring Roman reprisal on them all, for Pilate would think that Jesus might lead an insurrection larger than that of Barabbas. It is doubtful, however, that the crowd would be more concerned to forestall Roman reprisal than to gain the release of a favorite such as Jesus — and doubtful that the chief priests would regard the crowd as capable of such greater concern. More probably, then, the chief priests appeal to Barabbas's provenness as a freedom fighter and Jesus' unprovenness as such, indeed his having said to pay poll tax to Caesar (12:13-17).

C. E. B. Cranfield (451) wonders whether in v 12 Pilate hopes that the crowd will ask for the release of Jesus, too, whether if they do Pilate intends to show generosity by releasing Jesus as well as Barabbas, or whether Pilate hopes to persuade the crowd to alter their request. All that Pilate's question expresses, however, is puzzlement. Since in v 12 πάλιν means "again" (cf. v 9) and usually elsewhere as well, we should probably reject the translation "back" in v 13 ("but they shouted back"). In 11:3 an accompanying ὧδε, "here," clarified the meaning of "back" for πάλιν, but 15:13 has no ὧδε or equivalent. Nor on the supposition of an Aramaic substratum need we adopt the inferential translation "thereafter" (so M. Black, *Aramaic Approach* 112-13; see the foregoing comments). A prospective reference to the yelling of "Crucify him!" in v 14 has in its favor the repetitiousness of the shout and the non-mention of yelling in v 11 (so D. B. Peabody, *Mark as Composer* 146-47). But the basic meaning of πάλιν, "again," is retrospective, not prospective. In the comments we have noted an inexactitude of repetition in some other uses of πάλιν, and the modification of "yelled" by "vehemently" in v 14 leaves no need and little mental space for a carry-over from v 13. The normal translation "again" thus insures that Pilate is answering the crowd, as in v 9, not the chief priests. Besides, the chief priests have stirred up the crowd to ask for Barabbas's release, and he will release Barabbas to the crowd (v 15).

The crowd's yelling for Jesus' crucifixion may imply their expectation or knowledge that Barabbas is slated for crucifixion. Quite simply, then, they intend their yelling for Jesus' crucifixion instead of Barabbas's to confirm their desire for Barabbas's release. One could imagine that the crowd, perhaps stirred up again by the chief priests, cleverly ask for Jesus' crucifixion to prove that they do not belong to an insurrectionary movement led by Jesus and that therefore no Roman reprisal should come on them. But then the crowd would be too cleverly taking away the justification for Pilate's carrying out of their requests. Why should he release a proved insurrectionist and crucify someone who has neither rebelled nor captured the crowd's allegiance for the purpose of rebellion? It is better to think that they are unconscious of what Pilate may gather about Jesus from their requests. Mark does not say that the chief priests stirred up the crowd to yell for Jesus' crucifixion as they had stirred them up to yell for Barabbas's release.

In v 15, τὸ ἱκανὸν ποιῆσαι, "to do the sufficient thing," i.e. "to satisfy," may be a Latinism corresponding to *satis facere,* "to do enough" (BAGD s.v. ἱκανός 1c). H. Anderson (334) cites the disagreement of Pilate's offer to release Jesus with the stringencies that characterized Roman administration of justice, wonders how the chief priests would have had opportunity to incite the crowd during the trial, and misses a reference to formal sentencing. But we have seen that Pilate does not offer to release Jesus, but only tests the crowd's desire to have Jesus released. Furthermore, by the time Pilate tests their desire he has already examined Jesus and perceived the envy of the chief priests (there being no reason to doubt Mark's authorial omniscience concerning this envy); and administrators often fail to meet expectations attendant on their office. It is easy to imagine the chief priests' mingling with the crowd or using their servants to incite them. And to emphasize the fulfilment of Jesus' prediction in 10:33, Mark may substitute the statement that Pilate "gave him over" (v 15b) for one that Pilate sentenced Jesus. The release of Barabbas *to the crowd* spoils a picture of salvation through Jesus' suffering in Barabbas's place (against C. Maurer [in *Redaktion und Theologie des Passionsberichtes nach den Synoptikern* 126], who draws a parallel between the use of παραδίδωμι in Isa 53:6, 12 LXX for what happens to the suffering Servant of Yahweh and the use of the same verb in Mark 15:15 for what happens to Jesus).

On flogging as a preliminary to crucifixion, see Josephus *Ant.* 12.5.4 §256; idem *J.W.* 2.14.9 §§306, 308; 5.11.1 §449; 7.5.6 §154; 7.6.4 §§200, 202; 7.11.3 §450; Liv. 22.13.9; 28.37.3; 33.36.3; Cic. *Verr.* 5.62 §162; Sen. *De consol. ad Marc.* 26.3; Dion. Hal. *Ant. Rom.* 5.51.3; 7.69.1-2; Philo *Flac.* 9 §72; 10 §84; *Acts Pil.* 9:5; *Acta Justini et sociorum* 5.8 (cf. Diod. Sic. 18.16.3); on flogging in general, also Josephus *J.W.* 2.21.5 §612; 6.5.3 §304; Philo *Flac.* 10 §75; *T. Benj.* 2:2-3; *Digest* 48.19.8.3 (and see the discussion by H.-W. Kuhn in *ANRW* II 25/1. 745-58). Being tied to a stake and flogged, sometimes to death

(Dio Cass. 2, frg. 11.6; 16 after Zonar. 9.10.8; 30–35, frg. 104-6; 49.22.6), should be distinguished from being flogged prior to crucifixion. The flogging of a victim while he carried a cross-beam attached across his upper body (Dion. Hal. *Ant. Rom.* 7.69.1-2) seems to have been a regular practice. The crowd yelled that Pilate should crucify Jesus, not that he should let them crucify Jesus (v 13); and he released Barabbas to them, but is not said to have given Jesus over to them (v 15). Rather, the soldiers will take charge of Jesus' crucifixion (vv 16-24). Their leading Jesus away inside the courtyard which is a praetorium (v 16a), calling together the whole cohort (v 16b), hailing Jesus as Caesar would be hailed ("Ave, Caesar"), addressing Jesus as "king of the Jews" rather than as "king of Israel" (v 18; contrast v 32), requisitioning the Jew Simon of Cyrene (v 21), crucifying two bandits with Jesus (v 27), and apparently being under the command of a centurion (v 39) will all show them to have been Gentiles. As observed in the foregoing comments, the use of the Latinism φραγελλώσας (from *flagello*) for their flogging of Jesus suits a specifically Roman atmosphere (contrast μαστιγώσουσιν in 10:34).

Though Jews had used crucifixion from time to time (see, e.g., 11QTemple 1:6-13; 64:7-13; 4QNah 7-8; Josephus *J.W.* 1.4.6 §97; idem *Ant.* 13.14.2 §380; E. Stauffer, *Jerusalem und Rom* 125; Y. Yadin in *IEJ* 21 [1971] 1-12; J. M. Ford in *ExpTim* 87 [1975-76] 275-78; J. A. Fitzmyer in *CBQ* 40 [1978] 499-513; O. Betz in *SWJT* 30 [1988] 5-8), their use of it seems to have stopped from Herod the Great onward (M. Hengel, *Crucifixion* 84-85; cf. J. B. Baumgarten in *Harry M. Orlinsky Volume* 7-16). Furthermore, stoning was the prescribed method of execution for capital blasphemy (Lev 24:16; *m. Sanh.* 7:4); and the Sanhedrin condemned Jesus for such blasphemy (Mark 14:64). Jews would hardly have attached to Jesus' cross the inscription, "The King of the Jews" (v 26). If citing what they accused him of claiming for himself, they would have written "The King of Israel" (again see v 32). And Joseph of Arimathea has to ask Pilate, not the Sanhedrin, for Jesus' corpse (vv 42-45). Therefore we should reject the view that Jews, not Romans, crucified Jesus. Passages such as Acts 2:23, 36; 3:15; 4:10; 5:30; 7:52; 10:39; 1 Thess 2:15 mean that Jews induced Pilate to have Jesus crucified (so Luke 23:1-25, esp. 23:25: "but he [Pilate] gave Jesus over to their will").

THE FULFILMENT OF JESUS' PREDICTION THAT THE GENTILES WOULD MOCK HIM

15:16-20a *(Matt 27:27-31a; John 19:2-3)*

For the soldiers' mockery of Jesus, Mark first sets the stage (v 16) and then describes the mockery itself (vv 17-19), which subdivides into their dressing Jesus up like a king (v 27), saluting him (v 18), hitting him, spitting on him, and kneeling down to him (v 19), and finally indicates that they redressed him in his own clothes (v 20a).

15:16 *(Matt 27:27)* An adversative δέ, "but," and an advancement of the subject to a position before the verb signal a switch in subjects from Pilate (v 15) to the soldiers. Mark's audience will naturally understand that "the soldiers" to whom Pilate has given Jesus over for flogging and crucifixion (v 15) and who lead Jesus away "inside the court, i.e. praetorium" (cf. 14:54) are Gentiles (see the notes on v 15). As usual, the new pericope opens with a topographical shift. The soldiers now carry out the mockery to which Jesus predicted the Gentiles would subject him (10:34). Mark's returning to ἀπάγω, "lead away" (cf. 14:44, 53), instead of repeating the stronger ἀποφέρω, "take away" (cf. 15:1 with comments), implies that after his flogging Jesus was untied in preparation for his mockery. "Inside" (ἔσω) implies that Jesus' Jewish accusers have not entered Pilate's court (lest they defile themselves and not be fit to eat the Passover, according to John 18:28, which therefore raises a calendrical question). The "praetorium" (πραιτώριον, a Latin loanword) is the governor's official residence, or palace, in Jerusalem (see the notes on v 8). Τῆς αὐλῆς may refer more particularly to "the courtyard" surrounded by the buildings of the residence (see the following notes, but contrast BAGD s.v. αὐλή 4). The historical present tense in the statement, "And they call together the whole cohort," emphasizes the large scale on which the fulfilment of Jesus' prediction is taking place (cf. 14:55; 15:1 with comments). Attempts to make the statement more believable by scaling down the number of the cohort from its normal of about six hundred (though according to Josephus *J.W.* 3.4.2 §67 the number could run up to one thousand) to a maniple of about two hundred (as in Polyb. 11.23.1, 6), or by limiting the whole cohort to those present and supposing that some or many were elsewhere at the time, may or may not hit on the historical truth; but they certainly miss Mark's point of emphasis.

15:17-20a *(Matt 27:28-31a; John 19:2-3)* The details of the soldiers' mocking Jesus now add thoroughness of fulfilment to the large scale. Again the historical present tense in the twin statements, "And they dress him with purple [probably a soldier's red cloak in mock imitation of a royal robe] and, having woven a thorny crown [in mock imitation of Caesar's woven wreath], they put it around him [i.e. around his head]," stresses the detailedness of this fulfilment. The use of ἐνδιδύσκω (apparently a Doricism — BDF §73) instead of the more common ἐνδύω (to which v 20a returns) suits the speciality of Jesus' mock royal dress (cf. Luke 16:19). The salute, "Hail, king of the Jews!" (cf. vv 2, 9, 12, 26, 32), adds verbal mockery to sartorial mockery. And the soldiers' hitting Jesus on the head repeatedly with a reed (to heap insult on his thorny crown) and spitting on him (to heap insult on his royal robe) and kneeling before him (to heap insult on his falsely reported claim to kingship — the Greek verbs are all in the iterative imperfect) add physical mockery on top of sartorial and verbal mockeries. The spitting on Jesus fulfils a particularly mentioned detail in his prediction of the mockery (10:34; cf. 14:65 with comments and notes). Calling attention to this fulfilment are the vocalic-cum-consonantal assonance of ἔτυπτον, "they were hitting," and ἐνέπτυον, "they were spitting," and of κεφαλήν, "head," and καλάμῳ, "with a reed," the latter pair of which Mark highlights by advancing αὐτοῦ, "his," so as to put the assonant nouns cheek by jowl. The advanced αὐτοῦ does not emphasize Jesus as the owner of the head, then, but his head itself as the object of hitting with a reed (cf. the comments on 6:52). Also calling attention to the fulfilment of Jesus' prediction is the chiastic order of (a) robing Jesus, (b) crowning him, (b') hitting him on the head (where he is wearing the crown), and (a') spitting on him (where he is wearing the robe), each side of the chiasm being capped by homage, the first one verbal, the second one gesticular. "And when they had mocked him" summarizes the fulfilment of the prediction with the use of the same verb ἐμπαίζω, "mock," that appeared in Jesus' prediction (cf. also 15:31). The soldiers' taking the purple off him and putting his own clothes back on him prepare for the next episode, which will include their dividing up his clothes among themselves.

NOTES

Because v 20b ("in order that they might crucify him") picks up v 15 ("in order that he might be crucified") and because the soldiers' mocking of Jesus would more naturally precede his flogging (it is thought), vv 16-20a are widely regarded as a late insertion into the passion narrative (see, e.g., H. Anderson 338-39). But C. A. Evans (in *JBL* 101 [1982] 248-49) notes that the storytelling device of digression and resumption occurs in extra-NT literature where no one would detect a piecing together from different sources. That the soldiers' sport should follow Pilate's decision is no less likely than the Sanhedrin's venting spleen on Jesus after condemning him (14:65). Nor does a certain but by no means extensive similarity between these two mockings signal unhistoricity, as though one has been fabricated out of the other. The details of each are verisimilar (against H. Koester in *ANRW* II 25/2. 1525). The sorry state of a man just flogged would spice the soldiers' mockery with added pleasure (cf. the mocking of Jesus as he hangs on the cross — and *with regard to* his hanging there [vv 29-32]). John 19:1-3 advances the flogging and mockery to the middle of Jesus' Roman trial (cf. Luke 23:11), but the mockery still follows the flogging. Historical probability resists the Johannine order of flogging and mockery prior to Pilate's decision. There is no need to consider the mockery in Mark a secondary elaboration of the flogging (so R. Bultmann, *HST* 272). Why would flogging spark an elaboration in the form of mocking rather than in the more likely form of details concerning the flogging itself (cf. V. Taylor 584)? The different placements of the soldiers' mockery in Luke 23:11; John 19:2-3 does not prove it to be a free-floating and therefore originally independent tradition. For the mockery does not make sense outside the framework of Jesus' trial, and redactional shifts and different traditions of mockery provide equally good explanations of the different placements. It is less likely that the single mockery in *Gos. Pet.* 3:7-9 represents primitive tradition that Mark has multiplied (so Koester, loc. cit.; J. D. Crossan, *Four Other Gospels* 145-48) than that it represents an amalgamation of canonical materials. The Jewish judges, Herod Antipas, and Pilate are all brought together. Even Joseph of Arimathea is there in the role of Jesus' and Pilate's friend (1:1-2). And the Sanhedric and Roman forms of mockery are combined (3:6-9; cf. the simplifying that we see already in the fourth gospel, where the mockings in the Sanhedrin and at the cross are both eliminated). The surplus in Mark that is missing in the Gospel of Peter reflects the OT very little. Therefore it is *not* easier to believe that in the beginning there was only the belief that Jesus' death and resurrection happened according to the OT (1 Cor 15:3-4), the narrative of them only later being built out of the OT, than that a primitive narrative set Christians searching for OT precedents, which then influenced the narrative. Historical events themselves determined the structure of the narrative; and the preaching of the Cross as God's power for salvation must have forced someone like Peter, who according to Eus. *H.E.* 3.39.15 stands behind Mark, to tell the story of Jesus' death and resurrection in a fashion designed to counteract the shame of crucifixion.

J. D. Crossan (*Cross* 128) sees in the robing and crowning of Jesus an allusion to Zech 3:1-5, where Joshua (= Jesus) is supposed to have been similarly treated. But Joshua is undergoing trial, whereas Jesus' trial is over. Yahweh and Pilate do not correspond very well to each other in their capacities as the judges of Joshua and Jesus, respectively. Jesus is put in the role of a king, whom the chief priests have opposed, whereas Joshua is in fact the high priest, accused by the Satan. Yahweh's rebuke of the Satan contrasts with Pilate's having Jesus flogged and giving him over for crucifixion. Presumably, Jesus was undressed for the flogging; and the clothes that he had been wearing were unremarkable. But Joshua is wearing filthy garments, representing his iniquity. Yahweh takes it away, commanding him to be dressed and turbaned in clean, priestly garb. The soldiers mock Jesus with imitatively royal garb and then replace it with the everyday clothing that he had been wearing earlier. The number and width of these differences make it hard to imagine that the episode concerning Jesus even alludes to, much less grows out of, Zechariah's vision concerning Joshua.

The soldiers might be those stationed at the Fortress of Antonia or those who doubtless accompanied Pilate from Caesarea, where he lived most of the time (on Caesarea as his usual city of residence, see E. Schürer, G. Vermes, and F. Millar, *History* 1. 361). His staying now at Herod's palace in Jerusalem, if he is staying there rather than at the fortress (see again the notes on v 8), favors the latter possibility. The soldiers were not Roman in the strict sense, but recruits drawn from Gentiles living in the region. Jews were exempt from military service (ibid. 1. 362-67). Once called together, the whole cohort presumably joined in the mockery rather than spectating while the few of their number who had led Jesus from Pilate inside the courtyard staged the mockery for them.

If the buildings of Pilate's residence surrounded a courtyard, as favored by ἔσω, which doubles as an adverb, "inside," and as a substitute for the preposition εἰς, "into," τῆς αὐλῆς may keep its normal meaning "the courtyard" at the same time that it takes "praetorium" as a synonym; for then the courtyard belongs to the praetorium (H. A. W. Meyer 189; cf. Mark 14:54, 66, 68). The translation "palace" becomes unnecessary (though strongly favored by P. Benoit, *Jesus and the Gospels* 1. 180), as also the appeal to a misunderstood Aramaic substratum (דפרטורין, intended to mean "of the praetorium" but mistaken to mean "which [is] the praetorium" — mentioned and dismissed by F. Blass in *ExpTim* 10 [1898-99] 186). Of eight instances in the NT, only here is "praetorium" anarthrous. Because of this anarthrousness ὅ ἐστιν πραιτώριον, "i.e. praetorium," probably does not mean that τῆς αὐλῆς encompasses the whole of the praetorium, but that even though only a courtyard it has the identity of a praetorium.

The soldiers did not have to undress Jesus in preparation for putting imitatively royal garb on him. He was already undressed for the flogging. But Mark does not mention the undressing. Is he playing down the shame by omission? See BAGD s.v. πορφύρα; C. E. B. Cranfield 453; W. L. Lane 559; J. Blinzler, *Prozess* 326-27, nn. 27-29; *New Documents Illustrating Early Christianity . . . published in 1977*, p. 25, on the use of purple for royalty and for a soldier's red cloak. The word covers a range of colors from blue to red; so a soldier's red cloak would offer a handy imitation of royal purple. The weaving of a thorny crown imitates the woven wreath worn not only by Caesar but also by other rulers. On the possibility of a radiate crown, the spikes pointing outward, see H. St. J. Hart in *JTS* ns 3 [1952] 66-75; C. Bonner in *HTR* 46 [1953] 47-48 (with an apt citation of Apul. *Met.* 11.24); and, in general, W. Grundmann in *TDNT* 7. 632. With the mocking of Jesus as king, cf. Philo *Flac.* 6 §§36-39; V. A. Tcherikover and A. Fuks, eds., *Corpus Papyrorum Judaicarum* 2, nos. 154, 158; Plut. *Pomp.* 24; Dio Cass. 64.20.1-64.21.2; Dio Chrys. 4.67; also Josephus *J.W.* 4.3.8 §§155-57 (but with regard to the high priesthood rather than kingship) and R. Delbrueck in *ZNW* 41 (1942) 124-45. See V. Taylor 646-48 against the mockery as coming from a ritual drama common at the time. The use of a reed for hitting Jesus on the head indicates mockery of his thorny crown rather than infliction of pain by pounding the thorns into his skin. A reed is too fragile for effective pounding (cf. Isa 42:3; Matt 11:7 par. Luke 7:24; Matt 12:20).

W. L. Lane (560) suggests that the soldiers' spitting on Jesus parodies a kiss of homage. To H. Anderson (338) the soldiers' spitting on Jesus looks like an interpolation from the tradition reported in 14:65. But spitting is a common way of showing contempt; so it should come as no surprise that the soldiers as well as the Sanhedrists spit on Jesus. And as pointed out in the comments, the soldiers' spitting on Jesus suits their mockery of his imitatively royal robe just as their hitting him on the head with a reed suits their mockery of his thorny crown. This double suitability resists a theory of interpolation. F. J. Matera (*Kingship* 23-24) misses the chiasm noted in the foregoing comments when he cites awkward order as an argument for interpolation.

Τιθέντες τὰ γόνατα, "placing the knees, kneeling," probably represents the Latin *genua ponere* (BAGD s.v. τίθημι 11bα; C. F. D. Moule, *Idiom-Book* 192; BDF §5[3b]; H. Schlier in *TDNT* 1. 738). It is puzzling why V. Taylor (657, n. 1) should think that the evidence cited by Schlier is too slight. For a non-Latinism, Taylor cites Eur. *Tro.* 1307, γόνυ τίθημι γαίᾳ, "I put my knee to earth"; but the absence from Mark 15:19 of anything corresponding to γαίᾳ favors a Latinism. The suggestion that the soldiers did mock obeisance to Jesus as though he were divine, like a deified Caesar or an oriental divine king (ibid. 586), suffers from the lack of divine titles accompanying "the king of the Jews." Caesars and oriental potentates carried such titles. Since the crown of thorns represents royalty just as the purple does, the soldiers' taking the purple off Jesus before redressing him in his own clothes and leading him away to crucifixion (v 20a) suggests that they remove the crown of thorns at the same time. On the other hand, Mark's omitting to say that they removed this crown may imply that Jesus wore it right through his crucifixion.

THE WAY JESUS EXPIRED AS EVIDENCE OF HIS DIVINE SONSHIP

15:20b-41 (Matt 27:31b-56; Luke 23:26-49; John 19:16b-30)

As usual in Mark, a new pericope starts with an indication of topographical movement. Not till vv 42-43 will another such indication appear. Thus, as we would expect, the pericope dealing with Jesus' crucifixion is quite long. Preparations include the soldiers' taking Jesus out to be crucified (v 20b), requisitioning Simon of Cyrene to carry Jesus' cross (v 21), bringing Jesus to Golgotha (v 22), and offering him myrrhed wine (v 23). The execution includes their putting Jesus on a cross and dividing his clothes among themselves (vv 24-25), the wording of an inscription (v 26), and the crucifying of two bandits with him (v 27). The mockery at the cross includes blasphemous statements of passers-by (vv 29-30), ridiculing statements by the chief priests and scribes (vv 31-32a), and insulting statements by the bandits (v 32b). The death scene includes darkness (v 33), the cry of dereliction (v 34), an offer of sour wine (vv 35-36), expiration (v 37), a rending of the veil of the temple (v 38), the centurion's declaration (v 39), and observation by certain women (vv 40-41).

15:20b-23 *(Matt 27:31b-34; Luke 23:26-33a; John 19:16b-17)* The historical present tense in the statement, "And they lead him out in order that they might crucify him," headlines the fulfilment of Jesus' prediction that the Gentiles would kill him (10:33-34). The same emphasis comes out in the historical present tense of the further statement, "And they requisition a certain passer-by coming from a field, Simon a Cyrenian, the father of Alexander and Rufus, in order that he might take up his [Jesus'] cross," and of the yet further statement, "And they bring him to the Golgotha place, which is translated, 'Skull's place.' " The personal and place names add vividness to the already vivid use of the historical present tense. The personal names also imply that Alexander and Rufus are known to Mark's audience, to the audience of the pre-Marcan tradition, or to both of these audiences (and they might have been the same). The greater strength of the verb φέρουσιν, "bring" (v 22), as compared with ἀπήγαγον, "led away" (v 16), and ἐξάγουσιν, "lead out" (v 20b; cf. the comments on v 1), and the topographical terminology portend the imminent fulfilment of Jesus' predictions that he will be killed. In particular, the use of "Golgotha" to describe "the place" (N.B. the attributive position of "Golgotha" where Mark might have written a simple "to Golgotha"), the translation of "Golgotha" (Aramaic) by "Skull's" (contrast Mark's omitting to translate "Gethsemane" in 14:32), the repetition of "place," and the prominent positioning of "Skull's" before "place" (whereas Mark would normally have written "place of a Skull") all contribute to the sense of imminent fulfilment. The soldiers are leading Jesus out (ἐξάγουσιν); therefore "coming from a field" means that on requisition Simon has to reverse the direction of his travel. Historically, we might think that the soldiers have flogged Jesus so brutally that he cannot take up his cross, or if he has taken it up cannot carry it all the way to Golgotha, or at least cannot carry it as fast as the soldiers would like (cf. the quickness of his death only several hours later, which contrasts with other victims' hanging on their crosses for several days before dying). But Mark shows interest in Jesus' strength, not in his weakness (cf. his double emphasis on the loudness of Jesus' voice in vv 34, 37; also the comments on 14:39-42). More likely, then, it is to dignify Jesus that Mark notes the taking up of Jesus' cross by Simon of Cyrene. In Mark, Jesus does not even take up his cross, much less carry it. Somebody else takes it up (contrast 8:34 and esp. John 19:17). The use of ἄρῃ, "might take up," instead of φέρῃ, "might carry" (cf. φέρειν in Luke 23:26; also *portasse* in Iren. *Haer.* 1.24.4), sharpens the point. Omission of a reason for the requisition of Simon focuses attention on the dignifying of Jesus rather than on whatever weakness or suffering of his might have lain behind the requisition. The soldiers' trying to give him some wine spiced with myrrh (ἐδίδουν being a conative imperfect) adds to his dignity, for such wine is a delicacy (so, e.g., Plin. *HN* 14.15 §§92-93). An adversative δέ, "but," calls attention to his refusal to take the wine (contrast the switch to an aorist ἔδωκαν, "they gave," his tasting the wine, and only then refusing to drink it because gall, not myrrh, had been mixed with it — all in Matt 27:34). The refusal indicates a determination not to sleep on the cross (cf. his wakefulness in Gethsemane as Peter, James, and John slept). He will die awake and strong in flesh just as he prayed awake and strong in flesh.

15:24-27 *(Matt 27:35-38; Luke 23:33b-34; John 19:18-27)* Again Mark uses the historical present tense in the statement, "And they crucify him," to stress fulfilment of Jesus' prediction that the Gentiles would kill him (10:33-34; cf. the comments on 15:20b-23). Yet again we meet the historical present tense in the description of the soldiers' dividing Jesus' garments among themselves by casting lots. We should resist the temptation to think that Mark means to show the fulfilment of OT prophecy by borrowing phraseology from Ps 22:19(18) when he describes the division of Jesus' garments. He can assume his audience's knowledge of Jesus' predictions from his having recorded them earlier in order that the audience may note the fulfilment when it takes place. But he cannot assume his audience's knowledge of the OT, for they repeatedly need his explanation of all things Jewish. And he does not reveal to them here that he is borrowing from the OT; much less does he introduce its phraseology with a fulfilment-formula. It better suits his editorial purpose as evident elsewhere in the pericope to say that he dignifies Jesus again by showing the desirability of his garments, those garments which, as Mark's audience know, the woman with the flow of blood wanted to touch, and did touch, for her healing (5:27-28, 30) and which the sick in general sought to touch, even just the fringe of his garment ("and as many as touched it were being saved" — 6:56; cf. 2 Kgs 2:13-14; Acts 19:11-12). The soldiers' use of lots, the added clause, "who should take up what," and the superfluousness of this added clause (as shown by its omission in D *pc* it sy^s) emphasize the desirability of his garments (cf. executioners' claiming the last minimal possessions of their victims in Justinian's *Digest* 48.20.6). Thus the taking up of Jesus' garments parallels the taking up of Jesus' cross. Both instances of ἄρῃ, "take up," dignify him.

The notice of the third hour (c. 9 A.M.) as the hour of crucifixion gives three hours of daylight for the coming inscription, for the crucifixion of two others with Jesus, and for the mockery before the darkness that will blot out the shame of his crucifixion from the sixth to the ninth hours (v 33). Mark is starting a chronology that will show how little time Jesus spent on a cross (cf. the comments on vv 44-45). An adversative δέ, "but," sets this apologetic chronology against the crucifixion of Jesus and division of his garments; and the anarthrousness of "third hour" brings out the thirdness of the hour rather than the particularity of this third hour in order that emphasis may fall on the shortness of the Crucifixion. "And they crucified him" (v 25b) is repetitious of "and they crucify him" (v 24a) except that Mark switches to a past tense because of parallelism with the statement, "But it was [the] third hour" (v 25a). For the sake of the apologetic chronology, this repetitiousness (it forms an inclusion) and the use of a coordinate construction (we expect the subordinate construction, "*when* they crucified him") stress the Crucifixion as occurring right at the third hour, not at an earlier hour prior to the division of Jesus' garments. Mark does not want his audience to imagine that Jesus hung on a cross any longer than he actually did. The inscription of the charge against him, "The King of the Jews," and the crucifixion of two bandits with him, one on his right and one on his left, prepare for the following mockery. Mark's quoting the words of the inscription but not saying where it was put (contrast Matthew, Luke, and John) or whether it was paraded around (as in the extra-biblical passages cited in the following notes) shows that his interest lies in the title only as a charge that the chief priests and the scribes will take up in mockery. So also does the form of the charge as a phrase rather than a statement (cf. John, but contrast Matthew and Luke: "This (is) . . . ."); for Mark does not present Jesus as the king of the Jews (see the notes on 14:42; 15:2, 9, 12), the chief priests do not believe in his kingship, and the crowd have refused to acknowledge him as their king (15:9-14). According to 14:48-49, Jesus has already been mistreated as a bandit though he is not; so the crucifixion of two bandits on either side of him creates a foil for his innocence and dignifies him with a central position. Mark emphasizes these points by putting "with him [Jesus]" in a forward position and re-using the historical present tense in "they crucify" (cf. v 24). The mistreatment of Jesus as though he were a bandit gains further emphasis from his having called the traffickers in the temple "bandits" (11:17). Thus the temple-cleanser is crucified with bandits as though he were a temple-desecrator (cf. B. L. Mack, *Myth* 292).

15:29-32 *(Matt 27:39-44; Luke 23:35-43)* Mark now proceeds to another mockery of Jesus (cf. 14:65; 15:16-20), which continues to fulfil the passion predictions. The forward placement of οἱ παραπορευόμενοι, "the passers-by," shifts attention from the two bandits (cf. the forward placements of further subjects for similar purposes in vv 31a, 32b, 33, 35a, 37, 39a, 43a). "Shaking their heads," these passers-by vilify Jesus by bringing up the false charge that he predicted his destruction of the temple and building of another one in three days (cf. 14:58), by prefixing a scornful "Ha!" and by following up with a challenge that he save himself by coming down from the Cross. The double use of κατα- in καταλύων, "destroying," and καταβάς, "coming down," sharpens the vilification; and Mark identifies his own point of interest by describing the vilification as blasphemous. The one wrongly condemned for blasphemy has wrongly become its object. The passers-by address Jesus, but some of the chief priests and whole Sanhedrin have already addressed him (14:55, 60-65); so now the chief priests with the scribes speak to one another about him. They do not make use of the false charge brought up by the passers-by; for the chief priests and whole Sanhedrin threw that charge out of court, condemned Jesus on a Christological charge (14:55-64), and by implication converted this charge into a political charge with regard to kingship (15:1-20a). So now they say, "Others he saved [see 3:4; 5:23, 28, 34; 6:56; cf. 10:52]; himself he isn't able to save. Let the Christ, the king of Israel, come down now from the cross in order that we may see and believe [or, treating ἵνα as ecbatic, 'with the result that we will see and believe']" (cf. 8:11-12; John 8:30; Ps 42:11[10]). The forward positions of "others" and "himself" make an emphatic contrast. Where we expect "but" to introduce the statement that Jesus is unable to save himself, asyndeton sharpens the statement. The forward position of "the Christ, the king of Israel" emphasizes the rationale behind the challenge that he come down from the cross. The rationale is that a messianic king would not be hanging there. The reuse of κατα- in καταβάτω, "let . . . come down," revives the sharply vilifying wordplay with καταλύων. "Now" gives the challenge a temporal bite. "Likewise also" (ὁμοίως καί) shows that Mark regards this ridicule, too, as blasphemous. Because of their predominance, the chief priests take the lead over the scribes (cf. 15:1 with comments). Mark's use of ἐμπαίζω for the ridiculing shows fulfilment of Jesus' third passion prediction, where the same verb occurred (10:34; cf. 15:20 and see the excursus just following the comments on 8:31-32 that the scribes reappear here to further the motif of fulfilment). The Roman way of putting the charge against Jesus, "The King of the Jews," changes to a Jewish way of putting it: "the Christ, the king of Israel." These titles show why the scribes are mentioned in addition to the chief priests, for earlier the scribes have played a special role in Christological questions (2:6-7; 3:22; 9:11; 12:35). The insulting of Jesus by those who have been crucified with him puts the finishing touch on the fulfilment of this part of his passion predictions. The several mockeries concerning the temple, christhood, and kingship have followed the order of charges brought against him in 14:58, 61; 15:2; and a double dose of Marcan duality shows up in the order of material concerning (a) salvation, (b) coming down from the cross, (a') salvation; and (b') coming down from the cross. This duality adds to the emphasis on fulfilment of Jesus' prediction that he would be mocked. That even his co-victims insult him, and do so despite their deserving crucifixion and his not deserving it, highlights the extent to which the fulfilment goes.

15:33-39 *(Matt 27:45-54; Luke 23:44-48; John 19:28-30)* The interval between the third hour (midmorning), when Jesus was crucified (v 25), and the sixth hour (noon) has provided daylight for the wording of the inscription, the crucifixion of two bandits with Jesus, and the mockery (vv 26-32). Darkness now shrouds the whole earth from the sixth hour till Jesus' death at the ninth hour (midafternoon). The anarthrousness of "sixth hour" and "ninth hour" (v 33) brings out the sixthness and ninthness of the hours rather than the particularity of these hours in order that emphasis may again fall on the shortness of the Crucifixion (see also the comments on vv 25 and 44-45). The supernatural character of the darkness — it starts when the sun is at its highest and brightest and extends earth-wide — magnifies Mark's apologetic point: now that Jesus' prediction of mockery has reached complete fulfilment, God hides his Son from the blasphemers' leering.

The repetition of "ninth hour" (v 34), the prefixing of an anaphoric "the" (cf. v 33), and the forward placement of this temporal reference again stress the shortness of the Crucifixion. To portray Jesus at his death as strong — strong in flesh and superhumanly so (cf. the comments on 14:32-42, esp. 14:38b) — Mark mentions the loudness of Jesus' voice when he shouts, " 'Eloi, Eloi, lema sabachthani?' which is translated, 'My God, my God, why have you abandoned me?' " (Ps 22:2[1]; contrast *Gos. Pet.* 5:19, where with no mention of loudness Jesus laments his loss of strength: "My power, my power, you have abandoned me!" — aptly noted by G. Rossé, *Cry* 32-33; cf. ἰσχυρέ μου, "my Strong One," in Aquila's version of Ps 22:2, and see T. Boman, *Jesus-Überlieferung* 223, that ἡ δύναμις μου, "my power," is not a periphrasis for God's name). Twice before, Mark has noted "a loud voice" (1:26; 5:7). Each time the loudness represented superhuman strength. That Mark will shortly remention the loudness of Jesus' voice without quoting any words shows that he does not design the present mention of loudness to make the shout audible enough to be misunderstood. On the contrary, loudness should prevent misunderstanding. Rather, Mark designs the present as well as later mention of loudness to emphasize the superhuman strength of Jesus even as he expires. Mark's audience know that ordinarily victims of crucifixion weaken bit by bit and lapse into unconsciousness before dying. So shouting loudly at the last moment entails a remarkable exhibition of strength (cf. *1 Enoch* 71:11: "Thus I cried with a loud voice by the spirit of the power" [also 61:11]). How else would the Son of God expire (contrast 2 Cor 13:4 with Mark's way of presenting Jesus' death)?

To highlight this exhibition, Mark first uses the somewhat obsolescent ἐβόησεν, "he cried out," to introduce the shout with a certain formality that dignifies the loudness of Jesus' voice (see J. A. L. Lee in *NovT* 27 [1985] 25, and cf. βοάω and κράζω in a concordance). Next, Mark transliterates the Aramaic of the shout because the mystique of an oriental foreign language carries the connotation of power (cf. the comments and notes on 5:41; 7:34). Here, the power will turn out so superhuman that the breath-Spirit which Jesus exhales in shouting the Aramaic makes a wind strong enough to rend the veil of the temple (see the following comments on v 37-39). Enhancing this connotation of power are repetition, assonance, and alliteration (besides the obvious verbal repetition, N.B. the reversal of ἐλ- [bis] to λε-, the final ι [tris], and the fourfold α). Then Mark translates the transliteration to excite his audience's pity for Jesus as abandoned by God, abandoned to death, and as asking for what purpose (εἰς τί) God has abandoned him. The element -κατ- in ἐγκατέλιπες, "have you abandoned," carries on a wordplay begun in καταλύων, "destroying," καταβάς, "coming down," and καταβάτω, "let . . . come down" (vv 29, 30, 32). The possibilities of coming down from the cross and destroying the temple have now been replaced by the actuality of abandonment by God. Some bystanders' mistakenly thinking that Jesus is calling Elijah and the resultant running of someone, filling a sponge with sour wine, putting it around a reed, trying to make Jesus drink it (ἐπότιζεν — another conative imperfect; cf. v 23 and Ps 68:22 LXX[69:22 MT]; 1QH 4:11), and saying, "Permit we should see if Elijah comes to take him down," all make a dramatic foil to Jesus' expiring with a loud shout. The adversative δέ, "but," which introduces the second mention of Jesus' loud voice, signals this foil. The use of a reed with a sponge attached to its tip may dignify Jesus by putting him at a height otherwise impossible to reach, for no such reed and sponge were needed in the attempt to give him myrrhed wine prior to the Crucifixion (v 23).

We might think that the aorist tense in the circumstantial participial phrase ἀφεὶς φωνὴν μεγάλην indicates his "letting loose a loud voice" before he expired. But everywhere else in Mark the aorist circumstantial participle of ἀφίημι equates with the main verb of the clause. Simon and Andrew start following Jesus *by* leaving (letting loose) their nets (1:18). James and John go away behind Jesus *by* leaving (letting loose) their father (1:20). Taking Jesus along in a boat *entails* leaving (letting loose) the crowd (4:36). Leaving (letting loose) the commandment of God and holding fast the tradition of human beings form obverse sides of the *same* action; the one does not go before the other (7:8). And so on (8:13; 12:12; 13:34 [where the participle equates with the adjective ἀπόδημος, "away on a journey"]; 14:50). In the present text, therefore, Jesus' letting loose a loud voice equates with ἐξέπνευσεν, "he breathed out, expired." That is to say, his shout of superhuman strength *was* his last breath. No wonder the one who filled a sponge with sour wine and tried to make Jesus drink ran. But it was too late to revive Jesus. Dead men do not drink, and Jesus had expired with the shout (contrast his taking the sour wine in John 19:28-30 because there he has said, "I thirst," rather than expiring with a loud shout).

An adversative δέ, "but," distinguishes the one's running, filling a sponge, and so on from the mere talk of some bystanders. Asyndeton hurries the putting of the wine-soaked sponge around a reed in hope of reviving Jesus. The dropping of an epexegetic ἵνα, "that," after "permit" produces a terser and therefore stronger statement of imperative (cf. Matt 7:4 par. Luke 6:42; M. Reiser, *Syntax und Stil* 150-51). The imperative "permit" plus a direct object in "we should see . . ." is already stronger than a hortatory subjunctive, "Let's see . . . ," would have been. The futuristic present tense of "is coming" is stronger than the future tense of "will come" would have been. And the prefix καθ- in καθελεῖν, "to take down," adds to the wordplay with καταλύων, καταβάς, καταβάτω, and ἐγκατέλιπες (vv 29, 30, 32, 34). All this stylistic vigor makes for a better foil by which to emphasize Jesus' having already expired with a loud shout.

The Hebrew language speaks of giving a voice (Gen 45:2; Num 14:1), the Greek language of *letting loose* (ἀφίημι) a voice (cf. Dem. 18.218; Eur. *El.* 59; idem *Hipp.* 418; as well as passages cited in BAGD s.v. ἀφίημι 1aβ and numerous examples cited for the simplex ἵημι by LSJ s.v. 2). What power Jesus' voice will demonstrate when let loose is about to appear. The anarthrousness of "a loud voice," where we might have expected an anaphoric definite article, "the [afore-mentioned] loud voice," underlines the loud voice as such rather than its identity with the earlier one (though we should think of identity; for the failure of the attempt to make Jesus drink was not due to his refusal, as in v 23, but to his expiration, as shown by its introduction with an adversative δε, "but").

Ἐξέπνευσεν is "a poetic vocable reserved for solemn occasions" (E. K. Simpson, *Words* 14; see Soph. *Aj.* 1026; Josephus *Ant.* 12.9.1 §357; 19.8.3 §353; 19.9.1 §358; idem *J.W.* 1.13.10 §272; 1.23.6 §660; Plut. *Mor.* 347C, 597F; Babrius 60, for example). The use of it instead of the common ἀπέθανεν or ἐτελεύτησεν, "died," lends further dignity to Jesus' death. Mark's verb occurs especially for the deaths of important persons (M. Reiser in *Markus-Philologie* 157-58) and just possibly may hint at the impermanence of Jesus' death, for in *Chaereas and Callirhoe* 1.1.14; 3.9.1 Chariton uses it for fainting (cf. J. D. M. Derrett, *Making of Mark* 273-74). Furthermore, just as in 1:10, after the appearance of Elijah in the person of John the Baptizer (cf. 9:13) and at the beginning of Jesus' public ministry, the heavens were rent and the Spirit came down into Jesus, so now at the end of his public ministry and in the absence of Elijah Jesus' last breath consists in an exhalation of the Spirit, which is his breath. Ἐξέπνευσεν, "he expired, spirited out" (15:37), contrasts with τὸ πνεῦμα . . . καταβαῖνον εἰς αὐτόν, "the Spirit coming down into him" (1:10) — more particuarly, ἐξ- contrasts with εἰς and -έπνευσεν with πνεῦμα — just as the voice (φωνή) of Jesus asking God why he has abandoned him (15:34) has contrasted with the voice (φωνή) of God telling Jesus, "You are my beloved Son; in you I am well pleased" (1:11). And just as the force of the Spirit's coming down (κατα-) caused the heavens to be rent (σχιζομένους — 1:10), so the force of the Spirit's exhalation by Jesus causes the veil of the temple to be rent (ἐσχίσθη) from the top downward (κάτω; cf. the force of Jesus' expulsion by the Spirit into the wilderness — 1:12). This rending contrasts with the usual and graceful billowing "of the veil" (τοῦ . . . καταπετάσμα-τος) "from bottom . . . to the top" (ἀπ᾿ ἐδάφους . . . μέχρι τῆς ἄνω) because of the undercurrent "of the wind" (τοῦ πνεύματος — Ep. Arist. 86). Πνεῦμα means "breath," "wind," and "spirit," so that in his last breath Jesus exhales the wind of the Spirit that rends the veil (cf. Ezek 37:5-14 LXX and again 1 Enoch 71:11). The forward placement of τὸ καταπέτασμα τοῦ ναοῦ, "the veil of the temple," turns attention to the veil. "In two" stresses the completeness of its rending. "From top to bottom" (ἀπ᾿ ἄνωθεν ἕως κάτω) implies divine action, for the Spirit of Jesus is the Spirit of God that came down from heaven into Jesus inasmuch as he was God's Son (1:10-11, using κατα-), as now recognized by the centurion.

Just as the voice of God declared Jesus' divine sonship (1:11), the centurion, seeing that Jesus expired with such loud force that his last breath, the wind of the Spirit, completely rent the veil of the temple, declares that same divine sonship (see H. M. Jackson in NTS 33 [1987] 16-37, but disregard his interpretation of the veil-rending as a portent of destruction for the temple). Κάτω, "bottom, downward," makes a wordplay with καταπέτασμα, "veil, something spread down," extends the wordplay with καταλύων, καταβάς, καταβάτω, ἐγκατέλιπες, and καθελεῖν (vv 29, 30, 32, 34, 36; cf. M. A. Tolbert, Sowing the Gospel 282), and thus emphasizes the supernaturally forceful rending of the veil. Mark's omitting to specify which veil was rent, whether the outer or the inner (though the centurion's seeing the veil-rending requires the outer), concentrates attention on the single item of supernatural force, which points to Jesus' divine sonship. An adversative δέ, "but," now shifts attention to the centurion who is standing by. Mark is not content to describe the centurion merely as a bystander, however. No, he also describes him as standing opposite the temple. This description underscores that the centurion enjoys a full view of the veil-rending. This full view, in turn, lends great weight to his following declaration.

But Mark first gives a reason for the centurion's declaration: "seeing . . . that in this way Jesus expired." "Seeing" implies that the darkness has lifted and complements "hearing" (v 35), which went with the first mention of this shout. Whereas "hearing" pointed to the words that Jesus shouted, "seeing" points to the effect of his shout on the veil of the temple. "In this way" refers to the way in which the wind of the Spirit, exhaled when in his last breath Jesus let loose a loud shout, rent that veil in two from top to bottom. The veil-rending has not interrupted the two references in vv 37, 39 to Jesus' expiration, then, so much as it has detailed the visible effect of his expiration (thus we should interpret the paratactic καί, "and," at the start of v 38 as ecbatic: "with the result that") and thereby told what the centurion saw that evoked his declaration, "Truly this human being was Son of God" (cf. God's declaration, "You are my beloved Son . . . ," after Jesus saw the heavens being rent [1:10-11]; also the use of a loud voice in divine epiphanies, as discussed by O. Betz in TDNT 9. 293-94, and the statement of H. M. Jackson in NTS 33 [1987] 28: "What moved the centurion to confession was the simultaneous observation not only of the gigantic outer curtain of the Temple being torn in two from top to bottom but also of the fact that it was the powerful expulsion of Jesus' breath that caused the curtain to tear, . . .").

The centurion's declaration contrasts sharply with the high priest's charging Jesus with blasphemy for having declared, with some addition, that he himself was the Son of the Blessed One (14:61b-64). In the present Greek word order, "Son of God" comes before the copula for emphasis. "Truly" lends further emphasis to the identification. So also does the use of ἄνθρωπος, "human being," with οὗτος, "this," when οὗτος alone would have sufficed. "This human being" makes a foil of Jesus' humanity against which his deity as indicated in "Son of God" stands out. Whatever the centurion's meaning in the phrase υἱὸς θεοῦ, which in view of his presumed paganism might be translated "a son of a god" or "a son of God," and despite the imperfect tense of ἦν, "was," which naturally reflects Jesus' death but not his resurrection (an event yet to take place — cf. 11:32 for the use of ἦν concerning a past lifetime, and see E. S. Johnson, Jr., in *JSNT* 31 [1987] 7-8; J. D. Kingsbury, *Conflict in Mark* 54), Mark's use of this same phrase to express his own Christian point of view at the very start of the gospel (1:1) shows that he means it to be taken in the same way here, i.e. as meaning "Son of God" (against J. Delorme [in *Intertextuality in Biblical Writings* 39-40], who thinks that "was" makes the present declaration a mismatch with 1:1 [which, however, has no present tense to be mismatched by "was"]). As at the start, its double anarthrousness stresses the quality of Jesus' divine sonship (cf. the qualitative anarthrousness of Χριστοῦ in 1:1; 9:41; also the anarthrous occurrences of "Son of God" in Ign. *Eph.* 20:2 and *Smyrn.* 1:1 [mixed, as in Mark, with arthrous occurrences in *Magn.* 8:2 and the foreward to *Rom.*]; *Mart. Pol.* 17:3; *Barn.* 5:9; 7:9; 12:10 [again mixed, as in Mark, with arthrous occurrences in 5:11; 7:2] — against B. M. F. van Iersel in *NedTTs* 24 [1980] 32, n. 29; see further P. B. Harner in *JBL* 92 [1973] 79-81). The imperfect tense of ἦν implies that Jesus had been Son of God all along. An adversative δέ, "but," distinguishes the declaration of Jesus' divine sonship for special attention. That the declarer is not said to become a disciple — he remains only a military bystander, anonymous and unknown in the Christian community (contrast esp. v 21) — makes his declaration the more remarkable.

15:40-41 *(Matt 27:55-56; Luke 23:49; John 19:24b-27)* The male disciples have fled (14:50), and Peter is nursing his regret (14:72); so further to guarantee that Jesus had died in a way which evoked the centurion's declaration despite Jesus' crucifixion, Mark indicates that women were watching. He even lists the names of several of them ("Mary the Magdalene, and Mary the mother of James the little and of Joses, and Salome"). Historically, the distance from which they were watching may have been due to the Roman guard at the cross, female hesitancy in a male chauvinistic society, and dissociation from the mockers close to Jesus provide other possible reasons. But Mark may mention the distance to protect Jesus' nakedness (cf. v 24b) from close observation by the opposite sex (so J. M. Gundry-Volf in private communication). Mark also explains how it comes about that the women are watching (when Jesus was in Galilee they "used to follow him and wait on him" [cf. Luke 8:1-3]) and indicates that the named ones are far from alone (for there were "many others who had come up with him to Jerusalem" [cf. 10:32-34]). Thus Mark's apology shifts back to the earlier emphasis on Jesus' power of attraction over large numbers of people and enlists the present large number as fellow witnesses with the centurion to what he saw of the superhuman way in which Jesus expired. Though the named women will play a further role (see 15:47–16:8 and N.B. esp. that their having followed Jesus in Galilee prepares for the Galilean message that three of them are told to convey in 16:7), Mark's reference to their watching and his bringing in many other women as co-observers show that he is not merely preparing the ground for later events. He wants his audience to know that the centurion does not stand alone in seeing that Jesus died in the way he did. An adversative δέ, "but," distinguishes the women from the centurion; and the following καί, "also," presents them as further witnesses.

NOTES

The historical present tense in vv 20b, 21, 22a, 24, 27 does not represent a pre-Marcan source featuring Simon (as thought by W. Schenk, *Passionsbericht* 18-19, 24, with regard to vv 20b-22a, [23a?], 24, 27, 29b; cf. J. Schreiber, *Theologie des Vertrauens* 28-29; idem, *Kreuzigungsbericht* 87-90). Throughout his gospel Mark himself often uses the historical present tense for emphasis (so correctly F. J. Matera, *Kingship* 41-43). Nor do the numbered hours, the destruction and building of the temple, the darkness at midday, the loud shout of Jesus, and the rending of the veil represent a pre-Marcan apocalyptic tradition in vv 25, 26, 29a, 29c, 30, 33, 34a, 37-39 (again as thought by Schenk and Schreiber). The numbered hours stress the shortness of the time that Jesus spent on a cross (cf. v 44) rather than setting out an apocalyptic timetable. Three hours plus three more make far too short a period for such a timetable, anyway; and they do not give encouragement to the persecuted people of God as apocalyptic timetables are supposed to do. For three hours during the eschatological tribulation, says 4 Ezra 6:24, springs will stop flowing. But Mark's scheme begins with three hours devoid of prodigies; so it seems unlikely to have arisen out of apocalyptic. The destruction and building of the temple allude backward to a false charge, not forward to an apocalyptic event. The darkness from noon to midafternoon hides Jesus from the leer of blasphemers; it does not bring on them the judgment of the Day of the Lord. The loud shout of Jesus demonstrates his strength at the moment of expiration; it does not summon the dead from their graves and the living from their activities to meet Jesus (as in 1 Thess 4:16; cf. John 5:28; Matt 25:6). Nor does it strike a note of judgment. A shout of judgment would require words of judgment. There are none. It would be gratuitous to say that the words of abandonment have replaced words of judgment in an earlier version of the shout. And the rending of the veil does not desecrate and thereby desolate the temple (as predicted in 13:14); it demonstrates the force of Jesus' exhalation when he breathes his last.

T. A. Mohr (*Markus- und Johannespassion* 313-50) assigns vv 15, 20b-22a, 24, 26-27, 34a (without "at the ninth hour"), 36a, 37b, 40 to the original tradition, vv 23, 29-30, (32b?), 33, 38-39 to pre-Marcan redaction, and vv 22b, 25, 31-32a, 34b, 35, 36b, 37a ("leaving a loud voice"), 41, 34aα ("at the ninth hour") to Mark's redaction. Such assignments entail much guesswork. See J. Ernst 463-64 and F. J. Matera, *Kingship* 36-38, for summaries of them. J. Gnilka (2. 310-11), too, surveys other source critical views and notes that no verse fails to be attributed by someone to the oldest tradition, though some agreement exists that vv 20b-27, 34, 37 offer centers of gravity. R. Pesch (2. 476) sees main statements in those that tell about the leading of Jesus out to crucifixion, the bringing of him to Golgotha, and the Crucifixion itself, each followed respectively by subordinate statements about the requisitioning of Simon of Cyrene, the myrrhed wine, and the division of Jesus' garments (vv 20b-24). But parataxis dooms this scheme of super- and subordination. We are dealing with another scheme: Each of the first two independent clauses is followed by a ἵνα-clause (vv 20b-21). The third and fourth independent clauses are each followed by a relative clause (vv 22-23). In fact, this scheme probably determines the grammatically difficult relative construction ὃς δέ, "but who" (v 23b), where we would expect ὁ δέ, "but he" (as in a widespread v.l.). Verse 24 then begins a new subsection (dealing with the Crucifixion) that forsakes the foregoing scheme (which dealt with preparations).

The leading out in v 20b most naturally refers to a leading out from inside the courtyard, a praetorium (v 16). Other evidence favors in addition that Jesus was crucified just outside Jerusalem (John 19:20; Heb 13:12; Plaut. *Mil. Glor.* 2.4.6-7; Plut. *Mor.* 554A [cf. the stoning of people just outside a city — Lev 24:14, 23; Num 15:35-36; Deut 17:5; 1 Kgs 21:13; Acts 7:58; Josephus *Ant.* 4.8.24 §264; idem *J.W.* 4.6.1 §§359-60; also Lev 16:27]). Josephus *J.W.* 5.11.1 §§449-51 does not make a particularly good parallel, because there people are said to have been crucified before the wall of Jerusalem to frighten the rebels still holed up in the besieged city. The execution (though not crucifixion) outside a city in Tac. *Hist.* 4.11 does not make a good parallel at all, because the distance from the city was far so as to avoid attracting attention within the city.

See *New Documents Illustrating Early Christianity . . . published in 1976*, p. 42, that ἀγγαρεύουσιν, "they requisition," being an official term, does not necessarily strike a perjorative note; and on the right of soldiers to requisition subject peoples to carry loads and perform other services, see E. Hatch, *Essays* 37-38; MM s.v. ἀγγαρεύω; and BAGD s.v. for other literature). Simon came from Cyrene, capital city of the North African district of Cyrenaica (cf. Acts 2:10; 6:9; 11:20; 13:1; Josephus *Ag.Ap.* 2.4 §44; E. Schürer, G. Vermes, F. Millar, and M. Goodman, *History* 3/1. 60-62). We cannot tell whether he lived in Cyrenaica and was visiting Jerusalem as a pilgrim, or whether he had moved from Cyrenaica. His own name is Jewish (though often found among Greeks — BAGD s.v. Σίμων), his sons' names, Alexander and Rufus, Greek and Latin. Since he is identified by their names, Mark's audience and possibly that of pre-Marcan tradition do not seem to know him. The indefinite τινα, "a certain," before Simon's name carries the same implication more clearly yet. We cannot tell whether Simon or his sons were among the Cyrenians who opposed Stephen (Acts 6:9) or among the Cyrenians who belonged to Stephen's circle and fled to Syrian Antioch under persecution (Acts 11:19-20; 13:1). Paul had a Roman name as well as a Jewish one even though he was a Hebraist, born and bred of Hebraists (Phil 3:5). And he was such a Hebraist even though belonging to the Diaspora. So yet again we cannot be sure that the Greek and Latin names of Simon's sons make them (or him) Hellenists or that his Diasporan origin made him (or them) Hellenists. On the other hand, such possibilities are present, perhaps even probable. A burial cave located just outside Jerusalem on the southwest slope of the Kidron Valley and used prior to 70 C.E. by a Jewish family apparently of Cyrenian origin has yielded the inscription, "Alexander, [son] of Simon" (N. Avigad in *IEJ* 12 [1962] 1-12, esp. 9-11, 12; J. P. Kane in *JSS* 23 [1978] 278-79; B. Bagatti and J. T. Milik, *Gli scavi del "Dominus Flevit"* pt. 1, no. 9); and Rom 16:13 mentions a Rufus in the church at Rome (unless Romans 16 comes from a letter to a church located elsewhere — a view that has recently lost favor [for a summary, see J. D. G. Dunn, *Romans* 884-85]). Did the present Rufus move from Jerusalem to Rome and the present Alexander stay and die in Jerusalem? Peter, who stands behind Mark according to Papias's elder (Eus. *H.E.* 3.39.15), preached in both Jerusalem and Rome. It probably goes too far to conjecture from 2 Tim 4:14, which may emanate from Rome and mentions an Alexander who seems to be present at the place of writing, that Alexander as well as Rufus went to Rome and that subsequently Alexander returned to Jerusalem, died, and was interred in the aforementioned burial cave (cf. 1 Tim 1:20; also Phil 1:15-17 with 2 Tim 4:14 on his harmfulness to Paul, esp. if Philippians was written in Rome).

There is no indication that Simon of Cyrene has been working in a field. A worker would unlikely be coming home in midmorning (cf. Str-B 2. 828-29). The anarthrousness of ἀγροῦ may point to the countryside in general (cf. BAGD s.v. ἀγρός 2) rather than a particular field (contrast the arthrousness of ἀγρόν in 13:16, where a garment's having been laid aside seems to imply working in a particular field; and cf. M. Black, *Aramaic Approach* 133, n. 4). Or Simon may be staying or living in a hamlet nearby (see 5:14; 6:36, 56 for the use of ἀγρός possibly in this sense). So we have no convincing reason to think that Mark is attacking the Jews or Judaizing Christians by having a law-breaker do the honor of taking up Jesus' cross (see Exod 12:16; Lev 23:7; Num 28:18 for the prohibition of work on this day).

It is doubtful that Mark portrays Simon as a cross-taking disciple; for Jesus said that anyone wanting to follow behind him would have to deny himself, take up his own cross, and follow him (8:34) whereas Simon is requisitioned by others, takes up Jesus' cross, not his own, and is not said to follow behind Jesus. For all we know, he precedes Jesus. And taking up Jesus' cross does not make it Simon's; for Jesus, not Simon, is crucified on it, and 8:34 did not speak of taking up Jesus' cross to make it one's own (against K. Stock, *Boten* 169). Since Simon does not suffer or die with Jesus, we can hardly say that "his cross" carries a double meaning: Jesus' cross and Simon's, too (so W. Schmithals 685-86). To say that the requisitioning of Simon against his will teaches salvation as an unexpected gift, not as a human work or achievement (ibid. 687), is a tour de force owing more to explicit predestinarianism in Paul than to anything at all in Mark. Taking up a cross does not mean taking up two pieces of wood attached crossways to each other, and probably does not mean taking up the stake that will be put upright at the place of execution. Rather, it means taking up the cross-beam which will be affixed to an upright stake (Plaut. *Mil. Glor.* 2.4.6-7; Plut. *Mor.* 554A; Artem. *Oneir.* 2.56). The upright stake might or might not be a permanent fixture at the place of execution, and E. L. Martin (*Secrets* 169-83) suggests that Jesus' cross-beam was affixed to a living tree (cf. the use of ξύλον for a living tree in Luke 22:31; Rev 2:7; 22:2 [bis], 14, 19 with its use for Jesus' cross in Acts 5:30; 10:39; 13:29; Gal 3:13; 1 Pet 2:24) and indeed that the cross-beams of the two bandits crucified with Jesus were affixed to that same tree (cf. "with him" [Mark 15:27 par. Matt 27:38 par. John 19:18, 32 and esp. "in order that their bodies [plural] might not remain on the cross [singular] . . ." [John 19:31]). See M. Hengel, *Crucifixion* 22-32, for variety in the modes of crucifixion. The requisitioning of Simon to take up Jesus' cross might seem to imply that Mark portrays Jesus as the king of the Jews (so J. Gnilka 2. 311). But we have seen that elsewhere Mark does not do so (see esp. the notes on 14:42, but also the comments and notes on 15:2, 9, 12), and the dignifying of Jesus as God's Son (cf. esp. 15:39, but also 1:1, 11 et passim) gives at least as much point to Mark's mention of the requisitioning as an allusion to kingship over the Jews would have done.

Cicero (*Rab. Post.* 5 §16) mentions the executioner's hook for dragging condemned criminals to their place of execution. In view of Simon's carrying the cross of Jesus, does dragging by such a hook lie behind the switch from ἐξάγουσιν, "they lead out" (v 20b), to φέρουσιν, "they bring" (v 22), as though once Jesus is led out from "inside the courtyard, i.e. Praetorium" (cf. v 16), he is dragged to Golgotha? M. E. Boring (*Truly Human/Truly Divine* 53) suggests that though φέρουσιν (v 22) can mean "they bring," here it may mean "they carry" with reference to Jesus' weakness. But the parallel ἐξάγουσιν, "they lead," and Mark's emphasis on Jesus' strength undermine the suggestion. Elsewhere in Mark, the use of φέρω is fairly evenly distributed between "bring" and "carry." Against describing the antecedent of "him" in v 22 as unclear (so L. Schenke, *Der gekreuzigte Christus* 83), at the very end of v 21 "his" clearly refers to Jesus; and "they bring" (v 22) corresponds to "they lead away" (v 20a), to "they led away" (v 16), to "they brought away" (v 1), and to "they led away" (14:53), all of which have Jesus as their object. Furthermore, vv 23ff. go right on to use pronouns that indubitably refer to Jesus.

The Aramaicness of "Golgotha" points to an early date and Jerusalemite provenance for the tradition of the Crucifixion (cf. H. P. Rüger in *Markus-Philologie* 78). The neuter gender of ὅ, "which," disagrees with the masculine gender of τόν . . . τόπον, "the . . . place," and refers instead to "Golgotha," the name that Mark proceeds to translate. For Golgotha as so called because it was skull-shaped, and as such to be equated with what underlies the Church of the Holy Sepulchre, not with Gordon's Calvary, see B. E. Schein in *BA* 44 (1981) 21-26; R. M. Mackowski, *Jerusalem* 153-55; J. Ernst 466. The naming of the place according to its shape, not because of nearby graves or other ritual uncleanness, would render irrelevant the myth of Adam's skull and take away the basis of the view that Mark puts forward Jesus' death as abrogating the Jewish laws of ritual purity (against W. Schenk, *Passionsbericht* 30). Besides, the lack of reference to Jesus' sacrificial blood as cleansing the place undermines this view. Without such a reference, his death would seem to add further pollution; for corpses are defiling. But Golgotha may mean Skull's Place neither with respect to shape nor with respect to ritual uncleanness, but with respect to a place for counting heads, i.e. a polling place. For, as pointed out by E. L. Martin (*Secrets* 58-64), though "Golgotha" (גלגלת in Hebrew) refers in general to a human head (yet never to a dried out skull) in Judg 9:53; 2 Kgs 9:35; 1 Chr 10:10, its specific use in counting, or polling, predominates (see Exod 16:16; 38:26; Num 1:2, 18, 20, 22; 3:47; 1 Chr 23:3, 24). Furthermore, פקד, "count, muster," occurs extremely often in conjunction with this use of גלגלת; the מפקד altar was located on the Mount of Olives (ibid. 27-41, referring to Lev 4:12; 10:14; Num 19:1-22, esp. 9; Ezek 43:21; *m. Mid.* 1:3; 2:4; *m. Para* 3:6-7; *m. Ber.* 9:5; *m. Yoma* 7:2; *b. Zebah.* 105b; *b. Yoma* 68b in a discussion worth reading in full); and the location of Golgotha, a polling place, on the Mount of Olives would agree with the indication in Mark 15:38-39 that the centurion standing by the Cross was also standing opposite the temple and saw the rending of its veil (see both the foregoing comments and the following notes ad loc.).

C. Wiéner (in *La Pâque du Christ* 140-41) sees a concentric structure in vv 23-36: (a) the refusal of a drink in v 23; (b) an accomplishment of Psalm 22 at the third hour in vv 24-26; (c) the crucifixion of two bandits with Jesus in v 27; (d) the insulting of Jesus in vv 29-32a; (c′) the two bandits' mockery of Jesus in v 32b; (b′) another accomplishment of Psalm 22 in vv 33-34; and (a′) the acceptance of a drink in v 36. But the third hour is associated with Jesus' crucifixion, not with lot-casting for Jesus' garments in accordance with Psalm 22. The two bandits' mockery of Jesus should be separated off from the preceding mockery no more than within that preceding mockery the bypassers' blaspheming him and the chief priests' and scribes' making fun of him should be separated from each other. He does not accept a drink in vv 35-36, but more importantly the offer is of a piece with v 34. And it exacts too high a cost for concentricity to omit the Crucifixion as such, the three hours of darkness, and Jesus' expiration.

John and Luke omit the attempt to make Jesus drink wine prior to the Crucifixion and retain only the attempt at the end of the Crucifixion. *Gos. Pet.* 5:16 transfers the early attempt to the afternoon and amalgamates the two attempts (against H. Köster [in *ANRW* II 25/2. 1525], who regards the single attempt in *Gos. Pet.* 5:16 as more primitive than the double attempt in Mark and Matthew). Because of its greater closeness to "gall . . . sour wine" in Ps 69:22(21), J. D. Crossan (*Four Other Gospels* 138-39) considers "gall with sour wine" in *Gos. Pet.* 5:16 (cf. *Barn.* 7:3 ["sour wine and gall"], 5 ["gall with sour wine"]) to be "much more original" than "myrrhed wine" in Mark 15:23, which Matt 27:34 changes to "wine mixed with gall." One would think, however, that greater closeness to OT phraseology might just as well point to unoriginality. Here, it is easy to trace increasing assimilation to Ps 69:22(21). Mark 15:23 stands farthest away, mentioning wine and myrrh rather than sour wine and gall. Matt 27:34 introduces gall instead of myrrh. *Barn.* 7:3 replaces wine with sour wine and keeps the gall. *Barn.* 7:5 and *Gos. Pet.* 5:16 keep both the sour wine and the gall but reverse their order in accordance with Ps 69:22(21).

Since both before and after the attempt to give Jesus myrrhed wine in v 23 soldiers are the subject of all third person plural verbs in vv 16-22, 24-27, we have no reason to think that they are not the ones who try to give it to him. An indefinite third person plural would awkwardly interrupt the soldiers' other actions; and Mark could hardly expect his audience not to think of them as the subject of this action, too. Myrrhed wine does not at all correspond to the vinegar (MT), i.e. sour wine (LXX), of Ps 69(68):22; nor does it correspond to the frankincensed wine of *b. Sanh.* 43a and other rabbinic passages (Str-B 1. 1037-38; cf. Prov 31:6-7). Moreover, Gentile soldiers offer Jesus the myrrhed wine (see J.-P. Lémonon, *Pilate et le gouvernement de la Judée* 103-5, that they are non-Jewish recruits from Palestine), whereas Jewish women offered frankincensed wine. So the attempt to give Jesus myrrhed wine hardly grows out of Ps 69:22 or Jewish custom. That myrrhed wine was considered a delicacy makes the attempt to give it to Jesus a gesture of mockery in connection with his presumed kingship — but this only at the historical level, for Mark uses no vocabulary of mockery and directs attention only to the attempt to give Jesus a drink and his refusal to take it (cf. the notes on v 36). It reads too much into the text to describe the attempt as bad because the wine would alleviate Jesus' suffering, and then to contrast the attempt with a good act by Simon in taking up Jesus' cross (so J. Schreiber, *Theologie des Vertrauens* 62-66; see Dioscor. Ped. *De mater. med.* 1.64.3 for the soporific effect of myrrhed wine). The would-be wine-givers are criticized no more than Simon is commended, i.e. not at all. And if an attempt to alleviate Jesus' sufferings were to be considered bad, would not making him suffer — i.e. crucifying him — have to be considered good?

According to M. Wojciechowski (in *Bib* 65 [1984] 94-96), Jesus refuses to drink because he took a Nazirite vow in 14:25 (cf. Num 6:1-4; Judg 13:4-5; Amos 2:11-12). But what he said in 14:25 need not have consisted in a Nazirite vow; in fact, it represented abstinence only from the wine of Passover (see the notes ad loc.). On the ground that only in v 23 of the narrative concerning the Crucifixion does Jesus take action, J. Gnilka (2. 311-12) infers Mark's redaction for the purpose of setting forth Jesus as an example of accepting persecution. But refusal of wine makes a weak action by comparison with Jesus' shouting loudly (which Gnilka neglects), and what he shouts does not make a very good example of accepting persecution. The v.l. ὁ δέ, "but he" (A C L Θ Ψ 0250 f^{13} Majority Text sy^{p,h}), is easier and therefore less likely original than ὃς δέ, "but who."

For crucifixion in general, see esp. M. Hengel, *Crucifixion;* and on the remains of a Yohanan who was crucified during the Roman period and whose remains were discovered at Givʿat ha-Mivtar, see N. Haas in *IEJ* 20 (1970) 38-59; J. A. Fitzmyer in *CBQ* 40 (1978) 493-513; J. Zias and E. Sekeles in *IEJ* 35 (1985) 22-27; idem in *BA* 48 (1985) 190-91; H.-W. Kuhn in *ANRW* II 25/1. 745-58. The lot-casting for Jesus' garments implies that he was crucified naked (cf. Artem. *Oneir.* 2.61). H. Anderson (342) notes that though the garments of those condemned to death normally went to the executioners, no evidence favors a Roman practice of casting lots for the garments. The use of phraseology from Ps 22:19(18) might suggest that the lot-casting stems from the OT rather than from tradition or historical reminiscence. On the other hand, we should note, there is nothing inherently improbable in the lot-casting.

A. Mahoney (in *CBQ* 28 [1966] 292-99) associates the lot-casting with the third hour and delays the Crucifixion till the sixth hour. Mention of the Crucifixion prior to the mention of lot-casting and the third hour resists this opinion. According to Mahoney, the adversative δέ, "but," in v 25a indicates that the third hour of lot-casting differs from the time of the Crucifixion. But since the time of the Crucifixion has not yet come in view, the first side of the temporal contrast to which this argument ties δέ does not exist in the text. Δέ needs to introduce a contrast with something that precedes.

P. Parker (in *JBL* 100 [1981] 403) says that for a Gentile audience Mark may use a Roman method of counting hours, so that the third hour means noon rather than mid-morning. But neither the Romans nor other Gentiles started counting at midmorning (c. 9 am). If the Romans started counting at midnight, as is sometimes said, Mark's use of their method would put the Crucifixion c. 3 am. But see J. V. Miller in *JETS* 26 (1983) 158-63 against such a Roman practice. Miller himself harmonizes the third hour in Mark and "about the sixth hour" in John 19:14 by appealing to the looseness of ancient time-reckoning and by suggesting that Mark includes the preparatory scourging whereas John does not (ibid. 163-66). But the scourging lies quite far back in Mark's text (v 15) and occurred at the courtyard prior to the soldiers' mockery and leading of Jesus to Golgotha; and a leeway of three hours, a quarter of a day, stretches things. More likely, John shifts from the third hour to about the ninth to push Jesus' crucifixion entirely into the afternoon and thus correlate it with the slaying of the Passover sacrifices at that time, i.e. to make Jesus' crucifixion the true Passover sacrifice (cf. John 1:29, 36; 19:33, 36 with Exod 12:46; Num 9:12; Ps 34:21[20]). This possibility is also superior to positing a confusion of Γ (3) with Ϝ (6). Mark's use of τρίτη, "third," instead of Γ undermines the positing of a mistake.

To avoid disharmony with John 19:14, J. Blinzler (*Prozess* 416-22) and W. L. Lane (566-67) deny the originality of v 25 to Mark's text by appealing to the tardiness of the temporal note, to the repetitiousness of the reference to Jesus' crucifixion, and to the omissions by Matthew, Luke, and the Gospel of Peter. But the tardiness and repetitiousness only show to what extent Mark goes to start his emphasis on the shortness of time that Jesus spent on a cross. Repetitiousness translates into the duality that characterizes Mark's style. As often, the second mention adds greater specificity or a new feature — here, the third hour. Matthew drops this temporal note as irrelevant to his emphasis on persecution, and thus the reference to crucifixion as repetitious without reason (R. H. Gundry, *Matthew* 569). Luke and the Gospel of Peter may omit for similar reasons or may come under subsidiary influence from Matthew (idem in *The Four Gospels 1992*). See the foregoing comments that v 25 represents Mark's apologetic purpose. Textual tradition favors v 25 unanimously. Parataxis suits Mark's style. And the egregiousness of the parataxis in v 25b may have contributed to later omissions of the whole of v 25.

J. Schreiber (*Theologie des Vertrauens* 24) asks why the temporal note in v 25a is not integrated into v 24 (to produce "and at the third hour they crucify him") as another such note is integrated into v 33 ("and at the ninth hour Jesus cried out . . ."). The answer is that the subordination necessary to such an integration would not carry the emphasis which Mark thinks necessary to start his emphasis on the shortness of Jesus' time on a cross. Though Mark's hand may betray itself in the double reference to Jesus' crucifixion (vv 24a, 25b), the references do not necessarily imply fabrication of the intervening material. Mark may simply have positioned traditional material at this point (cf. C. A. Evans in *JBL* 101 [1982] 248-49 on the story-telling device of digression and resumption). We might consider the possibility that "and they crucified him" (v 25b) starts a new subsection leading to the inscription and the crucifixion of two bandits with Jesus just as "and they crucify him" (v 24a) started a new subsection leading to the division of Jesus' garments and the third hour. But the adversative δέ, "but," in v 25a distances the third hour from the preceding statements about crucifixion and division and throws the third hour together with the following restatement about crucifixion. J. Schreiber (*Kreuzigungsbericht* 55-56) denies Semitic parataxis in καί, i.e. denies that "and" means "when" with regard to Jesus' crucifixion at the third hour, and explains the double reference to Jesus' crucifixion by positing that Mark draws on two different traditions. This denial and explanation go against the grain of Marcan duality, however (cf. esp. the doubling of the ninth hour in vv 33-34), and fails to see in this instance of Marcan duality the beginning of an emphasis on the shortness of time that Jesus spent on a cross. That a temporal καί is not necessarily Semitic, see Pl. *Symp.* 220C and, for further references, M. Reiser, *Syntax und Stil* 119.

F. W. Danker (in *JBL* 85 [1966] 471) thinks it quite probable that in v 25b Mark repeats the statement about Jesus' crucifixion to portray the Crucifixion as Jesus' enthronement in line with Ps 21:29 LXX: "because the kingdom [is] the Lord's, and he himself is master (δεσπόζει) of the nations." The immediately following quotation of the inscribed charge against Jesus is supposed to favor this probability. But the inscription reads "the King of the Jews," not "the king of the nations"; and we have seen that neither Mark nor anyone in his gospel to whom he is sympathetic portrays Jesus as a king. Moreover, the restatement of Jesus' crucifixion goes with the mention of the third hour, the charge concerning kingship with the crucifixion of two bandits on either side of him. Kingship and banditry share rebelliousness against Roman authority.

Against treating the third, sixth, and ninth hours in vv 25a, 33-34 as redactional fabrications without a traditional or historical basis, D. C. Allison, Jr. (*End* 27), observes that elsewhere in Mark chronological notations lack the precision of these notations (though see 6:48 for a precise yet apparently traditional notation of time) and that since the passion narrative contains a heavier concentration of triads than characterizes the rest of Mark, this triad is traditional (cf. the three subsections devoted to Judas Iscariot's activity [14:10-11, 17-21, 43-47], Jesus' three returns to the three leading disciples [14:37, 40, 41], the high priest's three utterances [14:60, 61b, 63-64a], the three mockings of Jesus [14:65; 15:16-20a, 29-32], Peter's three denials [14:66-72], Pilate's three questions [15:9-14], and the three lists of female witnesses [15:40-41, 47; 16:1]). On the other hand, triads occur outside the passion narrative (F. Neirynck in *ETL* 55 [1979] 35-42); and we should distinguish between triadic events and authorial notations of triadism. Events may be triadic as well as singular, dyadic, etc.; and an author's narrative may reflect events with or without notations of their singular, dyadic, triadic, or other numerical character. Noting it, as is done with respect to Peter's denials, Jesus' returns to the leading disciples, and the hours of his crucifixion, exhibits authorial interest — and therefore a redactional point — but does not prove authorial fabrication, for which other evidence is needed.

According to John 19:19 the inscribed placard was attached to Jesus' cross, according to Matt 27:37 over his head (similarly Luke 23:38, which could also be understood to mean that the placard was hung on Jesus himself). Cf. Suet. *Calig.* 32.2; idem *Dom.* 10 §1; Dio Cass. 54.3.6-7; 73.16.5; Eus. H.E. 5.1.44. All these extra-biblical cross-references have to do with the inscription and parading of a charge prior to execution, and only in Dio Cass. 54.3.6-7 does the following execution take the form of crucifixion. We have, then, an occasional practice of variable application. D. E. Nineham (424) argues that Mark omits Jesus' name and origin, which would have been included in accordance with Matt 27:37; John 19:19. But of the extra-biblical cross-references, only Eus. *H.E.* 5.1.44 supports inclusion, and that only with respect to name. Matthew's support is likewise limited to name. Only John includes origin as well. So progressive addition looks more likely than subtraction. The oral and jurisprudential character of *m. Sanh.* 6:1 and the epistolary character of *m. Sanh.* 11:4, both of which passages include the name of the condemned, keep them from paralleling v 26. Besides, they deal with Jewish executions, v 26 with a Roman execution.

The present inscription need not imply that the historical Pilate judged or thought

Jesus guilty of insurrectionism, much less that Jesus really was guilty of it; for equally possibly, Pilate did not believe that Jesus claimed kingship over the Jews and could no longer suspect that the crowd called him their king, but yielded to their demand for his crucifixion and thus played along with the implied charge of the Sanhedrin that he claimed to be the king of the Jews. J. Gnilka (2. 319) argues that Mark would not record the inscription, "The King of the Jews," only to show that Jesus was crucified because of a misunderstanding. Perhaps not, but a positive portrayal of Jesus as the king of the Jews does not provide the only possible alternative. Mark may include this inscription to show that Jesus was crucified under a charge known on both sides, Jewish and Roman, to be false. The consequent injustice would feed into Mark's apology for the Cross.

Against the opinion that "the King of the Jews" is a historically impossible title because a political charge would read "the King of Judea" and a religious charge would read "the King of Israel," see Matt 2:2; Josephus *J.W.* 1.14.4 §282; idem *Ant.* 15.10.5 §373; 15.11.4 §409; 16.9.3 §291; 16.10.2 §311, in all of which passages "the King of the Jews" does occur. See M. Lowe (in *NovT* 18 [1976] 118-19) for the translation "the King of the Judeans" instead of "the King of the Jews." E. Linnemann (*Studien* 154) uses the non-mention of inscriptions for the two bandits to cast doubt on the historicity of the inscription for Jesus. But the focus of attention on Jesus may have caused Mark or a pre-Marcan traditioner to omit other inscriptions. Moreover, not each of the crucified needs to have had an inscription (the provision of one being only occasional); and "bandits" already implies what the two besides Jesus would have had on their inscriptions.

According to H. Anderson (342-43), v 27 would follow v 25 more naturally than it follows v 26, as indeed v 29 would follow v 26 more naturally than it follows v 28. But as every speaker and writer knows, wanted details often and necessarily interrupt the dominant threads of a narrative. Here, though the crucifixion of two bandits would follow that of Jesus very smoothly, the cost of breaking up the crucifixions is less than that of delaying the lot-casting for Jesus' garments, the hour of his crucifixion, and the inscription of the charge against him, all of which are tied more closely to his crucifixion than the crucifixion of the bandits is. Similarly, their crucifixion only appears at first to interrupt the narrative of Jesus' crucifixion; for their crucifixion is related to his not merely by virtue of crucifixion as such but by virtue of their positions on his right and left, and it would be out of place to mention their crucifixion between his and the lot-casting for his garments, the hour of his crucifixion, or the inscription, or to mention their crucifixion anachronistically after the bypassers' and Sanhedrists' mocking of Jesus, which occurs after the bandits' crucifixion as well as after Jesus's.

W. L. Lane (568) argues that since Roman law regarded neither theft (*furtum*) nor robbery (*rapina*, theft combined with violence) as a capital crime, the bandits crucified with Jesus were probably rebels. From Josephus's writings we know that the bandits who arose in first century Palestine did in fact resist Roman authority; and it would suit the crucifixion of Jesus as "the king of the Jews," i.e. as the would-be leader of a Jewish rebellion against Rome, to crucify two rebels with him. It would also suit the context to identify these two with the insurrectionists imprisoned with Barabbas, the switch from στασιαστῶν, "insurrectionists" (v 7), to λῃστάς, "bandits, rebels" (v 27), perhaps stemming from inscriptions designed to describe them as dangerous to society and thus to justify their crucifixion (D. Dormeyer, *Passion* 196; cf. Petr. *Sat.* 111-12). Literarily, on the other hand, the switch seems to break a connection between those insurrectionists and the present bandits and favor an allusion to the bandits who according to Jesus made the temple their cave (11:17; see the foregoing comments on 15:27). If so, any connection between the insurrectionists of 15:6 and the bandits of 15:27 may be limited to a traditional or historical substratum. For different answers to the question whether these bandits belonged to an existing political party of Zealots that became prominent during the Jewish War beginning in 66 C.E. or whether they had operated more or less independently as social bandits, the Zealot party originating not till the Jewish War, see M. Hengel, *Zealots* xiii-xvii et passim, and R. A. Horsley and J. S. Hanson, *Bandits* 48-87, respectively.

Among others, G. W. E. Nickelsburg (in *HTR* 73 [1980] 173) thinks that Mark pictures the cross as Jesus' throne, and the crucifixion of two bandits on Jesus' right and left as corresponding to 10:35-40, especially 10:40. But though 10:35-40 twice speaks of sitting and Mark might well have spoken of sitting on a cross (for crosses were often fitted with a peg enabling the victim to sit — see Sen. *Ep.* 101.11-12 [*ad Lucilium*]), he does not speak of Jesus or the two bandits as sitting on their crosses. Elsewhere, the NT speaks of hanging on a cross (Luke 23:39; Acts 5:30; 10:39; Gal 3:13). Though not incompatible with each other in connection with crucifixion, hanging and sitting do not equate. The glory of 10:37 is elsewhere associated with the Second Coming (8:38; 13:26), not with the Crucifixion (as in John). And the two for whom positions on Jesus' right and left have been prepared represent those who are able to share his fate inasmuch as they are disciples, not bandits. See the notes on 10:40 concerning the euphemism ἐξ εὐωνύμων, "on [the] left."

P. Rodgers (in *EvQ* 61 [1989] 81-84) argues for the acceptance of v 28 as original even though only L Θ 0112 0250 *f*[1,13] Majority Text lat sy[p,h] (bo[pt]) have it: though Luke 22:37 also quotes Isa 53:12, harmonistic influence on Mark is made unlikely by differences in contexts, in introductory formulas, and in speakers. Furthermore, the wording of the quotation differs from the LXX; and Or. *Cels.* 2.44 favors the originality of v 28 (cf. G. D. Kilpatrick in *Salvacion en la Palabra, Targum-Derash-Berith* 641-45). But the support of Origen weighs no more than other external evidence favoring inclusion. If Luke can carry a non-Septuagintal quotation, so also can a scribal interpolation in Mark. The difference in speakers may be due to interpolation into a new context. The crucifixion of two bandits with Jesus may have prompted an interpolation inasmuch as the quotation deals with being numbered with lawless people. Ἵνα πληρωθῶσιν αἱ γραφαί, "but in order that the Scriptures might be fulfilled" (14:49), may have led a scribe to change τοῦτο τὸ γεγραμμένον δεῖ τελεσθῆναι ἐν ἐμοί, "this that is inscripturated must be completed in me" (Luke 22:37), to καὶ ἐπληρώθη ἡ γραφὴ ἡ λέγουσα, "and the Scripture was fulfilled that says" (Mark 15:28). And in any case, if Luke can have moved and otherwise changed an original Mark 15:28, so also can a scribe have moved and otherwise changed Luke 22:37. The weightier external evidence of ℵ A B C D Ψ *pc* k sy[s] sa bo[pt] therefore decides the question in favor of omission.

"The ones passing by" (v 29) suggests the nearness of a road. See R. H. Gundry, *Use of the OT* 62-63, for possible echoes of Lam 2:15 in the passers-by and of Ps 22:8(7); Lam 2:15 in their head-shaking (cf. other passages cited by J. Schneider in *TDNT* 3. 718 and the apotropaic interpretation of head-shaking by H.-P. Müller in *THAT* 2. 704-5). V. Taylor (591) notes that except for an echo of Lam 2:15 Mark would probably have referred to bystanders, as in v 35 (cf. 14:47, 69, 70; 15:39), rather than to passers-by. D. Juel (*Messiah and Temple* 103 and *Messianic Exegesis* 95) suggests that Mark uses ἐβλασφήμουν, "were blaspheming," instead of ἐξεμυκτήρισαν, "ridiculed" (so Ps 21:8 LXX), to imply not just that the passers-by were slandering Jesus, but that those who condemned him for a blasphemy that he never uttered were themselves uttering blasphemy, really and truly. But the passers-by, who were blaspheming Jesus, differ from the Sanhedrists; and only the Sanhedrists condemned him as a blasphemer. Moreover, what the passers-by say by way of blasphemy does not allude to what Jesus said that the Sanhedrin condemned as blasphemous. What the Sanhedrists now say counts for blasphemy, too ("likewise also" — v 31); but the first instance of the present blasphemy, that of the passers-by, does not counteract the condemnation of Jesus for blasphemy.

To J. Schreiber (*Theologie des Vertrauens* 47) all the words of mockery carry irony, i.e. mean their opposite so far as Mark is concerned. For example, Jesus *does* destroy and rebuild the temple. W. C. Booth (*Rhetoric of Irony* 28-29), followed by R. M. Fowler (in *SBL 1983 Seminar Papers* 52-53), goes so far as to see double irony in that the mockers are themselves speaking ironically at the same time that Mark presents as true what they do not really mean. But no, Mark has described as false the testimony that Jesus said he would destroy and rebuild the temple (14:57-58). Irony here would contradict the description there.

The argument of R. J. McKelvey (*New Temple* 69) that v 29 has point "only if it represents an actual claim made by Jesus" neglects that mockers pay little attention to truth and that the mockery concerning the temple comes from passers-by, not from the chief priests and scribes, who themselves rejected as false the testimony concerning the temple and now mock him concerning the charges under which they condemned him for blasphemy and delivered him to Pilate (vv 31-32). Nor does v 29 refer to rebuilding the temple in the form of the church, not only because the passers-by know nothing of the church, but also because Jesus does not regather the disciples in three days after his death. He will do so not till they travel from Jerusalem to Galilee. That journey cannot start till the third day after his death and takes another three days (see the comments and notes on 14:58 for a more extensive discussion).

The scornfulness of "Ha! You who would destroy the temple . . ." and the challenge that Jesus save himself by coming down from the cross, not by confessing his sin, undermines the view that from a Jewish standpoint the passers-by are calling on Jesus to confess his sins in the hour of death (cf. *m. Sanh.* 6:2; 10:1; against O. Betz [in *SWJT* 30 (1988) 7], who cites *m. Sanh.* 6:2; 10:1 — but 10:1 is irrelevant; and 6:2 deals with an explicit exhortation to confess prior to execution as Mark 15:31-32 does not). According to J. R. Donahue (*Are You the Christ?* 197, n. 2), the main verb, "in this case *sōson* (present tense)," gives the participle ὁ καταλύων its temporal function — thus: "you who are destroying the temple" instead of the conative translation, "you who would destroy the temple." But the tense of σῶσον, "save," is *not* present. It is aorist. Hence, the rest of Donahue's interpretation falls, viz., that to make Jesus' mockers stand for Mark's ecclesiastical enemies, who teach that the destruction of the temple leads immediately to the Second Coming, Mark ascribes to Jesus' mockers a challenge that he come down from the cross now (again see the notes on 14:58).

That the chief priests and scribes do not address Jesus directly as the passers-by do discourages the thought of a doublet. Speaking to one another about Jesus reflects the chief priests' and scribes' co-membership in the Sanhedrin and suits their already having addressed him directly (14:65). The centering of their scepticism on Jesus' ability to save himself contrasts with the centering of scepticism on God's disposition to save the righteous sufferer in Wis 2:18 (see also the notes on 14:53-64 against a background in Wis 2:12-20; 5:1-7). The suggestion that the narrator of v 31b has in mind Jesus' saving others by not saving himself (J. Ernst 470) neglects that it is a question of Jesus' ability to save himself, not of his deciding whether to do so. Besides, he has already saved others without having saved himself. In the first instance, "saved others" refers to Jesus' healings; but for Mark and his audience, though not for the passers-by, the use of "save" for eternal salvation in 8:35b; 10:26; 13:13 suggests that meaning, too. H.-J. Steichele (*Der leidende Sohn Gottes* 270-71) notes that Jesus does not give a sign and to the end refuses to work the wonder of saving himself (cf. 8:11-12). True, he does not save himself; but Mark does not quote him as refusing to give a sign (contrast 8:11-12). Mark is bound by the historical fact of Jesus' death on a cross and is concerned to counteract the offense caused by that kind of death. He is not concerned to counteract a Christology of signs. Otherwise he would not have included the supernatural darkness of early afternoon, the superhuman loudness of Jesus' dying shout, and the rending of the veil.

G. W. E. Nickelsburg (in *HTR* 73 [1980] 173) considers the challenge that Jesus save himself a temptation, because the temptation in 1:12-13 did not reach a conclusion, because Jesus called Peter "Satan" for rebuking him on account of the first passion prediction in 8:31-33, and because tempting Jesus to come down from the cross parallels Satan's tempting him to cast himself down from the pinnacle of the temple in Matt 4:5-6 par. Luke 4:9. But though Mark used the vocabulary of temptation elsewhere (1:13; 8:11; 10:2; 12:15; 14:38), here he uses the vocabulary of mockery, not that of temptation. The temptation in 1:12-13 did not reach a conclusion because Mark was not interested in the temptation as such (see the comments and notes ad loc.). He called Peter's rebuke of Jesus just that — a rebuke, not a temptation. And it is methodologically illegitimate to interpret Mark by the Q-tradition of Jesus' temptation. Besides, to save himself by coming down from the cross would differ so radically from tempting God by casting himself from the pinnacle of the temple that the parallel breaks down even apart from methodological illegitimacy. On the sceptical side, H. Anderson (342-43) asserts that the chief priests and scribes would not have gone to Jesus' crucifixion or spoken of his having saved others and infers an idealized scene with theological meaning. But according to 3:22; 7:1, scribes went all the way from Jerusalem to Galilee to investigate Jesus. The outskirts of Jerusalem are not so far to go. We might also think that the chief priests and scribes, bent as they were on the death of Jesus, would go above all others to see his crucifixion — indeed, to make sure of its being carried out to the death. And Mark 3:22 says that the scribes from Jerusalem acknowledged his exorcisms. Even the Jewish Talmud acknowledges his supernatural powers (Str-B 1. 631).

The coming of mockery from three sources does not prove an expansion of originally sparer tradition; for redactors are just as likely to homogenize variegated tradition (cf. *Gos. Pet.* 1:1–3:9). And it is just as likely that different classes of mockers echoed one another with respect to Jesus' saving himself as that a composer or redactor made them do so. The combination of this similarity with differences in other respects strikes a realistic note, though realism can characterize fiction as well as fact. More particularly, Mark numbered Jesus' returns from praying in Gethsemane (14:41) and Peter's denials (14:72) but does not number the present classes of mockers or their acts of mockery; so there is no adequate reason to think that for a third mockery Mark adds to the tradition a new element of insulting remarks by the bandits crucified with Jesus. Nor do the triads of subsections about Judas Iscariot (14:10-11, 17-21, 43-47), utterances by the high priest (14:60, 61b, 63-64b), questions by Pilate (15:9-14), and lists of female witnesses (15:40-41, 47; 16:1) support such an addition; for again Mark does not number them, and his fondness for duality (F. Neirynck, *Duality*) should have made him satisfied with two mockeries at the cross if his tradition mentioned only two. The LXX of Pss 21:7; 30:12; 68:10 uses nouns that are cognate to Mark's verb ὠνείδιζον, "were insulting" (v 32b). But the differences between verb and noun and especially between being insulted by co-sufferers and being insulted by flourishing enemies cast doubt on a derivation of the bandits' insults from these psalms of righteous and not-so-righteous sufferers.

Because references to the third hour (vv 25-27) and the sixth (v 33) bracket the mockery (vv 29-32), F. J. Matera (*Kingship* 24-29) thinks that Mark has inserted the mockery to indicate passage of time, as he inserted the story of John the Baptizer's death (6:14-29) "between the time that Jesus sent his disciples on mission (6:7-13) and their return (6:30)." This analogy goes awry, however; for though the story of John's death filled space between Mark's notations of the disciples' mission and return, it told what had happened *before* the disciples' mission whereas the mockery of Jesus is presented as occurring *between* the crucifying of Jesus and the onset of darkness. At what other time could this mockery have occurred, presupposing as it does that Jesus is hanging on a cross ("let him now come down") and visible ("in order that we may see . . ."). Furthermore, it is not quite true to say that references to the third hour and the sixth bracket the mockery;

for a repeated reference to Jesus' crucifixion and references to the inscription and to the crucifixion of two bandits come between Mark's notation of the third hour and his description of the mockery.

Matera proceeds by saying that to shape the dialogue in this passage, Mark has (1) taken the destruction and rebuilding of the temple from 14:58; (2) transformed Jesus' command to take up one's own cross (8:34) and the going up to Jerusalem (10:32) into a challenge that Jesus come down from *his* cross; (3) made out of Jesus' observation that those who wish to save their lives will lose them, and vice versa (8:35), a contradictory challenge that Jesus save himself; (4) possibly borrowed "he is not able to save himself" from "who is able to be saved?" (10:26; cf. 10:27); and (5) possibly borrowed "in order that we may see" from "in order that they may see and not perceive" (4:12; cf. 8:11-13). But a topic that came up in court might well have come up in mockery, too. Jesus has not taken up his cross in Mark (see v 21); so challenging him to come down from it lacks any basis in his having followed the instructions given to others at 8:34. Coming down from the cross would not make a very good contrast with going up to Jerusalem, either; for Jesus would still be near Jerusalem if he were to come down. A borrowing from 8:35 would probably have included "wishes" with "to save," and "his life" instead of "himself" (though "life" can stand for "self," esp. in Semitic languages). Alternatively, at 8:35 Mark would already have changed "his life" to "himself," as the par. Luke 9:25 did. In 10:26 "is able" has to do with being saved by God (cf. 10:27), not with saving oneself. 15:32 uses ἴδωμεν for seeing, but 4:12 uses ἴδωσιν for failure to see and another verb (βλέπωσιν) for seeing. The synonymous use of "the Christ" and "the king of Israel" finds no parallel elsewhere in Mark. All in all, then, more tradition may underlie the passage than Matera allows for.

On the ground that repetition betrays a Marcan insertion, F. C. Synge in (*ExpTim* 92 [1980-81] 331) regards not the whole of the dialogue in vv 29-32 but everything between "from the Cross" at the end of v 29 and the same phrase in the middle of v 32 as a Marcan insertion designed to implicate the chief priests and scribes in the mockery of Jesus. But repetition has many more uses than transiting back to tradition; so this view stands on shaky ground.

In v 33 the temporal and geographical notations favor physical darkness over figurative darkness. Plut. *Pel.* 31 §§2-3 (295A) describes the apprehension and fear that people feel at a solar eclipse (cf. Jerome *Against John of Jerusalem* 42). *T. Adam* 3:6 says that the sun and moon darkened for seven days when Adam died, and *2 Enoch* 67:1-3 that darkness hid Enoch's translation from view. According to Cic. *Rep.* 2.10 §17; 6.22 §24; Liv. 1.16.1-3, Romulus was translated during a sudden darkening of the sun by a thick cloud and was consequently hailed as a god and a son of a god. Dion. Hal. *Ant. Rom.* 2.56.6 has Romulus dying, not translated, but puts at his death a total eclipse causing darkness like that of night over all the earth. Diog. Laert. 4.64 says that the moon was eclipsed as Carneades was dying. According to Josephus *Ant.* 17.6.4 §167, the moon was eclipsed on the night following the martyrdom of Matthias, a learned and zealous Jewish scholar (cf. Str-B 1. 1040-42 for similar phenomena at the deaths of other great scholars). Verg. *Geor.* 1.466-68 and Plin. *HN* 2.30 §98 say that the sun grew dark at the death of Julius Caesar, more specifically from the sixth hour till nighttime according to Pseudo-Servius (J. Wettstein 1. 538). Announcing the imminent death of Emperor Theodosius I, says Ambrose *De Obitu Theodosii Oration* 1, was a darkness denser than ordinary night and due apparently to thick clouds pouring down rain (tears of mourning); and Philo *Prov.* 2.50 says in general that eclipses announce the deaths of kings. In contrast with Luke 23:44-45a, however, Mark speaks only about darkness, not also about an eclipse (so his audience might think as well of a heavy cloud cover or a dust storm — cf. the darkening of the sun by smoke in Rev 9:2 and, because of parallelism with the moon's turning red, the probability of a similar darkening of the sun in Mark 13:24; also E. F. F. Bishop, *Jesus of Palestine* 250). Furthermore, darkness preceded the death of Jesus and ceased before it (as implied by the centurion's seeing the expiration of Jesus; contrast *Gos. Pet.* 6:21-22, where the sun shines again not till after his death and the pulling of the nails from his hands). Perhaps then the darkness does not announce his death as that of a king or another kind of divine man or represent the mourning of nature or of its creator over the death of God's Son Jesus so much as the darkness veils and thus counteracts the shame of crucifixion (see the foregoing comments; cf. Jer 4:27-28; Amos 8:10 with 8:9; *2 Apoc. Bar.* 10:12; *b. Sukk.* 29a; *Clem. Recogn.* 1.41; D. C. Allison, Jr., *End* 28-29).

Nor does it seem probable that the three hours of darkness allude to the three days of darkness that befell Egypt (Exod 10:21-23). Not only do hours differ from days; but also Mark does not make the darkness a plague on Jesus' persecutors as the Mosaic narrative makes darkness a plague on the Egyptian oppressors of Israel, and Jesus hangs in darkness whereas the Israelites enjoyed light while their oppressors suffered darkness. In Amos 8:9 the earth grows dark in broad daylight because the sun goes down at noon (cf. Jer 15:8-9). But the sun does not go down in Mark 15:33, the judgmental character of Amos 8:9 has no counterpart in Mark, and the phraseology of neither the Hebrew nor the LXX of Amos 8:9 carries over. Similar differences plague comparisons with 2 Sam 22:10; Isa 13:10; 24:23; 50:2-3; Jer 13:16; Joel 2:2, 10; 3:4(2:31); 4:15; Amos 5:18, 20; Mark 13:24; Rev 6:12-13; and numerous extra-biblical passages dealing with the consummation-Day of the Lord (see the references cited by Allison, *End* 29). See also the foregoing notes against an apocalyptic strain in the present passage (and therefore esp. against the view that for Mark the eschatological tribulation starts with Jesus' passion [ibid. 37-38]).

To K. Grayston (in *Theology* 55 [1952] 122-29), the darkness at Jesus' crucifixion recalls the primeval darkness and therefore presages a new creation. But for this thought, the coming of light after darkness would have been mentioned (cf. Revelation 21–22). As it is, Mark says nothing about its becoming light again at the ninth hour but leaves the restoration of daylight to be only inferred from the centurion's seeing the way Jesus expired. One might interpret the darkness as a sign of judgment, not on Jesus' enemies (as on the enemies of the helpless and needy in Amos 8:9 and its context), but on Jesus himself for bearing the sins of others (cf. God's abandoning him to die — v 34; so J. Schreiber, *Kreuzigungsbericht* 174-75). But nowhere in Mark is Jesus said to bear the sins of others; so Mark's audience could hardly be expected to interpret the darkness thus.

Gos. Pet. 5:15 says that darkness covered all Judea; and in Mark 15:33 ἐφ᾿ ὅλην τὴν γῆν could be translated "on the whole land," referring to Judea or Palestine. But out of eighteen instances of γῆ elsewhere in Mark, none has this narrow sense (see esp. 2:10; 9:3; 13:27, 31; against R. H. Gundry, *Matthew* 572-73). Elsewhere in the NT and the LXX ὅλη ἡ γῆ and the similar πᾶσα ἡ γῆ almost always mean the whole earth except when qualified by an additional phrase such as "of Egypt." Passover falls at the time of full moon; so a regular solar eclipse could not have occurred at the time and place of Jesus' death. But Mark is speaking of the supernatural, as in the rending of the veil; and regular solar eclipses do not include the whole earth or last for three hours even in one locality (fewer than eight minutes for a total eclipse, as a matter of fact), much less over the whole earth.

The third, sixth, and ninth hours have provided evenly spaced markers for a day of twelve hours. Jesus cries out to God at the ninth hour, the Jews' hour of prayer (Acts 3:1; for other evidence see E. von Severus in *RAC* 8. 1167). The timing of the outcry therefore joins its transliterated Aramaic to imply an early Jewish Christian origin of the tradition and, when joined also by the unlikelihood of Christians' putting a cry of despair on the lips of Jesus, the authenticity of the tradition. Mark does not describe the ninth hour as the hour of prayer, however, and cannot expect his audience, who require explanation of Jewish customs and translation of Semitic expressions, to recognize the hour as such; so the matter lies beneath the surface of this text.

Against seeing behind the third, sixth, and ninth hours a Christian celebration of Good Friday according to Jewish hours of prayer, or for that matter against seeing this temporal scheme as generated by Jewish hours of prayer, only for the ninth hour is anything like a prayer mentioned in the present passage; and the sixth hour was not a regular hour of prayer. Though Peter once prayed at about the sixth hour, others were preparing a meal at the time (Acts 10:9). On the Day of Pentecost the Spirit fell on the disciples at the third hour (Acts 2:15), and they may have been praying (Acts 1:14). But only the ninth hour is called "the hour of prayer" (Acts 3:1); and the first prayer of a day was offered early in the morning, though considerable leeway was allowed (*m. Ber.* 1.1; 4:1; E. Schürer, G. Vermes, F. Millar, and M. Black, *History* 2. 303, n. 40; Str-B 2. 696-702). Mark's omitting to say anything about the return of light at the ninth hour shows that he is not concerned to make a symbolic point with regard to Jesus' death as bringing the light of salvation.

The loudness of Jesus' voice does not indicate that he has fallen victim to demonic power (as thought by W. H. Kelber, *Mark's Story* 81) or that he has succeeded at the cost of his life in expelling a demon that possessed him (so F. W. Danker in *ZNW* 61 [1970] 48-69); for in 1:26 it was an unclean spirit, not its victim, who shouted with a loud voice, and in 5:6-8 the one who shouted with a loud voice, though at first appearing to be a demoniac, was addressed as an unclean spirit distinct from the demoniac. Though Jesus exorcized an unclean spirit in 1:26, the spirit gave a last demonstration of power over the demoniac by shouting with a loud voice and convulsing him. In 5:7 the loud voice of Legion contributed to a temporarily successful adjuration of Jesus (see the comments ad loc., and for the association of a loud voice with strength cf. also Rev 1:10 with 1:8; 5:2; 10:3 with 10:1; 18:2 in addition to *1 Enoch* 61:11; 71:11 [already cited]). That earlier in Mark a loud voice has twice and exclusively connoted strength weighs more than the varied use of a loud voice for prayer and praise, weeping and blessing, proclamation and command in cross-references such as Gen 39:14 LXX; 1 Kgs 8:55; 18:27-28; 2 Chr 32:18; Ezra 3:12; 1 Esdr 5:61; Neh 9:4; Esther 4:1 LXX; Job 2:12 LXX; Jdt 7:23, 29; 9:1; Isa 36:13; 40:9; 58:1; Ezek 8:18; 11:13; Sus 46 Theod; 1 Macc 3:54; 13:45; Luke 1:42; 17:15; 19:37; 23:23; John 11:43; Acts 7:57, 60; 8:7; 14:10; 16:28; 26:24; Rev 4:1; 6:10; 7:2, 10; 8:13; 11:12, 15; 12:10; 14:7, 9, 15, 18; 16:1, 17; 19:1, 17; 21:3.

Wherever OT phraseology appears in Jesus' words, to argue against authenticity that elsewhere he does not use such phraseology is to argue in a circle. The OT imbued first century Jewish culture so thoroughly (cf. the prominence of OT phraseology in 1QH, for example) that we should regard Jesus' use of OT phraseology as highly probable. From that standpoint, then, the use of Ps 22:2(1) does not call in question the authenticity of Mark 15:34. The practice of praying aloud even in private and Jesus' present inability to withdraw himself combine to blunt the argument against authenticity that he would not have prayed a private prayer in public as he does here (and in Gethsemane he appears to have prayed a private prayer within earshot of others).

To J. Schreiber (*Theologie des Vertrauens* 25-26), the cry of dereliction in v 34 offers a doublet of the wordless cry in v 37, the words in the doublet being drawn secondarily from Ps 21:2 LXX. The quotation differs from the LXX, however; and, more to the point, it is both unlikely that pre-Marcan Christians put a cry of despair on Jesus' lips and practically impossible that Mark, concerned everywhere else to stress Jesus' power, put such a cry on his lips. It is one thing to include the tradition of despair so as to excite pity for Jesus and then redact the tradition so as to overcome its offensiveness. It would be quite another thing to create a novum which by purchasing pity at the cost of Christological offensiveness requires further overcoming. The Crucifixion itself provides more than enough offensiveness. The motif of OT fulfilment is not present to make anyone suspect an event after the prophecy (as opposed to a prophecy after the event). The Greek translation differs from the LXX so as to rule out late fabrication in a Hellenistic setting. The transliterated Aramaic points to an early date. Luke 23:46 and John 19:30 substitute Christologically inoffensive last words of Jesus. In Mark 15:34, D c (i) k Porph substitute the less offensive ὠνείδισας, "have you insulted," for ἐγκατέλιπες, "have you abandoned." And the outgrowing confusion of "my God" with "Elijah" fastens on nothing in Christian thought, where Elijah does not play the role of helper to righteous sufferers. In Jewish tradition such sufferers do not die asking for what purpose God has abandoned them; so fabricating a cry of dereliction could scarcely prove to early Christians the status of Jesus as a righteous sufferer rather than striking them as Christologically offensive. What more is needed to establish the likelihood of authenticity for v 34, so that v 37 becomes a secondary back reference to it?

It might be thought that inclusion of the cry of dereliction disproves the interpretation of Mark as an attempt to overcome the scandal of the Cross rather than as an exposition of suffering discipleship. As with the rest of the Passion, however, Mark can hardly obliterate the tradition the offensiveness of which he is concerned to counteract. To ignore it would be to surrender to its offensiveness. So he must conquer it, scale, it, plant his flag on its peak. That is, he must retain the tradition in recognizable form but redact it in ways that make it an object of faith rather than an obstacle to faith. With respect to the cry of dereliction, he accomplishes this feat by means of a double emphasis on superhuman loudness, by framing the cry between the supernatural signs of darkness and veil-rending, and by citing the favorable effect on the centurion of the way in which Jesus expired.

The interrogativeness of Jesus' shout and the connotation of abandonment in ἐγκατέλιπες spoil the attempt of L. P. Trudinger (in *JETS* 17 [1974] 235-38) to transform the cry of dereliction into a cry of victory with respect to God's handing Jesus over as a sacrifice for sins. A. E. J. Rawlinson (236) argues that to Mark the cry of dereliction cannot imply God's abandonment of Jesus, for then Mark would not have included the cry. But this argument neglects that Mark translates the Aramaic in terms of abandonment and that in context abandonment means abandonment to death — and he is far from denying that Jesus died on a cross. The view of E. Best (*Temptation* lxiv-lxviii) that Jesus cries out in awareness of his bearing God's judgment on the sins of others rests on a wrongly judgmental interpretation of Jesus' cup and baptism in 10:38-39; 14:35-36 (see the notes ad loc.). According to M. Smith (*Clement* 222), the cry of dereliction shows Jesus thinking himself no longer possessed by the spirit that enabled him to practice magic (cf. *Gos. Pet.* 19 under the view that "my power" means "my demon"). But at this point the life of Jesus is at stake, not his ability to practice magic (if that is the correct way to put his former activities). And since nowhere else has he practiced magic for his own benefit, we can scarcely suppose that he despairs of practicing it to save his life on the present occasion.

Jesus' addressing God and saying "my God" (bis) in the address fail to disprove that he is despairing of life, for one may address God out of despair and other feelings besides hope. If out of despair, "my" adds pathos. Notably, Jesus does not address God as "Abba, Father," as he did in Gethsemane, where he still hoped for life instead of death (14:36). The suggestion that he quotes the first line of Psalm 22, not to express despair over God's abandoning him to death, but to imply confidence in the deliverance of which Ps 22:23-32(22-31) speaks has against it that elsewhere Jesus and NT writers select wanted quotations from the middle of OT passages. And the cry of despair in Ps 22:2(1) would be a singularly inapt pointer to a confidence spelled out in a wholly different kind of material many verses later in the psalm. The progression from the Sanhedrin's determination to destroy Jesus to Judas Iscariot's purpose to give him over to them, and then to the falling asleep of Peter, James, and John, the flight of the Twelve except for Judas, Peter's denials, the crowd's yielding to Sanhedric influence and Pilate's yielding to influence from the crowd, and now to God's abandoning Jesus to die — this progression, the double emphasis on the loudness of Jesus' shout, the Aramaic transliteration of the words that he shouted, and the translation of the transliteration all put emphasis on the cry of dereliction in its own right, not in a role merely of pointing beyond itself. Given these circumstances, not even a Jewish audience — much less Mark's Gentile audience — would hear the cry as pointing to a later salvific passage. The substitution of trustful and triumphant statements in Luke 23:46; John 19:30 reacts against the despairing cry in Mark 15:34 par. Matt 27:46. It does not interpret that cry in the light of later verses in Psalm 22, for then phraseology would have been drawn from them. The opposition of Jesus' will to the Father's (14:36) supports a cry of despair that God has abandoned Jesus to die (cf. 2 Cor 5:21; Gal 3:13). Εἰς τί means "why?" in the sense "for what purpose?" not in the sense "because of what?" Because Elijah went to heaven without dying (2 Kgs 2:11), Jews believed that he would come to save righteous sufferers (Str-B 4/2. 769-71; J. Jeremias in *TDNT* 2. 930, 935-36). The present text provides the earliest evidence of this belief, however. Though there is weight in the argument that no Christian would have fabricated the piece about Elijah because for Christians Elijah is Jesus' forerunner, not a helper of righteous sufferers, an early Jewish Christian might have kept the view of Elijah as helper alongside the view of Elijah as forerunner.

It is often said that Ἐλωΐ, "my God," does not come close enough to אֵלִיָּה or Ἠλίας, "Elijah," to provide a basis for misunderstanding the first as the second and that therefore either Ἐλωΐ represents an Aramaizing of the Hebrew אֵלִי, "my God," or some of the bystanders knowingly misinterpret Jesus' cry to God as a call to Elijah (for other views and the transliteration of the rest of Jesus' cry, see H. P. Rüger in *Markus-Philologie* 78-79; M. Wilcox in *ANRW* II 25/2. 1004-7; K. Beyer, *Die aramäischen Texte vom Toten Meer* 123; B. M. Metzger, *Textual Commentary* ad loc. Matt 27:46 and Mark 15:34; J. A. Fitzmyer in *NTS* 20 [1974] 393-94; R. H. Gundry, *Use of the OT* 63-66; D. J. Moo, *OT* 264-68; G. Rossé, *Cry* 42-44). But we should not dismiss the possibility that in the hubbub surrounding three simultaneous crucifixions Ἐλωΐ might be mistaken for אֵלִיָּה or Ἠλίας. The difference between the initial sounds is only one of the short versus the long of the same vowel. The immediately following liquid consonant l is exactly the same in both instances. The remainder of each, though differing somewhat, features a shared long i (in modern English, a long e) — and an accented one at that. Under the supposition that the Aramaic Ἐλωΐ gives no means by which a Greek reader could connect it with Ἠλίας so as to mistake "my God" for "Elijah," F. J. Matera (*Kingship* 31) argues for Mark's combining of divergent traditions, one that has Jesus quoting Ps 22:2(1) and another that has him calling for Elijah. As noted, however, the underlying supposition is questionable. Even if it were unquestionable, we would still have to ask, Why did some think that Jesus was calling Elijah unless Jesus was quoting Ps 22:2(1)? A general appeal to Jewish belief in Elijah as helper of righteous sufferers would provide an answer, but one so devoid of linguistic content as to prove unconvincing. Why think of Elijah as helper unless Jesus said something that sounded like Elijah's name?

J. Schreiber (*Kreuzigungsbericht* 174, n. 4) thinks that because Ἐλωΐ is not really mistakable for Ἠλίας, Mark is pointing to a radical failure to understand the necessity of the Cross. But those who fail to understand cannot be expected to understand. They are not disciples to whom Jesus has predicted his passion, but bystanders who have mocked him. If failure to understand the necessity of the Cross is in view, Jesus' "why?" exposes him equally, if not more, to Mark's criticism. And the supposition of unmistakability is again questionable.

Schreiber (op. cit. 190-93) further denies that Jesus called on the Elijah whom Jews regarded as a helper of righteous sufferers and affirms instead that Jesus called on the eschatological Elijah to help him. Mark then inserts vv 35-36 to show with v 37 that Jesus did not need help from the eschatological Elijah. But Jesus was not calling either Elijah.

He was only and mistakenly *thought* to be calling on Elijah, and this only in the supposedly inserted verses. The thinking of some bystanders that he was calling the eschatological Elijah would require either their own belief that the final tribulation had set in or their attributing such a belief to Jesus. For neither one of these requirements do we have evidence. And inasmuch as the bystanders wanted to see whether Elijah would come and take Jesus down from the cross before death occurred — yet it did occur; indeed, had already occurred (hence the failure to induce a drink) — Jesus did need, or had needed, the kind of help that the bystanders had in mind. These criticisms apply whether or not we treat the text historically or only literarily.

Since Elijah has already come and been put to death according to Scripture in the person of John the Baptizer (9:13), it is ironic that at the very time Jesus is suffering a similar fate (cf. 9:12), some bystanders think he is calling Elijah to come and take him down. But only half-ironic, and perhaps not at all ironic in Mark's intention; for though put to death in the person of John, Elijah is still coming first to restore all things (9:12), as John's violent end showed he did not do ("they did to him whatever things they wished" — 9:13b; cf. 6:14-29). The bystanders do not know that Elijah has already come; but even if they did, Jesus would need him to come again and take him down from the cross. Since Elijah is yet to come and restore all things, it is not so much the earlier coming of Elijah in the person of John as it is the passion predictions and the historical actuality of Jesus' death on a cross which keep Mark's audience from thinking that Elijah might come to take Jesus down (against F. J. Matera, *Kingship* 31-32).

The double offer of wine to Jesus (vv 23, 36) does not need to represent different developments of an originally single offer. The contrasts between a collective offer ("they," i.e. the soldiers) and an individual offer (τις, "a certain one"), between myrrhed wine (ἐσμυρνισμένον οἶνον) and sour wine (ὄξους), and between an honorific gesture and a cynical attempt to revive Jesus (N.B. the difference between ἐδίδουν, "were trying to *give*," and ἐπότιζεν, "was trying to *make* [him] drink") — these contrasts drive so wide a wedge between the two offers that it is easier to think of different episodes. One might hypothesize that the offer of sour wine represents an assimilation of the offer of myrrhed wine to Ps 69:22(21). But not only do the aforementioned contrasts favor different episodes. The use of a sponge and reed has no counterpart in Ps 69:22(21). Furthermore, sour wine was given the psalmist to insult him, if not to torture him, and he seems to have drunk it for lack of anything better; but the attempt to make Jesus drink sour wine has the purpose of reviving him, and he does not drink it because he is dead. So the coincidence of ὄξος, "sour wine," and ποτίζω, "cause to drink," may not signal an assimilation to Ps 69:22(21) any more than it signals a fabrication out of that passage.

As noted before, the centurion's seeing the way Jesus expired just before the attempt to revive him implies that daylight has returned; so the attempt does not contradict the darkness (as thought by W. Schenk, *Passionsbericht* 18-19). F. J. Matera (*Kingship* 29) considers the attempt an insertion framed by a quotation of Jesus' final shout and then another reference to it. But repetition does not guarantee insertion (again see C. A. Evans in *JBL* 101 [1982] 248-49). Nor does a different positioning of the sour wine in Luke 23:36 imply a free-floating tradition; rather, redaction by Luke. His replacement of the cry of dereliction, and consequently of the misunderstanding concerning Elijah, leaves the attempt to make Jesus drink sour wine occasionless and therefore leads Luke to advance the attempt to the morning mockery and to amalgamate the attempt with that mockery, so that "the king of Israel" changes to "the king of the Jews" now that non-Jewish soldiers are speaking as a result of the amalgamation. J. Gnilka (2. 312) thinks that originally the attempt had a purpose of increasing torture, not as in Mark of prolonging life, and that later introduction of bystanders and of Elijah shifted the purpose to one of prolonging Jesus' life so as to see whether Elijah would come and take him down. But sour wine would not increase torture except by prolonging Jesus' life, and Mark's text gives no indication that the attempt to make Jesus drink sour wine was originally devoid of the material concerning Elijah.

The parallel between the combination of seeing and taking down in v 36 and the same combination in the mockery at v 32a (though in reverse order) favors that traditionally and perhaps historically the attempt at reviving Jesus with sour wine to see if Elijah would come and take him down had the purpose of further mockery. But Mark does not use the vocabulary of mockery here, as he did in vv 29-32 ("blaspheme," "ha!" "ridicule," "insult"). Instead, emphasis falls on the expiration of Jesus so as to cut short the shame of his crucifixion. It is highly unlikely that Gentile soldiers would have known about Elijah or about the Jewish belief in his coming to deliver righteous sufferers (though cf. Xen. Eph. 4.2.1-7 for the deliverance of an innocent victim from the cross on which he had been crucified). In all probability, then, the bystanders are Jews. But Mark does not identify the one who runs and fills the sponge, etc., as a bystander. In this respect the contrast with 14:47 suggests that the fetcher of sour wine is a soldier whose reference to Elijah merely echoes the reference in the bystanders' statement. Though people besides soldiers might drink sour wine (cf. Num 6:3; Ruth 2:14), soldiers are well known to drink it (Plut. *Cat. Mai.* 1.13; Plaut. *Mil. Glor.* 836; idem, *Trucul.* 609; *PLond.* 1245. 9). Moreover, it was soldiers who offered Jesus myrrhed wine before his crucifixion (v 23). The possibility that a Roman soldier tried to make him drink sour wine disposes of the difficulty that no Jew would have approached the cross, or been allowed to approach it, with refreshment (against H. Anderson 346). It also disposes of any need to posit a combination of two different traditions consisting in the statements about Elijah (vv 35, 36b) and the attempt to make Jesus drink sour wine (v 36a) or to posit a redactional insertion of the attempt into a tradition devoted only to Elijah. Whether or not Ps 69:22(21) generated an unhistorical attempt to make Jesus drink sour wine, nothing about a tradition concerning Elijah would have suggested the insertion of such an attempt.

The absence of a ἵνα, "that," or an infinitival construction after ἄφετε has led some to interpret the verb as independent, "Allow [me]!" and ἴδωμεν as hortatory, "let's see" (v 36). But it is easier to regard the ἴδωμεν-clause as the expressed object of ἄφετε, an epexegetic ἵνα having dropped out, than to import "me" from nowhere (again cf. Matt 7:4 par. Luke 6:42). Wis 2:17 does not make a good parallel to Mark 15:36, for there the wicked wait to see whether the righteous man's prediction that God will preserve him from death at the hands of his enemies will indeed come to pass. To the bystanders, Jesus has predicted nothing of the sort; and to his disciples he has repeatedly predicted just the opposite (8:31; 9:31 et passim). Mark 15:39 will likewise contrast with Wis 2:18 (confession versus ridicule, a Gentile versus ungodly Jews, God's Son versus a son of God in the sense of a righteous man — see Z. Kato, *Völkermission* 172-73); but lacking the backdrop of a good parallel between Mark 15:36 and Wis 2:17, the contrast can hardly be regarded as deliberate.

It is possible to regard the shout in v 37 as Jesus' second (so Matt 27:50), just as wine is offered him twice, and to argue that remention in v 37 of the shout first mentioned in v 34 would have required an anaphoric definite article in v 37: "letting loose the [aforementioned] loud voice" (so J. D. Kingsbury, *Christology of Mark's Gospel* 131, n. 221). But the anarthrousness of "a loud voice" in v 37 has an explanation other than the introduction of a second loud voice (see the foregoing comments); and Mark's noting the loudness in both v 34 and v 37, providing no different words for the shout in v 37, and subordinating that shout to the new element of expiration all favor a back reference to the previously quoted shout, just as v 25b referred back to v 24a rather than implying a second crucifixion of Jesus. When using duality, Mark often adds a new element in back references. The present adding of expiration to the shout agrees with this practice and thereby supports a back reference rather than a second shout. The back reference integrates the expiration of Jesus with his shout so as to emphasize that he did not die in fleshly weakness, did not lapse into unconsciousness. This double emphasis on the loudness of his shout and therefore on his strength at the moment of expiration — an emphasis favored to be Mark's by its duality — helps disprove the hypothesis that Mark uses Jesus' passion to argue against divine man Christology (so T. J. Weeden, Sr., in *The Passion in Mark* 115-34). That the second emphasis on loudness evokes a declaration of Jesus' divine sonship proves the opposite hypothesis, viz., that Mark puts forward a divine man Christology to counteract the scandal of Jesus' passion. Ex hypothesi, remention in v 37 of the shout first mentioned in v 34 rules out distinguishing a shout of triumph in v 37 from a shout of despair in v 34 (so T. A. Mohr, *Markus- und Johannespassion* 327); and the absence in v 37 of any dominical words at all, much more the absence of triumphant dominical words, disfavors such a distinction. Again, there is no need to think that remention implies fabrication of the intervening episode (see the notes on v 25).

To S. Motyer (in *NTS* 33 [1987] 155-57), v 37 forms an inclusion with 1:9-11 and therefore represents a Marcan Pentecost, a proleptic bestowal of the Spirit, indicated by ἐξέπνευσεν, like that of Elijah to Elisha. Both passages do feature a declaration of Jesus' divine sonship, a downward motion (of the Spirit and of the veil-rending, respectively), the figure of Elijah, and cognates in πνεῦμα, "Spirit," and ἐξέπνευσεν, "he expired." But though John the Baptizer came as a new Elijah (cf. 1:6 and esp. 9:13) and though Jesus received the Spirit at his baptism by John, Jesus did not receive the spirit *of* John as Elisha had received the spirit *of* Elijah (2 Kgs 2:9-15). Nor did John bestow spirit; rather, he explicitly reserved that function for Jesus, the Stronger One (1:8). Nor had Elisha bestowed the Spirit as John predicted that Jesus would do. Nor does anyone at the Crucifixion receive the Spirit when Jesus breathes out (contrast John 20:22 as well as 2 Kgs 2:9-15). In Mark it is Jesus' public ministry that fulfills John's prediction that Jesus will baptize people in Holy Spirit (see the comments and notes on 1:8). To see in ἐξέπνευσεν a reference to baptism in the Holy Spirit would therefore be to impose a later Johannine interpretation on Mark 15:37 (contrast the phraseology of John 19:30 as well as the donative pneumatology that pervades the rest of the fourth gospel, too). On the other hand, to see in the verb an allusion to the release of Jesus' soul-substance in order that it might wend its way home to heaven (W. Schenk, *Passionsbericht* 45) is to impose an even later Gnostic interpretation.

Since the traditional site of Golgotha lies to the west end of the temple whereas only the east end was veiled (not to mention intervening obstacles to view), either tradition has misplaced Golgotha or the centurion's seeing of the veil-rending lacks historical substance. Partly because of 13:1-3, H. M. Jackson (in *NTS* 33 [1987] 24-25) suggests that Golgotha is thought to be located on the Mount of Olives, from which the temple is easily visible (see the notes on v 22 for evidence favoring this site and cf. E. L. Martin, *Secrets* 12-19). Jackson also thinks that "from top to bottom" tells how it was that the centurion could see the veil-rending from a distance (op. cit. 22). But Mark has not mentioned distance (contrast 5:6; 11:13), and reference to the bottom as well as the top implies that the centurion can see both.

The centurion did not see Jesus' loud voice (though Rev 1:12 speaks of seeing a voice), but saw the visible effect of the expiration which also produced an audible effect in that voice. According to Jackson (op. cit. 27), Jesus' breath, i.e. the Spirit of God which since baptism has become Jesus' own spirit, is ascending back to heaven from where it descended (1:10), and this in fulfilment of his prediction that he would sit at the right hand of the Power (14:62). But the present text says nothing of ascent. That the breath-wind-Spirit rends the veil from top to bottom tends in the opposite direction. The heavenly exaltation of Jesus presupposes his resurrection, but his resurrection will not occur till after three days. Even then he will go ahead of his disciples into Galilee (14:28; 16:7). From the judgmental use of the Lord's Spirit-wind-breath in the OT and later Jewish literature, Jackson argues for a portent of the destruction of the temple (op. cit. 29-30). But the favorable use of the Lord's Spirit-wind-breath in Ezek 37:5-14 exposes the weakness of this argument, and the comments and notes on Mark 11:11-25; 13:1-37; 14:58 have disproved a Marcan attack on the temple.

The outer veil of the temple had portrayed on it the starry heavens except for the signs of the Zodiac (Josephus *J.W.* 5.5.4 §213; idem *Ant.* 3.6.4 §132; 3.7.7 §183). This portrayal may contribute to the parallel between the rending of the veil here and the rending of the heavens in 1:10 (D. Ulansey in *JBL* 110 [1991] 123-25). But Mark's omitting both to specify the outer veil and to describe it as portraying the starry heavens combines with ignorance of Jewish things on the part of his audience — except for the present reference they would not know that the temple had any veil at all, much less an inner veil as well as an outer one (cf. esp. 7:2-4) — to keep this bit of background out of sight and concentrate attention on the rending itself as an act of power. The rending does not correspond to the dividing up of Jesus' garments (as thought by D. Dormeyer, *Sinn* 81), for the casting of lots avoided the rending of the garments for distribution (v 24). Nor does Mark present the rending of the veil as a profanation that opens the temple to public view and thereby abrogates the Jewish cult. There is no profanation when the temple is opened in Rev 11:19; 15:5; and Mark mentions no profanation here. He does not even mention an opening of the temple in consequence of the veil-rending or say that anyone looked into the temple. Thus the rending of the veil does not issue in a theophany or revelation of God's glory, as happens with the opening of the temple in Rev 11:19; 15:5-8.

Nor does the rending of the veil fulfil Jesus' prediction that the temple will be destroyed, or portend its fulfillment; for he predicted that destruction in terms of tumbled-down stones (13:2), for which the rending of the veil does not provide a good match, and by no means did the rending of the heavens in Mark's only other use of σχίζομαι, "be rent" (1:10), signify destruction (contrast also the use of ἱερόν for the temple-complex in 13:2 with the present use of ναός for the sanctuary). Something like a collapse of the lintel or columnar capitals of the temple (*Vit. Proph.* 12:12; *Gos. Naz.* 21, 36) would have provided a good match to portend the fulfilment of Jesus' prediction. The portents of destruction for the temple that we find in Josephus *J.W.* 6.5.3-4 §§288-315; Tac. *Hist.* 5.13; *b. Yoma* 39b; *y. Yoma* 6:3 do not include a veil-rending (the exceptions in *T. Levi* 10:3; *Vit. Proph.* 12:12 probably coming from Christian influence, as often in those books, and the removal of the veil in *2 Apoc. Bar.* 6:1-9 having the purpose of safe-keeping, just the opposite of destruction). Not even the opening by itself of the eastern gate into the inner court survives a close comparison; for according to Josephus that opening portended defenselessness in the face of enemy attack, whereas even an unrent veil provides no defense. Moreover, Tacitus and especially Josephus put this portent before the Jewish war apparently by just a bit, whereas the Talmud seems to extend it throughout the last forty years of the second temple. Since forty years appears stereotypically in the OT, the coincidence of forty years before the destruction of the temple and a possible year of Jesus' death holds doubtful significance (cf. the argument of Str-B 1. 1045-46 that the dating by Josephus, who wrote in the first century, deserves preference over the dating in the Talmud, written much later; against D. Juel, *Messiah and Temple* 140-42; also against E. L. Martin, *Secrets* 16-19, 229-30, where it is imagined that a stone lintel supported the veil, that the veil had the inner doors attached to it for stability, and that the collapse of the lintel made the veil tear in two from top to bottom and may also have forced the doors open). If the veil-rending does not portend the destruction of the temple, neither does it signal the eschatological end, as thought by D. C. Allison, Jr. (*End* 30-33), who interrelates rending and destruction to make a point of realized eschatology. The passages cited by Allison for destruction of the second temple and the building of a new one (*1 Enoch* 90:28-29; *Jub.* 1:27; Tob 13:16-18; 14:4-5;

11QTemple 29:8-10; 4QFlor 1:1-3; *Sib. Or.* 5:414-33; *Tg. Isa* 53:5; *Midr. Ps* 90:17; and perhaps *Mek.* Exod 15:17) do not so much as mention a veil of the temple (cf. the foregoing notes on 14:58).

Nor will Jesus build another temple in three days; so the rending of the veil does not fulfil 14:58 any more than it fulfils 13:2. Besides, Mark does not portray the centurion as a disciple of Jesus who might represent a newly built Christian community (see the foregoing comments); and 14:58 contained a falsely reported prediction, the fulfilment of which is therefore not to be expected (see the notes ad loc.). Though seeking testimony against Jesus, even the Sanhedrin did not judge the prediction to be reported truthfully. The declaration of the centurion (v 39) and the watching of women who had followed and served Jesus (vv 40-41) come too quickly to count as the building in three days of another temple understood as the Christian community (against which understanding revisit the notes on 14:58).

See T. J. Geddert, *Watchwords* 141-43, for thirty-five different interpretations of the veil-rending. H. Montefiore (*Josephus and the NT* 16-22) rejects its historicity on the grounds that the Jews could hardly have hushed up such a calamity and that Christians would have used it in anti-Jewish apologetics. But Christians did so use it, as his succeeding paragraph on NT uses of the veil-rending implies; so non-Christian Jews might naturally have expunged it from their own literature. The question therefore devolves on larger questions of historiography, legend, and the supernatural.

The centurion's declaration of Jesus' divine sonship does not count as a kind of entrance into the sanctuary, as though the rending opened it for entrance by Gentiles. For with the exception of priests and Levites, not even Jews could enter it; and not even Heb 10:19-20 makes entrance "through the veil" a privilege granted surprisingly to Gentile Christians. Furthermore, to make the veil-rending a sign of access to God by Gentile or Jew, Mark needs to have specified the inner veil, as does Heb 9:3 (cf. Heb 6:19 and again 10:20), whereas the centurion's seeing entails the only veil visible from outside the temple, i.e. the outer one. Yet a rending of the outer veil would not open the way to God, for he sits enthroned behind the inner veil. On the two veils, see C. Schneider in *TDNT* 3. 628-30; H. W. Attridge, *Hebrews* 184-85; R. H. Gundry, *Matthew* 575.

D. C. Allison, Jr. (*End* 33), suggests that since the outer veil looked like the heavens (see the earlier cited passages in Josephus and cf. the representation of the sky as a curtain or tent in Ps 104:2; Isa 40:22; *b. B. Meṣ.* 59a), the rending of the veil stands for the rending of the heavens on the Day of the Lord (Job 14:12 LXX; Ps 102:26; Isa 34:4; 63:19[64:1]; Hag 2:6, 21; *Sib. Or.* 3:82; 8:233, 413; Matt 24:29 par. Luke 21:25; 2 Pet 3:10; Rev 6:14). But Mark cannot expect an audience who require his explanation of Jewish matters to know the pictorial design embroidered on the outer veil of the Jewish temple. Had they known so much about the temple, he would have needed to specify the outer veil if they were to detect the suggested symbolism.

If the veil-rending represented God the Father as tearing his garments, so to speak, in sorrow over the death of his Son or in outrage over the crime of his Son Jesus's crucifixion, Mark would more likely have used διαρήσσω, "tear," instead of σχίζω, "rend" (cf. 14:63). So also Mark would probably have reused διαρήσσω to indicate that by tearing the veil God showed Jesus' crucifiers to be the real blasphemers, as opposed to the high priest's having torn his undergarments to show that Jesus had blasphemed (against a suggestion by D. Daube, *NTRJ* 24). Elisha tore his garments in two to show sorrow over Elijah's being swept heavenward (2 Kgs 2:12). But Jesus' dying and Elijah's translation contrast with each other; Jesus is thought to call Elijah for rescue; and 2 Kgdms 2:12 LXX uses διαρήσσω, not σχίζω. So we can hardly think that Jesus is cast as the antitype to Elijah (so another suggestion by Daube, op. cit. 23-26). Such a role for Jesus would also require the unlikelihood that in rending the veil of the temple God played the role of antitype to Elisha.

The verb ὁράω/ὄψομαι/εἶδον, "see," occurs about fifty times in Mark but carries a clearly eschatological association only several times (9:1; 13:14, 26; 14:62); so we need not attribute such a connotation to it in vv 32, 36, 39. The Latin loanword κεντυρίων occurs only at v 39 in the NT, which elsewhere uses ἑκατοντάρχης for "centurion." Though a foreign military term might circulate widely, the absence of this one elsewhere in the NT favors the tradition that Mark originated in Rome (see pp. 1041-45). Just as οἱ παραπορευόμενοι referred to people who were going by Jesus (v 29) and τινες τῶν παρεστώτων to some of those who were standing by him (v 35), so ὁ παρεστηκώς identifies the centurion as one of those who were standing by him (cf. 14:47, 69, 70 for similar uses of παρίστημι). Ἐξ ἐναντίας αὐτοῦ could mean "opposite him [Jesus]" instead of "opposite it [the temple or perhaps its veil]." Indeed, the supposition of a reference to Jesus has led to the conjecture that the veil-rending is a redactional insertion interrupting a back reference of αὐτοῦ to Jesus. G. Zuntz (in *Markus-Philologie* 216) even conjectures a post-Marcan scribal interpolation. But not only is there no need to see an interruption, for it makes good sense to say that the centurion was standing by Jesus opposite the temple or its veil. Standing *by* Jesus would contradict standing *opposite* him, and vice versa. In fact, Mark may write ἐξ ἐναντίας αὐτοῦ instead of κατέναντι αὐτοῦ to bring out the element of distance with ἐξ, "from" (so that a literal translation of the whole phrase would read "from opposite it"), and thus make clearer that αὐτοῦ does not refer to Jesus right here but to the temple over there (cf. the distancing of an opponent with ὁ ἐξ ἐναντίας in Tit 2:8 and contrast the compatibility of κατέναντι with proximity in Mark 12:41). Moreover, the centurion's seeing connects better with the visible effect on the temple of the way Jesus died, i.e. with the veil-rending, than with the audible effect of the way he died, i.e. his loud shout. Inattention to Mark's emphasis on the powerful effects of Jesus' dying shout mars the thesis that the centurion, a bearer of power, ironically declares Jesus to have been God's Son because he died a powerless death.

If we were to accept the v.l. κράξας, "shouting," in v 39, the point of Jesus' expiring with a superhuman burst of strength would gain yet further emphasis. This v.l. has strong and widespread external support in A C W Θ *f*¹,¹³ 33 lat sy and the Majority Text. Its omission has external support limited mainly to the Alexandrian family in ℵ B L Ψ 892 2148 co^(bo,sa,fay). Intervention of the veil-rending may have made a back reference to Jesus' shout seem out of place to Alexandrian scribes. We might reason that κράξας is unlikely to have crept into Mark 15:39 from Matt 27:50; for Matt 27:50 stands before, not after, the rending of the veil and thus parallels Mark 15:37 rather than Mark 15:39. Under the supposition of a relation between Mark 15:39 and Matt 27:50, κράξας in the latter might reflect κράξας in the former. And Mark's having written in 5:7 κράξας φωνῇ μεγάλῃ, "shouting with a loud voice," favors his use of κράξας here, too, in view of his having twice referred to "a loud voice" in vv 34 and 37. If we accept these arguments, οὕτως may modify κράξας instead of ἐξέπνευσεν to produce the meaning, "that shouting in this way, he expired," though οὕτως may still modify ἐξέπνευσεν to produce the meaning, "that shouting, he expired in this way."

Generally, on the other hand, we favor the shorter reading; and here κράξας looks like a scribal addition designed to interpret οὕτως as an allusion to Jesus' loud voice. The v.l. which has κράξας but not οὕτως (W Θ 565 sy^s) then follows the scribal insertion of κράξας, i.e. gets rid of οὕτως through recognition of its otiosity once scribes have inserted κράξας, which by definition indicates loudness of voice. The frequency of κράζω would have made its insertion easy, its omission unlikely (see also H. M. Jackson in *NTS* 33 [1987] 16-17, 33, nn. 3-4, against the originality of κράξας).

The centurion's seeing that Jesus has expired in a certain way may stand in some contrast with the wine-offerer's and bystanders' curiosity to see if Elijah is coming to take Jesus down. But since the centurion may not realize till the attempt to make Jesus drink sour wine has failed that he has expired, we should beware of drawing out of this contrast a further contrast between faith, which demands no sign, and unfaith, which does demand a sign (cf. W. Schenk, *Passionsbericht* 58). After all, the superhuman loudness of Jesus' dying shout and the rending of the veil by the breath-wind-Spirit exhaled in the shout make a kind of sign that evokes the centurion's declaration. Though the means differ, R. Bultmann (*HST* 274, n. 1) aptly compares the effect that a large serpent's coiling itself protectively around the face of Cleomenes' corpse had, viz., that a number of people thought him to be a child of the gods (Plut. *Cleom.* 39.1).

"Truly" falsifies the interpretation of υἱὸς θεοῦ as a merely pagan and therefore ironic "a son of God" in Mark's intention as well as in that of the centurion (so E. S. Johnson, Jr., in *JSNT* 31 [1987] 3-22, esp. 16-17). The argument that Mark's audience would not believe it possible for a professional soldier of the centurion's rank and experience to make a Christian-sounding declaration ("Son of God") concerning a victim of crucifixion — this argument also neglects the reference of "in this way" to the veil-rending exhalation of Jesus' last breath and fails to take seriously that so far as Mark is concerned the respect in which centurions were held could enhance a high Christology in this centurion's declaration rather than putting a pagan meaning on it.

To P. J. Achtemeier (61-62) the declaration that Jesus was God's Son (v 39) links up with the connection between Jesus' kingship and the Cross (vv 26, 32) to indicate that suffering defines that kingship. But the amazement which prompts the centurion to call Jesus God's Son so differs from the mockery which characterized the chief priests' and scribes' calling him the king of Israel and from the cynicism which underlay the inscription calling him the king of the Jews that we should not equate kingship and divine sonship. We have repeatedly seen that Jesus' suffering neither evokes nor defines the centurion's declaration. It is evoked and defined, rather, by the supernatural strength that enables Jesus at the moment of his death to shout with a superhumanly loud voice and with exhalant force so powerful that it rends the veil of the temple.

Likewise, to say that according to Mark only in the Cross can Jesus' identity as Son of God be adequately seen and confessed (among many others, see J. Gnilka 2. 324; J. L. Houlden, *Backward* 31-32; T. Söding, *Glaube* 251-80; J. Zmijewski in *SNTU* A/12. 11-13) is to overlook that the centurion does not declare Jesus' divine sonship because he sees Jesus die on a cross, but because he sees Jesus die there in a way that defies naturalistic explanation. It is Jesus' overcoming the weakness normally caused by crucifixion, not dying itself by crucifixion, which evokes the centurion's declaration (esp. against Söding [op. cit. 268-72], who incorrectly generalizes "in this way" with respect to the whole event of Jesus' death as the content of the gospel rather than interpreting "in this way" more naturally and contextually with respect to the manner of his expiration; similarly, P. J. Achtemeier in *Semeia* 11 [1978] 62). Mark does not present a Christology of the Cross to foster a theology of suffering, then, but the Christology of divine sonship to counteract the scandal of the Cross.

For this reason we should also reject the view of J. D. Crossan (*Four Other Gospels* 140-41) that Mark knew and used *Gos. Pet.* 11:45 but shifted the declaration about Jesus from the moment of his resurrection to the manner of his death and changed the declaration by the centurion's soldiers into a declaration by the centurion himself — all to serve a theology of the Cross according to which Mark portrays Jesus as God's Son in that he suffers and dies, not in that he rises from the dead, Mark closing his gospel, according to Crossan, without recording an appearance of the risen Jesus. Also standing against this thesis is the apparent influence on the Gospel of Peter from Matthew's post-Marcan addition of the guard at the tomb. It is easier to believe in a shift of the declaration from the Cross to the empty tomb than vice versa, especially in a book so florid as the Gospel of Peter, which looks like a conflation of Mark and

Matthew more than Matthew looks like a conflation of Mark and the Gospel of Peter (Crossan's view).

J. D. Kingsburg (*Christology of Mark's Gospel* 131) interprets "in this way" in terms of Jesus' dying as one who, having obeyed God, puts his total trust in God. But nowhere does Mark write about Jesus' dying with trust in God. For that, see Luke 23:46. On the contrary, Mark's quoting the cry of dereliction puts a question mark against Jesus' dying with such trust. In Gethsemane he resigned himself to the Father's will (14:35-36). But resignation is not quite the same as obedience, and "in *this* way" (οὕτως, the adverbial form of οὗτος, "this") demands a referent closer at hand than what Jesus prayed in Gethsemane. Moreover, it wrongly interprets the imperfect tense of ἦν, "was," to say that it points to his death as the "culmination" of his ministry (ibid. 131-32, 153). Regularly — and especially with a verb of being — this tense indicates linearity in past time, just the opposite of a culminative or any other point.

The centurion's declaration that Jesus was God's Son does not make the centurion a Christian either historically or literarily, for demons have likewise recognized the divine sonship of Jesus yet not converted (3:11; 5:7; cf. 1:24). Therefore it becomes irrelevant to cite other literature in which martyrdom causes conversions (see J. Pobee in *The Trial of Jesus* 101 for exemplary citations of this sort). Pobee (op. cit. 99-101) suggests that the centurion's declaration implies, "We Romans made a mistake in crucifying Jesus." On the historical level (if we presume historicity), the declaration does carry this implication; but the identification of Jesus as God's Son makes the declaration carry much weightier meaning on the historical and literary levels alike. The fulness of Christian meaning that Mark pours into "Son of God" is debatable, of course. To what degree does the title refer to Jesus' function? To what degree does it refer to his nature? What does it imply, if anything, about his origin, temporal or eternal, earthly or heavenly? Exactly what does it imply about his relation to God the Father and the Holy Spirit? Mark does not say, but he has made clear that it indicates Jesus' enjoyment of a unique relation to God (see the comments on 1:1, 11).

P. Hoffmann (in *Orientierung an Jesus* 199) suggests that in v 39 "human being, man," stands for "Son of man," so that "Son of man" turns out to be "Son of God." But elsewhere we see little or no transformation of "Son of man" into "human being, man"; and "this" points away from an origin in "Son of man," for elsewhere in the NT "Son of man" is not preceded by "this." In the sole exception of John 12:34 "this Son of man" refers back to a previous instance of "the Son of man" (cf. *1 Enoch* 37–71), whereas in Mark 15:39 there is no instance of "human being, man" (ἄνθρωπος) or "Son of man" preceding "this."

Against setting "the king of the Jews" (v 26), "the Christ, the king of Israel" (v 32), and "Son of God" (v 39) in a positive parallel with each other, the first arises out of a false charge, the second out of mockery, and only the third out of belief. "Son of God" occurs in the centurion's declaration but not in the Sanhedrists' mockery even though "the Christ" occurred in their mockery despite Mark's own favorable use of "Christ" alongside "Son of God" (1:1). This fact favors the use of tradition. Otherwise, Mark would probably have kept "the Christ" for the centurion's confession (thus to construct a parallel with the combination of "Christ" and "Son of God" in 1:1).

The adversative δέ, "but" in v 40 does not signal a new pericope shifting from the Crucifixion to the Resurrection, for which is needed an introduction of the women and the burial of Jesus (so R. H. Lightfoot, *History and Interpretation* 62-63). Δέ appears often in the middle of pericopes. In the middle of the present pericope, see examples at vv 23b, 25, 36, 37, 39, of which only the example in v 25 could possibly be made to start a new pericope by division of vv 20b-41 into smaller pericopes. And the women's seeing in vv 40-41 depends for its object on the immediately preceding verses.

Mark would hardly have included the women's distance if he had delayed mentioning them till now to show the true meaning of discipleship, i.e. following Jesus to the Cross
(as thought by E. S. Malbon in *Semeia* 28 [1983] 41-42). But does Mark or the tradition
he uses put them forward on the other hand as fellow guarantors with the centurion of
Jesus' death — against the charge of unbelievers that Jesus did not really die and therefore
only appeared to rise from the dead? Probably not; for no mention or hint of such a charge
appears elsewhere or otherwise in Mark, and according to the text the centurion saw *how*
Jesus expired ("in this way" — v 39), not just *that* he expired, and the centurion confirmed
to Pilate that Jesus had died *already* (vv 44-45), not just that he had *died*. Nor will the
switch from σῶμα, "body" (v 43), to πτῶμα, "corpse" (v 45), stress the reality of Jesus'
death; rather, the quickness with which he has died (see the comments ad loc.).

The "also" which helps introduce the women and the lack of an expressly stated
direct object for "watching" give the women the role of seeing exactly and only what
the centurion saw. Against the possibility that "from a distance" (ἀπὸ μακρόθεν) acts as
an adjective modifying "the women" rather than as an adverb modifying "watching"
(or "were . . . watching," if despite their separation ἦσαν and θεωροῦσαι form a periphrastic imperfect — but see the comments on 1:13), this same phrase has indubitably
acted as an adverb, not as an adjective, in 5:6; 8:3; 11:13; 14:54 (against a suggestion
by M. J. Selvidge in *CBQ* 45 [1983] 399). The women's watching only from a distance
forestalls a parallel with the surrounding of crucified men by their friends and relatives
(*y. Giṭ.* 7:1). The switch from εἶδον, "saw" (vv 32, 36, 39), to θεωρέω, "watch," suits
the distance that keeps the women from close involvement in what they observe. Cf. a
similar lack of close involvement in the other Marcan passages where θεωρέω occurs,
i.e. in 3:11; 5:15, 38; 12:41; 15:47; 16:4. In 3:11 lack of close involvement is supplemented by an attempt to forestall exorcism (see the comments ad loc.). In 5:15; 16:4
the lack of close involvement extends to the point of absence at the time of occurrence,
so that only the continuing result is seen.

R. Pesch (2. 505-7 and in *L'Évangile selon Marc* 377-78, 384-86) construes v 40
as listing four women: "Mary the Magdalene and Mary the [mother or wife] of James the
little, and Joses' mother and Salome" (cf. the insertion by Cod. B of another ἡ, "the,"
before Ἰωσῆτος, "of Joses," to go with μήτηρ, "mother"). But this construal produces an
unnatural ellipsis of "mother" or "wife" with the first-mentioned James before the use of
"mother" with the second-mentioned Joses. We would expect an ellipsis to follow the use,
as indeed ellipses of "mother" do follow in 15:47 and 16:1 once "mother" has been used
in 15:40. Furthermore, the listing of four women here would leave one of them anonymous
though the others are not. Worse yet, the anonymous mother of Joses in v 40 would turn
out to have the same name "Mary" that James's mother or wife has in v 47. Far easier,
then, to see one Mary as the mother of James and Joses, whose names stand in attributive
position (cf. the attributive position of Μαγδαληνή, "Magdalene"). Finally, to distinguish
between Mary the mother or wife of James the little and Joses' mother, who turns out to
be a third Mary when Mary the Magdalene is taken into account, produces a strange
alternation of omissions in 15:47 and 16:1: first an omission of Mary the mother or wife
of James, then of Mary the mother of Joses. As to 15:47, one could explain the omission
of Mary the mother or wife of James as well as the omission of Salome on the ground that
Mary the Magdalene and Mary the mother of Joses meet the minimal requirement of two
witnesses and that 15:40 has already made clear a surplus of witnesses in Mary the mother
or wife of James and in Salome and many other women. One could then explain the
replacement in 16:1 of the description "the [mother] of Joses" with the description "the
[mother or wife] of James" as compensation for the latter's omission in 15:47. But why
then does not Salome replace Mary the Magdalene in 16:1? It seems, rather, that in 16:1
Salome reappears for a full complement, James and Joses sharing one and the same mother.

See the comments on 15:47 for an explanation of Joses' sole mention in 15:47 versus James's sole mention in 16:1, and of the order of those sole mentions.

The three named women among many other women who followed Jesus correspond then to Peter, James, and John and provide witness to Jesus' death and burial and to the emptiness of the tomb. "Mary the Magdalene" means that this Mary comes from Magdala, a town near Tiberias on the west side of the Sea of Galilee (cf. Luke 8:2). The sons of the next Mary have the names of the first two of Jesus' four brothers as listed in 6:3, and in the same order as there. Since 6:3 also gives the name Mary to Jesus' mother, it seems likely that one and the same Mary was mother to Jesus, James, and Joses (and in 6:30 to Jude [not Iscariot] and Simon [not Peter or the Cananaean; cf. 3:16-19] as well — against the plea of J. W. Wenham in *EvQ* 47 [1975] 12 that two families *could* share so many names). Mark identifies her as the mother of Jesus' first two brothers rather than of Jesus himself (contrast the identification in 6:3 of Jesus but not James or Joses as her son) probably because the centurion has just identified Jesus as God's Son and Mark does not want Mary's being the mother of Jesus to lessen the emphasis in this passage on his divine sonship (a suggestion offered in *Mary in the NT* 70, n. 131). Ex hypothesi, Mark does not describe James as "the little" to distinguish him from James the brother of Jesus, and probably not to distinguish him from James the son of Alphaeus (for that James appeared farther back at 3:18) or from James the son of Zebedee (for the absence of that James's brother John, as well as of Peter, distinguishes him well enough from the present James inasmuch as elsewhere in Mark James the son of Zebedee never appears without his brother John and only twice, and in the same episode [10:35, 41], without Peter as well). Rather, Mark describes James as "the little" in reference to 6:3, i.e. as younger than his brother Jesus even though listed here before his brother Joses as though he (James) were the oldest son of Mary (see A. Deissmann, *Bible Studies* 144-45, for evidence favoring "the little" as an allusion to younger age rather than to smaller size in adulthood). The fact that "Joses" is a by-form of "Joseph," which is read by lat sy[s] and the par. Matt 27:56, suits a son of Joseph and Mary the mother of Jesus; i.e. Joses was named after his father (as often happened — see, e.g., Luke 1:59). The remaining brothers Jude and Simon drop out. Even without their inclusion, "the of-James-the-little-and-of-Joses mother" risks cumbersomeness; and from the cultural standpoint omission of the two youngest brothers is unexceptionable (cf. the neglect of David the youngest in 1 Sam 16:11). Mention of Jesus' older two brothers suffices to identify whose mother this Mary is.

Mary the Magdalene is mentioned first, perhaps because she takes some lead over the other women in the events of Jesus' burial and resurrection (cf. John 20:1-18), perhaps because the mother of James and Joses has only recently become a follower of Jesus (as also with regard to his brothers — cf. the mention of his mother and brothers not till after the mention of women in Acts 1:14). Along with his brothers, Mary the mother of Jesus stood outside the circle of disciples in 3:20-21, 31-35; but we have evidence from elsewhere that she and his brothers, above all James, later became disciples (see, e.g., Acts 15:13-21; 21:18; 1 Cor 9:5; Gal 1:19; 2:9, 12; Epistle of James; Hegesippus; Or. *Cels.* 1.47; Eus. *H.E.* 2.23.1-25). An inclusion of Mary the mother of Jesus' brothers among those women who were following him in Galilee and waiting on him there disfavors that Mark polemicizes against Jesus' family (against J. D. Crossan in *NovT* 15 [1973] 104-10; W. H. Kelber, *Oral and Written Gospel* 103-4). Of Salome, we know nothing more. Matt 27:56 replaces her with "the mother of Zebedee's sons" (see R. H. Gundry, *Matthew* 579, for the redactional character of this replacement, which is not to be understood as a description of Salome, for her name does not appear in Matthew's text; also the foregoing comments on Mark 10:46a with respect to the Secret Gospel of Mark).

The translation, "Mary the [wife] of James the younger and mother of Joses," identifies Mary by her husband as well as by her son, leaves "wife" but not "mother" to be supplied, makes the definite article modify an omitted "wife" as well as the stated "mother," and ignores the fraternal parallel in 6:3. P. Carrington (332) says that Mark betrays his youth by using sons instead of a husband or father to identify the second Mary. But Mark's youth was spent by the time he wrote his gospel, and the use of sons for identification has a satisfactory intratextual explanation in relation to 6:3. Because of 6:3, James the little and Joses need not be otherwise known to Mark's church. For following Jesus as an activity of discipleship, see 1:18; 2:14 et passim (though following him does not always carry this significance — see the comments and notes on 8:27; 10:32, 52). For waiting on Jesus, cf. 1:13, 31; and for going up to Jerusalem with him, see 10:32-33 (where following him in Judea and Transjordan on the road to Jerusalem [see 10:1] does not provide a close parallel, however, to following him in Galilee as per 15:41).

F. J. Matera (*Kingship* 52) uses the ambiguity of αἵ, "who" (v 41), to argue for Mark's insertion of the two Marys and Salome, and thence for his fabrication and insertion of vv 40-41 to introduce a larger insertion of the burial story into the passion narrative. But the ambiguity of αἵ would argue only for fabrication and insertion of the names into traditional material elsewhere in vv 40-41. Is αἵ ambiguous, however? Most naturally, it introduces a description of the women just named, whereas the "many others who came up with him [Jesus] to Jerusalem" switches back to the women in general for an a-b-b'-a' construction. It would also make easier sense if three rather than many women are said to have been following Jesus and waiting on him in Galilee.

Because the account of Jesus' crucifixion reached its climax in the centurion's declaration, L. Schenke (*Auferstehungsverkündigung* 21-27) thinks that Mark fabricated vv 40-41 out of v 47 and 16:1. See the comments and notes on the later verses, however, for changes which presuppose vv 40-41. That in both Jewish and Gentile courts the testimony of women is ordinarily suspect (Josephus *Ant.* 4.8.15 §219; *m. Roš. Haš.* 1:8; *m. Šebu.* 4:1; *y. Yoma* 6:2; *Num. Rab.* 10.5 on Num 6:2; *Sipre Deut.* 190; J. M. Baumgarten in *JBL* 76 [1957] 266-69; E. L. Bode, *First Easter Morning* 161; Str-B 2. 441; 3. 217, 251, 559-60[c]; PW s.v. "Martyria" and "Testimonium") makes it doubtful that Mark uses the women mentioned later to fabricate a cloud of witnesses for the way Jesus died. The extensive description of the women as Jesus' followers, ladies in waiting, and fellow travelers (cf. M. A. Tolbert, *Sowing the Gospel* 292-93) seems designed to make up for the social disadvantage of their sex; i.e. Mark seems bent on overcoming a cultural embarrassment in the tradition rather than on fabricating a culturally embarrassing fiction (cf. a defense of the women's historicity by W. Munro in *CBQ* 44 [1982] 234-41, though she wrongly accepts the view that in 16:1-8 Marcan redaction will do them ill). In the process, of course, Mark's style and emphases may shine through. D. Dormeyer (*Passion* 235-37) argues oppositely to Schenke that v 40 offers tradition, v 47 Mark's redaction, and 16:1 pre-Marcan redaction.

If tradition underlies vv 40-41, the argument that v 47 more naturally means "Mary the [daughter or wife] of Joses" and 16:1 "Mary the [daughter or wife] of James" falls to the ground. In accordance with v 40, the later ellipses become more naturally filled with "mother." It also becomes unnecessary to posit in v 40 a combination of different traditions from behind v 47 and 16:1, a combination that would entail a mistake in the equating of the Mary associated with Joses (v 47) and the Mary associated with James (16:1; see also J. D. Crossan [in *NovT* 15 (1973) 106], who asks why Mark would combine those traditions to produce v 40 and then show no interest in harmonizing v 47 and 16:1, and why he would mention James before Joses in v 40 against the order in which he later takes up the traditions mentioning them). The unusualness in Greek culture of distinguishing a woman by reference to her children is used to defend the greater naturalness of supplying "daughter" or "wife" in 15:47; 16:1 apart from 15:40. M.-J. Lagrange (439) counters by appealing to the modern Arab custom of distinguishing a woman by reference to her children. J. Ernst (474) thinks that an original accent fell on the distance from which the women were watching — this distance alluding to the desertion of a righteous sufferer by family and friends, as in 14:54 (with 14:50-52); Ps 38:12 LXX — and that Mark shifts the accent to the women's seeing. This view requires the substitution of something else for seeing in a hypothetically more original version, however; and a number of contrasts subvert an original as well as a current influence from Ps 38:12 LXX (καὶ οἱ ἔγγιστά μου ἀπὸ μακρόθεν ἔστησαν, "and my nearest ones [i.e. 'my closest relatives'] stood at a distance"): (1) standing versus watching; (2) aloofness versus concern (as it turns out in 15:47–16:1); (3) disease versus execution; and (4) deserved punishment by God versus miscarriage of human justice. On the ground that NT writers often violate the contextual meaning of OT passages, we might dismiss these contrasts as uninimical to an allusion. But Mark's using ἀπὸ μακρόθεν, "from a distance," also in a number of passages where no possibility of an allusion to Ps 38:12 LXX exists (5:6; 8:3; 11:13; 14:54) discounts the argumentative value of the closest similarity between Mark 15:40 and Ps 38:12 LXX. Because it has to do with seeing from a distance, 11:13 is especially comparable to 15:40. Because it has to do with discipleship, following from a distance in 14:54 is especially comparable to followers' watching from a distance in 15:40.

In 10:45, "to give his [the Son of man's] life a ransom in substitution for many" added a salvific meaning to the mundane meaning of "to serve" (διακονῆσαι) but did not erase its mundane meaning. This salvific meaning cannot apply to the Galilean activity of the present women. In 1:13 διακονέω probably carried its most common mundane meaning of waiting on table, serving food. In 1:31, which is like the present passage in having a woman as subject, the verb almost certainly carried this meaning. Despite attempts to broaden the meaning here, then, the women's waiting on Jesus probably consisted in serving him food. Even so, their discipleship is not brought into question (correctly, W. Munro in *CBQ* 44 [1982] 232-34). On the contrary, διακονέω suits very well whatever disciples may do on behalf of their teachers (W. D. Davies, *Setting* 422-23).

C. Wiéner (in *La Pâque du Christ* 142) finds a concentric structure in vv 40-47: (a) the women (vv 40-41); (b) Joseph of Arimathea and Pilate (vv 42-43); (c) Pilate and the centurion; (b') Joseph and Jesus' body; (a') the women. But the women's watching in vv 40-41 ties those verses to the preceding crucifixion (otherwise the women have nothing to watch), just as the women's watching in v 47 ties that verse to the preceding burial (as expressly stated, ". . . were watching where he [Jesus] was put," and otherwise they have nothing to watch that they have not already been said to have watched). Mark likes to start pericopes with topographical movement such as v 42 provides, thus breaking up the suggested concentric unity of vv 40-47. And though Joseph is not active in vv 44-45, his appearance there along with Pilate and the centurion tends against dividing those verses from their neighbors according to a different cast of characters.

THE DIGNIFYING OF JESUS' BODY IN BURIAL

15:42-47 (Matt 27:57-61; Luke 23:50-56; John 19:38-42)

The story of Jesus' burial starts with a request for his body by Joseph from Arimathea (vv 42-43), continues with Pilate's granting the request (vv 44-45), and reaches its climax in the entombment of the body (v 46). A notation that two women observe where the entombment takes place closes out the story (v 47).

15:42-43 *(Matt 27:57-58a; Luke 23:50-52; John 19:38a)* "And because it had already become late" (cf. 1:32; 4:35; 6:35, 47; 8:2; 11:11; 14:17) reminds readers that Jesus died at the ninth hour (halfway between noon and sundown), which counts for late in the day (vv 34-38). "Since it was Preparation, i.e. Pre-Sabbath" excludes a reference to evening (for at sundown the Sabbath itself begins) and sets a deadline for the burial of Jesus' body if it is not to hang disgracefully on the cross overnight and throughout the next day. *M. Sanh.* 6:5; *y. Ber.* 6:9 allow a delay of burial till the next day if time is lacking to treat the corpse with due honors, but in Jesus' case the corpse would have had to go unburied for yet another day, the Sabbath. The law against working on this day prohibits moving a corpse from sundown on Friday to sundown on Saturday. During this period *m. Šabb.* 23:5 allows the anointing and washing of a corpse, also the tying of the chin to keep it from dropping further and the removal of a mattress in order that the corpse might rest on sand for better preservation till the Sabbath ends and work on the corpse can proceed (cf. Mark's point that the corpse of Jesus did not hang exposed to deteriorative forces overnight and throughout the next day), but this mishnaic passage disallows the moving of any bodily member, even a closing of the eyelids and a tying of the chin higher (cf. the women's delaying till after the Sabbath their purchase of aromatics to anoint Jesus' corpse [16:1]; also the delay till nightfall of fetching a coffin and shroud for someone who has died on the Sabbath [*m. Šabb.* 23:4] and people's bringing their sick and demon-possessed not till Sabbath-closing sundown [1:32]; contrast the definition of the lateness in 1:32 as subsequent to sundown; see 1:32, 35; 4:35; 13:24; 14:12, 30; 16:2 for other examples of Mark's further temporal indications to refine the meaning of initial temporal indications, the notes on 14:17, and J. Jeremias, *Eucharistic Words* 17-18). The interpretation of "Preparation" by "Pre-Sabbath" points up the deadline.

To erase the shame of the Cross, Mark dignifies Jesus in burial as well as in death. Therefore he also notes that the one who comes to ask for Jesus' body — viz., Joseph from Arimathea — is "a distinguished councilor," and not only a man of political prominence but also one of religious devotion ("who also himself was waiting for the kingdom of God"; cf. 12:34; Luke 2:25, 38; 1QSb 5:21; the Qaddiš) and of derring-do ("taking a risk, he went in to Pilate and asked for the body of Jesus"). Καί, "also," emphasizes the religious devotion of Joseph as a distinct addition to his political prominence. Αὐτός, "himself," and the periphrastic construction of ἦν προσδεχόμενος, "was waiting for," intensify that emphasis (cf. S. E. Porter, *Verbal Aspect* 480). Τολμήσας, "taking a risk," is unnecessary except to dignify Jesus by drumming up admiration for his burier; and asyndeton punctuates this derring-do, as does also Mark's omitting to spell out the nature of the risk but dwelling only on the risk as such (cf. 12:34 for another example of an apparently Marcan τολμάω, "take a risk, dare"). It speaks well of Jesus that despite the disgraceful manner of his death such a man as Joseph should dangerously seek to bury his body. The compliment is especially powerful in that though Mark portrays Joseph as waiting for the kingdom of God, he does not portray him as a disciple of Jesus (contrast Matt 27:57; John 19:38). Rather, he identifies Joseph as a member of the very Sanhedrin which unanimously condemned Jesus (cf.

14:64 with 14:55). As a "councilor" (βουλευτής), Joseph belongs to that body the whole of which held a "consultation" (συμβούλιον) issuing in the delivery of Jesus to Pilate (15:1; contrast the denial in Luke 23:51 that Joseph consented to their counsel [βουλῇ] and action). Thus his political prominence, religious devotion, and personal bravery are all the more exceptional in comparison with the rest of the Sanhedrin and hence all the more complimentary of Jesus in relation to the Crucifixion.

15:44-47 *(Matt 27:58b-61; Luke 23:53-56; John 19:38b-42)* An adversative δέ, "but," and forward placement of ὁ . . . Πιλᾶτος, "the [aforementioned] Pilate," turn attention to Pilate. His marveling if Jesus "is already dead" (ἤδη τέθνηκεν, the adverb and perfect tense emphasizing a present state of death) stresses the shortness of time that he hung on a cross — another way in which Mark counteracts the shame of Jesus' crucifixion (see Sen. *Ep.* 101.10-14 [*ad Lucilium*] on death by crucifixion as normally taking a long time, and contrast the view of Augustine [*Ev. Joh.* 36.4] that Jesus' death was long and drawn out). Pilate's summoning the centurion and asking him if Jesus "died a while back" (πάλαι ἀπέθανεν, the adverb and aorist tense emphasizing a past event) reinforce the apologetic point, for Mark's repeated earlier temporal notations (vv 25, 33-34, 42) as well as the immediately preceding "already" (ἤδη) make clear in advance the answer: yes, Jesus did die a while back. Though a fairly well attested v.l. repeats ἤδη (so B D W Θ *pc* lat), Mark appears to switch to πάλαι for emphasis on the pastness of Jesus' death and therefore on the shortness of his stay on the Cross (see B. M. Metzger, *Textual Commentary* ad loc., on the text critical question and cf. BAGD s.v. πάλαι 2b for the rough equivalence of this adverb to ἤδη). Pilate's doubt that Jesus has died so quickly — a doubt accented by a double "if," one for his marveling and another for his inquiry — sharpens the point once the doubt is overcome. Confirmation from the centurion leads to Pilate's granting the request of Joseph. Δωρέομαι, "grant," occurs much less often than δίδωμι, "give" (in the NT, 3 times versus 415 times), and can carry a higher sounding connotation. The only other uses of δωρέομαι in the NT occur in Asianically, i.e. baroquely, styled 2 Peter at 1:3, 4. Here in Mark 14:45, then, the verb reverses Jesus' being given over (παραδίδωμι) to trial and crucifixion and dignifies Jesus' burial by connoting a formal donation of his corpse by Pilate to Joseph (contrast the indignity perpetrated on the executed by having their corpses sold — Cic. *Verr.* 2.5.45 §§119-20; 2.5.49-50 §§128-30; 2.5.51 §§134-35; cf. G. Scholz in *LingBib* 57 [1985] 84-85). According to the best attested reading, Mark switches from σῶμα, "body" (v 43), to πτῶμα, "corpse" (ℵ B D L Θ 565 sy^s; cf. 6:29), to put one last accent on Jesus' having died too soon to have spent very much time on a cross.

The purchase of a linen cloth dignifies Jesus with a brand new shroud. The asyndeton which introduces the taking down of Jesus highlights his avoiding the indignity of hanging on a cross overnight and throughout the Sabbath. So also does his proper wrapping in the linen cloth, and again his proper placement in a tomb (cf. 6:29), especially because Romans forbade such burial for those executed like Jesus under the charge of high treason (see the discussion of primary sources by R. E. Brown in *CBQ* 50 [1988] 234-36). Mark describes the tomb as "hewn out of a rock" (cf. Isa 22:16), not to prepare for entrance into the tomb at 16:5 and exit from it at 16:8 (for a tomb need not be so described to be understood as capable of entrance and exit [see John 19:41-42 with 20:3-8, for example] and might be a cave thus capable [see John 11:38, 43-44]), but to stress the propriety, indeed the dignity, of the burial (cf. L. E. Cox in *PEQ* 100 [1968] 133: "A monument hewn out of a rock" is a phrase that "can be most properly applied to a free standing monolith whether we think of the carving of the outside or of the cell"). Mark's omitting to say who owned the tomb (contrast Matt 27:60) rivets attention on its high grade.

Conspicuous by its absence is the usual Roman practice of leaving victims of crucifixion on their crosses for days while their corpses start decomposing in plain view and predatory animals and birds of carrion pick off their flesh (Or. *Matt* 27:54; Hor. *Epist.* 1.16.48; Petr. *Sat.* 111-112; Marc. Ann. Luc. 6.544-46; Plut. *Cleom.* 39.1). No such shame in Jesus' case (cf. the protecting of Cleomenes' corpse from birds of carrion — ibid.)! Instead, completing a wordplay with καταλύων, καταβάς, καταβάτω, ἐγκατέλιπες, καθελεῖν, καταπέτασμα, and κάτω (vv 29, 30, 32, 34, 36, 38 — see the comments ad loc.), the prefix καθ- in καθελών, "taking down," calls attention to removal from the cross. The wrapping of Jesus in a linen cloth probably implies that Joseph washed him and anointed him with oil in a characteristically Jewish manner. But a woman's having already myrrhed Jesus' body in preparation for burial (14:3-8) and the future intention of some women to anoint him with aromatics makes a washing and an anointing with mere oil unworthy of mention (see the comments and notes on 16:1). In rolling a stone to block entrance into the tomb, Joseph will have had the purpose of quarantining ritual pollution; but for Mark the blockage has the purpose of shielding Jesus' corpse from shameful predation and public exposure and prepares for the question, "Who will roll away the stone . . . ?" (16:3). Observation of the location by Mary the Magdalene and Mary the mother of Joses, to whom attention is shifted from Joseph by an adversative δε, "but," prepares for the women's coming to the tomb that Joseph has thus blocked. It seems that "Mary the [mother] of Joses" is shorthand for "Mary the mother of James the little and of Joses" (v 40), Joses being chosen as the last mentioned one of the pair of sons (cf. the apparently compensatory switch to James in 16:1). Salome and the many other women of vv 40-41 drop out, apparently because they do not stay with the two Marys beyond the Crucifixion to the burial.

NOTES

G. Scholz (in *LingBib* 57 [1985] 81-94) regards vv 42-47 as a fictive narrativizing of the theology of Jesus' being "given over." But the unknownness of Joseph outside the gospels and literature based on them tends in general toward historicity. See R. Pesch in *L'Évangile selon Marc* 367-70; L. Schenke, *Der gekreuzigte Christus* 77-83, against an original independence for vv 42-47.

Mark does not put the quick burial of Jesus in terms of the law that prohibits letting a corpse hang all night on a tree whether or not the Sabbath starts at sundown (Deut 21:22-23; Josh 10:26-27; 11QTemple 64:10-13; Josephus *J.W.* 4.5.2 §317; 3.8.5 §377; Philo *Spec.* 3.28 §151-52; *m. Sanh.* 6:5; *b. Sanh.* 46b). But J. D. Crossan (*Four Other Gospels* 152-57) traces a history of tradition starting, not with Mark 15:42; rather, with *Gos. Pet.* 5:15 (cf. 2:5a), which he thinks to be original. There, Jesus' enemies *are* concerned lest the law of Deut 21:22-23; Josh 10:26-27 et passim has been broken if the supernatural darkness means that the day has ended with Jesus' body hanging on a tree. In John 19:31, the problem still concerns his enemies; but in John 19:41-42 it concerns his friends, too — and in both passages the problem has shifted from that of a body hanging overnight on a tree to that of a body hanging on a cross through a Sabbath magnified by the Passover (cf. Philo *Flac.* 10 §83 on taking down bodies and giving them to relatives for burial to keep the festive sanctity of the emperor's birthday). By Mark 15:42 the problem has become residual in that only Joseph is concerned, and only with respect to the law of the Sabbath as such. The problem becomes even more residual in Matt 27:57, which does not so much as mention the Sabbath, much less the law against letting a dead man hang overnight on a tree. And to provide Luke 24:1 with background, Luke 23:54-56 transfers legal obedience in the face of imminent evening from Jesus' enemies and Joseph to faithful women.

Behind this reconstruction lies the hypothesis that *Gos. Pet.* 2:3-5a; 6:23-24 are late insertions to the effect that Joseph buried Jesus. In the original version of the Gospel of Peter, thinks Crossan, Jesus' enemies buried him. Mark then fabricated the burial by Joseph, who became an ambiguous and transitional figure leading from burial by Jesus' enemies to burial by his friends. Thus Mark provided Joseph but kept him in the Sanhedrin in deference to the original version of the Gospel of Peter, and kept Joseph's Christian credentials deliberately vague. Luke redeemed Joseph in the Sanhedrin, and Matthew and John removed Joseph completely from it and made him a full disciple of Jesus.

As traced, this development of Joseph looks true to the synoptic texts; but overall, a better history of the tradition concerning Jesus' burial starts with Mark 15:42. Here, Joseph buries Jesus out of traditional Jewish piety. Matt 27:57 transforms Joseph into a disciple and therefore makes his request one of personal allegiance to Jesus, an example of true discipleship. Then Luke 23:50-56 (Crossan errs in not taking vv 50-53 into account) shifts the emphasis to what good people Joseph and the women are in attending to the needs of Jesus' corpse, as throughout Luke-Acts emphasis falls on the goodness of Jesus and those attracted to him. Next, John 19:31-42 richly overlays the episode with theological motifs of Jesus as the Passover lamb, scriptural fulfilment, witness, regal glory, etc. Finally, *Gos. Pet.* 5:15 (cf. 2:5a) heightens the effect of the synoptics' supernatural darkness by making this darkness cause Jesus' crucifiers to think that the day may have ended prematurely with Jesus, not yet dead, still hanging on a cross in violation of the Law, and to the extent of making many of them go to bed thinking it was nighttime and others of them stumble because of the darkness (5:18). The subtraction of 2:3-5a; 6:23-24 leaves no burial at all in the Gospel of Peter. 6:21 says only that "the Jews drew the nails from the Lord's hands and laid him on the earth." The sun shines again in 6:22 and, skipping the supposedly inserted 6:23-24, the following verses do not describe a burial but merely allude to Jesus' being in a sepulchre. See R. E. Brown in *NTS* 33 (1987) 321-43; D. F. Wright in *Gospel Perspectives* 5. 221-27; F. Neirynck in *The NT in Early Christianity* 125, 127-28, 130-32, 140-57; J. B. Green in *JBL* 109 (1990) 356-58 against taking the Gospel of Peter as earlier than the synoptics and independent of them.

It should be inconceivable that the Mark who translates Aramaic and (whether hyperbolically or not) explains Jewish customs does not know that the Sabbath begins at sundown on Friday. Yet W. Schmithals (702-3) among others thinks so on the ground that ὀψίας must refer to evening. The word means "late," however, and need not refer to evening, though it usually does. The differing supplements to ὀψίας in 1:32; 15:42 favor that Mark uses the word variously and does know that the Sabbath begins at sundown on Friday. "Already" ties this lateness to the ninth hour, the hour of Jesus' expiration, and thereby forestalls the interpretation that Mark continues the earlier temporal scheme (vv 25, 33-34) by leaping ahead another three hours to evening and consequently wreaking havoc on the chronology of the Sabbath (so, e.g., T. A. Mohr, *Markus- und Johannespassion* 352-53). "Since (ἐπεί) it was preparation, i.e. Pre-Sabbath" does not retrospectively explain why it was late, but prospectively explains why Joseph went to Pilate to request Jesus' body. Thus the clause performs the same function that the preceding genitive absolute performed (in translation: "because it had already become late"). To say that it was late because it was Friday (i.e. Preparation, Pre-Sabbath) would make nonsense. Whenever the Sabbath starts, being Friday does not make the hour late. Lateness in the day depends on the time of day, not on the day of the week (esp. against J. Schreiber [*Theologie des Vertrauens* 88-91], who builds his case for anti-Judaistic polemic partly on a retrospective understanding of the ἐπεί-clause; see also R. E. Brown in *CBQ* 50 [1988] 238, n. 20, 239, n. 22, 240-41 against Schreiber, whose further arguments in *ZNW* 72 [1981] 141-57 often require Mark's Gentile audience to know Jewish laws as other parts of his book show they do not, or require him to write in disregard of their ignorance as other parts of his book show he does not).

Omission of the definite article before "from Arimathea" by B D Wᶜ 0112 28 *pc* syˢ boᵖᵗ opens the possibility but not necessity of construing the prepositional phrase adverbially ("coming from Arimathea") rather than adjectivally ("Joseph, the [one] from Arimathea"). The adverbial construal avoids redundancy in that ἐλθών then instances a journey to Jerusalem and εἰσῆλθεν an entrance into Pilate's presence. But as a councilor, a member of the Sanhedrin all of whom condemned Jesus, Joseph has been in Jerusalem from the start (as would be expected for the Passover, anyhow). So whether or not we read the definite article, the prepositional phrase acts adjectivally (cf. the comments on 1:9; also 3:7-8) and thus opens the possibility that though Joseph hails from Arimathea he does not live there (on its location, see S. F. Hunter and W. S. LaSor in *ISBE* [2nd ed.] 1. 290). As for redundancy, see 16:8 ("and going out, they fled from the tomb"); and ἐλθών might refer to Joseph's coming from Golgotha to the praetorium, and εἰσῆλθεν to his entrance into the praetorium (for examples of similar complementarity coming close to redundancy, see 1:29; 5:13; 6:1; 7:31; 9:30; 14:16). If sheer redundancy is to be found here, however, its cause probably lies in the length of the intervening material which identifies and describes Joseph.

The description of Joseph of Arimathea as a distinguished "councilor" (βουλευτής) favors his membership in the Sanhedrin — the great one in Jerusalem, not a local one in Arimathea — not only because Mark has recently written that the great Sanhedrin in Jerusalem made "a consultation" (συμβούλιον — v 1) but also because Josephus *J.W.* 2.17.1 §405 uses "councilors" (βουλευταί) for Sanhedrists. It escapes one why Joseph's being a minor character like Simon of Cyrene, the centurion, and the watching women should favor that Joseph belongs to a merely local Sanhedrin. That the high priest was another minor character did not exclude him from membership in the great Sanhedrin (against J. D. Kingsbury in *NTS* 36 [1990] 48-50). Mark's apparent inclusion of Joseph among those who condemned Jesus and gave him over to Pilate (14:55, 64; 15:1) raises questions about Joseph's behavior: Did he undergo a change of heart toward Jesus? Does Mark use hyperbole in assigning to all the Sanhedrists the condemnation of Jesus? And so on. Luke 23:50-51 makes Joseph into a Sanhedric exception, and Matt 27:57 changes him from a distinguished Sanhedrist into a wealthy disciple of Jesus. But Mark's desire to magnify the fulfilment of Jesus' passion predictions and the dignity of Jesus' burial overpowers any concern he might have had to clarify the role of Joseph (cf. the notes on v 46 for the possibility that genuine piety drove him both to vote for Jesus' condemnation and to bury Jesus' corpse). The difficulty of having Jesus' burier belong to the Sanhedrin which condemned Jesus argues for the traditionality of burial by Joseph (T. A. Mohr, *Markus- und Johannespassion* 353-54).

In view of Jesus' preaching and teaching about the kingdom, "waiting for the kingdom of God" might describe Joseph as having a specifically Christian hope rather than genuine Jewish piety (so, e.g., J. Wellhausen [2. Aufl.] 134; J. Blinzler in *Resurrexit* 58; J. D. Kingsbury in *NTS* 36 [1990] 48-50). But such a description would contradict his joining the rest of the Sanhedrin in condemning Jesus to death (14:64); and the phraseology of προσδέχομαι, "wait for," plus "the kingdom of God" occurs elsewhere neither in Mark nor in the rest of the NT for specifically Christian hope. Yet the phraseology does sound Jewish (G. Dalman, *Words* 109-10). Mark's stopping short of portraying the centurion and now Joseph as Jesus' disciples, or as becoming so, forestalls an interpretation of the centurion as a prototype of Gentile Christians and of Joseph as a prototype of Jewish Christians (against E. Wendling, *Entstehung* 174-76).

It may be true that only "a distinguished councilor" could go directly to Pilate and that only such a personage who had voted to condemn Jesus could risk asking for his corpse (a request that would rouse suspicions of insurrectionary sympathy with "the king of the Jews"). But if Mark were making these points, "taking a risk" would turn vapid and "who also himself was waiting for the kingdom of God" would become worse than irrelevant. For Pilate might take offense at Joseph's waiting for any kingdom that threatens to overturn the Roman Empire. According to Mark, moreover, Pilate knows the councilors who make up the Sanhedrin, distinguished or not, to have been envious of Jesus' popularity (v 10). The conjunction of Joseph's taking a risk and his entrance to Pilate works against relating the risk to the crowd or to the rest of the Sanhedrin, i.e. as possibly antagonizing those who yelled for Jesus' crucifixion or the judges who condemned Jesus, delivered him to Pilate, and incited the crowd to yell for Barabbas's release and possibly also for Jesus' crucifixion (so some suggestions canvassed by W. Grundmann [7. Aufl.] 440). Both groups were capable of casting suspicion on Joseph; but neither group makes an appearance in this episode, and hearing for himself the request of Joseph could easily suffice, without accusation from outside, to excite Pilate's suspicion of insurrectionary sympathy in Joseph. Better is the suggestion that the risk lay in asking for Jesus' body despite the Romans' prohibiting proper burial for a person executed, as Jesus was, under a charge of high treason (R. E. Brown in *CBQ* 50 [1988] 241). Jesus' disciples have fled, Peter has denied him, and Jewish women such as those who watched the Crucifixion from a distance will hardly have approached a Roman governor to ask for Jesus' body.

In 14:8 as well as in 15:43 σῶμα occurs for Jesus' body with respect to burial. But there is no allusion to the Lord's Supper in the mention of Jesus' body here any more than there was in 14:8. That the Lord's Supper mentions Jesus' body does not imply that every mention of his body alludes to the Lord's Supper.

In the NT "that" (ὅτι) follows "marvel" (θαυμάζω) more often than does "if" (εἰ). "If" echoes classical Greek (BDF §454[1]) and introduces an element of doubt ("expressed surprise that he was already dead, if he were" — C. F. D. Moule, *Idiom-Book* 154), which Pilate satisfies by inquiring of the centurion. The εἰ of Pilate's inquiry ("if he [Jesus] had died a while back"), parallels and defines the εἰ of his marveling. For dying, Mark follows the general practice of using the simplex θνήσκω in the perfect tense, the complex ἀποθνήσκω in other tenses (so v 44; also 5:35, 39; 9:26; 12:19, 20, 21, 22). J. Ernst (480) is correct to deny that Pilate's marveling implies a sense of the numinous (against J. Gnilka 2. 333), but not quite correct to declare that Pilate merely wants to make sure that Jesus has really died. Rather, he wants to make sure that Jesus has died so quickly. Mark does not present the quickness with which Jesus died as due to his willing to die when he did (as thought by G. Scholz in *LingBib* 57 [1985] 85), for the cry of dereliction which accompanies his death sounds a note disharmonious with voluntariness. Therefore Pilate's marveling at the quickness of Jesus' death has nothing to do with a Marcan messianic secret (again as thought ibid.). See C. J. Hemer in *Medicine and the Bible* 61-68 for a survey of medical opinions regarding Jesus' death, and E. L. Martin, *Secrets* 184-202, for the view that Jesus was stoned while hanging on the cross.

F. J. Matera (*Kingship* 53-55) argues for Mark's insertion of vv 44-45 from the characteristically Marcan chiasm of what F. Neirynck (*Duality* 121-22) calls "Request and Realization": (a) Joseph requests Jesus' body; (b) Pilate marvels if Jesus is already dead; (b') Pilate asks if Jesus died a while back; (a') Pilate grants the corpse. Matera finds further evidence of Mark's hand in the pairs of synonyms σῶμα and πτῶμα, "body" and "corpse," ἤδη and πάλαι, "already" and "a while back" (cf. the synonyms for "basket" in 8:18-21 [referring back to 6:43; 8:8], for "left [hand]" in 10:35-40, and for "see" or "watch" in 15:32, 36, 39, 40, 47; 16:4, 6). Matera correctly notes that a comparison of the phraseology in 15:46 with that of 6:29 shows the use of πτῶμα to draw a parallel between the burials of Jesus and John the Baptizer (see also 9:12b-13 and further details in Matera, op. cit. 97-100), that Pilate's marveling interrelates Jesus' burial to his trial (cf. 15:5), and that the mention of the centurion interrelates Jesus' burial to his crucifixion (cf. 15:39). But neither these interrelationships nor Marcan style proves fabrication and insertion. Notably, the chiasm to which Matera appeals starts before the supposed insertion (see v 43 for Joseph's request of Jesus' body), not to detail features of Marcan style (duality, introductory circumstantial participles, asyndeton, etc.) in vv 42-43, 46-47.

Pilate is the subject of v 45, Joseph of v 46 (as of v 43). But since Joseph appears as an indirect object at the very close of v 45, the shift in subjects takes place too naturally to support the theory that someone has interpolated vv 44-45. Verse 46 does not follow well on v 43, because without vv 44-45 the granting of Joseph's request has to be inferred and Pilate's willingness to grant it so soon goes unexplained. From that standpoint, then, there is no reason to view vv 44-45 as a fabrication by Mark (and we have repeatedly seen that even the ease of a jump over intervening material does not necessarily imply the fabrication of that material or its insertion from another tradition). One could imagine that pre-Marcan tradition contained Pilate's granting of the request, but his willingness to grant it so soon would remain problematic in a tradition lacking explanation of this willingness. See R. H. Gundry, *Matthew* 580-81, on Matthew's redactional reasons for omitting an explanation of Pilate's willingness (Matt 27:58) and on the secondary influence of Matthew in Luke's similar omission (Luke 23:52). Luke goes further by also omitting Pilate's grant of the request. These omissions do not represent a sparer pre-Marcan tradition. Mark puts the tradition underlying vv 44-46 to apologetic use, but this use does not belie traditionality.

Pilate's getting confirmation from the centurion that Jesus has died precludes that Jesus later comes back to consciousness without having died rather than coming back to life from death. Mark is not trying to prove that Jesus really died, however. "Already" and "a while back" point to quickness instead of reality. The reference to quickness opposes an anti-Gnostic apologetic, which would require a reference to reality (against J. Schreiber, *Theologie des Vertrauens* 47, n. 102).

For Joseph's purchasing a shroud on a festival day, when nothing but necessities were to be bought and sold, see J. Jeremias, *Eucharistic Words* 77-78. For burying the dead as a Jewish act of piety, see 2 Sam 21:8-14; Tob 1:17-19; 2:3-8; 12:12-13; Sir 7:33; 38:16; Josephus *J.W.* 3.8.5 §377. Such piety gives Jesus' saying, "Let the dead bury their own dead" (Luke 9:60), its shock-value and extends even to the burial of criminals executed by crucifixion (2 Sam 21:8-14; Josephus *J.W.* 3.8.5 §377; 4.5.2 §317). "And pious men [not Christians] buried Stephen and made loud lamentation over him" (Acts 8:2). Here lies a realistically possible harmonization of Joseph's participation in the condemnation of Jesus and his burial of Jesus' corpse: piety drove Joseph to both actions (cf. the attribution of Jesus' burial to the Jews who got him executed [Acts 13:27-29], Joseph apparently acting on their behalf [in view of Luke 23:50-53 and under the supposition that Luke-Acts is a well-integrated piece of literature]; also the attribution to the Jews of Jesus' removal from the Cross [John 19:31, 38 v.l.; *Gos. Pet.* 6:21; Justin *Dial.* 97.1]). There is no need to join R. E. Brown (in *CBQ* 50 [1988] 240) in appealing to the high priest's having to persuade the Sanhedrin against Jesus, as though Joseph was inclined in Jesus' favor and only acquiesced in the condemnation. The high priest exercised no persuasion. He did not have to. From the start, the whole Sanhedrin were seeking to put Jesus to death (see 14:55, 63-64). Joseph probably had the help of servants in the burying of Jesus' corpse (cf. Pilate's flogging Jesus in the sense of having him flogged [v 15] and before that the Sanhedrin's binding Jesus probably in the sense of having their servants bind him [v 1]; also F.-M. Braun in *RB* 45 [1936] 34-52, 184-200, 346-63; L. E. Cox in *PEQ* 100 [1968] 112-36; R. H. Smith in *BA* 30 [1967] 80-90 on the tomb).

The pedestrianness of ἐνείλησεν, "wrapped in" (contrast the elegance of ἐνετύλιξεν, "swathed in" — Matt 27:59; Luke 23:53) reflects Mark's lack of cultural sophistication, not any lack of purpose to dignify Jesus with a proper burial. Though Mark omits some details that he might have included to achieve this purpose (the washing of the corpse [cf. *Gos. Pet.* 24] and anointing it with oil — see the notes on 16:1 concerning the reason for omission), his mentioning the purchase of a brand new shroud and describing the tomb as hewn out of rock, not as a cave, much less as a hole dug in the ground, exhibit his dignifying purpose. On the other hand, the historical Joseph may have wanted only to get Jesus buried before sunset lest the law against letting corpses hang on a tree overnight be violated (ibid. 242-43).

B. Ketub. 8b is sometimes cited to prove the simplicity and inexpensiveness of a linen burial shroud and therefore the lack of honor in the shroud used for Jesus. Perhaps so to a Jewish audience used to sparing no expense to honor the dead. But Mark is writing for Gentiles, and they would regard a linen shroud as quite decent (cf. MM s.v. σινδών and the LXX of Judg 14:12, 13 [Cod. A]; Prov 31:24; 1 Macc 10:64 [Cod. A]). Since *b. Ketub.* 8b goes on to speak of using cheap rough cloth instead of linen for shrouds, we might wonder whether even there the later use of a linen shroud is meant to have carried over from earlier practice while other practices did not, rather than that at the time of Jesus the Jews customarily honored their dead with shrouds more expensive than linen.

D. Daube (*NTRJ* 310-11) suggests that Jesus was buried in one of the two plots used by the Sanhedrin for criminals, one plot for those who had been beheaded or strangled and the other for those who had been stoned or burned (*m. Sanh.* 6:5; *y. Ber.* 6:9; *t. Sanh.* 9:8-9); and that the evangelists other than Mark redactionally rid his burial of this disgrace. Mark's text allows such a burial, though the description "which was hewn out of rock" raises a doubt. Would the Sanhedrin have provided an architected site for the corpses of criminals (cf. J. Blinzler in *Resurrexit* 93-96 against burial in a common grave)? If not, we might suspect that Mark started the process of ridding Jesus' burial of disgrace. Whether or not Mark did, the later transfer of criminals' bones to family graves shows that the particular location of burial and the identity of the one buried there were kept in mind (cf. R. E. Brown in *CBQ* 50 [1988] 236-38). In the hewing of tombs out of rock, recesses and shelves were formed in order that corpses might be laid there (see G. Dalman, *SSW* 251, 366-81, on rock-tombs in the vicinity of Jerusalem; also E. L. Martin, *Secrets* 157-68). The absence of ἐλθοῦσαι, "coming," and the imperfect tense of ἐθεώρουν, "were watching" (v 47), disfavor that the women arrived at the scene of Jesus' burial not till after it had taken place (cf. Blinzler in *Resurrexit* 64-65). Thus the perfect tense of τέθειτο stresses the continuing result of a burial that had taken place while they were watching, not the precedence of a burial that had taken place before they started watching (against C. Masson,

Vers les sources d'eau vive 107); and the imperfect tense of ἐθεώϱουν, echoing as it does the periphrastic imperfect or present particle of this same verb in v 40, may even imply that the women were watching where Jesus was put from the same spot where they had been watching him expire (D. E. Nineham 435). We need not infer, then, that their watching where he was put rules out their watching the burial itself. The item of location has only the positive function of preparing for their visit to the tomb (16:1-8 — but it is too much to extrapolate that the church in Jerusalem held an annual celebration at the tomb [so L. Schenke, *Auferstehungsverkündigung* 98]). The further suggestion that they did not actually see where Jesus was put but were only trying to do so (ibid.) treats the imperfect as conative at the expense of making the women in 16:1 go to the correct tomb without knowing where it was.

The women's observing where Jesus was buried may but need not be intended to counteract a charge that they came to the wrong tomb Easter Sunday morning. Matt 27:62-66; 28:11-15 speaks of a Jewish charge that Jesus' disciples stole his body; but this charge requires the emptiness of the right tomb and Jewish acknowledgment of its emptiness, and nowhere does the NT reflect a charge that the women or other disciples went to the wrong tomb. Unless the story of the empty tomb developed late, unbelieving Jews might have shown the right tomb to be occupied by Jesus' body. They might have done so to refute the preaching of Jesus' resurrection apart from and prior to a late development of the story concerning the empty tomb, too. It is another question whether that story did develop late.

R. Mahoney (*Two Disciples* 107) pronounces v 47 superfluous in its present context, "not just because the names are repeated in 16.1, but because after 15.40f had put the women at the scene of the crucifixion, we would even without 15.47 have had no difficulty in accepting the fact that the women in 16.1f know where Jesus' tomb is to be found." But it does not go without saying that watching Jesus expire entails watching his burial. Nothing insures that he will be buried where the women who saw his expiration can also see his burial. Since the women saw where Jesus had been put, as Mahoney correctly notes, v 47 does not prepare for their question, "Who will roll away the stone from the door of the tomb for us?" (16:3). Rather, they know where to come on Sunday morning. But seeing where Jesus had been put would naturally entail seeing the stone at the mouth of the tomb where he had been put.

THE RESURRECTION OF JESUS AS A
FULFILMENT OF HIS PREDICTION

16:1-7 (Matt 28:1-7; Luke 23:56–24:8; John 20:1)

In the story of the empty tomb three women buy some aromatics (v 1) and come to the tomb (v 2). They ask one another who will roll away the stone (v 3) and see that it is already rolled away (v 4). Inside the tomb they see a young man (v 5). He announces Jesus' resurrection (v 6) and gives them a message to tell the disciples and Peter (v 7).

16:1-2 *(Matt 28:1; Luke 23:56–24:1; John 20:1a)* "And when the Sabbath had passed" relates back to Jesus' burial just before the onset of the Sabbath (15:42-47). Since the Sabbath ended at sundown on Saturday and since "very early in the morning" at the start of v 2 seems to indicate a temporal progression, Mark apparently wants his audience to think for the moment of Saturday evening.

The placement of "Mary the Magdalene and Mary the [mother] of the James and Salome" right after the opening genitive absolute (see the Greek text) helps link this pericope to the preceding one, which closed with a statement about the two Marys. The three women's buying aromatics that they might go anoint Jesus helps remove the disgrace of his crucifixion. Ordinarily, nobody would think to give a victim of crucifixion the dignity of an anointing. Moreover, this anointing would be of surpassing quality. The Jews customarily used oil, not aromatics (Str-B 2. 53). Only the burial of a king provides an exception in 2 Chr 16:14 LXX; and elsewhere in the LXX, too, aromatics always have an association with royalty (4 Kgdms 20:13; 1 Chr 9:29, 30; 2 Chr 9:1, 9 [bis]; 32:27; Esth 2:12; Cant 1:3; 4:10, 16; 5:1, 13; 6:1[2]; 8:14; Sir 24:15 [with the royal imagery of 24:4, 10-14]). Especially instructive is Cant 4:10 in that it contrasts the king's aromatics with the commoner's oils (MT) or garments (LXX). Correspondingly, at Cant 4:16; 5:1 aromatics represent the commoner's attractions as the king makes her his garden of sexual delight. In non-biblical literature, too, aromatics carry a royal or otherwise dignified association when used in reference to death and burial (Diod. Sic. 18.26.3 [for Alexander the Great]; Chariton 1.8.2; Plut. *Sull.* 38.2 [for Sulla the Roman dictator]; *1 Clem.* 25:2 [for the legendary Phoenix bird]; *Mart. Pol.* 15:2 [for the fragrance of a highly respected martyr's baking body]; *SIG* 3: 999. 17). Though not with reference to death and burial, aromatics are used for divine honor in *BGU* 149. 1 (cf. their use for a sacrifice in *POxy.* 1211. 10-11). The centurion has recently declared Jesus to have been God's Son (15:39). The Son of God deserves no less than a king, another great figure, or a deity would have gotten.

"Mary the Magdalene" echoes 15:40, 47. Since Mark called the other Mary "the [mother] of Joses" the last time he mentioned her (15:47), now he calls her "the [mother] of the James" (cf. 15:40). Just as after the initial full expression in 15:40 he used shorthand by mentioning only one of her sons at once in 15:47, so also he drops the initial designation of James as "the little" but alludes to it by prefixing "the" before "James" (not as in 15:40). His evident purpose to connect some women's observing the site of Jesus' burial (15:47) with their coming to anoint Jesus makes it unlikely that he means to distinguish a Mary the mother of the James from Mary the mother of Joses (and therefore unlikely that we should have translated 15:40 "Mary the [mother or sister] of James the little and Joses' mother" as well as unlikely that the women's names here in 16:1 imply this pericope's existence "at one time independent from the passion narrative" [W. L. Lane 585]). The fact that Salome comes back into the picture even though Mark did not mention her as one who was observing the site of Jesus' burial may seem to weaken this argument — but not really, for there is no apparent reason for Mark to have mentioned Mary the mother of Joses as one who was observing the site of Jesus' burial if she is not one who also comes to the tomb. Salome may not have seen the burial though she comes to the tomb with those who did see the burial.

"Very early in the morning on the first [day] of the week" implies that the purchase of aromatics must have taken place the preceding evening. The first position of λίαν, "very" (contrast 1:35 and cf. 15:1), emphasizes this implication. "On the first [day] of the week" seems otiose. *Of course* it is the first day of the week if the Sabbath has recently passed. Therefore the phrase may represent the special attention given by Christians to this day as the one on which Jesus was raised (besides the parallels in Matt 28:1; Luke 24:1; John 20:1, see also John 20:19; Acts 20:7; 1 Cor 16:2). Mark's pulse quickens at the thought that the women will discover the tomb empty; so he writes the historical present tense "are coming" with respect to their journey to the tomb. The pulse of his audience is expected to quicken, too. "When the sun had risen" keeps "very early in the morning" from being misunderstood as the last part of the night (cf. 1:35; 13:35) instead of a time right after sunrise (cf. the vv.ll.). Thus the women can see to come to the tomb and can see once they arrive (cf. vv 4, 6; contrast John 20:1).

16:3-4 *(Luke 24:2; John 20:1b)* The women's question, "Who will roll away the stone for us from the entrance of the tomb?" harks back to 15:46-47 and sets the stage for their "looking up" and seeing "that the stone *is* rolled away [ἀποκεκύλισται, perfect tense]." Who rolled it away? God? An angel? The resurrected Jesus? Even at the risk of letting his audience think first of graverobbers, Mark does not say (contrast Matt 28:2). He is interested only in the phenomenon as such. So he emphasizes it with the historical present tense in θεωροῦσιν, "they observe." The added statement, "for it was extremely large," does not give the reason why the women found the stone already rolled away; for its extremely large size would rather explain why they should *not* have found it already rolled away. Rather, the statement gives the reason why they were asking one another who would roll away the stone. But Mark cannot wait to mention the stone's having been rolled away already; so he puts it before his explanation of the reason for the women's question (cf. his stressing the discovery of nothing but leaves by putting it before an explanation of Jesus' going to find "something" on a fig tree [11:13] and his stressing Jesus' magnetic power by putting the Sanhedrin's fear of the crowd before a possible explanation of their seeking to kill him [12:12]; and contrast the v.l. here in 16:4, where D Θ 565 c ff² n [sys] Eus shift the explanation regarding the extremely large size of the stone to the beginning of v 4 — see F. Neirynck in *The NT in Early Christianity* 149-52 on this v.l.).

16:5-7 *(Matt 28:2-7; Luke 24:3-8)* On entering the tomb the women see "a young man." By implication he will turn out to be an angel (cf. the use of "young man" for "angel" in Tob 4:5-10 א; 2 Macc 3:26, 33; *Herm. Vis.* 3.1.6, 8; 3.2.5; 3.4.1), but Mark calls him a young man to recall the young man of 14:51-52 (for interpretation, see the comments ad loc.). That the present young man is "sitting on the right" both indicates his authority (cf. 10:37, 40; 12:36; 14:62), contrasts with the women's expectation of seeing Jesus' corpse lying prone, and makes the young man represent Jesus, who at the time of Mark's writing is sitting on the right hand of God (12:36; 14:62; Rom 8:34; Eph 1:20; Col. 3:1; Heb 1:3, 13; 8:1; 10:12; 12:2; 1 Pet 3:22). The plural of δεξιοῖς, "right," echoes 10:37, 40; 12:36; 14:62 and ultimately Ps 110:1 LXX (contrast the singular of δεξιᾷ in the just-listed epistolary passages), but the switch from ἐκ to ἐν for "on" echoes early Christian diction regarding the heavenly session of Jesus (again see the epistolary cross-references) and thereby betrays Mark's intention to make the young man represent Jesus, who is on the verge of heavenly exaltation. Addition of the definite article τοῖς makes up for the lack of a dependent genitive (contrast all the cross-references). "On the right" also augurs well, for the right side is the side of favor (for references, see W. Grundmann in *TDNT* 2. 37-40). "Wearing a white robe" contrasts with the linen cloth used for Jesus' corpse (15:46). Asyndeton underscores this contrast. The whiteness of the robe associates the young man with Jesus, whose garments turned an unearthly white at the Transfiguration (9:3), and begins to identify the young man as a heavenly figure, perhaps an angel, a messenger of Jesus (cf. Matt 28:3; Luke 24:4; John 20:12; Acts 1:10; Rev 6:11; 7:9, 13; Josephus *Ant.* 5.8.2-3 §§276-84). His proceeding to interpret the meaning of the empty tomb and to instruct the women what they should do completes his identification as an angel, for interpretation and instruction are standard functions of angels (cf. the very meaning of "angel," i.e. "messenger"; also the women's extreme amazement, the young man's telling them not to be extremely amazed, his knowing information that an angel but not a human being would typically know, and the authority with which he commands the women — all of which suit an angelophany; see, e.g., Gen 28:10-17; Dan 8:16-27; 9:20-27; Tob 12:6-22; Matt 1:20-21; 2:13, 19-20; Luke 1:11-17, 26-38; 2:8-14; Acts 5:19-20; 8:26; 10:3-6; 12:7-10; 27:23-24).

Before the interpretation, Mark notes the extreme amazement of the women to enhance the marvel of the scene, the unexpectedness of which forestalls suspicion that the women made it up. He uses the perfective ἐξ- with -εθαμβήθησαν to intensify the amazement (cf. the comments on 9:15). An adversative δέ, "but," shifts attention away from the young man to what he says. The historical present tense in "says" underlines his following words. "Stop being extremely amazed" implies that what has extremely amazed the women pales into insignificance by comparison with the announcement which he is about to make. "You're seeking Jesus the Nazarene, the crucified [one]" shifts attention to him whose power and glory the young man represents, extremely amazing though that representation has been, and prepares for an indication of Jesus' absence. In the word order of the Greek text, the first position of the direct object "Jesus," preceding its verb and separated by its verb from "the Nazarene," highlights the shift. So also does asyndeton. "The Nazarene" fits the way an angel just outside Jerusalem might refer to Jesus (cf. the similar speech of a demoniac in Capernaum [1:24], of people just outside Jericho [10:47], and of a servant girl in Jerusalem [14:67]). "The crucified [one]" makes all the more remarkable the following announcement, "He has been raised." The announcement echoes "after I have been raised" in 14:28 (N.B. esp. the shared use of ἐγείρω in the passive voice as against the use of ἀνίστημι in the active voice, "rise," at 8:31; 9:9, 31; 10:34) and negates the scandal of his crucifixion by noting its undoing in fulfilment of his prediction (cf. Paul's μᾶλλον δέ, "but rather," to introduce a reference to Jesus' resurrection after a reference to his death — Rom 8:34). Asyndeton reinforces this negation. Though the passive of ἐγείρω may be deponent, meaning "rise," the indubitably passive meaning of τὸν ἐσταυρωμένον, "the crucified [one]," and Jesus' being the object of others' action in "where they put him" give contextual support to the meaning "he has been raised" for ἠγέρθη. This passive meaning, in turn, suggests divine action: God has raised Jesus (cf. Acts 2:24; 3:15; 4:10; 5:30; 10:40; 13:30; Rom 4:24; 8:11; 10:9; 1 Cor 6:14; 15:15; 2 Cor 4:14; 1 Pet 1:21 for explicit statements to this effect). Asyndeton stresses the follow-up, "He is not here." This follow-up does more than draw the natural consequence of Jesus' having been raised, for he might have waited in the tomb. The follow-up leads toward the message, "He is going ahead of you into Galilee," with the result that the present tense of "is going ahead" will not mean that he is yet to go ahead (futuristic present). Rather, he is not here because he is already going ahead. The antithetical chiasm of (a) "you are seeking Jesus the Nazarene," (b) "the crucified [one]," (b′) "he has been raised," and (a′) "he is not here" gives the overall announcement a dramatic flair.

"Look, the place where they put him!" underscores Jesus' not being here, i.e. underscores that the fulfilment of his prediction in 14:28 has already started. The exclamatory use of "look" (N.B. that ἴδε is singular though the women are plural, and is not followed by an accusative of direct object) and of "the place where they put him" (N.B. that the nominative ὁ τόπος has no verb) and the asyndeton which introduces both "look" and "the place where they put him" intensify the emphasis. "Here" and "where they put him" hark back to the two Marys' "observing where he was put" (15:47). Mark likes indefinite third person plural verbs. Here, "they" betrays his hand; for though Joseph of Arimathea doubtless had help, 15:46 mentioned only Joseph as putting Jesus in the tomb (15:46).

Ἀλλά, "but," echoes 14:28 again and draws a contrast, not with the just-announced resurrection and absence of Jesus from the tomb; rather, between what the women were intending to do by way of anointing him and what the young man now tells them to do. "Go, tell his disciples" commissions the women to the Twelve minus Judas Iscariot and Peter. Asyndeton sharpens the command to tell. Judas has fallen out of discipleship. In an episode that led to Peter's denying Jesus three times, Peter separated from the other disciples (cf. 14:50 with 14:54, 66, 68, 72). Therefore he requires a separate report (cf. the separate appearances to him in Luke 24:34; 1 Cor 15:5), and the young man adds "and Peter." Therefore also this addition does not point forward to a restoration of Peter so much as it acts as a reminder that his denials fulfilled another prediction of Jesus at the expense of a prediction by Peter himself (14:30-31, 66-72). The mention of Peter after the disciples corresponds to the order of mention in 14:27-28 as well as to the order of the disciples' flight and Peter's following Jesus at a distance so as finally to deny him. "He [Jesus] is going ahead of you into Galilee" notes the continuing and complete fulfilment of Jesus' prediction in 14:28. If in a lost authentic ending of Mark Jesus appeared nearby to the women, as in Matt 28:8-10 (cf. John 20:11-17), his going ahead has not yet taken him far enough from the tomb to prevent that appearance. Since he has already started by leaving the tomb, the present tense ("is going ahead") replaces the future tense ("will go ahead" — so 14:28). And since the raising of Jesus that he predicted for himself in 14:28 has already formed the content of the young man's message to the women, only the remainder of Jesus' prediction in 14:28 — i.e. his going ahead of the disciples into Galilee — contributes to the message which the young man commands the women to give the disciples and Peter.

To make up for the absence of Jesus' resurrection from that message, indeed to substitute a visible proof of his resurrection for the mere announcement of it, the young man adds to the message, "There you will see him." Asyndeton dramatizes this prediction. "There" (Galilee) is opposed to "here" (the tomb), where "he is not." The first position of "there" emphasizes this opposition, which in turn emphasizes the fulfilment of Jesus' double prediction that he would be raised and go ahead of his disciples into Galilee. The placement of αὐτόν, "him," before its verb ὄψεσθε, "you will see," puts further emphasis on this fulfilment. The reference to seeing him in Galilee has the side-effect of defining "is going ahead of you" as "preceding you" rather than as "leading you"; for leading the disciples would entail their seeing the bodily resurrected Jesus all along the way to Galilee, not just on arrival there. An immortalizing of Jesus apart from bodily resurrection would have seemed impressive enough to Mark's audience of Hellenistic Gentiles. But no, compensation for crucifixion demands and gets more. The σῶμα, "body," the πτῶμα, "corpse," that was taken down from a cross and entombed has been raised to new life with the result that Jesus is going ahead of his disciples in re-embodied and therefore visible form. The alternation in 15:43, 45-46; 16:1 between the neuter nouns σῶμα and πτῶμα on the one hand and the masculine pronoun αὐτόν, "him," on the other hand have forestalled any thought of distinguishing between Jesus' person (as raised) and his body or corpse (as having merely disappeared or evaporated). The supposedly crude notion of a resuscitated corpse is exactly what Mark wants his readers to understand. But of course he would reject the descriptions "crude" and "resuscitated," the latter of which implies only a return to mortal life.

As though the fulfilment of Jesus' double prediction that he would be raised and go ahead of his disciples into Galilee has not gained enough emphasis, "according as he said to you" adds yet more. And as usual, the emphasis on fulfilment serves the apologetic point of supernatural ability to predict his own fate. Since 14:28 did not include a prediction of seeing him in Galilee, "according as he said to you" refers primarily and directly to his going ahead of the disciples into Galilee (cf. the delayed γάρ-clauses in 11:13; 12:12[?]; 16:4). Secondarily and indirectly, it refers to his resurrection, already subordinated in 14:28, in that seeing him there will demonstrate his having been raised. Since "according as he said to you" cannot include "there you will see him," the precedence of the latter clause at once puts initial emphasis on seeing Jesus as proof of his resurrection and, after this interruption, leaves a final emphasis to fall on the coming fulfilment of his prediction in 14:28.

NOTES

After canvassing possible pre-Marcan settings for the story of the empty tomb (preaching, apocalyptic haggadah, paschal liturgy, and anti-Jewish polemic), J. Kahmann (in *La Pâque du Christ* 127) proposes that Mark redacts the story so as to highlight a theology of the Cross in the reference to "the crucified [one]" (v 6; cf. 1 Cor 1:23; 2:2; Gal 3:1, which may reflect a tradition behind Mark as easily as provide a non-traditional source for Mark). On the contrary, a new event has outdated the Crucifixion: "he has been raised." The center of gravity has shifted to Jesus' resurrection.

J. D. G. Dunn (*Evidence* 66-67) appeals to archeological indications that in first century Palestine resurrection was popularly understood to entail some reuse of the dead body, in particular of its bones (cf. Matt 27:52-53; John 5:28-29; also Ezek 37:1-14; K. Bornhäuser, *Gebeine*), and argues from these indications that the preaching of Jesus' resurrection — a preaching that took place within a few weeks of his death and right in Jerusalem, on the outskirts of which he was crucified and buried — would have proved ineffective had the tomb not been empty (see also W. Pannenberg, *Jesus — God and Man* 100-105). A contrary view that the story of the empty tomb was fabricated because Jews could not conceptualize Jesus' victory over death except by thinking of a bodily resurrection overlooks the translations of Enoch and Elijah (Gen 5:24; 2 Kgs 2:1-14; Sir 44:16; 49:14; Heb 11:5; *1 Enoch* 70:1-4; *2 Enoch* 1 et passim; *3 Enoch* incipit; *Vit. Proph.* 21:15) and some Jews' having adopted a belief in the immortality of the soul or spirit apart from resurrection of the body (Wis 3:1-8; *Jub.* 23:31; *1 Enoch* 103:3-4; and probably QL, on which see R. H. Gundry, *Sōma* 100-106; see R. E. Brown, *Virginal Conception* 75-76; C. F. D. Moule in *The Significance of the Message of the Resurrection for Faith in Jesus Christ* 8-9).

It is true that in Hellenistic culture "a hero is recognized by the evidence of an empty grave" (W. L. Lane 586, n. 11; for evidence, see E. Bickermann in *ZNW* 23 [1924] 281-92; E. Rohde, *Psyche* 122, 129-30, 538, 568, n. 107; R. Pesch 2. 525). But this fact does not validate the hypothesis that Mark fabricated the story of the empty tomb partly to satisfy a Greco-Roman expectation of translation rather than of resurrection (so N. Q. Hamilton in *JBL* 84 [1965] 415-21). Translation would have made the rolling away of the stone unnecessary till the women arrived and needed to enter. An angelic young man would not have needed to roll it away for his own entry. The story features resurrection as well as absence (v 6); and inasmuch as resurrection entails the raising of an old body with improvements (1 Cor 15:35-49), not the creation ex nihilo of a brand new body, much less a mere disappearance of the corpse, the resurrection of Jesus to which the earlier NT epistles attest has already entailed the emptiness of his tomb (also against using epistolary omission of its emptiness to deny the present story an original connection with the story of Jesus' burial; in addition to the considerations that the epistolary listing of appearances would naturally not refer to the empty tomb, for apart from uniquely Johannine tradition no appearance takes place there, and that a late development of the story about the empty tomb would probably have incorporated a reference to the third day for linkage with that element in the early tradition). Cf. J. Kremer in *Resurrexit* 141-45; and see R. H. Gundry, *Sōma* 159-83; W. L. Craig in *Gospel Perspectives* 1. 47-74 against attempts to dematerialize the Resurrection, and the notes on 12:26-27 against seeing there a dematerialized view of resurrection (cf. the recognition of Bickermann [op. cit. 286] that the reference to resurrection in 16:6 does not really fit the notion of translation). G. Sellin (in *Kairos* 25 [1983] 250, n. 31) notes that "he has been raised" (v 6) does not imply a subsequent appearance on earth and concludes that the earthly appearance predicted in v 7 comes into the text by way of Mark's redaction. But the raising of Jesus was associated with following appearances on earth already before Paul (1 Cor 15:1, 4-7); so the present association is scarcely due to Mark's redaction. One could, of course, presume to describe the appearances in primitive tradition as staged from heaven (cf. 1 Cor 15:8 with Acts 9:3-5; 22:6-10; 26:12-18, though contrast Gal 1:16). But the preceding references to death and burial and Paul's own succeeding discussion of resurrection in bodily, even fleshly, terms recommend an earthly staging. Even if staged from heaven, the appearances would not sit well with the Hellenistic motif of translation, which emphasizes *dis*appearance.

For the theory that Mark fabricated vv 1-8 to attack a tradition of appearances by the resurrected Jesus in Jerusalem, see J. D. Crossan in *The Passion in Mark* 135-52 and critical remarks by J. E. Alsup in *SBL 1976 Seminar Papers* 263-67. For the historicity of the empty tomb, see E. Stauffer, *Jesus and His Story* 118-21; M. J. Harris, *Raised Immortal* 14-18, 38-40; W. L. Craig in *NTS* 31 (1985) 39-67; idem in *Gospel Perspectives* 2. 173-200, esp. 182-89; idem, *Historical Argument* passim; X. Léon-Dufour, *Resurrection* 210-11; R. H. Stein in *JETS* 20 (1977) 23-29; E. L. Bode, *First Easter Morning* 151-75, esp. 159-65. In favor of historicity it is argued that since emptiness does not prove resurrection and since the NT shows awareness of that fact (Matt 28:11-15; John 20:2, 13, 15), Christians had only a weak motive to fabricate the story of an empty tomb. On the other hand, bodily resurrection requires an empty tomb; therefore belief in the bodily resurrection of Jesus provided a strong motive for fabrication. Yet the risk of having the tomb opened and the body exposed would tend to forestall fabrication. Because opening the tomb after years and years had passed would make it difficult to identify the remains, a late date of fabrication would weaken the argument from risk of exposure. But as just noted, a late date would have incorporated the motif of the third day, already present in pre-Pauline tradition (1 Cor 15:4). Instead, we read of the first day of the week. Furthermore, discovery of the empty tomb less than two days after Jesus' death disagrees with resurrection after three days except under a Jewish method of reckoning (see the notes on 8:31). Since such a method is unlikely to have been used after the Gentilization of the church, the story of discovery less than two days afterward by non-Jewish reckoning must have originated early. Yet again, the distrust in women's testimony, especially in Jewish culture, bespeaks an early date. And quite apart from the question of date, fabrication is likely to have supplied culturally more credible witnesses to the emptiness of the tomb (for more details, see the following notes on v 7). Fabrication is also likely to have supplied a description of the resurrection itself, of the rolling away of the stone (as in Matt 28:2; *Gos. Pet.* 8:37), of Jesus' leaving the tomb (as in *Gos. Pet.* 8:39-42), of an appearance by Jesus at or near the tomb (as in John 20:11-17). Jewish Christians would have venerated the tomb had they thought it contained Jesus' remains (see the following notes). The lack of evidence that they did favors that from the start they knew it to be empty. Except for a knowledge of its emptiness, the pre-Pauline tradition would have omitted the raising of Jesus on the third day and skipped directly from his burial to his appearances.

See R. Pesch in *L'Évangile selon Marc* 370-74 for the interconnectedness of this story with that of Jesus' burial and therefore against an original independence of the present story. For an original independence R. Mahoney (*Two Disciples* 118, n. 46) argues that "if there had been time on Friday to buy a shroud, there was also time to buy aromatics." But after Jesus' death in mid-afternoon, Joseph of Arimathea went to Pilate and asked for Jesus' body. Pilate summoned the centurion for confirmation that Jesus had already died. The centurion came and gave the needed confirmation. Then Joseph bought a shroud, took Jesus' corpse down from its cross, wrapped it in the shroud, and buried it as the women watched. So it is hard to imagine that the hour had not grown too late for them to buy aromatics, the Sabbath starting at sunset. Besides, the women were not intent on preparing Jesus for burial; rather, on adding extraordinary honor to him after the completion of his burial (see the foregoing comments on aromatics versus oil).

15:46-37 did not say that the two Marys noticed a failure by Joseph to wash Jesus' corpse and anoint it with oil. Presumably the burial included those ordinary features. Otherwise Jesus would scarcely have been wrapped in linen cloth. It is not that the women regarded what Joseph did as incomplete; rather, as insufficient. For Mark, their intention to give Jesus extraordinary honor by anointing him with aromatics made the washing and anointing with oil unworthy of mention. Since that intention does not come out till now yet the omission of washing and anointing presupposed it, the stories of the burial and of the empty tomb probably circulated together. Since Jesus' resurrection formed part of the essential Christian gospel from the start and since resurrection usually goes with prior burial (an exception in Rev 11:7-11 only proves the rule by emphasizing a lack of burial), an originality of co-circulation is to have been expected anyway (against the possibility that because of the present intention to anoint Jesus, an anointing with oil was dropped from the story of his burial at a later uniting of that story with the story of the empty tomb). One might escape this argument by treating the buying and bringing of aromatics as a redactional addition designed to unite originally independent stories. But then the story of the empty tomb would lose the feature whose supposed disparity with the story of burial was thought to give evidence of original independence; i.e. the buying and bringing of aromatics is no longer present to disagree (as supposed) with the lack of indication that the women noticed any deficiency in the burial.

It is also argued that the women's names would not have been mentioned again in v 1 had the story of the empty tomb originally followed the story of Jesus' burial, for the burial story ended with their names (15:47). But it ended with mention of only the two Marys. Just as the failure of Salome and many other women to observe the burial (contrast 15:40-41) necessitated a second mention of the two Marys, who did observe it, so a failure of the many other women but not of the two Marys and Salome to observe the empty tomb requires a third mention of the two Marys and a second mention of Salome. As opposed to use of originally independent traditions, fabrication in whole or in part would likely have resulted in identical lists of names.

L. Schenke (*Auferstehungsverkündigung* 14, 30) argues that if the story of the empty tomb had originally followed the story of Jesus' burial, the story of the empty tomb would not have needed to remention the tomb time after time (vv 2, 3, 5, 8) and the women would not have waited so long before asking one another who would roll away the stone. But the repetition of "tomb" in 16:2 after its mention twice in 15:46 points to original independence from 15:46 no more than the repetitions in 16:3, 5, 8 point to original independence from 16:2. Mark delights in repetition (cf. the repetition of "tombs" in 5:2, 3, 5). He used "tomb" a second time in 15:46 to identify the door to which a stone was rolled. He repeats "tomb" in 16:2 to indicate arrival, not just journey, very early in the morning. He repeats it in 16:3 for antithetic parallelism with 15:46, in 16:5 to supplement "entering" (εἰσελθοῦσαι, which out of thirty occurrences in Mark lacks such a supplement only four times, 5:39 and 15:43 not counting as true exceptions [cf. 5:38 and πρὸς τὸν Πιλᾶτον, "to Pilate," respectively]), and in 16:8 to stress flight from the vicinity of the tomb in addition to exit from its interior (cf. 11:12).

Why would the women ask about the stone at all unless they observed it rolled to the door of the tomb at Jesus' burial? One could hypothesize that to link an originally independent story of the empty tomb with the story of Jesus' burial, Mark fabricates the women's question — and ex hypothesi their seeing the stone rolled away, too. Schenke (op. cit. 38) argues that they would have been surprised to see the stone rolled away if it had belonged to pre-Marcan tradition. This second hypothesis helps the first one that originally the story of the empty tomb circulated independently, but the need to add a second hypothesis does not recommend the first one, especially since we would expect such complementary stories to have co-circulated from the start. In fact, coming to Jesus' tomb favors that the story of its emptiness was originally told in connection with the story of Jesus' burial; for otherwise an audience would wonder how the women knew where to go. Their asking on arrival who will roll away the stone rather than taking along some help grows quite naturally out of the extreme earliness of the morning. One could ask why they did not arrange for help the evening before; but then they were busy buying aromatics, and the disciples had fled (14:50). Even an angelic commission will fail to make the women look up the disciples (16:7-8). Since the women ask their question only on arrival, they hope to find help in the vicinity of the tomb. Finding none and not yet noticing that the stone has been rolled away prompt the question. Historically, the women need not have regarded the rolling away of the stone as supernatural. They might easily have thought of transference or thievery (see John 20:2, 13, 15; cf. Matt 28:11-15). Therefore v 8 would not follow v 4 very well (as thought by some who regard vv 5-7 as a redactional insertion). For Mark flight, trembling, astonishment, dumbness, and fear do not grow out of a naturalistically explicable phenomenon; nor is it likely that a story like this one would ever have lacked the central Christian affirmation of v 6, "He has been raised." Narrativally and more importantly, to have noted the women's surprise at seeing the stone rolled away (if they were surprised) would have competed with the notation of their extreme amazement at what they saw inside the tomb; so the traditionality of the stone does not require a notation of surprise at its having been rolled away.

According to *Sem.* 8, everybody goes to view the dead at their place of burial for up to three days; and according to *Gen. Rab.* 100.7 on Gen 50:10, mourning peaks on the third day, the soul returning to the grave for three days in hope of reentering the body. But the later date of these traditions aside, they do not illuminate Mark 16:1; for it lacks the motif of three days and the elements of viewing and mourning the dead. Instead, it speaks of coming to anoint the dead. This intention militates against the suggestion of S. Safrai (in *The Jewish People in the First Century* 2. 784-85) that the women came to verify the death of Jesus because burial followed death so quickly that for three days after burial care was taken lest someone had been mistakenly buried alive. It also contrasts with the attempt in *PGM* XIII. 277-83 to conjure the resurrection of a dead body.

Against historicity it is often argued that coming to anoint a corpse two nights and a day after death makes nonsense. The stench of putrefaction, exacerbated by subtropical heat, would have forestalled such an intention (see, e.g., J. K. Elliott, *Questioning Christian Origins* 79; and cf. John 11:39, which relates to the fourth day after death, however). This argument forgets that Mark and his audience knew subtropical heat and the stench of putrefying corpses better than modern scholars do; yet the women's coming to anoint Jesus' corpse two nights and a day after burial makes sense to Mark, and he expects his audience to find the women's intention sensible. Otherwise he would not write about it. In fact, the buying of aromatics, not oil, implies the purpose of counteracting a stench, as in the use of aromatics to counteract the stench of Alexander's corpse (see Diod. Sic. 18.26.3 again, and cf. the foregoing comments). The women's intention to brave the stench in an attempt to counteract it adds to the honoring of Jesus. On the other hand, the high elevation of Jerusalem can make it cold at Passovertide. Peter's warming himself at a fire indicates such coldness (Mark 15:54). John 18:18 says outright, "It was cold," and includes others as warming themselves, too. A tomb hewn out of rock would enhance coldness. And two nights and a day do not make a long time. Therefore we should avoid overestimating the degree of putrefaction that had taken place (E. Dhanis in *Greg* 39 [1958] 383, n. 26; W. L. Craig in *Gospel Perspectives* 2. 184-85).

Does a woman's anticipative anointing of Jesus in preparation for his burial (14:3-9) cast in a negative light the women's present intention to anoint Jesus? One could just as well make a positive comparison: Jesus' commendation of the woman's anticipative anointing casts the present intention in a good light. It is the Resurrection, not the anticipative anointing, which negates the women's intention; and this negation is assuring, not critical. Mark has introduced the women very favorably (15:40-41; cf. T. E. Boomershine in *JBL* 100 [1981] 230-33). The young man does not berate them for coming to anoint Jesus again, but commissions them to announce the coming fulfilment of a Jesuanic prediction. The trembling, the astonishment, the fear, and, yes, even the dumbness with which they will flee from the tomb merit commendation inasmuch as those responses will highlight the awesomeness of Jesus' resurrection. The women cannot be faulted for having failed to believe the predictions of Jesus that he would rise. They had never heard those predictions, and neither here nor in 14:3-9 has Mark hinted at their knowing the remark of Jesus that the pouring of perfume on his head had amounted to an anticipatory preparation of his body for burial. Besides, differences in diction and substance make doubtful that Mark wished his audience to draw any sort of comparison between 14:3-9 and 16:1-8. The earlier passage spoke of pouring and perfuming; the present one speaks of anointing (ἀλείφω). The earlier passage spoke of narded perfume; the present one speaks of aromatics. The earlier passage spoke of preparation for burial; the present one follows burial, and not even the preceding story of burial used ἐνταφιασμός, "preparation for burial" (14:8), or any of its cognates, such as θάπτω, "bury." The earlier woman perfumed Jesus' body (σῶμα, neuter — 14:8), but the women intend to anoint him (αὐτόν, masculine — 16:1). At no point does Mark signal that he is comparing the women's intention unfavorably with the woman's act. By the same token, the differences between 16:1 and 14:3-9 weaken the argument (though they do not destroy it) that the earlier anointing leaves Mark with little reason to fabricate the women's present intention to anoint Jesus.

From the absence in 15:42-47; 16:2-8 of the women's purpose to anoint Jesus, L. Schenke (*Auferstehungsverkündigung* 35-37) argues that to provide a motive for coming to the tomb very early in the morning Mark fabricates the purchase of aromatics. But it would have been premature to mention the purpose of anointing in 15:42-47, and it is unnecessary to mention that purpose in 16:2-8 once 16:1 has mentioned it. Schenke (op. cit. 31, 51) correctly captures a distant implication in writing that v 1 explains the reason why the women did not come to the tomb right after sundown on Saturday: they had to buy aromatics, and by the time they did it was too late to come. Primarily, however, v 1 explains the reason why the women bought aromatics: they intended to anoint Jesus. Secondarily, the opening genitive absolute ("when the Sabbath had passed") implies the reason why they did not buy the aromatics before: the Sabbath prevented them. The further implication that the buying of aromatics used up the twilight between the end of Sabbath and the onset of darkness follows a distant third.

Though the definite article before James's name is anaphoric, referring back to the James whom 15:40 designated "the little," Joses had no such designation in 15:40; so his name did not get an anaphoric definite article in 15:47. The v.l. that leaves James's name anarthrous in 16:1 is probably due to an oversight of the back-reference, to parallel influence from the anarthrousness of Joses's name in 15:47, or to both. See the note on 5:23 concerning an Aramaic background for ἵνα ἐλθοῦσαι . . . , "in order that coming. . . ."

See E. C. Maloney, *Semitic Interference* 144-50, on the Semitic and Septuagintal background of τῇ μίᾳ τῶν σαββάτων, "on the first [day] of the week" (v 2; cf. בחד בשבתא, "on the first [day] of the week," in *Tg. Esth II* 2:9, for example). Mark's habit of adding specificity in the second half of a dual expression (see esp. 1:35; 14:12; 15:42) renders otiose the symbolic interpretation of "when the sun had risen" as an allusion to Mal 3:20, the rising of the sun representing the rising of Jesus as the "sun of righteousness." Also rendered otiose is the cultic interpretation according to which the mention of sunrise reflects an Easter sunrise service held annually by the Jerusalem church in or at the empty tomb (as thought by L. Schenke, *Auferstehungsverkündigung* 57-63, 79) or, less imaginatively, the weekly time of church and synagogue meetings (J. Ernst 485) or a daily time of Christian and Jewish prayers (E. von Severus in *RAC* 8. 1167). Luke seems to think that Mark unrealistically has the women buying aromatics before sunrise and therefore seems to shift the purchase back to late Friday (Luke 23:56; and see Jer 17:21-22; *m. Šabb.* 8:1 that carrying the aromatics to the tomb would have broken the Sabbath). This shift then allows a further shift of the women's coming to the tomb back from sunrise (Mark 16:2) to the crack of dawn (Luke 24:1). The latter shift enhances Luke's portrayal of the women (as well as of Jesus' other followers throughout Luke-Acts, and of Jesus himself) as full of personal and religious devotion. At the chronological level John 20:1, too, contradicts Mark 16:2 by saying that it was still dark; but we should take that darkness as John's symbol-producing redaction, with the result that just as Nicodemus came by night into the presence of Jesus the light of the world (i.e. the sun — John 3:2; cf. 8:12; 11:9-10) and just as Judas Iscariot departed from that light into the night of the darkness of sin and death (John 13:30; cf. 3:19-21), so Mary comes by darkness into the presence of that same light. There is no need, then, to distinguish between setting out before sunrise and arriving after sunrise, to labor over a supposed contradiction between "very early" and "when the sun had risen," to hypothesize a corruption of pre-Marcan tradition or of Mark's text through interpolation of "when the sun had risen" (see V. Taylor 605 for other suggested corruptions), or to posit the misunderstanding of an underlying Aramaic נגה, "shine," which might be taken for sunshine after sunrise instead of before, or vice versa. For a general discussion with extensive bibliography, see F. Neirynck, *Evangelica* 181-214, and Judg 9:33 LXX^A,B; 2 Kgdms 23:4 LXX; 4 Kgdms 3:22 LXX for other noncontradictory pairings of πρωί, "early," and sunrise; also the foregoing comments on v 2 for the strengthening of πρωί with λίαν, "very," not to indicate a time before sunrise but to help imply a purchase of the aromatics the preceding evening.

M.-J. Lagrange (445) defines ἀναβλέψασαι as "looking attentively." But for that meaning we should expect ἐμβλέψασαι or perhaps διαβλέψασαι (cf. 8:25; 10:21, 27; 14:67). The use of ἀναβλέπω in 6:41; 7:34; 8:24; 10:51, 52 suggests "looking up." But this meaning does not imply a location of the tomb on a promontory or at a high elevation. It means only that the women looked up from their path to see the tomb when it came into view (cf. Gen 29:1-10, esp. 29:1-2). If the very large size of the stone explains the reason why the women were asking one another who would roll it away (see the foregoing comments), we need not suppose that the angle of the women's approach combined with the magnitude of the stone to block the view of the tomb so completely as to prevent at first their detecting that the stone no longer stood before the door of the tomb (so E. Lohmeyer 353; W. Grundmann [7. Aufl.] 446).

Because the young man of vv 5-7 knows what was said at the Last Supper, argues J. H. McIndoe (in *ExpTim* 80 [1968-69] 125), we should identify him along with the young man of 14:51-52 with John Mark (cf. v 7 with 14:28-30; Acts 1:13; 12:12). But 14:17-25 gives no indication that anyone besides Jesus and the Twelve was present at the Last Supper; and the young man of 14:51-52 was following with Jesus from Gethsemane, not to Gethsemane from the Last Supper. If then one and the same young man is to be identified with John Mark, that identification lies beneath the surface of the text and he has undergone angelization and symbolization in the text of Mark (cf. the comments and notes on 14:51-52 as well as the comments on 16:5-7).

Since elsewhere Mark does not write of angelophanies, it can be argued that the present angelophany comes from pre-Marcan tradition (so J. Kremer in *Resurrexit* 152-53). But so far as we can tell, the pre-Marcan tradition that fed into 1:1–15:47 contained no angelophanies, either (1:13c hardly counting). So if any argument at all is to be made from the singularity of this one, that argument will tend toward historicity, not just toward traditionality.

Angels play numerous and prominent roles in apocalyptic literature, and this literature features resurrection. So the choice of an angelic figure to announce the resurrection of Jesus may indicate that his resurrection anticipates the final resurrection (W. L. Lane 587; cf. 8:38; 13:26-27). Blunting this interpretation, however, is the use of "young man," because it had no apocalyptic or eschatological associations in 14:51-52. Nor does the failure of the young man to relate Jesus' resurrection to a wider resurrection yet to come do this interpretation any good. Angels often convey special information outside apocalyptic literature, too. B. Rigaux (in *Resurrexit* 163) notes that though the young man's white robe looks apocalyptic, his designation as a young man rather than as an angel does not (and we might add that the use of אִישׁ, "man," for Gabriel and Michael in apocalyptic passages at Dan 9:21; 10:5 [cf. 12:5-7] is carefully qualified by descriptions of them as having the *appearance* of a גבר or אדם, "man," in Dan 8:15; 10:18). Nor does the present pericope convey a symbolic revelation, as apocalyptic does. The relation of the present young man to the one in 14:51-52, the use of "young man" rather than ἄγγελος, "messenger, angel," and in 1:2 the application of ἄγγελος to John the Baptizer also stand in the way of drawing a parallel between the present young man and John the Baptizer as messengers like those in the prologues and epilogues of Hellenistic dramas (so A. Stock 418 in dependence on B. M. F. van Iersel, *Reading Mark* 210-11).

G. R. Osborne (*Resurrection Narratives* 50) thinks that "young man" represents, not a correct identification by Mark, but the women's mistaking an angel for a young man. Thus Mark portrays the women as ignorant, like the disciples (cf. N. Perrin, *Resurrection* 29-30). But the text makes "young man" an identification by Mark which needs no correction. Furthermore, the women's extreme amazement suits the recognition of an angel having the appearance of a young man better than it suits a mistaking of the angel for merely a young man. Osborne says that the amazement strikes "when the women finally do begin to understand." But "finally" disagrees with the impression of instant amazement. The young man has not even spoken yet. With his sitting in the tomb, cf. *m. Ohol.* 15:8, which speaks of a forecourt; and against making him represent those who have just been baptized, see the excursus on the Secret Gospel of Mark following the notes on 10:46.

The use of ἐκθαμβέομαι in the command not to be extremely amazed (v 6) may look Marcan; for elsewhere in Mark this verb and its simplex form θαμβέομαι always occur in editorial comments, and ἐκθαμβέομαι has just occurred in such a comment (1:27; 9:15; 10:24, 32; 14:33; 16:5). One need not conclude that Mark creates the command out of thin air, however. He may change a traditional and standard "fear not," for example. Ἰησοῦν ζητεῖτε . . . might be punctuated as a question ("Do you seek Jesus . . . ?"), but a question would follow the command not to be amazed less well than a declaration would follow it. R. H. Lightfoot (*Locality* 57-58) and E. Lohmeyer (354-55) wrongly set the young man's saying that the women are seeking Jesus in contrast with the narrator's statement that they came to anoint Jesus (cf. v 1). Their seeking Jesus means simply that they expected to find him for the carrying out of their purpose but have found the young man instead, just as in 3:32 the finding of a crowd that makes Jesus unavailable to his mother and siblings likewise evoked the language of seeking. Failure to find turns an intention into a quest.

Though people seek with blameworthy purposes in 3:32; 8:11, 12; 11:18; 12:12; 14:1, 11, 55, the seeking for healings and exorcisms in 1:37 merits no blame. Otherwise Jesus would not have performed them. It goes too far, therefore, to say that the language of seeking in 16:6 tars the purpose of the women to anoint Jesus (against R. H. Lightfoot, *Gospel Message* 23-24). The most to be said is that their seeking him is useless. As elsewhere, context determines the connotation of the verb (cf. the foregoing notes on v 1).

The women's knowledge of Jesus does not make unsuitable the young man's identifying him as "the Nazarene, the crucified [one]." The purpose of this identification is not to inform the women about Jesus, but to inform them that the young man knows who Jesus is and what is their purpose in coming to the tomb. That Jesus is called a Nazarene at earlier times by those who speak merely from a standpoint distant from Nazareth (see the foregoing comments on v 6) makes doubtful an inclusion with his coming from Nazareth of Galilee in 1:9 or a lead into the announcement that he is going ahead to Galilee. One could suppose that "the Nazarene" hints at the spot in Galilee where the disciples will see him and links up with the tradition of the resurrected Christ's appearance to James, apparently James the brother of Jesus and resident of Nazareth (1 Cor 15:7; cf. Mark 6:3). Then the spot where the disciples will see Jesus would turn out to be not so vaguely defined and therefore ethereally unhistorical as is sometimes thought.

J. Kahmann (in *La Pâque du Christ* 122-24) notes that "the crucified [one]" does not carry a soteriological sense, for elsewhere in the NT we never read that Jesus "was crucified" for us or for our sins. The vocabulary of dying and sacrifice occurs in soteriological statements, and "for you" or "for your sins" is missing here. On the other hand, we might question Kahmann's interpretation of the perfect tense in ἐσταυρωμένον as stressing the permanent significance of the Cross (so also J. D. Kingsbury, *Christology of Mark's Gospel* 134). The immediately following statement that Jesus "has been raised" suggests instead that the perfect tense stresses the pastness of the Crucifixion. The perfect tense may also stress both past completion and continuing result, but here the negation of crucifixion (see also "he is not here" and following statements) favors only the pastness of a completed event over against the aorist tense of ἠγέρθη, "he has been raised," for an event that has just happened.

Kingsbury (op. cit. 134-35) sees in the switch from the active ἀνίστημι, "rise," of the passion-and-resurrection predictions (8:31; 9:9, 31; 10:34) to the passive ἠγέρθη, "has been raised," a pointer to the fulfilment of Ps 118:22-23, cited in Mark 12:10-11 (esp. 12:11a: "this is from the Lord"). But the following allusion in 16:7 to 14:28 makes ἠγέρθη in 16:6 refer far more easily to μετὰ τὸ ἐγερθῆναί με, "after I have been raised," in 14:28. Perhaps the switch to passive in 14:28 derived from Ps 118:22-23, then. In any case, Mark 12:10-11 supports a truly passive meaning of ἠγέρθη in both 14:28 and 16:6.

Among others, J. Kremer (*Osterevangelien* 38) thinks that the young man's announcement derives from an early Christian confessional formula such as we find in 1 Cor 15:3-4; 1 Thess 4:14; 1 Pet 3:18-22. Those passages speak of dying or suffering, however, not of being crucified; and only 1 Cor 15:3-4 speaks of being raised. The other two speak of rising. In addition, Matt 20:19 speaks of crucifying and being raised (and this by way of redaction); Acts 2:23-24 of nailing and causing to rise; Acts 2:36 of crucifying and making both Lord and Christ; Acts 3:14 of giving over, killing, and glorifying; Acts 3:15 of killing and raising; Acts 4:10-11 of crucifying and raising; Acts 5:30 of violent hands, hanging on a tree, and raising; Acts 10:39-40; 13:28, 30 of slaying, hanging on a tree, and raising; Rom 4:25 of being given over and raised; Rom 6:3-4 of dying and being raised; 2 Cor 13:4 of being crucified and living. No other passage speaks as the young man does of being crucified and being raised, both in the passive; and overall the terminology seems too varied for us to be confident of an underlying formula. The young man shapes his diction, rather, according to the event of Jesus' crucifixion and Jesus' own allusion in 14:28 to being raised. Likewise a formula, if such there was, may simply have reflected events. Otherwise, different contexts evoked varying diction in reference to the same events.

In the order of the young man's announcing the resurrection and then calling attention to the emptiness of the tomb, Kremer (op. cit. 38) sees the epiphanic pattern of a message followed by a sign, as in Gen 18:14; Exod 3:12; Judg 6:36-40; Isa 7:10-16; Luke 1:20, 36 (contrast Matt 28:6; Luke 24:6). We should add to this list Luke 1:26-35; 2:12. But except for Elisabeth's conception of John the Baptist in Luke 1:36, all the signs consist in future events; and Luke 1:36 may convey a further message rather than calling attention to a sign. So if we are to speak of a sign here, it will probably consist in the disciples' seeing Jesus in Galilee, a future event, more than in the emptiness of the tomb. It is stretching things to draw a parallel between this emptiness and the wilderness as a deserted place in 1:3-4 (so A. Stock 418 again in dependence on B. M. F. van Iersel, *Reading Mark* 199). Besides, the ordinarily deserted wilderness of 1:3-4 is stocked with crowds from all over.

Though the emptiness has a number of possible explanations besides Jesus' resurrection, it goes too far to deny that the emptiness contributes to belief in the Resurrection. Alone, the announcement of resurrection would lack credibility. The young man therefore cites the emptiness to support his announcement. To complete the circle of evidence, it will take the seeing of Jesus. Denying the evidential value of the present emptiness and future seeing (so A. Lindemann in *NTS* 26 [1979-80] 305 et al.) carries existentialist reaction against rationalism too far and neglects the evidential significance of "according as he told you." Granted, the young man does not tell the women to show the disciples the empty tomb. But the seeing of Jesus in Galilee will provide evidence so much stronger than that of the empty tomb that the disciples need not see the empty tomb now that the women have seen it.

According to H. F. von Campenhausen (*Tradition and Life* 69-77), vv 1-8 polemicize against those who say that the disciples stole Jesus' body. Not till later did the disciples come to know about the empty tomb, and the women's fearful silence prolonged the disciples' ignorance of it. A modern apologist may argue in this way, but it does not represent Mark's emphases. Among them are those that might even excite a suspicion of theft, viz., the stone's having been rolled away and the emptiness of the tomb. A convincing rebuttal of the theory of theft would require an appearance of the resurrected Jesus, preferably an appearance then and there rather than one yet to occur far away in Galilee (cf. John 20:1-2, 11-18).

The suggestion that "he is not here" may be designed to keep Christians from making pilgrimages to Jesus' tomb (E. Best, *Gospel as Story* 76) forgets that Christian pilgrims would not think of Jesus' corpse as there anyway. Furthermore, the absence of early Christian veneration for his tomb contrasts with Jewish veneration of the tombs of prophets and righteous people because their remains lay inside (cf. J. Jeremias, *Heiligengräber;* idem in *ZNW* 52 [1961] 95-101).

D. Whitaker (in *ExpTim* 81 [1969-70] 309-10) attributes the absence of Jesus' body to grave-robbing by non-disciples and cites in support the Nazareth inscription against grave-robbing. But see J. Irmscher in *ZNW* 42 (1949) 172-84 for a discussion of that inscription, a discussion that evacuates it of argumentative value by showing that it probably arose out of a narrow set of circumstances unrelated and inapplicable to Jesus' empty tomb. Besides, of what value to grave-robbers would his body be that they should take it away?

R. Pesch (2. 521) correctly notes that the symbiosis of revelation and commission in Jewish thought resists the hypothesis of a secondary expansion with v 7 (see also D. Dormeyer, *Passion* 224-26), but his downplaying of the women's role as witnesses (2. 538) pays too little attention to the triple use of θεωρέω, "observe, see," with them as the subject (15:40, 47; 16:4), to the young man's commanding them ἴδε, "look!" (16:6), and to their commission (16:7). As often noted, the suspicion with which the testimony of women was regarded (for references, see the notes on 15:40-41) favors the historicity of these women's seeing the tomb empty. Fabrication would likely have produced culturally more credible witnesses (cf. the limitation to males in the more polemical 1 Cor 15:5-8). True, *m. Yebam.* 16:7 allows the witness of a free woman, but its reliability falls far down the list, which begins with the firsthand witness of a free man and descends through the secondhand witness of a free man and the firsthand witness of a slave man to the firsthand witness of a free woman. Only the firsthand witness of a slave woman ranks lower; and R. Akiba is said not to have allowed the witness of any woman unless concrete evidence lent credibility to her word. Again, *m. Ketub.* 2:5; *m. 'Ed.* 3:6 allow the witness of a woman, but only when a self-damaging statement precedes a related self-serving statement. If other witnesses make the damaging statement, her related self-serving statement counts for nothing. Not only would fabrication have likely produced the witness of men. It would likely have produced many such witnesses to match earlier traditions such as we find in

1 Cor 15:5b ("to the Twelve"), 6 ("to over five hundred brothers at once"), 7 ("to all the apostles"), and might well have produced a story in which the Resurrection itself is observed (as in *Gos. Pet.* 9:35-42).

The probabilities that Mark wrote in Rome and that the Roman church had a special interest in Peter because of his ministry there (see pp. 1026-45) do not suffice to explain the separate mention of Peter as a recipient of the news which the women are commissioned to report. The links with other, uncomplimentary parts of Mark's narrative and with non-Roman traditions of Jesus' resurrection favor an explanation primarily in their terms (see the foregoing comments on v 7); and a presentation of Peter as chief of the apostles would probably have put his name before the reference to the disciples (thus: "Go say to Peter and the disciples, . . ."). In arguing that Peter's second position in v 7 puts emphasis on him because elsewhere in Mark he appears before his fellow disciples, J. D. Crossan (in *The Passion in Mark* 149) overlooks that in 14:27-30, a passage to which the present one alludes, Peter appeared second to his fellow disciples (cf. 14:50, 54).

The separate mention of Peter may combine with the collective mention of the disciples to imply that except for Peter the disciples had regrouped, presumably in Jerusalem. The implication would presuppose that in fleeing from Gethsemane (14:50) the disciples scattered individually rather than fleeing together (14:27). The implication would also presuppose that the women are not to hunt down the disciples in different locations. These presuppositions seem reasonable enough. Historically, we would expect the disciples to regroup after scattering for safety (cf. Luke 24:9-11, 33, 36; John 20:18-19). Psychologically, we can understand why Peter would keep to himself after denying Jesus three times (cf. 14:72c); and the tradition of a separate appearance to Peter (1 Cor 15:5; Luke 24:34) supports his apartness. Since he seems not to have been with the other disciples, there is no reason to translate the καί before his name "especially, particularly."

"And Peter" also opens the possibilities of Peter's traveling to Galilee by himself and of his seeing Jesus there in private. Matt 28:16-20 does not support these possibilities; but we cannot expect that passage to do so, for Matt 28:7 has already omitted "and Peter" (cf. Matt 28:10, too). Just as 1 Cor 15:5; Luke 24:34 support Peter's apartness in Jerusalem, so also they support the possibilities of his private travel and seeing. Of course, Luke 24:34 provides such support only under the supposition of a Lucan displacement to Jerusalem.

Because Mark 14:27-31 included Peter with the other disciples despite his attempt to distinguish himself from them (cf. 14:50), D. Catchpole (in *JTSA* 18 [1977] 4) seems to deny in 16:7 the commission of a separate report to Peter analogous to the separate appearance of the resurrected Jesus to Peter according to 1 Cor 15:5; Luke 24:34. Correctly, emphasis falls on the inclusion of Peter in the reception of a report. But 16:7 does not have to imply that Peter was with the other disciples any more than 14:27-31 implied that he was with them when he denied Jesus three times. He was not. As in the prediction of scandalization, so in the commission of a report the inclusion of Peter with the others carries no implication of topographical togetherness. Consequently, the topographical separation of Peter from them in 14:54, 66-72 combines with the absence of any indication that he has rejoined them, with his separate mention here, and with the tradition of his separate seeing of the resurrected Jesus to favor the commissioning of a separate report to him. The "you" which refers several times in v 7 to the disciples and Peter insures that ὅτι is recitative, introducing a direct quotation, rather than epexegetic, introducing an indirect quotation (which would read "they" and "them"). Yet the failure of Jesus' name to show up in the direct quotation exhibits an integration of the quotation into its narrative context.

E. Schweizer (367) suggests that the quotation may represent a pre-Marcan attempt to link the tradition of an empty tomb with that of Jesus' appearances in Galilee and at the same time to excuse the disciples' flight to Galilee by tracing it to his command. But if a tradition already had them fleeing to Galilee, nothing further was needed to put them there for the seeing of Jesus; and so far as Mark lets it shine through, tradition has not shown very much concern to excuse the disciples for their failures. Nothing has intimated that their flight from Gethsemane (14:50) entailed a return trip to Galilee. Peter's following Jesus at a distance into the high priest's courtyard (14:54) tends to limit the flight of the other disciples, too, as though all of them were fleeing arrest in Gethsemane without feeling that they also had to leave the environs of Jerusalem. And the historical presumption is that they would stay there for the week of Unleavened Bread before going back to Galilee. Notably, the message they are to hear carries no command that they go back, much less a command that they do so immediately, but only a declaration that they will see Jesus in Galilee (when they do go back, it is understood). The absence of a command to go back would leave a flight to Galilee unexcused even though we did have intimation of such a flight (cf. H. F. von Campenhausen, *Tradition and Life* 78-79; E. Dhanis in *Greg* 39 [1958] 387-88).

For that part of the quotation which echoes 14:28, assignment to Marcan fabrication is only as good as the assignment of 14:28 to Marcan fabrication. Ὑπάγετε, "go," which did not occur in 14:28, does not look especially Marcan (see the concordance s.v. ὑπάγω); and the commonness of εἴπατε, "tell," ἐκεῖ, "there," and ὄψεσθε, "you will see," makes them quite useless as arguments for or against traditionality. Peter and the other disciples belong to tradition. Ἀλλά, "but," echoes 14:28 and does not have to signal a redactional insertion (against D. Catchpole [in *JTSA* 18 (1977) 3-4], whose citation of 1:44a; 3:27; 9:13; 13:24 as passages where ἀλλά signals a seam overlooks not only 14:28 but a mass of other Marcan occurrences and the questionability of seams even in the cited passages — see the comments and notes ad loc.). But καθὼς εἶπεν ὑμῖν, "according as he said to you," matches the apparently editorial narrative statements in 11:6; 14:16 so closely and suits Mark's emphasis on the fulfilment of Jesus' predictions so well that we are bound to think it a strong possibility that Mark has added the clause, and if this clause perhaps also the preceding one on which it depends ("there you will see him"), leaving as traditional only that part of v 7 which echoes 14:28 (see the notes on 14:28 for the traditionality of that part, for "is preceding" rather than "is leading" as the meaning of προάγει, and against interpreting "Galilee" as the starting point of a world-wide mission to Gentiles).

Luke's fixation on Jerusalem exceeds any fixation on Galilee that Mark may display. Matthew supports Mark by narrating an appearance of the resurrected Jesus to the disciples in Galilee, and John narrates an appearance to them in Galilee as well as two appearances in Jerusalem. Therefore we have little reason to think of the reference to Galilee as coming from Mark's redaction.

By no means does Mark limit the secret revelations of Jesus to Galilee (8:27–9:13 and 9:28-29 with 9:30; 10:1 with 10:23-45; 11:20-26; 12:41–13:37; 14:17-31). Even a public revelation occurs outside Galilee in Jerusalem (14:61-62), where Jesus is also recognized as God's Son (15:39). So the theory that Mark or someone before him has fabricated the whole of v 7 to carry out a theology of secret revelations in Galilee as opposed to Jerusalem does not square with the data of the text (among others, see T. A. Burkill, *Mysterious Revelation* 252-57; R. H. Stein, *Proper Methodology* 209-13; W. L. Lane in *RevExp* 75 [1978] 609-10 for further indications that neither Mark nor his tradition draws a careful theological distinction between Galilee and Jerusalem).

Of course, one could say that whatever the extent of fabrication or traditionality, Mark inserts the whole of v 7 (just as one could say the same thing with regard to 14:28). But v 8 follows v 7 just as well as it would follow v 6. In fact, the initial clause of v 8 ("and coming out, they fled [ἔφυγον] from the tomb") loses another sharp contrastive point if not following v 7 ("go" [ὑπάγετε]); and the penultimate clause of v 8 ("and they said nothing to anyone") loses another sharp contrastive point if not following v 7 ("say to his disciples and Peter"). To maintain the insertion of v 7 one could therefore deny the traditionality of the initial and penultimate clauses in v 8 (and presumably also of the γάϱ-clauses depending on them ["for trembling and bewilderment was possessing them" and "for they were afraid"], for Mark likes γάϱ-clauses), but then the tradition would improbably end with no reaction to the news of Jesus' resurrection. To affirm that tradition underlies vv 7-8 is not to deny the presence of Marcanisms, however. Mark may write up tradition in his own way, i.e. by rewording it, subtracting from it, and adding to it. The possibility of rewording makes it difficult to be sure of addition, and the lack of pre-Marcan parallels makes it difficult to be sure of subtraction.

A cross-reference to *T. Job* 39–40 is not entirely apt. There, the bones of the dead are not to be found; but the dead are seen as glorified in heaven. The text does not attribute the absence of the bones to resurrection, and the seeing takes place then and there on the part of those who would fail to find the bones if they searched. (They are told it is useless to search.) By contrast, the young man in Mark attributes Jesus' absence to resurrection. Others than the searchers — i.e. others than the women — will see Jesus. They will see him on earth, not in heaven. Though resurrected, he will not be crowned with glory. At least the young man does not say so. The time of seeing will be later, and its locality distant.

L. Schenke (*Auferstehungsverkündigung* 43-44) treats v 7 as an insertion because of what he considers a sudden leap from the women to the disciples, because of the disciples' already knowing from 14:28 that after Jesus is raised he will go ahead of them to Galilee, because of the absence of his resurrection from the message to be conveyed to the disciples, and because of the anticlimax created by that absence as compared with the climactic announcement of resurrection in v 6. Schenke has failed to perceive, however, that "there you will see him" more than makes up for the absence by promising proof of resurrection instead of a report based on hearsay. In other words, seeing Jesus raised and traveled, both in accordance with his own prediction, heightens the climax reached in the announcement of his resurrection (see the foregoing comments). He has already told the disciples that after his resurrection he will go ahead of them into Galilee. But do they always know what they are told? For a negative answer, see 8:27-33; 9:9-10, 31-32; 10:32-45, including references to Jesus' resurrection (though 14:18-19, 27-31 imply a later knowledge of his passion). He will go ahead of them into Galilee — yes. But if they are not told that he has been raised in order that they may infer his going ahead, they need to be told of his going ahead in order that they may infer his resurrection. In that the women have entered the empty tomb, the announcement of Jesus' resurrection has more immediate pertinence for them than for the absent disciples. In that Jesus predicted to the disciples that he would go ahead of them into Galilee, an announcement that his going ahead is in progress has more immediate pertinence for them than for the women, and more immediate pertinence for the disciples than an announcement of the Resurrection would have had (cf. the subordination of the Resurrection in a prepositional phrase at 14:28). Besides, repetition belongs to the soul of communication, especially oral communication as in the life of Jesus, in dominical tradition, and in the reception of a book like Mark's gospel (originally more heard than read), and therefore need not indicate the insertion of extraneous material. Verse 7 leaps to the disciples but not away from the women, for they are to bear a message to the disciples. The integrity of a passage does not exclude the introduction of new personae in medias res, and such an introduction may entail a step but need not entail a leap. Here, the new personae do not even appear on stage, but only in a quotational allusion — a short step indeed (see also R. Pesch in *L'Évangile selon Marc* 382; and for a survey of redactional theories, F. Neirynck, *Evangelica* 239-72).

Schenke (op. cit. 49-52, n. 71) also thinks that Mark fabricated 16:7 as well as 14:28 to transfer appearances of the resurrected Jesus away from Jerusalem, headquarters of the Judaizers, whom Mark opposed. This view presupposes that Jesus did not appear in or near Jerusalem to the women in a lost authentic ending of Mark, as especially in Matt 28:8-10 (but see the following comments on Mark 16:8). Apart from the possibility of such an ending, the overall message of Mark shows little contact with the Judaizing controversy as we know it from Paul's letters and Acts (with respect to circumcision, works versus faith, etc.). A Judaizer might even draw some ammunition from 1:44; 7:6-13; 10:17-22; 12:28-34, though anti-Judaizers might draw their own from 2:15–3:6; 7:19; 10:2-12. And the favorable attention given to Peter in Mark 16:7 does not sit well with the unfavorable attention given to him in the anti-Judaistic passage Gal 2:11-21.

On the ground that Jesus went ahead of the disciples in their presence at 10:32 and that 16:7 corresponds to the pattern of other narratives dealing with heavenly travelers, D. Catchpole (in *JTSA* 18 [1977] 5-6) interprets 16:7 as meaning that Jesus will go ahead of the disciples in their presence but unseen by them till arrival in Galilee. The parallel with 10:32 fails, however; for there Jesus remained visible as he went ahead, and those who followed were afraid whereas in 16:7-8 it is the women, ahead of whom he will *not* be going, who are afraid. In Gen 16:1-2, 4-14, the angel of Yahweh found Hagar in the course of a journey; the angel was not traveling ahead of her. In Gen 18:1-16a; 19:1-23 Yahweh and two angels were traveling, but those to whom they appeared were not. In Mark 6:45-52 Jesus made the disciples go ahead of him (προάγειν). In Luke 24:13-35 he will join two travelers in mid-journey and accompany them visibly (though they will not recognize him till the end of the journey); he will not go ahead of them. The visibility and non-precedence of the angel Raphael as he traveled with Tobias in Tob 5:4–12:22 likewise differs from the scenario that Catchpole paints for Mark 16:7. The only passage in which a heavenly traveler goes ahead invisibly yet in companionship — viz., Gen 24:7 with 24:40 (cf. Exod 33:2) — does not issue in a seeing of him. Since Mark 6:45 has proved that προάγω need not imply the presence with each other of those going before and following, then, "there you will see him" favors that Jesus is going too far ahead of his disciples for them to see him till they catch up with him in Galilee rather than that he is going ahead of them so short a distance that they could see him except for his keeping himself invisible (cf. the observation of W. D. Davies, *The Gospel and the Land* 229-30, that προάγω does not occur in the LXX of Exod 13:21; Isa 52:12 for the Lord's going ahead of Israel). Elsewhere, the resurrected Jesus seems to become visible by joining his disciples and to become invisible by departing from them, but — except for the ongoing age of the church — not to stay invisible while still present with them.

At least two major roadblocks stand in the way of interpreting προάγει ὑμᾶς εἰς τὴν Γαλιλαίαν as meaning that Jesus will go ahead of his disciples *in* Galilee (so B. M. F. van Iersel in *ETL* 58 [1982] 365-70; idem, *Reading Mark* 206-7): (1) Since Jesus is not yet going ahead of his disciples in Galilee (otherwise no need would exist for a message to be conveyed), this interpretation requires προάγει to be taken as a futuristic present tense. Yet the switch to the present tense from the future tense of προάξω in 14:28 almost certainly indicates that what Jesus predicted earlier is now in process of fulfilment. (2) In the only other Marcan occurrence of προάγω εἰς the passage cannot tolerate the meaning "go ahead *in*" (see 6:45: "to get into the boat and go ahead *to* the other side toward Bethsaida"). This meaning will have prepared Mark's audience for the same meaning in 14:28 and here. Besides, he normally uses the spatial εἰς in the sense of "into" rather than "in" (see J. J. O'Rourke in *JBL* 85 [1966] 349-51).

According to B. M. F. van Iersel (*Reading Mark* 206-7 and in *ETL* 58 [1982] 369-70), seeing Jesus means understanding him, i.e. understanding what he did and taught in Galilee; and E. S. Malbon (in *BTB* 16 [1986] 11) argues that in 16:7 the disciples' seeing of Jesus will be no more literal than their blindness and deafness in 8:18 or than the seeing that enabled Bartimaeus to follow Jesus on the road in 10:52. But 4:12 (in particular, "seeing they may see . . . hearing they may hear") had already established the metaphorical character of blindness and deafness for 8:18 as well as in 4:12 itself. For the present passage, by contrast, we have no such indication of a metaphorical seeing. In 10:52 Bartimaeus's seeing and following and the road that he takes were all to be taken quite literally (see the comments and notes ad loc.). And the topographical expressions "going ahead," "Galilee," and "there" favor a literal meaning for the seeing of Jesus in 16:7. Likewise, the prediction that the disciples will see Jesus in Galilee subverts the suggestion that the young man symbolizes the resurrected Jesus and plays up his absence so as to avoid a glorious appearance of him (thus J. D. Crossan in *SBL 1972 Proceedings* 1. 58-59, n. 53).

P. Ricoeur (in *RSR* 73 [1985] 37-38) emphasizes the future tense in "there you will see him" to the extent of deducing that the narrative can proceed no further. Surely a false deduction! For the future tense in other predictions — take the passion-and-resurrection predictions, for example — did not forestall further narrative. Mark proceeded right on into the future with accounts of fulfilment. According to R. H. Fuller (*Formation* 61), "there you will see him" means that the disciples will find Jesus waiting to appear from heaven. But then he would not have gone ahead of them into Galilee. The prediction is earthbound.

The attempt to make the aorist passive of ὁράω, i.e. ὤφθην, the form used for appearances of the resurrected Jesus, to make the future middle deponent of ὁράω, i.e. ὄψομαι, the form used for seeing him come again, and thence to argue that in v 7 ὄψεσθε refers to seeing him come again — this attempt fails. Mark might easily have quoted the young man as saying that Jesus ascended and therefore is not here. Then the seeing of Jesus in Galilee would naturally relate to the Second Coming. But Mark does not quote the young man thus (E. Best, *Following Jesus* 239-40). And though the aorist passive occurs for past appearances of the resurrected Jesus in Luke 24:34; Acts 9:17; 13:31; 26:16 (bis); 1 Cor 15:5, 6, 7, 8; 1 Tim 3:16, the aorist active εἶδον occurs for past seeing of him in Matt 28:17; Luke 24:39 (bis); John 20:20, 25, 27; Acts 22:14, 18; 26:13, the perfect active ἑώρακα likewise in John 20:18, 25, 29; Acts 22:15; 1 Cor 9:1; and for future seeing of the resurrected Jesus the future middle deponent occurs in John 16:16, 17, 19; 19:37 (with 20:24-29). How else could a prediction of seeing the resurrected Jesus be expressed? Certainly not by the aorist passive! Furthermore, the aorist passive occurs for the past appearance of persons and things other than the resurrected Jesus in Mark 9:4 parr.; Luke 1:11; 22:43; Acts 2:3; 7:2, 26, 30, 35; Rev 11:19; 12:1, 3. Though the future middle deponent occurs for seeing Jesus come again in Mark 13:26 parr.; 14:62 par.; Heb 12:14(?); 1 John 3:2; Rev 1:7; 22:4, the future passive refers to the appearance of Jesus at his second coming in Heb 9:28, and the aorist active to seeing him come again in past visions at Rev 10:1(?); 14:14; 18:1(?); 19:11; 20:1(?). The aorist active also refers to seeing him on various occasions during his public ministry in Mark 5:6, 22; 6:49, 50; 9:8, 15, 20 (not to list extra-Marcan passages). The aorist passive is not to be expected in a prediction of seeing the resurrected Jesus, then. In fact, it is impossible. A variety of verbal forms, including the future middle deponent, refer to seeing the resurrected Jesus; and the future middle deponent does not necessarily signal a reference to seeing him come again.

Besides the matter of verbal forms, a private seeing of the resurrected Jesus in Galilee will not measure up to the public seeing of the Son of man coming in clouds with much power and glory (13:26; cf. 14:62) and with the holy angels (8:38), as though Mark intends the fulfilment of "there you will see him" (16:7) to count for the Second Coming. For since προάγει means that Jesus is preceding the disciples and Peter into Galilee, his arrival ahead of them precludes their seeing him coming in clouds with angels. If προάγει meant that he is leading the disciples and Peter into Galilee, they would still not see him coming in clouds with angels. And the Second Coming follows both the preaching of the gospel among all the nations and the unprecedented final tribulation (for details, see D. Catchpole in *JTSA* 18 [1977] 4-5), yet the Jewish war beginning in 66 C.E. did not fulfil Jesus' prediction of that tribulation (see 9:9 and esp. chap. 13 with comments and notes ad loc.) and Mark will hardly have put at the close of his gospel a Jesuanic prediction disproved by decades of non-fulfilment. The Second Coming did not occur in Galilee shortly after the Resurrection; chap. 13 has not located the Second Coming in Galilee; and the disciples, particularly Peter, have long since left Galilee by the time Mark writes (Acts 1–12 passim, 15; 1 Cor 9:5; 1 Pet 5:13). The switch from the future tense to the present of Jesus' going ahead (cf. 14:28) exacerbates this chronological problem. Jesus is already under way the very day of his resurrection (a point well made by E. Schweizer in *God's Christ and His People* 35). Though Peter enjoys a special connection with the Resurrection in 1 Cor 15:5, nowhere does he with the Second Coming. Though Galilee as well as Jerusalem enjoys a special connection with the Resurrection in Matt 28:16-20; John 21:1-23, nowhere does Galilee enjoy such a connection with the Second Coming. And according to Mark 13:37, all disciples are to watch for the Second Coming as an event yet to take place. The theory that 16:7 refers to the Second Coming but puts it soon after the destruction of Jerusalem and the temple in 70 C.E. (around which date and in view of which event Mark is supposed to have written; but again see the comments and notes on chap. 13) rather than soon after the Resurrection — this theory solves the foregoing chronological problem only to create another, viz., that even though Peter has died in Rome before the destruction, 16:7 includes him among those who will go to Galilee and see the Second Coming occur there after the destruction. Furthermore, you do not write a book of Mark's length and contents if you think that the Second Coming is about to occur. If Mark had wanted his audience to understand that the Resurrection predicted in 8:31; 9:9, 31; 10:34 would eventuate in the Second Coming rather than in private earthly appearances, the greater earliness of the tradition concerning those appearances (1 Cor 15:5-7) would have led him to clarify his rejection of them in favor of the Second Coming. A reference to Jesus' ascension would have done the trick, for example; but no such reference is to be found. For discussions on all sides, see esp. R. H. Lightfoot, *Locality* 62-65; E. Lohmeyer, *Galiläa und Jerusalem* 10-14; W. Marxsen, *Mark* 111-16; H.-W. Bartsch in *L'Évangile selon Marc* 411-33; N. Perrin in *Christology and a Modern Pilgrimage* 37-38; W. G. Kümmel, *Promise and Fulfillment* 77-79; R. H. Stein in *NTS* 20 (1973-74) 445-52; R. H. Fuller in *Critical History and Biblical Faith* 100; E. Best, *Temptation* 174-77; idem, *Gospel as Story* 74; B. M. F. van Iersel in *ETL* 58 (1982) 368-69; P. Pokorný in *ANRW* II 25/3. 1969-2035; G. Stemberger in W. D. Davies' *The Gospel and the Land* 409-38; T. J. Geddert, *Watchwords* 163-64.

To interpret v 7 as a command that Christians who have fled Jerusalem a while before its destruction should not return, but wait for the Second Coming in Galilee (so N. Q. Hamilton in *JBL* 84 [1965] 421), violates Jesus' going ahead of the disciples into Galilee and early Christians' fleeing from Jerusalem to Pella, in the Decapolis, not in Galilee. Neither Eusebius (*H.E.* 3.5.3) nor Epiphanius (*De mens. et pond.* 15 and *Haer.* 29.7; 30.2) associates the flight to Pella with the Second Coming or with an expectation thereof. See N. B. Stonehouse, *Witness of Matthew and Mark* 114-15, against seeing a reference to 13:26 in "according as he told you." Since the women will flee from the tomb, there is no need for a statement that the young man disappeared from their sight (cf. Luke 1:19-21; Acts 5:19-21; 9:3-8, 10-17; contrast Judg 6:20-21; 13:20; Tob 12:21; Luke 1:38; 2:15). Ordinarily, the recipients of a revelation act according to instructions. Here the women's silence will enhance the awesomeness of what they have seen and heard.

THE OVERAWING EFFECTS OF THE NEWS THAT
JESUS HAS BEEN RAISED

16:8 (Matt 28:8-10; Luke 24:9-11; John 20:2, 11-18)

From the standpoints of lower and higher criticism, we will have to consider the possibility of a lost ending for Mark. Canonically speaking, however, we first have to interpret Mark as ending with 16:8. Despite the addition of a long ending (vv 9-20) in the Textus Receptus, we should not think of that ending as canonical any more than we think of the myriad other inauthentic readings in the Textus Receptus as canonical. The canonizers may have mistaken inauthentic readings for the text of the autographs, but their purpose was to canonize the text of the early, apostolic writings — i.e. the autographs — not any and all later and often conflicting scribal additions, subtractions, and revisions as well.

The presently available canonical text brings Mark to a close on the reactions of the women to the news of Jesus' resurrection and of his going ahead of the disciples into Galilee and to the prediction of the disciples' seeing him there, i.e. on the women's flight because of trembling and astonishment and on their fear-caused dumbfoundedness. Their flight and dumbfoundedness do not characterize them as disobedient so much as they characterize the news of Jesus' resurrection, going ahead, etc., as overawing (cf. K. Tagawa, *Miracles et Évangile* 110-12). Mark's audience still expect the prediction that the disciples will see Jesus in Galilee to reach fulfilment despite the women's present failure to tell the disciples according to the instructions given them. Too many other predictions of Jesus have reached fulfilment in Mark to leave any doubt that this one will likewise reach fulfilment.

Critically speaking, v 8 is usually regarded nowadays as concluding a pericope that began with v 1 and as concluding Mark's whole gospel, too. But there are reasons to think that he is starting a new pericope, the rest of which is now lost:

(1) Mark has repeatedly and in detail narrated the fulfilments of Jesus' other predictions so far as those fulfilments occurred during Jesus' time on earth (a qualification missed by K. Aland in *L'Évangile selon Marc* 464-65; cf. the statement that v 8 appears "in the context, indeed at the climax, of the greatest density of closural satisfactions [i.e. fulfilments of Jesus' predictions] in the entire narrative [Mark 14–16]" [N. R. Petersen in *Int* 34 [1980] 155 — though Petersen disagrees with the conclusion drawn here]). They include the seeing of God's kingdom as having come with power at the Transfiguration, the finding of a colt, some disciples' being met by a man carrying a jar of water, the showing of the Upper Room, the betrayal of Jesus by one of the Twelve, the scattering of the rest of the Twelve, the denials of Jesus by Peter, and of course the Passion (including numerous details predicted by Jesus) and the Resurrection. Though Mark has quoted Jesus as predicting events to take place later, particularly just before the future coming of the Son of man and that coming itself, there remains one prediction whose fulfilment is to take place while Jesus is still on earth, the

prediction in 14:28 that after his resurrection he will go ahead of the disciples into Galilee. At 16:7 the young man in the empty tomb recalled this prediction and added to it both the enhancement, "and there you will see him," and an allusion to the reliability of Jesus' word: "according as he told you." It seems highly unlikely that Mark has included not only that prediction in its original setting but also a recollection of the prediction and two additions to it, the first one enhancing it, the second calling attention to its reliability (cf. the repetitions and elaborations of the passion-and-resurrection predictions in 8:31; 9:9, 12, 31; 10:32-34) only to omit a narrative of its fulfilment even though this fulfilment, like the others that he has narrated, took place during Jesus' time on earth. An omission would have mutilated Mark's apology for the Cross at the very point where he could and should have clinched it (contrast 1 Cor 15:5, the ending of Matthew, and — in a different way — the ending of Luke; also cf. the admission of A. M. Farrer [*Glass* 142-43], who argues for an ending at 16:8, that only a seeing of the resurrected Jesus in Galilee will suffice).

(2) The addition in v 7, "and there you will see him according as he told you," leads toward a narrative in which the disciples do see Jesus. A mere back reference to his prediction that he would go ahead into Galilee would not have included this enhancement of seeing Jesus, and a mere emphasis on the reliability of his prediction would not have added something that he did not say.

(3) For disobedience to the young man's command to tell the disciples and Peter and for a Marcan attack on the women for such disobedience, we would expect an adversative δέ, "but," to introduce either their flight or their going out and saying nothing to anyone, as elsewhere in every Marcan instance of disobedience, contradiction, refusal, and unresponsiveness (see 1:45; 7:36; 10:14, 22, 48; 15:23, 37). As it is, the two occurrences of καί, "and," combine with the two γάρ-clauses to suggest that the women are not disobedient so much as they are struck dumb with fright and therefore need and get reassurance and a second command from Jesus himself, as in Matt 28:9-10 (cf. John 20:11-17), and proceed to fulfil their commission, as in both Matt 28:11a with 28:16 and Luke 24:9 (cf. John 20:18).

(4) Since Matthew and Luke have been following Mark, their carrying on the story of the women favors common dependence on a lost continuation in Mark (cf. John 20:2, 11-18).

(5) More particularly, Luke 24:9 leaps from the empty tomb to an unidentified place where the women do carry out their commission: "and having returned from the tomb, they announced all these things to the eleven [Luke has written nothing about a commission to give Peter a separate report] and to all the rest." But Matt 28:9-10 says that Jesus meets the women on their way and commands them, "Go (ὑπάγετε) announce to my disciples that they should go into Galilee, and there they will see me," practically the same as what the angel in Matt 28:7 has already said to the women: "and going (πορευθεῖσαι) quickly, say to his [Jesus'] disciples, 'Behold, he is going ahead of you into Galilee; there you will see him.'" But the second commission of the women is not needed in Matthew, for Matt 28:8 has changed the women's fleeing and saying nothing to anyone (so Mark) into their running with great joy as well as fear to make the commissioned

announcement to Jesus' disciples. Hence, Matthew must have drawn the second commission from Mark, where the dumbfoundment of the women does require a second commission by Jesus in order that they may overcome their terror and carry the news to the disciples and Peter and in order that the prediction that the disciples will see Jesus in Galilee may thus reach fulfilment. In other words, the original ending of Mark has survived in redacted form outside Mark (G. W. Trompf in *NTS* 18 [1971-72] 317-18, 320; R. H. Gundry, *Matthew* 590-91; against F. Neirynck [*Evangelica* 287], whose view that Matthew fabricates his vv 9-10 to make the angel's promise [v 7] into a command to go into Galilee [v 10] neglects the possibilities of Matthew's inserting a command into Marcan material underlying vv 9-10, just as in 14:18 [contrast Mark 6:39] with anticipation of Mark 9:19 and just as in 26:27 with the change of an indicative ["they all drank" — Mark 14:23] into an imperative ["drink"]).

(6) Mark has regularly used notations of topographical movement preceded by "and" to start new pericopes, and we read just such a notation here ("and going out, they fled from the tomb"; cf. the beginning of new paragraphs in N-A²⁶ at v 8 and the parr. Matt 28:8; Luke 24:9).

(7) Though not always, very often Mark uses the aorist of ἐξέρχομαι, "go out" — almost half the time in participial form, as here — to introduce new pericopes (1:29, 35; 2:13; 6:1; 7:31; 8:27; 9:30; 11:11 [or 11:12]; 14:26). Ἐξέρχομαι also occurs at or toward the close of pericopes, but not so often as at the beginning (1:28 [but of a report, not people], 45; 2:12; 3:6; 14:16; see the comments ad loc. for making 6:14-29 part of a single pericope starting in 6:6b, so that ἐξελθόντες in 6:12 does not come toward the close; cf. Mark's use of ἀπέρχομαι, "go away," to end pericopes in 1:20; 5:12; 7:30; 10:22; 12:12; also the simplex ἔρχομαι, "go," in 6:29).

(8) Sometimes Mark closes a pericope on the note of fear (4:41; 9:32; 11:18; 12:12), but more usually he strikes this note earlier (5:33, 36; 6:20, 50; 9:6; 10:32; 11:32). So chances favor an original continuation beyond 16:8 (cf. the LXX of Gen 18:15; 45:3, where γάρ introduces fear and disturbance, respectively, and ends a clause but the paragraph continues; against T. E. Boomershine and G. L. Bartholomew in *JBL* 100 [1981] 213-23).

(9) Γάρ-clauses end pericopes in 1:38; 3:35; 6:52; 10:45; 11:18c; 12:44 (cf. 4:25), but these instances represent only a small fraction of the sixty-six γάρ-clauses scattered throughout the book. Again, then, chances favor an original continuation beyond 16:8.

(10) A sentence, paragraph, or section may end in γάρ, "for" (see the bibliography ibid. 213-14, n. 4). From that standpoint, then, one should avoid pressing the argument that γάρ could not have ended Mark's gospel and should avoid conjectural emendation of the present ending (for an example, see F. W. Danker in *CTM* 38 [1967] 26-27). Nonetheless, the failure of γάρ to turn up as the last word in any other book (with the possible exception of Plot. *Enn.* 5.5 — see P. W. van der Horst in *JTS* ns 23 [1972] 121-24) and the comparative rarity with which γάρ ends sentences, paragraphs, and sections still favor an original continuation beyond 16:8.

(11) At the same time that textual criticism, using both external evidence and internal criteria, rules out extant endings of Mark that go beyond v 8, the manuscript tradition betrays massive dissatisfaction with an ending at v 8, a dissatisfaction best explained by knowledge that Mark did not originally end there. For the more acceptable Mark's ending his gospel with ἐφοβοῦντο γάϱ, "for they were afraid," is shown to be, the less reason we have to think that scribes fabricated inauthentic endings apart from such knowledge; and — to explain scribal fabrication of inauthentic endings — the more unacceptable to scribes an ending in ἐφοβοῦντο γάϱ is shown to be, the less likely Mark ends his gospel with these words.

(12) "Since the fact of Resurrection appearances was clearly an element of the primitive preaching (cf. I Cor. xv.5ff., and also Acts i.22, ii.32, iii.15, x.41, xiii.31), it is highly improbable that Mark intended to conclude his gospel without at least one account of a Resurrection appearance" (C. E. B. Cranfield 471).

"And coming out" means exit from inside the tomb (cf. v 5). The women's fleeing from the tomb contrasts with the mere going (ὑπάγετε) that the young man commanded (v 7) and therefore calls for an explanation, which is that "trembling and astonishment was possessing them." Mark is emphasizing the overawing effect of what they have seen and heard. The duality of "trembling and astonishment" produces hendiadys, "tremulous astonishment," so as to intensify this emphasis. "And to no one did they say anything, for they were afraid" (cf. 9:6; also 5:15, 33; 9:32; 10:32; 11:18) reemphasizes the awesomeness of Jesus' resurrection as the climactic apology for the Cross (cf. 1 Sam 3:15; Dan 7:28; *Bib. Ant.* 53:12). The forward positions of οὐδενί and οὐδέν, "to no one" and "anything," and their double negativity (literally translated, "to no one" and "nothing") intensify this reemphasis.

NOTES

The non-apocalyptic settings of the women's present reactions elsewhere in Mark undermine an apocalyptic interpretation here in 16:8 (against R. Pesch 2. 528, with references to Daniel). Flight appears in an apocalyptic setting at 13:14, 18, but has appeared in other settings, too (see 5:14; 14:50, 52); and the women do not flee from an end-time danger as in the apocalyptic setting of 13:14, 18. A. M. Farrer (*Glass* 140-42) argues that the women's flight closes Mark's gospel as well as a pericope just as the flights of the disciples and of the young man in 14:50-52 closed a pericope (cf. also the young man of 16:5-7). But the closing of a pericope with 16:8 would not necessarily entail a closing of the gospel, and certain weaknesses in the parallel keep it from proving that 16:8 closes even a pericope. Flight came last in 14:50 and 14:52; but trembling, astonishment, silence, and fear all follow flight in 16:8. Furthermore, the present young man is wearing a white robe, not a linen cloth as did the young man of 14:51-52; and it is the women, not the present young man, who flee, whereas the earlier young man fled as had the disciples. To limit traditionality in v 8 to the women's flight leaves the flight without issue and therefore the preceding commission (v 7) without result (whether negative or ultimately positive), i.e. leaves the tradition without satisfactory closure.

T. A. Mohr (*Markus- und Johannespassion* 368) couples v 8ab with v 5b to demonstrate a redundancy of fear and cites v 6a to demonstrate a prohibition of fear. But distinctions need to be made. Extreme amazement (vv 5b, 6a) does not equate with fear, as shown by the fact that in the only other passage where Mark uses ἐκθαμβέομαι, "be extremely amazed," people ran toward the object of their extreme amazement and greeted him (9:15) whereas here the women flee away because of trembling astonishment (τρόμος καὶ ἔκστασις) and say nothing to anyone because of fear, not because of extreme amazement. Seeing the young man sitting in the opened tomb amazed them extremely. Hearing what he had to say shook, astonished, and frightened them. What we have, then, is not redundancy, but progression: from extreme amazement through tremulous astonishment to fear, each with a different outcome (explanation, flight, and silence, respectively).

In the failure of the women to say anything to anyone, N. Q. Hamilton (in *JBL* 84 [1965] 417) finds Mark to be explaining why the church did not know the story of the empty tomb till he fabricated and published it. The same theory could be applied to a pre-Marcan fabricator (cf. T. A. Burkill, *Mysterious Revelation* 250; and see F. Neirynck, *Evangelica* 247-51, for an extensive bibliography). For such an explanation, however, Mark or someone before him would probably have made the young man command the women to say that Jesus had been raised, that he was not in the tomb (cf. v 6). Instead, the young man commanded them to say that Jesus was going ahead to Galilee, where the disciples would see him just as he had said.

We should not attribute the silence of the women to a Marcan interest in secrecy. Elsewhere, silence is commanded (1:25, 44; 3:12; 5:43; 7:36; 8:30; 9:9; cf. 7:26). Here, speaking is commanded (as in 5:19). Elsewhere, silence is commanded only till the Resurrection (9:9). Here, the Resurrection has occurred. Elsewhere, speaking disobeys a command to silence (1:45; 7:36). Here, silence breaks a command to speak. Before his passion Jesus repeatedly spoke to the disciples about his resurrection (8:31; 9:9, 31; 10:34; 14:28); so we cannot think that his passion has made speakable to them what was formerly to be kept secret from them — and it is only to the disciples that the women are commanded to speak, though Jesus himself has already spoken even to non-disciples about his identity and exaltation (14:62; against M. Horstmann [*Studien* 133], who takes 16:8 as showing that secrecy is theologically constitutive even after the Resurrection).

J. Gnilka (2. 339) replies that the shift of movement back to Galilee accounts for the shift from broken commands to be silent to a broken command to speak. Just how and why the one shift accounts for the other remains unclear, however. All the commands to be silent, whether broken or not, were given well in advance of the journey to Jerusalem, which started not till 10:1. Silence does not characterize Mark's redaction in the first place. Nor does he impose silence on the women to make male disciples the first witnesses of the empty tomb. For the women remain its first witnesses to his audience whether or not the women told the original disciples (contrast 1 Cor 15:5-8).

The argument that the disciples lie outside οὐδενί, "to no one," because the narrator leads his audience to assume a telling of the story to him or to intermediaries by those who heard the women tell it (E. S. Malbon in *NovT* 28 [1986] 118, n. 27) — this argument neglects the phenomenon of an omniscient narrator whose knowledge does not have to rest on report or even appear to do so. The warning by E. Best (*Gospel as Story* 117-18) that not much of Mark can be attributed to the narrator's omniscience should not keep us from attributing some of Mark to that phenomenon (see 2:6-8a; 3:2, 5a et passim).

According to D. Catchpole (in *JTSA* 18 [1977] 6-7), juxtaposition of the command that the healed leper say nothing to anyone with the command that he go show himself to the priest (1:44) demonstrates that the women's silence relates only to the general public and therefore does not imply that the women were failing to tell the disciples what the young man commanded them to tell (cf. the comment of R. H. Smith in *CTM* 43 [1972] 526 that the healed leper cannot have shown himself for ritual cleansing without speaking to the priest about his former condition and purpose for coming). This interpretation needs some nuancing. Ultimately (i.e. in a lost ending or by implication outside Mark), the women may tell the disciples, as in the other gospels; but the command that the women tell the disciples contrasts with the absence of a command that the healed leper say something to the priest, and the command that the healed leper say nothing to anyone contrasts with the failure of the young man to command that the women say nothing except to the disciples. If the healed leper did say something to the priest, it need not have included an account of the way Jesus healed him; and it is *that* which Jesus commands him to say nothing about. The two cross-references 2 Kgs 4:29; Luke 10:4-5 (cited ibid.) do not help a delimitation of the women's silence to the general public, the disciples excepted. The first contains no commission to speak even on arrival. The second explicitly confines the commanded silence to the roadway. No such qualification attaches to the present silence of the women, and their fleeing (ἔφυγον) instead of going (ὑπάγετε — v 7) favors an unqualified silence. Though Catchpole correctly attributes the women's silence to commendable fear, then (op. cit. 7-10), the implication that Mark presents the silence as lasting only till they reach the disciples and Peter does not quite ring true. It would be better to say that though their fear suits the angelophany, their silence does not suit the angelic commission and therefore needs reversal by an assuring appearance of Jesus to them (again cf. Matt 28:8-10). Though in passages cited by Catchpole obedience issues from fear and trembling (Ps 2:11 LXX; 2 Cor 7:15; Eph 6:5; Phil 2:12), no silence contrasts with a command to speak, as it does in Mark 16:7-8.

According to G. R. Osborne (*Resurrection Narratives* 59), the implication in 9:9 that the Transfiguration may finally be related after the Resurrection calls for a continuation of Mark beyond 16:8. But only if the continuation carries a report of the Transfiguration by Peter, James, and John to those who had not seen it. For such a report, however, we have no ancillary evidence; and the report of the Transfiguration written by Mark after the Resurrection (9:2-8) makes any further report superfluous to his audience. Other arguments have to establish a continuation, then.

R. H. Fuller (*Formation* 64) says that the women remain silent because 9:9 made the male disciples proclaim the messianic secret after the Resurrection. But 9:9 had to do only with the Transfiguration ("the things that they had seen") and with only Peter, James, and John, and 16:7 only with Jesus' going ahead of all the disciples into Galilee and with their seeing him there. So the women might have conveyed their message without stealing thunder from Peter, James, and John.

D. E. Nineham (447) argues that the women's silence signals the end of the gospel by making a transition to further material *not*-to-be-expected (cf. Matthew's and Luke's omitting the silence to *add* further material). But the silence of Peter, James, and John in 9:9-10 did not prevent a transition to and addition of further material even though that silence was commanded. The women's silence goes against a command and thereby raises an expectation of further material that will keep the silence from frustrating a fulfilment of Jesus' prediction.

To justify an ending of Mark with v 8, A. Stock (*Call* 52-53) appeals to Aristotle that a tragedy ends appropriately in fear (*Poet.* 6.2; 9.11; 11.7; 13.2-4; 14.1-5; 19.4-5). But Aristotle is talking about the effect of a tragedy on its audience, not on a character or characters within the tragedy, as in the case of Mark's fearful women; and the Resurrection has turned Mark into a comedy, not a tragedy. The women's fear does not bring the gospel to a tragic climax. It merely explains why they are failing to carry out the commission given them. Mark's audience already know very well that somehow the news of the Resurrection got out. It must have, for they have barely finished hearing it read to them. So tragedy characterizes the disciples no more than it characterizes Jesus (cf. R. G. Walsh in *BTB* 19 [1989] 94-99).

T. W. Manson (*Servant-Messiah* 94) says that the women's silence grew out of fear for their own safety (cf. 13:9-20). But such fear would not have kept them from telling the disciples. Unlike the preaching of the good news among all the nations, the conveying of a private message to the disciples would not have endangered the women. The context points to fear of the supernatural, not to fear of persecution.

Though sometimes needing to be allayed, fear is always of a healthy sort elsewhere in Mark (see 4:41; 5:15, 33, 36; 6:20, 50; 9:6, 32; 10:32; 11:18, 32; 12:12; and the comments on 4:41), as are trembling (5:33) and astonishment (2:12; 5:42; 6:51 — with the understandable exception of 3:21, where ἔκστασις in the sense of berserkness is wrongly attributed to Jesus). Therefore Mark is not criticizing the women for their trembling, astonishment, and fear. Rather, he is using these reactions to highlight the supernaturalness of Jesus' resurrection.

A. T. Lincoln (in *JBL* 108 [1989] 285-87) disputes the healthiness of fear elsewhere in Mark by noting the juxtaposition of fear with unbelief in 4:40-41, with a request that Jesus leave in 5:15, 17, with lack of understanding and hardheartedness in 6:50, 52, with misunderstanding in 9:5-6, with ignorance in 9:32, with disregard of a passion prediction in 10:32ff., and with seeking to destroy Jesus in 11:18, 32; 12:12. Lincoln regards the fear in 6:20 as ambiguous and only the fear in 5:33 as positive, and even then not wholly so. Working backwards, we should ask why the fear in 5:33 should be considered only partly positive. It arises from recognition of a miracle and issues in coming to Jesus, falling before him, and telling him "all the truth" and in his pronouncement of salvation by faith. In 6:20 Herod's fear arises from knowledge that John the Baptizer is "a righteous and holy man." In 11:18, 32; 12:12 fear *keeps* the Sanhedrin from destroying Jesus. In 10:32a those who fear are those who follow Jesus; they are not those who disregard the passion prediction in 10:32b-34 (see esp. Jesus' taking along the latter ones for a private audience in 10:32b). In 9:32 fear neither causes ignorance nor arises from it, but keeps the disciples from asking Jesus about a passion prediction that they do not understand. We might describe this effect as negative, but it seems rather to reinforce their ignorance as a foil to Jesus' knowledge of his own fate; i.e. the fear plays a positive Christological role more than a negative discipular role. Similarly, the extreme fear in 9:6 plays up the awesomeness of the Transfiguration. In 6:50 fear plays up the awesomeness of Jesus' walking on the water. In 5:15 fear arises out of seeing the beneficial effects of an exorcism. It is the subsequent telling about the pigs which leads to a request that Jesus leave. And in 4:40-41 lack of faith is associated with cowardice in the face of a storm, great fear only with wonderment at the obedience of wind and sea to Jesus. Not bad.

Finding the Resurrection ambiguous in that Jesus is kept concealed despite it, D. O. Via (*Ethics* 55-56) interprets Mark to mean that there will be failure to understand after the Resurrection just as there was before it. We may grant that in 4:41 fear leads to a question, but a question based on understanding perfectly well what has happened, not on a failure to understand ("Who then is this one that even the wind and the sea obey him?"). In 6:50-52 fear and astonishment are based on failure to understand, but this failure has to do with an event (the feeding of the five thousand) completely different from the one which provoked the astonishment (the walking on the water and abatement of the wind). Ignorance concerning the meaning of a passion-and-resurrection prediction and fear to ask Jesus about it stand side by side in 9:32. But the ignorance does not engender the fear; rather, the fear prevents elimination of the ignorance. Whether the matter at hand be an exorcism, a healing, a resuscitation, a declaration of messiahship or divine sonship, a transfiguration, a prediction, a parable, an accusation, a real and present danger — elsewhere in Mark and outside 16:8 flight, trembling, astonishment, silence, and fear are predicated, as in 4:41, on understanding (1:24-25, 34, 44; 2:12; 3:11-12; 5:14-15, 33, 42-43; 6:20; 7:36; 8:26 v.l., 29-30 [see the comments and notes on 8:29-33 against describing the Christological confession as ignorant]; 9:9 [N.B. that the ignorance in 9:10 does not have to do with the event about which silence is to be temporarily maintained]; 10:32; 11:18, 32; 12:12; 13:14; 14:50, 52). Particularly instructive are 1:24-25, 34; 3:11-12 (in all of which Jesus told the demons not to speak, because they *knew* who he is); 5:33 (where a woman feared and trembled because she *knew* what had happened to her); 6:20 (where Herod feared John the Baptizer because he *knew* John to be a righteous and holy man); 12:12 (where the Sanhedrin feared the crowd because they *knew* that Jesus had spoken a parable against them). Here in 16:8 the women flee, tremble with astonishment, say nothing to anyone, and fear; but of ambiguity and failure to understand, Mark says not a syllable (see E. Linnemann in *ZTK* 66 [1969] 257).

Nor should we link a failure of the women to tell the disciples with a Marcan motif of ignorance on the part of the *disciples*. Elsewhere, the disciples betray ignorance, not for lack of hearing, but despite hearing (4:13; 6:52; 8:21, 32; 9:10, 32 et passim). Besides, the other gospels imply that the lost ending of Mark did not leave the disciples ignorant. Thus neither a motif of silence nor one of ignorance supports a denial that tradition underlies v 8.

Under the assumption that Mark wrote no further than v 8, W. H. Kelber (in *Discipleship in the NT* 31-32, 36, 39-40) finds Mark's theological point in the leaving of the disciples without an appearance of Jesus. It is that Jesus' earthly life was perfected in the Crucifixion, not directly in the Resurrection (cf. J. L. Magness, *Sense and Absence* 91). Why then did Mark not omit Jesus' prediction of going ahead into Galilee in 14:28 and end with the centurion's declaration at the Cross? Kelber would seem to answer that everything following the centurion's declaration leads up to 16:8, designed "to undercut the disciples' participation in the presence of the risen Lord"; for the failure of the women to carry out their commission implies that the disciples did not see Jesus in Galilee (cf. T. J. Weeden, *Traditions in Conflict* 44-51, 117). But Jesus himself had spoken directly to the disciples the first part of what the women were supposed to tell them (14:28), and the commission given to the women by the young man represents the will of God and of Jesus. Theologically, then, the disciples stand in a favorable light whatever the penultimate or ultimate failure of the women. Moreover, a failure of the disciples to see the resurrected Jesus in Galilee would make him into an unreliable character (for he predicted that he would go ahead of them into Galilee), yet the rest of Mark portrays him as utterly reliable (N. R. Petersen, *Literary Criticism* 77; idem in *Int* 34 [1980] 159-62).

Kelber goes on to compare the flight of the women with the disciples' flight from Gethsemane (14:50) and the women's fear with that of the disciples on several earlier occasions (4:41; 9:6, 32; 10:32) and to describe the flights and fears of all of them as dysfunctional (cf. D. O. Via, *Ethics* 50-53). But the women's flight from a friendly young man does not match very well the disciples' flight from a hostile gang. Nor was the disciples' fear in 4:41 dysfunctional (unless asking who Jesus is be so construed); nor was the fear of Jesus' followers in 10:32 dysfunctional. Kelber underestimates the positive role of the disciples as projected in 13:9-11 beyond the narrative and mistakes their negative role within the narrative of the whole gospel as representative of a false theology attacked by Mark. Rather, their negative role and now that of the women are designed to highlight the greatness and power of Jesus.

The original ending may have provided ἐφοβοῦντο, "they were fearing," with a direct object — but not necessarily so, for this verb does not require one (within Mark, e.g., see 5:15, 33, 36; 6:50; 10:32, though a direct object appears in 4:41; 6:20; 9:32 [in the form of an infinitival phrase]; 11:18, 32; 12:12; cf. R. H. Lightfoot, *Gospel Message* 86-87; idem, *Locality* 16-17). The imperfect tense of φοβέομαι, which we have in 16:8, lacks an object in 10:32, but has one in 6:20; 9:32; 11:18, 32. The possibility that here in 16:8 a direct object originally followed ἐφοβοῦντο takes some steam out of the argument that an accidental break is unlikely to have occurred right at the end of a sentence. So also does the ending of Cod. 2386 with v 8 even though the codex must originally have had one more page (as pointed out by K. Aland in *Neotestamentica et Semitica* 159-60 and in *ZTK* 67 [1970] 8, though he argues for Mark's ending with v 8). The last page of a codex is as liable to break off as the first page. But if the autograph or copy of Mark from which all our manuscripts stem took the form of a scroll, not a codex, it is still as easy to imagine a break occurring where it did in Cod. 2386. At first thought it may seem difficult to imagine that a break occurred at all; for the last segment of a scroll, by being innermost when the scroll is rolled up, is the most protected. But on second thought, when a scroll is not rolled up at the time of a break, the last segment is as liable to break off as is the first one — more so, in fact; for the last segment has been subjected to the most stress by being rolled up the most tightly, and deteriorative dampness may have been trapped in it when the scroll was rolled up.

By stopping with discovery of the empty tomb rather than going on to appearances of the resurrected Jesus, says D. Senior (*Passion of Jesus in the Gospel of Mark* 143-48), Mark shifts the weight of his gospel to Jesus' dying. Vindication and triumph are promised but not narrated. The emphasis falls on Jesus' setting for the disciples a pattern of suffering. Not so. Throughout, Mark has stressed Jesus' power, has done everything he could think of to counteract the shame of Jesus' crucifixion. It is no different now. Even in what we have of chap. 16, emphasis falls on the undoing of Jesus' death, on the imminent fulfilment of a prediction he made, and on the awesomeness of evident power, not on the hidden power of weakness as in 2 Cor 12:9.

P. J. Achtemeier (111-12) suggests that Mark omitted appearances of the resurrected Jesus to curtail the enthusiasm of over-realized eschatology. Similarly, A. Lindemann (in *NTS* 26 [1979-80] 314-17) attributes omission to a polemic against the theology of glory; and J. M. Robinson (in *The Bible and the Narrative Tradition* 103-5; cf. W. H. Kelber in *Discipleship in the NT* 40-42) suggests that Mark included no appearances because he disliked the gnostic connotation which had attached to the luminosity of those appearances available to him — and therefore he retrojected that luminosity to the transfiguration of the earthly Jesus in 9:2-8 (against which theory see the notes ad loc.). But Mark leaves no doubt: Jesus has already been raised. And the prediction of seeing him in Galilee can only excite enthusiasm and hold out the hope of glory (cf. the command in 13:37 that everybody watch for the coming of the Son of man with much power and glory [13:26; also 8:38]).

M. E. Boring (*Sayings* 201-3) suggests that in reaction against Christian prophecy spoken in the name of the resurrected, exalted Jesus and represented in Q but ungoverned by tradition concerning the earthly Jesus, Mark refuses to let Jesus speak after the Resurrection (cf. Boring's hypothesis that in the same reaction Mark puts the eschatological discourse of chap. 13 before Easter rather than after, where it would better fit as a farewell pointing to the future). This suggestion depends on Mark's ending with v 8 (or on an undemonstrable silence of Jesus in any lost ending). But even under the view that Mark ends with v 8, the prediction that the disciples will see the resurrected Jesus casts doubt on the suggestion. For that very prediction would play into the visionary claims of Christian prophets; and Mark's audience would assume that Jesus spoke to the disciples after they saw him, just as in 6:49-50 and in appearances of the resurrected Jesus as narrated elsewhere (Matt 28:17-20; Luke 24:13-32, 36-49; John 20:11-17, 19-23, 26-29; 21:1-23; Acts 1:3-8; 9:3-6, 10-17; 18:9-10; 22:6-10, 17-21; 26:12-18; Rev 1:9–3:22; cf. the normal pattern of seeing and hearing in theophanies and angelophanies).

G. Stemberger (in W. D. Davies' *The Gospel and the Land* 436-38) recognizes that to understand 14:28; 16:7 only of resurrection appearances, "one almost necessarily has to assume that the ending of Mark's gospel has been lost." Drawing back from this assumption, however, he says that Mark omitted the account of a resurrection appearance in order that he might teach his audience "that there is still something ahead, that Christ is still waiting for his believers, that the resurrection appearances are no privilege reserved to a few witnesses, but that the Risen Lord still appears." But the vagueness of the "something" that is still ahead in this interpretation, of the place to which believers are to go to see the waiting Christ, and of the character of his ongoing appearances in Mark's day would surely have led Mark to rid the words of the young man in v 7 of their concrete specificity.

E. Best (*Gospel as Story* 132-33) gives eloquent expression to a symbolic interpretation more specific than Stemberger's: "Where then is he [Jesus]? In Galilee at their [the disciples'] head. What does that mean? Listen to the story as a believer and work it out for yourself. It is like one of Jesus' own parables: the hearer is forced to go on thinking. . . . Jesus returns to Galilee whence he came in 1.9. . . . There is no resting place in the joy and triumph of the resurrection; we have always to return to the beginning in Galilee and advance forward again to the cross. It is a continual pilgrimage, . . . In that way the story is rounded off and we realise its unity." Thus, "Mark turns thought on the resurrection away from the idea of a number of isolated and discrete appearances to some or all of his historical disciples. He can be present at all times with all who believe in him" (ibid. 74). But physical separation from the historical disciples hardly represents or insures spiritual presence with later believers. Best's "joy and triumph of the resurrection" clashes with the trembling, astonishment, fear, and flight of Mark's women. An ending without further material leaves no journey of the disciples to Galilee whence to start another pilgrimage. And the topographical meaning of Jesus' being from Nazareth of Galilee in 1:9 favors a similarly topographical meaning for Galilee in 16:7 if a parallel is to be drawn between the two passages. A purely symbolic interpretation would not round off the story even though the details of the story did allow the suggested symbolism. If it be countered that the disciples' not going topographically to Galilee leaves Mark's audience to go symbolically to Galilee and thus fulfil the prediction of 14:28; 16:7 in the only remaining possible way (cf. the view of S. Ringe [in an unpublished paper read at the SBL meeting in Anaheim, CA, November 1989] that the lack of an appearance to the eleven in Galilee sends Mark's audience back to find Jesus there in a rereading of the gospel), then let it be shown that Galilee and going there carry symbolism (to the contrary, see the notes on 14:28 and cf. the quite topographical scattering of the disciples in 14:27). Besides, it is the eleven, not Mark's audience, who are to see Jesus in Galilee.

T. E. Boomershine and G. L. Bartholomew (in *JBL* 100 [1981] 216-17) recognize that an ending with v 8 leaves unanswered the question whether in view of the women's silence the disciples ever did see Jesus in Galilee, but argue that Mark has already tantalized his audience with γάρ-clauses that end pericopes and leave similarly unanswered questions in 6:52 (the disciples do not understand the meaning of the loaves, but what *is* their meaning?); 14:2 (the Sanhedrin determine to seize and kill Jesus before the festival, but what if the festival starts before they have opportunity?). Actually, however, these cross-references do not leave tantalizing questions unanswered. 6:52 means that because of a hardened heart the disciples do not understand a miracle to have taken place at the feeding of the five thousand (see the comments ad loc. and on 8:17-21); and 14:2 means that the Sanhedrin determine to seize and kill Jesus outside the festal assembly, a determination quickly accommodated by Judas Iscariot's offer to betray Jesus (14:10-11). Moreover, 14:2 does not end a pericope; and neither 6:52 nor 14:2 provides a parallel to the direct conflict between the command that the women speak and their silence.

Against the view that Mark ends suddenly because the whole book is only the beginning of the gospel (H. Baarlink, *Anfängliches Evangelium* 293-95), 1:1 does not cover the whole book (see the comments and notes ad loc.). J. L. Magness (*Sense and Absence*) cites numerous examples of sudden endings in ancient literature. Many of these examples represent the shortening rather than the omission of expected endings, however; and even the citation of omissions does not take into account Mark's practice of narrating the fulfilments of Jesus' predictions if those fulfilments occurred during his time on earth.

The suggestion that Mark stopped with v 8 because he had no traditional narratives of appearances, as distinguished from mere lists of appearances (so U. Wilckens, *Resurrection* 33; R. H. Fuller, *Formation* 66-67), does not reckon sufficiently with the implication of a narrative tradition in Jesus' going ahead into Galilee, or with the apparent reflection of Mark in Matthew's narratives of appearances to the fleeing women and to the disciples in Galilee. Apart from that reflection and the unlikelihood that fabrication of the appearance stories in Matthew, Luke, and John did not take place till after Mark wrote, he is likely to have known traditional narratives of appearances. "According as he told you" does not substitute the prediction of a reliable Jesus for a narrative of its fulfilment (as thought by R. P. Meye, *Jesus and the Twelve* 217-19 and in *BR* 14 [1969] 33-43), but predisposes Mark's audience to hear a following narrative as the fulfilment of Jesus' prediction.

For the same reason we should reject the view of R. C. Tannehill (in *Semeia* 16 [1979] 84) that Mark ends without a fulfilment of v 7 to show that just as Jesus' words have proved trustworthy in the past, they will so prove themselves in the future. After all, Mark writes far too late for this prediction to be considered still fulfillable; and to him and his audience the appeareance in Galilee, if it took place at all, belongs to the past. The audience need assurance that it did take place if the words of Jesus are to continue sounding trustworthy.

Or does Mark take for granted that his audience know a tradition of Jesus' Galilean appearance (so E. Best, *Gospel as Story* 73; A. Stock, *Call* 60-61)? From the start he took for granted that his audience knew about Jesus. Or did he? 1:1 identified Jesus by name, office, and divine title. 1:2-8 set the stage for his entry. 1:9a spelled out his geographical origin. 1:9b-11 narrated his initiation, and 1:12-13 his testing. Only then did an account of his public ministry start. Mark took little for granted. In greater detail, "Christ" has an understandable meaning in Greek ("anointed one"). "Son of God" would not fall strangely on non-Christian ears. Though they may never have heard the name "Isaiah" before, the text makes it clear to them that he was a prophet whose book is extant, as the text also makes clear who John was, what he did, and where he did it. An audience need not be acquainted with a book — here, the OT — to understand and appreciate a quotation from it. Allusions to that book may escape them, but those allusions may reflect only the background of the author, of an earlier traditioner, or of a historical subject — here, John the Baptizer as a new Elijah — rather than appealing to that of the audience as well. It may take a theologically instructed Christian to plumb the depths of "baptism," "the Spirit," "the good news," and "the rule of God"; but a non-Christian would understand these expressions well enough, and Mark provides the kind of contextual information necessary to sharpen that understanding: "of repentance for forgiveness of sins . . . in the Jordan" to define baptism, "coming down" from "heavens being split apart" to define "the Spirit," "of God" plus a directly quoted message to define "the good news," and pericope on pericope to define "the rule of God." Similarly, Mark describes Simon and Andrew as fishers and Judas Iscariot as Jesus' betrayer. It does not take prior knowledge of the betrayal to understand an early indication of betrayal. We may therefore doubt that the "ideal reader" of Mark is knowledgeable of dominical traditions in general (against Stock, op. cit. 39; D. Lührmann in *NTS* 27 [1980-81] 458; B. H. Branscomb xiv, among others) and that Mark takes for granted a knowledge of Jesus' Galilean appearance in particular. This book may be a gospel in the truest sense, a proclamation of good news to unbelievers who if they have heard anything at all have heard only that a Jesus in whom some people believe was crucified. Therefore the apologetic slant on the good news. The gradualness with which chap. 1 brings Jesus on stage also militates against the argument that 16:8 would end Mark no more abruptly than chap. 1 introduces him (so J. L. Magness, *Sense and Absence* 89).

For the possibility of Mark's ending without a fulfilment of the prediction that the disciples will see the resurrected Jesus in Galilee, cf. the argument of E. Best, *Gospel as Story* 120, that Mark also omits the fulfilments of 1:8, 17; 9:28-29; 14:21 even though those fulfilments have occurred by the time he writes. But see the comments on 1:8 that Mark has not omitted the fulfilment of the prediction that Jesus would baptize people in the Holy Spirit. The Spirit-empowered ministry of Jesus fulfilled it (see esp. 3:20-30). Besides, that prediction was John the Baptist's, not Jesus's; and even if we were to consider the filling with the Holy Spirit on the Day of Pentecost its fulfilment (Acts 2:1-4), the occurrence of that event after Jesus' time on earth would exclude it from Mark's narrative. The Galilean mission of the Twelve, recorded in 6:7-13, includes a fulfilment of 1:17: "I will make you to become fishers of human beings." No prediction is to be found in 9:28-29, but only a statement regarding exorcism and prayer. Likewise, 14:21 contains no prediction; rather, a woe — presumably to be realized in the hereafter. The argument still stands, therefore, that since elsewhere Mark has consistently recorded the fulfilments of Jesus' predictions so far as those fulfilments occurred during Jesus' time on earth, Mark almost surely recorded a fulfilment of the prediction made in 14:28 and revived and expanded in 16:7.

According to N. R. Peterson (*Literary Criticism* 76-78 and in *Int* 34 [1980] 155-59, 162-66) and J. G. Williams (*Gospel Against Parable* 105-6), so many of Jesus' predictions have already come to pass despite obstacles that the audience of Mark will infer a fulfilment by hook or crook of the prediction cited in v 7 even though the women say nothing to anybody and the narrative does not go on to include the fulfilment. A. T. Lincoln (in *JBL* 108 [1989] 291) adds that "the implied reader knows this because of the post-resurrection role ascribed to the disciples . . . in chap. 13, and the actual reader knows it because his or her acquaintance with the Christian message depends on such an event having taken place." Lincoln goes on to make a virtue out of necessity by saying that Mark's point lies in the unnarrated fulfilment: just as the women's failure did not thwart it, so the failures of persecuted Christians will not thwart the Second Coming (ibid. 297-98). But the women's flight has nothing to do with persecution; and Lincoln's view does not pay due to the climactic character of the fulfilment about to take place, to the repetition and expansion of the prediction in 16:7 as compared with 14:28, or to the consistency with which Mark has detailed the fulfilments which took place during the time of Jesus on earth — and his going ahead into Galilee and the disciples' seeing him there do keep the fulfilment of this prediction in his time on earth. Further narrative is needed, then. See the notes on v 7 against interpreting that verse as a prediction of the Second Coming, an interpretation which would forestall further narrative concerning a fulfilment of the prediction.

The brevity of some of Mark's γάǫ-clauses that do not end pericopes (1:16b ; 2:15c; 3:10a, 21b et passim) demolishes the argument that the brevity of the γάǫ-clause in 16:8d links up with Mark's using a short sentence to end a pericope more often than the other evangelists do (so T. E. Boomershine and G. L. Bartholomew in *JBL* 100 [1981] 219-22). The reflections of Mark's original ending in Matthew and Luke rule out the theory that for one reason or another (flight from persecution, death, etc.) Mark never finished his gospel. Moreover, this reflection favors the use of Mark's complete autograph (either where it was written or, because of circulation, elsewhere) or its entire destruction (say, in the fire that burned Rome during Nero's reign) plus loss of the original ending from the first copy before further copies were made either of the autograph or of the first copy. Otherwise, the original ending would likely have survived.

P. J. Achtemeier (104) argues that the wide divergence between Matthew and Luke after their parallels to Mark 16:8 imply that their copies of Mark ended at 16:8. In fact, however, the announcement to the apostles in Luke 24:9-10 seems related to Jesus' command to make such an announcement in Matt 28:9-10 (N.B. esp. the common use of ἀπαγγέλλω, "announce"). For the rest, Luke's well-known preoccupation with Jerusalem couples with use of non-Marcan tradition to explain the differences from Matthew. Already in material generally deriving from Mark 16:1-8, Luke has diverged in preparation for this other tradition (see Luke 24:6b-8 and, for the pros and cons of Galilee versus Jerusalem, B. Steinseifer in *ZNW* 62 [1971] 251-65).

One might ask why Luke does not give evidence of an appearance by Jesus to the women, as Matthew does, if Mark originally narrated it. The answer is that Luke has omitted the textually certain commission of the women, advanced their fear, and made substitutions of a different character for the women's flight, trembling, astonishment, and silence (cf. Luke 24:6-7 with Mark 16:7). No need remains for a recommissioning by Jesus himself, and the appearances to the Emmaus disciples and to Simon (Peter) can come by surprise.

Why did Mark not reproduce the ending once it was lost? More than one answer is possible. By moving away or dying, Mark may have passed off the scene before loss of the ending. At a distance, he may not have known of the loss. Nor may have others acquainted with the original ending, particularly if the loss occurred in transit or at a new location. In the precanonical period and with the writing of Matthew and Luke, it may not have seemed necessary to reproduce the lost ending.

See K. Aland in *L'Évangile selon Marc* 457-59; N. B. Stonehouse, *Witness of Matthew and Mark* 99-100, n. 15, and further literature cited there against the theory that Mark's original ending was suppressed because it contradicted other accounts as to the location and nature of Jesus' appearances. B. M. Metzger (*Textual Commentary* ad loc.) and K. Aland (in *L'Évangile selon Marc* 435-55 and in *Neotestamentica et Semitica* 157-80) discuss the vv.ll. that provide Mark with inauthentic endings. Text critically, those vv.ll. need discussion here no more than most other vv.ll. of their quality have needed it. See J. N. Birdsall in *JTS* ns 26 (1975) 151-60; J. T. Thomas in *JETS* 26 (1983) 409-12, 418 (2) against the defense of vv 9-20 by W. R. Farmer, *Last Twelve Verses*.

To reconstruct the lost ending of Mark, we should use Matt 28:9-10, 16-20 (but not 28:11-15, for it complements Matthew's redactional insertion in 27:62-66); Luke 24:9b-12 (but not 24:13-53, for it breathes the atmosphere of Jerusalem, whereas Mark 16:7 points to Galilee). Probably redactional elements will need omission or, more difficultly, replacement with characteristically Marcan diction (whether it represents tradition or redaction). For example, the following expressions in Matt 28:9-10 would seem to need omission or replacement: ἰδού, "behold"; προσελθοῦσαι, "approaching"; προσεκύνησαν, "they worshiped"; and τότε, "then." Presumably, the lost ending of Mark contained a version of the Great Commission, but one devoid of the characteristically Matthean contrast between heaven and earth, the characteristically Matthean diction πορευθέντες οὖν μαθητεύσατε, "going, therefore, make disciples," the Trinitarian addition of the Father and the Holy Spirit to the Son in the baptismal formula (Mark's version may have had a simple "my name"), and the characteristically Matthean references to teaching all Jesus' commandments and to his being with the disciples (cf. the unique "Immanuel" in Matt 1:23 and see R. H. Gundry, *Matthew* 590-91, 593-97). It would probably be foolhardy to speculate any further (but for such speculation, see W. C. Allen, *Matthew* 302-5; A. Strobel in *Verborum Veritas* 133-36; E. Linnemann in *ZTK* 66 [1969] 255-87; G. W. Trompf in *NTS* 18 [1971-72] 316-27; and against Linnemann, loc. cit., see K. Aland in *ZTK* 67 [1970] 3-13).

THE PURPOSE OF MARK

Now that Mark's text has passed before us, we can return better informed to the question, Why did he write this gospel? One could deny that it exhibits a unified authorial purpose (cf. J. Zmijewski in *SNTU* A/12. 6). But such a denial should be made only after every suggested such purpose has been weighed and found wanting; for it seems more likely that an author would write with a unified purpose than without one, and the foregoing pages of this commentary contain an interpretation that bids fair to fit the details of Mark's text nicely into the unified purpose of writing an apology for the Cross.

When weighed, other suggested purposes are found wanting. B. L. Mack (*Myth* 69-74, 166-67) suggests that in Jesus' teaching "the kingdom" carried a Cynic-Stoic meaning with reference to sage-kings, that "of God" was added to fit Jesus' Cynic-Stoic notion of sage-kings into the Semitic notion of God's rule, and that around this Jewishly apocalypticized kingdom of God Mark constructed a myth to justify the right of the Jesus-movement to exist apart from the synagogue. But why then the absence of evidence that Jesus originally identified himself as a sage-king (references to the kingdom of the Son of man being late, redactional, Semitic, and decidedly un-Cynic, un-Stoic)? And why then the absence of evidence that Jesus originally taught the possibility of his disciples' becoming autonomous kings in a sage-like sense instead of urging them to become non-autonomous subjects in a servant-like sense? Since "the kingdom of God" does not appear in Jewish apocalyptic literature and if "the kingdom" originally carried a non-apocalyptic, Cynic-Stoic meaning, why would Mark or a Christian before him have thought to apocalypticize the expression Judaistically? Neither Jewish apocalyptic nor Cynic-Stoic usage provides a motive or reason. To the extent that in the absence of either Jewish apocalyptic or Cynic-Stoic usage Mack is forced to appeal to Mark's supposed historical situation (the aftermath of the destruction of the temple in 70 C.E.), it seems unlikely that Mark gave a Jewish apocalyptic twist to Cynic-Stoic usage. We have also seen that chap. 13 does not reflect the destruction of the temple in 70 C.E., anyway (see the foregoing comments and notes ad loc.). And all in all, Mack's attribution of myth-making to Mark makes the large numbers and great zeal of early Christians inexplicable from the standpoint of sociology, the very standpoint from which Mack argues. NT Christianity exploded out of a volcano. Mack would have it pop out of a bubble (see further criticisms, esp. of a methodological sort, by A. Y. Collins in *JBL* 108 [1989] 726-29).

A view just opposite to that of Mack says that because of the deaths of eyewitnesses to Jesus' ministry and because of the spread of the gospel to regions uninhabited by any of those eyewitnesses, Mark writes to preserve Jesuanic tradition in a reliable form. But this view neglects both the evidence in Mark's text that he writes to put forward a point of view concerning Jesus' ministry and the indication in Eus. *H.E.* 3.39.3-4 that even a generation later Papias will regard oral traditions as more valuable than books (R. A. Guelich 1. xli). Papias's devaluation of books strikes also against the classical form critical and kerygmatic views that Mark writes to preserve oral traditions for their applicability to the life and witness of the Christian church rather than for their historical reliablity.

Against the view of W. H. Kelber (in *Discipleship in the NT* 40-42) that Mark writes a narrative to counteract an oral sayings tradition and to stall any further production of such tradition, not only is the assumption to be questioned that Mark was the first to put Jesuanic tradition in writing (cf. the possibilities that Q was written before Mark and that the "many" who wrote up Jesuanic tradition before Luke did so before Mark as well [Luke 1:1-4]) and not only were written texts read orally in private as well as in public, but also written texts were treated freely (cf. the targums, midrashim, and esp. Matthew's and Luke's treatments of Mark). So by writing qua writing Mark could hardly have hoped to stall the further production of oral tradition or to counteract what had already been produced to his dislike (cf. B. Gerhardssohn, *Gospel Tradition* 30-39; T. E. Boomershine in *Semeia* 39 [1987] 51-55; M. A. Tolbert, *Sowing the Gospel* 44-45, n. 36; D. Tannen in *Language* 58 [1982] 1-21).

Because the oral sayings tradition dislikeably lends itself to the portrayal of Jesus as a divine man and elevates his original disciples, suggests J. G. Williams (*Gospel Against Parable* 32-33; cf. M. E. Boring, *Sayings* 201-3), Mark writes up a narrative, neglects Q, teaches the necessity of suffering for the sake of Jesus and the Gospel, and ends at 16:8 in a way that leaves open whether the original disciples became authentic disciples. Likewise, J. M. Robinson (in *L'Évangile selon Marc* 18-19; idem, *Problem* 11-39) suggests that Mark wrote narrative to correct a gnosticizing emphasis on the risen Christ and his words (cf. W. H. Kelber in *Discipleship in the NT* 40-42). But the stories of miracles and exorcisms performed by Jesus, the notations of his magnetism, the exhibitions of his forensic, clairvoyant, and predictive powers, etc., make Mark's narrative just as contributory to the portrayal of a divine man as does the oral sayings tradition. Before saying that Mark neglected Q we need evidence that he knew Q, not just a few traditions that found their way into Q; and if he did know Q the minimalness of its suitability to an apology for the Cross could easily have led to his neglecting it. Even though the authority of Jesus had to do with his teaching prior to the Cross, Mark's emphasis on that authority runs against the grain of a purpose to pit deeds against words. World-wide evangelism by the original disciples in 13:9-13 forestalled any question whether they became authentic disciples after 16:8, and the gospel is not likely to have ended with 16:8.

The view that Mark writes to instruct catechumens concerning Jesus' life and ministry so far as Mark knows it (C. F. D. Moule in *Glaube und Eschatologie* 199-208) leaves unexplained the particular emphases made in Mark. For a catechetical purpose one would expect an emphasis on the teaching of Jesus that informs Christian doctrine and, above all, Christian morality (cf. the Didache). There is very little of that, however. Instead, we have found an apologetic emphasis on the various powers of Jesus. An appeal to Mark's ignorance of extensive doctrinal and moral teaching of Jesus would not only run afoul of the apologetic emphasis in the material which Mark does put forward. It would also amount to an admission that the catechetical theory has little basis in his text.

Theories that Mark has written a Christian lectionary, a cultic guidebook, an apocalyptic tract, an anti-apocalyptic tract, a gnosticizing portrayal of Jesus as the divine-human heavenly redeemer, or a revision of an earlier document or documents have deserved and attracted either too little attention or too much criticism to be treated here (for summaries and criticisms of these and other theories, both popular and unpopular, see S. P. Kealy, *Mark's Gospel: A History of Its Interpretation;* W. D. Davies, *Christian Origins* 67-95; J. Rohde, *Rediscovering* 113-40; E. Schweizer in *Neotestamentica et Semitica* 114-18; H. C. Kee in *Int* 32 [1978] 353-68; T. A. Burkill, *New Light* 180-264; A. Lindemann in *TRu* 49 [1984] 223-76, 311-71; D. O. Via, *Ethics* 72-75; P. Dschulnigg, *Sprache* 345-52, 411-84, 601-12; C. Breytenbach, *Nachfolge* 16-74; H. Baarlink, *Anfängliches Evangelium* 7-42; W. R. Telford in *The Interpretation of Mark* 1-41). In the final analysis, we are left once again with the competing views that Mark wrote to put forward a theology of suffering, a theology of glory, or a theology of both suffering and glory (cf. pp. 1-15).

As remarked briefly in the introduction to this commentary and with great detail throughout its comments and notes, a theology of glory pervades the Gospel of Mark (cf. John's going further by presenting the Cross itself as Jesus' glorification, whereas Mark presents other items as overcoming the shame of Jesus' crucifixion with glory), but a theology of suffering does not pervade the gospel. Even the tradition of suffering taken up by Mark is shot through with elements which overcome suffering with glory, perhaps the most dramatic example being the description of Jesus' dying cry of dereliction as so loud and forceful that the centurion at the cross declared him to be God's Son (15:39). Though in principle we should accept the possibility of a qualification of glory by suffering or of a dual emphasis on Son-of-God Christology and persecuted discipleship, Mark presents us in fact with neither a dual emphasis nor that qualification. Instead, he presents us with a qualification of suffering by glory. The little parenetic tradition that appears in his gospel he puts to the service of an apology for the Cross, perhaps the outstanding example being the addition to a call for cross-taking discipleship of a prediction that some will not taste death till they see God's kingdom as having come with power, and then a fulfilment of that prediction in the Transfiguration (8:34–9:8). If Mark were correcting glory with suffering or at least delaying glory till after suffering, we would expect him to have eliminated elements of glory from the traditions of Jesus' miracles, exorcisms, and predictions — statements of admiration, crowd-attraction, narratives of fulfilment, etc. — and we would expect him to have enriched the passion narrative with the detailed and sometimes lurid descriptions of physical torture that characterize the psalms of suffering righteous people, the prophecy concerning the suffering servant of Yahweh, and stories of martyrdom (for examples, see Ps 22:15-19; Isa 52:14; 53:2-3; 2 Macc 7:1-42). Instead, Mark spares us such details and dresses up the Passion in colors of fulfilment, decency, dignity, and the supernatural. And he lets non-disciples as well as disciples see these colors, so that we should not think in terms of secret epiphanies alone. It is public happenings which evoke from the centurion a declaration of Jesus' divine sonship, for example; and this declaration is unmatched even in anything said by disciples who had been privy to secret epiphanies.

Against a theology of glory, on the other hand, P. J. Achtemeier (in *CBQ* 37 [1975] 489-90) argues that since early Christians recognized the performance of miracles and exorcisms by others than Jesus and themselves (Mark 9:38-39 par. Luke 9:49-50; Matt 12:27 par. Luke 11:19), his miracles had "little if any probative value. . . . Those who observed such deeds could come to the conclusion that Jesus was in league with Satan (Mk 3:22 and par.) as easily as they could conclude that such deeds showed his relationship to God (e.g., Lk 5:8-9)" (so also R. P. Martin, *Mark* 170, with appeal to Mark 6:1-6a). But the ambiguity of miracles and exorcisms and a recognition of their performance by others do not eliminate the probative value of their performance by Jesus. Such ambiguity and recognition only imply that other criteria, too, need to be brought in play (cf. Deut 13:2-6). The blame for refusal to accept the probative value of Jesus' miracles and exorcisms falls on the stubbornness of unbelievers, not on the ambiguity of miracles and exorcisms (cf. Exod 7:8-13); and according to Mark 6:1-6a even a few of Jesus' miracles have so much probative value that unbelief in him is astounding. In view of the impossibility of Satan's casting out Satan, Jesus' exorcisms ought *not* to appear ambiguous — that is the point of 3:22-30. Not only do miracles and exorcisms have probative value with respect to the coming of God's kingdom (Matt 12:28 par. Luke 11:20). They also have such value with respect to the very person of Jesus (see esp. Mark 2:10-12 parr.; 4:39-41 parr.; Matt 11:2-6 par. Luke 7:18-23; Luke 7:11-17; John 20:30-31; 21:25; Acts 2:22; 10:38-39a; Justin *Dial.* 32–34; and, for a brief bibliography on miracle-stories as a well established tool of propaganda in the Greco-Roman world, D. L. Tiede in *ANRW* II 25/2. 1717-18). Jesus refused to give a sign from heaven, not because miracles and exorcisms lack probative value, much less because he opposed in principle the giving of evidence (again see Matt 11:2-6 par. Luke 7:18-23), but because those who were seeking such a sign had already received enough evidence (Mark 8:11-12 parr.). Nor does the ignorance of the disciples qualify Jesus' miracles and exorcisms as ambiguous; rather, it provides a foil against which his clairvoyance and prescience stand out. And as noted by F. Watson (in *JSNT* 24 [1985] 57-58), Marcan injunctions to secrecy concerning some of Jesus' miracles relativize those miracles no more than do Marcan injunctions to secrecy concerning Jesus' divine sonship relativize that prominent Christological theme.

Again on the other hand and for a Marcan stress on cross-taking discipleship instead of evidential glory, J. R. Donahue (*Theology and Setting* 7-12) argues that the first pericope following Mark's introduction deals with discipleship (1:16-20), that major sections of Mark thereafter start with pericopes dealing with discipleship (8:27-30; 11:1-10; 14:1-9, 10-11, 12-16), that the last-quoted words in Mark consist of a message to the disciples and Peter (16:7), and that the interchange in terms and functions between "the Twelve," "the disciples," etc., show a lack of fixation on the historical apostles. But 1:16-20 is not the first pericope following an introduction (see the comments and notes ad loc. on the preceding pericopes 1:1-8, 9-11, 12-13, and on 1:14-15 as introducing a pericope which 1:14-20 finishes out). Moreover, the point of 1:16-20 lies in Jesus' magnetic power, of 8:27-30 in his christhood, of 11:1-10; 14:1-9, 10-11, 12-16 in his predictive power and dignity. Furthermore, we will find reason to question that these pericopes start major sections. 16:7 contains a message for the disciples and Peter but does not deal with discipleship; rather, with the fulfilment of a prediction by Jesus. And the interchangeability in terms and functions between "the Twelve," "the disciples," etc., proves only that the Twelve came from among the disciples. As a matter of fact, the overlap between the Twelve and other disciples is incomplete: the Twelve alone carry the name "apostles," are with Jesus constantly, and are sent out to represent him in the preaching of repentance, in the casting out of demons, and in the healing of sick people (3:14-15; 6:7-13; cf. the comment of C. Breytenbach [*Nachfolge* 79-80] that Mark's gospel looks backward rather than sermonizing to the present Christian church).

Whereas a parenetic purpose with regard to Christian discipleship would explain only one small element in the contents of Mark and even then would misconstrue that element, an apologetic purpose with regard to the Cross provides a comprehensive explanation of all elements and, more especially, of the ways in which those elements are presented. Fitting together to form an apology for the Cross are not only the authority and radicalism of Jesus' teaching but also the fulfilment of his predictions, not only his power-packed miracles and exorcisms but also the supernatural manner and accompaniments of his death, not only his attraction of crowds but also his burial by a pious and brave member of the Sanhedrin, not only his baptismal approval by the Father and enduement with the Spirit but also his resurrection. No element has to be slighted or subsumed. Mark's taking for granted little if any knowledge of Jesus (see the notes on 16:8) favors that Mark writes apologetically not to keep Christians from apostatizing out of shame for the Cross (though Rom 1:16 implies the possibility of such shame) but to convert non-Christians despite the shame of the Cross (cf. the comments on 8:34-38 for Mark's redacting pre-Q tradition so as to aim at conversion rather than perseverance, and see M. A. Beavis, *Mark's Audience* 54-67, 170-76, on Mark as religious propaganda to be performed before interested listeners, i.e. as a missionary message to be read in public especially for non-Christians). So this gospel is for people who are afraid to believe in a world that despises weakness and esteems power. The Jesus of Mark is overpowering. Let the weak find in him their champion, the strong their conqueror.

THE ORIGIN OF MARK'S GOSPEL

The question of purpose leads naturally to questions of origin: Who wrote the Gospel of Mark? From what source or sources did its materials come? Where was it written? When? For answers to these questions we turn first to early traditions and then test the answers of those traditions against the contents of the gospel.

The earliest tradition concerning Mark's gospel is found in Eus. *H.E.*

3.39.15: καὶ τοῦθ' ὁ πρεσβύτερος ἔλεγεν· Μάρκος μὲν ἑρμηνευτὴς Πέτρου γενόμενος, ὅσα ἐμνημόνευσεν, ἀκριβῶς ἔγραψεν, οὐ μέντοι τάξει τὰ ὑπὸ τοῦ κυρίου ἢ
λεχθέντα ἢ πραχθέντα. οὔτε γὰρ ἤκουσεν τοῦ κυρίου οὔτε παρηκολούθησεν αὐτῷ,
ὕστερον δέ, ὡς ἔφην, Πέτρῳ· ὃς πρὸς τὰς χρείας ἐποιεῖτο τὰς διδασκαλίας, ἀλλ' οὐχ
ὥσπερ σύνταξιν τῶν κυριακῶν ποιούμενος λογίων, ὥστε οὐδὲν ἥμαρτεν Μάρκος
οὕτως ἔνια γράψας ὡς ἀπεμνημόνευσεν. ἑνὸς γὰρ ἐποιήσατο πρόνοιαν, τοῦ μηδὲν
ὧν ἤκουσεν παραλιπεῖν ἢ ψεύσασθαί τι ἐν αὐτοῖς, "And the elder was saying this:
'On the one hand, Mark, becoming Peter's interpreter, wrote accurately as many
things as he remembered. On the other hand, [he did] not [write] in order the
things either said or done by the Lord. For he had neither heard the Lord nor
followed him. But later, as I said, [he had followed] Peter, who was teaching in
accord with the anecdotes, yet not as it were arranging the Lord's oracles, so that
Mark did nothing wrong by writing some things as he related [them] from
memory. For he was thinking beforehand of one thing, [i.e.] to omit not a single
one of the things that he had heard or to falsify anything in them." We will take
up the date, meaning, and reliability of this tradition point by point, repeat some
arguments laid out in R. H. Gundry, *Matthew* 609-21, and add to those arguments.

The date of the tradition depends on the date of Papias's writing and on the
identity of the elder whom he quotes regarding Mark. Modern handbooks used
to put the date at ca. 130 C.E. or later (see the survey by R. W. Yarbrough in *JETS*
26 [1983] 181-82), but a consensus seems to be developing that Papias wrote
earlier by a quarter century or more, i.e. in the first decade of the second century.
Eusebius leads us to the early date by saying that Papias became famous during
the time of Polycarp and Ignatius, with whom he associates Clement of Rome
(*H.E.* 3.36.1-2; 3.39.1). Polycarp did not die till the middle of the second century;
but Ignatius died ca. 107 and Clement ca. 100. Eusebius's discussion of Papias's
writings comes right at this point, i.e. before Trajan's persecution, which started
ca. 110 and which Eusebius does not describe till Book 4 of his *Ecclesiastical
History* whereas the fragments of Papias appear in Book 3.

Furthermore, as pointed out by Yarbrough (op. cit. 186-90), Eusebius's
Chronicon puts together and in order the Apostle John, Papias, Polycarp, and
Ignatius and assigns the date 100 to this entry (R. Helm, *Chronik* 193-94); and
J. B. Orchard (in *The NT Age* 393-403) shows that Eusebius is following a
chronological order according to which all the events recorded in *H.E.* 3.34-39
take place during the bishopric of Evarestus at Rome (101-108 C.E.). Irenaeus,
writing ca. 180, describes Papias as an "ancient man" and as "the hearer of the
Apostle John" (*Haer.* 5.33.4; cf. Eus. *H.E.* 3.39.1, 13; cf. also R. H. Gundry,
Matthew 614-15). The failure of Irenaeus and Eusebius to quote Papias against
Gnosticism is best explained by Papias's having said nothing against Gnosticism
because he wrote before it became a serious threat, i.e. before 110 (cf. also
M. Hengel, *Studies* 152, n. 61). And the Papian fragments exhibit a general
similarity to the epistles of Ignatius and Polycarp, written early (for details, see
Yarbrough, op. cit. 188-90).

U. H. J. Körtner (*Papias* 225-26) agrees that Papias's polemics fit an early
rather than later date and adds that it is easier to think of an early date for Papias's

making inquiry of those who had heard "the elders" (Eus. *H.E.* 3.39.3-4), but it is hard to think of the Elder John and Aristion as still alive toward the middle of the second century. The present tense of λέγουσιν, "are saying" (ibid.), implies that they are still alive when Papias writes, however. It is also hard to believe that he lived so long as to have both had personal acquaintance with the daughters of "Philip the Apostle" in the middle of the first century (Eus. *H.E.* 3.39.9; cf. Acts 21:8-9) and written toward the middle of second century. Papias's use of "the Lord's disciples" and of "the elders" instead of "the apostles" for the guarantors of orthodoxy further favors an early date, i.e. a date before "the apostles" developed such a connotation; and Papias's lack of great attention to John's writings favors an early date, i.e. a date so soon after John had written that those writings did not yet command much attention. Finally, E. Stauffer (in *Neutestamentliche Aufsätze* 283-93) and H. H. Schmidt (in *TZ* 44 [1988] 135-46) have noted a large number of Semitisms in the Papian fragment on Mark, Semitisms favoring that the tradition of the Elder John had a very early and therefore likely reliable origin.

The only hard evidence favoring a late date consists in a statement by Philip of Side, who makes Papias refer to the reign of Hadrian (117-138; see the citation in Aland's *Synopsis* 531). But we have good reasons to distrust Philip's statement. He is notoriously unreliable and wrote approximately a century later than Eusebius did (Philip — ca. 430; Eusebius — ca. 324). Comparison of Philip's statement with Eusebius's favors that Philip depended on Eusebius but garbled the information he got. Eusebius mentions a Christian writer named Quadratus, who addressed an apology to Hadrian, the very emperor during whose reign Philip puts Papias's writings. The claim of Quadratus that some of the people whom Jesus healed and raised from the dead have lived up to his own day sounds something like the claim of Papias to have gotten information about the Lord's commands "from the living and abiding voice" of the elders and other disciples of the Lord (see Eus. *H.E.* 3.39.1-4 with 4.3.1-2). More strikingly, however, when Philip quotes Papias, the phraseology sounds more like Eusebius's quotations of Quadratus than of Papias; in other words, it looks as though Philip transferred what Quadratus wrote over to Papias. Thus, just as Eusebius associates Quadratus with Hadrian's reign and quotes Quadratus as referring to people raised from the dead by Jesus and still living, so Philip associates Papias with Hadrian's reign and writes that Papias referred to people raised from the dead by Jesus and still living. Furthermore, there appears to have been another Quadratus, who was a prophet, not an apologist. Eusebius discusses him in association with Jesus' original disciples and their immediate successors (*H.E.* 3.37.1). Philip probably confuses Quadratus the apologist with Quadratus the prophet. It was easy for him to do so, because he found Eusebius's similar discussion of Papias bounded by references to the name "Quadratus." A final cause of Philip's confusing Papias's writings with an apology by a Quadratus is Eusebius's associating this Quadratus with the daughters of Philip the evangelist (*H.E.* 3.37.1) just as Eusebius also associates Papias with them (*H.E.* 3.39.9). Poor Philip fell into a trap. In summary, a large number of considerations unite to disfavor a date of 130 or later in accordance with Philip of Side and to favor a date of 101-108 (see R. W. Yarbrough in *JETS* 26 [1983] 182-86 against arguments even less substantial than the one from Philip)

Now by his own testimony Papias is not surmising. He is passing on an earlier report by a certain elder. Properly speaking, the tradition does not go back merely to Papias, as most discussions leave the impression it does, but behind Papias to an elder. If Papias writes 101-108, then, the tradition that he passes on reaches back into the first century. We can say even more. It is usually thought that Papias stands twice removed from the apostles, whom he calls "the Lord's disciples"; i.e. he is separated from them both by supposedly non-apostolic elders and by those who heard such elders and told him what they had heard. But certain data in the text indicate that he claims to have listened often to those who had themselves heard some of the disciples speak; in other words, Papias stands only once removed from these original and closer disciples of Jesus (Eus. *H.E.* 3.39.3-4). We have, then, only three links, not four, in the chain of tradition: (1) the apostles; (2) those who heard the apostles; and (3) Papias. What are the data supporting this view?

First, Papias equates "the words of the elders" with "what Andrew or Peter or Philip or Thomas or James or John or Matthew or any other of the Lords' disciples had said." Why this equation? There are two possible, but mutually exclusive, reasons. One is that the elders are identical with the original disciples of Jesus, i.e. with the apostles. Another is that the elders are different from them but faithfully handed down their teaching. Against the view which sees a distinction, the passage quoted by Eusebius from Papias contains no apparent indication that Papias means to distinguish the elders from the disciples. The listing of the apostolic names under the designation "the Lord's disciples" certainly does not imply such a distinction, for Papias immediately identifies John "the elder" as one of "the Lord's disciples." Here he is using the two designations as synonyms. Their interchange so far as John is concerned points to their being synonymous so far as Andrew, Peter, Philip, Thomas, James, Matthew, and other disciples, too, are concerned.

Second, taking the two designations as synonymous conforms to the natural understanding of Papias's text. For if they are not synonymous, Papias jumps backward from second-generation elders to first-generation disciples without any warning only to turn around and use "elder" and "Lord's disciple" for one and the same man. This use of "elder" and "Lord's disciple" for John shows that we are not to regard the repeated τί as an accusative of general reference (the accusative of "last resort"), meaning "the words of the elders *concerning* what Andrew or Peter . . . had said," but as an appositive: "the words of the elders, i.e. what Andrew or Peter . . . had said." This use also shows that the expressions do not stand in apposition to each other because later elders repeated what earlier disciples had said; rather, what the Lord's disciples had said is identical with the words of the elders because the elders *were* the disciples Andrew, Peter, and the rest.

Third, though Eusebius distinguishes between John the disciple and John the elder for a tendentious reason yet to be exposed, the truth slips out in *H.E.*

3.39.7, where he writes that Papias "confesses that he had received the words of the apostles from those who had followed them." Here we find only one generation between the apostles and Papias. In a lapse, then, Eusebius himself implies that Papias used both the terms "elders" and "Lord's disciples" to mean "apostles."

Fourth, Papias emphasizes the elders' truthfulness in repeating the commandments given by the Lord. A supposedly earlier generation of disciples do not step in as obvious go-betweens to pass the commandments from Jesus to the elders. If Papias were distinguishing later elders from original disciples, we would have expected him to say outright that the elders got the Lord's commandments from the disciples. We might also have expected some emphasis on the truthfulness of the disciples as well as on that of the elders. The absence of such items means that we have no good reason to think that the elders differed from the disciples. On the other hand, Papias implies that he has not heard the elders; it is others who have heard them: "but if ever anyone came who had followed the elders, I inquired about the words of the elders." So it is easy to think that he did not hear the elders simply because they were the apostles and all of them except John had already died (cf. the use of "elder" for an apostle as well as for non-apostles in 1 Pet 5:1, and N.B. the close linkage of "apostles" and "elders" by the use of one definite article for them both in Acts 15:2; 16:4, though a second definite article in 15:4, 6, 22, 23 makes clear a distinction, perhaps because the apostles were not yet old enough to make "elders" a suitable designation for them). These third and fourth arguments undermine the view of L. Abramowski (in *Das Evangelium und die Evangelien* 348-49, n. 28) that the second occurrence of "Lord's disciples" in *H.E.* 3.39.4 is unoriginal, a view which if true would evacuate the first and second arguments.

An elder named John was still speaking. Since "elder" is being used as a synonym for "Lord's disciple" and "apostle," the Elder John is none other than the Apostle John; and Papias heard others who had heard his voice. To be sure, Eusebius distinguishes between the Apostle John and the Elder John (*H.E.* 3.39.6). But the distinction is tendentious. Eusebius does not like the Book of Revelation — the millenarianism that Papias, Irenaeus, and others have drawn from it seems crassly materialistic to him (*H.E.* 3.39.12-13) — so he wants to belittle the book by making it unapostolic, i.e. written by an elder named John as opposed to the apostle named John. Papias, however, not only pins the designation "the elders" on the apostles who had spoken in past times; he also repeats the term "elder" with John, yet not with Aristion. Why? The reason is that although Aristion was one of Jesus' original disciples, he was not an elder, i.e. not an apostle. Like John, however, Aristion was still speaking because he was still living. Papias did not mention him earlier because not till after all the apostles except John had died did what Aristion had to say attain great significance. Why go to Aristion when most of the apostles were still available? But after they had died, the fact that Aristion was an original disciple thrust him into prominence despite his not having been an apostle. Thus it appears that Papias repeats John's name because John is the last surviving elder and therefore one whose current statements Papias has been hearing by firsthand report. Since Papias uses the present tense concerning the elder's speaking and since the Apostle John, who is the elder, died at least by the end of the first century or the first few years of the second, Papias must have acquired this tradition before that time.

Some regard the change from the aorist εἶπεν, "said" or "had said," to the present λέγουσιν, "say" or "were saying," as awkward if the same John is in view. But, we may ask, how else could it be expressed in Greek that somebody has spoken and is still speaking? In English the perfect tense may indicate past action that continues in the present, as when a laborer says, "I have been working at this job for twenty years." But in Greek the perfect tense indicates action completed in the past; and Greek offers no other tense that covers both past and present action. Even in English we often juxtapose the past and present tenses, as in statements beginning, "She was, and is. . . ."

Papias delivers the statements about Mark and Matthew, not as his own, but as those of "the elder," apparently "the Elder John," since he has just designated John by that title (Eus. *H.E.* 3.39.14-16). There is no reason to take the phrase "as I said" in the statement concerning Mark as an intrusion by Papias into the elder's words; rather, the elder is referring to his own immediately preceding statement that Mark wrote as Peter's interpreter. Prior to the phrase nothing indicates that Papias has stopped quoting the elder and started giving his own comments. Moreover, the verb that Eusebius uses to introduce Papias's account, "sets out" (ἐκτέθειται), and the one that he uses to refer back to it, "are related" (ἱστόρηται, which has the connotation of narrating what one has learned by inquiry), appear to make Papias responsible only for relaying information from the elder, not for interpreting it as well. What we have, then, is a quotation by Papias from the elder clear to the end of the paragraph in Eus. *H.E.* 3.39.15.

A slight disjunction exists at the beginning of the next paragraph: "These things, then, are related by Papias concerning Mark; but concerning Matthew these things were said." Eusebius, however, is merely making an editorial transition. Consequently, Papias's quoting the elder not only extends throughout the statement concerning Mark, but also carries over to the one concerning Matthew. That no need was felt in the statement concerning Matthew to redescribe "the oracles" as "the Lord's" (as in the statement concerning Mark) confirms the original continuity in Papias's quotation from the elder, which Eusebius takes over. This is also confirmed by Eusebius's εἴρηται, "were said." If Eusebius meant to distinguish Papias as the speaker concerning Matthew from the elder quoted by Papias concerning Mark, instead of εἴρηται he would almost certainly have written φησί, "he [Papias] said." For this is the verb that he uses three times in the preceding context for Papias's speaking (Eus. *H.E.* 3.39.2, 7, 12). Furthermore, the perfect tense of εἴρηται suits especially well a speaking on the elder's part prior to the time of Papias's writing. A final confirmation of original continuity in Papias's quotation from the elder lies in οὖν at the beginning of the statement concerning Matthew, for this word links that statement to the one about Mark by nicely introducing the contrast between Matthew's orderliness and the previously mentioned disorderliness of Mark.

When recognized as referring back to the statement about Mark, οὖν contains an immensely important implication for synoptic studies. The word normally carries the inferential meaning "therefore." Nothing in the present context indicates that the unseen hand of divine providence is under consideration. Rather, Matthew's reason for writing is in view. So the elder, i.e. the Apostle John, is saying that Matthew wrote his gospel for the purpose of correcting Mark's lack of order. Thus we have astonishingly early external evidence that Mark wrote first and that Matthew knew Mark's gospel and wrote his own in view of it. (This evidence would be only slightly less impressive if the statement with οὖν came originally from Papias rather than from the elder; later patristic reversal of the order of writing was probably due to the emerging canonical order, which in turn depended on Matthew's greater suitability to liturgical reading — perhaps also on its beginning with a genealogy forming a link with the OT; cf. Clement of Alexandria's dating both Matthew and Luke before Mark expressly because of Jesus' genealogies in the first two [Eus. *H.E.* 6.14.5].)

Papias does not give any further or different identification of "the elder" who spoke concerning Mark. This fact suggests that in quoting Papias, Eusebius is following the order of a text which flows directly, not only from the section on Mark to that on Matthew, but also from the section where Papias identifies "the elder" as John to the section on Mark. If not, why the lack of further or different identification? If such an identification appeared in a different preceding context unknown to us but known to Eusebius because he had in his possession all Papias's "Exposition of the Lord's Oracles," Eusebius would surely have indicated a shift from the Elder John, who has just occupied his attention, to another elder. Since the Elder John seems to be none other than one of the Lord's disciples, i.e. the Apostle John, both the statements about Mark and Matthew come from an apostolic source. At the very least, they come from the generation before Papias's; and that is still so early as to fall within or right at the close of the apostolic period.

In the 180s Irenaeus designated Papias "the hearer of John" (*Haer.* 5.33.4; quoted by Eus. *H.E.* 3.39.1). From his own standpoint, Eusebius can accept this designation (*H.E.* 3.39.7) only because he distinguishes between the Apostle John and the Elder John (*H.E.* 3.39.5-6); otherwise, he could not heap scorn on Papias as a non-hearer of any apostle and on the Book of Revelation as an unapostolic document (*H.E.* 3.39.2, 8-14). But how should we evaluate his affirmation that Papias heard the Elder John? Papias himself does not say so in the statement which Eusebius quotes. That Papias often quotes the Elder John by name presents us with a non sequitur; for Eusebius quotes Papias as saying that he got the traditions of the elders by listening to *others* who had heard the elders and were still hearing the Elder John (and Aristion). Nowhere in the quotation does Papias claim to have heard any of them himself. Nevertheless, Irenaeus's designation and Eusebius's agreement with it suggests that Eusebius found in parts of Papias's "Exposition of the Lord's Oracles" no longer available to us indications that Papias had heard John. His hearing John could only strengthen the case for taking his quotation of the elder's statements about Mark and Matthew very seriously.

On the other hand, we need not take seriously Eusebius's inferring a distinction between the Apostle John and an Elder John from the story of two Ephesian tombs (as μνήματα is usually understood), both identified as John's. We might think that rival burial sites came into existence (cf. the ancient rivalry between the *Memoria Apostolorum ad Catacumbas* and the monuments on the Vatican hill and the Ostian way for the burial sites of Peter and Paul; also the modern rivalry between the Garden Tomb and the Church of the Holy Sepulchre as the place of Jesus' burial) and that the rival sites led to a distinguishing of persons in the story to which Eusebius appeals. Or it is possible that a second tomb may have belonged to a later Christian named John but quite unrelated to anyone Papias had in mind; for V. Schultze notes the frequency of ancient Christian graves in honor of elders who had NT names, such as John, Paul, Stephen et al. (*Altchristliche Städte und Landschaften. II. Kleinasien* 1.120). Better yet, T. Zahn notes that μνήματα may mean memorials or monuments of any kind, not only burial sites, and is able to cite church tradition to the effect that the two memorials in Ephesus both related to the Apostle John, one being the house where he had lived and a church had met, the other being the place where he was buried (*Acta Joannis* CLIV–CLXXII; also Schultze, op. cit. 2. 106, n. 4).

We need to keep in mind that Eusebius had an axe to grind concerning the Book of Revelation. He speaks vaguely concerning "the story of the ones who have said" and makes no claim that these storytellers linked the supposedly different men named John to Papias's text (*H.E.* 3.39.6). Finally and most damagingly, he quotes Dionysius of Alexandria as saying in the mid-third century, "But I think that there was a certain other [John] of those who came to be in Asia, since they say that there also came to be two memorials in Ephesus and that each is called John's" (*H.E.* 7.25.16). Dionysius's οἶμαι, "I think," is remarkably weak; and the vague "they say" anticipates Eusebius's expression, "the ones who have said." In fact, almost all Eusebius's phraseology echoes that of Dionysius exactly:

. . . τῶν ἐν ᾿Ασίᾳ γενομένων, ἐπεὶ καὶ δύο φασὶν
ἐν ᾿Εφέσῳ γενέσθαι μνήματα καὶ ἑκάτερον ᾿Ιωάννου
λέγεσθαι (Dionysius).

. . . τῶν δύο κατὰ τὴν ᾿Ασίαν ὁμωνυμία κεχρῆσθαι εἰρηκότων δύο τε
ἐν ᾿Εφέσῳ γενέσθαι μνήματα καὶ ἑκάτερον ᾿Ιωάννου ἔτι νῦν
λέγεσθαι (Eusebius).

To debunk the Book of Revelation, then, Eusebius apparently turns Dionysius's cautious inference, "I think there was another John," into a confident assertion, "there were two Johns." He then adds ἔτι νῦν, "still now," to strengthen the argument from two memorials and uses Dionysius's statement as a whole to distinguish an Elder John from the Apostle John in Papias's statement (cf. J. B.

Orchard in *The NT Age* 400, n. 7, for another use by Eusebius of Dionysius's vocabulary). But Dionysius himself would not have recognized this use of his statement; for in his own context he has just identified the elder who wrote 2–3 John with the Apostle John, and he has made no mention of the tradition passed on by Papias. In all likelihood, then, Eusebius gains the dubious honor of being first to make a false distinction between the Apostle John and the Elder John. Since the distinction is not only false, but also rests on an unnecessary inference from two memorials, the argument is doubly weak. Papias means to ascribe his information concerning Mark and Matthew to one and the same John, who was a disciple and elder, i.e. the famous apostle. For further discussion, see E. Gutwenger in *ZKT* 69 (1947) 385-416.

If Papias were setting Mark as an authoritative gospel over against Luke, which was captured and truncated by Marcion (so R. P. Martin, *Mark* 80-83), we would have expected a comparison between Mark and Luke. As it is, we have a comparison between Mark and Matthew. To be sure, there are some similarities between the statement of Papias's elder concerning Mark and certain terms in Luke 1:1-4, viz., ἀνατάξασθαι, παρέδοσαν, παρη-κολουθηκότι, ἀκριβῶς, and καθεξῆς; but there is no reason why the elder could not have known the Gospel of Luke and been influenced by the terminology of its prologue when making a defense of Mark over against Matthew, as he does. Apart from the possibility of such influence, any statement concerning the way tradition was written down is likely to contain the terms common to Luke 1:1-4 and Papias's elder. The elder's saying that Mark did not leave out anything that he had heard from Peter may defend Mark against the attractions of Matthew's greater fulness as easily as it might argue for Mark against Marcion's truncated Luke. Indeed, since the elder compares Mark with Matthew, his purpose may be to save Mark from being eclipsed by Matthew. Matthew gained greater favor in the early church, but the elder achieved his purpose (if such it was) to the extent that the canonization of Mark saved it from total eclipse. Against the insinuation that Papias has put his own words in the elder's mouth stand Papias's preoccupation with and devotion to "the living and abiding voice" of oral tradition and his emphasizing that he "learned well and remembered well" the things that came from the elders (Eus. *H.E.* 3.39.3). The possibility that Papias and Marcion confronted each other face-to-face (cf. the so-called Anti-Marcionite Prologue to John) need not have anything to do with the date of the elder's comparing Mark and Matthew; for the date of such a confrontation would remain uncertain, and the elder's statement is better understood against the rising popularity of Matthew than against Marcion's truncating of Luke.

Now that we have established the date of Papias's writing as during the period 101-108 C.E. and the identity of his elder as the Apostle John, the tradition that Mark wrote the gospel which bears his name looks as early and authoritative as one could wish. But since Mark was a very common name in the Roman empire, perhaps the most common, we must ask whether the Mark of Papias's elder is John Mark of the NT. According to Eus. *H.E.* 3.39.16, Papias knew 1 Peter. Since 1 Pet 5:13 describes Mark as Peter's "son," it is hard to think that Papias would have quoted the elder about another Mark as Peter's "interpreter" without making a distinction between the two. Moreover, Acts 12:11-17 puts Peter in John Mark's home on one occasion. That this same John Mark acted as helper to the pair Barnabas and Paul (Acts 12:25; 13:13), to Barnabas alone (Acts 15:36-41), and to Paul alone (Col 4:10; 2 Tim 4:11; Phlm 24) favors that he passed into the service of Peter, too, so that the NT speaks of only one Mark. According to Eus. *H.E.* 6.25.5, Origen identified Mark the evangelist with the Mark of 1 Pet 5:13; and Jerome (*Comm.* on Phlm 24 [PL 26.618A]) identifies Mark the evangelist with the Mark of Phlm 24. We know of no other Mark with credentials such as these that would qualify him to be the referent of Papias's elder.

But what does the elder mean by calling this Mark an interpreter of Peter? One might answer that Peter preached in Aramaic because he did not know Greek, or did not know it very well, so that Mark followed Peter in Peter's itineration outside Palestine (for which see Gal 2:11ff.; 1 Cor 1:12 with 9:5; and above all 1 Pet 5:13, which puts the two men together in Rome) and translated Peter's Aramaic, incomprehensible to most people in the Roman Empire, into Greek, the lingua franca of the empire. Alternatively, in Italy he translated Peter's Aramaic into Latin (again see 1 Pet 5:13, and cf. the numerous Latinisms in the Gospel of Mark — H. H. Schmidt in *TZ* 44 [1988] 137). But Greek as well as Latin was spoken in Italy. Paul wrote his epistle to the Romans in Greek, not in Latin. Clement of Rome wrote an epistle in Greek. The Roman emperor Marcus Aurelius wrote his *Meditations* in Greek. In Rome, Plutarch of Chaeronaea found his knowledge of Greek adequate. He did not know Latin (W. Barclay, *Introduction to the First Three Gospels* 122-23). And early tradition says that Mark wrote his gospel, a Greek one, in Rome for Romans (see the following discussion). The presence of numerous Latinisms in a Greek gospel implies a Latin substratum only to the extent that Mark used his supposed Latin translations of Peter's teachings as a basis for the gospel rather than going back to the supposed Aramaic original of Peter's teachings. No need exists, however, to say anything more than that a Roman provenance of the gospel led to the use of numerous Latinisms (again see the following discussion).

One might combine Latin translation in Italy or Rome with Greek translation elsewhere outside Palestine, but the more common theory of translation into Greek has its own problems. The greater the Hellenization of Palestine, more particularly of Galilee, and most particularly of Capernaum, located as it was on the major trade route known as the Via Maris, the less likely it seems that Peter, who came from Capernaum, would have needed anyone to translate his teachings into Greek. What we know of this Hellenization would lead us to believe that Peter knew Greek well enough to speak it for himself.

We might think, then, that before writing the gospel, Mark had become an oral expositor of Peter's teachings as he followed Peter about (cf. Paul's and Barnabas's regular use of subordinates, including Mark himself, in itinerant evangelism and subsequent pastoral ministry). Under this view the aorist tense of γενόμενος indicates action prior to that of the main verb ἔγραψεν, "having become [an interpreter of Peter] . . . he wrote," and the Gospel of Mark turns into a written version of Mark's earlier oral expositions. We cannot quarrel with the use of an aorist participle for prior action. This use is normal. And though representing the usage of Papias rather than that of the elder, Eus. *H.E.* 3.39.1, 3 equates ταῖς ἑρμηνείαις, "the interpretations," with ἐξηγήσεως, "exposition." This equation favors that Mark became Peter's expositor rather than translator. Otherwise, a shift from exposition to translation needs to have been noted (and see R. H. Gundry, *Matthew* 619-20, in dependence on J. Kürzinger for the non-translational meaning of "interpreted" in Eus. *H.E.* 3.39.16).

On the other hand, "the things that he had heard" points to the author Mark as a former listener rather than as a former expositor. Thus he became Peter's interpreter in writing the gospel as an exposition of Peter's oral teachings. The aorist participle γενόμενος then indicates action in conjunction with or, indeed, the same as that of the main verb ἔγραψεν (also a normal usage); and the elder's "as I said," which in the other views of his meaning makes Mark's following of Peter the background for his simultaneously becoming an oral interpreter of Peter *before* writing the gospel, now makes Mark's following of Peter the background for his later becoming an interpreter of Peter *in* the writing of the gospel (against H. H. Schmidt [in *TZ* 44 (1988) 136-37], whose argument that this meaning would require the present participle ὑπάρχων, "being," instead of γενόμενος, "becoming," neglects the historical bent of the elder's statement as well as the frequent use of an aorist participle for action in conjunction with or the same as that of the main verb).

"As many things as he remembered" and "as he related [them] from memory" (taking the prefix ἀπ- before -εμνημόνευσεν as adding to memory the idea of telling) allude to Peter's memory and telling, not to Mark's (cf. Justin *Dial.* 106.3 under the view that ἐν τοῖς ἀπομνημονεύμασιν αὐτοῦ refers to reminiscences concerning Jesus as told by Peter and written by Mark; also *SGM* and the reference in Clem. *Adumbr.* to 1 Pet 5:13 to Peter's many testimonies concerning Christ, though according to Eus. *H.E.* 6.14.6 Clement wrote that Mark remembered Peter's sayings). Otherwise the elder would be contradicting himself when saying that Mark "was thinking beforehand of one thing, [i.e.] to omit not a single one of the things that he had heard." Were Mark's memory in view, that statement would read that he "was thinking beforehand of one thing, [i.e.] to omit not a single one of the things that he *remembered.*" The placement of the clause ὅσα ἐμνημόνευσεν, "as many things as he remembered," before the verbal phrase of which it is the direct object — viz., ἀκριβῶς ἔγραψεν, "he wrote accurately" — draws the remembering close to the just-mentioned Peter so as to facilitate an identification of the rememberer as Peter rather than Mark. And ἔνια, "some things," agrees with the incompleteness implied by "as many things as he remembered" and by "as he related [them] from memory" just as these two clauses disagree with Mark's single-minded concern "to omit not a single one of the things that he had heard." Thus Peter remembered and related some but not all of Jesus' words and deeds, and Mark wrote accurately everything that he had heard in Peter's incomplete teachings (cf. the non-Marcan materials in Matthew, Luke, and John).

The elder describes Mark's writing as οὐ . . . τάξει, "not in order." Here it is important to observe that this description does not refer to chronological or topical disorder, but to interrupted order, i.e. to gaps. Τάξις is commonly used for a list, an inventory, a detailed enumeration (cf. J. A. Kleist, *Memoirs* 19-22; M. S.

Enslin in *ANRW* II 25/3. 2361-62). But that is what Mark is not. Mark is a small sampling, because it rests on the hit-and-miss tactics of Peter in his oral presentations. This lack of order as lack of fulness tallies both with the incompleteness of Peter's memory as seen in the clause "as many things as he remembered," in the expression "some things," and in the further clause "as he remembered [them]" and with the elder's drawing a contrast between Mark, a short gospel, and Matthew, a long one. This lack of order as lack of fulness also results in what Aristotle calls an episodic narrative of loose-knit anecdotes whose progression from one to another is ungoverned by the laws of inevitability or even of probability (*Poet.* 9.11-13; contrast the elder's going on to say that by contrast with Mark, Matthew "arranged [συνετάξατο] the oracles" [N.B. the prefixing of συν- to add close-knittedness to the fulness indicated by ταξ-] — Eus. *H.E.* 3.39.16 and the foregoing discussion that the elder puts Mark in contrast with Matthew rather than with Luke or John). The elder excuses Mark's lack of order on the ground that Mark, having neither heard Jesus nor followed him, was dependent on Peter. Subsidiarily, Peter is excused on the ground that he used anecdotes (as appropriate to oral teachings) rather than producing a full, close-knit arrangement. And to counteract the vice of Mark's gappiness, the elder stresses Mark's writing all that Peter remembered, taking care not to omit any of it, writing accurately, and falsifying nothing. (The interpretation of B. H. M. G. M. Standaert [*L'Évangile selon Marc* 448-51] starts off on the wrong foot by treating "not in order" as antithetical to "accurately," whereas these descriptions merely distinguish between Mark's not writing everything that Matthew wrote and the accuracy with which Mark wrote what he did write.)

The use of ποιέω in the middle voice with a direct object produces the verbal meaning of the direct object. Thus ἐποιεῖτο τὰς διδασκαλίας means "he was teaching on various occasions" (N.B. the plural), οὐχ ὥσπερ σύνταξιν . . . ποιούμενος means "not as it were arranging," and ἑνός . . . ἐποιήσατο πρόνοιαν means "he was thinking beforehand of one thing." The teaching was πρὸς τὰς χρείας, says the elder. Does this phrase mean that Peter suited his teachings "to the needs" of various occasions? Probably not, for three reasons: (1) no needs or needy people are identified by the elder; (2) the contents of Mark, which according to the elder reflect Peter's teachings, look apologetic of the Cross rather than helpful of audiences; (3) the translation of χρείας by "needs" does not suit the rhetorical tenor of the passage as established especially by τάξει, "order," and σύνταξιν, "arrangement" (J. Kürzinger, *Papias* passim). This tenor favors the rhetorical meaning "anecdotes" for χρείας. It is sometimes argued that πρός makes this meaning difficult to accept. But Luke 12:47 falsifies this argument with a use of πρός in the sense required here: "acting in accord with his will" (Luke 12:47). Thus, "teaching in accord with the anecdotes" (Eus. *H.E.* 3.39.15). "The anecdotes" refers back to "the things either said or done by the Lord" (see G. W. Buchanan, *Jesus* 43ff., that χρεία, "anecdote," carried its rhetorical meaning into the first and second centuries and could include deeds in addition to words, as here [against U. H. J. Körtner, *Papias* 158]). The strong adversatvie ἀλλ', "yet," the adverb ὥσπερ, "as it were," and the prefix σύν- before -ταξιν, "arrangement," emphasize that in his teachings Peter did not even come close to providing a close-knit and comprehensive narrative of "the Lord's oracles," which are "the things either said or done by the Lord" (see esp. H. H. Schmidt in *TZ* 44 [1988] 140-42) and thus not the Gospel of Mark itself but the Jesuanic subject matter of Peter's teachings that Mark wrote down in his gospel. The possibility that Papias added to the elder's statement Greek rhetorical terms in τάξει, χρείας, and σύνταξιν (on the rhetorical usage of which see J. Kürzinger, *Papias* passim, with significant argumentative support from Schmidt, op. cit. 138, n. 12) does not affect the argument from early, apostolic tradition for the Petrine origin of Mark's materials (though we should not discount the alternative possibility that John knew, or had come to know during his time in the province of Asia, Greek rhetorical terms and mixed them with Semitisms — against Schmidt, op. cit. 144). The elder does not deny that Mark drew from sources other than Peter's teachings. One may even regard as deliberate the absence of a statement that Mark added nothing to Peter's teachings (contrast Deut 4:2; 13:1[12:32]; Prov 30:6; Rev 22:18-19) and infer an implication on the elder's part that Mark did add non-Petrine materials to Peter's teachings. Nonetheless, it is hard to escape the impression that the elder is describing as Petrine the whole, or at least the bulk, of Mark's gospel.

For several reasons, however, the elder's report on the composition of Mark is widely regarded as at least overly simplistic and perhaps historically worthless (see esp. K. Niederwimmer in *ZNW* 58 [1967] 172-88): (1) Form criticism and redaction criticism have shown that Marcan materials went through more stages of growth and change than allowed by the straight, short line from Jesus through Peter to Mark. The needs of church life and evangelism shaped the materials; and the supernatural elements in stories such as those of Jesus' baptism, raising of Jairus's daughter, transfiguration, and resurrection, etc., are too fantastic to have come from someone so close to what really happened as Peter was. The narrative of Jesus' long day in Capernaum arises out of artistic manipulation of originally unrelated traditions, not out of the actuality of concatenated events as narrated by someone who was there; and Mark drew on earlier collections of controversy stories, miracle stories, sayings, and parables, and on an earlier passion narrative. (2) Mark commits several errors concerning Palestinian and Syrian topography that neither Peter nor Mark, both natives of the region, would have committed. (3) The Gospel of Mark betrays an ignorance of doublets in 6:35-44 with 8:1-9; 6:45-56 with 8:10; 7:31-37 with 8:22-26, betrays an equal ignorance of Palestinian Jewish customs, and reflects a non-Jewish standpoint. (4) Mark's stories about Peter do not differ in character from other stories in the gospel, as would be expected that they differ if Peter stands behind them. They include stories severely critical of Peter and exclude both the Aramaic form of his name — viz., "Cephas" — and the specially Petrine materials in Matt 14:28-31; 16:17-19; 17:24-27; Luke 8:45; 12:41; 22:8, 31; 24:12-35, as would not be expected if Peter stands behind Mark. (5) 1 Pet 5:13 provides a connection between Mark and Peter that Papias or his elder could have used to make Mark derivatively apostolic and thus more useful in a fight against Gnostics, who had their own gospels.

These reasons do not stand up under scrutiny. Both Peter and Mark could have shaped and developed Jesuanic materials. After all, Peter was a preacher as well as an eyewitness to most of what the Gospel of Mark contains; and the increasingly recognized homogeneity of style that characterizes Mark makes it difficult and probably impossible to prove the passage of Marcan materials through pre-Marcan non-Petrine stages. The supernatural element is a point at issue, i.e. a point to be argued *about,* not one to be argued *from.* Even otherwise, a greater openness to the supernatural than some moderns entertain would naturally affect the reporting of an eyewitness (cf. M. Hengel, *Studies* 11). We have repeatedly seen that Marcan materials are far less ecclesiastically relevant than is often claimed, that Mark himself (if not Peter before him) might have drawn together similar materials, and that a historical conjunction of some Marcanly conjoined events, sayings, etc., is not to be ruled out of court. Though some have cogently pointed out that topographical notations grow denser in materials set in and around Jerusalem, where Mark had lived, and that the worst supposed topographical error has to do with reaches far to the north, as might be expected of a Jerusalemite who like Mark had left Jerusalem long before and apparently never traveled to those northern reaches (cf. F. G. Lang in *ZDPV* 94 [1978] 145-60; J. Lambrecht, *Redaktion* 20; G. Lüderitz in *Markus-Philologie* 192, n. 67; M. Hengel, *Studies* 46; C. Breytenbach, *Nachfolge* 322-23), we have also seen that topographical errors are more apparent than real (e.g., see the comments and notes on 7:31; and for a list of supposed errors, some of them egregiously manufactured by hypercriticism, see P. Parker in *New Synoptic Studies* 68-70). The argument that a Palestinian would not have had occasion to distinguish a Syrophoenician from a Libophoenician, as is done in 7:23 (see K. Niederwimmer in *ZNW* 58 [1967] 182), overlooks that writing in Rome, as early tradition says Mark did, would have provided an occasion to make that distinction whatever his own geographical origin. For Libophoenicia, located on the coast of North Africa, lay closer to Rome than Syrophoenicia did; and the oldest evidence for the substantive "Syrophoenician" is to be found in Latin writers (M. Hengel, *Studies* 29, 137-38, n. 164; G. Theissen in *ZNW* 75 [1984] 222).

    The supposed doublets may not be doublets at all (see the comments and notes ad loc.). Even if they are, it is within the bounds of possibility — given the frequent looseness of ancient reportorial standards — that a Mark or a Peter doubled a single event for emphasis or multiple application. Mark's ignorance of Jewish customs has been much exaggerated (see esp. the comments and notes on 7:3-4, but also the notes on temporal and calendrical indicators scattered throughout Mark — e.g., on 14:12). What seems to reflect the standpoint of a non-Jewish author may equally well reflect the standpoint of a non-Jewish audience to which a Jewish author like Mark shows sensitivity (again see 7:3-4). The Jewishness of the author and his sensitivity to the non-Jewishness of his audience are much favored by his frequent citations of Aramaic and by his frequent translations of that same Aramaic into Greek (3:17-19; 5:41; 7:11, 34; 10:46; 11:9-10; 14:1, 32, 36, 45; 15:22, 34; cf. H. P. Rüger in *Markus-Philologie* 73-84). If in accordance with early tradition Mark wrote in Rome for Romans and Peter had ministered in Rome, and if in accordance with probability Peter had come to be known in Rome by that Greek form of his name rather than by its Aramaic form Cephas, no wonder this Aramaic form does not appear in Mark's gospel (and see the notes on 7:14-23 that that passage does not necessarily disagree with Acts 10:9-16). We would expect stories not about Peter to be similar to stories about him if both kinds of stories rested on his eyewitnessing, came from his lips, and passed through the sieve of Mark's composition. On the one hand, anybody who has heard the testimonies of former sinners and backsliders will not find it hard to believe that Peter told on himself the stories uncomplimentary to him. On the other hand, those same stories lessen the likelihood of Papias's, the elder's, or anyone else's guessing or inferring from 1 Pet 5:13 that Mark got his materials from Peter. The presence of good as well as bad concerning Peter supports the historical connection of Mark with Peter, for a redactional program would probably have produced a more consistently good or bad portrait of him (R. Feldmeier in M. Hengel's *Studies* 59-60; for the good, see 1:16-17; 5:37; 8:29; 9:2 with 9:1; 10:28 with 10:29-31; 11:21; 13:3-4 with 13:5-37, esp. 9-13, 21-23, 37; 14:72; 16:7). The specially Petrine notes and episodes to be found in Matthew and Luke but not in Mark may derive almost entirely from creative redaction, not from historical actuality, and therefore need not damage the case for Mark's writing of Peter's reminiscences (see R. H. Gundry, *Matthew* 299-300, 330-36, 355-57, and the standard commentaries on Luke ad loc.). Besides, we should not expect that in Mark's hearing, Peter told everything about his own special involvement with Jesus; and the amount of this kind of involvement that does appear in 1:16-17, 29-31, 36; 3:16; 5:37; 8:29, 32-33; 9:2, 5; 10:28; 11:21; 13:3; 14:29-31, 33-42, 54, 66-72; 16:7 agrees well enough with a Petrine origin of Mark's materials to support such an origin (cf. the ease with which C. H. Turner is able to turn Mark's "they" into a Petrine "we" [in *JTS* os 25 (1923-24) 377-86; 26 (1924-25) 225-40 and in *A New Commentary on Holy Scripture: NT* 48-49, 54; cf. T. W. Manson, *Studies* 40-43]).

We have already noted the lack of evidence for an anti-Gnostic thrust in the pre-Papian tradition. The Gospel of Mark does not seem especially suitable to anti-Gnostic use, anyway. Tending in the opposite direction are the supernatural powers of Mark's Jesus, the Transfiguration, Jesus' dying in a manner which evokes the declaration that he is God's Son, the emptiness of the tomb, and more generally the element of secrecy (cf. the modern interpretation of Mark as semi-Gnostic — J. Schreiber in *ZTK* 58 [1961] 154-83; S. Schulz, *Stunde*). Moreover, Papias's elder defends Mark against attack rather than using Mark as a weapon of attack. Nor does Papias shift the elder's tone from defensive to offensive. In fact, Papias's stated preference for oral tradition over books (Eus. *H.E.* 3.39.3-4) makes doubtful that he would have had any interest in elevating the Gospel of Mark from a non-apostolic book to a derivatively apostolic one. We do better, then, to regard 1 Pet 5:13 as supporting the Petrine and Roman traditions about Mark rather than as the foundation on which those traditions were fabricated. Further support for the Petrine side of the pre-Papian tradition, i.e. for Mark's writing down the reminiscences of Peter, derives from the unlikelihood that the Gospel of Mark, having been incorporated into the Gospels of Matthew and Luke, would have survived independently except for a primitive knowledge of its Petrine background. For Q, likewise incorporated into Matthew and Luke but apparently lacking a Petrine background, did not survive independently. Nor is anyone likely to have deduced from Mark that Peter stands behind this gospel (F. C. Grant, *Earliest Gospel* 36-37).

Support for the Marcan side of the pre-Papian tradition, i.e. for ascription of the gospel to Mark, derives from the unlikelihood of a false ascription to someone who was neither a famous apostle nor an apostle at all nor even a non-apostolic eyewitness of Jesus' ministry, but only a young helper of apostles — and one with a blemished record at that (Acts 13:13; 15:36-39; cf. the attempt to fill up these deficiencies by making Mark one of the seventy-two in Luke 10:1; so Adamantius *Dial. contra Marcion* [ed. Bakhuyzen, p. 10 — cited by T. Zahn, *Introduction to the NT* 2. 445, n. 3]; Epiph. *Haer.* 20.4; 51.6.10-11]). Further support for ascription to Mark comes from the early date of the titles given to Mark and the other canonical gospels. As pointed out by M. Hengel (*Studies* 64-84), these titles must have originated in the last third of the first century and therefore represent extremely early and likely reliable tradition. For the pre-Papian tradition, dating from 101-108 C.E., and the reference to the reminiscences of the apostles in Justin *Dial.* 106.1-3, dating from the middle of the second century, presuppose an already generally known ascription of the gospels to the apostles and their recorders (though our use of "gospel" for documents written by various people [thus, "the Gospel *of* Mark, the Gospel *of* Matthew, . . ."] is not equivalent to the early use of "gospel" for one message put in various written versions [thus, "the Gospel *according to* Mark, the Gospel *according to* Matthew, . . ."] — yet see Justin *1 Apol.* 66.3 [M. Hengel, *Studies* 65-67]). Moreover, book titles that included ascriptions of authorship were important from the start of circulation, and especially so in the early church; for the multiplicity of gospels, their circulation among widely scattered churches, the introduction of gospels into churches previously ignorant of them, the liturgical use of more than one gospel in one and the same church, and the proliferation of gospels beside those that came to be considered canonical — a proliferation that dates for the most part back to the second century — would have led to disagreements of ascription unless the ascriptions of the canonical gospels go back to the first century and reliable information (but see F. Bovon in *HTR* 81 [1988] 22-23; H. Koester in *NTS* 35 [1989] 373, n. 21, against making an argument from analogy out of a supposed uniformity of titles for the NT apocrypha). The early tradition that deals in particular with Mark exhibits a wealth of etiological detail. We might attribute this wealth to pious imagination; but the lack of similar detail concerning other gospels, even those that along with Mark became canonical, favors the reliability of the tradition concerning Mark. Otherwise we would expect pious imagination to have fabricated etiological details concerning the other canonical gospels, too. All these considerations combine with the apostolically Johannine source of the pre-Papian tradition to support authorship by John Mark and his taking of materials from Peter's teachings.

Traditions other than the pre-Papian one lead us also to matters of date and provenance, which thus far we have only anticipated. As to date, the foregoing comments and notes have shown that Mark 13 does not reflect the Jewish war which began in 66 C.E.; so we are free to date the writing of Mark before that war if evidence so favors. Indeed, the disparities between that war and chap. 13 favor an earlier date; for a date during or after the war would likely have brought about an assimilation of the contents of chap. 13 to the actualities of the war. Furthermore, Luke used Mark yet most likely ended the Book of Acts without telling the outcome of Paul's trial because that trial had not yet taken place (R. H. Gundry, *Matthew* 608-9). Alternatively, Luke wrote just after an acquittal and release of Paul (see the thorough and careful discussion by C. J. Hemer, *Book of Acts* 365-410). If then Luke wrote Acts before Paul's trial or just after his acquittal and release and therefore before his martyrdom in 64-67 and if Luke wrote his gospel before he wrote Acts, his use of Mark in writing the gospel requires that Mark have written not only before the Jewish war but also before the end of Paul's Roman imprisonment, the two years of which Acts 28:30 informs us are to be dated ca. 60-62. This dating of Mark agrees with and receives support from the early traditions that Mark died in Alexandria, Egypt, in the eighth year of Nero's reign (ca. 62; Jerome *De Vir. Inl.* 8; Eus. *Chron.* [R. Helm, *Chronik* 183]; idem *H.E.* 2.16, 24; see further references in M. Smith, *Clement* 280-81) and that Mark wrote in Rome before the death of Peter (ca. 64-67; Clement of Alexandria according to Eus. *H.E.* 6.14.5-7; idem *Adumbr.* to 1 Pet 5:13; idem *Letter to Theodore* containing *SGM;* Eus. *H.E.* 2.15.1-2; Recension 2 of the Latin so-called Anti-Marcionite Prologue to Mark; cf. the putting of Peter in Rome as early as Claudius's rule [41-54] by Eus. *H.E.* 2.14.6; 2.17.1; idem *Chron.* [which specifies the first or second year of Claudius's rule]; also T. W. Manson, *Studies* 38-40). D. L. Dungan (in *L'Évangile selon Marc* 200-201, n. 65) understands ὕστερον . . . Πέτρῳ in Eus. *H.E.* 3.39.15 to mean that Mark wrote "later than Peter," i.e. after Peter had died, and cites Recension 1 of the Latin Anti-Marcionite Prologue to Mark as understanding the pre-Papian tradition thus. But such a meaning would require the genitive Πέτρου. As it is, the dative Πέτρῳ stands in antithetic parallelism with the dative αὐτῷ, "him," for a contrast between following Jesus and following Peter (N.B. the adversative δέ, "but," and cf. the Greek text of the Anti-Marcionite Prologue to Luke). So although it is questionable that Recension 1 of the Latin Anti-Marcionite Prologue to Mark depended on the pre-Papian tradition in dating Mark after the death of Peter, such dependence would have entailed a misinterpretation of that tradition. And dating from no earlier than the juncture of the third and fourth centuries, the prologue cannot bear much weight. Iren. *Haer.* 3.1.1; Eus. *H.E.* 5.8.1-5 might seem to provide firmer support for Mark's writing after the death of Peter. But not only is it uncertain that ἔξοδον refers to the departure by death of Peter and Paul prior to Mark's writing. The word may refer to departure by travel. Also and more cogently, the perfect tense of ἐγγράφως, "having written," and of παραδέδωκεν, "he had delivered," means that by writing, Mark delivered the things being preached by Peter before Peter's and Paul's ἔξοδον (whatever this word means). Moreover, the present tense of the participle κηρυσσόμενα, "being preached," indicates that Peter was still preaching at the time Mark delivered Peter's subject matter by writing it. Besides denoting an action completed in the past, here prior to the departure of Peter and Paul, the perfect tense combines with a reference to the time following their departure to indicate that an abiding written deposit of Peter's preaching fills the temporal gap from his departure to Irenaeus's writing. If Recension 1 of the Latin Anti-Marcionite Prologue to Mark depends on the Irenaean tradition instead of the pre-Papian tradition, then, that dependence also entails a misinterpretation, presumably because of the translation of Irenaeus's original Greek into Latin and because of "the inadequacy of the Latin language to express exactly the meaning of the Greek perfect tense" (G. G. Gamba in *New Synoptic Studies* 31-33). Thus Irenaeus becomes a witness for the early date of Mark.

Other, later traditions might be canvassed; but the foregoing suffice to establish that the Gospel of Mark contains Peter's reminiscences of Jesus' words and deeds, that John Mark wrote it, that he wrote from having heard Peter tell anecdotes about Jesus, and that he wrote it in Rome while Peter was still preaching there and before two years of Paul's Roman imprisonment came to an end. Though the pre-Papian tradition could have provided the basis of later references to Mark as Peter's interpreter, later references to Mark's writing in Rome before Peter's death do not derive from that tradition and seem not to have arisen out of a late, inauthentic welding of 1 Pet 5:13 onto the pre-Papian tradition. They seem rather to have arisen out of independent historical memory, which therefore implies that later agreement with the pre-Papian tradition on the point of Mark's writing the reminiscences of Peter confirms that tradition more than relying on it. There is no progression from a date of writing after Peter's death to one before it; and though a Roman provenance is not to be found in the earliest traditions (the pre-Papian and the Irenaean), the placement of both Peter and Mark in Rome by the equally early if not earlier 1 Pet 5:13 makes the tradition of a Roman provenance credible. The theory of a tradition that grows from simple authorship by Mark to Petrine background, from a date after Peter's death to one before it, and then to a Roman provenance — all to give the gospel increasingly apostolic authority — looks neat in the abstract but does not fit the textual data when they are properly understood.

Supporting Clement's placement of Mark's writing in Rome (cf. the placement in Italy by both recensions of the Latin Anti-Marcionite Prologue to Mark, by both the Greek and the Latin texts of the Anti-Marcionite Prologue to Luke, and by the Monarchian Prologue to Luke) is the consideration that for the sake of his own Alexandrian Christianity Clement had reason to avoid a Roman provenance for Mark. The aforementioned tradition of John Mark's dying in Alexandria and the tradition of his having become the first bishop of Alexandria (Jerome *Prologus quattuor evangeliorum* [*Praefatio* in *Comm. Matt.;* cf. idem *Praefatio Marci*]; Recension 2 of the Latin Anti-Marcionite Prologue to Mark; Eus. *H.E.* 2.16.1; 2.24) would have oiled a setting in Alexandria. Indeed, Clement's setting the supposedly superior *SGM* in Alexandria betrays his bias (cf. the much later setting of canonical Mark in Egypt by Chrys. *Hom. on Matt.* 1.7). So it must have taken an early tradition of considerable weight to make Clement set the writing of Mark in Rome.

Though it does not prove a Roman provenance, the profusion of Latinisms in Mark supports the tradition of that provenance. These Latinisms include individual words (μόδιον = *modius* [4:21]; χόρτος = *herba* in the sense of a blade of grass [4:28]; λεγιών = *legio* [5:9, 15]; αἰτία = *causa* [5:33 v.l.]; σπεκουλάτωρ = *speculator* [6:27]; δηνάριον = *denarius* [6:37]; ξέστης = *sextarius* [7:4]; κῆνσος = *census* [12:14]; κοδράντης = *quadrans* [12:42]; φραγελλόω = *fragello* [15:15]; πραιτώριον = *praetorium* [15:16]; κεντυρίων = *centurio* [15:39, 44, 45]), turns of phrase (ὁδὸν ποιεῖν = *iter facere* [2:23]; Ἡρωδιανοί = *Herodiani,* like *praetoriani* [3:6; 12:13]; συμβούλιον ἐδίδουν = *consilium dederunt* [3:6]; ὅ ἐστιν = *hoc est* [3:17; 7:11, 34; 12:42; 15:16, 42]; ἐσχάτως ἔχει = *in extremis esse* [5:23]; εἶπεν δοθῆναι αὐτῇ φαγεῖν = similar to *duci eum iussit* [5:43]; πυγμῇ = *pugnus* [? — 7:3]; ἐκράτησεν = [*memoria*] *tenere* [? — 9:10]; κατακρινοῦσιν αὐτὸν θανάτῳ = *capite damnare* [? — 10:33]; εἶχον . . . ὅτι = *habere* [11:32]; ῥαπίσμασιν αὐτὸν ἔλαβον = *verberibus eum acceperunt* [14:65]; συμβούλιον ποιήσαντες = *consilium capere* [15:1]; τὸ ἱκανὸν ποιῆσαι = *satisfacere* [15:15]; τίθεντες τὰ γόνατα = *genua ponentes* [15:19]), possible Latin influence in word order and unusually frequent uses of ἵνα in a non-telic sense (P. Dschulnigg, *Sprache* 276-78), and a Latin name identical with that of a Christian known to have lived in Rome (15:21 — Rufus; cf. Rom 16:13). There was more than one Rufus, of course. Latinisms crop up elsewhere in the NT (see, e.g., δὸς ἐργασίαν in Luke 12:58, which has no parallel in Mark, however; so Mark did not delete the Latinism and may not have known this tradition). The Marcan Latinisms consisting of individual words are military, judicial, and economic, such as would naturally travel wherever Rome extended her rule and as a matter of fact do appear widely even in Aramaic and late Hebrew literature (H. J. Cadbury, *Making of Luke-Acts* 88-89). But the other kinds of Latinisms outnumber these and deal with much more than the military, judicial, and economic; and the unusual profusion of Latinisms in Mark favors a setting in Rome. Their attribution to pre-Marcan tradition rather than to Mark himself does not allow for the possibility of his suiting the tradition to a Roman setting, fails to appreciate that the explanation of Greek expressions by Latin ones in 12:42; 15:16 favors a Roman setting, and if true would imply that the pre-Marcan tradition took shape in Rome but not that Mark wrote elsewhere. The counter argument of W. H. Kelber (*Kingdom* 129, n. 1) that a Roman setting would have produced domestic, social, and religious Latinisms rather than military, judicial, and economic ones overlooks the many which do not fit the latter description and would have force only if the subject matter of Mark were set in Rome. On the contrary, that subject matter is set in Palestine, militarily, judicially, and economically dominated by Rome. It is a Roman setting of the writing of Mark that makes Latinisms especially suitable in description of what was happening in a Palestine occupied by the Romans (cf. the linguistic correspondences between Mark and the Shepherd of Hermas, written in Rome — Dschulnigg, op. cit. 281-83). Other suggested settings such as Galilee, the Decapolis, and Syria lack both support in early tradition and convincing internal support, though often appealing both to Mark's mention of those regions (as if Jesus' ministry in them did not suffice to explain their mention) and to a supposed correlation between chap. 13, the Jewish war, and apocalyptic fervor in those regions (against which correlation see the comments and notes ad loc.). G. Theissen (in *ZNW* 75 [1984] 222-23) argues that the use of "a Greek" as a cultural designation (7:31) fits an oriental standpoint better than it fits a Roman one, that the association of Idumeans with Syrophoenicians by the Roman Juvenal (*Sat.* 8.159) makes Mark's association of "a Greek" with "a Syrophoenician" look non-Roman, and that the mention of a Cyrenian in Mark 15:21 and of the presence of Cyrenians in the church at Antioch, Syria (Acts 11:20), favors a Syrian setting for Mark. But the use of "a Greek" to distinguish a person's culture from that same person's contrastive oriental lineage would make excellent sense to a Roman audience as well as fit Mark's own oriental standpoint. This use also makes irrelevant Juvenal's association of Idumeans with Syrophoenicians, for he is making no distinction between culture and lineage. And the presence of Cyrenians in the church at Antioch, Syria, is more than canceled out by the presence of a Rufus in the church at Rome (Rom 16:13) and Mark's mention of Rufus despite Rufus's playing no role in the story line. R. E. Brown (*Antioch and Rome* 197-201) finds the relation of Mark's theology to that of Romans, 1 Peter, and 1 Clement indecisive as to whether or not Mark was written in Rome.

It remains only to add that Clement of Alexandria has Mark writing at the request of Peter's many hearers (Eus. *H.E.* 6.24.5-7; so also Recension 2 of the Latin Anti-Marcionite Prologue to Mark), has Mark distributing the gospel to them, and has Peter coming to a knowledge of these activities and of the gospel itself only after the fact, and then neither forbidding the distribution urgently nor urging anyone to distribute it (presumably because his continued preaching made the distribution a matter of no consequence to him; contrast Eusebius's making Peter pleased and approving of Mark's gospel for use in churches [*H.E.* 2.15.1-2.16.1; so also Recension 2 of the Latin Anti-Marcionite Prologue to Mark]). The statement of Origen (Eus. *H.E.* 6.25.3-6) that Mark wrote as Peter instructed him need not contradict Clement's statement that Mark wrote without Peter's knowledge of what he was doing, for Peter's instruction may have consisted in showing Mark how to write by the way he (Peter) preached (cf. the pre-Papian tradition), not in a command to write the gospel. When followed by the dative, as here, the verb of instruction, ὑφηγήσατο, means "go just before, guide, lead" (LSJ s.v. ὑφηγέομαι), which would fit a showing by preaching. In Clement's *Adumbr.* to 1 Pet 5:13 we read more specifically that Mark wrote for Caesar's knights (*equitibus,* the middle rank of the Praetorium, both military and civil — cf. Phil 1:13; 4:22; B. Orchard, *Order of the Synoptics* 132). Especially in Rome, the center of power and culture, and more especially among these knights, representing Roman power and culture, death by crucifixion would be repugnant and an apology for the Cross, such as Mark's, would be called for.

THE OUTLINING OF MARK'S GOSPEL

The observation of Papias's elder that Mark did not write down the words and deeds of Jesus "in order" brings up the question of Mark's outline. We have already noted that "not in order," corresponding to Peter's "not as it were arranging the Lord's oracles," means that Mark wrote what Aristotle (*Poet.* 9.11-13) calls an episodic narrative, one in which episodes do not follow each other according to the laws of inevitability or even of probability. Because of gaps in the material, the connections are not "tight." On the other hand, modern scholars often argue that Mark did follow an outline and perhaps even wrote in imitation of Greek drama, particularly in imitation of Greek tragedy (for some surveys of proposed outlines, see H. Baarlink, *Anfängliches Evangelium* 68-107; H.-J. Steichele, *Der leidende Sohn Gottes* 299-302; F. J. Matera, *What Are They Saying About Mark?* 75-85; and for some of the more complicated outlines that attribute to Mark a fair amount of rhetorical sophistication, see G. G. Bilezikian, *Liberated Gospel;* F. G. Lang in *ZTK* 74 [1977] 1-24; B. H. M. G. M. Standaert, *L'Évangile selon Marc;* W. Stenger in *LingBib* 61 [1988] 7-56). Who is correct, then — these scholars or Papias's elder?

Modern outlines of Mark are legion, a fact which does not prove the incorrectness of them all but which does increase the burden on the person who would prove any one of them correct. Topographical outlines are encouraged by Mark's habit of introducing pericopes with the topographical movements of Jesus or of him with his disciples. Sometimes, on the other hand, Mark mentions no movement, only stationary location (1:2; 4:1; 12:35, 41; cf. 14:3). Sometimes topography does not enter the picture at all; we read only a temporal note (8:1; 14:1, 12; though N.B. that the increased frequency of temporal notes in chaps. 11–16 does not usually replace topographical movement, and that the temporal notes do not always come at the beginning of a pericope). Introductory topographical movement is not always on the part of Jesus or of him with his disciples (2:18; 6:30; 7:1; 10:13, 35; 12:13, 18, 28). Topographical movement occurs within pericopes, too (2:15; 4:10; 5:24, 38, 40; 6:32, 34, 48, 51, 55; 7:17; 9:9, 28; 10:10; 11:11b, 12, 20; 13:3; 14:3, 10, 13ff., 35, 37, 39, 40, 41; 15:22, 46), and is sometimes so vague as to provide little or no basis for outlining (2:18, 23; 6:30). Likewise, walking through Mark takes us hither and yon with little or no discernible pattern: the wilderness and Jordan River–Galilee (the seaside–Capernaum [the synagogue there–a house there]–synagogues throughout the region–Capernaum again [a house there]–the seaside again–grainfields–a synagogue again [in Capernaum?]–the seaside again–a mountain–a house again–the seaside again)–on the sea–the region of the Gergasenes–Galilee again, but without explicit mention (the seaside again–Jesus' hometown–surrounding villages–a mountain again and the sea again–Gennesaret)–the borders of Tyre (a house again)–Sidon–the borders of Decapolis–the sea again–the borders of Dalmanutha–on the sea again–Bethsaida–the villages of Philip's Caesarea–a mountain again–Galilee again (Capernaum again)–Transjordan and the borders of Judea ([reversing the order of their mention by Mark because of his putting the ultimate destination before the intermediate one] a road–Jericho–the neighborhood of Bethany, Bethphage, and Jerusalem [again reversing Mark's order]–Jerusalem [the temple]–Bethany again–Jerusalem again [the temple again]–Bethany again, but without explicit mention–Jerusalem again [the temple again–opposite the treasury within the temple]–the Mount of Olives–Jerusalem again [the Upper Room]–the Mount of Olives again [Gethsemane]–Jerusalem again, but without explicit mention [the high priest's palace–Pilate's palace–its inner court]–Golgotha–Jerusalem again, but without explicit mention [Pilate's palace again, but without explicit mention]–the tomb). These features of Marcan topography create problems for topographical outlines. The problems do not disappear if we take a larger view by assigning an introductory section to the wilderness and Jordan River (1:1-13), a first main section to Galilee (1:14–8:26), a second main section to a journey toward Jerusalem (8:27–10:52 [or 10:45 or 11:10]), and a last main section to Jerusalem (11:1 [or 10:46 or 11:11]–16:8). For prior to his journey to Jerusalem Jesus departs from Galilee only to go northward away from Jerusalem and then circuitously back to Galilee (7:24, 31; 8:10). At the time of his first passion-and-resurrection prediction he is on his way northward again, having already passed through Bethsaida and now going through the villages of Philip's Caesarea (8:22, 27); and even after this prediction he goes up a mountain (9:2), down it (9:9), and then into a house (9:28) — all outside Galilee — and then back through Galilee to Capernaum (9:30, 33) before heading out toward Jerusalem (10:1). That is to say, the departure for Jerusalem does not take place till after the first two passion-and-resurrection predictions in 8:31; 9:31 (or till after the first three if 9:9, 12 is also counted, as it should be).

We might then gravitate to a topical rather than topographical outline. In general, the first several pericopes introduce Jesus as the Christ, God's Son, endued with the Holy Spirit (1:1-8, 9-11, 12-13); and then Jesus speaks and acts with the authority and power of such a one. But except for the Transfiguration and the Burial, in which he plays only a passive role, his so speaking and acting cover the rest of the gospel and therefore provide no basis for an outline. Only by breaking down his words and deeds into various sorts do we begin to find an outline — yet so rudimentary a one that it hardly deserves the name. Jesus' miracles and exorcisms tend to congregate in the first half of the gospel, his predictions and their fulfilments in the second half. But we find an exorcism and a miracle in the second half (9:14-29; 10:46-52; cf. 9:2-13; 11:11-14, 19-25) and a prediction and its fulfilment in the first half (1:14-20 [esp. 17]; 6:6b-29 [esp. 6b-13, 30]). Moreover, the Transfiguration, the cursing and withering of the fig tree, the supernatural elements of the Passion — including the loudness and veil-rending force of Jesus' expiring shout — and the Resurrection all partake of the miraculous though occurring in the second half. The forensic victories of Jesus appear in both halves and congregate in 2:1–3:6; 11:27–12:40 but crop up also in 3:20-35; 7:1-23; 8:10-12; 10:1-12. His magnetism also appears in both halves even though we might not have expected to see it in the Passion-laden second half (for which see 9:15, 25, 30; 10:1, 13, 32, 46; 11:1-10, 18, 32; 12:12, 37c; 14:1-2; 15:10). Parables congregate in 4:1-34 but appear also in 3:23-27; 7:14-23; 12:1-12; 13:28-29, 33-37, and the non-parabolic yet explosively forceful teaching of Jesus congregates in 9:33–10:31 (not including 10:32-34, 35-45, which deal with prediction — see the comments and notes ad loc.) but appears also in 11:15-18, 22-25; 12:41-44.

Not even the widely accepted break between 8:26 and 8:27 passes muster very well. We have already noted that in 8:27 Jesus does not yet start on his way to Jerusalem for the Passion and Resurrection. We have also noted already that from 8:27 onward neither his forensic victories nor his magnetism nor the miraculous element ceases or even wanes (see the comments and notes on 9:14-29; 10:46-52 against depressing the exorcistic and miraculous elements of those passages in favor of discipular interpretations). He does not turn from the crowds to the disciples, but immediately upon predicting his passion and resurrection summons the crowd along with the disciples to take up their crosses and follow him (8:34-38) and speaks to them of God's kingdom (9:1). Jesus continues to teach and otherwise speak in public (10:1-9, 17-22; 11:17, 27–12:40) just as before 8:27 he taught the disciples in private (4:10-20, 34; 7:17-23; 8:14-21; cf. 6:8-11). To be sure, Peter confesses Jesus to be the Christ and the passion-and-resurrection predictions begin not till 8:27ff.; and demons no longer call Jesus the Son of God. If they had been calling him the Son of God right up to Peter's confession, the discontinuance of their calling him this from that confession onward might have given Peter's confession the significance of a fundamental break. But not so. The demons have not called Jesus the Son of God since 5:7. Besides, Peter's confessing Jesus to be the Christ does not equate with the demons' calling Jesus the Son of God so as to make their further such identification of him unnecessary. As to Mark's audience, they have known Jesus to be both the Christ and God's Son from the very start (1:1). For this reason, too, we may question whether Peter's confessing Jesus to be the Christ has so much significance as to signal a bifurcation of the gospel. Jesus has already suffered rejection (3:20-21, 31-35; 5:18-20; 6:1-6a) and encountered opposition (2:1–3:6, 22-30; 7:1-13; 8:11-13), even mortally dangerous opposition (3:1-6) of which he took cognizance in word (2:20) and action (3:7).

If even the widely accepted break between 8:26 and 8:27 stands in doubt, then, what shall we say of those outlines which deal in large-scale but fine-tuned chiasm and concentricity? The foregoing comments have noted chiasm and concentricity on a small scale; but the large scale invariably requires unnatural combinations of materials, unnatural divisions, strained correlations, arbitrary selectivity, and inconsistency of treatment. To take an example of the last, M. A. Beavis (*Mark's Audience* 128-29) treats 9:30–10:45 as a teaching scene but does not so treat 2:13-27 even though narrative and teaching alternate in both passages. Besides, ancient books were written for oral reading, a book like Mark's gospel for such reading to a group of listeners. The ear can catch small-scale chiasm and concentricity, but hardly those phenomena on a large scale; so Mark is unlikely to have used the latter.

Papias's elder was correct. Mark wrote down the words and deeds of Jesus "in order" no more than Peter "arranged" them when telling anecdotes about Jesus. Thus the Gospel of Mark presents only a loose disposition of materials governed by little more than the initiatory character of John the Baptizer's ministry and its locale in the wilderness at the Jordan River, the charismatic character and Galilean locale of the bulk of Jesus' ministry, and the finality of Jesus' passion and resurrection and their locale in Jerusalem (cf. B. Gerhardssohn in *Das Evangelium und die Evangelien* 100-101). Mark presents a collage, not a diptych or a triptych or any other carefully segmented portrayal of Jesus.

THE LITERARY GENRE OF MARK'S GOSPEL

The foregoing considerations of the earliest tradition concerning Mark and of Mark's outline have put us in a good position to consider the question of Mark's literary genre. The answers to this question swing from the artistic to the folkloristic, from the historical to the fictional, from the biographical (according to ancient norms) to the mythological; but a disintegration in the concept of literary genres has sharply diminished the importance of the question. As in other cultures, so much variety characterized books written in the Greco-Roman culture that we can hardly draw a line between the artistic and the folkloristic, between the historical and the fictional, between the biographical and the mythological. Yet only to the extent that these extremes can be kept from contaminating each other does the generic description of a book like Mark as one or the other provide an aid to interpretation. The stubborn fact is that between the extremes lie mixtures of the artistic and folkloristic, of the historical and fictional, of the biographical and mythological. So to describe Mark as biographical does not insulate it against mythology. To describe it as historical does not insulate it against fiction. To describe it as artistic does not insulate it against folklore. Or vice versa. In principle, Mark might stand somewhere in the middle of a continuum rather than at either end; for other literature of the period fills the continuum from end to end. Lacking clear lines of demarcation between literary genres, the literary description of Mark becomes less a heuristic device put to the service of interpretation and more a descriptive conclusion reached by an interpretation based on other factors.

For example, Mark's dealing with Jesus smacks of biography, but biography ranged from the sober and moralistic to the romantic and aretalogical. A description of Mark as biographical is therefore almost meaningless unless one defines what kind of biography Mark represents, and such a definition depends on disputed interpretations of Mark and of the particular biographies with which it is being compared as opposed to others with which it is not being compared. Furthermore, those comparisons break down. Mark's glorification of Jesus with stories of miracles, exorcisms, fulfilments of predictions, and such like brings the book close to aretalogical biographies; but by way of difference from such biographies, Jesus' miracles as described by Mark are notable for an absence of self-serving and self-glorification, for a failure of Jesus to perform them sometimes just for the sake of making an impression, and for their lack of curiosities, burlesque, and fantasy. And not as in aretalogies, Mark writes about a historical figure within living memory. The very genre of aretalogical biography stands in doubt. Works of literature allegedly belonging to it contain a diversity of materials that hinders our lumping those works together under that designation. Mark portrays Jesus as God's Son, but pagan parallels do not support apotheosis by ascription of miracles. Much less do the ascriptions of miracles to human beings in Jewish literature from the OT through the Talmud and the Midrashim. On the other hand, neither is Mark a biography of the moralistic sort known in the first century. Mark sets out good news about Jesus, not a moral example in Jesus (see 1:1). Yet again, the devotion of Mark's book solely to Jesus damages a comparison with biographical anecdotes about the patriarchs, Moses, Joshua, and others, including rabbis, in the OT and later Jewish literature. Nowhere in these bodies of literature do we find a whole book devoted to a single biographee, nor is that biographee portrayed as the Christ, God's Son.

We are reduced, then, to a variegated literary description of Mark according to partial parallels. Mark is biographical but evangelistic. The biographical mode is anecdotal but comprehensive of the book. The evangelistic mode is apologetic but narratival. The materials derive from Peter as remembered by Mark. Their arrangement is loose in detail but guided in general by the overall sweep of Jesus' ministry. Their historical reliability depends on the reliability of the pre-Papian tradition, of Mark's memory of and faithfulness to Peter's teachings, of Peter's memory of and faithfulness to Jesus' words and deeds. Naturally, philosophical presuppositions with regard to the possibility of the supernatural and the amount and quality of the evidence required to accept reports of the supernatural enter into consideration. So also do questions of cultural boundedness both in the first century and in our own, and in between as well. An artist might create a novum, but a non-artist is likely to follow a given cultural pattern fairly closely; so the unartistry of Mark combines with significant unlikenesses to any earlier book to suggest a large-scale derivation from brute facts about Jesus. The less reliable Mark is thought to be for philosophical reasons of a sceptical sort, the greater the need to reduce factuality by erasing the unlikenesses and to upset the earliest tradition about Mark's Petrine background. The more reliable Mark is thought to be out of respect for the unlikenesses and the tradition, the greater the need to relax a predisposition against the supernatural. At this point the disciplines of history and philosophy, both informed by psychology, sociology, and other disciplines, need to affect each other.

Since Mark drew from Peter's teachings, we can credit Mark with expanding the meaning of "gospel" to include the early ministry of Jesus in addition to the Cross and the Resurrection only if Peter's teachings are denied the description "gospel," only if the references to Jesus' early ministry in the evangelistic messages of Acts 2:22; 10:36-39a are denied the possibility of reflecting a homiletical use of anecdotes concerning the ministry, and only if Paul's concentration on the Cross and the Resurrection is universalized. None of these conditions seems likely to hold. Otherwise the preservation of tradition concerning Jesus' early ministry becomes hard to explain. In any case, Mark does not look like a wedding of that tradition with the Hellenistic or Pauline proclamation of Jesus as a descending and ascending redeemer from sin; for Mark's Jesus neither descends nor ascends, and the atoning value of his death receives little or no attention. Neither 10:45 nor 14:24 mentions sins (contrast Rom 3:23-26; 4:25; 8:1-4; 2 Cor 5:21; Gal

1:3-4). For much more discussion on the question of genre, see D. E. Aune in *Gospel Perspectives* 2. 9-60; idem, *The NT in its Literary Environment* 17-76; idem in *Greco-Roman Literature and the NT* 107-26; K. Berger in *ANRW* II 25/2. 1259-64; E. Best, *Story* 140-45; H. Cancik in *Markus-Philologie* 85-113, 115-30; A. Dihle in *Das Evangelium und die Evangelien* 384-411; idem in *ZTK* 80 (1983) 33-49; D. Dormeyer and H. Frankemölle in *ANRW* II 25/2. 1543-1704; D. Dormeyer, *Evangelium;* F. G. Downing in *Synoptic Studies: The Ampleforth Conferences of 1982 and 1983* 51-65; H. Frankemölle, *Evangelium;* R. A. Guelich in *Das Evangelium und die Evangelien* 183-129; R. H. Gundry in *New Dimensions in NT Study* 97-114 (with emphasis on theological influences on theories of genre); idem in *RJ* 33/6 (June, 1983) 28, 30; F. Hahn in *Der Erzähler des Evangeliums* 182-91; M. Hengel, *Acts and the History of Earliest Christianity* 3-34; F. J. Matera, *What Are They Saying About Mark?* 75-85; M. Reiser in *Markus-Philologie* 131-63; G. H. Stanton, *Jesus of Nazareth;* C. H. Talbert, *What Is a Gospel?;* idem in *Semeia* 43 (1988) 53-73; D. L. Tiede in *ANRW* II 25/2. 1705-29, esp. 1725-28; M. A. Tolbert, *Sowing the Gospel* 48-79; W. S. Vorster in *VF* 29 (1984) 2-25; J. G. Williams, *Gospel Against Parable* 201-14. In these discussions one will find references to many other discussions, too — especially earlier ones — and to primary literature.

Index of Modern Authors